PEARSON ALWAYS LEARNING

Finney • Demana • Waits • Kennedy

Calculus

A Complete Course

Second Custom Edition

Taken from:
Calculus: Graphical, Numerical, Algebraic (AP Edition)*, Fourth Edition
by Ross L. Finney, Franklin D. Demana, Bert K. Waits, and Daniel Kennedy

and

Calculus: A Complete Course, Second Edition
by Ross L. Finney, Franklin D. Demana, Bert K. Waits, and Daniel Kennedy

Cover image courtesy of: Steve and Karen Alexander/*Temporary Temples*

Taken from:

Calculus: Graphical, Numerical, Algebraic (AP Edition),* Fourth Edition (Chapters 1-11 in this edition)
by Ross L. Finney, Franklin D. Demana, Bert K. Waits, and Daniel Kennedy

Upper Saddle River, New Jersey, 07548.

Calculus: A Complete Course, Second Edition (Chapters 12-16 in this edition)
by Ross L. Finney, Franklin D. Demana, Bert K. Waits, and Daniel Kennedy

This special edition published in cooperation with Pearson Learning Solutions.

Pearson Learning Solutions, 501 Boylston Street, Suite 900, Boston, MA 02116
A Pearson Education Company
www.pearsoned.com

Printed in the United States of America

3 4 5 6 7 8 9 10 V357 16 15 14 13

000200010270756077

JH

PEARSON

ISBN 10: 1-256-06395-9
ISBN 13: 978-1-256-06395-7

To the Teacher

This second custom edition of *Calculus: A Complete Course* by Finney, Demana, Waits, and Kennedy completely supports the content, goals, and philosophy of the Advanced Placement (AP*) Calculus course (both AB and BC).

The following objectives reflect the goals of the AP* Calculus curriculum.

- Students should understand the meaning of the derivative in terms of rate of change and local linear approximations.
- Students should be able to work with functions represented graphically, numerically, analytically, or verbally, and should understand the connections among these representations.
- Students should understand the meaning of the definite integral both as a limit of Riemann sums and as a net accumulation of a rate of change, and understand the relationship between the derivative and integral.
- Students should be able to model problem situations with functions, differential equations, or integrals, and communicate both orally and in written form.
- Students should be able to represent differential equations with slope fields, solve separable differential equations analytically, and solve differential equations using numerical techniques such as Euler's method.
- Students should be able to interpret convergence and divergence of series using technology, and to use technology to help solve problems. They should be able to represent functions with series and find the Lagrange error bound for Taylor polynomials.

Calculus is explored through the interpretation of graphs and tables as well as analytic methods (multiple representation of functions). Derivatives are interpreted as rates of change and local linear approximation. Local linearity is used throughout the book. The definite integral is interpreted as total change over a specific interval and as a limit of Riemann sums. Problem situations are modeled with integrals. Chapter 7 focuses on the use of differential equations to model problems. We interpret differential equations using slope fields and then solve them analytically or numerically. Convergence and divergence of series are interpreted graphically and the Lagrange error bound is used to measure the accuracy of approximating functions with Taylor polynomials.

The use of technology has been enhanced and is integrated throughout the book to provide a balanced approach to the teaching and learning of calculus that involves algebraic, numerical, graphical, and verbal methods (the rule of four). Students are expected to use a multirepresentational approach to investigate and solve problems, to write about their conclusions, and often to work in groups to communicate mathematics orally. This book reflects what we have learned about the appropriate use of technology in the classroom during the last decade.

The visualizations and technological explorations pioneered by Demana and Waits are incorporated throughout the book. A steady focus on the goals of the Advanced Placement* Calculus curriculum has been skillfully woven into the material by Kennedy, a master high school calculus teacher. Suggestions from numerous teachers have helped us shape this modern, balanced, technological approach to the teaching and learning of calculus.

Philosophy on Technology Usage

When the AP Calculus committee, after consultation with leaders in mathematics and mathematics education, made the decision to require graphing calculators on the AP examinations, their intent was to enhance the teaching and learning of calculus in AP classrooms. In fact, that decision probably had an impact on the entire secondary mathematics curriculum, as teachers discovered that graphing utilities could make a deeper understanding of function behavior possible in earlier courses. The authors of this textbook have supported the use of this technology from its inception and, well aware of its potential for either facilitating or circumventing true understanding, have employed it carefully in our approach to problem solving. Indeed, longtime users of this textbook are well acquainted with our insistence on the distinction between **solving** the problem and **supporting** or **confirming** the solution, and how technology figures into each of those processes.

As hand-held graphing technology enters its fourth decade, we have come to realize that advances in technology and increased familiarity with calculators have gradually blurred some of the distinctions between solving and supporting that we had once assumed to be apparent. Textbook exercises that we had designed for a particular pedagogical purpose are now being solved with technology in ways that either side-step or obscure the learning we had hoped might take place. For example, students might find an equation of the line through two points by using linear regression, or they might match a set of differential equations with their slope fields by simply graphing each slope field. Now that calculators with computer algebra systems have arrived on the scene, exercises meant for practicing algebraic manipulations are being solved without the benefit of the practice. We do not want to retreat in any way from our support of modern technology, but we feel that the time has come to provide more guidance about the intent of the various exercises in our textbook.

Therefore, as a service to teachers and students alike, exercises in this textbook that **should be solved without calculators** will be identified with gray ovals around the exercise numbers. These will usually be exercises that demonstrate how various functions behave algebraically or how algebraic representations reflect graphical behavior and vice versa. Application problems will usually have no restrictions, in keeping with our emphasis on **modeling** and on bringing **all representations** to bear when confronting real-world problems.

Coincidentally, shortly before this edition went to press, the AP Calculus committee decided to change the number of noncalculator problems on the AP examinations from three to four (out of six). Their concern was related to test development rather than pedagogy, but, like our decision, it was informed by years of experience with the teachers, the students, and the technology. The goal today is the same as it was thirty years ago: to enhance the teaching and learning of mathematics.

Incidentally, we continue to encourage the use of calculators to **support** answers graphically or numerically after the problems have been solved with pencil and paper. Any time students can make those connections among the graphical, analytical, and numerical representations, they are doing good mathematics. We just don't want them to miss something along the way because they brought in their calculators too soon.

As a final note, we will freely admit that different teachers use our textbook in different ways, and some will probably override our no-calculator recommendations to fit with their pedagogical strategies. In the end, the teachers know what is best for their students, and we are just here to help.

Changes for This Edition

Mindful of the need to keep the applications of mathematics relevant to our students, we have changed many of the examples and exercises throughout the book to include the most current data available to us at the time of publication. We also looked carefully at the pedagogy of each section and added features to clarify (for students and teachers) where technology might interfere with the intended learning experience. We hope that the current edition retains our commitment to graphical, numerical, and algebraic representations, while reviving some of the algebraic emphasis that we never intended to lose.

In Chapter 2: Limits and Continuity, we revised the material on average rate of change and instantaneous rate of change to provide more clarity. We added more "solving analytically" and decreased (but did not eliminate) the "solve graphically" examples. Providing graphical support remains an important tool for the student when solving problems analytically. The concept of "difference quotient" was amplified with several analytic interpretations.

At the urging of many teachers who have used previous editions of our textbook, we have split the long chapter on techniques of differentiation into two chapters. The first part, Chapter 3: Derivatives, covers differentiability; the differentiation rules for sums, products, quotients, and integer powers of x; trigonometric derivatives; and the interpretation of the derivative as instantaneous change with respect to time. These topics appeared in the first five sections of Chapter 3 in the previous edition. A more intuitive proof of the Power Rule for positive integers, based on the Binomial Theorem, is used in this edition, and the section on the numerical derivative (which we continue to call NDER) has been updated to acknowledge the expanding use of traditional Leibniz notation in modern calculator displays. Examples and Explorations have also been updated to reflect the new notation.

This second chapter on the techniques of differentiation, Chapter 4: More Derivatives, begins with the Chain Rule, then proceeds through implicit differentiation and the derivatives of inverses, including separate sections on inverse trigonometric functions and exponential and logarithmic functions. These topics appeared in the last four sections of Chapter 3 in the previous edition. As a result of the chapter split, 86 brand-new Chapter Review exercises have been added to the textbook, along with an extra Quick Quiz for AP* Preparation.

In Chapter 5: Applications of Derivatives, we continued adding more emphasis on "solve analytically" and changed some "solve graphically" to "support graphically" after the analytic solution. At the suggestion of many teachers, we increased the use of sign charts in this chapter to assist student understanding. We also added the concept and definition of stationary point and added examples and exercises reflecting the addition. To better align the chapter with the AP* curriculum we shortened and moved "Newton's method" to the end of Section 5.5.

The material in Chapter 7: Differential Equations and Mathematical Modeling has been expanded to give students more practice with, and a better understanding of, slope fields. Ten new slope field exercises have been added to Section 7.1. In addition, the solution to Example 7: Newton's Law of Cooling has been clarified.

The opener to Chapter 10: Infinite Series has been updated to include some additional historical flavor. The treatment of the Lagrange error formula in Taylor's Theorem has been greatly expanded in the hope of making it less mysterious to students, and some old exercises were improved and some new exercises were added with the same end in mind. Exercises were also added to give students additional practice at finding (with justification) intervals of convergence and of absolute convergence.

At the suggestion of teachers, more examples of parametric functions and their applications were added to Chapter 11: Parametric, Vector, and Polar Functions.

While the Teacher's Edition continues to show answers in blue print next to the exercises wherever they fit, we have also included *all* answers for this edition in the back of the TE so that teachers will be able to find them all in one place (when, for example, grading student homework).

Continuing Features

Balanced Approach

A principal feature of this edition is the balance attained among the rule of four: analytic/algebraic, numerical, graphical, and verbal methods of representing problems. We believe that students must value all of these methods of representation, understand how they are connected in a given problem, and learn how to choose the one(s) most appropriate for solving a particular problem.

The Rule of Four

In support of the rule of four, we use a variety of techniques to solve problems. For instance, we obtain solutions algebraically or analytically, support our results graphically or numerically with technology, and then interpret the result in the original problem context. We have written exercises in which students are asked to solve problems by one method and then support or confirm their solutions by using another method. We want students to understand that technology can be used to support (but not prove) results, and that algebraic or analytic techniques are needed to prove results. We want students to understand that mathematics provides the foundation that allows us to use technology to solve problems.

Applications

The text includes a rich array of interesting applications from biology, business, chemistry, economics, engineering, finance, physics, the social sciences, and statistics. Some applications are based on real data from cited sources. Students are exposed to functions as mechanisms for modeling data and learn about how various functions can model real-life problems. They learn to analyze and model data, represent data graphically, interpret from graphs, and fit curves. Additionally, the tabular representations of data presented in the text highlight the concept that a function is a correspondence between numerical variables, helping students to build the connection between the numbers and the graphs.

Explorations

Students are expected to be actively involved in understanding calculus concepts and solving problems. Often the explorations provide a guided investigation of a concept. The explorations help build problem-solving ability by guiding students to develop a mathematical model of a problem, solve the mathematical model, support or confirm the solution, and interpret the solution. The ability to communicate their understanding is just as important to the learning process as reading or studying, not only in mathematics but also in every academic pursuit. Students can gain an entirely new perspective on their knowledge when they explain what they know in writing.

Graphing Utilities

The book assumes familiarity with a graphing utility that will produce the graph of a function within an arbitrary viewing window, find the zeros of a function, compute the derivative of a function numerically, and compute definite integrals numerically. Students are expected to recognize that a given graph is reasonable, identify all the important characteristics of a graph, interpret those characteristics, and confirm them using analytic methods. Toward that end, most graphs appearing in this book resemble students' actual grapher output or suggest hand-drawn sketches. This is one of the first calculus textbooks to take full advantage of graphing calculators, philosophically restructuring the course to teach new things in new ways to achieve new understanding, while (courageously) abandoning some old things and old ways that are no longer serving a purpose.

Exercise Sets

The exercise sets were updated for this edition, including many new ones. There are nearly 4000 exercises, with more than 80 Quick Quiz exercises and 560 Quick Review exercises. The different types of exercises included are:

Algebraic and analytic manipulation

Interpretation of graphs

Graphical representations

Numerical representations

Explorations

Writing to learn

Group activities

Data analyses

Descriptively titled applications

Extending the ideas

Each exercise set begins with the Quick Review feature, which can be used to introduce lessons, support Examples, and review prerequisite skills. The exercises that follow are graded from routine to challenging. Some exercises are also designed to be solved *without a calculator*; these exercises have numbers printed within a gray oval. Students are urged to **support** the answers to these (and all) exercises graphically or numerically, but only after they have solved them with pencil and paper. An additional block of exercises, Extending the Ideas, may be used in a variety of ways, including group work. We also provide Review Exercises and AP* Examination Preparation at the end of each chapter.

Print Supplements and Resources

For the Student

The following supplements are available for purchase:

AP* Test Prep Series: AP* Calculus

- Introduction to the AP* AB and BC Calculus Exams
- Precalculus Review of Calculus Prerequisites
- Review of AP* Calculus AB and Calculus BC Topics
- Practice Exams
- Answers and Solutions

Texas Instruments Graphing Calculator Manual

- An introduction to Texas Instruments' graphing calculators, as they are used for calculus
- Features the TI-84 Plus Silver Edition featuring MathPrint, TI-83 Plus Silver Edition, and the TI-89 Titanium.
- The keystrokes, menus and screens for the TI-84 Plus are similar to the TI-84 Plus Silver Edition, those for the TI-83 Plus are similar to the TI-83 Plus Silver Edition, and the TI-89, TI-92 Plus, and Voyage™ 200 are similar to the TI-89 Titanium.

For the Teacher

The following supplements are available to qualified adopters:

Annotated Teacher's Edition

- Answers included on the same page as the problem appears, for most exercises. All answers included in the back of the book.
- Solutions to Chapter Opening Problems, Teaching Notes, Common Errors, Notes on Examples and Exploration Extensions, and Assignment Guide included at the beginning of the book.

Solutions Manual

- Complete solutions for Quick Reviews, Exercises, Explorations, and Chapter Reviews

Technology Resources

The Second Custom Edition of Finney, Demana, Waits, Kennedy *Calculus: A Complete Course* is accompanied by an extensive range of technology resources designed to support students in practicing and learning the material, and to assist teachers in managing and delivering their courses.

Support for Students

MathXL® for School (optional, for purchase only)—access code required, www.MathXLforSchool.com

MathXL® for School is a powerful online homework, tutorial, and assessment system designed specifically for Pearson Education mathematics and statistics textbooks.

With MathXL for School, students:

- Do their homework and receive immediate feedback
- Get self-paced assistance on problems in a variety of ways (guided solutions, step-by-step examples, video clips, animations)
- Have a large number of practice problems to choose from—helping them master a topic
- Receive personalized study plans based on quiz and test results
- The MathXL for School course covers Chapters 1-11 of *Calculus: A Complete Course.*

Video Resources on DVD

This DVD-ROM features an engaging team of mathematics teachers who present comprehensive coverage of each section of the text. The lecturers' presentations include examples and exercises from the text and support an approach that emphasizes visualization and problem-solving. Available for purchase.

Support for Teachers

Most of the teacher supplements and resources for this book are available electronically upon adoption or to preview. For more information, please contact your Pearson School sales representative.

Downloadable Teacher's Resources

Please contact your Pearson School sales representative for download instructions.

- **Resources for AP* Exam Preparation and Practice** includes many resources to help prepare students for the AP* Calculus exam, including concepts worksheets, sample AB and BC exams, and answers to those exams.
- **AP* Calculus Implementation Guide** is a tool to help teachers manage class time and ensure the complete Advanced Placement* Calculus curriculum is covered. It includes pacing guides (for AB and BC Calculus), assignment guides, topic correlations, and lesson plans.
- **PowerPoint® Lecture Presentation** This time-saving resource includes classroom presentation slides that align to the topic sequence of the textbook.
- **Assessment Resources** include chapter quizzes, chapter tests, semester test, final tests, and alternate assessments.

MathXL® for School (optional, for purchase only)—access code required, www.MathXLforSchool.com

MathXL® for School is a powerful online homework, tutorial, and assessment system designed specifically for Pearson Education mathematics and statistics textbooks.

With MathXL for School, students:

- Do their homework and receive immediate feedback
- Get self-paced assistance on problems in a variety of ways (guided solutions, setp-by-step examples, video clips, animations)
- Have a large number of practice problems to choose from—helping them master a topic
- Receive personalized study plans based on quiz and test results

With MathXL for School, teachers:

- Quickly and easily create quizzes, tests and homework assignments
- Utilize automatic grading to rapidly assess student understanding
- Track both student and group performance in an online gradebook
- Prepare students for high-stakes testing
- Deliver quality instruction regardless of experience level
- The MathXL for School course covers Chapters 1-11 of *Calculus: A Complete Course.*

The Flash-based, platform- and browser-independent MathXL Player supports Firefox on Windows (XP, Vista and Windows 7), Safari and Firefox on the Macintosh, as well as Internet Explorer. For more information, visit our Web site at www.MathXLforSchool.com, or contact your Pearson School sales representative.

TestGen® CD-ROM

TestGen enables teachers to build, edit, print, and administer tests using a computerized bank of questions developed to cover all the objectives of the text. TestGen is algorithmically based, allowing teachers to create multiple but equivalent versions of the same question or test with the click of a button. Teachers can also modify test bank questions or add new questions. Tests can be printed or administered online.

To the AP* Student

We know that as you study for your AP* course, you're preparing along the way for the AP* exam. By tying the material in this book directly to AP* course goals and exam topics, we help you to focus your time most efficiently. And that's a good thing!

The AP* exam is an important milestone in your education. A high score will position you optimally for college acceptance—and possibly will give you college credits that put you a step ahead. Our primary commitment is to provide you with the tools you need to excel on the exam ... the rest is up to you!

Test-Taking Strategies for an Advanced Placement* Calculus Examination

You should approach the AP* Calculus Examination the same way you would any major test in your academic career. Just remember that it is a one-shot deal—you should be at your peak performance level on the day of the test. For that reason you should do everything that your "coach" tells you to do. In most cases your coach is your classroom teacher. It is very likely that your teacher has some experience, based on workshop information or previous students' performance, to share with you.

You should also analyze your own test-taking abilities. At this stage in your education, you probably know your strengths and weaknesses in test-taking situations. You may be very good at multiple choice questions but weaker in essays, or perhaps it is the other way around. Whatever your particular abilities are, evaluate them and respond accordingly. Spend more time on your weaker points. In other words, rather than spending time in your comfort zone where you need less work, try to improve your soft spots. In all cases, concentrate on clear communication of your strategies, techniques, and conclusions.

The following table presents some ideas in a quick and easy form.

General Strategies for AP* Examination Preparation

Time	Dos
Through the Year	• Register with your teacher/coordinator • Pay your fee (if applicable) on time • Take good notes • Work with others in study groups • Review on a regular basis • Evaluate your test-taking strengths and weaknesses—keep track of how successful you are when guessing
The Week Before	• Combine independent and group review • Get tips from your teacher • Do lots of mixed review problems • Check your exam date, time, and location • Review the appropriate AP* Calculus syllabus (AB or BC)
The Night Before	• Put new batteries in your calculator • Make sure your calculator is on the approved list • Lay out your clothes and supplies so that you are ready to go out the door • Do a short review • Go to bed at a reasonable hour
Exam Day	• Get up a little earlier than usual • Eat a good breakfast/lunch • Put some hard candy in your pocket in case you need an energy boost during the test • Get to your exam location 15 minutes early
Exam Night	• Relax—you earned it

Topics from the Advanced Placement* Curriculum for Calculus AB, Calculus BC

As an AP* Student, you are probably well aware of the good study habits that are needed to be a successful student in high school and college:

- attend all the classes
- ask questions (either during class or after)
- take clear and understandable notes
- make sure you understand the concepts rather than memorizing formulas
- do your homework; extend your test-prep time over several days or weeks, instead of cramming
- use all the resources—text and people—that are available to you.

No doubt this list of "good study habits" is one that you have seen or heard before. You should know that there is powerful research that suggests a few habits or routines will enable you to go beyond "knowing about" calculus, to more deeply "understanding" calculus. Here are three concrete actions for you to consider:

- Review your notes at least once a week and rewrite them in summary form.
- Verbally explain concepts (theorems, etc.) to a classmate.
- Form a study group that meets regularly to do homework and discuss reading and lecture notes.

Most of these tips boil down to one mantra, which all mathematicians believe in:

Math is not a spectator sport.

The AP* Calculus Examination is based on the following Topic Outline. For your convenience, we have noted all Calculus AB and Calculus BC objectives with clear indications of topics required only by the Calculus BC Exam. The outline cross-references each AP* Calculus objective with the appropriate chapters of this textbook.

Use this outline to track your progress through the AP* exam topics. Be sure to cover every topic associated with the exam you are taking. Check it off when you have studied and/or reviewed the topic.

Even as you prepare for your exam, I hope this book helps you map—and enjoy—your calculus journey!

—*John Brunsting*
Hinsdale Central High School

Topic Outline for AP* Calculus AB and AP* Calculus BC

(excerpted from the College Board's Course Description - Calculus: Calculus AB, Calculus BC, Fall 2010)

I.	Calculus Exam		Functions, Graphs, and Limits	*Calculus*
A	AB	BC	Analysis of graphs	1.2–1.6
B	AB	BC	Limits of functions (including one-sided limits)	
B1	AB	BC	An intuitive understanding of the limiting process	2.1, 2.2
B2	AB	BC	Calculating limits using algebra	2.1, 2.2
B3	AB	BC	Estimating limits from graphs or tables of data	2.1, 2.2
C	AB	BC	Asymptotic and unbounded behavior	
C1	AB	BC	Understanding asymptotes in terms of graphical behavior	2.2
C2	AB	BC	Describing asymptotic behavior in terms of limits involving infinity	2.2
C3	AB	BC	Comparing relative magnitudes of functions and their rates of change	2.2, 2.4, 9.3
D	AB	BC	Continuity as a property of functions	
D1	AB	BC	An intuitive understanding of continuity	2.3
D2	AB	BC	Understanding continuity in terms of limits	2.3
D3	AB	BC	Geometric understanding of graphs of continuous functions	2.3, 5.1–5.3
E		BC	Parametric, polar, and vector functions	11.1–11.3

II.	Calculus Exam		Derivatives	*Calculus*
A	AB	BC	Concept of the derivative	
A1	AB	BC	Derivative presented graphically, numerically, and analytically	2.4–5.5
A2	AB	BC	Derivative interpreted as an instantaneous rate of change	2.4
A3	AB	BC	Derivative defined as the limit of the difference quotient	2.4–3.1
A4	AB	BC	Relationship between differentiability and continuity	3.2
B	AB	BC	Derivative at a point	
B1	AB	BC	Slope of a curve at a point	2.4
B2	AB	BC	Tangent line to a curve at a point and local linear approximation	2.4, 5.5
B3	AB	BC	Instantaneous rate of change as the limit of average rate of change	2.4, 3.4
B4	AB	BC	Approximate rate of change from graphs and tables of values	2.4, 3.4
C	AB	BC	Derivative as a function	
C1	AB	BC	Corresponding characteristics of graphs of f and f'	3.1, 5.3
C2	AB	BC	Relationship between the increasing and decreasing behavior of f and the sign of f'	5.1, 5.3
C3	AB	BC	The Mean Value Theorem and its geometric consequences.	5.2
C4	AB	BC	Equations involving derivatives. Verbal descriptions are translated into equations involving derivatives and vice versa	3.4, 3.5, 5.6, 7.4, 7.5
D	AB	BC	Second Derivatives	
D1	AB	BC	Corresponding characteristics of graphs of f, f', and f''	5.3
D2	AB	BC	Relationship between the concavity of f and the sign of f''	5.3
D3	AB	BC	Points of inflection as places where concavity changes	5.3
E	AB	BC	Applications of derivatives	
E1	AB	BC	Analysis of curves, including the notions of monotonicity and concavity	5.1–5.3
E2		BC	Analysis of planar curves given in parametric form, polar form, and vector form, including velocity and acceleration vectors	11.1–11.3
E3	AB	BC	Optimization, both absolute (global) and relative (local) extrema	5.3, 5.4
E4	AB	BC	Modeling rates of change, including related rates problems	5.6
E5	AB	BC	Use of implicit differentiation to find the derivative of an inverse function	4.2

E6	AB	BC	Interpretation of the derivative as a rate of change in varied applied contexts, including velocity, speed, and acceleration	3.4
E7	AB	BC	Geometric interpretation of differential equations via slope fields and the relationship between slope fields and solution curves for differential equations	7.1
E8		BC	Numerical solution of differential equations using Euler's method	7.1
E9		BC	L'Hopital's Rule, including its use in determining limits and convergence of improper integrals and series	9.2, 10.5
F	AB	BC	Computation of derivatives	
F1	AB	BC	Knowledge of derivatives of basic functions, including power, exponential, logarithmic, trigonometric, and inverse trigonometric functions	3.3, 3.5, 4.3, 4.4
F2	AB	BC	Derivative rules for sums, products, and quotients of functions	3.3
F3	AB	BC	Chain rule and implicit differentiation	4.1, 4.2
F4		BC	Derivatives of parametric, polar, and vector functions	11.1–11.3

III.	**Calculus Exam**		**Integrals**	***Calculus***
A			Interpretations and properties of definite integrals	
A1	AB	BC	Definite integral as a limit of Riemann sums	6.1, 6.2
A2	AB	BC	Definite integral of the rate of change of a quantity over an interval interpreted as the change of the quantity over the closed interval: $\int_a^b f'(x)\,dx = f(b) - f(a)$.	6.1, 6.4
A3	AB	BC	Basic properties of definite integrals (Examples include additivity and linearity.)	6.2, 6.3
B			Applications of integrals	
B1a	AB	BC	Appropriate integrals are used in a variety of applications to model physical, biological, or economic situations. ... students should be able to adapt their knowledge and techniques. Emphasis is on using the method of setting up an approximating Riemann sum and representing its limit as a definite integral. ... specific applications should include using the integral of a rate of change to give accumulated change, finding the area of a region, the volume of a solid with known cross sections, the average value of a function, and the distance traveled by a particle along a line	6.4, 6.5, 7.4, 7.5, 8.1–8.5
B1b		BC	Appropriate integrals are used ... specific applications should include ... finding the area of a region bounded by polar curves ... and the length of a curve (including a curve given in parametric form)	8.4, 11.1, 11.3
C			Fundamental Theorem of Calculus	
C1	AB	BC	Use of the Fundamental Theorem to evaluate definite integrals	6.4
C2	AB	BC	Use of the Fundamental Theorem to represent a particular antiderivative, and the analytical and graphical analysis of functions so derived	6.4, 7.1
D			Techniques of antidifferentiation	
D1	AB	BC	Antiderivatives following directly from derivatives of basic functions	5.2, 7.1, 7.2
D2a	AB	BC	Antiderivatives by substitution of variables (including change of limits for definite integrals)	7.2
D2b		BC	Antiderivatives by ... parts, and simple partial fractions (nonrepeating linear factors only)	7.3, 7.5
D3		BC	Improper integrals (as limits of definite integrals)	9.3
E			Applications of antidifferentiation	
E1	AB	BC	Finding specific antiderivatives using initial conditions, including applications to motion along a line	7.1, 8.1
E2	AB	BC	Solving separable differential equations and using them in modeling In particular, studying the equations $y' = ky$ and exponential growth	7.4
E3		BC	Solving logistic differential equations and using them in modeling	7.5
F			Numerical approximations to definite integrals	
F1	AB	BC	Use of Riemann and trapezoidal sums to approximate definite integrals of functions represented algebraically, graphically, and by tables of values	6.2, 6.5

IV.	Calculus Exam	Polynomial Approximations and Series	*Calculus*
A		Concept of series	
A1	BC	A series is defined as a sequence of partial sums, and convergence is defined in terms of the limit of the sequence of partial sums. Technology can be used to explore convergence or divergence	10.1
B		Series of constants	
B1	BC	Motivating examples, including decimal expansion	10.1
B2	BC	Geometric series with applications	10.1
B3	BC	The harmonic series	10.5
B4	BC	Alternating series with error bound	10.5
B5	BC	Terms of series as areas of rectangles and their relationship to improper integrals, including the integral test and its use in testing the convergence of *p*-series	10.5
B6	BC	The ratio test for convergence or divergence	10.4
B7	BC	Comparing series to test for convergence and divergence	10.4
C		Taylor series	
C1	BC	Taylor polynomial approximation with graphical demonstration of convergence (For example, viewing graphs of various Taylor polynomials of the sine function approximating the sine curve.)	10.2
C2	BC	Maclaurin series and the general Taylor series centered at $x = a$	10.2
C3	BC	Maclaurin series for the functions e^x, $\sin x$, $\cos x$, and $\frac{1}{1-x}$	10.2
C4	BC	Formal manipulation of Taylor series and shortcuts to computing Taylor series, including substitution, differentiation, antidifferentiation, and the formation of new series from known series	10.1, 10.2
C5	BC	Functions defined by power series	10.1, 10.2
C6	BC	Radius and interval of convergence of power series	10.1, 10.4, 10.5
C7	BC	Lagrange error bound for Taylor polynomials	10.3

Upon publication, this text was correlated to the College Board's AP* Calculus AB and AP* Calculus BC Course Description dated Fall 2010. We continually monitor the College Board's AP* Course Description for updates to exam topics. For the most current AP* Exam Topic correlation for this textbook, visit PearsonSchool.com/AdvancedCorrelations.

Using the Book for Maximum Effectiveness

So, how can this book help you to join in the game of mathematics for a winning future? Let us show you some unique tools that we have included in the text to help prepare you not only for the AP* Calculus exam, but also for success beyond this course.

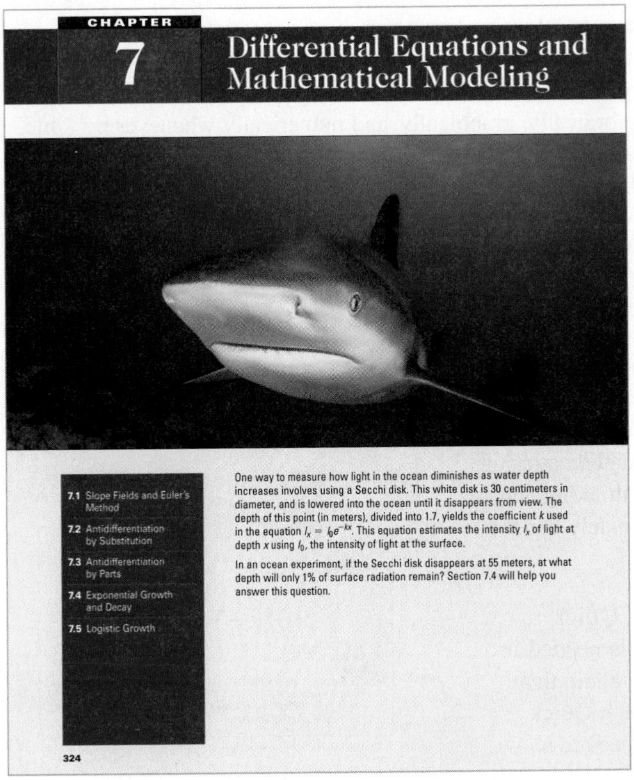

CHAPTER 7

Differential Equations and Mathematical Modeling

7.1 Slope Fields and Euler's Method
7.2 Antidifferentiation by Substitution
7.3 Antidifferentiation by Parts
7.4 Exponential Growth and Decay
7.5 Logistic Growth

One way to measure how light in the ocean diminishes as water depth increases involves using a Secchi disk. This white disk is 30 centimeters in diameter, and is lowered into the ocean until it disappears from view. The depth of this point (in meters), divided into 1.7, yields the coefficient k used in the equation $I_x = I_0 e^{-kx}$. This equation estimates the intensity I_x of light at depth x using I_0, the intensity of light at the surface.

In an ocean experiment, if the Secchi disk disappears at 55 meters, at what depth will only 1% of surface radiation remain? Section 7.4 will help you answer this question.

324

Chapter Openers provide a photograph and application to show you an example that illustrates the relevance of what you'll be learning in the chapter.

A **Chapter Overview** then follows to give you a sense of what you are going to learn. This overview provides a roadmap of the chapter as well as tells how the different topics in the chapter are connected under one big idea. It is always helpful to remember that mathematics isn't modular, but interconnected, and that the different skills you are learning throughout the course build on one another to help you understand more complex concepts.

CHAPTER 7 Overview

One of the early accomplishments of calculus was predicting the future position of a planet from its present position and velocity. Today this is just one of a number of occasions on which we deduce everything we need to know about a function from one of its known values and its rate of change. From this kind of information, we can tell how long a sample of radioactive polonium will last; whether, given current trends, a population will grow or become extinct; and how large major league baseball salaries are likely to be in the year 2015. In this chapter, we examine the analytic, graphical, and numerical techniques on which such predictions are based.

What you will learn about . . .

- Differential Equations
- Slope Fields
- Euler's Method

and why . . .

Differential equations have always been a prime motivation for the study of calculus and remain so to this day.

Similarly, the **What you will learn about . . . and why . . .** feature gives you the big ideas in each section and explains their purpose. You should read this as you begin the section and always review it after you have completed the section to make sure you understand all of the key topics that you have just studied.

Differential Equation Mode

If your calculator has a *differential equation mode* for graphing, it is intended for graphing slope fields. The usual "Y=" turns into a "dy/dx = " screen, and you can enter a function of x and/or y. The grapher draws a slope field for the differential equation when you press the GRAPH button.

Margin Notes appear throughout the book on various topics. Some notes provide more information on a key concept or an example. Other notes offer practical advice on using your graphing calculator to obtain the most accurate results.

Brief **Historical Notes** present the stories of people and the research that they have done to advance the study of mathematics. Reading these notes will often provide you with additional insight for solving problems that you can use later when doing the homework or completing the AP* Exam.

Charles Richard Drew (1904–1950)

Millions of people are alive today because of Charles Drew's pioneering work on blood plasma and the preservation of human blood for transfusion. After directing the Red Cross program that collected plasma for the Armed Forces in World War II, Dr. Drew went on to become Head of Surgery at Howard University and Chief of Staff at Freedmen's Hospital in Washington, D.C.

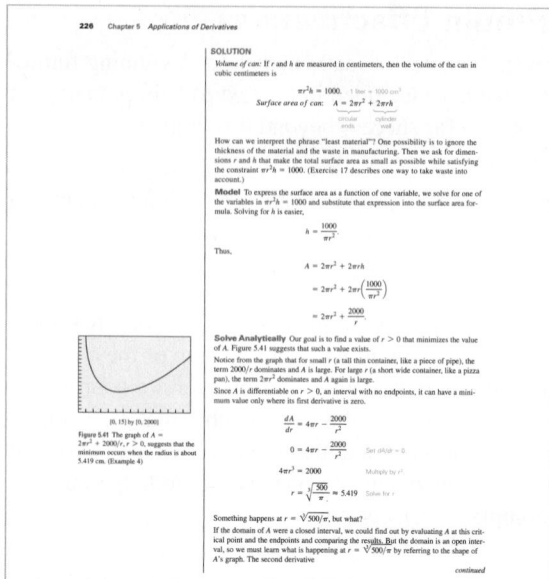

Many examples include solutions to **Solve Algebraically, Solve Graphically,** or **Solve Numerically**. You should be able to use different approaches for finding solutions to problems. For instance, you would obtain a solution algebraically when that is the most appropriate technique to use, and you would obtain solutions graphically or numerically when algebra is difficult or impossible to use. We urge you to solve problems by one method, then support or confirm your solution by using another method, and finally, interpret the results in the context of the problem. Doing so reinforces the idea that to understand a problem fully, you need to understand it algebraically, graphically, and numerically whenever possible.

226 Chapter 5 *Applications of Derivatives*

SOLUTION

Volume of can: If r and h are measured in centimeters, then the volume of the can in cubic centimeters is

$$\pi r^2 h = 1000. \quad \text{1 liter = 1000 cm}^3$$

$$\textit{Surface area of can:} \quad A = \underbrace{2\pi r^2}_{\text{circular ends}} + \underbrace{2\pi rh}_{\text{cylinder wall}}$$

How can we interpret the phrase "least material"? One possibility is to ignore the thickness of the material and the waste in manufacturing. Then we ask for dimensions r and h that make the total surface area as small as possible while satisfying the constraint $\pi r^2 h = 1000$. (Exercise 17 describes one way to take waste into account.)

Model To express the surface area as a function of one variable, we solve for one of the variables in $\pi r^2 h = 1000$ and substitute that expression into the surface area formula. Solving for h is easier,

$$h = \frac{1000}{\pi r^2}.$$

Thus,

$$A = 2\pi r^2 + 2\pi rh$$
$$= 2\pi r^2 + 2\pi r\left(\frac{1000}{\pi r^2}\right)$$
$$= 2\pi r^2 + \frac{2000}{r}.$$

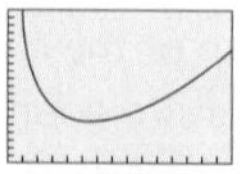

[0, 15] by [0, 2000]

Figure 5.41 The graph of $A = 2\pi r^2 + 2000/r$, $r > 0$, suggests that the minimum occurs when the radius is about 5.419 cm. (Example 4)

Solve Analytically Our goal is to find a value of $r > 0$ that minimizes the value of A. Figure 5.41 suggests that such a value exists.

Notice from the graph that for small r (a tall thin container, like a piece of pipe), the term $2000/r$ dominates and A is large. For large r (a short wide container, like a pizza pan), the term $2\pi r^2$ dominates and A again is large.

Since A is differentiable on $r > 0$, an interval with no endpoints, it can have a minimum value only where its first derivative is zero.

$$\frac{dA}{dr} = 4\pi r - \frac{2000}{r^2}$$
$$0 = 4\pi r - \frac{2000}{r^2} \quad \text{Set } dA/dr = 0.$$
$$4\pi r^3 = 2000 \quad \text{Multiply by } r^2.$$
$$r = \sqrt[3]{\frac{500}{\pi}} \approx 5.419 \quad \text{Solve for } r.$$

Something happens at $r = \sqrt[3]{500/\pi}$, but what?

If the domain of A were a closed interval, we could find out by evaluating A at this critical point and the endpoints and comparing the results. But the domain is an open interval, so we must learn what is happening at $r = \sqrt[3]{500/\pi}$ by referring to the shape of A's graph. The second derivative

continued

Each example ends with a suggestion to **Now Try** a related exercise. Working the suggested exercise is an easy way for you to check your comprehension of the material while reading each section, instead of waiting until the end of each section or chapter to see if you "got it." True comprehension of the textbook is essential for your success on the AP* Exam.

Explorations appear throughout the text and provide you with the perfect opportunity to become an active learner and discover mathematics on your own. Honing your critical thinking and problem-solving skills will ultimately benefit you on all of your AP* Exams.

EXPLORATION 1 Constructing Cones

A cone of height h and radius r is constructed from a flat, circular disk of radius 4 in. by removing a sector AOC of arc length x in. and then connecting the edges OA and OC. What arc length x will produce the cone of maximum volume, and what is that volume?

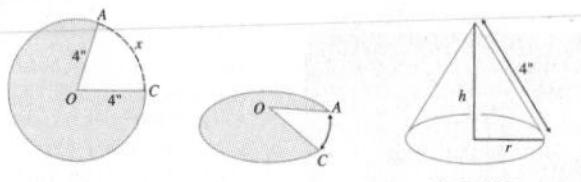

NOT TO SCALE

1. Show that

$$r = \frac{8\pi - x}{2\pi}, \quad h = \sqrt{16 - r^2}, \quad \text{and}$$
$$V(x) = \frac{\pi}{3}\left(\frac{8\pi - x}{2\pi}\right)^2 \sqrt{16 - \left(\frac{8\pi - x}{2\pi}\right)^2}$$

2. Show that the natural domain of V is $0 \le x \le 16\pi$. Graph V over this domain.
3. Explain why the restriction $0 \le x \le 8\pi$ makes sense in the problem situation. Graph V over this domain.
4. Use graphical methods to find where the cone has its maximum volume, and what that volume is.
5. Confirm your findings in part 4 analytically. [*Hint:* Use $V(x) = (1/3)\pi r^2 h$, $h^2 + r^2 = 16$, and the Chain Rule.]

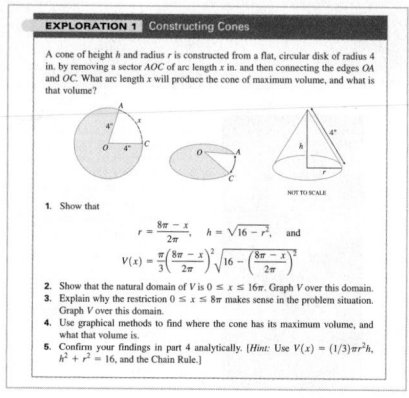

Each exercise set begins with a **Quick Review** to help you review skills needed in the exercise set, reminding you again that mathematics is not modular. Each Quick Review includes section references to show where these skills were covered earlier in the text. If you find these problems overly challenging, you should go back through the book and your notes to review the material covered in previous chapters. Remember, you need to *understand* the material from the *entire* calculus course for the AP* Calculus Exam, not just memorize the concepts from the last part of the course.

Quick Review 7.3 *(For help, go to Sections 4.3 and 4.4.)*

Exercise numbers with a gray background indicate problems that the authors have designed to be solved *without a calculator.*

In Exercises 1–4, find dy/dx.

1. $y = x^3 \sin 2x$
2. $y = e^{2x} \ln(3x + 1)$
3. $y = \tan^{-1} 2x$
4. $y = \sin^{-1}(x + 3)$

In Exercises 5 and 6, solve for x in terms of y.

5. $y = \tan^{-1} 3x$
6. $y = \cos^{-1}(x + 1)$
7. Find the area under the arch of the curve $y = \sin \pi x$ from $x = 0$ to $x = 1$.
8. Solve the differential equation $dy/dx = e^{2x}$.
9. Solve the initial value problem $dy/dx = x + \sin x$, $y(0) = 2$.
10. Use differentiation to confirm the integration formula

$$\int e^x \sin x \, dx = \frac{1}{2} e^x (\sin x - \cos x).$$

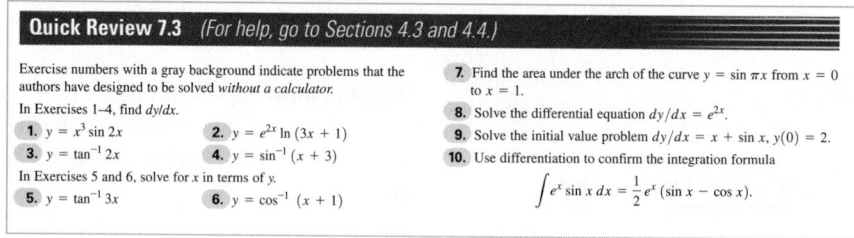

For exercises designed to be solved *without a calculator* the numbers of these exercises are printed in a grey oval. We encourage you to *support* the answers to these (and all) exercises graphically or numerically, but only after you have solved them with pencil and paper.

Standardized Test Questions

You may use a graphing calculator to solve the following problems.

61. **True or False** There is exactly one point in the plane with polar coordinates (2, 2). Justify your answer.
62. **True or False** The total area enclosed by the 3-petaled rose $r = \sin 3\theta$ is $\int_0^{2\pi} \frac{1}{2} \sin^2 3\theta d\theta$. Justify your answer.
63. **Multiple Choice** The area of the region enclosed by the polar graph of $r = \sqrt{3 + \cos \theta}$ is given by which integral?
(A) $\int_0^{2\pi} \sqrt{3 + \cos\theta}\, d\theta$ (B) $\int_0^{\pi} \sqrt{3 + \cos\theta}\, d\theta$
(C) $2\int_0^{\pi/2} (3 + \cos\theta)\, d\theta$ (D) $\int_0^{\pi} (3 + \cos\theta)\, d\theta$
(E) $\int_0^{\pi/2} \sqrt{3 + \cos\theta}\, d\theta$
64. **Multiple Choice** The area enclosed by one petal of the 3-petaled rose $r = 4\cos(3\theta)$ is given by which integral?
(A) $16\int_{-\pi/3}^{\pi/3} \cos(3\theta)\, d\theta$ (B) $8\int_{-\pi/6}^{\pi/6} \cos(3\theta)\, d\theta$
(C) $8\int_{-\pi/3}^{\pi/3} \cos^2(3\theta)\, d\theta$ (D) $16\int_{-\pi/6}^{\pi/6} \cos^2(3\theta)\, d\theta$
(E) $8\int_{-\pi/6}^{\pi/6} \cos^2(3\theta)\, d\theta$

Along with the standard types of exercises, including skill-based, application, writing, exploration, and extension questions, each exercise set includes a group of **Standardized Test Questions**. Each group includes two true-false with justifications and four multiple-choice questions, with instructions about the permitted use of your graphing calculator.

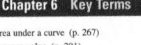

Chapter 6 Key Terms

area under a curve (p. 267)
average value (p. 291)
bounded function (p. 285)
cardiac output (p. 272)
characteristic function of the rationals (p. 286)
definite integral (p. 280)
differential calculus (p. 267)
dummy variable (p. 281)
error bounds (p. 315)
Fundamental Theorem of Calculus (p. 298)
integrable function (p. 280)
integral calculus (p. 267)
Integral Evaluation Theorem (p. 303)
integral of *f* from *a* to *b* (p. 280)
integral sign (p. 281)
integrand (p. 281)
lower bound (p. 290)
lower limit of integration (p. 281)
LRAM (p. 269)
mean value (p. 291)
Mean Value Theorem for Definite Integrals (p. 292)
MRAM (p. 269)
net area (p. 283)
NINT (p. 285)
norm of a partition (p. 279)
partition (p. 278)
Rectangular Approximation Method (RAM) (p. 269)
regular partition (p. 280)
Riemann sum (p. 278)
Riemann sum for *f* on the interval $[a, b]$ (p. 279)
RRAM (p. 269)
sigma notation (p. 278)
Simpson's Rule (p. 313)
subinterval (p. 279)
total area (p. 304)
Trapezoidal Rule (p. 311)
upper bound (p. 290)
upper limit of integration (p. 281)
variable of integration (p. 281)

Chapter 6 Review Exercises

Exercise numbers with a gray background indicate problems that the authors have designed to be solved *without a calculator.*

The collection of exercises marked in red could be used as a chapter test.

Exercises 1–6 refer to the region *R* in the first quadrant enclosed by the *x*-axis and the graph of the function $y = 4x - x^3$.

1. Sketch *R* and partition it into four subregions, each with a base of length $\Delta x = 1/2$.

6. Find the exact area of *R* by using the Fundamental Theorem of Calculus. 4

7. Use a calculator program to compute the RAM approximations in the following table for the area under the graph of $y = 1/x$ from $x = 1$ to $x = 5$.

n	LRAM_n	MRAM_n	RRAM_n
10	1.78204	1.60321	1.46204

Each chapter concludes with a list of **Key Terms**, with references back to where they are covered in the chapter, as well as **Chapter Review Exercises** to check your comprehension of the chapter material.

The **Quick Quiz for AP* Preparation** provides another opportunity to review your understanding as you progress through each chapter. A quiz appears after every two or three sections and asks you to answer questions about topics covered in those sections. Each quiz contains three multiple-choice questions and one free-response question of the AP* type. This continual reinforcement of ideas steers you away from rote memorization and toward the conceptual understanding needed for the AP* Calculus Exam.

Quick Quiz for AP* Preparation: Sections 5.4–5.6

You may use a graphing calculator to solve the following problems.

1. Multiple Choice If Newton's method is used to approximate the real root of $x^3 + 2x - 1 = 0$, what would the third approximation, x_3, be if the first approximation is $x_1 = 1$?
(A) 0.453 (B) 0.465 (C) 0.495 (D) 0.600 (E) 1.977

2. Multiple Choice The sides of a right triangle with legs *x* and *y* and hypotenuse *z* increase in such a way that $dz/dt = 1$ and $dx/dt = 3\,dy/dt$. At the instant when $x = 4$ and $y = 3$, what is dx/dt?
(A) $\frac{1}{3}$ (B) 1 (C) 2 (D) $\sqrt{5}$ (E) 5

3. Multiple Choice An observer 70 meters south of a railroad crossing watches an eastbound train traveling at 60 meters per second. At how many meters per second is the train moving away from the observer 4 seconds after it passes through the intersection?
(A) 57.60 (B) 57.88 (C) 59.20 (D) 60.00 (E) 67.40

4. Free Response (a) Approximate $\sqrt{26}$ by using the linearization of $y = \sqrt{x}$ at the point (25, 5). Show the computation that leads to your conclusion.
(b) Approximate $\sqrt{26}$ by using a first guess of 5 and one iteration of Newton's method to approximate the zero of $x^2 - 26$. Show the computation that leads to your conclusion.
(c) Approximate $\sqrt[3]{26}$ by using an appropriate linearization. Show the computation that leads to your conclusion.

AP* Examination Preparation

You may use a graphing calculator to solve the following problems.

53. Let *R* be the region in the first quadrant enclosed by the *y*-axis and the graphs of $y = 2 + \sin x$ and $y = \sec x$.
(a) Find the area of *R*.
(b) Find the volume of the solid generated when *R* is revolved about the *x*-axis.
(c) Find the volume of the solid whose base is *R* and whose cross sections cut by planes perpendicular to the *x*-axis are squares.

54. The temperature outside a house during a 24-hour period is given by

$$F(t) = 80 - 10\cos\left(\frac{\pi t}{12}\right), 0 \le t \le 24,$$

where $F(t)$ is measured in degrees Fahrenheit and *t* is measured in hours.
(a) Find the average temperature, to the nearest degree Fahrenheit, between $t = 6$ and $t = 14$.
(b) An air conditioner cooled the house whenever the outside temperature was at or above 78 degrees Fahrenheit. For what values of *t* was the air conditioner cooling the house?
(c) The cost of cooling the house accumulates at the rate of $0.05 per hour for each degree the outside temperature exceeds 78 degrees Fahrenheit. What was the total cost, to the nearest cent, to cool the house for this 24-hour period?

55. The rate at which people enter an amusement park on a given day is modeled by the function *E* defined by

$$E(t) = \frac{15600}{t^2 - 24t + 160}.$$

The rate at which people leave the same amusement park on the same day is modeled by the function *L* defined by

$$L(t) = \frac{9890}{t^2 - 38t + 370}.$$

Both $E(t)$ and $L(t)$ are measured in people per hour, and time *t* is measured in hours after midnight. These functions are valid for $9 \le t \le 23$, which are the hours that the park is open. At time $t = 9$, there are no people in the park.
(a) How many people have entered the park by 5:00 P.M. ($t = 17$)? Round your answer to the nearest whole number.
(b) The price of admission to the park is $15 until 5:00 P.M. ($t = 17$). After 5:00 P.M., the price of admission to the park is $11. How many dollars are collected from admissions to the park on the given day? Round your answer to the nearest whole number.
(c) Let $H(t) = \int_9^t (E(x) - L(x))\,dx$ for $9 \le t \le 23$. The value of $H(17)$ to the nearest whole number is 3725. Find the value of $H'(17)$ and explain the meaning of $H(17)$ and $H'(17)$ in the context of the park.
(d) At what time *t*, for $9 \le t \le 23$, does the model predict that the number of people in the park is a maximum?

An **AP* Examination Preparation** section appears at the end of each set of Chapter Review Exercises and includes three free-response questions of the AP* type. This set of questions, which also may or may not permit the use of your graphing calculator, gives you additional opportunity to practice skills and problem-solving techniques needed for the AP* Calculus Exam.

In addition to this text, *Pearson Education AP* Test Prep Series: AP* Calculus,* written by experienced AP* teachers, is also available to help you prepare for the AP* Calculus Exam. What does it include?

- **Text-specific correlations** between key AP* test topics and *Calculus: Graphical, Numerical, Algebraic*
- Reinforcement of the important **connections** between what you'll learn and what you'll be tested on in May
- 2 full **sample AB exams** & 2 **sample BC exams** including answers and explanation
- Test-Taking **strategies**

You can order *Pearson Education AP* Test Prep Series: AP* Calculus* by going online to PearsonSchool.com or calling 1-800-848-9500 and requesting ISBN 0-13-271121-4.

Contents

CHAPTER 3

CHAPTER 4

s swim serenely as seven swift sailb
Several silent swans swim serenely
ard to the sea. Several silent swans
ats sail southward to the sea. Several

CHAPTER 5

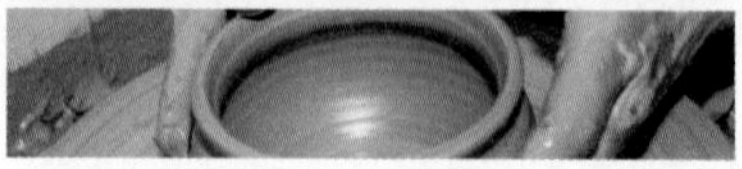

APPENDICES

CHAPTER 1 Prerequisites for Calculus

Exponential functions are used to model situations in which growth or decay changes dramatically. Such situations are found in nuclear power plants, which contain rods of plutonium-239, an extremely toxic radioactive isotope.

Operating at full capacity for one year, a 1000-megawatt power plant discharges about 435 lb of plutonium-239. With a half-life of 24,400 years, how much of the isotope will remain after 1000 years? This question can be answered with the mathematics covered in Section 1.3.

CHAPTER 1 Overview

This chapter reviews the most important things you need to know to start learning calculus. It also introduces the use of a graphing utility as a tool to investigate mathematical ideas, to support analytic work, and to solve problems with numerical and graphical methods. The emphasis is on functions and graphs, the main building blocks of calculus.

Functions and parametric equations are the major tools for describing the real world in mathematical terms, from temperature variations to planetary motions, from brain waves to business cycles, and from heartbeat patterns to population growth. Many functions have particular importance because of the behavior they describe. Trigonometric functions describe cyclic, repetitive activity; exponential, logarithmic, and logistic functions describe growth and decay; and polynomial functions can approximate these and most other functions.

1.1 Lines

What you will learn about . . .

- Increments
- Slope of a Line
- Parallel and Perpendicular Lines
- Equations of Lines
- Applications

and why . . .

Linear equations are used extensively in business and economic applications.

Increments

One reason calculus has proved to be so useful is that it is the right mathematics for relating the rate of change of a quantity to the graph of the quantity. Explaining that relationship is one goal of this book. It all begins with the slopes of lines.

When a particle in the plane moves from one point to another, the net changes or *increments* in its coordinates are found by subtracting the coordinates of its starting point from the coordinates of its stopping point.

DEFINITION Increments

If a particle moves from the point (x_1, y_1) to the point (x_2, y_2), the **increments** in its coordinates are

$$\Delta x = x_2 - x_1 \quad \text{and} \quad \Delta y = y_2 - y_1.$$

The symbols Δx and Δy are read "delta x" and "delta y." The letter Δ is a Greek capital d for "difference." Neither Δx nor Δy denotes multiplication; Δx is not "delta times x" nor is Δy "delta times y."

Increments can be positive, negative, or zero, as shown in Example 1.

EXAMPLE 1 Finding Increments

The coordinate increments from $(4, -3)$ to $(2, 5)$ are

$$\Delta x = 2 - 4 = -2, \quad \Delta y = 5 - (-3) = 8.$$

From $(5, 6)$ to $(5, 1)$, the increments are

$$\Delta x = 5 - 5 = 0, \quad \Delta y = 1 - 6 = -5.$$

Now Try Exercise 1.

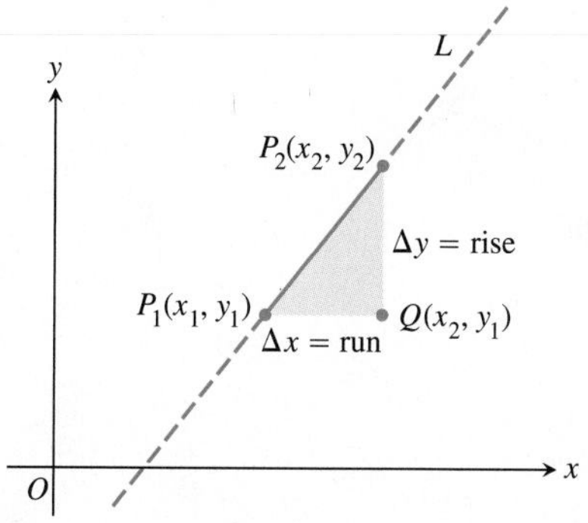

Figure 1.1 The slope of line L is

$$m = \frac{\text{rise}}{\text{run}} = \frac{\Delta y}{\Delta x}.$$

Slope of a Line

Each nonvertical line has a *slope,* which we can calculate from increments in coordinates.

Let L be a nonvertical line in the plane and $P_1(x_1, y_1)$ and $P_2(x_2, y_2)$ two points on L (Figure 1.1). We call $\Delta y = y_2 - y_1$ the **rise** from P_1 to P_2 and $\Delta x = x_2 - x_1$ the **run** from

P_1 to P_2. Since L is not vertical, $\Delta x \neq 0$ and we define the slope of L to be the amount of rise per unit of run. It is conventional to denote the slope by the letter m.

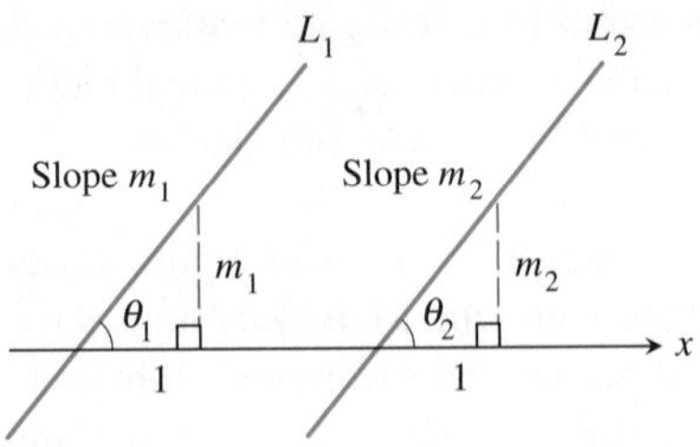

Figure 1.2 If $L_1 \| L_2$, then $\theta_1 = \theta_2$ and $m_1 = m_2$. Conversely, if $m_1 = m_2$, then $\theta_1 = \theta_2$ and $L_1 \| L_2$.

DEFINITION Slope

Let $P_1(x_1, y_1)$ and $P_2(x_2, y_2)$ be points on a nonvertical line, L. The **slope** of L is

$$m = \frac{\text{rise}}{\text{run}} = \frac{\Delta y}{\Delta x} = \frac{y_2 - y_1}{x_2 - x_1}.$$

A line that goes uphill as x increases has a positive slope. A line that goes downhill as x increases has a negative slope. A horizontal line has slope zero since all of its points have the same y-coordinate, making $\Delta y = 0$. For vertical lines, $\Delta x = 0$ and the ratio $\Delta y/\Delta x$ is undefined. We express this by saying that vertical lines *have no slope.*

Parallel and Perpendicular Lines

Parallel lines form equal angles with the x-axis (Figure 1.2). Hence, nonvertical parallel lines have the same slope. Conversely, lines with equal slopes form equal angles with the x-axis and are therefore parallel.

If two nonvertical lines L_1 and L_2 are perpendicular, their slopes m_1 and m_2 satisfy $m_1 m_2 = -1$, so each slope is the *negative reciprocal* of the other:

$$m_1 = -\frac{1}{m_2}, \quad m_2 = -\frac{1}{m_1}.$$

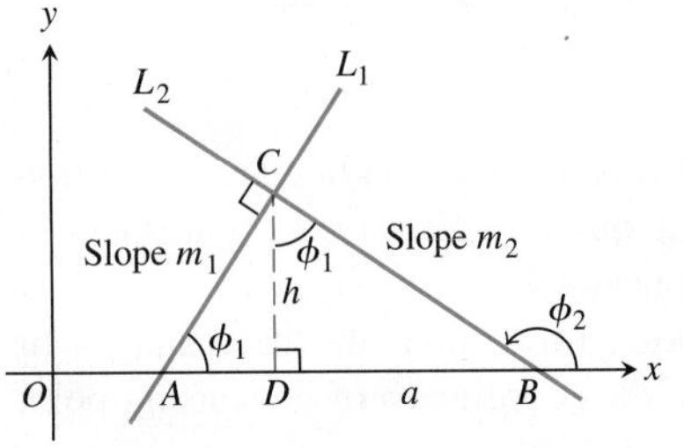

Figure 1.3 $\triangle ADC$ is similar to $\triangle CDB$. Hence ϕ_1 is also the upper angle in $\triangle CDB$, where $\tan \phi_1 = a/h$.

The argument goes like this: In the notation of Figure 1.3, $m_1 = \tan \phi_1 = a/h$, while $m_2 = \tan \phi_2 = -h/a$. Hence, $m_1 m_2 = (a/h)(-h/a) = -1$.

Equations of Lines

The vertical line through the point (a, b) has equation $x = a$ since every x-coordinate on the line has the value a. Similarly, the horizontal line through (a, b) has equation $y = b$.

EXAMPLE 2 Finding Equations of Vertical and Horizontal Lines

The vertical and horizontal lines through the point $(2, 3)$ have equations $x = 2$ and $y = 3$, respectively (Figure 1.4). ***Now Try Exercise 9.***

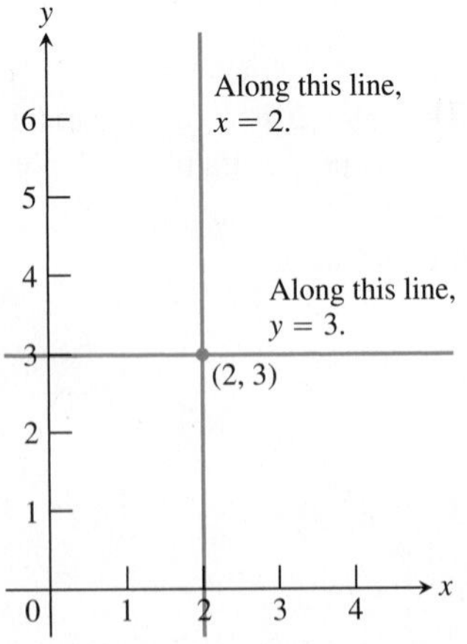

Figure 1.4 The standard equations for the vertical and horizontal lines through the point $(2, 3)$ are $x = 2$ and $y = 3$. (Example 2)

We can write an equation for any nonvertical line L if we know its slope m and the coordinates of one point $P_1(x_1, y_1)$ on it. If $P(x, y)$ is *any* other point on L, then

$$\frac{y - y_1}{x - x_1} = m,$$

so that

$$y - y_1 = m(x - x_1) \quad \text{or} \quad y = m(x - x_1) + y_1.$$

DEFINITION Point-Slope Equation

The equation

$$y = m(x - x_1) + y_1$$

is the **point-slope equation** of the line through the point (x_1, y_1) with slope m.

EXAMPLE 3 Using the Point-Slope Equation

Write the point-slope equation for the line through the point $(2, 3)$ with slope $-3/2$.

SOLUTION

We substitute $x_1 = 2$, $y_1 = 3$, and $m = -3/2$ into the point-slope equation and obtain

$$y = -\frac{3}{2}(x - 2) + 3 \quad \text{or} \quad y = -\frac{3}{2}x + 6.$$

Now Try Exercise 13.

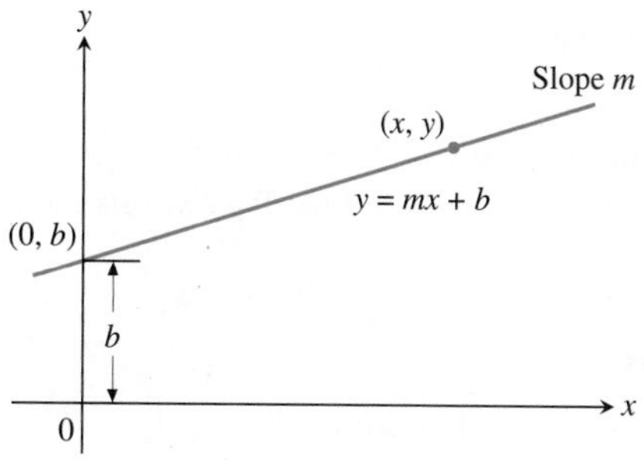

Figure 1.5 A line with slope m and y-intercept b.

The y-coordinate of the point where a nonvertical line intersects the y-axis is the **y-intercept** of the line. Similarly, the x-coordinate of the point where a nonhorizontal line intersects the x-axis is the **x-intercept** of the line. A line with slope m and **y-intercept** b passes through $(0, b)$ (Figure 1.5), so

$$y = m(x - 0) + b, \quad \text{or, more simply,} \quad y = mx + b.$$

DEFINITION Slope-Intercept Equation

The equation

$$y = mx + b$$

is the **slope-intercept equation** of the line with slope m and y-intercept b.

EXAMPLE 4 Writing the Slope-Intercept Equation

Write the slope-intercept equation for the line through $(-2, -1)$ and $(3, 4)$.

SOLUTION

The line's slope is

$$m = \frac{4 - (-1)}{3 - (-2)} = \frac{5}{5} = 1.$$

We can use this slope with either of the two given points in the point-slope equation. For $(x_1, y_1) = (-2, -1)$, we obtain

$$y = 1 \cdot (x - (-2)) + (-1)$$
$$y = x + 2 + (-1)$$
$$y = x + 1.$$

Now Try Exercise 17.

If A and B are not both zero, the graph of the equation $Ax + By = C$ is a line. Every line has an equation in this form, even lines with undefined slopes.

DEFINITION General Linear Equation

The equation

$$Ax + By = C \quad (A \text{ and } B \text{ not both } 0)$$

is a **general linear equation** in x and y.

Although the general linear form helps in the quick identification of lines, the slope-intercept form is the one to enter into a calculator for graphing.

$y = -\frac{8}{5}x + 4$

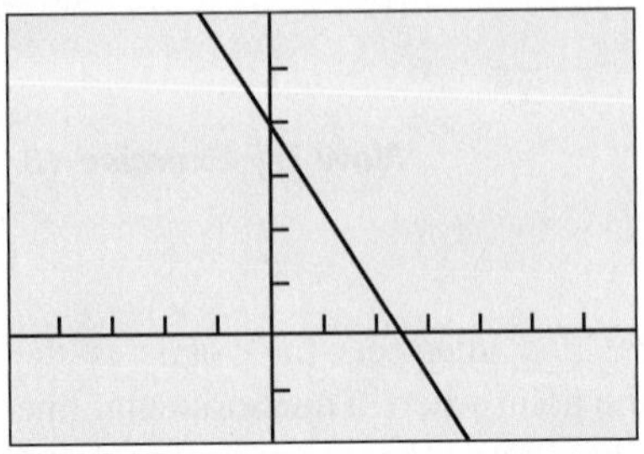

[–5, 7] by [–2, 6]

Figure 1.6 The line $8x + 5y = 20$. (Example 5)

EXAMPLE 5 Analyzing and Graphing a General Linear Equation

Find the slope and y-intercept of the line $8x + 5y = 20$. Graph the line.

SOLUTION

Solve the equation for y to put the equation in slope-intercept form:

$$8x + 5y = 20$$
$$5y = -8x + 20$$
$$y = -\frac{8}{5}x + 4$$

This form reveals the slope $(m = -8/5)$ and y-intercept $(b = 4)$, and puts the equation in a form suitable for graphing (Figure 1.6). ***Now Try Exercise 27.***

EXAMPLE 6 Writing Equations for Lines

Write an equation for the line through the point $(-1, 2)$ that is **(a)** parallel, and **(b)** perpendicular to the line L: $y = 3x - 4$.

SOLUTION

The line L, $y = 3x - 4$, has slope 3.

(a) The line $y = 3(x + 1) + 2$, or $y = 3x + 5$, passes through the point $(-1, 2)$, and is parallel to L because it has slope 3.

(b) The line $y = (-1/3)(x + 1) + 2$, or $y = (-1/3)x + 5/3$, passes through the point $(-1, 2)$, and is perpendicular to L because it has slope $-1/3$. ***Now Try Exercise 31.***

EXAMPLE 7 Determining a Function

The following table gives values for the linear function $f(x) = mx + b$. Determine m and b.

x	$f(x)$
-1	$14/3$
1	$-4/3$
2	$-13/3$

SOLUTION

The graph of f is a line. From the table we know that the following points are on the line: $(-1, 14/3)$, $(1, -4/3)$, $(2, -13/3)$.

Using the first two points, the slope m is

$$m = \frac{-4/3 - (14/3)}{1 - (-1)} = \frac{-6}{2} = -3.$$

So $f(x) = -3x + b$. Because $f(-1) = 14/3$, we have

$$f(-1) = -3(-1) + b$$
$$14/3 = 3 + b$$
$$b = 5/3.$$

continued

Thus, $m = -3$, $b = 5/3$, and $f(x) = -3x + 5/3$.

We can use either of the other two points determined by the table to check our work.

Now Try Exercise 35.

Applications

Many important variables are related by linear equations. For example, the relationship between Fahrenheit temperature and Celsius temperature is linear, a fact we use to advantage in the next example.

EXAMPLE 8 Temperature Conversion

Find the relationship between Fahrenheit and Celsius temperature. Then find the Celsius equivalent of 90°F and the Fahrenheit equivalent of -5°C.

SOLUTION

Because the relationship between the two temperature scales is linear, it has the form $F = mC + b$. The freezing point of water is $F = 32°$ or $C = 0°$, while the boiling point is $F = 212°$ or $C = 100°$. Thus,

$$32 = m \cdot 0 + b \quad \text{and} \quad 212 = m \cdot 100 + b,$$

so $b = 32$ and $m = (212 - 32)/100 = 9/5$. Therefore,

$$F = \frac{9}{5}C + 32, \quad \text{or} \quad C = \frac{5}{9}(F - 32).$$

These relationships let us find equivalent temperatures. The Celsius equivalent of 90°F is

$$C = \frac{5}{9}(90 - 32) \approx 32.2°.$$

The Fahrenheit equivalent of -5°C is

$$F = \frac{9}{5}(-5) + 32 = 23°.$$

Now Try Exercise 43.

Some graphing utilities have a feature that enables them to approximate the relationship between variables with a linear equation. We use this feature in Example 9.

It can be difficult to see patterns or trends in lists of paired numbers. For this reason, we sometimes begin by plotting the pairs (such a plot is called a **scatter plot**) to see whether the corresponding points lie close to a curve of some kind. If they do, and if we can find an equation $y = f(x)$ for the curve, then we have a formula that

1. summarizes the data with a simple expression, and
2. lets us predict values of y for other values of x.

The process of finding a curve to fit data is called **regression analysis** and the curve is called a **regression curve.**

There are many useful types of regression curves—power, exponential, logarithmic, sinusoidal, and so on. In the next example, we use the calculator's linear regression feature to fit the data in Table 1.1 with a line.

TABLE 1.1 World Population

Year	Population (millions)
1980	4454
1985	4853
1990	5285
1995	5696
2003	6305
2004	6378
2005	6450

Source: U.S. Bureau of the Census, *Statistical Abstract of the United States, 2004–2005 and 2010.*

EXAMPLE 9 Regression Analysis—Predicting World Population

Starting with the data in Table 1.1, build a linear model for the growth of the world population. Use the model to predict the world population in the year 2015, and compare this prediction with the Statistical Abstract prediction of 7229 million.

continued

Why Not Round the Decimals in Equation 1 Even More?

If we do, our final calculation will be way off. Using $y = 80x - 153{,}849$, for instance, gives $y = 7351$ when $x = 2015$, as compared to $y = 7265$, an increase of 86 million. The rule is: *Retain all decimal places while working a problem. Round only at the end.* We rounded the coefficients in Equation 1 enough to make it readable, but not enough to hurt the outcome. However, we knew how much we could safely round *only from first having done the entire calculation with numbers unrounded.*

SOLUTION

Model Upon entering the data into the grapher, we find the regression equation to be approximately

$$y = 79.957x - 153848.716, \tag{1}$$

where x represents the year and y the population *in millions.*

Figure 1.7a shows the scatter plot for Table 1.1 together with a graph of the regression line just found. You can see how well the line fits the data.

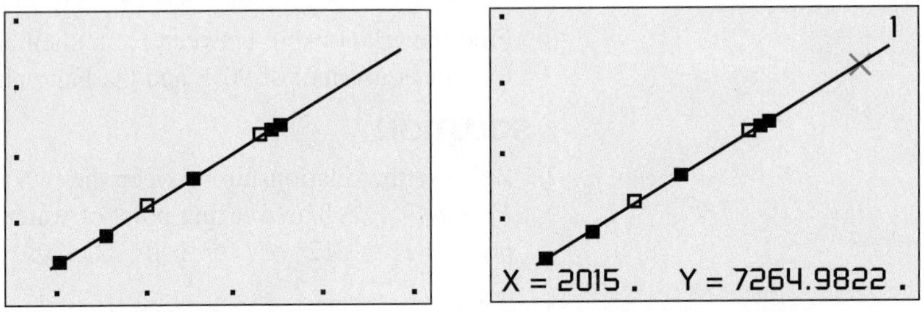

[1975, 2020] by [4000, 7500]

(a)

[1975, 2020] by [4000, 7500]

(b)

Figure 1.7 (Example 9)

Solve Graphically Our goal is to predict the population in the year 2015. Reading from the graph in Figure 1.7b, we conclude that when x is 2015, y is approximately 7265.

Confirm Algebraically Evaluating Equation 1 for $x = 2015$ gives

$$y = 79.957(2015) - 153848.716$$
$$\approx 7265.$$

Interpret The linear regression equation suggests that the world population in the year 2015 will be about 7265 million, or approximately 36 million more than the Statistical Abstract prediction of 7229 million. ***Now Try Exercise 45.***

Rounding Rule

Round your answer as appropriate, but do not round the numbers in the calculations that lead to it.

Regression Analysis

Regression analysis has four steps:

1. Plot the data (scatter plot).
2. Find the regression equation. For a line, it has the form $y = mx + b$.
3. Superimpose the graph of the regression equation on the scatter plot to see the fit.
4. Use the regression equation to predict y-values for particular values of x.

Quick Review 1.1 (For help, go to Section 1.1.)

Exercise numbers with a gray background indicate problems that the authors have designed to be solved *without a calculator.*

1. Find the value of y that corresponds to $x = 3$ in $y = -2 + 4(x - 3)$.

2. Find the value of x that corresponds to $y = 3$ in $y = 3 - 2(x + 1)$.

In Exercises 3 and 4, find the value of m that corresponds to the values of x and y.

3. $x = 5, \quad y = 2, \quad m = \dfrac{y - 3}{x - 4}$

4. $x = -1, \quad y = -3, \quad m = \dfrac{2 - y}{3 - x}$

In Exercises 5 and 6, determine whether the ordered pair is a solution to the equation.

5. $3x - 4y = 5$
(a) $(2, 1/4)$ **(b)** $(3, -1)$

6. $y = -2x + 5$
(a) $(-1, 7)$ **(b)** $(-2, 1)$

In Exercises 7 and 8, find the distance between the points.

7. $(1, 0), \quad (0, 1)$

8. $(2, 1), \quad (1, -1/3)$

In Exercises 9 and 10, solve for y in terms of x.

9. $4x - 3y = 7$

10. $-2x + 5y = -3$

Section 1.1 Exercises

Exercise numbers with a gray background indicate problems that the authors have designed to be solved *without a calculator.*

In Exercises 1–4, find the coordinate increments from A to B.

1. $A(1, 2), \ B(-1, -1)$

2. $A(-3, 2), \ B(-1, -2)$

3. $A(-3, 1), \ B(-8, 1)$

4. $A(0, 4), \ B(0, -2)$

In Exercises 5–8, let L be the line determined by points A and B.

(a) Plot A and B. **(b)** Find the slope of L.

(c) Draw the graph of L.

5. $A(1, -2), \quad B(2, 1)$

6. $A(-2, -1), \quad B(1, -2)$

7. $A(2, 3), \quad B(-1, 3)$

8. $A(1, 2), \quad B(1, -3)$

In Exercise 9–12, write an equation for **(a)** the vertical line and **(b)** the horizontal line through the point P.

9. $P(3, 2)$

10. $P(-1, 4/3)$

11. $P(0, -\sqrt{2})$

12. $P(-\pi, 0)$

In Exercises 13–16, write the point-slope equation for the line through the point P with slope m.

13. $P(1, 1), \quad m = 1$

14. $P(-1, 1), \quad m = -1$

15. $P(0, 3), \quad m = 2$

16. $P(-4, 0), \quad m = -2$

In Exercises 17–20, write the slope-intercept equation for the line with slope m and y-intercept b.

17. $m = 3, \quad b = -2$

18. $m = -1, \quad b = 2$

19. $m = -1/2, \quad b = -3$

20. $m = 1/3, \quad b = -1$

In Exercises 21–24, write a general linear equation for the line through the two points.

21. $(0, 0), \quad (2, 3)$

22. $(1, 1), \quad (2, 1)$

23. $(-2, 0), \quad (-2, -2)$

24. $(-2, 1), \quad (2, -2)$

In Exercises 25 and 26, the line contains the origin and the point in the upper right corner of the grapher screen. Write an equation for the line.

25.

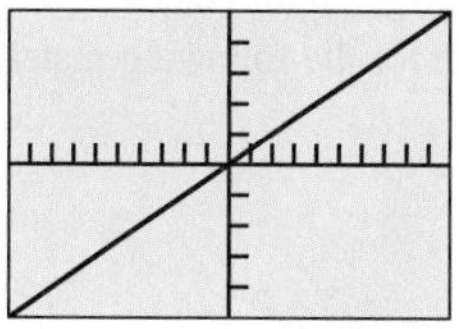

[–10, 10] by [–25, 25]

26.

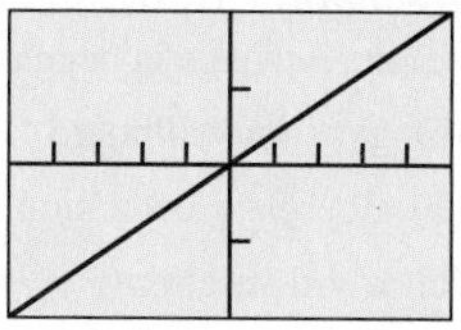

[–5, 5] by [–2, 2]

In Exercises 27–30, find the **(a)** slope and **(b)** y-intercept, and **(c)** graph the line.

27. $3x + 4y = 12$

28. $x + y = 2$

29. $\dfrac{x}{3} + \dfrac{y}{4} = 1$

30. $y = 2x + 4$

In Exercises 31–34, write an equation for the line through P that is **(a)** parallel to L, and **(b)** perpendicular to L.

31. $P(0, 0), \quad L: y = -x + 2$

32. $P(-2, 2), \quad L: 2x + y = 4$

33. $P(-2, 4), \quad L: x = 5$

34. $P(-1, 1/2), \quad L: y = 3$

In Exercises 35 and 36, a table of values is given for the linear function $f(x) = mx + b$. Determine m and b.

35.

x	$f(x)$
1	2
3	9
5	16

36.

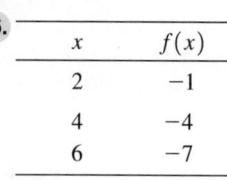

x	$f(x)$
2	−1
4	−4
6	−7

In Exercises 37 and 38, find the value of x or y for which the line through A and B has the given slope m.

37. $A(-2, 3),\quad B(4, y),\quad m = -2/3$

38. $A(-8, -2),\quad B(x, 2),\quad m = 2$

39. ***Revisiting Example 4*** Show that you get the same equation in Example 4 if you use the point $(3, 4)$ to write the equation.

40. **Writing to Learn *x- and y-intercepts***

(a) Explain why c and d are the x-intercept and y-intercept, respectively, of the line

$$\frac{x}{c} + \frac{y}{d} = 1.$$

(b) How are the x-intercept and y-intercept related to c and d in the line

$$\frac{x}{c} + \frac{y}{d} = 2?$$

41. ***Parallel and Perpendicular Lines*** For what value of k are the two lines $2x + ky = 3$ and $x + y = 1$ **(a)** parallel? **(b)** perpendicular?

Group Activity In Exercises 42–44, work in groups of two or three to solve the problem.

42. ***Insulation*** By measuring slopes in the figure below, find the temperature change in degrees per inch for the following materials.

(a) gypsum wallboard

(b) fiberglass insulation

(c) wood sheathing

(d) **Writing to Learn** Which of the materials in (a)–(c) is the best insulator? the poorest? Explain.

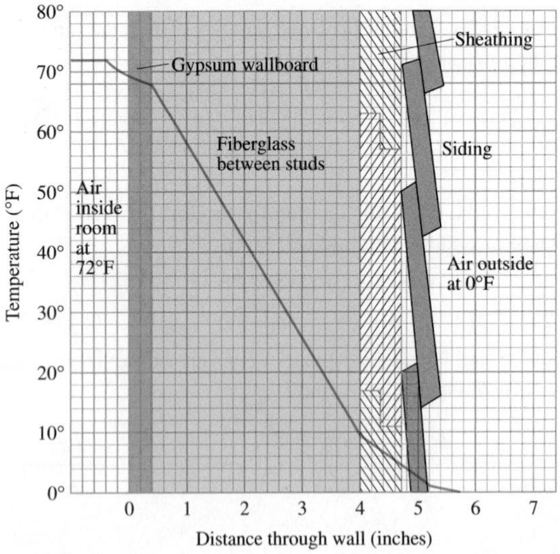

43. ***Pressure Under Water*** The pressure p experienced by a diver under water is related to the diver's depth d by an equation of the form $p = kd + 1$ (k a constant). When $d = 0$ meters, the pressure is 1 atmosphere. The pressure at 100 meters is 10.94 atmospheres. Find the pressure at 50 meters.

44. ***Modeling Distance Traveled*** A car starts from point P at time $t = 0$ and travels at 45 mph.

(a) Write an expression $d(t)$ for the distance the car travels from P.

(b) Graph $y = d(t)$.

(c) What is the slope of the graph in (b)? What does it have to do with the car?

(d) **Writing to Learn** Create a scenario in which t could have negative values.

(e) **Writing to Learn** Create a scenario in which the y-intercept of $y = d(t)$ could be 30.

In Exercises 45 and 46, use linear regression analysis.

45. Table 1.2 shows the mean annual compensation of construction workers.

TABLE 1.2 Construction Workers' Average Annual Compensation

Year	Annual Total Compensation (dollars)
1999	42,598
2000	44,764
2001	47,822
2002	48,966

Source: U.S. Bureau of the Census, *Statistical Abstract of the United States, 2004–2005.*

(a) Find the linear regression equation for the data.

(b) Find the slope of the regression line. What does the slope represent?

(c) Superimpose the graph of the linear regression equation on a scatter plot of the data.

(d) Use the regression equation to predict the construction workers' average annual compensation in the year 2008.

46. Table 1.3 lists the ages and weights of nine girls.

TABLE 1.3 Girls' Ages and Weights

Age (months)	Weight (pounds)
19	22
21	23
24	25
27	28
29	31
31	28
34	32
38	34
43	39

(a) Find the linear regression equation for the data.

(b) Find the slope of the regression line. What does the slope represent?

(c) Superimpose the graph of the linear regression equation on a scatter plot of the data.

(d) Use the regression equation to predict the approximate weight of a 30-month-old girl.

Standardized Test Questions

47. True or False The slope of a vertical line is zero. Justify your answer.

48. True or False The slope of a line perpendicular to the line $y = mx + b$ is $1/m$. Justify your answer.

49. Multiple Choice Which of the following is an equation of the line through $(-3, 4)$ with slope $1/2$?

(A) $y - 4 = \frac{1}{2}(x + 3)$ **(B)** $y + 3 = \frac{1}{2}(x - 4)$

(C) $y - 4 = -2(x + 3)$ **(D)** $y - 4 = 2(x + 3)$

(E) $y + 3 = 2(x - 4)$

50. Multiple Choice Which of the following is an equation of the vertical line through $(-2, 4)$?

(A) $y = 4$ **(B)** $x = 2$ **(C)** $y = -4$

(D) $x = 0$ **(E)** $x = -2$

51. Multiple Choice Which of the following is the x-intercept of the line $y = 2x - 5$?

(A) $x = -5$ **(B)** $x = 5$ **(C)** $x = 0$

(D) $x = 5/2$ **(E)** $x = -5/2$

52. Multiple Choice Which of the following is an equation of the line through $(-2, -1)$ parallel to the line $y = -3x + 1$?

(A) $y = -3x + 5$ **(B)** $y = -3x - 7$ **(C)** $y = \frac{1}{3}x - \frac{1}{3}$

(D) $y = -3x + 1$ **(E)** $y = -3x - 4$

Extending the Ideas

53. The median price of existing single-family homes has increased consistently during the past few years. However, the data in Table 1.4 show that there have been differences in various parts of the country.

TABLE 1.4 Median Price of Single-Family Homes

Year	South (dollars)	West (dollars)
1999	145,900	173,700
2000	148,000	196,400
2001	155,400	213,600
2002	163,400	238,500
2003	168,100	260,900

Source: U.S. Bureau of the Census, *Statistical Abstract of the United States, 2004–2005.*

(a) Find the linear regression equation for home cost in the South.

(b) What does the slope of the regression line represent?

(c) Find the linear regression equation for home cost in the West.

(d) Where is the median price increasing more rapidly, in the South or the West?

54. *Fahrenheit Versus Celsius* We found a relationship between Fahrenheit temperature and Celsius temperature in Example 8.

(a) Is there a temperature at which a Fahrenheit thermometer and a Celsius thermometer give the same reading? If so, what is it?

(b) Writing to Learn Graph $y_1 = (9/5)x + 32$, $y_2 = (5/9)(x - 32)$, and $y_3 = x$ in the same viewing window. Explain how this figure is related to the question in part (a).

55. *Parallelogram* Three different parallelograms have vertices at $(-1, 1)$, $(2, 0)$, and $(2, 3)$. Draw the three and give the coordinates of the missing vertices.

56. *Parallelogram* Show that if the midpoints of consecutive sides of any quadrilateral are connected, the result is a parallelogram.

57. *Tangent Line* Consider the circle of radius 5 centered at $(0, 0)$. Find an equation of the line tangent to the circle at the point $(3, 4)$.

58. Group Activity *Distance from a Point to a Line* This activity investigates how to find the distance from a point $P(a, b)$ to a line L: $Ax + By = C$.

(a) Write an equation for the line M through P perpendicular to L.

(b) Find the coordinates of the point Q in which M and L intersect.

(c) Find the distance from P to Q.

1.2 Functions and Graphs

What you will learn about . . .

- Functions
- Domains and Ranges
- Viewing and Interpreting Graphs
- Even Functions and Odd Functions—Symmetry
- Functions Defined in Pieces
- Absolute Value Function
- Composite Functions

and why . . .

Functions and graphs form the basis for understanding mathematics and applications.

Functions

The values of one variable often depend on the values for another:

- The temperature at which water boils depends on elevation (the boiling point drops as you go up).
- The amount by which your savings will grow in a year depends on the interest rate offered by the bank.
- The area of a circle depends on the circle's radius.

In each of these examples, the value of one variable quantity depends on the value of another. For example, the boiling temperature of water, b, depends on the elevation, e; the amount of interest, I, depends on the interest rate, r. We call b and I **dependent variables** because they are determined by the values of the variables e and r on which they depend. The variables e and r are **independent variables.**

A rule that assigns to each element in one set a unique element in another set is called a *function.* The sets may be sets of any kind and do not have to be the same. A function is like a machine that assigns a unique output to every allowable input. The inputs make up the **domain** of the function; the outputs make up the **range** (Figure 1.8).

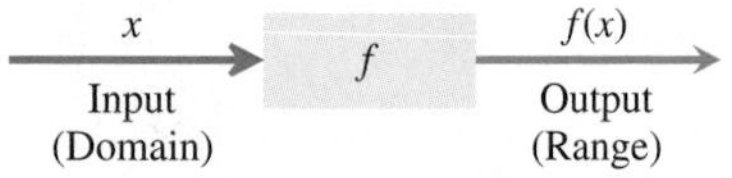

Figure 1.8 A "machine" diagram for a function.

DEFINITION Function

A **function** from a set D to a set R is a rule that assigns a unique element in R to each element in D.

In this definition, D is the domain of the function and R is a set *containing* the range (Figure 1.9).

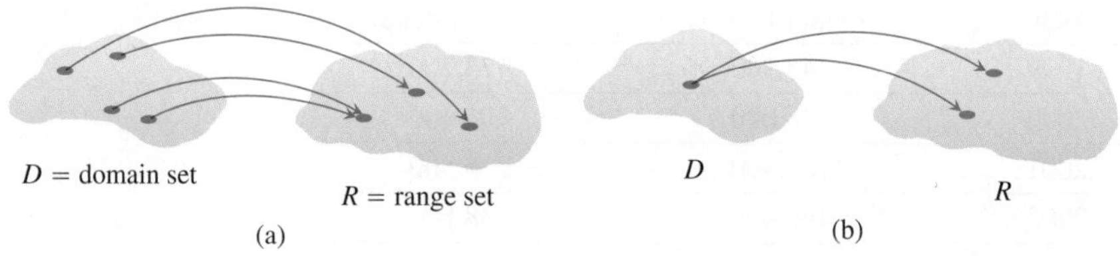

Figure 1.9 (a) A function from a set D to a set R. (b) *Not* a function. The assignment is not unique.

Leonhard Euler (1707–1783)

Leonhard Euler, the dominant mathematical figure of his century and the most prolific mathematician ever, was also an astronomer, physicist, botanist, and chemist, and an expert in oriental languages. His work was the first to give the function concept the prominence that it has in mathematics today. Euler's collected books and papers fill 72 volumes. This does not count his enormous correspondence to approximately 300 addresses. His introductory algebra text, written originally in German (Euler was Swiss), is still available in English translation.

Euler invented a symbolic way to say "y is a function of x":

$$y = f(x),$$

which we read as "y equals f of x." This notation enables us to give different functions different names by changing the letters we use. To say that the boiling point of water is a function of elevation, we can write $b = f(e)$. To say that the area of a circle is a function of the circle's radius, we can write $A = A(r)$, giving the function the same name as the dependent variable.

The notation $y = f(x)$ gives a way to denote specific values of a function. The value of f at a can be written as $f(a)$, read "f of a."

EXAMPLE 1 The Circle-Area Function

Write a formula that expresses the area of a circle as a function of its radius. Use the formula to find the area of a circle of radius 2 in.

SOLUTION

If the radius of the circle is r, then the area $A(r)$ of the circle can be expressed as $A(r) = \pi r^2$. The area of a circle of radius 2 can be found by evaluating the function $A(r)$ at $r = 2$.

$$A(2) = \pi(2)^2 = 4\pi$$

The area of a circle of radius 2 is 4π in^2. ***Now Try Exercise 3.***

Domains and Ranges

In Example 1, the domain of the function is restricted by context: The independent variable is a radius and must be positive. When we define a function $y = f(x)$ with a formula and the domain is not stated explicitly or restricted by context, the domain is assumed to be the largest set of x-values for which the formula gives real y-values—the so-called **natural domain.** If we want to restrict the domain, we must say so. The domain of $y = x^2$ is understood to be the entire set of real numbers. We must write "$y = x^2, x > 0$" if we want to restrict the function to positive values of x.

The domains and ranges of many real-valued functions of a real variable are intervals or combinations of intervals. The intervals may be open, closed, or half-open (Figures 1.10 and 1.11) and finite or infinite (Figure 1.12).

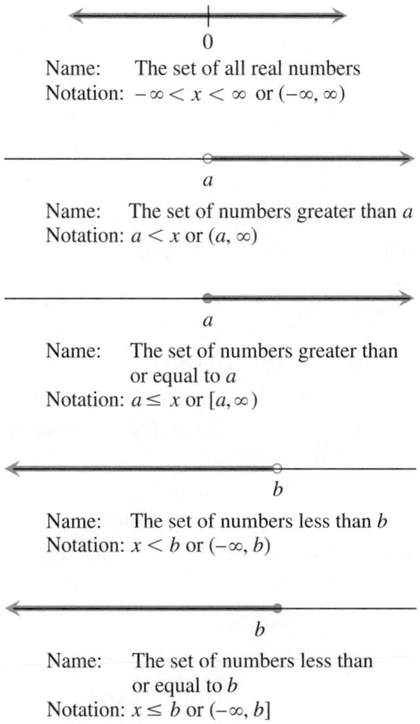

Figure 1.12 Infinite intervals—rays on the number line and the number line itself. The symbol ∞ (infinity) is used merely for convenience; it does not mean there is a number ∞.

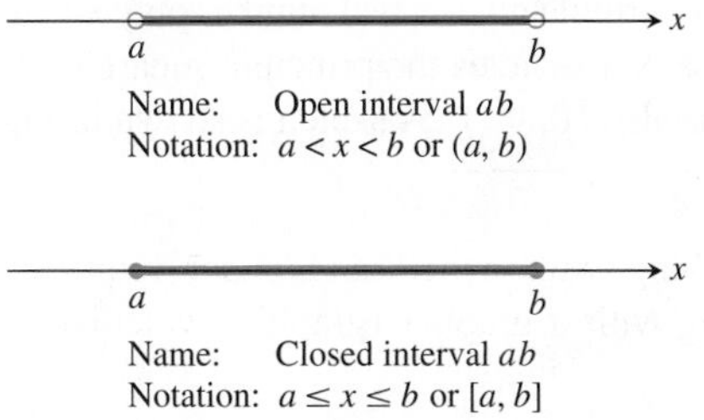

Figure 1.10 Open and closed finite intervals.

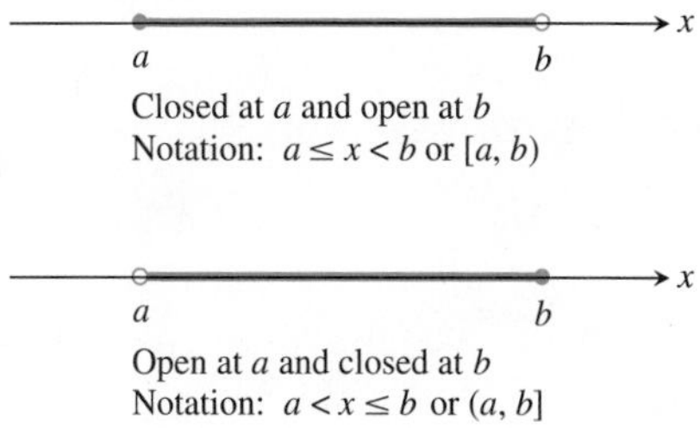

Figure 1.11 Half-open finite intervals.

The endpoints of an interval make up the interval's **boundary** and are called **boundary points.** The remaining points make up the interval's **interior** and are called **interior points. Closed intervals** contain their boundary points. **Open intervals** contain no boundary points. Every point of an open interval is an interior point of the interval.

Viewing and Interpreting Graphs

The points (x, y) in the plane whose coordinates are the input-output pairs of a function $y = f(x)$ make up the function's **graph.** The graph of the function $y = x + 2$, for example, is the set of points with coordinates (x, y) for which y equals $x + 2$.

EXAMPLE 2 Identifying Domain and Range of a Function

Identify the domain and range, and then sketch a graph of the function.

(a) $y = \dfrac{1}{x}$ **(b)** $y = \sqrt{x}$

SOLUTION

(a) The formula gives a real y-value for every real x-value except $x = 0$. (*We cannot divide any number by* 0.) The domain is $(-\infty, 0) \cup (0, \infty)$. The value y takes on every real number except $y = 0$. ($y = c \neq 0$ if $x = 1/c$). The range is also $(-\infty, 0) \cup (0, \infty)$. A sketch is shown in Figure 1.13a.

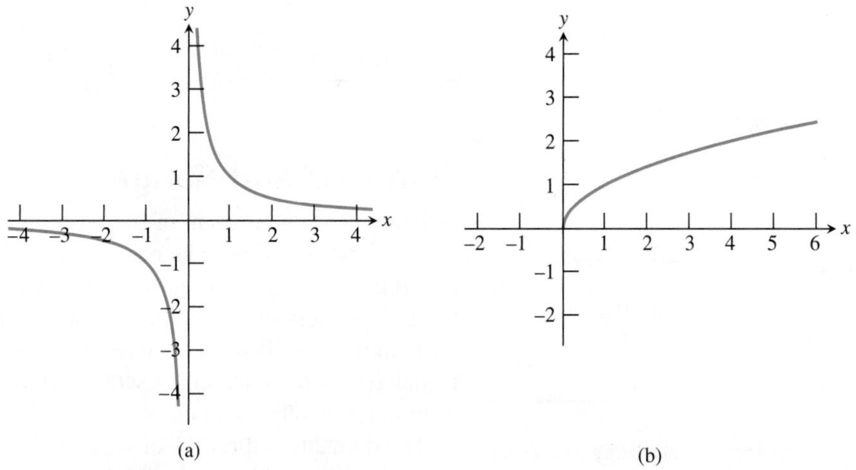

Figure 1.13 A sketch of the graph of (a) $y = 1/x$ and (b) $y = \sqrt{x}$. (Example 2)

(b) The formula gives a real number only when x is positive or zero. The domain is $[0, \infty)$. Because $\sqrt{x}$ denotes the principal square root of x, y is greater than or equal to zero. The range is also $[0, \infty)$. A sketch is shown in Figure 1.13b. ***Now Try Exercise 9.***

Graphing with pencil and paper requires that you develop graph *drawing* skills. Graphing with a grapher (graphing calculator) requires that you develop graph *viewing* skills.

Power Function

Any function that can be written in the form $f(x) = kx^a$, where k and a are nonzero constants, is a **power function.**

Graph Viewing Skills

1. Recognize that the graph is reasonable.
2. See all the important characteristics of the graph.
3. Interpret those characteristics.
4. Recognize grapher failure.

Being able to recognize that a graph is reasonable comes with experience. You need to know the basic functions, their graphs, and how changes in their equations affect the graphs.

Grapher failure occurs when the graph produced by a grapher is less than precise—or even incorrect—usually due to the limitations of the screen resolution of the grapher.

EXAMPLE 3 Identifying Domain and Range of a Function

Use a grapher to identify the domain and range, and then draw a graph of the function.

(a) $y = \sqrt{4 - x^2}$ **(b)** $y = x^{2/3}$

SOLUTION

(a) Figure 1.14a shows a graph of the function for $-4.7 \leq x \leq 4.7$ and $-3.1 \leq y \leq 3.1$, that is, the viewing window $[-4.7, 4.7]$ by $[-3.1, 3.1]$, with x-scale $= y$-scale $= 1$. The graph appears to be the upper half of a circle. The domain appears to be $[-2, 2]$. This observation is correct because we must have $4 - x^2 \geq 0$, or equivalently, $-2 \leq x \leq 2$. The range appears to be $[0, 2]$, which can also be verified algebraically.

Graphing $y = x^{2/3}$—Possible Grapher Failure

On some graphing calculators you need to enter this function as $y = (x^2)^{1/3}$ or $y = (x^{1/3})^2$ to obtain a correct graph. Try graphing this function on your grapher.

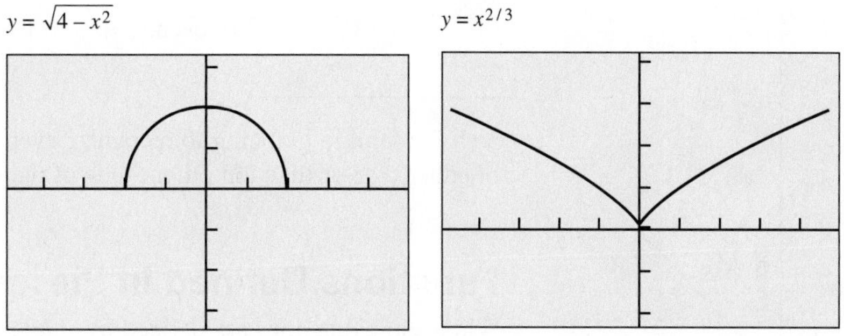

[–4.7, 4.7] by [–3.1, 3.1]

(a)

[–4.7, 4.7] by [–2, 4]

(b)

Figure 1.14 The graph of (a) $y = \sqrt{4 - x^2}$ and (b) $y = x^{2/3}$. (Example 3)

(b) Figure 1.14b shows a graph of the function in the viewing window $[-4.7, 4.7]$ by $[-2, 4]$, with x-scale $= y$-scale $= 1$. The domain appears to be $(-\infty, \infty)$, which we can verify by observing that $x^{2/3} = (\sqrt[3]{x})^2$. Also the range is $[0, \infty)$ by the same observation.

Now Try Exercise 15.

Even Functions and Odd Functions—Symmetry

The graphs of *even* and *odd* functions have important symmetry properties.

DEFINITIONS Even Function, Odd Function

A function $y = f(x)$ is an

even function of *x* if $f(-x) = f(x)$,

odd function of *x* if $f(-x) = -f(x)$,

for every x in the function's domain.

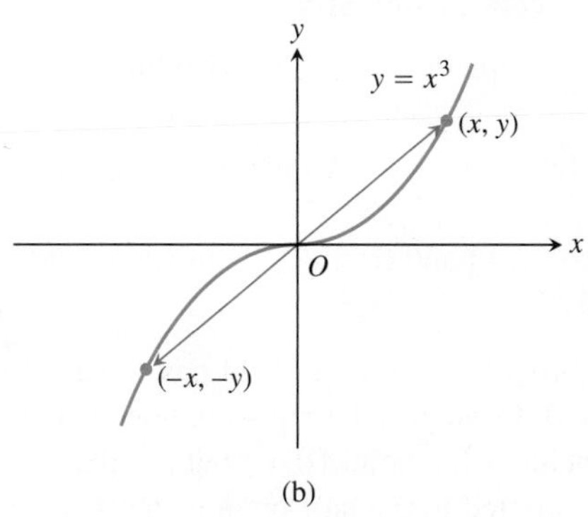

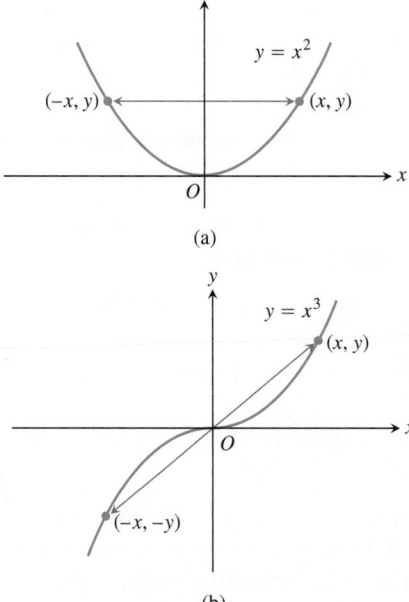

Figure 1.15 (a) The graph of $y = x^2$ (an even function) is symmetric about the y-axis. (b) The graph of $y = x^3$ (an odd function) is symmetric about the origin.

The names even and odd come from powers of x. If y is an even power of x, as in $y = x^2$ or $y = x^4$, it is an even function of x (because $(-x)^2 = x^2$ and $(-x)^4 = x^4$). If y is an odd power of x, as in $y = x$ or $y = x^3$, it is an odd function of x (because $(-x)^1 = -x$ and $(-x)^3 = -x^3$).

The graph of an even function is **symmetric about the *y*-axis.** Since $f(-x) = f(x)$, a point (x, y) lies on the graph if and only if the point $(-x, y)$ lies on the graph (Figure 1.15a).

The graph of an odd function is **symmetric about the origin.** Since $f(-x) = -f(x)$, a point (x, y) lies on the graph if and only if the point $(-x, -y)$ lies on the graph (Figure 1.15b).

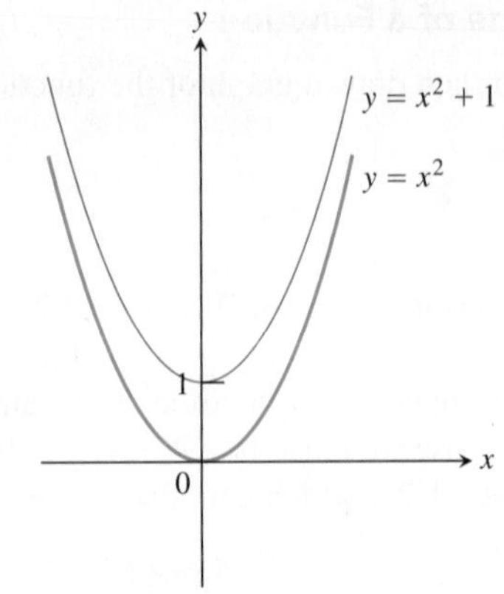

(a)

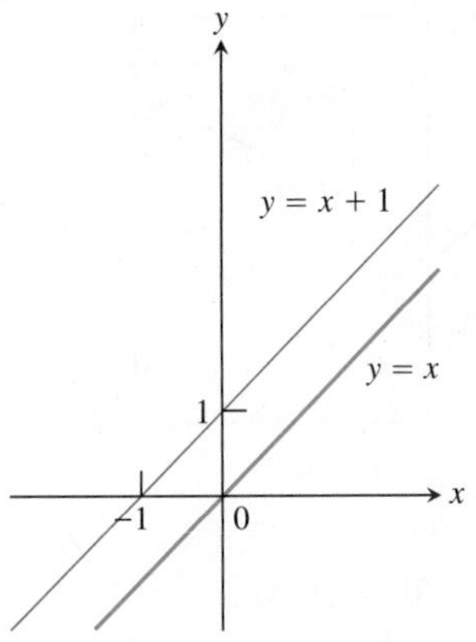

(b)

Figure 1.16 (a) When we add the constant term 1 to the function $y = x^2$, the resulting function $y = x^2 + 1$ is still even and its graph is still symmetric about the y-axis. (b) When we add the constant term 1 to the function $y = x$, the resulting function $y = x + 1$ is no longer odd. The symmetry about the origin is lost. (Example 4)

Equivalently, a graph is symmetric about the origin if a rotation of 180° about the origin leaves the graph unchanged.

EXAMPLE 4 Recognizing Even and Odd Functions

$f(x) = x^2$ Even function: $(-x)^2 = x^2$ for all x; symmetry about y-axis.

$f(x) = x^2 + 1$ Even function: $(-x)^2 + 1 = x^2 + 1$ for all x; symmetry about y-axis (Figure 1.16a).

$f(x) = x$ Odd function: $(-x) = -x$ for all x; symmetry about the origin.

$f(x) = x + 1$ Not odd: $f(-x) = -x + 1$, but $-f(x) = -x - 1$. The two are not equal.

Not even: $(-x) + 1 \neq x + 1$ for all $x \neq 0$ (Figure 1.16b).

Now Try Exercises 21 and 23.

It is useful in graphing to recognize even and odd functions. Once we know the graph of either type of function on one side of the y-axis, we know its graph on both sides.

Functions Defined in Pieces

While some functions are defined by single formulas, others are defined by applying different formulas to different parts of their domains.

EXAMPLE 5 Graphing Piecewise-Defined Functions

$$\text{Graph } y = f(x) = \begin{cases} -x, & x < 0 \\ x^2, & 0 \le x \le 1 \\ 1, & x > 1. \end{cases}$$

SOLUTION

The values of f are given by three separate formulas: $y = -x$ when $x < 0$, $y = x^2$ when $0 \le x \le 1$, and $y = 1$ when $x > 1$. However, the function is *just one function,* whose domain is the entire set of real numbers (Figure 1.17).

Now Try Exercise 33.

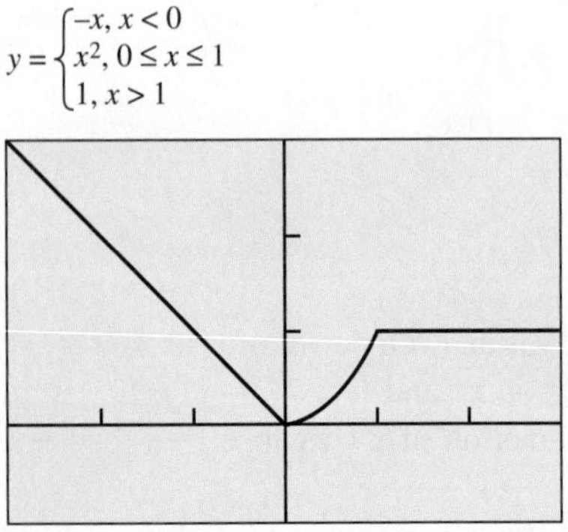

[–3, 3] by [–1, 3]

Figure 1.17 The graph of a piecewise-defined function. (Example 5)

EXAMPLE 6 Writing Formulas for Piecewise Functions

Write a formula for the function $y = f(x)$ whose graph consists of the two line segments in Figure 1.18.

SOLUTION

We find formulas for the segments from $(0, 0)$ to $(1, 1)$ and from $(1, 0)$ to $(2, 1)$ and piece them together in the manner of Example 5.

Segment from (0, 0) to (1, 1) The line through $(0, 0)$ and $(1, 1)$ has slope $m = (1 - 0)/(1 - 0) = 1$ and y-intercept $b = 0$. Its slope-intercept equation is $y = x$. The segment from $(0, 0)$ to $(1, 1)$ that includes the point $(0, 0)$ but not the point $(1, 1)$ is the graph of the function $y = x$ restricted to the half-open interval $0 \le x < 1$, namely,

$$y = x, \quad 0 \le x < 1.$$

continued

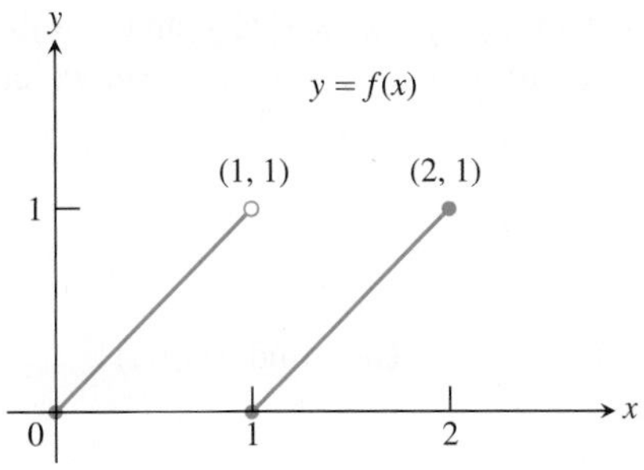

Figure 1.18 The segment on the left contains $(0, 0)$ but not $(1, 1)$. The segment on the right contains both of its endpoints. (Example 6)

Segment from (1, 0) to (2, 1) The line through $(1, 0)$ and $(2, 1)$ has slope $m = (1 - 0)/(2 - 1) = 1$ and passes through the point $(1, 0)$. The corresponding point-slope equation for the line is

$$y = 1(x - 1) + 0, \quad \text{or} \quad y = x - 1.$$

The segment from $(1, 0)$ to $(2, 1)$ that includes both endpoints is the graph of $y = x - 1$ restricted to the closed interval $1 \le x \le 2$, namely,

$$y = x - 1, \quad 1 \le x \le 2.$$

Piecewise Formula Combining the formulas for the two pieces of the graph, we obtain

$$f(x) = \begin{cases} x, & 0 \le x < 1 \\ x - 1, & 1 \le x \le 2. \end{cases}$$

Now Try Exercise 43.

Absolute Value Function

The **absolute value function** $y = |x|$ is defined piecewise by the formula

$$|x| = \begin{cases} -x, & x < 0 \\ x, & x \ge 0. \end{cases}$$

The function is even, and its graph (Figure 1.19) is symmetric about the y-axis.

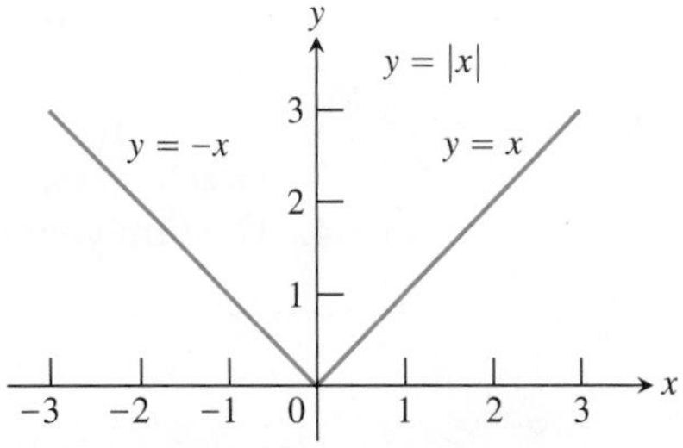

Figure 1.19 The absolute value function has domain $(-\infty, \infty)$ and range $[0, \infty)$.

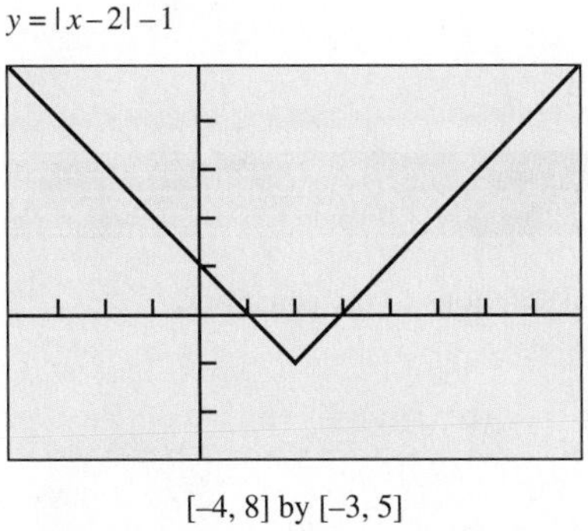

Figure 1.20 The lowest point of the graph of $f(x) = |x - 2| - 1$ is $(2, -1)$. (Example 7)

EXAMPLE 7 Using Transformations

Draw the graph of $f(x) = |x - 2| - 1$. Then find the domain and range.

SOLUTION

The graph of f is the graph of the absolute value function shifted 2 units horizontally to the right and 1 unit vertically downward (Figure 1.20). The domain of f is $(-\infty, \infty)$ and the range is $[-1, \infty)$.

Now Try Exercise 49.

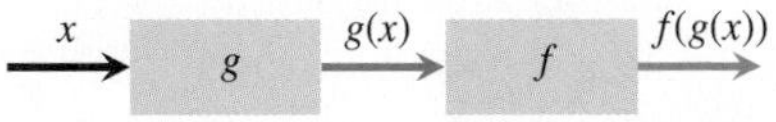

Figure 1.21 Two functions can be composed when a portion of the range of the first lies in the domain of the second.

Composite Functions

Suppose that some of the outputs of a function g can be used as inputs of a function f. We can then link g and f to form a new function whose inputs x are inputs of g and whose outputs are the numbers $f(g(x))$, as in Figure 1.21. We say that the function $f(g(x))$

(read "f of g of x") is the **composite of g and f.** It is made by *composing* g and f in the order of first g, then f. The usual "stand-alone" notation for this composite is $f \circ g$, which is read as "f of g." Thus, the value of $f \circ g$ at x is $(f \circ g)(x) = f(g(x))$.

EXAMPLE 8 Composing Functions

Find a formula for $f(g(x))$ if $g(x) = x^2$ and $f(x) = x - 7$. Then find $f(g(2))$.

SOLUTION

To find $f(g(x))$, we replace x in the formula $f(x) = x - 7$ by the expression given for $g(x)$.

$$f(x) = x - 7$$

$$f(g(x)) = g(x) - 7 = x^2 - 7$$

We then find the value of $f(g(2))$ by substituting 2 for x.

$$f(g(2)) = (2)^2 - 7 = -3$$

Now Try Exercise 51.

EXPLORATION 1 Composing Functions

Some graphers allow a function such as y_1 to be used as the independent variable of another function. With such a grapher, we can compose functions.

1. Enter the functions $y_1 = f(x) = 4 - x^2$, $y_2 = g(x) = \sqrt{x}$, $y_3 = y_2(y_1(x))$, and $y_4 = y_1(y_2(x))$. Which of y_3 and y_4 corresponds to $f \circ g$? to $g \circ f$?
2. Graph y_1, y_2, and y_3 and make conjectures about the domain and range of y_3.
3. Graph y_1, y_2, and y_4 and make conjectures about the domain and range of y_4.
4. Confirm your conjectures algebraically by finding formulas for y_3 and y_4.

Quick Review 1.2 *(For help, go to Appendix A1 and Section 1.2.)*

Exercise numbers with a gray background indicate problems that the authors have designed to be solved *without a calculator*.

In Exercises 1–6, solve for x.

1. $3x - 1 \le 5x + 3$

2. $x(x - 2) > 0$

3. $|x - 3| \le 4$

4. $|x - 2| \ge 5$

5. $x^2 < 16$

6. $9 - x^2 \ge 0$

In Exercises 7 and 8, describe how the graph of f can be transformed to the graph of g.

7. $f(x) = x^2, \quad g(x) = (x + 2)^2 - 3$

8. $f(x) = |x|, \quad g(x) = |x - 5| + 2$

In Exercises 9–12, find all real solutions to the equations.

9. $f(x) = x^2 - 5$

(a) $f(x) = 4$ **(b)** $f(x) = -6$

10. $f(x) = 1/x$

(a) $f(x) = -5$ **(b)** $f(x) = 0$

11. $f(x) = \sqrt{x + 7}$

(a) $f(x) = 4$ **(b)** $f(x) = 1$

12. $f(x) = \sqrt[3]{x - 1}$

(a) $f(x) = -2$ **(b)** $f(x) = 3$

Section 1.2 Exercises

Exercise numbers with a gray background indicate problems that the authors have designed to be solved *without a calculator.*

In Exercises 1–4, **(a)** write a formula for the function and **(b)** use the formula to find the indicated value of the function.

1. the area A of a circle as a function of its diameter d; the area of a circle of diameter 4 in.

2. the height h of an equilateral triangle as a function of its side length s; the height of an equilateral triangle of side length 3 m

3. the surface area S of a cube as a function of the length of the cube's edge e; the surface area of a cube of edge length 5 ft

4. the volume V of a sphere as a function of the sphere's radius r; the volume of a sphere of radius 3 cm

In Exercises 5–12, **(a)** identify the domain and range and **(b)** sketch the graph of the function.

5. $y = 4 - x^2$

6. $y = x^2 - 9$

7. $y = 2 + \sqrt{x - 1}$

8. $y = -\sqrt{-x}$

9. $y = \dfrac{1}{x - 2}$

10. $y = \sqrt[4]{-x}$

11. $y = 1 + \dfrac{1}{x}$

12. $y = 1 + \dfrac{1}{x^2}$

In Exercises 13–20, use a grapher to **(a)** identify the domain and range and **(b)** draw the graph of the function.

13. $y = \sqrt[3]{x}$

14. $y = 2\sqrt{3 - x}$

15. $y = \sqrt[3]{1 - x^2}$

16. $y = \sqrt{9 - x^2}$

17. $y = x^{2/5}$

18. $y = x^{3/2}$

19. $y = \sqrt[3]{x - 3}$

20. $y = \dfrac{1}{\sqrt{4 - x^2}}$

In Exercises 21–30, determine whether the function is even, odd, or neither. Try to answer without writing anything (except the answer).

21. $y = x^4$

22. $y = x + x^2$

23. $y = x + 2$

24. $y = x^2 - 3$

25. $y = \sqrt{x^2 + 2}$

26. $y = x + x^3$

27. $y = \dfrac{x^3}{x^2 - 1}$

28. $y = \sqrt[3]{2 - x}$

29. $y = \dfrac{1}{x - 1}$

30. $y = \dfrac{1}{x^2 - 1}$

In Exercises 31–34, graph the piecewise-defined functions.

31. $f(x) = \begin{cases} 3 - x, & x \le 1 \\ 2x, & 1 < x \end{cases}$

32. $f(x) = \begin{cases} 1, & x < 0 \\ \sqrt{x}, & x \ge 0 \end{cases}$

33. $f(x) = \begin{cases} 4 - x^2, & x < 1 \\ (3/2)x + 3/2, & 1 \le x \le 3 \\ x + 3, & x > 3 \end{cases}$

34. $f(x) = \begin{cases} x^2, & x < 0 \\ x^3, & 0 \le x \le 1 \\ 2x - 1, & x > 1 \end{cases}$

35. Writing to Learn The *vertical line test* to determine whether a curve is the graph of a function states: If every vertical line in the xy-plane intersects a given curve in at most one point, then the curve is the graph of a function. Explain why this is true.

36. Writing to Learn For a curve to be *symmetric about the x-axis,* the point (x, y) must lie on the curve if and only if the point $(x, -y)$ lies on the curve. Explain why a curve that is symmetric about the x-axis is not the graph of a function, unless the function is $y = 0$.

In Exercises 37–40, use the vertical line test (see Exercise 35) to determine whether the curve is the graph of a function.

37.

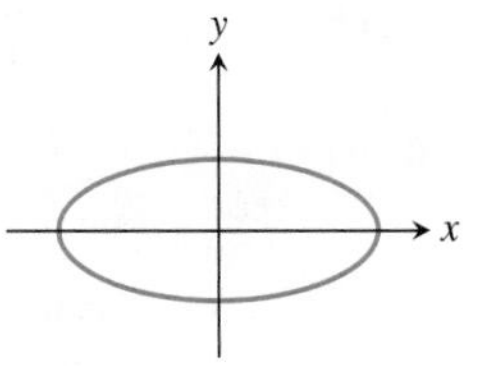

38.

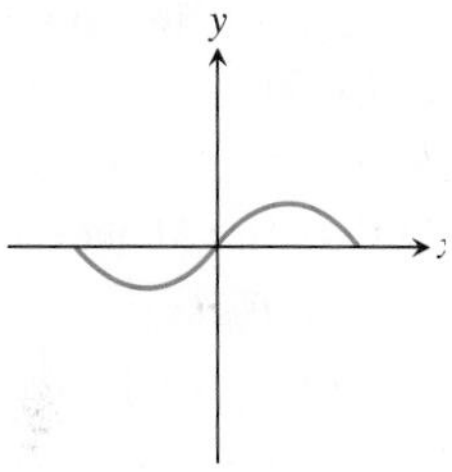

39.

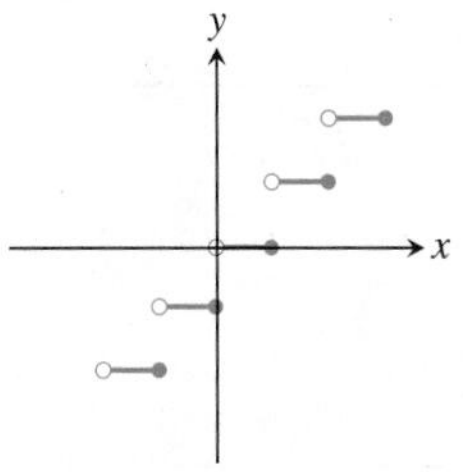

40.

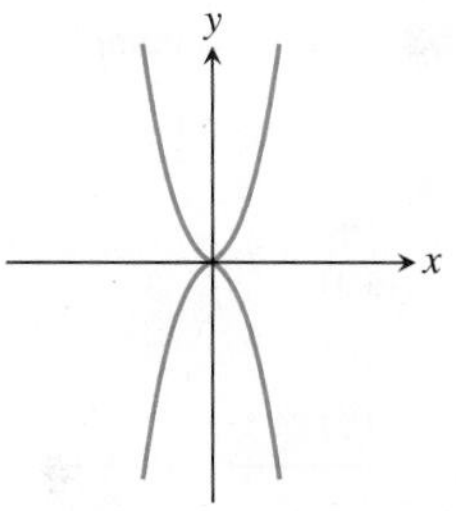

In Exercises 41–48, write a piecewise formula for the function.

41.

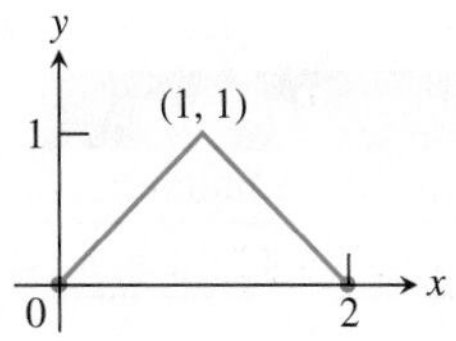

42.

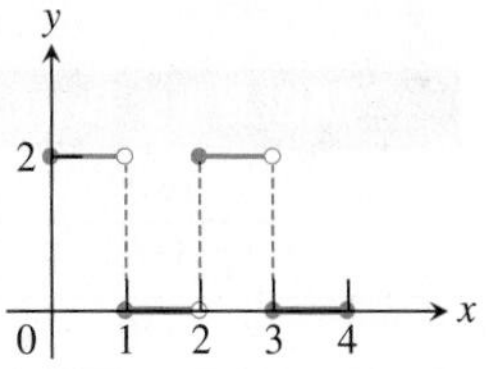

43.

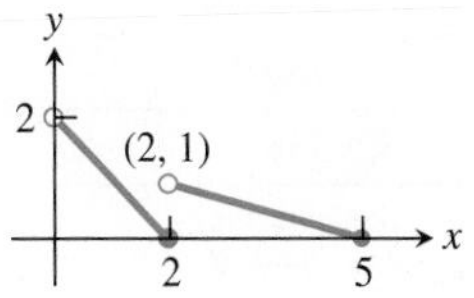

44.

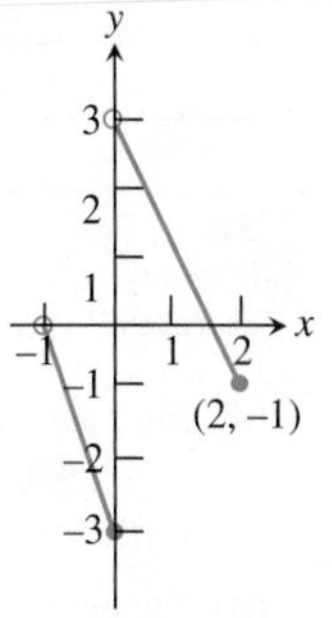

45.

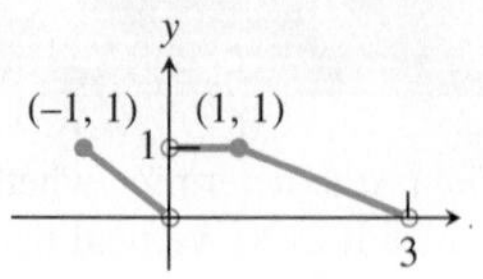

46.

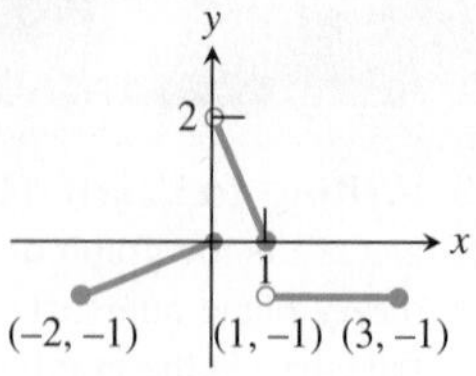

47.

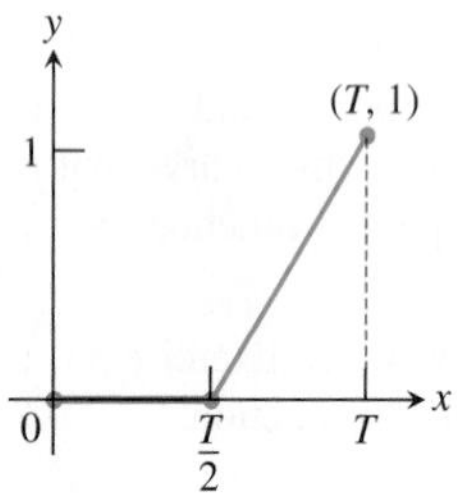

48.

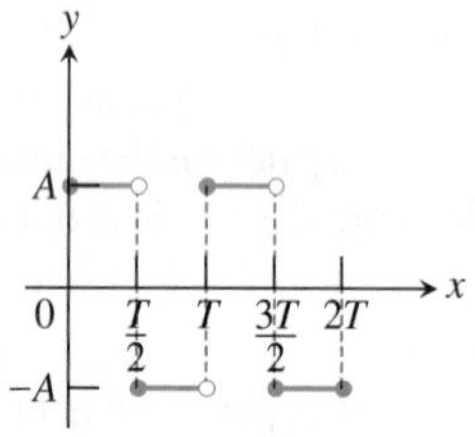

In Exercises 49 and 50, **(a)** draw the graph of the function. Then find its **(b)** domain and **(c)** range.

49. $f(x) = -|3 - x| + 2$ **50.** $f(x) = 2|x + 4| - 3$

In Exercises 51 and 52, find

(a) $f(g(x))$ **(b)** $g(f(x))$ **(c)** $f(g(0))$
(d) $g(f(0))$ **(e)** $g(g(-2))$ **(f)** $f(f(x))$

51. $f(x) = x + 5, \quad g(x) = x^2 - 3$

52. $f(x) = x + 1, \quad g(x) = x - 1$

53. Copy and complete the following table.

	$g(x)$	$f(x)$	$(f \circ g)(x)$
(a)	?	$\sqrt{x - 5}$	$\sqrt{x^2 - 5}$
(b)	?	$1 + 1/x$	x
(c)	$1/x$	?	x
(d)	$\sqrt{x}$	?	$\|x\|, x \geq 0$

54. ***Broadway Season Statistics*** Table 1.5 shows the gross revenue for the Broadway season in millions of dollars for several years.

TABLE 1.5 Broadway Season Revenue

Year	Amount ($ millions)
1994	406
1999	603
2004	769
2005	862
2006	939
2007	938

Source: The League of American Theatres and Producers, Inc., New York, NY, as reported in *The World Almanac and Book of Facts, 2009.*

(a) Find the quadratic regression for the data in Table 1.5. Let $x = 1990$ represent 1990, $x = 1991$ represent 1991, and so forth.

(b) Superimpose the graph of the quadratic regression equation on a scatter plot of the data.

(c) Use the quadratic regression to predict the amount of revenue in 2012.

(d) Now find the linear regression for the data and use it to predict the amount of revenue in 2012.

55. ***The Cone Problem*** Begin with a circular piece of paper with a 4-in. radius as shown in (a). Cut out a sector with an arc length of x. Join the two edges of the remaining portion to form a cone with radius r and height h, as shown in (b).

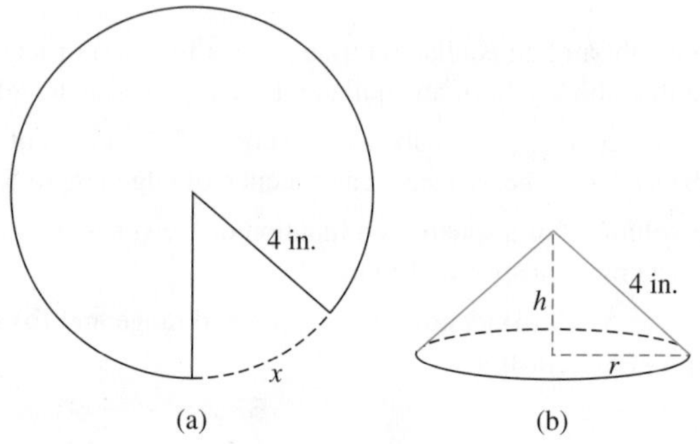

(a) Explain why the circumference of the base of the cone is $8\pi - x$.

(b) Express the radius r as a function of x.

(c) Express the height h as a function of x.

(d) Express the volume V of the cone as a function of x.

56. ***Industrial Costs*** Dayton Power and Light, Inc., has a power plant on the Miami River where the river is 800 ft wide. To lay a new cable from the plant to a location in the city 2 mi downstream on the opposite side costs \$180 per foot across the river and \$100 per foot along the land.

(a) Suppose that the cable goes from the plant to a point Q on the opposite side that is x ft from the point P directly opposite the plant. Write a function $C(x)$ that gives the cost of laying the cable in terms of the distance x.

(b) Generate a table of values to determine if the least expensive location for point Q is less than 2000 ft or greater than 2000 ft from point P.

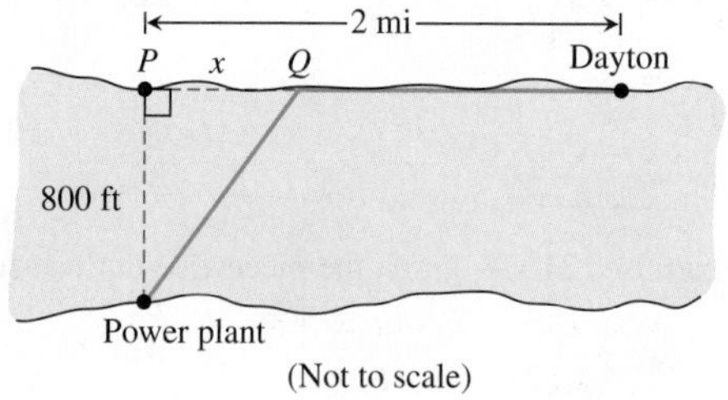

Standardized Test Questions

57. True or False The function $f(x) = x^4 + x^2 + x$ is an even function. Justify your answer.

58. True or False The function $f(x) = x^{-3}$ is an odd function. Justify your answer.

59. Multiple Choice Which of the following gives the domain of $f(x) = \dfrac{x}{\sqrt{9 - x^2}}$?

(A) $x \neq \pm 3$ (B) $(-3, 3)$ (C) $[-3, 3]$

(D) $(-\infty, -3) \cup (3, \infty)$ (E) $(3, \infty)$

60. Multiple Choice Which of the following gives the range of $f(x) = 1 + \dfrac{1}{x - 1}$?

(A) $(-\infty, 1) \cup (1, \infty)$ (B) $x \neq 1$ (C) all real numbers

(D) $(-\infty, 0) \cup (0, \infty)$ (E) $x \neq 0$

61. Multiple Choice If $f(x) = 2x - 1$ and $g(x) = x + 3$, which of the following gives $(f \circ g)(2)$?

(A) 2 (B) 6 (C) 7 (D) 9 (E) 10

62. Multiple Choice The length L of a rectangle is twice as long as its width W. Which of the following gives the area A of the rectangle as a function of its width?

(A) $A(W) = 3W$ (B) $A(W) = \frac{1}{2}W^2$ (C) $A(W) = 2W^2$

(D) $A(W) = W^2 + 2W$ (E) $A(W) = W^2 - 2W$

Explorations

In Exercises 63–66, **(a)** graph $f \circ g$ and $g \circ f$ and make a conjecture about the domain and range of each function. **(b)** Then confirm your conjectures by finding formulas for $f \circ g$ and $g \circ f$.

63. $f(x) = x - 7, \quad g(x) = \sqrt{x}$

64. $f(x) = 1 - x^2, \quad g(x) = \sqrt{x}$

65. $f(x) = x^2 - 3, \quad g(x) = \sqrt{x + 2}$

66. $f(x) = \dfrac{2x - 1}{x + 3}, \quad g(x) = \dfrac{3x + 1}{2 - x}$

Group Activity In Exercises 67–70, a portion of the graph of a function defined on $[-2, 2]$ is shown. Complete each graph assuming that the graph is **(a)** even, **(b)** odd.

67.

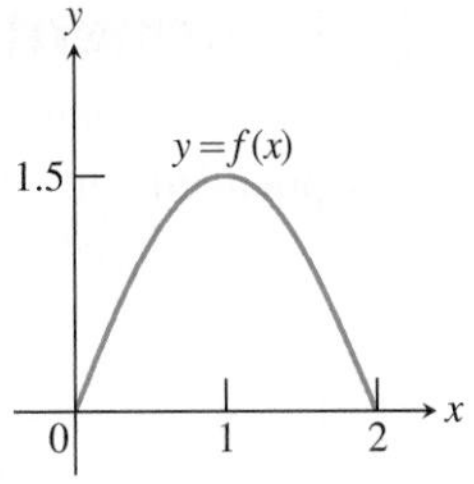

68.

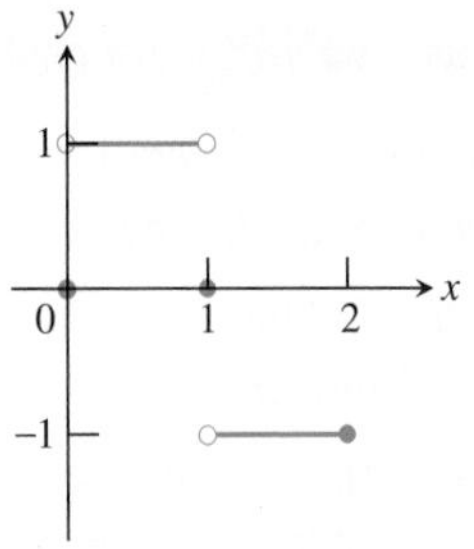

69.

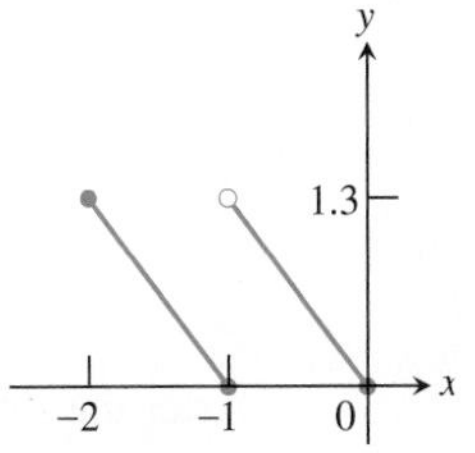

70.

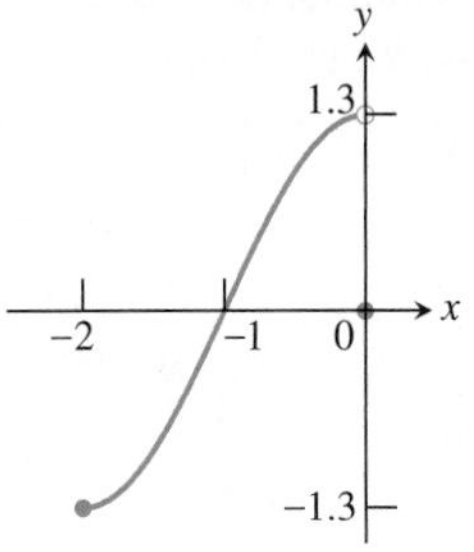

Extending the Ideas

71. Enter $y_1 = \sqrt{x}$, $y_2 = \sqrt{1 - x}$ and $y_3 = y_1 + y_2$ on your grapher.

(a) Graph y_3 in $[-3, 3]$ by $[-1, 3]$.

(b) Compare the domain of the graph of y_3 with the domains of the graphs of y_1 and y_2.

(c) Replace y_3 by

$$y_1 - y_2, \quad y_2 - y_1, \quad y_1 \cdot y_2, \quad y_1/y_2, \quad \text{and} \quad y_2/y_1,$$

in turn, and repeat the comparison of part (b).

(d) Based on your observations in (b) and (c), what would you conjecture about the domains of sums, differences, products, and quotients of functions?

72. *Even and Odd Functions*

(a) Must the product of two even functions always be even? Give reasons for your answer.

(b) Can anything be said about the product of two odd functions? Give reasons for your answer.

1.3 Exponential Functions

What you will learn about . . .

- Exponential Growth
- Exponential Decay
- Applications
- The Number *e*

and why . . .

Exponential functions model many growth patterns.

Exponential Growth

Table 1.6 shows the growth of \$100 invested in 1996 at an interest rate of 5.5%, compounded annually.

TABLE 1.6 Savings Account Growth

Year	Amount (dollars)	Increase (dollars)
1996	100	5.50
1997	$100(1.055) = 105.50$	5.80
1998	$100(1.055)^2 = 111.30$	6.12
1999	$100(1.055)^3 = 117.42$	6.46
2000	$100(1.055)^4 = 123.88$	

After the first year, the value of the account is always 1.055 times its value in the previous year. After n years, the value is $y = 100 \cdot (1.055)^n$.

Compound interest provides an example of *exponential growth* and is modeled by a function of the form $y = P \cdot a^x$, where P is the initial investment and a is equal to 1 plus the interest rate expressed as a decimal.

The equation $y = P \cdot a^x$, $a > 0$, $a \neq 1$, identifies a family of functions called *exponential functions.* Notice that the ratio of consecutive amounts in Table 1.6 is always the same: $111.30/105.30 = 117.42/111.30 = 123.88/117.42 \approx 1.055$. This fact is an important feature of exponential curves that has widespread application, as we will see.

$y = 2^x$

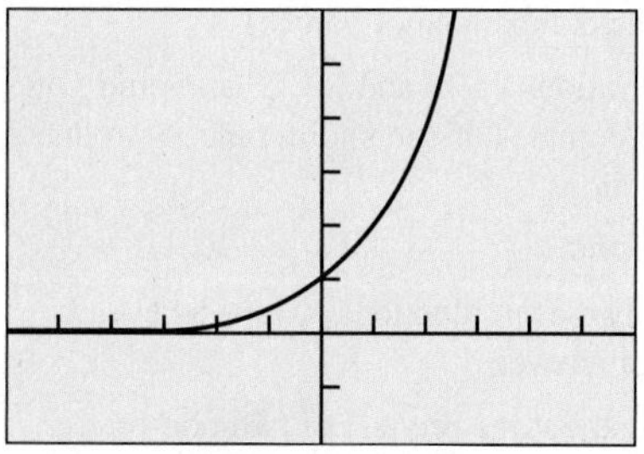

[–6, 6] by [–2, 6]

(a)

$y = 2^{-x}$

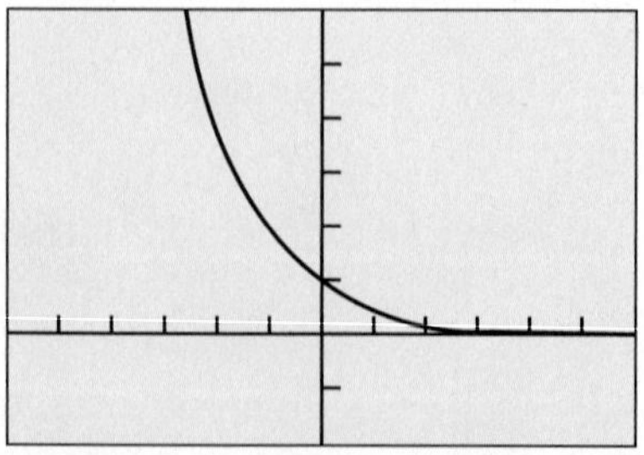

[–6, 6] by [–2, 6]

(b)

Figure 1.22 A graph of (a) $y = 2^x$ and (b) $y = 2^{-x}$.

EXPLORATION 1 Exponential Functions

1. Graph the function $y = a^x$ for $a = 2, 3, 5$, in a $[-5, 5]$ by $[-2, 5]$ viewing window.
2. For what values of x is it true that $2^x < 3^x < 5^x$?
3. For what values of x is it true that $2^x > 3^x > 5^x$?
4. For what values of x is it true that $2^x = 3^x = 5^x$?
5. Graph the function $y = (1/a)^x = a^{-x}$ for $a = 2, 3, 5$.
6. Repeat parts 2–4 for the functions in part 5.

DEFINITION Exponential Function

Let a be a positive real number other than 1. The function

$$f(x) = a^x$$

is the **exponential function with base *a*.**

The domain of $f(x) = a^x$ is $(-\infty, \infty)$ and the range is $(0, \infty)$. If $a > 1$, the graph of f looks like the graph of $y = 2^x$ in Figure 1.22a. If $0 < a < 1$, the graph of f looks like the graph of $y = 2^{-x}$ in Figure 1.22b.

EXAMPLE 1 Graphing an Exponential Function

Graph the function $y = 2(3^x) - 4$. State its domain and range.

continued

$y = 2(3^x) - 4$

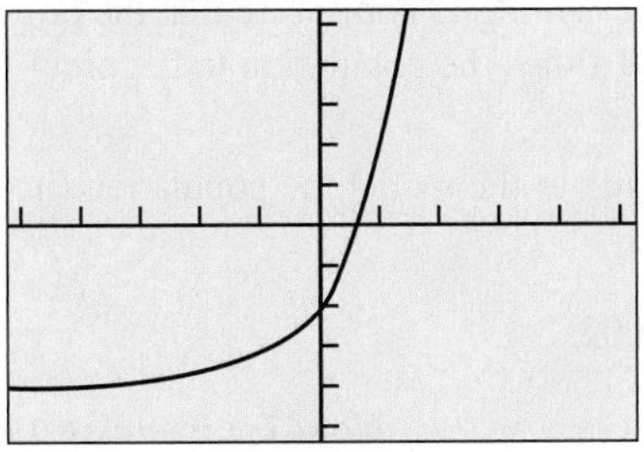

[−5, 5] by [−5, 5]

Figure 1.23 The graph of $y = 2(3^x) - 4$. (Example 1)

SOLUTION

Figure 1.23 shows the graph of the function y. It appears that the domain is $(-\infty, \infty)$. The range is $(-4, \infty)$ because $2(3^x) > 0$ for all x. ***Now Try Exercise 1.***

EXAMPLE 2 Finding Zeros

Find the zeros of $f(x) = 5 - 2.5^x$ graphically.

SOLUTION

Figure 1.24a suggests that f has a zero between $x = 1$ and $x = 2$, closer to 2. We can use our grapher to find that the zero is approximately 1.756 (Figure 1.24b). ***Now Try Exercise 9.***

$y = 5 - 2.5^x$

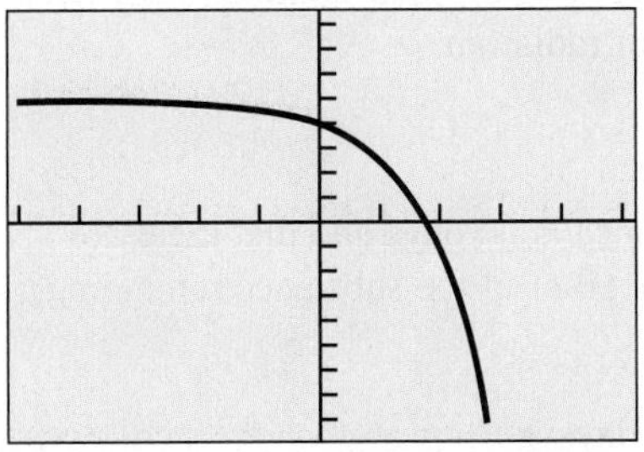

[−5, 5] by [−8, 8]

(a)

$y = 5 - 2.5^x$

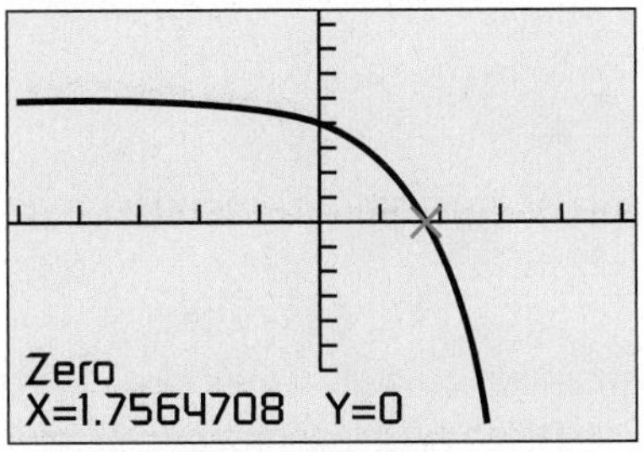

[−5, 5] by [−8, 8]

(b)

Figure 1.24 (a) A graph of $f(x) = 5 - 2.5^x$. (b) Showing the use of the ZERO feature to approximate the zero of f. (Example 2)

Exponential functions obey the rules for exponents.

Rules for Exponents

If $a > 0$ and $b > 0$, the following hold for all real numbers x and y.

1. $a^x \cdot a^y = a^{x+y}$ **2.** $\dfrac{a^x}{a^y} = a^{x-y}$ **3.** $(a^x)^y = (a^y)^x = a^{xy}$

4. $a^x \cdot b^x = (ab)^x$ **5.** $\left(\dfrac{a}{b}\right)^x = \dfrac{a^x}{b^x}$

In Table 1.6 we observed that the ratios of the amounts in consecutive years were always the same, namely the interest rate. Population growth can sometimes be modeled with an exponential function, as we see in Table 1.7 and Example 3.

Table 1.7 gives the United States population for several recent years. In this table we have divided the population in one year by the population in the previous year to get an idea of how the population is growing. These ratios are given in the third column.

TABLE 1.7 United States Population

Year	Population (millions)	Ratio
2002	287.9	$290.4/287.9 \approx 1.0087$
2003	290.4	$293.2/290.4 \approx 1.0096$
2004	293.2	$295.9/293.2 \approx 1.0092$
2005	295.9	$298.8/295.9 \approx 1.0098$
2006	298.8	$301.6/298.8 \approx 1.0094$
2007	301.6	

Source: Statistical Abstract of the United States, 2009.

EXAMPLE 3 Predicting United States Population

Use the data in Table 1.7 and an exponential model to predict the population of the United States in the year 2012.

continued

SOLUTION

Based on the third column of Table 1.7, we might be willing to conjecture that the population of the United States in any year is about 1.01 times the population in the previous year.

If we start with the population in 2002, then according to the model the population (in millions) in 2012 would be about

$$287.9(1.01)^{10} \approx 318.02,$$

or about 318.02 million people. *Now Try Exercise 19.*

Exponential Decay

Exponential functions can also model phenomena that produce a decrease over time, such as happens with radioactive decay. The **half-life** of a radioactive substance is the amount of time it takes for half of the substance to change from its original radioactive state to a nonradioactive state by emitting energy in the form of radiation.

EXAMPLE 4 Modeling Radioactive Decay

Suppose the half-life of a certain radioactive substance is 20 days and that there are 5 grams present initially. When will there be only 1 gram of the substance remaining?

SOLUTION

Model The number of grams remaining after 20 days is

$$5\left(\frac{1}{2}\right) = \frac{5}{2}.$$

The number of grams remaining after 40 days is

$$5\left(\frac{1}{2}\right)\left(\frac{1}{2}\right) = 5\left(\frac{1}{2}\right)^2 = \frac{5}{4}.$$

The function $y = 5(1/2)^{t/20}$ models the mass in grams of the radioactive substance after t days.

Solve Graphically Figure 1.25 shows that the graphs of $y_1 = 5(1/2)^{t/20}$ and $y_2 = 1$ (for 1 gram) intersect when t is approximately 46.44.

Interpret There will be 1 gram of the radioactive substance left after approximately 46.44 days, or about 46 days 10.5 hours. *Now Try Exercise 23.*

$y = 5\left(\frac{1}{2}\right)^{t/20}, y = 1$

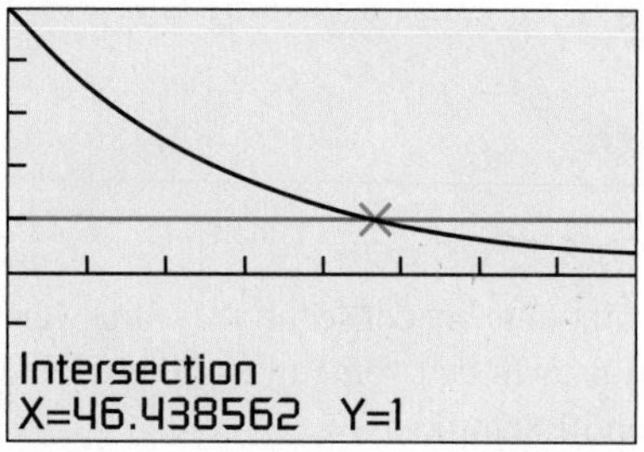

[0, 80] by [–3, 5]

Figure 1.25 (Example 4)

Compound interest investments, population growth, and radioactive decay are all examples of *exponential growth and decay.*

DEFINITIONS Exponential Growth, Exponential Decay

The function $y = k \cdot a^x, k > 0$ is a model for **exponential growth** if $a > 1$, and a model for **exponential decay** if $0 < a < 1$.

Applications

Most graphers have the exponential growth and decay model $y = k \cdot a^x$ built in as an exponential regression equation. We use this feature in Example 5 to analyze the U.S. population from the data in Table 1.8.

TABLE 1.8 U.S. Population

Year	Population (millions)
1880	50.2
1890	63.0
1900	76.2
1910	92.2
1920	106.0
1930	123.2
1940	132.1
1950	151.3
1960	179.3
1970	203.3
1980	226.5
1990	248.7

Source: The Statistical Abstract of the United States, 2004–2005.

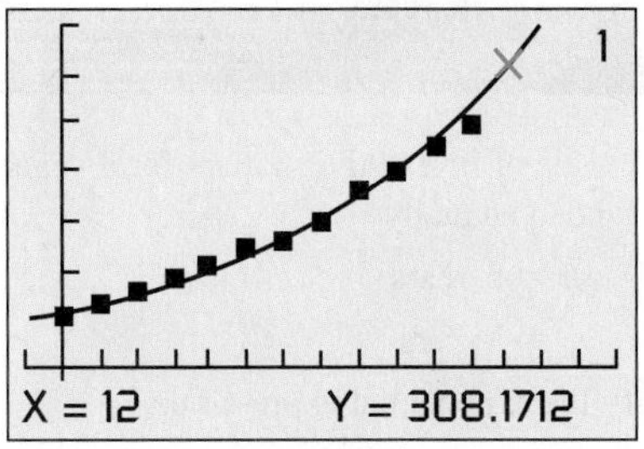

[–1, 15] by [–50, 350]

Figure 1.26 (Example 5)

EXAMPLE 5 Predicting the U.S. Population

Use the population data in Table 1.8 to estimate the population for the year 2000. Compare the result with the actual 2000 population of approximately 281.4 million.

SOLUTION

Model Let $x = 0$ represent 1880, $x = 1$ represent 1890, and so on. We enter the data into the grapher and find the exponential regression equation to be

$$f(x) = (56.4696)(1.1519)^x.$$

Figure 1.26 shows the graph of f superimposed on the scatter plot of the data.

Solve Graphically The year 2000 is represented by $x = 12$. Reading from the curve, we find

$$f(12) \approx 308.2.$$

The exponential model estimates the 2000 population to be 308.2 million, an overestimate of approximately 26.8 million, or about 9.5%.

Now Try Exercise 39(a, b).

EXAMPLE 6 Interpreting Exponential Regression

What *annual* rate of growth can we infer from the exponential regression equation in Example 5?

SOLUTION

Let r be the annual rate of growth of the U.S. population, expressed as a decimal. Because the time increments we used were 10-year intervals, we have

$$(1 + r)^{10} \approx 1.1519$$
$$r \approx \sqrt[10]{1.1519} - 1$$
$$r \approx 0.014$$

The annual rate of growth is about 1.4%. *Now Try Exercise 39(c).*

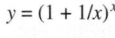

$y = (1 + 1/x)^x$

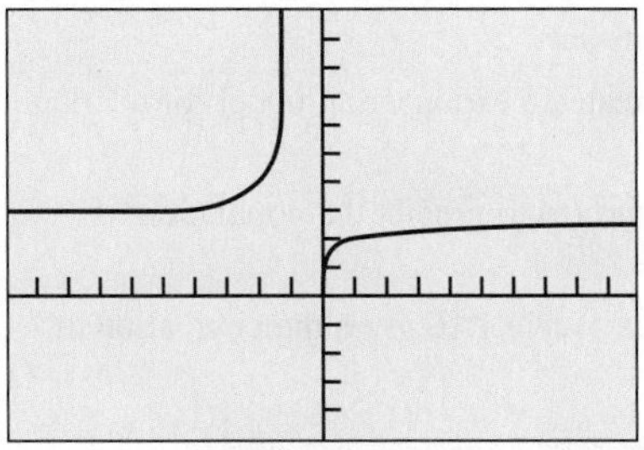

[–10, 10] by [–5, 10]

X	Y1
1000	2.7169
2000	2.7176
3000	2.7178
4000	2.7179
5000	2.718
6000	2.7181
7000	2.7181

Y1 = (1+1/X)^X

Figure 1.27 A graph and table of values for $f(x) = (1 + 1/x)^x$ both suggest that as $x \to \infty$, $f(x) \to e \approx 2.718$.

The Number *e*

Many natural, physical, and economic phenomena are best modeled by an exponential function whose base is the famous number e, which is 2.718281828 to nine decimal places. We can define e to be the number that the function $f(x) = (1 + 1/x)^x$ approaches as x approaches infinity. The graph and table in Figure 1.27 strongly suggest that such a number exists.

The exponential functions $y = e^x$ and $y = e^{-x}$ are frequently used as models of exponential growth or decay. For example, interest **compounded continuously** uses the model $y = P \cdot e^{rt}$, where P is the initial investment, r is the interest rate as a decimal, and t is time in years.

Quick Review 1.3 *(For help, go to Section 1.3.)*

Exercise numbers with a gray background indicate problems that the authors have designed to be solved *without a calculator.*

In Exercises 1–3, evaluate the expression. Round your answers to 3 decimal places.

1. $5^{2/3}$ **2.** $3^{\sqrt{2}}$

3. $3^{-1.5}$

In Exercises 4–6, solve the equation. Round your answers to 4 decimal places.

4. $x^3 = 17$ **5.** $x^5 = 24$

6. $x^{10} = 1.4567$

In Exercises 7 and 8, find the value of investing P dollars for n years with the interest rate r compounded annually.

7. $P = \$500, \quad r = 4.75\%, \quad n = 5$ years

8. $P = \$1000, \quad r = 6.3\%, \quad n = 3$ years

In Exercises 9 and 10, simplify the exponential expression.

9. $\dfrac{(x^{-3}y^2)^2}{(x^4y^3)^3}$ **10.** $\left(\dfrac{a^3b^{-2}}{c^4}\right)^2\left(\dfrac{a^4c^{-2}}{b^3}\right)^{-1}$

Section 1.3 Exercises

Exercise numbers with a gray background indicate problems that the authors have designed to be solved *without a calculator.*

In Exercises 1–4, graph the function. State its domain and range.

1. $y = -2^x + 3$ **2.** $y = e^x + 3$

3. $y = 3 \cdot e^{-x} - 2$ **4.** $y = -2^{-x} - 1$

In Exercises 5–8, rewrite the exponential expression to have the indicated base.

5. 9^{2x}, base 3 **6.** 16^{3x}, base 2

7. $(1/8)^{2x}$, base 2 **8.** $(1/27)^x$, base 3

In Exercises 9–12, use a graph to find the zeros of the function.

9. $f(x) = 2^x - 5$ **10.** $f(x) = e^x - 4$

11. $f(x) = 3^x - 0.5$ **12.** $f(x) = 3 - 2^x$

In Exercises 13–18, match the function with its graph. Try to do it without using your grapher.

13. $y = 2^x$ **14.** $y = 3^{-x}$ **15.** $y = -3^{-x}$

16. $y = -0.5^{-x}$ **17.** $y = 2^{-x} - 2$ **18.** $y = 1.5^x - 2$

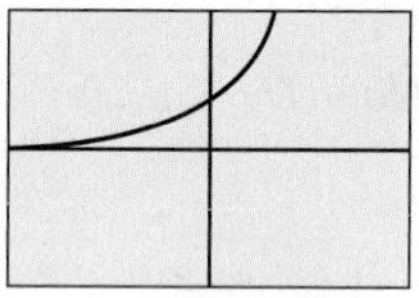

(a)

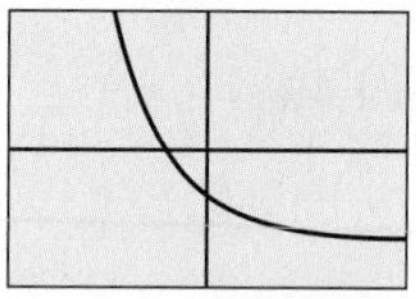

(b)

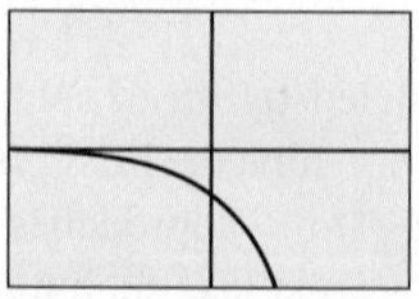

(c)

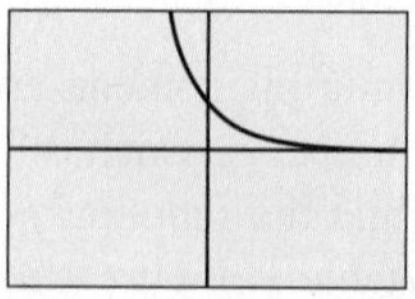

(d)

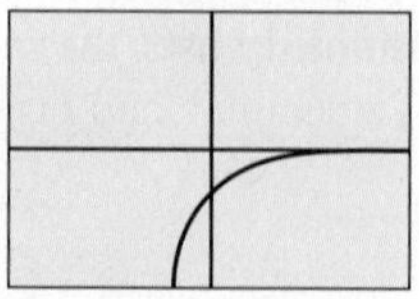

(e)

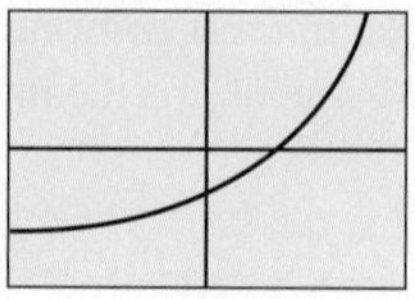

(f)

19. ***Population of Nevada*** Table 1.9 gives the population of Nevada for several years.

TABLE 1.9 Population of Nevada

Year	Population (thousands)
2002	2168
2003	2238
2004	2330
2005	2409
2006	2492
2007	2565

Source: Statistical Abstract of the United States, 2009.

(a) Compute the ratios of the population in one year by the population in the previous year.

(b) Based on part (a), create an exponential model for the population of Nevada.

(c) Use your model in part (b) to predict the population of Nevada in 2015.

20. ***Population of Virginia*** Table 1.10 gives the population of Virginia for several years.

TABLE 1.10 Population of Virginia

Year	Population (thousands)
2002	7282
2003	7371
2004	7464
2005	7558
2006	7640
2007	7712

Source: Statistical Abstract of the United States, 2009.

(a) Compute the ratios of the population in one year by the population in the previous year.

(b) Based on part (a), create an exponential model for the population of Virginia.

(c) Use your model in part (b) to predict the population of Virginia in 2012.

In Exercises 21–32, use an exponential model to solve the problem.

21. *Population Growth* The population of Knoxville is 500,000 and is increasing at the rate of 3.75% each year. Approximately when will the population reach 1 million?

22. *Population Growth* The population of Silver Run in the year 1890 was 6250. Assume the population increased at a rate of 2.75% per year.

(a) Estimate the population in 1915 and 1940.

(b) Approximately when did the population reach 50,000?

23. *Radioactive Decay* The half-life of phosphorus-32 is about 14 days. There are 6.6 grams present initially.

(a) Express the amount of phosphorus-32 remaining as a function of time t.

(b) When will there be 1 gram remaining?

24. *Finding Time* If John invests $2300 in a savings account with a 6% interest rate compounded annually, how long will it take until John's account has a balance of $4150?

25. *Doubling Your Money* Determine how much time is required for an investment to double in value if interest is earned at the rate of 6.25% compounded annually.

26. *Doubling Your Money* Determine how much time is required for an investment to double in value if interest is earned at the rate of 6.25% compounded monthly.

27. *Doubling Your Money* Determine how much time is required for an investment to double in value if interest is earned at the rate of 6.25% compounded continuously.

28. *Tripling Your Money* Determine how much time is required for an investment to triple in value if interest is earned at the rate of 5.75% compounded annually.

29. *Tripling Your Money* Determine how much time is required for an investment to triple in value if interest is earned at the rate of 5.75% compounded daily.

30. *Tripling Your Money* Determine how much time is required for an investment to triple in value if interest is earned at the rate of 5.75% compounded continuously.

31. *Cholera Bacteria* Suppose that a colony of bacteria starts with 1 bacterium and doubles in number every half hour. How many bacteria will the colony contain at the end of 24 h?

32. *Eliminating a Disease* Suppose that in any given year, the number of cases of a disease is reduced by 20%. If there are 10,000 cases today, how many years will it take

(a) to reduce the number of cases to 1000?

(b) to eliminate the disease; that is, to reduce the number of cases to less than 1?

Group Activity In Exercises 33–36, copy and complete the table for the function.

33. $y = 2x - 3$

x	y	Change (Δy)
1	?	
		?
2	?	
		?
3	?	
		?
4	?	

34. $y = -3x + 4$

x	y	Change (Δy)
1	?	
		?
2	?	
		?
3	?	
		?
4	?	

35. $y = x^2$

x	y	Change (Δy)
1	?	
		?
2	?	
		?
3	?	
		?
4	?	

36. $y = 3e^x$

x	y	Ratio (y_i/y_{i-1})
1	?	
		?
2	?	
		?
3	?	
		?
4	?	

37. Writing to Learn Explain how the change Δy is related to the slopes of the lines in Exercises 33 and 34. If the changes in x are constant for a linear function, what would you conclude about the corresponding changes in y?

38. *Bacteria Growth* The number of bacteria in a petri dish culture after t hours is

$$B = 100e^{0.693t}.$$

(a) What was the initial number of bacteria present?

(b) How many bacteria are present after 6 hours?

(c) Approximately when will the number of bacteria be 200? Estimate the doubling time of the bacteria.

39. *Population of Texas* Table 1.11 gives the population of Texas for several years.

TABLE 1.11 Population of Texas

Year	Population (thousands)
1980	14,229
1990	16,986
1995	18,959
1998	20,158
1999	20,558
2000	20,852

Source: Statistical Abstract of the United States, 2004–2005.

(a) Let $x = 0$ represent 1980, $x = 1$ represent 1981, and so forth. Find an exponential regression for the data, and superimpose its graph on a scatter plot of the data.

(b) Use the exponential regression equation to estimate the population of Texas in 2003. How close is the estimate to the actual population of 22,119,000 in 2003?

(c) Use the exponential regression equation to estimate the annual rate of growth of the population of Texas.

40. *Population of California* Table 1.12 gives the population of California for several years.

TABLE 1.12 Population of California

Year	Population (thousands)
1980	23,668
1990	29,811
1995	31,697
1998	32,988
1999	33,499
2000	33,872

Source: Statistical Abstract of the United States, 2004–2005.

(a) Let $x = 0$ represent 1980, $x = 1$ represent 1981, and so forth. Find an exponential regression for the data, and superimpose its graph on a scatter plot of the data.

(b) Use the exponential regression equation to estimate the population of California in 2003. How close is the estimate to the actual population of 35,484,000 in 2003?

(c) Use the exponential regression equation to estimate the annual rate of growth of the population of California.

Standardized Test Questions

You may use a graphing calculator to solve the following problems.

41. True or False The number 3^{-2} is negative. Justify your answer.

42. True or False If $4^3 = 2^a$, then $a = 6$. Justify your answer.

43. Multiple Choice John invests \$200 at 4.5% compounded annually. About how long will it take for John's investment to double in value?

(A) 6 yr (B) 9 yr (C) 12 yr (D) 16 yr (E) 20 yr

44. Multiple Choice Which of the following gives the domain of $y = 2e^{-x} - 3$?

(A) $(-\infty, \infty)$ (B) $[-3, \infty)$ (C) $[-1, \infty)$ (D) $(-\infty, 3]$ (E) $x \neq 0$

45. Multiple Choice Which of the following gives the range of $y = 4 - 2^{2x}$?

(A) $(-\infty, \infty)$ (B) $(-\infty, 4)$ (C) $[-4, \infty)$ (D) $(-\infty, 4]$ (E) all reals

46. Multiple Choice Which of the following gives the best approximation for the zero of $f(x) = 4 - e^x$?

(A) $x = -1.386$ (B) $x = 0.386$ (C) $x = 1.386$ (D) $x = 3$ (E) There are no zeros.

Exploration

47. Let $y_1 = x^2$ and $y_2 = 2^x$.

(a) Graph y_1 and y_2 in $[-5, 5]$ by $[-2, 10]$. How many times do you think the two graphs cross?

(b) Compare the corresponding changes in y_1 and y_2 as x changes from 1 to 2, 2 to 3, and so on. How large must x be for the changes in y_2 to overtake the changes in y_1?

(c) Solve for x: $x^2 = 2^x$.

(d) Solve for x: $x^2 < 2^x$.

Extending the Ideas

In Exercises 48 and 49, assume that the graph of the exponential function $f(x) = k \cdot a^x$ passes through the two points. Find the values of a and k.

48. $(1, 4.5), (-1, 0.5)$

49. $(1, 1.5), (-1, 6)$

Quick Quiz for AP* Preparation: Sections 1.1–1.3

You may use a graphing calculator to solve the following problems.

1. Multiple Choice Which of the following gives an equation for the line through $(3, -1)$ and parallel to the line $y = -2x + 1$?

(A) $= \frac{1}{2}x + \frac{7}{2}$ (B) $y = \frac{1}{2}x - \frac{5}{2}$ (C) $y = -2x + 5$ (D) $y = -2x - 7$ (E) $y = -2x + 1$

2. Multiple Choice If $f(x) = x^2 + 1$ and $g(x) = 2x - 1$, which of the following gives $f \circ g(2)$?

(A) 2 (B) 5 (C) 9 (D) 10 (E) 15

3. Multiple Choice The half-life of a certain radioactive substance is 8 hr. There are 5 grams present initially. Which of the following gives the best approximation when there will be 1 gram remaining?

(A) 2 (B) 10 (C) 15 (D) 16 (E) 19

4. Free Response Let $f(x) = e^{-x} - 2$.

(a) Find the domain of f. (b) Find the range of f.

(c) Find the zeros of f.

1.4 Parametric Equations

What you will learn about . . .

- Relations
- Circles
- Ellipses
- Lines and Other Curves

and why . . .

Parametric equations can be used to obtain graphs of relations and functions.

Relations

A **relation** is a set of ordered pairs (x, y) of real numbers. The **graph of a relation** is the set of points in the plane that correspond to the ordered pairs of the relation. If x and y are *functions* of a third variable t, called a *parameter*, then we can use the *parametric mode* of a grapher to obtain a graph of the relation.

EXAMPLE 1 Graphing Half a Parabola

Describe the graph of the relation determined by

$$x = \sqrt{t}, \quad y = t, \quad t \geq 0.$$

Indicate the direction in which the curve is traced. Find a Cartesian equation for a curve that contains the parametrized curve.

SOLUTION

Set $x_1 = \sqrt{t}$, $y_1 = t$, and use the parametric mode of the grapher to draw the graph in Figure 1.28. The graph appears to be the right half of the parabola $y = x^2$. Notice that there is no information about t on the graph itself. The curve appears to be traced to the upper right with starting point $(0, 0)$.

Confirm Algebraically Both x and y will be greater than or equal to zero because $t \geq 0$. Eliminating t we find that for every value of t,

$$y = t = (\sqrt{t})^2 = x^2.$$

Thus, the relation is the function $y = x^2$, $x \geq 0$.

Now Try Exercise 5.

$x = \sqrt{t}$, $y = t$

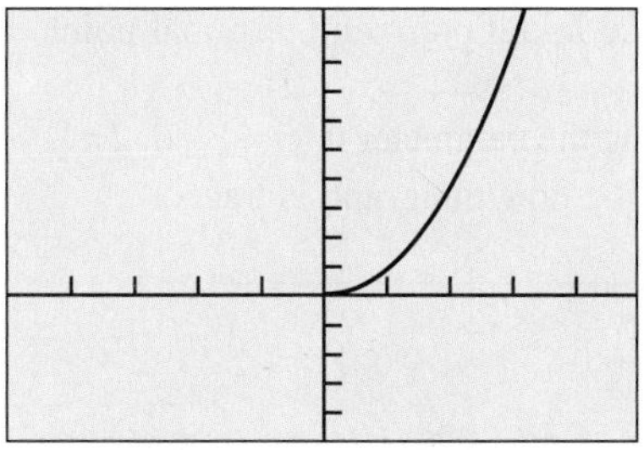

[–5, 5] by [–5, 10]

Figure 1.28 You must choose a *smallest* and *largest* value for t in parametric mode. Here we used 0 and 10, respectively. (Example 1)

DEFINITIONS Parametric Curve, Parametric Equations

If x and y are given as functions

$$x = f(t), \quad y = g(t)$$

over an interval of t-values, then the set of points $(x, y) = (f(t), g(t))$ defined by these equations is a **parametric curve**. The equations are **parametric equations** for the curve.

The variable t is a **parameter** for the curve and its domain I is the **parameter interval.** If I is a closed interval, $a \leq t \leq b$, the point $(f(a), g(a))$ is the **initial point of the curve** and the point $(f(b), g(b))$ is the **terminal point of the curve.** When we give parametric equations and a parameter interval for a curve, we say that we have **parametrized** the curve. The equations and interval constitute a **parametrization of the curve.**

In Example 1, the parameter interval is $[0, \infty)$, so $(0, 0)$ is the initial point and there is no terminal point.

A grapher can draw a parametrized curve only over a closed interval, so the portion it draws has endpoints even when the curve being graphed does not. Keep this in mind when you graph.

Circles

In applications, t often denotes time, an angle, or the distance a particle has traveled along its path from its starting point. In fact, parametric graphing can be used to simulate the motion of the particle.

EXPLORATION 1 Parametrizing Circles

Let $x = a \cos t$ and $y = a \sin t$.

1. Let $a = 1, 2,$ or 3 and graph the parametric equations in a *square viewing window* using the parameter interval $[0, 2\pi]$. How does changing a affect this graph?
2. Let $a = 2$ and graph the parametric equations using the following parameter intervals: $[0, \pi/2]$, $[0, \pi]$, $[0, 3\pi/2]$, $[2\pi, 4\pi]$, and $[0, 4\pi]$. Describe the role of the length of the parameter interval.
3. Let $a = 3$ and graph the parametric equations using the intervals $[\pi/2, 3\pi/2]$, $[\pi, 2\pi]$, $[3\pi/2, 3\pi]$, and $[\pi, 5\pi]$. What are the initial point and terminal point in each case?
4. Graph $x = 2 \cos(-t)$ and $y = 2 \sin(-t)$ using the parameter intervals $[0, 2\pi]$, $[\pi, 3\pi]$, and $[\pi/2, 3\pi/2]$. In each case, describe how the graph is traced.

For $x = a \cos t$ and $y = a \sin t$, we have

$$x^2 + y^2 = a^2 \cos^2 t + a^2 \sin^2 t = a^2(\cos^2 t + \sin^2 t) = a^2(1) = a^2,$$

using the identity $\cos^2 t + \sin^2 t = 1$. Thus, the curves in Exploration 1 were either circles or portions of circles, each with center at the origin.

EXAMPLE 2 Graphing a Circle

Describe the graph of the relation determined by

$$x = 2 \cos t, \quad y = 2 \sin t, \quad 0 \le t \le 2\pi.$$

Find the initial and terminal points, if any, and indicate the direction in which the curve is traced. Find a Cartesian equation for a curve that contains the parametrized curve.

SOLUTION

Figure 1.29 shows that the graph appears to be a circle with radius 2. By watching the graph develop we can see that the curve is traced exactly once counterclockwise. The initial point at $t = 0$ is $(2, 0)$, and the terminal point at $t = 2\pi$ is also $(2, 0)$.

Next we eliminate the variable t.

$$\begin{aligned} x^2 + y^2 &= 4 \cos^2 t + 4 \sin^2 t \\ &= 4(\cos^2 t + \sin^2 t) \\ &= 4 \qquad \text{Because } \cos^2 t + \sin^2 t = 1 \end{aligned}$$

The parametrized curve is a circle centered at the origin of radius 2.

Now Try Exercise 9.

$x = 2 \cos t, y = 2 \sin t$

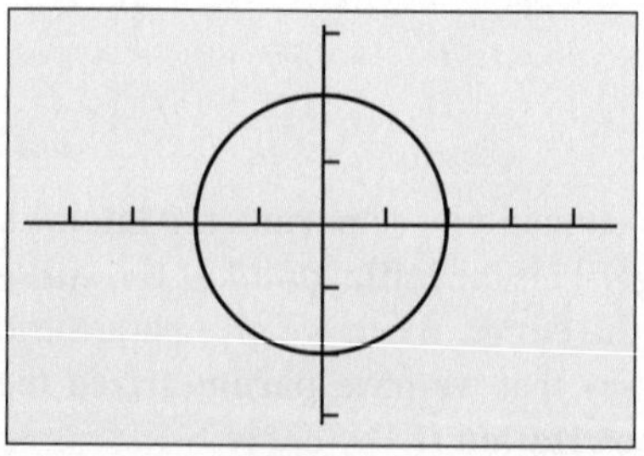

[–4.7, 4.7] by [–3.1, 3.1]

Figure 1.29 A graph of the parametric curve $x = 2 \cos t$, $y = 2 \sin t$, with Tmin $= 0$, Tmax $= 2\pi$, and Tstep $= \pi/24 \approx 0.131$. (Example 2)

Ellipses

Parametrizations of ellipses are similar to parametrizations of circles. Recall that the standard form of an ellipse centered at $(0, 0)$ is

$$\frac{x^2}{a^2} + \frac{y^2}{b^2} = 1.$$

EXAMPLE 3 Graphing an Ellipse

Graph the parametric curve $x = 3 \cos t$, $y = 4 \sin t$, $0 \leq t \leq 2\pi$.

Find a Cartesian equation for a curve that contains the parametric curve. What portion of the graph of the Cartesian equation is traced by the parametric curve? Indicate the direction in which the curve is traced and the initial and terminal points, if any.

SOLUTION

Figure 1.30 suggests that the curve is an ellipse. The Cartesian equation is

$$\left(\frac{x}{3}\right)^2 + \left(\frac{y}{4}\right)^2 = \cos^2 t + \sin^2 t = 1,$$

so the parametrized curve lies along an ellipse with major axis endpoints $(0, \pm 4)$ and minor axis endpoints $(\pm 3, 0)$. As t increases from 0 to 2π, the point $(x, y) = (3 \cos t, 4 \sin t)$ starts at $(3, 0)$ and traces the entire ellipse once counterclockwise. Thus, $(3, 0)$ is both the initial point and the terminal point.

Now Try Exercise 13.

$x = 3 \cos t$, $y = 4 \sin t$

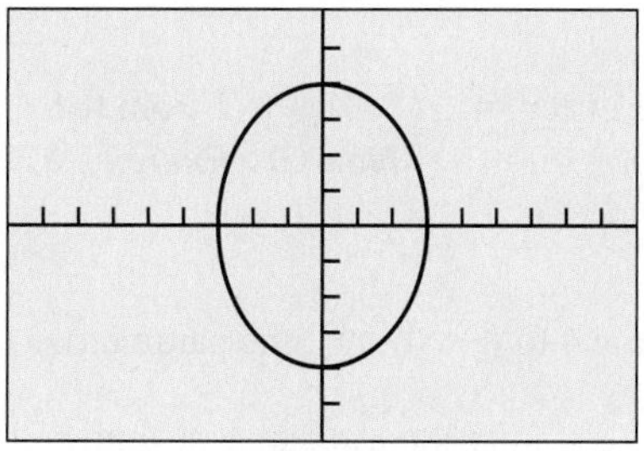

[–9, 9] by [–6, 6]

Figure 1.30 A graph of the parametric equations $x = 3 \cos t$, $y = 4 \sin t$ for $0 \leq t \leq 2\pi$. (Example 3)

EXPLORATION 2 Parametrizing Ellipses

Let $x = a \cos t$ and $y = b \sin t$.

1. Let $a = 2$ and $b = 3$. Then graph using the parameter interval $[0, 2\pi]$. Repeat, changing b to 4, 5, and 6.
2. Let $a = 3$ and $b = 4$. Then graph using the parameter interval $[0, 2\pi]$. Repeat, changing a to 5, 6, and 7.
3. Based on parts 1 and 2, how do you identify the axis that contains the major axis of the ellipse? the minor axis?
4. Let $a = 4$ and $b = 3$. Then graph using the parameter intervals $[0, \pi/2]$, $[0, \pi]$, $[0, 3\pi/2]$, and $[0, 4\pi]$. Describe the role of the length of the parameter interval.
5. Graph $x = 5 \cos(-t)$ and $y = 2 \sin(-t)$ using the parameter intervals $(0, 2\pi]$, $[\pi, 3\pi]$, and $[\pi/2, 3\pi/2]$. Describe how the graph is traced. What are the initial point and terminal point in each case?

For $x = a \cos t$ and $y = b \sin t$, we have $(x/a)^2 + (y/b)^2 = \cos^2 t + \sin^2 t = 1$. Thus, the curves in Exploration 2 were either ellipses or portions of ellipses, each with center at the origin.

In the exercises you will see how to graph hyperbolas parametrically.

Lines and Other Curves

Lines, line segments, and many other curves can be defined parametrically.

$x = 3t, y = 2 - 2t$

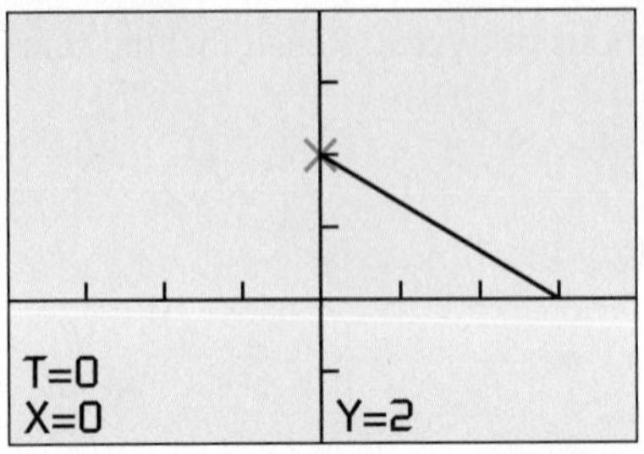

[–4, 4] by [–2, 4]

Figure 1.31 The graph of the line segment $x = 3t$, $y = 2 - 2t$, $0 \le t \le 1$, with trace on the initial point $(0, 2)$. (Example 4)

EXAMPLE 4 Graphing a Line Segment

Draw and identify the graph of the parametric curve determined by

$$x = 3t, \quad y = 2 - 2t, \quad 0 \le t \le 1.$$

SOLUTION

The graph (Figure 1.31) appears to be a line segment with endpoints $(0, 2)$ and $(3, 0)$.

Confirm Algebraically When $t = 0$, the equations give $x = 0$ and $y = 2$. When $t = 1$, they give $x = 3$ and $y = 0$. When we substitute $t = x/3$ into the y equation, we obtain

$$y = 2 - 2\left(\frac{x}{3}\right) = -\frac{2}{3}x + 2.$$

Thus, the parametric curve traces the segment of the line $y = -(2/3)x + 2$ from the point $(0, 2)$ to $(3, 0)$. ***Now Try Exercise 17.***

$x = 2 \cot t, y = 2 \sin^2 t$

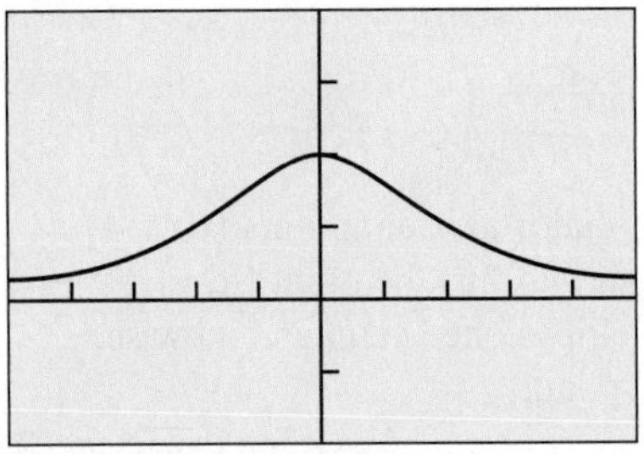

[–5, 5] by [–2, 4]

Figure 1.32 The witch of Agnesi. (Exploration 3)

If we change the parameter interval $[0, 1]$ in Example 4 to $(-\infty, \infty)$, the parametrization will trace the entire line $y = -(2/3)x + 2$.

The bell-shaped curve in Exploration 3 is the famous witch of Agnesi. You will find more information about this curve in Exercise 47.

EXPLORATION 3 Graphing the Witch of Agnesi

The witch of Agnesi is the curve

$$x = 2 \cot t, \quad y = 2 \sin^2 t, \quad 0 < t < \pi.$$

1. Draw the curve using the window in Figure 1.32. What did you choose as a closed parameter interval for your grapher? In what direction is the curve traced? How far to the left and right of the origin do you think the curve extends?
2. Graph the same parametric equations using the parameter intervals $(-\pi/2, \pi/2)$, $(0, \pi/2)$, and $(\pi/2, \pi)$. In each case, describe the curve you see and the direction in which it is traced by your grapher.
3. What happens if you replace $x = 2 \cot t$ by $x = -2 \cot t$ in the original parametrization? What happens if you use $x = 2 \cot(\pi - t)$?

Maria Agnesi (1718–1799)

The first text to include differential and integral calculus along with analytic geometry, infinite series, and differential equations was written in the 1740s by the Italian mathematician Maria Gaetana Agnesi. Agnesi, a gifted scholar and linguist whose Latin essay defending higher education for women was published when she was only 9 years old, was a well-published scientist by age 20, and an honorary faculty member of the University of Bologna by age 30.

Today, Agnesi is remembered chiefly for a bell-shaped curve called *the witch of Agnesi.* This name, found only in English texts, is the result of a mistranslation. Agnesi's own name for the curve was *versiera* or "turning curve." John Colson, a noted Cambridge mathematician, probably confused *versiera* with *avversiera*, which means "wife of the devil" and translated it into "witch."

EXAMPLE 5 Parametrizing a Line Segment

Find a parametrization for the line segment with endpoints $(-2, 1)$ and $(3, 5)$.

SOLUTION

Using $(-2, 1)$ we create the parametric equations

$$x = -2 + at, \qquad y = 1 + bt.$$

These represent a line, as we can see by solving each equation for t and equating to obtain

$$\frac{x + 2}{a} = \frac{y - 1}{b}.$$

continued

This line goes through the point $(-2, 1)$ when $t = 0$. We determine a and b so that the line goes through $(3, 5)$ when $t = 1$.

$$3 = -2 + a \quad \Rightarrow \quad a = 5 \qquad x = 3 \text{ when } t = 1.$$

$$5 = 1 + b \quad \Rightarrow \quad b = 4 \qquad y = 5 \text{ when } t = 1.$$

Therefore,

$$x = -2 + 5t, \quad y = 1 + 4t, \quad 0 \le t \le 1$$

is a parametrization of the line segment with initial point $(-2, 1)$ and terminal point $(3, 5)$.

Now Try Exercise 23.

Quick Review 1.4 *(For help, go to Section 1.1 and Appendix A1.)*

Exercise numbers with a gray background indicate problems that the authors have designed to be solved *without a calculator*.

In Exercises 1–3, write an equation for the line.

1. the line through the points $(1, 8)$ and $(4, 3)$

2. the horizontal line through the point $(3, -4)$

3. the vertical line through the point $(2, -3)$

In Exercises 4–6, find the x- and y-intercepts of the graph of the relation.

4. $\dfrac{x^2}{9} + \dfrac{y^2}{16} = 1$ **5.** $\dfrac{x^2}{16} - \dfrac{y^2}{9} = 1$

6. $2y^2 = x + 1$

In Exercises 7 and 8, determine whether the given points lie on the graph of the relation.

7. $2x^2y + y^2 = 3$

(a) $(1, 1)$ **(b)** $(-1, -1)$ **(c)** $(1/2, -2)$

8. $9x^2 - 18x + 4y^2 = 27$

(a) $(1, 3)$ **(b)** $(1, -3)$ **(c)** $(-1, 3)$

9. Solve for t.

(a) $2x + 3t = -5$ **(b)** $3y - 2t = -1$

10. For what values of a is each equation true?

(a) $\sqrt{a^2} = a$ **(b)** $\sqrt{a^2} = \pm a$

(c) $\sqrt{4a^2} = 2|a|$

Section 1.4 Exercises

In Exercises 1–4, match the parametric equations with their graph. State the approximate dimensions of the viewing window. Give a parameter interval that traces the curve exactly once.

1. $x = 3 \sin (2t), \quad y = 1.5 \cos t$

2. $x = \sin^3 t, \quad y = \cos^3 t$

3. $x = 7 \sin t - \sin (7t), \quad y = 7 \cos t - \cos (7t)$

4. $x = 12 \sin t - 3 \sin (6t), \quad y = 12 \cos t + 3 \cos (6t)$

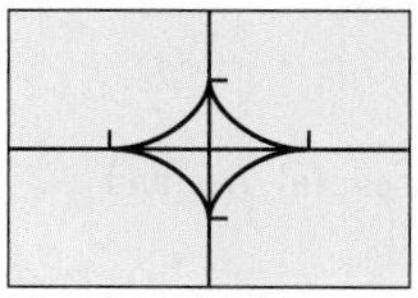

(a)

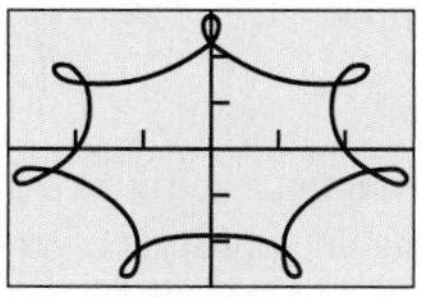

(b)

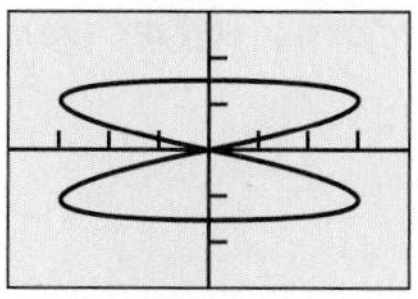

(c)

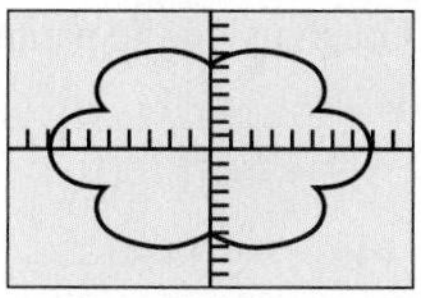

(d)

In Exercises 5–22, a parametrization is given for a curve.

(a) Graph the curve. What are the initial and terminal points, if any? Indicate the direction in which the curve is traced.

(b) Find a Cartesian equation for a curve that contains the parametrized curve. What portion of the graph of the Cartesian equation is traced by the parametrized curve?

5. $x = 3t, \quad y = 9t^2, \quad -\infty < t < \infty$

6. $x = -\sqrt{t}, \quad y = t, \quad t \ge 0$

7. $x = t, \quad y = \sqrt{t}, \quad t \ge 0$

8. $x = (\sec^2 t) - 1, \quad y = \tan t, \quad -\pi/2 < t < \pi/2$

9. $x = \cos t, \quad y = \sin t, \quad 0 \le t \le \pi$

10. $x = \sin (2\pi t), \quad y = \cos (2\pi t), \quad 0 \le t \le 1$

11. $x = \cos (\pi - t), \quad y = \sin (\pi - t), \quad 0 \le t \le \pi$

12. $x = 4 \cos t, \quad y = 2 \sin t, \quad 0 \le t \le 2\pi$

13. $x = 4 \sin t, \quad y = 2 \cos t, \quad 0 \le t \le \pi$

14. $x = 4 \sin t, \quad y = 5 \cos t, \quad 0 \le t \le 2\pi$

15. $x = 2t - 5, \quad y = 4t - 7, \quad -\infty < t < \infty$

16. $x = 1 - t, \quad y = 1 + t, \quad -\infty < t < \infty$

17. $x = t, \quad y = 1 - t, \quad 0 \le t \le 1$

18. $x = 3 - 3t, \quad y = 2t, \quad 0 \le t \le 1$

19. $x = 4 - \sqrt{t}, \quad y = \sqrt{t}, \quad 0 \le t$

20. $x = t^2, \quad y = \sqrt{4 - t^2}, \quad 0 \le t \le 2$

21. $x = \sin t, \quad y = \cos 2t, \quad -\infty < t < \infty$

22. $x = t^2 - 3, \quad y = t, \quad t \le 0$

In Exercises 23–28, find a parametrization for the curve.

23. the line segment with endpoints $(-1, -3)$ and $(4, 1)$

24. the line segment with endpoints $(-1, 3)$ and $(3, -2)$

25. the lower half of the parabola $x - 1 = y^2$

26. the left half of the parabola $y = x^2 + 2x$

27. the ray (half line) with initial point $(2, 3)$ that passes through the point $(-1, -1)$

28. the ray (half line) with initial point $(-1, 2)$ that passes through the point $(0, 0)$

Group Activity In Exercises 29–32, refer to the graph of

$$x = 3 - |t|, \quad y = t - 1, \quad -5 \le t \le 5,$$

shown in the figure. Find the values of t that produce the graph in the given quadrant.

29. Quadrant I

30. Quadrant II

31. Quadrant III

32. Quadrant IV

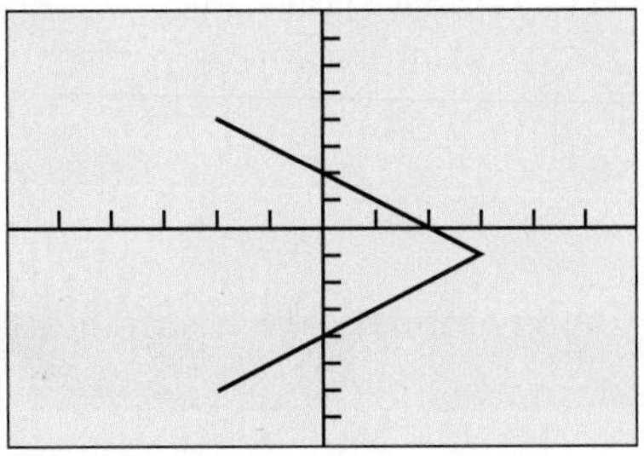

[–6, 6] by [–8, 8]

In Exercises 33 and 34, find a parametrization for the part of the graph that lies in Quadrant I.

33. $y = x^2 + 2x + 2$

34. $y = \sqrt{x + 3}$

35. ***Circles*** Find parametrizations to model the motion of a particle that starts at $(a, 0)$ and traces the circle $x^2 + y^2 = a^2, a > 0$, as indicated.

(a) once clockwise
(b) once counterclockwise
(c) twice clockwise
(d) twice counterclockwise

36. ***Ellipses*** Find parametrizations to model the motion of a particle that starts at $(-a, 0)$ and traces the ellipse

$$\left(\frac{x}{a}\right)^2 + \left(\frac{y}{b}\right)^2 = 1, \quad a > 0, b > 0,$$

as indicated.

(a) once clockwise
(b) once counterclockwise
(c) twice clockwise
(d) twice counterclockwise

Standardized Test Questions

You may use a graphing calculator to solve the following problems.

37. True or False The graph of the parametric curve $x = 3 \cos t$, $y = 4 \sin t$ is a circle. Justify your answer.

38. True or False The parametric curve $x = 2 \cos(-t)$, $y = 2 \sin(-t)$, $0 \le t \le 2\pi$ is traced clockwise. Justify your answer.

In Exercises 39 and 40, use the parametric curve $x = 5t$, $y = 3 - 3t$, $0 \le t \le 1$.

39. Multiple Choice Which of the following describes its graph?
(A) circle (B) parabola (C) ellipse
(D) line segment (E) line

40. Multiple Choice Which of the following is the initial point of the curve?
(A) $(-5, 6)$ (B) $(0, -3)$ (C) $(0, 3)$ (D) $(5, 0)$
(E) $(10, -3)$

41. Multiple Choice Which of the following describes the graph of the parametric curve $x = -3 \sin t$, $y = -3 \cos t$?
(A) circle (B) parabola (C) ellipse
(D) hyperbola (E) line

42. Multiple Choice Which of the following describes the graph of the parametric curve $x = 3t$, $y = 2t$, $t \ge 1$?
(A) circle (B) parabola (C) line segment
(D) line (E) ray

Explorations

43. ***Hyperbolas*** Let $x = a \sec t$ and $y = b \tan t$.

(a) **Writing to Learn** Let $a = 1, 2$, or 3, $b = 1, 2$, or 3, and graph using the parameter interval $(-\pi/2, \pi/2)$. Explain what you see, and describe the role of a and b in these parametric equations. (Caution: If you get what appear to be asymptotes, try using the approximation $[-1.57, 1.57]$ for the parameter interval.)

(b) Let $a = 2$, $b = 3$, and graph in the parameter interval $(\pi/2, 3\pi/2)$. Explain what you see.

(c) **Writing to Learn** Let $a = 2$, $b = 3$, and graph using the parameter interval $(-\pi/2, 3\pi/2)$. Explain why you must be careful about graphing in this interval or any interval that contains $\pm\pi/2$.

(d) Use algebra to explain why

$$\left(\frac{x}{a}\right)^2 - \left(\frac{y}{b}\right)^2 = 1.$$

(e) Let $x = a \tan t$ and $y = b \sec t$. Repeat (a), (b), and (d) using an appropriate version of (d).

44. ***Transformations*** Let $x = (2 \cos t) + h$ and $y = (2 \sin t) + k$.

(a) **Writing to Learn** Let $k = 0$ and $h = -2, -1, 1$, and 2, in turn. Graph using the parameter interval $[0, 2\pi]$. Describe the role of h.

(b) **Writing to Learn** Let $h = 0$ and $k = -2, -1, 1$, and 2, in turn. Graph using the parameter interval $[0, 2\pi]$. Describe the role of k.

(c) Find a parametrization for the circle with radius 5 and center at $(2, -3)$.

(d) Find a parametrization for the ellipse centered at $(-3, 4)$ with semimajor axis of length 5 parallel to the x-axis and semiminor axis of length 2 parallel to the y-axis.

In Exercises 45 and 46, a parametrization is given for a curve.

(a) Graph the curve. What are the initial and terminal points, if any? Indicate the direction in which the curve is traced.

(b) Find a Cartesian equation for a curve that contains the parametrized curve. What portion of the graph of the Cartesian equation is traced by the parametrized curve?

45. $x = -\sec t, \quad y = \tan t, \quad -\pi/2 < t < \pi/2$

46. $x = \tan t, \quad y = -2 \sec t, \quad -\pi/2 < t < \pi/2$

Extending the Ideas

47. *The Witch of Agnesi* The bell-shaped witch of Agnesi can be constructed as follows. Start with the circle of radius 1, centered at the point $(0, 1)$ as shown in the figure.

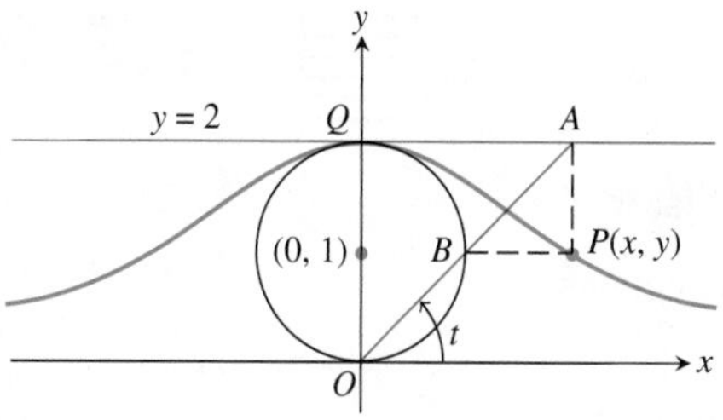

Choose a point A on the line $y = 2$, and connect it to the origin with a line segment. Call the point where the segment crosses the circle B. Let P be the point where the vertical line through A crosses the horizontal line through B. The witch is the curve traced by P as A moves along the line $y = 2$.

Find a parametrization for the witch by expressing the coordinates of P in terms of t, the radian measure of the angle that segment OA makes with the positive x-axis. The following equalities (which you may assume) will help:

(i) $x = AQ$ **(ii)** $y = 2 - AB \sin t$ **(iii)** $AB \cdot AO = (AQ)^2$

48. *Parametrizing Lines and Segments*

(a) Show that $x = x_1 + (x_2 - x_1)t, \quad y = y_1 + (y_2 - y_1)t$, $-\infty < t < \infty$ is a parametrization for the line through the points (x_1, y_1) and (x_2, y_2).

(b) Find a parametrization for the line segment with endpoints (x_1, y_1) and (x_2, y_2).

1.5 Functions and Logarithms

What you will learn about . . .

- One-to-One Functions
- Inverses
- Finding Inverses
- Logarithmic Functions
- Properties of Logarithms
- Applications

and why . . .

Logarithmic functions are used in many applications, including finding time in investment problems.

One-to-One Functions

As you know, a function is a rule that assigns a single value in its range to each point in its domain. Some functions assign the same output to more than one input. For example, $f(x) = x^2$ assigns the output 4 to both 2 and -2. Other functions never output a given value more than once. For example, the cubes of different numbers are always different.

If each output value of a function is associated with exactly one input value, the function is *one-to-one.*

Definition One-to-One Function

A function $f(x)$ is **one-to-one** on a domain D if $f(a) \neq f(b)$ whenever $a \neq b$.

The graph of a one-to-one function $y = f(x)$ can intersect any horizontal line at most once (the *horizontal line test*). If it intersects such a line more than once it assumes the same y-value more than once, and is therefore not one-to-one (Figure 1.33).

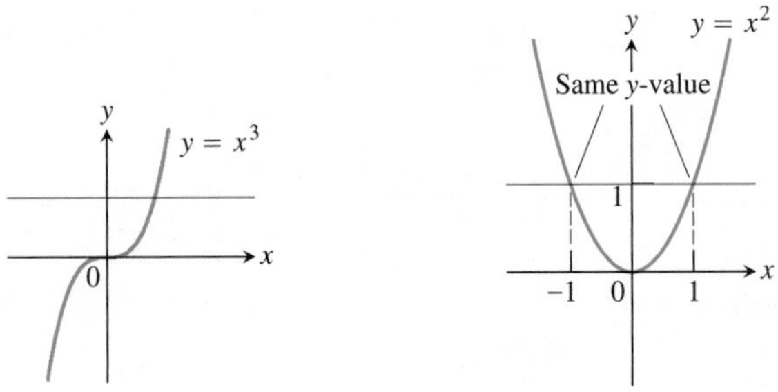

One-to-one: Graph meets each horizontal line once.

Not one-to-one: Graph meets some horizontal lines more than once.

Figure 1.33 Using the horizontal line test, we see that $y = x^3$ is one-to-one and $y = x^2$ is not.

$y = |x|$

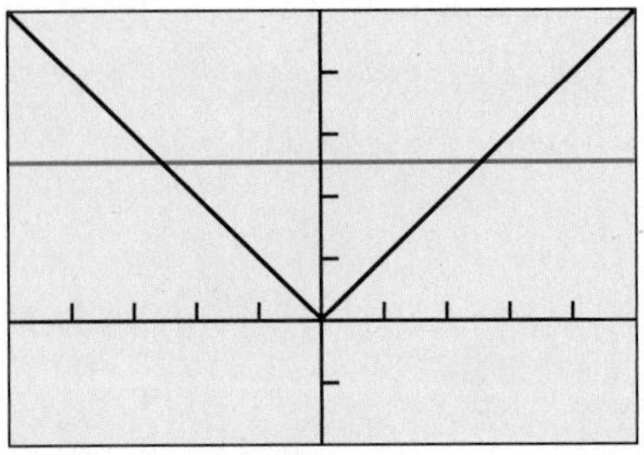

[–5, 5] by [–2, 5]

(a)

$y = \sqrt{x}$

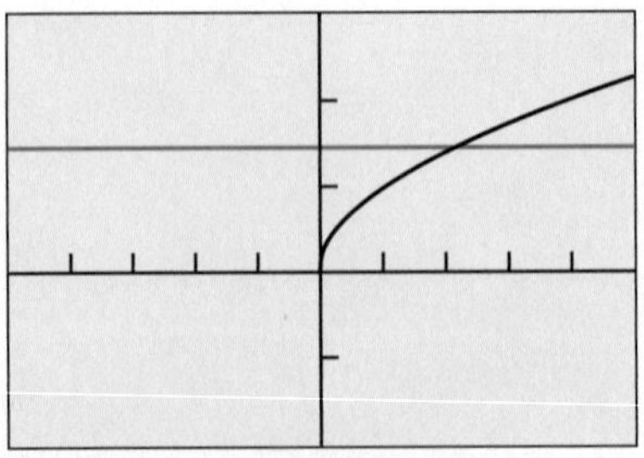

[–5, 5] by [–2, 3]

(b)

Figure 1.34 (a) The graph of $f(x) = |x|$ and a horizontal line. (b) The graph of $g(x) = \sqrt{x}$ and a horizontal line. (Example 1)

EXAMPLE 1 Using the Horizontal Line Test

Determine whether the functions are one-to-one.

(a) $f(x) = |x|$ **(b)** $g(x) = \sqrt{x}$

SOLUTION

(a) As Figure 1.34a suggests, each horizontal line $y = c$, $c > 0$, intersects the graph of $f(x) = |x|$ twice. So f is not one-to-one.

(b) As Figure 1.34b suggests, each horizontal line intersects the graph of $g(x) = \sqrt{x}$ either once or not at all. The function g is one-to-one.

Now Try Exercise 1.

Inverses

Since each output of a one-to-one function comes from just one input, a one-to-one function can be reversed to send outputs back to the inputs from which they came. The function defined by reversing a one-to-one function f is the **inverse of f.** The functions in Tables 1.13 and 1.14 are inverses of one another. The symbol for the inverse of f is f^{-1}, read "f inverse." The -1 in f^{-1} is not an exponent; $f^{-1}(x)$ does not mean $1/f(x)$.

TABLE 1.13 Rental Charge versus Time

Time x (hours)	Charge y (dollars)
1	5.00
2	7.50
3	10.00
4	12.50
5	15.00
6	17.50

TABLE 1.14 Time versus Rental Charge

Charge x (dollars)	Time y (hours)
5.00	1
7.50	2
10.00	3
12.50	4
15.00	5
17.50	6

As Tables 1.13 and 1.14 suggest, composing a function with its inverse in either order sends each output back to the input from which it came. In other words, the result of composing a function and its inverse in either order is the **identity function,** the function that assigns each number to itself. This gives a way to test whether two functions f and g are inverses of one another. Compute $f \circ g$ and $g \circ f$. If $(f \circ g)(x) = (g \circ f)(x) = x$, then f and g are inverses of one another; otherwise they are not. The functions $f(x) = x^3$ and $g(x) = x^{1/3}$ are inverses of one another because $(x^3)^{1/3} = x$ and $(x^{1/3})^3 = x$ for every number x.

EXPLORATION 1 Testing for Inverses Graphically

For each of the function pairs below,

(a) Graph f and g together in a square window.

(b) Graph $f \circ g$. **(c)** Graph $g \circ f$.

What can you conclude from the graphs?

1. $f(x) = x^3, \quad g(x) = x^{1/3}$

2. $f(x) = x, \quad g(x) = 1/x$

3. $f(x) = 3x, \quad g(x) = x/3$

4. $f(x) = e^x, \quad g(x) = \ln x$

Finding Inverses

How do we find the graph of the inverse of a function? Suppose, for example, that the function is the one pictured in Figure 1.35a. To read the graph, we start at the point x on the x-axis, go up to the graph, and then move over to the y-axis to read the value of y. If we start with y and want to find the x from which it came, we reverse the process (Figure 1.35b).

The graph of f is already the graph of f^{-1}, although the latter graph is not drawn in the usual way with the domain axis horizontal and the range axis vertical. For f^{-1}, the input-output pairs are reversed. To display the graph of f^{-1} in the usual way, we have to reverse the pairs by reflecting the graph across the 45° line $y = x$ (Figure 1.35c) and interchanging the letters x and y (Figure 1.35d). This puts the independent variable, now called x, on the horizontal axis and the dependent variable, now called y, on the vertical axis.

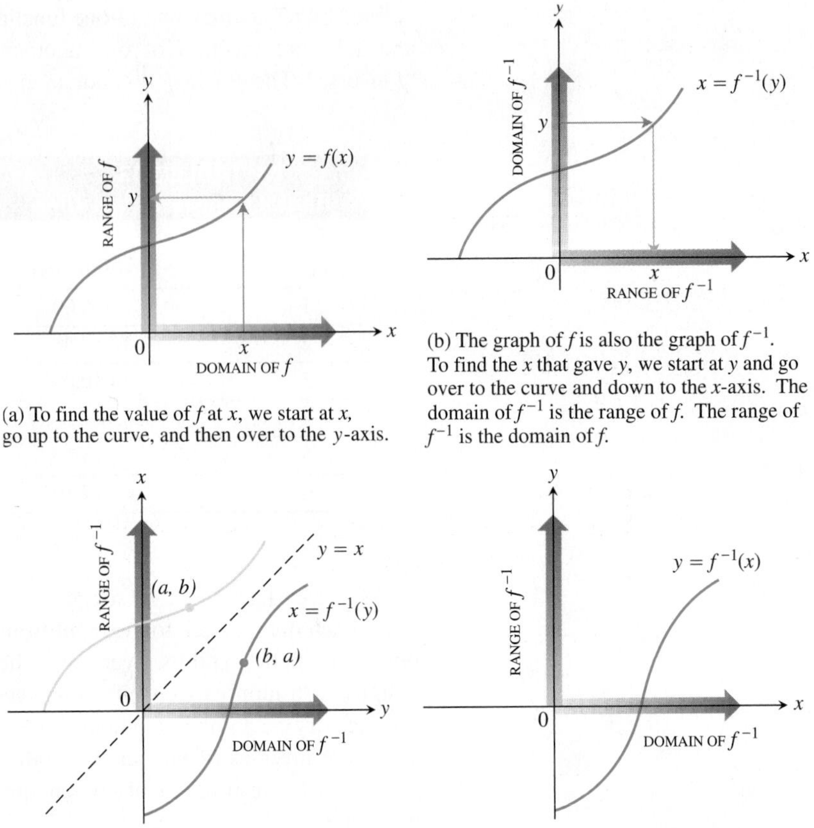

(a) To find the value of f at x, we start at x, go up to the curve, and then over to the y-axis.

(b) The graph of f is also the graph of f^{-1}. To find the x that gave y, we start at y and go over to the curve and down to the x-axis. The domain of f^{-1} is the range of f. The range of f^{-1} is the domain of f.

(c) To draw the graph of f^{-1} in the usual way, we reflect the system across the line $y = x$.

(d) Then we interchange the letters x and y. We now have a normal-looking graph of f^{-1} as a function of x.

Figure 1.35 The graph of $y = f^{-1}(x)$.

The fact that the graphs of f and f^{-1} are reflections of each other across the line $y = x$ is to be expected because the input-output pairs (a, b) of f have been reversed to produce the input-output pairs (b, a) of f^{-1}.

The pictures in Figure 1.35 tell us how to express f^{-1} as a function of x algebraically.

Writing f^{-1} as a Function of x

1. Solve the equation $y = f(x)$ for x in terms of y.
2. Interchange x and y. The resulting formula will be $y = f^{-1}(x)$.

EXAMPLE 2 Finding the Inverse Function

Show that the function $y = f(x) = -2x + 4$ is one-to-one and find its inverse function.

SOLUTION

Every horizontal line intersects the graph of f exactly once, so f is one-to-one and has an inverse.

Step 1:

Solve for x in terms of y: $y = -2x + 4$

$$x = -\frac{1}{2}y + 2$$

continued

Step 2:

Interchange x and y: $y = -\frac{1}{2}x + 2$

The inverse of the function $f(x) = -2x + 4$ is the function $f^{-1}(x) = -(1/2)x + 2$. We can verify that both composites are the identity function.

$$f^{-1}(f(x)) = -\frac{1}{2}(-2x + 4) + 2 = x - 2 + 2 = x$$

$$f(f^{-1}(x)) = -2\left(-\frac{1}{2}x + 2\right) + 4 = x - 4 + 4 = x$$

Now Try Exercise 13.

Graphing $y = f(x)$ and $y = f^{-1}(x)$ Parametrically

We can graph any function $y = f(x)$ as

$$x_1 = t, \quad y_1 = f(t).$$

Interchanging t and $f(t)$ produces parametric equations for the inverse:

$$x_2 = f(t), \quad y_2 = t.$$

We can use parametric graphing to graph the inverse of a function without finding an explicit rule for the inverse, as illustrated in Example 3.

EXAMPLE 3 Graphing the Inverse Parametrically

(a) Graph the one-to-one function $f(x) = x^2$, $x \geq 0$, together with its inverse and the line $y = x$, $x \geq 0$.

(b) Express the inverse of f as a function of x.

SOLUTION

(a) We can graph the three functions parametrically as follows:

Graph of f: $x_1 = t$, $y_1 = t^2$, $t \geq 0$

Graph of f^{-1}: $x_2 = t^2$, $y_2 = t$

Graph of $y = x$: $x_3 = t$, $y_3 = t$

Figure 1.36 shows the three graphs.

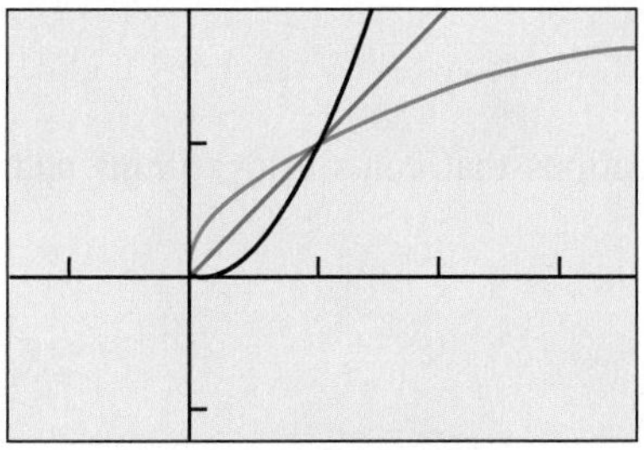

[–1.5, 3.5] by [–1, 2]

Figure 1.36 The graphs of f and f^{-1} are reflections of each other across the line $y = x$. (Example 3)

(b) Next we find a formula for $f^{-1}(x)$.

Step 1:

Solve for x in terms of y.

$$y = x^2$$
$$\sqrt{y} = \sqrt{x^2}$$
$$\sqrt{y} = x \qquad \text{Because } x \geq 0$$

Step 2:

Interchange x and y.

$$\sqrt{x} = y$$

Thus, $f^{-1}(x) = \sqrt{x}$.

Now Try Exercise 27.

Logarithmic Functions

If a is any positive real number other than 1, the base a exponential function $f(x) = a^x$ is one-to-one. It therefore has an inverse. Its inverse is called the *base a logarithm function.*

DEFINITION Base *a* Logarithm Function

The **base *a* logarithm function** $y = \log_a x$ is the inverse of the base a exponential function $y = a^x$ $(a > 0, a \neq 1)$.

The domain of $\log_a x$ is $(0, \infty)$, the range of a^x. The range of $\log_a x$ is $(-\infty, \infty)$, the domain of a^x.

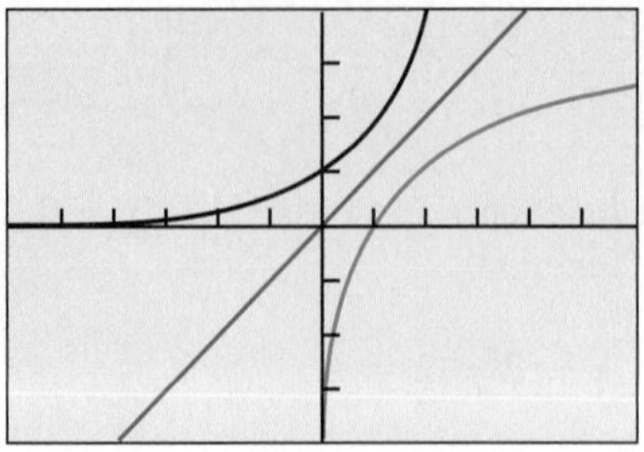

[–6, 6] by [–4, 4]

Figure 1.37 The graphs of $y = 2^x$ ($x_1 = t$, $y_1 = 2^t$), its inverse $y = \log_2 x$ ($x_2 = 2^t$, $y_2 = t$), and $y = x$ ($x_3 = t$, $y_3 = t$).

Because we have no technique for solving for x in terms of y in the equation $y = a^x$, we do not have an explicit formula for the logarithm function as a function of x. However, the graph of $y = \log_a x$ can be obtained by reflecting the graph of $y = a^x$ across the line $y = x$, or by using parametric graphing (Figure 1.37).

Logarithms with base e and base 10 are so important in applications that calculators have special keys for them. They also have their own special notation and names:

$$\log_e x = \ln x,$$
$$\log_{10} x = \log x$$

The function $y = \ln x$ is called the **natural logarithm function** and $y = \log x$ is often called the **common logarithm function.**

Properties of Logarithms

Because a^x and $\log_a x$ are inverses of each other, composing them in either order gives the identity function. This gives two useful properties.

Inverse Properties for a^x and $\log_a x$

1. Base a: $a^{\log_a x} = x$, $\log_a a^x = x$, $a > 1, x > 0$
2. Base e: $e^{\ln x} = x$, $\ln e^x = x$, $x > 0$

These properties help us with the solution of equations that contain logarithms and exponential functions.

EXAMPLE 4 Using the Inverse Properties

Solve for x: **(a)** $\ln x = 3t + 5$ **(b)** $e^{2x} = 10$

SOLUTION

(a) $\ln x = 3t + 5$

$e^{\ln x} = e^{3t+5}$ Exponentiate both sides.

$x = e^{3t+5}$ Inverse Property

(b) $e^{2x} = 10$

$\ln e^{2x} = \ln 10$ Take logarithms of both sides.

$2x = \ln 10$ Inverse Property

$x = \frac{1}{2} \ln 10 \approx 1.15$

Now Try Exercises 33 and 37.

The logarithm function has the following useful arithmetic properties.

Properties of Logarithms

For any real numbers $x > 0$ and $y > 0$,

1. *Product Rule:* $\log_a xy = \log_a x + \log_a y$
2. *Quotient Rule:* $\log_a \frac{x}{y} = \log_a x - \log_a y$
3. *Power Rule:* $\log_a x^y = y \log_a x$

EXPLORATION 2 Supporting the Product Rule

Let $y_1 = \ln(ax)$, $y_2 = \ln x$, and $y_3 = y_1 - y_2$.

1. Graph y_1 and y_2 for $a = 2, 3, 4$, and 5. How do the graphs of y_1 and y_2 appear to be related?
2. Support your finding by graphing y_3.
3. Confirm your finding algebraically.

The following formula allows us to evaluate $\log_a x$ for any base $a > 0$, $a \neq 1$, and to obtain its graph using the natural logarithm function on our grapher.

Change of Base Formula

$$\log_a x = \frac{\ln x}{\ln a}$$

$y = \frac{\ln x}{\ln 2}$

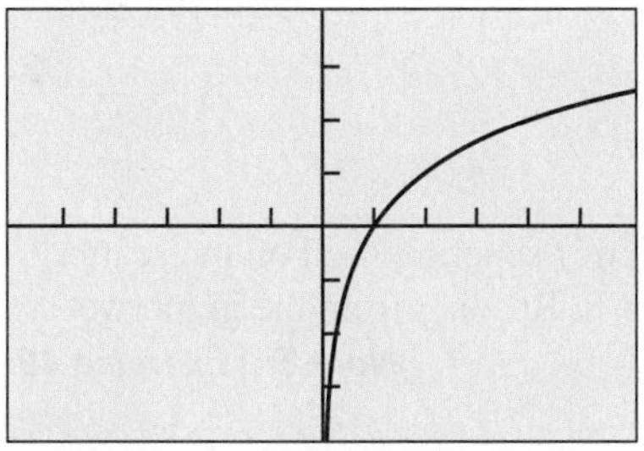

[–6, 6] by [–4, 4]

Figure 1.38 The graph of $f(x) = \log_2 x$ using $f(x) = (\ln x)/(\ln 2)$. (Example 5)

EXAMPLE 5 Graphing a Base *a* Logarithm Function

Graph $f(x) = \log_2 x$.

SOLUTION

We use the change of base formula to rewrite $f(x)$.

$$f(x) = \log_2 x = \frac{\ln x}{\ln 2}$$

Figure 1.38 gives the graph of *f*. ***Now Try Exercise 41.***

Applications

In Section 1.3 we used graphical methods to solve exponential growth and decay problems. Now we can use the properties of logarithms to solve the same problems algebraically.

EXAMPLE 6 Finding Time

Sarah invests \$1000 in an account that earns 5.25% interest compounded annually. How long will it take the account to reach \$2500?

SOLUTION

Model The amount in the account at any time *t* in years is $1000(1.0525)^t$, so we need to solve the equation

$$1000(1.0525)^t = 2500.$$

continued

TABLE 1.15 Saudi Arabia's Natural Gas Production

Year	Cubic Feet (trillions)
2002	2.00
2003	2.12
2004	2.32
2005	2.52
2006	2.59

Source: Statistical Abstract of the United States, 2010.

Solve Algebraically

$$(1.0525)^t = 2.5 \qquad \text{Divide by 1000.}$$

$$\ln (1.0525)^t = \ln 2.5 \qquad \text{Take logarithms of both sides.}$$

$$t \ln 1.0525 = \ln 2.5 \qquad \text{Power Rule}$$

$$t = \frac{\ln 2.5}{\ln 1.0525} \approx 17.9$$

Interpret The amount in Sarah's account will be \$2500 in about 17.9 years, or about 17 years and 11 months. ***Now Try Exercise 47.***

EXAMPLE 7 Estimating Natural Gas Production

Table 1.15 shows the annual number of cubic feet in trillions of natural gas produced by Saudi Arabia for several years.

Find the natural logarithm regression equation for the data in Table 1.15 and use it to estimate the number of cubic feet of natural gas produced by Saudi Arabia in 2008.

SOLUTION

Model We let $x = 0$ represent 2000, $x = 1$ represent 2001, and so forth. We compute the natural logarithm regression equation to be

$$f(x) = 1.558 + 0.571 \ln (x).$$

Solve Graphically Figure 1.39 shows the graph of f superimposed on the scatter plot of the data. The year 2008 is represented by $x = 8$. Reading from the graph we find $f(8) = 2.75$ trillion cubic feet. ***Now Try Exercise 49.***

$f(x) = 1.558 + (0.571) \ln x$

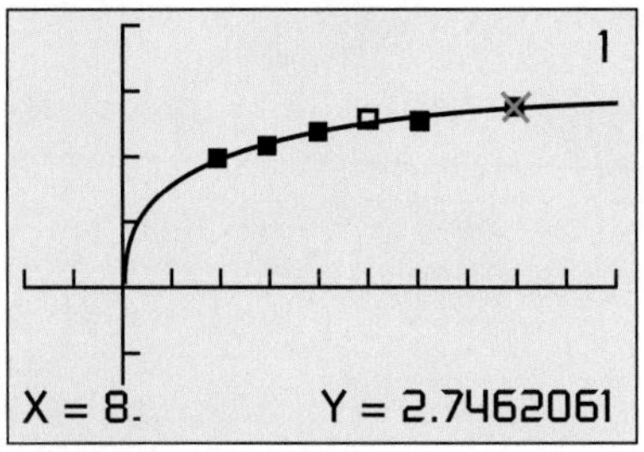

[–2, 10] by [–2, 4]

Figure 1.39 The value of f at $x = 8$ is about 2.75. (Example 7)

Quick Review 1.5 *(For help, go to Sections 1.2, 1.3, and 1.4.)*

Exercise numbers with a gray background indicate problems that the authors have designed to be solved *without a calculator*.

In Exercises 1–4, let $f(x) = \sqrt[3]{x - 1}$, $g(x) = x^2 + 1$, and evaluate the expression.

1. $(f \circ g)(1)$

2. $(g \circ f)(-7)$

3. $(f \circ g)(x)$

4. $(g \circ f)(x)$

In Exercises 5 and 6, choose parametric equations and a parameter interval to represent the function on the interval specified.

5. $y = \dfrac{1}{x - 1}, \quad x \geq 2$

6. $y = x, \quad x < -3$

In Exercises 7–10, find the points of intersection of the two curves. Round your answers to 2 decimal places.

7. $y = 2x - 3, \quad y = 5$

8. $y = -3x + 5, \quad y = -3$

9. **(a)** $y = 2^x, \quad y = 3$

(b) $y = 2^x, \quad y = -1$

10. **(a)** $y = e^{-x}, \quad y = 4$

(b) $y = e^{-x}, \quad y = -1$

Section 1.5 Exercises

In Exercises 1–6, determine whether the function is one-to-one.

1.

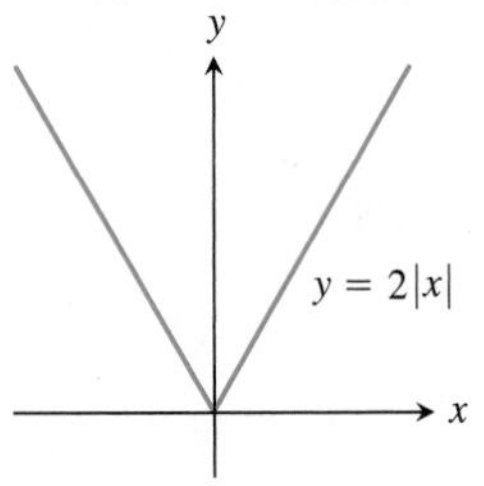

2.

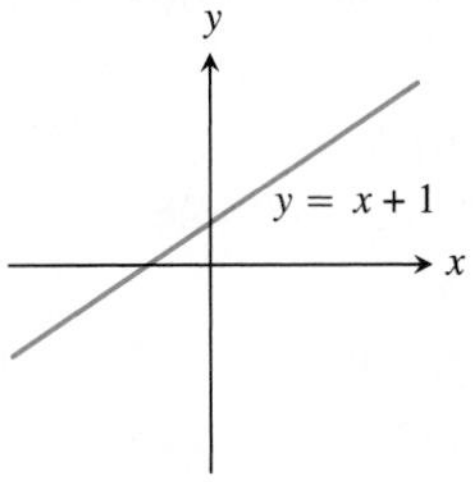

3.

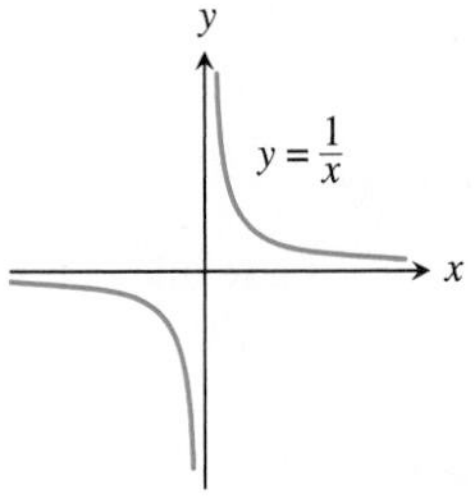

4.

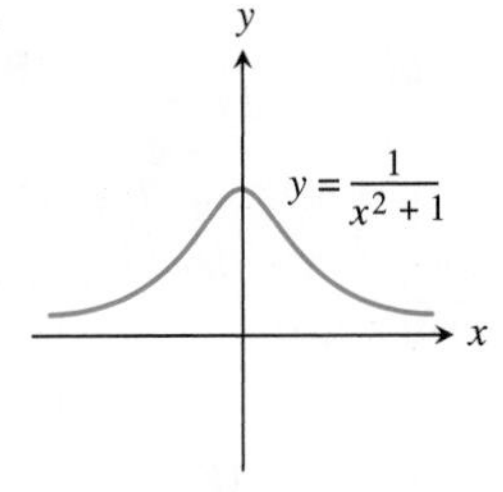

5.

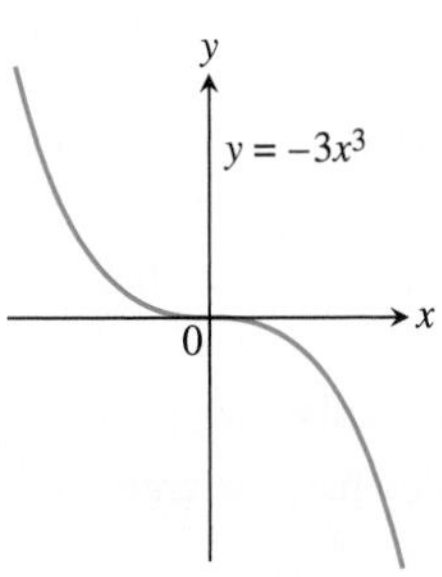

6.

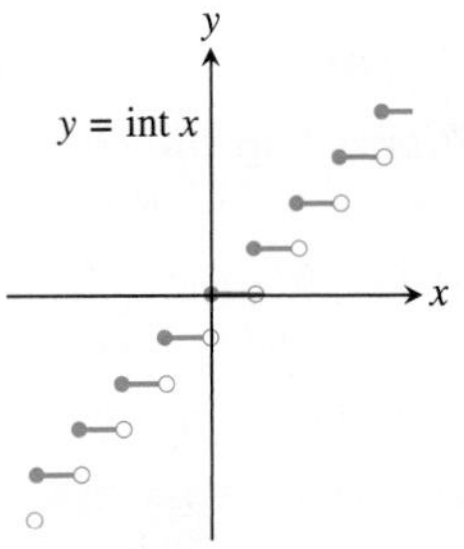

In Exercises 7–12, determine whether the function has an inverse function.

7. $y = \dfrac{3}{x-2} - 1$ **8.** $y = x^2 + 5x$ **9.** $y = x^3 - 4x + 6$

10. $y = x^3 + x$ **11.** $y = \ln x^2$ **12.** $y = 2^{3-x}$

In Exercises 13–24, find f^{-1} and verify that

$$(f \circ f^{-1})(x) = (f^{-1} \circ f)(x) = x.$$

13. $f(x) = 2x + 3$ **14.** $f(x) = 5 - 4x$

15. $f(x) = x^3 - 1$ **16.** $f(x) = x^2 + 1, \quad x \geq 0$

17. $f(x) = x^2, \quad x \leq 0$ **18.** $f(x) = x^{2/3}, \quad x \geq 0$

19. $f(x) = -(x-2)^2, \quad x \leq 2$

20. $f(x) = x^2 + 2x + 1, \quad x \geq -1$

21. $f(x) = \dfrac{1}{x^2}, \quad x > 0$ **22.** $f(x) = \dfrac{1}{x^3}$

23. $f(x) = \dfrac{2x+1}{x+3}$ **24.** $f(x) = \dfrac{x+3}{x-2}$

In Exercises 25–32, use parametric graphing to graph f, f^{-1}, and $y = x$.

25. $f(x) = e^x$ **26.** $f(x) = 3^x$ **27.** $f(x) = 2^{-x}$

28. $f(x) = 3^{-x}$ **29.** $f(x) = \ln x$ **30.** $f(x) = \log x$

31. $f(x) = \sin^{-1} x$ **32.** $f(x) = \tan^{-1} x$

In Exercises 33–36, solve the equation algebraically. Support your solution graphically.

33. $(1.045)^t = 2$ **34.** $e^{0.05t} = 3$

35. $e^x + e^{-x} = 3$ **36.** $2^x + 2^{-x} = 5$

In Exercises 37 and 38, solve for y.

37. $\ln y = 2t + 4$ **38.** $\ln (y - 1) - \ln 2 = x + \ln x$

In Exercises 39–42, draw the graph and determine the domain and range of the function.

39. $y = 2 \ln (3 - x) - 4$ **40.** $y = -3 \log (x + 2) + 1$

41. $y = \log_2 (x + 1)$ **42.** $y = \log_3 (x - 4)$

In Exercises 43 and 44, find a formula for f^{-1} and verify that $(f \circ f^{-1})(x) = (f^{-1} \circ f)(x) = x$.

43. $f(x) = \dfrac{100}{1 + 2^{-x}}$ **44.** $f(x) = \dfrac{50}{1 + 1.1^{-x}}$

45. ***Self-inverse*** Prove that the function f is its own inverse.

(a) $f(x) = \sqrt{1 - x^2}, \quad x \geq 0$ **(b)** $f(x) = 1/x$

46. ***Radioactive Decay*** The half-life of a certain radioactive substance is 12 hours. There are 8 grams present initially.

(a) Express the amount of substance remaining as a function of time t.

(b) When will there be 1 gram remaining?

47. ***Doubling Your Money*** Determine how much time is required for a \$500 investment to double in value if interest is earned at the rate of 4.75% compounded annually.

48. ***Population Growth*** The population of Glenbrook is 375,000 and is increasing at the rate of 2.25% per year. Predict when the population will be 1 million.

In Exercises 49 and 50, let $x = 0$ represent 1990, $x = 1$ represent 1991, and so forth.

49. ***Natural Gas Production***

(a) Find a natural logarithm regression equation for the data in Table 1.16 and superimpose its graph on a scatter plot of the data. Let $x = 0$ represent 2000.

TABLE 1.16
Iran's Natural Gas Production

Year	Cubic Feet (trillions)
2002	2.65
2003	2.86
2004	2.96
2005	3.56
2006	3.84

Source: Statistical Abstract of the United States, 2010.

(b) Estimate the number of cubic feet of natural gas produced by Iran in 2008.

(c) Using the model in part (b), predict when Iran's natural gas production reaches 4.2 trillion cubic feet.

50. ***Natural Gas Production***

(a) Find a natural logarithm regression equation for the data in Table 1.17 and superimpose its graph on a scatter plot of the data. Let $x = 0$ represent 2000.

TABLE 1.17 China's Natural Gas Production

Year	Cubic Feet (trillions)
2002	1.15
2003	1.21
2004	1.44
2005	1.76
2006	2.07

Source: Statistical Abstract of the United States, 2010.

(b) Estimate the number of cubic feet of natural gas produced by China in 2008.

(c) Using the model in part (b), predict when China's natural gas production reaches 2.25 trillion cubic feet.

51. Group Activity ***Inverse Functions*** Let $y = f(x) = mx + b$, $m \neq 0$.

(a) Writing to Learn Give a convincing argument that f is a one-to-one function.

(b) Find a formula for the inverse of f. How are the slopes of f and f^{-1} related?

(c) If the graphs of two functions are parallel lines with a nonzero slope, what can you say about the graphs of the inverses of the functions?

(d) If the graphs of two functions are perpendicular lines with a nonzero slope, what can you say about the graphs of the inverses of the functions?

Standardized Test Questions

52. True or False The function displayed in the graph below is one-to-one. Justify your answer.

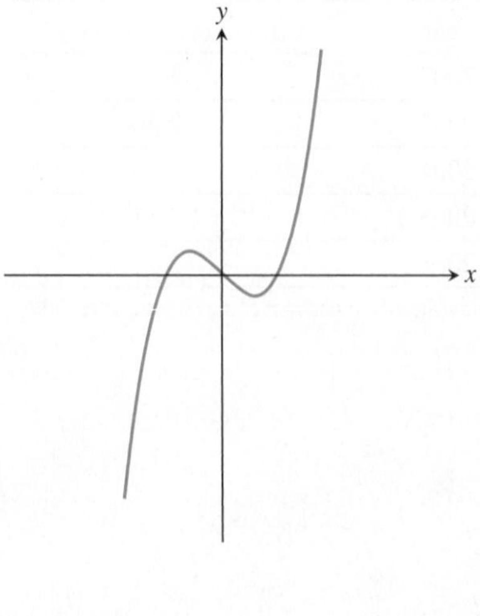

53. True or False If $(f \circ g)(x) = x$, then g is the inverse function of f. Justify your answer.

In Exercises 54 and 55, use the function $f(x) = 3 - \ln(x + 2)$.

54. Multiple Choice Which of the following is the domain of f?

(A) $x \neq -2$ **(B)** $(-\infty, \infty)$ **(C)** $(-2, \infty)$
(D) $[-1.9, \infty)$ **(E)** $(0, \infty)$

55. Multiple Choice Which of the following is the range of f?

(A) $(-\infty, \infty)$ **(B)** $(-\infty, 0)$ **(C)** $(-2, \infty)$
(D) $(0, \infty)$ **(E)** $(0, 5.3)$

56. Multiple Choice Which of the following is the inverse of $f(x) = 3x - 2$?

(A) $g(x) = \dfrac{1}{3x - 2}$ **(B)** $g(x) = x$ **(C)** $g(x) = 3x - 2$
(D) $g(x) = \dfrac{x - 2}{3}$ **(E)** $g(x) = \dfrac{x + 2}{3}$

57. Multiple Choice Which of the following is a solution of the equation $2 - 3^{-x} = -1$?

(A) $x = -2$ **(B)** $x = -1$ **(C)** $x = 0$
(D) $x = 1$ **(E)** There are no solutions.

Exploration

58. ***Supporting the Quotient Rule*** Let $y_1 = \ln(x/a)$, $y_2 = \ln x$, $y_3 = y_2 - y_1$, and $y_4 = e^{y_3}$.

(a) Graph y_1 and y_2 for $a = 2, 3, 4$, and 5. How are the graphs of y_1 and y_2 related?

(b) Graph y_3 for $a = 2, 3, 4$, and 5. Describe the graphs.

(c) Graph y_4 for $a = 2, 3, 4$, and 5. Compare the graphs to the graph of $y = a$.

(d) Use $e^{y_3} = e^{y_2 - y_1} = a$ to solve for y_1.

Extending the Ideas

59. ***One-to-One Functions*** If f is a one-to-one function, prove that $g(x) = -f(x)$ is also one-to-one.

60. ***One-to-One Functions*** If f is a one-to-one function and $f(x)$ is never zero, prove that $g(x) = 1/f(x)$ is also one-to-one.

61. ***Domain and Range*** Suppose that $a \neq 0$, $b \neq 1$, and $b > 0$. Determine the domain and range of the function.

(a) $y = a(b^{c-x}) + d$ **(b)** $y = a \log_b (x - c) + d$

62. Group Activity ***Inverse Functions***

Let $f(x) = \dfrac{ax + b}{cx + d}$, $c \neq 0$, $ad - bc \neq 0$.

(a) Writing to Learn Give a convincing argument that f is one-to-one.

(b) Find a formula for the inverse of f.

(c) Find the horizontal and vertical asymptotes of f.

(d) Find the horizontal and vertical asymptotes of f^{-1}. How are they related to those of f?

1.6 Trigonometric Functions

What you will learn about . . .

- Radian Measure
- Graphs of Trigonometric Functions
- Periodicity
- Even and Odd Trigonometric Functions
- Transformations of Trigonometric Graphs
- Inverse Trigonometric Functions

and why . . .

Trigonometric functions can be used to model periodic behavior and applications such as musical notes.

Radian Measure

The **radian measure** of the angle ACB at the center of the unit circle (Figure 1.40) equals the length of the arc that ACB cuts from the unit circle.

EXAMPLE 1 Finding Arc Length

Find the length of an arc subtended on a circle of radius 3 by a central angle of measure $2\pi/3$.

SOLUTION

According to Figure 1.40, if s is the length of the arc, then

$$s = r\theta = 3(2\pi/3) = 2\pi.$$

Now Try Exercise 1.

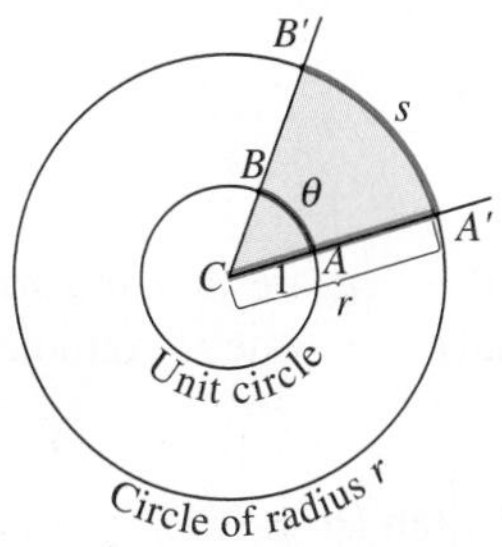

Figure 1.40 The radian measure of angle ACB is the length θ of arc AB on the unit circle centered at C. The value of θ can be found from any other circle, however, as the ratio s/r.

When an angle of measure θ is placed in *standard position* at the center of a circle of radius r (Figure 1.41), the six basic trigonometric functions of θ are defined as follows:

$$\textbf{sine: } \sin\theta = \frac{y}{r} \qquad \textbf{cosecant: } \csc\theta = \frac{r}{y}$$

$$\textbf{cosine: } \cos\theta = \frac{x}{r} \qquad \textbf{secant: } \sec\theta = \frac{r}{x}$$

$$\textbf{tangent: } \tan\theta = \frac{y}{x} \qquad \textbf{cotangent: } \cot\theta = \frac{x}{y}$$

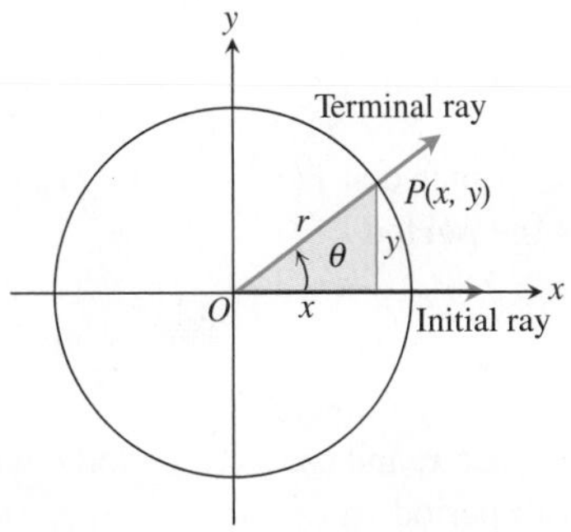

Figure 1.41 An angle θ in standard position.

Graphs of Trigonometric Functions

When we graph trigonometric functions in the coordinate plane, we usually denote the independent variable (radians) by x instead of θ. Figure 1.42 on the next page shows sketches of the six trigonometric functions. It is a good exercise for you to compare these with what you see in a grapher viewing window. (Some graphers have a "trig viewing window.")

EXPLORATION 1 Unwrapping Trigonometric Functions

Set your grapher in *radian mode,* parametric mode, and *simultaneous mode* (all three). Enter the parametric equations

$$x_1 = \cos t,\quad y_1 = \sin t \quad \text{and} \quad x_2 = t,\quad y_2 = \sin t.$$

1. Graph for $0 \le t \le 2\pi$ in the window $[-1.5, 2\pi]$ by $[-2.5, 2.5]$. Describe the two curves. (You may wish to make the viewing window square.)
2. Use TRACE to compare the y-values of the two curves.
3. Repeat part 2 in the window $[-1.5, 4\pi]$ by $[-5, 5]$, using the parameter interval $0 \le t \le 4\pi$.
4. Let $y_2 = \cos t$. Use TRACE to compare the x-values of curve 1 (the unit circle) with the y-values of curve 2 using the parameter intervals $[0, 2\pi]$ and $[0, 4\pi]$.
5. Set $y_2 = \tan t$, $\csc t$, $\sec t$, and $\cot t$. Graph each in the window $[-1.5, 2\pi]$ by $[-2.5, 2.5]$ using the interval $0 \le t \le 2\pi$. How is a y-value of curve 2 related to the corresponding point on curve 1? (Use TRACE to explore the curves.)

Angle Convention: Use Radians

From now on in this book it is assumed that all angles are measured in radians unless degrees or some other unit is stated explicitly. When we talk about the angle $\pi/3$, we mean $\pi/3$ radians (which is 60°), not $\pi/3$ degrees. When you do calculus, keep your calculator in radian mode.

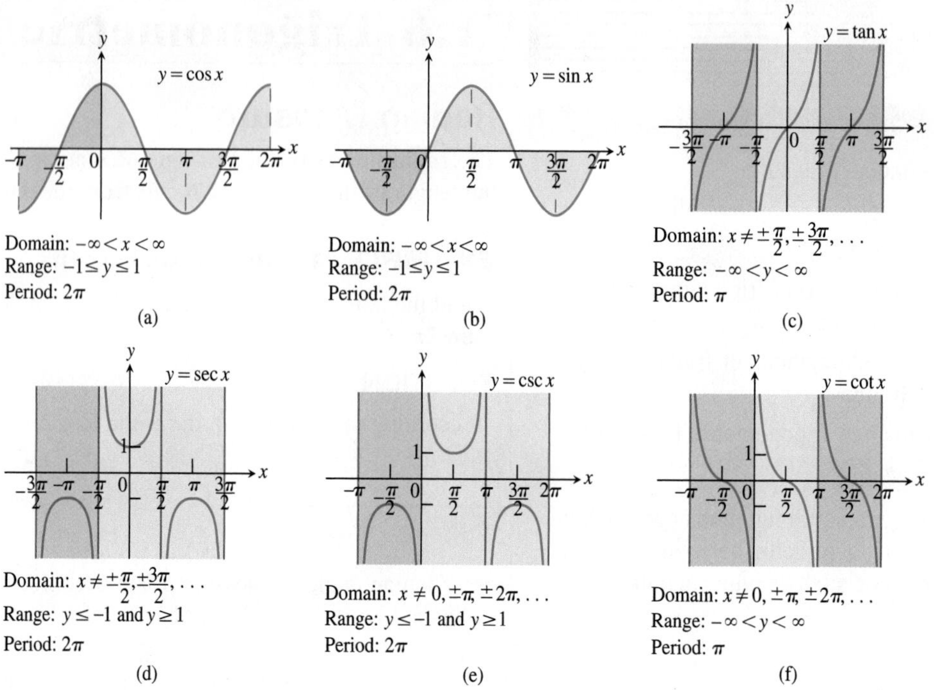

Figure 1.42 Graphs of the (a) cosine, (b) sine, (c) tangent, (d) secant, (e) cosecant, and (f) cotangent functions using radian measure.

Periods of Trigonometric Functions

Period π. $\tan(x + \pi) = \tan x$
$\cot(x + \pi) = \cot x$
Period 2π. $\sin(x + 2\pi) = \sin x$
$\cos(x + 2\pi) = \cos x$
$\sec(x + 2\pi) = \sec x$
$\csc(x + 2\pi) = \csc x$

Periodicity

When an angle of measure θ and an angle of measure $\theta + 2\pi$ are in standard position, their terminal rays coincide. The two angles therefore have the same trigonometric function values:

$$\begin{aligned} \cos(\theta + 2\pi) &= \cos\theta \quad \sin(\theta + 2\pi) = \sin\theta \quad \tan(\theta + 2\pi) = \tan\theta \\ \sec(\theta + 2\pi) &= \sec\theta \quad \csc(\theta + 2\pi) = \csc\theta \quad \cot(\theta + 2\pi) = \cot\theta \end{aligned} \tag{1}$$

Similarly, $\cos(\theta - 2\pi) = \cos\theta$, $\sin(\theta - 2\pi) = \sin\theta$, and so on.

We see the values of the trigonometric functions repeat at regular intervals. We describe this behavior by saying that the six basic trigonometric functions are *periodic*.

DEFINITION Periodic Function, Period

A function $f(x)$ is **periodic** if there is a positive number p such that $f(x + p) = f(x)$ for every value of x. The smallest such value of p is the **period** of f.

As we can see in Figure 1.42, the functions $\cos x$, $\sin x$, $\sec x$, and $\csc x$ are periodic with period 2π. The functions $\tan x$ and $\cot x$ are periodic with period π.

Even and Odd Trigonometric Functions

The graphs in Figure 1.42 suggest that $\cos x$ and $\sec x$ are even functions because their graphs are symmetric about the y-axis. The other four basic trigonometric functions are odd.

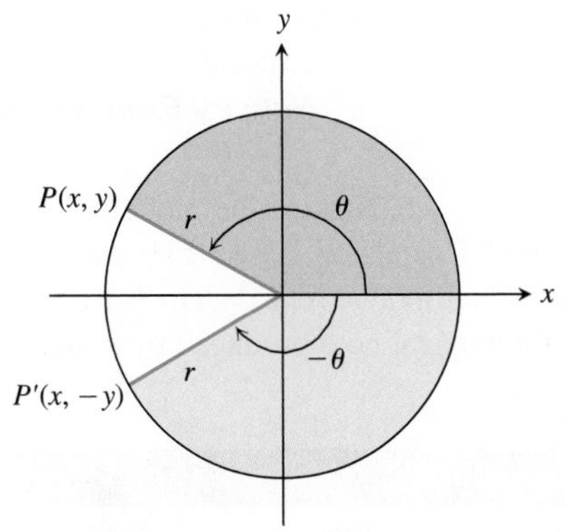

Figure 1.43 Angles of opposite sign. (Example 2)

EXAMPLE 2 Confirming Even and Odd

Show that cosine is an even function and sine is odd.

SOLUTION

From Figure 1.43 it follows that

$$\cos(-\theta) = \frac{x}{r} = \cos\theta, \quad \sin(-\theta) = \frac{-y}{r} = -\sin\theta,$$

so cosine is an even function and sine is odd. ***Now Try Exercise 5.***

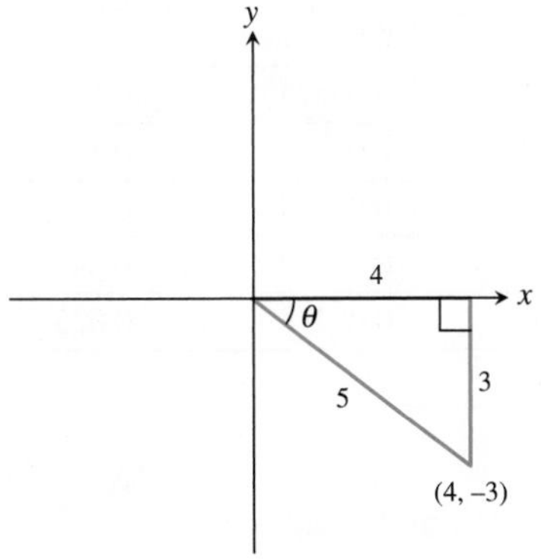

Figure 1.44 The angle θ in standard position. (Example 3)

EXAMPLE 3 Finding Trigonometric Values

Find all the trigonometric values of θ if $\sin\theta = -3/5$ and $\tan\theta < 0$.

SOLUTION

The angle θ is in the fourth quadrant, as shown in Figure 1.44, because its sine and tangent are negative. From this figure we can read that $\cos\theta = 4/5$, $\tan\theta = -3/4$, $\csc\theta = -5/3$, $\sec\theta = 5/4$, and $\cot\theta = -4/3$. ***Now Try Exercise 9.***

Transformations of Trigonometric Graphs

The rules for shifting, stretching, shrinking, and reflecting the graph of a function apply to the trigonometric functions. The following diagram will remind you of the controlling parameters.

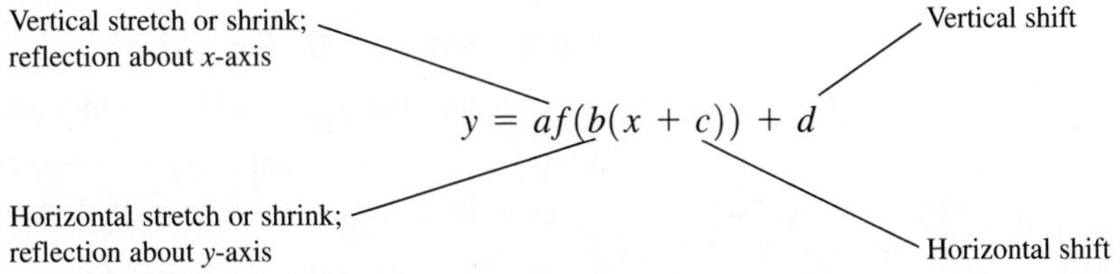

The general sine function or **sinusoid** can be written in the form

$$f(x) = A\sin\left[\frac{2\pi}{B}(x - C)\right] + D,$$

where $|A|$ is the *amplitude*, $|B|$ is the *period*, C is the *horizontal shift*, and D is the *vertical shift*.

EXAMPLE 4 Graphing a Trigonometric Function

Determine the **(a)** period, **(b)** domain, **(c)** range, and **(d)** draw the graph of the function $y = 3\cos(2x - \pi) + 1$.

SOLUTION

We can rewrite the function in the form

$$y = 3\cos\left[2\left(x - \frac{\pi}{2}\right)\right] + 1.$$

(a) The period is given by $2\pi/B$, where $2\pi/B = 2$. The period is π.

(b) The domain is $(-\infty, \infty)$.

(c) The graph is a basic cosine curve with amplitude 3 that has been shifted up 1 unit. Thus, the range is $[-2, 4]$.

continued

$y = 3\cos(2x - \pi) + 1$, $y = \cos x$

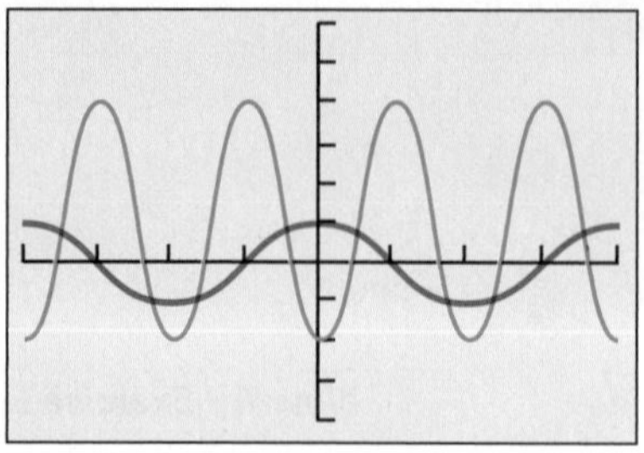

$[-2\pi, 2\pi]$ by $[-4, 6]$

Figure 1.45 The graph of $y = 3\cos(2x - \pi) + 1$ (blue) and the graph of $y = \cos x$ (red). (Example 4)

(d) The graph has been shifted to the right $\pi/2$ units. The graph is shown in Figure 1.45 together with the graph of $y = \cos x$. Notice that four periods of $y = 3\cos(2x - \pi) + 1$ are drawn in this window. ***Now Try Exercise 13.***

Musical notes are pressure waves in the air. The wave behavior can be modeled with great accuracy by general sine curves. Devices called Calculator Based Laboratory™ (CBL) systems can record these waves with the aid of a microphone. The data in Table 1.18 give pressure displacement versus time in seconds of a musical note produced by a tuning fork and recorded with a CBL system.

TABLE 1.18 Tuning Fork Data

Time	Pressure	Time	Pressure	Time	Pressure
0.00091	−0.080	0.00271	−0.141	0.00453	0.749
0.00108	0.200	0.00289	−0.309	0.00471	0.581
0.00125	0.480	0.00307	−0.348	0.00489	0.346
0.00144	0.693	0.00325	−0.248	0.00507	0.077
0.00162	0.816	0.00344	−0.041	0.00525	−0.164
0.00180	0.844	0.00362	0.217	0.00543	−0.320
0.00198	0.771	0.00379	0.480	0.00562	−0.354
0.00216	0.603	0.00398	0.681	0.00579	−0.248
0.00234	0.368	0.00416	0.810	0.00598	−0.035
0.00253	0.099	0.00435	0.827		

EXAMPLE 5 Finding the Frequency of a Musical Note

Consider the tuning fork data in Table 1.18.

(a) Find a sinusoidal regression equation (general sine curve) for the data and superimpose its graph on a scatter plot of the data.

(b) The *frequency* of a musical note, or wave, is measured in cycles per second, or hertz (1 Hz = 1 cycle per second). The frequency is the reciprocal of the *period* of the wave, which is measured in seconds per cycle. Estimate the frequency of the note produced by the tuning fork.

SOLUTION

(a) The sinusoidal regression equation produced by our calculator is approximately

$$y = 0.6\sin(2488.6x - 2.832) + 0.266.$$

Figure 1.46 shows its graph together with a scatter plot of the tuning fork data.

$y = 0.6\sin(2488.6x - 2.832) + 0.266$

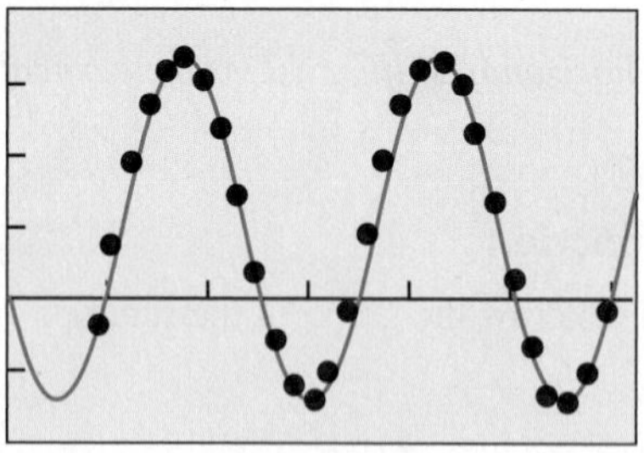

$[0, 0.0062]$ by $[-0.5, 1]$

Figure 1.46 A sinusoidal regression model for the tuning fork data in Table 1.18. (Example 5)

(b) The period is $\dfrac{2\pi}{2488.6}$ sec, so the frequency is $\dfrac{2488.6}{2\pi} \approx 396$ Hz.

Interpretation The tuning fork is vibrating at a frequency of about 396 Hz. On the pure tone scale, this is the note G above middle C. It is a few cycles per second different from the frequency of the G we hear on a piano's tempered scale, 392 Hz. ***Now Try Exercise 23.***

Inverse Trigonometric Functions

None of the six basic trigonometric functions graphed in Figure 1.42 is one-to-one. These functions do not have inverses. However, in each case the domain can be restricted to produce a new function that does have an inverse, as illustrated in Example 6.

$x = t, y = \sin t, -\frac{\pi}{2} \le t \le \frac{\pi}{2}$

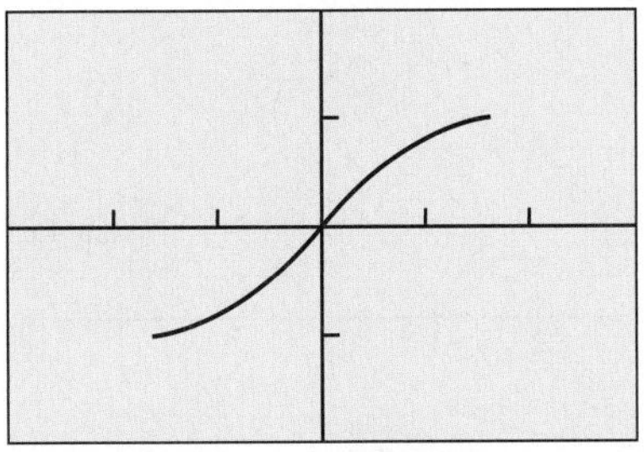

[–3, 3] by [–2, 2]

(a)

$x = \sin t, y = t, -\frac{\pi}{2} \le t \le \frac{\pi}{2}$

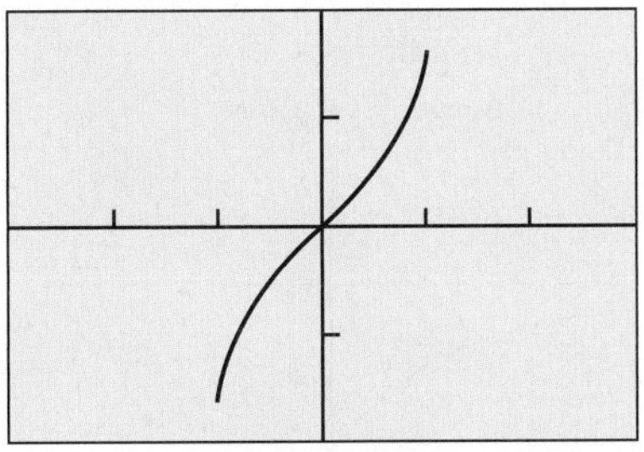

[–3, 3] by [–2, 2]

(b)

Figure 1.47 (a) A restricted sine function and (b) its inverse. (Example 6)

EXAMPLE 6 Restricting the Domain of the Sine

Show that the function $y = \sin x$, $-\pi/2 \le x \le \pi/2$, is one-to-one, and graph its inverse.

SOLUTION

Figure 1.47a shows the graph of this restricted sine function using the parametric equations

$$x_1 = t, \quad y_1 = \sin t, \quad -\frac{\pi}{2} \le t \le \frac{\pi}{2}.$$

This restricted sine function is one-to-one because it does not repeat any output values. It therefore has an inverse, which we graph in Figure 1.47b by interchanging the ordered pairs using the parametric equations

$$x_2 = \sin t, \quad y_2 = t, \quad -\frac{\pi}{2} \le t \le \frac{\pi}{2}.$$

Now Try Exercise 25.

The inverse of the restricted sine function of Example 6 is called the *inverse sine function*. The inverse sine of x is the angle whose sine is x. It is denoted by $\sin^{-1} x$ or arcsin x. Either notation is read "arcsine of x" or "the inverse sine of x."

The domains of the other basic trigonometric functions can also be restricted to produce a function with an inverse. The domains and ranges of the resulting inverse functions become parts of their definitions.

DEFINITIONS Inverse Trigonometric Functions

Function	Domain	Range
$y = \cos^{-1} x$	$-1 \le x \le 1$	$0 \le y \le \pi$
$y = \sin^{-1} x$	$-1 \le x \le 1$	$-\frac{\pi}{2} \le y \le \frac{\pi}{2}$
$y = \tan^{-1} x$	$-\infty < x < \infty$	$-\frac{\pi}{2} < y < \frac{\pi}{2}$
$y = \sec^{-1} x$	$\|x\| \ge 1$	$0 \le y \le \pi, y \ne \frac{\pi}{2}$
$y = \csc^{-1} x$	$\|x\| \ge 1$	$-\frac{\pi}{2} \le y \le \frac{\pi}{2}, y \ne 0$
$y = \cot^{-1} x$	$-\infty < x < \infty$	$0 < y < \pi$

The graphs of the six inverse trigonometric functions are shown in Figure 1.48.

EXAMPLE 7 Finding Angles in Degrees and Radians

Find the measure of $\cos^{-1}(-0.5)$ in degrees and radians.

SOLUTION

Put the calculator in degree mode and enter $\cos^{-1}(-0.5)$. The calculator returns 120, which means 120 degrees. Now put the calculator in radian mode and enter $\cos^{-1}(-0.5)$. The calculator returns 2.094395102, which is the measure of the angle in radians. You can check that $2\pi/3 \approx 2.094395102$.

Now Try Exercise 27.

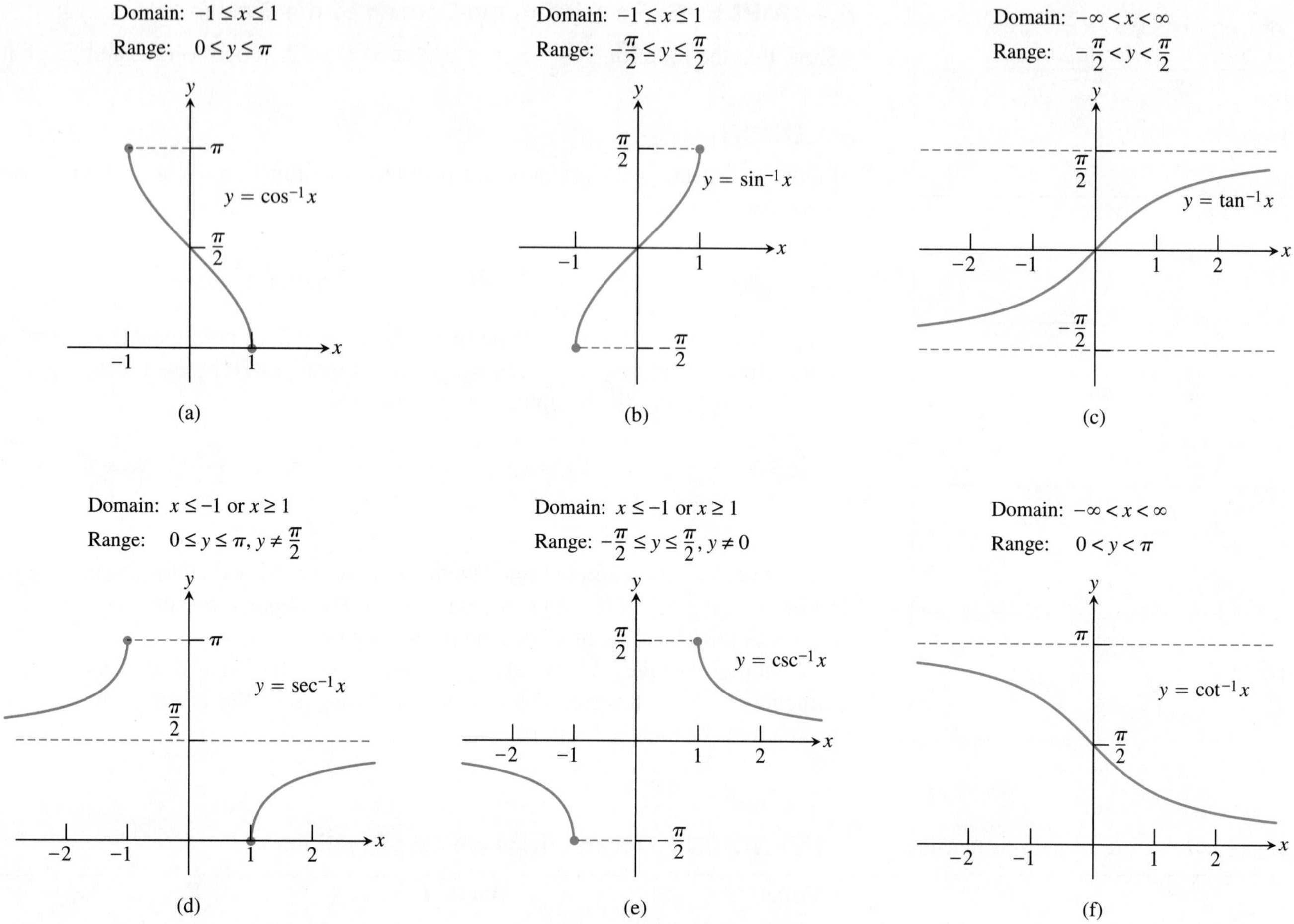

Figure 1.48 Graphs of (a) $y = \cos^{-1} x$, (b) $y = \sin^{-1} x$, (c) $y = \tan^{-1} x$, (d) $y = \sec^{-1} x$, (e) $y = \csc^{-1} x$, and (f) $y = \cot^{-1} x$.

EXAMPLE 8 Using the Inverse Trigonometric Functions

Solve for x.

(a) $\sin x = 0.7$ in $0 \le x < 2\pi$

(b) $\tan x = -2$ in $-\infty < x < \infty$

SOLUTION

(a) Notice that $x = \sin^{-1}(0.7) \approx 0.775$ is in the first quadrant, so 0.775 is one solution of this equation. The angle $\pi - x$ is in the second quadrant and has sine equal to 0.7. Thus two solutions in this interval are

$$\sin^{-1}(0.7) \approx 0.775 \quad \text{and} \quad \pi - \sin^{-1}(0.7) \approx 2.366.$$

(b) The angle $x = \tan^{-1}(2) \approx -1.107$ is in the fourth quadrant and is the only solution to this equation in the interval $-\pi/2 < x < \pi/2$ where $\tan x$ is one-to-one. Since $\tan x$ is periodic with period π, the solutions to this equation are of the form

$$\tan^{-1}(-2) + k\pi \approx -1.107 + k\pi$$

where k is any integer. ***Now Try Exercise 31.***

Quick Review 1.6 *(For help, go to Sections 1.2 and 1.6.)*

Exercise numbers with a gray background indicate problems that the authors have designed to be solved without a calculator.

In Exercises 1–4, convert from radians to degrees or degrees to radians.

1. $\pi/3$ **2.** -2.5 **3.** $-40°$ **4.** $45°$

In Exercises 5–7, solve the equation graphically in the given interval.

5. $\sin x = 0.6, \quad 0 \le x \le 2\pi$ **6.** $\cos x = -0.4, \quad 0 \le x \le 2\pi$

7. $\tan x = 1, \quad -\frac{\pi}{2} \le x < \frac{3\pi}{2}$

8. Show that $f(x) = 2x^2 - 3$ is an even function. Explain why its graph is symmetric about the y-axis.

9. Show that $f(x) = x^3 - 3x$ is an odd function. Explain why its graph is symmetric about the origin.

10. Give one way to restrict the domain of the function $f(x) = x^4 - 2$ to make the resulting function one-to-one.

Section 1.6 Exercises

In Exercises 1–4, the angle lies at the center of a circle and subtends an arc of the circle. Find the missing angle measure, circle radius, or arc length.

Angle	Radius	Arc Length
1. $5\pi/8$	2	?
2. 175°	?	10
3. ?	14	7
4. ?	6	$3\pi/2$

In Exercises 5–8, determine if the function is even or odd.

5. secant **6.** tangent

7. cosecant **8.** cotangent

In Exercises 9 and 10, find all the trigonometric values of θ with the given conditions.

9. $\cos\theta = -\frac{15}{17}, \quad \sin\theta > 0$

10. $\tan\theta = -1, \quad \sin\theta < 0$

In Exercises 11–14, determine **(a)** the period, **(b)** the domain, **(c)** the range, and **(d)** draw the graph of the function.

11. $y = 3\csc(3x + \pi) - 2$ **12.** $y = 2\sin(4x + \pi) + 3$

13. $y = -3\tan(3x + \pi) + 2$

14. $y = 2\sin\left(2x + \frac{\pi}{3}\right)$

In Exercises 15 and 16, choose an appropriate viewing window to display two complete periods of each trigonometric function in radian mode.

15. (a) $y = \sec x$ **(b)** $y = \csc x$ **(c)** $y = \cot x$

16. (a) $y = \sin x$ **(b)** $y = \cos x$ **(c)** $y = \tan x$

In Exercises 17–22, specify **(a)** the period, **(b)** the amplitude, and **(c)** identify the viewing window that is shown.

17. $y = 1.5\sin 2x$

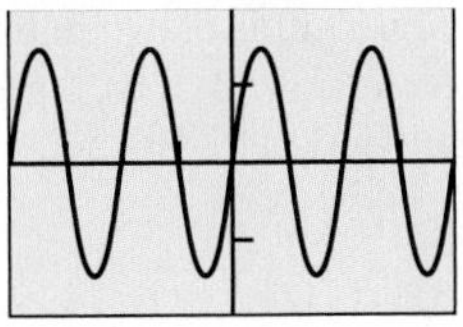

18. $y = 2\cos 3x$

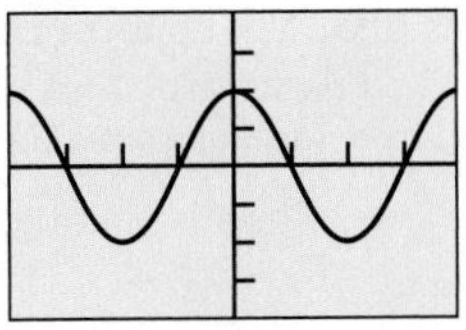

19. $y = -3\cos 2x$

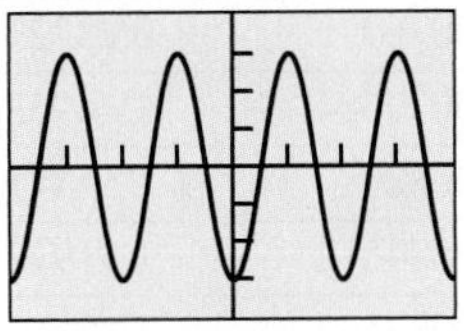

20. $y = 5\sin\frac{x}{2}$

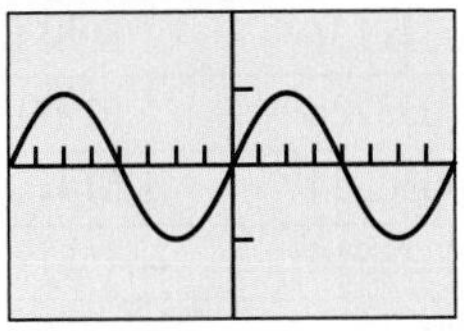

21. $y = -4\sin\frac{\pi}{3}x$

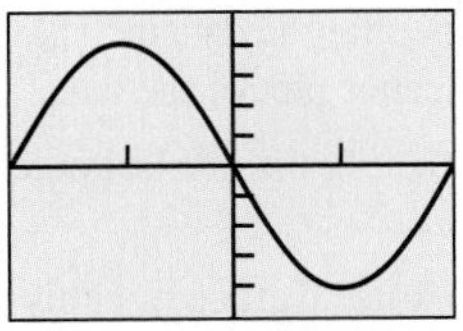

22. $y = \cos\pi x$

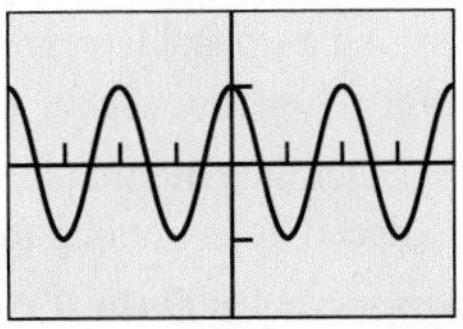

23. Group Activity A musical note like that produced with a tuning fork or pitch meter is a pressure wave. Table 1.19 gives frequencies (in Hz) of musical notes on the tempered scale. The pressure versus time tuning fork data in Table 1.20 were collected using a CBL™ and a microphone.

TABLE 1.19
Frequencies of Notes

Note	Frequency (Hz)
C	262
C# or D♭	277
D	294
D# or E♭	311
E	330
F	349
F# or G♭	370
G	392
G# or A♭	415
A	440
A# or B♭	466
B	494
C (next octave)	524

Source: CBL™ System Experimental Workbook, Texas Instruments, Inc., 1994.

TABLE 1.20 Tuning Fork Data

Time (s)	Pressure	Time (s)	Pressure
0.0002368	1.29021	0.0049024	−1.06632
0.0005664	1.50851	0.0051520	0.09235
0.0008256	1.51971	0.0054112	1.44694
0.0010752	1.51411	0.0056608	1.51411
0.0013344	1.47493	0.0059200	1.51971
0.0015840	0.45619	0.0061696	1.51411
0.0018432	−0.89280	0.0064288	1.43015
0.0020928	−1.51412	0.0066784	0.19871
0.0023520	−1.15588	0.0069408	−1.06072
0.0026016	−0.04758	0.0071904	−1.51412
0.0028640	1.36858	0.0074496	−0.97116
0.0031136	1.50851	0.0076992	0.23229
0.0033728	1.51971	0.0079584	1.46933
0.0036224	1.51411	0.0082080	1.51411
0.0038816	1.45813	0.0084672	1.51971
0.0041312	0.32185	0.0087168	1.50851
0.0043904	−0.97676	0.0089792	1.36298
0.0046400	−1.51971		

(a) Find a sinusoidal regression equation for the data in Table 1.20 and superimpose its graph on a scatter plot of the data.

(b) Determine the frequency of and identify the musical note produced by the tuning fork.

24. *Temperature Data* Table 1.21 gives the average monthly temperatures for St. Louis for a 12-month period starting with January. Model the monthly temperature with an equation of the form

$$y = a \sin [b(t - h)] + k,$$

y in degrees Fahrenheit, t in months, as follows:

TABLE 1.21 Temperature Data for St. Louis

Time (months)	Temperature (°F)
1	34
2	30
3	39
4	44
5	58
6	67
7	78
8	80
9	72
10	63
11	51
12	40

(a) Find the value of b assuming that the period is 12 months.

(b) How is the amplitude a related to the difference $80° - 30°$?

(c) Use the information in (b) to find k.

(d) Find h, and write an equation for y.

(e) Superimpose a graph of y on a scatter plot of the data.

In Exercises 25–26, show that the function is one-to-one, and graph its inverse.

25. $y = \cos x, \quad 0 \le x \le \pi$ **26.** $y = \tan x, \quad -\frac{\pi}{2} < x < \frac{\pi}{2}$

In Exercises 27–30, give the measure of the angle in radians and degrees. Give exact answers whenever possible.

27. $\sin^{-1}(0.5)$ **28.** $\sin^{-1}\left(-\frac{\sqrt{2}}{2}\right)$

29. $\tan^{-1}(-5)$ **30.** $\cos^{-1}(0.7)$

In Exercises 31–36, solve the equation in the specified interval.

31. $\tan x = 2.5, \quad 0 \le x \le 2\pi$

32. $\cos x = -0.7, \quad 2\pi \le x < 4\pi$

33. $\csc x = 2, \quad 0 < x < 2\pi$ **34.** $\sec x = -3, \quad -\pi \le x < \pi$

35. $\sin x = -0.5, \quad -\infty < x < \infty$

36. $\cot x = -1, \quad -\infty < x < \infty$

In Exercises 37–40, use the given information to find the values of the six trigonometric functions at the angle θ. Give exact answers.

37. $\theta = \sin^{-1}\left(\frac{8}{17}\right)$ **38.** $\theta = \tan^{-1}\left(-\frac{5}{12}\right)$

39. The point $P(-3, 4)$ is on the terminal side of θ.

40. The point $P(-2, 2)$ is on the terminal side of θ.

In Exercises 41 and 42, evaluate the expression.

41. $\sin\left(\cos^{-1}\left(\frac{7}{11}\right)\right)$

42. $\tan\left(\sin^{-1}\left(\frac{9}{13}\right)\right)$

43. *Temperatures in Fairbanks, Alaska* Find the **(a)** amplitude, **(b)** period, **(c)** horizontal shift, and **(d)** vertical shift of the model used in the figure below. **(e)** Then write the equation for the model.

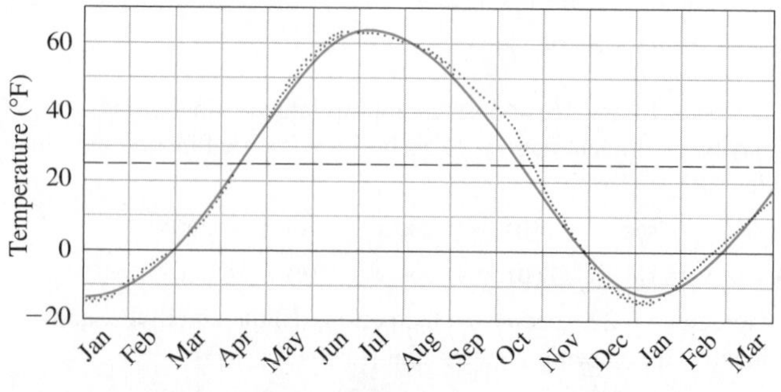

Normal mean air temperature for Fairbanks, Alaska, plotted as data points (red). The approximating sine function $f(x)$ is drawn in blue.

Source: "*Is the Curve of Temperature Variation a Sine Curve?*" by B. M. Lando and C. A. Lando, *The Mathematics Teacher, 76*, Fig. 2, p. 535 (Sept. 1977).

44. *Temperatures in Fairbanks, Alaska* Use the equation of Exercise 43 to approximate the answers to the following questions about the temperatures in Fairbanks, Alaska, shown in the figure in Exercise 43. Assume that the year has 365 days.

(a) What are the highest and lowest mean daily temperatures?

(b) What is the average of the highest and lowest mean daily temperatures? Why is this average the vertical shift of the function?

45. *Even-Odd*

(a) Show that $\cot x$ is an odd function of x.

(b) Show that the quotient of an even function and an odd function is an odd function.

46. *Even-Odd*

(a) Show that $\csc x$ is an odd function of x.

(b) Show that the reciprocal of an odd function is odd.

47. *Even-Odd* Show that the product of an even function and an odd function is an odd function.

48. *Finding the Period* Give a convincing argument that the period of $\tan x$ is π.

49. *Sinusoidal Regression* Table 1.22 gives the values of the function

$$f(x) = a \sin (bx + c) + d$$

accurate to two decimals.

TABLE 1.22
Values of a Function

x	$f(x)$
1	3.42
2	0.73
3	0.12
4	2.16
5	4.97
6	5.97

(a) Find a sinusoidal regression equation for the data.

(b) Rewrite the equation with a, b, c, and d rounded to the nearest integer.

Standardized Test Questions

You may use a graphing calculator to solve the following problems.

50. True or False The period of $y = \sin (x/2)$ is π. Justify your answer.

51. True or False The amplitude of $y = \frac{1}{2} \cos x$ is 1. Justify your answer.

In Exercises 52–54, $f(x) = 2 \cos (4x + \pi) - 1$.

52. Multiple Choice Which of the following is the domain of f?

(A) $[-\pi, \pi]$ (B) $[-3, 1]$ (C) $[-1, 4]$
(D) $(-\infty, \infty)$ (E) $x \neq 0$

53. Multiple Choice Which of the following is the range of f?

(A) $(-3, 1)$ (B) $[-3, 1]$ (C) $(-1, 4)$
(D) $[-1, 4]$ (E) $(-\infty, \infty)$

54. Multiple Choice Which of the following is the period of f?

(A) 4π (B) 3π (C) 2π (D) π (E) $\pi/2$

55. Multiple Choice Which of the following is the measure of $\tan^{-1}(-\sqrt{3})$ in degrees?

(A) $-60°$ (B) $-30°$ (C) $30°$ (D) $60°$ (E) $120°$

Exploration

56. *Trigonometric Identities* Let $f(x) = \sin x + \cos x$.

(a) Graph $y = f(x)$. Describe the graph.

(b) Use the graph to identify the amplitude, period, horizontal shift, and vertical shift.

(c) Use the formula

$$\sin \alpha \cos \beta + \cos \alpha \sin \beta = \sin (\alpha + \beta)$$

for the sine of the sum of two angles to confirm your answers.

Extending the Ideas

57. Exploration Let $y = \sin (ax) + \cos (ax)$.

Use the symbolic manipulator of a computer algebra system (CAS) to help you with the following:

(a) Express y as a sinusoid for $a = 2, 3, 4,$ and 5.

(b) Conjecture another formula for y for a equal to any positive integer n.

(c) Check your conjecture with a CAS.

(d) Use the formula for the sine of the sum of two angles (see Exercise 56c) to confirm your conjecture.

58. Exploration Let $y = a \sin x + b \cos x$.

Use the symbolic manipulator of a computer algebra system (CAS) to help you with the following:

(a) Express y as a sinusoid for the following pairs of values: $a = 2, b = 1$; $a = 1, b = 2$; $a = 5, b = 2$; $a = 2, b = 5$; $a = 3, b = 4$.

(b) Conjecture another formula for y for any pair of positive integers. Try other values if necessary.

(c) Check your conjecture with a CAS.

(d) Use the following formulas for the sine or cosine of a sum or difference of two angles to confirm your conjecture.

$$\sin \alpha \cos \beta \pm \cos \alpha \sin \beta = \sin (\alpha \pm \beta)$$

$$\cos \alpha \cos \beta \pm \sin \alpha \sin \beta = \cos (\alpha \mp \beta)$$

In Exercises 59 and 60, show that the function is periodic and find its period.

59. $y = \sin^3 x$ **60.** $y = |\tan x|$

In Exercises 61 and 62, graph one period of the function.

61. $f(x) = \sin (60x)$ **62.** $f(x) = \cos (60\pi x)$

Quick Quiz for AP* Preparation: Sections 1.4–1.6

1. Multiple Choice Which of the following is the domain of $f(x) = -\log_2(x+3)$?

(A) $(-\infty, \infty)$ **(B)** $(-\infty, 3)$ **(C)** $(-3, \infty)$

(D) $[-3, \infty)$ **(E)** $(-\infty, 3]$

2. Multiple Choice Which of the following is the range of $f(x) = 5\cos(x + \pi) + 3$?

(A) $(-\infty, \infty)$ **(B)** $[2, 4]$ **(C)** $[-8, 2]$

(D) $[-2, 8]$ **(E)** $\left[-\frac{2}{5}, \frac{8}{5}\right]$

3. Multiple Choice Which of the following gives the solution of $\tan x = -1$ in $\pi < x < \frac{3\pi}{2}$?

(A) $-\frac{\pi}{4}$ **(B)** $\frac{\pi}{4}$ **(C)** $\frac{\pi}{3}$ **(D)** $\frac{3\pi}{4}$ **(E)** $\frac{5\pi}{4}$

4. Free Response Let $f(x) = 5x - 3$.

(a) Find the inverse g of f.

(b) Compute $f \circ g(x)$. Show your work.

(c) Compute $g \circ f(x)$. Show your work.

Chapter 1 Key Terms

absolute value function (p. 17)
base a logarithm function (p. 39)
boundary of an interval (p. 13)
boundary points (p. 13)
change of base formula (p. 41)
closed interval (p. 13)
common logarithm function (p. 40)
composing (p. 18)
composite function (p. 17)
compounded continuously (p. 25)
cosecant function (p. 45)
cosine function (p. 45)
cotangent function (p. 45)
dependent variable (p. 12)
domain (p. 12)
even function (p. 15)
exponential decay (p. 24)
exponential function base a (p. 22)
exponential growth (p. 24)
function (p. 12)
general linear equation (p. 5)
graph of a function (p. 13)
graph of a relation (p. 29)
grapher failure (p. 15)
half-life (p. 24)
half-open interval (p. 13)
identity function (p. 37)
increments (p. 3)
independent variable (p. 12)
initial point of parametrized curve (p. 29)
interior of an interval (p. 13)
interior points of an interval (p. 13)
inverse cosecant function (p. 49)
inverse cosine function (p. 49)
inverse cotangent function (p. 49)
inverse function (p. 37)
inverse properties for a^x and $\log_a x$ (p. 40)
inverse secant function (p. 49)
inverse sine function (p. 49)
inverse tangent function (p. 49)
linear regression (p. 7)
natural domain (p. 13)
natural logarithm function (p. 40)
odd function (p. 15)
one-to-one function (p. 36)
open interval (p. 13)
parallel lines (p. 4)
parameter (p. 29)
parameter interval (p. 29)
parametric curve (p. 29)
parametric equations (p. 29)
parametrization of a curve (p. 29)
parametrize (p. 29)
period of a function (p. 46)
periodic function (p. 46)
perpendicular lines (p. 4)
piecewise-defined function (p. 16)
point-slope equation (p. 4)
power rule for logarithms (p. 40)
product rule for logarithms (p. 40)
quotient rule for logarithms (p. 40)
radian measure (p. 45)
range (p. 12)
regression analysis (p. 7)
regression curve (p. 7)
relation (p. 29)
rise (p. 3)
rules for exponents (p. 23)
run (p. 3)
scatter plot (p. 7)
secant function (p. 45)
sine function (p. 45)
sinusoid (p. 47)
sinusoidal regression (p. 48)
slope (p. 4)
slope-intercept equation (p. 5)
symmetry about the origin (p. 15)
symmetry about the y-axis (p. 15)
tangent function (p. 45)
terminal point of parametrized curve (p. 29)
witch of Agnesi (p. 32)
x-intercept (p. 5)
y-intercept (p. 5)

Chapter 1 Review Exercises

Exercise numbers with a gray background indicate problems that the authors have designed to be solved without a calculator.

The collection of exercises marked in red could be used as a chapter test.

In Exercises 1–14, write an equation for the specified line.

1. through $(1, -6)$ with slope 3

2. through $(-1, 2)$ with slope $-1/2$

3. the vertical line through $(0, -3)$

4. through $(-3, 6)$ and $(1, -2)$

5. the horizontal line through $(0, 2)$

6. through $(3, 3)$ and $(-2, 5)$

7. with slope -3 and y-intercept 3

8. through $(3, 1)$ and parallel to $2x - y = -2$

9. through $(4, -12)$ and parallel to $4x + 3y = 12$

10. through $(-2, -3)$ and perpendicular to $3x - 5y = 1$

11. through $(-1, 2)$ and perpendicular to $\frac{1}{2}x + \frac{1}{3}y = 1$

12. with x-intercept 3 and y-intercept -5

13. the line $y = f(x)$, where f has the following values:

x	-2	2	4
$f(x)$	4	2	1

14. through $(4, -2)$ with x-intercept -3

In Exercises 15–18, determine whether the graph of the function is symmetric about the y-axis, the origin, or neither.

15. $y = x^{1/5}$ **16.** $y = x^{2/5}$

17. $y = x^2 - 2x - 1$ **18.** $y = e^{-x^2}$

In Exercises 19–26, determine whether the function is even, odd, or neither.

19. $y = x^2 + 1$ **20.** $y = x^5 - x^3 - x$

21. $y = 1 - \cos x$ **22.** $y = \sec x \tan x$

23. $y = \dfrac{x^4 + 1}{x^3 - 2x}$ **24.** $y = 1 - \sin x$

25. $y = x + \cos x$ **26.** $y = \sqrt{x^4 - 1}$

In Exercises 27–38, find the **(a)** domain and **(b)** range, and **(c)** graph the function.

27. $y = |x| - 2$ **28.** $y = -2 + \sqrt{1 - x}$

29. $y = \sqrt{16 - x^2}$ **30.** $y = 3^{2-x} + 1$

31. $y = 2e^{-x} - 3$ **32.** $y = \tan(2x - \pi)$

33. $y = 2\sin(3x + \pi) - 1$ **34.** $y = x^{2/5}$

35. $y = \ln(x - 3) + 1$ **36.** $y = -1 + \sqrt[3]{2 - x}$

37. $y = \begin{cases} \sqrt{-x}, & -4 \le x \le 0 \\ \sqrt{x}, & 0 < x \le 4 \end{cases}$ **38.** $y = \begin{cases} -x - 2, & -2 \le x \le -1 \\ x, & -1 < x \le 1 \\ -x + 2, & 1 < x \le 2 \end{cases}$

In Exercises 39 and 40, write a piecewise formula for the function.

39.

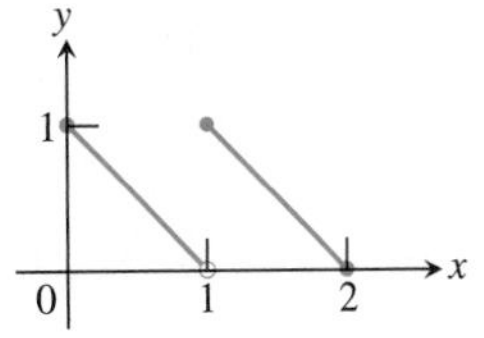

40.

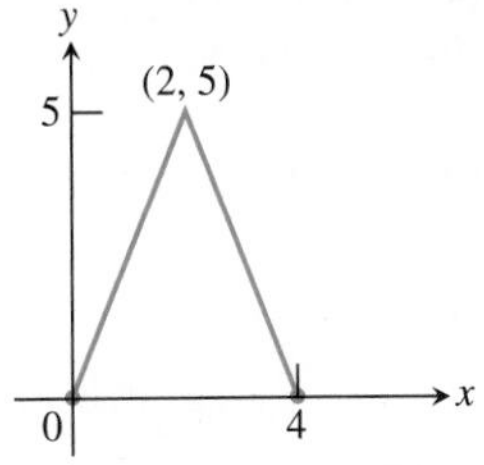

In Exercises 41 and 42, find

(a) $(f \circ g)(-1)$ **(b)** $(g \circ f)(2)$ **(c)** $(f \circ f)(x)$ **(d)** $(g \circ g)(x)$

41. $f(x) = \dfrac{1}{x}$, $g(x) = \dfrac{1}{\sqrt{x + 2}}$

42. $f(x) = 2 - x$, $g(x) = \sqrt[3]{x + 1}$

In Exercises 43 and 44, **(a)** write a formula for $f \circ g$ and $g \circ f$ and find the **(b)** domain and **(c)** range of each.

43. $f(x) = 2 - x^2$, $g(x) = \sqrt{x + 2}$

44. $f(x) = \sqrt{x}$, $g(x) = \sqrt{1 - x}$

In Exercises 45–48, a parametrization is given for a curve.

(a) Graph the curve. Identify the initial and terminal points, if any. Indicate the direction in which the curve is traced.

(b) Find a Cartesian equation for a curve that contains the parametrized curve. What portion of the graph of the Cartesian equation is traced by the parametrized curve?

45. $x = 5\cos t$, $y = 2\sin t$, $0 \le t \le 2\pi$

46. $x = 4\cos t$, $y = 4\sin t$, $\pi/2 \le t < 3\pi/2$

47. $x = 2 - t$, $y = 11 - 2t$, $-2 \le t \le 4$

48. $x = 1 + t$, $y = \sqrt{4 - 2t}$, $t \le 2$

In Exercises 49–52, give a parametrization for the curve.

49. the line segment with endpoints $(-2, 5)$ and $(4, 3)$

50. the line through $(-3, -2)$ and $(4, -1)$

51. the ray with initial point $(2, 5)$ that passes through $(-1, 0)$

52. $y = x(x - 4)$, $x \le 2$

Group Activity In Exercises 53 and 54, do the following.

(a) Find f^{-1} and show that $(f \circ f^{-1})(x) = (f^{-1} \circ f)(x) = x$.

(b) Graph f and f^{-1} in the same viewing window.

53. $f(x) = 2 - 3x$ **54.** $f(x) = (x + 2)^2$, $x \ge -2$

In Exercises 55 and 56, find the measure of the angle in radians and degrees.

55. $\sin^{-1}(0.6)$ **56.** $\tan^{-1}(-2.3)$

57. Find the six trigonometric values of $\theta = \cos^{-1}(3/7)$. Give exact answers.

58. Solve the equation $\sin x = -0.2$ in the following intervals.

(a) $0 \le x < 2\pi$ **(b)** $-\infty < x < \infty$

59. Solve for x: $e^{-0.2x} = 4$

60. The graph of f is shown. Draw the graph of each function.

(a) $y = f(-x)$
(b) $y = -f(x)$
(c) $y = -2f(x + 1) + 1$
(d) $y = 3f(x - 2) - 2$

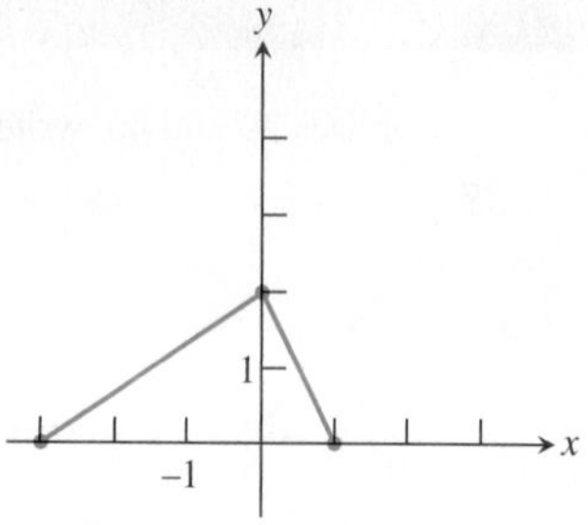

61. A portion of the graph of a function defined on $[-3, 3]$ is shown. Complete the graph assuming that the function is

(a) even.
(b) odd.

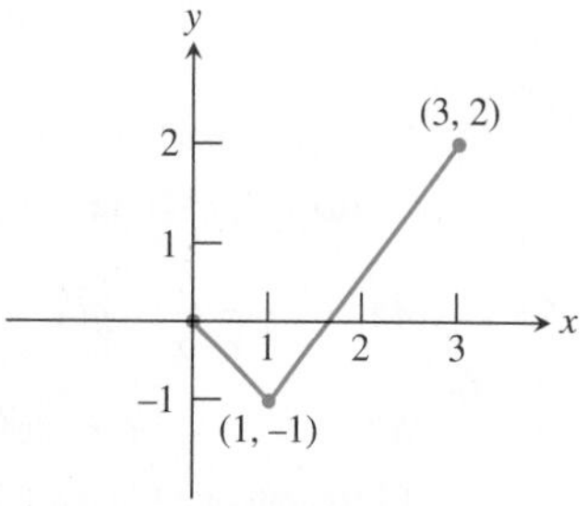

62. *Depreciation* Smith Hauling purchased an 18-wheel truck for \$100,000. The truck depreciates at the constant rate of \$10,000 per year for 10 years.

(a) Write an expression that gives the value y after x years.
(b) When is the value of the truck \$55,000?

63. *Drug Absorption* A drug is administered intravenously for pain. The function

$$f(t) = 90 - 52 \ln (1 + t), \quad 0 \le t \le 4$$

gives the number of units of the drug in the body after t hours.

(a) What was the initial number of units of the drug administered?
(b) How much is present after 2 hours?
(c) Draw the graph of f.

64. *Finding Time* If Joenita invests \$1500 in a retirement account that earns 8% compounded annually, how long will it take this single payment to grow to \$5000?

65. *Guppy Population* The number of guppies in Susan's aquarium doubles every day. There are four guppies initially.

(a) Write the number of guppies as a function of time t.
(b) How many guppies were present after 4 days? after 1 week?
(c) When will there be 2000 guppies?
(d) **Writing to Learn** Give reasons why this might not be a good model for the growth of Susan's guppy population.

66. *Doctoral Degrees* Table 1.23 shows the number of doctoral degrees earned by Hispanic students for several years. Let $x = 0$ represent 1990, $x = 1$ represent 1991, and so forth.

TABLE 1.23
Doctorates Earned by Hispanic Americans

Year	Number of Degrees
1990	780
2000	1305
2005	1824
2006	1882
2007	2035

Source: Statistical Abstract of the United States, 2010.

(a) Find a linear regression equation for the data and superimpose its graph on a scatter plot of the data.
(b) Use the regression equation in part (a) to predict the number of doctoral degrees earned by Hispanic Americans in 2009.
(c) **Writing to Learn** Find the slope of the regression line. What does the slope represent?

67. *Population of New York* Table 1.24 shows the population of New York State for several years. Let $x = 0$ represent 2000, $x = 1$ represent 2001, and so forth.

TABLE 1.24
Population of New York State

Year	Population (thousands)
2003	19,231
2004	19,301
2005	19,336
2006	19,367
2007	19,429
2008	19,490

Source: Statistical Abstract of the United States, 2010.

(a) Find the exponential regression equation for the data and superimpose its graph on a scatter plot of the data.
(b) Use the regression equation to predict the population in 2009.
(c) Use the exponential regression equation to estimate the annual rate of growth of the population of New York State.

AP* Examination Preparation

You may use a graphing calculator to solve the following problems.

68. Consider the point $P(-2, 1)$ and the line L: $x + y = 2$.

(a) Find the slope of L.
(b) Write an equation for the line through P and parallel to L.
(c) Write an equation for the line through P and perpendicular to L.
(d) What is the x-intercept of L?

69. Let $f(x) = 1 - \ln (x - 2)$.

(a) What is the domain of f? (b) What is the range of f?
(c) What are the x-intercepts of the graph of f?
(d) Find f^{-1}. (e) Confirm your answer algebraically in part (d).

70. Let $f(x) = 1 - 3 \cos (2x)$.

(a) What is the domain of f? (b) What is the range of f?
(c) What is the period of f?
(d) Is f an even function, odd function, or neither?
(e) Find all the zeros of f in $\pi/2 \le x \le \pi$.

CHAPTER

2 Limits and Continuity

An Economic Injury Level (EIL) is a measurement of the fewest number of insect pests that will cause economic damage to a crop or forest. It has been estimated that monitoring pest populations and establishing EILs can reduce pesticide use by 30%–50%.

Accurate population estimates are crucial for determining EILs. A population density of one insect pest can be approximated by

$$D(t) = \frac{t^2}{90} + \frac{t}{3}$$

pests per plant, where t is the number of days since initial infestation. What is the rate of change of this population density when the population density is equal to the EIL of 20 pests per plant? Section 2.4 can help answer this question.

CHAPTER 2 Overview

The concept of limit is one of the ideas that distinguish calculus from algebra and trigonometry.

In this chapter, we show how to define and calculate limits of function values. The calculation rules are straightforward, and most of the limits we need can be found by substitution, graphical investigation, numerical approximation, algebra, or some combination of these.

One of the uses of limits is to test functions for continuity. Continuous functions arise frequently in scientific work because they model such an enormous range of natural behavior. They also have special mathematical properties, not otherwise guaranteed.

2.1 Rates of Change and Limits

What you will learn about . . .

- Average and Instantaneous Speed
- Definition of Limit
- Properties of Limits
- One-Sided and Two-Sided Limits
- Sandwich Theorem

and why . . .

Limits can be used to describe continuity, the derivative, and the integral: the ideas giving the foundation of calculus.

Average and Instantaneous Speed

Average speed of a moving body during an interval of time is found by dividing the distance covered by the elapsed time. More precisely, if $y = f(t)$ is a distance or position function of a moving body at time t, then the **average rate of change** (or **average speed**) is the ratio

$$\frac{f(t+h) - f(t)}{h}$$

where the elapsed time is the interval of time from t to $t + h$, or simply h. Often we call the numerator Δy, the change in $y = f(t)$, and the denominator Δt, the change in elapsed time t, where Δy is read "delta y" and Δt is read "delta t." Thus we often write the ratio as

$$\frac{\Delta y}{\Delta t} = \frac{f(t+h) - f(t)}{h}.$$

Free Fall

Near the surface of the earth, all bodies fall with the same constant acceleration. The distance a body falls after it is released from rest is a constant multiple of the square of the time fallen. At least, that is what happens when a body falls in a vacuum, where there is no air to slow it down. The square-of-time rule also holds for dense, heavy objects like rocks, ball bearings, and steel tools during the first few seconds of fall through air, before the velocity builds up to where air resistance begins to matter. When air resistance is absent or insignificant and the only force acting on a falling body is the force of gravity, we call the way the body falls *free fall.*

EXAMPLE 1 Finding an Average Speed

A rock breaks loose from the top of a tall cliff. What is its average speed during the first 2 seconds of fall?

SOLUTION

Experiments show that a dense solid object dropped from rest to fall freely near the surface of the earth will fall

$$y = 16t^2$$

feet in the first t seconds. The average speed of the rock over any given time interval is the distance traveled, Δy, divided by the length of the interval Δt. For the first 2 seconds of fall, from $t = 0$ to $t = 2$, we have

$$\frac{\Delta y}{\Delta t} = \frac{16(2)^2 - 16(0)^2}{2 - 0} = 32\,\frac{\text{ft}}{\text{sec}}.$$

Now Try Exercise 1.

A moving body's **instantaneous speed** is the speed of the moving object at a *given instant of time*. The major issue is *how* to compute this speed, since the "elapsed time" seems to be zero, as we explain in Example 2. We show after this example that we need the mathematical concept of a *limit* to understand and compute instantaneous speed.

TABLE 2.1 Average Speeds over Short Time Intervals Starting at $t = 2$

$$\frac{\Delta y}{\Delta t} = \frac{16(2 + h)^2 - 16(2)^2}{h}$$

Length of Time Interval, h (sec)	Average Speed for Interval $\Delta y/\Delta t$ (ft/sec)
1	80
0.1	65.6
0.01	64.16
0.001	64.016
0.0001	64.0016
0.00001	64.00016

EXAMPLE 2 Finding an Instantaneous Speed

Find the speed of the rock in Example 1 at the instant $t = 2$.

SOLUTION

Solve Numerically We can calculate the average speed of the rock over the interval from time $t = 2$ to any slightly later time $t = 2 + h$ as

$$\frac{\Delta y}{\Delta t} = \frac{16(2 + h)^2 - 16(2)^2}{h}. \qquad (1)$$

We cannot use this formula to calculate the speed at the exact instant $t = 2$ because that would require taking $h = 0$, and $0/0$ is undefined. However, we can get a good idea of what is happening at $t = 2$ by evaluating the formula at values of h *close* to 0. When we do, we see a clear pattern (Table 2.1). As h approaches 0, the average speed approaches the limiting value 64 ft/sec.

Confirm Algebraically If we expand the numerator of Equation 1 and simplify, we find that

$$\frac{\Delta y}{\Delta t} = \frac{16(2 + h)^2 - 16(2)^2}{h} = \frac{16(4 + 4h + h^2) - 64}{h}$$

$$= \frac{64h + 16h^2}{h} = 64 + 16h.$$

For values of h different from 0, the expressions on the right and left are equivalent and the average speed is $64 + 16h$ ft/sec. We can now see why the average speed has the limiting value $64 + 16(0) = 64$ ft/sec as h approaches 0. ***Now Try Exercise 3.***

Formal Definition of Limit

You may want to look over the examples in Appendix A3, pp. 577–584, which provide illustrations of the formal limit definition of a function ***f* that has limit *L* as *x* approaches *c*.**

Definition of Limit

As in the preceding example, most limits of interest in the real world can be viewed as numerical limits of values of functions. And this is where a graphing utility and calculus come in. A calculator can suggest the limits, and calculus can give the mathematics for confirming the limits analytically.

Limits give us a language for describing how the outputs of a function behave as the inputs approach some particular value. In Example 2, the average speed was not defined at $h = 0$ but approached the limit 64 as h approached 0. We were able to see this numerically and to confirm it algebraically by eliminating h from the denominator. But we cannot always do that. For instance, we can see both graphically and numerically (Figure 2.1) that the values of $f(x) = (\sin x)/x$ approach 1 as x approaches 0.

We cannot eliminate the x from the denominator of $(\sin x)/x$ to confirm the observation algebraically. We need to use a theorem about limits to make that confirmation, as you will see in Exercise 77.

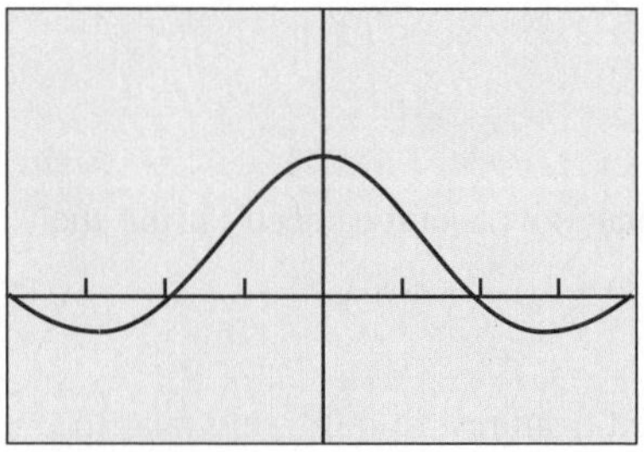

$[-2\pi, 2\pi]$ by $[-1, 2]$

(a)

X	Y1
-.3	.98507
-.2	.99335
-.1	.99833
0	ERROR
.1	.99833
.2	.99335
.3	.98507

Y1 = sin(X)/X

(b)

Figure 2.1 (a) A graph and (b) table of values for $f(x) = (\sin x)/x$ that suggest the limit of f as x approaches 0 is 1.

DEFINITION Limit

Assume f is defined in a neighborhood of c and let c and L be real numbers. The function ***f* has limit *L* as *x* approaches *c*** if, given any positive number ε, there is a positive number δ such that for all x,

$$0 < |x - c| < \delta \Rightarrow |f(x) - L| < \varepsilon.$$

We write

$$\lim_{x \to c} f(x) = L.$$

The sentence $\lim_{x \to c} f(x) = L$ is read, "The limit of f of x as x approaches c equals L." The notation means that the values $f(x)$ of the function f approach or equal L as the values of x approach *(but do not equal)* c. Appendix A3 provides practice applying the definition of limit.

We saw in Example 2 that $\lim_{h \to 0} (64 + 16h) = 64$.

As suggested in Figure 2.1,

$$\lim_{x \to 0} \frac{\sin x}{x} = 1.$$

Figure 2.2 illustrates the fact that the existence of a limit as $x \to c$ never depends on how the function may or may not be defined at c. The function f has limit 2 as $x \to 1$ even though f is not defined at 1. The function g has limit 2 as $x \to 1$ even though $g(1) \neq 2$. The function h is the only one whose limit as $x \to 1$ equals its value at $x = 1$.

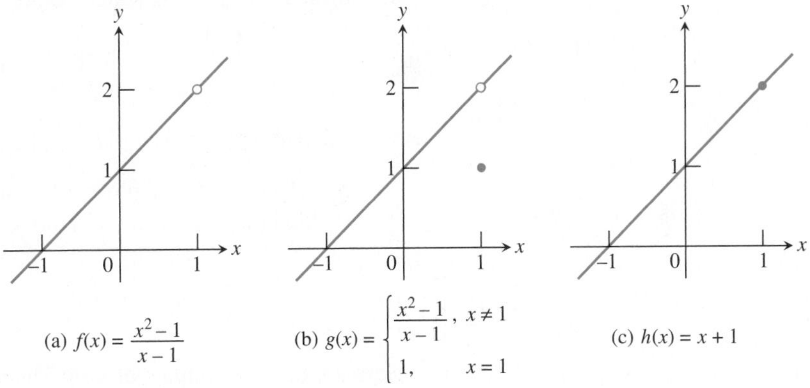

Figure 2.2 $\lim_{x \to 1} f(x) = \lim_{x \to 1} g(x) = \lim_{x \to 1} h(x) = 2$.

Properties of Limits

By applying six basic facts about limits, we can calculate many unfamiliar limits from limits we already know. For instance, from knowing that

$$\lim_{x \to c} (k) = k$$ Limit of the function with constant value k

and

$$\lim_{x \to c} (x) = c,$$ Limit of the identity function at $x = c$

we can calculate the limits of all polynomial and rational functions. The facts are listed in Theorem 1.

THEOREM 1 Properties of Limits

If L, M, c, and k are real numbers and

$$\lim_{x \to c} f(x) = L \quad \text{and} \quad \lim_{x \to c} g(x) = M, \text{ then}$$

1. *Sum Rule:* $$\lim_{x \to c} (f(x) + g(x)) = L + M$$

   The limit of the sum of two functions is the sum of their limits.

2. *Difference Rule:* $$\lim_{x \to c} (f(x) - g(x)) = L - M$$

   The limit of the difference of two functions is the difference of their limits.

continued

3. *Product Rule:* $\lim_{x\to c} (f(x)\cdot g(x)) = L\cdot M$

The limit of a product of two functions is the product of their limits.

4. *Constant Multiple Rule:* $\lim_{x\to c} (k\cdot f(x)) = k\cdot L$

The limit of a constant times a function is the constant times the limit of the function.

5. *Quotient Rule:* $\lim_{x\to c} \frac{f(x)}{g(x)} = \frac{L}{M},\ M \neq 0$

The limit of a quotient of two functions is the quotient of their limits, provided the limit of the denominator is not zero.

6. *Power Rule:* If r and s are integers, $s \neq 0$, then

$$\lim_{x\to c} (f(x))^{r/s} = L^{r/s}$$

provided that $L^{r/s}$ is a real number.

The limit of a rational power of a function is that power of the limit of the function, provided the latter is a real number.

Here are some examples of how Theorem 1 can be used to find limits of polynomial and rational functions.

Using Analytic Methods

We remind the student that *unless otherwise stated* all examples and exercises are to be done using analytic algebraic methods *without* the use of graphing calculators or computer algebra systems.

EXAMPLE 3 Using Properties of Limits

Use the observations $\lim_{x\to c} k = k$ and $\lim_{x\to c} x = c$, and the properties of limits to find the following limits.

(a) $\lim_{x\to c} (x^3 + 4x^2 - 3)$ **(b)** $\lim_{x\to c} \frac{x^4 + x^2 - 1}{x^2 + 5}$

SOLUTION

(a) $\lim_{x\to c} (x^3 + 4x^2 - 3) = \lim_{x\to c} x^3 + \lim_{x\to c} 4x^2 - \lim_{x\to c} 3$ Sum and Difference Rules

$= c^3 + 4c^2 - 3$ Product and Constant Multiple Rules

(b) $\lim_{x\to c} \frac{x^4 + x^2 - 1}{x^2 + 5} = \frac{\lim_{x\to c} (x^4 + x^2 - 1)}{\lim_{x\to c} (x^2 + 5)}$ Quotient Rule

$= \frac{\lim_{x\to c} x^4 + \lim_{x\to c} x^2 - \lim_{x\to c} 1}{\lim_{x\to c} x^2 + \lim_{x\to c} 5}$ Sum and Difference Rules

$= \frac{c^4 + c^2 - 1}{c^2 + 5}$ Product Rule

Now Try Exercises 5 and 6.

Example 3 shows the remarkable strength of Theorem 1. From the two simple observations that $\lim_{x\to c} k = k$ and $\lim_{x\to c} x = c$, we can immediately work our way to limits of polynomial functions and most rational functions using substitution.

THEOREM 2 Polynomial and Rational Functions

1. If $f(x) = a_n x^n + a_{n-1} x^{n-1} + \cdots + a_0$ is any polynomial function and c is any real number, then

$$\lim_{x \to c} f(x) = f(c) = a_n c^n + a_{n-1} c^{n-1} + \cdots + a_0.$$

2. If $f(x)$ and $g(x)$ are polynomials and c is any real number, then

$$\lim_{x \to c} \frac{f(x)}{g(x)} = \frac{f(c)}{g(c)}, \quad \text{provided that } g(c) \neq 0.$$

EXAMPLE 4 Using Theorem 2

(a) $\lim_{x \to 3} [x^2(2 - x)] = (3)^2(2 - 3) = -9$

(b) $\lim_{x \to 2} \frac{x^2 + 2x + 4}{x + 2} = \frac{(2)^2 + 2(2) + 4}{2 + 2} = \frac{12}{4} = 3$

Now Try Exercises 9 and 11.

As with polynomials, limits of many familiar functions can be found by substitution at points where they are defined. This includes trigonometric functions, exponential and logarithmic functions, and composites of these functions. Feel free to use these properties.

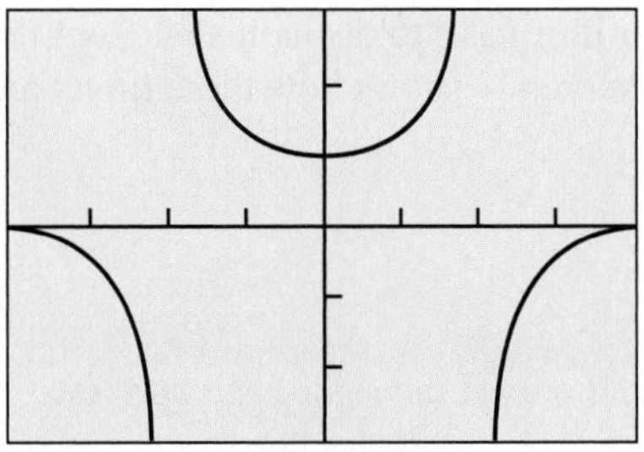

[$-\pi$, π] by [-3, 3]

Figure 2.3 The graph of

$$f(x) = (\tan x)/x$$

suggests that $f(x) \to 1$ as $x \to 0$. (Example 5)

EXAMPLE 5 Using the Product Rule

Determine $\lim_{x \to 0} \frac{\tan x}{x}$.

SOLUTION

Solve Analytically Using the analytic result of Exercise 77, we have

$$\lim_{x \to 0} \frac{\tan x}{x} = \lim_{x \to 0} \left(\frac{\sin x}{x} \cdot \frac{1}{\cos x} \right) \qquad \tan x = \frac{\sin x}{\cos x}$$

$$= \lim_{x \to 0} \frac{\sin x}{x} \cdot \lim_{x \to 0} \frac{1}{\cos x} \qquad \text{Product Rule}$$

$$= 1 \cdot \frac{1}{\cos 0} = 1 \cdot \frac{1}{1} = 1.$$

Support Graphically The graph of $f(x) = (\tan x)/x$ in Figure 2.3 suggests that the limit exists and is about 1.

Now Try Exercise 33.

Sometimes we can use a graph to discover that limits do not exist, as illustrated by Example 6.

EXAMPLE 6 Exploring a Nonexistent Limit

Use a graph to show that

$$\lim_{x \to 2} \frac{x^3 - 1}{x - 2}$$

does not exist.

continued

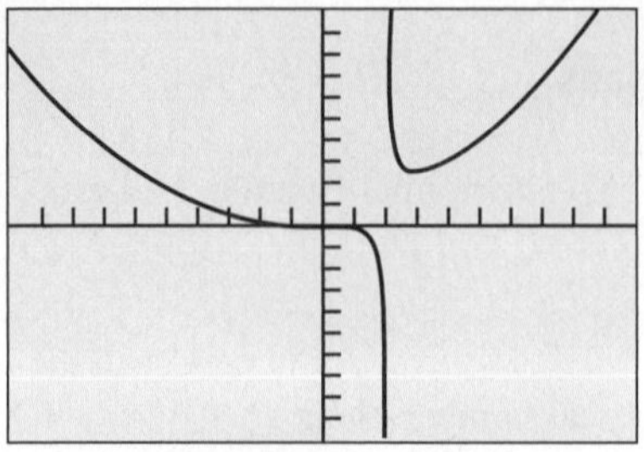

[–10, 10] by [–100, 100]

Figure 2.4 The graph of $f(x) = (x^3 - 1)/(x - 2)$. (Example 6)

SOLUTION

Notice that the denominator is 0 when x is replaced by 2, so we cannot use substitution to determine the limit. The graph in Figure 2.4 of $f(x) = (x^3 - 1)/(x - 2)$ strongly suggests that as $x \to 2$ from either side, the absolute values of the function values get very large. This, in turn, suggests that the limit does not exist.

Now Try Exercise 35.

One-Sided and Two-Sided Limits

Sometimes the values of a function f tend to different limits as x approaches a number c from opposite sides. When this happens, we call the limit of f as x approaches c from the right the **right-hand limit** of f at c and the limit as x approaches c from the left the **left-hand limit** of f at c. Here is the notation we use:

right-hand: $\lim_{x \to c^+} f(x)$ *The limit of f as x approaches c from the right.*

left-hand: $\lim_{x \to c^-} f(x)$ *The limit of f as x approaches c from the left.*

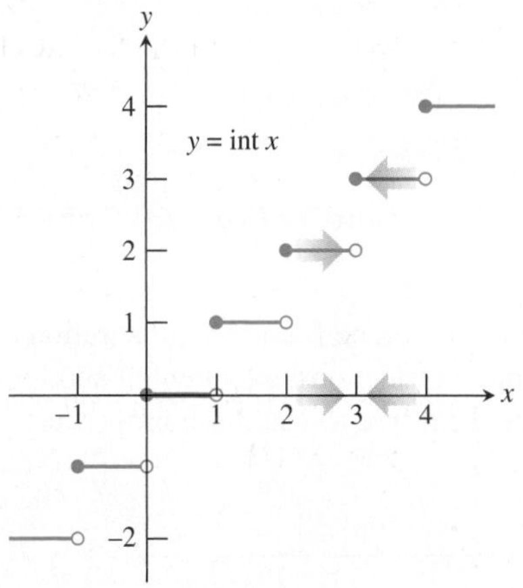

Figure 2.5 At each integer, the greatest integer function $y = \text{int } x$ has different right-hand and left-hand limits. (Example 7)

EXAMPLE 7 Function Values Approach Two Numbers

The greatest integer function $f(x) = \text{int } x$ has different right-hand and left-hand limits at each integer, as we can see in Figure 2.5. For example,

$$\lim_{x \to 3^+} \text{int } x = 3 \quad \text{and} \quad \lim_{x \to 3^-} \text{int } x = 2.$$

The limit of int x as x approaches an integer n from the right is n, while the limit as x approaches n from the left is $n - 1$.

Now Try Exercises 37 and 38.

We sometimes call $\lim_{x \to c} f(x)$ the **two-sided limit** of f at c to distinguish it from the *one-sided* right-hand and left-hand limits of f at c. Theorem 3 shows how these limits are related.

On the Far Side

If f is not defined to the left of $x = c$, then f does not have a left-hand limit at c. Similarly, if f is not defined to the right of $x = c$, then f does not have a right-hand limit at c.

THEOREM 3 One-Sided and Two-Sided Limits

A function $f(x)$ has a limit as x approaches c if and only if the right-hand and left-hand limits at c exist and are equal. In symbols,

$$\lim_{x \to c} f(x) = L \Leftrightarrow \lim_{x \to c^+} f(x) = L \quad \text{and} \quad \lim_{x \to c^-} f(x) = L.$$

Thus, the greatest integer function $f(x) = \text{int } x$ of Example 7 does not have a limit as $x \to 3$ even though each one-sided limit exists.

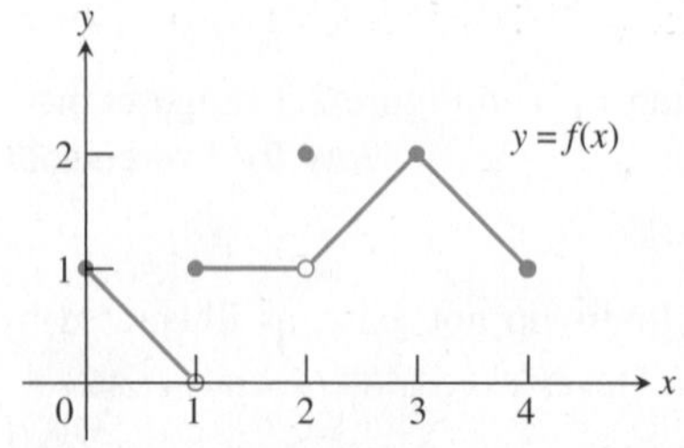

Figure 2.6 The graph of the function

$$f(x) = \begin{cases} -x + 1, & 0 \le x < 1 \\ 1, & 1 \le x < 2 \\ 2, & x = 2 \\ x - 1, & 2 < x \le 3 \\ -x + 5, & 3 < x \le 4. \end{cases}$$

(Example 8)

EXAMPLE 8 Exploring Right- and Left-Hand Limits

All the following statements about the function $y = f(x)$ graphed in Figure 2.6 are true.

At $x = 0$: $\lim_{x \to 0^+} f(x) = 1$.

At $x = 1$: $\lim_{x \to 1^-} f(x) = 0$ even though $f(1) = 1$,

$\lim_{x \to 1^+} f(x) = 1$,

f has no limit as $x \to 1$. (The right- and left-hand limits at 1 are not equal, so $\lim_{x \to 1} f(x)$ does not exist.)

continued

At $x = 2$: $\lim_{x\to 2^-} f(x) = 1$,

$\lim_{x\to 2^+} f(x) = 1$,

$\lim_{x\to 2} f(x) = 1$ even though $f(2) = 2$.

At $x = 3$: $\lim_{x\to 3^-} f(x) = \lim_{x\to 3^+} f(x) = 2 = f(3) = \lim_{x\to 3} f(x)$.

At $x = 4$: $\lim_{x\to 4^-} f(x) = 1$.

At noninteger values of c between 0 and 4, f has a limit as $x \to c$.

Now Try Exercise 43.

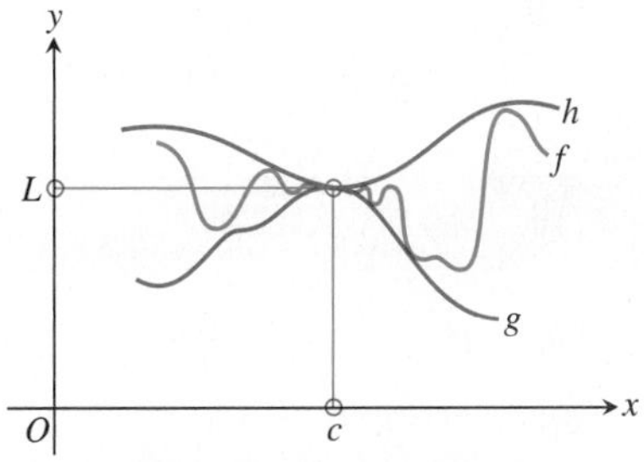

Figure 2.7 Sandwiching f between g and h forces the limiting value of f to be between the limiting values of g and h.

Sandwich Theorem

If we cannot find a limit directly, we may be able to find it indirectly with the Sandwich Theorem. The theorem refers to a function f whose values are sandwiched between the values of two other functions, g and h. If g and h have the same limit as $x \to c$, then f has that limit too, as suggested by Figure 2.7.

THEOREM 4 The Sandwich Theorem

If $g(x) \le f(x) \le h(x)$ for all $x \ne c$ in some interval about c, and

$$\lim_{x\to c} g(x) = \lim_{x\to c} h(x) = L,$$

then

$$\lim_{x\to c} f(x) = L.$$

EXAMPLE 9 Using the Sandwich Theorem

Show that $\lim_{x\to 0} [x^2 \sin(1/x)] = 0$.

SOLUTION

We know that the values of the sine function lie between -1 and 1. So, it follows that

$$\left|x^2 \sin\frac{1}{x}\right| = |x^2| \cdot \left|\sin\frac{1}{x}\right| \le |x^2| \cdot 1 = x^2$$

and

$$-x^2 \le x^2 \sin\frac{1}{x} \le x^2.$$

Because $\lim_{x\to 0} (-x^2) = \lim_{x\to 0} x^2 = 0$, the Sandwich Theorem gives

$$\lim_{x\to 0}\left(x^2 \sin\frac{1}{x}\right) = 0.$$

The graphs in Figure 2.8 support this result.

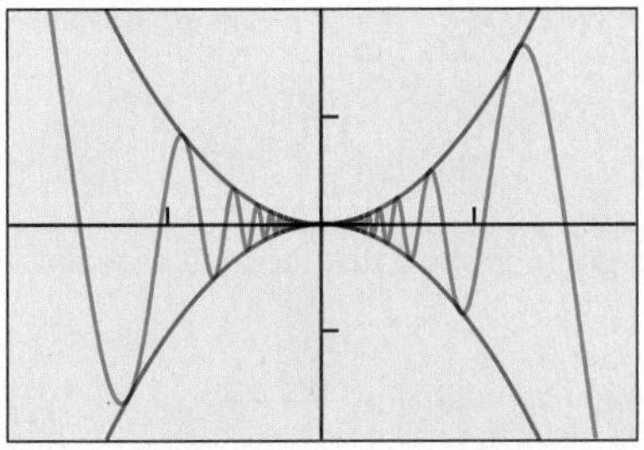

[-0.2, 0.2] by [-0.02, 0.02]

Figure 2.8 The graphs of $y_1 = x^2$, $y_2 = x^2 \sin(1/x)$, and $y_3 = -x^2$. Notice that $y_3 \le y_2 \le y_1$. (Example 9)

Quick Review 2.1 *(For help, go to Section 1.2.)*

Exercise numbers with a gray background indicate problems that the authors have designed to be solved *without a calculator.*

In Exercises 1–4, find $f(2)$.

1. $f(x) = 2x^3 - 5x^2 + 4$

2. $f(x) = \dfrac{4x^2 - 5}{x^3 + 4}$

3. $f(x) = \sin\left(\pi \dfrac{x}{2}\right)$

4. $f(x) = \begin{cases} 3x - 1, & x < 2 \\ \dfrac{1}{x^2 - 1}, & x \geq 2 \end{cases}$

In Exercises 5–8, write the inequality in the form $a < x < b$.

5. $|x| < 4$

6. $|x| < c^2$

7. $|x - 2| < 3$

8. $|x - c| < d^2$

In Exercises 9 and 10, write the fraction in reduced form.

9. $\dfrac{x^2 - 3x - 18}{x + 3}$

10. $\dfrac{2x^2 - x}{2x^2 + x - 1}$

Section 2.1 Exercises

In Exercises 1–4, an object dropped from rest from the top of a tall building falls $y = 16t^2$ feet in the first t seconds.

1. Find the average speed during the first 3 seconds of fall.

2. Find the average speed during the first 4 seconds of fall.

3. Find the speed of the object at $t = 3$ seconds and confirm your answer algebraically.

4. Find the speed of the object at $t = 4$ seconds and confirm your answer algebraically.

In Exercises 5 and 6, use $\lim_{x\to c} k = k$, $\lim_{x\to c} x = c$, and the properties of limits to find the limit.

5. $\lim\limits_{x\to c} (2x^3 - 3x^2 + x - 1)$

6. $\lim\limits_{x\to c} \dfrac{x^4 - x^3 + 1}{x^2 + 9}$

In Exercises 7–14, determine the limit by substitution. Support graphically.

7. $\lim\limits_{x\to -1/2} 3x^2(2x - 1)$

8. $\lim\limits_{x\to -4} (x + 3)^{1998}$

9. $\lim\limits_{x\to 1} (x^3 + 3x^2 - 2x - 17)$

10. $\lim\limits_{y\to 2} \dfrac{y^2 + 5y + 6}{y + 2}$

11. $\lim\limits_{y\to -3} \dfrac{y^2 + 4y + 3}{y^2 - 3}$

12. $\lim\limits_{x\to 1/2} \text{int } x$

13. $\lim\limits_{x\to -2} (x - 6)^{2/3}$

14. $\lim\limits_{x\to 2} \sqrt{x + 3}$

In Exercises 15–20, complete the following tables and state what you believe $\lim_{x\to 0} f(x)$ to be.

(a)

x	−0.1	−0.01	−0.001	−0.0001	...
$f(x)$	?	?	?	?	

(b)

x	0.1	0.01	0.001	0.0001	...
$f(x)$	?	?	?	?	

15. $f(x) = \dfrac{x^2 + 6x + 2}{x + 1}$

16. $f(x) = \dfrac{x^2 - x}{x}$

17. $f(x) = x \sin \dfrac{1}{x}$

18. $f(x) = \sin \dfrac{1}{x}$

19. $f(x) = \dfrac{10^x - 1}{x}$

20. $f(x) = x \sin(\ln |x|)$

In Exercises 21–24, explain why you cannot use substitution to determine the limit. Find the limit if it exists.

21. $\lim\limits_{x\to -2} \sqrt{x - 2}$

22. $\lim\limits_{x\to 0} \dfrac{1}{x^2}$

23. $\lim\limits_{x\to 0} \dfrac{|x|}{x}$

24. $\lim\limits_{x\to 0} \dfrac{(4 + x)^2 - 16}{x}$

In Exercises 25–34, determine the limit graphically. Confirm algebraically.

25. $\lim\limits_{x\to 1} \dfrac{x - 1}{x^2 - 1}$

26. $\lim\limits_{t\to 2} \dfrac{t^2 - 3t + 2}{t^2 - 4}$

27. $\lim\limits_{x\to 0} \dfrac{5x^3 + 8x^2}{3x^4 - 16x^2}$

28. $\lim\limits_{x\to 0} \dfrac{\frac{1}{2 + x} - \frac{1}{2}}{x}$

29. $\lim\limits_{x\to 0} \dfrac{(2 + x)^3 - 8}{x}$

30. $\lim\limits_{x\to 0} \dfrac{\sin 2x}{x}$

31. $\lim\limits_{x\to 0} \dfrac{\sin x}{2x^2 - x}$

32. $\lim\limits_{x\to 0} \dfrac{x + \sin x}{x}$

33. $\lim\limits_{x\to 0} \dfrac{\sin^2 x}{x}$

34. $\lim\limits_{x\to 5} \dfrac{x^3 - 125}{x - 5}$

In Exercises 35 and 36, use a graph to show that the limit does not exist.

35. $\lim\limits_{x\to 1} \dfrac{x^2 - 4}{x - 1}$

36. $\lim\limits_{x\to 2} \dfrac{x + 1}{x^2 - 4}$

In Exercises 37–42, determine the limit.

37. $\lim\limits_{x\to 0^+} \text{int } x$

38. $\lim\limits_{x\to 0^-} \text{int } x$

39. $\lim_{x \to 0.01} \text{int } x$

40. $\lim_{x \to 2^-} \text{int } x$

41. $\lim_{x \to 0^+} \frac{x}{|x|}$

42. $\lim_{x \to 0^-} \frac{x}{|x|}$

In Exercises 43 and 44, which of the statements are true about the function $y = f(x)$ graphed there, and which are false?

43.

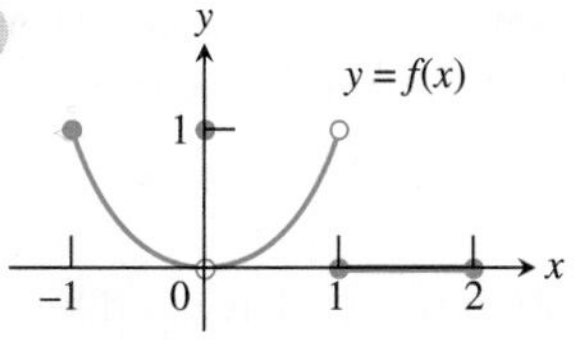

(a) $\lim_{x \to -1^+} f(x) = 1$

(b) $\lim_{x \to 0^-} f(x) = 0$

(c) $\lim_{x \to 0^-} f(x) = 1$

(d) $\lim_{x \to 0^-} f(x) = \lim_{x \to 0^+} f(x)$

(e) $\lim_{x \to 0} f(x)$ exists

(f) $\lim_{x \to 0} f(x) = 0$

(g) $\lim_{x \to 0} f(x) = 1$

(h) $\lim_{x \to 1} f(x) = 1$

(i) $\lim_{x \to 1} f(x) = 0$

(j) $\lim_{x \to 2^-} f(x) = 2$

44.

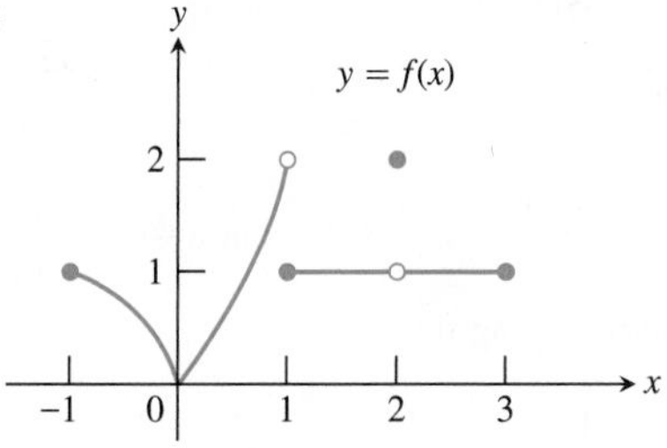

(a) $\lim_{x \to -1^+} f(x) = 1$

(b) $\lim_{x \to 2} f(x)$ does not exist.

(c) $\lim_{x \to 2} f(x) = 2$

(d) $\lim_{x \to 1^-} f(x) = 2$

(e) $\lim_{x \to 1^+} f(x) = 1$

(f) $\lim_{x \to 1} f(x)$ does not exist.

(g) $\lim_{x \to 0^+} f(x) = \lim_{x \to 0^-} f(x)$

(h) $\lim_{x \to c} f(x)$ exists at every c in $(-1, 1)$.

(i) $\lim_{x \to c} f(x)$ exists at every c in $(1, 3)$.

In Exercises 45–50, use the graph to estimate the limits and value of the function, or explain why the limits do not exist.

45.

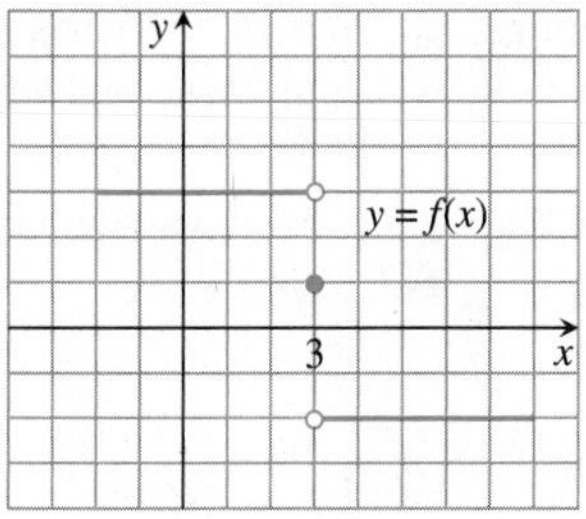

(a) $\lim_{x \to 3^-} f(x)$

(b) $\lim_{x \to 3^+} f(x)$

(c) $\lim_{x \to 3} f(x)$

(d) $f(3)$

46.

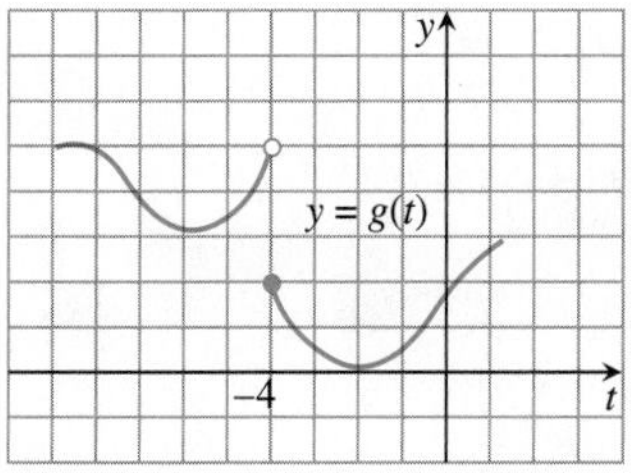

(a) $\lim_{t \to -4^-} g(t)$

(b) $\lim_{t \to -4^+} g(t)$

(c) $\lim_{t \to -4} g(t)$

(d) $g(-4)$

47.

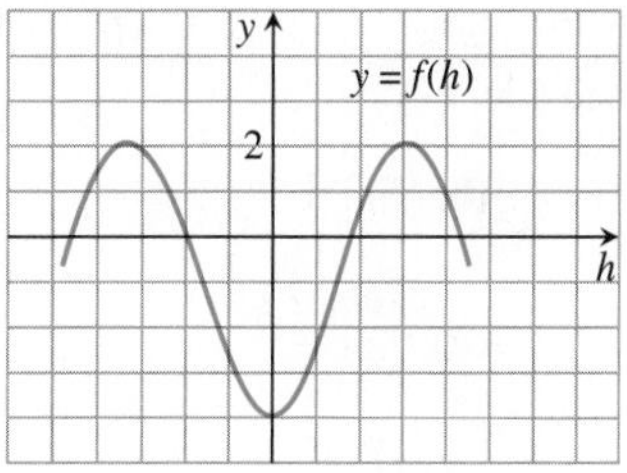

(a) $\lim_{h \to 0^-} f(h)$

(b) $\lim_{h \to 0^+} f(h)$

(c) $\lim_{h \to 0} f(h)$

(d) $f(0)$

48.

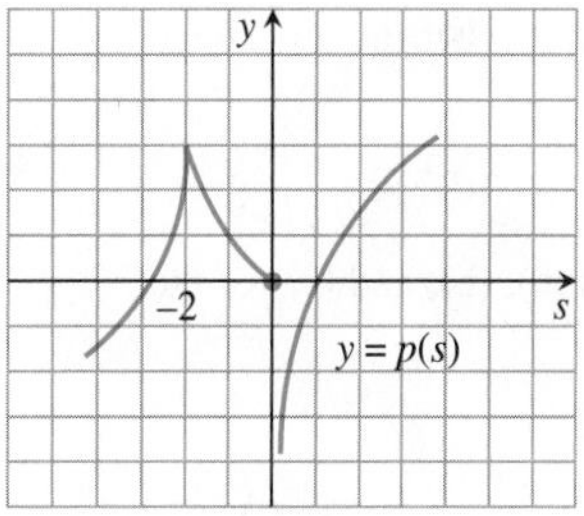

(a) $\lim_{s \to -2^-} p(s)$

(b) $\lim_{s \to -2^+} p(s)$

(c) $\lim_{s \to -2} p(s)$

(d) $p(-2)$

49.

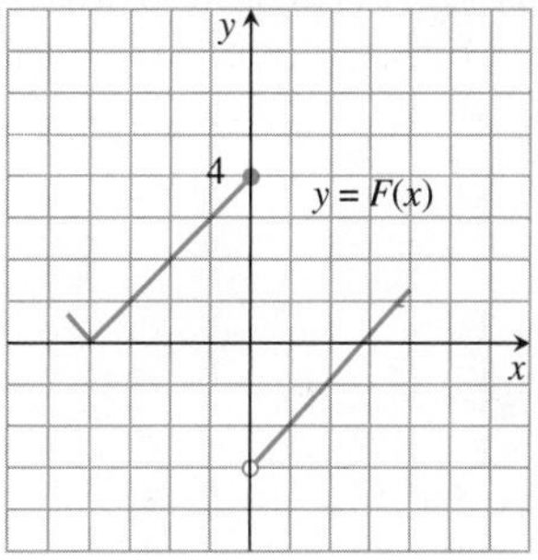

(a) $\lim_{x \to 0^-} F(x)$

(b) $\lim_{x \to 0^+} F(x)$

(c) $\lim_{x \to 0} F(x)$

(d) $F(0)$

50.

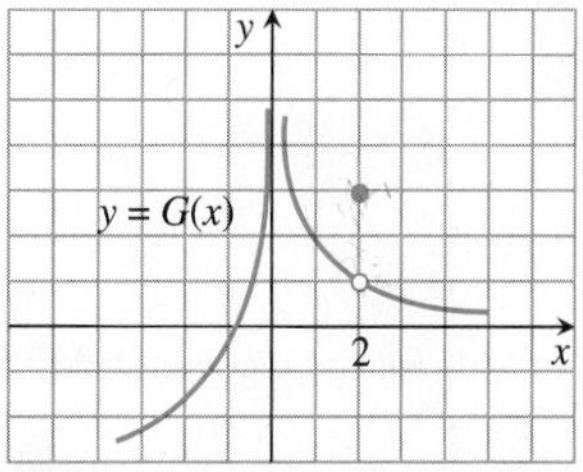

(a) $\lim_{x \to 2^-} G(x)$

(b) $\lim_{x \to 2^+} G(x)$

(c) $\lim_{x \to 2} G(x)$

(d) $G(2)$

In Exercises 51–54, match the function with the table.

51. $y_1 = \frac{x^2 + x - 2}{x - 1}$

52. $y_1 = \frac{x^2 - x - 2}{x - 1}$

53. $y_1 = \frac{x^2 - 2x + 1}{x - 1}$

54. $y_1 = \frac{x^2 + x - 2}{x + 1}$

X	Y_1
.7	−.4765
.8	−.3111
.9	−.1526
1	0
1.1	.14762
1.2	.29091
1.3	.43043

X = .7

(a)

X	Y_1
.7	7.3667
.8	10.8
.9	20.9
1	ERROR
1.1	−18.9
1.2	−8.8
1.3	−5.367

X = .7

(b)

X	Y_1
.7	2.7
.8	2.8
.9	2.9
1	ERROR
1.1	3.1
1.2	3.2
1.3	3.3

X = .7

(c)

X	Y_1
.7	−.3
.8	−.2
.9	−.1
1	ERROR
1.1	.1
1.2	.2
1.3	.3

X = .7

(d)

In Exercises 55 and 56, determine the limit.

55. Assume that $\lim_{x\to 4} f(x) = 0$ and $\lim_{x\to 4} g(x) = 3$.

(a) $\lim_{x\to 4} (g(x) + 3)$ (b) $\lim_{x\to 4} x f(x)$

(c) $\lim_{x\to 4} g^2(x)$ (d) $\lim_{x\to 4} \dfrac{g(x)}{f(x) - 1}$

56. Assume that $\lim_{x\to b} f(x) = 7$ and $\lim_{x\to b} g(x) = -3$.

(a) $\lim_{x\to b} (f(x) + g(x))$ (b) $\lim_{x\to b} (f(x)\cdot g(x))$

(c) $\lim_{x\to b} 4\, g(x)$ (d) $\lim_{x\to b} \dfrac{f(x)}{g(x)}$

In Exercises 57–60, complete parts (a), (b), and (c) for the piecewise-defined function.

(a) Draw the graph of f.

(b) Determine $\lim_{x\to c^+} f(x)$ and $\lim_{x\to c^-} f(x)$.

(c) **Writing to Learn** Does $\lim_{x\to c} f(x)$ exist? If so, what is it? If not, explain.

57. $c = 2,\ f(x) = \begin{cases} 3 - x, & x < 2 \\ \dfrac{x}{2} + 1, & x > 2 \end{cases}$

58. $c = 2,\ f(x) = \begin{cases} 3 - x, & x < 2 \\ 2, & x = 2 \\ x/2, & x > 2 \end{cases}$

59. $c = 1,\ f(x) = \begin{cases} \dfrac{1}{x - 1}, & x < 1 \\ x^3 - 2x + 5, & x \ge 1 \end{cases}$

60. $c = -1,\ f(x) = \begin{cases} 1 - x^2, & x \ne -1 \\ 2, & x = -1 \end{cases}$

In Exercises 61–64, complete parts (a)–(d) for the piecewise-defined function.

(a) Draw the graph of f.

(b) At what points c in the domain of f does $\lim_{x\to c} f(x)$ exist?

(c) At what points c does only the left-hand limit exist?

(d) At what points c does only the right-hand limit exist?

61. $f(x) = \begin{cases} \sin x, & -2\pi \le x < 0 \\ \cos x, & 0 \le x \le 2\pi \end{cases}$

62. $f(x) = \begin{cases} \cos x, & -\pi \le x < 0 \\ \sec x, & 0 \le x \le \pi \end{cases}$

63. $f(x) = \begin{cases} \sqrt{1 - x^2}, & 0 \le x < 1 \\ 1, & 1 \le x < 2 \\ 2, & x = 2 \end{cases}$

64. $f(x) = \begin{cases} x, & -1 \le x < 0, \text{ or } 0 < x \le 1 \\ 1, & x = 0 \\ 0, & x < -1, \text{ or } x > 1 \end{cases}$

In Exercises 65–68, find the limit graphically. Use the Sandwich Theorem to confirm your answer.

65. $\lim_{x\to 0} x \sin x$ **66.** $\lim_{x\to 0} x^2 \sin x$

67. $\lim_{x\to 0} x^2 \sin \dfrac{1}{x^2}$ **68.** $\lim_{x\to 0} x^2 \cos \dfrac{1}{x^2}$

69. ***Free Fall*** A water balloon dropped from a window high above the ground falls $y = 4.9t^2$ m in t sec. Find the balloon's

(a) average speed during the first 3 sec of fall.

(b) speed at the instant $t = 3$.

70. ***Free Fall on a Small Airless Planet*** A rock released from rest to fall on a small airless planet falls $y = gt^2$ m in t sec, g a constant. Suppose that the rock falls to the bottom of a crevasse 20 m below and reaches the bottom in 4 sec.

(a) Find the value of g.

(b) Find the average speed for the fall.

(c) With what speed did the rock hit the bottom?

Standardized Test Questions

71. True or False If $\lim_{x\to c^-} f(x) = 2$ and $\lim_{x\to c^+} f(x) = 2$, then $\lim_{x\to c} f(x) = 2$. Justify your answer.

72. True or False $\lim_{x\to 0} \dfrac{x + \sin x}{x} = 2$. Justify your answer.

In Exercises 73–76, use the following function.

$$f(x) = \begin{cases} 2 - x, & x \le 1 \\ \dfrac{x}{2} + 1, & x > 1 \end{cases}$$

73. Multiple Choice What is the value of $\lim_{x\to 1^-} f(x)$?

(A) 5/2 (B) 3/2 (C) 1 (D) 0 (E) does not exist

74. Multiple Choice What is the value of $\lim_{x\to 1^+} f(x)$?

(A) 5/2 (B) 3/2 (C) 1 (D) 0 (E) does not exist

75. Multiple Choice What is the value of $\lim_{x\to 1} f(x)$?

(A) 5/2 (B) 3/2 (C) 1 (D) 0 (E) does not exist

76. Multiple Choice What is the value of $f(1)$?

(A) 5/2 (B) 3/2 (C) 1 (D) 0 (E) does not exist

77. Group Activity To prove that $\lim_{\theta\to 0} (\sin\theta)/\theta = 1$ when θ is measured in radians, the plan is to show that the right- and left-hand limits are both 1.

(a) To show that the right-hand limit is 1, explain why we can restrict our attention to $0 < \theta < \pi/2$.

(b) Use the figure to show that

$$\text{area of } \Delta OAP = \frac{1}{2}\sin\theta,$$

$$\text{area of sector } OAP = \frac{\theta}{2},$$

$$\text{area of } \Delta OAT = \frac{1}{2}\tan\theta.$$

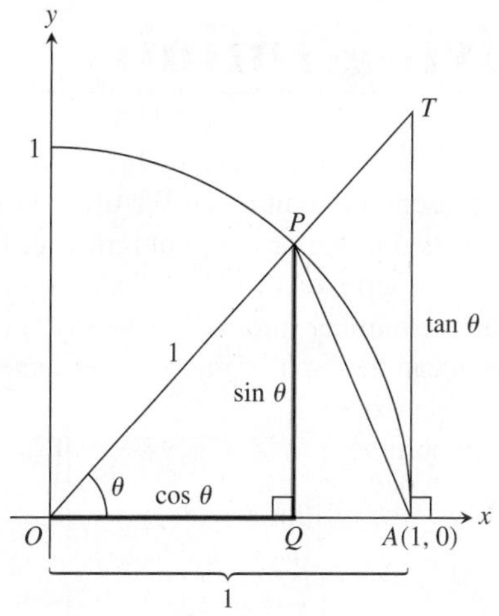

(c) Use part (b) and the figure to show that for $0 < \theta < \pi/2$,

$$\frac{1}{2}\sin\theta < \frac{1}{2}\theta < \frac{1}{2}\tan\theta.$$

(d) Show that for $0 < \theta < \pi/2$ the inequality of part (c) can be written in the form

$$1 < \frac{\theta}{\sin\theta} < \frac{1}{\cos\theta}.$$

(e) Show that for $0 < \theta < \pi/2$ the inequality of part (d) can be written in the form

$$\cos\theta < \frac{\sin\theta}{\theta} < 1.$$

(f) Use the Sandwich Theorem to show that

$$\lim_{\theta\to 0^+} \frac{\sin\theta}{\theta} = 1.$$

(g) Show that $(\sin\theta)/\theta$ is an even function.

(h) Use part (g) to show that

$$\lim_{\theta\to 0^-} \frac{\sin\theta}{\theta} = 1.$$

(i) Finally, show that

$$\lim_{\theta\to 0} \frac{\sin\theta}{\theta} = 1.$$

Extending the Ideas

78. *Controlling Outputs* Let $f(x) = \sqrt{3x - 2}$.

(a) Show that $\lim_{x\to 2} f(x) = 2 = f(2)$.

(b) Use a graph to estimate values for a and b so that $1.8 < f(x) < 2.2$ provided $a < x < b$.

(c) Use a graph to estimate values for a and b so that $1.99 < f(x) < 2.01$ provided $a < x < b$.

79. *Controlling Outputs* Let $f(x) = \sin x$.

(a) Find $f(\pi/6)$.

(b) Use a graph to estimate an interval (a, b) about $x = \pi/6$ so that $0.3 < f(x) < 0.7$ provided $a < x < b$.

(c) Use a graph to estimate an interval (a, b) about $x = \pi/6$ so that $0.49 < f(x) < 0.51$ provided $a < x < b$.

80. *Limits and Geometry* Let $P(a, a^2)$ be a point on the parabola $y = x^2$, $a > 0$. Let O be the origin and $(0, b)$ the y-intercept of the perpendicular bisector of line segment OP. Find $\lim_{P\to O} b$.

2.2 Limits Involving Infinity

What you will learn about . . .

- Finite Limits as $x \to \pm\infty$
- Sandwich Theorem Revisited
- Infinite Limits as $x \to a$
- End Behavior Models
- "Seeing" Limits as $x \to \pm\infty$

and why . . .

Limits can be used to describe the behavior of functions for numbers large in absolute value.

Finite Limits as $x \to \pm\infty$

The symbol for infinity (∞) does not represent a real number. We use ∞ to describe the behavior of a function when the values in its domain or range outgrow all finite bounds. For example, when we say "the limit of *f* as *x* approaches infinity" we mean the limit of *f* as *x* moves increasingly far to the right on the number line. When we say "the limit of *f* as *x* approaches negative infinity $(-\infty)$" we mean the limit of *f* as *x* moves increasingly far to the left. (The limit in each case may or may not exist.)

Looking at $f(x) = 1/x$ (Figure 2.9), we observe

(a) as $x \to \infty$, $(1/x) \to 0$ and we write

$$\lim_{x\to\infty} (1/x) = 0,$$

(b) as $x \to -\infty$, $(1/x) \to 0$ and we write

$$\lim_{x\to-\infty} (1/x) = 0.$$

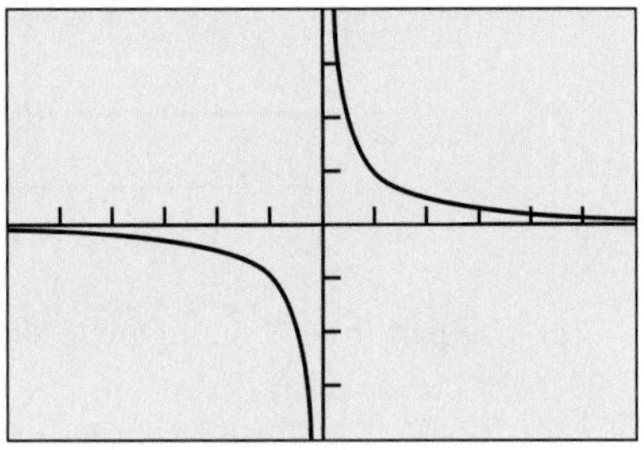

[–6, 6] by [–4, 4]

Figure 2.9 The graph of $f(x) = 1/x$.

We say that the line $y = 0$ is a *horizontal asymptote* of the graph of *f*.

DEFINITION Horizontal Asymptote

The line $y = b$ is a **horizontal asymptote** of the graph of a function $y = f(x)$ if either

$$\lim_{x\to\infty} f(x) = b \quad \text{or} \quad \lim_{x\to-\infty} f(x) = b.$$

The graph of $f(x) = 2 + (1/x)$ has the single horizontal asymptote $y = 2$ because

$$\lim_{x\to\infty}\left(2 + \frac{1}{x}\right) = 2 \quad \text{and} \quad \lim_{x\to-\infty}\left(2 + \frac{1}{x}\right) = 2.$$

A function can have more than one horizontal asymptote, as Example 1 demonstrates.

EXAMPLE 1 Looking for Horizontal Asymptotes

Use graphs and tables to find $\lim_{x\to\infty} f(x)$, $\lim_{x\to-\infty} f(x)$, and identify all horizontal asymptotes of $f(x) = x/\sqrt{x^2 + 1}$.

SOLUTION

Solve Graphically Figure 2.10a shows the graph for $-10 \le x \le 10$. The graph climbs rapidly toward the line $y = 1$ as *x* moves away from the origin to the right. On our calculator screen, the graph soon becomes indistinguishable from the line. Thus $\lim_{x\to\infty} f(x) = 1$. Similarly, as *x* moves away from the origin to the left, the graph drops rapidly toward the line $y = -1$ and soon appears to overlap the line. Thus $\lim_{x\to-\infty} f(x) = -1$. The horizontal asymptotes are $y = 1$ and $y = -1$.

continued

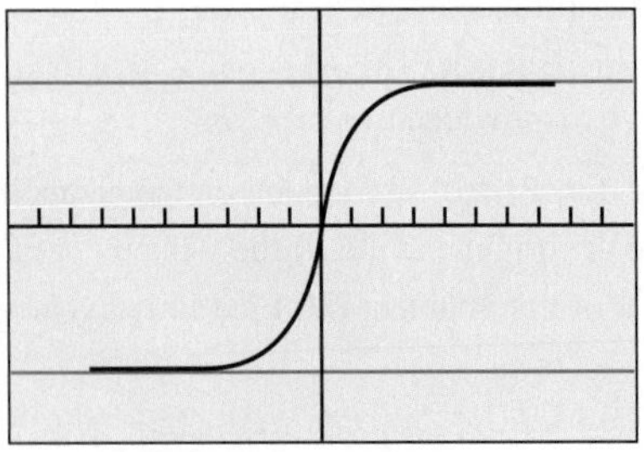

[–10, 10] by [–1.5, 1.5]

(a)

X	Y1	
0	0	
1	.7071	
2	.8944	
3	.9487	
4	.9701	
5	.9806	
6	.9864	

Y1 = X/√(X² + 1)

X	Y1	
-6	-.9864	
-5	-.9806	
-4	-.9701	
-3	-.9487	
-2	-.8944	
-1	-.7071	
0	0	

Y1 = X/√(X² + 1)

(b)

Figure 2.10 (a) The graph of $f(x) = x/\sqrt{x^2 + 1}$ has two horizontal asymptotes, $y = -1$ and $y = 1$. (b) Selected values of *f*. (Example 1)

Confirm Numerically The table in Figure 2.10b confirms the rapid approach of $f(x)$ toward 1 as $x \to \infty$. Since f is an odd function of x, we can expect its values to approach -1 in a similar way as $x \to -\infty$. ***Now Try Exercise 5.***

Sandwich Theorem Revisited

The Sandwich Theorem also holds for limits as $x \to \pm\infty$.

EXAMPLE 2 Finding a Limit as x Approaches ∞

Find $\lim_{x\to\infty} f(x)$ for $f(x) = \frac{\sin x}{x}$.

SOLUTION

Solve Graphically and Numerically The graph and table of values in Figure 2.11 suggest that $y = 0$ is the horizontal asymptote of f.

Confirm Analytically We know that $-1 \le \sin x \le 1$. So, for $x > 0$ we have

$$-\frac{1}{x} \le \frac{\sin x}{x} \le \frac{1}{x}.$$

Therefore, by the Sandwich Theorem,

$$0 = \lim_{x\to\infty}\left(-\frac{1}{x}\right) = \lim_{x\to\infty}\frac{\sin x}{x} = \lim_{x\to\infty}\frac{1}{x} = 0.$$

Since $(\sin x)/x$ is an even function of x, we can also conclude that

$$\lim_{x\to\infty}\frac{\sin x}{x} = 0.$$

Now Try Exercise 9.

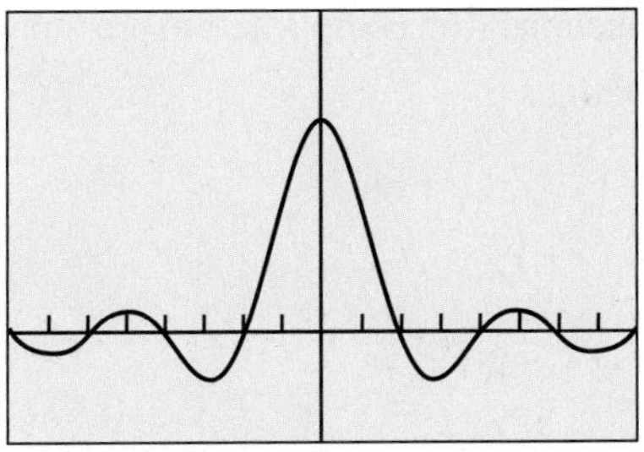

$[-4\pi, 4\pi]$ by $[-0.5, 1.5]$

(a)

X	Y1	
100	-.0051	
200	-.0044	
300	-.0033	
400	-.0021	
500	-9E-4	
600	7.4E-5	
700	7.8E-4	

Y1 = sin(X)/X

(b)

Figure 2.11 (a) The graph of $f(x) = (\sin x)/x$ oscillates about the x-axis. The amplitude of the oscillations decreases toward zero as $x \to \pm\infty$. (b) A table of values for f that suggests $f(x) \to 0$ as $x \to \infty$. (Example 2)

Limits at infinity have properties similar to those of finite limits.

THEOREM 5 Properties of Limits as $x \to \pm\infty$

If L, M, and k are real numbers and

$$\lim_{x\to\pm\infty} f(x) = L \quad \text{and} \quad \lim_{x\to\pm\infty} g(x) = M, \text{ then}$$

1. *Sum Rule:* $\lim_{x\to\pm\infty}(f(x) + g(x)) = L + M$
2. *Difference Rule:* $\lim_{x\to\pm\infty}(f(x) - g(x)) = L - M$
3. *Product Rule:* $\lim_{x\to\pm\infty}(f(x)\cdot g(x)) = L\cdot M$
4. *Constant Multiple Rule:* $\lim_{x\to\pm\infty}(k\cdot f(x)) = k\cdot L$
5. *Quotient Rule:* $\lim_{x\to\pm\infty}\frac{f(x)}{g(x)} = \frac{L}{M}, M \neq 0$
6. *Power Rule:* If r and s are integers, $s \neq 0$, then

$$\lim_{x\to\pm\infty}(f(x))^{r/s} = L^{r/s}$$

provided that $L^{r/s}$ is a real number.

We can use Theorem 5 to find limits at infinity of functions with complicated expressions, as illustrated in Example 3.

EXAMPLE 3 Using Theorem 5

Find $\lim_{x\to\infty} \frac{5x + \sin x}{x}$.

SOLUTION

Notice that

$$\frac{5x + \sin x}{x} = \frac{5x}{x} + \frac{\sin x}{x} = 5 + \frac{\sin x}{x}.$$

So,

$$\lim_{x\to\infty} \frac{5x + \sin x}{x} = \lim_{x\to\infty} 5 + \lim_{x\to\infty} \frac{\sin x}{x} \quad \text{Sum Rule}$$

$$= 5 + 0 = 5. \quad \text{Known values}$$

Now Try Exercise 25.

EXPLORATION 1 Exploring Theorem 5

We must be careful how we apply Theorem 5.

1. (Example 3 again) Let $f(x) = 5x + \sin x$ and $g(x) = x$. Do the limits as $x \to \infty$ of f and g exist? Can we apply the Quotient Rule to $\lim_{x\to\infty} f(x)/g(x)$? Explain. Does the limit of the quotient exist?
2. Let $f(x) = \sin^2 x$ and $g(x) = \cos^2 x$. Describe the behavior of f and g as $x \to \infty$. Can we apply the Sum Rule to $\lim_{x\to\infty} (f(x) + g(x))$? Explain. Does the limit of the sum exist?
3. Let $f(x) = \ln(2x)$ and $g(x) = \ln(x + 1)$. Find the limits as $x \to \infty$ of f and g. Can we apply the Difference Rule to $\lim_{x\to\infty} (f(x) - g(x))$? Explain. Does the limit of the difference exist?
4. Based on parts 1–3, what advice might you give about applying Theorem 5?

Infinite Limits as $x \to a$

If the values of a function $f(x)$ outgrow all positive bounds as x approaches a finite number a, we say that $\lim_{x\to a} f(x) = \infty$. If the values of f become large and negative, exceeding all negative bounds as $x \to a$, we say that $\lim_{x\to a} f(x) = -\infty$.

Looking at $f(x) = 1/x$ (Figure 2.9, page 70), we observe that

$$\lim_{x\to 0^+} 1/x = \infty \quad \text{and} \quad \lim_{x\to 0^-} 1/x = -\infty.$$

We say that the line $x = 0$ is a *vertical asymptote* of the graph of f.

DEFINITION Vertical Asymptote

The line $x = a$ is a **vertical asymptote** of the graph of a function $y = f(x)$ if either

$$\lim_{x\to a^+} f(x) = \pm\infty \quad \text{or} \quad \lim_{x\to a^-} f(x) = \pm\infty.$$

EXAMPLE 4 Finding Vertical Asymptotes

Find the vertical asymptotes of $f(x) = \frac{1}{x^2}$. Describe the behavior to the left and right of each vertical asymptote.

SOLUTION

The values of the function approach ∞ on either side of $x = 0$.

$$\lim_{x \to 0^+} \frac{1}{x^2} = \infty \quad \text{and} \quad \lim_{x \to 0^-} \frac{1}{x^2} = \infty.$$

The line $x = 0$ is the only vertical asymptote. ***Now Try Exercise 27.***

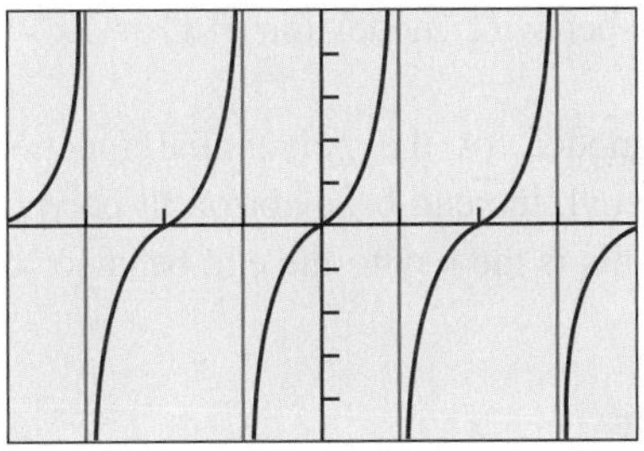

$[-2\pi, 2\pi]$ by $[-5, 5]$

Figure 2.12 The graph of $f(x) = \tan x$ has a vertical asymptote at

$$\ldots, -\frac{3\pi}{2}, -\frac{\pi}{2}, \frac{\pi}{2}, \frac{3\pi}{2}, \ldots. \text{ (Example 5)}$$

We can also say that $\lim_{x \to 0} (1/x^2) = \infty$. We can make no such statement about $1/x$.

EXAMPLE 5 Finding Vertical Asymptotes

The graph of $f(x) = \tan x = (\sin x)/(\cos x)$ has infinitely many vertical asymptotes, one at each point where the cosine is zero. If a is an odd multiple of $\pi/2$, then

$$\lim_{x \to a^+} \tan x = -\infty \quad \text{and} \quad \lim_{x \to a^-} \tan x = \infty,$$

as suggested by Figure 2.12. ***Now Try Exercise 31.***

You might think that the graph of a quotient always has a vertical asymptote where the denominator is zero, but that need not be the case. For example, we observed in Section 2.1 that $\lim_{x \to 0} (\sin x)/x = 1$.

$y = 3x^4 - 2x^3 + 3x^2 - 5x + 6$

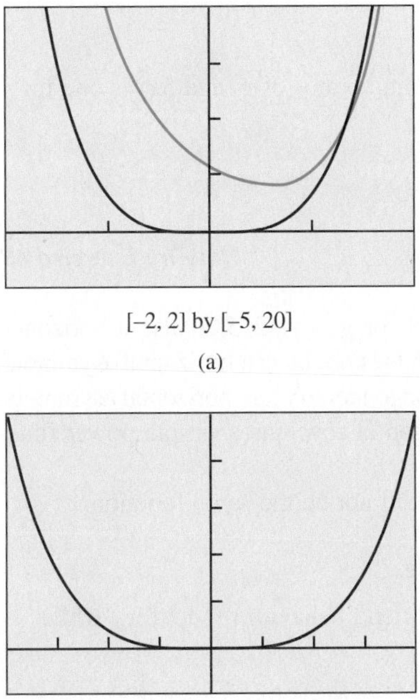

$[-2, 2]$ by $[-5, 20]$

(a)

$[-20, 20]$ by $[-100000, 500000]$

(b)

Figure 2.13 The graphs of f and g, (a) distinct for $|x|$ small, are (b) nearly identical for $|x|$ large. (Example 6)

End Behavior Models

For numerically large values of x, we can sometimes model the behavior of a complicated function by a simpler one that acts virtually in the same way.

EXAMPLE 6 Modeling Functions For $|x|$ Large

Let $f(x) = 3x^4 - 2x^3 + 3x^2 - 5x + 6$ and $g(x) = 3x^4$. Show that while f and g are quite different for numerically small values of x, they are virtually identical for $|x|$ large.

SOLUTION

Solve Graphically The graphs of f and g (Figure 2.13a), quite different near the origin, are virtually identical on a larger scale (Figure 2.13b).

Confirm Analytically We can test the claim that g models f for numerically large values of x by examining the ratio of the two functions as $x \to \pm\infty$. We find that

$$\begin{aligned} \lim_{x \to \pm\infty} \frac{f(x)}{g(x)} &= \lim_{x \to \pm\infty} \frac{3x^4 - 2x^3 + 3x^2 - 5x + 6}{3x^4} \\ &= \lim_{x \to \pm\infty} \left(1 - \frac{2}{3x} + \frac{1}{x^2} - \frac{5}{3x^3} + \frac{2}{x^4}\right) \\ &= 1, \end{aligned}$$

convincing evidence that f and g behave alike for $|x|$ large. ***Now Try Exercise 39.***

DEFINITION End Behavior Model

The function g is

(a) a **right end behavior model** for f if and only if $\lim_{x\to\infty} \frac{f(x)}{g(x)} = 1.$

(b) a **left end behavior model** for f if and only if $\lim_{x\to-\infty} \frac{f(x)}{g(x)} = 1.$

If one function provides both a left and right end behavior model, it is simply called an **end behavior model.** Thus, $g(x) = 3x^4$ is an end behavior model for $f(x) = 3x^4 - 2x^3 + 3x^2 - 5x + 6$ (Example 6).

In general, $g(x) = a_n x^n$ is an end behavior model for the polynomial function $f(x) = a_n x^n + a_{n-1}x^{n-1} + \cdots + a_0$, $a_n \neq 0$. Overall, the end behavior of all polynomials behave like the end behavior of monomials. This is the key to the end behavior of rational functions, as illustrated in Example 7.

EXAMPLE 7 Finding End Behavior Models

Find an end behavior model for

(a) $f(x) = \dfrac{2x^5 + x^4 - x^2 + 1}{3x^2 - 5x + 7}$ **(b)** $g(x) = \dfrac{2x^3 - x^2 + x - 1}{5x^3 + x^2 + x - 5}$

SOLUTION

(a) Notice that $2x^5$ is an end behavior model for the numerator of f, and $3x^2$ is one for the denominator. This makes

$$\frac{2x^5}{3x^2} = \frac{2}{3}x^3$$

an end behavior model for f.

(b) Similarly, $2x^3$ is an end behavior model for the numerator of g, and $5x^3$ is one for the denominator of g. This makes

$$\frac{2x^3}{5x^3} = \frac{2}{5}$$

an end behavior model for g. ***Now Try Exercise 43.***

Notice in Example 7b that the end behavior model for g, $y = 2/5$, is also a horizontal asymptote of the graph of g, while in 7a, the graph of f does not have a horizontal asymptote. We can use the end behavior model of a rational function to identify any horizontal asymptote.

We can see from Example 7 that a rational function always has a simple power function as an end behavior model.

A function's right and left end behavior models need not be the same function.

EXAMPLE 8 Finding End Behavior Models

Let $f(x) = x + e^{-x}$. Show that $g(x) = x$ is a right end behavior model for f while $h(x) = e^{-x}$ is a left end behavior model for f.

SOLUTION

On the right,

$$\lim_{x\to\infty} \frac{f(x)}{g(x)} = \lim_{x\to\infty} \frac{x + e^{-x}}{x} = \lim_{x\to\infty} \left(1 + \frac{e^{-x}}{x}\right) = 1 \text{ because } \lim_{x\to\infty} \frac{e^{-x}}{x} = 0.$$

continued

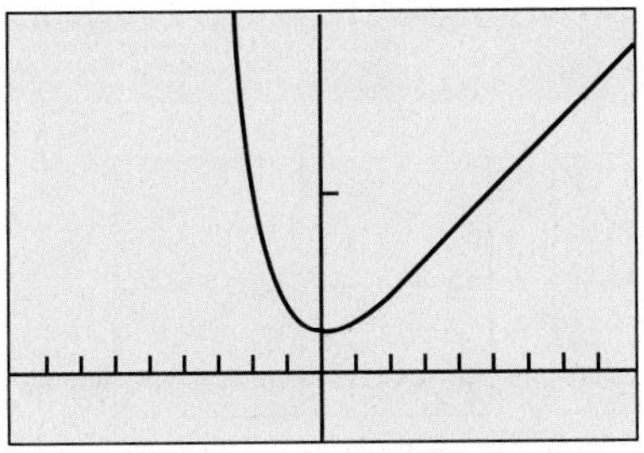

[–9, 9] by [–2, 10]

Figure 2.14 The graph of $f(x) = x + e^{-x}$ looks like the graph of $g(x) = x$ to the right of the y-axis, and like the graph of $h(x) = e^{-x}$ to the left of the y-axis. (Example 8)

On the left,

$$\lim_{x\to-\infty} \frac{f(x)}{h(x)} = \lim_{x\to-\infty} \frac{x + e^{-x}}{e^{-x}} = \lim_{x\to-\infty} \left(\frac{x}{e^{-x}} + 1\right) = 1 \text{ because } \lim_{x\to-\infty} \frac{x}{e^{-x}} = 0.$$

The graph of f in Figure 2.14 supports these end behavior conclusions.

Now Try Exercise 45.

"Seeing" Limits as $x \to \pm\infty$

We can investigate the graph of $y = f(x)$ as $x \to \pm\infty$ by investigating the graph of $y = f(1/x)$ as $x \to 0$.

EXAMPLE 9 Using Substitution

Find $\lim_{x\to\infty} \sin(1/x)$.

SOLUTION

Figure 2.15a suggests that the limit is 0. Indeed, replacing $\lim_{x\to\infty} \sin(1/x)$ by the equivalent $\lim_{x\to0^+} \sin x = 0$ (Figure 2.15b), we find

$$\lim_{x\to\infty} \sin 1/x = \lim_{x\to0^+} \sin x = 0.$$

Now Try Exercise 49.

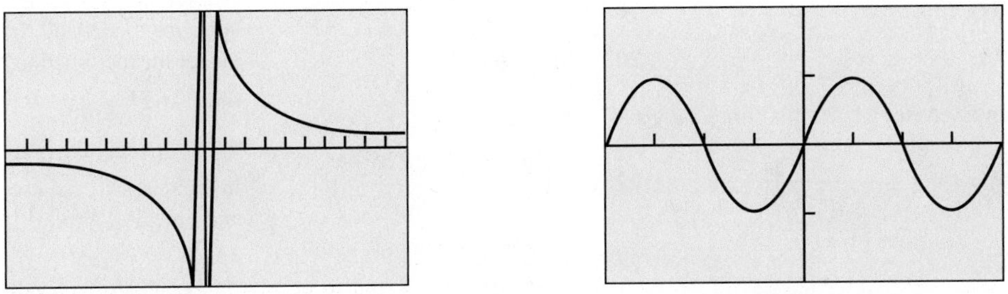

[–10, 10] by [–1, 1]

(a)

[-2π, 2π] by [–2, 2]

(b)

Figure 2.15 The graphs of (a) $f(x) = \sin(1/x)$ and (b) $g(x) = f(1/x) = \sin x$. (Example 9)

Quick Review 2.2 *(For help, go to Sections 1.2 and 1.5.)*

Exercise numbers with a gray background indicate problems that the authors have designed to be solved *without a calculator.*

In Exercises 1–4, find f^{-1} and graph f, f^{-1}, and $y = x$ in the same square viewing window.

1. $f(x) = 2x - 3$

2. $f(x) = e^x$

3. $f(x) = \tan^{-1} x$

4. $f(x) = \cot^{-1} x$

In Exercises 5 and 6, find the quotient $q(x)$ and remainder $r(x)$ when $f(x)$ is divided by $g(x)$.

5. $f(x) = 2x^3 - 3x^2 + x - 1, \quad g(x) = 3x^3 + 4x - 5$

6. $f(x) = 2x^5 - x^3 + x - 1, \quad g(x) = x^3 - x^2 + 1$

In Exercises 7–10, write a formula for **(a)** $f(-x)$ and **(b)** $f(1/x)$. Simplify where possible.

7. $f(x) = \cos x$

8. $f(x) = e^{-x}$

9. $f(x) = \dfrac{\ln x}{x}$

10. $f(x) = \left(x + \dfrac{1}{x}\right) \sin x$

Section 2.2 Exercises

In Exercises 1–8, use graphs and tables to find **(a)** $\lim_{x\to\infty} f(x)$ and **(b)** $\lim_{x\to-\infty} f(x)$. **(c)** Identify all horizontal asymptotes.

1. $f(x) = \cos\left(\dfrac{1}{x}\right)$ **2.** $f(x) = \dfrac{\sin 2x}{x}$

3. $f(x) = \dfrac{e^{-x}}{x}$ **4.** $f(x) = \dfrac{3x^3 - x + 1}{x + 3}$

5. $f(x) = \dfrac{3x + 1}{|x| + 2}$ **6.** $f(x) = \dfrac{2x - 1}{|x| - 3}$

7. $f(x) = \dfrac{x}{|x|}$ **8.** $f(x) = \dfrac{|x|}{|x| + 1}$

In Exercises 9–12, find the limit and confirm your answer using the Sandwich Theorem.

9. $\lim_{x\to\infty} \dfrac{1 - \cos x}{x^2}$ **10.** $\lim_{x\to-\infty} \dfrac{1 - \cos x}{x^2}$

11. $\lim_{x\to-\infty} \dfrac{\sin x}{x}$ **12.** $\lim_{x\to\infty} \dfrac{\sin(x^2)}{x}$

In Exercises 13–20, use graphs and tables to find the limits.

13. $\lim_{x\to 2^+} \dfrac{1}{x - 2}$ **14.** $\lim_{x\to 2^-} \dfrac{x}{x - 2}$

15. $\lim_{x\to -3^-} \dfrac{1}{x + 3}$ **16.** $\lim_{x\to -3^+} \dfrac{x}{x + 3}$

17. $\lim_{x\to 0^+} \dfrac{\text{int } x}{x}$ **18.** $\lim_{x\to 0^-} \dfrac{\text{int } x}{x}$

19. $\lim_{x\to 0^+} \csc x$ **20.** $\lim_{x\to(\pi/2)^+} \sec x$

In Exercises 21–26, find $\lim_{x\to\infty} y$ and $\lim_{x\to-\infty} y$.

21. $y = \left(2 - \dfrac{x}{x + 1}\right)\left(\dfrac{x^2}{5 + x^2}\right)$ **22.** $y = \left(\dfrac{2}{x} + 1\right)\left(\dfrac{5x^2 - 1}{x^2}\right)$

23. $y = \dfrac{\cos(1/x)}{1 + (1/x)}$ **24.** $y = \dfrac{2x + \sin x}{x}$

25. $y = \dfrac{\sin x}{2x^2 + x}$ **26.** $y = \dfrac{x \sin x + 2 \sin x}{2x^2}$

In Exercises 27–34, **(a)** find the vertical asymptotes of the graph of $f(x)$. **(b)** Describe the behavior of $f(x)$ to the left and right of each vertical asymptote.

27. $f(x) = \dfrac{1}{x^2 - 4}$ **28.** $f(x) = \dfrac{x^2 - 1}{2x + 4}$

29. $f(x) = \dfrac{x^2 - 2x}{x + 1}$ **30.** $f(x) = \dfrac{1 - x}{2x^2 - 5x - 3}$

31. $f(x) = \cot x$ **32.** $f(x) = \sec x$

33. $f(x) = \dfrac{\tan x}{\sin x}$ **34.** $f(x) = \dfrac{\cot x}{\cos x}$

In Exercises 35–38, match the function with the graph of its end behavior model.

35. $y = \dfrac{2x^3 - 3x^2 + 1}{x + 3}$ **36.** $y = \dfrac{x^5 - x^4 + x + 1}{2x^2 + x - 3}$

37. $y = \dfrac{2x^4 - x^3 + x^2 - 1}{2 - x}$ **38.** $y = \dfrac{x^4 - 3x^3 + x^2 - 1}{1 - x^2}$

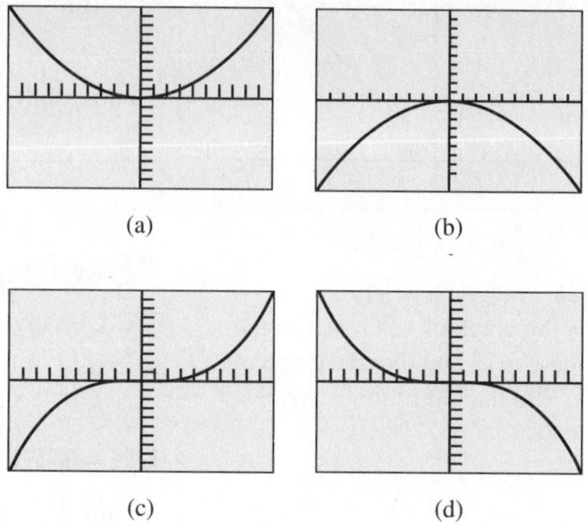

(a) (b) (c) (d)

In Exercises 39–44, **(a)** find a power function end behavior model for *f*. **(b)** Identify any horizontal asymptotes.

39. $f(x) = 3x^2 - 2x + 1$ **40.** $f(x) = -4x^3 + x^2 - 2x - 1$

41. $f(x) = \dfrac{x - 2}{2x^2 + 3x - 5}$ **42.** $f(x) = \dfrac{3x^2 - x + 5}{x^2 - 4}$

43. $f(x) = \dfrac{4x^3 - 2x + 1}{x - 2}$ **44.** $f(x) = \dfrac{-x^4 + 2x^2 + x - 3}{x^2 - 4}$

In Exercises 45–48, find **(a)** a simple basic function as a right end behavior model and **(b)** a simple basic function as a left end behavior model for the function.

45. $y = e^x - 2x$ **46.** $y = x^2 + e^{-x}$

47. $y = x + \ln|x|$ **48.** $y = x^2 + \sin x$

In Exercises 49–52, use the graph of $y = f(1/x)$ to find $\lim_{x\to\infty} f(x)$ and $\lim_{x\to-\infty} f(x)$.

49. $f(x) = xe^x$ **50.** $f(x) = x^2e^{-x}$

51. $f(x) = \dfrac{\ln|x|}{x}$ **52.** $f(x) = x \sin\dfrac{1}{x}$

In Exercises 53 and 54, find the limit of $f(x)$ as **(a)** $x \to -\infty$, **(b)** $x \to \infty$, **(c)** $x \to 0^-$, and **(d)** $x \to 0^+$.

53. $f(x) = \begin{cases} 1/x, & x < 0 \\ -1, & x \geq 0 \end{cases}$

54. $f(x) = \begin{cases} \dfrac{x - 2}{x - 1}, & x \leq 0 \\ 1/x^2, & x > 0 \end{cases}$

Group Activity In Exercises 55 and 56, sketch a graph of a function $y = f(x)$ that satisfies the stated conditions. Include any asymptotes.

55. $\lim_{x\to 1} f(x) = 2$, $\lim_{x\to 5^-} f(x) = \infty$, $\lim_{x\to 5^+} f(x) = \infty$,
$\lim_{x\to\infty} f(x) = -1$, $\lim_{x\to -2^+} f(x) = -\infty$,
$\lim_{x\to -2^-} f(x) = \infty$, $\lim_{x\to-\infty} f(x) = 0$

56. $\lim_{x\to 2} f(x) = -1$, $\lim_{x\to 4^+} f(x) = -\infty$, $\lim_{x\to 4^-} f(x) = \infty$,
$\lim_{x\to\infty} f(x) = \infty$, $\lim_{x\to-\infty} f(x) = 2$

57. Group Activity ***End Behavior Models*** Suppose that $g_1(x)$ is a right end behavior model for $f_1(x)$ and that $g_2(x)$ is a right end behavior model for $f_2(x)$. Explain why this makes $g_1(x)/g_2(x)$ a right end behavior model for $f_1(x)/f_2(x)$.

58. Writing to Learn Let L be a real number, $\lim_{x\to c} f(x) = L$, and $\lim_{x\to c} g(x) = \infty$ or $-\infty$. Can $\lim_{x\to c} (f(x) + g(x))$ be determined? Explain.

Standardized Test Questions

59. True or False It is possible for a function to have more than one horizontal asymptote. Justify your answer.

60. True or False If $f(x)$ has a vertical asymptote at $x = c$, then either $\lim_{x\to c^-} f(x) = \lim_{x\to c^+} f(x) = \infty$ or $\lim_{x\to c^-} f(x) = \lim_{x\to c^+} f(x) = -\infty$. Justify your answer.

61. Multiple Choice $\lim_{x\to 2^-} \dfrac{x}{x-2} =$

(A) $-\infty$ **(B)** ∞ **(C)** 1 **(D)** $-1/2$ **(E)** -1

You may use a graphing calculator to solve the following problems.

62. Multiple Choice $\lim_{x\to 0} \dfrac{\cos(2x)}{x} =$

(A) 1/2 **(B)** 1 **(C)** 2 **(D)** cos 2 **(E)** does not exist

63. Multiple Choice $\lim_{x\to 0} \dfrac{\sin(3x)}{x} =$

(A) 1/3 **(B)** 1 **(C)** 3 **(D)** sin 3 **(E)** does not exist

64. Multiple Choice Which of the following is an end behavior for

$$f(x) = \frac{2x^3 - x^2 + x + 1}{x^3 - 1}?$$

(A) x^3 **(B)** $2x^3$ **(C)** $1/x^3$ **(D)** 2 **(E)** 1/2

Exploration

65. ***Exploring Properties of Limits*** Find the limits of f, g, and fg as $x \to c$.

(a) $f(x) = \dfrac{1}{x}$, $g(x) = x$, $c = 0$

(b) $f(x) = -\dfrac{2}{x^3}$, $g(x) = 4x^3$, $c = 0$

(c) $f(x) = \dfrac{3}{x-2}$, $g(x) = (x-2)^3$, $c = 2$

(d) $f(x) = \dfrac{5}{(3-x)^4}$, $g(x) = (x-3)^2$, $c = 3$

(e) Writing to Learn Suppose that $\lim_{x\to c} f(x) = 0$ and $\lim_{x\to c} g(x) = \infty$. Based on your observations in parts (a)–(d), what can you say about $\lim_{x\to c} (f(x) \cdot g(x))$?

Extending the Ideas

66. ***The Greatest Integer Function***

(a) Show that

$$\frac{x-1}{x} < \frac{\text{int } x}{x} \le 1 \ (x > 0) \text{ and } \frac{x-1}{x} > \frac{\text{int } x}{x} \ge 1 \ (x < 0).$$

(b) Determine $\lim_{x\to\infty} \dfrac{\text{int } x}{x}$.

(c) Determine $\lim_{x\to-\infty} \dfrac{\text{int } x}{x}$.

67. ***Sandwich Theorem*** Use the Sandwich Theorem to confirm the limit as $x \to \infty$ found in Exercise 3.

68. Writing to Learn Explain why there is no value L for which $\lim_{x\to\infty} \sin x = L$.

In Exercises 69–71, find the limit. Give a convincing argument that the value is correct.

69. $\lim_{x\to\infty} \dfrac{\ln x^2}{\ln x}$

70. $\lim_{x\to\infty} \dfrac{\ln x}{\log x}$

71. $\lim_{x\to\infty} \dfrac{\ln(x+1)}{\ln x}$

Quick Quiz for AP* Preparation: Sections 2.1 and 2.2

1. Multiple Choice Find $\lim_{x\to 3} \dfrac{x^2 - x - 6}{x - 3}$, if it exists.

(A) -1 **(B)** 1 **(C)** 2 **(D)** 5 **(E)** does not exist

2. Multiple Choice Find $\lim_{x\to 2^+} f(x)$, if it exists, where

$$f(x) = \begin{cases} 3x + 1, & x < 2 \\ \dfrac{5}{x+1}, & x \ge 2 \end{cases}$$

(A) 5/3 **(B)** 13/3 **(C)** 7 **(D)** ∞ **(E)** does not exist

3. Multiple Choice Which of the following lines is a horizontal asymptote for

$$f(x) = \frac{3x^3 - x^2 + x - 7}{2x^3 + 4x - 5}?$$

(A) $y = \frac{3}{2}x$ **(B)** $y = 0$ **(C)** $y = 2/3$ **(D)** $y = 7/5$ **(E)** $y = 3/2$

4. Free Response Let $f(x) = \dfrac{\cos x}{x}$.

(a) Find the domain and range of f.

(b) Is f even, odd, or neither? Justify your answer.

(c) Find $\lim_{x\to\infty} f(x)$.

(d) Use the Sandwich Theorem to justify your answer to part (c).

2.3 Continuity

What you will learn about . . .

- Continuity at a Point
- Continuous Functions
- Algebraic Combinations
- Composites
- Intermediate Value Theorem for Continuous Functions

and why . . .

Continuous functions are used to describe how a body moves through space and how the speed of a chemical reaction changes with time.

Continuity at a Point

When we plot function values generated in the laboratory or collected in the field, we often connect the plotted points with an unbroken curve to show what the function's values are likely to have been at the times we did not measure (Figure 2.16). In doing so, we are assuming that we are working with a *continuous function,* a function whose outputs vary continuously with the inputs and do not jump from one value to another without taking on the values in between. Any function $y = f(x)$ whose graph can be sketched in one continuous motion without lifting the pencil is an example of a continuous function.

Continuous functions are those we use to find a planet's closest point of approach to the sun or the peak concentration of antibodies in blood plasma. They are also the functions we use to describe how a body moves through space or how the speed of a chemical reaction changes with time. In fact, so many physical processes proceed continuously that throughout the 18th and 19th centuries it rarely occurred to anyone to look for any other kind of behavior. It came as a surprise when the physicists of the 1920s discovered that light comes in particles and that heated atoms emit light at discrete frequencies (Figure 2.17). As a result of these and other discoveries, and because of the heavy use of discontinuous functions in computer science, statistics, and mathematical modeling, the issue of continuity has become one of practical as well as theoretical importance.

To understand continuity, we need to consider a function like the one in Figure 2.18, whose limits we investigated in Example 8, Section 2.1.

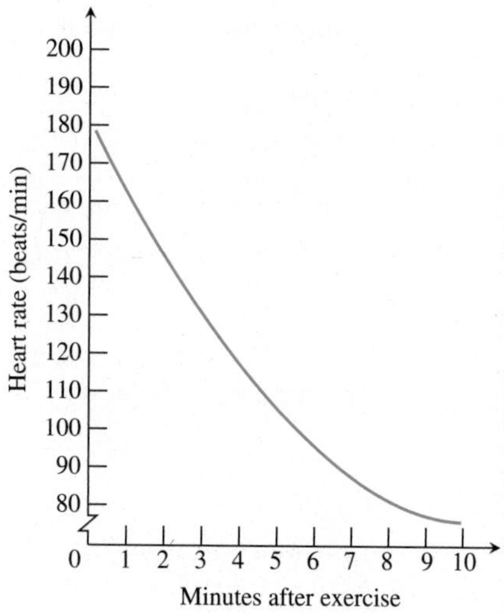

Figure 2.16 How the heartbeat returns to a normal rate after running.

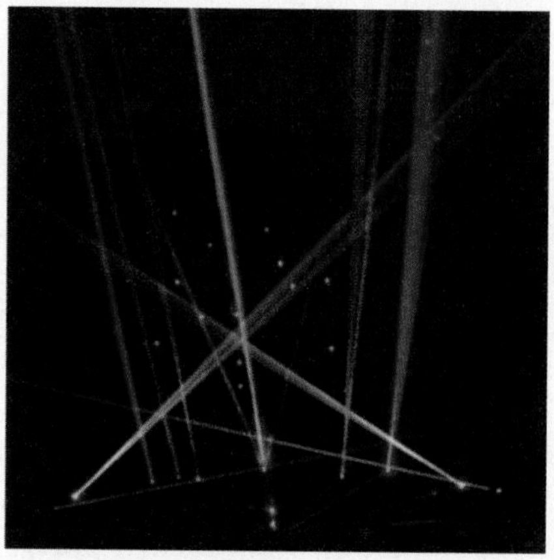

Figure 2.17 The laser was developed as a result of an understanding of the nature of the atom.

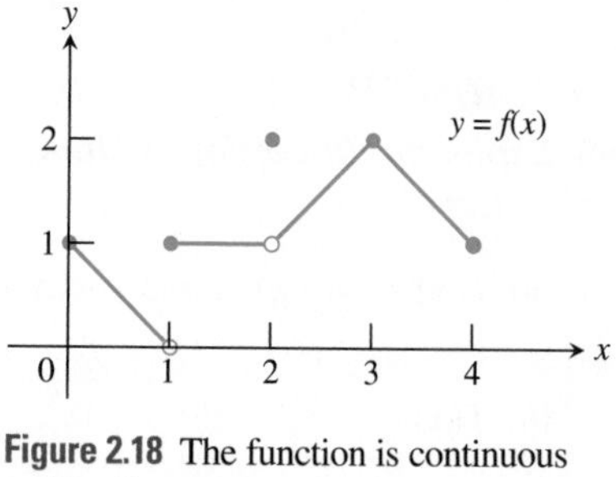

Figure 2.18 The function is continuous on $[0, 4]$ except at $x = 1$ and $x = 2$. (Example 1)

EXAMPLE 1 Investigating Continuity

Find the points at which the function f in Figure 2.18 is continuous, and the points at which f is discontinuous.

SOLUTION

The function f is continuous at every point in its domain $[0, 4]$ except at $x = 1$ and $x = 2$. At these points there are breaks in the graph. Note the relationship between the limit of f and the value of f at each point of the function's domain.

Points at which f is continuous:

At $x = 0$, $\lim_{x\to 0^+} f(x) = f(0)$.

At $x = 4$, $\lim_{x\to 4^-} f(x) = f(4)$.

At $0 < c < 4,\ c \neq 1, 2,$ $\lim_{x\to c} f(x) = f(c)$.

continued

Points at which f is discontinuous:

At $x = 1$, $\lim_{x \to 1} f(x)$ does not exist.

At $x = 2$, $\lim_{x \to 2} f(x) = 1$, but $1 \neq f(2)$.

At $c < 0, c > 4$, these points are not in the domain of f.

Now Try Exercise 5.

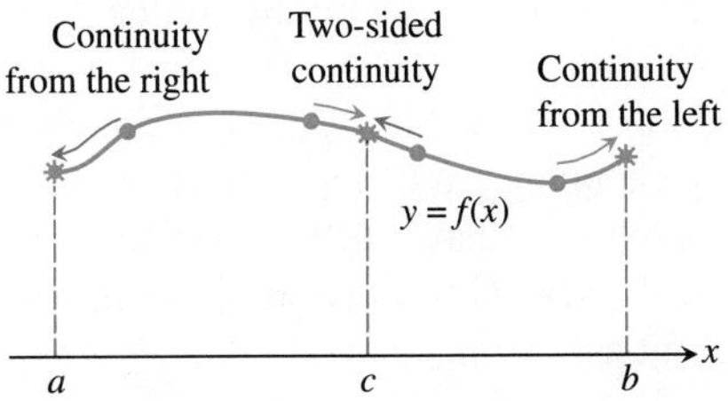

Figure 2.19 Continuity at points a, b, and c for a function $y = f(x)$ that is continuous on the interval $[a, b]$.

To define continuity at a point in a function's domain, we need to define continuity at an interior point (which involves a two-sided limit) and continuity at an endpoint (which involves a one-sided limit) (Figure 2.19).

DEFINITION Continuity at a Point

Interior Point: A function $y = f(x)$ is **continuous at an interior point c** of its domain if

$$\lim_{x \to c} f(x) = f(c).$$

Endpoint: A function $y = f(x)$ is **continuous at a left endpoint a** or is **continuous at a right endpoint b** of its domain if

$$\lim_{x \to a^+} f(x) = f(a) \quad \text{or} \quad \lim_{x \to b^-} f(x) = f(b), \quad \text{respectively.}$$

If a function f is not continuous at a point c, we say that f is **discontinuous** at c and c is a **point of discontinuity** of f. Note that c need not be in the domain of f.

EXAMPLE 2 Finding Points of Continuity and Discontinuity

Find the points of continuity and the points of discontinuity of the greatest integer function (Figure 2.20).

SOLUTION

For the function to be continuous at $x = c$, the limit as $x \to c$ must exist and must equal the value of the function at $x = c$. The greatest integer function is discontinuous at every integer. For example,

$$\lim_{x \to 3^-} \text{int } x = 2 \quad \text{and} \quad \lim_{x \to 3^+} \text{int } x = 3$$

so the limit as $x \to 3$ does not exist. Notice that int $3 = 3$. In general, if n is any integer,

$$\lim_{x \to n^-} \text{int } x = n - 1 \quad \text{and} \quad \lim_{x \to n^+} \text{int } x = n,$$

so the limit as $x \to n$ does not exist.

The greatest integer function is continuous at every other real number. For example,

$$\lim_{x \to 1.5} \text{int } x = 1 = \text{int } 1.5.$$

In general, if $n - 1 < c < n$, n an integer, then

$$\lim_{x \to c} \text{int } x = n - 1 = \text{int } c.$$

Now Try Exercise 7.

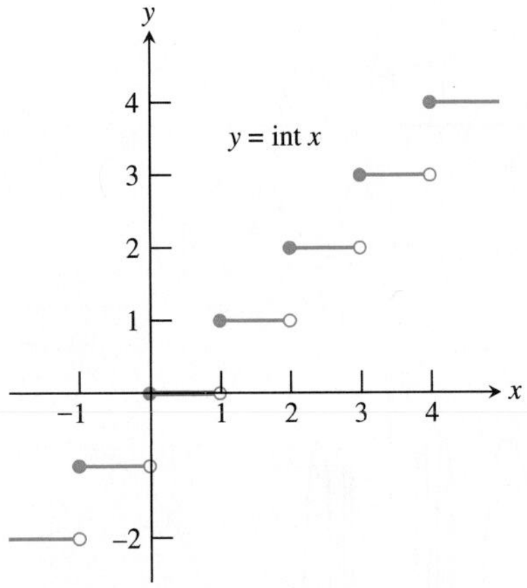

Figure 2.20 The function int x is continuous at every noninteger point. (Example 2)

Shirley Ann Jackson (1946–)

Distinguished scientist Shirley Jackson credits her interest in science to her parents and excellent mathematics and science teachers in high school. She studied physics, and in 1973, became the first African American woman to earn a Ph.D. at the Massachusetts Institute of Technology. Since then, Dr. Jackson has done research on topics relating to theoretical material sciences, has received numerous scholarships and honors, and has published more than 100 scientific articles.

Figure 2.21 is a catalog of discontinuity types. The function in (a) is continuous at $x = 0$. The function in (b) would be continuous if it had $f(0) = 1$. The function in (c) would be continuous if $f(0)$ were 1 instead of 2. The discontinuities in (b) and (c) are **removable.** Each function has a limit as $x \to 0$, and we can remove the discontinuity by setting $f(0)$ equal to this limit.

The discontinuities in (d)–(f) of Figure 2.21 are more serious: $\lim_{x\to 0} f(x)$ does not exist and there is no way to improve the situation by changing f at 0. The step function in (d) has a **jump discontinuity:** The one-sided limits exist but have different values. The function $f(x) = 1/x^2$ in (e) has an **infinite discontinuity.** The function in (f) has an **oscillating discontinuity:** It oscillates and has no limit as $x \to 0$.

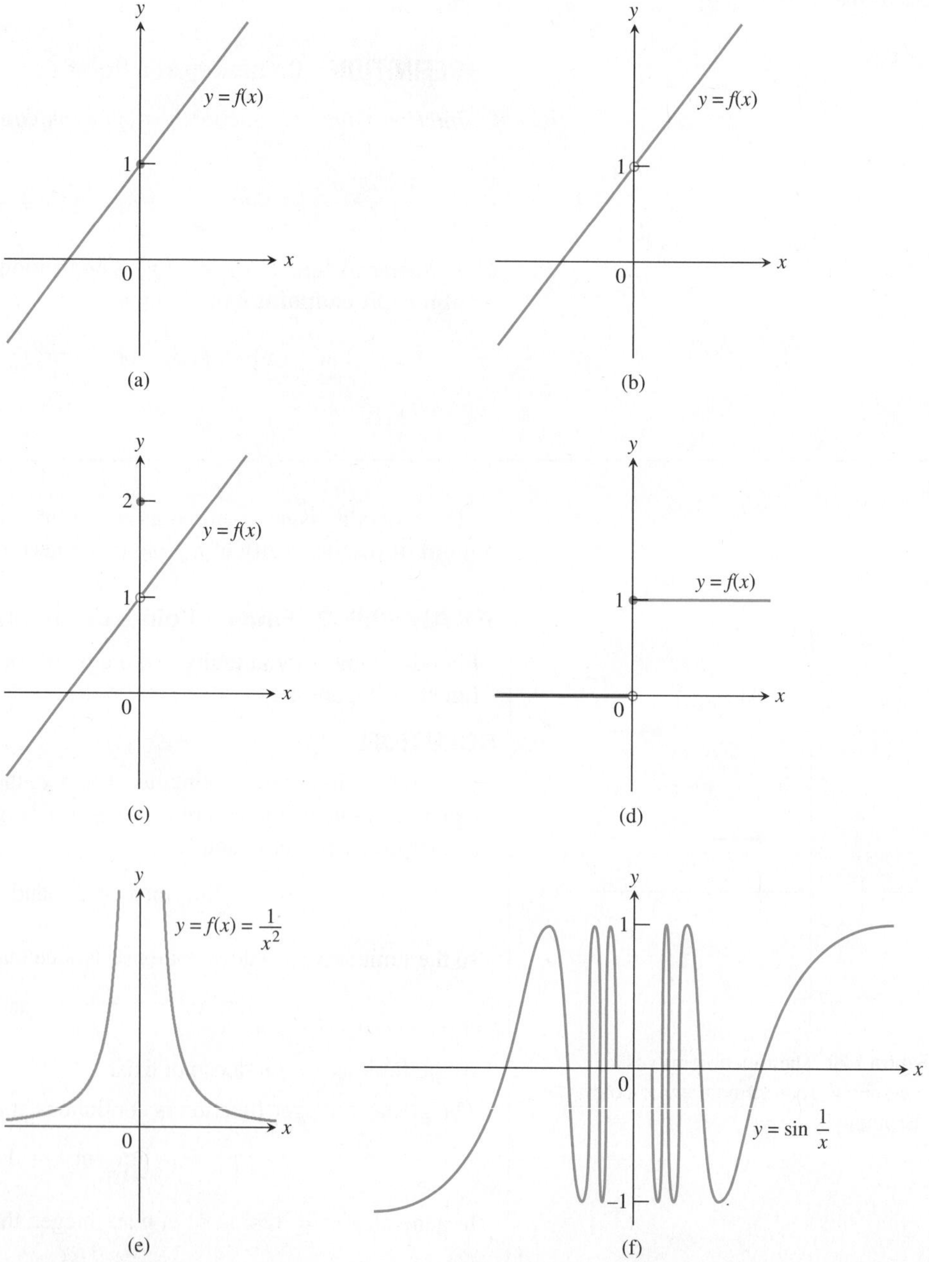

Figure 2.21 The function in part (a) is continuous at $x = 0$. The functions in parts (b)–(f) are not.

EXPLORATION 1 Removing a Discontinuity

Let $f(x) = \dfrac{x^3 - 7x - 6}{x^2 - 9}$.

1. Factor the denominator. What is the domain of f?
2. Investigate the graph of f around $x = 3$ to see that f has a removable discontinuity at $x = 3$.
3. How should f be defined at $x = 3$ to remove the discontinuity? Use ZOOM-IN and tables as necessary.
4. Show that $(x - 3)$ is a factor of the numerator of f, and remove all common factors. Now compute the limit as $x \to 3$ of the reduced form for f.
5. Show that the *extended function*

$$g(x) = \begin{cases} \dfrac{x^3 - 7x - 6}{x^2 - 9}, & x \neq 3 \\ 10/3, & x = 3 \end{cases}$$

is continuous at $x = 3$. The function g is the **continuous extension** of the original function f to include $x = 3$.

Now Try Exercise 25.

Continuous Functions

A function is **continuous on an interval** if and only if it is continuous at every point of the interval. A **continuous function** is one that is continuous at every point of its domain. A continuous function need not be continuous on every interval. For example, $y = 1/x$ is not continuous on $[-1, 1]$.

EXAMPLE 3 Identifying Continuous Functions

The reciprocal function $y = 1/x$ (Figure 2.22) is a continuous function because it is continuous at every point of its domain. However, it has a point of discontinuity at $x = 0$ because it is not defined there.

Now Try Exercise 31.

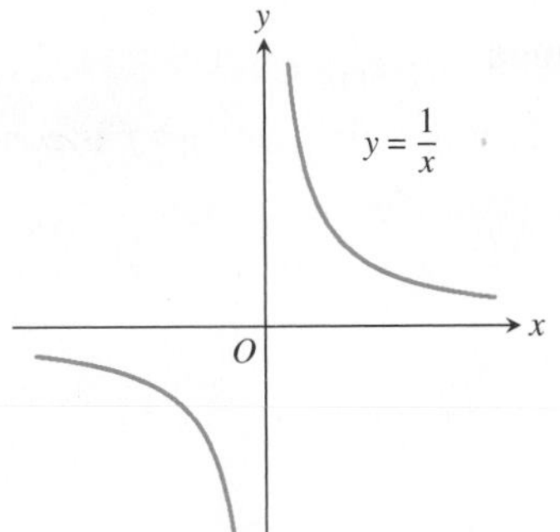

Figure 2.22 The function $y = 1/x$ is continuous at every value of x except $x = 0$. It has a point of discontinuity at $x = 0$. (Example 3)

Polynomial functions f are continuous at every real number c because $\lim_{x\to c} f(x) = f(c)$. Rational functions are continuous at every point of their domains. They have points of discontinuity at the zeros of their denominators. The absolute value function $y = |x|$ is continuous at every real number. The exponential functions, logarithmic functions, trigonometric functions, and radical functions like $y = \sqrt[n]{x}$ (n a positive integer greater than 1) are continuous at every point of their domains. All of these functions are continuous functions.

Algebraic Combinations

As you may have guessed, algebraic combinations of continuous functions are continuous wherever they are defined.

THEOREM 6 Properties of Continuous Functions

If the functions f and g are continuous at $x = c$, then the following combinations are continuous at $x = c$.

1. *Sums:* $f + g$
2. *Differences:* $f - g$
3. *Products:* $f \cdot g$
4. *Constant multiples:* $k \cdot f$, for any number k
5. *Quotients:* f/g, provided $g(c) \neq 0$

Composites

All composites of continuous functions are continuous. This means composites like

$$y = \sin (x^2) \quad \text{and} \quad y = |\cos x|$$

are continuous at every point at which they are defined. The idea is that if $f(x)$ is continuous at $x = c$ and $g(x)$ is continuous at $x = f(c)$, then $g \circ f$ is continuous at $x = c$ (Figure 2.23). In this case, the limit as $x \to c$ is $g(f(c))$.

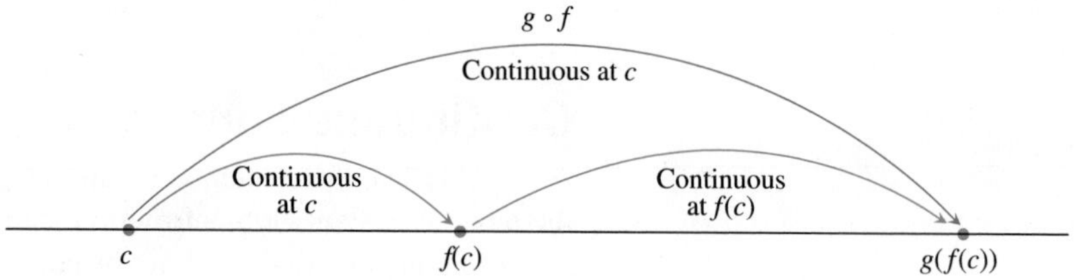

Figure 2.23 Composites of continuous functions are continuous.

THEOREM 7 Composite of Continuous Functions

If f is continuous at c and g is continuous at $f(c)$, then the composite $g \circ f$ is continuous at c.

EXAMPLE 4 Using Theorem 7

Show that $y = \left|\dfrac{x \sin x}{x^2 + 2}\right|$ is continuous.

SOLUTION

The graph (Figure 2.24) of $y = |(x \sin x)/(x^2 + 2)|$ suggests that the function is continuous at every value of x. By letting

$$g(x) = |x| \quad \text{and} \quad f(x) = \frac{x \sin x}{x^2 + 2},$$

we see that y is the composite $g \circ f$.

We know that the absolute value function g is continuous. The function f is continuous by Theorem 6. Their composite is continuous by Theorem 7. ***Now Try Exercise 33.***

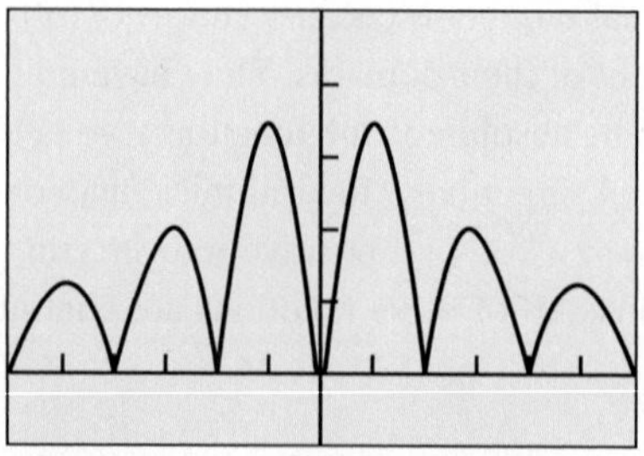

$[-3\pi, 3\pi]$ by $[-0.1, 0.5]$

Figure 2.24 The graph suggests that $y = |(x \sin x)/(x^2 + 2)|$ is continuous. (Example 4)

Intermediate Value Theorem for Continuous Functions

Functions that are continuous on intervals have properties that make them particularly useful in mathematics and its applications. One of these is the *intermediate value property.* A function is said to have the **intermediate value property** if it never takes on two values without taking on all the values in between.

THEOREM 8 The Intermediate Value Theorem for Continuous Functions

A function $y = f(x)$ that is continuous on a closed interval $[a, b]$ takes on every value between $f(a)$ and $f(b)$. In other words, if y_0 is between $f(a)$ and $f(b)$, then $y_0 = f(c)$ for some c in $[a, b]$.

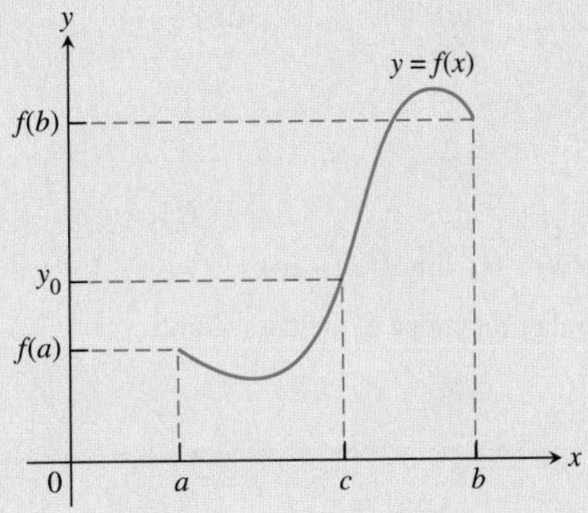

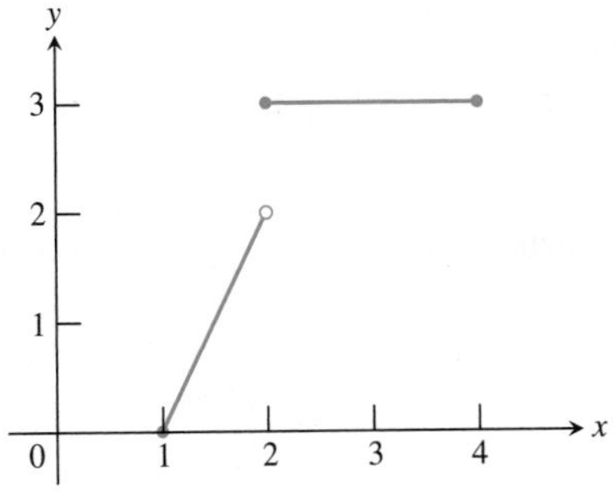

Figure 2.25 The function

$$f(x) = \begin{cases} 2x - 2, & 1 \le x < 2 \\ 3, & 2 \le x \le 4 \end{cases}$$

does not take on all values between $f(1) = 0$ and $f(4) = 3$; it misses all the values between 2 and 3.

The continuity of f on the interval is essential to Theorem 8. If f is discontinuous at even one point of the interval, the theorem's conclusion may fail, as it does for the function graphed in Figure 2.25.

A Consequence for Graphing: Connectivity Theorem 8 is the reason why the graph of a function continuous on an interval cannot have any breaks. The graph will be **connected,** a single, unbroken curve, like the graph of $\sin x$. It will not have jumps like those in the graph of the greatest integer function int x, or separate branches like we see in the graph of $1/x$.

Most graphers can plot points *(dot mode)*. Some can turn on pixels between plotted points to suggest an unbroken curve *(connected mode)*. For functions, the connected format basically assumes that outputs *vary continuously* with inputs and do not jump from one value to another without taking on all values in between.

Grapher Failure

In connected mode, a grapher may conceal a function's discontinuities by portraying the graph as a connected curve when it is not. To see what we mean, graph = $y =$ int (x) in a $[-10, 10]$ by $[-10, 10]$ window in both connected and dot modes. A knowledge of where to expect discontinuities will help you recognize this form of grapher failure.

EXAMPLE 5 Using Theorem 8

Is any real number exactly 1 less than its cube? Compute any such value accurate to three decimal places.

SOLUTION

We answer this question by applying the Intermediate Value Theorem in the following way. Any such number must satisfy the equation $x = x^3 - 1$ or, equivalently, $x^3 - x - 1 = 0$. Hence, we are looking for a zero value of the continuous function $f(x) = x^3 - x - 1$ (Figure 2.26). The function changes sign between 1 and 2, so there must be a point c between 1 and 2 where $f(c) = 0$.

There are a variety of methods for numerically computing the value of c to be accurate to as many decimal places as your technology allows. For example, a simple application of ZOOM (box) and TRACE using a graphing calculator will quickly give the result of $c = 1.324$ accurate to three decimal places. Most calculators have a numerical zero finder that will give an immediate solution as well. ***Now Try Exercise 46.***

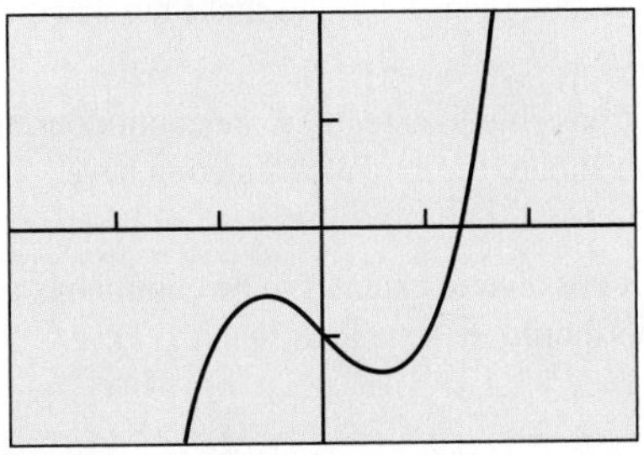

[–3, 3] by [–2, 2]

Figure 2.26 The graph of $f(x) = x^3 - x - 1$. (Example 5)

Can you find the *exact* value of c such that $f(c) = c^3 - c - 1 = 0$ and that you know exists by the application of the Intermediate Value Theorem? Discuss your answer with your fellow students and your teacher.

Quick Review 2.3 *(For help, go to Sections 1.2 and 2.1.)*

Exercise numbers with a gray background indicate problems that the authors have designed to be solved *without a calculator.*

1. Find $\lim_{x\to -1} \frac{3x^2 - 2x + 1}{x^3 + 4}$.

2. Let $f(x) = \text{int } x$. Find each limit.

(a) $\lim_{x\to -1^-} f(x)$ **(b)** $\lim_{x\to -1^+} f(x)$ **(c)** $\lim_{x\to -1} f(x)$ **(d)** $f(-1)$

3. Let $f(x) = \begin{cases} x^2 - 4x + 5, & x < 2 \\ 4 - x, & x \geq 2. \end{cases}$

Find each limit.

(a) $\lim_{x\to 2^-} f(x)$ **(b)** $\lim_{x\to 2^+} f(x)$ **(c)** $\lim_{x\to 2} f(x)$ **(d)** $f(2)$

In Exercises 4–6, find the remaining functions in the list of functions: $f, g, f \circ g, g \circ f$.

4. $f(x) = \frac{2x - 1}{x + 5}$, $g(x) = \frac{1}{x} + 1$

5. $f(x) = x^2$, $(g \circ f)(x) = \sin x^2$, domain of $g = [0, \infty)$

6. $g(x) = \sqrt{x - 1}$, $(g \circ f)(x) = 1/x$, $x > 0$

7. Use factoring to solve $2x^2 + 9x - 5 = 0$.

8. Use graphing to solve $x^3 + 2x - 1 = 0$.

In Exercises 9 and 10, let

$$f(x) = \begin{cases} 5 - x, & x \leq 3 \\ -x^2 + 6x - 8, & x > 3. \end{cases}$$

9. Solve the equation $f(x) = 4$.

10. Find a value of c for which the equation $f(x) = c$ has no solution.

Section 2.3 Exercises

In Exercises 1–10, find the points of continuity and the points of discontinuity of the function. Identify each type of discontinuity.

1. $y = \frac{1}{(x + 2)^2}$

2. $y = \frac{x + 1}{x^2 - 4x + 3}$

3. $y = \frac{1}{x^2 + 1}$

4. $y = |x - 1|$

5. $y = \sqrt{2x + 3}$

6. $y = \sqrt[3]{2x - 1}$

7. $y = |x|/x$

8. $y = \cot x$

9. $y = e^{1/x}$

10. $y = \ln (x + 1)$

In Exercises 11–18, use the function f defined and graphed below to answer the questions.

$$f(x) = \begin{cases} x^2 - 1, & -1 \leq x < 0 \\ 2x, & 0 < x < 1 \\ 1, & x = 1 \\ -2x + 4, & 1 < x < 2 \\ 0, & 2 < x < 3 \end{cases}$$

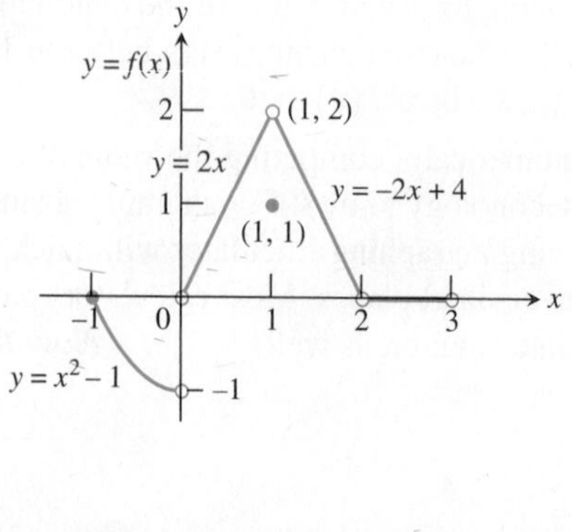

11. (a) Does $f(-1)$ exist?

(b) Does $\lim_{x\to -1^+} f(x)$ exist?

(c) Does $\lim_{x\to -1^+} f(x) = f(-1)$?

(d) Is f continuous at $x = -1$?

12. (a) Does $f(1)$ exist?

(b) Does $\lim_{x\to 1} f(x)$ exist?

(c) Does $\lim_{x\to 1} f(x) = f(1)$?

(d) Is f continuous at $x = 1$?

13. (a) Is f defined at $x = 2$? (Look at the definition of f.)

(b) Is f continuous at $x = 2$?

14. At what values of x is f continuous?

15. What value should be assigned to $f(2)$ to make the extended function continuous at $x = 2$?

16. What new value should be assigned to $f(1)$ to make the new function continuous at $x = 1$?

17. Writing to Learn Is it possible to extend f to be continuous at $x = 0$? If so, what value should the extended function have there? If not, why not?

18. Writing to Learn Is it possible to extend f to be continuous at $x = 3$? If so, what value should the extended function have there? If not, why not?

In Exercises 19–24, **(a)** find each point of discontinuity. **(b)** Which of the discontinuities are removable? not removable? Give reasons for your answers.

19. $f(x) = \begin{cases} 3 - x, & x < 2 \\ \dfrac{x}{2} + 1, & x > 2 \end{cases}$

20. $f(x) = \begin{cases} 3 - x, & x < 2 \\ 2, & x = 2 \\ x/2, & x > 2 \end{cases}$

21. $f(x) = \begin{cases} \dfrac{1}{x - 1}, & x < 1 \\ x^3 - 2x + 5, & x \geq 1 \end{cases}$

22. $f(x) = \begin{cases} 1 - x^2, & x \neq -1 \\ 2, & x = -1 \end{cases}$

23.

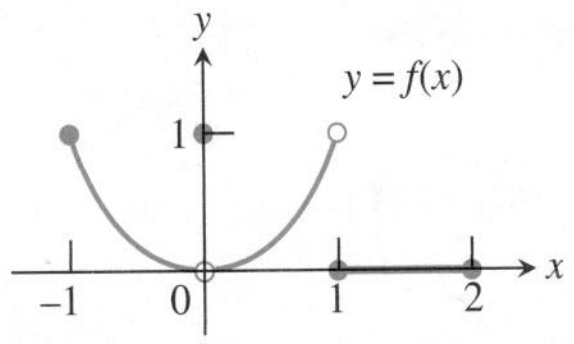

24.

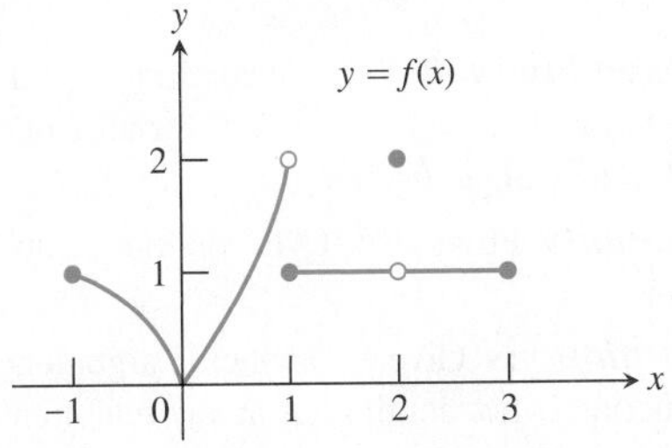

In Exercises 25–30, give a formula for the extended function that is continuous at the indicated point.

25. $f(x) = \dfrac{x^2 - 9}{x + 3}, \quad x = -3$

26. $f(x) = \dfrac{x^3 - 1}{x^2 - 1}, \quad x = 1$

27. $f(x) = \dfrac{\sin x}{x}, \quad x = 0$

28. $f(x) = \dfrac{\sin 4x}{x}, \quad x = 0$

29. $f(x) = \dfrac{x - 4}{\sqrt{x} - 2}, \quad x = 4$

30. $f(x) = \dfrac{x^3 - 4x^2 - 11x + 30}{x^2 - 4}, \quad x = 2$

In Exercises 31 and 32, explain why the given function is continuous.

31. $f(x) = \dfrac{1}{x - 3}$

32. $g(x) = \dfrac{1}{\sqrt{x - 1}}$

In Exercises 33–36, use Theorem 7 to show that the given function is continuous.

33. $f(x) = \sqrt{\left(\dfrac{x}{x + 1}\right)}$

34. $f(x) = \sin(x^2 + 1)$

35. $f(x) = \cos(\sqrt[3]{1 - x})$

36. $f(x) = \tan\left(\dfrac{x^2}{x^2 + 4}\right)$

Group Activity In Exercises 37–40, verify that the function is continuous and state its domain. Indicate which theorems you are using, and which functions you are assuming to be continuous.

37. $y = \dfrac{1}{\sqrt{x + 2}}$

38. $y = x^2 + \sqrt[3]{4 - x}$

39. $y = |x^2 - 4x|$

40. $y = \begin{cases} \dfrac{x^2 - 1}{x - 1}, & x \neq 1 \\ 2, & x = 1 \end{cases}$

In Exercises 41–44, sketch a possible graph for a function f that has the stated properties.

41. $f(3)$ exists but $\lim_{x \to 3} f(x)$ does not.

42. $f(-2)$ exists, $\lim_{x \to -2^+} f(x) = f(-2)$, but $\lim_{x \to -2} f(x)$ does not exist.

43. $f(4)$ exists, $\lim_{x \to 4} f(x)$ exists, but f is not continuous at $x = 4$.

44. $f(x)$ is continuous for all x except $x = 1$, where f has a nonremovable discontinuity.

45. ***Solving Equations*** Is any real number exactly 1 less than its fourth power? Give any such values accurate to 3 decimal places.

46. ***Solving Equations*** Is any real number exactly 2 more than its cube? Give any such values accurate to 3 decimal places.

47. ***Continuous Function*** Find a value for a so that the function

$$f(x) = \begin{cases} x^2 - 1, & x < 3 \\ 2ax, & x \geq 3 \end{cases}$$

is continuous.

48. ***Continuous Function*** Find a value for a so that the function

$$f(x) = \begin{cases} 2x + 3, & x \leq 2 \\ ax + 1, & x > 2 \end{cases}$$

is continuous.

49. ***Continuous Function*** Find a value for a so that the function

$$f(x) = \begin{cases} 4 - x^2, & x < -1 \\ ax^2 - 1, & x \geq -1 \end{cases}$$

is continuous.

50. ***Continuous Function*** Find a value for a so that the function

$$f(x) = \begin{cases} x^2 + x + a, & x < 1 \\ x^3, & x \geq 1 \end{cases}$$

is continuous.

51. Writing to Learn Explain why the equation $e^{-x} = x$ has at least one solution.

52. ***Salary Negotiation*** A welder's contract promises a 3.5% salary increase each year for 4 years and Luisa has an initial salary of \$36,500.

(a) Show that Luisa's salary is given by

$$y = 36{,}500(1.035)^{\text{int}\, t},$$

where t is the time, measured in years, since Luisa signed the contract.

(b) Graph Luisa's salary function. At what values of t is it continuous?

53. *Airport Parking* Valuepark charge \$1.10 per hour or fraction of an hour for airport parking. The maximum charge per day is \$7.25.

(a) Write a formula that gives the charge for x hours with $0 \le x \le 24$. (*Hint:* See Exercise 52.)

(b) Graph the function in part (a). At what values of x is it continuous?

Standardized Test Questions

You may use a graphing calculator to solve the following problems.

54. True or False A continuous function cannot have a point of discontinuity. Justify your answer.

55. True or False It is possible to extend the definition of a function f at a jump discontinuity $x = a$ so that f is continuous at $x = a$. Justify your answer.

56. Multiple Choice On which of the following intervals is $f(x) = \dfrac{1}{\sqrt{x}}$ not continuous?

(A) $(0, \infty)$ **(B)** $[0, \infty)$ **(C)** $(0, 2)$
(D) $(1, 2)$ **(E)** $[1, \infty)$

57. Multiple Choice Which of the following points is not a point of discontinuity of $f(x) = \sqrt{x - 1}$?

(A) $x = -1$ **(B)** $x = -1/2$ **(C)** $x = 0$
(D) $x = 1/2$ **(E)** $x = 1$

58. Multiple Choice Which of the following statements about the function

$$f(x) = \begin{cases} 2x, & 0 < x < 1 \\ 1, & x = 1 \\ -x + 3, & 1 < x < 2 \end{cases}$$

is not true?

(A) $f(1)$ does not exist.

(B) $\lim_{x\to 0^+} f(x)$ exists.

(C) $\lim_{x\to 2^-} f(x)$ exists.

(D) $\lim_{x\to 1} f(x)$ exists.

(E) $\lim_{x\to 1} f(x) \neq f(1)$

59. Multiple Choice Which of the following points of discontinuity of

$$f(x) = \frac{x(x-1)(x-2)^2(x+1)^2(x-3)^2}{x(x-1)(x-2)(x+1)^2(x-3)^3}$$

is not removable?

(A) $x = -1$ **(B)** $x = 0$ **(C)** $x = 1$
(D) $x = 2$ **(E)** $x = 3$

Exploration

60. Let $f(x) = \left(1 + \dfrac{1}{x}\right)^x$.

(a) Find the domain of f. **(b)** Draw the graph of f.

(c) Writing to Learn Explain why $x = -1$ and $x = 0$ are points of discontinuity of f.

(d) Writing to Learn Are either of the discontinuities in part (c) removable? Explain.

(e) Use graphs and tables to estimate $\lim_{x\to\infty} f(x)$.

Extending the Ideas

61. *Continuity at a Point* Show that $f(x)$ is continuous at $x = a$ if and only if

$$\lim_{h\to 0} f(a + h) = f(a).$$

62. *Continuity on Closed Intervals* Let f be continuous and never zero on $[a, b]$. Show that either $f(x) > 0$ for all x in $[a, b]$ or $f(x) < 0$ for all x in $[a, b]$.

63. *Properties of Continuity* Prove that if f is continuous on an interval, then so is $|f|$.

64. *Everywhere Discontinuous* Give a convincing argument that the following function is not continuous at any real number.

$$f(x) = \begin{cases} 1, & \text{if } x \text{ is rational} \\ 0, & \text{if } x \text{ is irrational} \end{cases}$$

2.4 Rates of Change and Tangent Lines

What you will learn about . . .

- Average Rates of Change
- Tangent to a Curve
- Slope of a Curve
- Normal to a Curve
- Speed Revisited

and why . . .

The tangent line determines the direction of a body's motion at every point along its path.

Average Rates of Change

We encounter average rates of change in such forms as average speed (in miles per hour), growth rates of populations (in percent per year), and average monthly rainfall (in inches per month). The **average rate of change** of a quantity over a period of time is the amount of change divided by the time it takes. In general, the *average rate of change* of a function over an interval is the amount of change divided by the length of the interval.

EXAMPLE 1 Finding Average Rate of Change

Find the average rate of change of $f(x) = x^3 - x$ over the interval $[1, 3]$.

SOLUTION

Since $f(1) = 0$ and $f(3) = 24$, the average rate of change over the interval $[1, 3]$ is

$$\frac{f(3) - f(1)}{3 - 1} = \frac{24 - 0}{2} = 12.$$

Now Try Exercise 1.

Experimental biologists often want to know the rates at which populations grow under controlled laboratory conditions. Figure 2.27 shows how the number of fruit flies (*Drosophila*) grew in a controlled 50-day experiment. The graph was made by counting flies at regular intervals, plotting a point for each count, and drawing a smooth curve through the plotted points.

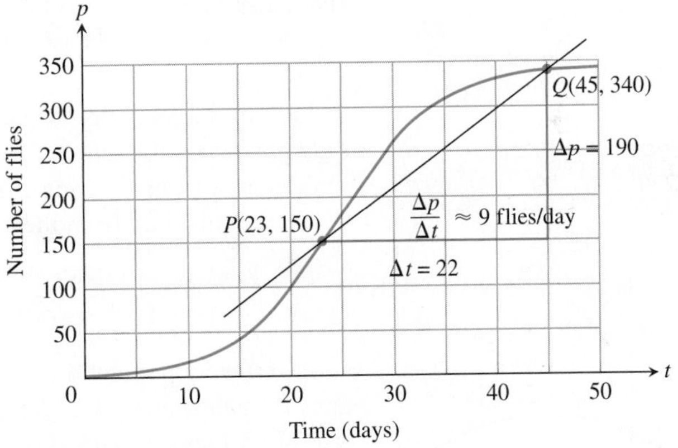

Figure 2.27 Growth of a fruit fly population in a controlled experiment.
Source: Elements of Mathematical Biology. (Example 2)

Secant to a Curve

A line through two points on a curve is a **secant to the curve.**

EXAMPLE 2 Growing *Drosophila* in a Laboratory

Use the points $P(23, 150)$ and $Q(45, 340)$ in Figure 2.27 to compute the average rate of change and the slope of the secant line PQ.

SOLUTION

There were 150 flies on day 23 and 340 flies on day 45. This gives an increase of $340 - 150 = 190$ flies in $45 - 23 = 22$ days.

The average rate of change in the population p from day 23 to day 45 was

$$\textit{Average rate of change:}\quad \frac{\Delta p}{\Delta t} = \frac{340 - 150}{45 - 23} = \frac{190}{22} \approx 8.6 \text{ flies/day},$$

or about 9 flies per day.

continued

Marjorie Lee Browne (1914–1979)

When Marjorie Browne graduated from the University of Michigan in 1949, she was one of the first two African American women to be awarded a Ph.D. in Mathematics. Browne went on to become chairperson of the mathematics department at North Carolina Central University, and succeeded in obtaining grants for retraining high school mathematics teachers.

This average rate of change is also the slope of the secant line through the two points P and Q on the population curve. We can calculate the slope of the secant PQ from the coordinates of P and Q.

$$\text{Secant slope: } \frac{\Delta p}{\Delta t} = \frac{340 - 150}{45 - 23} = \frac{190}{22} \approx 8.6 \text{ flies/day}$$

Now Try Exercise 7.

As suggested by Example 2, *we can always think of an average rate of change as the slope of a secant line.*

In addition to knowing the average rate at which the population grew from day 23 to day 45, we may also want to know how fast the population was growing on day 23 itself. To find out, we can watch the slope of the secant PQ change as we back Q along the curve toward P. The results for four positions of Q are shown in Figure 2.28.

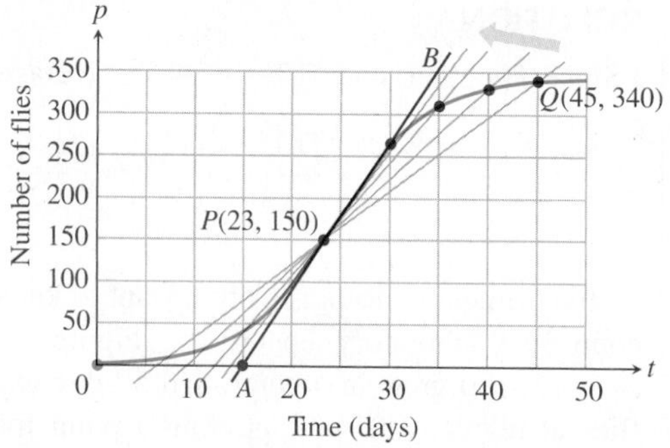

(a)

Q	Slope of $PQ = \Delta p/\Delta t$ (flies/day)
(45, 340)	(340 – 150)/(45 – 23) ≈ 8.6
(40, 330)	(330 – 150)/(40 – 23) ≈ 10.6
(35, 310)	(310 – 150)/(35 – 23) ≈ 13.3
(30, 265)	(265 – 150)/(30 – 23) ≈ 16.4

(b)

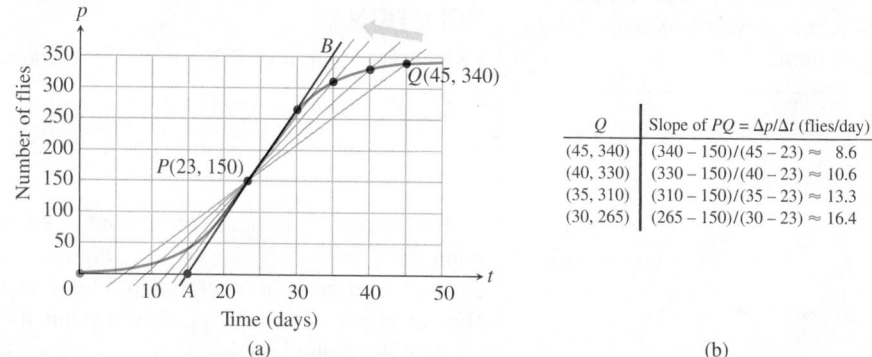

Figure 2.28 (a) Four secants to the fruit fly graph of Figure 2.27, through the point $P(23, 150)$. (b) The slopes of the four secants.

In terms of geometry, what we see as Q approaches P along the curve is this: The secant PQ approaches the tangent line AB that we drew by eye at P. This means that within the limitations of our drawing, the slopes of the secants approach the slope of the tangent, which we calculate from the coordinates of A and B to be

$$\frac{350 - 0}{35 - 15} = 17.5 \text{ flies/day.}$$

In terms of population, what we see as Q approaches P is this: The average growth rates for increasingly smaller time intervals approach the slope of the tangent to the curve at P (17.5 flies per day). The slope of the tangent line is therefore the number we take as the rate at which the fly population was growing on day $t = 23$.

Tangent to a Curve

The moral of the fruit fly story would seem to be that we should define the rate at which the value of the function $y = f(x)$ is changing with respect to x at any particular value $x = a$ to be the slope of the tangent to the curve $y = f(x)$ at $x = a$. But how are we to define the tangent line at an arbitrary point P on the curve and find its slope from the formula $y = f(x)$? The problem here is that we know only one point. Our usual definition of slope requires two points.

The solution that mathematician Pierre Fermat found in 1629 proved to be one of that century's major contributions to calculus. We still use his method of defining tangents to produce formulas for slopes of curves and rates of change:

1. We start with what we can calculate, namely, the slope of a secant through P and a point Q nearby on the curve.

Why Find Tangents to Curves?

In mechanics, the tangent determines the direction of a body's motion at every point along its path.

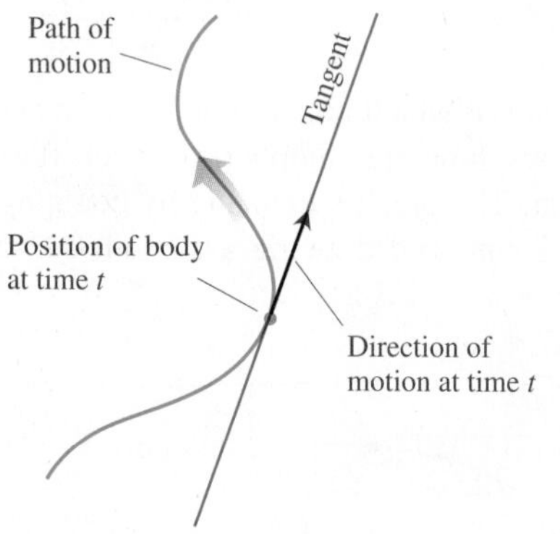

In geometry, the tangents to two curves at a point of intersection determine the angle at which the curves intersect.

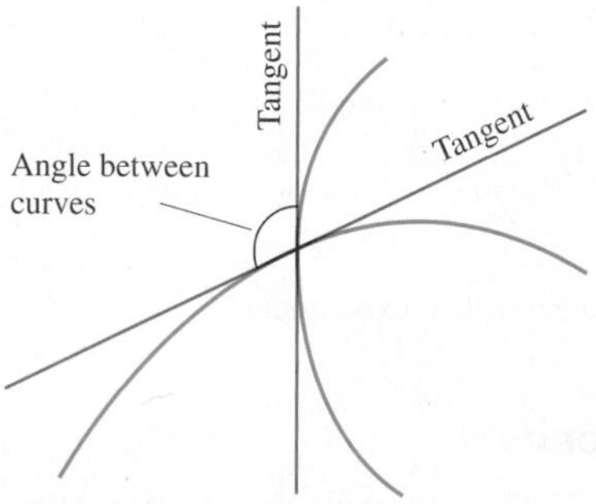

In optics, the tangent determines the angle at which a ray of light enters a curved lens (more about this in Section 4.2). The problem of how to find a tangent to a curve became the dominant mathematical problem of the early 17th century, and it is hard to overestimate how badly the scientists of the day wanted to know the answer. Descartes went so far as to say that the problem was the most useful and most general problem not only that he knew but that he had any desire to know.

2. We find the limiting value of the secant slope (if it exists) as Q approaches P along the curve.

3. We define the *slope of the curve* at P to be this number and define the *tangent to the curve* at P to be the line through P with this slope.

EXAMPLE 3 Finding Slope and Tangent Line

Find the slope of the parabola $y = x^2$ at the point $P(2, 4)$. Write an equation for the tangent to the parabola at this point.

SOLUTION

We begin with a secant line through $P(2, 4)$ and a nearby point $Q(2 + h, (2 + h)^2)$ on the curve (Figure 2.29).

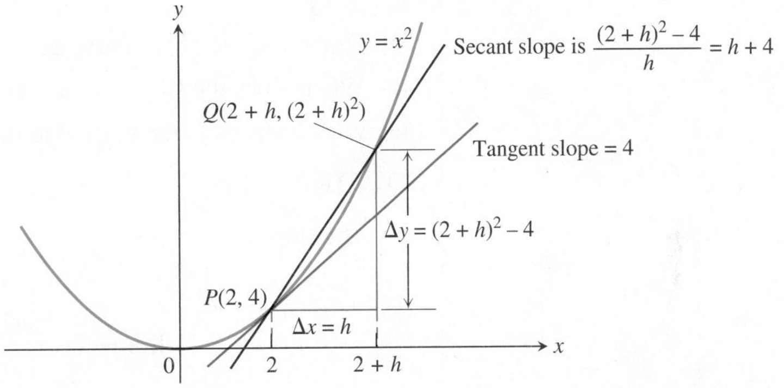

Figure 2.29 The slope of the tangent to the parabola $y = x^2$ at $P(2, 4)$ is 4.

We then write an expression for the slope of the secant line and find the limiting value of this slope as Q approaches P along the curve.

$$\text{Secant slope} = \frac{\Delta y}{\Delta x} = \frac{(2 + h)^2 - 4}{h}$$
$$= \frac{h^2 + 4h + 4 - 4}{h}$$
$$= \frac{h^2 + 4h}{h} = h + 4$$

The limit of the secant slope as Q approaches P along the curve is

$$\lim_{Q \to P} (\text{secant slope}) = \lim_{h \to 0} (h + 4) = 4.$$

Thus, the slope of the parabola at P is 4.

The tangent to the parabola at P is the line through $P(2, 4)$ with slope $m = 4$.

$$y - 4 = 4(x - 2)$$
$$y = 4x - 8 + 4$$
$$y = 4x - 4$$

Now Try Exercise 11 (a, b).

Pierre de Fermat (1601–1665)

The dynamic approach to tangency, invented by Fermat in 1629, proved to be one of the 17th century's major contributions to calculus. Fermat, a skilled linguist and one of his century's greatest mathematicians, tended to confine his writing to professional correspondence and to papers written for personal friends. He rarely wrote completed descriptions of his work, even for his personal use. His name slipped into relative obscurity until the late 1800s, and it was only from a four-volume edition of his works published at the beginning of this century that the true importance of his many achievements became clear.

Slope of a Curve

To find the tangent to a curve $y = f(x)$ at a point $P(a, f(a))$ we use the same dynamic procedure. We calculate the slope of the secant line through P and a point $Q(a + h, f(a + h))$. We then investigate the limit of the slope as $h \to 0$ (Figure 2.30). If the limit exists, it is the slope of the curve at P and we define the tangent at P to be the line through P having this slope.

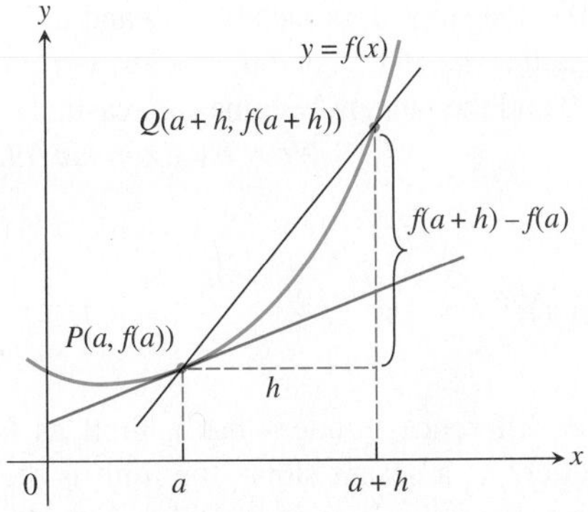

Figure 2.30 The tangent slope is

$$\lim_{h \to 0} \frac{f(a + h) - f(a)}{h}.$$

DEFINITION Slope of a Curve at a Point

The **slope of the curve** $y = f(x)$ at the point $P(a, f(a))$ is the number

$$m = \lim_{h \to 0} \frac{f(a + h) - f(a)}{h},$$

provided the limit exists.

The **tangent line to the curve** at P is the line through P with this slope.

EXAMPLE 4 Exploring Slope and Tangent

Let $f(x) = 1/x$.

(a) Find the slope of the curve at $x = a$.

(b) Where does the slope equal $-1/4$?

(c) What happens to the tangent to the curve at the point $(a, 1/a)$ for different values of a?

SOLUTION

(a) The slope at $x = a$ is

$$\lim_{h \to 0} \frac{f(a + h) - f(a)}{h} = \lim_{h \to 0} \frac{\frac{1}{a+h} - \frac{1}{a}}{h}$$

$$= \lim_{h \to 0} \frac{1}{h} \cdot \frac{a - (a + h)}{a(a + h)}$$

$$= \lim_{h \to 0} \cdot \frac{-h}{ha(a + h)}$$

$$= \lim_{h \to 0} \frac{-1}{a(a + h)} = -\frac{1}{a^2}.$$

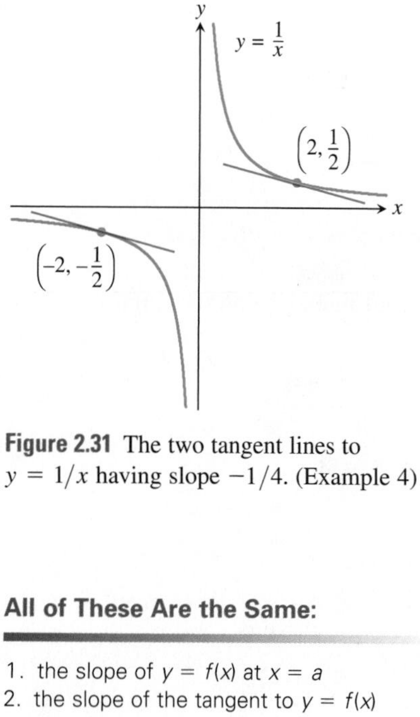

Figure 2.31 The two tangent lines to $y = 1/x$ having slope $-1/4$. (Example 4)

(b) The slope will be $-1/4$ if

$$-\frac{1}{a^2} = -\frac{1}{4}$$

$$a^2 = 4 \quad \text{Multiply by } -4a^2.$$

$$a = \pm 2.$$

The curve has the slope $-1/4$ at the two points $(2, 1/2)$ and $(-2, -1/2)$ (Figure 2.31).

(c) The slope $-1/a^2$ is always negative. As $a \to 0^+$, the slope approaches $-\infty$ and the tangent becomes increasingly steep. We see this again as $a \to 0^-$. As a moves away from the origin in either direction, the slope approaches 0 and the tangent becomes increasingly horizontal.

Now Try Exercise 19.

All of These Are the Same:

1. the slope of $y = f(x)$ at $x = a$
2. the slope of the tangent to $y = f(x)$ at $x = a$
3. the (instantaneous) rate of change of $f(x)$ with respect to x at $x = a$
4. $\lim_{h \to 0} \frac{f(a + h) - f(a)}{h}$

The expression

$$\frac{f(a + h) - f(a)}{h}$$

is the **difference quotient of f at a.** Suppose the difference quotient has a limit as h approaches zero. If we interpret the difference quotient as a secant slope, the limit is the slope of both the curve and the tangent to the curve at the point $x = a$. If we interpret the difference quotient as an average rate of change, the limit is the function's rate of change with respect to x at the point $x = a$. This limit is one of the two most important mathematical objects considered in calculus. We will begin a thorough study of it in Chapter 3.

An Alternate Form

In Chapter 3, we will introduce the expression

$$\frac{f(x) - f(a)}{x - a}$$

as an important and useful alternate form of the **difference quotient of f at a.** (See Exercise 55.)

Normal to a Curve

The **normal line** to a curve at a point is the line perpendicular to the tangent at that point.

EXAMPLE 5 Finding a Normal Line

Write an equation for the normal to the curve $f(x) = 4 - x^2$ at $x = 1$.

SOLUTION

The slope of the tangent to the curve at $x = 1$ is

$$\begin{aligned}\lim_{h\to 0}\frac{f(1+h)-f(1)}{h} &= \lim_{h\to 0}\frac{4-(1+h)^2-3}{h}\\ &= \lim_{h\to 0}\frac{4-1-2h-h^2-3}{h}\\ &= \lim_{h\to 0}\frac{-h(2+h)}{h} = -2.\end{aligned}$$

Thus, the slope of the normal is $1/2$, the negative reciprocal of -2. The normal to the curve at $(1, f(1)) = (1, 3)$ is the line through $(1, 3)$ with slope $m = 1/2$.

$$\begin{aligned}y - 3 &= \frac{1}{2}(x-1)\\ y &= \frac{1}{2}x - \frac{1}{2} + 3\\ y &= \frac{1}{2}x + \frac{5}{2}\end{aligned}$$

You can support this result by drawing the graphs in a square viewing window.

Now Try Exercise 11 (c, d).

About the Word *Normal*

When analytic geometry was developed in the 17th century, European scientists still wrote about their work and ideas in Latin, the one language that all educated Europeans could read and understand. The Latin word *normalis*, which scholars used for *perpendicular*, became *normal* when they discussed geometry in English.

Speed Revisited

The function $y = 16t^2$ that gave the distance fallen by the rock in Example 1, Section 2.1, was the rock's *position function.* A body's average speed along a coordinate axis (here, the y-axis) for a given period of time is the average rate of change of its *position* $y = f(t)$. Its *instantaneous speed* at any time t is the **instantaneous rate of change** of position with respect to time at time t, or

$$\lim_{h\to 0}\frac{f(t+h)-f(t)}{h}.$$

We saw in Example 1, Section 2.1, that the rock's instantaneous speed at $t = 2$ sec was 64 ft/sec.

Particle Motion

We only have considered objects moving in one direction in this chapter. In Chapter 3, we will deal with more complicated motion.

EXAMPLE 6 Finding Instantaneous Rate of Change

Find

$$\lim_{h\to 0}\frac{f(t+h)-f(t)}{h}$$

for the function $f(t) = 2t^2 - 1$ at $t = 2$. Interpret the answer if $f(t)$ represents a position function in feet of an object at time t seconds.

continued

SOLUTION

$$\lim_{h\to 0}\frac{f(t+h)-f(t)}{h} = \lim_{h\to 0}\frac{2(2+h)^2-1-(2\cdot 2^2-1)}{h}$$
$$= \lim_{h\to 0}\frac{8+8h+2h^2-1-7}{h}$$
$$= \lim_{h\to 0}\frac{8h+2h^2}{h}$$
$$= \lim_{h\to 0}(8+2h) = 8$$

The instantaneous rate of change of the object is 8 ft/sec.

Now Try Exercise 23.

EXAMPLE 7 Investigating Free Fall

Find the speed of the falling rock in Example 1, Section 2.1, at $t = 1$ sec.

SOLUTION

The position function of the rock is $f(t) = 16t^2$. The average speed of the rock over the interval between $t = 1$ and $t = 1 + h$ sec was

$$\frac{f(1+h)-f(1)}{h} = \frac{16(1+h)^2-16(1)^2}{h} = \frac{16(h^2+2h)}{h} = 16(h+2).$$

The rock's speed at the instant $t = 1$ was

$$\lim_{h\to 0} 16(h+2) = 32 \text{ ft/sec.}$$

Now Try Exercise 31.

Quick Review 2.4 *(For help, go to Section 1.1.)*

Exercise numbers with a gray background indicate problems that the authors have designed to be solved *without a calculator.*

In Exercises 1 and 2, find the increments Δx and Δy from point A to point B.

1. $A(-5, 2),\ \ B(3, 5)$

2. $A(1, 3),\ \ B(a, b)$

In Exercises 3 and 4, find the slope of the line determined by the points.

3. $(-2, 3),\ \ (5, -1)$

4. $(-3, -1),\ \ (3, 3)$

In Exercises 5–9, write an equation for the specified line.

5. through $(-2, 3)$ with slope $= 3/2$

6. through $(1, 6)$ and $(4, -1)$

7. through $(1, 4)$ and parallel to $y = -\frac{3}{4}x + 2$

8. through $(1, 4)$ and perpendicular to $y = -\frac{3}{4}x + 2$

9. through $(-1, 3)$ and parallel to $2x + 3y = 5$

10. For what value of b will the slope of the line through $(2, 3)$ and $(4, b)$ be $5/3$?

Section 2.4 Exercises

In Exercises 1–6, find the average rate of change of the function over each interval.

1. $f(x) = x^3 + 1$
(a) $[2, 3]$ **(b)** $[-1, 1]$

2. $f(x) = \sqrt{4x + 1}$
(a) $[0, 2]$ **(b)** $[10, 12]$

3. $f(x) = e^x$
(a) $[-2, 0]$ **(b)** $[1, 3]$

4. $f(x) = \ln x$
(a) $[1, 4]$ **(b)** $[100, 103]$

5. $f(x) = \cot x$
(a) $[\pi/4, 3\pi/4]$ **(b)** $[\pi/6, \pi/2]$

6. $f(x) = 2 + \cos x$
(a) $[0, \pi]$ **(b)** $[-\pi, \pi]$

In Exercises 7 and 8, a distance-time graph is shown.

(a) Estimate the slopes of the secants PQ_1, PQ_2, PQ_3, and PQ_4, arranging them in order in a table. What is the appropriate unit for these slopes?

(b) Estimate the speed at point P.

7. *Accelerating from a Standstill* The figure shows the distance-time graph for a 1994 Ford® Mustang Cobra™ accelerating from a standstill.

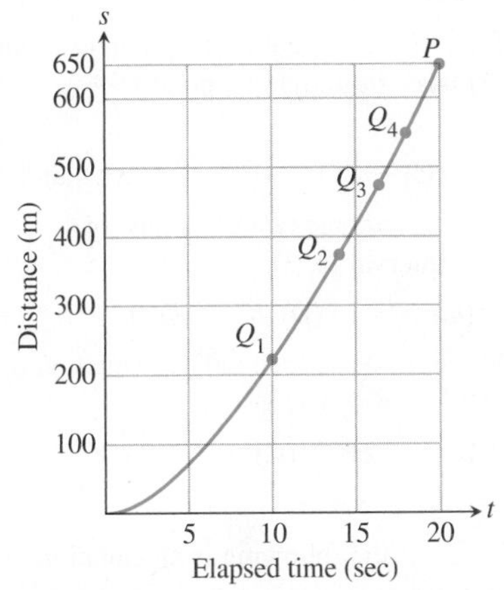

8. *Lunar Data* The accompanying figure shows a distance-time graph for a wrench that fell from the top platform of a communication mast on the moon to the station roof 80 m below.

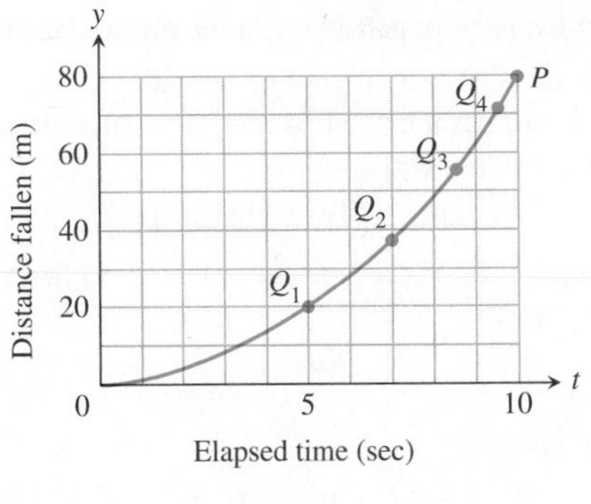

In Exercises 9–12, at the indicated point find

(a) the slope of the curve,

(b) an equation of the tangent, and

(c) an equation of the normal.

(d) Then draw a graph of the curve, tangent line, and normal line in the same square viewing window.

9. $y = x^2$ at $x = -2$

10. $y = x^2 - 4x$ at $x = 1$

11. $y = \dfrac{1}{x-1}$ at $x = 2$

12. $y = x^2 - 3x - 1$ at $x = 0$

In Exercises 13 and 14, find the slope of the curve at the indicated point.

13. $f(x) = |x|$ at **(a)** $x = 2$ **(b)** $x = -3$

14. $f(x) = |x - 2|$ at $x = 1$

In Exercises 15–18, determine whether the curve has a tangent at the indicated point. If it does, give its slope. If not, explain why not.

15. $f(x) = \begin{cases} 2 - 2x - x^2, & x < 0 \\ 2x + 2, & x \geq 0 \end{cases}$ at $x = 0$

16. $f(x) = \begin{cases} -x, & x < 0 \\ x^2 - x, & x \geq 0 \end{cases}$ at $x = 0$

17. $f(x) = \begin{cases} 1/x, & x \leq 2 \\ \dfrac{4 - x}{4}, & x > 2 \end{cases}$ at $x = 2$

18. $f(x) = \begin{cases} \sin x, & 0 \leq x < 3\pi/4 \\ \cos x, & 3\pi/4 \leq x \leq 2\pi \end{cases}$ at $x = 3\pi/4$

In Exercises 19–22, **(a)** find the slope of the curve at $x = a$.
(b) Writing to Learn Describe what happens to the tangent at $x = a$ as a changes.

19. $y = x^2 + 2$

20. $y = 2/x$

21. $y = \dfrac{1}{x-1}$

22. $y = 9 - x^2$

Find the instantaneous rate of change of the position function $y = f(t)$ in feet at the given time t in seconds.

23. $f(t) = 3t - 7, \quad t = 1$

24. $f(t) = 3t^2 + 2t, \quad t = 3$

25. $f(t) = \dfrac{t+1}{t}, \quad t = 2$

26. $f(t) = t^3 - 1, \quad t = 2$

27. *Free Fall* An object is dropped from the top of a 100-m tower. Its height above ground after t sec is $100 - 4.9t^2$ m. How fast is it falling 2 sec after it is dropped?

28. *Rocket Launch* At t sec after lift-off, the height of a rocket is $3t^2$ ft. How fast is the rocket climbing after 10 sec?

29. *Area of Circle* What is the rate of change of the area of a circle with respect to the radius when the radius is $r = 3$ in.?

30. *Volume of Sphere* What is the rate of change of the volume of a sphere with respect to the radius when the radius is $r = 2$ in.?

31. *Free Fall on Mars* The equation for free fall at the surface of Mars is $s = 1.86t^2$ m with t in seconds. Assume a rock is dropped from the top of a 200-m cliff. Find the speed of the rock at $t = 1$ sec.

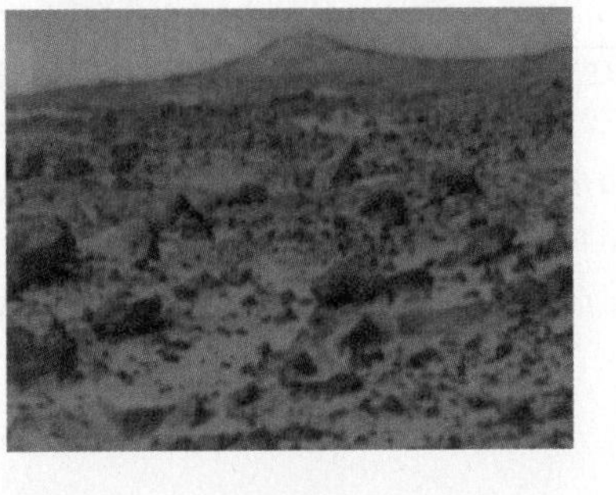

32. *Free Fall on Jupiter* The equation for free fall at the surface of Jupiter is $s = 11.44t^2$ m with t in seconds. Assume a rock is dropped from the top of a 500-m cliff. Find the speed of the rock at $t = 2$ sec.

33. *Horizontal Tangent* At what point is the tangent to $f(x) = x^2 + 4x - 1$ horizontal?

34. *Horizontal Tangent* At what point is the tangent to $f(x) = 3 - 4x - x^2$ horizontal?

35. *Finding Tangents and Normals*

(a) Find an equation for each tangent to the curve $y = 1/(x - 1)$ that has slope -1. (See Exercise 21.)

(b) Find an equation for each normal to the curve $y = 1/(x - 1)$ that has slope 1.

36. *Finding Tangents* Find the equations of all lines tangent to $y = 9 - x^2$ that pass through the point $(1, 12)$.

37. Table 2.2 gives the total amount of U.S. exported wheat products in metric tons for several years.

TABLE 2.2 U.S. Exported Wheat Products

Year	Exported Wheat Products (metric tons)
2000	844
2004	381
2005	313
2006	281
2007	448
2008	389

Source: U.S. Department of Agriculture, Economic Research Service, *Foreign Agricultural Trade of the United States, (FATUS)*, Table 820.

(a) Let $x = 0$ represent 2000, $x = 1$ represent 2001, and so forth. Make a scatter plot of the data.

(b) Let P represent the point corresponding to 2008, Q_1 the point corresponding to 2004, Q_2 the point corresponding to 2005, and Q_3 the point corresponding to 2007. Find the slope of the secant line PQ_i for $i = 1, 2, 3$.

38. Table 2.3 gives the amount of federal spending in billions of dollars for national defense for several years.

TABLE 2.3 National Defense Spending

Year	National Defense Spending ($ billions)
2003	404.8
2004	455.8
2005	495.3
2006	521.8
2007	551.3
2008	616.1
2009	690.3

Source: U.S. Office of Management and Budget, *Budget Authority by Function and Subfunction, Outlay by Function and Subfunction*, Table 492.

(a) Find the average rate of change in spending from 2003 to 2009.

(b) Find the average rate of change in spending from 2005 to 2008.

(c) Find the average rate of change in spending from 2008 to 2009.

(d) Writing to Learn Explain why someone might be hesitant to make predictions about the rate of change of national defense spending based on the data given in Table 2.3.

Standardized Test Questions

39. True or False If the graph of a function has a tangent line at $x = a$, then the graph also has a normal line at $x = a$. Justify your answer.

40. True or False The graph of $f(x) = |x|$ has a tangent line at $x = 0$. Justify your answer.

41. Multiple Choice If the line L tangent to the graph of a function f at the point $(2, 5)$ passes through the point $(-1, -3)$, what is the slope of L?

(A) $-3/8$ **(B)** $3/8$ **(C)** $-8/3$ **(D)** $8/3$ **(E)** undefined

42. Multiple Choice Find the average rate of change of $f(x) = x^2 + x$ over the interval $[1, 3]$.

(A) -5 **(B)** $1/5$ **(C)** $1/4$ **(D)** 4 **(E)** 5

43. Multiple Choice Which of the following is an equation of the tangent to the graph of $f(x) = 2/x$ at $x = 1$?

(A) $y = -2x$ **(B)** $y = 2x$ **(C)** $y = -2x + 4$
(D) $y = -x + 3$ **(E)** $y = x + 3$

44. Multiple Choice Which of the following is an equation of the normal to the graph of $f(x) = 2/x$ at $x = 1$?

(A) $y = \frac{1}{2}x + \frac{3}{2}$ **(B)** $y = -\frac{1}{2}x$ **(C)** $y = \frac{1}{2}x + 2$
(D) $y = -\frac{1}{2}x + 2$ **(E)** $y = 2x + 5$

Explorations

In Exercises 45 and 46, complete the following for the function.

(a) Compute the difference quotient

$$\frac{f(1 + h) - f(1)}{h}.$$

(b) Use graphs and tables to estimate the limit of the difference quotient in part (a) as $h \to 0$.

(c) Compare your estimate in part (b) with the given number.

(d) Writing to Learn Based on your computations, do you think the graph of f has a tangent at $x = 1$? If so, estimate its slope. If not, explain why not.

45. $f(x) = e^x$, e

46. $f(x) = 2^x$, $\ln 4$

Group Activity In Exercises 47–50, the curve $y = f(x)$ has a **vertical tangent** at $x = a$ if

$$\lim_{h \to 0} \frac{f(a + h) - f(a)}{h} = \infty$$

or if

$$\lim_{h \to 0} \frac{f(a + h) - f(a)}{h} = -\infty.$$

In each case, the right- and left-hand limits are required to be the same: both $+\infty$ or both $-\infty$.

Use graphs to investigate whether the curve has a vertical tangent at $x = 0$.

47. $y = x^{2/5}$

48. $y = x^{3/5}$

49. $y = x^{1/3}$

50. $y = x^{2/3}$

Extending the Ideas

In Exercises 51 and 52, determine whether the graph of the function has a tangent at the origin. Explain your answer.

51. $f(x) = \begin{cases} x^2 \sin \dfrac{1}{x}, & x \neq 0 \\ 0, & x = 0 \end{cases}$

52. $f(x) = \begin{cases} x \sin \dfrac{1}{x}, & x \neq 0 \\ 0, & x = 0 \end{cases}$

53. *Sine Function* Estimate the slope of the curve $y = \sin x$ at $x = 1$. (*Hint:* See Exercises 45 and 46.)

54. Consider the function f given in Example 1. Explain how the average rate of change of f over the interval $[3, 3 + h]$ is the same as the difference quotient of f at $a = 3$.

55. (a) Let $x = a + h$. Show algebraically how the difference quotient of f at a,

$$\frac{f(a+h) - f(a)}{h},$$

is equivalent to an alternate form given by

$$\frac{f(x) - f(a)}{x - a}.$$

(b) Writing to Learn Why do you think we discuss two forms of the difference quotient of f at a?

Quick Quiz for AP* Preparation: Sections 2.3 and 2.4

You may use a calculator with these problems.

1. Multiple Choice Which of the following values is the average rate of $f(x) = \sqrt{x + 1}$ over the interval $(0, 3)$?

(A) -3 **(B)** -1 **(C)** $-1/3$ **(D)** $1/3$ **(E)** 3

2. Multiple Choice Which of the following statements is false for the function

$$f(x) = \begin{cases} \dfrac{3}{4}x, & 0 \le x < 4 \\ 2, & x = 4 \\ -x + 7, & 4 < x \le 6 \\ 1, & 6 < x < 8? \end{cases}$$

(A) $\lim_{x \to 4} f(x)$ exists **(B)** $f(4)$ exists

(C) $\lim_{x \to 6} f(x)$ exists **(D)** $\lim_{x \to 8^-} f(x)$ exists

(E) f is continuous at $x = 4$

3. Multiple Choice Which of the following is an equation for the tangent line to $f(x) = 9 - x^2$ at $x = 2$?

(A) $y = \frac{1}{4}x + \frac{9}{2}$ **(B)** $y = -4x + 13$

(C) $y = -4x - 3$ **(D)** $y = 4x - 3$

(E) $y = 4x + 13$

4. Free Response Let $f(x) = 2x - x^2$.

(a) Find $f(3)$. **(b)** Find $f(3 + h)$.

(c) Find $\dfrac{f(3+h) - f(3)}{h}$.

(d) Find the instantaneous rate of change of f at $x = 3$.

Chapter 2 Key Terms

average rate of change (p. 87)
average speed (p. 59)
composite of continuous functions (p. 82)
connected graph (p. 83)
Constant Multiple Rule for Limits (p. 61)
continuity at a point (p. 78)
continuous at an endpoint (p. 79)
continuous at an interior point (p. 79)
continuous extension (p. 81)
continuous function (p. 81)
continuous on an interval (p. 81)
difference quotient (p. 90)
Difference Rule for Limits (p. 61)
discontinuous (p. 79)
end behavior model (p. 74)
free fall (p. 91)
horizontal asymptote (p. 70)
infinite discontinuity (p. 80)
instantaneous rate of change (p. 91)
instantaneous speed (p. 91)
intermediate value property (p. 83)
Intermediate Value Theorem for Continuous Functions (p. 83)
jump discontinuity (p. 80)
left end behavior model (p. 74)
left-hand limit (p. 64)
limit of a function (p. 60)
normal to a curve (p. 91)
oscillating discontinuity (p. 80)
point of discontinuity (p. 79)
Power Rule for Limits (p. 71)
Product Rule for Limits (p. 61)
Properties of Continuous Functions (p. 82)
Quotient Rule for Limits (p. 61)
removable discontinuity (p. 80)
right end behavior model (p. 74)
right-hand limit (p. 64)
Sandwich Theorem (p. 65)
secant to a curve (p. 87)
slope of a curve (p. 89)
Sum Rule for Limits (p. 61)
tangent line to a curve (p. 88)
two-sided limit (p. 64)
vertical asymptote (p. 72)
vertical tangent (p. 94)

Chapter 2 Review Exercises

Exercise numbers with a gray background indicate problems that the authors have designed to be solved *without a calculator*.

The collection of exercises marked in red could be used as a chapter test.

In Exercises 1–14, find the limits.

1. $\lim_{x\to -2}(x^3 - 2x^2 + 1)$

2. $\lim_{x\to -2}\dfrac{x^2+1}{3x^2-2x+5}$

3. $\lim_{x\to 4}\sqrt{1-2x}$

4. $\lim_{x\to 5}\sqrt[4]{9-x^2}$

5. $\lim_{x\to 0}\dfrac{\dfrac{1}{2+x}-\dfrac{1}{2}}{x}$

6. $\lim_{x\to\pm\infty}\dfrac{2x^2+3}{5x^2+7}$

7. $\lim_{x\to\pm\infty}\dfrac{x^4+x^3}{12x^3+128}$

8. $\lim_{x\to 0}\dfrac{\sin 2x}{4x}$

9. $\lim_{x\to 0}\dfrac{x\csc x+1}{x\csc x}$

10. $\lim_{x\to 0} e^x \sin x$

11. $\lim_{x\to 7/2^+}\text{int}\,(2x-1)$

12. $\lim_{x\to 7/2^-}\text{int}\,(2x-1)$

13. $\lim_{x\to\infty} e^{-x}\cos x$

14. $\lim_{x\to\infty}\dfrac{x+\sin x}{x+\cos x}$

In Exercises 15–20, determine whether the limit exists on the basis of the graph of $y = f(x)$. The domain of f is the set of real numbers.

15. $\lim_{x\to d} f(x)$

16. $\lim_{x\to c^+} f(x)$

17. $\lim_{x\to c^-} f(x)$

18. $\lim_{x\to c} f(x)$

19. $\lim_{x\to b} f(x)$

20. $\lim_{x\to a} f(x)$

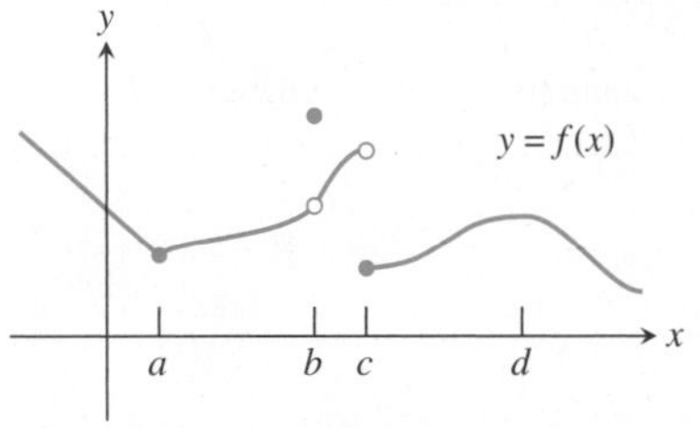

In Exercises 21–24, determine whether the function f used in Exercises 15–20 is continuous at the indicated point.

21. $x = a$

22. $x = b$

23. $x = c$

24. $x = d$

In Exercises 25 and 26, use the graph of the function with domain $-1 \le x \le 3$.

25. Determine

(a) $\lim_{x\to 3^-} g(x)$. (b) $g(3)$.

(c) whether $g(x)$ is continuous at $x = 3$.

(d) the points of discontinuity of $g(x)$.

(e) **Writing to Learn** whether any points of discontinuity are removable. If so, describe the new function. If not, explain why not.

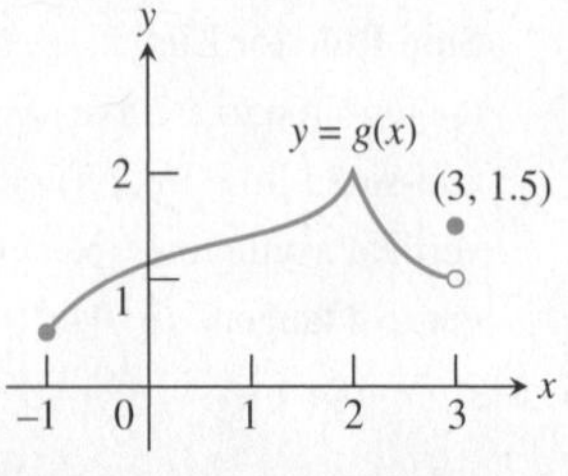

26. Determine

(a) $\lim_{x\to 1^-} k(x)$. (b) $\lim_{x\to 1^+} k(x)$. (c) $k(1)$.

(d) whether $k(x)$ is continuous at $x = 1$.

(e) the points of discontinuity of $k(x)$.

(f) **Writing to Learn** whether any points of discontinuity are removable. If so, describe the new function. If not, explain why not.

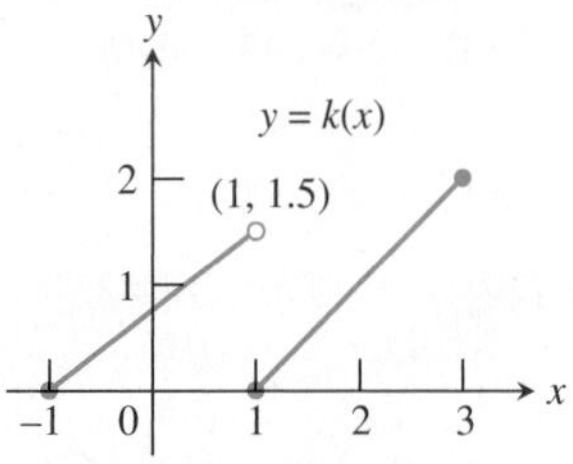

In Exercises 27 and 28, **(a)** find the vertical asymptotes of the graph of $y = f(x)$, and **(b)** describe the behavior of $f(x)$ to the left and right of any vertical asymptote.

27. $f(x) = \dfrac{x+3}{x+2}$

28. $f(x) = \dfrac{x-1}{x^2(x+2)}$

In Exercises 29 and 30, answer the questions for the piecewise-defined function.

29. $f(x) = \begin{cases} 1, & x \le -1 \\ -x, & -1 < x < 0 \\ 1, & x = 0 \\ -x, & 0 < x < 1 \\ 1, & x \ge 1 \end{cases}$

(a) Find the right-hand and left-hand limits of f at $x = -1, 0$, and 1.

(b) Does f have a limit as x approaches -1? 0? 1? If so, what is it? If not, why not?

(c) Is f continuous at $x = -1$? 0? 1? Explain.

30. $f(x) = \begin{cases} |x^3 - 4x|, & x < 1 \\ x^2 - 2x - 2, & x \ge 1 \end{cases}$

(a) Find the right-hand and left-hand limits of f at $x = 1$.

(b) Does f have a limit as $x \to 1$? If so, what is it? If not, why not?

(c) At what points is f continuous?

(d) At what points is f discontinuous?

In Exercises 31 and 32, find all points of discontinuity of the function.

31. $f(x) = \dfrac{x+1}{4-x^2}$

32. $g(x) = \sqrt[3]{3x+2}$

In Exercises 33–36, find **(a)** a power function end behavior model and **(b)** any horizontal asymptotes.

33. $f(x) = \dfrac{2x+1}{x^2-2x+1}$

34. $f(x) = \dfrac{2x^2+5x-1}{x^2+2x}$

35. $f(x) = \dfrac{x^3-4x^2+3x+3}{x-3}$

36. $f(x) = \dfrac{x^4-3x^2+x-1}{x^3-x+1}$

In Exercises 37 and 38, find **(a)** a right end behavior model and **(b)** a left end behavior model for the function.

37. $f(x) = x + e^x$

38. $f(x) = \ln|x| + \sin x$

Group Activity In Exercises 39 and 40, what value should be assigned to k to make f a continuous function?

39. $f(x) = \begin{cases} \dfrac{x^2 + 2x - 15}{x - 3}, & x \neq 3 \\ k, & x = 3 \end{cases}$

40. $f(x) = \begin{cases} \dfrac{\sin x}{2x}, & x \neq 0 \\ k, & x = 0 \end{cases}$

Group Activity In Exercises 41 and 42, sketch a graph of a function f that satisfies the given conditions.

41. $\lim_{x\to\infty} f(x) = 3, \quad \lim_{x\to-\infty} f(x) = \infty,$
$\lim_{x\to 3^+} f(x) = \infty, \quad \lim_{x\to 3^-} f(x) = -\infty$

42. $\lim_{x\to 2} f(x)$ does not exist, $\lim_{x\to 2^+} f(x) = f(2) = 3$

43. ***Average Rate of Change*** Find the average rate of change of $f(x) = 1 + \sin x$ over the interval $[0, \pi/2]$.

44. ***Rate of Change*** Find the instantaneous rate of change of the volume $V = (1/3)\pi r^2 H$ of a cone with respect to the radius r at $r = a$ if the height H does not change.

45. ***Rate of Change*** Find the instantaneous rate of change of the surface area $S = 6x^2$ of a cube with respect to the edge length x at $x = a$.

46. ***Slope of a Curve*** Find the slope of the curve $y = x^2 - x - 2$ at $x = a$.

47. ***Tangent and Normal*** Let $f(x) = x^2 - 3x$ and $P = (1, f(1))$. Find **(a)** the slope of the curve $y = f(x)$ at P, **(b)** an equation of the tangent at P, and **(c)** an equation of the normal at P.

48. ***Horizontal Tangents*** At what points, if any, are the tangents to the graph of $f(x) = x^2 - 3x$ horizontal? (See Exercise 47.)

49. ***Bear Population*** The number of bears in a federal wildlife reserve is given by the population equation

$$p(t) = \frac{200}{1 + 7e^{-0.1t}},$$

where t is in years.

(a) **Writing to Learn** Find $p(0)$. Give a possible interpretation of this number.

(b) Find $\lim_{t\to\infty} p(t)$.

(c) **Writing to Learn** Give a possible interpretation of the result in part (b).

50. ***Taxi Fares*** Bluetop Cab charges \$3.20 for the first mile and \$1.35 for each additional mile or part of a mile.

(a) Write a formula that gives the charge for x miles with $0 \leq x \leq 20$.

(b) Graph the function in (a). At what values of x is it discontinuous?

51. Table 2.4 gives the population of Florida for several years. All data was collected on July 1 of the given year.

(a) Let $x = 0$ represent 2000, $x = 1$ represent 2001, and so forth. Make a scatter plot for the data.

(b) Let P represent the point corresponding to 2009, Q_1 the point corresponding to 2002, Q_2 the point corresponding to 2004, and Q_3 the point corresponding to 2008. Find the slope of the secant the PQ_i for $i = 1, 2,$ and 3.

TABLE 2.4 Population of Florida

Year	Population (in thousands)
2000	16,047
2002	16,341
2004	17,314
2006	18,019
2008	18,328
2009	18,538

Source: U.S. Census Bureau, *Statistical Abstract of the United States; 2009–2010.*

(c) Using the same information given in part (b), find the average rates of change from Q_i to P.

(d) Estimate the instantaneous rate of change of the population on July 1, 2009.

(e) **Writing to Learn** Assuming the population growth in Table 2.4 *is linear*, estimate the population of Florida in 2020. Explain why linear growth may or may not be a bad assumption over longer periods of time.

52. ***Limit Properties*** Assume that

$$\lim_{x\to c} [f(x) + g(x)] = 2,$$
$$\lim_{x\to c} [f(x) - g(x)] = 1,$$

and that $\lim_{x\to c} f(x)$ and $\lim_{x\to c} g(x)$ exist. Find $\lim_{x\to c} f(x)$ and $\lim_{x\to c} g(x)$.

AP* Examination Preparation

53. Free Response Let $f(x) = \dfrac{x}{|x^2 - 9|}$.

(a) Find the domain of f.

(b) Write an equation for each vertical asymptote of the graph of f.

(c) Write an equation for each horizontal asymptote of the graph of f.

(d) Is f odd, even, or neither? Justify your answer.

(e) Find all values of x for which f is discontinuous and classify each discontinuity as removable or nonremovable.

54. Free Response Let $f(x) = \begin{cases} x^2 - a^2 x & \text{if } x < 2, \\ 4 - 2x^2 & \text{if } x \geq 2. \end{cases}$

(a) Find $\lim_{x\to 2^-} f(x)$.

(b) Find $\lim_{x\to 2^+} f(x)$.

(c) Find all values of a that make f continuous at 2. Justify your answer.

55. Free Response Let $f(x) = \dfrac{x^3 - 2x^2 + 1}{x^2 + 3}$.

(a) Find all zeros of f.

(b) Find a right end behavior model $g(x)$ for f.

(c) Determine $\lim_{x\to\infty} f(x)$ and $\lim_{x\to\infty} \dfrac{f(x)}{g(x)}$.

CHAPTER

3 Derivatives

Shown here is the pain reliever acetaminophen in crystalline form, photographed under a transmitted light microscope. While acetaminophen relieves pain with few side effects, it is toxic in large doses. One study found that only 30% of parents who gave acetaminophen to their children could accurately calculate and measure the correct dose.

One rule for calculating the dosage (mg) of acetaminophen for children ages 1 to 12 years old is $D(t) = 750t/(t + 12)$, where t is age in years. What is an expression for the rate of change of a child's dosage with respect to the child's age? How does the rate of change of the dosage relate to the growth rate of children? This problem can be solved with the information covered in Section 3.4.

CHAPTER 3 Overview

In Chapter 2, we learned how to find the slope of a tangent to a curve as the limit of the slopes of secant lines. In Example 4 of Section 2.4, we derived a formula for the slope of the tangent at an arbitrary point $(a, 1/a)$ on the graph of the function $f(x) = 1/x$ and showed that it was $-1/a^2$.

This seemingly unimportant result is more powerful than it might appear at first glance, as it gives us a simple way to calculate the instantaneous rate of change of f at any point. The study of rates of change of functions is called *differential calculus,* and the formula $-1/a^2$ was our first look at a *derivative.* The derivative was the 17th-century breakthrough that enabled mathematicians to unlock the secrets of planetary motion and gravitational attraction—of objects changing position over time. We will learn many uses for derivatives in Chapter 5, but first, in the next two chapters, we will focus on what derivatives are and how they work.

3.1 Derivative of a Function

What you will learn about . . .

- Definition of Derivative
- Notation
- Relationships Between the Graphs of f and f'
- Graphing the Derivative from Data
- One-sided Derivatives

and why . . .

The derivative is the key to modeling instantaneous change mathematically.

Definition of Derivative

In Section 2.4, we defined the slope of a curve $y = f(x)$ at the point where $x = a$ to be

$$m = \lim_{h \to 0} \frac{f(a + h) - f(a)}{h}.$$

When it exists, this limit is called the **derivative of f at a.** In this section, we investigate the derivative as a *function* derived from f by considering the limit at each point of the domain of f.

DEFINITION Derivative

The **derivative** of the function f with respect to the variable x is the function f' whose value at x is

$$f'(x) = \lim_{h \to 0} \frac{f(x + h) - f(x)}{h}, \qquad (1)$$

provided the limit exists.

The domain of f', the set of points in the domain of f for which the limit exists, may be smaller than the domain of f. If $f'(x)$ exists, we say that f **has a derivative (is differentiable)** at x. A function that is differentiable at every point of its domain is a **differentiable function.**

EXAMPLE 1 Applying the Definition

Differentiate (that is, find the derivative of) $f(x) = x^3$.

continued

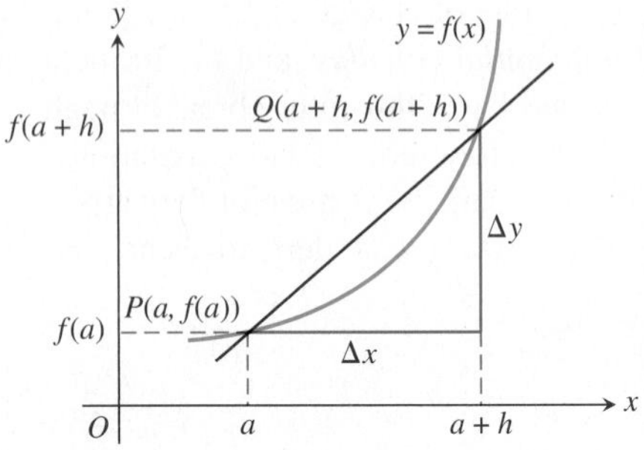

Figure 3.1 The slope of the secant line PQ is

$$\frac{\Delta y}{\Delta x} = \frac{f(a+h) - f(a)}{(a+h) - a} = \frac{f(a+h) - f(a)}{h}.$$

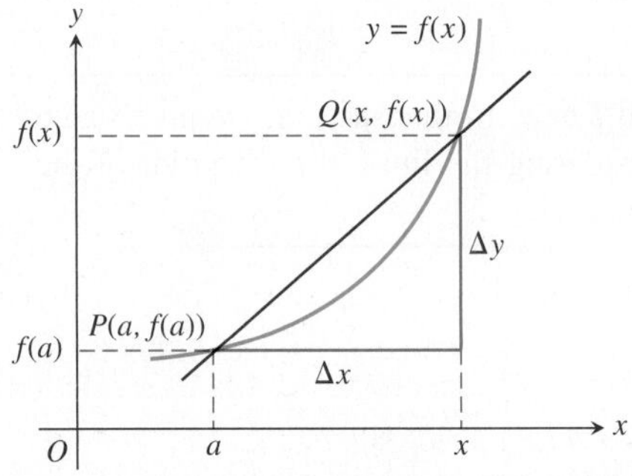

Figure 3.2 The slope of the secant line PQ is

$$\frac{\Delta y}{\Delta x} = \frac{f(x) - f(a)}{x - a}.$$

SOLUTION

Applying the definition, we have

$$\begin{aligned} f'(x) &= \lim_{h\to 0} \frac{f(x+h) - f(x)}{h} \\ &= \lim_{h\to 0} \frac{(x+h)^3 - x^3}{h} && \text{Eq. 1 with } f(x) = x^3,\ f(x+h) = (x+h)^3 \\ &= \lim_{h\to 0} \frac{(x^3 + 3x^2h + 3xh^2 + h^3) - x^3}{h} && (x+h)^3 \text{ expanded} \\ &= \lim_{h\to 0} \frac{(3x^3 + 3xh + h^2)h}{h} && x^3 \text{ terms cancelled, } h \text{ factored out} \\ &= \lim_{h\to 0} (3x^2 + 3xh + h^2) = 3x^2. \end{aligned}$$

Now Try Exercise 1.

The derivative of $f(x)$ at a point where $x = a$ is found by taking the limit as $h \to 0$ of slopes of secant lines, as shown in Figure 3.1.

By relabeling the picture as in Figure 3.2, we arrive at a useful alternate formula for calculating the derivative. This time, the limit is taken as x approaches a.

DEFINITION (ALTERNATE) Derivative at a Point

The **derivative** of the function ***f* at the point *x* = *a*** is the limit

$$f'(a) = \lim_{x\to a} \frac{f(x) - f(a)}{x - a}, \tag{2}$$

provided the limit exists.

After we find the derivative of f at a point $x = a$ using the alternate form, we can find the derivative of f as a function by applying the resulting formula to an arbitrary x in the domain of f.

EXAMPLE 2 Applying the Alternate Definition

Differentiate $f(x) = \sqrt{x}$ using the alternate definition.

SOLUTION

At the point $x = a$,

$$\begin{aligned} f'(a) &= \lim_{x\to a} \frac{f(x) - f(a)}{x - a} \\ &= \lim_{x\to a} \frac{\sqrt{x} - \sqrt{a}}{x - a} && \text{Eq. 2 with } f(x) = \sqrt{x} \\ &= \lim_{x\to a} \frac{\sqrt{x} - \sqrt{a}}{x - a} \cdot \frac{\sqrt{x} + \sqrt{a}}{\sqrt{x} + \sqrt{a}} && \text{Rationalize...} \\ &= \lim_{x\to a} \frac{x - a}{(x - a)(\sqrt{x} + \sqrt{a})} && \text{...the numerator.} \\ &= \lim_{x\to a} \frac{1}{\sqrt{x} + \sqrt{a}} && \text{We can now take the limit.} \\ &= \frac{1}{2\sqrt{a}}. \end{aligned}$$

Applying this formula to an arbitrary $x > 0$ in the domain of f identifies the derivative as the function $f'(x) = 1/(2\sqrt{x})$ with domain $(0, \infty)$. ***Now Try Exercise 5.***

Why all the notation?

The "prime" notations y' and f' come from notations that Newton used for derivatives. The d/dx notations are similar to those used by Leibniz. Each has its advantages and disadvantages.

Notation

There are many ways to denote the derivative of a function $y = f(x)$. Besides $f'(x)$, the most common notations are these:

y'	"y prime"	Nice and brief, but does not name the independent variable.
$\dfrac{dy}{dx}$	"$dy\ dx$" or "the derivative of y with respect to x"	Names both variables and uses d for derivative.
$\dfrac{df}{dx}$	"$df\ dx$" or "the derivative of f with respect to x"	Emphasizes the function's name.
$\dfrac{d}{dx}f(x)$	"$d\ dx$ of f at x" or "the derivative of f at x"	Emphasizes the idea that differentiation is an operation performed on f.

Relationships Between the Graphs of *f* and *f′*

When we have the explicit formula for $f(x)$, we can derive a formula for $f'(x)$ using methods like those in Examples 1 and 2. We have already seen, however, that functions are encountered in other ways: graphically, for example, or in tables of data.

Because we can think of the derivative at a point in graphical terms as *slope,* we can get a good idea of what the graph of the function f' looks like by *estimating the slopes* at various points along the graph of f.

EXAMPLE 3 Graphing *f′* from *f*

Graph the derivative of the function f whose graph is shown in Figure 3.3a. Discuss the behavior of f in terms of the signs and values of f'.

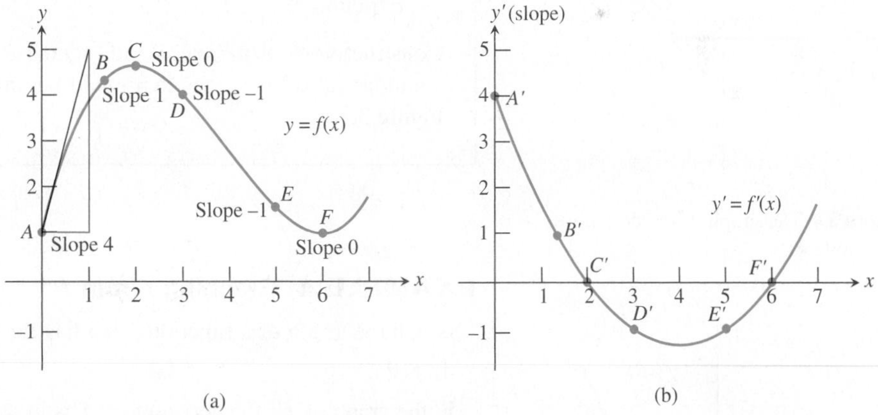

Figure 3.3 By plotting the slopes at points on the graph of $y = f(x)$, we obtain a graph of $y' = f'(x)$. The slope at point A of the graph of f in part (a) is the y-coordinate of point A' on the graph of f' in part (b), and so on. (Example 3)

SOLUTION

First, we draw a pair of coordinate axes, marking the horizontal axis in x-units and the vertical axis in slope units (Figure 3.3b). Next, we estimate the slope of the graph of f at various points, plotting the corresponding slope values using the new axes. At $A(0, f(0))$, the graph of f has slope 4, so $f'(0) = 4$. At B, the graph of f has slope 1, so $f' = 1$ at B', and so on.

continued

We complete our estimate of the graph of f' by connecting the plotted points with a smooth curve.

Although we do not have a formula for either f or f', the graph of each reveals important information about the behavior of the other. In particular, notice that f is decreasing where f' is negative and increasing where f' is positive. Where f' is zero, the graph of f has a horizontal tangent, changing from increasing to decreasing at point C and from decreasing to increasing at point F. **Now Try Exercise 23.**

EXPLORATION 1 Reading the Graphs

Suppose that the function f in Figure 3.3a represents the depth y (in inches) of water in a ditch alongside a dirt road as a function of time x (in days). How would you answer the following questions?

1. What does the graph in Figure 3.3b represent? What units would you use along the y'-axis?
2. Describe as carefully as you can what happened to the water in the ditch over the course of the 7-day period.
3. Can you describe the weather during the 7 days? When was it the wettest? When was it the driest?
4. How does the graph of the derivative help in finding when the weather was wettest or driest?
5. Interpret the significance of point C in terms of the water in the ditch. How does the significance of point C' reflect that in terms of rate of change?
6. It is tempting to say that it rains right up until the beginning of the second day, but that overlooks a fact about rainwater that is important in flood control. Explain.

Construct your own "real-world" scenario for the function in Example 3, and pose a similar set of questions that could be answered by considering the two graphs in Figure 3.3.

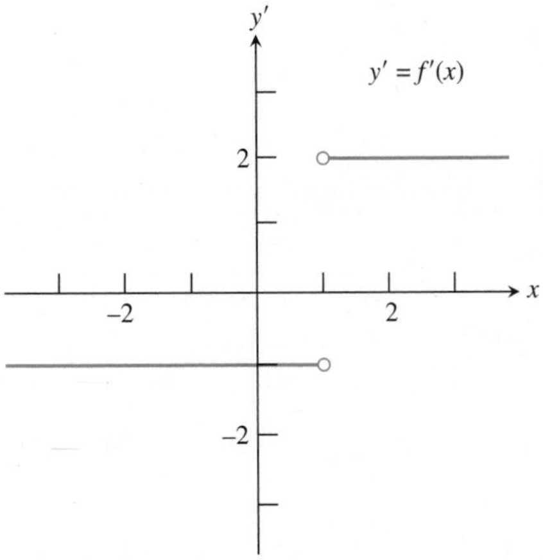

Figure 3.4 The graph of the derivative. (Example 4)

EXAMPLE 4 Graphing f from f'

Sketch the graph of a function f that has the following properties:

i. $f(0) = 0$;

ii. the graph of f', the derivative of f, is as shown in Figure 3.4;

iii. f is continuous for all x.

SOLUTION

To satisfy property (i), we begin with a point at the origin.

To satisfy property (ii), we consider what the graph of the derivative tells us about slopes. To the left of $x = 1$, the graph of f has a constant slope of -1; therefore we draw a line with slope -1 to the left of $x = 1$, making sure that it goes through the origin.

To the right of $x = 1$, the graph of f has a constant slope of 2, so it must be a line with slope 2. There are infinitely many such lines but only one—the one that meets the left side of the graph at $(1, -1)$—will satisfy the continuity requirement. The resulting graph is shown in Figure 3.5. **Now Try Exercise 27.**

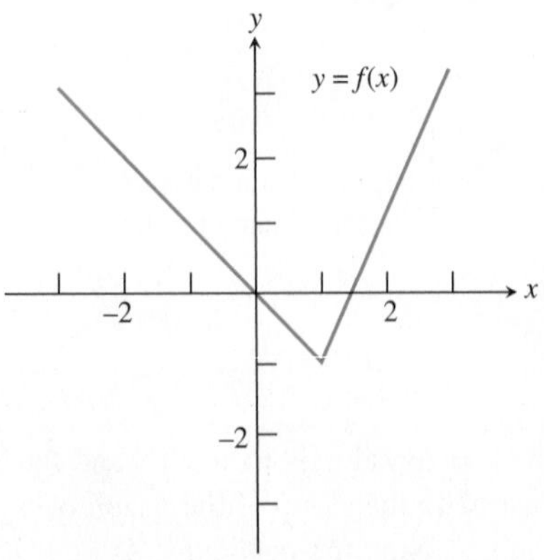

Figure 3.5 The graph of f, constructed from the graph of f' and two other conditions. (Example 4)

What's happening at $x = 1$?

Notice that f in Figure 3.5 is defined at $x = 1$, while f' is not. It is the continuity of f that enables us to conclude that $f(1) = -1$. Looking at the graph of f, can you see why f' could not possibly be defined at $x = 1$? We will explore the reason for this in Example 6.

David H. Blackwell (1919–2010)

By the age of 22, David Blackwell had earned a Ph.D. in Mathematics from the University of Illinois. He taught at Howard University, where his research included statistics, Markov chains, and sequential analysis. He then went on to teach and continue his research at the University of California at Berkeley. Dr. Blackwell served as president of the American Statistical Association and was the first African American mathematician of the National Academy of Sciences.

Graphing the Derivative from Data

Discrete points plotted from sets of data do not yield a continuous curve, but we have seen that the shape and pattern of the graphed points (called a scatter plot) can be meaningful nonetheless. It is often possible to fit a curve to the points using regression techniques. If the fit is good, we could use the curve to get a graph of the derivative visually, as in Example 3. However, it is also possible to get a scatter plot of the derivative numerically, directly from the data, by computing the slopes between successive points, as in Example 5.

EXAMPLE 5 Estimating the Probability of Shared Birthdays

Suppose 30 people are in a room. What is the probability that two of them share the same birthday? Ignore the year of birth.

SOLUTION

It may surprise you to learn that the probability of a shared birthday among 30 people is at least 0.706, well above two-thirds! In fact, if we assume that no one day is more likely to be a birthday than any other day, the probabilities shown in Table 3.1 are not hard to determine (see Exercise 45).

TABLE 3.1 Probabilities of Shared Birthdays

People in Room (x)	Probability (y)
0	0
5	0.027
10	0.117
15	0.253
20	0.411
25	0.569
30	0.706
35	0.814
40	0.891
45	0.941
50	0.970
55	0.986
60	0.994
65	0.998
70	0.999

TABLE 3.2 Estimates of Slopes on the Probability Curve

Midpoint of Interval (x)	Change (Slope $\Delta y/\Delta x$)
2.5	0.0054
7.5	0.0180
12.5	0.0272
17.5	0.0316
22.5	0.0316
27.5	0.0274
32.5	0.0216
37.5	0.0154
42.5	0.0100
47.5	0.0058
52.5	0.0032
57.5	0.0016
62.5	0.0008
67.5	0.0002

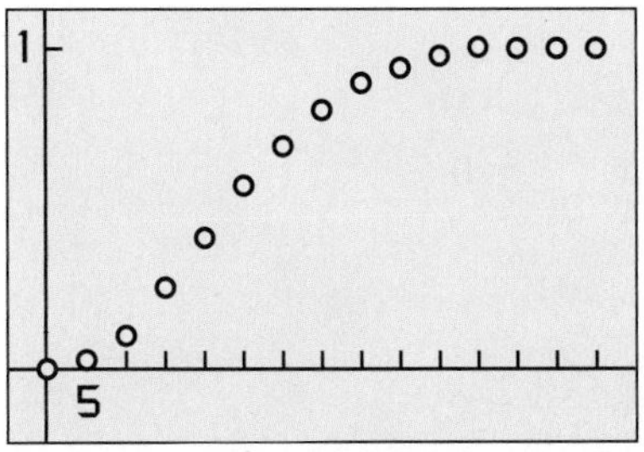

[–5, 75] by [–0.2, 1.1]

Figure 3.6 Scatter plot of the probabilities (y) of shared birthdays among x people, for $x = 0, 5, 10, \ldots, 70$. (Example 5)

A scatter plot of the data in Table 3.1 is shown in Figure 3.6.

Notice that the probabilities grow slowly at first, then faster, then much more slowly past $x = 45$. At which x are they growing the fastest? To answer the question, we need the graph of the derivative.

Using the data in Table 3.1, we compute the slopes between successive points on the probability plot. For example, from $x = 0$ to $x = 5$ the slope is

$$\frac{0.027 - 0}{5 - 0} = 0.0054.$$

We make a new table showing the slopes, beginning with slope 0.0054 on the interval $[0, 5]$ (Table 3.2). A logical x-value to use to represent the interval is its midpoint, 2.5.

continued

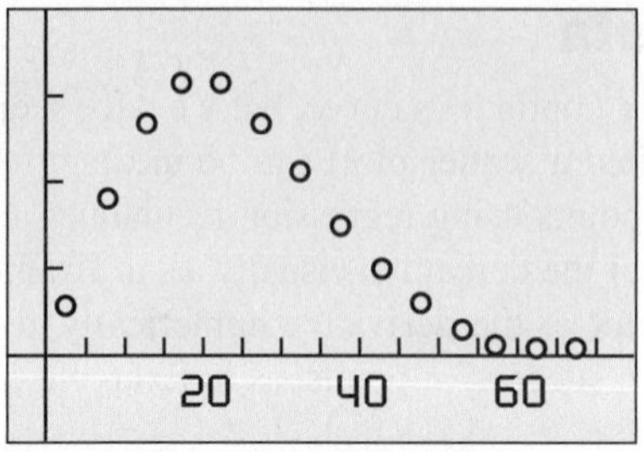

[–5, 75] by [–0.01, 0.04]

Figure 3.7 A scatter plot of the derivative data in Table 3.2. (Example 5)

A scatter plot of the derivative data in Table 3.2 is shown in Figure 3.7.

From the derivative plot, we can see that the rate of change peaks near $x = 20$. You can impress your friends with your "psychic powers" by predicting a shared birthday in a room of just 25 people (since you will be right about 57% of the time), but the derivative warns you to be cautious: A few less people can make quite a difference. On the other hand, going from 40 people to 100 people will not improve your chances much at all.

Now Try Exercise 29.

Generating shared birthday probabilities: If you know a little about probability, you might try generating the probabilities in Table 3.1. Extending the Idea Exercise 45 at the end of this section shows how to generate them on a calculator.

One-Sided Derivatives

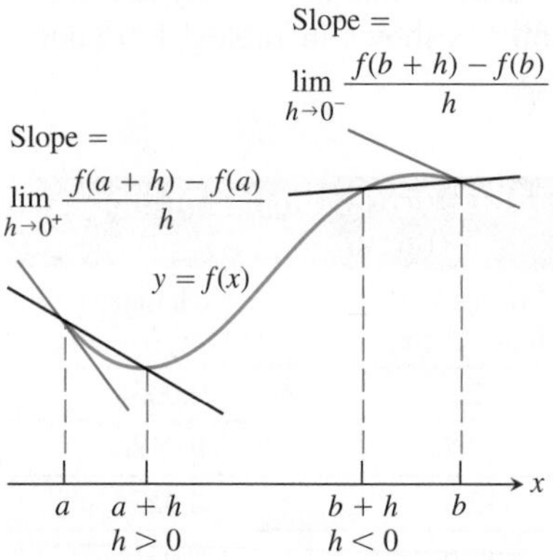

Figure 3.8 Derivatives at endpoints are one-sided limits.

A function $y = f(x)$ is **differentiable on a closed interval $[a, b]$** if it has a derivative at every interior point of the interval, and if the limits

$$\lim_{h\to 0^+} \frac{f(a+h) - f(a)}{h} \quad \text{[the \textbf{right-hand derivative at } \boldsymbol{a}\text{]}}$$

$$\lim_{h\to 0^-} \frac{f(b+h) - f(b)}{h} \quad \text{[the \textbf{left-hand derivative at } \boldsymbol{b}\text{]}}$$

exist at the endpoints. In the right-hand derivative, h is positive and $a + h$ approaches a from the right. In the left-hand derivative, h is negative and $b + h$ approaches b from the left (Figure 3.8).

Right-hand and left-hand derivatives may be defined at any point of a function's domain.

The usual relationship between one-sided and two-sided limits holds for derivatives. Theorem 3, Section 2.1, allows us to conclude that a function has a (two-sided) derivative at a point if and only if the function's right-hand and left-hand derivatives are defined and equal at that point.

EXAMPLE 6 One-Sided Derivatives Can Differ at a Point

Show that the following function has left-hand and right-hand derivatives at $x = 0$, but no derivative there (Figure 3.9).

$$y = \begin{cases} x^2, & x \le 0 \\ 2x, & x > 0 \end{cases}$$

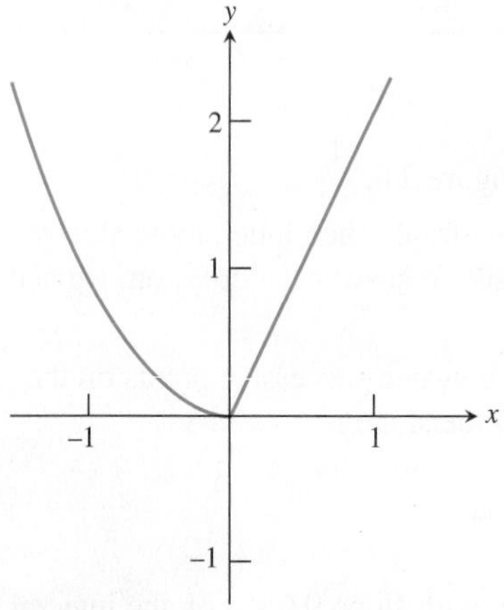

Figure 3.9 A function with different one-sided derivatives at $x = 0$. (Example 6)

SOLUTION

We verify the existence of the left-hand derivative:

$$\lim_{h\to 0^-} \frac{(0+h)^2 - 0^2}{h} = \lim_{h\to 0^-} \frac{h^2}{h} = 0.$$

We verify the existence of the right-hand derivative:

$$\lim_{h\to 0^+} \frac{2(0+h) - 0^2}{h} = \lim_{h\to 0^+} \frac{2h}{h} = 2.$$

Since the left-hand derivative equals zero and the right-hand derivative equals 2, the derivatives are not equal at $x = 0$. The function does not have a derivative at 0.

Now Try Exercise 31.

Quick Review 3.1 *(For help, go to Sections 2.1 and 2.4.)*

Exercise numbers with a gray background indicate problems that the authors have designed to be solved *without a calculator.*

In Exercises 1–4, evaluate the indicated limit algebraically.

1. $\lim_{h \to 0} \dfrac{(2+h)^2 - 4}{h}$

2. $\lim_{x \to 2^+} \dfrac{x+3}{2}$

3. $\lim_{y \to 0^-} \dfrac{|y|}{y}$

4. $\lim_{x \to 4} \dfrac{2x - 8}{\sqrt{x} - 2}$

5. Find the slope of the line tangent to the parabola $y = x^2 + 1$ at its vertex.

6. By considering the graph of $f(x) = x^3 - 3x^2 + 2$, find the intervals on which f is increasing.

In Exercises 7–10, let

$$f(x) = \begin{cases} x + 2, & x \le 1 \\ (x-1)^2, & x > 1. \end{cases}$$

7. Find $\lim_{x \to 1^+} f(x)$ and $\lim_{x \to 1^-} f(x)$.

8. Find $\lim_{h \to 0^+} f(1 + h)$.

9. Does $\lim_{x \to 1} f(x)$ exist? Explain.

10. Is f continuous? Explain.

Section 3.1 Exercises

In Exercises 1–4, use the definition

$$f'(a) = \lim_{h \to 0} \frac{f(a+h) - f(a)}{h}$$

to find the derivative of the given function at the given value of a.

1. $f(x) = 1/x,\ a = 2$

2. $f(x) = x^2 + 4,\ a = 1$

3. $f(x) = 3 - x^2,\ a = -1$

4. $f(x) = x^3 + x,\ a = 0$

In Exercises 5–8, use the definition

$$f'(a) = \lim_{x \to a} \frac{f(x) - f(a)}{x - a}$$

to find the derivative of the given function at the given value of a.

5. $f(x) = 1/x,\ a = 2$

6. $f(x) = x^2 + 4,\ a = 1$

7. $f(x) = \sqrt{x + 1},\ a = 3$

8. $f(x) = 2x + 3,\ a = -1$

9. Find $f'(x)$ if $f(x) = 3x - 12$.

10. Find dy/dx if $y = 7x$.

11. Find $\dfrac{d}{dx}(x^2)$.

12. Find $\dfrac{d}{dx} f(x)$ if $f(x) = 3x^2$.

In Exercises 13–16, match the graph of the function with the graph of the derivative shown here:

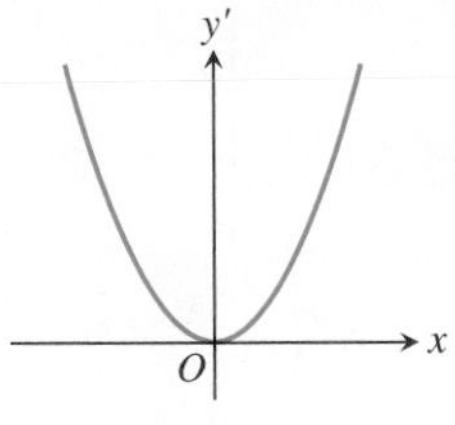

(a)

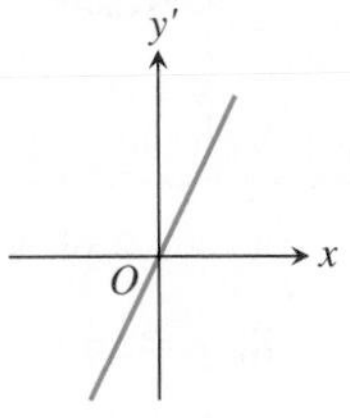

(b)

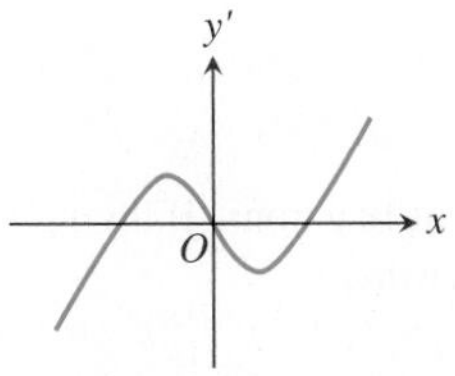

(c)

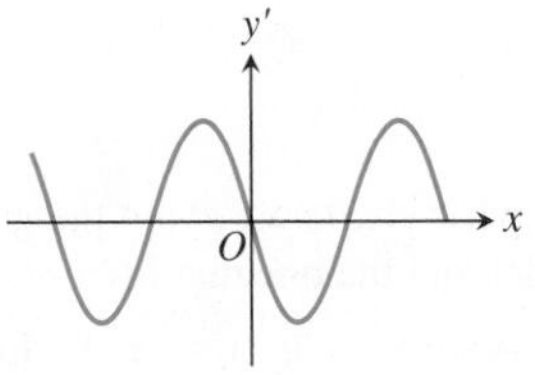

(d)

13.

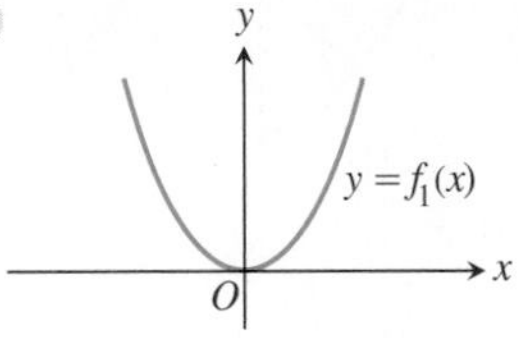

14.

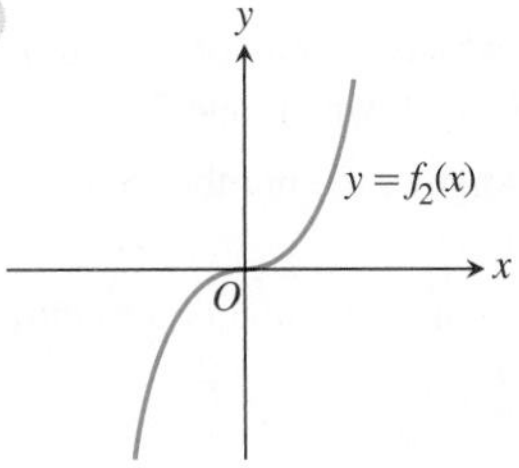

15.

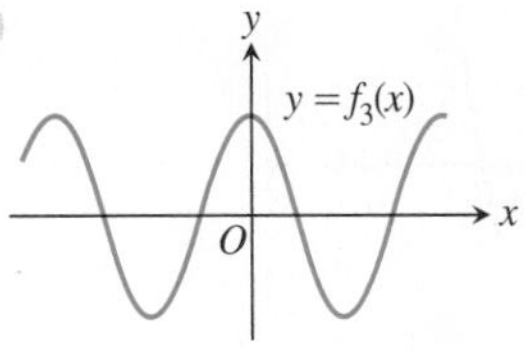

16.

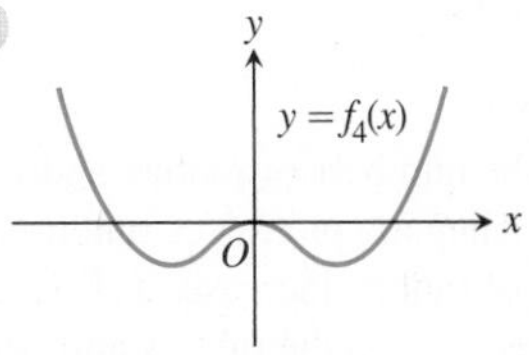

17. If $f(2) = 3$ and $f'(2) = 5$, find an equation of **(a)** the *tangent* line, and **(b)** the *normal* line to the graph of $y = f(x)$ at the point where $x = 2$.
[*Hint:* Recall that the normal line is perpendicular to the tangent line.]

18. Find the derivative of the function $y = 2x^2 - 13x + 5$ and use it to find an equation of the line tangent to the curve at $x = 3$.

19. Find the lines that are **(a)** tangent and **(b)** normal to the curve $y = x^3$ at the point $(1, 1)$.

20. Find the lines that are (a) tangent and **(b)** normal to the curve $y = \sqrt{x}$ at $x = 4$.

21. ***Daylight in Fairbanks*** The viewing window below shows the number of hours of daylight in Fairbanks, Alaska, on each day for a typical 365-day period from January 1 to December 31. Answer the following questions by estimating slopes on the graph in hours per day. For the purposes of estimation, assume that each month has 30 days.

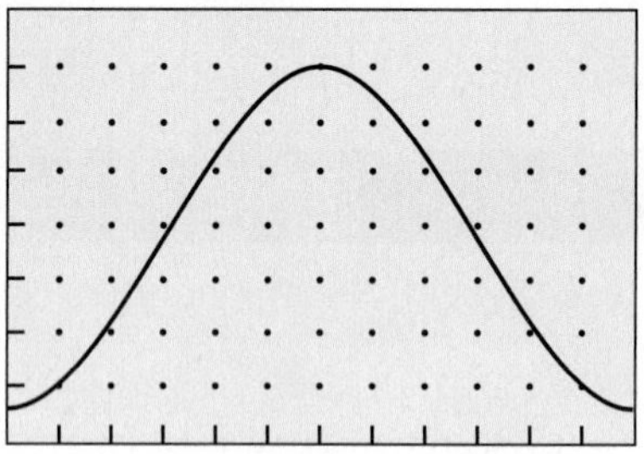

[0, 365] by [0, 24]

(a) On about what date is the amount of daylight increasing at the fastest rate? What is that rate?

(b) Do there appear to be days on which the rate of change in the amount of daylight is zero? If so, which ones?

(c) On what dates is the rate of change in the number of daylight hours positive? negative?

22. ***Graphing f′ from f*** Given the graph of the function *f* below, sketch a graph of the *derivative* of *f*.

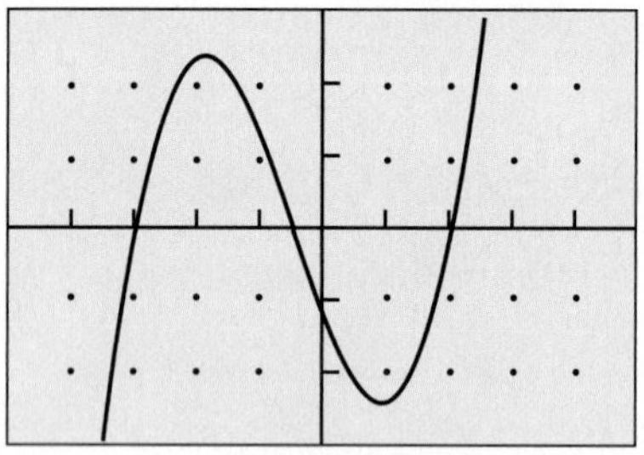

[–5, 5] by [–3, 3]

23. The graphs in Figure 3.10a show the numbers of rabbits and foxes in a small arctic population. They are plotted as functions of time for 200 days. The number of rabbits increases at first, as the rabbits reproduce. But the foxes prey on the rabbits and, as the number of foxes increases, the rabbit population levels off and then drops. Figure 3.10b shows the graph of the derivative of the rabbit population. We made it by plotting slopes, as in Example 3.

(a) What is the value of the derivative of the rabbit population in Figure 3.10 when the number of rabbits is largest? smallest?

(b) What is the size of the rabbit population in Figure 3.10 when its derivative is largest? smallest?

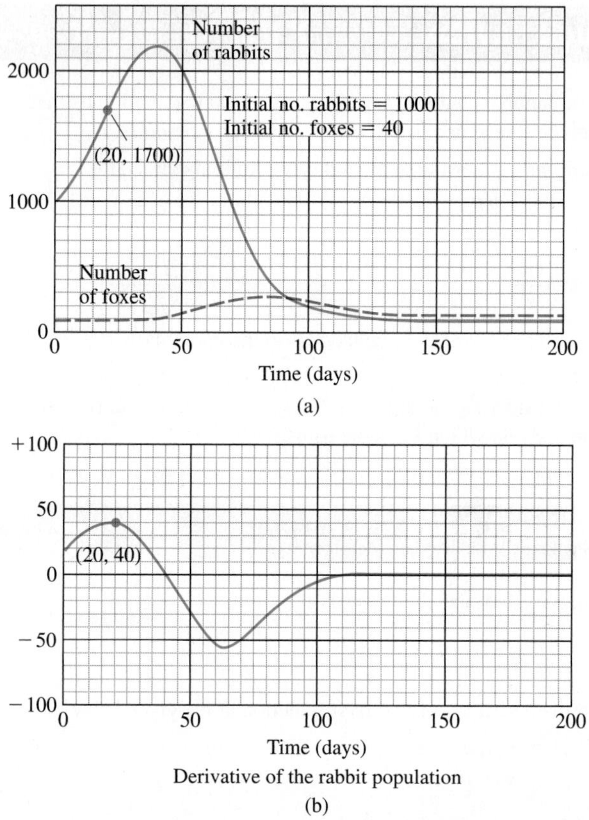

Figure 3.10 Rabbits and foxes in an arctic predator-prey food chain. *Source: Differentiation* by W. U. Walton et al., Project CALC, Education Development Center, Inc., Newton, MA, 1975, p. 86.

24. Shown below is the graph of $f(x) = x \ln x - x$. From what you know about the graphs of functions (i) through (v), pick out the one that is the *derivative* of *f* for $x > 0$.

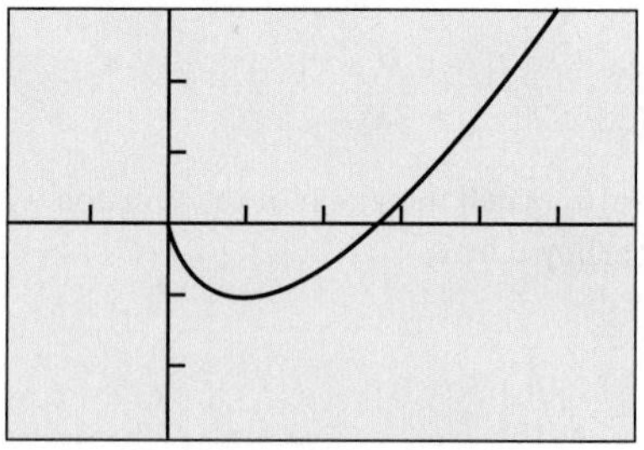

[–2, 6] by [–3, 3]

i. $y = \sin x$ **ii.** $y = \ln x$ **iii.** $y = \sqrt{x}$
iv. $y = x^2$ **v.** $y = 3x - 1$

25. From what you know about the graphs of functions (i) through (v), pick out the one that is *its own derivative.*

i. $y = \sin x$ **ii.** $y = x$ **iii.** $y = \sqrt{x}$
iv. $y = e^x$ **v.** $y = x^2$

26. The graph of the function $y = f(x)$ shown here is made of line segments joined end to end.

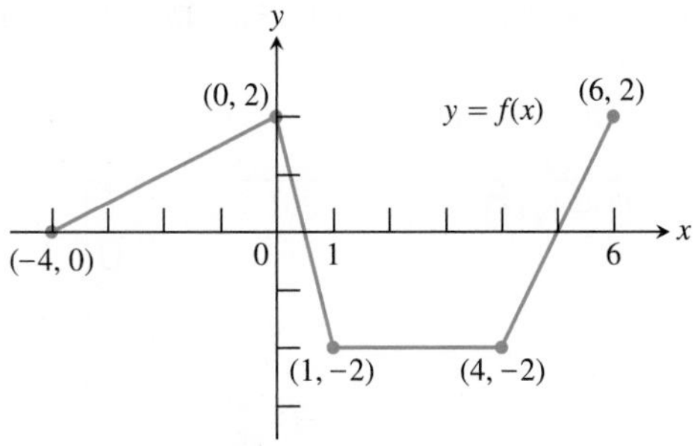

(a) Graph the function's derivative.

(b) At what values of x between $x = -4$ and $x = 6$ is the function not differentiable?

27. *Graphing f from f′* Sketch the graph of a continuous function f with $f(0) = -1$ and

$$f'(x) = \begin{cases} 1, & x < -1 \\ -2, & x > -1. \end{cases}$$

28. *Graphing f from f′* Sketch the graph of a continuous function f with $f(0) = 1$ and

$$f'(x) = \begin{cases} 2, & x < 2 \\ -1, & x > 2. \end{cases}$$

In Exercises 29 and 30, use the data to answer the questions.

29. *A Downhill Skier* Table 3.3 gives the approximate distance traveled by a downhill skier after t seconds for $0 \le t \le 10$. Use the method of Example 5 to sketch a graph of the derivative; then answer the following questions:

(a) What does the derivative represent?

(b) In what units would the derivative be measured?

(c) Can you guess an equation of the derivative by considering its graph?

TABLE 3.3 Skiing Distances

Time t (seconds)	Distance Traveled (feet)
0	0
1	3.3
2	13.3
3	29.9
4	53.2
5	83.2
6	119.8
7	163.0
8	212.9
9	269.5
10	332.7

30. *A Whitewater River* Bear Creek, a Georgia river known to kayaking enthusiasts, drops more than 770 feet over one stretch of 3.24 miles. By reading a contour map, one can estimate the elevations (y) at various distances (x) downriver from the start of the kayaking route (Table 3.4).

TABLE 3.4 Elevations Along Bear Creek

Distance Downriver (miles)	River Elevation (feet)
0.00	1577
0.56	1512
0.92	1448
1.19	1384
1.30	1319
1.39	1255
1.57	1191
1.74	1126
1.98	1062
2.18	998
2.41	933
2.64	869
3.24	805

(a) Sketch a graph of elevation (y) as a function of distance downriver (x).

(b) Use the technique of Example 5 to get an approximate graph of the derivative, dy/dx.

(c) The average change in elevation over a given distance is called a *gradient*. In this problem, what units of measure would be appropriate for a gradient?

(d) In this problem, what units of measure would be appropriate for the derivative?

(e) How would you identify the most dangerous section of the river (ignoring rocks) by analyzing the graph in (a)? Explain.

(f) How would you identify the most dangerous section of the river by analyzing the graph in (b)? Explain.

31. Using one-sided derivatives, show that the function

$$f(x) = \begin{cases} x^2 + x, & x \le 1 \\ 3x - 2, & x > 1 \end{cases}$$

does not have a derivative at $x = 1$.

32. Using one-sided derivatives, show that the function

$$f(x) = \begin{cases} x^3, & x \le 1 \\ 3x, & x > 1 \end{cases}$$

does not have a derivative at $x = 1$.

33. Writing to Learn Graph $y = \sin x$ and $y = \cos x$ in the same viewing window. Which function could be the derivative of the other? Defend your answer in terms of the behavior of the graphs.

34. In Example 2 of this section we showed that the derivative of $y = \sqrt{x}$ is a function with domain $(0, \infty)$. However, the function $y = \sqrt{x}$ itself has domain $[0, \infty)$, so it could have a right-hand derivative at $x = 0$. Prove that it does not.

35. Writing to Learn Use the concept of the derivative to define what it might mean for two parabolas to be parallel. Construct equations for two such parallel parabolas and graph them. Are the parabolas "everywhere equidistant," and if so, in what sense?

Standardized Test Questions

36. True or False If $f(x) = x^2 + x$, then $f'(x)$ exists for every real number x. Justify your answer.

37. True or False If the left-hand derivative and the right-hand derivative of f exist at $x = a$, then $f'(a)$ exists. Justify your answer.

38. Multiple Choice Let $f(x) = 4 - 3x$. Which of the following is equal to $f'(-1)$?

(A) -7 (B) 7 (C) -3 (D) 3 (E) does not exist

39. Multiple Choice Let $f(x) = 1 - 3x^2$. Which of the following is equal to $f'(1)$?

(A) -6 (B) -5 (C) 5 (D) 6 (E) does not exist

In Exercises 40 and 41, let

$$f(x) = \begin{cases} x^2 - 1, & x < 0 \\ 2x - 1, & x \geq 0. \end{cases}$$

40. Multiple Choice Which of the following is equal to the left-hand derivative of f at $x = 0$?

(A) -2 (B) 0 (C) 2 (D) ∞ (E) $-\infty$

41. Multiple Choice Which of the following is equal to the right-hand derivative of f at $x = 0$?

(A) -2 (B) 0 (C) 2 (D) ∞ (E) $-\infty$

Explorations

42. Let $f(x) = \begin{cases} x^2, & x \leq 1 \\ 2x, & x > 1. \end{cases}$

(a) Find $f'(x)$ for $x < 1$.

(b) Find $f'(x)$ for $x > 1$.

(c) Find $\lim_{x \to 1^-} f'(x)$.

(d) Find $\lim_{x \to 1^+} f'(x)$.

(e) Does $\lim_{x \to 1} f'(x)$ exist? Explain.

(f) Use the definition to find the left-hand derivative of f at $x = 1$ if it exists.

(g) Use the definition to find the right-hand derivative of f at $x = 1$ if it exists.

(h) Does $f'(1)$ exist? Explain.

43. Group Activity Using graphing calculators, have each person in your group do the following:

(a) pick two numbers a and b between 1 and 10;

(b) graph the function $y = (x - a)(x + b)$;

(c) graph the *derivative* of your function (it will be a line with slope 2);

(d) find the y-intercept of your derivative graph.

(e) Compare your answers and determine a simple way to predict the y-intercept, given the values of a and b. Test your result.

Extending the Ideas

44. Find the unique value of k that makes the function

$$f(x) = \begin{cases} x^3, & x \leq 1 \\ 3x + k, & x > 1 \end{cases}$$

differentiable at $x = 1$.

45. *Generating the Birthday Probabilities* Example 5 of this section concerns the probability that, in a group of n people, at least two people will share a common birthday. You can generate these probabilities on your calculator for values of n from 1 to 365.

Step 1: Set the values of N and P to zero:

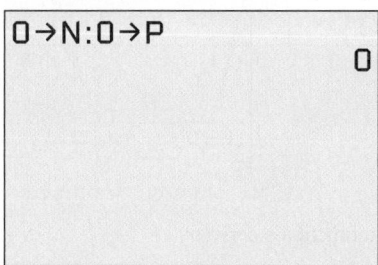

```
0→N:0→P
                    0
```

Step 2: Type in this single, multi-step command:

```
N+1→N:1–(1–P)(366
–N)/365→P: {N,P}
```

Now each time you press the ENTER key, the command will print a new value of N (the number of people in the room) alongside P (the probability that at least two of them share a common birthday):

```
                 {1 0}
      {2 .002739726}
     {3 .0082041659}
     {4 .0163559125}
     {5 .0271355737}
     {6 .0404624836}
     {7 .0562357031}
```

If you have some experience with probability, try to answer the following questions without looking at the table:

(a) If there are three people in the room, what is the probability that they all have *different* birthdays? (Assume that there are 365 possible birthdays, all of them equally likely.)

(b) If there are three people in the room, what is the probability that at least two of them share a common birthday?

(c) Explain how you can use the answer in part (b) to find the probability of a shared birthday when there are *four* people in the room. (This is how the calculator statement in Step 2 generates the probabilities.)

(d) Is it reasonable to assume that all calendar dates are equally likely birthdays? Explain your answer.

3.2 Differentiability

What you will learn about . . .

- How $f'(a)$ Might Fail to Exist
- Differentiability Implies Local Linearity
- Numerical Derivatives on a Calculator
- Differentiability Implies Continuity
- Intermediate Value Theorem for Derivatives

and why . . .

Graphs of differentiable functions can be approximated by their tangent lines at points where the derivative exists.

How $f'(a)$ Might Fail to Exist

A function will not have a derivative at a point $P(a, f(a))$ where the slopes of the secant lines,

$$\frac{f(x) - f(a)}{x - a},$$

fail to approach a limit as x approaches a. Figures 3.11–3.14 illustrate four different instances where this occurs. For example, a function whose graph is otherwise smooth will fail to have a derivative at a point where the graph has

1. a *corner*, where the one-sided derivatives differ; Example: $f(x) = |x|$

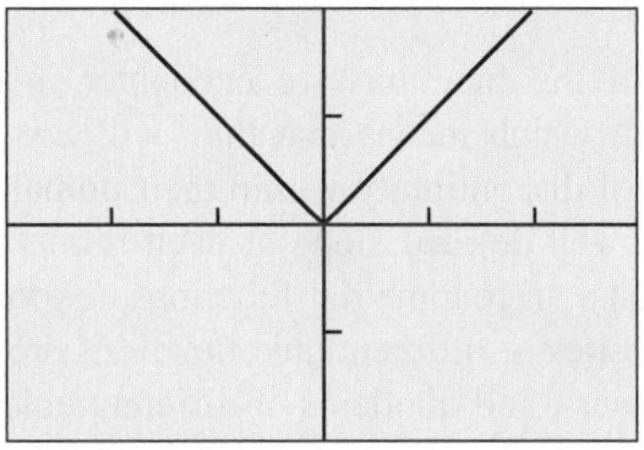

[–3, 3] by [–2, 2]

Figure 3.11 There is a "corner" at $x = 0$.

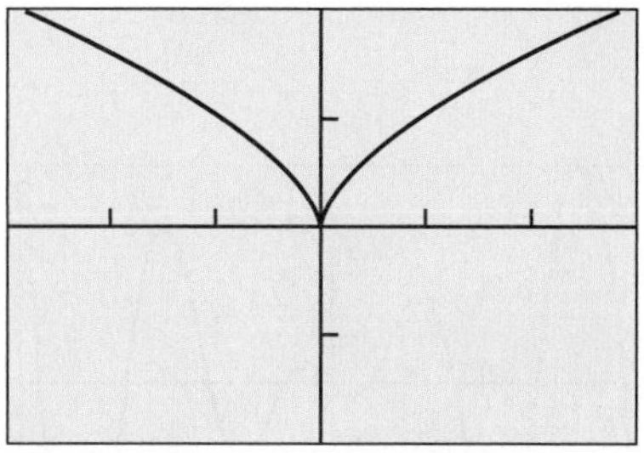

[–3, 3] by [–2, 2]

Figure 3.12 There is a "cusp" at $x = 0$.

2. a *cusp*, where the slopes of the secant lines approach ∞ from one side and $-\infty$ from the other (an extreme case of a corner); Example: $f(x) = x^{2/3}$

3. a *vertical tangent*, where the slopes of the secant lines approach either ∞ or $-\infty$ from both sides (in this example, ∞); Example: $f(x) = \sqrt[3]{x}$

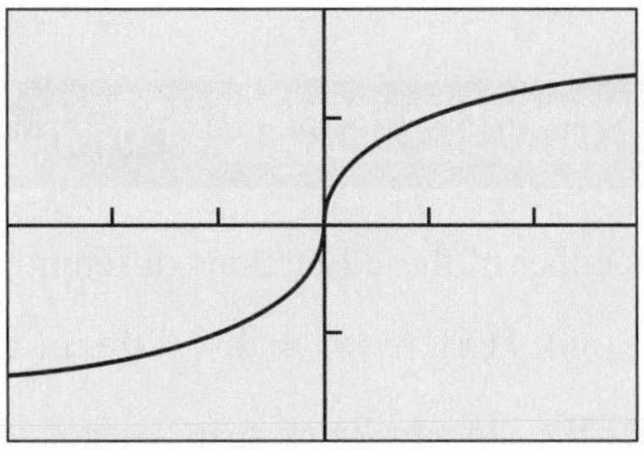

[–3, 3] by [–2, 2]

Figure 3.13 There is a vertical tangent line at $x = 0$.

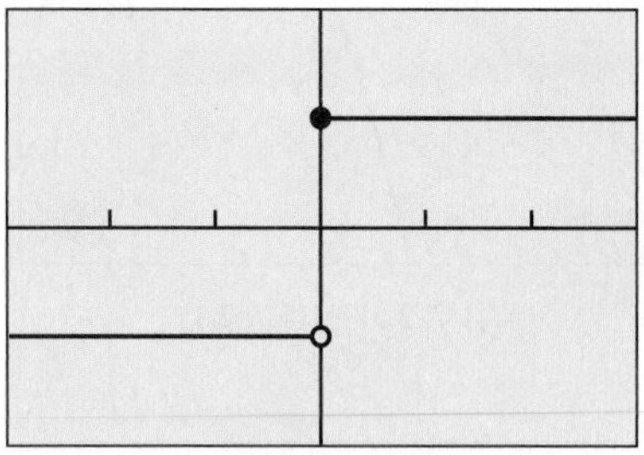

[–3, 3] by [–2, 2]

Figure 3.14 There is a discontinuity at $x = 0$.

4. a *discontinuity* (which will cause one or both of the one-sided derivatives to be nonexistent). Example: The *Unit Step Function*

$$U(x) = \begin{cases} -1, & x < 0 \\ 1, & x \geq 0 \end{cases}$$

In this example, the left-hand derivative fails to exist:

$$\lim_{h \to 0^-} \frac{U(0 + h) - U(0)}{h} = \lim_{h \to 0^-} \frac{(-1) - (1)}{h} = \lim_{h \to 0^-} \frac{-2}{h} = \infty.$$

How rough can the graph of a continuous function be?

The graph of the absolute value function fails to be differentiable at a single point. If you graph $y = \sin^{-1}(\sin(x))$ on your calculator, you will see a continuous function with an *infinite* number of points of nondifferentiability. But can a continuous function fail to be differentiable at *every* point?

The answer, surprisingly enough, is yes, as Karl Weierstrass showed in 1872. One of his formulas (there are many like it) was

$$f(x) = \sum_{n=0}^{\infty} \left(\frac{2}{3}\right)^n \cos(9^n \pi x),$$

a formula that expresses f as an infinite (but converging) sum of cosines with increasingly higher frequencies. By adding wiggles to wiggles infinitely many times, so to speak, the formula produces a function whose graph is too bumpy in the limit to have a tangent anywhere!

Later in this section we will prove a theorem that states that a function *must* be continuous at a to be differentiable at a. This theorem would provide a quick and easy verification that U is not differentiable at $x = 0$.

EXAMPLE 1 Finding Where a Function Is Not Differentiable

Find all points in the domain of $f(x) = |x - 2| + 3$ where f is not differentiable.

SOLUTION

Think graphically! The graph of this function is the same as that of $y = |x|$, translated 2 units to the right and 3 units up. This puts the corner at the point $(2, 3)$, so this function is not differentiable at $x = 2$.

At every other point, the graph is (locally) a straight line and f has derivative $+1$ or -1 (again, just like $y = |x|$). ***Now Try Exercise 1.***

Most of the functions we encounter in calculus are differentiable wherever they are defined, which means that they will *not* have corners, cusps, vertical tangent lines, or points of discontinuity within their domains. Their graphs will be unbroken and smooth, with a well-defined slope at each point. Polynomials are differentiable, as are rational functions, trigonometric functions, exponential functions, and logarithmic functions. Composites of differentiable functions are differentiable, and so are sums, products, integer powers, and quotients of differentiable functions, where defined. We will see why all of this is true as Chapters 3 and 4 unfold.

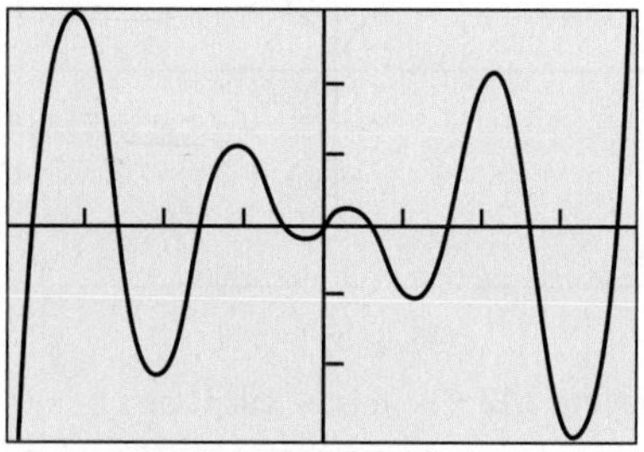

[–4, 4] by [–3, 3]
(a)

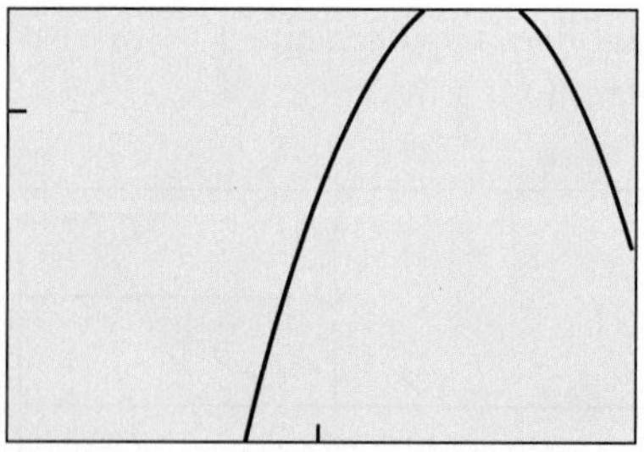

[1.7, 2.3] by [1.7, 2.1]
(b)

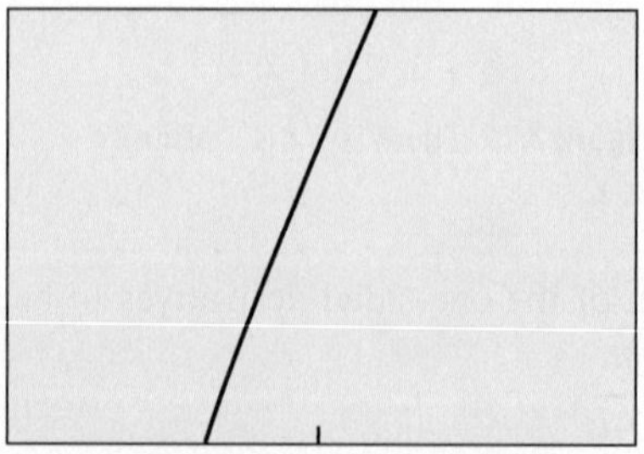

[1.93, 2.07] by [1.85, 1.95]
(c)

Figure 3.15 Three different views of the differentiable function $f(x) = x \cos(3x)$. We have zoomed in here at the point $(2, 1.9)$.

Differentiability Implies Local Linearity

A good way to think of differentiable functions is that they are **locally linear;** that is, a function that is differentiable at a closely resembles its own tangent line very close to a. In the jargon of graphing calculators, differentiable curves will "straighten out" when we zoom in on them at a point of differentiability. (See Figure 3.15.)

EXPLORATION 1 Zooming in to "See" Differentiability

Is either of these functions differentiable at $x = 0$?

(a) $f(x) = |x| + 1$ **(b)** $g(x) = \sqrt{x^2 + 0.0001} + 0.99$

1. We already know that f is not differentiable at $x = 0$; its graph has a corner there. Graph f and zoom in at the point $(0, 1)$ several times. Does the corner show signs of straightening out?
2. Now do the same thing with g. Does the graph of g show signs of straightening out? We will learn a quick way to differentiate g in Section 3.6, but for now suffice it to say that it *is* differentiable at $x = 0$, and in fact has a horizontal tangent there.
3. How many zooms does it take before the graph of g looks exactly like a horizontal line?
4. Now graph f and g *together* in a standard square viewing window. They appear to be identical until you start zooming in. The differentiable function eventually straightens out, while the nondifferentiable function remains impressively unchanged.

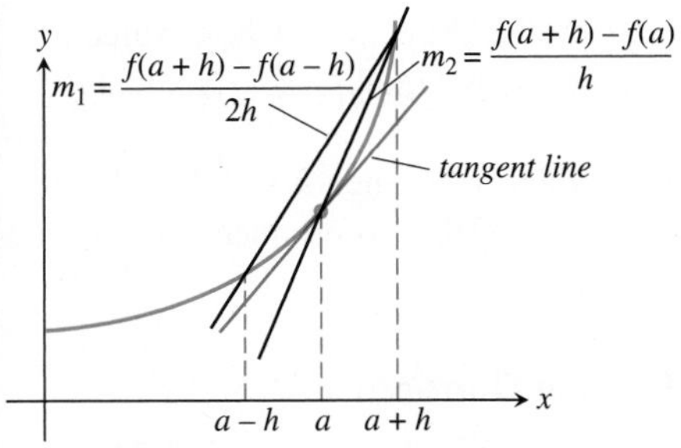

Figure 3.16 The symmetric difference quotient (slope m_1) usually gives a better approximation of the derivative for a given value of h than does the regular difference quotient (slope m_2), which is why the symmetric difference quotient is used in the numerical derivative.

Numerical Derivatives on a Calculator

For small values of h, the difference quotient

$$\frac{f(a+h) - f(a)}{h}$$

is often a good numerical approximation of $f'(a)$. However, as suggested by Figure 3.16, the same value of h will usually yield a *better* approximation of $f'(a)$ if we use the **symmetric difference quotient**

$$\frac{f(a+h) - f(a-h)}{2h}$$

to compute the slope between two nearby points on opposite sides of a. In fact, this approximation (which calculators can easily compute) is close enough to be used as a substitute for the derivative at a point in most applications.

DEFINITION The Numerical Derivative

The **numerical derivative of f at a,** which we will denote NDER $(f(x), a)$, is the *number*

$$\frac{f(a+0.001) - f(a-0.001)}{0.002}.$$

The **numerical derivative of f,** which we will denote NDER $(f(x), x)$, is the *function*

$$\frac{f(x+0.001) - f(x-0.001)}{0.002}.$$

Some calculators have a name for the numerical derivative, like nDeriv$(f(x), x, a)$, which is similar to the one we use in the definition. Others use the Leibniz notation for the actual derivative at a:

$$\frac{d}{dx}(f(x))\bigg|_{x=a}.$$

We do not want to suggest that the numerical derivative and the derivative are the same, so we will continue to use our generic term NDER when referring to the numerical derivative. Thus, in this textbook,

$$\text{NDER}(f(x), a) = \frac{f(a+0.001) - f(a-0.001)}{0.002},$$

while

$$\frac{d}{dx}(f(x))\bigg|_{x=a} = \lim_{h \to 0} \frac{f(a+h) - f(a)}{h}.$$

Be aware, however, that $\frac{d}{dx}(f(x))\bigg|_{x=a}$ on your calculator might well refer to the numerical derivative.

EXAMPLE 2 Computing a Numerical Derivative

If $f(x) = x^3$, use the numerical derivative to approximate $f'(2)$.

SOLUTION

$$f'(2) = \frac{d}{dx}(x^3)\bigg|_{x=2} \approx \text{NDER}(x^3, 2) = \frac{(2.001)^3 - (1.999)^3}{0.002} = 12.000001.$$

Now Try Exercise 17.

In Example 1 of Section 3.1, we found the derivative of x^3 to be $3x^2$, whose value at $x = 2$ is $3(2)^2 = 12$. The numerical derivative is accurate to 5 decimal places. Not bad for the push of a button.

Example 2 gives dramatic evidence that NDER is very accurate when $h = 0.001$. Such accuracy is usually the case, although it is also possible for NDER to produce some surprisingly inaccurate results, as in Example 3.

EXAMPLE 3 Fooling the Symmetric Difference Quotient

Compute NDER $(|x|, 0)$, the numerical derivative of $|x|$ at $x = 0$.

SOLUTION

We saw at the start of this section that $y = |x|$ is not differentiable at $x = 0$, since its right-hand and left-hand derivatives at $x = 0$ are not the same. Nonetheless,

$$\begin{aligned}\text{NDER}(|x|, 0) &= \frac{|0 + 0.001| - |0 - 0.001|}{2(0.001)} \\ &= \frac{0.001 - 0.001}{0.002} \\ &= 0\end{aligned}$$

Even in the limit,

$$\lim_{h \to 0} \frac{|0 + h| - |0 - h|}{2h} = \lim_{h \to 0} \frac{0}{2h} = 0.$$

This proves that the derivative *cannot* be defined as the limit of the symmetric difference quotient. The symmetric difference quotient, which works on opposite sides of 0, has no chance of detecting the corner! ***Now Try Exercise 23.***

In light of Example 3, it is worth repeating here that the symmetric difference quotient actually does approach $f'(a)$ *when* $f'(a)$ *exists,* and in fact approximates it quite well (as in Example 2).

EXPLORATION 2 Looking at the Symmetric Difference Quotient Analytically

Let $f(x) = x^2$ and let $h = 0.01$.

1. Find
$$\frac{f(10 + h) - f(10)}{h}.$$
How close is it to $f'(10)$?
2. Find
$$\frac{f(10 + h) - f(10 - h)}{2h}.$$
How close is it to $f'(10)$?
3. Repeat this comparison for $f(x) = x^3$.

EXAMPLE 4 Graphing a Derivative Using NDER

Let $f(x) = \ln x$. Use NDER to graph $y = f'(x)$. Can you guess what function $f'(x)$ is by analyzing its graph?

continued

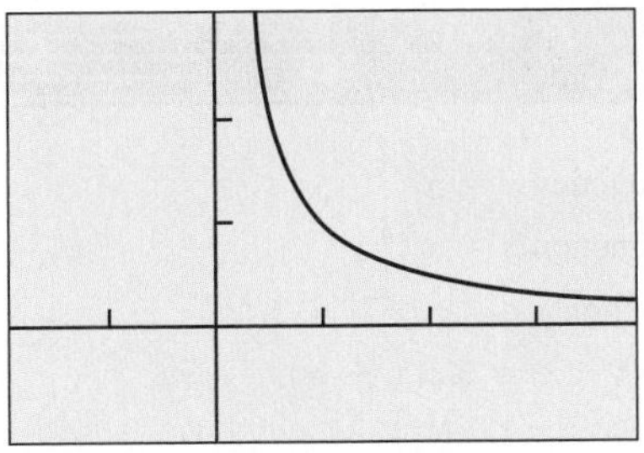

[–2, 4] by [–1, 3]

(a)

X	Y1
.1	10
.2	5
.3	3.3333
.4	2.5
.5	2
.6	1.6667
.7	1.4286

X = .1

(b)

Figure 3.17 (a) The graph of NDER $(\ln(x), x)$ and (b) a table of values. What graph could this be? (Example 4)

SOLUTION

The graph is shown in Figure 3.17a. The shape of the graph suggests, and the table of values in Figure 3.17b supports, the conjecture that this is the graph of $y = 1/x$. We will prove in Section 3.9 (using analytic methods) that this is indeed the case.

Now Try Exercise 27.

Differentiability Implies Continuity

We began this section with a look at the typical ways that a function could fail to have a derivative at a point. As one example, we indicated graphically that a discontinuity in the graph of f would cause one or both of the one-sided derivatives to be nonexistent. It is actually not difficult to give an analytic proof that continuity is an essential condition for the derivative to exist, so we include that as a theorem here.

THEOREM 1 Differentiability Implies Continuity

If f has a derivative at $x = a$, then f is continuous at $x = a$.

Proof Our task is to show that $\lim_{x \to a} f(x) = f(a)$, or, equivalently, that

$$\lim_{x \to a}[f(x) - f(a)] = 0.$$

Using the Limit Product Rule (and noting that $x - a$ is not zero), we can write

$$\begin{aligned}
\lim_{x \to a}[f(x) - f(a)] &= \lim_{x \to a}\left[(x - a)\frac{f(x) - f(a)}{x - a}\right] \\
&= \lim_{x \to a}(x - a) \cdot \lim_{x \to a}\frac{f(x) - f(a)}{x - a} \\
&= 0 \cdot f'(a) \\
&= 0.
\end{aligned}$$

■

The converse of Theorem 1 is false, as we have already seen. A continuous function might have a corner, a cusp, or a vertical tangent line, and hence not be differentiable at a given point.

Intermediate Value Theorem for Derivatives

Not every function can be a derivative. A derivative must have the Intermediate Value Property, as stated in the following theorem (the proof of which can be found in advanced texts).

THEOREM 2 Intermediate Value Theorem for Derivatives

If a and b are any two points in an interval on which f is differentiable, then f' takes on every value between $f'(a)$ and $f'(b)$.

EXAMPLE 5 Applying Theorem 2

Does any function have the Unit Step Function (see Figure 3.14) as its derivative?

SOLUTION

No. Choose some $a < 0$ and some $b > 0$. Then $U(a) = -1$ and $U(b) = 1$, but U does not take on any value between -1 and 1.

Now Try Exercise 37.

The question of when a function is a derivative of some function is one of the central questions in all of calculus. The answer, found by Newton and Leibniz, would revolutionize the world of mathematics. We will see what that answer is when we reach Chapter 6.

Quick Review 3.2 (For help, go to Sections 1.2 and 2.1.)

Exercise numbers with a gray background indicate problems that the authors have designed to be solved *without a calculator.*

In Exercises 1–5, tell whether the limit could be used to define $f'(a)$ (assuming that f is differentiable at a).

1. $\lim_{h\to 0} \dfrac{f(a+h)-f(a)}{h}$

2. $\lim_{h\to 0} \dfrac{f(a+h)-f(h)}{h}$

3. $\lim_{x\to a} \dfrac{f(x)-f(a)}{x-a}$

4. $\lim_{x\to a} \dfrac{f(a)-f(x)}{a-x}$

5. $\lim_{h\to 0} \dfrac{f(a+h)+f(a-h)}{h}$

6. Find the domain of the function $y = x^{4/3}$.

7. Find the domain of the function $y = x^{3/4}$.

8. Find the range of the function $y = |x-2| + 3$.

9. Find the slope of the line $y - 5 = 3.2(x + \pi)$.

10. If $f(x) = 5x$, find

$$\frac{f(3+0.001) - f(3-0.001)}{0.002}.$$

Section 3.2 Exercises

In Exercises 1–4, compare the right-hand and left-hand derivatives to show that the function is not differentiable at the point P. Find all points where f is not differentiable.

1.

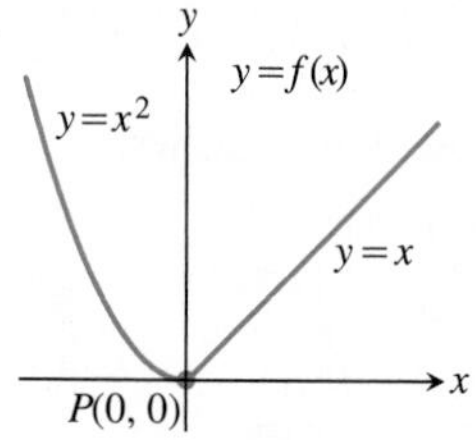

2.

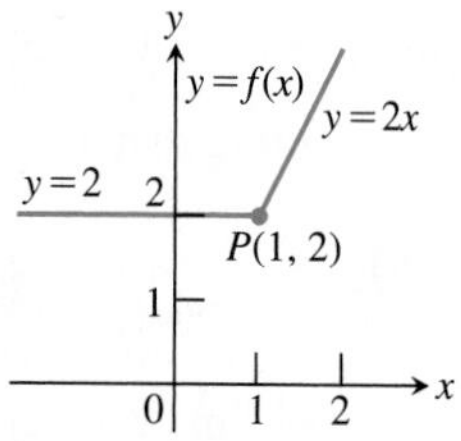

3.

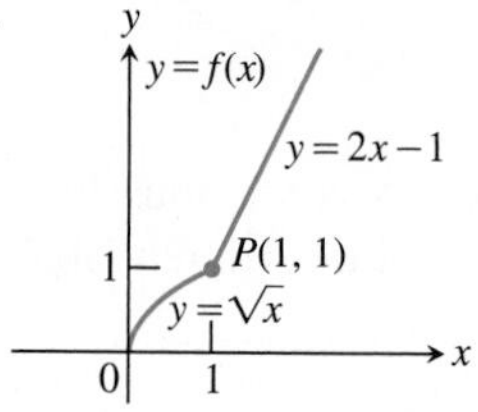

4.

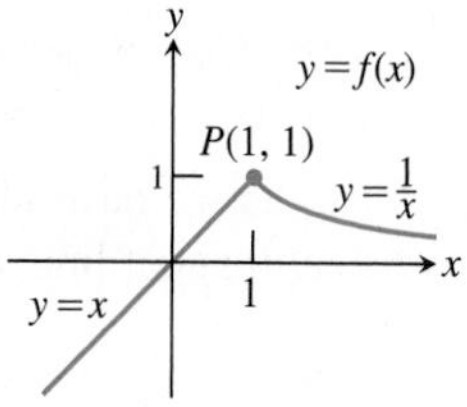

In Exercises 5–10, the graph of a function over a closed interval D is given. At what domain points does the function appear to be

(a) differentiable? **(b)** continuous but not differentiable?

(c) neither continuous nor differentiable?

5.

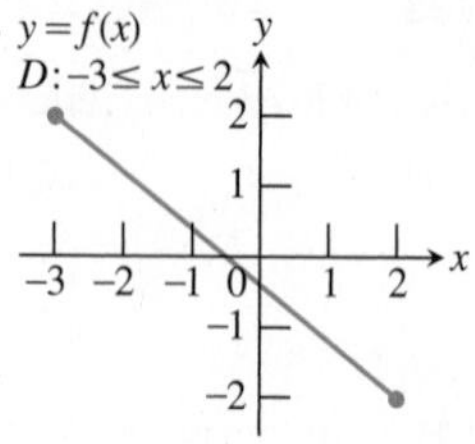

6.

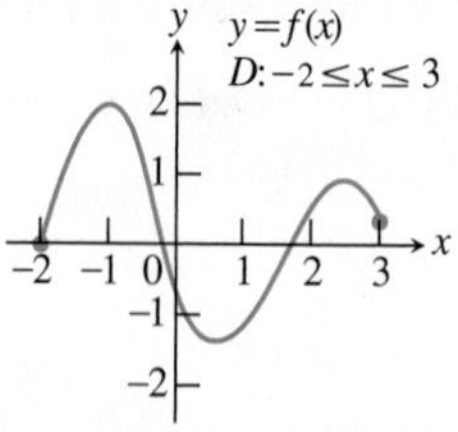

7.

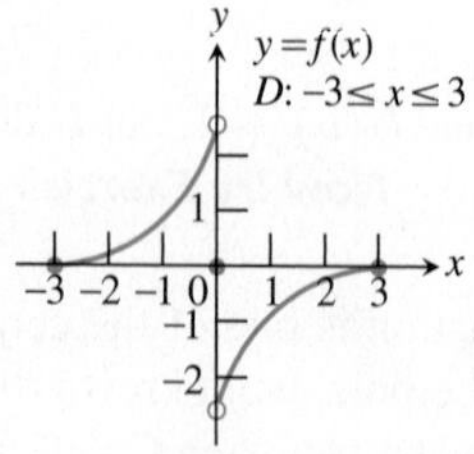

8.

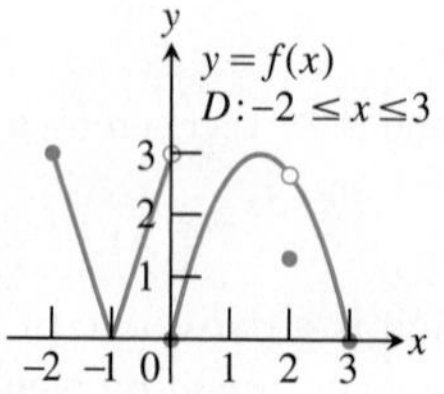

9.

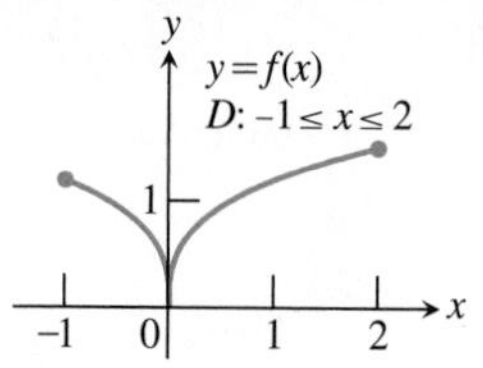

10.

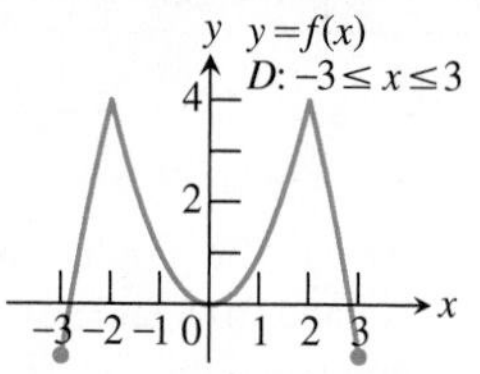

In Exercises 11–16, the function fails to be differentiable at $x = 0$. Tell whether the problem is a corner, a cusp, a vertical tangent, or a discontinuity.

11. $y = \begin{cases} \tan^{-1} x, & x \neq 0 \\ 1, & x = 0 \end{cases}$

12. $y = x^{4/5}$

13. $y = x + \sqrt{x^2} + 2$

14. $y = 3 - \sqrt[3]{x}$

15. $y = 3x - 2|x| - 1$

16. $y = \sqrt[3]{|x|}$

In Exercises 17–26, find the numerical derivative of the given function at the indicated point. Use $h = 0.001$. Is the function differentiable at the indicated point?

17. $f(x) = 4x - x^2, x = 0$

18. $f(x) = 4x - x^2, x = 3$

19. $f(x) = 4x - x^2, x = 1$

20. $f(x) = x^3 - 4x, x = 0$

21. $f(x) = x^3 - 4x, x = -2$

22. $f(x) = x^3 - 4x, x = 2$

23. $f(x) = x^{2/3}, x = 0$

24. $f(x) = |x - 3|, x = 3$

25. $f(x) = x^{2/5}, x = 0$

26. $f(x) = x^{4/5}, x = 0$

Group Activity In Exercises 27–30, use NDER to graph the derivative of the function. If possible, identify the derivative function by looking at the graph.

27. $y = -\cos x$

28. $y = 0.25x^4$

29. $y = \dfrac{x|x|}{2}$

30. $y = -\ln|\cos x|$

In Exercises 31–36, find all values of x for which the function is differentiable.

31. $f(x) = \dfrac{x^3 - 8}{x^2 - 4x - 5}$

32. $h(x) = \sqrt[3]{3x - 6} + 5$

33. $P(x) = \sin(|x|) - 1$

34. $Q(x) = 3\cos(|x|)$

35. $g(x) = \begin{cases} (x+1)^2, & x \leq 0 \\ 2x + 1, & 0 < x < 3 \\ (4 - x)^2, & x \geq 3 \end{cases}$

36. $C(x) = x|x|$

37. Show that the function

$$f(x) = \begin{cases} 0, & -1 \le x < 0 \\ 1, & 0 \le x \le 1 \end{cases}$$

is not the derivative of any function on the interval $-1 \le x \le 1$.

38. Writing to Learn Recall that the numerical derivative (NDER) can give meaningless values at points where a function is not differentiable. In this exercise, we consider the numerical derivatives of the functions $1/x$ and $1/x^2$ at $x = 0$.

(a) Explain why neither function is differentiable at $x = 0$.

(b) Find NDER at $x = 0$ for each function.

(c) By analyzing the definition of the symmetric difference quotient, explain why NDER returns wrong responses that are so different from each other for these two functions.

39. Let f be the function defined as

$$f(x) = \begin{cases} 3 - x, & x < 1 \\ ax^2 + bx, & x \ge 1 \end{cases}$$

where a and b are constants.

(a) If the function is continuous for all x, what is the relationship between a and b?

(b) Find the unique values for a and b that will make f both continuous and differentiable.

Standardized Test Questions

You may use a graphing calculator to solve the following problems.

40. True or False If f has a derivative at $x = a$, then f is continuous at $x = a$. Justify your answer.

41. True or False If f is continuous at $x = a$, then f has a derivative at $x = a$. Justify your answer.

42. Multiple Choice Which of the following is true about the graph of $f(x) = x^{4/5}$ at $x = 0$?

(A) It has a corner.

(B) It has a cusp.

(C) It has a vertical tangent.

(D) It has a discontinuity.

(E) $f(0)$ does not exist.

43. Multiple Choice Let $f(x) = \sqrt[3]{x} - 1$. At which of the following points is $f'(a) \ne$ NDER $(f(x), x, a)$?

(A) $a = 1$ **(B)** $a = -1$ **(C)** $a = 2$ **(D)** $a = -2$
(E) $a = 0$

In Exercises 44 and 45, let

$$f(x) = \begin{cases} 2x + 1, & x \le 0 \\ x^2 + 1, & x > 0. \end{cases}$$

44. Multiple Choice Which of the following is equal to the left-hand derivative of f at $x = 0$?

(A) $2x$ **(B)** 2 **(C)** 0 **(D)** $-\infty$ **(E)** ∞

45. Multiple Choice Which of the following is equal to the right-hand derivative of f at $x = 0$?

(A) $2x$ **(B)** 2 **(C)** 0 **(D)** $-\infty$ **(E)** ∞

Explorations

46. (a) Enter the expression "$x < 0$" into Y1 of your calculator using "<" from the TEST menu. Graph Y1 in DOT MODE in the window $[-4.7, 4.7]$ by $[-3.1, 3.1]$.

(b) Describe the graph in part (a).

(c) Enter the expression "$x \ge 0$" into Y1 of your calculator using "≥" from the TEST menu. Graph Y1 in DOT MODE in the window $[-4.7, 4.7]$ by $[-3.1, 3.1]$.

(d) Describe the graph in part (c).

47. *Graphing Piecewise Functions on a Calculator* Let

$$f(x) = \begin{cases} x^2, & x \le 0 \\ 2x, & x > 0. \end{cases}$$

(a) Enter the expression "(X²)(X≤0)+(2X)(X>0)" into Y1 of your calculator and draw its graph in the window $[-4.7, 4.7]$ by $[-3, 5]$.

(b) Explain why the values of Y1 and $f(x)$ are the same.

(c) Enter the numerical derivative of Y1 into Y2 of your calculator and draw its graph in the same window. Turn off the graph of Y1.

(d) Use TRACE to calculate NDER(Y1, x, -0.1), NDER(Y1, x, 0), and NDER(Y1, x, 0.1). Compare with Section 3.1, Example 6.

Extending the Ideas

48. *Oscillation* There is another way that a function might fail to be differentiable, and that is by *oscillation*. Let

$$f(x) = \begin{cases} x \sin \dfrac{1}{x}, & x \ne 0 \\ 0, & x = 0. \end{cases}$$

(a) Show that f is continuous at $x = 0$.

(b) Show that

$$\frac{f(0 + h) - f(0)}{h} = \sin \frac{1}{h}.$$

(c) Explain why

$$\lim_{h \to 0} \frac{f(0 + h) - f(0)}{h}$$

does not exist.

(d) Does f have either a left-hand or right-hand derivative at $x = 0$?

(e) Now consider the function

$$g(x) = \begin{cases} x^2 \sin \dfrac{1}{x}, & x \ne 0 \\ 0, & x = 0. \end{cases}$$

Use the definition of the derivative to show that g is differentiable at $x = 0$ and that $g'(0) = 0$.

3.3 Rules for Differentiation

What you will learn about . . .

- Positive Integer Powers, Multiples, Sums, and Differences
- Products and Quotients
- Negative Integer Powers of x
- Second and Higher Order Derivatives

and why . . .

These rules help us find derivatives of functions analytically more efficiently.

Positive Integer Powers, Multiples, Sums, and Differences

The first rule of differentiation is that the derivative of every constant function is the zero function.

RULE 1 Derivative of a Constant Function

If f is the function with the constant value c, then

$$\frac{df}{dx} = \frac{d}{dx}(c) = 0.$$

Proof of Rule 1 If $f(x) = c$ is a function with a constant value c, then

$$\lim_{h \to 0} \frac{f(x + h) - f(x)}{h} = \lim_{h \to 0} \frac{c - c}{h} = \lim_{h \to 0} 0 = 0. \quad \blacksquare$$

The next rule is a first step toward a rule for differentiating any polynomial.

RULE 2 Power Rule for Positive Integer Powers of x

If n is a positive integer, then

$$\frac{d}{dx}(x^n) = nx^{n-1}.$$

Proof of Rule 2 If $f(x) = x^n$, then

$$\frac{d}{dx}(x^n) = \lim_{h \to 0} \frac{(x + h)^n - x^n}{h}.$$

We can expand $(x + h)^n$ using the Binomial Theorem as follows:

$$\begin{aligned}(x + h)^n &= x^n + n \cdot x^{n-1}h + \frac{n(n-1)}{2} \cdot x^{n-2}h^2 + \cdots + n \cdot xh^{n-1} + h^n \\ &= x^n + n \cdot x^{n-1}h + h^2 \cdot [\text{stuff}]\end{aligned}$$

Notice that after the first two terms of the expansion, every term has a factor of h to a power greater than or equal to 2. This means we can factor h^2 out of all the remaining terms (leaving a polynomial expression we have chosen to call "stuff" since its particulars become irrelevant). Now we can complete the proof.

$$\begin{aligned}\frac{d}{dx}(x^n) &= \lim_{h \to 0} \frac{(x + h)^n - x^n}{h} \\ &= \lim_{h \to 0} \frac{x^n + n \cdot x^{n-1}h + h^2 \cdot [\text{stuff}] - x^n}{h} \\ &= \lim_{h \to 0} \frac{n \cdot x^{n-1}h + h^2 \cdot [\text{stuff}]}{h} \\ &= \lim_{h \to 0} (n \cdot x^{n-1} + h \cdot [\text{stuff}]) \\ &= nx^{n-1} + 0 \cdot [\text{stuff}] \\ &= nx^{n-1}\end{aligned} \quad \blacksquare$$

The Power Rule says: To differentiate x^n, multiply by n and subtract 1 from the exponent. For example, the derivatives of x^2, x^3, and x^4 are $2x^1$, $3x^2$, and $4x^3$, respectively.

RULE 3 The Constant Multiple Rule

If u is a differentiable function of x and c is a constant, then

$$\frac{d}{dx}(cu) = c\frac{du}{dx}.$$

Proof of Rule 3

$$\begin{aligned}\frac{d}{dx}(cu) &= \lim_{h\to 0}\frac{cu(x+h)-cu(x)}{h}\\ &= c\lim_{h\to 0}\frac{u(x+h)-u(x)}{h}\\ &= c\frac{du}{dx}\end{aligned}$$

■

Rule 3 says that if a differentiable function is multiplied by a constant, then its derivative is multiplied by the same constant. Combined with Rule 2, it enables us to find the derivative of any monomial quickly; for example, the derivative of $7x^4$ is $7(4x^3) = 28x^3$.

To find the derivatives of polynomials, we need to be able to differentiate sums and differences of monomials. We can accomplish this by applying the Sum and Difference Rule.

Denoting Functions by *u* and *v*

The functions we work with when we need a differentiation formula are likely to be denoted by letters like *f* and *g*. When we apply the formula, we do not want to find the formula using these same letters in some other way. To guard against this, we denote the functions in differentiation rules by letters like *u* and *v* that are not likely to be already in use.

RULE 4 The Sum and Difference Rule

If u and v are differentiable functions of x, then their sum and difference are differentiable at every point where u and v are differentiable. At such points,

$$\frac{d}{dx}(u \pm v) = \frac{du}{dx} \pm \frac{dv}{dx}.$$

Proof of Rule 4

We use the difference quotient for $f(x) = u(x) + v(x)$.

$$\begin{aligned}\frac{d}{dx}[u(x)+v(x)] &= \lim_{h\to 0}\frac{[u(x+h)+v(x+h)]-[u(x)+v(x)]}{h}\\ &= \lim_{h\to 0}\left[\frac{u(x+h)-u(x)}{h}+\frac{v(x+h)-v(x)}{h}\right]\\ &= \lim_{h\to 0}\frac{u(x+h)-u(x)}{h}+\lim_{h\to 0}\frac{v(x+h)-v(x)}{h}\\ &= \frac{du}{dx}+\frac{dv}{dx}\end{aligned}$$

The proof of the rule for the difference of two functions is similar. ■

EXAMPLE 1 Differentiating a Polynomial

Find $\frac{dp}{dt}$ if $p = t^3 + 6t^2 - \frac{5}{3}t + 16$.

SOLUTION

By Rule 4 we can differentiate the polynomial term-by-term, applying Rules 1 through 3 as we go.

$$\frac{dp}{dt} = \frac{d}{dt}(t^3) + \frac{d}{dt}(6t^2) - \frac{d}{dt}\left(\frac{5}{3}t\right) + \frac{d}{dt}(16) \quad \text{Sum and Difference Rule}$$

$$= 3t^2 + 6 \cdot 2t - \frac{5}{3} + 0 \quad \text{Constant and Power Rules}$$

$$= 3t^2 + 12t - \frac{5}{3}$$

Now Try Exercise 5.

EXAMPLE 2 Finding Horizontal Tangents

Does the curve $y = x^4 - 2x^2 + 2$ have any horizontal tangents? If so, where?

SOLUTION

The horizontal tangents, if any, occur where the slope dy/dx is zero. To find these points, we

(a) calculate dy/dx:

$$\frac{dy}{dx} = \frac{d}{dx}(x^4 - 2x^2 + 2) = 4x^3 - 4x.$$

(b) solve the equation $dy/dx = 0$ for x:

$$4x^3 - 4x = 0$$
$$4x(x^2 - 1) = 0$$
$$x = 0, 1, -1.$$

The curve has horizontal tangents at $x = 0$, 1, and -1. The corresponding points on the curve (found from the equation $y = x^4 - 2x^2 + 2$) are $(0, 2)$, $(1, 1)$, and $(-1, 1)$. You might wish to graph the curve to see where the horizontal tangents go.

Now Try Exercise 7.

The derivative in Example 2 was easily factored, making an algebraic solution of the equation $dy/dx = 0$ correspondingly simple. When a simple algebraic solution is not possible, the solutions to $dy/dx = 0$ can still be found to a high degree of accuracy by using the SOLVE capability of your calculator.

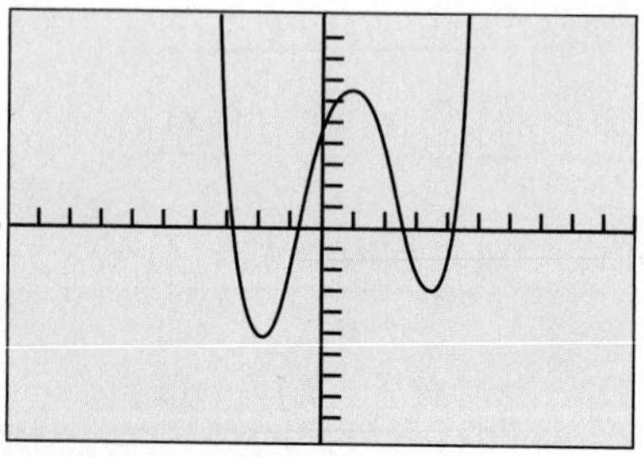

[–10, 10] by [–10, 10]

Figure 3.18 The graph of

$$y = 0.2x^4 - 0.7x^3 - 2x^2 + 5x + 4$$

has three horizontal tangents. (Example 3)

EXAMPLE 3 Using Calculus and Calculator

As can be seen in the viewing window $[-10, 10]$ by $[-10, 10]$, the graph of $y = 0.2x^4 - 0.7x^3 - 2x^2 + 5x + 4$ has three horizontal tangents (Figure 3.18). At what points do these horizontal tangents occur?

continued

SOLUTION

First we find the derivative

$$\frac{dy}{dx} = 0.8x^3 - 2.1x^2 - 4x + 5.$$

Using the calculator solver, we find that $0.8x^3 - 2.1x^2 - 4x + 5 = 0$ when $x \approx -1.862$, 0.9484, and 3.539. We use the calculator again to evaluate the original function at these x-values and find the corresponding points to be approximately $(-1.862, -5.321)$, $(0.9484, 6.508)$, and $(3.539, -3.008)$. ***Now Try Exercise 11.***

On Rounding Calculator Values

Notice in Example 3 that we rounded the *x*-values to four significant digits when we presented the answers. The calculator actually presented many more digits, but there was no practical reason for writing all of them. When we used the calculator to compute the corresponding *y*-values, however, we *used the x-values stored in the calculator,* not the rounded values. We then rounded the *y*-values to four significant digits when we presented the ordered pairs. Significant "round-off errors" can accumulate in a problem if you use rounded intermediate values for doing additional computations, so avoid rounding until the final answer.

Products and Quotients

While the derivative of the sum of two functions is the sum of their derivatives and the derivative of the difference of two functions is the difference of their derivatives, the derivative of the product of two functions is *not* the product of their derivatives.

For instance,

$$\frac{d}{dx}(x \cdot x) = \frac{d}{dx}(x^2) = 2x, \qquad \text{while} \qquad \frac{d}{dx}(x) \cdot \frac{d}{dx}(x) = 1 \cdot 1 = 1.$$

The derivative of a product is actually the sum of *two* products, as we now explain.

Formula Tip

You can remember the Product Rule with the phrase "the first times the derivative of the second plus the second times the derivative of the first."

RULE 5 The Product Rule

The product of two differentiable functions u and v is differentiable, and

$$\frac{d}{dx}(uv) = u\frac{dv}{dx} + v\frac{du}{dx}.$$

Proof of Rule 5 We begin, as usual, by applying the definition.

$$\frac{d}{dx}(uv) = \lim_{h \to 0} \frac{u(x+h)v(x+h) - u(x)v(x)}{h}$$

To change the fraction into an equivalent one that contains difference quotients for the derivatives of u and v, we subtract and add $u(x+h)v(x)$ in the numerator. Then,

$$\frac{d}{dx}(uv) = \lim_{h \to 0} \frac{u(x+h)v(x+h) - u(x+h)v(x) + u(x+h)v(x) - u(x)v(x)}{h}$$

$$= \lim_{h \to 0} \left[u(x+h)\frac{v(x+h) - v(x)}{h} + v(x)\frac{u(x+h) - u(x)}{h} \right] \qquad \text{Factor and separate.}$$

$$= \lim_{h \to 0} u(x+h) \cdot \lim_{h \to 0} \frac{v(x+h) - v(x)}{h} + v(x) \cdot \lim_{h \to 0} \frac{u(x+h) - u(x)}{h}.$$

As h approaches 0, $u(x+h)$ approaches $u(x)$ because u, being differentiable at x, is continuous at x. The two fractions approach the values of dv/dx and du/dx, respectively, at x. Therefore

$$\frac{d}{dx}(uv) = u\frac{dv}{dx} + v\frac{du}{dx}. \qquad ■$$

Gottfried Wilhelm Leibniz (1646–1716)

The method of limits used in this book was not discovered until nearly a century after Newton and Leibniz, the discoverers of calculus, had died.

To Leibniz, the key idea was the *differential,* an infinitely small quantity that was almost like zero, but which—unlike zero—could be used in the denominator of a fraction. Thus, Leibniz thought of the derivative *dy*/*dx* as the quotient of two differentials, *dy* and *dx*.

The problem was explaining why these differentials sometimes became zero and sometimes did not! See Exercise 59.

Some 17th-century mathematicians were confident that the calculus of Newton and Leibniz would eventually be found to be fatally flawed because of these mysterious quantities. It was only after later generations of mathematicians had found better ways to prove their results that the calculus of Newton and Leibniz was accepted by the entire scientific community.

EXAMPLE 4 Differentiating a Product

Find $f'(x)$ if $f(x) = (x^2 + 1)(x^3 + 3)$.

SOLUTION

From the Product Rule with $u = x^2 + 1$ and $v = x^3 + 3$, we find

$$f'(x) = \frac{d}{dx}[(x^2 + 1)(x^3 + 3)] = (x^2 + 1)(3x^2) + (x^3 + 3)(2x)$$
$$= 3x^4 + 3x^2 + 2x^4 + 6x$$
$$= 5x^4 + 3x^2 + 6x.$$

Now Try Exercise 13.

We could also have done Example 4 by multiplying out the original expression and then differentiating the resulting polynomial. That alternate strategy will not work, however, on a product like $x^2 \sin x$.

Just as the derivative of the product of two differentiable functions is not the product of their derivatives, the derivative of a quotient of two functions is not the quotient of their derivatives. What happens instead is this:

Formula Tip

Since order is important in subtraction, be sure to set up the numerator of the Quotient Rule correctly:

v times the derivative of *u*

minus

u times the derivative of *v*.

You can remember the Quotient Rule with the phrase "bottom times the derivative of the top minus the top times the derivative of the bottom, all over the bottom squared."

RULE 6 The Quotient Rule

At a point where $v \neq 0$, the quotient $y = u/v$ of two differentiable functions is differentiable, and

$$\frac{d}{dx}\left(\frac{u}{v}\right) = \frac{v\dfrac{du}{dx} - u\dfrac{dv}{dx}}{v^2}.$$

Proof of Rule 6

$$\frac{d}{dx}\left(\frac{u}{v}\right) = \lim_{h\to 0} \frac{\dfrac{u(x+h)}{v(x+h)} - \dfrac{u(x)}{v(x)}}{h}$$

$$= \lim_{h\to 0} \frac{v(x)u(x+h) - u(x)v(x+h)}{hv(x+h)v(x)}$$

To change the last fraction into an equivalent one that contains the difference quotients for the derivatives of u and v, we subtract and add $v(x)u(x)$ in the numerator. This allows us to continue with

$$\frac{d}{dx}\left(\frac{u}{v}\right) = \lim_{h\to 0} \frac{v(x)u(x+h) - v(x)u(x) + v(x)u(x) - u(x)v(x+h)}{hv(x+h)v(x)}$$

$$= \lim_{h\to 0} \frac{v(x)\dfrac{u(x+h) - u(x)}{h} - u(x)\dfrac{v(x+h) - v(x)}{h}}{v(x+h)v(x)}.$$

Taking the limits in both the numerator and denominator now gives us the Quotient Rule. ■

EXAMPLE 5 Supporting Computations Graphically

Differentiate $f(x) = \dfrac{x^2 - 1}{x^2 + 1}$. Support graphically.

continued

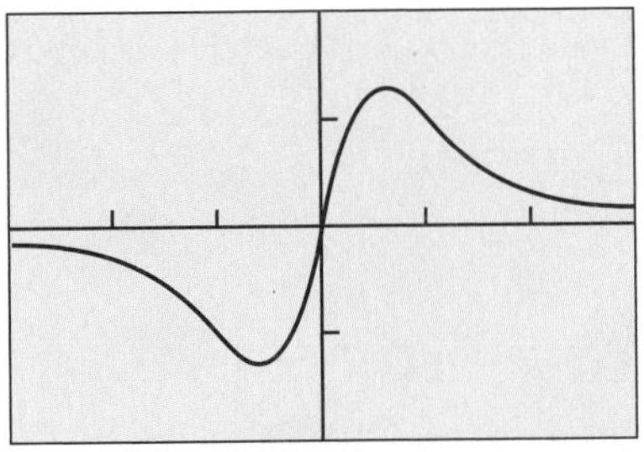

[−3, 3] by [−2, 2]

Figure 3.19 The graph of

$$y = \frac{4x}{(x^2+1)^2}$$

and the graph of

$$y = \text{NDER}\left(\frac{x^2-1}{x^2+1}, x\right)$$

appear to be the same. (Example 5)

SOLUTION

We apply the Quotient Rule with $u = x^2 - 1$ and $v = x^2 + 1$:

$$f'(x) = \frac{(x^2+1)\cdot 2x - (x^2-1)\cdot 2x}{(x^2+1)^2} \qquad \frac{v(du/dx) - u(dv/dx)}{v^2}$$

$$= \frac{2x^3 + 2x - 2x^3 + 2x}{(x^2+1)^2}$$

$$= \frac{4x}{(x^2+1)^2}.$$

The graphs of $y_1 = f'(x)$ calculated above and of $y_2 = \text{NDER}\,(f(x), x)$ are shown in Figure 3.19. The fact that they appear to be identical provides strong graphical support that our calculations are indeed correct. ***Now Try Exercise 19.***

EXAMPLE 6 Working with Numerical Values

Let $y = uv$ be the product of the functions u and v. Find $y'(2)$ if

$$u(2) = 3, \quad u'(2) = -4, \quad v(2) = 1, \quad \text{and} \quad v'(2) = 2.$$

SOLUTION

From the Product Rule, $y' = (uv)' = uv' + vu'$. In particular,

$$y'(2) = u(2)v'(2) + v(2)u'(2)$$
$$= (3)(2) + (1)(-4)$$
$$= 2.$$

Now Try Exercise 23.

Negative Integer Powers of *x*

The rule for differentiating negative powers of x is the same as Rule 2 for differentiating positive powers of x, although our proof of Rule 2 does not work for negative values of n. We can now extend the Power Rule to negative integer powers by a clever use of the Quotient Rule.

RULE 7 Power Rule for Negative Integer Powers of *x*

If n is a negative integer and $x \neq 0$, then

$$\frac{d}{dx}(x^n) = nx^{n-1}.$$

Proof of Rule 7 If n is a negative integer, then $n = -m$, where m is a positive integer. Hence, $x^n = x^{-m} = 1/x^m$, and

$$\frac{d}{dx}(x^n) = \frac{d}{dx}\left(\frac{1}{x^m}\right) = \frac{x^m \cdot \frac{d}{dx}(1) - 1 \cdot \frac{d}{dx}(x^m)}{(x^m)^2}$$

$$= \frac{0 - mx^{m-1}}{x^{2m}}$$

$$= -mx^{-m-1}$$

$$= nx^{n-1}.$$

■

EXAMPLE 7 Using the Power Rule

Find an equation for the line tangent to the curve

$$y = \frac{x^2 + 3}{2x}$$

at the point $(1, 2)$. Support your answer graphically.

SOLUTION

We could find the derivative by the Quotient Rule, but it is easier to first simplify the function as a sum of two powers of x.

$$\frac{dy}{dx} = \frac{d}{dx}\left(\frac{x^2}{2x} + \frac{3}{2x}\right)$$
$$= \frac{d}{dx}\left(\frac{1}{2}x + \frac{3}{2}x^{-1}\right)$$
$$= \frac{1}{2} - \frac{3}{2}x^{-2}$$

The slope at $x = 1$ is

$$\left.\frac{dy}{dx}\right|_{x=1} = \left[\frac{1}{2} - \frac{3}{2}x^{-2}\right]_{x=1} = \frac{1}{2} - \frac{3}{2} = -1.$$

The line through $(1, 2)$ with slope $m = -1$ is

$$y - 2 = (-1)(x - 1)$$
$$y = -x + 1 + 2$$
$$y = -x + 3.$$

We graph $y = (x^2 + 3)/2x$ and $y = -x + 3$ (Figure 3.20), observing that the line appears to be tangent to the curve at $(1, 2)$. Thus, we have graphical support that our computations are correct.

Now Try Exercise 27.

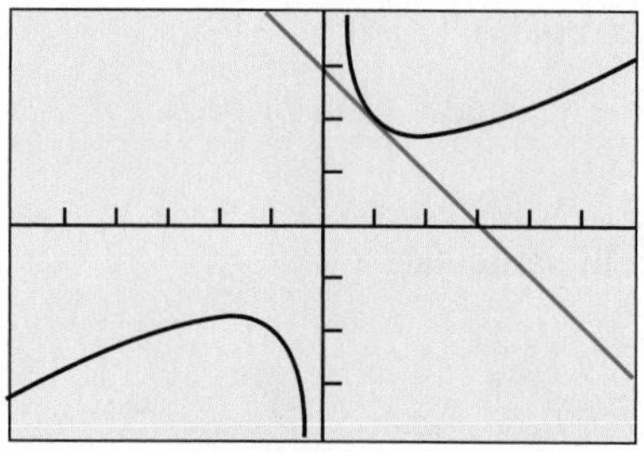

[–6, 6] by [–4, 4]

Figure 3.20 The line $y = -x + 3$ appears to be tangent to the graph of

$$y = \frac{x^2 + 3}{2x}$$

at the point $(1, 2)$. (Example 7)

Second and Higher Order Derivatives

The derivative $y' = dy/dx$ is called the *first derivative* of y with respect to x. The first derivative may itself be a differentiable function of x. If so, its derivative,

$$y'' = \frac{dy'}{dx} = \frac{d}{dx}\left(\frac{dy}{dx}\right) = \frac{d^2y}{dx^2},$$

is called the *second derivative* of y with respect to x. If y'' ("y double-prime") is differentiable, its derivative,

$$y''' = \frac{dy''}{dx} = \frac{d^3y}{dx^3},$$

is called the *third derivative* of y with respect to x. The names continue as you might expect they would, except that the multiple-prime notation begins to lose its usefulness after about three primes. We use

$$y^{(n)} = \frac{d}{dx}y^{(n-1)} \quad \text{"}y\text{ super }n\text{"}$$

to denote the ***n*th derivative** of y with respect to x. (We also use d^ny/dx^n.) Do not confuse $y^{(n)}$ with the nth power of y, which is y^n.

Technology Tip

HIGHER ORDER DERIVATIVES WITH NDER

Some graphers will allow the *nesting* of the NDER function,

NDER (NDER($f(x)$, x), a),

but such nesting, in general, is safe only to the second derivative. Beyond that, the error buildup in the algorithm makes the results unreliable.

EXAMPLE 8 Finding Higher Order Derivatives

Find the first four derivatives of $y = x^3 - 5x^2 + 2$.

SOLUTION

The first four derivatives are:

First derivative:	$y' = 3x^2 - 10x;$
Second derivative:	$y'' = 6x - 10;$
Third derivative:	$y''' = 6;$
Fourth derivative:	$y^{(4)} = 0.$

This function has derivatives of all orders, the fourth and higher order derivatives all being zero. ***Now Try Exercise 33.***

EXAMPLE 9 Finding Instantaneous Rate of Change

An orange farmer currently has 200 trees yielding an average of 15 bushels of oranges per tree. She is expanding her farm at the rate of 15 trees per year, while improved husbandry is improving her average annual yield by 1.2 bushels per tree. What is the current (instantaneous) rate of increase of her total annual production of oranges?

SOLUTION

Let the functions t and y be defined as follows.

$$t(x) = \text{the number of trees } x \text{ years from now.}$$
$$y(x) = \text{yield per tree } x \text{ years from now.}$$

Then $p(x) = t(x)y(x)$ is the total production of oranges in year x. We know the following values.

$$t(0) = 200, \quad y(0) = 15$$
$$t'(0) = 15, \quad y'(0) = 1.2$$

We need to find $p'(0)$, where $p = ty$.

$$\begin{aligned} p'(0) &= t(0)y'(0) + y(0)t'(0) \\ &= (200)(1.2) + (15)(15) \\ &= 465 \end{aligned}$$

The rate we seek is 465 bushels per year. ***Now Try Exercise 51.***

Quick Review 3.3 *(For help, go to Sections 1.2 and 3.1.)*

Exercise numbers with a gray background indicate problems that the authors have designed to be solved *without a calculator.*

In Exercises 1–6, write the expression as a sum of powers of x.

1. $(x^2 - 2)(x^{-1} + 1)$

2. $\left(\dfrac{x}{x^2 + 1}\right)^{-1}$

3. $3x^2 - \dfrac{2}{x} + \dfrac{5}{x^2}$

4. $\dfrac{3x^4 - 2x^3 + 4}{2x^2}$

5. $(x^{-1} + 2)(x^{-2} + 1)$

6. $\dfrac{x^{-1} + x^{-2}}{x^{-3}}$

7. Find the positive roots of the equation

$$2x^3 - 5x^2 - 2x + 6 = 0$$

and evaluate the function $y = 500x^6$ at each root. Round your answers to the nearest integer, but only in the final step.

8. If $f(x) = 7$ for all real numbers x, find

(a) $f(10)$. **(b)** $f(0)$.

(c) $f(x + h)$. **(d)** $\lim_{x\to 0} \dfrac{f(x) - f(a)}{x - a}$.

9. Find the derivatives of these functions with respect to x.

(a) $f(x) = \pi$ **(b)** $f(x) = \pi^2$ **(c)** $f(x) = \pi^{15}$

10. Find the derivatives of these functions with respect to x using the definition of the derivative.

(a) $f(x) = \dfrac{x}{\pi}$ **(b)** $f(x) = \dfrac{\pi}{x}$

Section 3.3 Exercises

In Exercises 1–6, find dy/dx.

1. $y = -x^2 + 3$ **2.** $y = \dfrac{x^3}{3} - x$

3. $y = 2x + 1$ **4.** $y = x^2 + x + 1$

5. $y = \dfrac{x^3}{3} + \dfrac{x^2}{2} + x$ **6.** $y = 1 - x + x^2 - x^3$

In Exercises 7–12, find the horizontal tangents of the curve.

7. $y = x^3 - 2x^2 + x + 1$ **8.** $y = x^3 - 4x^2 + x + 2$

9. $y = x^4 - 4x^2 + 1$ **10.** $y = 4x^3 - 6x^2 - 1$

11. $y = 5x^3 - 3x^5$ **12.** $y = x^4 - 7x^3 + 2x^2 + 15$

13. Let $y = (x + 1)(x^2 + 1)$. Find dy/dx **(a)** by applying the Product Rule, and **(b)** by multiplying the factors first and then differentiating.

14. Let $y = (x^2 + 3)/x$. Find dy/dx **(a)** by using the Quotient Rule, and **(b)** by first dividing the terms in the numerator by the denominator and then differentiating.

In Exercises 15–22, find dy/dx. (You can support your answer graphically.)

15. $(x^3 + x + 1)(x^4 + x^2 + 1)$ **16.** $(x^2 + 1)(x^3 + 1)$

17. $y = \dfrac{2x + 5}{3x - 2}$ **18.** $y = \dfrac{x^2 + 5x - 1}{x^2}$

19. $y = \dfrac{(x - 1)(x^2 + x + 1)}{x^3}$ **20.** $y = (1 - x)(1 + x^2)^{-1}$

21. $y = \dfrac{x^2}{1 - x^3}$ **22.** $y = \dfrac{(x + 1)(x + 2)}{(x - 1)(x - 2)}$

23. Suppose u and v are functions of x that are differentiable at $x = 0$, and that $u(0) = 5$, $u'(0) = -3$, $v(0) = -1$, $v'(0) = 2$. Find the values of the following derivatives at $x = 0$.

(a) $\dfrac{d}{dx}(uv)$ **(b)** $\dfrac{d}{dx}\left(\dfrac{u}{v}\right)$

(c) $\dfrac{d}{dx}\left(\dfrac{u}{v}\right)$ **(d)** $\dfrac{d}{dx}(7v - 2u)$

24. Suppose u and v are functions of x that are differentiable at $x = 2$ and that $u(2) = 3$, $u'(2) = -4$, $v(2) = 1$, and $v'(2) = 2$. Find the values of the following derivatives at $x = 2$.

(a) $\dfrac{d}{dx}(uv)$ **(b)** $\dfrac{d}{dx}\left(\dfrac{u}{v}\right)$

(c) $\dfrac{d}{dx}\left(\dfrac{u}{v}\right)$ **(d)** $\dfrac{d}{dx}(3u - 2v + 2uv)$

25. Which of the following numbers is the slope of the line tangent to the curve $y = x^2 + 5x$ at $x = 3$?

i. 24 **ii.** $-5/2$ **iii.** 11 **iv.** 8

26. Which of the following numbers is the slope of the line $3x - 2y + 12 = 0$?

i. 6 **ii.** 3 **iii.** $3/2$ **iv.** $2/3$

In Exercises 27 and 28, find an equation for the line tangent to the curve at the given point.

27. $y = \dfrac{x^3 + 1}{2x}$, $x = 1$ **28.** $y = \dfrac{x^4 + 2}{x^2}$, $x = -1$

In Exercises 29–32, find dy/dx.

29. $y = 4x^{-2} - 8x + 1$

30. $y = \dfrac{x^{-4}}{4} - \dfrac{x^{-3}}{3} + \dfrac{x^{-2}}{2} - x^{-1} + 3$

31. $y = \dfrac{\sqrt{x} - 1}{\sqrt{x} + 1}$ **32.** $y = 2\sqrt{x} - \dfrac{1}{\sqrt{x}}$

In Exercises 33–36, find the first four derivatives of the function.

33. $y = x^4 + x^3 - 2x^2 + x - 5$ **34.** $y = x^2 + x + 3$

35. $y = x^{-1} + x^2$ **36.** $y = \dfrac{x + 1}{x}$

37. Find an equation of the line perpendicular to the tangent to the curve $y = x^3 - 3x + 1$ at the point $(2, 3)$

38. Find the tangents to the curve $y = x^3 + x$ at the points where the slope is 4. What is the smallest slope of the curve? At what value of x does the curve have this slope?

39. Find the points on the curve $y = 2x^3 - 3x^2 - 12x + 20$ where the tangent is parallel to the x-axis.

40. Find the x- and y-intercepts of the line that is tangent to the curve $y = x^3$ at the point $(-2, -8)$.

41. Find the tangents to *Newton's serpentine,*

$$y = \frac{4x}{x^2 + 1},$$

at the origin and the point $(1, 2)$.

42. Find the tangent to the *witch of Agnesi,*

$$y = \frac{8}{4 + x^2},$$

at the point $(2, 1)$.

43. Use the definition of derivative (given in Section 3.1, Equation 1) to show that

(a) $\dfrac{d}{dx}(x) = 1.$

(b) $\dfrac{d}{dx}(-u) = -\dfrac{du}{dx}.$

44. Use the Product Rule to show that

$$\frac{d}{dx}(c \cdot f(x)) = c \cdot \frac{d}{dx} f(x)$$

for any constant c.

45. Devise a rule for $\dfrac{d}{dx}\left(\dfrac{1}{f(x)}\right)$.

When we work with functions of a single variable in mathematics, we often call the independent variable x and the dependent variable y. Applied fields use many different letters, however. Here are some examples.

46. *Cylinder Pressure* If gas in a cylinder is maintained at a constant temperature T, the pressure P is related to the volume V by a formula of the form

$$P = \frac{nRT}{V - nb} - \frac{an^2}{V^2},$$

in which a, b, n, and R are constants. Find dP/dV.

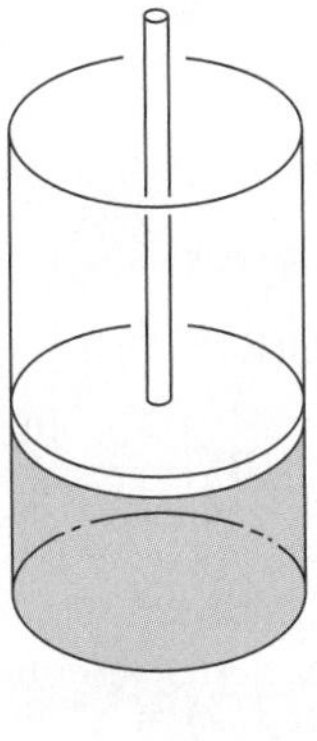

47. *Free Fall* When a rock falls from rest near the surface of the earth, the distance it covers during the first few seconds is given by the equation

$$s = 4.9t^2.$$

In this equation, s is the distance in meters and t is the elapsed time in seconds. Find ds/dt and d^2s/dt^2.

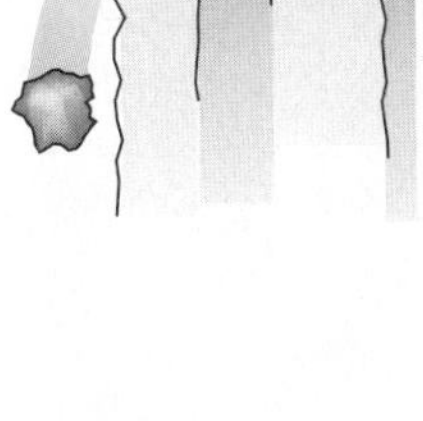

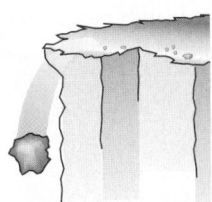

Group Activity In Exercises 48–52, *work in groups of two or three* to solve the problems.

48. *The Body's Reaction to Medicine* The reaction of the body to a dose of medicine can often be represented by an equation of the form

$$R = M^2\left(\frac{C}{2} - \frac{M}{3}\right),$$

where C is a positive constant and M is the amount of medicine absorbed in the blood. If the reaction is a change in blood pressure, R is measured in millimeters of mercury. If the reaction is a change in temperature, R is measured in degrees, and so on.

Find dR/dM. This derivative, as a function of M, is called the sensitivity of the body to medicine. In Chapter 5, we shall see how to find the amount of medicine to which the body is most sensitive. *Source: Some Mathematical Models in Biology,* Revised Edition, December 1967, PB-202 364, p. 221; distributed by N.T.I.S., U.S. Department of Commerce.

49. Writing to Learn Recall that the area A of a circle with radius r is πr^2 and that the circumference C is $2\pi r$. Notice that $dA/dr = C$. Explain in terms of geometry why the instantaneous rate of change of the area with respect to the radius should equal the circumference.

50. Writing to Learn Recall that the volume V of a sphere of radius r is $(4/3)\pi r^3$ and that the surface area A is $4\pi r^2$. Notice that $dV/dr = A$. Explain in terms of geometry why the instantaneous rate of change of the volume with respect to the radius should equal the surface area.

51. *Orchard Farming* An apple farmer currently has 156 trees yielding an average of 12 bushels of apples per tree. He is expanding his farm at a rate of 13 trees per year, while improved husbandry is boosting his average annual yield by 1.5 bushels per tree. What is the current (instantaneous) rate of increase of his total annual production of apples? Answer in appropriate units of measure.

52. *Picnic Pavilion Rental* The members of the Blue Boar society always divide the pavilion rental fee for their picnics equally among the members. Currently there are 65 members and the pavilion rents for \$250. The pavilion cost is increasing at a rate of \$10 per year, while the Blue Boar membership is increasing at a rate of 6 members per year. What is the current (instantaneous) rate of change in each member's share of the pavilion rental fee? Answer in appropriate units of measure.

Standardized Test Questions

53. True or False $\dfrac{d}{dx}(\pi^3) = 3\pi^2$. Justify your answer.

54. True or False The graph of $f(x) = 1/x$ has no horizontal tangents. Justify your answer.

55. Multiple Choice Let $y = uv$ be the product of the functions u and v. Find $y'(1)$ if $u(1) = 2$, $u'(1) = 3$, $v(1) = -1$, and $v'(1) = 1$.

(A) -4 (B) -1 (C) 1 (D) 4 (E) 7

56. Multiple Choice Let $f(x) = x - \frac{1}{x}$. Find $f''(x)$.

(A) $1 + \frac{1}{x^2}$ (B) $1 - \frac{1}{x^2}$ (C) $\frac{2}{x^3}$

(D) $-\frac{2}{x^3}$ (E) does not exist

57. Multiple Choice Which of the following is $\frac{d}{dx}\left(\frac{x+1}{x-1}\right)$?

(A) $\frac{2}{(x-1)^2}$ (B) 0 (C) $-\frac{x^2+1}{x^2}$

(D) $2x - \frac{1}{x^2} - 1$ (E) $-\frac{2}{(x-1)^2}$

58. Multiple Choice Assume $f(x) = (x^2 - 1)(x^2 + 1)$. Which of the following gives the number of horizontal tangents of f?

(A) 0 (B) 1 (C) 2 (D) 3 (E) 4

Extending the Ideas

59. *Leibniz's Proof of the Product Rule* Here's how Leibniz explained the Product Rule in a letter to his colleague John Wallis:

It is useful to consider quantities infinitely small such that when their ratio is sought, they may not be considered zero, but which are rejected as often as they occur with quantities incomparably greater. Thus if we have $x + dx$, dx is rejected. Similarly we cannot have xdx and $dxdx$ standing together, as xdx is incomparably greater than $dxdx$. Hence if we are to differentiate uv, we write

$$\begin{aligned} d(uv) &= (u + du)(v + dv) - uv \\ &= uv + vdu + udv + dudv - uv \\ &= vdu + udv. \end{aligned}$$

Answer the following questions about Leibniz's proof.

(a) What does Leibniz mean by a quantity being "rejected"?

(b) What happened to $dudv$ in the last step of Leibniz's proof?

(c) Divide both sides of Leibniz's formula

$$d(uv) = vdu + udv$$

by the differential dx. What formula results?

(d) Why would the critics of Leibniz's time have objected to dividing both sides of the equation by dx?

(e) Leibniz had a similar simple (but not-so-clean) proof of the Quotient Rule. Can you reconstruct it?

Quick Quiz for AP* Preparation: Sections 3.1–3.3

1. Multiple Choice Let $f(x) = |x + 1|$. Which of the following statements about f are true?

I. f is continuous at $x = -1$.

II. f is differentiable at $x = -1$.

III. f has a corner at $x = -1$.

(A) I only (B) II only (C) III only

(D) I and III only (E) I and II only

2. Multiple Choice If the line normal to the graph of f at the point $(1, 2)$ passes through the point $(-1, 1)$, then which of the following gives the value of $f'(1) = ?$

(A) -2 (B) 2 (C) $-1/2$ (D) $1/2$ (E) 3

3. Multiple Choice Find dy/dx if $y = \frac{4x-3}{2x+1}$.

(A) $\frac{10}{(4x-3)^2}$ (B) $-\frac{10}{(4x-3)^2}$ (C) $\frac{10}{(2x+1)^2}$

(D) $-\frac{10}{(2x+1)^2}$ (E) 2

4. Free Response Let $f(x) = x^4 - 4x^2$.

(a) Find all the points where f has horizontal tangents.

(b) Find an equation of the tangent line at $x = 1$.

(c) Find an equation of the normal line at $x = 1$.

3.4 Velocity and Other Rates of Change

What you will learn about . . .

- Instantaneous Rates of Change
- Motion Along a Line
- Sensitivity to Change
- Derivatives in Economics

and why . . .

Derivatives give the rates at which things change in the world.

Instantaneous Rates of Change

In this section we examine some applications in which derivatives as functions are used to represent the rates at which things change in the world around us. It is natural to think of change as change with respect to time, but other variables can be treated in the same way. For example, a physician may want to know how change in dosage affects the body's response to a drug. An economist may want to study how the cost of producing steel varies with the number of tons produced.

If we interpret the difference quotient

$$\frac{f(x+h)-f(x)}{h}$$

as the average rate of change of the function f over the interval from x to $x+h$, we can interpret its limit as h approaches 0 to be the rate at which f is changing at the point x.

DEFINITION Instantaneous Rate of Change

The **(instantaneous) rate of change** of f with respect to x at a is the derivative

$$f'(a) = \lim_{h\to 0} \frac{f(a+h)-f(a)}{h},$$

provided the limit exists.

It is conventional to use the word *instantaneous* even when x does not represent time. The word, however, is frequently omitted in practice. When we say *rate of change,* we mean *instantaneous rate of change*.

EXAMPLE 1 Enlarging Circles

(a) Find the rate of change of the area A of a circle with respect to its radius r.

(b) Evaluate the rate of change of A at $r = 5$ and at $r = 10$.

(c) If r is measured in inches and A is measured in square inches, what units would be appropriate for dA/dr?

SOLUTION

The area of a circle is related to its radius by the equation $A = \pi r^2$.

(a) The (instantaneous) rate of change of A with respect to r is

$$\frac{dA}{dr} = \frac{d}{dr}(\pi r^2) = \pi \cdot 2r = 2\pi r.$$

(b) At $r = 5$, the rate is 10π (about 31.4). At $r = 10$, the rate is 20π (about 62.8).

Notice that the rate of change gets bigger as r gets bigger. As can be seen in Figure 3.21, the same change in radius brings about a bigger change in area as the circles grow radially away from the center.

(c) The appropriate units for dA/dr are square inches (of area) per inch (of radius).

Now Try Exercise 1.

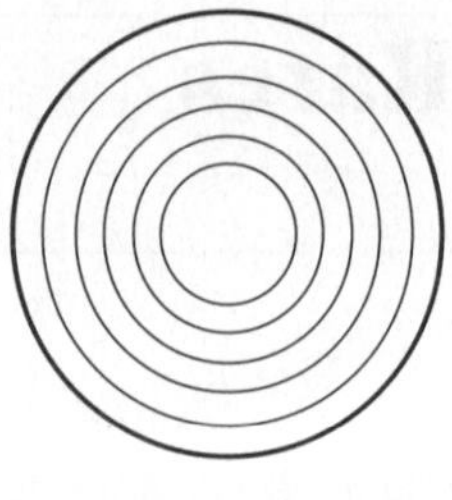

Figure 3.21 The same change in radius brings about a larger change in area as the circles grow radially away from the center. (Example 1, Exploration 1)

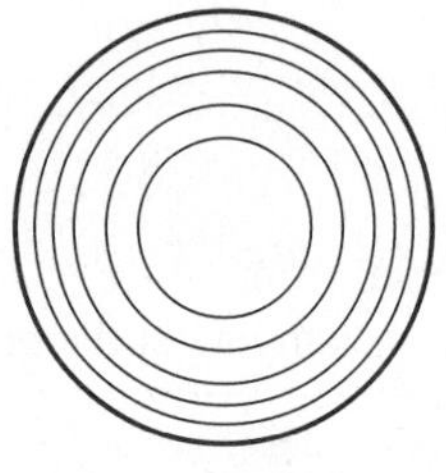

Figure 3.22 Which is the more appropriate model for the growth of rings in a tree—the circles here or those in Figure 3.21? (Exploration 1)

EXPLORATION 1 Growth Rings on a Tree

The phenomenon observed in Example 1, that the rate of change in area of a circle with respect to its radius gets larger as the radius gets larger, is reflected in nature in many ways. When trees grow, they add layers of wood directly under the inner bark during the growing season, then form a darker, protective layer for protection during the winter. This results in concentric rings that can be seen in a cross-sectional slice of the trunk. The age of the tree can be determined by counting the rings.

1. Look at the concentric rings in Figure 3.21 and Figure 3.22. Which is a better model for the pattern of growth rings in a tree? Is it likely that a tree could find the nutrients and light necessary to increase its amount of growth every year?
2. Considering how trees grow, explain why the change in *area* of the rings remains relatively constant from year to year.
3. If the change in area is constant, and if

$$\frac{dA}{dr} = \frac{\text{change in area}}{\text{change in radius}} = 2\pi r,$$

explain why the change in radius must get smaller as r gets bigger.

Motion Along a Line

Suppose that an object is moving along a coordinate line (say an s-axis) so that we know its position s on that line as a function of time t:

$$s = f(t).$$

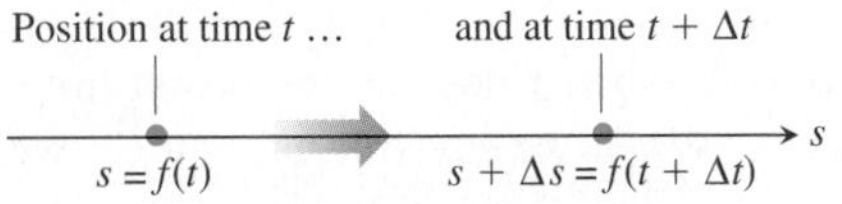

Figure 3.23 The positions of an object moving along a coordinate line at time t and shortly later at time $t + \Delta t$.

The **displacement** of the object over the time interval from t to $t + \Delta t$ is

$$\Delta s = f(t + \Delta t) - f(t)$$

(Figure 3.23) and the **average velocity** of the object over that time interval is

$$v_{\text{av}} = \frac{\text{displacement}}{\text{travel time}} = \frac{\Delta s}{\Delta t} = \frac{f(t + \Delta t) - f(t)}{\Delta t}.$$

To find the object's velocity at the exact instant t, we take the limit of the average velocity over the interval from t to $t + \Delta t$ as Δt shrinks to zero. The limit is the derivative of f with respect to t.

DEFINITION Instantaneous Velocity

The **(instantaneous) velocity** is the derivative of the position function $s = f(t)$ with respect to time. At time t the velocity is

$$v(t) = \frac{ds}{dt} = \lim_{\Delta t \to 0} \frac{f(t + \Delta t) - f(t)}{\Delta t}.$$

EXAMPLE 2 Finding the Velocity of a Race Car

Figure 3.24 shows the time-to-distance graph of a 1996 Riley & Scott Mk III-Olds WSC race car. The slope of the secant PQ is the average velocity for the 3-second interval from $t = 2$ to $t = 5$ sec, in this case, about 100 ft/sec or 68 mph. The slope of the tangent at P is the speedometer reading at $t = 2$ sec, about 57 ft/sec or 39 mph. The acceleration for the period shown is a nearly constant 28.5 ft/sec during each second, which is about $0.89g$ where g is the acceleration due to gravity. The race car's top speed is an estimated 190 mph. *Source: Road and Track,* March 1997.

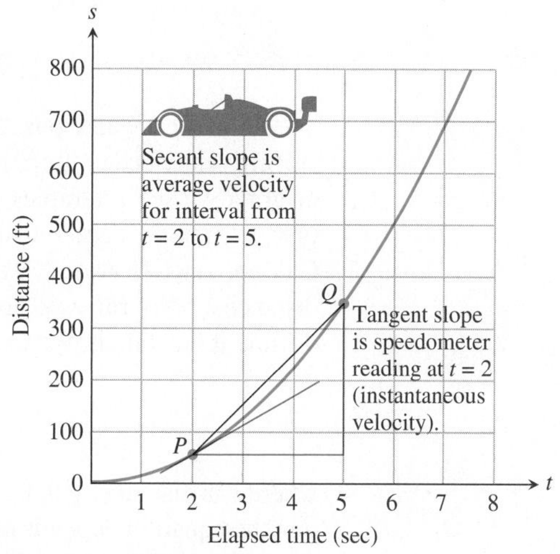

Figure 3.24 The time-to-distance graph for Example 2. ***Now Try Exercise 7.***

Besides telling how fast an object is moving, velocity tells the direction of motion. When the object is moving forward (when s is increasing), the velocity is positive; when the object is moving backward (when s is decreasing), the velocity is negative.

If we drive to a friend's house and back at 30 mph, the speedometer will show 30 on the way over but will not show -30 on the way back, even though our distance from home is decreasing. The speedometer always shows *speed,* which is the absolute value of velocity. Speed measures the rate of motion regardless of direction.

DEFINITION Speed

Speed is the absolute value of velocity.

$$\text{Speed} = |v(t)| = \left|\frac{ds}{dt}\right|$$

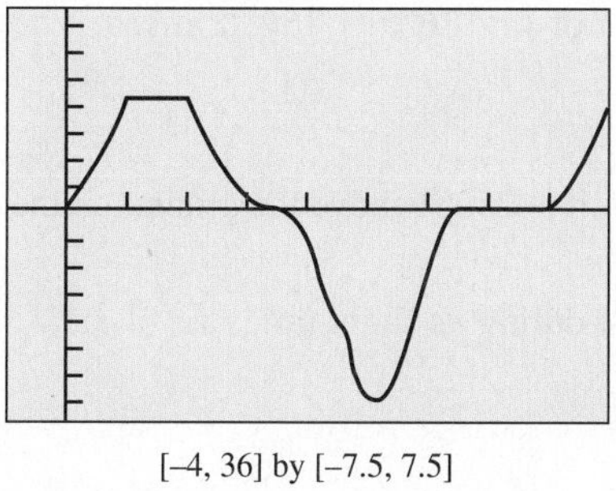

[–4, 36] by [–7.5, 7.5]

Figure 3.25 A student's velocity graph from data recorded by a motion detector. (Example 3)

EXAMPLE 3 Reading a Velocity Graph

A student walks around in front of a motion detector that records her velocity at 1-second intervals for 36 seconds. She stores the data in her graphing calculator and uses it to generate the time-velocity graph shown in Figure 3.25. Describe her motion as a function of time by reading the velocity graph. When is her *speed* a maximum?

SOLUTION

The student moves forward for the first 14 seconds, moves backward for the next 12 seconds, stands still for 6 seconds, and then moves forward again. She achieves her maximum speed at $t \approx 20$, while moving backward. ***Now Try Exercise 9.***

The rate at which a body's velocity changes is called the body's *acceleration*. The acceleration measures how quickly the body picks up or loses speed.

DEFINITION Acceleration

Acceleration is the derivative of velocity with respect to time. If a body's velocity at time t is $v(t) = ds/dt$, then the body's acceleration at time t is

$$a(t) = \frac{dv}{dt} = \frac{d^2s}{dt^2}.$$

The earliest questions that motivated the discovery of calculus were concerned with velocity and acceleration, particularly the motion of freely falling bodies under the force of gravity. (See Examples 1 and 2 in Section 2.1.) The mathematical description of this type of motion captured the imagination of many great scientists, including Aristotle, Galileo, and Newton. Experimental and theoretical investigations revealed that the distance a body released from rest falls freely is proportional to the square of the amount of time it has fallen. We express this by saying that

$$s = \frac{1}{2}gt^2,$$

where s is distance, g is the acceleration due to Earth's gravity, and t is time. The value of g in the equation depends on the units used to measure s and t. With t in seconds (the usual unit), we have the following values:

Free-fall Constants (Earth)

English units: $g = 32\frac{\text{ft}}{\text{sec}^2}$, $s = \frac{1}{2}(32)t^2 = 16t^2$ (s in feet)

Metric units: $g = 9.8\frac{\text{m}}{\text{sec}^2}$, $s = \frac{1}{2}(9.8)t^2 = 4.9t^2$ (s in meters)

The abbreviation ft/sec^2 is read "feet per second squared" or "feet per second per second," and m/sec^2 is read "meters per second squared."

EXAMPLE 4 Modeling Vertical Motion

A dynamite blast propels a heavy rock straight up with a launch velocity of 160 ft/sec (about 109 mph) (Figure 3.26a). It reaches a height of $s = 160t - 16t^2$ ft after t seconds.

(a) How high does the rock go?

(b) What is the velocity and speed of the rock when it is 256 ft above the ground on the way up? on the way down?

(c) What is the acceleration of the rock at any time t during its flight (after the blast)?

(d) When does the rock hit the ground?

SOLUTION

In the coordinate system we have chosen, s measures height from the ground up, so velocity is positive on the way up and negative on the way down.

continued

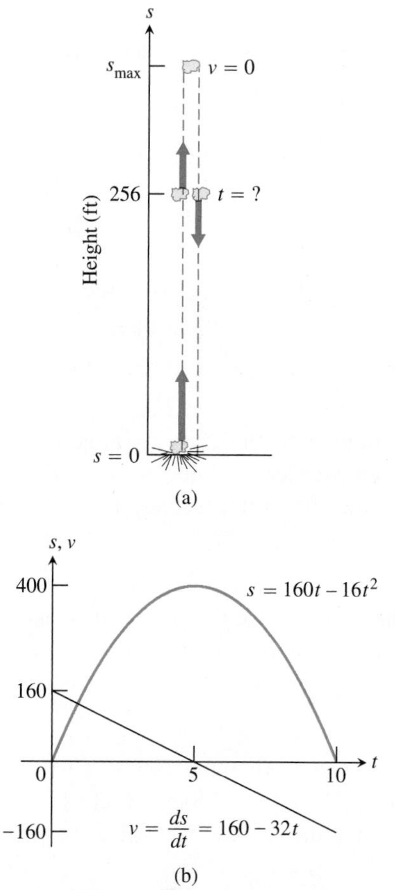

Figure 3.26 (a) The rock in Example 4. (b) The graphs of s and v as functions of time t, showing that s is largest when $v = ds/dt = 0$. (The graph of s is *not* the path of the rock; it is a plot of height as a function of time.) (Example 4)

(a) The instant when the rock is at its highest point is the one instant during the flight when the velocity is 0. At any time t, the velocity is

$$v = \frac{ds}{dt} = \frac{d}{dt}(160t - 16t^2) = 160 - 32t \text{ ft/sec.}$$

The velocity is zero when $160 - 32t = 0$, or at $t = 5$ sec.

The maximum height is the height of the rock at $t = 5$ sec. That is,

$$s_{max} = s(5) = 160(5) - 16(5)^2 = 400 \text{ ft.}$$

See Figure 3.26b.

(b) To find the velocity when the height is 256 ft, we determine the two values of t for which $s(t) = 256$ ft.

$$\begin{aligned} s(t) = 160t - 16t^2 &= 256 \\ 16t^2 - 160t + 256 &= 0 \\ 16(t^2 - 10t + 16) &= 0 \\ (t - 2)(t - 8) &= 0 \\ t = 2 \text{ sec} \quad \text{or} \quad t &= 8 \text{ sec} \end{aligned}$$

The velocity of the rock at each of these times is

$$v(2) = 160 - 32(2) = 96 \text{ ft/sec,}$$
$$v(8) = 160 - 32(8) = -96 \text{ ft/sec.}$$

At both instants, the speed of the rock is 96 ft/sec.

(c) At any time during its flight after the explosion, the rock's acceleration is

$$a = \frac{dv}{dt} = \frac{d}{dt}(160 - 32t) = -32 \text{ ft/sec}^2.$$

The acceleration is always downward. When the rock is rising, it is slowing down; when it is falling, it is speeding up.

(d) The rock hits the ground at the positive time for which $s = 0$. The equation $160t - 16t^2 = 0$ has two solutions: $t = 0$ and $t = 10$. The blast initiated the flight of the rock from ground level at $t = 0$. The rock returned to the ground 10 seconds later.

Now Try Exercise 13.

EXAMPLE 5 Studying Particle Motion

A particle moves along a line so that its position at any time $t \geq 0$ is given by the function $s(t) = t^2 - 4t + 3$, where s is measured in meters and t is measured in seconds.

(a) Find the displacement of the particle during the first 2 seconds.

(b) Find the average velocity of the particle during the first 4 seconds.

(c) Find the instantaneous velocity of the particle when $t = 4$.

(d) Find the acceleration of the particle when $t = 4$.

(e) Describe the motion of the particle. At what values of t does the particle change directions?

(f) Use parametric graphing to view the motion of the particle on the horizontal line $y = 2$.

continued

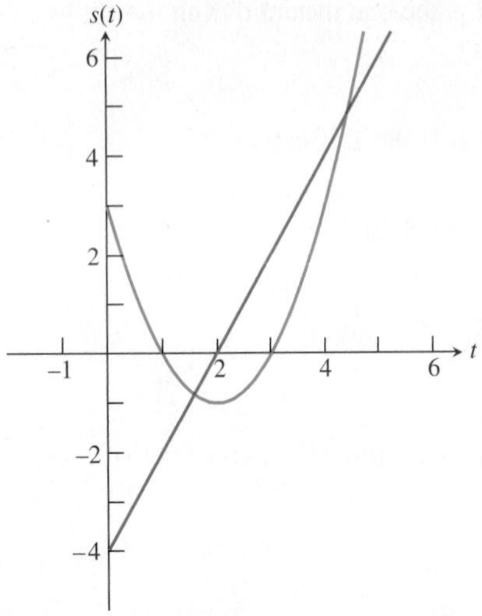

Figure 3.27 The graphs of $s(t) = t^2 - 4t + 3, t \geq 0$ (blue) and its derivative $v(t) = 2t - 4, t \geq 0$ (red). (Example 5)

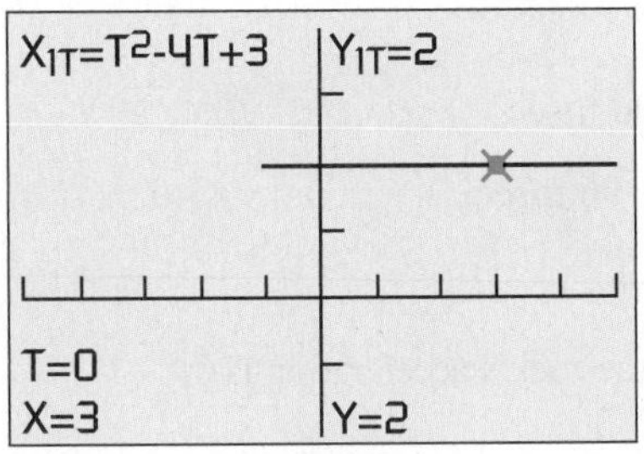

[−5, 5] by [−2, 4]

Figure 3.28 The graph of $X_{1T} = T^2 - 4T + 3$, $Y_{1T} = 2$ in parametric mode. (Example 5)

SOLUTION

(a) The displacement is given by $s(2) - s(0) = (-1) - 3 = -4$. This value means that the particle is 4 units left of where it started.

(b) The average velocity we seek is

$$\frac{s(4) - s(0)}{4 - 0} = \frac{3 - 3}{4} = 0 \text{ m/sec.}$$

(c) The velocity $v(t)$ at any time t is $v(t) = ds/dt = 2t - 4$. So $v(4) = 4$ m/sec

(d) The acceleration $a(t)$ at any time t is $a(t) = dv/dt = 2$ m/sec^2. So $a(4) = 2$.

(e) The graphs of $s(t) = t^2 - 4t + 3$ for $t \geq 0$ and its derivative $v(t) = 2t - 4$ shown in Figure 3.27 will help us analyze the motion.

For $0 \leq t < 2$, $v(t) < 0$, so the particle is moving to the left. Notice that $s(t)$ is decreasing. The particle starts ($t = 0$) at $s = 3$ and moves left, arriving at the origin $t = 1$ when $s = 0$. The particle continues moving to the left until it reaches the point $s = -1$ at $t = 2$.

At $t = 2$, $v = 0$, so the particle is at rest.

For $t > 2$, $v(t) > 0$, so the particle is moving to the right. Notice that $s(t)$ is increasing. In this interval, the particle starts at $s = -1$, moving to the right through the origin and continuing to the right for the rest of time.

The particle changes direction at $t = 2$ when $v = 0$.

(f) Enter $X_{1T}=T^2-4T+3$, $Y_{1T} = 2$ in parametric mode and graph in the window $[-5, 5]$ by $[-2, 4]$ with Tmin = 0, Tmax = 10 (it really should be ∞), and Xscl=Yscl=1 (Figure 3.28). By using TRACE you can follow the path of the particle. You will learn more ways to visualize motion in Explorations 2 and 3.

Now Try Exercise 19.

EXPLORATION 2 Modeling Horizontal Motion

The position (x-coordinate) of a particle moving on the horizontal line $y = 2$ is given by $x(t) = 4t^3 - 16t^2 + 15t$ for $t \geq 0$.

1. Graph the parametric equations $x_1(t) = 4t^3 - 16t^2 + 15t$, $y_1(t) = 2$ in $[-4, 6]$ by $[-3, 5]$. Use TRACE to support that the particle starts at the point $(0, 2)$, moves to the right, then to the left, and finally to the right. At what times does the particle reverse direction?
2. Graph the parametric equations $x_2(t) = x_1(t)$, $y_2(t) = t$ in the same viewing window. Explain how this graph shows the back and forth motion of the particle. Use this graph to find when the particle reverses direction.
3. Graph the parametric equations $x_3(t) = t$, $y_3(t) = x_1(t)$ in the same viewing window. Explain how this graph shows the back and forth motion of the particle. Use this graph to find when the particle reverses direction.
4. Use the methods in parts 1, 2, and 3 to represent and describe the *velocity* of the particle.

EXPLORATION 3 Seeing Motion on a Graphing Calculator

The graphs in Figure 3.26b give us plenty of information about the flight of the rock in Example 4, but neither graph shows the path of the rock in flight. We can simulate the moving rock by graphing the parametric equations

$$x_1(t) = 3(t < 5) + 3.1(t \geq 5), \quad y_1(t) = 160t - 16t^2$$

in dot mode.

This will show the upward flight of the rock along the vertical line $x = 3$, and the downward flight of the rock along the line $x = 3.1$.

1. To see the flight of the rock from beginning to end, what should we use for *t*Min and *t*Max in our graphing window?
2. Set *x*Min = 0, *x*Max = 6, and *y*Min = −10. Use the results from Example 4 to determine an appropriate value for *y*Max. (You will want the entire flight of the rock to fit within the vertical range of the screen.)
3. Set *t*Step initially at 0.1. (A higher number will make the simulation move faster. A lower number will slow it down.)
4. Can you explain why the grapher actually slows down when the rock would slow down, and speeds up when the rock would speed up?

Sensitivity to Change

When a small change in x produces a large change in the value of a function $f(x)$, we say that the function is relatively **sensitive** to changes in x. The derivative $f'(x)$ is a measure of this sensitivity.

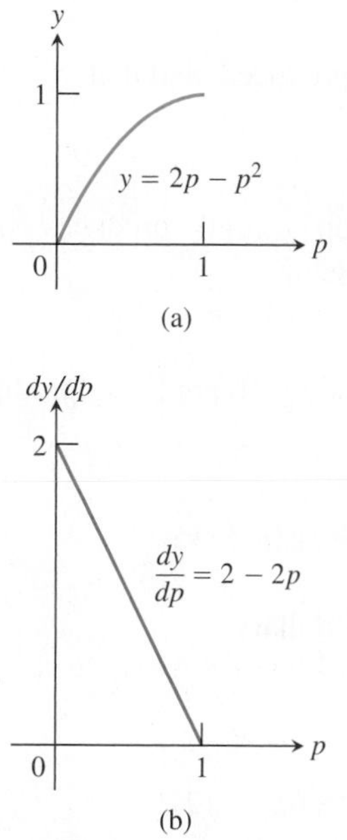

Figure 3.29 (a) The graph of $y = 2p - p^2$ describing the proportion of smooth-skinned peas. (b) The graph of dy/dp. (Example 6)

EXAMPLE 6 Sensitivity to Change

The Austrian monk Gregor Johann Mendel (1822–1884), working with garden peas and other plants, provided the first scientific explanation of hybridization. His careful records showed that if p (a number between 0 and 1) is the relative frequency of the gene for smooth skin in peas (dominant) and $(1 - p)$ is the relative frequency of the gene for wrinkled skin in peas (recessive), then the proportion of smooth-skinned peas in the next generation will be

$$y = 2p(1 - p) + p^2 = 2p - p^2.$$

Compare the graphs of y and dy/dp to determine what values of y are more sensitive to a change in p. The graph of y versus p in Figure 3.29a suggests that the value of y is more sensitive to a change in p when p is small than it is to a change in p when p is large. Indeed, this is borne out by the derivative graph in Figure 3.29b, which shows that dy/dp is close to 2 when p is near 0 and close to 0 when p is near 1.

Now Try Exercise 25.

Derivatives in Economics

Engineers use the terms *velocity* and *acceleration* to refer to the derivatives of functions describing motion. Economists, too, have a specialized vocabulary for rates of change and derivatives. They call them *marginals.*

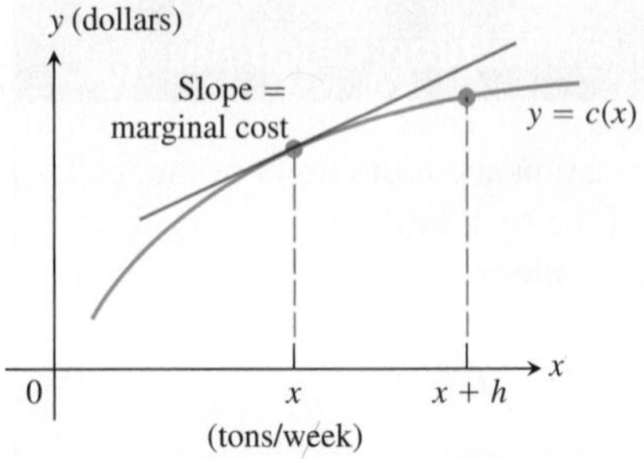

Figure 3.30 Weekly steel production: $c(x)$ is the cost of producing x tons per week. The cost of producing an additional h tons per week is $c(x + h) - c(x)$.

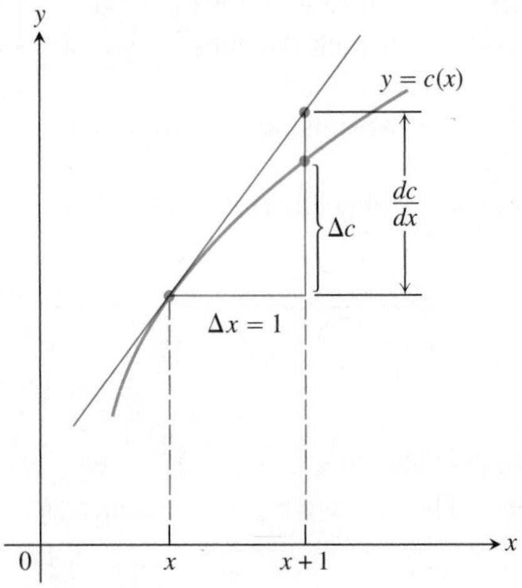

Figure 3.31 Because dc/dx is the slope of the tangent at x, the marginal cost dc/dx approximates the extra cost Δc of producing $\Delta x = 1$ more unit.

In a manufacturing operation, *the cost of production* $c(x)$ is a function of x, the number of units produced. The *marginal cost of production* is the rate of change of cost with respect to the level of production, so it is dc/dx.

Suppose $c(x)$ represents the dollars needed to produce x tons of steel in one week. It costs more to produce $x + h$ tons per week, and the cost difference divided by h is the average cost of producing each additional ton.

$$\frac{c(x+h) - c(x)}{h} = \begin{cases} \text{the average cost of each of the} \\ \text{additional } h \text{ tons produced} \end{cases}$$

The limit of this ratio as $h \to 0$ is the **marginal cost** of producing more steel per week when the current production is x tons (Figure 3.30).

$$\frac{dc}{dx} = \lim_{h \to 0} \frac{c(x+h) - c(x)}{h} = \text{marginal cost of production}$$

Sometimes the marginal cost of production is loosely defined to be the extra cost of producing one more unit,

$$\frac{\Delta c}{\Delta x} = \frac{c(x+1) - c(x)}{1},$$

which is approximated by the value of dc/dx at x. This approximation is acceptable if the slope of c does not change quickly near x, for then the difference quotient is close to its limit dc/dx even if $\Delta x = 1$ (Figure 3.31). The approximation works best for large values of x.

EXAMPLE 7 Marginal Cost and Marginal Revenue

Suppose it costs

$$c(x) = x^3 - 6x^2 + 15x$$

dollars to produce x radiators when 8 to 10 radiators are produced, and that

$$r(x) = x^3 - 3x^2 + 12x$$

gives the dollar revenue from selling x radiators. Your shop currently produces 10 radiators a day. Find the marginal cost and **marginal revenue.**

SOLUTION

The marginal cost of producing one more radiator a day when 10 are being produced is $c'(10)$.

$$c'(x) = \frac{d}{dx}(x^3 - 6x^2 + 15x) = 3x^2 - 12x + 15$$

$$c'(10) = 3(100) - 12(10) + 15 = 195 \text{ dollars}$$

The marginal revenue is

$$r'(x) = \frac{d}{dx}(x^3 - 3x^2 + 12x) = 3x^2 - 6x + 12,$$

so,

$$r'(10) = 3(100) - 6(10) + 12 = 252 \text{ dollars.}$$

Now Try Exercises 27 and 28.

Quick Review 3.4 (For help, go to Sections 1.2, 3.1, and 3.3.)

Exercise numbers with a gray background indicate problems that the authors have designed to be solved *without a calculator.*

In Exercises 1–10, answer the questions about the graph of the quadratic function $y = f(x) = -16x^2 + 160x - 256$ by analyzing the equation algebraically. Then support your answers graphically.

1. Does the graph open upward or downward?
2. What is the y-intercept?
3. What are the x-intercepts?
4. What is the range of the function?
5. What point is the vertex of the parabola?
6. At what x-values does $f(x) = 80$?
7. For what x-value does $dy/dx = 100$?
8. On what interval is $dy/dx > 0$?
9. Find $\lim_{h \to 0} \frac{f(3 + h) - f(3)}{h}$.
10. Find d^2y/dx^2 at $x = 7$.

Section 3.4 Exercises

1. (a) Write the volume V of a cube as a function of the side length s.
   (b) Find the (instantaneous) rate of change of the volume V with respect to a side s.
   (c) Evaluate the rate of change of V at $s = 1$ and $s = 5$.
   (d) If s is measured in inches and V is measured in cubic inches, what units would be appropriate for dV/ds?
2. (a) Write the area A of a circle as a function of the circumference C.
   (b) Find the (instantaneous) rate of change of the area A with respect to the circumference C.
   (c) Evaluate the rate of change of A at $C = \pi$ and $C = 6\pi$.
   (d) If C is measured in inches and A is measured in square inches, what units would be appropriate for dA/dC?
3. (a) Write the area A of an equilateral triangle as a function of the side length s.
   (b) Find the (instantaneous) rate of change of the area A with respect to a side s.
   (c) Evaluate the rate of change of A at $s = 2$ and $s = 10$.
   (d) If s is measured in inches and A is measured in square inches, what units would be appropriate for dA/ds?
4. A square of side length s is inscribed in a circle of radius r.
   (a) Write the area A of the square as a function of the radius r of the circle.
   (b) Find the (instantaneous) rate of change of the area A with respect to the radius r of the circle.
   (c) Evaluate the rate of change of A at $r = 1$ and $r = 8$.
   (d) If r is measured in inches and A is measured in square inches, what units would be appropriate for dA/dr?

Group Activity In Exercises 5 and 6, the coordinates s of a moving body for various values of t are given. **(a)** Plot s versus t on coordinate paper, and sketch a smooth curve through the given points. **(b)** Assuming that this smooth curve represents the motion of the body, estimate the velocity at $t = 1.0$, $t = 2.5$, and $t = 3.5$.

5.

t (sec)	0	0.5	1.0	1.5	2.0	2.5	3.0	3.5	4.0
s (ft)	12.5	26	36.5	44	48.5	50	48.5	44	36.5

6.

t (sec)	0	0.5	1.0	1.5	2.0	2.5	3.0	3.5	4.0
s (ft)	3.5	−4	−8.5	−10	−8.5	−4	3.5	14	27.5

7. **Group Activity *Fruit Flies*** *(Example 2, Section 2.4 continued)* Populations starting out in closed environments grow slowly at first, when there are relatively few members, then more rapidly as the number of reproducing individuals increases and resources are still abundant, then slowly again as the population reaches the carrying capacity of the environment.
   (a) Use the graphical technique of Section 3.1, Example 3, to graph the derivative of the fruit fly population introduced in Section 2.4. The graph of the population is reproduced below. What units should be used on the horizontal and vertical axes for the derivative's graph?
   (b) During what days does the population seem to be increasing fastest? slowest?

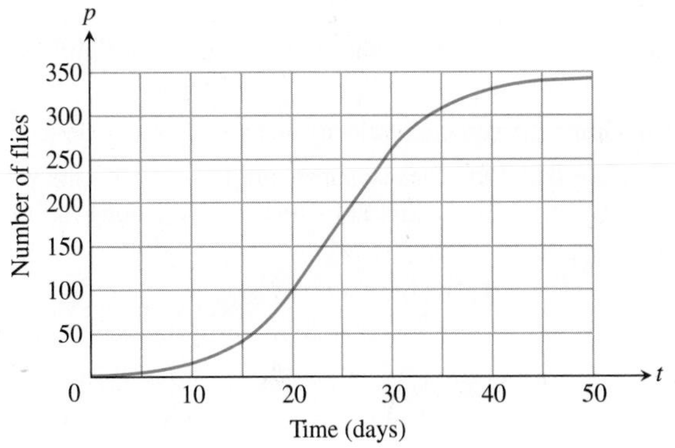

8. *Draining a Tank* The number of gallons of water in a tank t minutes after the tank has started to drain is $Q(t) = 200(30 - t)^2$. How fast is the water running out at the end of 10 min? What is the average rate at which the water flows out during the first 10 min?

9. *Particle Motion* The accompanying figure shows the velocity $v = f(t)$ of a particle moving on a coordinate line.

(a) When does the particle move forward? move backward? speed up? slow down?

(b) When is the particle's acceleration positive? negative? zero?

(c) When does the particle move at its greatest speed?

(d) When does the particle stand still for more than an instant?

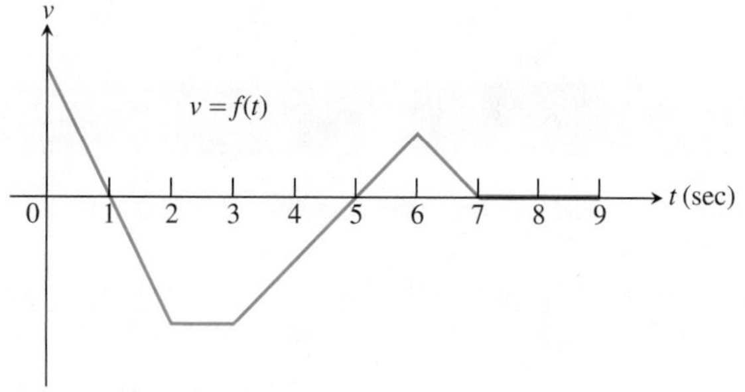

10. *Particle Motion* A particle P moves on the number line shown in part (a) of the accompanying figure. Part (b) shows the position of P as a function of time t.

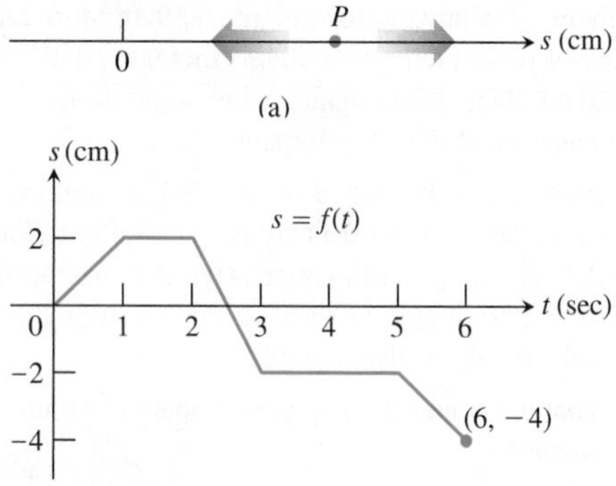

(a) When is P moving to the left? moving to the right? standing still?

(b) Graph the particle's velocity and speed (where defined).

11. *Particle Motion* The accompanying figure shows the velocity $v = ds/dt = f(t)$ (m/sec) of a body moving along a coordinate line.

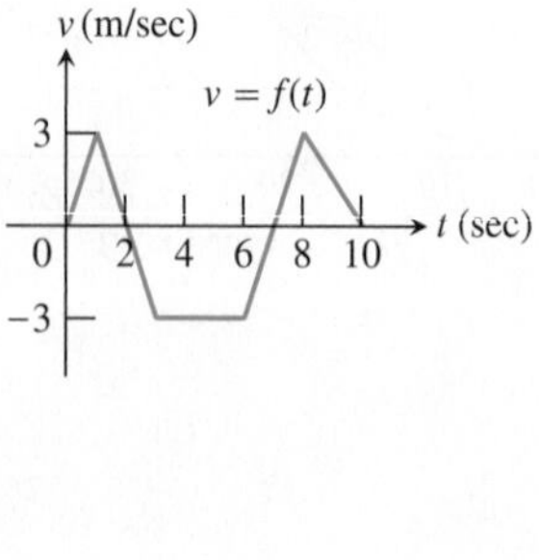

(a) When does the body reverse direction?

(b) When (approximately) is the body moving at a constant speed?

(c) Graph the body's speed for $0 \le t \le 10$.

(d) Graph the acceleration, where defined.

12. *Thoroughbred Racing* A racehorse is running a 10-furlong race. (A furlong is 220 yards, although we will use furlongs and seconds as our units in this exercise.) As the horse passes each furlong marker (F), a steward records the time elapsed (t) since the beginning of the race, as shown in the table below:

F	0	1	2	3	4	5	6	7	8	9	10
t	0	20	33	46	59	73	86	100	112	124	135

(a) How long does it take the horse to finish the race?

(b) What is the average speed of the horse over the first 5 furlongs?

(c) What is the approximate speed of the horse as it passes the 3-furlong marker?

(d) During which portion of the race is the horse running the fastest?

(e) During which portion of the race is the horse accelerating the fastest?

13. *Lunar Projectile Motion* A rock thrown vertically upward from the surface of the moon at a velocity of 24 m/sec (about 86 km/h) reaches a height of $s = 24t - 0.8t^2$ meters in t seconds.

(a) Find the rock's velocity and acceleration as functions of time. (The acceleration in this case is the acceleration of gravity on the moon.)

(b) How long did it take the rock to reach its highest point?

(c) How high did the rock go?

(d) When did the rock reach half its maximum height?

(e) How long was the rock aloft?

14. *Free Fall* The equations for free fall near the surfaces of Mars and Jupiter (s in meters, t in seconds) are: Mars, $s = 1.86t^2$; Jupiter, $s = 11.44t^2$. How long would it take a rock falling from rest to reach a velocity of 16.6 m/sec (about 60 km/h) on each planet?

15. *Projectile Motion* On Earth, in the absence of air, the rock in Exercise 13 would reach a height of $s = 24t - 4.9t^2$ meters in t seconds. How high would the rock go?

16. *Speeding Bullet* A bullet fired straight up from the moon's surface would reach a height of $s = 832t - 2.6t^2$ ft after t sec. On Earth, in the absence of air, its height would be $s = 832t - 16t^2$ ft after t sec. How long would it take the bullet to get back down in each case?

17. *Parametric Graphing* Devise a grapher simulation of the problem situation in Exercise 16. Use it to support the answers obtained analytically.

18. ***Launching a Rocket*** When a model rocket is launched, the propellant burns for a few seconds, accelerating the rocket upward. After burnout, the rocket coasts upward for a while and then begins to fall. A small explosive charge pops out a parachute shortly after the rocket starts downward. The parachute slows the rocket to keep it from breaking when it lands. This graph shows velocity data from the flight.

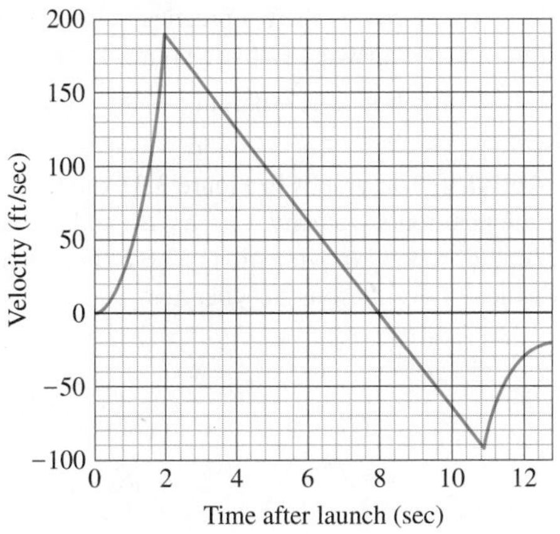

Use the graph to answer the following.

(a) How fast was the rocket climbing when the engine stopped?

(b) For how many seconds did the engine burn?

(c) When did the rocket reach its highest point? What was its velocity then?

(d) When did the parachute pop out? How fast was the rocket falling then?

(e) How long did the rocket fall before the parachute opened?

(f) When was the rocket's acceleration greatest? When was the acceleration constant?

19. ***Particle Motion*** A particle moves along a line so that its position at any time $t \geq 0$ is given by the function

$$s(t) = t^2 - 3t + 2,$$

where s is measured in meters and t is measured in seconds.

(a) Find the displacement during the first 5 seconds.

(b) Find the average velocity during the first 5 seconds.

(c) Find the instantaneous velocity when $t = 4$.

(d) Find the acceleration of the particle when $t = 4$.

(e) At what values of t does the particle change direction?

(f) Where is the particle when s is a minimum?

20. ***Particle Motion*** A particle moves along a line so that its position at any time $t \geq 0$ is given by the function $s(t) = -t^3 + 7t^2 - 14t + 8$ where s is measured in meters and t is measured in seconds.

(a) Find the instantaneous velocity at any time t.

(b) Find the acceleration of the particle at any time t.

(c) When is the particle at rest?

(d) Describe the motion of the particle. At what values of t does the particle change directions?

21. ***Particle Motion*** A particle moves along a line so that its position at any time $t \geq 0$ is given by the function $s(t) = (t - 2)^2(t - 4)$ where s is measured in meters and t is measured in seconds.

(a) Find the instantaneous velocity at any time t.

(b) Find the acceleration of the particle at any time t.

(c) When is the particle at rest?

(d) Describe the motion of the particle. At what values of t does the particle change directions?

22. ***Particle Motion*** A particle moves along a line so that its position at any time $t \geq 0$ is given by the function $s(t) = t^3 - 6t^2 + 8t + 2$ where s is measured in meters and t is measured in seconds.

(a) Find the instantaneous velocity at any time t.

(b) Find the acceleration of the particle at any time t.

(c) When is the particle at rest?

(d) Describe the motion of the particle. At what values of t does the particle change directions?

23. ***Particle Motion*** The position of a body at time t sec is $s = t^3 - 6t^2 + 9t$ m. Find the body's acceleration each time the velocity is zero.

24. ***Finding Speed*** A body's velocity at time t sec is $v = 2t^3 - 9t^2 + 12t - 5$ m/sec. Find the body's speed each time the acceleration is zero.

25. ***Draining a Tank*** It takes 12 hours to drain a storage tank by opening the valve at the bottom. The depth y of fluid in the tank t hours after the valve is opened is given by the formula

$$y = 6\left(1 - \frac{t}{12}\right)^2 \text{ m.}$$

(a) Find the rate dy/dt (m/h) at which the water level is changing at time t.

(b) When is the fluid level in the tank falling fastest? slowest? What are the values of dy/dt at these times?

(c) Graph y and dy/dt together and discuss the behavior of y in relation to the signs and values of dy/dt.

26. ***Moving Truck*** The graph here shows the position s of a truck traveling on a highway. The truck starts at $t = 0$ and returns 15 hours later at $t = 15$.

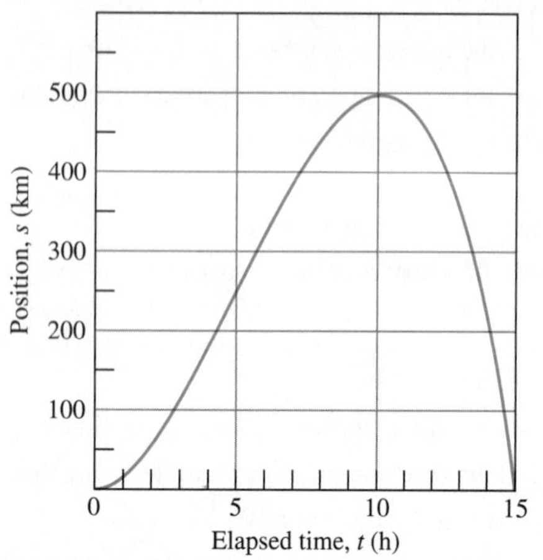

(a) Use the technique described in Section 3.1, Example 3, to graph the truck's velocity $v = ds/dt$ for $0 \le t \le 15$. Then repeat the process, with the velocity curve, to graph the truck's acceleration dv/dt.

(b) Suppose $s = 15t^2 - t^3$. Graph ds/dt and d^2s/dt^2, and compare your graphs with those in part (a).

27. ***Marginal Cost*** Suppose that the dollar cost of producing x washing machines is $c(x) = 2000 + 100x - 0.1x^2$.

(a) Find the average cost of producing 100 washing machines.

(b) Find the marginal cost when 100 machines are produced.

(c) Show that the marginal cost when 100 washing machines are produced is approximately the cost of producing one more washing machine after the first 100 have been made, by calculating the latter cost directly.

28. ***Marginal Revenue*** Suppose the weekly revenue in dollars from selling x custom-made office desks is

$$r(x) = 2000\left(1 - \frac{1}{x + 1}\right).$$

(a) Draw the graph of r. What values of x make sense in this problem situation?

(b) Find the marginal revenue when x desks are sold.

(c) Use the function $r'(x)$ to estimate the increase in revenue that will result from increasing sales from 5 desks a week to 6 desks a week.

(d) **Writing to Learn** Find the limit of $r'(x)$ as $x \to \infty$. How would you interpret this number?

29. ***Finding Profit*** The monthly profit (in thousands of dollars) of a software company is given by

$$P(x) = \frac{10}{1 + 50 \cdot 2^{5-0.1x}},$$

where x is the number of software packages sold.

(a) Graph $P(x)$.

(b) What values of x make sense in the problem situation?

(c) Use NDER to graph $P'(x)$. For what values of x is P relatively sensitive to changes in x?

(d) What is the profit when the marginal profit is greatest?

(e) What is the marginal profit when 50 units are sold? 100 units, 125 units, 150 units, 175 units, and 300 units?

(f) What is $\lim_{x\to\infty} P(x)$? What is the maximum profit possible?

(g) **Writing to Learn** Is there a practical explanation to the maximum profit answer? Explain your reasoning.

30. In Step 1 of Exploration 2, at what time is the particle at the point $(5, 2)$?

31. **Group Activity** The graphs in Figure 3.31 show as functions of time t the position s, velocity $v = ds/dt$, and acceleration $a = d^2s/dt^2$ of a body moving along a coordinate line. Which graph is which? Give reasons for your answers.

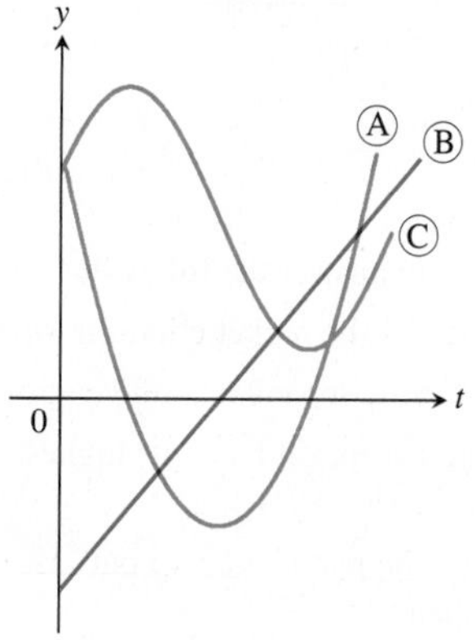

Figure 3.32 The graphs for Exercise 31.

32. **Group Activity** The graphs in Figure 3.33 show as functions of time t the position s, the velocity $v = ds/dt$, and the acceleration $a = d^2s/dt^2$ of a body moving along a coordinate line. Which graph is which? Give reasons for your answers.

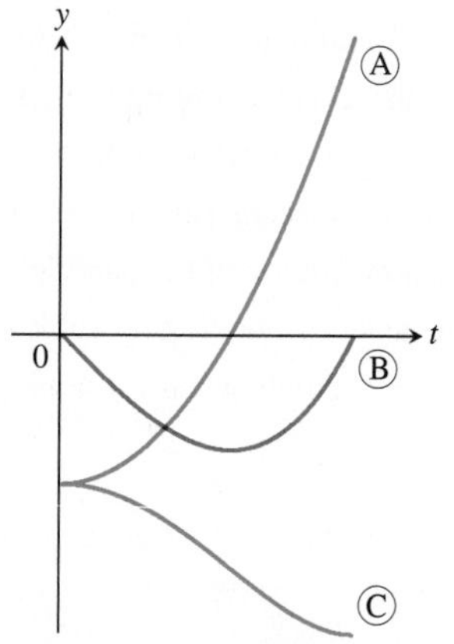

Figure 3.33 The graphs for Exercise 32.

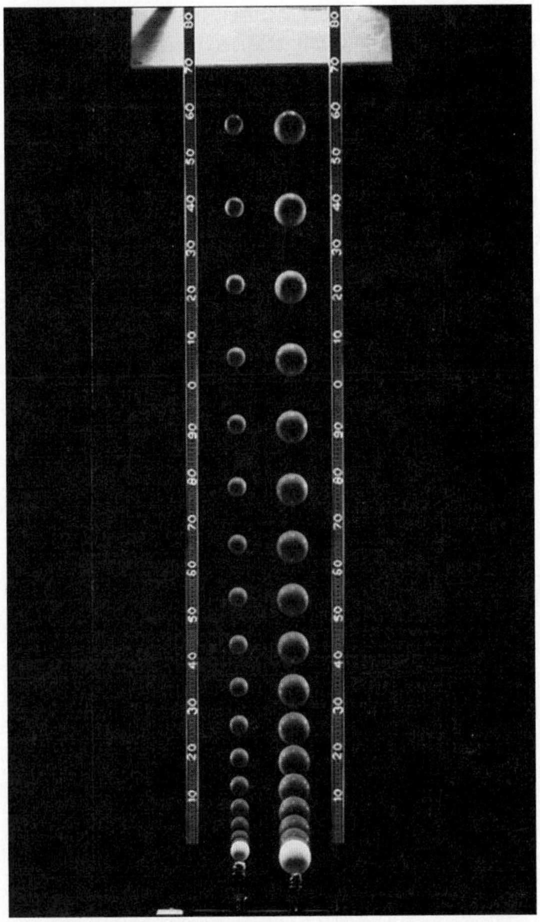

Figure 3.34 Two balls falling from rest. (Exercise 38)

33. ***Pisa by Parachute*** *(continuation of Exercise 18)* In 1988, Mike McCarthy parachuted 179 ft from the top of the Tower of Pisa. Make a rough sketch to show the shape of the graph of his downward velocity during the jump.

34. ***Inflating a Balloon*** The volume $V = (4/3)\pi r^3$ of a spherical balloon changes with the radius.

(a) At what rate does the volume change with respect to the radius when $r = 2$ ft?

(b) By approximately how much does the volume increase when the radius changes from 2 to 2.2 ft?

35. ***Volcanic Lava Fountains*** Although the November 1959 Kilauea Iki eruption on the island of Hawaii began with a line of fountains along the wall of the crater, activity was later confined to a single vent in the crater's floor, which at one point shot lava 1900 ft straight into the air (a world record). What was the lava's exit velocity in feet per second? in miles per hour? [*Hint:* If v_0 is the exit velocity of a particle of lava, its height t seconds later will be $s = v_0t - 16t^2$ feet. Begin by finding the time at which $ds/dt = 0$. Neglect air resistance.]

36. **Writing to Learn** Suppose you are looking at a graph of velocity as a function of time. How can you estimate the acceleration at a given point in time?

37. ***Particle Motion*** The position (x-coordinate) of a particle moving on the line $y = 2$ is given by $x(t) = 2t^3 - 13t^2 + 22t - 5$ where t is time in seconds.

(a) Describe the motion of the particle for $t \geq 0$.

(b) When does the particle speed up? slow down?

(c) When does the particle change direction?

(d) When is the particle at rest?

(e) Describe the velocity and speed of the particle.

(f) When is the particle at the point $(5, 2)$?

38. ***Falling Objects*** The multiflash photograph in Figure 3.34 shows two balls falling from rest. The vertical rulers are marked in centimeters. Use the equation $s = 490t^2$ (the free-fall equation for s in centimeters and t in seconds) to answer the following questions.

(a) How long did it take the balls to fall the first 160 cm? What was their average velocity for the period?

(b) How fast were the balls falling when they reached the 160-cm mark? What was their acceleration then?

(c) About how fast was the light flashing (flashes per second)?

39. **Writing to Learn** Explain how the Sum and Difference Rule (Rule 4 in Section 3.3) can be used to derive a formula for *marginal profit* in terms of marginal revenue and marginal cost.

Standardized Test Questions

You may use a graphing calculator to solve the following problems.

40. **True or False** The speed of a particle at $t = a$ is given by the value of the velocity at $t = a$. Justify your answer.

41. **True or False** The acceleration of a particle is the second derivative of the position function. Justify your answer.

42. **Multiple Choice** Find the instantaneous rate of change of $f(x) = x^2 - 2/x + 4$ at $x = -1$.

(A) -7 (B) -4 (C) 0 (D) 4 (E) 7

43. **Multiple Choice** Find the instantaneous rate of change of the volume of a cube with respect to a side length x.

(A) x (B) $3x$ (C) $6x$ (D) $3x^2$ (E) x^3

In Exercises 44 and 45, a particle moves along a line so that its position at any time $t \geq 0$ is given by $s(t) = 2 + 7t - t^2$.

44. **Multiple Choice** At which of the following times is the particle moving to the left?

(A) $t = 0$ (B) $t = 1$ (C) $t = 2$ (D) $t = 7/2$ (E) $t = 4$

45. **Multiple Choice** When is the particle at rest?

(A) $t = 1$ (B) $t = 2$ (C) $t = 7/2$ (D) $t = 4$ (E) $t = 5$

Explorations

46. ***Bacterium Population*** When a bactericide was added to a nutrient broth in which bacteria were growing, the bacterium population continued to grow for a while but then stopped growing and began to decline. The size of the population at time t (hours) was $b(t) = 10^6 + 10^4t - 10^3t^2$. Find the growth rates at $t = 0$, $t = 5$, and $t = 10$ hours.

47. *Finding f from f′* Let $f'(x) = 3x^2$.

(a) Compute the derivatives of $g(x) = x^3$, $h(x) = x^3 - 2$, and $t(x) = x^3 + 3$.

(b) Graph the numerical derivatives of g, h, and t.

(c) Describe a *family* of functions, $f(x)$, that have the property that $f'(x) = 3x^2$.

(d) Is there a function f such that $f'(x) = 3x^2$ and $f(0) = 0$? If so, what is it?

(e) Is there a function f such that $f'(x) = 3x^2$ and $f(0) = 3$? If so, what is it?

48. *Airplane Takeoff* Suppose that the distance an aircraft travels along a runway before takeoff is given by $D = (10/9)t^2$, where D is measured in meters from the starting point and t is measured in seconds from the time the brakes are released. If the aircraft will become airborne when its speed reaches 200 km/h, how long will it take to become airborne, and what distance will it have traveled by that time?

Extending the Ideas

49. *Even and Odd Functions*

(a) Show that if f is a differentiable even function, then f' is an odd function.

(b) Show that if f is a differentiable odd function, then f' is an even function.

50. *Extended Product Rule* Derive a formula for the derivative of the product fgh of three differentiable functions.

3.5 Derivatives of Trigonometric Functions

What you will learn about . . .

- Derivative of the Sine Function
- Derivative of the Cosine Function
- Simple Harmonic Motion
- Jerk
- Derivatives of the Other Basic Trigonometric Functions

and why . . .

The derivatives of sines and cosines play a key role in describing periodic change.

Derivative of the Sine Function

Trigonometric functions are important because so many of the phenomena we want information about are periodic (heart rhythms, earthquakes, tides, weather). It is known that continuous periodic functions can always be expressed in terms of sines and cosines, so the derivatives of sines and cosines play a key role in describing periodic change. This section introduces the derivatives of the six basic trigonometric functions.

EXPLORATION 1 Making a Conjecture by Graphing the Derivative

In the window $[-2\pi, 2\pi]$ by $[-4, 4]$, graph $y_1 = \sin x$ and $y_2 = \frac{d}{dx}(\sin x)$ (Figure 3.35). If your calculator does not recognize $\frac{d}{dx}(\sin x)$, use the numerical derivative.

1. When the graph of $y_1 = \sin x$ is increasing, what is true about the graph of $y_2 = \frac{d}{dx}(\sin x)$?
2. When the graph of $y_1 = \sin x$ is decreasing, what is true about the graph of $y_2 = \frac{d}{dx}(\sin x)$?
3. When the graph of $y_1 = \sin x$ stops increasing and starts decreasing, what is true about the graph of $y_2 = \frac{d}{dx}(\sin x)$?
4. At the places where $y_2 = \frac{d}{dx}(\sin x) = \pm 1$, what appears to be the slope of the graph of $y_1 = \sin x$?
5. Make a conjecture about what function the derivative of sine might be. Test your conjecture by graphing your function and $y_2 = \frac{d}{dx}(\sin x)$ in the same viewing window.
6. Now let $y_1 = \cos x$ and $y_2 = \frac{d}{dx}(\cos x)$. Answer questions (1) through (5) *without* looking at the graph of $y_2 = \frac{d}{dx}(\cos x)$ until you are ready to test your conjecture about what function the derivative of cosine might be.

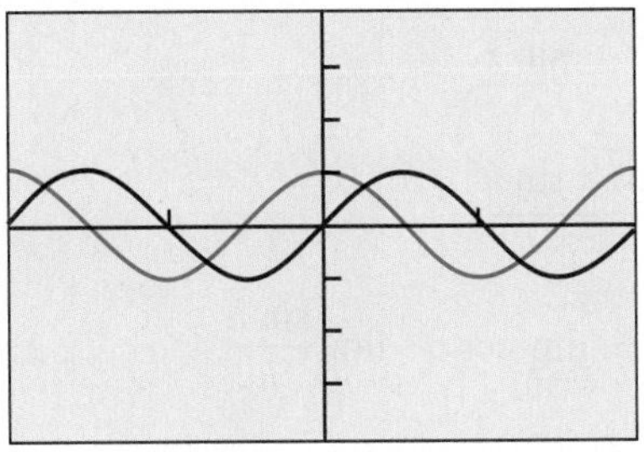

$[-2\pi, 2\pi]$ by $[-4, 4]$

Figure 3.35 Sine and its derivative. What is the derivative? (Exploration 1)

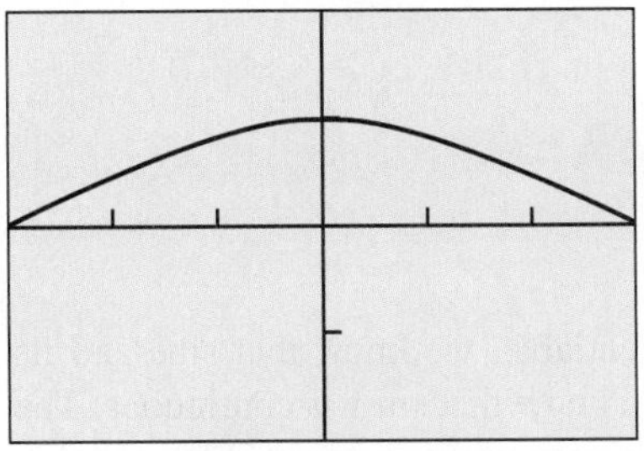

$[-3, 3]$ by $[-2, 2]$

(a)

X	Y1
−.03	.99985
−.02	.99993
−.01	.99998
0	ERROR
.01	.99998
.02	.99993
.03	.99985

Y1 = sin (X)/X

(b)

Figure 3.36 (a) Graphical and (b) tabular support that $\lim_{h\to 0} \frac{\sin(h)}{h} = 1$.

If you conjectured that the derivative of the sine function is the cosine function, then you are right. We will confirm this analytically, but first we appeal to technology one more time to evaluate two limits needed in the proof (see Figure 3.36 in the margin and Figure 3.37 on the next page):

A Word on Notation

In Exploration 1, a CAS calculator will accept the notation $y_2 = \frac{d}{dx}(\sin x)$ and graph the true derivative. Non-CAS users should use $y_2 =$ NDER(sin x, x), which works just as well as a visualization. In either case, you will be using your graph to make conjectures about the true derivative.

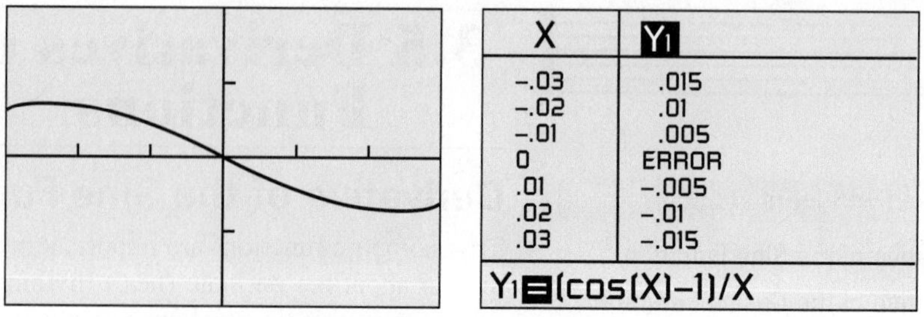

X
Y1
−.03
−.02
−.01
0
.01
.02
.03
.015
.01
.005
ERROR
−.005
−.01
−.015
Y1=(cos(X)−1)/X

[−3, 3] by [−2, 2]

(a)

(b)

Figure 3.37 (a) Graphical and (b) tabular support that $\lim_{h\to 0} \frac{\cos(h) - 1}{h} = 0$.

Confirm Analytically

(Also, see Section 2.1, Exercise 77.) Now, let $y = \sin x$. Then

$$\begin{aligned}
\frac{dy}{dx} &= \lim_{h\to 0} \frac{\sin(x+h) - \sin x}{h} \\
&= \lim_{h\to 0} \frac{\sin x \cos h + \cos x \sin h - \sin x}{h} \qquad \text{Angle sum identity} \\
&= \lim_{h\to 0} \frac{(\sin x)(\cos h - 1) + \cos x \sin h}{h} \\
&= \lim_{h\to 0} \sin x \cdot \lim_{h\to 0} \frac{(\cos h - 1)}{h} + \lim_{h\to 0} \cos x \cdot \lim_{h\to 0} \frac{\sin h}{h} \\
&= \sin x \cdot 0 + \cos x \cdot 1 \\
&= \cos x.
\end{aligned}$$

In short, the derivative of the sine is the cosine.

$$\frac{d}{dx} \sin x = \cos x$$

Now that we know that the sine function is differentiable, we know that sine and its derivative obey all the rules for differentiation. We also know that $\sin x$ is continuous. The same holds for the other trigonometric functions in this section. Each one is differentiable at every point in its domain, so each one is continuous at every point in its domain, and the differentiation rules apply for each one.

Derivative of the Cosine Function

If you conjectured in Exploration 1 that the derivative of the cosine function is the negative of the sine function, you were correct. You can confirm this analytically in Exercise 24.

$$\frac{d}{dx} \cos x = -\sin x$$

Radian Measure in Calculus

In case you have been wondering why calculus uses radian measure instead of degrees, you are now ready to understand the answer. The derivative of sin *x* is cos *x* *only* if *x* is measured in radians! If you look at the analytic confirmation, you will note that the derivative comes down to

$$\cos x \text{ times } \lim_{h\to 0} \frac{\sin h}{h}.$$

We saw that

$$\lim_{h\to 0} \frac{\sin h}{h} = 1$$

in Figure 3.36, but only because the graph in Figure 3.36 is in *radian mode.* If you look at the limit of the same function in *degree* mode you will get a very different limit (and hence a different derivative for sine). See Exercise 50.

EXAMPLE 1 Revisiting the Differentiation Rules

Find the derivatives of **(a)** $y = x^2 \sin x$ and **(b)** $u = \cos x/(1 - \sin x)$.

SOLUTION

(a) $$\frac{dy}{dx} = x^2 \cdot \frac{d}{dx}(\sin x) + \sin x \cdot \frac{d}{dx}(x^2) \qquad \text{Product Rule}$$
$$= x^2 \cos x + 2x \sin x$$

(b) $$\frac{du}{dx} = \frac{(1 - \sin x)\cdot \frac{d}{dx}(\cos x) - \cos x \cdot \frac{d}{dx}(1 - \sin x)}{(1 - \sin x)^2} \qquad \text{Quotient Rule}$$
$$= \frac{(1 - \sin x)(-\sin x) - \cos x\,(0 - \cos x)}{(1 - \sin x)^2}$$
$$= \frac{-\sin x + \sin^2 x + \cos^2 x}{(1 - \sin x)^2}$$
$$= \frac{1 - \sin x}{(1 - \sin x)^2} \qquad \sin^2 x + \cos^2 x = 1$$
$$= \frac{1}{1 - \sin x}$$

Now Try Exercises 5 and 9.

Simple Harmonic Motion

The motion of a weight bobbing up and down on the end of a spring is an example of **simple harmonic motion.** Example 2 describes a case in which there are no opposing forces like friction or buoyancy to slow down the motion.

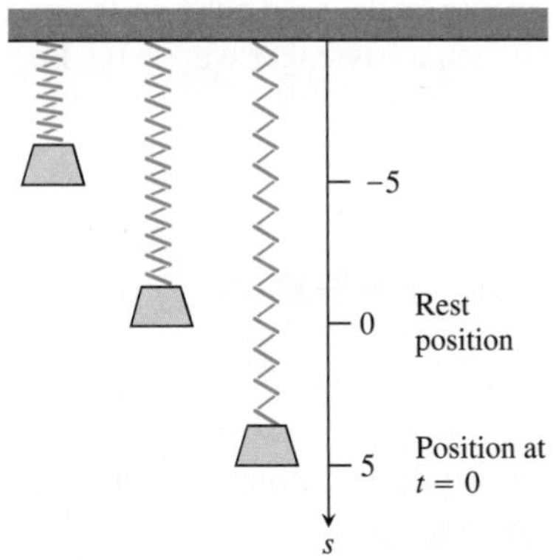

Figure 3.38 The weighted spring in Example 2.

EXAMPLE 2 The Motion of a Weight on a Spring

A weight hanging from a spring (Figure 3.38) is stretched 5 units beyond its rest position $(s = 0)$ and released at time $t = 0$ to bob up and down. Its position at any later time *t* is

$$s = 5 \cos t.$$

What are its velocity and acceleration at time *t*? Describe its motion.

SOLUTION We have:

Position: $s = 5 \cos t;$

Velocity: $v = \frac{ds}{dt} = \frac{d}{dt}(5 \cos t) = -5 \sin t;$

Acceleration: $a = \frac{dv}{dt} = \frac{d}{dt}(-5 \sin t) = -5 \cos t.$

Notice how much we can learn from these equations:

1. As time passes, the weight moves down and up between $s = -5$ and $s = 5$ on the *s*-axis. The amplitude of the motion is 5. The period of the motion is 2π.
2. The velocity $v = -5 \sin t$ attains its greatest magnitude, 5, when $\cos t = 0$, as the graphs show in Figure 3.39. Hence the speed of the weight, $|v| = 5\,|\sin t|$, is greatest when $\cos t = 0$, that is, when $s = 0$ (the rest position). The speed of the weight is zero when $\sin t = 0$. This occurs when $s = 5 \cos t = \pm 5$, at the endpoints of the interval of motion.
3. The acceleration value is always the exact opposite of the position value. When the weight is above the rest position, gravity is pulling it back down; when the weight is below the rest position, the spring is pulling it back up. *continued*

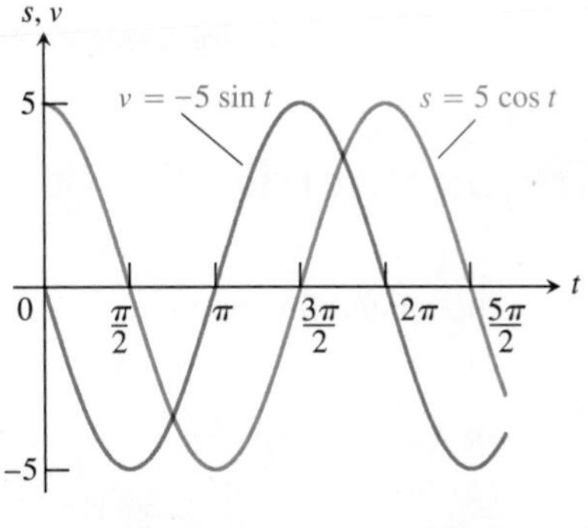

Figure 3.39 Graphs of the position and velocity of the weight in Example 2.

4. The acceleration, $a = -5\cos t$, is zero only at the rest position where $\cos t = 0$ and the force of gravity and the force from the spring offset each other. When the weight is anywhere else, the two forces are unequal and acceleration is nonzero. The acceleration is greatest in magnitude at the points farthest from the rest position, where $\cos t = \pm 1$.

Now Try Exercise 11.

Jerk

A sudden change in acceleration is called a "jerk." When a ride in a car or a bus is jerky, it is not that the accelerations involved are necessarily large but that the changes in acceleration are abrupt. Jerk is what spills your soft drink. The derivative responsible for jerk is the *third* derivative of position.

DEFINITION Jerk

Jerk is the derivative of acceleration. If a body's position at time t is $s(t)$, the body's jerk at time t is

$$j(t) = \frac{da}{dt} = \frac{d^3s}{dt^3}.$$

Tests have shown that motion sickness comes from accelerations whose changes in magnitude or direction take us by surprise. Keeping an eye on the road helps us to see the changes coming. A driver is less likely to become sick than a passenger who is reading in the back seat.

EXAMPLE 3 A Couple of Jerks

(a) The jerk caused by the constant acceleration of gravity ($g = -32$ ft/sec^2) is zero:

$$j = \frac{d}{dt}(g) = 0.$$

This explains why we don't experience motion sickness while just sitting around.

(b) The jerk of the simple harmonic motion in Example 2 is

$$j = \frac{da}{dt} = \frac{d}{dt}(-5\cos t)$$
$$= 5\sin t.$$

It has its greatest magnitude when $\sin t = \pm 1$. This does not occur at the extremes of the displacement, but at the rest position, where the acceleration changes direction and sign.

Now Try Exercise 19.

Derivatives of the Other Basic Trigonometric Functions

Because $\sin x$ and $\cos x$ are differentiable functions of x, the related functions

$$\tan x = \frac{\sin x}{\cos x}, \qquad \sec x = \frac{1}{\cos x},$$

$$\cot x = \frac{\cos x}{\sin x}, \qquad \csc x = \frac{1}{\sin x}$$

are differentiable at every value of x for which they are defined. Their derivatives (Exercises 25 and 26) are given by the following formulas.

$$\frac{d}{dx}\tan x = \sec^2 x, \qquad \frac{d}{dx}\sec x = \sec x \tan x$$

$$\frac{d}{dx}\cot x = -\csc^2 x, \qquad \frac{d}{dx}\csc x = -\csc x \cot x$$

EXAMPLE 4 Finding Tangent and Normal Lines

Find equations for the lines that are tangent and normal to the graph of

$$f(x) = \frac{\tan x}{x}$$

at $x = 2$. Support graphically.

SOLUTION

Solve Numerically Since we will be using a calculator approximation for $f(2)$ anyway, this is a good place to use NDER.

We compute $(\tan 2)/2$ on the calculator and store it as k. The slope of the tangent line at $(2, k)$ is

$$\text{NDER}\left(\frac{\tan x}{x}, 2\right),$$

which we compute and store as m. The equation of the tangent line is $y - k = m(x - 2)$, or

$$y = mx + k - 2m.$$

Only after we have found m and $k - 2m$ do we round the coefficients, giving the tangent line as

$$y = 3.43x - 7.96.$$

The equation of the normal line is

$$y - k = -\frac{1}{m}(x - 2), \text{ or}$$

$$y = -\frac{1}{m}x + k + \frac{2}{m}.$$

Again we wait until the end to round the coefficients, giving the normal line as

$$y = -0.291x - 0.51.$$

$y_1 = \tan(x)/x$
$y_2 = 3.43x - 7.96$
$y_3 = -0.291x - 0.51$

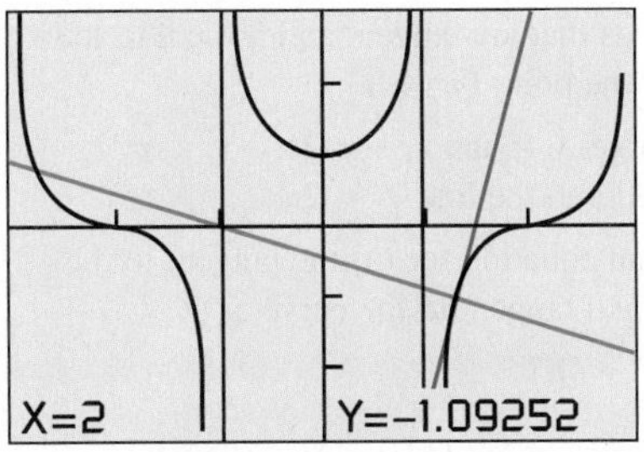

$[-3\pi/2, 3\pi/2]$ by $[-3, 3]$

Figure 3.40 Graphical support for Example 4.

Support Graphically Figure 3.40, showing the original function and the two lines, supports our computations. ***Now Try Exercise 23.***

EXAMPLE 5 A Trigonometric Second Derivative

Find y'' if $y = \sec x$.

SOLUTION

$$\begin{aligned}
y &= \sec x \\
y' &= \sec x \tan x \\
y'' &= \frac{d}{dx}(\sec x \tan x) \\
&= \sec x \frac{d}{dx}(\tan x) + \tan x \frac{d}{dx}(\sec x) \\
&= \sec x (\sec^2 x) + \tan x (\sec x \tan x) \\
&= \sec^3 x + \sec x \tan^2 x
\end{aligned}$$

Now Try Exercise 36.

Quick Review 3.5 (For help, go to Sections 1.6, 3.1, and 3.4.)

Exercise numbers with a gray background indicate problems that the authors have designed to be solved *without a calculator.*

1. Convert 135 degrees to radians.

2. Convert 1.7 radians to degrees.

3. Find the exact value of $\sin(\pi/3)$ without a calculator.

4. State the domain and the range of the cosine function.

5. State the domain and the range of the tangent function.

6. If $\sin a = -1$, what is $\cos a$?

7. If $\tan a = -1$, what are two possible values of $\sin a$?

8. Verify the identity:

$$\frac{1-\cos h}{h} = \frac{\sin^2 h}{h(1+\cos h)}.$$

9. Find an equation of the line tangent to the curve $y = 2x^3 - 7x^2 + 10$ at the point $(3, 1)$.

10. A particle moves along a line with velocity $v = 2t^3 - 7t^2 + 10$ for time $t \geq 0$. Find the acceleration of the particle at $t = 3$.

Section 3.5 Exercises

In Exercises 1–10, find dy/dx. Use your grapher to support your analysis if you are unsure of your answer.

1. $y = 1 + x - \cos x$

2. $y = 2\sin x - \tan x$

3. $y = \dfrac{1}{x} + 5\sin x$

4. $y = x \sec x$

5. $y = 4 - x^2 \sin x$

6. $y = 3x + x\tan x$

7. $y = \dfrac{4}{\cos x}$

8. $y = \dfrac{x}{1+\cos x}$

9. $y = \dfrac{\cot x}{1+\cot x}$

10. $y = \dfrac{\cos x}{1+\sin x}$

In Exercises 11 and 12, a weight hanging from a spring (see Figure 3.38) bobs up and down with position function $s = f(t)$ (s in meters, t in seconds). What are its velocity and acceleration at time t? Describe its motion.

11. $s = 5\sin t$

12. $s = 7\cos t$

In Exercises 13–16, a body is moving in simple harmonic motion with position function $s = f(t)$ (s in meters, t in seconds).

(a) Find the body's velocity, speed, and acceleration at time t.

(b) Find the body's velocity, speed, and acceleration at time $t = \pi/4$.

(c) Describe the motion of the body.

13. $s = 2 + 3\sin t$

14. $s = 1 - 4\cos t$

15. $s = 2\sin t + 3\cos t$

16. $s = \cos t - 3\sin t$

In Exercises 17–20, a body is moving in simple harmonic motion with position function $s = f(t)$ (s in meters, t in seconds). Find the jerk at time t.

17. $s = 2\cos t$

18. $s = 1 + 2\cos t$

19. $s = \sin t - \cos t$

20. $s = 2 + 2\sin t$

21. Find equations for the lines that are tangent and normal to the graph of $y = \sin x + 3$ at $x = \pi$.

22. Find equations for the lines that are tangent and normal to the graph of $y = \sec x$ at $x = \pi/4$.

23. Find equations for the lines that are tangent and normal to the graph of $y = x^2 \sin x$ at $x = 3$.

24. Use the definition of the derivative to prove that $(d/dx)(\cos x) = -\sin x$. (You will need the limits found at the beginning of this section.)

25. Assuming that $(d/dx)(\sin x) = \cos x$ and $(d/dx)(\cos x) = -\sin x$, prove each of the following.

(a) $\dfrac{d}{dx}\tan x = \sec^2 x$ **(b)** $\dfrac{d}{dx}\sec x = \sec x \tan x$

26. Assuming that $(d/dx)(\sin x) = \cos x$ and $(d/dx)(\cos x) = -\sin x$, prove each of the following.

(a) $\dfrac{d}{dx}\cot x = -\csc^2 x$ **(b)** $\dfrac{d}{dx}\csc x = -\csc x \cot x$

27. Show that the graphs of $y = \sec x$ and $y = \cos x$ have horizontal tangents at $x = 0$.

28. Show that the graphs of $y = \tan x$ and $y = \cot x$ have no horizontal tangents.

29. Find equations for the lines that are tangent and normal to the curve $y = \sqrt{2}\cos x$ at the point $(\pi/4, 1)$.

30. Find the points on the curve $y = \tan x$, $-\pi/2 < x < \pi/2$, where the tangent is parallel to the line $y = 2x$.

In Exercises 31 and 32, find an equation for **(a)** the tangent to the curve at P and **(b)** the horizontal tangent to the curve at Q.

31.

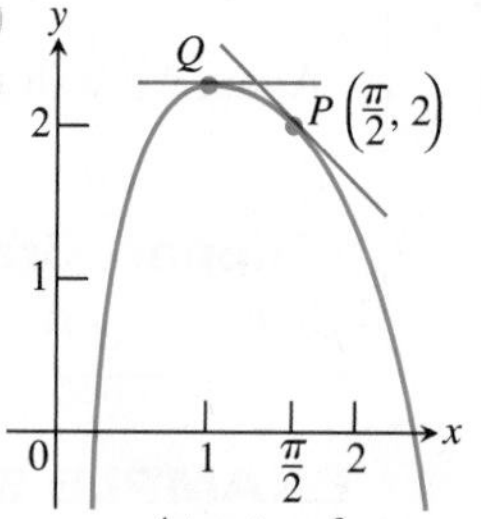

$y = 4 + \cot x - 2\csc x$

32.

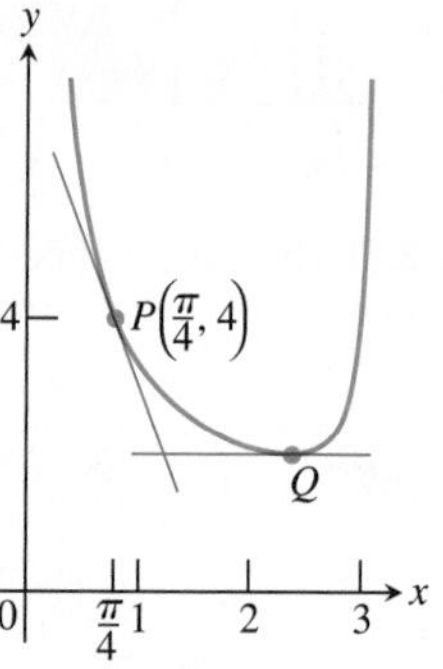

$y = 1 + \sqrt{2}\csc x + \cot x$

Group Activity In Exercises 33 and 34, a body is moving in simple harmonic motion with position $s = f(t)$ (s in meters, t in seconds).

(a) Find the body's velocity, speed, acceleration, and jerk at time t.

(b) Find the body's velocity, speed, acceleration, and jerk at time $t = \pi/4$ sec.

(c) Describe the motion of the body.

33. $s = 2 - 2 \sin t$

34. $s = \sin t + \cos t$

35. Find y'' if $y = \csc x$.

36. Find y'' if $y = \theta \tan \theta$.

37. Writing to Learn Is there a value of b that will make

$$g(x) = \begin{cases} x + b, & x < 0 \\ \cos x, & x \geq 0 \end{cases}$$

continuous at $x = 0$? differentiable at $x = 0$? Give reasons for your answers.

38. Find $\dfrac{d^{999}}{dx^{999}}(\cos x)$.

39. Find $\dfrac{d^{725}}{dx^{725}}(\sin x)$.

40. *Local Linearity* This is the graph of the function $y = \sin x$ close to the origin. Since $\sin x$ is differentiable, this graph resembles a line. Find an equation for this line.

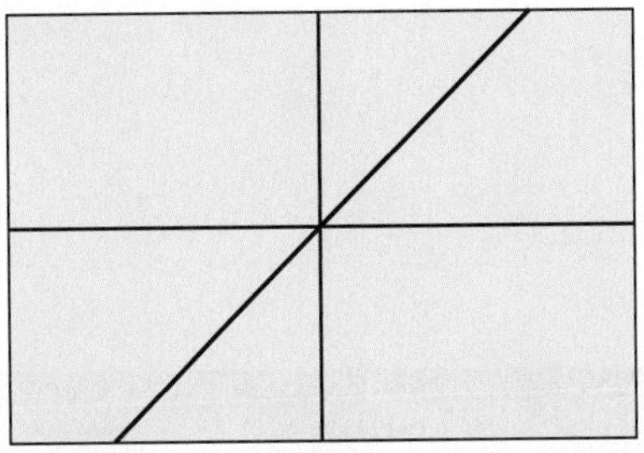

41. *(Continuation of Exercise 40)* For values of x close to 0, the linear equation found in Exercise 40 gives a good approximation of $\sin x$.

(a) Use this fact to estimate $\sin(0.12)$.

(b) Find $\sin(0.12)$ with a calculator. How close is the approximation in part (a)?

42. Use the identity $\sin 2x = 2 \sin x \cos x$ to find the derivative of $\sin 2x$. Then use the identity $\cos 2x = \cos^2 x - \sin^2 x$ to express that derivative in terms of $\cos 2x$.

43. Use the identity $\cos 2x = \cos x \cos x - \sin x \sin x$ to find the derivative of $\cos 2x$. Express the derivative in terms of $\sin 2x$.

Standardized Test Questions

You may use a graphing calculator to solve the following problems.

In Exercises 44 and 45, a spring is bobbing up and down on the end of a spring according to $s(t) = -3 \sin t$.

44. True or False The spring is traveling upward at $t = 3\pi/4$. Justify your answer.

45. True or False The velocity and speed of the particle are the same at $t = \pi/4$. Justify your answer.

46. Multiple Choice Which of the following is an equation of the tangent line to $y = \sin x + \cos x$ at $x = \pi$?

(A) $y = -x + \pi - 1$ **(B)** $y = -x + \pi + 1$

(C) $y = -x - \pi + 1$ **(D)** $y = -x - \pi - 1$

(E) $y = x - \pi + 1$

47. Multiple Choice Which of the following is an equation of the normal line to $y = \sin x + \cos x$ at $x = \pi$?

(A) $y = -x + \pi - 1$ **(B)** $y = x - \pi - 1$

(C) $y = x - \pi + 1$ **(D)** $y = x + \pi + 1$

(E) $y = x + \pi - 1$

48. Multiple Choice Find y'' if $y = x \sin x$.

(A) $-x \sin x$ **(B)** $x \cos x + \sin x$ **(C)** $-x \sin x + 2 \cos x$

(D) $x \sin x$ **(E)** $-\sin x + \cos x$

49. Multiple Choice A body is moving in simple harmonic motion with position $s = 3 + \sin t$. At which of the following times is the velocity zero?

(A) $t = 0$ **(B)** $t = \pi/4$ **(C)** $t = \pi/2$

(D) $t = \pi$ **(E)** none of these

Exploration

50. *Radians vs. Degrees* What happens to the derivatives of $\sin x$ and $\cos x$ if x is measured in degrees instead of radians? To find out, take the following steps.

(a) With your grapher in degree mode, graph

$$f(h) = \frac{\sin h}{h}$$

and estimate $\lim_{h \to 0} f(h)$. Compare your estimate with $\pi/180$. Is there any reason to believe the limit should be $\pi/180$?

(b) With your grapher in degree mode, estimate

$$\lim_{h \to 0} \frac{\cos h - 1}{h}.$$

(c) Now go back to the derivation of the formula for the derivative of $\sin x$ in the text and carry out the steps of the derivation using degree-mode limits. What formula do you obtain for the derivative?

(d) Derive the formula for the derivative of $\cos x$ using degree-mode limits.

(e) The disadvantages of the degree-mode formulas become apparent as you start taking derivatives of higher order. What are the second and third degree-mode derivatives of $\sin x$ and $\cos x$?

Extending the Ideas

51. Use analytic methods to show that

$$\lim_{h \to 0} \frac{\cos h - 1}{h} = 0.$$

[*Hint:* Multiply numerator and denominator by $(\cos h + 1)$.]

52. Find A and B in $y = A \sin x + B \cos x$ so that $y'' - y = \sin x$.

Quick Quiz for AP* Preparation: Sections 3.4–3.5

1. Multiple Choice If the line tangent to the graph of the function f at the point $(1, 6)$ passes through the point $(-1, -4)$, then $f'(1)$ is

(A) -1 (B) 1 (C) 5 (D) 6 (E) undefined

2. Multiple Choice Which of the following gives y'' for $y = \cos x + \tan x$?

(A) $-\cos x + 2\sec^2 x \tan x$ (B) $\cos x + 2\sec^2 x \tan x$

(C) $-\sin x + \sec^2 x$ (D) $-\cos x + \sec^2 x \tan x$

(E) $\cos x + \sec^2 x \tan x$

3. Multiple Choice If $y = \dfrac{3x + 2}{2x + 3}$, then $\dfrac{dy}{dx} =$

(A) $\dfrac{12x - 13}{(2x + 3)^2}$ (B) $\dfrac{12x - 13}{(2x + 3)^2}$ (C) $\dfrac{-5}{(2x + 3)^2}$

(D) $\dfrac{5}{(2x + 3)^2}$ (E) $\dfrac{2}{3}$

4. Free Response A particle moves along a line so that its position at any time $t \geq 0$ is given by $s(t) = -t^2 + t + 2$, where s is measured in meters and t is measured in seconds.

(a) What is the initial position of the particle?

(b) Find the initial velocity of the particle at any time t.

(c) When is the particle moving to the right?

(d) Find the acceleration of the particle at any time t.

(e) Find the speed of the particle at the moment when $s(t) = 0$.

Chapter 3 Key Terms

acceleration (p. 130)
average velocity (p. 128)
Constant Multiple Rule (p. 117)
Derivative of a Constant Function (p. 116)
derivative of f at a (p. 99)
differentiable function (p. 99)
differentiable on a closed interval (p. 104)
displacement (p. 128)
free-fall constants (p. 130)
instantaneous rate of change (p. 127)
instantaneous velocity (p. 128)
Intermediate Value Theorem for Derivatives (p. 113)
jerk (p. 144)
left-hand derivative (p. 104)
local linearity (p. 110)
marginal cost (p. 134)
marginal revenue (p. 134)
nth derivative (p. 122)
numerical derivative (NDER) (p. 111)
Power Rule for Negative Integer Powers of x (p. 121)
Power Rule for Positive Integer Powers of x (p. 116)
Product Rule (p. 119)
Quotient Rule (p. 120)
right-hand derivative (p. 104)
sensitivity to change (p. 133)
simple harmonic motion (p. 143)
speed (p. 129)
Sum and Difference Rule (p. 117)
symmetric difference quotient (p. 111)
velocity (p. 128)

Chapter 3 Review Exercises

Exercise numbers with a gray background indicate problems that the authors have designed to be solved *without a calculator.*

The collection of exercises marked in red could be used as a chapter test.

In Exercises 1–30, find the derivative of the function.

1. $y = x^5 - \dfrac{1}{8}x^2 + \dfrac{1}{4}x$

2. $y = 3 - 7x^3 + 3x^7$

3. $y = 2 \sin x \cos x$

4. $y = \dfrac{2x + 1}{2x - 1}$

5. $s = (t^2 - 1)(t^2 + 1)$

6. $s = \dfrac{t^2 + 1}{1 - t^2}$

7. $y = \sqrt{x} + 1 + \dfrac{1}{\sqrt{x}}$

8. $y = (x^5 + 1)(3x^2 - x)$

9. $r = 5\theta^2 \sec \theta$

10. $r = \dfrac{\tan \theta}{\theta^3 + \theta + 1}$

11. $y = x^2 \sin x + x \cos x$

12. $y = x^2 \sin x - x \cos x$

13. $y = \dfrac{\tan x}{2x^3}$

14. $y = \tan x - \cot x$

15. $y = \dfrac{1}{\sin x + \cos x}$

16. $y = \dfrac{1}{\sin x} + \dfrac{1}{\cos x}$

17. $V = \dfrac{4}{3}\pi r^3 + 8\pi r^2$

18. $A = \dfrac{\sqrt{3}}{4}s^2 + \dfrac{3\pi}{8}s^2$

19. $s = \dfrac{1 + \sin t}{1 + \tan t}$

20. $s = \dfrac{1 + \sin t}{1 + \cos t}$

21. $s = \dfrac{t^{-1} + t^{-2}}{t^{-3}}$

22. $y = x^{-2} \cos x - 4x^{-3}$

23. $y = \dfrac{\sin u}{\csc u} + \dfrac{\cos u}{\sec u}$

24. $y = \dfrac{\cot u}{\tan u} - \dfrac{\csc u}{\sin u}$

25. $y = 2x^{-2}(x^5 - x^3)$

26. $y = 4x^2(x^{-1} + 3x^{-4})$

27. $y = \dfrac{t^2}{\pi^3} - \dfrac{\pi^2}{t^3}$

28. $y = \dfrac{t^3}{\pi^2} - \dfrac{\pi^3}{t^2}$

29. $y = \sec x \tan x \cos x$

30. $y = \dfrac{\sin x \cot x}{\cos x}$

In Exercises 31–34, find all values of x for which the function is differentiable.

31. $y = \dfrac{\sin x}{x}$

32. $y = \sin x - x \cos x$

33. $y = \dfrac{3 \cos x}{x - 2}$

34. $y = (2x - 7)^{-1}(x + 5)$

In Exercises 35–38, find the slope of the curve at $x = \pi$.

35. $y = \sec x$

36. $y = \sin x \cos x$

37. $y = \dfrac{\cos x}{x}$

38. $y = \dfrac{x}{x + \sin x}$

In Exercises 39–42, find $\dfrac{d^2y}{dx^2}$.

39. $y = \dfrac{1}{\cos x}$

40. $y = \csc x$

41. $y = x \sin x$

42. $y = x - x \cos x$

In Exercises 43 and 44, find all derivatives of the function.

43. $y = \dfrac{x^4}{2} - \dfrac{3}{2}x^2 - x$

44. $y = \dfrac{x^5}{120}$

In Exercises 45–48, find an equation for the **(a)** tangent and **(b)** normal to the curve at the indicated point.

45. $y = 8x^{-2}, \quad x = 2$

46. $y = 4 + \cot x - 2 \csc x, \quad x = \pi/2$

47. $y = \sin x + \cos x, \quad x = \dfrac{\pi}{4}$

48. $y = 2x^2 + \dfrac{1}{x^4}, \quad x = 1$

In Exercises 49–52, find the coordinates of all points on the curve at which the tangent line has slope 6. If no such point exists, write "none."

49. $y = 2x^3$

50. $y = \dfrac{2x^3 - 3x^2}{6}$

51. $y = \dfrac{6x}{x + 1}$

52. $y = 2 \sin x$

53. Writing to Learn

(a) Graph the function

$$f(x) = \begin{cases} x, & 0 \le x \le 1 \\ 2 - x, & 1 < x \le 2. \end{cases}$$

(b) Is f continuous at $x = 1$? Explain.

(c) Is f differentiable at $x = 1$? Explain.

54. Writing to Learn For what values of the constant m is

$$f(x) = \begin{cases} 2\sin x, & x \le 0 \\ mx, & x > 0 \end{cases}$$

(a) continuous at $x = 0$? Explain.

(b) differentiable at $x = 0$? Explain.

In Exercises 55–58, determine where the function is **(a)** differentiable, **(b)** continuous but not differentiable, and **(c)** neither continuous nor differentiable.

55. $f(x) = x^{4/5}$

56. $y = x^{3/5}$

57. $f(x) = \begin{cases} 2x - 3, & -1 \le x < 0 \\ x - 3, & 0 \le x \le 4 \end{cases}$

58. $g(x) = \begin{cases} \dfrac{x - 1}{x}, & -2 \le x < 0 \\ \dfrac{x + 1}{x}, & 0 \le x \le 2 \end{cases}$

In Exercises 59 and 60, use the graph of f to sketch the graph of f'.

59. ***Sketching f' from f***

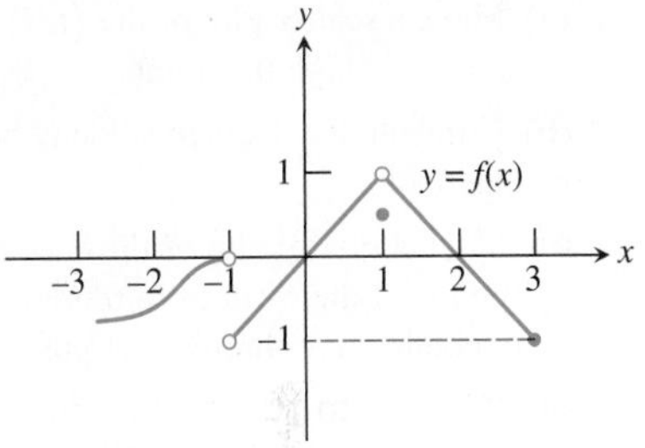

60. ***Sketching f' from f***

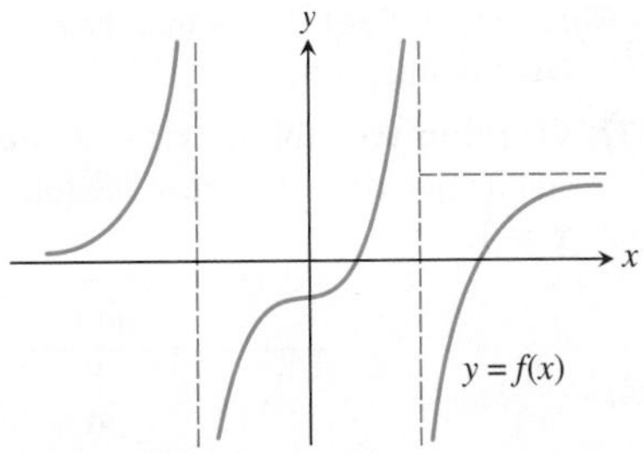

61. ***Recognizing Graphs*** The following graphs show the distance traveled, velocity, and acceleration for each second of a 2-minute automobile trip. Which graph shows

(a) distance? **(b)** velocity? **(c)** acceleration?

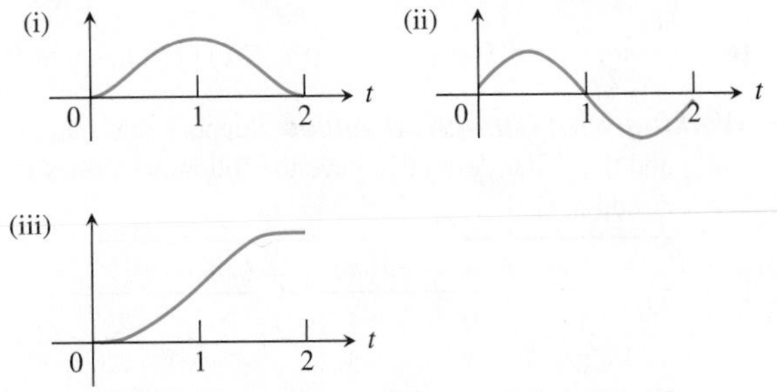

62. ***Sketching f from f'*** Sketch the graph of a continuous function f with $f(0) = 5$ and

$$f'(x) = \begin{cases} -2, & x < 2 \\ -0.5, & x > 2. \end{cases}$$

63. ***Sketching f from f'*** Sketch the graph of a continuous function f with $f(-1) = 2$ and

$$f'(x) = \begin{cases} -2, & x < 1 \\ 1, & 1 < x < 4 \\ -1, & 4 < x < 6. \end{cases}$$

64. Which of the following statements could be true if $f''(x) = x^{1/3}$?

i. $f(x) = \frac{9}{28}x^{7/3} + 9$ **ii.** $f'(x) = \frac{9}{28}x^{7/3} - 2$

iii. $f'(x) = \frac{3}{4}x^{4/3} + 6$ **iv.** $f(x) = \frac{3}{4}x^{4/3} - 4$

A. i only **B.** iii only

C. ii and iv only **D.** i and iii only

65. *Derivative from Data* The following data give the coordinates of a moving body for various values of t.

t (sec)	0	0.5	1	1.5	2	2.5	3	3.5	4
s (ft)	10	38	58	70	74	70	58	38	10

(a) Make a scatter plot of the (t, s) data and sketch a smooth curve through the points.

(b) Compute the average velocity between consecutive points of the table.

(c) Make a scatter plot of the data in part (b) using the midpoints of the t values to represent the data. Then sketch a smooth curve through the points.

(d) Writing to Learn Why does the curve in part (c) approximate the graph of ds/dt?

66. Factorial Fact Prove that the nth derivative of x^n is $n!$ for any positive integer n.

67. Working with Numerical Values Suppose that a function f and its first derivative have the following values at $x = 0$ and $x = 1$.

x	$f(x)$	$f'(x)$
0	9	−2
1	−3	4

Find the first derivative of the following functions at the given value of x.

(a) $3f(x),\quad x = 1$ **(b)** $xf(x),\quad x = 1$

(c) $x^2f(x),\quad x = 1$ **(d)** $\frac{f(x)}{x},\quad x = 1$

(e) $\frac{f(x)}{x^2 + 2},\quad x = 0$ **(f)** $f(x) \cdot f(x),\quad x = 0$

68. *Working with Numerical Values* Suppose that function f and g and their first derivative have the following values at $x = -1$ and $x = 0$.

x	$f(x)$	$g(x)$	$f'(x)$	$g'(x)$
−1	0	−1	2	1
0	−1	−3	−2	4

Find the first derivative of the following combinations at the given value of x.

(a) $3f(x) - g(x),\quad x = -1$ **(b)** $f(x)g(x),\quad x = 0$

(c) $f(x)g(x),\quad x = -1$ **(d)** $\frac{f(x)}{g(x)},\quad x = 0$

(e) $\frac{f(x)}{g(x)},\quad x = -1$ **(f)** $\frac{f(x)}{g(x) + 2},\quad x = 0$

69. If two functions f and g have positive slopes at $x = 0$, must the function $f + g$ have a positive slope at $x = 0$? Justify your answer.

70. If two functions f and g have positive slopes at $x = 0$, must the function $f \cdot g$ have a positive slope at $x = 0$? Justify your answer.

71. *Vertical Motion* On Earth, if you shoot a paper clip 64 ft straight up into the air with a rubber band, the paper clip will be $s(t) = 64t - 16t^2$ feet above your hand at t sec after firing.

(a) Find ds/dt and d^2s/dt^2.

(b) How long does it take the paper clip to reach its maximum height?

(c) With what velocity does it leave your hand?

(d) On the moon, the same force will send the paper clip to a height of $s(t) = 64t - 2.6t^2$ ft in t sec. About how long will it take the paper clip to reach its maximum height, and how high will it go?

72. *Free Fall* Suppose two balls are falling from rest at a certain height in centimeters above the ground. Use the equation $s = 490t^2$ to answer the following questions.

(a) How long does it take the balls to fall the first 160 cm? What is their average velocity for the period?

(b) How fast are the balls falling when they reach the 160-cm mark? What is their acceleration then?

73. *Filling a Bowl* If a hemispherical bowl of radius 10 in. is filled with water to a depth of x in., the volume of water is given by $V = \pi[10 - (x/3)]x^2$. Find the rate of increase of the volume per inch increase of depth.

74. *Marginal Revenue* A bus will hold 60 people. The fare charged (p dollars) is related to the number x of people who use the bus by the formula $p = [3 - (x/40)]^2$.

(a) Write a formula for the total revenue per trip received by the bus company.

(b) What number of people per trip will make the marginal revenue equal to zero? What is the corresponding fare?

(c) Writing to Learn Do you think the bus company's fare policy is good for its business?

75. *Searchlight* The figure shows a boat 1km offshore sweeping the shore with a searchlight. The light turns at a constant rate, $d\theta/dt = -0.6$ rad/sec.

(a) How fast is the light moving along the shore when it reaches point A?

(b) How many revolutions per minute is 0.6 rad/sec?

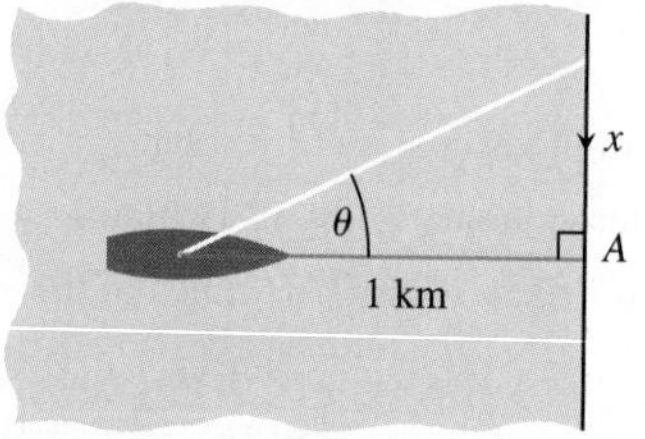

76. *Calculator Exploration* Use your calculator to graph the functions

$$y_1 = \cos^{-1}(\cos(x)) \text{ and } y_2 = \frac{|\sin(x)|}{\sin(x)}.$$

(a) Based on the graphical information, find a relationship between these two functions that involves the derivative.

(b) Can you find a find a function y_2 that relates to the function $y_1 = \sin^{-1}(\sin(x))$ in the same way?

77. ***Finding a Range*** The range of the function $y = \dfrac{3x}{x^4 + 6}$ is the interval $[-a, a]$, where a is a certain irrational number. Use a calculator to graph the function, and then find the exact value of a algebraically. [*Hint:* Do you see how solving the equation $\dfrac{dy}{dx} = 0$ might be useful for finding the exact value of a?]

78. ***Finding a Range*** The range of the function $y = \dfrac{4x}{x^2 + 2}$ is the interval $[-a, a]$, where a is a certain irrational number. Use a calculator to graph the function, and then find the exact value of a algebraically.

79. Graph the function $f(x) = \tan^{-1}(\tan 2x)$ in the window $[-\pi, \pi]$ by $[-4, 4]$. Then answer the following questions.

(a) What is the domain of f?

(b) What is the range of f?

(c) At which points is f not differentiable?

(d) Describe the graph of f'.

80. ***Fundamental Frequency of a Vibrating Piano String*** We measure the frequencies at which wires vibrate in cycles (trips back and forth) per sec. The unit of measure is a *hertz:* 1 cycle per sec. Middle A on a piano has a frequency 440 hertz. For any given wire, the fundamental frequency y is a function of four variables:

r: the radius of the wire;

l: the length;

d: the density of the wire;

T: the tension (force) holding the wire taut.

With r and l in centimeters, d in grams per cubic centimeter, and T in dynes (it takes about 100,000 dynes to lift an apple), the fundamental frequency of the wire is

$$y = \frac{1}{2rl}\sqrt{\frac{T}{\pi d}}.$$

If we keep all the variables fixed except one, then y can be alternatively thought of as four different functions of one variable, $y(r)$, $y(l)$, $y(d)$, and $y(T)$. How would changing each variable affect the string's fundamental frequency? To find out, calculate $y'(r)$, $y'(l)$, $y'(d)$, and $y'(T)$.

AP* Examination Preparation

You may use a graphing calculator to solve the following problems.

81. A particle moves along the x-axis so that at any time $t \geq 0$ its position is given by $x(t) = t^3 - 12t + 5$.

(a) Find the velocity of the particle at any time t.

(b) Find the acceleration of the particle at any time t.

(c) Find all values of t for which the particle is at rest.

(d) Find the speed of the particle when its acceleration is zero.

(e) Is the particle moving toward the origin or away from the origin when $t = 3$? Justify your answer.

82. The function f is differentiable for all real numbers and satisfies the conditions in the table below. The function g is defined by

$$g(x) = \frac{f(x)}{f(x) - 3}.$$

x	$g(x)$	$f'(x)$
2	−1	3
4	3	5

(a) Write an equation of the line tangent to the graph of f at $x = 4$.

(b) Is f continuous at $x = 3$? Justify your answer.

(c) Is there a zero of f in the interval $[2, 4]$? Justify your answer.

(d) Find $g'(2)$.

(e) Explain why g is not differentiable at $x = 4$.

83. Let $f(x) = \dfrac{\cos(x)}{\cos(x) - 2}$ for $-2\pi \leq x \leq 2\pi$.

(a) Sketch a graph of f in the window $[-2\pi, 2\pi]$ by $[-2, 2]$.

(b) Find $f'(x)$.

(c) Find all values in the domain of f for which $f'(x) = 0$.

(d) Use information obtained from parts (a) and (c) to find the range of f.

CHAPTER

4 More Derivatives

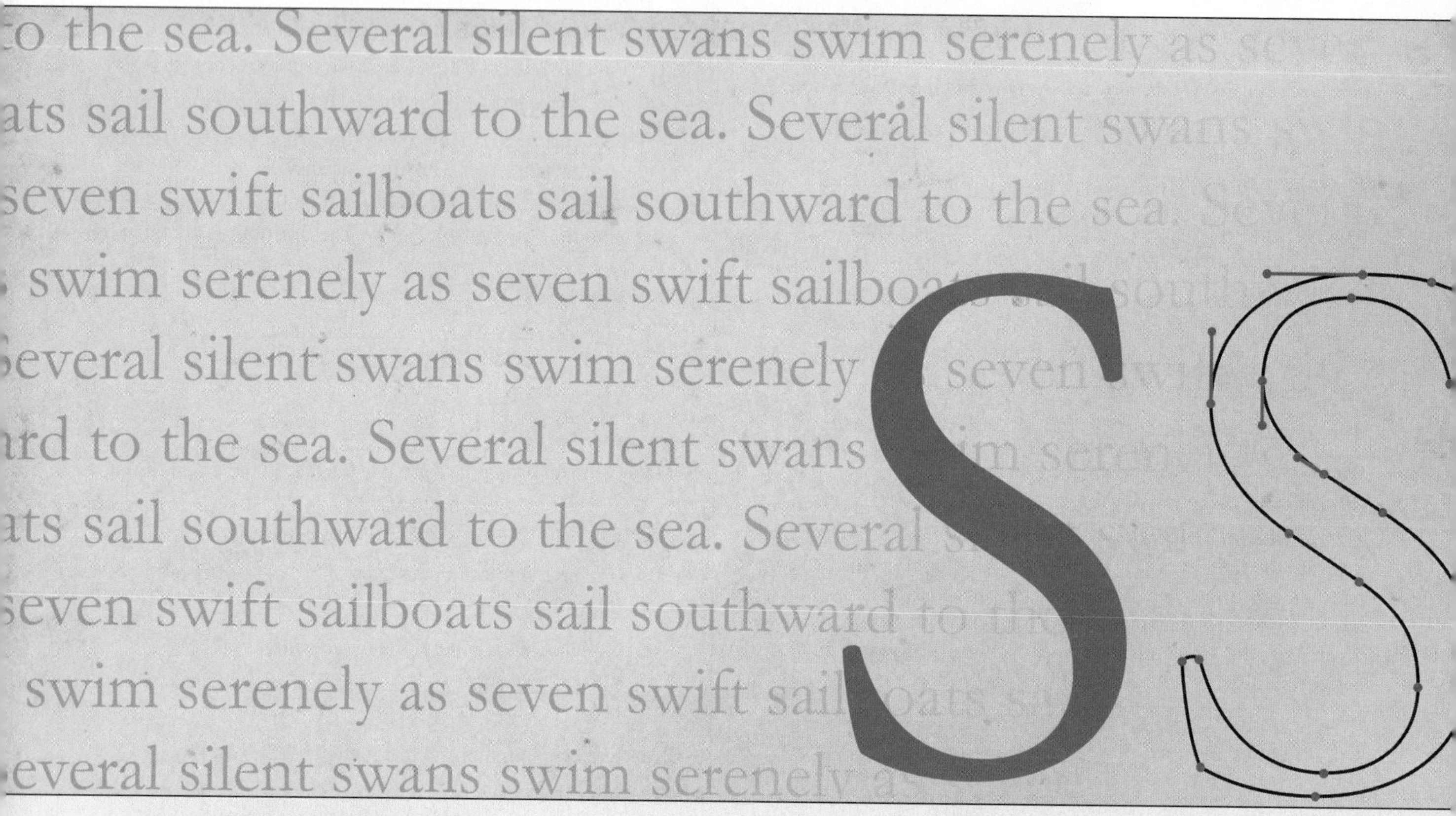

the sea. Several silent swans swim serenely as
sail southward to the sea. Several silent
swift sailboats sail southward to the
swim serenely as seven swift
silent swans swim serenely
to the sea. Several silent swans
sail southward to the sea. Several
swift sailboats sail
swim serenely as seven swift
silent swans swim

The letter S above is pieced together from curves joined at the red dots. Each piece of the outline is defined by parametric equations $x = f(t)$ and $y = g(t)$, where f and g are cubic polynomials and the parameter t runs from 0 to 1. In a font design program such as Fontlab™ you can drag the control points (blue dots) to change the shape of each piece of the outline. (We show control points for just two pieces of the outline.) As you drag the control points, you are actually changing the coefficients of the polynomials f and g. Using the techniques of Example 6 in Section 4.1 you can show that as long as a joint (or *node*) lies on the line joining its adjacent control points, the two curves that meet at the node will have the same slope there, making a smooth transition. When you send the letter to an output device like a printer, it uses the parametric equations to render the outline at the highest possible resolution.

4.1 Chain Rule

What you will learn about . . .

- Derivative of a Composite Function
- "Outside-Inside" Rule
- Repeated Use of the Chain Rule
- Slopes of Parametrized Curves
- Power Chain Rule

and why . . .

The Chain Rule is the most widely used differentiation rule in mathematics.

Derivative of a Composite Function

We now know how to differentiate $\sin x$ and $x^2 - 4$, but how do we differentiate a composite like $\sin(x^2 - 4)$? The answer is with the Chain Rule, which is probably the most widely used differentiation rule in mathematics. This section describes the rule and how to use it.

EXAMPLE 1 Relating Derivatives

The function $y = 6x - 10 = 2(3x - 5)$ is the composite of the functions $y = 2u$ and $u = 3x - 5$. How are the derivatives of these three functions related?

SOLUTION

We have

$$\frac{dy}{dx} = 6, \quad \frac{dy}{du} = 2, \quad \frac{du}{dx} = 3.$$

Since $6 = 2 \cdot 3$,

$$\frac{dy}{dx} = \frac{dy}{du} \cdot \frac{du}{dx}.$$

Now Try Exercise 1.

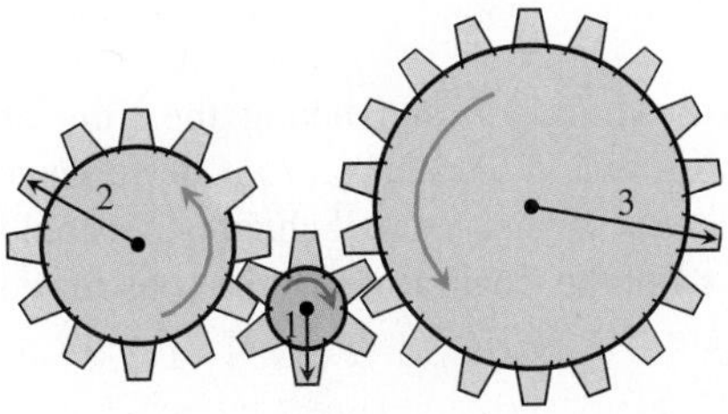

Figure 4.1 When gear A makes x turns, gear B makes u turns, and gear C makes y turns. By comparing circumferences or counting teeth, we see that $y = u/2$ and $u = 3x$, so $y = 3x/2$. Thus $dy/du = 1/2$, $du/dx = 3$, and $dy/dx = 3/2 = (dy/du)(du/dx)$.

Is it an accident that $dy/dx = dy/du \cdot du/dx$?

If we think of the derivative as a rate of change, our intuition allows us to see that this relationship is reasonable. For $y = f(u)$ and $u = g(x)$, if y changes twice as fast as u and u changes three times as fast as x, then we expect y to change six times as fast as x. This is much like the effect of a multiple gear train (Figure 4.1).

Let us try again on another function.

EXAMPLE 2 Relating Derivatives

The polynomial $y = 9x^4 + 6x^2 + 1 = (3x^2 + 1)^2$ is the composite of $y = u^2$ and $u = 3x^2 + 1$. Calculating derivatives, we see that

$$\begin{aligned}\frac{dy}{du} \cdot \frac{du}{dx} &= 2u \cdot 6x \\ &= 2(3x^2 + 1) \cdot 6x \\ &= 36x^3 + 12x.\end{aligned}$$

Also,

$$\begin{aligned}\frac{dy}{dx} &= \frac{d}{dx}(9x^4 + 6x^2 + 1) \\ &= 36x^3 + 12x.\end{aligned}$$

Once again,

$$\frac{dy}{du} \cdot \frac{du}{dx} = \frac{dy}{dx}.$$

Now Try Exercise 5.

The derivative of the composite function $f(g(x))$ at x is the derivative of f at $g(x)$ times the derivative of g at x (Figure 4.2). This is known as the Chain Rule.

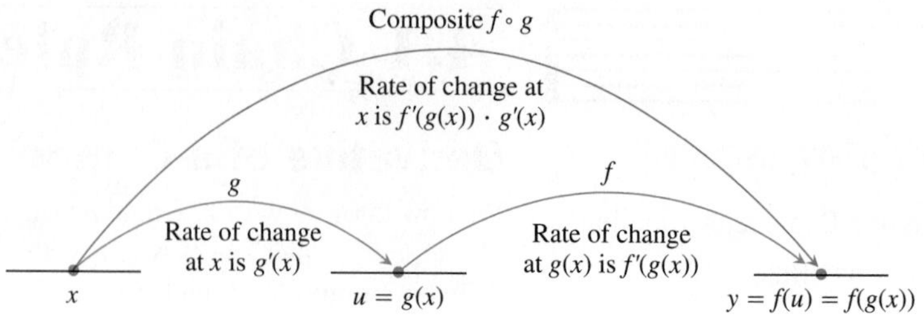

Figure 4.2 Rates of change multiply: the derivative of $f \circ g$ at x is the derivative of f at the point $g(x)$ times the derivative of g at x.

RULE 8 The Chain Rule

If f is differentiable at the point $u = g(x)$, and g is differentiable at x, then the composite function $(f \circ g)(x) = f(g(x))$ is differentiable at x, and

$$(f \circ g)'(x) = f'(g(x)) \cdot g'(x).$$

In Leibniz notation, if $y = f(u)$ and $u = g(x)$, then

$$\frac{dy}{dx} = \frac{dy}{du} \cdot \frac{du}{dx},$$

where dy/du is evaluated at $u = g(x)$.

It would be tempting to try to prove the Chain Rule by writing

$$\frac{\Delta y}{\Delta x} = \frac{\Delta y}{\Delta u} \cdot \frac{\Delta u}{\Delta x}$$

(a true statement about fractions with nonzero denominators) and taking the limit as $\Delta x \to 0$. This is essentially what is happening, and it would work as a proof if we knew that Δu, the change in u, was nonzero; but we do not know this. A small change in x could conceivably produce no change in u. An air-tight proof of the Chain Rule can be constructed through a different approach, but we will omit it here.

EXAMPLE 3 Applying the Chain Rule

An object moves along the x-axis so that its position at any time $t \geq 0$ is given by $x(t) = \cos(t^2 + 1)$. Find the velocity of the object as a function of t.

SOLUTION

We know that the velocity is dx/dt. In this instance, x is a composite function: $x = \cos(u)$ and $u = t^2 + 1$. We have

$$\frac{dx}{du} = -\sin(u) \qquad x = \cos(u)$$

$$\frac{du}{dt} = 2t. \qquad u = t^2 + 1$$

By the Chain Rule,

$$\begin{aligned} \frac{dx}{dt} &= \frac{dx}{du} \cdot \frac{du}{dt} \\ &= -\sin(u) \cdot 2t \\ &= -\sin(t^2 + 1) \cdot 2t \\ &= -2t \sin(t^2 + 1). \end{aligned}$$

Now Try Exercise 9.

"Outside-Inside" Rule

It sometimes helps to think about the Chain Rule this way: If $y = f(g(x))$, then

$$\frac{dy}{dx} = f'(g(x)) \cdot g'(x).$$

In words, differentiate the "outside" function f and evaluate it at the "inside" function $g(x)$ left alone; then multiply by the derivative of the "inside function."

EXAMPLE 4 Differentiating from the Outside In

Differentiate $\sin(x^2 + x)$ with respect to x.

SOLUTION

$$\frac{d}{dx}\sin(\underbrace{x^2 + x}_{\text{inside}}) = \cos(\underbrace{x^2 + x}_{\text{inside left alone}}) \cdot (\underbrace{2x + 1}_{\text{derivative of the inside}})$$

Now Try Exercise 13.

Repeated Use of the Chain Rule

We sometimes have to use the Chain Rule two or more times to find a derivative. Here is an example:

EXAMPLE 5 A Three-Link "Chain"

Find the derivative of $g(t) = \tan(5 - \sin 2t)$.

SOLUTION

Notice here that tan is a function of $5 - \sin 2t$, while sin is a function of $2t$, which is itself a function of t. Therefore, by the Chain Rule,

$$\begin{aligned} g'(t) &= \frac{d}{dt}(\tan(5 - \sin 2t)) \\ &= \sec^2(5 - \sin 2t) \cdot \frac{d}{dt}(5 - \sin 2t) && \text{Derivative of } \tan u \text{ with } u = 5 - \sin 2t \\ &= \sec^2(5 - \sin 2t) \cdot \left(0 - \cos 2t \cdot \frac{d}{dt}(2t)\right) && \text{Derivative of } 5 - \sin u \text{ with } u = 2t \\ &= \sec^2(5 - \sin 2t) \cdot (-\cos 2t) \cdot 2 \\ &= -2(\cos 2t)\sec^2(5 - \sin 2t). \end{aligned}$$

Now Try Exercise 23.

Slopes of Parametrized Curves

A parametrized curve $(x(t), y(t))$ is *differentiable at t* if x and y are differentiable at t. At a point on a differentiable parametrized curve where y is also a differentiable function of x, the derivatives dy/dt, dx/dt, and dy/dx are related by the Chain Rule:

$$\frac{dy}{dt} = \frac{dy}{dx} \cdot \frac{dx}{dt}.$$

If $dx/dt \neq 0$, we may divide both sides of this equation by dx/dt to solve for dy/dx.

Finding *dy/dx* Parametrically

If all three derivatives exist and $dx/dt \neq 0$,

$$\frac{dy}{dx} = \frac{dy/dt}{dx/dt}. \tag{1}$$

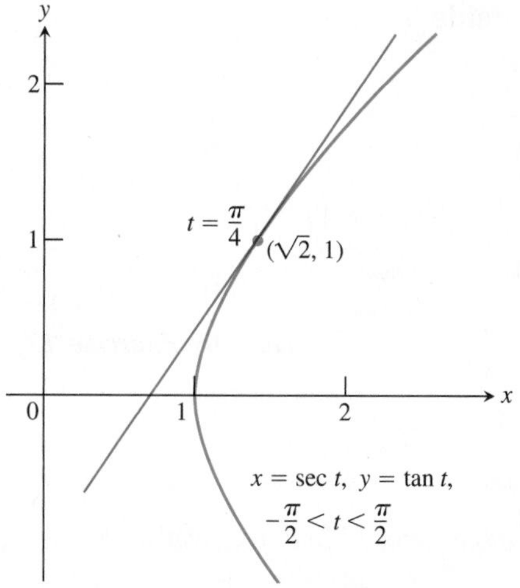

Figure 4.3 The hyperbola branch in Example 6. Equation 1 applies for every point on the graph except $(1, 0)$. Can you state why Equation 1 fails at $(1, 0)$?

EXAMPLE 6 Differentiating with a Parameter

Find the line tangent to the right-hand hyperbola branch defined parametrically by

$$x = \sec t, \quad y = \tan t, \quad -\frac{\pi}{2} < t < \frac{\pi}{2}$$

at the point $(\sqrt{2}, 1)$, where $t = \pi/4$ (Figure 4.3).

SOLUTION

All three of the derivatives in Equation 1 exist and $dx/dt = \sec t \tan t \neq 0$ at the indicated point. Therefore, Equation 1 applies and

$$\begin{aligned}\frac{dy}{dx} &= \frac{dy/dt}{dx/dt}\\ &= \frac{\sec^2 t}{\sec t \tan t}\\ &= \frac{\sec t}{\tan t}\\ &= \csc t.\end{aligned}$$

Setting $t = \pi/4$ gives

$$\left.\frac{dy}{dx}\right|_{t=\pi/4} = \csc(\pi/4) = \sqrt{2}.$$

The equation of the tangent line is

$$\begin{aligned}y - 1 &= \sqrt{2}(x - \sqrt{2})\\ y &= \sqrt{2}x - 2 + 1\\ y &= \sqrt{2}x - 1.\end{aligned}$$

Now Try Exercise 41.

Power Chain Rule

If f is a differentiable function of u, and u is a differentiable function of x, then substituting $y = f(u)$ into the Chain Rule formula

$$\frac{dy}{dx} = \frac{dy}{du} \cdot \frac{du}{dx}$$

leads to the formula

$$\frac{d}{dx}f(u) = f'(u)\frac{du}{dx}.$$

Here's an example of how it works: If n is an integer and $f(u) = u^n$, the Power Rules (Rules 2 and 7) tell us that $f'(u) = nu^{n-1}$. If u is a differentiable function of x, then we can use the Chain Rule to extend this to the **Power Chain Rule:**

$$\frac{d}{dx}u^n = nu^{n-1}\frac{du}{dx}. \qquad \frac{d}{du}(u^n) = nu^{n-1}$$

EXAMPLE 7 Finding Slope

(a) Find the slope of the line tangent to the curve $y = \sin^5 x$ at the point where $x = \pi/3$.

(b) Show that the slope of every line tangent to the curve $y = 1/(1 - 2x)^3$ is positive.

SOLUTION

(a)
$$\frac{dy}{dx} = 5\sin^4 x \cdot \frac{d}{dx}\sin x \qquad \text{Power Chain Rule with } u = \sin x,\ n = 5$$
$$= 5\sin^4 x \cos x$$

The tangent line has slope

$$\left.\frac{dy}{dx}\right|_{x=\pi/3} = 5\left(\frac{\sqrt{3}}{2}\right)^4\left(\frac{1}{2}\right) = \frac{45}{32}.$$

(b)
$$\frac{dy}{dx} = \frac{d}{dx}(1 - 2x)^{-3}$$
$$= -3(1 - 2x)^{-4} \cdot \frac{d}{dx}(1 - 2x) \qquad \text{Power Chain Rule with } u = (1 - 2x),\ n = -3$$
$$= -3(1 - 2x)^{-4} \cdot (-2)$$
$$= \frac{6}{(1 - 2x)^4}$$

At any point (x, y) on the curve, $x \neq 1/2$ and the slope of the tangent line is

$$\frac{dy}{dx} = \frac{6}{(1 - 2x)^4},$$

the quotient of two positive numbers. ***Now Try Exercise 53.***

EXAMPLE 8 Radians Versus Degrees

It is important to remember that the formulas for the derivatives of both sin x and cos x were obtained under the assumption that x is measured in radians, *not* degrees. The Chain Rule gives us new insight into the difference between the two. Since $180° = \pi$ radians, $x° = \pi x/180$ radians. By the Chain Rule,

$$\frac{d}{dx}\sin(x°) = \frac{d}{dx}\sin\left(\frac{\pi x}{180}\right) = \frac{\pi}{180}\cos\left(\frac{\pi x}{180}\right) = \frac{\pi}{180}\cos(x°).$$

See Figure 4.4.

The factor $\pi/180$, annoying in the first derivative, would compound with repeated differentiation. We see at a glance the compelling reason for the use of radian measure.

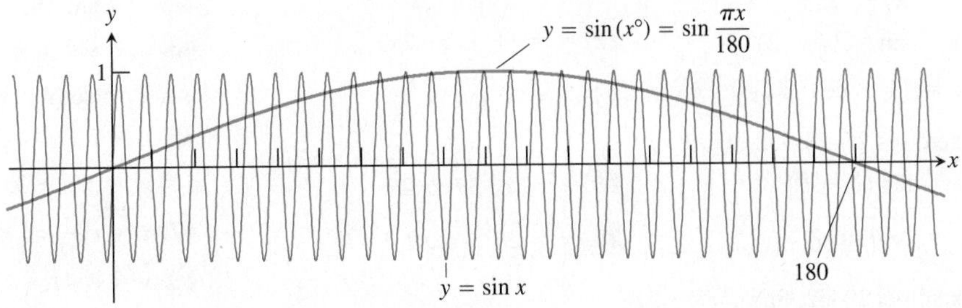

Figure 4.4 sin $(x°)$ oscillates only $\pi/180$ times as often as sin x oscillates. Its maximum slope is $\pi/180$. (Example 8)

Quick Review 4.1 (For help, go to Sections 1.2 and 1.6.)

Exercise numbers with a gray background indicate problems that the authors have designed to be solved *without a calculator.*

In Exercises 1–5, let $f(x) = \sin x$, $g(x) = x^2 + 1$, and $h(x) = 7x$. Write a simplified expression for the composite function.

1. $f(g(x))$
2. $f(g(h(x)))$
3. $(g \circ h)(x)$
4. $(h \circ g)(x)$
5. $f\left(\frac{g(x)}{h(x)}\right)$

In Exercises 6–10, let $f(x) = \cos x$, $g(x) = \sqrt{x + 2}$, and $h(x) = 3x^2$. Write the given function as a composite of two or more of f, g, and h. For example, $\cos 3x^2$ is $f(h(x))$.

6. $\sqrt{\cos x + 2}$
7. $\sqrt{3\cos^2 x + 2}$
8. $3\cos x + 6$
9. $\cos 27x^4$
10. $\cos\sqrt{2 + 3x^2}$

Section 4.1 Exercises

In Exercises 1–8, use the given substitution and the Chain Rule to find dy/dx.

1. $y = \sin(3x + 1), u = 3x + 1$
2. $y = \sin(7 - 5x), u = 7 - 5x$
3. $y = \cos(\sqrt{3}x), u = \sqrt{3}x$
4. $y = \tan(2x - x^3), u = 2x - x^3$
5. $y = \left(\frac{\sin x}{1 + \cos x}\right)^2, \quad u = \frac{\sin x}{1 + \cos x}$
6. $y = 5\cot\left(\frac{2}{x}\right), u = \frac{2}{x}$
7. $y = \cos(\sin x), u = \sin x$
8. $y = \sec(\tan x), u = \tan x$

In Exercises 9–12, an object moves along the x-axis so that its position at any time $t \geq 0$ is given by $x(t) = s(t)$. Find the velocity of the object as a function of t.

9. $s = \cos\left(\frac{\pi}{2} - 3t\right)$
10. $s = t\cos(\pi - 4t)$
11. $s = \frac{4}{3\pi}\sin 3t + \frac{4}{5\pi}\cos 5t$
12. $s = \sin\left(\frac{3\pi}{2}t\right) + \cos\left(\frac{7\pi}{4}t\right)$

In Exercises 13–24, find dy/dx. If you are unsure of your answer, use NDER to support your computation.

13. $y = (x + \sqrt{x})^{-2}$
14. $y = (\csc x + \cot x)^{-1}$
15. $y = \sin^{-5} x - \cos^3 x$
16. $y = x^3(2x - 5)^4$
17. $y = \sin^3 x \tan 4x$
18. $y = 4\sqrt{\sec x + \tan x}$
19. $y = \frac{3}{\sqrt{2x + 1}}$
20. $y = \frac{x}{\sqrt{1 + x^2}}$
21. $y = \sin^2(3x - 2)$
22. $y = (1 + \cos 2x)^2$
23. $y = (1 + \cos^2 7x)^3$
24. $y = \sqrt{\tan 5x}$

In Exercises 25–28 find $dr/d\theta$.

25. $r = \tan(2 - \theta)$
26. $r = \sec 2\theta \tan 2\theta$
27. $r = \sqrt{\theta \sin \theta}$
28. $r = 2\theta\sqrt{\sec \theta}$

In Exercises 29–32, find y''.

29. $y = \tan x$
30. $y = \cot x$
31. $y = \cot(3x - 1)$
32. $y = 9\tan(x/3)$

In Exercises 33–38, find the value of $(f \circ g)'$ at the given value of x.

33. $f(u) = u^5 + 1, \quad u = g(x) = \sqrt{x}, \quad x = 1$
34. $f(u) = 1 - \frac{1}{u}, \quad u = g(x) = \frac{1}{1 - x}, \quad x = -1$
35. $f(u) = \cot\frac{\pi u}{10}, \quad u = g(x) = 5\sqrt{x}, \quad x = 1$
36. $f(u) = u + \frac{1}{\cos^2 u}, \quad u = g(x) = \pi x, \quad x = \frac{1}{4}$
37. $f(u) = \frac{2u}{u^2 + 1}, \quad u = g(x) = 10x^2 + x + 1, \quad x = 0$
38. $f(u) = \left(\frac{u - 1}{u + 1}\right)^2, \quad u = g(x) = \frac{1}{x^2} - 1, \quad x = -1$

What happens if you can write a function as a composite in different ways? Do you get the same derivative each time? The Chain Rule says you should. Try it with the functions in Exercises 39 and 40.

39. Find dy/dx if $y = \cos(6x + 2)$ by writing y as a composite with
    (a) $y = \cos u$ and $u = 6x + 2$.
    (b) $y = \cos 2u$ and $u = 3x + 1$.
40. Find dy/dx if $y = \sin(x^2 + 1)$ by writing y as a composite with
    (a) $y = \sin(u + 1)$ and $u = x^2$.
    (b) $y = \sin u$ and $u = x^2 + 1$.

In Exercises 41–48, find the equation of the line tangent to the curve at the point defined by the given value of t.

41. $x = 2\cos t, \quad y = 2\sin t, \quad t = \pi/4$
42. $x = \sin 2\pi t, \quad y = \cos 2\pi t, \quad t = -1/6$
43. $x = \sec^2 t - 1, \quad y = \tan t, \quad t = -\pi/4$
44. $x = \sec t, \quad y = \tan t, \quad t = \pi/6$
45. $x = t, \quad y = \sqrt{t}, \quad t = 1/4$
46. $x = 2t^2 + 3, \quad y = t^4, \quad t = -1$
47. $x = t - \sin t, \quad y = 1 - \cos t, \quad t = \pi/3$
48. $x = \cos t, \quad y = 1 + \sin t, \quad t = \pi/2$

49. Let $x = t^2 + t$, and let $y = \sin t$.

(a) Find dy/dx as a function of t.

(b) Find $\frac{d}{dt}\left(\frac{dy}{dx}\right)$ as a function of t.

(c) Find $\frac{d}{dx}\left(\frac{dy}{dx}\right)$ as a function of t.

Use the Chain Rule and your answer from part (b).

(d) Which of the expressions in parts (b) and (c) is d^2y/dx^2?

50. A circle of radius 2 and center $(0, 0)$ can be parametrized by the equations $x = 2\cos t$ and $y = 2\sin t$. Show that for any value of t, the line tangent to the circle at $(2\cos t, 2\sin t)$ is perpendicular to the radius.

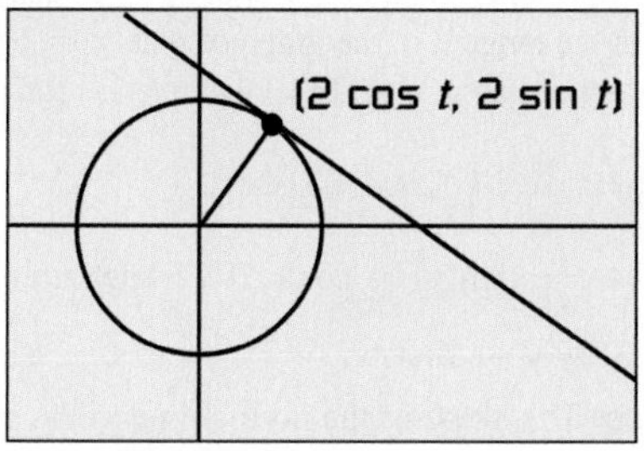

51. Let $s = \cos\theta$. Evaluate ds/dt when $\theta = 3\pi/2$ and $d\theta/dt = 5$.

52. Let $y = x^2 + 7x - 5$. Evaluate dy/dt when $x = 1$ and $dx/dt = 1/3$.

53. What is the largest value possible for the slope of the curve $y = \sin(x/2)$?

54. Write an equation for the tangent to the curve $y = \sin mx$ at the origin.

55. Find the lines that are tangent and normal to the curve $y = 2\tan(\pi x/4)$ at $x = 1$. Support your answer graphically.

56. ***Working with Numerical Values*** Suppose that functions f and g and their derivatives have the following values at $x = 2$ and $x = 3$.

x	$f(x)$	$g(x)$	$f'(x)$	$g'(x)$
2	8	2	1/3	−3
3	3	−4	2π	5

Evaluate the derivatives with respect to x of the following combinations at the given value of x.

(a) $2f(x)$ at $x = 2$ (b) $f(x) + g(x)$ at $x = 3$

(c) $f(x) \cdot g(x)$ at $x = 3$ (d) $f(x)/g(x)$ at $x = 2$

(e) $f(g(x))$ at $x = 2$ (f) $\sqrt{f(x)}$ at $x = 2$

(g) $1/g^2(x)$ at $x = 3$ (h) $\sqrt{f^2(x) + g^2(x)}$ at $x = 2$

57. ***Extension of Example 8*** Show that $\frac{d}{dx}\cos(x°)$ is $-\frac{\pi}{180}\sin(x°)$.

58. ***Working with Numerical Values*** Suppose that the functions f and g and their derivatives with respect to x have the following values at $x = 0$ and $x = 1$.

x	$f(x)$	$g(x)$	$f'(x)$	$g'(x)$
0	1	1	5	1/3
1	3	−4	−1/3	−8/3

Evaluate the derivatives with respect to x of the following combinations at the given value of x.

(a) $5f(x) - g(x)$, $x = 1$ (b) $f(x)g^3(x)$, $x = 0$

(c) $\frac{f(x)}{g(x) + 1}$, $x = 1$ (d) $f(g(x))$, $x = 0$

(e) $g(f(x))$, $x = 0$ (f) $(g(x) + f(x))^{-2}$, $x = 1$

(g) $f(x + g(x))$, $x = 0$

59. ***Orthogonal Curves*** Two curves are said to cross at right angles if their tangents are perpendicular at the crossing point. The technical word for "crossing at right angles" is **orthogonal.** Show that the curves $y = \sin 2x$ and $y = -\sin(x/2)$ are orthogonal at the origin. Draw both graphs and both tangents in a square viewing window.

60. Writing to Learn Explain why the Chain Rule formula

$$\frac{dy}{dx} = \frac{dy}{du} \cdot \frac{du}{dx}$$

is not simply the well-known rule for multiplying fractions.

61. ***Running Machinery Too Fast*** Suppose that a piston is moving straight up and down and that its position at time t seconds is

$$s = A\cos(2\pi bt),$$

with A and b positive. The value of A is the amplitude of the motion, and b is the frequency (number of times the piston moves up and down each second). What effect does doubling the frequency have on the piston's velocity, acceleration, and jerk? (Once you find out, you will know why machinery breaks when you run it too fast.)

Figure 4.5 The internal forces in the engine get so large that they tear the engine apart when the velocity is too great.

62. Group Activity *Temperatures in Fairbanks, Alaska.* The graph in Figure 4.6 shows the average Fahrenheit temperature in Fairbanks, Alaska, during a typical 365-day year. The equation that approximates the temperature on day x is

$$y = 37 \sin\left[\frac{2\pi}{365}(x - 101)\right] + 25.$$

(a) On what day is the temperature increasing the fastest?

(b) About how many degrees per day is the temperature increasing when it is increasing at its fastest?

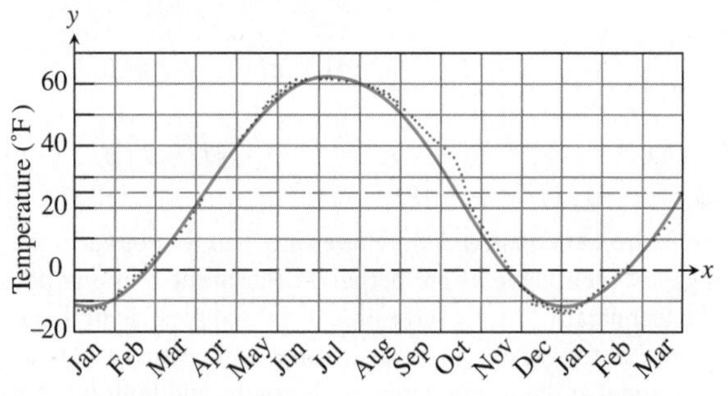

Figure 4.6 Normal mean air temperatures at Fairbanks, Alaska, plotted as data points, and the approximating sine function (Exercise 62).

63. *Particle Motion* The position of a particle moving along a coordinate line is $s = \sqrt{1 + 4t}$, with s in meters and t in seconds. Find the particle's velocity and acceleration at $t = 6$ sec.

64. *Constant Acceleration* Suppose the velocity of a falling body is $v = k\sqrt{s}$ m/sec (k a constant) at the instant the body has fallen s meters from its starting point. Show that the body's acceleration is constant.

65. *Falling Meteorite* The velocity of a heavy meteorite entering the earth's atmosphere is inversely proportional to $\sqrt{s}$ when it is s kilometers from the earth's center. Show that the meteorite's acceleration is inversely proportional to s^2.

66. *Particle Acceleration* A particle moves along the x-axis with velocity $dx/dt = f(x)$. Show that the particle's acceleration is $f(x)f'(x)$.

67. *Temperature and the Period of a Pendulum* For oscillations of small amplitude (short swings), we may safely model the relationship between the period T and the length L of a simple pendulum with the equation

$$T = 2\pi\sqrt{\frac{L}{g}},$$

where g is the constant acceleration of gravity at the pendulum's location. If we measure g in centimeters per second squared, we measure L in centimeters and T in seconds. If the pendulum is made of metal, its length will vary with temperature, either increasing or decreasing at a rate that is roughly proportional to L. In symbols, with u being temperature and k the proportionality constant,

$$\frac{dL}{du} = kL.$$

Assuming this to be the case, show that the rate at which the period changes with respect to temperature is $kT/2$.

68. Writing to Learn *Chain Rule* Suppose that $f(x) = x^2$ and $g(x) = |x|$. Then the composites

$$(f \circ g)(x) = |x|^2 = x^2 \quad \text{and} \quad (g \circ f)(x) = |x^2| = x^2$$

are both differentiable at $x = 0$ even though g itself is not differentiable at $x = 0$. Does this contradict the Chain Rule? Explain.

69. *Tangents* Suppose that $u = g(x)$ is differentiable at $x = 1$ and that $y = f(u)$ is differentiable at $u = g(1)$. If the graph of $y = f(g(x))$ has a horizontal tangent at $x = 1$, can we conclude anything about the tangent to the graph of g at $x = 1$ or the tangent to the graph of f at $u = g(1)$? Give reasons for your answer.

Standardized Test Questions

70. True or False $\frac{d}{dx}(\sin x) = \cos x$, if x is measured in degrees or radians. Justify your answer.

71. True or False The slope of the normal line to the curve $x = 3\cos t$, $y = 3\sin t$ at $t = \pi/4$ is -1. Justify your answer.

72. Multiple Choice Which of the following is dy/dx if $y = \tan(4x)$?

(A) $4\sec(4x)\tan(4x)$ **(B)** $\sec(4x)\tan(4x)$ **(C)** $4\cot(4x)$
(D) $\sec^2(4x)$ **(E)** $4\sec^2(4x)$

73. Multiple Choice Which of the following is dy/dx if $y = \cos^2(x^3 + x^2)$?

(A) $-2(3x^2 + 2x)$
(B) $-(3x^2 + 2x)\cos(x^3 + x^2)\sin(x^3 + x^2)$
(C) $-2(3x^2 + 2x)\cos(x^3 + x^2)\sin(x^3 + x^2)$
(D) $2(3x^2 + 2x)\cos(x^3 + x^2)\sin(x^3 + x^2)$
(E) $2(3x^2 + 2x)$

In Exercises 74 and 75, use the curve defined by the parametric equations $x = t - \cos t$, $y = -1 + \sin t$.

74. Multiple Choice Which of the following is an equation of the tangent line to the curve at $t = 0$?

(A) $y = x$ **(B)** $y = -x$ **(C)** $y = x + 2$
(D) $y = x - 2$ **(E)** $y = -x - 2$

75. Multiple Choice At which of the following values of t is $dy/dx = 0$?

(A) $t = \pi/4$ **(B)** $t = \pi/2$ **(C)** $t = 3\pi/4$
(D) $t = \pi$ **(E)** $t = 2\pi$

Explorations

76. *The Derivative of sin 2x* Graph the function $y = 2\cos 2x$ for $-2 \le x \le 3.5$. Then, on the same screen, graph

$$y = \frac{\sin 2(x+h) - \sin 2x}{h}$$

for $h = 1.0$, 0.5, and 0.2. Experiment with other values of h, including negative values. What do you see happening as $h \to 0$? Explain this behavior.

77. *The Derivative of cos (x²)* Graph $y = -2x\sin(x^2)$ for $-2 \le x \le 3$. Then, on screen, graph

$$y = \frac{\cos[(x+h)^2] - \cos(x)^2}{h}$$

for $h = 1.0$, 0.7, and 0.3. Experiment with other values of h. What do you see happening as $h \to 0$? Explain this behavior.

Extending the Ideas

78. *Absolute Value Functions* Let u be a differentiable function of x.

(a) Show that $\frac{d}{dx}|u| = u'\frac{u}{|u|}$.

(b) Use part (a) to find the derivatives of $f(x) = |x^2 - 9|$ and $g(x) = |x|\sin x$.

79. *Geometric and Arithmetic Mean* The geometric mean of u and v is $G = \sqrt{uv}$ and the arithmetic mean is $A = (u+v)/2$. Show that if $u = x$, $v = x + c$, c a real number, then

$$\frac{dG}{dx} = \frac{A}{G}.$$

4.2 Implicit Differentiation

What you will learn about . . .

- Implicitly Defined Functions
- Lenses, Tangents, and Normal Lines
- Derivatives of Higher Order
- Rational Powers of Differentiable Functions

and why . . .

Implicit differentiation allows us to find derivatives of functions that are not defined or written explicitly as a function of a single variable.

Implicitly Defined Functions

The graph of the equation $x^3 + y^3 - 9xy = 0$ (Figure 4.7) has a well-defined slope at nearly every point because it is the union of the graphs of the functions $y = f_1(x)$, $y = f_2(x)$, and $y = f_3(x)$, which are differentiable except at O and A. But how do we find the slope when we cannot conveniently solve the equation to find the functions? The answer is to treat y as a differentiable function of x and differentiate both sides of the equation with respect to x, using the differentiation rules for sums, products, and quotients, and the Chain Rule. Then solve for dy/dx in terms of x and y *together* to obtain a formula that calculates the slope at any point (x, y) on the graph from the values of x and y.

The process by which we find dy/dx is called **implicit differentiation.** The phrase derives from the fact that the equation

$$x^3 + y^3 - 9xy = 0$$

defines the functions f_1, f_2, and f_3 implicitly (i.e., hidden inside the equation), without giving us *explicit* formulas to work with.

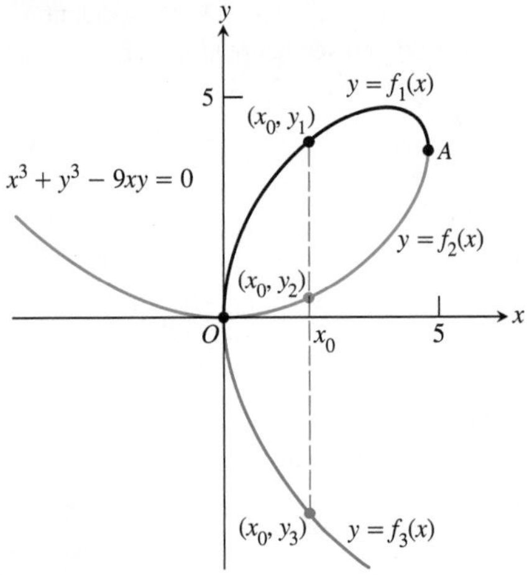

Figure 4.7 The graph of $x^3 + y^3 - 9xy = 0$ (called a *folium*). Although not the graph of a function, it is the union of the graphs of three separate functions. This particular curve dates to Descartes in 1638.

EXAMPLE 1 Differentiating Implicitly

Find dy/dx if $y^2 = x$.

SOLUTION

To find dy/dx, we simply differentiate both sides of the equation $y^2 = x$ with respect to x, treating y as a differentiable function of x and applying the Chain Rule:

$$y^2 = x$$

$$2y\frac{dy}{dx} = 1 \qquad \frac{d}{dx}(y^2) = \frac{d}{dy}(y^2)\cdot\frac{dy}{dx}$$

$$\frac{dy}{dx} = \frac{1}{2y}.$$

Now Try Exercise 3.

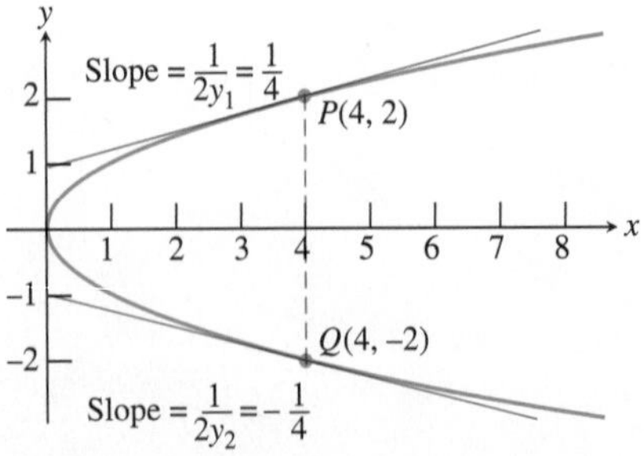

Figure 4.8 The derivative found in Example 1 gives the slope for the tangent lines at both P and Q, because it is a function of y.

In the previous example we differentiated with respect to x, and yet the derivative we obtained appeared as a function of y. Not only is this acceptable, it is actually quite useful. Figure 4.8, for example, shows that the curve has two different tangent lines when $x = 4$: one at the point $(4, 2)$ and the other at the point $(4, -2)$. Since the formula for dy/dx depends on y, our single formula gives the slope in both cases.

Implicit differentiation will frequently yield a derivative that is expressed in terms of both x and y, as in Example 2.

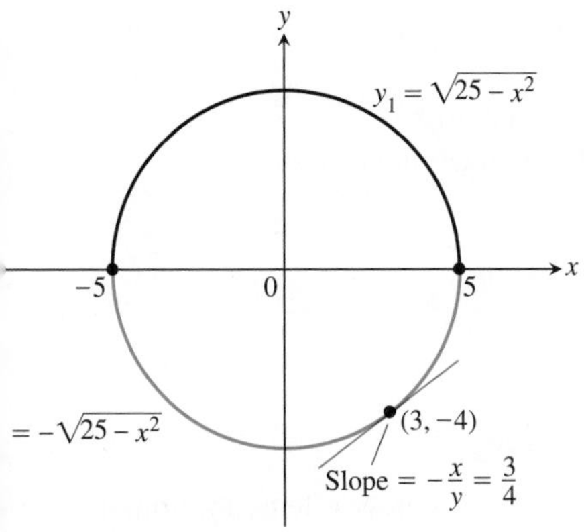

Figure 4.9 The circle combines the graphs of two functions. The graph of y_2 is the lower semicircle and passes through $(3, -4)$. (Example 2)

EXAMPLE 2 Finding Slope on a Circle

Find the slope of the circle $x^2 + y^2 = 25$ at the point $(3, -4)$.

SOLUTION

The circle is not the graph of a single function of x, but it is the union of the graphs of two differentiable functions, $y_1 = \sqrt{25 - x^2}$ and $y_2 = -\sqrt{25 - x^2}$ (Figure 4.9). The point $(3, -4)$ lies on the graph of y_2, so it is possible to find the slope by calculating explicitly:

$$\left.\frac{dy_2}{dx}\right|_{x=3} = -\left.\frac{-2x}{2\sqrt{25 - x^2}}\right|_{x=3} = -\frac{-6}{2\sqrt{25 - 9}} = \frac{3}{4}.$$

But we can also find this slope more easily by differentiating both sides of the equation of the circle implicitly with respect to x:

$$\frac{d}{dx}(x^2 + y^2) = \frac{d}{dx}(25) \qquad \text{Differentiate both sides with respect to } x.$$

$$2x + 2y\frac{dy}{dx} = 0$$

$$\frac{dy}{dx} = -\frac{x}{y}.$$

The slope at $(3, -4)$ is

$$-\left.\frac{x}{y}\right|_{(3,-4)} = -\frac{3}{-4} = \frac{3}{4}.$$

The implicit solution, besides being computationally easier, yields a formula for dy/dx that applies at any point on the circle (except, of course, $(\pm 5, 0)$, where slope is undefined). The explicit solution derived from the formula for y_2 applies only to the lower half of the circle.

Now Try Exercise 11.

To calculate the derivatives of other implicitly defined functions, we proceed as in Examples 1 and 2. We treat y as a differentiable function of x and apply the usual rules to differentiate both sides of the defining equation.

EXAMPLE 3 Solving for *dy/dx*

Show that the slope dy/dx is defined at every point on the graph of $2y = x^2 + \sin y$.

SOLUTION

First we need to know dy/dx, which we find by implicit differentiation:

$$2y = x^2 + \sin y$$

$$\frac{d}{dx}(2y) = \frac{d}{dx}(x^2 + \sin y) \qquad \text{Differentiate both sides with respect to } x \ldots$$

$$= \frac{d}{dx}(x^2) + \frac{d}{dx}(\sin y)$$

$$2\frac{dy}{dx} = 2x + \cos y \frac{dy}{dx} \qquad \ldots \text{treating } y \text{ as a function of } x \text{ and using the Chain Rule.}$$

$$2\frac{dy}{dx} - (\cos y)\frac{dy}{dx} = 2x \qquad \text{Collect terms with } dy/dx$$

$$(2 - \cos y)\frac{dy}{dx} = 2x \qquad \text{and factor out } dy/dx.$$

$$\frac{dy}{dx} = \frac{2x}{2 - \cos y}. \qquad \text{Solve for } dy/dx \text{ by dividing.}$$

The formula for dy/dx is defined at every point (x, y), except for those points at which $\cos y = 2$. Since $\cos y$ cannot be greater than 1, this never happens.

Now Try Exercise 13.

Ellen Ochoa (1958–)

After earning a doctorate degree in electrical engineering from Stanford University, Ellen Ochoa became a research engineer and, within a few years, received three patents in the field of optics. In 1990, Ochoa joined the NASA astronaut program, and, three years later, became the first Hispanic female to travel in space. Ochoa's message to young people is: "If you stay in school you have the potential to achieve what you want in the future."

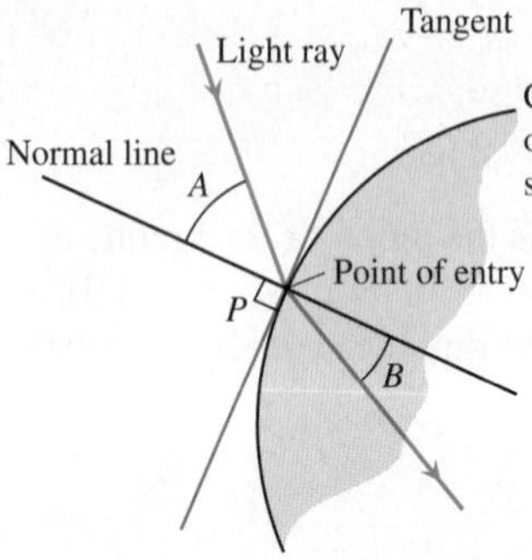

Figure 4.10 The profile of a lens, showing the bending (refraction) of a ray of light as it passes through the lens surface.

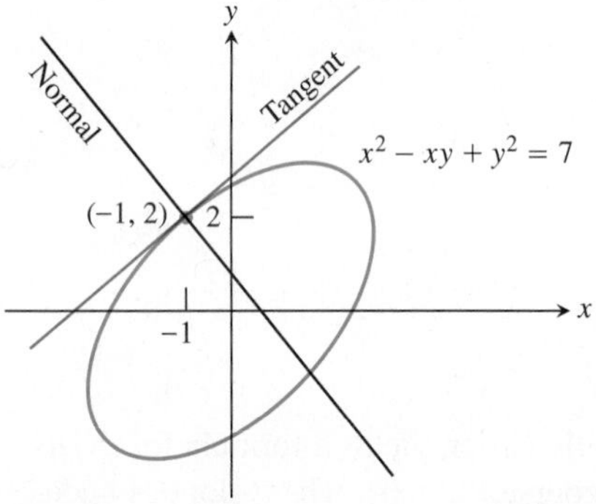

Figure 4.11 Tangent and normal lines to the ellipse $x^2 - xy + y^2 = 7$ at the point $(-1, 2)$. (Example 4)

Implicit Differentiation Process

1. Differentiate both sides of the equation with respect to x.
2. Collect the terms with dy/dx on one side of the equation.
3. Factor out dy/dx.
4. Solve for dy/dx.

Lenses, Tangents, and Normal Lines

In the law that describes how light changes direction as it enters a lens, the important angles are the angles the light makes with the line perpendicular to the surface of the lens at the point of entry (angles A and B in Figure 4.10). This line is called the *normal to the surface* at the point of entry. In a profile view of a lens like the one in Figure 4.10, the normal is a line perpendicular to the tangent to the profile curve at the point of entry.

Profiles of lenses are often described by quadratic curves (see Figure 4.11). When they are, we can use implicit differentiation to find the tangents and normals.

EXAMPLE 4 Tangent and normal to an ellipse

Find the tangent and normal to the ellipse $x^2 - xy + y^2 = 7$ at the point $(-1, 2)$. (See Figure 4.11.)

SOLUTION

We first use implicit differentiation to find dy/dx:

$$x^2 - xy + y^2 = 7$$

$$\frac{d}{dx}(x^2) - \frac{d}{dx}(xy) + \frac{d}{dx}(y^2) = \frac{d}{dx}(7) \qquad \text{Differentiate both sides with respect to } x\ldots$$

$$2x - \left(x\frac{dy}{dx} + y\frac{dx}{dx}\right) + 2y\frac{dy}{dx} = 0 \qquad \ldots\text{treating } xy \text{ as a product and } y \text{ as a function of } x.$$

$$(2y - x)\frac{dy}{dx} = y - 2x \qquad \text{Collect terms.}$$

$$\frac{dy}{dx} = \frac{y - 2x}{2y - x}. \qquad \text{Solve for } dy/dx.$$

We then evaluate the derivative at $x = -1$, $y = 2$ to obtain

$$\left.\frac{dy}{dx}\right|_{(-1,2)} = \left.\frac{y - 2x}{2y - x}\right|_{(-1,2)} = \frac{2 - 2(-1)}{2(2) - (-1)} = \frac{4}{5}.$$

The tangent to the curve at $(-1, 2)$ is

$$y - 2 = \frac{4}{5}(x - (-1))$$

$$y = \frac{4}{5}x + \frac{14}{5}.$$

continued

The normal to the curve at $(-1, 2)$ is

$$y - 2 = -\frac{5}{4}(x + 1)$$

$$y = -\frac{5}{4}x + \frac{3}{4}.$$

Now Try Exercise 17.

Derivatives of Higher Order

Implicit differentiation can also be used to find derivatives of higher order. Here is an example.

EXAMPLE 5 Finding a Second Derivative Implicitly

Find d^2y/dx^2 if $2x^3 - 3y^2 = 8$.

SOLUTION

To start, we differentiate both sides of the equation with respect to x in order to find $y' = dy/dx$.

$$\frac{d}{dx}(2x^3 - 3y^2) = \frac{d}{dx}(8)$$

$$6x^2 - 6yy' = 0$$

$$x^2 - yy' = 0$$

$$y' = \frac{x^2}{y}, \text{ when } y \neq 0$$

We now apply the Quotient Rule to find y''.

$$y'' = \frac{d}{dx}\left(\frac{x^2}{y}\right) = \frac{2xy - x^2y'}{y^2} = \frac{2x}{y} - \frac{x^2}{y^2} \cdot y'$$

Finally, we substitute $y' = x^2/y$ to express y'' in terms of x and y.

$$y'' = \frac{2x}{y} - \frac{x^2}{y^2}\left(\frac{x^2}{y}\right) = \frac{2x}{y} - \frac{x^4}{y^3}, \text{ when } y \neq 0$$

Now Try Exercise 29.

EXPLORATION 1 An Unexpected Derivative

Consider the set of all points (x, y) satisfying the equation $x^2 - 2xy + y^2 = 4$. What does the graph of the equation look like? You can find out in two ways in this Exploration.

1. Use implicit differentiation to find dy/dx. Are you surprised by this derivative?
2. Knowing the derivative, what do you conjecture about the graph?
3. What are the possible values of y when $x = 0$? Does this information enable you to refine your conjecture about the graph?
4. The original equation can be written as $(x - y)^2 - 4 = 0$. By factoring the expression on the left, write two equations whose graphs combine to give the graph of the original equation. Then sketch the graph.
5. Explain why your graph is consistent with the derivative found in part 1.

Rational Powers of Differentiable Functions

We know that the Power Rule

$$\frac{d}{dx}x^n = nx^{n-1}$$

holds for any integer n (Rules 2 and 7). We can now prove that it holds when n is any rational number.

RULE 9 Power Rule for Rational Powers of *x*

If n is any rational number, then

$$\frac{d}{dx}x^n = nx^{n-1}.$$

If $n < 1$, then the derivative does not exist at $x = 0$.

Proof Let p and q be integers with $q > 0$ and suppose that $y = \sqrt[q]{x^p} = x^{p/q}$. Then

$$y^q = x^p.$$

Since p and q are integers (for which we already have the Power Rule), we can differentiate both sides of the equation with respect to x and obtain

$$qy^{q-1}\frac{dy}{dx} = px^{p-1}.$$

If $y \neq 0$, we can divide both sides of the equation by qy^{q-1} to solve for dy/dx, obtaining

$$\begin{aligned}
\frac{dy}{dx} &= \frac{px^{p-1}}{qy^{q-1}} \\
&= \frac{p}{q} \cdot \frac{x^{p-1}}{(x^{p/q})^{q-1}} && y = x^{p/q} \\
&= \frac{p}{q} \cdot \frac{x^{p-1}}{x^{p-p/q}} && \frac{p}{q}(q-1) = p - \frac{p}{q} \\
&= \frac{p}{q} \cdot x^{(p-1)-(p-p/q)} && \text{A law of exponents} \\
&= \frac{p}{q} \cdot x^{(p/q)-1}.
\end{aligned}$$

This proves the rule. ■

By combining this result with the Chain Rule, we get an extension of the Power Chain Rule to rational powers of u:

If n is a rational number and u is a differentiable function of x, then u^n is a differentiable function of x and

$$\frac{d}{dx}u^n = nu^{n-1}\frac{du}{dx},$$

provided that $u \neq 0$ if $n < 1$.

The restriction that $u \neq 0$ when $n < 1$ is necessary because 0 might be in the domain of u^n but not in the domain of u^{n-1}, as we see in the first two parts of Example 6.

EXAMPLE 6 Using the Rational Power Rule

(a) $\dfrac{d}{dx}(\sqrt{x}) = \dfrac{d}{dx}(x^{1/2}) = \dfrac{1}{2}x^{-1/2} = \dfrac{1}{2\sqrt{x}}$

Notice that $\sqrt{x}$ is defined at $x = 0$, but $1/(2\sqrt{x})$ is not.

(b) $\dfrac{d}{dx}(x^{2/3}) = \dfrac{2}{3}(x^{-1/3}) = \dfrac{2}{3x^{1/3}}$

The original function is defined for all real numbers, but the derivative is undefined at $x = 0$. Recall Figure 3.12, which showed that this function's graph has a *cusp* at $x = 0$.

(c)
$$\frac{d}{dx}(\cos x)^{-1/5} = -\frac{1}{5}(\cos x)^{-6/5}\cdot\frac{d}{dx}(\cos x)$$
$$= -\frac{1}{5}(\cos x)^{-6/5}(-\sin x)$$
$$= \frac{1}{5}\sin x(\cos x)^{-6/5}$$

Now Try Exercise 33.

Quick Review 4.2 *(For help, go to Section 1.2 and Appendix A.5.)*

Exercise numbers with a gray background indicate problems that the authors have designed to be solved *without a calculator.*

In Exercises 1–5, sketch the curve defined by the equation and find two functions y_1 and y_2 whose graphs will combine to give the curve.

1. $x - y^2 = 0$

2. $4x^2 + 9y^2 = 36$

3. $x^2 - 4y^2 = 0$

4. $x^2 + y^2 = 9$

5. $x^2 + y^2 = 2x + 3$

In Exercises 6–8, solve for y' in terms of y and x.

6. $x^2y' - 2xy = 4x - y$

7. $y'\sin x - x\cos x = xy' + y$

8. $x(y^2 - y') = y'(x^2 - y)$

In Exercises 9 and 10, find an expression for the function using rational powers rather than radicals.

9. $\sqrt{x}(x - \sqrt[3]{x})$

10. $\dfrac{x + \sqrt[3]{x^2}}{\sqrt{x^3}}$

Section 4.2 Exercises

In Exercises 1–8, find dy/dx.

1. $x^2y + xy^2 = 6$

2. $x^3 + y^3 = 18xy$

3. $y^2 = \dfrac{x - 1}{x + 1}$

4. $x^2 = \dfrac{x - y}{x + y}$

5. $x = \tan y$

6. $x = \sin y$

7. $x + \tan(xy) = 0$

8. $x + \sin y = xy$

In Exercises 9–12, find dy/dx and find the slope of the curve at the indicated point.

9. $x^2 + y^2 = 13,\quad (-2, 3)$

10. $x^2 + y^2 = 9,\quad (0, 3)$

11. $(x - 1)^2 + (y - 1)^2 = 13,\quad (3, 4)$

12. $(x + 2)^2 + (y + 3)^2 = 25,\ (1, -7)$

In Exercises 13–16, find where the slope of the curve is defined.

13. $x^2y - xy^2 = 4$

14. $x = \cos y$

15. $x^3 + y^3 = xy$

16. $x^2 + 4xy + 4y^2 - 3x = 6$

In Exercises 17–26, find the lines that are **(a)** tangent and **(b)** normal to the curve at the given point.

17. $x^2 + xy - y^2 = 1,\quad (2, 3)$

18. $x^2 + y^2 = 25,\quad (3, -4)$

19. $x^2y^2 = 9,\ (-1, 3)$

20. $y^2 - 2x - 4y - 1 = 0,\quad (-2, 1)$

21. $6x^2 + 3xy + 2y^2 + 17y - 6 = 0,\quad (-1, 0)$

22. $x^2 - \sqrt{3}xy + 2y^2 = 5,\quad (\sqrt{3}, 2)$

23. $2xy + \pi\sin y = 2\pi,\quad (1, \pi y/2)$

24. $x\sin 2y = y\cos 2x,\quad (\pi/4, \pi/2)$

25. $y = 2\sin(\pi x - y),\quad (1, 0)$

26. $x^2\cos^2 y - \sin y = 0,\quad (0, \pi)$

In Exercises 27–30, use implicit differentiation to find dy/dx and then d^2y/dx^2.

27. $x^2 + y^2 = 1$

28. $x^{2/3} + y^{2/3} = 1$

29. $y^2 = x^2 + 2x$

30. $y^2 + 2y = 2x + 1$

In Exercises 31–42, find dy/dx.

31. $y = x^{9/4}$

32. $y = x^{-3/5}$

33. $y = \sqrt[3]{x}$

34. $y = \sqrt[4]{x}$

35. $y = (2x + 5)^{-1/2}$

36. $y = (1 - 6x)^{2/3}$

37. $y = x\sqrt{x^2 + 1}$

38. $y = \dfrac{x}{\sqrt{x^2 + 1}}$

39. $y = \sqrt{1 - \sqrt{x}}$

40. $y = 3(2x^{-1/2} + 1)^{-1/3}$

41. $y = 3(\csc x)^{3/2}$

42. $y = [\sin(x + 5)]^{5/4}$

43. Which of the following could be true if $f''(x) = x^{-1/3}$?

(a) $f(x) = \frac{3}{2}x^{2/3} - 3$ **(b)** $f(x) = \frac{9}{10}x^{5/3} - 7$

(c) $f'''(x) = -\frac{1}{3}x^{-4/3}$ **(d)** $f'(x) = \frac{3}{2}x^{2/3} + 6$

44. Which of the following could be true if $g''(t) = 1/t^{3/4}$?

(a) $g'(t) = 4\sqrt[4]{t} - 4$ **(b)** $g'''(t) = -4/\sqrt[4]{t}$

(c) $g(t) = t - 7 + (16/5)t^{5/4}$ **(d)** $g'(t) =)1/4)t^{1/4}$

45. *The Eight Curve* **(a)** Find the slopes of the figure-eight-shaped curve

$$y^4 = y^2 - x^2$$

at the two points shown on the graph that follows.

(b) Use parametric mode and the two pairs of parametric equations

$$x_1(t) = \sqrt{t^2 - t^4}, \quad y_1(t) = t,$$
$$x_2(t) = -\sqrt{t^2 - t^4}, \quad y_2(t) = t,$$

to graph the curve. Specify a window and a parameter interval.

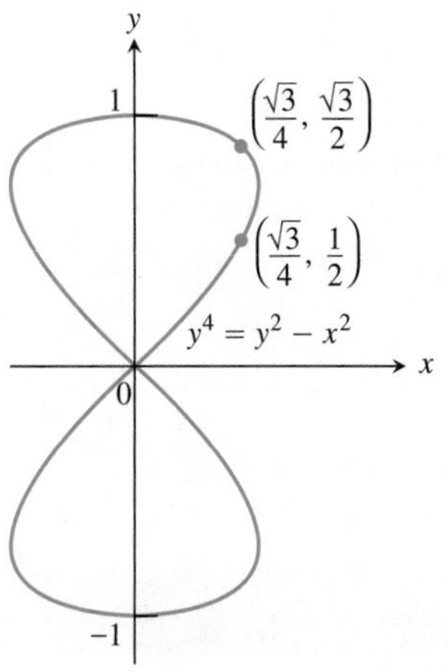

46. *The Cissoid of Diocles (dates from about 200 B.C.E.)*

(a) Find equations for the tangent and normal to the cissoid of Diocles,

$$y^2(2 - x) = x^3,$$

at the point $(1, 1)$ as pictured below.

(b) Explain how to reproduce the graph on a grapher.

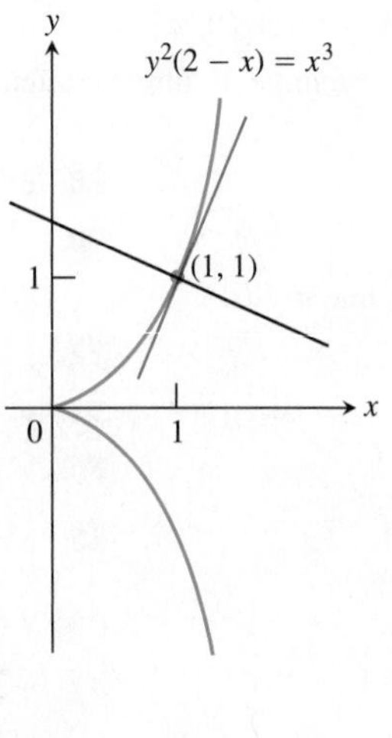

47. **(a)** Confirm that $(-1, 1)$ is on the curve defined by $x^3y^2 = \cos(\pi y)$.

(b) Use part (a) to find the slope of the line tangent to the curve at $(-1, 1)$.

48. Group Activity

(a) Show that the relation

$$y^3 - xy = -1$$

cannot be a function of x by showing that there is more than one possible y-value when $x = 2$.

(b) On a small enough square with center $(2, 1)$, the part of the graph of the relation within the square will define a function $y = f(x)$. For this function, find $f'(2)$ and $f''(2)$.

49. Find the two points where the curve $x^2 + xy + y^2 = 7$ crosses the x-axis, and show that the tangents to the curve at these points are parallel. What is the common slope of these tangents?

50. Find points on the curve $x^2 + xy + y^2 = 7$ **(a)** where the tangent is parallel to the x-axis and **(b)** where the tangent is parallel to the y-axis. (In the latter case, dy/dx is not defined, but dx/dy is. What value does dx/dy have at these points?)

51. *Orthogonal Curves* Two curves are *orthogonal* at a point of intersection if their tangents at that point cross at right angles. Show that the curves $2x^2 + 3y^2 = 5$ and $y^2 = x^3$ are orthogonal at $(1, 1)$ and $(1, -1)$. Use parametric mode to draw the curves and to show the tangent lines.

52. The position of a body moving along a coordinate line at time t is $s = (4 + 6t)^{3/2}$, with s in meters and t in seconds. Find the body's velocity and acceleration when $t = 2$ sec.

53. The velocity of a falling body is $v = 8\sqrt{s - t} + 1$ feet per second at the instant t (sec) the body has fallen s feet from its starting point. Show that the body's acceleration is 32 ft/sec².

54. *The Devil's Curve (Gabriel Cramer [the Cramer of Cramer's Rule], 1750)* Find the slopes of the devil's curve $y^4 - 4y^2 = x^4 - 9x^2$ at the four indicated points.

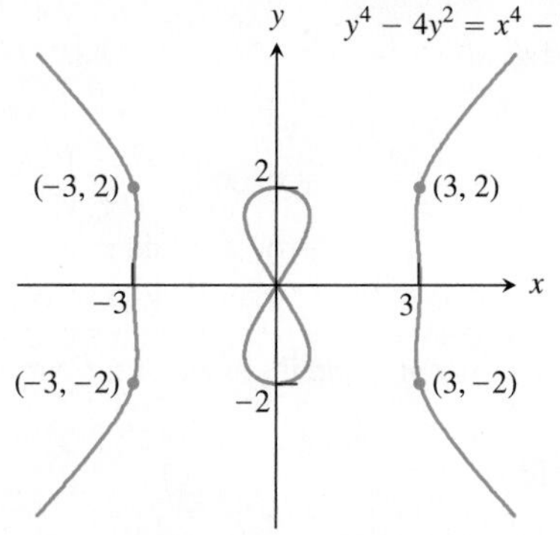

55. *The Folium of Descartes* (See Figure 4.7 on page 162)

(a) Find the slope of the folium of Descartes, $x^3 + y^3 - 9xy = 0$ at the points $(4, 2)$ and $(2, 4)$.

(b) At what point other than the origin does the folium have a horizontal tangent?

(c) Find the coordinates of point A in Figure 4.7, where the folium has a vertical tangent.

56. The line that is normal to the curve $x^2 + 2xy - 3y^2 = 0$ at $(1, 1)$ intersects the curve at what other point?

57. Find the normals to the curve $xy + 2x - y = 0$ that are parallel to the line $2x + y = 0$.

58. Show that if it is possible to draw these three normals from the point $(a, 0)$ to the parabola $x = y^2$ shown here, then a must be greater than $1/2$. One of the normals is the x-axis. For what value of a are the other two normals perpendicular?

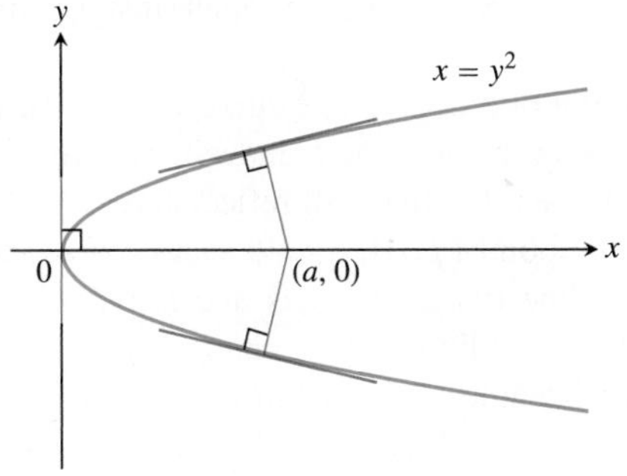

Standardized Test Questions

59. True or False The slope of $xy^2 + x = 1$ at $(1/2, 1)$ is 2. Justify your answer.

60. True or False The derivative of $y = \sqrt[3]{x}$ is $\dfrac{1}{3x^{2/3}}$. Justify your answer.

In Exercises 61 and 62, use the curve $x^2 - xy + y^2 = 1$.

61. Multiple Choice Which of the following is equal to dy/dx?

(A) $\dfrac{y - 2x}{2y - x}$ **(B)** $\dfrac{y + 2x}{2y - x}$ **(C)** $\dfrac{2x}{x - 2y}$

(D) $\dfrac{2x + y}{x - 2y}$ **(E)** $\dfrac{y + 2x}{x}$

62. Multiple Choice Which of the following is equal to $\dfrac{d^2y}{dx^2}$?

(A) $-\dfrac{6}{(2y - x)^3}$ **(B)** $\dfrac{10y^2 - 10x^2 - 10xy}{(2y - x)^3}$

(C) $\dfrac{8x^2 - 4xy + 8y^2}{(x - 2y)^3}$ **(D)** $\dfrac{10x^2 + 10y^2}{(x - 2y)^3}$ **(E)** $\dfrac{2}{x}$

63. Multiple Choice Which of the following is equal to dy/dx if $y = x^{3/4}$?

(A) $\dfrac{3x^{1/3}}{4}$ **(B)** $\dfrac{4x^{1/4}}{3}$ **(C)** $\dfrac{3x^{1/4}}{4}$ **(D)** $\dfrac{4}{3x^{1/4}}$ **(E)** $\dfrac{3}{4x^{1/4}}$

64. Multiple Choice Which of the following is equal to the slope of the tangent to $y^2 - x^2 = 1$ at $(1, \sqrt{2})$?

(A) $-\dfrac{1}{\sqrt{2}}$ **(B)** $-\sqrt{2}$ **(C)** $\dfrac{1}{\sqrt{2}}$ **(D)** $\sqrt{2}$ **(E)** 0

Extending the Ideas

65. *Finding Tangents*

(a) Show that the tangent to the ellipse

$$\frac{x^2}{a^2} + \frac{y^2}{b^2} = 1$$

at the point (x_1, y_1) has equation

$$\frac{x_1x}{a^2} + \frac{y_1y}{b^2} = 1.$$

(b) Find an equation for the tangent to the hyperbola

$$\frac{x^2}{a^2} - \frac{y^2}{b^2} = 1$$

at the point (x_1, y_1).

66. *End Behavior Model* Consider the hyperbola

$$\frac{x^2}{a^2} - \frac{y^2}{b^2} = 1.$$

Show that

(a) $y = \pm\dfrac{b}{a}\sqrt{x^2 - a^2}$.

(b) $g(x) = (b/a)|x|$ is an end behavior model for

$$f(x) = (b/a)\sqrt{x^2 - a^2}.$$

(c) $g(x) = -(b/a)|x|$ is an end behavior model for

$$f(x) = -(b/a)\sqrt{x^2 - a^2}.$$

Quick Quiz for AP* Preparation: Sections 4.1–4.2

1. Multiple Choice Which of the following gives $\dfrac{dy}{dx}$ for $y = \sin^4(3x)$?

(A) $4\sin^3(3x)\cos(3x)$ **(B)** $12\sin^3(3x)\cos(3x)$

(C) $12\sin(3x)\cos(3x)$ **(D)** $12\sin^3(3x)$

(E) $-12\sin^3(3x)\cos(3x)$

2. Multiple Choice What is the slope of the line tangent to the curve $2x^2 - 3y^2 = 2xy - 6$ at the point $(3, 2)$?

(A) 0 **(B)** $\dfrac{4}{9}$ **(C)** $\dfrac{7}{9}$ **(D)** $\dfrac{6}{7}$ **(E)** $\dfrac{5}{3}$

3. Multiple Choice Which of the following gives $\dfrac{dy}{dx}$ for the parametric curve $x = 3\sin t$, $y = 2\cos t$?

(A) $-\dfrac{3}{2}\cos t$ **(B)** $\dfrac{3}{2}\cos t$ **(C)** $-\dfrac{2}{3}\tan t$

(D) $\dfrac{2}{3}\tan t$ **(E)** $\tan t$

4. Free Response A curve in the xy-plane is defined by $xy^2 - x^3y = 6$.

(a) Find $\dfrac{dy}{dx}$.

(b) Find an equation for the tangent line at each point on the curve with x-coordinate 1.

(c) Find the x-coordinate of each point on the curve where the tangent line is vertical.

4.3 Derivatives of Inverse Trigonometric Functions

What you will learn about . . .

- Derivatives of Inverse Functions
- Derivative of the Arcsine
- Derivative of the Arctangent
- Derivative of the Arcsecant
- Derivatives of the Other Three

and why . . .

The relationship between the graph of a function and its inverse allows us to see the relationship between their derivatives.

Derivatives of Inverse Functions

In Section 1.5 we learned that the graph of the inverse of a function f can be obtained by reflecting the graph of f across the line $y = x$. If we combine that with our understanding of what makes a function differentiable, we can gain some quick insights into the differentiability of inverse functions.

As Figure 4.12 suggests, the reflection of a continuous curve with no cusps or corners will be another continuous curve with no cusps or corners. Indeed, if there is a tangent line to the graph of f at the point $(a, f(a))$, then that line will reflect across $y = x$ to become a tangent line to the graph of f^{-1} at the point $(f(a), a)$. We can even see geometrically that the *slope* of the reflected tangent line (when it exists and is not zero) will be the *reciprocal* of the slope of the original tangent line, since a change in y becomes a change in x in the reflection, and a change in x becomes a change in y.

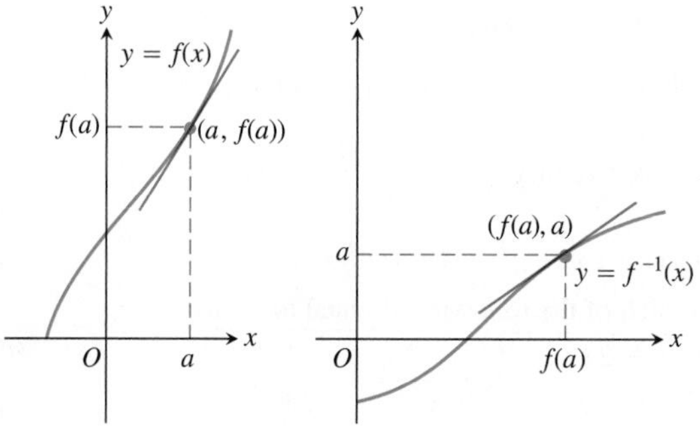

The slopes are reciprocal: $\left.\dfrac{df^{-1}}{dx}\right|_{f(a)} = \dfrac{1}{\left.\dfrac{df}{dx}\right|_{a}}$

Figure 4.12 The graphs of a function and its inverse. Notice that the tangent lines have reciprocal slopes.

All of this serves as an introduction to the following theorem, which we will assume as we proceed to find derivatives of inverse functions. Although the essentials of the proof are illustrated in the geometry of Figure 4.12, a careful analytic proof is more appropriate for an advanced calculus text and will be omitted here.

THEOREM 1 Derivatives of Inverse Functions

If f is differentiable at every point of an interval I and df/dx is never zero on I, then f has an inverse and f^{-1} is differentiable at every point of the interval $f(I)$.

EXPLORATION 1 Finding a Derivative on an Inverse Graph Geometrically

Let $f(x) = x^5 + 2x - 1$. Since the point $(1, 2)$ is on the graph of f, it follows that the point $(2, 1)$ is on the graph of f^{-1}. Can you find

$$\frac{df^{-1}}{dx}(2),$$

the value of df^{-1}/dx at 2, without knowing a formula for f^{-1}?

1. Graph $f(x) = x^5 + 2x - 1$. A function must be one-to-one to have an inverse function. Is this function one-to-one?
2. Find $f'(x)$. How could this derivative help you to conclude that f has an inverse?
3. Reflect the graph of f across the line $y = x$ to obtain a graph of f^{-1}.
4. Sketch the tangent line to the graph of f^{-1} at the point $(2, 1)$. Call it L.
5. Reflect the line L across the line $y = x$. At what point is the reflection of L tangent to the graph of f?
6. What is the slope of the reflection of L?
7. What is the slope of L?
8. What is $\dfrac{df^{-1}}{dx}(2)$?

Derivative of the Arcsine

We know that the function $x = \sin y$ is differentiable in the open interval $-\pi/2 < y < \pi/2$ and that its derivative, the cosine, is positive there. Theorem 1 therefore assures us that the inverse function $y = \sin^{-1}(x)$ (the *arcsine* of x) is differentiable throughout the interval $-1 < x < 1$. We cannot expect it to be differentiable at $x = -1$ or $x = 1$, however, because the tangents to the graph are vertical at these points (Figure 4.13).

We find the derivative of $y = \sin^{-1}(x)$ as follows:

$$y = \sin^{-1} x$$

$$\sin y = x \qquad \text{Inverse function relationship}$$

$$\frac{d}{dx}(\sin y) = \frac{d}{dx}x \qquad \text{Differentiate both sides.}$$

$$\cos y \frac{dy}{dx} = 1 \qquad \text{Implicit differentiation}$$

$$\frac{dy}{dx} = \frac{1}{\cos y}$$

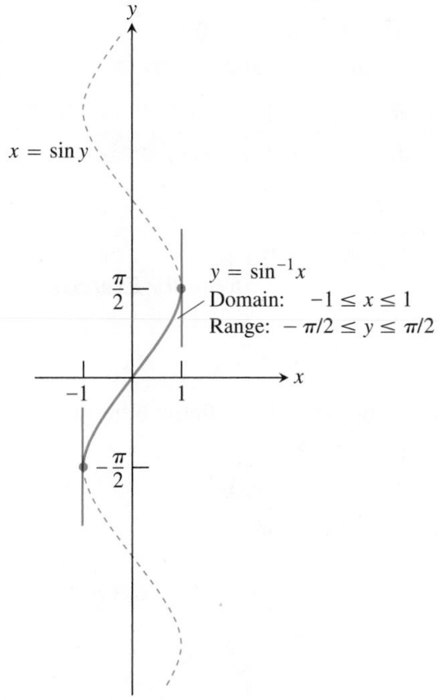

Figure 4.13 The graph of $y = \sin^{-1} x$ has vertical tangents $x = -1$ and $x = 1$.

The division in the last step is safe because $\cos y \neq 0$ for $-\pi/2 < y < \pi/2$. In fact, $\cos y$ is *positive* for $-\pi/2 < y < \pi/2$, so we can replace $\cos y$ with $\sqrt{1 - (\sin y)^2}$, which is $\sqrt{1 - x^2}$. Thus

$$\frac{d}{dx}(\sin^{-1} x) = \frac{1}{\sqrt{1 - x^2}}.$$

If u is a differentiable function of x with $|u| < 1$, we apply the Chain Rule to get

$$\frac{d}{dx}\sin^{-1} u = \frac{1}{\sqrt{1 - u^2}}\frac{du}{dx}, \quad |u| < 1.$$

EXAMPLE 1 Applying the Formula

$$\frac{d}{dx}(\sin^{-1} x^2) = \frac{1}{\sqrt{1 - (x^2)^2}} \cdot \frac{d}{dx}(x^2) = \frac{2x}{\sqrt{1 - x^4}}$$

Now Try Exercise 3.

Derivative of the Arctangent

Although the function $y = \sin^{-1}(x)$ has a rather narrow domain of $[-1, 1]$, the function $y = \tan^{-1} x$ is defined for all real numbers, and is differentiable for all real numbers, as we will now see. The differentiation proceeds exactly as with the arcsine function.

$$y = \tan^{-1} x$$

$$\tan y = x \qquad \text{Inverse function relationship}$$

$$\frac{d}{dx}(\tan y) = \frac{d}{dx}x$$

$$\sec^2 y \frac{dy}{dx} = 1 \qquad \text{Implicit differentiation}$$

$$\frac{dy}{dx} = \frac{1}{\sec^2 y}$$

$$= \frac{1}{1 + (\tan y)^2} \qquad \text{Trig identity: } \sec^2 y = 1 + \tan^2 y$$

$$= \frac{1}{1 + x^2}$$

The derivative is defined for all real numbers. If u is a differentiable function of x, we get the Chain Rule form:

$$\frac{d}{dx}\tan^{-1} u = \frac{1}{1 + u^2}\frac{du}{dx}.$$

EXAMPLE 2 A Moving Particle

A particle moves along the x-axis so that its position at any time $t \ge 0$ is $x(t) = \tan^{-1}\sqrt{t}$. What is the velocity of the particle when $t = 16$?

SOLUTION $v(t) = \frac{d}{dt}\tan^{-1}\sqrt{t} = \frac{1}{1 + (\sqrt{t})^2} \cdot \frac{d}{dt}\sqrt{t} = \frac{1}{1 + t} \cdot \frac{1}{2\sqrt{t}}$

When $t = 16$, the velocity is $v(16) = \frac{1}{1 + 16} \cdot \frac{1}{2\sqrt{16}} = \frac{1}{136}$.

Now Try Exercise 11.

Derivative of the Arcsecant

We find the derivative of $y = \sec^{-1} x$, $|x| > 1$, beginning as we did with the other inverse trigonometric functions.

$$y = \sec^{-1} x$$

$$\sec y = x \qquad \text{Inverse function relationship}$$

$$\frac{d}{dx}(\sec y) = \frac{d}{dx}x$$

$$\sec y \tan y \frac{dy}{dx} = 1$$

$$\frac{dy}{dx} = \frac{1}{\sec y \tan y} \qquad \text{Since } |x| > 1,\ y \text{ lies in } (0, \pi/2) \cup (\pi/2, \pi) \text{ and } \sec y \tan y \ne 0.$$

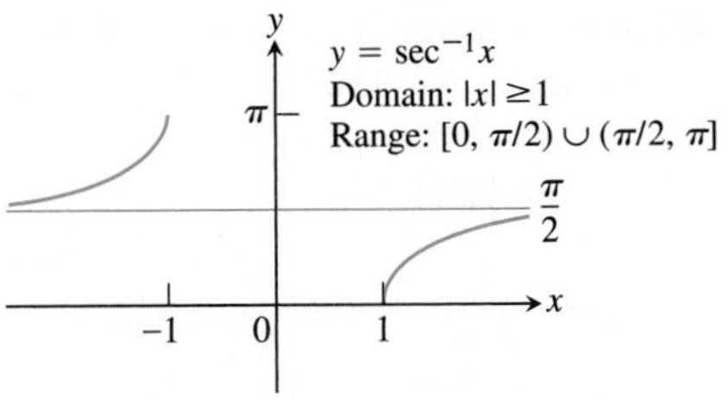

Figure 4.14 The slope of the curve $y = \sec^{-1} x$ is positive for both $x < -1$ and $x > 1$.

To express the result in terms of x, we use the relationships

$$\sec y = x \quad \text{and} \quad \tan y = \pm\sqrt{\sec^2 y - 1} = \pm\sqrt{x^2 - 1}$$

to get

$$\frac{dy}{dx} = \pm\frac{1}{x\sqrt{x^2 - 1}}.$$

Can we do anything about the $\pm$ sign? A glance at Figure 4.14 shows that the slope of the graph $y = \sec^{-1} x$ is always positive. That must mean that

$$\frac{d}{dx}\sec^{-1} x = \begin{cases} +\dfrac{1}{x\sqrt{x^2 - 1}} & \text{if } x > 1 \\ -\dfrac{1}{x\sqrt{x^2 - 1}} & \text{if } x < -1. \end{cases}$$

With the absolute value symbol we can write a single expression that eliminates the "$\pm$" ambiguity:

$$\frac{d}{dx}\sec^{-1} x = \frac{1}{|x|\sqrt{x^2 - 1}}.$$

If u is a differentiable function of x with $|u| > 1$, we have the formula

$$\frac{d}{dx}\sec^{-1} u = \frac{1}{|u|\sqrt{u^2 - 1}}\frac{du}{dx}, \quad |u| > 1.$$

EXAMPLE 3 Using the Formula

$$\begin{aligned} \frac{d}{dx}\sec^{-1}(5x^4) &= \frac{1}{|5x^4|\sqrt{(5x^4)^2 - 1}}\frac{d}{dx}(5x^4) \\ &= \frac{1}{5x^4\sqrt{25x^8 - 1}}(20x^3) \\ &= \frac{4}{x\sqrt{25x^8 - 1}} \end{aligned}$$

Now Try Exercise 17.

Derivatives of the Other Three

We could use the same technique to find the derivatives of the other three inverse trigonometric functions—arccosine, arccotangent, and arccosecant—but there is a much easier way, thanks to the following identities.

Inverse Function–Inverse Cofunction Identities

$$\cos^{-1} x = \pi/2 - \sin^{-1} x$$
$$\cot^{-1} x = \pi/2 - \tan^{-1} x$$
$$\csc^{-1} x = \pi/2 - \sec^{-1} x$$

It follows easily that the derivatives of the inverse cofunctions are the negatives of the derivatives of the corresponding inverse functions (see Exercises 32–34).

You have probably noticed by now that most calculators do not have buttons for $\cot^{-1}$, $\sec^{-1}$, or $\csc^{-1}$. They are not needed because of the following identities:

Calculator Conversion Identities

$$\sec^{-1} x = \cos^{-1}(1/x)$$
$$\cot^{-1} x = \pi/2 - \tan^{-1} x$$
$$\csc^{-1} x = \sin^{-1}(1/x)$$

Notice that we do not use $\tan^{-1}(1/x)$ as an identity for $\cot^{-1} x$. A glance at the graphs of $y = \tan^{-1}(1/x)$ and $y = \pi/2 - \tan^{-1} x$ reveals the problem (Figure 4.15).

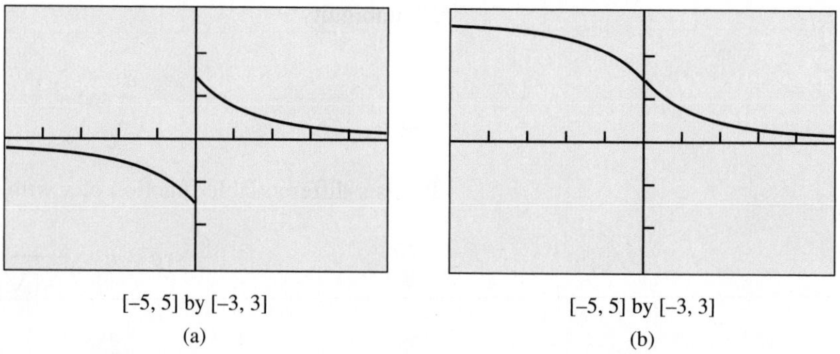

Figure 4.15 The graphs of (a) $y = \tan^{-1}(1/x)$ and (b) $y = \pi/2 - \tan^{-1} x$. The graph in (b) is the same as the graph of $y = \cot^{-1} x$.

We cannot replace $\cot^{-1} x$ by the function $y = \tan^{-1}(1/x)$ in the identity for the inverse functions and inverse cofunctions, and so it is not the function we want for $\cot^{-1} x$. The ranges of the inverse trigonometric functions have been chosen in part to make the two sets of identities above hold.

EXAMPLE 4 A Tangent Line to the Arccotangent Curve

Find an equation for the line tangent to the graph of $y = \cot^{-1} x$ at $x = -1$.

SOLUTION

First, we note that

$$\cot^{-1}(-1) = \pi/2 - \tan^{-1}(-1) = \pi/2 - (-\pi/4) = 3\pi/4.$$

The slope of the tangent line is

$$\left.\frac{dy}{dx}\right|_{x=-1} = -\left.\frac{1}{1 + x^2}\right|_{x=-1} = -\frac{1}{1 + (-1)^2} = -\frac{1}{2}.$$

So the tangent line has equation $y - 3\pi/4 = (-1/2)(x + 1)$.

Now Try Exercise 23.

Quick Review 4.3 *(For help, go to Sections 1.2, 1.5, and 1.6.)*

Exercise numbers with a gray background indicate problems that the authors have designed to be solved *without a calculator.*

In Exercises 1–5, give the *domain* and *range* of the function, and evaluate the function at $x = 1$.

1. $y = \sin^{-1} x$

2. $y = \cos^{-1} x$

3. $y = \tan^{-1} x$;

4. $y = \sec^{-1} x$

5. $y = \tan(\tan^{-1} x)$

In Exercises 6–10, find the inverse of the given function.

6. $y = 3x - 8$

7. $y = \sqrt[3]{x + 5}$

8. $y = \dfrac{8}{x}$

9. $y = \dfrac{3x - 2}{x}$

10. $y = \arctan(x/3)$

Section 4.3 Exercises

In Exercises 1–8, find the derivative of y with respect to the appropriate variable.

1. $y = \cos^{-1}(x^2)$

2. $y = \cos^{-1}(1/x)$

3. $y = \sin^{-1}\sqrt{2}t$

4. $y = \sin^{-1}(1 - t)$

5. $y = \sin^{-1}\dfrac{3}{t^2}$

6. $y = s\sqrt{1 - s^2} + \cos^{-1} s$

7. $y = x\sin^{-1} x + \sqrt{1 - x^2}$

8. $y = \dfrac{1}{\sin^{-1}(2x)}$

In Exercises 9–12, a particle moves along the x-axis so that its position at any time $t \geq 0$ is given by $x(t)$. Find the velocity at the indicated value of t.

9. $x(t) = \sin^{-1}\left(\dfrac{t}{4}\right)$, $t = 3$

10. $x(t) = \sin^{-1}\left(\dfrac{\sqrt{t}}{4}\right)$, $t = 4$

11. $x(t) = \tan^{-1} t$, $t = 2$

12. $x(t) = \tan^{-1}(t^2)$, $t = 1$

In Exercises 13–22, find the derivatives of y with respect to the appropriate variable.

13. $y = \sec^{-1}(2s + 1)$

14. $y = \sec^{-1} 5s$

15. $y = \csc^{-1}(x^2 + 1)$, $x > 0$

16. $y = \csc^{-1} x/2$

17. $y = \sec^{-1}\dfrac{1}{t}$, $0 < t < 1$

18. $y = \cot^{-1}\sqrt{t}$

19. $y = \cot^{-1}\sqrt{t - 1}$

20. $y = \sqrt{s^2 - 1} - \sec^{-1} s$

21. $y = \tan^{-1}\sqrt{x^2 - 1} + \csc^{-1} x$, $x > 1$,

22. $y = \cot^{-1}\dfrac{1}{x} - \tan^{-1} x$

In Exercises 23–26, find an equation for the tangent to the graph of y at the indicated point.

23. $y = \sec^{-1} x$, $x = 2$

24. $y = \tan^{-1} x$, $x = 2$

25. $y = \sin^{-1}\left(\dfrac{x}{4}\right)$, $x = 3$

26. $y = \tan^{-1}(x^2)$, $x = 1$

27. **(a)** Find an equation for the line tangent to the graph of $y = \tan x$ at the point $(\pi/4, 1)$.

(b) Find an equation for the line tangent to the graph of $y = \tan^{-1} x$ at the point $(1, \pi/4)$.

28. Let $f(x) = x^5 + 2x^3 + x - 1$.

(a) Find $f(1)$ and $f'(1)$.

(b) Find $f^{-1}(3)$ and $(f^{-1})'(3)$.

29. Let $f(x) = \cos x + 3x$.

(a) Show that f has a differentiable inverse.

(b) Find $f(0)$ and $f'(0)$.

(c) Find $f^{-1}(1)$ and $(f^{-1})'(1)$.

30. Group Activity Graph the function $f(x) = \sin^{-1}(\sin x)$ in the viewing window $[-2\pi, 2\pi]$ by $[-4, 4]$. Then answer the following questions:

(a) What is the domain of f?

(b) What is the range of f?

(c) At which points is f not differentiable?

(d) Sketch a graph of $y = f'(x)$ without using NDER or computing the derivative.

(e) Find $f'(x)$ algebraically. Can you reconcile your answer with the graph in part (d)?

31. Group Activity A particle moves along the x-axis so that its position at any time $t \geq 0$ is given by $x = \arctan t$.

(a) Prove that the particle is always moving to the right.

(b) Prove that the particle is always decelerating.

(c) What is the limiting position of the particle as t approaches infinity?

In Exercises 32–34, use the inverse function–inverse cofunction identities to derive the formula for the derivative of the function.

32. arccosine

33. arccotangent

34. arccosecant

Standardized Test Questions

You may use a graphing calculator to solve the following problems.

35. True or False The domain of $y = \sin^{-1} x$ is $-1 \le x \le 1$. Justify your answer.

36. True or False The domain of $y = \tan^{-1} x$ is $-1 \le x \le 1$. Justify your answer.

37. Multiple Choice Which of the following is $\frac{d}{dx}\sin^{-1}\left(\frac{x}{2}\right)$?

(A) $-\frac{2}{\sqrt{4-x^2}}$ (B) $-\frac{1}{\sqrt{4-x^2}}$ (C) $\frac{2}{4+x^2}$

(D) $\frac{2}{\sqrt{4-x^2}}$ (E) $\frac{1}{\sqrt{4-x^2}}$

38. Multiple Choice Which of the following is $\frac{d}{dx}\tan^{-1}(3x)$?

(A) $-\frac{3}{1+9x^2}$ (B) $-\frac{1}{1+9x^2}$ (C) $\frac{1}{1+9x^2}$

(D) $\frac{3}{1+9x^2}$ (E) $\frac{3}{\sqrt{1-9x^2}}$

39. Multiple Choice Which of the following is $\frac{d}{dx}\sec^{-1}(x^2)$?

(A) $\frac{2}{x\sqrt{x^4-1}}$ (B) $\frac{2}{x\sqrt{x^2-1}}$ (C) $\frac{2}{x\sqrt{1-x^4}}$

(D) $\frac{2}{x\sqrt{1-x^2}}$ (E) $\frac{2x}{\sqrt{1-x^4}}$

40. Multiple Choice Which of the following is the slope of the tangent line to $y = \tan^{-1}(2x)$ at $x = 1$?

(A) $-2/5$ (B) $1/5$ (C) $2/5$ (D) $5/2$ (E) 5

Explorations

In Exercises 41–46, find **(a)** the right end behavior model, **(b)** the left end behavior model, and **(c)** any horizontal tangents for the function if they exist.

41. $y = \tan^{-1} x$

42. $y = \cot^{-1} x$

43. $y = \sec^{-1} x$

44. $y = \csc^{-1} x$

45. $y = \sin^{-1} x$

46. $y = \cos^{-1} x$

Extending the Ideas

47. *Identities* Confirm the following identities for $x > 0$.

(a) $\cos^{-1} x + \sin^{-1} x = \pi/2$

(b) $\tan^{-1} x + \cot^{-1} x = \pi/2$

(c) $\sec^{-1} x + \csc^{-1} x = \pi/2$

48. *Proof Without Words* The figure gives a proof without words that $\tan^{-1} 1 + \tan^{-1} 2 + \tan^{-1} 3 = \pi$. Explain what is going on.

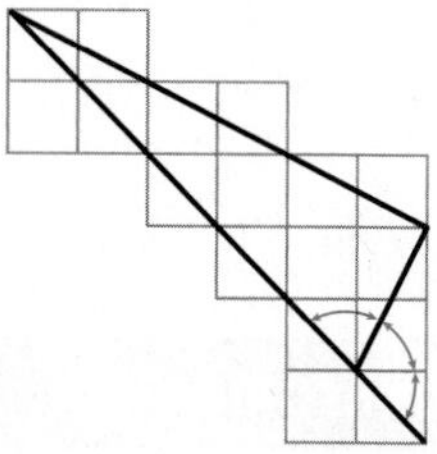

49. *(Continuation of Exercise 48)* Here is a way to construct $\tan^{-1} 1$, $\tan^{-1} 2$, and $\tan^{-1} 3$ by folding a square of paper. Try it and explain what is going on.

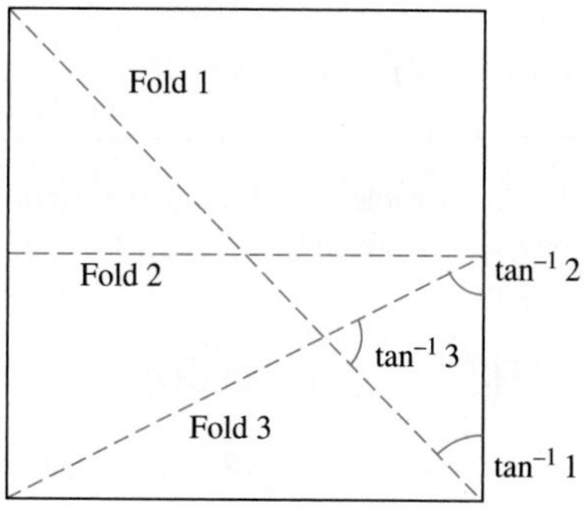

4.4 Derivatives of Exponential and Logarithmic Functions

What you will learn about . . .

- Derivative of e^x
- Derivative of a^x
- Derivative of ln x
- Derivative of $\log_a x$
- Power Rule for Arbitrary Real Powers

and why . . .

Exponential functions are involved in the modeling of growth rates in the real world.

Derivative of e^x

At the end of the brief review of exponential functions in Section 1.3, we mentioned that the function $y = e^x$ was a particularly important function for modeling exponential growth. The number e was defined in that section to be the limit of $(1 + 1/x)^x$ as $x \to \infty$. This intriguing number shows up in other interesting limits as well, but the one with the most interesting implications for the *calculus* of exponential functions is this one:

$$\lim_{h \to 0} \frac{e^h - 1}{h} = 1.$$

(The graph and the table in Figure 4.16 provide strong support for this limit being 1. A formal algebraic proof that begins with our limit definition of e would require some rather subtle limit arguments, so we will not include one here.)

The fact that the limit is 1 creates a remarkable relationship between the function e^x and its derivative, as we will now see.

$$\begin{aligned}\frac{d}{dx}(e^x) &= \lim_{h \to 0} \frac{e^{x+h} - e^x}{h} \\ &= \lim_{h \to 0} \frac{e^x \cdot e^h - e^x}{h} \\ &= \lim_{h \to 0} \left(e^x \cdot \frac{e^h - 1}{h}\right) \\ &= e^x \cdot \lim_{h \to 0} \left(\frac{e^h - 1}{h}\right) \\ &= e^x \cdot 1 \\ &= e^x\end{aligned}$$

In other words, the derivative of this particular function is itself!

$$\frac{d}{dx}(e^x) = e^x$$

If u is a differentiable function of x, then we have

$$\frac{d}{dx}e^u = e^u \frac{du}{dx}.$$

We will make extensive use of this formula when we study exponential growth and decay in Chapter 7.

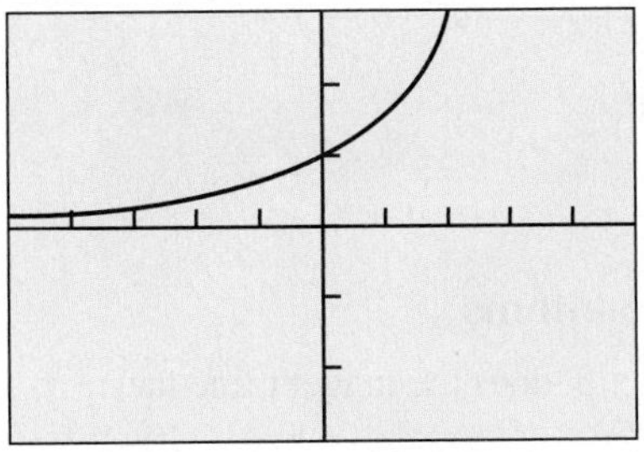

[−4.9, 4.9] by [−2.9, 2.9]

(a)

X	Y1	
−.03	.98515	
−.02	.99007	
−.01	.99502	
0	ERROR	
.01	1.005	
.02	1.0101	
.03	1.0152	
X=0		

(b)

Figure 4.16 (a) The graph and (b) the table support the conclusion that

$$\lim_{h \to 0} \frac{e^h - 1}{h} = 1.$$

EXAMPLE 1 Using the Formula

Find dy/dx if $y = e^{(x+x^2)}$.

SOLUTION

Let $u = x + x^2$ and $y = e^u$. Then

$$\frac{dy}{dx} = e^u \frac{du}{dx}, \quad \text{and} \quad \frac{du}{dx} = 1 + 2x.$$

Thus, $\dfrac{dy}{dx} = e^u \dfrac{du}{dx} = e^{(x+x^2)}(1 + 2x)$.

Now Try Exercise 9.

Is any other function its own derivative?

The zero function is also its own derivative, but this hardly seems worth mentioning. (Its value is always 0 and its slope is always 0.) In addition to e^x, however, we can also say that any constant *multiple* of e^x is its own derivative:

$$\frac{d}{dx}(c \cdot e^x) = c \cdot e^x.$$

The next obvious question is whether there are still *other* functions that are their own derivatives, and this time the answer is no. The only functions that satisfy the condition $dy/dx = y$ are functions of the form $y = ke^x$ (and notice that the zero function can be included in this category). We will prove this significant fact in Chapter 7.

Derivative of a^x

What about an exponential function with a base other than e? We will assume that the base is positive and different from 1, since negative numbers to arbitrary real powers are not always real numbers, and $y = 1^x$ is a constant function.

If $a > 0$ and $a \neq 1$, we can use the properties of logarithms to write a^x in terms of e^x. The formula for doing so is

$$a^x = e^{x \ln a}. \qquad e^{x \ln a} = e^{\ln(a^x)} = a^x$$

We can then find the derivative of a^x with the Chain Rule.

$$\frac{d}{dx}a^x = \frac{d}{dx}e^{x \ln a} = e^{x \ln a} \cdot \frac{d}{dx}(x \ln a) = e^{x \ln a} \cdot \ln a = a^x \ln a$$

Thus, if u is a differentiable function of x, we get the following rule.

For $a > 0$ and $a \neq 1$,

$$\frac{d}{dx}(a^u) = a^u \ln a \frac{du}{dx}.$$

EXAMPLE 2 Reviewing the Algebra of Logarithms

At what point on the graph of the function $y = 2^t - 3$ does the tangent line have slope 21?

SOLUTION

The slope is the derivative:

$$\frac{d}{dt}(2^t - 3) = 2^t \cdot \ln 2 - 0 = 2^t \ln 2.$$

We want the value of t for which $2^t \ln 2 = 21$. We could use the solver on the calculator, but we will use logarithms for the sake of review.

$$2^t \ln 2 = 21$$

$$2^t = \frac{21}{\ln 2}$$

$$\ln 2^t = \ln\left(\frac{21}{\ln 2}\right) \qquad \text{Logarithm of both sides}$$

$$t \cdot \ln 2 = \ln 21 - \ln(\ln 2) \qquad \text{Properties of logarithms}$$

$$t = \frac{\ln 21 - \ln(\ln 2)}{\ln 2}$$

$$t \approx 4.921$$

$$y = 2^t - 3 \approx 27.297 \qquad \text{Using the stored value of } t$$

The point is approximately $(4.9, 27.3)$.

Now Try Exercise 29.

EXPLORATION 1 Leaving Milk on the Counter

A glass of cold milk from the refrigerator is left on the counter on a warm summer day. Its temperature y (in degrees Fahrenheit) after sitting on the counter t minutes is

$$y = 72 - 30(0.98)^t.$$

Answer the following questions by interpreting y and dy/dt.

1. What is the temperature of the refrigerator? How can you tell?
2. What is the temperature of the room? How can you tell?
3. When is the milk warming up the fastest? How can you tell?
4. Determine algebraically when the temperature of the milk reaches 55°F.
5. At what rate is the milk warming when its temperature is 55°F? Answer with an appropriate unit of measure.

Derivative of ln x

Now that we know the derivative of e^x, it is relatively easy to find the derivative of its inverse function, ln x.

$$y = \ln x$$

$$e^y = x \qquad \text{Inverse function relationship}$$

$$\frac{d}{dx}(e^y) = \frac{d}{dx}(x) \qquad \text{Differentiate implicitly.}$$

$$e^y\frac{dy}{dx} = 1$$

$$\frac{dy}{dx} = \frac{1}{e^y} = \frac{1}{x}$$

This equation answers what was once a perplexing problem: Is there a function with derivative x^{-1}? All of the other power functions follow the Power Rule,

$$\frac{d}{dx}x^n = nx^{n-1}.$$

However, this formula is not much help if one is looking for a function with x^{-1} as its derivative! Now we know why: The function we should be looking for is not a power function at all; it is the natural logarithm function.

If u is a differentiable function of x and $u > 0$,

$$\frac{d}{dx}\ln u = \frac{1}{u}\frac{du}{dx}.$$

EXAMPLE 3 A Tangent Through the Origin

A line with slope m passes through the origin and is tangent to the graph of $y = \ln x$. What is the value of m?

SOLUTION

This problem is a little harder than it looks, since we do not know the point of tangency. However, we do know two important facts about that point:

1. it has coordinates $(a, \ln a)$ for some positive a, and
2. the tangent line there has slope $m = 1/a$ (Figure 4.17).

Since the tangent line passes through the origin, its slope is

$$m = \frac{\ln a - 0}{a - 0} = \frac{\ln a}{a}.$$

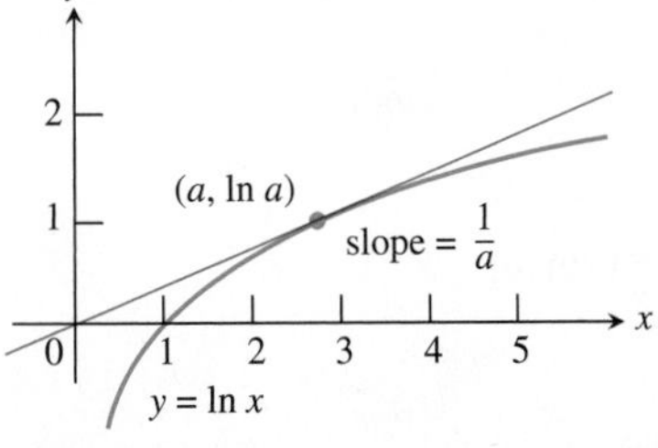

Figure 4.17 The tangent line intersects the curve at some point $(a, \ln a)$, where the slope of the curve is $1/a$. (Example 3)

continued

Setting these two formulas for m equal to each other, we have

$$\frac{\ln a}{a} = \frac{1}{a}$$
$$\ln a = 1$$
$$e^{\ln a} = e^1$$
$$a = e$$
$$m = \frac{1}{e}.$$

Now Try Exercise 31.

Derivative of $\log_a x$

To find the derivative of $\log_a x$ for an arbitrary base $(a > 0, a \neq 1)$, we use the change-of-base formula for logarithms to express $\log_a x$ in terms of natural logarithms, as follows:

$$\log_a x = \frac{\ln x}{\ln a}.$$

The rest is easy:

$$\frac{d}{dx}\log_a x = \frac{d}{dx}\left(\frac{\ln x}{\ln a}\right)$$
$$= \frac{1}{\ln a} \cdot \frac{d}{dx}\ln x \quad \text{Since } \ln a \text{ is a constant}$$
$$= \frac{1}{\ln a} \cdot \frac{1}{x}$$
$$= \frac{1}{x \ln a}.$$

So, if u is a differentiable function of x and $u > 0$, the formula is as follows.

For $a > 0$ and $a \neq 1$,

$$\frac{d}{dx}\log_a u = \frac{1}{u \ln a}\frac{du}{dx}.$$

EXAMPLE 4 Going the Long Way with the Chain Rule

Find dy/dx if $y = \log_a a^{\sin x}$.

SOLUTION

Carefully working from the outside in, we apply the Chain Rule to get:

$$\frac{d}{dx}(\log_a a^{\sin x}) = \frac{1}{a^{\sin x} \ln a} \cdot \frac{d}{dx}(a^{\sin x}) \quad \log_a u,\ u = a^{\sin x}$$
$$= \frac{1}{a^{\sin x} \ln a} \cdot a^{\sin x} \ln a \cdot \frac{d}{dx}(\sin x) \quad a^u,\ u = \sin x$$
$$= \frac{a^{\sin x} \ln a}{a^{\sin x} \ln a} \cdot \cos x$$
$$= \cos x.$$

Now Try Exercise 23.

We could have saved ourselves a lot of work in Example 4 if we had noticed at the beginning that $\log_a a^{\sin x}$, being the composite of inverse functions, is equal to $\sin x$. It is always a good idea to simplify functions *before* differentiating, wherever possible. On the other hand, it is comforting to know that all these rules do work if applied correctly.

Power Rule for Arbitrary Real Powers

We are now ready to prove the Power Rule in its final form. As long as $x > 0$, we can write any real power of x as a power of e, specifically

$$x^n = e^{n \ln x}.$$

This enables us to differentiate x^n for any real power n, as follows:

$$\begin{aligned}
\frac{d}{dx}(x^n) &= \frac{d}{dx}(e^{n \ln x}) \\
&= e^{n \ln x} \cdot \frac{d}{dx}(n \ln x) \qquad e^u,\ u = n \ln x \\
&= e^{n \ln x} \cdot \frac{n}{x} \\
&= x^n \cdot \frac{n}{x} \\
&= nx^{n-1}.
\end{aligned}$$

The Chain Rule extends this result to the Power Rule's final form.

RULE 10 Power Rule for Arbitrary Real Powers

If u is a positive differentiable function of x and n is any real number, then u^n is a differentiable function of x, and

$$\frac{d}{dx}u^n = nu^{n-1}\frac{du}{dx}.$$

EXAMPLE 5 Using the Power Rule in All Its Power

(a) If $y = x^{\sqrt{2}}$, then

$$\frac{dy}{dx} = \sqrt{2}x^{(\sqrt{2}-1)}.$$

(b) If $y = (2 + \sin 3x)^\pi$, then

$$\begin{aligned}
\frac{d}{dx}(2 + \sin 3x)^\pi &= \pi(2 + \sin 3x)^{\pi-1}(\cos 3x) \cdot 3 \\
&= 3\pi(2 + \sin 3x)^{\pi-1}(\cos 3x).
\end{aligned}$$

Now Try Exercise 35.

EXAMPLE 6 Finding Domain

If $f(x) = \ln(x - 3)$, find $f'(x)$. State the domain of f'.

SOLUTION

The domain of f is $(3, \infty)$ and

$$f'(x) = \frac{1}{x - 3}.$$

continued

The domain of f' appears to be all $x \neq 3$. However, since f is not defined for $x < 3$, neither is f'. Thus,

$$f'(x) = \frac{1}{x-3}, \quad x > 3.$$

That is, the domain of f' is $(3, \infty)$. **Now Try Exercise 37.**

Sometimes the properties of logarithms can be used to simplify the differentiation process, even if we must introduce the logarithms ourselves as a step in the process. Example 7 shows a clever way to differentiate $y = x^x$ for $x > 0$.

EXAMPLE 7 Logarithmic Differentiation

Find dy/dx for $y = x^x$, $x > 0$.

SOLUTION

$$y = x^x$$

$$\ln y = \ln x^x \qquad \text{Logs of both sides}$$

$$\ln y = x \ln x \qquad \text{Property of logs}$$

$$\frac{d}{dx}(\ln y) = \frac{d}{dx}(x \ln x) \qquad \text{Differentiate implicitly.}$$

$$\frac{1}{y}\frac{dy}{dx} = 1 \cdot \ln x + x \cdot \frac{1}{x}$$

$$\frac{dy}{dx} = y(\ln x + 1)$$

$$\frac{dy}{dx} = x^x(\ln x + 1)$$

Now Try Exercise 43.

EXAMPLE 8 How Fast Does a Flu Spread?

The spread of a flu in a certain school is modeled by the equation

$$P(t) = \frac{100}{1 + e^{3-t}},$$

where $P(t)$ is the total number of students infected t days after the flu was first noticed. Many of them may already be well again at time t.

(a) Estimate the initial number of students infected with the flu.

(b) How fast is the flu spreading after 3 days?

(c) When will the flu spread at its maximum rate? What is this rate?

SOLUTION

The graph of P as a function of t is shown in Figure 4.18.

(a) $P(0) = 100/(1 + e^3) = 5$ students (to the nearest whole number).

continued

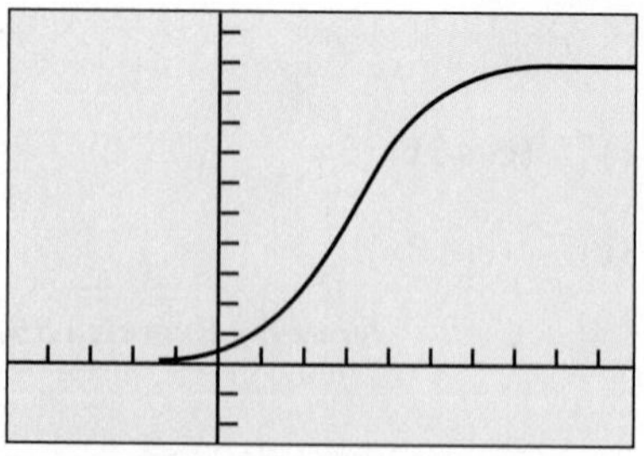

[–5, 10] by [–25, 120]

Figure 4.18 The graph of

$$P(t) = \frac{100}{1 + e^{3-t}},$$

modeling the spread of a flu. (Example 8)

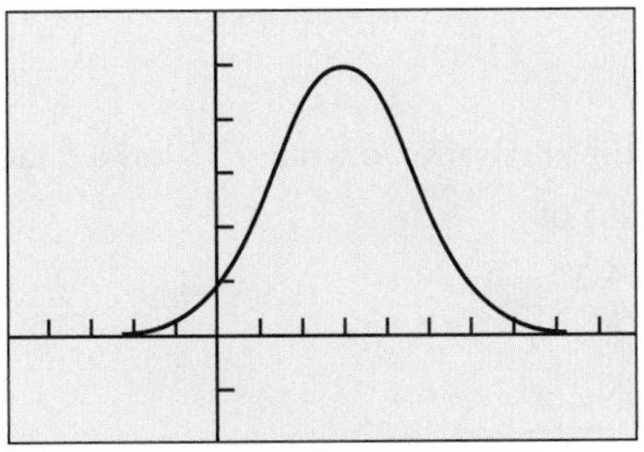

[–5, 10] by [–10, 30]

Figure 4.19 The graph of dP/dt, the rate of spread of the flu in Example 8. The graph of P is shown in Figure 4.18.

(b) To find the rate at which the flu spreads, we find dP/dt. To find dP/dt, we need to invoke the Chain Rule twice:

$$\begin{aligned}\frac{dP}{dt} &= \frac{d}{dt}(100(1 + e^{3-t})^{-1}) = 100\cdot(-1)(1 + e^{3-t})^{-2}\cdot\frac{d}{dt}(1 + e^{3-t})\\ &= -100(1 + e^{3-t})^{-2}\cdot(0 + e^{3-t}\cdot\frac{d}{dt}(3 - t))\\ &= -100(1 + e^{3-t})^{-2}(e^{3-t}\cdot(-1))\\ &= \frac{100e^{3-t}}{(1 + e^{3-t})^2}.\end{aligned}$$

At $t = 3$, then, $dP/dt = 100/4 = 25$. The flu is spreading to 25 students per day.

(c) We could estimate when the flu is spreading the fastest by seeing where the graph of $y = P(t)$ has the steepest upward slope, but we can answer both the "when" and the "what" parts of this question most easily by finding the maximum point on the graph of the derivative (Figure 4.19).

We see by tracing on the curve that the maximum rate occurs at about 3 days, when (as we have just calculated) the flu is spreading at a rate of 25 students per day.

Now Try Exercise 51.

Quick Review 4.4 *(For help, go to Sections 1.3 and 1.5.)*

Exercise numbers with a gray background indicate problems that the authors have designed to be solved *without a calculator.*

1. Write $\log_5 8$ in terms of natural logarithms.

2. Write 7^x as a power of e.

In Exercises 3–7, simplify the expression using properties of exponents and logarithms.

3. $\ln(e^{\tan x})$

4. $\ln(x^2 - 4) - \ln(x - 2)$

5. $\log_2(8^{x-5})$

6. $(\log_4 x^{15})/(\log_4 x^{12})$

7. $3\ln x - \ln 3x + \ln(12x^2)$

In Exercises 8–10, solve the equation algebraically using logarithms. Give an *exact* answer, such as $(\ln 2)/3$, and also an approximate answer to the nearest hundredth.

8. $3^x = 19$

9. $5^t \ln 5 = 18$

10. $3^{x+1} = 2^x$

Section 4.4 Exercises

In Exercises 1–28, find dy/dx.

1. $y = 2e^x$

2. $y = e^{2x}$

3. $y = e^{-x}$

4. $y = e^{-5x}$

5. $y = e^{2x/3}$

6. $y = e^{-x/4}$

7. $y = xe^2 - e^x$

8. $y = x^2e^x - xe^x$

9. $y = e^{\sqrt{x}}$

10. $y = e^{(x^2)}$

11. $y = 8^x$

12. $y = 9^{-x}$

13. $y = 3^{\csc x}$

14. $y = 3^{\cot x}$

15. $y = \ln(x^2)$

16. $y = (\ln x)^2$

17. $y = \ln(1/x)$

18. $y = \ln(10/x)$

19. $y = \ln(\ln x)$

20. $y = x\ln x - x$

21. $y = \log_4 x^2$

22. $y = \log_5 \sqrt{x}$

23. $y = \log_2(1/x)$

24. $y = 1/\log_2 x$

25. $y = \ln 2\cdot\log_2 x$

26. $y = \log_3(1 + x\ln 3)$

27. $y = \log_{10} e^x$

28. $y = \ln 10^x$

29. At what point on the graph of $y = 3^x + 1$ is the tangent line parallel to the line $y = 5x - 1$?

30. At what point on the graph of $y = 2e^x - 1$ is the tangent line perpendicular to the line $y = -3x + 2$?

31. A line with slope m passes through the origin and is tangent to $y = \ln(2x)$. What is the value of m?

32. A line with slope m passes through the origin and is tangent to $y = \ln(x/3)$. What is the value of m?

In Exercises 33–36, find dy/dx.

33. $y = x^{\pi}$

34. $y = x^{1+\sqrt{2}}$

35. $y = x^{-\sqrt{2}}$

36. $y = x^{1-e}$

In Exercises 37–42, find $f'(x)$ and state the domain of f'.

37. $f(x) = \ln(x + 2)$

38. $f(x) = \ln(2x + 2)$

39. $f(x) = \ln(2 - \cos x)$

40. $f(x) = \ln(x^2 + 1)$

41. $f(x) = \log_2(3x + 1)$

42. $f(x) = \log_{10}\sqrt{x + 1}$

Group Activity In Exercises 43–48, use the technique of logarithmic differentiation to find dy/dx.

43. $y = (\sin x)^x, \quad 0 < x < \pi/2$

44. $y = x^{\tan x}, \quad x > 0$

45. $y = \sqrt[5]{\dfrac{(x - 3)^4(x^2 + 1)}{(2x + 5)^3}}$

46. $y = \dfrac{x\sqrt{x^2 + 1}}{(x + 1)^{2/3}}$

47. $y = x^{\ln x}$ **48.** $y = x^{(1/\ln x)}$

49. Find an equation for a line that is tangent to the graph of $y = e^x$ and goes through the origin.

50. Find an equation for a line that is normal to the graph of $y = xe^x$ and goes through the origin.

51. *Spread of a Rumor* The spread of a rumor in a certain school is modeled by the equation

$$P(t) = \frac{300}{1 + 2^{4-t}},$$

where $P(t)$ is the total number of students who have heard the rumor t days after the rumor first started to spread.

(a) Estimate the initial number of students who first heard the rumor.

(b) How fast is the rumor spreading after 4 days?

(c) When will the rumor spread at its maximum rate? What is that rate?

52. *Spread of Flu* The spread of flu in a certain school is modeled by the equation

$$P(t) = \frac{200}{1 + e^{5-t}},$$

where $P(t)$ is the total number of students infected t days after the flu first started to spread.

(a) Estimate the initial number of students infected with this flu.

(b) How fast is the flu spreading after 4 days?

(c) When will the flu spread at its maximum rate? What is that rate?

53. *Radioactive Decay* The amount A (in grams) of radioactive plutonium remaining in a 20-gram sample after t days is given by the formula

$$A = 20 \cdot (1/2)^{t/140}.$$

At what rate is the plutonium decaying when $t = 2$ days? Answer in appropriate units.

54. For any positive constant k, the derivative of $\ln(kx)$ is $1/x$. Prove this fact

(a) by using the Chain Rule.

(b) by using a property of logarithms and differentiating.

55. Let $f(x) = 2^x$.

(a) Find $f'(0)$.

(b) Use the definition of the derivative to write $f'(0)$ as a limit.

(c) Deduce the exact value of

$$\lim_{h \to 0} \frac{2^h - 1}{h}.$$

(d) What is the exact value of

$$\lim_{h \to 0} \frac{7^h - 1}{h}?$$

56. Writing to Learn The graph of $y = \ln x$ looks as though it might be approaching a horizontal asymptote. Write an argument based on the graph of $y = e^x$ to explain why it does not.

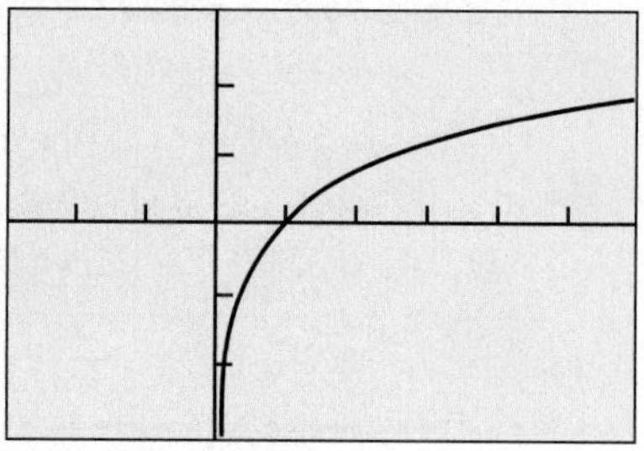

[–3, 6] by [–3, 3]

Standardized Test Questions

57. True or False The derivative of $y = 2^x$ is 2^x. Justify your answer.

58. True or False The derivative of $y = e^{2x}$ is $2(\ln 2)e^{2x}$. Justify your answer.

59. Multiple Choice If a flu is spreading at the rate of

$$P(t) = \frac{150}{1 + e^{4-t}},$$

which of the following is the initial number of persons infected?

(A) 1 **(B)** 3 **(C)** 7 **(D)** 8 **(E)** 75

60. Multiple Choice Which of the following is the domain of $f'(x)$ if $f(x) = \log_2(x + 3)$?

(A) $x < -3$ **(B)** $x \le 3$ **(C)** $x \ne -3$

(D) $x > -3$ **(E)** $x \ge -3$

61. Multiple Choice Which of the following gives dy/dx if $y = \log_{10}(2x - 3)$?

(A) $\dfrac{2}{(2x - 3)\ln 10}$ **(B)** $\dfrac{2}{2x - 3}$ **(C)** $\dfrac{1}{(2x - 3)\ln 10}$

(D) $\dfrac{1}{2x - 3}$ **(E)** $\dfrac{1}{2x}$

62. Multiple Choice Which of the following gives the slope of the tangent line to the graph of $y = 2^{1-x}$ at $x = 2$?

(A) $-\dfrac{1}{2}$ **(B)** $\dfrac{1}{2}$ **(C)** -2 **(D)** 2 **(E)** $-\dfrac{\ln 2}{2}$

Exploration

63. Let $y_1 = a^x$, $y_2 = \text{NDER}(y_1, x)$ $y_3 = y_2/y_1$, and $y_4 = e^{y_3}$.

(a) Describe the graph of y_4 for $a = 2, 3, 4, 5$. Generalize your description to an arbitrary $a > 1$.

(b) Describe the graph of y_3 for $a = 2, 3, 4, 5$. Compare a table of values for y_3 for $a = 2, 3, 4, 5$ with $\ln a$. Generalize your description to an arbitrary $a > 1$.

(c) Explain how parts (a) and (b) support the statement

$$\frac{d}{dx}a^x = a^x \quad \text{if and only if} \quad a = e.$$

(d) Show algebraically that $y_1 = y_2$ if and only if $a = e$.

Extending the Ideas

64. ***Orthogonal Families of Curves*** Prove that all curves in the family

$$y = -\frac{1}{2}x^2 + k$$

(k any constant) are perpendicular to all curves in the family $y = \ln x + c$ (c any constant) at their points of intersection. (See accompanying figure.)

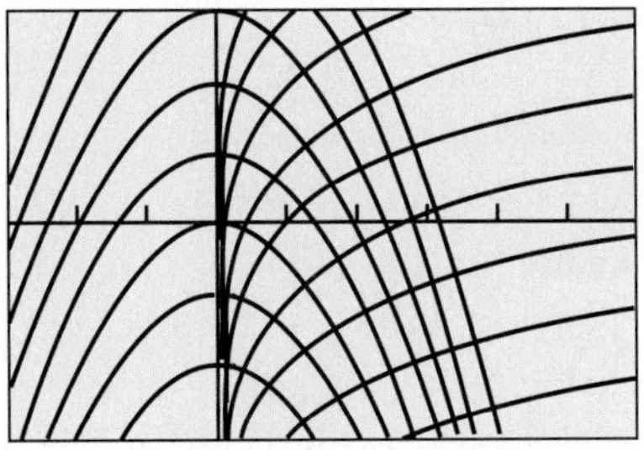

[–3, 6] by [–3, 3]

65. ***Which is Bigger, π^e or e^π?*** Calculators have taken some of the mystery out of this once-challenging question. (Go ahead and check; you will see that it is a surprisingly close call.) You can answer the question without a calculator, though, by using the result from Example 3 of this section.

Recall from that example that the line through the origin tangent to the graph of $y = \ln x$ has slope $1/e$.

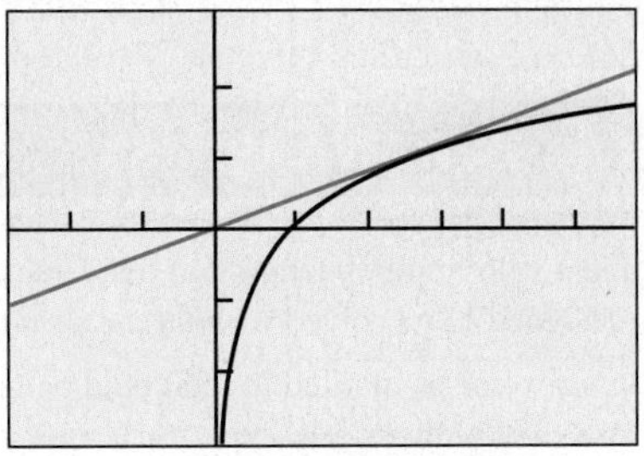

[–3, 6] by [–3, 3]

(a) Find an equation for this tangent line.

(b) Give an argument based on the graphs of $y = \ln x$ and the tangent line to explain why $\ln x < x/e$ for all positive $x \neq e$.

(c) Show that $\ln(x^e) < x$ for all positive $x \neq e$.

(d) Conclude that $x^e < e^x$ for all positive $x \neq e$.

(e) So which is bigger, π^e or e^π?

Quick Quiz for AP* Preparation: Sections 4.3–4.4

1. Multiple Choice If $f(x) = \ln(x + 4 + e^{-3x})$, then $f'(0)$ is

(A) $-\frac{2}{5}$ **(B)** $\frac{1}{5}$ **(C)** $\frac{1}{4}$ **(D)** $\frac{2}{5}$ **(E)** nonexistent

2. Multiple Choice Let f be the function defined by $f(x) = x^3 + x$. If $g(x) = f^{-1}(x)$ and $g(2) = 1$, what is the value of $g'(2)$?

(A) $\frac{1}{13}$ **(B)** $\frac{1}{4}$ **(C)** $\frac{7}{4}$ **(D)** 4 **(E)** 13

3. Multiple Choice Which of the following gives $\frac{dy}{dx}$ if $y = \sin^{-1}(2x)$?

(A) $-\frac{2}{\sqrt{1-4x^2}}$ **(B)** $-\frac{1}{\sqrt{1-4x^2}}$ **(C)** $\frac{2}{\sqrt{1-4x^2}}$

(D) $\frac{1}{\sqrt{1-4x^2}}$ **(E)** $\frac{2x}{1+4x^2}$

4. Free Response A particle moves along the x-axis with position at time t given by $x(t) = e^t \sin t$ for $0 \le t \le 2\pi$.

(a) Find each time t, $0 \le t \le 2\pi$, for which the particle is at rest.

(b) Find the value of the constant A for which $Ax''(t) + x'(t) = x(t)$ for $0 \le t \le 2\pi$.

Chapter 4 Key Terms

Chain Rule (p. 154)
implicit differentiation (p. 162)
inverse function–inverse cofunction identities (p. 173)
logarithmic differentiation (p. 182)
normal to the surface (p. 164)
orthogonal curves (p. 159)
orthogonal families (p. 185)
Power Chain Rule (p. 156)
Power Rule for Arbitrary Real Powers (p. 181)
Power Rule for Rational Powers of x (p. 166)

Chapter 4 Review Exercises

Exercise numbers with a gray background indicate problems that the authors have designed to be solved *without a calculator.*

The collection of exercises marked in red could be used as a chapter test.

In Exercises 1–30, find the derivative of the function.

1. $y = e^{3x-7}$ **2.** $y = \tan(e^x)$

3. $y = \sin^3 x$ **4.** $y = \ln(\csc x)$

5. $s = \cos(1 - 2t)$ **6.** $s = \cot \dfrac{2}{t}$

7. $y = \sqrt{1 + \cos x}$ **8.** $y = x\sqrt{2x + 1}$

9. $r = \sec(1 + 3\theta)$ **10.** $r = \tan^2(3 - \theta^2)$

11. $y = x^2 \csc 5x$ **12.** $y = \ln \sqrt{x}$

13. $y = \ln(1 + e^x)$ **14.** $y = xe^{-x}$

15. $y = e^{(1+\ln x)}$ **16.** $y = \ln(\sin x)$

17. $r = \ln(\cos^{-1} x)$ **18.** $r = \log_2(\theta^2)$

19. $s = \log_5(t - 7)$ **20.** $s = 8^{-t}$

21. $y = x^{\ln x}$ **22.** $y = \dfrac{(2x)2^x}{\sqrt{x^2 + 1}}$

23. $y = e^{\tan^{-1} x}$ **24.** $y = \sin^{-1}\sqrt{1 - u^2}$

25. $y = t \sec^{-1} t - \dfrac{1}{2}\ln t$ **26.** $y = (1 + t^2)\cot^{-1} 2t$

27. $y = z\cos^{-1} z - \sqrt{1 - z^2}$ **28.** $y = 2\sqrt{x - 1}\csc^{-1}\sqrt{x}$

29. $y = \csc^{-1}(\sec x), 0 \le x < \dfrac{\pi}{2}$

30. $r = \left(\dfrac{1 + \sin\theta}{1 - \cos\theta}\right)^2$

In Exercises 31–34, find all values of x for which the function is differentiable.

31. $y = \ln x^2$ **32.** $y = \sin(e^{2x})$

33. $y = \sqrt{\dfrac{1 - x}{1 + x^2}}$ **34.** $y = \dfrac{1}{1 - e^x}$

In Exercises 35–38, find dy/dx.

35. $xy + 2x + 3y = 1$ **36.** $5x^{4/5} + 10y^{6/5} = 15$

37. $\sqrt{xy} = 1$ **38.** $y^2 = \dfrac{x}{x + 1}$

In Exercises 39–42, find d^2y/dx^2 by implicit differentiation.

39. $x^3 + y^3 = 1$ **40.** $y^2 = 1 - \dfrac{2}{x}$

41. $y^3 + y = 2\cos x$ **42.** $x^{1/3} + y^{1/3} = 4$

In Exercises 43 and 44, find $\dfrac{d^{40}y}{dx^{40}}$.

43. $y = e^{\sqrt[8]{2x}}$ **44.** $y = \sin(\sqrt[8]{2x})$

In Exercises 45–48, find an equation for the **(a)** tangent and **(b)** normal to the curve at the indicated point.

45. $y = \sqrt{x^2 - 2x}, \quad x = 3$ **46.** $y = \tan 2x, \quad x = \pi/3$

47. $x^2 + 2y^2 = 9, \quad (1, 2)$ **48.** $x + \sqrt{xy} = 6, \quad (4, 1)$

In Exercises 49–52, find an equation for the line tangent to the curve at the point defined by the given value of t.

49. $x = 2\sin t, \quad y = 2\cos t, \quad t = 3\pi/4$

50. $x = 3\cos t, \quad y = 4\sin t, \quad t = 3\pi/4$

51. $x = 3\sec t, \quad y = 5\tan t, \quad t = \pi/6$

52. $x = \cos t, \quad y = t + \sin t, \quad t = -\pi/4$

53. Writing to Learn

Let $f(x) = \begin{cases} \sin ax + b\cos x, & x < 0 \\ 5x + 3, & x \ge 0 \end{cases}$.

(a) If f is continuous at $x = 0$, find the value of b. Justify your answer.

(b) If f is differentiable at $x = 0$, find the value of a. Justify your answer.

(c) Is f differentiable at $x = 0$ if $a = 5$ and $b = 4$? Justify your answer.

54. Writing to Learn For what values of the constant m is

$$f(x) = \begin{cases} \sin 2x, & x \le 0 \\ mx, & x > 0 \end{cases}$$

(a) continuous at $x = 0$? Explain.

(b) differentiable at $x = 0$? Explain.

In Exercises 55–58, determine where the function is **(a)** differentiable, **(b)** continuous but not differentiable, and **(c)** neither continuous nor differentiable.

55. $f(x) = \sqrt[5]{(x - 1)^3}$ **56.** $g(x) = \sin(x^2 + 1)$

57. $f(x) = \begin{cases} \sqrt{x^2 + 3}, & -1 \le x < 1 \\ x + 1, & 1 \le x < 3 \end{cases}$

58. $g(x) = \begin{cases} \sin 2x, & -3 \le x < 0 \\ x^2 + 2x, & 0 \le x \le 3 \end{cases}$

59. Simplify, Simplify Find the derivative of each function easily by simplifying the expression before differentiating.

(a) $y = (\sqrt{3 - \sin x})^2$ **(b)** $y = \ln(3e^{7x^2 - 13x + 5})$

(c) $s = \tan(\tan^{-1}(t^2 - 3t))$ **(d)** $s = \sqrt[3]{t^6} - 5(\sin(\sin^{-1} t))^6$

60. Simplify, Simplify Find the derivative of each function relatively easily by simplifying the expression before differentiating.

(a) $y = \ln\left(\frac{2x+7}{3x+2}\right)$ (b) $y = \frac{(x^2-1)^2}{(x^2-2x+1)(x+1))}$

(c) $s = \sin^2(\cos^{-1} t)$ (d) $s = \left(\frac{2\sqrt{t}}{\sqrt[3]{t}}\right)^5$

61. Hitting the Slopes A differentiable function f has the property that $f'(x) > 0$ for all x. The line $y = 3x - 2$ is tangent to the graph of f at the point where $x = 2$.

(a) Find the equation of the line normal to the graph of f at the point where $x = 2$.

(b) Find the equation of the line tangent to the graph of f^{-1} at the point where $y = 2$.

(c) Find the equation of the line tangent to the graph of $y = \frac{f(x)}{x}$ at the point where $x = 2$.

62. Hitting the Slopes Again A differentiable function g has the property that $g'(x) < 0$ for all x. The line $y = 5 - 2x$ is tangent to the graph of g at the point where $x = 1$.

(a) Find the equation of the line normal to the graph of g at the point where $x = 1$.

(b) Find the equation of the line tangent to the graph of g^{-1} at the point where $y = 1$.

(c) Find the equation of the line tangent to the graph of $y = g(x^2)$ at the point where $x = 1$.

63. Logarithmic Differentiation Use the technique of logarithmic differentiation to find $\frac{dy}{dx}$ when

$y = \frac{(x+2)^5(2x-3)^4}{(x+17)^2}$. (See Example 7 of Section 4.4.)

64. Logarithmic Differentiation Use the technique of logarithmic differentiation to find $\frac{dy}{dx}$ when $y = (x^2+2)^{x+5}$. (See Example 7 of Section 4.4.)

65. Differential Equations Equations that involve derivatives are called *differential equations.* We will have much more to say about them in Chapter 7, but meanwhile try to use what you have learned in Chapters 3 and 4 to find at least one nonzero function that satisfies each of these differential equations.

(a) $f'(x) = x$ (b) $f'(x) = f(x)$ (c) $f'(x) = -f(x)$

(d) $f''(x) = f(x)$ (e) $f''(x) = -f(x)$

66. *Working with Numerical Values* Suppose that a function f and its first derivative have the following values at $x = 0$ and $x = 1$.

x	$f(x)$	$f'(x)$
0	9	−2
1	−3	1/5

Find the first derivative of the following combinations at the given value of x.

(a) $\sqrt{x}f(x)$, $x = 1$ (b) $\sqrt{f(x)}$, $x = 0$

(c) $f(\sqrt{x})$, $x = 1$ (d) $f(1 - 5\tan x)$, $x = 0$

(e) $\frac{f(x)}{2 + \cos x}$, $x = 0$ (f) $10\sin\left(\frac{\pi x}{2}\right)f^2(x)$, $x = 1$

67. *Working with Numerical Values* Suppose that functions f and g and their first derivatives have the following values at $x = -1$ and $x = 0$.

x	$f(x)$	$g(x)$	$f'(x)$	$g'(x)$
−1	0	−1	2	1
0	−1	−3	−2	4

Find the first derivative of the following combinations at the given value of x.

(a) $\frac{f(2x)}{x-1}$, $x = 0$ (b) $f^2(x)g^3(x)$, $x = 0$

(c) $g(f(x))$, $x = -1$ (d) $f(g(x))$, $x = -1$

(e) $f(g(2x-1))$, $x = 0$ (f) $g(x + f(x))$, $x = 0$

68. Find the value of dw/ds at $s = 0$ if $w = \sin(\sqrt{r} - 2)$ and $r = 8\sin(s + \pi/6)$.

69. Find the value of dr/dt at $t = 0$ if $r = (\theta^2 + 7)^{1/3}$ and $\theta^2 t + \theta = 1$.

70. *Particle Motion* The position at time $t \geq 0$ of a particle moving along the s-axis is

$$s(t) = 10\cos(t + \pi/4).$$

(a) Give parametric equations that can be used to simulate the motion of the particle.

(b) What is the particle's initial position ($t = 0$)?

(c) What points reached by the particle are farthest to the left and right of the origin?

(d) When does the particle first reach the origin? What are its velocity, speed, and acceleration then?

71. Implicit Hyperbola The hyperbola shown in the graph is defined implicitly by the equation $4x^2 + 8xy + y^2 + 3 = 0$.

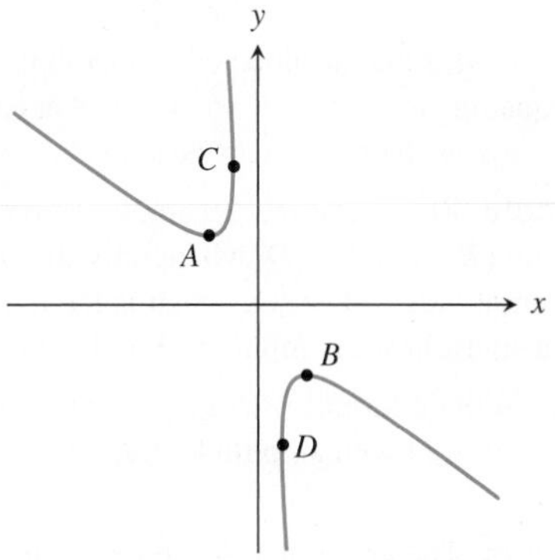

(a) Find the coordinates of points A and B, where the tangent lines are horizontal.

(b) Find the coordinates of points C and D, where the tangent lines are vertical.

72. Implicit Ellipse The ellipse shown in the graph is defined implicitly by the equation $2x^2 - 2xy + y^2 - 4 = 0$.

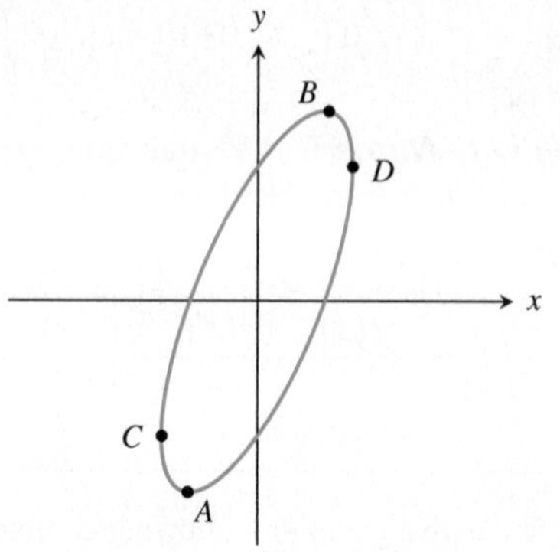

(a) Find the coordinates of points A and B, where the tangent lines are horizontal.

(b) Find the coordinates of points C and D, where the tangent lines are vertical.

73. Implicit Parabola The parabola shown in the graph is defined implicitly by the equation $x^2 - 2xy + y^2 - 4x = 8$.

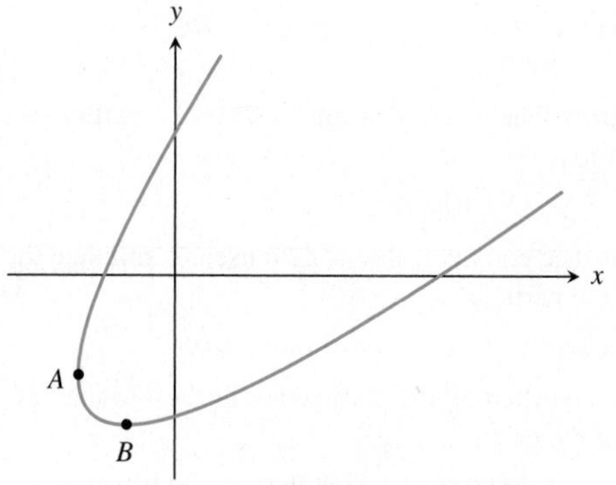

(a) Find the coordinates of point A, where the tangent line is vertical.

(b) Find the coordinates of point B, where the tangent line is horizontal.

74. Problem 73 Revisited Find the slope of the parabola defined implicitly by the equation $x^2 - 2xy + y^2 - 4x = 8$ at each of the points where it crosses the coordinate axes.

75. Slope of a Sinusoid Recall that the general equation of a sinusoid is $y = A \sin(Bx + C) + D$, where only the constants A and B affect the amplitude and period. What is the maximum possible slope for a sinusoid with amplitude 3 and period π?

76. Writing to Learn Write a formula that gives the maximum possible slope for a sinusoid with amplitude A and period p. Justify your answer.

77. Horizontal Tangents The graph of $y = \sin(x - \sin x)$ appears to have horizontal tangents at the x-axis. Does it?

78. *Spread of Measles* The spread of measles in a certain school is given by

$$P(t) = \frac{200}{1 + e^{5-t}},$$

where t is the number of days since the measles first appeared, and $P(t)$ is the total number of students who have caught the measles to date.

(a) Estimate the initial number of students infected with measles.

(b) About how many students in all will get the measles?

(c) When will the rate of spread of measles be greatest? What is this rate?

79. If $x^2 + 2xy + 2y^2 = 5$, find

(a) $\dfrac{dy}{dx}$ at the point $(1, 1)$;

(b) $\dfrac{d^2y}{dx^2}$ at the point $(1, 1)$.

80. If $x^2 - y^2 = 1$, find d^2y/dx^2 at the point $(2, \sqrt{3})$.

AP* Examination Preparation

81. A function f and its first and second derivatives are defined for all real numbers, and it is given that $f(0) = 2$, $f'(0) = 3$, and $f''(0) = -1$.

(a) Define a function g by $g(x) = e^{kx} + f(x)$, where k is a constant. Find $g'(0)$ and $g''(0)$ in terms of k. Show your work.

(b) Define a function h by $h(x) = \cos(bx)\, f(x)$, where b is a constant. Find $h'(x)$ and write an equation for the line tangent to the graph of h at $x = 0$.

82. Let $\dfrac{e^x + e^{-x}}{2}$.

(a) Find $\dfrac{dy}{dx}$.

(b) Find $\dfrac{d^2y}{dx^2}$.

(c) Find an equation of the line tangent to the curve at $x = 1$.

(d) Find an equation of the line normal to the curve at $x = 1$.

(e) Find any points where the tangent line is horizontal.

83. Let $f(x) = \ln(1 - x^2)$.

(a) State the domain of f.

(b) Find $f'(x)$.

(c) State the domain of f'.

(d) Prove that $f''(x) < 0$ for all x in the domain of f.

CHAPTER

5 Applications of Derivatives

An automobile's gas mileage is a function of many variables, including road surface, tire type, velocity, fuel octane rating, road angle, and the speed and direction of the wind. If we look only at velocity's effect on gas mileage, the mileage of a certain car can be approximated by

$$m(v) = 0.00015v^3 - 0.032v^2 + 1.8v + 1.7$$

(where v is velocity).

At what speed should you drive this car to obtain the best gas mileage? The ideas in Section 5.1 will help you find the answer.

CHAPTER 5 Overview

In the past, when virtually all graphing was done by hand—often laboriously—derivatives were the key tool used to sketch the graph of a function. Now we can graph a function quickly, and usually correctly, using a grapher. However, confirmation of much of what we see and conclude true from a grapher view must still come from calculus.

This chapter shows how to draw conclusions from derivatives about the extreme values of a function and about the general shape of a function's graph. We will also see how a tangent line captures the shape of a curve near the point of tangency, how to deduce rates of change we cannot measure from rates of change we already know, and how to find a function when we know only its first derivative and its value at a single point. The key to recovering functions from derivatives is the Mean Value Theorem, a theorem whose corollaries provide the gateway to *integral calculus,* which we begin in Chapter 6.

5.1 Extreme Values of Functions

What you will learn about . . .

- Absolute (Global) Extreme Values
- Local (Relative) Extreme Values
- Finding Extreme Values

and why . . .

Finding maximum and minimum values of functions, called optimization, is an important issue in real-world problems.

Absolute (Global) Extreme Values

One of the most useful things we can learn from a function's derivative is whether the function assumes any maximum or minimum values on a given interval and where these values are located if it does. Once we know how to find a function's extreme values, we will be able to answer such questions as "What is the most effective size for a dose of medicine?" and "What is the least expensive way to pipe oil from an offshore well to a refinery down the coast?" We will see how to answer questions like these in Section 5.4.

DEFINITION Absolute Extreme Values

Let f be a function with domain D. Then $f(c)$ is the

(a) absolute maximum value on D if and only if $f(x) \le f(c)$ for all x in D.
(b) absolute minimum value on D if and only if $f(x) \ge f(c)$ for all x in D.

Absolute (or **global**) maximum and minimum values are also called **absolute extrema** (plural of the Latin *extremum*). We often omit the term "absolute" or "global" and just say maximum and minimum.

Example 1 shows that extreme values can occur at interior points or endpoints of intervals.

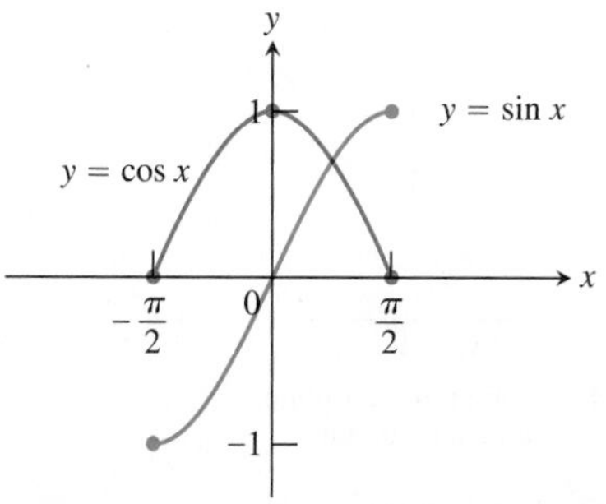

Figure 5.1 (Example 1)

EXAMPLE 1 Exploring Extreme Values

On $[-\pi/2, \pi/2]$, $f(x) = \cos x$ takes on a maximum value of 1 (once) and a minimum value of 0 (twice). The function $g(x) = \sin x$ takes on a maximum value of 1 and a minimum value of -1 (Figure 5.1). ***Now Try Exercise 1.***

Functions with the same defining rule can have different extrema, depending on the domain.

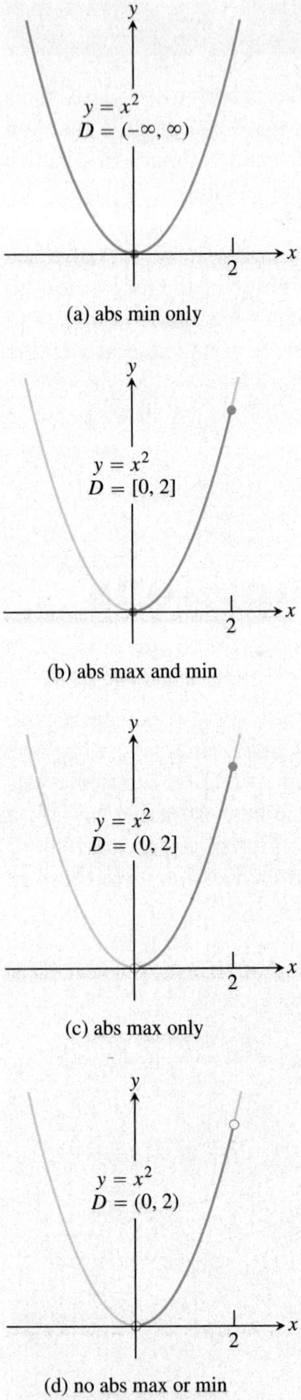

Figure 5.2 (Example 2)

EXAMPLE 2 Exploring Absolute Extrema

The absolute extrema of the following functions on their domains can be seen in Figure 5.2.

	Function Rule	Domain D	Absolute Extrema on D
(a)	$y = x^2$	$(-\infty, \infty)$	No absolute maximum Absolute minimum of 0 at $x = 0$
(b)	$y = x^2$	$[0, 2]$	Absolute maximum of 4 at $x = 2$ Absolute minimum of 0 at $x = 0$
(c)	$y = x^2$	$(0, 2]$	Absolute maximum of 4 at $x = 2$ No absolute minimum
(d)	$y = x^2$	$(0, 2)$	No absolute extrema

Now Try Exercise 3.

Example 2 shows that a function may fail to have a maximum or minimum value. This cannot happen with a continuous function on a finite closed interval.

THEOREM 1 The Extreme Value Theorem

If f is continuous on a closed interval $[a, b]$, then f has both a maximum value and a minimum value on the interval. (Figure 5.3)

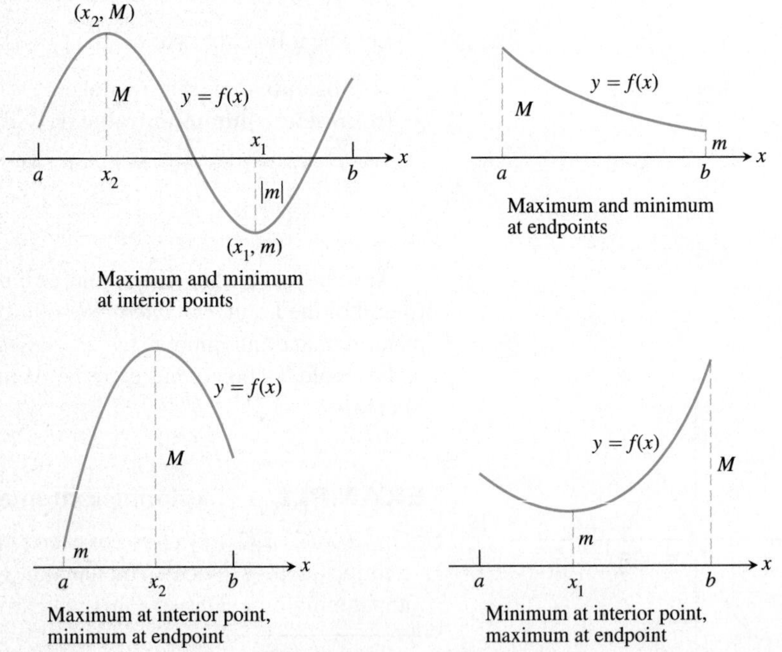

Figure 5.3 Some possibilities for a continuous function's maximum (M) and minimum (m) on a closed interval $[a, b]$.

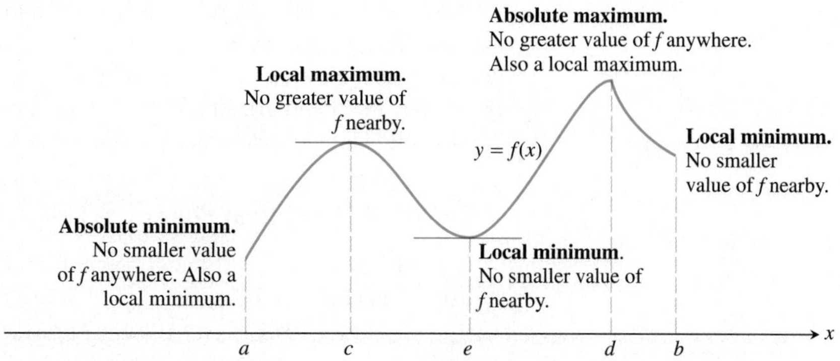

Figure 5.4 Classifying extreme values.

Local (Relative) Extreme Values

Figure 5.4 shows a graph with five points where a function has extreme values on its domain $[a, b]$. The function's absolute minimum occurs at a even though at e the function's value is smaller than at any other point *nearby*. The curve rises to the left and falls to the right around c, making $f(c)$ a maximum locally. The function attains its absolute maximum at d.

DEFINITION Local Extreme Values

Let c be an interior point of the domain of the function f. Then $f(c)$ is a

(a) **local maximum value** at c if and only if $f(x) \leq f(c)$ for all x in some open interval containing c.
(b) **local minimum value** at c if and only if $f(x) \geq f(c)$ for all x in some open interval containing c.

A function f has a local maximum or local minimum *at an endpoint* c if the appropriate inequality holds for all x in some half-open domain interval containing c.

Local extrema are also called **relative extrema.**

An **absolute extremum** is also a local extremum, because being an extreme value overall makes it an extreme value in its immediate neighborhood. Hence, *a list of local extrema will automatically include absolute extrema if there are any.*

Finding Extreme Values

The interior domain points where the function in Figure 5.4 has local extreme values are points where either f' is zero or f' does not exist. This is generally the case, as we see from the following theorem.

THEOREM 2 Local Extreme Values

If a function f has a local maximum value or a local minimum value at an interior point c of its domain, and if f' exists at c, then

$$f'(c) = 0.$$

Because of Theorem 2, we usually need to look at only a few points to find a function's extrema. These consist of the interior domain points where $f' = 0$ or f' does not exist (the domain points covered by the theorem) and the domain endpoints (the domain points not covered by the theorem). At all other domain points, $f' > 0$ or $f' < 0$.

The following definition helps us summarize these findings.

DEFINITION Critical Point

A point in the interior of the domain of a function f at which $f' = 0$ or f' does not exist is a **critical point** of f.

Thus, in summary, extreme values occur only at critical points and endpoints.

DEFINITION Stationary Point

A point in the interior of the domain of a function f at which $f' = 0$ is called a ***stationary point*** of f.

A stationary point can be a minimum, a maximum, or an inflection point. Note that critical points and stationary points of a function f are *not necessarily* the same. See Examples 3 and 5.

EXAMPLE 3 Finding Absolute Extrema

Find the absolute maximum and minimum values of $f(x) = x^{2/3}$ on the interval $[-2, 3]$.

SOLUTION

Solve Analytically We evaluate the function at the critical points and endpoints and take the largest and smallest of the resulting values.

The first derivative

$$f'(x) = \frac{2}{3}x^{-1/3} = \frac{2}{3\sqrt[3]{x}}$$

has no zeros but is undefined at $x = 0$. The values of f at this one critical point and at the endpoints are

Critical point value: $f(0) = 0$;

Endpoint values: $f(-2) = (-2)^{2/3} = \sqrt[3]{4}$;

$f(3) = (3)^{2/3} = \sqrt[3]{9}$.

We can see from this list that the function's absolute maximum value is $\sqrt[3]{9} \approx 2.08$, and occurs at the right endpoint $x = 3$. The absolute minimum value is 0, and occurs at the interior point $x = 0$.

Support Graphically The graph in Figure 5.5 suggests that f has an absolute maximum value of about 2 at $x = 3$ and an absolute minimum value of 0 at $x = 0$. The critical point $(0, 0)$ is **not** a stationary point. ***Now Try Exercise 11.***

$y = x^{2/3}$

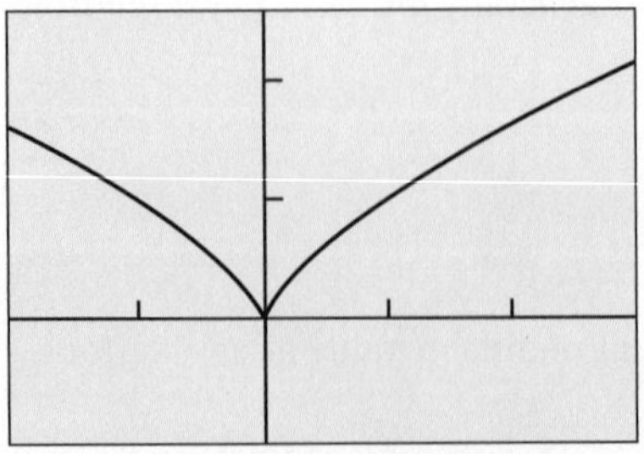

[–2, 3] by [–1, 2.5]

Figure 5.5 (Example 3)

In Example 4, we investigate the reciprocal of the function whose graph was drawn in Example 3 of Section 1.2 to illustrate "grapher failure."

EXAMPLE 4 Finding Extreme Values

Find the extreme values of $f(x) = \dfrac{1}{\sqrt{4 - x^2}}$.

continued

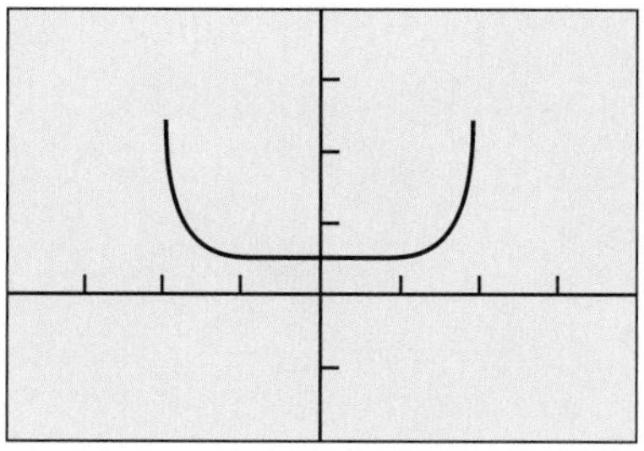

[–4, 4] by [–2, 4]

Figure 5.6 The graph of

$$f(x) = \frac{1}{\sqrt{4 - x^2}}.$$

(Example 4)

SOLUTION

Solve Graphically Figure 5.6 suggests that f has an absolute minimum of about 0.5 at $x = 0$. There also appear to be local maxima at $x = -2$ and $x = 2$. However, f is not defined at these points and there do not appear to be maxima anywhere else.

Confirm Analytically The function f is defined only for $4 - x^2 > 0$, so its domain is the open interval $(-2, 2)$. The domain has no endpoints, so all the extreme values must occur at critical points. We rewrite the formula for f to find f':

$$f(x) = \frac{1}{\sqrt{4 - x^2}} = (4 - x^2)^{-1/2}$$

Thus,

$$f'(x) = -\frac{1}{4}(4 - x^2)^{-3/2}(-2x) = \frac{x}{(4 - x^2)^{3/2}}.$$

The only critical point in the domain $(-2, 2)$ is $x = 0$. The value

$$f(0) = \frac{1}{\sqrt{4 - 0^2}} = \frac{1}{2}$$

is therefore the sole candidate for an extreme value.

To determine whether $1/2$ is an extreme value of f, we examine the formula

$$f(x) = \frac{1}{\sqrt{4 - x^2}}.$$

As x moves away from 0 on either side, the denominator gets smaller, the values of f increase, and the graph rises. We have a minimum value at $x = 0$, and the minimum is absolute.

The function has no maxima, either local or absolute. This does not violate Theorem 1 (The Extreme Value Theorem) because here f is defined on an *open* interval. To invoke Theorem 1's guarantee of extreme points, the interval must be closed. ***Now Try Exercise 25.***

While a function's extrema can occur only at critical points and endpoints, not every critical point or endpoint signals the presence of an extreme value. Figure 5.7 illustrates this for interior points. Exercise 55 describes a function that fails to assume an extreme value at an endpoint of its domain.

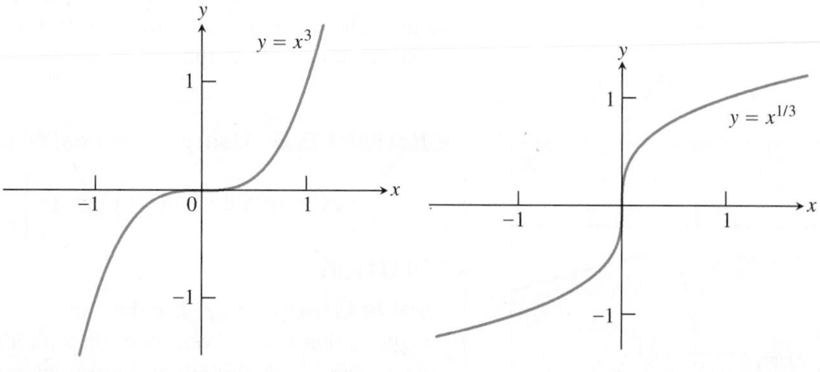

(a) (b)

Figure 5.7 Critical points without extreme values. (a) $y' = 3x^2$ is 0 at $x = 0$, but $y = x^3$ has no extremum there. (b) $y' = (1/3)x^{-2/3}$ is undefined at $x = 0$, but $y = x^{1/3}$ has no extremum there.

EXAMPLE 5 Finding Extreme Values

Find the extreme values of

$$f(x) = \begin{cases} 5 - 2x^2, & x \leq 1 \\ x + 2, & x > 1. \end{cases}$$

SOLUTION

Solve Analytically For $x \neq 1$, the derivative is

$$f'(x) = \begin{cases} \dfrac{d}{dx}(5 - 2x^2) = -4x, & x < 1 \\ \dfrac{d}{dx}(x + 2) = 1, & x > 1. \end{cases}$$

The only point where $f' = 0$ is $x = 0$. What happens at $x = 1$?

At $x = 1$, the right- and left-hand derivatives are, respectively,

$$\lim_{h \to 0^+} \frac{f(1 + h) - f(1)}{h} = \lim_{h \to 0^+} \frac{(1 + h) + 2 - 3}{h} = \lim_{h \to 0^+} \frac{h}{h} = 1.$$

$$\lim_{h \to 0^-} \frac{f(1 + h) - f(1)}{h} = \lim_{h \to 0^-} \frac{5 - 2(1 + h)^2 - 3}{h}$$

$$= \lim_{h \to 0^-} \frac{-2h(2 + h)}{h} = -4.$$

Since these one-sided derivatives differ, f has no derivative at $x = 1$, and 1 is a second critical point of f.

The domain $(-\infty, \infty)$ has no endpoints, so the only values of f that might be local extrema are those at the critical points:

$$f(0) = 5 \quad \text{and} \quad f(1) = 3$$

From the formula for f, we see that the values of f immediately to either side of $x = 0$ are less than 5, so 5 is a local maximum. Similarly, the values of f immediately to either side of $x = 1$ are greater than 3, so 3 is a local minimum.

Support Graphically The graph in Figure 5.8 suggests that $f'(0) = 0$ and that $f'(1)$ does not exist. There appears to be a local maximum value of 5 at $x = 0$ and a local minimum value of 3 at $x = 1$. The point $(0, 50)$ is the only stationary point. ***Now Try Exercise 41.***

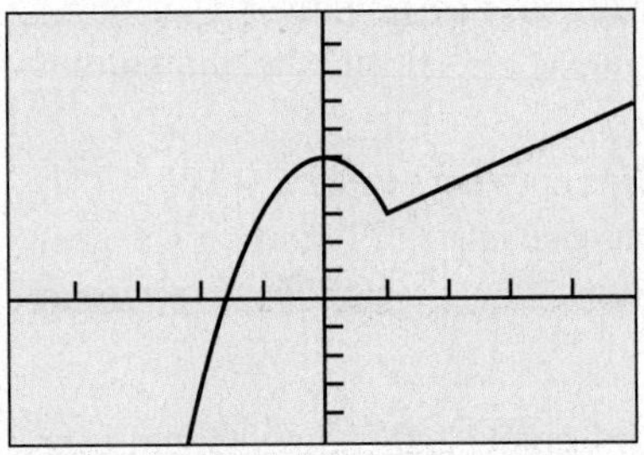

[–5, 5] by [–5, 10]

Figure 5.8 The function in Example 5.

Most graphing calculators have built-in methods to find the coordinates of points where extreme values occur. We must, of course, be sure that we use correct graphs to find these values. The calculus that you learn in this chapter should make you feel more confident about working with graphs.

EXAMPLE 6 Using Graphical Methods

Find the extreme values of $f(x) = \text{In}\left|\dfrac{x}{1 + x^2}\right|$.

SOLUTION

Solve Graphically The domain of f is the set of all nonzero real numbers. Figure 5.9 suggests that f is an even function with a maximum value at two points. The coordinates found in this window suggest an extreme value of about -0.69 at approximately $x = 1$. Because f is even, there is another extreme of the same value at approximately $x = -1$. The figure also suggests a minimum value at $x = 0$, but f is not defined there.

continued

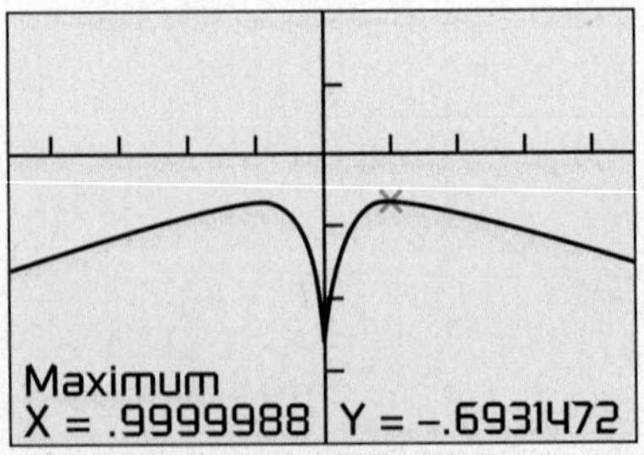

[–4.5, 4.5] by [–4, 2]

Figure 5.9 The function in Example 6.

Confirm Analytically The derivative

$$f'(x) = \frac{1 - x^2}{x(1 + x^2)}$$

is defined at every point of the function's domain. The critical points where $f'(x) = 0$ are $x = 1$ and $x = -1$. The corresponding values of f are both $\ln(1/2) = -\ln 2 \approx -0.69$.

Now Try Exercise 37.

EXPLORATION 1 Finding Extreme Values

Let $f(x) = \left|\frac{x}{x^2 + 1}\right|, -2 \le x \le 2.$

1. Determine graphically the extreme values of f and where they occur. Find f' at these values of x.
2. Graph f and f' (or NDER $(f(x), x, x)$) in the same viewing window. Comment on the relationship between the graphs.
3. Find a formula for $f'(x)$.

Quick Review 5.1 *(For help, go to Sections 1.2, 2.1, 3.5, and 4.1.)*

Exercise numbers with a gray background indicate problems that the authors have designed to be solved *without a calculator.*

In Exercises 1–4, find the first derivative of the function.

1. $f(x) = \sqrt{4 - x}$

2. $f(x) = \frac{2}{\sqrt{9 - x^2}}$

3. $g(x) = \cos(\ln x)$

4. $h(x) = e^{2x}$

In Exercises 5–8, match the table with a graph of $f(x)$.

5.

x	$f'(x)$
a	0
b	0
c	5

6.

x	$f'(x)$
a	0
b	0
c	−5

7.

x	$f'(x)$
a	does not exist
b	0
c	−2

8.

x	$f'(x)$
a	does not exist
b	does not exist
c	−1.7

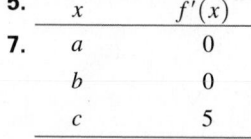

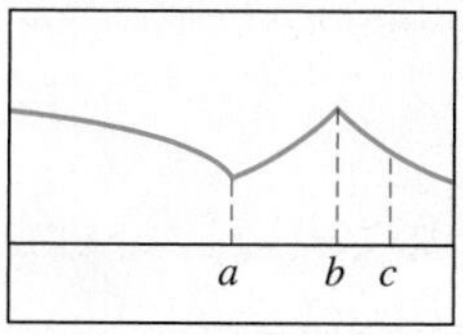

(a)

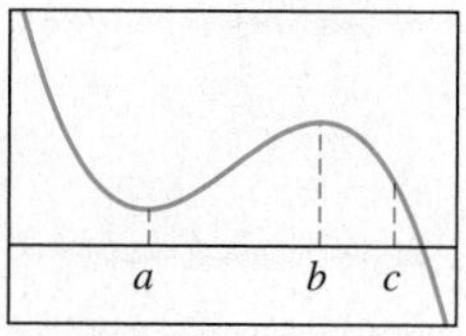

(b)

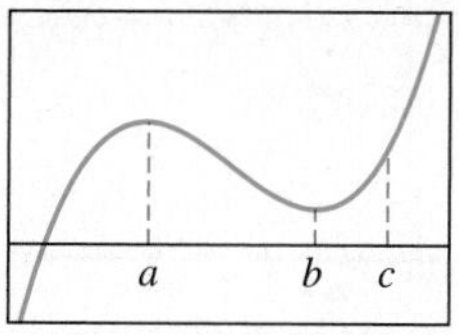

(c)

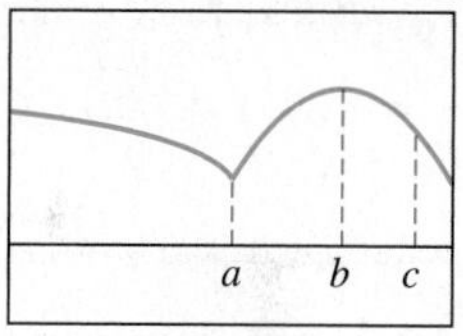

(d)

In Exercises 9 and 10, find the limit for

$$f(x) = \frac{2}{\sqrt{9 - x^2}}.$$

9. $\lim_{x \to 3^-} f(x)$

10. $\lim_{x \to -3^+} f(x)$

In Exercises 11 and 12, let

$$f(x) = \begin{cases} x^3 - 2x, & x \le 2 \\ x + 2, & x > 2. \end{cases}$$

11. Find **(a)** $f'(1)$, **(b)** $f'(3)$, **(c)** $f'(2)$.

12. **(a)** Find the domain of f'.

(b) Write a formula for $f'(x)$.

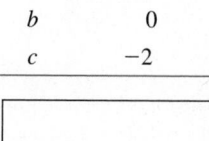

Section 5.1 Exercises

In Exercises 1–4, find the extreme values and where they occur.

1.

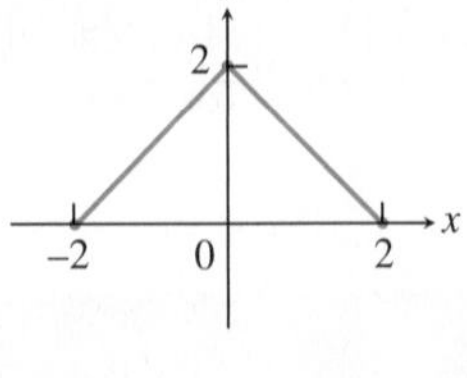

2.

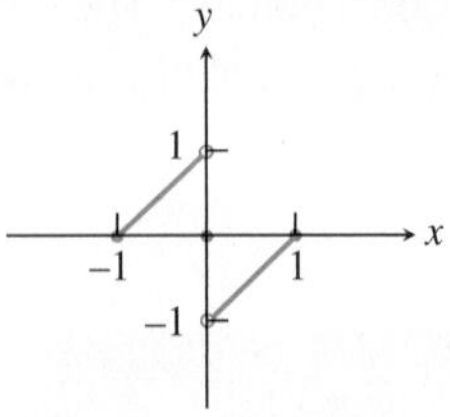

3.

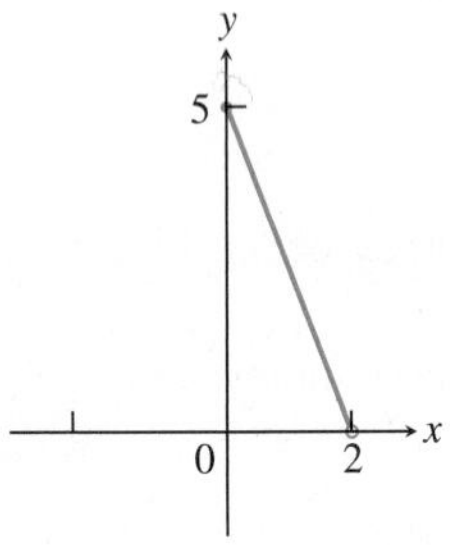

4.

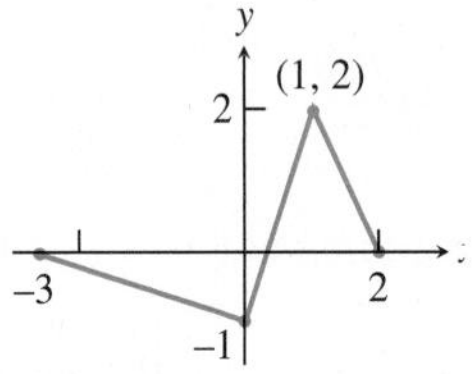

In Exercises 5–10, identify each x-value at which any absolute extreme value occurs. Explain how your answer is consistent with the Extreme Value Theorem.

5.

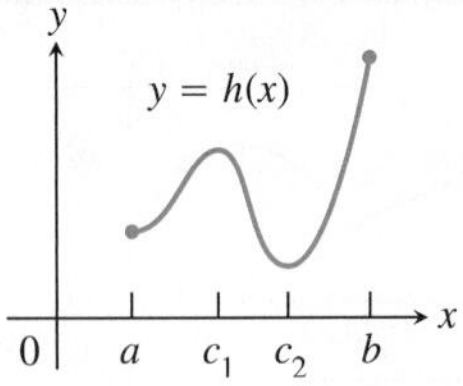

6.

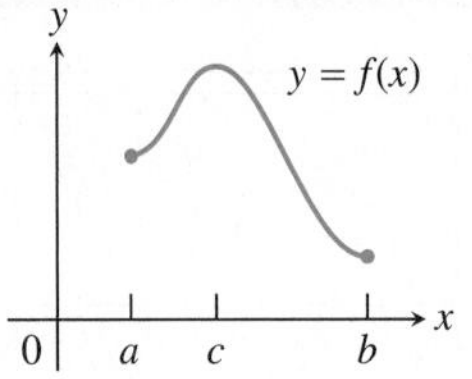

7.

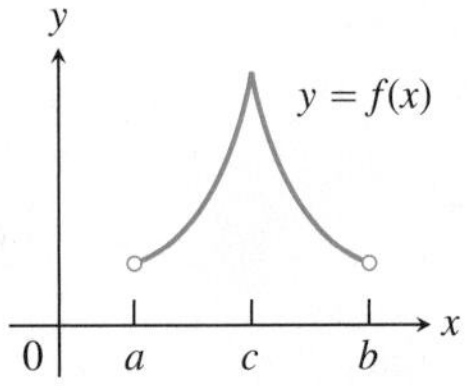

8.

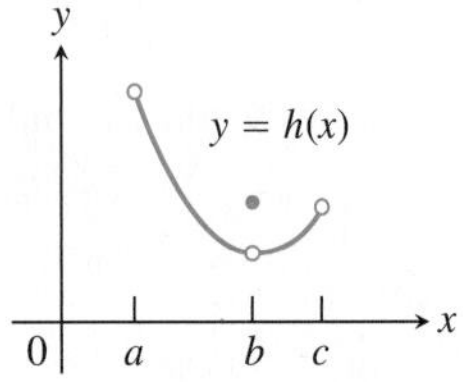

9.

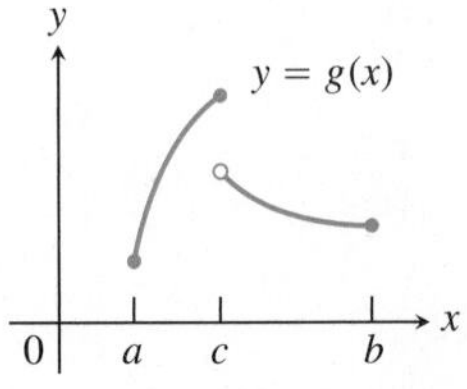

10.

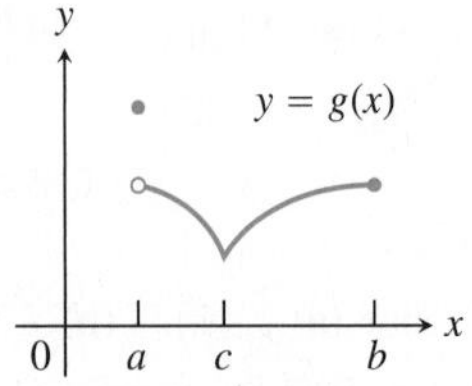

In Exercises 11–18, use analytic methods to find the extreme values of the function on the interval and where they occur. Identify any critical points that are *not* stationary points.

11. $f(x) = \dfrac{1}{x} + \text{In}\, x, \quad 0.5 \le x \le 4$

12. $g(x) = e^{-x}, \quad -1 \le x \le 1$

13. $h(x) = \text{In}\,(x+1), \quad 0 \le x \le 3$

14. $k(x) = e^{-x^2}, \quad -\infty < x < \infty$

15. $f(x) = \sin\left(x + \dfrac{\pi}{4}\right), \quad 0 \le x \le \dfrac{7\pi}{4}$

16. $g(x) = \sec x, \quad -\dfrac{\pi}{2} < x < \dfrac{3\pi}{2}$

17. $f(x) = x^{2/5}, \quad -3 \le x < 1$

18. $f(x) = x^{3/5}, \quad -2 < x \le 3$

In Exercises 19–30, find the extreme values of the function and where they occur.

19. $y = 2x^2 - 8x + 9$

20. $y = x^3 - 2x + 4$

21. $y = x^3 + x^2 - 8x + 5$

22. $y = x^3 - 3x^2 + 3x - 2$

23. $y = \sqrt{x^2 - 1}$

24. $y = \dfrac{1}{x^2 - 1}$

25. $y = \dfrac{1}{\sqrt{1 - x^2}}$

26. $y = \dfrac{1}{\sqrt[3]{1 - x^2}}$

27. $y = \sqrt{3 + 2x - x^2}$

28. $y = \dfrac{3}{2}x^4 + 4x^3 - 9x^2 + 10$

29. $y = \dfrac{x}{x^2 + 1}$

30. $y = \dfrac{x + 1}{x^2 + 2x + 2}$

Group Activity In Exercises 31–34, find the extreme values of the function on the interval and where they occur.

31. $f(x) = |x - 2| + |x + 3|, \quad -5 \le x \le 5$

32. $g(x) = |x - 1| - |x - 5|, \quad -2 \le x \le 7$

33. $h(x) = |x + 2| - |x - 3|, \quad -\infty < x < \infty$

34. $k(x) = |x + 1| + |x - 3|, \quad -\infty < x < \infty$

In Exercises 35–42, identify the critical points and determine the local extreme values. Identify which critical points are *not* stationary points.

35. $y = x^{2/3}(x + 2)$

36. $y = x^{2/3}(x^2 - 4)$

37. $y = x\sqrt{4 - x^2}$

38. $y = x^2\sqrt{3 - x}$

39. $y = \begin{cases} 4 - 2x, & x \le 1 \\ x + 1, & x > 1 \end{cases}$

40. $y = \begin{cases} 3 = x, & x < 0 \\ 3 + 2x - x^2, & x \ge 0 \end{cases}$

41. $y = \begin{cases} -x^2 - 2x + 4, & x \le 1 \\ -x^2 + 6x - 4, & x > 1 \end{cases}$

42. $y = \begin{cases} -\dfrac{1}{4}x^2 - \dfrac{1}{2}x + \dfrac{15}{4}, & x \le 1 \\ x^3 - 6x^2 + 8x, & x > 1 \end{cases}$

43. Writing to Learn The function

$$V(x) = x(10 - 2x)(16 - 2x), \quad 0 < x < 5.$$

models the volume of a box.

(a) Find the extreme values of V.

(b) Interpret any values found in (a) in terms of volume of the box.

(c) Support your analytic answer to part (a) graphically.

44. Writing to Learn The function

$$P(x) = 2x + \frac{200}{x}, \quad 0 < x < \infty,$$

models the perimeter of a rectangle of dimensions x by $100/x$.

(a) Find any extreme values of P.

(b) Give an interpretation in terms of perimeter of the rectangle for any values found in (a).

Standardized Test Questions

45. True or False If $f(c)$ is a local maximum of a continuous function f on an open interval (a, b), then $f'(c) = 0$. Justify your answer.

46. True or False If m is a local minimum and M is a local maximum of a continuous function f on (a, b), then $m < M$. Justify your answer.

47. Multiple Choice Which of the following values is the absolute maximum of the function $f(x) = 4x - x^2 + 6$ on the interval $[0, 4]$?

(A) 0 **(B)** 2 **(C)** 4 **(D)** 6 **(E)** 10

48. Multiple Choice If f is a continuous, decreasing function on $[0, 10]$ with a critical point at $(4, 2)$, which of the following statements *must be false*?

(A) $f(10)$ is an absolute minimum of f on $[0, 10]$.

(B) $f(4)$ is neither a relative maximum nor a relative minimum.

(C) $f'(4)$ does not exist.

(D) $f'(4) = 0$

(E) $f'(4) < 0$

49. Multiple Choice Which of the following functions has exactly two local extrema on its domain?

(A) $f(x) = |x - 2|$

(B) $f(x) = x^3 - 6x + 5$

(C) $f(x) = x^3 + 6x - 5$

(D) $f(x) = \tan x$

(E) $f(x) = x + \ln x$

50. Multiple Choice If an even function f with domain all real numbers has a local maximum at $x = a$, then $f(-a)$

(A) is a local minimum.

(B) is a local maximum.

(C) is both a local minimum and a local maximum.

(D) could be either a local minimum or a local maximum.

(E) is neither a local minimum nor a local maximum.

Explorations

In Exercises 51 and 52, give reasons for your answers.

51. Writing to Learn Let $f(x) = (x - 2)^{2/3}$.

(a) Does $f'(2)$ exist?

(b) Show that the only local extreme value of f occurs at $x = 2$.

(c) Does the result in (b) contradict the Extreme Value Theorem?

(d) Repeat parts (a) and (b) for $f(x) = (x - a)^{2/3}$, replacing 2 by a.

52. Writing to Learn Let $f(x) = |x^3 - 9x|$.

(a) Does $f'(0)$ exist?

(b) Does $f'(3)$ exist?

(c) Does $f'(-3)$ exist?

(d) Determine all extrema of f.

Extending the Ideas

53. *Cubic Functions* Consider the cubic function

$$f(x) = ax^3 + bx^2 + cx + d.$$

(a) Show that f can have 0, 1, or 2 critical points. Give examples and graphs to support your argument.

(b) How many local extreme values can f have?

54. *Proving Theorem 2* Assume that the function f has a local maximum value at the interior point c of its domain and that $f'(c)$ exists.

(a) Show that there is an open interval containing c such that $f(x) - f(c) \le 0$ for all x in the open interval.

(b) Writing to Learn Now explain why we may say

$$\lim_{x \to c^+} \frac{f(x) - f(c)}{x - c} \le 0.$$

(c) Writing to Learn Now explain why we may say

$$\lim_{x \to c^-} \frac{f(x) - f(c)}{x - c} \ge 0.$$

(d) Writing to Learn Explain how parts (b) and (c) allow us to conclude $f'(c) = 0$.

(e) Writing to Learn Give a similar argument if f has a local minimum value at an interior point.

55. *Functions with No Extreme Values at Endpoints*

(a) Graph the function

$$f(x) = \begin{cases} \sin\dfrac{1}{x}, & x > 0 \\ 0, & x = 0. \end{cases}$$

Explain why $f(0) = 0$ is not a local extreme value of f.

(b) Group Activity Construct a function of your own that fails to have an extreme value at a domain endpoint.

5.2 Mean Value Theorem

What you will learn about . . .

- Mean Value Theorem
- Physical Interpretation
- Increasing and Decreasing Functions
- Other Consequences

and why . . .

The Mean Value Theorem is an important theoretical tool to connect the average and instantaneous rates of change.

Mean Value Theorem

The Mean Value Theorem connects the average rate of change of a function over an interval with the instantaneous rate of change of the function at a point within the interval. Its powerful corollaries lie at the heart of some of the most important applications of the calculus.

The theorem says that somewhere between points A and B on a differentiable curve, there is at least one tangent line parallel to chord AB (Figure 5.10).

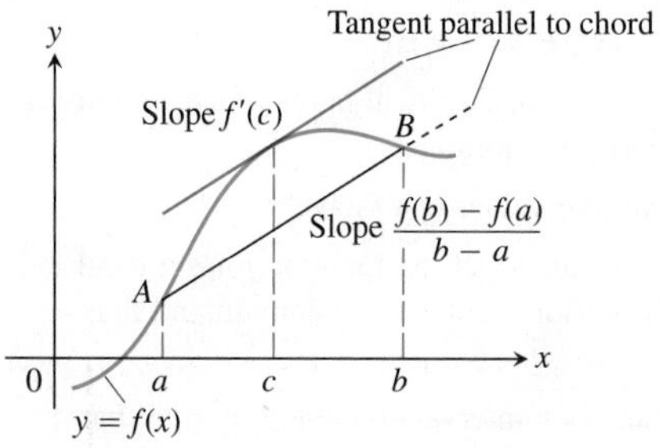

Figure 5.10 Figure for the Mean Value Theorem.

THEOREM 3 Mean Value Theorem for Derivatives

If $y = f(x)$ is continuous at every point of the closed interval $[a, b]$ and differentiable at every point of its interior (a, b), then there is at least one point c in (a, b) at which

$$f'(c) = \frac{f(b) - f(a)}{b - a}.$$

The hypotheses of Theorem 3 cannot be relaxed. If they fail at even one point, the graph may fail to have a tangent parallel to the chord. For instance, the function $f(x) = |x|$ is continuous on $[-1, 1]$ and differentiable at every point of the interior $(-1, 1)$ except $x = 0$. The graph has no tangent parallel to chord AB (Figure 5.11a). The function $g(x) = \text{int}\,(x)$ is differentiable at every point of $(1, 2)$ and continuous at every point of $[1, 2]$ except $x = 2$. Again, the graph has no tangent parallel to chord AB (Figure 5.11b).

The Mean Value Theorem is an *existence theorem.* It tells us the number c exists without telling how to find it. We can sometimes satisfy our curiosity about the value of c but the real importance of the theorem lies in the surprising conclusions we can draw from it.

Rolle's Theorem

The first version of the Mean Value Theorem was proved by French mathematician Michel Rolle (1652–1719). His version had $f(a) = f(b) = 0$. and was proved only for polynomials, using algebra and geometry.

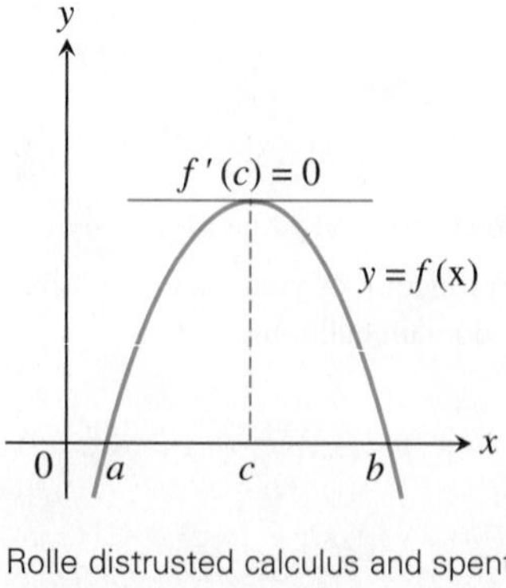

Rolle distrusted calculus and spent most of his life denouncing it. It is ironic that he is known today only for an unintended contribution to a field he tried to suppress.

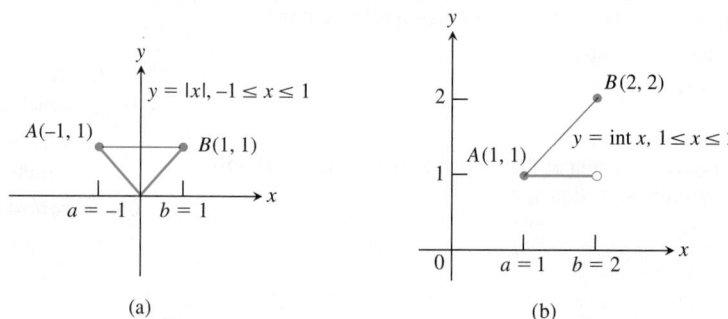

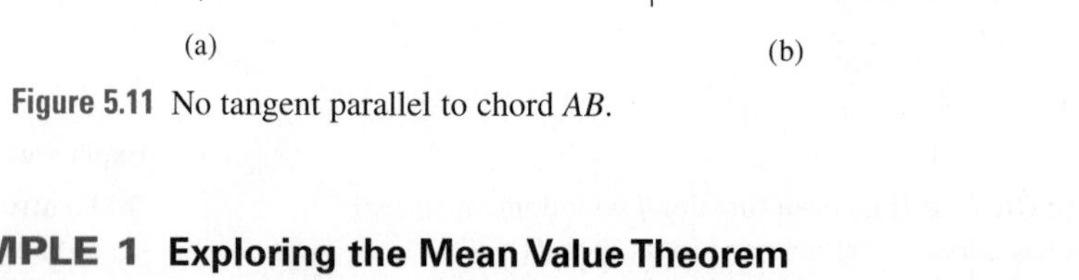

Figure 5.11 No tangent parallel to chord AB.

EXAMPLE 1 Exploring the Mean Value Theorem

Show that the function $f(x) = x^2$ satisfies the hypotheses of the Mean Value Theorem on the interval $[0, 2]$. Then find a solution c to the equation

$$f'(c) = \frac{f(b) - f(a)}{b - a}$$

on this interval.

continued

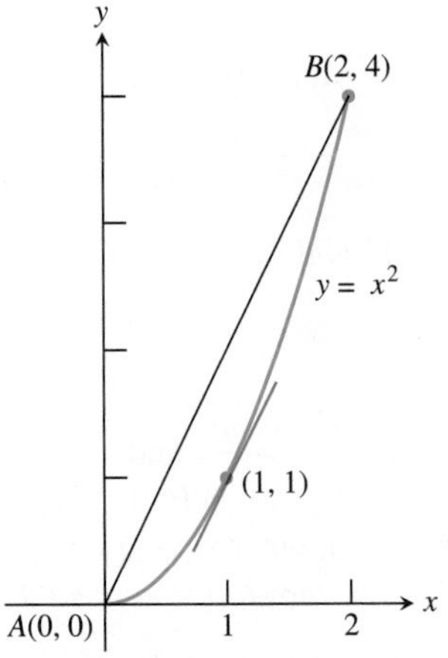

Figure 5.12 (Example 1)

SOLUTION

The function $f(x) = x^2$ is continuous on $[0, 2]$ and differentiable on $(0, 2)$. Since $f(0) = 0$ and $f(2) = 4$, the Mean Value Theorem guarantees a point c in the interval $(0, 2)$ for which

$$f'(c) = \frac{f(b) - f(a)}{b - a}$$

$$2c = \frac{f(2) - f(0)}{2 - 0} = 2 \quad f'(x) = 2x$$

$$c = 1.$$

Interpret The tangent line to $f(x) = x^2$ at $x = 1$ has slope 2 and is parallel to the chord joining $A(0, 0)$ and $B(2, 4)$ (Figure 5.12). ***Now Try Exercise 1.***

EXAMPLE 2 Exploring the Mean Value Theorem

Explain why each of the following functions fails to satisfy the conditions of the Mean Value Theorem on the interval $[-1, 1]$.

(a) $f(x) = \sqrt{x^2 + 1}$ **(b)** $f(x) = \begin{cases} x^3 + 3 & \text{for } x < 1 \\ x^2 + 1 & \text{for } x \geq 1 \end{cases}$

SOLUTION

(a) Note that $\sqrt{x^2 + 1} = |x| + 1$, so this is just a vertical shift of the absolute value function, which has a nondifferentiable "corner" at $x = 0$. (See Section 3.2.) The function f is not differentiable on $(-1, 1)$.

(b) Since $\lim_{x\to1^-} f(x) \lim_{x\to1^-} x^3 + 3 = 4$ and $\lim_{x\to1^+} f(x) = \lim_{x\to1^+} x^2 + 1 = 2$, the function has a discontinuity at $x = 1$. The function f is not continuous on $[-1, 1]$.

If the two functions given had satisfied the necessary conditions, the *conclusion* of the Mean Value Theorem would have guaranteed the existence of a number c in $(-1, 1)$ such that $f'(c) = \dfrac{f(1) - f(-1)}{1 - (-1)} = 0$. Such a number c does not exist for the function in part (a), but one happens to exist for the function in part (b) (Figure 5.13).

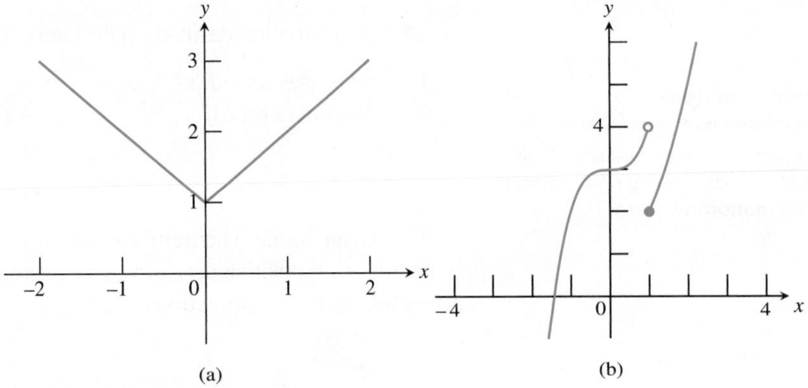

Figure 5.13 For both functions in Example 2, $\dfrac{f(1) - f(-1)}{1 - (-1)} = 0$ but neither function satisfies the conditions of the Mean Value Theorem on the interval $[-1, 1]$. For the function in Example 2(a), there is no number c such that $f'(c) = 0$. It happens that $f'(0) = 0$ in Example 2(b). ***Now Try Exercise 3.***

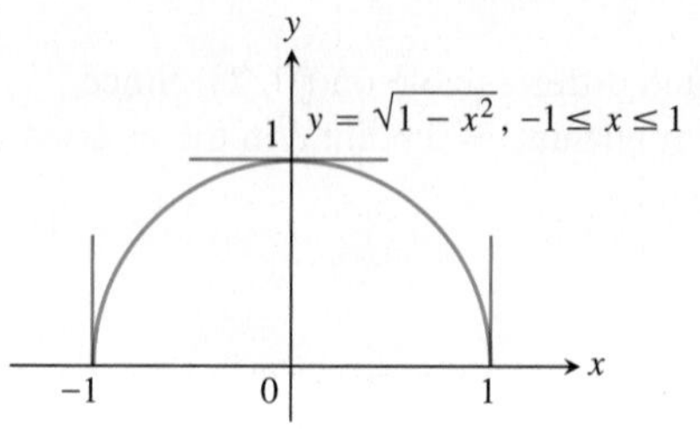

Figure 5.14 (Example 3)

EXAMPLE 3 Applying the Mean Value Theorem

Let $f(x) = \sqrt{1 - x^2}$, $A = (-1, f(-1))$, and $B = (1, f(1))$. Find a tangent to f in the interval $(-1, 1)$ that is parallel to the secant AB.

SOLUTION

The function f (Figure 5.14) is continuous on the interval $[-1, 1]$ and

$$f'(x) = \frac{-x}{\sqrt{1 - x^2}}$$

is defined on the interval $(-1, 1)$. The function is not differentiable at $x = -1$ and $x = 1$, but it does not need to be for the theorem to apply. Since $f(-1) = f(1) = 0$, the tangent we are looking for is horizontal. We find that $f' = 0$ at $x = 0$, where the graph has the horizontal tangent $y = 1$. ***Now Try Exercise 9.***

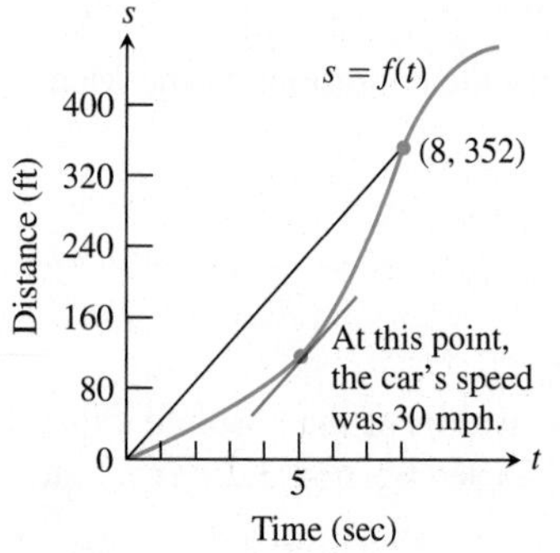

Figure 5.15 (Example 4)

Physical Interpretation

If we think of the difference quotient $(f(b) - f(a))/(b - a)$ as the average change in f over $[a, b]$ and $f'(c)$ as an instantaneous change, then the Mean Value Theorem says that the instantaneous change at some interior point must equal the average change over the entire interval.

EXAMPLE 4 Interpreting the Mean Value Theorem

If a car accelerating from zero takes 8 sec to go 352 ft, its average velocity for the 8-sec interval is $352/8 = 44$ft/sec, or 30 mph. At some point during the acceleration, the theorem says, the speedometer must read exactly 30 mph (Figure 5.15). ***Now Try Exercise 11.***

Increasing and Decreasing Functions

Our first use of the Mean Value Theorem will be its application to increasing and decreasing functions.

DEFINITIONS Increasing Function, Decreasing Function

Let f be a function defined on an interval I and let x_1 and x_2 be any two points in I.

1. f **increases** on I if $x_1 < x_2 \Rightarrow f(x_1) < f(x_2)$.
2. f **decreases** on I if $x_1 < x_2 \Rightarrow f(x_1) > f(x_2)$.

Monotonic Functions

A function that is always increasing on an interval or always decreasing on an interval is said to be **monotonic** there.

The Mean Value Theorem allows us to identify exactly where graphs rise and fall. Functions with positive derivatives are increasing functions; functions with negative derivatives are decreasing functions.

COROLLARY 1 Increasing and Decreasing Functions

Let f be continuous on $[a, b]$ and differentiable on (a, b).

1. If $f' > 0$ at each point of (a, b), then f increases on $[a, b]$.
2. If $f' < 0$ at each point of (a, b), then f decreases on $[a, b]$.

Proof Let x_1 and x_2 be any two points in $[a, b]$ with $x_1 < x_2$. The Mean Value Theorem applied to f on $[x_1, x_2]$ gives

$$f(x_2) - f(x_1) = f'(c)(x_2 - x_1)$$

for some c between x_1 and x_2. The sign of the right-hand side of this equation is the same as the sign of $f'(c)$ because $x_2 - x_1$ is positive. Therefore,

(a) $f(x_1) < f(x_2)$ if $f' > 0$ on (a, b) (f is increasing), or

(b) $f(x_1) > f(x_2)$ if $f' < 0$ on (a, b) (f is decreasing). ■

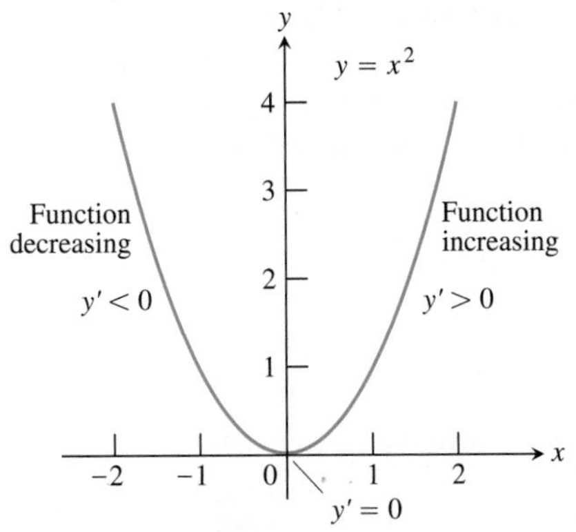

Figure 5.16 (Example 5)

EXAMPLE 5 Determining Where Graphs Rise or Fall

The function $y = x^2$ (Figure 5.16) is

(a) decreasing on $(-\infty, 0)$ because $y' = 2x < 0$ on $(-\infty, 0)$.

(b) increasing on $[0, \infty)$ because $y' = 2x > 0$ on $(0, \infty)$. ***Now Try Exercise 15.***

What's Happening at Zero?

Note that 0 appears in both intervals in Example 5, which is consistent both with the definition and with Corollary 1. Does this mean that the function $y = x^2$ is both increasing and decreasing at $x = 0$? No! This is because a function can only be described as increasing or decreasing on an *interval* with more than one point (see the definition). Saying that $y = x^2$ is "increasing at $x = 2$" is not really proper either, but you will often see that statement used as a short way of saying $y = x^2$ is "increasing on an interval containing 2."

EXAMPLE 6 Determining Where Graphs Rise or Fall

Where is the function $f(x) = x^3 - 4x$ increasing and where is it decreasing?

SOLUTION

Solve Analytically The function is increasing where $f'(x) > 0$.

$$3x^2 - 4 > 0$$

$$x^2 > \frac{4}{3}$$

$$x < -\sqrt{\frac{4}{3}} \quad \text{or} \quad x > \sqrt{\frac{4}{3}}$$

The function is decreasing where $f'(x) < 0$.

$$3x^2 - 4 < 0$$

$$x^2 < \frac{4}{3}$$

$$-\sqrt{\frac{4}{3}} < x < \sqrt{\frac{4}{3}}$$

In interval notation, f is increasing on $(-\infty, -\sqrt{4/3}]$, decreasing on $[-\sqrt{4/3}, \sqrt{4/3}]$, and increasing on $[\sqrt{4/3}, \infty)$. See Figure 5.17 for graphical support of the analytic solution. ***Now Try Exercise 27.***

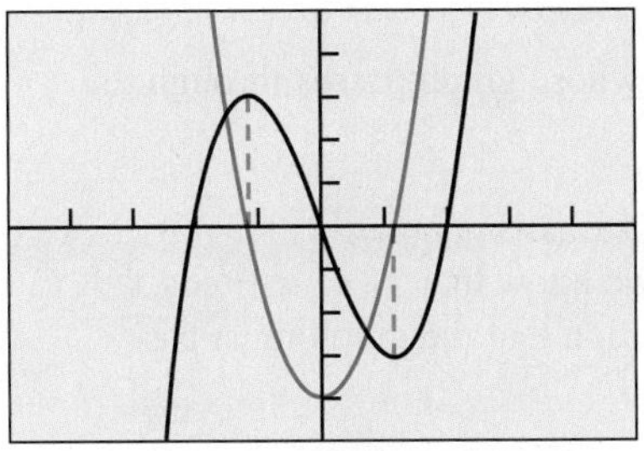

[–5, 5] by [–5, 5]

Figure 5.17 By comparing the graphs of $f(x) = x^3 - 4x$ and $f'(x) = 3x^2 - 4$ we can relate the increasing and decreasing behavior of f to the sign of f'. (Example 6)

Other Consequences

We know that constant functions have the zero function as their derivative. We can now use the Mean Value Theorem to show conversely that the only functions with the zero function as derivative are constant functions.

COROLLARY 2 Functions with $f' = 0$ Are Constant

If $f'(x) = 0$ at each point of an interval I, then there is a constant C for which $f(x) = C$ for all x in I.

Proof Our plan is to show that $f(x_1) = f(x_2)$ for any two points x_1 and x_2 in I. We can assume the points are numbered so that $x_1 < x_2$. Since f is differentiable at every point of $[x_1, x_2]$ it is continuous at every point as well. Thus, f satisfies the hypotheses of the Mean Value Theorem on $[x_1, x_2]$. Therefore, there is a point c between x_1 and x_2 for which

$$f'(c) = \frac{f(x_2) - f(x_1)}{x_2 - x_1}.$$

Because $f'(c) = 0$, it follows that $f(x_1) = f(x_2)$. ■

We can use Corollary 2 to show that if two functions have the same derivative, they differ by a constant.

COROLLARY 3 Functions with the Same Derivative Differ by a Constant

If $f'(x) = g'(x)$ at each point of an interval I, then there is a constant C such that $f(x) = g(x) + C$ for all x in I.

Proof Let $h = f - g$. Then for each point x in I,

$$h'(x) = f'(x) - g'(x) = 0.$$

It follows from Corollary 2 that there is a constant C such that $h(x) = C$ for all x in I. Thus, $h(x) = f(x) - g(x) = C$, or $f(x) = g(x) + C$. ■

We know that the derivative of $f(x) = x^2$ is $2x$ on the interval $(-\infty, \infty)$. So, any other function $g(x)$ with derivative $2x$ on $(-\infty, \infty)$ must have the formula $g(x) = x^2 + C$ for some constant C.

EXAMPLE 7 Applying Corollary 3

Find the function $f(x)$ whose derivative is $\sin x$ and whose graph passes through the point $(0, 2)$.

SOLUTION

Since f has the same derivative as $g(x) = -\cos x$, we know that $f(x) = -\cos x + C$, for some constant C. To identify C, we use the condition that the graph must pass through $(0, 2)$. This is equivalent to saying that

$$\begin{aligned} f(0) &= 2 \\ -\cos(0) + C &= 2 \quad f(x) = -\cos x + C \\ -1 + C &= 2 \\ C &= 3. \end{aligned}$$

The formula for f is $f(x) = -\cos x + 3$. ***Now Try Exercise 35.***

In Example 7 we were given a derivative and asked to find a function with that derivative. This type of function is so important that it has a name.

DEFINITION Antiderivative

A function $F(x)$ is an **antiderivative** of a function $f(x)$ if $F'(x) = f(x)$ for all x in the domain of f. The process of finding an antiderivative is **antidifferentiation.**

We know that if f has one antiderivative F then it has infinitely many antiderivatives, each differing from F by a constant. Corollary 3 says these are all there are. In Example 7, we found the particular antiderivative of $\sin x$ whose graph passed through the point $(0, 2)$.

EXAMPLE 8 Finding Velocity and Position

Find the velocity and position functions of a body falling freely from a height of 0 meters under each of the following sets of conditions:

(a) The acceleration is 9.8 m/sec² and the body falls from rest.

(b) The acceleration is 9.8 m/sec² and the body is propelled downward with an initial velocity of 1 m/sec.

SOLUTION

(a) ***Falling from rest.*** We measure distance fallen in meters and time in seconds, and assume that the body is released from rest at time $t = 0$.

Velocity: We know that the velocity $v(t)$ is an antiderivative of the constant function 9.8. We also know that $g(t) = 9.8t$ is an antiderivative of 9.8. By Corollary 3,

$$v(t) = 9.8t + C$$

for some constant C. Since the body falls from rest, $v(0) = 0$. Thus,

$$9.8(0) + C = 0 \quad \text{and} \quad C = 0.$$

The body's velocity function is $v(t) = 9.8t$

Position: We know that the position $s(t)$ is an antiderivative of $9.8t$. We also know that $h(t) = 4.9t^2$ is an antiderivative of $9.8t$. By Corollary 3,

$$s(t) = 4.9t^2 + C$$

for some constant C. Since $s(0) = 0$,

$$4.9(0)^2 + C = 0 \quad \text{and} \quad C = 0.$$

The body's position function is $s(t) = 4.9t^2$.

(b) ***Propelled downward.*** We measure distance fallen in meters and time in seconds, and assume that the body is propelled downward with velocity of 1 m/sec at time $t = 0$.

Velocity: The velocity function still has the form $9.8t + C$, but instead of being zero, the initial velocity (velocity at $t = 0$) is now 1 m/sec. Thus,

$$9.8(0) + C = 1 \quad \text{and} \quad C = 1.$$

The body's velocity function is $v(t) = 9.8t + 1$.

Position: We know that the position $s(t)$ is an antiderivative of $9.8t + 1$. We also know that $k(t) = 4.9t^2 + t$ is an antiderivative of $9.8t + 1$. By Corollary 3,

$$s(t) = 4.9t^2 + t + C$$

for some constant C. Since $s(0) = 0$,

$$4.9(0)^2 + 0 + C = 0 \quad \text{and} \quad C = 0.$$

The body's position function is $s(t) = 4.9t^2 + t$. ***Now Try Exercise 43.***

Quick Review 5.2 (For help, go to Sections 1.2, 2.3, and 3.2.)

Exercise numbers with a gray background indicate problems that the authors have designed to be solved *without a calculator.*

In Exercises 1 and 2, find exact solutions to the inequality.

1. $2x^2 - 6 < 0$

2. $3x^2 - 6 > 0$

In Exercises 3–5, let $f(x) = \sqrt{8 - 2x^2}$.

3. Find the domain of *f*.

4. Where is *f* continuous?

5. Where is *f* differentiable?

In Exercises 6–8, let $f(x) = \dfrac{x}{x^2 - 1}$.

6. Find the domain of *f*.

7. Where is *f* continuous?

8. Where is *f* differentiable?

In Exercises 9 and 10, find *C* so that the graph of the function *f* passes through the specified point.

9. $f(x) = -2x + C, \quad (-2, 7)$

10. $g(x) = x^2 + 2x + C, \quad (1, -1)$

Section 5.2 Exercises

In Exercises 1–8, **(a)** state whether or not the function satisfies the hypotheses of the Mean Value Theorem on the given interval, and **(b)** if it does, find each value of *c* in the interval (a, b) that satisfies the equation

$$f'(c) = \frac{f(b) - f(a)}{b - a}.$$

1. $f(x) = x^2 + 2x - 1$ on $[0, 1]$

2. $f(x) = x^{2/3}$ on $[0, 1]$

3. $f(x) = x^{1/3}$ on $[-1, 1]$

4. $f(x) = |x - 1|$ on $[0, 4]$

5. $f(x) = \sin^{-1} x$ on $[-1, 1]$

6. $f(x) = \text{In}\,(x - 1)$ on $[2, 4]$

7. $f(x) = \begin{cases} \cos x, & 0 \le x < \pi/2 \\ \sin x, & \pi/2 \le x \le \pi \end{cases}$ on $[0, \pi]$

8. $f(x) = \begin{cases} \sin^{-1} x, & -1 \le x < 1 \\ x/2 + 1, & 1 \le x \le 3 \end{cases}$ on $[-1, 3]$

In Exercises 9 and 10, the interval $a \le x \le b$ is given. Let $A = (a, f(a))$ and $B = (b, f(b))$. Write an equation for

(a) the secant line *AB*.

(b) a tangent line to *f* in the interval (a, b) that is parallel to *AB*.

9. $f(x) = x + \dfrac{1}{x}, \quad 0.5 \le x \le 2$

10. $f(x) = \sqrt{x - 1}, \quad 1 \le x \le 3$

11. *Speeding* A trucker handed in a ticket at a toll booth showing that in 2 h she had covered 159 mi on a toll road with speed limit 65 mph. The trucker was cited for speeding. Why?

12. *Temperature Change* It took 20 sec for the temperature to rise from 0°F to 212°F when a thermometer was taken from a freezer and placed in boiling water. Explain why at some moment in that interval the mercury was rising at exactly 10.6°F/sec.

13. *Triremes* Classical accounts tell us that a 170-oar trireme (ancient Greek or Roman warship) once covered 184 sea miles in 24 h. Explain why at some point during this feat the trireme's speed exceeded 7.5 knots (sea miles per hour).

14. *Running a Marathon* A marathoner ran the 26.2-mi New York City Marathon in 2.2 h. Show that at least twice, the marathoner was running at exactly 11 mph.

In Exercises 15–22, use analytic methods to find **(a)** the local extrema, **(b)** the intervals on which the function is increasing, and **(c)** the intervals on which the function is decreasing.

15. $f(x) = 5x - x^2$

16. $g(x) = x^2 - x - 12$

17. $h(x) = \dfrac{2}{x}$

18. $k(x) = \dfrac{1}{x^2}$

19. $f(x) = e^{2x}$

20. $f(x) = e^{-0.5x}$

21. $y = 4 - \sqrt{x + 2}$

22. $y = x^4 - 10x^2 + 9$

In Exercises 23–28, find **(a)** the local extrema, **(b)** the intervals on which the function is increasing, and **(c)** the intervals on which the function is decreasing.

23. $f(x) = x\sqrt{4 - x}$ **24.** $g(x) = x^{1/3}(x + 8)$

25. $h(x) = \dfrac{-x}{x^2 + 4}$ **26.** $k(x) = \dfrac{x}{x^2 - 4}$

27. $f(x) = x^3 - 2x - 2\cos x$ **28.** $g(x) = 2x + \cos x$

In Exercises 29–34, find all possible functions f with the given derivative.

29. $f'(x) = x$ **30.** $f'(x) = 2$

31. $f'(x) = 3x^2 - 2x + 1$ **32.** $f'(x) = \sin x$

33. $f'(x) = e^x$ **34.** $f'(x) = \dfrac{1}{x - 1}, \quad x > 1$

In Exercises 35–38, find the function with the given derivative whose graph passes through the point P.

35. $f'(x) = -\dfrac{1}{x^2}, \quad x > 0, \quad P(2, 1)$

36. $f'(x) = \dfrac{1}{4x^{3/4}}, \quad P(1, -2)$

37. $f'(x) = \dfrac{1}{x + 2}, \quad x > -2, \quad P(-1, 3)$

38. $f'(x) = 2x + 1 - \cos x, \quad P(0, 3),$

Group Activity In Exercises 39–42, sketch a graph of a differentiable function $y = f(x)$ that has the given properties.

39. **(a)** local minimum at $(1,1)$, local maximum at $(3, 3)$

(b) local minima at $(1,1)$ and $(3, 3)$

(c) local maxima at $(1,1)$ and $(3, 3)$

40. $f(2) = 3, \quad f'(2) = 0,$ and

(a) $f'(x) > 0$ for $x < 2$, $f'(x) < 0$ for $x > 2$.

(b) $f'(x) < 0$ for $x < 2$, $f'(x) > 0$ for $x > 2$.

(c) $f'(x) < 0$ for $x \neq 2$.

(d) $f'(x) > 0$ for $x \neq 2$.

41. $f'(-1) = f'(1) = 0$, $f'(x) > 0$ on $(-1, 1)$, $f'(x) < 0$ for $x < -1$, $f'(x) > 0$ for $x > 1$.

42. A local minimum value that is greater than one of its local maximum values.

43. ***Free Fall*** On the moon, the acceleration due to gravity is 1.6 m/sec^2.

(a) If a rock is dropped into a crevasse, how fast will it be going just before it hits bottom 30 sec later?

(b) How far below the point of release is the bottom of the crevasse?

(c) If instead of being released from rest, the rock is thrown into the crevasse from the same point with a downward velocity of 4 m/sec, when will it hit the bottom and how fast will it be going when it does?

44. ***Diving*** **(a)** With what velocity will you hit the water if you step off from a 10-m diving platform?

(b) With what velocity will you hit the water if you dive off the platform with an upward velocity of 2 m/sec?

45. **Writing to Learn** The function

$$f(x) = \begin{cases} x, & 0 \le x < 1 \\ 0, & x = 1 \end{cases}$$

is zero at $x = 0$ and at $x = 1$. Its derivative is equal to 1 at every point between 0 and 1, so f' is never zero between 0 and 1, and the graph of f has no tangent parallel to the chord from $(0, 0)$ to $(1, 0)$. Explain why this does not contradict the Mean Value Theorem.

46. **Writing to Learn** Explain why there is a zero of $y = \cos x$ between every two zeros of $y = \sin x$.

47. ***Unique Solution*** Assume that f is continuous on $[a, b]$ and differentiable on (a, b). Also assume that $f(a)$ and $f(b)$ have opposite signs and $f' \neq 0$ between a and b. Show that $f(x) = 0$ exactly once between a and b.

In Exercises 48 and 49, show that the equation has exactly one solution in the interval. [*Hint:* See Exercise 47.]

48. $x^4 + 3x + 1 = 0, \qquad -2 \le x \le -1$

49. $x + \text{In}\,(x + 1) = 0, \qquad 0 \le x \le 3$

50. ***Parallel Tangents*** Assume that f and g are differentiable on $[a, b]$ and that $f(a) = g(a)$ and $f(b) = g(b)$. Show that there is at least one point between a and b where the tangents to the graphs of f and g are parallel or the same line. Illustrate with a sketch.

Standardized Test Questions

You may use a graphing calculator to solve the following problems.

51. **True or False** If f is differentiable and increasing on (a, b), then $f'(c) > 0$ for every c in (a, b). Justify your answer.

52. **True or False** If f is differentiable and $f'(c) > 0$ for every c in (a, b), then f is increasing on (a, b). Justify your answer.

53. Multiple Choice If $f(x) = \cos x$, then the Mean Value Theorem guarantees that somewhere between 0 and $\pi/3$, $f'(x) =$

(A) $-\frac{3}{2\pi}$ (B) $-\frac{\sqrt{3}}{2}$ (C) -1 (D) 0 (E) $\frac{1}{2}$

54. Multiple Choice On what interval is the function $g(x) = e^{x^3-6x^2+8}$ decreasing?

(A) $(-\infty, 2]$ (B) $[0, 4]$ (C) $[2, 4]$

(D) $(4, \infty)$ (E) no interval

55. Multiple Choice Which of the following functions is an antiderivative of $\frac{1}{\sqrt{x}}$?

(A) $-\frac{1}{\sqrt{2x^3}}$ (B) $-\frac{2}{\sqrt{x}}$ (C) $\frac{\sqrt{x}}{2}$

(D) $\sqrt{x} + 5$ (E) $2\sqrt{x} - 10$

56. Multiple Choice All of the following functions satisfy the conditions of the Mean Value Theorem on the interval $[-1, 1]$ *except*

(A) $\sin x$ (B) $\sin^{-1}x$ (C) $x^{5/3}$ (D) $x^{3/5}$ (E) $\frac{x}{x-2}$

Explorations

57. *Analyzing Derivative Data* Assume that f is continuous on $[-2, 2]$ and differentiable on $(-2, 2)$. The table gives some values of $f'(x)$.

x	$f'(x)$	x	$f'(x)$
−2	7	0.25	−4.81
−1.75	4.19	0.5	−4.25
−1.5	1.75	0.75	−3.31
−1.25	−0.31	1	−2
−1	−2	1.25	−0.31
−0.75	−3.31	1.5	1.75
−0.5	−4.25	1.75	4.19
−0.25	−4.81	2	7
0	−5		

(a) Estimate where f is increasing, decreasing, and has local extrema.

(b) Find a quadratic regression equation for the data in the table and superimpose its graph on a scatter plot of the data.

(c) Use the model in part (b) for f' and find a formula for f that satisfies $f(0) = 0$.

58. *Analyzing Motion Data* Priya's distance D in meters from a motion detector is given by the data in Table 5.1.

TABLE 5.1 Motion Detector Data

t (sec)	D (m)	t (sec)	D (m)
0.0	3.36	4.5	3.59
0.5	2.61	5.0	4.15
1.0	1.86	5.5	3.99
1.5	1.27	6.0	3.37
2.0	0.91	6.5	2.58
2.5	1.14	7.0	1.93
3.0	1.69	7.5	1.25
3.5	2.37	8.0	0.67
4.0	3.01		

(a) Estimate when Priya is moving toward the motion detector; away from the motion detector.

(b) **Writing to Learn** Give an interpretation of any local extreme values in terms of this problem situation.

(c) Find a cubic regression equation $D = f(t)$ for the data in Table 5.1 and superimpose its graph on a scatter plot of the data.

(d) Use the model in (c) for f to find a formula for f'. Use this formula to estimate the answers to (a).

Extending the Ideas

59. *Geometric Mean* The **geometric mean** of two positive numbers a and b is $\sqrt{ab}$. Show that for $f(x) = 1/x$ on any interval $[a, b]$ of positive numbers, the value of c in the conclusion of the Mean Value Theorem is $c = \sqrt{ab}$.

60. *Arithmetic Mean* The **arithmetic mean** of two numbers a and b is $(a + b)/2$. Show that for $f(x) = x^2$ on any interval $[a, b]$, the value of c in the conclusion of the Mean Value Theorem is $c = (a + b)/2$.

61. *Upper Bounds* Show that for any numbers a and b $|\sin b - \sin a| \le |b - a|$.

62. *Sign of f'* Assume that f is differentiable on $a \le x \le b$ and that $f(b) < f(a)$. Show that f' is negative at some point between a and b.

63. *Monotonic Functions* Show that monotonic increasing and decreasing functions are one-to-one.

5.3 Connecting f' and f'' with the Graph of f

What you will learn about . . .

- First Derivative Test for Local Extrema
- Concavity
- Points of Inflection
- Second Derivative Test for Local Extrema
- Learning About Functions from Derivatives

and why . . .

Differential calculus is a powerful problem-solving tool precisely because of its usefulness for analyzing functions.

First Derivative Test for Local Extrema

As we see once again in Figure 5.18, a function f may have local extrema at some critical points while failing to have local extrema at others. The key is the sign of f' in a critical point's immediate vicinity. As x moves from left to right, the values of f increase where $f' > 0$ and decrease where $f' < 0$.

At the points where f has a minimum value, we see that $f' < 0$ on the interval immediately to the left and $f' > 0$ on the interval immediately to the right. (If the point is an endpoint, there is only the interval on the appropriate side to consider.) This means that the curve is falling (values decreasing) on the left of the minimum value and rising (values increasing) on its right. Similarly, at the points where f has a maximum value, $f' > 0$ on the interval immediately to the left and $f' < 0$ on the interval immediately to the right. This means that the curve is rising (values increasing) on the left of the maximum value and falling (values decreasing) on its right.

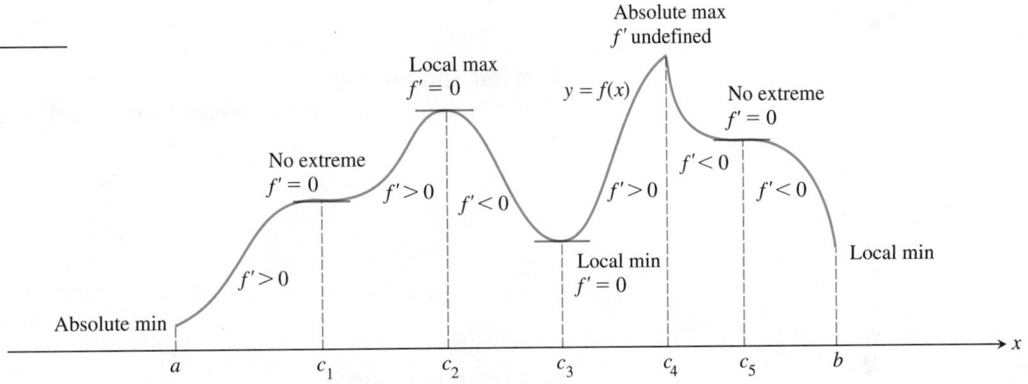

Figure 5.18 A function's first derivative tells how the graph rises and falls.

THEOREM 4 First Derivative Test for Local Extrema

The following test applies to a continuous function $f(x)$.

At a critical point c:

1. If f' changes sign from positive to negative at c ($f' > 0$ for $x < c$ and $f' < 0$ for $x > c$), then f has a local maximum value at c.

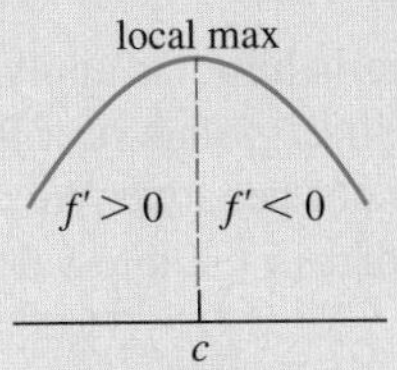

(a) $f'(c) = 0$

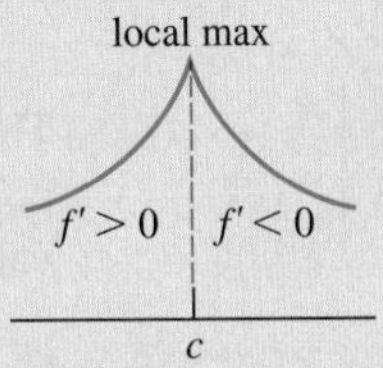

(b) $f'(c)$ undefined

continued

2. If f' changes sign from negative to positive at c $(f' < 0$ for $x < c$ and $f' > 0$ for $x > c)$ then f has a local minimum value at c.

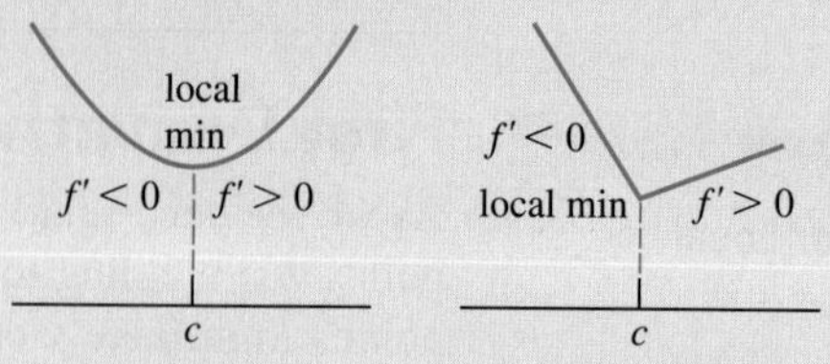

(a) $f'(c) = 0$ (b) $f'(c)$ undefined

3. If f' does not change sign at c $(f'$ has the same sign on both sides of $c)$, then f has no local extreme value at c.

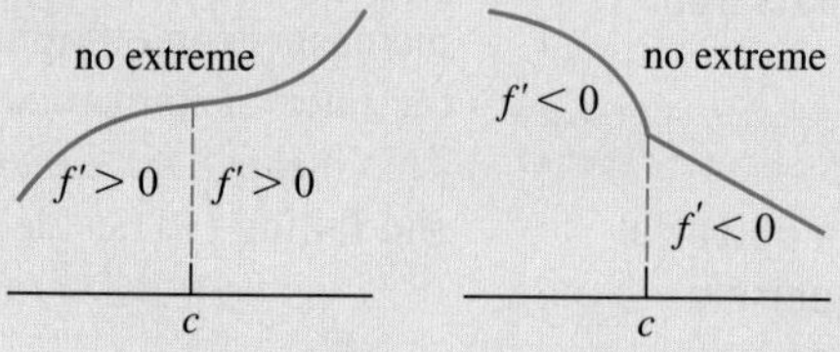

(a) $f'(c) = 0$ (b) $f'(c)$ undefined

At a left endpoint *a*:

If $f' < 0$ $(f' > 0)$ for $x > a$, then f has a local maximum (minimum) value at a.

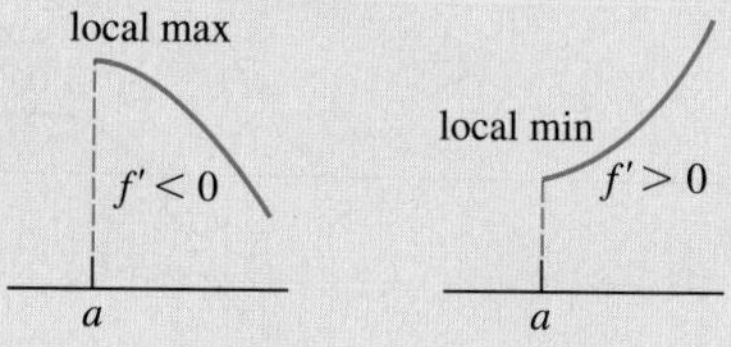

At a right endpoint *b*:

If $f' < 0$ $(f' > 0)$ for $x < b$, then f has a local minimum (maximum) value at b.

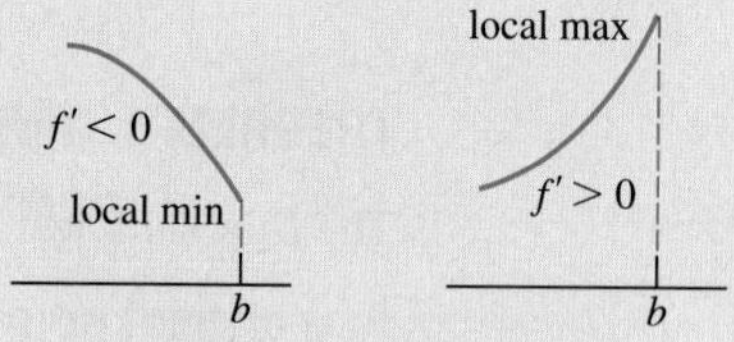

Here is how we apply the First Derivative Test to find the local extrema of a function. The critical points of a function f partition the x-axis into intervals on which f' is either positive or negative. We determine the sign of f' in each interval by evaluating f' for one value of x in the interval. Then we apply Theorem 4 as shown in Examples 1 and 2.

EXAMPLE 1 Using the First Derivative Test

For each of the following functions, use the First Derivative Test to find the local extreme values. Identify any absolute extrema.

(a) $f(x) = x^3 - 12x - 5$ **(b)** $g(x) = (x^2 - 3)e^x$

continued

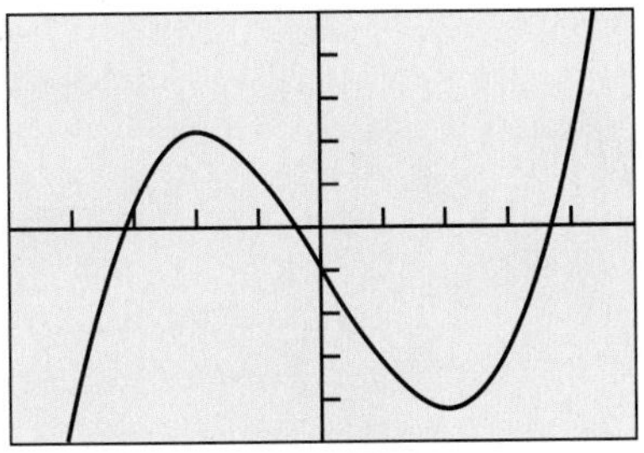

[–5, 5] by [–25, 25]

Figure 5.19 The graph of $f(x) = x^3 - 12x - 5$.

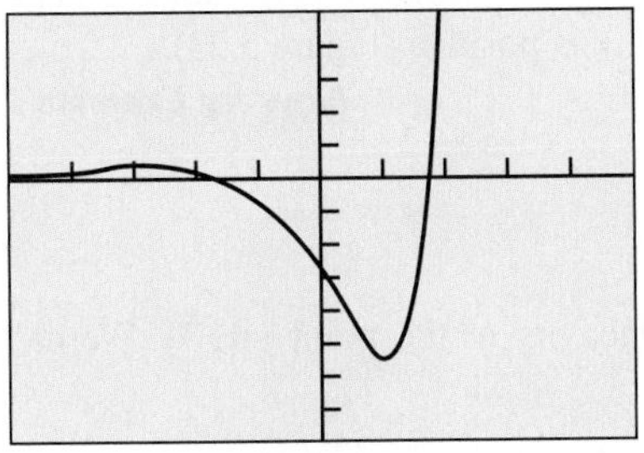

[–5, 5] by [–8, 5]

Figure 5.20 The graph of $g(x) = (x^2 - 3)e^x$.

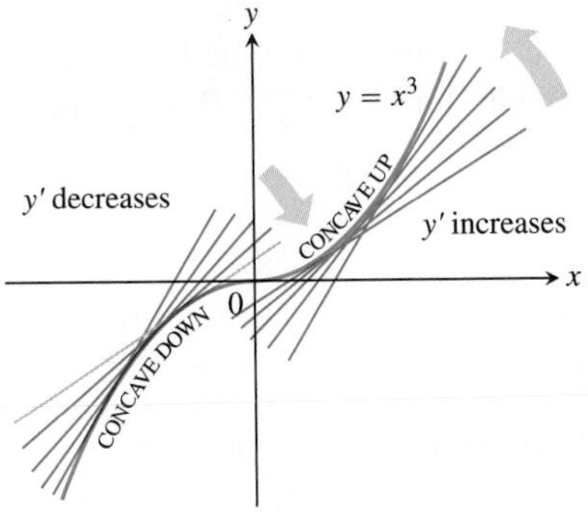

Figure 5.21 The graph of $y = x^3$ is concave down on $(-\infty, 0)$ and concave up on $(0, \infty)$.

SOLUTION

(a) Since f is differentiable for all real numbers, the only possible critical points are the zeros of f'. Solving $f'(x) = 3x^2 - 12 = 0$, we find the zeros to be $x = 2$ and $x = -2$. The zeros partition the x-axis into three intervals, as shown below:

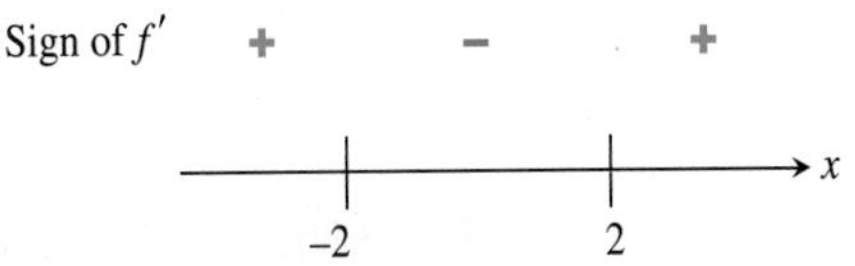

Using the First Derivative Test, we can see from the sign of f' on each interval that there is a local maximum at $x = -2$ and a local minimum at $x = 2$. The local maximum value is $f(-2) = 11$, and the local minimum value is $f(2) = -21$. There are no absolute extrema, as the function has range $(-\infty, \infty)$ (Figure 5.19).

(b) Since g is differentiable for all real numbers, the only possible critical points are the zeros of g'. Since $g'(x) = (x^2 - 3) \bullet e^x + (2x) \bullet e^x = (x^2 + 2x - 3) \bullet e^x$, we find the zeros of g' to be $x = 1$ and $x = -3$. The zeros partition the x-axis into three intervals, as shown below:

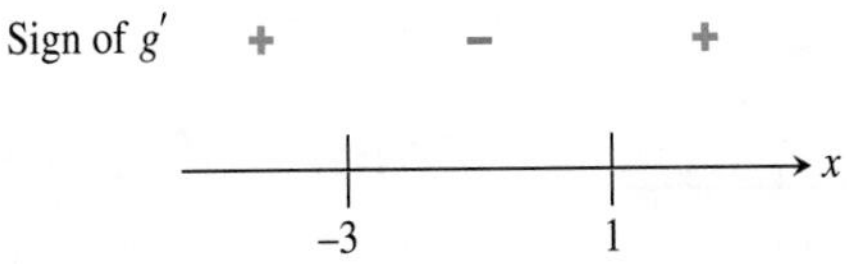

Using the First Derivative Test, we can see from the sign of f' on each interval that there is a local maximum at $x = -3$ and a local minimum at $x = 1$. The local maximum value is $g(-3) = 6e^{-3} \approx 0.299$, and the local minimum value is $g(1) = -2e \approx -5.437$. Although this function has the same increasing–decreasing–increasing pattern as f, its left end behavior is quite different. We see that $\lim_{x \to -\infty} g(x) = 0$, so the graph approaches the y-axis asymptotically and is therefore bounded below. This makes $g(1)$ an *absolute* minimum. Since $\lim_{x \to \infty} g(x) = \infty$, there is no absolute maximum (Figure 5.20).

Now Try Exercise 3.

Concavity

As you can see in Figure 5.21, the function $y = x^3$ rises as x increases, but the portions defined on the intervals $(-\infty, 0)$ and $(0, \infty)$ *turn* in different ways. Looking at tangents as we scan from left to right, we see that the slope y' of the curve decreases on the interval $(-\infty, 0)$ and then increases on the interval $(0, \infty)$. The curve $y = x^3$ is *concave down* on $(-\infty, 0)$ and *concave up* on $(0, \infty)$. The curve lies below the tangents where it is concave down, and above the tangents where it is concave up.

DEFINITION Concavity

The graph of a differentiable function $y = f(x)$ is

(a) concave up on an open interval I if y' is increasing on I.

(b) concave down on an open interval I if y' is decreasing on I.

If a function $y = f(x)$ has a second derivative, then we can conclude that y' increases if $y'' > 0$ and y' decreases if $y'' < 0$.

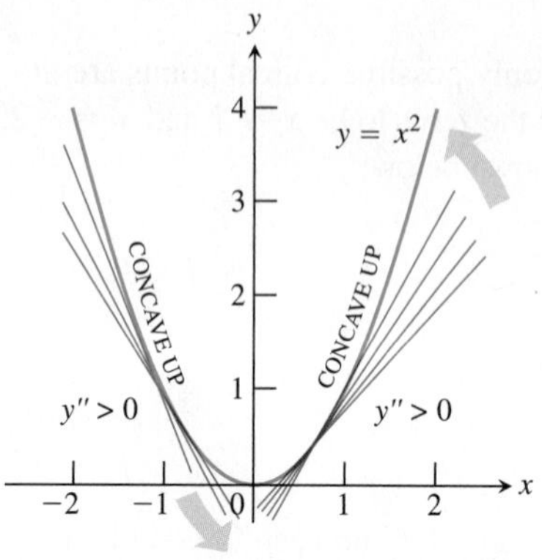

Figure 5.22 The graph of $y = x^2$ is concave up on any interval. (Example 2)

$y_1 = 3 + \sin x$, $y_2 = -\sin x$

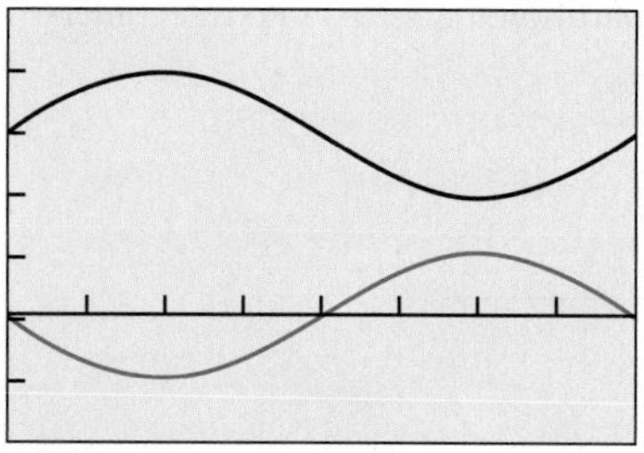

[0, 2π] by [–2, 5]

Figure 5.23 Using the graph of y'' to determine the concavity of y. (Example 2)

Concavity Test

The graph of a twice-differentiable function $y = f(x)$ is

(a) concave up on any interval where $y'' > 0$.

(b) concave down on any interval where $y'' < 0$.

EXAMPLE 2 Determining Concavity

Use the Concavity Test to determine the concavity of the given functions on the given intervals:

(a) $y = x^2$ on $(3, 10)$ **(b)** $y = 3 + \sin x$ on $(0, 2\pi)$

SOLUTION

(a) Since $y'' = 2$ is always positive, the graph of $y = x^2$ is concave up on *any* interval. In particular, it is concave up on $(3, 10)$ (Figure 5.22).

(b) The graph of $y = 3 + \sin x$ is concave down on $(0, \pi)$, where $y'' = -\sin x$ is negative. It is concave up on $(\pi, 2\pi)$, where $y'' = -\sin x$ is positive (Figure 5.23).

Now Try Exercise 7.

Points of Inflection

The curve $y = 3 + \sin x$ in Example 2 changes concavity at the point $(\pi, 3)$. We call $(\pi, 3)$ a *point of inflection* of the curve.

DEFINITION Point of Inflection

A point where the graph of a function has a tangent line and where the concavity changes is a **point of inflection.**

A point on a curve where y'' is positive on one side and negative on the other is a point of inflection. At such a point, y'' is either zero (because derivatives have the Intermediate Value Property) or undefined. If y is a twice differentiable function, $y'' = 0$ at a point of inflection and y' has a local maximum or minimum.

EXAMPLE 3 Finding Points of Inflection

Find all points of inflection of the graph of $y = e^{-x^2}$.

SOLUTION

First we find the second derivative, recalling the Chain and Product Rules:

$$\begin{aligned} y &= e^{-x^2} \\ y' &= e^{-x^2} \cdot (-2x) \\ y'' &= e^{-x^2} \cdot (-2x) \cdot (-2x) + e^{-x^2} \cdot (-2) \\ &= e^{-x^2}(4x^2 - 2) \end{aligned}$$

The factor e^{-x^2} is always positive, while the factor $(4x^2 - 2)$ changes sign at $-\sqrt{1/2}$ and at $\sqrt{1/2}$. Since y'' must also change sign at these two numbers, the points of inflection are $(-\sqrt{1/2}, 1/\sqrt{e})$ and $(\sqrt{1/2}, 1/\sqrt{e})$. We confirm our solution graphically by observing the changes of curvature in Figure 5.24.

Now Try Exercise 13.

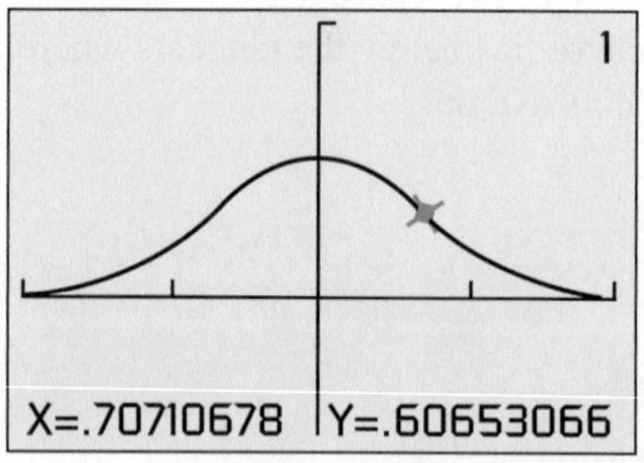

[–2, 2] by [–1, 2]

Figure 5.24 Graphical confirmation that the graph of $y = e^{-x^2}$ has a point of inflection at $x = \sqrt{1/2}$ (and hence also at $x = -\sqrt{1/2}$. (Example 3)

EXAMPLE 4 Reading the Graph of the Derivative

The graph of the *derivative* of a function *f* on the interval $[-4, 4]$ is shown in Figure 5.25. Answer the following questions about *f*, justifying each answer with information obtained from the graph of f'.

(a) On what intervals is *f* increasing?

(b) On what intervals is the graph of *f* concave up?

(c) At which *x*-coordinates does *f* have local extrema?

(d) What are the *x*-coordinates of all inflection points of the graph of *f*?

(e) Sketch a possible graph of *f* on the interval $[-4, 4]$.

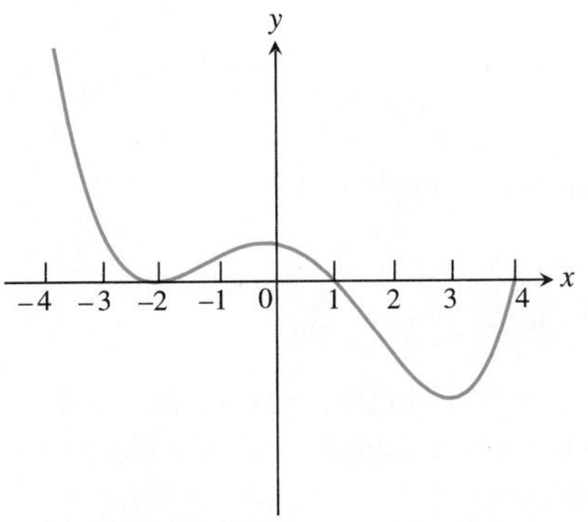

Figure 5.25 The graph of f' the derivative of *f*, on the interval $[-4, 4]$.

SOLUTION

Often, making a chart showing where f' is positive and negative and where f' is increasing and decreasing helps to understand the behavior of the function *f* (whose derivative is f'). The following chart is based on Figure 5.25.

Intervals	$-4 \le x < -2$	$-2 < x \le 0$	$0 < x \le 1$	$1 < x \le 3$	$3 < x \le 4$
Sign of f'	positive	positive	positive	negative	negative
Graph of f'	decreasing	increasing	decreasing	decreasing	increasing

(a) Since $f' > 0$ on the intervals $[-4, -2)$ and $(-2, 1)$, the function *f* must be increasing on the entire interval $[-4, 1]$ with a horizontal tangent at $x = -2$ (a "shelf point").

(b) The graph of *f* is concave up on the intervals where f' is increasing. We see from the graph that f' is increasing on the intervals $(-2, 0)$ and $(3, 4)$.

(c) By the First Derivative Test, there is a local maximum at $x = 1$ because the sign of f' changes from positive to negative there. Note that there is no extremum at $x = -2$, since f' does not change sign. Because the function increases from the left endpoint and decreases to the right endpoint, there are local minima at the endpoints $x = -4$ and $x = 4$.

(d) The inflection points of the graph of *f* have the same *x*-coordinates as the turning points of the graph of f', namely -2, 0, and 3.

(e) A possible graph satisfying all the conditions is shown in Figure 5.26.

Now Try Exercise 23.

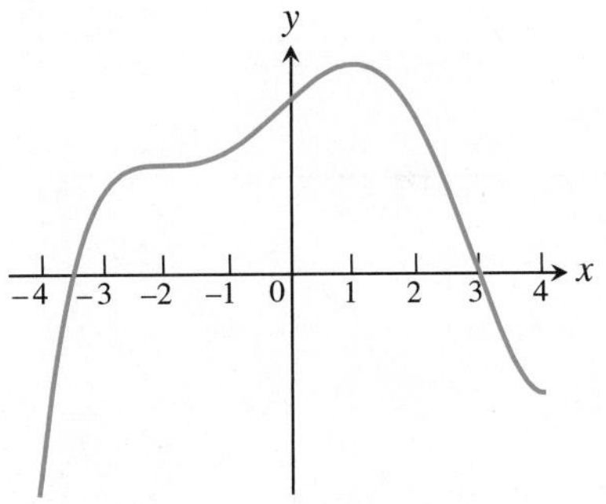

Figure 5.26 A possible graph of *f*. (Example 4)

Caution: It is tempting to oversimplify a point of inflection as a point where the second derivative is zero, but that can be wrong for two reasons:

1. *The second derivative can be zero at a noninflection point.* For example, consider the function $f(x) = x^4$ (Figure 5.27). Since $f''(x) = 12x^2$, we have $f''(0) = 0$; however, $(0, 0)$ is not an inflection point. Note that f' does not *change sign* at $x = 0$.
2. *The second derivative need not be zero at an inflection point.* For example, consider the function $f(x) = \sqrt[3]{x}$ (Figure 5.28). The concavity changes at $x = 0$, but there is a *vertical* tangent line, so both $f'(0)$ and $f''(0)$ fail to exist.

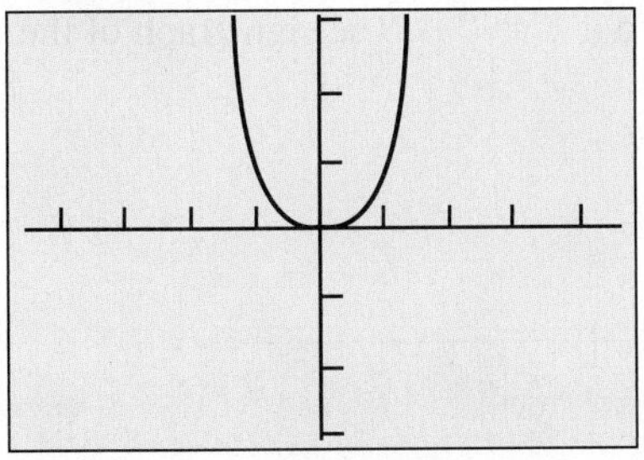

[−4.7, 4.7] by [−3.1, 3.1]

Figure 5.27 The function $f(x) = x^4$ does not have a point of inflection at the origin, even though $f''(0) = 0$.

Therefore, the only safe way to test algebraically for a point of inflection is to confirm a sign change of the second derivative. This *could* occur at a point where the second derivative is zero, but it also could occur at a point where the second derivative fails to exist.

To study the motion of a body moving along a line, we often graph the body's position as a function of time. One reason for doing so is to reveal where the body's acceleration, given by the second derivative, changes sign. On the graph, these are the points of inflection.

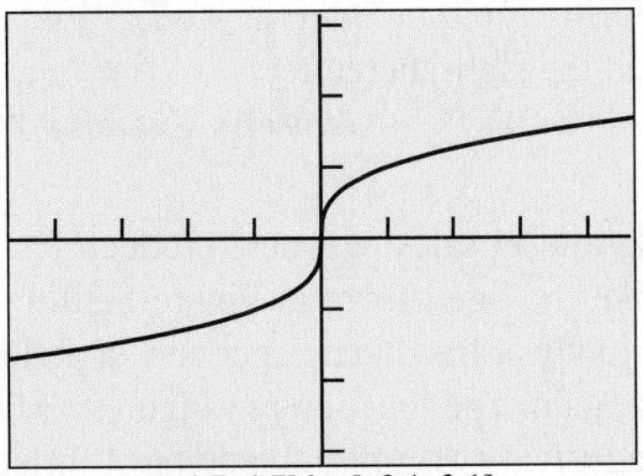

[−4.7, 4.7] by [−3.1, 3.1]

Figure 5.28 The function $f(x) = \sqrt[3]{x}$ has a point of inflection at the origin, even though $f''(0) \neq 0$.

EXAMPLE 5 Studying Motion Along a Line

A particle is moving along the *x*-axis with position function

$$x(t) = 2t^3 - 14t^2 + 22t - 5, \quad t \ge 0.$$

Find the velocity and acceleration, and describe the motion of the particle.

continued

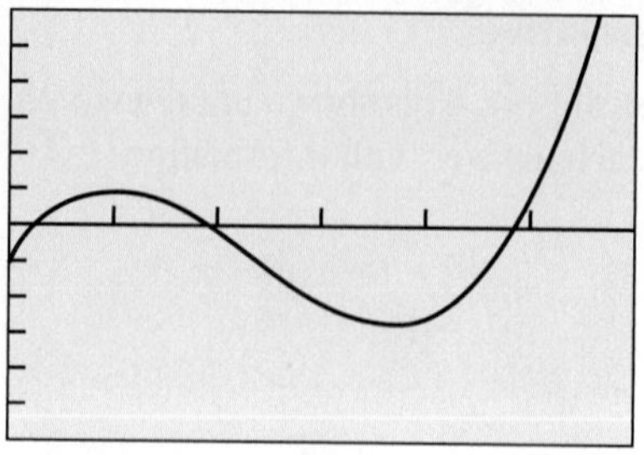

[0, 6] by [–30, 30]
(a)

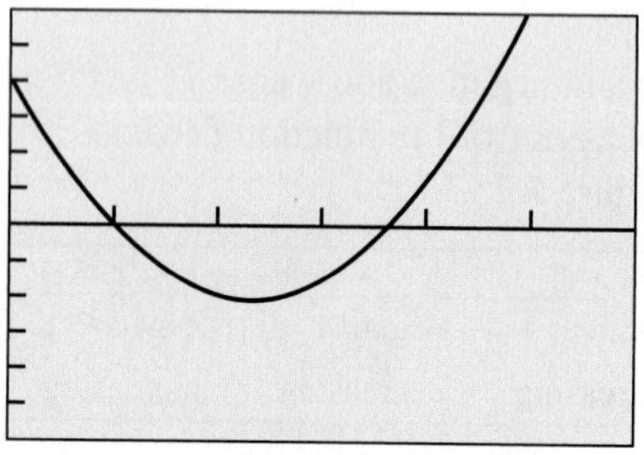

[0, 6] by [–30, 30]
(b)

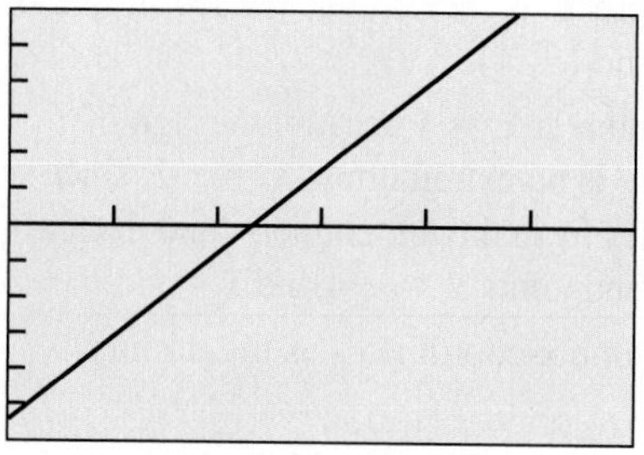

[0, 6] by [–30, 30]
(c)

Figure 5.29 The graph of
(a) $x(t) = 2t^3 - 14t^2 + 22t - 5, t \geq 0$,
(b) $x'(t) = 6t^2 - 28t + 22$, and
(c) $x''(t) = 12t - 28$. (Example 5)

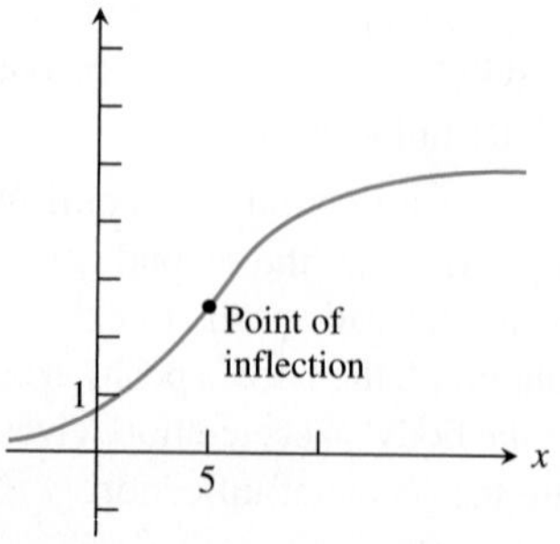

Figure 5.30 A logistic curve

$$y = \frac{c}{1 + ae^{-bx}}.$$

SOLUTION

Solve Analytically

The velocity is

$$v(t) = x'(t) = 6t^2 - 28t + 22 = 2(t - 1)(3t - 11),$$

and the acceleration is

$$a(t) = v'(t) = x''(t) = 12t - 28 = 4(3t - 7).$$

When the function $x(t)$ is increasing, the particle is moving to the right on the x-axis; when $x(t)$ is decreasing, the particle is moving to the left. Figure 5.29 shows the graphs of the position, velocity, and acceleration of the particle.

Notice that the first derivative ($v = x'$) is zero when $t = 1$ and $t = 11/3$. These zeros partition the t-axis into three intervals, as shown in the sign graph of v below:

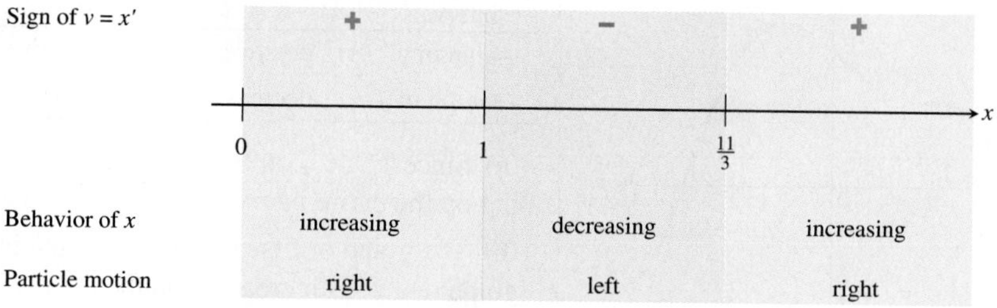

The particle is moving to the right in the time intervals $[0, 1)$ and $(11/3, \infty)$ and moving to the left in $(1, 11/3)$.

The acceleration $a(t) = 12t - 28$ has a single zero at $t = 7/3$. The sign graph of the acceleration is shown below:

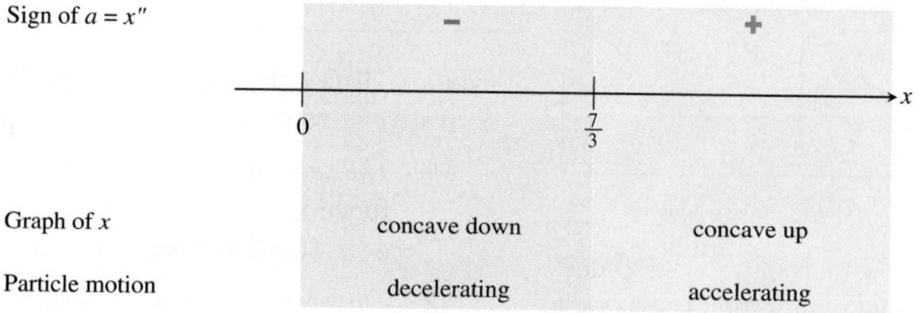

The accelerating force is directed toward the left during the time interval $[0, 7/3]$, is momentarily zero at $t = 7/3$, and is directed toward the right thereafter.

Now Try Exercise 25.

The growth of an individual company, of a population, in sales of a new product, or of salaries often follows a ***logistic*** or ***life cycle curve*** like the one shown in Figure 5.30. For example, sales of a new product will generally grow slowly at first, then experience a period of rapid growth. Eventually, sales growth slows down again. The function f in Figure 5.30 is increasing. Its rate of increase, f', is at first increasing ($f'' > 0$) up to the point of inflection, and then its rate of increase, f', is decreasing ($f'' < 0$). This is, in a sense, the opposite of what happens in Figure 5.21.

Some graphers have the logistic curve as a built-in regression model. We use this feature in Example 6.

TABLE 5.2 Population of Alaska

Years Since 1900	Population
30	59,278
40	75,524
50	128,643
60	226,167
70	302,583
80	401,851
90	550,043
100	626,932
109	698,473

Source: Bureau of the Census, U.S. Chamber of Commerce; www.quickfacts.census.gov.

EXAMPLE 6 Population Growth in Alaska

Table 5.2 shows the population of Alaska from 1930 to 2009 in years since 1900.

(a) Find the logistic regression for the data.

(b) Use the regression equation to predict the Alaskan population in the 2020 census.

(c) Find the inflection point of the regression equation. What significance does the inflection point have in terms of population growth in Alaska?

(d) What does the regression equation indicate about the population of Alaska in the long run?

SOLUTION

(a) Using years since 1900 as the independent variable and population as the dependent variable, the logistic regression equation is approximately

$$y = \frac{846003}{1 + 80.902e^{-0.0547x}}$$

Its graph is superimposed on a scatter plot of the data in Figure 5.31(a). Store the regression equation as Y1 in your calculator.

(b) The calculator reports Y1(120) to be approximately 759,204.094. (Given the uncertainty of this kind of extrapolation, it is probably more reasonable to say "approximately 759,200.")

(c) The inflection point will occur where y'' changes sign. Finding y'' algebraically would be tedious, but we can graph the numerical derivative of the numerical derivative and find the zero graphically. Figure 5.31(b) shows the graph of y'', which is nDeriv(nDeriv(Y1,X,X),X,X) in calculator syntax. The zero is approximately 80, so the inflection point occurred in 1980, when the population was about 402,000 and growing the fastest.

(d) Notice that $\lim_{x\to\infty} \frac{846003}{1 + 80.902e^{-0.0547x}} = 846003$, so the regression equation indicates that the population of Alaska will stabilize at about 846,003 in the long run. Do not put too much faith in this number, however, as human population is dependent on too many variables that can, and will, change over time.

Now Try Exercise 31.

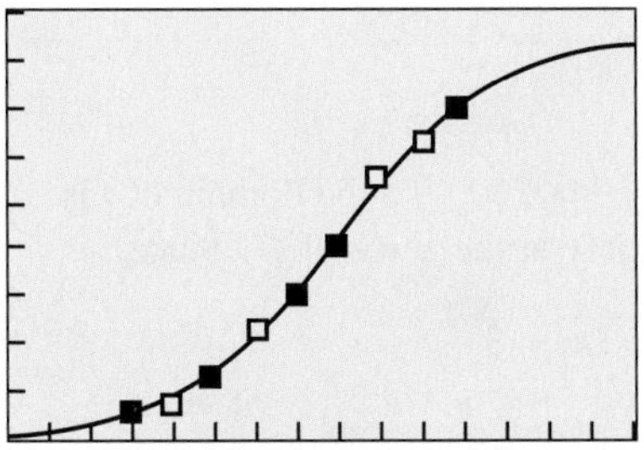

[0, 150] by [0, 900000]
(a)

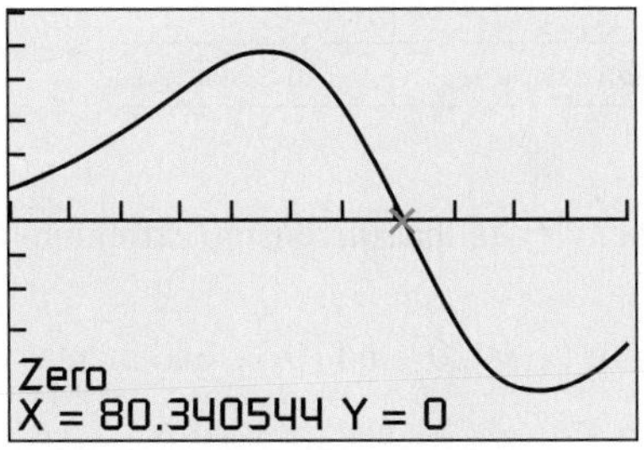

[10, 120] by [−300, 300]
(b)

Figure 5.31 (a) The logistic regression curve

$$y = \frac{846003}{1 + 80.902e^{-0.0547x}}$$

superimposed on the population data from Table 5.2, and (b) the graph of y'' showing a zero at about $x = 80.341$.

Second Derivative Test for Local Extrema

Instead of looking for sign changes in y' at critical points, we can sometimes use the following test to determine the presence of local extrema.

THEOREM 5 Second Derivative Test for Local Extrema

1. If $f'(c) = 0$ and $f''(c) < 0$, then f has a local maximum at $x = c$.
2. If $f'(c) = 0$ and $f''(c) > 0$, then f has a local minimum at $x = c$.

This test requires us to know f'' *only at c itself* and not in an interval about c. This makes the test easy to apply. That's the good news. The bad news is that the test fails if $f''(c) = 0$ or if $f''(c)$ fails to exist. When this happens, go back to the First Derivative Test for local extreme values.

In Example 7, we apply the Second Derivative Test to the function in Example 1.

EXAMPLE 7 Using the Second Derivative Test

Find the local extreme values of $f(x) = x^3 - 12x - 5$.

SOLUTION

We have

$$f'(x) = 3x^2 - 12 = 3(x^2 - 4)$$
$$f''(x) = 6x.$$

Testing the critical points $x = \pm 2$ (there are no endpoints), we find

$$f''(-2) = -12 < 0 \Rightarrow f \text{ has a local maximum at } x = -2 \text{ and}$$
$$f''(2) = 12 > 0 \Rightarrow f \text{ has a local minimum at } x = 2.$$

Now Try Exercise 35.

EXAMPLE 8 Using f' and f'' to Graph f

Let $f'(x) = 4x^3 - 12x^2$.

(a) Identify where the extrema of f occur.

(b) Find the intervals on which f is increasing and the intervals on which f is decreasing.

(c) Find where the graph of f is concave up and where it is concave down.

(d) Sketch a possible graph for f.

SOLUTION

f is continuous since f' exists. The domain of f' is $(-\infty, \infty)$, so the domain of f is also $(-\infty, \infty)$. Thus, the critical points of f occur only at the zeros of f'. Since

$$f'(x) = 4x^3 - 12x^2 = 4x^2(x - 3),$$

the first derivative is zero at $x = 0$ and $x = 3$.

Intervals	$x < 0$	$0 < x < 3$	$3 < x$
Sign of f'	$-$	$-$	$+$
Behavior of f	decreasing	decreasing	increasing

(a) Using the First Derivative Test and the table above, we see that there is no extremum at $x = 0$ and a local minimum at $x = 3$.

(b) Using the table above, we see that f is decreasing in $(-\infty, 0]$ and $[0,3]$, and increasing in $[3, \infty)$.

(c) $f''(x) = 12x^2 - 24x = 12x(x - 2)$ is zero at $x = 0$ and $x = 2$.

Intervals	$x < 0$	$0 < x < 2$	$2 < x$
Sign of f''	$+$	$-$	$+$
Behavior of f	concave up	concave down	concave up

Note

The *Second Derivative Test* does not apply at $x = 0$ because $f''(0) = 0$. We need the First Derivative Test to see that there is no local extremum at $x = 0$.

We see that f is concave up on the intervals $(-\infty, 0)$ and $(2, \infty)$, and concave down on $(0, 2)$.

continued

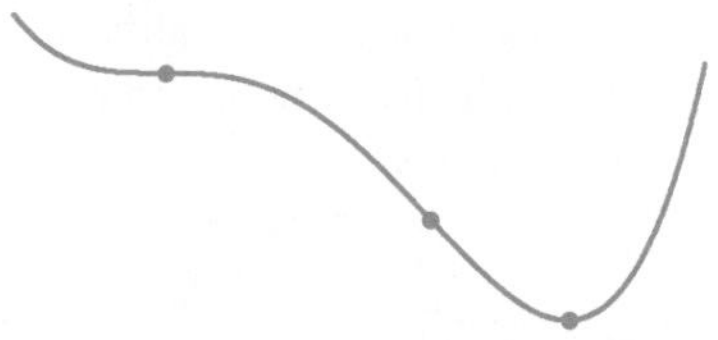

Figure 5.32 The graph for f has no extremum but has points of inflection where $x = 0$ and $x = 2$, and a local minimum where $x = 3$. (Example 8)

(d) Summarizing the information in the two tables above, we obtain

$x < 0$	$0 < x < 2$	$0 < x < 3$	$x < 3$
decreasing	decreasing	decreasing	increasing
concave up	concave down	concave up	concave up

Figure 5.32 shows one possibility for the graph of f. ***Now Try Exercise 39***

EXPLORATION 1 Finding f from f'

Let $f'(x) = 4x^3 - 12x^2$.

1. Find three different functions with derivative equal to $f'(x)$. How are the graphs of the three functions related?
2. Compare their behavior with the behavior found in Example 8.

Learning About Functions from Derivatives

We have seen in Example 8 and Exploration 1 that we are able to recover almost everything we need to know about a differentiable function $y = f(x)$ by examining y'. We can find where the graph rises and falls and where any local extrema are assumed. We can differentiate y' to learn how the graph bends as it passes over the intervals of rise and fall. We can determine the shape of the function's graph. The only information we cannot get from the derivative is how to place the graph in the xy-plane. As we discovered in Section 5.2, the only additional information we need to position the graph is the value of f at one point.

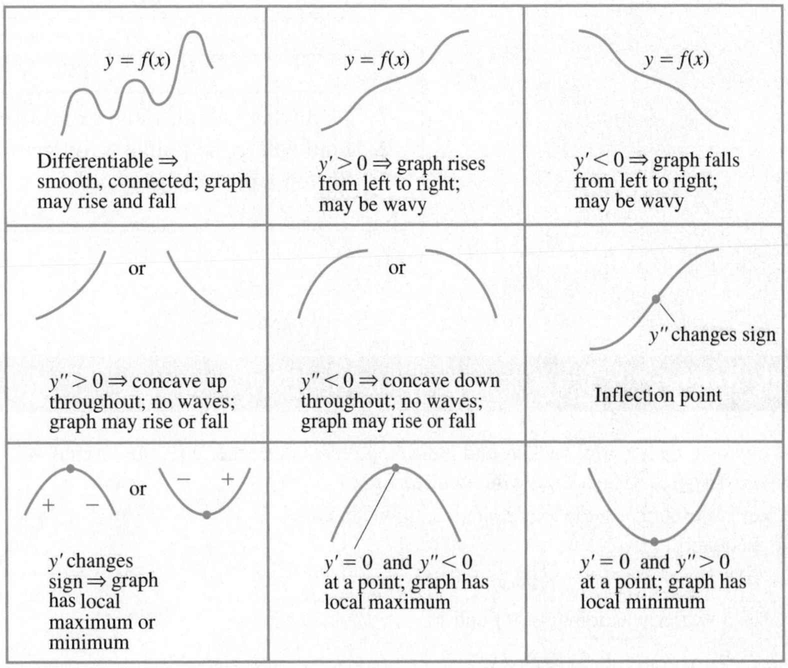

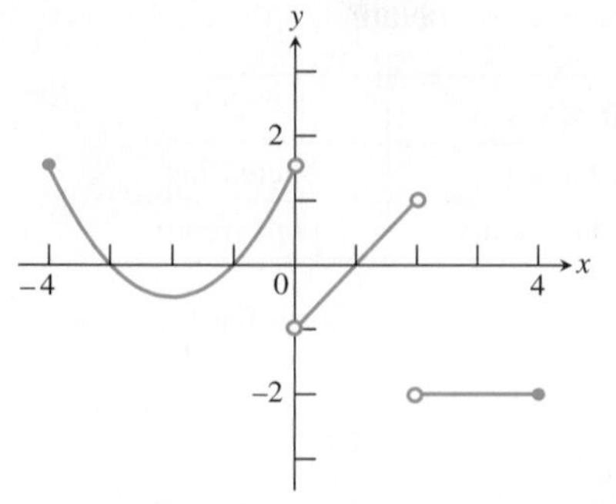

Figure 5.33 The graph of f', a discontinuous derivative.

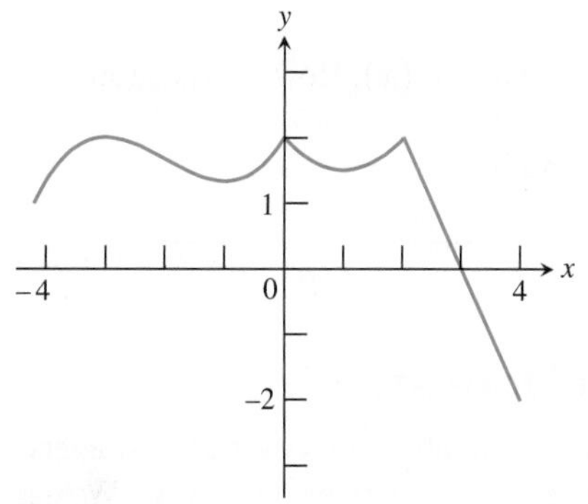

Figure 5.34 A possible graph of f. (Example 9)

Note

Because sign charts are very helpful, you will want to use and analyze them on a regular basis.

Remember also that a function can be continuous and still have points of nondifferentiability (cusps, corners, and points with vertical tangent lines). Thus, a noncontinuous graph of f' could lead to a continuous graph of f, as Example 9 shows.

EXAMPLE 9 Analyzing a Discontinuous Derivative

A function f is continuous on the interval $[-4, 4]$. The discontinuous function f', with domain $[-4, 0) \cup (0, 2) \cup (2, 4)]$, is shown in the graph to the left (Figure 5.33).
(a) Find the x-coordinates of all local extrema and points of inflection of f.
(b) Sketch a possible graph of f.

SOLUTION

(a) For extrema, we look for places where f' changes sign. There are local maxima at $x = -3$, 0, and 2 (where f' goes from positive to negative) and local minima at $x = -1$ and 1 (where f' goes from negative to positive). There are also local minima at the two endpoints $x = -4$ and 4, because f' starts positive at the left endpoint and ends negative at the right endpoint.

For points of inflection, we look for places where f'' changes sign, that is, where the graph of f' changes direction. This occurs only at $x = -2$.

(b) A possible graph of f is shown in Figure 5.34. The derivative information determines the shape of the three components, and the continuity condition determines that the three components must be linked together. ***Now Try Exercises 49 and 53.***

EXPLORATION 2 Finding f from f' and f''

A function f is continuous on its domain $[-2, 4]$, $f(-2) = 5$, $f(4) = 1$, and f' and f'' have the following properties.

x	$-2 < x < 0$	$x = 0$	$0 < x < 2$	$x = 2$	$2 < x < 4$
f'	+	does not exist	−	0	−
f''	+	does not exist	+	0	−

1. Find where all absolute extrema of f occur.
2. Find where the points of inflection of f occur.
3. Sketch a possible graph of f.

Quick Review 5.3 *(For help, go to Sections 1.3, 2.2, 3.3, and 4.4.)*

Exercise numbers with a gray background indicate problems that the authors have designed to be solved *without a calculator.*

In Exercises 1 and 2, factor the expression and use sign charts to solve the inequality.

1. $x^2 - 9 < 0$ **2.** $x^3 - 4x > 0$

In Exercises 3–6, find the domains of f and f'.

3. $f(x) = xe^x$ **4.** $f(x) = x^{3/5}$

5. $f(x) = \dfrac{x}{x - 2}$ **6.** $f(x) = x^{2/5}$

In Exercises 7–10, find the horizontal asymptotes of the function's graph.

7. $y = (4 - x^2)e^x$ **8.** $y = (x^2 - x)e^{-x}$

9. $y = \dfrac{200}{1 + 10e^{-0.5x}}$ **10.** $y = \dfrac{750}{2 + 5e^{-0.1x}}$

Section 5.3 Exercises

In Exercises 1–6, use the **First Derivative Test** to determine the local extreme values of the function, and identify any absolute extrema. Support your answers graphically.

1. $y = x^2 - x - 1$

2. $y = -2x^3 + 6x^2 - 3$

3. $y = 2x^4 - 4x^2 + 1$

4. $y = xe^{1/x}$

5. $y = x\sqrt{8 - x^2}$

6. $y = \begin{cases} 3 - x^2, & x < 0 \\ x^2 + 1, & x \geq 0 \end{cases}$

In Exercises 7–12, use the Concavity Test to determine the intervals on which the graph of the function is **(a)** concave up and **(b)** concave down.

7. $y = 4x^3 + 21x^2 + 36x - 20$

8. $y = -x^4 + 4x^3 - 4x + 1$

9. $y = 2x^{1/5} + 3$

10. $y = 5 - x^{1/3}$

11. $y = \begin{cases} 2x, & x < 1 \\ 2 - x^2, & x \geq 1 \end{cases}$

12. $y = e^x, \quad 0 \leq x \leq 2\pi$

In Exercises 13 –20, find all points of inflection of the function.

13. $y = xe^x$

14. $y = x\sqrt{9 - x^2}$

15. $y = \tan^{-1} x$

16. $y = x^3(4 - x)$

17. $y = x^{1/3}(x - 4)$

18. $y = x^{1/2}(x + 3)$

19. $y = \dfrac{x^3 - 2x^2 + x - 1}{x - 2}$

20. $y = \dfrac{x}{x^2 + 1}$

In Exercises 21 and 22, use the graph of the function f to estimate where **(a)** f' and **(b)** f'' are 0, positive, and negative.

21.

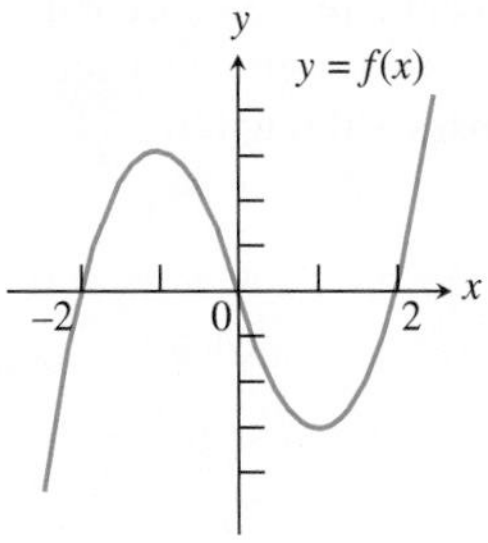

22.

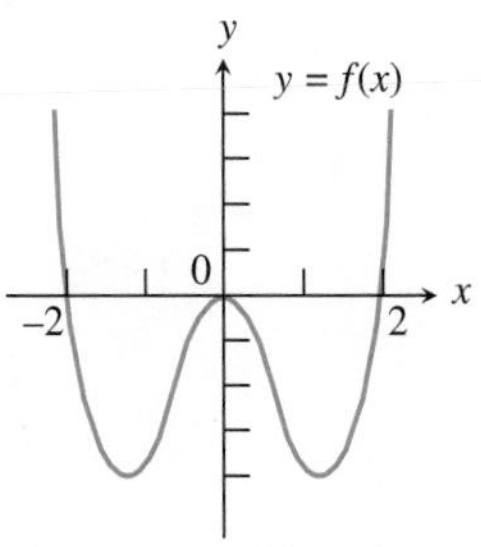

In Exercises 23 and 24, use the graph of the function f' to estimate the intervals on which the function f is **(a)** increasing or **(b)** decreasing. Also, **(c)** estimate the x-coordinates of all local extreme values.

23.

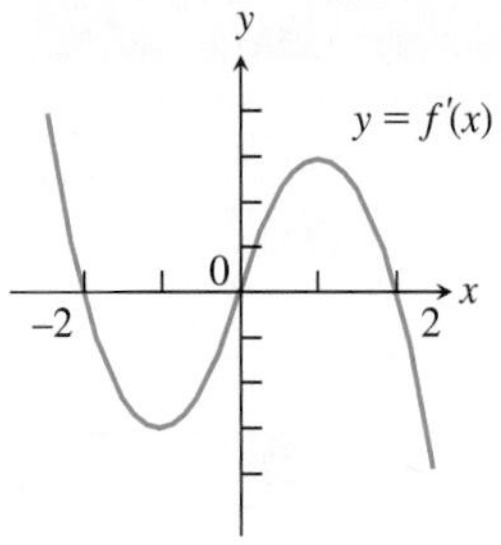

24.

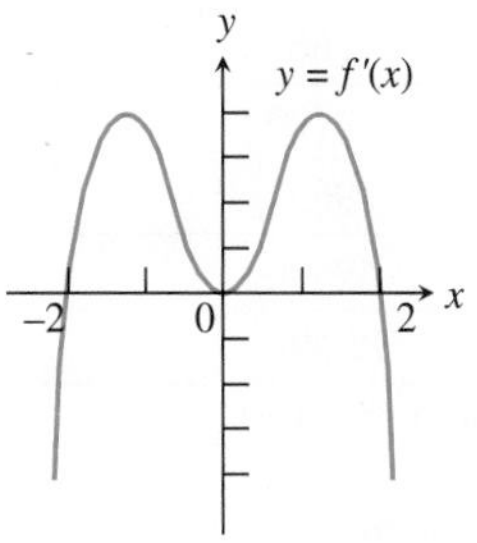

In Exercises 25–28, a particle is moving along the x-axis with position function $x(t)$. Find the **(a)** velocity and **(b)** acceleration, and **(c)** describe the motion of the particle for $t \geq 0$.

25. $x(t) = t^2 - 4t + 3$

26. $x(t) = 6 - 2t - t^2$

27. $x(t) = t^3 - 3t + 3$

28. $x(t) = 3t^2 - 2t^3$

In Exercises 29 and 30, the graph of the position function $y = s(t)$ of a particle moving along a line is given. At approximately what times is the particle's **(a)** velocity equal to zero? **(b)** acceleration equal to zero?

29.

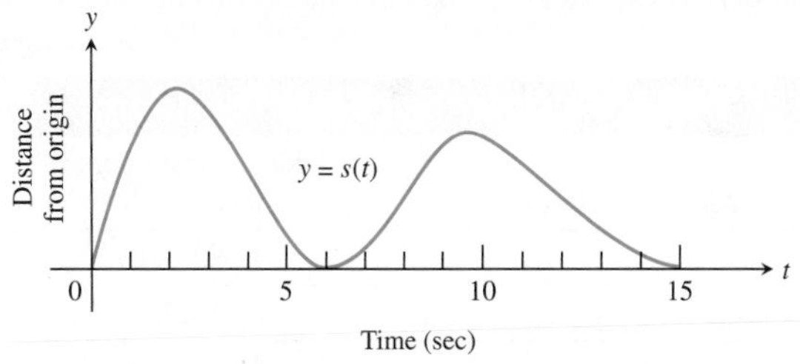

30.

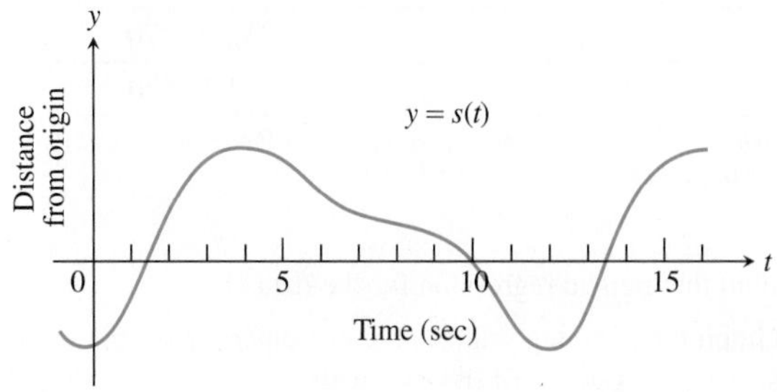

31. Table 5.3 shows the population of Pennsylvania in each 10-year census between 1830 and 1950.

TABLE 5.3 Population of Pennsylvania

Years Since 1820	Population in Thousands
10	1348
20	1724
30	2312
40	2906
50	3522
60	4283
70	5258
80	6302
90	7665
100	8720
110	9631
120	9900
130	10,498

Source: Bureau of the Census, U.S. Chamber of Commerce.

(a) Find the logistic regression for the data.

(b) Graph the data in a scatter plot and superimpose the regression curve.

(c) Use the regression equation to predict the Pennsylvania population in the 2000 census.

(d) In what year was the Pennsylvania population growing the fastest? What significant behavior does the graph of the regression equation exhibit at that point?

(e) What does the regression equation indicate about the population of Pennsylvania in the long run?

32. In 1977, there were 12,168,450 basic cable television subscribers in the United States. Table 5.4 shows the cumulative number of subscribers added to that baseline number from 1978 to 1985.

TABLE 5.4 Growth of Cable Television

Years Since 1977	Added Subscribers Since 1977
1	1,391,910
2	2,814,380
3	5,671,490
4	11,219,200
5	17,340,570
6	22,113,790
7	25,290,870
8	27,872,520

Source: Nielsen Media Research, as reported in *The World Almanac and Book of Facts 2004.*

(a) Find the logistic regression for the data.

(b) Graph the data in a scatter plot and superimpose the regression curve. Does it fit the data well?

(c) In what year between 1977 and 1985 were basic cable TV subscriptions growing the fastest? What significant behavior does the graph of the regression equation exhibit at that point?

(d) What does the regression equation indicate about the number of basic cable television subscribers in the long run? (Be sure to add the baseline 1977 number.)

(e) **Writing to Learn** In fact, the long-run number of basic cable subscribers predicted by the regression equation falls short of the actual 2010 number by more than 20 million. What circumstances changed to render the earlier model so ineffective?

In Exercises 33–38, use the Second Derivative Test to find the local extrema for the function.

33. $y = 3x - x^3 + 5$

34. $y = x^5 - 80 + 100$

35. $y = x^3 + 3x^2 - 2$

36. $y = 3x^5 - 25x^3 + 60x + 20$

37. $y = xe^x$

38. $y = xe^{-x}$

In Exercises 39 and 40, use the derivative of the function $y = f(x)$ to find the points at which f has a

(a) local maximum, **(b)** local minimum, or

(c) point of inflection.

39. $y' = (x - 1)^2(x - 2)$

40. $y' = (x - 1)^2(x - 2)(x - 4)$

Exercises 41 and 42 show the graphs of the first and second derivatives of a function $y = f(x)$. Copy the figure and add a sketch of a possible graph of f that passes through the point P.

41.

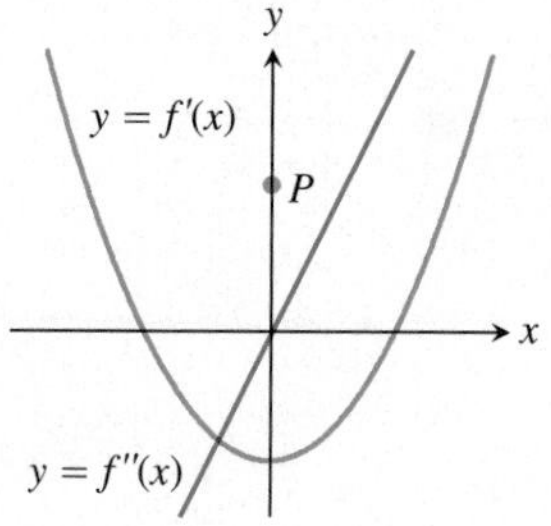

42.

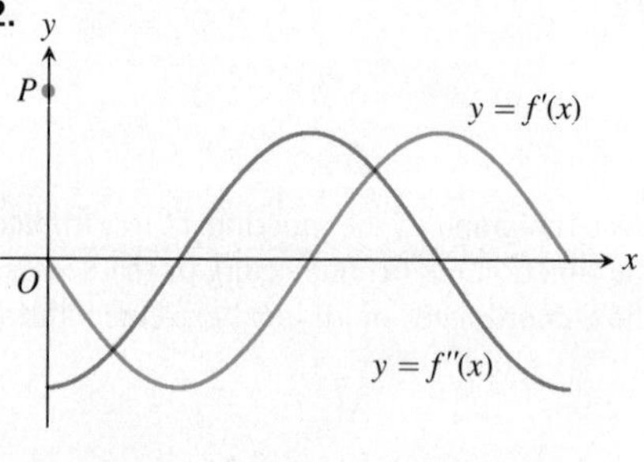

43. Writing to Learn If $f(x)$ is a differentiable function and $f'(c) = 0$ at an interior point c of f's domain, must f have a local maximum or minimum at $x = c$? Explain.

44. Writing to Learn If $f(x)$ is a twice-differentiable function and $f''(c) = 0$ at an interior point c of f's domain, must f have an inflection point at $x = c$? Explain.

45. *Connecting f and f′* Sketch a smooth curve $y = f(x)$ through the origin with the properties that $f'(x) < 0$ for $x < 0$ and $f'(x) > 0$ for $x > 0$.

46. *Connecting f and f″* Sketch a smooth curve $y = f(x)$ through the origin with the properties that $f''(x) < 0$ for $x < 0$ and $f''(x) > 0$ for $x > 0$.

47. *Connecting f, f′, and f″* Sketch a continuous curve $y = f(x)$ with the following properties. Label coordinates where possible.

$f(-2) = 8$	$f'(x) > 0$ for) $\|x\| > 2$
$f(0) = 4$	$f'(x) < 0$ for) $\|x\| < 2$
$f(2) = 0$	$f''(x) < 0$ for $x < 0$
$f'(2) = f'(-2) = 0$	$f''(x) > 0$ for $x > 0$

48. *Using Behavior to Sketch* Sketch a continuous curve $y = f(x)$ with the following properties. Label coordinates where possible.

x	y	Curve
$x < 2$		falling, concave up
2	1	horizontal tangent
$2 < x < 4$		rising, concave up
4	4	inflection point
$4 < x < 6$		rising, concave down
6	7	horizontal tangent
$x > 6$		falling, concave down

In Exercises 49 and 50, use the graph of f' to estimate the intervals on which the function f is **(a)** increasing or **(b)** decreasing. Also, **(c)** estimate the x-coordinates of all local extreme values. (Assume that the function f is continuous, even at the points where f' is undefined.)

49. The domain of f' is $[0,4) \cup (4,6]$.

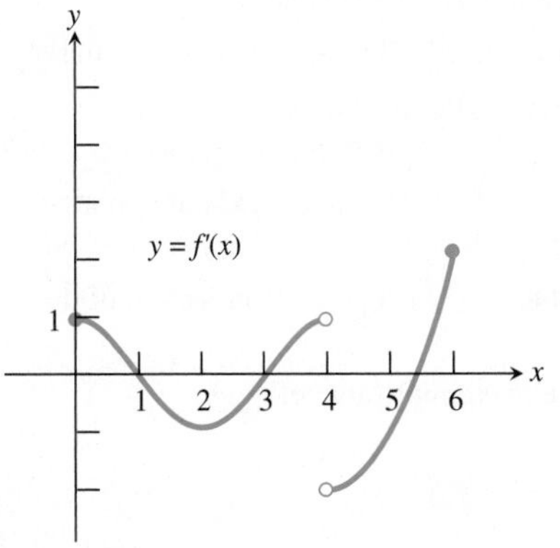

50. The domain of f' is $[0,1) \cup (1,2) \cup (2,3]$.

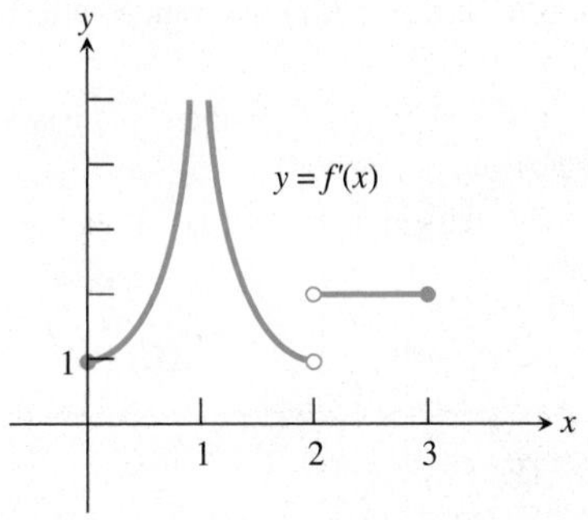

Group Activity In Exercises 51 and 52, do the following.

(a) Find the absolute extrema of f and where they occur.

(b) Find any points of inflection.

(c) Sketch a possible graph of f.

51. f is continuous on $[0, 3]$ and satisfies the following.

x	0	1	2	3
f	0	2	0	−2
f'	3	0	does not exist	−3
f''	0	−1	does not exist	0

x	$0 < x < 1$	$1 < x < 2$	$2 < x < 3$
f	+	+	−
f'	+	−	−
f''	−	−	−

52. f is an even function, continuous on $[-3, 3]$, and satisfies the following.

x	0	1	2
f	2	0	−1
f'	does not exist	0	does not exist
f''	does not exist	0	does not exist

x	$0 < x < 1$	$1 < x < 2$	$2 < x < 3$
f	+	−	−
f'	−	−	+
f''	+	−	−

(d) What can you conclude about $f(3)$ and $f(-3)$?

Group Activity In Exercises 53 and 54, sketch a possible graph of a continuous function f that has the given properties.

53. Domain $[0, 6]$, graph of f' given in Exercise 49, and $f(0) = 2$.

54. Domain $[0, 3]$, graph of f' given in Exercise 50, and $f(0) = -3$.

Standardized Test Questions

55. True or False If $f''(c) = 0$, then $(c, f(c))$ is a point of inflection. Justify your answer.

56. True or False If $f'(c) = 0$ and $f''(c) < 0$, then $f(c)$ is a local maximum. Justify your answer.

57. Multiple Choice If $a < 0$, the graph of $y = ax^3 + 3x^2 + 4x + 5$ is concave up on

(A) $\left(-\infty, -\frac{1}{a}\right)$ **(B)** $\left(-\infty, \frac{1}{a}\right)$ **(C)** $\left(-\frac{1}{a}, \infty\right)$

(D) $\left(\frac{1}{a}, \infty\right)$ **(E)** $(-\infty, -1)$

58. Multiple Choice If $f(0) = f'(0) = f''(0) = 0$, which of the following *must be true*?

(A) There is a local maximum of f at the origin.

(B) There is a local minimum of f at the origin.

(C) There is no local extremum of f at the origin.

(D) There is a point of inflection of the graph of f at the origin.

(E) There is a horizontal tangent to the graph of f at the origin.

59. Multiple Choice The x-coordinates of the points of inflection of the graph of $y = x^5 - 5x^4 + 3x + 7$ are

(A) 0 only **(B)** 1 only **(C)** 3 only **(D)** 0 and 3 **(E)** 0 and 1

60. Multiple Choice Which of the following conditions would enable you to conclude that the graph of f has a point of inflection at $x = c$?

(A) There is a local maximum of f' at $x = c$.

(B) $f''(c) = 0$.

(C) $f''(c)$ does not exist.

(D) The sign of f' changes at $x = c$.

(E) f is a cubic polynomial and $C = 0$.

Exploration

61. *Graphs of Cubics* There is almost no leeway in the locations of the inflection point and the extrema of $f(x) = ax^3 + bx^2 + cx + d$, $a \neq 0$, because the one inflection point occurs at $x = -b/(3a)$ and the extrema, if any, must be located symmetrically about this value of x. Check this out by examining **(a)** the cubic in Exercise 7 and **(b)** the cubic in Exercise 2. Then **(c)** prove the general case.

Extending the Ideas

In Exercises 62 and 63, feel free to use a CAS (computer algebra system), if you have one, to solve the problem.

62. *Logistic Functions* Let $f(x) = c/(1 + ae^{-bx})$ with $a > 0$, $abc \neq 0$.

(a) Show that f is increasing on the interval $(-\infty, \infty)$ if $abc > 0$, and decreasing if $abc < 0$.

(b) Show that the point of inflection of f occurs at $x = (\text{In } |a|)/b$.

63. *Quartic Polynomial Functions* Let $f(x) = ax^4 + bx^3 + cx^2 + dx + e$ with $a \neq 0$.

(a) Show that the graph of f has 0 or 2 points of inflection.

(b) Write a condition that must be satisfied by the coefficients if the graph of f has 0 or 2 points of inflection.

Quick Quiz for AP* Preparation: Sections 5.1–5.3

1. Multiple Choice How many critical points does the function $f(x) = (x - 2)^5 (x + 3)^4$ have?

(A) One **(B)** Two **(C)** Three **(D)** Five **(E)** Nine

2. Multiple Choice For what value of x does the function $f(x) = (x - 2)(x - 3)^2$ have a relative maximum?

(A) -3 **(B)** $-\frac{7}{3}$ **(C)** $-\frac{5}{2}$ **(D)** $\frac{7}{3}$ **(E)** $\frac{5}{2}$

3. Multiple Choice If g is a differentiable function such that $g(x) < 0$ for all real numbers x, and if $f'(x) = (x^2 - 9)g(x)$, which of the following is true?

(A) f has a relative maximum at $x = -3$ and a relative minimum at $x = 3$.

(B) f has a relative minimum at $x = -3$ and a relative maximum at $x = 3$.

(C) f has relative minima at $x = -3$ and at $x = 3$.

(D) f has relative maxima at $x = -3$ and at $x = 3$.

(E) It cannot be determined if f has any relative extrema.

4. Free Response Let f be the function given by $f(x) = 3 \text{ In } (x^2 + 2) - 2x$ with domain $[-2, 4]$.

(a) Find the coordinate of each relative maximum point and each relative minimum point of f. Justify your answer.

(b) Find the x-coordinate of each point of inflection of the graph of f.

(c) Find the absolute maximum value of $f(x)$.

5.4 Modeling and Optimization

What you will learn about . . .

- Examples from Mathematics
- Examples from Business and Industry
- Examples from Economics
- Modeling Discrete Phenomena with Differentiable Functions

and why . . .

Historically, optimization problems were among the earliest applications of what we now call differential calculus.

Examples from Mathematics

While today's graphing technology makes it easy to find extrema without calculus, the algebraic methods of differentiation were understandably more practical, and certainly more accurate, when graphs had to be rendered by hand. Indeed, one of the oldest applications of what we now call "differential calculus" (pre-dating Newton and Leibniz) was to find maximum and minimum values of functions by finding where horizontal tangent lines might occur. We will use both algebraic and graphical methods in this section to solve "max-min" problems in a variety of contexts, but the emphasis will be on the *modeling* process that both methods have in common. Here is a strategy you can use:

Strategy for Solving Max-Min Problems

1. **Understand the Problem** Read the problem carefully. Identify the information you need to solve the problem.
2. **Develop a Mathematical Model of the Problem** Draw pictures and label the parts that are important to the problem. Introduce a variable to represent the quantity to be maximized or minimized. Using that variable, write a function whose extreme value gives the information sought.
3. **Graph the Function** Find the domain of the function. Determine what values of the variable make sense in the problem.
4. **Identify the Critical Points and Endpoints** Find where the derivative is zero or fails to exist.
5. **Solve the Mathematical Model** If unsure of the result, support or confirm your solution with another method.
6. **Interpret the Solution** Translate your mathematical result into the problem setting and decide whether the result makes sense.

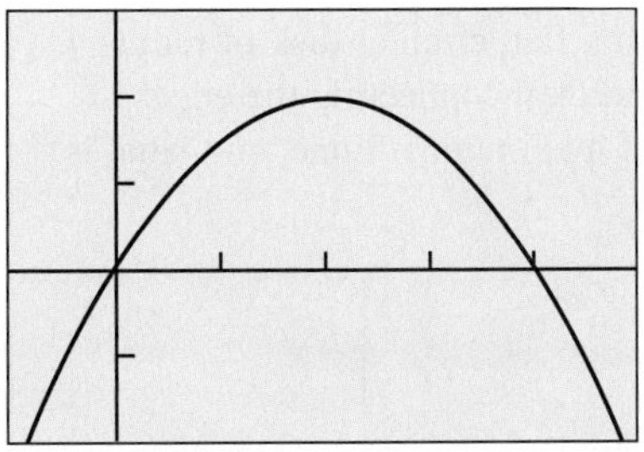

[–5, 25] by [–100, 150]

Figure 5.35 The graph of $f(x) = x(20 - x)$ with domain $(-\infty, \infty)$ has an absolute maximum of 100 at $x = 10$. (Example 1)

EXAMPLE 1 Using the Strategy

Find two numbers whose sum is 20 and whose product is as large as possible.

SOLUTION

Model If one number is x, the other is $(20 - x)$, and their product is $f(x) = x(20 - x)$.

Solve Graphically We can see from the graph of f in Figure 5.35 that there is a maximum. From what we know about parabolas, the maximum occurs at $x = 10$.

Confirm Analytically When $x = 10$, $f'(x) = 20 - 2x = 0$. Since $f''(x) = -2$ (always negative), the maximum occurs at $x = 10$. The other number is $20 - x = 10$.

Interpret The two numbers we seek are $x = 10$ and $20 - x = 10$.

Now Try Exercise 1.

Sometimes we find it helpful to use both analytic and graphical methods together, as in Example 2.

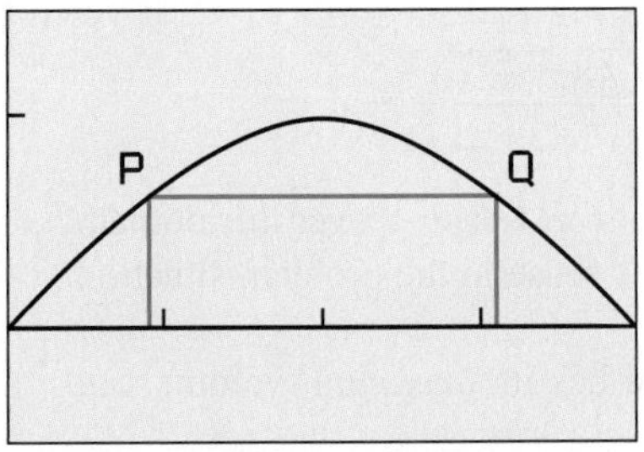

[0, π] by [–0.5, 1.5]

Figure 5.36 A rectangle inscribed under one arch of $y = \sin x$. (Example 2)

EXAMPLE 2 Inscribing Rectangles

A rectangle is to be inscribed under one arch of the sine curve (Figure 5.36). What is the largest area the rectangle can have, and what dimensions give that area?

continued

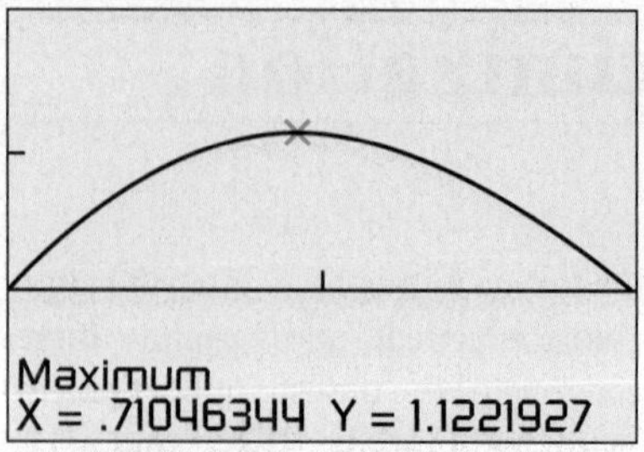

[0, $\pi/2$] by [–1, 2]

(a)

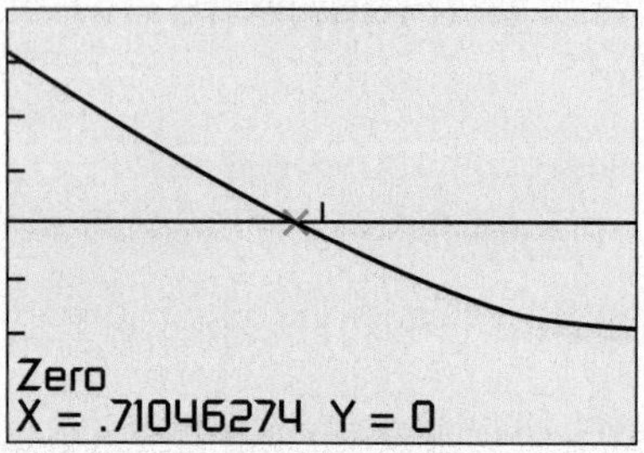

[0, $\pi/2$] by [–4, 4]

(b)

Figure 5.37 The graph of (a) $A(x) = (\pi - 2x)\sin x$ and (b) A' in the interval $0 \le x \le \pi/2$. (Example 2)

SOLUTION

Model Let $(x, \sin x)$ be the coordinates of point P in Figure 5.36. From what we know about the sine function the x-coordinate of point Q is $(\pi - x)$. Thus,

$$\pi - 2x = \text{length of rectangle}$$

and

$$\sin x = \text{height of rectangle.}$$

The area of the rectangle is

$$A(x) = (\pi - 2x)\sin x.$$

Solve Analytically and Graphically We can assume that $0 \le x \le \pi/2$. Notice that $A = 0$ at the endpoints $x = 0$ and $x = \pi/2$. Since A is differentiable, the only critical points occur at the zeros of the first derivative,

$$A'(x) = -2\sin x + (\pi - 2x)\cos x.$$

It is not possible to solve the equation $A'(x) = 0$ using algebraic methods. We can use the graph of A (Figure 5.37a) to find the maximum value and where it occurs. Or, we can use the graph of A' (Figure 5.37b) to find where the derivative is zero, and then evaluate A at this value of x to find the maximum value. The two x-values appear to be the same, as they should.

Interpret The rectangle has a maximum area of about 1.122 square units when $x \approx 0.710$. At this point, the rectangle is $\pi - 2x \approx 1.721$ units long by $\sin x \approx 0.652$ unit high.

Now Try Exercise 5.

EXPLORATION 1 Constructing Cones

A cone of height h and radius r is constructed from a flat, circular disk of radius 4 in. by removing a sector AOC of arc length x in. and then connecting the edges OA and OC. What arc length x will produce the cone of maximum volume, and what is that volume?

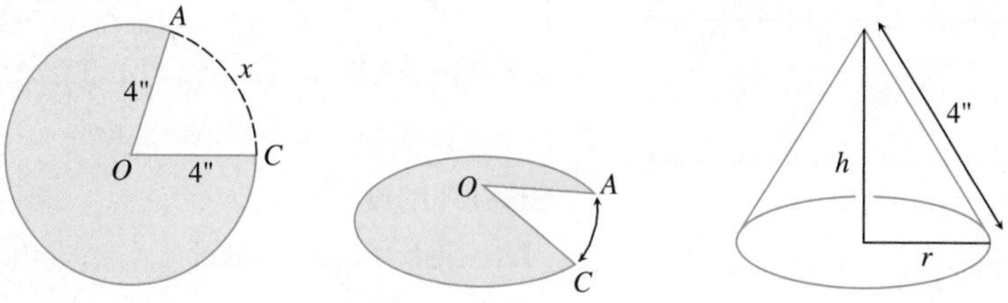

NOT TO SCALE

1. Show that

$$r = \frac{8\pi - x}{2\pi}, \quad h = \sqrt{16 - r^2}, \quad \text{and}$$

$$V(x) = \frac{\pi}{3}\left(\frac{8\pi - x}{2\pi}\right)^2\sqrt{16 - \left(\frac{8\pi - x}{2\pi}\right)^2}$$

2. Show that the natural domain of V is $0 \le x \le 16\pi$. Graph V over this domain.
3. Explain why the restriction $0 \le x \le 8\pi$ makes sense in the problem situation. Graph V over this domain.
4. Use graphical methods to find where the cone has its maximum volume, and what that volume is.
5. Confirm your findings in part 4 analytically. [*Hint:* Use $V(x) = (1/3)\pi r^2 h$, $h^2 + r^2 = 16$, and the Chain Rule.]

Examples from Business and Industry

To *optimize* something means to maximize or minimize some aspect of it. What is the size of the most profitable production run? What is the least expensive shape for an oil can? What is the stiffest rectangular beam we can cut from a 12-inch log? We usually answer such questions by finding the greatest or smallest value of some function that we have used to model the situation.

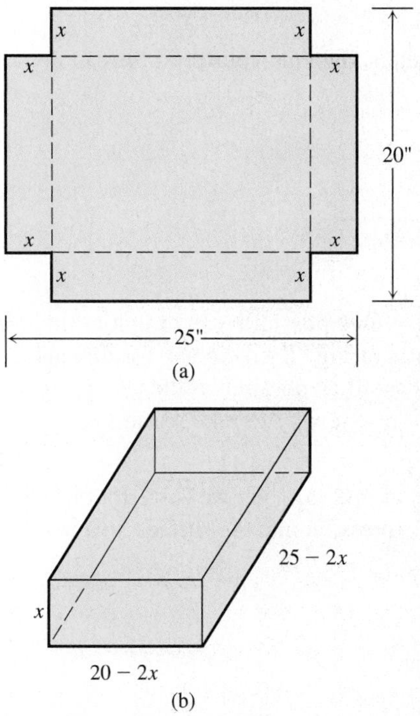

Figure 5.38 An open box made by cutting the corners from a piece of tin. (Example 3)

EXAMPLE 3 Fabricating a Box

An open-top box is to be made by cutting congruent squares of side length x from the corners of a 20- by 25-inch sheet of tin and bending up the sides (Figure 5.38). How large should the squares be to make the box hold as much as possible? What is the resulting maximum volume?

SOLUTION

Model The height of the box is x, and the other two dimensions are $(20 - 2x)$ and $(25 - 2x)$. Thus, the volume of the box is

$$V(x) = x(20 - 2x)(25 - 2x).$$

Solve Analytically Expanding, we obtain $V(x) = 4x^3 - 90x^2 + 500x$. The first derivative of V is

$$V'(x) = 12x^2 - 180x + 500.$$

The two solutions of the quadratic equation $V'(x) = 0$ are

$$c_1 = \frac{180 - \sqrt{180^2 - 48(500)}}{24} \approx 3.681 \quad \text{and}$$

$$c_2 = \frac{180 + \sqrt{180^2 - 48(500)}}{24} \approx 11.317.$$

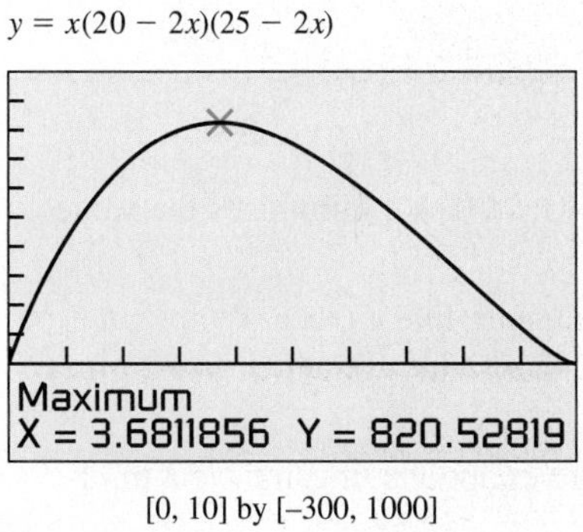

Figure 5.39 We chose the -300 in $-300 \le y \le 1000$ so that the coordinates of the local maximum at the bottom of the screen would not interfere with the graph. (Example 3)

Only c_1 is in the domain $[0, 10]$ of V. The values of V at this one critical point and the two endpoints are

Critical point value: $V(c_1) \approx 820.528$

Endpoint values: $V(0) = 0, \quad V(10) = 0.$

Support Graphically Because $2x$ cannot exceed 20, we have $0 \le x \le 10$. Figure 5.39 suggests that the maximum value of V is about 820.528 and occurs at $x \approx 3.681$.

Interpret Cutout squares that are about 3.681 in. on a side give the maximum volume, about 820.528 in^3.

Now Try Exercise 7.

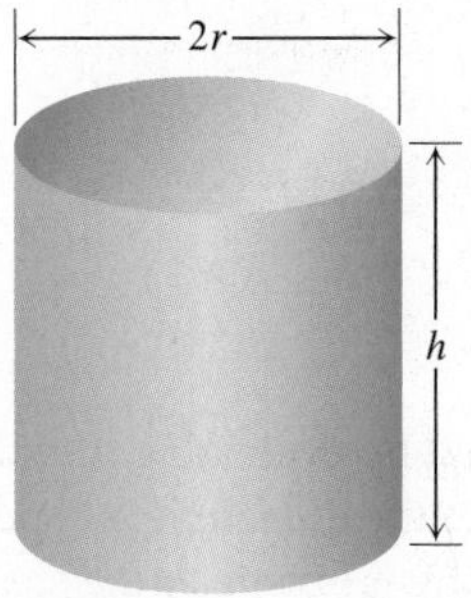

Figure 5.40 This one-liter can uses the least material when $h = 2r$. (Example 4)

EXAMPLE 4 Designing a Can

You have been asked to design a one-liter oil can shaped like a right circular cylinder (see Figure 5.40). What dimensions will use the least material?

continued

SOLUTION

Volume of can: If r and h are measured in centimeters, then the volume of the can in cubic centimeters is

$$\pi r^2 h = 1000. \quad \text{1 liter = 1000 cm}^3$$

$$\textit{Surface area of can:} \quad A = \underbrace{2\pi r^2}_{\text{circular ends}} + \underbrace{2\pi rh}_{\text{cylinder wall}}$$

How can we interpret the phrase "least material"? One possibility is to ignore the thickness of the material and the waste in manufacturing. Then we ask for dimensions r and h that make the total surface area as small as possible while satisfying the constraint $\pi r^2 h = 1000$. (Exercise 17 describes one way to take waste into account.)

Model To express the surface area as a function of one variable, we solve for one of the variables in $\pi r^2 h = 1000$ and substitute that expression into the surface area formula. Solving for h is easier,

$$h = \frac{1000}{\pi r^2}.$$

Thus,

$$\begin{aligned} A &= 2\pi r^2 + 2\pi rh \\ &= 2\pi r^2 + 2\pi r\left(\frac{1000}{\pi r^2}\right) \\ &= 2\pi r^2 + \frac{2000}{r}. \end{aligned}$$

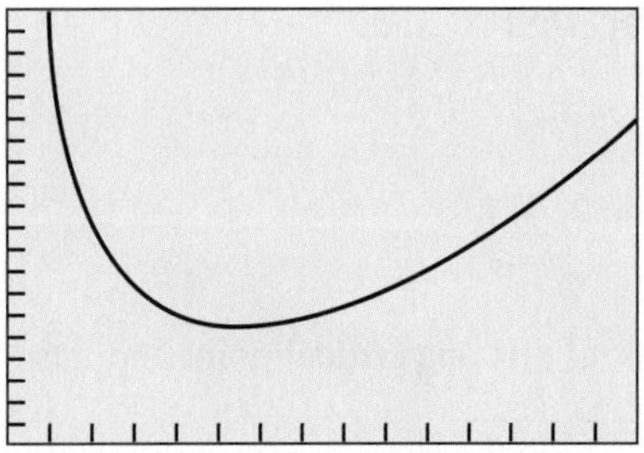

[0, 15] by [0, 2000]

Figure 5.41 The graph of $A = 2\pi r^2 + 2000/r$, $r > 0$, suggests that the minimum occurs when the radius is about 5.419 cm. (Example 4)

Solve Analytically Our goal is to find a value of $r > 0$ that minimizes the value of A. Figure 5.41 suggests that such a value exists.

Notice from the graph that for small r (a tall thin container, like a piece of pipe), the term $2000/r$ dominates and A is large. For large r (a short wide container, like a pizza pan), the term $2\pi r^2$ dominates and A again is large.

Since A is differentiable on $r > 0$, an interval with no endpoints, it can have a minimum value only where its first derivative is zero.

$$\frac{dA}{dr} = 4\pi r - \frac{2000}{r^2}$$

$$0 = 4\pi r - \frac{2000}{r^2} \quad \text{Set } dA/dr = 0.$$

$$4\pi r^3 = 2000 \quad \text{Multiply by } r^2.$$

$$r = \sqrt[3]{\frac{500}{\pi}} \approx 5.419 \quad \text{Solve for } r.$$

Something happens at $r = \sqrt[3]{500/\pi}$, but what?

If the domain of A were a closed interval, we could find out by evaluating A at this critical point and the endpoints and comparing the results. But the domain is an open interval, so we must learn what is happening at $r = \sqrt[3]{500/\pi}$ by referring to the shape of A's graph. The second derivative

continued

$$\frac{d^2A}{dr^2} = 4\pi + \frac{4000}{r^3}$$

is positive throughout the domain of A. The graph is therefore concave up and the value of A at $r = \sqrt[3]{500/\pi}$ an absolute minimum.
The corresponding value of h (after a little algebra) is

$$h = \frac{1000}{\pi r^2} = 2\sqrt[3]{\frac{500}{\pi}} = 2r.$$

Interpret The one-liter can that uses the least material has height equal to the diameter, with $r \approx 5.419$ cm and $h \approx 10.839$ cm. ***Now Try Exercise 11.***

Examples from Economics

Here we want to point out two more places where calculus makes a contribution to economic theory. The first has to do with maximizing profit. The second has to do with minimizing average cost.

Suppose that

$$\begin{aligned} r(x) &= \text{the revenue from selling } x \text{ items,} \\ c(x) &= \text{the cost of producing the } x \text{ items,} \\ p(x) &= r(x) - c(x) = \text{the profit from selling } x \text{ items.} \end{aligned}$$

The marginal revenue, marginal cost, and marginal profit at this production level (x items) are

$$\frac{dr}{dx} = \text{marginal revenue,} \qquad \frac{dc}{dx} = \text{marginal cost,} \qquad \frac{dp}{dx} = \text{marginal profit.}$$

The first observation is about the relationship of p to these derivatives.

Marginal Analysis

Because differentiable functions are locally linear, we can use the marginals to approximate the extra revenue, cost, or profit resulting from selling or producing one more item. Using these approximations is referred to as *marginal analysis.*

THEOREM 6 Maximum Profit

Maximum profit (if any) occurs at a production level at which marginal revenue equals marginal cost.

Proof We assume that $r(x)$ and $c(x)$ are differentiable for all $x > 0$, so if $p(x) = r(x) - c(x)$ has a maximum value, it occurs at a production level at which $p'(x) = 0$. Since $p'(x) = r'(x) - c'(x)$, $p'(x) = 0$ implies that

$$r'(x) - c'(x) = 0 \quad \text{or} \quad r'(x) = c'(x). \qquad \blacksquare$$

Figure 5.42 gives more information about this situation.

What guidance do we get from this observation? We know that a production level at which $p'(x) = 0$ need not be a level of maximum profit. It might be a level of minimum

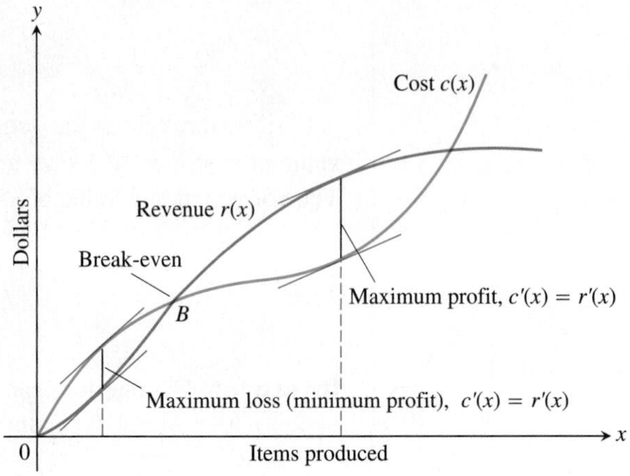

Figure 5.42 The graph of a typical cost function starts concave down and later turns concave up. It crosses the revenue curve at the break-even point B. To the left of B, the company operates at a loss. To the right, the company operates at a profit, the maximum profit occurring where $r'(x) = c'(x)$. Farther to the right, cost exceeds revenue (perhaps because of a combination of market saturation and rising labor and material costs) and production levels become unprofitable again.

profit, for example. But if we are making financial projections for our company, we should look for production levels at which marginal cost seems to equal marginal revenue. If there is a most profitable production level, it will be one of these.

EXAMPLE 5 Maximizing Profit

Suppose that $r(x) = 9x$ and $c(x) = x^3 - 6x^2 + 15x$, where x represents thousands of units. Is there a production level that maximizes profit? If so, what is it?

SOLUTION

Notice that $r'(x) = 9$ and $c'(x) = 3x^2 - 12x + 15$.

$$3x^2 - 12x + 15 = 9 \quad \text{Set } c'(x) = r'(x).$$
$$3x^2 - 12x + 6 = 0$$

The two solutions of the quadratic equation are

$$x_1 = \frac{12 - \sqrt{72}}{6} = 2 - \sqrt{2} \approx 0.586 \quad \text{and}$$

$$x_2 = \frac{12 + \sqrt{72}}{6} = 2 + \sqrt{2} \approx 3.414.$$

The possible production levels for maximum profit are $x \approx 0.586$ thousand units or $x \approx 3.414$ thousand units. The graphs in Figure 5.43 show that maximum profit occurs at about $x = 3.414$ and maximum loss occurs at about $x = 0.586$.

Another way to look for optimal production levels is to look for levels that minimize the average cost of the units produced. Theorem 7 helps us find them. ***Now Try Exercise 23.***

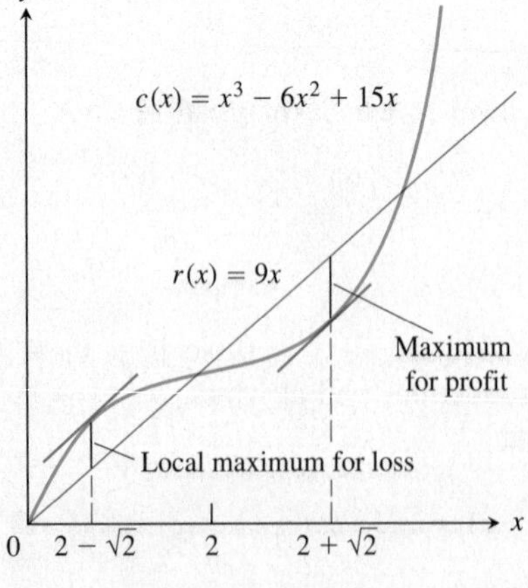

Figure 5.43 The cost and revenue curves for Example 5.

THEOREM 7 Minimizing Average Cost

The production level (if any) at which average cost is smallest is a level at which the average cost equals the marginal cost.

Proof We assume that $c(x)$ is differentiable.

$$c(x) = \text{cost of producing } x \text{ items, } x > 0.$$

$$\frac{c(x)}{x} = \text{average cost of producing } x \text{ items}$$

If the average cost can be minimized, it will be a production level at which

$$\frac{d}{dx}\left(\frac{c(x)}{x}\right) = 0$$

$$\frac{xc'(x) - c(x)}{x^2} = 0 \quad \text{Quotient Rule}$$

$$xc'(x) - c(x) = 0 \quad \text{Multiply by } x^2.$$

$$\underbrace{c'(x)}_{\text{marginal cost}} = \underbrace{\frac{c(x)}{x}}_{\text{average cost}}.$$

■

Again we have to be careful about what Theorem 7 does and does not say. It does not say that there is a production level of minimum average cost—it says where to look to see if there is one. Look for production levels at which average cost and marginal cost are equal. Then check to see if any of them gives a minimum average cost.

EXAMPLE 6 Minimizing Average Cost

Suppose $c(x) = x^3 - 6x^2 + 15x$, where x represents thousands of units. Is there a production level that minimizes average cost? If so, what is it?

SOLUTION

We look for levels at which average cost equals marginal cost.

$$\text{Marginal cost: } c'(x) = 3x^2 - 12x + 15$$

$$\text{Average cost: } \frac{c(x)}{x} = x^2 - 6x + 15$$

$$3x^2 - 12x + 15 = x^2 - 6x + 15 \quad \text{Marginal cost = Average cost}$$

$$2x^2 - 6x = 0$$

$$2x(x - 3) = 0$$

$$x = 0 \quad \text{or} \quad x = 3$$

Since $x > 0$, the only production level that might minimize average cost is $x = 3$ thousand units.

We use the Second Derivative Test.

$$\frac{d}{dx}\left(\frac{c(x)}{x}\right) = 2x - 6$$

$$\frac{d^2}{dx^2}\left(\frac{c(x)}{x}\right) = 2 > 0$$

The second derivative is positive for all $x > 0$, so $x = 3$ gives an absolute minimum.

Now Try Exercise 25.

Modeling Discrete Phenomena with Differentiable Functions

In case you are wondering how we can use differentiable functions $c(x)$ and $r(x)$ to describe the cost and revenue that comes from producing a number of items x that can only be an integer, here is the rationale.

When x is large, we can reasonably fit the cost and revenue data with smooth curves $c(x)$ and $r(x)$ that are defined not only at integer values of x but also at the values in between just as we do when we use regression equations. Once we have these differentiable functions, which are supposed to behave like the real cost and revenue when x is an integer, we can apply calculus to draw conclusions about their values. We then translate these mathematical conclusions into inferences about the real world that we hope will have predictive value. When they do, as is the case with the economic theory here, we say that the functions give a good model of reality.

What do we do when our calculus tells us that the best production level is a value of x that isn't an integer, as it did in Example 5? We use the nearest convenient integer. For $x \approx 3.414$ thousand units in Example 5, we might use 3414, or perhaps 3410 or 3420 if we ship in boxes of 10.

Quick Review 5.4 *(For help, go to Sections 1.6, 5.1, and Appendix A.1.)*

Exercise numbers with a gray background indicate problems that the authors have designed to be solved *without a calculator.*

1. Use the First Derivative Test to identify the local extrema of $y = x^3 - 6x^2 + 12x - 8$.

2. Use the Second Derivative Test to identify the local extrema of $y = 2x^3 + 3x^2 - 12x - 3$.

3. Find the volume of a cone with radius 5 cm and height 8 cm.

4. Find the dimensions of a right circular cylinder with volume 1000 cm^3 and surface area 600 cm^2.

In Exercises 5–8, rewrite the expression as a trigonometric function of the angle α.

5. $\sin(-\alpha)$ **6.** $\cos(-\alpha)$

7. $\sin(\pi - \alpha)$ **8.** $\cos(\pi - \alpha)$

In Exercises 9 and 10, use substitution to find the exact solutions of the system of equations.

9. $\begin{cases} x^2 + y^2 = 4 \\ y = \sqrt{3x} \end{cases}$

10. $\begin{cases} \dfrac{x^2}{4} + \dfrac{y^2}{9} = 1 \\ y = x + 3 \end{cases}$

Section 5.4 Exercises

In Exercises 1–10, solve the problem analytically. Support your answer graphically.

1. ***Finding Numbers*** The sum of two nonnegative numbers is 20. Find the numbers if

(a) the sum of their squares is as large as possible; as small as possible.

(b) one number plus the square root of the other is as large as possible; as small as possible.

2. ***Maximizing Area*** What is the largest possible area for a right triangle whose hypotenuse is 5 cm long, and what are its dimensions?

3. ***Maximizing Perimeter*** What is the smallest perimeter possible for a rectangle whose area is 16 in^2, and what are its dimensions?

4. ***Finding Area*** Show that among all rectangles with an 8-m perimeter, the one with largest area is a square.

5. ***Inscribing Rectangles*** The figure shows a rectangle inscribed in an isosceles right triangle whose hypotenuse is 2 units long.

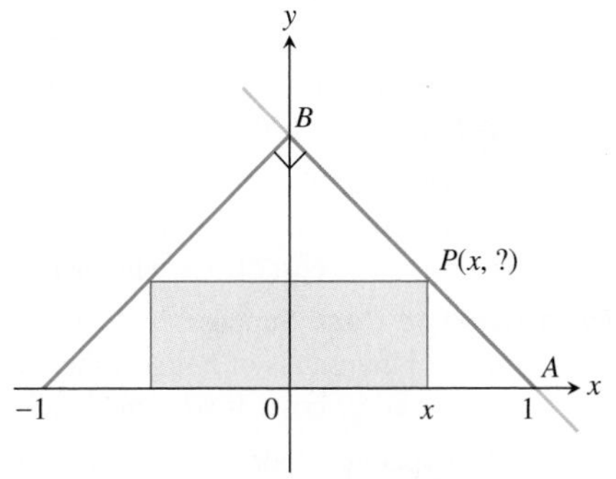

(a) Express the y-coordinate of P in terms of x. [*Hint:* Write an equation for the line AB.]

(b) Express the area of the rectangle in terms of x.

(c) What is the largest area the rectangle can have, and what are its dimensions?

6. ***Largest Rectangle*** A rectangle has its base on the x-axis and its upper two vertices on the parabola $y = 12 - x^2$. What is the largest area the rectangle can have, and what are its dimensions?

7. ***Optimal Dimensions*** You are planning to make an open rectangular box from an 8- by 15-in. piece of cardboard by cutting congruent squares from the corners and folding up the sides. What are the dimensions of the box of largest volume you can make this way, and what is its volume?

8. ***Closing Off the First Quadrant*** You are planning to close off a corner of the first quadrant with a line segment 20 units long running from $(a, 0)$ to $(0, b)$. Show that the area of the triangle enclosed by the segment is largest when $a = b$.

9. ***The Best Fencing Plan*** A rectangular plot of farmland will be bounded on one side by a river and on the other three sides by a single-strand electric fence. With 800 m of wire at your disposal, what is the largest area you can enclose, and what are its dimensions?

10. ***The Shortest Fence*** A 216-m^2 rectangular pea patch is to be enclosed by a fence and divided into two equal parts by another fence parallel to one of the sides. What dimensions for the outer rectangle will require the smallest total length of fence? How much fence will be needed?

11. ***Designing a Tank*** Your iron works has contracted to design and build a 500-ft^3, square-based, open-top, rectangular steel holding tank for a paper company. The tank is to be made by welding thin stainless steel plates together along their edges. As the production engineer, your job is to find dimensions for the base and height that will make the tank weigh as little as possible.

(a) What dimensions do you tell the shop to use?

(b) **Writing to Learn** Briefly describe how you took weight into account.

12. ***Catching Rainwater*** A 1125-ft^3 open-top rectangular tank with a square base x ft on a side and y ft deep is to be built with its top flush with the ground to catch runoff water. The costs associated with the tank involve not only the material from which the tank is made but also an excavation charge proportional to the product xy.

(a) If the total cost is

$$c = 5(x^2 + 4xy) + 10xy,$$

what values of x and y will minimize it?

(b) **Writing to Learn** Give a possible scenario for the cost function in (a).

13. ***Designing a Poster*** You are designing a rectangular poster to contain 50 in^2 of printing with a 4-in. margin at the top and bottom and a 2-in. margin at each side. What overall dimensions will minimize the amount of paper used?

14. ***Vertical Motion*** The height of an object moving vertically is given by

$$s = -16t^2 + 96t + 112,$$

with s in ft and t in sec. Find **(a)** the object's velocity when $t = 0$, **(b)** its maximum height and when it occurs, and **(c)** its velocity when $s = 0$.

15. ***Finding an Angle*** Two sides of a triangle have lengths a and b, and the angle between them is θ. What value of θ will maximize the triangle's area? [*Hint:* $A = (1/2)\, ab \sin \theta$.]

16. ***Designing a Can*** What are the dimensions of the lightest open-top right circular cylindrical can that will hold a volume of 1000 cm^3? Compare the result here with the result in Example 4.

17. ***Designing a Can*** You are designing a 1000-cm^3 right circular cylindrical can whose manufacture will take waste into account. There is no waste in cutting the aluminum for the side, but the top and bottom of radius r will be cut from squares that measure $2r$ units on a side. The total amount of aluminum used up by the can will therefore be

$$A = 8r^2 + 2\pi rh$$

rather than the $A = 2\pi r^2 + 2\pi rh$ in Example 4. In Example 4 the ratio of h to r for the most economical can was 2 to 1. What is the ratio now?

18. ***Designing a Box with Lid*** A piece of cardboard measures 10 in. by 15 in. Two equal squares are removed from the corners of a 10-in. side as shown in the figure. Two equal rectangles are removed from the other corners so that the tabs can be folded to form a rectangular box with lid.

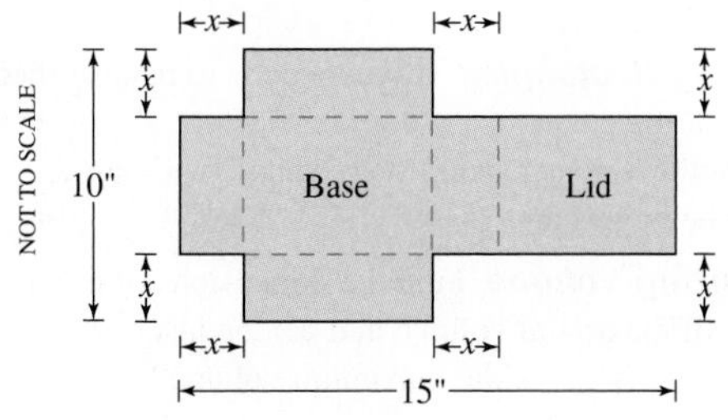

(a) Write a formula $V(x)$ for the volume of the box.

(b) Find the domain of V for the problem situation and graph V over this domain.

(c) Use a graphical method to find the maximum volume and the value of x that gives it.

(d) Confirm your result in part (c) analytically.

19. *Designing a Suitcase* A 24- by 36-in. sheet of cardboard is folded in half to form a 24- by 18-in. rectangle as shown in the figure. Then four congruent squares of side length x are cut from the corners of the folded rectangle. The sheet is unfolded, and the six tabs are folded up to form a box with sides and a lid.

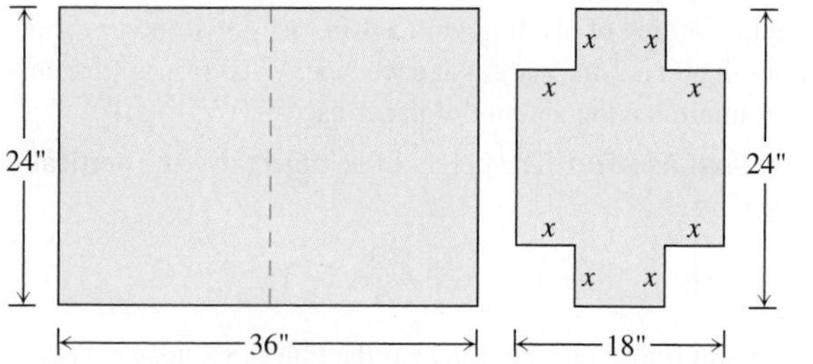

The sheet is then unfolded.

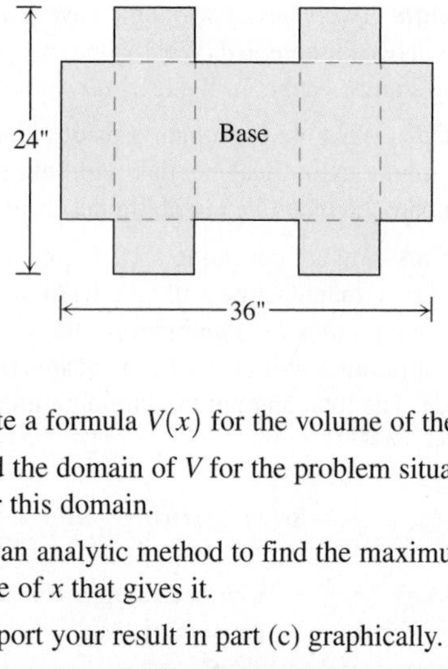

(a) Write a formula $V(x)$ for the volume of the box.

(b) Find the domain of V for the problem situation and graph V over this domain.

(c) Use an analytic method to find the maximum volume and the value of x that gives it.

(d) Support your result in part (c) graphically.

(e) Find a value of x that yields a volume of 1120 in^3.

(f) **Writing to Learn** Write a paragraph describing the issues that arise in part (b).

20. *Quickest Route* Jane is 2 mi offshore in a boat and wishes to reach a coastal village 6 mi down a straight shoreline from the point nearest the boat. She can row 2 mph and can walk 5 mph. Where should she land her boat to reach the village in the least amount of time?

21. *Inscribing Rectangles* A rectangle is to be inscribed under the arch of the curve $y = 4\cos(0.5x)$ from $x = -\pi$ to $x = \pi$. What are the dimensions of the rectangle with largest area, and what is the largest area?

22. *Maximizing Volume* Find the dimensions of a right circular cylinder of maximum volume that can be inscribed in a sphere of radius 10 cm. What is the maximum volume?

23. *Maximizing Profit* Suppose $r(x) = 8\sqrt{x}$ represents revenue and $c(x) = 2x^2$ represents cost, with x measured in thousands of units. Is there a production level that maximizes profit? If so, what is it?

24. *Maximizing Profit* Suppose $r(x) = x^2/(x^2 + 1)$ represents revenue and $c(x) = (x - 1)^3/3 - 1/3$ represents cost, with x measured in thousands of units. Is there a production level that maximizes profit? If so, what is it?

25. *Minimizing Average Cost* Suppose $c(x) = x^3 - 10x^2 - 30x$, where x is measured in thousands of units. Is there a production level that minimizes average cost? If so, what is it?

26. *Minimizing Average Cost* Suppose $c(x) = xe^x - 2x^2$, where x is measured in thousands of units. Is there a production level that minimizes average cost? If so, what is it?

27. *Tour Service* You operate a tour service that offers the following rates:

- \$200 per person if 50 people (the minimum number to book the tour) go on the tour.
- For each additional person, up to a maximum of 80 people total, the rate per person is reduced by \$2.

It costs \$6000 (a fixed cost) plus \$32 per person to conduct the tour. How many people does it take to maximize your profit?

28. Group Activity The figure shows the graph of $f(x) = xe^{-x}$, $x \geq 0$.

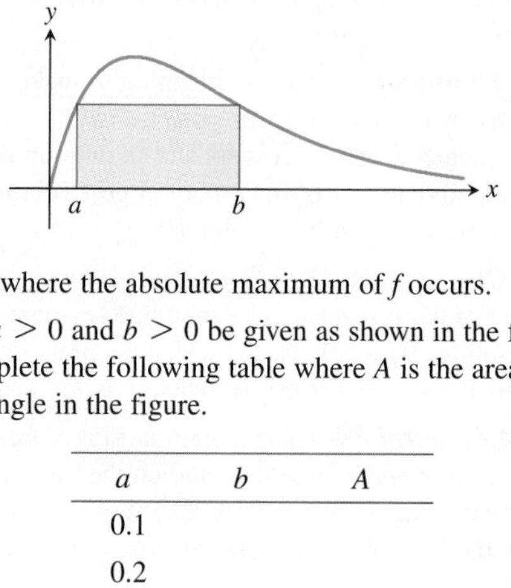

(a) Find where the absolute maximum of f occurs.

(b) Let $a > 0$ and $b > 0$ be given as shown in the figure. Complete the following table where A is the area of the rectangle in the figure.

a	b	A
0.1		
0.2		
0.3		
⋮		
1		

(c) Draw a scatter plot of the data (a, A).

(d) Find the quadratic, cubic, and quartic regression equations for the data in part (b), and superimpose their graphs on a scatter plot of the data.

(e) Use each of the regression equations in part (d) to estimate the maximum possible value of the area of the rectangle.

29. *Cubic Polynomial Functions*

Let $f(x) = ax^3 + bx^2 + cx + d$, $a \neq 0$.

(a) Show that f has either 0 or 2 local extrema.

(b) Give an example of each possibility in part (a).

30. *Shipping Packages* The U.S. Postal Service will accept a box for domestic shipment only if the sum of its length and girth (distance around), as shown in the figure, does not exceed 108 in. What dimensions will give a box with a square end the largest possible volume?

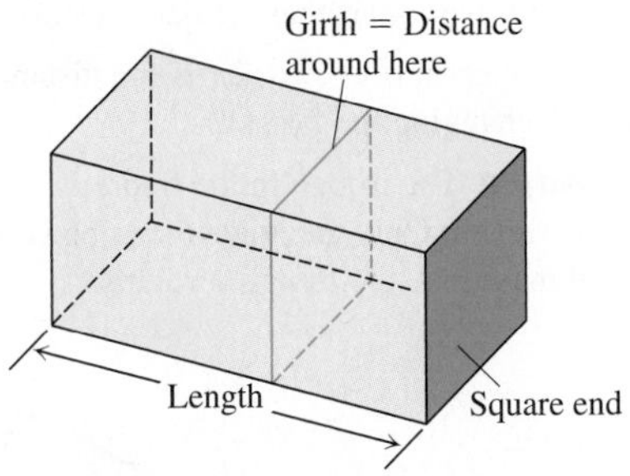

31. *Constructing Cylinders* Compare the answers to the following two construction problems.

(a) A rectangular sheet of perimeter 36 cm and dimensions x cm by y cm is to be rolled into a cylinder as shown in part (a) of the figure. What values of x and y give the largest volume?

(b) The same sheet is to be revolved about one of the sides of length y to sweep out the cylinder as shown in part (b) of the figure. What values of x and y give the largest volume?

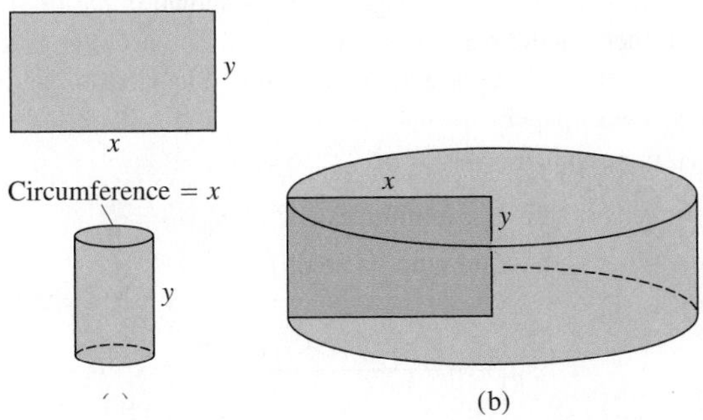

32. *Constructing Cones* A right triangle whose hypotenuse is $\sqrt{3}$ m long is revolved about one of its legs to generate a right circular cone. Find the radius, height, and volume of the cone of greatest volume that can be made this way.

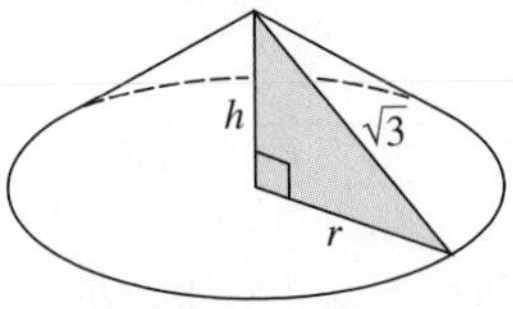

33. *Finding Parameter Values* What value of a makes $f(x) = x^2 + (a/x)$ have **(a)** a local minimum at $x = 2$? **(b)** a point of inflection at $x = 1$?

34. *Finding Parameter Values* Show that $f(x) = x^2 + (a/x)$ cannot have a local maximum for any value of a.

35. *Finding Parameter Values* What values of a and b make $f(x) = x^3 + ax^2 + bx$ have **(a)** a local maximum at $x = -1$ and a local minimum at $x = 3$? **(b)** a local minimum at $x = 4$ and a point of inflection at $x = 1$?

36. *Inscribing a Cone* Find the volume of the largest right circular cone that can be inscribed in a sphere of radius 3.

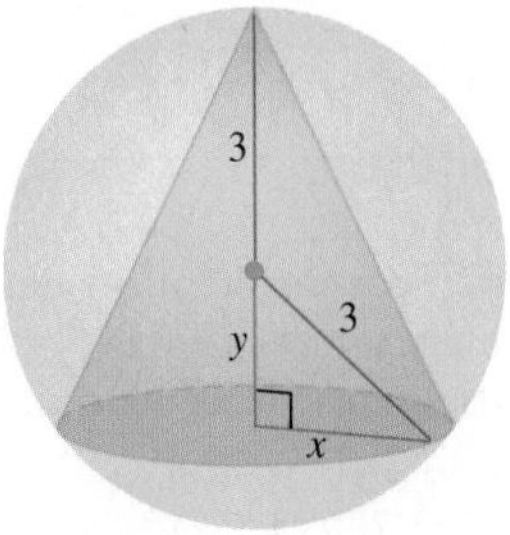

37. *Strength of a Beam* The strength S of a rectangular wooden beam is proportional to its width times the square of its depth.

(a) Find the dimensions of the strongest beam that can be cut from a 12-in.-diameter cylindrical log.

(b) **Writing to Learn** Graph S as a function of the beam's width w, assuming the proportionality constant to be $k = 1$. Reconcile what you see with your answer in part (a).

(c) **Writing to Learn** On the same screen, graph S as a function of the beam's depth d, again taking $k = 1$. Compare the graphs with one another and with your answer in part (a). What would be the effect of changing to some other value of k? Try it.

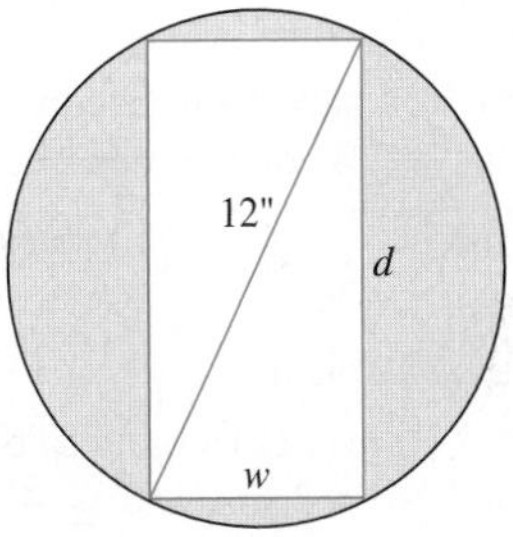

38. *Stiffness of a Beam* The stiffness S of a rectangular beam is proportional to its width times the cube of its depth.

(a) Find the dimensions of the stiffest beam that can be cut from a 12-in.-diameter cylindrical log.

(b) **Writing to Learn** Graph S as a function of the beam's width w, assuming the proportionality constant to be $k = 1$. Reconcile what you see with your answer in part (a).

(c) **Writing to Learn** On the same screen, graph S as a function of the beam's depth d, again taking $k = 1$. Compare the graphs with one another and with your answer in part (a). What would be the effect of changing to some other value of k? Try it.

39. *Frictionless Cart* A small frictionless cart, attached to the wall by a spring, is pulled 10 cm from its rest position and released at time $t = 0$ to roll back and forth for 4 sec. Its position at time t is $s = 10 \cos \pi t$.

(a) What is the cart's maximum speed? When is the cart moving that fast? Where is it then? What is the magnitude of the acceleration then?

(b) Where is the cart when the magnitude of the acceleration is greatest? What is the cart's speed then?

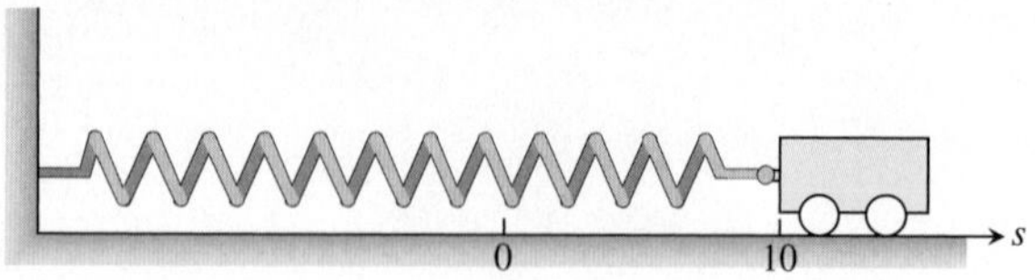

40. ***Electrical Current*** Suppose that at any time t (sec) the current i (amp) in an alternating current circuit is $i = 2\cos t + 2\sin t$. What is the peak (largest magnitude) current for this circuit?

41. ***Calculus and Geometry*** How close does the curve $y = \sqrt{x}$ come to the point $(3/2, 0)$? [*Hint:* If you minimize the *square* of the distance, you can avoid square roots.]

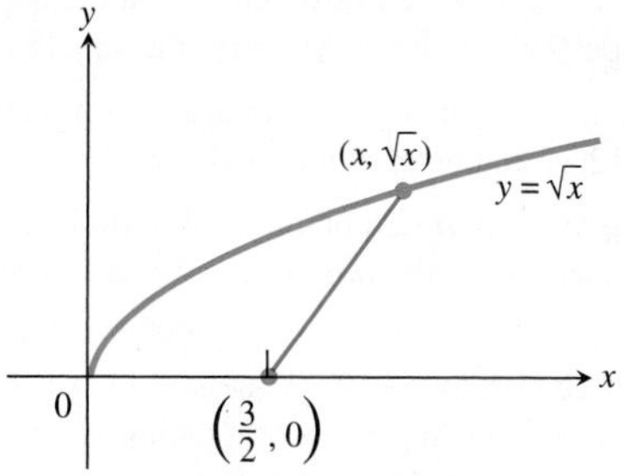

42. ***Calculus and Geometry*** How close does the semicircle $y = \sqrt{16 - x^2}$ come to the point $(1, \sqrt{3})$?

43. **Writing to Learn** Is the function $f(x) = x^2 - x + 1$ ever negative? Explain.

44. **Writing to Learn** You have been asked to determine whether the function $f(x) = 3 + 4\cos x + \cos 2x$ is ever negative.

(a) Explain why you need to consider values of x only in the interval $[0, 2\pi]$.

(b) Is f ever negative? Explain.

45. ***Vertical Motion*** Two masses hanging side by side from springs have positions $s_1 = 2\sin t$ and $s_2 = \sin 2t$, respectively, with s_1 and s_2 in meters and t in seconds.

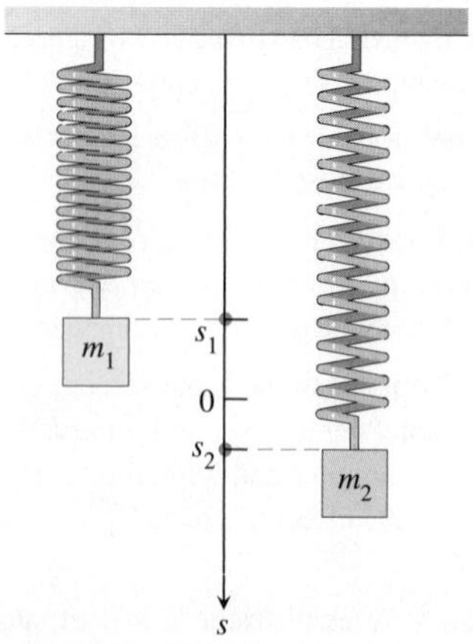

(a) At what times in the interval $t > 0$ do the masses pass each other? [*Hint:* $\sin 2t = 2\sin t\cos t$.]

(b) When in the interval $0 \le t \le 2\pi$ is the vertical distance between the masses the greatest? What is this distance? [*Hint:* $\cos 2t = 2\cos^2 t - 1$.]

46. ***Motion on a Line*** The positions of two particles on the s-axis are $s_1 = \sin t$ and $s_2 = \sin(t + \pi/3)$, with s_1 and s_2 in meters and t in seconds.

(a) At what time(s) in the interval $0 \le t \le 2\pi$ do the particles meet?

(b) What is the farthest apart that the particles ever get?

(c) When in the interval $0 \le t \le 2\pi$ is the distance between the particles changing the fastest?

47. ***Finding an Angle*** The trough in the figure is to be made to the dimensions shown. Only the angle θ can be varied. What value of θ will maximize the trough's volume?

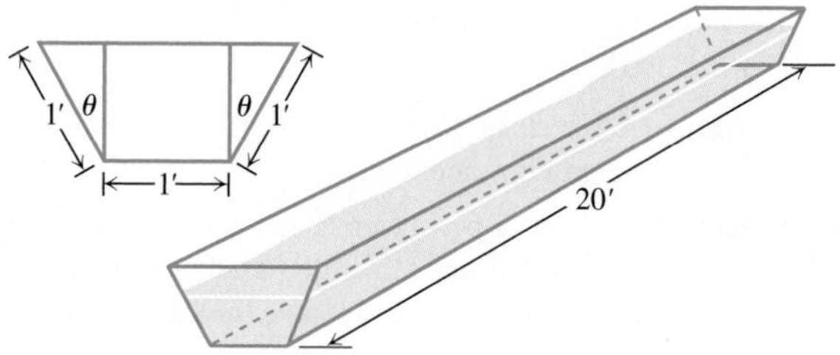

48. **Group Activity** ***Paper Folding*** A rectangular sheet of 8 1/2- by 11-in. paper is placed on a flat surface. One of the corners is placed on the opposite longer edge, as shown in the figure, and held there as the paper is smoothed flat. The problem is to make the length of the crease as small as possible. Call the length L. Try it with paper.

(a) Show that $L^2 = 2x^3/(2x - 8.5)$.

(b) What value of x minimizes L^2?

(c) What is the minimum value of L?

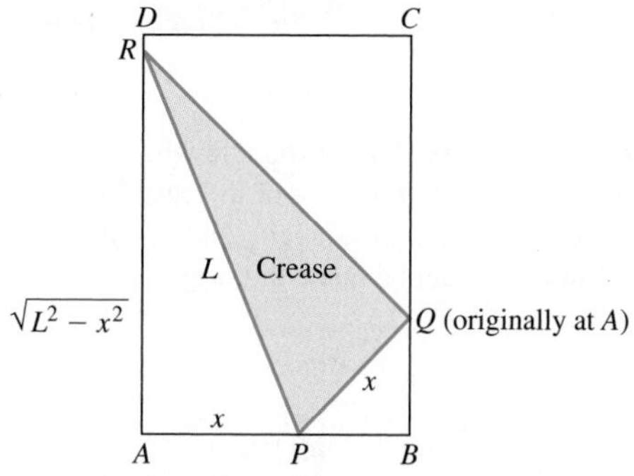

49. ***Sensitivity to Medicine*** (*continuation of Exercise 48, Section 3.3*) Find the amount of medicine to which the body is most sensitive by finding the value of M that maximizes the derivative dR/dM.

50. ***Selling Backpacks*** It costs you c dollars each to manufacture and distribute backpacks. If the backpacks sell at x dollars each, the number sold is given by

$$n = \frac{a}{x - c} + b(100 - x),$$

where a and b are certain positive constants. What selling price will bring a maximum profit?

Standardized Test Questions

You may use a graphing calculator to solve the following problems.

51. True or False A continuous function on a closed interval must attain a maximum value on that interval. Justify your answer.

52. True or False If $f'(c) = 0$ and $f(c)$ is not a local maximum, then $f(c)$ is a local minimum. Justify your answer.

53. Multiple Choice Two positive numbers have a sum of 60. What is the maximum product of one number times the square of the second number?

(A) 3481

(B) 3600

(C) 27,000

(D) 32,000

(E) 36,000

54. Multiple Choice A continuous function f has domain $[1, 25]$ and range $[3, 30]$. If $f'(x) < 0$ for all x between 1 and 25, what is $f(25)$?

(A) 1

(B) 3

(C) 25

(D) 30

(E) impossible to determine from the information given

55. Multiple Choice What is the maximum area of a right triangle with hypotenuse 10?

(A) 24 (B) 25 (C) $25\sqrt{2}$ (D) 48 (E) 50

56. Multiple Choice A rectangle is inscribed between the parabolas $y = 4x^2$ and $y = 30 - x^2$ as shown below:

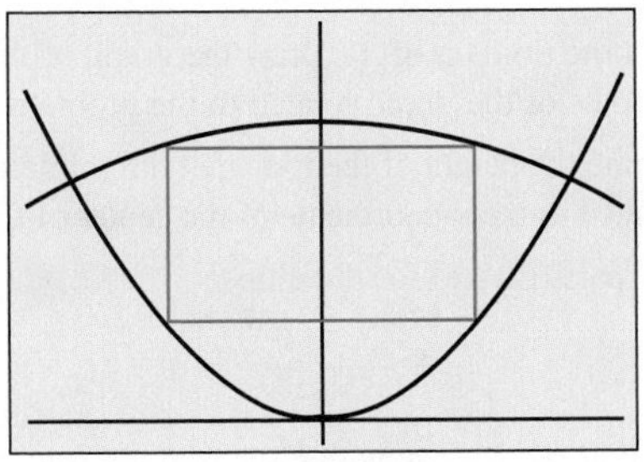

[–3, 3] by [–2, 40]

What is the maximum area of such a rectangle?

(A) $20\sqrt{2}$ (B) 40 (C) $30\sqrt{2}$ (D) 50 (E) $40\sqrt{2}$

Explorations

57. *Fermat's Principle in Optics* Fermat's principle in optics states that light always travels from one point to another along a path that minimizes the travel time. Light from a source A is reflected by a plane mirror to a receiver at point B, as shown in the figure. Show that for the light to obey Fermat's principle, the angle of incidence must equal the angle of reflection, both measured from the line normal to the reflecting surface. (This result can also be derived without calculus. There is a purely geometric argument, which you may prefer.)

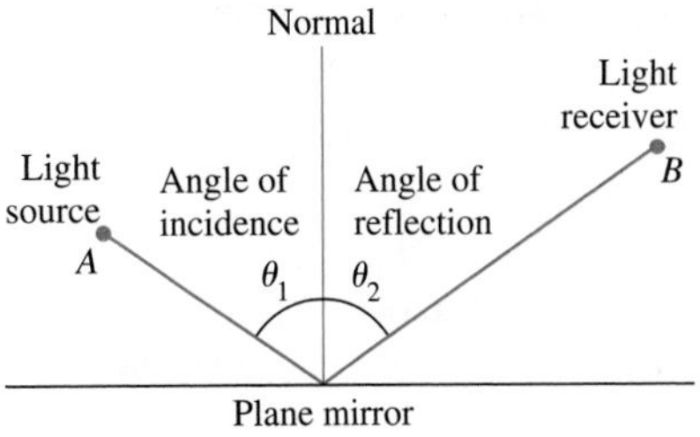

58. *Tin Pest* When metallic tin is kept below 13.2°C, it slowly becomes brittle and crumbles to a gray powder. Tin objects eventually crumble to this gray powder spontaneously if kept in a cold climate for years. The Europeans who saw tin organ pipes in their churches crumble away years ago called the change *tin pest* because it seemed to be contagious. And indeed it was, for the gray powder is a catalyst for its own formation.

A *catalyst* for a chemical reaction is a substance that controls the rate of reaction without undergoing any permanent change in itself. An *autocatalytic reaction* is one whose product is a catalyst for its own formation. Such a reaction may proceed slowly at first if the amount of catalyst present is small and slowly again at the end, when most of the original substance is used up. But in between, when both the substance and its catalyst product are abundant, the reaction proceeds at a faster pace.

In some cases it is reasonable to assume that the rate $v = dx/dt$ of the reaction is proportional both to the amount of the original substance present and to the amount of product. That is, v may be considered to be a function of x alone, and

$$v = kx(a - x) = kax - kx^2,$$

where

x = the amount of product,

a = the amount of substance at the beginning,

k = a positive constant.

At what value of x does the rate v have a maximum? What is the maximum value of v?

59. *How We Cough* When we cough, the trachea (windpipe) contracts to increase the velocity of the air going out. This raises the question of how much it should contract to maximize the velocity and whether it really contracts that much when we cough.

Under reasonable assumptions about the elasticity of the tracheal wall and about how the air near the wall is slowed by friction, the average flow velocity v (in cm/sec) can be modeled by the equation

$$v = c(r_0 - r)r^2, \quad \frac{r_0}{2} \le r \le r_0,$$

where r_0 is the rest radius of the trachea in cm and c is a positive constant whose value depends in part on the length of the trachea.

(a) Show that v is greatest when $r = (2/3)r_0$, that is, when the trachea is about 33% contracted. The remarkable fact is that X-ray photographs confirm that the trachea contracts about this much during a cough.

(b) Take r_0 to be 0.5 and c to be 1, and graph v over the interval $0 \le r \le 0.5$. Compare what you see to the claim that v is a maximum when $r = (2/3)r_0$.

60. *Wilson Lot Size Formula* One of the formulas for inventory management says that the average weekly cost of ordering, paying for, and holding merchandise is

$$A(q) = \frac{km}{q} + cm + \frac{hq}{2},$$

where q is the quantity you order when things run low (shoes, radios, brooms, or whatever the item might be), k is the cost of placing an order (the same, no matter how often you order), c is the cost of one item (a constant), m is the number of items sold each week (a constant), and h is the weekly holding cost per item (a constant that takes into account things such as space, utilities, insurance, and security).

(a) Your job, as the inventory manager for your store, is to find the quantity that will minimize $A(q)$. What is it? (The formula you get for the answer is called the *Wilson lot size formula.*)

(b) Shipping costs sometimes depend on order size. When they do, it is more realistic to replace k by $k + bq$, the sum of k and a constant multiple of q. What is the most economical quantity to order now?

61. *Production Level* Show that if $r(x) = 6x$ and $c(x) = x^3 - 6x^2 + 15x$ are your revenue and cost functions, then the best you can do is break even (have revenue equal cost).

62. *Production Level* Suppose $c(x) = x^3 - 20x^2 + 20{,}000x$ is the cost of manufacturing x items. Find a production level that will minimize the average cost of making x items.

Extending the Ideas

63. *Airplane Landing Path* An airplane is flying at altitude H when it begins its descent to an airport runway that is at horizontal ground distance L from the airplane, as shown in the figure. Assume that the landing path of the airplane is the graph of a cubic polynomial function $y = ax^3 + bx^2 + cx + d$ where $y(-L) = H$ and $y(0) = 0$.

(a) What is dy/dx at $x = 0$?

(b) What is dy/dx at $x = -L$?

(c) Use the values for dy/dx at $x = 0$ and $x = -L$ together with $y(0) = 0$ and $y(-L) = H$ to show that

$$y(x) = H\left[2\left(\frac{x}{L}\right)^3 + 3\left(\frac{x}{L}\right)^2\right].$$

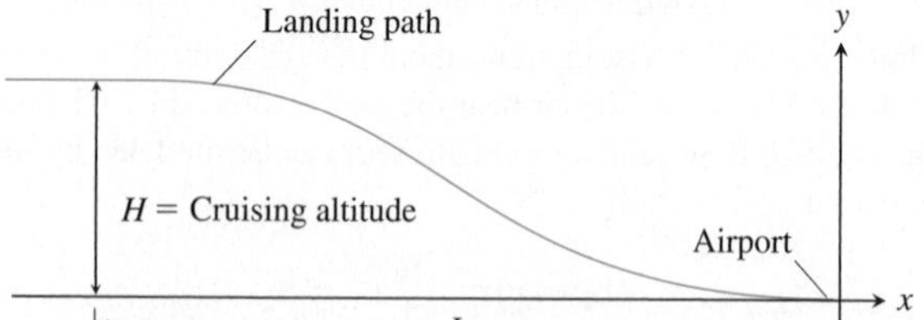

In Exercises 64 and 65, you might find it helpful to use a CAS.

64. *Generalized Cone Problem* A cone of height h and radius r is constructed from a flat, circular disk of radius a in. as described in Exploration 1.

(a) Find a formula for the volume V of the cone in terms of x and a.

(b) Find r and h in the cone of maximum volume for $a = 4$, 5, 6, 8.

(c) Writing to Learn Find a simple relationship between r and h that is independent of a for the cone of maximum volume. Explain how you arrived at your relationship.

65. *Circumscribing an Ellipse* Let $P(x, a)$ and $Q(-x, a)$ be two points on the upper half of the ellipse

$$\frac{x^2}{100} + \frac{(y-5)^2}{25} = 1$$

centered at $(0, 5)$. A triangle RST is formed by using the tangent lines to the ellipse at Q and P as shown in the figure.

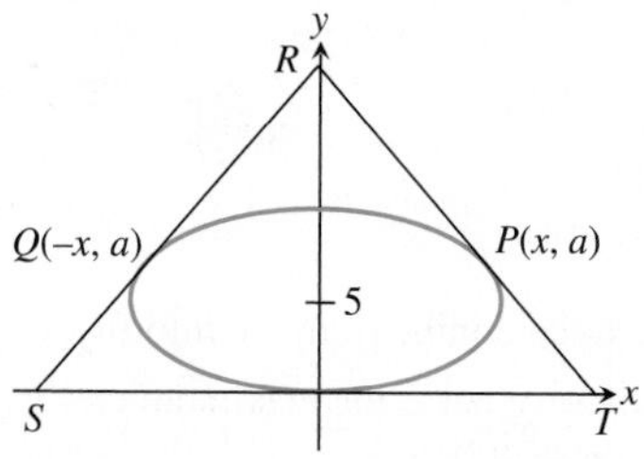

(a) Show that the area of the triangle is

$$A(x) = -f'(x)\left[x - \frac{f(x)}{f'(x)}\right]^2,$$

where $y = f(x)$ is the function representing the upper half of the ellipse.

(b) What is the domain of A? Draw the graph of A. How are the asymptotes of the graph related to the problem situation?

(c) Determine the height of the triangle with minimum area. How is it related to the y-coordinate of the center of the ellipse?

(d) Repeat parts (a)–(c) for the ellipse

$$\frac{x^2}{C^2} + \frac{(y-B)^2}{B^2} = 1$$

centered at $(0, B)$. Show that the triangle has minimum area when its height is $3B$.

5.5 Linearization and Differentials

What you will learn about . . .

- Linear Approximation
- Differentials
- Estimating Change with Differentials
- Absolute, Relative, and Percentage Change
- Sensitivity to Change
- Newton's Method

and why . . .

Engineering and science depend on approximations in most practical applications; it is important to understand how approximation techniques work.

Linear Approximation

In our study of the derivative we have frequently referred to the "tangent line to the curve" at a point. What makes that tangent line so important mathematically is that it provides a *useful representation of the curve itself* if we stay close enough to the point of tangency. We say that differentiable curves are always **locally linear,** a fact that can best be appreciated graphically by zooming in at a point on the curve, as Exploration 1 shows.

EXPLORATION 1 Appreciating Local Linearity

The function $f(x) = (x^2 + 0.0001)^{1/4} + 0.9$ is differentiable at $x = 0$ and hence "locally linear" there. Let us explore the significance of this fact with the help of a graphing calculator.

1. Graph $y = f(x)$ in the "ZoomDecimal" window. What appears to be the behavior of the function at the point $(0, 1)$?
2. Show algebraically that f is differentiable at $x = 0$. What is the equation of the tangent line at $(0, 1)$?
3. Now zoom in repeatedly, keeping the cursor at $(0, 1)$. What is the long-range outcome of repeated zooming?
4. The graph of $y = f(x)$ eventually looks like the graph of a line. What line is it?

We hope that this exploration gives you a new appreciation for the tangent line. As you zoom in on a differentiable function, its graph at that point actually seems to *become* the graph of the tangent line! This observation—that even the most complicated differentiable curve behaves locally like the simplest graph of all, a straight line—is the basis for most of the applications of differential calculus. It is what allows us, for example, to refer to the derivative as the "slope of the curve" or as "the velocity at time t_0."

Algebraically, the principle of local linearity means that the *equation* of the tangent line defines a function that can be used to *approximate* a differentiable function near the point of tangency. In recognition of this fact, we give the equation of the tangent line a new name: the *linearization of f at a.* Recall that the tangent line at $(a, f(a))$ has point-slope equation $y - f(a) = f'(x)(x - a)$ (Figure 5.44).

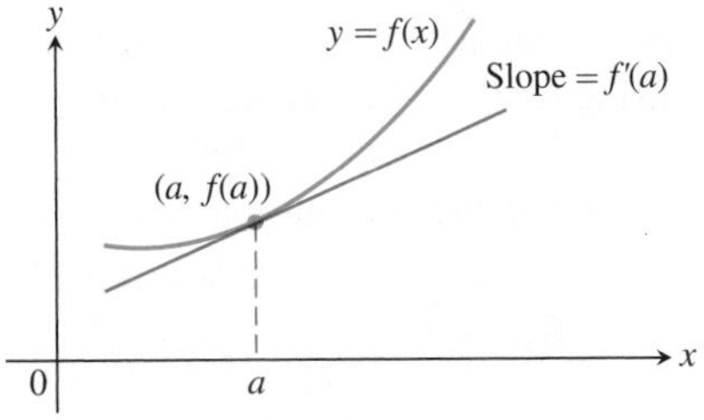

Figure 5.44 The tangent to the curve $y = f(x)$ at $x = a$ is the line $y = f(a) + f'(a)(x - a)$.

DEFINITION Linearization

If f is differentiable at $x = a$, then the equation of the tangent line,

$$L(x) = f(a) + f'(a)(x - a),$$

defines the **linearization of f at a.** The approximation $f(x) \approx L(x)$ is the **standard linear approximation of f at a.** The point $x = a$ is the **center** of the approximation.

EXAMPLE 1 Finding a Linearization

Find the linearization of $f(x) = \sqrt{1 + x}$ at $x = 0$, and use it to approximate $\sqrt{1.02}$ without a calculator. Then use a calculator to determine the accuracy of the approximation.

continued

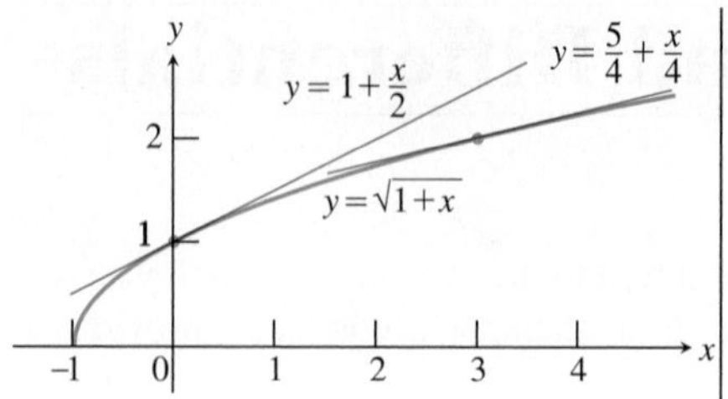

Figure 5.45 The graph of $f(x) = \sqrt{1 + x}$ and its linearization at $x = 0$ and $x = 3$. (Example 1)

SOLUTION

Since $f(0) = 1$, the point of tangency is $(0, 1)$. Since $f'(x) = \frac{1}{2}(1 + x)^{-1/2}$, the slope of the tangent line is $f'(0) = \frac{1}{2}$. Thus

$$L(x) = 1 + \frac{1}{2}(x - 0) = 1 + \frac{x}{2}. \qquad \text{(Figure 5.45)}$$

To approximate $\sqrt{1.02}$, we use $x = 0.02$:

$$\sqrt{1.02} = f(0.02) \approx L(0.02) = 1 + \frac{0.20}{2} = 1.01$$

The calculator gives $\sqrt{1.02} = 1.009950494$, so the approximation error is $|1.009950494 - 1.01| \approx 4.05 \times 10^{-5}$. We report that the error is less than 10^{-4}.

Now Try Exercise 1.

Why not just use a calculator?

We readily admit that linearization will never replace a calculator when it comes to finding square roots. Indeed, historically it was the other way around. Understanding linearization, however, brings you one step closer to understanding how the calculator finds those square roots so easily. You will get many steps closer when you study Taylor polynomials in Chapter 10. (A linearization is just a Taylor polynomial of degree 1.)

Look at how accurate the approximation $\sqrt{1 + x} \approx 1 + \frac{x}{2}$ is for values of x near 0.

Approximation	|True Value – Approximation|
$\sqrt{1.002} \approx 1 + \frac{0.002}{2} = 1.001$	$<10^{-6}$
$\sqrt{1.02} \approx 1 + \frac{0.02}{2} = 1.01$	$<10^{-4}$
$\sqrt{1.2} \approx 1 + \frac{0.2}{2} = 1.1$	$<10^{-2}$

As we move away from zero (the center of the approximation), we lose accuracy and the approximation becomes less useful. For example, using $L(2) = 2$ as an approximation for $f(2) = \sqrt{3}$ is not even accurate to one decimal place. We could do slightly better using $L(2)$ to approximate $f(2)$ if we were to use 3 as the center of our approximation (Figure 5.45).

EXAMPLE 2 Finding a Linearization

Find the linearization of $f(x) = \cos x$ at $x = \pi/2$ and use it to approximate cos 1.75 without a calculator. Then use a calculator to determine the accuracy of the approximation.

SOLUTION

Since $f(\pi/2) = \cos(\pi/2) = 0$, the point of tangency is $(\pi/2, 0)$. The slope of the tangent line is $f'(\pi/2) = -\sin(\pi/2) = -1$. Thus

$$L(x) = 0 + (-1)\left(x - \frac{\pi}{2}\right) = -x + \frac{\pi}{2}. \qquad \text{(Figure 5.46)}$$

To approximate $\cos(1.75)$, we use $x = 1.75$:

$$\cos 1.75 = f(1.75) \approx L(1.75) = -1.75 + \frac{\pi}{2}$$

The calculator gives $\cos 1.75 = -0.1782460556$, so the approximation error is $|-0.1782460556 - (-1.75 + \pi/2)| \approx 9.57 \times 10^{-4}$. We report that the error is less than 10^{-3}.

Now Try Exercise 5.

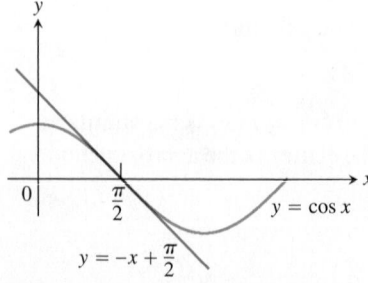

Figure 5.46 The graph of $f(x) = \cos x$ and its linearization at $x = \pi/2$. Near $x = \pi/2$, $\cos x \approx -x + (\pi/2)$. (Example 2)

EXAMPLE 3 Approximating Binomial Powers

Example 1 introduces a special case of a general linearization formula that applies to powers of $1 + x$ for small values of x:

$$(1 + x)^k \approx 1 + kx$$

If k is a positive integer this follows from the Binomial Theorem, but the formula actually holds for *all* real values of k. (We leave the justification to you as Exercise 7.) Use this formula to find polynomials that will approximate the following functions for values of x close to zero:

(a) $\sqrt[3]{1 - x}$ **(b)** $\dfrac{1}{1 - x}$ **(c)** $\sqrt{1 + 5x^4}$ **(d)** $\dfrac{1}{\sqrt{1 - x^2}}$

SOLUTION

We change each expression to the form $(1 + y)^k$, where k is a real number and y is a function of x that is close to 0 when x is close to zero. The approximation is then given by $1 + ky$.

(a) $\sqrt[3]{1 - x} = (1 + (-x))^{1/3} \approx 1 + \dfrac{1}{3}(-x) = 1 - \dfrac{x}{3}$

(b) $\dfrac{1}{1 - x} = (1 + (-x))^{-1} \approx 1 + (-1)(-x) = 1 + x$

(c) $\sqrt{1 + 5x^4} = ((1 + 5x^4))^{1/2} \approx 1 + \dfrac{1}{2}(5x^4) = 1 + \dfrac{5}{2}x^4$

(d) $\dfrac{1}{\sqrt{1 - x^2}} = ((1 + (-x^2))^{-1/2} \approx 1 + \left(-\dfrac{1}{2}\right)(-x^2) = 1 + \dfrac{1}{2}x^2$

Now Try Exercise 9.

EXAMPLE 4 Approximating Roots

Use linearizations to approximate **(a)** $\sqrt{123}$ and **(b)** $\sqrt[3]{123}$.

SOLUTION

Part of the analysis is to decide where to center the approximations.

(a) Let $f(x) = \sqrt{x}$. The closest perfect square to 123 is 121, so we center the linearization at $x = 121$. The tangent line at $(121, 11)$ has slope

$$f'(121) = \frac{1}{2}(121)^{-1/2} = \frac{1}{2}\cdot\frac{1}{\sqrt{121}} = \frac{1}{22}.$$

So

$$\sqrt{121} \approx L(121) = 11 + \frac{1}{22}(123 - 121) = 11.\overline{09}.$$

(b) Let $f(x) = \sqrt[3]{x}$. The closest perfect cube to 123 is 125, so we center the linearization at $x = 125$. The tangent line at $(125, 5)$ has slope

$$f'(125) = \frac{1}{3}(125)^{-2/3} = \frac{1}{3}\cdot\frac{1}{(\sqrt[3]{125})^2} = \frac{1}{75}.$$

So

$$\sqrt[3]{123} \approx L(123) = 5 + \frac{1}{75}(123 - 125) = 4.97\overline{3}.$$

A calculator shows both approximations to be within 10^{-3} of the actual values.

Now Try Exercise 11.

Differentials

Leibniz used the notation dy/dx to represent the derivative of y with respect to x. The notation *looks* like a quotient of real numbers, but it is really a *limit* of quotients in which both numerator and denominator go to zero (without actually equaling zero). That makes it tricky to define dy and dx as separate entities. (See the margin note, "Leibniz and His Notation.") Since we really only need to define dy and dx as formal variables, we define them in terms of each other so that their quotient must be the derivative.

Leibniz and His Notation

Although Leibniz did most of his calculus using *dy* and *dx* as separable entities, he never quite settled the issue of what they were. To him, they were "infinitesimals"—nonzero numbers, but infinitesimally small. There was much debate about whether such things could exist in mathematics, but luckily for the early development of calculus it did not matter: Thanks to the Chain Rule, *dy/dx behaved* like a quotient whether it was one or not.

DEFINITION Differentials

Let $y = f(x)$ be a differentiable function. The **differential dx** is an independent variable. The **differential dy** is

$$dy = f'(x)\,dx.$$

Unlike the independent variable dx, the variable dy is always a dependent variable. It depends on both x and dx.

EXAMPLE 5 Finding the Differential *dy*

Find the differential dy and evaluate dy for the given values of x and dx.

(a) $y = x^5 + 37x, \quad x = 1, \quad dx = 0.01$ **(b)** $y = \sin 3x, \quad x = \pi, \quad dx = -0.02$

(c) $x + y = xy, \quad x = 2, \quad dx = 0.05$

SOLUTION

(a) $dy = (5x^4 + 37)\,dx$. When $x = 1$ and $dx = 0.01$, $dy = (5 + 37)(0.01) = 0.42$.

(b) $dy = (3\cos 3x)\,dx$. When $x = \pi$ and $dx = -0.02$,
$dy = (3\cos 3\pi)(-0.02) = 0.06$.

(c) We could solve explicitly for y before differentiating, but it is easier to use implicit differentiation:

$$d(x + y) = d(xy)$$

$$dx + dy = xdy + ydx \quad \text{Sum and Product Rules in differential form}$$

$$dy(1 - x) = (y - 1)dx$$

$$dy = \frac{(y - 1)dx}{1 - x}$$

When $x = 2$ in the original equation, $2 + y = 2y$, so y is also 2. Therefore

$$dy = \frac{(2 - 1)(0.05)}{(1 - 2)} = -0.05.$$

Now Try Exercise 15.

Fan Chung Graham (1949–)

"Don't be intimidated!" is Dr. Fan Chung Graham's advice to young women considering careers in mathematics. Fan Chung Graham came to the United States from Taiwan to earn a Ph.D. in Mathematics from the University of Pennsylvania. She worked in the field of combinatorics at Bell Labs and Bellcore, and then, in 1994, returned to her alma mater as a Professor of Mathematics. Her research interests include spectral graph theory, discrete geometry, algorithms, and communication networks.

If $dx \neq 0$, then the quotient of the differential dy by the differential dx is equal to the derivative $f'(x)$ because

$$\frac{dy}{dx} = \frac{f'(x)dx}{dx} = f'(x).$$

We sometimes write

$$df = f'(x)\,dx$$

in place of $dy = f'(x)\,dx$, calling df the **differential of f**. For instance, if $f(x) = 3x^2 - 6$, then

$$df = d(3x^2 - 6) = 6x\,dx.$$

Every differentiation formula like

$$\frac{d(u+v)}{dx} = \frac{du}{dx} + \frac{dv}{dx} \quad \text{or} \quad \frac{d(\sin u)}{dx} = \cos u \frac{du}{dx}$$

has a corresponding differential form like

$$d(u+v) = du + dv \quad \text{or} \quad d(\sin u) = \cos u\, du.$$

EXAMPLE 6 Finding Differentials of Functions

(a) $d(\tan 2x) = \sec^2(2x)\, d(2x) = 2\sec^2 2x\, dx$

(b) $d\left(\frac{x}{x+1}\right) = \frac{(x+1)\,dx - x\,d(x+1)}{(x+1)^2} = \frac{x\,dx + dx - x\,dx}{(x+1)^2} = \frac{dx}{(x+1)^2}$

Now Try Exercise 23.

Estimating Change with Differentials

Suppose we know the value of a differentiable function $f(x)$ at a point a and we want to predict how much this value will change if we move to a nearby point $a + dx$. If dx is small, f and its linearization L at a will change by nearly the same amount (Figure 5.47). Since the values of L are simple to calculate, calculating the change in L offers a practical way to estimate the change in f.

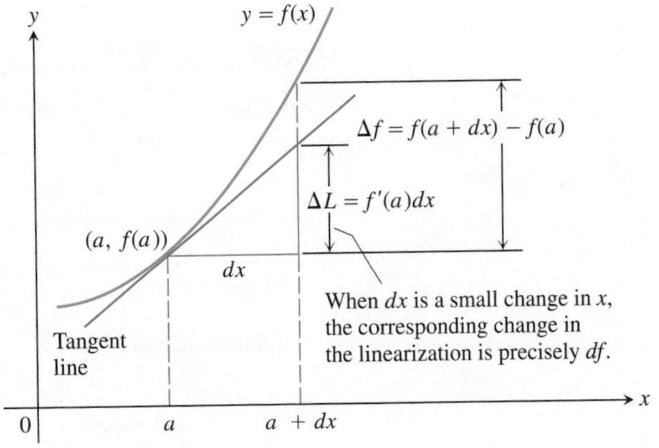

Figure 5.47 Approximating the change in the function f by the change in the linearization of f.

In the notation of Figure 5.47, the change in f is

$$\Delta f = f(a+dx) - f(a).$$

The corresponding change in L is

$$\begin{aligned}\Delta L &= L(a+dx) - L(a)\\ &= \underbrace{f(a) + f'(a)[(a+dx) - a]}_{L(a+dx)} - \underbrace{f(a)}_{L(a)}\\ &= f'(a)\,dx.\end{aligned}$$

Thus, the differential $df = f'(x)\,dx$ has a geometric interpretation: The value of df at $x = a$ is ΔL, the change in the linearization of f corresponding to the change dx.

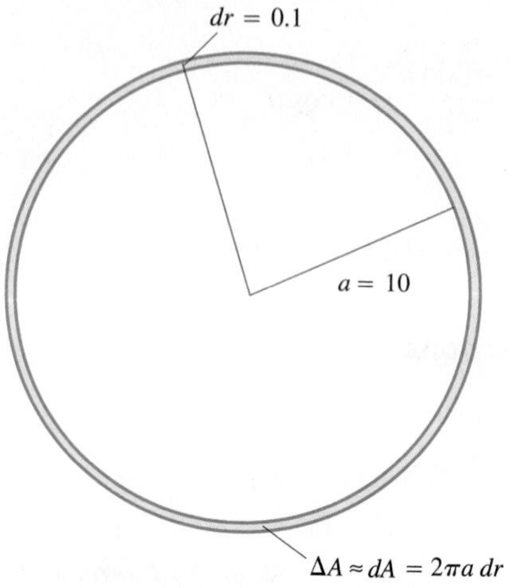

Figure 5.48 When dr is small compared with a, as it is when $dr = 0.1$ and $a = 10$, the differential $dA = 2\pi a\, dr$ gives a good estimate of ΔA. (Example 7)

Differential Estimate of Change

Let $f(x)$ be differentiable at $x = a$. The approximate change in the value of f when x changes from a to $a + dx$ is

$$df = f'(a)\, dx.$$

EXAMPLE 7 Estimating Change with Differentials

The radius r of a circle increases from $a = 10$ m to 10.1 m (Figure 5.48). Use dA to estimate the increase in the circle's area A. Compare this estimate with the true change ΔA, and find the approximation error.

SOLUTION

Since $A = \pi r^2$, the estimated increase is

$$dA = A'(a)\, dr = 2\pi a\, dr = 2\pi(10)(0.1) = 2\pi \text{ m}^2.$$

The true change is

$$\Delta A = \pi(10.1)^2 - \pi(10)^2 = (102.01 - 100)\pi = 2.01\pi \text{ m}^2.$$

The approximation error is $\Delta A - dA = 2.01\pi - 2\pi = 0.01\pi \text{ m}^2$.

Now Try Exercise 27.

Absolute, Relative, and Percentage Change

As we move from a to a nearby point $a + dx$, we can describe the change in f in three ways:

	True	Estimated
Absolute change	$\Delta f = f(a + dx) - f(a)$	$df = f'(a)\, dx$
Relative change	$\dfrac{\Delta f}{f(a)}$	$\dfrac{df}{f(a)}$
Percentage change	$\dfrac{\Delta f}{f(a)} \times 100$	$\dfrac{df}{f(a)} \times 100$

EXAMPLE 8 Changing Tires

Inflating a bicycle tire changes its radius from 12 inches to 13 inches. Use differentials to estimate the absolute change, the relative change, and the percentage change in the perimeter of the tire.

SOLUTION

Perimeter $P = 2\pi r$, so $\Delta P \approx dP = 2\pi dr = 2\pi(1) = 2\pi \approx 6.28$.

The absolute change is approximately 6.3 inches.

The relative change (when $P(12) = 24\pi$) is approximately $2\pi/24\pi \approx 0.08$.

The percentage change is approximately 8 percent.

Now Try Exercise 31.

Why It's Easy to Estimate Change in Perimeter

Note that the *true* change in Example 8 is $P(13) - P(12) = 26\pi - 24\pi = 2\pi$, so the differential estimate in this case is perfectly accurate! Why? Since $P = 2\pi r$ is a linear function of r, the linearization of P is the same as P itself. It is useful to keep in mind that local linearity is what makes estimation by differentials work.

Another way to interpret the change in $f(x)$ resulting from a change in x is the effect that an error in estimating x has on the estimation of $f(x)$. We illustrate this in Example 9.

EXAMPLE 9 Estimating the Earth's Surface Area

Suppose the earth were a perfect sphere and we determined its radius to be 3959 ± 0.1 miles. What effect would the tolerance of ± 0.1 mi have on our estimate of the earth's surface area?

SOLUTION

The surface area of a sphere of radius r is $S = 4\pi r^2$. The uncertainty in the calculation of S that arises from measuring r with a tolerance of dr miles is

$$dS = 8\pi r\, dr.$$

With $r = 3959$ and $dr = 0.1$, our estimate of S could be off by as much as

$$dS = 8\pi(3959)(0.1) \approx 9950 \text{ mi}^2,$$

to the nearest square mile, which is about the area of the state of Maryland.

Now Try Exercise 37.

EXAMPLE 10 Determining Tolerance

About how accurately should we measure the radius r of a sphere to calculate the surface area $S = 4\pi r^2$ within 1% of its true value?

SOLUTION

We want any inaccuracy in our measurement to be small enough to make the corresponding increment ΔS in the surface area satisfy the inequality

$$|\Delta S| \le \frac{1}{100}S = \frac{4\pi r^2}{100}.$$

We replace ΔS in this inequality by its approximation

$$dS = \left(\frac{ds}{dr}\right)dr = 8\pi r\, dr.$$

This gives

$$|8\pi r\, dr| \le \frac{4\pi r^2}{100}, \quad \text{or} \quad |dr| \le \frac{1}{8\pi r}\cdot\frac{4\pi r^2}{100} = \frac{1}{2}\cdot\frac{r}{100} = 0.005r.$$

We should measure r with an error dr that is no more than 0.5% of the true value.

Now Try Exercise 45.

Angiography

An opaque dye is injected into a partially blocked artery to make the inside visible under X-rays. This reveals the location and severity of the blockage.

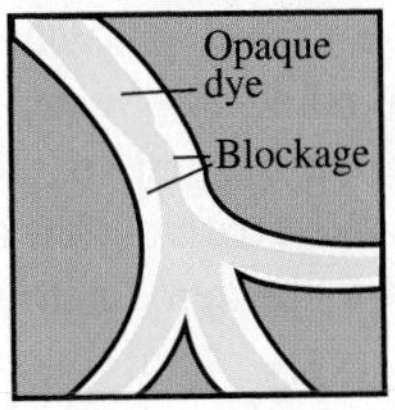

Angioplasty

A balloon-tipped catheter is inflated inside the artery to widen it at the blockage site.

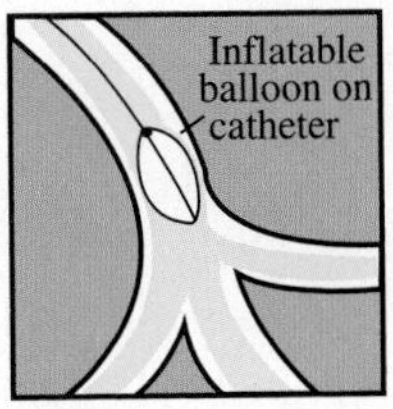

EXAMPLE 11 Unclogging Arteries

In the late 1830s, the French physiologist Jean Poiseuille ("pwa-ZOY") discovered the formula we use today to predict how much the radius of a partially clogged artery has to be expanded to restore normal flow. His formula,

$$V = kr^4,$$

says that the volume V of fluid flowing through a small pipe or tube in a unit of time at a fixed pressure is a constant times the fourth power of the tube's radius r. How will a 10% increase in r affect V?

SOLUTION

The differentials of r and V are related by the equation

$$dV = \frac{dV}{dr}\,dr = 4kr^3\, dr.$$

continued

The relative change in V is

$$\frac{dV}{V} = \frac{4kr^3dr}{kr^4} = 4\frac{dr}{r}.$$

The relative change in V is 4 times the relative change in r, so a 10% increase in r will produce a 40% increase in the flow. **Now Try Exercise 47.**

Sensitivity to Change

The equation $df = f'(x)\,dx$ tells how *sensitive* the output of f is to a change in input at different values of x. The larger the value of f' at x, the greater the effect of a given change dx.

EXAMPLE 12 Finding Depth of a Well

You want to calculate the depth of a well from the equation $s = 16t^2$ by timing how long it takes a heavy stone you drop to splash into the water below. How sensitive will your calculations be to a 0.1-sec error in measuring the time?

SOLUTION

The size of ds in the equation

$$ds = 32t\,dt$$

depends on how big t is. If $t = 2$ sec, the error caused by $dt = 0.1$ is only

$$ds = 32(2)(0.1) = 6.4 \text{ ft.}$$

Three seconds later at $t = 5$ sec, the error caused by the same dt is

$$ds = 32(5)(0.1) = 16 \text{ ft.}$$

Now Try Exercise 49.

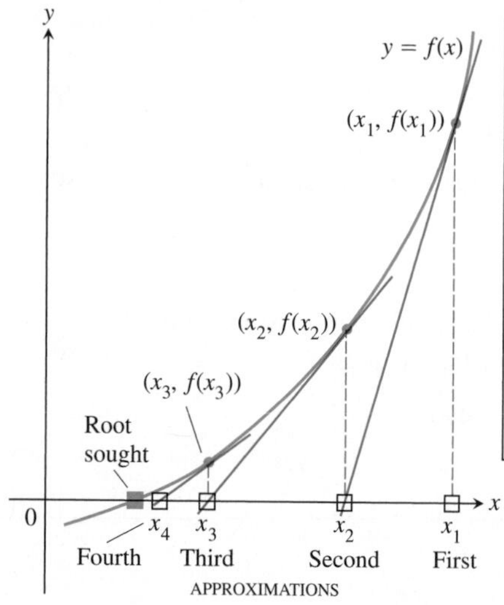

Figure 5.49 Usually the approximations rapidly approach an actual zero of $y = f(x)$.

Newton's Method

Newton's method is a numerical technique for approximating a zero of a function with zeros of its linearizations. Under favorable circumstances, the zeros of the linearizations *converge* rapidly to an accurate approximation. Many calculators use the method because it applies to a wide range of functions and usually gets results in only a few steps. Here is how it works.

To find a solution of an equation $f(x) = 0$, we begin with an initial estimate x_1, found either by looking at a graph or by simply guessing. Then we use the tangent to the curve $y = f(x)$ at $(x_1, f(x_1))$ to approximate the curve (Figure 5.49). The point where the tangent crosses the x-axis is the next approximation x_2. The number x_2 is usually a better approximation to the solution than is x_1. The point where the tangent to the curve at $(x_2, f(x_2))$ crosses the x-axis is the next approximation x_3. We continue on, using each approximation to generate the next, until we are close enough to the zero to stop.

There is a formula for finding the $(n + 1)$st approximation x_{n+1} from the nth approximation x_n, which is shown in the following procedure for Newton's method.

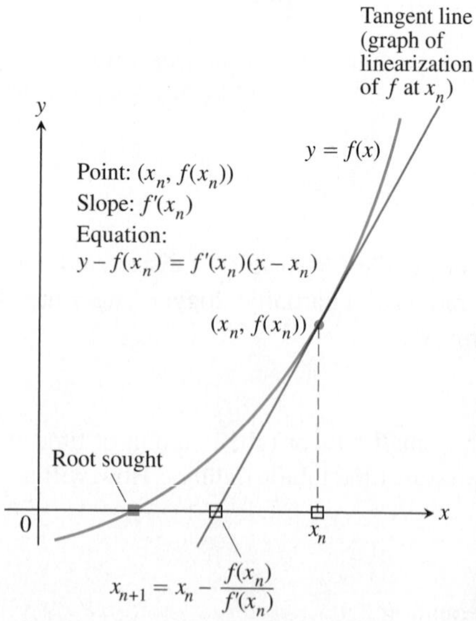

Figure 5.50 From x_n we go up to the curve and follow the tangent line down to find x_{n+1}.

Procedure for Newton's Method

1. Guess a first approximation to a solution of the equation $f(x) = 0$. A graph of $y = f(x)$ may help.
2. Use the first approximation to get a second, the second to get a third, and so on, using the formula

$$x_{n+1} = x_n - \frac{f(x_n)}{f'(x_n)}.$$

See Figure 5.50.

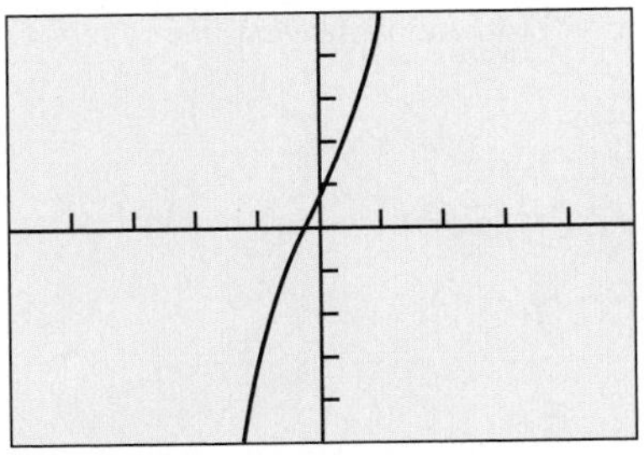

Figure 5.51 A calculator graph of $y = x^3 + 3x + 1$ suggests that -0.3 is a good first guess at the zero to begin Newton's method. (Example 13)

EXAMPLE 13 Using Newton's Method

Use Newton's method to solve $x^3 + 3x + 1 = 0$.

SOLUTION

Let $f(x) = x^3 + 3x + 1$, then $f'(x) = 3x^2 + 3$ and

$$x_{n+1} = x_n - \frac{f(x_n)}{f'(x_n)} = x_n - \frac{x_n^3 + 3x_n + 1}{3x_n^2 + 3}.$$

The graph of f in Figure 5.51 suggests that $x_1 = -0.3$ is a good first approximation to the zero of f in the interval $-1 \le x \le 0$. Then,

$$x_1 = -0.3,$$
$$x_2 = -0.322324159,$$
$$x_3 = -0.3221853603,$$
$$x_4 = -0.3221853546.$$

The x_n for $n \ge 5$ all appear to equal x_4 on the calculator we used for our computations. We conclude that the solution to the equation $x^3 + 3x + 1 = 0$ is about-0.3221853546. *Now Try Exercise 53.*

Newton's Method May Fail

Newton's method does not work if $f'(x_1) = 0$. In that case, choose a new starting point.

Newton's method does not always converge. For instance (see Figure 5.52), successive approximations $r - h$ and $r + h$ can go back and forth between these two values, and no amount of iteration will bring us any closer to the zero r.

If Newton's method does converge, it converges to a zero of f. However, the method may converge to a zero that is different from the expected one if the starting value is not close enough to the zero sought. Figure 5.53 shows how this might happen.

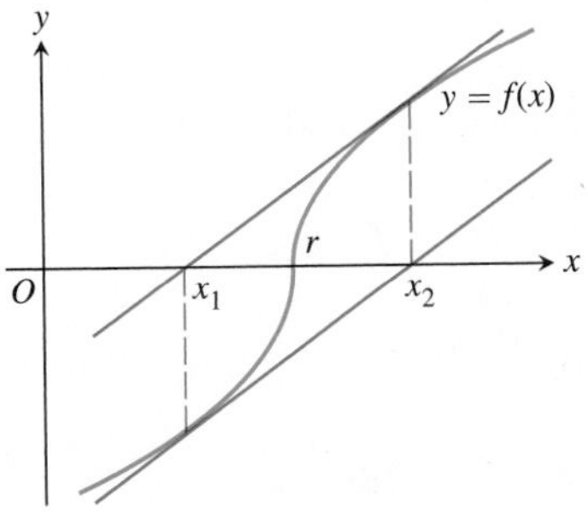

Figure 5.52 The graph of the function

$$f(x) = \begin{cases} -\sqrt{r - x}, & x < r \\ \sqrt{x - r}, & x \ge r. \end{cases}$$

If $x_1 = r - h$, then $x_2 = r + h$. Successive approximations go back and forth between these two values, and Newton's method fails to converge.

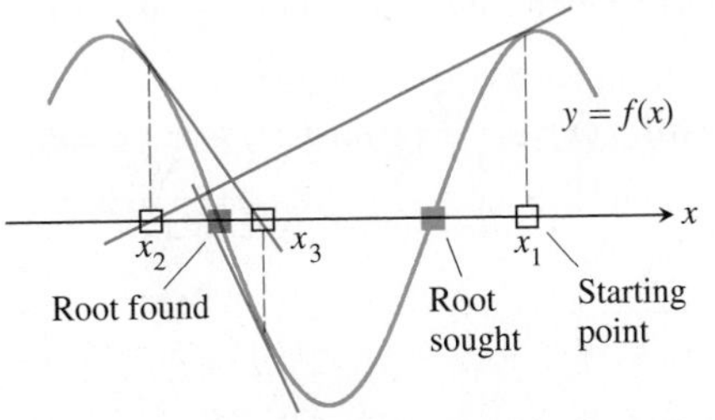

Figure 5.53 Newton's method may miss the zero you want if you start too far away.

Quick Review 5.5 *(For help, go to Sections 3.3, 4.1, and 4.4.)*

Exercise numbers with a gray background indicate problems that the authors have designed to be solved *without a calculator.*

In Exercises 1 and 2, find dy/dx.

1. $y = \sin(x^2 + 1)$ **2.** $y = \dfrac{x + \cos x}{x + 1}$

In Exercises 3 and 4, solve the equation graphically.

3. $xe^{-x} + 1 = 0$ **4.** $x^3 + 3x + 1 = 0$

In Exercises 5 and 6, let $f(x) = xe^{-x} + 1$. Write an equation for the line tangent to f at $x = c$.

5. $c = 0$ **6.** $c = -1$

7. Find where the tangent line in **(a)** Exercise 5 and **(b)** Exercise 6 crosses the x-axis.

8. Let $g(x)$ be the function whose graph is the tangent line to the graph of $f(x) = x^3 - 4x + 1$ at $x = 1$. Complete the table.

x	$f(x)$	$g(x)$
0.7		
0.8		
0.9		
1		
1.1		
1.2		
1.3		

In Exercises 9 and 10, graph $y = f(x)$ and its tangent line at $x = c$.

9. $c = 1.5, \quad f(x) = \sin x$

10. $c = 4, \quad f(x) = \begin{cases} -\sqrt{3 - x}, & x < 3 \\ \sqrt{x - 3}, & x \geq 3 \end{cases}$

Section 5.5 Exercises

In Exercises 1–6, **(a)** find the linearization $L(x)$ of $f(x)$ at $x = a$. **(b)** How accurate is the approximation $L(a + 0.1) \approx f(a + 0.1)$? See the comparisons following Example 1.

1. $f(x) = x^3 - 2x + 3, \quad a = 2$

2. $f(x) = \sqrt{x^2 + 9}, \quad a = -4$

3. $f(x) = x + \dfrac{1}{x}, \quad a = 1$

4. $f(x) = \ln(x + 1), \quad a = 0$

5. $f(x) = \tan x, \quad a = \pi$

6. $f(x) = \cos^{-1} x, \quad a = 0$

7. Show that the linearization of $f(x) = (1 + x)^k$ at $x = 0$ is $L(x) = 1 + kx$

8. Use the linearization $(1 + x)^k \approx 1 + kx$ to approximate the following. State how accurate your approximation is.

(a) $(1.002)^{100}$ **(b)** $\sqrt[3]{1.009}$

In Exercises 9 and 10, use the linear approximation $(1 + x)^k \approx 1 + kx$ to find an approximation for the function $f(x)$ for values of x near zero.

9. **(a)** $f(x) = (1 - x)^6$ **(b)** $f(x) = \dfrac{2}{1 - x}$ **(c)** $f(x) = \dfrac{1}{\sqrt{1 + x}}$

10. **(a)** $f(x) = (4 + 3x)^{1/3}$ **(b)** $f(x) = \sqrt{2 + x^2}$

(c) $f(x) = \sqrt[3]{\left(1 - \dfrac{1}{2 + x}\right)^2}$

In Exercises 11–14, approximate the root by using a linearization centered at an appropriate nearby number.

11. $\sqrt{101}$ **12.** $\sqrt[3]{26}$

13. $\sqrt[3]{998}$ **14.** $\sqrt{80}$

In Exercises 15–22, **(a)** find dy, and **(b)** evaluate dy for the given value of x and dx.

15. $y = x^3 - 3x, \quad x = 2, \quad dx = 0.05$

16. $y = \dfrac{2x}{1 + x^2}, \quad x = -2, \quad dx = 0.1$

17. $y = x^2 \ln x, \quad x = 1, \quad dx = 0.01$

18. $y = x\sqrt{1 - x^2}, \quad x = 0, \quad dx = -0.2$

19. $y = e^{\sin x}, \quad x = \pi, \quad dx = -0.1$

20. $y = 3 \csc\left(1 - \dfrac{x}{3}\right), \quad x = 1, \quad dx = 0.1$

21. $y + xy - x = 0, \quad x = 0, \quad dx = 0.01$

22. $2y = x^2 - xy, \quad x = 2, \quad dx = -0.05$

In Exercises 23–26, find the differential.

23. $d(\sqrt{1 - x^2})$

24. $d(e^{5x} + x^5)$

25. $d(\arctan 4x)$

26. $d(8^x + x^8)$

In Exercises 27–30, the function f changes value when x changes from a to $a + dx$. Find

(a) the true change $\Delta f = f(a + dx) - f(a)$.

(b) the estimated change $df = f'(a)\,dx$.

(c) the approximation error $|\Delta f - df|$.

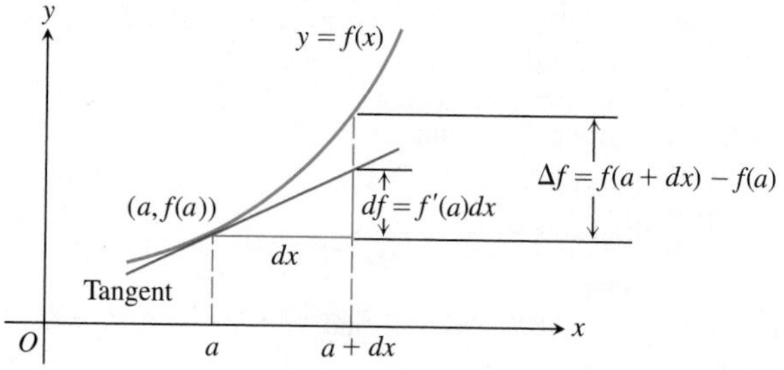

27. $f(x) = x^2 + 2x, \quad a = 0, \quad dx = 0.1$

28. $f(x) = x^3 - x, \quad a = 1, \quad dx = 0.1$

29. $f(x) = x^{-1}, \quad a = 0.5, \quad dx = 0.05$

30. $f(x) = x^4, \quad a = 1, \quad dx = 0.01$

In Exercises 31–36, write a differential formula that estimates the given change in volume or surface area. Then use the formula to estimate the change when the dependent variable changes from 10 cm to 10.05 cm.

31. ***Volume*** The change in the volume $V = (4/3)\pi r^3$ of a sphere when the radius changes from a to $a + dr$

32. ***Surface Area*** The change in the surface area $S = 4\pi r^2$ of a sphere when the radius changes from a to $a + dr$

$V = \frac{4}{3}\pi r^3, \quad S = 4\pi r^2$

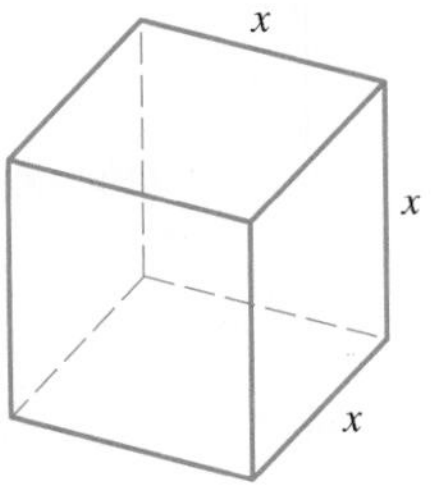

$V = x^3, \quad S = 6x^2$

33. ***Volume*** The change in the volume $V = x^3$ of a cube when the edge lengths change from a to $a + dx$

34. ***Surface Area*** The change in the surface area $S = 6x^2$ of a cube when the edge lengths change from a to $a + dx$

35. ***Volume*** The change in the volume $V = \pi r^2 h$ of a right circular cylinder when the radius changes from a to $a + dr$ and the height does not change

36. ***Surface Area*** The change in the lateral surface area $S = 2\pi rh$ of a right circular cylinder when the height changes from a to $a + dh$ and the radius does not change

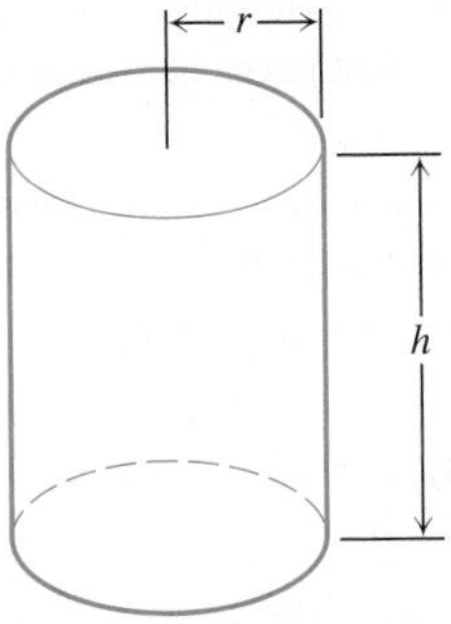

$V = \pi r^2 h, \quad S = 2\pi rh$

In Exercises 37–40, use differentials to estimate the maximum error in measurement resulting from the tolerance of error in the dependent variable. Express answers to the nearest tenth, since that is the precision used to express the tolerance.

37. The area of a circle with radius 10 ± 0.1 in.

38. The volume of a sphere with radius 8 ± 0.3 in.

39. The volume of a cube with side 15 ± 0.2 cm.

40. The area of an equilateral triangle with side 20 ± 0.5 cm.

41. ***Linear Approximation*** Let f be a function with $f(0) = 1$ and $f'(x) = \cos(x^2)$.

(a) Find the linearization of f at $x = 0$.

(b) Estimate the value of f at $x = 0.1$.

(c) **Writing to Learn** Do you think the actual value of f at $x = 0.1$ is greater than or less than the estimate in part (b)? Explain.

42. ***Expanding Circle*** The radius of a circle is increased from 2.00 to 2.02 m.

(a) Estimate the resulting change in area.

(b) Estimate as a percentage of the circle's original area.

43. ***Growing Tree*** The diameter of a tree was 10 in. During the following year, the circumference increased 2 in. About how much did the tree's diameter increase? the tree's cross-section area?

44. ***Percentage Error*** The edge of a cube is measured as 10 cm with an error of 1%. The cube's volume is to be calculated from this measurement. Estimate the percentage error in the volume calculation.

45. ***Tolerance*** About how accurately should you measure the side of a square to be sure of calculating the area to within 2% of its true value?

46. ***Tolerance*** **(a)** About how accurately must the interior diameter of a 10-m-high cylindrical storage tank be measured to calculate the tank's volume to within 1% of its true value?

(b) About how accurately must the tank's exterior diameter be measured to calculate the amount of paint it will take to paint the side of the tank to within 5% of the true amount?

47. ***Minting Coins*** A manufacturer contracts to mint coins for the federal government. The coins must weigh within 0.1% of their ideal weight, so the volume must be within 0.1% of the ideal volume. Assuming the thickness of the coins does not change, what is the percentage change in the volume of the coin that would result from a 0.1% increase in the radius?

48. ***Tolerance*** The height and radius of a right circular cylinder are equal, so the cylinder's volume is $V = \pi h^3$. The volume is to be calculated with an error of no more than 1% of the true value. Find approximately the greatest error that can be tolerated in the measurement of h, expressed as a percentage of h.

49. ***Estimating Volume*** You can estimate the volume of a sphere by measuring its circumference with a tape measure, dividing by 2π to get the radius, then using the radius in the volume formula. Find how sensitive your volume estimate is to a 1/8-in. error in the circumference measurement by filling in the table below for spheres of the given sizes. Use differentials when filling in the last column.

Sphere Type	True Radius	Tape Error	Radius Error	Volume Error
Orange	2 in.	1/8 in.		
Melon	4 in.	1/8 in.		
Beach Ball	7 in.	1/8 in.		

50. ***Estimating Surface Area*** Change the heading in the last column of the table in Exercise 49 to "Surface Area Error" and find how sensitive the measure of surface area is to a 1/8-in. error in estimating the circumference of the sphere.

51. ***The Effect of Flight Maneuvers on the Heart*** The amount of work done by the heart's main pumping chamber, the left ventricle, is given by the equation

$$W = PV + \frac{V\delta v^2}{2g},$$

where W is the work per unit time, P is the average blood pressure, V is the volume of blood pumped out during the unit of time, δ ("delta") is the density of the blood, v is the average velocity of the exiting blood, and g is the acceleration of gravity.

When P, V, δ, and v remain constant, W becomes a function of g, and the equation takes the simplified form

$$W = a + \frac{b}{g} \quad (a, b \text{ constant}).$$

As a member of NASA's medical team, you want to know how sensitive W is to apparent changes in g caused by flight maneuvers, and this depends on the initial value of g. As part of your investigation, you decide to compare the effect on W of a given change dg on the moon, where $g = 5.2$ ft/sec^2, with the effect the same change dg would have on Earth, where $g = 32$ ft/sec^2. Use the simplified equation above to find the ratio of dW_{moon} to dW_{Earth}.

52. ***Measuring Acceleration of Gravity*** When the length L of a clock pendulum is held constant by controlling its temperature, the pendulum's period T depends on the acceleration of gravity g. The period will therefore vary slightly as the clock is moved from place to place on the earth's surface, depending on the change in g. By keeping track of ΔT, we can estimate the variation in g from the equation $T = 2\pi(L/g)^{1/2}$ that relates T, g, and L.

(a) With L held constant and g as the independent variable, calculate dT and use it to answer parts (b) and (c).

(b) **Writing to Learn** If g increases, will T increase or decrease? Will a pendulum clock speed up or slow down? Explain.

(c) A clock with a 100-cm pendulum is moved from a location where $g = 980$ cm/sec^2 to a new location. This increases the period by $dT = 0.001$ sec. Find dg and estimate the value of g at the new location.

Using Newton's Method on Your Calculator

A nice way to get your calculator to perform the calculations in Newton's method. Try it with the function $f(x) = x^3 + 3x + 1$ from Example 5.

1. Enter the function in Y1 and its derivative in Y2.
2. On the home screen, store the initial guess into x. For example, using the initial guess in Example 5, you would type $-.3 \to X$.
3. Type X−Y1/Y2 → X and press the ENTER key over and over. Watch as the numbers converge to the zero of f. When the values stop changing, it means that your calculator has found the zero to the extent of its displayed digits, as shown in the following figure.

```
-.3→X
                    -.3
X-Y1/Y2→X
           -.322324159
          -.3221853603
          -.3221853546
          -.3221853546
```

4. Experiment with different initial guesses and repeat Steps 2 and 3.
5. Experiment with different functions and repeat Steps 1 through 3. Compare each final value you find with the value given by your calculator's built-in zero-finding feature.

In Exercises 53–56, use Newton's method to estimate all real solutions of the equation. Make your answers accurate to 6 decimal places.

53. $x^3 + x - 1 = 0$

54. $x^4 + x - 3 = 0$

55. $x^2 - 2x + 1 = \sin x$

56. $x^4 - 2 = 0$

Standardized Test Questions

You may use a graphing calculator to solve the following problems.

57. True or False Newton's method will not find the zero of $f(x) = x/(x^2 + 1)$ if the first guess is greater than 1. Justify your answer.

58. True or False If u and v are differentiable functions, then $d(uv) = du\, dv$. Justify your answer.

59. Multiple Choice What is the linearization of $f(x) = e^x$ at $x = 1$?

(A) $y = e$ (B) $y = ex$ (C) $y = e^x$
(D) $y = x - e$ (E) $y = e(x - 1)$

60. Multiple Choice If $y = \tan x$, $x = \pi$, and $dx = 0.5$, what does dy equal?

(A) -0.25 (B) -0.5 (C) 0 (D) 0.5 (E) 0.25

61. Multiple Choice If Newton's method is used to find the zero of $f(x) = x - x^3 + 2$, what is the third estimate if the first estimate is 1?

(A) $-\frac{3}{4}$ (B) $\frac{3}{2}$ (C) $\frac{8}{5}$ (D) $\frac{18}{11}$ (E) 3

62. Multiple Choice If the linearization of $y = \sqrt[3]{x}$ at $x = 64$ is used to approximate $\sqrt[3]{66}$, what is the percentage error?

(A) 0.01% (B) 0.04% (C) 0.4% (D) 1% (E) 4%

Explorations

63. ***Newton's Method*** Suppose your first guess in using Newton's method is lucky in the sense that x_1 is a root of $f(x) = 0$. What happens to x_2 and later approximations?

64. ***Oscillation*** Show that if $h > 0$, applying Newton's method to

$$f(x) = \begin{cases} \sqrt{x}, & x \ge 0 \\ \sqrt{-x}, & x < 0 \end{cases}$$

leads to $x_2 = -h$ if $x_1 = h$, and to $x_2 = h$ if $x_1 = -h$. Draw a picture that shows what is going on.

65. *Approximations That Get Worse and Worse* Apply Newton's method to $f(x) = x^{1/3}$ with $x_1 = 1$, and calculate x_2, x_3, x_4, and x_5. Find a formula for $|x_n|$. What happens to $|x_n|$ as $n \to \infty$? Draw a picture that shows what is going on.

66. *Quadratic Approximations*

(a) Let $Q(x) = b_0 + b_1(x - a) + b_2(x - a)^2$ be a quadratic approximation to $f(x)$ at $x = a$ with the properties:

i. $Q(a) = f(a)$,

ii. $Q'(a) = f'(a)$,

iii. $Q''(a) = f''(a)$.

Determine the coefficients b_0, b_1, and b_2.

(b) Find the quadratic approximation to $f(x) = 1/(1 - x)$ at $x = 0$.

(c) Graph $f(x) = 1/(1 - x)$ and its quadratic approximation at $x = 0$. Then ZOOM IN on the two graphs at the point $(0, 1)$. Comment on what you see.

(d) Find the quadratic approximation to $g(x) = 1/x$ at $x = 1$. Graph g and its quadratic approximation together. Comment on what you see.

(e) Find the quadratic approximation to $h(x) = \sqrt{1 + x}$ at $x = 0$. Graph h and its quadratic approximation together. Comment on what you see.

(f) What are the linearizations of f, g, and h at the respective points in parts (b), (d), and (e)?

67. *Multiples of Pi* Store any number as X in your calculator. Then enter the command X − tan(X) → X and press the ENTER key repeatedly until the displayed value stops changing. The result is always an integral multiple of π. Why is this so? [*Hint:* These are zeros of the sine function.]

Extending the Ideas

68. *Formulas for Differentials* Verify the following formulas.

(a) $d(c) = 0$ (c a constant)

(b) $d(cu) = c\,du$ (c a constant)

(c) $d(u + v) = du + dv$

(d) $d(u \cdot v) = u\,dv + v\,du$

(e) $d\left(\frac{u}{v}\right) = \frac{v\,du - u\,dv}{v^2}$

(f) $d(u^n) = nu^{n-1}\,du$

69. *Linearization* Show that the approximation of tan x by its linearization at the origin must improve as $x \to 0$ by showing that

$$\lim_{x \to 0} \frac{\tan x}{x} = 1.$$

70. *The Linearization Is the Best Linear Approximation* Suppose that $y = f(x)$ is differentiable at $x = a$ and that $g(x) = m(x - a) + c$ (m and c constants). If the error $E(x) = f(x) - g(x)$ were small enough near $x = a$, we might think of using g as a linear approximation of f instead of the linearization $L(x) = f(a) + f'(a)(x - a)$. Show that if we impose on g the conditions

i. $E(a) = 0$,

ii. $\lim_{x \to a} \frac{E(x)}{x - a} = 0$,

then $g(x) = f(a) + f'(a)(x - a)$. Thus, the linearization gives the only linear approximation whose error is both zero at $x = a$ and negligible in comparison with $(x - a)$.

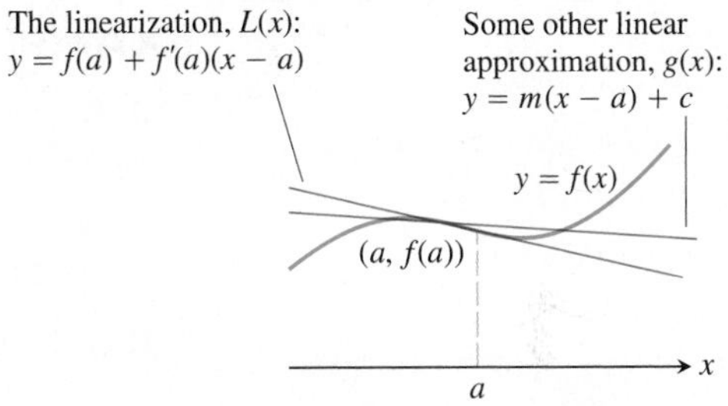

71. Writing to Learn Find the linearization of $f(x) = \sqrt{x + 1} + \sin x$ at $x = 0$. How is it related to the individual linearizations for $\sqrt{x + 1}$ and $\sin x$?

72. *Formula for Newton's Method* Derive the formula for finding the $(n + 1)$st approximation x_{n+1} from the nth approximation x_n. [*Hint:* Write the point-slope equation for the tangent line to the curve at $(x_n, f(x_n))$. See Figure 5.50 on page 244. Then set $y = 0$ and solve for x.]

5.6 Related Rates

What you will learn about . . .

- Related Rate Equations
- Solution Strategy
- Simulating Related Motion

and why . . .

Related rate problems are at the heart of Newtonian mechanics; it was essentially to solve such problems that calculus was invented.

Related Rate Equations

Suppose that a particle $P(x, y)$ is moving along a curve C in the plane so that its coordinates x and y are differentiable functions of time t. If D is the distance from the origin to P, then using the Chain Rule we can find an equation that relates dD/dt, dx/dt, and dy/dt.

$$D = \sqrt{x^2 + y^2}$$

$$\frac{dD}{dt} = \frac{1}{2}(x^2 + y^2)^{-1/2}\left(2x\frac{dx}{dt} + 2y\frac{dy}{dt}\right)$$

Any equation involving two or more variables that are differentiable functions of time t can be used to find an equation that relates their corresponding rates.

EXAMPLE 1 Finding Related Rate Equations

(a) Assume that the radius r of a sphere is a differentiable function of t and let V be the volume of the sphere. Find an equation that relates dV/dt and dr/dt.

(b) Assume that the radius r and height h of a cone are differentiable functions of t and let V be the volume of the cone. Find an equation that relates dV/dt, dr/dt, and dh/dt.

SOLUTION

(a) $V = \dfrac{4}{3}\pi r^3$ Volume formula for a sphere

$$\frac{dV}{dt} = 4\pi r^2 \frac{dr}{dt}$$

(b) $V = \dfrac{\pi}{3} r^2 h$ Cone volume formula

$$\frac{dV}{dt} = \frac{\pi}{3}\left(r^2 \cdot \frac{dh}{dt} + 2r\frac{dr}{dt} \cdot h\right) = \frac{\pi}{3}\left(r^2\frac{dh}{dt} + 2rh\frac{dr}{dt}\right)$$

Now Try Exercise 3.

Solution Strategy

What has always distinguished calculus from algebra is its ability to deal with variables that change over time. Example 1 illustrates how easy it is to move from a formula relating static variables to a formula that relates their rates of change: Simply differentiate the formula implicitly with respect to t. This introduces an important category of problems called *related rate problems* that still constitutes one of the most important applications of calculus.

We introduce a strategy for solving related rate problems, similar to the strategy we introduced for max-min problems earlier in this chapter.

Strategy for Solving Related Rate Problems

1. **Understand the problem.** In particular, identify the variable whose rate of change you *seek* and the variable (or variables) whose rate of change you *know*.
2. **Develop a mathematical model of the problem.** Draw a picture (many of these problems involve geometric figures) and label the parts that are important to the problem. *Be sure to distinguish constant quantities from variables that change over time.* Only constant quantities can be assigned numerical values at the start.

continued

3. **Write an equation relating the variable whose rate of change you seek with the variable(s) whose rate of change you know.** The formula is often geometric, but it could come from a scientific application.
4. **Differentiate both sides of the equation implicitly with respect to time *t*.** Be sure to follow all the differentiation rules. The Chain Rule will be especially critical, as you will be differentiating with respect to the parameter t.
5. **Substitute values for any quantities that depend on time.** Notice that it is only safe to do this *after* the differentiation step. Substituting too soon "freezes the picture" and makes changeable variables behave like constants, with zero derivatives.
6. **Interpret the solution.** Translate your mathematical result into the problem setting (with appropriate units) and decide whether the result makes sense.

We illustrate the strategy in Example 2.

EXAMPLE 2 A Rising Balloon

A hot-air balloon rising straight up from a level field is tracked by a range finder 500 feet from the lift-off point. At the moment the range finder's elevation angle is $\pi/4$, the angle is increasing at the rate of 0.14 radians per minute. How fast is the balloon rising at that moment?

SOLUTION

We will carefully identify the six steps of the strategy in this first example.

Step 1: Let h be the height of the balloon and let θ be the elevation angle.

We seek: dh/dt

We know: $d\theta/dt = 0.14$ rad/min

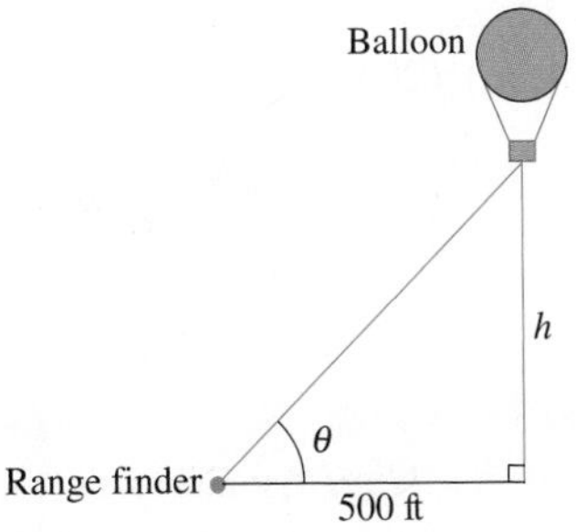

Figure 5.54 The picture shows how h and θ are related geometrically. We seek dh/dt when $\theta = \pi/4$ and $d\theta/dt = 0.14$ rad/min. (Example 2)

Step 2: We draw a picture (Figure 5.54). We label the horizontal distance "500 ft" because it does not change over time. We label the height "h" and the angle of elevation "θ." Notice that we do not label the angle "$\pi/4$," as that would freeze the picture.

Step 3: We need a formula that relates h and θ. Since $\frac{h}{500} = \tan\theta$, we get $h = 500\tan\theta$.

Step 4: Differentiate implicitly:

$$\frac{d}{dt}(h) = \frac{d}{dt}(500\tan\theta)$$

$$\frac{dh}{dt} = 500\sec^2\theta\,\frac{d\theta}{dt}$$

Step 5: Let $d\theta/dt = 0.14$ and let $\theta = \pi/4$. (Note that it is now safe to specify our moment in time.)

$$\frac{dh}{dt} = 500\sec^2\left(\frac{\pi}{4}\right)(0.14) = 500(\sqrt{2})^2(0.14) = 140.$$

Step 6: At the moment in question, the balloon is rising at the rate of 140 ft/min.

Now Try Exercise 11.

Unit Analysis in Example 2

A careful analysis of the units in Example 2 gives

$$dh/dt = (500\text{ ft})(\sqrt{2})^2\,(0.14\text{ rad/min})$$
$$= 140\text{ ft}\cdot\text{rad/min}.$$

Remember that radian measure is actually dimensionless, adaptable to whatever unit is applied to the "unit" circle. The linear units in Example 2 are measured in feet, so "ft • rad " is simply "ft."

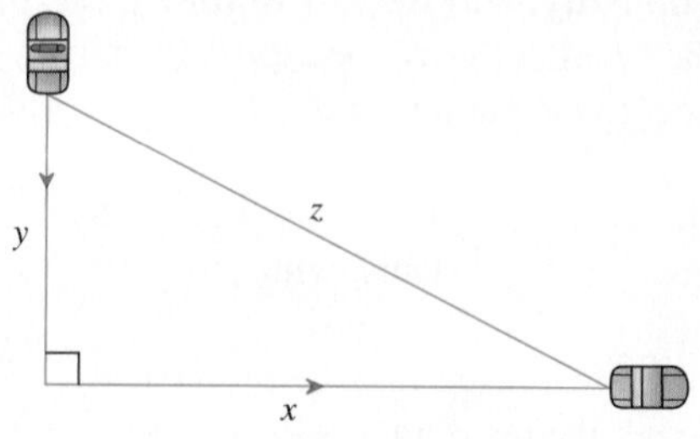

Figure 5.55 A sketch showing the variables in Example 3. We know dy/dt and dz/dt, and we seek dx/dt. The variables x, y, and z are related by the Pythagorean Theorem: $x^2 + y^2 = z^2$.

EXAMPLE 3 A Highway Chase

A police cruiser, approaching a right-angled intersection from the north, is chasing a speeding car that has turned the corner and is now moving straight east. When the cruiser is 0.6 mi north of the intersection and the car is 0.8 mi to the east, the police determine with radar that the distance between them and the car is increasing at 20 mph. If the cruiser is moving at 60 mph at the instant of measurement, what is the speed of the car?

SOLUTION

We carry out the steps of the strategy.

Let x be the distance of the speeding car from the intersection, let y be the distance of the police cruiser from the intersection, and let z be the distance between the car and the cruiser. Distances x and z are increasing, but distance y is decreasing; so dy/dt is negative.

We seek: dx/dt

We know: $dz/dt = 20$ mph and $dy/dt = -60$ mph

A sketch (Figure 5.55) shows that x, y, and z form three sides of a right triangle. We need to relate those three variables, so we use the Pythagorean Theorem:

$$x^2 + y^2 = z^2$$

Differentiating implicitly with respect to t, we get

$$2x\frac{dx}{dt} + 2y\frac{dy}{dt} = 2z\frac{dz}{dt}, \text{ which reduces to } x\frac{dx}{dt} + y\frac{dy}{dt} = z\frac{dz}{dt}.$$

We now substitute the numerical values for x, y, dz/dt, dy/dt, and z (which equals $\sqrt{x^2 + y^2}$):

$$(0.8)\frac{dx}{dt} + (0.6)(-60) = \sqrt{(0.8)^2 + (0.6)^2}(20)$$

$$(0.8)\frac{dx}{dt} - 36 = (1)(20)$$

$$\frac{dx}{dt} = 70$$

At the moment in question, the car's speed is 70 mph. ***Now Try Exercise 13.***

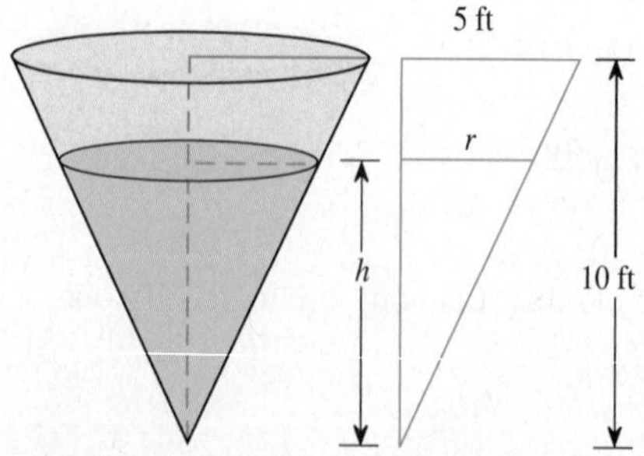

Figure 5.56 In Example 4, the cone of water is increasing in volume inside the reservoir. We know dV/dt and we seek dh/dt. Similar triangles enable us to relate V directly to h.

EXAMPLE 4 Filling a Conical Tank

Water runs into a conical tank at the rate of 9 ft³/min. The tank stands point down and has a height of 10 ft and a base radius of 5 ft. How fast is the water level rising when the water is 6 ft deep?

SOLUTION 1

We carry out the steps of the strategy. Figure 5.56 shows a partially filled conical tank. The tank itself does not change over time; what we are interested in is the changing cone of *water* inside the tank. Let V be the volume, r the radius, and h the height of the cone of water.

We seek: dh/dt

We know: $dV/dt = 9 \text{ ft}^3/\text{min}$

continued

We need to relate V and h. The volume of the cone of water is $V = \frac{1}{3}\pi r^2 h$, but this formula also involves the variable r, whose rate of change is not given. We need to either find dr/dt (see Solution 2) or eliminate r from the equation, which we can do by using the similar triangles in Figure 5.56 to relate r and h:

$$\frac{r}{h} = \frac{5}{10}, \text{ or simply } r = \frac{h}{2}$$

Therefore,

$$V = \frac{1}{3}\pi\left(\frac{h}{2}\right)^2 h = \frac{\pi}{12}h^3.$$

Differentiate with respect to t:

$$\frac{dV}{dt} = \frac{\pi}{12} \cdot 3h^2 \frac{dh}{dt} = \frac{\pi}{4}h^2 \frac{dh}{dt}$$

Let $h = 6$ and $dV/dt = 9$; then solve for dh/dt:

$$9 = \frac{\pi}{4}(6)^2 \frac{dh}{dt}$$

$$\frac{dh}{dt} = \frac{1}{\pi} \approx 0.32$$

At the moment in question, the water level is rising at 0.32 ft/min.

SOLUTION 2

The similar triangle relationship

$$r = \frac{h}{2} \text{ also implies that } \frac{dr}{dt} = \frac{1}{2}\frac{dh}{dt}$$

and that $r = 3$ when $h = 6$. So, we could have left all three variables in the formula $V = \frac{1}{3}\pi r^2 h$ and proceeded as follows:

$$\frac{dV}{dt} = \frac{1}{3}\pi\left(2r\frac{dr}{dt}h + r^2\frac{dh}{dt}\right)$$

$$= \frac{1}{3}\pi\left(2r\left(\frac{1}{2}\frac{dh}{dt}\right)h + r^2\frac{dh}{dt}\right)$$

$$9 = \frac{1}{3}\pi\left(2(3)\left(\frac{1}{2}\frac{dh}{dt}\right)(6) + (3)^2\frac{dh}{dt}\right)$$

$$9 = 9\pi\frac{dh}{dt}$$

$$\frac{dh}{dt} = \frac{1}{\pi}$$

This is obviously more complicated than the one-variable approach. In general, it is computationally easier to simplify expressions as much as possible *before* you differentiate.

Now Try Exercise 17.

Simulating Related Motion

Parametric mode on a grapher can be used to simulate the motion of moving objects when the motion of each can be expressed as a function of time. In a classic related rate problem, the top end of a ladder slides vertically down a wall as the bottom end is pulled horizontally away from the wall at a steady rate. Exploration 1 shows how you can use your grapher to simulate the related movements of the two ends of the ladder.

EXPLORATION 1 The Sliding Ladder

A 10-foot ladder leans against a vertical wall. The base of the ladder is pulled away from the wall at a constant rate of 2 ft/sec.

1. Explain why the motion of the two ends of the ladder can be represented by the parametric equations given below.

$$\begin{aligned} X1T &= 2T \\ Y1T &= 0 \\ X2T &= 0 \\ Y2T &= \sqrt{10^2 - (2T)^2} \end{aligned}$$

2. What minimum and maximum values of T make sense in this problem?
3. Put your grapher in parametric and simultaneous modes. Enter the parametric equations and change the graphing style to "0" (the little ball) if your grapher has this feature. Set Tmin=0, Tmax=5, Tstep=5/20, Xmin=−1, Xmax=17, Xscl=0, Ymin=−1, Ymax=11, and Yscl=0. You can speed up the action by making the denominator in the Tstep smaller or slow it down by making it larger.
4. Press GRAPH and watch the two ends of the ladder move as time changes. Do both ends seem to move at a constant rate?
5. To see the simulation again, enter "ClrDraw" from the DRAW menu.
6. If y represents the vertical height of the top of the ladder and x the distance of the bottom from the wall, relate y and x and find dy/dt in terms of x and y. (Remember that $dx/dt = 2$.)
7. Find dy/dt when $t = 3$ and interpret its meaning. Why is it negative?
8. In theory, how fast is the top of the ladder moving as it hits the ground?

Figure 5.57 shows you how to write a calculator program that animates the falling ladder as a line segment.

```
PROGRAM:LADDER
:For (A, 0, 5, .25)
:ClrDraw
:Line(2,2+√ (100–
(2A)²), 2+2A, 2)
:If A=0:Pause
:End
```

```
WINDOW
 Xmin=2
 Xmax=20
 Xscl=0
 Ymin=1
 Ymax=13
 Yscl=0
 Xres=1
```

Figure 5.57 This 5-step program (with the viewing window set as shown) will animate the ladder in Exploration 1. Be sure any functions in the "Y=" register are turned off. Run the program and the ladder appears against the wall; push ENTER to start the bottom moving away from the wall.

For an enhanced picture, you can insert the commands ":Pt-On(2,2+$\sqrt{(100 - (2A)^2)}$,2)" and ":Pt-On(2+2A,2,2)" on either side of the middle line of the program.

Quick Review 5.6 (For help, go to Sections 1.1, 1.4, and 4.2.)

Exercise numbers with a gray background indicate problems that the authors have designed to be solved *without a calculator*.

In Exercises 1 and 2, find the distance between the points A and B.

1. $A(0, 5),\ B(7, 0)$ **2.** $A(0, a), B(b, 0)$

In Exercises 3–6, find dy/dx.

3. $2xy + y^2 = x + y$

4. $x \sin y = 1 - xy$

5. $x^2 = \tan y$ **6.** $\ln(x + y) = 2x$

In Exercises 7 and 8, find a parametrization for the line segment with endpoints A and B.

7. $A(-2, 1), B(4, -3)$ **8.** $A(0, -4), B(5, 0)$

In Exercises 9 and 10, let $x = 2 \cos t$, $y = 2 \sin t$. Find a parameter interval that produces the indicated portion of the graph.

9. The portion in the second and third quadrants, including the points on the axes.

10. The portion in the fourth quadrant, including the points on the axes.

Section 5.6 Exercises

In Exercises 1–41, assume all variables are differentiable functions of t.

1. *Area* The radius r and area A of a circle are related by the equation $A = \pi r^2$. Write an equation that relates dA/dt to dr/dt.

2. *Surface Area* The radius r and surface area S of a sphere are related by the equation $S = 4\pi r^2$. Write an equation that relates dS/dt to dr/dt.

3. *Volume* The radius r, height h, and volume V of a right circular cylinder are related by the equation $V = \pi r^2 h$.

(a) How is dV/dt related to dh/dt if r is constant?

(b) How is dV/dt related to dr/dt if h is constant?

(c) How is dV/dt related to dr/dt and dh/dt if neither r nor h is constant?

4. *Electrical Power* The power P (watts) of an electric circuit is related to the circuit's resistance R (ohms) and current I (amperes) by the equation $P = RI^2$.

(a) How is dP/dt related to dR/dt and dI/dt?

(b) How is dR/dt related to dI/dt if P is constant?

5. *Diagonals* If x, y, and z are lengths of the edges of a rectangular box, the common length of the box's diagonals is $s = \sqrt{x^2 + y^2 + z^2}$. How is ds/dt related to dx/dt, dy/dt, and dz/dt?

6. *Area* If a and b are the lengths of two sides of a triangle, and θ the measure of the included angle, the area A of the triangle is $A = (1/2)\, ab \sin \theta$. How is dA/dt related to da/dt, db/dt, and $d\theta/dt$?

7. *Changing Voltage* The voltage V (volts), current I (amperes), and resistance R (ohms) of an electric circuit like the one shown here are related by the equation $V = IR$. Suppose that V is increasing at the rate of 1 volt/sec while I is decreasing at the rate of $1/3$ amp/sec. Let t denote time in sec.

(a) What is the value of dV/dt?

(b) What is the value of dI/dt?

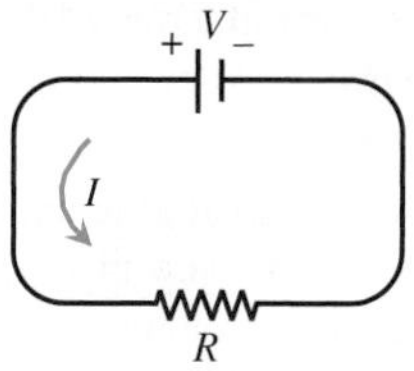

(c) Write an equation that relates dR/dt to dV/dt and dI/dt.

(d) **Writing to Learn** Find the rate at which R is changing when $V = 12$ volts and $I = 2$ amp. Is R increasing or decreasing? Explain.

8. *Heating a Plate* When a circular plate of metal is heated in an oven, its radius increases at the rate of 0.01 cm/sec. At what rate is the plate's area increasing when the radius is 50 cm?

9. *Changing Dimensions in a Rectangle* The length l of a rectangle is decreasing at the rate of 2 cm/sec while the width w is increasing at the rate of 2 cm/sec. When $l = 12$ cm and $w = 5$ cm, find the rates of change of.

(a) the area, (b) the perimeter, and

(c) the length of a diagonal of the rectangle.

(d) **Writing to Learn** Which of these quantities are decreasing, and which are increasing? Explain.

10. *Changing Dimensions in a Rectangular Box* Suppose that the edge lengths x, y, and z of a closed rectangular box are changing at the following rates:

$$\frac{dx}{dt} = 1 \text{ m/sec}, \quad \frac{dy}{dt} = -2 \text{ m/sec}, \quad \frac{dz}{dt} = 1 \text{ m/sec}$$

Find the rates at which the box's (a) volume, (b) surface area, and (c) diagonal length $s = \sqrt{x^2 + y^2 + z^2}$ are changing at the instant when $x = 4$, $y = 3$, and $z = 2$.

11. *Inflating Balloon* A spherical balloon is inflated with helium at the rate of $100\pi\ \text{ft}^3/\text{min}$.

(a) How fast is the balloon's radius increasing at the instant the radius is 5 ft?

(b) How fast is the surface area increasing at that instant?

12. *Growing Raindrop* Suppose that a droplet of mist is a perfect sphere and that, through condensation, the droplet picks up moisture at a rate proportional to its surface area. Show that under these circumstances the droplet's radius increases at a constant rate.

13. *Air Traffic Control* An airplane is flying at an altitude of 7 mi and passes directly over a radar antenna as shown in the figure. When the plane is 10 mi from the antenna ($s = 10$), the radar detects that the distance s is changing at the rate of 300 mph. What is the speed of the airplane at that moment?

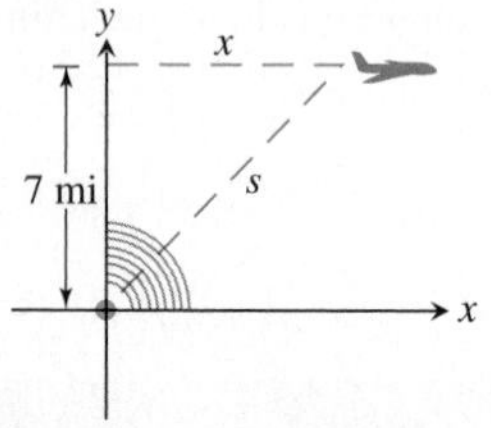

14. *Flying a Kite* Inge flies a kite at a height of 300 ft, the wind carrying the kite horizontally away at a rate of 25 ft/sec. How fast must she let out the string when the kite is 500 ft away from her?

15. *Boring a Cylinder* The mechanics at Lincoln Automotive are reboring a 6-in.-deep cylinder to fit a new piston. The machine they are using increases the cylinder's radius one-thousandth of an inch every 3 min. How rapidly is the cylinder volume increasing when the bore (diameter) is 3.800 in.?

16. *Growing Sand Pile* Sand falls from a conveyor belt at the rate of 10 m^3/min onto the top of a conical pile. The height of the pile is always three-eighths of the base diameter. How fast are the **(a)** height and **(b)** radius changing when the pile is 4 m high? Give your answer in cm/min.

17. *Draining Conical Reservoir* Water is flowing at the rate of 50 m^3/min from a concrete conical reservoir (vertex down) of base radius 45 m and height 6 m. **(a)** How fast is the water level falling when the water is 5 m deep? **(b)** How fast is the radius of the water's surface changing at that moment? Give your answer in cm/min.

18. *Draining Hemispherical Reservoir* Water is flowing at the rate of 6 m^3/min from a reservoir shaped like a hemispherical bowl of radius 13 m, shown here in profile. Answer the following questions given that the volume of water in a hemispherical bowl of radius R is $V = (\pi/3)y^2(3R - y)$ when the water is y units deep.

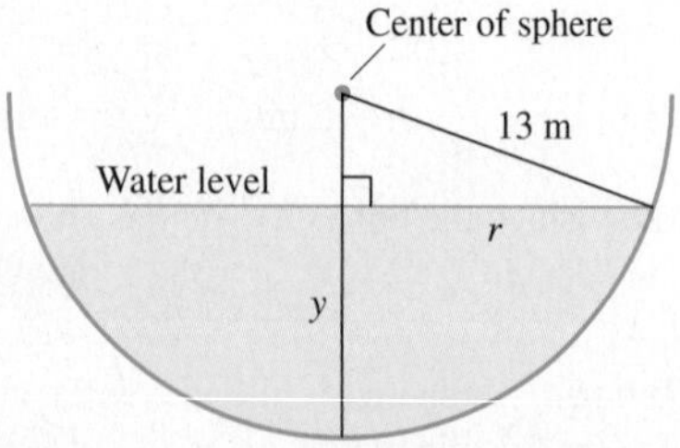

(a) At what rate is the water level changing when the water is 8 m deep?

(b) What is the radius r of the water's surface when the water is y m deep?

(c) At what rate is the radius r changing when the water is 8 m deep?

19. *Sliding Ladder* A 13-ft ladder is leaning against a house (see figure) when its base starts to slide away. By the time the base is 12 ft from the house, the base is moving at the rate of 5 ft/sec.

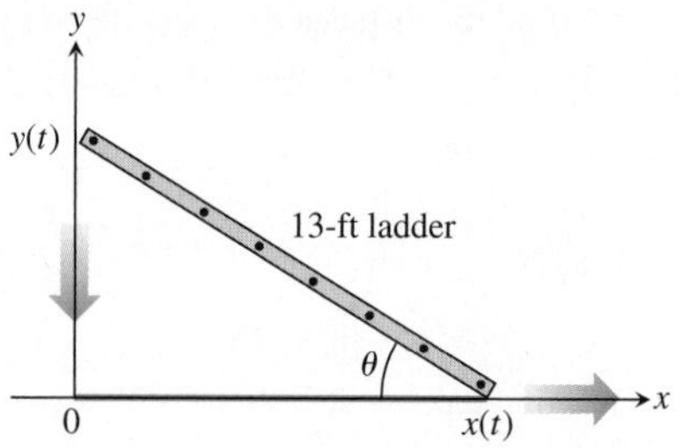

(a) How fast is the top of the ladder sliding down the wall at that moment?

(b) At what rate is the area of the triangle formed by the ladder, wall, and ground changing at that moment?

(c) At what rate is the angle θ between the ladder and the ground changing at that moment?

20. *Filling a Trough* A trough is 15 ft long and 4 ft across the top, as shown in the figure. Its ends are isosceles triangles with height 3 ft. Water runs into the trough at the rate of 2.5 ft^3/min. How fast is the water level rising when it is 2 ft deep?

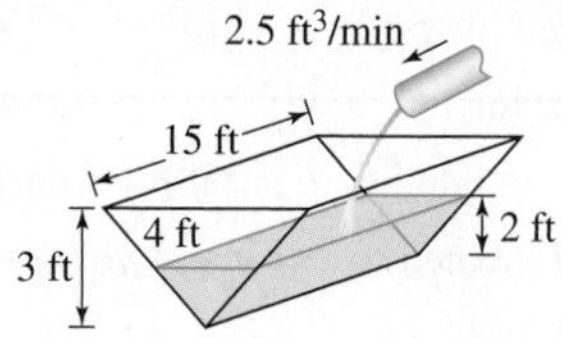

21. *Hauling in a Dinghy* A dinghy is pulled toward a dock by a rope from the bow through a ring on the dock 6 ft above the bow, as shown in the figure. The rope is hauled in at the rate of 2 ft/sec.

(a) How fast is the boat approaching the dock when 10 ft of rope are out?

(b) At what rate is angle θ changing at that moment?

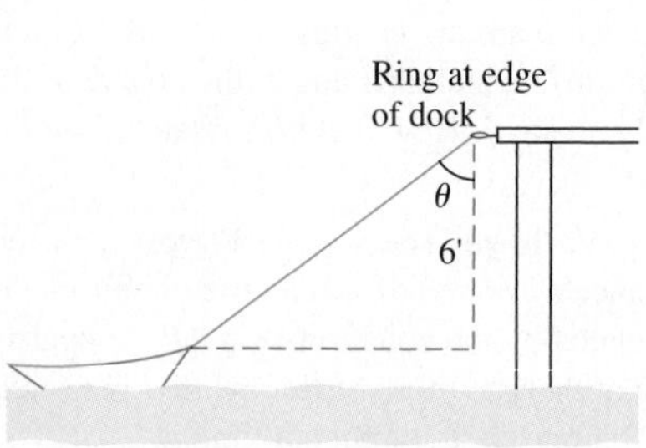

22. *Rising Balloon* A balloon is rising vertically above a level, straight road at a constant rate of 1 ft/sec. Just when the balloon is 65 ft above the ground, a bicycle moving at a constant rate of 17 ft/sec passes under it. How fast is the distance between the bicycle and balloon increasing 3 sec later (see figure)?

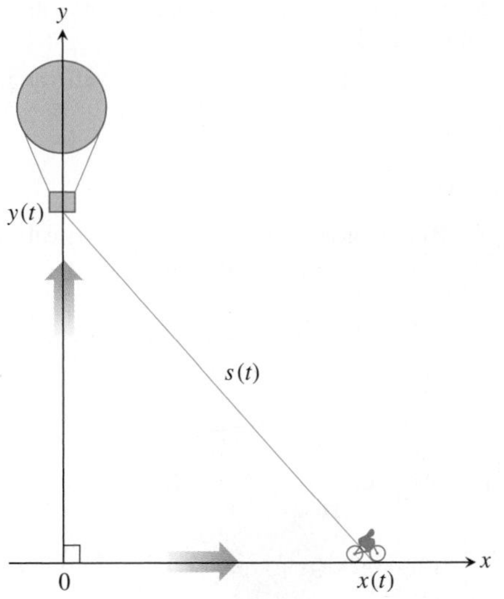

In Exercises 23 and 24, a particle is moving along the curve $y = f(x)$.

23. Let $y = f(x) = \dfrac{10}{1 + x^2}$.

If $dx/dt = 3$ cm/sec, find dy/dt at the point where

(a) $x = -2$. **(b)** $x = 0$. **(c)** $x = 20$.

24. Let $y = f(x) = x^3 - 4x$.

If $dx/dt = -2$ cm/sec, find dy/dt at the point where

(a) $x = -3$. **(b)** $x = 1$. **(c)** $x = 4$.

25. *Particle Motion* A particle moves along the parabola $y = x^2$ in the first quadrant in such a way that its x-coordinate (in meters) increases at a constant rate of 10 m/sec. How fast is the angle of inclination θ of the line joining the particle to the origin changing when $x = 3$?

26. *Particle Motion* A particle moves from right to left along the parabolic curve $y = \sqrt{-x}$ in such a way that its x-coordinate (in meters) decreases at the rate of 8 m/sec. How fast is the angle of inclination θ of the line joining the particle to the origin changing when $x = -4$?

27. *Melting Ice* A spherical iron ball is coated with a layer of ice of uniform thickness. If the ice melts at the rate of 8 mL/min, how fast is the outer surface area of ice decreasing when the outer diameter (ball plus ice) is 20 cm?

28. *Particle Motion* A particle $P(x, y)$ is moving in the coordinate plane in such a way that $dx/dt = -1$ m/sec and $dy/dt = -5$ m/sec. How fast is the particle's distance from the origin changing as it passes through the point $(5, 12)$?

29. *Moving Shadow* A man 6 ft tall walks at the rate of 5 ft/sec toward a streetlight that is 16 ft above the ground. At what rate is the length of his shadow changing when he is 10 ft from the base of the light?

30. *Moving Shadow* A light shines from the top of a pole 50 ft high. A ball is dropped from the same height from a point 30 ft away from the light, as shown below. How fast is the ball's shadow moving along the ground 1/2 sec later? (Assume the ball falls a distance $s = 16t^2$ in t sec.)

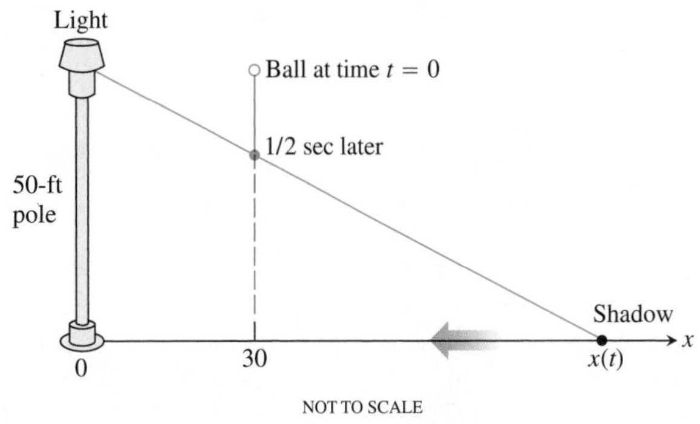

31. *Moving Race Car* You are videotaping a race from a stand 132 ft from the track, following a car that is moving at 180 mph (264 ft/sec), as shown in the figure. About how fast will your camera angle θ be changing when the car is right in front of you? a half second later?

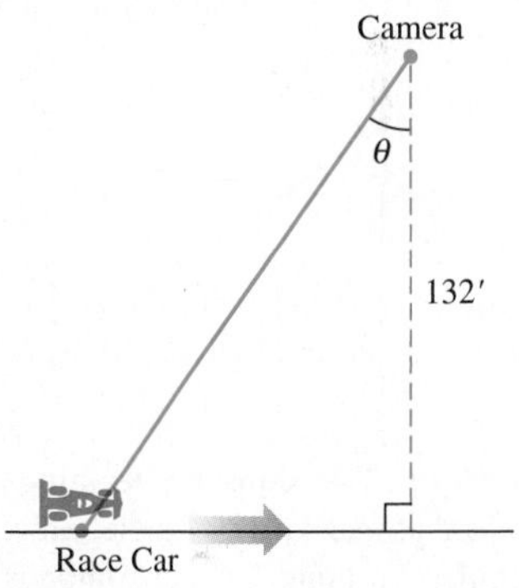

32. *Speed Trap* A highway patrol airplane flies 3 mi above a level, straight road at a constant rate of 120 mph. The pilot sees an oncoming car and with radar determines that at the instant the line-of-sight distance from plane to car is 5 mi the line-of-sight distance is decreasing at the rate of 160 mph. Find the car's speed along the highway.

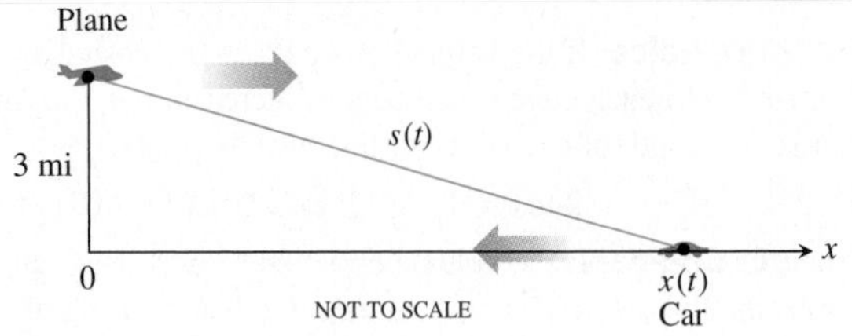

33. *Building's Shadow* On a morning of a day when the sun will pass directly overhead, the shadow of an 80-ft building on level ground is 60 ft long, as shown in the figure. At the moment in question, the angle θ the sun makes with the ground is increasing at the rate of 0.27°/min. At what rate is the shadow length decreasing? Express your answer in in./min, to the nearest tenth. (Remember to use radians.)

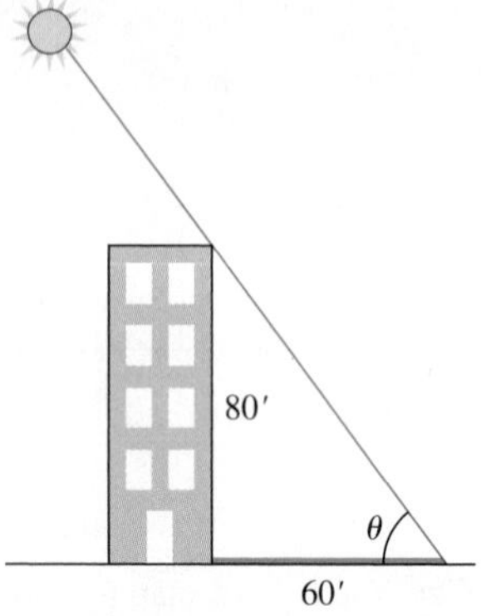

34. ***Walkers*** A and B are walking on straight streets that meet at right angles. A approaches the intersection at 2 m/sec and B moves away from the intersection at 1 m/sec, as shown in the figure. At what rate is the angle θ changing when A is 10 m from the intersection and B is 20 m from the intersection? Express your answer in degrees per second to the nearest degree.

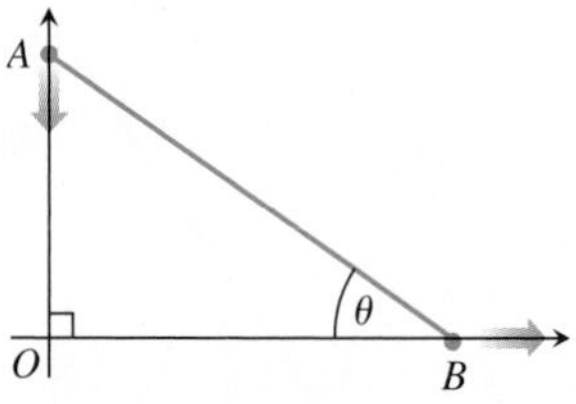

35. ***Moving Ships*** Two ships are steaming away from a point O along routes that make a 120° angle. Ship A moves at 14 knots (nautical miles per hour; a nautical mile is 2000 yards). Ship B moves at 21 knots. How fast are the ships moving apart when $OA = 5$ and $OB = 3$ nautical miles?

Standardized Test Questions

You may use a graphing calculator to solve the following problems.

36. **True or False** If the radius of a circle is expanding at a constant rate, then its circumference is increasing at a constant rate. Justify your answer.

37. **True or False** If the radius of a circle is expanding at a constant rate, then its area is increasing at a constant rate. Justify your answer.

38. **Multiple Choice** If the volume of a cube is increasing at 24 in^3/min and each edge of the cube is increasing at 2 in./min, what is the length of each edge of the cube?
(A) 2 in. **(B)** $2\sqrt{2}$ in. **(C)** $\sqrt[3]{12}$ in **(D)** 4 in. **(E)** 8 in.

39. **Multiple Choice** If the volume of a cube is increasing at 24 in^3/min and the surface area of the cube is increasing at 12 in^2/ min, what is the length of each edge of the cube?
(A) 2 in. **(B)** $2\sqrt{2}$ in. **(C)** $\sqrt[3]{12}$ in. **(D)** 4 in. **(E)** 8 in.

40. **Multiple Choice** A particle is moving around the unit circle (the circle of radius 1 centered at the origin). At the point (0.6, 0.8) the particle has horizontal velocity $dx/dt = 3$. What is its vertical velocity dy/dt at that point?
(A) −3.875 **(B)** −3.75 **(C)** −2.25 **(D)** 3.75 **(E)** 3.875

41. **Multiple Choice** A cylindrical rubber cord is stretched at a constant rate of 2 cm per second. Assuming its volume does not change, how fast is its radius shrinking when its length is 100 cm and its radius is 1 cm?
(A) 0 cm/sec **(B)** 0.01 cm/sec **(C)** 0.02 cm/sec
(D) 2 cm/sec **(E)** 3.979 cm/sec

Explorations

42. **Making Coffee** Coffee is draining from a conical filter into a cylindrical coffeepot at the rate of 10 in^3/min.

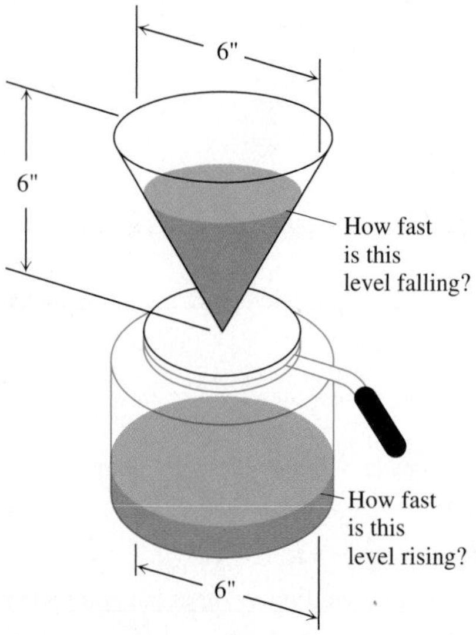

(a) How fast is the level in the pot rising when the coffee in the cone is 5 in. deep?
(b) How fast is the level in the cone falling at that moment?

43. ***Cost, Revenue, and Profit*** A company can manufacture x items at a cost of $c(x)$ dollars, a sales revenue of $r(x)$ dollars, and a profit of $p(x) = r(x) - c(x)$ dollars (all amounts in thousands). Find dc/dt, dr/dt, and dp/dt for the following values of x and dx/dt.
(a) $r(x) = 9x$, $c(x) = x^3 - 6x^2 + 15x$, and $dx/dt = 0.1$ when $x = 2$.
(b) $r(x) = 70x$, $c(x) = x^3 - 6x^2 + 45/x$, and $dx/dt = 0.05$ when $x = 1.5$.

44. **Group Activity *Cardiac Output*** In the late 1860s, Adolf Fick, a professor of physiology in the Faculty of Medicine in Würtzberg, Germany, developed one of the methods we use today for measuring how much blood your heart pumps in a minute. Your cardiac output as you read this sentence is probably about 7 liters a minute. At rest it is likely to be a bit under 6 L/min. If you are a trained marathon runner running a marathon, your cardiac output can be as high as 30 L/min.

Your cardiac output can be calculated with the formula

$$y = \frac{Q}{D},$$

where Q is the number of milliliters of CO_2 you exhale in a minute and D is the difference between the CO_2 concentration (mL/L) in the blood pumped to the lungs and the CO_2 concentration in the blood returning from the lungs. With $Q = 233$ mL/min and $D = 97 - 56 = 41$ mL/L,

$$y = \frac{233 \text{ mL/min}}{41 \text{ mL/L}} \approx 5.68 \text{ L/min},$$

fairly close to the 6 L/min that most people have at basal (resting) conditions. (Data courtesy of J. Kenneth Herd, M.D., Quillan College of Medicine, East Tennessee State University.)

Suppose that when $Q = 233$ and $D = 41$, we also know that D is decreasing at the rate of 2 units a minute but that Q remains unchanged. What is happening to the cardiac output?

Extending the Ideas

45. *Motion Along A Circle* A wheel of radius 2 ft makes 8 revolutions about its center every second.

(a) Explain how the parametric equations

$$x = 2 \cos \theta, \quad y = 2 \sin \theta$$

can be used to represent the motion of the wheel.

(b) Express θ as a function of time t.

(c) Find the rate of horizontal movement and the rate of vertical movement of a point on the edge of the wheel when it is at the position given by $\theta = \pi/4, \pi/2$, and π.

46. *Ferris Wheel* A Ferris wheel with radius 30 ft makes one revolution every 10 sec.

(a) Assume that the center of the Ferris wheel is located at the point $(0, 40)$, and write parametric equations to model its motion. [*Hint:* See Exercise 45.]

(b) At $t = 0$ the point P on the Ferris wheel is located at $(30, 40)$. Find the rate of horizontal movement, and the rate of vertical movement of the point P when $t = 5$ sec and $t = 8$ sec.

47. *Industrial Production* (a) Economists often use the expression "rate of growth" in relative rather than absolute terms. For example, let $u = f(t)$ be the number of people in the labor force at time t in a given industry. (We treat this function as though it were differentiable even though it is an integer-valued step function.)

Let $v = g(t)$ be the average production per person in the labor force at time t. The total production is then $y = uv$. If the labor force is growing at the rate of 4% per year $(du/dt = 0.04u)$ and the production per worker is growing at the rate of 5% per year $(dv/dt = 0.05v)$, find the rate of growth of the total production, y.

(b) Suppose that the labor force in part (a) is decreasing at the rate of 2% per year while the production per person is increasing at the rate of 3% per year. Is the total production increasing, or is it decreasing, and at what rate?

Quick Quiz for AP* Preparation: Sections 5.4–5.6

You may use a graphing calculator to solve the following problems.

1. Multiple Choice If Newton's method is used to approximate the real root of $x^3 + 2x - 1 = 0$, what would the third approximation, x_3, be if the first approximation is $x_1 = 1$?

(A) 0.453 (B) 0.465 (C) 0.495 (D) 0.600 (E) 1.977

2. Multiple Choice The sides of a right triangle with legs x and y and hypotenuse z increase in such a way that $dz/dt = 1$ and $dx/dt = 3\, dy/dt$. At the instant when $x = 4$ and $y = 3$, what is dx/dt?

(A) $\frac{1}{3}$ (B) 1 (C) 2 (D) $\sqrt{5}$ (E) 5

3. Multiple Choice An observer 70 meters south of a railroad crossing watches an eastbound train traveling at 60 meters per second. At how many meters per second is the train moving away from the observer 4 seconds after it passes through the intersection?

(A) 57.60 (B) 57.88 (C) 59.20 (D) 60.00 (E) 67.40

4. Free Response (a) Approximate $\sqrt{26}$ by using the linearization of $y = \sqrt{x}$ at the point $(25, 5)$. Show the computation that leads to your conclusion.

(b) Approximate $\sqrt{26}$ by using a first guess of 5 and one iteration of Newton's method to approximate the zero of $x^2 - 26$. Show the computation that leads to your conclusion.

(c) Approximate $\sqrt[3]{26}$ by using an appropriate linearization. Show the computation that leads to your conclusion.

Chapter 5 Key Terms

absolute change (p. 242)
absolute maximum value (p. 191)
absolute minimum value (p. 191)
antiderivative (p. 204)
antidifferentiation (p. 204)
arithmetic mean (p. 208)
average cost (p. 228)
center of linear approximation (p. 237)
concave down (p. 211)
concave up (p. 211)
Concavity Test (p. 212)
critical point (p. 194)
decreasing function (p. 202)
differential (p. 240)
differential estimate of change (p. 242)
differential of a function (p. 240)
extrema (p. 191)
Extreme Value Theorem (p. 192)

First Derivative Test (p. 209)
First Derivative Test for Local Extrema (p. 209)
geometric mean (p. 208)
global maximum value (p. 187)
global minimum value (p. 187)
increasing function (p. 202)
linear approximation (p. 237)
linearization (p. 237)
local linearity (p. 237)
local maximum value (p. 193)
local minimum value (p. 193)
logistic or life cycle curve (p. 214)
logistic regression (p. 215)
marginal analysis (p. 227)
marginal cost and revenue (p. 227)
Mean Value Theorem (p. 200)
monotonic function (p. 208)
Newton's method (p. 244)
optimization (p. 223)
percentage change (p. 242)
point of inflection (p. 212)
profit (p. 227)
quadratic approximation (p. 249)
related rates (p. 250)
relative change (p. 242)
relative extrema (p. 193)
Rolle's Theorem (p. 200)
Second Derivative Test for Local Extrema (p. 215)
standard linear approximation (p. 237)
stationary point (p. 194)

Chapter 5 Review Exercises

Exercise numbers with a gray background indicate problems that the authors have designed to be solved *without a calculator*.

The collection of exercises marked in red could be used as a chapter test.

In Exercises 1 and 2, use analytic methods to find the global extreme values of the function on the interval and state where they occur.

1. $y = x\sqrt{2 - x}, \quad -2 \le x \le 2$

2. $y = x^3 - 9x^2 - 21x - 11, \quad -\infty < x < \infty$

In Exercises 3 and 4, use analytic methods. Find the intervals on which the function is

(a) increasing, **(b)** decreasing,
(c) concave up, **(d)** concave down.

Then find any

(e) local extreme values, **(f)** inflection points.

3. $y = x^2 e^{1/x^2}$ **4.** $y = x\sqrt{4 - x^2}$

In Exercises 5–16, use analytic methods to find the intervals on which the function is

(a) increasing, **(b)** decreasing,
(c) concave up, **(d)** concave down.

Support your answers graphically. Then find any

(e) local extreme values, **(f)** inflection points.

5. $y = 1 + x - x^2 - x^4$ **6.** $y = e^{x-1} - x$

7. $y = \dfrac{1}{\sqrt[4]{1 - x^2}}$. **8.** $y = \dfrac{x}{x^3 - 1}$

9. $y = \cos^{-1} x$ **10.** $y = \dfrac{x}{x^2 + 2x + 3}$

11. $y = \ln|x|, -2 \le x \le 2, \quad x \ne 0$

12. $y = \sin 3x + \cos 4x, \quad 0 \le x \le 2\pi$

13. $y = \begin{cases} e^{-x}, & x \le 0 \\ 4x - x^3, & x > 0 \end{cases}$

14. $y = -x^5 + \dfrac{7}{3}x^3 + 5x^2 + 4x + 2$

15. $y = x^{4/5}(2 - x)$

16. $y = \dfrac{5 - 4x + 4x^2 - x^3}{x - 2}$

In Exercises 17 and 18, use the derivative of the function $y = f(x)$ to find the points at which f has a

(a) local maximum, **(b)** local minimum, or
(c) point of inflection.

17. $y' = 6(x + 1)(x - 2)^2$ **18.** $y' = 6(x + 1)(x - 2)$

In Exercises 19–22, find all possible functions with the given derivative.

19. $f'(x) = x^{-5} + e^{-x}$ **20.** $f'(x) = \sec x \tan x$

21. $f'(x) = \dfrac{2}{x} + x^2 + 1, \ x > 0$ **22.** $f'(x) = \sqrt{x} + \dfrac{1}{\sqrt{x}}$

In Exercises 23 and 24, find the function with the given derivative whose graph passes through the point P.

23. $f'(x) = \sin x + \cos x, \quad P(\pi, 3)$

24. $f'(x) = x^{1/3} + x^2 + x + 1, \quad P(1, 0)$

In Exercises 25 and 26, the velocity v or acceleration a of a particle is given. Find the particle's position s at time t.

25. $v = 9.8t + 5, \ s = 10$ when $t = 0$

26. $a = 32, \ v = 20$ and $s = 5$ when $t = 0$

In Exercises 27–30, find the linearization $L(x)$ of $f(x)$ at $x = a$.

27. $f(x) = \tan x, \quad a = -\pi/4$ **28.** $f(x) = \sec x, \quad a = \pi/4$

29. $f(x) = \dfrac{1}{1 + \tan x}, \quad a = 0$ **30.** $f(x) = e^x + \sin x, \ a = 0$

In Exercises 31–34, use the graph to answer the questions.

31. Identify any global extreme values of f and the values of x at which they occur.

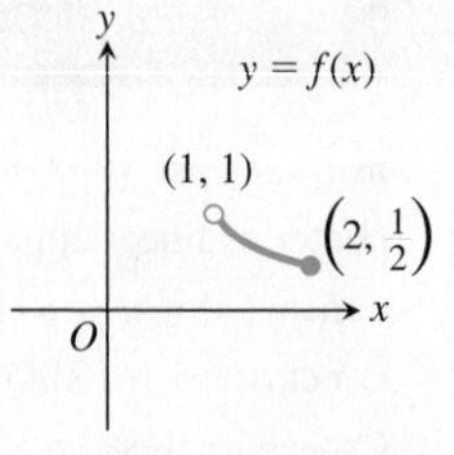

Figure for Exercise 31

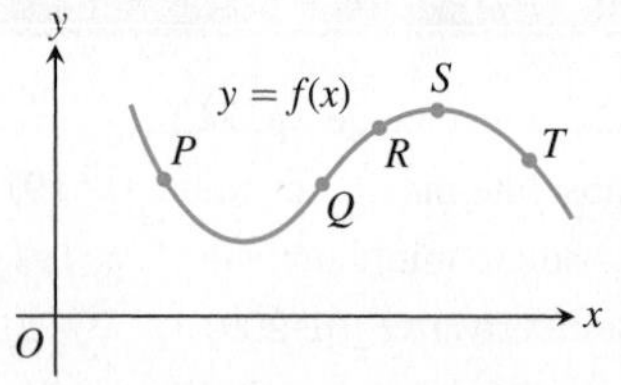

Figure for Exercise 32

32. At which of the five points on the graph of $y = f(x)$ shown here

(a) are y' and y'' both negative?

(b) is y' negative and y'' positive?

33. Estimate the intervals on which the function $y = f(x)$ is **(a)** increasing; **(b)** decreasing. **(c)** Estimate any local extreme values of the function and where they occur.

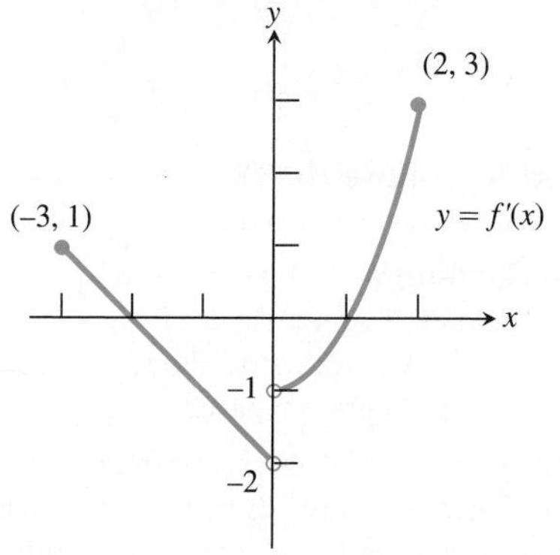

34. Here is the graph of the fruit fly population from Section 2.4, Example 2. On approximately what day did the population's growth rate change from increasing to decreasing?

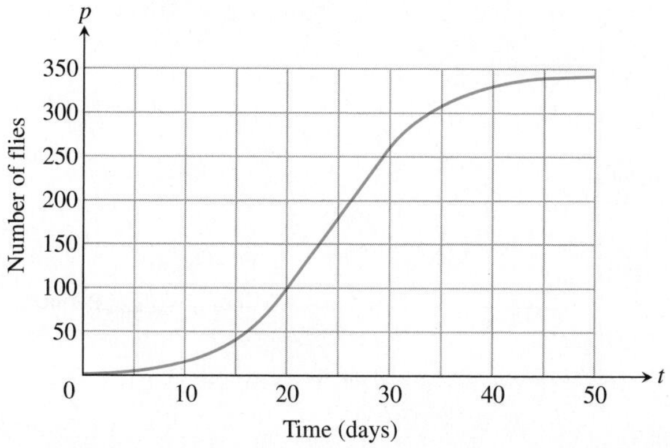

35. *Connecting f and f′* The graph of f' is shown in Exercise 33. Sketch a possible graph of f given that it is continuous with domain $[-3, 2]$ and $f(-3) = 0$.

36. *Connecting f, f′, and f″* The function f is continuous on $[0, 3]$ and satisfies the following.

x	0	1	2	3
f	0	-2	0	3
f'	-3	0	does not exist	4
f''	0	1	does not exist	0

x	$0 < x < 1$	$1 < x < 2$	$2 < x < 3$
f	$-$	$-$	$+$
f'	$-$	$+$	$+$
f''	$+$	$+$	$+$

(a) Find the absolute extrema of f and where they occur.

(b) Find any points of inflection.

(c) Sketch a possible graph of f.

37. *Mean Value Theorem* Let $f(x) = x \ln x$.

(a) Writing to Learn Show that f satisfies the hypotheses of the Mean Value Theorem on the interval $[a, b] = [0.5, 3]$.

(b) Find the value(s) of c in (a, b) for which

$$f'(c) = \frac{f(b) - f(a)}{b - a}.$$

(c) Write an equation for the secant line AB where $A = (a, f(a))$ and $B = (b, f(b))$.

(d) Write an equation for the tangent line that is parallel to the secant line AB.

38. *Motion along a Line* A particle is moving along a line with position function $s(t) = 3 + 4t - 3t^2 - t^3$. Find the **(a)** velocity and **(b)** acceleration, and **(c)** describe the motion of the particle for $t \geq 0$.

39. *Approximating Functions* Let f be a function with $f'(x) = \sin x^2$ and $f(0) = -1$.

(a) Find the linearization of f at $x = 0$.

(b) Approximate the value of f at $x = 0.1$.

(c) Writing to Learn Is the actual value of f at $x = 0.1$ greater than or less than the approximation in (b)?

40. *Differentials* Let $y = x^2 e^{-x}$. Find **(a)** dy and **(b)** evaluate dy for $x = 1$ and $dx = 0.01$.

41. Table 5.5 shows the growth of the U.S. population from 1790 to 2000 in 30-year increments and includes the growth in 2010.

TABLE 5.5 U.S. Population Growth

Year	Growth
1790	3929
1820	9638
1850	23,192
1880	50,189
1910	92,228
1940	132,165
1970	203,302
2000	281,422
2010	309,447

Source: http://www.census.gov/population/censusdata/table-4.pdf US Census Bureau; (2010) http://www.census.gov/

(a) Find the logistic regression for the data.

(b) Graph the data in a scatter plot and superimpose the regression curve.

(c) Use the regression equation to predict the U.S. population in 2050.

(d) About what year is the U.S. population growing the fastest? What significant behavior does the graph of the regression equation exhibit at that point?

(e) What does the regression equation indicate about the U.S. population in the long run?

(f) Writing to Learn Is your answer to part (e) reasonable?

42. ***Newton's Method*** Use Newton's method to estimate all real solutions to $2\cos x - \sqrt{1 + x} = 0$. State your answers accurate to 6 decimal places.

43. ***Rocket Launch*** A rocket lifts off the surface of Earth with a constant acceleration of 20 m/sec^2. How fast will the rocket be going 1 min later?

44. ***Launching on Mars*** The acceleration of gravity near the surface of Mars is 3.72 m/sec^2. If a rock is blasted straight up from the surface with an initial velocity of 93 m/sec (about 208 mph), how high does it go?

45. ***Area of Sector*** If the perimeter of the circular sector shown here is fixed at 100 ft, what values of r and s will give the sector the greatest area?

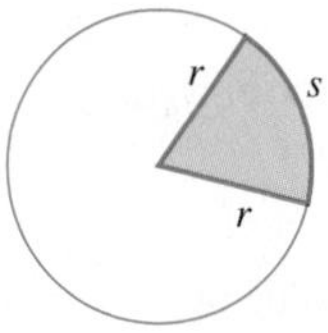

46. ***Area of Triangle*** An isosceles triangle has its vertex at the origin and its base parallel to the x-axis with the vertices above the axis on the curve $y = 27 - x^2$. Find the largest area the triangle can have.

47. ***Storage Bin*** Find the dimensions of the largest open-top storage bin with a square base and vertical sides that can be made from 108 ft^2 of sheet steel. (Neglect the thickness of the steel and assume that there is no waste.)

48. ***Designing a Vat*** You are to design an open-top rectangular stainless-steel vat. It is to have a square base and a volume of 32 ft^3, to be welded from quarter-inch plate, and weigh no more than necessary. What dimensions do you recommend?

49. ***Inscribing a Cylinder*** Find the height and radius of the largest right circular cylinder that can be put into a sphere of radius $\sqrt{3}$, as described in the figure.

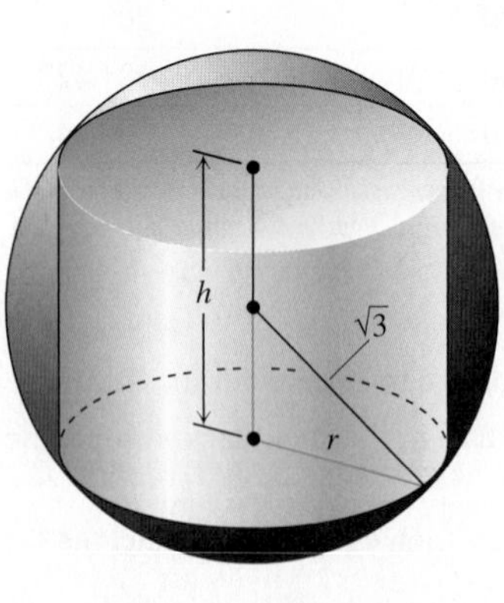

50. ***Cone in a Cone*** The figure shows two right circular cones, one upside down inside the other. The two bases are parallel, and the vertex of the smaller cone lies at the center of the larger cone's base. What values of r and h will give the smaller cone the largest possible volume?

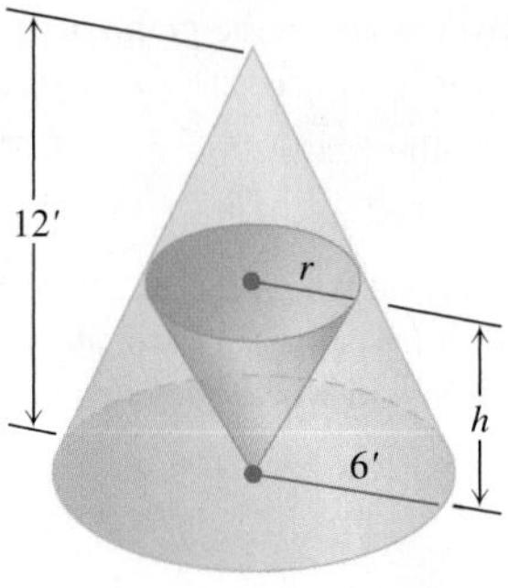

51. ***Box with Lid*** Repeat Exercise 18 of Section 5.4 but this time remove the two equal squares from the corners of a 15-in. side.

52. ***Inscribing a Rectangle*** A rectangle is inscribed under one arch of $y = 8\cos(0.3x)$ with its base on the x-axis and its upper two vertices on the curve symmetric about the y-axis. What is the largest area the rectangle can have?

53. ***Oil Refinery*** A drilling rig 12 mi offshore is to be connected by a pipe to a refinery onshore, 20 mi down the coast from the rig, as shown in the figure. If underwater pipe costs \$40,000 per mile and land-based pipe costs \$30,000 per mile, what values of x and y give the least expensive connection?

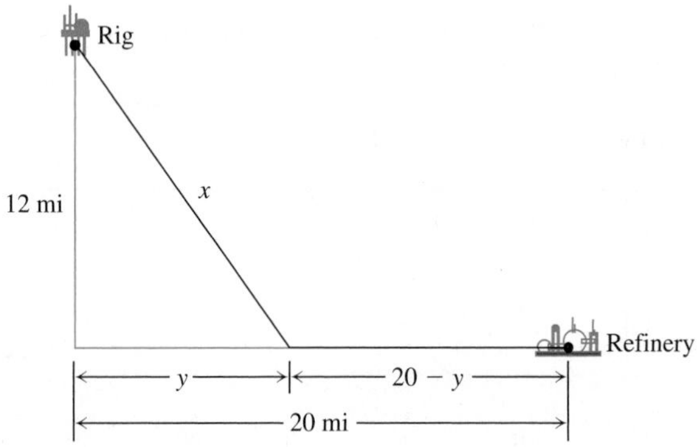

54. ***Designing an Athletic Field*** An athletic field is to be built in the shape of a rectangle x units long capped by semicircular regions of radius r at the two ends. The field is to be bounded by a 400-m running track. What values of x and r will give the rectangle the largest possible area?

55. ***Manufacturing Tires*** Your company can manufacture x hundred grade A tires and y hundred grade B tires a day, where $0 \le x \le 4$ and

$$y = \frac{40 - 10x}{5 - x}.$$

Your profit on a grade A tire is twice your profit on a grade B tire. What is the most profitable number of each kind to make?

56. ***Particle Motion*** The positions of two particles on the s-axis are $s_1 = \cos t$ and $s_2 = \cos(t + \pi/4)$.

(a) What is the farthest apart the particles ever get?

(b) When do the particles collide?

57. ***Open-top Box*** An open-top rectangular box is constructed from a 10-by 16-in. piece of cardboard by cutting squares of equal side length from the corners and folding up the sides. Find

analytically the dimensions of the box of largest volume and the maximum volume. Support your answers graphically.

58. *Changing Area* The radius of a circle is changing at the rate of $-2/\pi$ m/sec. At what rate is the circle's area changing when $r = 10$ m?

59. *Particle Motion* The coordinates of a particle moving in the plane are differentiable functions of time t with $dx/dt = -1$ m/sec and $dy/dt = -5$ m/sec. How fast is the particle approaching the origin as it passes through the point $(5, 12)$?

60. *Changing Cube* The volume of a cube is increasing at the rate of 1200 cm^3/min at the instant its edges are 20 cm long. At what rate are the edges changing at that instant?

61. *Particle Motion* A point moves smoothly along the curve $y = x^{3/2}$ in the first quadrant in such a way that its distance from the origin increases at the constant rate of 11 units per second. Find dx/dt when $x = 3$.

62. *Draining Water* Water drains from the conical tank shown in the figure at the rate of 5 ft^3/min.

(a) What is the relation between the variables h and r?

(b) How fast is the water level dropping when $h = 6$ ft?

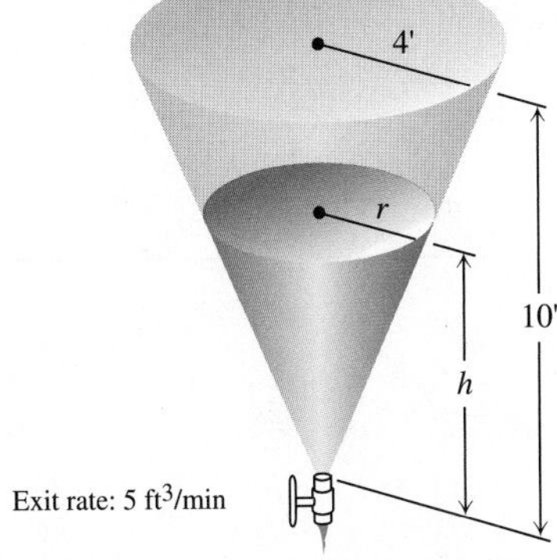

63. *Stringing Telephone Cable* As telephone cable is pulled from a large spool to be strung from the telephone poles along a street, it unwinds from the spool in layers of constant radius, as suggested in the figure. If the truck pulling the cable moves at a constant rate of 6 ft/sec, use the equation $s = r\theta$ to find how fast (in rad/sec) the spool is turning when the layer of radius 1.2 ft is being unwound.

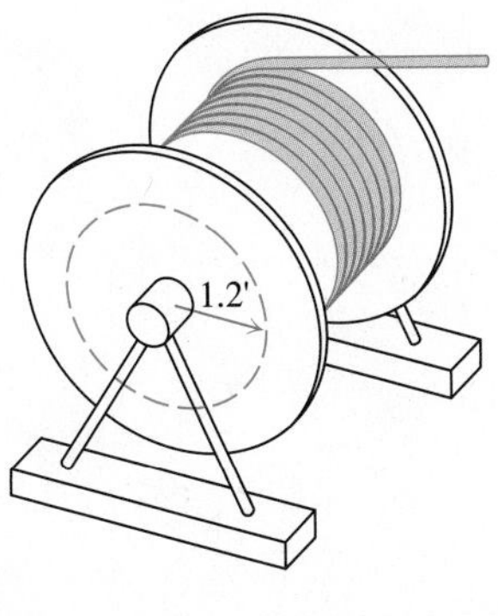

64. *Throwing Dirt* You sling a shovelful of dirt up from the bottom of a 17-ft hole with an initial velocity of 32 ft/sec. Is that enough speed to get the dirt out of the hole, or had you better duck?

65. *Estimating Change* Write a formula that estimates the change that occurs in the volume of a right circular cone (see figure) when the radius changes from a to $a + dr$ and the height does not change.

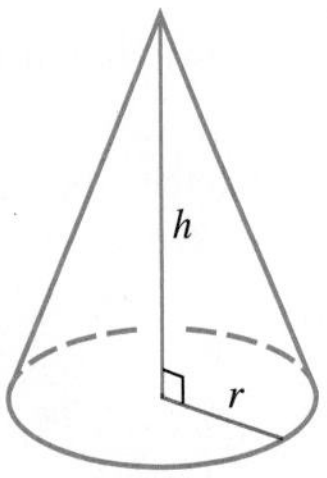

$V = \frac{1}{3}\pi r^2 h$

66. *Controlling Error*

(a) How accurately should you measure the edge of a cube to be reasonably sure of calculating the cube's surface area with an error of no more than 2%?

(b) Suppose the edge is measured with the accuracy required in part (a). About how accurately can the cube's volume be calculated from the edge measurement? To find out, estimate the percentage error in the volume calculation that might result from using the edge measurement.

67. *Compounding Error* The circumference of the equator of a sphere is measured as 10 cm with a possible error of 0.4 cm. This measurement is used to calculate the radius. The radius is then used to calculate the surface area and volume of the sphere. Estimate the percentage errors in the calculated values of **(a)** the radius, **(b)** the surface area, and **(c)** the volume.

68. *Finding Height* To find the height of a lamppost (see figure), you stand a 6-ft pole 20 ft from the lamp and measure the length a of its shadow, finding it to be 15 ft, give or take an inch. Calculate the height of the lamppost using the value $a = 15$, and estimate the possible error in the result.

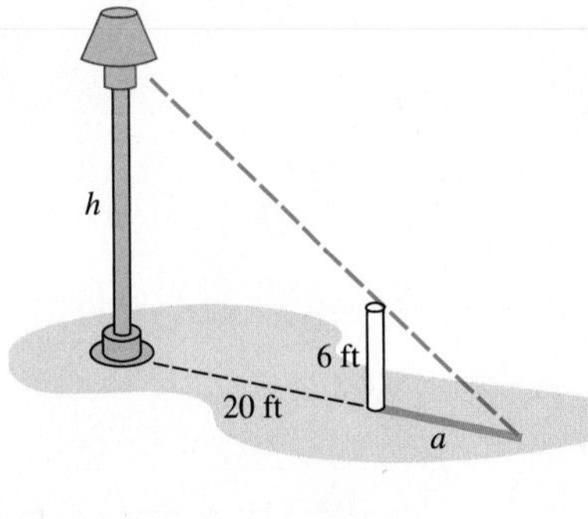

69. *Decreasing Function* Show that the function $y = \sin^2 x - 3x$ decreases on every interval in its domain.

AP Examination Preparation

70. The accompanying figure shows the graph of the derivative of a function f. The domain of f is the closed interval $[-3, 3]$.

(a) For what values of x in the open interval $(-3, 3)$ does f have a relative maximum? Justify your answer.

(b) For what values of x in the open interval $(-3, 3)$ does f have a relative minimum? Justify your answer.

(c) For what values of x is the graph of f concave up? Justify your answer.

(d) Suppose $f(-3) = 0$. Sketch a possible graph of f on the domain $[-3, 3]$.

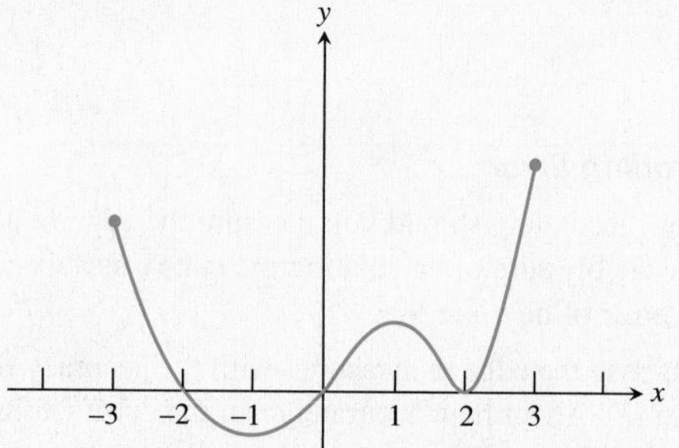

71. The volume V of a cone $(V = \frac{1}{3}\pi r^2 h)$ is increasing at the rate of 4π cubic inches per second. At the instant when the radius of the cone is 2 inches, its volume is 8π cubic inches and the radius is increasing at $1/3$ inch per second.

(a) At the instant when the radius of the cone is 2 inches, what is the rate of change of the area of its base?

(b) At the instant when the radius of the cone is 2 inches, what is the rate of change of its height h?

(c) At the instant when the radius of the cone is 2 inches, what is the instantaneous rate of change of the area of its base with respect to its height h?

72. A piece of wire 60 inches long is cut into six sections, two of length a and four of length b. Each of the two sections of length a is bent into the form of a circle, and the circles are then joined by the four sections of length b to make a frame for a model of a right circular cylinder, as shown in the accompanying figure.

(a) Find the values of a and b that will make the cylinder of maximum volume.

(b) Use differential calculus to justify your answer in part (a).

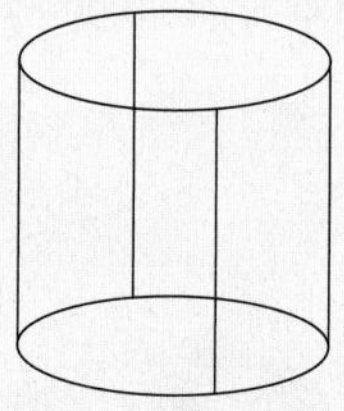

CHAPTER

6 The Definite Integral

The 1995 Reader's Digest Sweepstakes grand prize winner is being paid a total of \$5,010,000 over 30 years. If invested, the winnings plus the interest earned generate an amount defined by

$$A = e^{rT}\int_0^T mPe^{-rt}\,dt.$$

(r = interest rate, P = size of payment, T = term in years, m = number of payments per year.)

Would the prize have a different value if it were paid in 15 annual installments of \$334,000 instead of 30 annual installments of \$167,000? Section 6.4 can help you compare the total amounts.

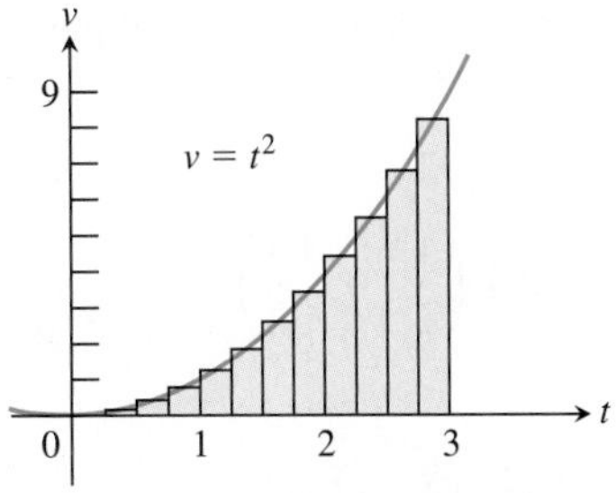

Figure 6.6 These rectangles have approximately the same areas as the strips in Figure 6.4. Each rectangle has height m_i^2, where m_i is the midpoint of its base. (Example 1)

The area of this narrow rectangle approximates the distance traveled over the time subinterval. Adding all the areas (distances) gives an approximation of the total area under the curve (total distance traveled) from $t = 0$ to $t = 3$ (Figure 6.6).

Computing this sum of areas is straightforward. Each rectangle has a base of length $\Delta t = 1/4$, while the height of each rectangle can be found by evaluating the function at the midpoint of the subinterval. Table 6.1 shows the computations for the first four rectangles.

TABLE 6.1

Subinterval	$\left[0, \frac{1}{4}\right]$	$\left[\frac{1}{4}, \frac{1}{2}\right]$	$\left[\frac{1}{2}, \frac{3}{4}\right]$	$\left[\frac{3}{4}, 1\right]$
Midpoint m_i	$\frac{1}{8}$	$\frac{3}{8}$	$\frac{5}{8}$	$\frac{7}{8}$
Height $= (m_i)^2$	$\frac{1}{64}$	$\frac{9}{64}$	$\frac{25}{64}$	$\frac{49}{64}$
Area $= (1/4)(m_i)^2$	$\frac{1}{256}$	$\frac{9}{256}$	$\frac{25}{256}$	$\frac{49}{256}$

Continuing in this manner, we derive the area $(1/4)(m_i)^2$ for each of the twelve subintervals and add them:

$$\frac{1}{256} + \frac{9}{256} + \frac{25}{256} + \frac{49}{256} + \frac{81}{256} + \frac{121}{256} + \frac{169}{256} + \frac{225}{256}$$

$$+ \frac{289}{256} + \frac{361}{256} + \frac{441}{256} + \frac{529}{256} = \frac{2300}{256} \approx 8.98$$

Since this number approximates the area and hence the total distance traveled by the particle, we conclude that the particle has moved approximately 9 units in 3 seconds. If it starts at $x = 0$, then it is very close to $x = 9$ when $t = 3$. ***Now Try Exercise 3.***

Approximation by Rectangles

Approximating irregularly shaped regions by regularly shaped regions for the purpose of computing areas is not new. Archimedes used the idea more than 2200 years ago to find the area of a circle, demonstrating in the process that π was located between 3.140845 and 3.142857. He also used approximations to find the area under a parabolic arch, anticipating the answer to an important 17-century question nearly 2000 years before anyone thought to ask it. The fact that we still measure the area of anything—even a circle—in "square units" is obvious testimony to the historical effectiveness of using rectangles for approximating areas.

To make it easier to talk about approximations with rectangles, we now introduce some new terminology.

Rectangular Approximation Method (RAM)

In Example 1 we used the *Midpoint Rectangular Approximation Method* (MRAM) to approximate the area under the curve. The name suggests the choice we made when determining the heights of the approximating rectangles: We evaluated the function at the midpoint of each subinterval. If instead we had evaluated the function at the left-hand endpoint we would have obtained the *LRAM* approximation, and if we had used the right-hand endpoints we would have obtained the *RRAM* approximation. Figure 6.7 shows what the three approximations look like graphically when we approximate the area under the curve $y = x^2$ from $x = 0$ to $x = 3$ with six subintervals.

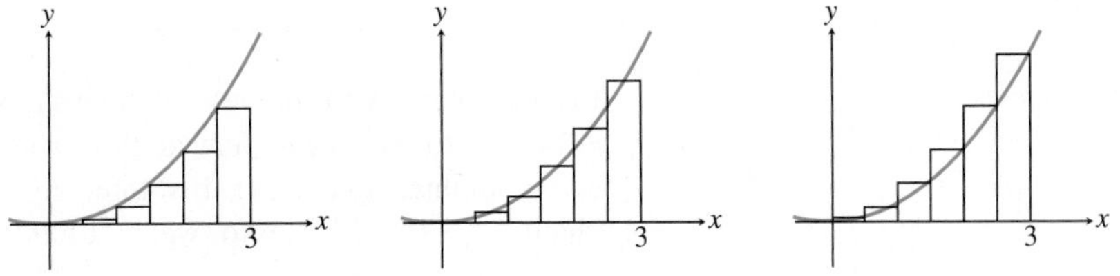

Figure 6.7 LRAM, MRAM, and RRAM approximations to the area under the graph of $y = x^2$ from $x = 0$ to $x = 3$.

No matter which RAM approximation we compute, we are adding products of the form $f(x_i) \cdot \Delta x$, or, in this case, $(x_i)^2 \cdot (3/6)$.

LRAM:

$$\left(0\right)^2\left(\frac{1}{2}\right) + \left(\frac{1}{2}\right)^2\left(\frac{1}{2}\right) + \left(1\right)^2\left(\frac{1}{2}\right) + \left(\frac{3}{2}\right)^2\left(\frac{1}{2}\right) + \left(2\right)^2\left(\frac{1}{2}\right) + \left(\frac{5}{2}\right)^2\left(\frac{1}{2}\right) = 6.875$$

MRAM:

$$\left(\frac{1}{4}\right)^2\left(\frac{1}{2}\right) + \left(\frac{3}{4}\right)^2\left(\frac{1}{2}\right) + \left(\frac{5}{4}\right)^2\left(\frac{1}{2}\right) + \left(\frac{7}{4}\right)^2\left(\frac{1}{2}\right) + \left(\frac{9}{4}\right)^2\left(\frac{1}{2}\right) + \left(\frac{11}{4}\right)^2\left(\frac{1}{2}\right) = 8.9375$$

RRAM:

$$\left(\frac{1}{2}\right)^2\left(\frac{1}{2}\right) + \left(1\right)^2\left(\frac{1}{2}\right) + \left(\frac{3}{2}\right)^2\left(\frac{1}{2}\right) + \left(2\right)^2\left(\frac{1}{2}\right) + \left(\frac{5}{2}\right)^2\left(\frac{1}{2}\right) + \left(3\right)^2\left(\frac{1}{2}\right) = 11.375$$

As we can see from Figure 6.7, LRAM is smaller than the true area and RRAM is larger. MRAM appears to be the closest of the three approximations. However, observe what happens as the number n of subintervals increases:

n	LRAM_n	MRAM_n	RRAM_n
6	6.875	8.9375	11.375
12	7.90625	8.984375	10.15625
24	8.4453125	8.99609375	9.5703125
48	8.720703125	8.999023438	9.283203125
100	8.86545	8.999775	9.13545
1000	8.9865045	8.99999775	9.0135045

We computed the numbers in this table using a graphing calculator and a summing program called RAM. A version of this program for most graphing calculators can be found in the *Technology Resource Manual* that accompanies this textbook. *All three sums* approach the same number (in this case, 9).

EXAMPLE 2 Estimating Area Under the Graph of a Nonnegative Function

Figure 6.8 shows the graph of $f(x) = x^2 \sin x$ on the interval $[0, 3]$. Estimate the area under the curve from $x = 0$ to $x = 3$.

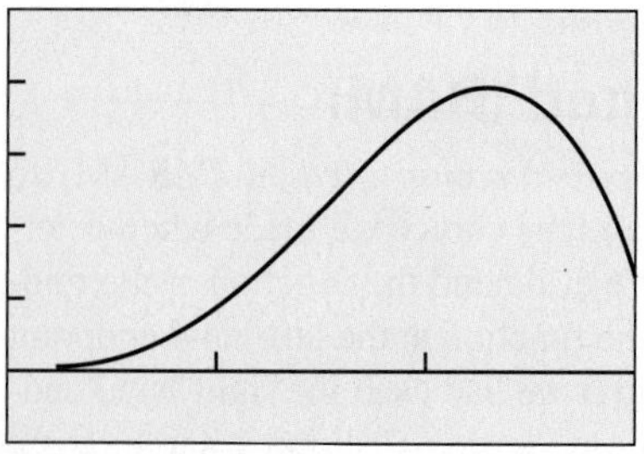

[0, 3] by [–1, 5]

Figure 6.8 The graph of $y = x^2 \sin x$ over the interval $[0, 3]$. (Example 2)

SOLUTION

We apply our RAM program to get the numbers in this table.

n	LRAM_n	MRAM_n	RRAM_n
5	5.15480	5.89668	5.91685
10	5.52574	5.80685	5.90677
25	5.69079	5.78150	5.84320
50	5.73615	5.77788	5.81235
100	5.75701	5.77697	5.79511
1000	5.77476	5.77667	5.77857

It is not necessary to compute all three sums each time just to approximate the area, but we wanted to show again how all three sums approach the same number. With 1000 subintervals, all three agree in the first three digits. (The *exact* area is $-7\cos 3 + 6\sin 3 - 2$, which is 5.77666752456 to twelve digits.) ***Now Try Exercise 7.***

EXPLORATION 1 Which RAM Is the Biggest?

You might think from the previous two RAM tables that LRAM is always a little low and RRAM a little high, with MRAM somewhere in between. That, however, depends on n and on the shape of the curve.

1. Graph $y = 5 - 4\sin(x/2)$ in the window $[0, 3]$ by $[0, 5]$. Copy the graph on paper and sketch the rectangles for the LRAM, MRAM, and RRAM sums with $n = 3$. Order the three approximations from greatest to smallest.
2. Graph $y = 2\sin(5x) + 3$ in the same window. Copy the graph on paper and sketch the rectangles for the LRAM, MRAM, and RRAM sums with $n = 3$. Order the three approximations from greatest to smallest.
3. If a positive, continuous function is increasing on an interval, what can we say about the relative sizes of LRAM, MRAM, and RRAM? Explain.
4. If a positive, continuous function is decreasing on an interval, what can we say about the relative sizes of LRAM, MRAM, and RRAM? Explain.

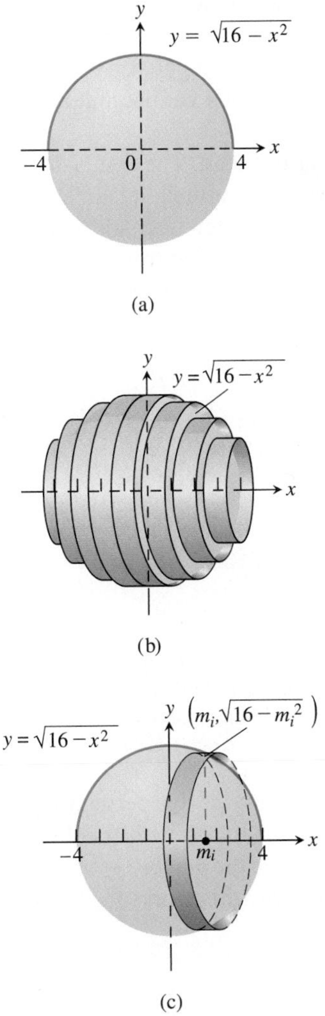

Figure 6.9 (a) The semicircle $y = \sqrt{16 - x^2}$ revolved about the x-axis to generate a sphere. (b) Slices of the solid sphere approximated with cylinders (drawn for $n = 8$). (c) The typical approximating cylinder has radius $f(m_i) = \sqrt{16 - m_i^2}$. (Example 3)

Volume of a Sphere

Although the visual representation of RAM approximation focuses on area, remember that our original motivation for looking at sums of this type was to find distance traveled by an object moving with a nonconstant velocity. The connection between Examples 1 and 2 is that in each case, we have a function f defined on a closed interval and estimate what we want to know with a sum of function values multiplied by interval lengths. Many other physical quantities can be estimated this way.

EXAMPLE 3 Estimating the Volume of a Sphere

Estimate the volume of a solid sphere of radius 4.

SOLUTION

We picture the sphere as if its surface were generated by revolving the graph of the function $f(x) = \sqrt{16 - x^2}$ about the x-axis (Figure 6.9a). We partition the interval $-4 \le x \le 4$ into n subintervals of equal length $\Delta x = 8/n$. We then slice the sphere with planes perpendicular to the x-axis at the partition points, cutting it like a round loaf of bread into n parallel slices of width Δx. When n is large, each slice can be approximated by a cylinder, a familiar geometric shape of known volume, $\pi r^2 h$. In our case, the cylinders lie on their sides and h is Δx while r varies according to where we are on the x-axis (Figure 6.9b). A logical radius to choose for each cylinder is $f(m_i) = \sqrt{16 - m_i^2}$, where m_i is the midpoint of the interval where the ith slice intersects the x-axis (Figure 6.9c).

We can now approximate the volume of the sphere by using MRAM to sum the cylinder volumes,

$$\pi r^2 h = \pi\left(\sqrt{16 - m_i^2}\right)^2 \Delta x.$$

The function we use in the RAM program is $\pi\left(\sqrt{16 - x^2}\right)^2 = \pi(16 - x^2)$. The interval is $[-4, 4]$.

Number of Slices (n)	MRAM_n
10	269.42299
25	268.29704
50	268.13619
100	268.09598
1000	268.08271

continued

Keeping Track of Units

Notice in Example 3 that we are summing products of the form $\pi(16 - x^2)$ (a cross-section area, measured in square units) times Δx (a length, measured in units). The products are therefore measured in cubic units, which are the correct units for volume.

The value for $n = 1000$ compares *very* favorably with the true volume,

$$V = \frac{4}{3}\pi r^3 = \frac{4}{3}\pi(4)^3 = \frac{256\pi}{3} \approx 268.0825731.$$

Even for $n = 10$ the difference between the MRAM approximation and the true volume is a small percentage of V:

$$\frac{|\text{MRAM}_{10} - V|}{V} = \frac{\text{MRAM}_{10} - 256\pi/3}{256\pi/3} \leq 0.005$$

That is, the error percentage is about one half of one percent! **Now Try Exercise 13.**

Cardiac Output

So far we have seen applications of the RAM process to finding distance traveled and volume. These applications hint at the usefulness of this technique. To suggest its versatility we will present an application from human physiology.

The number of liters of blood your heart pumps in a fixed time interval is called your *cardiac output*. For a person at rest, the rate might be 5 or 6 liters per minute. During strenuous exercise the rate might be as high as 30 liters per minute. It might also be altered significantly by disease. How can a physician measure a patient's cardiac output without interrupting the flow of blood?

One technique is to inject a dye into a main vein near the heart. The dye is drawn into the right side of the heart and pumped through the lungs and out the left side of the heart into the aorta, where its concentration can be measured every few seconds as the blood flows past. The data in Table 6.2 and the plot in Figure 6.10 (obtained from the data) show the response of a healthy, resting patient to an injection of 5.6 mg of dye.

TABLE 6.2 Dye Concentration Data

Seconds After Injection t	Dye Concentration (adjusted for recirculation) c
5	0
7	3.8
9	8.0
11	6.1
13	3.6
15	2.3
17	1.45
19	0.91
21	0.57
23	0.36
25	0.23
27	0.14
29	0.09
31	0

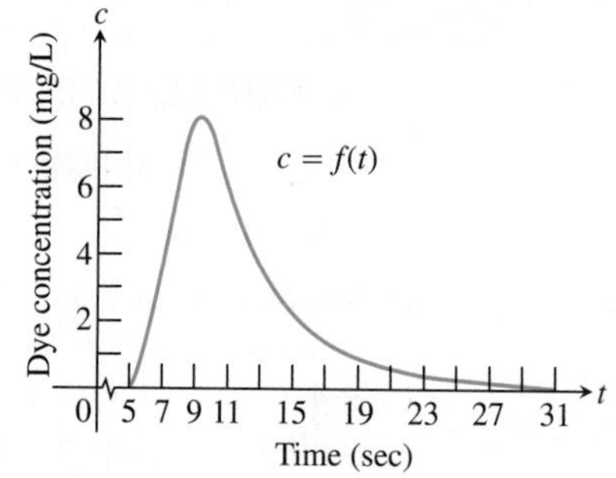

Figure 6.10 The dye concentration data from Table 6.2, plotted and fitted with a smooth curve. Time is measured with $t = 0$ at the time of injection. The dye concentration is zero at the beginning while the dye passes through the lungs. It then rises to a maximum at about $t = 9$ sec and tapers to zero by $t = 31$ sec.

The graph shows dye concentration (measured in milligrams of dye per liter of blood) as a function of time (in seconds). How can we use this graph to obtain the cardiac output (measured in liters of blood per second)? The trick is to divide the *number of mg of dye* by the *area under the dye concentration curve.* You can see why this works if you consider what happens to the units:

$$\frac{\text{mg of dye}}{\text{units of area under curve}} = \frac{\text{mg of dye}}{\dfrac{\text{mg of dye}}{\text{L of blood}} \cdot \text{sec}} = \frac{\text{mg of dye}}{\text{sec}} \cdot \frac{\text{L of blood}}{\text{mg of dye}} = \frac{\text{L of blood}}{\text{sec}}$$

So you are now ready to compute like a cardiologist.

Charles Richard Drew (1904–1950)

Millions of people are alive today because of Charles Drew's pioneering work on blood plasma and the preservation of human blood for transfusion. After directing the Red Cross program that collected plasma for the Armed Forces in World War II, Dr. Drew went on to become Head of Surgery at Howard University and Chief of Staff at Freedmen's Hospital in Washington, D.C.

EXAMPLE 4 Computing Cardiac Output from Dye Concentration

Estimate the cardiac output of the patient whose data appear in Table 6.2 and Figure 6.10. Give the estimate in liters per minute.

SOLUTION

We have seen that we can obtain the cardiac output by dividing the amount of dye (5.6 mg for our patient) by the area under the curve in Figure 6.10. Now we need to find the area. Our geometry formulas do not apply to this irregularly shaped region, and the RAM program is useless without a formula for the function. Nonetheless, we can draw the MRAM rectangles ourselves and estimate their heights from the graph.

In Figure 6.11 each rectangle has a base 2 units long and a height $f(m_i)$ equal to the height of the curve above the midpoint of the base.

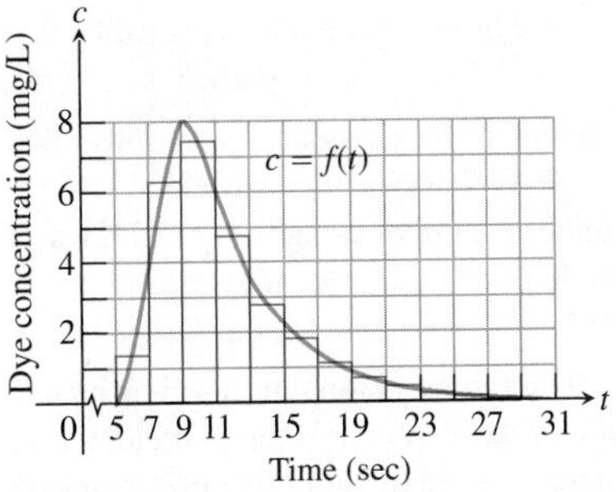

Figure 6.11 The region under the concentration curve of Figure 6.10 is approximated with rectangles. We ignore the portion from $t = 29$ to $t = 31$; its concentration is negligible. (Example 4)

The area of each rectangle, then, is $f(m_i)$ times 2, and the sum of the rectangular areas is the MRAM estimate for the area under the curve:

$$\begin{aligned}\text{Area} &\approx f(6)\cdot 2 + f(8)\cdot 2 + f(10)\cdot 2 + \cdots + f(28)\cdot 2\\ &\approx 2\cdot(1.4 + 6.3 + 7.5 + 4.8 + 2.8 + 1.9 + 1.1\\ &\qquad + 0.7 + 0.5 + 0.3 + 0.2 + 0.1)\\ &= 2\cdot(27.6) = 55.2\ (\text{mg/L})\cdot\text{sec}\end{aligned}$$

Dividing 5.6 mg by this figure gives an estimate for cardiac output in liters per second. Multiplying by 60 converts the estimate to liters per minute:

$$\frac{5.6\text{ mg}}{55.2\text{ mg}\cdot\text{sec/L}}\cdot\frac{60\text{ sec}}{1\text{ min}} \approx 6.09\text{ L/min}$$

Now Try Exercise 15.

Quick Review 6.1

Exercise numbers with a gray background indicate problems that the authors have designed to be solved *without a calculator.*

As you answer the questions in Exercises 1–10, try to associate the answers with area, as in Figure 6.1.

1. A train travels at 80 mph for 5 hours. How far does it travel?

2. A truck travels at an average speed of 48 mph for 3 hours. How far does it travel?

3. Beginning at a standstill, a car maintains a constant acceleration of 10 ft/sec^2 for 10 seconds. What is its velocity after 10 seconds? Give your answer in ft/sec and then convert it to mi/h.

4. In a vacuum, light travels at a speed of 300,000 kilometers per second. How many kilometers does it travel in a year? (This distance equals one *light-year.*)

5. A long distance runner ran a race in 5 hours, averaging 6 mph for the first 3 hours and 5 mph for the last 2 hours. How far did she run?

6. A pump working at 20 gallons/minute pumps for an hour. How many gallons are pumped?

7. At 8:00 P.M. the temperature began dropping at a rate of 1 degree Celsius per hour. Twelve hours later it began rising at a rate of 1.5 degrees per hour for six hours. What was the net change in temperature over the 18-hour period?

8. Water flows over a spillway at a steady rate of 300 cubic feet per second. How many cubic feet of water pass over the spillway in one day?

9. A city has a population density of 350 people per square mile in an area of 50 square miles. What is the population of the city?

10. A hummingbird in flight beats its wings at a rate of 70 times per second. How many times does it beat its wings in an hour if it is in flight 70% of the time?

Section 6.1 Exercises

1. A particle starts at $x = 0$ and moves along the x-axis with velocity $v(t) = 5$ for time $t \geq 0$. Where is the particle at $t = 4$?

2. A particle starts at $x = 0$ and moves along the x-axis with velocity $v(t) = 2t + 1$ for time $t \geq 0$. Where is the particle at $t = 4$?

3. A particle starts at $x = 0$ and moves along the x-axis with velocity $v(t) = t^2 + 1$ for time $t \geq 0$. Where is the particle at $t = 4$? Approximate the area under the curve using four rectangles of equal width and heights determined by the midpoints of the intervals, as in Example 1.

4. A particle starts at $x = 0$ and moves along the x-axis with velocity $v(t) = t^2 + 1$ for time $t \geq 0$. Where is the particle at $t = 5$? Approximate the area under the curve using five rectangles of equal width and heights determined by the midpoints of the intervals, as in Example 1.

Exercises 5–8 refer to the region R enclosed between the graph of the function $y = 2x - x^2$ and the x-axis for $0 \leq x \leq 2$.

5. **(a)** Sketch the region R.

(b) Partition $[0, 2]$ into 4 subintervals and show the four rectangles that LRAM uses to approximate the area of R. Compute the LRAM sum without a calculator.

6. Repeat Exercise 5(b) for RRAM and MRAM.

7. Using a calculator program, find the RAM sums that complete the following table.

n	LRAM_n	MRAM_n	RRAM_n
10			
50			
100			
500			

8. Make a conjecture about the area of the region R.

In Exercises 9–12, use RAM to estimate the area of the region enclosed between the graph of f and the x-axis for $a \leq x \leq b$.

9. $f(x) = x^2 - x + 3, \quad a = 0, \quad b = 3$

10. $f(x) = \dfrac{1}{x}, \quad a = 1, \quad b = 3$

11. $f(x) = e^{-x^2}, \quad a = 0, \quad b = 2$

12. $f(x) = \sin x, \quad a = 0, \quad b = \pi$

13. *(Continuation of Example 3)* Use the slicing technique of Example 3 to find the MRAM sums that approximate the volume of a sphere of radius 5. Use $n = 10, 20, 40, 80$, and 160.

14. *(Continuation of Exercise 13)* Use a geometry formula to find the volume V of the sphere in Exercise 13 and find **(a)** the error and **(b)** the percentage error in the MRAM approximation for each value of n given.

15. ***Cardiac Output*** The following table gives dye concentrations for a dye-concentration cardiac-output determination like the one in Example 4. The amount of dye injected in this patient was 5 mg instead of 5.6 mg. Use rectangles to estimate the area under the dye concentration curve and then go on to estimate the patient's cardiac output.

Seconds After Injection t	Dye Concentration (adjusted for recirculation) c
2	0
4	0.6
6	1.4
8	2.7
10	3.7
12	4.1
14	3.8
16	2.9
18	1.7
20	1.0
22	0.5
24	0

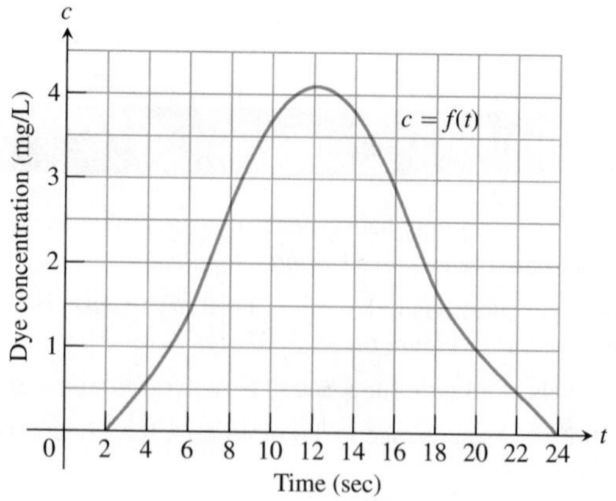

16. *Distance Traveled* The table below shows the velocity of a model train engine moving along a track for 10 sec. Estimate the distance traveled by the engine, using 10 subintervals of length 1 with **(a)** left-endpoint values (LRAM) and **(b)** right-endpoint values (RRAM).

Time (sec)	Velocity (in./sec)	Time (sec)	Velocity (in./sec)
0	0	6	11
1	12	7	6
2	22	8	2
3	10	9	6
4	5	10	0
5	13		

17. *Distance Traveled Upstream* You are walking along the bank of a tidal river watching the incoming tide carry a bottle upstream. You record the velocity of the flow every 5 minutes for an hour, with the results shown in the table below. About how far upstream does the bottle travel during that hour? Find the **(a)** LRAM and **(b)** RRAM estimates using 12 subintervals of length 5.

Time (min)	Velocity (m/sec)	Time (min)	Velocity (m/sec)
0	1	35	1.2
5	1.2	40	1.0
10	1.7	45	1.8
15	2.0	50	1.5
20	1.8	55	1.2
25	1.6	60	0
30	1.4		

18. *Length of a Road* You and a companion are driving along a twisty stretch of dirt road in a car whose speedometer works but whose odometer (mileage counter) is broken. To find out how long this particular stretch of road is, you record the car's velocity at 10-sec intervals, with the results shown in the table below. (The velocity was converted from mi/h to ft/sec using 30 mi/h = 44 ft/sec.) Estimate the length of the road by averaging the LRAM and RRAM sums.

Time (sec)	Velocity (ft/sec)	Time (sec)	Velocity (ft/sec)
0	0	70	15
10	44	80	22
20	15	90	35
30	35	100	44
40	30	110	30
50	44	120	35
60	35		

19. *Distance from Velocity Data* The table below gives data for the velocity of a vintage sports car accelerating from 0 to 142 mi/h in 36 sec (10 thousandths of an hour).

Time (h)	Velocity (mi/h)	Time (h)	Velocity (mi/h)
0.0	0	0.006	116
0.001	40	0.007	125
0.002	62	0.008	132
0.003	82	0.009	137
0.004	96	0.010	142
0.005	108		

(a) Use rectangles to estimate how far the car traveled during the 36 sec it took to reach 142 mi/h.

(b) Roughly how many seconds did it take the car to reach the halfway point? About how fast was the car going then?

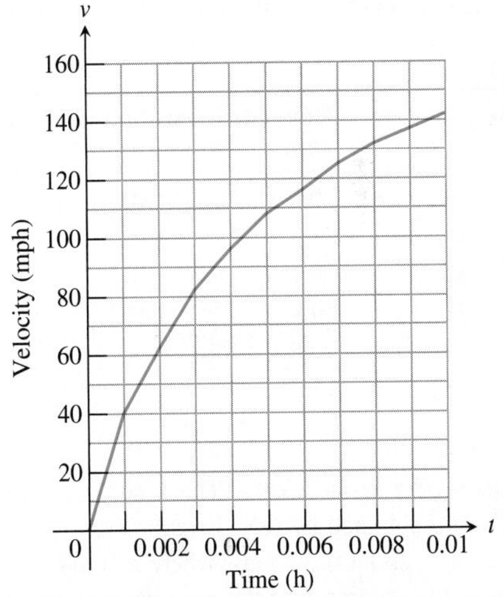

20. *Volume of a Solid Hemisphere* To estimate the volume of a solid hemisphere of radius 4, imagine its axis of symmetry to be the interval $[0, 4]$ on the x-axis. Partition $[0, 4]$ into eight subintervals of equal length and approximate the solid with cylinders based on the circular cross sections of the hemisphere perpendicular to the x-axis at the subintervals' left endpoints. (See the accompanying profile view.)

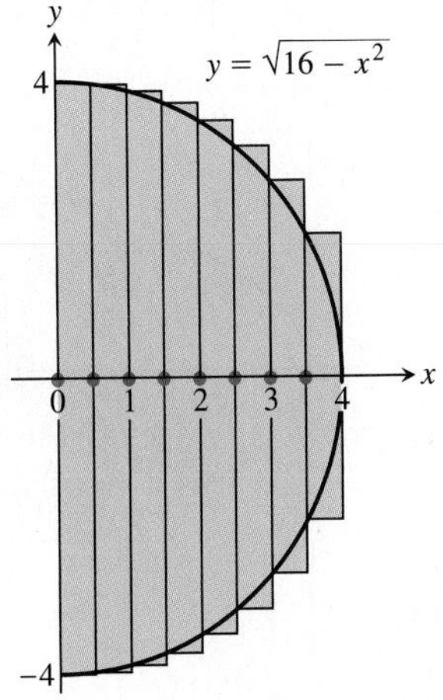

(a) Writing to Learn Find the sum S_8 of the volumes of the cylinders. Do you expect S_8 to overestimate V? Give reasons for your answer.

(b) Express $|V - S_8|$ as a percentage of V to the nearest percent.

21. Repeat Exercise 20 using cylinders based on cross sections at the right endpoints of the subintervals.

22. *Volume of Water in a Reservoir* A reservoir shaped like a hemispherical bowl of radius 8 m is filled with water to a depth of 4 m.

(a) Find an estimate S of the water's volume by approximating the water with eight circumscribed solid cylinders.

(b) It can be shown that the water's volume is $V = (320\pi)/3\ \text{m}^3$. Find the error $|V - S|$ as a percentage of V to the nearest percent.

23. *Volume of Water in a Swimming Pool* A rectangular swimming pool is 30 ft wide and 50 ft long. The table below shows the depth $h(x)$ of the water at 5-ft intervals from one end of the pool to the other. Estimate the volume of water in the pool using **(a)** left-endpoint values and **(b)** right-endpoint values.

Position (ft) x	Depth (ft) $h(x)$	Position (ft) x	Depth (ft) $h(x)$
0	6.0	30	11.5
5	8.2	35	11.9
10	9.1	40	12.3
15	9.9	45	12.7
20	10.5	50	13.0
25	11.0		

24. *Volume of a Nose Cone* The nose "cone" of a rocket is a *paraboloid* obtained by revolving the curve $y = \sqrt{x}$, $0 \le x \le 5$ about the x-axis, where x is measured in feet. Estimate the volume V of the nose cone by partitioning $[0, 5]$ into five subintervals of equal length, slicing the cone with planes perpendicular to the x-axis at the subintervals' left endpoints, constructing cylinders of height 1 based on cross sections at these points, and finding the volumes of these cylinders. (See the accompanying figure.)

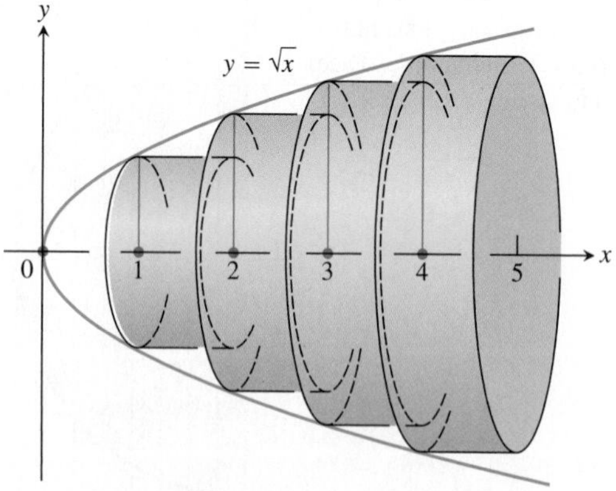

25. *Volume of a Nose Cone* Repeat Exercise 24 using cylinders based on cross sections at the *midpoints* of the subintervals.

26. *Free Fall with Air Resistance* An object is dropped straight down from a helicopter. The object falls faster and faster but its acceleration (rate of change of its velocity) decreases over time because of air resistance. The acceleration is measured in ft/sec² and recorded every second after the drop for 5 sec, as shown in the table below.

t	0	1	2	3	4	5
a	32.00	19.41	11.77	7.14	4.33	2.63

(a) Use LRAM_5 to find an upper estimate for the speed when $t = 5$.

(b) Use RRAM_5 to find a lower estimate for the speed when $t = 5$.

(c) Use upper estimates for the speed during the first second, second second, and third second to find an upper estimate for the distance fallen when $t = 3$.

27. *Distance Traveled by a Projectile* An object is shot straight upward from sea level with an initial velocity of 400 ft/sec.

(a) Assuming gravity is the only force acting on the object, give an upper estimate for its velocity after 5 sec have elapsed. Use $g = 32\ \text{ft/sec}^2$ for the gravitational constant.

(b) Use RRAM_5 to find a lower estimate for the height attained after 5 sec.

28. *Water Pollution* Oil is leaking out of a tanker damaged at sea. The damage to the tanker is worsening, as evidenced by the increased leakage each hour, recorded in the table below.

Time (h)	0	1	2	3	4
Leakage (gal/h)	50	70	97	136	190

Time (h)	5	6	7	8
Leakage (gal/h)	265	369	516	720

(a) Give an upper and lower estimate of the total quantity of oil that has escaped after 5 hours.

(b) Repeat part (a) for the quantity of oil that has escaped after 8 hours.

(c) The tanker continues to leak 720 gal/h after the first 8 hours. If the tanker originally contained 25,000 gal of oil, approximately how many more hours will elapse in the worst case before all of the oil has leaked? in the best case?

29. *Air Pollution* A power plant generates electricity by burning oil. Pollutants produced by the burning process are removed by scrubbers in the smokestacks. Over time the scrubbers become less efficient and eventually must be replaced when the amount of pollutants released exceeds government standards. Measurements taken at the end of each month determine the rate at which pollutants are released into the atmosphere, as recorded in the table below.

Month	Jan	Feb	Mar	Apr	May	Jun
Pollutant Release Rate (tons/day)	0.20	0.25	0.27	0.34	0.45	0.52

Month	Jul	Aug	Sep	Oct	Nov	Dec
Pollutant Release Rate (tons/day)	0.63	0.70	0.81	0.85	0.89	0.95

(a) Assuming a 30-day month and that new scrubbers allow only 0.05 ton/day released, give an upper estimate of the total tonnage of pollutants released by the end of June. What is a lower estimate?

(b) In the best case, approximately when will a total of 125 tons of pollutants have been released into the atmosphere?

30. Writing to Learn The graph shows the sales record for a company over a 10-year period. If sales are measured in millions of units per year, explain what information can be obtained from the area of the region, and why.

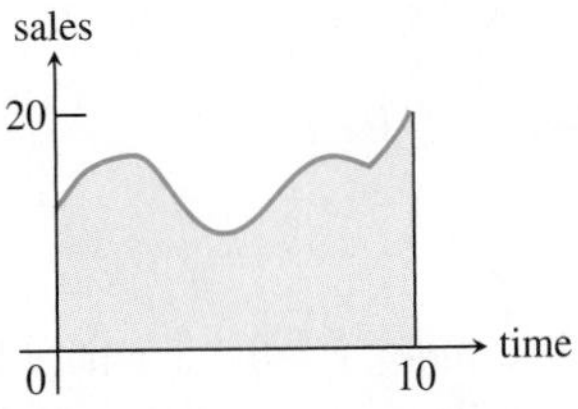

Standardized Test Questions

31. True or False If f is a positive, continuous, increasing function on $[a, b]$, then LRAM gives an area estimate that is less than the true area under the curve. Justify your answer.

32. True or False For a given number of rectangles, MRAM always gives a more accurate approximation to the true area under the curve than RRAM or LRAM. Justify your answer.

33. Multiple Choice If an MRAM sum with four rectangles of equal width is used to approximate the area enclosed between the x-axis and the graph of $y = 4x - x^2$, the approximation is

(A) 10 **(B)** 10.5 **(C)** $10.\overline{6}$ **(D)** 10.75 **(E)** 11

34. Multiple Choice If f is a positive, continuous function on an interval $[a, b]$, which of the following rectangular approximation methods has a limit equal to the actual area under the curve from a to b as the number of rectangles approaches infinity?

I. LRAM

II. RRAM

III. MRAM

(A) I and II only

(B) III only

(C) I and III only

(D) I, II, and III

(E) None of these

35. Multiple Choice An LRAM sum with 4 equal subdivisions is used to approximate the area under the sine curve from $x = 0$ to $x = \pi$. What is the approximation?

(A) $\frac{\pi}{4}\left(0 + \frac{\pi}{4} + \frac{\pi}{2} + \frac{3\pi}{4}\right)$ **(B)** $\frac{\pi}{4}\left(0 + \frac{1}{2} + \frac{\sqrt{3}}{2} + 1\right)$

(C) $\frac{\pi}{4}\left(0 + \frac{\sqrt{2}}{2} + 1 + \frac{\sqrt{2}}{2}\right)$ **(D)** $\frac{\pi}{4}\left(0 + \frac{1}{2} + \frac{\sqrt{2}}{2} + \frac{\sqrt{3}}{2}\right)$

(E) $\frac{\pi}{4}\left(\frac{1}{2} + \frac{\sqrt{2}}{2} + \frac{\sqrt{3}}{2} + 1\right)$

36. Multiple Choice A truck moves with positive velocity $v(t)$ from time $t = 3$ to time $t = 15$. The area under the graph of $y = v(t)$ between 3 and 15 gives

(A) the velocity of the truck at $t = 15$.

(B) the acceleration of the truck at $t = 15$.

(C) the position of the truck at $t = 15$.

(D) the distance traveled by the truck from $t = 3$ to $t = 15$.

(E) the average position of the truck in the interval from $t = 3$ to $t = 15$.

Exploration

37. Group Activity ***Area of a Circle*** Inscribe a regular n-sided polygon inside a circle of radius 1 and compute the area of the polygon for the following values of n.

(a) 4 (square) **(b)** 8 (octagon) **(c)** 16

(d) Compare the areas in parts (a), (b), and (c) with the area of the circle.

Extending the Ideas

38. *Rectangular Approximation Methods* Prove or disprove the following statement: MRAM_n is always the average of LRAM_n and RRAM_n.

39. *Rectangular Approximation Methods* Show that if f is a nonnegative function on the interval $[a, b]$ and the line $x = (a + b)/2$ is a line of symmetry of the graph of $y = f(x)$, then $\text{LRAM}_n\, f = \text{RRAM}_n\, f$ for every positive integer n.

40. *(Continuation of Exercise 37)*

(a) Inscribe a regular n-sided polygon inside a circle of radius 1 and compute the area of one of the n congruent triangles formed by drawing radii to the vertices of the polygon.

(b) Compute the limit of the area of the inscribed polygon as $n \to \infty$.

(c) Repeat the computations in parts (a) and (b) for a circle of radius r.

6.2 Definite Integrals

What you will learn about . . .

- Riemann Sums
- Terminology and Notation of Integration
- Definite Integral and Area
- Constant Functions
- Integrals on a Calculator
- Discontinuous Integrable Functions

and why . . .

The definite integral is the basis of integral calculus, just as the derivative is the basis of differential calculus.

Riemann Sums

In the preceding section, we estimated distances, areas, and volumes with finite sums. The terms in the sums were obtained by multiplying selected function values by the lengths of intervals. In this section we move beyond finite sums to see what happens in the limit, as the terms become infinitely small and their number infinitely large.

Sigma notation enables us to express a large sum in compact form:

$$\sum_{k=1}^{n} a_k = a_1 + a_2 + a_3 + \cdots + a_{n-1} + a_n$$

The Greek capital letter Σ (sigma) stands for "sum." The index k tells us where to begin the sum (at the number below the Σ) and where to end (at the number above). If the symbol ∞ appears above the Σ, it indicates that the terms go on indefinitely.

The sums in which we will be interested are called *Riemann* ("*ree*-mahn") *sums,* after Georg Friedrich Bernhard Riemann (1826–1866). LRAM, MRAM, and RRAM in the previous section are all examples of Riemann sums—not because they estimated area, but because they were constructed in a particular way. We now describe that construction formally, in a more general context that does not confine us to nonnegative functions.

We begin with an arbitrary continuous function $f(x)$ defined on a closed interval $[a, b]$. Like the function graphed in Figure 6.12, it may have negative values as well as positive values.

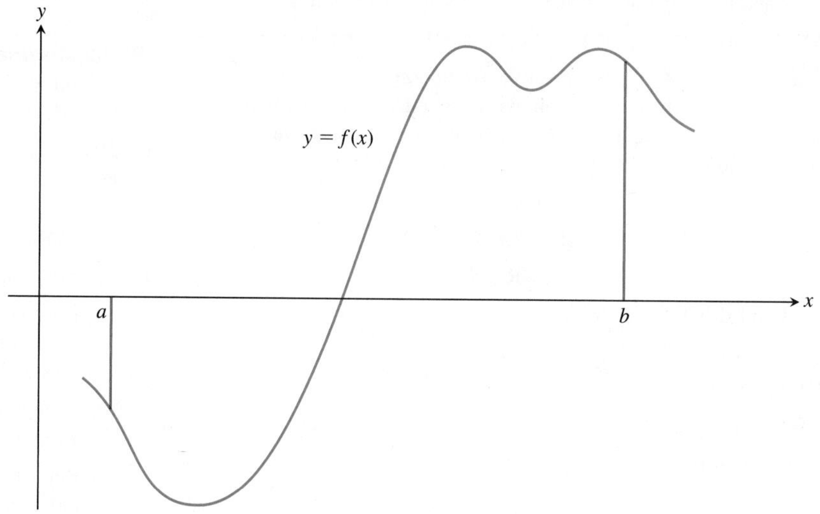

Figure 6.12 The graph of a typical function $y = f(x)$ over a closed interval $[a, b]$.

We then partition the interval $[a, b]$ into n subintervals by choosing $n - 1$ points, say $x_1, x_2, \cdots, x_{n-1}$, between a and b subject only to the condition that

$$a < x_1 < x_2 < \cdots < x_{n-1} < b.$$

To make the notation consistent, we denote a by x_0 and b by x_n. The set

$$P = \{x_0, x_1, x_2, \cdots, x_n\}$$

is called a **partition** of $[a, b]$.

The partition P determines n closed **subintervals,** as shown in Figure 6.13. The kth subinterval is $[x_{k-1}, x_k]$, which has length $\Delta x_k = x_k - x_{k-1}$.

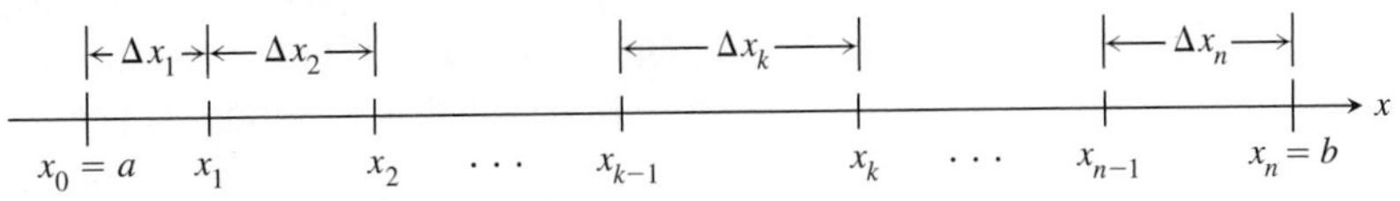

Figure 6.13 The partition $P = \{a = x_0, x_1, x_2, \cdots, x_n = b\}$ divides $[a, b]$ into n subintervals of lengths $\Delta x_1, \Delta x_2, \cdots, \Delta x_n$. The kth subinterval has length Δx_k.

In each subinterval we select some number. Denote the number chosen from the kth subinterval by c_k.

Then, on each subinterval we stand a vertical rectangle that reaches from the x-axis to touch the curve at $(c_k, f(c_k))$. These rectangles could lie either above or below the x-axis (Figure 6.14).

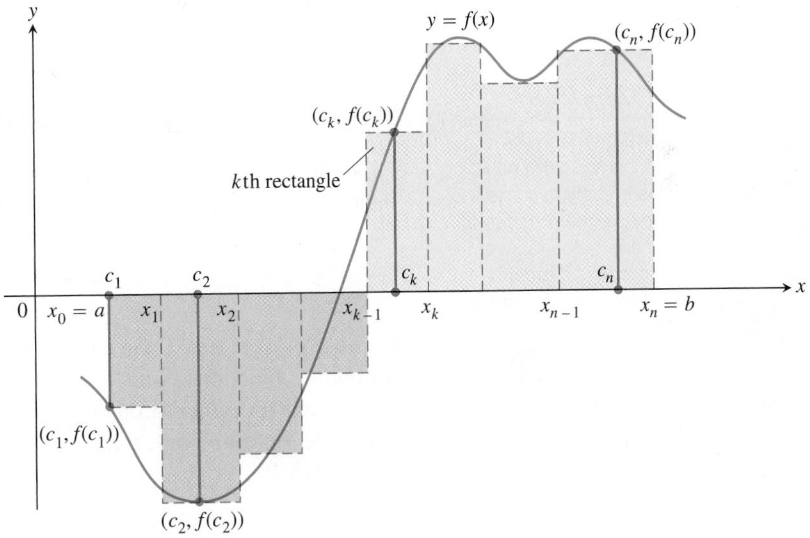

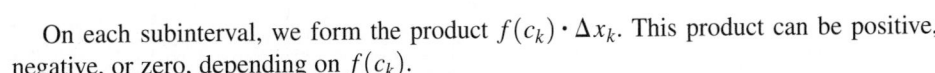

Figure 6.14 Rectangles extending from the x-axis to intersect the curve at the points $(c_k, f(c_k))$. The rectangles approximate the region between the x-axis and the graph of the function.

On each subinterval, we form the product $f(c_k) \cdot \Delta x_k$. This product can be positive, negative, or zero, depending on $f(c_k)$.

Finally, we take the sum of these products:

$$S_n = \sum_{k=1}^{n} f(c_k) \cdot \Delta x_k$$

This sum, which depends on the partition P and the choice of the numbers c_k, is a **Riemann sum for f on the interval $[a, b]$.**

As the partitions of $[a, b]$ become finer and finer, we would expect the rectangles defined by the partitions to approximate the region between the x-axis and the graph of f with increasing accuracy (Figure 6.15).

Just as LRAM, MRAM, and RRAM in our earlier examples converged to a common value in the limit, *all* Riemann sums for a given function on $[a, b]$ converge to a common value, as long as the lengths of the subintervals all tend to zero. This latter condition is assured by requiring the longest subinterval length (called the **norm** of the partition and denoted by $||P||$) to tend to zero.

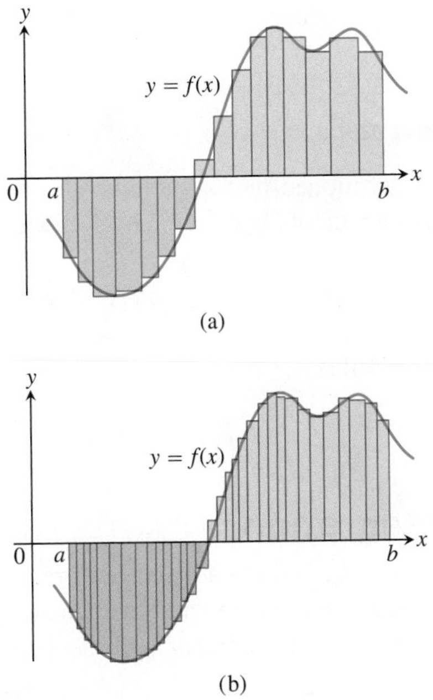

Figure 6.15 The curve of Figure 6.12 with rectangles from finer partitions of $[a, b]$. Finer partitions create more rectangles, with shorter bases.

DEFINITION The Definite Integral as a Limit of Riemann Sums

Let f be a function defined on a closed interval $[a, b]$. For any partition P of $[a, b]$, let the numbers c_k be chosen arbitrarily in the subintervals $[x_{k-1}, x_k]$.

If there exists a number I such that

$$\lim_{\|P\| \to 0} \sum_{k=1}^{n} f(c_k)\Delta x_k = I$$

no matter how P and the c_k's are chosen, then f is **integrable** on $[a, b]$ and I is the **definite integral** of f over $[a, b]$.

Despite the potential for variety in the sums $\Sigma f(c_k)\Delta x_k$ as the partitions change and as the c_k's are chosen arbitrarily in the intervals of each partition, the sums always have the same limit as $\|P\| \to 0$ as long as f is *continuous* on $[a, b]$.

Georg Riemann (1826–1866)

The mathematicians of the 17th and 18th centuries blithely assumed the existence of limits of Riemann sums (as we admittedly did in our RAM explorations of the last section), but the existence was not established mathematically until Georg Riemann proved Theorem 1 in 1854. You can find a current version of Riemann's proof in most advanced calculus books.

THEOREM 1 The Existence of Definite Integrals

All continuous functions are integrable. That is, if a function f is continuous on an interval $[a, b]$, then its definite integral over $[a, b]$ exists.

Because of Theorem 1, we can get by with a simpler construction for definite integrals of continuous functions. Since we know for these functions that the Riemann sums tend to the same limit for *all* partitions in which $\|P\| \to 0$, we need only to consider the limit of the so-called **regular partitions,** in which all the subintervals have the same length.

The Definite Integral of a Continuous Function on $[a, b]$

Let f be continuous on $[a, b]$, and let $[a, b]$ be partitioned into n subintervals of equal length $\Delta x = (b - a)/n$. Then the definite integral of f over $[a, b]$ is given by

$$\lim_{n \to \infty} \sum_{k=1}^{n} f(c_k)\Delta x,$$

where each c_k is chosen arbitrarily in the kth subinterval.

Terminology and Notation of Integration

Leibniz's clever choice of notation for the derivative, dy/dx, had the advantage of retaining an identity as a "fraction" even though both numerator and denominator had tended to zero. Although not really fractions, derivatives can *behave* like fractions, so the notation makes profound results like the Chain Rule

$$\frac{dy}{dx} = \frac{dy}{du} \cdot \frac{du}{dx}$$

seem almost simple.

The notation that Leibniz introduced for the definite integral was equally inspired. In his derivative notation, the Greek letters ("Δ" for "difference") switch to Roman letters ("d" for "differential") in the limit,

$$\lim_{\Delta x \to 0} \frac{\Delta y}{\Delta x} = \frac{dy}{dx}.$$

In his definite integral notation, the Greek letters again become Roman letters in the limit,

$$\lim_{n \to \infty} \sum_{k=1}^{n} f(c_k)\Delta x = \int_a^b f(x)\, dx.$$

Notice that the difference Δx has again tended to zero, becoming a differential dx. The Greek "Σ" has become an elongated Roman "S," so that the integral can retain its identity as a "sum." The c_k's have become so crowded together in the limit that we no longer think of a choppy selection of x-values between a and b, but rather of a continuous, unbroken sampling of x-values from a to b. It is as if we were summing *all* products of the form $f(x)dx$ as x goes from a to b, so we can abandon the k and the n used in the finite sum expression.

The symbol

$$\int_a^b f(x)\, dx$$

is read as "the integral from a to b of f of x dee x," or sometimes as "the integral from a to b of f of x with respect to x." The component parts also have names:

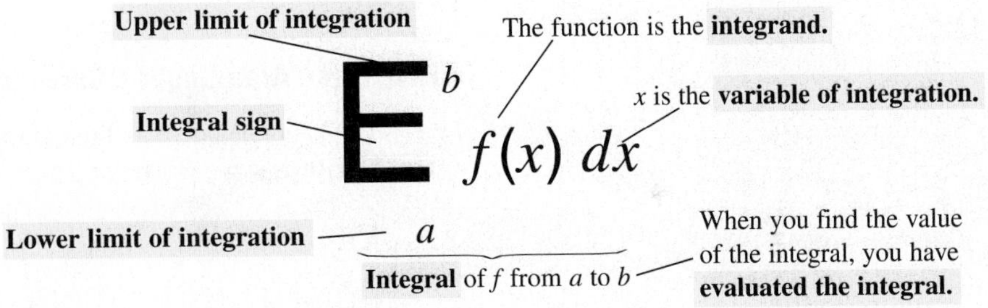

The value of the definite integral of a function over any particular interval depends on the function and not on the letter we choose to represent its independent variable. If we decide to use t or u instead of x, we simply write the integral as

$$\int_a^b f(t)\, dt \quad \text{or} \quad \int_a^b f(u)\, du \quad \text{instead of} \quad \int_a^b f(x)\, dx.$$

No matter how we represent the integral, it is the same *number*, defined as a limit of Riemann sums. Since it does not matter what letter we use to run from a to b, the variable of integration is called a **dummy variable.**

EXAMPLE 1 Using the Notation

The interval $[-1, 3]$ is partitioned into n subintervals of equal length $\Delta x = 4/n$. Let m_k denote the midpoint of the kth subinterval. Express the limit

$$\lim_{n \to \infty} \sum_{k=1}^{n} (3(m_k)^2 - 2m_k + 5)\, \Delta x$$

as an integral.

continued

SOLUTION

Since the midpoints m_k have been chosen from the subintervals of the partition, this expression is indeed a limit of Riemann sums. (The points chosen did not have to be midpoints; they could have been chosen from the subintervals in any arbitrary fashion.) The function being integrated is $f(x) = 3x^2 - 2x + 5$ over the interval $[-1, 3]$. Therefore,

$$\lim_{n\to\infty} \sum_{k=1}^{n} (3(m_k)^2 - 2m_k + 5)\,\Delta x = \int_{-1}^{3} (3x^2 - 2x + 5)\,dx.$$

Now Try Exercise 5.

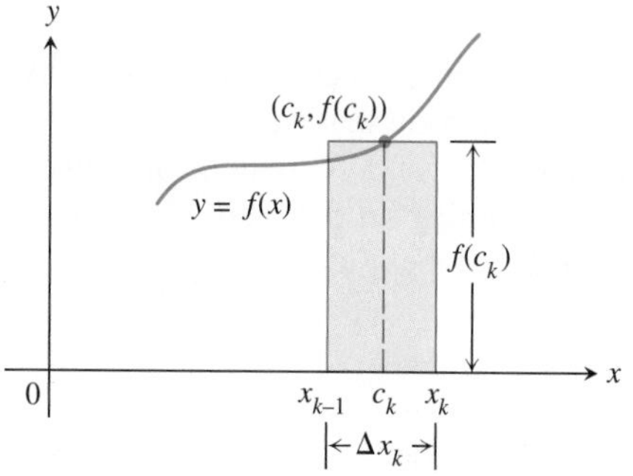

Figure 6.16 A term of a Riemann sum $\Sigma f(c_k)\Delta x_k$ for a nonnegative function f is either zero or the area of a rectangle such as the one shown.

Definite Integral and Area

If an integrable function $y = f(x)$ is nonnegative throughout an interval $[a, b]$, each nonzero term $f(c_k)\Delta x_k$ is the area of a rectangle reaching from the x-axis up to the curve $y = f(x)$. (See Figure 6.16.)

The Riemann sum

$$\sum f(c_k)\,\Delta x_k,$$

which is the sum of the areas of these rectangles, gives an estimate of the area of the region between the curve and the x-axis from a to b. Since the rectangles give an increasingly good approximation of the region as we use partitions with smaller and smaller norms, we call the limiting value the area under the curve.

DEFINITION Area Under a Curve (as a Definite Integral)

If $y = f(x)$ is nonnegative and integrable over a closed interval $[a, b]$, then the **area under the curve $y = f(x)$ from a to b** is the integral of f from a to b,

$$A = \int_a^b f(x)\,dx.$$

This definition works both ways: We can use integrals to calculate areas *and* we can use areas to calculate integrals.

EXAMPLE 2 Revisiting Area Under a Curve

Evaluate the integral $\int_{-2}^{2} \sqrt{4 - x^2}\,dx$.

SOLUTION

We recognize $f(x) = \sqrt{4 - x^2}$ as a function whose graph is a semicircle of radius 2 centered at the origin (Figure 6.17).

The area between the semicircle and the x-axis from -2 to 2 can be computed using the geometry formula

$$\text{Area} = \frac{1}{2}\cdot \pi r^2 = \frac{1}{2}\cdot \pi(2)^2 = 2\pi.$$

Because the area is also the value of the integral of f from -2 to 2,

$$\int_{-2}^{2} \sqrt{4 - x^2}\,dx = 2\pi.$$

Now Try Exercise 15.

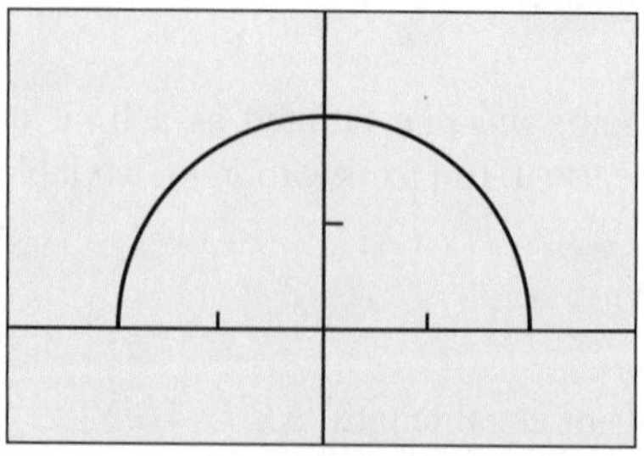

[-3, 3] by [-1, 3]

Figure 6.17 A square viewing window on $y = \sqrt{4 - x^2}$. The graph is a semicircle because $y = \sqrt{4 - x^2}$ is the same as $y^2 = 4 - x^2$, or $x^2 + y^2 = 4$, with $y \geq 0$. (Example 2)

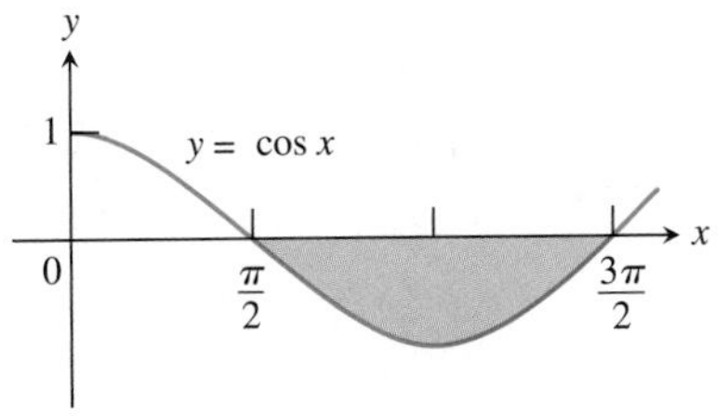

Figure 6.18 Because $f(x) = \cos x$ is nonpositive on $[\pi/2, 3\pi/2]$, the integral of f is a negative number. The area of the shaded region is the opposite of this integral,

$$\text{Area} = -\int_{\pi/2}^{3\pi/2} \cos x \, dx.$$

If an integrable function $y = f(x)$ is nonpositive, the nonzero terms $f(c_k)\Delta x_k$ in the Riemann sums for f over an interval $[a, b]$ are negatives of rectangle areas. The limit of the sums, the integral of f from a to b, is therefore the *negative* of the area of the region between the graph of f and the x-axis (Figure 6.18).

$$\int_a^b f(x) \, dx = -(\text{the area}) \quad \text{if} \quad f(x) \le 0.$$

Or, turning this around,

$$\text{Area} = -\int_a^b f(x) \, dx \quad \text{when} \quad f(x) \le 0.$$

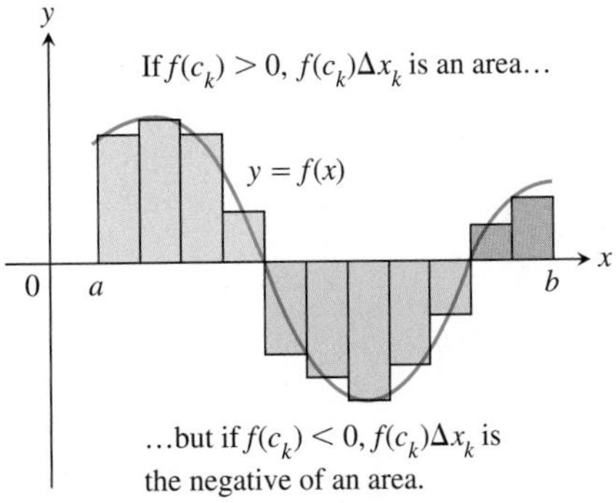

Figure 6.19 An integrable function f with negative as well as positive values.

If an integrable function $y = f(x)$ has both positive and negative values on an interval $[a, b]$, then the Riemann sums for f on $[a, b]$ add areas of rectangles that lie above the x-axis to the negatives of areas of rectangles that lie below the x-axis, as in Figure 6.19. The resulting cancellations mean that the limiting value is a number whose magnitude is less than the total area between the curve and the x-axis. The value of the integral is the area above the x-axis minus the area below.

For any integrable function,

$$\int_a^b f(x) \, dx = (\text{area above the } x\text{-axis}) - (\text{area below the } x\text{-axis}).$$

Net Area

Sometimes $\int_a^b f(x)\,dx$ is called the *net area* of the region determined by the curve $y = f(x)$ and the x-axis between $x = a$ and $x = b$.

EXPLORATION 1 Finding Integrals by Signed Areas

It is a fact (which we will revisit) that $\int_0^\pi \sin x \, dx = 2$ (Figure 6.20). With that information, what you know about integrals and areas, what you know about graphing curves, and sometimes a bit of intuition, determine the values of the following integrals. Give as convincing an argument as you can for each value, based on the graph of the function.

1. $\displaystyle\int_\pi^{2\pi} \sin x \, dx$ **2.** $\displaystyle\int_0^{2\pi} \sin x \, dx$ **3.** $\displaystyle\int_0^{\pi/2} \sin x \, dx$

4. $\displaystyle\int_0^{\pi} (2 + \sin x) \, dx$ **5.** $\displaystyle\int_0^{\pi} 2 \sin x \, dx$ **6.** $\displaystyle\int_2^{\pi+2} \sin (x - 2) \, dx$

7. $\displaystyle\int_{-\pi}^{\pi} \sin u \, du$ **8.** $\displaystyle\int_0^{2\pi} \sin (x/2) \, dx$ **9.** $\displaystyle\int_0^{\pi} \cos x \, dx$

10. Suppose k is *any* positive number. Make a conjecture about $\int_{-k}^{k} \sin x \, dx$ and support your conjecture.

y = sin x

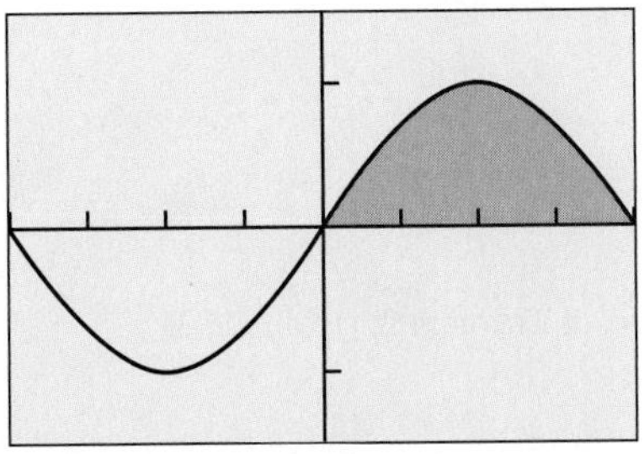

[−π, π] by [−1.5, 1.5]

Figure 6.20

$$\int_0^\pi \sin x \, dx = 2. \text{ (Exploration 1)}$$

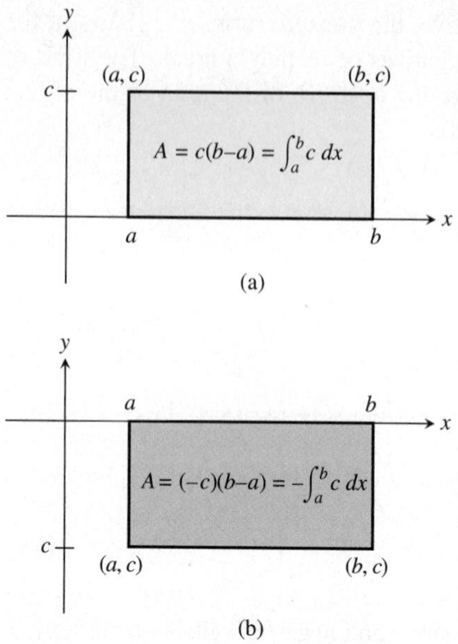

Figure 6.21 (a) If c is a positive constant, then $\int_a^b c\,dx$ is the area of the rectangle shown. (b) If c is negative, then $\int_a^b c\,dx$ is the opposite of the area of the rectangle.

Constant Functions

Integrals of constant functions are easy to evaluate. Over a closed interval, they are simply the constant times the length of the interval (Figure 6.21).

THEOREM 2 The Integral of a Constant

If $f(x) = c$, where c is a constant, on the interval $[a, b]$, then

$$\int_a^b f(x)\,dx = \int_a^b c\,dx = c(b - a).$$

Proof A constant function is continuous, so the integral exists, and we can evaluate it as a limit of Riemann sums with subintervals of equal length $(b - a)/n$. Any such sum looks like

$$\sum_{k=1}^{n} f(c_k) \cdot \Delta x, \quad \text{which is} \quad \sum_{k=1}^{n} c \cdot \frac{b - a}{n}.$$

Then

$$\begin{aligned}\sum_{k=1}^{n} c \cdot \frac{b - a}{n} &= c \cdot (b - a) \sum_{k=1}^{n} \frac{1}{n} \\ &= c(b - a) \cdot n\left(\frac{1}{n}\right) \\ &= c(b - a).\end{aligned}$$

Since the sum is *always* $c(b - a)$ for any value of n, it follows that the limit of the sums, the integral to which they converge, is also $c(b - a)$. ■

EXAMPLE 3 Revisiting the Train Problem

A train moves along a track at a steady 75 miles per hour from 7:00 A.M. to 9:00 A.M. Express its total distance traveled as an integral. Evaluate the integral using Theorem 2.

SOLUTION

(See Figure 6.22.)

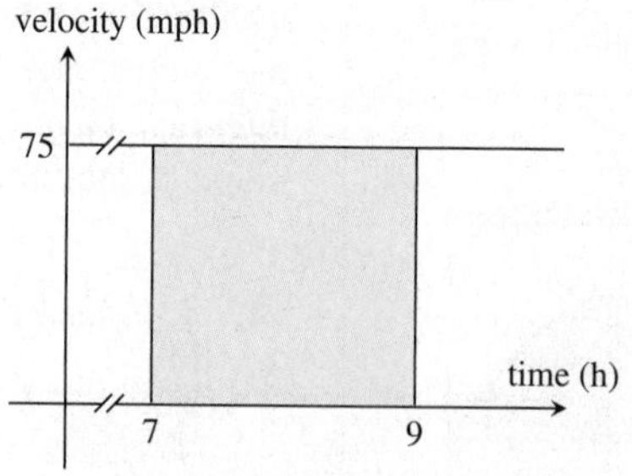

Figure 6.22 The area of the rectangle is a special case of Theorem 2. (Example 3)

$$\text{Distance traveled} = \int_7^9 75\,dt = 75 \cdot (9 - 7) = 150$$

Since the 75 is measured in miles/hour and the $(9 - 7)$ is measured in hours, the 150 is measured in miles. The train traveled 150 miles. ***Now Try Exercise 29.***

Integrals on a Calculator

You do not have to know much about your calculator to realize that finding the limit of a Riemann sum is exactly the kind of thing that it does best. We have seen how effectively it can approximate areas using MRAM, but most modern calculators have sophisticated built-in programs that converge to integrals with much greater speed and precision than that. We will assume that your calculator has such a numerical integration capability, which we will denote as **NINT.** In particular, we will use NINT $(f(x), x, a, b)$ to denote a calculator (or computer) approximation of $\int_a^b f(x)\,dx$. When we write

$$\int_a^b f(x)\,dx = \text{NINT}\,(f(x), x, a, b),$$

we do so with the understanding that the right-hand side of the equation is an approximation of the left-hand side.

EXAMPLE 4 Using NINT

Evaluate the following integrals numerically.

(a) $\int_{-1}^{2} x \sin x\,dx$ **(b)** $\int_0^1 \frac{4}{1 + x^2}\,dx$ **(c)** $\int_0^5 e^{-x^2}\,dx$

SOLUTION

(a) NINT $(x \sin x, x, -1, 2) \approx 2.04$

(b) NINT $(4/(1 + x^2), x, 0, 1) \approx 3.14$

(c) NINT $(e^{-x^2}, x, 0, 5) \approx 0.89$

Now Try Exercise 33.

We will eventually be able to confirm that the exact value for the integral in Example 4a is $-2\cos 2 + \sin 2 - \cos 1 + \sin 1$. You might want to conjecture for yourself what the exact answer to Example 4b might be. As for Example 4c, no explicit *exact* value has ever been found for this integral! The best we can do in this case (and in many like it) is to approximate the integral numerically. Here, technology is not only useful, it is essential.

Bounded Functions

We say a function is *bounded* on a given domain if its range is confined between some minimum value *m* and some maximum value *M*. That is, given any *x* in the domain, $m \le f(x) \le M$. Equivalently, the graph of $y = f(x)$ lies between the horizontal lines $y = m$ and $y = M$.

Discontinuous Integrable Functions

Theorem 1 guarantees that all continuous functions are integrable. But some functions with discontinuities are also integrable. For example, a bounded function (see margin note) that has a finite number of points of discontinuity on an interval $[a, b]$ will still be integrable on the interval if it is continuous everywhere else.

$y = |x|/x$

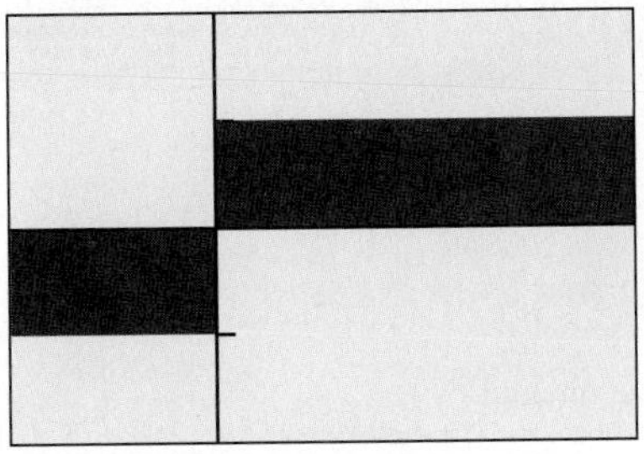

[−1, 2] by [−2, 2]

Figure 6.23 A discontinuous integrable function:

$$\int_{-1}^{2} \frac{|x|}{x}\,dx = -(\text{area below } x\text{-axis}) + (\text{area above } x\text{-axis}).$$

(Example 5)

EXAMPLE 5 Integrating a Discontinuous Function

Find $\int_{-1}^{2} \frac{|x|}{x}\,dx.$

SOLUTION

This function has a discontinuity at $x = 0$, where the graph jumps from $y = -1$ to $y = 1$. The graph, however, determines two rectangles, one below the x-axis and one above (Figure 6.23).

Using the idea of net area, we have

$$\int_{-1}^{2} \frac{|x|}{x}\,dx = -1 + 2 = 1.$$

Now Try Exercise 37.

A Nonintegrable Function

How "bad" does a function have to be before it is *not* integrable? One way to defeat integrability is to be unbounded (like $y = 1/x$ near $x = 0$), which can prevent the Riemann sums from tending to a finite limit. Another, more subtle, way is to be bounded but badly discontinuous, like the *characteristic function of the rationals:*

$$f(x) = \begin{cases} 1 & \text{if } x \text{ is rational} \\ 0 & \text{if } x \text{ is irrational.} \end{cases}$$

No matter what partition we take of the closed interval $[0, 1]$, every subinterval contains both rational and irrational numbers. That means that we can always form a Riemann sum with all rational c_k's (a Riemann sum of 1) or all irrational c_k's (a Riemann sum of 0). The sums can therefore never tend toward a unique limit.

EXPLORATION 2 More Discontinuous Integrands

1. Explain why the function

$$f(x) = \frac{x^2 - 4}{x - 2}$$

is not continuous on $[0, 3]$. What kind of discontinuity occurs?

2. Use areas to show that

$$\int_0^3 \frac{x^2 - 4}{x - 2}\,dx = 10.5.$$

3. Use areas to show that

$$\int_0^5 \text{int}\,(x)\,dx = 10.$$

Quick Review 6.2

Exercise numbers with a gray background indicate problems that the authors have designed to be solved *without a calculator.*

In Exercises 1–3, evaluate the sum.

1. $\sum_{n=1}^{5} n^2$

2. $\sum_{k=0}^{4} (3k - 2)$

3. $\sum_{j=0}^{4} 100\,(j + 1)^2$

In Exercises 4–6, write the sum in sigma notation.

4. $1 + 2 + 3 + \cdots + 98 + 99$

5. $0 + 2 + 4 + \cdots + 48 + 50$

6. $3(1)^2 + 3(2)^2 + \cdots + 3(500)^2$

In Exercises 7 and 8, write the expression as a single sum in sigma notation.

7. $2\sum_{x=1}^{50} x^2 + 3\sum_{x=1}^{50} x$

8. $\sum_{k=0}^{8} x^k + \sum_{k=9}^{20} x^k$

9. Find $\sum_{k=0}^{n} (-1)^k$ if n is odd.

10. Find $\sum_{k=0}^{n} (-1)^k$ if n is even.

Section 6.2 Exercises

In Exercises 1–6, each c_k is chosen from the kth subinterval of a regular partition of the indicated interval into n subintervals of length Δx. Express the limit as a definite integral.

1. $\lim_{n\to\infty} \sum_{k=1}^{n} c_k^{\,2}\Delta x, \quad [0, 2]$

2. $\lim_{n\to\infty} \sum_{k=1}^{n} (c_k^{\,2} - 3c_k)\Delta x, \quad [-7, 5]$

3. $\lim_{n\to\infty} \sum_{k=1}^{n} \frac{1}{c_k}\Delta x, \quad [1, 4]$

4. $\lim_{n\to\infty} \sum_{k=1}^{n} \frac{1}{1 - c_k}\Delta x, \quad [2, 3]$

5. $\lim_{n\to\infty} \sum_{k=1}^{n} \sqrt{4 - c_k^{\,2}}\,\Delta x, \quad [0, 1]$

6. $\lim_{n\to\infty} \sum_{k=1}^{n} (\sin^3 c_k)\,\Delta x, \quad [-\pi, \pi]$

In Exercises 7–12, evaluate the integral.

7. $\int_{-2}^{1} 5\,dx$

8. $\int_{3}^{7} (-20)\,dx$

9. $\int_{0}^{3} (-160)\,dt$

10. $\int_{-4}^{-1} \frac{\pi}{2}\,d\theta$

11. $\int_{-2.1}^{3.4} 0.5\,ds$

12. $\int_{\sqrt{2}}^{\sqrt{18}} \sqrt{2}\,dr$

In Exercises 13–22, use the graph of the integrand and areas to evaluate the integral.

13. $\int_{-2}^{4}\left(\frac{x}{2}+3\right)dx$

14. $\int_{1/2}^{3/2}(-2x+4)\,dx$

15. $\int_{-3}^{3}\sqrt{9-x^2}\,dx$

16. $\int_{-4}^{0}\sqrt{16-x^2}\,dx$

17. $\int_{-2}^{1}|x|\,dx$

18. $\int_{-1}^{1}(1-|x|)\,dx$

19. $\int_{-1}^{1}(2-|x|)\,dx$

20. $\int_{-1}^{1}(1+\sqrt{1-x^2})\,dx$

21. $\int_{\pi}^{2\pi}\theta\,d\theta$

22. $\int_{\sqrt{2}}^{5\sqrt{2}}r\,dr$

In Exercises 23–28, use areas to evaluate the integral.

23. $\int_{0}^{b}x\,dx,\quad b>0$

24. $\int_{0}^{b}4x\,dx,\quad b>0$

25. $\int_{a}^{b}2s\,ds,\quad 0<a<b$

26. $\int_{a}^{b}3t\,dt,\quad 0<a<b$

27. $\int_{a}^{2a}x\,dx,\quad a>0,$

28. $\int_{a}^{\sqrt{3}a}x\,dx,\quad a>0$

In Exercises 29–32, express the desired quantity as a definite integral and evaluate the integral using Theorem 2.

29. Find the distance traveled by a train moving at 87 mph from 8:00 A.M. to 11:00 A.M.

30. Find the output from a pump producing 25 gallons per minute during the first hour of its operation.

31. Find the calories burned by a walker burning 300 calories per hour between 6:00 P.M. and 7:30 P.M.

32. Find the amount of water lost from a bucket leaking 0.4 liters per hour between 8:30 A.M. and 11:00 A.M.

In Exercises 33–36, use NINT to evaluate the expression.

33. $\int_{0}^{5}\frac{x}{x^2+4}\,dx$

34. $3+2\int_{0}^{\pi/3}\tan x\,dx$

35. Find the area enclosed between the x-axis and the graph of $y=4-x^2$ from $x=-2$ to $x=2$.

36. Find the area enclosed between the x-axis and the graph of $y=x^2e^{-x}$ from $x=-1$ to $x=3$.

In Exercises 37–40, **(a)** find the points of discontinuity of the integrand on the interval of integration, and **(b)** use area to evaluate the integral.

37. $\int_{-2}^{3}\frac{x}{|x|}\,dx$

38. $\int_{-6}^{5}2\,\text{int}\,(x-3)\,dx$

39. $\int_{-3}^{4}\frac{x^2-1}{x+1}\,dx$

40. $\int_{-5}^{6}\frac{9-x^2}{x-3}\,dx$

Standardized Test Questions

41. True or False If $\int_a^b f(x)\,dx>0$, then $f(x)$ is positive for all x in $[a,b]$. Justify your answer.

42. True or False If $f(x)$ is positive for all x in $[a,b]$, then $\int_a^b f(x)\,dx>0$. Justify your answer.

43. Multiple Choice If $\int_2^5 f(x)\,dx=18$, then $\int_2^5(f(x)+4)\,dx=$

(A) 20 (B) 22 (C) 23 (D) 25 (E) 30

44. Multiple Choice $\int_{-4}^{4}(4-|x|)\,dx=$

(A) 0 (B) 4 (C) 8 (D) 16 (E) 32

45. Multiple Choice If the interval $[0,\pi]$ is divided into n subintervals of length π/n and c_k is chosen from the kth subinterval, which of the following is a Riemann sum?

(A) $\sum_{k=1}^{n}\sin(c_k)$ (B) $\sum_{k=1}^{\infty}\sin(c_k)$ (C) $\sum_{k=1}^{n}\sin(c_k)\left(\frac{\pi}{n}\right)$

(D) $\sum_{k=1}^{n}\sin\left(\frac{\pi}{n}\right)(c_k)$ (E) $\sum_{k=1}^{n}\sin(c_k)\left(\frac{\pi}{k}\right)$

46. Multiple Choice Which of the following quantities would *not* be represented by the definite integral $\int_0^8 70\,dt$?

(A) The distance traveled by a train moving at 70 mph for 8 minutes.

(B) The volume of ice cream produced by a machine making 70 gallons per hour for 8 hours.

(C) The length of a track left by a snail traveling at 70 cm per hour for 8 hours.

(D) The total sales of a company selling \$70 of merchandise per hour for 8 hours.

(E) The amount the tide has risen 8 minutes after low tide if it rises at a rate of 70 mm per minute during that period.

Explorations

In Exercises 47–56, use graphs, your knowledge of area, and the fact that

$$\int_0^1 x^3\,dx=\frac{1}{4}$$

to evaluate the integral.

47. $\int_{-1}^{1}x^3\,dx$

48. $\int_{0}^{1}(x^3+3)\,dx$

49. $\int_{2}^{3}(x-2)^3\,dx$

50. $\int_{-1}^{1}|x|^3\,dx$

51. $\int_{0}^{1}(1-x^3)\,dx$

52. $\int_{-1}^{2}(|x|-1)^3\,dx$

53. $\int_{0}^{2}\left(\frac{x}{2}\right)^3dx$

54. $\int_{-8}^{8}x^3\,dx$

55. $\int_{0}^{1}(x^3-1)\,dx$

56. $\int_{0}^{1}\sqrt[3]{x}\,dx$

Extending the Ideas

57. Writing to Learn The function

$$f(x) = \begin{cases} \dfrac{1}{x^2}, & 0 < x \le 1 \\ 0, & x = 0 \end{cases}$$

is defined on $[0, 1]$ and has a single point of discontinuity at $x = 0$.

(a) What happens to the graph of f as x approaches 0 from the right?

(b) The function f is not integrable on $[0, 1]$. Give a convincing argument based on Riemann sums to explain why it is not.

58. It can be shown by mathematical induction (see Appendix 2) that

$$\sum_{k=1}^{n} k^2 = \frac{n(n+1)(2n+1)}{6}.$$

Use this fact to give a formal proof that

$$\int_0^1 x^2\,dx = \frac{1}{3}$$

by following the steps given in the next column.

(a) Partition $[0, 1]$ into n subintervals of length $1/n$. Show that the RRAM Riemann sum for the integral is

$$\sum_{k=1}^{n}\left(\left(\frac{k}{n}\right)^2 \cdot \frac{1}{n}\right).$$

(b) Show that this sum can be written as

$$\frac{1}{n^3} \cdot \sum_{k=1}^{n} k^2.$$

(c) Show that the sum can therefore be written as

$$\frac{(n+1)(2n+1)}{6n^2}.$$

(d) Show that

$$\lim_{n\to\infty} \sum_{k=1}^{n}\left(\left(\frac{k}{n}\right)^2 \cdot \frac{1}{n}\right) = \frac{1}{3}.$$

(e) Explain why the equation in part (d) proves that

$$\int_0^1 x^2\,dx = \frac{1}{3}.$$

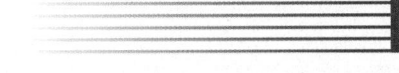

6.3 Definite Integrals and Antiderivatives

What you will learn about . . .

- Properties of Definite Integrals
- Average Value of a Function
- Mean Value Theorem for Definite Integrals
- Connecting Differential and Integral Calculus

and why . . .

Working with the properties of definite integrals helps us to understand better the definite integral. Connecting derivatives and definite integrals sets the stage for the Fundamental Theorem of Calculus.

Properties of Definite Integrals

In defining $\int_a^b f(x)$ as a limit of sums $\Sigma c_k \Delta x_k$, we moved from left to right across the interval $[a, b]$. What would happen if we integrated in the *opposite direction*? The integral would become $\int_b^a f(x)\,dx$—again a limit of sums of the form $\Sigma f(c_k)\Delta x_k$—but this time each of the Δx_k's would be negative as the x-values *decreased* from b to a. This would change the signs of all the terms in each Riemann sum, and ultimately the sign of the definite integral. This suggests the rule

$$\int_b^a f(x)\,dx = -\int_a^b f(x)\,dx.$$

Since the original definition did not apply to integrating backwards over an interval, we can treat this rule as a logical extension of the definition.

Although $[a, a]$ is technically not an interval, another logical extension of the definition is that $\int_a^a f(x)\,dx = 0$.

These are the first two rules in Table 6.3. The others are inherited from rules that hold for Riemann sums. However, the limit step required to *prove* that these rules hold in the limit (as the norms of the partitions tend to zero) places their mathematical verification beyond the scope of this course. They should make good sense nonetheless.

TABLE 6.3 Rules for Definite Integrals

1. *Order of Integration:* $\int_b^a f(x)\,dx = -\int_a^b f(x)\,dx$ A definition

2. *Zero:* $\int_a^a f(x)\,dx = 0$ Also a definition

3. *Constant Multiple:* $\int_a^b kf(x)\,dx = k\int_a^b f(x)\,dx$ Any number k

   $\int_a^b -f(x)\,dx = -\int_a^b f(x)\,dx$ $k = -1$

4. *Sum and Difference:* $\int_a^b (f(x) \pm g(x))\,dx = \int_a^b f(x)\,dx \pm \int_a^b g(x)\,dx$

5. *Additivity:* $\int_a^b f(x)\,dx + \int_b^c f(x)\,dx = \int_a^c f(x)\,dx$

6. *Max-Min Inequality:* If max f and min f are the maximum and minimum values of f on $[a, b]$, then

$$\min f \cdot (b - a) \le \int_a^b f(x)\,dx \le \max f \cdot (b - a).$$

7. *Domination:* $f(x) \ge g(x)$ on $[a, b] \Rightarrow \int_a^b f(x)\,dx \ge \int_a^b g(x)\,dx$

   $f(x) \ge 0$ on $[a, b] \Rightarrow \int_a^b f(x)\,dx \ge 0$ $g = 0$

EXAMPLE 1 Using the Rules for Definite Integrals

Suppose

$$\int_{-1}^{1} f(x)\,dx = 5, \quad \int_{1}^{4} f(x)\,dx = -2, \quad \text{and} \quad \int_{-1}^{1} h(x)\,dx = 7.$$

Find each of the following integrals, if possible.

(a) $\int_{4}^{1} f(x)\,dx$ **(b)** $\int_{-1}^{4} f(x)\,dx$ **(c)** $\int_{-1}^{1} [2f(x) + 3h(x)]\,dx$

(d) $\int_{0}^{1} f(x)\,dx$ **(e)** $\int_{-2}^{2} h(x)\,dx$ **(f)** $\int_{-1}^{4} [f(x) + h(x)]\,dx$

SOLUTION

(a) $\int_{4}^{1} f(x)\,dx = -\int_{1}^{4} f(x)\,dx = -(-2) = 2$

(b) $\int_{-1}^{4} f(x)\,dx = \int_{-1}^{1} f(x)\,dx + \int_{1}^{4} f(x)\,dx = 5 + (-2) = 3$

(c) $\int_{-1}^{1} [2f(x) + 3h(x)]\,dx = 2\int_{-1}^{1} f(x)\,dx + 3\int_{-1}^{1} h(x)\,dx = 2(5) + 3(7) = 31$

(d) Not enough information given. (We cannot assume, for example, that integrating over half the interval would give half the integral!)

(e) Not enough information given. (We have no information about the function h outside the interval $[-1, 1]$.)

(f) Not enough information given (same reason as in part (e)). ***Now Try Exercise 1.***

EXAMPLE 2 Finding Bounds for an Integral

Show that the value of $\int_0^1 \sqrt{1 + \cos x}\,dx$ is less than $3/2$.

SOLUTION

The Max-Min Inequality for definite integrals (Rule 6) says that $\min f \cdot (b - a)$ is a *lower bound* for the value of $\int_a^b f(x)\,dx$ and that $\max f \cdot (b - a)$ is an *upper bound.* The maximum value of $\sqrt{1 + \cos x}$ on $[0, 1]$ is $\sqrt{2}$, so

$$\int_0^1 \sqrt{1 + \cos x}\,dx \le \sqrt{2} \cdot (1 - 0) = \sqrt{2}.$$

Since $\int_0^1 \sqrt{1 + \cos x}\,dx$ is bounded above by $\sqrt{2}$ (which is 1.414...), it is less than $3/2$. ***Now Try Exercise 7.***

Average Value of a Function

The *average* of n numbers is the sum of the numbers divided by n. How would we define the average value of an arbitrary function f over a closed interval $[a, b]$? As there are infinitely many values to consider, adding them and then dividing by infinity is not an option.

Consider, then, what happens if we take a large *sample* of n numbers from regular subintervals of the interval $[a, b]$. One way would be to take some number c_k from each of the n subintervals of length

$$\Delta x = \frac{b - a}{n}.$$

The average of the n sampled values is

$$\frac{f(c_1) + f(c_2) + \cdots + f(c_n)}{n} = \frac{1}{n} \cdot \sum_{k=1}^{n} f(c_k)$$

$$= \frac{\Delta x}{b - a} \sum_{k=1}^{n} f(c_k) \qquad \frac{1}{n} = \frac{\Delta x}{b - a}$$

$$= \frac{1}{b - a} \cdot \sum_{k=1}^{n} f(c_k) \Delta x.$$

Does this last sum look familiar? It is $1/(b - a)$ times a Riemann sum for f on $[a, b]$. That means that when we consider this averaging process as $n \to \infty$, we find it *has a limit,* namely $1/(b - a)$ times the integral of f over $[a, b]$. We are led by this remarkable fact to the following definition.

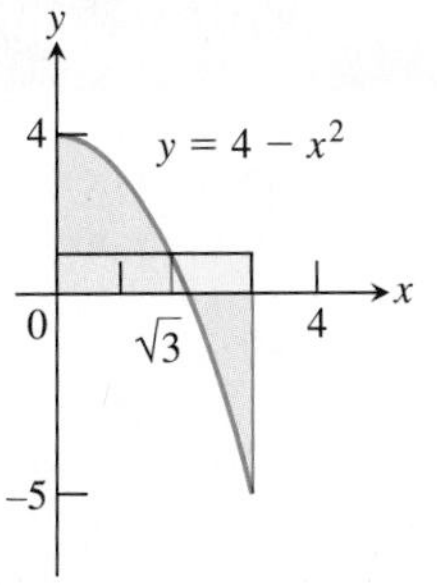

Figure 6.24 The rectangle with base $[0, 3]$ and with height equal to 1 (the average value of the function $f(x) = (4 - x^2)$ has area equal to the net area between f and the x-axis from 0 to 3. (Example 3)

DEFINITION Average (Mean) Value

If f is integrable on $[a, b]$, its **average (mean) value** on $[a, b]$ is

$$av(f) = \frac{1}{b - a} \int_a^b f(x)\,dx.$$

EXAMPLE 3 Applying the Definition

Find the average value of $f(x) = 4 - x^2$ on $[0, 3]$. Does f actually take on this value at some point in the given interval?

SOLUTION

$$av(f) = \frac{1}{b - a} \int_a^b f(x)\,dx$$

$$= \frac{1}{3 - 0} \int_0^3 (4 - x^2)\,dx$$

$$= \frac{1}{3 - 0} \cdot 3 \qquad \text{Using NINT}$$

$$= 1$$

The average value of $f(x) = 4 - x^2$ over the interval $[0, 3]$ is 1. The function assumes this value when $4 - x^2 = 1$ or $x = \pm\sqrt{3}$. Since $x = \sqrt{3}$ lies in the interval $[0, 3]$, the function does assume its average value in the given interval (Figure 6.24).

Now Try Exercise 11.

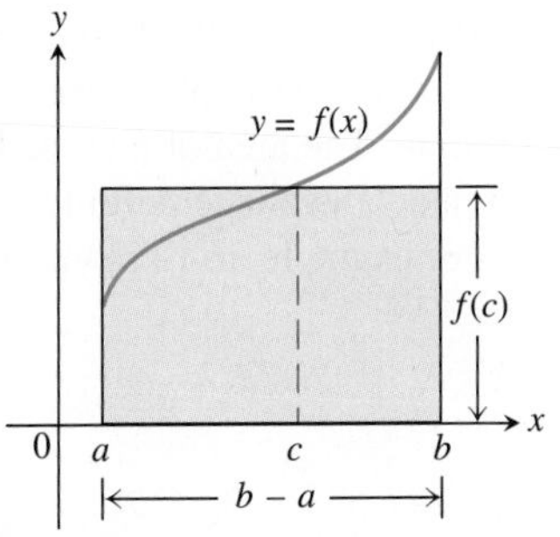

Figure 6.25 The value $f(c)$ in the Mean Value Theorem is, in a sense, the average (or *mean*) height of f on $[a, b]$. When $f \geq 0$, the area of the shaded rectangle

$$f(c)(b - a) = \int_a^b f(x)\,dx,$$

is the area under the graph of f from a to b.

Mean Value Theorem for Definite Integrals

It was no mere coincidence that the function in Example 3 took on its average value at some point in the interval. Look at the graph in Figure 6.25 and imagine rectangles with base $(b - a)$ and heights ranging from the minimum of f (a rectangle too small to give the integral) to the maximum of f (a rectangle too large). Somewhere in between there is a "just right" rectangle, and its topside will intersect the graph of f if f is continuous. The statement that a continuous function on a closed interval *always* assumes its average value at least once in the interval is known as the Mean Value Theorem for Definite Integrals.

THEOREM 3 The Mean Value Theorem for Definite Integrals

If f is continuous on $[a, b]$, then at some point c in $[a, b]$,

$$f(c) = \frac{1}{b-a}\int_a^b f(x)\,dx.$$

EXPLORATION 1 How Long is the Average Chord of a Circle?

Suppose we have a circle of radius r centered at the origin. We want to know the average length of the chords perpendicular to the diameter $[-r, r]$ on the x-axis.

1. Show that the length of the chord at x is $2\sqrt{r^2 - x^2}$ (Figure 6.26).
2. Set up an integral expression for the average value of $2\sqrt{r^2 - x^2}$ over the interval $[-r, r]$.
3. Evaluate the integral by identifying its value as an area.
4. So, what is the average length of a chord of a circle of radius r?
5. Explain how we can use the Mean Value Theorem for Definite Integrals (Theorem 3) to show that the function assumes the value in step 4.

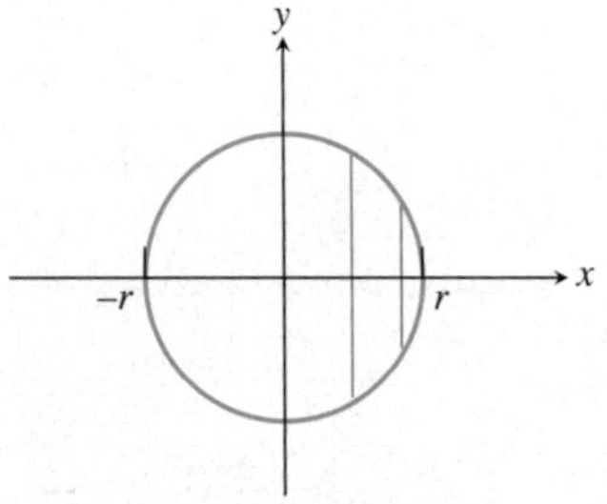

Figure 6.26 Chords perpendicular to the diameter $[-r, r]$ in a circle of radius r centered at the origin. (Exploration 1)

Connecting Differential and Integral Calculus

Before we move on to the next section, let us pause for a moment of historical perspective that can help you to appreciate the power of the theorem that you are about to encounter. In Example 3 we used NINT to find the integral, and in Section 6.2, Example 2, we were fortunate that we could use our knowledge of the area of a circle. The area of a circle has been around for a long time, but NINT has not; so how did people evaluate definite integrals when they could not apply some known area formula? For example, in Exploration 1 of the previous section we used the fact that

$$\int_0^{\pi} \sin x\,dx = 2.$$

Would Newton and Leibniz have known this fact? How?

They did know that *quotients of infinitely small quantities,* as they put it, could be used to get velocity functions from position functions, and that *sums of infinitely thin "rectangle areas"* could be used to get position functions from velocity functions. In some way, then, there had to be a connection between these two seemingly different processes. Newton and Leibniz were able to picture that connection, and it led them to the Fundamental Theorem of Calculus. Can you picture it? Try Exploration 2.

EXPLORATION 2 Finding the Derivative of an Integral

Group Activity Suppose we are given the graph of a continuous function f, as in Figure 6.27.

1. Copy the graph of f onto your own paper. Choose any x greater than a in the interval $[a, b]$ and mark it on the x-axis.
2. Using only *vertical line segments,* shade in the region between the graph of f and the x-axis from a to x. (Some shading might be below the x-axis.)
3. Your shaded region represents a definite integral. Explain why this integral can be written as $\int_a^x f(t)\,dt$. (Why don't we write it as $\int_a^x f(x)\,dx$?)
4. Compare your picture with others produced by your group. Notice how your integral (a real number) depends on which x you chose in the interval $[a, b]$. The integral is therefore a *function of* x on $[a, b]$. Call it F.
5. Recall that $F'(x)$ is the limit of $\Delta F/\Delta x$ as Δx gets smaller and smaller. Represent ΔF in your picture by drawing *one more vertical shading segment* to the right of the last one you drew in step 2. ΔF is the (signed) *area* of your vertical segment.
6. Represent Δx in your picture by moving x to beneath your newly drawn segment. That small change in Δx is the *thickness* of your vertical segment.
7. What is now the *height* of your vertical segment?
8. Can you see why Newton and Leibniz concluded that $F'(x) = f(x)$?

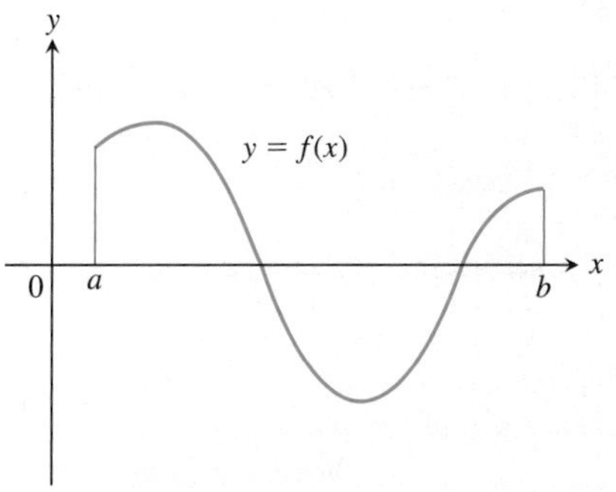

Figure 6.27 The graph of the function in Exploration 2.

If all went well in Exploration 2, you concluded that the derivative with respect to x of the integral of f from a to x is simply f. Specifically,

$$\frac{d}{dx}\int_a^x f(t)\,dt = f(x).$$

This means that the integral is an *antiderivative* of f, a fact we can exploit in the following way.

If F is any antiderivative of f, then

$$\int_a^x f(t)\,dt = F(x) + C$$

for some constant C. Setting x in this equation equal to a gives

$$\int_a^a f(t)\,dt = F(a) + C$$

$$0 = F(a) + C$$

$$C = -F(a).$$

Putting it all together,

$$\int_a^x f(t)\,dt = F(x) - F(a).$$

The implications of the previous last equation were enormous for the discoverers of calculus. It meant that they could evaluate the definite integral of f from a to any number x simply by computing $F(x) - F(a)$, where F *is any antiderivative of* f.

EXAMPLE 4 Finding an Integral Using Antiderivatives

Find $\int_0^{\pi} \sin x \, dx$ using the formula $\int_a^x f(t)\,dt = F(x) - F(a)$.

SOLUTION

Since $\sin x$ is the rate of change of the quantity $F(x) = -\cos x$, that is $F'(x) = \sin x$

$$\int_0^{\pi} \sin x \, dx = -\cos(\pi) - (-\cos(0))$$

$$= -(-1) - (-1)$$

$$= 2.$$

This explains how we obtained the value for Exploration 1 of the previous section.

Now Try Exercise 21.

Quick Review 6.3 *(For help, go to Sections 4.1, 4.3, and 4.4.)*

Exercise numbers with a gray background indicate problems that the authors have designed to be solved *without a calculator.*

In Exercises 1–10, find dy/dx.

1. $y = -\cos x$
2. $y = \sin x$
3. $y = \ln(\sec x)$
4. $y = \ln(\sin x)$
5. $y = \ln(\sec x + \tan x)$
6. $y = x \ln x - x$
7. $y = \dfrac{x^{n+1}}{n+1} \quad (n \neq -1)$
8. $y = \dfrac{1}{2^x + 1}$
9. $y = xe^x$
10. $y = \tan^{-1} x$

Section 6.3 Exercises

The exercises in this section are designed to reinforce your understanding of the definite integral from the algebraic and geometric points of view. For this reason, you should not use the numerical integration capability of your calculator (NINT) except perhaps to support an answer.

1. Suppose that f and g are continuous functions and that

$$\int_1^2 f(x)\,dx = -4, \quad \int_1^5 f(x)\,dx = 6, \quad \int_1^5 g(x)\,dx = 8.$$

Use the rules in Table 6.3 to find each integral.

(a) $\int_2^2 g(x)\,dx$ **(b)** $\int_5^1 g(x)\,dx$

(c) $\int_1^2 3f(x)\,dx$ **(d)** $\int_2^5 f(x)\,dx$

(e) $\int_1^5 [f(x) - g(x)]\,dx$ **(f)** $\int_1^5 [4f(x) - g(x)]\,dx$

2. Suppose that f and h are continuous functions and that

$$\int_1^9 f(x)\,dx = -1, \quad \int_7^9 f(x)\,dx = 5, \quad \int_7^9 h(x)\,dx = 4.$$

Use the rules in Table 6.3 to find each integral.

(a) $\int_1^9 -2f(x)\,dx$ **(b)** $\int_7^9 [f(x) + h(x)]\,dx$

(c) $\int_7^9 [2f(x) - 3h(x)]\,dx$ **(d)** $\int_9^1 f(x)\,dx$

(e) $\int_1^7 f(x)\,dx$ **(f)** $\int_9^7 [h(x) - f(x)]\,dx$

3. Suppose that $\int_1^2 f(x)\,dx = 5$. Find each integral.

(a) $\int_1^2 f(u)\,du$ **(b)** $\int_1^2 \sqrt{3} f(z)\,dz$

(c) $\int_2^1 f(t)\,dt$ **(d)** $\int_1^2 [-f(x)]\,dx$

4. Suppose that $\int_{-3}^0 g(t)\,dt = \sqrt{2}$. Find each integral.

(a) $\int_0^{-3} g(t)\,dt$ **(b)** $\int_{-3}^0 g(u)\,du$

(c) $\int_{-3}^0 [-g(x)]\,dx$ **(d)** $\int_{-3}^0 \dfrac{g(r)}{\sqrt{2}}\,dr$

5. Suppose that f is continuous and that

$$\int_0^3 f(z)\,dz = 3 \quad \text{and} \quad \int_0^4 f(z)\,dz = 7.$$

Find each integral.

(a) $\int_3^4 f(z)\,dz$ **(b)** $\int_4^3 f(t)\,dt$

6. Suppose that h is continuous and that

$$\int_{-1}^1 h(r)\,dr = 0 \quad \text{and} \quad \int_{-1}^3 h(r)\,dr = 6.$$

Find each integral.

(a) $\int_1^3 h(r)\,dr$ **(b)** $-\int_3^1 h(u)\,du$

7. Show that the value of $\int_0^1 \sin(x^2)\,dx$ cannot possibly be 2.

8. Show that the value of $\int_0^1 \sqrt{x+8}\,dx$ lies between $2\sqrt{2} \approx 2.8$ and 3.

9. *Integrals of Nonnegative Functions* Use the Max-Min Inequality to show that if f is integrable then

$$f(x) \geq 0 \text{ on } [a, b] \Rightarrow \int_a^b f(x)\,dx \geq 0.$$

10. *Integrals of Nonpositive Functions* Show that if f is integrable then

$$f(x) \leq 0 \text{ on } [a, b] \Rightarrow \int_a^b f(x)\,dx \leq 0.$$

In Exercises 11–14, use NINT to find the average value of the function on the interval. At what point(s) in the interval does the function assume its average value?

11. $y = x^2 - 1,\ [0, \sqrt{3}]$ **12.** $y = -\dfrac{x^2}{2},\ [0, 3]$

13. $y = -3x^2 - 1,\ [0, 1]$ **14.** $y = (x-1)^2,\ [0, 3]$

In Exercises 15–18, find the average value of the function on the interval without integrating, by appealing to the geometry of the region between the graph and the x-axis.

15. $f(x) = \begin{cases} x + 4, & -4 \leq x \leq -1, \\ -x + 2, & -1 < x \leq 2, \end{cases}$ on $[-4, 2]$

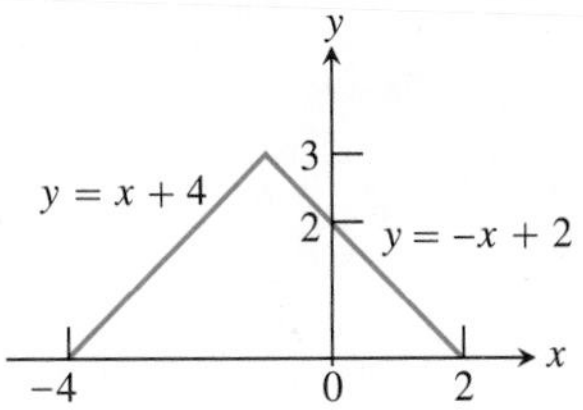

16. $f(t) = 1 - \sqrt{1 - t^2},\ [-1, 1]$

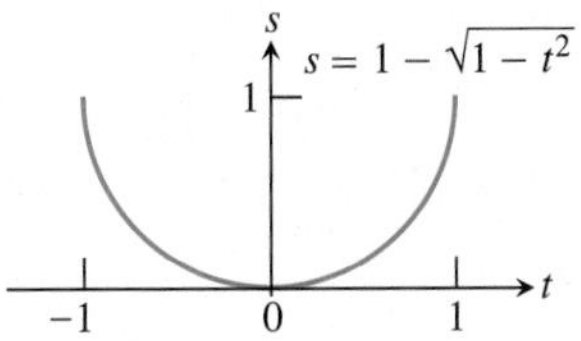

17. $f(t) = \sin t,\ [0, 2\pi]$

18. $f(\theta) = \tan\theta,\ \left[-\dfrac{\pi}{4}, \dfrac{\pi}{4}\right]$

In Exercises 19–30, interpret the integrand as the rate of change of a quantity and evaluate the integral using the antiderivative of the quantity, as in Example 4.

19. $\int_\pi^{2\pi} \sin x\,dx$ **20.** $\int_0^{\pi/2} \cos x\,dx$

21. $\int_0^1 e^x\,dx$ **22.** $\int_0^{\pi/4} \sec^2 x\,dx$

23. $\int_1^4 2x\,dx$ **24.** $\int_{-1}^2 3x^2\,dx$

25. $\int_{-2}^6 5\,dx$ **26.** $\int_3^7 8\,dx$

27. $\int_{-1}^1 \dfrac{1}{1+x^2}\,dx$ **28.** $\int_0^{1/2} \dfrac{1}{\sqrt{1-x^2}}\,dx$

29. $\int_1^e \dfrac{1}{x}\,dx$ **30.** $\int_1^4 -x^{-2}\,dx$

In Exercises 31–36, find the average value of the function on the interval, using antiderivatives to compute the integral.

31. $y = \sin x,\ [0, \pi]$ **32.** $y = \dfrac{1}{x},\ [e, 2e]$

33. $y = \sec^2 x,\ \left[0, \dfrac{\pi}{4}\right]$ **34.** $y = \dfrac{1}{1+x^2},\ [0, 1]$

35. $y = 3x^2 + 2x,\ [-1, 2]$ **36.** $y = \sec x \tan x,\ \left[0, \dfrac{\pi}{3}\right]$

37. Group Activity Use the Max-Min Inequality to find upper and lower bounds for the value of

$$\int_0^1 \frac{1}{1+x^4}\,dx.$$

38. Group Activity *(Continuation of Exercise 37)* Use the Max-Min Inequality to find upper and lower bounds for the values of

$$\int_0^{0.5} \frac{1}{1+x^4}\,dx \quad \text{and} \quad \int_{0.5}^1 \frac{1}{1+x^4}\,dx.$$

Add these to arrive at an improved estimate for

$$\int_0^1 \frac{1}{1+x^4}\,dx.$$

39. Writing to Learn If $av(f)$ really is a typical value of the integrable function $f(x)$ on $[a, b]$, then the number $av(f)$ should have the same integral over $[a, b]$ that f does. Does it? That is, does

$$\int_a^b av(f)\,dx = \int_a^b f(x)\,dx?$$

Give reasons for your answer.

40. Writing to Learn A driver averaged 30 mph on a 150-mile trip and then returned over the same 150 miles at the rate of 50 mph. He figured that his average speed was 40 mph for the entire trip.

(a) What was his total distance traveled?

(b) What was his total time spent for the trip?

(c) What was his average speed for the trip?

(d) Explain the error in the driver's reasoning.

41. Writing to Learn A dam released 1000 m^3 of water at 10 m^3/min and then released another 1000 m^3 at 20 m^3/min. What was the average rate at which the water was released? Give reasons for your answer.

42. Use the inequality $\sin x \leq x$, which holds for $x \geq 0$, to find an upper bound for the value of $\int_0^1 \sin x\, dx$.

43. The inequality $\sec x \geq 1 + (x^2/2)$ holds on $(-\pi/2, \pi/2)$. Use it to find a lower bound for the value of $\int_0^1 \sec x\, dx$.

44. Show that the average value of a linear function $L(x)$ on $[a, b]$ is

$$\frac{L(a) + L(b)}{2}.$$

[*Caution*: This simple formula for average value does *not* work for functions in general!]

Standardized Test Questions

You may use a graphing calculator to solve the following problems.

45. True or False The average value of a function f on $[a, b]$ always lies between $f(a)$ and $f(b)$. Justify your answer.

46. True or False If $\int_a^b f(x)\,dx = 0$, then $f(a) = f(b)$. Justify your answer.

47. Multiple Choice If $\int_3^7 f(x)\,dx = 5$ and $\int_3^7 g(x)\,dx = 3$, then all of the following must be true *except*

(A) $\int_3^7 f(x)g(x)\,dx = 15$

(B) $\int_3^7 [f(x) + g(x)]\,dx = 8$

(C) $\int_3^7 2f(x)\,dx = 10$

(D) $\int_3^7 [f(x) - g(x)]\,dx = 2$

(E) $\int_7^3 [g(x) - f(x)]\,dx = 2$

48. Multiple Choice If $\int_2^5 f(x)\,dx = 12$ and $\int_5^8 f(x)\,dx = 4$, then all of the following must be true *except*

(A) $\int_2^8 f(x)\,dx = 16$

(B) $\int_2^5 f(x)\,dx - \int_5^8 3f(x)\,dx = 0$

(C) $\int_5^2 f(x)\,dx = -12$

(D) $\int_{-5}^{-8} f(x)\,dx = -4$

(E) $\int_2^6 f(x)\,dx + \int_6^8 f(x)\,dx = 16$

49. Multiple Choice What is the average value of the cosine function on the interval $[1, 5]$?

(A) -0.990 (B) -0.450 (C) -0.128

(D) 0.412 (E) 0.998

50. Multiple Choice If the average value of the function f on the interval $[a, b]$ is 10, then $\int_a^b f(x)\,dx =$

(A) $\frac{10}{b-a}$ (B) $\frac{f(a) + f(b)}{10}$ (C) $10b - 10a$

(D) $\frac{b-a}{10}$ (E) $\frac{f(b) + f(a)}{20}$

Exploration

51. *Comparing Area Formulas* Consider the region in the first quadrant under the curve $y = (h/b)x$ from $x = 0$ to $x = b$ (see figure).

(a) Use a geometry formula to calculate the area of the region.

(b) Find all antiderivatives of y.

(c) Use an antiderivative of y to evaluate $\int_0^b y(x)\,dx$.

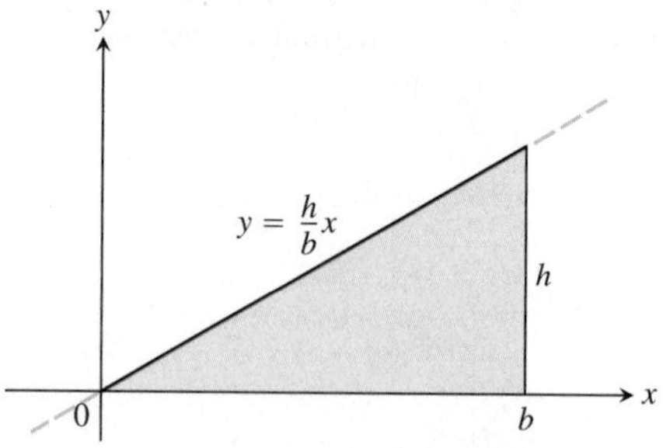

Extending the Ideas

52. ***Graphing Calculator Challenge*** If $k > 1$, and if the average value of x^k on $[0, k]$ is k, what is k? Check your result with a CAS if you have one available.

53. Show that if $F'(x) = G'(x)$ on $[a, b]$, then

$$F(b) - F(a) = G(b) - G(a).$$

Quick Quiz for AP* Preparation: Sections 6.1–6.3

1. **Multiple Choice** If $\int_a^b f(x)\,dx = a + 2b$, then $\int_a^b (f(x) + 3)\,dx =$

   (A) $a + 2b + 3$ (B) $3b - 3a$
   (C) $4a - b$ (D) $5b - 2a$
   (E) $5b - 3a$

2. **Multiple Choice** The expression

$$\frac{1}{20}\left(\sqrt{\frac{1}{20}} + \sqrt{\frac{2}{20}} + \sqrt{\frac{3}{20}} + \cdots + \sqrt{\frac{20}{20}}\right)$$

   is a Riemann sum approximation for

   (A) $\int_0^1 \sqrt{\frac{x}{20}}\,dx$ (B) $\int_0^1 \sqrt{x}\,dx$
   (C) $\frac{1}{20}\int_0^1 \sqrt{\frac{x}{20}}\,dx$ (D) $\frac{1}{20}\int_0^1 \sqrt{x}\,dx$
   (E) $\frac{1}{20}\int_0^{20} \sqrt{x}\,dx$

3. **Multiple Choice** What are all values of k for which $\int_2^k x^2\,dx = 0$?

   (A) -2 (B) 0 (C) 2
   (D) -2 and 2 (E) -2, 0, and 2

4. **Free Response** Let f be a function such that $f''(x) = 6x + 12$.

   (a) Find $f(x)$ if the graph of f is tangent to the line $4x - y = 5$ at the point $(0, -5)$.

   (b) Find the average value of $f(x)$ on the closed interval $[-1, 1]$.

6.4 Fundamental Theorem of Calculus

What you will learn about . . .

- Fundamental Theorem, Part 1
- Graphing the Function $\int_a^x f(t)\,dt$
- Fundamental Theorem, Part 2
- Area Connection
- Analyzing Antiderivatives Graphically

and why . . .

The Fundamental Theorem of Calculus is a triumph of mathematical discovery and the key to solving many problems.

Sir Isaac Newton (1642–1727)

Sir Isaac Newton is considered to be one of the most influential mathematicians of all time. Moreover, by the age of 25, he had also made revolutionary advances in optics, physics, and astronomy.

Fundamental Theorem, Part 1

This section presents the discovery by Newton and Leibniz of the astonishing connection between integration and differentiation. This connection started the mathematical development that fueled the scientific revolution for the next 200 years, and is still regarded as the most important computational discovery in the history of mathematics: The Fundamental Theorem of Calculus.

The Fundamental Theorem comes in two parts, both of which were previewed in Exploration 2 of the previous section. The first part says that the definite integral of a continuous function is a differentiable function of its upper limit of integration. Moreover, it tells us what that derivative is. The second part says that the definite integral of a continuous function from a to b can be found from any one of the function's antiderivatives F as the number $F(b) - F(a)$.

THEOREM 4 The Fundamental Theorem of Calculus, Part 1

If f is continuous on $[a, b]$, then the function

$$F(x) = \int_a^x f(t)\,dt$$

has a derivative at every point x in $[a, b]$, and

$$\frac{dF}{dx} = \frac{d}{dx}\int_a^x f(t)\,dt = f(x).$$

Proof The geometric exploration at the end of the previous section contained the idea of the proof, but it glossed over the necessary limit arguments. Here we will be more precise. Apply the definition of the derivative directly to the function F. That is,

$$\begin{aligned}\frac{dF}{dx} &= \lim_{h\to 0}\frac{F(x+h)-F(x)}{h}\\ &= \lim_{h\to 0}\frac{\int_a^{x+h} f(t)\,dt - \int_a^x f(t)\,dt}{h}\\ &= \lim_{h\to 0}\frac{\int_x^{x+h} f(t)\,dt}{h}\\ &= \lim_{h\to 0}\left[\frac{1}{h}\int_x^{x+h} f(t)\,dt\right].\end{aligned}$$

Rules for integrals, Section 6.3

The expression in brackets in the last line is the average value of f from x to $x + h$. We know from the Mean Value Theorem for Definite Integrals (Theorem 3, Section 6.3) that f, being continuous, takes on its average value at least once in the interval; that is,

$$\frac{1}{h}\int_x^{x+h} f(t)\,dt = f(c) \quad \text{for some } c \text{ between } x \text{ and } x + h.$$

We can therefore continue our proof, letting $(1/h)\int_x^{x+h} f(t)\,dt = f(c)$,

$$\frac{dF}{dx} = \lim_{h\to 0} \frac{1}{h}\int_x^{x+h} f(t)\,dt$$

$$= \lim_{h\to 0} f(c), \quad \text{where } c \text{ lies between } x \text{ and } x + h.$$

What happens to c as h goes to zero? As $x + h$ gets closer to x, it carries c along with it like a bead on a wire, forcing c to approach x. Since f is continuous, this means that $f(c)$ approaches $f(x)$:

$$\lim_{h\to 0} f(c) = f(x).$$

Putting it all together,

$$\frac{dF}{dx} = \lim_{h\to 0} \frac{F(x + h) - F(x)}{h} \qquad \text{Definition of derivatives}$$

$$= \lim_{h\to 0} \frac{\int_x^{x+h} f(t)\,dt}{h} \qquad \text{Rules for integrals}$$

$$= \lim_{h\to 0} f(c) \quad \text{for some } c \text{ between } x \text{ and } x + h.$$

$$= f(x). \qquad \text{Because } f \text{ is continuous}$$

This concludes the proof. ■

It is difficult to overestimate the power of the equation

$$\frac{d}{dx}\int_a^x f(t)\,dt = f(x). \qquad (1)$$

It says that every continuous function f is the derivative of some other function, namely $\int_a^x f(t)\,dt$. It says that every continuous function has an antiderivative. And it says that the processes of integration and differentiation are inverses of one another. If any equation deserves to be called the Fundamental Theorem of Calculus, this equation is surely the one.

EXAMPLE 1 Applying the Fundamental Theorem

Find

$$\frac{d}{dx}\int_{-\pi}^x \cos t\,dt \quad \text{and} \quad \frac{d}{dx}\int_0^x \frac{1}{1 + t^2}\,dt$$

by using the Fundamental Theorem.

SOLUTION

$$\frac{d}{dx}\int_{-\pi}^x \cos t\,dt = \cos x \qquad \text{Eq. 1 with } f(t) = \cos t$$

$$\frac{d}{dx}\int_0^x \frac{1}{1 + t^2}\,dt = \frac{1}{1 + x^2} \qquad \text{Eq. 1 with } f(t) = \frac{1}{1 + t^2}$$

Now Try Exercise 3.

EXAMPLE 2 The Fundamental Theorem with the Chain Rule

Find dy/dx if $y = \int_1^{x^2} \cos t\, dt$.

SOLUTION

The upper limit of integration is not x but x^2. This makes y a composite of

$$y = \int_1^u \cos t\, dt \quad \text{and} \quad u = x^2.$$

We must therefore apply the Chain Rule when finding dy/dx.

$$\begin{aligned}
\frac{dy}{dx} &= \frac{dy}{du} \cdot \frac{du}{dx} \\
&= \left(\frac{d}{du} \int_1^u \cos t\, dt \right) \cdot \frac{du}{dx} \\
&= \cos u \cdot \frac{du}{dx} \\
&= \cos(x^2) \cdot 2x \\
&= 2x \cos x^2
\end{aligned}$$

Now Try Exercise 9.

EXAMPLE 3 Variable Lower Limits of Integration

Find dy/dx.

(a) $y = \displaystyle\int_x^5 3t \sin t\, dt$ **(b)** $y = \displaystyle\int_{2x}^{x^2} \frac{1}{2 + e^t}\, dt$

SOLUTION

The rules for integrals set these up for the Fundamental Theorem.

(a)
$$\begin{aligned}
\frac{d}{dx} \int_x^5 3t \sin t\, dt &= \frac{d}{dx}\left(-\int_5^x 3t \sin t\, dt \right) \\
&= -\frac{d}{dx} \int_5^x 3t \sin t\, dt \\
&= -3x \sin x
\end{aligned}$$

(b)
$$\begin{aligned}
\frac{d}{dx} \int_{2x}^{x^2} \frac{1}{2 + e^t}\, dt &= \frac{d}{dx}\left(\int_0^{x^2} \frac{1}{2 + e^t}\, dt - \int_0^{2x} \frac{1}{2 + e^t}\, dt \right) \\
&= \frac{1}{2 + e^{x^2}} \frac{d}{dx}(x^2) - \frac{1}{2 + e^{2x}} \frac{d}{dx}(2x) \qquad \text{Chain Rule} \\
&= \frac{1}{2 + e^{x^2}} \cdot 2x - \frac{1}{2 + e^{2x}} \cdot 2 \\
&= \frac{2x}{2 + e^{x^2}} - \frac{2}{2 + e^{2x}}
\end{aligned}$$

Now Try Exercise 19.

EXAMPLE 4 Constructing a Function with a Given Derivative and Value

Find a function $y = f(x)$ with derivative

$$\frac{dy}{dx} = \tan x$$

that satisfies the condition $f(3) = 5$.

SOLUTION

The Fundamental Theorem makes it easy to construct a function with derivative tan *x:*

$$y = \int_3^x \tan t \, dt.$$

Since $y(3) = 0$, we have only to add 5 to this function to construct one with derivative tan x whose value at $x = 3$ is 5:

$$f(x) = \int_3^x \tan t \, dt + 5.$$

Now Try Exercise 25.

Although the solution to the problem in Example 4 satisfies the two required conditions, you might question whether it is in a useful form. Not many years ago, this form might have posed a computation problem. Indeed, for such problems much effort has been expended over the centuries trying to find solutions that do not involve integrals. We will see some in Chapter 7, where we will learn (for example) how to write the solution in Example 4 as

$$y = \ln\left|\frac{\cos 3}{\cos x}\right| + 5.$$

However, now that computers and calculators are capable of evaluating integrals, the form given in Example 4 is not only useful, but in some ways preferable. It is certainly easier to find and is always available.

Graphing the Function $\int_a^x f(t)\,dt$

Consider for a moment the two forms of the function we have just been discussing,

$$F(x) = \int_3^x \tan t \, dt + 5 \quad \text{and} \quad F(x) = \ln\left|\frac{\cos 3}{\cos x}\right| + 5.$$

With which expression is it easier to evaluate, say, $F(4)$? From the time of Newton almost to the present, there has been no contest: the expression on the right. At least it provides something to compute, and there have always been tables or slide rules or calculators to facilitate that computation. The expression on the left involved at best a tedious summing process and almost certainly an increased opportunity for error.

Today we can find $F(4)$ from either expression on the same machine. The choice is between NINT $(\tan x, x, 3, 4) + 5$ and $\ln(\text{abs}(\cos(3)/\cos(4))) + 5$. Both calculations give 5.415135083 in approximately the same amount of time.

We can even use NINT to graph the function. This modest technology feat would have absolutely dazzled the mathematicians of the 18th and 19th centuries, who knew how the solutions of differential equations, such as $dy/dx = \tan x$, could be written as integrals, but for whom integrals were of no practical use computationally unless they could be written in exact form. Since so few integrals could, in fact, be written in exact form, NINT would have spared generations of scientists much frustration.

Nevertheless, one must not proceed blindly into the world of calculator computation. Exploration 1 will demonstrate the need for caution.

EXPLORATION 1 Graphing NINT f

Let us use NINT to attempt to graph the function we just discussed,

$$F(x) = \int_3^x \tan t\, dt + 5.$$

1. Graph the function $y = F(x)$ in the window $[-10, 10]$ by $[-10, 10]$. You will probably wait a long time and see no graph. Break out of the graphing program if necessary.
2. Recall that the graph of the function $y = \tan x$ has vertical asymptotes. Where do they occur on the interval $[-10, 10]$?
3. When attempting to graph the function $F(x) = \int_3^x \tan t\, dt + 5$ on the interval $[-10, 10]$, your grapher begins by trying to find $F(-10)$. Explain why this might cause a problem for your calculator.
4. Set your viewing window so that your calculator graphs only over the domain of the continuous branch of the tangent function that contains the point (3, tan 3).
5. What is the domain in step 4? Is it an open interval or a closed interval?
6. What is the domain of $F(x)$? Is it an open interval or a closed interval?
7. Your calculator graphs over the closed interval $[x_{\min}, x_{\max}]$. Find a viewing window that will give you a good look at the graph of F and produce the graph on your calculator.
8. Describe the graph of F.

Graphing NINT f

Some graphers can graph the numerical integral $y =$ NINT $(f(x), x, a, x)$ directly as a function of x. Others will require a toolbox program such as the one called NINTGRAF provided in the *Technology Resource Manual.*

You have probably noticed that your grapher moves slowly when graphing NINT. This is because it must compute each value as a limit of sums—comparatively slow work even for a microprocessor. Here are some ways to speed up the process:

1. Change the *tolerance* on your grapher. The smaller the tolerance, the more accurate the calculator will try to be when finding the limiting value of each sum (and the longer it will take to do so). The default value is usually quite small (like 0.00001), but a value as large as 1 can be used for graphing in a typical viewing window.

2. Change the *x-resolution.* The default resolution is 1, which means that the grapher will compute a function value for every vertical column of pixels. At resolution 2 it computes only every second value, and so on. With higher resolutions, some graph smoothness is sacrificed for speed.

3. Switch to parametric mode. To graph $y =$ NINT $(f(x), x, a, x)$ in parametric mode, let $x(t) = t$ and let $y(t) =$ NINT $(f(t), t, a, t)$. You can then control the speed of the grapher by changing the t-step. (Choosing a bigger t-step has the same effect as choosing a larger x-resolution.)

EXPLORATION 2 The Effect of Changing a in $\int_a^x f(t)\,dt$

The first part of the Fundamental Theorem of Calculus asserts that the derivative of $\int_a^x f(t)\,dt$ is $f(x)$, regardless of the value of a.

1. Graph NDER (NINT $(x^2, x, 0, x)$).
2. Graph NDER (NINT $(x^2, x, 5, x)$).
3. Without graphing, tell what the x-intercept of NINT $(x^2, x, 0, x)$ is. Explain.
4. Without graphing, tell what the x-intercept of NINT $(x^2, x, 5, x)$ is. Explain.
5. How does changing a affect the graph of $y = (d/dx)\int_a^x f(t)\,dt$?
6. How does changing a affect the graph of $y = \int_a^x f(t)\,dt$?

Fundamental Theorem, Part 2

The second part of the Fundamental Theorem of Calculus shows how to evaluate definite integrals directly from antiderivatives.

THEOREM 4 (continued) The Fundamental Theorem of Calculus, Part 2

If f is continuous at every point of $[a, b]$, and if F is any antiderivative of f on $[a, b]$, then

$$\int_a^b f(x)\,dx = F(b) - F(a).$$

This part of the Fundamental Theorem is also called the **Integral Evaluation Theorem.**

Proof Part 1 of the Fundamental Theorem tells us that an antiderivative of f exists, namely

$$G(x) = \int_a^x f(t)\,dt.$$

Thus, if F is *any* antiderivative of f, then $F(x) = G(x) + C$ for some constant C (by Corollary 3 of the Mean Value Theorem for Derivatives, Section 5.2).

Evaluating $F(b) - F(a)$, we have

$$\begin{aligned} F(b) - F(a) &= [G(b) + C] - [G(a) + C] \\ &= G(b) - G(a) \\ &= \int_a^b f(t)\,dt - \int_a^a f(t)\,dt \\ &= \int_a^b f(t)\,dt - 0 \\ &= \int_a^b f(t)\,dt. \end{aligned}$$

■

At the risk of repeating ourselves: It is difficult to overestimate the power of the simple equation

$$\int_a^b f(x)\,dx = F(b) - F(a).$$

It says that any definite integral of any continuous function f can be calculated without taking limits, without calculating Riemann sums, and often without effort—so long as an antiderivative of f can be found. If you can imagine what it was like before this theorem (and before computing machines), when approximations by tedious sums were the only alternative for solving many real-world problems, then you can imagine what a miracle calculus was thought to be. If any equation deserves to be called the Fundamental Theorem of Calculus, this equation is surely the (second) one.

Integral Evaluation Notation

The usual notation for $F(b) - F(a)$ is

$$F(x)\Big]_a^b \quad \text{or} \quad \Big[F(x)\Big]_a^b,$$

depending on whether F has one or more terms. This notation provides a compact "recipe" for the evaluation, allowing us to show the antiderivative in an intermediate step.

EXAMPLE 5 Evaluating an Integral

Evaluate $\int_{-1}^{3}(x^3 + 1)\,dx$ using an antiderivative.

SOLUTION

Solve Analytically A simple antiderivative of $x^3 + 1$ is $(x^4/4) + x$. Therefore,

$$\int_{-1}^{3}\left(x^3 + 1\right)dx = \left[\frac{x^4}{4} + x\right]_{-1}^{3}$$

$$= \left(\frac{81}{4} + 3\right) - \left(\frac{1}{4} - 1\right)$$

$$= 24.$$

Support Numerically NINT $(x^3 + 1, x, -1, 3) = 24.$ ***Now Try Exercise 29.***

Area Connection

In Section 6.2 we saw that the definite integral could be interpreted as the net area between the graph of a function and the x-axis. We can therefore compute areas using antiderivatives, but we must again be careful to distinguish net area (in which area below the x-axis is counted as negative) from total area. The unmodified word "area" will be taken to mean *total area.*

EXAMPLE 6 Finding Area Using Antiderivatives

Find the area of the region between the curve $y = 4 - x^2$, $0 \le x \le 3$, and the x-axis.

SOLUTION

The curve crosses the x-axis at $x = 2$, partitioning the interval $[0, 3]$ into two subintervals, on each of which $f(x) = 4 - x^2$ will not change sign.

We can see from the graph (Figure 6.28) that $f(x) > 0$ on $[0, 2)$ and $f(x) < 0$ on $(2, 3]$.

Over $[0, 2]$: $\displaystyle\int_0^2 (4 - x^2)\,dx = \left[4x - \frac{x^3}{3}\right]_0^2 = \frac{16}{3}.$

Over $[2, 3]$: $\displaystyle\int_2^3 (4 - x^2)\,dx = \left[4x - \frac{x^3}{3}\right]_2^3 = -\frac{7}{3}.$

The area of the region is $\left|\frac{16}{3}\right| + \left|-\frac{7}{3}\right| = \frac{23}{3}.$ ***Now Try Exercise 41.***

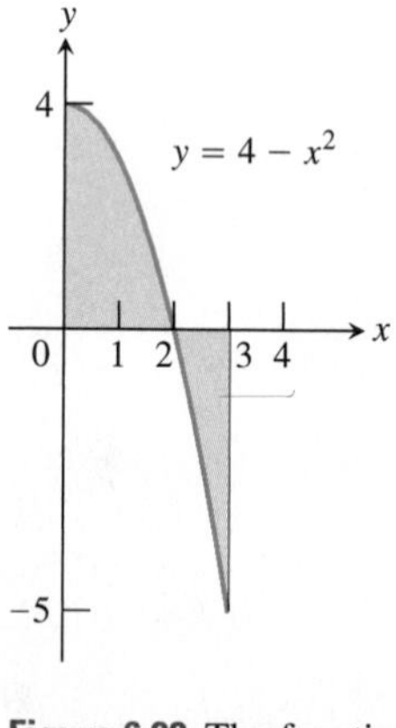

Figure 6.28 The function $f(x) = 4 - x^2$ changes sign only at $x = 2$ on the interval $[0, 3]$. (Example 6)

How to Find Total Area Analytically

To find the area between the graph of $y = f(x)$ and the x-axis over the interval $[a, b]$ analytically,

1. partition $[a, b]$ with the zeros of f,
2. integrate f over each subinterval,
3. add the absolute values of the integrals.

We can find area numerically by using NINT to integrate the *absolute value* of the function over the given interval. There is no need to partition. By taking absolute values, we automatically reflect the negative portions of the graph across the x-axis to count all area as positive (Figure 6.29).

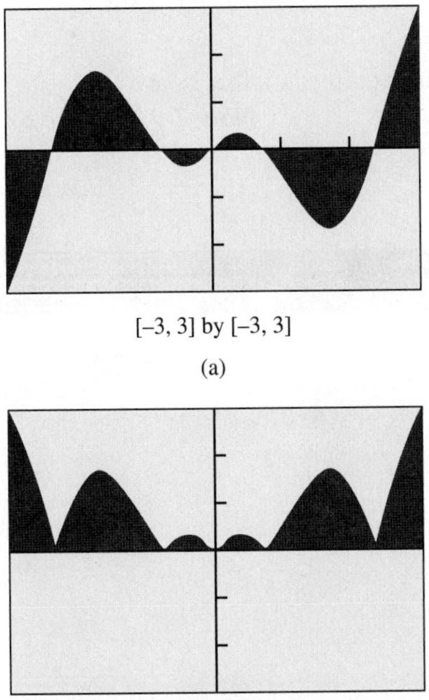
[−3, 3] by [−3, 3]

(a)

[−3, 3] by [−3, 3]

(b)

Figure 6.29 The graphs of (a) $y = x\cos 2x$ and (b) $y = |x\cos 2x|$ over $[-3, 3]$. The shaded regions have the same area.

EXAMPLE 7 Finding Area Using NINT

Find the area of the region between the curve $y = x\cos 2x$ and the x-axis over the interval $-3 \le x \le 3$ (Figure 6.29).

SOLUTION

Rounded to two decimal places, we have

$$\text{NINT}\,(|x\cos 2x|, x, -3, 3) = 5.43.$$

Now Try Exercise 51.

How to Find Total Area Numerically

To find the area between the graph of $y = f(x)$ and the x-axis over the interval $[a, b]$ numerically, evaluate

$$\text{NINT}\,(|f(x)|, x, a, b).$$

Analyzing Antiderivatives Graphically

A good way to put several calculus concepts together at this point is to start with the graph of a function f and consider a new function h defined as a definite integral of f. If $h(x) = \int_a^x f(t)\,dt$, for example, the Fundamental Theorem guarantees that $h'(x) = f(x)$, so the graph of f is also the graph of h'. We can therefore make conclusions about the behavior of h by considering the graphical behavior of its derivative f, just as we did in Section 5.3.

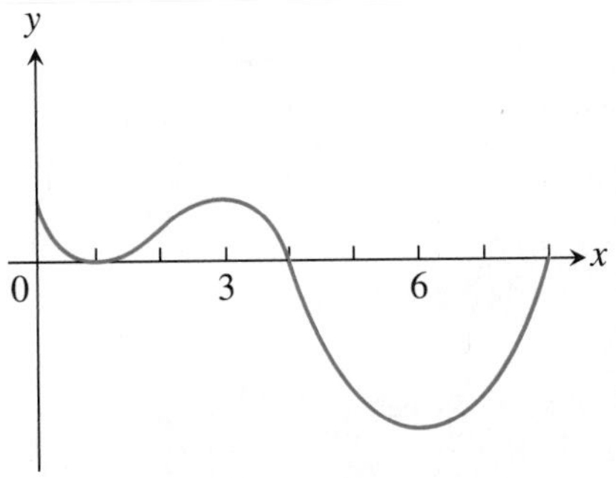

Figure 6.30 The graph of f in Example 8, in which questions are asked about the function $h(x) = \int_1^x f(t)\,dt$.

EXAMPLE 8 Using the Graph of f to Analyze $h(x) = \int_a^x f(t)\,dt$

The graph of a continuous function f with domain $[0, 8]$ is shown in Figure 6.30. Let h be the function defined by $h(x) = \int_1^x f(t)\,dt$.

(a) Find $h(1)$.

(b) Is $h(0)$ positive or negative? Justify your answer.

(c) Find the value of x for which $h(x)$ is a maximum.

(d) Find the value of x for which $h(x)$ is a minimum.

(e) Find the x-coordinates of all points of inflections of the graph of $y = h(x)$.

continued

SOLUTION

First, we note that $h'(x) = f(x)$, so the graph of f is also the graph of the derivative of h. Also, h is continuous because it is differentiable.

(a) $h(1) = \int_1^1 f(t)\,dt = 0$.

(b) $h(0) = \int_1^0 f(t)\,dt < 0$, because we are integrating from right to left under a positive function.

(c) The derivative of h is positive on $(0, 1)$, positive on $(1, 4)$, and negative on $(4, 8)$, so the continuous function h is increasing on $[0, 4]$ and decreasing on $[4, 8]$. Thus $f(4)$ is a maximum.

(d) The sign analysis of the derivative above shows that the minimum value occurs at an endpoint of the interval $[0, 8]$. We see by comparing areas that $h(0) = \int_1^0 f(t)\,dt \approx -0.5$, while $h(8) = \int_1^8 f(t)\,dt$ is a negative number considerably less than -1. Thus $f(8)$ is a minimum.

(e) The points of inflection occur where $h' = f$ changes direction, that is, at $x = 1$, $x = 3$, and $x = 6$.

Now Try Exercise 57.

Quick Review 6.4 *(For help, go to Sections 4.1, 4.2, and 4.4.)*

Exercise numbers with a gray background indicate problems that the authors have designed to be solved *without a calculator.*

In Exercises 1–10, find dy/dx.

1. $y = \sin(x^2)$

2. $y = (\sin x)^2$

3. $y = \sec^2 x - \tan^2 x$

4. $y = \ln(3x) - \ln(7x)$

5. $y = 2^x$

6. $y = \sqrt{x}$

7. $y = \dfrac{\cos x}{x}$

8. $y = \sin t$ and $x = \cos t$

9. $xy + x = y^2$

10. $dx/dy = 3x$

Section 6.4 Exercises

In Exercises 1–20, find dy/dx.

1. $y = \displaystyle\int_0^x (\sin^2 t)\,dt$

2. $y = \displaystyle\int_2^x (3t + \cos t^2)\,dt$

3. $y = \displaystyle\int_0^x (t^3 - t)^5\,dt$

4. $y = \displaystyle\int_{-2}^x \sqrt{1 + e^{5t}}\,dt$

5. $y = \displaystyle\int_2^x (\tan^3 u)\,du$

6. $y = \displaystyle\int_4^x e^u \sec u\,du$

7. $y = \displaystyle\int_7^x \frac{1 + t}{1 + t^2}\,dt$

8. $y = \displaystyle\int_{-\pi}^x \frac{2 - \sin t}{3 + \cos t}\,dt$

9. $y = \displaystyle\int_0^{x^2} e^{t^2}\,dt$

10. $y = \displaystyle\int_6^{x^2} \cot 3t\,dt$

11. $y = \displaystyle\int_2^{5x} \frac{\sqrt{1 + u^2}}{u}\,du$

12. $y = \displaystyle\int_\pi^{\pi - x} \frac{1 + \sin^2 u}{1 + \cos^2 u}\,du$

13. $y = \displaystyle\int_x^6 \ln(1 + t^2)\,dt$

14. $y = \displaystyle\int_x^7 \sqrt{2t^4 + t + 1}\,dt$

15. $y = \displaystyle\int_{x^3}^5 \frac{\cos t}{t^2 + 2}\,dt$

16. $y = \displaystyle\int_{5x^2}^{25} \frac{t^2 - 2t + 9}{t^3 + 6}\,dt$

17. $y = \displaystyle\int_{\sqrt{x}}^x \sin(r^2)\,dr$

18. $y = \displaystyle\int_{3x^2}^{5x} \ln(2 + p^2)\,dp$

19. $\displaystyle\int_{x^2}^{x^3} \cos(2t)\,dt$

20. $y = \displaystyle\int_{\sin x}^{\cos x} t^2\,dt$

In Exercises 21–26, construct a function of the form $y = \int_a^x f(t)\,dt + C$ that satisfies the given conditions.

21. $\dfrac{dy}{dx} = \sin^3 x$, and $y = 0$ when $x = 5$.

22. $\dfrac{dy}{dx} = e^x \tan x$, and $y = 0$ when $x = 8$.

23. $\dfrac{dy}{dx} = \ln(\sin x + 5)$, and $y = 3$ when $x = 2$.

24. $\dfrac{dy}{dx} = \sqrt{3 - \cos x}$, and $y = 4$ when $x = -3$.

25. $\dfrac{dy}{dx} = \cos^2 5x$, and $y = -2$ when $x = 7$.

26. $\dfrac{dy}{dx} = e^{\sqrt{x}}$, and $y = 1$ when $x = 0$.

In Exercises 27–40, evaluate each integral using Part 2 of the Fundamental Theorem. Support your answer with NINT if you are unsure.

27. $\displaystyle\int_{1/2}^{3} \left(2 - \frac{1}{x}\right) dx$

28. $\displaystyle\int_{2}^{-1} 3^x \, dx$

29. $\displaystyle\int_{0}^{1} (x^2 + \sqrt{x})\, dx$

30. $\displaystyle\int_{0}^{5} x^{3/2}\, dx$

31. $\displaystyle\int_{1}^{32} x^{-6/5}\, dx$

32. $\displaystyle\int_{-2}^{-1} \frac{2}{x^2}\, dx$

33. $\displaystyle\int_{0}^{\pi} \sin x \, dx$

34. $\displaystyle\int_{0}^{\pi} (1 + \cos x)\, dx$

35. $\displaystyle\int_{0}^{\pi/3} 2\sec^2 \theta \, d\theta$

36. $\displaystyle\int_{\pi/6}^{5\pi/6} \csc^2 \theta \, d\theta$

37. $\displaystyle\int_{\pi/4}^{3\pi/4} \csc x \cot x \, dx$

38. $\displaystyle\int_{0}^{\pi/3} 4 \sec x \tan x \, dx$

39. $\displaystyle\int_{-1}^{1} (r + 1)^2\, dr$

40. $\displaystyle\int_{0}^{4} \frac{1 - \sqrt{u}}{\sqrt{u}}\, du$

In Exercises 41–44, find the total area of the region between the curve and the x-axis.

41. $y = 2 - x, \quad 0 \le x \le 3$

42. $y = 3x^2 - 3, \quad -2 \le x \le 2$

43. $y = x^3 - 3x^2 + 2x, \quad 0 \le x \le 2$

44. $y = x^3 - 4x, \quad -2 \le x \le 2$

In Exercises 45–48, find the area of the shaded region.

45.

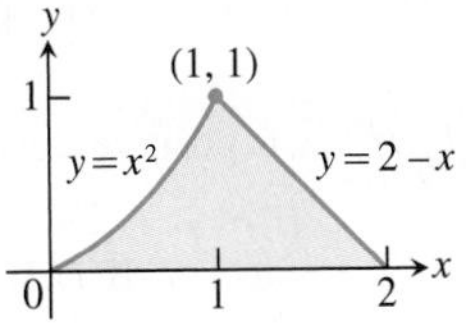

46.

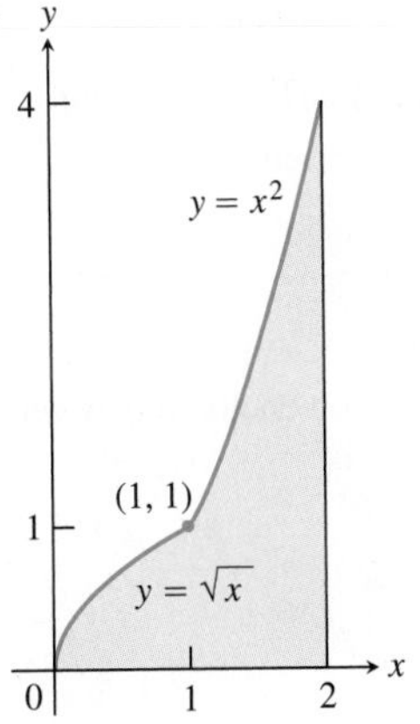

47.

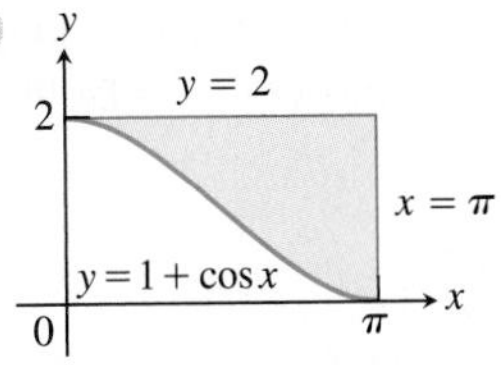

48.

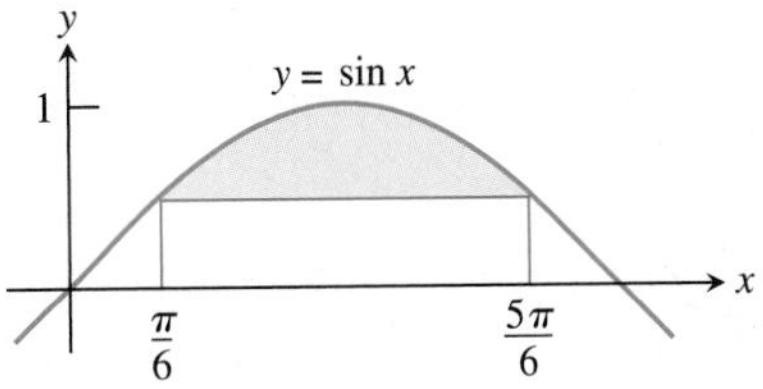

In Exercises 49–54, use NINT to solve the problem.

49. Evaluate $\displaystyle\int_{0}^{10} \frac{1}{3 + 2\sin x}\, dx$.

50. Evaluate $\displaystyle\int_{-0.8}^{0.8} \frac{2x^4 - 1}{x^4 - 1}\, dx$.

51. Find the area of the semielliptical region between the x-axis and the graph of $y = \sqrt{8 - 2x^2}$.

52. Find the average value of $\sqrt{\cos x}$ on the interval $[-1, 1]$.

53. For what value of x does $\int_0^x e^{-t^2}\, dt = 0.6$?

54. Find the area of the region in the first quadrant enclosed by the coordinate axes and the graph of $x^3 + y^3 = 1$.

In Exercises 55 and 56, find K so that

$$\int_a^x f(t)\, dt + K = \int_b^x f(t)\, dt.$$

55. $f(x) = x^2 - 3x + 1; \quad a = -1; \quad b = 2$

56. $f(x) = \sin^2 x; \quad a = 0; \quad b = 2$

57. Let

$$H(x) = \int_0^x f(t)\, dt,$$

where f is the continuous function with domain $[0, 12]$ graphed here.

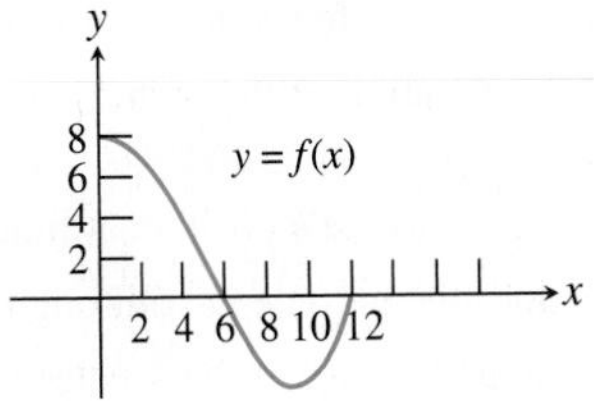

(a) Find $H(0)$.

(b) On what interval is H increasing? Explain.

(c) On what interval is the graph of H concave up? Explain.

(d) Is $H(12)$ positive or negative? Explain.

(e) Where does H achieve its maximum value? Explain.

(f) Where does H achieve its minimum value? Explain.

In Exercises 58 and 59, f is the differentiable function whose graph is shown in the given figure. The position at time t (sec) of a particle moving along a coordinate axis is

$$s = \int_0^t f(x)\,dx$$

meters. Use the graph to answer the questions. Give reasons for your answers.

58.

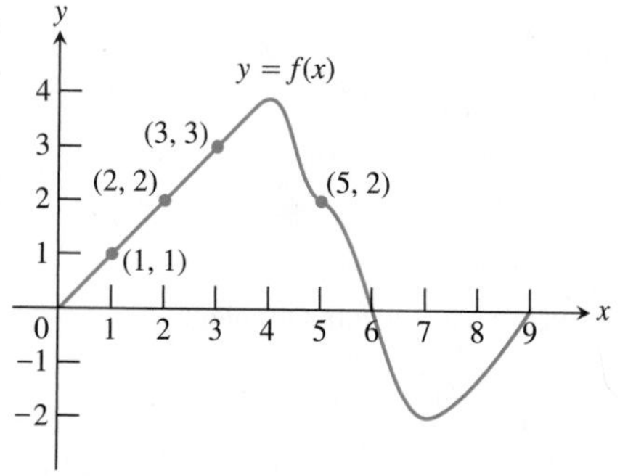

(a) What is the particle's velocity at time $t = 5$?

(b) Is the acceleration of the particle at time $t = 5$ positive or negative?

(c) What is the particle's position at time $t = 3$?

(d) At what time during the first 9 sec does s have its largest value?

(e) Approximately when is the acceleration zero?

(f) When is the particle moving toward the origin? away from the origin?

(g) On which side of the origin does the particle lie at time $t = 9$?

59.

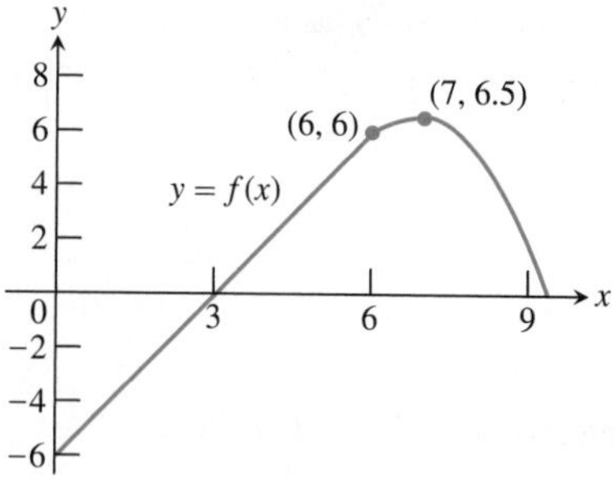

(a) What is the particle's velocity at time $t = 3$?

(b) Is the acceleration of the particle at time $t = 3$ positive or negative?

(c) What is the particle's position at time $t = 3$?

(d) When does the particle pass through the origin?

(e) Approximately when is the acceleration zero?

(f) When is the particle moving toward the origin? away from the origin?

(g) On which side of the origin does the particle lie at time $t = 9$?

60. Suppose $\int_1^x f(t)\,dt = x^2 - 2x + 1$. Find $f(x)$.

61. *Linearization* Find the linearization of

$$f(x) = 2 + \int_0^x \frac{10}{1+t}\,dt \quad \text{at} \quad x = 0.$$

62. Find $f(4)$ if $\int_0^x f(t)\,dt = x\cos \pi x$.

63. *Finding Area* Show that if k is a positive constant, then the area between the x-axis and one arch of the curve $y = \sin kx$ is always $2/k$.

64. *Archimedes' Area Formula for Parabolas* Archimedes (287–212 B.C.), inventor, military engineer, physicist, and the greatest mathematician of classical times, discovered that the area under a parabolic arch like the one shown here is always two-thirds the base times the height.

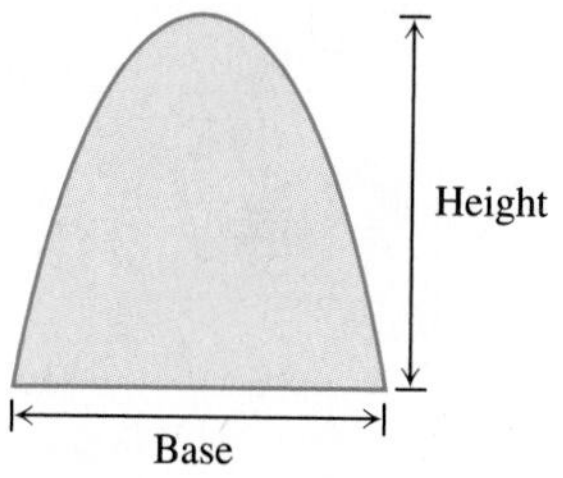

(a) Find the area under the parabolic arch

$$y = 6 - x - x^2, \quad -3 \le x \le 2.$$

(b) Find the height of the arch.

(c) Show that the area is two-thirds the base times the height.

Standardized Test Questions

You may use a graphing calculator to solve the following problems.

65. True or False If f is continuous on an open interval I containing a, then F defined by $F(x) = \int_a^x f(t)\,dt$ is continuous on I. Justify your answer.

66. True or False If $b > a$, then $\dfrac{d}{dx}\int_a^b e^{x^2}\,dx$ is positive. Justify your answer.

67. Multiple Choice Let $f(x) = \int_a^x \ln(2 + \sin t)\,dt$. If $f(3) = 4$, then $f(5) =$

(A) 0.040 **(B)** 0.272 **(C)** 0.961 **(D)** 4.555 **(E)** 6.667

68. Multiple Choice What is $\lim\limits_{h\to 0} \dfrac{1}{h}\int_x^{x+h} f(t)\,dt$?

(A) 0 **(B)** 1 **(C)** $f'(x)$ **(D)** $f(x)$ **(E)** nonexistent

69. Multiple Choice At $x = \pi$, the linearization of $f(x) = \int_\pi^x \cos^3 t\,dt$ is

(A) $y = -1$ **(B)** $y = -x$ **(C)** $y = \pi$

(D) $y = x - \pi$ **(E)** $y = \pi - x$

70. Multiple Choice The area of the region enclosed between the graph of $y = \sqrt{1 - x^4}$ and the x-axis is

(A) 0.886 **(B)** 1.253 **(C)** 1.414

(D) 1.571 **(E)** 1.748

Explorations

71. *The Sine Integral Function* The sine integral function

$$\mathrm{Si}(x) = \int_0^x \frac{\sin t}{t}\,dt$$

is one of the many useful functions in engineering that are defined as integrals. Although the notation does not show it, the function being integrated is

$$f(t) = \begin{cases} \dfrac{\sin t}{t}, & t \neq 0 \\ 1, & t = 0, \end{cases}$$

the continuous extension of $(\sin t)/t$ to the origin.

(a) Show that $\mathrm{Si}(x)$ is an odd function of x.

(b) What is the value of $\mathrm{Si}(0)$?

(c) Find the values of x at which $\mathrm{Si}(x)$ has a local extreme value.

(d) Use NINT to graph $\mathrm{Si}(x)$.

72. *Cost from Marginal Cost* The marginal cost of printing a poster when x posters have been printed is

$$\frac{dc}{dx} = \frac{1}{2\sqrt{x}}$$

dollars. Find

(a) $c(100) - c(1)$, the cost of printing posters 2 to 100.

(b) $c(400) - c(100)$, the cost of printing posters 101 to 400.

73. *Revenue from Marginal Revenue* Suppose that a company's marginal revenue from the manufacture and sale of eggbeaters is

$$\frac{dr}{dx} = 2 - \frac{2}{(x+1)^2},$$

where r is measured in thousands of dollars and x in thousands of units. How much money should the company expect from a production run of $x = 3$ thousand eggbeaters? To find out, integrate the marginal revenue from $x = 0$ to $x = 3$.

74. *Average Daily Holding Cost* Solon Container receives 450 drums of plastic pellets every 30 days. The inventory function (drums on hand as a function of days) is $I(x) = 450 - x^2/2$.

(a) Find the average daily inventory (that is, the average value of $I(x)$ for the 30-day period).

(b) If the holding cost for one drum is \$0.02 per day, find the average daily holding cost (that is, the per-drum holding cost times the average daily inventory).

75. Suppose that f has a negative derivative for all values of x and that $f(1) = 0$. Which of the following statements must be true of the function

$$h(x) = \int_0^x f(t)\,dt?$$

Give reasons for your answers.

(a) h is a twice-differentiable function of x.

(b) h and dh/dx are both continuous.

(c) The graph of h has a horizontal tangent at $x = 1$.

(d) h has a local maximum at $x = 1$.

(e) h has a local minimum at $x = 1$.

(f) The graph of h has an inflection point at $x = 1$.

(g) The graph of dh/dx crosses the x-axis at $x = 1$.

Extending the Ideas

76. Writing to Learn If f is an odd continuous function, give a graphical argument to explain why $\int_0^x f(t)\,dt$ is even.

77. Writing to Learn If f is an even continuous function, give a graphical argument to explain why $\int_0^x f(t)\,dt$ is odd.

78. Writing to Learn Explain why we can conclude from Exercises 76 and 77 that every even continuous function is the derivative of an odd continuous function and vice versa.

79. Give a convincing argument that the equation

$$\int_0^x \frac{\sin t}{t}\,dt = 1$$

has exactly one solution. Give its approximate value.

6.5 Trapezoidal Rule

What you will learn about . . .

- Trapezoidal Approximations
- Other Algorithms
- Error Analysis

and why . . .

Some definite integrals are best found by numerical approximations, and rectangles are not always the most efficient figures to use.

Trapezoidal Approximations

You probably noticed in Section 6.1 that MRAM was generally more efficient in approximating integrals than either LRAM or RRAM, even though all three RAM approximations approached the same limit. All three RAM approximations, however, depend on the areas of rectangles. Are there other geometric shapes with known areas that can do the job more efficiently? The answer is yes, and the most obvious one is the trapezoid.

As shown in Figure 6.31, if $[a, b]$ is partitioned into n subintervals of equal length $h = (b - a)/n$, the graph of f on $[a, b]$ can be approximated by a straight line segment over each subinterval.

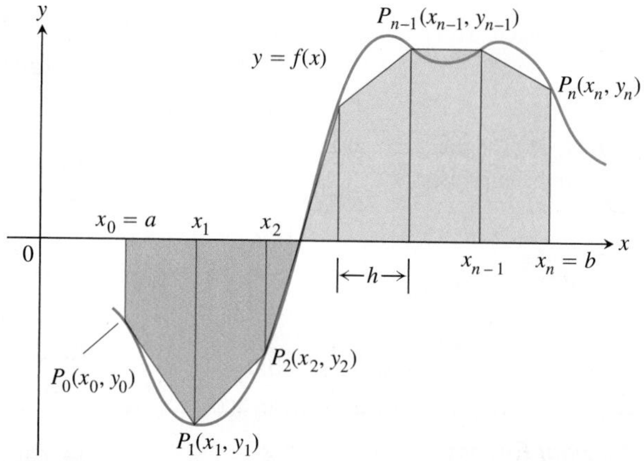

Figure 6.31 The trapezoidal rule approximates short stretches of the curve $y = f(x)$ with line segments. To approximate the integral of f from a to b, we add the "signed" areas of the trapezoids made by joining the ends of the segments to the x-axis.

The region between the curve and the x-axis is then approximated by the trapezoids, the area of each trapezoid being the length of its horizontal "altitude" times the average of its two vertical "bases." That is,

$$\int_a^b f(x)\,dx \approx h\cdot\frac{y_0 + y_1}{2} + h\cdot\frac{y_1 + y_2}{2} + \cdots + h\cdot\frac{y_{n-1} + y_n}{2}$$

$$= h\left(\frac{y_0}{2} + y_1 + y_2 + \cdots + y_{n-1} + \frac{y_n}{2}\right)$$

$$= \frac{h}{2}\left(y_0 + 2y_1 + 2y_2 + \cdots + 2y_{n-1} + y_n\right),$$

where

$$y_0 = f(a),\quad y_1 = f(x_1),\quad \ldots,\quad y_{n-1} = f(x_{n-1}),\quad y_n = f(b).$$

This is algebraically equivalent to finding the numerical average of LRAM and RRAM; indeed, that is how some texts define the Trapezoidal Rule.

The Trapezoidal Rule

To approximate $\int_a^b f(x)\,dx$, use

$$T = \frac{h}{2}\left(y_0 + 2y_1 + 2y_2 + \cdots + 2y_{n-1} + y_n\right),$$

where $[a, b]$ is partitioned into n subintervals of equal length $h = (b - a)/n$.

Equivalently,

$$T = \frac{\text{LRAM}_n + \text{RRAM}_n}{2},$$

where LRAM_n and RRAM_n are the Riemann sums using the left and right endpoints, respectively, for f for the partition.

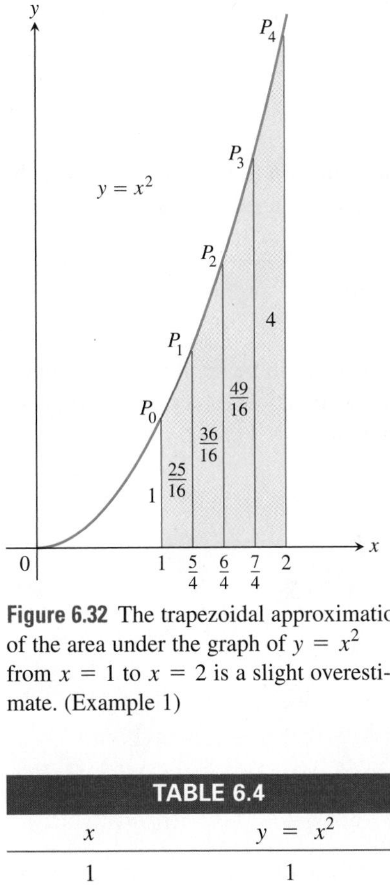

Figure 6.32 The trapezoidal approximation of the area under the graph of $y = x^2$ from $x = 1$ to $x = 2$ is a slight overestimate. (Example 1)

TABLE 6.4

x	$y = x^2$
1	1
$\frac{5}{4}$	$\frac{25}{16}$
$\frac{6}{4}$	$\frac{36}{16}$
$\frac{7}{4}$	$\frac{49}{16}$
2	4

EXAMPLE 1 Applying the Trapezoidal Rule

Use the Trapezoidal Rule with $n = 4$ to estimate $\int_1^2 x^2\,dx$. Compare the estimate with the value of NINT $(x^2, x, 1, 2)$ and with the exact value.

SOLUTION

Partition $[1, 2]$ into four subintervals of equal length (Figure 6.32). Then evaluate $y = x^2$ at each partition point (Table 6.4).

Using these y values, $n = 4$, and $h = (2 - 1)/4 = 1/4$ in the Trapezoidal Rule, we have

$$\begin{aligned} T &= \frac{h}{2}\left(y_0 + 2y_1 + 2y_2 + 2y_3 + y_4\right) \\ &= \frac{1}{8}\left(1 + 2\left(\frac{25}{16}\right) + 2\left(\frac{36}{16}\right) + 2\left(\frac{49}{16}\right) + 4\right) \\ &= \frac{75}{32} = 2.34375. \end{aligned}$$

The value of NINT $(x^2, x, 1, 2)$ is 2.333333333.

The exact value of the integral is

$$\int_1^2 x^2\,dx = \left.\frac{x^3}{3}\right]_1^2 = \frac{8}{3} - \frac{1}{3} = \frac{7}{3}.$$

The T approximation overestimates the integral by about half a percent of its true value of $7/3$. The percentage error is $(2.34375 - 7/3)/(7/3) \approx 0.446\%$.

Now try Exercise 3.

We could have predicted that the Trapezoidal Rule would overestimate the integral in Example 1 by considering the geometry of the graph in Figure 6.32. Since the parabola is concave *up,* the approximating segments lie above the curve, giving each trapezoid slightly more area than the corresponding strip under the curve. In Figure 6.31 we see that the straight segments lie *under* the curve on those intervals where the curve is concave *down,* causing the Trapezoidal Rule to *underestimate* the integral on those intervals. The interpretation of "area" changes where the curve lies below the x-axis but it is still the case that the higher y-values give the greater signed area. So we can always say that T overestimates the integral where the graph is concave up and underestimates the integral where the graph is concave down.

EXAMPLE 2 Averaging Temperatures

An observer measures the outside temperature every hour from noon until midnight, recording the temperatures in the following table.

Time	N	1	2	3	4	5	6	7	8	9	10	11	M
Temp	63	65	66	68	70	69	68	68	65	64	62	58	55

What was the average temperature for the 12-hour period?

SOLUTION

We are looking for the average value of a continuous function (temperature) for which we know values at discrete times that are one unit apart. We need to find

$$av(f) = \frac{1}{b-a}\int_a^b f(x)\,dx,$$

without having a formula for $f(x)$. The integral, however, can be approximated by the Trapezoidal Rule, using the temperatures in the table as function values at the points of a 12-subinterval partition of the 12-hour interval (making $h = 1$).

$$\begin{aligned} T &= \frac{h}{2}\left(y_0 + 2y_1 + 2y_2 + \cdots + 2y_{11} + y_{12}\right) \\ &= \frac{1}{2}\left(63 + 2\cdot 65 + 2\cdot 66 + \cdots + 2\cdot 58 + 55\right) \\ &= 782 \end{aligned}$$

Using T to approximate $\int_a^b f(x)\,dx$, we have

$$av(f) \approx \frac{1}{b-a}\cdot T = \frac{1}{12}\cdot 782 \approx 65.17.$$

Rounding to be consistent with the data given, we estimate the average temperature as 65 degrees.

Now Try Exercise 7.

Other Algorithms

LRAM, MRAM, RRAM, and the Trapezoidal Rule all give reasonable approximations to the integral of a continuous function over a closed interval. The Trapezoidal Rule is more efficient, giving a better approximation for small values of n, which makes it a faster algorithm for numerical integration.

Indeed, the only shortcoming of the Trapezoidal Rule seems to be that it depends on approximating curved arcs with straight segments. You might think that an algorithm that approximates the curve with *curved* pieces would be even more efficient (and hence faster for machines), and you would be right. All we need to do is find a geometric figure with a straight base, straight sides, and a curved top that has a known area. You might not know one, but the ancient Greeks did; it is one of the things they knew about parabolas.

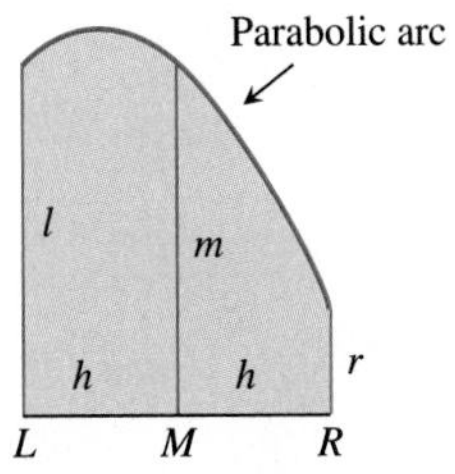

Figure 6.33 The area under the parabolic arc can be computed from the length of the base *LR* and the lengths of the altitudes constructed at *L*, *R* and midpoint *M*. (Exploration 1)

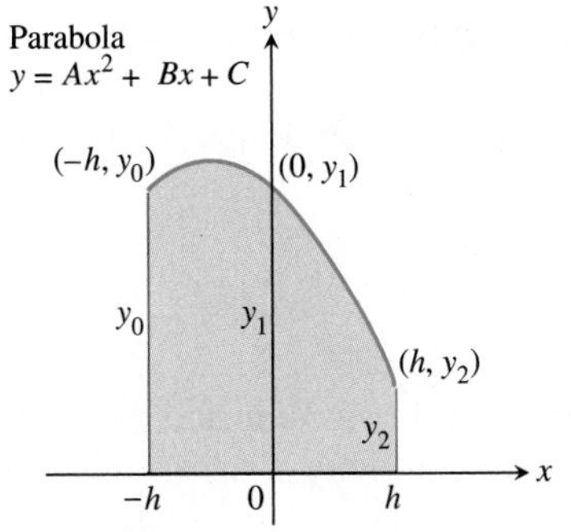

Figure 6.34 A convenient coordinatization of Figure 6.33. The parabola has equation $y = Ax^2 + Bx + C$, and the midpoint of the base is at the origin. (Exploration 1)

EXPLORATION 1 Area Under a Parabolic Arc

The area A_p of a figure having a horizontal base, vertical sides, and a parabolic top (Figure 6.33) can be computed by the formula

$$A_p = \frac{h}{3}\left(l + 4m + r\right),$$

where h is half the length of the base, l and r are the lengths of the left and right sides, and m is the altitude at the midpoint of the base. This formula, once a profound discovery of ancient geometers, is readily verified today with calculus.

1. Coordinatize Figure 6.33 by centering the base at the origin, as shown in Figure 6.34. Let $y = Ax^2 + Bx + C$ be the equation of the parabola. Using this equation, show that $y_0 = Ah^2 - Bh + C$, $y_1 = C$, and $y_2 = Ah^2 + Bh + C$.
2. Show that $y_0 + 4y_1 + y_2 = 2Ah^2 + 6C$.
3. Integrate to show that the area A_p is

$$\frac{h}{3}(2Ah^2 + 6C).$$

4. Combine these results to derive the formula

$$A_P = \frac{h}{3}\left(y_0 + 4y_1 + y_2\right).$$

This last formula leads to an efficient rule for approximating integrals numerically. Partition the interval of integration into an even number of subintervals, apply the formula for A_p to successive interval pairs, and add the results. This algorithm is known as Simpson's Rule.

What's in a Name?

The formula that underlies Simpson's Rule (see Exploration 1) was discovered long before Thomas Simpson (1720–1761) was born. Just as Pythagoras did not discover the Pythagorean Theorem, Simpson did not discover Simpson's Rule. It is another of history's beautiful quirks that one of the ablest mathematicians of 18th-century England is remembered not for his successful textbooks and his contributions to mathematical analysis, but for a rule that was never his, that he never laid claim to, and that bears his name only because he happened to mention it in one of his books.

Simpson's Rule

To approximate $\int_a^b f(x)\,dx$, use

$$S = \frac{h}{3}\left(y_0 + 4y_1 + 2y_2 + 4y_3 + \cdots + 2y_{n-2} + 4y_{n-1} + y_n\right),$$

where $[a, b]$ is partitioned into an *even* number n of subintervals of equal length $h = (b - a)/n$.

EXAMPLE 3 Applying Simpson's Rule

Use Simpson's Rule with $n = 4$ to approximate $\int_0^2 5x^4\,dx$.

SOLUTION

Partition $[0, 2]$ into four subintervals and evaluate $y = 5x^4$ at the partition points. (See Table 6.5 on the next page.)

continued

TABLE 6.5

x	$y = 5x^4$
0	0
$\frac{1}{2}$	$\frac{5}{16}$
1	5
$\frac{3}{2}$	$\frac{405}{16}$
2	80

Then apply Simpson's Rule with $n = 4$ and $h = 1/2$:

$$S = \frac{h}{3}\left(y_0 + 4y_1 + 2y_2 + 4y_3 + y_4\right)$$

$$= \frac{1}{6}\left(0 + 4\left(\frac{5}{16}\right) + 2(5) + 4\left(\frac{405}{16}\right) + 80\right)$$

$$= \frac{385}{12}$$

This estimate differs from the exact value (32) by only $1/12$, a percentage error of less than three-tenths of one percent—and this was with just 4 subintervals.

Now Try Exercise 17.

There are still other algorithms for approximating definite integrals, most of them involving fancy numerical analysis designed to make the calculations more efficient for high-speed computers. Some are kept secret by the companies that design the machines. In any case, we will not deal with them here.

Error Analysis

After finding that the trapezoidal approximation in Example 1 overestimated the integral, we pointed out that this could have been predicted from the concavity of the curve we were approximating.

Knowing something about the error in an approximation is more than just an interesting sidelight. Despite what your years of classroom experience might have suggested, exact answers are not always easy to find in mathematics. It is fortunate that for all *practical* purposes exact answers are also rarely necessary. (For example, a carpenter who computes the need for a board of length $\sqrt{34}$ feet will happily settle for an approximation when cutting the board.)

Suppose that an exact answer really *cannot* be found, but that we know that an approximation within 0.001 unit is good enough. How can we tell that our approximation is within 0.001 if we do not know the exact answer? This is where knowing something about the error is critical.

Since the Trapezoidal Rule approximates curves with straight lines, it seems reasonable that the error depends on how "curvy" the graph is. This suggests that the error depends on the second derivative. It is also apparent that the error depends on the length h of the subintervals. It can be shown that if f'' is continuous the error in the trapezoidal approximation, denoted E_T, satisfies the inequality

$$|E_T| \le \frac{b-a}{12} h^2 M_{f''},$$

where $[a, b]$ is the interval of integration, h is the length of each subinterval, and $M_{f''}$ is the maximum value of $|f''|$ on $[a, b]$.

It can also be shown that the error E_S in Simpson's Rule depends on h and the *fourth* derivative. It satisfies the inequality

$$|E_S| \le \frac{b-a}{180} h^4 M_{f^{(4)}},$$

where $[a, b]$ is the interval of integration, h is the length of each subinterval, and $M_{f^{(4)}}$ is the maximum value of $|f^{(4)}|$ on $[a, b]$, provided that $f^{(4)}$ is continuous.

For comparison's sake, if all the assumptions hold, we have the following *error bounds*.

Error Bounds

If T and S represent the approximations to $\int_a^b f(x)\,dx$ given by the Trapezoidal Rule and Simpson's Rule, respectively, then the errors E_T and E_S satisfy

$$|E_T| \le \frac{b-a}{12} h^2 M_{f''} \quad \text{and} \quad |E_S| \le \frac{b-a}{180} h^4 M_{f^{(4)}}.$$

If we disregard possible differences in magnitude between $M_{f''}$ and $M_{f^{(4)}}$, we notice immediately that $(b-a)/180$ is one-fifteenth the size of $(b-a)/12$, giving S an obvious advantage over T as an approximation. That, however, is almost insignificant when compared to the fact that the trapezoid error varies as the *square* of h, while Simpson's error varies as the *fourth power* of h. (Remember that h is already a small number in most partitions.)

Table 6.6 shows T and S values for approximations of $\int_1^2 1/x\,dx$ using various values of n. Notice how Simpson's Rule dramatically improves over the Trapezoidal Rule. In particular, notice that when we double the value of n (thereby halving the value of h), the T error is divided by 2 *squared,* while the S error is divided by 2 *to the fourth.*

TABLE 6.6 Trapezoidal Rule Approximations (T_n) and Simpson's Rule Approximations (S_n) of ln 2 = $\int_1^2 (1/x)\,dx$

n	T_n	|Error| less than ...	S_n	|Error| less than ...
10	0.6937714032	0.0006242227	0.6931502307	0.0000030502
20	0.6933033818	0.0001562013	0.6931473747	0.0000001942
30	0.6932166154	0.0000694349	0.6931472190	0.0000000385
40	0.6931862400	0.0000390595	0.6931471927	0.0000000122
50	0.6931721793	0.0000249988	0.6931471856	0.0000000050
100	0.6931534305	0.0000062500	0.6931471809	0.0000000004

This has a dramatic effect as h gets very small. The Simpson approximation for $n = 50$ rounds accurately to seven places, and for $n = 100$ agrees to nine decimal places (billionths)!

We close by showing you the values (Table 6.7) we found for $\int_1^5 (\sin x)/x\,dx$ by six different calculator methods. The exact value of this integral to six decimal places is 0.603848, so both Simpson's method with 50 subintervals and NINT give results accurate to at least six places (millionths).

TABLE 6.7 Approximations of $\int_1^5 (\sin x)/x\,dx$

Method	Subintervals	Value
LRAM	50	0.6453898
RRAM	50	0.5627293
MRAM	50	0.6037425
TRAP	50	0.6040595
SIMP	50	0.6038481
NINT	Tol = 0.00001	0.6038482

Quick Review 6.5 *(For help, go to Sections 4.4 and 5.3.)*

Exercise numbers with a gray background indicate problems that the authors have designed to be solved *without a calculator.*

In Exercises 1–10, tell whether the curve is concave up or concave down on the given interval.

1. $y = \cos x$ on $[-1, 1]$
2. $y = x^4 - 12x - 5$ on $[8, 17]$
3. $y = 4x^3 - 3x^2 + 6$ on $[-8, 0]$
4. $y = \sin(x/2)$ on $[48\pi, 50\pi]$
5. $y = e^{2x}$ on $[-5, 5]$
6. $y = \ln x$ on $[100, 200]$
7. $y = \dfrac{1}{x}$ on $[3, 6]$
8. $y = \csc x$ on $[0, \pi]$
9. $y = 10^{10} - 10x^{10}$ on $[10, 10^{10}]$
10. $y = \sin x - \cos x$ on $[1, 2]$

Section 6.5 Exercises

In Exercises 1–6, **(a)** use the Trapezoidal Rule with $n = 4$ to approximate the value of the integral. **(b)** Use the concavity of the function to predict whether the approximation is an overestimate or an underestimate. Finally, **(c)** find the integral's exact value to check your answer.

1. $\int_0^2 x\,dx$

2. $\int_0^2 x^2\,dx$

3. $\int_0^2 x^3\,dx$

4. $\int_1^2 \frac{1}{x}\,dx$

5. $\int_0^4 \sqrt{x}\,dx$

6. $\int_0^{\pi} \sin x\,dx$

7. Use the function values in the following table and the Trapezoidal Rule with $n = 6$ to approximate $\int_0^6 f(x)\,dx$.

x	0	1	2	3	4	5	6
$f(x)$	12	10	9	11	13	16	18

8. Use the function values in the following table and the Trapezoidal Rule with $n = 6$ to approximate $\int_2^8 f(x)\,dx$.

x	2	3	4	5	6	7	8
$f(x)$	16	19	17	14	13	16	20

9. ***Volume of Water in a Swimming Pool*** A rectangular swimming pool is 30 ft wide and 50 ft long. The table below shows the depth $h(x)$ of the water at 5-ft intervals from one end of the pool to the other. Estimate the volume of water in the pool using the Trapezoidal Rule with $n = 10$, applied to the integral

$$V = \int_0^{50} 30 \cdot h(x)\,dx.$$

Position (ft) x	Depth (ft) $h(x)$	Position (ft) x	Depth (ft) $h(x)$
0	6.0	30	11.5
5	8.2	35	11.9
10	9.1	40	12.3
15	9.9	45	12.7
20	10.5	50	13.0
25	11.0		

10. ***Stocking a Fish Pond*** As the fish and game warden of your township, you are responsible for stocking the town pond with fish before the fishing season. The average depth of the pond is 20 feet. Using a scaled map, you measure distances across the pond at 200-foot intervals, as shown in the diagram.

(a) Use the Trapezoidal Rule to estimate the volume of the pond.

(b) You plan to start the season with one fish per 1000 cubic feet. You intend to have at least 25% of the opening day's fish population left at the end of the season. What is the maximum number of licenses the town can sell if the average seasonal catch is 20 fish per license?

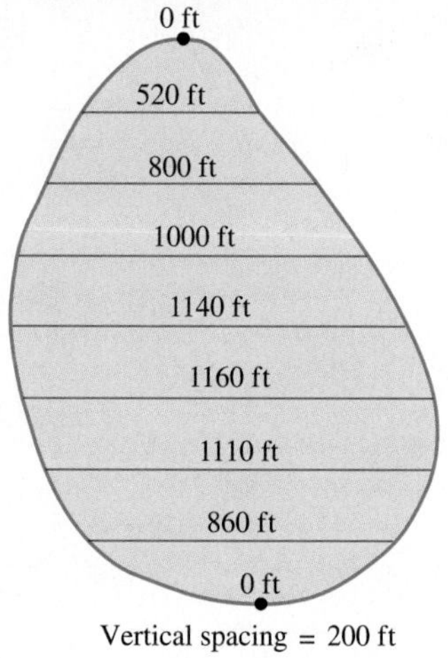

11. ***Scarpellone Panther I*** The The accompanying table shows time-to-speed data for a 2011 Scarpellone Panther I accelerating from rest to 130 mph. How far had the Panther I traveled by the time it reached this speed? (Use trapezoids to estimate the area under the velocity curve, but be careful: the time intervals vary in length.)

Speed Change: Zero to	Time (sec)
30 mph	1.8
40 mph	3.1
50 mph	4.2
60 mph	5.5
70 mph	7.4
80 mph	9.2
90 mph	11.5
100 mph	14.6
120 mph	20.9
130 mph	25.7

Source: DK Track Times (Abstract), December 2010.

12. The table below records the velocity of a bobsled at 1-second intervals for the first eight seconds of its run. Use the Trapezoidal Rule to approximate the distance the bobsled travels during that 8-second interval. (Give your final answer in feet.)

Time (seconds)	Speed (miles/hr)
0	0
1	3
2	7
3	12
4	17
5	25
6	33
7	41
8	48

In Exercises 13–18, **(a)** use Simpson's Rule with $n = 4$ to approximate the value of the integral and **(b)** find the exact value of the integral to check your answer. (Note that these are the same integrals as Exercises 1–6, so you can also compare it with the Trapezoidal Rule approximation.)

13. $\int_0^2 x\,dx$

14. $\int_0^2 x^2\,dx$

15. $\int_0^2 x^3\,dx$

16. $\int_1^2 \frac{1}{x}\,dx$

17. $\int_0^4 \sqrt{x}\,dx$

18. $\int_0^{\pi} \sin x\,dx$

19. Consider the integral $\int_{-1}^{3}(x^3 - 2x)\,dx$.

(a) Use Simpson's Rule with $n = 4$ to approximate its value.

(b) Find the exact value of the integral. What is the error, $|E_S|$?

(c) Explain how you could have predicted what you found in (b) from knowing the error-bound formula.

(d) Writing to Learn Is it possible to make a general statement about using Simpson's Rule to approximate integrals of cubic polynomials? Explain.

20. Writing to Learn In Example 2 (before rounding) we found the average temperature to be 65.17 degrees when we used the integral approximation, yet the average of the 13 discrete temperatures is only 64.69 degrees. Considering the shape of the temperature curve, explain why you would expect the average of the 13 discrete temperatures to be less than the average value of the temperature function on the entire interval.

21. *(Continuation of Exercise 20)*

(a) In the Trapezoidal Rule, every function value in the sum is doubled except for the two endpoint values. Show that if you double the endpoint values, you get 70.08 for the average temperature.

(b) Explain why it makes more sense to not double the endpoint values if we are interested in the average temperature over the entire 12-hour period.

22. Group Activity For most functions, Simpson's Rule gives a better approximation to an integral than the Trapezoidal Rule for a given value of n. Sketch the graph of a function on a closed interval for which the Trapezoidal Rule obviously gives a better approximation than Simpson's Rule for $n = 4$.

In Exercises 23–26, use a calculator program to find the Simpson's Rule approximations with $n = 50$ and $n = 100$.

23. $\int_{-1}^{1} 2\sqrt{1 - x^2}\,dx$

24. $\int_0^1 \sqrt{1 + x^4}\,dx$

25. $\int_0^{\pi/2} \frac{\sin x}{x}\,dx$

26. $\int_0^{\pi/2} \sin(x^2)\,dx$

27. Consider the integral $\int_0^{\pi} \sin x\,dx$.

(a) Use a calculator program to find the Trapezoidal Rule approximations for $n = 10,\ 100,$ and 1000.

(b) Record the errors with as many decimal places of accuracy as you can.

(c) What pattern do you see?

(d) Writing to Learn Explain how the error bound for E_T accounts for the pattern.

28. *(Continuation of Exercise 27)* Repeat Exercise 27 with Simpson's Rule and E_S.

29. *Aerodynamic Drag* A vehicle's aerodynamic drag is determined in part by its cross-section area, so, all other things being equal, engineers try to make this area as small as possible. Use Simpson's Rule to estimate the cross-section area of the body of James Worden's solar-powered Solectria® automobile at M.I.T. from the diagram below.

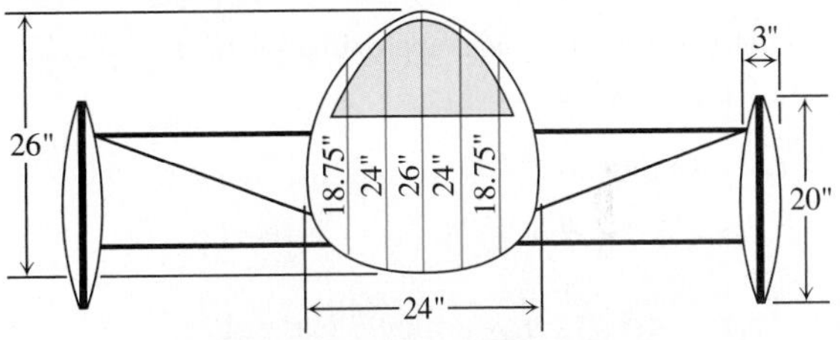

30. *Wing Design* The design of a new airplane requires a gasoline tank of constant cross-section area in each wing. A scale drawing of a cross section is shown here. The tank must hold 5000 lb of gasoline, which has a density of 42 lb/ft^3. Estimate the length of the tank.

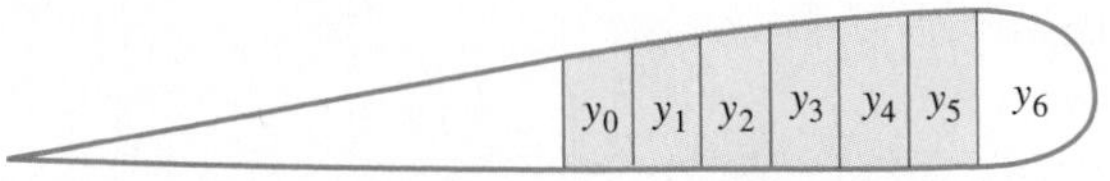

$y_0 = 1.5$ ft, $y_1 = 1.6$ ft, $y_2 = 1.8$ ft, $y_3 = 1.9$ ft,
$y_4 = 2.0$ ft, $y_5 = y_6 = 2.1$ ft Horizontal spacing = 1 ft

Standardized Test Questions

31. True or False The Trapezoidal Rule will underestimate $\int_a^b f(x)\,dx$ if the graph of f is concave up on $[a, b]$. Justify your answer.

32. True or False For a given value of n, the Trapezoidal Rule with n subdivisions will always give a more accurate estimate of $\int_a^b f(x)\,dx$ than a right Riemann sum with n subdivisions. Justify your answer.

33. Multiple Choice Using 8 equal subdivisions of the interval $[2, 12]$, the LRAM approximation of $\int_2^{12} f(x)\,dx$ is 16.6 and the trapezoidal approximation is 16.4. What is the RRAM approximation?

(A) 16.2 **(B)** 16.5

(C) 16.6 **(D)** 16.8

(E) It cannot be determined from the given information.

34. Multiple Choice If three equal subdivisions of $[-2, 4]$ are used, what is the trapezoidal approximation of $\int_{-2}^{4} \frac{e^x}{2}\,dx$?

(A) $e^4 + e^2 + e^0 + e^{-2}$

(B) $e^4 + 2e^2 + 2e^0 + e^{-2}$

(C) $\frac{1}{2}(e^4 + e^2 + e^0 + e^{-2})$

(D) $\frac{1}{2}(e^4 + 2e^2 + 2e^0 + e^{-2})$

(E) $\frac{1}{4}(e^4 + 2e^2 + 2e^0 + e^{-2})$

35. Multiple Choice The trapezoidal approximation of $\int_0^{\pi} \sin x\,dx$ using 4 equal subdivisions of the interval of integration is

(A) $\frac{\pi}{2}$

(B) π

(C) $\frac{\pi}{4}(1 + \sqrt{2})$

(D) $\frac{\pi}{2}(1 + \sqrt{2})$

(E) $\frac{\pi}{4}(2 + \sqrt{2})$

36. Multiple Choice Suppose f, f', and f'' are all positive on the interval $[a, b]$, and suppose we compute LRAM, RRAM, and trapezoidal approximations of $I = \int_a^b f(x)\,dx$ using the same number of equal subdivisions of $[a, b]$. If we denote the three approximations of I as L, R, and T respectively, which of the following is true?

(A) $R < T < I < L$ **(B)** $R < I < T < L$

(C) $L < I < T < R$ **(D)** $L < T < I < R$

(E) $L < I < R < T$

Explorations

37. Consider the integral $\int_{-1}^{1} \sin(x^2)\,dx$.

(a) Find f'' for $f(x) = \sin(x^2)$.

(b) Graph $y = f''(x)$ in the viewing window $[-1, 1]$ by $[-3, 3]$.

(c) Explain why the graph in part (b) suggests that $|f''(x)| \le 3$ for $-1 \le x \le 1$.

(d) Show that the error estimate for the Trapezoidal Rule in this case becomes

$$|E_T| \le \frac{h^2}{2}.$$

(e) Show that the Trapezoidal Rule error will be less than or equal to 0.01 if $h \le 0.1$.

(f) How large must n be for $h \le 0.1$?

38. Consider the integral $\int_{-1}^{1} \sin(x^2)\,dx$.

(a) Find $f^{(4)}$ for $f^{(x)} = \sin(x^2)$. (You may want to check your work with a CAS if you have one available.)

(b) Graph $y = f^{(4)}(x)$ in the viewing window $[-1, 1]$ by $[-30, 10]$.

(c) Explain why the graph in part (b) suggests that $|f^{(4)}(x)| \le 30$ for $-1 \le x \le 1$.

(d) Show that the error estimate for Simpson's Rule in this case becomes

$$|E_S| \le \frac{h^4}{3}.$$

(e) Show that the Simpson's Rule error will be less than or equal to 0.01 if $h \le 0.4$.

(f) How large must n be for $h \le 0.4$?

Extending the Ideas

39. Using the definitions, prove that, in general,

$$T_n = \frac{\text{LRAM}_n + \text{RRAM}_n}{2}.$$

40. Using the definitions, prove that, in general,

$$S_{2n} = \frac{\text{MRAM}_n + 2T_{2n}}{3}.$$

Quick Quiz for AP* Preparation: Sections 6.4 and 6.5

You may use a graphing calculator to solve the following problems.

1. **Multiple Choice** The function f is continuous on the closed interval $[1, 7]$ and has values that are given in the table below.

x	1	4	6	7
$f(x)$	10	30	40	20

Using the subintervals $[1, 4]$, $[4, 6]$, and $[6, 7]$, what is the trapezoidal approximation of $\int_1^7 f(x)\,dx$?

(A) 110 **(B)** 130 **(C)** 160 **(D)** 190 **(E)** 210

2. **Multiple Choice** Let $F(x)$ be an antiderivative of $\sin^3 x$. If $F(1) = 0$, then $F(8) =$

(A) 0.00 **(B)** 0.021 **(C)** 0.373 **(D)** 0.632 **(E)** 0.968

3. **Multiple Choice** Let $f(x) = \int_{-2}^{x^2-3x} e^{t^2}\,dt$. At what value of x is $f(x)$ a minimum?

(A) For no value of x **(B)** $\frac{1}{2}$ **(C)** $\frac{3}{2}$ **(D)** 2 **(E)** 3

4. **Free Response** Let $F(x) = \int_0^x \sin(t^2)\,dt$ for $0 \le x \le 3$.

(a) Use the Trapezoidal Rule with four equal subdivisions of the closed interval $[0, 2]$ to approximate $F(2)$.

(b) On what interval or intervals is F increasing? Justify your answer.

(c) If the average rate of change of F on the closed interval $[0, 3]$ is k, find $\int_0^3 \sin(t^2)\,dt$ in terms of k.

Chapter 6 Key Terms

Chapter 6 Review Exercises

Exercise numbers with a gray background indicate problems that the authors have designed to be solved *without a calculator.*

The collection of exercises marked in red could be used as a chapter test.

Exercises 1–6 refer to the region R in the first quadrant enclosed by the x-axis and the graph of the function $y = 4x - x^3$.

1. Sketch R and partition it into four subregions, each with a base of length $\Delta x = 1/2$.

2. Sketch the rectangles and compute (by hand) the area for the $LRAM_4$ approximation.

3. Sketch the rectangles and compute (by hand) the area for the $MRAM_4$ approximation.

4. Sketch the rectangles and compute (by hand) the area for the $RRAM_4$ approximation.

5. Sketch the trapezoids and compute (by hand) the area for the T_4 approximation.

6. Find the exact area of R by using the Fundamental Theorem of Calculus.

7. Use a calculator program to compute the RAM approximations in the following table for the area under the graph of $y = 1/x$ from $x = 1$ to $x = 5$.

n	$LRAM_n$	$MRAM_n$	$RRAM_n$
10			
20			
30			
50			
100			
1000			

8. *(Continuation of Exercise 7)* Use the Fundamental Theorem of Calculus to determine the value to which the sums in the table are converging.

9. Suppose

$$\int_{-2}^{2} f(x)\,dx = 4, \quad \int_{2}^{5} f(x)\,dx = 3, \quad \int_{-2}^{5} g(x)\,dx = 2.$$

Which of the following statements are true, and which, if any, are false?

(a) $\int_{5}^{2} f(x)\,dx = -3$

(b) $\int_{-2}^{5} [f(x) + g(x)]\,dx = 9$

(c) $f(x) \le g(x)$ on the interval $-2 \le x \le 5$

10. The region under one arch of the curve $y = \sin x$ is revolved around the x-axis to form a solid. **(a)** Use the method of Example 3, Section 5.1, to set up a Riemann sum that approximates the volume of the solid. **(b)** Find the volume using NINT.

11. The accompanying graph shows the velocity (m/sec) of a body moving along the s-axis during the time interval from $t = 0$ to $t = 10$ sec. **(a)** About how far did the body travel during those 10 seconds?

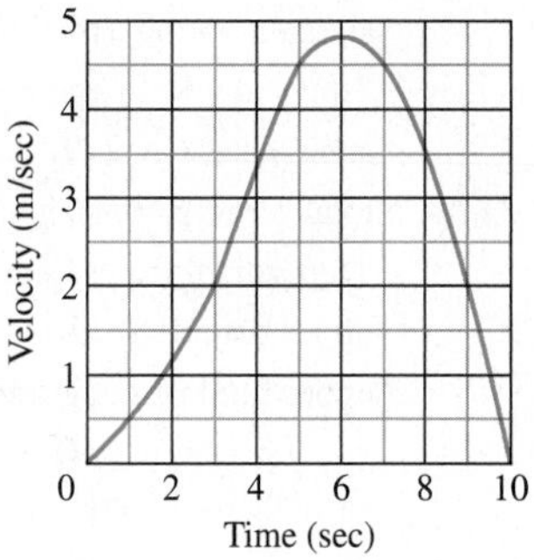

(b) Sketch a graph of position (s) as a function of time (t) for $0 \le t \le 10$, assuming $s(0) = 0$.

12. The interval $[0, 10]$ is partitioned into n subintervals of length $\Delta x = 10/n$. We form the following Riemann sums, choosing each c_k in the kth subinterval. Write the limit as $n \to \infty$ of each Riemann sum as a definite integral.

(a) $\sum_{k=1}^{n} (c_k)^3 \Delta x$

(b) $\sum_{k=1}^{n} c_k(\sin c_k)\Delta x$

(c) $\sum_{k=1}^{n} c_k(3c_k - 2)^2 \Delta x$

(d) $\sum_{k=1}^{n} (1 + c_k^2)^{-1} \Delta x$

(e) $\sum_{k=1}^{n} \pi(9 - \sin^2(\pi c_k/10))\Delta x$

In Exercises 13 and 14, find the total area between the curve and the x-axis.

13. $y = 4 - x, \quad 0 \le x \le 6$

14. $y = \cos x, \quad 0 \le x \le \pi$

In Exercises 15–24, evaluate the integral analytically by using the Integral Evaluation Theorem (Part 2 of the Fundamental Theorem, Theorem 4).

15. $\int_{-2}^{2} 5\,dx$

16. $\int_{2}^{5} 4x\,dx$

17. $\int_{0}^{\pi/4} \cos x\,dx$

18. $\int_{-1}^{1} (3x^2 - 4x + 7)\,dx$

19. $\int_{0}^{1} (8s^3 - 12s^2 + 5)\,ds$

20. $\int_{1}^{2} \frac{4}{x^2}\,dx$

21. $\int_{1}^{27} y^{-4/3}\,dy$

22. $\int_{1}^{4} \frac{dt}{t\sqrt{t}}$

23. $\int_{0}^{\pi/3} \sec^2 \theta\,d\theta$

24. $\int_{1}^{e} (1/x)\,dx$

In Exercises 25–29, evaluate the integral.

25. $\int_{0}^{1} \frac{36}{(2x + 1)^3}\,dx$

26. $\int_{1}^{2} \left(x + \frac{1}{x^2}\right) dx$

27. $\int_{-\pi/3}^{0} \sec x \tan x\,dx$

28. $\int_{-1}^{1} 2x \sin(1 - x^2)\,dx$

29. $\int_{0}^{2} \frac{2}{y + 1}\,dy$

In Exercises 30–32, evaluate the integral by interpreting it as area and using formulas from geometry.

30. $\int_{0}^{2} \sqrt{4 - x^2}\,dx$

31. $\int_{-4}^{8} |x|\,dx$

32. $\int_{-8}^{8} 2\sqrt{64 - x^2}\,dx$

33. ***Oil Consumption on Pathfinder Island*** A diesel generator runs continuously, consuming oil at a gradually increasing rate until it must be temporarily shut down to have the filters replaced.

Day	Oil Consumption Rate (liters/hour)
Sun	0.019
Mon	0.020
Tue	0.021
Wed	0.023
Thu	0.025
Fri	0.028
Sat	0.031
Sun	0.035

(a) Give an upper estimate and a lower estimate for the amount of oil consumed by the generator during that week.

(b) Use the Trapezoidal Rule to estimate the amount of oil consumed by the generator during that week.

34. *Rubber-Band–Powered Sled* A sled powered by a wound rubber band moves along a track until friction and the unwinding of the rubber band gradually slow it to a stop. A speedometer in the sled monitors its speed, which is recorded at 3-second intervals during the 27-second run.

Time (sec)	Speed (ft/sec)
0	5.30
3	5.25
6	5.04
9	4.71
12	4.25
15	3.66
18	2.94
21	2.09
24	1.11
27	0

(a) Give an upper estimate and a lower estimate for the distance traveled by the sled.

(b) Use the Trapezoidal Rule to estimate the distance traveled by the sled.

35. Writing to Learn Your friend knows how to compute integrals but never could understand what difference the "dx" makes, claiming that it is irrelevant. How would you explain to your friend why it is necessary?

36. The function

$$f(x) = \begin{cases} x^2, & x \geq 0 \\ x - 2, & x < 0 \end{cases}$$

is discontinuous at 0, but integrable on $[-4, 4]$. Find $\int_{-4}^{4} f(x)\,dx$.

37. Show that $0 \leq \int_0^1 \sqrt{1 + \sin^2 x}\,dx \leq \sqrt{2}$.

38. Find the average value of

(a) $y = \sqrt{x}$ over the interval $[0, 4]$.

(b) $y = a\sqrt{x}$ over the interval $[0, a]$.

In Exercises 39–42, find dy/dx.

39. $y = \displaystyle\int_2^x \sqrt{2 + \cos^3 t}\,dt$

40. $y = \displaystyle\int_2^{7x^2} \sqrt{2 + \cos^3 t}\,dt$

41. $y = \displaystyle\int_x^1 \frac{6}{3 + t^4}\,dt$

42. $y = \displaystyle\int_x^{2x} \frac{1}{t^2 + 1}\,dt$

43. *Printing Costs* Including start-up costs, it costs a printer \$50 to print 25 copies of a newsletter, after which the marginal cost at x copies is

$$\frac{dc}{dx} = \frac{2}{\sqrt{x}} \text{ dollars per copy.}$$

Find the total cost of printing 2500 newsletters.

44. *Average Daily Inventory* Rich Wholesale Foods, a manufacturer of cookies, stores its cases of cookies in an air-conditioned warehouse for shipment every 14 days. Rich tries to keep 600 cases on reserve to meet occasional peaks in demand, so a typical 14-day inventory function is $I(t) = 600 + 600t$, $0 \leq t \leq 14$. The holding cost for each case is 4¢ per day. Find Rich's average daily inventory and average daily holding cost (that is, the average of $I(x)$ for the 14-day period, and this average multiplied by the holding cost).

45. Solve for x: $\int_0^x (t^3 - 2t + 3)dt = 4$.

46. Suppose $f(x)$ has a positive derivative for all values of x and that $f(1) = 0$. Which of the following statements must be true of

$$g(x) = \int_0^x f(t)\,dt?$$

(a) g is a differentiable function of x.

(b) g is a continuous function of x.

(c) The graph of g has a horizontal tangent line at $x = 1$.

(d) g has a local maximum at $x = 1$.

(e) g has a local minimum at $x = 1$.

(f) The graph of g has an inflection point at $x = 1$.

(g) The graph of dg/dx crosses the x-axis at $x = 1$.

47. Suppose $F(x)$ is an antiderivative of $f(x) = \sqrt{1 + x^4}$. Express $\int_0^1 \sqrt{1 + x^4}\,dx$ in terms of F.

48. Express the function $y(x)$ with

$$\frac{dy}{dx} = \frac{\sin x}{x} \quad \text{and} \quad y(5) = 3$$

as a definite integral.

49. Show that $y = x^2 + \int_1^x 1/t\,dt + 1$ satisfies both of the following conditions:

i. $y'' = 2 - \dfrac{1}{x^2}$

ii. $y = 2$ and $y' = 3$ when $x = 1$.

50. Writing to Learn Which of the following is the graph of the function whose derivative is $dy/dx = 2x$ and whose value at $x = 1$ is 4? Explain your answer.

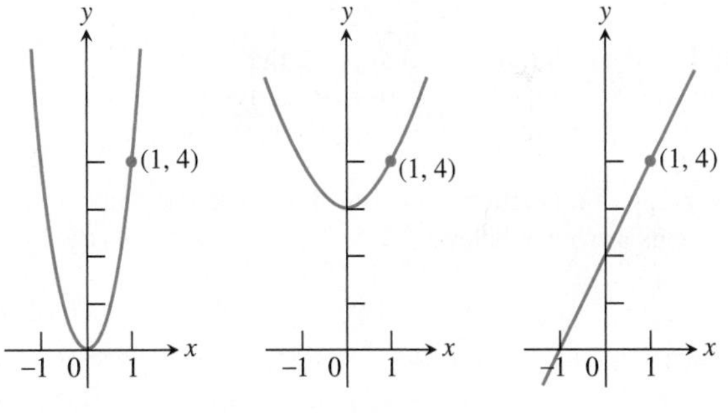

(a) (b) (c)

51. *Fuel Efficiency* An automobile computer gives a digital readout of fuel consumption in gallons per hour. During a trip, a passenger recorded the fuel consumption every 5 minutes for a full hour of travel.

time	gal/h	time	gal/lh
0	2.5	35	2.5
5	2.4	40	2.4
10	2.3	45	2.3
15	2.4	50	2.4
20	2.4	55	2.4
25	2.5	60	2.3
30	2.6		

(a) Use the Trapezoidal Rule to approximate the total fuel consumption during the hour.

(b) If the automobile covered 60 miles in the hour, what was its fuel efficiency (in miles per gallon) for that portion of the trip?

52. *Skydiving* Skydivers A and B are in a helicopter hovering at 6400 feet. Skydiver A jumps and descends for 4 sec before opening her parachute. The helicopter then climbs to 7000 feet and hovers there. Forty-five seconds after A leaves the aircraft, B jumps and descends for 13 sec before opening her parachute. Both skydivers descend at 16 ft/sec with parachutes open. Assume that the skydivers fall freely (with acceleration -32 ft/sec^2) before their parachutes open.

(a) At what altitude does A's parachute open?

(b) At what altitude does B's parachute open?

(c) Which skydiver lands first?

53. *Relating Simpson's Rule, MRAM, and T* The figure below shows an interval of length $2h$ with a trapezoid, a midpoint rectangle, and a parabolic region on it.

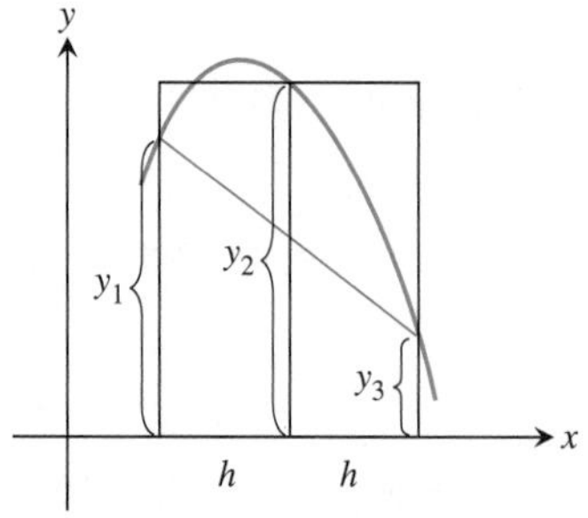

(a) Show that the area of the trapezoid plus twice the area of the rectangle equals

$$h(y_1 + 4y_2 + y_3).$$

(b) Use the result in part (a) to prove that

$$S_{2_n} = \frac{2 \cdot \text{MRAM}_n + T_n}{3}.$$

54. The graph of a function f consists of a semicircle and two line segments as shown below.

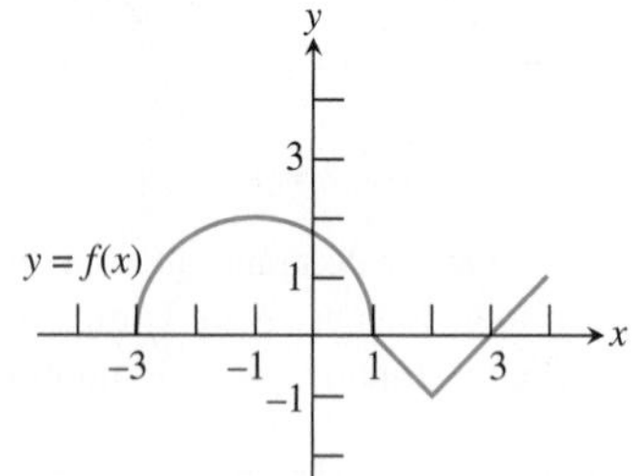

Let $g(x) = \int_1^x f(t)\,dt$.

(a) Find $g(1)$.

(b) Find $g(3)$.

(c) Find $g(-1)$.

(d) Find all values of x on the open interval $(-3, 4)$ at which g has a relative maximum.

(e) Write an equation for the line tangent to the graph of g at $x = -1$.

(f) Find the x-coordinate of each point of inflection of the graph of g on the open interval $(-3, 4)$.

(g) Find the range of g.

55. What is the total area under the curve $y = e^{-x^2/2}$?

The graph approaches the x-axis as an asymptote both to the left and the right, but quickly enough so that the total area is a finite number. In fact,

$$\text{NINT}\,(e^{-x^2/2}, x, -10, 10)$$

computes all but a negligible amount of the area.

(a) Find this number on your calculator. Verify that NINT $(e^{-x^2/2}, x, -20, 20)$ does not increase the number enough for the calculator to distinguish the difference.

(b) This area has an interesting relationship to π. Perform various (simple) algebraic operations on the number to discover what it is.

56. *Filling a Swamp* A town wants to drain and fill the small polluted swamp shown below. The swamp averages 5 ft deep. About how many cubic yards of dirt will it take to fill the area after the swamp is drained?

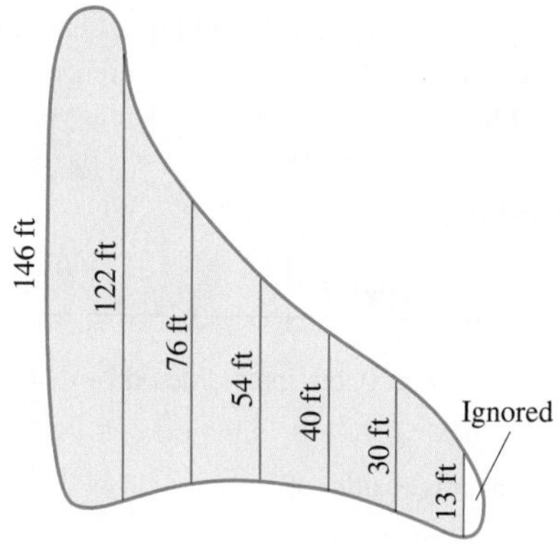

Horizontal spacing = 20 ft

57. *Household Electricity* We model the voltage V in our homes with the sine function

$$V = V_{\max} \sin(120\,\pi t),$$

which expresses V in volts as a function of time t in seconds. The function runs through 60 cycles each second. The number $V_{\max}$ is the *peak voltage.*

To measure the voltage effectively, we use an instrument that measures the square root of the average value of the square of the voltage over a 1-second interval:

$$V_{\text{rms}} = \sqrt{(V^2)_{\text{av}}}$$

The subscript "rms" stands for "root mean square." It turns out that

$$V_{\text{rms}} = \frac{V_{\max}}{\sqrt{2}}. \qquad (1)$$

The familiar phrase "115 volts ac" means that the rms voltage is 115. The peak voltage, obtained from Equation 1 as $V_{\max} = 115\sqrt{2}$, is about 163 volts.

(a) Find the average value of V^2 over a 1-sec interval. Then find V_{rms}, and verify Equation 1.

(b) The circuit that runs your electric stove is rated 240 volts rms. What is the peak value of the allowable voltage?

AP *Examination Preparation

You may use a graphing calculator to solve the following problems.

58. The rate at which water flows out of a pipe is given by a differentiable function R of time t. The table below records the rate at 4-hour intervals for a 24-hour period.

t (hours)	$R(t)$ (gallons per hour)
0	9.6
4	10.3
8	10.9
12	11.1
16	10.9
20	10.5
24	9.6

(a) Use the Trapezoidal Rule with 6 subdivisions of equal length to approximate $\int_0^{24} R(t)\,dt$. Explain the meaning of your answer in terms of water flow, using correct units.

(b) Is there some time t between 0 and 24 such that $R'(t) = 0$? Justify your answer.

(c) Suppose the rate of water flow is approximated by $Q(t) = 0.01(950 + 25x - x^2)$. Use $Q(t)$ to approximate the average rate of water flow during the 24-hour period. Indicate units of measure.

59. Let f be a differentiable function with the following properties.

i. $f'(x) = ax^2 + bx$ **ii.** $f'(1) = -6$ and $f''(x) = 6$

iii. $\int_1^2 f(x)\,dx = 14$

Find $f(x)$. Show your work.

60. The graph of the function f, consisting of three line segments, is shown below.

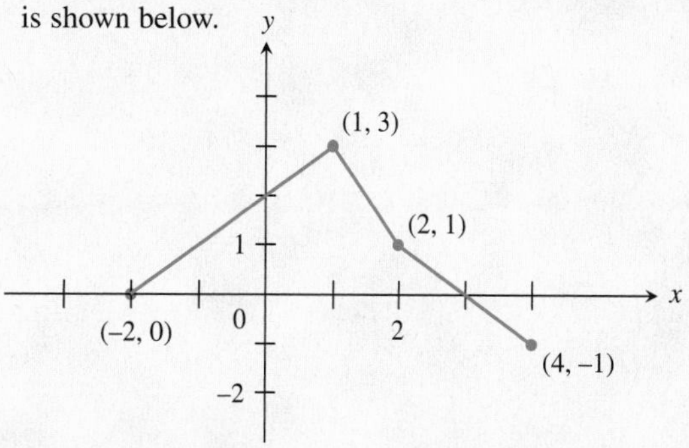

Let $g(x) = \int_1^x f(t)\,dt$.

(a) Compute $g(4)$ and $g(-2)$.

(b) Find the instantaneous rate of change of g, with respect to x, at $x = 2$.

(c) Find the absolute minimum value of g on the closed interval $[-2, 4]$. Justify your answer.

(d) The second derivative of g is not defined at $x = 1$ and $x = 2$. Which of these values are x-coordinates of points of inflection of the graph of g? Justify your answer.

CHAPTER

7 Differential Equations and Mathematical Modeling

One way to measure how light in the ocean diminishes as water depth increases involves using a Secchi disk. This white disk is 30 centimeters in diameter, and is lowered into the ocean until it disappears from view. The depth of this point (in meters), divided into 1.7, yields the coefficient k used in the equation $I_x = I_0e^{-kx}$. This equation estimates the intensity I_x of light at depth x using I_0, the intensity of light at the surface.

In an ocean experiment, if the Secchi disk disappears at 55 meters, at what depth will only 1% of surface radiation remain? Section 7.4 will help you answer this question.

CHAPTER 7 Overview

One of the early accomplishments of calculus was predicting the future position of a planet from its present position and velocity. Today this is just one of a number of occasions on which we deduce everything we need to know about a function from one of its known values and its rate of change. From this kind of information, we can tell how long a sample of radioactive polonium will last; whether, given current trends, a population will grow or become extinct; and how large major league baseball salaries are likely to be in the year 2015. In this chapter, we examine the analytic, graphical, and numerical techniques on which such predictions are based.

7.1 Slope Fields and Euler's Method

What you will learn about . . .

- Differential Equations
- Slope Fields
- Euler's Method

and why . . .

Differential equations have always been a prime motivation for the study of calculus and remain so to this day.

Differential Equations

We have already seen how the discovery of calculus enabled mathematicians to solve problems that had befuddled them for centuries because the problems involved moving objects. Leibniz and Newton were able to model these problems of motion by using equations involving derivatives—what we call *differential equations* today, after the notation of Leibniz. Much energy and creativity has been spent over the years on techniques for solving such equations, which continue to arise in all areas of applied mathematics.

DEFINITION Differential Equation

An equation involving a derivative is called a **differential equation.** The **order of a differential equation** is the order of the highest derivative involved in the equation.

EXAMPLE 1 Solving a Differential Equation

Find all functions y that satisfy $dy/dx = \sec^2 x + 2x + 5$.

SOLUTION

We first encountered this sort of differential equation (called *exact* because it gives the derivative exactly) in Chapter 5. The solution can be any antiderivative of $\sec^2 x + 2x + 5$, which can be any function of the form $y = \tan x + x^2 + 5x + C$. That family of functions is the *general* solution to the differential equation.

Now Try Exercise 1.

Notice that we cannot find a unique solution to a differential equation unless we are given further information. If the general solution to a first-order differential equation is continuous, the only additional information needed is the value of the function at a single point, called an *initial condition.* A differential equation with an initial condition is called an *initial value problem.* It has a unique solution, called the *particular solution* to the differential equation.

EXAMPLE 2 Solving an Initial Value Problem

Find the particular solution to the equation $dy/dx = e^x - 6x^2$ whose graph passes through the point $(1, 0)$.

SOLUTION

The general solution is $y = e^x - 2x^3 + C$. Applying the initial condition, we have $0 = e - 2 + C$, from which we conclude that $C = 2 - e$. Therefore, the particular solution is $y = e^x - 2x^3 + 2 - e$.

Now Try Exercise 13.

An initial condition determines a particular solution by requiring that a solution curve pass through a given point. If the curve is continuous, this pins down the solution on the entire domain. If the curve is discontinuous, the initial condition only pins down the continuous *piece of the curve* that passes through the given point. In this case, the domain of the solution must be specified.

EXAMPLE 3 Handling Discontinuity in an Initial Value Problem

Find the particular solution to the equation $dy/dx = 2x - \sec^2 x$ whose graph passes through the point $(0, 3)$.

SOLUTION

The general solution is $y = x^2 - \tan x + C$. Applying the initial condition, we have $3 = 0 - 0 + C$, from which we conclude that $C = 3$. Therefore, the particular solution is $y = x^2 - \tan x + 3$. Since the point $(0, 3)$ only pins down the continuous piece of the general solution over the interval $(-\pi/2, \pi/2)$, we add the domain stipulation $-\pi/2 < x < \pi/2$.

Now Try Exercise 15.

Sometimes we are unable to find an antiderivative to solve an initial value problem, but we can still find a solution using the Fundamental Theorem of Calculus.

EXAMPLE 4 Using the Fundamental Theorem to Solve an Initial Value Problem

Find the solution to the differential equation $f'(x) = e^{-x^2}$ for which $f(7) = 3$.

SOLUTION

This almost seems too simple, but $f(x) = \int_7^x e^{-t^2}\,dt + 3$ has both of the necessary properties! Clearly, $f(7) = \int_7^7 e^{-t^2}\,dt + 3 = 0 + 3 = 3$, and $f'(x) = e^{x^2}$ by the Fundamental Theorem. The integral form of the solution in Example 4 might seem less desirable than the explicit form of the solutions in Examples 2 and 3, but (thanks to modern technology) it does enable us to find $f(x)$ for any x. For example, $f(-2) = \int_7^{-2} e^{-t^2}\,dt + 3 = \text{NINT}\,(e\wedge(-t^2), t, 7, -2) + 3 \approx 1.2317$.

Now Try Exercise 21.

EXAMPLE 5 Graphing a General Solution

Graph the family of functions that solve the differential equation $dy/dx = \cos x$.

SOLUTION

Any function of the form $y = \sin x + C$ solves the differential equation. We cannot graph them all, but we can graph enough of them to see what a family of solutions would look like. The command $\{-3, -2, -1, 0, 1, 2, 3,\} \rightarrow L_1$ stores seven values of C in the list L_1. Figure 7.1 shows the result of graphing the function $Y_1 = \sin(x) + L_1$.

Now Try Exercises 25–28.

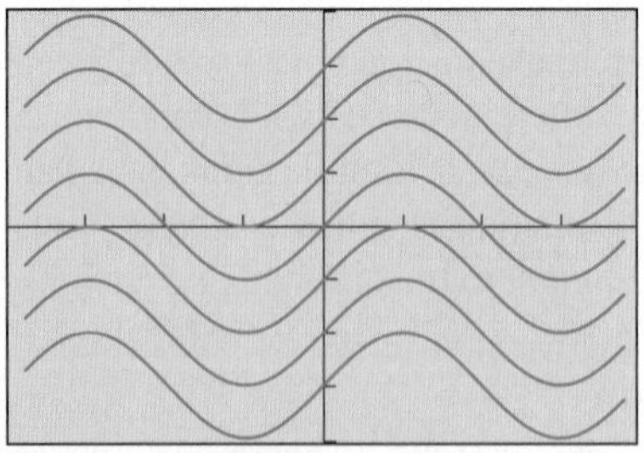

$[-2\pi, 2\pi]$ by $[-4, 4]$

Figure 7.1 A graph of the family of functions $Y_1 = \sin(x) + L_1$, where $L_1 = \{-3, -2, -1, 0, 1, 2, 3\}$. This graph shows some of the functions that satisfy the differential equation $dy/dx = \cos x$. (Example 5)

Notice that the graph in Figure 7.1 consists of a family of parallel curves. This should come as no surprise, since functions of the form $\sin(x) + C$ are all vertical translations of the basic sine curve. It might be less obvious that we could have predicted the appearance of this family of curves from *the differential equation itself.* Exploration 1 gives you a new way to look at the solution graph.

Exploration 1 suggests the interesting possibility that we could have produced the family of curves in Figure 7.1 without even solving the differential equation, simply by looking carefully at slopes. That is exactly the idea behind *slope fields*.

EXPLORATION 1 Seeing the Slopes

Figure 7.1 shows the general solution to the exact differential equation $dy/dx = \cos x$.

1. Since $\cos x = 0$ at odd multiples of $\pi/2$, we should "see" that $dy/dx = 0$ at the odd multiples of $\pi/2$ in Figure 7.1. Is that true? How can you tell?
2. Algebraically, the y-coordinate does not affect the value of $dy/dx = \cos x$. Why not?
3. Does the graph show that the y-coordinate does not affect the value of dy/dx? How can you tell?
4. According to the differential equation $dy/dx = \cos x$, what should be the slope of the solution curves when $x = 0$? Can you see this in the graph?
5. According to the differential equation $dy/dx = \cos x$, what should be the slope of the solution curves when $x = \pi$? Can you see this in the graph?
6. Since $\cos x$ is an even function, the slope at any point should be the same as the slope at its reflection across the y-axis. Is this true? How can you tell?

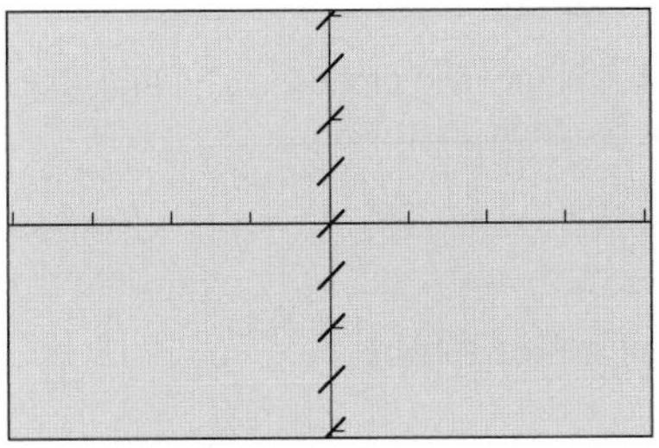

$[-2\pi, 2\pi]$ by $[-4, 4]$

(a)

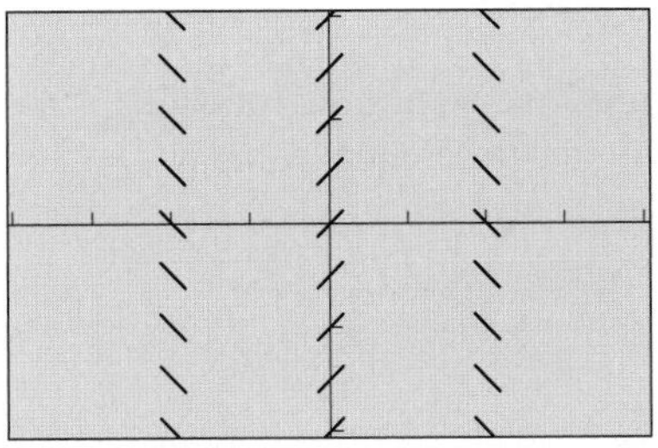

$[-2\pi, 2\pi]$ by $[-4, 4]$

(b)

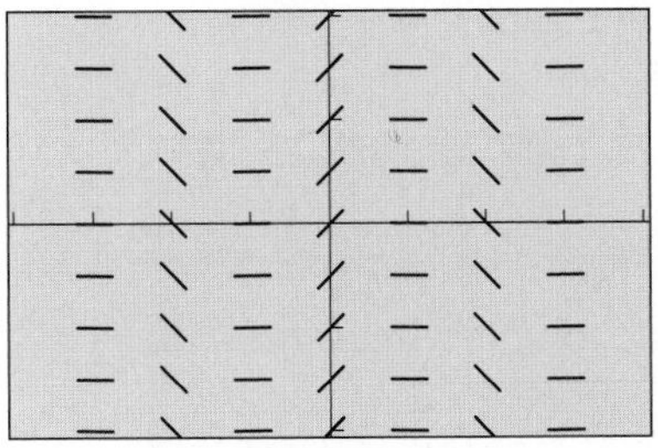

$[-2\pi, 2\pi]$ by $[-4, 4]$

(c)

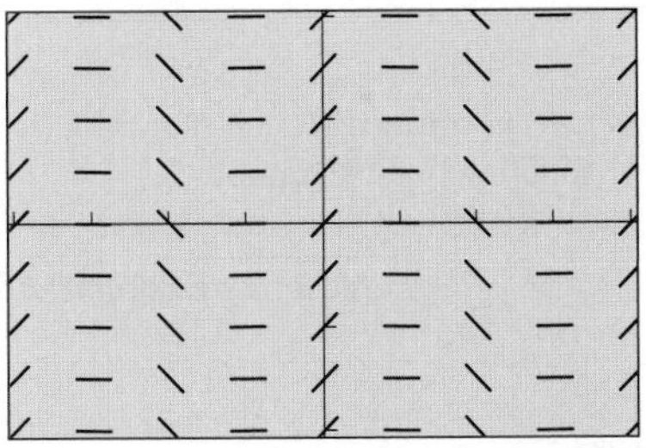

$[-2\pi, 2\pi]$ by $[-4, 4]$

(d)

Figure 7.2 The steps in constructing a slope field for the differential equation $dy/dx = \cos x$. (Example 6)

Slope Fields

Suppose we want to produce Figure 7.1 without actually solving the differential equation $dy/dx = \cos x$. Since the differential equation gives the *slope* at any point (x, y), we can use that information to draw a small piece of the linearization at that point, which (thanks to local linearity) approximates the solution curve that passes through that point. Repeating that process at many points yields an approximation of Figure 7.1 called a slope field. Example 6 shows how this is done.

EXAMPLE 6 Constructing a Slope Field

Construct a slope field for the differential equation $dy/dx = \cos x$.

SOLUTION

We know that the slope at any point $(0, y)$ will be $\cos 0 = 1$, so we can start by drawing tiny segments with slope 1 at several points along the y-axis (Figure 7.2a). Then, since the slope at any point (π, y) or $(-\pi, y)$ will be -1, we can draw tiny segments with slope -1 at several points along the vertical lines $x = \pi$ and $x = -\pi$ (Figure 7.2b). The slope at all odd multiples of $\pi/2$ will be zero, so we draw tiny horizontal segments along the lines $x = \pm\pi/2$ and $x = \pm 3\pi/2$ (Figure 7.2c). Finally, we add tiny segments of slope 1 along the lines $x = \pm 2\pi$ (Figure 7.2d).

Now Try Exercise 29.

To illustrate how a family of solution curves conforms to a slope field, we superimpose the solutions in Figure 7.1 on the slope field in Figure 7.2d. The result is shown in Figure 7.3 on the next page.

We could get a smoother-looking slope field by drawing shorter line segments at more points, but that can get tedious. Happily, the algorithm is simple enough to be programmed into a graphing calculator. One such program, using a lattice of 150 sample points, produced in a matter of seconds the graph in Figure 7.4 on the next page.

It is also possible to produce slope fields for differential equations that are not of the form $dy/dx = f(x)$. We will study analytic techniques for solving certain types of these nonexact differential equations later in this chapter, but you should keep in mind that you can graph the general solution with a slope field even if you cannot find it analytically.

Differential Equation Mode

If your calculator has a *differential equation mode* for graphing, it is intended for graphing slope fields. The usual "Y=" turns into a "$dy/dx =$ " screen, and you can enter a function of x and/or y. The grapher draws a slope field for the differential equation when you press the GRAPH button.

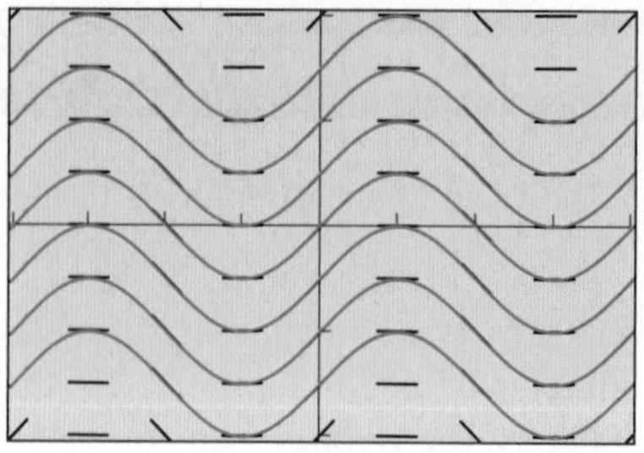

$[-2\pi, 2\pi]$ by $[-4, 4]$

Figure 7.3 The graph of the general solution in Figure 7.1 conforms nicely to the slope field of the differential equation. (Example 6)

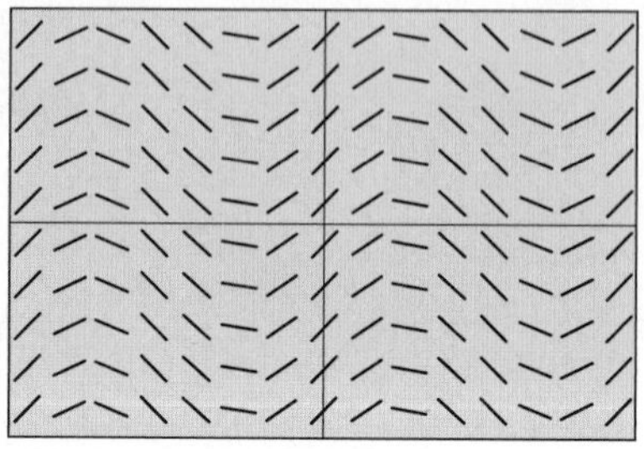

$[-2\pi, 2\pi]$ by $[-4, 4]$

Figure 7.4 A slope field produced by a graphing calculator program.

Can We Solve the Differential Equation in Example 7?

Although it looks harmless enough, the differential equation $dy/dx = x + y$ is not easy to solve until you have seen how it is done. It is an example of a *first-order linear differential equation,* and its general solution is

$$y = Ce^x - x - 1$$

(which you can easily check by verifying that $dy/dx = x + y$). We will defer the analytic solution of such equations to a later course.

EXAMPLE 7 Constructing a Slope Field for a Nonexact Differential Equation

Use a calculator to construct a slope field for the differential equation $dy/dx = x + y$ and sketch a graph of the particular solution that passes through the point $(2, 0)$.

SOLUTION

The calculator produces a graph like the one in Figure 7.5a. Notice the following properties of the graph, all of them easily predictable from the differential equation:

1. The slopes are zero along the line $x + y = 0$.
2. The slopes are -1 along the line $x + y = -1$.
3. The slopes get steeper as x increases.
4. The slopes get steeper as y increases.

The particular solution can be found by drawing a smooth curve through the point $(2, 0)$ that follows the slopes in the slope field, as shown in Figure 7.5b.

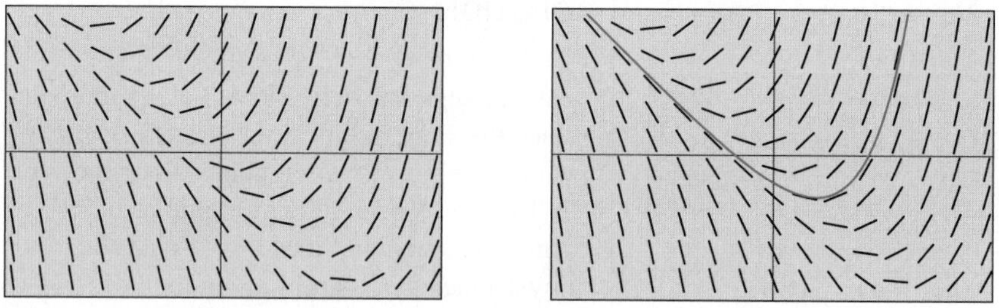

$[-4.7, 4.7]$ by $[-3.1, 3.1]$
(a)

$[-4.7, 4.7]$ by $[-3.1, 3.1]$
(b)

Figure 7.5 (a) A slope field for the differential equation $dy/dx = x + y$, and (b) the same slope field with the graph of the particular solution through $(2, 0)$ superimposed. (Example 7)

Now Try Exercise 35.

EXAMPLE 8 Matching Slope Fields with Differential Equations

Use slope analysis to match each of the following differential equations with one of the slope fields (a) through (d). (Do not use your graphing calculator.)

1. $\dfrac{dy}{dx} = x - y$ **2.** $\dfrac{dy}{dx} = xy$ **3.** $\dfrac{dy}{dx} = \dfrac{x}{y}$ **4.** $\dfrac{dy}{dx} = \dfrac{y}{x}$

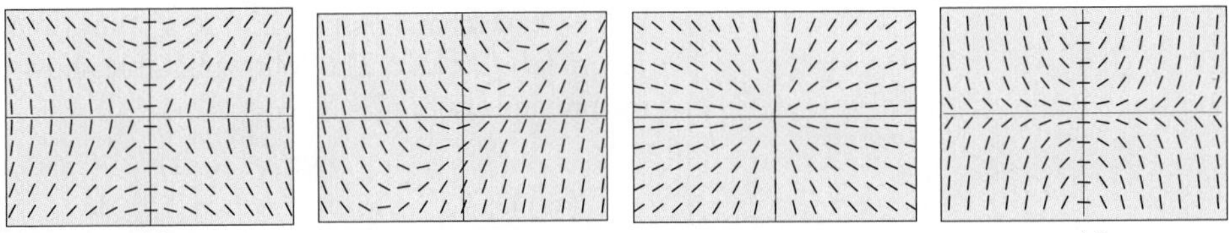

(a) (b) (c) (d)

SOLUTION

To match Equation 1, we look for a graph that has zero slope along the line $x - y = 0$. That is graph (b).

To match Equation 2, we look for a graph that has zero slope along both axes. That is graph (d).

To match Equation 3, we look for a graph that has horizontal segments when $x = 0$ and vertical segments when $y = 0$. That is graph (a).

To match Equation 4, we look for a graph that has vertical segments when $x = 0$ and horizontal segments when $y = 0$. That is graph (c).

Now Try Exercise 39.

Euler's Method

In Example 7 we graphed the particular solution to an initial value problem by first producing a slope field and then finding a smooth curve through the slope field that passed through the given point. In fact, we could have graphed the particular solution directly, by starting at the given point and piecing together little line segments to build a continuous approximation of the curve. This clever application of local linearity to graph a solution without knowing its equation is called **Euler's Method.**

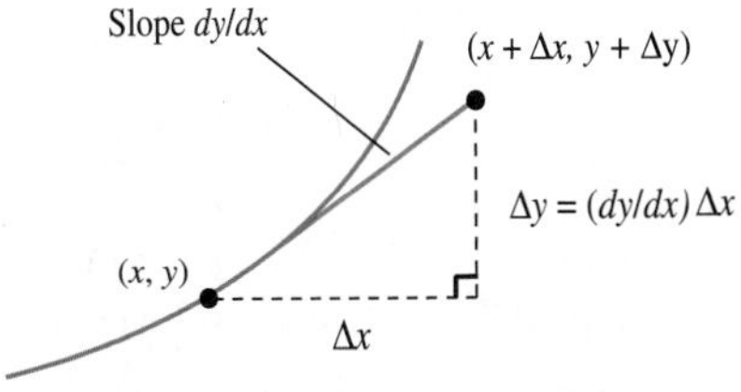

Figure 7.6 How Euler's Method moves along the linearization at the point (x, y) to define a new point $(x + \Delta x, y + \Delta y)$. The process is then repeated, starting with the new point.

Euler's Method for Graphing a Solution to an Initial Value Problem

1. Begin at the point (x, y) specified by the initial condition. This point will be on the graph, as required.
2. Use the differential equation to find the slope dy/dx at the point.
3. Increase x by a small amount Δx. Increase y by a small amount Δy, where $\Delta y = (dy/dx)\Delta x$. This defines a new point $(x + \Delta x, y + \Delta y)$ that lies along the linearization (Figure 7.6).
4. Using this new point, return to step 2. Repeating the process constructs the graph to the right of the initial point.
5. To construct the graph moving to the left from the initial point, repeat the process using negative values for Δx.

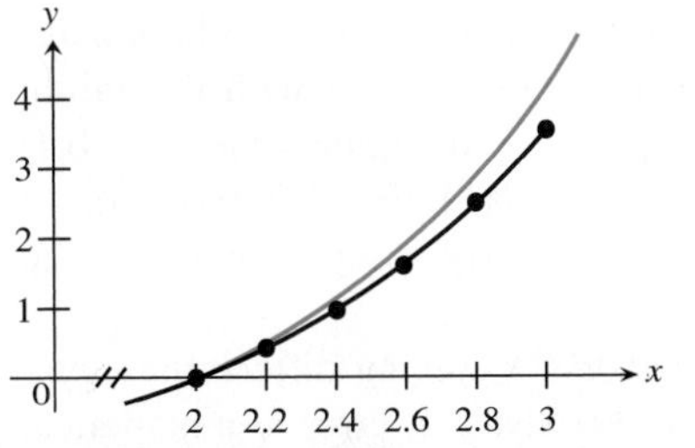

Figure 7.7 Euler's Method is used to construct an approximate solution to an initial value problem between $x = 2$ and $x = 3$. (Example 9)

We illustrate the method in Example 9.

EXAMPLE 9 Applying Euler's Method

Let f be the function that satisfies the initial value problem in Example 6 (that is, $dy/dx = x + y$ and $f(2) = 0$). Use Euler's Method and increments of $\Delta x = 0.2$ to approximate $f(3)$.

SOLUTION

We use Euler's Method to construct an approximation of the curve from $x = 2$ to $x = 3$, pasting together five small linearization segments (Figure 7.7). Each segment will extend from a point (x, y) to a point $(x + \Delta x, y + \Delta y)$, where $\Delta x = 0.2$ and $\Delta y = (dy/dx)\Delta x$. The following table shows how we construct each new point from the previous one.

(x, y)	$dy/dx = x + y$	Δx	$\Delta y = (dy/dx)\Delta x$	$(x + \Delta x, y + \Delta y)$
(2, 0)	2	0.2	0.4	(2.2, 0.4)
(2.2, 0.4)	2.6	0.2	0.52	(2.4, 0.92)
(2.4, 0.92)	3.32	0.2	0.664	(2.6, 1.584)
(2.6, 1.584)	4.184	0.2	0.8368	(2.8, 2.4208)
(2.8, 2.4208)	5.2208	0.2	1.04416	(3, 3.46496)

Euler's Method leads us to an approximation $f(3) \approx 3.46496$, which we would more reasonably report as $f(3) \approx 3.465$.

Now Try Exercise 51.

You can see from Figure 7.7 that Euler's Method leads to an underestimate when the curve is concave up, just as it will lead to an overestimate when the curve is concave down. You can also see that the error increases as the distance from the original point increases. In fact, the true value of $f(3)$ is about 4.155, so the approximation error is about 16.6%. We could increase the accuracy by taking smaller increments—a reasonable option if we have a calculator program to do the work. For example, 100 increments of 0.01 give an estimate of 4.1144, cutting the error to about 1%.

EXAMPLE 10 Moving Backward with Euler's Method

If $dy/dx = 2x - y$ and if $y = 3$ when $x = 2$, use Euler's Method with five equal steps to approximate y when $x = 1.5$.

SOLUTION

Starting at $x = 2$, we need five equal steps of $\Delta x = -0.1$.

(x, y)	$dy/dx = 2x - y$	Δx	$\Delta y = (dy/dx)\Delta x$	$(x + \Delta x, y + \Delta y)$
(2, 3)	1	−0.1	−0.1	(1.9, 2.9)
(1.9, 2.9)	0.9	−0.1	−0.09	(1.8, 2.81)
(1.8, 2.81)	0.79	−0.1	−0.079	(1.7, 2.731)
(1.7, 2.731)	0.669	−0.1	−0.0669	(1.6, 2.6641)
(1.6, 2.6641)	0.5359	−0.1	−0.05359	(1.5, 2.61051)

The value at $x = 1.5$ is approximately 2.61. (The actual value is about 2.649, so the percentage error in this case is about 1.4%.) ***Now Try Exercise 55.***

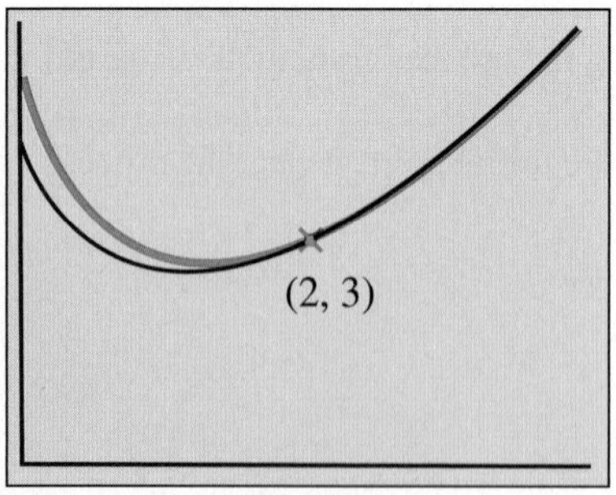

[0, 4] by [0, 6]

Figure 7.8 A grapher program using Euler's Method and increments of 0.1 produced this approximation to the solution curve for the initial value problem in Example 10. The actual solution curve is shown in red.

If we program a grapher to do the work of finding the points, Euler's Method can be used to graph (approximately) the solution to an initial value problem without actually solving it. For example, a graphing calculator program starting with the initial value problem in Example 9 produced the graph in Figure 7.8, using increments of 0.1. The graph of the actual solution is shown in red. Notice that Euler's Method does a better job of approximating the curve when the curve is nearly straight, as should be expected.

Euler's Method is one example of a *numerical method* for solving differential equations. The table of values is the *numerical solution*. The analysis of error in a numerical solution and the investigation of methods to reduce it are important, but appropriate for a more advanced course (which would also describe more accurate numerical methods than the one shown here).

Quick Review 7.1

Exercise numbers with a gray background indicate problems that the authors have designed to be solved *without a calculator.*

In Exercises 1–8, determine whether or not the function y satisfies the differential equation.

1. $\dfrac{dy}{dx} = y \qquad y = e^x$

2. $\dfrac{dy}{dx} = 4y \qquad y = e^{4x}$

3. $\dfrac{dy}{dx} = 2xy \qquad y = x^2 e^x$

4. $\dfrac{dy}{dx} = 2xy \qquad y = e^{x^2}$

5. $\dfrac{dy}{dx} = 2xy \qquad y = e^{x^2} + 5$

6. $\dfrac{dy}{dx} = \dfrac{1}{y} \qquad y = \sqrt{2x}$

7. $\dfrac{dy}{dx} = y \tan x \qquad y = \sec x$

8. $\dfrac{dy}{dx} = y^2 \qquad y = x^{-1}$

In Exercises 9–12, find the constant C.

9. $y = 3x^2 + 4x + C$ and $y = 2$ when $x = 1$

10. $y = 2 \sin x - 3 \cos x + C$ and $y = 4$ when $x = 0$

11. $y = e^{2x} + \sec x + C$ and $y = 5$ when $x = 0$

12. $y = \tan^{-1} x + \ln(2x - 1) + C$ and $y = \pi$ when $x = 1$

Section 7.1 Exercises

In Exercises 1–10, find the general solution to the exact differential equation.

1. $\dfrac{dy}{dx} = 5x^4 - \sec^2 x$

2. $\dfrac{dy}{dx} = \sec x \tan x - e^x$

3. $\dfrac{dy}{dx} = \sin x - e^{-x} + 8x^3$

4. $\dfrac{dy}{dx} = \dfrac{1}{x} - \dfrac{1}{x^2} \; (x > 0)$

5. $\dfrac{dy}{dx} = 5^x \ln 5 + \dfrac{1}{x^2 + 1}$

6. $\dfrac{dy}{dx} = \dfrac{1}{\sqrt{1 - x^2}} - \dfrac{1}{\sqrt{x}}$

7. $\dfrac{dy}{dt} = 3t^2 \cos(t^3)$

8. $\dfrac{dy}{dt} = (\cos t)\, e^{\sin t}$

9. $\dfrac{du}{dx} = (\sec^2 x^5)(5x^4)$

10. $\dfrac{dy}{du} = 4 (\sin u)^3 (\cos u)$

In Exercises 11–20, solve the initial value problem explicitly.

11. $\dfrac{dy}{dx} = 3 \sin x$ and $y = 2$ when $x = 0$

12. $\dfrac{dy}{dx} = 2e^x - \cos x$ and $y = 3$ when $x = 0$

13. $\dfrac{du}{dx} = 7x^6 - 3x^2 + 5$ and $u = 1$ when $x = 1$

14. $\dfrac{dA}{dx} = 10x^9 + 5x^4 - 2x + 4$ and $A = 6$ when $x = 1$

15. $\dfrac{dy}{dx} = -\dfrac{1}{x^2} - \dfrac{3}{x^4} + 12$ and $y = 3$ when $x = 1$

16. $\dfrac{dy}{dx} = 5 \sec^2 x - \dfrac{3}{2}\sqrt{x}$ and $y = 7$ when $x = 0$

17. $\dfrac{dy}{dt} = \dfrac{1}{1 + t^2} + 2^t \ln 2$ and $y = 3$ when $t = 0$

18. $\dfrac{dx}{dt} = \dfrac{1}{t} - \dfrac{1}{t^2} + 6$ and $x = 0$ when $t = 1$

19. $\dfrac{dv}{dt} = 4 \sec t \tan t + e^t + 6t$ and $v = 5$ when $t = 0$

20. $\dfrac{ds}{dt} = t(3t - 2)$ and $s = 0$ when $t = 1$

In Exercises 21–24, solve the initial value problem using the Fundamental Theorem. (Your answer will contain a definite integral.)

21. $\dfrac{dy}{dx} = \sin(x^2)$ and $y = 5$ when $x = 1$

22. $\dfrac{du}{dx} = \sqrt{2 + \cos x}$ and $u = -3$ when $x = 0$

23. $F'(x) = e^{\cos x}$ and $F(2) = 9$

24. $G'(s) = \sqrt[3]{\tan s}$ and $G(0) = 4$

In Exercises 25–28, match the differential equation with the graph of a family of functions (a)–(d) that solve it. Use slope analysis, not your graphing calculator.

25. $\dfrac{dy}{dx} = (\sin x)^2$

26. $\dfrac{dy}{dx} = (\sin x)^3$

27. $\dfrac{dy}{dx} = (\cos x)^2$

28. $\dfrac{dy}{dx} = (\cos x)^3$

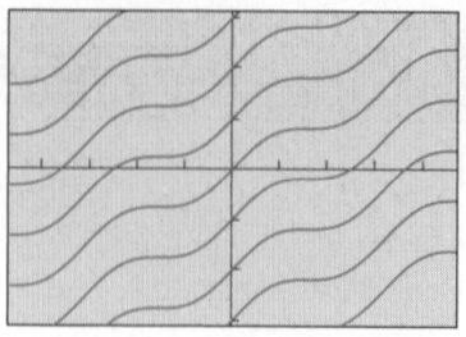
(a)

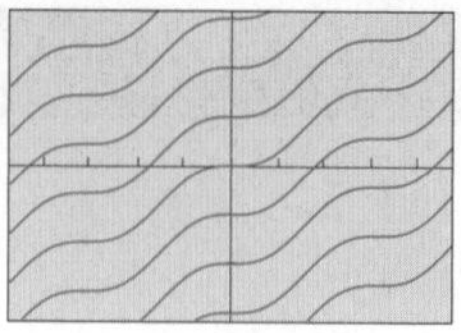
(b)

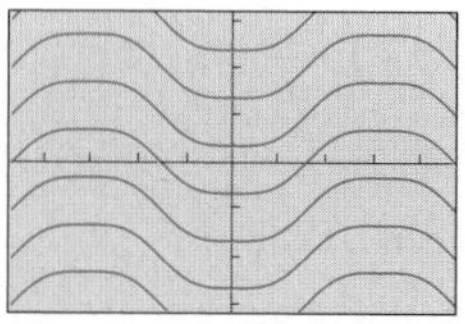
(c)

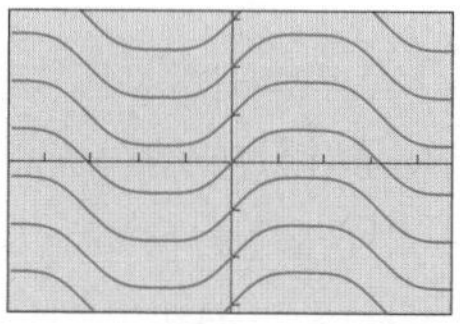
(d)

In Exercises 29–34, construct a slope field for the differential equation. In each case, copy the graph at the right and draw tiny segments through the twelve lattice points shown in the graph. Use slope analysis, not your graphing calculator.

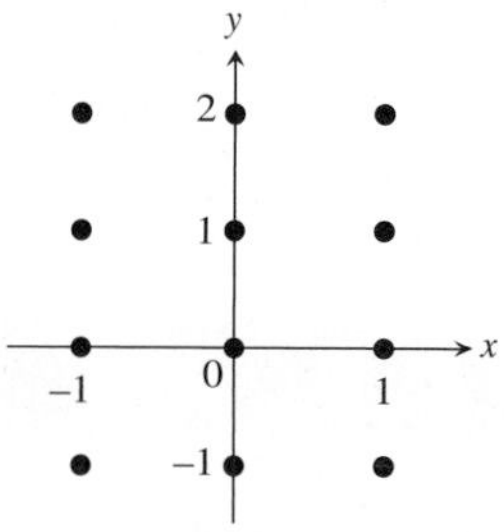

29. $\frac{dy}{dx} = x$ **30.** $\frac{dy}{dx} = y$ **31.** $\frac{dy}{dx} = 2x + y$

32. $\frac{dy}{dx} = 2x - y$ **33.** $\frac{dy}{dx} = x + 2y$ **34.** $\frac{dy}{dx} = x - 2y$

In Exercises 35–40, match the differential equation with the appropriate slope field. Then use the slope field to sketch the graph of the particular solution through the highlighted point (3, 2). (All slope fields are shown in the window $[-6, 6]$ by $[-4, 4]$.)

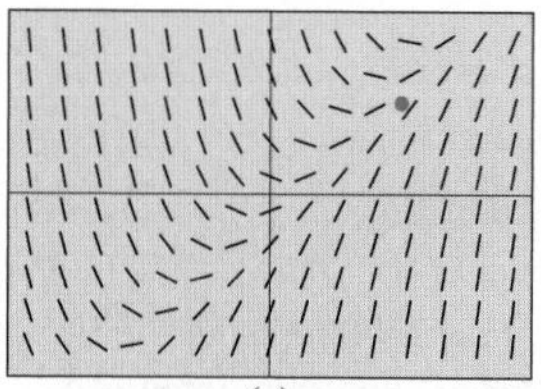
(a)

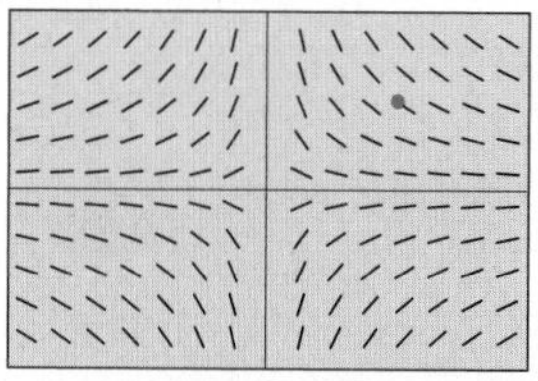
(b)

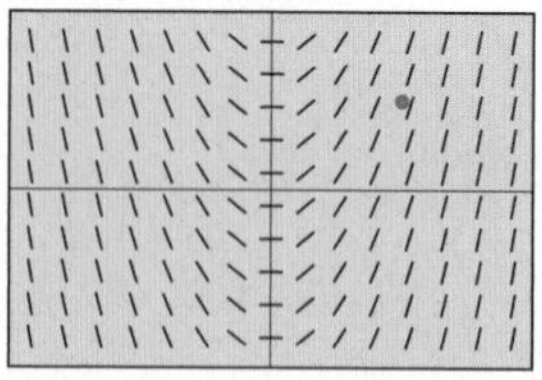
(c)

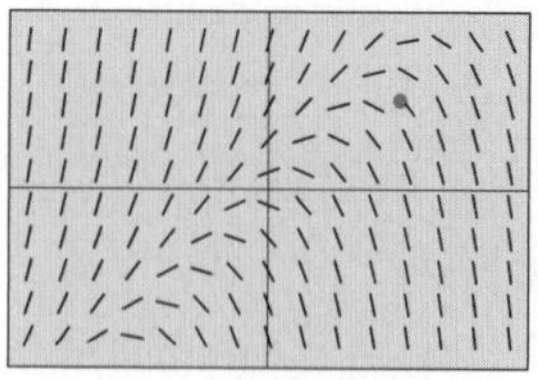
(d)

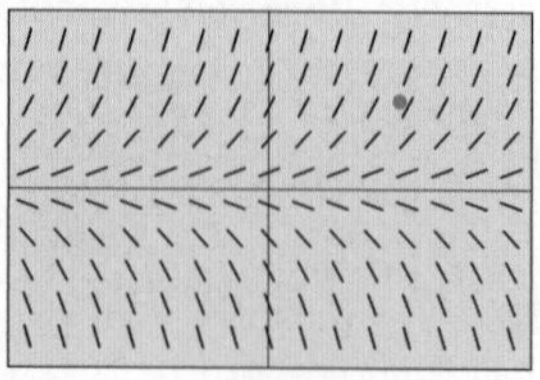
(e)

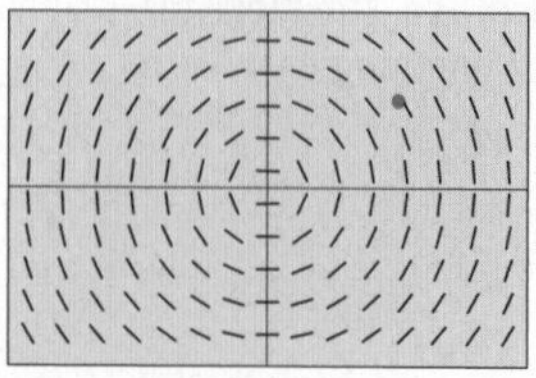
(f)

35. $\frac{dy}{dx} = x$ **36.** $\frac{dy}{dx} = y$

37. $\frac{dy}{dx} = x - y$ **38.** $\frac{dy}{dx} = y - x$

39. $\frac{dy}{dx} = -\frac{y}{x}$ **40.** $\frac{dy}{dx} = -\frac{x}{y}$

In Exercises 41–46, match the differential equation with the appropriate slope field. Then use the slope field to sketch the graph of the particular solution through the highlighted point (0, 2). (All slope fields are shown in the window $[-6, 6]$ by $[-4, 4]$.)

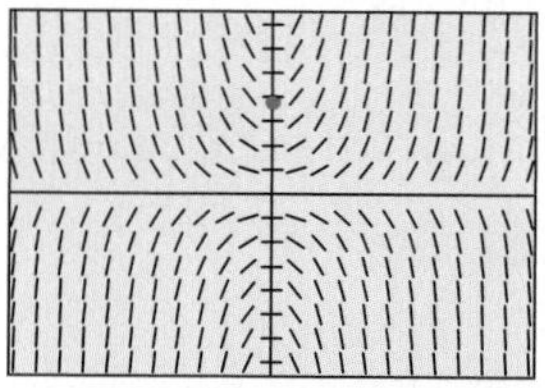
(a)

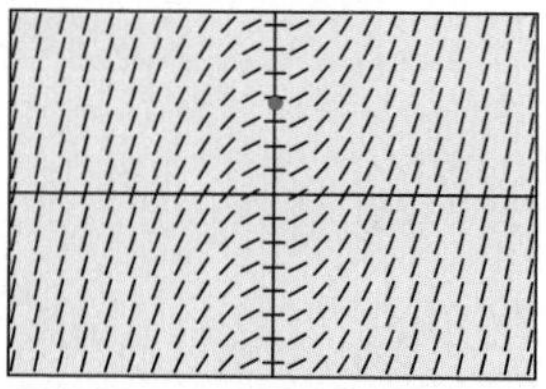
(b)

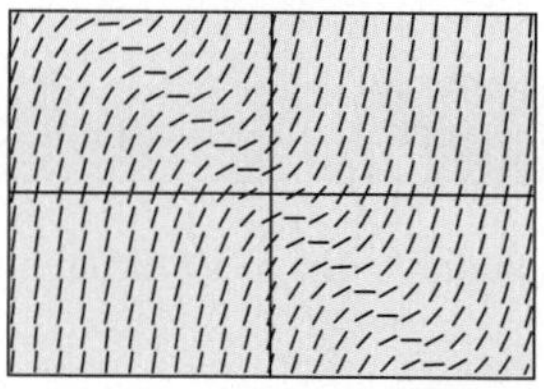
(c)

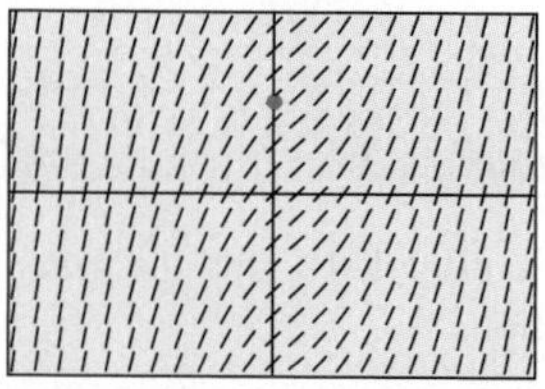
(d)

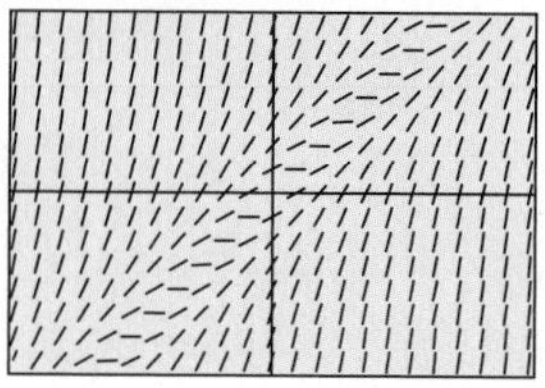
(e)

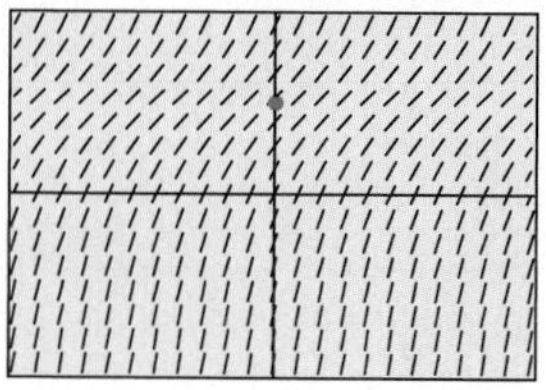
(f)

41. $\frac{dy}{dx} = \sqrt{x^2 - x + 1}$ **42.** $\frac{dy}{dx} = \sqrt{y^2 - 4y + 5}$

43. $\frac{dy}{dx} = |x + y|$ **44.** $\frac{dy}{dx} = |x - y|$

45. $\frac{dy}{dx} = |x|$ **46.** $\frac{dy}{dx} = xy$

47. **(a)** Sketch a graph of the solution to the initial value problem

$$\frac{dy}{dx} = \sec^2 x \text{ and } y = 1 \text{ when } x = \pi.$$

(b) Writing to Learn A student solved part (a) and used a graphing calculator to produce the following graph:

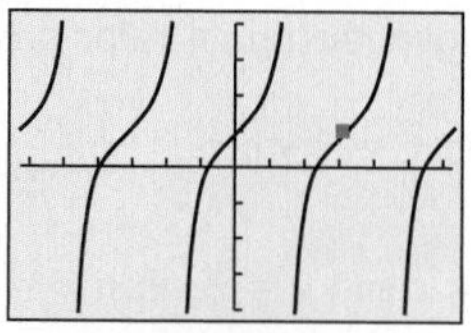
$[-2\pi, 2\pi]$ by $[-4, 4]$

How would you explain to this student why this graph is *not* the correct answer to part (a)?

48. **(a)** Sketch a graph of the solution to the initial value problem

$$\frac{dy}{dx} = -x^{-2} \text{ and } y = 1 \text{ when } x = 1.$$

(b) Writing to Learn A student solved part (a) and used a graphing calculator to produce the following graph:

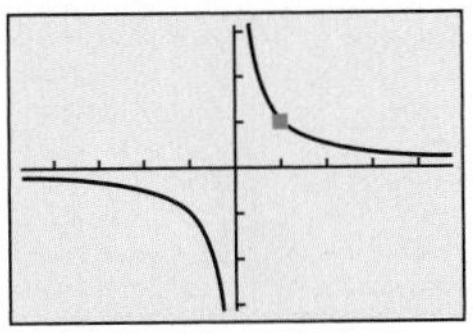

[−4.7, 4.7] by [−3.1, 3.1]

How would you explain to this student why this graph is *not* the correct answer to part (a)?

49. *Left Field Line* A single line from the slope field for $\frac{dy}{dx} = 2y + x$ is shown in the second quadrant of one of the following three graphs. Choose the only possible graph and draw a line for the same slope field through the reflected point in the first quadrant. All graphs are shown in the window $[-4.7, 4.7]$ by $[-3.1, 3.1]$.

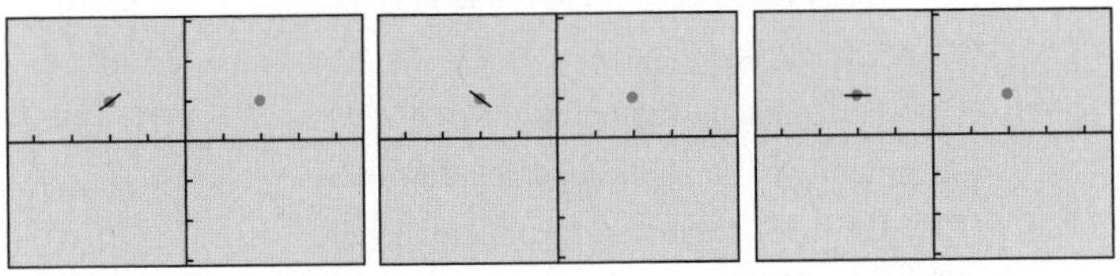

(a) (b) (c)

50. *Right Field Line* A single line from the slope field for $\frac{dy}{dx} = y^2 - x$ is shown in the first quadrant of one of the following three graphs. Choose the only possible graph and draw a line for the same slope field through the reflected point in the second quadrant. All graphs are shown in the window $[-4.7, 4.7]$ by $[-3.1, 3.1]$.

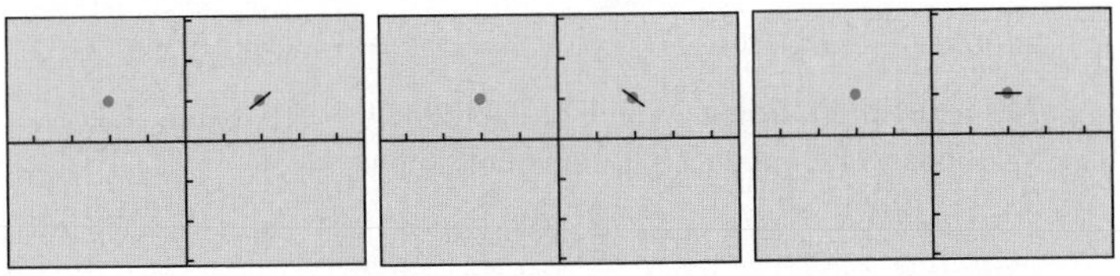

(a) (b) (c)

In Exercises 51–54, use Euler's Method with increments of $\Delta x = 0.1$ to approximate the value of y when $x = 1.3$.

51. $\frac{dy}{dx} = x - 1$ and $y = 2$ when $x = 1$

52. $\frac{dy}{dx} = y - 1$ and $y = 3$ when $x = 1$

53. $\frac{dy}{dx} = y - x$ and $y = 2$ when $x = 1$

54. $\frac{dy}{dx} = 2x - y$ and $y = 0$ when $x = 1$

In Exercises 55–58, use Euler's Method with increments of $\Delta x = -0.1$ to approximate the value of y when $x = 1.7$.

55. $\frac{dy}{dx} = 2 - x$ and $y = 1$ when $x = 2$

56. $\frac{dy}{dx} = 1 + y$ and $y = 0$ when $x = 2$

57. $\frac{dy}{dx} = x - y$ and $y = 2$ when $x = 2$

58. $\frac{dy}{dx} = x - 2y$ and $y = 1$ when $x = 2$

In Exercises 59 and 60, **(a)** determine which graph shows the solution of the initial value problem without actually solving the problem.

(b) Writing to Learn Explain how you eliminated two of the possibilities.

59. $\frac{dy}{dx} = \frac{1}{1 + x^2}, \quad y(0) = \frac{\pi}{2}$

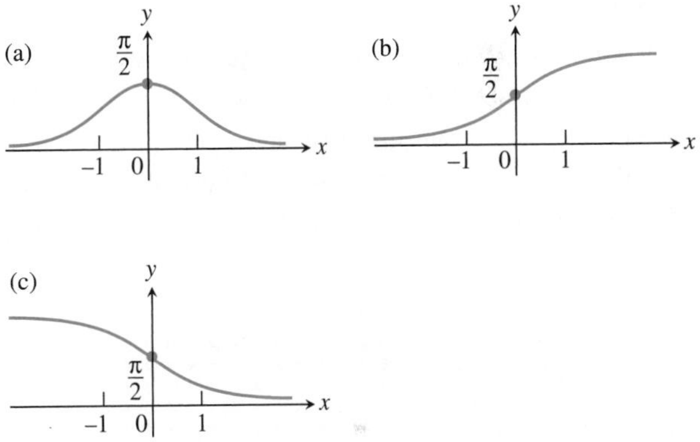

60. $\frac{dy}{dx} = -x, \; y(-1) = 1$

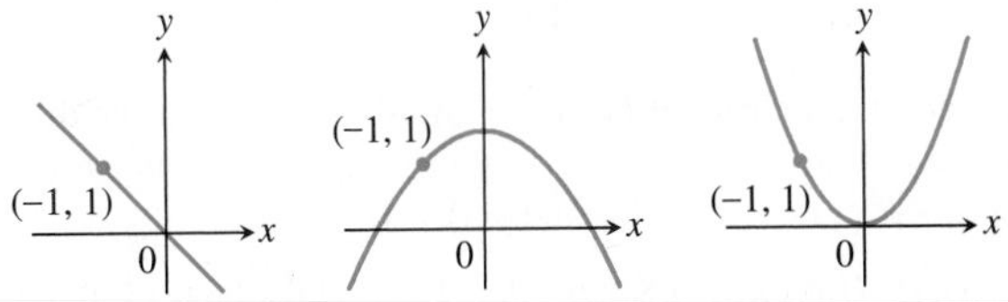

(a) (b) (c)

61. Writing to Learn Explain why $y = x^2$ could not be a solution to the differential equation with slope field shown below.

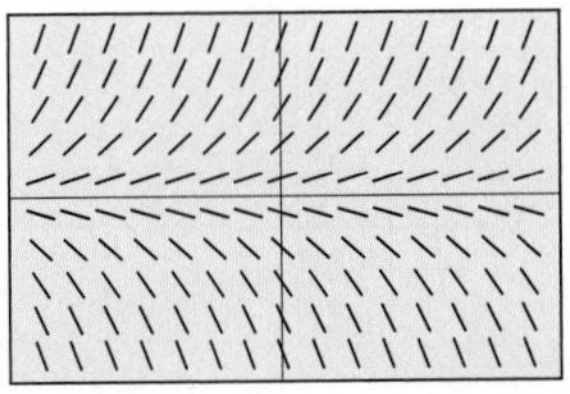

[−4.7, 4.7] by [−3.1, 3.1]

62. Writing to Learn Explain why $y = \sin x$ could not be a solution to the differential equation with slope field shown below.

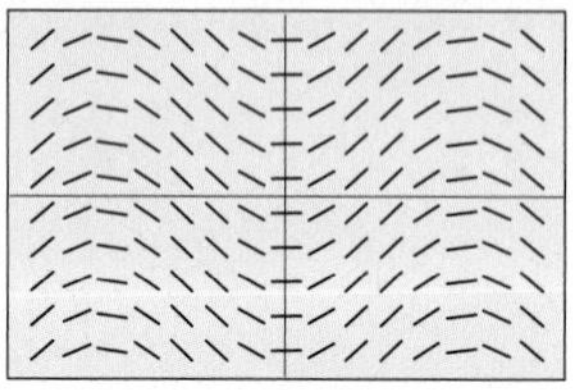

$[-4.7, 4.7]$ by $[-3.1, 3.1]$

63. *Percentage Error* Let $y = f(x)$ be the solution to the initial value problem $dy/dx = 2x + 1$ such that $f(1) = 3$. Find the percentage error if Euler's Method with $\Delta x = 0.1$ is used to approximate $f(1.4)$.

64. *Percentage Error* Let $y = f(x)$ be the solution to the initial value problem $dy/dx = 2x - 1$ such that $f(2) = 3$. Find the percentage error if Euler's Method with $\Delta x = -0.1$ is used to approximate $f(1.6)$.

65. *Perpendicular Slope Fields* The figure below shows the slope fields for the differential equations $dy/dx = e^{(x-y)/2}$ and $dy/dx = -e^{(y-x)/2}$ superimposed on the same grid. It appears that the slope lines are perpendicular wherever they intersect. Prove algebraically that this must be so.

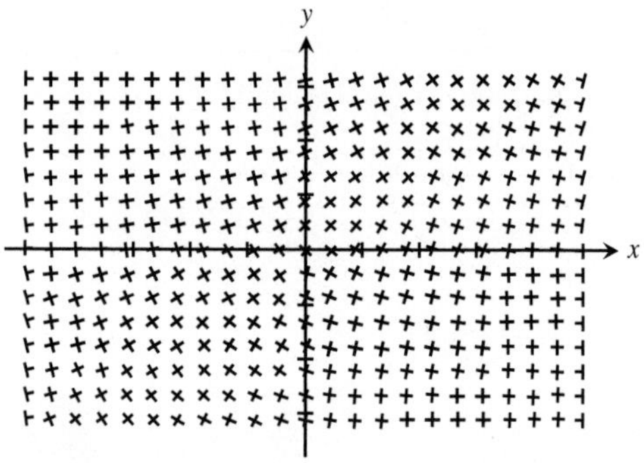

66. *Perpendicular Slope Fields* If the slope fields for the differential equations $dy/dx = \sec x$ and $dy/dx = g(x)$ are perpendicular (as in Exercise 65), find $g(x)$.

67. *Plowing Through a Slope Field* The slope field for the differential equation $dy/dx = \csc x$ is shown below. Find a function that will be *perpendicular* to every line it crosses in the slope field. [*Hint:* First find a differential equation that will produce a perpendicular slope field.]

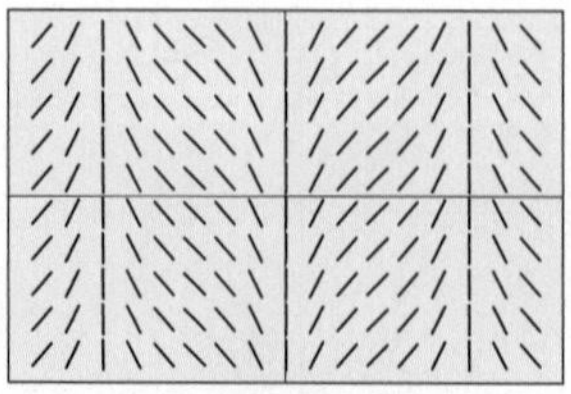

$[-4.7, 4.7]$ by $[-3.1, 3.1]$

68. *Plowing Through a Slope Field* The slope field for the differential equation $dy/dx = 1/x$ is shown below. Find a function that will be *perpendicular* to every line it crosses in the slope field. [*Hint:* First find a differential equation that will produce a perpendicular slope field.]

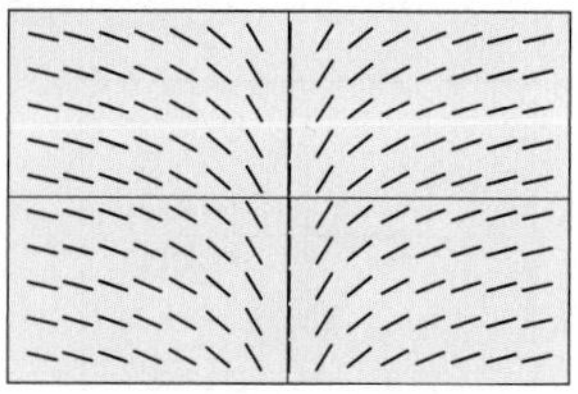

$[-4.7, 4.7]$ by $[-3.1, 3.1]$

Standardized Test Questions

69. True or False Any two solutions to the differential equation $dy/dx = 5$ are parallel lines. Justify your answer.

70. True or False If $f(x)$ is a solution to $dy/dx = 2x$, then $f^{-1}(x)$ is a solution to $dy/dx = 2y$. Justify your answer.

71. Multiple Choice A slope field for the differential equation $dy/dx = 42 - y$ will show

(A) a line with slope -1 and y-intercept 42.

(B) a vertical asymptote at $x = 42$.

(C) a horizontal asymptote at $y = 42$.

(D) a family of parabolas opening downward.

(E) a family of parabolas opening to the left.

72. Multiple Choice For which of the following differential equations will a slope field show nothing but negative slopes in the fourth quadrant?

(A) $\dfrac{dy}{dx} = -\dfrac{x}{y}$ **(B)** $\dfrac{dy}{dx} = xy + 5$ **(C)** $\dfrac{dy}{dx} = xy^2 - 2$

(D) $\dfrac{dy}{dx} = \dfrac{x^3}{x^2}$ **(E)** $\dfrac{dy}{dx} = \dfrac{y}{x^2} - 3$

73. Multiple Choice If $dy/dx = 2xy$ and $y = 1$ when $x = 0$, then $y =$

(A) y^{2x} **(B)** e^{x^2} **(C)** x^2y **(D)** $x^2y + 1$ **(E)** $\dfrac{x^2y^2}{2} + 1$

74. Multiple Choice Which of the following differential equations would produce the slope field shown below?

(A) $\dfrac{dy}{dx} = y - |x|$ **(B)** $\dfrac{dy}{dx} = |y| - x$

(C) $\dfrac{dy}{dx} = |y - x|$ **(D)** $\dfrac{dy}{dx} = |y + x|$

(E) $\dfrac{dy}{dx} = |y| - |x|$

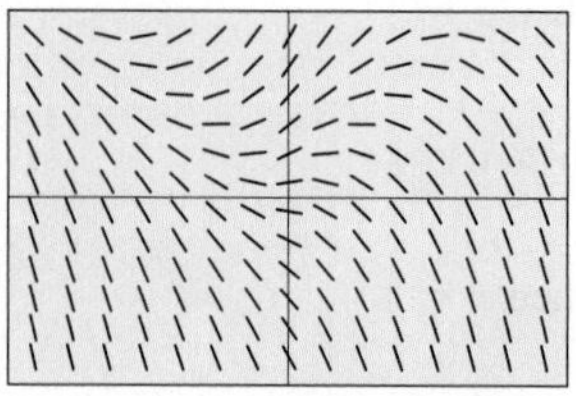

$[-3, 3]$ by $[-1.98, 1.98]$

Explorations

75. *Solving Differential Equations* Let $\frac{dy}{dx} = x - \frac{1}{x^2}$.

(a) Find a solution to the differential equation in the interval $(0, \infty)$ that satisfies $y(1) = 2$.

(b) Find a solution to the differential equation in the interval $(-\infty, 0)$ that satisfies $y(-1) = 1$.

(c) Show that the following piecewise function is a solution to the differential equation for any values of C_1 and C_2.

$$y = \begin{cases} \frac{1}{x} + \frac{x^2}{2} + C_1 & x < 0 \\ \frac{1}{x} + \frac{x^2}{2} + C_2 & x > 0 \end{cases}$$

(d) Choose values for C_1 and C_2 so that the solution in part (c) agrees with the solutions in parts (a) and (b).

(e) Choose values for C_1 and C_2 so that the solution in part (c) satisfies $y(2) = -1$ and $y(-2) = 2$.

76. *Solving Differential Equations* Let $\frac{dy}{dx} = \frac{1}{x}$.

(a) Show that $y = \ln x + C$ is a solution to the differential equation in the interval $(0, \infty)$.

(b) Show that $y = \ln(-x) + C$ is a solution to the differential equation in the interval $(-\infty, 0)$.

(c) Writing to Learn Explain why $y = \ln|x| + C$ is a solution to the differential equation in the domain $(-\infty, 0) \cup (0, \infty)$.

(d) Show that the function

$$y = \begin{cases} \ln(-x) + C_1, & x < 0 \\ \ln x + C_2, & x > 0 \end{cases}$$

is a solution to the differential equation for any values of C_1 and C_2.

Extending the Ideas

77. *Second-Order Differential Equations* Find the general solution to each of the following second-order differential equations by first finding dy/dx and then finding y. The general solution will have two unknown constants.

(a) $\frac{d^2y}{dx^2} = 12x + 4$ **(b)** $\frac{d^2y}{dx^2} = e^x + \sin x$

(c) $\frac{d^2y}{dx^2} = x^3 + x^{-3}$

78. *Second-Order Differential Equations* Find the specific solution to each of the following second-order initial value problems by first finding dy/dx and then finding y.

(a) $\frac{d^2y}{dx^2} = 24x^2 - 10$. When $x = 1$, $\frac{dy}{dx} = 3$ and $y = 5$.

(b) $\frac{d^2y}{dx^2} = \cos x - \sin x$. When $x = 0$, $\frac{dy}{dx} = 2$ and $y = 0$

(c) $\frac{d^2y}{dx^2} = e^x - x$. When $x = 0$, $\frac{dy}{dx} = 0$ and $y = 1$.

79. *Differential Equation Potpourri* For each of the following differential equations, find at least one particular solution. You will need to call on past experience with functions you have differentiated. For a greater challenge, find the general solution.

(a) $y' = x$ **(b)** $y' = -x$ **(c)** $y' = y$

(d) $y' = -y$ **(e)** $y' = xy$

80. *Second-Order Potpourri* For each of the following second-order differential equations, find at least one particular solution. You will need to call on past experience with functions you have differentiated. For a significantly greater challenge, find the general solution (which will involve two unknown constants).

(a) $y'' = x$ **(b)** $y'' = -x$ **(c)** $y'' = -\sin x$

(d) $y'' = y$ **(e)** $y'' = -y$

7.2 Antidifferentiation by Substitution

What you will learn about . . .

- Indefinite Integrals
- Leibniz Notation and Antiderivatives
- Substitution in Indefinite Integrals
- Substitution in Definite Integrals

and why . . .

Antidifferentiation techniques were historically crucial for applying the results of calculus.

Indefinite Integrals

If $y = f(x)$ we can denote the derivative of f by either dy/dx or $f'(x)$. What can we use to denote the *antiderivative* of f? We have seen that the general solution to the differential equation $dy/dx = f(x)$ actually consists of an infinite family of functions of the form $F(x) + C$, where $F'(x) = f(x)$. Both the name for this family of functions and the symbol we use to denote it are closely related to the definite integral because of the Fundamental Theorem of Calculus.

DEFINITION Indefinite Integral

The family of all antiderivatives of a function $f(x)$ is the **indefinite integral of f with respect to x** and is denoted by $\int f(x)dx$.

If F is any function such that $F'(x) = f(x)$, then $\int f(x)dx = F(x) + C$, where C is an arbitrary constant, called the **constant of integration.**

As in Chapter 6, the symbol $\int$ is an **integral sign,** the function f is the **integrand** of the integral, and x is the **variable of integration.**

Notice that an indefinite integral is not at all like a definite integral, despite the similarities in notation and name. A definite integral is a *number*, the limit of a sequence of Riemann sums. An indefinite integral is a *family of functions* having a common derivative. If the Fundamental Theorem of Calculus had not provided such a dramatic link between antiderivatives and integration, we would surely be using a different name and symbol for the general antiderivative today.

EXAMPLE 1 Evaluating an Indefinite Integral

Evaluate $\int (x^2 - \sin x)\, dx$.

SOLUTION

Evaluating this indefinite integral is just like solving the differential equation $dy/dx = x^2 - \sin x$. Our past experience with derivatives leads us to conclude that

$$\int (x^2 - \sin x)\, dx = \frac{x^3}{3} + \cos x + C$$

(as you can check by differentiating).

Now Try Exercise 3.

You have actually been finding antiderivatives since Section 6.3, so Example 1 should hardly have seemed new. Indeed, each derivative formula in Chapters 3 and 4 could be turned around to yield a corresponding indefinite integral formula. We list some of the most useful such indefinite integral formulas on the next page. Be sure to familiarize yourself with these before moving on to the next section, in which function composition becomes an issue. (Incidentally, it is in anticipation of the next section that we give some of these formulas in terms of the variable u rather than x.)

Properties of Indefinite Integrals

$$\int k\,f(x)dx = k\int f(x)\,dx \quad \text{for any constant } k$$

$$\int (f(x) \pm g(x))\,dx = \int f(x)\,dx \pm \int g(x)\,dx$$

Power Formulas

$$\int u^n\,du = \frac{u^{n+1}}{n+1} + C \text{ when } n \neq -1$$

$$\int u^{-1}\,du = \int \frac{1}{u}\,du = \ln|u| + C$$

(see Example 2)

Trigonometric Formulas

$$\int \cos u\,du = \sin u + C \qquad \int \sin u\,du = -\cos u + C$$

$$\int \sec^2 u\,du = \tan u + C \qquad \int \csc^2 u\,du = -\cot u + C$$

$$\int \sec u \tan u\,du = \sec u + C \qquad \int \csc u \cot u\,du = -\csc u + C$$

Exponential and Logarithmic Formulas

$$\int e^u\,du = e^u + C \qquad \int a^u\,du = \frac{a^u}{\ln a} + C$$

$$\int \ln u\,du = u \ln u - u + C \quad \text{(See Example 2)}$$

$$\int \log_a u\,du = \int \frac{\ln u}{\ln a}\,du = \frac{u \ln u - u}{\ln a} + C$$

A Note on Absolute Value

Since the indefinite integral does not specify a domain, you should always use the absolute value when finding $\int 1/u\,du$. The function $\ln u + C$ is only defined on positive u-intervals, while the function $\ln|u| + C$ is defined on both the positive *and* negative intervals in the domain of $1/u$ (see Example 2).

EXAMPLE 2 Verifying Antiderivative Formulas

Verify the antiderivative formulas:

(a) $\int u^{-1}\,du = \int \frac{1}{u}\,du = \ln|u| + C$ **(b)** $\int \ln u\,du = u \ln u - u + C$

SOLUTION

We can verify antiderivative formulas by differentiating.

(a) For $u > 0$, we have $\frac{d}{du}(\ln|u| + C) = \frac{d}{du}(\ln u + C) = \frac{1}{u} + 0 = \frac{1}{u}$.

For $u < 0$, we have $\frac{d}{du}(\ln|u| + C) = \frac{d}{du}(\ln(-u) + C) = \frac{1}{-u}(-1) + 0 = \frac{1}{u}$.

Since $\frac{d}{du}(\ln|u| + C) = \frac{1}{u}$ in either case, $\ln|u| + C$ is the general antiderivative of the function $\frac{1}{u}$ on its entire domain.

(b) $\frac{d}{du}(u \ln u - u + C) = 1 \cdot \ln u + u\left(\frac{1}{u}\right) - 1 + 0 = \ln u + 1 - 1 = \ln u.$

Now Try Exercise 11.

Leibniz Notation and Antiderivatives

The appearance of the differential "dx" in the definite integral $\int_a^b f(x)\,dx$ is easily explained by the fact that it is the limit of a Riemann sum of the form $\sum_{k=1}^{n} f(x_k)\cdot\Delta x$ (see Section 6.2). The same "dx" almost seems unnecessary when we use the indefinite integral $\int f(x)dx$ to represent the general antiderivative of f, but in fact it is quite useful for *dealing with the effects of the Chain Rule* when function composition is involved. Exploration 1 will show you why this is an important consideration.

EXPLORATION 1 Are $\int f(u)\,du$ and $\int f(u)\,dx$ the Same Thing?

Let $u = x^2$ and let $f(u) = u^3$.

1. Find $\int f(u)\,du$ as a function of u.
2. Use your answer to question 1 to write $\int f(u)\,du$ as a function of x.
3. Show that $f(u) = x^6$ and find $\int f(u)\,dx$ as a function of x.
4. Are the answers to questions 2 and 3 the same?

Exploration 1 shows that the notation $\int f(u)$ is not sufficient to describe an antiderivative when u is a function of another variable. Just as du/du is different from du/dx when differentiating, $\int f(u)\,du$ is different from $\int f(u)\,dx$ when antidifferentiating. We will use this fact to our advantage in the next section, where the importance of "dx" or "du" in the integral expression will become even more apparent.

EXAMPLE 3 Paying Attention to the Differential

Let $f(x) = x^3 + 1$ and let $u = x^2$. Find each of the following antiderivatives in terms of x:

(a) $\displaystyle\int f(x)\,dx$ **(b)** $\displaystyle\int f(u)\,du$ **(c)** $\displaystyle\int f(u)\,dx$

SOLUTION

(a) $$\int f(x)\,dx = \int (x^3+1)\,dx = \frac{x^4}{4} + x + C$$

(b) $$\int f(u)\,du = \int (u^3+1)\,du = \frac{u^4}{4} + u + C = \frac{(x^2)^4}{4} + x^2 + C = \frac{x^8}{4} + x^2 + C$$

(c) $$\int f(u)\,dx = \int (u^3+1)\,dx = \int ((x^2)^3+1)\,dx = \int (x^6+1)\,dx = \frac{x^7}{7} + x + C$$

Now Try Exercise 15.

Substitution in Indefinite Integrals

A change of variables can often turn an unfamiliar integral into one that we can evaluate. The important point to remember is that it is *not sufficient* to change an integral of the form $\int f(x)\,dx$ into an integral of the form $\int g(u)\,dx$. The differential matters. A complete substitution changes the integral $\int f(x)\,dx$ into an integral of the form $\int g(u)\,du$.

EXAMPLE 4 Using Substitution

Evaluate $\int \sin x\, e^{\cos x}\,dx$.

continued

SOLUTION

Let $u = \cos x$. Then $du/dx = -\sin x$, from which we conclude that $du = -\sin x\, dx$. We rewrite the integral and proceed as follows:

$$\int \sin x\, e^{\cos x}\, dx = -\int (-\sin x)e^{\cos x}\, dx$$
$$= -\int e^{\cos x} \cdot (-\sin x)\, dx$$
$$= -\int e^{u}\, du \quad \text{Substitute } u \text{ for } \cos x \text{ and } du \text{ for } -\sin x\, dx.$$
$$= -e^{u} + C$$
$$= -e^{\cos x} + C \quad \text{Re-substitute } \cos x \text{ for } u \text{ after antidifferentiating.}$$

Now Try Exercise 19.

If you differentiate $-e^{\cos x} + C$, you will find that a factor of $-\sin x$ appears when you apply the Chain Rule. The technique of *antidifferentiation by substitution* reverses that effect by absorbing the $-\sin x$ into the differential du when you change $\int \sin x\, e^{\cos x}\, dx$ into $-\int e^{u}\, du$. That is why a "u-substitution" always involves a "du-substitution" to convert the integral into a form ready for antidifferentiation.

EXAMPLE 5 Using Substitution

Evaluate $\int x^2\sqrt{5 + 2x^3}\, dx$.

SOLUTION

This integral invites the substitution $u = 5 + 2x^3$, $du = 6x^2\, dx$.

$$\int x^2 \sqrt{5 + 2x^3}\, dx. = \int (5 + 2x^3)^{1/2} \cdot x^2\, dx$$
$$= \frac{1}{6}\int (5 + 2x^3)^{1/2} \cdot 6x^2\, dx \quad \text{Set up the substitution with a factor of 6.}$$
$$= \frac{1}{6}\int u^{1/2}\, du \quad \text{Substitute } u \text{ for } 5 + 2x^3 \text{ and } du \text{ for } 6x^2\, dx.$$
$$= \frac{1}{6}\left(\frac{2}{3}\right)u^{3/2} + C$$
$$= \frac{1}{9}(5 + 2x^3)^{3/2} + C \quad \text{Re-substitute after antidifferentiating.}$$

Now Try Exercise 27.

EXAMPLE 6 Using Substitution

Evaluate $\int \cot 7x\, dx$.

SOLUTION

We do not recall a function whose derivative is $\cot 7x$, but a basic trigonometric identity changes the integrand into a form that invites the substitution $u = \sin 7x$, $du = 7\cos 7x\, dx$. We rewrite the integrand as shown below.

$$\int \cot 7x\, dx = \int \frac{\cos 7x}{\sin 7x}\, dx \quad \text{Trigonometric identity}$$
$$= \frac{1}{7}\int \frac{7\cos 7x\, dx}{\sin 7x} \quad \text{Note that } du = 7\cos 7x\, dx \text{ when } u = \sin 7x. \text{ We multiply by } \frac{1}{7}\cdot 7\text{, or 1.}$$

continued

$$= \frac{1}{7}\int \frac{du}{u}$$ Substitute u for 7 sin x and du for 7 cos 7x dx.

$$= \frac{1}{7}\ln |u| + C$$ Notice the absolute value!

$$= \frac{1}{7}\ln |\sin 7x| + C$$ Resubstitute sin 7x for u after antidifferentiating.

Now Try Exercise 29.

EXAMPLE 7 Setting Up a Substitution with a Trigonometric Identity

Find the indefinite integrals. In each case you can use a trigonometric identity to set up a substitution.

(a) $\int \frac{dx}{\cos^2 2x}$ **(b)** $\int \cot^2 3x\, dx$ **(c)** $\int \cos^3 x\, dx$

SOLUTION

(a) $\int \frac{dx}{\cos^2 2x} = \int \sec^2 2x\, dx = \frac{1}{2}\int \sec^2 2x \cdot 2dx$

$$= \frac{1}{2}\int \sec^2 u\, du$$ Let $u = 2x$ and $du = 2\,dx$.

$$= \frac{1}{2}\tan u + C$$

$$= \frac{1}{2}\tan 2x + C$$ Resubstitute after antidifferentiating.

(b) $\int \cot^2 3x\, dx = \int (\csc^2 3x - 1)\, dx$

$$= \frac{1}{3}\int (\csc^2 3x - 1) \cdot 3\, dx$$

$$= \frac{1}{3}\int (\csc^2 u - 1) \cdot du$$ Let $u = 3x$ and $du = 3\,dx$.

$$= \frac{1}{3}(-\cot u - u) + C$$

$$= \frac{1}{3}(-\cot 3x - 3x) + C$$

$$= -\frac{1}{3}\cot 3x - x + C$$ Resubstitute after antidifferentiation.

(c) $\int \cos^3 x\, dx = \int (\cos^2 x) \cos x\, dx$

$$= \int (1 - \sin^2 x) \cos x\, dx$$

$$= \int (1 - u^2)\, du$$ Let $u = \sin x$ and $du = \cos x\, dx$.

$$= u - \frac{u^3}{3} + C$$

$$= \sin x - \frac{\sin^3 x}{3} + C$$ Resubstitute after antidifferentiating.

Now Try Exercise 47.

Substitution in Definite Integrals

Antiderivatives play an important role when we evaluate a definite integral by the Fundamental Theorem of Calculus, and so, consequently, does substitution. In fact, if we make full use of our substitution of variables and change the interval of integration to match the u-substitution in the integrand, we can avoid the "resubstitution" step in the previous four examples.

EXAMPLE 8 Evaluating a Definite Integral by Substitution

Evaluate $\int_0^{\pi/3} \tan x \sec^2 x\, dx$.

SOLUTION

Let $u = \tan x$ and $du = \sec^2 x\, dx$.

Note also that $u(0) = \tan 0 = 0$ and $u(\pi/3) = \tan(\pi/3) = \sqrt{3}$.

So

$$\int_0^{\pi/3} \tan x \sec^2 x\, dx = \int_0^{\sqrt{3}} u\, du \qquad \text{Substitute } u\text{-interval for } x\text{-interval.}$$

$$= \frac{u^2}{2}\bigg|_0^{\sqrt{3}} = \frac{3}{2} - 0 = \frac{3}{2}.$$

Now Try Exercise 55.

EXAMPLE 9 That Absolute Value Again

Evaluate $\int_0^1 \frac{x}{x^2 - 4}\, dx$.

SOLUTION

Let $u = x^2 - 4$ and $du = 2x\, dx$. Then $u(0) = 0^2 - 4 = -4$ and $u(1) = 1^2 - 4 = -3$.

So

$$\int_0^1 \frac{x}{x^2 - 4}\, dx = \frac{1}{2}\int_0^1 \frac{2x\, dx}{x^2 - 4}$$

$$= \frac{1}{2}\int_{-4}^{-3} \frac{du}{u} \qquad \text{Substitute } u\text{-interval for } x\text{-interval.}$$

$$= \frac{1}{2} \ln|u| \bigg|_{-4}^{-3}$$

$$= \frac{1}{2}(\ln 3 - \ln 4) = \frac{1}{2} \ln\left(\frac{3}{4}\right).$$

Notice that $\ln u$ would not have existed over the interval of integration $[-4, -3]$. The absolute value in the antiderivative is important.

Now Try Exercise 63.

Finally, consider this historical note. The technique of u-substitution derived its importance from the fact that it was a powerful tool for antidifferentiation. Antidifferentiation derived its importance from the Fundamental Theorem, which established it as the way to evaluate definite integrals. Definite integrals derived their importance from real-world applications. While the applications are no less important today, the fact that the definite integrals can be easily evaluated by technology has made the world less reliant on antidifferentiation, and hence less reliant on u-substitution. Consequently, you have seen in this book only a sampling of the substitution tricks calculus students would have routinely studied in the past. You may see more of them in a differential equations course.

Quick Review 7.2 *(For help, go to Sections 4.1 and 4.4.)*

Exercise numbers with a gray background indicate problems that the authors have designed to be solved *without a calculator.*

In Exercises 1 and 2, evaluate the definite integral.

1. $\int_0^2 x^4\,dx$ **2.** $\int_1^5 \sqrt{x-1}\,dx$

In Exercises 3–10, find dy/dx.

3. $y = \int_2^x 3^t\,dt$ **4.** $y = \int_0^x 3^t\,dt$

5. $y = (x^3 - 2x^2 + 3)^4$

6. $y = \sin^2(4x - 5)$

7. $y = \ln \cos x$

8. $y = \ln \sin x$

9. $y = \ln(\sec x + \tan x)$

10. $y = \ln(\csc x + \cot x)$

Section 7.2 Exercises

In Exercises 1–6, find the indefinite integral.

1. $\int (\cos x - 3x^2)\,dx$ **2.** $\int x^{-2}\,dx$

3. $\int \left(t^2 - \frac{1}{t^2}\right) dt$ **4.** $\int \frac{dt}{t^2 + 1}$

5. $\int (3x^4 - 2x^{-3} + \sec^2 x)\,dx$

6. $\int (2e^x + \sec x \tan x - \sqrt{x})\,dx$

In Exercises 7–12, use differentiation to verify the antiderivative formula.

7. $\int \csc^2 u\,du = -\cot u + C$ **8.** $\int \csc u \cot u = -\csc u + C$

9. $\int e^{2x}\,dx = \frac{1}{2}e^{2x} + C$ **10.** $\int 5^x\,dx = \frac{1}{\ln 5}5^x + C$

11. $\int \frac{1}{1+u^2}\,du = \tan^{-1} u + C$ **12.** $\int \frac{1}{\sqrt{1-u^2}}\,du = \sin^{-1} u + C$

In Exercises 13–16, verify that $\int f(u)\,du \neq \int f(u)\,dx$

13. $f(u) = \sqrt{u}$ and $u = x^2\ (x > 0)$

14. $f(u) = u^2$ and $u = x^5$

15. $f(u) = e^u$ and $u = 7x$ **16.** $f(u) = \sin u$ and $u = 4x$

In Exercises 17–24, use the indicated substitution to evaluate the integral. Confirm your answer by differentiation.

17. $\int \sin 3x\,dx, \quad u = 3x$

18. $\int x\cos(2x^2)\,dx, \quad u = 2x^2$

19. $\int \sec 2x \tan 2x\,dx, \quad u = 2x$

20. $\int 28(7x - 2)^3\,dx, \quad u = 7x - 2$

21. $\int \frac{dx}{x^2 + 9}, \quad u = \frac{x}{3}$ **22.** $\int \frac{9r^2\,dr}{\sqrt{1 - r^3}}, \quad u = 1 - r^3$

23. $\int \left(1 - \cos\frac{t}{2}\right)^2 \sin\frac{t}{2}\,dt, \quad u = 1 - \cos\frac{t}{2}$

24. $\int 8(y^4 + 4y^2 + 1)^2(y^3 + 2y)\,dy, \quad u = y^4 + 4y^2 + 1$

In Exercises 25–46, use substitution to evaluate the integral.

25. $\int \frac{dx}{(1-x)^2}$ **26.** $\int \sec^2(x + 2)\,dx$

27. $\int \sqrt{\tan x}\,\sec^2 x\,dx$

28. $\int \sec\left(\theta + \frac{\pi}{2}\right)\tan\left(\theta + \frac{\pi}{2}\right)d\theta$

29. $\int \tan(4x + 2)\,dx$ **30.** $\int 3(\sin x)^{-2}\,dx$

31. $\int \cos(3z + 4)\,dz$ **32.** $\int \sqrt{\cot x}\,\csc^2 x\,dx$

33. $\int \frac{\ln^6 x}{x}\,dx$ **34.** $\int \tan^7\left(\frac{x}{2}\right)\sec^2\left(\frac{x}{2}\right)dx$

35. $\int s^{1/3}\cos(s^{4/3} - 8)\,ds$ **36.** $\int \frac{dx}{\sin^2 3x}$

37. $\int \frac{\sin(2t + 1)}{\cos^2(2t + 1)}\,dt$ **38.** $\int \frac{6\cos t}{(2 + \sin t)^2}\,dt$

39. $\int \frac{dx}{x \ln x}$ **40.** $\int \tan^2 x \sec^2 x\,dx$

41. $\displaystyle\int \frac{x\,dx}{x^2+1}$

42. $\displaystyle\int \frac{40\,dx}{x^2+25}$

43. $\displaystyle\int \frac{dx}{\cot 3x}$

44. $\displaystyle\int \frac{dx}{\sqrt{5x+8}}$

45. $\displaystyle\int \sec x\,dx$ [*Hint:* Multiply the integrand by

$$\frac{\sec x + \tan x}{\sec x + \tan x}$$

and then use a substitution to integrate the result.]

46. $\displaystyle\int \csc x\,dx$ [*Hint:* Multiply the integrand by

$$\frac{\csc x + \cot x}{\csc x + \cot x}$$

and then use a substitution to integrate the result.]

In Exercises 47–52, use the given trigonometric identity to set up a u-substitution and then evaluate the indefinite integral.

47. $\displaystyle\int \sin^3 2x\,dx,\quad \sin^2 2x = 1 - \cos^2 2x$

48. $\displaystyle\int \sec^4 x\,dx,\quad \sec^2 x = 1 + \tan^2 x$

49. $\displaystyle\int 2\sin^2 x\,dx,\quad \cos 2x = 1 - 2\sin^2 x$

50. $\displaystyle\int 4\cos^2 x\,dx,\quad \cos 2x = 2\cos^2 x - 1$

51. $\displaystyle\int \tan^4 x\,dx,\quad \tan^2 x = \sec^2 x - 1$

52. $\displaystyle\int (\cos^4 x - \sin^4 x)dx,\quad \cos 2x = \cos^2 x - \sin^2 x$

In Exercises 53–66, make a u-substitution and integrate from $u(a)$ to $u(b)$.

53. $\displaystyle\int_0^3 \sqrt{y+1}\,dy$

54. $\displaystyle\int_0^1 r\sqrt{1-r^2}\,dr$

55. $\displaystyle\int_{-\pi/4}^0 \tan x \sec^2 x\,dx$

56. $\displaystyle\int_{-1}^1 \frac{5r}{(4+r^2)^2}\,dr$

57. $\displaystyle\int_0^1 \frac{10\sqrt{\theta}}{(1+\theta^{3/2})^2}\,d\theta$

58. $\displaystyle\int_{-\pi}^{\pi} \frac{\cos x}{\sqrt{4+3\sin x}}\,dx$

59. $\displaystyle\int_0^1 \sqrt{t^5+2t}\,(5t^4+2)\,dt$

60. $\displaystyle\int_0^{\pi/6} \cos^{-3} 2\theta \sin 2\theta\,d\theta$

61. $\displaystyle\int_0^7 \frac{dx}{x+2}$

62. $\displaystyle\int_2^5 \frac{dx}{2x-3}$

63. $\displaystyle\int_1^2 \frac{dt}{t-3}$

64. $\displaystyle\int_{\pi/4}^{3\pi/4} \cot x\,dx$

65. $\displaystyle\int_{-1}^3 \frac{x\,dx}{x^2+1}$

66. $\displaystyle\int_0^2 \frac{e^x\,dx}{3+e^x}$

Two Routes to the Integral In Exercises 67 and 68, make a substitution $u = \cdots$ (an expression in x), $du = \cdots$. Then

(a) integrate with respect to u from $u(a)$ to $u(b)$.

(b) find an antiderivative with respect to u, replace u by the expression in x, then evaluate from a to b.

67. $\displaystyle\int_0^1 \frac{x^3}{\sqrt{x^4+9}}\,dx$

68. $\displaystyle\int_{\pi/6}^{\pi/3} (1-\cos 3x)\sin 3x\,dx$

69. Show that

$$y = \ln\left|\frac{\cos 3}{\cos x}\right| + 5$$

is the solution to the initial value problem

$$\frac{dy}{dx} = \tan x,\quad f(3) = 5.$$

(See the discussion following Example 4, Section 6.4.)

70. Show that

$$y = \ln\left|\frac{\sin x}{\sin 2}\right| + 6$$

is the solution to the initial value problem

$$\frac{dy}{dx} = \cot x,\quad f(2) = 6.$$

Standardized Test Questions

71. True or False By u-substitution, $\int_0^{\pi/4} \tan^3 x \sec^2 x\,dx = \int_0^{\pi/4} u^3\,du$. Justify your answer.

72. True or False If f is positive and differentiable on $[a, b]$, then

$$\int_a^b \frac{f'(x)dx}{f(x)} = \ln\left(\frac{f(b)}{f(a)}\right).$$ Justify your answer.

73. Multiple Choice $\int \tan x\,dx =$

(A) $\dfrac{\tan^2 x}{2} + C$ **(B)** $\ln|\cot x| + C$ **(C)** $\ln|\cos x| + C$

(D) $-\ln|\cos x| + C$ **(E)** $-\ln|\cot x| + C$

74. Multiple Choice $\int_0^2 e^{2x}\,dx =$

(A) $\dfrac{e^4}{2}$ **(B)** $e^4 - 1$ **(C)** $e^4 - 2$ **(D)** $2e^4 - 2$ **(E)** $\dfrac{e^4 - 1}{2}$

75. Multiple Choice If $\int_3^5 f(x-a)\,dx = 7$ where a is a constant, then $\int_{3-a}^{5-a} f(x)\,dx =$

(A) $7 + a$ **(B)** 7 **(C)** $7 - a$ **(D)** $a - 7$ **(E)** -7

76. Multiple Choice If the differential equation $dy/dx = f(x)$ leads to the slope field shown below, which of the following could be $\int f(x)\,dx$?

(A) $\sin x + C$ **(B)** $\cos x + C$ **(C)** $-\sin x + C$

(D) $-\cos x + C$ **(E)** $\dfrac{\sin x}{2} + C$

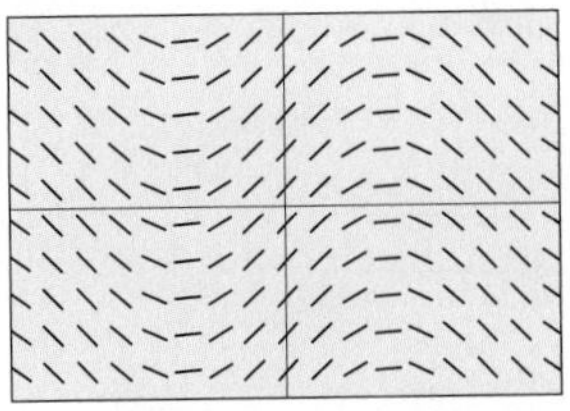

Explorations

77. *Constant of Integration* Consider the integral

$$\int \sqrt{x+1}\,dx.$$

(a) Show that $\int \sqrt{x+1}\,dx = \frac{2}{3}(x+1)^{3/2} + C.$

(b) Writing to Learn Explain why

$$y_1 = \int_0^x \sqrt{t+1}\,dt \quad \text{and} \quad y_2 = \int_3^x \sqrt{t+1}\,dt$$

are antiderivatives of $\sqrt{x+1}$.

(c) Use a table of values for $y_1 - y_2$ to find the value of C for which $y_1 = y_2 + C$.

(d) Writing to Learn Give a convincing argument that

$$C = \int_0^3 \sqrt{x+1}\,dx.$$

78. Group Activity *Making Connections* Suppose that

$$\int f(x)\,dx = F(x) + C.$$

(a) Explain how you can use the derivative of $F(x) + C$ to confirm the integration is correct.

(b) Explain how you can use a slope field of f and the graph of $y = F(x)$ to support your evaluation of the integral.

(c) Explain how you can use the graphs of $y_1 = F(x)$ and $y_2 = \int_0^x f(t)\,dt$ to support your evaluation of the integral.

(d) Explain how you can use a table of values for $y_1 - y_2$, y_1 and y_2 defined as in part (c), to support your evaluation of the integral.

(e) Explain how you can use graphs of f and NDER of $F(x)$ to support your evaluation of the integral.

(f) Illustrate parts (a)–(e) for $f(x) = \dfrac{x}{\sqrt{x^2+1}}$.

79. *Different Solutions?* Consider the integral $\int 2 \sin x \cos x\,dx$.

(a) Evaluate the integral using the substitution $u = \sin x$.

(b) Evaluate the integral using the substitution $u = \cos x$.

(c) Writing to Learn Explain why the different-looking answers in parts (a) and (b) are actually equivalent.

80. *Different Solutions?* Consider the integral $\int 2 \sec^2 x \tan x\,dx$.

(a) Evaluate the integral using the substitution $u = \tan x$.

(b) Evaluate the integral using the substitution $u = \sec x$.

(c) Writing to Learn Explain why the different-looking answers in parts (a) and (b) are actually equivalent.

Extending the Ideas

81. *Trigonometric Substitution* Suppose $u = \sin^{-1} x$. Then $\cos u > 0$.

(a) Use the substitution $x = \sin u$, $dx = \cos u\,du$ to show that

$$\int \frac{dx}{\sqrt{1-x^2}} = \int 1\,du.$$

(b) Evaluate $\int 1\,du$ to show that $\int \frac{dx}{\sqrt{1-x^2}} = \sin^{-1} x + C.$

82. *Trigonometric Substitution* Suppose $u = \tan^{-1} x$.

(a) Use the substitution $x = \tan u$, $dx = \sec^2 u\,du$ to show that

$$\int \frac{dx}{1+x^2} = \int 1\,du.$$

(b) Evaluate $\int 1\,du$ to show that $\int \frac{dx}{1+x^2} = \tan^{-1} x + C.$

83. *Trigonometric Substitution* Suppose $\sqrt{x} = \sin y$.

(a) Use the substitution $x = \sin^2 y$, $dx = 2 \sin y \cos y\,dy$ to show that

$$\int_0^{1/2} \frac{\sqrt{x}\,dx}{\sqrt{1-x}} = \int_0^{\pi/4} 2 \sin^2 y\,dy.$$

(b) Use the identity given in Exercise 49 to evaluate the definite integral without a calculator.

84. *Trigonometric Substitution* Suppose $u = \tan^{-1} x$.

(a) Use the substitution $x = \tan u$, $dx = \sec^2 u\,du$ to show that

$$\int_0^{\sqrt{3}} \frac{dx}{\sqrt{1+x^2}} = \int_0^{\pi/3} \sec u\,du.$$

(b) Use the hint in Exercise 45 to evaluate the definite integral without a calculator.

7.3 Antidifferentiation by Parts

What you will learn about . . .

- Product Rule in Integral Form
- Solving for the Unknown Integral
- Tabular Integration
- Inverse Trigonometric and Logarithmic Functions

and why . . .

The Product Rule relates to derivatives as the technique of parts relates to antiderivatives.

Product Rule in Integral Form

When u and v are differentiable functions of x, the Product Rule for differentiation tells us that

$$\frac{d}{dx}(uv) = u\frac{dv}{dx} + v\frac{du}{dx}.$$

Integrating both sides with respect to x and rearranging leads to the integral equation

$$\int\left(u\frac{dv}{dx}\right)dx = \int\left(\frac{d}{dx}(uv)\right)dx - \int\left(v\frac{du}{dx}\right)dx$$
$$= uv - \int\left(v\frac{du}{dx}\right)dx.$$

When this equation is written in the simpler differential notation we obtain the following formula.

Integration by Parts Formula

$$\int u\,dv = uv - \int v\,du$$

LIPET

If you are wondering what to choose for *u*, here is what we usually do. Our first choice is a natural logarithm (L), if there is one. If there isn't, we look for an inverse trigonometric function (I). If there isn't one of these either, look for a polynomial (P). Barring that, look for an exponential (E) or a trigonometric function (T). That's the preference order: **L I P E T**.

In general, we want *u* to be something that simplifies when differentiated, and *dv* to be something that remains manageable when integrated.

This formula expresses one integral, $\int u\,dv$, in terms of a second integral, $\int v\,du$. With a proper choice of u and v, the second integral may be easier to evaluate than the first. This is the reason for the importance of the formula. When faced with an integral that we cannot handle analytically, we can replace it by one with which we might have more success.

EXAMPLE 1 Using Integration by Parts

Evaluate $\int x \cos x\,dx$.

SOLUTION

We use the formula $\int u\,dv = uv - \int v\,du$ with

$$u = x, \quad dv = \cos x\,dx.$$

To complete the formula, we take the differential of u and find the simplest antiderivative of $\cos x$.

$$du = dx \quad v = \sin x$$

Then,

$$\int \overset{u}{x}\,\overbrace{\cos x\,dx}^{dv} = \overset{u}{x}\,\overset{v}{\sin x} - \int \overset{v}{\sin x}\,\overset{du}{dx} = x\sin x + \cos x + C.$$

Now Try Exercise 1.

The goal of integration by parts is to go from an integral $\int u\,dv$ that we don't see how to evaluate to an integral $\int v\,du$ that we can evaluate. Keep in mind that integration by parts does not always work.

Let's examine the choices available for u and v in Example 1.

EXPLORATION 1 Choosing the Right u and dv

Not every choice of u and dv leads to success in antidifferentiation by parts. There is always a trade-off when we replace $\int u\,dv$ with $\int v\,du$, and we gain nothing if $\int v\,du$ is no easier to find than the integral we started with. Let us look at the other choices we might have made in Example 1 to find $\int x\cos x\,dx$.

1. Apply the parts formula to $\int x\cos x\,dx$, letting $u = 1$ and $dv = x\cos x\,dx$. Analyze the result to explain why the choice of $u = 1$ is never a good one.
2. Apply the parts formula to $\int x\cos x\,dx$, letting $u = x\cos x$ and $dv = dx$. Analyze the result to explain why this is not a good choice for this integral.
3. Apply the parts formula to $\int x\cos x\,dx$, letting $u = \cos x$ and $dv = x\,dx$. Analyze the result to explain why this is not a good choice for this integral.
4. What makes x a good choice for u and $\cos x\,dx$ a good choice for dv?

Sometimes we have to use integration by parts more than once to evaluate an integral.

EXAMPLE 2 Repeated Use of Integration by Parts

Evaluate $\int x^2 e^x\,dx$.

SOLUTION

With $u = x^2$, $dv = e^x\,dx$, $du = 2x\,dx$, and $v = e^x$, we have

$$\int \overset{u}{x^2}\,\overbrace{e^x\,dx}^{dv} = \overset{u}{x^2}\,\overset{v}{e^x} - \int \overset{v}{e^x}\,\overbrace{2x\,dx}^{du}$$

$$= x^2 e^x - 2\int x\,e^x\,dx.$$

The new integral is less complicated than the original because the exponent of x is reduced by one. To evaluate the integral on the right, we integrate by parts again, with $u = x$, $dv = e^x\,dx$. Then $du = dx$, $v = e^x$, and

$$\int \overset{u}{x}\,\overbrace{e^x\,dx}^{dv} = \overset{u}{x}\,\overset{v}{e^x} - \int \overset{v}{e^x}\,\overset{du}{dx} = x\,e^x - e^x + C.$$

Hence,

$$\int x^2 e^x\,dx = x^2e^x - 2\int xe^x\,dx$$

$$= x^2e^x - 2xe^x + 2e^x + C.$$

The technique of Example 2 can be applied repeatedly for any integral of the form $\int x^n e^x\,dx$ in which n is a positive integer, because differentiating x^n will eventually reduce the exponent to zero and lead to a final integral involving only e^x. Repeated integration by parts can be done most easily by the method of *tabular integration*, covered later in this section.

Now Try Exercise 5.

EXAMPLE 3 Solving an Initial Value Problem

Solve the differential equation $dy/dx = x\ln(x)$ subject to the initial condition $y = -1$ when $x = 1$. Confirm the solution graphically by showing that it conforms to the slope field.

continued

SOLUTION

We find the antiderivative of $x \ln(x)$ by using parts. It is usually a better idea to differentiate $\ln(x)$ than to antidifferentiate it. (Do you see why?) So we let $u = \ln(x)$ and $dv = x\,dx$.

$$y = \int x \ln(x)\,dx = \int \overset{u}{\ln(x)}\,\overbrace{x\,dx}^{dv}$$

$$= \overset{u}{\ln(x)}\overset{v}{\left(\frac{x^2}{2}\right)} - \int \overset{v}{\left(\frac{x^2}{2}\right)}\overbrace{\left(\frac{1}{x}\right)dx}^{du}$$

$$= \left(\frac{x^2}{2}\right)\ln(x) - \int \left(\frac{x}{2}\right)dx$$

$$= \left(\frac{x^2}{2}\right)\ln(x) - \frac{x^2}{4} + C$$

Using the initial condition,

$$-1 = \left(\frac{1}{2}\right)\ln(1) - \frac{1}{4} + C$$

$$-\frac{3}{4} = 0 + C$$

$$C = -\frac{3}{4}.$$

Thus

$$y = \left(\frac{x^2}{2}\right)\ln(x) - \frac{x^2}{4} - \frac{3}{4}.$$

Figure 7.9 shows a graph of this function superimposed on a slope field for $dy/dx = x\ln(x)$, to which it conforms nicely. ***Now Try Exercise 11.***

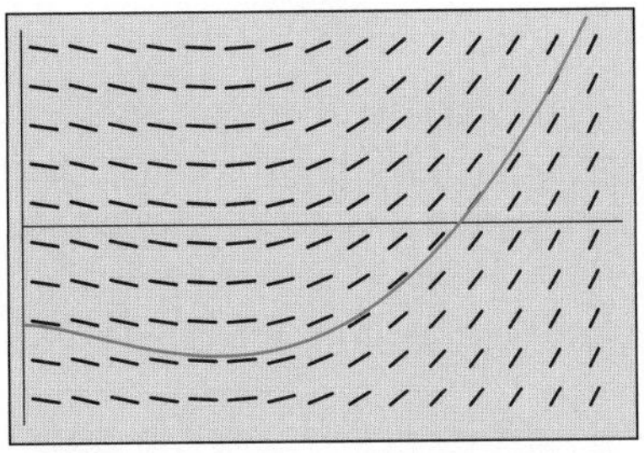

[0, 3] by [–1.5, 1.5]

Figure 7.9 The solution to the initial value problem in Example 3 conforms nicely to a slope field of the differential equation. (Example 3)

Solving for the Unknown Integral

Integrals like the one in the next example occur in electrical engineering. Their evaluation requires two integrations by parts, followed by solving for the unknown integral.

EXAMPLE 4 Solving for the Unknown Integral

Evaluate $\int e^x \cos x\,dx$.

SOLUTION

Let $u = e^x$, $dv = \cos x\,dx$. Then $du = e^x\,dx$, $v = \sin x$, and

$$\int \overset{u}{e^x}\,\overbrace{\cos x\,dx}^{dv} = \overset{u}{e^x}\,\overset{v}{\sin x} - \int \overset{v}{\sin x}\,\overbrace{e^x\,dx}^{du}$$

$$= e^x \sin x - \int e^x \sin x\,dx.$$

The second integral is like the first, except it has $\sin x$ in place of $\cos x$. To evaluate it, we use integration by parts again, with

$$u = e^x, \quad dv = \sin x\,dx, \quad v = -\cos x, \quad du = e^x\,dx.$$

continued

Then

$$\int e^x \cos x\,dx = e^x \sin x - \int \overset{u}{e^x}\,\overbrace{\sin x\,dx}^{dv}$$

$$= e^x \sin x - \left(\overset{u}{e^x}\overset{v}{(-\cos x)} - \int \overset{v}{(-\cos x)}\overbrace{e^x\,dx}^{du}\right)$$

$$= e^x \sin x + e^x \cos x - \int e^x \cos x\,dx.$$

The unknown integral now appears on both sides of the equation. Adding the integral to both sides gives

$$2\int e^x \cos x\,dx = e^x \sin x + e^x \cos x + C.$$

Dividing by 2 and renaming the constant of integration gives

$$\int e^x \cos x\,dx = \frac{e^x \sin x + e^x \cos x}{2} + C.$$

Now Try Exercise 17.

When making repeated use of integration by parts in circumstances like Example 4, once a choice for u and dv is made, it is usually not a good idea to switch choices in the second stage of the problem. Doing so will result in undoing the work. For example, if we had switched to the substitution $u = \sin x$, $dv = e^x\,dx$ in the second integration, we would have obtained

$$\int e^x \cos x\,dx = e^x \sin x - \int \overset{u}{\sin x}\,\overbrace{e^x\,dx}^{dv}$$

$$= e^x \sin x - \left(\overset{u}{\sin x}\,\overset{v}{e^x} - \int \overset{v}{e^x} - \overbrace{\cos x\,dx}^{du}\right)$$

$$= \int e^x \cos x\,dx,$$

undoing the first integration by parts.

Tabular Integration

We have seen that integrals of the form $\int f(x)g(x)dx$, in which f can be differentiated repeatedly to become zero and g can be integrated repeatedly without difficulty, are natural candidates for integration by parts. However, if many repetitions are required, the calculations can be cumbersome. In situations like this, there is a way to organize the calculations that saves a great deal of work. It is **tabular integration,** as shown in Examples 5 and 6.

Tic-Tac-Toe Method

A scene in the 1988 movie *Stand and Deliver* showed calculus teacher Jaime Escalante (played by Edward James Olmos) referring to this tabular method as the "Tic-Tac-Toe" method. Although the connection to the classic X-and-O grid game is not readily apparent, the name has endured in many classrooms ever since.

EXAMPLE 5 Using Tabular Integration

Evaluate $\int x^2 e^x\,dx$.

SOLUTION

With $f(x) = x^2$ and $g(x) = e^x$, we list:

$f(x)$ and its derivatives		$g(x)$ and its integrals
x^2	$(+)$	e^x
$2x$	$(-)$	e^x
2	$(+)$	e^x
0		e^x

We combine the products of the functions connected by the arrows according to the operation signs above the arrows to obtain

$$\int x^2 e^x\,dx = x^2 e^x - 2xe^x + 2e^x + C.$$

Compare this with the result in Example 2. **_Now Try Exercise 21._**

EXAMPLE 6 Using Tabular Integration

Evaluate $\int x^3 \sin x\,dx$.

SOLUTION

With $f(x) = x^3$ and $g(x) = \sin x$, we list:

$f(x)$ and its derivatives		$g(x)$ and its integrals
x^3	$(+)$	$\sin x$
$3x^2$	$(-)$	$-\cos x$
$6x$	$(+)$	$-\sin x$
6	$(-)$	$\cos x$
0		$\sin x$

Again we combine the products of the functions connected by the arrows according to the operation signs above the arrows to obtain

$$\int x^3 \sin x\,dx = -x^3\cos x + 3x^2 \sin x + 6x\cos x - 6\sin x + C.$$

Now Try Exercise 23.

Inverse Trigonometric and Logarithmic Functions

The method of parts is useful only when the integrand can be written as a product of two functions (u and dv). In fact, *any* integrand $f(x)\,dx$ satisfies that requirement, since we can let $u = f(x)$ and $dv = dx$. There are not many antiderivatives of the form $\int f(x)\,dx$ that you would want to find by parts, but there are some, most notably the antiderivatives of logarithmic and inverse trigonometric functions.

EXAMPLE 7 Antidifferentiating ln *x*

Find $\int \ln x\,dx$.

SOLUTION

If we want to use parts, we have little choice but to let $u = \ln x$ and $dv = dx$.

$$\int \overset{u}{\ln x}\,\overset{dv}{dx} = \overset{u}{(\ln x)}\overset{v}{(x)} - \int \overbrace{(x)\left(\frac{1}{x}\right)dx}^{v\quad du}$$

$$= x\ln x - \int 1\,dx$$

$$= x\ln x - x + C$$

EXAMPLE 8 Antidifferentiating $\sin^{-1} x$

Find the solution to the differential equation $dy/dx = \sin^{-1} x$ if the graph of the solution passes through the point (0, 0).

SOLUTION

We find $\int \sin^{-1} x\, dx$, letting $u = \sin^{-1} x$, $dv = dx$.

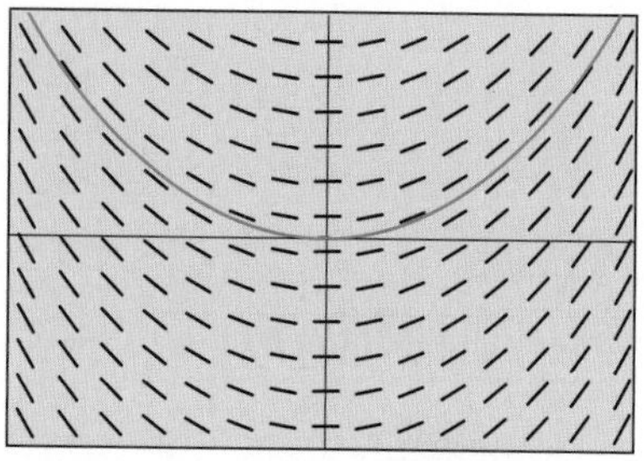

[−1, 1] by [−0.5, 0.5]

Figure 7.10 The solution to the initial value problem in Example 8 conforms nicely to the slope field of the differential equation. (Example 8)

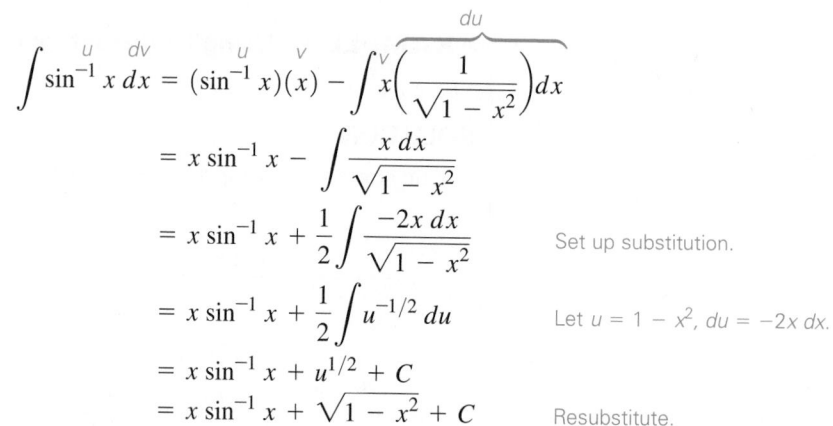

$$\int \overset{u}{\sin^{-1} x}\, \overset{dv}{dx} = \overset{u}{(\sin^{-1} x)}\overset{v}{(x)} - \int \overset{v}{x}\overset{du}{\left(\frac{1}{\sqrt{1-x^2}}\right)dx}$$

$$= x \sin^{-1} x - \int \frac{x\, dx}{\sqrt{1-x^2}}$$

$$= x \sin^{-1} x + \frac{1}{2}\int \frac{-2x\, dx}{\sqrt{1-x^2}} \qquad \text{Set up substitution.}$$

$$= x \sin^{-1} x + \frac{1}{2}\int u^{-1/2}\, du \qquad \text{Let } u = 1 - x^2,\ du = -2x\, dx.$$

$$= x \sin^{-1} x + u^{1/2} + C$$

$$= x \sin^{-1} x + \sqrt{1-x^2} + C \qquad \text{Resubstitute.}$$

Applying the initial condition $y = 0$ when $x = 0$, we conclude that the particular solution is $y = x \sin^{-1} x + \sqrt{1-x^2} - 1$.

A graph of $y = x \sin^{-1} x + \sqrt{1-x^2} - 1$ conforms nicely to the slope field for $dy/dx = \sin^{-1} x$, as shown in Figure 7.10.

Quick Review 7.3 *(For help, go to Sections 4.3 and 4.4.)*

Exercise numbers with a gray background indicate problems that the authors have designed to be solved *without a calculator.*

In Exercises 1–4, find dy/dx.

1. $y = x^3 \sin 2x$
2. $y = e^{2x} \ln(3x + 1)$
3. $y = \tan^{-1} 2x$
4. $y = \sin^{-1}(x + 3)$

In Exercises 5 and 6, solve for x in terms of y.

5. $y = \tan^{-1} 3x$
6. $y = \cos^{-1}(x + 1)$
7. Find the area under the arch of the curve $y = \sin \pi x$ from $x = 0$ to $x = 1$.
8. Solve the differential equation $dy/dx = e^{2x}$.
9. Solve the initial value problem $dy/dx = x + \sin x$, $y(0) = 2$.
10. Use differentiation to confirm the integration formula

$$\int e^x \sin x\, dx = \frac{1}{2} e^x (\sin x - \cos x).$$

Section 7.3 Exercises

In Exercises 1–10, find the indefinite integral.

1. $\int x \sin x\, dx$
2. $\int x e^x\, dx$
3. $\int 3t e^{2t}\, dt$
4. $\int 2t \cos(3t) dt$
5. $\int x^2 \cos x\, dx$
6. $\int x^2 e^{-x}\, dx$
7. $\int 3x^2 e^{2x}\, dx$
8. $\int x^2 \cos\left(\frac{x}{2}\right) dx$
9. $\int y \ln y\, dy$
10. $\int t^2 \ln t\, dt$

In Exercises 11–16, solve the initial value problem. (Then you can confirm your answer by checking that it conforms to the slope field of the differential equation.)

11. $\frac{dy}{dx} = (x + 2) \sin x$ and $y = 2$ when $x = 0$
12. $\frac{dy}{dx} = 2xe^{-x}$ and $y = 3$ when $x = 0$
13. $\frac{du}{dx} = x \sec^2 x$ and $u = 1$ when $x = 0$
14. $\frac{dz}{dx} = x^3 \ln x$ and $z = 5$ when $x = 1$

15. $\dfrac{dy}{dx} = x\sqrt{x - 1}$ and $y = 2$ when $x = 1$

16. $\dfrac{dy}{dx} = 2x\sqrt{x + 2}$ and $y = 0$ when $x = -1$

In Exercises 17–20, use parts and solve for the unknown integral.

17. $\displaystyle\int e^x \sin x\, dx$ **18.** $\displaystyle\int e^{-x} \cos x\, dx$

19. $\displaystyle\int e^x \cos 2x\, dx$ **20.** $\displaystyle\int e^{-x} \sin 2x\, dx$

In Exercises 21–24, use tabular integration to find the antiderivative.

21. $\displaystyle\int x^4 e^{-x}\, dx$ **22.** $\displaystyle\int (x^2 - 5x)e^x\, dx$

23. $\displaystyle\int x^3 e^{-2x}\, dx$ **24.** $\displaystyle\int x^3 \cos 2x\, dx$

In Exercises 25–28, evaluate the integral analytically. Support your answer using NINT.

25. $\displaystyle\int_0^{\pi/2} x^2 \sin 2x\, dx$ **26.** $\displaystyle\int_0^{\pi/2} x^3 \cos 2x\, dx$

27. $\displaystyle\int_{-2}^{3} e^{2x} \cos 3x\, dx$ **28.** $\displaystyle\int_{-3}^{2} e^{-2x} \sin 2x\, dx$

In Exercises 29–32, solve the differential equation.

29. $\dfrac{dy}{dx} = x^2 e^{4x}$ **30.** $\dfrac{dy}{dx} = x^2 \ln x$

31. $\dfrac{dy}{d\theta} = \theta \sec^{-1} \theta,\quad \theta > 1$ **32.** $\dfrac{dy}{d\theta} = \theta \sec \theta \tan \theta$

33. ***Finding Area*** Find the area of the region enclosed by the x-axis and the curve $y = x \sin x$ for

(a) $0 \le x \le \pi$, **(b)** $\pi \le x \le 2\pi$, **(c)** $0 \le x \le 2\pi$.

34. ***Finding Area*** Find the area of the region enclosed by the y-axis and the curves $y = x^2$ and $y = (x^2 + x + 1)e^{-x}$.

35. ***Average Value*** A retarding force, symbolized by the dashpot in the figure, slows the motion of the weighted spring so that the mass's position at time t is

$$y = 2e^{-t} \cos t, \quad t \ge 0.$$

Find the average value of y over the interval $0 \le t \le 2\pi$.

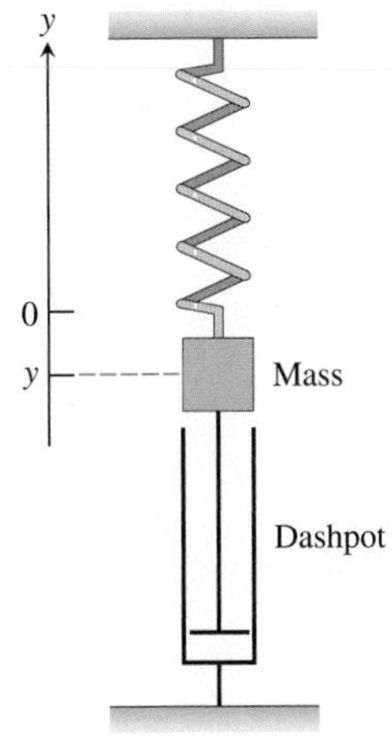

Standardized Test Questions

36. **True or False** If $f'(x) = g(x)$, then $\int x\, g(x)\, dx = x\, f(x) - \int f(x)\, dx$. Justify your answer.

37. **True or False** If $f'(x) = g(x)$, then $\int x^2 g(x)\, dx = x^2 f(x) - 2\int x\, f(x)\, dx$. Justify your answer.

38. **Multiple Choice** If $\int x^2 \cos x\, dx = h(x) - \int 2x \sin x\, dx$, then $h(x) =$

(A) $2 \sin x + 2x \cos x + C$

(B) $x^2 \sin x + C$

(C) $2x \cos x - x^2 \sin x + C$

(D) $4 \cos x - 2x \sin x + C$

(E) $(2 - x^2) \cos x - 4 \sin x + C$

39. **Multiple Choice** $\int x \sin(5x)\, dx =$

(A) $-x \cos (5x) + \sin (5x) + C$

(B) $-\dfrac{x}{5} \cos (5x) + \dfrac{1}{25} \sin (5x) + C$

(C) $-\dfrac{x}{5} \cos (5x) + \dfrac{1}{5} \sin (5x) + C$

(D) $\dfrac{x}{5} \cos (5x) + \dfrac{1}{25} \sin (5x) + C$

(E) $5x \cos (5x) - \sin (5x) + C$

40. **Multiple Choice** $\int x \csc^2 x\, dx =$

(A) $\dfrac{x^2 \csc^3 x}{6} + C$

(B) $x \cot x - \ln |\sin x| + C$

(C) $-x \cot x + \ln |\sin x| + C$

(D) $-x \cot x - \ln |\sin x| + C$

(E) $-x \sec^2 x - \tan x + C$

41. **Multiple Choice** The graph of $y = f(x)$ conforms to the slope field for the differential equation $dy/dx = 4x \ln x$, as shown in the graph below. Which of the following could be $f(x)$?

(A) $2x^2 (\ln x)^2 + 3$

(B) $x^3 \ln x + 3$

(C) $2x^2 \ln x - x^2 + 3$

(D) $(2x^2 + 3) \ln x - 1$

(E) $2x(\ln x)^2 - \dfrac{4}{3}(\ln x)^3 + 3$

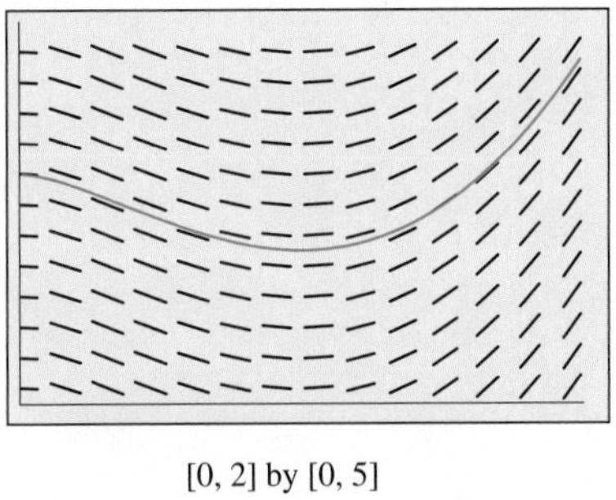

[0, 2] by [0, 5]

Explorations

42. Consider the integral $\int x^n e^x \, dx$. Use integration by parts to evaluate the integral if

(a) $n = 1$.

(b) $n = 2$.

(c) $n = 3$.

(d) Conjecture the value of the integral for any positive integer n.

(e) Writing to Learn Give a convincing argument that your conjecture in part (d) is true.

In Exercises 43–46, evaluate the integral by using a substitution prior to integration by parts.

43. $\int \sin \sqrt{x} \, dx$

44. $\int e^{\sqrt{3x+9}} \, dx$

45. $\int x^7 e^{x^2} \, dx$

46. $\int \sin (\ln r) \, dr$

In Exercises 47–50, use integration by parts to establish the *reduction formula*.

47. $\int x^n \cos x \, dx = x^n \sin x - n \int x^{n-1} \sin x \, dx$

48. $\int x^n \sin x \, dx = -x^n \cos x + n \int x^{n-1} \cos x \, dx$

49. $\int x^n e^{ax} \, dx = \dfrac{x^n e^{ax}}{a} - \dfrac{n}{a} \int x^{n-1} e^{ax} \, dx, \; a \neq 0$

50. $\int (\ln x)^n \, dx = x(\ln x)^n - n \int (\ln x)^{n-1} \, dx$

Extending the Ideas

51. *Integrating Inverse Functions* Assume that the function f has an inverse.

(a) Show that $\int f^{-1}(x) \, dx = \int y f'(y) \, dy$. [*Hint:* Use the substitution $y = f^{-1}(x)$.]

(b) Use integration by parts on the second integral in part (a) to show that

$$\int f^{-1}(x) \, dx = \int y f'(y) \, dy = x f^{-1}(x) - \int f(y) \, dy.$$

52. *Integrating Inverse Functions* Assume that the function f has an inverse. Use integration by parts directly to show that

$$\int f^{-1}(x) \, dx = x f^{-1}(x) - \int x \left(\frac{d}{dx} f^{-1}(x) \right) dx.$$

In Exercises 53–56, evaluate the integral using

(a) the technique of Exercise 51.

(b) the technique of Exercise 52.

(c) Show that the expressions (with $C = 0$) obtained in parts (a) and (b) are the same.

53. $\int \sin^{-1} x \, dx$

54. $\int \tan^{-1} x \, dx$

55. $\int \cos^{-1} x \, dx$

56. $\int \log_2 x \, dx$

57. *A Challenging Antiderivative* Use integration by parts to find $\int \sec^3 x \, dx$. [*Hint:* Start with $\int \sec^3 x \, dx = \int \sec x \cdot \sec^2 x \, dx$. Eventually you might want to look at Exercise 45 in the previous section.]

58. *An Equally Challenging Antiderivative* Use integration by parts to find $\int \csc^3 x \, dx$. [*Hint:* Start with $\int \csc^3 x \, dx = \int \csc x \cdot \csc^2 x \, dx$. Eventually you might want to look at Exercise 46 in the previous section.]

Quick Quiz for AP* Preparation: Sections 7.1–7.3

1. Multiple Choice Which of the following differential equations would produce the slope field shown below?

(A) $\dfrac{dy}{dx} = y - 3x$ (B) $\dfrac{dy}{dx} = y - \dfrac{x}{3}$

(C) $\dfrac{dy}{dx} = y + \dfrac{x}{3}$ (D) $\dfrac{dy}{dx} = y + \dfrac{x}{3}$

(E) $\dfrac{dy}{dx} = x - \dfrac{y}{3}$

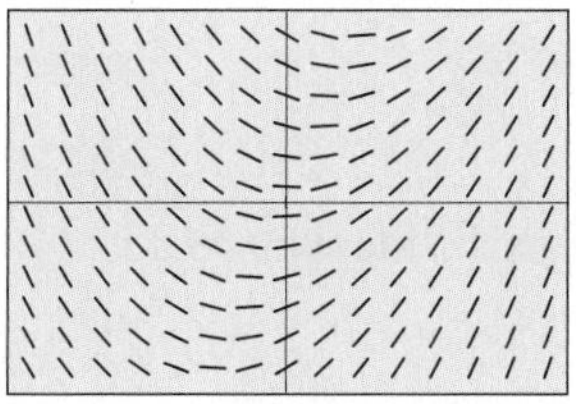

2. Multiple Choice If the substitution $\sqrt{x} = \sin y$ is made in the integrand of $\displaystyle\int_0^{1/2} \frac{\sqrt{x}}{\sqrt{1-x}}\,dx$, the resulting integral is

(A) $\displaystyle\int_0^{1/2} \sin^2 y\,dy$ (B) $\displaystyle 2\int_0^{1/2} \frac{\sin^2 y}{\cos y}\,dy$

(C) $\displaystyle 2\int_0^{\pi/4} \sin^2 y\,dy$ (D) $\displaystyle\int_0^{\pi/4} \sin^2 y\,dy$

(E) $\displaystyle 2\int_0^{\pi/6} \sin^2 y\,dy$

3. Multiple Choice $\int x\,e^{2x}\,dx =$

(A) $\dfrac{x\,e^{2x}}{2} - \dfrac{e^{2x}}{4} + C$ (B) $\dfrac{x\,e^{2x}}{2} - \dfrac{e^{2x}}{2} + C$

(C) $\dfrac{x\,e^{2x}}{2} + \dfrac{e^{2x}}{4} + C$ (D) $\dfrac{x\,e^{2x}}{2} + \dfrac{e^{2x}}{2} + C$

(E) $\dfrac{x^2\,e^{2x}}{4} + C$

4. Free Response Consider the differential equation $dy/dx = 2y - 4x$.

(a) The slope field for the differential equation is shown below. Sketch the solution curve that passes through the point $(0, 1)$ and sketch the solution curve that goes through the point $(0, -1)$.

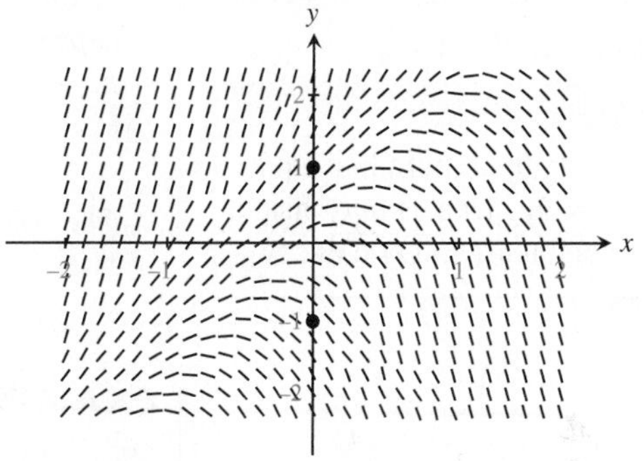

(b) There is a value of b for which $y = 2x + b$ is a solution to the differential equation. Find this value of b. Justify your answer.

(c) Let g be the function that satisfies the given differential equation with the initial condition $g(0) = 0$. It appears from the slope field that g has a local maximum at the point $(0, 0)$. Using the differential equation, prove analytically that this is so.

7.4 Exponential Growth and Decay

What you will learn about . . .

- Separable Differential Equations
- Law of Exponential Change
- Continuously Compounded Interest
- Radioactivity
- Modeling Growth with Other Bases
- Newton's Law of Cooling

and why . . .

Understanding the differential equation $dy/dx = ky$ gives us new insight into exponential growth and decay.

Separable Differential Equations

Before we revisit the topic of exponential growth (last seen as a precalculus topic in Chapter 1), we need to introduce the concept of separable differential equations.

DEFINITION Separable Differential Equation

A differential equation of the form $dy/dx = f(y)g(x)$ is called **separable.** We **separate the variables** by writing it in the form

$$\frac{1}{f(y)}\,dy = g(x)\,dx.$$

The solution is found by antidifferentiating each side with respect to its thusly isolated variable.

EXAMPLE 1 Solving by Separation of Variables

Solve for y if $dy/dx = (xy)^2$ and $y = 1$ when $x = 1$.

SOLUTION

The equation is separable because it can be written in the form $dy/dx = y^2x^2$, where $f(y) = y^2$ and $g(x) = x^2$. We separate the variables and antidifferentiate as follows.

$$y^{-2}\,dy = x^2\,dx \qquad \text{Separate the variables.}$$

$$\int y^{-2}\,dy = \int x^2\,dx \qquad \text{Prepare to antidifferentiate.}$$

$$-y^{-1} = \frac{x^3}{3} + C \qquad \text{Note that only one constant is needed.}$$

We then apply the initial condition to find C.

$$-1 = \frac{1}{3} + C \Rightarrow C = -\frac{4}{3}$$

$$-y^{-1} = \frac{x^3}{3} - \frac{4}{3}$$

$$y^{-1} = \frac{4 - x^3}{3}$$

$$y = \frac{3}{4 - x^3}$$

This solution is valid for the continuous section of the function that goes through the point $(1, 1)$, that is, on the domain $(-\infty, \sqrt[3]{4})$.

It is apparent that $y = 1$ when $x = 1$, but it is worth checking that $dy/dx = (xy)^2$.

$$y = \frac{3}{4 - x^3}$$

$$\frac{dy}{dx} = -3(4 - x^3)^{-2}(-3x^2)$$

$$\frac{dy}{dx} = \frac{9x^2}{(4 - x^3)^2} = x^2\left(\frac{3}{4 - x^3}\right)^2 = x^2y^2 = (xy)^2$$

Now Try Exercise 1.

Law of Exponential Change

You have probably solved enough exponential growth problems by now to recognize that they involve growth in which the rate of change is proportional to the amount present. The more bacteria in the dish, the faster they multiply. The more radioactive material present, the faster it decays. The greater your bank account (assuming it earns compounded interest), the faster it grows.

The differential equation that describes this growth is $dy/dt = ky$, where k is the *growth constant* (if positive) or the *decay constant* (if negative). We can solve this equation by separating the variables.

$$\frac{dy}{dt} = ky$$

$$\frac{1}{y}\,dy = k\,dt \qquad \text{Separate the variables.}$$

$$\ln|y| = kt + C \qquad \text{Antidifferentiate both sides.}$$

$$|y| = e^{kt+C} \qquad \text{Exponentiate both sides.}$$

$$|y| = e^C e^{kt} \qquad \text{Property of exponents.}$$

$$y = \pm e^C e^{kt} \qquad \text{Definition of absolute value.}$$

$$y = Ae^{kt} \qquad \text{Let } A = \pm e^C.$$

What if $A = 0$?

If $A = 0$, then the solution to $dy/dt = ky$ is the constant function $y = 0$. This function is technically of the form $y = Ae^{kt}$, but we do not consider it to be an exponential function. The initial condition in this case leads to a "trivial" solution.

This solution shows that the *only* growth function that results in a growth rate proportional to the amount present is, in fact, exponential. Note that the constant A is the amount present when $t = 0$, so it is usually denoted y_0.

The Law of Exponential Change

If y changes at a rate proportional to the amount present (that is, if $dy/dt = ky$), and if $y = y_0$ when $t = 0$, then

$$y = y_0 e^{kt}.$$

The constant k is the **growth constant** if $k > 0$ or the **decay constant** if $k < 0$.

Now Try Exercise 11.

Continuously Compounded Interest

Suppose that A_0 dollars are invested at a fixed annual interest rate r (expressed as a decimal). If interest is added to the account k times a year, the amount of money present after t years is

$$A(t) = A_0\left(1 + \frac{r}{k}\right)^{kt}.$$

The interest might be added ("compounded," bankers say) monthly $(k = 12)$, weekly $(k = 52)$, daily $(k = 365)$, or even more frequently, by the hour or by the minute.

If, instead of being added at discrete intervals, the interest is added continuously at a rate proportional to the amount in the account, we can model the growth of the account with the initial value problem.

Differential equation: $\dfrac{dA}{dt} = rA$

Initial condition: $A(0) = A_0$

It can be shown that

$$\lim_{k\to\infty} A_0\left(1+\frac{r}{k}\right)^{kt} = A_0e^{rt}.$$

We will see how this limit is evaluated in Section 9.2, Exercise 57.

The amount of money in the account after t years is then

$$A(t) = A_0e^{rt}.$$

Interest paid according to this formula is said to be **compounded continuously.** The number r is the **continuous interest rate.**

EXAMPLE 2 Compounding Interest Continuously

Suppose you deposit \$800 in an account that pays 6.3% annual interest. How much will you have 8 years later if the interest is **(a)** compounded continuously? **(b)** compounded quarterly?

SOLUTION

Here $A_0 = 800$ and $r = 0.063$. The amount in the account to the nearest cent after 8 years is

(a) $A(8) = 800e^{(0.063)(8)} = 1324.26.$

(b) $A(8) = 800\left(1+\dfrac{0.063}{4}\right)^{(4)(8)} = 1319.07.$

You might have expected to generate more than an additional \$5.19 with interest compounded continuously. ***Now Try Exercise 19.***

For radium-226, which used to be painted on watch dials to make them glow at night (a dangerous practice for the painters, who licked their brush-tips), t is measured in years and $k = 4.3 \times 10^{-4}$. For radon-222 gas, t is measured in days and $k = 0.18$. The decay of radium in the earth's crust is the source of the radon we sometimes find in our basements.

Radioactivity

When an atom emits some of its mass as radiation, the remainder of the atom re-forms to make an atom of some new element. This process of radiation and change is **radioactive decay,** and an element whose atoms go spontaneously through this process is **radioactive.** Radioactive carbon-14 decays into nitrogen. Radium, through a number of intervening radioactive steps, decays into lead.

Experiments have shown that at any given time the rate at which a radioactive element decays (as measured by the number of nuclei that change per unit of time) is approximately proportional to the number of radioactive nuclei present. Thus, the decay of a radioactive element is described by the equation $dy/dt = -ky$, $k > 0$. If y_0 is the number of radioactive nuclei present at time zero, the number still present at any later time t will be

$$y = y_0e^{-kt}, \quad k > 0.$$

Convention

It is conventional to use $-k$ ($k > 0$) here instead of k ($k < 0$) to emphasize that y is decreasing.

The **half-life** of a radioactive element is the time required for half of the radioactive nuclei present in a sample to decay. Example 3 shows the surprising fact that the half-life is a constant that depends only on the radioactive substance and not on the number of radioactive nuclei present in the sample.

EXAMPLE 3 Finding Half-Life

Find the half-life of a radioactive substance with decay equation $y = y_0e^{-kt}$ and show that the half-life depends only on k.

SOLUTION

Model The half-life is the solution to the equation

$$y_0e^{-kt} = \frac{1}{2}y_0.$$

continued

Solve Algebraically

$$e^{-kt} = \frac{1}{2} \qquad \text{Divide by } y_0.$$

$$-kt = \ln \frac{1}{2} \qquad \text{Take ln of both sides.}$$

$$t = -\frac{1}{k} \ln \frac{1}{2} = \frac{\ln 2}{k} \qquad \ln \frac{1}{a} = -\ln a$$

Interpret This value of t is the half-life of the element. It depends only on the value of k. Note that the number y_0 does not appear. ***Now Try Exercise 21.***

DEFINITION Half-life

The **half-life** of a radioactive substance with rate constant k $(k > 0)$ is

$$\text{half-life} = \frac{\ln 2}{k}.$$

Modeling Growth with Other Bases

As we have seen, the differential equation $dy/dt = ky$ leads to the exponential solution

$$y = y_0\, e^{kt},$$

where y_0 is the value of y at $t = 0$. We can also write this solution in the form

$$y = y_0\, b^{ht},$$

where b is any positive number not equal to 1, and h is another rate constant, related to k by the equation $k = h \ln b$. This means that exponential growth can be modeled in *any* positive base not equal to 1, enabling us to choose a convenient base to fit a given growth pattern, as the following exploration shows.

EXPLORATION 1 Choosing a Convenient Base

A certain population y is growing at a continuous rate so that the population doubles every 5 years.

1. Let $y = y_0\, 2^{ht}$. Since $y = 2\, y_0$ when $t = 5$, what is h? What is the relationship of h to the doubling period?
2. How long does it take for the population to triple?

A certain population y is growing at a continuous rate so that the population triples every 10 years.

3. Let $y = y_0\, 3^{ht}$. Since $y = 3\, y_0$ when $t = 10$, what is h? What is the relationship of h to the tripling period?
4. How long does it take for the population to double?

A certain isotope of sodium (Na-24) has a half-life of 15 hours. That is, half the atoms of Na-24 disintegrate into another nuclear form in fifteen hours.

5. Let $A = A_0(1/2)^{ht}$. Since $y = (1/2)\, y_0$ when $t = 15$, what is h? What is the relationship of h to the half-life?
6. How long does it take for the amount of radioactive material to decay to 10% of the original amount?

It is important to note that while the exponential growth model $y = y_0\, b^{ht}$ satisfies the differential equation $dy/dt = ky$ for any positive base b, it is only when $b = e$ that the growth constant k appears in the exponent as the coefficient of t. In general, the coefficient of t is the reciprocal of the time period required for the population to grow (or decay) by a factor of b.

EXAMPLE 4 Choosing a Base

At the beginning of the summer, the population of a hive of bald-faced hornets (which are actually wasps) is growing at a rate proportional to the population. From a population of 10 on May 1, the number of hornets grows to 50 in thirty days. If the growth continues to follow the same model, how many days after May 1 will the population reach 100?

SOLUTION

Since $dy/dt = ky$, the growth is exponential. Noting that the population grows by a factor of 5 in 30 days, we model the growth in base 5: $y = 10 \times 5^{(1/30)t}$. Now we need only solve the equation $100 = 10 \times 5^{(1/30)t}$ for t:

$$100 = 10 \times 5^{(1/30)t}$$
$$10 = 5^{(1/30)t}$$
$$\ln 10 = (1/30)t \ln 5$$
$$t = 30\left(\frac{\ln 10}{\ln 5}\right) = 42.920$$

Approximately 43 days will pass after May 1 before the population reaches 100.

Now Try Exercise 23.

EXAMPLE 5 Using Carbon-14 Dating

Scientists who use carbon-14 dating use 5700 years for its half-life. Find the age of a sample in which 10% of the radioactive nuclei originally present have decayed.

SOLUTION

We model the exponential decay in base 1/2: $A = A_0(1/2)^{t/5700}$. We seek the value of t for which $0.9A_0 = A_0(1/2)^{t/5700}$, or $(1/2)^{t/5700} = 0.9$.

Solving algebraically with logarithms,

$$(1/2)^{t/5700} = 0.9$$
$$(t/5700)\ln(1/2) = \ln(0.9)$$
$$t = 5700\left(\frac{\ln(0.9)}{\ln(0.5)}\right)$$
$$t \approx 866.$$

Interpreting the answer, we conclude that the sample is about 866 years old.

Now Try Exercise 25.

Newton's Law of Cooling

Soup left in a cup cools to the temperature of the surrounding air. A hot silver ingot immersed in water cools to the temperature of the surrounding water. In situations like these, the rate at which an object's temperature is changing at any given time is roughly proportional to the difference between its temperature and the temperature of the surrounding medium.

Hornets Aplenty

The hornet population in Example 4 can grow exponentially for a while, but the ecosystem cannot sustain such growth all summer. The model will eventually become logistic, as we will see in the next section. Nevertheless, given the right conditions, a bald-faced hornet nest can grow to be bigger than a basketball and house more than 600 workers.

Carbon-14 Dating

The decay of radioactive elements can sometimes be used to date events from Earth's past. The ages of rocks more than 2 billion years old have been measured by the extent of the radioactive decay of uranium (half-life 4.5 billion years!). In a living organism, the ratio of radioactive carbon, carbon-14, to ordinary carbon stays fairly constant during the lifetime of the organism, being approximately equal to the ratio in the organism's surroundings at the time. After the organism's death, however, no new carbon is ingested, and the proportion of carbon-14 decreases as the carbon-14 decays. It is possible to estimate the ages of fairly old organic remains by comparing the proportion of carbon-14 they contain with the proportion assumed to have been in the organism's environment at the time it lived. Archeologists have dated shells (which contain $CaCO_3$), seeds, and wooden artifacts this way. The estimate of 15,500 years for the age of the cave paintings at Lascaux, France, is based on carbon-14 dating. After generations of controversy, the Shroud of Turin, long believed by many to be the burial cloth of Christ, was shown by carbon-14 dating in 1988 to have been made after 1200 C.E.

J. Ernest Wilkins, Jr. (1923–)

By the age of nineteen, J. Ernest Wilkins had earned a Ph.D. degree in Mathematics from the University of Chicago. He then taught, served on the Manhattan project (the goal of which was to build the first atomic bomb), and worked as a mathematician and physicist for several corporations. In 1970, Dr. Wilkins joined the faculty at Howard University and served as head of the electrical engineering, physics, chemistry, and mathematics departments before retiring. He is currently working as Distinguished Professor of Applied Mathematics and Mathematical Physics at Clark Atlanta University.

This observation is *Newton's Law of Cooling,* although it applies to warming as well, and there is an equation for it.

If T is the temperature of the object at time t, and T_s is the surrounding temperature, then

$$\frac{dT}{dt} = -k(T - T_s). \qquad (1)$$

Since $dT = d(T - T_s)$, Equation 1 can be written as

$$\frac{d}{dt}(T - T_s) = -k(T - T_s).$$

Its solution, by the law of exponential change, is

$$T - T_s = (T_0 - T_s)e^{-kt},$$

where T_0 is the temperature at time $t = 0$. This equation also bears the name **Newton's Law of Cooling.**

EXAMPLE 6 Using Newton's Law of Cooling

A hard-boiled egg at 98°C is put in a pan under running 18°C water to cool. After 5 minutes, the egg's temperature is found to be 38°C. How much longer will it take the egg to reach 20°C?

SOLUTION

Model Using Newton's Law of Cooling with $T_S = 18$ and $T_0 = 98$, we have

$$T - 18 = (98 - 18)e^{-kt} \quad \text{or} \quad T = 18 + 80e^{-kt}.$$

To find k we use the information that $T = 38$ when $t = 5$.

$$38 = 18 + 80e^{-5k}$$
$$e^{-5k} = \frac{1}{4}$$
$$-5k = \ln\frac{1}{4} = -\ln 4$$
$$k = \frac{1}{5}\ln 4$$

The egg's temperature at time t is $T = 18 + 80e^{-(0.2 \ln 4)t}$.

Solve Graphically We can now use a grapher to find the time when the egg's temperature is 20°C. Figure 7.11 shows that the graphs of

$$y = 20 \quad \text{and} \quad y = T = 18 + 80e^{-(0.2 \ln 4)t}$$

intersect at about $t = 13.3$.

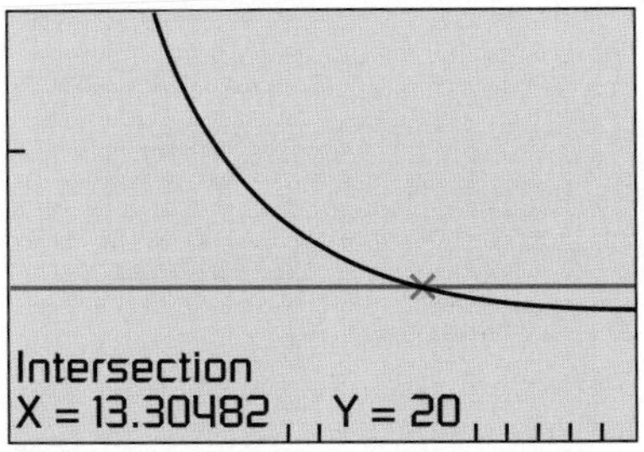

[0, 20] by [10, 40]

Figure 7.11 The egg will reach 20°C about 13.3 min after being placed in the pan to cool. (Example 6)

Interpret The egg's temperature will reach 20°C in about 13.3 min after it is put in the pan under running water to cool. Because it took 5 min to reach 38°C, it will take slightly more than 8 additional minutes to reach 20°C.

Now Try Exercise 31.

The next example shows how to use exponential regression to fit a function to real data. A CBL™ temperature probe was used to collect the data.

TABLE 7.1 Experimental Data

Time (sec)	T (°C)	$T - T_s$ (°C)
2	64.8	60.3
5	49.0	44.5
10	31.4	26.9
15	22.0	17.5
20	16.5	12.0
25	14.2	9.7
30	12.0	7.5

EXAMPLE 7 Using Newton's Law of Cooling

A temperature probe (thermometer) is removed from a cup of coffee and placed in water that has a temperature of $T_s = 4.5$°C. Temperature readings T, as recorded in Table 7.1, are taken after 2 sec, 5 sec, and every 5 sec thereafter. Estimate

(a) the coffee's temperature at the time the temperature probe was removed.

(b) the time when the temperature probe reading will be 8°C.

SOLUTION

In this case, Newton's Law of Cooling predicts that $T - 4.5 = (T_0 - 4.5)e^{-kt}$. Notice that T itself is not an exponential function of time, but $T - 4.5$ is. For this reason we have added a third column to Table 7.1 to show the values of $T - 4.5$.

We use exponential regression to model the list in column 3 as an exponential function of the list in column 1, resulting in the exponential model

$$T - 4.5 = 61.66(0.9277^t).$$

Thus,

$$T = 4.5 + 61.66(0.9277^t)$$

gives a model for temperature T as a function of time t. Figure 7.12 shows a graph of this equation superimposed on the scatter plot for the (t, T) data. As expected, the fit is quite good.

(a) At time $t = 0$, when the probe was removed, the temperature was

$$T = 4.5 + 61.66(0.9277^0) \approx 66.16°C.$$

(b) Solve Graphically Figure 7.12b shows that the graphs of

$$y = 8 \quad \text{and} \quad y = T = 4.5 + 61.66(0.9277^t)$$

intersect at about $t = 38$.

Interpret The temperature of the coffee was about 66.2°C when the temperature probe was removed. The temperature probe will reach 8°C about 38 sec after it is removed from the coffee and placed in the water.

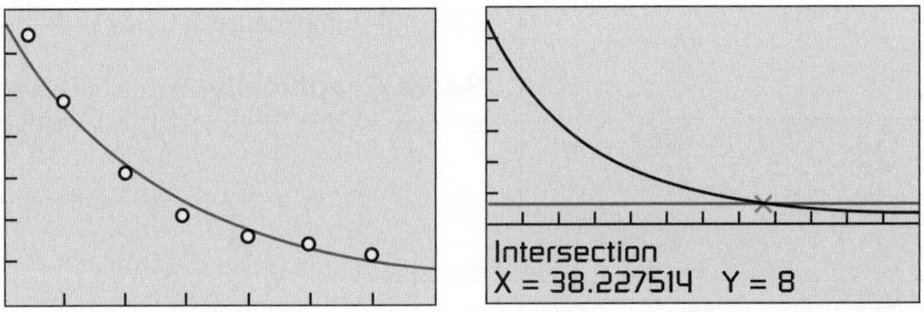

[0, 35] by [0, 70]

(a)

[0, 60] by [–20, 70]

(b)

Figure 7.12 (Example 7)

Now Try Exercise 33.

Quick Review 7.4

Exercise numbers with a gray background indicate problems that the authors have designed to be solved *without a calculator.*

In Exercises 1 and 2, rewrite the equation in exponential form or logarithmic form.

1. $\ln a = b$
2. $e^c = d$

In Exercises 3–8, solve the equation.

3. $\ln(x + 3) = 2$
4. $100e^{2x} = 600$
5. $0.85^x = 2.5$
6. $2^{k+1} = 3^k$
7. $1.1^t = 10$
8. $e^{-2t} = \frac{1}{4}$

In Exercises 9 and 10, solve for y.

9. $\ln(y + 1) = 2x - 3$
10. $\ln|y + 2| = 3t - 1$

Section 7.4 Exercises

In Exercises 1–10, use separation of variables to solve the initial value problem. Indicate the domain over which the solution is valid.

1. $\frac{dy}{dx} = \frac{x}{y}$ and $y = 2$ when $x = 1$
2. $\frac{dy}{dx} = -\frac{x}{y}$ and $y = 3$ when $x = 4$
3. $\frac{dy}{dx} = \frac{y}{x}$ and $y = 2$ when $x = 2$
4. $\frac{dy}{dx} = 2xy$ and $y = 3$ when $x = 0$
5. $\frac{dy}{dx} = (y + 5)(x + 2)$ and $y = 1$ when $x = 0$
6. $\frac{dy}{dx} = \cos^2 y$ and $y = 0$ when $x = 0$
7. $\frac{dy}{dx} = (\cos x)e^{y+\sin x}$ and $y = 0$ when $x = 0$
8. $\frac{dy}{dx} = e^{x-y}$ and $y = 2$ when $x = 0$
9. $\frac{dy}{dx} = -2xy^2$ and $y = 0.25$ when $x = 1$
10. $\frac{dy}{dx} = \frac{4\sqrt{y}\ln x}{x}$ and $y = 1$ when $x = e$

In Exercises 11–14, find the solution of the differential equation $dy/dt = ky$, k a constant, that satisfies the given conditions.

11. $k = 1.5,\ y(0) = 100$
12. $k = -0.5,\ y(0) = 200$
13. $y(0) = 50,\ y(5) = 100$
14. $y(0) = 60,\ y(10) = 30$

In Exercises 15–18, complete the table for an investment if interest is compounded continuously.

	Initial Deposit ($)	Annual Rate (%)	Doubling Time (yr)	Amount in 30 yr ($)
15.	1000	8.6		
16.	2000		15	
17.		5.25		2898.44
18.	1200			10,405.37

In Exercises 19 and 20, find the amount of time required for a \$2000 investment to double if the annual interest rate r is compounded **(a)** annually, **(b)** monthly, **(c)** quarterly, and **(d)** continuously.

19. $r = 4.75\%$
20. $r = 8.25\%$

21. ***Half-Life*** The radioactive decay of Sm-151 (an isotope of samarium) can be modeled by the differential equation $dy/dt = -0.0077y$, where t is measured in years. Find the half-life of Sm-151.

22. ***Half-Life*** An isotope of neptunium (Np-240) has a half-life of 65 minutes. If the decay of Np-240 is modeled by the differential equation $dy/dt = -ky$, where t is measured in minutes, what is the decay constant k?

23. ***Growth of Cholera Bacteria*** Suppose that the cholera bacteria in a colony grow unchecked according to the Law of Exponential Change. The colony starts with 1 bacterium and doubles in number every half hour.
    (a) How many bacteria will the colony contain at the end of 24 h?
    (b) **Writing to Learn** Use part (a) to explain why a person who feels well in the morning may be dangerously ill by evening even though, in an infected person, many bacteria are destroyed.

24. ***Bacterial Growth*** A colony of bacteria is grown under ideal conditions in a laboratory so that the population increases exponentially with time. At the end of 3 h there are 10,000 bacteria. At the end of 5 h there are 40,000 bacteria. How many bacteria were present initially?

25. ***Radon-222*** The decay equation for radon-222 gas is known to be $y = y_0e^{-0.18t}$, with t in days. About how long will it take the amount of radon in a sealed sample of air to decay to 90% of its original value?

26. ***Polonium-210*** The number of radioactive atoms remaining after t days in a sample of polonium-210 that starts with y_0 radioactive atoms is $y = y_0e^{-0.005t}$.
    (a) Find the element's half-life.
    (b) Your sample will not be useful to you after 95% of the radioactive nuclei present on the day the sample arrives have disintegrated. For about how many days after the sample arrives will you be able to use the polonium?

In Exercises 27 and 28, find the exponential function $y = y_0 e^{kt}$ whose graph passes through the two points.

27.

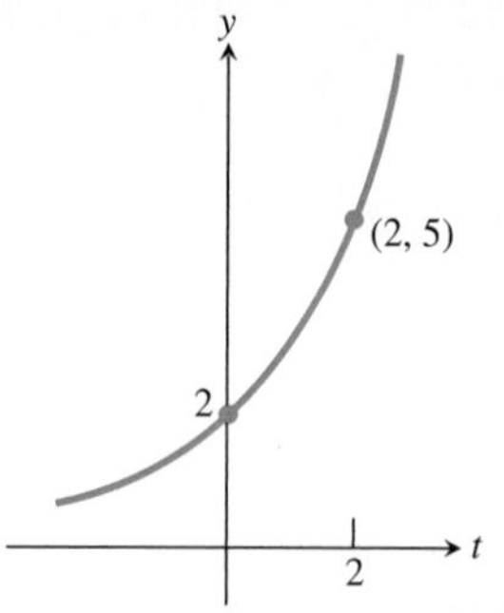

28.

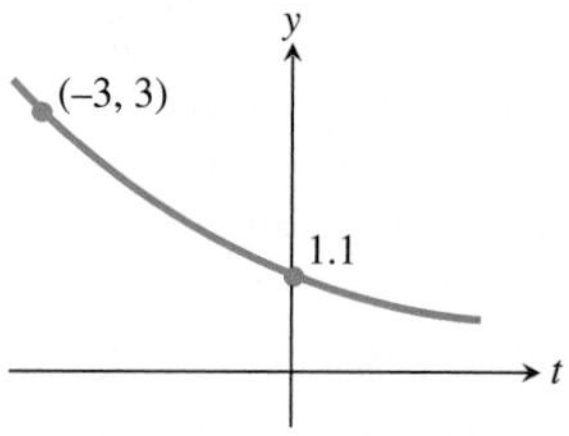

29. *Mean Life of Radioactive Nuclei* Physicists using the radioactive decay equation $y = y_0 e^{-kt}$ call the number $1/k$ the *mean life* of a radioactive nucleus. The mean life of a radon-222 nucleus is about $1/0.18 \approx 5.6$ days. The mean life of a carbon-14 nucleus is more than 8000 years. Show that 95% of the radioactive nuclei originally present in any sample will disintegrate within three mean lifetimes, that is, by time $t = 3/k$. Thus, the mean life of a nucleus gives a quick way to estimate how long the radioactivity of a sample will last.

30. *Finding the Original Temperature of a Beam* An aluminum beam was brought from the outside cold into a machine shop where the temperature was held at 65°F. After 10 min, the beam warmed to 35°F and after another 10 min its temperature was 50°F. Use Newton's Law of Cooling to estimate the beam's initial temperature.

31. *Cooling Soup* Suppose that a cup of soup cooled from 90°C to 60°C in 10 min in a room whose temperature was 20°C. Use Newton's Law of Cooling to answer the following questions.

(a) How much longer would it take the soup to cool to 35°C?

(b) Instead of being left to stand in the room, the cup of 90°C soup is put into a freezer whose temperature is −15°C. How long will it take the soup to cool from 90°C to 35°C?

32. *Cooling Silver* The temperature of an ingot of silver is 60°C above room temperature right now. Twenty minutes ago, it was 70°C above room temperature. How far above room temperature will the silver be

(a) 15 minutes from now?

(b) 2 hours from now?

(c) When will the silver be 10°C above room temperature?

33. *Temperature Experiment* A temperature probe is removed from a cup of coffee and placed in water whose temperature (T_s) is 10°C. The data in Table 7.2 were collected over the next 30 sec with a CBL™ temperature probe.

TABLE 7.2 Experimental Data

Time (sec)	T (°C)	$T - T_s$ (°C)
2	80.47	70.47
5	69.39	59.39
10	49.66	39.66
15	35.26	25.26
20	28.15	18.15
25	23.56	13.56
30	20.62	10.62

(a) Find an exponential regression equation for the $(t, T - T_s)$ data.

(b) Use the regression equation in part (a) to find a model for the (t, T) data. Superimpose the graph of the model on a scatter plot of the (t, T) data.

(c) Estimate when the temperature probe will read 12°C.

(d) Estimate the coffee's temperature when the temperature probe was removed.

34. *A Very Cool Experiment* A temperature probe is removed from a cup of hot chocolate and placed in ice water (temperature $T_S = 0°C$). The data in Table 7.3 were collected over the next 30 seconds.

TABLE 7.3 Experimental Data

Time (sec)	Temperature (°C)
2	74.68
5	61.99
10	34.89
15	21.95
20	15.36
25	11.89
30	10.02

(a) Writing to Learn Explain why temperature in this experiment can be modeled as an exponential function of time.

(b) Use exponential regression to find the best exponential model. Superimpose a graph of the model on a scatter plot of the (*time, temperature*) data.

(c) Estimate when the probe will reach 5°C.

(d) Estimate the temperature of the hot chocolate when the probe was removed.

35. *Dating Crater Lake* The charcoal from a tree killed in the volcanic eruption that formed Crater Lake in Oregon contained 44.5% of the carbon-14 found in living matter. About how old is Crater Lake?

36. *Carbon-14 Dating Measurement Sensitivity* To see the effect of a relatively small error in the estimate of the amount of carbon-14 in a sample being dated, answer the following questions about this hypothetical situation.

(a) A fossilized bone found in central Illinois in the year 2000 C.E. contains 17% of its original carbon-14 content. Estimate the year the animal died.

(b) Repeat part (a) assuming 18% instead of 17%.

(c) Repeat part (a) assuming 16% instead of 17%.

37. What is the half-life of a substance that decays to 1/3 of its original radioactive amount in 5 years?

38. A savings account earning compound interest triples in value in 10 years. How long will it take for the original investment to quadruple?

39. ***The Inversion of Sugar*** The processing of raw sugar has an "inversion" step that changes the sugar's molecular structure. Once the process has begun, the rate of change of the amount of raw sugar is proportional to the amount of raw sugar remaining. If 1000 kg of raw sugar reduces to 800 kg of raw sugar during the first 10 h, how much raw sugar will remain after another 14 h?

40. ***Oil Depletion*** Suppose the amount of oil pumped from one of the canyon wells in Whittier, California, decreases at the continuous rate of 10% per year. When will the well's output fall to one-fifth of its present level?

41. ***Atmospheric Pressure*** Earth's atmospheric pressure p is often modeled by assuming that the rate dp/dh at which p changes with the altitude h above sea level is proportional to p. Suppose that the pressure at sea level is 1013 millibars (about 14.7 lb/in^2) and that the pressure at an altitude of 20 km is 90 millibars.

(a) Solve the initial value problem

Differential equation: $\dfrac{dp}{dh} = kp,$

Initial condition: $p = p_0$ when $h = 0,$

to express p in terms of h. Determine the values of p_0 and k from the given altitude-pressure data.

(b) What is the atmospheric pressure at $h = 50$ km?

(c) At what altitude does the pressure equal 900 millibars?

42. ***First-Order Chemical Reactions*** In some chemical reactions the rate at which the amount of a substance changes with time is proportional to the amount present. For the change of δ-glucono lactone into gluconic acid, for example,

$$\frac{dy}{dt} = -0.6y$$

when y is measured in grams and t is measured in hours. If there are 100 grams of a δ-glucono lactone present when $t - 0$, how many grams will be left after the first hour?

43. ***Discharging Capacitor Voltage*** Suppose that electricity is draining from a capacitor at a rate proportional to the voltage V across its terminals and that, if t is measured in seconds,

$$\frac{dV}{dt} = -\frac{1}{40}V.$$

(a) Solve this differential equation for V, using V_0 to denote the value of V when $t = 0$.

(b) How long will it take the voltage to drop to 10% of its original value?

44. ***John Napier's Answer*** John Napier (1550–1617), the Scottish laird who invented logarithms, was the first person to answer the question, "What happens if you invest an amount of money at 100% yearly interest, compounded continuously?"

(a) **Writing to Learn** What does happen? Explain.

(b) How long does it take to triple your money?

(c) **Writing to Learn** How much can you earn in a year?

45. ***Benjamin Franklin's Will*** The Franklin Technical Institute of Boston owes its existence to a provision in a codicil to Benjamin Franklin's will. In part the codicil reads:

> I wish to be useful even after my Death, if possible, in forming and advancing other young men that may be serviceable to their Country in both Boston and Philadelphia. To this end I devote Two thousand Pounds Sterling, which I give, one thousand thereof to the Inhabitants of the Town of Boston in Massachusetts, and the other thousand to the inhabitants of the City of Philadelphia, in Trust and for the Uses, Interests and Purposes hereinafter mentioned and declared.

Franklin's plan was to lend money to young apprentices at 5% interest with the provision that each borrower should pay each year along

> . . . with the yearly Interest, one tenth part of the Principal, which sums of Principal and Interest shall be again let to fresh Borrowers. ... If this plan is executed and succeeds as projected without interruption for one hundred Years, the Sum will then be one hundred and thirty-one thousand Pounds of which I would have the Managers of the Donation to the Inhabitants of the Town of Boston, then lay out at their discretion one hundred thousand Pounds in Public Works. ... The remaining thirty-one thousand Pounds, I would have continued to be let out on Interest in the manner above directed for another hundred Years. ... At the end of this second term if no unfortunate accident has prevented the operation the sum will be Four Millions and Sixty-one Thousand Pounds.

It was not always possible to find as many borrowers as Franklin had planned, but the managers of the trust did the best they could. At the end of 100 years from the receipt of the Franklin gift, in January 1894, the fund had grown from 1000 pounds to almost 90,000 pounds. In 100 years the original capital had multiplied about 90 times instead of the 131 times Franklin had imagined.

(a) What annual rate of interest, compounded continuously for 100 years, would have multiplied Benjamin Franklin's original capital by 90?

(b) In Benjamin Franklin's estimate that the original 1000 pounds would grow to 131,000 in 100 years, he was using an annual rate of 5% and compounding once each year. What rate of interest per year when compounded continuously for 100 years would multiply the original amount by 131?

46. *Rules of 70 and 72* The rules state that it takes about $70/i$ or $72/i$ years for money to double at i percent, compounded continuously, using whichever of 70 or 72 is easier to divide by i.

(a) Show that it takes $t = (\ln 2)/r$ years for money to double if it is invested at annual interest rate r (in decimal form) compounded continuously.

(b) Graph the functions

$$y_1 = \frac{\ln 2}{r}, \quad y_2 = \frac{70}{100\,r}, \quad \text{and} \quad y_3 = \frac{72}{100r}$$

in the $[0, 0.1]$ by $[0, 100]$ viewing window.

(c) Writing to Learn Explain why these two rules of thumb for mental computation are reasonable.

(d) Use the rules to estimate how long it takes to double money at 5% compounded continuously.

(e) Invent a rule for estimating the number of years needed to triple your money.

Standardized Test Questions

You may use a graphing calculator to solve the following problems.

47. True or False If $dy/dx = ky$, then $y = e^{kx} + C$. Justify your answer.

48. True or False The general solution to $dy/dt = 2y$ can be written in the form $y = C(3^{kt})$ for some constants C and k. Justify your answer.

49. Multiple Choice A bank account earning continuously compounded interest doubles in value in 7.0 years. At the same interest rate, how long would it take the value of the account to triple?

(A) 4.4 years **(B)** 9.8 years **(C)** 10.5 years
(D) 11.1 years **(E)** 21.0 years

50. Multiple Choice A sample of Ce-143 (an isotope of cerium) loses 99% of its radioactive matter in 199 hours. What is the half-life of Ce-143?

(A) 4 hours **(B)** 6 hours **(C)** 30 hours
(D) 100.5 hours **(E)** 143 hours

51. Multiple Choice In which of the following models is dy/dt directly proportional to y?

I. $y = e^{kt} + C$
II. $y = Ce^{kt}$
III. $y = 28^{kt}$

(A) I only **(B)** II only **(C)** I and II only
(D) II and III only **(E)** I, II, and III

52. Multiple Choice An apple pie comes out of the oven at 425°F and is placed on a counter in a 68°F room to cool. In 30 minutes it has cooled to 195°F. According to Newton's Law of Cooling, how many additional minutes must pass before it cools to 100°F?

(A) 12.4 **(B)** 15.4 **(C)** 25.0 **(D)** 35.0 **(E)** 40.0

Explorations

53. *Resistance Proportional to Velocity* It is reasonable to assume that the air resistance encountered by a moving object, such as a car coasting to a stop, is proportional to the object's velocity. The resisting force on an object of mass m moving with velocity v is thus $-kv$ for some positive constant k.

(a) Use the law *Force* = *Mass* × *Acceleration* to show that the velocity of an object slowed by air resistance (and no other forces) satisfies the differential equation.

$$m\frac{dy}{dt} = -kv.$$

(b) Solve the differential equation to show that $v = v_0\,e^{-(k/m)t}$, where v_0 is the velocity of the object at time $t = 0$.

(c) If k is the same for two objects of different masses, which one will slow to half its starting velocity in the shortest time? Justify your answer.

54. *Coasting to a Stop* Assume that the resistance encountered by a moving object is proportional to the object's velocity so that its velocity is $v = v_0 e^{-(k/m)t}$.

(a) Integrate the velocity function with respect to t to obtain the distance function s. Assume that $s(0) = 0$ and show that

$$s(t) = \frac{v_0 m}{k}\left(1 - e^{-(k/m)t}\right).$$

(b) Show that the total coasting distance traveled by the object as it coasts to a complete stop is $v_0 m/k$.

55. *Coasting to a Stop* Table 7.4 shows the distance s (meters) coasted on in-line skates in terms of time t (seconds) by Kelly Schmitzer. Find a model for her position in the form given in Exercise 54(a) and superimpose its graph on a scatter plot of the data. Her initial velocity was $v_0 = 0.80$ m/sec, her mass $m = 49.90$ kg (110 lb), and her total coasting distance was 1.32 m.

TABLE 7.4 Kelly Schmitzer Skating Data

t (sec)	s (m)	t (sec)	s (m)	t (sec)	s (m)
0	0	1.5	0.89	3.1	1.30
0.1	0.07	1.7	0.97	3.3	1.31
0.3	0.22	1.9	1.05	3.5	1.32
0.5	0.36	2.1	1.11	3.7	1.32
0.7	0.49	2.3	1.17	3.9	1.32
0.9	0.60	2.5	1.22	4.1	1.32
1.1	0.71	2.7	1.25	4.3	1.32
1.3	0.81	2.9	1.28	4.5	1.32

Source: Valerie Sharritts, St. Francis de Sales H.S., Columbus, OH.

56. *Coasting to a Stop* Table 7.5 shows the distance s (meters) coasted on in-line skates in t seconds by Johnathon Krueger. Find a model for his position in the form given in Exercise 54(a) and superimpose its graph on a scatter plot of the data. His initial velocity was $v_0 = 0.86$ m/sec, his mass $m = 30.84$ kg (he weighed 68 lb), and his total coasting distance 0.97 m.

TABLE 7.5 Johnathon Krueger Skating Data

t (sec)	s (m)	t (sec)	s (m)	t (sec)	s (m)
0	0	0.93	0.61	1.86	0.93
0.13	0.08	1.06	0.68	2.00	0.94
0.27	0.19	1.20	0.74	2.13	0.95
0.40	0.28	1.33	0.79	2.26	0.96
0.53	0.36	1.46	0.83	2.39	0.96
0.67	0.45	1.60	0.87	2.53	0.97
0.80	0.53	1.73	0.90	2.66	0.97

Source: Valerie Sharritts, St. Francis de Sales H.S., Columbus, OH.

Extending the Ideas

57. *Continuously Compounded Interest*

(a) Use tables to give a numerical argument that

$$\lim_{x\to\infty}\left(1+\frac{1}{x}\right)^x = e.$$

Support your argument graphically.

(b) For several different values of r, give numerical and graphical evidence that

$$\lim_{x\to\infty}\left(1+\frac{r}{x}\right)^x = e^r.$$

(c) Writing to Learn Explain why compounding interest over smaller and smaller periods of time leads to the concept of interest compounded continuously.

58. *Skydiving* If a body of mass m falling from rest under the action of gravity encounters an air resistance proportional to the square of the velocity, then the body's velocity $v(t)$ is modeled by the initial value problem

Differential equation: $m\dfrac{dv}{dt} = mg - kv^2,$

Initial condition: $v(0) = 0,$

where t represents time in seconds, g is the acceleration due to gravity, and k is a constant that depends on the body's aerodynamic properties and the density of the air. (We assume that the fall is short enough so that variation in the air's density will not affect the outcome.)

(a) Show that the function

$$v(t) = \sqrt{\frac{mg}{k}}\,\frac{e^{at} - e^{-at}}{e^{at} + e^{-at}},$$

where $a = \sqrt{gk/m}$, is a solution of the initial value problem.

(b) Find the body's limiting velocity, $\lim_{t\to\infty} v(t)$.

(c) For a 160-lb skydiver $(mg = 160)$, and with time in seconds and distance in feet, a typical value for k is 0.005. What is the diver's limiting velocity in feet per second? in miles per hour?

Skydivers can vary their limiting velocities by changing the amount of body area opposing the fall. Their velocities can vary from 94 to 321 miles per hour.

7.5 Logistic Growth

What you will learn about . . .

- How Populations Grow
- Partial Fractions
- The Logistic Differential Equation
- Logistic Growth Models

and why . . .

Populations in the real world tend to grow logistically over extended periods of time.

How Populations Grow

In Section 7.4 we showed that when the rate of change of a population is directly proportional to the size of the population, the population grows exponentially. This seems like a reasonable model for population growth in the short term, but populations in nature cannot sustain exponential growth for very long. Available food, habitat, and living space are just a few of the constraints that will eventually impose limits on the growth of any real-world population.

EXPLORATION 1 Exponential Growth Revisited

Almost any algebra book will include a problem like this: A culture of bacteria in a Petri dish is doubling every hour. If there are 100 bacteria at time $t = 0$, how many bacteria will there be in 12 hours?

1. Answer the algebra question.
2. Suppose a textbook editor, seeking to add a little unit conversion to the problem to satisfy a reviewer, changes "12 hours" to "12 days" in the second edition of the textbook. What is the answer to the revised question?
3. Is the new answer reasonable? [*Hint:* It has been estimated that there are about 10^{79} atoms in the entire universe.]
4. Suppose the maximal sustainable population of bacteria in this Petri dish is 500,000 bacteria. How many hours will it take the bacteria to reach this population if the exponential model continues to hold?
5. The graph below shows what the graph of the population would look like if it were to remain exponential until hitting 500,000. Draw a more reasonable graph that shows how the population might approach 500,000 after growing exponentially up to the marked point.

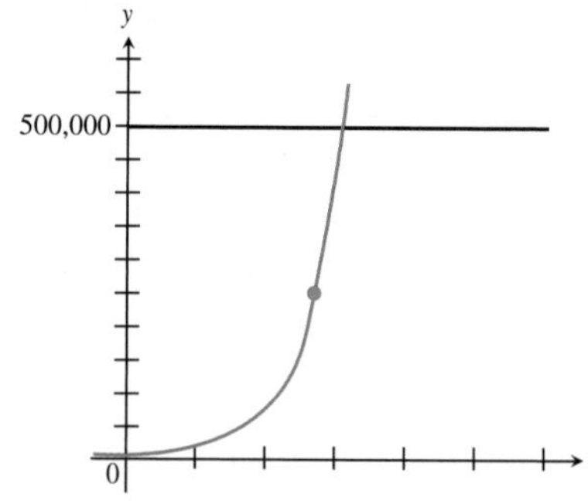

You might recall that we introduced *logistic* curves in Section 5.3 to illustrate points of inflection. Logistic growth, which starts off exponentially and then changes concavity to approach a maximal sustainable population, is a better model for real-world populations, for all the reasons mentioned above.

Partial Fractions

Before we introduce the differential equation that describes logistic growth, we need to review a bit of algebra that is needed to solve it.

Partial Fraction Decomposition with Distinct Linear Denominators

If $f(x) = \dfrac{P(x)}{Q(x)}$, where P and Q are polynomials with the degree of P less than the degree of Q, and if $Q(x)$ can be written as a product of distinct linear factors, then $f(x)$ can be written as a sum of rational functions with distinct linear denominators.

We will illustrate this principle with examples.

A Question of Degree

Note that the technique of partial fractions only applies to rational functions of the form

$$\frac{P(x)}{Q(x)}$$

where P and Q are polynomials with the degree of P less than the degree of Q. Such a fraction is called *proper.* Example 2 will show you how to handle an *improper* fraction.

A Little on the Heaviside

The substitution technique used to find A and B in Example 1 (and in subsequent examples) is often called the **Heaviside Method** after English engineer Oliver Heaviside (1850–1925).

EXAMPLE 1 Finding a Partial Fraction Decomposition

Write the function $f(x) = \dfrac{x - 13}{2x^2 - 7x + 3}$ as a sum of rational functions with linear denominators.

SOLUTION

Since $f(x) = \dfrac{x - 13}{(2x - 1)(x - 3)}$, we will find numbers A and B so that

$f(x) = \dfrac{A}{2x - 1} + \dfrac{B}{x - 3}.$

Note that $\dfrac{A}{2x - 1} + \dfrac{B}{x - 3} = \dfrac{A(x - 3) + B(2x - 1)}{(2x - 1)(x - 3)}$, so it follows that

$$A(x - 3) + B(2x - 1) = x - 13. \qquad (1)$$

Setting $x = 3$ in equation (1), we get

$$A(0) + B(5) = -10, \text{ so } B = -2.$$

Setting $x = \dfrac{1}{2}$ in equation (1), we get

$$A\left(-\frac{5}{2}\right) + B(0) = -\frac{25}{2}, \text{ so } A = 5.$$

Therefore $f(x) = \dfrac{x - 13}{(2x - 1)(x - 3)} = \dfrac{5}{2x - 1} - \dfrac{2}{x - 3}.$

Now Try Exercise 3.

You might already have guessed that partial fraction decomposition can be of great value when antidifferentiating rational functions.

EXAMPLE 2 Antidifferentiating with Partial Fractions

Find $\displaystyle\int \frac{3x^4 + 1}{x^2 - 1}\,dx.$

SOLUTION

First we note that the degree of the denominator is not less than the degree of the numerator. We use the division algorithm to find the quotient and remainder:

$$\begin{array}{r l}
 & 3x^2 + 3 \\
x^2 - 1\,\big) & 3x^4 \qquad\; + 1 \\
 & \underline{3x^4 - 3x^2} \\
 & \qquad 3x^2 + 1 \\
 & \qquad \underline{3x^2 - 3} \\
 & \qquad\qquad\;\; 4
\end{array}$$

continued

Thus

$$\int \frac{3x^4 + 1}{x^2 - 1}\,dx = \int \left(3x^2 + 3 + \frac{4}{x^2 - 1}\right) dx$$
$$= x^3 + 3x + \int \frac{4}{(x - 1)(x + 1)}\,dx$$
$$= x^3 + 3x + \int \left(\frac{A}{x - 1} + \frac{B}{x + 1}\right) dx.$$

We know that $A(x + 1) + B(x - 1) = 4$.

Setting $x = 1$,

$$A(2) + B(0) = 4, \text{ so } A = 2.$$

Setting $x = -1$,

$$A(0) + B(-2) = 4, \text{ so } B = -2.$$

Thus

$$\int \frac{3x^4 + 1}{x^2 - 1}\,dx = x^3 + 3x + \int \left(\frac{2}{x - 1} + \frac{-2}{x + 1}\right) dx$$
$$= x^3 + 3x + 2\ln|x - 1| - 2\ln|x + 1| + C$$
$$= x^3 + 3x + 2\ln\left|\frac{x - 1}{x + 1}\right| + C.$$

Now Try Exercise 7.

EXAMPLE 3 Finding Three Partial Fractions

This example will be our most laborious problem.

Find the general solution to $\dfrac{dy}{dx} = \dfrac{6x^2 - 8x - 4}{(x^2 - 4)(x - 1)}$.

SOLUTION

$$y = \int \frac{6x^2 - 8x - 4}{(x - 2)(x + 2)(x - 1)}\,dx = \int \left(\frac{A}{x - 2} + \frac{B}{x + 2} + \frac{C}{x - 1}\right) dx.$$

We know that $A(x + 2)(x - 1) + B(x - 2)(x - 1) + C(x - 2)(x + 2) = 6x^2 - 8x - 4$.

Setting $x = 2$:

$$A(4)(1) + B(0) + C(0) = 4, \text{ so } A = 1.$$

Setting $x = -2$:

$$A(0) + B(-4)(-3) + C(0) = 36, \text{ so } B = 3.$$

Setting $x = 1$,

$$A(0) + B(0) + C(-1)(3) = -6, \text{ so } C = 2.$$

Thus

$$\int \frac{6x^2 - 8x - 4}{(x - 2)(x + 2)(x - 1)}\,dx = \int \left(\frac{1}{x - 2} + \frac{3}{x + 2} + \frac{2}{x - 1}\right) dx$$
$$= \ln|x - 2| + 3\ln|x + 2| + 2\ln|x - 1| + C$$
$$= \ln\left(|x - 2||x + 2|^3|x - 1|^2\right) + C.$$

Now Try Exercise 17.

The technique of partial fractions can actually be extended to apply to all rational functions, but the method has to be adapted slightly if there are repeated linear factors or irreducible quadratic factors in the denominator. Both of these cases lead to partial fractions with quadratic denominators, and we will not deal with them in this book.

The Logistic Differential Equation

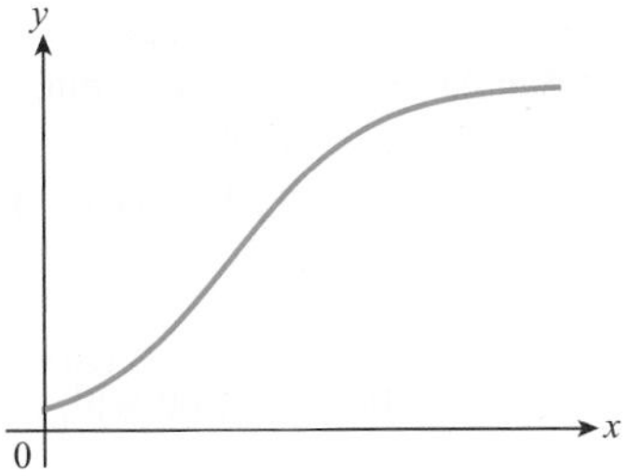

Figure 7.13 A logistic curve.

Now consider the case of a population P with a growth curve as a function of time that begins increasing and concave up (as in exponential growth), then turns increasing and concave down as it approaches the carrying capacity of its habitat. A **logistic curve,** like the one shown in Figure 7.13, has the shape to model this growth.

We have seen that the exponential growth at the beginning can be modeled by the differential equation

$$\frac{dP}{dt} = kP \text{ for some } k > 0.$$

If we want the growth rate to approach zero as P approaches a maximal **carrying capacity** M, we can introduce a limiting factor of $M - P$:

$$\frac{dP}{dt} = kP(M - P)$$

This is the **logistic differential equation.** Before we find its general solution, let us see how much we can learn about logistic growth just by studying the differential equation itself.

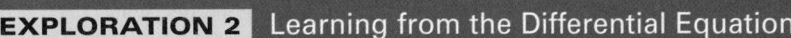

EXPLORATION 2 Learning from the Differential Equation

Consider a (positive) population P that satisfies $dP/dt = kP(M - P)$, where k and M are positive constants.

1. For what values of P will the growth rate dP/dt be close to zero?
2. As a function of P, $y = kP(M - P)$ has a graph that is an upside-down parabola. What is the value of P at the vertex of that parabola?
3. Use the answer to part (2) to explain why the growth rate is maximized when the population reaches half the carrying capacity.
4. If the initial population is less than M, is the initial growth rate positive or negative?
5. If the initial population is greater than M, is the initial growth rate positive or negative?
6. If the initial population equals M, what is the initial growth rate?
7. What is $\lim_{t \to \infty} P(t)$? Does it depend on the initial population?

You can use the results of Exploration 2 in the following example.

EXAMPLE 4

The growth rate of a population P of bears in a newly established wildlife preserve is modeled by the differential equation $dP/dt = 0.008P(100 - P)$, where t is measured in years.

(a) What is the carrying capacity for bears in this wildlife preserve?

(b) What is the bear population when the population is growing the fastest?

(c) What is the rate of change of the population when it is growing the fastest?

continued

SOLUTION

(a) The carrying capacity is 100 bears.

(b) The bear population is growing the fastest when it is half the carrying capacity, 50 bears.

(c) When $P = 50$, $dP/dt = 0.008(50)(100 - 50) = 20$ bears per year. Although the derivative represents the instantaneous growth rate, it is reasonable to say that the population grows by about 20 bears that year.

Now Try Exercise 25.

In this next example we will find the solution to a logistic differential equation with an initial condition.

EXAMPLE 5 Tracking a Moose Population

In 1985 and 1987, the Michigan Department of Natural Resources airlifted 61 moose from Algonquin Park, Ontario to Marquette County in the Upper Peninsula. It was originally hoped that the population P would reach carrying capacity in about 25 years with a growth rate of

$$\frac{dP}{dt} = 0.0003P(1000 - P).$$

(a) According to the model, what is the carrying capacity?

(b) With a calculator, generate a slope field for the differential equation.

(c) Solve the differential equation with the initial condition $P(0) = 61$ and show that it conforms to the slope field.

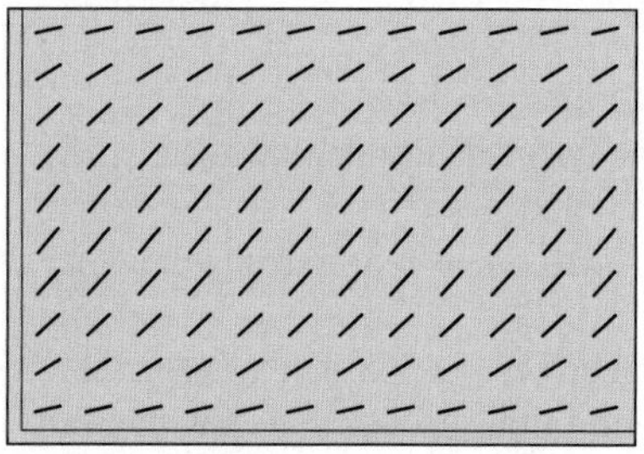

[0, 25] by [0, 1000]

Figure 7.14 The slope field for the moose differential equation in Example 5.

SOLUTION

(a) The carrying capacity is 1000 moose.

(b) The slope field is shown in Figure 7.14. Since the population approaches a horizontal asymptote at 1000 in about 25 years, we use the window [0, 25] by [0, 1000].

(c) After separating the variables, we encounter an antiderivative to be found using partial fractions.

$$\frac{dP}{P(1000 - P)} = 0.0003\,dt$$

$$\int \frac{1}{P(1000 - P)}\,dP = \int 0.0003\,dt$$

$$\int \left(\frac{A}{P} + \frac{B}{1000 - P}\right) dP = \int 0.0003\,dt$$

We know that $A(1000 - P) + B(P) = 1$.

Setting $P = 0$: $A(1000) + B(0) = 1$, so $A = 0.001$.

Setting $P = 1000$: $A(0) + B(1000) = 1$, so $B = 0.001$.

continued

$$\int\left(\frac{0.001}{P} + \frac{0.001}{1000 - P}\right) dP = \int 0.0003\, dt$$

$$\int\left(\frac{1}{P} + \frac{1}{1000 - P}\right) dP = \int 0.3\, dt \qquad \text{Multiplied both integrals by 1000}$$

$$\ln P - \ln(1000 - P) = 0.3t + C$$

$$\ln(1000 - P) - \ln P = -0.3t - C$$

$$\ln\left(\frac{1000 - P}{P}\right) = -0.3t - C$$

$$\frac{1000}{P} - 1 = e^{-0.3t-C}$$

$$\frac{1000}{P} = 1 + e^{-0.3t}\,e^{-C}$$

Setting $P = 61$ and $t = 0$, we find that $e^{-C} \approx 15.393$. Thus

$$\frac{1000}{P} = 1 + 15.393e^{-0.3t}$$

$$P = \frac{1000}{1 + 15.393e^{-0.3t}}.$$

The graph conforms nicely to the slope field, as shown in Figure 7.15.

Now Try Exercise 29.

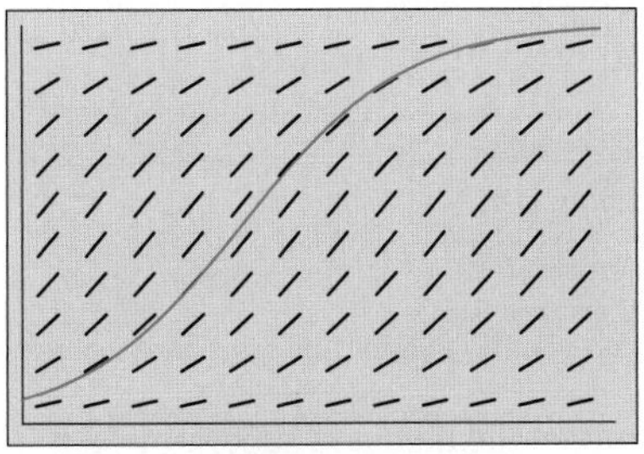

[0, 25] by [0, 1000]

Figure 7.15 The particular solution

$$P = \frac{1000}{1 + 15.393e^{-0.3t}}$$

conforms nicely to the slope field for $dP/dt = 0.0003P\,(1000 - P)$. (Example 5)

Logistic Growth Models

We could solve many more logistic differential equations and the algebra would look the same every time. In fact, it is almost as simple to solve the equation using letters for all the constants, thereby arriving at a general formula. In Exercise 35 we will ask you to verify the result in the box below.

The General Logistic Formula

The solution of the general logistic differential equation

$$\frac{dP}{dt} = kP(M - P)$$

is

$$P = \frac{M}{1 + Ae^{-(Mk)t}}$$

where A is a constant determined by an appropriate initial condition. The **carrying capacity** M and the **growth constant** k are positive constants.

We introduced logistic regression in Example 6 of Section 5.3. We close this section with another logistic regression example that makes use of our additional understanding.

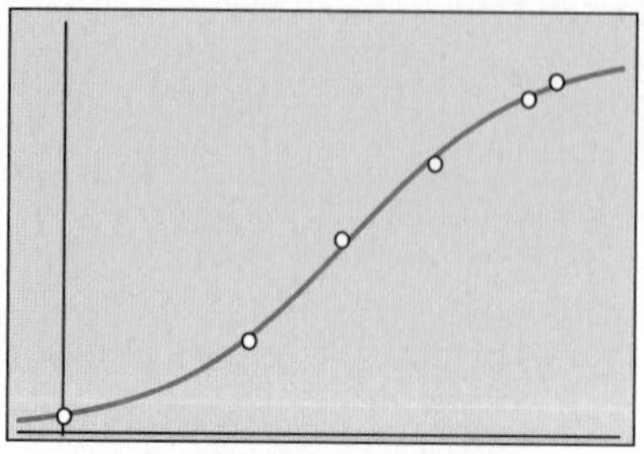

[–5, 60] by [–3600, 337000]

Figure 7.16 The logistic regression curve fitted to the data for population growth in Aurora, CO, from 1950 to 2003. (Example 6)

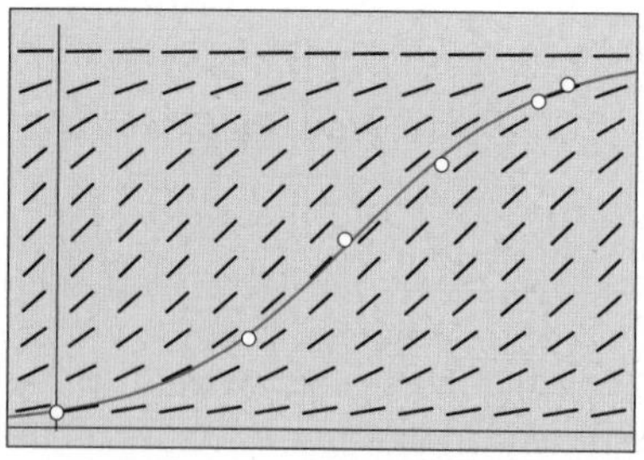

[–5, 60] by [–3600, 337000]

Figure 7.17 The slope field for the differential equation derived from the regression curve fits the data and the regression curve nicely. (Example 6)

Graphing Calculator Logistics

Unfortunately, some graphing calculators allow for a *vertical shift* when fitting a logistic curve to a set of data points. The regression equation for such a curve would have the form

$$y = \frac{c}{1 + ae^{-bx}} + d.$$

While the curve might fit the data better, this function cannot be a solution to the logistic differential equation if d is not zero. Since our definition of a logistic function begins with the differential equation, we will consistently use only logistic regression equations of the form

$$y = \frac{c}{1 + ae^{-bx}}.$$

EXAMPLE 6 Using Logistic Regression

Table 7.6 shows the population of Aurora, CO, for selected years between 1950 and 2003.

TABLE 7.6 Population of Aurora, CO

Years After 1950	Population
0	11,421
20	74,974
30	158,588
40	222,103
50	275,923
53	290,418

Source: Bureau of the Census, U.S. Department of Commerce, as reported in The World Almanac and Book of Facts, 2005.

(a) Use logistic regression to find a logistic curve to model the data and superimpose it on a scatter plot of population against years after 1950.

(b) Based on the regression equation, what will the Aurora population approach in the long run?

(c) Based on the regression equation, when would the population of Aurora first exceed 300,000 people?

(d) Write a logistic differential equation in the form $dP/dt = kP(M - P)$ that models the growth of the Aurora data in Table 7.6.

SOLUTION

(a) The regression equation is

$$P = \frac{316440.7}{1 + 23.577e^{-0.1026t}}.$$

The graph is shown superimposed on the scatter plot in Figure 7.16. The fit is almost perfect.

(b) Approximately 316,441 people. (The carrying capacity is the numerator of the regression equation.)

(c) Set

$$\frac{316440.7}{1 + 23.577e^{-0.1026t}} = 300{,}000.$$

The regression line crosses the 300,000 mark sometime in the 59th year, that is, in 2009. (Incidentally, as if to demonstrate the limitations of real-world growth modeling, the city of Aurora had a population boom from 2004 to 2008. According to www.IDcide.com, they actually passed the 300,000 mark in 2006.)

(d) We see from the regression equation that $M = 316440.7$ and $Mk = 0.1026$. Therefore $k \approx 3.24 \times 10^{-7}$. The logistic growth model is

$$\frac{dP}{dt} = (3.24 \times 10^{-7})\,P(316440.7 - P).$$

Figure 7.17 shows the slope field for this differential equation superimposed on the scatter plot and the regression equation. ***Now Try Exercise 37.***

We caution readers once again not to assume that logistic models work perfectly in all real-world, population-growth problems; there are too many unpredictable variables that can and will change the growth conditions over time.

Quick Review 7.5 (For help, go to Sections 2.2 and 2.3.)

Exercise numbers with a gray background indicate problems that the authors have designed to be solved *without a calculator.*

In Exercises 1–4, use the polynomial division algorithm (as in Example 2 of this section) to write the rational function in the form $Q(x) + \frac{R(x)}{D(x)}$, where the degree of R is less than the degree of D.

1. $\frac{x^2}{x-1}$

2. $\frac{x^2}{x^2-4}$

3. $\frac{x^2+x+1}{x^2+x-2}$

4. $\frac{x^3-5}{x^2-1}$

In Exercises 5–10, let $f(x) = \frac{60}{1+5e^{-0.1x}}$.

5. Find where f is continuous.

6. Find $\lim_{x\to\infty} f(x)$.

7. Find $\lim_{x\to\infty} f(x)$.

8. Find the y-intercept of the graph of f.

9. Find all horizontal asymptotes of the graph of f.

10. Draw the graph of $y = f(x)$.

Section 7.5 Exercises

In Exercises 1–4, find the values of A and B that complete the partial fraction decomposition.

1. $\frac{x-12}{x^2-4x} = \frac{A}{x} + \frac{B}{x-4}$

2. $\frac{2x+16}{x^2+x-6} = \frac{A}{x+3} + \frac{B}{x-2}$

3. $\frac{16-x}{x^2+3x-10} = \frac{A}{x-2} + \frac{B}{x+5}$

4. $\frac{3}{x^2-9} = \frac{A}{x-3} + \frac{B}{x+3}$

In Exercises 5–14, evaluate the integral.

5. $\int \frac{x-12}{x^2-4x}\,dx$

6. $\int \frac{2x+16}{x^2+x-6}\,dx$

7. $\int \frac{2x^3}{x^2-4}\,dx$

8. $\int \frac{x^2-6}{x^2-9}\,dx$

9. $\int \frac{2\,dx}{x^2+1}$

10. $\int \frac{3\,dx}{x^2+9}$

11. $\int \frac{7\,dx}{2x^2-5x-3}$

12. $\int \frac{1-3x}{3x^2-5x+2}\,dx$

13. $\int \frac{8x-7}{2x^2-x-3}\,dx$

14. $\int \frac{5x+14}{x^2+7x}\,dx$

In Exercises 15–18, solve the differential equation.

15. $\frac{dy}{dx} = \frac{2x-6}{x^2-2x}$

16. $\frac{du}{dx} = \frac{2}{x^2-1}$

17. $F'(x) = \frac{2}{x^3-x}$

18. $G'(t) = \frac{2t^3}{t^3-t}$

In Exercises 19–22, find the integral *without* using the technique of partial fractions.

19. $\int \frac{2x}{x^2-4}\,dx$

20. $\int \frac{4x-3}{2x^2-3x+1}\,dx$

21. $\int \frac{x^2+x-1}{x^2-x}\,dx$

22. $\int \frac{2x^3}{x^2-1}\,dx$

In Exercises 23–26, the logistic equation describes the growth of a population P, where t is measured in years. In each case, find **(a)** the carrying capacity of the population, **(b)** the size of the population when it is growing the fastest, and **(c)** the rate at which the population is growing when it is growing the fastest.

23. $\frac{dP}{dt} = 0.006P(200-P)$

24. $\frac{dP}{dt} = 0.0008P(700-P)$

25. $\frac{dP}{dt} = 0.0002P(1200-P)$

26. $\frac{dP}{dt} = 10^{-5}P(5000-P)$

In Exercises 27–30, solve the initial value problem using partial fractions. Use a graphing utility to generate a slope field for the differential equation and verify that the solution conforms to the slope field.

27. $\frac{dP}{dt} = 0.006P(200-P)$ and $P = 8$ when $t = 0$.

28. $\frac{dP}{dt} = 0.0008P(700-P)$ and $P = 10$ when $t = 0$.

29. $\frac{dP}{dt} = 0.0002P(1200-P)$ and $P = 20$ when $t = 0$.

30. $\frac{dP}{dt} = 10^{-5}P(5000-P)$ and $P = 50$ when $t = 0$.

In Exercises 31 and 32, a population function is given.

(a) Show that the function is a solution of a logistic differential equation. Identify k and the carrying capacity.

(b) Writing to Learn Estimate $P(0)$. Explain its meaning in the context of the problem.

31. ***Rabbit Population*** A population of rabbits is given by the formula

$$P(t) = \frac{1000}{1+e^{4.8-0.7t}},$$

where t is the number of months after a few rabbits are released.

32. ***Spread of Measles*** The number of students infected by measles in a certain school is given by the formula

$$P(t) = \frac{200}{1+e^{5.3-t}},$$

where t is the number of days after students are first exposed to an infected student.

33. ***Guppy Population*** A 2000-gallon tank can support no more than 150 guppies. Six guppies are introduced into the tank. Assume that the rate of growth of the population is

$$\frac{dP}{dt} = 0.0015P(150 - P),$$

where time t is in weeks.

(a) Find a formula for the guppy population in terms of t.

(b) How long will it take for the guppy population to be 100? 125?

34. ***Gorilla Population*** A certain wild animal preserve can support no more than 250 lowland gorillas. Twenty-eight gorillas were known to be in the preserve in 1970. Assume that the rate of growth of the population is

$$\frac{dP}{dt} = 0.0004P(250 - P),$$

where time t is in years.

(a) Find a formula for the gorilla population in terms of t.

(b) How long will it take for the gorilla population to reach the carrying capacity of the preserve?

35. ***Logistic Differential Equation*** Show that the solution of the differential equation

$$\frac{dP}{dt} = kP(M - P) \quad \text{is} \quad P = \frac{M}{1 + Ae^{-Mkt}},$$

where A is a constant determined by an appropriate initial condition.

36. ***Limited Growth Equation*** Another differential equation that models limited growth of a population P in an environment with carrying capacity M is $dP/dt = k(M - P)$ (where $k > 0$ and $M > 0$).

(a) Show that $P = M - Ae^{-kt}$, where A is a constant determined by an appropriate initial condition.

(b) What is $\lim_{t \to \infty} P(t)$?

(c) For what time $t \geq 0$ is the population growing the fastest?

(d) **Writing to Learn** How does the growth curve in this model differ from the growth curve in the logistic model?

37. ***Population Growth*** Table 7.7 shows the population of Laredo, Texas for selected years between 1950 and 2003.

TABLE 7.7 Population of Laredo, TX

Years After 1950	Population
0	10,571
20	81,437
30	138,857
40	180,650
50	215,794
53	218,027

Source: Bureau of the Census, U.S. Department of Commerce, as reported in The World Almanac and Book of Facts, 2005.

(a) Use logistic regression to find a curve to model the data and superimpose it on a scatter plot of population against years after 1950.

(b) Based on the regression equation, what number will the Laredo population approach in the long run?

(c) Based on the regression equation, when would the Laredo population first exceed 225,000 people?

(d) Write a logistic differential equation in the form $dP/dt = kP(M - P)$ that models the growth of the Laredo data in Table 7.7.

38. ***Population Growth*** Table 7.8 shows the population of Virginia Beach, VA, for selected years between 1950 and 2003.

TABLE 7.8 Population of Virginia Beach

Years After 1950	Population
0	5,390
20	172,106
30	262,199
40	393,069
50	425,257
53	439,467

Source: Bureau of the Census, U.S. Department of Commerce, as reported in The World Almanac and Book of Facts, 2005.

(a) Use logistic regression to find a curve to model the data and superimpose it on a scatter plot of population against years after 1950.

(b) Based on the regression equation, what number will the Virginia Beach population approach in the long run?

(c) Based on the regression equation, when would the Virginia Beach population first exceed 450,000 people?

(d) Write a logistic differential equation in the form $dP/dt = kP(M - P)$ that models the growth of the Virginia Beach data in Table 7.8.

Standardized Test Questions

39. **True or False** For small values of t, the solution to logistic differential equation $dP/dt = kP(100 - P)$ that passes through the point (0, 10) resembles the solution to the differential equation $dP/dt = kP$ that passes through the point (0, 10). Justify your answer.

40. **True or False** If $0 < P(0) < M$, then the graph of the solution to the differential equation $dP/dt = kP(100 - P)$ has asymptotes $y = 0$ and $y = 100$. Justify your answer.

41. **Multiple Choice** The spread of a disease through a community can be modeled with the logistic equation

$$y = \frac{600}{1 + 59e^{-0.1t}},$$

where y is the number of people infected after t days. How many people are infected when the disease is spreading the fastest?

(A) 10 (B) 59 (C) 60 (D) 300 (E) 600

42. Multiple Choice The spread of a disease through a community can be modeled with the logistic equation

$$y = \frac{0.9}{1 + 45e^{-0.15t}},$$

where y is the proportion of people infected after t days. According to the model, what percentage of the people in the community will not become infected?

(A) 2% (B) 10% (C) 15% (D) 45% (E) 90%

43. Multiple Choice $\int_2^3 \frac{3}{(x-1)(x+2)}\,dx =$

(A) $-\frac{33}{20}$ (B) $-\frac{9}{20}$ (C) $\ln\left(\frac{5}{2}\right)$ (D) $\ln\left(\frac{8}{5}\right)$ (E) $\ln\left(\frac{2}{5}\right)$

44. Multiple Choice Which of the following differential equations would produce the slope field shown below?

(A) $\frac{dy}{dx} = 0.01x(120 - x)$ (B) $\frac{dy}{dx} = 0.01y(120 - y)$

(C) $\frac{dy}{dx} = 0.01y(100 - x)$ (D) $\frac{dy}{dx} = \frac{120}{1 + 60e^{-1.2x}}$

(E) $\frac{dy}{dx} = \frac{120}{1 + 60e^{-1.2y}}$

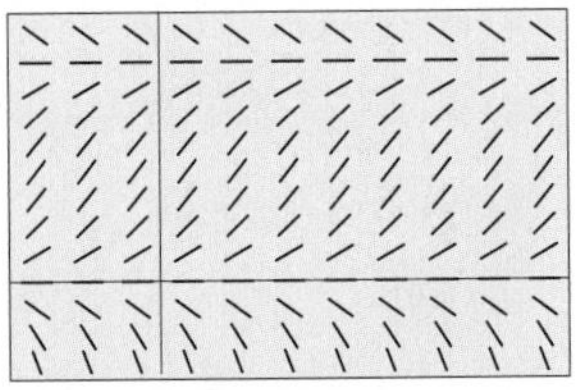

[-3, 8] by [-50, 150]

Explorations

45. *Extinct Populations* One theory states that if the size of a population falls below a minimum m, the population will become extinct. This condition leads to the *extended* logistic differential equation

$$\frac{dP}{dt} = kP\left(1 - \frac{P}{M}\right)\left(1 - \frac{m}{P}\right) = \frac{k}{M}(M - P)(P - m),$$

with $k > 0$ the proportionality constant and M the population maximum.

(a) Show that dP/dt is positive for $m < P < M$ and negative if $P < m$ or $P > M$.

(b) Let $m = 100$, $M = 1200$, and assume that $m < P < M$. Show that the differential equation can be rewritten in the form

$$\left[\frac{1}{1200 - P} + \frac{1}{P - 100}\right]\frac{dP}{dt} = \frac{11}{12}k.$$

Use a procedure similar to that used in Example 5 in Section 7.5 to solve this differential equation.

(c) Find the solution to part (b) that satisfies $P(0) = 300$.

(d) Superimpose the graph of the solution in part (c) with $k = 0.1$ on a slope field of the differential equation.

(e) Solve the general extended differential equation with the restriction $m < P < M$.

46. *Integral Tables* Antiderivatives of various generic functions can be found as formulas in *integral tables*. See if you can derive the formulas that would appear in an integral table for the following functions. (Here, a is an arbitrary constant.)

(a) $\int \frac{dx}{a^2 + x^2}$ **(b)** $\int \frac{dx}{a^2 - x^2}$ **(c)** $\int \frac{dx}{(a + x)^2}$

Extending the Ideas

47. *Partial Fractions with Repeated Linear Factors*

If

$$f(x) = \frac{P(x)}{(x - r)^m}$$

is a rational function with the degree of P less than m, then the partial fraction decomposition of f is

$$f(x) = \frac{A_1}{x - r} + \frac{A_2}{(x - r)^2} + \cdots + \frac{A_m}{(x - r)^m}.$$

For example,

$$\frac{4x}{(x - 2)^2} = \frac{4}{x - 2} + \frac{8}{(x - 2)^2}.$$

Use partial fractions to find the following integrals:

(a) $\int \frac{5x}{(x + 3)^2}\,dx$

(b) $\int \frac{5x}{(x + 3)^3}\,dx$ [*Hint:* Use part (a).]

48. *More on Repeated Linear Factors* The Heaviside Method is not very effective at finding the unknown numerators for partial fraction decompositions with repeated linear factors, but here is another way to find them.

(a) If $\frac{x^2 + 3x + 5}{(x - 1)^3} = \frac{A}{x - 1} + \frac{B}{(x - 1)^2} + \frac{C}{(x - 1)^3}$, show that

$A(x - 1)^2 + B(x - 1) + C = x^2 + 3x + 5.$

(b) Expand and equate coefficients of like terms to show that $A = 1$, $-2A + B = 3$, and $A - B + C = 5$. Then find A, B, and C.

(c) Use partial fractions to evaluate $\int \frac{x^2 + 3x + 5}{(x - 1)^3}\,dx.$

Quick Quiz: Sections 7.4 and 7.5

You may use a graphing calculator to solve the following problems.

1. **Multiple Choice** The rate at which acreage is being consumed by a plot of kudzu is proportional to the number of acres already consumed at time t. If there are 2 acres consumed when $t = 1$ and 3 acres consumed when $t = 5$, how many acres will be consumed when $t = 8$?

   (A) 3.750 **(B)** 4.000 **(C)** 4.066 **(D)** 4.132 **(E)** 4.600

2. **Multiple Choice** Let $F(x)$ be an antiderivative of $\cos(x^2)$. If $F(1) = 0$, then $F(5) =$

   (A) -0.099 **(B)** -0.153 **(C)** -0.293 **(D)** -0.992 **(E)** -1.833

3. **Multiple Choice** $\displaystyle\int \frac{dx}{(x-1)(x+3)} =$

   (A) $\dfrac{1}{4}\ln\left|\dfrac{x-1}{x+3}\right| + C$ **(B)** $\dfrac{1}{4}\ln\left|\dfrac{x+3}{x-1}\right| + C$

   (C) $\dfrac{1}{2}\ln|(x-1)(x+3)| + C$ **(D)** $\dfrac{1}{2}\ln\left|\dfrac{2x+2}{(x-1)(x+3)}\right| + C$

   (E) $\ln|(x-1)(x+3)| + C$

4. **Free Response** A population is modeled by a function P that satisfies the logistic differential equation

$$\frac{dP}{dt} = \frac{P}{5}\left(1 - \frac{P}{10}\right).$$

   (a) If $P(0) = 3$, what is $\lim_{t\to\infty} P(t)$?

   (b) If $P(0) = 20$, what is $\lim_{t\to\infty} P(t)$?

   (c) A different population is modeled by a function Y that satisfies the separable differential equation

$$\frac{dY}{dt} = \frac{Y}{5}\left(1 - \frac{t}{10}\right).$$

   Find $Y(t)$ if $Y(0) = 3$.

   (d) For the function Y found in part (c), what is $\lim_{t\to\infty} Y(t)$?

Chapter 7 Key Terms

antidifferentiation by parts (p. 345)
antidifferentiation by substitution (p. 339)
arbitrary constant of integration (p. 336)
carbon-14 dating (p. 358)
carrying capacity (p. 371)
compounded continuously (p. 356)
constant of integration (p. 336)
continuous interest rate (p. 356)
decay constant (p. 355)
differential equation (p. 325)
direction field (p. 327)
Euler's Method (p. 329)
evaluate an integral (p. 336)
exact differential equation (p. 325)
general solution to a differential equation (p. 325)
growth constant (p. 355)
first-order differential equation (p. 325)
first-order linear differential equation (p. 328)
graphical solution of a differential equation (p. 326)
half-life (p. 356)
Heaviside method (p. 367)
indefinite integral (p. 336)
initial condition (p. 325)
initial value problem (p. 325)
integral sign (p. 336)
integrand (p. 336)
integration by parts (p. 345)
Law of Exponential Change (p. 355)
Leibniz notation for integrals (p. 338)
logistic differential equation (p. 369)
logistic growth model (p. 371)
logistic regression (p. 369)
Newton's Law of Cooling (p. 358)
numerical method (p. 330)
numerical solution of a differential equation (p. 330)
order of a differential equation (p. 325)
partial fraction decomposition (p. 367)
particular solution (p. 325)
proper rational function (p. 367)
properties of indefinite integrals (p. 337)
radioactive (p. 356)
radioactive decay (p. 356)
resistance proportional to velocity (p. 364)
second-order differential equation (p. 335)
separable differential equations (p. 354)
separation of variables (p. 354)
slope field (p. 327)
solution of a differential equation (p. 325)
substitution in definite integrals (p. 341)
tabular integration (p. 348)
variable of integration (p. 336)

Chapter 7 Review Exercises

Exercise numbers with a gray background indicate problems that the authors have designed to be solved *without a calculator.*

The collection of exercises marked in red could be used as a chapter test.

In Exercises 1–10, evaluate the integral analytically. You may use NINT to support your result.

1. $\displaystyle\int_0^{\pi/3} \sec^2 \theta \, d\theta$

2. $\displaystyle\int_1^2 \left(x + \frac{1}{x^2}\right) dx$

3. $\displaystyle\int_0^1 \frac{36\, dx}{(2x+1)^3}$

4. $\displaystyle\int_{-1}^1 2x \sin(1 - x^2)\, dx$

5. $\displaystyle\int_0^{\pi/2} 5 \sin^{3/2} x \cos x \, dx$

6. $\displaystyle\int_{1/2}^4 \frac{x^2 + 3x}{x}\, dx$

7. $\displaystyle\int_0^{\pi/4} e^{\tan x} \sec^2 x \, dx$

8. $\displaystyle\int_1^e \frac{\sqrt{\ln r}}{r}\, dr$

9. $\displaystyle\int_0^1 \frac{x}{x^2 + 5x + 6}\, dx$

10. $\displaystyle\int_1^2 \frac{2x + 6}{x^2 - 3x}\, dx$

In Exercises 11–24, evaluate the integral.

11. $\displaystyle\int \frac{\cos x}{2 - \sin x}\, dx$

12. $\displaystyle\int \frac{dx}{\sqrt[3]{3x+4}}$

13. $\displaystyle\int \frac{t\, dt}{t^2 + 5}$

14. $\displaystyle\int \frac{1}{\theta^2} \sec \frac{1}{\theta} \tan \frac{1}{\theta}\, d\theta$

15. $\displaystyle\int \frac{\tan(\ln y)}{y}\, dy$

16. $\displaystyle\int e^x \sec(e^x)\, dx$

17. $\displaystyle\int \frac{dx}{x \ln x}$

18. $\displaystyle\int \frac{dt}{t\sqrt{t}}$

19. $\displaystyle\int x^3 \cos x \, dx$

20. $\displaystyle\int x^4 \ln x \, dx$

21. $\displaystyle\int e^{3x} \sin x \, dx$

22. $\displaystyle\int x^2 e^{-3x}\, dx$

23. $\displaystyle\int \frac{25}{x^2 - 25}\, dx$

24. $\displaystyle\int \frac{5x + 2}{2x^2 + x - 1}\, dx$

In Exercises 25–34, solve the initial value problem analytically. Support your solution by overlaying its graph on a slope field of the differential equation.

25. $\dfrac{dy}{dx} = 1 + x + \dfrac{x^2}{2}, \quad y(0) = 1$

26. $\dfrac{dy}{dx} = \left(x + \dfrac{1}{x}\right)^2, \quad y(1) = 1$

27. $\dfrac{dy}{dt} = \dfrac{1}{t+4}, \quad y(-3) = 2$

28. $\dfrac{dy}{d\theta} = \csc 2\theta \cot 2\theta, \quad y(\pi/4) = 1$

29. $\dfrac{d^2y}{dx^2} = 2x - \dfrac{1}{x^2}, \quad x > 0, \quad y'(1) = 1, \quad y(1) = 0$

30. $\dfrac{d^3r}{dt^3} = -\cos t, \quad r''(0) = r'(0) = r(0) = -1$

31. $\dfrac{dy}{dx} = y + 2, \quad y(0) = 2$

32. $\dfrac{dy}{dx} = (2x+1)(y+1), \quad y(-1) = 1$

33. $\dfrac{dy}{dt} = y(1 - y), \quad y(0) = 0.1$

34. $\dfrac{dy}{dx} = 0.001y(100 - y), \quad y(0) = 5$

35. Find an integral equation $y = \int_a^x f(t)dt + b$ such that $dy/dx = \sin^3 x$ and $y = 5$ when $x = 4$.

36. Find an integral equation $y = \int_a^x f(t)dt + b$ such that $dy/dx = \sqrt{1 + x^4}$ and $y = 2$ when $x = 1$.

In Exercises 37 and 38, construct a slope field for the differential equation. In each case, copy the graph shown and draw tiny segments through the twelve lattice points shown in the graph. Use slope analysis, not your graphing calculator.

37. $\dfrac{dy}{dx} = -x$

38. $\dfrac{dy}{dx} = 1 - y$

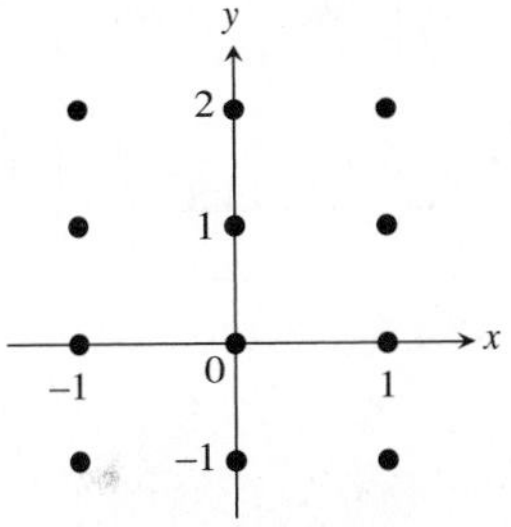

In Exercises 39–42, match the differential equation with the appropriate slope field. (All slope fields are shown in the window $[-6, 6]$ by $[-4, 4]$.)

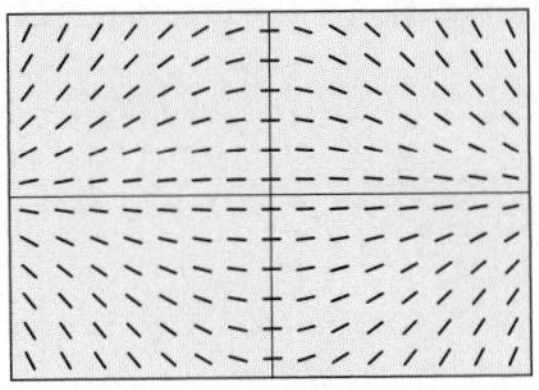
(a)

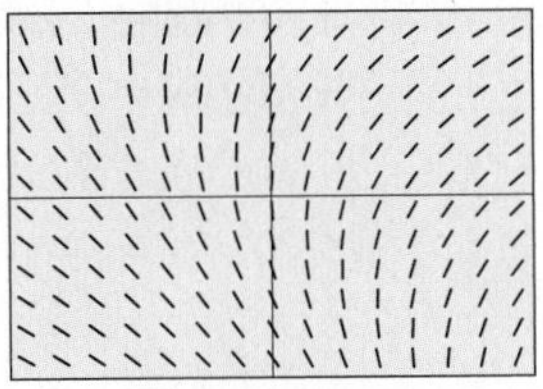
(b)

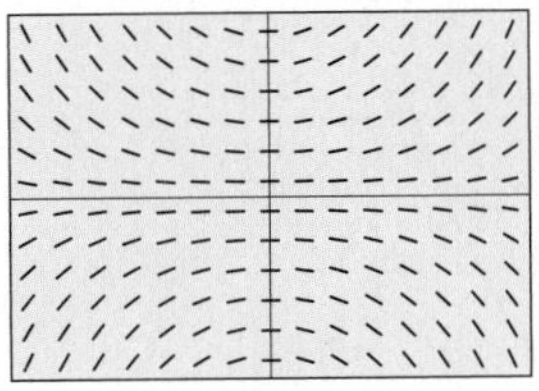
(c)

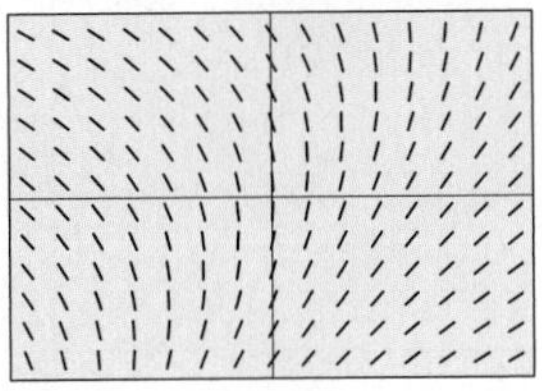
(d)

39. $\dfrac{dy}{dx} = \dfrac{5}{x + y}$

40. $\dfrac{dy}{dx} = \dfrac{5}{x - y}$

41. $\dfrac{dy}{dx} = \dfrac{xy}{10}$

42. $\dfrac{dy}{dx} = -\dfrac{xy}{10}$

43. Suppose $dy/dx = x + y - 1$ and $y = 1$ when $x = 1$. Use Euler's Method with increments of $\Delta x = 0.1$ to approximate the value of y when $x = 1.3$.

44. Suppose $dy/dx = x - y$ and $y = 2$ when $x = 1$. Use Euler's Method with increments of $\Delta x = -0.1$ to approximate the value of y when $x = 0.7$.

In Exercises 45 and 46, match the indefinite integral with the graph of one of the antiderivatives of the integrand.

45. $\int \frac{\sin x}{x}\,dx$

46. $\int e^{-x^2}\,dx$

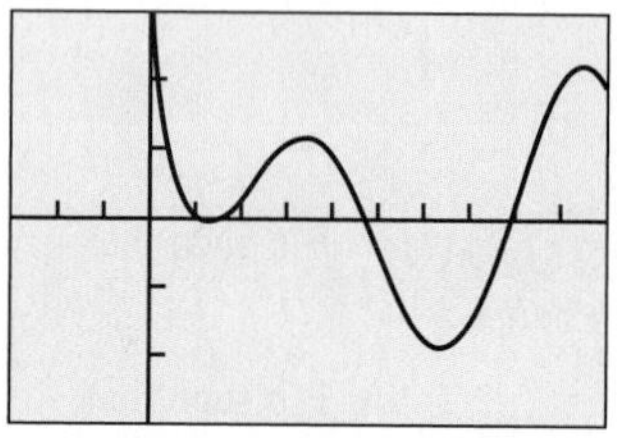

[–3, 10] by [–3, 3]

(a)

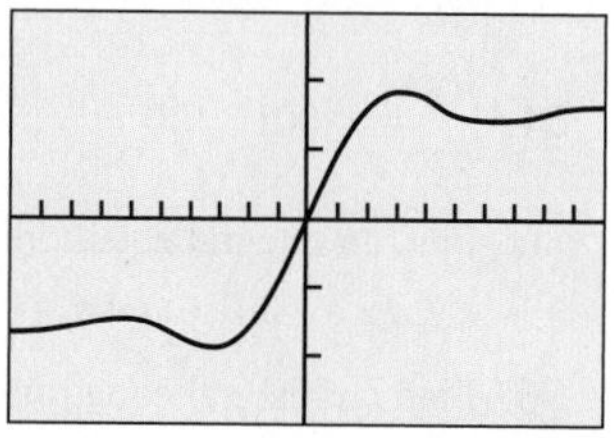

[–10, 10] by [–3, 3]

(b)

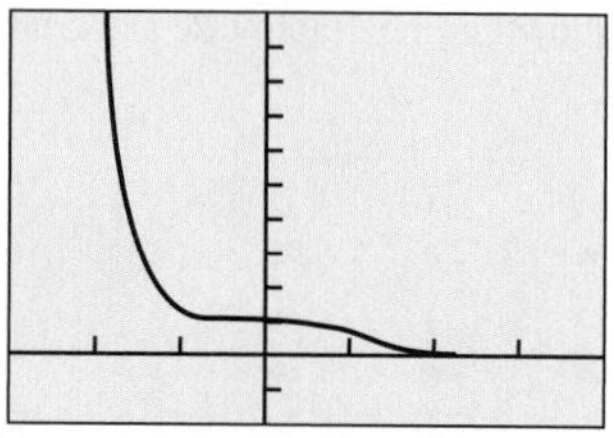

[–3, 4] by [–2, 10]

(c)

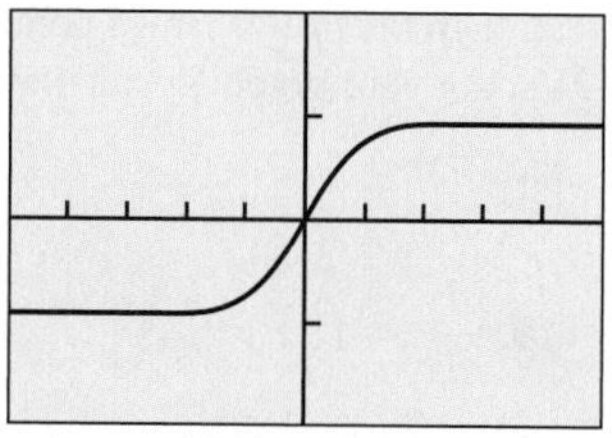

[–5, 5] by [–2, 2]

(d)

47. Writing to Learn The figure shows the graph of the function $y = f(x)$ that is the solution of one of the following initial value problems. Which one? How do you know?

i. $dy/dx = 2x, \quad y(1) = 0$

ii. $dy/dx = x^2, \quad y(1) = 1$

iii. $dy/dx = 2x + 2, \quad y(1) = 1$

iv. $dy/dx = 2x, \quad y(1) = 1$

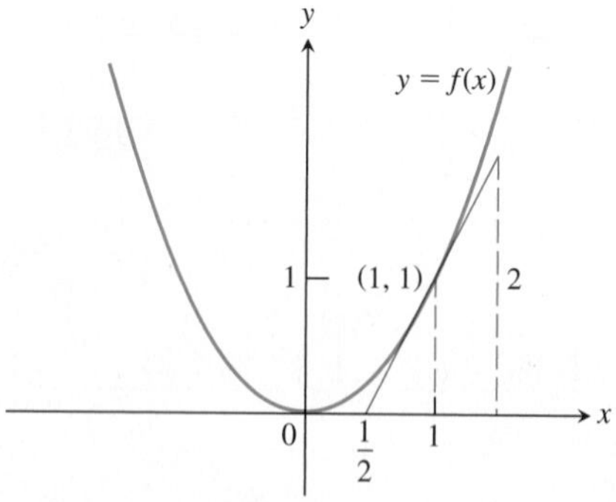

48. Writing to Learn Does the following initial value problem have a solution? Explain.

$$\frac{d^2y}{dx^2} = 0, \quad y'(0) = 1, \quad y(0) = 0$$

49. *Moving Particle* The acceleration of a particle moving along a coordinate line is

$$\frac{d^2s}{dt^2} = 2 + 6t \text{ m/sec}^2.$$

At $t = 0$ the velocity is 4 m/sec.

(a) Find the velocity as a function of time t.

(b) How far does the particle move during the first second of its trip, from $t = 0$ to $t = 1$?

50. *Sketching Solutions* Draw a possible graph for the function $y = f(x)$ with slope field given in the figure that satisfies the initial condition $y(0) = 0$.

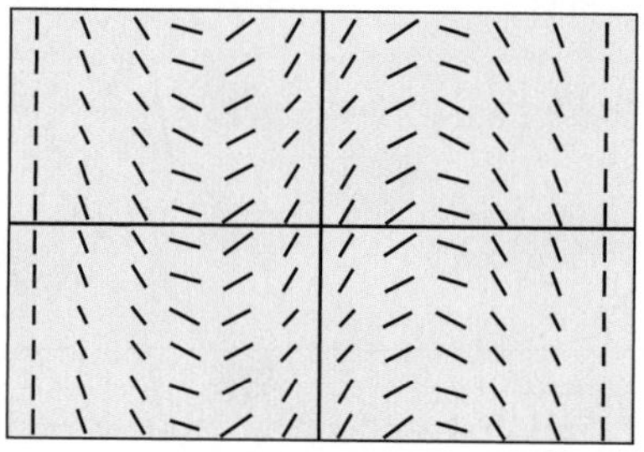

[–10, 10] by [–10, 10]

51. *Californium-252* What costs \$27 million per gram and can be used to treat brain cancer, analyze coal for its sulfur content, and detect explosives in luggage? The answer is californium-252, a radioactive isotope so rare that only about 8 g of it have been made in the Western world since its discovery by Glenn Seaborg in 1950. The half-life of the isotope is 2.645 years—long enough for a useful service life and short enough to have a high radioactivity per unit mass. One microgram of the isotope releases 170 million neutrons per second.

(a) What is the value of k in the decay equation for this isotope?

(b) What is the isotope's mean life? (See Exercise 19, Section 7.4.)

52. *Cooling a Pie* A deep-dish apple pie, whose internal temperature was 220°F when removed from the oven, was set out on a 40°F breezy porch to cool. Fifteen minutes later, the pie's internal temperature was 180°F. How long did it take the pie to cool from there to 70°F?

53. *Finding Temperature* A pan of warm water (46°C) was put into a refrigerator. Ten minutes later, the water's temperature was 39°C; 10 minutes after that, it was 33°C. Use Newton's Law of Cooling to estimate how cold the refrigerator was.

54. *Art Forgery* A painting attributed to Vermeer (1632–1675), which should contain no more than 96.2% of its original carbon-14, contains 99.5% instead. About how old is the forgery?

55. *Carbon-14* What is the age of a sample of charcoal in which 90% of the carbon-14 that was originally present has decayed?

56. *Appreciation* A violin made in 1785 by John Betts, one of England's finest violin makers, cost \$250 in 1924 and sold for \$7500 in 1988. Assuming a constant relative rate of appreciation, what was that rate?

57. **Working Underwater** The intensity $L(x)$ of light x feet beneath the surface of the ocean satisfies the differential equation

$$\frac{dL}{dx} = -kL,$$

where k is a constant. As a diver you know from experience that diving to 18 ft in the Caribbean Sea cuts the intensity in half. You cannot work without artificial light when the intensity falls below a tenth of the surface value. About how deep can you expect to work without artificial light?

58. ***Transport Through a Cell Membrane*** Under certain conditions, the result of the movement of a dissolved substance across a cell's membrane is described by the equation

$$\frac{dy}{dt} = k\frac{A}{V}(c - y),$$

where y is the concentration of the substance inside the cell, and dy/dt is the rate with which y changes over time. The letters k, A, V, and c stand for constants, k being the *permeability coefficient* (a property of the membrane), A the surface area of the membrane, V the cell's volume, and c the concentration of the substance outside the cell. The equation says that the rate at which the concentration changes within the cell is proportional to the difference between it and the outside concentration.

(a) Solve the equation for $y(t)$, using $y_0 = y(0)$.

(b) Find the steady-state concentration, $\lim_{t\to\infty} y(t)$.

59. ***Logistic Equation*** The spread of flu in a certain school is given by the formula

$$P(t) = \frac{150}{1 + e^{4.3-t}},$$

where t is the number of days after students are first exposed to infected students.

(a) Show that the function is a solution of a logistic differential equation. Identify k and the carrying capacity.

(b) **Writing to Learn** Estimate $P(0)$. Explain its meaning in the context of the problem.

(c) Estimate the number of days it will take for a total of 125 students to become infected.

60. ***Confirming a Solution*** Show that

$$y = \int_0^x \sin(t^2)\,dt + x^3 + x + 2$$

is the solution of the initial value problem.

Differential equation: $y'' = 2x\cos(x^2) + 6x$

Initial conditions: $y'(0) = 1, \quad y(0) = 2$

61. ***Finding an Exact Solution*** Use analytic methods to find the exact solution to

$$\frac{dP}{dt} = 0.002P\left(1 - \frac{P}{800}\right), \quad P(0) = 50.$$

62. ***Supporting a Solution*** Give two ways to provide graphical support for the integral formula

$$\int x^2 \ln x\,dx = \frac{x^3}{3}\ln x - \frac{x^3}{9} + C.$$

63. ***Doubling Time*** Find the amount of time required for \$10,000 to double if the 6.3% annual interest is compounded **(a)** annually, **(b)** continuously.

64. ***Constant of Integration*** Let

$$f(x) = \int_0^x u(t)\,dt \quad \text{and} \quad g(x) = \int_3^x u(t)\,dt.$$

(a) Show that f and g are antiderivatives of $u(x)$.

(b) Find a constant C so that $f(x) = g(x) + C$.

65. ***Population Growth*** Table 7.9 shows the population of Anchorage, AK for selected years between 1950 and 2003.

TABLE 7.9 Population of Anchorage, AK

Years After 1950	Population
0	11,254
20	48,081
30	174,431
53	270,951

Source: Bureau of the Census, U.S. Department of Commerce, as reported in The World Almanac and Book of Facts, 2005

(a) Use logistic regression to find a curve to model the data and superimpose it on a scatter plot of population against years after 1950.

(b) Based on the regression equation, what number will the Anchorage population approach in the long run?

(c) Write a logistic differential equation in the form $dp/dt = kP(M - P)$ that models the growth of the Anchorage data in Table 7.9.

(d) **Writing to Learn** The population of Anchorage in 2000 was 260,283. If this point is included in the data, how does it affect carrying capacity predicted by the regression equation? Is there reason to be concerned about our model?

66. ***Temperature Experiment*** A temperature probe is removed from a cup of hot chocolate and placed in water whose temperature (T_s) is 0°C. The data in Table 7.10 were collected over the next 30 sec with a CBL™ temperature probe.

TABLE 7.10 Experimental Data

Time t (sec)	T (°C)
2	74.68
5	61.99
10	34.89
15	21.95
20	15.36
25	11.89
30	10.02

(a) Find an exponential regression equation for the (t, T) data. Superimpose its graph on a scatter plot of the data.

(b) Estimate when the temperature probe will read 40°C.

(c) Estimate the hot chocolate's temperature when the temperature probe was removed.

AP* Examination Preparation

You may use a graphing calculator to solve the following problems.

67. The spread of a rumor through a small town is modeled by $dy/dt = 1.2y(1 - y)$, where y is the proportion of the townspeople who have heard the rumor at time t in days. At time $t = 0$, ten percent of the townspeople have heard the rumor.

(a) What proportion of the townspeople have heard the rumor when it is spreading the fastest?

(b) Find y explicitly as a function of t.

(c) At what time t is the rumor spreading the fastest?

68. A population P of wolves at time t years $(t \geq 0)$ is increasing at a rate directly proportional to $600 - P$, where the constant of proportionality is k.

(a) If $P(0) = 200$, find $P(t)$ in terms of t and k.

(b) If $P(2) = 500$, find k.

(c) Find $\lim_{t\to\infty} P(t)$.

69. Let $v(t)$ be the velocity, in feet per second, of a skydiver at time t seconds, $t \geq 0$. After her parachute opens, her velocity satisfies the differential equation $dv/dt = -2(v + 17)$, with initial condition $v(0) = -47$.

(a) Use separation of variables to find an expression for v in terms of t, where t is measured in seconds.

(b) Terminal velocity is defined as $\lim_{t\to\infty} v(t)$. Find the terminal velocity of the skydiver to the nearest foot per second.

(c) It is safe to land when her speed is 20 feet per second. At what time t does she reach this speed?

CHAPTER

8 Applications of Definite Integrals

The art of pottery developed independently in many ancient civilizations and still exists in modern times. The desired shape of the side of a pottery vase can be described by

$$y = 5.0 + 2\sin(x/4) \ (0 \le x \le 8\pi),$$

where x is the height and y is the radius at height x (in inches).

A base for the vase is preformed and placed on a potter's wheel. How much clay should be added to the base to form this vase if the inside radius is always 1 inch less than the outside radius? Section 8.3 contains the needed mathematics.

CHAPTER 8 Overview

By this point it should be apparent that finding the limits of Riemann sums is not just an intellectual exercise; it is a natural way to calculate mathematical or physical quantities that appear to be irregular when viewed as a whole, but which can be fragmented into regular pieces. We calculate values for the regular pieces using known formulas, then sum them to find a value for the irregular whole. This approach to problem solving was around for thousands of years before calculus came along, but it was tedious work and the more accurate you wanted to be the more tedious it became.

With calculus it became possible to get *exact* answers for these problems with almost no effort, because in the limit these sums became definite integrals and definite integrals could be evaluated with antiderivatives. With calculus, the challenge became one of fitting an integrable function to the situation at hand (the "modeling" step) and then finding an antiderivative for it.

Today we can finesse the antidifferentiation step (occasionally an insurmountable hurdle for our predecessors) with programs like NINT, but the modeling step is no less crucial. Ironically, it is the modeling step that is thousands of years old. Before either calculus or technology can be of assistance, we must still break down the irregular whole into regular parts and set up a function to be integrated. We have already seen how the process works with area, volume, and average value, for example. Now we will focus more closely on the underlying modeling step: how to set up the function to be integrated.

8.1 Integral as Net Change

What you will learn about . . .

- Linear Motion Revisited
- General Strategy
- Consumption over Time
- Net Change from Data
- Work

and why . . .

The integral is a tool that can be used to calculate net change and total accumulation.

Linear Motion Revisited

In many applications, the integral is viewed as net change over time. The classic example of this kind is distance traveled, a problem we discussed in Chapter 6.

EXAMPLE 1 Interpreting a Velocity Function

Figure 8.1 shows the velocity

$$\frac{ds}{dt} = v(t) = t^2 - \frac{8}{(t+1)^2} \quad \frac{\text{cm}}{\text{sec}}$$

of a particle moving along a horizontal s-axis for $0 \le t \le 5$. Describe the motion.

SOLUTION

Solve Graphically The graph of v (Figure 8.1) starts with $v(0) = -8$, which we interpret as saying that the particle has an initial velocity of 8 cm/sec to the left. It slows to a halt at about $t = 1.25$ sec, after which it moves to the right $(v > 0)$ with increasing speed, reaching a velocity of $v(5) \approx 24.8$ cm/sec at the end. ***Now Try Exercise 1(a).***

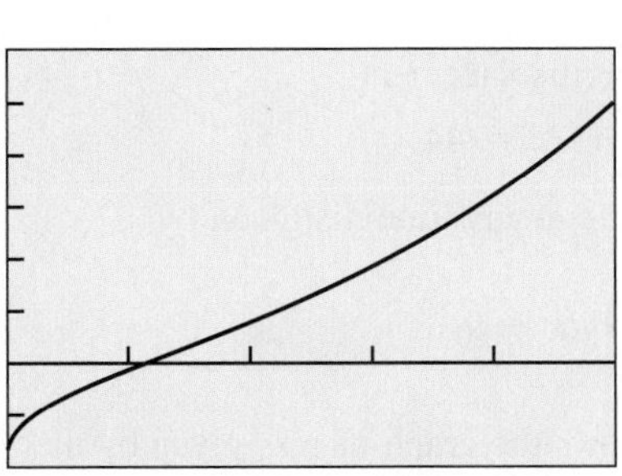

[0, 5] by [–10, 30]

Figure 8.1 The velocity function in Example 1.

EXAMPLE 2 Finding Position from Displacement

Suppose the initial position of the particle in Example 1 is $s(0) = 9$. What is the particle's position at **(a)** $t = 1$ sec? **(b)** $t = 5$ sec?

SOLUTION

Solve Analytically

(a) The position at $t = 1$ is the initial position $s(0)$ plus the displacement (the amount, Δs, that the position changed from $t = 0$ to $t = 1$). When velocity is

continued

Reminder from Section 3.4

A change in position is a **displacement.** If $s(t)$ is a body's position at time t, the displacement over the time interval from t to $t + \Delta t$ is $s(t + \Delta t) - s(t)$. The displacement may be positive, negative, or zero, depending on the motion.

constant during a motion, we can find the displacement (change in position) with the formula

$$\text{Displacement} = \text{rate of change} \times \text{time.}$$

But in our case the velocity varies, so we resort instead to partitioning the time interval $[0, 1]$ into subintervals of length Δt so short that the velocity is effectively constant on each subinterval. If t_k is any time in the kth subinterval, the particle's velocity throughout that interval will be close to $v(t_k)$. The change in the particle's position during the brief time this constant velocity applies is

$$v(t_k)\Delta t. \quad \text{Rate of change} \times \text{time}$$

If $v(t_k)$ is negative, the displacement is negative and the particle will move left. If $v(t_k)$ is positive, the particle will move right. The sum

$$\sum v(t_k)\Delta t$$

of all these small position changes approximates the displacement for the time interval $[0, 1]$.

The sum $\sum v(t_k)\Delta t$ is a Riemann sum for the continuous function $v(t)$ over $[0, 1]$. As the norms of the partitions go to zero, the approximations improve and the sums converge to the integral of v over $[0, 1]$, giving

$$\begin{aligned} \text{Displacement} &= \int_0^1 v(t)\,dt \\ &= \int_0^1 \left(t^2 - \frac{8}{(t+1)^2}\right) dt \\ &= \left[\frac{t^3}{3} + \frac{8}{t+1}\right]_0^1 \\ &= \frac{1}{3} + \frac{8}{2} - 8 = -\frac{11}{3}. \end{aligned}$$

During the first second of motion, the particle moves $11/3$ cm to the left. It starts at $s(0) = 9$, so its position at $t = 1$ is

$$\text{New position} = \text{initial position} + \text{displacement} = 9 - \frac{11}{3} = \frac{16}{3}.$$

(b) If we model the displacement from $t = 0$ to $t = 5$ in the same way, we arrive at

$$\text{Displacement} = \int_0^5 v(t)\,dt = \left[\frac{t^3}{3} + \frac{8}{t+1}\right]_0^5 = 35.$$

The motion has the net effect of displacing the particle 35 cm to the right of its starting point. The particle's final position is

$$\begin{aligned} \text{Final position} &= \text{initial position} + \text{displacement} \\ &= s(0) + 35 = 9 + 35 = 44. \end{aligned}$$

Support Graphically The position of the particle at any time t is given by

$$s(t) = \int_0^t \left[u^2 - \frac{8}{(u+1)^2}\right] du + 9,$$

because $s'(t) = v(t)$ and $s(0) = 9$. Figure 8.2 shows the graph of $s(t)$ given by the parametrization

$$x(t) = \text{NINT}\,(v(u), u, 0, t) + 9, \quad y(t) = t, \quad 0 \le t \le 5.$$

continued

(a) Figure 8.2a supports that the position of the particle at $t = 1$ is $16/3$.

(b) Figure 8.2b shows the position of the particle is 44 at $t = 5$. Therefore, the displacement is $44 - 9 = 35$.

Now Try Exercise 1(b).

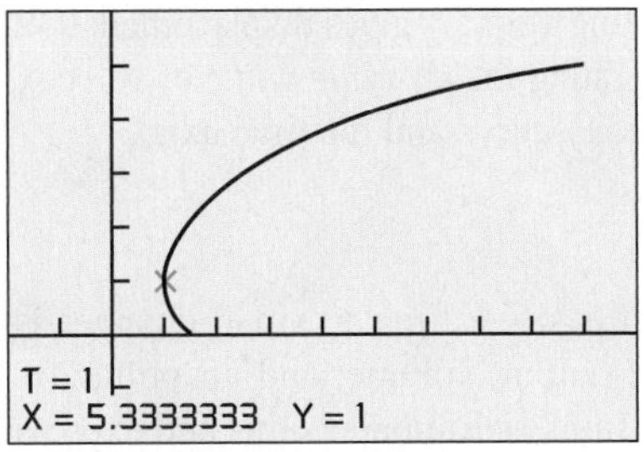

[–10, 50] by [–2, 6]

(a)

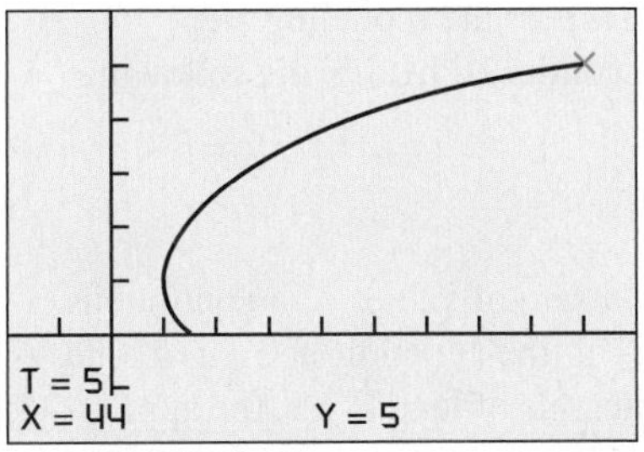

[–10, 50] by [–2, 6]

(b)

Figure 8.2 Using TRACE and the parametrization in Example 2 you can "see" the left and right motion of the particle.

The reason for our method in Example 2 was to illustrate the *modeling step* that will be used throughout this chapter. We can also solve Example 2 using the techniques of Chapter 7 as shown in Exploration 1.

EXPLORATION 1 Revisiting Example 2

The velocity of a particle moving along a horizontal s-axis for $0 \le t \le 5$ is

$$\frac{ds}{dt} = t^2 - \frac{8}{(t+1)^2}.$$

1. Use the indefinite integral of ds/dt to find the solution of the initial value problem

$$\frac{ds}{dt} = t^2 - \frac{8}{(t+1)^2}, \qquad s(0) = 9.$$

2. Determine the position of the particle at $t = 1$. Compare your answer with the answer to Example 2a.
3. Determine the position of the particle at $t = 5$. Compare your answer with the answer to Example 2b.

We know now that the particle in Example 1 was at $s(0) = 9$ at the beginning of the motion and at $s(5) = 44$ at the end. But it did not travel from 9 to 44 directly—it began its trip by moving to the left (Figure 8.2). How much distance did the particle actually travel? We find out in Example 3.

EXAMPLE 3 Calculating Total Distance Traveled

Find the *total distance traveled* by the particle in Example 1.

SOLUTION

Solve Analytically We partition the time interval as in Example 2 but record every position shift as *positive* by taking absolute values. The Riemann sum approximating total distance traveled is

$$\sum |v(t_k)| \Delta t,$$

and we are led to the integral

$$\text{Total distance traveled} = \int_0^5 |v(t)|\, dt = \int_0^5 \left| t^2 - \frac{8}{(t+1)^2} \right| dt.$$

Evaluate Numerically We have

$$\text{NINT}\left(\left| t^2 - \frac{8}{(t+1)^2} \right|, t, 0, 5 \right) \approx 42.59.$$

Now Try Exercise 1(c).

What we learn from Examples 2 and 3 is this: Integrating velocity gives displacement (net area between the velocity curve and the time axis). Integrating the *absolute value* of velocity gives total distance traveled (total area between the velocity curve and the time axis).

General Strategy

The idea of fragmenting net effects into finite sums of easily estimated small changes is not new. We used it in Section 6.1 to estimate cardiac output, volume, and air pollution. What *is* new is that we can now identify many of these sums as Riemann sums and express their limits as integrals. The advantages of doing so are twofold. First, we can evaluate one of these integrals to get an accurate result in less time than it takes to crank out even the crudest estimate from a finite sum. Second, the integral itself becomes a formula that enables us to solve similar problems without having to repeat the modeling step.

The strategy that we began in Section 6.1 and have continued here is the following:

Strategy for Modeling with Integrals

1. *Approximate what you want to find as a Riemann sum* of values of a continuous function multiplied by interval lengths. If $f(x)$ is the function and $[a, b]$ the interval, and you partition the interval into subintervals of length Δx, the approximating sums will have the form $\sum f(c_k)\Delta x$ with c_k a point in the kth subinterval.
2. *Write a definite integral,* here $\int_b^a f(x)\,dx$, to express the limit of these sums as the norms of the partitions go to zero.
3. *Evaluate the integral* numerically or with an antiderivative.

EXAMPLE 4 Modeling the Effects of Acceleration

A car moving with initial velocity of 5 mph accelerates at the rate of $a(t) = 2.4t$ mph per second for 8 seconds.

(a) How fast is the car going when the 8 seconds are up?

(b) How far did the car travel during those 8 seconds?

SOLUTION

(a) We first model the effect of the acceleration on the car's velocity.

Step 1:

Approximate the net change in velocity as a Riemann sum. When acceleration is constant,

$$\text{velocity change} = \text{acceleration} \times \text{time applied}. \qquad \text{Rate of change} \times \text{time}$$

To apply this formula, we partition $[0, 8]$ into short subintervals of length Δt. On each subinterval the acceleration is nearly constant, so if t_k is any point in the kth subinterval, the change in velocity imparted by the acceleration in the subinterval is approximately

$$a(t_k)\,\Delta t \text{ mph.} \qquad \frac{\text{mph}}{\text{sec}} \times \text{sec}$$

The net change in velocity for $0 \le t \le 8$ is approximately

$$\sum a(t_k)\,\Delta t \text{ mph.}$$

Step 2:

Write a definite integral. The limit of these sums as the norms of the partitions go to zero is

$$\int_0^8 a(t)\,dt.$$

continued

Step 3:

Evaluate the integral. Using an antiderivative, we have

$$\text{Net velocity change} = \int_0^8 2.4t\,dt = 1.2t^2\Big]_0^8 = 76.8\text{ mph.}$$

So, how fast is the car going when the 8 seconds are up? Its initial velocity is 5 mph and the acceleration adds another 76.8 mph for a total of 81.8 mph.

(b) There is nothing special about the upper limit 8 in the preceding calculation. Applying the acceleration for any length of time t adds

$$\int_0^t 2.4u\,du\text{ mph}$$ *u* is just a dummy variable here.

to the car's velocity, giving

$$v(t) = 5 + \int_0^t 2.4u\,du = 5 + 1.2t^2\text{ mph.}$$

The distance traveled from $t = 0$ to $t = 8$ sec is

$$\int_0^8 |v(t)|\,dt = \int_0^8 (5 + 1.2t^2)\,dt$$ Extension of Example 3

$$= \Big[5t + 0.4t^3\Big]_0^8$$

$$= 244.8\text{ mph} \times \text{seconds.}$$

Miles-per-hour second is not a distance unit that we normally work with! To convert to miles we multiply by hours/second $= 1/3600$, obtaining

$$244.8 \times \frac{1}{3600} = 0.068\text{ mile.}$$ $\frac{\text{mi}}{\text{h}} \times \text{sec} \times \frac{\text{h}}{\text{sec}} = \text{mi}$

The car traveled 0.068 mi during the 8 seconds of acceleration. ***Now Try Exercise 9.***

Consumption over Time

The integral is a natural tool to calculate net change and total accumulation of more quantities than just distance and velocity. Integrals can be used to calculate growth, decay, and, as in the next example, consumption. Whenever you want to find the cumulative effect of a varying rate of change, integrate it.

EXAMPLE 5 Potato Consumption

From 1970 to 1980, the rate of potato consumption in a particular country was $C(t) = 2.2 + 1.1^t$ millions of bushels per year, with t being years since the beginning of 1970. How many bushels were consumed from the beginning of 1972 to the end of 1973?

SOLUTION

We seek the cumulative effect of the consumption rate for $2 \le t \le 4$.

Step 1:

Riemann sum. We partition $[2, 4]$ into subintervals of length Δt and let t_k be a time in the kth subinterval. The amount consumed during this interval is approximately

$$C(t_k)\Delta t\text{ million bushels.}$$

The consumption for $2 \le t \le 4$ is approximately

$$\sum C(t_k)\Delta t\text{ million bushels.}$$

continued

Step 2:

Definite integral. The amount consumed from $t = 2$ to $t = 4$ is the limit of these sums as the norms of the partitions go to zero.

$$\int_2^4 C(t)\,dt = \int_2^4 (2.2 + 1.1^t)\,dt \text{ million bushels}$$

Step 3:

Evaluate. Evaluating numerically, we obtain

$$\text{NINT}\,(2.2 + 1.1^t, t, 2, 4) \approx 7.066 \text{ million bushels.}$$

Now Try Exercise 21.

Net Change from Data

Many real applications begin with data, not a fully modeled function. In the next example, we are given data on the rate at which a pump operates in consecutive 5-minute intervals and asked to find the total amount pumped.

TABLE 8.1 Pumping Rates

Time (min)	Rate (gal/min)
0	58
5	60
10	65
15	64
20	58
25	57
30	55
35	55
40	59
45	60
50	60
55	63
60	63

EXAMPLE 6 Finding Gallons Pumped from Rate Data

A pump connected to a generator operates at a varying rate, depending on how much power is being drawn from the generator to operate other machinery. The rate (gallons per minute) at which the pump operates is recorded at 5-minute intervals for one hour as shown in Table 8.1. How many gallons were pumped during that hour?

SOLUTION

Let $R(t)$, $0 \leq t \leq 60$, be the pumping rate as a continuous function of time for the hour. We can partition the hour into short subintervals of length Δt on which the rate is nearly constant and form the sum $\sum R(t_k)\,\Delta t$ as an approximation to the amount pumped during the hour. This reveals the integral formula for the number of gallons pumped to be

$$\text{Gallons pumped} = \int_0^{60} R(t)\,dt.$$

We have no formula for R in this instance, but the 13 equally spaced values in Table 8.1 enable us to estimate the integral with the Trapezoidal Rule:

$$\int_0^{60} R(t)\,dt \approx \frac{60}{2 \cdot 12}\left[58 + 2(60) + 2(65) + \cdots + 2(63) + 63\right]$$
$$= 3582.5.$$

The total amount pumped during the hour is about 3580 gal. ***Now Try Exercise 27.***

Joules

The **joule**, abbreviated J and pronounced "jewel," is named after the English physicist James Prescott Joule (1818–1889). The defining equation is

1 joule = (1 newton)(1 meter).

In symbols, $1\text{ J} = 1\text{ N}\cdot\text{m}$.

It takes a force of about 1 N to lift an apple from a table. If you lift it 1 m you have done about 1 J of work on the apple. If you eat the apple, you will have consumed about 80 food calories, the heat equivalent of nearly 335,000 joules. If this energy were directly useful for mechanical work (it's not), it would enable you to lift 335,000 more apples up 1 m.

Work

In everyday life, *work* means an activity that requires muscular or mental effort. In science, the term refers specifically to a force acting on a body and the body's subsequent displacement. When a body moves a distance d along a straight line as a result of the action of a force of constant magnitude F in the direction of motion, the **work** done by the force is

$$W = Fd.$$

The equation $W = Fd$ is the **constant-force formula** for work.

The units of work are force × distance. In the metric system, the unit is the newton-meter, which, for historical reasons, is called a joule (see margin note). In the U.S. customary system, the most common unit of work is the **foot-pound.**

Hooke's Law for springs says that the force it takes to stretch or compress a spring x units from its natural (unstressed) length is a constant times x. In symbols,

$$F = kx,$$

where k, measured in force units per unit length, is a characteristic of the spring called the **force constant.**

EXAMPLE 7 A Bit of Work

It takes a force of 10 N to stretch a spring 2 m beyond its natural length. How much work is done in stretching the spring 4 m from its natural length?

SOLUTION

We let $F(x)$ represent the force in newtons required to stretch the spring x meters from its natural length. By Hooke's Law, $F(x) = kx$ for some constant k. We are told that

$$F(2) = 10 = k \cdot 2,$$ The force required to stretch the spring 2 m is 10 newtons.

so $k = 5$ N/m and $F(x) = 5x$ for this particular spring.

We construct an integral for the work done in applying F over the interval from $x = 0$ to $x = 4$.

Step 1:

Riemann sum. We partition the interval into subintervals on each of which F is so nearly constant that we can apply the constant-force formula for work. If x_k is any point in the kth subinterval, the value of F throughout the interval is approximately $F(x_k) = 5x_k$. The work done by F across the interval is approximately $5x_k\,\Delta x$, where Δx is the length of the interval. The sum

$$\sum F(x_k)\,\Delta x = \sum 5x_k\,\Delta x$$

approximates the work done by F from $x = 0$ to $x = 4$.

Steps 2 and 3:

Integrate. The limit of these sums as the norms of the partitions go to zero is

$$\int_0^4 F(x)\,dx = \int_0^4 5x\,dx = 5\frac{x^2}{2}\Big]_0^4 = 40 \text{ N} \cdot \text{m}.$$

Now Try Exercise 29.

Numerically, work is the area under the force graph.

We will revisit work in Section 8.5.

Quick Review 8.1 *(For help, go to Section 1.2.)*

Exercise numbers with a gray background indicate problems that the authors have designed to be solved *without a calculator.*

In Exercises 1–10, find all values of x (if any) at which the function changes sign on the given interval. Sketch a number line graph of the interval, and indicate the sign of the function on each subinterval.

Example: $f(x) = x^2 - 1$ on $[-2, 3]$

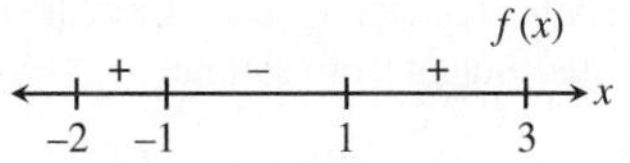

Changes sign at $x = \pm 1$.

1. $\sin 2x$ on $[-3, 2]$

2. $x^2 - 3x + 2$ on $[-2, 4]$

3. $x^2 - 2x + 3$ on $[-4, 2]$

4. $2x^3 - 3x^2 + 1$ on $[-2, 2]$

5. $x \cos 2x$ on $[0, 4]$

6. xe^{-x} on $[0, \infty)$

7. $\dfrac{x}{x^2 + 1}$ on $[-5, 30]$

8. $\dfrac{x^2 - 2}{x^2 - 4}$ on $[-3, 3]$

9. $\sec(1 + \sqrt{1 - \sin^2 x})$ on $(-\infty, \infty)$

10. $\sin(1/x)$ on $[0.1, 0.2]$

Section 8.1 Exercises

In Exercises 1–8, the function $v(t)$ is the velocity in m/sec of a particle moving along the x-axis. Use analytic methods to do each of the following:

(a) Determine when the particle is moving to the right, to the left, and stopped.

(b) Find the particle's displacement for the given time interval. If $s(0) = 3$, what is the particle's final position?

(c) Find the total distance traveled by the particle.

1. $v(t) = 5\cos t, \quad 0 \le t \le 2\pi$

2. $v(t) = 6\sin 3t, \quad 0 \le t \le \pi/2$

3. $v(t) = 49 - 9.8t, \quad 0 \le t \le 10$

4. $v(t) = 6t^2 - 18t + 12, \quad 0 \le t \le 2$

5. $v(t) = 5\sin^2 t\cos t, \quad 0 \le t \le 2\pi$

6. $v(t) = \sqrt{4 - t}, \quad 0 \le t \le 4$

7. $v(t) = e^{\sin t}\cos t, \quad 0 \le t \le 2\pi$

8. $v(t) = \dfrac{t}{1 + t^2}, \quad 0 \le t \le 3$

9. An automobile accelerates from rest at $1 + 3\sqrt{t}$ mph/sec for 9 seconds.

(a) What is its velocity after 9 seconds?

(b) How far does it travel in those 9 seconds?

10. A particle travels with velocity

$$v(t) = (t - 2)\sin t \text{ m/sec}$$

for $0 \le t \le 4$ sec.

(a) What is the particle's displacement?

(b) What is the total distance traveled?

11. ***Projectile*** Recall that the acceleration due to Earth's gravity is 32 ft/sec^2. From ground level, a projectile is fired straight upward with velocity 90 feet per second.

(a) What is its velocity after 3 seconds?

(b) When does it hit the ground?

(c) When it hits the ground, what is the net distance it has traveled?

(d) When it hits the ground, what is the total distance it has traveled?

In Exercises 12–16, a particle moves along the x-axis (units in cm). Its initial position at $t = 0$ sec is $x(0) = 15$. The figure shows the graph of the particle's velocity $v(t)$. The numbers are the *areas* of the enclosed regions.

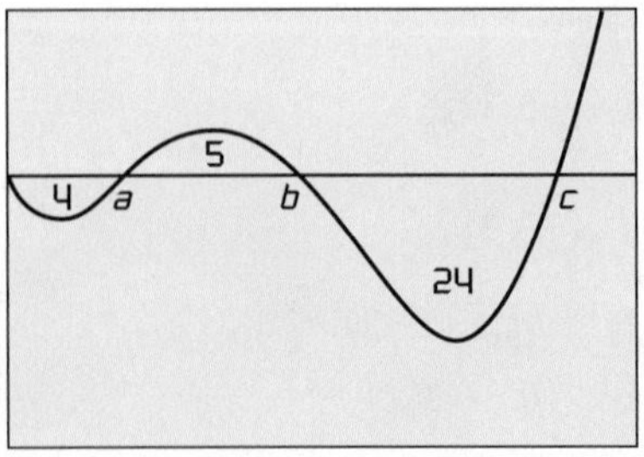

12. What is the particle's displacement between $t = 0$ and $t = c$?

13. What is the total distance traveled by the particle in the same time period?

14. Give the positions of the particle at times a, b, and c.

15. Approximately where does the particle achieve its greatest positive acceleration on the interval $[0, b]$?

16. Approximately where does the particle achieve its greatest positive acceleration on the interval $[0, c]$?

In Exercises 17–20, the graph of the velocity of a particle moving on the x-axis is given. The particle starts at $x = 2$ when $t = 0$.

(a) Find where the particle is at the end of the trip.

(b) Find the total distance traveled by the particle.

17.

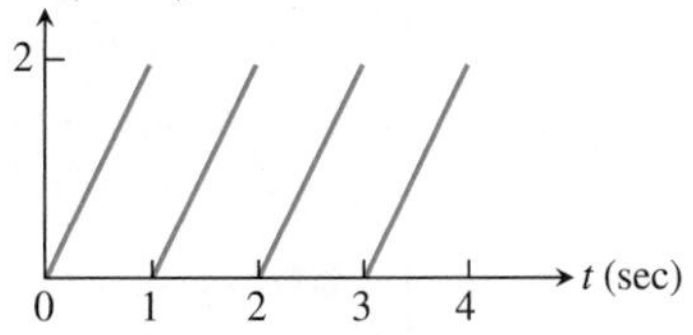

18.

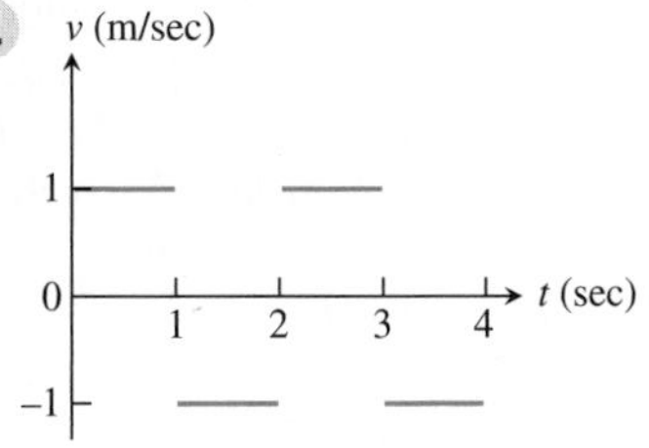

19.

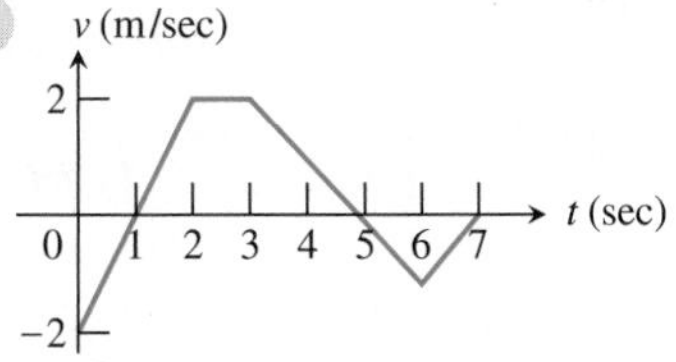

20.

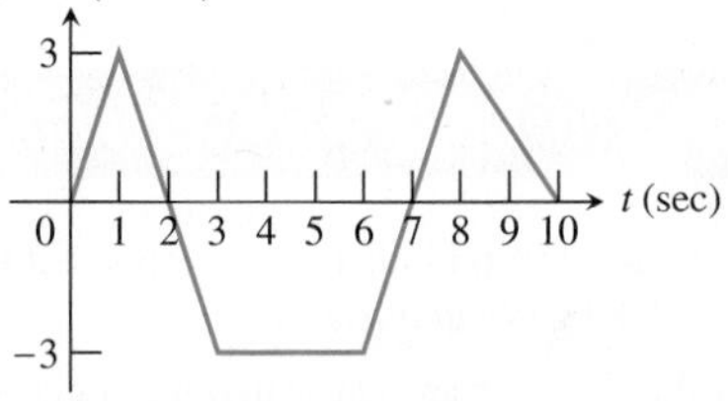

21. ***U.S. Oil Consumption*** The rate of consumption of oil in the United States during the 1980s (in billions of barrels per year) is modeled by the function $C = 27.08 \cdot e^{t/25}$, where t is the number of years after January 1, 1980. Find the total consumption of oil in the United States from January 1, 1980, to January 1, 1990.

22. ***Home Electricity Use*** The rate at which your home consumes electricity is measured in kilowatts. If your home consumes electricity at the rate of 1 kilowatt for 1 hour, you will be charged for 1 "kilowatt-hour" of electricity. Suppose that the average consumption rate for a certain home is modeled by the function $C(t) = 3.9 - 2.4 \sin(\pi t/12)$, where $C(t)$ is measured in kilowatts and t is the number of hours past midnight. Find the average daily consumption for this home, measured in kilowatt-hours.

23. ***Population Density*** Population density measures the number of people per square mile inhabiting a given living area. Washerton's population density, which decreases as you move away from the city center, can be approximated by the function $10{,}000(2 - r)$ at a distance r miles from the city center.

(a) If the population density approaches zero at the edge of the city, what is the city's radius?

(b) A thin ring around the center of the city has thick ness Δr and radius r. If you straighten it out, it suggests a rectangular strip. Approximately what is its area?

(c) **Writing to Learn** Explain why the population of the ring in part (b) is approximately

$$10{,}000(2 - r)(2\pi r)\Delta r.$$

(d) Estimate the total population of Washerton by setting up and evaluating a definite integral.

24. ***Oil Flow*** Oil flows through a cylindrical pipe of radius 3 inches, but friction from the pipe slows the flow toward the outer edge. The speed at which the oil flows at a distance r inches from the center is $8(10 - r^2)$ inches per second.

(a) In a plane cross section of the pipe, a thin ring with thickness Δr at a distance r inches from the center approximates a rectangular strip when you straighten it out. What is the area of the strip (and hence the approximate area of the ring)?

(b) Explain why we know that oil passes through this ring at approximately $8(10 - r^2)(2\pi r)\Delta r$ cubic inches per second.

(c) Set up and evaluate a definite integral that will give the rate (in cubic inches per second) at which oil is flowing through the pipe.

25. **Group Activity *Bagel Sales*** From 1995 to 2005, the Konigsberg Bakery noticed a consistent increase in annual sales of its bagels. The annual sales (in thousands of bagels) are shown below.

Year	Sales (thousands)
1995	5
1996	8.9
1997	16
1998	26.3
1999	39.8
2000	56.5
2001	76.4
2002	99.5
2003	125.8
2004	155.3
2005	188

(a) What was the total number of bagels sold over the 11-year period? (This is not a calculus question!)

(b) Use quadratic regression to model the annual bagel sales (in thousands) as a function $B(x)$, where x is the number of years after 1995.

(c) Integrate $B(x)$ over the interval $[0, 11]$ to find total bagel sales for the 11-year period.

(d) Explain graphically why the answer in part (a) is smaller than the answer in part (c).

26. **Group Activity** *(Continuation of Exercise 25)*

(a) Integrate $B(x)$ over the interval $[-0.5, 10.5]$ to find total bagel sales for the 11-year period.

(b) Explain graphically why the answer in part (a) is better than the answer in 25(c).

27. ***Filling Milk Cartons*** A machine fills milk cartons with milk at an approximately constant rate, but backups along the assembly line cause some variation. The rates (in cases per hour) are recorded at hourly intervals during a 10-hour period, from 8:00 A.M. to 6:00 P.M.

Time	Rate (cases/h)
8	120
9	110
10	115
11	115
12	119
1	120
2	120
3	115
4	112
5	110
6	121

Use the Trapezoidal Rule with $n = 10$ to determine approximately how many cases of milk were filled by the machine over the 10-hour period.

28. **Writing to Learn** As a school project, Anna accompanies her mother on a trip to the grocery store and keeps a log of the car's speed at 10-second intervals. Explain how she can use the data to estimate the distance from her home to the store. What is the connection between this process and the definite integral?

29. ***Hooke's Law*** A certain spring requires a force of 6 N to stretch it 3 cm beyond its natural length.

(a) What force would be required to stretch the string 9 cm beyond its natural length?

(b) What would be the work done in stretching the string 9 cm beyond its natural length?

30. ***Hooke's Law*** Hooke's Law also applies to *compressing* springs; that is, it requires a force of kx to compress a spring a distance x from its natural length. Suppose a 10,000-lb force compressed a spring from its natural length of 12 inches to a length of 11 inches. How much work was done in compressing the spring

(a) the first half-inch? (b) the second half-inch?

Standardized Test Questions

You may use a graphing calculator to solve the following problems.

31. True or False The figure below shows the velocity for a particle moving along the x-axis. The displacement for this particle is negative. Justify your answer.

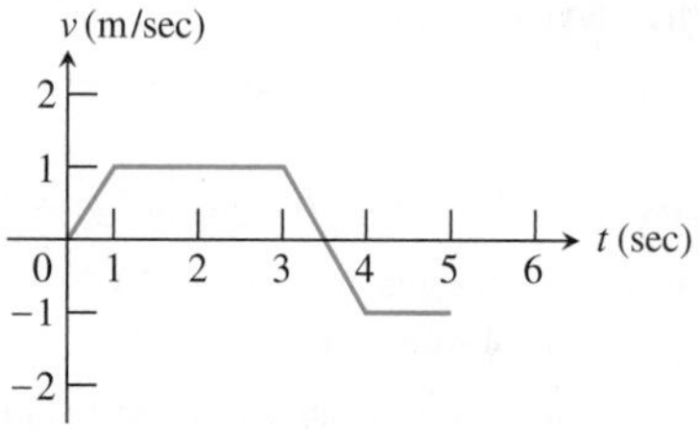

32. True or False If the velocity of a particle moving along the x-axis is always positive, then the displacement is equal to the total distance traveled. Justify your answer.

33. Multiple Choice The graph below shows the rate at which water is pumped from a storage tank. Approximate the total gallons of water pumped from the tank in 24 hours.

(A) 600 **(B)** 2400 **(C)** 3600 **(D)** 4200 **(E)** 4800

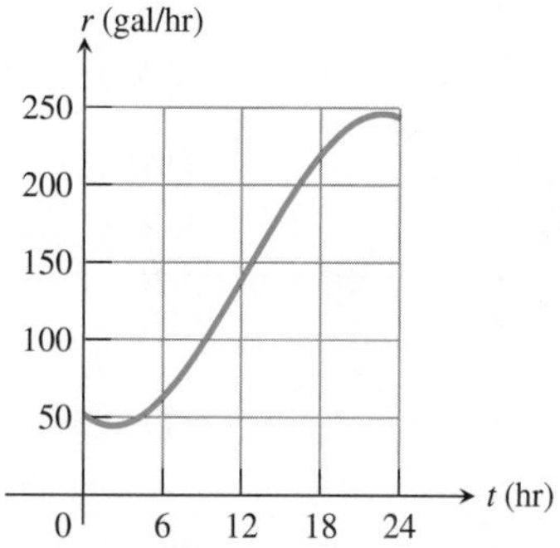

34. Multiple Choice The data for the acceleration $a(t)$ of a car from 0 to 15 seconds are given in the table below. If the velocity at $t = 0$ is 5 ft/sec, which of the following gives the approximate velocity at $t = 15$ using the Trapezoidal Rule?

(A) 47 ft/sec **(B)** 52 ft/sec **(C)** 120 ft/sec

(D) 125 ft/sec **(E)** 141 ft/sec

t (sec)	0	3	6	9	12	15
$a(t)$ (ft/sec^2)	4	8	6	9	10	10

35. Multiple Choice The rate at which customers arrive at a counter to be served is modeled by the function F defined by $F(t) = 12 + 6\cos\left(\frac{t}{\pi}\right)$ for $0 \le t \le 60$, where $F(t)$ is measured in customers per minute and t is measured in minutes. To the nearest whole number, how many customers arrive at the counter over the 60-minute period?

(A) 720 **(B)** 725 **(C)** 732 **(D)** 744 **(E)** 756

36. Multiple Choice Pollution is being removed from a lake at a rate modeled by the function $y = 20e^{-0.5t}$ tons/yr, where t is the number of years since 1995. Estimate the amount of pollution removed from the lake between 1995 and 2005. Round your answer to the nearest ton.

(A) 40 **(B)** 47 **(C)** 56 **(D)** 61 **(E)** 71

Extending the Ideas

37. *Inflation* Although the economy is continuously changing, we analyze it with discrete measurements. The following table records the *annual* inflation rate as measured each month for 13 con secutive months. Use the Trapezoidal Rule with $n = 12$ to find the overall inflation rate for the year.

Month	Annual Rate
January	0.04
February	0.04
March	0.05
April	0.06
May	0.05
June	0.04
July	0.04
August	0.05
September	0.04
October	0.06
November	0.06
December	0.05
January	0.05

38. *Inflation Rate* The table below shows the *monthly* inflation rate (in *thousandths*) for energy prices for thirteen consecutive months. Use the Trapezoidal Rule with $n = 12$ to approximate the *annual* inflation rate for the 12-month period running from the middle of the first month to the middle of the last month.

Month	Monthly Rate (in thousandths)
January	3.6
February	4.0
March	3.1
April	2.8
May	2.8
June	3.2
July	3.3
August	3.1
September	3.2
October	3.4
November	3.4
December	3.9
January	4.0

39. *Center of Mass* Suppose we have a finite collection of masses in the coordinate plane, the mass m_k located at the point (x_k, y_k) as shown in the figure.

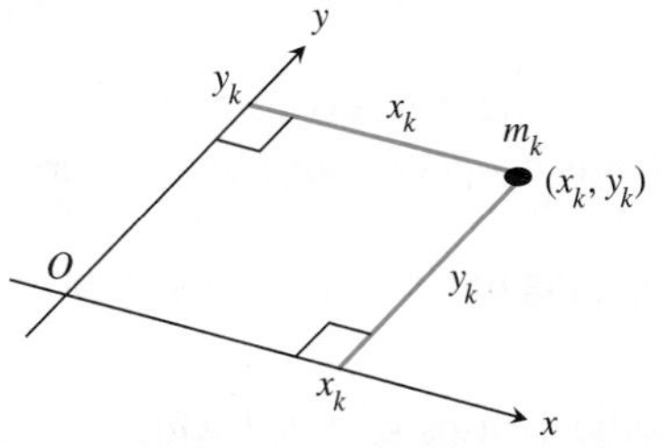

Each mass m_k has **moment $m_k y_k$ with respect to the x-axis** and **moment $m_k x_k$ about the y-axis.** The moments of the entire system with respect to the two axes are

$$\text{Moment about } x\text{-axis: } M_x = \sum m_k y_k,$$

$$\text{Moment about } y\text{-axis: } M_y = \sum m_k x_k.$$

The **center of mass** is $(\bar{x}, \bar{y})$ where

$$\bar{x} = \frac{M_y}{M} = \frac{\Sigma\, m_k x_k}{\Sigma\, m_k} \quad \text{and} \quad \bar{y} = \frac{M_x}{M} = \frac{\Sigma\, m_k x_k}{\Sigma\, m_k}.$$

Suppose we have a thin, flat plate occupying a region in the plane.

(a) Imagine the region cut into thin strips parallel to the y-axis. Show that

$$\bar{x} = \frac{\int x\, dm}{\int dm},$$

where $dm = \delta\, dA$, $\delta =$ density (mass per unit area), and $A =$ area of the region.

(b) Imagine the region cut into thin strips parallel to the x-axis. Show that

$$\bar{y} = \frac{\int y\, dm}{\int dm},$$

where $dm = \delta\, dA$, $\delta =$ density, and $A =$ area of the region.

In Exercises 40 and 41, use Exercise 39 to find the center of mass of the region with given density.

40. the region bounded by the parabola $y = x^2$ and the line $y = 4$ with constant density δ

41. the region bounded by the lines $y = x$, $y = -x$, $x = 2$ with constant density δ

8.2 Areas in the Plane

What you will learn about . . .

- Area Between Curves
- Area Enclosed by Intersecting Curves
- Boundaries with Changing Functions
- Integrating with Respect to y
- Saving Time with Geometric Formulas

and why . . .

The techniques of this section allow us to compute areas of complex regions of the plane.

Area Between Curves

We know how to find the area of a region between a curve and the x-axis but many times we want to know the area of a region that is bounded above by one curve, $y = f(x)$, and below by another, $y = g(x)$ (Figure 8.3).

We find the area as an integral by applying the first two steps of the modeling strategy developed in Section 8.1.

1. We partition the region into vertical strips of equal width Δx and approximate each strip with a rectangle with base parallel to $[a, b]$ (Figure 8.4). Each rectangle has area

$$[f(c_k) - g(c_k)]\Delta x$$

for some c_k in its respective subinterval (Figure 8.5). This expression will be nonnegative even if the region lies below the x-axis. We approximate the area of the region with the Riemann sum

$$\sum [f(c_k) - g(c_k)]\Delta x.$$

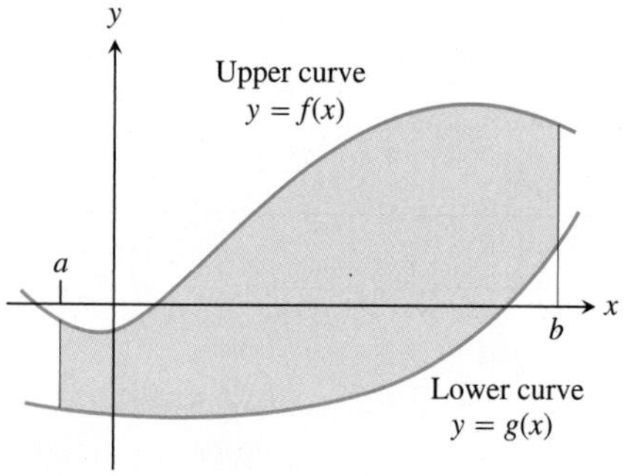

Figure 8.3 The region between $y = f(x)$ and $y = g(x)$ and the lines $x = a$ and $x = b$.

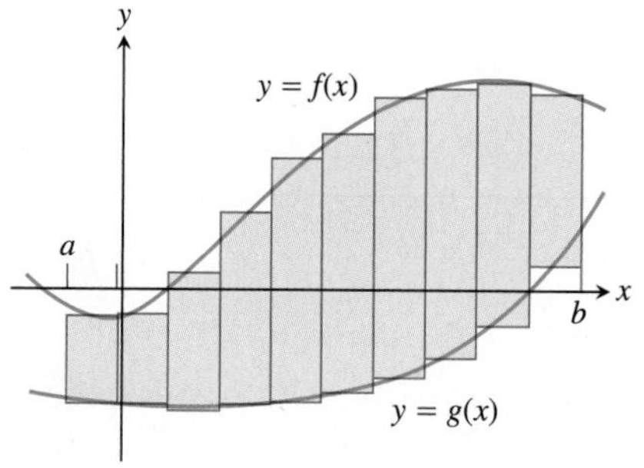

Figure 8.4 We approximate the region with rectangles perpendicular to the x-axis.

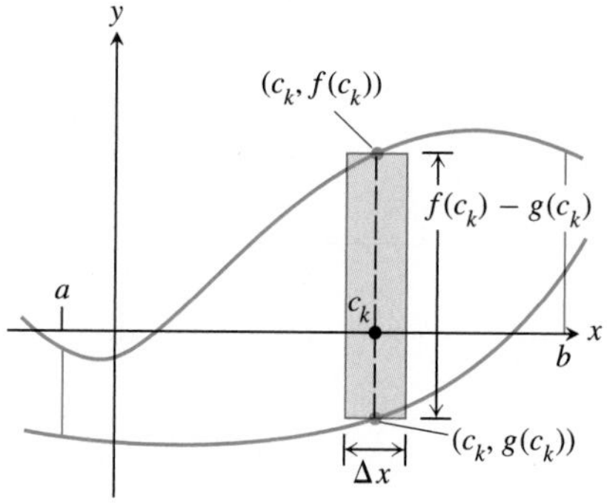

Figure 8.5 The area of a typical rectangle is $[f(c_k) - g(c_k)]\Delta x$.

2. The limit of these sums as $\Delta x \to 0$ is

$$\int_a^b [f(x) - g(x)]\, dx.$$

This approach to finding area captures the properties of area, so it can serve as a definition.

DEFINITION Area Between Curves

If f and g are continuous with $f(x) \geq g(x)$ throughout $[a, b]$, then the **area between the curves $y = f(x)$ and $y = g(x)$ from a to b** is the integral of $[f - g]$ from a to b,

$$A = \int_a^b [f(x) - g(x)]\, dx.$$

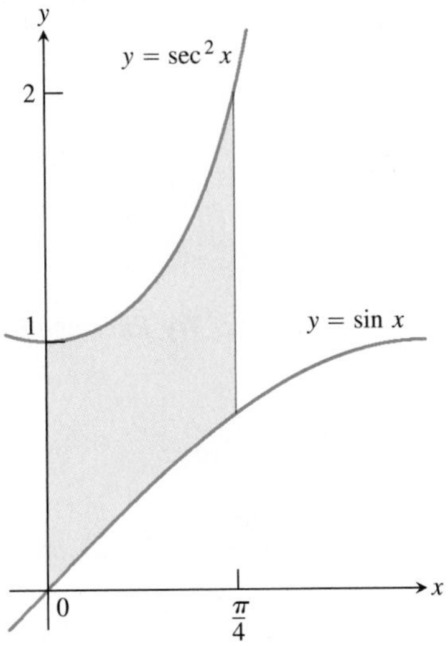

Figure 8.6 The region in Example 1.

EXAMPLE 1 Applying the Definition

Find the area of the region between $y = \sec^2 x$ and $y = \sin x$ from $x = 0$ to $x = \pi/4$.

SOLUTION

We graph the curves (Figure 8.6) to find their relative positions in the plane, and see that $y = \sec^2 x$ lies *above* $y = \sin x$ on $[0, \pi/4]$. The area is therefore

$$A = \int_0^{\pi/4} [\sec^2 x - \sin x]\,dx$$

$$= \Big[\tan x + \cos x\Big]_0^{\pi/4}$$

$$= \frac{\sqrt{2}}{2} \text{ units squared.}$$

Now Try Exercise 1.

EXPLORATION 1 A Family of Butterflies

For each positive integer k, let A_k denote the area of the butterfly-shaped region enclosed between the graphs of $y = k \sin kx$ and $y = 2k - k \sin kx$ on the interval $[0, \pi/k]$. The regions for $k = 1$ and $k = 2$ are shown in Figure 8.7.

1. Find the areas of the two regions in Figure 8.7.
2. Make a conjecture about the areas A_k for $k \geq 3$.
3. Set up a definite integral that gives the area A_k. Can you make a simple u-substitution that will transform this integral into the definite integral that gives the area A_1?
4. What is $\lim_{k\to\infty} A_k$?
5. If P_k denotes the perimeter of the kth butterfly-shaped region, what is $\lim_{k\to\infty} P_k$? (You can answer this question without an explicit formula for P_k.)

$y_1 = 2k - k \sin kx$
$y_2 = k \sin kx$

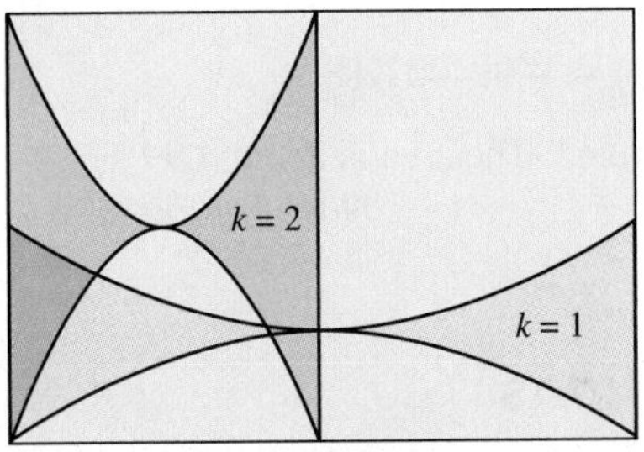

$[0, \pi]$ by $[0, 4]$

Figure 8.7 Two members of the family of butterfly-shaped regions described in Exploration 1.

Area Enclosed by Intersecting Curves

When a region is enclosed by intersecting curves, the intersection points give the limits of integration.

EXAMPLE 2 Area of an Enclosed Region

Find the area of the region enclosed by the parabola $y = 2 - x^2$ and the line $y = -x$.

SOLUTION

We graph the curves to view the region (Figure 8.8).

The limits of integration are found by solving the equation

$$2 - x^2 = -x$$

either algebraically or by calculator. The solutions are $x = -1$ and $x = 2$.

continued

$y_1 = 2 - x^2$
$y_2 = -x$

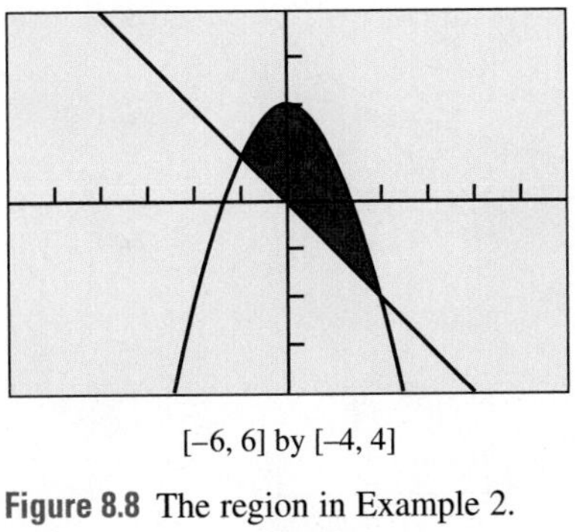

$[-6, 6]$ by $[-4, 4]$

Figure 8.8 The region in Example 2.

Since the parabola lies above the line on $[-1, 2]$, the area integrand is $2 - x^2 - (-x)$.

$$\begin{aligned} A &= \int_{-1}^{2} [2 - x^2 - (-x)]\, dx \\ &= \left[2x - \frac{x^3}{3} + \frac{x^2}{2}\right]_{-1}^{2} \\ &= \frac{9}{2} \text{ units squared} \end{aligned}$$

Now Try Exercise 5.

EXAMPLE 3 Using a Calculator

Find the area of the region enclosed by the graphs of $y = 2\cos x$ and $y = x^2 - 1$.

SOLUTION

The region is shown in Figure 8.9.

Using a calculator, we solve the equation

$$2\cos x = x^2 - 1$$

to find the x-coordinates of the points where the curves intersect. These are the limits of integration. The solutions are $x = \pm 1.265423706$. We store the negative value as A and the positive value as B. The area is

$$\text{NINT}\,(2\cos x - (x^2 - 1), x, A, B) \approx 4.994907788.$$

This is the final calculation, so we are now free to round. The area is about 4.99.

Now Try Exercise 7.

$y_1 = 2\cos x$
$y_2 = x^2 - 1$

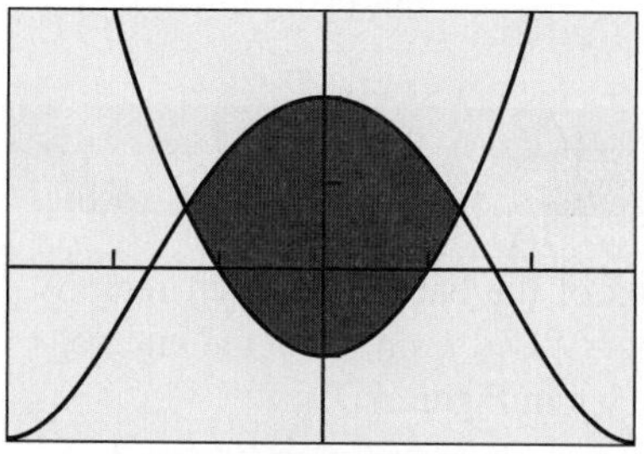

[–3, 3] by [–2, 3]

Figure 8.9 The region in Example 3.

Finding Intersections by Calculator

The coordinates of the points of intersection of two curves are sometimes needed for other calculations. To take advantage of the accuracy provided by calculators, use them to solve for the values and *store* the ones you want.

Boundaries with Changing Functions

If a boundary of a region is defined by more than one function, we can partition the region into subregions that correspond to the function changes and proceed as usual.

EXAMPLE 4 Finding Area Using Subregions

Find the area of the region R in the first quadrant that is bounded above by $y = \sqrt{x}$ and below by the x-axis and the line $y = x - 2$.

SOLUTION

The region is shown in Figure 8.10.

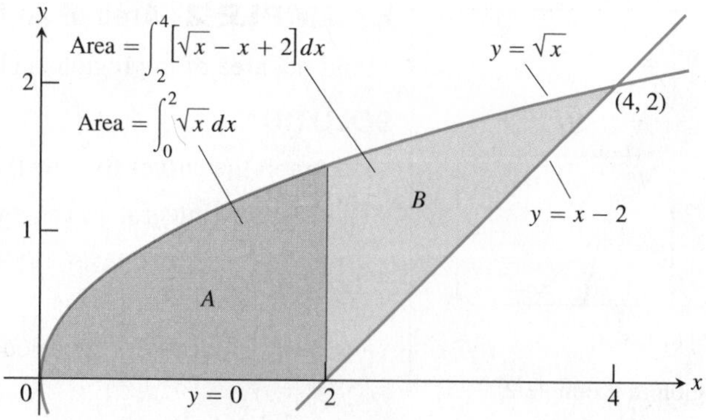

Figure 8.10 Region R split into subregions A and B. (Example 4)

continued

While it appears that no single integral can give the area of R (the bottom boundary is defined by two different curves), we can split the region at $x = 2$ into two regions A and B. The area of R can be found as the sum of the areas of A and B.

$$\text{Area of } R = \underbrace{\int_0^2 \sqrt{x}\,dx}_{\text{area of } A} + \underbrace{\int_2^4 [\sqrt{x} - (x-2)]\,dx}_{\text{area of } B}$$

$$= \left[\frac{2}{3}x^{3/2}\right]_0^2 + \left[\frac{2}{3}x^{3/2} - \frac{x^2}{2} + 2x\right]_2^4$$

$$= \frac{10}{3} \text{ units squared}$$

Now Try Exercise 9.

Integrating with Respect to *y*

Sometimes the boundaries of a region are more easily described by functions of y than by functions of x. We can use approximating rectangles that are horizontal rather than vertical and the resulting basic formula has y in place of x.

For regions like these

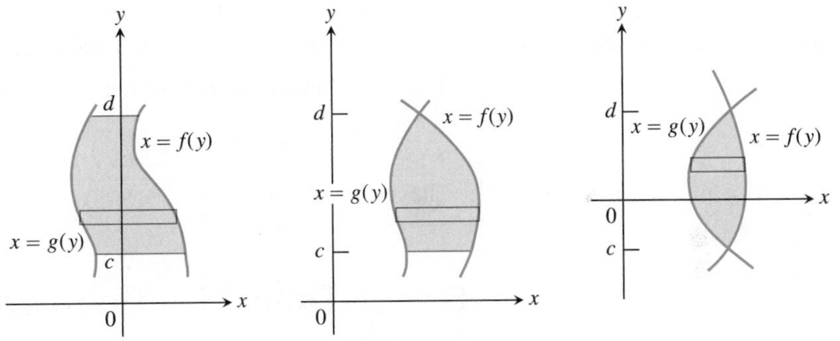

use this formula

$$A = \int_c^d [f(y) - g(y)]\,dy.$$

EXAMPLE 5 Integrating with Respect to *y*

Find the area of the region in Example 4 by integrating with respect to y.

SOLUTION

We remarked in solving Example 4 that "it appears that no single integral can give the area of R," but notice how appearances change when we think of our rectangles being summed over y. The interval of integration is $[0, 2]$, and the rectangles run between the same two curves on the entire interval. There is no need to split the region (Figure 8.11).

We need to solve for x in terms of y in both equations:

$$y = x - 2 \quad \text{becomes} \quad x = y + 2,$$

$$y = \sqrt{x} \quad \text{becomes} \quad x = y^2, \quad y \geq 0.$$

continued

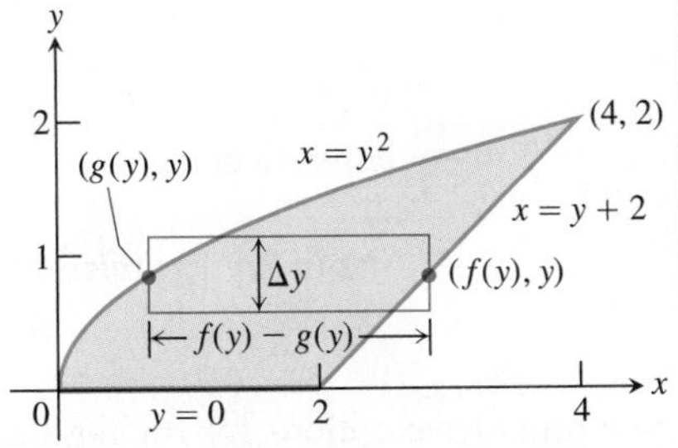

Figure 8.11 It takes two integrations to find the area of this region if we integrate with respect to x. It takes only one if we integrate with respect to y. (Example 5)

$y_1 = x^3, y_2 = \sqrt{x+2}, y_3 = -\sqrt{x+2}$

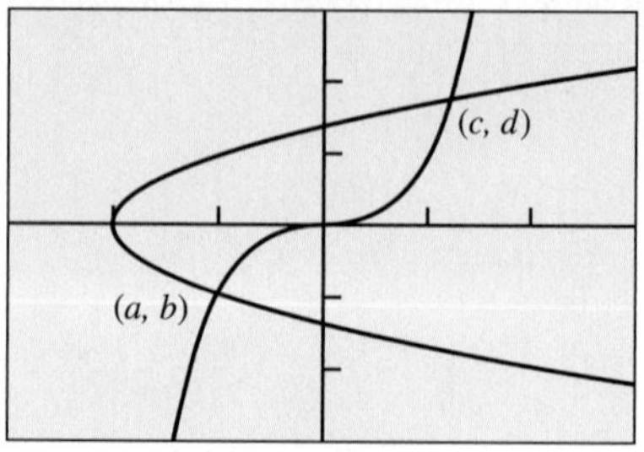

[–3, 3] by [–3, 3]

Figure 8.12 The region in Example 6.

We must still be careful to subtract the lower number from the higher number when forming the integrand. In this case, the higher numbers are the higher x-values, which are on the line $x = y + 2$ because the line lies to the *right* of the parabola. So,

$$\text{Area of } R = \int_0^2 (y + 2 - y^2)\,dy = \left[\frac{y^2}{2} + 2y - \frac{y^3}{3}\right]_0^2 = \frac{10}{3} \text{ units squared.}$$

Now Try Exercise 11.

EXAMPLE 6 Making the Choice

Find the area of the region enclosed by the graphs of $y = x^3$ and $x = y^2 - 2$.

SOLUTION

We can produce a graph of the region on a calculator by graphing the three curves $y = x^3$, $y = \sqrt{x + 2}$, and $y = -\sqrt{x + 2}$ (Figure 8.12).

This conveniently gives us all of our bounding curves as functions of x. If we integrate in terms of x, however, we need to split the region at $x = a$ (Figure 8.13).

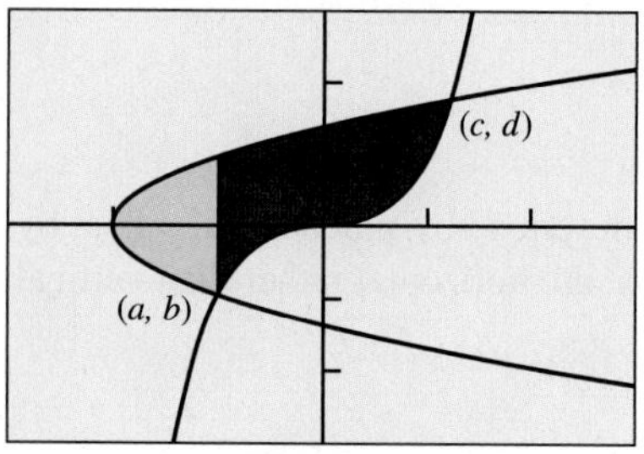

[–3, 3] by [–3, 3]

Figure 8.13 If we integrate with respect to x in Example 6, we must split the region at $x = a$.

On the other hand, we can integrate from $y = b$ to $y = d$ and handle the entire region at once. We solve the cubic for x in terms of y:

$$y = x^3 \quad \text{becomes} \quad x = y^{1/3}$$

To find the limits of integration, we solve $y^{1/3} = y^2 - 2$. It is easy to see that the lower limit is $b = -1$, but a calculator is needed to find that the upper limit $d = 1.793003715$. We store this value as D.

The cubic lies to the right of the parabola, so

$$\text{Area} = \text{NINT}\,(y^{1/3} - (y^2 - 2), y, -1, \text{D}) = 4.214939673.$$

The area is about 4.21.

Now Try Exercise 27.

Saving Time with Geometry Formulas

Here is yet another way to handle Example 4.

EXAMPLE 7 Using Geometry

Find the area of the region in Example 4 by subtracting the area of the triangular region from the area under the square root curve.

SOLUTION

Figure 8.14 illustrates the strategy, which enables us to integrate with respect to x without splitting the region.

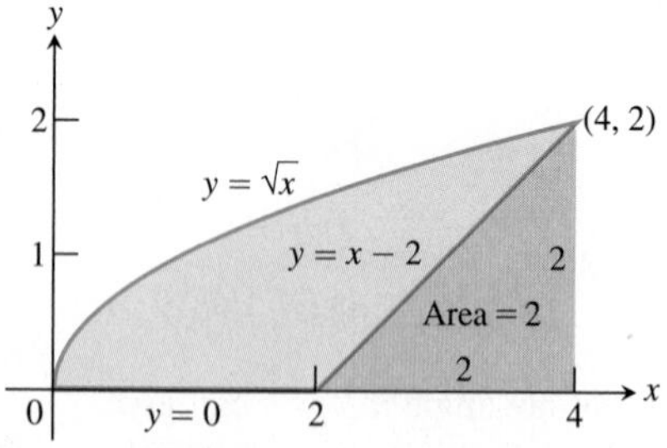

Figure 8.14 The area of the blue region is the area under the parabola $y = \sqrt{x}$ minus the area of the triangle. (Example 7)

$$\text{Area} = \int_0^4 \sqrt{x}\,dx - \frac{1}{2}(2)(2) = \frac{2}{3}x^{3/2}\Big]_0^4 - 2 = \frac{10}{3} \text{ units squared}$$

Now Try Exercise 35.

The moral behind Examples 4, 5, and 7 is that you often have options for finding the area of a region, some of which may be easier than others. You can integrate with respect to x or with respect to y, you can partition the region into subregions, and sometimes you can even use traditional geometry formulas. Sketch the region first and take a moment to determine the best way to proceed.

Quick Review 8.2 *(For help, go to Sections 1.2 and 6.1.)*

Exercise numbers with a gray background indicate problems that the authors have designed to be solved *without a calculator*.

In Exercises 1–5, find the area between the x-axis and the graph of the given function over the given interval.

1. $y = \sin x$ over $[0, \pi]$

2. $y = e^{2x}$ over $[0, 1]$

3. $y = \sec^2 x$ over $[-\pi/4, \pi/4]$

4. $y = 4x - x^3$ over $[0, 2]$

5. $y = \sqrt{9 - x^2}$ over $[-3, 3]$

In Exercises 6–10, find the x- and y-coordinates of all points where the graphs of the given functions intersect. If the curves never intersect, write "NI."

6. $y = x^2 - 4x$ and $y = x + 6$

7. $y = e^x$ and $y = x + 1$

8. $y = x^2 - \pi x$ and $y = \sin x$

9. $y = \dfrac{2x}{x^2 + 1}$ and $y = x^3$

10. $y = \sin x$ and $y = x^3$

Section 8.2 Exercises

In Exercises 1–6, find the area of the shaded region analytically.

1.

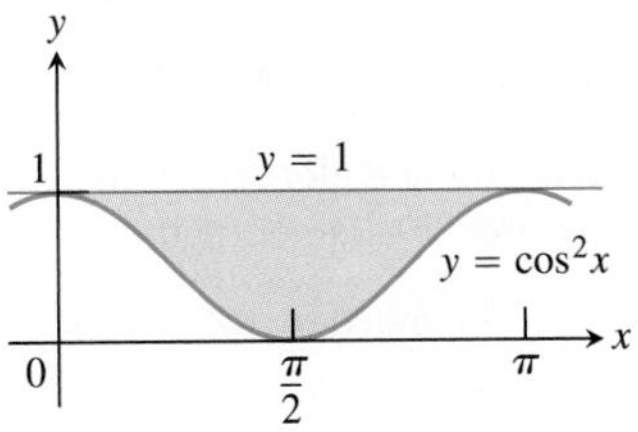

2.

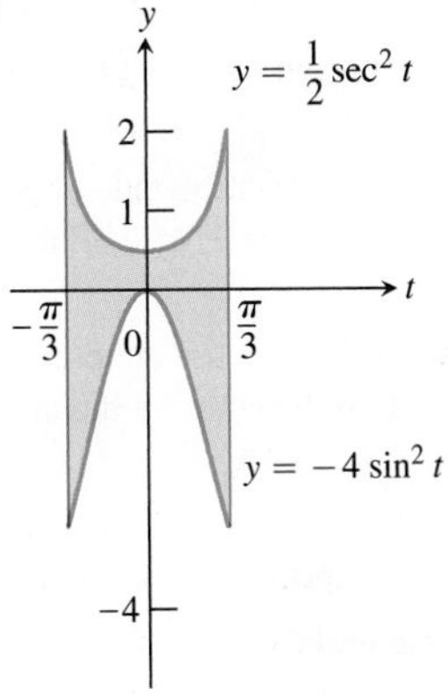

3.

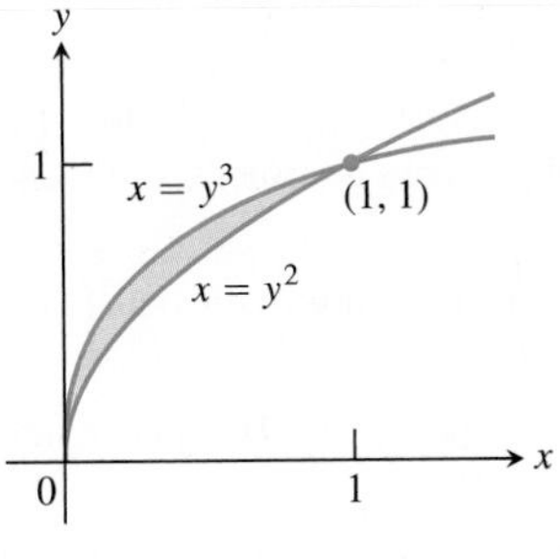

4.

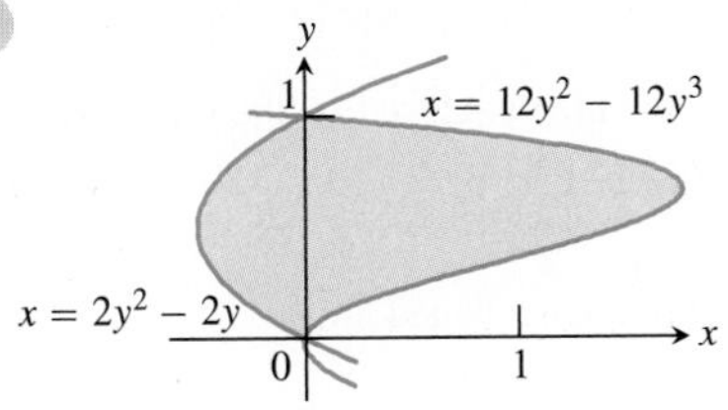

5.

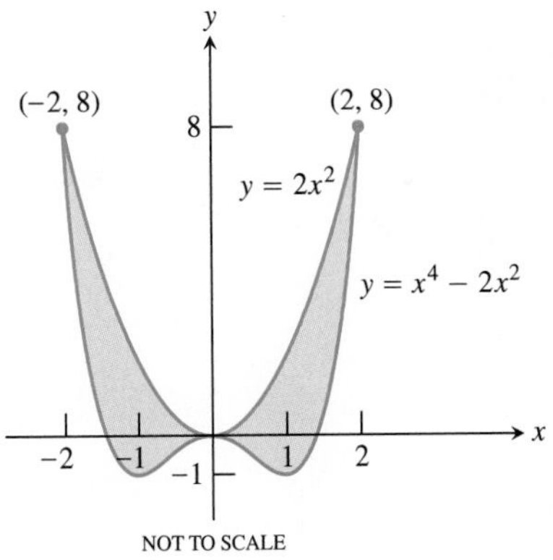

6.

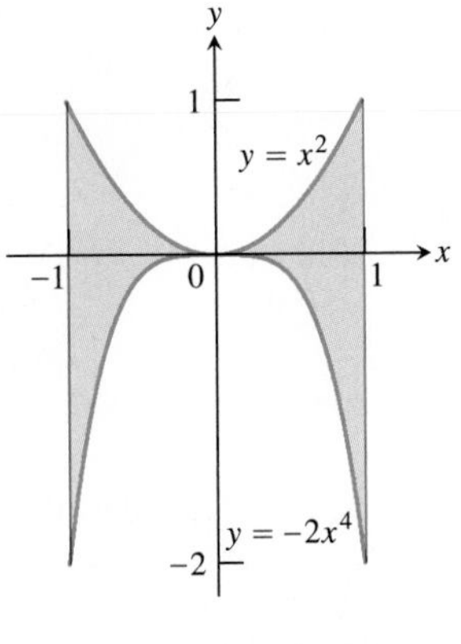

In Exercises 7 and 8, use a calculator to find the area of the region enclosed by the graphs of the two functions.

7. $y = \sin x, y = 1 - x^2$ **8.** $y = \cos(2x), y = x^2 - 2$

In Exercises 9 and 10, find the area of the shaded region analytically.

9.

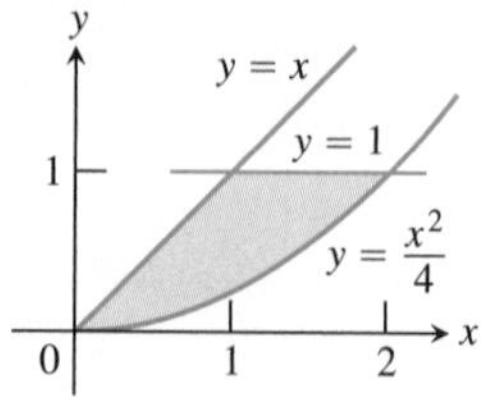

10.

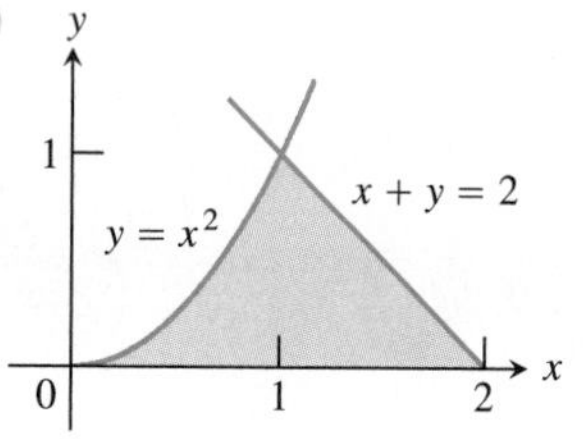

In Exercises 11 and 12, find the area enclosed by the graphs of the two curves by integrating with respect to y.

11. $y^2 = x + 1, y^2 = 3 - x$ **12.** $y^2 = x + 3, y = 2x$

In Exercises 13 and 14, find the total shaded area.

13.

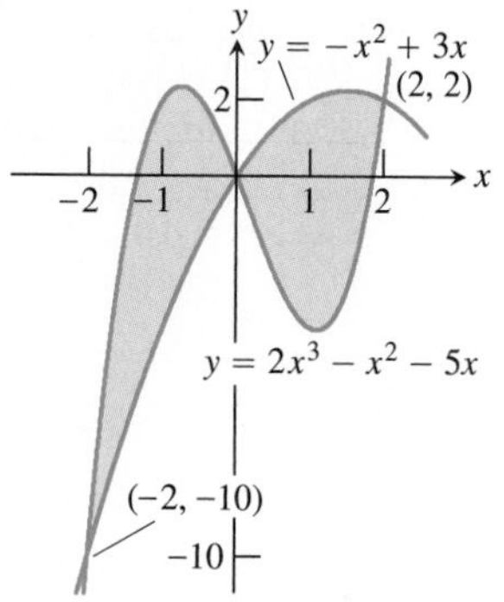

14.

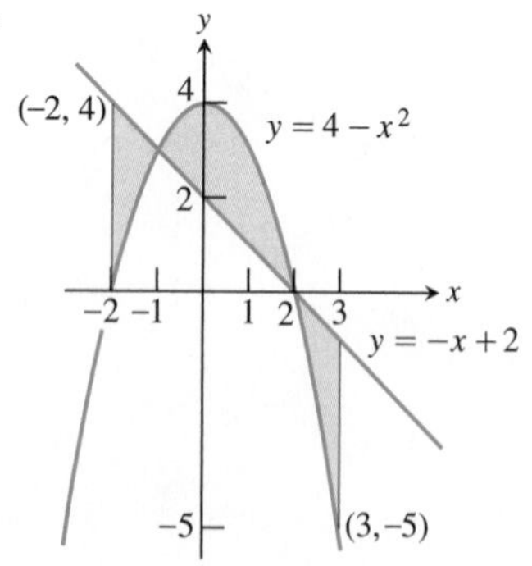

In Exercises 15–34, find the area of the regions enclosed by the lines and curves.

15. $y = x^2 - 2$ and $y = 2$

16. $y = 2x - x^2$ and $y = -3$

17. $y = 7 - 2x^2$ and $y = x^2 + 4$

18. $y = x^4 - 4x^2 + 4$ and $y = x^2$

19. $y = x\sqrt{a^2 - x^2}, \quad a > 0,$ and $y = 0$

20. $y = \sqrt{|x|}$ and $5y = x + 6$
(How many intersection points are there?)

21. $y = |x^2 - 4|$ and $y = (x^2/2) + 4$

22. $x = y^2$ and $x = y + 2$

23. $y^2 - 4x = 4$ and $4x - y = 16$

24. $x - y^2 = 0$ and $x + 2y^2 = 3$

25. $x + y^2 = 0$ and $x + 3y^2 = 2$

26. $4x^2 + y = 4$ and $x^4 - y = 1$

27. $x + y^2 = 3$ and $4x + y^2 = 0$

28. $y = 2\sin x$ and $y = \sin 2x, \quad 0 \le x \le \pi$

29. $y = 8\cos x$ and $y = \sec^2 x, \quad -\pi/3 \le x \le \pi/3$

30. $y = \cos(\pi x/2)$ and $y = 1 - x^2$

31. $y = \sin(\pi x/2)$ and $y = x$

32. $y = \sec^2 x, \quad y = \tan^2 x, \quad x = -\pi/4, \quad x = \pi/4$

33. $x = \tan^2 y$ and $x = -\tan^2 y, \quad -\pi/4 \le y \le \pi/4$

34. $x = 3\sin y\sqrt{\cos y}$ and $x = 0, \quad 0 \le y \le \pi/2$

In Exercises 35 and 36, find the area of the region by subtracting the area of a triangular region from the area of a larger region.

35. The region on or above the x-axis bounded by the curves $y^2 = x + 3$ and $y = 2x$

36. The region on or above the x-axis bounded by the curves $y = 4 - x^2$ and $y = 3x$

37. Find the area of the propeller-shaped region enclosed by the curve $x - y^3 = 0$ and the line $x - y = 0$.

38. Find the area of the region in the first quadrant bounded by the line $y = x$, the line $x = 2$, the curve $y = 1/x^2$, and the x-axis.

39. Find the area of the "triangular" region in the first quadrant bounded on the left by the y-axis and on the right by the curves $y = \sin x$ and $y = \cos x$.

40. Find the area of the region between the curve $y = 3 - x^2$ and the line $y = -1$ by integrating with respect to **(a)** x, **(b)** y.

41. The region bounded below by the parabola $y = x^2$ and above by the line $y = 4$ is to be partitioned into two subsections of equal area by cutting across it with the horizontal line $y = c$.

(a) Sketch the region and draw a line $y = c$ across it that looks about right. In terms of c, what are the coordinates of the points where the line and parabola intersect? Add them to your figure.

(b) Find c by integrating with respect to y. (This puts c in the limits of integration.)

(c) Find c by integrating with respect to x. (This puts c into the integrand as well.)

42. Find the area of the region in the first quadrant bounded on the left by the y-axis, below by the line $y = x/4$, above left by the curve $y = 1 + \sqrt{x}$, and above right by the curve $y = 2/\sqrt{x}$.

43. The figure here shows triangle AOC inscribed in the region cut from the parabola $y = x^2$ by the line $y = a^2$. Find the limit of the ratio of the area of the triangle to the area of the parabolic region as a approaches zero.

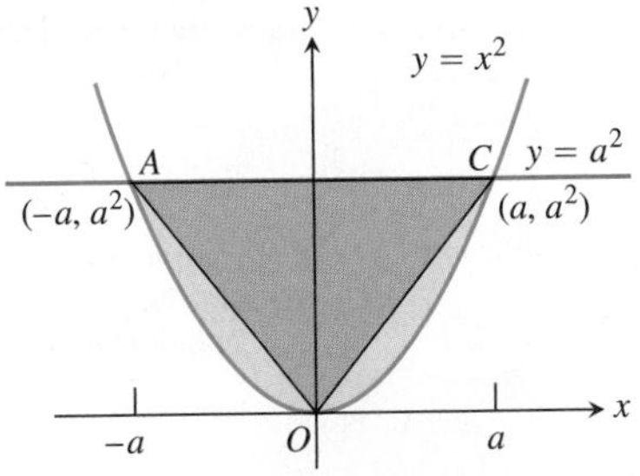

44. Suppose the area of the region between the graph of a positive continuous function f and the x-axis from $x = a$ to $x = b$ is 4 square units. Find the area between the curves $y = f(x)$ and $y = 2f(x)$ from $x = a$ to $x = b$.

45. Writing to Learn Which of the following integrals, if either, calculates the area of the shaded region shown here? Give reasons for your answer.

i. $\displaystyle\int_{-1}^{1} (x - (-x))\,dx = \int_{-1}^{1} 2x\,dx$

ii. $\displaystyle\int_{-1}^{1} (-x - (x))\,dx = \int_{-1}^{1} -2x\,dx$

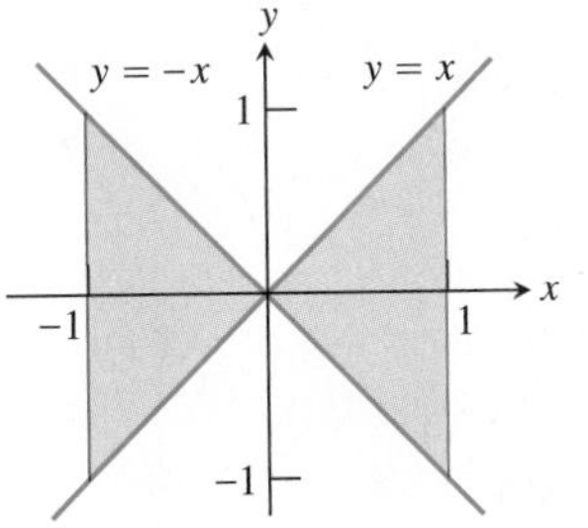

46. Writing to Learn Is the following statement true, sometimes true, or never true? The area of the region between the graphs of the continuous functions $y = f(x)$ and $y = g(x)$ and the vertical lines $x = a$ and $x = b$ $(a < b)$ is

$$\int_a^b [f(x) - g(x)]\,dx.$$

Give reasons for your answer.

47. Find the area of the propeller-shaped region enclosed between the graphs of

$$y = \frac{2x}{x^2 + 1} \quad \text{and} \quad y = x^3.$$

48. Find the area of the propeller-shaped region enclosed between the graphs of $y = \sin x$ and $y = x^3$.

49. Find the positive value of k such that the area of the region enclosed between the graph of $y = k \cos x$ and the graph of $y = kx^2$ is 2.

Standardized Test Questions

50. True or False The area of the region enclosed by the graph of $y = x^2 + 1$ and the line $y = 10$ is 36. Justify your answer.

51. True or False The area of the region in the first quadrant enclosed by the graphs of $y = \cos x$, $y = x$, and the y-axis is given by the definite integral $\int_0^{0.739} (x - \cos x)\,dx$. Justify your answer.

52. Multiple Choice Let R be the region in the first quadrant bounded by the x-axis, the graph of $x = y^2 + 2$, and the line $x = 4$. Which of the following integrals gives the area of R?

(A) $\displaystyle\int_0^{\sqrt{2}} [4 - (y^2 + 2)]\,dy$ **(B)** $\displaystyle\int_0^{\sqrt{2}} [(y^2 + 2) - 4]\,dy$

(C) $\displaystyle\int_{-\sqrt{2}}^{\sqrt{2}} [4 - (y^2 + 2)]\,dy$ **(D)** $\displaystyle\int_{-\sqrt{2}}^{\sqrt{2}} [(y^2 + 2) - 4]\,dy$

(E) $\displaystyle\int_2^4 [4 - (y^2 + 2)]\,dy$

53. Multiple Choice Which of the following gives the area of the region between the graphs of $y = x^2$ and $y = -x$ from $x = 0$ to $x = 3$?

(A) 2 **(B)** 9/2 **(C)** 13/2 **(D)** 13 **(E)** 27/2

54. Multiple Choice Let R be the shaded region enclosed by the graphs of $y = e^{-x^2}$, $y = -\sin(3x)$, and the y-axis as shown in the figure below. Which of the following gives the approximate area of the region R? You may use a calculator on this problem.

(A) 1.139 **(B)** 1.445 **(C)** 1.869 **(D)** 2.114 **(E)** 2.340

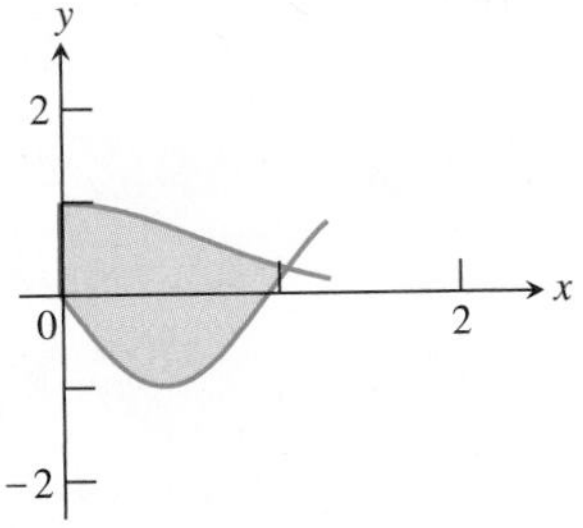

55. Multiple Choice Let f and g be the functions given by $f(x) = e^x$ and $g(x) = 1/x$. Which of the following gives the area of the region enclosed by the graphs of f and g between $x = 1$ and $x = 2$?

(A) $e^2 - e - \ln 2$

(B) $\ln 2 - e^2 + e$

(C) $e^2 - \dfrac{1}{2}$

(D) $e^2 - e - \dfrac{1}{2}$

(E) $\dfrac{1}{e} - \ln 2$

Exploration

56. Group Activity ***Area of Ellipse***

An ellipse with major axis of length $2a$ and minor axis of length $2b$ can be coordinatized with its center at the origin and its major axis horizontal, in which case it is defined by the equation

$$\frac{x^2}{a^2} + \frac{y^2}{b^2} = 1.$$

(a) Find the equations that define the upper and lower semi-ellipses as functions of x.

(b) Write an integral expression that gives the area of the ellipse.

(c) With your group, use NINT to find the areas of ellipses for various lengths of a and b.

(d) There is a simple formula for the area of an ellipse with major axis of length $2a$ and minor axis of length $2b$. Can you tell what it is from the areas you and your group have found?

(e) Work with your group to write a *proof* of this area formula by showing that it is the exact value of the integral expression in part (b).

Extending the Ideas

57. *Cavalieri's Theorem* Bonaventura Cavalieri (1598–1647) discovered that if two plane regions can be arranged to lie over the same interval of the x-axis in such a way that they have identical vertical cross sections at every point (see figure), then the regions have the same area. Show that this theorem is true.

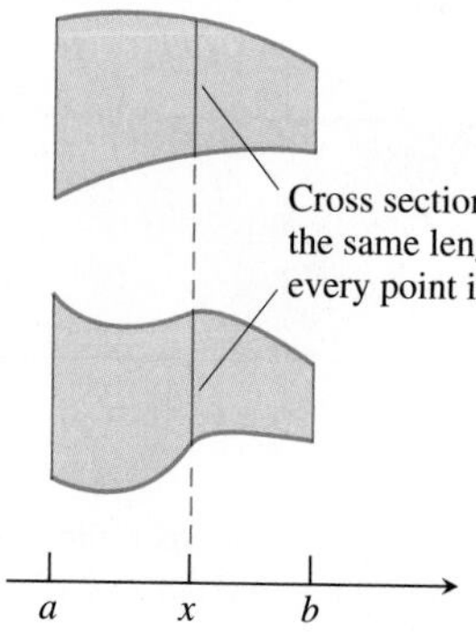
Cross sections have
the same length at
every point in [a, b].
a
x
b

58. Find the area of the region enclosed by the curves

$$y = \frac{x}{x^2 + 1} \quad \text{and} \quad y = mx, \quad 0 < m < 1.$$

8.3 Volumes

What you will learn about . . .

- Volume As an Integral
- Square Cross Sections
- Circular Cross Sections
- Cylindrical Shells
- Other Cross Sections

and why . . .

The techniques of this section allow us to compute volumes of certain solids in three dimensions.

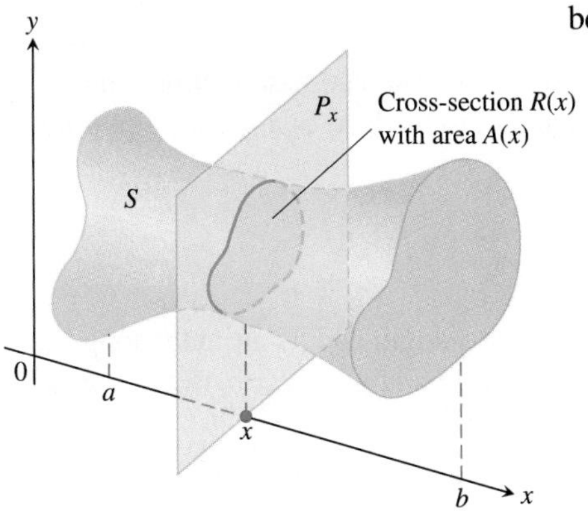

Figure 8.15 The cross section of an arbitrary solid at point x.

Volume As an Integral

In Section 6.1, Example 3, we estimated the volume of a sphere by partitioning it into thin slices that were nearly cylindrical and summing the cylinders' volumes using MRAM. MRAM sums are Riemann sums, and had we known how at the time, we could have continued on to express the volume of the sphere as a definite integral.

Starting the same way, we can now find the volumes of a great many solids by integration. Suppose we want to find the volume of a solid like the one in Figure 8.15. The cross section of the solid at each point x in the interval $[a, b]$ is a region $R(x)$ of area $A(x)$. If A is a continuous function of x, we can use it to define and calculate the volume of the solid as an integral in the following way.

We partition $[a, b]$ into subintervals of length Δx and slice the solid, as we would a loaf of bread, by planes perpendicular to the x-axis at the partition points. The kth slice, the one between the planes at x_{k-1} and x_k, has approximately the same volume as the cylinder between the two planes based on the region $R(x_k)$ (Figure 8.16).

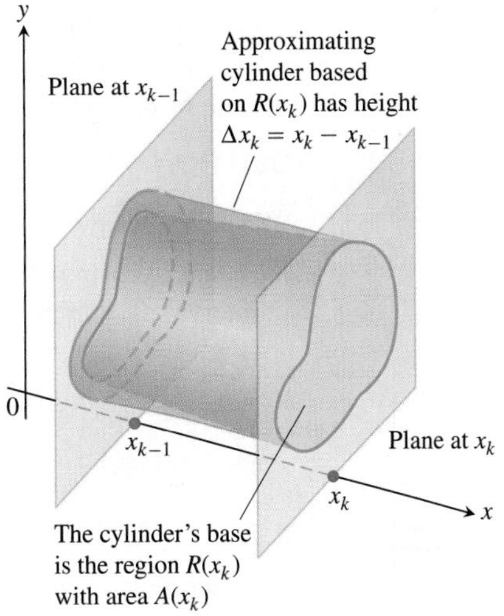

Figure 8.16 Enlarged view of the slice of the solid between the planes at x_{k-1} and x_k.

The volume of the cylinder is

$$V_k = \text{base area} \times \text{height} = A(x_k) \times \Delta x.$$

The sum

$$\sum V_k = \sum A(x_k) \times \Delta x$$

approximates the volume of the solid.

This is a Riemann sum for $A(x)$ on $[a, b]$. We expect the approximations to improve as the norms of the partitions go to zero, so we define their limiting integral to be the *volume of the solid.*

DEFINITION Volume of a Solid

The **volume of a solid** of known integrable cross-section area $A(x)$ from $x = a$ to $x = b$ is the integral of A from a to b,

$$V = \int_a^b A(x)\, dx.$$

To apply the formula in the previous definition, we proceed as follows.

How to Find Volume by the Method of Slicing

1. Sketch the solid and a typical cross section.
2. Find a formula for $A(x)$.
3. Find the limits of integration.
4. Integrate $A(x)$ to find the volume.

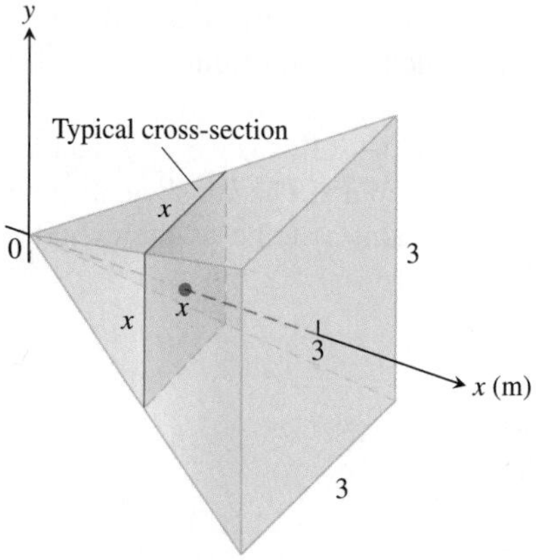

Figure 8.17 A cross section of the pyramid in Example 1.

Square Cross Sections

Let us apply the volume formula to a solid with square cross sections.

EXAMPLE 1 A Square-Based Pyramid

A pyramid 3 m high has congruent triangular sides and a square base that is 3 m on each side. Each cross section of the pyramid parallel to the base is a square. Find the volume of the pyramid.

SOLUTION

We follow the steps for the method of slicing.

1. *Sketch.* We draw the pyramid with its vertex at the origin and its altitude along the interval $0 \le x \le 3$. We sketch a typical cross section at a point x between 0 and 3 (Figure 8.17).
2. *Find a formula for $A(x)$.* The cross section at x is a square x meters on a side, so
$$A(x) = x^2.$$
3. *Find the limits of integration.* The squares go from $x = 0$ to $x = 3$.
4. *Integrate to find the volume.*
$$V = \int_0^3 A(x)\,dx = \int_0^3 x^2\,dx = \left.\frac{x^3}{3}\right]_0^3 = 9 \text{ m}^3$$

Now Try Exercise 3.

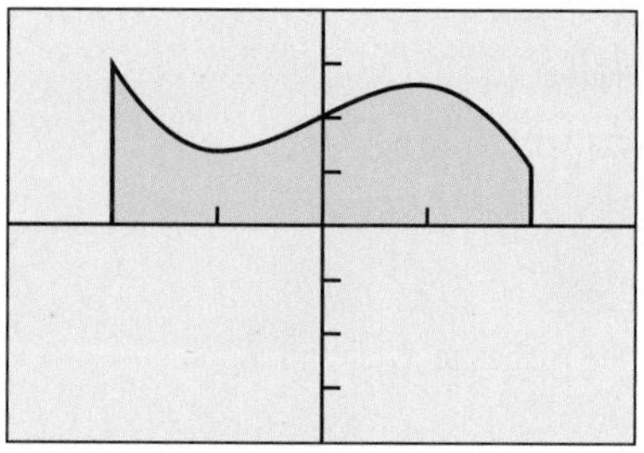

[−3, 3] by [−4, 4]

Figure 8.18 The region in Example 2.

Circular Cross Sections

The only thing that changes when the cross sections of a solid are circular is the formula for $A(x)$. Many such solids are **solids of revolution,** as in the next example.

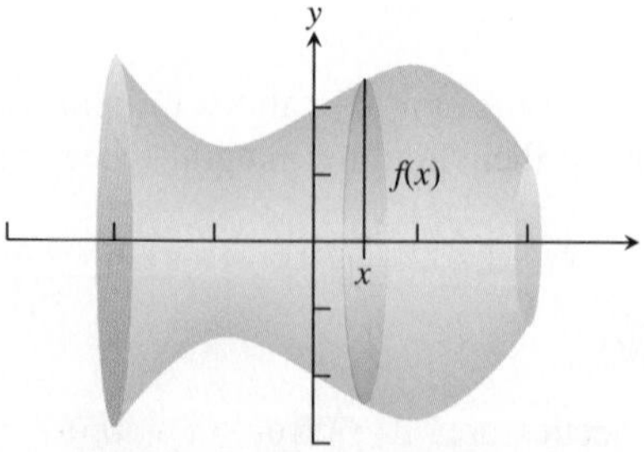

Figure 8.19 The region in Figure 8.18 is revolved about the x-axis to generate a solid. A typical cross section is circular, with radius $f(x) = 2 + x \cos x$. (Example 2)

EXAMPLE 2 A Solid of Revolution

The region between the graph of $f(x) = 2 + x \cos x$ and the x-axis over the interval $[-2, 2]$ is revolved about the x-axis to generate a solid. Find the volume of the solid.

SOLUTION

Revolving the region (Figure 8.18) about the x-axis generates the vase-shaped solid in Figure 8.19. The cross section at a typical point x is circular, with radius equal to $f(x)$. Its area is

$$A(x) = \pi(f(x))^2.$$

continued

The volume of the solid is

$$V = \int_{-2}^{2} A(x)\,dx$$

$$\approx \text{NINT}\,(\pi(2 + x\cos x)^2, x, -2, 2) \approx 52.43 \text{ units cubed.}$$

Now Try Exercise 7.

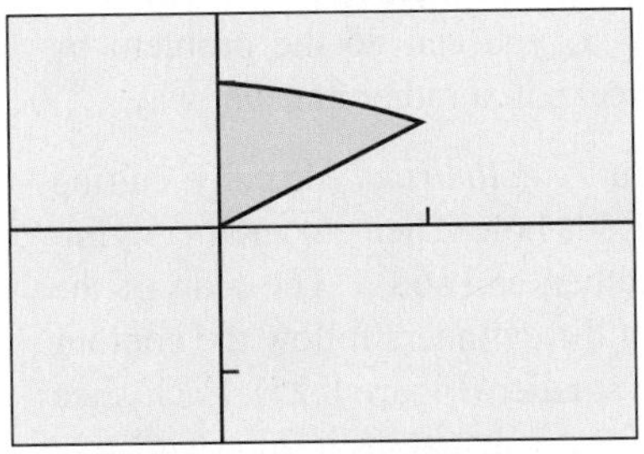

Figure 8.20 The region in Example 3.

EXAMPLE 3 Washer Cross Sections

The region in the first quadrant enclosed by the y-axis and the graphs of $y = \cos x$ and $y = \sin x$ is revolved about the x-axis to form a solid. Find its volume.

SOLUTION

The region is shown in Figure 8.20.

We revolve it about the x-axis to generate a solid with a cone-shaped cavity in its center (Figure 8.21).

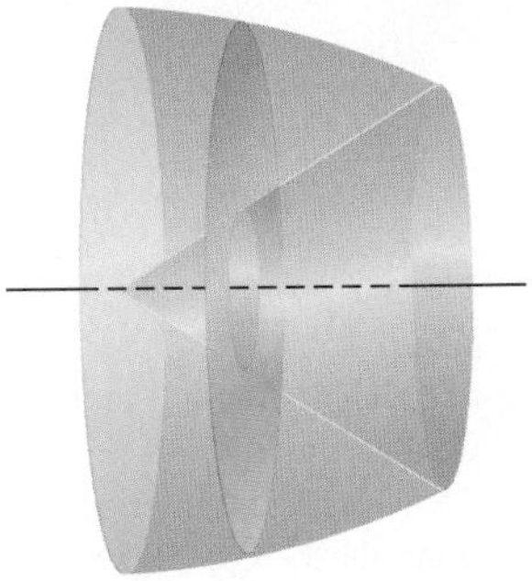

Figure 8.21 The solid generated by revolving the region in Figure 8.20 about the x-axis. A typical cross section is a washer: a circular region with a circular region cut out of its center. (Example 3)

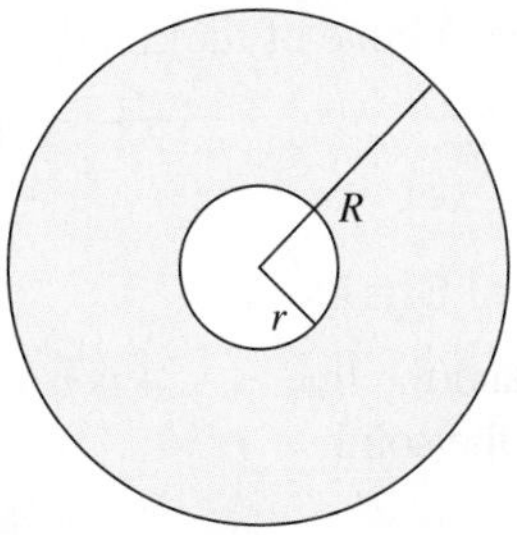

Figure 8.22 The area of a washer is $\pi R^2 - \pi r^2$. (Example 3)

Caution!

The area of a washer is $\pi R^2 - \pi r^2$, which you can simplify to $\pi(R^2 - r^2)$, but *not* to $\pi(R - r)^2$. No matter how tempting it is to make the latter simplification, it's wrong. Don't do it.

This time each cross section perpendicular to the *axis of revolution* is a *washer,* a circular region with a circular region cut from its center. The area of a washer can be found by subtracting the inner area from the outer area (Figure 8.22).

In our region the cosine curve defines the outer radius, and the curves intersect at $x = \pi/4$. The volume is

$$V = \int_0^{\pi/4} \pi(\cos^2 x - \sin^2 x)\,dx$$

$$= \pi \int_0^{\pi/4} \cos 2x\,dx \quad \text{identity: } \cos^2 x - \sin^2 x = \cos 2x$$

$$= \pi\left[\frac{\sin 2x}{2}\right]_0^{\pi/4} = \frac{\pi}{2} \text{ units cubed.}$$

Now Try Exercise 17.

We could have done the integration in Example 3 with NINT, but we wanted to demonstrate how a trigonometric identity can be useful under unexpected circumstances in calculus. The double-angle identity turned a difficult integrand into an easy one and enabled us to get an exact answer by antidifferentiation.

Cylindrical Shells

There is another way to find volumes of solids of rotation that can be useful when the axis of revolution is perpendicular to the axis containing the natural interval of integration. Instead of summing volumes of thin slices, we sum volumes of thin cylindrical shells that grow outward from the axis of revolution like tree rings.

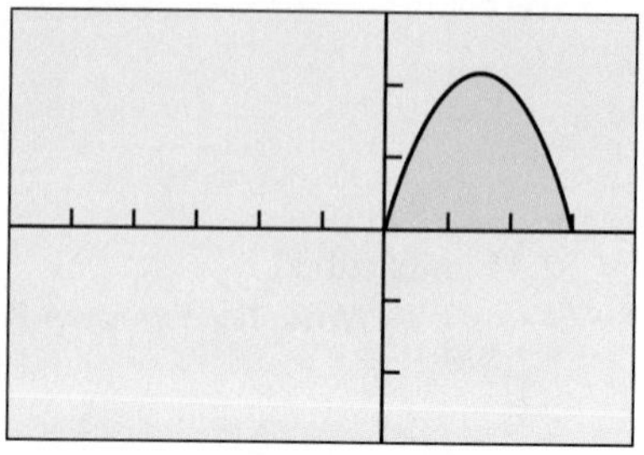

[–6, 4] by [–3, 3]

Figure 8.23 The graph of the region in Exploration 1, before revolution.

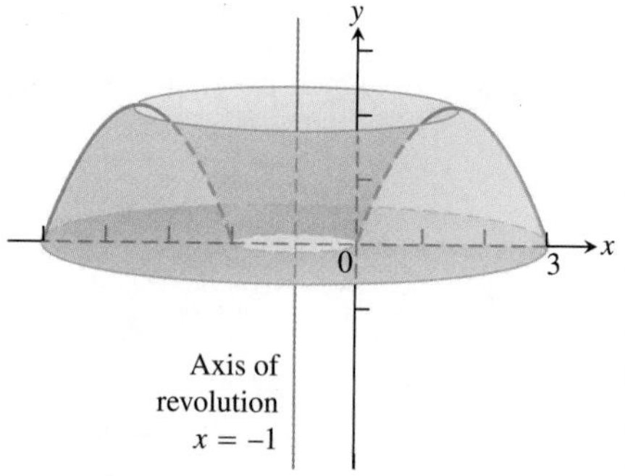

Figure 8.24 The region in Figure 8.23 is revolved about the line $x = -1$ to form a solid cake. The natural interval of integration is along the x-axis, perpendicular to the axis of revolution. (Exploration 1)

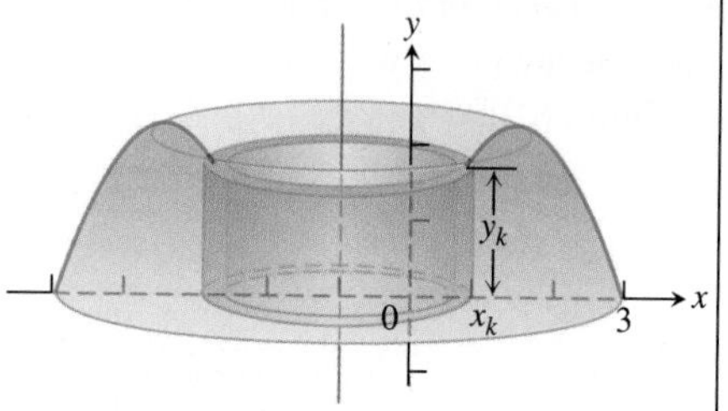

Figure 8.25 Cutting the cake into thin cylindrical slices, working from the inside out. Each slice occurs at some x_k between 0 and 3 and has thickness Δx. (Exploration 1)

EXPLORATION 1 Volume by Cylindrical Shells

The region enclosed by the x-axis and the parabola $y = f(x) = 3x - x^2$ is revolved about the line $x = -1$ to generate the shape of a cake (Figures 8.23, 8.24). (Such a cake is often called a bundt cake.) What is the volume of the cake?

Integrating with respect to y would be awkward here, as it is not easy to get the original parabola in terms of y. (Try finding the volume by washers and you will soon see what we mean.) To integrate with respect to x, you can do the problem by *cylindrical shells,* which requires that you cut the cake in a rather unusual way.

1. Instead of cutting the usual wedge shape, cut a *cylindrical* slice by cutting straight down all the way around close to the inside hole. Then cut another cylindrical slice around the enlarged hole, then another, and so on. The radii of the cylinders gradually increase, and the heights of the cylinders follow the contour of the parabola: smaller to larger, then back to smaller (Figure 8.25). Each slice is sitting over a subinterval of the x-axis of length Δx. Its radius is approximately $(1 + x_k)$. What is its height?
2. If you unroll the cylinder at x_k and flatten it out, it becomes (essentially) a rectangular slab with thickness Δx. Show that the volume of the slab is approximately $2\pi(x_k + 1)(3x_k - x_k^2)\Delta x$.
3. $\sum 2\pi(x_k + 1)(3x_k - x_k^2)\Delta x$ is a Riemann sum. What is the limit of these Riemann sums as $\Delta x \to 0$?
4. Evaluate the integral you found in step 3 to find the volume of the cake!

EXAMPLE 4 Finding Volumes Using Cylindrical Shells

The region bounded by the curve $y = \sqrt{x}$, the x-axis, and the line $x = 4$ is revolved about the x-axis to generate a solid. Find the volume of the solid.

SOLUTION

1. Sketch the region and draw a line segment across it parallel to the axis of revolution (Figure 8.26). Label the segment's length (shell height) and distance from the axis of revolution (shell radius). The width of the segment is the shell thickness dy. (We drew the shell in Figure 8.27, but you need not do that.)

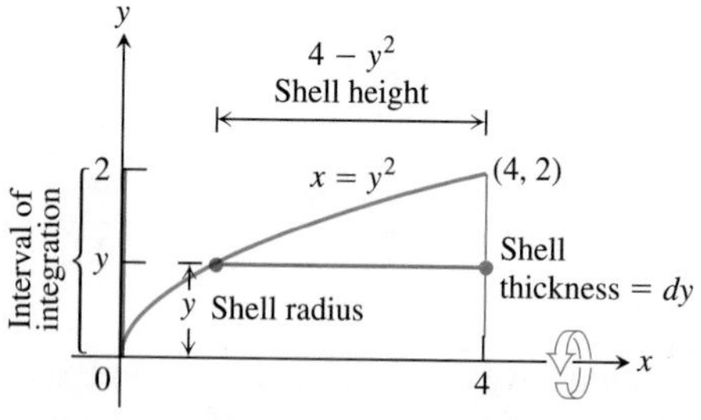

Figure 8.26 The region, shell dimensions, and interval of integration in Example 4.

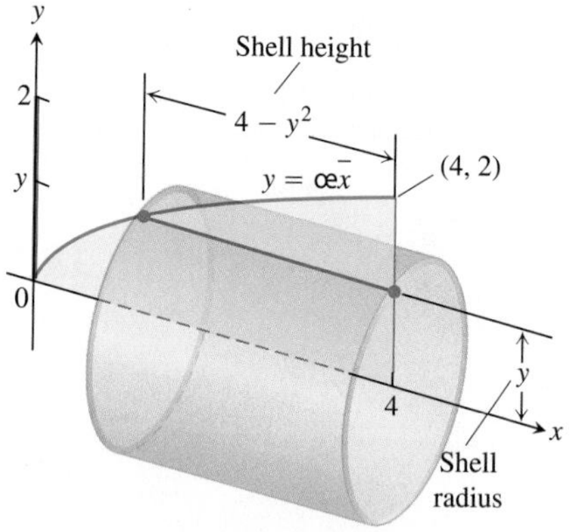

Figure 8.27 The shell swept out by the line segment in Figure 8.26.

2. Identify the limits of integration: y runs from 0 to 2.
3. Integrate to find the volume.

continued

$$V = \int_0^2 2\pi \begin{pmatrix}\text{shell}\\ \text{radius}\end{pmatrix}\begin{pmatrix}\text{shell}\\ \text{height}\end{pmatrix} dy$$

$$= \int_0^2 2\pi(y)(4 - y^2)\, dy$$

$$= 2\pi \int (4y - y^3)\, dy$$

$$= 2\pi\left[2y^2 - \frac{y^4}{4}\right]_0^2 = 8\pi$$

Now Try Exercise 33(a).

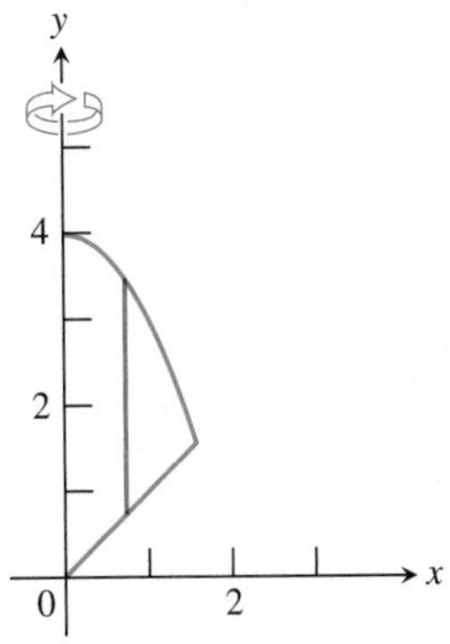

Figure 8.28 The region and the height of a typical shell in Example 5.

EXAMPLE 5 Finding Volumes Using Cylindrical Shells

The region bounded by the curves $y = 4 - x^2$, $y = x$, and $x = 0$ is revolved about the y-axis to form a solid. Use cylindrical shells to find the volume of the solid.

SOLUTION

1. Sketch the region and draw a line segment across it parallel to the y-axis (Figure 8.28). The segment's length (shell height) is $4 - x^2 - x$. The distance of the segment from the axis of revolution (shell radius) is x.
2. Identify the limits of integration: The x-coordinate of the point of intersection of the curves $y = 4 - x^2$ and $y = x$ in the first quadrant is about 1.562. So x runs from 0 to 1.562.
3. Integrate to find the volume.

$$V = \int_0^{1.562} 2\pi \begin{pmatrix}\text{shell}\\ \text{radius}\end{pmatrix}\begin{pmatrix}\text{shell}\\ \text{height}\end{pmatrix} dx$$

$$= \int_0^{1.562} 2\pi(x)(4 - x^2 - x)\, dx$$

$$= 2\pi \int_0^{1.562} (4x - x^3 - x^2)\, dx$$

$$= 2\pi\left[2x^2 - \frac{x^4}{4} - \frac{x^3}{3}\right]_0^{1.562}$$

$$\approx 13.327$$

Now Try Exercise 35.

EXAMPLE 6 Comparing Different Methods for Finding a Volume

We found the volume of the solid in Example 4 by using cylindrical shells. Use circular cross sections (or disks) to find the volume of the same solid.

SOLUTION

The following sketch shows drawing a line segment across the region bounded by $y = \sqrt{x}$, the x-axis, and the line $x = 4$ perpendicular to the axis of revolution.

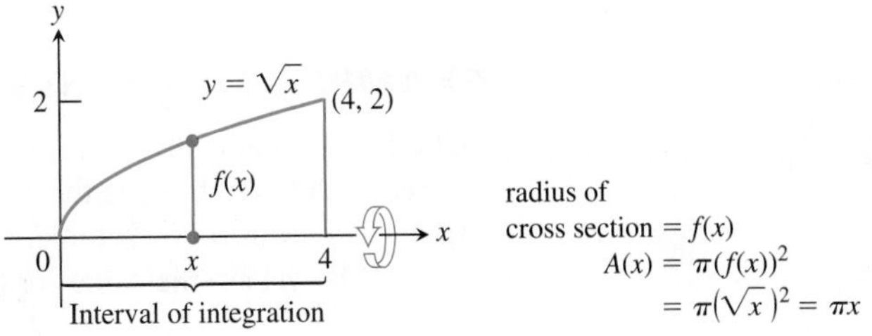

continued

The volume of the solid is

$$V = \int_0^4 A(x)\,dx = \int_0^4 \pi x\,dx = \pi\left[\frac{x^2}{2}\right]_0^4 = 8\pi$$

Either method gives the same volume, 8π. **Now Try Exercise 37.**

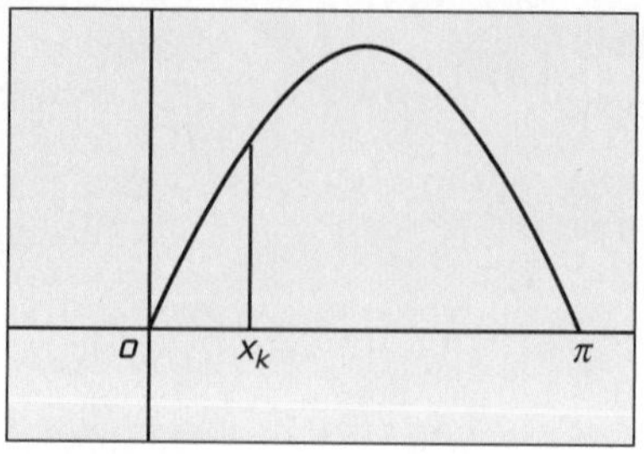

[–1, 3.5] by [–0.8, 2.2]

Figure 8.29 The base of the paperweight in Example 7. The segment perpendicular to the x-axis at x_k is the diameter of a semicircle that is perpendicular to the base.

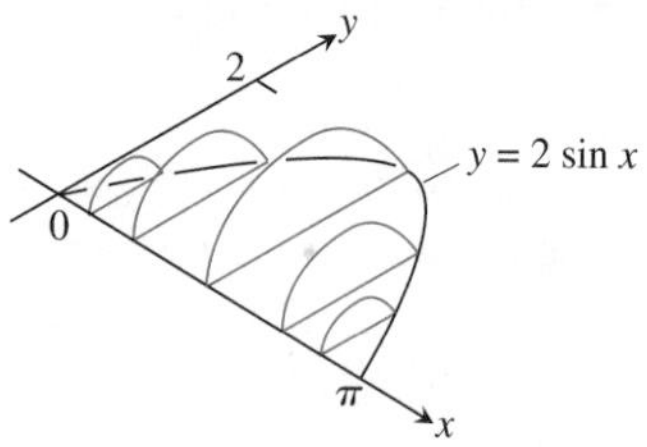

Figure 8.30 Cross sections perpendicular to the region in Figure 8.29 are semicircular. (Example 7)

Other Cross Sections

The method of cross-section slicing can be used to find volumes of a wide variety of unusually shaped solids, so long as the cross sections have areas that we can describe with some formula. Admittedly, it does take a special artistic talent to *draw* some of these solids, but a crude picture is usually enough to suggest how to set up the integral.

EXAMPLE 7 A Mathematician's Paperweight

A mathematician has a paperweight made so that its base is the shape of the region between the x-axis and one arch of the curve $y = 2 \sin x$ (linear units in inches). Each cross section cut perpendicular to the x-axis (and hence to the xy-plane) is a semicircle whose diameter runs from the x-axis to the curve. (Think of the cross section as a semicircular fin sticking up out of the plane.) Find the volume of the paperweight.

SOLUTION

The paperweight is not easily drawn, but we know what it looks like. Its base is the region in Figure 8.29, and the cross sections perpendicular to the base are semicircular fins like those in Figure 8.30.

The semicircle at each point x has

$$\text{radius} = \frac{2 \sin x}{2} = \sin x \quad \text{and area} \quad A(x) = \frac{1}{2}\pi(\sin x)^2.$$

The volume of the paperweight is

$$\begin{aligned} V &= \int_0^{\pi} A(x)\,dx \\ &= \frac{\pi}{2}\int_0^{\pi} (\sin x)^2\,dx \\ &\approx \frac{\pi}{2}\,\text{NINT}\left((\sin x)^2, x, 0, \pi\right) \\ &\approx \frac{\pi}{2}(1.570796327). \end{aligned}$$

The number in parentheses looks like half of π, an observation that can be confirmed analytically, and which we support numerically by dividing by π to get 0.5. The volume of the paperweight is

$$\frac{\pi}{2}\cdot\frac{\pi}{2} = \frac{\pi^2}{4} \approx 2.47 \text{ in}^3.$$

Now Try Exercise 39(a).

Bonaventura Cavalieri (1598–1647)

Cavalieri, a student of Galileo, discovered that if two plane regions can be arranged to lie over the same interval of the x-axis in such a way that they have identical vertical cross sections at every point, then the regions have the same area. This theorem and a letter of recommendation from Galileo were enough to win Cavalieri a chair at the University of Bologna in 1629. The solid geometry version in Example 8, which Cavalieri never proved, was named after him by later geometers.

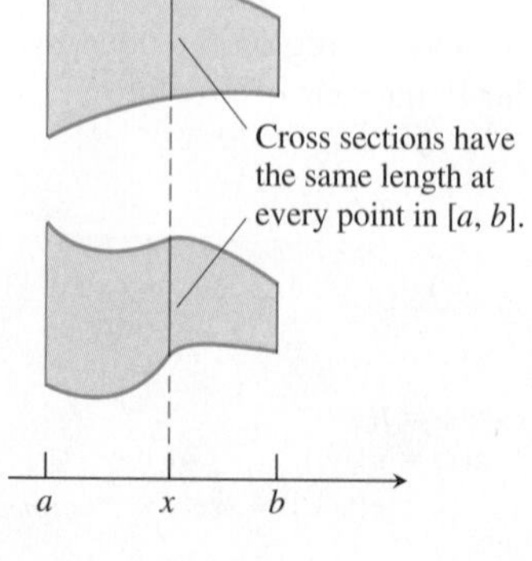

EXAMPLE 8 Cavalieri's Volume Theorem

Cavalieri's volume theorem says that solids with equal altitudes and identical cross-section areas at each height have the same volume (Figure 8.31). This follows immediately from the definition of volume, because the cross section area function $A(x)$ and the interval $[a, b]$ are the same for both solids.

continued

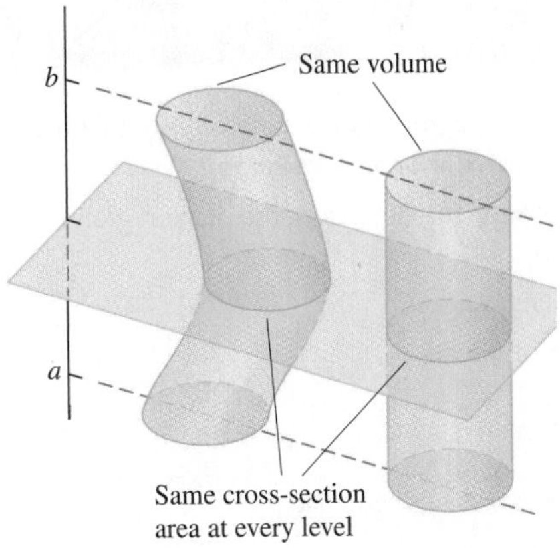

Figure 8.31 *Cavalieri's volume theorem:* These solids have the same volume. You can illustrate this yourself with stacks of coins. (Example 8)

Now Try Exercise 43.

EXPLORATION 2 Surface Area

We know how to find the volume of a solid of revolution, but how would we find the *surface area*? As before, we partition the solid into thin slices, but now we wish to form a Riemann sum of approximations to *surface areas of slices* (rather than of volumes of slices).

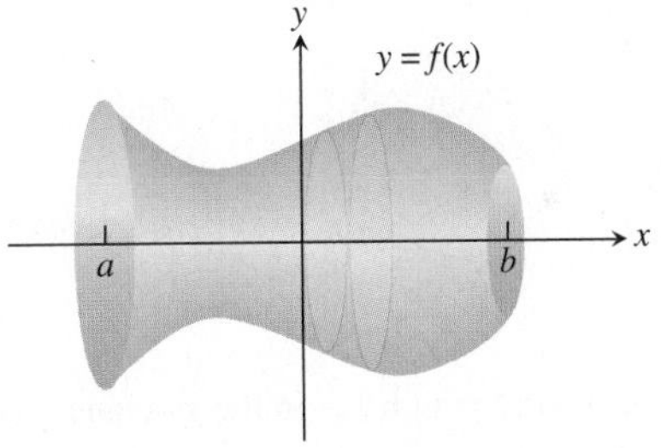

A typical slice has a surface area that can be approximated by $2\pi \cdot f(x) \cdot \Delta s$, where Δs is the tiny *slant height* of the slice. We will see in Section 8.4, when we study arc length, that $\Delta s = \sqrt{\Delta x^2 + \Delta y^2}$, and that this can be written as $\Delta s = \sqrt{1 + (f'(x_k))^2}\,\Delta x$.

Thus, the surface area is approximated by the Riemann sum

$$\sum_{k=1}^{n} 2\pi\, f(x_k)\sqrt{1 + (f'(x_k))^2}\,\Delta x.$$

1. Write the limit of the Riemann sums as a definite integral from a to b. When will the limit exist?
2. Use the formula from part 1 to find the surface area of the solid generated by revolving a single arch of the curve $y = \sin x$ about the x-axis.
3. The region enclosed by the graphs of $y^2 = x$ and $x = 4$ is revolved about the x-axis to form a solid. Find the surface area of the solid.

Quick Review 8.3 (For help, go to Section 1.2.)

Exercise numbers with a gray background indicate problems that the authors have designed to be solved *without a calculator*.

In Exercises 1–10, give a formula for the area of the plane region in terms of the single variable x.

1. a square with sides of length x
2. a square with diagonals of length x
3. a semicircle of radius x
4. a semicircle of diameter x
5. an equilateral triangle with sides of length x
6. an isosceles right triangle with legs of length x
7. an isosceles right triangle with hypotenuse x
8. an isosceles triangle with two sides of length $2x$ and one side of length x
9. a triangle with sides $3x$, $4x$, and $5x$
10. a regular hexagon with sides of length x

Section 8.3 Exercises

In Exercises 1 and 2, find a formula for the area $A(x)$ of the cross sections of the solid that are perpendicular to the x-axis.

1. The solid lies between planes perpendicular to the x-axis at $x = -1$ and $x = 1$. The cross sections perpendicular to the x-axis between these planes run from the semicircle $y = -\sqrt{1 - x^2}$ to the semicircle $y = \sqrt{1 - x^2}$.

(a) The cross sections are circular disks with diameters in the xy-plane.

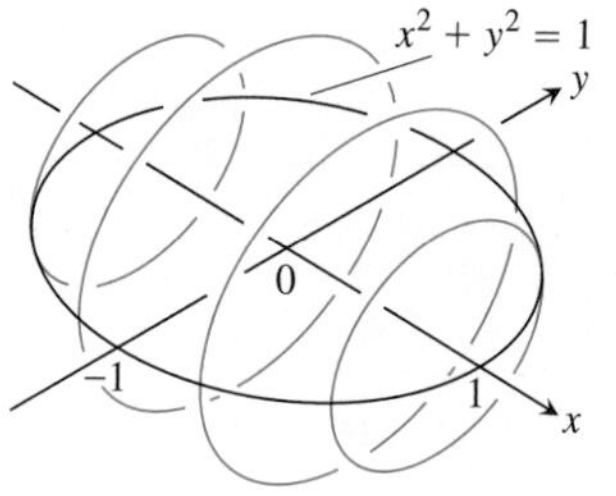

(b) The cross sections are squares with bases in the xy-plane.

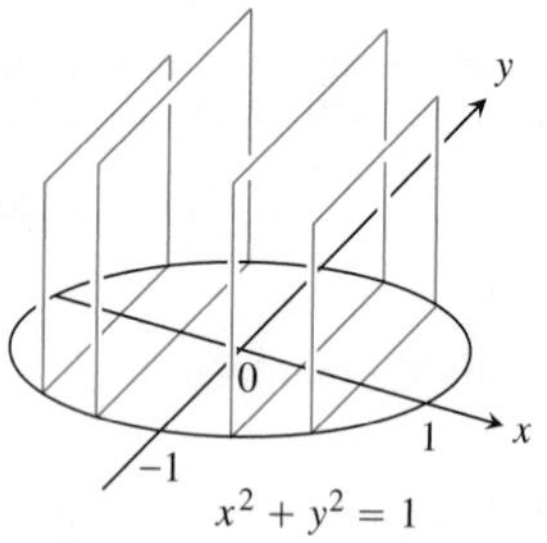

(c) The cross sections are squares with diagonals in the xy-plane. (The length of a square's diagonal is $\sqrt{2}$ times the length of its sides.)

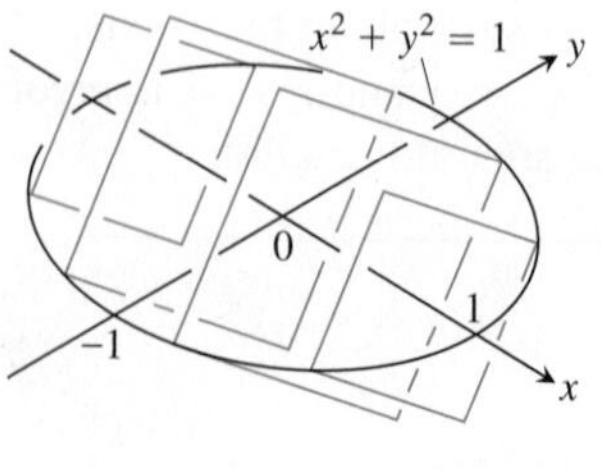

(d) The cross sections are equilateral triangles with bases in the xy-plane.

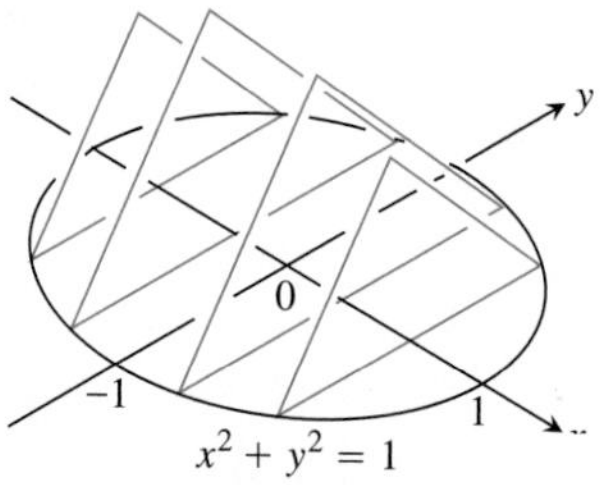

2. The solid lies between planes perpendicular to the x-axis at $x = 0$ and $x = 4$. The cross sections perpendicular to the x-axis between these planes run from $y = -\sqrt{x}$ to $y = \sqrt{x}$.

(a) The cross sections are circular disks with diameters in the xy-plane.

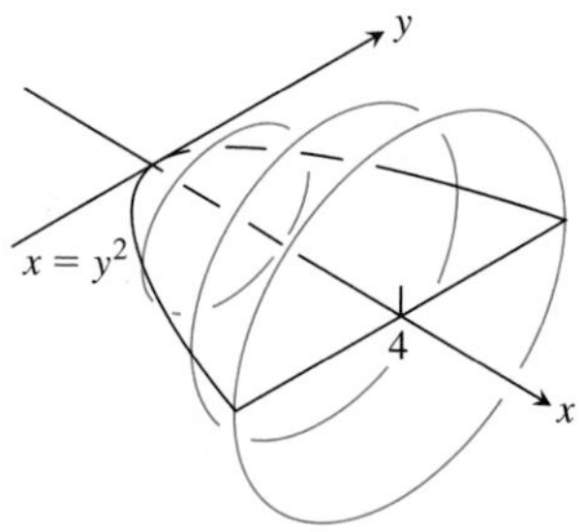

(b) The cross sections are squares with bases in the xy-plane.

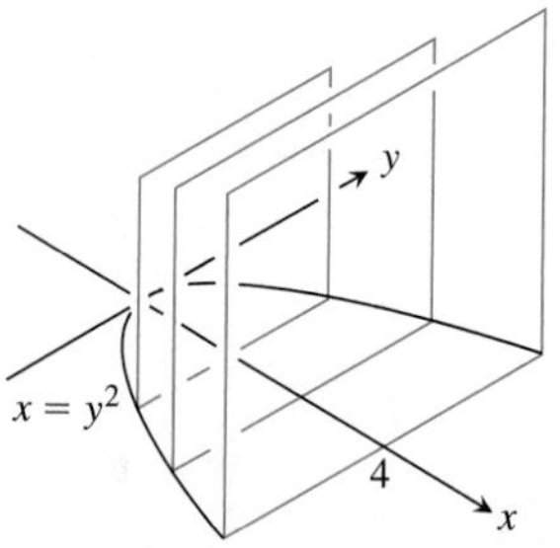

(c) The cross sections are squares with diagonals in the xy-plane.

(d) The cross sections are equilateral triangles with bases in the xy-plane.

In Exercises 3–6, find the volume of the solid analytically.

3. The solid lies between planes perpendicular to the x-axis at $x = 0$ and $x = 4$. The cross sections perpendicular to the axis on the interval $0 \le x \le 4$ are squares whose diagonals run from $y = -\sqrt{x}$ to $y = \sqrt{x}$.

4. The solid lies between planes perpendicular to the x-axis at $x = -1$ and $x = 1$. The cross sections perpendicular to the x-axis are circular disks whose diameters run from the parabola $y = x^2$ to the parabola $y = 2 - x^2$.

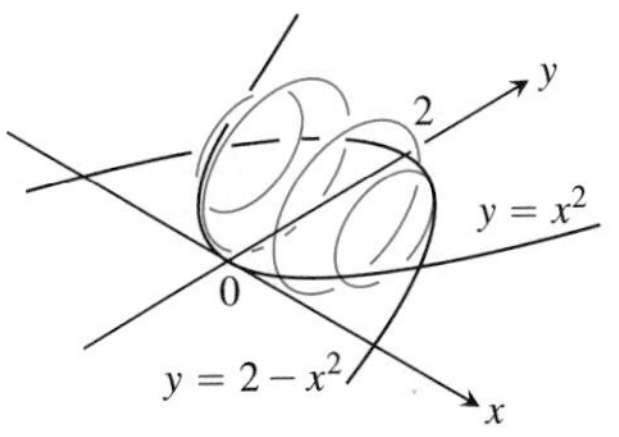

5. The solid lies between planes perpendicular to the x-axis at $x = -1$ and $x = 1$. The cross sections perpendicular to the x-axis between these planes are squares whose bases run from the semicircle $y = -\sqrt{1 - x^2}$ to the semicircle $y = \sqrt{1 - x^2}$.

6. The solid lies between planes perpendicular to the x-axis at $x = -1$ and $x = 1$. The cross sections perpendicular to the x-axis between these planes are squares whose diagonals run from the semicircle $y = -\sqrt{1 - x^2}$ to the semicircle $y = \sqrt{1 - x^2}$.

In Exercises 7–10, find the volume of the solid generated by revolving the shaded region about the given axis.

7. about the x-axis

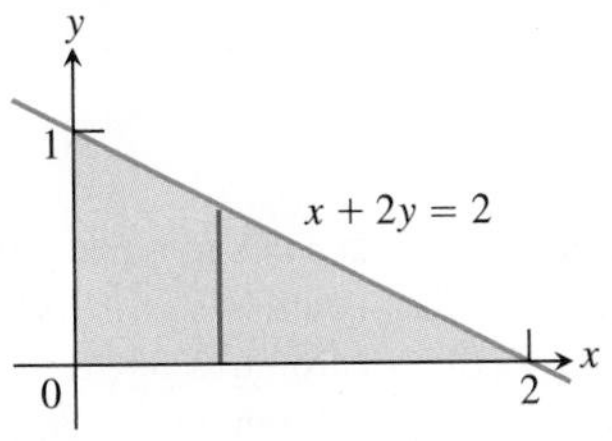

8. about the y-axis

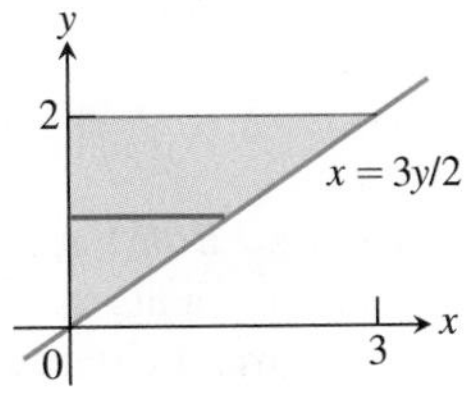

9. about the y-axis

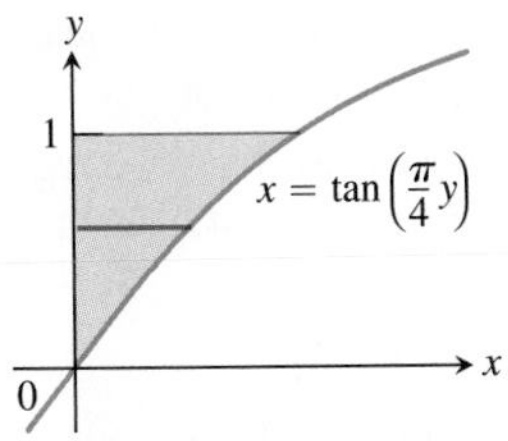

10. about the x-axis

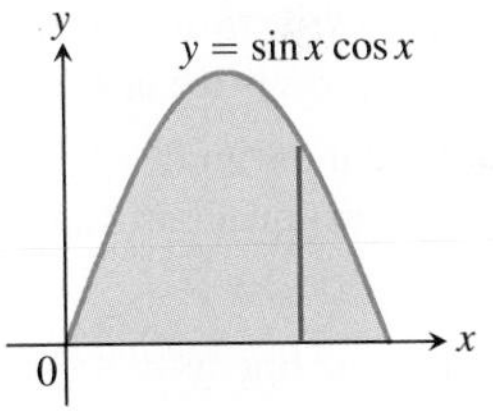

In Exercises 11–20, find the volume of the solid generated by revolving the region bounded by the lines and curves about the x-axis.

11. $y = x^2, \quad y = 0, \quad x = 2$

12. $y = x^3, \quad y = 0, \quad x = 2$

13. $y = \sqrt{9 - x^2}, \quad y = 0$

14. $y = x - x^2, \quad y = 0$

15. $y = x, \quad y = 1, \quad x = 0$

16. $y = 2x, \quad y = x, \quad x = 1$

17. $y = x^2 + 1, \quad y = x + 3$

18. $y = 4 - x^2, \quad y = 2 - x$

19. $y = \sec x, \quad y = \sqrt{2}, \quad -\pi/4 \le x \le \pi/4$

20. $y = -\sqrt{x}, \quad y = -2, \quad x = 0$

In Exercises 21 and 22, find the volume of the solid generated by revolving the region about the given line.

21. the region in the first quadrant bounded above by the line $y = \sqrt{2}$, below by the curve $y = \sec x \tan x$, and on the left by the y-axis, about the line $y = \sqrt{2}$

22. the region in the first quadrant bounded above by the line $y = 2$, below by the curve $y = 2 \sin x$, $0 \le x \le \pi/2$, and on the left by the y-axis, about the line $y = 2$

In Exercises 23–28, find the volume of the solid generated by revolving the region about the y-axis.

23. the region enclosed by $x = \sqrt{5}y^2, \quad x = 0, \quad y = -1, \quad y = 1$

24. the region enclosed by $x = y^{3/2}, \quad x = 0, \quad y = 2$

25. the region enclosed by the triangle with vertices $(1, 0)$, $(2, 1)$, and $(1, 1)$

26. the region enclosed by the triangle with vertices $(0, 1)$, $(1, 0)$, and $(1, 1)$

27. the region in the first quadrant bounded above by the parabola $y = x^2$, below by the x-axis, and on the right by the line $x = 2$

28. the region bounded above by the curve $y = \sqrt{x}$ and below by the line $y = x$

Group Activity In Exercises 29–32, find the volume of the solid described.

29. Find the volume of the solid generated by revolving the region bounded by $y = \sqrt{x}$ and the lines $y = 2$ and $x = 0$ about

(a) the x-axis. **(b)** the y-axis.

(c) the line $y = 2$. **(d)** the line $x = 4$.

30. Find the volume of the solid generated by revolving the triangular region bounded by the lines $y = 2x$, $y = 0$, and $x = 1$ about

(a) the line $x = 1$. **(b)** the line $x = 2$.

31. Find the volume of the solid generated by revolving the region bounded by the parabola $y = x^2$ and the line $y = 1$ about

(a) the line $y = 1$. **(b)** the line $y = 2$.

(c) the line $y = -1$.

32. By integration, find the volume of the solid generated by revolving the triangular region with vertices $(0, 0)$, $(b, 0)$, $(0, h)$ about

(a) the x-axis. **(b)** the y-axis.

In Exercises 33 and 34, use the cylindrical shell method to find the volume of the solid generated by revolving the shaded region about the indicated axis.

33. **(a)** the x-axis **(b)** the line $y = 1$

(c) the line $y = 8/5$ **(d)** the line $y = -2/5$

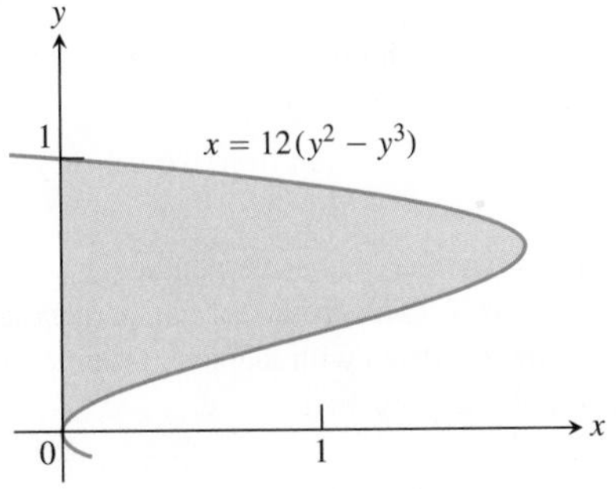

34. **(a)** the x-axis **(b)** the line $y = 2$

(c) the line $y = 5$ **(d)** the line $y = -5/8$

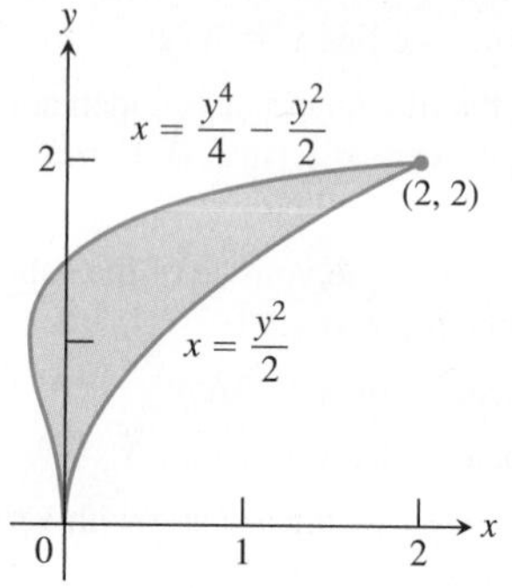

In Exercises 35–38, use the cylindrical shell method to find the volume of the solid generated by revolving the region bounded by the curves about the y-axis.

35. $y = x, \quad y = -x/2, \quad x = 2$

36. $y = x^2, \quad y = 2 - x, \quad x = 0, \quad \text{for} \quad x \geq 0$

37. $y = \sqrt{x}, \quad y = 0, \quad x = 4$

38. $y = 2x - 1, \quad y = \sqrt{x}, \quad x = 0$

In Exercises 39–42, find the volume of the solid analytically.

39. The base of a solid is the region between the curve $y = 2\sqrt{\sin x}$ and the interval $[0, \pi]$ on the x-axis. The cross sections perpendicular to the x-axis are

(a) equilateral triangles with bases running from the x-axis to the curve as shown in the figure.

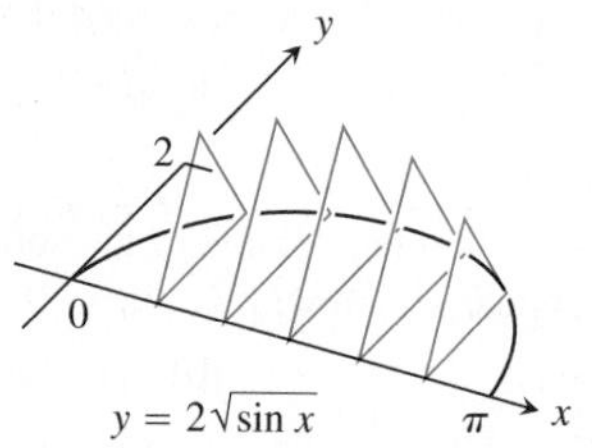

(b) squares with bases running from the x-axis to the curve.

40. The solid lies between planes perpendicular to the x-axis at $x = -\pi/3$ and $x = \pi/3$. The cross sections perpendicular to the x-axis are

(a) circular disks with diameters running from the curve $y = \tan x$ to the curve $y = \sec x$.

(b) squares whose bases run from the curve $y = \tan x$ to the curve $y = \sec x$.

41. The solid lies between planes perpendicular to the y-axis at $y = 0$ and $y = 2$. The cross sections perpendicular to the y-axis are circular disks with diameters running from the y-axis to the parabola $x = \sqrt{5}y^2$.

42. The base of the solid is the disk $x^2 + y^2 \leq 1$. The cross sections by planes perpendicular to the y-axis between $y = -1$ and $y = 1$ are isosceles right triangles with one leg in the disk.

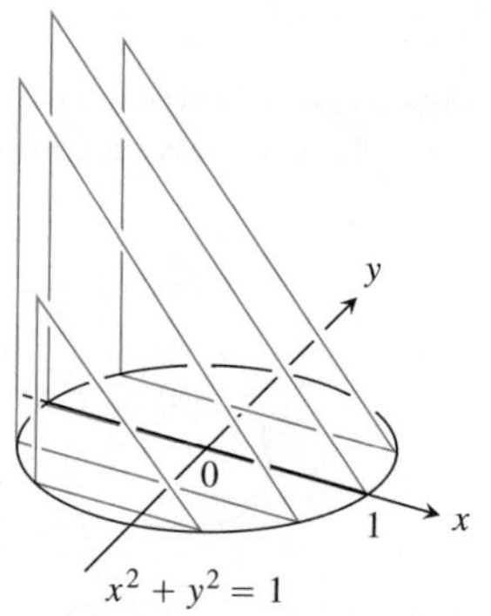

43. Writing to Learn A solid lies between planes perpendicular to the x-axis at $x = 0$ and $x = 12$. The cross sections by planes perpendicular to the x-axis are circular disks whose diameters run from the line $y = x/2$ to the line $y = x$ as shown in the figure. Explain why the solid has the same volume as a right circular cone with base radius 3 and height 12.

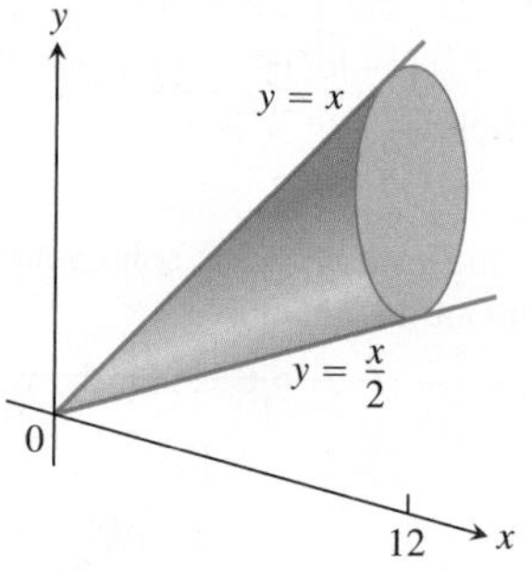

44. ***A Twisted Solid*** A square of side length s lies in a plane perpendicular to a line L. One vertex of the square lies on L. As this square moves a distance h along L, the square turns one revolution about L to generate a corkscrew-like column with square cross sections.

(a) Find the volume of the column.

(b) **Writing to Learn** What will the volume be if the square turns twice instead of once? Give reasons for your answer.

45. Find the volume of the solid generated by revolving the region in the first quadrant bounded by $y = x^3$ and $y = 4x$ about

(a) the x-axis,

(b) the line $y = 8$.

46. Find the volume of the solid generated by revolving the region bounded by $y = 2x - x^2$ and $y = x$ about

(a) the y-axis,

(b) the line $x = 1$.

47. The region in the first quadrant that is bounded above by the curve $y = 1/\sqrt{x}$, on the left by the line $x = 1/4$, and below by the line $y = 1$ is revolved about the y-axis to generate a solid. Find the volume of the solid by **(a)** the washer method and **(b)** the cylindrical shell method.

48. Let $f(x) = \begin{cases} (\sin x)/x, & 0 < x \le \pi \\ 1, & x = 0. \end{cases}$

(a) Show that $x f(x) = \sin x, \quad 0 \le x \le \pi$.

(b) Find the volume of the solid generated by revolving the shaded region about the y-axis.

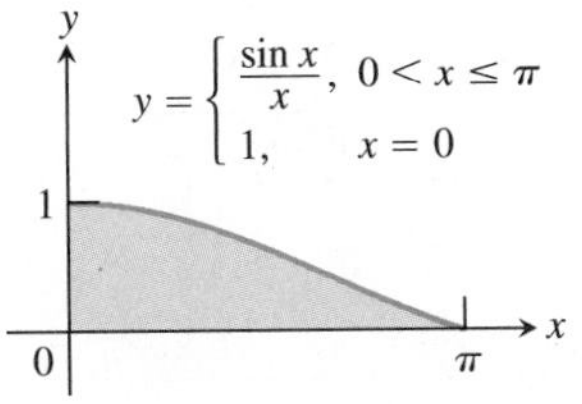

49. *Designing a Plumb Bob* Having been asked to design a brass plumb bob that will weigh in the neighborhood of 190 g, you decide to shape it like the solid of revolution shown here.

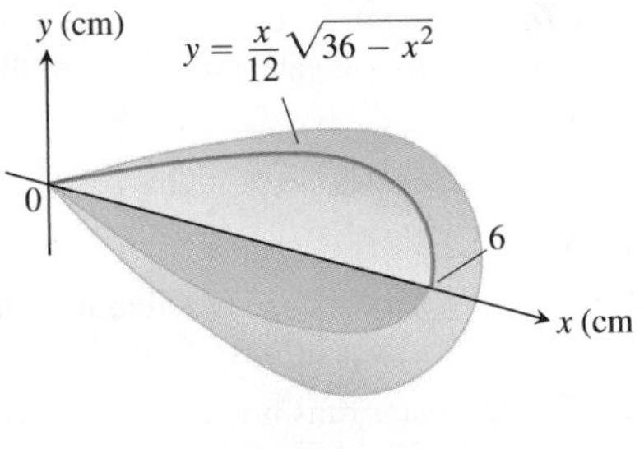

(a) Find the plumb bob's volume.

(b) If you specify a brass that weighs 8.5 g/cm^3, how much will the plumb bob weigh to the nearest gram?

50. *Volume of a Bowl* A bowl has a shape that can be generated by revolving the graph of $y = x^2/2$ between $y = 0$ and $y = 5$ about the y-axis.

(a) Find the volume of the bowl.

(b) If we fill the bowl with water at a constant rate of 3 cubic units per second, how fast will the water level in the bowl be rising when the water is 4 units deep?

51. *The Classical Bead Problem* A round hole is drilled through the center of a spherical solid of radius r. The resulting cylindrical hole has height 4 cm.

(a) What is the volume of the solid that remains?

(b) What is unusual about the answer?

52. Writing to Learn Explain how you could estimate the volume of a solid of revolution by measuring the shadow cast on a table parallel to its axis of revolution by a light shining directly above it.

53. *Same Volume About Each Axis* The region in the first quadrant enclosed between the graph of $y = ax - x^2$ and the x-axis generates the same volume whether it is revolved about the x-axis or the y-axis. Find the value of a.

54. *(Continuation of Exploration 2)* Let $x = g(y) > 0$ have a continuous first derivative on $[c, d]$. Show that the area of the surface generated by revolving the curve $x = g(y)$ about the y-axis is

$$S = \int_c^d 2\pi\, g(y)\sqrt{1 + (g'(y))^2}\, dy.$$

In Exercises 55–62, find the area of the surface generated by revolving the curve about the indicated axis.

55. $x = \sqrt{y}, \quad 0 \le y \le 2; \quad y\text{-axis}$

56. $x = y^3/3, \quad 0 \le y \le 1; \quad y\text{-axis}$

57. $x = y^{1/2} - (1/3)^{3/2}, \quad 1 \le y \le 3; \quad y\text{-axis}$

58. $x = \sqrt{2y - 1}, \quad (5/8) \le y \le 1; \quad y\text{-axis}$

59. $y = x^2, \quad 0 \le x \le 2; \quad x\text{-axis}$

60. $y = 3x - x^2, \quad 0 \le x \le 3; \quad x\text{-axis}$

61. $y = \sqrt{2x - x^2}, \quad 0.5 \le x \le 1.5; \quad x\text{-axis}$

62. $y = \sqrt{x + 1}, \quad 1 \le x \le 5; \quad x\text{-axis}$

Standardized Test Questions

You may use a graphing calculator to solve the following problems.

63. True or False The volume of a solid of a known integrable cross section area $A(x)$ from $x = a$ to $x = b$ is $\int_a^b A(x)\, dx$. Justify your answer.

64. True or False If the region enclosed by the y-axis, the line $y = 2$, and the curve $y = \sqrt{x}$ is revolved about the y-axis, the volume of the solid is given by the definite integral $\int_0^2 \pi y^2\, dy$. Justify your answer.

65. Multiple Choice The base of a solid S is the region enclosed by the graph of $y = \ln x$, the line $x = e$, and the x-axis. If the cross sections of S perpendicular to the x-axis are squares, which of the following gives the best approximation of the volume of S?

(A) 0.718 **(B)** 1.718 **(C)** 2.718 **(D)** 3.171 **(E)** 7.388

66. Multiple Choice Let R be the region in the first quadrant bounded by the graph of $y = 8 - x^{3/2}$, the x-axis, and the y-axis. Which of the following gives the best approximation of the volume of the solid generated when R is revolved about the x-axis?

(A) 60.3 **(B)** 115.2 **(C)** 225.4 **(D)** 319.7 **(E)** 361.9

67. Multiple Choice Let R be the region enclosed by the graph of $y = x^2$, the line $x = 4$, and the x-axis. Which of the following gives the best approximation of the volume of the solid generated when R is revolved about the y-axis?

(A) 64π **(B)** 128π **(C)** 256π **(D)** 360 **(E)** 512

68. Multiple Choice Let R be the region enclosed by the graphs of $y = e^{-x}$, $y = e^x$, and $x = 1$. Which of the following gives the volume of the solid generated when R is revolved about the x-axis?

(A) $\int_0^1 (e^x - e^{-x})\, dx$

(B) $\int_0^1 (e^{2x} - e^{-2x})\, dx$

(C) $\int_0^1 (e^x - e^{-x})^2\, dx$

(D) $\pi \int_0^1 (e^{2x} - e^{-2x})\, dx$

(E) $\pi \int_0^1 (e^x - e^{-x})^2\, dx$

Explorations

69. *Max-Min* The arch $y = \sin x, 0 \le x \le \pi$, is revolved about the line $y = c, 0 \le c \le 1$, to generate the solid in the figure.

(a) Find the value of c that minimizes the volume of the solid. What is the minimum volume?

(b) What value of c in $[0, 1]$ maximizes the volume of the solid?

(c) Writing to Learn Graph the solid's volume as a function of c, first for $0 \le c \le 1$ and then on a larger domain. What happens to the volume of the solid as c moves away from $[0, 1]$? Does this make sense physically? Give reasons for your answers.

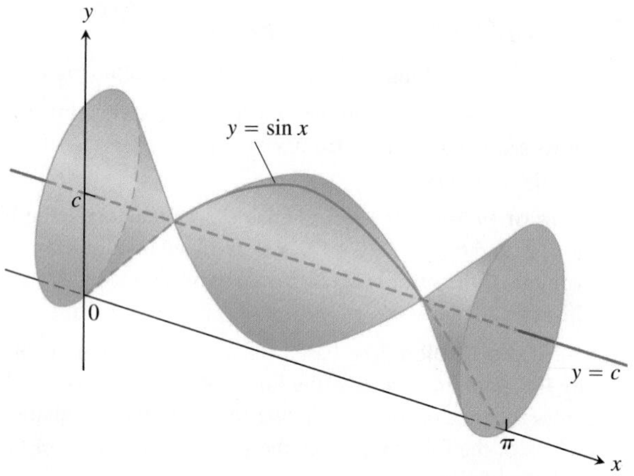

70. *A Vase* We wish to estimate the volume of a flower vase using only a calculator, a string, and a ruler. We measure the height of the vase to be 6 inches. We then use the string and the ruler to find circumferences of the vase (in inches) at half-inch intervals. (We list them from the top down to correspond with the picture of the vase.)

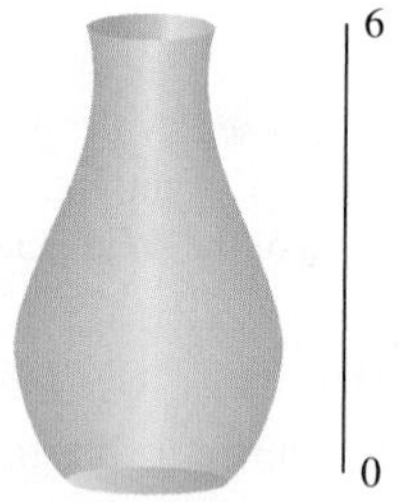

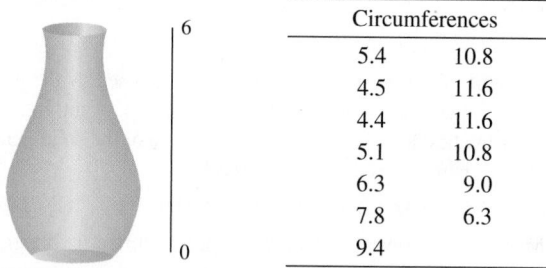

Circumferences	
5.4	10.8
4.5	11.6
4.4	11.6
5.1	10.8
6.3	9.0
7.8	6.3
9.4	

(a) Find the areas of the cross sections that correspond to the given circumferences.

(b) Express the volume of the vase as an integral with respect to y over the interval $[0, 6]$.

(c) Approximate the integral using the Trapezoidal Rule with $n = 12$.

Extending the Ideas

71. *Volume of a Hemisphere* Derive the formula $V = (2/3)\pi R^3$ for the volume of a hemisphere of radius R by com paring its cross sections with the cross sections of a solid right cir cular cylinder of radius R and height R from which a solid right circular cone of base radius R and height R has been removed, as suggested by the figure.

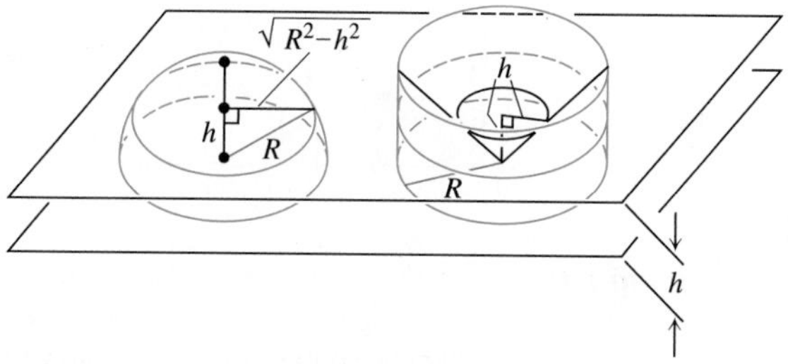

72. *Volume of a Torus* The disk $x^2 + y^2 \le a^2$ is revolved about the line $x = b\ (b > a)$ to generate a solid shaped like a doughnut, called a *torus*. Find its volume. [*Hint:* $\int_{-a}^{a} \sqrt{a^2 - y^2}\, dy = \pi a^2/2$, since it is the area of a semicircle of radius a.]

73. *Filling a Bowl*

(a) *Volume* A hemispherical bowl of radius a contains water to a depth h. Find the volume of water in the bowl.

(b) *Related Rates* Water runs into a sunken concrete hemispherical bowl of radius 5 m at a rate of 0.2 m^3/sec. How fast is the water level in the bowl rising when the water is 4 m deep?

74. *Consistency of Volume Definitions* The volume formulas in calculus are consistent with the standard formulas from geometry in the sense that they agree on objects to which both apply.

(a) As a case in point, show that if you revolve the region enclosed by the semicircle $y = \sqrt{a^2 - x^2}$ and the x-axis about the x-axis to generate a solid sphere, the calculus formula for volume at the beginning of the section will give $(4/3)\pi a^3$ for the volume just as it should.

(b) Use calculus to find the volume of a right circular cone of height h and base radius r.

Quick Quiz for AP* Preparation: Sections 8.1–8.3

You may use a graphing calculator to solve the following problems.

1. Multiple Choice The base of a solid is the region in the first quadrant bounded by the x-axis, the graph of $y = \sin^{-1} x$, and the vertical line $x = 1$. For this solid, each cross section perpendicular to the x-axis is a square. What is the volume?

(A) 0.117 **(B)** 0.285 **(C)** 0.467 **(D)** 0.571 **(E)** 1.571

2. Multiple Choice Let R be the region in the first quadrant bounded by the graph of $y = 3x - x^2$ and the x-axis. A solid is generated when R is revolved about the vertical line $x = -1$. Set up, but do not evaluate, the definite integral that gives the volume of this solid.

(A) $\displaystyle\int_0^3 2\pi(x + 1)(3x - x^2)\,dx$

(B) $\displaystyle\int_{-1}^3 2\pi(x + 1)(3x - x^2)\,dx$

(C) $\displaystyle\int_0^3 2\pi(x)(3x - x^2)\,dx$

(D) $\displaystyle\int_0^3 2\pi(3x - x^2)^2\,dx$

(E) $\displaystyle\int_0^3 (3x - x^2)\,dx$

3. Multiple Choice A developing country consumes oil at a rate given by $r(t) = 20e^{0.2t}$ million barrels per year, where t is time measured in years, for $0 \le t \le 10$. Which of the following expressions gives the amount of oil consumed by the country during the time interval $0 \le t \le 10$?

(A) $r(10)$

(B) $r(10) - r(0)$

(C) $\displaystyle\int_0^{10} r'(t)\,dt$

(D) $\displaystyle\int_0^{10} r(t)\,dt$

(E) $10 \cdot r(10)$

4. Free Response Let R be the region bounded by the graphs of $y = \sqrt{x}$, $y = e^{-x}$, and the y-axis.

(a) Find the area of R.

(b) Find the volume of the solid generated when R is revolved about the horizontal line $y = -1$.

(c) The region R is the base of a solid. For this solid, each cross section perpendicular to the x-axis is a semicircle whose diameter runs from the graph of $y = \sqrt{x}$ to the graph of $y = e^{-x}$. Find the volume of this solid.

8.4 Lengths of Curves

What you will learn about . . .

- A Sine Wave
- Length of a Smooth Curve
- Vertical Tangents, Corners, and Cusps

and why . . .

The length of a smooth curve can be found using a definite integral.

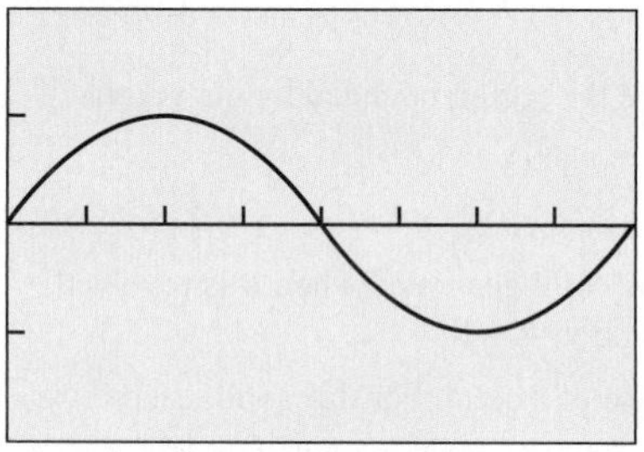

[0, 2π] by [–2, 2]

Figure 8.32 One wave of a sine curve has to be longer than 2π.

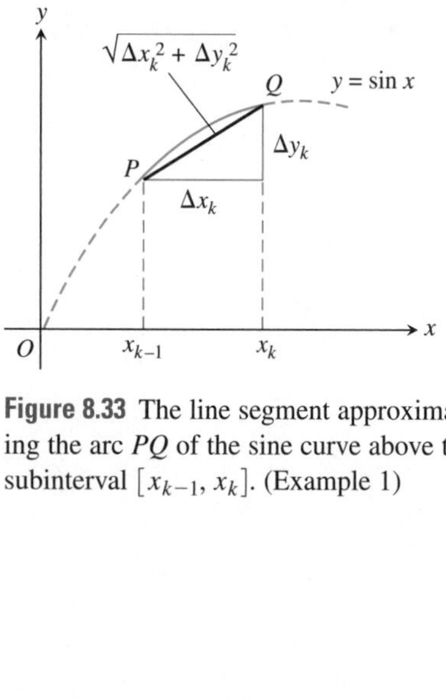

Figure 8.33 The line segment approximating the arc PQ of the sine curve above the subinterval $[x_{k-1}, x_k]$. (Example 1)

Group Exploration

Later in this section we will use an integral to find the length of the sine wave with great precision. But there are ways to get good approximations without integrating. Take five minutes to come up with a written estimate of the curve's length. No fair looking ahead.

A Sine Wave

How long is a sine wave (Figure 8.32)?

The usual meaning of *wavelength* refers to the fundamental period, which for $y = \sin x$ is 2π. But how long is the curve itself? If you straightened it out like a piece of string along the positive x-axis with one end at 0, where would the other end be?

EXAMPLE 1 The Length of a Sine Wave

What is the length of the curve $y = \sin x$ from $x = 0$ to $x = 2\pi$?

SOLUTION

We answer this question with integration, following our usual plan of breaking the whole into measurable parts. We partition $[0, 2\pi]$ into intervals so short that the pieces of curve (call them "arcs") lying directly above the intervals are nearly straight. That way, each arc is nearly the same as the line segment joining its two ends and we can take the length of the segment as an approximation to the length of the arc.

Figure 8.33 shows the segment approximating the arc above the subinterval $[x_{k-1}, x_k]$. The length of the segment is $\sqrt{\Delta x_k^2 + \Delta y_k^2}$. The sum

$$\sum \sqrt{\Delta x_k^2 + \Delta y_k^2}$$

over the entire partition approximates the length of the curve. All we need now is to find the limit of this sum as the norms of the partitions go to zero. That's the usual plan, but this time there is a problem. Do you see it?

The problem is that the sums as written are not Riemann sums. They do not have the form $\sum f(c_k)\Delta x$. We can rewrite them as Riemann sums if we multiply and divide each square root by Δx_k.

$$\sum \sqrt{\Delta x_k^2 + \Delta y_k^2} = \sum \frac{\sqrt{(\Delta x_k)^2 + (\Delta y_k)^2}}{\Delta x_k} \Delta x_k$$

$$= \sum \sqrt{1 + \left(\frac{\Delta y_k}{\Delta x_k}\right)^2} \Delta x_k$$

This is better, but we still need to write the last square root as a function evaluated at some c_k in the kth subinterval. For this, we call on the Mean Value Theorem for differentiable functions (Section 5.2), which says that since $\sin x$ is continuous on $[x_{k-1}, x_k]$ and is differentiable on (x_{k-1}, x_k) there is a point c_k in $[x_{k-1}, x_k]$ at which $\Delta y_k / \Delta x_k = \sin' c_k$ (Figure 8.34). That gives us

$$\sum \sqrt{1 + (\sin' c_k)^2}\, \Delta x_k,$$

which *is* a Riemann sum.

Now we take the limit as the norms of the subdivisions go to zero and find that the length of one wave of the sine function is

$$\int_0^{2\pi} \sqrt{1 + (\sin' x)^2}\, dx = \int_0^{2\pi} \sqrt{1 + \cos^2 x}\, dx \approx 7.64. \quad \text{Using NINT}$$

How close was your estimate?

Now Try Exercise 9.

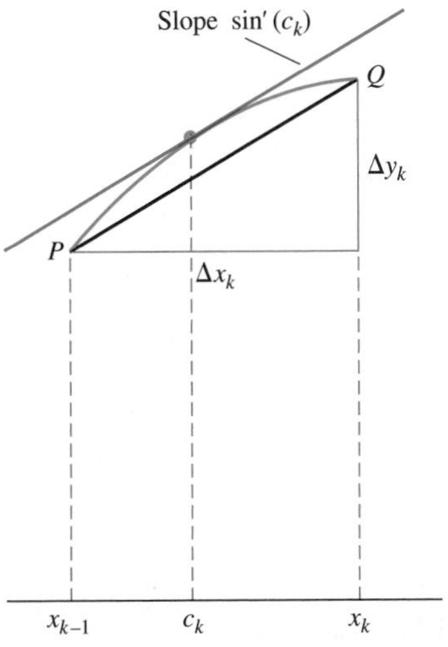

Figure 8.34 The portion of the sine curve above $[x_{k-1}, x_k]$. At some c_k in the interval, $\sin'(c_k) = \Delta y_k/\Delta x_k$, the slope of segment PQ. (Example 1)

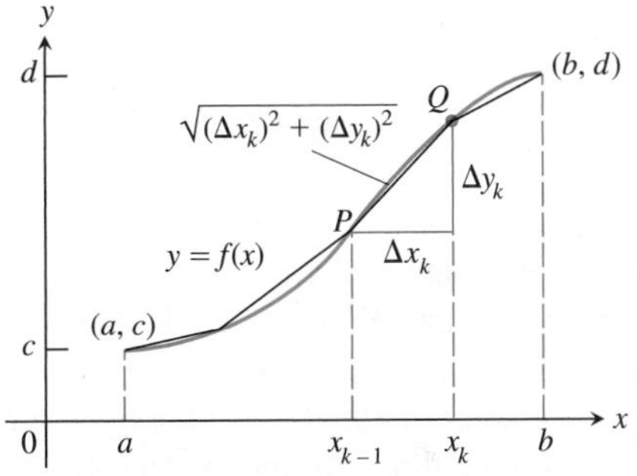

Figure 8.35 The graph of f, approximated by line segments.

Length of a Smooth Curve

We are almost ready to define the length of a curve as a definite integral, using the procedure of Example 1. We first call attention to two properties of the sine function that came into play along the way.

We obviously used *differentiability* when we invoked the Mean Value Theorem to replace $\Delta y_k/\Delta x_k$ by $\sin'(c_k)$ for some c_k in the interval $[x_{k-1}, x_k]$. Less obviously, we used the continuity of the derivative of sine in passing from $\sum\sqrt{1 + (\sin'(c_k))^2}\,\Delta x_k$ to the Riemann integral. The requirement for finding the length of a curve by this method, then, is that the function have a continuous first derivative. We call this property **smoothness.** A function with a continuous first derivative is **smooth** and its graph is a **smooth curve.**

Let us review the process, this time with a general smooth function $f(x)$. Suppose the graph of f begins at the point (a, c) and ends at (b, d), as shown in Figure 8.35. We partition the interval $a \le x \le b$ into subintervals so short that the arcs of the curve above them are nearly straight. The length of the segment approximating the arc above the subinterval $[x_{k-1}, x_k]$ is $\sqrt{\Delta x_k^2 + \Delta y_k^2}$. The sum $\sum\sqrt{\Delta x_k^2 + \Delta y_k^2}$ approximates the length of the curve. We apply the Mean Value Theorem to f on each subinterval to rewrite the sum as a Riemann sum,

$$\sum\sqrt{\Delta x_k^2 + \Delta y_k^2} = \sum\sqrt{1 + \left(\frac{\Delta y_k}{\Delta x_k}\right)^2}\,\Delta x_k$$

$$= \sum\sqrt{1 + (f'(c_k))^2}\,\Delta x_k.$$

For some point c_k in (x_{k-1}, x_k)

Passing to the limit as the norms of the subdivisions go to zero gives the length of the curve as

$$L = \int_a^b \sqrt{1 + (f'(x))^2}\,dx = \int_a^b \sqrt{1 + \left(\frac{dy}{dx}\right)^2}\,dx.$$

We could as easily have transformed $\sum\sqrt{\Delta x_k^2 + \Delta y_k^2}$ into a Riemann sum by dividing and multiplying by Δy_k, giving a formula that involves x as a function of y (say, $x = g(y)$) on the interval $[c, d]$:

$$L \approx \sum\frac{\sqrt{(\Delta x_k)^2 + (\Delta y_k)^2}}{\Delta y_k}\Delta y_k = \sum\sqrt{1 + \left(\frac{\Delta x_k}{\Delta y_k}\right)^2}\,\Delta y_k$$

$$= \sum\sqrt{1 + (g'(c_k))^2}\,\Delta y_k.$$

For some c_k in (y_{k-1}, y_k)

The limit of these sums, as the norms of the subdivisions go to zero, gives another reasonable way to calculate the curve's length,

$$L = \int_c^d \sqrt{1 + (g'(y))^2}\,dy = \int_c^d \sqrt{1 + \left(\frac{dx}{dy}\right)^2}\,dy.$$

Putting these two formulas together, we have the following definition for the length of a smooth curve.

DEFINITION Arc Length: Length of a Smooth Curve

If a smooth curve begins at (a, c) and ends at (b, d), $a < b$, $c < d$, then the **length (arc length) of the curve** is

$$L = \int_a^b \sqrt{1 + \left(\frac{dy}{dx}\right)^2}\,dx \quad \text{if } y \text{ is a smooth function of } x \text{ on } [a, b];$$

$$L = \int_c^d \sqrt{1 + \left(\frac{dx}{dy}\right)^2}\,dy \quad \text{if } x \text{ is a smooth function of } y \text{ on } [c, d].$$

EXAMPLE 2 Applying the Definition

Find the *exact* length of the curve

$$y = \frac{4\sqrt{2}}{3}x^{3/2} - 1 \quad \text{for} \quad 0 \le x \le 1.$$

SOLUTION

$$\frac{dy}{dx} = \frac{4\sqrt{2}}{3} \cdot \frac{3}{2}x^{1/2} = 2\sqrt{2}\, x^{1/2},$$

which is continuous on $[0, 1]$. Therefore,

$$\begin{aligned} L &= \int_0^1 \sqrt{1 + \left(\frac{dy}{dx}\right)^2}\, dx \\ &= \int_0^1 \sqrt{1 + \left(2\sqrt{2}x^{1/2}\right)^2}\, dx \\ &= \int_0^1 \sqrt{1 + 8x}\, dx \\ &= \frac{2}{3} \cdot \frac{1}{8}(1 + 8x)^{3/2}\Big]_0^1 \\ &= \frac{13}{6}. \end{aligned}$$

Now Try Exercise 11.

We asked for an exact length in Example 2 to take advantage of the rare opportunity it afforded of taking the antiderivative of an arc length integrand. When you add 1 to the square of the derivative of an arbitrary smooth function and then take the square root of that sum, the result is rarely antidifferentiable by reasonable methods. We know a few more functions that give "nice" integrands, but we are saving those for the exercises.

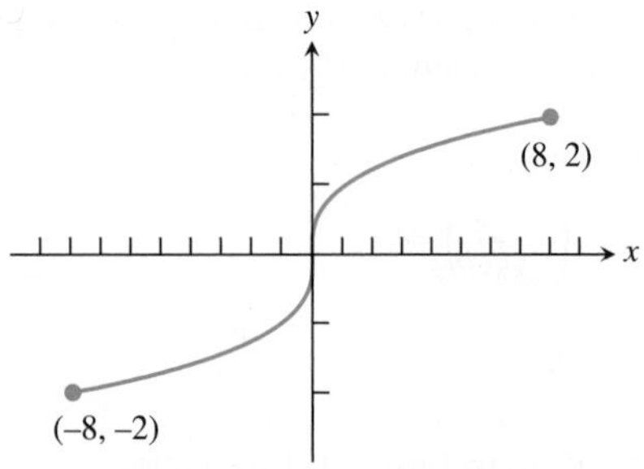

Figure 8.36 The graph of $y = x^{1/3}$ has a vertical tangent line at the origin where dy/dx does not exist. (Example 3)

Vertical Tangents, Corners, and Cusps

Sometimes a curve has a vertical tangent, corner, or cusp where the derivative we need to work with is undefined. We can sometimes get around such a difficulty in ways illustrated by the following examples.

EXAMPLE 3 A Vertical Tangent

Find the length of the curve $y = x^{1/3}$ between $(-8, -2)$ and $(8, 2)$.

SOLUTION

The derivative

$$\frac{dy}{dx} = \frac{1}{3}x^{-2/3} = \frac{1}{3x^{2/3}}$$

is not defined at $x = 0$. Graphically, there is a vertical tangent at $x = 0$ where the derivative becomes infinite (Figure 8.36). If we change to x as a function of y, the tangent at the origin will be horizontal (Figure 8.37) and the derivative will be zero instead of undefined. Solving $y = x^{1/3}$ for x gives $x = y^3$, and we have

$$L = \int_{-2}^{2} \sqrt{1 + \left(\frac{dx}{dy}\right)^2}\, dy = \int_{-2}^{2} \sqrt{1 + (3y^2)^2}\, dy \approx 17.26. \quad \text{Using NINT}$$

Now Try Exercise 25.

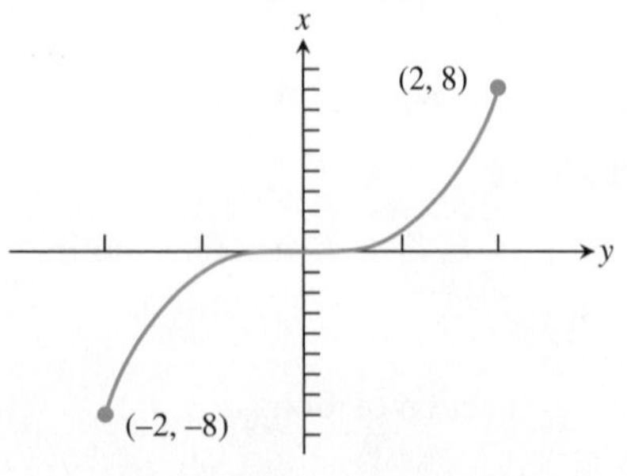

Figure 8.37 The curve in Figure 8.36 plotted with x as a function of y. The tangent at the origin is now horizontal. (Example 3)

What happens if you fail to notice that dy/dx is undefined at $x = 0$ and ask your calculator to compute

$$\text{NINT}\left(\sqrt{1 + \left((1/3)\, x^{-2/3}\right)^2},\, x, -8, 8\right)?$$

This actually depends on your calculator. If, in the process of its calculations, it tries to evaluate the function at $x = 0$, then some sort of domain error will result. If it tries to find convergent Riemann sums near $x = 0$, it might get into a long, futile loop of computations that you will have to interrupt. Or it might actually produce an answer—in which case you hope it would be sufficiently bizarre for you to realize that it should not be trusted.

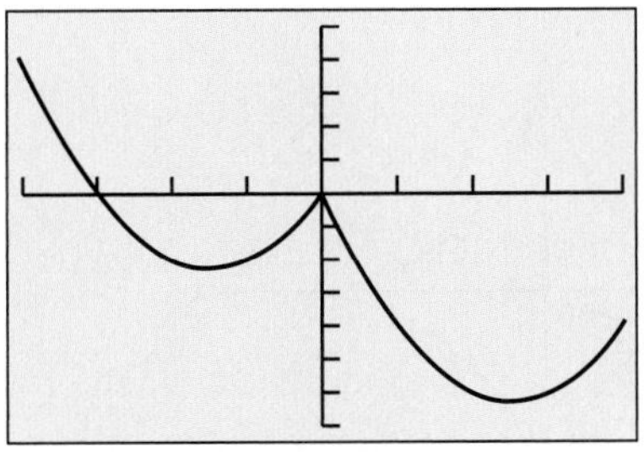

[−4, 4] by [−7, 5]

Figure 8.38 The graph of

$y = x^2 - 4|x| - x,\ -4 \le x \le 4,$

has a corner at $x = 0$ where neither dy/dx nor dx/dy exists. We find the lengths of the two smooth pieces and add them together. (Example 4)

EXAMPLE 4 Getting Around a Corner

Find the length of the curve $y = x^2 - 4|x| - x$ from $x = -4$ to $x = 4$.

SOLUTION

We should always be alert for abrupt slope changes when absolute value is involved. We graph the function to check (Figure 8.38).

There is clearly a corner at $x = 0$ where neither dy/dx nor dx/dy can exist. To find the length, we split the curve at $x = 0$ to write the function *without* absolute values:

$$x^2 - 4|x| - x = \begin{cases} x^2 + 3x & \text{if } x < 0, \\ x^2 - 5x & \text{if } x \ge 0. \end{cases}$$

Then,

$$L = \int_{-4}^{0} \sqrt{1 + (2x + 3)^2}\, dx + \int_{0}^{4} \sqrt{1 + (2x - 5)^2}\, dx$$

$$\approx 19.56. \quad \text{By NINT}$$

Now Try Exercise 27.

Finally, cusps are handled the same way corners are: split the curve into smooth pieces and add the lengths of those pieces.

Quick Review 8.4 *(For help, go to Sections 1.3 and 3.2.)*

Exercise numbers with a gray background indicate problems that the authors have designed to be solved *without a calculator.*

In Exercises 1–5, simplify the function.

1. $\sqrt{1 + 2x + x^2}$ on $[1, 5]$
2. $\sqrt{1 - x + \dfrac{x^2}{4}}$ on $[-3, -1]$
3. $\sqrt{1 + (\tan x)^2}$ on $[0, \pi/3]$
4. $\sqrt{1 + (x/4 - 1/x)^2}$ on $[4, 12]$
5. $\sqrt{1 + \cos 2x}$ on $[0, \pi/2]$

In Exercises 6–10, identify all values of x for which the function fails to be differentiable.

6. $f(x) = |x - 4|$
7. $f(x) = 5x^{2/3}$
8. $f(x) = \sqrt[5]{x + 3}$
9. $f(x) = \sqrt{x^2 - 4x + 4}$
10. $f(x) = 1 + \sqrt[3]{\sin x}$

Section 8.4 Exercises

In Exercises 1–10,

(a) set up an integral for the length of the curve;

(b) graph the curve to see what it looks like;

(c) use NINT to find the length of the curve.

1. $y = x^2, \quad -1 \le x \le 2$

2. $y = \tan x, \quad -\pi/3 \le x \le 0$

3. $x = \sin y, \quad 0 \le y \le \pi$

4. $x = \sqrt{1 - y^2}, \quad -1/2 \le y \le 1/2$

5. $y^2 + 2y = 2x + 1$, from $(-1, -1)$ to $(7, 3)$

6. $y = \sin x - x \cos x, \quad 0 \le x \le \pi$

7. $y = \int_0^x \tan t\, dt, \quad 0 \le x \le \pi/6$

8. $x = \int_0^y \sqrt{\sec^2 t - 1}\, dt, \quad -\pi/3 \le y \le \pi/4$

9. $y = \sec x, \quad -\pi/3 \le x \le \pi/3$

10. $y = (e^x + e^{-x})/2, \quad -3 \le x \le 3$

In Exercises 11–18, find the exact length of the curve analytically by antidifferentiation. You will need to simplify the integrand algebraically before finding an antiderivative.

11. $y = (1/3)(x^2 + 2)^{3/2}$ from $x = 0$ to $x = 3$

12. $y = x^{3/2}$ from $x = 0$ to $x = 4$

13. $x = (y^3/3) + 1/(4y)$ from $y = 1$ to $y = 3$
[*Hint:* $1 + (dx/dy)^2$ is a perfect square.]

14. $x = (y^4/4) + 1/(8y^2)$ from $y = 1$ to $y = 2$
[*Hint:* $1 + (dx/dy)^2$ is a perfect square.]

15. $x = (y^3/6) + 1/(2y)$ from $y = 1$ to $y = 2$
[*Hint:* $1 + (dx/dy)^2$ is a perfect square.]

16. $y = (x^3/3) + x^2 + x + 1/(4x + 4), \quad 0 \le x \le 2$

17. $x = \int_0^y \sqrt{\sec^4 t - 1}\, dt, \quad -\pi/4 \le y \le \pi/4$

18. $y = \int_{-2}^x \sqrt{3t^4 - 1}\, dt, \quad -2 \le x \le -1$

19. (a) Group Activity Find a curve through the point $(1, 1)$ whose length integral is

$$L = \int_1^4 \sqrt{1 + \frac{1}{4x}}\, dx.$$

(b) Writing to Learn How many such curves are there? Give reasons for your answer.

20. (a) Group Activity Find a curve through the point $(0, 1)$ whose length integral is

$$L = \int_1^2 \sqrt{1 + \frac{1}{y^4}}\, dy.$$

(b) Writing to Learn How many such curves are there? Give reasons for your answer.

21. Find the length of the curve

$$y = \int_0^x \sqrt{\cos 2t}\, dt$$

from $x = 0$ to $x = \pi/4$.

22. *The Length of an Astroid* The graph of the equation $x^{2/3} + y^{2/3} = 1$ is one of the family of curves called *astroids* (not "asteroids") because of their starlike appearance (see figure). Find the length of this particular astroid by finding the length of half the first quadrant portion, $y = (1 - x^{2/3})^{3/2}$, $\sqrt{2}/4 \le x \le 1$, and multiplying by 8.

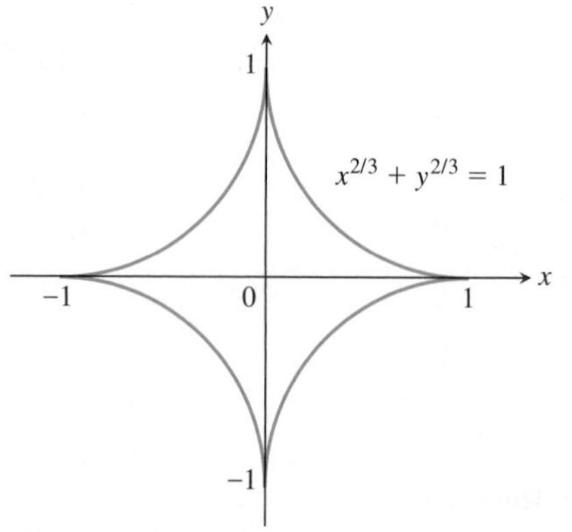

23. *Fabricating Metal Sheets* Your metal fabrication company is bidding for a contract to make sheets of corrugated steel roofing like the one shown here. The cross sections of the corrugated sheets are to conform to the curve

$$y = \sin\left(\frac{3\pi}{20}x\right), \quad 0 \le x \le 20 \text{ in.}$$

If the roofing is to be stamped from flat sheets by a process that does not stretch the material, how wide should the original material be? Give your answer to two decimal places.

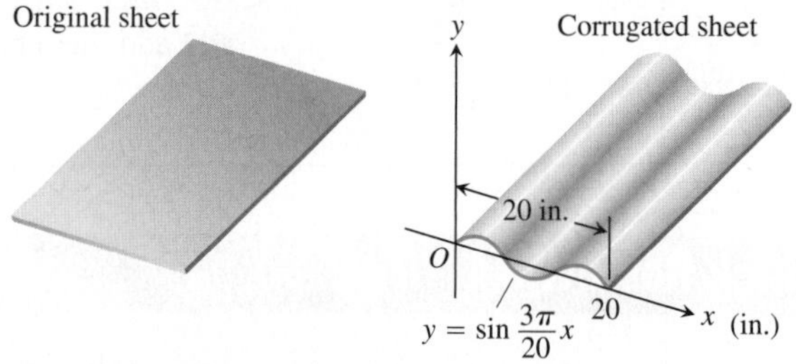

24. *Tunnel Construction* Your engineering firm is bidding for the contract to construct the tunnel shown on the next page. The tunnel is 300 ft long and 50 ft wide at the base. The cross section is shaped like one arch of the curve $y = 25\cos(\pi x/50)$. Upon completion, the tunnel's inside surface (excluding the roadway) will be treated with a waterproof sealer that costs \$1.75 per square foot to apply. How much will it cost to apply the sealer?

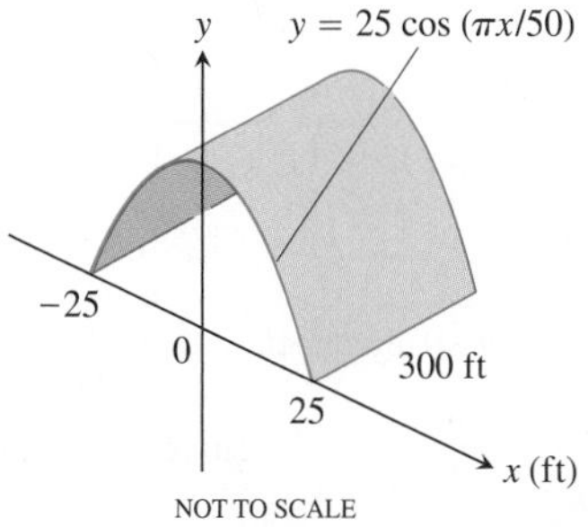

In Exercises 25 and 26, find the length of the curve.

25. $f(x) = x^{1/3} + x^{2/3}, \quad 0 \le x \le 2$

26. $f(x) = \dfrac{x-1}{4x^2+1}, \quad -\dfrac{1}{2} \le x \le 1$

In Exercises 27–29, find the length of the nonsmooth curve.

27. $y = x^3 + 5|x|$ from $x = -2$ to $x = 1$

28. $\sqrt{x} + \sqrt{y} = 1$

29. $y = \sqrt[4]{x}$ from $x = 0$ to $x = 16$

30. Writing to Learn Explain geometrically why it does not work to use short *horizontal* line segments to approximate the lengths of small arcs when we search for a Riemann sum that leads to the formula for arc length.

31. Writing to Learn A curve is totally contained inside the square with vertices $(0, 0)$, $(1, 0)$, $(1, 1)$, and $(0, 1)$. Is there any limit to the possible length of the curve? Explain.

Standardized Test Questions

32. True or False If a function $y = f(x)$ is continuous on an interval $[a, b]$, then the length of its curve is given by

$\int_a^b \sqrt{1 + \left(\dfrac{dy}{dx}\right)^2}\, dx$. Justify your answer.

33. True or False If a function $y = f(x)$ is differentiable on an interval $[a, b]$, then the length of its curve is given by

$\int_a^b \sqrt{1 + \left(\dfrac{dy}{dx}\right)^2}\, dx$. Justify your answer.

34. Multiple Choice Which of the following gives the best approximation of the length of the arc of $y = \cos(2x)$ from $x = 0$ to $x = \pi/4$?

(A) 0.785 (B) 0.955 (C) 1.0 (D) 1.318 (E) 1.977

35. Multiple Choice Which of the following expressions gives the length of the graph of $x = y^3$ from $y = -2$ to $y = 2$?

(A) $\int_{-2}^{2} (1 + y^6)\, dy$ (B) $\int_{-2}^{2} \sqrt{1 + y^6}\, dy$

(C) $\int_{-2}^{2} \sqrt{1 + 9y^4}\, dy$ (D) $\int_{-2}^{2} \sqrt{1 + x^2}\, dx$

(E) $\int_{-2}^{2} \sqrt{1 + x^4}\, dx$

36. Multiple Choice Find the length of the curve described by $y = \dfrac{2}{3}x^{3/2}$ from $x = 0$ to $x = 8$.

(A) $\dfrac{26}{3}$ (B) $\dfrac{52}{3}$ (C) $\dfrac{512\sqrt{2}}{15}$

(D) $\dfrac{512\sqrt{2}}{15} + 8$ (E) 96

37. Multiple Choice Which of the following expressions should be used to find the length of the curve $y = x^{2/3}$ from $x = -1$ to $x = 1$?

(A) $2\int_0^1 \sqrt{1 + \dfrac{9}{4}y}\, dy$ (B) $\int_{-1}^{1} \sqrt{1 + \dfrac{9}{4}y}\, dy$

(C) $\int_0^1 \sqrt{1 + y^3}\, dy$ (D) $\int_0^1 \sqrt{1 + y^6}\, dy$

(E) $\int_0^1 \sqrt{1 + y^{9/4}}\, dy$

Exploration

38. *Modeling Running Tracks* Two lanes of a running track are modeled by the semiellipses as shown. The equation for lane 1 is $y = \sqrt{100 - 0.2x^2}$, and the equation for lane 2 is $y = \sqrt{150 - 0.2x^2}$. The starting point for lane 1 is at the negative x-intercept $(-\sqrt{500}, 0)$. The finish points for both lanes are the positive x-intercepts. Where should the starting point be placed on lane 2 so that the two lane lengths will be equal (running clockwise)?

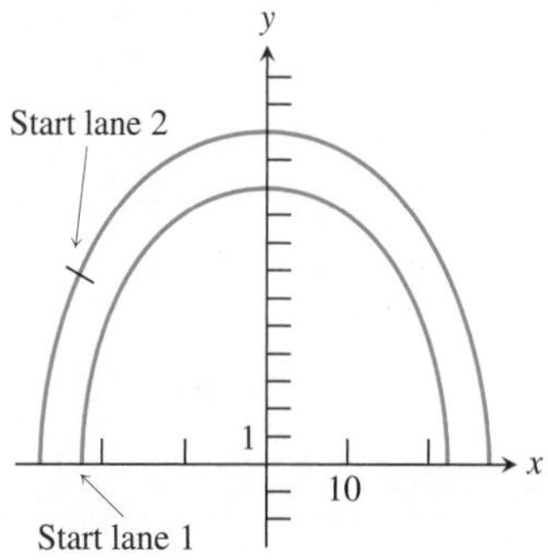

Extending the Ideas

39. *Using Tangent Fins to Find Arc Length* Assume f is smooth on $[a, b]$ and partition the interval $[a, b]$ in the usual way. In each subinterval $[x_{k-1}, x_k]$ construct the *tangent fin* at the point $(x_{k-1}, f(x_{k-1}))$ as shown in the figure.

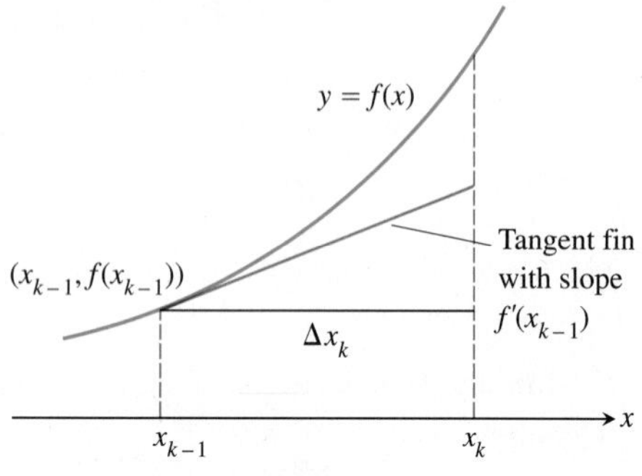

(a) Show that the length of the kth tangent fin over the interval $[x_{k-1}, x_k]$ equals

$$\sqrt{(\Delta x_k)^2 + (f'(x_{k-1})\Delta x_k)^2}.$$

(b) Show that

$$\lim_{n\to\infty} \sum_{k=1}^{n} (\text{length of } k\text{th tangent fin}) = \int_a^b \sqrt{1 + (f'(x))^2}\, dx,$$

which is the length L of the curve $y = f(x)$ from $x = a$ to $x = b$.

40. Is there a smooth curve $y = f(x)$ whose length over the interval $0 \le x \le a$ is always $a\sqrt{2}$? Give reasons for your answer.

8.5 Applications from Science and Statistics

What you will learn about . . .

- Work Revisited
- Fluid Force and Fluid Pressure
- Normal Probabilities

and why . . .

It is important to see applications of integrals as various accumulation functions.

Our goal in this section is to hint at the diversity of ways in which the definite integral can be used. The contexts may be new to you, but we will explain what you need to know as we go along.

Work Revisited

Recall from Section 8.1 that *work* is defined as force (in the direction of motion) times displacement. A familiar example is to move against the force of gravity to lift an object. The object has to move, incidentally, before "work" is done, no matter how tired you get *trying*.

If the force $F(x)$ is not constant, then the work done in moving an object from $x = a$ to $x = b$ is the definite integral $W = \int_a^b F(x)\,dx$.

4.4 newtons ≈ 1 lb

(1 newton)(1 meter) = 1 N·m = 1 Joule

EXAMPLE 1 Finding the Work Done by a Force

Find the work done by the force $F(x) = \cos(\pi x)$ newtons along the x-axis from $x = 0$ meters to $x = 1/2$ meter.

SOLUTION

$$W = \int_0^{1/2} \cos(\pi x)\,dx$$

$$= \frac{1}{\pi}\sin(\pi x)\Big|_0^{1/2}$$

$$= \frac{1}{\pi}\left(\sin\left(\frac{\pi}{2}\right) - \sin(0)\right)$$

$$= \frac{1}{\pi} \approx 0.318$$

Now Try Exercise 1.

EXAMPLE 2 Work Done Lifting

A leaky bucket weighs 22 newtons (N) empty. It is lifted from the ground at a constant rate to a point 20 m above the ground by a rope weighing 0.4 N/m. The bucket starts with 70 N (approximately 7.1 liters) of water, but it leaks at a constant rate and just finishes draining as the bucket reaches the top. Find the amount of work done

(a) lifting the bucket alone;

(b) lifting the water alone;

(c) lifting the rope alone;

(d) lifting the bucket, water, and rope together.

SOLUTION

(a) *The bucket alone.* This is easy because the bucket's weight is constant. To lift it, you must exert a force of 22 N through the entire 20-meter interval.

$$\text{Work} = (22\text{ N}) \times (20\text{ m}) = 440\text{ N}\cdot\text{m} = 440\text{ J}$$

Figure 8.39 shows the graph of force vs. distance applied. The work corresponds to the area under the force graph.

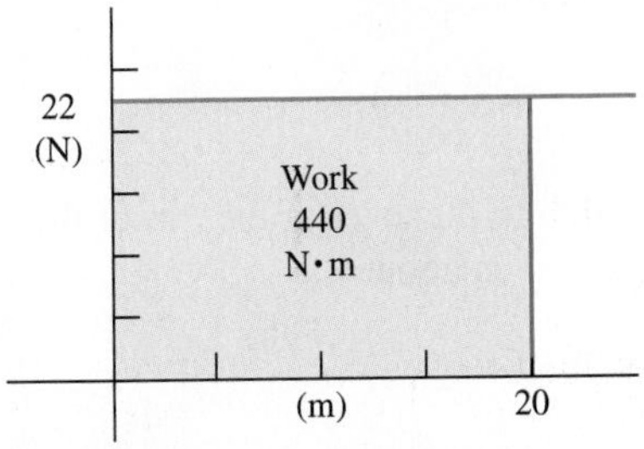

Figure 8.39 The work done by a constant 22-N force lifting a bucket 20 m is 440 N · m. (Example 2)

continued

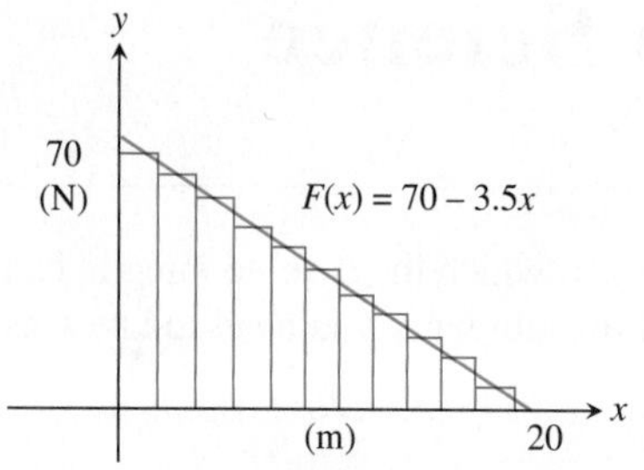

Figure 8.40 The force required to lift the water varies with distance but the work still corresponds to the area under the force graph. (Example 2)

(b) *The water alone.* The force needed to lift the water is equal to the water's weight, which decreases steadily from 70 N to 0 N over the 20-m lift. When the bucket is x m off the ground, the water weighs

$$F(x) = 70\left(\frac{20 - x}{20}\right) = 70\left(1 - \frac{x}{20}\right) = 70 - 3.5x \text{ N.}$$

original weight of water — proportion left at elevation x

The work done is (Figure 8.40)

$$W = \int_a^b F(x)\,dx$$

$$= \int_0^{20} (70 - 3.5x)\,dx = \Big[70x - 1.75x^2\Big]_0^{20} = 1400 - 700 = 700 \text{ J.}$$

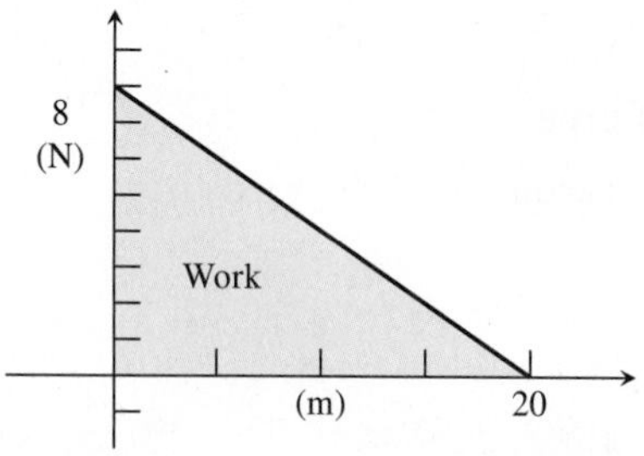

Figure 8.41 The work done lifting the rope to the top corresponds to the area of another triangle. (Example 2)

(c) *The rope alone.* The force needed to lift the rope is also variable, starting at $(0.4)(20) = 8$ N when the bucket is on the ground and ending at 0 N when the bucket and rope are all at the top. As with the leaky bucket, the rate of decrease is constant. At elevation x meters, the $(20 - x)$ meters of rope still there to lift weigh $F(x) = (0.4)(20 - x)$ N. Figure 8.41 shows the graph of F. The work done lifting the rope is

$$\int_0^{20} F(x)\,dx = \int_0^{20} (0.4)(20 - x)\,dx$$

$$= \Big[8x - 0.2x^2\Big]_0^{20} = 160 - 80 = 80 \text{ N} \cdot \text{m} = 80 \text{ J.}$$

(d) *The bucket, water, and rope together.* The total work is

$$440 + 700 + 80 = 1220 \text{ J.}$$

Now Try Exercise 5.

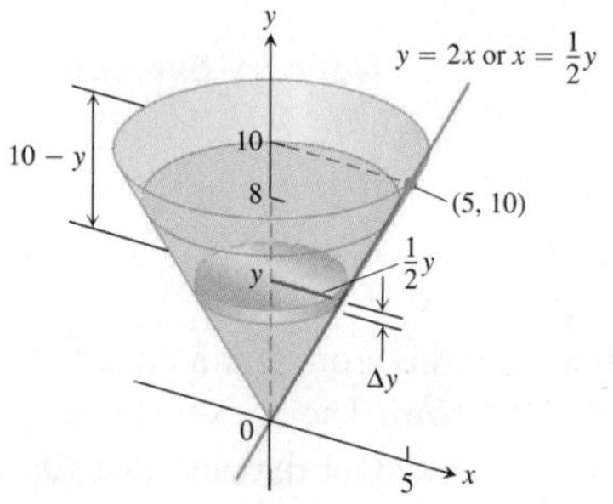

Figure 8.42 The conical tank in Example 3.

EXAMPLE 3 Work Done Pumping

The conical tank in Figure 8.42 is filled to within 2 ft of the top with olive oil weighing 57 lb/ft^3. How much work does it take to pump the oil to the rim of the tank?

SOLUTION

We imagine the oil partitioned into thin slabs by planes perpendicular to the y-axis at the points of a partition of the interval $[0, 8]$. (The 8 represents the top of the oil, not the top of the tank.)

The typical slab between the planes at y and $y + \Delta y$ has a volume of about

$$\Delta V = \pi(\text{radius})^2(\text{thickness}) = \pi\left(\frac{1}{2}y\right)^2 \Delta y = \frac{\pi}{4}y^2 \Delta y \text{ ft}^3.$$

The force $F(y)$ required to lift this slab is equal to its weight,

$$F(y) = 57\,\Delta V = \frac{57\pi}{4}y^2 \Delta y \text{ lb.} \qquad \text{Weight} = \left(\begin{matrix}\text{weight per}\\ \text{unit volume}\end{matrix}\right) \times \text{volume}$$

The distance through which $F(y)$ must act to lift this slab to the level of the rim of the cone is about $(10 - y)$ ft, so the work done lifting the slab is about

$$\Delta W = \frac{57\pi}{4}(10 - y)y^2\,\Delta y \text{ ft} \cdot \text{lb.}$$

The work done lifting all the slabs from $y = 0$ to $y = 8$ to the rim is approximately

$$W \approx \sum \frac{57\pi}{4}(10 - y)y^2\,\Delta y \text{ ft} \cdot \text{lb.}$$

continued

This is a Riemann sum for the function $(57\pi/4)(10 - y)y^2$ on the interval from $y = 0$ to $y = 8$. The work of pumping the oil to the rim is the limit of these sums as the norms of the partitions go to zero.

$$W = \int_0^8 \frac{57\pi}{4}(10 - y)y^2\,dy = \frac{57\pi}{4}\int_0^8 (10y^2 - y^3)\,dy$$

$$= \frac{57\pi}{4}\left[\frac{10y^3}{3} - \frac{y^4}{4}\right]_0^8 \approx 30{,}561 \text{ ft}\cdot\text{lb}$$

Now Try Exercise 17.

Fluid Force and Fluid Pressure

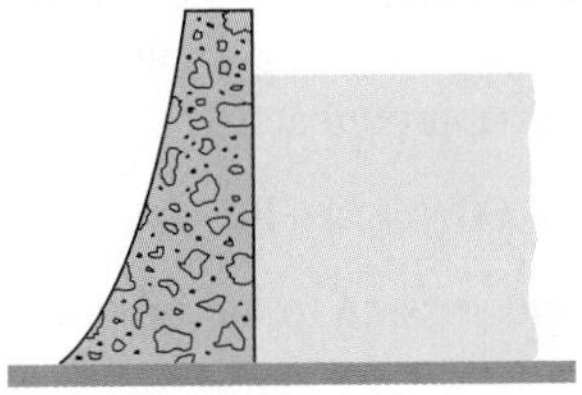

Figure 8.43 To withstand the increasing pressure, dams are built thicker toward the bottom.

We make dams thicker at the bottom than at the top (Figure 8.43) because the pressure against them increases with depth. It is a remarkable fact that the pressure at any point on a dam depends only on how far below the surface the point lies and not on how much water the dam is holding back. In any liquid, the **fluid pressure** p (force per unit area) at depth h is

$$p = wh, \qquad \text{Dimensions check: } \frac{\text{lb}}{\text{ft}^2} = \frac{\text{lb}}{\text{ft}^3} \times \text{ft, for example}$$

where w is the *weight-density* (weight per unit volume) of the liquid.

Typical Weight-densities (lb/ft^3)

Gasoline	42
Mercury	849
Milk	64.5
Molasses	100
Seawater	64
Water	62.4

EXAMPLE 4 The Great Molasses Flood of 1919

At 1:00 P.M. on January 15, 1919 (an unseasonably warm day), a 90-ft-high, 90-foot-diameter cylindrical metal tank in which the Puritan Distilling Company stored molasses at the corner of Foster and Commercial streets in Boston's North End exploded. Molasses flooded the streets 30 feet deep, trapping pedestrians and horses, knocking down buildings, and oozing into homes. It was eventually tracked all over town and even made its way into the suburbs via trolley cars and people's shoes. It took weeks to clean up.

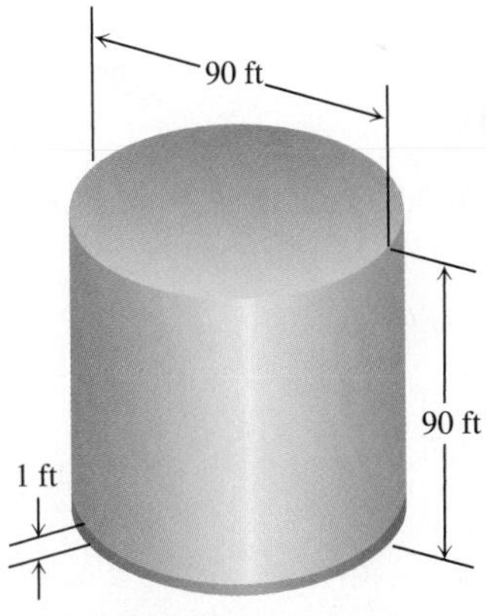

Figure 8.44 The molasses tank of Example 4.

(a) Given that the tank was full of molasses weighing 100 lb/ft^3, what was the total force exerted by the molasses on the bottom of the tank at the time it ruptured?

(b) What was the total force against the bottom foot-wide band of the tank wall (Figure 8.44)?

continued

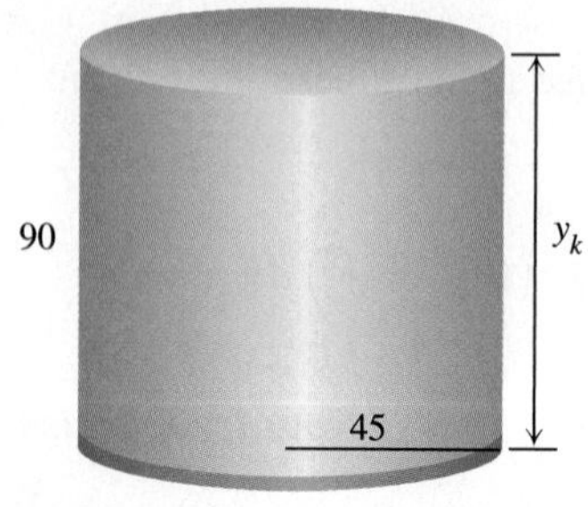

Figure 8.45 The 1-ft band at the bottom of the tank wall can be partitioned into thin strips on which the pressure is approximately constant. (Example 4)

SOLUTION

(a) At the bottom of the tank, the molasses exerted a constant pressure of

$$p = wh = \left(100\,\frac{\text{lb}}{\text{ft}^3}\right)(90\text{ ft}) = 9000\,\frac{\text{lb}}{\text{ft}^2}.$$

Since the area of the base was $\pi(45)^2$, the total force on the base was

$$\left(9000\,\frac{\text{lb}}{\text{ft}^2}\right)(2025\,\pi\text{ ft}^2) \approx 57{,}255{,}526\text{ lb}.$$

(b) We partition the band from depth 89 ft to depth 90 ft into narrower bands of width Δy and choose a depth y_k in each one. The pressure at this depth y_k is $p = wh = 100\,y_k$ lb/ft^2 (Figure 8.45). The force against each narrow band is approximately

$$\text{pressure} \times \text{area} = (100y_k)(90\pi\,\Delta y) = 9000\pi\,y_k\,\Delta y\text{ lb}.$$

Adding the forces against all the bands in the partition and passing to the limit as the norms go to zero, we arrive at

$$F = \int_{89}^{90} 9000\pi y\,dy = 9000\pi\int_{89}^{90} y\,dy \approx 2{,}530{,}553\text{ lb}$$

for the force against the bottom foot of tank wall. *Now Try Exercise 25.*

Normal Probabilities

Suppose you find an old clock in the attic. What is the probability that it has stopped somewhere between 2:00 and 5:00?

If you imagine time being measured continuously over a 12-hour interval, it is easy to conclude that the answer is 1/4 (since the interval from 2:00 to 5:00 contains one-fourth of the time), and that is correct. Mathematically, however, the situation is not quite that clear because both the 12-hour interval and the 3-hour interval contain an *infinite* number of times. In what sense does the ratio of one infinity to another infinity equal 1/4?

The easiest way to resolve that question is to look at area. We represent the total probability of the 12-hour interval as a rectangle of area 1 sitting above the interval (Figure 8.46).

Not only does it make perfect sense to say that the rectangle over the time interval $[2, 5]$ has an area that is one-fourth the area of the total rectangle, the area actually *equals* 1/4, since the total rectangle has area 1. That is why mathematicians represent probabilities as areas, and that is where definite integrals enter the picture.

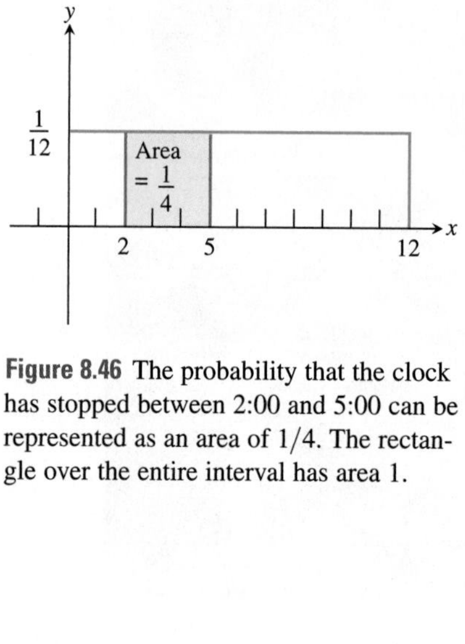

Figure 8.46 The probability that the clock has stopped between 2:00 and 5:00 can be represented as an area of 1/4. The rectangle over the entire interval has area 1.

DEFINITION Probability Density Function (pdf)

A **probability density function** is a function $f(x)$ with domain all reals such that

$$f(x) \geq 0 \text{ for all } x \quad \text{and} \quad \int_{-\infty}^{\infty} f(x)\,dx = 1.$$

Then the probability associated with an interval $[a, b]$ is

$$\int_a^b f(x)\,dx.$$

Improper Integrals

More information about improper integrals like $\int_{-\infty}^{\infty} f(x)\,dx$ can be found in Section 9.3. (You will not need that information here.)

Probabilities of events, such as the clock stopping between 2:00 and 5:00, are integrals of an appropriate pdf.

EXAMPLE 5 Probability of the Clock Stopping

Find the probability that the clock stopped between 2:00 and 5:00.

SOLUTION

The pdf of the clock is

$$f(t) = \begin{cases} 1/12, & 0 \le t \le 12 \\ 0, & \text{otherwise.} \end{cases}$$

The probability that the clock stopped at some time t with $2 \le t \le 5$ is

$$\int_2^5 f(t)\, dt = \frac{1}{4}.$$

Now Try Exercise 27.

By far the most useful kind of pdf is the *normal* kind. ("Normal" here is a technical term, referring to a curve with the shape in Figure 8.47.) The **normal curve,** often called the "bell curve," is one of the most significant curves in applied mathematics because it enables us to describe entire populations based on the statistical measurements taken from a reasonably sized sample. The measurements needed are the *mean* (μ) and the *standard deviation* (σ), which your calculators will approximate for you from the data. The symbols on the calculator will probably be $\bar{x}$ and s (see your *Owner's Manual*), but go ahead and use them as μ and σ, respectively. Once you have the numbers, you can find the curve by using the following remarkable formula discovered by Karl Friedrich Gauss.

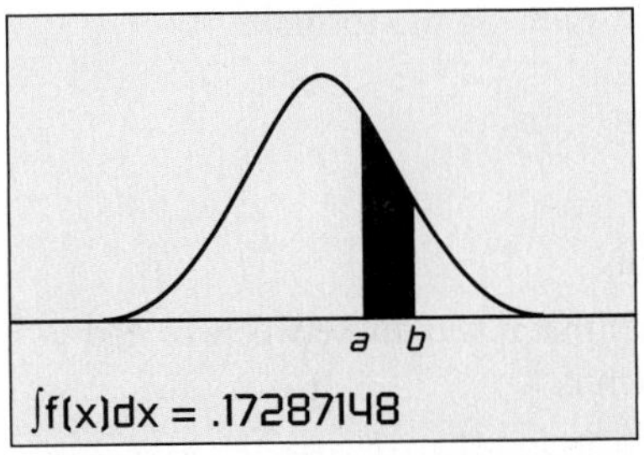

Figure 8.47 A normal probability density function. The probability associated with the interval $[a, b]$ is the area under the curve, as shown.

DEFINITION Normal Probability Density Function (pdf)

The **normal probability density function (Gaussian curve)** for a population with mean μ and standard deviation σ is

$$f(x) = \frac{1}{\sigma\sqrt{2\pi}} e^{-(x-\mu)^2/(2\sigma^2)}.$$

The **mean** μ represents the average value of the variable x. The **standard deviation** σ measures the "scatter" around the mean. For a normal curve, the mean and standard deviation tell you where most of the probability lies. The rule of thumb, illustrated in Figure 8.48, is this:

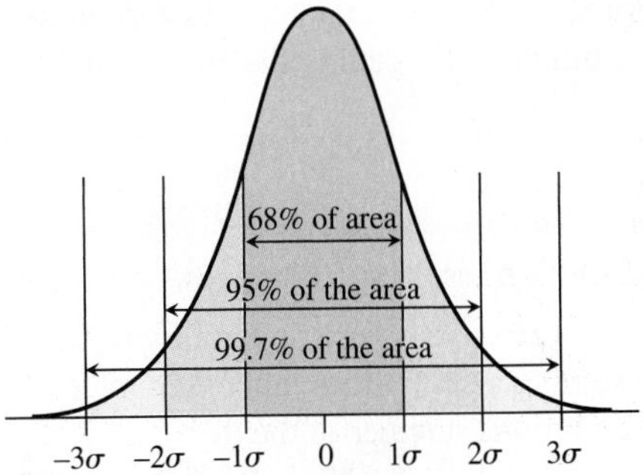

Figure 8.48 The 68-95-99.7 rule for normal distributions.

The 68-95-99.7 Rule for Normal Distributions

Given a normal curve,

- 68% of the area will lie within σ of the mean μ,
- 95% of the area will lie within 2σ of the mean μ,
- 99.7% of the area will lie within 3σ of the mean μ.

Even with the 68-95-99.7 rule, the area under the curve can spread quite a bit, depending on the size of σ Figure 8.49 shows three normal pdfs with mean $\mu = 2$ and standard deviations equal to 0.5, 1, and 2.

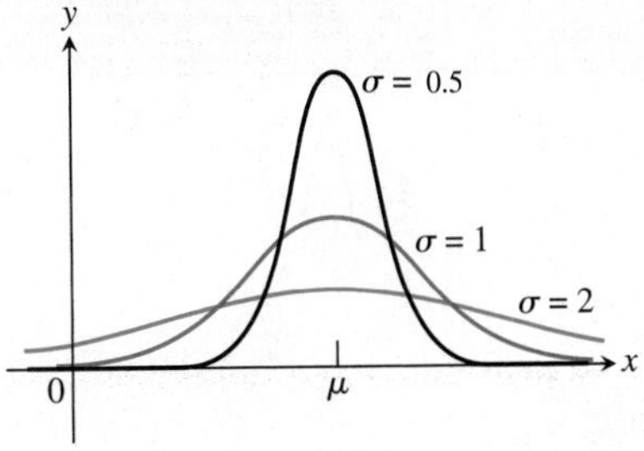

Figure 8.49 Normal pdf curves with mean $\mu = 2$ and $\sigma = 0.5$, 1, and 2.

EXAMPLE 6 A Telephone Help Line

Suppose a telephone help line takes a mean of 2 minutes to answer calls. If the standard deviation is $\sigma = 0.5$, then 68% of the calls are answered in the range of 1.5 to 2.5 minutes and 99.7% of the calls are answered in the range of 0.5 to 3.5 minutes. Assume that the time to answer calls is normally distributed. **Now Try Exercise 29.**

EXAMPLE 7 Weights of Spinach Boxes

Suppose that frozen spinach boxes marked as "10 ounces" of spinach have a mean weight of 10.3 ounces and a standard deviation of 0.2 ounce. Assume that the weights of the spinach boxes are normally distributed

(a) What percentage of *all* such spinach boxes can be expected to weigh between 10 and 11 ounces?

(b) What percentage would we expect to weigh less than 10 ounces?

(c) What is the probability that a box weighs *exactly* 10 ounces?

SOLUTION

Assuming that some person or machine is *trying* to pack 10 ounces of spinach into these boxes, we expect that most of the weights will be around 10, with probabilities tailing off for boxes being heavier or lighter. We expect, in other words, that a normal pdf will model these probabilities. First, we define $f(x)$ using the formula

$$f(x) = \frac{1}{0.2\sqrt{2\pi}} e^{-(x-10.3)^2/(0.08)}.$$

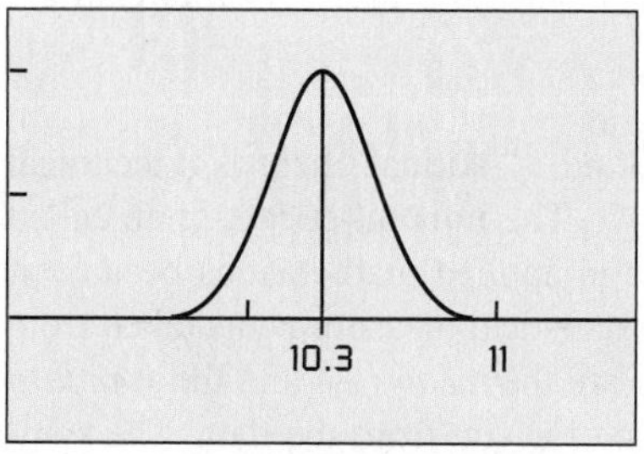

[9, 11.5] by [−1, 2.5]

Figure 8.50 The normal pdf for the spinach weights in Example 7. The mean is at the center.

The graph (Figure 8.50) has the look we are expecting.

(a) For an arbitrary box of this spinach, the probability that it weighs between 10 and 11 ounces is the area under the curve from 10 to 11, which is

$$\text{NINT}\,(f(x), x, 10, 11) \approx 0.933.$$

So without doing any more measuring, we can predict that about 93.3% of all such spinach boxes will weigh between 10 and 11 ounces.

(b) For the probability that a box weighs less than 10 ounces, we use the entire area under the curve to the left of $x = 10$. The curve actually approaches the x-axis as an asymptote, but you can see from the graph (Figure 8.50) that $f(x)$ approaches zero quite quickly. Indeed, $f(9)$ is only slightly larger than a billionth. So getting the area from 9 to 10 should do it:

$$\text{NINT}\,(f(x), x, 9, 10) \approx 0.067.$$

We would expect only about 6.7% of the boxes to weigh less than 10 ounces.

(c) This would be the integral from 10 to 10, which is zero. This zero probability might seem strange at first, but remember that we are assuming a continuous, unbroken interval of possible spinach weights, and 10 is but one of an infinite number of them.

Now Try Exercise 31.

Quick Review 8.5 *(For help, go to Section 6.2.)*

Exercise numbers with a gray background indicate problems that the authors have designed to be solved *without a calculator.*

In Exercises 1–5, find the definite integral by **(a)** antiderivatives and **(b)** using NINT.

1. $\int_0^1 e^{-x}\,dx$

2. $\int_0^1 e^x\,dx$

3. $\int_{\pi/4}^{\pi/2} \sin x\,dx$

4. $\int_0^3 (x^2 + 2)\,dx$

5. $\int_1^2 \frac{x^2}{x^3 + 1}\,dx$

In Exercises 6–10 find, but do not evaluate, the definite integral that is the limit as the norms of the partitions go to zero of the Riemann sums on the closed interval $[0, 7]$.

6. $\sum 2\pi(x_k + 2)(\sin x_k)\,\Delta x$

7. $\sum (1 - x_k^2)(2\pi\, x_k)\,\Delta x$

8. $\sum \pi(\cos x_k)^2\,\Delta x$

9. $\sum \pi\left(\frac{y_k}{2}\right)^2(10 - y_k)\,\Delta y$

10. $\sum \frac{\sqrt{3}}{4}(\sin^2 x_k)\,\Delta x$

Section 8.5 Exercises

In Exercises 1–4, find the work done by the force of $F(x)$ newtons along the x-axis from $x = a$ meters to $x = b$ meters.

1. $F(x) = xe^{-x/3}, \quad a = 0, \quad b = 5$

2. $F(x) = x\sin(\pi x/4), \quad a = 0, \quad b = 3$

3. $F(x) = x\sqrt{9 - x^2}, \quad a = 0, \quad b = 3$

4. $F(x) = e^{\sin x}\cos x + 2, \quad a = 0, \quad b = 10$

5. *Leaky Bucket* The workers in Example 2 changed to a larger bucket that held 50 L (490 N) of water, but the new bucket had an even larger leak so that it too was empty by the time it reached the top. Assuming the water leaked out at a steady rate, how much work was done lifting the water to a point 20 meters above the ground? (Do not include the rope and bucket.)

6. *Leaky Bucket* The bucket in Exercise 5 is hauled up more quickly so that there is still 10 L (98 N) of water left when the bucket reaches the top. How much work is done lifting the water this time? (Do not include the rope and bucket.)

7. *Leaky Sand Bag* A bag of sand originally weighing 144 lb was lifted at a constant rate. As it rose, sand leaked out at a constant rate. The sand was half gone by the time the bag had been lifted 18 ft. How much work was done lifting the sand this far? (Neglect the weights of the bag and lifting equipment.)

8. *Stretching a Spring* A spring has a natural length of 10 in. An 800-lb force stretches the spring to 14 in.

(a) Find the force constant.

(b) How much work is done in stretching the spring from 10 in. to 12 in.?

(c) How far beyond its natural length will a 1600-lb force stretch the spring?

9. *Subway Car Springs* It takes a force of 21,714 lb to compress a coil spring assembly on a New York City Transit Authority subway car from its free height of 8 in. to its fully compressed height of 5 in.

(a) What is the assembly's force constant?

(b) How much work does it take to compress the assembly the first half-inch? the second half-inch? Answer to the nearest inch-pound.

(*Source:* Data courtesy of Bombardier, Inc., Mass Transit Division, for spring assemblies in subway cars delivered to the New York City Transit Authority from 1985 to 1987.)

10. *Bathroom Scale* A bathroom scale is compressed $1/16$ in. when a 150-lb person stands on it. Assuming the scale behaves like a spring that obeys Hooke's Law,

(a) how much does someone who compresses the scale $1/8$ in. weigh?

(b) how much work is done in compressing the scale $1/8$ in.?

11. *Hauling a Rope* A mountain climber is about to haul up a 50-m length of hanging rope. How much work will it take if the rope weighs 0.624 N/m?

12. *Compressing Gas* Suppose that gas in a circular cylinder of cross-section area A is being compressed by a piston (see figure).

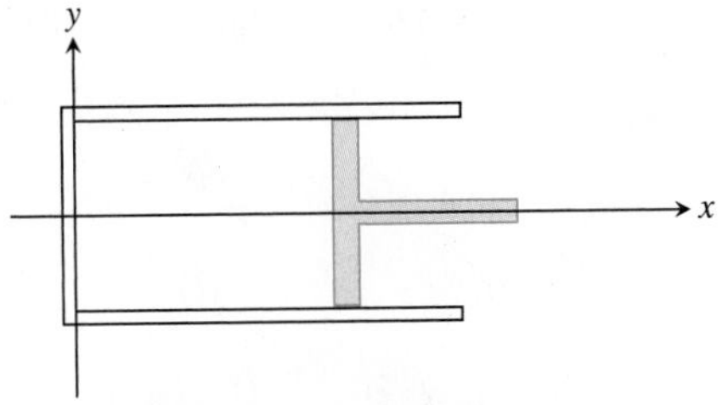

(a) If p is the pressure of the gas in pounds per square inch and V is the volume in cubic inches, show that the work done in compressing the gas from state (p_1, V_1) to state (p_2, V_2) is given by the equation

$$\text{Work} = \int_{(p_1, V_1)}^{(p_2, V_2)} p\,dV \text{ in.} \cdot \text{lb},$$

where the force against the piston is pA.

(b) Find the work done in compressing the gas from $V_1 = 243 \text{ in.}^3$ to $V_2 = 32 \text{ in.}^3$ if $p_1 = 50 \text{ lb/in.}^3$ and p and V obey the gas law $pV^{1.4} = \text{constant}$ (for adiabatic processes).

Group Activity In Exercises 13–16, the vertical end of a tank containing water (blue shading) weighing 62.4 lb/ft^3 has the given shape.

(a) Writing to Learn Explain how to approximate the force against the end of the tank by a Riemann sum.

(b) Find the force as an integral and evaluate it.

13. semicircle

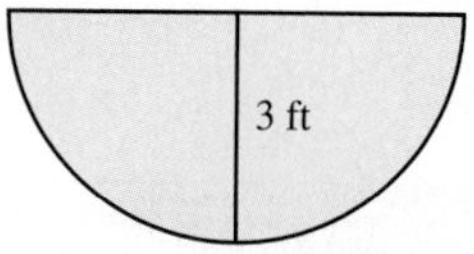

14. semiellipse

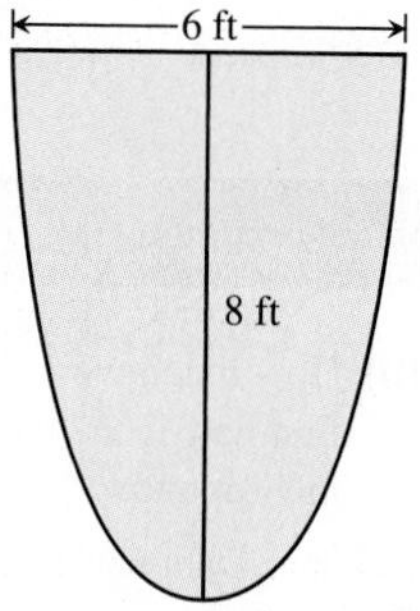

15. triangle

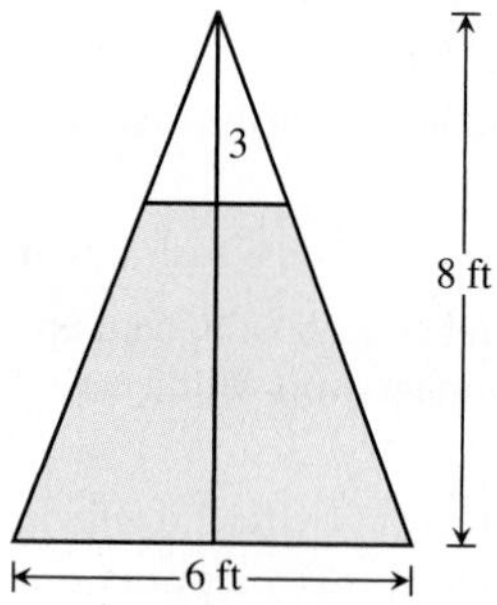

16. parabola

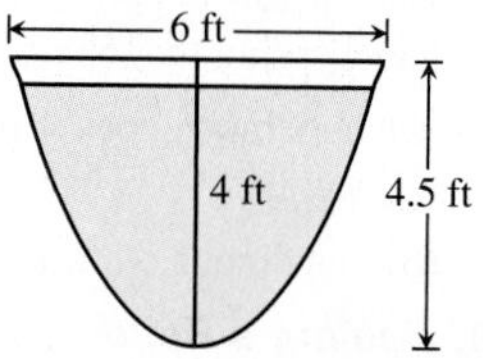

17. *Pumping Water* The rectangular tank shown here, with its top at ground level, is used to catch runoff water. Assume that the water weighs 62.4 lb/ft^3.

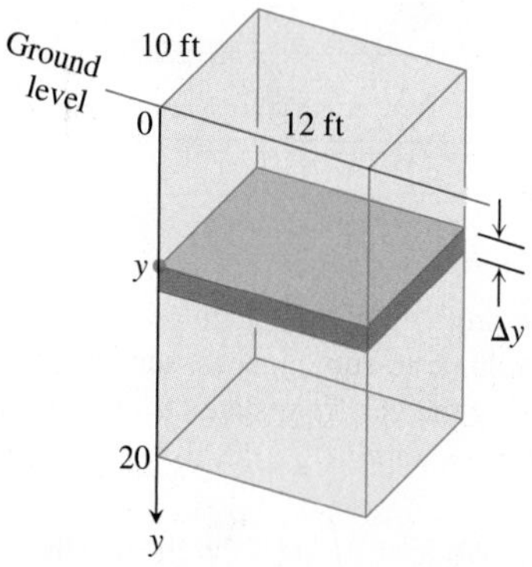

(a) How much work does it take to empty the tank by pumping the water back to ground level once the tank is full?

(b) If the water is pumped to ground level with a (5/11)-horsepower motor (work output 250 ft · lb/sec), how long will it take to empty the full tank (to the nearest minute)?

(c) Show that the pump in part (b) will lower the water level 10 ft (halfway) during the first 25 min of pumping.

(d) *The Weight of Water* Because of differences in the strength of Earth's gravitational field, the weight of a cubic foot of water at sea level can vary from as little as 62.26 lb at the equator to as much as 62.59 lb near the poles, a variation of about 0.5%. A cubic foot of water that weighs 62.4 lb in Melbourne or New York City will weigh 62.5 lb in Juneau or Stockholm. What are the answers to parts (a) and (b) in a location where water weighs 62.26 lb/ft^3? 62.5 lb/ft^3?

18. *Emptying a Tank* A vertical right cylindrical tank measures 30 ft high and 20 ft in diameter. It is full of kerosene weighing 51.2 lb/ft^3. How much work does it take to pump the kerosene to the level of the top of the tank?

19. Writing to Learn The cylindrical tank shown here is to be filled by pumping water from a lake 15 ft below the bottom of the tank. There are two ways to go about this. One is to pump the water through a hose attached to a valve in the bottom of the tank. The other is to attach the hose to the rim of the tank and let the water pour in. Which way will require less work? Give reasons for your answer.

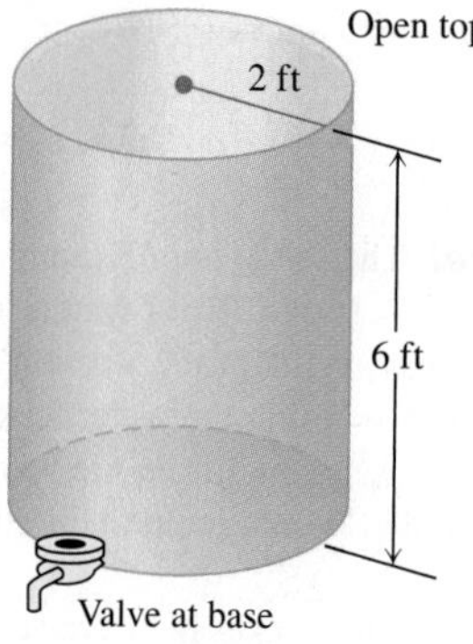

20. *Drinking a Milkshake* The truncated conical container shown here is full of strawberry milkshake that weighs (4/9) oz/in^3. As you can see, the container is 7 in. deep, 2.5 in. across at the base, and 3.5 in. across at the top (a standard size at Brigham's in Boston). The straw sticks up an inch above the top. About how much work does it take to drink the milkshake through the straw (neglecting friction)? Answer in inch-ounces.

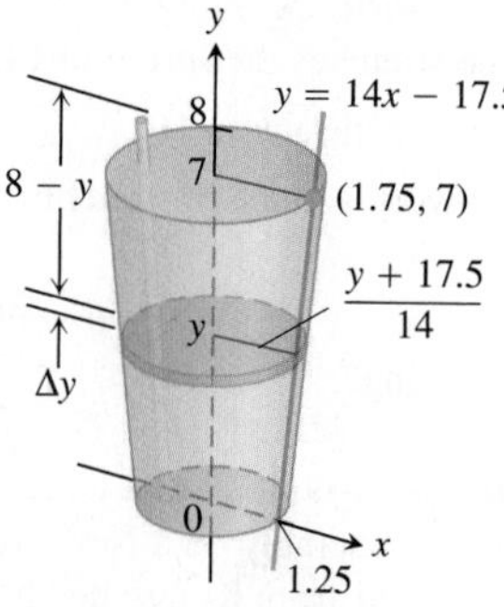

Dimensions in inches

21. *Revisiting Example 3* How much work will it take to pump the oil in Example 3 to a level 3 ft above the cone's rim?

22. *Pumping Milk* Suppose the conical tank in Example 3 contains milk weighing 64.5 lb/ft^3 instead of olive oil. How much work will it take to pump the contents to the rim?

23. Writing to Learn You are in charge of the evacuation and repair of the storage tank shown here. The tank is a hemisphere of radius 10 ft and is full of benzene weighing 56 lb/ft^3.

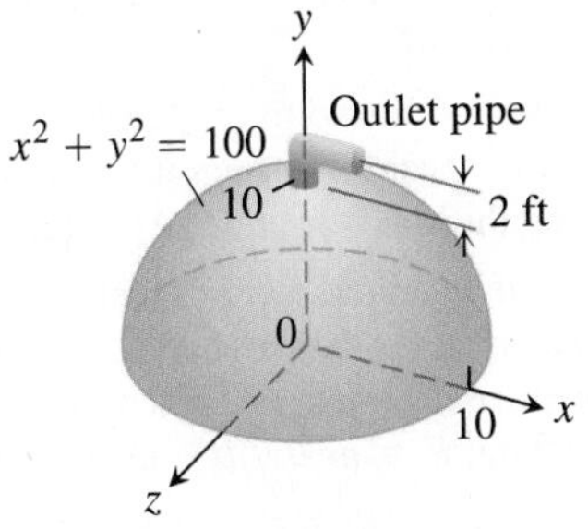

A firm you contacted says it can empty the tank for 1/2 cent per foot-pound of work. Find the work required to empty the tank by pumping the benzene to an outlet 2 ft above the tank. If you have budgeted $5000 for the job, can you afford to hire the firm?

24. *Water Tower* Your town has decided to drill a well to increase its water supply. As the town engineer, you have determined that a water tower will be necessary to provide the pressure needed for distribution, and you have designed the system shown here. The water is to be pumped from a 300-ft well through a vertical 4-in. pipe into the base of a cylindrical tank 20 ft in diameter and 25 ft high. The base of the tank will be 60 ft above ground. The pump is a 3-hp pump, rated at 1650 ft • lb/sec. To the nearest hour, how long will it take to fill the tank the first time? (Include the time it takes to fill the pipe.) Assume water weighs 62.4 lb/ft^3.

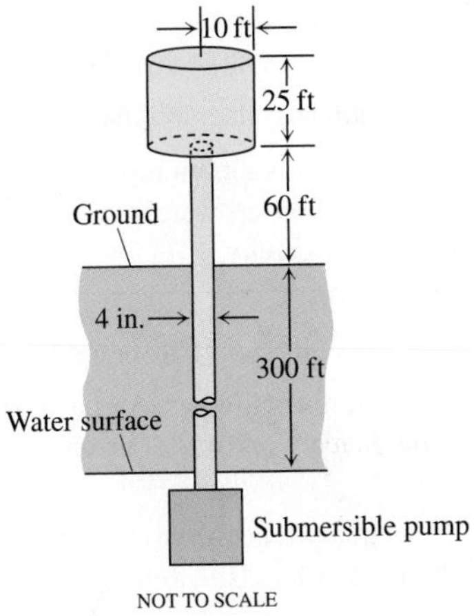

25. *Fish Tank* A rectangular freshwater fish tank with base 2×4 ft and height 2 ft (interior dimensions) is filled to within 2 in. of the top.

(a) Find the fluid force against each end of the tank.

(b) Suppose the tank is sealed and stood on end (without spilling) so that one of the square ends is the base. What does that do to the fluid forces on the rectangular sides?

26. *Milk Carton* A rectangular milk carton measures 3.75 in. by 3.75 in. at the base and is 7.75 in. tall. Find the force of the milk (weighing 64.5 lb/ft^3) on one side when the carton is full.

27. Find the probability that a clock stopped between 1:00 and 5:00.

28. Find the probability that a clock stopped between 3:00 and 6:00.

For problems 29, 30, and 31, assume a normal distribution.

29. Suppose a telephone help line takes a mean of 2 minutes to answer calls. If the standard deviation is $\sigma = 2$, what percentage of the calls are answered in the range of 0 to 4 minutes?

30. *Test Scores* The mean score on a national aptitude test is 498 with a standard deviation of 100 points.

(a) What percentage of the population has scores between 400 and 500?

(b) If we sample 300 test-takers at random, about how many should have scores above 700?

31. *Heights of Females* The mean height of an adult female in New York City is estimated to be 63.4 inches with a standard deviation of 3.2 inches. What proportion of the adult females in New York City are

(a) less than 63.4 inches tall?

(b) between 63 and 65 inches tall?

(c) taller than 6 feet?

(d) exactly 5 feet tall?

32. Writing to Learn Exercises 30 and 31 are subtly different, in that the heights in Exercise 31 are measured *continuously* and the scores in Exercise 30 are measured *discretely.* The discrete probabilities determine rectangles above the individual test scores, so that there actually is a nonzero probability of scoring, say, 560. The rectangles would look like the figure below, and would have total area 1.

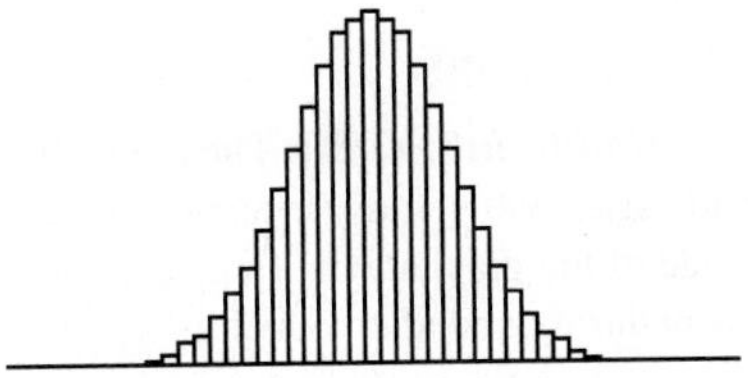

Explain why integration gives a good estimate for the probability, even in the discrete case.

33. Writing to Learn Suppose that $f(t)$ is the probability density function for the lifetime of a certain type of lightbulb where t is in hours. What is the meaning of the integral

$$\int_{100}^{800} f(t)\,dt?$$

Standardized Test Questions

You may use a graphing calculator to solve the following problems.

34. True or False A force is applied to compress a spring several inches. Assume the spring obeys Hooke's Law. Twice as much work is required to compress the spring the second inch than is required to compress the spring the first inch. Justify your answer.

35. True or False An aquarium contains water weighing 62.4 lb/ft^3. The aquarium is in the shape of a cube where the length of each edge is 3 ft. Each side of the aquarium is engineered to withstand 1000 pounds of force. This should be sufficient to withstand the force from water pressure. Justify your answer.

36. Multiple Choice A force of $F(x) = 350x$ newtons moves a particle along a line from $x = 0$ m to $x = 5$ m. Which of the following gives the best approximation of the work done by the force?

(A) 1750 J (B) 2187.5 J (C) 2916.67 J
(D) 3281.25 J (E) 4375 J

37. Multiple Choice A leaky bag of sand weighs 50 N. It is lifted from the ground at a constant rate, to a height of 20 m above the ground. The sand leaks at a constant rate and just finishes draining as the bag reaches the top. Which of the following gives the work done to lift the sand to the top? (Neglect the bag.)

(A) 50 J (B) 100 J (C) 250 J (D) 500 J (E) 1000 J

38. Multiple Choice A spring has a natural length of 0.10 m. A 200-N force stretches the spring to a length of 0.15 m. Which of the following gives the work done in stretching the spring from 0.10 m to 0.15 m?

(A) 0.05 J (B) 5 J (C) 10 J (D) 200 J (E) 4000 J

39. Multiple Choice A vertical right cylindrical tank measures 12 ft high and 16 ft in diameter. It is full of water weighing 62.4 lb/ft^3. How much work does it take to pump the water to the level of the top of the tank? Round your answer to the nearest ft-lb.

(A) 149,490 ft-lb

(B) 285,696 ft-lb

(C) 360,240 ft-lb

(D) 448,776 ft-lb

(E) 903,331 ft-lb

Extending the Ideas

40. *Putting a Satellite into Orbit* The strength of Earth's gravitational field varies with the distance r from Earth's center, and the magnitude of the gravitational force experienced by a satellite of mass m during and after launch is

$$F(r) = \frac{mMG}{r^2}.$$

Here, $M = 5.975 \times 10^{24}$ kg is Earth's mass, $G = 6.6726 \times 10^{-11}\ \mathrm{N \cdot m^2\,kg^{-2}}$ is the *universal gravitational constant*, and r is measured in meters. The work it takes to lift a 1000-kg satellite from Earth's surface to a circular orbit 35,780 km above Earth's center is therefore given by the integral

$$\text{Work} = \int_{6{,}370{,}000}^{35{,}780{,}000} \frac{1000\, MG}{r^2}\, dr \text{ joules.}$$

The lower limit of integration is Earth's radius in meters at the launch site. Evaluate the integral. (This calculation does not take into account energy spent lifting the launch vehicle or energy spent bringing the satellite to orbit velocity.)

41. *Forcing Electrons Together* Two electrons r meters apart repel each other with a force of

$$F = \frac{23 \times 10^{-29}}{r^2} \text{ newton.}$$

(a) Suppose one electron is held fixed at the point $(1, 0)$ on the x-axis (units in meters). How much work does it take to move a second electron along the x-axis from the point $(-1, 0)$ to the origin?

(b) Suppose an electron is held fixed at each of the points $(-1, 0)$ and $(1, 0)$. How much work does it take to move a third electron along the x-axis from $(5, 0)$ to $(3, 0)$?

42. *Kinetic Energy* If a variable force of magnitude $F(x)$ moves a body of mass m along the x-axis from x_1 to x_2, the body's velocity v can be written as dx/dt (where t represents time). Use Newton's second law of motion, $F = m(dv/dt)$, and the Chain Rule

$$\frac{dv}{dt} = \frac{dv}{dx}\frac{dx}{dt} = v\frac{dv}{dx}$$

to show that the net work done by the force in moving the body from x_1 to x_2 is

$$W = \int_{x_1}^{x_2} F(x)\, dx = \frac{1}{2}mv_2^2 - \frac{1}{2}mv_1^2, \qquad (1)$$

where v_1 and v_2 are the body's velocities at x_1 and x_2. In physics the expression $(1/2)mv^2$ is the *kinetic energy* of the body moving with velocity v. Therefore, *the work done by the force equals the change in the body's kinetic energy,* and we can find the work by calculating this change.

> **Weight vs. Mass**
>
> Weight is the force that results from gravity pulling on a mass. The two are related by the equation in Newton's second law,
>
> weight = mass × acceleration.
>
> Thus,
>
> newtons = kilograms × m/sec^2,
>
> pounds = slugs × ft/sec^2.
>
> To convert mass to weight, multiply by the acceleration of gravity. To convert weight to mass, divide by the acceleration of gravity.

In Exercises 43–49, use Equation 1 from Exercise 42.

43. *Tennis* A 2-oz tennis ball was served at 160 ft/sec (about 109 mph). How much work was done on the ball to make it go this fast?

44. *Baseball* How many foot-pounds of work does it take to throw a baseball 90 mph? A baseball weighs 5 oz = 0.3125 lb.

45. *Golf* A 1.6-oz golf ball is driven off the tee at a speed of 280 ft/sec (about 191 mph). How many foot-pounds of work are done getting the ball into the air?

46. *Tennis* During the match in which Pete Sampras won the 1990 U.S. Open men's tennis championship, Sampras hit a serve that was clocked at a phenomenal 124 mph. How much work did Sampras have to do on the 2-oz ball to get it to that speed?

47. ***Football*** A quarterback threw a 14.5-oz football 88 ft/sec (60 mph). How many foot-pounds of work were done on the ball to get it to that speed?

48. ***Softball*** How much work has to be performed on a 6.5-oz softball to pitch it at 132 ft/sec (90 mph)?

49. ***A Ball Bearing*** A 2-oz steel ball bearing is placed on a vertical spring whose force constant is $k = 18$ lb/ft. The spring is compressed 3 in. and released. About how high does the ball bearing go? (*Hint:* The kinetic (compression) energy, mgh, of a spring is $\frac{1}{2}ks^2$, where s is the distance the spring is compressed, m is the mass, g is the acceleration of gravity, and h is the height.)

Quick Quiz for AP* Preparation: Sections 8.4 and 8.5

1. **Multiple Choice** The length of a curve from $x = 0$ to $x = 1$ is given by $\int_0^1 \sqrt{1 + 16x^6}\, dx$. If the curve contains the point (1, 4), which of the following could be an equation for this curve?

(A) $y = x^4 + 3$

(B) $y = x^4 + 1$

(C) $y = 1 + 16x^6$

(D) $y = \sqrt{1 + 16x^6}$

(E) $y = x + \frac{x^7}{7}$

2. **Multiple Choice** Which of the following gives the length of the path described by the parametric equations $x = \frac{1}{4}t^4$ and $y = t^3$, where $0 \le t \le 2$?

(A) $\int_0^2 t^6 + 9t^4\, dt$

(B) $\int_0^2 \sqrt{t^6 + 1}\, dt$

(C) $\int_0^2 \sqrt{1 + 9t^4}\, dt$

(D) $\int_0^2 \sqrt{t^6 + 9t^4}\, dt$

(E) $\int_0^2 \sqrt{t^3 + 3t^2}\, dt$

3. **Multiple Choice** The base of a solid is a circle of radius 2 inches. Each cross section perpendicular to a certain diameter is a square with one side lying in the circle. The volume of the solid in cubic inches is

(A) 16

(B) 16π

(C) $\frac{128}{3}$

(D) $\frac{128\pi}{3}$

(E) 32π

4. **Free Response** The front of a fish tank is rectangular in shape and measures 2 ft wide by 1.5 ft tall. The water in the tank exerts pressure on the front of the tank. The pressure at any point on the front of the tank depends only on how far below the surface the point lies and is given by the equation $p = 62.4h$, where h is depth below the surface measured in feet and p is pressure measured in pounds/ft^2.

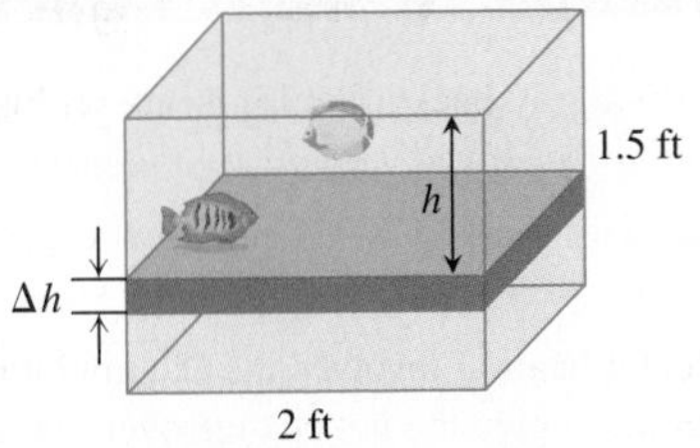

The front of the tank can be partitioned into narrow horizontal bands of height Δh. The force exerted by the water on a band at depth h_i is approximately

$$\text{pressure} \cdot \text{area} = 62.4h_i \cdot 2\Delta h.$$

(a) Write the Riemann sum that approximates the force exerted on the entire front of the tank.

(b) Use the Riemann sum from part (a) to write and evaluate a definite integral that gives the force exerted on the front of the tank. Include correct units.

(c) Find the total force exerted on the front of the tank if the front (and back) are semicircles with diameter 2 ft. Include correct units.

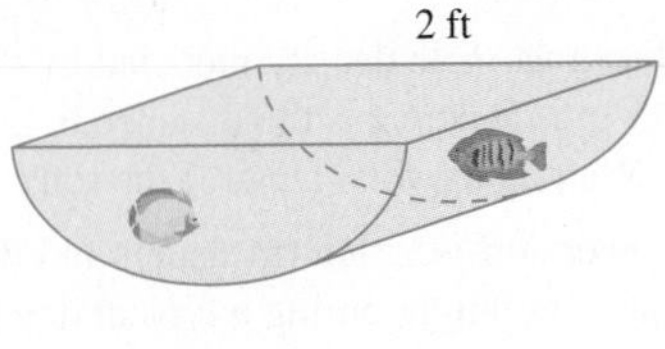

Chapter 8 Key Terms

arc length (p. 417)
area between curves (p. 394)
Cavalieri's theorems (p. 408)
center of mass (p. 393)
constant-force formula (p. 388)
cylindrical shells (p. 406)
displacement (p. 384)
fluid force (p. 425)
fluid pressure (p. 425)
foot-pound (p. 388)
force constant (p. 389)
Gaussian curve (p. 427)
Hooke's Law (p. 389)
inflation rate (p. 392)
joule (p. 388)
length of a curve (p. 417)
mean (p. 427)
moment (p. 393)
net change (p. 383)
newton (p. 388)
normal curve (p. 427)
normal pdf (p. 427)
probability density function (pdf) (p. 426)
68-95-99.7 rule (p. 427)
smooth curve (p. 417)
smooth function (p. 417)
solid of revolution (p. 404)
standard deviation (p. 427)
surface area (p. 409)
total distance traveled (p. 385)
universal gravitational constant (p. 432)
volume by cylindrical shells (p. 406)
volume by slicing (p. 404)
volume of a solid (p. 403)
weight-density (p. 425)
work (p. 388)

Chapter 8 Review Exercises

Exercise numbers with a gray background indicate problems that the authors have designed to be solved *without a calculator*.

The collection of exercises marked in red could be used as a chapter test.

In Exercises 1–5, the application involves the accumulation of small changes over an interval to give the net change over that entire interval. Set up an integral to model the accumulation and evaluate it to answer the question.

1. A toy car slides down a ramp and coasts to a stop after 5 sec. Its velocity from $t = 0$ to $t = 5$ is modeled by $v(t) = t^2 - 0.2t^3$ ft/sec. How far does it travel?

2. The fuel consumption of a diesel motor between weekly maintenance periods is modeled by the function $c(t) = 4 + 0.001t^4$ gal/day, $0 \le t \le 7$. How many gallons does it consume in a week?

3. The number of billboards per mile along a 100-mile stretch of an interstate highway approaching a certain city is modeled by the function $B(x) = 21 - e^{0.03x}$, where x is the distance from the city in miles. About how many billboards are along that stretch of highway?

4. A 2-meter rod has a variable density modeled by the function $\rho(x) = 11 - 4x$ g/m, where x is the distance in meters from the base of the rod. What is the total mass of the rod?

5. The electrical power consumption (measured in kilowatts) at a factory t hours after midnight during a typical day is modeled by $E(t) = 300(2 - \cos(\pi t/12))$. How many kilowatt-hours of electrical energy does the company consume in a typical day?

In Exercises 6–19, find the area of the region enclosed by the lines and curves. You may use a graphing calculator to graph the functions.

6. $y = x, \quad y = 0, \quad y = 1/x^2, \quad x = 2$

7. $y = x + 1, \quad y = 3 - x^2$

8. $\sqrt{x} + \sqrt{y} = 1, \quad x = 0, \quad y = 0$

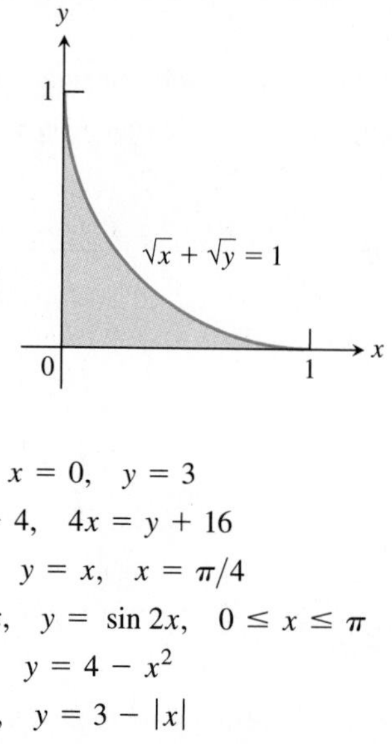

9. $x = 2y^2, \quad x = 0, \quad y = 3$

10. $4x = y^2 - 4, \quad 4x = y + 16$

11. $y = \sin x, \quad y = x, \quad x = \pi/4$

12. $y = 2\sin x, \quad y = \sin 2x, \quad 0 \le x \le \pi$

13. $y = \cos x, \quad y = 4 - x^2$

14. $y = \sec^2 x, \quad y = 3 - |x|$

15. ***The Necklace*** one of the smaller bead-shaped regions enclosed by the graphs of $y = 1 + \cos x$ and $y = 2 - \cos x$

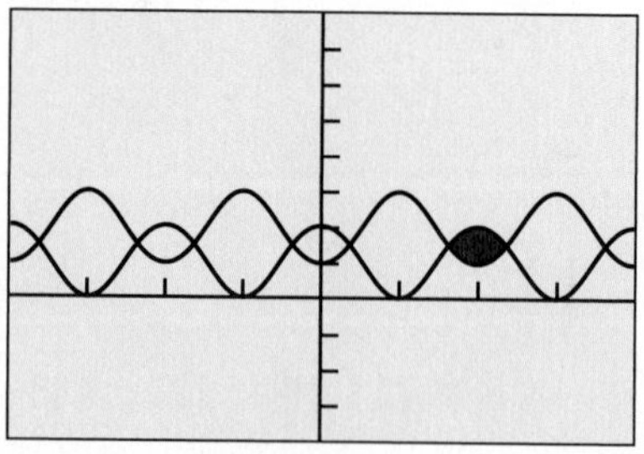

$[-4\pi, 4\pi]$ by $[-4, 8]$

16. one of the larger bead-shaped regions enclosed by the curves in Exercise 15

17. ***The Bow Tie*** the region enclosed by the graphs of

$$y = x^3 - x \quad \text{and} \quad y = \frac{x}{x^2 + 1}$$

(shown in the next column).

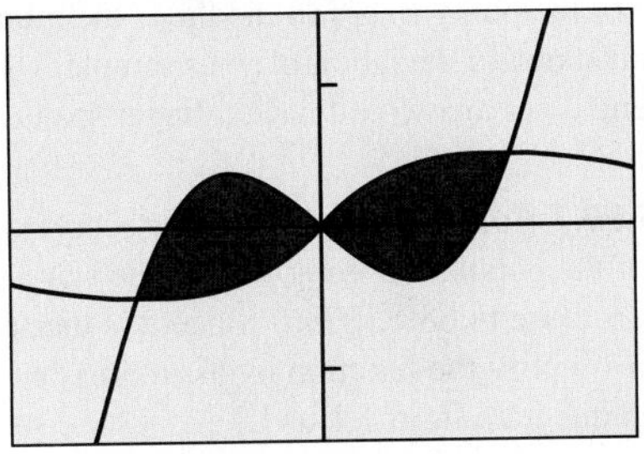

[–2, 2] by [–1.5, 1.5]

18. ***The Bell*** the region enclosed by the graphs of

$$y = 3^{1-x^2} \quad \text{and} \quad y = \frac{x^2 - 3}{10}$$

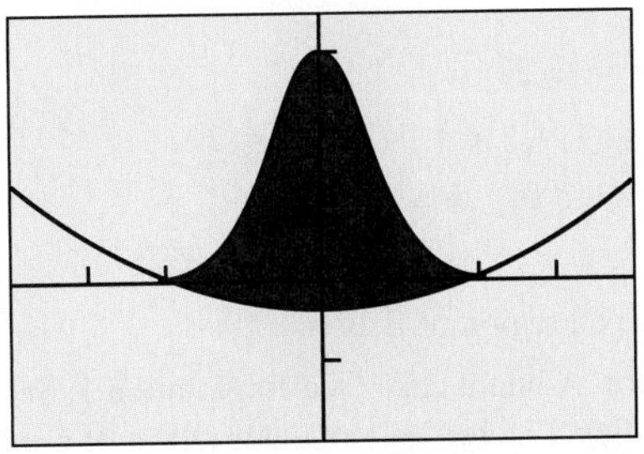

[–4, 4] by [–2, 3.5]

19. ***The Kissing Fish*** the region enclosed between the graphs of $y = x \sin x$ and $y = -x \sin x$ over the interval $[-\pi, \pi]$

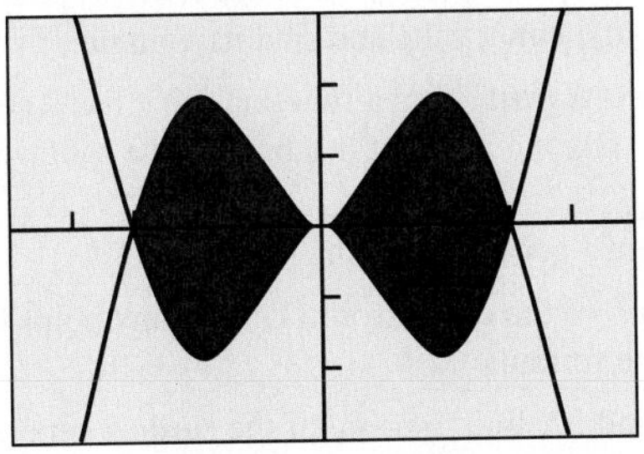

[–5, 5] by [–3, 3]

20. Find the volume of the solid generated by revolving the region bounded by the x-axis, the curve $y = 3x^4$, and the lines $x = -1$ and $x = 1$ about the x-axis.

21. Find the volume of the solid generated by revolving the region enclosed by the parabola $y^2 = 4x$ and the line $y = x$ about

(a) the x-axis. **(b)** the y-axis.

(c) the line $x = 4$. **(d)** the line $y = 4$.

22. The section of the parabola $y = x^2/2$ from $y = 0$ to $y = 2$ is revolved about the y-axis to form a bowl.

(a) Find the volume of the bowl.

(b) Find how much the bowl is holding when it is filled to a depth of k units $(0 < k < 2)$.

(c) If the bowl is filled at a rate of 2 cubic units per second, how fast is the depth k increasing when $k = 1$?

23. The profile of a football resembles the ellipse shown here (all dimensions in inches). Find the volume of the football to the nearest cubic inch.

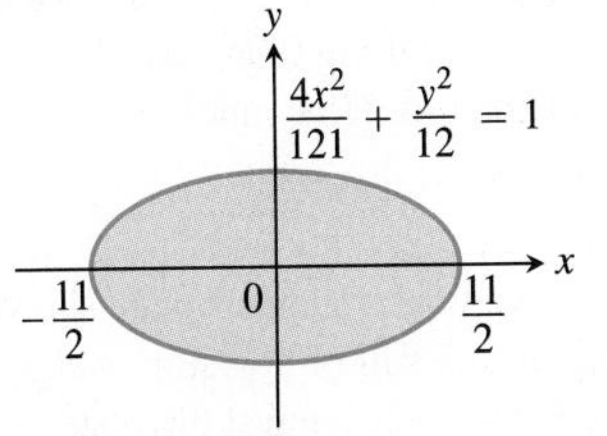

24. The base of a solid is the region enclosed between the graphs of $y = \sin x$ and $y = -\sin x$ from $x = 0$ to $x = \pi$. Each cross section perpendicular to the x-axis is a semicircle with diameter connecting the two graphs. Find the volume of the solid.

25. The region enclosed by the graphs of $y = e^{x/2}$, $y = 1$, and $x = \ln 3$ is revolved about the x-axis. Find the volume of the solid generated.

26. A round hole of radius $\sqrt{3}$ feet is bored through the center of a sphere of radius 2 feet. Find the volume of the piece cut out.

27. Find the length of the arch of the parabola $y = 9 - x^2$ that lies above the x-axis.

28. Find the *perimeter* of the bow-tie-shaped region enclosed between the graphs of $y = x^3 - x$ and $y = x - x^3$.

29. A particle travels at 2 units per second along the curve $y = x^3 - 3x^2 + 2$. How long does it take to travel from the local maximum to the local minimum?

30. **Group Activity** One of the following statements is true for all $k > 0$ and one is false. Which is which? Explain.

(a) The graphs of $y = k \sin x$ and $y = \sin kx$ have the same length on the interval $[0, 2\pi]$.

(b) The graph of $y = k \sin x$ is k times as long as the graph of $y = \sin x$ on the interval $[0, 2\pi]$.

31. Let $F(x) = \int_1^x \sqrt{t^4 - 1}\, dt$. Find the *exact* length of the graph of F from $x = 2$ to $x = 5$ without using a calculator.

32. ***Rock Climbing*** A rock climber is about to haul up 100 N (about 22.5 lb) of equipment that has been hanging beneath her on 40 m of rope weighing 0.8 N/m. How much work will it take to lift

(a) the equipment? **(b)** the rope?

(c) the rope and equipment together?

33. ***Hauling Water*** You drove an 800-gallon tank truck from the base of Mt. Washington to the summit and discovered on arrival that the tank was only half full. You had started out with a full tank of water, had climbed at a steady rate, and had taken 50 minutes to accomplish the 4750-ft elevation change. Assuming that the water leaked out at a steady rate, how much work was spent in carrying the water to the summit? Water weighs 8 lb/gal. (Do not count the work done getting you and the truck to the top.)

34. *Stretching a Spring* If a force of 80 N is required to hold a spring 0.3 m beyond its unstressed length, how much work does it take to stretch the spring this far? How much work does it take to stretch the spring an additional meter?

35. Writing to Learn It takes a lot more effort to roll a stone up a hill than to roll the stone down the hill, but the weight of the stone and the distance it covers are the same. Does this mean that the same amount of work is done? Explain.

36. *Emptying a Bowl* A hemispherical bowl with radius 8 inches is filled with punch (weighing 0.04 pound per cubic inch) to within 2 inches of the top. How much work is done emptying the bowl if the contents are pumped just high enough to get over the rim?

37. *Fluid Force* The vertical triangular plate shown below is the end plate of a feeding trough full of hog slop, weighing 80 pounds per cubic foot. What is the force against the plate?

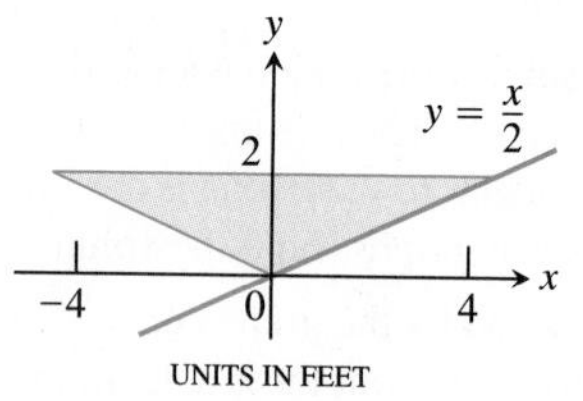

38. *Fluid Force* A standard olive oil can measures 5.75 in. by 3.5 in. by 10 in. Find the fluid force against the base and each side of the can when it is full. (Olive oil has a weight-density of 57 pounds per cubic foot.)

39. *Volume* A solid lies between planes perpendicular to the x-axis at $x = 0$ and at $x = 6$. The cross sections between the planes are squares whose bases run from the x-axis up to the curve $\sqrt{x} + \sqrt{y} = \sqrt{6}$. Find the volume of the solid.

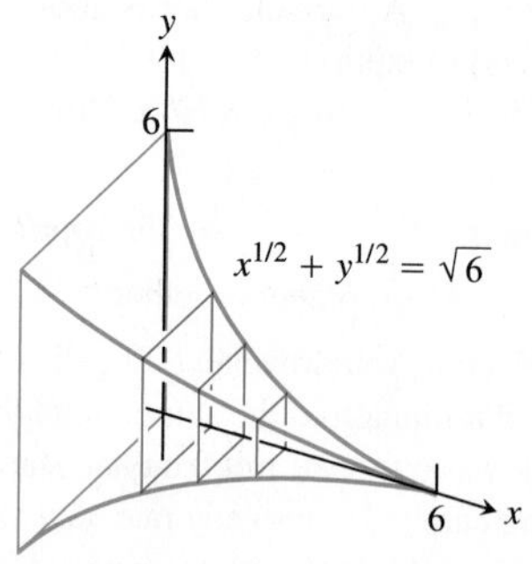

40. *Yellow Perch* A researcher measures the lengths of 3-year-old yellow perch in a fish hatchery and finds that they have a mean length of 17.2 cm with a standard deviation of 3.4 cm. What proportion of 3-year-old yellow perch raised under similar conditions can be expected to reach a length of 20 cm or more?

41. Group Activity Using as large a sample of classmates as possible, measure the span of each person's fully stretched hand, from the tip of the pinky finger to the tip of the thumb. Based on the mean and standard deviation of your sample, what percentage of students your age would have a finger span of more than 10 inches?

42. *The 68-95-99.7 Rule* **(a)** Verify that for every normal pdf, the proportion of the population lying within one standard deviation of the mean is close to 68%. [*Hint:* Since it is the same for every pdf, you can simplify the function by assuming that $\mu = 0$ and $\sigma = 1$. Then integrate from -1 to 1.]

(b) Verify the two remaining parts of the rule.

43. Writing to Learn Explain why the area under the graph of a probability density function has to equal 1.

In Exercises 44–48, use the cylindrical shell method to find the volume of the solid generated by revolving the region bounded by the curves about the y-axis.

44. $y = 2x, \quad y = x/2, \quad x = 1$

45. $y = 1/x, \quad y = 0, \quad x = 1/2, \quad x = 2$

46. $y = \sin x, \quad y = 0, \quad 0 \le x \le \pi$

47. $y = x - 3, \quad y = x^2 - 3x$

48. The bell-shaped region in Exercise 18

49. *Bundt Cake* A bundt cake (see Exploration 1, Section 8.3) has a hole of radius 2 inches and an outer radius of 6 inches at the base. It is 5 inches high, and each cross-sectional slice is parabolic.

(a) Model a typical slice by finding the equation of the parabola with y-intercept 5 and x-intercepts ± 2.

(b) Revolve the parabolic region about an appropriate line to generate the bundt cake and find its volume.

50. *Finding a Function* Find a function f that has a continuous derivative on $(0, \infty)$ and that has both of the following properties:

i. The graph of f goes through the point $(1, 1)$.

ii. The length L of the curve from $(1, 1)$ to any point $(x, f(x))$ is given by the formula $L = \ln x + f(x) - 1$.

In Exercises 51 and 52, find the area of the surface generated by revolving the curve about the indicated axis.

51. $y = \tan x, \quad 0 \le x \le \pi/4; \quad x$-axis

52. $xy = 1, \quad 1 \le y \le 2; \quad y$-axis

AP* Examination Preparation

You may use a graphing calculator to solve the following problems.

53. Let R be the region in the first quadrant enclosed by the y-axis and the graphs of $y = 2 + \sin x$ and $y = \sec x$.

(a) Find the area of R.

(b) Find the volume of the solid generated when R is revolved about the x-axis.

(c) Find the volume of the solid whose base is R and whose cross sections cut by planes perpendicular to the x-axis are squares.

54. The temperature outside a house during a 24-hour period is given by

$$F(t) = 80 - 10\cos\left(\frac{\pi t}{12}\right),\ 0 \le t \le 24,$$

where $F(t)$ is measured in degrees Fahrenheit and t is measured in hours.

(a) Find the average temperature, to the nearest degree Fahrenheit, between $t = 6$ and $t = 14$.

(b) An air conditioner cooled the house whenever the outside temperature was at or above 78 degrees Fahrenheit. For what values of t was the air conditioner cooling the house?

(c) The cost of cooling the house accumulates at the rate of \$0.05 per hour for each degree the outside temperature exceeds 78 degrees Fahrenheit. What was the total cost, to the nearest cent, to cool the house for this 24-hour period?

55. The rate at which people enter an amusement park on a given day is modeled by the function E defined by

$$E(t) = \frac{15600}{t^2 - 24t + 160}.$$

The rate at which people leave the same amusement park on the same day is modeled by the function L defined by

$$L(t) = \frac{9890}{t^2 - 38t + 370}.$$

Both $E(t)$ and $L(t)$ are measured in people per hour, and time t is measured in hours after midnight. These functions are valid for $9 \le t \le 23$, which are the hours that the park is open. At time $t = 9$, there are no people in the park.

(a) How many people have entered the park by 5:00 P.M. ($t = 17$)? Round your answer to the nearest whole number.

(b) The price of admission to the park is \$15 until 5:00 P.M. ($t = 17$). After 5:00 P.M., the price of admission to the park is \$11. How many dollars are collected from admissions to the park on the given day? Round your answer to the nearest whole number.

(c) Let $H(t) = \int_9^t (E(x) - L(x))\,dx$ for $9 \le t \le 23$. The value of $H(17)$ to the nearest whole number is 3725. Find the value of $H'(17)$ and explain the meaning of $H(17)$ and $H'(17)$ in the context of the park.

(d) At what time t, for $9 \le t \le 23$, does the model predict that the number of people in the park is a maximum?

CHAPTER

9 Sequences, L'Hôpital's Rul[e] and Improper Integrals

NASA's Mars Pathfinder collected and transmitted scientific data and photographs back to Earth.

How much work must be done against gravity for the 2000-pound Pathfinder to escape Earth's gravity, that is, to be lifted an infinite distance above the surface of Earth? Assume that the force due to gravity on an object of weight w, r miles from the center of Earth, is

$$F = 16{,}000{,}000\, w/(r^2) \quad (r \geq 4000) \text{ (in pounds).}$$

The radius of Earth is approximately 4000 miles. The concepts in Section 9.4 will help you solve this problem.

CHAPTER 9 Overview

In the late 17th century, John Bernoulli discovered a rule for calculating limits of fractions whose numerators and denominators both approach zero. The rule is known today as l'Hôpital's Rule, after Guillaume François Antoine de l'Hôpital (1661–1704), Marquis de St. Mesme, a French nobleman who wrote the first differential calculus text, where the rule first appeared in print. We will also use l'Hôpital's Rule to compare the rates at which functions of x grow as $|x|$ becomes large.

In Chapter 6 we saw how to evaluate definite integrals of continuous functions and bounded functions with a finite number of discontinuities on finite closed intervals. These ideas are extended to integrals where one or both limits of integration are infinite, and to integrals whose integrands become unbounded on the interval of integration. Sequences are introduced in preparation for the study of infinite series in Chapter 10.

9.1 Sequences

What you will learn about . . .

- Defining a Sequence
- Arithmetic and Geometric Sequences
- Graphing a Sequence
- Limit of a Sequence

and why . . .

Sequences arise frequently in mathematics and applied fields.

Defining a Sequence

We have seen sequences before, such as sequences $x_0, x_1, \ldots, x_n, \ldots$ of numerical approximations generated by Newton's method in Chapter 5. A **sequence** $\{a_n\}$ is a list of numbers written in an explicit order. For example, in the sequence

$$\{a_n\} = \{a_1, a_2, a_3, \ldots, a_n, \ldots\},$$

a_1 is the *first term,* a_2 is the *second term,* a_3 is the *third term,* and so forth. The numbers $a_1, a_2, a_3, \ldots, a_n, \ldots$ are the **terms** of the sequence and a_n is the ***n*th term** of the sequence. We may also think of the sequence $\{a_1, a_2, a_3, \ldots, a_n, \ldots\}$ as a function with domain the set of positive integers and range $\{a_1, a_2, a_3, \ldots, a_n, \ldots\}$.

Any real-valued function with domain a subset of the set of positive integers is considered a sequence. If the domain is finite, then the sequence is a **finite sequence.** Generally we will concentrate on **infinite sequences,** that is, sequences with domains that are infinite subsets of the positive integers.

EXAMPLE 1 Defining a Sequence Explicitly

Find the first six terms and the 100th term of the sequence $\{a_n\}$ where

$$a_n = \frac{(-1)^n}{n^2 + 1}.$$

SOLUTION

Set n equal to 1, 2, 3, 4, 5, 6, and we obtain

$$a_1 = \frac{(-1)^1}{1^2 + 1} = -\frac{1}{2}, a_2 = \frac{(-1)^2}{2^2 + 1} = \frac{1}{5}, a_3 = -\frac{1}{10}, a_4 = \frac{1}{17}, a_5 = -\frac{1}{26}, a_6 = \frac{1}{37}.$$

For $n = 100$ we find

$$a_{100} = \frac{1}{100^2 + 1} = \frac{1}{10001}.$$

Now Try Exercise 1.

The sequence of Example 1 is defined **explicitly** because the formula for a_n is defined in terms of n. Another way to define a sequence is **recursively** by giving a formula for a_n relating it to previous terms, as shown in Example 2.

EXAMPLE 2 Defining a Sequence Recursively

Find the first four terms and the eighth term for the sequence defined recursively by the following conditions:

$$b_1 = 4$$
$$b_n = b_{n-1} + 2 \quad \text{for all} \quad n \geq 2$$

SOLUTION

We proceed one term at a time, starting with $b_1 = 4$ and obtaining each succeeding term by adding 2 to the term just before it:

$$b_1 = 4$$
$$b_2 = b_1 + 2 = 6$$
$$b_3 = b_2 + 2 = 8$$
$$b_4 = b_3 + 2 = 10$$
and so forth

Continuing in this way we arrive at $b_8 = 18$. *Now Try Exercise 5.*

Explicit and Recursive Formulas for Arithmetic Sequences

From the sequence $\{a, a + d, a + 2d, \ldots, a + (n - 1)d, \ldots\}$ we have $a_1 = a$ and $a_n = a + (n - 1)d$ for any positive integer n. So, for any arithmetic sequence, we have an explicit formula and a recursive formula for a_n.

Arithmetic and Geometric Sequences

There are a variety of rules by which we can construct sequences, but two particular types of sequence are dominant in mathematical applications: those in which pairs of successive terms all have a *common difference* (*arithmetic sequences*), and those in which pairs of successive terms all have a *common quotient*, or *common ratio* (*geometric sequences*).

DEFINITION Arithmetic Sequence

A sequence $\{a_n\}$ is an **arithmetic sequence** if it can be written in the form

$$\{a, a + d, a + 2d, \ldots, a + (n - 1)d, \ldots\}$$

for some constant d. The number d is the **common difference.**

Each term in an arithmetic sequence can be obtained recursively from its preceding term by adding d:

$$a_n = a_{n-1} + d \quad \text{for all} \quad n \geq 2$$

EXAMPLE 3 Defining Arithmetic Sequences

For each of the following arithmetic sequences, find **(a)** the common difference, **(b)** the ninth term, **(c)** a recursive rule for the nth term, and **(d)** an explicit rule for the nth term.

Sequence 1: $-5, -2, 1, 4, 7, \ldots$ **Sequence 2:** $\ln 2, \ln 6, \ln 18, \ln 54, \ldots$

SOLUTION

Sequence 1

(a) The difference between successive terms is 3.

(b) $a_9 = -5 + (9 - 1)(3) = 19$

(c) The sequence is defined recursively by $a_1 = -5$ and $a_n = a_{n-1} + 3$ for all $n \geq 2$.

(d) The sequence is defined explicitly by $a_n = -5 + (n - 1)(3) = 3n - 8$.

Sequence 2

(a) The difference between the first two terms is $\ln 6 - \ln 2 = \ln(6/2) = \ln 3$. You can check that $\ln 18 - \ln 6 = \ln 54 - \ln 18$ are also equal to $\ln 3$.

continued

(b) $a_9 = \ln 2 + (9 - 1)(\ln 3) = \ln 2 + 8 \ln 3 = \ln(2 \cdot 3^8) = \ln 13{,}122$

(c) The sequence is defined recursively by $a_1 = \ln 2$ and $a_n = a_{n-1} + \ln 3$ for all $n \geq 2$.

(d) The sequence is defined explicitly by $a_n = \ln 2 + (n - 1)(\ln 3) = \ln(2 \cdot 3^{n-1})$.

Now Try Exercise 13.

DEFINITION Geometric Sequence

A sequence $\{a_n\}$ is an **geometric sequence** if it can be written in the form

$$\{a, a \cdot r, a \cdot r^2, \ldots, a \cdot r^{n-1}, \ldots\}$$

for some nonzero constant r. The number r is the **common ratio.**

Each term in a geometric sequence can be obtained recursively from its preceding term by multiplying by r:

$$a_n = a_{n-1} \cdot r \quad \text{for all} \quad n \geq 2.$$

EXAMPLE 4 Defining Geometric Sequences

For each of the following geometric sequences, find **(a)** the common ratio, **(b)** the tenth term, **(c)** a recursive rule for the nth term, and **(d)** an explicit rule for the nth term.

Sequence 1: 1, −2, 4, −8, 16, ... **Sequence 2:** $10^{-2}, 10^{-1}, 1, 10, 10^2, \ldots$

SOLUTION

Sequence 1

(a) The ratio between successive terms is −2.

(b) $a_{10} = (1) \cdot (-2)^9 = -512$

(c) The sequence is defined recursively by $a_1 = 1$ and $a_n = (-2)a_{n-1}$ for $n \geq 2$.

(d) The sequence is defined explicitly by $a_n = (1) \cdot (-2)^{n-1} = (-2)^{n-1}$.

Sequence 2

(a) The ratio between successive terms is 10.

(b) $a_{10} = (10^{-2}) \cdot (10^9) = 10^7$

(c) The sequence is defined recursively by $a_1 = 10^{-2}$ and $a_n = (10)a_{n-1}$ for $n \geq 2$.

(d) The sequence is defined explicitly by $a_n = (10^{-2}) \cdot (10^{n-1}) = 10^{n-3}$.

Now Try Exercise 17.

EXAMPLE 5 Constructing a Sequence

The second and fifth terms of a geometric sequence are 6 and −48, respectively. Find the first term, common ratio, and an explicit rule for the nth term.

SOLUTION

Because the sequence is geometric the second term is $a_1 \cdot r$ and the fifth term is $a_1 \cdot r^4$, where a_1 is the first term and r is the common ratio. Dividing, we have

$$\frac{a_1 \cdot r^4}{a_1 \cdot r} = -\frac{48}{6}$$
$$r^3 = -8$$
$$r = -2.$$

continued

Then $a_1 \cdot r = 6$ implies that $a_1 = -3$. The sequence is defined explicitly by

$$a_n = (-3)(-2)^{n-1} = (-1)^n(3)(2^{n-1}).$$

Now Try Exercise 21.

Graphing a Sequence

As with other kinds of functions, it helps to represent a sequence geometrically with its graph. One way to produce a graph of a sequence on a graphing calculator is to use parametric mode, as shown in Example 6.

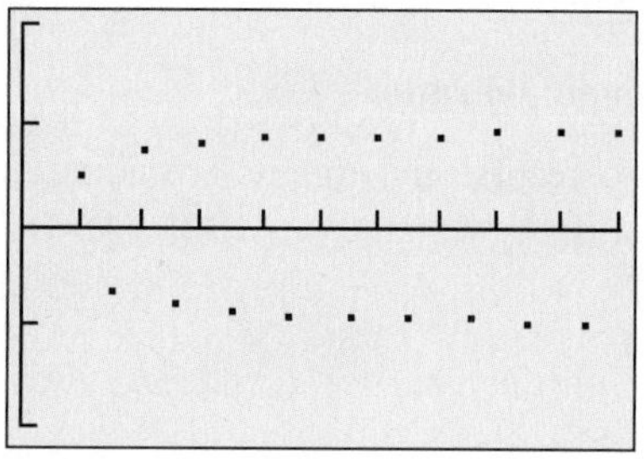

[0, 20] by [–2, 2]

Figure 9.1 The sequence of Example 6.

EXAMPLE 6 Graphing a Sequence Using Parametric Mode

Draw a graph of the sequence $\{a_n\}$ with $a_n = (-1)^n \dfrac{n-1}{n}$, $n = 1, 2, \ldots$.

SOLUTION

Let $X_{1T} = T$, $Y_{1T} = (-1)^T \dfrac{T-1}{T}$, and graph in dot mode. Set Tmin = 1, Tmax = 20, and Tstep = 1. Even though the domain of the sequence is all positive integers, we are required to choose a value for Tmax to use parametric graphing mode. Finally, we choose Xmin = 0, Xmax = 20, Xscl = 2, Ymin = –2, Ymax = 2, Yscl = 1, and draw the graph (Figure 9.1).

Now Try Exercise 23.

Some graphing calculators have a built-in sequence graphing mode that makes it easy to graph sequences defined recursively. The function names used in this mode are u, v, and w. We will use this procedure to graph the sequence of Example 7.

EXAMPLE 7 Graphing a Sequence Using Sequence Graphing Mode

Graph the sequence defined recursively by

$$b_1 = 4$$
$$b_n = b_{n-1} + 2 \quad \text{for all} \quad n \geq 2.$$

SOLUTION

We set the calculator in Sequence graphing mode and dot mode (Figure 9.2a). Replace b_n by $u(n)$. Then select nMin = 1, $u(n) = u(n-1) + 2$, and $u(n\text{Min}) = \{4\}$ (Figure 9.2b).

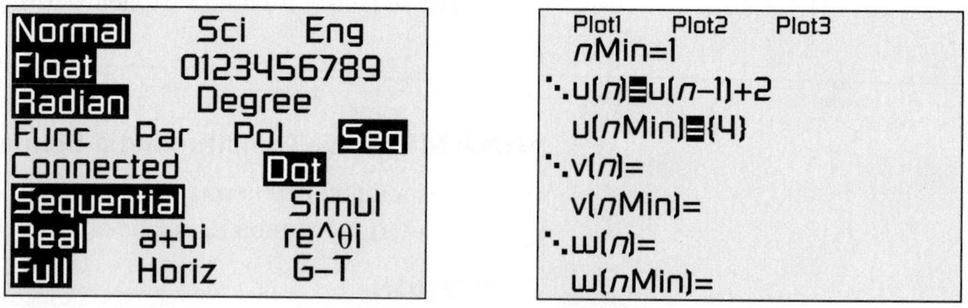

(a) (b)

Figure 9.2 (a) Setting sequence mode and dot mode on the calculator, and (b) entering the sequence of Example 7 in the calculator.

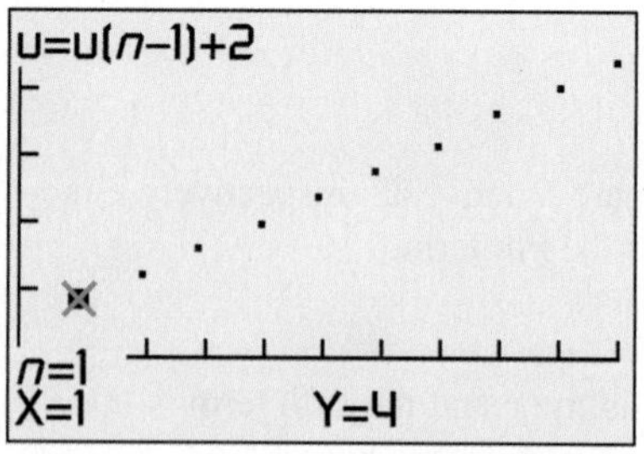

[0, 10] by [–5, 25]

Figure 9.3 The graph of the sequence of Example 7. The TRACE feature shows the coordinates of the first point (1, 4) of the sequence,

$b_1 = 4, b_n = b_{n-1} + 2, n \geq 2.$

Then set nMin = 1, nMax = 10, PlotStart = 1, PlotStep = 1, and graph in the [0, 10] by [–5, 25] viewing window (Figure 9.3). We have also activated TRACE in Figure 9.3.

Now Try Exercise 27.

Limit of a Sequence

The sequence $\{1, 2, 3, \ldots, n, \ldots\}$ of positive integers has no limit. As with functions, we can use a grapher to suggest what a limiting value may be, and then we can confirm the limit analytically with theorems based on a formal definition, as we did in Chapter 2.

DEFINITION Limit

Let L be a real number. The sequence $\{a_n\}$ has **limit L as n approaches ∞** if, given any positive number ϵ, there is a positive number M such that for all $n > M$ we have

$$|a_n - L| < \epsilon.$$

We write $\lim_{n\to\infty} a_n = L$ and say that the sequence **converges to L.** Sequences that do not have limits **diverge.**

Just as in Chapter 2, there are important properties of limits that help us compute limits of sequences.

THEOREM 1 Properties of Limits

If L and M are real numbers and $\lim_{n\to\infty} a_n = L$ and $\lim_{n\to\infty} b_n = M$, then

1. *Sum Rule:*
   $\lim_{n\to\infty} (a_n + b_n) = L + M$
2. *Difference Rule:*
   $\lim_{n\to\infty} (a_n - b_n) = L - M$
3. *Product Rule:*
   $\lim_{n\to\infty} (a_n b_n) = L \cdot M$
4. *Constant Multiple Rule:*
   $\lim_{n\to\infty} (c \cdot a_n) = c \cdot L$
5. *Quotient Rule:*
   $\lim_{n\to\infty} \frac{a_n}{b_n} = \frac{L}{M}, \quad M \neq 0$

EXAMPLE 8 Finding the Limit of a Sequence

Determine whether the sequence converges or diverges. If it converges, find its limit.

$$a_n = \frac{2n - 1}{n}$$

SOLUTION

It appears from the graph of the sequence in Figure 9.4 that the limit exists. Analytically, using Properties of Limits we have

$$\lim_{n\to\infty} \frac{2n-1}{n} = \lim_{n\to\infty}\left(2 - \frac{1}{n}\right)$$

$$= \lim_{n\to\infty}(2) - \lim_{n\to\infty}\left(\frac{1}{n}\right)$$

$$= 2 - 0 = 2.$$

The sequence converges and its limit is 2. ***Now Try Exercise 31.***

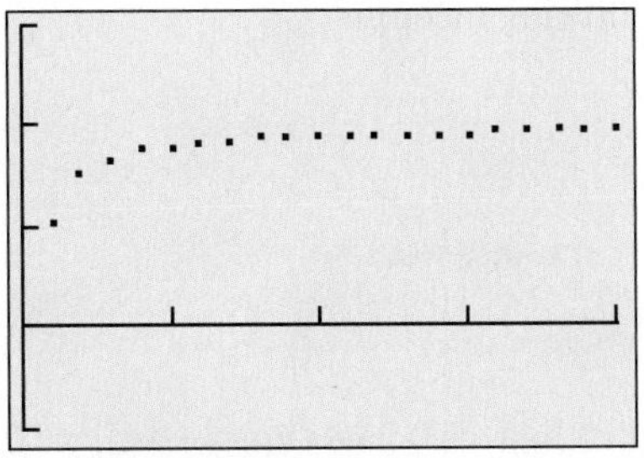

[0, 20] by [–1, 3]

Figure 9.4 The graph of the sequence in Example 8.

EXAMPLE 9 Determining Convergence or Divergence

Determine whether the sequence with given nth term converges or diverges. If it converges, find its limit.

(a) $a_n = (-1)^n \dfrac{n-1}{n}, n = 1, 2, \ldots$ **(b)** $b_1 = 4, b_n = b_{n-1} + 2$ for all $n \geq 2$

SOLUTION

(a) This is the sequence of Example 6 with graph shown in Figure 9.1. This sequence diverges. In fact, we can see that the terms with n even approach 1 while the terms with n odd approach -1.

(b) This is the sequence of Example 7 with graph shown in Figure 9.3. This sequence also diverges. In fact, we can say that $\lim_{n\to\infty} b_n = \infty$. ***Now Try Exercise 35.***

An important theorem that can be rewritten for sequences is the Sandwich Theorem from Chapter 2.

THEOREM 2 The Sandwich Theorem for Sequences

If $\lim_{n\to\infty} a_n = \lim_{n\to\infty} c_n = L$ and if there is an integer N for which $a_n \leq b_n \leq c_n$ for all $n > N$, then $\lim_{n\to\infty} b_n = L$.

EXAMPLE 10 Using the Sandwich Theorem

Show that the sequence $\left\{\dfrac{\cos n}{n}\right\}$ converges, and find its limit.

SOLUTION

Because $|\cos x| \leq 1$ for all x, it follows that

$$\left|\frac{\cos n}{n}\right| \leq \frac{|\cos n|}{|n|} \leq \frac{1}{n}$$

for all integers $n \geq 1$. Thus,

$$-\frac{1}{n} \leq \frac{\cos n}{n} \leq \frac{1}{n}.$$

Then, $\lim_{n\to\infty} \dfrac{\cos n}{n} = 0$ because $\lim_{n\to\infty}\left(-\dfrac{1}{n}\right) = \lim_{n\to\infty}\left(\dfrac{1}{n}\right) = 0$ and the sequence $\left\{\dfrac{\cos n}{n}\right\}$ converges. ***Now Try Exercise 41.***

We can use the Sandwich Theorem to prove the following theorem.

THEOREM 3 Absolute Value Theorem

Consider the sequence $\{a_n\}$. If $\lim_{n\to\infty} |a_n| = 0$, then $\lim_{n\to\infty} a_n = 0$.

Proof We know that $-|a_n| \leq a_n \leq |a_n|$. Thus, $\lim_{n\to\infty} |a_n| = 0$ and $\lim_{n\to\infty} -|a_n| = 0$ implies that $\lim_{n\to\infty} a_n = 0$ because of the Sandwich Theorem. ■

Another way to state the Absolute Value Theorem is that if the absolute value sequence converges to 0, then the original sequence also converges to 0.

Quick Review 9.1 *(For help, go to Sections 1.2, 2.1, and 2.2.)*

Exercise numbers with a gray background indicate problems that the authors have designed to be solved *without a calculator.*

In Exercises 1 and 2, let $f(x) = \dfrac{x}{x+3}$. Find the values of f.

1. $f(5)$ **2.** $f(-2)$

In Exercises 3 and 4, evaluate the expression $a + (n-1)d$ for the given values of a, n, and d.

3. $a = -2,\ n = 3,\ d = 1.5$

4. $a = -7,\ n = 5,\ d = 3$

In Exercises 5 and 6, evaluate the expression ar^{n-1} for the given values of a, r, and n.

5. $a = 1.5,\ r = 2,\ n = 4$ **6.** $a = -2,\ r = 1.5,\ n = 3$

In Exercises 7–10, find the value of the limit.

7. $\displaystyle\lim_{x\to\infty} \frac{5x^3 + 2x^2}{3x^4 + 16x^2}$ **8.** $\displaystyle\lim_{x\to 0} \frac{\sin(3x)}{x}$

9. $\displaystyle\lim_{x\to\infty} \left(x \sin\left(\frac{1}{x}\right)\right)$ **10.** $\displaystyle\lim_{x\to\infty} \frac{2x^3 + x^2}{x+1}$

Section 9.1 Exercises

In Exercises 1–4, find the first six terms and the 50th term of the sequence with specified nth term.

1. $a_n = \dfrac{n}{n+1}$ **2.** $b_n = 3 - \dfrac{1}{n}$

3. $c_n = \left(1 + \dfrac{1}{n}\right)^n$ **4.** $d_n = n^2 - 3n$

In Exercises 5–10, find the first four terms and the eighth term of the recursively defined sequence.

5. $a_1 = 3,\ a_n = a_{n-1} - 2$ for all $n \ge 2$

6. $b_1 = -2,\ b_n = b_{n-1} + 1$ for all $n \ge 2$

7. $c_1 = 2,\ c_n = 2c_{n-1}$ for all $n \ge 2$

8. $d_1 = 10,\ d_n = 1.1d_{n-1}$ for all $n \ge 2$

9. $u_1 = 1,\ u_2 = 1,\ u_n = u_{n-1} + u_{n-2}$ for all $n \ge 3$

10. $v_1 = -3,\ v_2 = 2,\ v_n = v_{n-1} + v_{n-2}$ for all $n \ge 3$

In Exercises 11–14, the sequences are arithmetic. Find

(a) the common difference,

(b) the eighth term,

(c) a recursive rule for the nth term, and

(d) an explicit rule for the nth term.

11. $-2, 1, 4, 7, \ldots$ **12.** $15, 13, 11, 9, \ldots$

13. $1, 3/2, 2, 5/2, \ldots$ **14.** $3, 3.1, 3.2, 3.3, \ldots$

In Exercises 15–18, the sequences are geometric. Find

(a) the common ratio,

(b) the ninth term,

(c) a recursive rule for the nth term, and

(d) an explicit rule for the nth term.

15. $8, 4, 2, 1, \ldots$ **16.** $1, 1.5, 2.25, 3.375, \ldots$

17. $-3, 9, -27, 81, \ldots$ **18.** $5, -5, 5, -5, \ldots$

19. The second and fifth terms of an arithmetic sequence are -2 and 7, respectively. Find the first term and a recursive rule for the nth term.

20. The fifth and ninth terms of an arithmetic sequence are 5 and -3, respectively. Find the first term and an explicit rule for the nth term.

21. The fourth and seventh terms of a geometric sequence are 3010 and 3,010,000, respectively. Find the first term, common ratio, and an explicit rule for the nth term.

22. The second and seventh terms of a geometric sequence are $-1/2$ and 16, respectively. Find the first term, common ratio, and an explicit rule for the nth term.

In Exercises 23–30, draw a graph of the sequence $\{a_n\}$.

23. $a_n = \dfrac{n}{n^2+1},\quad n = 1, 2, 3, \ldots$

24. $a_n = \dfrac{n-2}{n+2},\quad n = 1, 2, 3, \ldots$

25. $a_n = (-1)^n \dfrac{2n+1}{n},\quad n = 1, 2, 3, \ldots$

26. $a_n = \left(1 + \dfrac{2}{n}\right)^n,\quad n = 1, 2, 3, \ldots$

27. $u_1 = 2,\quad u_n = 3u_{n-1}\quad$ for all $n \ge 2$

28. $u_1 = 2,\quad u_n = u_{n-1} + 3\quad$ for all $n \ge 2$

29. $u_1 = 3,\quad u_n = 5 - \dfrac{1}{2}u_{n-1}\quad$ for all $n \ge 2$

30. $u_1 = 5,\quad u_n = u_{n-1} - 2\quad$ for all $n \ge 2$

In Exercises 31–40, determine the convergence or divergence of the sequence with given nth term. If the sequence converges, find its limit.

31. $a_n = \dfrac{3n+1}{n}$ **32.** $a_n = \dfrac{2n}{n+3}$

33. $a_n = \dfrac{2n^2 - n - 1}{5n^2 + n + 2}$ **34.** $a_n = \dfrac{n}{n^2+1}$

35. $a_n = (-1)^n \dfrac{n-1}{n+3}$ **36.** $a_n = (-1)^n \dfrac{n+1}{n^2+2}$

37. $a_n = (1.1)^n$ **38.** $a_n = (0.9)^n$

39. $a_n = n \sin\left(\dfrac{1}{n}\right)$ **40.** $a_n = \cos\left(n\dfrac{\pi}{2}\right)$

In Exercises 41–44, use the Sandwich Theorem to show that the sequence with given nth term converges and find its limit.

41. $a_n = \dfrac{\sin n}{n}$ **42.** $a_n = \dfrac{1}{2^n}$

43. $a_n = \dfrac{1}{n!}$ **44.** $a_n = \dfrac{\sin^2 n}{2^n}$

In Exercises 45–48, match the graph or table with the sequence with given nth term.

45. $a_n = \dfrac{2n - 1}{n}$

46. $b_n = (-1)^n \dfrac{3n + 1}{n + 3}$

47. $c_n = \dfrac{n + 1}{n}$

48. $d_n = \dfrac{4}{n + 2}$

n	u(n)
1	1.3333
2	1
3	.8
4	.66667
5	.57143
6	.5
7	.44444

n = 1

(a)

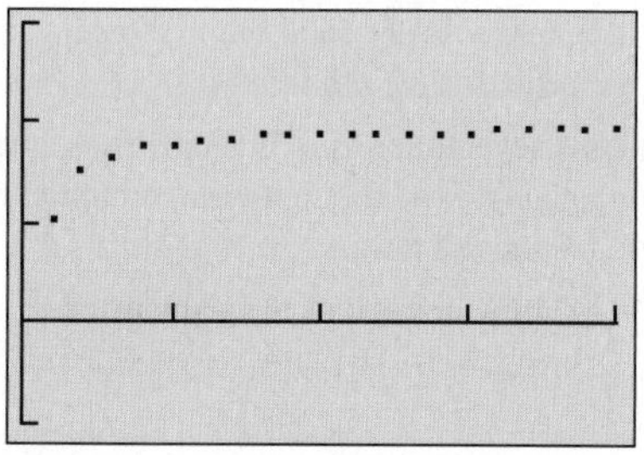

[0, 20] by [–1, 3]

(b)

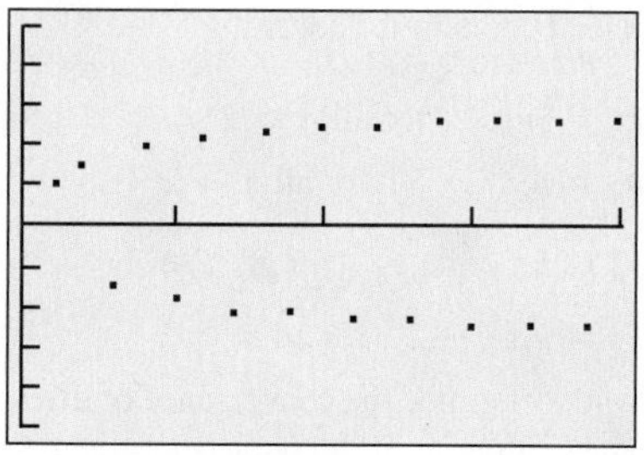

[0, 20] by [–5, 5]

(c)

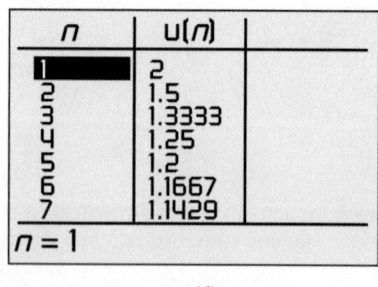

n	u(n)
1	2
2	1.5
3	1.3333
4	1.25
5	1.2
6	1.1667
7	1.1429

n = 1

(d)

Standardized Test Questions

49. True or False If the first two terms of an arithmetic sequence are negative, then all its terms are negative. Justify your answer.

50. True or False If the first two terms of a geometric sequence are positive, then all its terms are positive. Justify your answer.

51. Multiple Choice The first and third terms of an arithmetic sequence are -1 and 5, respectively. Which of the following is the sixth term?

(A) -25 **(B)** 11 **(C)** 14 **(D)** 29 **(E)** 3125

52. Multiple Choice The second and third terms of a geometric sequence are 2.5 and 1.25, respectively. Which of the following is the first term?

(A) -5 **(B)** -2.5 **(C)** 0.625 **(D)** 3.75 **(E)** 5

53. Multiple Choice Which of the following is the limit of the sequence with nth term $a_n = n \sin\left(\dfrac{3\pi}{n}\right)$?

(A) 1 **(B)** π **(C)** 2π **(D)** 3π **(E)** 4π

54. Multiple Choice Which of the following is the limit of the sequence with nth term $a_n = (-1)^n \dfrac{3n - 1}{n + 2}$?

(A) -3 **(B)** 0 **(C)** 2 **(D)** 3 **(E)** diverges

Explorations

55. *Connecting Geometry and Sequences* In the sequence of diagrams that follow, regular polygons are inscribed in unit circles with at least one side of each polygon perpendicular to the x-axis.

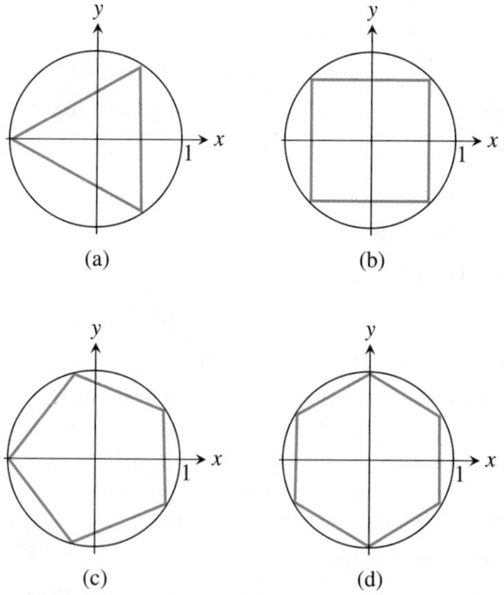

(a) Prove that the perimeter of each polygon in the sequence is given by $a_n = 2n \sin(\pi/n)$, where n is the number of sides in the polygon.

(b) Determine $\lim_{n\to\infty} a_n$.

56. ***Fibonacci Sequence*** The **Fibonacci Sequence** can be defined recursively by $a_1 = 1$, $a_2 = 1$, and $a_n = a_{n-2} + a_{n-1}$ for all integers $n \geq 3$.

(a) Write out the first 10 terms of the sequence.

(b) Draw a graph of the sequence using the Sequence Graphing mode on your grapher. Enter $\mathrm{u}(n) = \mathrm{u}(n-1) + \mathrm{u}(n-2)$ and $\mathrm{u}(n\mathrm{Min}) = \{1, 1\}$.

Extending the Ideas

57. Writing to Learn If $\{a_n\}$ is a geometric sequence with all positive terms, explain why $\{\log a_n\}$ must be arithmetic.

58. Writing to Learn If $\{a_n\}$ is an arithmetic sequence, explain why $\{10^{a_n}\}$ must be geometric.

59. ***Proving Limits*** Use the formal definition of limit to prove that

$$\lim_{n \to \infty} \frac{1}{n} = 0.$$

9.2 L'Hôpital's Rule

What you will learn about . . .

- Indeterminate Form $0/0$
- Indeterminate Forms ∞/∞, $\infty \cdot 0$, $\infty - \infty$
- Indeterminate Forms 1^{∞}, 0^0, ∞^0

and why . . .

Limits can be used to describe the behavior of functions, and l'Hôpital's Rule is an important technique for finding limits.

Indeterminate Form 0/0

If functions $f(x)$ and $g(x)$ are both zero at $x = a$, then

$$\lim_{x \to a} \frac{f(x)}{g(x)}$$

cannot be found by substituting $x = a$. The substitution produces $0/0$, a meaningless expression known as an **indeterminate form.** Our experience so far has been that limits that lead to indeterminate forms may or may not be hard to find algebraically. It took a lot of analysis in Exercise 75 of Section 2.1 to find $\lim_{x\to 0} (\sin x)/x$. But we have had remarkable success with the limit

$$f'(a) = \lim_{x \to a} \frac{f(x) - f(a)}{x - a},$$

from which we calculate derivatives and which always produces the equivalent of $0/0$. L'Hôpital's Rule enables us to draw on our success with derivatives to evaluate limits that otherwise lead to indeterminate forms.

THEOREM 4 L'Hôpital's Rule (First Form)

Suppose that $f(a) = g(a) = 0$, that $f'(a)$ and $g'(a)$ exist, and that $g'(a) \neq 0$. Then

$$\lim_{x \to a} \frac{f(x)}{g(x)} = \frac{f'(a)}{g'(a)}.$$

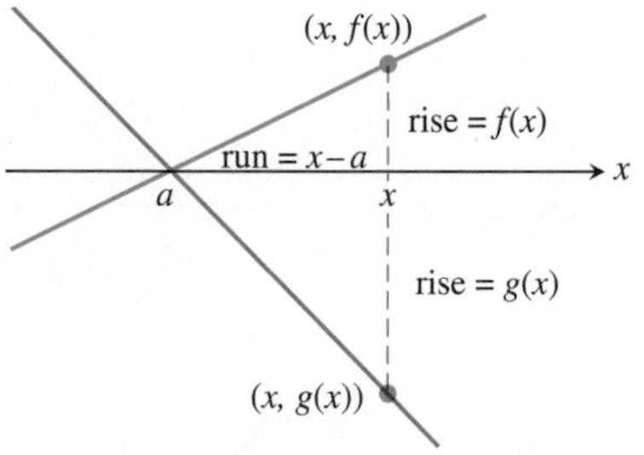

Figure 9.5 A zoom-in view of the graphs of the differentiable functions f and g at $x = a$. (Theorem 4)

Proof

Graphical Argument

If we zoom in on the graphs of f and g at $(a, f(a)) = (a, g(a)) = (a, 0)$, the graphs (Figure 9.5) appear to be straight lines because differentiable functions are locally linear. Let m_1 and m_2 be the slopes of the lines for f and g, respectively. Then for x near a,

$$\frac{f(x)}{g(x)} = \frac{\dfrac{f(x)}{x-a}}{\dfrac{g(x)}{x-a}} = \frac{m_1}{m_2}.$$

As $x \to a$, m_1 and m_2 approach $f'(a)$ and $g'(a)$, respectively. Therefore,

$$\lim_{x \to a} \frac{f(x)}{g(x)} = \lim_{x \to a} \frac{m_1}{m_2} = \frac{f'(a)}{g'(a)}.$$

Confirm Analytically

Working backward from $f'(a)$ and $g'(a)$, which are themselves limits, we have

$$\frac{f'(a)}{g'(a)} = \frac{\displaystyle\lim_{x\to a} \frac{f(x) - f(a)}{x - a}}{\displaystyle\lim_{x\to a} \frac{g(x) - g(a)}{x - a}} = \lim_{x \to a} \frac{\dfrac{f(x) - f(a)}{x - a}}{\dfrac{g(x) - g(a)}{x - a}}$$

$$= \lim_{x \to a} \frac{f(x) - f(a)}{g(x) - g(a)} = \lim_{x \to a} \frac{f(x) - 0}{g(x) - 0} = \lim_{x \to a} \frac{f(x)}{g(x)}. \quad \blacksquare$$

Bernard A. Harris Jr. (1956–)

Bernard Harris, M.D., became an astronaut in 1991. In 1995, as the Payload Commander on the STS-63 mission, he became the first African American to walk in space. During this mission, which included a rendezvous with the Russian Space Station, Mir, Harris traveled over 2.9 million miles. Dr. Harris left NASA in 1996 to become Vice President of Microgravity and Life Sciences for SPACEHAB Incorporated.

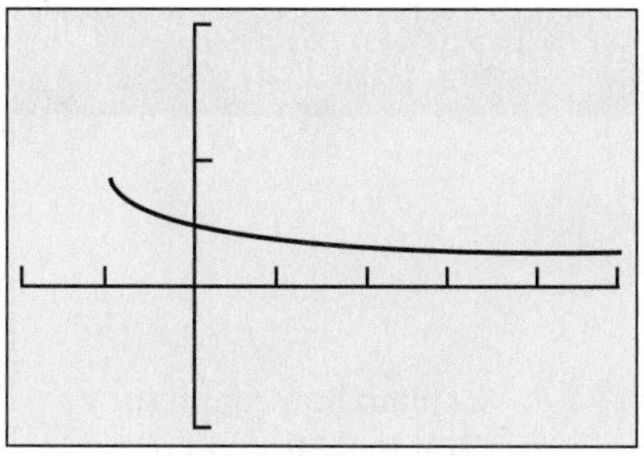

[–2, 5] by [–1, 2]

Figure 9.6 The graph of $y = \dfrac{\sqrt{1+x}-1}{x}$. (Example 1)

EXAMPLE 1 Indeterminate Form 0/0

Estimate the limit graphically and then use l'Hôpital's Rule to find the limit.

$$\lim_{x\to 0} \frac{\sqrt{1+x}-1}{x}$$

SOLUTION

From the graph in Figure 9.6 we can estimate the limit to be about $1/2$. If we set $f(x) = \sqrt{1+x} - 1$ and $g(x) = x$ we have $f(0) = g(0) = 0$. Thus, l'Hôpital's Rule applies in this case. Because $f'(x) = (1/2)(1+x)^{-1/2}$ and $g'(x) = 1$ it follows that

$$\lim_{x\to 0} \frac{\sqrt{1+x}-1}{x} = \lim_{x\to 0} \frac{(1/2)(1+x)^{-1/2}}{1} = \frac{1}{2}.$$

Now Try Exercise 3.

Sometimes after differentiation the new numerator and denominator both equal zero at $x = a$, as we will see in Example 2. In these cases we apply a stronger form of l'Hôpital's Rule.

Augustin-Louis Cauchy (1789–1857)

An engineer with a genius for mathematics and mathematical modeling, Cauchy created an early modeling of surface wave propagation that is now a classic in hydrodynamics. Cauchy (pronounced "CO-she") invented our notion of continuity and proved the Intermediate Value Theorem for continuous functions. He invented modern limit notation and was the first to prove the convergence of $(1 + 1/n)^n$. His Mean Value Theorem, the subject of Exercise 71, is the key to proving the stronger form of l'Hôpital's Rule. His work advanced not only calculus and mathematical analysis, but also the fields of complex function theory, error theory, differential equations, and celestial mechanics.

THEOREM 5 L'Hôpital's Rule (Stronger Form)

Suppose that $f(a) = g(a) = 0$, that f and g are differentiable on an open interval I containing a, and that $g'(x) \neq 0$ on I if $x \neq a$. Then

$$\lim_{x\to a} \frac{f(x)}{g(x)} = \lim_{x\to a} \frac{f'(x)}{g'(x)},$$

if the latter limit exists.

When you apply l'Hôpital's Rule, look for a change from $0/0$ into something else. This is where the limit is revealed.

EXAMPLE 2 Applying a Stronger Form of l'Hôpital's Rule

Evaluate $\displaystyle\lim_{x\to 0} \frac{\sqrt{1+x}-1-x/2}{x^2}$.

SOLUTION

Substituting $x = 0$ leads to the indeterminate form $0/0$ because the numerator and denominator of the fraction are 0 when 0 is substituted for x. So we apply l'Hôpital's Rule.

$$\lim_{x\to 0} \frac{\sqrt{1+x}-1-x/2}{x^2} = \lim_{x\to 0} \frac{(1/2)(1+x)^{-1/2}-1/2}{2x} \qquad \text{Differentiate numerator and denominator}$$

Substituting 0 for x leads to 0 in both the numerator and denominator of the second fraction, so we differentiate again.

$$\lim_{x\to 0} \frac{\sqrt{1+x}-1-x/2}{x^2} = \lim_{x\to 0} \frac{(1/2)(1+x)^{-1/2}-1/2}{2x} = \lim_{x\to 0} \frac{-(1/4)(1+x)^{-3/2}}{2}$$

The third limit in the above line is $-1/8$. Thus,

$$\lim_{x\to 0} \frac{\sqrt{1+x}-1-x/2}{x^2} = -\frac{1}{8}.$$

Now Try Exercise 5.

EXPLORATION 1 Exploring L'Hôpital's Rule Graphically

Consider the function $f(x) = \dfrac{\sin x}{x}$.

1. Use l'Hôpital's Rule to find $\lim_{x\to 0} f(x)$.
2. Let $y_1 = \sin x,\ y_2 = x,\ y_3 = y_1/y_2,\ y_4 = y_1'/y_2'$. Explain how graphing y_3 and y_4 in the same viewing window provides support for l'Hôpital's Rule in part 1.
3. Let $y_5 = y_3'$. Graph y_3, y_4, and y_5 in the same viewing window. Based on what you see in the viewing window, make a statement about what l'Hôpital's Rule does *not* say.

L'Hôpital's Rule applies to one-sided limits as well.

EXAMPLE 3 Using L'Hôpital's Rule with One-Sided Limits

Evaluate the following limits using l'Hôpital's Rule:

(a) $\displaystyle\lim_{x\to 0^+} \frac{\sin x}{x^2}$ **(b)** $\displaystyle\lim_{x\to 0^-} \frac{\sin x}{x^2}$

Support your answer graphically.

SOLUTION

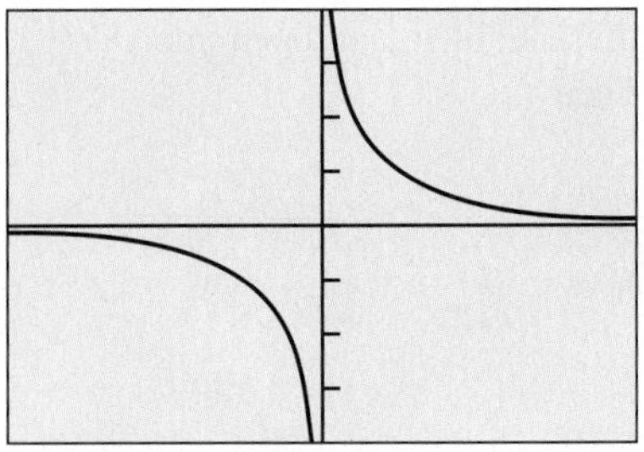

[−1, 1] by [−20, 20]

Figure 9.7 The graph of $f(x) = (\sin x)/x^2$. (Example 3)

(a) Substituting $x = 0$ leads to the indeterminate form $0/0$. Apply l'Hôpital's Rule by differentiating numerator and denominator.

$$\lim_{x\to 0^+} \frac{\sin x}{x^2} = \lim_{x\to 0^+} \frac{\cos x}{2x} \qquad \frac{1}{0}$$
$$= \infty$$

(b)
$$\lim_{x\to 0^-} \frac{\sin x}{x^2} = \lim_{x\to 0^-} \frac{\cos x}{2x} \qquad -\frac{1}{0}$$
$$= -\infty$$

Figure 9.7 supports the results. ***Now Try Exercise 11.***

When we reach a point where one of the derivatives approaches 0, as in Example 3, and the other does not, then the limit in question is 0 (if the numerator approaches 0) or $\pm$ infinity (if the denominator approaches 0).

Indeterminate Forms ∞/∞, $\infty \cdot 0$, $\infty - \infty$

A version of l'Hôpital's Rule also applies to quotients that lead to the indeterminate form ∞/∞. If $f(x)$ and $g(x)$ both approach infinity as $x \to a$, then

$$\lim_{x\to a} \frac{f(x)}{g(x)} = \lim_{x\to a} \frac{f'(x)}{g'(x)},$$

provided the latter limit exists. The a here (and in the indeterminate form $0/0$) may itself be finite or infinite, and may be an endpoint of the interval I of Theorem 5.

EXAMPLE 4 Working with Indeterminate Form ∞/∞

Identify the indeterminate form and evaluate the limit using l'Hôpital's Rule. Support your answer graphically.

$$\lim_{x\to \pi/2} \frac{\sec x}{1 + \tan x}$$

continued

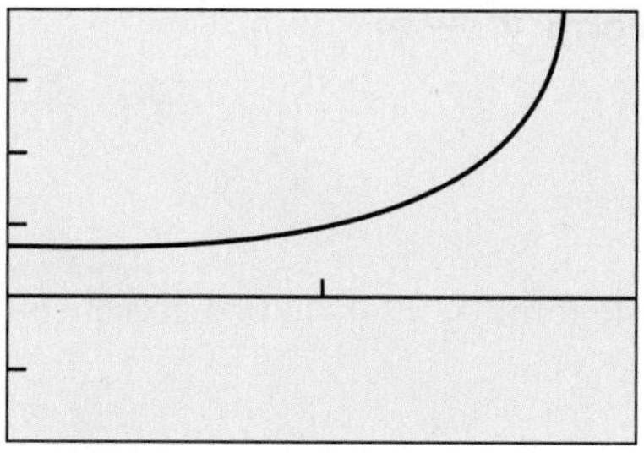

$[\pi/4, 3\pi/4]$ by $[-2, 4]$

Figure 9.8 The graph of $y = (\sec x)/(1 + \tan x)$. (Example 4)

SOLUTION

The numerator and denominator are discontinuous at $x = \pi/2$, so we investigate the one-sided limits there. To apply l'Hôpital's Rule we can choose I to be any open interval containing $x = \pi/2$.

$$\lim_{x\to(\pi/2)^-} \frac{\sec x}{1 + \tan x} \qquad \frac{\infty}{\infty} \text{ from the left}$$

Next differentiate the numerator and denominator.

$$\lim_{x\to(\pi/2)^-} \frac{\sec x}{1 + \tan x} = \lim_{x\to(\pi/2)^-} \frac{\sec x \tan x}{\sec^2 x} = \lim_{x\to(\pi/2)^-} \sin x = 1$$

The right-hand limit is 1 also, with $(-\infty)/(-\infty)$ as the indeterminate form. Therefore, the two-sided limit is equal to 1. The graph of $(\sec x)/(1 + \tan x)$ in Figure 9.8 appears to pass right through the point $(\pi/2, 1)$ and supports the work above.

Now Try Exercise 13.

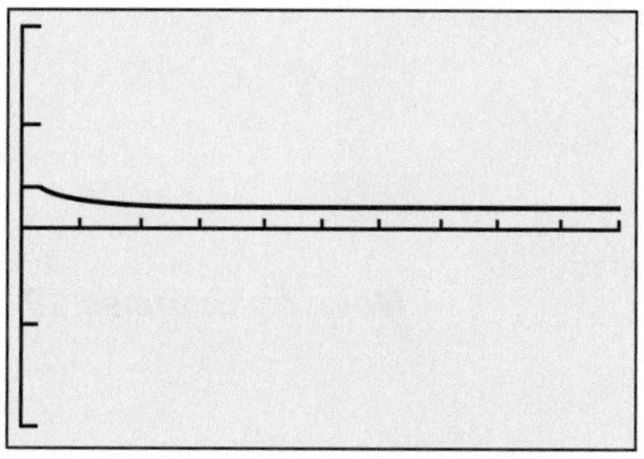

$[0, 1000]$ by $[-2, 2]$

Figure 9.9 A graph of $y = (\ln x)/(2\sqrt{x})$. (Example 5)

EXAMPLE 5 Working with Indeterminate Form ∞/∞

Identify the indeterminate form and evaluate the limit using l'Hôpital's Rule. Support your answer graphically.

$$\lim_{x\to\infty} \frac{\ln x}{2\sqrt{x}}$$

SOLUTION

$$\frac{\infty}{\infty}$$

$$\lim_{x\to\infty} \frac{\ln x}{2\sqrt{x}} = \lim_{x\to\infty} \frac{1/x}{1/\sqrt{x}} = \lim_{x\to\infty} \frac{1}{\sqrt{x}} = 0$$

The graph in Figure 9.9 supports the result. *Now Try Exercise 15.*

We can sometimes handle the indeterminate forms $\infty \cdot 0$ and $\infty - \infty$ by using algebra to get $0/0$ or ∞/∞ instead. Here again we do not mean to suggest that there is a number $\infty \cdot 0$ or $\infty - \infty$ any more than we mean to suggest that there is a number $0/0$ or ∞/∞. These forms are not numbers but descriptions of function behavior.

EXAMPLE 6 Working with Indeterminate Form $\infty \cdot 0$

Find **(a)** $\lim_{x\to\infty}\left(x \sin \frac{1}{x}\right)$ **(b)** $\lim_{x\to-\infty}\left(x \sin \frac{1}{x}\right)$.

SOLUTION

Figure 9.10 suggests that the limits exist.

(a)

$$\lim_{x\to\infty}\left(x \sin \frac{1}{x}\right) \qquad \infty \cdot 0$$

$$= \lim_{h\to 0^+}\left(\frac{1}{h} \sin h\right) \qquad \text{Let } h = 1/x.$$

$$= 1$$

(b) Similarly,

$$\lim_{x\to-\infty}\left(x \sin \frac{1}{x}\right) = 1.$$

Now Try Exercise 17.

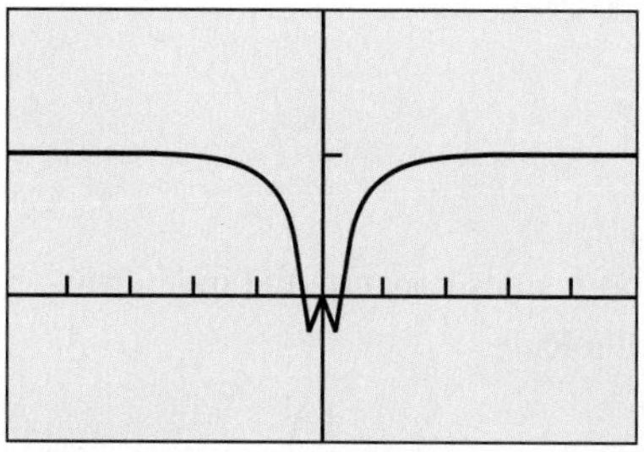

$[-5, 5]$ by $[-1, 2]$

Figure 9.10 The graph of $y = x \sin (1/x)$. (Example 6)

EXAMPLE 7 Working with Indeterminate Form $\infty - \infty$

Find $\lim_{x \to 1} \left(\frac{1}{\ln x} - \frac{1}{x - 1} \right)$.

SOLUTION

Combining the two fractions converts the indeterminate form $\infty - \infty$ to 0/0, to which we can apply l'Hôpital's Rule.

$$\lim_{x \to 1} \left(\frac{1}{\ln x} - \frac{1}{x - 1} \right) \qquad \infty - \infty$$

$$= \lim_{x \to 1} \frac{x - 1 - \ln x}{(x - 1) \ln x} \qquad \text{Now } \frac{0}{0}$$

$$= \lim_{x \to 1} \frac{1 - 1/x}{\frac{x - 1}{x} + \ln x}$$

$$= \lim_{x \to 1} \frac{x - 1}{x \ln x + x - 1} \qquad \text{Still } \frac{0}{0}$$

$$= \lim_{x \to 1} \frac{1}{2 + \ln x}$$

$$= \frac{1}{2}$$

Now Try Exercise 19.

Indeterminate Forms 1^{∞}, 0^0, ∞^0

Limits that lead to the indeterminate forms 1^{∞}, 0^0, and ∞^0 can sometimes be handled by taking logarithms first. We use l'Hôpital's Rule to find the limit of the logarithm and then exponentiate to reveal the original function's behavior.

Since $b = e^{\ln b}$ for every positive number b, we can write $f(x)$ as

$$f(x) = e^{\ln f(x)}$$

for any positive functions $f(x)$.

$$\lim_{x \to a} \ln f(x) = L \quad \Rightarrow \quad \lim_{x \to a} f(x) = \lim_{x \to a} e^{\ln f(x)} = e^L$$

Here a can be finite or infinite.

In Section 1.3 we used graphs and tables to investigate the values of $f(x) = (1 + 1/x)^x$ as $x \to \infty$. Now we find this limit with l'Hôpital's Rule.

EXAMPLE 8 Working with Indeterminate Form 1^{∞}

Find $\lim_{x \to \infty} \left(1 + \frac{1}{x} \right)^x$.

SOLUTION

Let $f(x) = (1 + 1/x)^x$. Then taking logarithms of both sides converts the indeterminate form 1^{∞} to 0/0, to which we can apply l'Hôpital's Rule.

$$\ln f(x) = \ln \left(1 + \frac{1}{x} \right)^x = x \ln \left(1 + \frac{1}{x} \right) = \frac{\ln \left(1 + \frac{1}{x} \right)}{\frac{1}{x}}$$

continued

We apply l'Hôpital's Rule to the previous expression.

$$\lim_{x\to\infty} \ln f(x) = \lim_{x\to\infty} \frac{\ln\left(1+\frac{1}{x}\right)}{\frac{1}{x}} \qquad \frac{0}{0}$$

$$= \lim_{x\to\infty} \frac{\frac{1}{1+\frac{1}{x}}\left(-\frac{1}{x^2}\right)}{-\frac{1}{x^2}} \qquad \text{Differentiate numerator and denominator}$$

$$= \lim_{x\to\infty} \frac{1}{1+\frac{1}{x}} = 1$$

Therefore,

$$\lim_{x\to\infty}\left(1+\frac{1}{x}\right)^x = \lim_{x\to\infty} f(x) = \lim_{x\to\infty} e^{\ln f(x)} = e^1 = e.$$

Now Try Exercise 21.

EXAMPLE 9 Working with Indeterminate Form 0^0

Determine whether $\lim_{x\to 0^+} x^x$ exists and find its value if it does.

SOLUTION

Investigate Graphically Figure 9.11 suggests that the limit exists and has a value near 1.

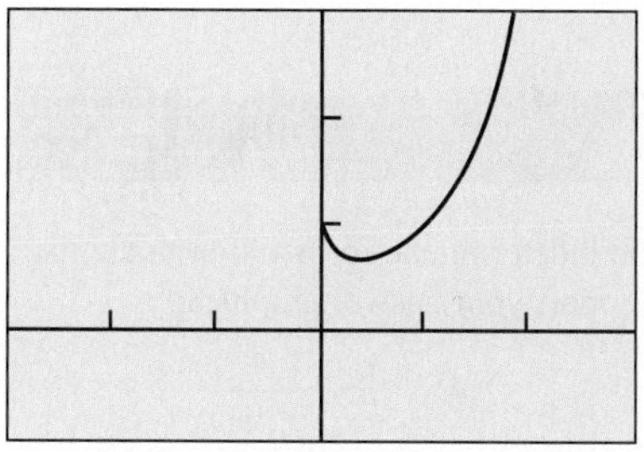

[–3, 3] by [–1, 3]

Figure 9.11 The graph of $y = x^x$. (Example 9)

Solve Analytically The limit leads to the indeterminate form 0^0. To convert the problem to one involving $0/0$, we let $f(x) = x^x$ and take the logarithm of both sides.

$$\ln f(x) = x \ln x = \frac{\ln x}{1/x}$$

Applying l'Hôpital's Rule to $(\ln x/)(1/x)$ we obtain

$$\lim_{x\to 0^+} \ln f(x) = \lim_{x\to 0^+} \frac{\ln x}{1/x} \qquad \frac{-\infty}{\infty}$$

$$= \lim_{x\to 0^+} \frac{1/x}{-1/x^2} \qquad \text{Differentiate.}$$

$$= \lim_{x\to 0^+} (-x) = 0.$$

Therefore,

$$\lim_{x\to 0^+} x^x = \lim_{x\to 0^+} f(x) = \lim_{x\to 0^+} e^{\ln f(x)} = e^0 = 1.$$

Now Try Exercise 23.

EXAMPLE 10 Working with Indeterminate Form ∞^0

Find $\lim_{x\to\infty} x^{1/x}$.

SOLUTION

Let $f(x) = x^{1/x}$. Then

$$\ln f(x) = \frac{\ln x}{x}.$$

continued

Applying l'Hôpital's Rule to $\ln f(x)$ we obtain

$$\begin{aligned}\lim_{x\to\infty} \ln f(x) &= \lim_{x\to\infty} \frac{\ln x}{x} && \frac{\infty}{\infty}\\ &= \lim_{x\to\infty} \frac{1/x}{1} && \text{Differentiate.}\\ &= \lim_{x\to\infty} \frac{1}{x} = 0.\end{aligned}$$

Therefore,

$$\lim_{x\to\infty} x^{1/x} = \lim_{x\to\infty} f(x) = \lim_{x\to\infty} e^{\ln f(x)} = e^0 = 1.$$

Now Try Exercise 25.

Quick Review 9.2 *(For help, go to Sections 2.1 and 2.2.)*

Exercise numbers with a gray background indicate problems that the authors have designed to be solved *without a calculator*

In Exercises 1 and 2, use tables to estimate the value of the limit.

1. $\lim_{x\to\infty} \left(1 + \frac{0.1}{x}\right)^x$ **2.** $\lim_{x\to 0^+} x^{1/(\ln x)}$

In Exercises 3–8, use graphs or tables to estimate the value of the limit.

3. $\lim_{x\to 0^-} \left(1 - \frac{1}{x}\right)^x$ **4.** $\lim_{x\to -1^-} \left(1 + \frac{1}{x}\right)^x$

5. $\lim_{t\to 1} \frac{t-1}{\sqrt{t}-1}$ **6.** $\lim_{x\to\infty} \frac{\sqrt{4x^2+1}}{x+1}$

7. $\lim_{x\to 0} \frac{\sin 3x}{x}$ **8.** $\lim_{\theta\to\pi/2} \frac{\tan\theta}{2+\tan\theta}$

In Exercises 9 and 10, substitute $x = 1/h$ to express y as a function of h.

9. $y = x \sin \frac{1}{x}$ **10.** $y = \left(1 + \frac{1}{x}\right)^x$

Section 9.2 Exercises

In Exercises 1–4, estimate the limit graphically and then use l'Hôpital's Rule to find the limit.

1. $\lim_{x\to 2} \frac{x-2}{x^2-4}$ **2.** $\lim_{x\to 0} \frac{\sin(5x)}{x}$

3. $\lim_{x\to 2} \frac{\sqrt{2+x}-2}{x-2}$ **4.** $\lim_{x\to 1} \frac{\sqrt[3]{x}-1}{x-1}$

In Exercises 5–8, apply the stronger form of l'Hôpital's Rule to find the limit.

5. $\lim_{x\to 0} \frac{1-\cos x}{x^2}$ **6.** $\lim_{\theta\to\pi/2} \frac{1-\sin\theta}{1+\cos(2\theta)}$

7. $\lim_{t\to 0} \frac{\cos t - 1}{e^t - t - 1}$ **8.** $\lim_{x\to 2} \frac{x^2-4x+4}{x^3-12x+16}$

In Exercises 9–12, use l'Hôpital's Rule to evaluate the one-sided limits. Support your answer graphically.

9. (a) $\lim_{x\to 0^-} \frac{\sin 4x}{\sin 2x}$ **(b)** $\lim_{x\to 0^+} \frac{\sin 4x}{\sin 2x}$

10. (a) $\lim_{x\to 0^-} \frac{\tan x}{x}$ **(b)** $\lim_{x\to 0^+} \frac{\tan x}{x}$

11. (a) $\lim_{x\to 0^-} \frac{\sin x}{x^3}$ **(b)** $\lim_{x\to 0^+} \frac{\sin x}{x^3}$

12. (a) $\lim_{x\to 0^-} \frac{\tan x}{x^2}$ **(b)** $\lim_{x\to 0^+} \frac{\tan x}{x^2}$

In Exercises 13–16, identify the indeterminate form and evaluate the limit using l'Hôpital's Rule. Support your answer graphically.

13. $\lim_{x\to\pi} \frac{\csc x}{1+\cot x}$ **14.** $\lim_{x\to\pi/2} \frac{1+\sec x}{\tan x}$

15. $\lim_{x\to\infty} \frac{\ln(x+1)}{\log_2 x}$

16. $\lim_{x\to\infty} \frac{5x^2-3x}{7x^2+1}$

In Exercises 17–26, identify the indeterminate form and evaluate the limit using l'Hôpital's Rule.

17. $\lim_{x\to 0^+} (x \ln x)$ **18.** $\lim_{x\to\infty} \left(x \tan \frac{1}{x}\right)$

19. $\lim_{x\to 0^+} (\csc x - \cot x + \cos x)$ **20.** $\lim_{x\to\infty} (\ln(2x) - \ln(x+1))$

21. $\lim_{x\to 0} (e^x + x)^{1/x}$ **22.** $\lim_{x\to 1} x^{1/(x-1)}$

23. $\lim_{x\to 1} (x^2 - 2x + 1)^{x-1}$ **24.** $\lim_{x\to 0^+} (\sin x)^x$

25. $\lim_{x\to 0^+} \left(1 + \frac{1}{x}\right)^x$ **26.** $\lim_{x\to\infty} (\ln x)^{1/x}$

In Exercises 27 and 28, **(a)** complete the table and estimate the limit. **(b)** Use l'Hôpital's Rule to confirm your estimate.

27. $\lim_{x\to\infty} f(x),\ f(x) = \frac{\ln x^5}{x}$

x	10	10^2	10^3	10^4	10^5
$f(x)$					

28. $\lim_{x\to 0^+} f(x),\ f(x) = \dfrac{x - \sin x}{x^3}$

x	10^0	10^{-1}	10^{-2}	10^{-3}	10^{-4}
$f(x)$					

In Exercises 29–32, use tables to estimate the limit. Confirm your estimate using l'Hôpital's Rule.

29. $\lim_{\theta\to 0} \dfrac{\sin 3\theta}{\sin 4\theta}$

30. $\lim_{t\to 0}\left(\dfrac{1}{\sin t} - \dfrac{1}{t}\right)$

31. $\lim_{x\to\infty} (1 + x)^{1/x}$

32. $\lim_{x\to\infty} \dfrac{x - 2x^2}{3x^2 + 5x}$

In Exercises 33–52, use l'Hôpital's Rule to evaluate the limit.

33. $\lim_{\theta\to 0} \dfrac{\sin \theta^2}{\theta}$

34. $\lim_{t\to 1} \dfrac{t - 1}{\ln t - \sin \pi t}$

35. $\lim_{x\to\infty} \dfrac{\log_2 x}{\log_3 (x + 3)}$

36. $\lim_{y\to 0^+} \dfrac{\ln (y^2 + 2y)}{\ln y}$

37. $\lim_{y\to\pi/2}\left(\dfrac{\pi}{2} - y\right)\tan y$

38. $\lim_{x\to 0^+} (\ln x - \ln \sin x)$

39. $\lim_{x\to 0^+}\left(\dfrac{1}{x} - \dfrac{1}{\sqrt{x}}\right)$

40. $\lim_{x\to 0}\left(\dfrac{1}{x^2}\right)^x$

41. $\lim_{x\to\pm\infty} \dfrac{3x - 5}{2x^2 - x + 2}$

42. $\lim_{x\to 0} \dfrac{\sin 7x}{\tan 11x}$

43. $\lim_{x\to\infty} (1 + 2x)^{1/(2 \ln x)}$

44. $\lim_{x\to(\pi/2)^-} (\cos x)^{\cos x}$

45. $\lim_{x\to 0^+} (1 + x)^{1/x}$

46. $\lim_{x\to 0^+} (\sin x)^{\tan x}$

47. $\lim_{x\to 1^+} x^{1/(1-x)}$

48. $\lim_{x\to\infty} \displaystyle\int_x^{2x} \frac{dt}{t}$

49. $\lim_{x\to 1} \dfrac{x^3 - 1}{4x^3 - x - 3}$

50. $\lim_{x\to\infty} \dfrac{2x^2 + 3x}{x^3 + x + 1}$

51. $\lim_{x\to 1} \dfrac{\int_1^x \cos t\, dt}{x^2 - 1}$

52. $\lim_{x\to 1} \dfrac{\int_1^x \frac{dt}{t}}{x^3 - 1}$

Group Activity In Exercises 53 and 54, do the following.

(a) Writing to Learn Explain why l'Hôpital's Rule does not help you to find the limit.

(b) Use a graph to estimate the limit.

(c) Evaluate the limit analytically, using the techniques of Chapter 2.

53. $\lim_{x\to\infty} \dfrac{\sqrt{9x + 1}}{\sqrt{x + 1}}$

54. $\lim_{x\to\pi/2} \dfrac{\sec x}{\tan x}$

55. ***Continuous Extension*** Find a value of c that makes the function

$$f(x) = \begin{cases} \dfrac{9x - 3 \sin 3x}{5x^3}, & x \neq 0 \\ c, & x = 0 \end{cases}$$

continuous at $x = 0$. Explain why your value of c works.

56. ***Continuous Extension*** Let $f(x) = |x|^x,\ x \neq 0$. Show that f has a removable discontinuity at $x = 0$ and extend the definition of f to $x = 0$ so that the extended function is continuous there.

57. ***Interest Compounded Continuously***

(a) Show that $\lim_{k\to\infty} A_0\left(1 + \dfrac{r}{k}\right)^{kt} = A_0 e^{rt}$.

(b) Writing to Learn Explain how the limit in part (a) connects interest compounded k times per year with interest compounded continuously.

58. ***L'Hôpital's Rule*** Let

$$f(x) = \begin{cases} x + 2, & x \neq 0 \\ 0, & x = 0 \end{cases} \quad \text{and} \quad g(x) = \begin{cases} x + 1, & x \neq 0 \\ 0, & x = 0. \end{cases}$$

(a) Show that

$$\lim_{x\to 0} \frac{f'(x)}{g'(x)} = 1 \quad \text{but} \quad \lim_{x\to 0} \frac{f(x)}{g(x)} = 2.$$

(b) Writing to Learn Explain why this does not contradict l'Hôpital's Rule.

59. ***Solid of Revolution*** Let $A(t)$ be the area of the region in the first quadrant enclosed by the coordinate axes, the curve $y = e^{-x}$, and the line $x = t > 0$ as shown in the figure. Let $V(t)$ be the volume of the solid generated by revolving the region about the x-axis. Find the following limits.

(a) $\lim_{t\to\infty} A(t)$ **(b)** $\lim_{t\to\infty} \dfrac{V(t)}{A(t)}$ **(c)** $\lim_{t\to 0^+} \dfrac{V(t)}{A(t)}$

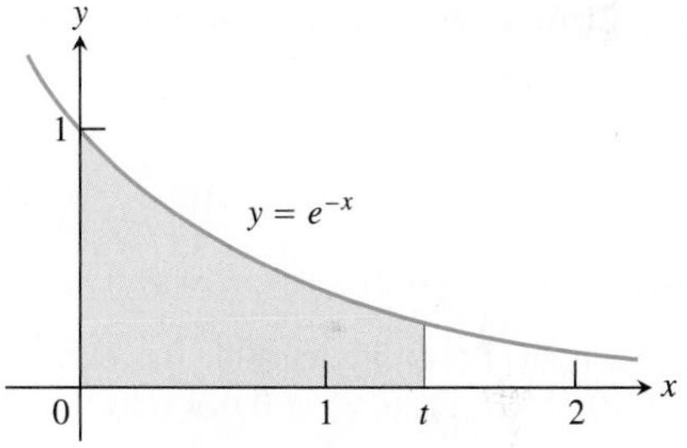

60. ***L'Hôpital's Trap*** Let $f(x) = \dfrac{1 - \cos x}{x + x^2}$.

(a) Use graphs or tables to estimate $\lim_{x\to 0} f(x)$.

(b) Find the error in the following incorrect application of l'Hôpital's Rule.

$$\lim_{x\to 0} \frac{1 - \cos x}{x + x^2} = \lim_{x\to 0} \frac{\sin x}{1 + 2x} = \lim_{x\to 0} \frac{\cos x}{2} = \frac{1}{2}$$

61. ***Exponential Functions*** **(a)** Use the equation

$$a^x = e^{x \ln a}$$

to find the domain of

$$f(x) = \left(1 + \frac{1}{x}\right)^x.$$

(b) Find $\lim_{x\to -1^-} f(x)$.

(c) Find $\lim_{x\to -\infty} f(x)$.

Standardized Test Questions

62. True or False If $f(a) = g(a) = 0$ and $f'(a)$ and $g'(a)$ exist, then

$\lim_{x \to a} \frac{f(x)}{g(x)} = \frac{f'(a)}{g'a}$. Justify your answer.

63. True or False $\lim_{x \to 0^+} x^x$ does not exist. Justify your answer.

64. Multiple Choice Which of the following gives the value of

$$\lim_{x \to 0} \frac{x}{\tan x}?$$

(A) -1 (B) 0 (C) 1 (D) π (E) Does not exist

65. Multiple Choice Which of the following gives the value of

$$\lim_{x \to 1} \frac{1 - \frac{1}{x}}{1 - \frac{1}{x^2}}?$$

(A) Does not exist (B) 2 (C) 1 (D) 1/2 (E) 0

66. Multiple Choice Which of the following gives the value of

$$\lim_{x \to \infty} \frac{\log_2 x}{\log_3 x}?$$

(A) 1 (B) $\frac{\ln 3}{\ln 2}$ (C) $\frac{\ln 2}{\ln 3}$ (D) $\ln\left(\frac{3}{2}\right)$ (E) $\ln\left(\frac{2}{3}\right)$

67. Multiple Choice Which of the following gives the value of

$$\lim_{x \to \infty} \left(1 + \frac{1}{x}\right)^{3x}?$$

(A) 0 (B) 1 (C) e (D) e^2 (E) e^3

Explorations

68. Give an example of two differentiable functions f and g with $\lim_{x \to 3} f(x) = \lim_{x \to 3} g(x) = 0$ that satisfy the following.

(a) $\lim_{x \to 3} \frac{f(x)}{g(x)} = 7$ (b) $\lim_{x \to 3} \frac{f(x)}{g(x)} = 0$

(c) $\lim_{x \to 3} \frac{f(x)}{g(x)} = \infty$

69. Give an example of two differentiable functions f and g with $\lim_{x \to \infty} f(x) = \lim_{x \to \infty} g(x) = \infty$ that satisfy the following.

(a) $\lim_{x \to \infty} \frac{f(x)}{g(x)} = 3$ (b) $\lim_{x \to \infty} \frac{f(x)}{g(x)} = 0$

(c) $\lim_{x \to \infty} \frac{f(x)}{g(x)} = \infty$

Extending the Ideas

70. *Grapher Precision* Let $f(x) = \frac{1 - \cos x^6}{x^{12}}$.

(a) Explain why some graphs of f may give false information about $\lim_{x \to 0} f(x)$. (*Hint:* Try the window $[-1, 1]$ by $[-0.5, 1]$.)

(b) Explain why tables may give false information about $\lim_{x \to 0} f(x)$. (*Hint:* Try tables with increments of 0.01.)

(c) Use l'Hôpital's Rule to find $\lim_{x \to 0} f(x)$.

(d) **Writing to Learn** This is an example of a function for which graphers do not have enough precision to give reliable information. Explain this statement in your own words.

71. *Cauchy's Mean Value Theorem* Suppose that functions f and g are continuous on $[a, b]$ and differentiable throughout (a, b) and suppose also that $g' \neq 0$ throughout (a, b). Then there exists a number c in (a, b) at which

$$\frac{f'(c)}{g'(c)} = \frac{f(b) - f(a)}{g(b) - g(a)}.$$

Find all values of c in (a, b) that satisfy this property for the following given functions and intervals.

(a) $f(x) = x^3 + 1$, $g(x) = x^2 - x$, $[a, b] = [-1, 1]$

(b) $f(x) = \cos x$, $g(x) = \sin x$, $[a, b] = [0, \pi/2]$

72. *Why 0^∞ and $0^{-\infty}$ Are Not Indeterminate Forms* Assume that $f(x)$ is nonnegative in an open interval containing c and $\lim_{x \to 0} f(x) = 0$.

(a) If $\lim_{x \to c} g(x) = \infty$, show that $\lim_{x \to c} f(x)^{g(x)} = 0$.

(b) If $\lim_{x \to c} g(x) = -\infty$, show that $\lim_{x \to c} f(x)^{g(x)} = \infty$.

Quick Quiz for AP* Preparation: Sections 9.1 and 9.2

1. Multiple Choice Which of the following gives the value of

$$\lim_{x \to 0} \frac{(x + 1)^{4/3} - (4/3)x - 1}{x^2}?$$

(A) $-1/3$ (B) 0 (C) $2/9$
(D) $4/9$ (E) Does not exist

2. Multiple Choice Which of the following gives the value of $\lim_{x \to 0^+} (3x^{2x})$?

(A) 0 (B) 1 (C) 2
(D) 3 (E) Does not exist

3. Multiple Choice Which of the following gives the value of

$$\lim_{x \to 2} \frac{\int_2^x \sin t \, dt}{x^2 - 4}$$

(A) $-\frac{\sin 2}{4}$ (B) $\frac{\sin 2}{4}$ (C) $-\frac{\sin 2}{4}$
(D) $\frac{\sin 2}{4}$ (E) Does not exist

4. Free Response The second and fifth terms of a geometric sequence are -4 and $1/2$, respectively. Find

(a) the first term, (b) the common ratio,

(c) an explicit rule for the nth term, and

(d) a recursive rule for the nth term.

9.3 Relative Rates of Growth

What you will learn about . . .

- Comparing Rates of Growth
- Using L'Hôpital's Rule to Compare Growth Rates
- Sequential Versus Binary Search

and why . . .

Understanding growth rates as $x \to \infty$ is an important feature in understanding the behavior of functions.

$y = e^x$
$y = \ln x$
$y = x$

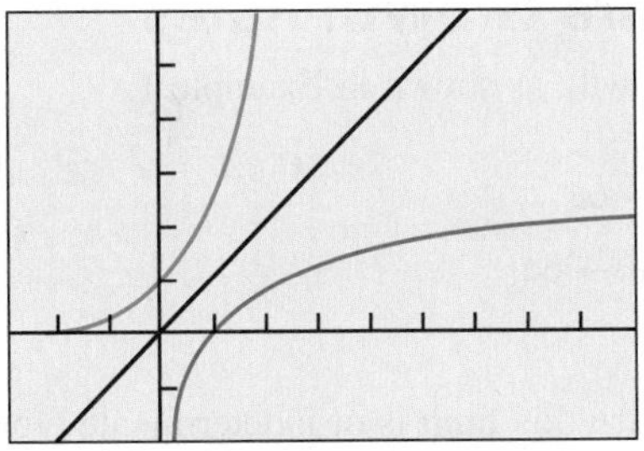

[–3, 9] by [–2, 6]

Figure 9.12 The graphs of $y = e^x$, $y = \ln x$, and $y = x$.

Comparing Rates of Growth

We restrict our attention to functions whose values eventually become and remain positive as $x \to \infty$.

The exponential function e^x grows so rapidly and the logarithm function $\ln x$ grows so slowly that they set standards by which we can judge the growth of other functions. The graphs (Figure 9.12) of e^x, $\ln x$, and x suggest how rapidly and slowly e^x and $\ln x$, respectively, grow in comparison to x.

In fact, all the functions a^x, $a > 1$, grow faster (eventually) than any power of x, even $x^{1{,}000{,}000}$ (Exercise 39), and hence faster (eventually) than any polynomial function.

To get a feeling for how rapidly the values of e^x grow with increasing x, think of graphing the function on a large blackboard, with the axes scaled in centimeters. At $x = 1$ cm, the graph is $e^1 \approx 3$ cm above the x-axis. At $x = 6$ cm, the graph is $e^6 \approx 403$ cm ≈ 4 m high. (It is about to go through the ceiling if it hasn't done so already.) At $x = 10$ cm, the graph is $e^{10} \approx 22{,}026$ cm ≈ 220 m high, higher than most buildings. At $x = 24$ cm, the graph is more than halfway to the moon, and at $x = 43$ cm from the origin, the graph is high enough to reach well past the sun's closest stellar neighbor, the red dwarf star Proxima Centauri:

$$\begin{aligned} e^{43} &\approx 4.7 \times 10^{18} \text{ cm} \\ &= 4.7 \times 10^{13} \text{ km} \\ &\approx 1.57 \times 10^{8} \text{ light-seconds} \\ &\approx 5.0 \text{ light-years} \end{aligned}$$

Light travels about 300,000 km/sec in a vacuum.

The distance to Proxima Centauri is 4.2 light-years. Yet with $x = 43$ cm from the origin, the graph is still less than 2 feet to the right of the y-axis.

In contrast, the logarithm function $\ln x$ grows more slowly as $x \to \infty$ than any positive power of x, even $x^{1/1{,}000{,}000}$ (Exercise 41). Because $\ln x$ and e^x are inverse functions, the calculations above show that with axes scaled in centimeters, you have to go nearly 5 light-years out on the x-axis to find where the graph of $\ln x$ is even 43 cm high.

In fact, all the functions $\log_a x$, $a > 1$, grow slower (eventually) than any positive power of x.

These comparisons of exponential, polynomial, and logarithmic functions can be made precise by defining what it means for a function $f(x)$ to *grow faster* than another function $g(x)$ as $x \to \infty$.

DEFINITIONS Faster, Slower, Same-Rate Growth as $x \to \infty$

Let $f(x)$ and $g(x)$ be positive for x sufficiently large.

1. f **grows faster** than g (and g **grows slower** than f) as $x \to \infty$ if

$$\lim_{x\to\infty} \frac{f(x)}{g(x)} = \infty, \quad \text{or, equivalently, if} \quad \lim_{x\to\infty} \frac{g(x)}{f(x)} = 0.$$

2. f and g **grow at the same rate** as $x \to \infty$ if

$$\lim_{x\to\infty} \frac{f(x)}{g(x)} = L \neq 0.$$

L finite and not zero

According to these definitions, $y = 2x$ does not grow faster than $y = x$ as $x \to \infty$. The two functions grow at the same rate because

$$\lim_{x\to\infty} \frac{2x}{x} = \lim_{x\to\infty} 2 = 2,$$

Grace Murray Hopper (1906–1992)

Computer scientists use function comparisons like the ones in this section to measure the relative efficiencies of computer programs. The pioneering work of Rear Admiral Grace Murray Hopper in the field of computer technology led the navy, and the country, into the computer age. Hopper graduated from Yale in 1934 with a Ph.D. in Mathematics. During World War II she joined the navy and became director of a project that resulted in the development of COBOL, a computer language that enabled computers to "talk to one another." On September 6, 1997, the navy commissioned a multi-mission ship the USS *Hopper*.

which is a finite nonzero limit. The reason for this apparent disregard of common sense is that we want "f grows faster than g" to mean that for large x-values, g is negligible in comparison to f.

If $L = 1$ in part 2 of the definition, then f and g are right end behavior models for each other (Section 2.2). If f grows faster than g, then

$$\lim_{x\to\infty} \frac{f(x) + g(x)}{f(x)} = \lim_{x\to\infty}\left(1 + \frac{g(x)}{f(x)}\right) = 1 + 0 = 1,$$

so f is a right end behavior model for $f + g$. Thus, for large x-values, g can be ignored in the sum $f + g$. This explains why, for large x-values, we can ignore the terms

$$g(x) = a_{n-1}x^{n-1} + \cdots + a_0$$

in

$$f(x) = a_n x^n + a_{n-1}x^{n-1} + \cdots + a_0;$$

that is, why $a_n x^n$ is an end behavior model for

$$a_n x^n + a_{n-1}x^{n-1} + \cdots + a_0.$$

Using L'Hôpital's Rule to Compare Growth Rates

L'Hôpital's Rule can help us to compare rates of growth, as shown in Example 1.

EXAMPLE 1 Comparing e^x and x^2 as $x \to \infty$

Show that the function e^x grows faster than x^2 as $x \to \infty$.

SOLUTION

We need to show that $\lim_{x\to\infty} (e^x/x^2) = \infty$. Notice this limit is of indeterminate type ∞/∞, so we can apply l'Hôpital's Rule and take the derivative of the numerator and the derivative of the denominator. In fact, we have to apply l'Hôpital's Rule twice.

$$\lim_{x\to\infty} \frac{e^x}{x^2} = \lim_{x\to\infty} \frac{e^x}{2x} = \lim_{x\to\infty} \frac{e^x}{1} = \infty$$

Now Try Exercise 1.

EXPLORATION 1 Comparing Rates of Growth as $x \to \infty$

1. Show that a^x, $a > 1$, grows faster than x^2 as $x \to \infty$.
2. Show that 3^x grows faster than 2^x as $x \to \infty$.
3. If $a > b > 1$, show that a^x grows faster than b^x as $x \to \infty$.

EXAMPLE 2 Comparing ln x with x and x^2 as $x \to \infty$

Show that ln x grows slower than **(a)** x and **(b)** x^2 as $x \to \infty$.

SOLUTION

(a) Solve Analytically

$$\lim_{x\to\infty} \frac{\ln x}{x} = \lim_{x\to\infty} \frac{1/x}{1} \quad \text{l'Hôpital's Rule}$$

$$= \lim_{x\to\infty} \frac{1}{x} = 0$$

continued

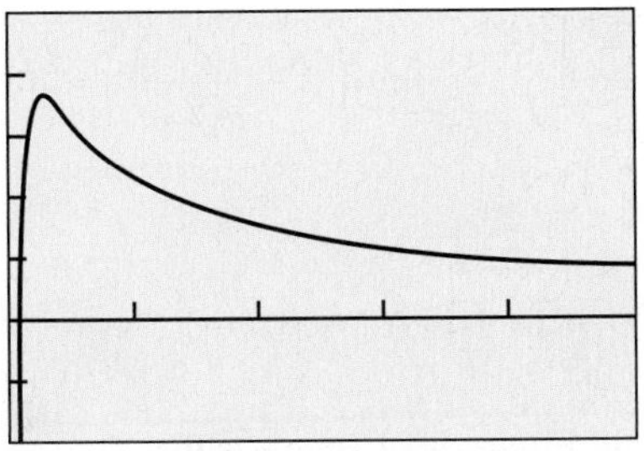

[0, 50] by [–0.2, 0.5]

Figure 9.13 The x-axis is a horizontal asymptote of the function $f(x) = (\ln x)/x$. (Example 2)

Support Graphically Figure 9.13 suggests that the graph of the function $f(x) = (\ln x)/x$ drops dramatically toward the x-axis as x outstrips $\ln x$.

(b) $$\lim_{x\to\infty} \frac{\ln x}{x^2} = \lim_{x\to\infty}\left(\frac{\ln x}{x}\cdot\frac{1}{x}\right) = 0\cdot 0 = 0$$

Now Try Exercise 5.

EXAMPLE 3 Comparing x with $x + \sin x$ as $x \to \infty$

Show that x grows at the same rate as $x + \sin x$ as $x \to \infty$.

SOLUTION

We need to show that $\lim_{x\to\infty} ((x + \sin x)/x)$ is finite and not 0. The limit can be computed directly.

$$\lim_{x\to\infty} \frac{x + \sin x}{x} = \lim_{x\to\infty}\left(1 + \frac{\sin x}{x}\right) = 1$$

Now Try Exercise 9.

EXAMPLE 4 Comparing Logarithmic Functions as $x \to \infty$

Let a and b be numbers greater than 1. Show that $\log_a x$ and $\log_b x$ grow at the same rate as $x \to \infty$.

SOLUTION

$$\lim_{x\to\infty} \frac{\log_a x}{\log_b x} = \lim_{x\to\infty} \frac{\ln x/\ln a}{\ln x/\ln b} = \frac{\ln b}{\ln a}$$

The limiting value is finite and nonzero. *Now Try Exercise 13.*

Growing at the same rate is a *transitive relation.*

Transitivity of Growing Rates

If f grows at the same rate as g as $x \to \infty$ and g grows at the same rate as h as $x \to \infty$, then f grows at the same rate as h as $x \to \infty$.

The reason is that

$$\lim_{x\to\infty} \frac{f}{g} = L \quad \text{and} \quad \lim_{x\to\infty} \frac{g}{h} = M$$

together imply that

$$\lim_{x\to\infty} \frac{f}{h} = \lim_{x\to\infty}\left(\frac{f}{g}\cdot\frac{g}{h}\right) = LM.$$

If L and M are finite and nonzero, then so is LM.

EXAMPLE 5 Growing at the Same Rate as $x \to \infty$

Show that $f(x) = \sqrt{x^2 + 5}$ and $g(x) = (2\sqrt{x} - 1)^2$ grow at the same rate as $x \to \infty$.

SOLUTION

Solve Analytically We show that f and g grow at the same rate by showing that they both grow at the same rate as $h(x) = x$.

$$\lim_{x\to\infty} \frac{f(x)}{h(x)} = \lim_{x\to\infty} \frac{\sqrt{x^2 + 5}}{x} = \lim_{x\to\infty} \sqrt{1 + \frac{5}{x^2}} = 1$$

and

continued

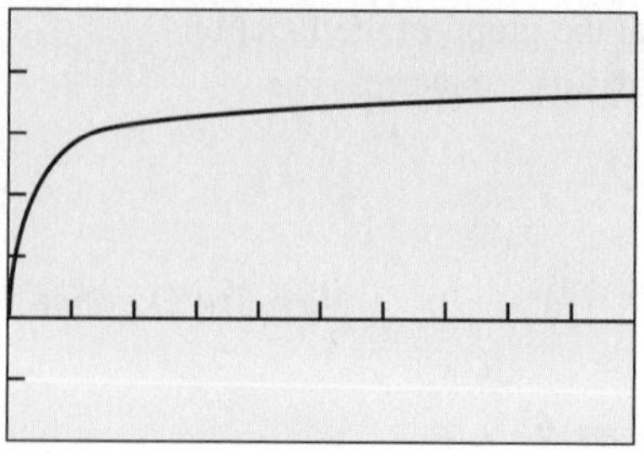

[0, 100] by [–2, 5]

Figure 9.14 The graph of g/f appears to have the line $y = 4$ as a horizontal asymptote. (Example 5)

$$\lim_{x\to\infty}\frac{g(x)}{h(x)} = \lim_{x\to\infty}\frac{(2\sqrt{x}-1)^2}{x} = \lim_{x\to\infty}\left(\frac{2\sqrt{x}-1}{\sqrt{x}}\right)^2 = \lim_{x\to\infty}\left(2-\frac{1}{\sqrt{x}}\right)^2 = 4$$

Thus,

$$\lim_{x\to\infty}\frac{f}{g} = \lim_{x\to\infty}\left(\frac{f}{h}\cdot\frac{h}{g}\right) = 1\cdot\frac{1}{4} = \frac{1}{4},$$

and f and g grow at the same rate as $x \to \infty$.

Support Graphically The graph of $y = g/f$ in Figure 9.14 suggests that the quotient g/f is an increasing function with horizontal asymptote $y = 4$. This supports that f and g grow at the same rate.

Now Try Exercise 31.

Sequential Versus Binary Search

Computer scientists sometimes measure the efficiency of an algorithm by counting the number of steps a computer must take to make the algorithm do something (Figure 9.15). (Your graphing calculator works according to algorithms programmed into it.) There can be significant differences in how efficiently algorithms perform, even if they are designed to accomplish the same task. Here is an example.

Webster's *Third New International Dictionary* lists about 26,000 words that begin with the letter *a*. One way to look up a word, or to learn if it is not there, is to read through the list one word at a time until you either find the word or determine that it is not there. This **sequential search** method makes no particular use of the words' alphabetical arrangement. You are sure to get an answer, but it might take about 26,000 steps.

Note

You would not use a sequential search method to find a word, but you might program a computer to search for a word using this technique.

Another way to find the word or to learn that it is not there is to go straight to the middle of the list (give or take a few words). If you do not find the word, then go to the middle of the half that would contain it and forget about the half that would not. (You know which half would contain it because you know the list is ordered alphabetically.) This **binary search** method eliminates roughly 13,000 words in this first step. If you do not find the word on the second try, then jump to the middle of the half that would contain it. Continue this way until you have found the word or divided the list in half so many times that there are no words left. How many times do you have to divide the list to find the word or learn that it is not there? At most 15, because

$$\frac{26{,}000}{2^{15}} < 1.$$

This certainly beats a possible 26,000 steps.

For a list of length n, a sequential search algorithm takes on the order of n steps to find a word or determine that it is not in the list.

Figure 9.15 Computer scientists look for the most efficient algorithms when they program searches.

EXAMPLE 6 Finding the Order of a Binary Search

For a list of length n, how many steps are required for a binary search?

SOLUTION

A binary search takes on the order of $\log_2 n$ steps. The reason is if $2^{m-1} < n \le 2^m$, then $m - 1 < \log_2 n \le m$, and the number of bisections required to narrow the list to one word will be at most m, the smallest integer greater than or equal to $\log_2 n$.

Now Try Exercise 43.

On a list of length n, there is a big difference between a sequential search (order n) and a binary search (order $\log_2 n$) because n grows faster than $\log_2 n$ as $n \to \infty$. In fact,

$$\lim_{n\to\infty}\frac{n}{\log_2 n} = \lim_{n\to\infty}\frac{1}{1/(n\ln 2)} = \infty.$$

Quick Review 9.3 *(For help, go to Sections 2.2 and 5.1.)*

Exercise numbers with a gray background indicate problems that the authors have designed to be solved *without a calculator.*

In Exercises 1–4, evaluate the limit.

1. $\lim_{x\to\infty} \frac{\ln x}{e^x}$ **2.** $\lim_{x\to\infty} \frac{e^x}{x^3}$

3. $\lim_{x\to-\infty} \frac{x^2}{e^{2x}}$ **4.** $\lim_{x\to\infty} \frac{x^2}{e^{2x}}$

In Exercises 5 and 6, find an end behavior model (Section 2.2) for the function.

5. $f(x) = -3x^4 + 5x^3 - x + 1$

6. $f(x) = \frac{2x^3 - 3x + 1}{x + 2}$

In Exercises 7 and 8, show that g is a right end behavior model for f.

7. $g(x) = x, \quad f(x) = x + \ln x$

8. $g(x) = 2x, \quad f(x) = \sqrt{4x^2 + 5x}$

9. Let $f(x) = \frac{e^x + x^2}{e^x}$. Find the

(a) local extreme values of f and where they occur.

(b) intervals on which f is increasing.

(c) intervals on which f is decreasing.

10. Let $f(x) = \frac{x + \sin x}{x}$.

Find the absolute maximum value of f and where it occurs.

Section 9.3 Exercises

In Exercises 1–4, show that e^x grows faster than the given function.

1. $x^3 - 3x + 1$ **2.** x^{20}

3. $e^{\cos x}$ **4.** $(5/2)^x$

In Exercises 5–8, show that $\ln x$ grows slower than the given function.

5. $x - \ln x$ **6.** $\sqrt{x}$

7. $\sqrt[3]{x}$ **8.** x^3

In Exercises 9–12, show that x^2 grows at the same rate as the given function.

9. $x^2 + 4x$ **10.** $\sqrt{x^4 + 5x}$

11. $\sqrt[3]{x^6 + x^2}$ **12.** $x^2 + \sin x$

In Exercises 13 and 14, show that the two functions grow at the same rate.

13. $\ln x, \log \sqrt{x}$ **14.** e^{x+1}, e^x

In Exercises 15–20, determine whether the function grows faster than e^x, at the same rate as e^x, or slower than e^x as $x \to \infty$.

15. $\sqrt{1 + x^4}$ **16.** 4^x

17. $x \ln x - x$ **18.** xe^x

19. x^{1000} **20.** $(e^x + e^{-x})/2$

In Exercises 21–24, determine whether the function grows faster than x^2, at the same rate as x^2, or slower than x^2 as $x \to \infty$.

21. $x^3 + 3$ **22.** $15x + 3$

23. $\ln x$ **24.** 2^x

In Exercises 25–28, determine whether the function grows faster than $\ln x$, at the same rate as $\ln x$, or slower than $\ln x$ as $x \to \infty$.

25. $\log_2 x^2$ **26.** $1/\sqrt{x}$

27. e^{-x} **28.** $5 \ln x$

In Exercises 29 and 30, order the functions from slowest-growing to fastest-growing as $x \to \infty$.

29. $e^x, \quad x^x, \quad (\ln x)^x, \quad e^{x/2}$

30. $2^x, \quad x^2, \quad (\ln 2)^x, \quad e^x$

In Exercises 31–34, show that the three functions grow at the same rate as $x \to \infty$.

31. $f_1(x) = \sqrt{x}, \quad f_2(x) = \sqrt{10x + 1}, \quad f_3(x) = \sqrt{x + 1}$

32. $f_1(x) = x^2, \quad f_2(x) = \sqrt{x^4 + x}, \quad f_3(x) = \sqrt{x^4 - x^3}$

33. $f_1(x) = 3^x, \quad f_2(x) = \sqrt{9^x + 2^x}, \quad f_3(x) = \sqrt{9^x - 4^x}$

34. $f_1(x) = x^3, \quad f_2(x) = \frac{x^4 + 2x^2 - 1}{x + 1}, \quad f_3(x) = \frac{2x^5 - 1}{x^2 + 1}$

In Exercises 35–38, only one of the following is true.

i. f grows faster than g.

ii. g grows faster than f.

iii. f and g grow at the same rate.

Use the given graph of f/g to determine which one is true.

35.

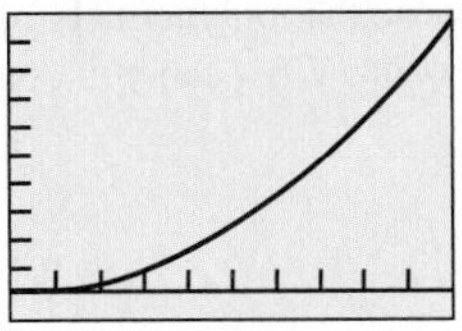

[0, 100] by [–1000, 10000]

36.

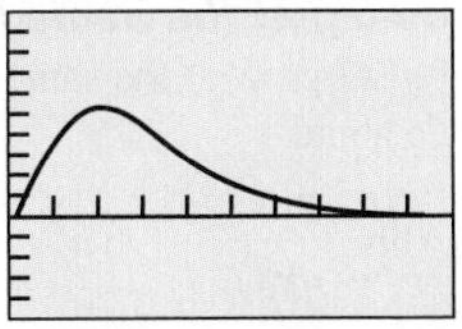

[0, 10] by [–0.5, 1]

37.

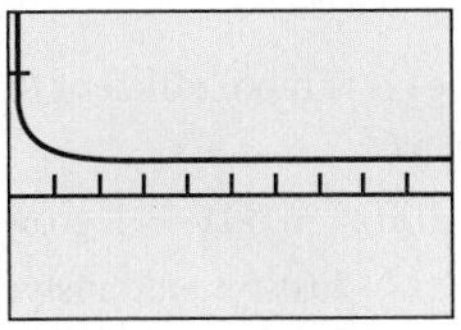

[0, 100] by [–1, 1.5]

38.

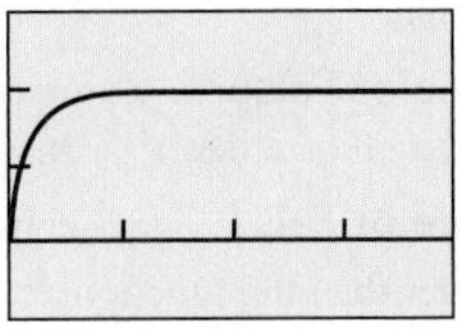

[0, 20] by [–1, 3]

Group Activity In Exercises 39–41, do the following comparisons.

39. ***Comparing Exponential and Power Functions***

(a) Writing to Learn Explain why e^x grows faster than x^n as $x \to \infty$ for any positive integer n, even $n = 1{,}000{,}000$. (*Hint:* What is the nth derivative of x^n?)

(b) Writing to Learn Explain why a^x, $a > 1$, grows faster than x^n as $x \to \infty$ for any positive integer n.

40. *Comparing Exponential and Polynomial Functions*

(a) Writing to Learn Show that e^x grows faster than any polynomial

$$a_n x^n + a_{n-1}x^{n-1} + \cdots + a_1 x + a_0,\ a_n > 0,$$

as $x \to \infty$. Explain.

(b) Writing to Learn Show that a^x, $a > 1$, grows faster than any polynomial

$$a_n x^n + a_{n-1}x^{n-1} + \cdots + a_1 x + a_0,\ a_n > 0,$$

as $x \to \infty$. Explain.

41. *Comparing Logarithm and Power Functions*

(a) Writing to Learn Show that $\ln x$ grows slower than $x^{1/n}$ as $x \to \infty$ for any positive integer n, even $n = 1{,}000{,}000$. Explain.

(b) Writing to Learn Show that for any number $a > 0$, $\ln x$ grows slower than x^a as $x \to \infty$. Explain.

42. *Comparing Logarithm and Polynomial Functions* Show that $\ln x$ grows slower than any nonconstant polynomial

$$a_n x^n + a_{n-1}x^{n-1} + \cdots + a_1 x + a_0,\ a_n > 0,$$

as $x \to \infty$.

43. *Search Algorithms* Suppose you have three different algorithms for solving the same problem and each algorithm provides for a number of steps that is of order of one of the functions listed here.

$$n \log_2 n,\ n^{3/2},\ n(\log_2 n)^2$$

Which of the algorithms is likely the most efficient in the long run? Give reasons for your answer.

44. *Sequential and Binary Search* Suppose you are looking for an item in an ordered list one million items long. How many steps might it take to find the item with **(a)** a sequential search? **(b)** a binary search?

45. *Growing at the Same Rate* Suppose that polynomials $p(x)$ and $q(x)$ grow at the same rate as $x \to \infty$. What can you conclude about

(a) $\lim_{x\to\infty} \dfrac{p(x)}{q(x)}$? **(b)** $\lim_{x\to-\infty} \dfrac{p(x)}{q(x)}$?

Standardized Test Questions

You may use a graphing calculator to solve the following problems.

46. True or False A search of order $n \log_2 n$ is more efficient than a search of order $n^{3/2}$. Justify your answer.

47. True or False The function $f(x) = 100x^2 + 50x + 1$ grows faster than the function $x^2 + 1$ as $x \to \infty$. Justify your answer.

48. Multiple Choice Which of the following functions grows faster than $x^5 + x^2 + 1$ as $x \to \infty$?

(A) $x^2 + 1$ **(B)** $x^3 + 2$ **(C)** $x^4 - x^2$ **(D)** x^5 **(E)** $x^6 + 1$

49. Multiple Choice Which of the following functions grows faster than $\log_{13} x$ as $x \to \infty$?

(A) e^{-x} **(B)** $\log_2 x$ **(C)** $\ln x$ **(D)** $\log x$ **(E)** $x \ln x$

50. Multiple Choice Which of the following functions grows at the same rate as e^x as $x \to \infty$?

(A) e^{2x} **(B)** e^{3x} **(C)** e^{x+2} **(D)** e^{-x} **(E)** e^{-x+1}

51. Multiple Choice Which of the following functions grows at the same rate as $\sqrt{x^8 + x^4}$ as $x \to \infty$?

(A) x **(B)** x^2 **(C)** x^3 **(D)** x^4 **(E)** x^5

Explorations

52. Let

$$f(x) = a_n x^n + a_{n-1}x^{n-1} + \cdots + a_1 x + a_0$$

and

$$g(x) = b_m x^m + b_{m-1}x^{m-1} + \cdots + b_1 x + b_0$$

be any two polynomial functions with $a_n > 0$, $b_m > 0$.

(a) Compare the rates of growth of x^5 and x^2 as $x \to \infty$.

(b) Compare the rates of growth of $5x^3$ and $2x^3$ as $x \to \infty$.

(c) If x^m grows faster than x^n as $x \to \infty$, what can you conclude about m and n?

(d) If x^m grows at the same rate as x^n as $x \to \infty$, what can you conclude about m and n?

(e) If $g(x)$ grows faster than $f(x)$ as $x \to \infty$, what can you conclude about their degrees?

(f) If $g(x)$ grows at the same rate as $f(x)$ as $x \to \infty$, what can you conclude about their degrees?

Extending the Ideas

53. Suppose that the values of the functions $f(x)$ and $g(x)$ eventually become and remain negative as $x \to \infty$. We say that

i. f **decreases faster** than g as $x \to \infty$ if

$$\lim_{x\to\infty} \frac{f(x)}{g(x)} = \infty.$$

ii. f and g **decrease at the same rate** as $x \to \infty$ if

$$\lim_{x\to\infty} \frac{f(x)}{g(x)} = L \neq 0.$$

(a) Show that if f decreases faster than g as $x \to \infty$, then $|f|$ grows faster than $|g|$ as $x \to \infty$.

(b) Show that if f and g decrease at the same rate as $x \to \infty$, then $|f|$ and $|g|$ grow at the same rate as $x \to \infty$.

54. Suppose that the values of the functions $f(x)$ and $g(x)$ eventually become and remain positive as $x \to -\infty$. We say that

i. f **grows faster** than g as $x \to -\infty$ if

$$\lim_{x\to-\infty} \frac{f(x)}{g(x)} = \infty.$$

ii. f and g **grow at the same rate** as $x \to -\infty$ if

$$\lim_{x\to-\infty} \frac{f(x)}{g(x)} = L \neq 0.$$

(a) Show that if f grows faster than g as $x \to -\infty$, then $f(-x)$ grows faster than $g(-x)$ as $x \to \infty$.

(b) Show that if f and g grow at the same rate as $x \to -\infty$, then $f(-x)$ and $g(-x)$ grow at the same rate as $x \to \infty$.

9.4 Improper Integrals

What you will learn about . . .

- Infinite Limits of Integration
- Integrands with Infinite Discontinuities
- Test for Convergence and Divergence
- Applications

and why . . .

The techniques of this section allow us to extend integration techniques to cases where the interval of integration $[a, b]$ is not finite or where integrands are not continuous.

Infinite Limits of Integration

Consider the infinite region that lies under the curve $y = e^{-x/2}$ in the first quadrant (Figure 9.16a). You might think this region has infinite area, but we will see that it is finite. Here is how we assign a value to the area. First we find the area $A(b)$ of the portion of the region that is bounded on the right by $x = b$ (Figure 9.16b).

$$A(b) = \int_0^b e^{-x/2}\,dx = -2e^{-x/2}\Big]_0^b = -2e^{-b/2} + 2$$

Then we find the limit of $A(b)$ as $b \to \infty$.

$$\lim_{b\to\infty} A(b) = \lim_{b\to\infty} (-2e^{-b/2} + 2) = 2$$

The area under the curve from 0 to ∞ is

$$\int_0^\infty e^{-x/2}\,dx = \lim_{b\to\infty} \int_0^b e^{-x/2}\,dx = 2.$$

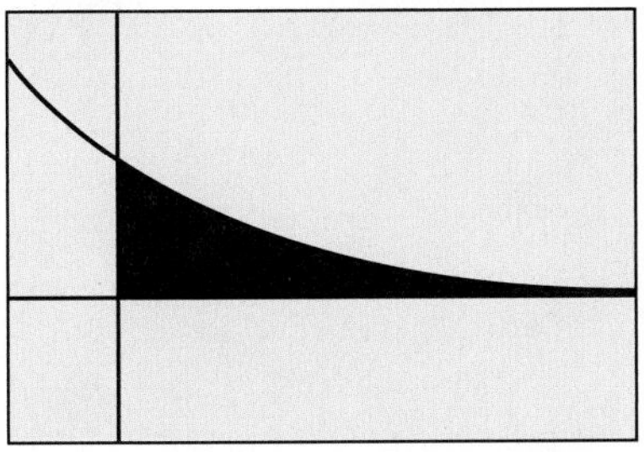

(a)

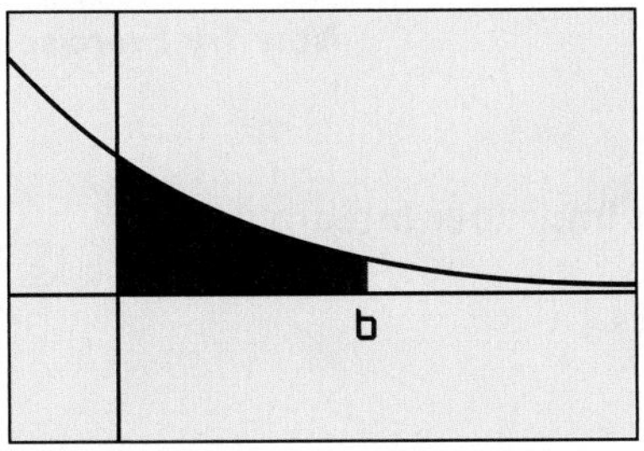

(b)

Figure 9.16 (a) The area in the first quadrant under the curve $y = e^{-x/2}$ is (b)

$$\lim_{b\to\infty} \int_0^b e^{-x/2}\,dx.$$

DEFINITION Improper Integrals with Infinite Integration Limits

Integrals with infinite limits of integration are **improper integrals.**

1. If $f(x)$ is continuous on $[a, \infty)$, then
$$\int_a^\infty f(x)\,dx = \lim_{b\to\infty} \int_a^b f(x)\,dx.$$
2. If $f(x)$ is continuous on $(-\infty, b]$, then
$$\int_{-\infty}^b f(x)\,dx = \lim_{a\to-\infty} \int_a^b f(x)\,dx.$$
3. If $f(x)$ is continuous on $(-\infty, \infty)$, then
$$\int_{-\infty}^\infty f(x)\,dx = \int_{-\infty}^c f(x)\,dx + \int_c^\infty f(x)\,dx,$$
where c is any real number.

In parts 1 and 2, if the limit is finite the improper integral **converges** and the limit is the **value** of the improper integral. If the limit fails to exist, the improper integral **diverges.** In part 3, the integral on the left-hand side of the equation **converges** if both improper integrals on the right-hand side converge; otherwise it **diverges** and has no value. It can be shown that the choice of c in part 3 is unimportant. We can evaluate or determine the convergence or divergence of $\int_{-\infty}^\infty f(x)\,dx$ with any convenient choice.

EXAMPLE 1 Writing Improper Integrals as Limits

Express the improper integral $\int_{-\infty}^\infty e^x\,dx$ in terms of limits of definite integrals and then evaluate the integral.

continued

SOLUTION

Choosing $c = 0$ in part 3 of the definition we can write the integral as

$$\int_{-\infty}^{\infty} e^x\,dx = \lim_{b\to-\infty}\int_b^0 e^x\,dx + \lim_{b\to\infty}\int_0^b e^x\,dx.$$

Next we evaluate the definite integrals and compute the corresponding limits.

$$\begin{aligned}\int_{-\infty}^{\infty} e^x\,dx &= \lim_{b\to-\infty}\int_b^0 e^x\,dx + \lim_{b\to\infty}\int_0^b e^x\,dx\\ &= \lim_{b\to-\infty}(1 - e^b) + \lim_{b\to\infty}(e^b - 1)\\ &= 1 + \infty\end{aligned}$$

The integral diverges because the second part diverges. ***Now Try Exercise 3.***

EXAMPLE 2 Evaluating an Improper Integral on [1, ∞)

Does the improper integral $\int_1^{\infty}\frac{dx}{x}$ converge or diverge?

SOLUTION

$$\begin{aligned}\int_1^{\infty}\frac{dx}{x} &= \lim_{b\to\infty}\int_1^b\frac{dx}{x} && \text{Definition}\\ &= \lim_{b\to\infty}\ln x\Big]_1^b\\ &= \lim_{b\to\infty}(\ln b - \ln 1) = \infty\end{aligned}$$

Thus, the integral diverges. ***Now Try Exercise 5.***

EXAMPLE 3 Using Partial Fractions with Improper Integrals

Evaluate $\int_0^{\infty}\frac{2\,dx}{x^2 + 4x + 3}$ or state that it diverges.

SOLUTION

By definition, $\int_0^{\infty}\frac{2\,dx}{x^2 + 4x + 3} = \lim_{b\to\infty}\int_0^b\frac{2\,dx}{x^2 + 4x + 3}$. We use partial fractions to integrate the definite integral. Set

$$\frac{2}{x^2 + 4x + 3} = \frac{A}{x + 1} + \frac{B}{x + 3}$$

and solve for A and B.

$$\begin{aligned}\frac{2}{x^2 + 4x + 3} &= \frac{A(x + 3)}{(x + 1)(x + 3)} + \frac{B(x + 1)}{(x + 3)(x + 1)}\\ &= \frac{(A + B)x + (3A + B)}{(x + 1)(x + 3)}\end{aligned}$$

continued

Thus, $A + B = 0$ and $3A + B = 2$. Solving, we find $A = 1$ and $B = -1$. Therefore,

$$\frac{2}{x^2 + 4x + 3} = \frac{1}{x + 1} - \frac{1}{x + 3}$$

and

$$\begin{aligned}\int_0^b \frac{2\,dx}{x^2 + 4x + 3} &= \int_0^b \frac{dx}{x + 1} - \int_0^b \frac{dx}{x + 3}\\ &= \ln(x + 1)\Big]_0^b - \ln(x + 3)\Big]_0^b\\ &= \ln(b + 1) - \ln(b + 3) + \ln 3\\ &= \ln\frac{b + 1}{b + 3} + \ln 3\end{aligned}$$

So,

$$\lim_{b\to\infty}\left[\ln\left(\frac{b + 1}{b + 3}\right) + \ln 3\right] = \lim_{b\to\infty}\left[\ln\left(\frac{1 + 1/b}{1 + 3/b}\right) + \ln 3\right] = \ln 3.$$

Thus, $\displaystyle\int_0^\infty \frac{2\,dx}{x^2 + 4x + 3} = \ln 3.$

Now Try Exercise 13.

In Example 4 we use l'Hô1pital's Rule to help evaluate the improper integral.

EXAMPLE 4 Using L'Hôpital's Rule with Improper Integrals

Evaluate $\int_1^\infty xe^{-x}\,dx$ or state that it diverges.

SOLUTION

By definition $\int_1^\infty xe^{-x}\,dx = \lim_{b\to\infty} \int_1^b xe^{-x}\,dx$. We use integration by parts to evaluate the definite integral. Let

$$u = x \qquad dv = e^{-x}\,dx$$

$$du = dx \qquad v = -e^{-x}.$$

Then

$$\begin{aligned}\int_1^b xe^{-x}\,dx &= \Big[-xe^{-x}\Big]_1^b + \int_1^b e^{-x}\,dx\\ &= \Big[-xe^{-x} - e^{-x}\Big]_1^b\\ &= \Big[-(x + 1)e^{-x}\Big]_1^b\\ &= -(b + 1)e^{-b} + 2e^{-1}.\end{aligned}$$

So,

$$\begin{aligned}\lim_{b\to\infty}\left[-(b + 1)e^{-b} + 2e^{-1}\right] &= \lim_{b\to\infty}\frac{-(b + 1)}{e^b} + \frac{2}{e}\\ &= \lim_{b\to\infty}\frac{-1}{e^b} + \frac{2}{e}\\ &= \frac{2}{e}.\end{aligned}$$

Thus $\int_1^\infty xe^{-x}\,dx = 2/e$.

Now Try Exercise 17.

EXAMPLE 5 Evaluating an Integral on $(-\infty, \infty)$

Evaluate $\displaystyle\int_{-\infty}^{\infty} \frac{dx}{1 + x^2}$.

SOLUTION

According to the definition (part 3) we can write

$$\int_{-\infty}^{\infty} \frac{dx}{1 + x^2} = \int_{-\infty}^{0} \frac{dx}{1 + x^2} + \int_{0}^{\infty} \frac{dx}{1 + x^2}.$$

Next, we evaluate each improper integral on the right-hand side of the equation above.

$$\begin{aligned}\int_{-\infty}^{0} \frac{dx}{1 + x^2} &= \lim_{a \to -\infty} \int_{a}^{0} \frac{dx}{1 + x^2} \\ &= \lim_{a \to -\infty} \tan^{-1} x \Big]_{a}^{0} \\ &= \lim_{a \to -\infty} (\tan^{-1} 0 - \tan^{-1} a) = 0 - \left(-\frac{\pi}{2}\right) = \frac{\pi}{2}\end{aligned}$$

$$\begin{aligned}\int_{0}^{\infty} \frac{dx}{1 + x^2} &= \lim_{b \to \infty} \int_{0}^{b} \frac{dx}{1 + x^2} \\ &= \lim_{b \to \infty} \tan^{-1} x \Big]_{0}^{b} \\ &= \lim_{b \to \infty} (\tan^{-1} b - \tan^{-1} 0) = \frac{\pi}{2} - 0 = \frac{\pi}{2}\end{aligned}$$

Thus, $$\int_{-\infty}^{\infty} \frac{dx}{1 + x^2} = \frac{\pi}{2} + \frac{\pi}{2} = \pi.$$

Now Try Exercise 21.

Integrands with Infinite Discontinuities

Another type of improper integral arises when the integrand has a vertical asymptote—an infinite discontinuity—at a limit of integration or at some point between the limits of integration.

Consider the infinite region in the first quadrant that lies under the curve $y = 1/\sqrt{x}$ from $x = 0$ to $x = 1$ (Figure 9.17a). First we find the area of the portion from a to 1 (Figure 9.17b).

$$\int_{a}^{1} \frac{dx}{\sqrt{x}} = 2\sqrt{x}\Big]_{a}^{1} = 2 - 2\sqrt{a}$$

Then, we find the limit of this area as $a \to 0^+$.

$$\lim_{a \to 0^+} \int_{a}^{1} \frac{dx}{\sqrt{x}} = \lim_{a \to 0^+} (2 - 2\sqrt{a}) = 2$$

The area under the curve from 0 to 1 is

$$\int_{0}^{1} \frac{dx}{\sqrt{x}} = \lim_{a \to 0^+} \int_{a}^{1} \frac{dx}{\sqrt{x}} = 2.$$

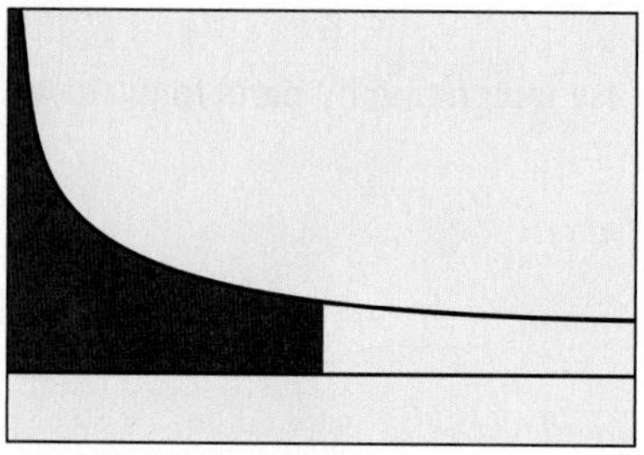

[0, 2] by [–1, 5]

(a)

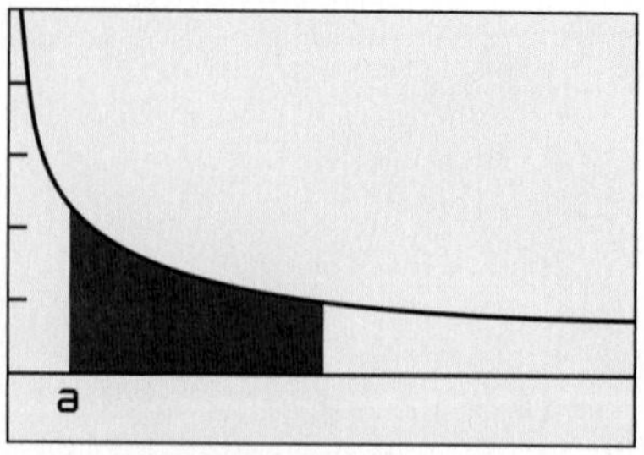

[0, 2] by [–1, 5]

(b)

Figure 9.17 (a) The area under the curve $y = 1/\sqrt{x}$ from $x = 0$ to $x = 1$ is (b)

$$\lim_{a \to 0^+} \int_{a}^{1} (1/\sqrt{x})\, dx.$$

DEFINITION Improper Integrals with Infinite Discontinuities

Integrals of functions that become infinite at a point within the interval of integration are **improper integrals.**

1. If $f(x)$ is continuous on $(a, b]$, then

$$\int_a^b f(x)\,dx = \lim_{c\to a^+} \int_c^b f(x)\,dx.$$

2. If $f(x)$ is continuous on $[a, b)$, then

$$\int_a^b f(x)\,dx = \lim_{c\to b^-} \int_a^c f(x)\,dx.$$

3. If $f(x)$ is continuous on $[a, c) \cup (c, b]$, then

$$\int_a^b f(x)\,dx = \int_a^c f(x)\,dx + \int_c^b f(x)\,dx.$$

In parts 1 and 2, if the limit is finite the improper integral **converges** and the limit is the **value** of the improper integral. If the limit fails to exist, the improper integral **diverges.** In part 3, the integral on the left-hand side of the equation **converges** if both integrals on the right-hand side have values; otherwise it **diverges.**

EXPLORATION 1 Investigation of $\int_0^1 \frac{dx}{x^p}$

1. Explain why these integrals are improper if $p > 0$.
2. Show that the integral diverges if $p = 1$.
3. Show that the integral diverges if $p > 1$.
4. Show that the integral converges if $0 < p < 1$.

EXAMPLE 6 Infinite Discontinuity at an Interior Point

Evaluate $\displaystyle\int_0^3 \frac{dx}{(x-1)^{2/3}}$.

SOLUTION

The integrand has a vertical asymptote at $x = 1$ and is continuous on $[0, 1)$ and $(1, 3]$. Thus, by part 3 of the definition above

$$\int_0^3 \frac{dx}{(x-1)^{2/3}} = \int_0^1 \frac{dx}{(x-1)^{2/3}} + \int_1^3 \frac{dx}{(x-1)^{2/3}}.$$

Next, we evaluate each improper integral on the right-hand side of this equation.

$$\begin{aligned}\int_0^1 \frac{dx}{(x-1)^{2/3}} &= \lim_{c\to 1^-} \int_0^c \frac{dx}{(x-1)^{2/3}}\\ &= \lim_{c\to 1^-} 3(x-1)^{1/3}\Big]_0^c\\ &= \lim_{c\to 1^-} [3(c-1)^{1/3} + 3] = 3\end{aligned}$$

continued

$$\int_1^3 \frac{dx}{(x-1)^{2/3}} = \lim_{c \to 1^+} \int_c^3 \frac{dx}{(x-1)^{2/3}}$$

$$= \lim_{c \to 1^+} 3(x-1)^{1/3}\Big]_c^3$$

$$= \lim_{c \to 1^+} [3(3-1)^{1/3} - 3(c-1)^{1/3}] = 3\sqrt[3]{2}$$

We conclude that

$$\int_0^3 \frac{dx}{(x-1)^{2/3}} = 3 + 3\sqrt[3]{2}$$

Now Try Exercise 25.

EXAMPLE 7 Infinite Discontinuity at an Endpoint

Evaluate $\displaystyle\int_1^2 \frac{dx}{(x-2)}$.

SOLUTION

The integrand has an infinite discontinuity at $x = 2$ and is continuous on $[1, 2)$. Thus,

$$\int_1^2 \frac{dx}{x-2} = \lim_{c \to 2^-} \int_1^c \frac{dx}{x-2}$$

$$= \lim_{c \to 2^-} \ln|x-2|\Big]_1^c$$

$$= \lim_{c \to 2^-} (\ln|c-2| - \ln|-1|) = -\infty.$$

The original integral diverges and has no value. *Now Try Exercise 29.*

Test for Convergence and Divergence

When we cannot evaluate an improper integral directly (often the case in practice) we first try to determine whether it converges or diverges. If the integral diverges, that's the end of the story. If it converges, we can then use numerical methods to approximate its value. In such cases the following theorem is useful.

THEOREM 6 Comparison Test

Let f and g be continuous on $[a, \infty)$ with $0 \le f(x) \le g(x)$ for all $x \ge a$. Then

1. $\displaystyle\int_a^\infty f(x)\,dx$ converges if $\displaystyle\int_a^\infty g(x)\,dx$ converges.
2. $\displaystyle\int_a^\infty g(x)\,dx$ diverges if $\displaystyle\int_a^\infty f(x)\,dx$ diverges.

EXAMPLE 8 Investigating Convergence

Does the integral $\int_1^\infty e^{-x^2}\,dx$ converge?

SOLUTION

Solve Analytically By definition, $\displaystyle\int_1^\infty e^{-x^2}\,dx = \lim_{b \to \infty} \int_1^b e^{-x^2}\,dx.$

continued

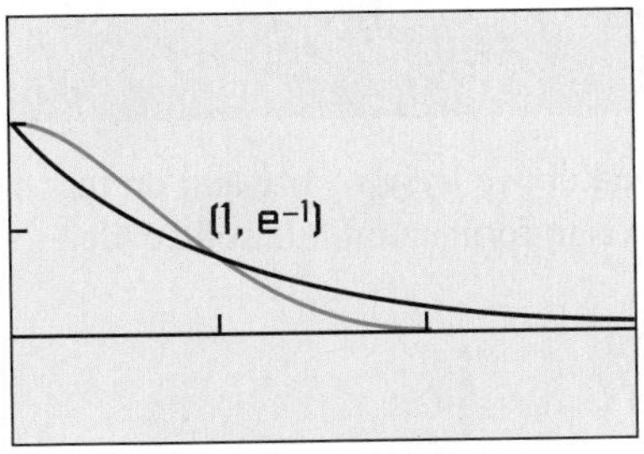

[0, 3] by [–0.5, 1.5]

Figure 9.18 The graph of $y = e^{-x^2}$ lies below the graph of $y = e^{-x}$ for $x > 1$. (Example 8)

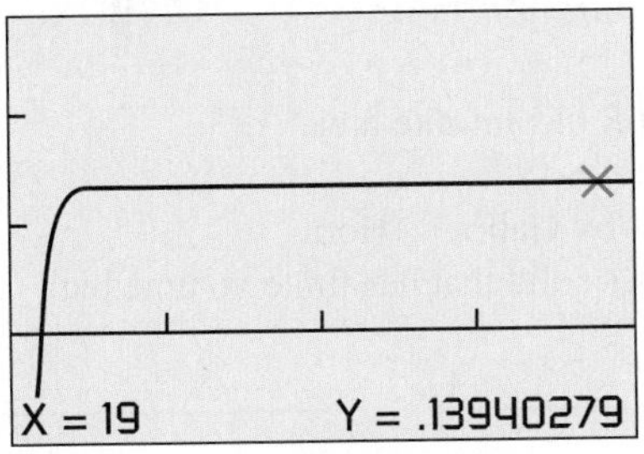

[0, 20] by [–0.1, 0.3]

Figure 9.19 The graph of NINT $(e^{-x^2}, x, 1, x)$. (Example 8)

We cannot evaluate the latter integral directly because there is no simple formula for the antiderivative of e^{-x^2}. We must therefore determine its convergence or divergence some other way. Because $e^{-x^2} > 0$ for all x, $\int_1^b e^{-x^2} dx$ is an increasing function of b. Therefore, as $b \to \infty$, the integral either becomes infinite as $b \to \infty$ or it is bounded from above and is forced to converge (have a finite limit).

The two curves $y = e^{-x^2}$ and $y = e^{-x}$ intersect at $(1, e^{-1})$, and $0 < e^{-x^2} \le e^{-x}$ for $x \ge 1$ (Figure 9.18). Thus, for any $b > 1$,

$$0 < \int_1^b e^{-x^2} dx \le \int_1^b e^{-x} dx = -e^{-b} + e^{-1} < e^{-1} \approx 0.368.$$

Rounded up to be safe

As an increasing function of b bounded above by 0.368, the integral $\int_1^\infty e^{-x^2} dx$ must converge. This does not tell us much about the value of the improper integral, however, except that it is positive and less than 0.368.

Support Graphically The graph of NINT $(e^{-x^2}, x, 1, x)$ is shown in Figure 9.19. The value of the integral rises rapidly as x first moves away from 1 but changes little past $x = 3$. Values sampled along the curve suggest a limit of about 0.13940 as $x \to \infty$. (Exercise 57 shows how to confirm the accuracy of this estimate.)

Now Try Exercise 31.

Applications

EXAMPLE 9 Finding Circumference

Use the arc length formula (Section 8.4) to show that the circumference of the circle $x^2 + y^2 = 4$ is 4π.

SOLUTION

One fourth of this circle is given by $y = \sqrt{4 - x^2}$, $0 \le x \le 2$. Its arc length is

$$L = \int_0^2 \sqrt{1 + (y')^2}\, dx, \quad \text{where} \quad y' = -\frac{x}{\sqrt{4 - x^2}}.$$

The integral is improper because y' is not defined at $x = 2$. We evaluate it as a limit.

$$\begin{aligned} L = \int_0^2 \sqrt{1 + (y')^2}\, dx &= \int_0^2 \sqrt{1 + \frac{x^2}{4 - x^2}}\, dx \\ &= \int_0^2 \sqrt{\frac{4}{4 - x^2}}\, dx \\ &= \lim_{b \to 2^-} \int_0^b \sqrt{\frac{4}{4 - x^2}}\, dx \\ &= \lim_{b \to 2^-} \int_0^b \sqrt{\frac{1}{1 - (x/2)^2}}\, dx \\ &= \lim_{b \to 2^-} 2 \sin^{-1} \frac{x}{2} \bigg]_0^b \\ &= \lim_{b \to 2^-} 2 \left[\sin^{-1} \frac{b}{2} - 0 \right] = \pi \end{aligned}$$

The circumference of the quarter circle is π; the circumference of the circle is 4π.

Now Try Exercise 47.

EXPLORATION 2 Gabriel's Horn

Consider the region R in the first quadrant bounded above by $y = 1/x$ and on the left by $x = 1$. The region is revolved about the x-axis to form an infinite solid called Gabriel's Horn, which is shown in the figure.

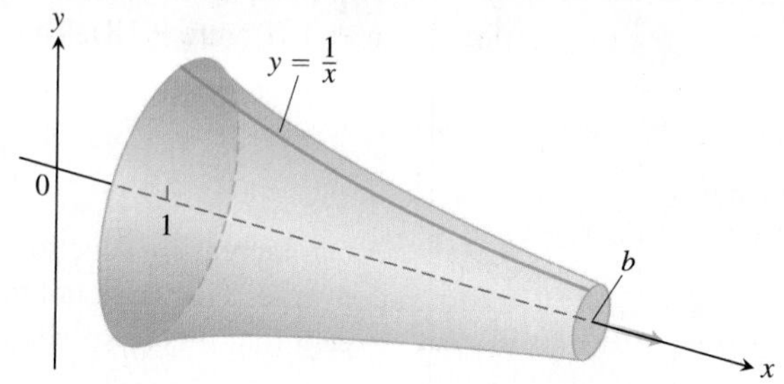

1. Explain how Example 2 shows that the region R has infinite area.
2. Find the volume of the solid.
3. Find the area of the shadow that would be cast by Gabriel's Horn.
4. Why is Gabriel's Horn sometimes described as a solid that has finite volume but casts an infinite shadow?

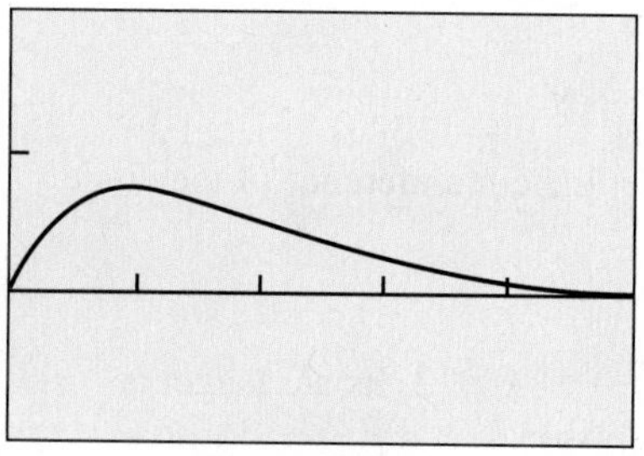

[0, 5] by [–0.5, 1]

Figure 9.20 The graph of $y = xe^{-x}$. (Example 10)

EXAMPLE 10 Finding the Volume of an Infinite Solid

Find the volume of the solid obtained by revolving the curve $y = xe^{-x}, 0 \le x < \infty$ about the x-axis.

SOLUTION

Figure 9.20 shows a portion of the region to be revolved about the x-axis. The area of a typical cross section of the solid is

$$\pi(\text{radius})^2 = \pi y^2 = \pi x^2 e^{-2x}.$$

The volume of the solid is

$$V = \pi \int_0^{\infty} x^2 e^{-2x}\,dx = \pi \lim_{b\to\infty} \int_0^b x^2 e^{-2x}\,dx.$$

Integrating by parts twice we obtain the following.

$$\int x^2 e^{-2x}\,dx = -\frac{x^2}{2}e^{-2x} + \int xe^{-2x}\,dx \qquad u = x^2,\ dv = e^{-2x}\,dx,\ du = 2x\,dx,\ v = -\tfrac{1}{2}e^{-2x}$$

$$= -\frac{x^2}{2}e^{-2x} - \frac{x}{2}e^{-2x} + \frac{1}{2}\int e^{-2x}\,dx \qquad u = x,\ dv = e^{-2x}\,dx,\ du = dx,\ v = -\tfrac{1}{2}e^{-2x}$$

$$= -\frac{x^2}{2}e^{-2x} - \frac{x}{2}e^{-2x} + \frac{1}{4}e^{-2x} + C$$

$$= -\frac{2x^2 + 2x + 1}{4e^{2x}} + C$$

Thus,

$$V = \pi \lim_{b\to\infty}\left[-\frac{2x^2 + 2x + 1}{4e^{2x}}\right]_0^b$$

$$= \pi \lim_{b\to\infty}\left[-\frac{2b^2 + 2b + 1}{4e^{2b}} + \frac{1}{4}\right] = \frac{\pi}{4},$$

and the volume of the solid is $\pi/4$.

Now Try Exercise 55.

Quick Review 9.4 (For help, go to Sections 1.2, 6.3, and 9.2.)

Exercise numbers with a gray background indicate problems that the authors have designed to be solved *without a calculator.*

In Exercises 1–4, evaluate the integral.

1. $\int_0^3 \frac{dx}{x+3}$

2. $\int_{-1}^1 \frac{x\,dx}{x^2+1}$

3. $\int \frac{dx}{x^2+4}$

4. $\int \frac{dx}{x^4}$

In Exercises 5 and 6, find the domain of the function.

5. $g(x) = \frac{1}{\sqrt{9-x^2}}$

6. $h(x) = \frac{1}{\sqrt{x-1}}$

In Exercises 7 and 8, confirm the inequality.

7. $\left|\frac{\cos x}{x^2}\right| \le \frac{1}{x^2}, \quad -\infty < x < \infty$

8. $\frac{1}{\sqrt{x^2-1}} \ge \frac{1}{x}, \quad x > 1$

In Exercises 9 and 10, show that the functions f and g grow at the same rate as $x \to \infty$.

9. $f(x) = 4e^x - 5, \quad g(x) = 3e^x + 7$

10. $f(x) = \sqrt{2x-1}, \quad g(x) = \sqrt{x+3}$

Section 9.4 Exercises

In Exercises 1–4, **(a)** express the improper integral as a limit of definite integrals, and **(b)** evaluate the integral.

1. $\int_0^\infty \frac{2x}{x^2+1}\,dx$

2. $\int_1^\infty \frac{dx}{x^{1/3}}$

3. $\int_{-\infty}^\infty \frac{2x}{(x^2+1)^2}\,dx$

4. $\int_1^\infty \frac{dx}{\sqrt{x}}$

In Exercises 5–24, evaluate the improper integral or state that it diverges.

5. $\int_1^\infty \frac{dx}{x^4}$

6. $\int_1^\infty \frac{2\,dx}{x^3}$

7. $\int_1^\infty \frac{dx}{\sqrt[3]{x}}$

8. $\int_1^\infty \frac{dx}{\sqrt[4]{x}}$

9. $\int_{-\infty}^{-1} \frac{dx}{x^2}$

10. $\int_{-\infty}^{0} \frac{dx}{(x-2)^3}$

11. $\int_{-\infty}^{-2} \frac{2\,dx}{x^2-1}$

12. $\int_2^\infty \frac{3\,dx}{x^2-x}$

13. $\int_{-1}^\infty \frac{dx}{x^2+5x+6}$

14. $\int_{-\infty}^{0} \frac{2\,dx}{x^2-4x+3}$

15. $\int_1^\infty \frac{5x+6}{x^2+2x}\,dx$

16. $\int_{-2}^{-\infty} \frac{2\,dx}{x^2-2x}$

17. $\int_1^\infty xe^{-2x}\,dx$

18. $\int_{-\infty}^{0} x^2e^x\,dx$

19. $\int_1^\infty x\ln(x)\,dx$

20. $\int_0^\infty (x+1)e^{-x}\,dx$

21. $\int_{-\infty}^\infty e^{-|x|}\,dx$

22. $\int_{-\infty}^\infty 2xe^{-x^2}\,dx$

23. $\int_{-\infty}^\infty \frac{dx}{e^x+e^{-x}}$

24. $\int_{-\infty}^\infty e^{2x}\,dx$

In Exercises 25–30, **(a)** state why the integral is improper. Then **(b)** evaluate the integral or state that it diverges.

25. $\int_0^2 \frac{dx}{1-x^2}$

26. $\int_0^1 \frac{dx}{\sqrt{1-x^2}}$

27. $\int_0^1 \frac{x+1}{\sqrt{x^2+2x}}\,dx$

28. $\int_0^4 \frac{e^{-\sqrt{x}}}{\sqrt{x}}\,dx$

29. $\int_0^1 x\ln(x)\,dx$

30. $\int_{-1}^4 \frac{dx}{\sqrt{|x|}}$

In Exercises 31–34, use the Comparison Test to determine whether the integral converges or diverges.

31. $\int_1^\infty \frac{dx}{1+e^x}$

32. $\int_1^\infty \frac{dx}{x^3+1}$

33. $\int_\pi^\infty \frac{2+\cos x}{x}\,dx$

34. $\int_{-\infty}^\infty \frac{dx}{\sqrt{x^4+1}}$

In Exercises 35–42, evaluate the integral or state that it diverges.

35. $\int_0^{\ln 2} y^{-2}e^{1/y}\,dy$

36. $\int_0^4 \frac{dr}{\sqrt{4-r}}$

37. $\int_0^\infty \frac{ds}{(1+s)\sqrt{s}}$

38. $\int_1^2 \frac{du}{u\sqrt{u^2-1}}$

39. $\int_0^\infty \frac{16\tan^{-1} v}{1+v^2}\,dv$

40. $\int_{-\infty}^0 \theta e^\theta\,d\theta$

41. $\int_0^2 \frac{dt}{1-t}$

42. $\int_{-1}^1 \ln(|w|)\,dw$

In Exercises 43 and 44, find the area of the region in the first quadrant that lies under the given curve.

43. $y = \frac{\ln x}{x^2}$

44. $y = \frac{\ln x}{x}$

45. **Group Activity**

(a) Show that if f is an even function and the necessary integrals exist, then

$$\int_{-\infty}^\infty f(x)\,dx = 2\int_0^\infty f(x)\,dx.$$

(b) Show that if f is odd and the necessary integrals exist, then

$$\int_{-\infty}^\infty f(x)\,dx = 0.$$

46. Writing to Learn

(a) Show that the integral $\int_0^{\infty} \frac{2x\,dx}{x^2+1}$ diverges.

(b) Explain why we can conclude from part (a) that

$$\int_{-\infty}^{\infty} \frac{2x\,dx}{x^2+1} \text{ diverges.}$$

(c) Show that $\lim_{b\to\infty} \int_{-b}^{b} \frac{2x\,dx}{x^2+1} = 0.$

(d) Explain why the result in part (c) does not contradict part (b).

47. *Finding Perimeter* Find the perimeter of the 4-sided figure $x^{2/3} + y^{2/3} = 1$.

Standardized Test Questions

You may use a graphing calculator to solve the following problems.

In Exercises 48 and 49, let f and g be continuous on $[a, \infty)$ with $0 \le f(x) \le g(x)$ for all $x \ge a$.

48. True or False If $\int_a^{\infty} f(x)dx$ converges then $\int_a^{\infty} g(x)dx$ converges. Justify your answer.

49. True or False If $\int_a^{\infty} g(x)dx$ converges then $\int_a^{\infty} f(x)dx$ converges. Justify your answer.

50. Multiple Choice Which of the following gives the value of the integral $\int_1^{\infty} \frac{dx}{x^{1.01}}$?

(A) 1 (B) 10 (C) 100 (D) 1000 (E) diverges

51. Multiple Choice Which of the following gives the value of the integral $\int_0^{1} \frac{dx}{x^{0.5}}$?

(A) 1 (B) 2 (C) 3 (D) 4 (E) diverges

52. Multiple Choice Which of the following gives the value of the integral $\int_0^{1} \frac{dx}{x-1}$?

(A) -1 (B) $-1/2$ (C) 0 (D) 1 (E) diverges

53. Multiple Choice Which of the following gives the value of the area under the curve $y = 1/(x^2+1)$ in the first quadrant?

(A) $\pi/4$ (B) 1 (C) $\pi/2$ (D) π (E) diverges

Explorations

54. *The Integral* $\int_1^{\infty} \frac{dx}{x^p}$.

(a) Evaluate the integral for $p = 0.5$.

(b) Evaluate the integral for $p = 1$.

(c) Evaluate the integral for $p = 1.5$.

(d) Show that $\int_1^{\infty} \frac{dx}{x^p} = \lim_{b\to\infty}\left[\frac{1}{1-p}\left(\frac{1}{b^{p-1}} - 1\right)\right]$

(e) Use part (d) to show that $\int_1^{\infty} \frac{dx}{x^p} = \begin{cases} \frac{1}{p-1}, & p > 1 \\ \infty, & p < 1. \end{cases}$

(f) For what values of p does the integral converge? diverge?

55. Each cross section of the solid infinite horn shown in the figure cut by a plane perpendicular to the x-axis for $-\infty < x \le \ln 2$ is a circular disc with one diameter reaching from the x-axis to the curve $y = e^x$.

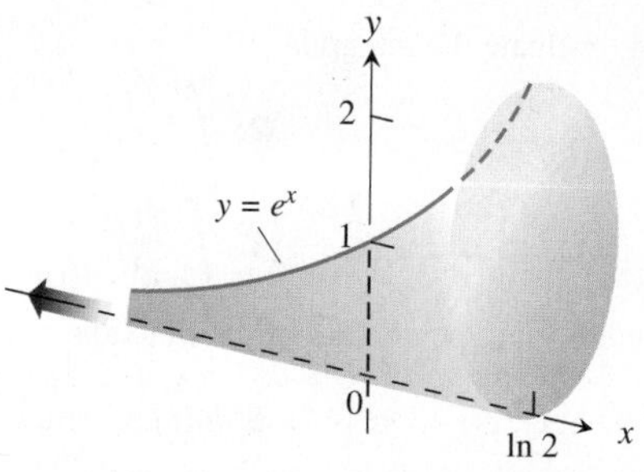

(a) Find the area of a typical cross section.

(b) Express the volume of the horn as an improper integral.

(c) Find the volume of the horn.

56. *Normal Probability Distribution Function* In Section 8.5, we encountered the bell-shaped normal distribution curve that is the graph of

$$f(x) = \frac{1}{\sigma\sqrt{2\pi}} e^{-\frac{1}{2}\left(\frac{x-\mu}{\sigma}\right)^2},$$

the normal probability density function with mean μ and standard deviation σ. The number μ tells where the distribution is centered, and σ measures the "scatter" around the mean.

From the theory of probability, it is known that

$$\int_{-\infty}^{\infty} f(x)\,dx = 1.$$

In what follows, let $\mu = 0$ and $\sigma = 1$.

(a) Draw the graph of f. Find the intervals on which f is increasing, the intervals on which f is decreasing, and any local extreme values and where they occur.

(b) Evaluate $\int_{-n}^{n} f(x)\,dx$ for $n = 1, 2, 3$.

(c) Give a convincing argument that $\int_{-\infty}^{\infty} f(x)\,dx = 1.$

[*Hint:* Show that $0 < f(x) < e^{-x/2}$ for $x > 1$, and for $b > 1$,

$$\int_b^{\infty} e^{-x/2}\,dx \to 0 \quad \text{as} \quad b \to \infty.]$$

57. *Approximating the Value of* $\int_1^{\infty} e^{-x^2}\,dx$

(a) Show that $\int_6^{\infty} e^{-x^2}\,dx \le \int_0^{\infty} e^{-6x}\,dx < 4 \times 10^{-17}$.

(b) **Writing to Learn** Explain why

$$\int_1^{\infty} e^{-x^2}\,dx \approx \int_1^{6} e^{-x^2}\,dx$$

with error of at most 4×10^{-17}.

(c) Use the approximation in part (b) to estimate the value of $\int_1^{\infty} e^{-x^2}\,dx$. Compare this estimate with the value displayed in Figure 9.19.

(d) Writing to Learn Explain why

$$\int_0^{\infty} e^{-x^2}\,dx \approx \int_1^{3} e^{-x^2}\,dx$$

with error of at most 0.000042.

Extending the Ideas

58. Use properties of integrals to give a convincing argument that Theorem 6 is true.

59. Consider the integral

$$f(n+1) = \int_0^{\infty} x^n e^{-x}\,dx$$

where $n \geq 0$.

(a) Show that $\int_0^{\infty} x^n e^{-x}\,dx$ converges for $n = 0, 1, 2$.

(b) Use integration by parts to show that $f(n+1) = nf(n)$.

(c) Give a convincing argument that $\int_0^{\infty} x^n e^{-x}\,dx$ converges for all integers $n \geq 0$.

60. Let $f(x) = \int_0^{x} \frac{\sin t}{t}\,dt$.

(a) Use graphs and tables to investigate the values of $f(x)$ as $x \to \infty$.

(b) Does the integral $\int_0^{\infty} (\sin x)/x\,dx$ converge? Give a convincing argument.

61. (a) Show that we get the same value for the improper integral in Example 5 if we express

$$\int_{-\infty}^{\infty} \frac{dx}{1+x^2} = \int_{-\infty}^{1} \frac{dx}{1+x^2} + \int_{1}^{\infty} \frac{dx}{1+x^2},$$

and then evaluate these two integrals.

(b) Show that it doesn't matter what we choose for c in (Improper Integrals with Infinite Integration Limits, part 3)

$$\int_{-\infty}^{\infty} f(x)\,dx = \int_{-\infty}^{c} f(x)\,dx + \int_{c}^{\infty} f(x)\,dx.$$

Quick Quiz for AP* Preparation: Sections 9.3 and 9.4

You may use a graphing calculator to solve the following problems.

1. Multiple Choice Which of the following functions grows faster than x^2 as $x \to \infty$?

(A) e^{-x} **(B)** $\ln(x)$ **(C)** $7x + 10$ **(D)** $2x^2 - 3x$ **(E)** $0.1x^3$

2. Multiple Choice Find all the values of p for which the integral converges $\int_1^{\infty} \frac{dx}{x^{p+1}}$.

(A) $p < -1$ **(B)** $p < 0$ **(C)** $p > 0$
(D) $p > 1$ **(E)** diverges for all p

3. Multiple Choice Find all the values of p for which the integral converges $\int_0^{1} \frac{dx}{x^{p+1}}$.

(A) $p < -1$ **(B)** $p < 0$ **(C)** $p > 0$
(D) $p > 1$ **(E)** diverges for all p

4. Free Response Consider the region R in the first quadrant under the curve $y = \frac{2\ln(x)}{x^2}$.

(a) Write the area of R as an improper integral.

(b) Express the integral in part (a) as a limit of a definite integral.

(c) Find the area of R.

Chapter 9 Key Terms

Absolute Value Theorem for Sequences (p. 444)
arithmetic sequence (p. 440)
binary search (p. 460)
common difference (p. 440)
common ratio (p. 441)
comparison test (p. 468)
constant multiple rule for limits (p. 443)
convergence of improper integral (p. 463)
convergent sequence (p. 443)
difference rule for limits (p. 443)
divergence of improper integral (p. 463)
divergent sequence (p. 443)
explicitly defined sequence (p. 439)
finite sequence (p. 439)
geometric sequence (p. 441)
grows at the same rate (p. 437)
grows faster (p. 457)
grows slower (p. 457)
improper integral (pp. 463)
indeterminate form (p. 448)
infinite sequence (p. 439)
l'Hôpital's Rule, first form (p. 448)
l'Hôpital's Rule, stronger form (p. 449)
limit of a sequence (p. 443)
nth term of a sequence (p. 439)
product rule for limits (p. 443)
quotient rule for limits (p. 443)
recursively defined sequence (p. 439)
Sandwich Theorem for Sequences (p. 444)
sequence (p. 439)
sequential search (p. 460)
sum rule for limits (p. 443)
terms of sequence (p. 439)
transitivity of growing rates (p. 459)
value of improper integral (p. 463)

Chapter 9 Review Exercises

Exercise numbers with a gray background indicate problems that the authors have designed to be solved *without a calculator.*

The collection of exercises marked in red could be used as a Chapter Test.

In Exercises 1 and 2, find the first four terms and the fortieth term of the given sequence.

1. $a_n = (-1)^n \dfrac{n+1}{n+3}$ for all $n \geq 1$

2. $a_1 = -3,\ a_n = 2a_{n-1}$ for all $n \geq 2$

3. The sequence $-1, 1/2, 2, 7/2, \ldots$ is arithmetic. Find **(a)** the common difference, **(b)** the tenth term, and **(c)** an explicit rule for the nth term.

4. The sequence $1/2, -2, 8, -32, \ldots$ is geometric. Find **(a)** the common ratio, **(b)** the seventh term, and **(c)** an explicit rule for the nth term.

In Exercises 5 and 6, draw a graph of the sequence with given nth term.

5. $a_n = \dfrac{2^{n+1} + (-1)^n}{2^n},\ n = 1, 2, 3, \ldots$

6. $a_n = (-1)^{n-1} \dfrac{n-1}{n}$

In Exercises 7 and 8, determine the convergence or divergence of the sequence with given nth term. If the sequence converges, find its limit.

7. $a_n = \dfrac{3n^2 - 1}{2n^2 + 1}$

8. $a_n = (-1)^n \dfrac{3n - 1}{n + 2}$

In Exercises 9–22, find the limit.

9. $\displaystyle\lim_{t\to 0} \frac{t - \ln(1 + 2t)}{t^2}$

10. $\displaystyle\lim_{t\to 0} \frac{\tan 3t}{\tan 5t}$

11. $\displaystyle\lim_{x\to 0} \frac{x \sin x}{1 - \cos x}$

12. $\displaystyle\lim_{x\to 1} x^{1/(1-x)}$

13. $\displaystyle\lim_{x\to\infty} x^{1/x}$

14. $\displaystyle\lim_{x\to\infty} \left(1 + \frac{3}{x}\right)^x$

15. $\displaystyle\lim_{r\to\infty} \frac{\cos r}{\ln r}$

16. $\displaystyle\lim_{\theta\to\pi/2} \left(\theta - \frac{\pi}{2}\right) \sec \theta$

17. $\displaystyle\lim_{x\to 1} \left(\frac{1}{x - 1} - \frac{1}{\ln x}\right)$

18. $\displaystyle\lim_{x\to 0^+} \left(1 + \frac{1}{x}\right)^x$

19. $\displaystyle\lim_{\theta\to 0^+} (\tan \theta)^\theta$

20. $\displaystyle\lim_{\theta\to\infty} \theta^2 \sin\left(\frac{1}{\theta}\right)$

21. $\displaystyle\lim_{x\to\infty} \frac{x^3 - 3x^2 + 1}{2x^2 + x - 3}$

22. $\displaystyle\lim_{x\to\infty} \frac{3x^2 - x + 1}{x^4 - x^3 + 2}$

In Exercises 23–34, determine whether f grows faster than, slower than, or at the same rate as g as $x \to \infty$. Give reasons for your answer.

23. $f(x) = x,\quad g(x) = 5x$

24. $f(x) = \log_2 x,\quad g(x) = \log_3 x$

25. $f(x) = x,\quad g(x) = x + \dfrac{1}{x}$

26. $f(x) = \dfrac{x}{100},\quad g(x) = xe^{-x}$

27. $f(x) = x,\quad g(x) = \tan^{-1} x$

28. $f(x) = \csc^{-1} x,\quad g(x) = \dfrac{1}{x}$

29. $f(x) = x^{\ln x},\quad g(x) = x \log_2 x$

30. $f(x) = 3^{-x},\quad g(x) = 2^{-x}$

31. $f(x) = \ln 2x,\quad g(x) = \ln x^2$

32. $f(x) = 10x^3 + 2x^2,\quad g(x) = e^x$

33. $f(x) = \tan^{-1} \dfrac{1}{x},\quad g(x) = \dfrac{1}{x}$

34. $f(x) = \sin^{-1} \dfrac{1}{x},\quad g(x) = \dfrac{1}{x^2}$

In Exercises 35 and 36,

(a) show that f has a removable discontinuity at $x = 0$.

(b) define f at $x = 0$ so that it is continuous there.

35. $f(x) = \dfrac{2^{\sin x} - 1}{e^x - 1}$

36. $f(x) = x \ln x$

In Exercises 37–48, evaluate the improper integral or state that it diverges.

37. $\displaystyle\int_1^\infty \frac{dx}{x^{3/2}}$

38. $\displaystyle\int_1^\infty \frac{dx}{x^2 + 7x} + 12$

39. $\displaystyle\int_{-\infty}^{-1} \frac{3dx}{3x - x^2}$

40. $\displaystyle\int_0^3 \frac{dx}{\sqrt{9 - x^2}}$

41. $\displaystyle\int_0^1 \ln(x)\, dx$

42. $\displaystyle\int_{-1}^1 \frac{dy}{y^{2/3}}$

43. $\displaystyle\int_{-2}^0 \frac{d\theta}{(\theta + 1)^{3/5}}$

44. $\displaystyle\int_3^\infty \frac{2dx}{x^2 - 2x}$

45. $\displaystyle\int_0^\infty x^2 e^{-x}\, dx$

46. $\displaystyle\int_{-\infty}^0 xe^{3x}\, dx$

47. $\displaystyle\int_{-\infty}^\infty \frac{dx}{e^x + e^{-x}}$

48. $\displaystyle\int_{-\infty}^\infty \frac{4dx}{x^2 + 16}$

In Exercises 49 and 50, use the comparison test to determine whether the improper integral converges or diverges.

49. $\displaystyle\int_1^\infty \frac{\ln z}{z}\, dz$

50. $\displaystyle\int_1^\infty \frac{e^{-t}}{\sqrt{t}}\, dt$

51. The second and fifth terms of a geometric sequence are -3 and $-3/8$, respectively. Find **(a)** the first term, **(b)** the common ratio, and **(c)** an explicit formula for the nth term.

52. The second and sixth terms of an arithmetic sequence are 11.5 and 5.5, respectively. Find **(a)** the first term, **(b)** the common difference, and **(c)** an explicit formula for the nth term.

53. Consider the improper $\int_{\infty}^{\infty} e^{-2|x|}\, dx$.

(a) Express the improper integral as a limit of definite integrals.

(b) Evaluate the integral.

54. ***Infinite Solid*** The infinite region bounded by the coordinate axes and the curve $y = -\ln x$ in the first quadrant (see figure) is revolved about the x-axis to generate a solid. Find the volume of the solid.

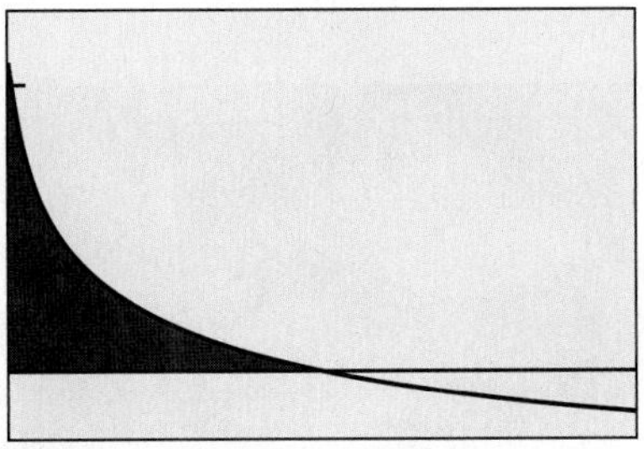

[0, 2] by [–1, 5]

55. ***Infinite Region*** Find the area of the region in the first quadrant under the curve $y = xe^{-x}$ (see figure).

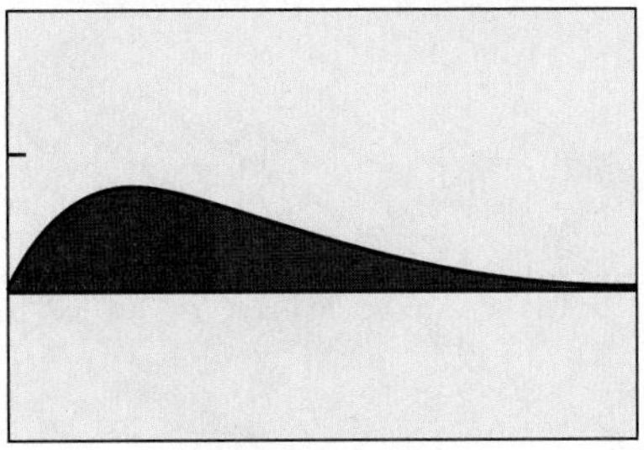

[0, 5] by [–0.5, 1]

AP* Examination Preparation

56. Consider the infinite region R in the first quadrant under the curve $y = xe^{-x/2}$.

(a) Write the area of R as an improper integral.

(b) Express the integral in part (a) as a limit of a definite integral.

(c) Find the area of R.

57. The infinite region in the first quadrant bounded by the coordinate axes and the curve $y = \dfrac{1}{x} - 1$ is revolved about the y-axis to generate a solid.

(a) Write the volume of the solid as an improper integral.

(b) Express the integral in part (a) as a limit of a definite integral.

(c) Find the volume of the solid.

58. Determine whether or not $\int_0^\infty xe^{-x}\,dx$ converges. If it converges, give its value. Show your reasoning.

CHAPTER

10 Infinite Series

One of the infinite processes that calculus helped to clarify was the summing of infinite series. For example, mathematicians had long known that the infinite "*p*-series" $\frac{1}{1^2} + \frac{1}{2^2} + \frac{1}{3^2} + \frac{1}{4^2} + \cdots$ had a finite sum, but it took calculus (and the mind of the great 18th-century mathematician Leonhard Euler) to prove that it had the surprising sum $\frac{\pi^2}{6}$. The convergence is unfortunately slow, though; the error after summing n terms is still about $\frac{1}{n}$.

Shown here is a close-up of a high speed microprocessor chip. If a computer adds 1,000,000 terms of the *p*-series in one second, how many places of accuracy will it achieve in 24 hours? Section 10.5 provides a discussion of *p*-series.

CHAPTER 10 Overview

One consequence of the early and dramatic successes that scientists enjoyed when using calculus to explain natural phenomena was that there suddenly seemed to be no limits, so to speak, on how infinite processes might be exploited. There was still considerable mystery about "infinite sums" and "division by infinitely small quantities" in the years after Newton and Leibniz, but even mathematicians normally insistent on rigorous proof were inclined to throw caution to the wind while things were working. The result was a century of unprecedented progress in understanding the physical universe. (Moreover, we can note happily in retrospect, the proofs eventually followed.)

One infinite process that had puzzled mathematicians for centuries was the summing of infinite series. Sometimes an infinite series of terms added up to a number, as in

$$\frac{1}{2}+\frac{1}{4}+\frac{1}{8}+\frac{1}{16}+\cdots=1.$$

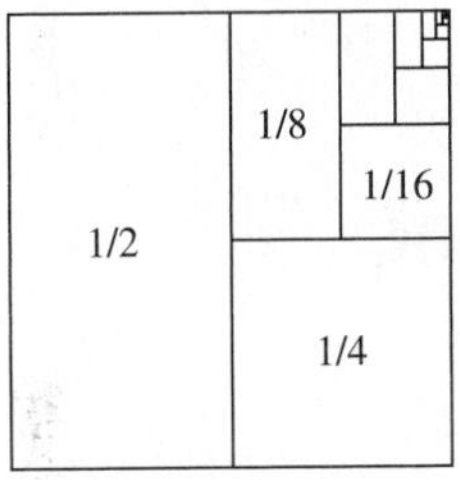

(You can see this by adding the areas in the "infinitely halved" unit square at the right.) But sometimes the infinite sum was infinite, as in

$$\frac{1}{1}+\frac{1}{2}+\frac{1}{3}+\frac{1}{4}+\frac{1}{5}+\cdots=\infty$$

(although this is far from obvious), and sometimes the infinite sum was difficult to pin down, as in

$$1-1+1-1+1-1+\cdots$$

(Is it 0? Is it 1? Is it neither?).

Nonetheless, mathematicians like Gauss and Euler successfully used infinite series to derive previously inaccessible results. Laplace used infinite series to prove the stability of the solar system (although that does not stop some people from worrying about it today when they feel that "too many" planets have swung to the same side of the sun). It was years later that careful analysts like Cauchy developed the theoretical foundation for series computations, sending many mathematicians (including Laplace) back to their desks to verify their results.

Our approach in this chapter will be to discover the calculus of infinite series as the pioneers of calculus did: proceeding intuitively, accepting what works and rejecting what does not. Toward the end of the chapter we will return to the crucial question of convergence and take a careful look at it.

10.1 Power Series

What you will learn about . . .

- Geometric Series
- Representing Functions by Series
- Differentiation and Integration
- Identifying a Series

and why . . .

Power series are important in understanding the physical universe and can be used to represent functions.

Geometric Series

The first thing to get straight about an infinite series is that it is not simply an example of addition. Addition of real numbers is a *binary* operation, meaning that we really add numbers two at a time. The only reason that $1 + 2 + 3$ makes sense as "addition" is that we can *group* the numbers and then add them two at a time. The associative property of addition guarantees that we get the same sum no matter how we group them:

$$1+(2+3)=1+5=6 \quad \text{and} \quad (1+2)+3=3+3=6.$$

In short, a *finite sum* of real numbers always produces a real number (the result of a finite number of binary additions), but an *infinite sum* of real numbers is something else entirely. That is why we need the following definition.

DEFINITION Infinite Series

An **infinite series** is an expression of the form

$$a_1 + a_2 + a_3 + \cdots + a_n + \cdots, \qquad \text{or} \qquad \sum_{k=1}^{\infty} a_k.$$

The numbers $a_1, a_2, \ldots$ are the **terms** of the series; a_n is the ***n*th term.**

The **partial sums** of the series form a sequence

$$\begin{aligned} s_1 &= a_1 \\ s_2 &= a_1 + a_2 \\ s_3 &= a_1 + a_2 + a_3 \\ &\vdots \\ s_n &= \sum_{k=1}^{n} a_k \\ &\vdots \end{aligned}$$

of real numbers, each defined as a finite sum. If the sequence of partial sums has a limit S as $n \to \infty$, we say the series **converges** to the sum S, and we write

$$a_1 + a_2 + a_3 + \cdots + a_n + \cdots = \sum_{k=1}^{\infty} a_k = S.$$

Otherwise, we say the series **diverges.**

EXAMPLE 1 Identifying a Divergent Series

Does the series $1 - 1 + 1 - 1 + 1 - 1 + \cdots$ converge?

SOLUTION

You might be tempted to pair the terms as

$$(1 - 1) + (1 - 1) + (1 - 1) + \cdots.$$

That strategy, however, requires an *infinite* number of pairings, so it cannot be justified by the associative property of addition. This is an infinite series, not a finite sum, so if it has a sum it *has to be* the limit of its sequence of partial sums,

$$1, 0, 1, 0, 1, 0, 1, \ldots.$$

Since this sequence has no limit, the series has no sum. It diverges. ***Now Try Exercise 7.***

EXAMPLE 2 Identifying a Convergent Series

Does the series

$$\frac{3}{10} + \frac{3}{100} + \frac{3}{1000} + \cdots + \frac{3}{10^n} + \cdots$$

converge?

SOLUTION

Here is the sequence of partial sums, written in decimal form.

$$0.3, 0.33, 0.333, 0.3333, \ldots$$

This sequence has a limit $0.\overline{3}$, which we recognize as the fraction $1/3$. The series converges to the sum $1/3$. ***Now Try Exercise 9.***

There is an easy way to identify some divergent series. In Exercise 62 you are asked to show that whenever an infinite series $\sum_{k=1}^{\infty} a_k$ converges, the limit of the nth term as $n \to \infty$ must be zero.

If the **infinite series**

$$\sum_{k=1}^{\infty} a_k = a_1 + a_2 + \cdots + a_k + \cdots$$

converges, then $\lim_{k\to\infty} a_k = 0$.

This means that if $\lim_{k\to\infty} a_k \neq 0$ the series must diverge.

The series in Example 2 is a **geometric series** because each term is obtained from its preceding term by multiplying by the same number r—in this case, $r = 1/10$. (The series of areas for the infinitely halved square at the beginning of this chapter is also geometric.) The convergence of geometric series is one of the few infinite processes with which mathematicians were reasonably comfortable prior to calculus. You may have already seen the following result in a previous course.

The **geometric series**

$$a + ar + ar^2 + ar^3 + \cdots + ar^{n-1} + \cdots = \sum_{n=1}^{\infty} ar^{n-1}$$

converges to the sum $a/(1 - r)$ if $|r| < 1$, and diverges if $|r| \geq 1$.

This completely settles the issue for geometric series. We know which ones converge and which ones diverge, and for the convergent ones we know what the sums must be. The interval $-1 < r < 1$ is the **interval of convergence.**

EXAMPLE 3 Analyzing Geometric Series

Tell whether each series converges or diverges. If it converges, give its sum.

(a) $\displaystyle\sum_{n=1}^{\infty} 3\left(\frac{1}{2}\right)^{n-1}$

(b) $\displaystyle 1 - \frac{1}{2} + \frac{1}{4} - \frac{1}{8} + \cdots + \left(-\frac{1}{2}\right)^{n-1} + \cdots$

(c) $\displaystyle\sum_{k=0}^{\infty} \left(\frac{3}{5}\right)^{k}$

(d) $\displaystyle\frac{\pi}{2} + \frac{\pi^2}{4} + \frac{\pi^3}{8} + \cdots$

SOLUTION

(a) First term is $a = 3$ and $r = 1/2$. The series converges to

$$\frac{3}{1 - (1/2)} = 6.$$

(b) First term is $a = 1$ and $r = -1/2$. The series converges to

$$\frac{1}{1 - (-1/2)} = \frac{2}{3}.$$

continued

Partial Sums

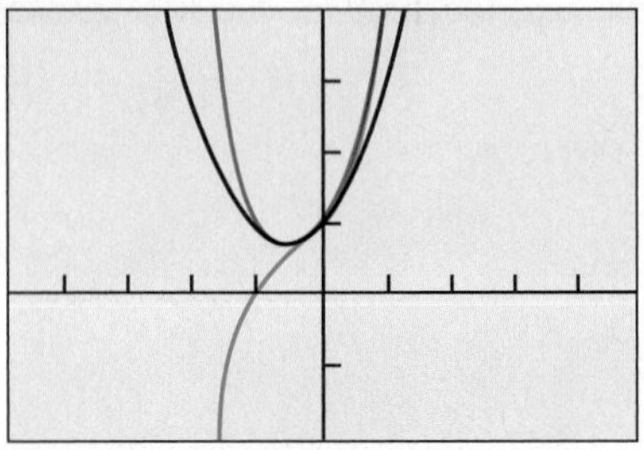

[–4.7, 4.7] by [–2, 4]

(a)

$y = 1/(1-x)$

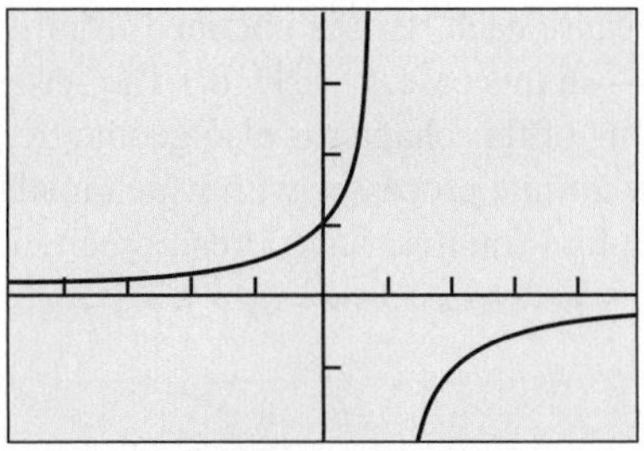

[–4.7, 4.7] by [–2, 4]

(b)

Figure 10.1 (a) Partial sums converging to $1/(1-x)$ on the interval $(0, 1)$. The partial sums graphed here are $1 + x + x^2$, $1 + x + x^2 + x^3$, and $1 + x + x^2 + x^3 + x^4$. (b) Notice how the graphs in (a) resemble the graph of $1/(1-x)$ on the interval $(-1, 1)$ but are not even close when $|x| \geq 1$.

(c) First term is $a = (3/5)^0 = 1$ and $r = 3/5$. The series converges to

$$\frac{1}{1-(3/5)} = \frac{5}{2}.$$

(d) In this series, $r = \pi/2 > 1$. The series diverges. ***Now Try Exercises 11 and 19.***

We have hardly begun our study of infinite series, but knowing everything there is to know about the convergence and divergence of an *entire class* of series (geometric) is an impressive start. Like the Renaissance mathematicians, we are ready to explore where this might lead. We are ready to bring in x.

Representing Functions by Series

If $|x| < 1$, then the geometric series formula assures us that

$$1 + x + x^2 + x^3 + \cdots + x^n + \cdots = \frac{1}{1-x}.$$

Consider this statement for a moment. The expression on the right defines a function whose domain is the set of all numbers $x \neq 1$. The expression on the left defines a function whose domain is the interval of convergence, $|x| < 1$. The equality is understood to hold only on this latter domain, where both sides of the equation are defined. On this domain, the series *represents* the function $1/(1-x)$.

The partial sums of the infinite series on the left are all polynomials, so we can graph them (Figure 10.1). As expected, we see that the convergence is strong in the interval $(-1, 1)$ but breaks down when $|x| \geq 1$.

The expression $\sum_{n=0}^{\infty} x^n$ is like a polynomial in that it is a sum of coefficients times powers of x, but polynomials have *finite* degrees and do not suffer from divergence for the wrong values of x. Just as an infinite series of numbers is not a mere sum, this series of powers of x is not a mere polynomial.

When we set $x = 0$ in the expression

$$\sum_{n=0}^{\infty} c_n x^n = c_0 + c_1 x + c_2 x^2 + \cdots + c_n x^n + \cdots,$$

we get c_0 on the right but $c_0 \cdot 0^0$ on the left. Since 0^0 is not a number, this is a slight flaw in the notation, which we agree to overlook. The same situation arises when we set

$$x = a \text{ in } \sum_{n=0}^{\infty} c_n (x-a)^n.$$

In either case, we agree that the expression will equal c_0. (It really *should* equal c_0, so we are not compromising the mathematics; we are clarifying the notation we use to convey the mathematics.)

DEFINITION Power Series

An expression of the form

$$\sum_{n=0}^{\infty} c_n x^n = c_0 + c_1 x + c_2 x^2 + \cdots + c_n x^n + \cdots$$

is a **power series centered at $x = 0$.** An expression of the form

$$\sum_{n=0}^{\infty} c_n (x-a)^n = c_0 + c_1(x-a) + c_2(x-a)^2 + \cdots + c_n(x-a)^n + \cdots$$

is a **power series centered at $x = a$.** The term $c_n(x-a)^n$ is the ***n*th term;** the number a is the **center.**

The geometric series

$$\sum_{n=0}^{\infty} x^n = 1 + x + x^2 + \cdots + x^n + \cdots$$

is a power series centered at $x = 0$. It converges on the interval $-1 < x < 1$, also centered at $x = 0$. This is typical behavior, as we will see in Section 10.4. A power series either converges for all x, converges on a finite interval with the same center as the series, or converges only at the center itself.

We have seen that the power series $\sum_{n=0}^{\infty} x^n$ represents the function $1/(1 - x)$ on the domain $(-1, 1)$. Can we find power series to represent other functions?

EXPLORATION 1 Finding Power Series for Other Functions

1. Given that $1/(1 - x)$ is represented by the power series

$$1 + x + x^2 + \cdots + x^n + \cdots$$

on the interval $(-1, 1)$,

(a) find a power series that represents $1/(1 + x)$ on $(-1, 1)$.
(b) find a power series that represents $x/(1 + x)$ on $(-1, 1)$.
(c) find a power series that represents $1/(1 - 2x)$ on $(-1/2, 1/2)$.
(d) find a power series that represents

$$\frac{1}{x} = \frac{1}{1 + (x - 1)}$$

on $(0, 2)$.

Could you have found the intervals of convergence yourself?

2. Find a power series that represents

$$\frac{1}{3x} = \frac{1}{3} \cdot \left(\frac{1}{1 + (x - 1)}\right)$$

and give its interval of convergence.

Differentiation and Integration

So far we have only represented functions by power series that happen to be geometric. The partial sums that converge to those power series, however, are *polynomials,* and we can apply calculus to polynomials. It would seem logical that the calculus of polynomials (the first rules we encountered in Chapter 3) would also apply to power series.

EXAMPLE 4 Finding a Power Series by Differentiation

Given that $1/(1 - x)$ is represented by the power series

$$1 + x + x^2 + \cdots + x^n + \cdots$$

on the interval $(-1, 1)$, find a power series to represent $1/(1 - x)^2$.

SOLUTION

Notice that $1/(1 - x)^2$ is the derivative of $1/(1 - x)$. To find the power series, we differentiate both sides of the equation

$$\frac{1}{1 - x} = 1 + x + x^2 + x^3 + \cdots + x^n + \cdots.$$

$$\frac{d}{dx}\left(\frac{1}{1 - x}\right) = \frac{d}{dx}(1 + x + x^2 + x^3 + \cdots + x^n + \cdots)$$

$$\frac{1}{(1 - x)^2} = 1 + 2x + 3x^2 + 4x^3 + \cdots + nx^{n-1} + \cdots$$

continued

What about the interval of convergence? Since the original series converges for $-1 < x < 1$, it would seem that the differentiated series ought to converge on the same open interval. Graphs (Figure 10.2) of the partial sums $1 + 2x + 3x^2$, $1 + 2x + 3x^2 + 4x^3$, and $1 + 2x + 3x^2 + 4x^3 + 5x^4$ suggest that this is the case (although such empirical evidence does not constitute a proof). ***Now Try Exercise 27.***

Partial Sums

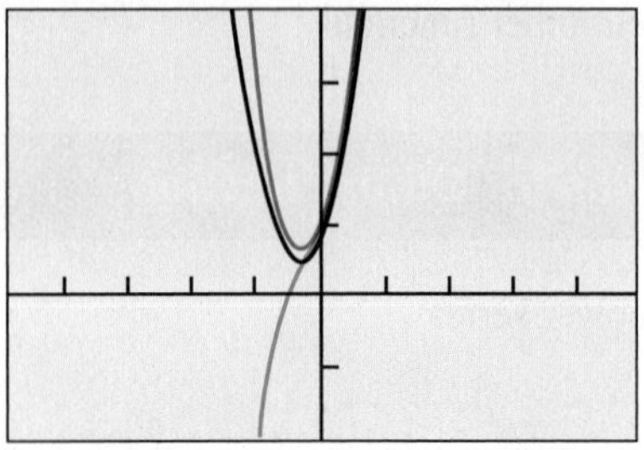

[–4.7, 4.7] by [–2, 4]

(a)

$y = 1/(1-x)^2$

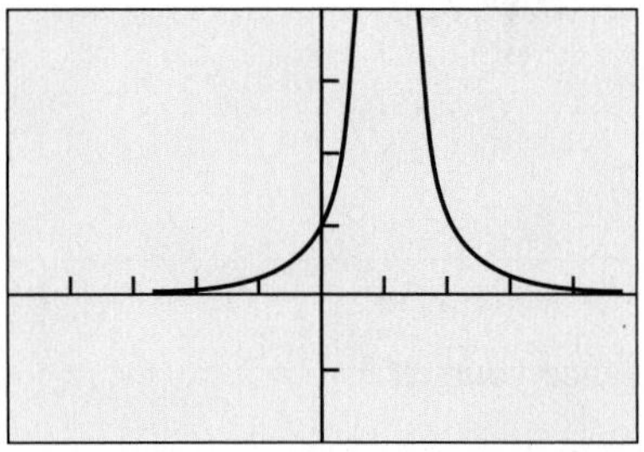

[–4.7, 4.7] by [–2, 4]

(b)

Figure 10.2 (a) The polynomial partial sums of the power series we derived for (b) $1/(1 - x)^2$ seem to converge on the open interval $(-1, 1)$. (Example 4)

The basic theorem about differentiating power series is the following.

THEOREM 1 Term-by-Term Differentiation

If $f(x) = \sum_{n=0}^{\infty} c_n(x-a)^n = c_0 + c_1(x-a) + c_2(x-a)^2 + \cdots + c_n(x-a)^n + \cdots$

converges for $|x - a| < R$, then the series

$$\sum_{n=1}^{\infty} nc_n(x-a)^{n-1} = c_1 + 2c_2(x-a) + 3c_3(x-a)^2 + \cdots + nc_n(x-a)^{n-1} + \cdots,$$

obtained by differentiating the series for f term by term, converges for $|x - a| < R$ and represents $f'(x)$ on that interval. If the series for f converges for all x, then so does the series for f'.

Theorem 1 says that if a power series is differentiated term by term, the new series will converge on the same interval to the derivative of the function represented by the original series. This gives a way to generate new connections between functions and series.

Another way to reveal new connections between functions and series is by integration.

EXAMPLE 5 Finding a Power Series by Integration

Given that

$$\frac{1}{1+x} = 1 - x + x^2 - x^3 + \cdots + (-x)^n + \cdots, \quad -1 < x < 1$$

(Exploration 1, part 1), find a power series to represent $\ln(1 + x)$.

SOLUTION

Recall that $1/(1 + x)$ is the derivative of $\ln(1 + x)$. We can therefore integrate the series for $1/(1 + x)$ to obtain a series for $\ln(1 + x)$ (no absolute value bars are necessary because $(1 + x)$ is positive for $-1 < x < 1$).

$$\frac{1}{1+x} = 1 - x + x^2 - x^3 + \cdots + (-x)^n + \cdots$$
$$= 1 - x + x^2 - x^3 + \cdots + (-1)^n x^n + \cdots$$

$$\int_0^x \frac{1}{1+t}\,dt = \int_0^x (1 - t + t^2 - t^3 + \cdots + (-1)^n t^n + \cdots)\,dt$$

t is a dummy variable.

$$\ln(1+t)\Big]_0^x = \left[t - \frac{t^2}{2} + \frac{t^3}{3} - \frac{t^4}{4} + \cdots + (-1)^n \frac{t^{n+1}}{n+1} + \cdots\right]_0^x$$

$$\ln(1+x) = x - \frac{x^2}{2} + \frac{x^3}{3} - \frac{x^4}{4} + \cdots + (-1)^n \frac{x^{n+1}}{n+1} + \cdots$$

continued

It would seem logical for the new series to converge where the original series converges, on the open interval $(-1, 1)$. The graphs of the partial sums in Figure 10.3 support this idea. ***Now Try Exercise 33.***

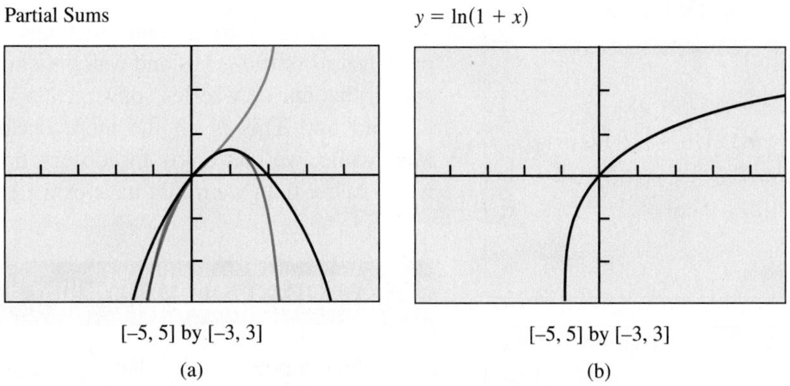

Figure 10.3 (a) The graphs of the partial sums

$$x - \frac{x^2}{2}, \qquad x - \frac{x^2}{2} + \frac{x^3}{3}, \qquad \text{and} \qquad x - \frac{x^2}{2} + \frac{x^3}{3} - \frac{x^4}{4}$$

closing in on (b) the graph of $\ln(1 + x)$ over the interval $(-1, 1)$. (Example 5)

The idea that the integrated series in Example 5 converges to $\ln(1 + x)$ for all x between -1 and 1 is confirmed by the following theorem.

THEOREM 2 Term-by-Term Integration

If $f(x) = \sum_{n=0}^{\infty} c_n(x - a)^n = c_0 + c_1(x - a) + c_2(x - a)^2 + \cdots + c_n(x - a)^n + \cdots$

converges for $|x - a| < R$, then the series

$$\sum_{n=0}^{\infty} c_n \frac{(x - a)^{n+1}}{n + 1} = c_0(x - a) + c_1 \frac{(x - a)^2}{2} + c_2 \frac{(x - a)^3}{3} + \cdots + c_n \frac{(x - a)^{n+1}}{n + 1} + \cdots,$$

obtained by integrating the series for f term by term, converges for $|x - a| < R$ and represents $\int_a^x f(t)\,dt$ on that interval. If the series for f converges for all x, then so does the series for the integral.

Theorem 2 says that if a power series is integrated term by term, the new series will converge on the same interval to the integral of the function represented by the original series.

There is still more to be learned from Example 5. The original equation

$$\frac{1}{1 + x} = 1 - x + x^2 - x^3 + \cdots + (-x)^n + \cdots$$

clearly diverges at $x = 1$ (see Example 1). The behavior is not so apparent, however, for the equation we obtained by integrating:

$$\ln(1 + x) = x - \frac{x^2}{2} + \frac{x^3}{3} - \frac{x^4}{4} + \cdots + (-1)^n \frac{x^{n+1}}{n + 1} + \cdots$$

Some calculators have a *sequence mode* that enables you to generate a sequence of partial sums, but you can also do it with simple commands on the home screen. Try entering the two multiple-step commands shown on the first screen below.

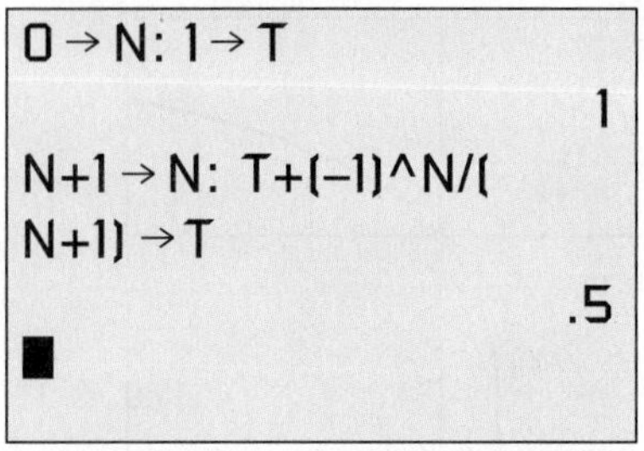

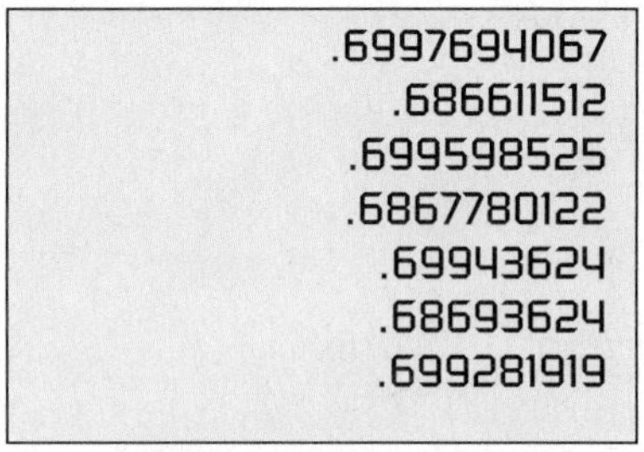

If you are successful, then every time you hit ENTER, the calculator will display the next partial sum of the series

$$1 - \frac{1}{2} + \frac{1}{3} - \frac{1}{4} + \cdots + \frac{(-1)^n}{n+1} + \cdots.$$

The second screen shows the result of about 80 ENTERs. The sequence certainly seems to be converging to $\ln 2 = 0.6931471806\ldots$.

If we let $x = 1$ on both sides of this equation, we get

$$\ln 2 = 1 - \frac{1}{2} + \frac{1}{3} - \frac{1}{4} + \cdots + \frac{(-1)^n}{n+1} + \cdots,$$

which looks like a reasonable statement. It looks even more reasonable if you look at the partial sums of the series and watch them converge toward ln 2 (see margin note). It would appear that our new series converges at 1 despite the fact that we obtained it from a series that did not! This is all the more reason to take a careful look at convergence later. Meanwhile, we can enjoy the observation that we have created a series that apparently works better than we might have expected and better than Theorem 2 could guarantee.

EXPLORATION 2 Finding a Power Series for $\tan^{-1} x$

1. Find a power series that represents $1/(1 + x^2)$ on $(-1, 1)$.
2. Use the technique of Example 5 to find a power series that represents $\tan^{-1} x$ on $(-1, 1)$.
3. Graph the first four partial sums. Do the graphs suggest convergence on the open interval $(-1, 1)$?
4. Do you think that the series for $\tan^{-1} x$ converges at $x = 1$? Can you support your answer with evidence?

Identifying a Series

So far we have been finding power series to represent functions. Let us now try to find the function that a given power series represents.

EXPLORATION 3 A Series with a Curious Property

Define a function *f* by a power series as follows:

$$f(x) = 1 + x + \frac{x^2}{2!} + \frac{x^3}{3!} + \frac{x^4}{4!} + \cdots + \frac{x^n}{n!} + \cdots$$

1. Find $f'(x)$.
2. Find $f(0)$.
3. What well-known function do you suppose *f* is?
4. Use your responses to parts 1 and 2 to set up an initial value problem that the function *f* must solve. You will need a differential equation and an initial condition.
5. Solve the initial value problem to prove your conjecture in part 3.
6. Graph the first three partial sums. What appears to be the interval of convergence?
7. Graph the next three partial sums. Did you underestimate the interval of convergence?

The correct answer to part 7 in Exploration 3 above is "yes," unless you had the keen insight (or reckless bravado) to answer "all real numbers" in part 6. You will be able to prove the remarkable fact that this series converges *for all x* by using the Remainder Estimation Theorem, which you will see in Section 10.3.

Quick Review 10.1 (For help, go to Section 9.1.)

In Exercises 1 and 2, find the first four terms and the 30th term of the sequence

$$\{u_n\}_{n=1}^{\infty} = \{u_1, u_2, \ldots, u_n, \ldots\}.$$

1. $u_n = \dfrac{4}{n+2}$ **2.** $u_n = \dfrac{(-1)^n}{n}$

In Exercises 3 and 4, the sequences are geometric ($a_{n+1}/a_n = r$, a constant). Find

(a) the common ratio r. **(b)** the tenth term.

(c) a rule for the nth term.

3. $\{2, 6, 18, 54, \ldots\}$ **4.** $\{8, -4, 2, -1, \ldots\}$

In Exercises 5–10,

(a) graph the sequence $\{a_n\}$.

(b) determine $\lim_{n\to\infty} a_n$.

5. $a_n = \dfrac{1-n}{n^2}$ **6.** $a_n = \left(1+\dfrac{1}{n}\right)^n$

7. $a_n = (-1)^n$ **8.** $a_n = \dfrac{1-2n}{1+2n}$

9. $a_n = 2 - \dfrac{1}{n}$ **10.** $a_n = \dfrac{\ln(n+1)}{n}$

Section 10.1 Exercises

Exercise numbers with a gray background indicate problems that the authors have designed to be solved *without a calculator.*

1. Replace the $*$ with an expression that will generate the series

$$1 - \frac{1}{4} + \frac{1}{9} - \frac{1}{16} + \cdots.$$

(a) $\sum_{n=1}^{\infty} (-1)^{n-1}\left(\dfrac{1}{*}\right)$ **(b)** $\sum_{n=0}^{\infty} (-1)^{n}\left(\dfrac{1}{*}\right)$

(c) $\sum_{n=*}^{\infty} (-1)^{n}\left(\dfrac{-1}{(n-2)^2}\right)$

2. Write an expression for the nth term, a_n

(a) $\sum_{n=0}^{\infty} a_n = 1 + \dfrac{1}{3} + \dfrac{1}{9} + \dfrac{1}{27} + \dfrac{1}{81} + \cdots$

(b) $\sum_{n=1}^{\infty} a_n = 1 - \dfrac{1}{2} + \dfrac{1}{3} - \dfrac{1}{4} + \dfrac{1}{5} - \cdots$

(c) $\sum_{n=0}^{\infty} a_n = 5 + 0.5 + 0.05 + 0.005 + 0.0005 + \cdots$

In Exercises 3–6, tell whether the series is the same as

$$\sum_{n=1}^{\infty}\left(-\frac{1}{2}\right)^{n-1}.$$

3. $\sum_{n=1}^{\infty} -\left(\dfrac{1}{2}\right)^{n-1}$ **4.** $\sum_{n=0}^{\infty}\left(-\dfrac{1}{2}\right)^{n}$

5. $\sum_{n=0}^{\infty} (-1)^n\left(\dfrac{1}{2}\right)^{n}$ **6.** $\sum_{n=1}^{\infty} \dfrac{(-1)^n}{2^{n-1}}$

In Exercises 7–10, compute the limit of the partial sums to determine whether the series converges or diverges.

7. $1 + 1.1 + 1.11 + 1.111 + 1.1111 + \cdots$

8. $2 - 1 + 1 - 1 + 1 - 1 + \cdots$

9. $\dfrac{1}{2} + \dfrac{1}{4} + \dfrac{1}{8} + \cdots + \dfrac{1}{2^k} + \cdots$

10. $3 + 0.5 + 0.05 + 0.005 + 0.0005 + \cdots$

In Exercises 11–20, tell whether the series converges or diverges. If it converges, give its sum.

11. $1 + \dfrac{2}{3} + \left(\dfrac{2}{3}\right)^2 + \left(\dfrac{2}{3}\right)^3 + \cdots + \left(\dfrac{2}{3}\right)^n + \cdots$

12. $1 - 2 + 3 - 4 + 5 - \cdots + (-1)^n(n+1) + \cdots$

13. $\sum_{n=0}^{\infty}\left(\dfrac{5}{4}\right)\left(\dfrac{2}{3}\right)^n$ **14.** $\sum_{n=0}^{\infty}\left(\dfrac{2}{3}\right)\left(\dfrac{5}{4}\right)^n$

15. $\sum_{n=0}^{\infty} \cos(n\pi)$

16. $3 - 0.3 + 0.03 - 0.003 + 0.0003 - \cdots + 3(-0.1)^n + \cdots$

17. $\sum_{n=0}^{\infty} \sin^n\left(\dfrac{\pi}{4} + n\pi\right)$

18. $\dfrac{1}{2} + \dfrac{2}{3} + \dfrac{3}{4} + \dfrac{4}{5} + \cdots + \dfrac{n}{n+1} + \cdots$

19. $\sum_{n=1}^{\infty}\left(\dfrac{e}{\pi}\right)^n$ **20.** $\sum_{n=0}^{\infty} \dfrac{5^n}{6^{n+1}}$

In Exercises 21–24, find the interval of convergence and the function of x represented by the geometric series.

21. $\sum_{n=0}^{\infty} 2^n x^n$ **22.** $\sum_{n=0}^{\infty} (-1)^n (x+1)^n$

23. $\sum_{n=0}^{\infty}\left(-\dfrac{1}{2}\right)^n (x-3)^n$ **24.** $\sum_{n=0}^{\infty} 3\left(\dfrac{x-1}{2}\right)^n$

In Exercises 25 and 26, find the values of x for which the geometric series converges and find the function of x it represents.

25. $\sum_{n=0}^{\infty} \sin^n x$ **26.** $\sum_{n=0}^{\infty} \tan^n x$

In Exercises 27–30, use the series and the function $f(x)$ that it represents from the indicated exercise to find a power series for $f'(x)$.

27. Exercise 21 **28.** Exercise 22

29. Exercise 23 **30.** Exercise 24

In Exercises 31–34, use the series centered at a and the function it represents to find a power series for $\int_a^x f(t)\,dt$.

31. Exercise 21 **32.** Exercise 22

33. Exercise 23 **34.** Exercise 24

35. Writing to Learn Each of the following series diverges in a slightly different way. Explain what is happening to the sequence of partial sums in each case.

(a) $\sum_{n=1}^{\infty} 2n$ **(b)** $\sum_{n=0}^{\infty} (-1)^n$ **(c)** $\sum_{n=1}^{\infty} (-1)^n(2n)$

36. Prove that $\sum_{n=0}^{\infty} \frac{e^{n\pi}}{\pi^{ne}}$ diverges.

37. Solve for x: $\sum_{n=0}^{\infty} x^n = 20$.

38. Writing to Learn Explain how it is possible, given any real number at all, to construct an infinite series of non-zero terms that converges to it.

39. Make up a geometric series Σar^{n-1} that converges to the number 5 if

(a) $a = 2$ **(b)** $a = 13/2$

In Exercises 40 and 41, express the repeating decimal as a geometric series and find its sum.

40. $0.\overline{21}$ **41.** $0.\overline{234}$

In Exercises 42–47, express the number as the ratio of two integers.

42. $0.\overline{7} = 0.7777\ldots$

43. $0.\overline{d} = 0.dddd\ldots,$ where d is a digit

44. $0.0\overline{6} = 0.06666\ldots$ **45.** $1.\overline{414} = 1.414\,414\,414\ldots$

46. $1.24\overline{123} = 1.24\,123\,123\,123\ldots$

47. $3.\overline{142857} = 3.142857\,142857\ldots$

48. *Bouncing Ball* A ball is dropped from a height of 4 m. Each time it strikes the pavement after falling from a height of h m, it rebounds to a height of $0.6h$ m. Find the total distance the ball travels up and down.

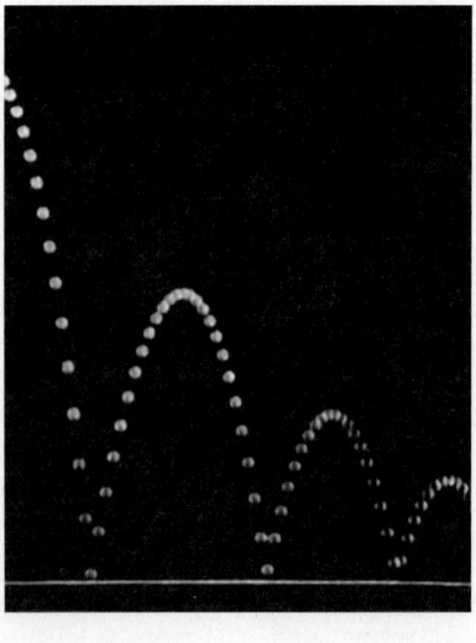

49. *(Continuation of Exercise 48)* Find the total number of seconds that the ball in Exercise 48 travels. [*Hint:* A freely falling ball travels $4.9t^2$ meters in t seconds, so it will fall h meters in $\sqrt{h/4.9}$ seconds. Bouncing from ground to apex takes the same time as falling from apex to ground.]

50. *Summing Areas* The figure below shows the first five of an infinite sequence of squares. The outermost square has an area of 4 m^2. Each of the other squares is obtained by joining the midpoints of the sides of the preceding square. Find the sum of the areas of all the squares.

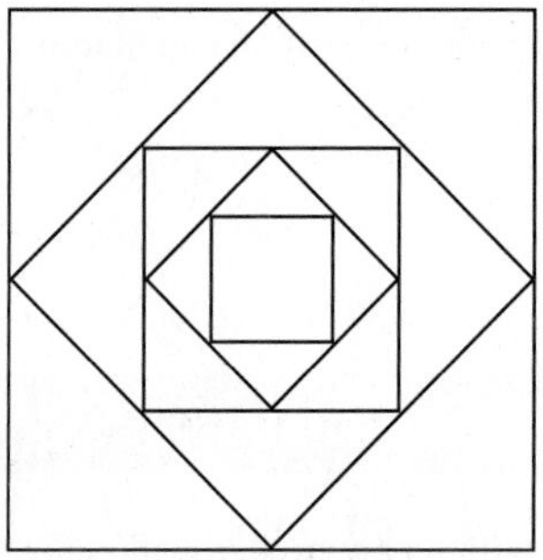

51. *Summing Areas* The accompanying figure shows the first three rows and part of the fourth row of a sequence of rows of semicircles. There are 2^n semicircles in the nth row, each of radius $1/(2^n)$. Find the sum of the areas of all the semicircles.

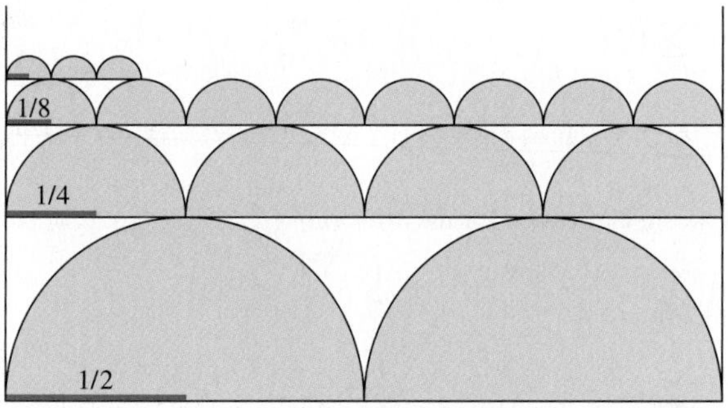

52. *Sum of a Finite Geometric Progression* Let a and r be real numbers with $r \neq 1$, and let

$$S = a + ar + ar^2 + ar^3 + \cdots + ar^{n-1}.$$

(a) Find $S - rS$.

(b) Use the result in part (a) to show that $S = \frac{a - ar^n}{1 - r}$.

53. *Sum of a Convergent Geometric Series* Exercise 52 gives a formula for the nth partial sum of an infinite geometric series. Use this formula to show that $\sum_{n=1}^{\infty} ar^{n-1}$ diverges when $|r| \geq 1$ and converges to $a/(1 - r)$ when $|r| < 1$.

In Exercises 54–59, find a power series to represent the given function and identify its interval of convergence. When writing the power series, include a formula for the nth term.

54. $\frac{1}{1 + 3x}$ **55.** $\frac{x}{1 - 2x}$

56. $\frac{3}{1 - x^3}$ **57.** $\frac{1}{1 + (x - 4)}$

58. $\frac{1}{4x} = \frac{1}{4}\left(\frac{1}{1 + (x - 1)}\right)$ **59.** $\frac{1}{2 - x}$ [*Hint:* Rewrite $2 - x$.]

60. Find the value of b for which $1 + e^b + e^{2b} + e^{3b} + \cdots = 9$.

61. Let S be the series $\sum_{n=0}^{\infty}\left(\frac{t}{1+t}\right)^n, \quad t \neq 0.$

(a) Find the value to which S converges when $t = 1$.

(b) Determine all values of t for which S converges.

(c) Find all values of t that make the sum of S greater than 10.

62. *nth Term Test* Assume that the series $\sum_{k=1}^{\infty} a_k$ converges to S.

(a) Writing to Learn Explain why $\lim_{n\to\infty} \sum_{k=1}^{k=n} a_k = S$.

(b) Show that $S_n = S_{n-1} + a_n$, where S_n denotes the nth partial sum of the series.

(c) Show that $\lim_{n\to\infty} a_n = 0$.

63. *A Series for ln x* Starting with the power series found for $1/x$ in Exploration 1, Part 4, find a power series for $\ln x$ centered at $(x - 1) = 1$.

64. *Differentiation* Use differentiation to find a series for $f(x) = 2/(1 - x)^3$. What is the interval of convergence of your series?

65. Group Activity *Intervals of Convergence* How much can the interval of convergence of a power series be changed by integration or differentiation? To be specific, suppose that the power series

$$f(x) = c_0 + c_1x + c_2x^2 + \cdots + c_nx^n + \cdots$$

converges for $-1 < x < 1$ and diverges for all other values of x.

(a) Writing to Learn Could the series obtained by integrating the series for f term by term possibly converge for $-2 < x < 2$? Explain. [*Hint:* Apply Theorem 1, not Theorem 2.]

(b) Writing to Learn Could the series obtained by differentiating the series for f term by term possibly converge for $-2 < x < 2$? Explain.

Standardized Test Questions

66. True or False The series

$$\frac{1}{2} + \frac{1.01}{2} + \frac{(1.01)^2}{2} + \cdots + \frac{(1.01)^n}{2} + \cdots$$

converges. Justify your answer.

67. True or False The series $1 + \frac{1}{2} + \frac{1}{4} + \frac{1}{8} + \frac{1}{16} + \cdots$ diverges. Justify your answer.

68. Multiple Choice To which of the following numbers does the series $1 + \frac{1}{3} + \frac{1}{9} + \frac{1}{27} + \cdots$ converge?

(A) 2/3 **(B)** 9/8 **(C)** 3/2 **(D)** 2 **(E)** It diverges

In Exercises 69–71, use the geometric series $\sum_{n=0}^{\infty}(x - 1)^n$, which represents the function $f(x)$.

69. Multiple Choice Find the values of x for which the series converges.

(A) $0 < x < 2$ **(B)** $0 < x < 1$ **(C)** $-1 < x < 0$

(D) $-1 < x < 1$ **(E)** $-2 < x < 0$

70. Multiple Choice Which of the following is the function that the power series represents?

(A) $\frac{1}{x-1}$ **(B)** $\frac{1}{1-2x}$ **(C)** $-\frac{1}{x}$ **(D)** $\frac{1}{x-2}$ **(E)** $\frac{1}{2-x}$

71. Multiple Choice Which of the following is a function that $\int_0^x f(t)\,dt$ represents?

(A) $-\ln\left(\frac{x-2}{2}\right)$ **(B)** $\ln\left(\frac{x-2}{2}\right)$ **(C)** $\frac{1}{(x-2)^2}$

(D) $-\ln\left(\frac{|x-2|}{2}\right)$ **(E)** $\ln\left(\frac{|x-2|}{2}\right)$

Exploration

72. Let $f(t) = \frac{4}{1+t^2}$ and $G(x) = \int_0^x f(t)\,dt$.

(a) Find the first four nonzero terms and the general term for a power series for $f(t)$ centered at $t = 0$.

(b) Find the first four nonzero terms and the general term for a power series for $G(x)$ centered at $x = 0$.

(c) Find the interval of convergence of the power series in part (a).

(d) The interval of convergence of the power series in part (b) is almost the same as the interval in part (c), but includes two more numbers. What are the numbers?

Extending the Ideas

The sequence $\{a_n\}$ **converges** to the number L if to every positive number ε there corresponds an integer N such that for all n,

$$n > N \Rightarrow |a_n - L| < \varepsilon.$$

L is the **limit** of the sequence and we write $\lim_{n\to\infty} a_n = L$. If no such number L exists, we say that $\{a_n\}$ **diverges.**

73. *Tail of a Sequence* Prove that if $\{a_n\}$ is a convergent sequence, then to every positive number ε there corresponds an integer N such that for all m and n,

$$m > N \text{ and } n > N \Rightarrow |a_m - a_n| < \varepsilon.$$

[*Hint:* Let $\lim_{n\to\infty} a_n = L$. As the terms approach L, how far apart can they be?]

74. *Uniqueness of Limits* Prove that limits of sequences are unique. That is, show that if L_1 and L_2 are numbers such that $\lim_{n\to\infty} a_n = L_1$ and $\lim_{n\to\infty} a_n = L_2$, then $L_1 = L_2$.

75. *Limits and Subsequences* Prove that if two subsequences of a sequence $\{a_n\}$ have different limits $L_1 \neq L_2$, then $\{a_n\}$ diverges.

76. *Limits and Asymptotes*

(a) Show that the sequence with nth term $a_n = (3n + 1)/(n + 1)$ converges.

(b) If $\lim_{n\to\infty} a_n = L$, explain why $y = L$ is a horizontal asymptote of the graph of the function

$$f(x) = \frac{3x+1}{x+1}$$

obtained by replacing n by x in the nth term.

10.2 Taylor Series

What you will learn about . . .

- Constructing a Series
- Series for sin *x* and cos *x*
- Beauty Bare
- Maclaurin and Taylor Series
- Combining Taylor Series
- Table of Maclaurin Series

and why . . .

The partial sums of a Taylor series are polynomials that can be used to approximate the function represented by the series.

Constructing a Series

A comprehensive understanding of geometric series served us well in Section 10.1, enabling us to find power series to represent certain functions, and functions that are equivalent to certain power series (all of these equivalencies being subject to the condition of convergence). In this section we learn a more general technique for constructing power series, one that makes good use of the tools of calculus.

Let us start by constructing a polynomial.

EXPLORATION 1 Designing a Polynomial to Specifications

Construct a polynomial $P(x) = a_0 + a_1x + a_2x^2 + a_3x^3 + a_4x^4$ with the following behavior at $x = 0$:

$$\begin{aligned} P(0) &= 5, \\ P'(0) &= 7, \\ P''(0) &= 11, \\ P'''(0) &= 13, \text{ and} \\ P^{(4)}(0) &= 17. \end{aligned}$$

This task might look difficult at first, but when you try it you will find that the predictability of differentiation when applied to polynomials makes it straightforward. (Be sure to check this out before you move on.)

There is nothing special about the number of derivatives in Exploration 1. We could have prescribed the value of the polynomial and its first n derivatives at $x = 0$ for any n and found a polynomial of degree at most n to match. Our plan now is to use the technique of Exploration 1 to construct polynomials that approximate functions by emulating their behavior at 0.

EXAMPLE 1 Approximating ln (1 + *x*) by a Polynomial

Construct a polynomial $P(x) = a_0 + a_1x + a_2x^2 + a_3x^3 + a_4x^4$ that matches the behavior of $\ln(1 + x)$ at $x = 0$ through its first four derivatives. That is,

$$\begin{aligned} P(0) &= \ln(1 + x) && \text{at } x = 0, \\ P'(0) &= (\ln(1 + x))' && \text{at } x = 0, \\ P''(0) &= (\ln(1 + x))'' && \text{at } x = 0, \\ P'''(0) &= (\ln(1 + x))''' && \text{at } x = 0, \text{ and} \\ P^{(4)}(0) &= (\ln(1 + x))^{(4)} && \text{at } x = 0. \end{aligned}$$

SOLUTION

This is just like Exploration 1, except that first we need to find out what the numbers are.

$$P(0) = \ln(1 + x)\Big|_{x=0} = 0$$

$$P'(0) = \frac{1}{1 + x}\Big|_{x=0} = 1$$

continued

$$P''(0) = -\frac{1}{(1+x)^2}\bigg|_{x=0} = -1$$

$$P'''(0) = \frac{2}{(1+x)^3}\bigg|_{x=0} = 2$$

$$P^{(4)}(0) = -\frac{6}{(1+x)^4}\bigg|_{x=0} = -6$$

In working through Exploration 1, you probably noticed that the coefficient of the term x^n in the polynomial we seek is $P^{(n)}(0)$ divided by $n!$. The polynomial is

$$P(x) = 0 + x - \frac{x^2}{2} + \frac{x^3}{3} - \frac{x^4}{4}.$$

Now Try Exercise 1.

We have just constructed the fourth-order **Taylor polynomial** for the function $\ln(1 + x)$ at $x = 0$. You might recognize it as the beginning of the power series we discovered for $\ln(1 + x)$ in Example 5 of Section 10.1, when we came upon it by integrating a geometric series. If we keep going, of course, we will gradually reconstruct that entire series one term at a time, improving the approximation near $x = 0$ with every term we add. The series is called the **Taylor series** generated by the function $\ln(1 + x)$ at $x = 0$.

You might also recall Figure 10.3, which shows how the polynomial approximations converge nicely to $\ln(1 + x)$ near $x = 0$, but then gradually peel away from the curve as x gets farther away from 0 in either direction. Given that the coefficients are totally determined by specifying behavior at $x = 0$, that is exactly what we ought to expect.

Series for sin *x* and cos *x*

We can use the technique of Example 1 to construct Taylor series about $x = 0$ for any function, as long as we can keep taking derivatives there. Two functions that are particularly well suited for this treatment are the sine and cosine.

EXAMPLE 2 Constructing a Power Series for sin *x*

Construct the seventh-order Taylor polynomial and the Taylor series for $\sin x$ at $x = 0$.

SOLUTION

We need to evaluate $\sin x$ and its first seven derivatives at $x = 0$. Fortunately, this is not hard to do.

$$\begin{aligned}
\sin(0) &= 0 \\
\sin'(0) &= \cos(0) = 1 \\
\sin''(0) &= -\sin(0) = 0 \\
\sin'''(0) &= -\cos(0) = -1 \\
\sin^{(4)}(0) &= \sin(0) = 0 \\
\sin^{(5)}(0) &= \cos(0) = 1 \\
&\vdots
\end{aligned}$$

The pattern 0, 1, 0, -1 will keep repeating forever.

continued

The unique seventh-order Taylor polynomial that matches all these derivatives at $x = 0$ is

$$P_7(x) = 0 + 1x - 0x^2 - \frac{1}{3!}x^3 + 0x^4 + \frac{1}{5!}x^5 - 0x^6 - \frac{1}{7!}x^7$$

$$= x - \frac{x^3}{3!} + \frac{x^5}{5!} - \frac{x^7}{7!}.$$

P_7 is the seventh-order Taylor polynomial for $\sin x$ at $x = 0$. (It also happens to be of seventh degree, but that does not always happen. For example, you can see that P_8 for $\sin x$ will be the same polynomial as P_7.)

To form the Taylor series, we just keep on going:

$$x - \frac{x^3}{3!} + \frac{x^5}{5!} - \frac{x^7}{7!} + \frac{x^9}{9!} - \cdots = \sum_{n=0}^{\infty} (-1)^n \frac{x^{2n+1}}{(2n+1)!}$$

Now Try Exercise 3.

EXPLORATION 2 A Power Series for the Cosine

Group Activity

1. Construct the sixth-order Taylor polynomial and the Taylor series at $x = 0$ for $\cos x$.
2. Compare your method for attacking part 1 with the methods of other groups. Did anyone find a shortcut?

Beauty Bare

Edna St. Vincent Millay, an early 20-century American poet, referring to the experience of simultaneously seeing and understanding the geometric underpinnings of nature, wrote, "Euclid alone has looked on Beauty bare." In case you have never experienced that sort of reverie when gazing upon something geometric, we intend to give you that opportunity now.

In Example 2 we constructed a power series for $\sin x$ by matching the behavior of $\sin x$ at $x = 0$. Let us graph the first nine partial sums together with $y = \sin x$ to see how well we did (Figure 10.4).

Behold what is occurring here! These polynomials were constructed to mimic the behavior of $\sin x$ near $x = 0$. The *only* information we used to construct the coefficients of these polynomials was information about the sine function and its derivatives at 0. Yet, somehow, the information at $x = 0$ is producing a series whose graph not only looks like sine near the origin, but appears to be a clone of the *entire* sine curve. This is no deception, either; we will show in Section 10.3, Example 3, that the Taylor series for $\sin x$ does, in fact, converge to $\sin x$ over the entire real line. We have managed to construct an entire function by knowing its behavior at a single point! (The same is true about the series for $\cos x$ found in Exploration 2.)

We still must remember that convergence is an infinite process. Even the one-billionth–order Taylor polynomial begins to peel away from $\sin x$ as we move away from 0, although imperceptibly at first, and eventually becomes unbounded, as any polynomial must. Nonetheless, we can approximate the sine of *any* number to whatever accuracy we want if we just have the patience to work out enough terms of this series!

This kind of dramatic convergence does not occur for all Taylor series. The Taylor polynomials for $\ln(1 + x)$ do not converge outside the interval from -1 to 1, no matter how many terms we add.

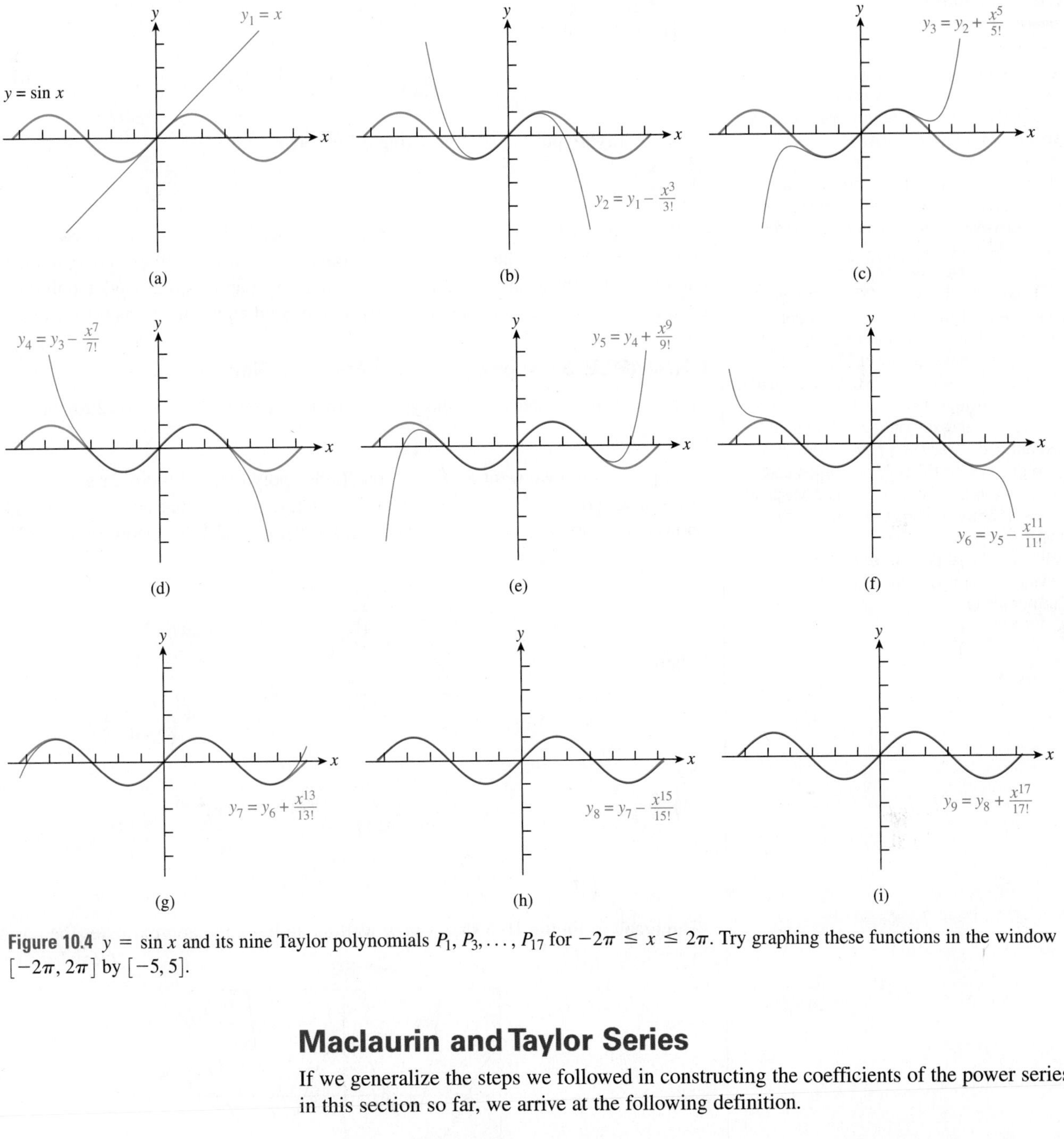

Figure 10.4 $y = \sin x$ and its nine Taylor polynomials $P_1, P_3, \ldots, P_{17}$ for $-2\pi \le x \le 2\pi$. Try graphing these functions in the window $[-2\pi, 2\pi]$ by $[-5, 5]$.

Maclaurin and Taylor Series

If we generalize the steps we followed in constructing the coefficients of the power series in this section so far, we arrive at the following definition.

DEFINITION Taylor Series Generated by *f* at $x = 0$ (Maclaurin Series)

Let f be a function with derivatives of all orders throughout some open interval containing 0. Then the **Taylor series generated by f at $x = 0$** is

$$f(0) + f'(0)x + \frac{f''(0)}{2!}x^2 + \cdots + \frac{f^{(n)}(0)}{n!}x^n + \cdots = \sum_{k=0}^{\infty} \frac{f^{(k)}(0)}{k!}x^k.$$

This series is also called the **Maclaurin series generated by f.**

continued

Who invented Taylor series?

Brook Taylor (1685–1731) did not invent Taylor series, and Maclaurin series were not developed by Colin Maclaurin (1698–1746). James Gregory was already working with Taylor series when Taylor was only a few years old, and he published the Maclaurin series for tan *x*, sec *x*, arctan *x*, and arcsec *x* ten years before Maclaurin was born. Nicolaus Mercator discovered the Maclaurin series for ln (1 + *x*) at about the same time.

Taylor was unaware of Gregory's work when he published his book *Methodus Incrementorum Directa et Inversa* in 1715, containing what we now call Taylor series. Maclaurin quoted Taylor's work in a calculus book he wrote in 1742. The book popularized series representations of functions, and although Maclaurin never claimed to have discovered them, Taylor series centered at *x* = 0 became known as Maclaurin series. History evened things up in the end. Maclaurin, a brilliant mathematician, was the original discoverer of the rule for solving systems of equations that we call Cramer's rule.

The partial sum

$$P_n(x) = \sum_{k=0}^{n} \frac{f^{(k)}(0)}{k!} x^k$$

is the **Taylor polynomial of order n for f at $x = 0$.**

We use $f^{(0)}$ to mean f. *Every* power series constructed in this way converges to the function f at $x = 0$, but we have seen that the convergence might well extend to an interval containing 0, or even to the entire real line. When this happens, the Taylor polynomials that form the partial sums of a Taylor series provide good approximations for f near 0.

EXAMPLE 3 Approximating a Function Near 0

Find the fourth-order Taylor polynomial that approximates $y = \cos 2x$ near $x = 0$.

SOLUTION

The polynomial we want is $P_4(x)$, the Taylor polynomial for $\cos 2x$ at $x = 0$. Before we go cranking out derivatives, though, remember that we can use a known power series to generate another, as we did in Section 10.1. We know from Exploration 2 that

$$\cos x = 1 - \frac{x^2}{2!} + \frac{x^4}{4!} - \cdots + (-1)^n \frac{x^{2n}}{(2n)!} + \cdots.$$

Therefore,

$$\cos 2x = 1 - \frac{(2x)^2}{2!} + \frac{(2x)^4}{4!} - \cdots + (-1)^n \frac{(2x)^{2n}}{(2n)!} + \cdots.$$

So,

$$\begin{aligned} P_4(x) &= 1 - \frac{(2x)^2}{2!} + \frac{(2x)^4}{4!} \\ &= 1 - 2x^2 + (2/3)x^4. \end{aligned}$$

The graph in Figure 10.5 shows how well the polynomial approximates the cosine near $x = 0$.

Now Try Exercise 5.

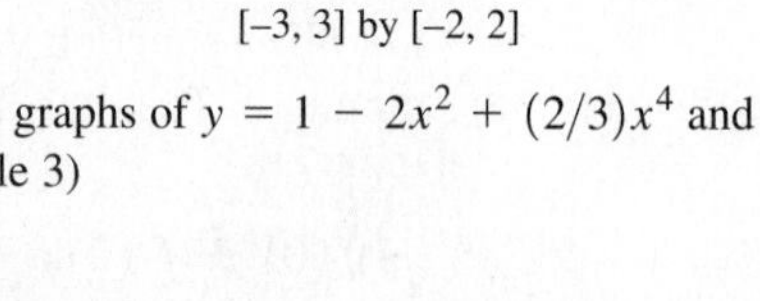

[–3, 3] by [–2, 2]

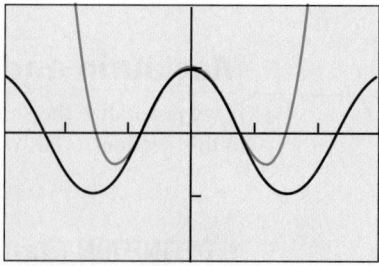

Figure 10.5 The graphs of $y = 1 - 2x^2 + (2/3)x^4$ and $y = \cos 2x$ near $x = 0$. (Example 3)

These polynomial approximations can be useful in a variety of ways. For one thing, it is easy to do calculus with polynomials. For another thing, polynomials are built using only the two basic operations of addition and multiplication, so computers can handle them easily.

EXPLORATION 3 Approximating sin 13

How many terms of the series

$$\sum_{n=0}^{\infty} (-1)^n \frac{x^{2n+1}}{(2n+1)!}$$

are required to approximate sin 13 accurate to the third decimal place?

1. Find sin 13 on your calculator (radians, of course).
2. Enter these two multiple-step commands on your home screen. They will give you the first-order and second-order Taylor polynomial approximations for sin 13. Notice that the second-order approximation, in particular, is not very good.

```
0→N: 13→T
                        13
N+1→N: T+(-1)^N*1
3^(2N+1)/(2N+1)!
→T
              -353.1666667
```

3. Continue to hit ENTER. Each time you will add one more term to the Taylor polynomial approximation. Be patient; things will get worse before they get better.
4. How many terms are required before the polynomial approximations stabilize in the thousandths place for $x = 13$?

This strategy for approximation would be of limited practical value if we were restricted to power series at $x = 0$—but we are not. We can match a power series with f in the same way at *any* value $x = a$, provided we can take the derivatives. In fact, we can get a formula for doing that by simply "shifting horizontally" the formula we already have.

DEFINITION Taylor Series Generated by f at $x = a$

Let f be a function with derivatives of all orders throughout some open interval containing a. Then the **Taylor series generated by f at $x = a$** is

$$f(a) + f'(a)(x-a) + \frac{f''(a)}{2!}(x-a)^2 + \cdots + \frac{f^{(n)}(a)}{n!}(x-a)^n + \cdots$$
$$= \sum_{k=0}^{\infty} \frac{f^{(k)}(a)}{k!}(x-a)^k.$$

The partial sum

$$P_n(x) = \sum_{k=0}^{n} \frac{f^{(k)}(a)}{k!}(x-a)^k$$

is the **Taylor polynomial of order n for f at $x = a$.**

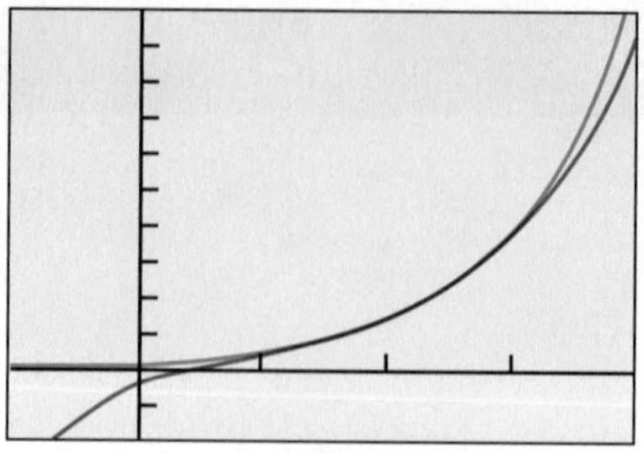

[−1, 4] by [−10, 50]

Figure 10.6 The graphs of $y = e^x$ and $y = P_3(x)$ (the third-order Taylor polynomial for e^x at $x = 2$). (Example 4)

EXAMPLE 4 A Taylor Series at $x = 2$

Find the Taylor series generated by $f(x) = e^x$ at $x = 2$.

SOLUTION

We first observe that $f(2) = f'(2) = f''(2) = \cdots = f^{(n)}(2) = e^2$. The series, therefore, is

$$e^x = e^2 + e^2(x-2) + \frac{e^2}{2!}(x-2)^2 + \cdots + \frac{e^2}{n!}(x-2)^n + \cdots$$
$$= \sum_{k=0}^{\infty}\left(\frac{e^2}{k!}\right)(x-2)^k.$$

We illustrate the convergence near $x = 2$ by sketching the graphs of $y = e^x$ and $y = P_3(x)$ in Figure 10.6. ***Now Try Exercise 13.***

EXAMPLE 5 A Taylor Polynomial for a Polynomial

Find the third-order Taylor polynomial for $f(x) = 2x^3 - 3x^2 + 4x - 5$

(a) at $x = 0$. **(b)** at $x = 1$.

SOLUTION

(a) This is easy. This polynomial is already written in powers of x and is of degree three, so it is its own third-order (and fourth-order, etc.) Taylor polynomial at $x = 0$.

(b) This would also be easy if we could quickly rewrite the formula for f as a polynomial in powers of $x - 1$, but that would require some messy tinkering. Instead, we apply the Taylor series formula.

$$f(1) = 2x^3 - 3x^2 + 4x - 5\Big|_{x=1} = -2$$

$$f'(1) = 6x^2 - 6x + 4\Big|_{x=1} = 4$$

$$f''(1) = 12x - 6\Big|_{x=1} = 6$$

$$f'''(1) = 12$$

So,

$$P_3(x) = -2 + 4(x-1) + \frac{6}{2!}(x-1)^2 + \frac{12}{3!}(x-1)^3$$
$$= 2(x-1)^3 + 3(x-1)^2 + 4(x-1) - 2.$$

This polynomial function agrees with f at every value of x (as you can verify by multiplying it out) but it is written in powers of $(x - 1)$ instead of x. ***Now Try Exercise 15.***

Combining Taylor Series

On the intersection of their intervals of convergence, Taylor series can be added, subtracted, and multiplied by constants and powers of x, and the results are once again Taylor series. The Taylor series for $f(x) + g(x)$ is the sum of the Taylor series for $f(x)$ and the

Taylor series for $g(x)$ because the nth derivative of $f + g$ is $f^{(n)} + g^{(n)}$, and so on. We can obtain the Maclaurin series for $(1 + \cos 2x)/2$ by substituting $2x$ in the Maclaurin series for $\cos x$, adding 1, and dividing the result by 2. The Maclaurin series for $\sin x + \cos x$ is the term-by-term sum of the series for $\sin x$ and $\cos x$. We obtain the Maclaurin series for $x \sin x$ by multiplying all the terms of the Maclaurin series for $\sin x$ by x.

Table of Maclaurin Series

We conclude the section by listing some of the most useful Maclaurin series, all of which have been derived in one way or another in the first two sections of this chapter. The exercises will ask you to use these series as basic building blocks for constructing other series (e.g., $\tan^{-1} x^2$ or $7xe^x$). We also list the intervals of convergence, although rigorous proofs of convergence are deferred until we develop convergence tests in Sections 10.4 and 10.5.

Maclaurin Series (Taylor Series at $x = 0$)

$$\frac{1}{1-x} = 1 + x + x^2 + \cdots + x^n + \cdots = \sum_{n=0}^{\infty} x^n \qquad (|x| < 1)$$

$$\frac{1}{1+x} = 1 - x + x^2 - \cdots + (-x)^n + \cdots = \sum_{n=0}^{\infty} (-1)^n x^n \qquad (|x| < 1)$$

$$e^x = 1 + x + \frac{x^2}{2!} + \cdots + \frac{x^n}{n!} + \cdots = \sum_{n=0}^{\infty} \frac{x^n}{n!} \qquad \text{(all real } x\text{)}$$

$$\sin x = x - \frac{x^3}{3!} + \frac{x^5}{5!} - \cdots + (-1)^n \frac{x^{2n+1}}{(2n+1)!} + \cdots$$

$$= \sum_{n=0}^{\infty} (-1)^n \frac{x^{2n+1}}{(2n+1)!} \qquad \text{(all real } x\text{)}$$

$$\cos x = 1 - \frac{x^2}{2!} + \frac{x^4}{4!} - \cdots + (-1)^n \frac{x^{2n}}{(2n)!} + \cdots$$

$$= \sum_{n=0}^{\infty} (-1)^n \frac{x^{2n}}{(2n)!} \qquad \text{(all real } x\text{)}$$

$$\ln(1+x) = x - \frac{x^2}{2} + \frac{x^3}{3} - \cdots + (-1)^{n-1} \frac{x^n}{n} + \cdots$$

$$= \sum_{n=1}^{\infty} (-1)^{n-1} \frac{x^n}{n} \qquad (-1 < x \le 1)$$

$$\tan^{-1} x = x - \frac{x^3}{3} + \frac{x^5}{5} - \cdots + (-1)^n \frac{x^{2n+1}}{2n+1} + \cdots$$

$$= \sum_{n=0}^{\infty} (-1)^n \frac{x^{2n+1}}{2n+1} \qquad (|x| \le 1)$$

Quick Review 10.2 (For help, go to Sections 3.3 and 4.1.)

Exercise numbers with a gray background indicate problems that the authors have designed to be solved *without a calculator*.

In Exercises 1–5, find a formula for the *n*th derivative of the function.

1. e^{2x}

2. $\dfrac{1}{x-1}$

3. 3^x

4. $\ln x$

5. x^n

In Exercises 6–10, find dy/dx. (Assume that letters other than x represent constants.)

6. $y = \dfrac{x^n}{n!}$

7. $y = \dfrac{2^n(x-a)^n}{n!}$

8. $y = (-1)^n \dfrac{x^{2n+1}}{(2n+1)!}$

9. $y = \dfrac{(x+a)^{2n}}{(2n)!}$

10. $y = \dfrac{(1-x)^n}{n!}$

Section 10.2 Exercises

In Exercises 1 and 2, use the formula in the definition to construct the fourth-order Taylor polynomial at $x = 0$ for the function.

1. $f(x) = \sqrt{1+x^2}$

2. $f(x) = e^{2x}$

In Exercises 3 and 4, use the formula in the definition to construct the fifth-order Taylor polynomial and the Taylor series for the function at $x = 0$.

3. $f(x) = \dfrac{1}{x+2}$

4. $f(x) = e^{1-x}$

In Exercises 5–12, *use the table of Maclaurin series on the preceding page*. Construct the first three nonzero terms and the general term of the Maclaurin series generated by the function and give the interval of convergence.

5. $\sin 2x$

6. $\ln(1-x)$

7. $\tan^{-1} x^2$

8. $7x\, e^x$

9. $\cos\left(\dfrac{x}{2}\right)$

10. $x^2 \cos x$

11. $\dfrac{x}{1-x^3}$

12. e^{-2x}

In Exercises 13 and 14, find the Taylor series generated by the function at the given point.

13. $f(x) = \dfrac{1}{x+1}, \quad x = 2$

14. $f(x) = e^{x/2}, \quad x = 1$

In Exercises 15–17, use the methods of Example 5 to find the Taylor polynomial of order 3 generated by f

(a) at $x = 0$; **(b)** at $x = 1$.

15. $f(x) = x^3 - 2x + 4$

16. $f(x) = 2x^3 + x^2 + 3x - 8$

17. $f(x) = x^4$

In Exercises 18–21, find the Taylor polynomials of orders 0, 1, 2, and 3 generated by f at $x = a$.

18. $f(x) = \dfrac{1}{x}, \quad a = 2$

19. $f(x) = \sin x, \quad a = \pi/4$

20. $f(x) = \cos x, \quad a = \pi/4$

21. $f(x) = \sqrt{x}, \quad a = 4$

22. Let f be a function that has derivatives of all orders for all real numbers. Assume $f(0) = 4$, $f'(0) = 5$, $f''(0) = -8$, and $f'''(0) = 6$.

(a) Write the third-order Taylor polynomial for f at $x = 0$ and use it to approximate $f(0.2)$.

(b) Write the second-order Taylor polynomial for f', the derivative of f, at $x = 0$ and use it to approximate $f'(0.2)$.

23. Let f be a function that has derivatives of all orders for all real numbers. Assume $f(1) = 4$, $f'(1) = -1$, $f''(1) = 3$, and $f'''(1) = 2$.

(a) Write the third-order Taylor polynomial for f at $x = 1$ and use it to approximate $f(1.2)$.

(b) Write the second-order Taylor polynomial for f', the derivative of f, at $x = 1$ and use it to approximate $f'(1.2)$.

24. The Maclaurin series for $f(x)$ is

$$f(x) = 1 + \frac{x}{2!} + \frac{x^2}{3!} + \frac{x^3}{4!} + \cdots + \frac{x^n}{(n+1)!} + \cdots.$$

(a) Find $f'(0)$ and $f^{(10)}(0)$.

(b) Let $g(x) = xf(x)$. Write the Maclaurin series for $g(x)$, showing the first three nonzero terms and the general term.

(c) Write $g(x)$ in terms of a familiar function without using series.

25. (a) Write the first three nonzero terms and the general term of the Taylor series generated by $e^{x/2}$ at $x = 0$.

(b) Write the first three nonzero terms and the general term of a power series to represent

$$g(x) = \frac{e^x - 1}{x}.$$

(c) For the function g in part (b), find $g'(1)$ and use it to show that

$$\sum_{n=1}^{\infty} = \frac{n}{(n+1)!} = 1.$$

26. Let

$$f(t) = \frac{2}{1-t^2} \quad \text{and} \quad G(x) = \int_0^x f(t)\, dt.$$

(a) Find the first four terms and the general term for the Maclaurin series generated by f.

(b) Find the first four nonzero terms and the Maclaurin series for G.

27. (a) Find the first four nonzero terms in the Taylor series generated by $f(x) = \sqrt{1 + x}$ at $x = 0$.

(b) Use the results found in part (a) to find the first four nonzero terms in the Taylor series for $g(x) = \sqrt{1 + x^2}$ at $x = 0$.

(c) Find the first four nonzero terms in the Taylor series at $x = 0$ for the function h such that $h'(x) = \sqrt{1 + x^2}$ and $h(0) = 5$.

28. Consider the power series

$$\sum_{n=0}^{\infty} a_n x^n, \text{ where } a_0 = 1 \text{ and } a_n = \left(\frac{3}{n}\right) a_{n-1} \text{ for } n \geq 1.$$

(This defines the coefficients *recursively*.)

(a) Find the first four terms and the general term of the series.

(b) What function f is represented by this power series?

(c) Find the exact value of $f'(1)$.

29. Use the technique of Exploration 3 to determine the number of terms of the Maclaurin series for $\cos x$ that are needed to approximate the value of cos 18 accurate to within 0.001 of the true value.

30. **Writing to Learn** Based on what you know about polynomial functions, explain why no Taylor polynomial of any order could actually equal $\sin x$.

31. **Writing to Learn** Your friend has memorized the Maclaurin series for both $\sin x$ and $\cos x$ but is having a hard time remembering which is which. Assuming that your friend knows the trigonometric functions well, what are some tips you could give that would help match $\sin x$ and $\cos x$ with their correct series?

32. What is the coefficient of x^5 in the Maclaurin series generated by $\sin 3x$?

33. What is the coefficient of $(x - 2)^3$ in the Taylor series generated by $\ln x$ at $x = 2$?

34. **Writing to Learn** Review the definition of the *linearization* of a differentiable function f at a in Chapter 5. What is the connection between the linearization of f and Taylor polynomials?

35. ***Linearizations at Inflection Points***

(a) As the figure below suggests, linearizations fit particularly well at inflection points. As another example, graph *Newton's serpentine* $f(x) = 4x/(x^2 + 1)$ together with its linearizations at $x = 0$ and $x = \sqrt{3}$.

(b) Show that if the graph of a twice-differentiable function $f(x)$ has an inflection point at $x = a$, then the linearization of f at $x = a$ is also the second-order Taylor polynomial of f at $x = a$. This explains why tangent lines fit so well at inflection points.

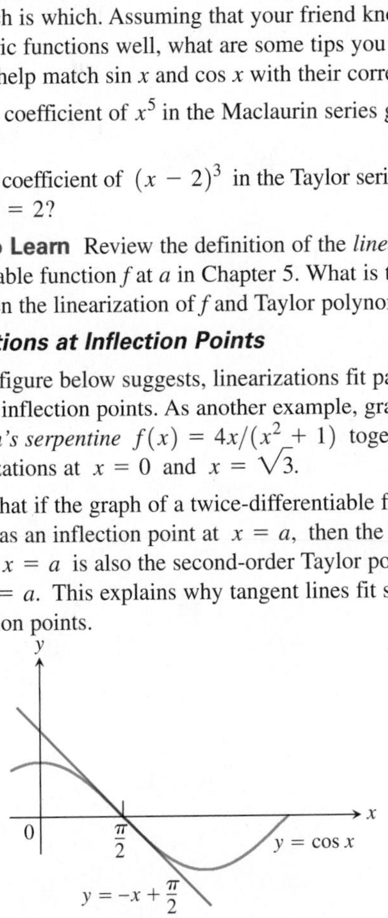

The graph of $f(x) = \cos x$ and its linearization at $\pi/2$. (Exercise 35)

36. According to the table of Maclaurin series, the power series

$$x - \frac{x^3}{3} + \frac{x^5}{5} - \cdots + (-1)^n \frac{x^{2n+1}}{2n+1} + \cdots$$

converges at $x = \pm 1$. To what number does it converge when $x = 1$? To what number does it converge when $x = -1$?

Standardized Test Questions

In Exercises 37 and 38, the Taylor series generated by $f(x)$ at $x = 0$ is

$$x - \frac{x^3}{3} + \frac{x^5}{5} - \cdots + (-1)^n \frac{x^{2n+1}}{2n+1} + \cdots.$$

37. **True or False** $f(0) = 0$. Justify your answer.

38. **True or False** $f'''(0) = -1/3$. Justify your answer.

39. **Multiple Choice** If $f(0) = 0$, $f'(0) = 1$, $f''(0) = 0$, and $f'''(0) = 2$, then which of the following is the third-order Taylor polynomial generated by $f(x)$ at $x = 0$?

(A) $2x^3 + x$ (B) $\frac{1}{3}x^3 + \frac{1}{2}x$ (C) $\frac{2}{3}x^3 + x$

(D) $2x^3 - x$ (E) $\frac{1}{3}x^3 + x$

40. **Multiple Choice** Which of the following is the coefficient of x^4 in the Maclaurin series generated by $\cos(3x)$?

(A) 27/8 (B) 9 (C) 1/24 (D) 0 (E) −27/8

In Exercises 41 and 42, let $f(x) = \sin x$.

41. **Multiple Choice** Which of the following is the fourth-order Taylor polynomial generated by $f(x)$ at $x = \pi/2$?

(A) $(x - \pi/2) - \frac{(x - \pi/2)^2}{2!} + \frac{(x - \pi/2)^4}{4!}$

(B) $1 + \frac{(x - \pi/2)^2}{2!} + \frac{(x - \pi/2)^4}{4!}$

(C) $1 - \frac{(x - \pi/2)^2}{2!} + \frac{(x - \pi/2)^4}{4!}$

(D) $1 - (x - \pi/2)^2 + (x - \pi/2)^4$

(E) $1 + (x - \pi/2)^2 + (x - \pi/2)^4$

42. **Multiple Choice** Which of the following is the Taylor series generated by $f(x)$ at $x = \pi/2$?

(A) $\sum_{n=0}^{\infty} (-1)^n \frac{(x - \pi/2)^{2n}}{(2n)!}$

(B) $\sum_{n=0}^{\infty} (-1)^n \frac{(x - \pi/2)^{2n+1}}{(2n)!}$

(C) $\sum_{n=0}^{\infty} \frac{(x - \pi/2)^{2n}}{(2n)!}$

(D) $\sum_{n=0}^{\infty} (-1)^n (x - \pi/2)^{2n}$

(E) $\sum_{n=0}^{\infty} (x - \pi/2)^{2n}$

Explorations

43. **(a)** Using the table of Maclaurin series, find a power series to represent $f(x) = (\sin x)/x$.

(b) The power series you found in part (a) is not quite a Maclaurin series for *f*, because *f* is technically not eligible to have a Maclaurin series. Why not?

(c) If we redefine *f* as follows, then the power series in part (a) *will* be a Maclaurin series for *f*. What is the value of *k*?

$$f(x) = \begin{cases} \dfrac{\sin x}{x}, & x \neq 0, \\ k, & x = 0 \end{cases}$$

44. Group Activity Find a function *f* whose Maclaurin series is

$$1x^1 + 2x^2 + 3x^3 + \cdots + nx^n + \cdots.$$

Extending the Ideas

45. ***The Binomial Series*** Let $f(x) = (1 + x)^m$ for some nonzero constant *m*.

(a) Show that $f'''(x) = m(m - 1)(m - 2)(1 + x)^{m-3}$.

(b) Extend the result of part (a) to show that

$$f^{(k)}(0) = m(m - 1)(m - 2) \cdots (m - k + 1).$$

(c) Find the coefficient of x^k in the Maclaurin series generated by *f*.

(d) We define the symbol $\binom{m}{k}$ as follows:

$$\binom{m}{k} = \frac{m(m - 1)(m - 2) \cdots (m - k + 1)}{k!},$$

with the understanding that

$$\binom{m}{0} = 1 \quad \text{and} \quad \binom{m}{1} = m.$$

With this notation, show that the Maclaurin series generated by $f(x) = (1 + x)^m$ is

$$\sum_{k=0}^{\infty} \binom{m}{k} x^k.$$

This is called the **binomial series.**

46. ***(Continuation of Exercise 45)*** If *m* is a positive integer, explain why the Maclaurin series generated by *f* is a polynomial of degree *m*. (This means that

$$(1 + x)^m = \sum_{k=0}^{m} \binom{m}{k} x^k.$$

You may recognize this result as the **Binomial Theorem** from algebra.)

10.3 Taylor's Theorem

What you will learn about . . .

- Taylor Polynomials
- The Remainder
- Bounding the Remainder
- Euler's Formula

and why . . .

If we approximate a function represented by a power series by its Taylor polynomials, it is important to know how to determine the error in the approximation.

Taylor Polynomials

While there is a certain unspoiled beauty in the exactness of a convergent Taylor series, it is the inexact Taylor polynomials that essentially do all the work. It is satisfying to know, for example, that $\sin x$ can be found *exactly* by summing an infinite Taylor series, but if we want to use that information to find sin 3, we will have to evaluate Taylor polynomials until we arrive at an *approximation* with which we are satisfied. Even a computer must deal with finite sums.

EXAMPLE 1 Approximating a Function to Specifications

Find a Taylor polynomial that will serve as an adequate substitute for $\sin x$ on the interval $[-\pi, \pi]$.

SOLUTION

You do not have to be a professional mathematician to appreciate the imprecision of this problem as written. We are simply unable to proceed until someone decides what an "adequate" substitute is! We will revisit this issue shortly, but for now let us accept the following clarification of "adequate."

By "adequate," we mean that the polynomial should differ from $\sin x$ by less than 0.0001 anywhere on the interval.

Now we have a clear mission: Choose $P_n(x)$ so that $|P_n(x) - \sin x| < 0.0001$ for every x in the interval $[-\pi, \pi]$. How do we do this?

Recall the nine graphs of the partial sums of the Maclaurin series for $\sin x$ in Section 10.2. They show that the approximations get worse as x moves away from 0, suggesting that if we can make $|P_n(\pi) - \sin \pi| < 0.0001$, then P_n will be adequate throughout the interval. Since $\sin \pi = 0$, this means that we need to make $|P_n(\pi)| < 0.0001$.

We evaluate the partial sums at $x = \pi$, adding a term at a time, eventually arriving at the following:

```
π−π³/3!+π^5/5!−π
^7/7!+π^9/9!−π^1
1/11!+π^13/13!
    2.114256749E⁻5
```

As graphical support that the polynomial $P_{13}(x)$ is adequate throughout the interval, we graph the *absolute error* of the approximation, namely $|P_{13}(x) - \sin x|$, in the window $[-\pi, \pi]$ by $[-0.00004, 0.00004]$ (Figure 10.7). ***Now Try Exercise 11.***

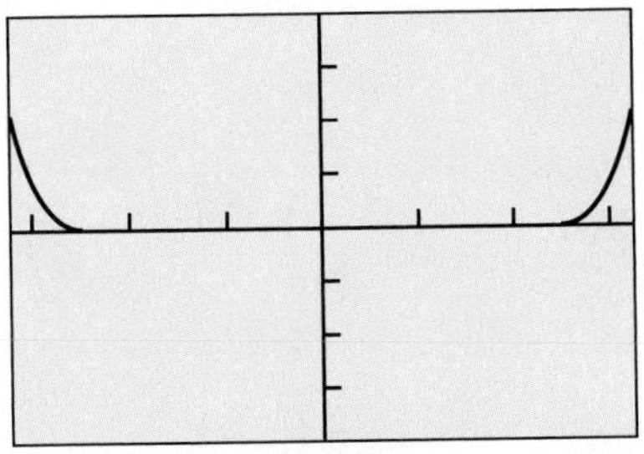

$[-\pi, \pi]$ by $[-0.00004, 0.00004]$

Figure 10.7 The graph shows that $|P_{13}(x) - \sin x| < 0.00010$ throughout the interval $[-\pi, \pi]$. (Example 1)

In practical terms, then, we would like to be able to use Taylor polynomials to approximate functions over the intervals of convergence of the Taylor series, and we would like to keep the error of the approximation within specified bounds. Since the error results from *truncating* the series down to a polynomial (that is, cutting it off after some number of terms), we call it the **truncation error.**

EXAMPLE 2 Truncation Error for a Geometric Series

Find a formula for the truncation error if we use $1 + x^2 + x^4 + x^6$ to approximate $1/(1 - x^2)$ over the interval $(-1, 1)$.

SOLUTION

We recognize this polynomial as the fourth partial sum of the geometric series for $1/(1 - x^2)$. Since this series converges to $1/(1 - x^2)$ on $(-1, 1)$, the truncation error is the absolute value of the part that we threw away, namely

$$|x^8 + x^{10} + \cdots + x^{2n} + \cdots|.$$

This is the absolute value of a geometric series with first term x^8 and $r = x^2$. Therefore,

$$|x^8 + x^{10} + \cdots + x^{2n} + \cdots| = \left|\frac{x^8}{1 - x^2}\right| = \frac{x^8}{1 - x^2}.$$

Figure 10.8 shows that the error is small near 0, but increases as x gets closer to 1 or -1.

Now Try Exercise 13.

$y = x^8/(1 - x^2)$

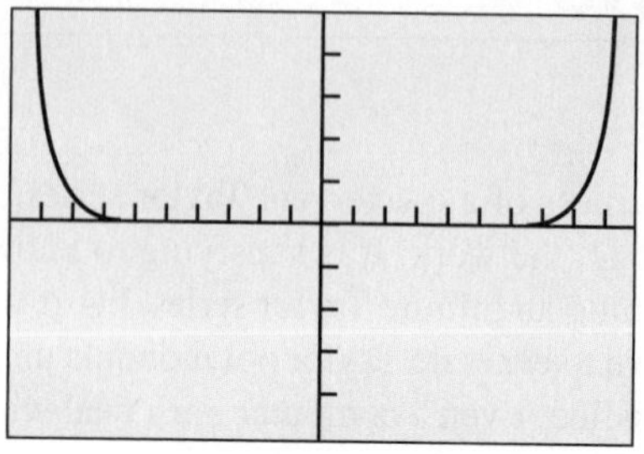

[–1, 1] by [–5, 5]

Figure 10.8 A graph of the truncation error on $(-1, 1)$ if $P_6(x)$ is used to approximate $1/(1 - x^2)$. (Example 2)

You can probably infer from our solution in Example 2 that the truncation error after 5 terms would be $x^{10}/(1 - x^2)$, and after n terms would be $x^{2n}/(1 - x^2)$. Figure 10.9 shows how these errors get closer to 0 on the interval $(-1, 1)$ as n gets larger, and that they still get worse as we approach -1 and 1.

It was fortunate for our error analysis that this series was geometric, since the error was consequently a geometric series itself. This enabled us to write it as a (nonseries) function and study it exactly. But how could we handle the error if we were to truncate a *nongeometric* series? That practical question sets the stage for Taylor's Theorem.

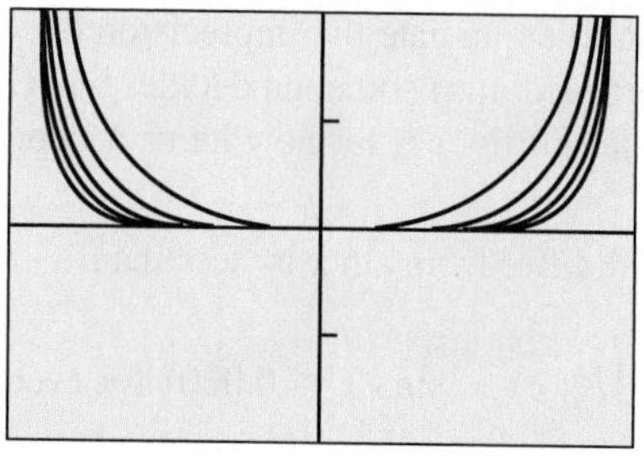

[–1, 1] by [–2, 2]

Figure 10.9 The truncation errors for $n = 2, 4, 6, 8, 10$, when we approximate $1/(1 - x^2)$ by its Taylor polynomials of higher and higher order. (The errors for the higher-order polynomials are on the bottom.)

The Remainder

Every truncation splits a Taylor series into two equally significant pieces: the Taylor polynomial $P_n(x)$ that gives us the approximation, and the *remainder* $R_n(x)$ that tells us whether the approximation is any good. Taylor's Theorem is about both pieces.

THEOREM 3 Taylor's Theorem with Remainder

If f has derivatives of all orders in an open interval I containing a, then for each positive integer n and for each x in I,

$$f(x) = f(a) + f'(a)(x - a) + \frac{f''(a)}{2!}(x - a)^2 + \cdots + \frac{f^{(n)}(a)}{n!}(x - a)^n + R_n(x),$$

where

$$R_n(x) = \frac{f^{(n+1)}(c)}{(n + 1)!}(x - a)^{n+1}$$

for some c between a and x.

Pause for a moment to consider how remarkable this theorem is. If we wish to approximate f by a polynomial of degree n over an interval I, the theorem gives us both a formula for the *polynomial* and a formula for the *error* involved in using that approximation over the interval I.

The first equation in Taylor's Theorem is **Taylor's formula.** The function $R_n(x)$ is the **remainder of order n** or the **error term** for the approximation of f by $P_n(x)$ over I. It is also called the **Lagrange form** of the remainder, and bounds on $R_n(x)$ found using this form are **Lagrange error bounds.**

The introduction of $R_n(x)$ finally gives us a mathematically precise way to define what we mean when we say that a Taylor series converges to a function on an interval. If $R_n(x) \to 0$ as $n \to \infty$ for all x in I, we say that the Taylor series generated by f at $x = a$ **converges to f** on I, and we write

$$f(x) = \sum_{k=0}^{\infty} \frac{f^{(k)}(a)}{k!}(x - a)^k.$$

EXAMPLE 3 Proving Convergence of a Maclaurin Series

Prove that the series

$$\sum_{k=0}^{\infty} (-1)^k \frac{x^{2k+1}}{(2k + 1)!}$$

converges to $\sin x$ for all real x.

SOLUTION

We need to consider what happens to $R_n(x)$ as $n \to \infty$.

By Taylor's Theorem,

$$R_n(x) = \frac{f^{(n+1)}(c)}{(n + 1)!}(x - 0)^{n+1},$$

where $f^{(n+1)}(c)$ is the $(n + 1)$st derivative of $\sin x$ evaluated at some c between x and 0. This does not seem at first glance to give us much information, but *for this particular function* we can say something very significant about $f^{(n+1)}(c)$: It lies between -1 and 1 inclusive. Therefore, no matter what x is, we have

$$\begin{aligned} |R_n(x)| &= \left| \frac{f^{(n+1)}(c)}{(n + 1)!}(x - 0)^{n+1} \right| \\ &= \frac{|f^{(n+1)}(c)|}{(n + 1)!}|x^{n+1}| \\ &\le \frac{1}{(n + 1)!}|x^{n+1}| = \frac{|x|^{n+1}}{(n + 1)!}. \end{aligned}$$

What happens to $|x|^{n+1}/(n + 1)!$ as $n \to \infty$? The numerator is a product of $n + 1$ factors, all of them $|x|$. The denominator is a product of $n + 1$ factors, the largest of which eventually exceed $|x|$ and keep on growing as $n \to \infty$. The factorial growth in the denominator, therefore, eventually outstrips the exponential growth in the numerator, and we have $|x|^{n+1}/(n + 1)! \to 0$ for all x. This means that $R_n(x) \to 0$ for all x, which completes the proof.

Now Try Exercise 15.

EXPLORATION 1 Your Turn

Modify the steps of the proof in Example 3 to prove that

$$\sum_{k=0}^{\infty} (-1)^k \frac{x^{2k}}{(2k)!}$$

converges to $\cos x$ for all real x.

Bounding the Remainder

Notice in Example 3 and Exploration 1 that we were able to use the remainder formula in Taylor's Theorem to verify the convergence of two Taylor series to their generating functions ($\sin x$ and $\cos x$) for all real numbers, and yet in neither case did we have to find an actual value for $f^{(n+1)}(c)$. Let us take a closer look at the error term to see how we might generalize this approach.

Behavior as $n \to \infty$ depends on f and c.

Gets bigger exponentially if $|x - a| > 1$, but gets smaller exponentially if $|x - a| < 1$.

$$R_n(x) = f^{(n+1)}(c)\frac{(x-a)^{n+1}}{(n+1)!}$$

Gets bigger no matter what, and factorial growth outstrips exponential growth.

The Lagrange formula for the error suggests that $\lim_{n\to\infty} R_n(x)$ will be zero *unless* the $f^{(n+1)}(c)$ factor grows without bound. In fact, it will still be zero if the $f^{(n+1)}(c)$ factor only contributes more exponential growth to the numerator. That is the idea conveyed in the following Remainder Estimation Theorem.

Name That Theorem

The Remainder Estimation Theorem should probably be called the Remainder Bounding Theorem. The *estimation* involved is really the Lagrange error formula given in Taylor's Theorem. The Remainder Estimation Theorem just provides (for some functions) a convenient *bound* for the Lagrange error term that goes to zero as n goes to infinity.

THEOREM 4 Remainder Estimation Theorem

If there are positive constants M and r such that $|f^{(n+1)}(t)| \le Mr^{n+1}$ for all t between a and x, then the remainder $R_n(x)$ in Taylor's Theorem satisfies the inequality

$$|R_n(x)| \le M\frac{r^{n+1}|x-a|^{n+1}}{(n+1)!}.$$

If these conditions hold for every n and all the other conditions of Taylor's Theorem are satisfied by f, then the series converges to $f(x)$.

It does not matter if M and r are huge; the important thing is that they do not get any *more huge* as $n \to \infty$. This allows the factorial growth to outstrip the exponential growth and thereby sweep $R_n(x)$ to zero.

EXAMPLE 4 Proving Convergence with the Remainder Estimation Theorem

The Maclaurin series for e^{7x} is $\sum_{n=0}^{\infty} \frac{(7x)^n}{n!}$. Prove that it converges to e^{7x} for all x.

SOLUTION

First, note that if $f(t) = e^{7t}$, then $f^{(n+1)}(t) = 7^{n+1}e^{7t}$. On any interval $[0, x]$, the increasing function e^{7t} is bounded by $M = e^{7x}$, so $|f^{(n+1)}(t)| \le M \cdot 7^{n+1}$ for all t between 0 and x. On any interval $[x, 0]$, the increasing function e^{7t} is bounded by $M = 1$, so again $|f^{(n+1)}(t)| \le M \cdot 7^{n+1}$ for all t between 0 and x. By the Remainder Estimation Theorem, the series converges to e^{7x} in either case. Since x is arbitrary, the series therefore converges for all x.

Now Try Exercise 17.

EXAMPLE 5 Estimating a Remainder

The approximation $\ln(1 + x) \approx x - (x^2/2)$ is used when x is small. Use the Lagrange form of the remainder to get a bound for the maximum error when $|x| \le 0.1$. Support the answer graphically.

continued

$y = \ln(1 + x) - (x - x^2/2)$

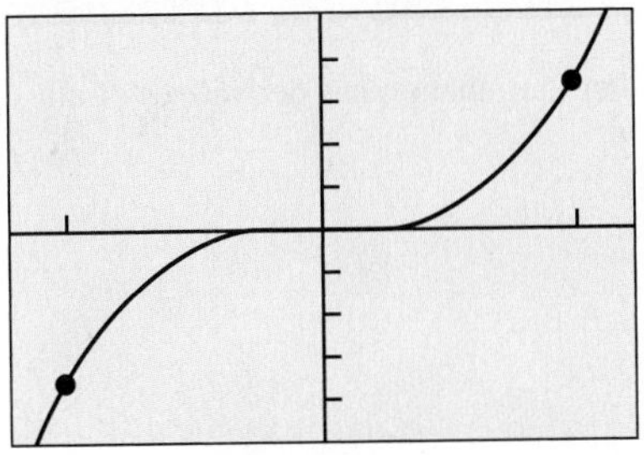

[–0.12, 0.12] by [–0.0005, 0.0005]

Figure 10.10 The graph of the error term $R_2(x)$ in Example 5. Maximum error for $|x| \le 0.1$ occurs at the left-hand endpoint of the interval.

SOLUTION

In the notation of the Remainder Estimation Theorem, $f(x) = \ln(1 + x)$, the polynomial is $P_2(x)$, and we need a bound for $|R_2(x)|$. On the interval $[-0.1, 0.1]$, the function $|f^{(3)}(t)| = 2/(1 + t)^3$ is strictly decreasing, achieving its maximum value at the left-hand endpoint, -0.1. We can therefore bound $|f^{(3)}(t)|$ by

$$M = \left|\frac{2}{(1 + (-0.1))^3}\right| = \frac{2000}{729}.$$

We can let $r = 1$.

By the Remainder Estimation Theorem, we may conclude that

$$|R_2(x)| \le \frac{2000}{729} \cdot \frac{|x|^3}{3!} \le \frac{2000}{729} \cdot \frac{|\pm 0.1|^3}{3!} < 4.6 \times 10^{-4}.$$ Rounded up, to be safe

Since $R_2(x) = \ln(1 + x) - (x - x^2/2)$, it is an easy matter to produce a graph to *observe* the behavior of the error on the interval $[-0.1, 0.1]$ (Figure 10.10).

The graph almost appears to have odd-function symmetry, but evaluation shows that $R_2(-0.1) \approx -3.605 \times 10^{-4}$ and $R_2(0.1) \approx 3.102 \times 10^{-4}$. The maximum *absolute* error on the interval is 3.605×10^{-4}, which is indeed less than the bound, 4.6×10^{-4}.

Now Try Exercise 23.

Euler's Formula

We have seen that sin x, cos x, and e^x equal their respective Maclaurin series for all real numbers x. It can also be shown that this is true for all *complex* numbers, although we would need to extend our concept of limit to know what convergence would mean in that context. Accept for the moment that we can substitute complex numbers into these power series, and let us see where that might lead.

We mentioned at the beginning of the chapter that Leonhard Euler had derived some powerful results using infinite series. One of the most impressive was the surprisingly simple relationship he discovered that connects the exponential function e^x to the trigonometric functions sin x and cos x. You do not need a deep understanding of complex numbers to understand what Euler did, but you do need to recall the powers of $i = \sqrt{-1}$.

$i^1 = i$	$i^5 = i$
$i^2 = -1$	$i^6 = -1$
$i^3 = -i$	$i^7 = -i$
$i^4 = 1$	$i^8 = 1$ etc.

Now try this exploration!

Srinivasa Ramanujan (1887–1920)

Ramanujan, from southern India, wrote with amazing originality and depth on a wide range of topics in mathematics, including infinite series, prime and composite numbers, integers as the sum of squares, function theory, and combinatorics. His theorems have influenced medical research and statistical mechanics. One of his identities has been used by computer programmers to calculate the decimal expansion of pi to millions of digits. There are still areas of his work that have not been explored. Ramanujan was largely self taught and, although he worked with the British mathematician G. H. Hardy of Cambridge, he never graduated from college because he neglected his other studies for mathematics.

EXPLORATION 2 Euler's Formula

Assume that e^x, cos x, and sin x equal their Maclaurin series (as in the table in Section 10.2) for complex numbers as well as for real numbers.

1. Find the Maclaurin series for e^{ix}.
2. Use the result of part 1 and the Maclaurin series for cos x and sin x to prove that $e^{ix} = \cos x + i \sin x$. This equation is known as **Euler's formula.**
3. Use Euler's formula to prove that $e^{i\pi} + 1 = 0$. This beautiful equation, which brings together the five most celebrated numbers in mathematics in such a stunningly unexpected way, is also widely known as Euler's formula. (There are still others. The prolific Euler had more than his share.)

Quick Review 10.3 (For help, go to Sections 3.3 and 4.1.)

Exercise numbers with a gray background indicate problems that the authors have designed to be solved *without a calculator.*

In Exercises 1–5, find the smallest number M that bounds $|f|$ from above on the interval I (that is, find the smallest M such that $|f(x)| \leq M$ for all x in I).

1. $f(x) = 2\cos(3x), \quad I = [-2\pi, 2\pi]$
2. $f(x) = x^2 + 3, \quad I = [1, 2]$
3. $f(x) = 2^x, \quad I = [-3, 0]$
4. $f(x) = \dfrac{x}{x^2 + 1}, \quad I = [-2, 2]$
5. $f(x) = \begin{cases} 2 - x^2, & x \leq 1, \\ 2x - 1, & x > 1, \end{cases} \quad I = [-3, 3]$

In Exercises 6–10, tell whether the function has derivatives of all orders at the given value of a.

6. $\dfrac{x}{x + 1}, \quad a = 0$
7. $|x^2 - 4|, \quad a = 2$
8. $\sin x + \cos x, \quad a = \pi$
9. $e^{-x}, \quad a = 0$
10. $x^{3/2}, \quad a = 0$

Section 10.3 Exercises

In Exercises 1–5, find the Taylor polynomial of order four for the function at $x = 0$, and use it to approximate the value of the function at $x = 0.2$.

1. e^{-2x}
2. $\cos(\pi x/2)$
3. $5\sin(-x)$
4. $\ln(1 + x^2)$
5. $(1 - x)^{-2}$

In Exercises 6–10, find the Maclaurin series for the function.

6. $\sin x - x + \dfrac{x^3}{3!}$
7. xe^x
8. $\cos^2 x \left(= \dfrac{1 + \cos 2x}{2}\right)$
9. $\sin^2 x$
10. $\dfrac{x^2}{1 - 2x}$

11. Use graphs to find a Taylor polynomial $P_n(x)$ for $\ln(1 + x)$ so that $|P_n(x) - \ln(1 + x)| < 0.001$ for every x in $[-0.5, 0.5]$.

12. Use graphs to find a Taylor polynomial $P_n(x)$ for $\cos x$ so that $|P_n(x) - \cos x| < 0.001$ for every x in $[-\pi, \pi]$.

13. Find a formula for the truncation error if we use $P_6(x)$ to approximate $\dfrac{1}{1 - 2x}$ on $(-1/2, 1/2)$.

14. Find a formula for the truncation error if we use $P_9(x)$ to approximate $\dfrac{1}{1 - x}$ on $(-1, 1)$.

In Exercises 15–18, use the Remainder Estimation Theorem to prove that the Maclaurin series for the function coverages for all real x.

15. $\cos x$
16. $\sin 5x$
17. $\cos 8x$
18. e^{5x}

19. For approximately what values of x can you replace $\sin x$ by $x - (x^3/6)$ with an error magnitude no greater than 5×10^{-4}? Give reasons for your answer.

20. If $\cos x$ is replaced by $1 - (x^2/2)$ and $|x| < 0.5$, what estimate can be made of the error? Does $1 - (x^2/2)$ tend to be too large or too small? Support your answer graphically.

21. How close is the approximation $\sin x \approx x$ when $|x| < 10^{-3}$? For which of these values of x is $x < \sin x$? Support your answer graphically.

22. The approximation $\sqrt{1 + x} \approx 1 + (x/2)$ is used when x is small. Estimate the maximum error when $|x| < 0.01$.

23. The approximation $e^x \approx 1 + x + (x^2/2)$ is used when x is small. Estimate the error when $|x| < 0.1$.

24. ***Hyperbolic sine and cosine*** The hyperbolic sine and hyperbolic cosine functions, denoted sinh and cosh respectively, are defined as

$$\sinh x = \frac{e^x - e^{-x}}{2} \quad \text{and} \quad \cosh x = \frac{e^x + e^{-x}}{2}.$$

(Appendix A6 gives more information about hyperbolic functions.)

Find the Maclaurin series generated by $\sinh x$ and $\cosh x$.

25. ***(Continuation of Exercise 24)*** Use the Remainder Estimation Theorem to prove that $\cosh x$ equals its Maclaurin series for all real numbers x.

26. **Writing to Learn** Review the statement of the Mean Value Theorem (Section 5.2) and explain its relationship to Taylor's Theorem.

Quadratic Approximations Just as we call the Taylor polynomial of order 1 generated by f at $x = a$ the *linearization* of f at a, we call the Taylor polynomial of order 2 generated by f at $x = a$ the *quadratic approximation* of f at a.

In Exercises 27–31, find **(a)** the linearization and **(b)** the quadratic approximation of f at $x = 0$. Then **(c)** graph the function and its linear and quadratic approximations together around $x = 0$ and comment on how the graphs are related.

27. $f(x) = \ln(\cos x)$

28. $f(x) = e^{\sin x}$

29. $f(x) = 1/\sqrt{1 - x^2}$

30. $f(x) = \sec x$

31. $f(x) = \tan x$

32. Use the Taylor polynomial of order 2 to find the quadratic approximation of $f(x) = (1 + x)^k$ at $x = 0$ (k a constant). If $k = 3$, for approximately what values of x in the interval $[0, 1]$ will the magnitude of the error in the quadratic approximation be less than $1/100$?

33. *A Cubic Approximation of e^x* The approximation

$$e^x \approx 1 + x + \frac{x^2}{2} + \frac{x^3}{6}$$

is used on small intervals about the origin. Estimate the magnitude of the approximation error for $|x| \le 0.1$.

34. *A Cubic Approximation* Use the Taylor polynomial of order 3 to find the *cubic approximation* of $f(x) = 1/(1 - x)$ at $x = 0$. Give an upper bound for the magnitude of the approximation error for $|x| \le 0.1$.

35. Consider the initial value problem,

$$\frac{dy}{dx} = e^{-x^2} \quad \text{and} \quad y = 2 \quad \text{when } x = 0.$$

(a) Can you find a formula for the function y that does not involve any integrals?

(b) Can you represent y by a power series?

(c) For what values of x does this power series actually equal the function y? Give a reason for your answer.

36. (a) Construct the Maclaurin series for $\ln(1 - x)$.

(b) Use this series and the series for $\ln(1 + x)$ to construct a Maclaurin series for

$$\ln \frac{1 + x}{1 - x}.$$

37. *Identifying Graphs* Which well-known functions are approximated on the interval $(-\pi/2, \pi/2)$ by the following Taylor polynomials?

(a) $x + \dfrac{x^3}{3} + \dfrac{2x^5}{15} + \dfrac{17x^7}{315} + \dfrac{62x^9}{2835}$

(b) $1 + \dfrac{x^2}{2} + \dfrac{5x^4}{24} + \dfrac{61x^6}{720} + \dfrac{277x^8}{8064}$

Standardized Test Questions

You may use a graphing calculator to solve the following problems.

38. True or False The degree of the linearization of a function f at $x = a$ must be 1. Justify your answer.

39. True or False If $\sum_{n=0}^{\infty} \dfrac{x^{n+1}}{n!} = x + x^2 + \dfrac{x^3}{2!} + \cdots$ is the Maclaurin series for the function $f(x)$, then $f'(0) = 1$. Justify your answer.

40. Multiple Choice Which of the following gives the Taylor polynomial of order 5 approximation to $\sin(1.5)$?

(A) 0.965 **(B)** 0.985 **(C)** 0.997 **(D)** 1.001 **(E)** 1.005

41. Multiple Choice Let $\sum_{n=0}^{\infty} \dfrac{x^{n+1}}{n!} = x + x^2 + \dfrac{x^3}{2!} + \cdots$ be the Maclaurin series for $f(x)$. Which of the following is $f^{(12)}(0)$, the 12th derivative of f at $x = 0$?

(A) $1/11!$ **(B)** $1/12!$ **(C)** 0 **(D)** 1 **(E)** 12

42. Multiple Choice Let $\sum_{n=0}^{\infty} (-1)^n \dfrac{x^{2n}}{(2n)!} = 1 - \dfrac{x^2}{2!} + \dfrac{x^4}{4!} - \cdots$ be the Maclaurin series for $\cos x$. Which of the following gives the smallest value of n for which $|P_n(x) - \cos x| < 0.01$ for all x in the interval $[-\pi, \pi]$?

(A) 12 **(B)** 10 **(C)** 8 **(D)** 6 **(E)** 4

43. Multiple Choice Which of the following is the quadratic approximation for $f(x) = e^{-x}$ at $x = 0$?

(A) $1 - x + \dfrac{1}{2}x^2$ **(B)** $1 - x - \dfrac{1}{2}x^2$

(C) $1 + x + \dfrac{1}{2}x^2$ **(D)** $1 + x$ **(E)** $1 - x$

Explorations

44. Group Activity Try to reinforce each other's ideas and verify your computations at each step.

(a) Use the identity

$$\sin^2 x = \frac{1}{2}(1 - \cos 2x)$$

to obtain the Maclaurin series for $\sin^2 x$.

(b) Differentiate this series to obtain the Maclaurin series for $2 \sin x \cos x$.

(c) Verify that this is the series for $\sin 2x$.

45. *Improving Approximations to π*

(a) Let P be an approximation of π accurate to n decimal places. Check with a calculator to see that $P + \sin P$ gives an approximation correct to at least $3n$ decimal places!

(b) Use the Remainder Estimation Theorem and the Maclaurin series for $\sin x$ to explain what is happening in part (a). [*Hint:* Let $P = \pi + x$, where x is the error of the estimate. Why should $(P + \sin P) - \pi$ be less than x^3?]

46. *Euler's Identities* Use Euler's formula to show that

(a) $\cos\theta = \dfrac{e^{i\theta} + e^{-i\theta}}{2}$, and

(b) $\sin\theta = \dfrac{e^{i\theta} - e^{-i\theta}}{2i}$.

47. *A Divergent Remainder* Recall that the Maclaurin series for $f(x) = \dfrac{1}{1-x}$ converges only if $|x| < 1$. By analyzing partial sums of the series, find a formula for the remainder $R_n(x)$ when $x = -1$ and show that $\lim_{n\to\infty} R_n(x) \neq 0$.

48. *Follow-up to Exercise 47* Show that the value of c in the Lagrange error formula that will yield the error $R_n(-1)$ found in Exercise 47 is $c = 1 - 2^{\left(\frac{1}{n+2}\right)}$.

Extending the Ideas

49. When a and b are real numbers, we define $e^{(a+ib)x}$ with the equation

$$e^{(a+ib)x} = e^{ax} \cdot e^{ibx} = e^{ax}(\cos bx + i \sin bx).$$

Differentiate the right-hand side of this equation to show that

$$\frac{d}{dx} e^{(a+ib)x} = (a + ib)\, e^{(a+ib)x}.$$

Thus, the familiar rule

$$\frac{d}{dx} e^{kx} = ke^{kx}$$

holds for complex values of k as well as for real values.

50. *(Continuation of Exercise 49)*

(a) Confirm the antiderivative formula

$$\int e^{(a+ib)x} dx = \frac{a - ib}{a^2 + b^2} e^{(a+ib)x} + C$$

by differentiating both sides. (In this case, $C = C_1 + iC_2$ is a complex constant of integration.)

(b) Two complex numbers $a + ib$ and $c + id$ are equal if and only if $a = c$ and $b = d$. Use this fact and the formula in part (a) to evaluate $\int e^{ax} \cos bx\, dx$ and $\int e^{ax} \sin bx\, dx$.

Quick Quiz for AP* Preparation: Sections 10.1–10.3

1. Multiple Choice Which of the following is the sum of the series $\sum_{n=0}^{\infty} \dfrac{\pi^n}{e^{2n}}$?

(A) $\dfrac{e}{e - \pi}$ **(B)** $\dfrac{\pi}{\pi - e}$ **(C)** $\dfrac{\pi}{\pi - e^2}$

(D) $\dfrac{e^2}{e^2 - \pi}$ **(E)** The series diverges.

2. Multiple Choice Assume that f has derivatives of all orders for all real numbers x, $f(0) = 2$, $f'(0) = -1$, $f''(0) = 6$, and $f'''(0) = 12$. Which of the following is the third-order Taylor polynomial for f at $x = 0$?

(A) $2 - x + 3x^2 + 2x^3$ **(B)** $2 - x + 6x^2 + 12x^3$

(C) $2 - \frac{1}{2}x + 3x^2 + 2x^3$ **(D)** $-2 + x - 3x^2 - 2x^3$

(E) $2 - x + 6x^2$

3. Multiple Choice Which of the following is the Taylor series generated by $f(x) = 1/x$ at $x = 1$?

(A) $\sum_{n=0}^{\infty} (x-1)^n$ **(B)** $\sum_{n=0}^{\infty} (-1)^n x^n$

(C) $\sum_{n=0}^{\infty} (-1)^n (x+1)^n$ **(D)** $\sum_{n=0}^{\infty} (-1)^n \dfrac{(x-1)^n}{n!}$

(E) $\sum_{n=0}^{\infty} (-1)^n (x-1)^n$

4. Free Response Let f be the function defined by

$$f(x) = \sum_{n=0}^{\infty} 2\left(\frac{x+2}{3}\right)^n$$

for all values of x for which the series converges.

(a) Find the interval of convergence for the series.

(b) Find the function that the series represents.

10.4 Radius of Convergence

What you will learn about . . .

- Convergence
- *n*th-Term Test
- Comparing Nonnegative Series
- Ratio Test
- Endpoint Convergence

and why . . .

It is important to develop a strategy for finding the interval of convergence of a power series and to obtain some tests that can be used to determine convergence of a series.

Convergence

Throughout our explorations of infinite series we stressed the importance of convergence. In terms of numbers, the difference between a convergent series and a divergent series could hardly be more stark: A convergent series is a number and may be treated as such; a divergent series is not a number and must not be treated as one.

Recall that the symbol "=" means many different things in mathematics.

1. $1 + 1 = 2$ signifies *equality of real numbers.* It is a true sentence.
2. $2(x - 3) = 2x - 6$ signifies *equivalent expressions.* It is a true sentence.
3. $x^2 + 3 = 7$ is an *equation.* It is an *open sentence,* because it can be true or false, depending on whether x is a solution to the equation.
4. $(x^2 - 1)/(x + 1) = x - 1$ is an *identity.* It is a true sentence (very much like the equation in (2)), but with the important qualification that *x must be in the domain of both expressions.* If either side of the equality is undefined, the sentence is meaningless. Substituting -1 into both sides of the equation in (3) gives a sentence that is mathematically false (i.e., $4 = 7$); substituting -1 into both sides of this identity gives a sentence that is meaningless.

$y = \dfrac{1}{1 + x^2}$

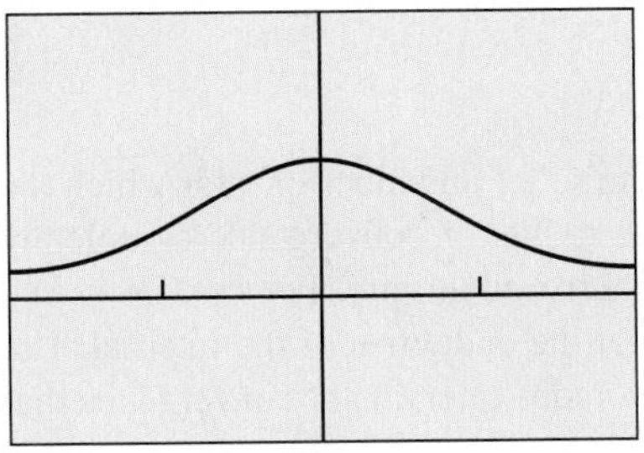

[–2, 2] by [–1, 2]

(a)

Partial Sums

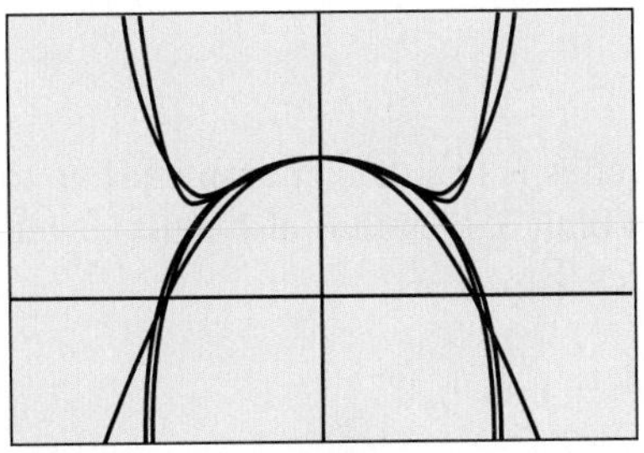

[–2, 2] by [–1, 2]

(b)

Figure 10.11 (a) The graph of $y = 1/(1 + x^2)$ and (b) the graphs of the Taylor polynomials $P_2(x)$, $P_4(x)$, $P_6(x)$, $P_8(x)$, and $P_{10}(x)$. The approximations become better and better, but only over the interval of convergence $(-1, 1)$. (Example 1)

EXAMPLE 1 The Importance of Convergence

Consider the sentence

$$\frac{1}{1 + x^2} = 1 - x^2 + x^4 - x^6 + \cdots + (-1)^n x^{2n} + \cdots.$$

For what values of x is this an identity?

SOLUTION

The function on the left has domain all real numbers. The function on the right can be viewed as a limit of Taylor polynomials. Each Taylor polynomial has domain all real numbers, but the polynomial values *converge* only when $|x| < 1$, so the *series* has the domain $(-1, 1)$. If we graph the Taylor polynomials (Figure 10.11), we can see the dramatic convergence to $1/(1 + x^2)$ over the interval $(-1, 1)$. The divergence is just as dramatic for $|x| \geq 1$.

For values of x outside the interval, the statement in this example is meaningless. The Taylor series on the right diverges, so it is not a number. The sentence is an identity for x in $(-1, 1)$.

Now Try Exercise 1.

Seki Kowa (1642–1708)

Child prodigy, brilliant mathematician, and inspirational teacher, Seki Kowa was born into a samurai warrior family in Fujioka, Kozuke, Japan, and adopted by the family of an accountant. Among his contributions were an improved method of solving higher-degree equations, the use of determinants in solving simultaneous equations, and a form of calculus known in Japan as *yenri.* It is difficult to know the full extent of his work because the samurai code demanded great modesty. Seki Kowa is credited with awakening in Japan a scientific spirit that continues to this day.

As convincing as these graphs are, they do not *prove* convergence or divergence as $n \to \infty$. The series in Example 1 happens to be geometric, so we do have an analytic proof that it converges for $|x| < 1$ and diverges for $|x| \geq 1$, but for nongeometric series we do not have such undeniable assurance about convergence (yet).

In this section we develop a strategy for finding the interval of convergence of an arbitrary power series and backing it up with proof. We begin by noting that any power series of the form $\sum_{n=0}^{\infty} c_n(x - a)^n$ always converges at $x = a$, thus assuring us of at least one coordinate on the real number line where the series must converge. We have encountered power series that converge for all real numbers (the Maclaurin series for $\sin x$, $\cos x$, and e^x), and we have encountered power series like the series in Example 1 that converge only on a finite interval centered at a. A useful fact about power series is that those are the only possibilities, as the following theorem attests.

THEOREM 5 The Convergence Theorem for Power Series

There are three possibilities for $\sum_{n=0}^{\infty} c_n(x - a)^n$ with respect to convergence:

1. There is a positive number R such that the series diverges for $|x - a| > R$ but converges for $|x - a| < R$. The series may or may not converge at either of the endpoints $x = a - R$ and $x = a + R$.
2. The series converges for every x $(R = \infty)$.
3. The series converges at $x = a$ and diverges elsewhere $(R = 0)$.

The number R is the **radius of convergence,** and the set of all values of x for which the series converges is the **interval of convergence.** The radius of convergence completely determines the interval of convergence if R is either zero or infinite. For $0 < R < \infty$, however, there remains the question of what happens at the endpoints of the interval. The table of Maclaurin series at the end of Section 10.2 includes intervals of convergence that are open, half-open, and closed.

We will learn how to find the radius of convergence first, and then we will settle the endpoint question in Section 10.5.

*n*th-Term Test

The most obvious requirement for convergence of a series is that the nth term must go to zero as $n \to \infty$. If the partial sums are approaching a limit S, then they also must be getting close to one another, so that for a convergent series $\sum a_n$,

$$\lim_{n\to\infty} a_n = \lim_{n\to\infty} (S_n - S_{n-1}) = S - S = 0.$$

This gives a handy test for divergence:

THEOREM 6 The *n*th-Term Test for Divergence

$\sum_{n=1}^{\infty} a_n$ diverges if $\lim_{n\to\infty} a_n$ fails to exist or is different from zero.

Comparing Nonnegative Series

An effective way to show that a series $\sum a_n$ of nonnegative numbers *converges* is to compare it term by term with a known convergent series $\sum c_n$.

THEOREM 7 The Direct Comparison Test

Let $\sum a_n$ be a series with no negative terms.

(a) $\sum a_n$ converges if there is a convergent series $\sum c_n$ with $a_n \leq c_n$ for all $n > N$, for some integer N.

(b) $\sum a_n$ diverges if there is a divergent series $\sum d_n$ of nonnegative terms with $a_n \geq d_n$ for all $n > N$, for some integer N.

If we can show that $\sum a_n$, $a_n \geq 0$ is eventually dominated by a convergent series, that will establish the convergence of $\sum a_n$. If we can show that $\sum a_n$ eventually dominates a divergent series of nonnegative terms, that will establish the divergence of $\sum a_n$.

We leave the proof to Exercises 61 and 62.

EXAMPLE 2 Proving Convergence by Comparison

Prove that $\displaystyle\sum_{n=0}^{\infty} \frac{x^{2n}}{(n!)^2}$ converges for all real x.

SOLUTION

Let x be any real number. The series

$$\sum_{n=0}^{\infty} \frac{x^{2n}}{(n!)^2}$$

has no negative terms.

For any n, we have

$$\frac{x^{2n}}{(n!)^2} \leq \frac{x^{2n}}{n!} = \frac{(x^2)^n}{n!}.$$

We recognize

$$\sum_{n=0}^{\infty} \frac{(x^2)^n}{n!}$$

as the Taylor series for e^{x^2}, which we know converges to e^{x^2} for all real numbers. Since the e^{x^2} series dominates

$$\sum_{n=0}^{\infty} \frac{x^{2n}}{(n!)^2}$$

term by term, the latter series must also converge for all real numbers by the Direct Comparison Test. ***Now Try Exercise 3.***

For the Direct Comparison Test to apply, the terms of the unknown series must be *nonnegative*. The fact that $\sum a_n$ is dominated by a convergent positive series means nothing if $\sum a_n$ diverges to $-\infty$. You might think that the requirement of nonnegativity would limit the usefulness of the Direct Comparison Test, but in practice this does not turn out to be the case. We can apply our test to $\sum |a_n|$ (which certainly has no negative terms); if $\sum |a_n|$ converges, then $\sum a_n$ converges.

DEFINITION Absolute Convergence

If the series $\sum |a_n|$ of absolute values converges, then $\sum a_n$ **converges absolutely.**

THEOREM 8 Absolute Convergence Implies Convergence

If $\sum |a_n|$ converges, then $\sum a_n$ converges.

Proof For each n,

$$-|a_n| \le a_n \le |a_n|, \qquad \text{so} \qquad 0 \le a_n + |a_n| \le 2|a_n|.$$

If $\sum |a_n|$ converges, then $\sum 2|a_n|$ converges, and by the Direct Comparison Test, the non-negative series $\sum(a_n + |a_n|)$ converges. The equality $a_n = (a_n + |a_n|) - |a_n|$ now allows us to express $\sum a_n$ as the difference of two convergent series:

$$\sum a_n = \sum (a_n + |a_n| - |a_n|) = \sum (a_n + |a_n|) - \sum |a_n|.$$

Therefore, $\sum a_n$ converges. ■

EXAMPLE 3 Using Absolute Convergence

Show that

$$\sum_{n=0}^{\infty} \frac{(\sin x)^n}{n!}$$

converges for all x.

SOLUTION

Let x be any real number. The series

$$\sum_{n=0}^{\infty} \frac{|\sin x|^n}{n!}$$

has no negative terms, and it is term-by-term less than or equal to the series $\sum_{n=0}^{\infty} (1/n!)$, which we know converges to e. Therefore,

$$\sum_{n=0}^{\infty} \frac{|\sin x|^n}{n!}$$

converges by direct comparison. Since

$$\sum_{n=0}^{\infty} \frac{(\sin x)^n}{n!}$$

converges absolutely, it converges. ***Now Try Exercise 5.***

Ratio Test

Our strategy for finding the radius of convergence for an arbitrary power series will be to check for absolute convergence using a powerful test called the *Ratio Test.*

THEOREM 9 The Ratio Test

Let $\sum a_n$ be a series with positive terms, and with

$$\lim_{n\to\infty} \frac{a_{n+1}}{a_n} = L.$$

Then,

(a) the series *converges* if $L < 1$,
(b) the series *diverges* if $L > 1$,
(c) the test is *inconclusive* if $L = 1$.

L'Hôpital's rule is occasionally helpful in determining the limits that arise here.

Proof

(a) $L < 1$:

Choose some number r such that $L < r < 1$. Since

$$\lim_{n\to\infty} \frac{a_{n+1}}{a_n} = L,$$

we know that there is some N large enough so that a_{n+1}/a_n is arbitrarily close to L for all $n \geq N$. In particular, we can guarantee that for some N large enough, $(a_{n+1}/a_n) < r$ for all $n \geq N$. (See Figure 10.12.)

Thus,

$$\frac{a_{N+1}}{a_N} < r \quad \text{so} \quad a_{N+1} < ra_N$$

$$\frac{a_{N+2}}{a_{N+1}} < r \quad \text{so} \quad a_{N+2} < ra_{N+1} < r^2 a_N$$

$$\frac{a_{N+3}}{a_{N+2}} < r \quad \text{so} \quad a_{N+3} < ra_{N+2} < r^3 a_N$$

$$\vdots$$

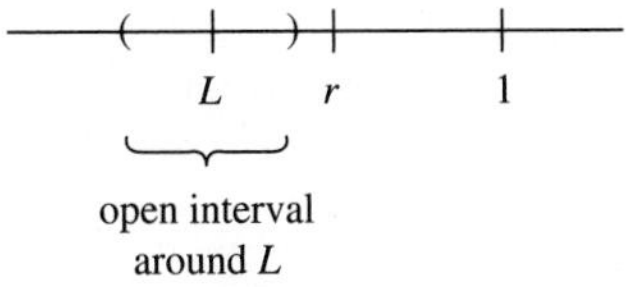

Figure 10.12 Since

$$\lim_{n\to\infty} \frac{a_{n+1}}{a_n} = L,$$

there is some N large enough so that a_{n+1}/a_n lies inside this open interval around L for all $n \geq N$. This guarantees that $a_{n+1}/a_n < r < 1$ for all $n \geq N$.

This shows that for $n \geq N$ we can dominate $\sum a_n$ by $a_N(1 + r + r^2 + \cdots)$. Since $0 < r < 1$, this latter series is a convergent geometric series, and so $\sum a_n$ converges by the Direct Comparison Test.

(b) $L > 1$:

From some index M,

$$\frac{a_{n+1}}{a_n} > 1$$

for all $n \geq M$. In particular,

$$a_M < a_{M+1} < a_{M+2} < \cdots.$$

The terms of the series do not approach 0, so $\sum a_n$ diverges by the nth-Term Test.

(c) $L = 1$:

In Exploration 1 you will finish the proof by showing that the Ratio Test is inconclusive when $L = 1$. ■

A Note on Absolute Convergence: The proof of the Ratio Test shows that the convergence of a power series inside its radius of convergence is *absolute* convergence, a stronger result than we first stated in Theorem 5. We will learn more about the distinction between convergence and absolute convergence in Section 10.5.

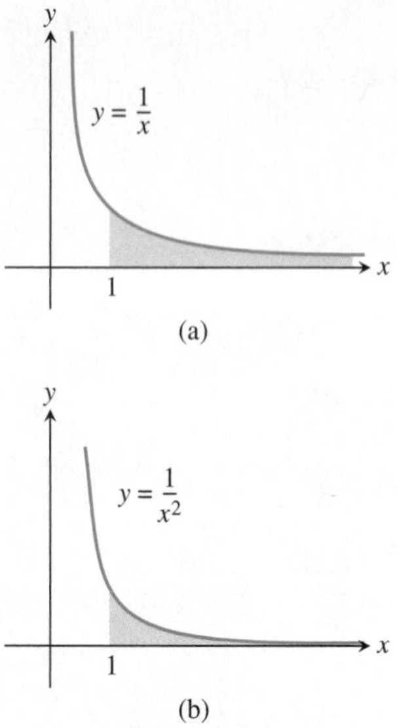

Figure 10.13 Find these areas. (Exploration 1)

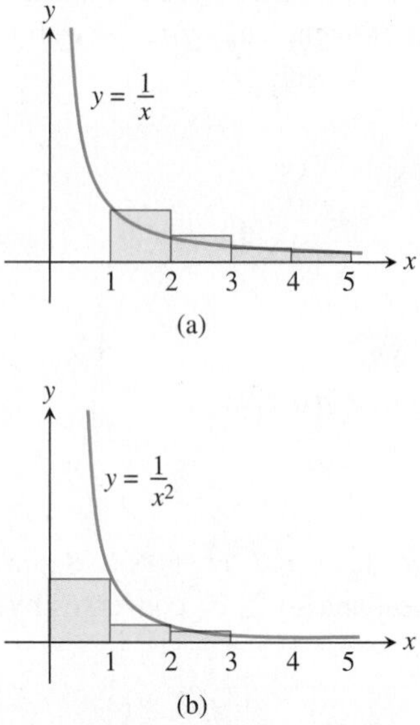

Figure 10.14 The areas of the rectangles form a series in each case. (Exploration 1)

EXPLORATION 1 Finishing the Proof of the Ratio Test

Consider

$$\sum_{n=1}^{\infty} \frac{1}{n} \quad \text{and} \quad \sum_{n=1}^{\infty} \frac{1}{n^2}.$$

(We will refer to them hereafter in this exploration as $\Sigma 1/n$ and $\Sigma 1/n^2$.)

1. Show that the Ratio Test yields $L = 1$ for both series.
2. Use improper integrals to find the areas shaded in Figures 10.13a and 10.13b for $1 \le x < \infty$.
3. Explain how Figure 10.14a shows that $\Sigma 1/n$ diverges, while Figure 10.14b shows that $\Sigma 1/n^2$ converges.
4. Explain how this proves the last part of the Ratio Test.

EXAMPLE 4 Finding the Radius of Convergence

Find the radius of convergence of

$$\sum_{n=0}^{\infty} \frac{nx^n}{10^n}.$$

SOLUTION

We check for absolute convergence using the Ratio Test.

$$\lim_{n\to\infty} \frac{|a_{n+1}|}{|a_n|} = \lim_{n\to\infty} \frac{(n+1)\,|x^{n+1}|}{10^{n+1}} \cdot \frac{10^n}{n|x^n|}$$

$$= \lim_{n\to\infty} \left(\frac{n+1}{n}\right) \frac{|x|}{10} = \frac{|x|}{10}$$

Setting $|x|/10 < 1$, we see that the series converges absolutely (and hence converges) for $-10 < x < 10$. The series diverges for $|x| > 10$, which means (by Theorem 5, the Convergence Theorem for Power Series) that it diverges for $x > 10$ and for $x < -10$. The radius of convergence is 10.

Now Try Exercise 9.

EXAMPLE 5 A Series with Radius of Convergence 0

Find the radius of convergence of the series $\sum_{n=0}^{\infty} n!x^n$.

SOLUTION

We check for absolute convergence using the Ratio Test.

$$\lim_{n\to\infty} \frac{|a_{n+1}|}{|a_n|} = \lim_{n\to\infty} \frac{(n+1)!|x|^{n+1}}{n!|x|^n}$$

$$= \lim_{n\to\infty} (n+1)|x|$$

$$= \infty, \qquad x \neq 0$$

The series converges only for $x = 0$. The radius of convergence is $R = 0$.

Now Try Exercise 17.

Endpoint Convergence

The Ratio Test, which is really a test for absolute convergence, establishes the radius of convergence for $\sum |c_n(x - a)^n|$. Theorem 5 guarantees that this is the same as the radius of convergence of $\sum c_n(x - a)^n$. Therefore, all that remains to be resolved about the convergence of an arbitrary power series is the question of convergence at the endpoints of the convergence interval when the radius of convergence is a finite, nonzero number.

EXPLORATION 2 Revisiting a Maclaurin Series

For what values of x does the series

$$x - \frac{x^2}{2} + \frac{x^3}{3} - \cdots + (-1)^{n-1}\frac{x^n}{n} + \cdots$$

converge?

1. Apply the Ratio Test to determine the radius of convergence.
2. Substitute the left-hand endpoint of the interval into the power series. Use Figure 10.14a of Exploration 1 to help you decide whether the resulting series converges or diverges.
3. Substitute the right-hand endpoint of the interval into the power series. You should get

$$1 - \frac{1}{2} + \frac{1}{3} - \frac{1}{4} + \cdots + \frac{(-1)^{n-1}}{n} + \cdots.$$

Chart the progress of the partial sums of this series geometrically on a number line as follows: Start at 0. Go forward 1. Go back 1/2. Go forward 1/3. Go back 1/4. Go forward 1/5, and so on.
4. Does the series converge at the right-hand endpoint? Give a convincing argument based on your geometric journey in part 3.
5. Does the series converge *absolutely* at the right-hand endpoint?

EXAMPLE 6 Determining Convergence of a Series

Determine the convergence or divergence of the series $\displaystyle\sum_{n=0}^{\infty} \frac{3^n}{5^n + 1}$.

SOLUTION

We use the Ratio Test.

$$\lim_{n\to\infty} \frac{a_{n+1}}{a_n} = \lim_{n\to\infty} \frac{\dfrac{3^{n+1}}{5^{n+1}+1}}{\dfrac{3^n}{5^n+1}} = \lim_{n\to\infty}\left(\frac{3^{n+1}}{5^{n+1}+1}\right)\left(\frac{5^n+1}{3^n}\right)$$

$$= \lim_{n\to\infty} 3\left(\frac{5^n+1}{5^{n+1}+1}\right)$$

$$= \lim_{n\to\infty} 3\,\frac{1 + \dfrac{1}{5^n}}{5 + \dfrac{1}{5^n}}$$ Divide numerator and denominator by 5^n.

$$= \frac{3}{5}$$

The series converges because the ratio $3/5 < 1$. ***Now Try Exercise 31.***

The question of convergence of a power series at an endpoint is really a question about the convergence of a series of numbers. If the series is geometric with first term a and common ratio r, then the series converges to $a/(1-r)$ if $|r|<1$ and diverges if $|r| \geq 1$. Another type of series whose sums are easily found are **telescoping series,** as illustrated in Example 7.

EXAMPLE 7 Summing a Telescoping Series

Find the sum of $\displaystyle\sum_{n=1}^{\infty} \frac{1}{n(n+1)}$.

SOLUTION

Use partial fractions to rewrite the nth term.

$$\frac{1}{n(n+1)} = \frac{1}{n} - \frac{1}{n+1}$$

We compute a few partial sums to find a general formula.

$$s_1 = 1 - \frac{1}{2}$$

$$s_2 = \left(1 - \frac{1}{2}\right) + \left(\frac{1}{2} - \frac{1}{3}\right) = 1 - \frac{1}{3}$$

$$s_3 = \left(1 - \frac{1}{2}\right) + \left(\frac{1}{2} - \frac{1}{3}\right) + \left(\frac{1}{3} - \frac{1}{4}\right) = 1 - \frac{1}{4}$$

We can see that, in general,

$$s_n = 1 - \frac{1}{n},$$

because all the terms between the first and last cancel when the parentheses are removed. Therefore, the sum of the series is

$$S = \lim_{n\to\infty} s_n = 1.$$

Now Try Exercise 48.

Telescoping Series

We call the series in Example 7 a *telescoping series* because its partial sums collapse like an old handheld telescope.

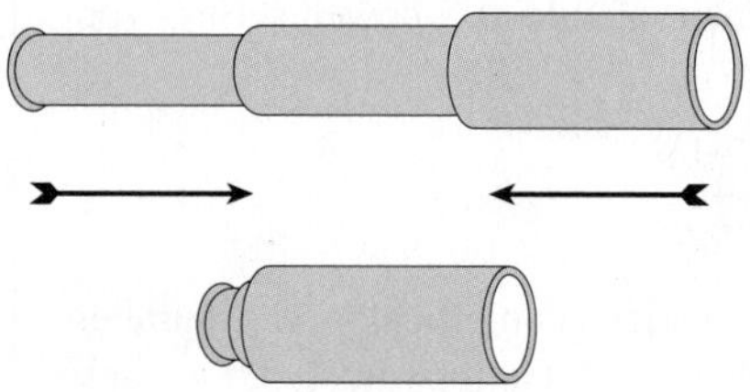

The final section of this chapter will formalize some of the strategies used in Exploration 2 and Example 7 and will develop additional tests that can be used to determine series behavior at endpoints.

Quick Review 10.4 *(For help, go to Sections 2.2 and 10.1.)*

Exercise numbers with a gray background indicate problems that the authors have designed to be solved *without a calculator.*

In Exercises 1–5, find the limit of the expression as $n \to \infty$. Assume x remains fixed as n changes.

1. $\dfrac{n|x|}{n+1}$

2. $\dfrac{n^2|x-3|}{n(n-1)}$

3. $\dfrac{|x|^n}{n!}$

4. $\dfrac{(n+1)^4x^2}{(2n)^4}$

5. $\dfrac{|2x+1|^{n+1}2^n}{2^{n+1}|2x+1|^n}$

In Exercises 6–10, the terms of one of the series (call it $\sum a_n$) will eventually be greater than the terms of the other series (call it $\sum b_n$). Identify which series is which, and find the smallest positive integer N for which $a_n > b_n$ for all $n \geq N$.

6. $\sum 5n, \quad \sum n^2$

7. $\sum n^5, \quad \sum 5^n$

8. $\sum \ln n, \quad \sum \sqrt{n},$

9. $\sum \dfrac{1}{10^n}, \quad \sum \dfrac{1}{n!}$

10. $\sum \dfrac{1}{n^2}, \quad \sum n^{-3}$

Section 10.4 Exercises

In Exercises 1 and 2, find the values of x for which the equation is an identity. Support your answer graphically.

1. $\dfrac{-1}{x+4} = 1 + (x+5) + (x+5)^2 + (x+5)^3 + \cdots$

2. $\dfrac{1}{1-x} = 1 + x + x^2 + x^3 + \cdots$

In Exercises 3 and 4, use a comparison test to show that the series converges for all x.

3. $\displaystyle\sum_{n=0}^{\infty} \frac{x^{3n}}{2n! + 1}$ **4.** $\displaystyle\sum_{n=0}^{\infty} \frac{x^{2n}}{n! + 2}$

In Exercises 5 and 6, show that the series converges absolutely.

5. $\displaystyle\sum_{n=0}^{\infty} \frac{(\cos x)^n}{n! + 1}$ **6.** $\displaystyle\sum_{n=0}^{\infty} \frac{2(\sin x)^n}{n! + 3}$

In Exercises 7–22, find the *radius* of convergence of the power series.

7. $\displaystyle\sum_{n=0}^{\infty} x^n$ **8.** $\displaystyle\sum_{n=0}^{\infty} (x+5)^n$

9. $\displaystyle\sum_{n=0}^{\infty} (-1)^n(4x+1)^n$ **10.** $\displaystyle\sum_{n=1}^{\infty} \frac{(3x-2)^n}{n}$

11. $\displaystyle\sum_{n=0}^{\infty} \frac{(x-2)^n}{10^n}$ **12.** $\displaystyle\sum_{n=0}^{\infty} \frac{nx^n}{n+2}$

13. $\displaystyle\sum_{n=1}^{\infty} \frac{x^n}{n\sqrt{n}\,3^n}$ **14.** $\displaystyle\sum_{n=0}^{\infty} \frac{x^{2n+1}}{n!}$

15. $\displaystyle\sum_{n=0}^{\infty} \frac{n(x+3)^n}{5^n}$ **16.** $\displaystyle\sum_{n=0}^{\infty} \frac{nx^n}{4^n(n^2+1)}$

17. $\displaystyle\sum_{n=0}^{\infty} n!(x-4)^n$ **18.** $\displaystyle\sum_{n=0}^{\infty} \frac{\sqrt{n}\,x^n}{3^n}$

19. $\displaystyle\sum_{n=0}^{\infty} (-2)^n(n+1)(x-1)^n$ **20.** $\displaystyle\sum_{n=1}^{\infty} \frac{(4x-5)^{2n+1}}{n^{3/2}}$

21. $\displaystyle\sum_{n=1}^{\infty} \frac{(x+\pi)^n}{\sqrt{n}}$ **22.** $\displaystyle\sum_{n=0}^{\infty} \frac{(x-\sqrt{2})^{2n+1}}{2^n}$

In Exercises 23–28, find the *interval* of convergence of the series and, within this interval, the sum of the series as a function of x.

23. $\displaystyle\sum_{n=0}^{\infty} \frac{(x-1)^{2n}}{4^n}$ **24.** $\displaystyle\sum_{n=0}^{\infty} \frac{(x+1)^{2n}}{9^n}$

25. $\displaystyle\sum_{n=0}^{\infty} \left(\frac{\sqrt{x}}{2} - 1\right)^n$ **26.** $\displaystyle\sum_{n=0}^{\infty} (\ln x)^n$

27. $\displaystyle\sum_{n=0}^{\infty} \left(\frac{x^2-1}{3}\right)^n$ **28.** $\displaystyle\sum_{n=0}^{\infty} \left(\frac{\sin x}{2}\right)^n$

In Exercises 29–44, determine the convergence or divergence of the series. Identify the test (or tests) you use. There may be more than one correct way to determine convergence or divergence of a given series.

29. $\displaystyle\sum_{n=1}^{\infty} \frac{n}{n+1}$ **30.** $\displaystyle\sum_{n=1}^{\infty} \frac{2^n}{n+1}$

31. $\displaystyle\sum_{n=1}^{\infty} \frac{n^2-1}{2^n}$ **32.** $\displaystyle\sum_{n=1}^{\infty} -\frac{1}{8^n}$

33. $\displaystyle\sum_{n=1}^{\infty} \frac{2^n}{3^n+1}$ **34.** $\displaystyle\sum_{n=1}^{\infty} n\sin\left(\frac{1}{n}\right)$

35. $\displaystyle\sum_{n=0}^{\infty} n^2e^{-n}$ **36.** $\displaystyle\sum_{n=0}^{\infty} \frac{n^{10}}{10^n}$

37. $\displaystyle\sum_{n=1}^{\infty} \frac{(n+3)!}{3!n!3^n}$ **38.** $\displaystyle\sum_{n=1}^{\infty} \left(1+\frac{1}{n}\right)^n$

39. $\displaystyle\sum_{n=0}^{\infty} \frac{(-2)^n}{3^n}$ **40.** $\displaystyle\sum_{n=1}^{\infty} n!e^{-n}$

41. $\displaystyle\sum_{n=1}^{\infty} \frac{3n}{n^3 2^n}$ **42.** $\displaystyle\sum_{n=1}^{\infty} \frac{n\ln n}{2^n}$

43. $\displaystyle\sum_{n=1}^{\infty} \frac{n!}{(2n+1)!}$

44. $\displaystyle\sum_{n=1}^{\infty} \frac{n!}{n^n}$ [*Hint:* If you do not recognize L, try recognizing the reciprocal of L.]

45. Give an example to show that the converse of the nth-Term Test is false. That is, $\sum a_n$ might diverge even though $\lim_{n\to\infty} a_n = 0$.

46. Find two convergent series $\sum a_n$ and $\sum b_n$ such that $\sum(a_n/b_n)$ diverges

47. Writing to Learn We reviewed in Section 10.1 how to find the interval of convergence for the geometric series $\sum_{n=0}^{\infty} x^n$. Can we find the interval of convergence of a geometric series by using the Ratio Test? Explain.

In Exercises 48–54, find the sum of the telescoping series.

48. $\displaystyle\sum_{n=1}^{\infty} \frac{4}{(4n-3)(4n+1)}$ **49.** $\displaystyle\sum_{n=1}^{\infty} \frac{6}{(2n-1)(2n+1)}$

50. $\displaystyle\sum_{n=1}^{\infty} \frac{40n}{(2n-1)^2(2n+1)^2}$ **51.** $\displaystyle\sum_{n=1}^{\infty} \frac{2n+1}{n^2(n+1)^2}$

52. $\displaystyle\sum_{n=1}^{\infty} \left(\frac{1}{\sqrt{n}} - \frac{1}{\sqrt{n+1}}\right)$

53. $\displaystyle\sum_{n=1}^{\infty} \left(\frac{1}{\ln(n+2)} - \frac{1}{\ln(n+1)}\right)$

54. $\displaystyle\sum_{n=1}^{\infty} (\tan^{-1}(n) - \tan^{-1}(n+1))$

Standardized Test Questions

You may use a graphing calculator to solve the following problems.

55. True or False If a series converges absolutely, then it converges. Justify your answer.

56. True or False If the radius of convergence of a power series is 0, then the series diverges for all real numbers. Justify your answer.

57. Multiple Choice Which of the following gives $\lim_{n\to\infty} \frac{a_{n+1}}{a_n}$ for the series $\sum_{n=0}^{\infty} \frac{2^n}{(-3)^n}$?

(A) 3/2 (B) 2/3 (C) 1 (D) 0 (E) ∞

58. Multiple Choice Which of the following gives the radius of convergence of the series $\sum_{n=1}^{\infty} \frac{(2x-3)^n}{n}$?

(A) 2 (B) 1 (C) 1/2 (D) 0 (E) ∞

59. Multiple Choice Which of the following describes the behavior of the series $\sum_{n=1}^{\infty} \frac{(\sin x)^n}{2^n n^2}$?

I. diverges
II. converges
III. converges absolutely

(A) I only (B) II only (C) III only
(D) I & II only (E) II & III only

60. Multiple Choice Which of the following gives the sum of the telescoping series $\sum_{n=1}^{\infty} \frac{3}{(3n-1)(3n+2)}$?

(A) 3/10 (B) 3/8 (C) 9/22 (D) 1/2 (E) The series diverges.

Explorations

Group Activity *Nondecreasing Sequences* As you already know, a nondecreasing (or increasing) function $f(x)$ that is bounded from above on an interval $[a, \infty)$ has a limit as $x \to \infty$ that is less than or equal to the bound. The same is true of sequences of numbers. If $s_1 \le s_2 \le s_3 \le \ldots \le s_n \ldots$ and there is a number M such that $|s_n| \le M$ for all n, then the sequence converges to a limit $S \le M$. You will need this fact as you work through Exercises 61 and 62.

61. *Proof of the Direct Comparison Test, Part a* Let $\sum a_n$ be a series with no negative terms, and let $\sum c_n$ be a convergent series such that $a_n \le c_n$ for all $n \ge N$, for some integer N.

(a) Show that the partial sums of $\sum a_n$ are bounded above by

$$a_1 + \cdots + a_N + \sum_{n=N+1}^{\infty} c_n.$$

(b) Explain why this shows that $\sum a_n$ must converge.

62. *Proof of the Direct Comparison Test, Part b* Let $\sum a_n$ be a series with no negative terms, and let $\sum d_n$ be a divergent series of nonnegative terms such that $a_n \ge d_n$ for all $n \ge N$, for some integer N.

(a) Show that the partial sums of $\sum d_n$ are bounded above by

$$d_1 + \cdots + d_N + \sum_{n=N+1}^{\infty} a_n.$$

(b) Explain why this leads to a contradiction if we assume that $\sum a_n$ converges.

63. Group Activity Within your group, have each student make up a power series with radius of convergence equal to one of the numbers $1, 2, \ldots, n$. Then exchange series with another group and match the other group's series with the correct radii of convergence.

Extending the Ideas

64. We can show that the series

$$\sum_{n=0}^{\infty} \frac{n^2}{2^n}$$

converges by the Ratio Test, but what is its sum?

To find out, express $1/(1-x)$ as a geometric series. Differentiate both sides of the resulting equation with respect to x, multiply both sides of the result by x, differentiate again, multiply by x again, and set x equal to $1/2$. What do you get? (*Source:* David E. Dobbs's letter to the editor, *Illinois Mathematics Teacher,* Vol. 33, Issue 4, 1982, p. 27.)

10.5 Testing Convergence at Endpoints

What you will learn about . . .

- Integral Test
- Harmonic Series and p-series
- Comparison Tests
- Alternating Series
- Absolute and Conditional Convergence
- Intervals of Convergence
- A Word of Caution

and why . . .

Additional tests for convergence of series are introduced in this section.

Integral Test

In Exploration 1 of Section 10.4, you showed that $\sum 1/n$ *diverges* by modeling it as a sum of rectangle areas that contain the area under the curve $y = 1/x$ from 1 to ∞. You also showed that $\sum 1/n^2$ *converges* by modeling it as a sum of rectangle areas contained by the area under the curve $y = 1/x^2$ from 1 to ∞. This area-based convergence test in its general form is known as the *Integral Test.*

THEOREM 10 The Integral Test

Let $\{a_n\}$ be a sequence of positive terms. Suppose that $a_n = f(n)$, where f is a continuous, positive, decreasing function of x for all $x \geq N$ (N a positive integer). Then the series $\sum_{n=N}^{\infty} a_n$ and the integral $\int_N^{\infty} f(x)\,dx$ either both converge or both diverge.

Proof We will illustrate the proof for $N = 1$ to keep the notation simple, but the illustration can be shifted horizontally to any value of N without affecting the logic of the proof.

The proof is entirely contained in these two pictures (Figure 10.15):

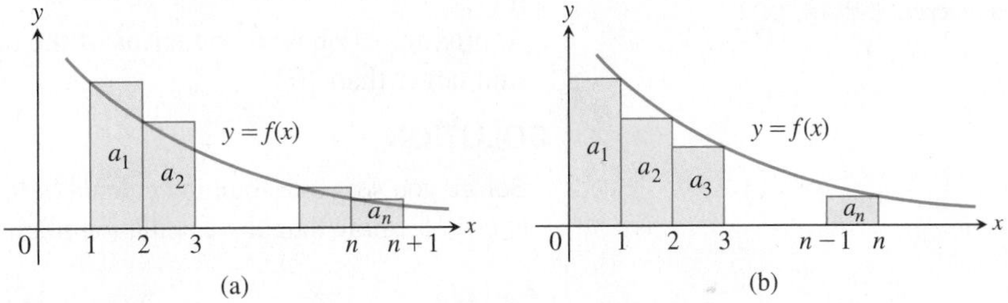

Figure 10.15 (a) The sum $a_1 + a_2 + \cdots + a_n$ provides an upper bound for $\int_1^{n+1} f(x)\,dx$. (b) The sum $a_2 + a_3 + \cdots + a_n$ provides a lower bound for $\int_1^{n} f(x)\,dx$. (Theorem 10)

We leave it to you (in Exercise 52) to supply the words. ■

EXAMPLE 1 Applying the Integral Test

Does $\displaystyle\sum_{n=1}^{\infty} \frac{1}{n\sqrt{n}}$ converge?

SOLUTION

The Integral Test applies because

$$f(x) = \frac{1}{x\sqrt{x}}$$

is a continuous, positive, decreasing function of x for $x > 1$.

We have

$$\int_1^{\infty} \frac{1}{x\sqrt{x}}\,dx = \lim_{k\to\infty} \int_1^{k} x^{-3/2}\,dx = \lim_{k\to\infty} \left[-2x^{-1/2}\right]_1^k$$

$$= \lim_{k\to\infty} \left(-\frac{2}{\sqrt{k}} + 2\right) = 2.$$

Since the integral converges, so must the series. *Now Try Exercise 1.*

Caution

The series and the integral in the Integral Test need not have the same value in the convergent case. Although the integral converges to 2 in Example 1, the series might have a quite different sum. If you use your calculator to compute or graph partial sums for the series, you can see that the 11th partial sum is already greater than 2.

Harmonic Series and *p*-series

The Integral Test can be used to settle the question of convergence for any series of the form $\sum_{n=1}^{\infty} = (1/n^p)$, p a real constant. (The series in Example 1 had this form, with $p = 3/2$.) Such a series is called a ***p*-series.**

EXPLORATION 1 The *p*-Series Test

1. Use the Integral Test to prove that $\sum_{n=1}^{\infty} (1/n^p)$ converges if $p > 1$.
2. Use the Integral Test to prove that $\sum_{n=1}^{\infty} (1/n^p)$ diverges if $p < 1$.
3. Use the Integral Test to prove that $\sum_{n=1}^{\infty} (1/n^p)$ diverges if $p = 1$.

What is harmonic about the harmonic series?

The terms in the harmonic series correspond to the nodes on a vibrating string that produce multiples of the fundamental frequency. For example, 1/2 produces the harmonic that is twice the fundamental frequency, 1/3 produces a frequency that is three times the fundamental frequency, and so on. The fundamental frequency is the lowest note or pitch we hear when a string is plucked. (Figure 10.17)

The p-series with $p = 1$ is the **harmonic series,** and it is probably the most famous divergent series in mathematics. The p-Series Test shows that the harmonic series is just *barely* divergent; if we increase p to 1.000000001, for instance, the series converges!

The slowness with which the harmonic series approaches infinity is most impressive. Consider the following example.

EXAMPLE 2 The Slow Divergence of the Harmonic Series

Approximately how many terms of the harmonic series are required to form a partial sum larger than 20?

SOLUTION

Before you set your graphing calculator to the task of finding this number, you might want to estimate how long the calculation might take. The graphs tell the story (Figure 10.16).

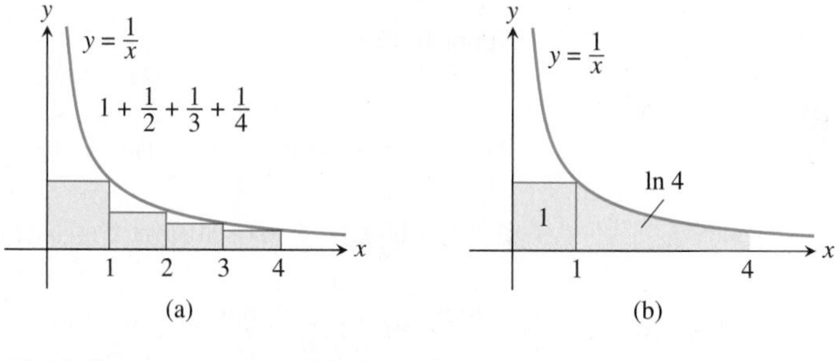

Figure 10.16 Finding an upper bound for one of the partial sums of the harmonic series. (Example 2)

Let H_n denote the nth partial sum of the harmonic series. Comparing the two graphs, we see that $H_4 < (1 + \ln 4)$ and (in general) that $H_n \leq (1 + \ln n)$. If we wish H_n to be greater than 20, then

$$\begin{aligned} 1 + \ln n > H_n &> 20 \\ 1 + \ln n &> 20 \\ \ln n &> 19 \\ n &> e^{19}. \end{aligned}$$

The exact value of e^{19} rounds up to 178,482,301. It will take *at least* that many terms of the harmonic series to move the partial sums beyond 20. It would take your calculator several weeks to compute a partial sum of this many terms. Nonetheless, the harmonic series really does diverge!

Now Try Exercise 3.

Figure 10.17 On a guitar, the second harmonic note is produced when the finger is positioned halfway between the bridge and nut of the string while the string is plucked with the other hand.

Comparison Tests

The p-Series Test tells everything there is to know about the convergence or divergence of series of the form $\Sigma(1/n^p)$. This is admittedly a rather narrow class of series, but we can test many other kinds (including those in which the nth term is any rational function of n) by *comparing* them to p-series.

The Direct Comparison Test (Theorem 7, Section 10.4) is one method of comparison, but the *Limit Comparison Test* is another.

THEOREM 11 The Limit Comparison Test (LCT)

Suppose that $a_n > 0$ and $b_n > 0$ for all $n \geq N$ (N a positive integer).

1. If $\lim_{n\to\infty} \dfrac{a_n}{b_n} = c, 0 < c < \infty$, then $\Sigma\, a_n$ and $\Sigma\, b_n$ both converge or both diverge.
2. If $\lim_{n\to\infty} \dfrac{a_n}{b_n} = 0$ and $\Sigma\, b_n$ converges, then $\Sigma\, a_n$ converges.
3. If $\lim_{n\to\infty} \dfrac{a_n}{b_n} = \infty$ and $\Sigma\, b_n$ diverges, then $\Sigma\, a_n$ diverges.

We omit the proof.

EXAMPLE 3 Using the Limit Comparison Test

Determine whether the series converge or diverge.

(a) $\dfrac{3}{4} + \dfrac{5}{9} + \dfrac{7}{16} + \dfrac{9}{25} + \cdots = \displaystyle\sum_{n=1}^{\infty} \frac{2n+1}{(n+1)^2}$

(b) $\dfrac{1}{1} + \dfrac{1}{3} + \dfrac{1}{7} + \dfrac{1}{15} + \cdots = \displaystyle\sum_{n=1}^{\infty} \frac{1}{2^n - 1}$

(c) $\dfrac{8}{4} + \dfrac{11}{21} + \dfrac{14}{56} + \dfrac{17}{115} + \cdots = \displaystyle\sum_{n=2}^{\infty} \frac{3n+2}{n^3 - 2n}$

(d) $\sin 1 + \sin\dfrac{1}{2} + \sin\dfrac{1}{3} + \cdots = \displaystyle\sum_{n=1}^{\infty} \sin\left(\frac{1}{n}\right)$

SOLUTION

(a) For n large, $\dfrac{2n+1}{(n+1)^2}$ behaves like $\dfrac{2n}{n^2} = \dfrac{2}{n}$,

so we compare terms of the given series to terms of $\Sigma\,(1/n)$ and try the LCT.

$$\lim_{n\to\infty} \frac{a_n}{b_n} = \lim_{n\to\infty} \frac{(2n+1)/(n+1)^2}{1/n}$$

$$= \lim_{n\to\infty} \frac{2n+1}{(n+1)^2} \cdot \frac{n}{1}$$

Applying l'Hôpital's rule, $\displaystyle\lim_{n\to\infty} \frac{2n^2+n}{(n+1)^2} = \lim_{n\to\infty} \frac{4n+1}{2(n+1)} = 2.$

Since the limit is positive and $\Sigma\,(1/n)$ diverges,

$$\sum_{n=1}^{\infty} \frac{2n+1}{(n+1)^2}$$

also diverges.

continued

(b) For n large, $1/(2^n - 1)$ behaves like $1/2^n$, so we compare the given series to $\Sigma\,(1/2^n)$.

$$\lim_{n\to\infty}\frac{a_n}{b_n} = \lim_{n\to\infty}\frac{1}{2^n - 1}\cdot\frac{2^n}{1}$$

$$= \lim_{n\to\infty}\frac{2^n}{2^n - 1}$$

$$= \lim_{n\to\infty}\frac{1}{1 - (1/2^n)} = 1$$

Since $\Sigma\,(1/2^n)$ converges (geometric, $r = 1/2$), the LCT guarantees that

$$\sum_{n=1}^{\infty}\frac{1}{2^n - 1}$$

also converges.

(c) For n large,

$$\frac{3n + 2}{n^3 - 2n}$$

behaves like $3/n^2$, so we compare the given series to $\Sigma\,(1/n^2)$.

$$\lim_{n\to\infty}\frac{a_n}{b_n} = \lim_{n\to\infty}\frac{3n + 2}{n^3 - 2n}\cdot\frac{n^2}{1}$$

$$= \lim_{n\to\infty}\frac{3n^3 + 2n^2}{n^3 - 2n} = 3$$

Since $\Sigma\,(1/n^2)$ converges by the p-Series Test,

$$\sum_{n=2}^{\infty}\frac{3n + 2}{n^3 - 2n}$$

also converges (by the LCT).

(d) Recall that

$$\lim_{x\to 0}\frac{\sin x}{x} = 1,$$

so we try the LCT by comparing the given series to $\Sigma\,(1/n)$.

$$\lim_{n\to\infty}\frac{a_n}{b_n} = \lim_{n\to\infty}\frac{\sin(1/n)}{(1/n)} = 1$$

Since $\Sigma\,(1/n)$ diverges, $\Sigma_{n=1}^{\infty}\sin(1/n)$ also diverges. ***Now Try Exercise 5.***

As Example 3 suggests, applying the Limit Comparison Test has strong connections to analyzing end behavior in functions. In part (c) of Example 3, we could have reached the same conclusion if a_n had been *any* linear polynomial in n divided by *any* cubic polynomial in n, since any such rational function "in the end" will grow like $1/n^2$.

Alternating Series

A series in which the terms are alternately positive and negative is an **alternating series.**

Here are three examples.

$$1 - \frac{1}{2} + \frac{1}{3} - \frac{1}{4} + \frac{1}{5} - \cdots + \frac{(-1)^{n+1}}{n} + \cdots \tag{1}$$

$$-2 + 1 - \frac{1}{2} + \frac{1}{4} - \frac{1}{8} + \cdots + \frac{(-1)^n 4}{2^n} + \cdots \tag{2}$$

$$1 - 2 + 3 - 4 + 5 - 6 + \cdots + (-1)^{n+1} n + \cdots \tag{3}$$

Series 1, called the **alternating harmonic series,** converges, as we will see shortly. (You may have come to this conclusion already in Exploration 2 of Section 10.4.) Series 2, a geometric series with $a = -2$, $r = -1/2$, converges to $-2/[1 + (1/2)] = -4/3$. Series 3 diverges by the nth-Term Test.

We prove the convergence of the alternating harmonic series by applying the following test.

THEOREM 12 The Alternating Series Test (Leibniz's Theorem)

The series

$$\sum_{n=1}^{\infty} (-1)^{n+1} u_n = u_1 - u_2 + u_3 - u_4 + \cdots$$

converges if all three of the following conditions are satisfied:

1. each u_n is positive;
2. $u_n \geq u_{n+1}$ for all $n \geq N$, for some integer N;
3. $\lim_{n\to\infty} u_n = 0$.

Figure 10.18 illustrates the convergence of the partial sums to their limit L.

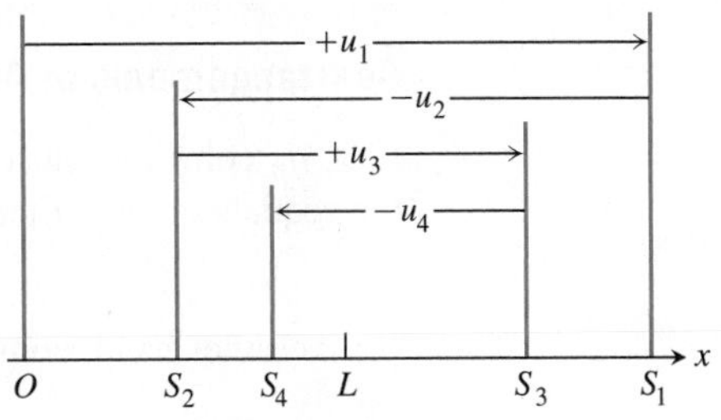

Figure 10.18 Closing in on the sum of a convergent alternating series. (Theorem 12)

The figure that proves the Alternating Series Test actually proves more than the *fact* of convergence; it also shows the *way* that an alternating series converges when it satisfies the conditions of the test. The partial sums keep "overshooting" the limit as they go back and forth on the number line, gradually closing in as the terms tend to zero. If we stop at the nth partial sum, we know that the next term $(\pm u_{n+1})$ will again cause us to overshoot the limit in the positive direction or negative direction, depending on the sign carried by u_{n+1}. This gives us a convenient bound for the truncation error, which we state as another theorem.

THEOREM 13 The Alternating Series Estimation Theorem

If the alternating series $\sum_{n=1}^{\infty}(-1)^{n+1}u_n$ satisfies the conditions of Theorem 12, then the truncation error for the nth partial sum is less than u_{n+1} and has the same sign as the first unused term.

EXAMPLE 4 The Alternating Harmonic Series

Prove that the alternating harmonic series is convergent, but not absolutely convergent. Find a bound for the truncation error after 99 terms.

SOLUTION

The terms are strictly alternating in sign and decrease in absolute value from the start:

$$1 > \frac{1}{2} > \frac{1}{3} > \cdots. \quad \text{Also,} \quad \frac{1}{n} \to 0.$$

By the Alternating Series Test,

$$\sum_{n=1}^{\infty} \frac{(-1)^{n+1}}{n}$$

converges.

On the other hand, the series $\sum_{n=1}^{\infty}(1/n)$ of absolute values is the harmonic series, which diverges, so the alternating harmonic series is not absolutely convergent.

The Alternating Series Estimation Theorem guarantees that the truncation error after 99 terms is less than $u_{99+1} = 1/(99 + 1) = 1/100$. ***Now Try Exercise 23.***

A Note on the Error Bound

Theorem 13 does not give a *formula* for the truncation error, but a *bound* for the truncation error. The bound might be fairly conservative. For example, the first 99 terms of the alternating harmonic series add to about 0.6981721793, while the series itself has a sum of $\ln 2 \approx 0.6931471806$. That makes the actual truncation error very close to 0.005, about half the size of the bound of 0.01 given by Theorem 13.

Absolute and Conditional Convergence

Because the alternating harmonic series is convergent but not absolutely convergent, we say it is **conditionally convergent** (or **converges conditionally**).

We take it for granted that we can rearrange the terms of a *finite* sum without affecting the sum. We can also rearrange a *finite number* of terms of an infinite series without affecting the sum. But if we rearrange an infinite number of terms of an infinite series, we can be sure of leaving the sum unaltered *only if it converges absolutely.*

Rearrangements of Absolutely Convergent Series

If $\sum a_n$ converges absolutely, and if $b_1, b_2, b_3, \ldots, bn, \ldots$ is any rearrangement of the sequence $\{a_n\}$, then $\sum b_n$ converges absolutely and $\sum_{n=1}^{\infty} b_n = \sum_{n=1}^{\infty} a_n$.

On the other hand, consider this:

Rearrangements of Conditionally Convergent Series

If $\sum a_n$ converges conditionally, then the terms can be rearranged to form a divergent series. The terms can also be rearranged to form a series that converges to *any* preassigned sum.

This seems incredible, but it is a logical consequence of the definition of the sum as the *limit of the sequence of partial sums.* A conditionally convergent series consists of positive terms that sum to ∞ and negative terms that sum to $-\infty$, so we can manipulate the partial sums to do virtually anything we wish. We illustrate the technique with the alternating harmonic series.

EXAMPLE 5 Rearranging the Alternating Harmonic Series

Show how to rearrange the terms of

$$\sum_{n=1}^{\infty} \frac{(-1)^{n+1}}{n}$$

to form

(a) a divergent series; **(b)** a series that converges to π.

SOLUTION

The series of positive terms,

$$1 + \frac{1}{3} + \frac{1}{5} + \cdots + \frac{1}{2n+1} + \cdots,$$

diverges to ∞, while the series of negative terms,

$$-\frac{1}{2} - \frac{1}{4} - \frac{1}{6} - \cdots - \frac{1}{2n} - \cdots,$$

diverges to $-\infty$. No matter what finite number of terms we use, the remaining positive terms or negative terms still diverge. So, we build our series as follows:

(a) Start by adding positive terms until the partial sum is greater than 1. Then add negative terms until the partial sum is less than -2. Then add positive terms until the sum is greater than 3. Then add negative terms until the sum is less than -4. Continue in this manner indefinitely, so that the sequence of partial sums swings arbitrarily far in both directions and hence diverges.

(b) Start by adding positive terms until the partial sum is greater than π. Then add negative terms until the partial sum is less than π. Then add positive terms until the sum is greater than π. Continue in this manner indefinitely, always closing in on π. Since the positive and negative terms of the original series both approach zero, the amount by which the partial sums exceed or fall short of π approaches zero. ***Now Try Exercise 33.***

Intervals of Convergence

Our purpose in this section has been to develop tests for convergence that can be used at the endpoints of the intervals of absolute convergence of power series. There are three possibilities at each endpoint: The series could diverge, it could converge absolutely, or it could converge conditionally.

How to Test a Power Series $\sum_{n=0}^{\infty} c_n(x-a)^n$ for Convergence

1. Use the Ratio Test to find the values of x for which the series converges absolutely. Ordinarily, this is an open interval

$$a - R < x < a + R.$$

In some instances, the series converges for all values of x. In rare cases, the series converges only at $x = a$.

continued

2. If the interval of absolute convergence is finite, test for convergence or divergence at each endpoint. The Ratio Test fails at these points. Use a comparison test, the Integral Test, or the Alternating Series Test.
3. If the interval of absolute convergence is $a - R < x < a + R$, conclude that the series diverges (it does not even converge conditionally) for $|x - a| > R$, because for those values of x the nth term does not approach zero.

EXAMPLE 6 The Convergence of Your Knowledge About Convergence

For each of the following series, find (a) the radius of convergence and (b) the interval of convergence. Then identify the values of x for which the series converges (c) absolutely and (d) conditionally.

(a) $\displaystyle\sum_{n=1}^{\infty}(-1)^{n+1}\frac{x^{2n}}{2n} = \frac{x^2}{2} - \frac{x^4}{4} + \frac{x^6}{6} - \cdots$

(b) $\displaystyle\sum_{n=0}^{\infty}\frac{(10x)^n}{n!} = 1 + 10x + \frac{100x^2}{2!} + \frac{1000x^3}{3!} + \cdots$

(c) $\displaystyle\sum_{n=0}^{\infty} n!(x+1)^n = 1 + (x+1) + 2!(x+1)^2 + 3!(x+1)^3 + \cdots$

(d) $\displaystyle\sum_{n=1}^{\infty}\frac{(x-3)^n}{2n} = \frac{(x-3)}{2} + \frac{(x-3)^2}{4} + \frac{(x-3)^3}{6} + \cdots$

SOLUTION

The strategy is to apply the Ratio Test to determine the interval of absolute convergence, then check the endpoints for conditional convergence (but not with the Ratio Test!).

Series (A):

First, apply the Ratio Test for absolute convergence:

$$\begin{aligned}\lim_{n\to\infty}\left|\frac{u_{n+1}}{u_n}\right| &= \lim_{n\to\infty}\frac{x^{2n+2}}{2n+2}\cdot\frac{2n}{x^{2n}}\\ &= \lim_{n\to\infty}\left(\frac{2n}{2n+2}\right)x^2\\ &= \lim_{n\to\infty}\left(\frac{2}{2}\right)x^2 \qquad \text{L'Hopital's Rule}\\ &= x^2\end{aligned}$$

The series converges absolutely for $x^2 < 1$, i.e., on the interval $(-1, 1)$. Now check the endpoints:

At $x = \pm 1$, the series is $\displaystyle\sum_{n=1}^{\infty}\frac{(-1)^{n+1}}{2n}$, which converges conditionally by the Alternating Series Test. (In fact, it is half the alternating harmonic series.) Thus, for series (A) we have **(a)** $r = 1$; **(b)** $[-1, 1]$; **(c)** $(-1, 1)$; and **(d)** $x = \pm 1$.

continued

Series (B):
First, apply the Ratio Test for absolute convergence:

$$\begin{aligned}\lim_{n\to\infty}\left|\frac{u_{n+1}}{u_n}\right| &= \lim_{n\to\infty}\frac{|10x|^{n+1}}{(n+1)!}\cdot\frac{n!}{|10x|^n}\\ &= \lim_{n\to\infty}\frac{|10x|}{n+1}\\ &= 0\end{aligned}$$

The series converges absolutely for all x. There are no endpoints to check. Thus, for series (B) we have **(a)** $r = \infty$; **(b)** $(-\infty, \infty)$; **(c)** $(-\infty, \infty)$; and **(d)** no values of x.

Series (C):
First, apply the Ratio Test for absolute convergence:

$$\begin{aligned}\lim_{n\to\infty}\left|\frac{u_{n+1}}{u_n}\right| &= \lim_{n\to\infty}\frac{(n+1)!(x+1)^{n+1}}{n!(x+1)^n}\\ &= \lim_{n\to\infty}(n+1)|x+1|\\ &= \begin{cases}\infty & \text{if } x \neq -1\\ 0 & \text{if } x = -1.\end{cases}\end{aligned}$$

The series converges absolutely at $x = 0$ and diverges for all other x. There are no endpoints to check.
Thus, for series (C) we have **(a)** $r = 0$; **(b)** $\{-1\}$; **(c)** $\{-1\}$; and **(d)** no values of x.

Series (D):
First, apply the Ratio Test for absolute convergence:

$$\begin{aligned}\lim_{n\to\infty}\left|\frac{u_{n+1}}{u_n}\right| &= \lim_{n\to\infty}\frac{|x-3|^{n+1}}{2n+2}\cdot\frac{2n}{|x-3|^n}\\ &= \lim_{n\to\infty}\left(\frac{2n}{2n+2}\right)|x-3|\\ &= \lim_{n\to\infty}\left(\frac{2}{2}\right)|x-3| \qquad \text{L'Hopital's Rule}\\ &= |x-3|\end{aligned}$$

The series converges absolutely for $|x - 3| < 1$, i.e., on the interval $(2, 4)$.
Now check the endpoints:

At $x = 2$, the series is $\sum_{n=1}^{\infty}\frac{(-1)^n}{2n}$, which converges conditionally by the Alternating Series Test.

At $x = 4$, the series is $\sum_{n=1}^{\infty}\frac{1}{2n}$, which converges by limit comparison with the harmonic series.

Thus, for series (D) we have **(a)** $r = 1$; **(b)** $[2, 4)$; **(c)** $(2, 4)$; and **(d)** $x = 2$.

Now Try Exercise 41.

To facilitate testing convergence at endpoints we can use the following flowchart.

Procedure for Determining Convergence

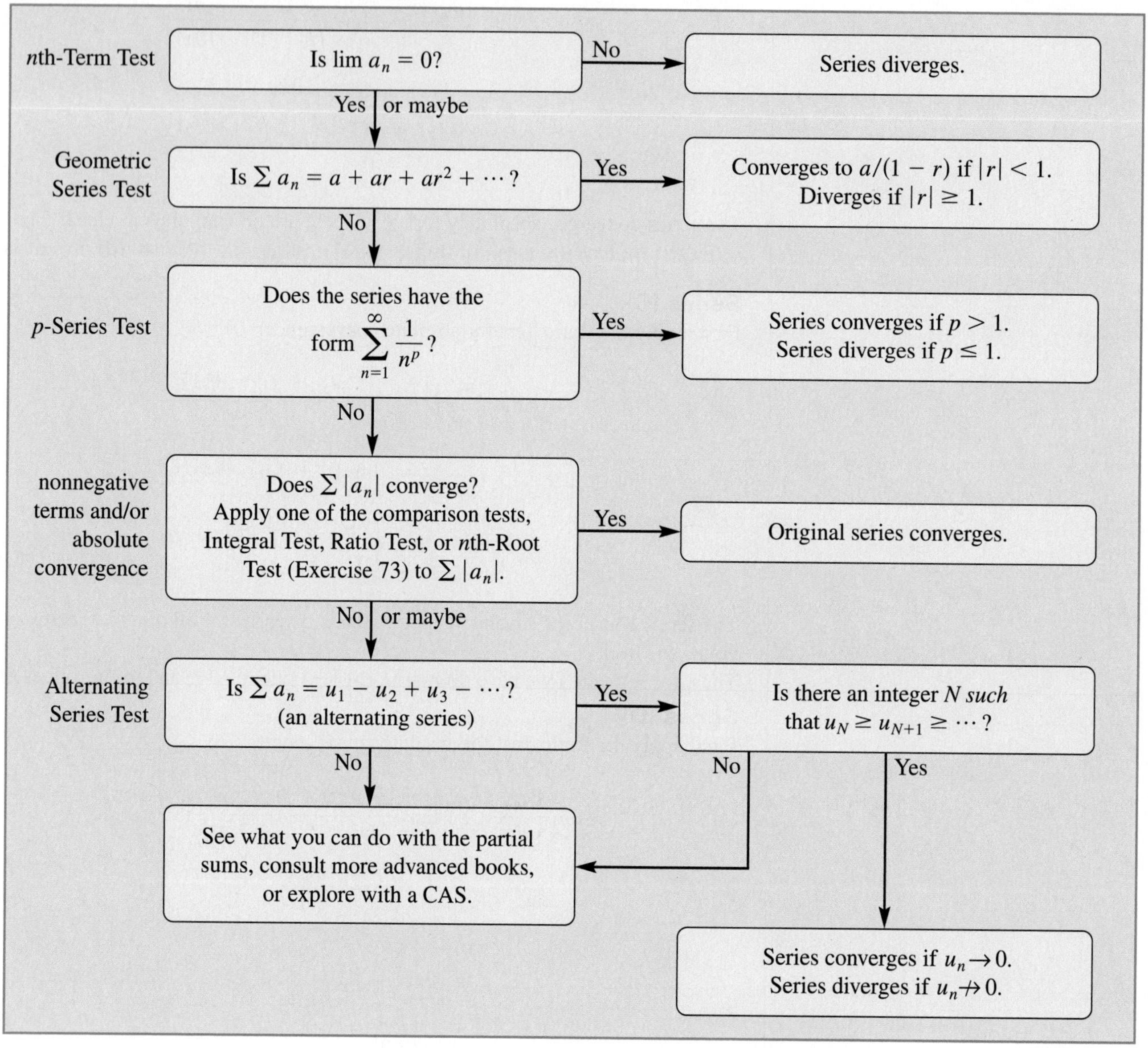

A Word of Caution

Although we can use the tests we have developed to find where a given power series converges, they do not tell us what function that power series is converging *to.* Even if the series is known to be a Maclaurin series generated by a function *f*, we cannot automatically conclude that the series converges *to the function f* on its interval of convergence. That is why it is so important to estimate the error.

For example, we can use the Ratio Test to show that the Maclaurin series for $\sin x$, $\cos x$, and e^x all converge absolutely for all real numbers. However, the reason we know that they converge to $\sin x$, $\cos x$, and e^x is that we used the Remainder Estimation Theorem to show that the respective truncation errors went to zero.

The following exploration shows what can happen with a strange function.

EXPLORATION 2 The Maclaurin Series of a Strange Function

Let $f(x) = \begin{cases} 0, & x = 0 \\ e^{-1/x^2}, & x \neq 0. \end{cases}$

It can be shown (although not easily) that f (Figure 10.19) has derivatives of all orders at $x = 0$ and that $f^{(n)}(0) = 0$ for all n. Use this fact as you proceed with the exploration.

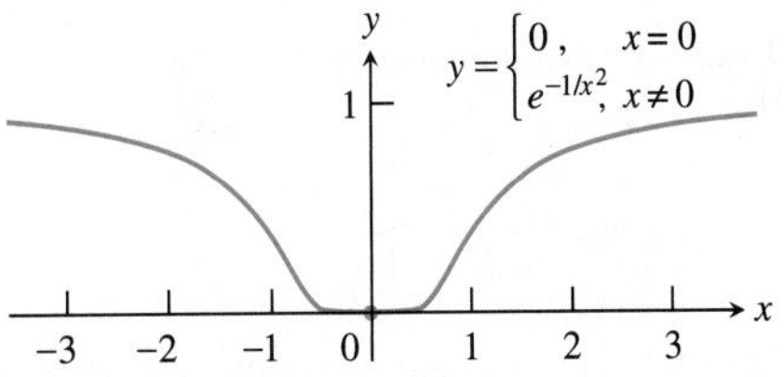

Figure 10.19 The graph of the continuous extension of $y = e^{-1/x^2}$ is so flat at the origin that all of its derivatives there are zero.

1. Construct the Maclaurin series for f.
2. For what values of x does this series converge?
3. Find all values of x for which the series actually converges to $f(x)$.

If you are surprised by the behavior of the series in Exploration 2, remember that we identified it up front as a strange function. It was fortunate for the early history of calculus that the functions that modeled physical behavior in the Newtonian world were much more predictable, enabling the early theories to enjoy encouraging successes before they could be lost in detail. When the subtleties of convergence emerged later, the theory was prepared to confront them.

Quick Review 10.5 *(For help, go to Sections 1.2 and 9.3.)*

Exercise numbers with a gray background indicate problems that the authors have designed to be solved *without a calculator.*

In Exercises 1–5, determine whether the improper integral converges or diverges. Give reasons for your answer. (You do not need to evaluate the integral.)

1. $\int_1^\infty \frac{1}{x^{4/3}}\,dx$

2. $\int_1^\infty \frac{x^2}{x^3+1}\,dx$

3. $\int_1^\infty \frac{\ln x}{x}\,dx$

4. $\int_1^\infty \frac{1+\cos x}{x^2}\,dx$

5. $\int_1^\infty \frac{\sqrt{x}}{x+1}\,dx$

In Exercises 6–10, determine whether the function is both positive and decreasing on some interval (N, ∞). (You do not need to identify N.)

6. $f(x) = \frac{3}{x}$

7. $f(x) = \frac{7x}{x^2 - 8}$

8. $f(x) = \frac{3 + x^2}{3 - x^2}$

9. $f(x) = \frac{\sin x}{x^5}$

10. $f(x) = \ln(1/x)$

Section 10.5 Exercises

In Exercises 1and 2, use the Integral Test to determine convergence or divergence of the series.

1. $\sum_{n=1}^{\infty} \frac{1}{\sqrt[3]{n}}$

2. $\sum_{n=1}^{\infty} n^{-3/2}$

3. Find the first six partial sums of $\sum_{n=1}^{\infty} \frac{1}{n}$.

4. If S_k is the k-th partial sum of $\sum_{n=1}^{\infty} \frac{1}{n}$, find the first value of k for which $S_k > 4$.

In Exercises 5 and 6, use the Limit Comparison Test to determine convergence or divergence of the series.

5. $\sum_{n=1}^{\infty} \frac{3n - 1}{n^2 + 1}$

6. $\sum_{n=0}^{\infty} \frac{2^n}{3^n + 1}$

In Exercises 7–22, determine whether the series converges or diverges. There may be more than one correct way to determine convergence or divergence of a given series.

7. $\sum_{n=1}^{\infty} \frac{5}{n + 1}$

8. $\sum_{n=1}^{\infty} \frac{3}{\sqrt{n}}$

9. $\sum_{n=1}^{\infty} \frac{\ln n}{n}$

10. $\sum_{n=1}^{\infty} \frac{1}{2n - 1}$

11. $\sum_{n=1}^{\infty} \frac{1}{(\ln 2)^n}$

12. $\sum_{n=1}^{\infty} \frac{1}{(\ln 3)^n}$

13. $\sum_{n=1}^{\infty} n \sin\left(\frac{1}{n}\right)$

14. $\sum_{n=0}^{\infty} \frac{e^n}{1 + e^{2n}}$

15. $\sum_{n=1}^{\infty} \frac{\sqrt{n}}{n^2 + 1}$

16. $\sum_{n=1}^{\infty} \frac{5n^3 - 3n}{n^2(n + 2)(n^2 + 5)}$

17. $\sum_{n=1}^{\infty} \frac{3^{n-1} + 1}{3^n}$

18. $\sum_{n=2}^{\infty} (-1)^{n+1} \frac{1}{\ln n}$

19. $\sum_{n=1}^{\infty} (-1)^{n+1} \frac{10^n}{n^{10}}$

20. $\sum_{n=1}^{\infty} (-1)^{n+1} \frac{\sqrt{n} + 1}{n + 1}$

21. $\sum_{n=1}^{\infty} (-1)^{n+1} \frac{\ln n}{\ln n^2}$

22. $\sum_{n=1}^{\infty} \left(\frac{1}{n} - \frac{1}{n^2}\right)$

In Exercises 23–26, determine whether the series converges absolutely, converges conditionally, or diverges. Give reasons for your answer. Find a bound for the truncation error after 99 terms.

23. $\sum_{n=1}^{\infty} (-1)^{n+1} \frac{1 + n}{n^2}$

24. $\sum_{n=1}^{\infty} (-1)^{n+1} (0.1)^n$

25. $\sum_{n=2}^{\infty} (-1)^{n+1} \frac{1}{n \ln n}$

26. $\sum_{n=1}^{\infty} (-1)^n n^2 \left(\frac{2}{3}\right)^n$

In Exercises 27–32, determine whether the series converges absolutely, converges conditionally, or diverges. Give reasons for your answers.

27. $\sum_{n=1}^{\infty} (-1)^{n+1} \frac{n!}{2^n}$

28. $\sum_{n=1}^{\infty} (-1)^{n+1} \frac{\sin n}{n^2}$

29. $\sum_{n=1}^{\infty} \frac{(-1)^n}{1 + \sqrt{n}}$

30. $\sum_{n=1}^{\infty} \frac{\cos n\pi}{n\sqrt{n}}$

31. $\sum_{n=1}^{\infty} \frac{\cos n\pi}{n}$

32. $\sum_{n=1}^{\infty} \frac{(-1)^n}{\sqrt{n} + \sqrt{n + 1}}$

In Exercises 33 and 34, explain how to rearrange the terms of the series from the specified exercise to form **(a)** a divergent series, and **(b)** a series that converges to 4.

33. Exercise 23

34. Exercise 25

In Exercises 35–50, find **(a)** the *interval* of convergence of the series. For what values of x does the series converge **(b)** absolutely, **(c)** conditionally?

35. $\sum_{n=0}^{\infty} x^n$

36. $\sum_{n=0}^{\infty} (x + 5)^n$

37. $\sum_{n=0}^{\infty} (-1)^n (4x + 1)^n$

38. $\sum_{n=1}^{\infty} \frac{(3x - 2)^n}{n}$

39. $\sum_{n=0}^{\infty} \frac{(x - 2)^n}{10^n}$

40. $\sum_{n=0}^{\infty} \frac{nx^n}{n + 2}$

41. $\sum_{n=1}^{\infty} \frac{x^n}{n\sqrt{n}3^n}$

42. $\sum_{n=0}^{\infty} \frac{x^{2n+1}}{n!}$

43. $\sum_{n=0}^{\infty} \frac{n(x + 3)^n}{5^n}$

44. $\sum_{n=0}^{\infty} \frac{nx^n}{4^n(n^2 + 1)}$

45. $\sum_{n=0}^{\infty} \frac{\sqrt{n}x^n}{3^n}$

46. $\sum_{n=0}^{\infty} n!(x - 4)^n$

47. $\sum_{n=0}^{\infty} (-2)^n (n + 1)(x - 1)^n$

48. $\sum_{n=1}^{\infty} \frac{(4x - 5)^{2n+1}}{n^{3/2}}$

49. $\sum_{n=1}^{\infty} \frac{(x + \pi)^n}{\sqrt{n}}$

50. $\sum_{n=0}^{\infty} (\ln x)^n$

51. Not only do the figures in Example 2 show that the nth partial sum of the harmonic series is less than $1 + \ln n$; they also show that it is *greater* than $\ln(n + 1)$. Suppose you had started summing the harmonic series with $S_1 = 1$ at the time the universe was formed, 13 billion years ago. If you had been able to add a term every *second* since then, about how large would your partial sum be today? (Assume a 365-day year.)

52. Writing to Learn Write out a proof of the Integral Test (Theorem 10) for $N = 1$, explaining what you see in Figure 10.15.

53. ***(Continuation of Exercise 52)*** Relabel the pictures for an arbitrary N and explain why the same conclusions about convergence can be drawn.

54. In each of the following cases, decide whether the infinite series converges. Justify your answer.

(a) $\sum_{k=1}^{\infty} \frac{1}{\sqrt{2k+7}}$ (b) $\sum_{k=1}^{\infty} \left(1+\frac{1}{k}\right)^k$

(c) $\sum_{k=1}^{\infty} \frac{\cos k}{k^2+\sqrt{k}}$ (d) $\sum_{k=3}^{\infty} \frac{18}{k(\ln k)}$

In Exercises 55 and 56, find the *radius* of convergence of the series.

55. $\sum_{n=1}^{\infty} \frac{n^n(x+2)^n}{3^n n!}$ **56.** $\sum_{n=1}^{\infty} \frac{n!x^n}{n^n 5^n}$

57. Construct a series that diverges more slowly than the harmonic series. Justify your answer.

58. Let $a_k = (-1)^{k+1} \int_0^{1/k} 6(kx)^2\, dx$.

(a) Evaluate a_k.

(b) Show that $\sum_{k=1}^{\infty} a_k$ converges.

(c) Show that

$$1 \le \sum_{k=1}^{\infty} a_k \le \frac{3}{2}.$$

59. (a) Determine whether the series

$$A = \sum_{n=1}^{\infty} \frac{n}{3n^2+1}$$

converges or diverges. Justify your answer.

(b) If S is the series formed by multiplying the nth term in A by the nth term in $\sum_{n=1}^{\infty}(3/n)$, write an expression using summation notation for S and determine whether S converges or diverges.

60. (a) Find the Taylor series generated by $f(x) = \ln(1+x)$ at $x = 0$. Include an expression for the general term.

(b) For what values of x does the series in part (a) converge?

(c) Use Theorem 13 to find a bound for the error in evaluating $\ln(3/2)$ by using only the first five nonzero terms of the series in part (a).

(d) Use the result found in part (a) to determine the logarithmic function whose Taylor series is

$$\sum_{n=1}^{\infty} \frac{(-1)^{n+1}x^{2n}}{2n}.$$

61. Determine all values of x for which the series

$$\sum_{k=0}^{\infty} \frac{2^k x^k}{\ln(k+2)}$$

converges. Justify your answer.

62. Consider the series $\sum_{n=2}^{\infty} \frac{1}{n^p \ln n}$, where $p \ge 0$.

(a) Show that the series converges for $p > 1$.

(b) **Writing to Learn** Determine whether the series converges or diverges for $p = 1$. Show your analysis.

(c) Show that the series diverges for $0 \le p < 1$.

63. The Maclaurin series for $1/(1+x)$ converges for $-1 < x < 1$, but when we integrate it term by term, the resulting series for $\ln|1+x|$ converges for $-1 < x \le 1$. Verify the convergence at $x = 1$.

64. The Maclaurin series for $1/(1+x^2)$ converges for $-1 < x < 1$, but when we integrate it term by term, the resulting series for $\arctan x$ converges for $-1 \le x \le 1$. Verify the convergence at $x = 1$ and $x = -1$.

65. (a) The series

$$\frac{1}{3} - \frac{1}{2} + \frac{1}{9} - \frac{1}{4} + \frac{1}{27} - \frac{1}{8} + \cdots + \frac{1}{3^n} - \frac{1}{2^n} + \cdots$$

fails to satisfy one of the conditions of the Alternating Series Test. Which one?

(b) Find the sum of the series in part (a).

Standardized Test Questions

You may use a graphing calculator to solve the following problems.

66. True or False The series

$$\sum_{n=1}^{\infty} (-1)^{n+1} \frac{x^{2n}}{2n}$$

converges on a closed interval. Justify your answer.

67. True or False If S_{100} is used to estimate the sum of the series

$$\sum_{n=1}^{\infty} \frac{(-1)^n}{n^2},$$

the estimate is an overestimate. Justify your answer.

In Exercises 68 and 69, use the series $\sum_{n=0}^{\infty} \frac{n(2x-5)^n}{n+2}$.

68. Multiple Choice Which of the following is the radius of convergence of the series?

(A) 1 (B) 1/2 (C) 3/2 (D) 2 (E) 5/2

69. Multiple Choice Which of the following is the interval of convergence of the series?

(A) $2 < x < 3$ (B) $4 < x < 6$ (C) $-\frac{1}{2} < x < \frac{1}{2}$

(D) $-3 < x < -2$ (E) $-6 < x < -4$

70. Multiple Choice Which of the following series converge?

I. $\sum_{n=1}^{\infty} \frac{4}{\sqrt{n}}$ II. $\sum_{n=1}^{\infty} \frac{1}{(\ln 4)^n}$ III. $\sum_{n=1}^{\infty} \frac{(-1)^n}{n^2}$

(A) I only (B) II only (C) III only

(D) I & II only (E) II & III only

71. Multiple Choice Which of the following gives the truncation error if S_{100} is used to approximate the sum of the series

$$\sum_{n=1}^{\infty} \frac{(-1)^n}{2^n}$$

(A) $\frac{1}{3 \cdot 2^{101}}$ **(B)** $\frac{1}{3 \cdot 2^{100}}$ **(C)** $\frac{1}{2^{101}}$

(D) $\frac{3}{2^{101}}$ **(E)** $\frac{3}{2^{100}}$

Exploration

72. Group Activity Within your group, have each student construct a series that converges to one of the numbers $1, \ldots, n$. Then exchange your series with another group and try to figure out which number is matched with which series.

Extending the Ideas

Here is a test called the *nth-Root Test.*

> ***nth*-Root Test** Let $\sum a_n$ be a series with $a_n \geq 0$ for $n \geq N$, and suppose that $\lim_{n\to\infty} \sqrt[n]{a_n} = L$.
>
> Then,
>
> **(a)** the series *converges* if $L < 1$,
>
> **(b)** the series *diverges* if $L > 1$ or L is infinite,
>
> **(c)** the test is *inconclusive* if $L = 1$.

73. Use the *n*th-Root Test and the fact that $\lim_{n\to\infty} \sqrt[n]{n} = 1$ to test the following series for convergence or divergence.

(a) $\sum_{n=1}^{\infty} \frac{n^2}{2^n}$

(b) $\sum_{n=1}^{\infty} \left(\frac{n}{2n-1}\right)^n$

(c) $\sum_{n=1}^{\infty} a_n$, where $a_n = \begin{cases} n/2^n, & n \text{ is odd} \\ 1/2^n, & n \text{ is even} \end{cases}$

74. Use the *n*th-Root Test and whatever else you need to find the intervals of convergence of the following series.

(a) $\sum_{n=0}^{\infty} \frac{(x-1)^n}{4^n}$

(b) $\sum_{n=1}^{\infty} \frac{(x-2)^n}{n \cdot 3^n}$

(c) $\sum_{n=1}^{\infty} 2^n x^n$

(d) $\sum_{n=0}^{\infty} (\ln x)^n$

Quick Quiz for AP* Preparation: Sections 10.4 and 10.5

You may use a graphing calculator to solve the following problems.

1. Multiple Choice Which of the following series converge?

I. $\sum_{n=0}^{\infty} \frac{2}{n^2+1}$ II. $\sum_{n=1}^{\infty} \frac{2^n-1}{3^n+1}$ III. $\sum_{n=1}^{\infty} \frac{\sqrt[4]{n}}{n}$

(A) I only **(B)** II only **(C)** III only

(D) II & III only **(E)** I & II only

2. Multiple Choice Which of the following is the sum of the telescoping series

$$\sum_{n=1}^{\infty} \frac{2}{(n+1)(n+2)}?$$

(A) $1/3$ **(B)** $1/2$ **(C)** $3/5$ **(D)** $2/3$ **(E)** 1

3. Multiple Choice Which of the following describes the behavior of the series

$$\sum_{n=1}^{\infty} (-1)^n \frac{\ln n}{n}?$$

I. converges II. diverges III. converges conditionally

(A) I only **(B)** II only **(C)** III only

(D) I & III only **(E)** II & III only

4. Free Response Consider the power series

$$\sum_{n=0}^{\infty} \frac{n(2x+3)^n}{n+2}.$$

(a) Find all values of x for which the series converges absolutely. Justify your answer.

(b) Find all values of x for which the series converges conditionally. Justify your answer.

Chapter 10 Key Terms

absolute convergence (p. 510)
alternating harmonic series (p. 521)
alternating series (p. 521)
Alternating Series Estimation Theorem (p. 522)
Alternating Series Test (p. 521)
binomial series (p. 498)
Binomial Theorem (p. 498)
center of power series (p. 480)
conditional convergence (p. 522)
convergent sequence (p. 487)
converges absolutely (p. 510)
Convergence Theorem for Power Series (p. 508)
convergent series (p. 478)
differentiation of series (p. 481)
Direct Comparison Test (p. 509)
divergent sequence (p. 487)
divergent series (p. 478)
error term (p. 500)
Euler's formula (p. 503)
Euler's identities (p. 505)
finite sum (p. 477)
geometric series (p. 479)
harmonic series (p. 518)
hyperbolic sine and cosine (p. 504)
identity (p. 507)
infinite series (p. 478)
Integral Test (p. 517)
integration of series (p. 482)
interval of convergence (p. 479)
Lagrange error bound (p. 500)
Lagrange form of the remainder (p. 500)
Leibniz's Theorem (p. 521)
Limit Comparison Test (p. 519)
limit of a sequence (p. 487)
Maclaurin series (pp. 491, 495)
*n*th-Root Test (p. 530)
*n*th term of a series (p. 478)
*n*th-Term Test for divergence (p. 508)
partial sum (p. 478)
power series centered at $x = a$ (p. 480)
p-series (p. 518)
p-Series Test (p. 518)
quadratic approximation (p. 504)
radius of convergence (p. 508)
Ratio Test (p. 511)
rearrangement of series (p. 522)
Remainder Estimation Theorem (p. 502)
remainder of order n (p. 500)
representing functions by series (p. 480)
sum of a series (p. 477)
Taylor polynomial (p. 489)
Taylor polynomial of order n at $x = a$ (p. 489)
Taylor series (p. 491)
Taylor series at $x = a$ (p. 493)
Taylor's formula (p. 500)
Taylor's Theorem with Remainder (p. 500)
telescoping series (p. 514)
Term-by-Term Differentiation Theorem (p. 482)
Term-by-Term Integration Theorem (p. 483)
terms of a series (p. 478)
truncation error (p. 499)

Chapter 10 Review Exercises

Exercise numbers with a gray background indicate problems that the authors have designed to be solved *without a calculator*.

The collection of exercises marked in red could be used as a chapter test.

In Exercises 1–16, find **(a)** the radius of convergence for the series and **(b)** its interval of convergence. Then identify the values of x for which the series converges **(c)** absolutely and **(d)** conditionally.

1. $\displaystyle\sum_{n=0}^{\infty} \frac{(-x)^n}{n!}$

2. $\displaystyle\sum_{n=1}^{\infty} \frac{(x+4)^n}{n3^n}$

3. $\displaystyle\sum_{n=0}^{\infty} \left(\frac{2}{3}\right)^n (x-1)^n$

4. $\displaystyle\sum_{n=1}^{\infty} \frac{(x-1)^{2n-2}}{(2n-1)!}$

5. $\displaystyle\sum_{n=1}^{\infty} \frac{(-1)^{n-1}(3x-1)^n}{n^2}$

6. $\displaystyle\sum_{n=0}^{\infty} (n+1)x^{3n}$

7. $\displaystyle\sum_{n=0}^{\infty} \frac{(n+1)(2x+1)^n}{(2n+1)2^n}$

8. $\displaystyle\sum_{n=1}^{\infty} \frac{x^n}{n^n}$

9. $\displaystyle\sum_{n=1}^{\infty} \frac{x^n}{\sqrt{n}}$

10. $\displaystyle\sum_{n=1}^{\infty} \frac{e^n}{n^e} x^n$

11. $\displaystyle\sum_{n=0}^{\infty} \frac{(n+1)x^{2n-1}}{3^n}$

12. $\displaystyle\sum_{n=0}^{\infty} \frac{(-1)^n(x-1)^{2n+1}}{2n+1}$

13. $\displaystyle\sum_{n=1}^{\infty} \frac{n!}{2^n} x^{2n}$

14. $\displaystyle\sum_{n=2}^{\infty} \frac{(10x)^n}{\ln n}$

15. $\displaystyle\sum_{n=1}^{\infty} (n+1)!x^n$

16. $\displaystyle\sum_{n=1}^{\infty} \left(\frac{x^2-1}{2}\right)^n$

In Exercises 17–22, the series is the value of the Maclaurin series of a function $f(x)$ at a particular point. What function and what point? What is the sum of the series?

17. $1 - \frac{1}{4} + \frac{1}{16} - \cdots + (-1)^n \frac{1}{4^n} + \cdots$

18. $\frac{2}{3} - \frac{4}{18} + \frac{8}{81} - \cdots + (-1)^{n-1} \frac{2^n}{n3^n} + \cdots$

19. $\pi - \frac{\pi^3}{3!} + \frac{\pi^5}{5!} - \cdots + (-1)^n \frac{\pi^{2n+1}}{(2n+1)!} + \cdots$

20. $1 - \frac{\pi^2}{9 \cdot 2!} + \frac{\pi^4}{81 \cdot 4!} - \cdots + (-1)^n \frac{\pi^{2n}}{3^{2n}(2n)!} + \cdots$

21. $1 + \ln 2 + \frac{(\ln 2)^2}{2!} + \cdots + \frac{(\ln 2)^n}{n!} + \cdots$

22. $\frac{1}{\sqrt{3}} - \frac{1}{9\sqrt{3}} + \frac{1}{45\sqrt{3}} - \cdots + (-1)^{n-1} \frac{1}{(2n-1)(\sqrt{3})^{2n-1}} + \cdots$

In Exercises 23–36, find a Maclaurin series for the function.

23. $\dfrac{1}{1-6x}$

24. $\dfrac{1}{1-x^3}$

25. $x^9 - 2x^2 + 1$

26. $\dfrac{4x}{1-x}$

27. $\sin \pi x$

28. $-\sin \dfrac{2x}{3}$

29. $-x + \sin x$

30. $\dfrac{e^x + e^{-x}}{2}$

31. $\cos \sqrt{5x}$

32. $e^{(\pi x/2)}$

33. xe^{-x^2}

34. $\tan^{-1} 3x$

35. $\ln(1-2x)$

36. $x \ln(1-x)$

In Exercises 37–40, find the first four nonzero terms and the general term of the Taylor series generated by f at $x = a$.

37. $f(x) = \dfrac{1}{3-x}, \quad a = 2$

38. $f(x) = x^3 - 2x^2 + 5, \quad a = -1$

39. $f(x) = \dfrac{1}{x}, \quad a = 3$

40. $f(x) = \sin x, \quad a = \pi$

In Exercises 41–52, determine if the series converges absolutely, converges conditionally, or diverges. Give reasons for your answer.

41. $\displaystyle\sum_{n=1}^{\infty} \frac{-5}{n}$

42. $\displaystyle\sum_{n=1}^{\infty} \frac{(-1)^n}{\sqrt{n}}$

43. $\displaystyle\sum_{n=1}^{\infty} \frac{\ln n}{n^3}$

44. $\displaystyle\sum_{n=1}^{\infty} \frac{n+1}{n!}$

45. $\displaystyle\sum_{n=1}^{\infty} \frac{(-1)^n}{\ln(n+1)}$

46. $\displaystyle\sum_{n=2}^{\infty} \frac{1}{n(\ln n)^2}$

47. $\displaystyle\sum_{n=1}^{\infty} \frac{(-3)^n}{n!}$

48. $\displaystyle\sum_{n=1}^{\infty} \frac{2^n 3^n}{n^n}$

49. $\displaystyle\sum_{n=1}^{\infty} \frac{(-1)^n(n^2+1)}{2n^2+n-1}$

50. $\displaystyle\sum_{n=1}^{\infty} \frac{1}{\sqrt{n(n+1)(n+2)}}$

51. $\displaystyle\sum_{n=2}^{\infty} \frac{1}{n\sqrt{n^2-1}}$

52. $\displaystyle\sum_{n=1}^{\infty} \left(\frac{n}{n+1}\right)^n$

In Exercises 53 and 54, find the sum of the series.

53. $\displaystyle\sum_{n=3}^{\infty} \frac{1}{(2n-3)(2n-1)}$

54. $\displaystyle\sum_{n=2}^{\infty} \frac{-2}{n(n+1)}$

55. Let f be a function that has derivatives of all orders for all real numbers. Assume that $f(3) = 1$, $f'(3) = 4$, $f''(3) = 6$, and $f'''(3) = 12$.

(a) Write the third-order Taylor polynomial for f at $x = 3$ and use it to approximate $f(3.2)$.

(b) Write the second-order Taylor polynomial for f' at $x = 3$ and use it to approximate $f'(2.7)$.

(c) Does the linearization of f underestimate or overestimate the values of $f(x)$ near $x = 3$? Justify your answer.

56. Let

$$P_4(x) = 7 - 3(x-4) + 5(x-4)^2 - 2(x-4)^3 + 6(x-4)^4$$

be the Taylor polynomial of order 4 for the function f at $x = 4$. Assume f has derivatives of all orders for all real numbers.

(a) Find $f(4)$ and $f'''(4)$.

(b) Write the second-order Taylor polynomial for f' at $x = 4$ and use it to approximate $f'(4.3)$.

(c) Write the fourth-order Taylor polynomial for $g(x) = \int_4^x f(t)\,dt$ at $x = 4$.

(d) Can the exact value of $f(3)$ be determined from the information given? Justify your answer.

57. (a) Write the first three nonzero terms and the general term of the Taylor series generated by $f(x) = 5\sin(x/2)$ at $x = 0$.

(b) What is the interval of convergence for the series found in (a)? Show your method.

(c) **Writing to Learn** What is the minimum number of terms of the series in (a) needed to approximate $f(x)$ on the interval $(-2, 2)$ with an error not exceeding 0.1 in magnitude? Show your method.

58. Let $f(x) = 1/(1-2x)$.

(a) Write the first four terms and the general term of the Taylor series generated by $f(x)$ at $x = 0$.

(b) What is the interval of convergence for the series found in part (a)? Show your method.

(c) Find $f(-1/4)$. How many terms of the series are adequate for approximating $f(-1/4)$ with an error not exceeding one percent in magnitude? Justify your answer.

59. Let $f(x) = \displaystyle\sum_{n=1}^{\infty} \frac{x^n n^n}{n!}$

for all x for which the series converges.

(a) Find the radius of convergence of this series.

(b) Use the first three terms of this series to approximate $f(-1/3)$.

(c) Estimate the error involved in the approximation in part (b). Justify your answer.

60. Let $f(x) = 1/(x-2)$.

(a) Write the first four terms and the general term of the Taylor series generated by $f(x)$ at $x = 3$.

(b) Use the result from part (a) to find the first four terms and the general term of the series generated by $\ln|x-2|$ at $x = 3$.

(c) Use the series in part (b) to compute a number that differs from $\ln(3/2)$ by less than 0.05. Justify your answer.

61. Let $f(x) = e^{-2x^2}$.

(a) Find the first four nonzero terms and the general term for the power series generated by $f(x)$ at $x = 0$.

(b) Find the interval of convergence of the series generated by $f(x)$ at $x = 0$. Show the analysis that leads to your conclusion.

(c) **Writing to Learn** Let g be the function defined by the sum of the first four nonzero terms of the series generated by $f(x)$. Show that $|f(x) - g(x)| < 0.02$ for $-0.6 \le x \le 0.6$.

62. (a) Find the Maclaurin series generated by $f(x) = x^2/(1 + x)$.

(b) Does the series converge at $x = 1$? Explain.

63. ***Evaluating Nonelementary Integrals*** Maclaurin series can be used to express nonelementary integrals in terms of series.

(a) Express $\int_0^x \sin t^2\, dt$ as a power series.

(b) According to the Alternating Series Estimation Theorem, how many terms of the series in part (a) should you use to estimate $\int_0^1 \sin x^2\, dx$ with an error of less than 0.001?

(c) Use NINT to approximate $\int_0^1 \sin x^2\, dx$.

(d) How close to the answer in part (c) do you get if you use four terms of the series in part (a)?

64. ***Estimating an Integral*** Suppose you want a quick noncalculator estimate for the value of $\int_0^1 x^2 e^x\, dx$. There are several ways to get one.

(a) Use the Trapezoidal Rule with $n = 2$ to estimate $\int_0^1 x^2 e^x\, dx$.

(b) Write the first three nonzero terms of the Maclaurin series for x^2e^x to obtain the fourth-order Maclaurin polynomial $P_4(x)$ for x^2e^x. Use $\int_0^1 P_4(x)\, dx$ to obtain another estimate of $\int_0^1 x^2 e^x\, dx$.

(c) **Writing to Learn** The second derivative of $f(x) = x^2e^x$ is positive for all $x > 0$. Explain why this enables you to conclude that the Trapezoidal Rule estimate obtained in part (a) is too large.

(d) **Writing to Learn** All the derivatives of $f(x) = x^2e^x$ are positive for $x > 0$. Explain why this enables you to conclude that all Maclaurin series approximations to $f(x)$ for x in $[0, 1]$ will be too small. [*Hint:* $f(x) = P_n(x) + R_n(x)$.]

(e) Use integration by parts to evaluate $\int_0^1 x^2 e^x\, dx$.

65. ***Perpetuities*** Suppose you want to give a favorite school or charity \$1000 a year forever. This kind of gift is called a *perpetuity.* Assume you can earn 8% annually on your money, i.e., that a payment of a_n today will be worth $a_n\,(1.08)^n$ in n years.

(a) Show that the amount you must invest today to cover the nth \$1000 payment in n years is $1000(1.08)^{-n}$.

(b) Construct an infinite series that gives the amount you must invest today to cover *all* the payments in the perpetuity.

(c) Show that the series in part (b) converges and find its sum. This sum is called the *present value* of the perpetuity. What does it represent?

66. ***(Continuation of Exercise 65)*** Find the present value of a \$1000-per-year perpetuity at 6% annual interest.

67. ***Expected Payoff*** How much would you expect to win playing the following game?

Toss a *fair* coin (heads and tails equally likely). Every time it comes up heads you win a dollar, but the game is over as soon as it comes up tails.

(a) The *expected payoff* of the game is computed by summing all possible payoffs times their respective probabilities. If the probability of tossing the first tail on the nth toss is $(1/2)^n$, express the expected payoff of this game as an infinite series.

(b) Differentiate both sides of

$$\frac{1}{1-x} = 1 + x + x^2 + \cdots + x^n + \cdots$$

to get a series for $1/(1 - x)^2$.

(c) Use the series in part (b) to get a series for $x^2/(1 - x)^2$.

(d) Use the series in part (c) to evaluate the expected payoff of the game.

68. ***Punching out Triangles*** This exercise refers to the "right side up" equilateral triangle with sides of length $2b$ in the accompanying figure.

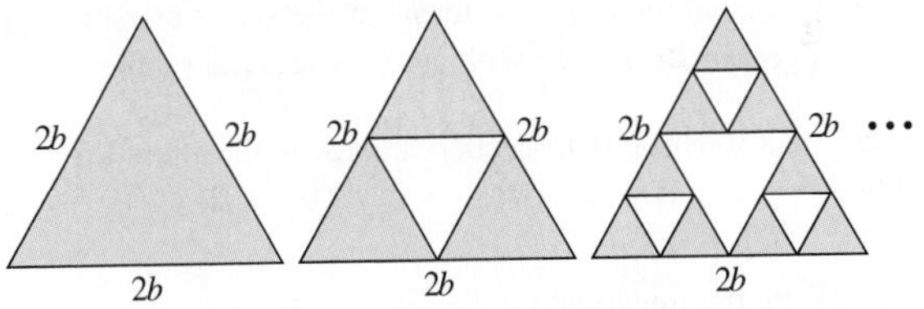

"Upside down" equilateral triangles are removed from the original triangle as the sequence of pictures suggests. The sum of the areas removed from the original triangle forms an infinite series.

(a) Find this infinite series.

(b) Find the sum of this infinite series and hence find the total area removed from the original triangle.

(c) Is every point on the original triangle removed? Explain why or why not.

69. ***Nicole Oresme's (pronounced "O-rem's") Theorem*** Prove Nicole Oresme's Theorem that

$$1 + \frac{1}{2}\cdot 2 + \frac{1}{4}\cdot 3 + \cdots + \frac{n}{2^{n-1}} + \cdots = 4.$$

[*Hint:* Differentiate both sides of the equation $1/(1 - x) = 1 + \sum_{n=1}^{\infty} x^n$.]

70. (a) Show that

$$\sum_{n=1}^{\infty} \frac{n(n+1)}{x^n} = \frac{2x^2}{(x-1)^3}$$

for $|x| > 1$ by differentiating the identity

$$\sum_{n=1}^{\infty} x^{n+1} = \frac{x^2}{1-x}$$

twice, multiplying the result by x, and then replacing x by $1/x$.

(b) Use part (a) to find the real solution greater than 1 of the equation

$$x = \sum_{n=1}^{\infty} \frac{n(n+1)}{x^n}.$$

AP* Examination Preparation

You may use a graphing calculator to solve the following problems.

71. Let $f(x) = \dfrac{1}{x+1}$.

(a) Find the first three terms and the general term for the Taylor series for f at $x = 1$.

(b) Find the interval of convergence for the series in part (a). Justify your answer.

(c) Find the third-order Taylor polynomial for f at $x = 1$, and use it to approximate $f(0.5)$.

72. Let $f(x) = \sum_{n=0}^{\infty} \dfrac{nx^n}{2^n}$.

(a) Find the interval of convergence of the series. Justify your answer.

(b) Show that the first nine terms of the series are sufficient to approximate $f(-1)$ with an error less than 0.01.

73. Let f be a function that has derivatives of all orders for all real numbers. Assume that $f(0) = -1$, $f'(0) = 2$, $f''(0) = -3$, and $f'''(0) = 4$.

(a) Write the linearization for f at $x = 0$.

(b) Write the quadratic approximation for f at $x = 0$.

(c) Write the third-degree Taylor approximation $P_3(x)$ for f at $x = 0$.

(d) Use $P_3(x)$ to approximate $f(0.7)$.

CHAPTER

11 Parametric, Vector, and Polar Functions

In 1935, air traffic control was conducted with a system of teletype machines, wall-sized blackboards, large table maps, and movable markers representing airplanes. Today's radar data processing includes an automatic display of aircraft identification, speed, altitude, and velocity vectors.

A DC-10 plane flying due west at 600 mph enters a region with a steady air current coming from the southwest at 100 mph. How should the pilot adjust the airplane's course and speed to maintain its original velocity vector? This type of problem is covered in Section 11.2.

CHAPTER 11 Overview

The material in this book is generally described as the calculus of a single variable, since it deals with functions of one independent variable (usually x or t). In this chapter you will apply your understanding of single-variable calculus in three kinds of two-variable contexts, enabling you to analyze some new kinds of curves (parametrically defined and polar) and to analyze motion in the plane that does not proceed along a straight line. Interestingly enough, this will not require the tools of multi-variable calculus, which you will probably learn in your next calculus course. We will simply use single-variable calculus in some new and interesting ways.

11.1 Parametric Functions

What you will learn about . . .

- Parametric Curves in the Plane
- Slope and Concavity
- Arc Length
- Cycloids

and why . . .

Parametric equations enable us to define some interesting and important curves that would be difficult or impossible to define in the form $y = f(x)$.

Parametric Curves in the Plane

We reviewed parametrically defined functions in Section 1.4. Instead of defining the points (x, y) on a planar curve by relating y directly to x, we can define both coordinates as functions of a parameter t. The resulting set of points may or may not define y as a function of x (that is, the parametric curve might fail the vertical line test).

EXAMPLE 1 Reviewing Some Parametric Curves

Sketch the parametric curves and identify those which define y as a function of x. In each case, eliminate the parameter to find an equation that relates x and y directly.

(a) $x = \cos t$ and $y = \sin t$ for t in the interval $[0, 2\pi)$

(b) $x = 3\cos t$ and $y = 2\sin t$ for t in the interval $[0, 4\pi]$

(c) $x = \sqrt{t}$ and $y = t - 2$ for t in the interval $[0, 4]$

SOLUTION

(a) This is probably the best-known parametrization of all. The curve is the unit circle (Figure 11.1a), and it does not define y as a function of x. To eliminate the parameter, we use the identity $(\cos t)^2 + (\sin t)^2 = 1$ to write $x^2 + y^2 = 1$.

(b) This parametrization stretches the unit circle by a factor of 3 horizontally and by a factor of 2 vertically. The result is an ellipse (Figure 11.1b), which is traced twice as t covers the interval $[0, 4\pi]$. (In fact, the point $(3, 0)$ is visited three times.) It does not define y as a function of x. We use the same identity as in part (a) to write $\left(\frac{x}{3}\right)^2 + \left(\frac{y}{2}\right)^2 = 1.$

(c) This parametrization produces a segment of a parabola (Figure 11.1c). It does define y as a function of x. Since $t = x^2$, we write $y = x^2 - 2$. *Now Try Exercise 1.*

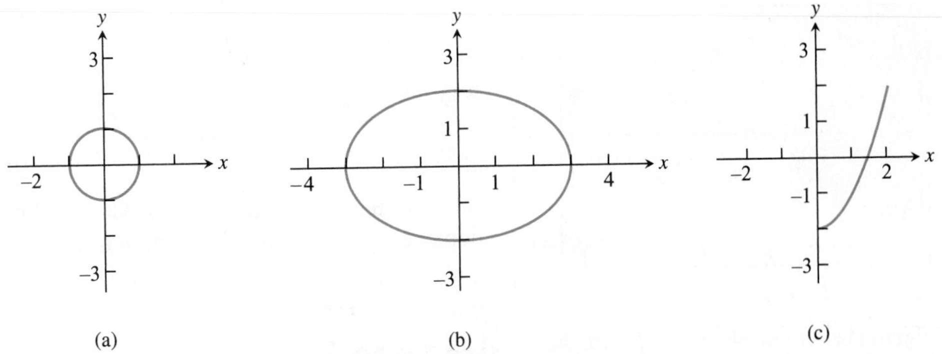

Figure 11.1 A collection of parametric curves (Example 1). Each point (x, y) is determined by parametric functions of t, but only the parametrization in graph (c) determines y as a function of x.

Slope and Concavity

We can analyze the slope and concavity of parametric curves just as we can with explicitly-defined curves. The slope of the curve is still dy/dx, and the concavity still depends on d^2y/dx^2, so all that is needed is a way of differentiating with respect to x when everything is given in terms of t. The required parametric differentiation formulas are straightforward applications of the Chain Rule.

Parametric Differentiation Formulas

If x and y are both differentiable functions of t and if $dx/dt \neq 0$, then

$$\frac{dy}{dx} = \frac{dy/dt}{dx/dt}.$$

If $y' = dy/dx$ is also a differentiable function of t, then

$$\frac{d^2y}{dx^2} = \frac{d}{dx}(y') = \frac{dy'/dt}{dx/dt}.$$

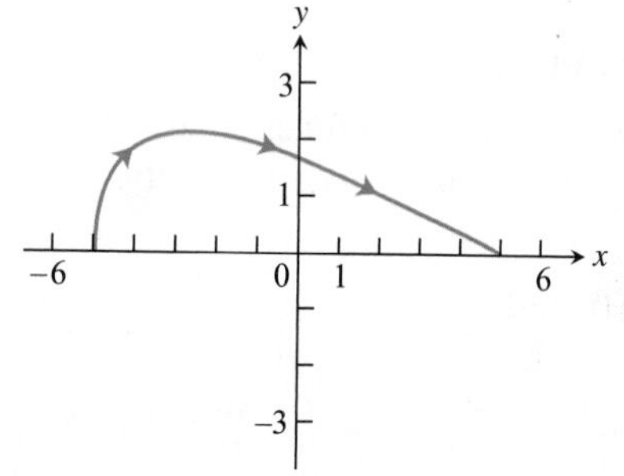

Figure 11.2 The parametric curve defined in Example 2.

EXAMPLE 2 Analyzing a Parametric Curve

Consider the curve defined parametrically by $x = t^2 - 5$ and $y = 2 \sin t$ for $0 \leq t \leq \pi$.

(a) Sketch a graph of the curve in the viewing window $[-7, 7]$ by $[-4, 4]$. Indicate the direction in which it is traced.

(b) Find the highest point on the curve. Justify your answer.

(c) Find all points of inflection on the curve. Justify your answer.

SOLUTION

(a) The curve is shown in Figure 11.2.

(b) We seek to maximize y as a function of t, so we compute $dy/dt = 2 \cos t$. Since dy/dt is positive for $0 \leq t < \pi/2$ and negative for $\pi/2 < t \leq \pi$, the maximum occurs when $t = \pi/2$. Substituting this t-value into the parametrization, we find the highest point to be approximately $(-2.533, 2)$.

(c) First we compute d^2y/dx^2.

$$\frac{dy}{dx} = \frac{dy/dt}{dx/dt} = \frac{2 \cos t}{2t} = \frac{\cos t}{t}$$

$$\frac{d^2y}{dx^2} = \frac{dy'/dt}{dx/dt} = \frac{\dfrac{(-\sin t)(t) - (1)(\cos t)}{t^2}}{2t} = -\frac{t \sin t + \cos t}{2t^3}$$

A graph of

$$y = -\frac{t \sin t + \cos t}{2t^3} \text{ on the interval } [0, \pi] \text{ (Figure 11.3)}$$

shows a sign change at $t = 2.798386\ldots$. Substituting this t value into the parametrization, we find the point of inflection to be approximately $(2.831, 0.673)$.

Now Try Exercise 19.

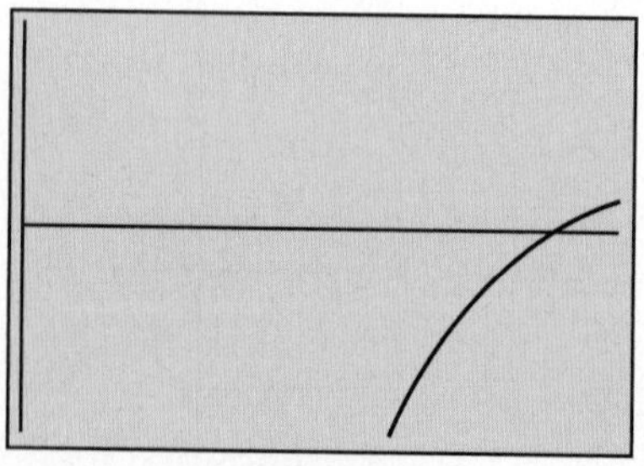

$[0, \pi]$ by $[-0.1, 0.1]$

Figure 11.3 The graph of d^2y/dx^2 for the parametric curve in Example 2 shows a sign change at $t = 2.798386\ldots$, indicating a point of inflection on the curve. (Example 2)

Arc Length

In Section 8.4 we derived two different formulas for arc length, each of them based on an approximation of the curve by tiny straight line segments with length $\sqrt{\Delta x_k^2 + \Delta y_k^2}$. (See Figure 11.4.)

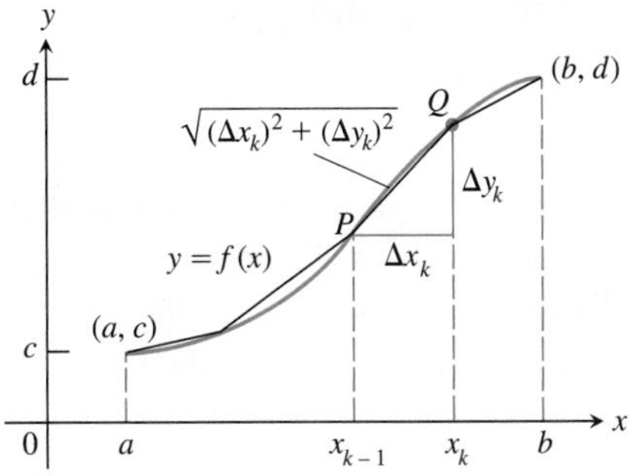

Figure 11.4 The graph of f, approximated by line segments.

Here is a third formula based on the same approximation.

Arc Length of a Parametrized Curve

Let L be the length of a parametric curve that is traversed exactly once as t increases from t_1 to t_2.

If dx/dt and dy/dt are continuous functions of t, then

$$L = \int_{t_1}^{t_2} \sqrt{\left(\frac{dx}{dt}\right)^2 + \left(\frac{dy}{dt}\right)^2}\, dt.$$

EXAMPLE 3 Measuring a Parametric Curve

Find the length of the astroid (Figure 11.5)

$$x = \cos^3 t, \quad y = \sin^3 t, \quad 0 \le t \le 2\pi.$$

$x = \cos^3 t,\ y = \sin^3 t,\ 0 \le t \le 2\pi$

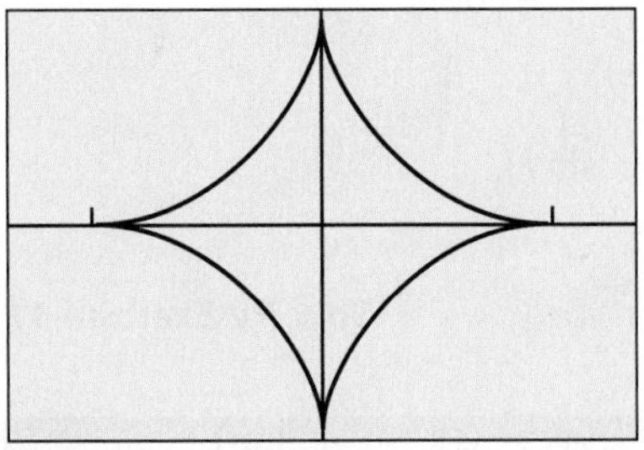

Figure 11.5 The astroid in Example 3.

SOLUTION

Solve Analytically The curve is traced once as t goes from 0 to 2π. Because of the curve's symmetry with respect to the coordinate axes, its length is four times the length of the first quadrant portion. We have

$$\left(\frac{dx}{dt}\right)^2 = \left((3\cos^2 t)(-\sin t)\right)^2 = 9\cos^4 t \sin^2 t$$

$$\left(\frac{dy}{dt}\right)^2 = \left((3\sin^2 t)(\cos t)\right)^2 = 9\sin^4 t \cos^2 t$$

$$\sqrt{\left(\frac{dx}{dt}\right)^2 + \left(\frac{dy}{dt}\right)^2} = \sqrt{9\cos^2 t \sin^2 t\,\underbrace{(\cos^2 t + \sin^2 t)}_{1}}$$

$$= \sqrt{9\cos^2 t \sin^2 t}$$

$$= 3|\cos t \sin t|.$$

Thus, the length of the first quadrant portion of the curve is

$$\int_0^{\pi/2} 3|\cos t \sin t|\, dt = 3\int_0^{\pi/2} \cos t \sin t\, dt \qquad \cos t \sin t \ge 0,\ 0 \le t \le \pi/2$$

$$= \frac{3}{2}\sin^2 t\Big]_0^{\pi/2} \qquad u = \sin t,\ du = \cos t\, dt$$

$$= \frac{3}{2}.$$

The length of the astroid is $4(3/2) = 6$.

Support Numerically NINT $(3|\cos t \sin t|, t, 0, 2\pi) = 6$. ***Now Try Exercise 29.***

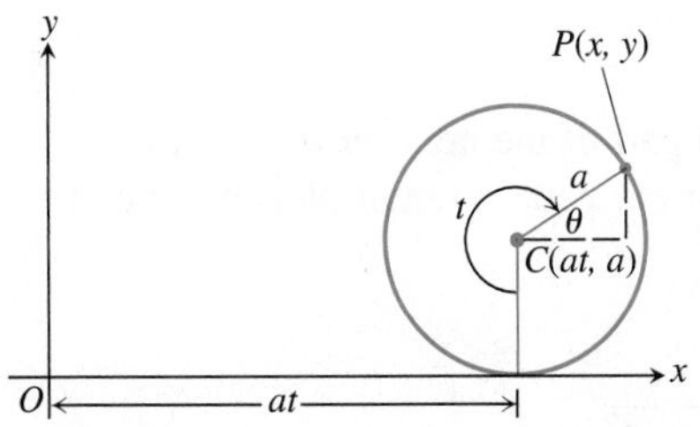

Figure 11.6 The position of $P(x, y)$ on the edge of the wheel when the wheel has turned t radians. (Example 4)

Cycloids

Suppose that a wheel of radius a rolls along a horizontal line without slipping (see Figure 11.6). The path traced by a point P on the wheel's edge is a **cycloid**, where P is originally at the origin.

Huygens's Clock
The problem with a pendulum clock whose bob swings in a circular arc is that the frequency of the swing depends on the amplitude of the swing. The wider the swing, the longer it takes the bob to return to center.

This does not happen if the bob can be made to swing in a cycloid. In 1673, Christiaan Huygens (1629–1695), the Dutch mathematician, physicist, and astronomer who discovered the rings of Saturn, designed a pendulum clock whose bob would swing in a cycloid. Driven by a need to make accurate determinations of longitude at sea, he hung the bob from a fine wire constrained by guards that caused it to draw up as it swung away from center. How were the guards shaped? They were cycloids, too.

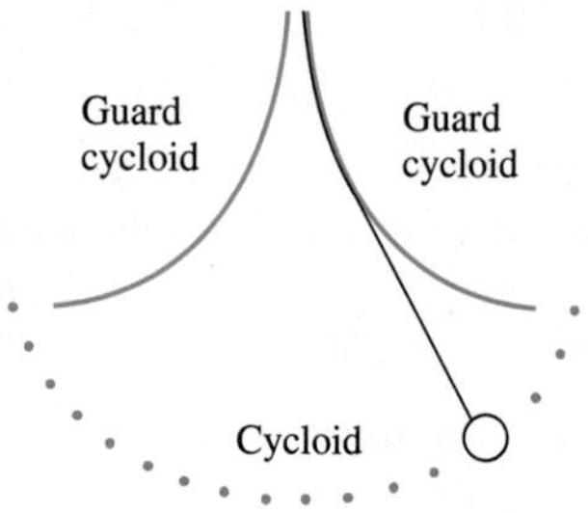

EXAMPLE 4 Finding Parametric Equations for a Cycloid

Find parametric equations for the path of the point P in Figure 11.6.

SOLUTION

We suppose that the wheel rolls to the right, P being at the origin when the turn angle t equals 0. Figure 11.6 shows the wheel after it has turned t radians. The base of the wheel is at distance at from the origin. The wheel's center is at (at, a), and the coordinates of P are

$$x = at + a\cos\theta, \quad y = a + a\sin\theta.$$

To express θ in terms of t, we observe that $t + \theta = 3\pi/2 + 2k\pi$ for some integer k, so

$$\theta = \frac{3\pi}{2} - t + 2k\pi.$$

Thus,

$$\cos\theta = \cos\left(\frac{3\pi}{2} - t + 2k\pi\right) = -\sin t,$$

$$\sin\theta = \sin\left(\frac{3\pi}{2} - t + 2k\pi\right) = -\cos t.$$

Therefore,

$$x = at - a\sin t = a(t - \sin t),$$
$$y = a - a\cos t = a(1 - \cos t).$$

Now Try Exercise 41.

EXPLORATION 1 Investigating Cycloids

Consider the cycloids with parametric equations

$$x = a(t - \sin t), \qquad y = a(1 - \cos t), \qquad a > 0.$$

1. Graph the equations for $a = 1, 2,$ and 3.
2. Find the x-intercepts.
3. Show that $y \geq 0$ for all t.
4. Explain why the arches of a cycloid are congruent.
5. What is the maximum value of y? Where is it attained?
6. Describe the graph of a cycloid.

EXAMPLE 5 Finding Length

Find the length of one arch of the cycloid

$$x = a(t - \sin t), \qquad y = a(1 - \cos t), \qquad a > 0.$$

SOLUTION

Figure 11.7 shows the first arch of the cycloid and part of the next for $a = 1$. In Exploration 1 you found that the x-intercepts occur at t equal to multiples of 2π and that the arches are congruent.

The length of the first arch is

$$\int_0^{2\pi} \sqrt{\left(\frac{dx}{dt}\right)^2 + \left(\frac{dy}{dt}\right)^2}\, dt.$$

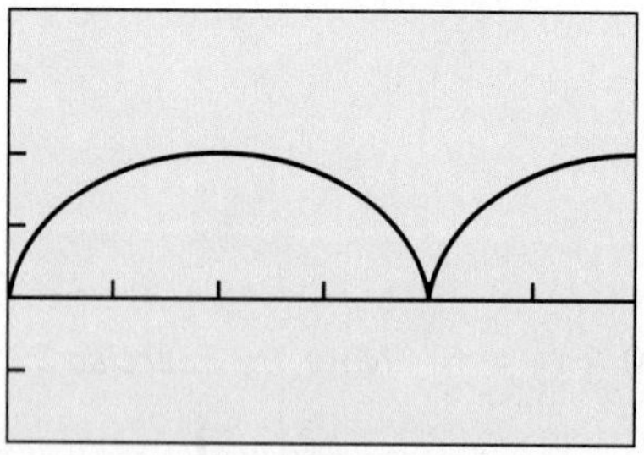

$[0, 3\pi]$ by $[-2, 4]$

Figure 11.7 The graph of the cycloid $x = t - \sin t$, $y = 1 - \cos t$, $t \geq 0$. (Example 5)

We have

$$\left(\frac{dx}{dt}\right)^2 = [a(1 - \cos t)]^2 = a^2(1 - 2\cos t + \cos^2 t)$$

$$\left(\frac{dy}{dt}\right)^2 = [a \sin t]^2 = a^2 \sin^2 t$$

$$\sqrt{\left(\frac{dx}{dt}\right)^2 + \left(\frac{dy}{dt}\right)^2} = a\sqrt{2 - 2\cos t}. \qquad a > 0, \sin^2 t + \cos^2 t = 1$$

Therefore,

$$\int_0^{2\pi} \sqrt{\left(\frac{dx}{dt}\right)^2 + \left(\frac{dy}{dt}\right)^2}\, dt = a\int_0^{2\pi} \sqrt{2 - 2\cos t}\, dt = 8a. \qquad \text{Using NINT}$$

The length of one arch of the cycloid is $8a$.

Now Try Exercise 43.

Quick Review 11.1 *(For help, go to Appendix A.1.)*

Exercise numbers with a gray background indicate problems that the authors have designed to be solved *without a calculator.*

Use algebra or a trig identity to write an equation relating x and y.

1. $x = t + 1$ and $y = 2t + 3$

2. $x = 3t$ and $y = 54t^3 - 3$

3. $x = \sin t$ and $y = \cos t$

4. $x = \sin t \cos t$ and $y = \sin(2t)$

5. $x = \tan\theta$ and $y = \sec\theta$

6. $x = \csc\theta$ and $y = \cot\theta$

7. $x = \cos\theta$ and $y = \cos(2\theta)$

8. $x = \sin\theta$ and $y = \cos(2\theta)$

9. $x = \cos\theta$ and $y = \sin\theta$ $(0 \le \theta \le \pi)$

10. $x = \cos\theta$ and $y = \sin\theta$ $(\pi \le \theta \le 2\pi)$

Section 11.1 Exercises

In Exercises 1–6, sketch the parametric curves and identify those which define y as a function of x. In each case, eliminate the parameter to find an equation that relates x and y directly.

1. $x = 2t + 3$ and $y = 4t - 3$ for t in the interval $[0, 3]$

2. $x = \sqrt{t - 2}$ and $y = \dfrac{t + 5}{4}$ for t in the interval $[3, 11]$

3. $x = \tan t$ and $y = \sec t$ for t in the interval $[0, \pi/4]$

4. $x = \sin t$ and $y = 2\cos t$ for t in the interval $[0, \pi]$

5. $x = \sin t$ and $y = \cos(2t)$ for t in the interval $[0, 2\pi]$

6. $x = \sin 6t$ and $y = 2t$ for t in the interval $[0, \pi/2]$

In Exercises 7–16, find **(a)** dy/dx and **(b)** d^2y/dx^2 in terms of t.

7. $x = 4\sin t, \quad y = 2\cos t$

8. $x = \cos t, \quad y = \sqrt{3}\cos t$

9. $x = -\sqrt{t + 1}, \quad y = \sqrt{3t}$

10. $x = 1/t, \quad y = -2 + \ln t$

11. $x = t^2 - 3t, \quad y = t^3$

12. $x = t^2 + t, \quad y = t^2 - t$

13. $x = \tan t, \quad y = \sec t$

14. $x = 2\cos t, \quad y = \cos(2t)$

15. $x = \ln(2t), \quad y = \ln(3t)^4$

16. $x = \ln(5t), \quad y = e^{5t}$

In Exercises 17–22,

(a) sketch the curve over the given t-interval, indicating the direction in which it is traced,

(b) identify the requested point, and

(c) justify that you have found the requested point by analyzing an appropriate derivative. (You may use a grapher, as was done in Example 2, part (c).

17. $x = t + 1, \quad y = t^2 + t, \quad -2 \le t \le 2$ — Lowest point

18. $x = t^2 + 2t, \quad y = t^2 - 2t + 3, \quad -2 \le t \le 3$ — Leftmost point

19. $x = 2\sin t, \quad y = \cos t, \quad 0 \le t \le \pi$ — Rightmost point

20. $x = \tan t, \quad y = 2\sec t, \quad -1 \le t \le 1$ — Lowest point

21. $x = 2\sin t, \quad y = \cos(2t), \quad 1.5 \le t \le 4.5$ — Highest point

22. $x = \ln(5t), \quad y = \ln(4t^2), \quad 0 < t \le 10$ — Rightmost point

In Exercises 23–26, find the points at which the tangent line to the curve is **(a)** horizontal or **(b)** vertical.

23. $x = 2 + \cos t, \quad y = -1 + \sin t$

24. $x = \sec t, \quad y = \tan t$

25. $x = 2 - t, \quad y = t^3 - 4t$

26. $x = -2 + 3\cos t, \quad y = 1 + 3\sin t$

In Exercises 27–34, find the length of the curve. (For an algebraic challenge, evaluate the integrals in Exercises 29–34 without a calculator.)

27. $x = \cos t,\quad y = \sin t,\quad 0 \le t \le 2\pi$

28. $x = 3\sin t,\quad y = 3\cos t,\quad 0 \le t \le \pi$

29. $x = 8\cos t + 8t\sin t,\quad y = 8\sin t - 8t\cos t,\quad 0 \le t \le \pi/2$

30 $x = 2\cos^3 t,\quad y = 2\sin^3 t,\quad 0 \le t \le 2\pi$

31. $x = \dfrac{(2t+3)^{3/2}}{3},\quad y = t + \dfrac{t^2}{2},\quad 0 \le t \le 3$

32. $x = \dfrac{(8t+8)^{3/2}}{12},\quad y = t^2 + t,\quad 0 \le t \le 2$

33. $x = \dfrac{1}{3}t^3,\quad y = \dfrac{1}{2}t^2,\quad 0 \le t \le 1$

34. $x = \ln(\sec t + \tan t) - \sin t,\quad y = \cos t,\quad 0 \le t \le \pi/3$

35. *Length Is Independent of Parametrization* To illustrate the fact that the numbers we get for length do not usually depend on the way we parametrize our curves, calculate the length of the semicircle $y = \sqrt{1 - x^2}$ with these two different parametrizations.

(a) $x = \cos 2t,\quad y = \sin 2t,\quad 0 \le t \le \pi/2$

(b) $x = \sin \pi t,\quad y = \cos \pi t,\quad -1/2 \le t \le 1/2$

36. *Perimeter of an Ellipse* Find the length of the ellipse

$$x = 3\cos t,\quad y = 4\sin t,\quad 0 \le t \le 2\pi.$$

37. *Cartesian Length Formula* The graph of a function $y = f(x)$ over an interval $[a, b]$ automatically has the parametrization

$$x = x,\quad y = f(x),\quad a \le x \le b.$$

The parameter in this case is x itself. Show that for this parametrization, the length formula

$$L = \int_a^b \sqrt{\left(\frac{dx}{dt}\right)^2 + \left(\frac{dy}{dt}\right)^2}\, dt$$

reduces to the Cartesian formula

$$L = \int_a^b \sqrt{1 + \left(\frac{dy}{dx}\right)^2}\, dx$$

derived in Section 8.4.

38. *(Continuation of Exercise 37)* Show that the Cartesian formula

$$L = \int_c^d \sqrt{1 + \left(\frac{dx}{dy}\right)^2}\, dy$$

for the length of the curve $x = g(y),\ c \le y \le d$, from Section 8.4 is a special case of the parametric length formula

$$L = \int_a^b \sqrt{\left(\frac{dx}{dt}\right)^2 + \left(\frac{dy}{dt}\right)^2}\, dt.$$

Exercises 39 and 40 refer to the region bounded by the x-axis and one arch of the cycloid

$$x = a(t - \sin t),\quad y = a(1 - \cos t)$$

that is shaded in the figure shown at the top of the next column.

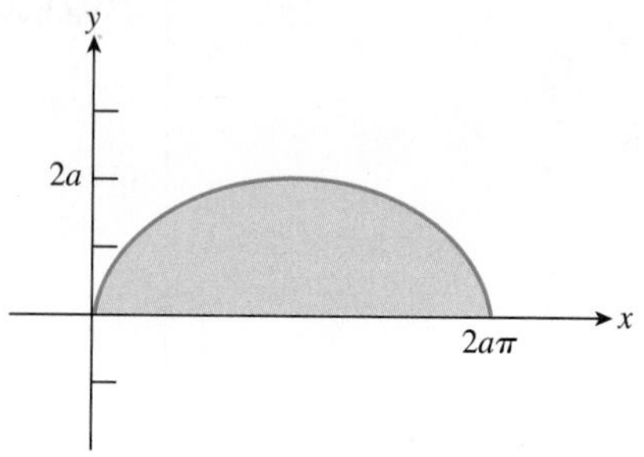

39. Find the area of the shaded region. [*Hint:* $dx = (dx/dt)\, dt$]

40. Find the volume swept out by revolving the region about the x-axis. [*Hint:* $dV = \pi y^2\, dx = \pi y^2 (dx/dt)\, dt$]

41. *Curtate Cycloid* Modify Example 4 slightly to find the parametric equations for the motion of a point in the *interior* of a wheel of radius a as the wheel rolls along the horizontal line without slipping. Assume that the point is at distance b from the center of the wheel, where $0 < b < a$. This curve, known as a *curtate cycloid,* has been used by artisans in designing the arches of violins (*Source:* mathworld.wolfram.com).

42. *Prolate Cycloid* Modify Example 4 slightly to find the parametric equations for the motion of a point on the *exterior* of a wheel of radius a as the wheel rolls along the horizontal line without slipping. Assume that the point is at distance b from the center of the wheel, where $a < b < 2a$. This curve, known as a *prolate cycloid,* is traced out by a point on the outer edge of a train's flanged wheel as the train moves along a track. (If you graph a prolate cycloid, you can see why they say that there is always part of a forward-moving train that is moving backwards!)

43. *Arc Length* Find the length of one arch (that is, the curve over one period) of the curtate cycloid defined parametrically by $x = 3t - 2\sin t$ and $y = 3 - 2\cos t$.

44. *Arc Length* Find the length of one arch (that is, the curve over one period) of the prolate cycloid defined parametrically by $x = 2t - 3\sin t$ and $y = 2 - 3\cos t$.

Standardized Test Questions

45. True or False In a parametrization, if x is a continuous function of t and y is a continuous function of t, then y is a continuous function of x. Justify your answer.

46. True or False If f is a function with domain all real numbers, then the graph of f can be defined parametrically by $x = t$ and $y = f(t)$ for $-\infty < t\, \infty$. Justify your answer.

47. Multiple Choice For which of the following parametrizations of the unit circle will the circle be traversed clockwise?

(A) $x = \cos t,\quad y = \sin t,\quad 0 \le t \le 2\pi$

(B) $x = \sin t,\quad y = \cos t,\quad 0 \le t \le 2\pi$

(C) $x = -\cos t,\quad y = -\sin t,\quad 0 \le t \le 2\pi$

(D) $x = -\sin t,\quad y = \cos t,\quad 0 \le t \le 2\pi$

(E) $x = \sin t,\quad y = -\cos t,\quad 0 \le t \le 2\pi$

48. Multiple Choice A parametric curve is defined by $x = \sin t$ and $y = \csc t$ for $0 < t < \pi/2$. This curve is

(A) increasing and concave up.

(B) increasing and concave down.

(C) decreasing and concave up.

(D) decreasing and concave down.

(E) decreasing with a point of inflection.

49. Multiple Choice The parametric curve defined by $x = \ln(t)$, $y = t$ for $t > 0$ is identical to the graph of the function

(A) $y = \ln x$ for all real x.

(B) $y = \ln^x$ for $x > 0$.

(C) $y = e^x$ for all real x.

(D) $y = e^x$ for $x > 0$.

(E) $y = \ln(e^x)$ for $x > 0$.

50. Multiple Choice The curve parametrized by

$$x = 6\sin t - 3\sin(7t) \text{ and } y = 6\cos t - 3\cos(7t),$$

as shown in the diagram below, is traversed exactly once as t increases from 0 to 2π. The total length of the curve is given by

(A) $\int_0^{2\pi} \sqrt{(6\sin t - 3\sin(7t))^2 + (6\cos t - 3\cos(7t))^2}\,dt$

(B) $\int_0^{2\pi} \sqrt{(6\cos t - 3\cos(7t))^2 + (6\sin t - 3\sin(7t))^2}\,dt$

(C) $\int_0^{2\pi} \sqrt{(6\cos t - 21\cos(7t))^2 - (6\sin t - 21\sin(7t))^2}\,dt$

(D) $\int_0^{2\pi} \sqrt{(6\cos t - 21\cos(7t))^2 + (-6\sin t + 21\sin(7t))^2}\,dt$

(E) $\int_0^{2\pi} \sqrt{(6\cos t - 3\cos(7t))^2 + (6\sin t + 3\sin(3t))^2}\,dt$

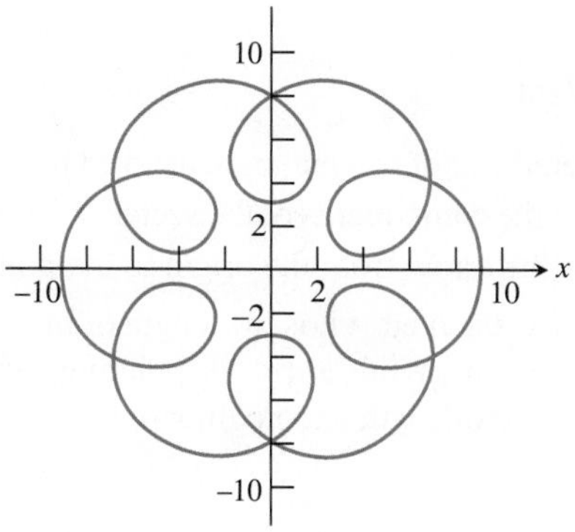

Explorations

51. Group Activity ***Involute of a Circle*** If a string wound around a fixed circle is unwound while being held taut in the plane of the circle, its end P traces an *involute* of the circle as suggested by the diagram below. In the diagram, the circle is the unit circle in the xy-plane, and the initial position of the tracing point is the point (1,0) on the x-axis. The unwound portion of the string is tangent to the circle at Q, and t is the radian measure of the angle from the positive x-axis to the segment OQ.

(a) Derive parametric equations for the involute by expressing the coordinates x and y of P in terms of t for $t \geq 0$.

(b) Find the length of the involute for $0 \leq t \leq 2\pi$.

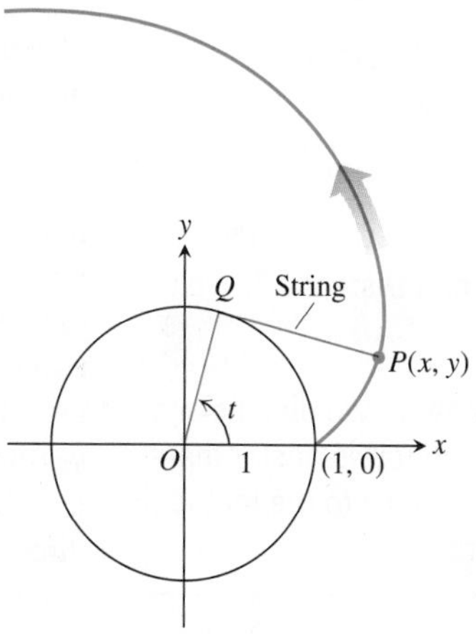

52. *(Continuation of Exercise 51)* Repeat Exercise 51 using the circle of radius a centered at the origin, $x^2 + y^2 = a^2$.

In Exercises 53–56, a projectile is launched over horizontal ground at an angle θ with the horizontal and with initial velocity v_0 ft/sec. Its path is given by the parametric equations

$$x = (v_0 \cos\theta)t, \quad y = (v_0 \sin\theta)t - 16t^2.$$

(a) Find the length of the path traveled by the projectile.

(b) Estimate the maximum height of the projectile.

53. $\theta = 20°$, $v_0 = 150$

54. $\theta = 30°$, $v_0 = 150$

55. $\theta = 60°$, $v_0 = 150$

56. $\theta = 90°$, $v_0 = 150$

Extending the Ideas

If dx/dt and dy/dt are continuous, the parametric curve defined by $(x(t), y(t))$ for $a \leq t \leq b$ is called *smooth*. If the curve is traversed exactly once as t increases from a to b, and if y is a positive function of x, then the curve can be revolved about the x-axis to form a solid of revolution (see Section 8.3). The *surface area* of such a solid is given by

$$S = \int_a^b 2\pi y \sqrt{\left(\frac{dx}{dt}\right)^2 + \left(\frac{dy}{dt}\right)^2}\,dt.$$

Apply this formula in Exercises 57–60 to find the surface area when the parametric curve is revolved about the x-axis.

57. $x = \cos t$, $y = 2 + \sin t$, $0 \leq t \leq 2\pi$

58. $x = 2\sqrt{t}$, $y = (2/3)t^{3/2}$, $0 \leq t \leq 2$

59. $x = t^2 + 2$, $y = t + 1$, $0 \leq t \leq 3$

60. $x = \ln(\sec t + \tan t) - \sin t$, $y = \cos t$, $0 \leq t \leq \pi/3$

11.2 Vectors in the Plane

What you will learn about . . .

- Two-Dimensional Vectors
- Vector Operations
- Modeling Planar Motion
- Velocity, Acceleration, and Speed
- Displacement and Distance Traveled

and why . . .

The jump from one to two dimensions (and eventually higher) is easier than one might think, thanks to the mathematics of vectors.

Two-Dimensional Vectors

When an object moves *along a straight line*, its velocity can be determined by a single number that represents both magnitude and direction (forward if the number is positive, backward if it is negative). The speed of an object moving on a path *in a plane* can still be represented by a number, but how can we represent its direction when there are an infinite number of directions possible? Fortunately, we can represent both magnitude and direction with just two numbers, just as we can represent any point in the plane with just two coordinates (which is possible essentially for the same reason). This representation is what two-dimensional vectors were designed to do.

While the pair (a, b) determines a point in the plane, it also determines a **directed line segment** (or **arrow**) with its tail at the origin and its head at (a, b) (Figure 11.8). The length of this arrow represents magnitude, while the direction in which it points represents direction. In this way, the ordered pair (a, b) represents a mathematical object with both magnitude and direction, called the **position vector of (a, b)**.

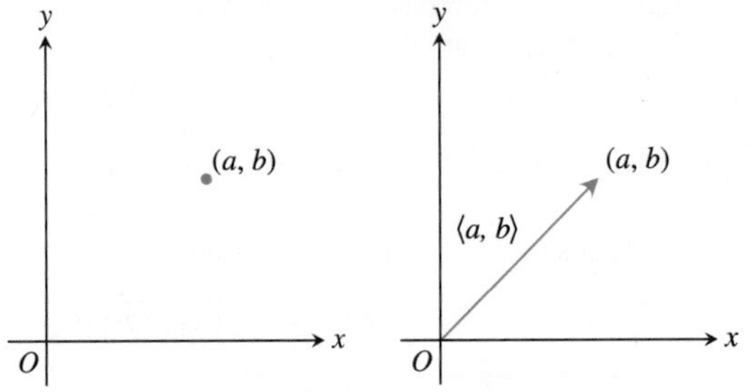

Figure 11.8 The point represents the ordered pair (a, b). The arrow (directed line segment) represents the vector $\langle a, b\rangle$.

DEFINITION Two-Dimensional Vector

A **two-dimensional vector v** is an ordered pair of real numbers, denoted in **component form** as $\langle a, b\rangle$. The numbers a and b are the **components** of the vector **v**. The **standard representation** of the vector $\langle a, b\rangle$ is the arrow from the origin to the point (a, b). The **magnitude** (or **absolute value**) of **v**, denoted $|\mathbf{v}|$, is the length of the arrow, and the **direction of v** is the direction in which the arrow is pointing. The vector $\mathbf{0} = \langle 0, 0\rangle$, called the **zero vector**, has zero length and no direction.

The distance formula in the plane gives a simple computational formula for magnitude.

Magnitude of a Vector

The **magnitude** or **absolute value** of the vector $\langle a, b\rangle$ is the nonnegative real number $|\langle a, b\rangle| = \sqrt{a^2 + b^2}$.

Direction can be quantified in several ways; for example, navigators use bearings from compass points. The simplest choice for us is to measure direction as we do with the trigonometric functions, using the usual position angle formed with the positive x-axis as the initial ray and the vector as the terminal ray. In this way, every nonzero vector determines a unique **direction angle** θ satisfying (in degrees) $0 \leq \theta < 360$ or (in radians) $0 \leq \theta < 2\pi$. (See Figure 11.10 for an example.)

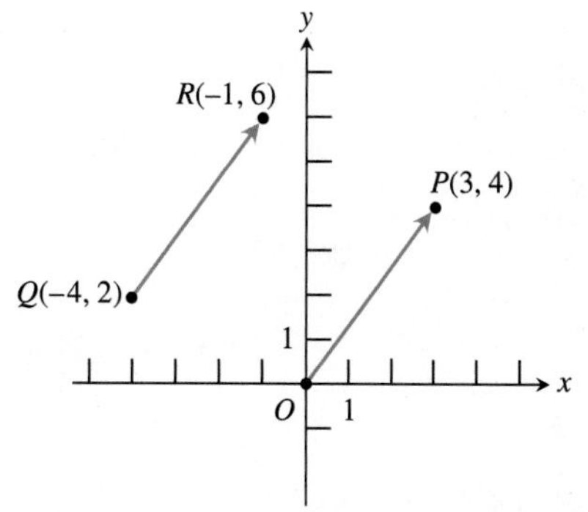

Figure 11.9 The arrows $\overrightarrow{QR}$ and $\overrightarrow{OP}$ both represent the vector $\langle 3, 4 \rangle$, as would any arrow with the same length pointing in the same direction. Such arrows are called *equivalent*.

Direction Angle of a Vector

The **direction angle** of a nonzero vector **v** is the smallest nonnegative angle θ formed with the positive x-axis as the initial ray and the standard representation of **v** as the terminal ray.

This textbook uses boldface variables to represent vectors (for example, **u** and **v**) to distinguish them from numbers. In handwritten form it is customary to distinguish vector variables by arrows (for example, $\vec{u}$ and $\vec{v}$). We also use angled brackets to distinguish a vector $\langle x, y \rangle$ from a point (x, y) in the plane, although it is not uncommon to see (x, y) used for both, especially in handwritten form.

It is often convenient in applications to represent vectors with arrows that begin at points other than the origin. The important thing to remember is that *any two arrows with the same length and pointing in the same direction represent the same vector*. In Figure 11.9, for example, the vector $\langle 3, 4 \rangle$ is shown represented by $\overrightarrow{QR}$, an arrow with **initial point** Q and **terminal point** R, as well as by its standard representation $\overrightarrow{OP}$. Two arrows that represent the same vector are said to be **equivalent**.

The quick way to associate arrows with the vectors they represent is to use the following rule.

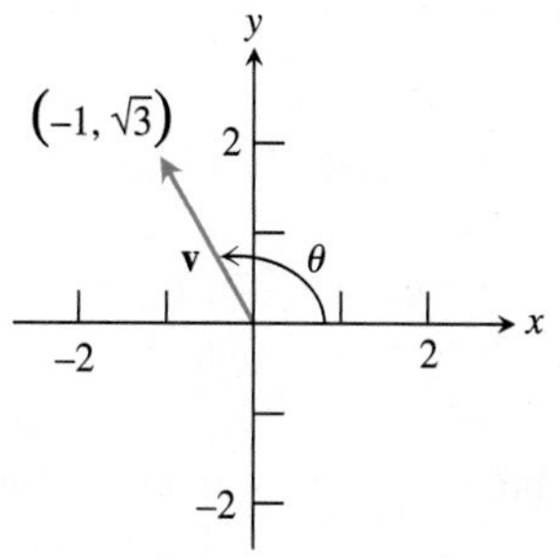

Figure 11.10 The vector **v** in Example 1 is represented by an arrow from the origin to the point $(-1, \sqrt{3})$.

Head Minus Tail (HMT) Rule

If an arrow has initial point (x_1, y_1) and terminal point (x_2, y_2), it represents the vector $\langle x_2 - x_1, y_2 - y_1 \rangle$.

EXAMPLE 1 Finding Magnitude and Direction

Find the magnitude and the direction angle θ of the vector $\mathbf{v} = \langle -1, \sqrt{3} \rangle$ (Figure 11.10).

SOLUTION

The magnitude of **v** is $|\mathbf{v}| = \sqrt{(-1-0)^2 + (\sqrt{3}-0)^2} = 2$. Using triangle ratios, we see that the direction angle θ satisfies $\cos\theta = -1/2$ and $\sin\theta = \sqrt{3}/2$, so $\theta = 120°$ or $2\pi/3$ radians.

Now Try Exercise 5.

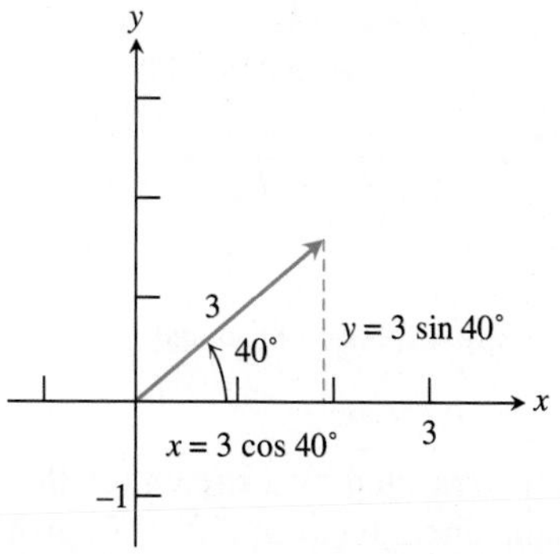

Figure 11.11 The vector in Example 2 is represented by an arrow from the origin to the point $(3 \cos 40°, 3 \sin 40°)$.

EXAMPLE 2 Finding Component Form

Find the component form of a vector with magnitude 3 and direction angle 40°.

SOLUTION

The components of the vector, found trigonometrically, are $x = 3 \cos 40°$ and $y = 3 \sin 40°$ (Figure 11.11).

The vector is $\langle 3 \cos 40°, 3 \sin 40° \rangle \approx \langle 2.298, 1.928 \rangle$.

Now Try Exercise 13.

Why Not Use Slope for Direction?

Notice that *slope* is inadequate for determining the direction of a vector, since two vectors with the same slope could be pointing in opposite directions. Moreover, vectors are still useful in dimensions higher than 2, while slope is not.

Vector Operations

The algebra of vectors sometimes involves working with vectors and numbers at the same time. In this context, we refer to the numbers as **scalars**. The two most basic algebraic operations involving vectors are *vector addition* (adding a vector to a vector) and *scalar multiplication* (multiplying a vector by a number). Both operations are easily represented geometrically.

DEFINITION Vector Addition and Scalar Multiplication

Let $\mathbf{u} = \langle u_1, u_2 \rangle$ and $\mathbf{v} = \langle v_1, v_2 \rangle$ be vectors and let k be a real number (scalar).

The **sum** (or **resultant**) **of the vectors u and v** is the vector

$$\mathbf{u} + \mathbf{v} = \langle u_1 + v_1, u_2 + v_2 \rangle.$$

The **product of the scalar k and the vector u** is

$$k\mathbf{u} = k\langle u_1, u_2 \rangle = \langle ku_1, ku_2 \rangle.$$

The **opposite of a vector v** is $-\mathbf{v} = (-1)\mathbf{v}$. We define vector subtraction by

$$\mathbf{u} - \mathbf{v} = \mathbf{u} + (-\mathbf{v}).$$

The vector $\dfrac{\mathbf{v}}{|\mathbf{v}|}$ is a vector of magnitude 1, called a **unit vector**. Its component form is $\langle \cos \theta, \sin \theta \rangle$, where θ is the direction angle of **v**. For this reason, $\dfrac{\mathbf{v}}{|\mathbf{v}|}$ is sometimes called the **direction vector** of **v**.

The sum of two vectors **u** and **v** can be represented geometrically by arrows in two ways. In the **tail-to-head representation**, the arrow from the origin to (u_1, u_2) is the standard representation of **u**, the arrow from (u_1, u_2) to $(u_1 + v_1, u_2 + v_2)$, represents **v** (as you can verify by the HMT Rule), and the arrow from the origin to $(u_1 + v_1, u_2 + v_2)$ then is the standard representation of $u + v$ (Figure 11.12a).

In the **parallelogram representation**, the standard representations of **u** and **v** determine a parallelogram whose diagonal is the standard representation of $\mathbf{u} + \mathbf{v}$ (Figure 11.12b).

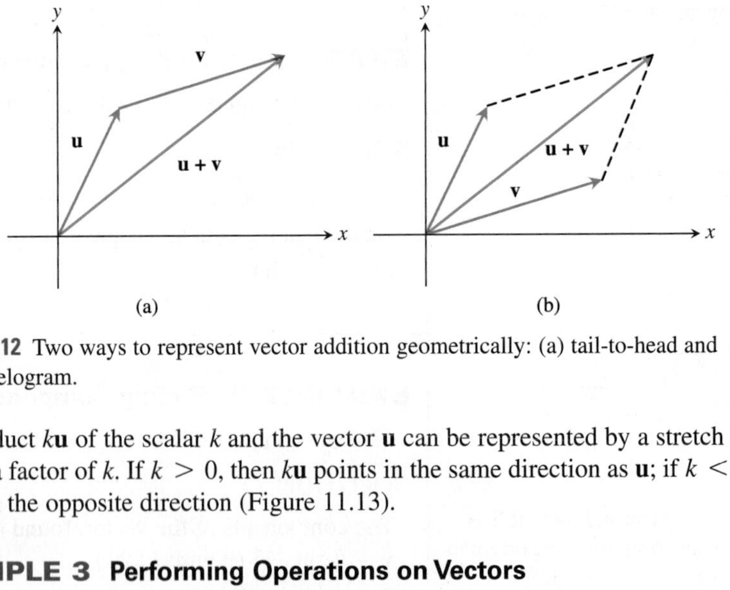

Figure 11.12 Two ways to represent vector addition geometrically: (a) tail-to-head and (b) parallelogram.

The product $k\mathbf{u}$ of the scalar k and the vector **u** can be represented by a stretch (or shrink) of **u** by a factor of k. If $k > 0$, then $k\mathbf{u}$ points in the same direction as **u**; if $k < 0$, then $k\mathbf{u}$ points in the opposite direction (Figure 11.13).

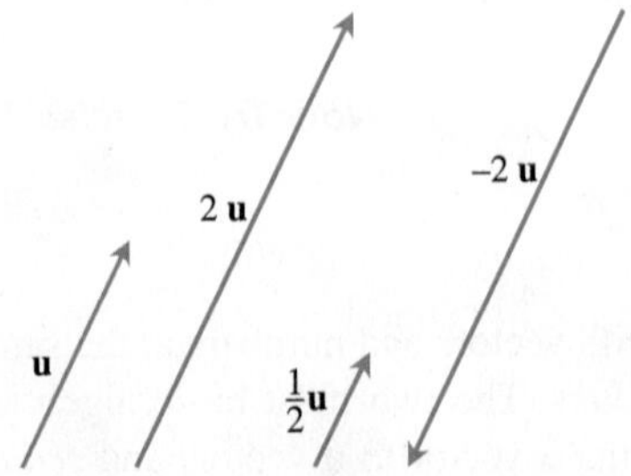

Figure 11.13 Representations of **u** and several scalar multiples of **u**.

EXAMPLE 3 Performing Operations on Vectors

Let $\mathbf{u} = \langle -1, 3 \rangle$ and $\mathbf{v} = \langle 4, 7 \rangle$. Find the following.

(a) $2\mathbf{u} + 3\mathbf{v}$ **(b)** $\mathbf{u} - \mathbf{v}$ **(c)** $\left| \dfrac{1}{2}\mathbf{u} \right|$

SOLUTION

(a) $2\mathbf{u} + 3\mathbf{v} = 2\langle -1, 3 \rangle + 3\langle 4, 7 \rangle$

$= \langle 2(-1) + 3(4), 2(3) + 3(7) \rangle = \langle 10, 27 \rangle$

continued

(b) $\mathbf{u} - \mathbf{v} = \langle -1, 3 \rangle - \langle 4, 7 \rangle$

$= \langle -1 - 4, 3 - 7 \rangle = \langle -5, -4 \rangle$

(c) $\left| \frac{1}{2}\mathbf{u} \right| = \left| \left\langle -\frac{1}{2}, \frac{3}{2} \right\rangle \right| = \sqrt{\left(-\frac{1}{2}\right)^2 + \left(\frac{3}{2}\right)^2} = \frac{1}{2}\sqrt{10}$

Now Try Exercise 21.

Vector operations have many of the properties of their real-number counterparts.

Properties of Vector Operations

Let **u**, **v**, **w** be vectors and a, b be scalars.

1. $\mathbf{u} + \mathbf{v} = \mathbf{v} + \mathbf{u}$
2. $(\mathbf{u} + \mathbf{v}) + \mathbf{w} = \mathbf{u} + (\mathbf{v} + \mathbf{w})$
3. $\mathbf{u} + \mathbf{0} = \mathbf{u}$
4. $\mathbf{u} + (-\mathbf{u}) = \mathbf{0}$
5. $0\mathbf{u} = \mathbf{0}$
6. $1\mathbf{u} = \mathbf{u}$
7. $a(b\mathbf{u}) = (ab)\mathbf{u}$
8. $a(\mathbf{u} + \mathbf{v}) = a\mathbf{u} + a\mathbf{v}$
9. $(a + b)\mathbf{u} = a\mathbf{u} + b\mathbf{u}$

Modeling Planar Motion

Although vectors are used in many other physical applications, our primary reason for introducing them into this course is to model the motion of objects moving in a coordinate plane. You may have seen vector problems of the following type in a physics or mechanics course.

EXAMPLE 4 Finding Ground Speed and Direction

A Boeing® 727® airplane, flying due east at 500 mph in still air, encounters a 70-mph tail wind acting in the direction 60° north of east. The airplane holds its compass heading due east but, because of the wind, acquires a new ground speed and direction. What are they?

SOLUTION

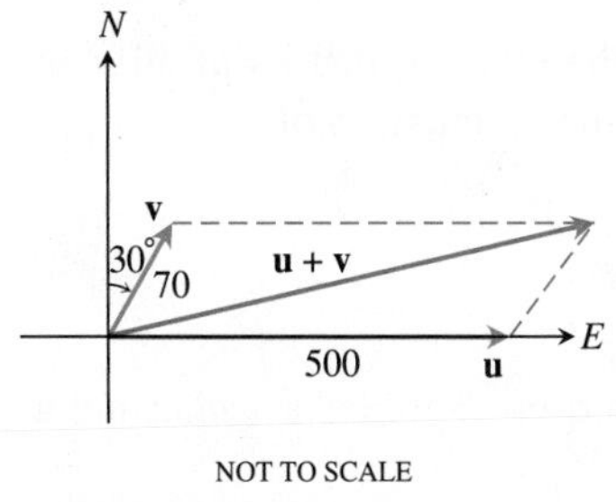

Figure 11.14 Vectors representing the velocities of the airplane and tail wind in Example 4.

If $\mathbf{u}$ = the velocity of the airplane alone and $\mathbf{v}$ = the velocity of the tail wind, then $|\mathbf{u}| = 500$ and $|\mathbf{v}| = 70$ (Figure 11.14).

We need to find the magnitude and direction of the *resultant vector* $\mathbf{u} + \mathbf{v}$. If we let the positive x-axis represent east and the positive y-axis represent north, then the component forms of **u** and **v** are

$$\mathbf{u} = \langle 500, 0 \rangle \quad \text{and} \quad \mathbf{v} = \langle 70 \cos 60°, 70 \sin 60° \rangle = \langle 35, 35\sqrt{3} \rangle.$$

Therefore,

$$\mathbf{u} + \mathbf{v} = \langle 535, 35\sqrt{3} \rangle,$$

$$|\mathbf{u} + \mathbf{v}| = \sqrt{535^2 + (35\sqrt{3})^2} \approx 538.4,$$

and

$$\theta = \tan^{-1} \frac{35\sqrt{3}}{535} \approx 6.5°.$$

Interpret The new ground speed of the airplane is about 538.4 mph, and its new direction is about 6.5° north of east.

Now Try Exercise 25.

Recall that if the position x of an object moving along a line is given as a function of time t, then the velocity of the object is dx/dt and the acceleration of the object is d^2x/dt^2. It is almost as simple to relate position, velocity, and acceleration for an object moving in the plane, because we can model those functions with vectors and treat *the components of the vectors as separate linear models*. Example 5 shows how simple this modeling actually is.

EXAMPLE 5 Doing Calculus Componentwise

A particle moves in the plane so that its position at any time $t \geq 0$ is given by $(\sin t, t^2/2)$.

(a) Find the position vector of the particle at time t.

(b) Find the velocity vector of the particle at time t.

(c) Find the acceleration of the particle at time t.

(d) Describe the position and motion of the particle at time $t = 6$.

SOLUTION

(a) The position vector, which has the same components as the position point, is $\langle \sin t, t^2/2 \rangle$. In fact, it could also be represented as $(\sin t, t^2/2)$, since the context would identify it as a vector.

(b) Differentiate each component of the position vector to get $\langle \cos\ t, t \rangle$.

(c) Differentiate each component of the velocity vector to get $\langle -\sin t, 1 \rangle$.

(d) The particle is at the point $(\sin 6, 18)$, with velocity $\langle \cos 6, 6 \rangle$ and acceleration $\langle -\sin 6, 1 \rangle$.

You can graph the path of this particle parametrically, letting $x = \sin(t)$ and $y = t^2/2$. In Figure 11.15 we show the path of the particle from $t = 0$ to $t = 6$. The red arrow at the point $(\sin 6, 18)$ represents the velocity vector $(\cos 6, 6)$. It shows both the magnitude and direction of the velocity at that moment in time.

Now Try Exercise 31.

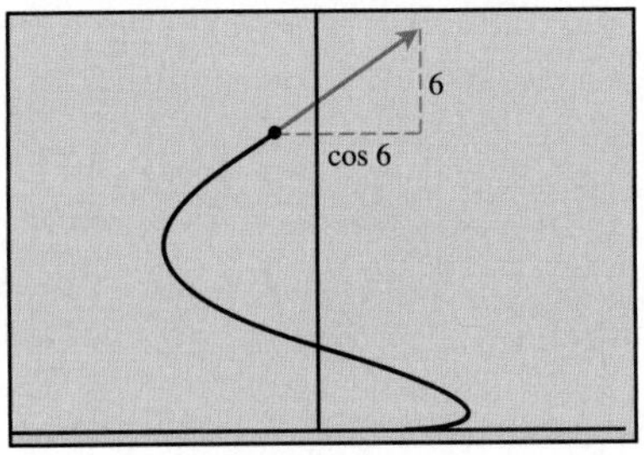

[–2, 2] by [0, 25]

$0 \leq t \leq 6$

Figure 11.15 The path of the particle in Example 5 from $t = 0$ to $t = 6$. The red arrow shows the velocity vector at $t = 6$.

Velocity, Acceleration, and Speed

We are now ready to give some definitions.

DEFINITIONS Velocity, Speed, Acceleration, and Direction of Motion

Suppose a particle moves along a smooth curve in the plane so that its position at any time t is $(x(t)), y(t)$, where x and y are differentiable functions of t.

1. The particle's **position vector** is $\mathbf{r}(t) = \langle x(t), y(t) \rangle$.
2. The particle's **velocity vector** is $\mathbf{v}(t) = \left\langle \frac{dx}{dt}, \frac{dy}{dt} \right\rangle$.
3. The particle's **speed** is the magnitude of $\mathbf{v}$, denoted $|\mathbf{v}|$. Speed is a *scalar*, not a vector.
4. The particle's **acceleration vector** is $\mathbf{a}(t) = \left\langle \frac{d^2x}{dt^2}, \frac{d^2y}{dt^2} \right\rangle$.
5. The particle's **direction of motion** is the **direction vector** $\frac{\mathbf{v}}{|\mathbf{v}|}$.

A Word About Differentiability

Our definitions can be expanded to a **calculus of vectors**, in which (for example) $d\mathbf{v}/dt = \mathbf{a}(t)$, but it is not our intention to get into that here. We have therefore finessed the fine point of vector differentiability by requiring the path of our particle to be "smooth." The path can have vertical tangents, fail the vertical line test, and loop back on itself, but corners and cusps are still problematic.

EXAMPLE 6 Catching a Fly Ball

A baseball leaves a batter's bat at an angle of 60° from the horizontal, traveling at 110 feet per second. A fielder, who is standing in the direct line of the hit with his glove at a vertical reach of 8 feet, catches the ball for the out. His feet do not leave the ground.

continued

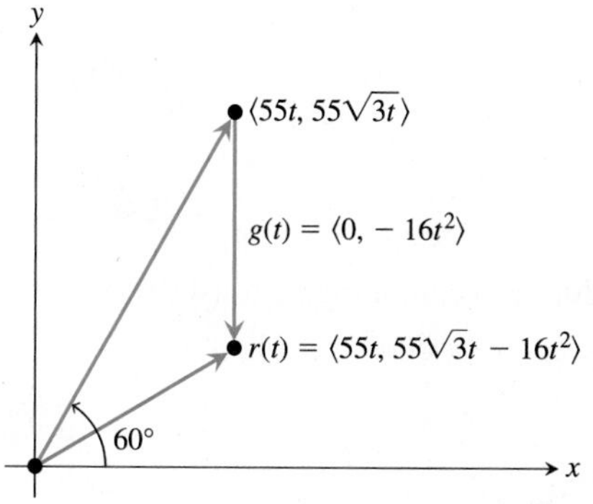

Figure 11.16 A vector diagram showing $\mathbf{r}(t)$, the position vector of a baseball hit by a bat, and the effect of gravity. (Example 6)

(a) Find the position vector of the baseball at time t (in seconds).

(b) Find the velocity vector of the baseball at time t (in seconds).

(c) At what time t does the fielder catch the ball, and how far is he from home plate?

(d) How fast is the ball traveling when he catches the ball?

SOLUTION

(a) From elementary physics we know that the position vector of the ball at any time t is $\mathbf{r}(t) = \langle x(t), y(t)\rangle$, where $x(t) = 110t \cos 60° = 55t$ and $y(t) = 110t \sin 60° - 16t^2 = 55\sqrt{3}t - 16t^2$. See Figure 11.16.

Note that we ignore the height of the batter (the ball is hit a few feet off the ground), air resistance, and wind effects. We consider only gravity in this model of the motion of a baseball hit by a bat.

(b) The velocity vector is $\mathbf{v}(t) = \left\langle \frac{dx}{dt}, \frac{dy}{dt} \right\rangle$. Evaluating the derivatives, we get $\mathbf{v}(t) = \langle 55, 55\sqrt{3} - 32t\rangle$.

(c) Note that the *vertical component* of the desired position vector must be 8 (feet). So, $y(t) = 55\sqrt{3}t - 16t^2 = 8$. Next, solving for $t(t > 0)$, we have

$16t^2 - 55\sqrt{3}t + 8 = 0$, which gives $t = \dfrac{55\sqrt{3} + \sqrt{(55\sqrt{3})^2 - 4 \cdot 16 \cdot 8}}{32}$, or

$t \approx 5.869$ seconds. Thus, the fielder catches the ball in the air 5.869 seconds after the ball was hit. The *horizontal component* of the position vector is $x(t) = 55t$, which gives $x(t) = 55(5.869) \approx 322.780$ feet. So, the fielder is standing about 323 feet from home plate when he catches the ball.

(d) The speed of the ball at any time t is $|\mathbf{v}(t)|$. So, we evaluate $|\mathbf{v}(t)|$ at $t = 5.869$, found in part (c):

$$|\mathbf{v}(t)| = \sqrt{55^2 + (55\sqrt{3} - 32t)^2}$$

$$|\mathbf{v}(5.869)| = \sqrt{55^2 + (55\sqrt{3} - 32 \cdot 5.869)^2} \approx 107.655 \text{ ft/sec, or } 73.402 \text{ mph}$$

So, the ball is traveling at about 73 mph when the fielder catches the ball.

Now Try Exercise 33.

EXAMPLE 7 Studying Planar Motion

A particle moves in the plane with position vector $\mathbf{r}(t) = \langle \sin(3t), \cos(5t)\rangle$. Find the velocity and acceleration vectors and determine the path of the particle.

SOLUTION

$$\text{Velocity } \mathbf{v}(t) = \left\langle \frac{d}{dt}(\sin(3t)), \frac{d}{dt}(\cos(5t)) \right\rangle = \langle 3\cos(3t), -5\sin(5t)\rangle.$$

$$\text{Acceleration } \mathbf{a}(t) = \left\langle \frac{d}{dt}(3\cos(3t)), \frac{d}{dt}(-5\sin(5t)) \right\rangle = \langle -9\sin(3t), -25\cos(5t)\rangle.$$

The path of the particle is found by graphing (in parametric mode) the curve defined by $x = \sin(3t)$ and $y = \cos(5t)$ (Figure 11.17).

Now Try Exercise 35.

[–1.6, 1.6] by [–1.1, 1.1]

$0 \le t \le 6.3$

Figure 11.17 The path of the busy particle in Example 7.

EXAMPLE 8 Studying Planar Motion

A particle moves in an elliptical path so that its position at any time $t \geq 0$ is given by $(4 \sin t, 2 \cos t)$.

(a) Find the velocity and acceleration vectors.

(b) Find the velocity, acceleration, speed, and direction of motion at $t = \pi/4$.

(c) Sketch the path of the particle and show the velocity vector at the point $(4, 0)$.

(d) Does the particle travel clockwise or counterclockwise around the origin?

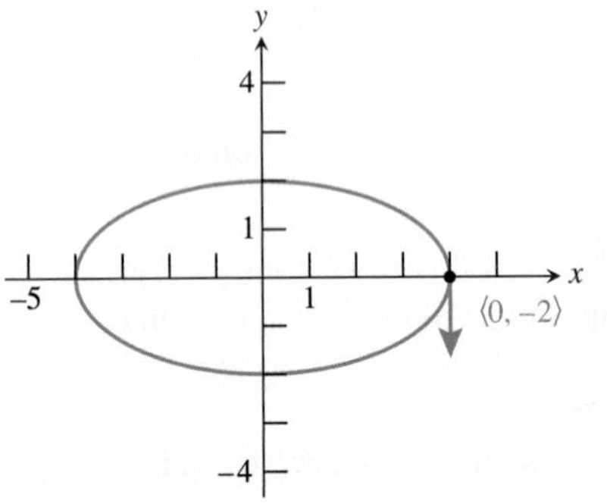

Figure 11.18 The ellipse on which the particle travels in Example 8. The velocity vector at the point $(4, 0)$ is $\langle 0, -2 \rangle$, represented by an arrow tangent to the ellipse at $(4, 0)$ and pointing down. The direction of the velocity at that point indicates that the particle travels clockwise around the origin.

SOLUTION

(a) Velocity $\mathbf{v}(t) = \left\langle \frac{d}{dt}(4 \sin t), \frac{d}{dt}(2 \cos t) \right\rangle = \langle 4 \cos t, -2 \sin t \rangle$

Acceleration $\mathbf{a}(t) = \left\langle \frac{d}{dt}(4 \cos t), \frac{d}{dt}(-2 \sin t) \right\rangle = \langle -4 \sin t, -2 \cos t \rangle$

(b) Velocity $\mathbf{v}(\pi/4) = \langle 4 \cos(\pi/4), -2 \sin(\pi/4) \rangle = \langle 2\sqrt{2}, -\sqrt{2} \rangle$

Acceleration $\mathbf{a}(\pi/4) = \langle -4 \sin(\pi/4), -2 \cos(\pi/4) \rangle = \langle -2\sqrt{2}, -\sqrt{2} \rangle$

Speed $= |\mathbf{v}(\pi/4)| = |\langle 2\sqrt{2}, -\sqrt{2} \rangle| = \sqrt{(2\sqrt{2})^2 + (-\sqrt{2})^2} = \sqrt{10}$

(c) The ellipse defined parametrically by $x = 4 \sin t$ and $y = 2 \cos t$ is shown in Figure 11.18. At the point $(4, 0)$, $\sin t = 1$ and $\cos t = 0$, so $\mathbf{v}(t) = \langle 4 \cos t, -2 \sin t \rangle = \langle 0, -2 \rangle$. The vector $\langle 0, -2 \rangle$ is drawn tangent to the curve at $(4, 0)$.

(d) As the vector in Figure 11.18 shows, the particle travels clockwise around the origin.

Now Try Exercise 37.

Displacement and Distance Traveled

Recall that when a particle moves along a line with velocity $v(t)$, the displacement (or net distance traveled) from time $t = a$ to time $t = b$ is given by $\int_a^b v(t)\,dt$, while the (total) distance traveled in that time interval is given by $\int_a^b |v(t)|\,dt$. When a particle moves in the plane with velocity vector $\mathbf{v}(t)$, displacement and distance traveled can be found by applying the same integrals to the vector $\mathbf{v}$, although in slightly different ways.

DEFINITIONS Displacement and Distance Traveled

Suppose a particle moves along a path in the plane so that its velocity at any time t is $\mathbf{v}(t) = (v_1(t), v_2(t))$, where v_1 and v_2 are integrable functions of t.

The **displacement** from $t = a$ to $t = b$ is given by the vector

$$\left\langle \int_a^b v_1(t)\,dt, \int_a^b v_2(t)\,dt \right\rangle.$$

The preceding vector is added to the position at time $t = a$ to get the position at time $t = b$.

The **distance traveled** from $t = a$ to $t = b$ is

$$\int_a^b |\mathbf{v}(t)|\,dt = \int_a^b \sqrt{(v_1(t))^2 + (v_2(t))^2}\,dt.$$

There are two things worth noting about the formula for distance traveled. First of all, it is a nice example of the integral as an accumulator, since we are summing up bits of speed multiplied by bits of time, which equals bits of positive distance. Second, it is actually a new look at an old formula. Substitute dx/dt for $v_1(t)$ and dy/dt for $v_2(t)$ and you get the arc length formula for a curve defined parametrically (Section 11.1). This formula makes sense, since the distance the particle travels is precisely the length of the path along which it moves.

EXAMPLE 9 Finding Displacement and Distance Traveled

A particle moves in the plane with velocity vector $\mathbf{v}(t) = \langle t - 3\pi \cos \pi t, 2t - \pi \sin \pi t \rangle$. At $t = 0$, the particle is at the point $(1, 5)$.

(a) Find the position of the particle at $t = 4$.

(b) What is the total distance traveled by the particle from $t = 0$ to $t = 4$?

SOLUTION

(a) Displacement $= \left\langle \int_0^4 (t - 3\pi \cos \pi t)dt, \int_0^4 (2t - \pi \sin \pi t)dt \right\rangle = \langle 8, 16 \rangle$.

The particle is at the point $(1 + 8, 5 + 16) = (9, 21)$.

(b) Distance traveled $= \int_0^4 \sqrt{(t - 3\pi \cos \pi t)^2 + (2t - \pi \sin \pi t)^2}\, dt \approx 33.533$.

Now Try Exercise 39.

EXAMPLE 10 Finding the Path of the Particle

Determine the path that the particle in Example 9 travels going from (1, 5) to (9, 21).

SOLUTION

The velocity vector and the position at $t = 0$ combine to give us the vector equivalent of an initial value problem. We simply find the components of the position vector separately.

$$\frac{dx}{dt} = t - 3\pi \cos \pi t$$

$$x = \frac{t^2}{2} - 3 \sin \pi t + C \qquad \text{Antidifferentiate.}$$

$$x = \frac{t^2}{2} - 3 \sin \pi t + 1 \qquad x = 1 \text{ when } t = 0.$$

$$\frac{dy}{dt} = 2t - \pi \sin \pi t$$

$$y = t^2 + \cos \pi t + C \qquad \text{Antidifferentiate.}$$

$$y = t^2 + \cos \pi t + 4 \qquad y = 5 \text{ when } t = 0.$$

We then graph the position $\langle t^2/2 - 3 \sin \pi t + 1, t^2 + \cos \pi t + 4 \rangle$ parametrically from $t = 0$ to $t = 4$. The path is shown in Figure 11.19.

Now Try Exercise 43.

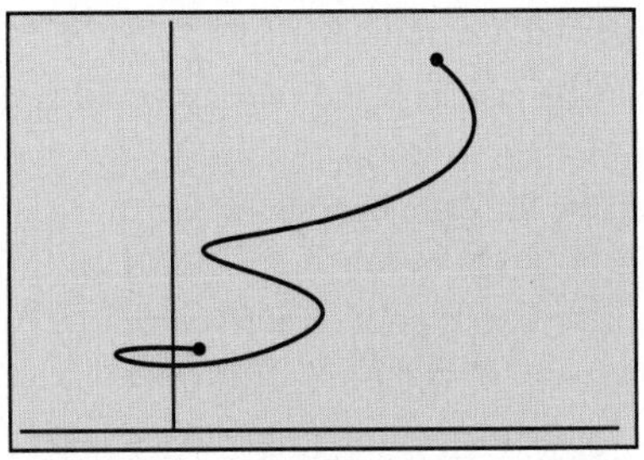

[–5, 15] by [0, 23]
$0 \le t \le 4$

Figure 11.19 The path traveled by the particle in Example 9 as it goes from (1, 5) to (9, 21) in four seconds. (Example 9)

Quick Review 11.2 *(For help, go to Sections 1.1, 5.3, and 11.1.)*

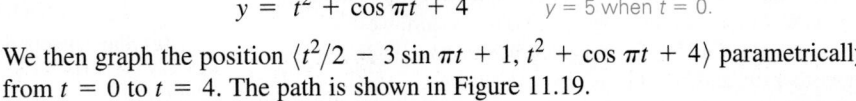

Exercise numbers with a gray background indicate problems that the authors have designed to be solved *without a calculator.*

In Exercises 1–4, let $P = (1, 2)$ and $Q = (5, 3)$.

1. Find the distance between the points P and Q.

2. Find the slope of the line segment PQ.

3. If $R = (3, b)$, determine b so that segments PQ and RQ are collinear.

4. If $R = (3, b)$, determine b so that segments PQ and RQ are perpendicular.

In Exercises 5 and 6, determine the missing coordinate so that the four points form a parallelogram $ABCD$.

5. $A = (0, 0), \quad B = (1, 3), \quad C = (5, 3), \quad D = (a, 0)$

6. $A = (1, 1), \quad B = (3, 5), \quad C = (8, b), \quad D = (6, 2)$

7. Find the velocity and acceleration of a particle moving along a line if its position at time t is given by $x(t) = t \sin t$.

8. A particle moves along the x-axis with velocity $v(t) = 3t^2 - 12t$ for $t \ge 0$. If its position is $x = 40$ when $t = 0$, where is the particle when $t = 4$?

9. A particle moves along the x-axis with velocity $v(t) = 3t^2 - 12t$ for $t \ge 0$. What is the total distance traveled by the particle from $t = 0$ to $t = 4$?

10. Find the length of the curve defined parametrically by $x = \sin(2t)$ and $y = \cos(3t)$ for $0 \le t \le 2\pi$.

Section 11.2 Exercises

In Exercises 1–4, find the component form of the vector.

1. the vector from the origin to the point $A = (2, 3)$

2. the vector from the point $A = (2, 3)$ to the origin

3. the vector $\overrightarrow{PQ}$, where $P = (1, 3)$ and $Q = (2, -1)$

4. the vector $\overrightarrow{OP}$, where O is the origin and P is the midpoint of the segment RS connecting $R = (2, -1)$ and $S = (-4, 3)$.

In Exercises 5–10, find the magnitude of the vector and the direction angle θ it forms with the positive x-axis $(0 < \theta < 360°)$.

5. $\langle 2, 2 \rangle$

6. $\langle -\sqrt{2}, \sqrt{2} \rangle$

7. $\langle \sqrt{3}, 1 \rangle$

8. $\langle -2, -2\sqrt{3} \rangle$

9. $\langle -5, 0 \rangle$

10. $\langle 0, 4 \rangle$

In Exercises 11–16, find the component form of the vector with the given magnitude that forms the given directional angle with the positive x-axis.

11. 4, 180°

12. 6, 270°

13. 5, 100°

14. 13, 200°

15. $3\sqrt{2}$, $\pi/4$ radians

16. $2\sqrt{3}$, $\pi/6$ radians

In Exercises 17–24, let $\mathbf{u} = \langle 3, -2 \rangle$ and $\mathbf{v} = \langle -2, 5 \rangle$ Find the **(a)** component form and **(b)** magnitude of the vector.

17. $3\mathbf{u}$

18. $-2\mathbf{v}$

19. $\mathbf{u} + \mathbf{v}$

20. $\mathbf{u} - \mathbf{v}$

21. $2\mathbf{u} - 3\mathbf{v}$

22. $-2\mathbf{u} + 5\mathbf{v}$

23. $\frac{3}{5}\mathbf{u} + \frac{4}{5}\mathbf{v}$

24. $-\frac{5}{13}\mathbf{u} + \frac{12}{13}\mathbf{v}$

25. ***Navigation*** An airplane, flying in the direction 20° east of north at 325 mph in still air, encounters a 40-mph tail wind acting in the direction 40° west of north. The airplane maintains its compass heading but, because of the wind, acquires a new ground speed and direction. What are they?

26. A river is flowing due east at 2 mph. A canoeist paddles across the river at 4 mph with his bow aimed directly northwest (a direction angle of 135°). What is the true direction angle of the canoeist's path, and how fast is the canoe going?

In Exercises 27–32, a particle travels in the plane with position vector $\mathbf{r}(t)$. Find **(a)** the velocity vector $\mathbf{v}(t)$ and **(b)** the acceleration vector $\mathbf{a}(t)$.

27. $\mathbf{r}(t) = \langle 3t^2, 2t^3 \rangle$

28. $\mathbf{r}(t) = \langle \sin 2t, 2\cos t \rangle$

29. $\mathbf{r}(t) = \langle te^{-t}, e^{-t} \rangle$

30. $\mathbf{r}(t) = \langle 2\cos 3t, 2\sin 4t \rangle$

31. $\mathbf{r}(t) = \langle t^2 + \sin 2t, t^2 - \cos 2t \rangle$

32. $\mathbf{r}(t) = \langle t\sin t, t\cos t \rangle$

33. A baseball leaves the bat at an angle of 55° from the horizontal traveling at 90 feet per second. A 20-foot boundary fence is 230 feet from the batter in a direct line of where the baseball is hit.

(a) Find the position vector of the baseball at time t (in seconds).

(b) Find the velocity vector of the baseball at time t (in seconds).

(c) Is the hit a home run?

(d) At what time t does the ball hit the fence or clear it for a home run? Illustrate with a graph and explain why the graph supports your solution.

(e) How fast is the ball traveling when it either hits the fence or passes over it?

34. Football A player punts the ball from his own 30-yard line at an angle of 57 degrees from horizontal, traveling at 81 feet per second. A 6-foot player from the opposing team is standing on his own 10-yard line to receive the punt.

(a) Find the position vector of the football at time t in seconds. Assume a 100-yard playing field.

(b) Find the velocity vector of the football at time t in seconds.

(c) About what time t is the football "over" the player on the 10-yard line?

(d) Can the 6-ft player call for a "fair catch" and likely catch the ball while standing on the 10-yard line downfield? Explain your reasoning and your assumptions.

35. A particle moves in the plane with position vector $\langle \cos 3t, \sin 2t \rangle$. Find the velocity and acceleration vectors and determine the path of the particle.

36. A particle moves in the plane with position vector $\langle \sin 4t, \cos 3t \rangle$. Find the velocity and acceleration vectors and determine the path of the particle.

37. A particle moves in the plane so that its position at any time $t \geq 0$ is given by $x = \sin 4t \cos t$ and $y = \sin 2t$.

(a) Find the velocity and speed of the particle when $t = 5\pi/4$.

(b) Draw the path of the particle and show the velocity vector at $t = 5\pi/4$.

(c) Is the particle moving to the left or to the right when $t = 5\pi/4$?

38. A particle moves in the plane so that its position at any time $t \geq 0$ is given by $x = e^t + e^{-t}$ and $y = e^t - e^{-t}$.

(a) Find the velocity vector.

(b) Find $\displaystyle\lim_{t\to\infty} \frac{dy/dt}{dx/dt}$.

(c) Show algebraically that the particle moves on the hyperbola $x^2 - y^2 = 4$.

(d) Sketch the path of the particle, showing the velocity vector at $t = 0$.

In Exercises 39–42, the velocity $\mathbf{v}(t)$ of a particle moving in the plane is given, along with the position of the particle at time $t = 0$. Find **(a)** the position of the particle at time $t = 3$, and **(b)** the distance the particle travels from $t = 0$ to $t = 3$.

39. $\mathbf{v}(t) = \langle 3t^2 - 2t, 1 + \cos \pi t \rangle$; $(2, 6)$

40. $\mathbf{v}(t) = \langle 2\pi\cos 4\pi t, 4\pi\sin 2\pi t \rangle$; $(7, 2)$

41. $\mathbf{v}(t) = \langle (t+1)^{-1}, (t+2)^{-2} \rangle$; $(3, -2)$

42. $\mathbf{v}(t) = \langle e^t - t, e^t + t \rangle$; $(1, 1)$

43. Sketch the path that the particle travels in Exercise 39.

44. Sketch the path that the particle travels in Exercise 40.

45. A point moves in the plane so that $x = 5\cos(\pi t/6)$ and $y = 3\sin(\pi t/6)$.

(a) Find the speed of the point at $t = 2$.

(b) Find the acceleration vector at $t = 2$.

(c) Eliminate the parameter and find an equation in x and y that defines the curve on which the point moves.

46. A particle moves with position vector $\langle \sec \pi t, \tan \pi t \rangle$ for $0 \le t < 1/2$.

(a) Find the velocity and speed of the particle at $t = 1/4$.

(b) The particle moves along a hyperbola. Eliminate the parameter to find an equation of the hyperbola in terms of x and y.

(c) Sketch the path of the particle over the time interval $0 \le t < 1/2$.

47. A particle moves on the circle $x^2 + y^2 = 1$ so that its position vector at any time $t \ge 0$ is $\left\langle \frac{1 - t^2}{1 + t^2}, \frac{2t}{1 + t^2} \right\rangle$.

(a) Find the velocity vector.

(b) Is the particle ever at rest? Justify your answer.

(c) Give the coordinates of the point that the particle approaches as t increases without bound.

48. A particle moves in the plane so that its position at any time t, $0 \le t \le 2\pi$, is given parametrically by $x = \sin t$ and $y = \cos(2t)$.

(a) Find the velocity vector for the particle.

(b) For what values of t is the particle at rest?

(c) Write an equation for the path of the particle in terms of x and y that does not involve trigonometric functions.

(d) Sketch the path of the particle.

49. A particle moves in the plane so that its position at any time t, $0 \le t \le 2\pi$, is given parametrically by $x = e^t \sin t$ and $y = e^t \cos t$.

(a) Find the slope of the path of the particle at time $t = \pi/2$.

(b) Find the speed of the particle when $t = 1$.

(c) Find the distance traveled by the particle along the path from $t = 0$ to $t = 1$.

50. The position of a particle at any time $t \ge 0$ is given by $x(t) = t^2 - 3$ and $y(t) = \frac{2}{3}t^3$.

(a) Find the magnitude of the velocity vector at $t = 4$.

(b) Find the total distance traveled by the particle from $t = 0$ to $t = 4$.

(c) Find dy/dx as a function of x.

51. An object moving along a curve in the xy-plane has position $(x(t), y(t))$ at time $t \ge 0$ with $dx/dt = 2 + \sin(t^2)$. The derivative dy/dt is not explicitly given. At time $t = 2$, the object is at position $(3, 5)$.

(a) Find the x-coordinate of the position of the object at time $t = 4$.

(b) At time $t = 2$, the value of dy/dt is -6. Write an equation for the line tangent to the curve at the point $(x(2), y(2))$.

(c) Find the speed of the object at time $t = 2$.

(d) For $t \ge 3$, the line tangent to the curve at $(x(t), y(t))$ has a slope of $2t - 1$. Find the acceleration vector of the object at time $t = 4$.

52. For $0 \le t \le 3$, an object moving along a curve in the xy-plane has position $(x(t), y(t))$ with $dx/dt = \sin(t^3)$ and $dy/dt = 3\cos(t^2)$. At time $t = 2$, the object is at position $(4, 5)$.

(a) Write an equation for the line tangent to the curve at $(4, 5)$.

(b) Find the speed of the object at time $t = 2$.

(c) Find the total distance traveled by the object over the time interval $0 \le t \le 1$.

(d) Find the position of the object at time $t = 3$.

Standardized Test Questions

You may use a graphing calculator to solve the following problems.

53. **True or False** A scalar multiple of a vector **v** has the same direction as **v**. Justify your answer.

54. **True or False** If a vector with direction angle 0° is added to a vector with direction angle 90°, the result is a vector with direction angle 45°. Justify your answer.

55. **Multiple Choice** The position of a particle in the xy-plane is given by $x = t^2 + 1$ and $y = \ln(2t + 3)$ for all $t \ge 0$. The acceleration vector of the particle is

(A) $\left(2t, \frac{2}{2t + 3}\right)$. **(B)** $\left(2t, -\frac{4}{(2t + 3)^2}\right)$. **(C)** $\left(2, \frac{4}{(2t + 3)^2}\right)$.

(D) $\left(2, \frac{2}{(2t + 3)^2}\right)$. **(E)** $\left(2, -\frac{4}{(2t + 3)^2}\right)$.

56. **Multiple Choice** An object moving along a curve in the xy-plane has position $(x(t), y(t))$ with $dx/dt = \cos(t^2)$ and $dy/dt = \sin(t^3)$. At time $t = 0$, the object is at position $(4, 7)$. Where is the particle when $t = 2$?

(A) $\langle -0.654, 0.989 \rangle$ **(B)** $\langle 0.461, 0.452 \rangle$ **(C)** $\langle 3.346, 7.989 \rangle$

(D) $\langle 4.461, 7.452 \rangle$ **(E)** $\langle 5.962, 8.962 \rangle$

57. **Multiple Choice** A vector with magnitude 7 and direction angle 40° is added to a vector with magnitude 4 and direction angle 140°. The result is a vector with magnitude

(A) 4.684. **(B)** 7.435. **(C)** 8.062. **(D)** 9.369. **(E)** 11.

58. **Multiple Choice** The path of a particle moving in the plane is defined parametrically as a function of time t by $x = \sin 2t$ and $y = \cos 5t$. What is the speed of the particle when $t = 2$?

(A) 1.130 **(B)** 3.018 **(C)** $\langle -1.307, 2.720 \rangle$

(D) $\langle 0.757, 0.839 \rangle$ **(E)** $\langle 1.307, 2.720 \rangle$

Explorations

Two nonzero vectors are said to be *orthogonal* if they are perpendicular to each other. The zero vector is considered to be orthogonal to every vector.

59. ***Orthogonal vectors*** A particle with coordinates (x, y) moves along a curve in the first quadrant in such a way that $dx/dt = -x$ and $dy/dt = \sqrt{1 - x^2}$ for every $t \ge 0$. Find the acceleration vector in terms of x and show that it is orthogonal to the corresponding velocity vector.

60. ***Orthogonal vectors*** A particle moves around the unit circle with position vector $\langle \cos t, \sin t \rangle$. Use vectors to show that the particle's velocity is always orthogonal to both its position and its acceleration.

61. ***Colliding particles*** The paths of two particles for $t \geq 0$ are given by the position vectors

$$\mathbf{r}_1(t) = \langle t - 3, (t - 3)^2 \rangle$$

$$\mathbf{r}_2(t) = \left\langle \frac{3t}{2} - 4, \frac{3t}{2} - 2 \right\rangle.$$

(a) Determine the exact time(s) at which the particles collide.

(b) Find the direction of motion of each particle at the time(s) of collision.

62. ***A Satellite in Circular Orbit*** A satellite of mass m is moving at a constant speed v around a planet of mass M in a circular orbit of radius r_0, as measured from the planet's center of mass. Determine the satellite's orbital period T (the time to complete one full orbit), as follows:

(a) Coordinatize the orbital plane by placing the origin at the planet's center of mass, with the satellite on the x-axis at $t = 0$ and moving counterclockwise, as in the accompanying figure.

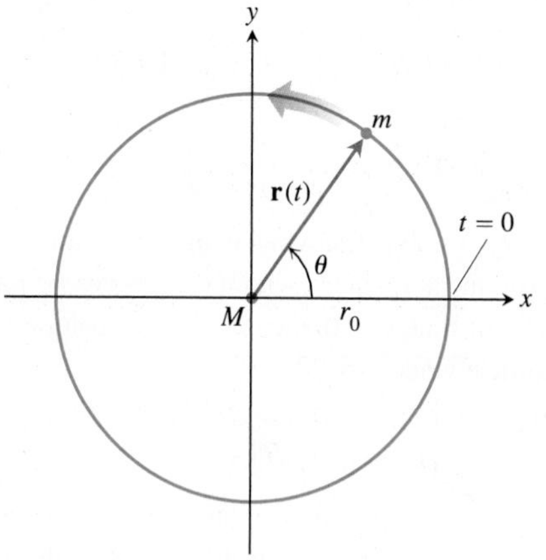

Let $\mathbf{r}(t)$ be the satellite's position vector at time t. Show that $\theta = vt/r_0$ and hence that

$$\mathbf{r}(t) = \left\langle r_0 \cos \frac{vt}{r_0}, r_0 \sin \frac{vt}{r_0} \right\rangle$$

(b) Find the acceleration of the satellite.

(c) According to Newton's law of gravitation, the gravitational force exerted on the satellite by the planet is directed toward the origin and is given by

$$\mathbf{F} = \left(-\frac{GmM}{r_0^2} \right) \frac{\mathbf{r}}{r_0},$$

where G is the universal constant of gravitation. Using Newton's second law, $\mathbf{F} = m\mathbf{a}$, show that $v^2 = GM/r_0$.

(d) Show that the orbital period T satisfies $vT = 2\pi r_0$.

(e) From parts (c) and (d), deduce that

$$T^2 = \frac{4\pi^2}{GM} r_0^3;$$

that is, the square of the period of a satellite in circular orbit is proportional to the cube of the radius from the orbital center.

63. Use the parametric graphing mode on your calculator to simulate the baseball problem in Example 6. Set $X_{1T} = 110T \cos(60°)$ and $Y_{1T} = 110T \sin(60°)$. Use TRACE to support the analytic results found in the example. [*Hint:* Use a $[0, 350]$ by $[-50, 200]$ window with Tstep = 0.001. Note that it will take a few minutes to fully graph with such a small Tstep increment.] Then use TRACE repeatedly (input 5 for 5 seconds, 5.5, 5.65, and so forth). Look at the y-coordinate after each TRACE input.

Extending the Ideas

Let $\mathbf{u} = \langle u_1, u_2 \rangle$ and $\mathbf{v} = \langle v_1, v_2 \rangle$ be vectors in the plane. The **dot product** or **inner product** $\mathbf{u} \cdot \mathbf{v}$ is a scalar defined by

$$\mathbf{u} \cdot \mathbf{v} = \langle u_1, u_2 \rangle \cdot \langle v_1, v_2 \rangle = u_1 v_1 + u_2 v_2.$$

64. ***Using the Dot Product*** Show that the dot product of two perpendicular vectors is zero.

65. ***An Alternate Formula for Dot Product*** Let $\mathbf{u} = \langle u_1, u_2 \rangle$ and $\mathbf{v} = \langle v_1, v_2 \rangle$ be vectors in the plane, and let $\mathbf{w} = \mathbf{u} - \mathbf{v}$.

(a) Explain why $\mathbf{w}$ can be represented by the arrow in the accompanying diagram.

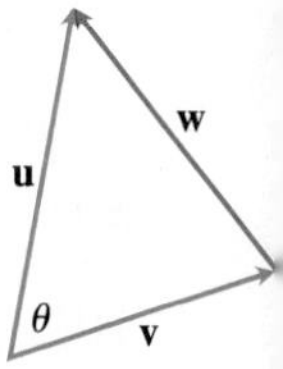

(b) Explain why $|\mathbf{w}|^2 = |\mathbf{u}|^2 + |\mathbf{v}|^2 - 2|\mathbf{u}||\mathbf{v}| \cos \theta$, where θ is the angle between vectors $\mathbf{u}$ and $\mathbf{v}$.

(c) Find the component form of $\mathbf{w}$ and use it to prove that

$$|\mathbf{u}|^2 + |\mathbf{v}|^2 - |\mathbf{w}|^2 = 2(u_1 v_1 + u_2 v_2).$$

(d) Finally, prove that $\mathbf{u} \cdot \mathbf{v} = |\mathbf{u}||\mathbf{v}| \cos \theta$, where θ is the angle between vectors $\mathbf{u}$ and $\mathbf{v}$.

11.3 Polar Functions

What you will learn about . . .

- Polar Coordinates
- Polar Curves
- Slopes of Polar Curves
- Areas Enclosed by Polar Curves
- A Small Polar Gallery

and why . . .

Polar equations enable us to define some interesting and important curves that would be difficult or impossible to define in the form $y = f(x)$.

Polar Coordinates

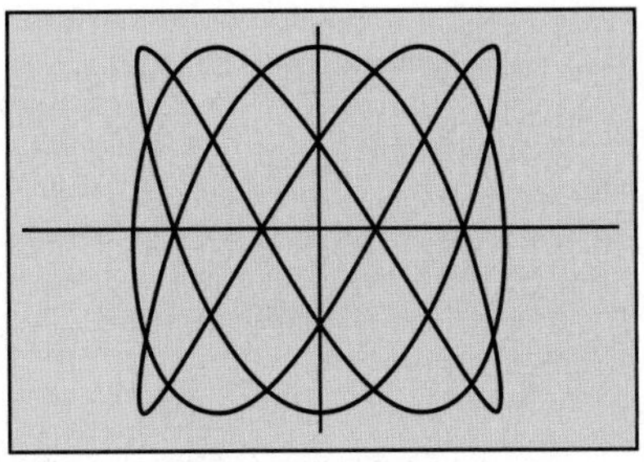

If you graph the two functions $y = \sin 3x$ and $y = \cos 5x$ on the same pair of axes, you will get two sinusoids. But if you graph the curve defined *parametrically* by $x = \sin 3t$ and $y = \cos 5t$, you will get the figure shown. Parametric graphing opens up a whole new world of curves that can be defined using our familiar basic functions.

Another way to enter that world is to use a different coordinate system. In **polar coordinates** we identify the origin O as the **pole** and the positive x-axis as the **initial ray** of angles measured in the usual trigonometric way. We can then identify each point P in the plane by polar coordinates (r, θ), where r gives the directed distance from O to P and θ gives the directed angle from the initial ray to the ray $\overrightarrow{OP}$. In Figure 11.20 we see that the point P with rectangular (Cartesian) coordinates $(2, 2)$ has polar coordinates $(2\sqrt{2}, \pi/4)$.

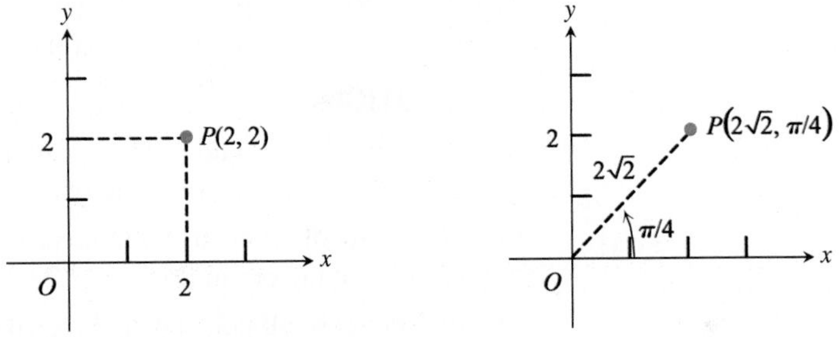

Rectangular coordinates

Polar coordinates

Figure 11.20 Point P has rectangular coordinates $(2, 2)$ and polar coordinates $(2\sqrt{2}, \pi/4)$.

As you would expect, we can also coordinatize point P with the polar coordinates $(2\sqrt{2}, 9\pi/4)$ or $(2\sqrt{2}, -7\pi/4)$, since those angles determine the same ray $\overrightarrow{OP}$. Less obviously, we can also coordinatize P with polar coordinates $(-2\sqrt{2}, -3\pi/4)$, since the *directed* distance $-2\sqrt{2}$ in the $-3\pi/4$ direction is the same as the directed distance $2\sqrt{2}$ in the $\pi/4$ direction (Figure 11.21). So, although each pair (r, θ) determines a unique point in the plane, each point in the plane can be coordinatized by an infinite number of polar ordered pairs.

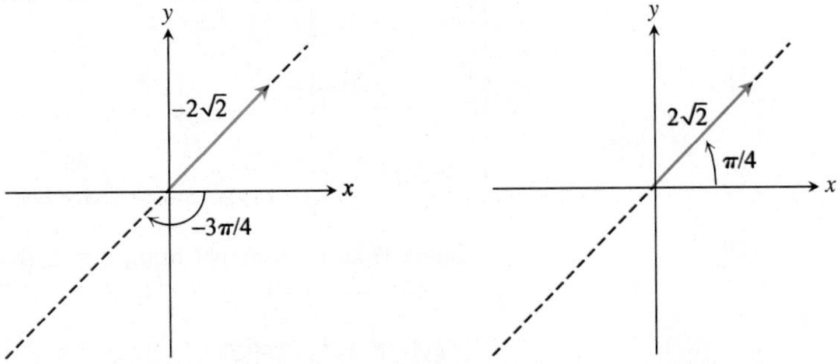

Figure 11.21 The directed *negative* distance $-2\sqrt{2}$ in the $-3\pi/4$ direction is the same as the directed *positive* distance $2\sqrt{2}$ in the $\pi/4$ direction. Thus the polar coordinates $(-2\sqrt{2}, -3\pi/4)$ and $(2\sqrt{2}, \pi/4)$ determine the same point.

EXAMPLE 1 Rectangular and Polar Coordinates

(a) Find rectangular coordinates for the points with given polar coordinates.

(i) $(4, \pi/2)$ **(ii)** $(-3, \pi)$ **(iii)** $(16, 5\pi/6)$ **(iv)** $(-\sqrt{2}, -\pi/4)$

(b) Find two different sets of polar coordinates for the points with given rectangular coordinates.

(i) $(1, 0)$ **(ii)** $(-3, 3)$ **(iii)** $(0, -4)$ **(iv)** $(1, \sqrt{3})$

SOLUTION

(a) (i) $(0, 4)$ **(ii)** $(3, 0)$ **(iii)** $(-8\sqrt{3}, 8)$ **(iv)** $(-1, 1)$

(b) A point has infinitely many sets of polar coordinates, so here we list just two typical examples for each given point.

(i) $(1, 0), (1, 2\pi)$ **(ii)** $(3\sqrt{2}, 3\pi/4), (-3\sqrt{2}, -\pi/4)$

(iii) $(4, -\pi/2), (4, 3\pi/2)$ **(iv)** $(2, \pi/3), (-2, 4\pi/3)$

Now Try Exercises 1 and 3.

EXAMPLE 2 Graphing with Polar Coordinates

Graph all points in the plane that satisfy the given polar equation

(a) $r = 2$ **(b)** $r = -2$ **(c)** $\theta = \pi/6$

SOLUTION

First, note that we do *not* label our axes r and θ. We are graphing *polar* equations in the usual xy-plane, not renaming our rectangular variables!

(a) The set of all points with directed distance 2 units from the pole is a circle of radius 2 centered at the origin (Figure 11.22a).

(b) The set of all points with directed distance -2 units from the pole is also a circle of radius 2 centered at the origin (Figure 11.22b).

(c) The set of all points of positive or negative directed distance from the pole in the $\pi/6$ direction is a line through the origin with slope $\tan(\pi/6)$ (Figure 11.22c).

Now Try Exercise 7.

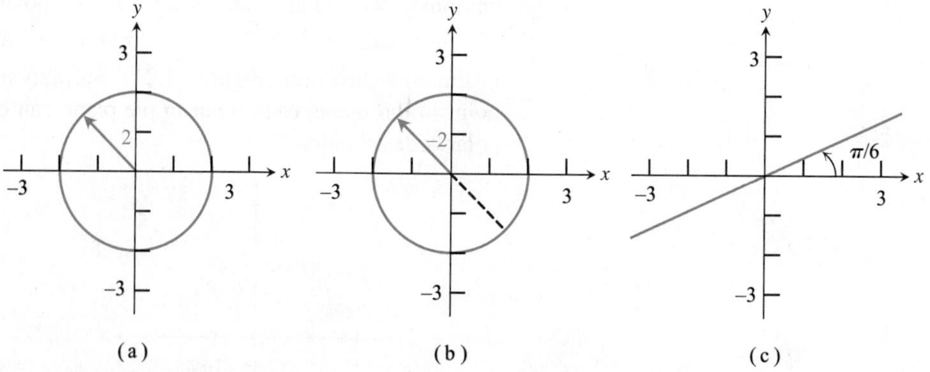

Figure 11.22 Polar graphs of (a) $r = 2$, (b) $r = -2$, and (c) $\theta = \pi/6$. (Example 2)

Polar Curves

The curves in Example 2 are a start, but we would not introduce a new coordinate system just to graph circles and lines; there are far more interesting polar curves to study. In the past it was hard work to produce reasonable polar graphs by hand, but today, thanks to graphing technology, it is just a matter of finding the right window and pushing the right buttons. Our intent in this section is to use the technology to produce the graphs and then concentrate on how calculus can be used to give us further information.

EXAMPLE 3 Polar Graphing with Technology

Find an appropriate graphing window and produce a graph of the polar curve.

(a) $r = \sin 6\theta$ **(b)** $r = 1 - 2\cos\theta$ **(c)** $r = 4\sin\theta$

SOLUTION

For all these graphs, set your calculator to POLAR mode.

(a) First we find the window. Notice that $|r| = |\sin 6\theta| \le 1$ for all θ, so points on the graph are all within 1 unit from the pole. We want a window at least as large as $[-1, 1]$ by $[-1, 1]$, but we choose the window $[-1.5, 1.5]$ by $[-1, 1]$ in order to keep the *aspect ratio* close to the screen dimensions, which have a ratio of 3:2. We choose a θ-range of $0 \le \theta \le 2\pi$ to get a full rotation around the graph, after which we know that $\sin 6\theta$ will repeat the same graph periodically. Choose θ step $= 0.05$. The result is shown in Figure 11.23a.

(b) In this graph we notice that $|r| = |1 - 2\cos\theta| \le 3$, so we choose $[-3, 3]$ for our y-range and, to get the right aspect ratio, $[-4.5, 4.5]$ for our x-range. Due to the cosine's period, $0 \le \theta \le 2\pi$ again suffices for our θ-range. The graph is shown in Figure 11.23b.

(c) Since $|r| = |4\sin\theta| \le 4$, we choose $[-4, 4]$ for our y-range and $[-6, 6]$ for our x-range. Due to the sine's period, $0 \le \theta \le 2\pi$ again suffices for our θ-range. The graph is shown in Figure 11.23c.

Now Try Exercise 13.

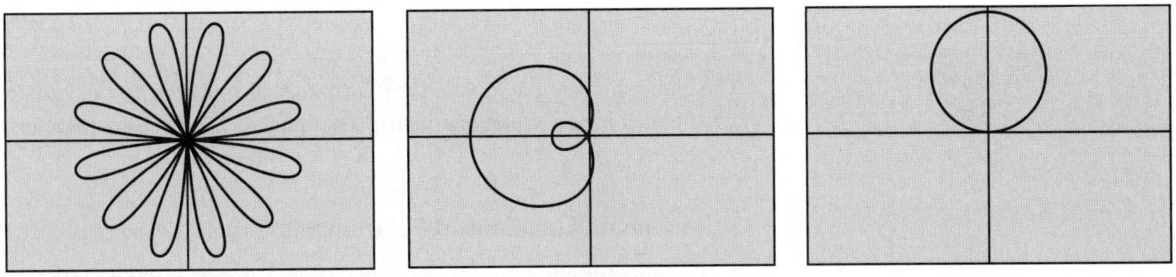

[−1.5, 1.5] by [−1, 1]
$0 \le \theta \le 2\pi$

(a)

[−4.5, 4.5] by [−3, 3]
$0 \le \theta \le 2\pi$

(b)

[−6, 6] by [−4, 4]
$0 \le \theta \le 2\pi$

(c)

Figure 11.23 The graphs of the three polar curves in Example 3. The curves are (a) a 12-petaled rose, (b) a limaçon, and (c) a circle.

A Rose is a Rose

The graph in Figure 11.23a is called a 12-petaled rose, because it looks like a flower and some flowers are roses. The graph in Figure 11.23b is called a limaçon (LEE-ma-sohn) from an old French word for *snail.* We will have more names for you at the end of the section.

With a little experimentation, it is possible to improve on the "safe" windows we chose in Example 3 (at least in parts (b) and (c)), but it is always a good idea to keep a 3:2 ratio of the x-range to the y-range so that shapes do not become distorted. Also, an astute observer may have noticed that the graph in part (c) was traversed *twice* as θ went from 0 to 2π, so a range of $0 \le \theta \le \pi$ would have sufficed to produce the entire graph. From 0 to π, the circle is swept out by positive r-values; then from π to 2π, the same circle is swept out by negative r-values.

Although the graph in Figure 11.23c certainly looks like a circle, how can we tell for sure that it really is? One way is to convert the polar equation to a Cartesian equation and verify that it is the equation of a circle. Trigonometry gives us a simple way to convert polar equations to rectangular equations and vice versa.

Polar–Rectangular Conversion Formulas

$$x = r\cos\theta \qquad r^2 = x^2 + y^2$$

$$y = r\sin\theta \qquad \tan\theta = \frac{y}{x}$$

EXAMPLE 4 Converting Polar to Rectangular

Use the polar–rectangular conversion formulas to show that the polar graph of $r = 4\sin\theta$ is a circle.

SOLUTION

To facilitate the substitutions, multiply both sides of the original equation by r. (This could introduce extraneous solutions with $r = 0$, but the pole is the only such point, and we notice that it is already on the graph.)

$$r = 4\sin\theta$$

$$r^2 = 4r\sin\theta \qquad \text{Multiply by } r.$$

$$x^2 + y^2 = 4y \qquad \text{Polar–rectangular conversion}$$

$$x^2 + y^2 - 4y = 0$$

$$x^2 + y^2 - 4y + 4 = 4 \qquad \text{Completing the square}$$

$$x^2 + (y-2)^2 = 2^2 \qquad \text{Circle in standard form}$$

Sure enough, the graph is a circle centered at (0, 2) with radius 2. See Figure 11.23c for graphing calculator support of the analytic solution.

Now Try Exercise 25.

The polar–rectangular conversion formulas also reveal the calculator's secret to polar graphing: It is really just parametric graphing with θ as the parameter.

Parametric Equations of Polar Curves

The polar graph of $r = f(\theta)$ is the curve defined parametrically by:

$$x = r\cos\theta = f(\theta)\cos\theta$$

$$y = r\sin\theta = f(\theta)\sin\theta$$

EXPLORATION 1 Graphing Polar Curves Parametrically

Switch your grapher to parametric mode and enter the equations

$$x = \sin(6t)\cos t$$

$$y = \sin(6t)\sin t.$$

1. Set an appropriate window and see if you can reproduce the polar graph in Figure 11.23a.
2. Then produce the graphs in Figures 11.23b and 11.23c in the same way.

Slopes of Polar Curves

Since polar curves are drawn in the *xy*-plane, the *slope* of a polar curve is still the slope of the tangent line, which is dy/dx. The polar–rectangular conversion formulas enable us to write x and y as functions of θ, so we can find dy/dx as we did with parametrically defined functions:

$$\frac{dy}{dx} = \frac{dy/d\theta}{dx/d\theta}.$$

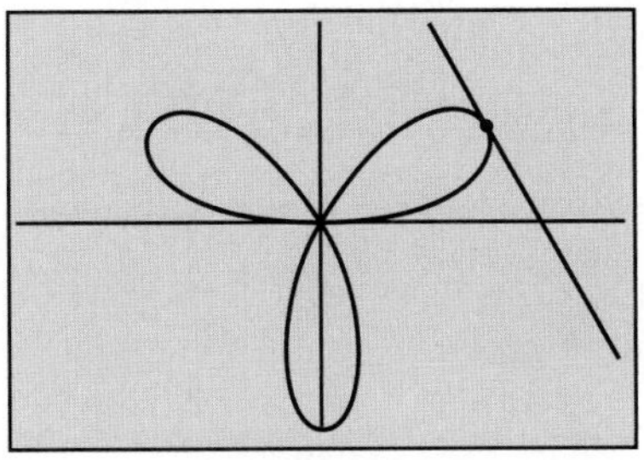

[–3, 3] by [–2, 2]
$0 \le \theta \le \pi$

Figure 11.24 The 3-petaled rose curve $r = 2 \sin 3\theta$. Example 5 shows how to find the tangent line to the curve at $\theta = \pi/6$.

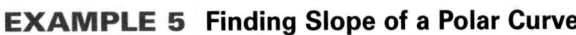

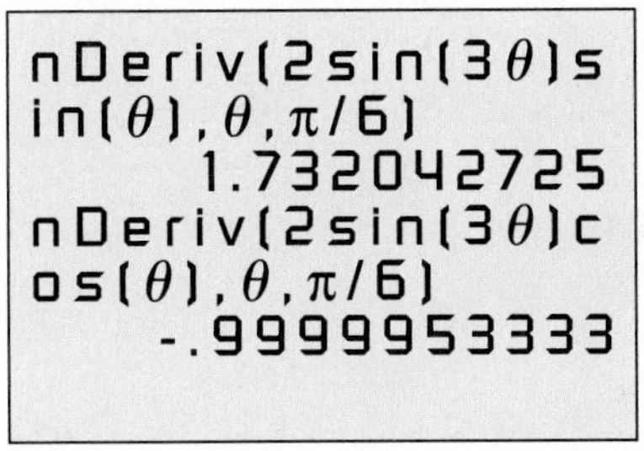

Figure 11.25 NDER (Section 3.2) applied to $\frac{dy/d\theta}{dx/d\theta}$ and evaluated at $\theta = \frac{\pi}{6}$ supports numerically that the slope of $r = 2 \sin 3\theta$ at $\theta = \pi/6$ is $-1.7320\ldots$, or $-\sqrt{3}$.

EXAMPLE 5 Finding Slope of a Polar Curve

Find the slope of the rose curve $r = 2 \sin 3\theta$ at the point where $\theta = \pi/6$ and use it to find the equation of the tangent line (Figure 11.24).

SOLUTION

By substitution using the parametric representation of the polar equation $r = 2 \sin 3\theta$, we have

$$x = r \cos \theta = 2 \sin 3\theta \cos \theta$$
$$y = r \sin \theta = 2 \sin 3\theta \sin \theta.$$

So, the slope is

$$\left.\frac{dy}{dx}\right|_{\theta=\frac{\pi}{6}} = \left.\frac{dy/d\theta}{dx/d\theta}\right|_{\theta=\frac{\pi}{6}} = \left.\frac{\frac{d}{d\theta}(2 \sin 3\theta \sin\theta)}{\frac{d}{d\theta}(2 \sin 3\theta \cos\theta)}\right|_{\theta=\frac{\pi}{6}}$$

Using the derivative product rule on both the numerator and denominator, you can compute analytically that the slope is $-\sqrt{3}$. See Figure 11.25 for numerical support.

When $\theta = \pi/6$,

$$x = 2 \sin(\pi/2) \cos(\pi/6) = \sqrt{3} \quad \text{and} \quad y = 2 \sin(\pi/2) \sin(\pi/6) = 1.$$

So the tangent line has equation $y - 1 = -\sqrt{3}\,(x - \sqrt{3})$.

Now Try Exercise 39.

Areas Enclosed by Polar Curves

We would like to be able to use numerical integration to find areas enclosed by polar curves just as we did with curves defined by their rectangular coordinates. Converting the equations to rectangular coordinates is not a reasonable option for most polar curves, so we would like to have a formula involving small changes in θ rather than small changes in x. While a small change Δx produces a thin *rectangular* strip of area, a small change $\Delta\theta$ produces a thin *circular sector* of area (Figure 11.26).

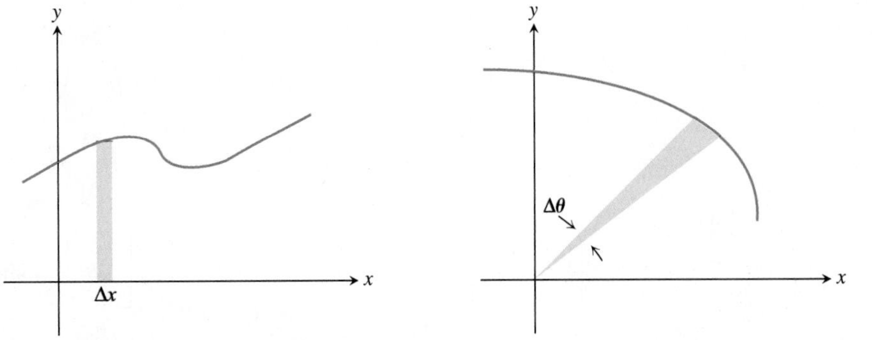

Figure 11.26 A small change in x produces a rectangular strip of area, while a small change in θ produces a thin *sector* of area.

Recall from geometry that the area of a sector of a circle is $\frac{1}{2}r^2\theta$, where r is the radius and θ is the central angle measured in radians. If we replace θ by the differential $d\theta$, we get the **area differential** $dA = \frac{1}{2}r^2 d\theta$ (Figure 11.27), which is exactly the quantity that we need to integrate to get an area in polar coordinates.

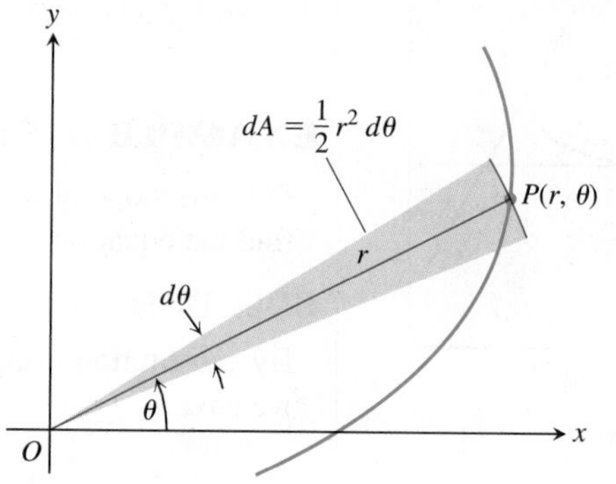

Figure 11.27 The area differential dA.

Area in Polar Coordinates

The area of the region between the origin and the curve $r = f(\theta)$ for $\alpha \le \theta \le \beta$ is

$$A = \int_{\alpha}^{\beta} \frac{1}{2} r^2 d\theta = \int_{\alpha}^{\beta} \frac{1}{2}(f(\theta))^2\,d\theta.$$

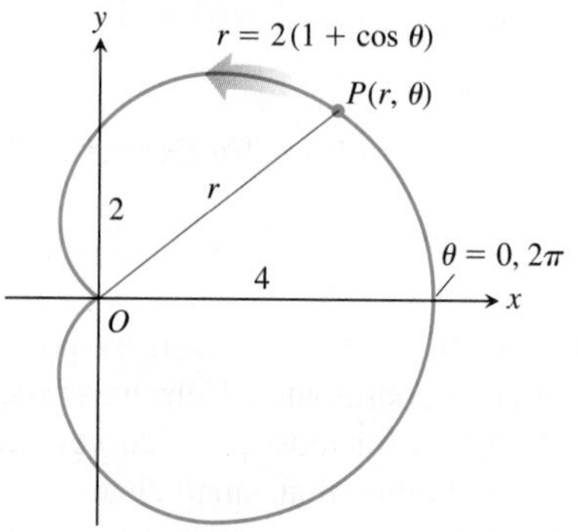

Figure 11.28 The cardioid in Example 6.

EXAMPLE 6 Finding Area

Find the area of the region in the plane enclosed by the cardioid $r = 2(1 + \cos\theta)$.

SOLUTION

We graph the cardioid (Figure 11.28) and determine that the *radius OP* sweeps out the region exactly once as θ runs from 0 to 2π.

Solve Analytically The area is therefore

$$\int_{\theta=0}^{\theta=2\pi} \frac{1}{2}r^2\,d\theta = \int_0^{2\pi} \frac{1}{2}\cdot 4(1+\cos\theta)^2\,d\theta$$

$$= \int_0^{2\pi} 2(1 + 2\cos\theta + \cos^2\theta)\,d\theta$$

$$= \int_0^{2\pi} \left(2 + 4\cos\theta + 2\frac{1+\cos 2\theta}{2}\right) d\theta$$

$$= \int_0^{2\pi} (3 + 4\cos\theta + \cos 2\theta)\,d\theta$$

$$= \left[3\theta + 4\sin\theta + \frac{\sin 2\,\theta}{2}\right]_0^{2\pi} = 6\pi - 0 = 6\pi.$$

Support Numerically NINT $(2(1 + \cos\theta)^2, \theta, 0, 2\pi) = 18.84955592$, which agrees with 6π to eight decimal places.

Now Try Exercise 43.

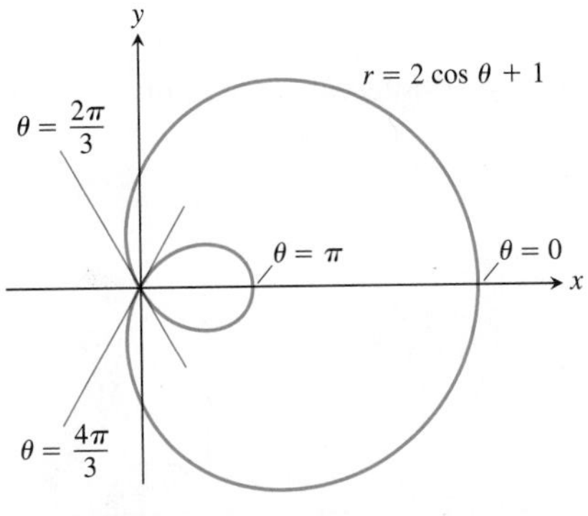

Figure 11.29 The limaçon in Example 7.

EXAMPLE 7 Finding Area

Find the area inside the smaller loop of the limaçon $r = 2\cos\theta + 1$.

SOLUTION

After watching the grapher generate the curve over the interval $0 \le \theta \le 2\pi$ (Figure 11.29), we see that the smaller loop is traced by the point (r, θ) as θ increases from $\theta = 2\pi/3$ to $\theta = 4\pi/3$ (the values for which $r = 2\cos\theta + 1 = 0$). The area we seek is

$$A = \int_{2\pi/3}^{4\pi/3} \frac{1}{2} r^2 \, d\theta = \frac{1}{2} \int_{2\pi/3}^{4\pi/3} (2\cos\theta + 1)^2 \, d\theta.$$

Solve Numerically

$$\frac{1}{2}\text{NINT}\left((2\cos\theta + 1)^2, \theta, 2\pi/3, 4\pi/3\right) \approx 0.544.$$

Now Try Exercise 47.

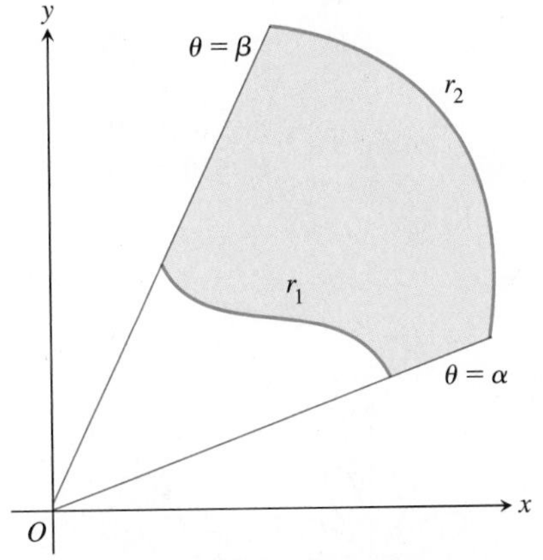

Figure 11.30 The area of the shaded region is calculated by subtracting the area of the region between r_1 and the origin from the area of the region between r_2 and the origin.

To find the area of a region like the one in Figure 11.30, which lies between two polar curves $r_1 = r_1(\theta)$ and $r_2 = r_2(\theta)$ from $\theta = \alpha$ to $\theta = \beta$, we subtract the integral of $(1/2)r_1^2$ from the integral of $(1/2)r_2^2$. This leads to the following formula.

Area Between Polar Curves

The area of the region between $r_1(\theta)$ and $r_2(\theta)$ for $\alpha \le \theta \le \beta$ is

$$A = \int_\alpha^\beta \frac{1}{2} r_2^2 \, d\theta - \int_\alpha^\beta \frac{1}{2} r_1^2 \, d\theta = \int_\alpha^\beta \frac{1}{2}(r_2^2 - r_1^2)\, d\theta.$$

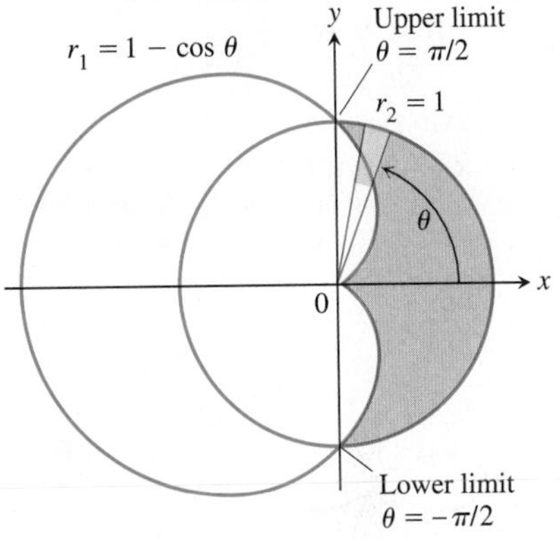

Figure 11.31 The region and limits of integration in Example 8.

EXAMPLE 8 Finding Area Between Curves

Find the area of the region that lies inside the circle $r = 1$ and outside the cardioid $r = 1 - \cos\theta$.

SOLUTION

The region is shown in Figure 11.31. The outer curve is $r_2 = 1$, the inner curve is $r_1 = 1 - \cos\theta$, and θ runs from $-\pi/2$ to $\pi/2$. Using the formula for the area between polar curves, the area is

$$A = \int_{-\pi/2}^{\pi/2} \frac{1}{2}(r_2^2 - r_1^2)\, d\theta$$

$$= 2\int_0^{\pi/2} \frac{1}{2}(r_2^2 - r_1^2)\, d\theta \qquad \text{Symmetry}$$

$$= \int_0^{\pi/2} (1 - (1 - 2\cos\theta + \cos^2\theta))\, d\theta$$

$$= \int_0^{\pi/2} \left(2\cos\theta - \left(\frac{1 + \cos 2\theta}{2}\right)\right) d\theta$$

$$= 2\sin\theta - \left(\frac{\theta}{2} + \frac{\sin 2\theta}{4}\right)\Bigg|_0^{\pi/2} = 2 - \frac{\pi}{4} \approx 1.215$$

The analytic solution can be numerically supported using NINT on a calculator, as shown in Figure 11.32.

Now Try Exercise 53.

Figure 11.32 NINT (Section 6.2) applied to the integrand and limits of integration given in Example 8.

A SMALL POLAR GALLERY

Here are a few of the more common polar graphs and the θ-intervals that can be used to produce them.

CIRCLES

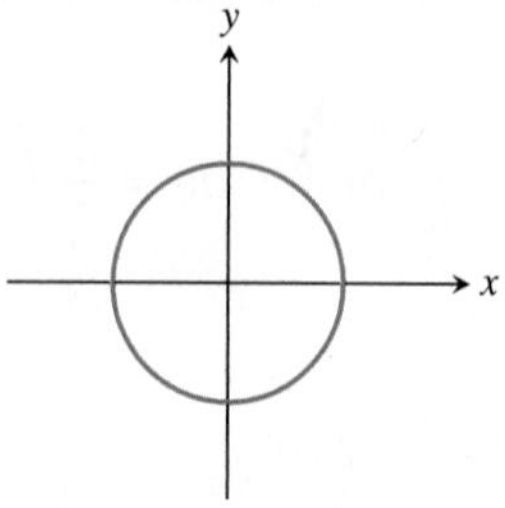

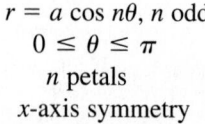

$r =$ constant
$0 \le \theta \le 2\pi$

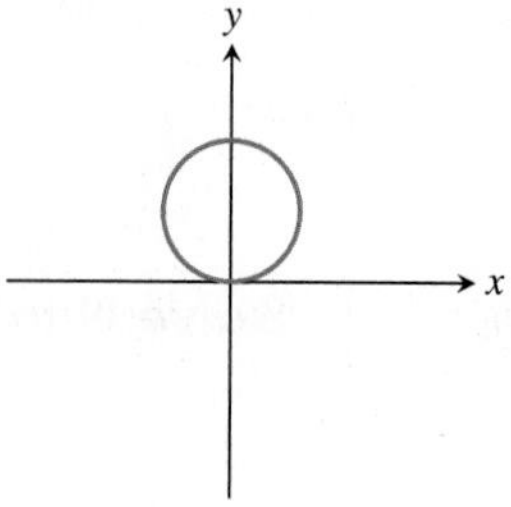

$r = a \sin \theta$
$0 \le \theta \le \pi$

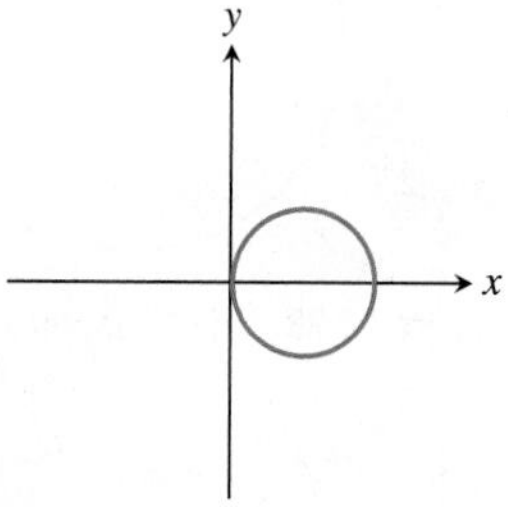

$r = a \cos \theta$
$0 \le \theta \le \pi$

ROSE CURVES

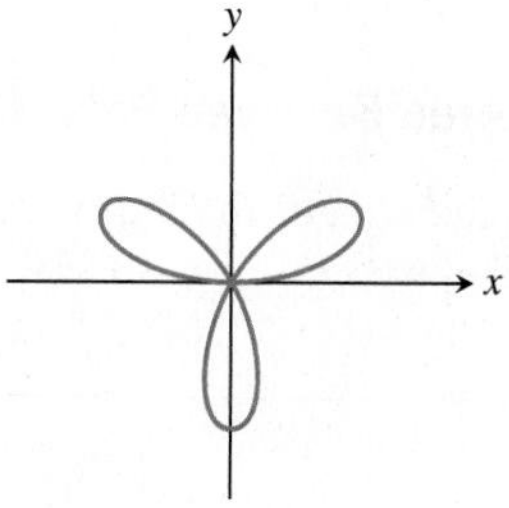

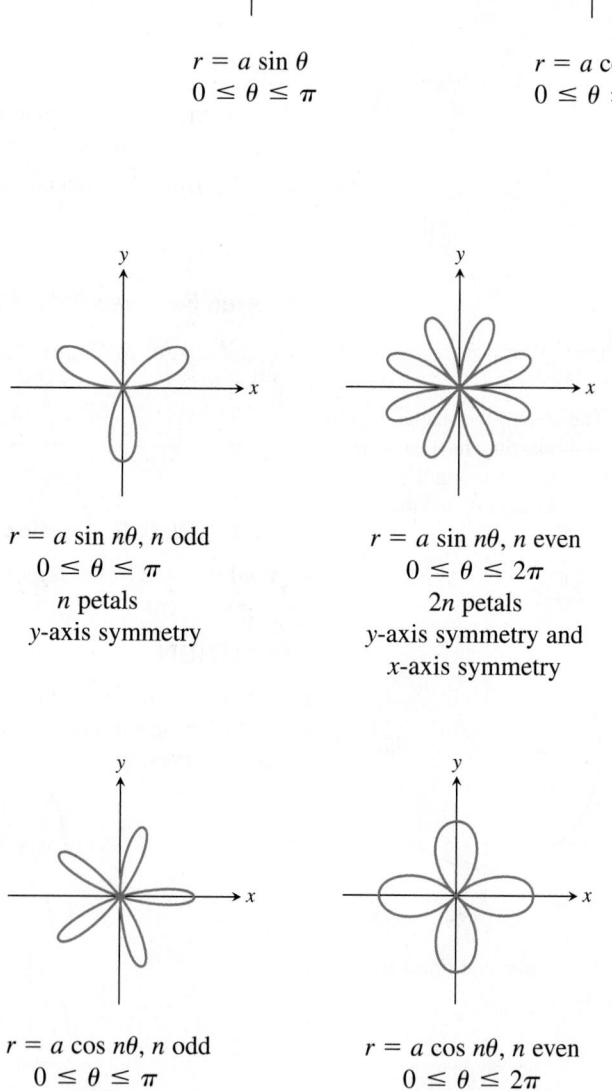

$r = a \sin n\theta$, n odd
$0 \le \theta \le \pi$
n petals
y-axis symmetry

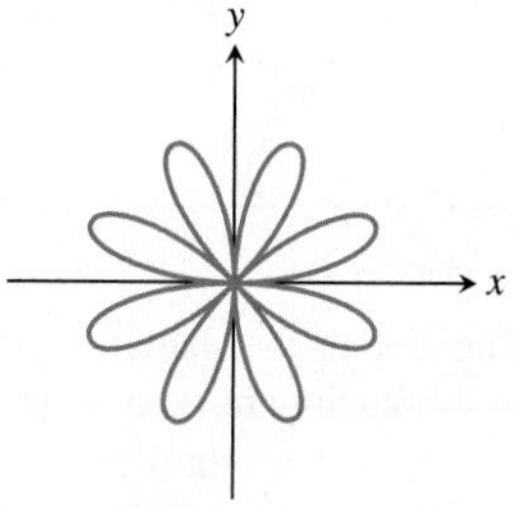

$r = a \sin n\theta$, n even
$0 \le \theta \le 2\pi$
$2n$ petals
y-axis symmetry and
x-axis symmetry

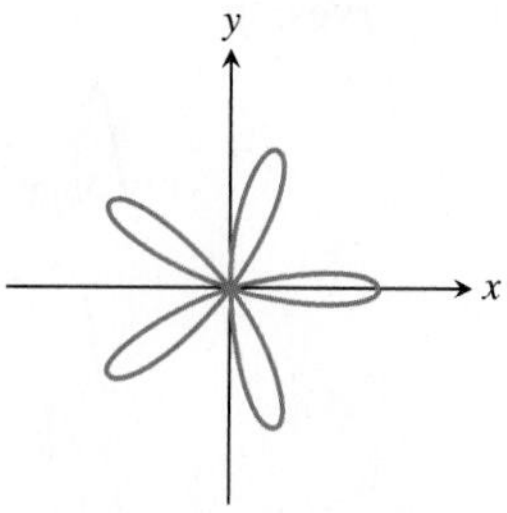

$r = a \cos n\theta$, n odd
$0 \le \theta \le \pi$
n petals
x-axis symmetry

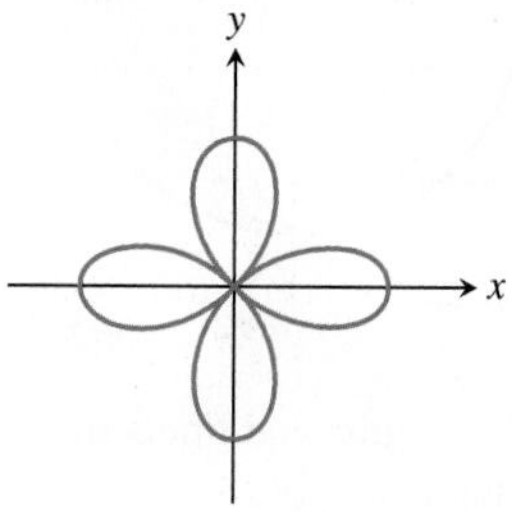

$r = a \cos n\theta$, n even
$0 \le \theta \le 2\pi$
$2n$ petals
y-axis symmetry and
x-axis symmetry

LIMAÇON CURVES

$r = a \pm b \sin \theta$ or $r = a \pm b \cos \theta$ with $a > 0$ and $b > 0$
($r = a \pm b \sin \theta$ has y-axis symmetry; $r = a \pm b \cos \theta$ has x-axis symmetry.)

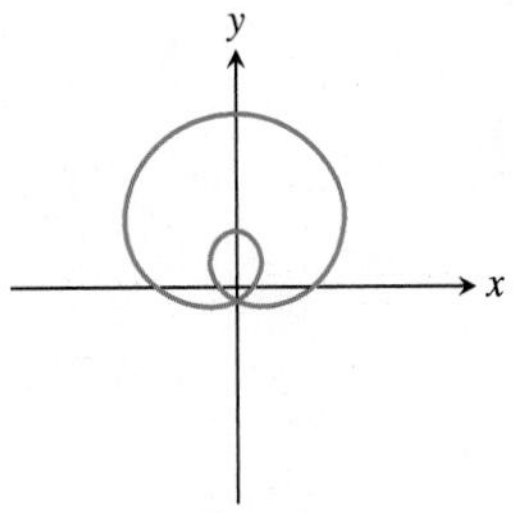

$\frac{a}{b} < 1$
$0 \leq \theta \leq 2\pi$
Limaçon with loop

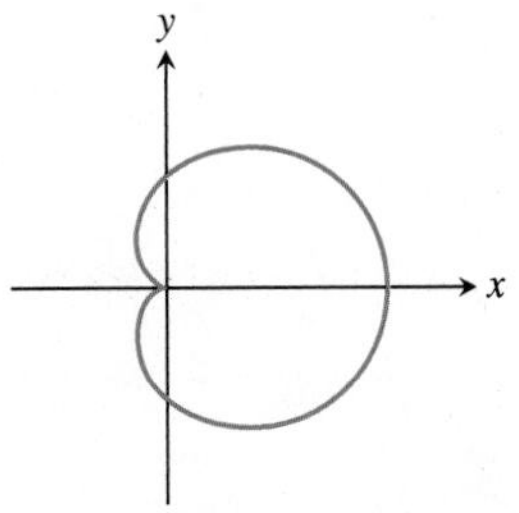

$\frac{a}{b} = 1$
$0 \leq \theta \leq 2\pi$
Cardioid

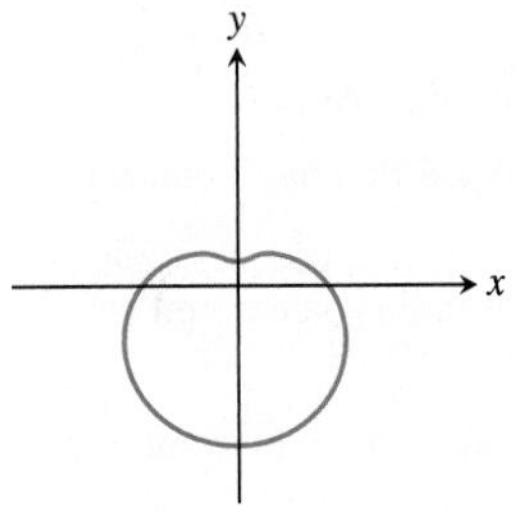

$1 < \frac{a}{b} < 2$
$0 \leq \theta \leq \pi$
Dimpled limaçon

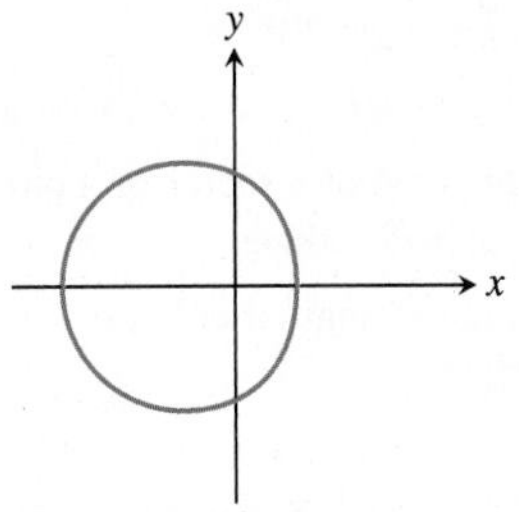

$\frac{a}{b} \geq 2$
$0 \leq \theta \leq 2\pi$
Convex limaçon

LEMNISCATE CURVES

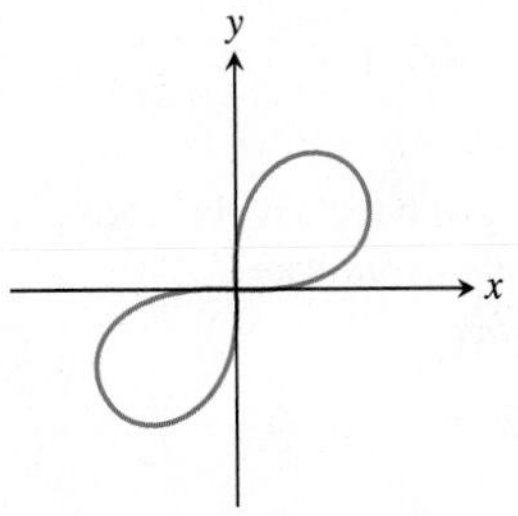

$r^2 = a^2 \sin 2\theta$
$0 \leq \theta \leq \pi$

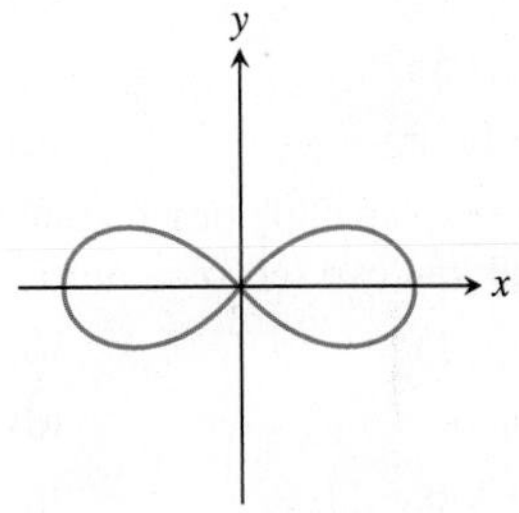

$r^2 = a^2 \sin 2\theta$
$0 \leq \theta \leq \pi$

Spiral of Archimedes

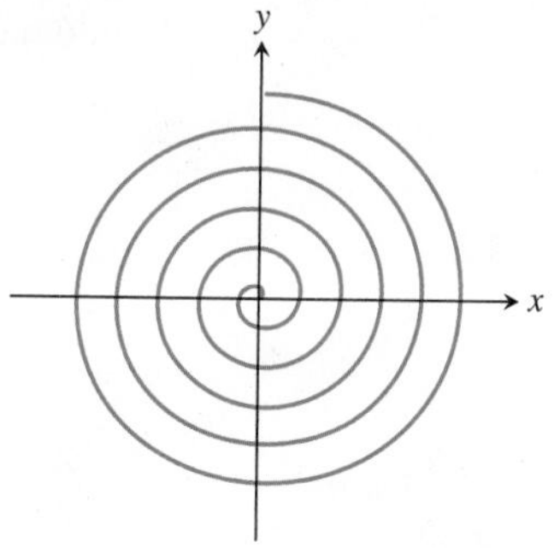

$r = \theta > 0$

Quick Review 11.3 *(For help, go to Sections 11.1 and 11.2.)*

Exercise numbers with a gray background indicate problems that the authors have designed to be solved *without a calculator*.

1. Find the component form of a vector with magnitude 4 and direction angle 30°.

2. Find the area of a 30° sector of a circle of radius 6.

3. Find the area of a sector of a circle of radius 8 that has a central angle of $\pi/8$ radians.

4. Find the rectangular equation of a circle of radius 5 centered at the origin.

5. Explain how to use your calculator in function mode to graph the curve $x^2 + 3y^2 = 4$.

Exercises 6–10 refer to the parametrized curve

$$x = 3\cos t,\ y = 5\sin t,\ 0 \le t \le 2\pi.$$

6. Find dy/dx.

7. Find the slope of the curve at $t = 2$.

8. Find the points on the curve where the slope is zero.

9. Find the points on the curve where the slope is undefined.

10. Find the length of the curve from $t = 0$ to $t = \pi$.

Section 11.3 Exercises

In Exercises 1 and 2, plot each point with the given polar coordinates and find the corresponding rectangular coordinates.

1. **(a)** $(\sqrt{2}, \pi/4)$ **(b)** $(1, 0)$
(c) $(0, \pi/2)$ **(d)** $(-\sqrt{2}, \pi/4)$

2. **(a)** $(-3, 5\pi/6)$ **(b)** $(5, \tan^{-1}(4/3))$
(c) $(-1, 7\pi)$ **(d)** $(2\sqrt{3}, 2\pi/3)$

In Exercises 3 and 4, plot each point with the given rectangular coordinates and find two sets of corresponding polar coordinates.

3. **(a)** $(-1, 1)$ **(b)** $(1, -\sqrt{3})$
(c) $(0, 3)$ **(d)** $(-1, 0)$

4. **(a)** $(-\sqrt{3}, -1)$ **(b)** $(3, 4)$
(c) $(0, -2)$ **(d)** $(2, 0)$

In Exercises 5–10, graph the set of points whose polar coordinates satisfy the given equation.

5. $r = 3$ **6.** $r = -3$

7. $r^2 = 4$ **8.** $\theta = -\pi/4$

9. $|\theta| = \pi/6$ **10.** $r^2 + 8 = 6r$

In Exercises 11–20, find an appropriate window and use a graphing calculator to produce the polar curve. Then sketch the complete curve and identify the type of curve by name.

11. $r = 1 + \cos\theta$ **12.** $r = 2 - 2\cos\theta$

13. $r = 2\cos 3\theta$ **14.** $r = -3\sin 2\theta$

15. $r = 1 - 2\sin\theta$ **16.** $r = 3/2 + \cos\theta$

17. $r^2 = 4\cos 2\theta$ **18.** $r^2 = \sin 2\theta$

19. $r = 4\sin\theta$ **20.** $r = 3\cos\theta$

In Exercises 21–30, use analytic methods to replace the polar equation by an equivalent Cartesian (rectangular) equation. Then identify or describe the graph without using a grapher.

21. $r = 4\csc\theta$ **22.** $r = -3\sec\theta$

23. $r\cos\theta + r\sin\theta = 1$ **24.** $r^2 = 1$

25. $r = \dfrac{5}{\sin\theta - 2\cos\theta}$ **26.** $r^2\sin 2\theta = 2$

27. $\cos^2\theta = \sin^2\theta$ **28.** $r^2 = -4r\cos\theta$

29. $r = 8\sin\theta$ **30.** $r = 2\cos\theta + 2\sin\theta$

In Exercises 31–38, find an appropriate window and use a graphing calculator to produce the polar curve. Then sketch the complete curve and identify the type of curve by name. (*Note*: You won't find these in the Polar Gallery.)

31. $r = \sec\theta\tan\theta$

32. $r = -\csc\theta\cot\theta$

33. $r = \dfrac{1}{1+\cos\theta}$

34. $r = \dfrac{2}{1-\sin\theta}$

35. $r = \dfrac{14}{5+9\cos\theta}$

36. $r = \dfrac{12}{8+6\cos\theta}$

37. $r = \dfrac{1}{1-0.8\cos\theta}$

38. $r = \dfrac{1}{1-1.3\cos\theta}$

In Exercises 39–42, find the slope of the curve at each indicated point.

39. $r = -1 + \sin\theta,\ \theta = \theta,\ \pi$

40. $r = \cos 2\theta,\ \theta = 0,\ \pm\pi/2\ ,\ \pi$

41. $r = 2 - 3\sin\theta$

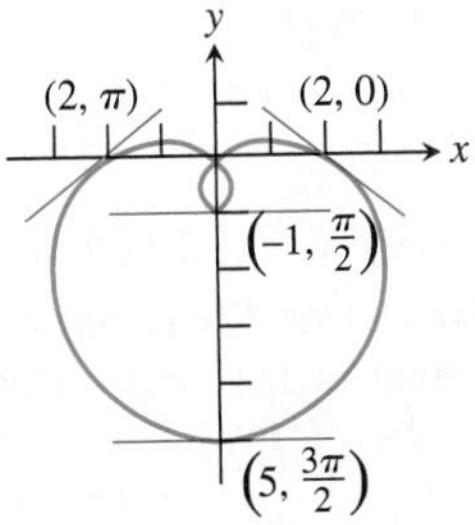

42. $r = 3(1 - \cos\theta)$

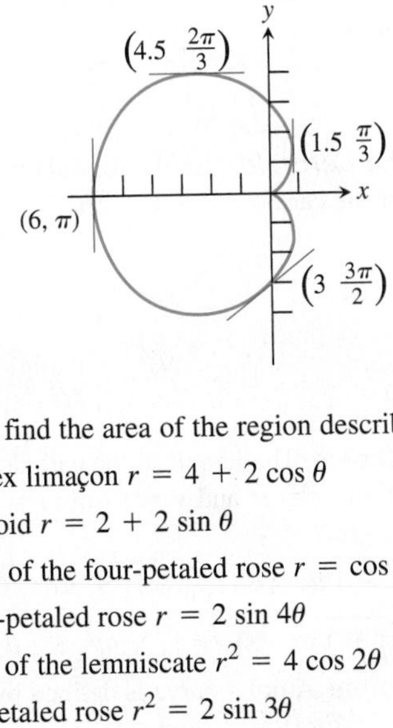

In Exercises 43–56, find the area of the region described.

43. inside the convex limaçon $r = 4 + 2\cos\theta$

44. inside the cardioid $r = 2 + 2\sin\theta$

45. inside one petal of the four-petaled rose $r = \cos 2\theta$

46. inside the eight-petaled rose $r = 2\sin 4\theta$

47. inside one loop of the lemniscate $r^2 = 4\cos 2\theta$

48. inside the six-petaled rose $r^2 = 2\sin 3\theta$

49. inside the dimpled limaçon $r = 3 - 2\cos\theta$

50. inside the inner loop of the limaçon $r = 2\sin\theta - 1$

51. shared by the circles $r = 2\cos\theta$ and $r = 2\sin\theta$

52. shared by the circles $r = 1$ and $r = 2\sin\theta$

53. shared by the circle $r = 2$ and the cardioid $r = 2\,(1 - \cos\theta)$

54. shared by the cardioids $r = 2(1 + \cos\theta)$ and $r = 2\,(1 - \cos\theta)$

55. inside the circle $r = 2$ and outside the cardioid $r = 2\,(1 - \sin\theta)$

56. inside the four-petaled rose $r = 4\cos 2\theta$ and outside the circle $r = 2$

57. Sketch the polar curves $r = 3\cos\theta$ and $r = 1 + \cos\theta$ and find the area that lies inside the circle and outside the cardioid.

58. Sketch the polar curves $r = 2$ and $r = 2(1 - \sin\theta)$ and find the area that lies inside the circle and outside the cardioid.

59. Sketch the polar curve $r = 2\sin 3\theta$. Find the area enclosed by the curve and find the slope of the curve at the point where $\theta = \pi/4$.

60. The accompanying figure shows the parts of the graphs of the line $x = \frac{5}{3}y$ and the curve $x = \sqrt{1+y^2}$ that lie in the first quadrant. Region R is enclosed by the line, the curve, and the x-axis.

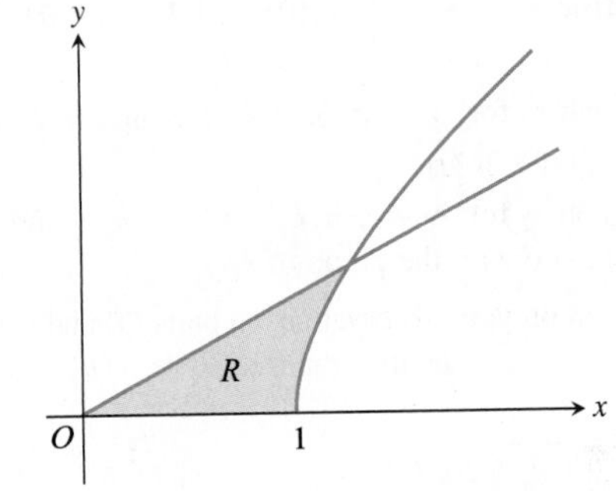

(a) Set up and evaluate an integral expression with respect to y that gives the area of R.

(b) Show that the curve $x = \sqrt{1+y^2}$ can be described in polar coordinates by $r^2 = \dfrac{1}{\cos^2\theta - \sin^2\theta}$.

(c) Use the polar equation in part (b) to set up an integral expression with respect to θ that gives the area of R.

Standardized Test Questions

You may use a graphing calculator to solve the following problems.

61. True or False There is exactly one point in the plane with polar coordinates (2, 2). Justify your answer.

62. True or False The total area enclosed by the 3-petaled rose $r = \sin 3\theta$ is $\int_0^{2\pi}\frac{1}{2}\sin^2 3\theta d\theta$. Justify your answer.

63. Multiple Choice The area of the region enclosed by the polar graph of $r = \sqrt{3+\cos\theta}$ is given by which integral?

(A) $\int_0^{2\pi}\sqrt{3+\cos\theta}\,d\theta$ **(B)** $\int_0^{\pi}\sqrt{3+\cos\theta}\,d\theta$

(C) $2\int_0^{\pi/2}(3+\cos\theta)\,d\theta$ **(D)** $\int_0^{\pi}(3+\cos\theta)\,d\theta$

(E) $\int_0^{\pi/2}\sqrt{3+\cos\theta}\,d\theta$

64. Multiple Choice The area enclosed by one petal of the 3-petaled rose $r = 4\cos(3\theta)$ is given by which integral?

(A) $16\int_{-\pi/3}^{\pi/3}\cos(3\theta)\,d\theta$ **(B)** $8\int_{-\pi/6}^{\pi/6}\cos(3\theta)\,d\theta$

(C) $8\int_{-\pi/3}^{\pi/3}\cos^2(3\theta)\,d\theta$ **(D)** $16\int_{-\pi/6}^{\pi/6}\cos^2(3\theta)\,d\theta$

(E) $8\int_{-\pi/6}^{\pi/6}\cos^2(3\theta)\,d\theta$

65. Multiple Choice If $a \neq 0$ and $\theta \neq 0$, all of the following must necessarily represent the same point in polar coordinates *except* which ordered pair?

(A) (a, θ) (B) $(-a, -\theta)$ (C) $(-a, \theta - \pi)$

(D) $(-a, \theta + \pi)$ (E) $(a, \theta - 2\pi)$

66. Multiple Choice Which of the following gives the slope of the polar curve $r = f(\theta)$ graphed in the xy-plane?

(A) $\dfrac{dr}{d\theta}$ (B) $\dfrac{dy}{d\theta}$ (C) $\dfrac{dx}{d\theta}$ (D) $\dfrac{dy/d\theta}{dx/d\theta}$ (E) $\dfrac{dy}{dx}\dfrac{dr}{d\theta}$

Explorations

67. *Rotating Curves* Let $r_1(\theta) = 3(1 - \cos\theta)$ and $r_2(\theta) = r_1(\theta - \alpha)$.

(a) Graph r_2 for $\alpha = \pi/6, \pi/4, \pi/3$, and $\pi/2$ and compare with the graph of r_1.

(b) Graph r_2 for $\alpha = -\pi/6, -\pi/4, -\pi/3$, and $-\pi/2$ and compare with the graph of r_1.

(c) Based on your observations in parts (a) and (b), describe the relationship between the graphs of $r_1 = f(\theta)$ and $r_2 = f(\theta - \alpha)$.

68. Let $r = \dfrac{2}{1 + k\cos\theta}$.

(a) Graph r in a square viewing window for $k = 0.1, 0.3, 0.5, 0.7$, and 0.9. Describe the graphs.

(b) Based on your observations in part (a), conjecture what happens to the graphs for $0 < k < 1$ and $k \to 0^+$.

69. Let $r = \dfrac{2}{1 + k\cos\theta}$.

(a) Graph r in a square viewing window for $k = 1.1, 1.3, 1.5, 1.7$, and 1.9. Describe the graphs.

(b) Based on your observations in part (a), conjecture what happens to the graphs for $k > 1$ and $k \to 1^+$.

70. Let $r = \dfrac{k}{1 + \cos\theta}$.

(a) Graph r in a square viewing window for $k = 1, 3, 5, 7$, and 9. Describe the graphs.

(b) Based on your observations in part (a), conjecture what happens to the graphs for $k > 0$ and $k \to 0^+$.

Extending the Ideas

71. *Distance Formula* Show that the distance between two points (r_1, θ_1) and (r_2, θ_2) in polar coordinates is

$$d = \sqrt{r_1^2 + r_2^2 - 2r_1r_2\cos(\theta_1 - \theta_2)}.$$

72. *Average Value* If f is continuous, the average value of the polar coordinate r over the curve $r = f(\theta)$, $\alpha \le \theta \le \beta$, with respect to θ is

$$r_{av} = \frac{1}{\beta - \alpha}\int_\alpha^\beta f(\theta)\,d\theta.$$

Use this formula to find the average value of r with respect to θ over the following curves $(a > 0)$.

(a) the cardioid $r = a(1 - \cos\theta)$

(b) the circle $r = a$

(c) the circle $r = a\cos\theta$, $-\pi/2 \le \theta \le \pi/2$

73. *Length of a Polar Curve* The parametric form of the arc length formula (Section 11.1) gives the length of a polar curve as

$$L = \int_\alpha^\beta \sqrt{\left(\frac{dx}{d\theta}\right)^2 + \left(\frac{dy}{d\theta}\right)^2}\,d\theta.$$

Assuming that the necessary derivatives are continuous, show that the substitutions $x = r\cos\theta$ and $y = r\sin\theta$ transform this expression into

$$L = \int_\alpha^\beta \sqrt{r^2 + \left(\frac{dr}{d\theta}\right)^2}\,d\theta.$$

74. *Length of a Cardioid* Use the formula in Exercise 73 to find the length of the cardioid $r = 1 + \cos\theta$.

Quick Quiz for AP* Preparation: Sections 11.1–11.3

You may use a graphing calculator to solve the following problems.

1. Multiple Choice Which of the following is equal to the area of the region inside the polar curve $r = 2\cos\theta$ and outside the polar curve $r = \cos\theta$?

(A) $3\int_0^{\pi/2}\cos^2\theta\,d\theta$ (B) $3\int_0^{\pi}\cos^2\theta\,d\theta$

(C) $\frac{3}{2}\int_0^{\pi/2}\cos^2\theta\,d\theta$ (D) $3\int_0^{\pi/2}\cos\theta\,d\theta$

(E) $3\int_0^{\pi}\cos\theta\,d\theta$

2. Multiple Choice For what values of t does the curve given by the parametric equations $x = t^3 - t^2 - 1$ and $y = t^4 + 2t^2 - 8t$ have a vertical tangent?

(A) 0 only (B) 1 only

(C) 0 and 2/3 only (D) 0, 2/3, and 1

(E) No value

3. Multiple Choice The length of the path described by the parametric equations $x = t^2$ and $y = t$ from $t = 0$ to $t = 4$ is given by which integral?

(A) $\int_0^4\sqrt{4t + 1}\,dt$ (B) $2\int_0^4\sqrt{t^2 + 1}\,dt$ (C) $\int_0^4\sqrt{2t^2 + 1}\,dt$

(D) $\int_0^4\sqrt{4t^2 + 1}\,dt$ (E) $2\pi\int_0^4\sqrt{4t^2 + 1}\,dt$

4. Free Response A polar curve is defined by the equation $r = \theta + \sin 2\theta$ for $0 \le \theta \le \pi$.

(a) Find the area bounded by the curve and the x-axis.

(b) Find the angle θ that corresponds to the point on the curve where $x = -2$.

(c) For $\dfrac{\pi}{3} < \theta < \dfrac{2\pi}{3}$, $\dfrac{dr}{d\theta}$ is negative. How can this be seen from the graph?

(d) At what angle θ in the interval $0 \le \theta \le \pi/2$ is the curve farthest away from the origin? Justify your answer.

Chapter 11 Key Terms

Absolute value of a vector (p. 544)
Acceleration vector (p. 548)
Archimedes spiral (p. 564)
Arc length of a parametrized curve (p. 539)
Arc length of a polar curve (p. 566)
Area between polar curves (p. 561)
Area differential (p. 560)
Area in polar coordinates (p. 560)
Arrow (p. 544)
Cardioid (p. 563)
Cartesian equation of a curve (p. 557)
Component form of a vector (p. 545)
Components of a vector (p. 544)
Convex limaçon (p. 563)
Cycloid (p. 539)
Dimpled limaçon (p. 563)
Directed distance (p. 555)
Directed line segment (p. 544)
Direction angle of a vector (p. 545)
Direction of motion (p. 548)
Direction vector (p. 544)
Displacement (p. 550)
Distance traveled (p. 550)
Dot product of vectors (p. 554)
Equivalent arrows (p. 545)
Head Minus Tail Rule (p. 545)
Huygens's clock (p. 540)
Initial point of an arrow (p. 545)
Initial ray of angle of direction (p. 555)
Lemniscate (p. 563)
Limaçon (p. 563)
Limaçon with inner loop (p. 563)
Magnitude of a vector (p. 544)
Opposite of a vector (p. 546)
Orthogonal vectors (p. 553)
Parallelogram representation of vector addition (p. 546)
Parametric equations of a polar curve (p. 558)
Parametric formula for dy/dx (p. 538)
Parametric formula for d^2y/dx^2 (p. 538)
Path of a particle (p. 548)
Polar coordinates (p. 555)
Polar equation of a curve (p. 556)
Polar graphing (p. 556)
Polar–rectangular conversion formulas (p. 558)
Pole (p. 555)
Position of a particle (p. 548)
Position vector (p. 544)
Properties of vectors (p. 547)
Rectangular coordinates (p. 552)
Resultant vector (p. 546)
Rose curve (p. 562)
Scalar (p. 545)
Scalar multiple of a vector (p. 546)
Speed (p. 548)
Standard representation of a vector (p. 544)
Sum of vectors (p. 546)
Tail-to-head representation of vector addition (p. 546)
Terminal point of an arrow (p. 545)
Unit vector (p. 546)
Vector (p. 544)
Vector addition (p. 545)
Velocity vector (p. 548)
Zero vector (p. 544)

Chapter 11 Review Exercises

In Exercises 1–4, let $\mathbf{u} = \langle -3, 4\rangle$ and $\mathbf{v} = \langle 2, -5\rangle$. Find **(a)** the component form of the vector and **(b)** its magnitude.

1. $3\mathbf{u} - 4\mathbf{v}$ **2.** $\mathbf{u} + \mathbf{v}$ **3.** $-2\mathbf{u}$ **4.** $5\mathbf{v}$

In Exercises 5–8, find the component form of the vector.

5. the vector obtained by rotating $\langle 0, 1\rangle$ through an angle of $2\pi/3$ radians

6. the unit vector that makes an angle of $\pi/6$ radian with the positive x-axis

7. the vector 2 units long in the direction $4\mathbf{i} - \mathbf{j}$

8. the vector 5 units long in the direction opposite to the direction of $\langle 3/5, 4/5\rangle$

In Exercises 9 and 10, **(a)** find an equation for the tangent to the curve at the point corresponding to the given value of t, and **(b)** find the value of d^2y/dx^2 at this point.

9. $x = (1/2)\tan t,\ y = (1/2)\sec t;\ t = \pi/3$

10. $x = 1 + 1/t^2,\ y = 1 - 3/t;\ t = 2$

In Exercises 11–14, find the points at which the tangent to the curve is **(a)** horizontal; **(b)** vertical.

11. $x = (1/2)\tan t,\ y = (1/2)\sec t$

12. $x = -2\cos t,\ y = 2\sin t$

13. $x = -\cos t,\ y = \cos^2 t$ **14.** $x = 4\cos t,\ y = 9\sin t$

In Exercises 15–20, find an appropriate window and graph the polar curve on a graphing calculator. Then sketch the curve on paper and identify the type of curve.

15. $r = 1 - \sin\theta$ **16.** $r = 2 + \cos\theta$

17. $r = \cos 2\theta$ **18.** $r\cos\theta = 1$

19. $r^2 = \sin 2\theta$ **20.** $r = -\sin\theta$

In Exercises 21 and 22, find the slope of the tangent lines at the point where $\theta = \pi/3$.

21. $r = \cos 2\theta$ **22.** $r = 2 + \cos 2\theta$

In Exercises 23 and 24, find equations for the horizontal and vertical tangent lines to the curves.

23. $r = 1 - \cos(\theta/2),\ 0 \le \theta \le 4\pi$

24. $r = 2(1 - \sin\theta),\ 0 \le \theta \le 2\pi$

25. Find equations for the lines that are tangent to the tips of the petals of the four-petaled rose $r = \sin 2\theta$.

26. Find equations for the lines that are tangent to the cardioid $r = 1 + \sin\theta$ at the points where it crosses the x-axis.

In Exercises 27–30, replace the polar equation by an equivalent Cartesian equation. Then identify or describe the graph.

27. $r\cos\theta = r\sin\theta$ **28.** $r = 3\cos\theta$

29. $r = 4\tan\theta\sec\theta$ **30.** $r\cos(\theta + \pi/3) = 2\sqrt{3}$

In Exercises 31–34, replace the Cartesian equation by an equivalent polar equation.

31. $x^2 + y^2 + 5y = 0$ **32.** $x^2 + y^2 - 2y = 0$

33. $x^2 + 4y^2 = 16$ **34.** $(x + 2)^2 + (y - 5)^2 = 16$

In Exercises 35–38, find the area of the region described.

35. enclosed by the limaçon $r = 2 - \cos\theta$

36. enclosed by one petal of the three-petaled rose $r = \sin 3\theta$

37. inside the "figure eight" $r = 1 + \cos 2\theta$ and outside the circle $r = 1$

38. inside the cardioid $r = 2(1 + \sin\theta)$ and outside the circle $r = 2\sin\theta$

In Exercises 39 and 40, $\mathbf{r}(t)$ is the position vector of a particle moving in the plane at time t. Find **(a)** the velocity and acceleration vectors, and **(b)** the speed at the given value of t.

39. $\mathbf{r}(t) = \langle 4\cos t, \sqrt{2}\sin t\rangle,\ t = \pi/4$

40. $\mathbf{r}(t) = \langle \sqrt{3}\sec t, \sqrt{3}\tan t\rangle, t = 0$

41. The position of a particle in the plane at time t is

$\mathbf{r} = \left\langle \frac{1}{\sqrt{1 + t^2}}, \frac{t}{\sqrt{1 + t^2}} \right\rangle$. Find the particle's maximum speed.

42. *Writing to Learning* Suppose that $\mathbf{r}(t) = \langle e^t\cos t, e^t\sin t\rangle$. Show that the angle between $\mathbf{r}$ and the acceleration vector $\mathbf{a}$ never changes. What is the angle?

In Exercises 43–46, find the position vector.

43. $\mathbf{v}(t) = \langle -\sin t, \cos t\rangle$ and $\mathbf{r}(0) = \langle 0, 1\rangle$

44. $\mathbf{v}(t) = \left\langle \frac{1}{t^2 + 1}, \frac{t}{\sqrt{t^2 + 1}} \right\rangle$ and $\mathbf{r}(0) = \langle 1, 1\rangle$

45. $\mathbf{a}(t) = \langle 0, 2\rangle$ and $\mathbf{v}(0) = \langle 0, 0\rangle$ and $\mathbf{r}(0) = \langle 1, 0\rangle$,

46. $\mathbf{a}(t) = \langle -2, -2\rangle$ and $\mathbf{v}(1) = \langle 4, 0\rangle$ and $\mathbf{r}(1) = \langle 3, 3\rangle$

47. *Particle Motion* A particle moves in the plane in such a manner that its coordinates at time t are

$$x = 3\cos\frac{\pi}{4}t,\quad y = 5\sin\frac{\pi}{4}t.$$

(a) Find the length of the velocity vector at $t = 3$.
(b) Find the x- and y-components of the acceleration of the particle at $t = 3$.
(c) Find a single equation in x and y for the path of the particle.

48. *Particle Motion* At time t, $0 \le t \le 4$, the position of a particle moving along a path in the plane is given by the parametric equations

$$x = e^t\cos t,\quad y = e^t\sin t.$$

(a) Find the slope of the path of the particle at time $t = \pi$.
(b) Find the speed of the particle when $t = 3$.
(c) Find the distance traveled by the particle along the path from $t = 0$ to $t = 3$.

49. *Particle Motion* The position of a particle at any time $t \ge 0$ is given by

$$x(t) = t^2 - 2,\quad y(t) = \frac{2}{5}t^3.$$

(a) Find the magnitude of the velocity vector at $t = 4$.
(b) Find the total distance traveled by the particle from $t = 0$ to $t = 4$.
(c) Find dy/dx as a function of x.

50. *Navigation* An airplane, flying in the direction 80° east of north at 540 mph in still air, encounters a 55-mph tail wind acting in the direction 100° east of north. The airplane holds its compass heading but, because of the wind, acquires a different ground speed and direction. What are they?

AP* Examination Preparation

You may use a graphing calculator to solve the following problems.

51. A particle moves along the graph of $y = \cos x$ so that its x-component of acceleration is always 2. At time $t = 0$, the particle is at the point $(\pi, -1)$ and the velocity of the particle is $\langle 0, 0\rangle$.

(a) Find the position vector of the particle.
(b) Find the speed of the particle when it is at the point $(4, \cos 4)$.

52. Two particles move in the xy-plane. For time $t \ge 0$, the position of particle A is given by $x = t - 2$ and $y = (t - 2)^2$, and the position of particle B is given by $x = \frac{3}{2}t - 4$ and $y = \frac{3}{2}t - 2$.

(a) Find the velocity vector for each particle at time $t = 3$.
(b) Find the distance traveled by particle A from $t = 0$ to $t = 3$.
(c) Determine the exact time when the particles collide.

53. A region R in the xy-plane is bounded below by the x-axis and above by the polar curve defined by $r = \frac{4}{1 + \sin\theta}$ for $0 \le \theta \le \pi$.

(a) Find the area of R by evaluating an integral in polar coordinates.
(b) The curve resembles an arch of the parabola $8y = 16 - x^2$. Convert the polar equation to rectangular coordinates and prove that the curves are the same.
(c) Set up an integral in rectangular coordinates that gives the area of R.

Chapter 12

Vectors and Analytic Geometry in Space

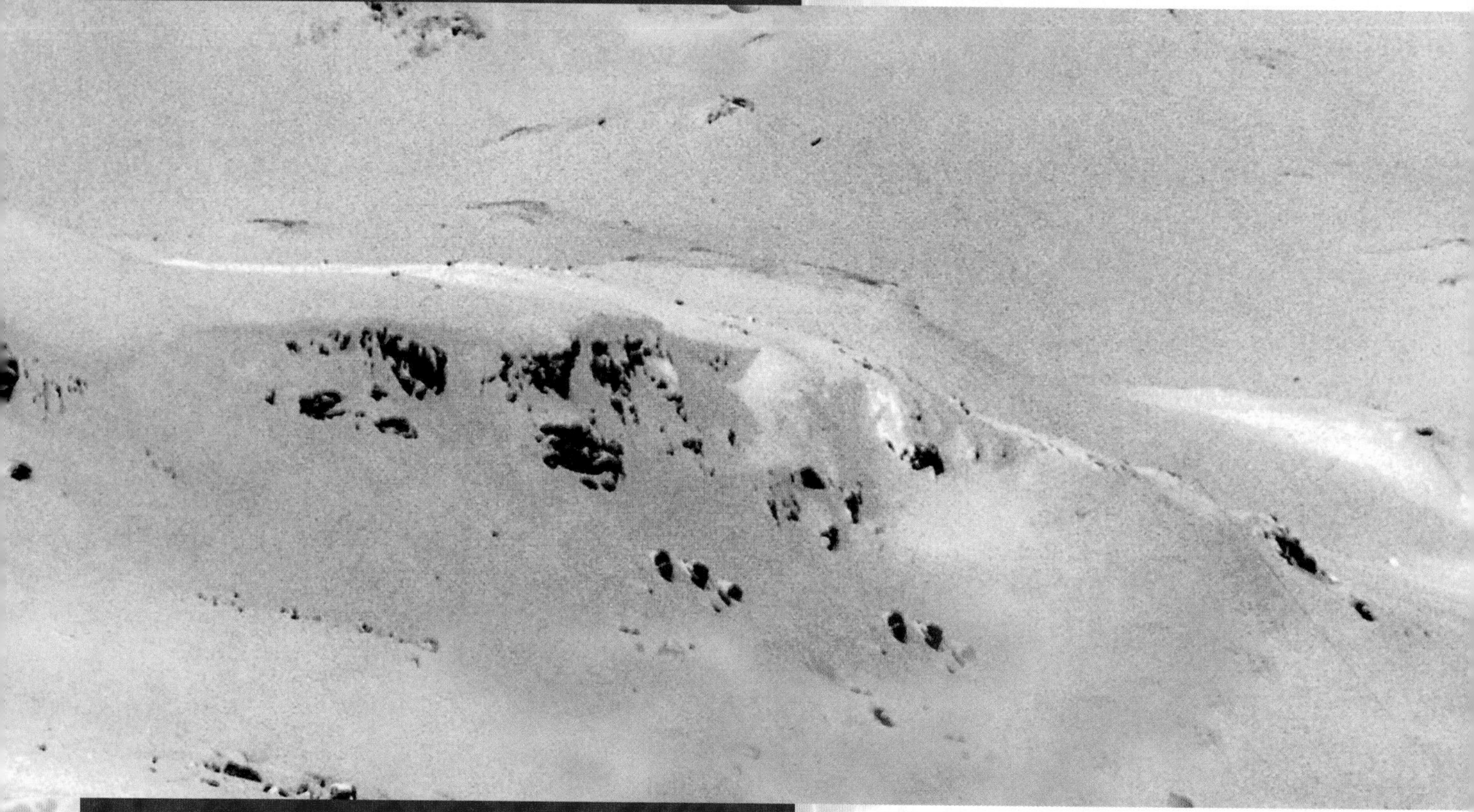

Long before sled dog racing became a formal sport, Alaskan natives trained sled dogs to pull loads and help with chores. During the 1925 "Great Race of Mercy to Nome," sled dogs carried diphtheria antitoxin serum 674 miles in less than six days, saving many lives.

A child on a sled is pulled from point (0, 0, 0) to point (12, 16, 0) by two dogs. The forces exerted by the dogs are given by $7\mathbf{i} + 8\mathbf{j} + \mathbf{k}$ and $6\mathbf{i} + 9\mathbf{j} + 2\mathbf{k}$. If distances are in feet and forces are in pounds, find the amount of work done by the dogs. Section 12.2 covers the mathematics you need to answer this question.

Chapter 12 Overview

This chapter introduces three-dimensional vector operations and coordinate systems. We define distance, practice with the arithmetic of vectors in space, and make connections between sets of points and equations and inequalities. Just as the coordinate plane is the natural place to study functions of a single variable, coordinate space is the place to study functions of two variables (or more). We establish coordinates in space by adding a third axis that measures distance above and below the *xy*-plane.

12.1 Cartesian (Rectangular) Coordinates and Vectors in Space

What you'll learn about

- Cartesian Coordinates
- Vectors in Space
- Magnitude
- Zero and Unit Vectors
- Magnitude and Direction
- Distance and Spheres in Space
- Midpoints of Line Segments

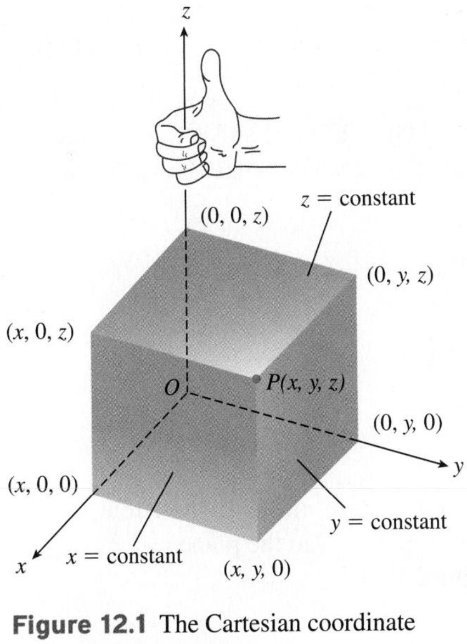

Figure 12.1 The Cartesian coordinate system is right-handed.

Cartesian Coordinates

To locate points in space, we use three mutually perpendicular coordinate axes, arranged as in Figure 12.1. The x-, y-, and z-axes shown there make a **right-handed coordinate frame:** When you hold your right hand so that the fingers curl from the positive x-axis toward the positive y-axis, your thumb points along the positive z-axis.

The **Cartesian coordinates** (x, y, z) **of a point** P in space are the numbers at which the planes through P perpendicular to the axes cut the axes.

Points on the x-axis have y- and z-coordinates equal to zero. That is, they have coordinates of the form $(x, 0, 0)$. Similarly, points on the y-axis have coordinates of the form $(0, y, 0)$. Points on the z-axis have coordinates of the form $(0, 0, z)$.

The points in a plane perpendicular to the x-axis all have the same x-coordinate, this being the number at which that plane cuts the x-axis. The y- and z-coordinates can be any numbers. Similarly, the points in a plane perpendicular to the y-axis have a common y-coordinate and the points in a plane perpendicular to the z-axis have a common z-coordinate. To write equations for these planes, we name the common coordinate's value. The plane $x = 2$ is the plane perpendicular to the x-axis at $x = 2$. The plane $y = 3$ is the plane perpendicular to the y-axis at $y = 3$. The plane $z = 5$ is the plane perpendicular to the z-axis at $z = 5$. Figure 12.2 shows the planes $x = 2$, $y = 3$, and $z = 5$, together with their intersection point $(2, 3, 5)$.

The planes $x = 2$ and $y = 3$ in Figure 12.2 intersect in a line parallel to the z-axis. This line is described by the *pair* of equations $x = 2$, $y = 3$. A point (x, y, z) lies on the line if and only if $x = 2$ and $y = 3$. Similarly, the line of intersection of the planes $y = 3$ and $z = 5$ is described by the equation pair $y = 3$, $z = 5$. This line runs parallel to the x-axis. The line of intersection of the planes $x = 2$ and $z = 5$, parallel to the y-axis, is described by the equation pair $x = 2$, $z = 5$.

The three planes determined by the coordinate axes are the ***xy*-plane,** whose standard equation is $z = 0$; the ***yz*-plane,** whose standard equation is $x = 0$; and the ***xz*-plane,** whose standard equation is $y = 0$. They meet at the **origin** $(0, 0, 0)$ (Figure 12.3).

The three **coordinate planes** $x = 0$, $y = 0$, and $z = 0$ divide space into eight cells called **octants.** The octant in which the point coordinates are all nonnegative is the **first octant;** there is no conventional numbering for the other seven octants.

Cartesian coordinates for space are also called **rectangular coordinates** because the axes that define them meet at right angles.

In the following examples, we match coordinate equations and inequalities with the sets of points they define in space.

EXAMPLE 1 Interpreting Equations and Inequalities

(a) $z \geq 0$ The half-space consisting of the points on and above the *xy*-plane.

(b) $x = -3$ The plane perpendicular to the x-axis at $x = -3$. This plane parallels the *yz*-plane and lies 3 units behind it.

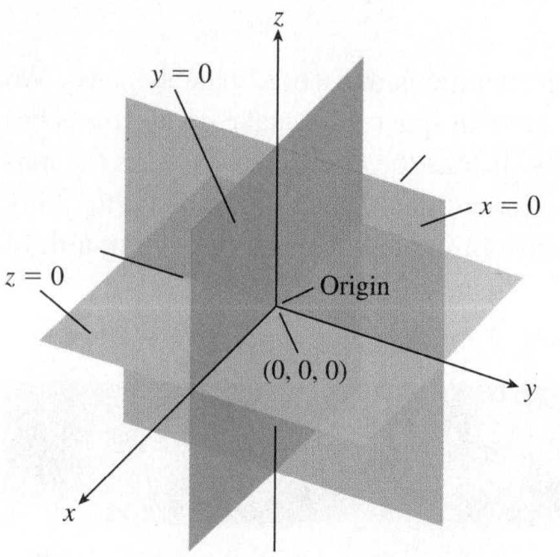

Figure 12.3 The planes $x = 0$, $y = 0$, and $z = 0$ divide space into eight octants.

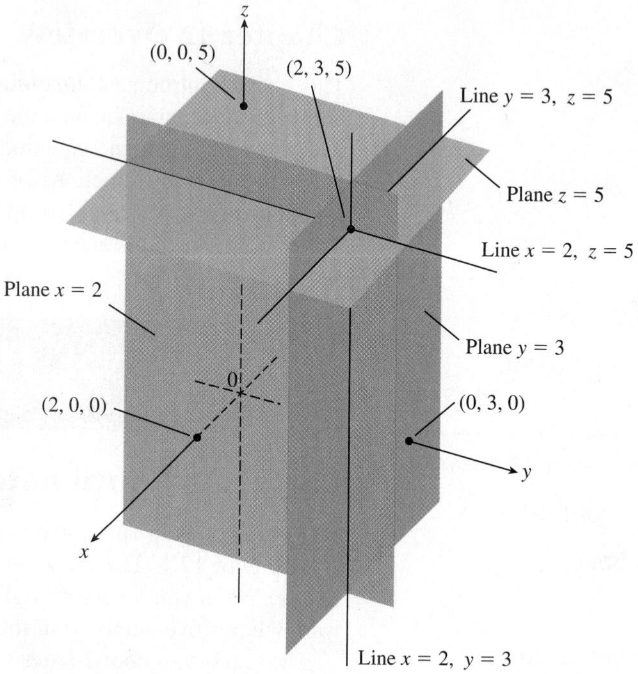

Figure 12.2 The planes $x = 2$, $y = 3$, and $z = 5$ determine three lines through the point (2, 3, 5).

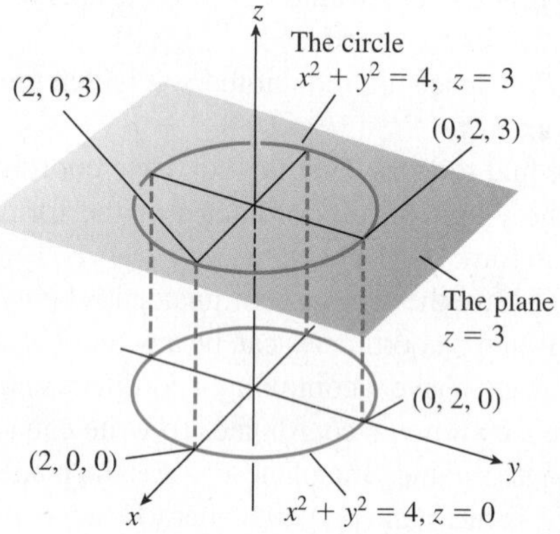

Figure 12.4 The circle $x^2 + y^2 = 4$, $z = 3$. (Example 2)

(c) $z = 0, x \leq 0, y \geq 0$	The second quadrant of the xy-plane.
(d) $x \geq 0, y \geq 0, z \geq 0$	The first octant.
(e) $-1 \leq y \leq 1$	The slab between the planes $y = -1$ and $y = 1$, including the planes.
(f) $y = -2, z = 2$	The line in which the planes $y = -2$ and $z = 2$ intersect. Alternatively, the line through the point $(0, -2, 2)$ parallel to the x-axis.

Recall that two vectors are *equal* (or the *same*) if they have the same length and direction.

EXAMPLE 2 Graphing Equations

What points $P(x, y, z)$ satisfy the equations

$$x^2 + y^2 = 4 \quad \text{and} \quad z = 3?$$

SOLUTION

The points lie in the horizontal plane $z = 3$ and, in this plane, make up the circle $x^2 + y^2 = 4$. We call this set of points "the circle $x^2 + y^2 = 4$ in the plane $z = 3$" or, more simply, "the circle $x^2 + y^2 = 4$, $z = 3$" (Figure 12.4).

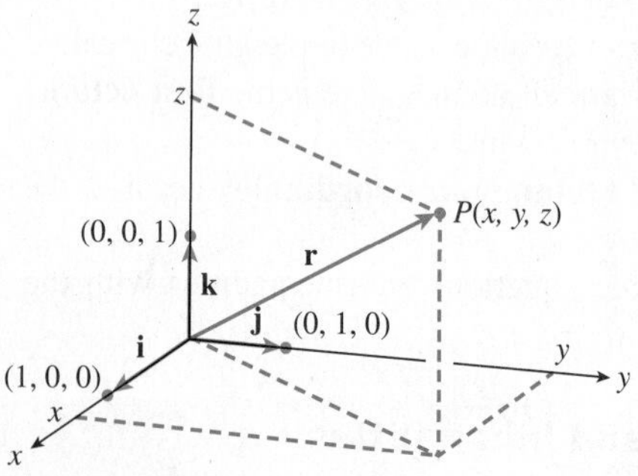

Figure 12.5 The position vector of a point in space.

Vectors in Space

The sets of equivalent directed line segments that we use to represent forces, displacements, and velocities are called vectors, just as in the plane (see Section 10.2).

The vectors represented by the directed line segments from the origin to the points (1, 0, 0), (0, 1, 0), and (0, 0, 1) are the **standard unit vectors i, j,** and **k** (Figure 12.5). The **position vector r** from the origin O to the typical point $P(x, y, z)$ is

$$\mathbf{r} = \overrightarrow{OP} = x\mathbf{i} + y\mathbf{j} + z\mathbf{k}.$$

The definitions of addition, subtraction, and scalar multiplication are the same as in the plane.

DEFINITIONS Vector Operations

Let $\mathbf{A} = a_1\mathbf{i} + a_2\mathbf{j} + a_3\mathbf{k}$ and $\mathbf{B} = b_1\mathbf{i} + b_2\mathbf{j} + b_3\mathbf{k}$ be vectors with k a scalar (real number).

Addition: $\mathbf{A} + \mathbf{B} = (a_1 + b_1)\mathbf{i} + (a_2 + b_2)\mathbf{j} + (a_3 + b_3)\mathbf{k}$

Subtraction: $\mathbf{A} - \mathbf{B} = (a_1 - b_1)\mathbf{i} + (a_2 - b_2)\mathbf{j} + (a_3 - b_3)\mathbf{k}$

Scalar multiplication: $k\mathbf{A} = (ka_1)\mathbf{i} + (ka_2)\mathbf{j} + (ka_3)\mathbf{k}$

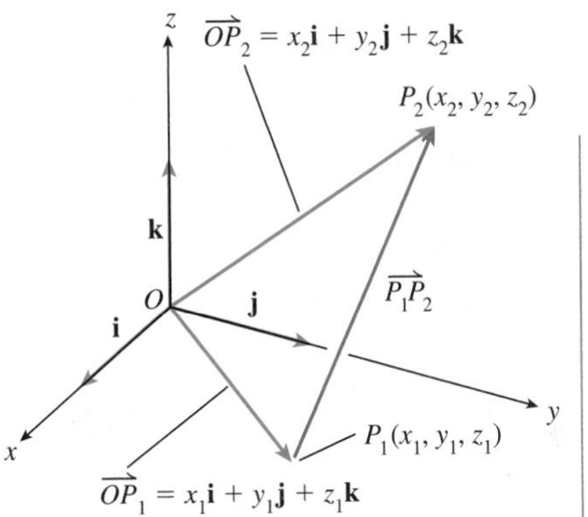

Figure 12.6 The vector from P_1 to P_2 is $\overrightarrow{P_1P_2} = (x_2 - x_1)\mathbf{i} + (y_2 - y_1)\mathbf{j} + (z_2 - z_1)\mathbf{k}$. (Example 3)

EXAMPLE 3 Finding the Vector from One Point to Another

Show that the vector from $P_1(x_1, y_1, z_1)$ to $P_2(x_2, y_2, z_2)$ is

$$\overrightarrow{P_1P_2} = (x_2 - x_1)\mathbf{i} + (y_2 - y_1)\mathbf{j} + (z_2 - z_1)\mathbf{k}.$$

SOLUTION

Since $\overrightarrow{OP_1} + \overrightarrow{P_1P_2} = \overrightarrow{OP_2}$ (Figure 12.6), we have

$$\begin{aligned}\overrightarrow{P_1P_2} &= \overrightarrow{OP_2} - \overrightarrow{OP_1}\\ &= (x_2\mathbf{i} + y_2\mathbf{j} + z_2\mathbf{k}) - (x_1\mathbf{i} + y_1\mathbf{j} + z_1\mathbf{k})\\ &= (x_2 - x_1)\mathbf{i} + (y_2 - y_1)\mathbf{j} + (z_2 - z_1)\mathbf{k}.\end{aligned}$$

Magnitude

As always, the important features of a vector are its magnitude and direction. We find a formula for the magnitude (length) of $a_1\mathbf{i} + a_2\mathbf{j} + a_3\mathbf{k}$ by applying the Pythagorean Theorem to the right triangles in Figure 12.7. From triangle ABC,

$$|\overrightarrow{AC}| = \sqrt{a_1^2 + a_2^2},$$

and from triangle ACD,

$$|a_1\mathbf{i} + a_2\mathbf{j} + a_3\mathbf{k}| = |\overrightarrow{AD}| = \sqrt{|\overrightarrow{AC}|^2 + |\overrightarrow{CD}|^2} = \sqrt{a_1^2 + a_2^2 + a_3^2}.$$

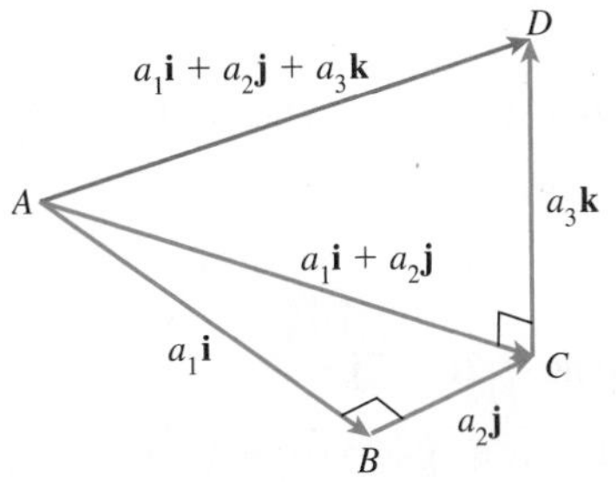

Figure 12.7 The length of $\overrightarrow{AC}$ is $\sqrt{a_1^2 + a_2^2}$ and the length of $\overrightarrow{AD}$ is $\sqrt{a_1^2 + a_2^2 + a_3^2}$.

DEFINITION Magnitude (Length) of a Vector

The **magnitude (length) of A** $= a_1\mathbf{i} + a_2\mathbf{j} + a_3\mathbf{k}$ is

$$|\mathbf{A}| = |a_1\mathbf{i} + a_2\mathbf{j} + a_3\mathbf{k}| = \sqrt{a_1^2 + a_2^2 + a_3^2}$$

Zero and Unit Vectors

The **zero vector** in space is the vector $\mathbf{0} = 0\mathbf{i} + 0\mathbf{j} + 0\mathbf{k}$. As in the plane, $\mathbf{0}$ has length zero and no direction.

A **unit vector** in space is a vector of length 1. The equations

$$\begin{aligned}|\mathbf{i}| &= |1\mathbf{i} + 0\mathbf{j} + 0\mathbf{k}| = \sqrt{1^2 + 0^2 + 0^2} = 1,\\ |\mathbf{j}| &= |0\mathbf{i} + 1\mathbf{j} + 0\mathbf{k}| = \sqrt{0^2 + 1^2 + 0^2} = 1,\\ |\mathbf{k}| &= |0\mathbf{i} + 0\mathbf{j} + 1\mathbf{k}| = \sqrt{0^2 + 0^2 + 1^2} = 1,\end{aligned}$$

show that the standard unit vectors are indeed unit vectors.

Magnitude and Direction

If $\mathbf{A} \neq \mathbf{0}$, then $\mathbf{A}/|\mathbf{A}|$ is a unit vector in the direction of **A**. We can use the equation

$$\mathbf{A} = |\mathbf{A}| \frac{\mathbf{A}}{|\mathbf{A}|}$$

to express **A** as a product of its magnitude and direction.

EXAMPLE 4 Writing a Vector as Length Times Direction

Express $\mathbf{A} = \mathbf{i} - 2\mathbf{j} + 3\mathbf{k}$ as a product of its magnitude and direction.

SOLUTION

$\mathbf{A}/|\mathbf{A}|$ is a unit vector in the direction of **A**. The magnitude of **A** is

$$|\mathbf{A}| = \sqrt{(1)^2 + (-2)^2 + (3)^2} = \sqrt{1 + 4 + 9} = \sqrt{14}.$$

Thus,

$$\begin{aligned} \mathbf{A} &= |\mathbf{A}| \cdot \frac{\mathbf{A}}{|\mathbf{A}|} \\ &= \sqrt{14} \cdot \frac{\mathbf{i} - 2\mathbf{j} + 3\mathbf{k}}{\sqrt{14}} \\ &= \sqrt{14} \cdot \left(\frac{1}{\sqrt{14}}\mathbf{i} - \frac{2}{\sqrt{14}}\mathbf{j} + \frac{3}{\sqrt{14}}\mathbf{k} \right) \\ &= (\text{length of } \mathbf{A}) \cdot (\text{direction of } \mathbf{A}). \end{aligned}$$

EXAMPLE 5 Finding a Unit Vector

Find a unit vector **u** in the direction of the vector from $P_1(1, 0, 1)$ to $P_2(3, 2, 0)$.

SOLUTION

We divide $\overrightarrow{P_1P_2}$ by its length:

$$\overrightarrow{P_1P_2} = (3 - 1)\mathbf{i} + (2 - 0)\mathbf{j} + (0 - 1)\mathbf{k} = 2\mathbf{i} + 2\mathbf{j} - \mathbf{k}$$

$$|\overrightarrow{P_1P_2}| = \sqrt{(2)^2 + (2)^2 + (-1)^2} = \sqrt{4 + 4 + 1} = \sqrt{9} = 3$$

$$\mathbf{u} = \frac{\overrightarrow{P_1P_2}}{|\overrightarrow{P_1P_2}|} = \frac{2\mathbf{i} + 2\mathbf{j} - \mathbf{k}}{3} = \frac{2}{3}\mathbf{i} + \frac{2}{3}\mathbf{j} - \frac{1}{3}\mathbf{k}.$$

EXAMPLE 6 Finding a Vector with given Magnitude and Direction

Find a vector 6 units long in the direction of $\mathbf{A} = 2\mathbf{i} + 2\mathbf{j} - \mathbf{k}$.

SOLUTION

The vector we want is

$$6\frac{\mathbf{A}}{|\mathbf{A}|} = 6\frac{2\mathbf{i} + 2\mathbf{j} - \mathbf{k}}{\sqrt{2^2 + 2^2 + (-1)^2}} = 6\frac{2\mathbf{i} + 2\mathbf{j} - \mathbf{k}}{3} = 4\mathbf{i} + 4\mathbf{j} - 2\mathbf{k}.$$

Distance and Spheres in Space

The distance between two points P_1 and P_2 in space is the length of $\overrightarrow{P_1P_2}$.

> **Distance Between Points**
>
> The distance between $P_1(x_1, y_1, z_1)$ and $P_2(x_2, y_2, z_2)$ is
>
> $$|\overrightarrow{P_1P_2}| = \sqrt{(x_2 - x_1)^2 + (y_2 - y_1)^2 + (z_2 - z_1)^2}.$$

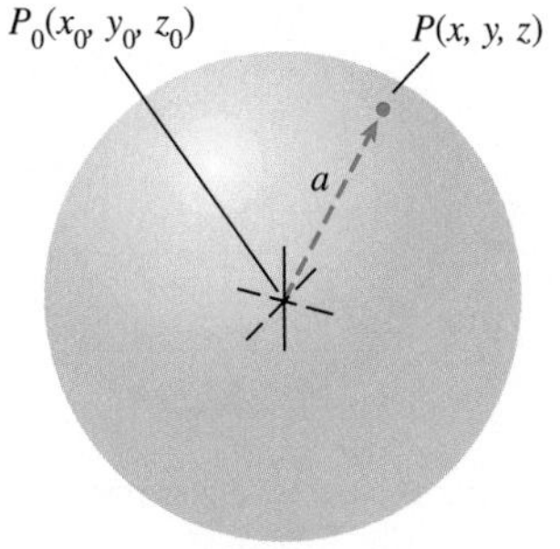

Figure 12.8 The sphere of radius a centered at (x_0, y_0, z_0).

EXAMPLE 7 Finding Distance Between Points

The distance between $P_1(2, 1, 5)$ and $P_2(-2, 3, 0)$ is

$$\begin{aligned} |\overrightarrow{P_1P_2}| &= \sqrt{(-2 - 2)^2 + (3 - 1)^2 + (0 - 5)^2} \\ &= \sqrt{16 + 4 + 25} = \sqrt{45} \approx 6.708. \end{aligned}$$

We use the distance formula to write equations for spheres in space (Figure 12.8). A *sphere* is the set of all points $P(x, y, z)$ in space a fixed distance from a fixed point $P_0(x_0, y_0, z_0)$. A point $P(x, y, z)$ lies on the sphere of radius a centered at $P_0(x_0, y_0, z_0)$ precisely when $|\overrightarrow{P_0P}| = a$ or

$$(x - x_0)^2 + (y - y_0)^2 + (z - z_0)^2 = a^2.$$

> **Standard Equation for the Sphere of Radius *a* and Center (x_0, y_0, z_0)**
>
> $$(x - x_0)^2 + (y - y_0)^2 + (z - z_0)^2 = a^2$$

Drawing Lesson
How to Draw Three-Dimensional Objects to Look Three-Dimensional

1. *Break lines.* When one line passes behind another, break it to show that it doesn't touch and that part of it is hidden.

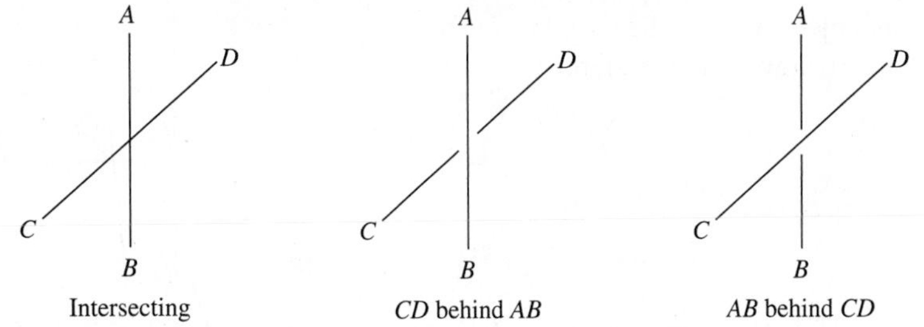

2. Make the angle between the positive x-axis and the positive y-axis large enough.

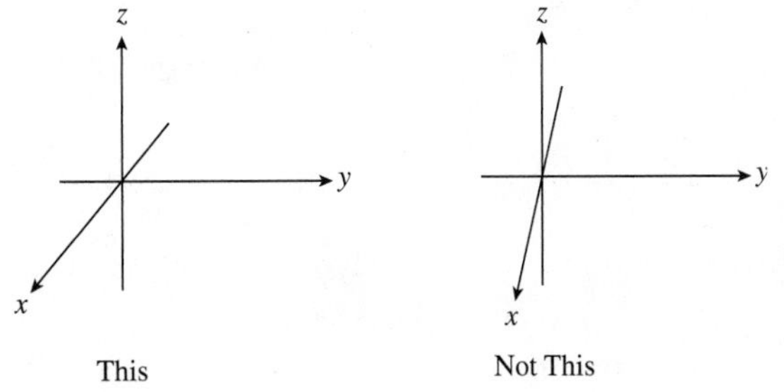

3. Draw planes parallel to the coordinate planes as if they were rectangles with sides parallel to the coordinate axes.

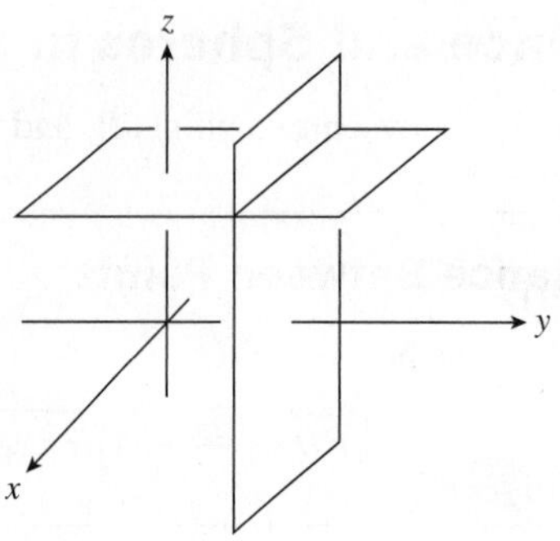

4. Dash or omit hidden portions of lines. Don't let the line touch the boundary of the parallelogram that represents the plane, unless the line lies in the plane.

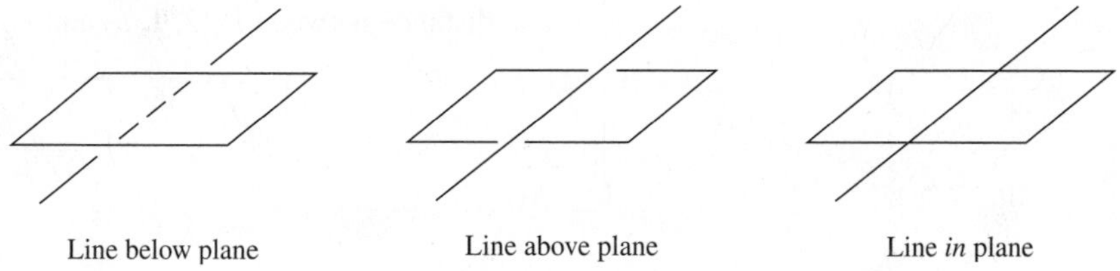

5. *Spheres.* Draw the sphere first (outine and equator); draw axes, if any, later. Use line breaks and dashed lines.

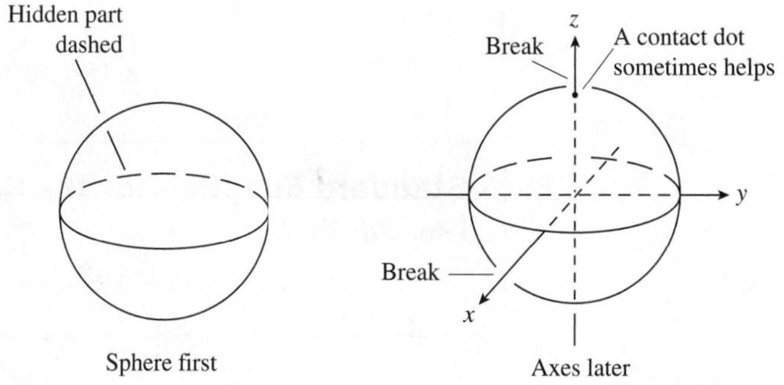

6. A general rule for perspective: Draw the object as if it lies some distance away, below, and to the left.

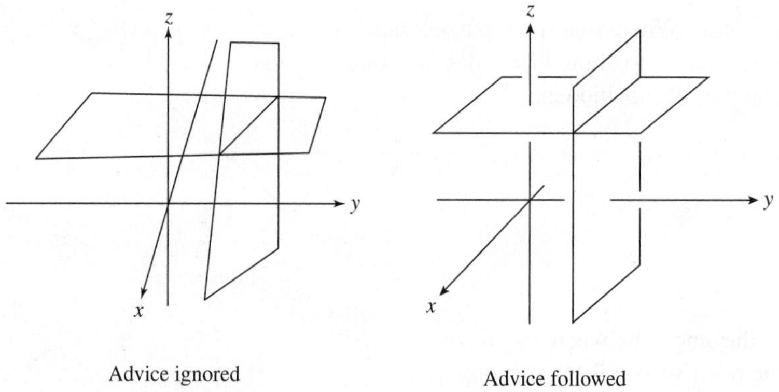

7. To draw a plane that crosses all three coordinate axes, follow the steps shown here. (a) Sketch the axes and mark the intercepts. (b) Connect the intercepts to form two sides of a parallelogram. (c) Complete the parallelogram and enlarge it by drawing lines parallel to its sides. (d) Darken the exposed parts, break hidden lines, and, if desired, dash hidden portions of the axes. You may wish to erase the smaller parallelogram at this point.

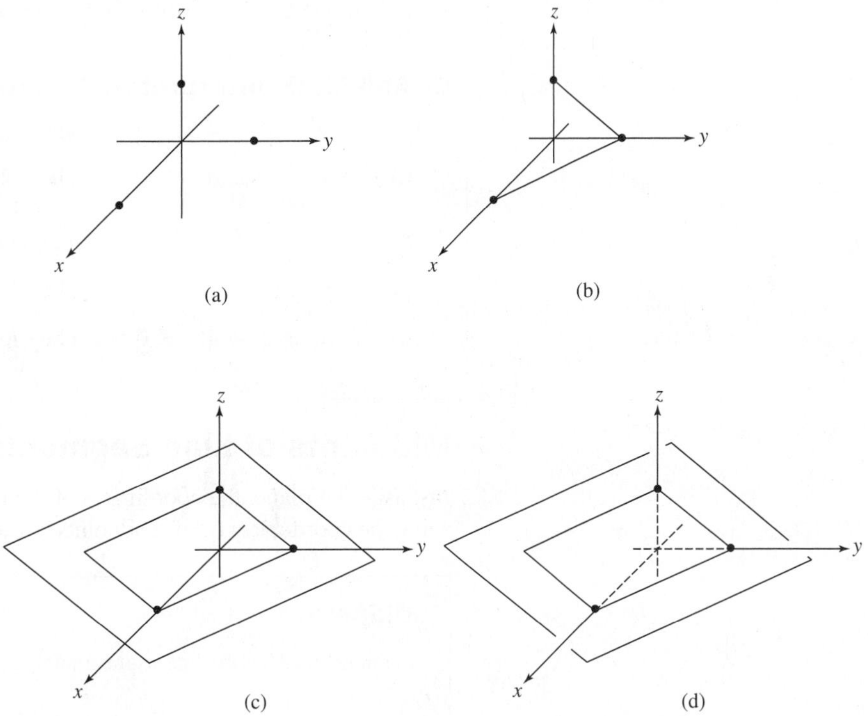

EXAMPLE 8 Finding the Center and Radius of a Sphere

Find the center and radius of the sphere

$$x^2 + y^2 + z^2 + 3x - 4z + 1 = 0.$$

SOLUTION

We find the center and radius of a sphere the way we find the center and radius of a circle: Complete the squares on the x-, y-, and z-terms as necessary and write each quadratic as a squared linear expression. Then, from the equation in standard form, read off the center and radius. For the sphere here we have

$$x^2 + y^2 + z^2 + 3x - 4z + 1 = 0$$

$$(x^2 + 3x) + y^2 + (z^2 - 4z) = -1$$

$$\left(x^2 + 3x + \left(\frac{3}{2}\right)^2\right) + y^2 + \left(z^2 - 4z + \left(\frac{-4}{2}\right)^2\right) = -1 + \left(\frac{3}{2}\right)^2 + \left(\frac{-4}{2}\right)^2$$

$$\left(x + \frac{3}{2}\right)^2 + y^2 + (z - 2)^2 = -1 + \frac{9}{4} + 4 = \frac{21}{4}.$$

From this standard form we read that $x_0 = -3/2$, $y_0 = 0$, $z_0 = 2$, and $a = \sqrt{21}/2$. The center is $(-3/2, 0, 2)$. The radius is $\sqrt{21}/2$.

In Example 9 we describe sets that are bounded by spheres or portions of spheres.

EXAMPLE 9 Interpreting Equations and Inequalities

(a) $x^2 + y^2 + z^2 < 4$ The interior of the sphere $x^2 + y^2 + z^2 = 4$.

(b) $x^2 + y^2 + z^2 \le 4$ The solid ball bounded by the sphere $x^2 + y^2 + z^2 = 4$. Alternatively, the sphere $x^2 + y^2 + z^2 = 4$ together with its interior.

(c) $x^2 + y^2 + z^2 > 4$ The exterior of the sphere $x^2 + y^2 + z^2 = 4$.

(d) $x^2 + y^2 + z^2 = 4, z \le 0$ The lower hemisphere cut from the sphere $x^2 + y^2 + z^2 = 4$ by the xy-plane (the plane $z = 0$).

Midpoints of Line Segments

Just as in the plane, the coordinates of the midpoints of a line segment are found by averaging the coordinates of the endpoints of the segment.

Midpoint

The midpoint M of the line segment joining points $P_1(x_1, y_1, z_1)$ and $P_2(x_2, y_2, z_2)$ is the point

$$\left(\frac{x_1 + x_2}{2}, \frac{y_1 + y_2}{2}, \frac{z_1 + z_2}{2}\right).$$

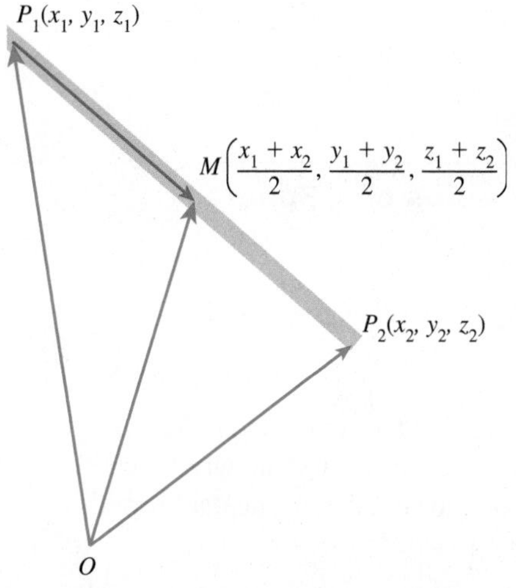

Figure 12.9 The coordinates of the midpoint are the averages of the coordinates of P_1 and P_2.

To see why, observe (Figure 12.9) that

$$\begin{aligned}\overrightarrow{OM} &= \overrightarrow{OP_1} + \frac{1}{2}\left(\overrightarrow{P_1P_2}\right) = \overrightarrow{OP_1} + \frac{1}{2}\left(\overrightarrow{OP_2} - \overrightarrow{OP_1}\right)\\ &= \frac{1}{2}\left(\overrightarrow{OP_1} + \overrightarrow{OP_2}\right)\\ &= \frac{x_1 + x_2}{2}\mathbf{i} + \frac{y_1 + y_2}{2}\mathbf{j} + \frac{z_1 + z_2}{2}\mathbf{k}.\end{aligned}$$

EXAMPLE 10 Finding a Midpoint

The midpoint of the line segment joining $P_1(3, -2, 0)$ and $P_2(7, 4, 4)$ is

$$\left(\frac{3 + 7}{2}, \frac{-2 + 4}{2}, \frac{0 + 4}{2}\right) = (5, 1, 2).$$

Quick Review 12.1

In Exercises 1 and 2, let $P_1(-2, 3)$ and $P_2(5, 2)$ be two points in the xy-plane.

1. Find the distance between the points P_1 and P_2.

2. Find the midpoint of the line segment P_1P_2.

In Exercises 3–5, let $\mathbf{u} = \langle 2, 3\rangle = 2\mathbf{i} + 3\mathbf{j}$ be a vector in the xy-plane.

3. Find the magnitude of $\mathbf{u}$.

4. Find a unit vector in the direction of $\mathbf{u}$.

5. Find a vector 3 units long in the direction of $-\mathbf{u}$.

In Exercises 6 and 7, give a geometric description of the set of points in the xy-plane whose coordinates satisfy the equation or inequality.

6. $\frac{x^2}{4} + \frac{y^2}{9} = 1$

7. $\frac{x^2}{4} + \frac{y^2}{9} + \le 1$

8. Write an equation for the circle in the xy-plane with center $(2, -3)$ and radius 3 units.

9. Find the center and radius of the circle in the xy-plane: $x^2 + y^2 + 6x - 2y = -6$.

10. Find the vector in the xy-plane from the point $P_1(-2, 3)$ to the point $P_2(3, -1)$.

Section 12.1 Exercises

In Exercises 1–10, give a geometric description of the set of points in space whose coordinates satisfy the pair of equations.

1. $x = 2,\ y = 3$

2. $x = -1,\ z = 0$

3. $y = 0,\ z = 0$

4. $x = 1,\ y = 0$

5. $x^2 + y^2 = 4,\ z = -2$

6. $x^2 + z^2 = 4,\ y = 0$

7. $y^2 + z^2 = 1,\ x = 0$

8. $x^2 + y^2 + z^2 = 25,\ y = -4.$

9. $x^2 + y^2 + (z + 3)^2 = 25,\ z = 0$

10. $x^2 + (y - 1)^2 + z^2 = 4,\ y = 0$

In Exercises 11–16, describe the set of points in space whose coordinates satisfy the given inequalities or combination of equations and inequalities.

11. **(a)** $x \geq 0,\ y \geq 0,\ z = 0$ **(b)** $x \geq 0,\ y \leq 0,\ z = 0$

12. **(a)** $0 \leq x \leq 1$ **(b)** $0 \leq x \leq 1,\ 0 \leq y \leq 1$
(c) $0 \leq x \leq 1,\ 0 \leq y \leq 1,\ 0 \leq z \leq 1$

13. **(a)** $x^2 + y^2 + z^2 \leq 1$ **(b)** $x^2 + y^2 + z^2 > 1$

14. **(a)** $x^2 + y^2 \leq 1,\ z = 0$ **(b)** $x^2 + y^2 \leq 1,\ z = 3$
(c) $x^2 + y^2 \leq 1$, no restriction on z

15. **(a)** $x^2 + y^2 + z^2 = 1,\ z \geq 0$ **(b)** $x^2 + y^2 + z^2 \leq 1,\ z \geq 0$

16. **(a)** $x = y,\ z = 0$ **(b)** $x = y$, no restriction on z

In Exercises 17–26, describe the given set with a single equation or a pair of equations.

17. The plane perpendicular to the
(a) x-axis at $(3, 0, 0)$ **(b)** y-axis at $(0, -1, 0)$
(c) z-axis at $(0, 0, -2)$

18. The plane through the point $(3, -1, 2)$ perpendicular to the
(a) x-axis **(b)** y-axis **(c)** z-axis

19. The plane through the point $(3, -1, 1)$ parallel to the
(a) xy-plane **(b)** yz-plane **(c)** xz-plane

20. The circle of radius 2 centered at $(0, 0, 0)$ and lying in the
(a) xy-plane **(b)** yz-plane **(c)** xz-plane

21. The circle of radius 2 centered at $(0, 2, 0)$ and lying in the
(a) xy-plane **(b)** yz-plane **(c)** plane $y = 2$

22. The circle of radius 1 centered at $(-3, 4, 1)$ and lying in a plane parallel to the
(a) xy-plane **(b)** yz-plane **(c)** xz-plane

23. The line through the point $(1, 3, -1)$ parallel to the
(a) x-axis **(b)** y-axis **(c)** z-axis

24. The set of points in space equidistant from the origin and the point $(0, 2, 0)$

25. The circle in which the plane through the point $(1, 1, 3)$ perpendicular to the z-axis meets the sphere of radius 5 centered at the origin

26. The set of points in space that lie 2 units from the point $(0, 0, 1)$ and, at the same time, 2 units from the point $(0, 0, -1)$

In Exercises 27–32, write inequalities to describe the set.

27. The slab bounded by the planes $z = 0$ and $z = 1$ (planes included)

28. The solid cube in the first octant bounded by the coordinate planes and the planes $x = 2$, $y = 2$, and $z = 2$

29. The half-space consisting of the points on and below the xy-plane

30. The upper hemisphere of the sphere of radius 1 centered at the origin

31. The **(a)** interior and **(b)** exterior of the sphere of radius 1 centered at the point $(1, 1, 1)$

32. The closed region bounded by the spheres of radius 1 and radius 2 centered at the origin. (*Closed* means the spheres are to be included. Had we wanted the spheres left out, we would have asked for the *open* region bounded by the spheres. This is analogous to the way we use *closed* and *open* to described intervals: *Closed* means endpoints included, *open* means endpoints left out. Closed sets include boundaries; open sets leave them out.)

In Exercises 33–38, express the vector as a product of its length and direction.

33. $2\mathbf{i} + \mathbf{j} - 2\mathbf{k}$

34. $9\mathbf{i} - 2\mathbf{j} + 6\mathbf{k}$

35. $5\mathbf{k}$

36. $\frac{3}{5}\mathbf{i} + \frac{4}{5}\mathbf{k}$

37. $\frac{1}{\sqrt{6}}\mathbf{i} - \frac{1}{\sqrt{6}}\mathbf{j} - \frac{1}{\sqrt{6}}\mathbf{k}$

38. $\frac{\mathbf{i}}{\sqrt{3}} + \frac{\mathbf{j}}{\sqrt{3}} + \frac{\mathbf{k}}{\sqrt{3}}$

In Exercises 39 and 40, find the vector whose length and direction are given. Try to do the calculation mentally.

39.

Length	Direction
(a) 2	$\mathbf{i}$
(b) $\sqrt{3}$	$-\mathbf{k}$
(c) $\frac{1}{2}$	$\frac{3}{5}\mathbf{j} + \frac{4}{5}\mathbf{k}$
(d) 7	$\frac{6}{7}\mathbf{i} - \frac{2}{7}\mathbf{j} + \frac{3}{7}\mathbf{k}$

40.

	Length	Direction
(a)	7	$-\mathbf{j}$
(b)	$\sqrt{2}$	$-\frac{3}{5}\mathbf{i} - \frac{4}{5}\mathbf{k}$
(c)	$\frac{13}{12}$	$\frac{3}{13}\mathbf{i} - \frac{4}{13}\mathbf{j} - \frac{12}{13}\mathbf{k}$
(d)	$a > 0$	$\frac{1}{\sqrt{2}}\mathbf{i} + \frac{1}{\sqrt{3}}\mathbf{j} - \frac{1}{\sqrt{6}}\mathbf{k}$

41. Find a vector of magnitude 7 in the direction of $\mathbf{A} = 12\mathbf{i} - 5\mathbf{k}$.

42. Find a vector of magnitude 3 in the direction opposite to the direction of $\mathbf{A} = (1/2)\mathbf{i} - (1/2)\mathbf{j} - (1/2)\mathbf{k}$.

In Exercises 43–46, find

(a) the distance between the points P_1 and P_2,

(b) the direction of $\overrightarrow{P_1P_2}$,

(c) the midpoint of line segment P_1P_2.

43. $P_1(-1, 1, 5), P_2(2, 5, 0)$ **44.** $P_1(1, 4, 5), P_2(4, -2, 7)$

45. $P_1(3, 4, 5), P_2(2, 3, 4)$ **46.** $P_1(0, 0, 0), P_2(2, -2, -2)$

In Exercises 47 and 48, find the center and radius of the sphere.

47. $(x + 2)^2 + y^2 + (z - 2)^2 = 8$

48. $x^2 + \left(y + \frac{1}{3}\right)^2 + \left(z - \frac{1}{3}\right)^2 = \frac{29}{9}$

In Exercises 49 and 50, find an equation for the sphere with given center and radius.

49. Center: $(1, 2, 3)$, radius: $\sqrt{14}$

50. Center: $(0, -1, 5)$, radius: 2

In Exercises 51–54, find the center and radius of the sphere.

51. $x^2 + y^2 + z^2 + 4x - 4z = 0$ **52.** $x^2 + y^2 + z^2 - 6y + 8z = 0$

53. $2x^2 + 2y^2 + 2z^2 + x + y + z = 9$

54. $3x^2 + 3y^2 + 3z^2 + 2y - 2z = 9$

In Exercises 55–58, *work in groups of two or three.*

55. If $\overrightarrow{AB} = \mathbf{i} + 4\mathbf{j} - 2\mathbf{k}$ and B is the point $(5, 1, 3)$, find A.

56. If $\overrightarrow{AB} = -7\mathbf{i} + 3\mathbf{j} + 8\mathbf{k}$ and A is the point $(-2, -3, 6)$, find B.

57. Find a formula for the distance from the point $P(x, y, z)$ to the

(a) x-axis (b) y-axis (c) z-axis

58. Find a formula for the distance from the point $P(x, y, z)$ to the

(a) xy-plane (b) yz-plane (c) xz-plane

59. *Writing to Learn* Let $ABCD$ be a general, not necessarily planar, quadrilateral in space. Show that the two segments joining the midpoints of opposite sides of $ABCD$ bisect each other.

60. *Writing to Learn* Suppose A, B, and C are vertices of a triangle and a, b, and c are, respectively, the midpoints of the opposite sides.

Show that $\overrightarrow{Aa} + \overrightarrow{Bb} + \overrightarrow{Cc} = 0$

61. Using only vectors, show that $P_1P_2P_3P_4$ form a parallelogram where $P_1 = (0, 0, 0)$, $P_2 = (1, 2, 3)$, $P_3 = (3, 5, 7)$, and $P_4 = (2, 3, 4)$.

Explorations

62. *Cross Sections of Sphere*

(a) Find the cross sections of the sphere

$$x^2 + y^2 + z^2 = 16$$

formed by its intersection with the planes $z = 0$, $z = -2$, and $z = 3$.

(b) Graph the three curves in part (a) in a two-dimensional coordinate system.

(c) Show how to set up your grapher to graph the cross section of the sphere for any value of z.

(d) For each value of z, what is the area A_z of the cross section?

(e) How is $\int_{-4}^{4} A_z dz$ related to the sphere?

63. *Cross Sections of Sphere*

(a) Find the cross sections of the sphere

$$x^2 + y^2 + z^2 = 9$$

formed by its intersection with the planes $x = -1$, $x = 0$, and $x = 2$.

(b) Graph the three curves in part (a) in a two-dimensional coordinate system.

(c) Show how to set up your grapher to graph the cross section of the sphere for any value of x.

(d) For each value of x, what is the area A_x of the cross section?

(e) How is $\int_{-3}^{3} A_x dx$ related to the sphere?

Extending The Ideas

64. *Medians of a Triangle* Suppose A, B, and C are the corners of the thin triangular plate of constant density shown here.

(a) Find the vector from C to the midpoint M of side AB.

(b) Find the vector from C to the point that lies two-thirds of the way from C to M on the median CM.

(c) Find the coordinates of the point in which the medians of ΔABC intersect. (This point is the plate's center of mass (c.m.).)

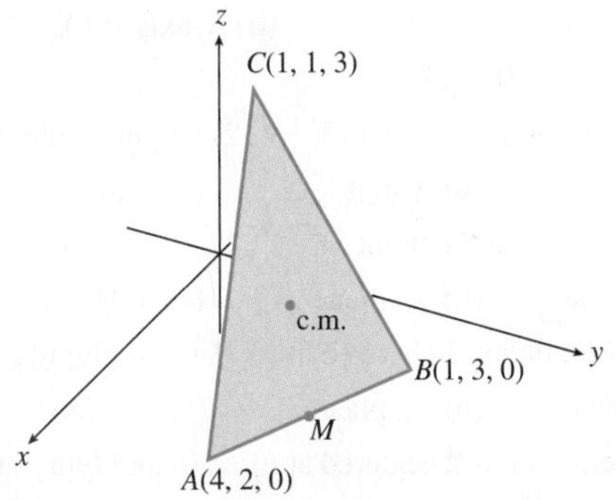

65. *Medians of a Triangle* Find the vector from the origin to the point of intersection of the medians of the triangle whose vertices are $A(1, -1, 2)$, $B(2, 1, 3)$, and $C(-1, 2, -1)$.

66. *Regular Polygons* Vectors are drawn from the center of a regular n-sided polygon in the plane to the vertices of the polygon. Show that the sum of the vectors is zero. (*Hint:* What happens to the sum if you rotate the polygon about its center?)

12.2 Dot Products

What you'll learn about

- Component Form
- Properties of the Dot Product
- Perpendicular (Orthogonal) Vectors and Projections
- Writing a Vector as a Sum of Orthogonal Vectors
- Work

Component Form

The dot product (or inner product) of two vectors in space is defined in the same way as for vectors in the plane. When two nonzero vectors **A** and **B** are placed so their initial points coincide, they form an angle θ of measure $0 \le \theta \le \pi$.

DEFINITION Dot Product (Inner Product)

The **dot product** (or **inner product**) $\mathbf{A} \cdot \mathbf{B}$ ("**A** dot **B**") of vectors **A** and **B** is the number

$$\mathbf{A} \cdot \mathbf{B} = |\mathbf{A}||\mathbf{B}| \cos \theta,$$

where θ is the angle between **A** and **B**.

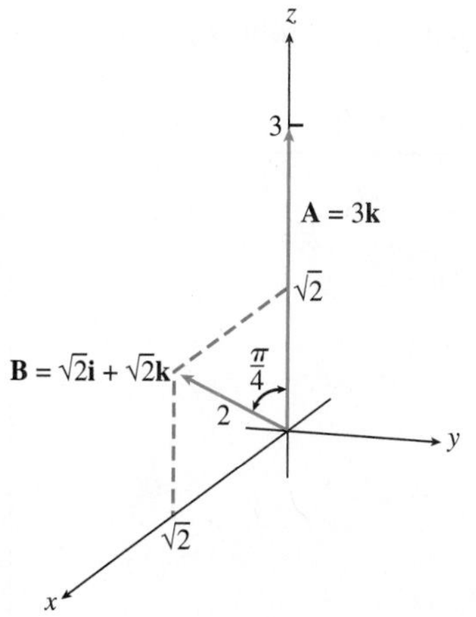

Figure 12.10 The vectors in Example 1.

EXAMPLE 1 Computing a Dot Product

If $\mathbf{A} = 3\mathbf{k}$ and $\mathbf{B} = \sqrt{2}\mathbf{i} + \sqrt{2}\mathbf{k}$ (Figure 12.10), then

$$\mathbf{A} \cdot \mathbf{B} = |\mathbf{A}||\mathbf{B}| \cos \theta = (3)(2) \cos \frac{\pi}{4} = 6 \cdot \frac{\sqrt{2}}{2} = 3\sqrt{2}.$$

We also proved (see Theorem 1) that the dot product can be expressed using the components of the vectors. The same proof yields the following formula.

If $\mathbf{A} = a_1\mathbf{i} + a_2\mathbf{j} + a_3\mathbf{k}$ and $\mathbf{B} = b_1\mathbf{i} + b_2\mathbf{j} + b_3\mathbf{k}$, then

$$\mathbf{A} \cdot \mathbf{B} = a_1 b_1 + a_2 b_2 + a_3 b_3.$$

Solving for θ in the definition of dot product gives a formula for finding angles between vectors.

The angle between two nonzero vectors **A** and **B** is

$$\theta = cos^{-1}\left(\frac{\mathbf{A} \cdot \mathbf{B}}{|\mathbf{A}||\mathbf{B}|}\right).$$

EXAMPLE 2 Finding the Angle Between Vectors

Find the angle between $\mathbf{A} = \mathbf{i} - 2\mathbf{j} - 2\mathbf{k}$ and $\mathbf{B} = 6\mathbf{i} + 3\mathbf{j} + 2\mathbf{k}$.

SOLUTION

Using the formula above, we have

$$\begin{aligned}
\mathbf{A} \cdot \mathbf{B} &= (1)(6) + (-2)(3) + (-2)(2) = -4 \\
|\mathbf{A}| &= \sqrt{(1)^2 + (-2)^2 + (-2)^2} = \sqrt{9} = 3 \\
|\mathbf{B}| &= \sqrt{(6)^2 + (3)^2 + (2)^2} = \sqrt{49} = 7 \\
\theta &= \cos^{-1}\left(\frac{\mathbf{A} \cdot \mathbf{B}}{|\mathbf{A}||\mathbf{B}|}\right) \\
&= \cos^{-1}\left(\frac{-4}{(3)(7)}\right) \approx 1.762 \text{ radians}
\end{aligned}$$

Properties of the Dot Product

We can use the component form of the dot product to establish the following properties (see Exercise 45).

Properties of the Dot Product

Let **A, B, C,** and **D** be vectors and c any number (scalar).

1. $\mathbf{A} \cdot \mathbf{B} = \mathbf{B} \cdot \mathbf{A}$
2. $(c\mathbf{A}) \cdot \mathbf{B} = \mathbf{A} \cdot (c\mathbf{B}) = c(\mathbf{A} \cdot \mathbf{B})$
3. $\mathbf{A} \cdot (\mathbf{B} + \mathbf{C}) = \mathbf{A} \cdot \mathbf{B} + \mathbf{A} \cdot \mathbf{C}$
4. $(\mathbf{A} + \mathbf{B}) \cdot \mathbf{C} = \mathbf{A} \cdot \mathbf{C} + \mathbf{B} \cdot \mathbf{C}$
5. $(\mathbf{A} + \mathbf{B}) \cdot (\mathbf{C} + \mathbf{D}) = \mathbf{A} \cdot \mathbf{C} + \mathbf{A} \cdot \mathbf{D} + \mathbf{B} \cdot \mathbf{C} + \mathbf{B} \cdot \mathbf{D}$
6. $\mathbf{A} \cdot \mathbf{A} = |\mathbf{A}|^2$

Perpendicular (Orthogonal) Vectors and Projections

Two nonzero vectors **A** and **B** are **perpendicular** or **orthogonal** if the angle between them is $\pi/2$. For such vectors, we automatically have $\mathbf{A} \cdot \mathbf{B} = 0$ because $\cos(\pi/2) = 0$. The converse is also true. If **A** and **B** are nonzero vectors with $\mathbf{A} \cdot \mathbf{B} = |\mathbf{A}||\mathbf{B}| \cos \theta = 0$, then $\cos \theta = 0$ and $\theta = \cos^{-1} 0 = \pi/2$.

THEOREM 1 Perpendicular Vectors

Nonzero vectors **A** and **B** are perpendicular (orthogonal) if and only if $\mathbf{A} \cdot \mathbf{B} = 0$

EXAMPLE 3 Showing Vectors Perpendicular

The nonzero vectors $\mathbf{A} = 3\mathbf{i} - 2\mathbf{j} + \mathbf{k}$ and $\mathbf{B} = 2\mathbf{j} + 4\mathbf{k}$ are orthogonal because

$$\mathbf{A} \cdot \mathbf{B} = (3)(0) + (-2)(2) + (1)(4) = 0.$$

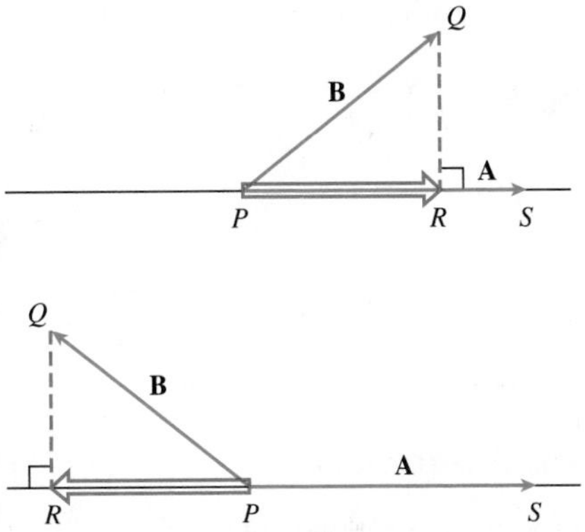

Figure 12.11 The vector projection of **B** onto **A**.

The **vector projection** of $\mathbf{B} = \overrightarrow{PQ}$ onto a nonzero vector $\mathbf{A} = \overrightarrow{PS}$ (Figure 12.11) is the vector $\overrightarrow{PR}$ determined by dropping a perpendicular from Q to the line PS. The notation for this vector is

$$\text{proj}_{\mathbf{A}}\mathbf{B} \quad \text{("the vector projection of } \mathbf{B} \text{ onto } \mathbf{A}\text{").}$$

If **B** represents a force, then $\text{proj}_{\mathbf{A}}\mathbf{B}$ represents the effective force in the direction of **A** (Figure 12.12).

If the angle θ between **A** and **B** is acute, $\text{proj}_{\mathbf{A}}\mathbf{B}$ has length $|\mathbf{B}|\cos\theta$ and direction $\mathbf{A}/|\mathbf{A}|$ (Figure 12.13). If θ is obtuse, $\cos\theta < 0$ and $\text{proj}_{\mathbf{A}}\mathbf{B}$ has length $-|\mathbf{B}|\cos\theta$ and direction $-\mathbf{A}/|\mathbf{A}|$. In either case,

$$\begin{aligned}
\text{proj}_{\mathbf{A}}\mathbf{B} &= (|\mathbf{B}|\cos\theta)\frac{\mathbf{A}}{|\mathbf{A}|} \\
&= \left(\frac{\mathbf{A}\cdot\mathbf{B}}{|\mathbf{A}|}\right)\frac{\mathbf{A}}{|\mathbf{A}|} \\
&= \left(\mathbf{B}\cdot\frac{\mathbf{A}}{|\mathbf{A}|}\right)\frac{\mathbf{A}}{|\mathbf{A}|}
\end{aligned}$$

$|\mathbf{B}|\cos\theta = \dfrac{|\mathbf{A}||\mathbf{B}|\cos\theta}{|\mathbf{A}|} = \dfrac{\mathbf{A}\cdot\mathbf{B}}{|\mathbf{A}|}$

This is **B** "dotted" with the direction of **A**, times the direction of **A**.

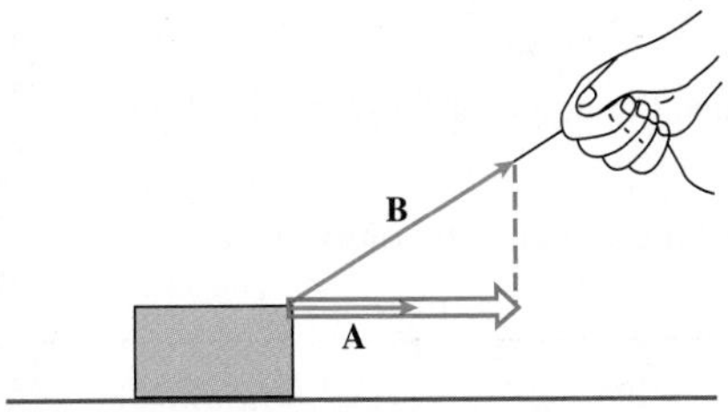

Figure 12.12 If we pull on a box with force **B,** the effective force in the direction of **A** is the vector projection of **B** onto **A.**

Projection of B onto A

$$\text{proj}_{\mathbf{A}}\mathbf{B} = \left(\mathbf{B}\cdot\frac{\mathbf{A}}{|\mathbf{A}|}\right)\frac{\mathbf{A}}{|\mathbf{A}|} = \left(\frac{\mathbf{B}\cdot\mathbf{A}}{\mathbf{A}\cdot\mathbf{A}}\right)\mathbf{A} \qquad (1)$$

The number $|\mathbf{B}|\cos\theta$ is the **scalar component of B in the direction of A.** Since

$$|\mathbf{B}|\cos\theta = \mathbf{B}\cdot\frac{\mathbf{A}}{|\mathbf{A}|}, \qquad (2)$$

we can find the scalar component by "dotting" **B** with the direction of **A.** Equation (1) says that the vector projection of **B** onto **A** is the scalar component of **B** in the direction of **A** times the direction of **A.**

Although the first part of Equation (1) describes the effect of **B** in the direction of **A,** the second part is better for calculations because it avoids square roots.

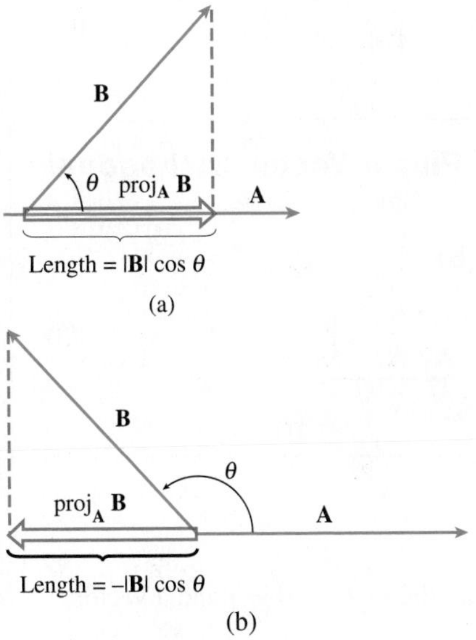

Figure 12.13 The length of $\text{proj}_{\mathbf{A}}\mathbf{B}$ is (a) $|\mathbf{B}|\cos\theta \geq 0$ and (b) $-|\mathbf{B}|\cos\theta$ if $\cos\theta < 0$.

EXAMPLE 4 Using the Projection Formula (Eq. (1))

Find the vector projection of $\mathbf{B} = 6\mathbf{i} + 3\mathbf{j} + 2\mathbf{k}$ onto $\mathbf{A} = \mathbf{i} - 2\mathbf{j} - 2\mathbf{k}$ and the scalar component of **B** in the direction of **A.**

SOLUTION

We find $\text{proj}_{\mathbf{A}}\mathbf{B}$ from Equation (1):

$$\text{proj}_{\mathbf{A}}\mathbf{B} = \frac{\mathbf{B}\cdot\mathbf{A}}{\mathbf{A}\cdot\mathbf{A}}\mathbf{A} = \frac{6 - 6 - 4}{1 + 4 + 4}(\mathbf{i} - 2\mathbf{j} - 2\mathbf{k}) = -\frac{4}{9}\mathbf{i} + \frac{8}{9}\mathbf{j} + \frac{8}{9}\mathbf{k}.$$

We find the scalar component of **B** in the direction of **A** from Equation (2):

$$|\mathbf{B}|\cos\theta = \mathbf{B}\cdot\frac{\mathbf{A}}{|\mathbf{A}|} = (6\mathbf{i} + 3\mathbf{j} + 2\mathbf{k})\cdot\left(\frac{1}{3}\mathbf{i} - \frac{2}{3}\mathbf{j} - \frac{2}{3}\mathbf{k}\right)$$

$$= 2 - 2 - \frac{4}{3} = -\frac{4}{3}.$$

EXPLORATION 1 Proving a Theorem in Solid Geometry

1. Let P and Q be two endpoints of a diameter of a sphere centered at the origin. If P has coordinates (a, b, c), find the coordinates of Q.
2. Let $X = (x, y, z)$ be any other point on the sphere. Use the equation of a sphere to show that $x^2 + y^2 + z^2 = a^2 + b^2 + c^2$.
3. Find the components of vectors $\overrightarrow{PX}$ and $\overrightarrow{QX}$.
4. Compute the dot product of $\overrightarrow{PX}$ and $\overrightarrow{QX}$ and use the equation in step 2 to show that it is zero.
5. What can you conclude about angle PXQ? What geometric theorem have you proved?

Writing a Vector as a Sum of Orthogonal Vectors

In mechanics, we often need to express a vector **B** as a sum of a vector parallel to a vector **A** and a vector orthogonal to **A**. We can accomplish this with the equation

$$\mathbf{B} = \text{proj}_{\mathbf{A}}\mathbf{B} + (\mathbf{B} - \text{proj}_{\mathbf{A}}\mathbf{B}),$$

shown in Figure 12.14.

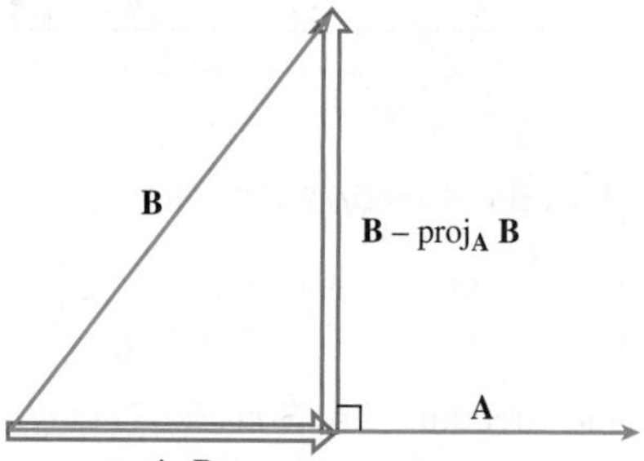

Figure 12.14 Writing **B** as the sum of vectors parallel and orthogonal to **A**.

Writing B as a Vector Parallel to A Plus a Vector Orthogonal to A

$$\mathbf{B} = \text{proj}_{\mathbf{A}}\mathbf{B} + (\mathbf{B} - \text{proj}_{\mathbf{A}}\mathbf{B})$$

$$= \underbrace{\left(\frac{\mathbf{B}\cdot\mathbf{A}}{\mathbf{A}\cdot\mathbf{A}}\right)\mathbf{A}}_{\text{parallel to A}} + \underbrace{\left(\mathbf{B} - \left(\frac{\mathbf{B}\cdot\mathbf{A}}{\mathbf{A}\cdot\mathbf{A}}\right)\mathbf{A}\right)}_{\text{orthogonal to A}} \qquad (3)$$

EXAMPLE 5 Decomposing a Vector

Express $\mathbf{B} = 2\mathbf{i} + \mathbf{j} - 3\mathbf{k}$ as the sum of a vector parallel to $\mathbf{A} = 3\mathbf{i} - \mathbf{j}$ and a vector orthogonal to **A**.

SOLUTION

We use Equation (3). With

$$\mathbf{A}\cdot\mathbf{B} = 6 - 1 = 5 \text{ and } \mathbf{A}\cdot\mathbf{A} = 9 + 1 = 10,$$

Equation (3) gives

$$\mathbf{B} = \frac{\mathbf{B}\cdot\mathbf{A}}{\mathbf{A}\cdot\mathbf{A}}\mathbf{A} + \left(\mathbf{B} - \frac{\mathbf{B}\cdot\mathbf{A}}{\mathbf{A}\cdot\mathbf{A}}\mathbf{A}\right)$$

$$= \frac{5}{10}(3\mathbf{i} - \mathbf{j}) + \left(2\mathbf{i} + \mathbf{j} - 3\mathbf{k} - \frac{5}{10}(3\mathbf{i} - \mathbf{j})\right)$$

$$= \left(\frac{3}{2}\mathbf{i} - \frac{1}{2}\mathbf{j}\right) + \left(\frac{1}{2}\mathbf{i} + \frac{3}{2}\mathbf{j} - 3\mathbf{k}\right).$$

To check this result, notice that the first vector is parallel to **A** because it is (1/2)**A.** The second vector in the sum is orthogonal to **A** because

$$\left(\frac{1}{2}\mathbf{i} + \frac{3}{2}\mathbf{j} - 3\mathbf{k}\right)\cdot(3\mathbf{i} - \mathbf{j}) = \frac{3}{2} - \frac{3}{2} = 0.$$

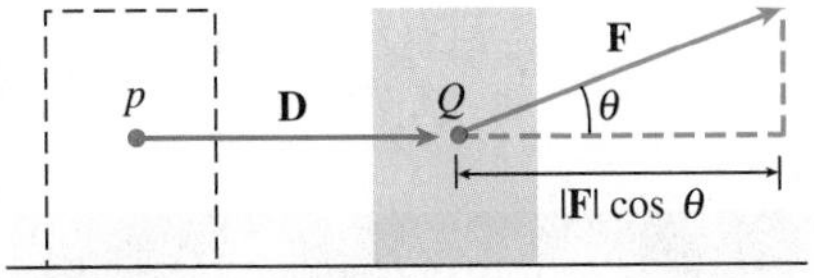

Figure 12.15 The work done by a constant force **F** during a displacement **D** is $(|\mathbf{F}|\cos\theta)|\mathbf{D}|$.

Work

We calculated the work done by a constant force of magnitude F in moving an object through a distance d as $W = Fd$. That formula holds only if the force is directed along the line of motion. If a force **F** moving an object through a displacement $\mathbf{D} = \overrightarrow{PQ}$ has some other direction, the work is performed by the component of **F** in the direction of **D.** If θ is the angle between **F** and **D** (Figure 12.15), then

$$\text{Work} = \begin{pmatrix}\text{scalar component of } \mathbf{F} \\ \text{in the direction of } \mathbf{D}\end{pmatrix}(\text{length of } \mathbf{D})$$

$$= (|\mathbf{F}|\cos\theta)|\mathbf{D}|$$

$$= \mathbf{F}\cdot\mathbf{D}$$

DEFINITION Work

The **work** done by a constant force **F** acting through a displacement $\mathbf{D} = \overrightarrow{PQ}$ is

$$W = \mathbf{F}\cdot\mathbf{D} = |\mathbf{F}||\mathbf{D}|\cos\theta,$$

where θ is the angle between **F** and **D.**

The standard units of work are the foot-pound and the newton-meter, both force-distance units. The newton-meter is usually called a *joule*.

EXAMPLE 6 Finding Work Done by a Force

If $|\mathbf{F}| = 40$ N (newtons), $|\mathbf{D}| = 3$ m, and $\theta = 60°$, the work done by **F** in acting from P to Q is

$$\text{Work} = |\mathbf{F}||\mathbf{D}|\cos\theta = (40)(3)\cos 60°$$

$$= (120)(1/2) = 60 \text{ J (joules)}.$$

We will encounter more interesting work problems in Chapter 15 when we can find the work done by a variable force along a path in space.

Quick Review 12.2

In Exercises 1–3, let $\mathbf{A} = \mathbf{i} + \mathbf{j}$ and $\mathbf{B} = \mathbf{i} - \mathbf{j}$.

1. Find $\mathbf{A} \cdot \mathbf{B}$.

2. Find the angle between **A** and **B**.

3. Find $\mathbf{A} \cdot \mathbf{i}$.

In Exercises 4 and 5, write an equation for the line in the xy-plane that passes through the point (3, 2) and satisfies the given condition.

4. Parallel to $\mathbf{i} - \mathbf{j}$.

5. Perpendicular to $\mathbf{i} - \mathbf{j}$.

In Exercises 6 and 7, let $y = \sin x$.

6. Find the two unit vectors that are tangent to the curve at $x = \pi/6$.

7. Find the two unit vectors that are normal to the curve at $x = \pi/6$.

In Exercises 8 and 9, let $x = 5 \cos t$ and $y = 3 \sin t$.

8. Find the two unit vectors that are tangent to the curve at $t = 3\pi/4$.

9. Find the two unit vectors that are normal to the curve at $t = 3\pi/4$.

10. Find the work done by a force of 50 N moving along the x-axis from $x = -2$ to $x = 3$.

Section 12.2 Exercises

In Exercises 1–6, find

(a) $\mathbf{A} \cdot \mathbf{B}, |\mathbf{A}|, |\mathbf{B}|$;

(b) the angle between **A** and **B**;

(c) the scalar component of **B** in the direction of **A**;

(d) the vector $\text{proj}_{\mathbf{A}}\mathbf{B}$.

1. $\mathbf{A} = 2\mathbf{i} - 4\mathbf{j} + \sqrt{5}\mathbf{k}, \mathbf{B} = -2\mathbf{i} + 4\mathbf{j} - \sqrt{5}\mathbf{k}$

2. $\mathbf{A} = (3/5)\mathbf{i} + (4/5)\mathbf{k}, \mathbf{B} = 5\mathbf{i} + 12\mathbf{j}$

3. $\mathbf{A} = 10\mathbf{i} + 11\mathbf{j} - 2\mathbf{k}, \mathbf{B} = 3\mathbf{j} + 4\mathbf{k}$

4. $\mathbf{A} = 2\mathbf{i} + 10\mathbf{j} - 11\mathbf{k}, \mathbf{B} = 2\mathbf{i} + 2\mathbf{j} + \mathbf{k}$

5. $\mathbf{A} = 5\mathbf{j} - 3\mathbf{k}, \mathbf{B} = \mathbf{i} + \mathbf{j} + \mathbf{k}$

6. $\mathbf{A} = -\mathbf{i} + \mathbf{j}, \mathbf{B} = \sqrt{2}\mathbf{i} + \sqrt{3}\mathbf{j} + 2\mathbf{k}$

In Exercises 7–9, write **B** as the sum of a vector parallel to **A** and a vector orthogonal to **A**.

7. $\mathbf{B} = 3\mathbf{j} + 4\mathbf{k}, \mathbf{A} = \mathbf{i} + \mathbf{j}$

8. $\mathbf{B} = \mathbf{j} + \mathbf{k}, \mathbf{A} = \mathbf{i} + \mathbf{j}$

9. $\mathbf{B} = 8\mathbf{i} + 4\mathbf{j} - 12\mathbf{k}, \mathbf{A} = \mathbf{i} + 2\mathbf{j} - \mathbf{k}$

10. ***Sum of Vectors*** $\mathbf{B} = \mathbf{i} + (\mathbf{j} + \mathbf{k})$ is already the sum of a vector parallel to **i** and a vector orthogonal to **i**. If you use Equation (3) with $\mathbf{A} = \mathbf{i}$, do you get $\mathbf{B}_1 = \mathbf{i}$ and $\mathbf{B}_2 = \mathbf{j} + \mathbf{k}$? Try it and find out.

11. **Writing to Learn** ***Orthogonal Sums and Differences*** In the accompanying figure, it looks as if $\mathbf{v}_1 + \mathbf{v}_2$ and $\mathbf{v}_1 - \mathbf{v}_2$ are orthogonal. Is this mere coincidence, or are there circumstances under which we may expect the sum of two vectors to be orthogonal to their differences? Give reasons for your answer.

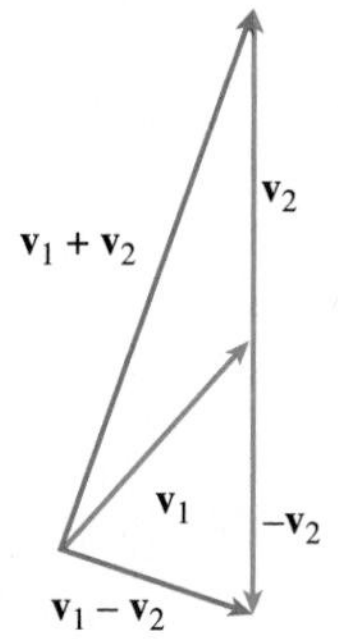

12. ***Work in Groups of Two or Three*** The accompanying figure shows a pyramid $OABCD$ with a square base whose sides are 1 unit long. The pyramid's height is also 1 unit, and the point D stands directly above the midpoint of the diagonal OB. Find the angle between $\overrightarrow{OB}$ and $\overrightarrow{OD}$.

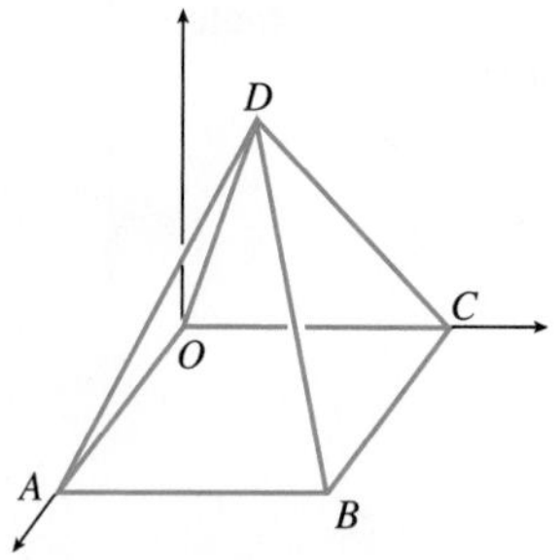

Exploration

13. ***Direction Angles and Direction Cosines*** The **direction angles** α, β, and γ of a vector $\mathbf{v} = a\mathbf{i} + b\mathbf{j} + c\mathbf{k}$ are defined as follows:

α is the angle between $\mathbf{v}$ and the positive x-axis $(0 \le \alpha \le \pi)$,

β is the angle between $\mathbf{v}$ and the positive y-axis $(0 \le \beta \le \pi)$,

γ is the angle between $\mathbf{v}$ and the positive z-axis $(0 \le \gamma \le \pi)$.

(a) Show that

$$\cos\alpha = \frac{a}{|\mathbf{v}|}, \qquad \cos\beta = \frac{b}{|\mathbf{v}|}, \qquad \cos\gamma = \frac{c}{|\mathbf{v}|},$$

and $\cos^2\alpha + \cos^2\beta + \cos^2\gamma = 1$. These cosines are the direction cosines of $\mathbf{v}$.

(b) Show that if $\mathbf{v} = a\mathbf{i} + b\mathbf{j} + c\mathbf{k}$ is a unit vector, then a, b, and c are the direction cosines of $\mathbf{v}$.

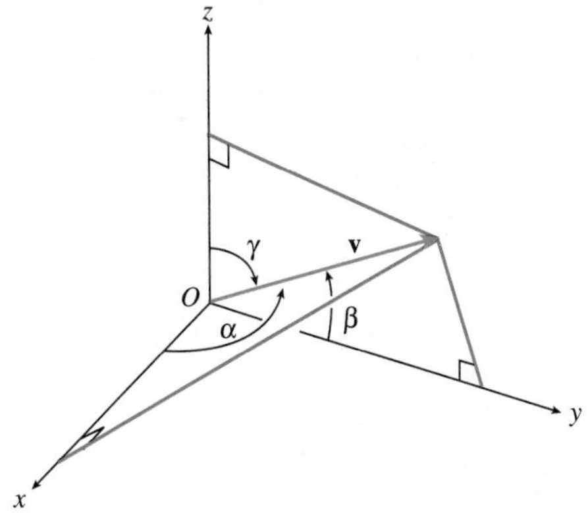

14. ***Interior Angles of a Triangle*** Find the interior angles of the triangle ABC whose vertices are $A(-1, 0, 2)$, $B(2, 1, -1)$, and $C(1, -2, 2)$.

15. ***Diagonal of a Cube*** Find the angle between the diagonal of a cube and the diagonal of one of its faces. (*Hint:* Use a cube whose edges represent **i, j,** and **k.**)

16. ***Grade*** A water main is to be constructed with a 20% grade in the north direction and a 10% grade in the east direction as shown in the figure. Determine the angle θ required in the water main for the turn from north to east.

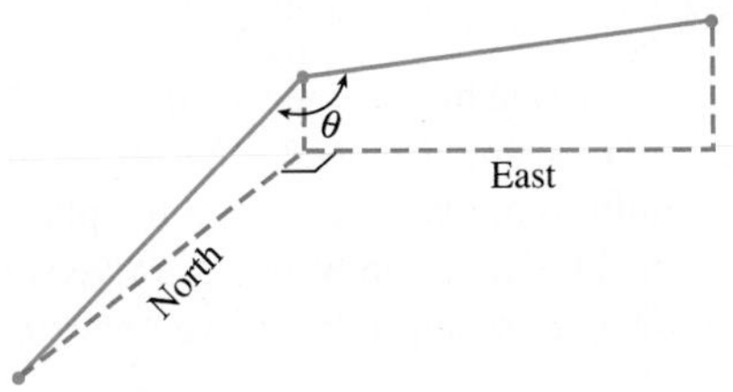

17. ***Orthogonal Unit Vectors*** If $\mathbf{u}_1$ and $\mathbf{u}_2$ are orthogonal unit vectors and $\mathbf{v} = a\mathbf{u}_1 + b\mathbf{u}_2$, find $\mathbf{v} \cdot \mathbf{u}_1$.

18. **Writing to Learn** ***Cancellation in Dot Product*** In real-number multiplication, if $ab_1 = ab_2$ and a is not zero, we can cancel the a and conclude that $b_1 = b_2$. Does the same rule hold for vector multiplication: If $\mathbf{A} \cdot \mathbf{B}_1 = \mathbf{A} \cdot \mathbf{B}_2$ and $\mathbf{A} \ne \mathbf{0}$, can you conclude that $\mathbf{B}_1 = \mathbf{B}_2$? Give reasons for your answer.

19. ***Linear Combinations of Orthogonal Vectors*** Suppose **A, B,** and **C** are mutually orthogonal vectors. Let $\mathbf{D} = 5\mathbf{A} - 6\mathbf{B} + 3\mathbf{C}$.

(a) If **A, B,** and **C** are unit vectors, find $|\mathbf{D}|$, the magnitude of **D.**

(b) If $|\mathbf{A}| = 2$, $|\mathbf{B}| = 3$, and $|\mathbf{C}| = 4$, find $|\mathbf{D}|$.

20. ***Linear Combinations of Orthogonal Vectors*** Suppose **A, B,** and **C** are mutually orthogonal vectors. If **D** is a vector such that $\mathbf{D} = \alpha\mathbf{A} + \beta\mathbf{B} + \gamma\mathbf{C}$ where α, β, and γ are scalars, prove that $\alpha = \mathbf{D} \cdot \mathbf{A}$, $\beta = \mathbf{D} \cdot \mathbf{B}$, and $\gamma = \mathbf{D} \cdot \mathbf{C}$.

21. ***Work Along a Line in Space*** Find the work done by a force $\mathbf{F} = 5\mathbf{k}$ (magnitude 5 N) in moving an object along the line from the origin to the point (1, 1, 1) (distance in meters).

22. ***The Locomotive Big Boy*** The Union Pacific's *Big Boy* locomotive could pull 6000-ton trains with a tractive effort (pull) of 602,148 N (135,368 lb). At this level of effort, about how much work did *Big Boy* do on the (approximately straight) 605-km journey from San Francisco to Los Angeles?

23. ***Work Sliding a Crate*** How much work does it take to slide a crate 20 m along a loading dock by pulling on it with a 200-N force at an angle of 30° from the horizontal?

24. ***Wind at Work*** The wind passing over a boat's sail exerted a 1000-lb magnitude force **F** as shown here. How much work did the wind perform in moving the boat forward 1 mi? Answer in foot-pounds.

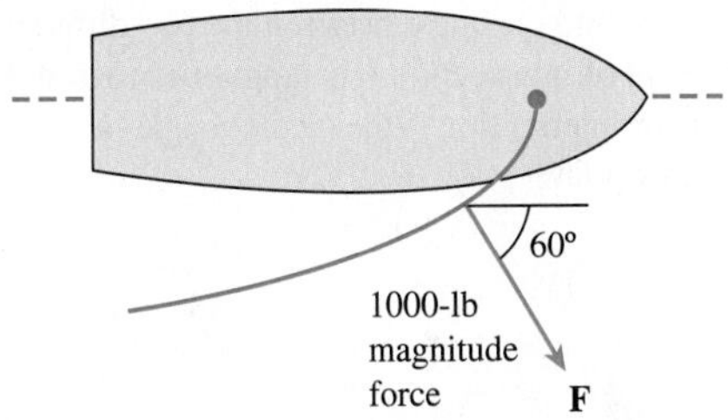

25. ***Vector Perpendicular to a Line*** Show that the vector $\mathbf{v} = a\mathbf{i} + b\mathbf{j}$ is perpendicular to the line $ax + by = c$ by establishing that the slope of any line segment representing $\mathbf{v}$ is the negative reciprocal of the slope of the line.

26. ***Vector Parallel to a Line*** Show that the vector $\mathbf{v} = a\mathbf{i} + b\mathbf{j}$ is parallel to the line $bx - ay = c$ by establishing that the slope of any line segment representing $\mathbf{v}$ is the same as the slope of the line.

In Exercises 27–30, use the result of Exercise 25 to find an equation for the line through P perpendicular to **v.** Then sketch the line. Include **v** in your sketch *as a vector starting at the origin.*

27. $P(2, 1)$, $\mathbf{v} = \mathbf{i} + 2\mathbf{j}$

28. $P(-1, 2)$, $\mathbf{v} = -2\mathbf{i} - \mathbf{j}$

29. $P(-2, -7)$, $\mathbf{v} = -2\mathbf{i} + \mathbf{j}$

30. $P(11, 10)$, $\mathbf{v} = 2\mathbf{i} - 3\mathbf{j}$

In Exercises 31–34, use the result of Exercise 26 to find an equation for the line through P parallel to **v.** Then sketch the line. Include **v** in your sketch *as a vector starting at the origin.*

31. $P(-2, 1)$, $\mathbf{v} = \mathbf{i} - \mathbf{j}$

32. $P(0, -2)$, $\mathbf{v} = 2\mathbf{i} + 3\mathbf{j}$

33. $P(1, 2)$, $\mathbf{v} = -\mathbf{i} - 2\mathbf{j}$

34. $P(1, 3)$, $\mathbf{v} = 3\mathbf{i} - 2\mathbf{j}$

In Exercises 35–40, *work in groups of two or three.* The **acute angle between intersecting lines in the plane** that do not cross at right angles is the same as the angle determined by vectors normal to the lines or by vectors parallel to the lines as shown in the figure. Use this fact and the results of Exercises 25 and 26 to find the acute angle between the given lines.

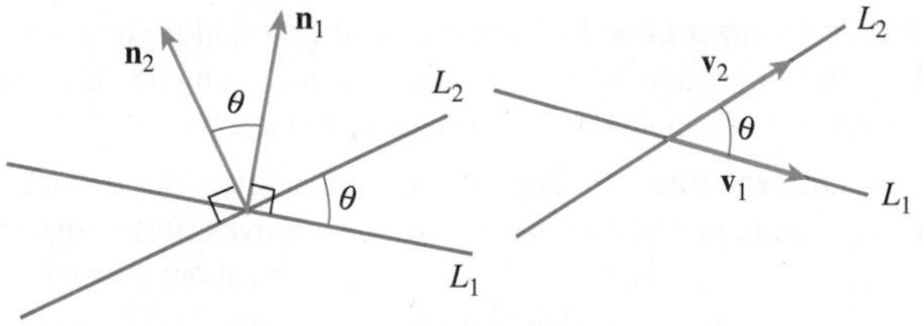

35. $3x + y = 5, \quad 2x - y = 4$

36. $y = \sqrt{3}x - 1, \quad y = -\sqrt{3}x + 2$

37. $\sqrt{3}x - y = -2, \quad x - \sqrt{3}y = 1$

38. $x + \sqrt{3}y = 1, \quad (1 - \sqrt{3})x + (1 + \sqrt{3})y = 8$

39. $3x - 4y = 3, \quad x - y = 7$

40. $12x + 5y = 1, \quad 2x - 2y = 3$

In Exercises 41–44, find the angle between the two differentiable curves at each point of intersection. The **angle between differentiable curves** at a point of intersection is the (acute) angle between the curves' tangent lines at this point.

41. $y = \frac{3}{2} - x^2, \quad y = x^2$

42. $x = \frac{3}{4} - y^2, \quad x = y^2 - \frac{3}{4}$

43. $y = x^3, \quad x = y^2$

44. $y = -x^2, \quad y = \sqrt[3]{x}$

45. ***Properties of the Dot Product*** Let $\mathbf{A}$, $\mathbf{B}$, $\mathbf{C}$, and $\mathbf{D}$ be vectors and c any scalar. Use the component form of the dot product to establish the following properties.

(a) $\mathbf{A} \cdot \mathbf{B} = \mathbf{B} \cdot \mathbf{A}$

(b) $(c\mathbf{A}) \cdot \mathbf{B} = \mathbf{A} \cdot (c\mathbf{B}) = c(\mathbf{A} \cdot \mathbf{B})$

(c) $\mathbf{A} \cdot (\mathbf{B} + \mathbf{C}) = \mathbf{A} \cdot \mathbf{B} + \mathbf{A} \cdot \mathbf{C}$

(d) $(\mathbf{A} + \mathbf{B}) \cdot \mathbf{C} = \mathbf{A} \cdot \mathbf{C} + \mathbf{B} \cdot \mathbf{C}$

(e) $(\mathbf{A} + \mathbf{B}) \cdot (\mathbf{C} + \mathbf{D}) = \mathbf{A} \cdot \mathbf{C} + \mathbf{A} \cdot \mathbf{D} + \mathbf{B} \cdot \mathbf{C} + \mathbf{B} \cdot \mathbf{D}$

(f) $\mathbf{A} \cdot \mathbf{A} = |\mathbf{A}|^2$

Extending the Ideas

46. (a) Use the equation $\mathbf{u} \cdot \mathbf{v} = |\mathbf{u}||\mathbf{v}| \cos \theta$ to show that the inequality $|\mathbf{u} \cdot \mathbf{v}| \le |\mathbf{u}||\mathbf{v}|$ holds for any vectors $\mathbf{u}$ and $\mathbf{v}$.

(b) **Writing to Learn** Under what circumstances, if any, does $|\mathbf{u} \cdot \mathbf{v}|$ equal $|\mathbf{u}||\mathbf{v}|$? Give reasons for your answer.

47. Copy the axes and vector shown here. Then shade in the points (x, y) for which $(x\mathbf{i} + y\mathbf{j}) \cdot \mathbf{v} \le 0$. Justify your answer.

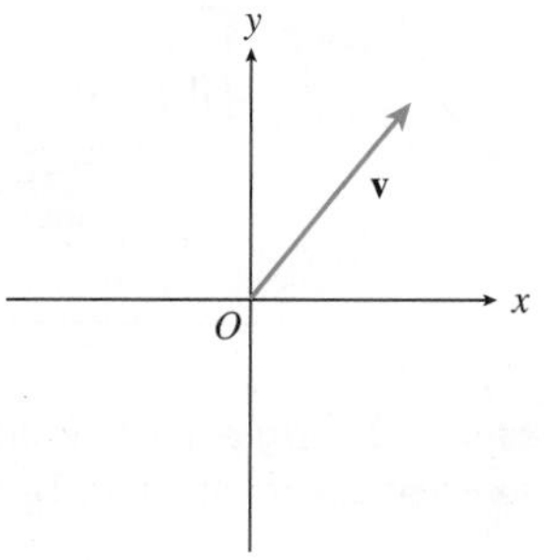

12.3 Cross Products

What you'll learn about

- Definition of Cross Product
- Are Cross Products Commutative?
- $|\mathbf{A} \times \mathbf{B}|$ Is the Area of a Parallelogram
- Torque
- Associative and Distributive Laws
- Determinant Formula for $\mathbf{A} \times \mathbf{B}$
- Triple Scalar or Box Product

Definition of Cross Product

In studying lines in the plane, we needed to describe how a line was tilting. We did so with the notions of slope and angle of inclination. In space, we need to be able to describe how a plane is tilting. We accomplish this by multiplying two vectors in the plane together to get a third vector perpendicular to the plane. The direction of this third vector tells us the "inclination" of the plane. The product we use to multiply the vectors together is the *vector* or *cross product.*

We start with two nonzero vectors $\mathbf{A}$ and $\mathbf{B}$ in space. If $\mathbf{A}$ and $\mathbf{B}$ are not parallel, they determine a plane. We select a unit vector $\mathbf{n}$ perpendicular to the plane by the **right-hand rule.** This means we choose $\mathbf{n}$ to be the unit (normal) vector that points the way your right thumb points when your fingers curl through the angle θ from $\mathbf{A}$ to $\mathbf{B}$ (Figure 12.16).

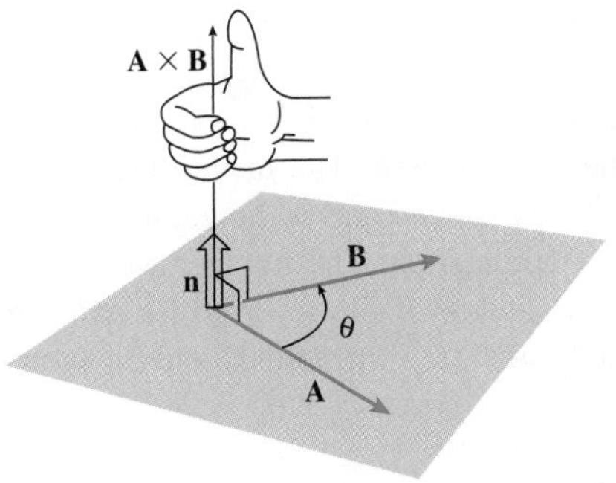

Figure 12.16 The construction of $\mathbf{A} \times \mathbf{B}$.

> **DEFINITION Vector Product A × B**
>
> The **vector product** $\mathbf{A} \times \mathbf{B}$ **("A cross B") of A and B** is the vector
>
> $$\mathbf{A} \times \mathbf{B} = (|\mathbf{A}||\mathbf{B}|\sin\theta)\mathbf{n}.$$

We sometimes call the dot product a **scalar product** to distinguish it from the vector product. The vector $\mathbf{A} \times \mathbf{B}$ is orthogonal to both $\mathbf{A}$ and $\mathbf{B}$ because it is a scalar multiple of $\mathbf{n}$. The vector product of $\mathbf{A}$ and $\mathbf{B}$ is often called the **cross product** of $\mathbf{A}$ and $\mathbf{B}$ because of the cross in the notation $\mathbf{A} \times \mathbf{B}$.

Since the sines of 0 and π are both zero, it makes sense to define the cross product of two parallel nonzero vectors to be $\mathbf{0}$.

If one or both of $\mathbf{A}$ and $\mathbf{B}$ are zero, we also define $\mathbf{A} \times \mathbf{B}$ to be zero. This way, the cross product of two vectors $\mathbf{A}$ and $\mathbf{B}$ is zero if and only if $\mathbf{A}$ and $\mathbf{B}$ are parallel or one or both of them are zero.

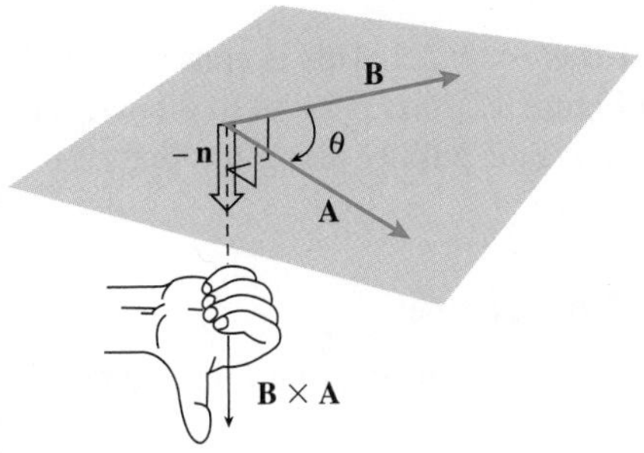

Figure 12.17 The construction of $\mathbf{B} \times \mathbf{A}$.

> Nonzero vectors $\mathbf{A}$ and $\mathbf{B}$ are parallel if and only if $\mathbf{A} \times \mathbf{B} = \mathbf{0}$.

Are Cross Products Commutative?

Reversing the order of the factors in a nonzero cross product reverses the direction of the product. When the fingers of our right hand curl through the angle θ from $\mathbf{B}$ to $\mathbf{A}$, our thumb points the opposite way and the unit vector we choose in forming $\mathbf{B} \times \mathbf{A}$ is the negative of the one we choose in forming $\mathbf{A} \times \mathbf{B}$ (Figure 12.17). Thus, for all vectors $\mathbf{A}$ and $\mathbf{B}$,

> $$\mathbf{B} \times \mathbf{A} = -(\mathbf{A} \times \mathbf{B}).$$

Unlike the dot product, the cross product is not commutative.

When we apply the definition to calculate the pairwise cross products of $\mathbf{i}$, $\mathbf{j}$, and $\mathbf{k}$, we find (Figure 12.18)

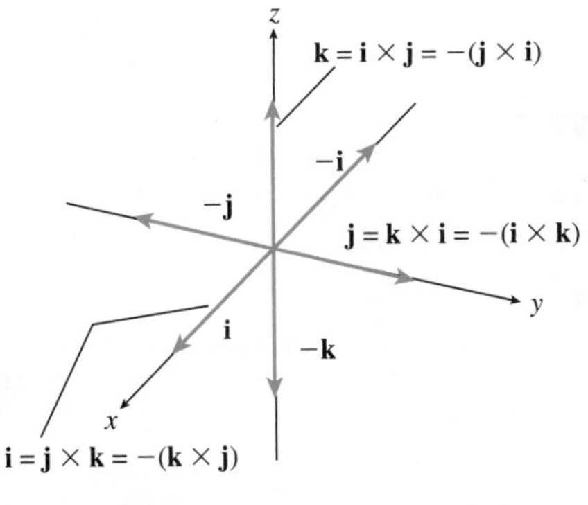

Figure 12.18 The pairwise cross products of $\mathbf{i}$, $\mathbf{j}$, and $\mathbf{k}$.

$$\mathbf{i} \times \mathbf{j} = -(\mathbf{j} \times \mathbf{i}) = \mathbf{k}$$
$$\mathbf{j} \times \mathbf{k} = -(\mathbf{k} \times \mathbf{j}) = \mathbf{i}$$
$$\mathbf{k} \times \mathbf{i} = -(\mathbf{i} \times \mathbf{k}) = \mathbf{j}$$

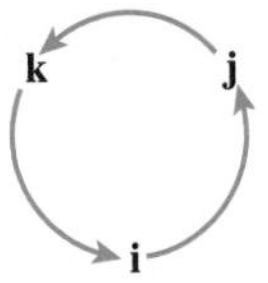

Diagram for recalling these products.

and

$$\mathbf{i} \times \mathbf{i} = \mathbf{j} \times \mathbf{j} = \mathbf{k} \times \mathbf{k} = \mathbf{0}.$$

$|\mathbf{A} \times \mathbf{B}|$ Is the Area of a Parallelogram

Because $\mathbf{n}$ is a unit vector, the magnitude of $\mathbf{A} \times \mathbf{B}$ is

> $$|\mathbf{A} \times \mathbf{B}| = |\mathbf{A}||\mathbf{B}||\sin\theta||\mathbf{n}| = |\mathbf{A}||\mathbf{B}||\sin\theta|.$$

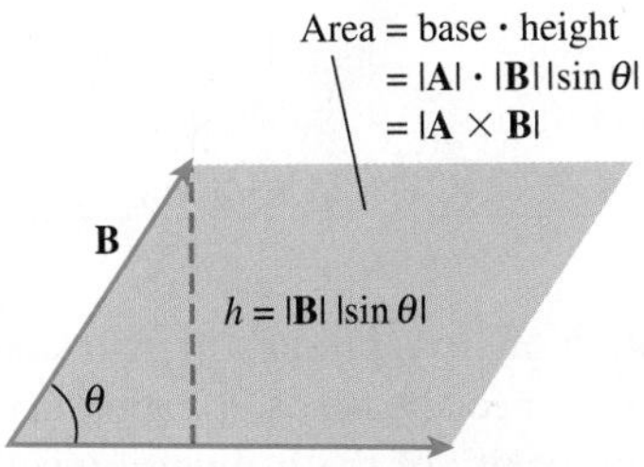

Figure 12.19 The parallelogram determined by $\mathbf{A}$ and $\mathbf{B}$.

This is the area of the parallelogram determined by $\mathbf{A}$ and $\mathbf{B}$ (Figure 12.19), $|\mathbf{A}|$ being the base of the parallelogram and $|\mathbf{B}||\sin\theta|$ the height.

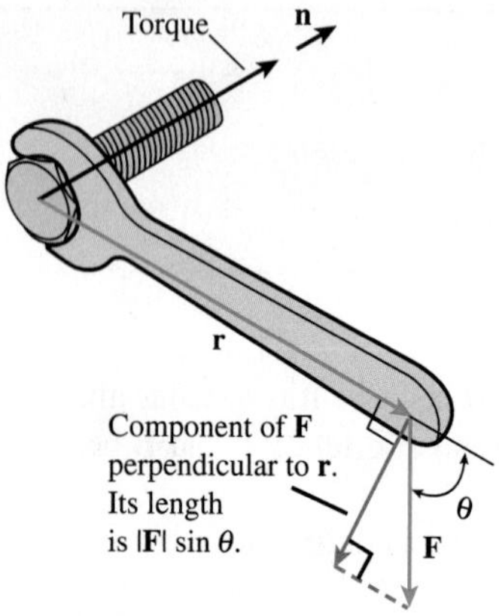

Figure 12.20 The torque vector describes the tendency of the force **F** to drive the bolt forward.

Torque

When we tighten a bolt by applying a force **F** to a wrench (Figure 12.20), the torque we produce acts along the axis of the bolt to drive the bolt forward. The magnitude of the torque depends on how far out on the wrench the force is applied and on how much of the force is perpendicular to the wrench at the point of application. The number we use to measure the torque's magnitude is the product of the length of the lever arm **r** and the scalar component of **F** perpendicular to **r.** The usual units are foot-pounds and Newton-meters, the same units as work.

In the notation of Figure 12.20,

$$\text{Magnitude of torque vector} = |\mathbf{r}||\mathbf{F}| \sin\theta,$$

or $|\mathbf{r} \times \mathbf{F}|$. If we let **n** be a unit vector along the axis of the bolt in the direction of the torque, then a complete description of the torque vector is $\mathbf{r} \times \mathbf{F}$, or

$$\text{Torque vector} = (|\mathbf{r}||\mathbf{F}| \sin\theta)\mathbf{n}.$$

Recall that we defined $\mathbf{A} \times \mathbf{B}$ to be $\mathbf{0}$ when **A** and **B** are parallel. This is consistent with the torque interpretation as well. If the force **F** in Figure 12.20 is parallel to the wrench, meaning that we are trying to turn the bolt by pushing or pulling along the line of the wrench's handle, the torque produced is zero.

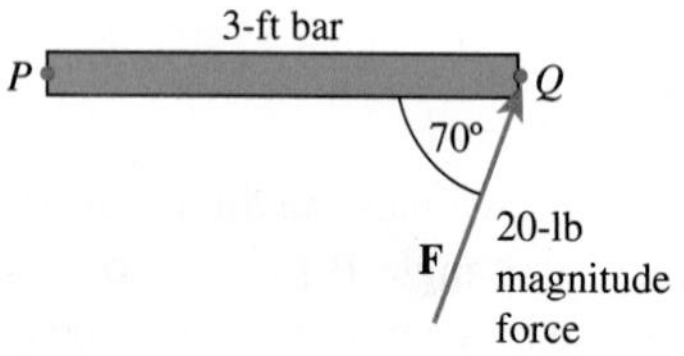

Figure 12.21 The figure for Example 1.

EXAMPLE 1 Finding the Magnitude of a Torque

The magnitude of the torque exerted by the force **F** about the pivot point P in Figure 12.21 is

$$|\overrightarrow{PQ} \times \mathbf{F}| = |\overrightarrow{PQ}||\mathbf{F}| \sin 70°$$
$$\approx (3)(20)(0.94) = 56.4 \text{ ft-lb}$$

Associative and Distributive Laws

As a rule, cross-product multiplication is *not associative* because $(\mathbf{A} \times \mathbf{B}) \times \mathbf{C}$ lies in the plane of **A** and **B** whereas $\mathbf{A} \times (\mathbf{B} \times \mathbf{C})$ lies in the plane of **B** and **C.** However, the following properties do hold.

Properties of the Cross Product
Scalar Distributive Laws

$$(r\mathbf{A}) \times (s\mathbf{B}) = (rs)(\mathbf{A} \times \mathbf{B}) \tag{1}$$

$$(-\mathbf{A}) \times \mathbf{B} = \mathbf{A} \times (-\mathbf{B}) = -(\mathbf{A} \times \mathbf{B}) \tag{2}$$

Vector Distributive Laws

$$\mathbf{A} \times (\mathbf{B} + \mathbf{C}) = \mathbf{A} \times \mathbf{B} + \mathbf{A} \times \mathbf{C} \tag{3}$$

$$(\mathbf{B} + \mathbf{C}) \times \mathbf{A} = \mathbf{B} \times \mathbf{A} + \mathbf{C} \times \mathbf{A} \tag{4}$$

Equation (1) can be verified by applying the definition of cross product to both sides of the equation and comparing the results. Equation (2) is a special case of Equation (1). We will skip the proof of Equation (3) because of the complexity of the geometry involved. Equation (4) follows from Equation (3) by multiplying both sides of Equation (3) by -1 and reversing the orders of the products.

Determinant Formula for A × B

Our next objective is to calculate $\mathbf{A} \times \mathbf{B}$ from the components of $\mathbf{A}$ and $\mathbf{B}$ relative to a Cartesian coordinate system.

Suppose

$$\mathbf{A} = a_1\mathbf{i} + a_2\mathbf{j} + a_3\mathbf{k}, \mathbf{B} = b_1\mathbf{i} + b_2\mathbf{j} + b_3\mathbf{k}.$$

Then the distributive laws and the rules for multiplying **i, j,** and **k** tell us that

$$\begin{aligned}\mathbf{A} \times \mathbf{B} &= (a_1\mathbf{i} + a_2\mathbf{j} + a_3\mathbf{k}) \times (b_1\mathbf{i} + b_2\mathbf{j} + b_3\mathbf{k}) \\ &= a_1b_1\mathbf{i} \times \mathbf{i} + a_1b_2\mathbf{i} \times \mathbf{j} + a_1b_3\mathbf{i} \times \mathbf{k} \\ &\quad + a_2b_1\mathbf{j} \times \mathbf{i} + a_2b_2\mathbf{j} \times \mathbf{j} + a_2b_3\mathbf{j} \times \mathbf{k} \\ &\quad + a_3b_1\mathbf{k} \times \mathbf{i} + a_3b_2\mathbf{k} \times \mathbf{j} + a_3b_3\mathbf{k} \times \mathbf{k} \\ &= (a_2b_3 - a_3b_2)\mathbf{i} - (a_1b_3 - a_3b_1)\mathbf{j} + (a_1b_2 - a_2b_1)\mathbf{k}.\end{aligned}$$

The terms in the last line are the same as the terms in the expansion of the symbolic determinant

$$\begin{vmatrix} \mathbf{i} & \mathbf{j} & \mathbf{k} \\ a_1 & a_2 & a_3 \\ b_1 & b_2 & b_3 \end{vmatrix}.$$

We therefore have the following formula.

Determinants

LS(For more information, see Appendix 8.)

$$\begin{vmatrix} a & b \\ c & d \end{vmatrix} = ad - bc$$

Example

$$\begin{vmatrix} 2 & 1 \\ -4 & 3 \end{vmatrix} = (2)(3) - (1)(-4)$$
$$= 6 + 4 = 10$$

$$\begin{vmatrix} a_1 & a_2 & a_3 \\ b_1 & b_2 & b_3 \\ c_1 & c_2 & c_3 \end{vmatrix}$$
$$= a_1\begin{vmatrix} b_2 & b_3 \\ c_2 & c_3 \end{vmatrix} - a_2\begin{vmatrix} b_1 & b_2 \\ c_1 & c_3 \end{vmatrix} + a_3\begin{vmatrix} b_1 & b_2 \\ c_1 & c_2 \end{vmatrix}$$

Example

$$\begin{vmatrix} -5 & 3 & 1 \\ 2 & 1 & 1 \\ -4 & 3 & 1 \end{vmatrix}$$
$$= (-5)\begin{vmatrix} 1 & 1 \\ 3 & 1 \end{vmatrix} - (3)\begin{vmatrix} 2 & 1 \\ -4 & 1 \end{vmatrix}$$
$$+ (1)\begin{vmatrix} 2 & 1 \\ -4 & 3 \end{vmatrix}$$
$$= -5(1 - 3) - 3(2 + 4) + 1(6 + 4)$$
$$= 10 - 18 + 10 = 2$$

Evaluating Cross Products Using Determinants

If $\mathbf{A} = a_1\mathbf{i} + a_2\mathbf{j} + a_3\mathbf{k}$ and $\mathbf{B} = b_1\mathbf{i} + b_2\mathbf{j} + b_3\mathbf{k}$, then

$$\mathbf{A} \times \mathbf{B} = \begin{vmatrix} \mathbf{i} & \mathbf{j} & \mathbf{k} \\ a_1 & a_2 & a_3 \\ b_1 & b_2 & b_3 \end{vmatrix}.$$

EXAMPLE 2 Computing Cross Products with Determinants

Find $\mathbf{A} \times \mathbf{B}$ and $\mathbf{B} \times \mathbf{A}$ if

$$\mathbf{A} = 2\mathbf{i} + \mathbf{j} + \mathbf{k}, \qquad \mathbf{B} = -4\mathbf{i} + 3\mathbf{j} + \mathbf{k}.$$

SOLUTION

$$\mathbf{A} \times \mathbf{B} = \begin{vmatrix} \mathbf{i} & \mathbf{j} & \mathbf{k} \\ 2 & 1 & 1 \\ -4 & 3 & 1 \end{vmatrix} = \begin{vmatrix} 1 & 1 \\ 3 & 1 \end{vmatrix}\mathbf{i} - \begin{vmatrix} 2 & 1 \\ -4 & 1 \end{vmatrix}\mathbf{j} + \begin{vmatrix} 2 & 1 \\ -4 & 3 \end{vmatrix}\mathbf{k}$$

$$= -2\mathbf{i} - 6\mathbf{j} + 10\mathbf{k}$$

$$\mathbf{B} \times \mathbf{A} = -(\mathbf{A} \times \mathbf{B}) = 2\mathbf{i} + 6\mathbf{j} - 10\mathbf{k}$$

EXAMPLE 3 Finding Vectors Perpendicular to a Plane

Find a vector perpendicular to the plane of $P(1, -1, 0)$, $Q(2, 1, -1)$, and $R(-1, 1, 2)$.

SOLUTION

The vector $\overrightarrow{PQ} \times \overrightarrow{PR}$ is perpendicular to the plane because it is perpendicular to both vectors. In terms of components,

$$\overrightarrow{PQ} = (2 - 1)\mathbf{i} + (1 + 1)\mathbf{j} + (-1 - 0)\mathbf{k} = \mathbf{i} + 2\mathbf{j} - \mathbf{k}$$

$$\overrightarrow{PR} = (-1 - 1)\mathbf{i} + (1 + 1)\mathbf{j} + (2 - 0)\mathbf{k} = -2\mathbf{i} + 2\mathbf{j} + 2\mathbf{k}$$

$$\overrightarrow{PQ} \times \overrightarrow{PR} = \begin{vmatrix} \mathbf{i} & \mathbf{j} & \mathbf{k} \\ 1 & 2 & -1 \\ -2 & 2 & 2 \end{vmatrix} = \begin{vmatrix} 2 & -1 \\ 2 & 2 \end{vmatrix}\mathbf{i} - \begin{vmatrix} 1 & -1 \\ -2 & 2 \end{vmatrix}\mathbf{j} + \begin{vmatrix} 1 & 2 \\ -2 & 2 \end{vmatrix}\mathbf{k}$$

$$= 6\mathbf{i} + 6\mathbf{k}.$$

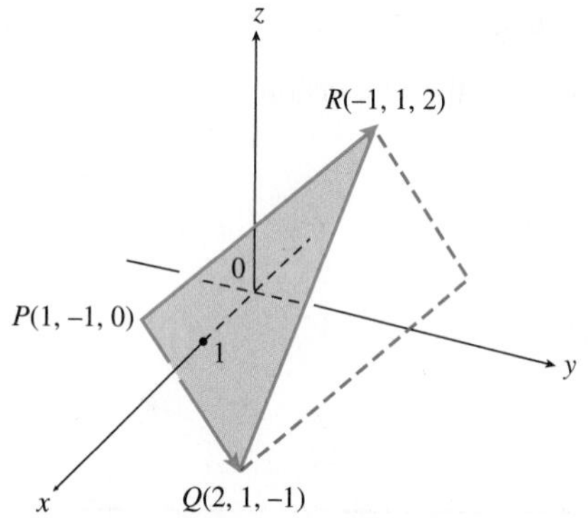

Figure 12.22 The area of the triangle PQR is half of $|\overrightarrow{PQ} \times \overrightarrow{PR}|$. (Example 4)

EXAMPLE 4 Finding the Area of a Triangle

Find the area of the triangle with vertices $P(1, -1, 0)$, $Q(2, 1, -1)$, and $R(-1, 1, 2)$ (Figure 12.22).

SOLUTION

The area of the parallelogram determined by P, Q, and R is

$$|\overrightarrow{PQ} \times \overrightarrow{PR}| = |6\mathbf{i} + 6\mathbf{k}|$$
$$= \sqrt{6^2 + 6^2} = 6\sqrt{2}.$$

The triangle's area is half of this, or $3\sqrt{2}$ units squared.

EXAMPLE 5 Finding a Unit Normal to a Plane

Find a unit vector perpendicular to the plane containing $P(1, -1, 0)$, $Q(2, 1, -1)$, and $R(-1, 1, 2)$.

SOLUTION

Since $\overrightarrow{PQ} \times \overrightarrow{PR}$ is perpendicular to the plane, its direction $\mathbf{n}$ is a unit vector perpendicular to the plane. Taking values from Examples 3 and 4, we have

$$\mathbf{n} = \frac{\overrightarrow{PQ} \times \overrightarrow{PR}}{|\overrightarrow{PQ} \times \overrightarrow{PR}|} = \frac{6\mathbf{i} + 6\mathbf{k}}{6\sqrt{2}} = \frac{1}{\sqrt{2}}\mathbf{i} + \frac{1}{\sqrt{2}}\mathbf{k}.$$

Triple Scalar or Box Product

The product $(\mathbf{A} \times \mathbf{B}) \cdot \mathbf{C}$ is the **triple scalar product** of **A, B,** and **C** (in that order). As you can see from the formula

$$|(\mathbf{A} \times \mathbf{B}) \cdot \mathbf{C}| = |\mathbf{A} \times \mathbf{B}||\mathbf{C}||\cos\theta|,$$

the absolute value of the product is the volume of the parallelepiped (parallelogram-sided box) determined by **A, B,** and **C** (Figure 12.23). The number $|\mathbf{A} \times \mathbf{B}|$ is the area of the base parallelogram. The number $|\mathbf{C}||\cos\theta|$ is the parallelepiped's height. Because of this geometry, $(\mathbf{A} \times \mathbf{B}) \cdot \mathbf{C}$ is also called the **box product** of **A, B,** and **C.**

By treating the planes of **B** and **C** and of **C** and **A** as the base planes of the parallelepiped determined by **A, B,** and **C,** we see that

$$(\mathbf{A} \times \mathbf{B}) \cdot \mathbf{C} = (\mathbf{B} \times \mathbf{C}) \cdot \mathbf{A} = (\mathbf{C} \times \mathbf{A}) \cdot \mathbf{B}.$$

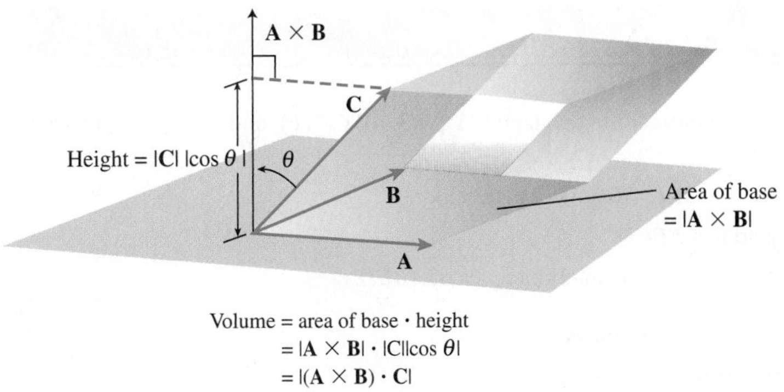

Figure 12.23 The number $|(\mathbf{A} \times \mathbf{B}) \cdot \mathbf{C}|$ is the volume of a parallelepiped.

Triple Scalar Product

The dot and cross may be interchanged in a triple scalar product without altering its value.

Since the dot product is commutative, the equation above also gives

$$(\mathbf{A} \times \mathbf{B}) \cdot \mathbf{C} = \mathbf{A} \cdot (\mathbf{B} \times \mathbf{C}).$$

The triple scalar product can be evaluated as a determinant:

$$\begin{aligned}\mathbf{A} \cdot (\mathbf{B} \times \mathbf{C}) &= \mathbf{A} \cdot \left[\begin{vmatrix} b_2 & b_3 \\ c_2 & c_3 \end{vmatrix} \mathbf{i} - \begin{vmatrix} b_1 & b_3 \\ c_1 & c_3 \end{vmatrix} \mathbf{j} + \begin{vmatrix} b_1 & b_2 \\ c_1 & c_2 \end{vmatrix} \mathbf{k} \right] \\ &= a_1 \begin{vmatrix} b_2 & b_3 \\ c_2 & c_3 \end{vmatrix} - a_2 \begin{vmatrix} b_1 & b_3 \\ c_1 & c_3 \end{vmatrix} + a_3 \begin{vmatrix} b_1 & b_2 \\ c_1 & c_2 \end{vmatrix} \\ &= \begin{vmatrix} a_1 & a_2 & a_3 \\ b_1 & b_2 & b_3 \\ c_1 & c_2 & c_3 \end{vmatrix}\end{aligned}$$

Triple Scalar Product

$$\mathbf{A} \cdot (\mathbf{B} \times \mathbf{C}) = (\mathbf{A} \times \mathbf{B}) \cdot \mathbf{C} = \begin{vmatrix} a_1 & a_2 & a_3 \\ b_1 & b_2 & b_3 \\ c_1 & c_2 & c_3 \end{vmatrix} \quad (5)$$

EXAMPLE 6 Finding the Volume of a Parallelepiped

Find the volume of the box (parallelepiped) determined by $\mathbf{A} = \mathbf{i} + 2\mathbf{j} - \mathbf{k}$, $\mathbf{B} = -2\mathbf{i} + 3\mathbf{k}$, and $\mathbf{C} = 7\mathbf{j} - 4\mathbf{k}$.

SOLUTION

Using a calculator, we find

$$\mathbf{A} \cdot (\mathbf{B} \times \mathbf{C}) = \begin{vmatrix} 1 & 2 & -1 \\ -2 & 0 & 3 \\ 0 & 7 & -4 \end{vmatrix} = -23.$$

The volume is $|\mathbf{A} \cdot (\mathbf{B} \times \mathbf{C})| = 23$ units cubed.

Quick Review 12.3

In Exercises 1–3, consider the points $A(1, 1)$, $B(3, 4)$, $C(7, 6)$, and $D(5, 3)$.

1. Show that the figure $ABCD$ is a parallelogram.

2. Find the area of $ABCD$.

3. Find the measure of the interior angles of $ABCD$.

In Exercises 4 and 5, solve the equation.

4. $\sin 2x = 0, 0 \le x \le 2\pi$

5. $\cos 2x = 0, 0 \le x \le 2\pi$

In Exercises 6–10, evaluate the determinants.

6. $\begin{vmatrix} 2 & 3 \\ -1 & 1 \end{vmatrix}$ **7.** $\begin{vmatrix} -3 & 4 \\ 0 & 1 \end{vmatrix}$

8. $\begin{vmatrix} 2 & 3 & -1 \\ -1 & 2 & 4 \\ 1 & 0 & 3 \end{vmatrix}$ **9.** $\begin{vmatrix} -1 & 0 & 1 \\ 1 & 1 & 1 \\ 0 & 1 & -1 \end{vmatrix}$

10. $\begin{vmatrix} 2 & -1 & 3 \\ 4 & 0 & -2 \\ -6 & 1 & -1 \end{vmatrix}$

Section 12.3 Exercises

In Exercises 1–8, find the length and direction (when defined) of $\mathbf{A} \times \mathbf{B}$ and $\mathbf{B} \times \mathbf{A}$.

1. $\mathbf{A} = 2\mathbf{i} - 2\mathbf{j} - \mathbf{k}, \mathbf{B} = \mathbf{i} - \mathbf{k}$

2. $\mathbf{A} = 2\mathbf{i} - 3\mathbf{j}, \mathbf{B} = -\mathbf{i} + \mathbf{j}$

3. $\mathbf{A} = 2\mathbf{i} - 2\mathbf{j} + 4\mathbf{k}, \mathbf{B} = -\mathbf{i} + \mathbf{j} - 2\mathbf{k}$

4. $\mathbf{A} = \mathbf{i} + \mathbf{j} - \mathbf{k}, \mathbf{B} = \mathbf{0}$

5. $\mathbf{A} = 2\mathbf{i}, \mathbf{B} = -3\mathbf{j}$

6. $\mathbf{A} = \mathbf{i} \times \mathbf{j}, \mathbf{B} = \mathbf{j} \times \mathbf{k}$

7. $\mathbf{A} = -8\mathbf{i} - 2\mathbf{j} - 4\mathbf{k}, \mathbf{B} = 2\mathbf{i} + 2\mathbf{j} + \mathbf{k}$

8. $\mathbf{A} = \frac{3}{2}\mathbf{i} - \frac{1}{2}\mathbf{j} + \mathbf{k}, \mathbf{B} = \mathbf{i} + \mathbf{j} + \mathbf{k}$

In Exercises 9–14, sketch the coordinate axes and then include the vectors $\mathbf{A}$, $\mathbf{B}$, and $\mathbf{A} \times \mathbf{B}$ as vectors starting at the origin.

9. $\mathbf{A} = \mathbf{i}, \mathbf{B} = \mathbf{j}$ **10.** $\mathbf{A} = \mathbf{i} - \mathbf{k}, \mathbf{B} = \mathbf{j}$

11. $\mathbf{A} = \mathbf{i} - \mathbf{k}, \mathbf{B} = \mathbf{j} + \mathbf{k}$

12. $\mathbf{A} = 2\mathbf{i} - \mathbf{j}, \mathbf{B} = \mathbf{i} + 2\mathbf{j}$

13. $\mathbf{A} = \mathbf{i} + \mathbf{j}, \mathbf{B} = \mathbf{i} - \mathbf{j}$ **14.** $\mathbf{A} = \mathbf{j} + 2\mathbf{k}, \mathbf{B} = \mathbf{i}$

In Exercises 15–18, find

(a) the area of the triangle determined by the points P, Q, and R.

(b) a unit vector perpendicular to plane PQR.

15. $P(1, -1, 2), Q(2, 0, -1), R(0, 2, 1)$

16. $P(1, 1, 1), Q(2, 1, 3), R(3, -1, 1)$

17. $P(2, -2, 1), Q(3, -1, 2), R(3, -1, 1)$

18. $P(-2, 2, 0), Q(0, 1, -1), R(-1, 2, -2)$

19. Writing to Learn Let $\mathbf{A} = 5\mathbf{i} - \mathbf{j} + \mathbf{k}, \mathbf{B} = \mathbf{j} - 5\mathbf{k}$, and $\mathbf{C} = -15\mathbf{i} + 3\mathbf{j} - 3\mathbf{k}$. Which vectors, if any, are **(a)** perpendicular, **(b)** parallel? Give reasons for your answers.

20. Writing to Learn Let $\mathbf{A} = \mathbf{i} + 2\mathbf{j} - \mathbf{k}, \mathbf{B} = -\mathbf{i} + \mathbf{j} + \mathbf{k}, \mathbf{C} = \mathbf{i} + \mathbf{k}$, and $\mathbf{D} = -(\pi/2)\mathbf{i} - \pi\mathbf{j} + (\pi/2)\mathbf{k}$. Which vectors, if any, are **(a)** perpendicular, **(b)** parallel? Give reasons for your answers.

In Exercises 21 and 22, *work in groups of two or three.* Find the magnitude of the torque exerted by $\mathbf{F}$ on the bolt at P if $|\overrightarrow{PQ}| = 8$ in. and $|\mathbf{F}| = 30$ lb. Answer in foot-pounds.

21.

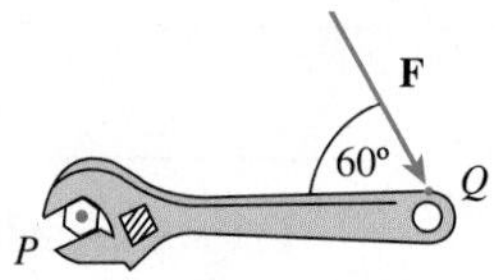

22.

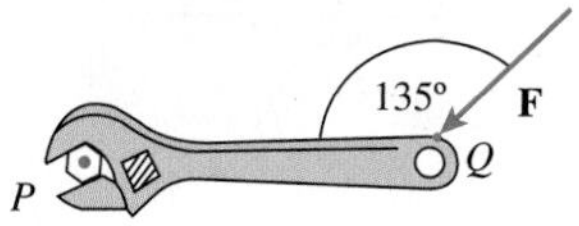

In Exercises 23–26, verify that $(\mathbf{A} \times \mathbf{B}) \cdot \mathbf{C} = (\mathbf{B} \times \mathbf{C}) \cdot \mathbf{A} = (\mathbf{C} \times \mathbf{A}) \cdot \mathbf{B}$ and find the volume of the parallelepiped (box) determined by $\mathbf{A}$, $\mathbf{B}$, and $\mathbf{C}$.

	A	**B**	**C**
23.	$2\mathbf{i}$	$2\mathbf{j}$	$2\mathbf{k}$
24.	$\mathbf{i} - \mathbf{j} + \mathbf{k}$	$2\mathbf{i} + \mathbf{j} - 2\mathbf{k}$	$-\mathbf{i} + 2\mathbf{j} - \mathbf{k}$
25.	$2\mathbf{i} + \mathbf{j}$	$2\mathbf{i} - \mathbf{j} + \mathbf{k}$	$\mathbf{i} + 2\mathbf{k}$
26.	$\mathbf{i} + \mathbf{j} - 2\mathbf{k}$	$-\mathbf{i} - \mathbf{k}$	$2\mathbf{i} + 4\mathbf{j} - 2\mathbf{k}$

Explorations

27. Which of the following are *always true* and which are *not always true?* Give reasons for your answers.

(a) $|\mathbf{A}| = \sqrt{\mathbf{A} \cdot \mathbf{A}}$ **(b)** $\mathbf{A} \cdot \mathbf{A} = |\mathbf{A}|$

(c) $\mathbf{A} \times \mathbf{0} = \mathbf{0} \times \mathbf{A} = 0$ **(d)** $\mathbf{A} \times (-\mathbf{A}) = \mathbf{0}$

(e) $\mathbf{A} \times \mathbf{B} = \mathbf{B} \times \mathbf{A}$

(f) $\mathbf{A} \times (\mathbf{B} + \mathbf{C}) = \mathbf{A} \times \mathbf{B} + \mathbf{A} \times \mathbf{C}$

(g) $(\mathbf{A} \times \mathbf{B}) \cdot \mathbf{B} = 0$

(h) $(\mathbf{A} \times \mathbf{B}) \cdot \mathbf{C} = \mathbf{A} \cdot (\mathbf{B} \times \mathbf{C})$

28. Which of the following are *always true* and which are *not always true?* Give reasons for your answers.

(a) $\mathbf{A} \cdot \mathbf{B} = \mathbf{B} \cdot \mathbf{A}$

(b) $\mathbf{A} \times \mathbf{B} = -(\mathbf{B} \times \mathbf{A})$

(c) $(-\mathbf{A}) \times \mathbf{B} = -(\mathbf{A} \times \mathbf{B})$

(d) $(c\mathbf{A}) \cdot \mathbf{B} = \mathbf{A} \cdot (c\mathbf{B}) = c(\mathbf{A} \cdot \mathbf{B})$, c any number

(e) $c(\mathbf{A} \times \mathbf{B}) = (c\mathbf{A}) \times \mathbf{B} = \mathbf{A} \times (c\mathbf{B})$, c any number

(f) $\mathbf{A} \cdot \mathbf{A} = |\mathbf{A}|^2$

(g) $(\mathbf{A} \times \mathbf{A}) \cdot \mathbf{A} = 0$

(h) $(\mathbf{A} \times \mathbf{B}) \cdot \mathbf{A} = \mathbf{B} \cdot (\mathbf{A} \times \mathbf{B})$

29. Given nonzero vectors **A, B,** and **C,** use dot-product and cross-product notation, as appropriate, to describe the following.

(a) The vector projection of **A** onto **B**

(b) A vector orthogonal to **A** and **B**

(c) A vector orthogonal to $\mathbf{A} \times \mathbf{B}$ and **C**

(d) The volume of the parallelepiped determined by **A, B,** and **C**

30. Given nonzero vectors **A, B,** and **C,** use dot-product and cross-product notation to describe the following.

(a) A vector orthogonal to $\mathbf{A} \times \mathbf{B}$ and $\mathbf{A} \times \mathbf{C}$

(b) A vector orthogonal to $\mathbf{A} + \mathbf{B}$ and $\mathbf{A} - \mathbf{B}$

(c) A vector of length $|\mathbf{A}|$ in the direction of **B**

(d) The area of the parallelogram determined by **A** and **C**

31. Writing to Learn Let **A, B,** and **C** be vectors. Which of the following make sense, and which do not? Give reasons for your answers.

(a) $(\mathbf{A} \times \mathbf{B}) \cdot \mathbf{C}$ **(b)** $\mathbf{A} \times (\mathbf{B} \cdot \mathbf{C})$

(c) $\mathbf{A} \times (\mathbf{B} \times \mathbf{C})$ **(d)** $\mathbf{A} \cdot (\mathbf{B} \cdot \mathbf{C})$

32. Writing to Learn Show that except in degenerate cases, $(\mathbf{A} \times \mathbf{B}) \times \mathbf{C}$ lies in the plane of **A** and **B** whereas $\mathbf{A} \times (\mathbf{B} \times \mathbf{C})$ lies in the plane of **B** and **C.** What are the degenerate cases?

In Exercises 33–36, find the area of the parallelogram whose vertices are given.

33. $A(1, 0)$, $B(0, 1)$, $C(-1, 0)$, $D(0, -1)$

34. $A(0, 0)$, $B(7, 3)$, $C(9, 8)$, $D(2, 5)$

35. $A(-1, 2)$, $B(2, 0)$, $C(7, 1)$, $D(4, 3)$

36. $A(-6, 0)$, $B(1, -4)$, $C(3, 1)$, $D(-4, 5)$

In Exercises 37–40, find the area of the triangle whose vertices are given.

37. $A(0, 0)$, $B(-2, 3)$, $C(3, 1)$

38. $A(-1, -1)$, $B(3, 3)$, $C(2, 1)$

39. $A(-5, 3)$, $B(1, -2)$, $C(6, -2)$

40. $A(-6, 0)$, $B(10, -5)$, $C(-2, 4)$

Extending the Ideas

41. Writing to Learn Find a formula for the area of the triangle in the xy-plane with vertices at $(0, 0)$, (a_1, a_2), and (b_1, b_2). Explain your work.

42. Find a concise formula for the area of a triangle in the xy-plane with vertices (a_1, a_2), (b_1, b_2), and (c_1, c_2).

43. ***Cancellation in Cross Products*** If $\mathbf{A} \times \mathbf{B} = \mathbf{A} \times \mathbf{C}$ and $\mathbf{A} \neq \mathbf{0}$, then does $\mathbf{B} = \mathbf{C}$? Give reasons for your answer.

44. ***Double Cancellation*** If $\mathbf{A} \neq \mathbf{0}$ and if $\mathbf{A} \times \mathbf{B} = \mathbf{A} \times \mathbf{C}$ and $\mathbf{A} \cdot \mathbf{B} = \mathbf{A} \cdot \mathbf{C}$, then does $\mathbf{B} = \mathbf{C}$? Give reasons for your answer.

12.4 Lines and Planes in Space

- Lines and Line Segments in Space
- Equations for Planes in Space
- Lines of Intersection

Lines and Line Segments in Space

Suppose L is a line in space passing through a point $P_0(x_0, y_0, z_0)$ parallel to a vector $\mathbf{v} = A\mathbf{i} + B\mathbf{j} + C\mathbf{k}$. Then L is the set of all points $P(x, y, z)$ for which $\overrightarrow{P_0P}$ is parallel to $\mathbf{v}$ (Figure 12.24). That is, P lies on L if and only if $\overrightarrow{P_0P}$ is a scalar multiple of $\mathbf{v}$.

Vector Equation for a Line

A vector equation for the line through $P_0(x_0, y_0, z_0)$ parallel to $\mathbf{v}$ is

$$\overrightarrow{P_0P} = t\mathbf{v}, \qquad -\infty < t < \infty. \qquad (1)$$

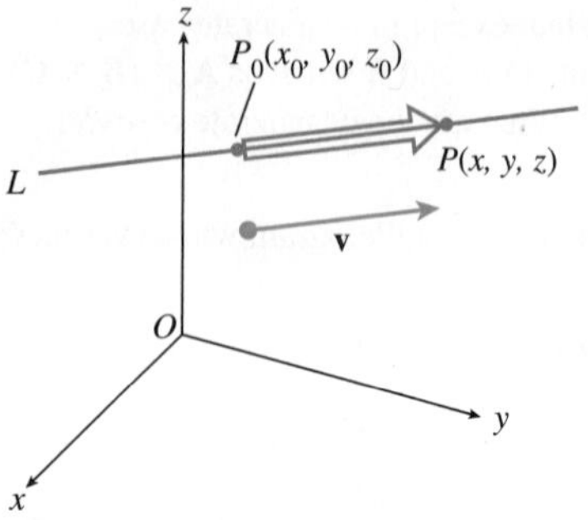

Figure 12.24 A point P lies on the line through P_0 parallel to **v** if and only if $\overrightarrow{P_0P}$ is a scalar multiple of **v**.

Equating the corresponding components of the two sides of Equation (1) gives three scalar equations involving the parameter t:

$$(x - x_0)\mathbf{i} + (y - y_0)\mathbf{j} + (z - z_0)\mathbf{k} = t(A\mathbf{i} + B\mathbf{j} + C\mathbf{k}) \qquad \text{Eq. (1) expanded}$$

$$x - x_0 = tA, \qquad y - y_0 = tB, \qquad z - z_0 = tC. \qquad \text{Components equated}$$

When rearranged, these equations give the standard parametrization of the line for the parameter interval $-\infty < t < \infty$.

Parametric Equations for a Line

The standard parametrization of the line through $P_0(x_0, y_0, z_0)$ parallel to $\mathbf{v} = A\mathbf{i} + B\mathbf{j} + C\mathbf{k}$ is

$$x = x_0 + tA, \qquad y = y_0 + tB, \qquad z = z_0 + tC, \qquad -\infty < t < \infty. \tag{2}$$

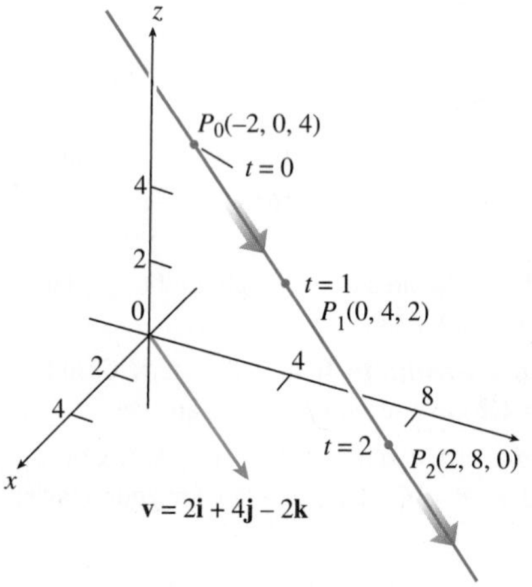

Figure 12.25 Selected points and parameter values on the line of Example 1. The arrows show the direction of increasing t.

EXAMPLE 1 Parametrizing a Line Passing Through a Point Parallel to a Vector

Find parametric equations for the line through $(-2, 0, 4)$ parallel to $\mathbf{v} = 2\mathbf{i} + 4\mathbf{j} - 2\mathbf{k}$ (Figure 12.25).

SOLUTION

With $P_0(x_0, y_0, z_0)$ equal to $(-2, 0, 4)$ and $A\mathbf{i} + B\mathbf{j} + C\mathbf{k}$ equal to $2\mathbf{i} + 4\mathbf{j} - 2\mathbf{k}$, Equations (2) become

$$x = -2 + 2t, \qquad y = 4t, \qquad z = 4 - 2t.$$

EXAMPLE 2 Parametrizing a Line Through Two Points

Find parametric equations for the line through $P(-3, 2, -3)$ and $Q(1, -1, 4)$.

SOLUTION

The vector

$$\begin{aligned}\overrightarrow{PQ} &= (1 - (-3))\,\mathbf{i} + (-1 - 2)\mathbf{j} + (4 - (-3))\mathbf{k} \\ &= 4\mathbf{i} - 3\mathbf{j} + 7\mathbf{k}\end{aligned}$$

is parallel to the line, and Equations (2) with $(x_0, y_0, z_0) = (-3, 2, -3)$ give

$$x = -3 + 4t, \qquad y = 2 - 3t, \qquad z = -3 + 7t.$$

We could have chosen $Q(1, -1, 4)$ as the "base point" and written

$$x = 1 + 4t, \qquad y = -1 - 3t, \qquad z = 4 + 7t.$$

These equations serve as well as the first; they simply place you at a different point for a given value of t.

Just as in the plane, parametrizations are not unique.

To parametrize a line segment joining two points, we first parametrize the line through the points just as we did in the plane. We then find the t-values for the endpoints and restrict t to lie in the closed interval bounded by these values. The line equations together with this added restriction parametrize the segment, as illustrated in Example 3.

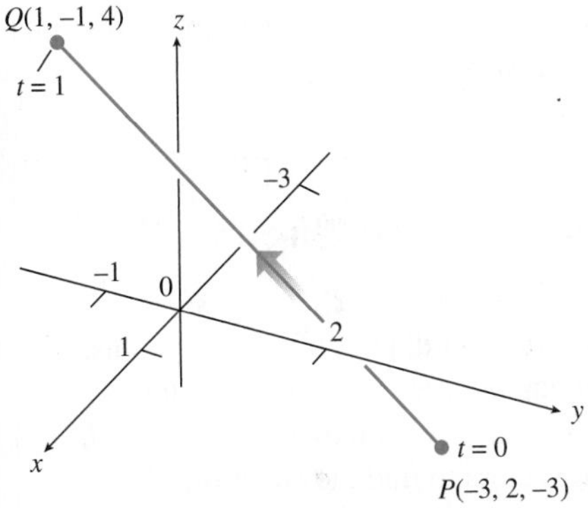

Figure 12.26 Example 3 derives a parametrization of line segment PQ. The arrow shows the direction of increasing t.

EXAMPLE 3 Parametrizing a Line Segment

Parametrize the line segment joining the points $P(-3, 2, -3)$ and $Q(1, -1, 4)$ (Figure 12.26).

SOLUTION

We begin with equations for the line through P and Q, taking them, in this case, from Example 2:

$$x = -3 + 4t, \qquad y = 2 - 3t, \qquad z = -3 + 7t.$$

We observe that the point

$$(x, y, z) = (-3 + 4t, 2 - 3t, -3 + 7t)$$

passes through $P(-3, 2, -3)$ at $t = 0$ and $Q(1, -1, 4)$ at $t = 1$. We add the restriction $0 \le t \le 1$ to parametrize the segment:

$$x = -3 + 4t, \qquad y = 2 - 3t, \qquad z = -3 + 7t, \qquad 0 \le t \le 1.$$

Equations for Planes in Space

Suppose plane M passes through a point $P_0(x_0, y_0, z_0)$ and is normal (perpendicular) to the nonzero vector $\mathbf{n} = A\mathbf{i} + B\mathbf{j} + C\mathbf{k}$. Then M is the set of all points $P(x, y, z)$ for which $\overrightarrow{P_0P}$ is orthogonal to $\mathbf{n}$ (Figure 12.27). That is, P lies on M if and only if $\mathbf{n} \cdot \overrightarrow{P_0P} = 0$. This equation is equivalent to

$$(A\mathbf{i} + B\mathbf{j} + C\mathbf{k}) \cdot [(x - x_0)\mathbf{i} + (y - y_0)\mathbf{j} + (z - z_0)\mathbf{k}] = 0$$

or

$$A(x - x_0) + B(y - y_0) + C(z - z_0) = 0.$$

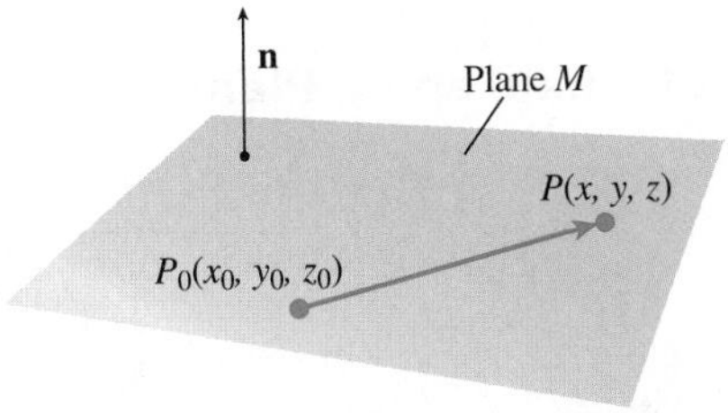

Figure 12.27 The standard equation for a plane in space is defined in terms of a vector normal to the plane: A point P lies in the plane through P_0 normal to $\mathbf{n}$ if and only if $\mathbf{n} \cdot \overrightarrow{P_0P} = 0$.

Equations for a Plane

The **plane through $P_0(x_0, y_0, z_0)$ normal to $\mathbf{n} = A\mathbf{i} + B\mathbf{j} + C\mathbf{k}$** has

Vector equation:	$\mathbf{n} \cdot \overrightarrow{P_0P} = 0$
Component equation:	$A(x - x_0) + B(y - y_0) + C(z - z_0) = 0$
Component equation simplified:	$Ax + By + Cz = D$, where $D = Ax_0 + By_0 + Cz_0$

EXAMPLE 4 Finding an Equation for a Plane

Find an equation for the plane through $P_0(-3, 0, 7)$ perpendicular to $\mathbf{n} = 5\mathbf{i} + 2\mathbf{j} - \mathbf{k}$.

SOLUTION

The component equation is

$$5(x - (-3)) + 2(y - 0) + (-1)(z - 7) = 0.$$

Simplifying, we obtain

$$5x + 15 + 2y - z + 7 = 0$$

$$5x + 2y - z = -22.$$

$A\mathbf{i} + B\mathbf{j} + C\mathbf{k}$ is normal to the plane $Ax + By + Cz = D$.

Notice in Example 4 how the components of $\mathbf{n} = 5\mathbf{i} + 2\mathbf{j} - \mathbf{k}$ became the coefficients of x, y, and z in the equation $5x + 2y - z = -22$, and $D = Ax_0 + By_0 + Cz_0 = -22$.

EXPLORATION 1 Finding an Equation for the Plane Through Three Points

Two points in the xy-plane determine a line. Given the coordinates of the two points, we can easily determine the corresponding linear equation $ax + by = c$. Similarly, three points in xyz-space determine a plane with a linear equation $ax + by + cz = d$. Given the coordinates of three points, we can use vectors to find the equation, as in this exploration.

1. Given the three points $A(0, 0, 1)$, $B(2, 0, 0)$, and $C(0, 3, 0)$, find the vectors $\overrightarrow{AB}$ and $\overrightarrow{AC}$ in component form.
2. Use the cross product to find a vector perpendicular to both $\overrightarrow{AB}$ and $\overrightarrow{AC}$. Call it $\mathbf{v}$.
3. Find an equation of the plane through A perpendicular to $\mathbf{v}$.

EXAMPLE 5 Finding the Intersection of a Line and a Plane

Find the point where the line

$$x = \frac{8}{3} + 2t, \qquad y = -2t, \qquad z = 1 + t$$

intersects the plane $3x + 2y + 6z = 6$.

SOLUTION

The point

$$\left(\frac{8}{3} + 2t,\ -2t,\ 1 + t\right)$$

lies in the plane if its coordinates satisfy the equation of the plane; that is, if

$$3\left(\frac{8}{3} + 2t\right) + 2(-2t) + 6(1 + t) = 6,$$

or

$$\begin{aligned} 8 + 6t - 4t + 6 + 6t &= 6 \\ 8t &= -8 \\ t &= -1. \end{aligned}$$

The point of intersection is

$$(x, y, z)\big|_{t=-1} = \left(\frac{8}{3} - 2, 2, 1 - 1\right) = \left(\frac{2}{3}, 2, 0\right)$$

Lines of Intersection

Two planes that are not parallel intersect in a line.

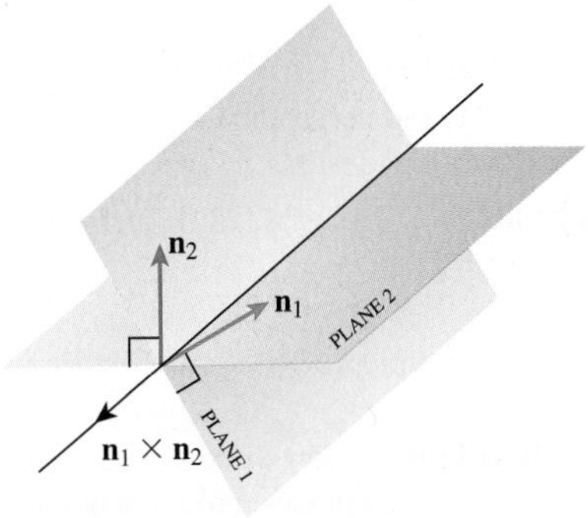

Figure 12.28 How the line of intersection of two planes is related to the planes' normal vectors. (Example 6)

EXAMPLE 6 Finding a Vector Parallel to the Line of Intersection of Two Planes

Find a vector parallel to the line of intersection of the planes $3x - 6y - 2z = 15$ and $2x + y - 2z = 5$.

SOLUTION

The line of intersection of two planes is perpendicular to the planes' normal vectors $\mathbf{n}_1$ and $\mathbf{n}_2$ (Figure 12.28) and therefore parallel to $\mathbf{n}_1 \times \mathbf{n}_2$. Turning this around, $\mathbf{n}_1 \times \mathbf{n}_2$ is a vector parallel to the planes' line of intersection. In our case,

$$\mathbf{n}_1 \times \mathbf{n}_2 = \begin{vmatrix} \mathbf{i} & \mathbf{j} & \mathbf{k} \\ 3 & -6 & -2 \\ 2 & 1 & -2 \end{vmatrix} = 14\mathbf{i} + 2\mathbf{j} + 15\mathbf{k}.$$

Any nonzero scalar multiple of $\mathbf{n}_1 \times \mathbf{n}_2$ will do as well.

EXAMPLE 7 Parametrizing the Line of Intersection of Two Planes

Find parametric equations for the line in which the planes $3x - 6y - 2z = 15$ and $2x + y - 2z = 5$ intersect.

SOLUTION

We find a vector parallel to the line and a point on the line and use Equations (2).

Example 6 identifies $\mathbf{v} = 14\mathbf{i} + 2\mathbf{j} + 15\mathbf{k}$ as a vector parallel to the line. To find a point on the line, we can take any point common to the two planes. Substituting $z = 0$ in the planes' equations and solving for x and y simultaneously identifies one of the points as $(3, -1, 0)$. The line is

$$x = 3 + 14t, \qquad y = -1 + 2t, \qquad z = 15t.$$

Quick Review 12.4

1. Which of the following points are solutions of the equation $2x - y + 3z = -3$?
   (a) $(1, 2, -1)$ (b) $(3, 1, 2)$
   (c) $(-1, 3, -4)$ (d) $(5, 0, 4)$

In Exercises 2–4, find a parametrization for the curve.

2. The line through $(-2, -3)$ and $(3, 1)$
3. The line segment with endpoints $(-2, -3)$ and $(3, 1)$
4. The line through $(1, 2)$ and parallel to the line $2x + 3y = 1$

In Exercise 5 and 6, solve the system of equations.

5. $x - 2y = -1$
   $2x + y = 2$
6. $3x + 2y = 1$
   $4x - 3y = -1$
7. Find a unit vector in the direction of $\mathbf{v} = -2\mathbf{i} + \mathbf{j} + 2\mathbf{k}$.

In Exercises 8–10, let $\mathbf{v}_1 = 3\mathbf{i} - 2\mathbf{j} + \mathbf{k}$ and $\mathbf{v}_2 = -\mathbf{i} + \mathbf{j} - 2\mathbf{k}$.

8. Find $\mathbf{u} = \mathbf{v}_1 \times \mathbf{v}_2$ and $\mathbf{w} = \mathbf{v}_2 \times \mathbf{v}_1$.
9. Show that $\mathbf{u} \cdot \mathbf{v}_1 = \mathbf{w} \cdot \mathbf{v}_1 = 0$.
10. Show that $\mathbf{u} \cdot \mathbf{v}_2 = \mathbf{w} \cdot \mathbf{v}_2 = 0$.

Section 12.4 Exercises

In Exercises 1–10, find parametric equations for the line.

1. The line through the point $P(3, -4, -1)$ parallel to the vector $\mathbf{i} + \mathbf{j} + \mathbf{k}$
2. The line through $P(1, 2, -1)$ and $Q(-1, 0, 1)$
3. The line through $P(-2, 0, 3)$ and $Q(3, 5, -2)$
4. The line through the origin parallel to the vector $2\mathbf{j} + \mathbf{k}$
5. The line through the point $(3, -2, 1)$ parallel to the line $x = 1 + 2t,\ y = 2 - t,\ z = 3t$
6. The line through $(1, 1, 1)$ parallel to the z-axis
7. The line through $(2, 4, 5)$ perpendicular to the plane $3x + 7y - 5z = 21$
8. The line through $(0, -7, 0)$ perpendicular to the plane $x + 2y + 2z = 13$
9. The line through $(2, 3, 0)$ perpendicular to the vectors $\mathbf{A} = \mathbf{i} + 2\mathbf{j} + 3\mathbf{k}$ and $\mathbf{B} = 3\mathbf{i} + 4\mathbf{j} + 5\mathbf{k}$
10. The x-axis

In Exercises 11–14, find parametrizations for the line segment joining the points. Draw coordinate axes and sketch each segment, indicating the direction of increasing t for your parametrization.

11. $(0, 0, 0), (1, 1, 3/2)$
12. $(1, 0, 0), (1, 1, 0)$
13. $(0, 1, 1), (0, -1, 1)$
14. $(1, 0, -1), (0, 3, 0)$

In Exercises 15–20, find an equation for the plane.

15. The plane through $P_0(0, 2, -1)$ normal to $\mathbf{n} = 3\mathbf{i} - 2\mathbf{j} - \mathbf{k}$
16. The plane through $(1, -1, 3)$ parallel to the plane $3x + y + z = 7$
17. The plane through $(1, 1, -1)$, $(2, 0, 2)$, and $(0, -2, 1)$
18. The plane through $(2, 4, 5)$, $(1, 5, 7)$, and $(-1, 6, 8)$
19. The plane through $P_0(2, 4, 5)$ perpendicular to the line $x = 5 + t,\ y = 1 + 3t,\ z = 4t$
20. The plane through $A(1, -2, 1)$ perpendicular to the vector from the origin to A
21. Find the point of intersection of the lines $x = 2t + 1,\ y = 3t + 2,\ z = 4t + 3$, and $x = s + 2,\ y = 2s + 4,\ z = -4s - 1$, and then find the plane determined by these lines.
22. Find the point of intersection of the lines $x = t,\ y = -t + 2,\ z = t + 1$, and $x = 2s + 2,\ y = s + 3,\ z = 5s + 6$, and then find the plane determined by these lines.

In Exercises 23 and 24, find the plane determined by the intersecting lines.

23. L_1: $x = -1 + t,\ y = 2 + t,\ z = 1 - t,\ -\infty < t < \infty$
    L_2: $x = 1 - 4s,\ y = 1 + 2s,\ z = 2 - 2s,\ -\infty < s < \infty$
24. L_1: $x = t,\ y = 3 - 3t,\ z = -2 - t,\ -\infty < t < \infty$
    L_2: $x = 1 + s,\ y = 4 + s,\ z = -1 + s,\ -\infty < s < \infty$
25. Find a plane through $P_0(2, 1, -1)$ and perpendicular to the line of intersection of the planes $2x + y - z = 3,\ x + 2y + z = 2$.
26. Find a plane through the points $P_1(1, 2, 3)$, $P_2(3, 2, 1)$ and perpendicular to the plane $4x - y + 2z = 7$.

Exploration

27. ***Distance from a Point to a Line*** Follow these steps to find the distance from a point S to a line that passes through a point P parallel to a vector $\mathbf{v}$ as shown in the figure.

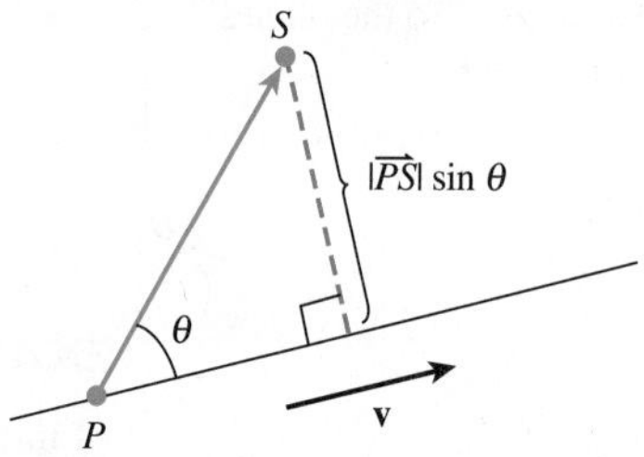

(a) Show that the length of the component of $\overrightarrow{PS}$ normal to the line is $|\overrightarrow{PS}| \sin\theta$.

(b) Show that the distance d from S to the line through P parallel to $\mathbf{v}$ is

$$d = \frac{|\overrightarrow{PS} \times \mathbf{v}|}{|\mathbf{v}|}.$$

In Exercises 28–30, use the result of Exercise 27 to find the distance from the point to the line.

28. $(0, 0, 0)$; $x = 5 + 3t,\ y = 5 + 4t,\ z = -3 - 5t$
29. $(2, 1, 3)$; $x = 2 + 2t,\ y = 1 + 6t,\ z = 3$
30. $(3, -1, 4)$; $x = 4 - t,\ y = 3 + 2t,\ z = -5 + 3t$

Explorations

31. ***Distance from a Point to a Plane*** Follow these steps to find the distance d from a point S to a plane $Ax + By + Cz = D$.

(a) Find a point P on the plane.

(b) Find $\overrightarrow{PS}$.

(c) Show that the distance is

$$d = \left| \overrightarrow{PS} \cdot \frac{\mathbf{n}}{|\mathbf{n}|} \right|,$$

where $\mathbf{n} = A\mathbf{i} + B\mathbf{j} + C\mathbf{k}$.

In Exercises 32–34, use the result of Exercise 31 to find the distance from the point to the plane.

32. $(2, -3, 4)$, $x + 2y + 2z = 13$

33. $(0, 1, 1)$, $4y + 3z = -12$

34. $(0, -1, 0)$, $2x + y + 2z = 4$

35. Find the distance from the plane $x + 2y + 6z = 1$ to the plane $x + 2y + 6z = 10$.

36. Find the distance from the line $x = 2 + t$, $y = 1 + t$, $z = -(1/2) - (1/2)t$ to the plane $x + 2y + 6z = 10$.

Exploration

37. *Angle Between Planes* The **angle between two intersecting planes** is defined to be the (acute) angle determined by the normal vectors as shown in the figure.

(a) If $\mathbf{n}_1$ and $\mathbf{n}_2$ are the normals to two planes, show that the angle between the planes is

$$\theta = \cos^{-1}\left(\frac{|\mathbf{n}_1 \cdot \mathbf{n}_2|}{|\mathbf{n}_1||\mathbf{n}_2|}\right).$$

(b) Show that the angle between the planes $3x - 6y - 2z = 15$ and $2x + y - 2z = 5$ is about 1.38 radians.

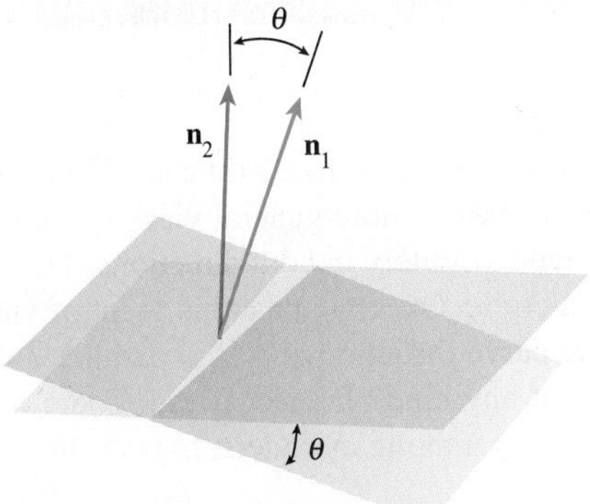

In Exercises 38–40, use the result of Exercise 37 to find the acute angle between the planes.

38. $x + y + z = 1$, $z = 0$

39. $2x + 2y - z = 3$, $x + 2y + z = 2$

40. $4y + 3z = -12$, $3x + 2y + 6z = 6$

In Exercises 41–44, find the point in which the line meets the plane.

41. $x = 1 - t$, $y = 3t$, $z = 1 + t$; $2x - y + 3z = 6$

42. $x = 2$, $y = 3 + 2t$, $z = -2 - 2t$; $6x + 3y - 4z = -12$

43. $x = 1 + 2t$, $y = 1 + 5t$, $z = 3t$; $x + y + z = 2$

44. $x = -1 + 3t$, $y = -2$, $z = 5t$; $2x - 3z = 7$

In Exercises 45–48, find a parametrization for the line in which the planes intersect.

45. $x + y + z = 1$, $x + y = 2$

46. $3x - 6y - 2z = 3$, $2x + y - 2z = 2$

47. $x - 2y + 4z = 2$, $x + y - 2z = 5$

48. $5x - 2y = 11$, $4y - 5z = -17$

In Exercises 49 and 50, *work in groups of two or three.* Given two lines in space, either they are parallel, or they intersect, or they are skew (imagine, for example, the flight paths of two airplanes in the sky). Determine whether the lines, taken two at a time, are parallel, intersect, or are skew. If they intersect, find the point of intersection.

49. $L_1: x = 3 + 2t$, $y = -1 + 4t$, $z = 2 - t$, $-\infty < t < \infty$
$L_2: x = 1 + 4s$, $y = 1 + 2s$, $z = -3 + 4s$, $-\infty < s < \infty$
$L_3: x = 3 + 2r$, $y = 2 + r$, $z = -2 + 2r$, $-\infty < r < \infty$

50. $L_1: x = 1 + 2t$, $y = -1 - t$, $z = 3t$, $-\infty < t < \infty$
$L_2: x = 2 - s$, $y = 3s$, $z = 1 + s$, $-\infty < s < \infty$
$L_3: x = 5 + 2r$, $y = 1 - r$, $z = 8 + 3r$, $-\infty < r < \infty$

51. Use Equations (2) to generate a parametrization of the line through $P_1(2, -4, 7)$ parallel to $\mathbf{v}_1 = 2\mathbf{i} - \mathbf{j} + 3\mathbf{k}$. Then generate another parametrization of the line using the point $P_2(-2, -2, 1)$ and the vector $\mathbf{v}_2 = -\mathbf{i} + (1/2)\mathbf{j} - (3/2)\mathbf{k}$.

52. Use the component form to generate an equation for the plane through $P_1(4, 1, 5)$ normal to $\mathbf{n}_1 = \mathbf{i} - 2\mathbf{j} + \mathbf{k}$. Then generate another equation for the same plane using the point $P_2(3, -2, 0)$ and the normal vector $\mathbf{n}_2 = -\sqrt{2}\mathbf{i} + 2\sqrt{2}\mathbf{j} - \sqrt{2}\mathbf{k}$.

53. Writing to Learn Find the points in which the line $x = 1 + 2t$, $y = -1 - t$, $z = 3t$ meets the coordinate planes. Describe the reasoning behind your answer.

54. Writing to Learn Find equations for the line in the plane $z = 3$ that makes an angle of $\pi/6$ rad with $\mathbf{i}$ and an angle of $\pi/3$ rad with $\mathbf{j}$. Describe the reasoning behind your answer.

55. Writing to Learn Is the line $x = 1 - 2t$, $y = 2 + 5t$, $z = -3t$ parallel to the plane $2x + y - z = 8$? Give reasons for your answer.

56. Writing to Learn How can you tell when two planes $A_1x + B_1y + C_1z = D_1$ and $A_2x + B_2y + C_2z = D_2$ are parallel? Perpendicular? Give reasons for your answer.

57. Find two different planes whose intersection is the line $x = 1 + t$, $y = 2 - t$, $z = 3 + 2t$. Write equations for each plane in the form $Ax + By + Cz = D$.

58. Writing to Learn Find a plane through the origin that meets the plane $M: 2x + 3y + z = 12$ in a right angle. How do you know that your plane is perpendicular to M?

59. Writing to Learn For any nonzero numbers a, b, and c, the graph of $(x/a) + (y/b) + (z/c) = 1$ is a plane. Which planes have an equation of this form?

60. Writing to Learn Suppose L_1 and L_2 are disjoint (nonintersecting) nonparallel lines. Is it possible for a nonzero vector to be perpendicular to both L_1 and L_2? Give reasons for your answer.

Extending the Ideas

61. ***Perspective in Computer Graphics*** In computer graphics and perspective drawing, we need to represent objects seen by the eye in space as images on a two-dimensional plane. Suppose the eye is at $E(x_0, 0, 0)$ as shown here and we want to represent a point $P_1(x_1, y_1, z_1)$ as a point on the yz-plane. We do this by projecting P_1 onto the plane with a ray from E. The point P_1 will be portrayed as the point $P(0, y, z)$. The problem for us as graphics designers is to find y and z given E and P_1.

    (a) Write a vector equation that holds between $\overrightarrow{EP}$ and $\overrightarrow{EP_1}$. Use the equation to express y and z in terms of x_0, x_1, y_1, and z_1.

    (b) Test the formula obtained for y and z in part (a) by investigating their behavior at $x_1 = 0$ and $x_1 = x_0$ and by seeing what happens as $x_0 \to \infty$.

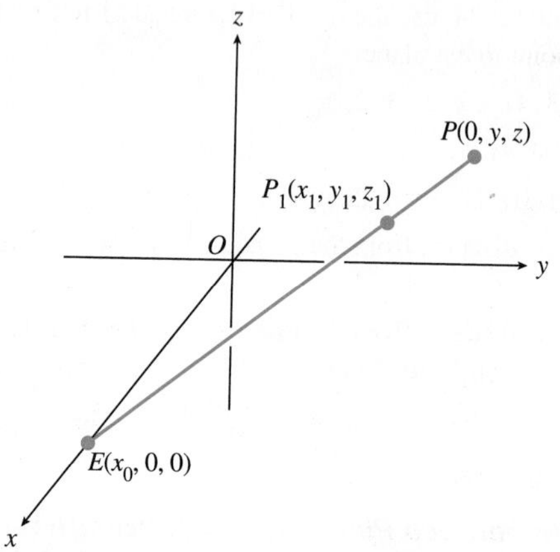

62. ***Hidden Lines*** Here is another typical problem in computer graphics. Your eye is at (4, 0, 0). You are looking at a triangular plate whose vertices are (1, 0, 1), (1, 1, 0), and (−2, 2, 2). The line segment from (1, 0, 0) to (0, 2, 2) passes through the plate. What portion of the line segment is hidden from your view by the plane?

12.5 Cylinders and Cylindrical Coordinates

What you'll learn about

- Cylinders
- Cylindrical Coordinates

Cylinders

We normally think of a circular cylinder as something like a tin can. When we do geometry with coordinates in space, however, we take a more general view. Cylinders no longer have tops or bottoms, and their sides extend infinitely in both directions. They are surfaces made of parallel lines passing through a circle. Once we take this point of view, it is easy to generalize still further. Why does the curve through which the parallel lines pass have to be a circle? Why can't it be a curve of any kind? Indeed, it can. There can be elliptical cylinders (generating curve an ellipse), parabolic cylinders, hyperbolic cylinders, and so on.

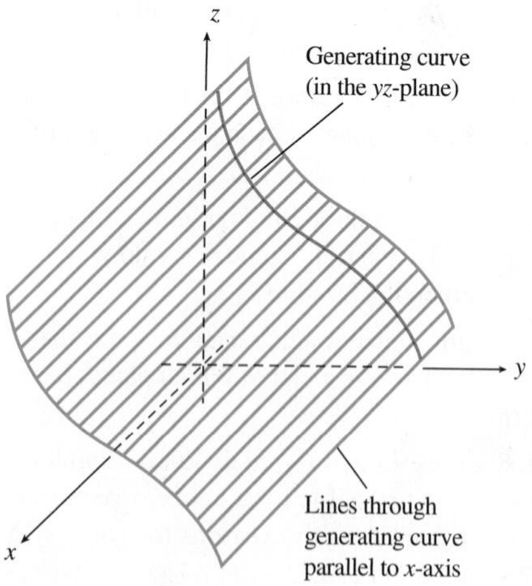

Figure 12.29 A cylinder and generating curve.

DEFINITION Cylinder and Generating Curve

A **cylinder** is a surface composed of the lines that pass through a given plane curve parallel to a given line in space. The curve is a **generating curve** for the cylinder. See Figure 12.29.

EXAMPLE 1 Finding an Equation for a Parabolic Cylinder

Find an equation for the cylinder composed of the lines that pass through the curve $y = x^2$, $z = 0$ parallel to the z-axis (Figure 12.30).

SOLUTION

If the point $P_0(x_0, x_0^2, 0)$ lies on the parabola in the xy-plane, then the point $Q(x_0, x_0^2, z)$ will lie on the cylinder because it lies on the line $x = x_0$, $y = x_0^2$ through P_0 parallel to the z-axis. Conversely, any point $Q(x_0, x_0^2, z)$ whose y-coordinate is the square of its x-coordinate will lie on the cylinder because it lies on the line $x = x_0$, $y = x_0^2$ through

P_0 parallel to the z-axis. Regardless of the value of their z-coordinate, the points on the surface are the points whose x- and y-coordinates satisfy the equation $y = x^2$ (Figure 12.31). This is the equation we seek.

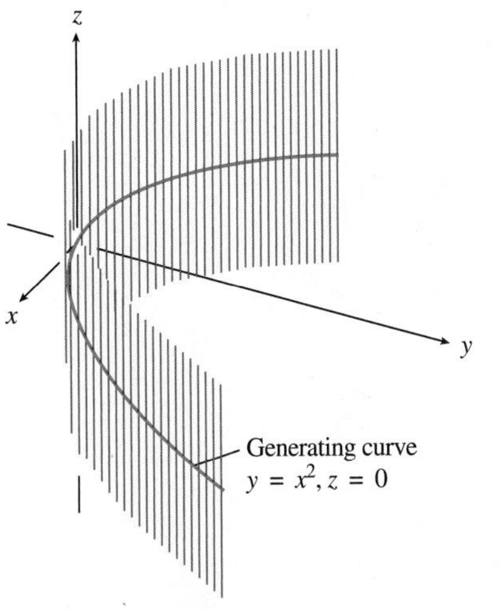

Figure 12.30 The cylinder of lines through the parabola $y = x^2$ in the xy-plane parallel to the z-axis. (Example 1)

EXAMPLE 2 Sketching Cylinders

Identify and sketch the cylinders **(a)** $x^2 + y^2 = 1$ and **(b)** $z = y^2$.

SOLUTION

(a) The cylinder $x^2 + y^2 = 1$: Since the equation places no restriction on z, the cylinder consists of all the points in space lying directly above or below points of the unit circle in the xy-plane. The cylinder is the circular cylinder of radius 1 with axis the z-axis. See the drawing lesson on page 596 for how to sketch it.

(b) The cylinder $z = y^2$: This time there is no restriction on the coordinate x. The cylinder consists of all the points lying on lines through the parabola $z = y^2$ in the yz-plane parallel to the x-axis, the points whose y- and z-coordinates satisfy the equation $z = y^2$ regardless of the value of x. (See the drawing lesson on page 596.) The graph in Figure 12.32 supports this conclusion.

As the examples suggest, any curve $f(x, y) = c$ in the xy-plane defines a cylinder parallel to the z-axis whose equation is also $f(x, y) = c$. Similarly, an equation in x and z defines a cylinder parallel to the y-axis, and an equation in y and z defines a cylinder parallel to the x-axis. See Figures 12.33 and 12.34.

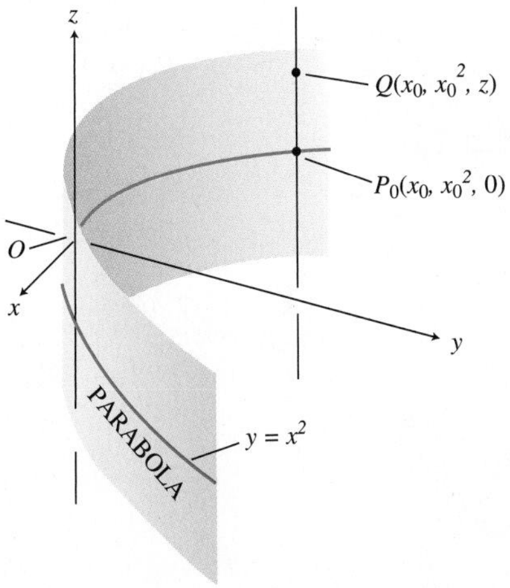

Figure 12.31 The cylinder $y = x^2$.

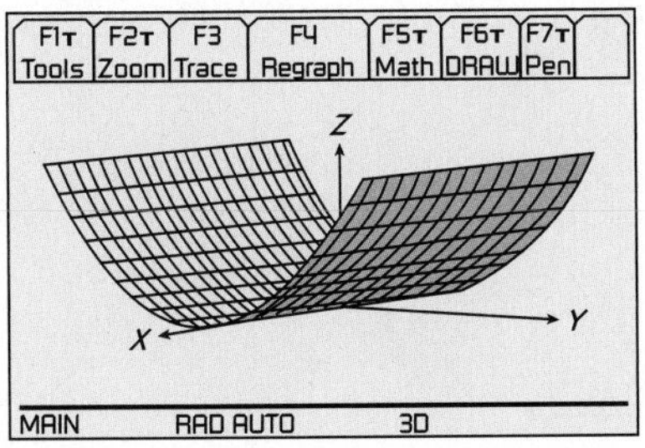

Figure 12.32 $z = y^2$. (Example 2)

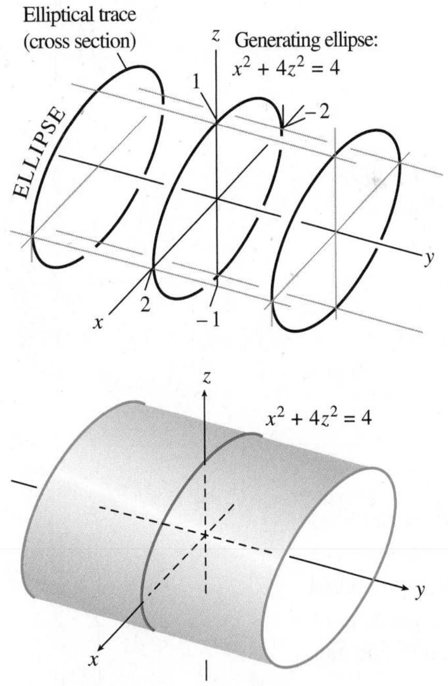

Figure 12.33 The elliptical cylinder $x^2 + 4z^2 = 4$ is made of lines parallel to the y-axis through the ellipse $x^2 + 4z^2 = 4$ in the xz-plane. The cross sections or "traces" of the cylinder in planes perpendicular to the y-axis are ellipses congruent to the generating ellipse. The cylinder extends along the entire y-axis.

Drawing Lesson
How to Draw Cylinders Parallel to the Coordinate Axes

1. Sketch all three coordinate axes *very lightly.*

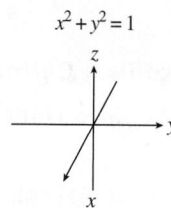

$x^2 + y^2 = 1$

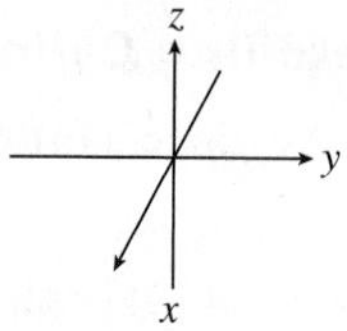

$z = y^2$

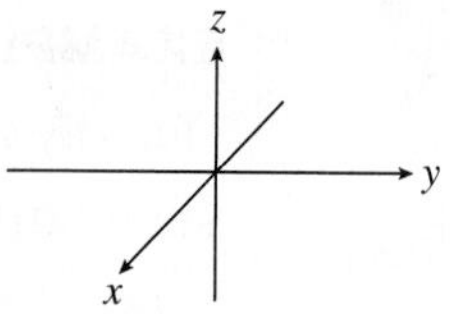

2. Sketch the trace of the cylinder in the coordinate plane of the two variables that appear in the cylinder's equation. Sketch *very lightly.*

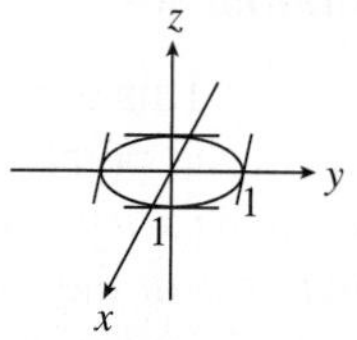

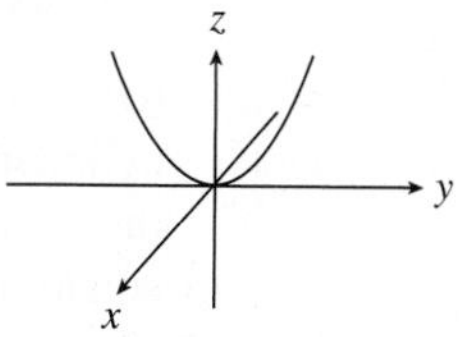

3. Sketch traces in parallel planes on either side (again, *lightly*).

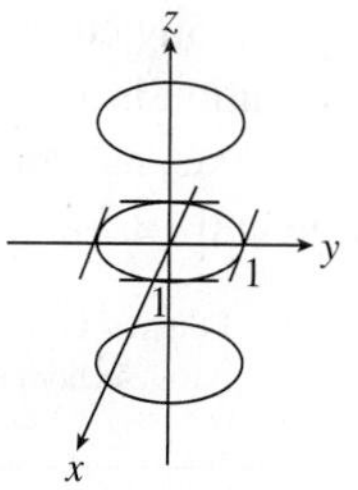

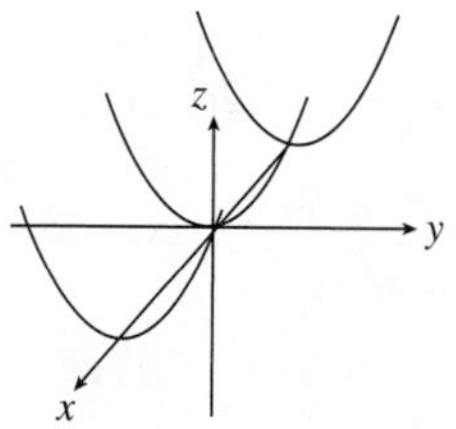

4. Add parallel outer edges to give the shape definition.

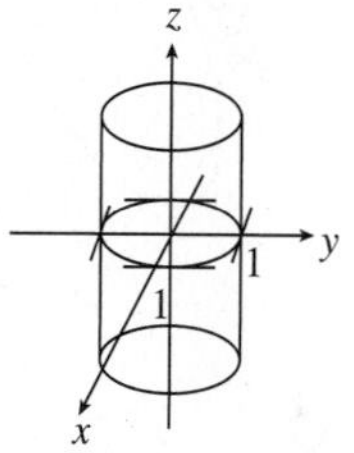

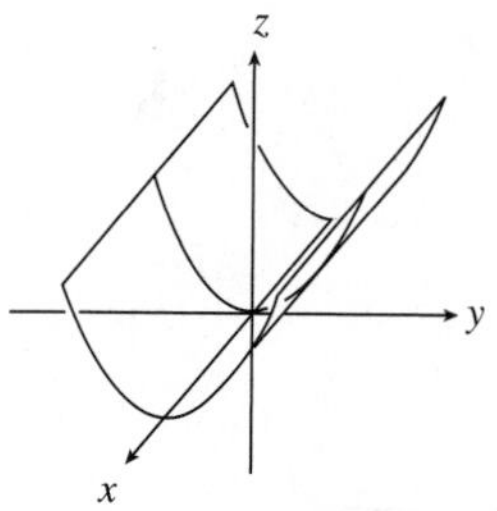

5. If more definition is required, darken the parts of the lines that are exposed to view. Leave the hidden parts light. Use line breaks when you can.

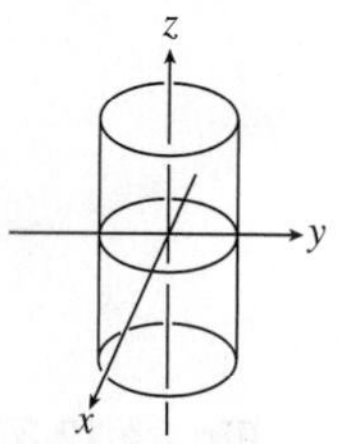

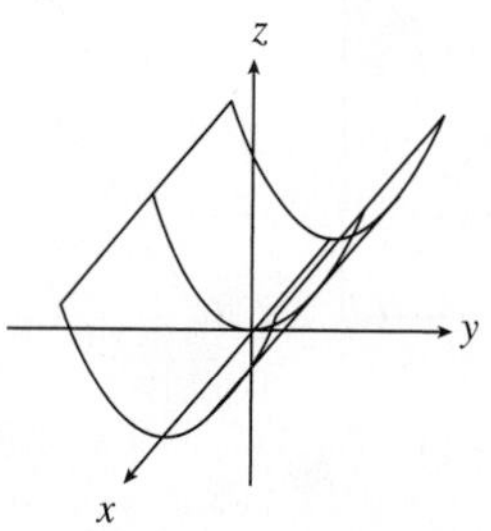

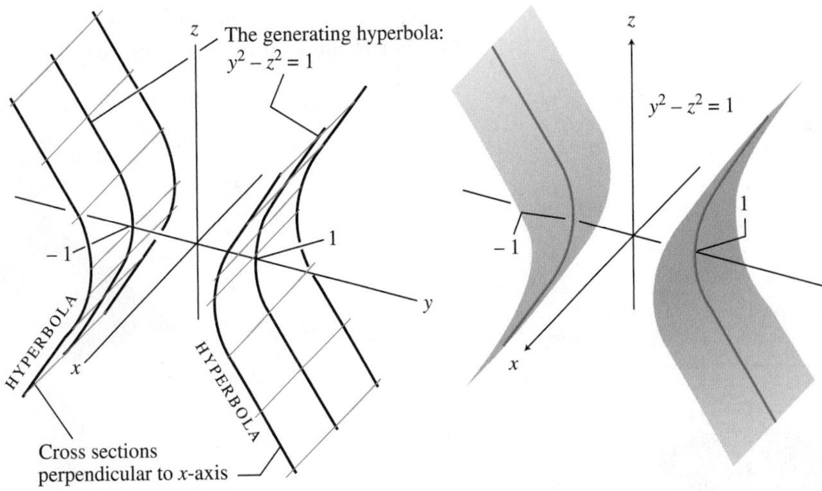

Figure 12.34 The hyperbolic cylinder $y^2 - z^2 = 1$ is made of lines parallel to the x-axis through the hyperbola $y^2 - z^2 = 1$ in the yz-plane. The cross sections perpendicular to the x-axis are hyperbolas congruent to the generating hyperbola.

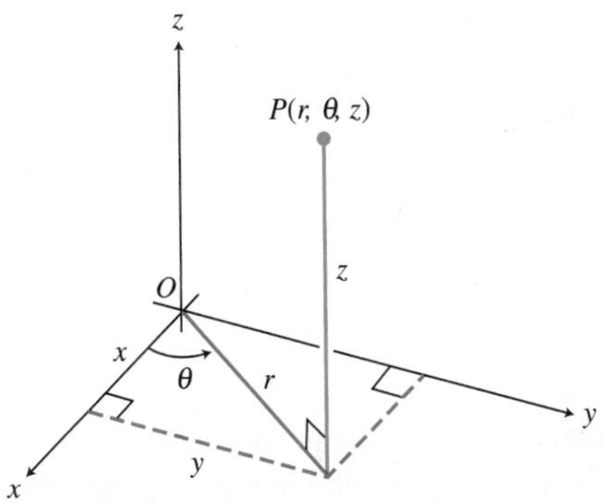

Figure 12.35 The cylindrical coordinates of the point P are r, θ, and z.

Cylindrical Coordinates

We obtain cylindrical coordinates for space by replacing the Cartesian coordinates in the xy-plane by polar coordinates. This assigns to every point in space one or more coordinate triples of the form (r, θ, z), as shown in Figure 12.35.

> **DEFINITION Cylindrical Coordinates**
>
> **Cylindrical coordinates** represent a point P in space by ordered triples (r, θ, z) in which
>
> **1.** r and θ are polar coordinates for the vertical projection of P on the xy-plane, and
>
> **2.** z is the rectangular vertical coordinate.

The values of x, y, r, and θ are related by the usual equations.

> **Equations Relating Rectangular and Cylindrical Coordinates**
>
> $$x = r\cos\theta, \qquad y = r\sin\theta, \qquad z = z$$
> $$r^2 = x^2 + y^2 \qquad \tan\theta = y/x \tag{1}$$

In cylindrical coordinates, the equation $r = a$, $a > 0$ describes not just a circle of radius a in the plane but an entire cylinder about the z-axis (see Figure 12.36). The simplicity of this equation is one reason for the popularity of cylindrical coordinates. Another is the efficiency cylindrical coordinates bring to descriptions of planetary motion (Section 12.4).

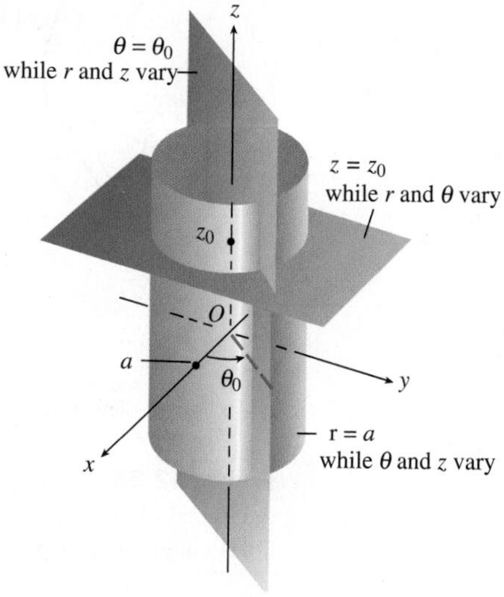

Figure 12.36 Constant-coordinate equations in cylindrical coordinates define cylinders and planes.

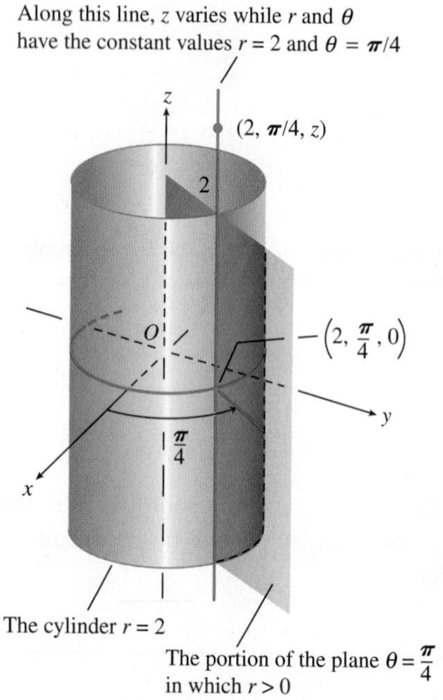

Figure 12.37 The points whose first two cylindrical coordinates are $r = 2$ and $\theta = \pi/4$ form a line parallel to the z-axis. (Example 3)

EXAMPLE 3 Identifying a Vertical Line

What points satisfy the equations

$$r = 2, \qquad \theta = \frac{\pi}{4}?$$

SOLUTION

These points make up the line in which the cylinder $r = 2$ cuts the portion of the plane $\theta = \pi/4$ where r is positive (Figure 12.37). This is the line through the point $(2, \pi/4, 0)$ parallel to the z-axis.

EXPLORATION 1 Easy as Pi

1. A point has cylindrical coordinates (π, π, π). What are its rectangular coordinates?
2. A point has rectangular coordinates (π, π, π). What are its cylindrical coordinates?
3. Describe the graph of the equation $r = \pi$.
4. Describe the graph of the equation $\theta = \pi$.
5. Describe the graph formed by the intersection of the graphs in parts 3 and 4.
6. Describe the graph of all points satisfying the simultaneous equations $r = \pi$ and $\theta = \pi$.
7. Why are the answers to parts 5 and 6 different?

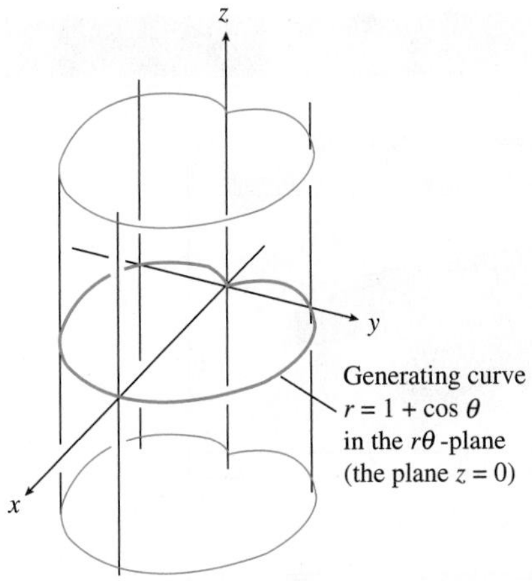

Figure 12.38 The equation $r = 1 + \cos\theta$ defines a cylinder in space whose cross sections perpendicular to the z-axis are cardioids. (Example 4)

EXAMPLE 4 Sketching a Surface in Cylindrical Coordinates

Sketch the surface $r = 1 + \cos\theta$.

SOLUTION

The equation involves only r and θ; the variable z can take on any value. Therefore, the surface is a cylinder of lines that pass through the cardioid $r = 1 + \cos\theta$ in the $r\theta$-plane parallel to the z-axis. The rules for sketching the cylinder are the same as before: Sketch the x-, y-, and z-axes, draw a few cross sections, connect the cross sections with parallel lines, and darken the exposed parts (Figure 12.38).

EXAMPLE 5 Changing from Cylindrical to Cartesian Coordinates

Find a Cartesian equation for the cylinder $r = 3/2$.

SOLUTION

Using Equations (1), we have

$$r = \frac{3}{2}$$

$$\sqrt{x^2 + y^2} = \frac{3}{2} \qquad \text{Substitute } \sqrt{x^2 + y^2} \text{ for } r.$$

$$4x^2 + 4y^2 = 9 \qquad \text{Square and multiply both sides by 4.}$$

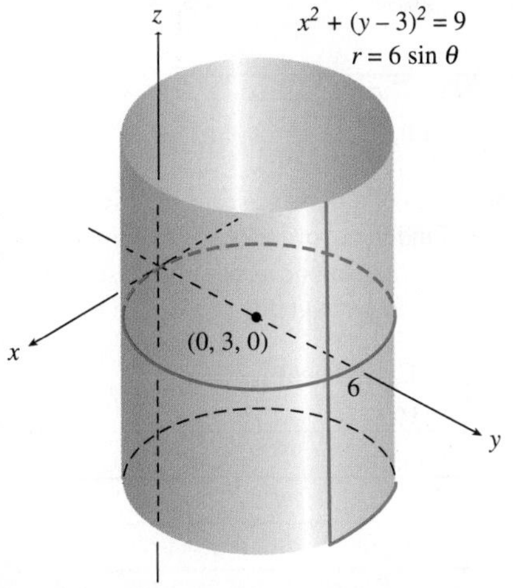

Figure 12.39 The cylinder in Example 6.

EXAMPLE 6 Changing from Cartesian to Cylindrical Coordinates

Find a cylindrical-coordinate equation for the cylinder $x^2 + (y - 3)^2 = 9$ (Figure 12.39).

SOLUTION

The equation for the cylinder in cylindrical coordinates is the same as the polar equation for the cylinder's trace (cross section) in the xy-plane, namely $r = 6\sin\theta$.

Quick Review 12.5

In Exercises 1–4, graph the equation in the xy-plane and identify the graph.

1. **(a)** $x^2 + 2x + y^2 = 0$ **(b)** $x^2 + y^2 - 4y = 0$

2. **(a)** $x^2 + 2y^2 = 8$ **(b)** $4x^2 + y^2 = 36$

3. **(a)** $xy = 4$ **(b)** $x^2 - 4y^2 = 36$

4. **(a)** $y = x^2 - 1$ **(b)** $x = 4 - y^2$

In Exercises 5–8, find a polar equation for the circle. Then graph the circle in the polar-coordinate plane.

5. $x^2 + y^2 = 9$

6. $(x - 1)^2 + y^2 = 1$

7. $x^2 + (y + 2)^2 = 4$

8. $(x + 3)^2 + y^2 = 9$

In Exercises 9 and 10, graph the equation in the polar-coordinate plane and identify the graph.

9. **(a)** $r = 1 + \cos\theta$ **(b)** $r = \sin\theta - 1$

10. **(a)** $r = 2\csc\theta$ **(b)** $r = -\sec\theta$

Section 12.5 Exercises

In Exercises 1 and 2, match the equation with the cylinder it defines. What kinds of cylinders are these?

1. $9y^2 + z^2 = 16$ **2.** $x^2 + 2z^2 = 8$

(a)

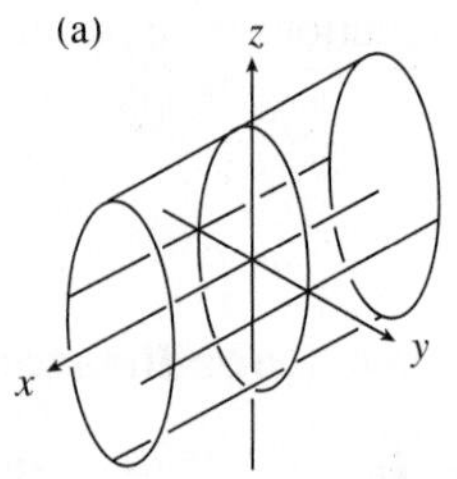

(b)

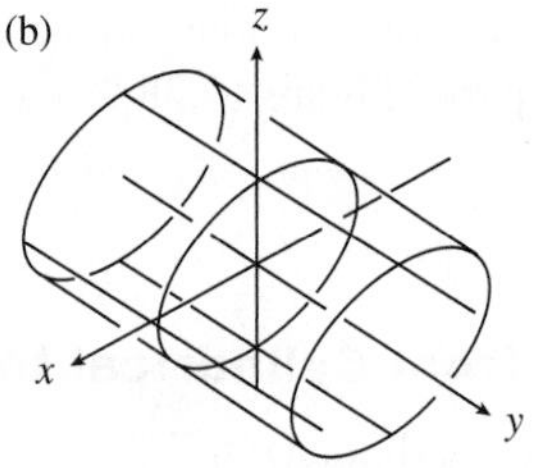

In Exercises 3–12, *work in groups of two or three* to sketch the surface.

3. $x^2 + y^2 = 4$ **4.** $x^2 + z^2 = 4$

5. $z^2 - y^2 = 1$ **6.** $x = y^2$

7. $x^2 + 4z^2 = 16$ **8.** $4x^2 + y^2 = 36$

9. $16x^2 + 4y^2 = 1$ **10.** $x = 4 - y^2$

11. $z^2 + 4y^2 = 9$ **12.** $x^2 - 4y^2 = 1$

In Exercises 13–16, match the equation with its graph.

13. $z = y^2 - 1$ **14.** $yz = 1$

15. $x^2z = 1$ **16.** $z = 1 - x^2$

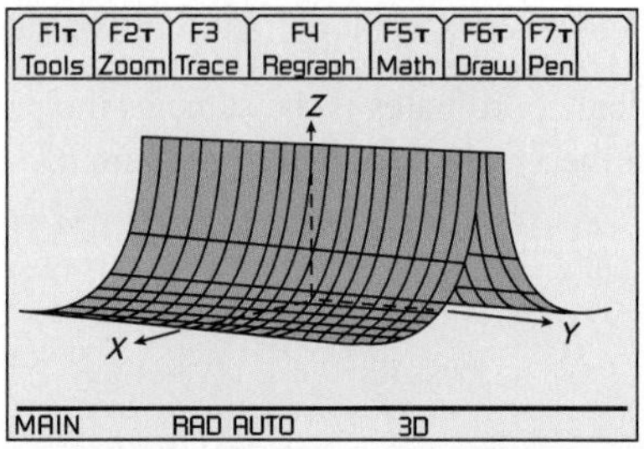

(a)

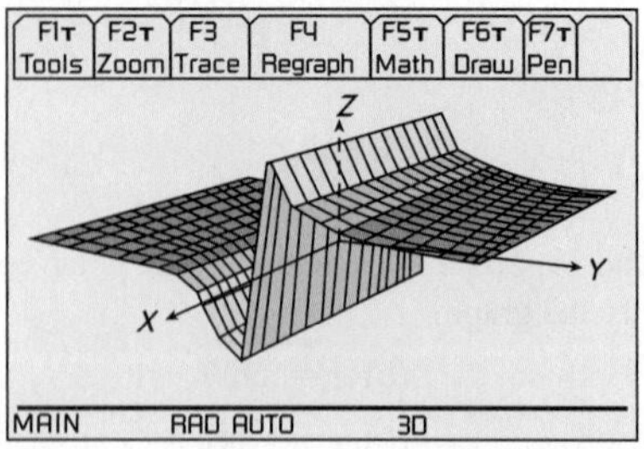

(b)

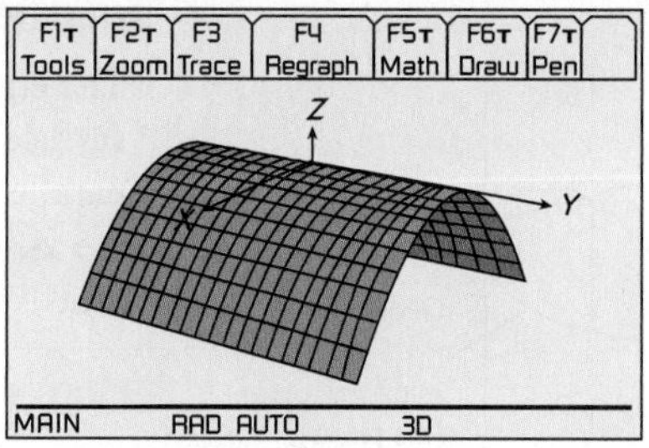

(c)

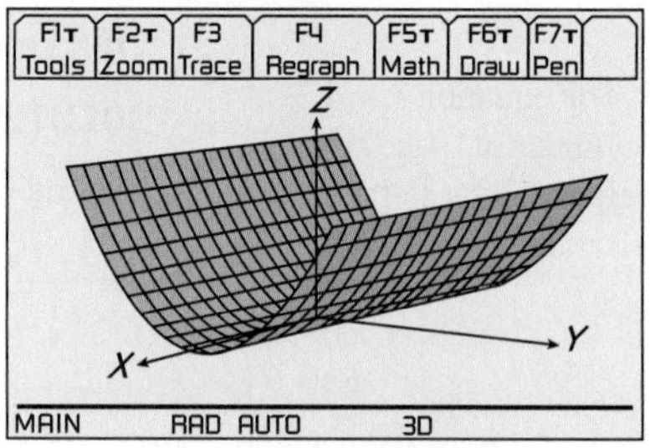

(d)

In Exercises 17–24, the coordinates of a point in space are given in one of two coordinate systems. Find the coordinates of the point in the other system. There may be more than one answer because points in cylindrical coordinates can have more than one coordinate triple.

	Rectangular (x, y, z)	**Cylindrical** (r, θ, z)
17.	(0, 0, 0)	
18.	(1, 0, 0)	
19.	(0, 1, 0)	
20.	(0, 0, 1)	
21.		(1, 0, 0)
22.		$(\sqrt{2}, 0, 1)$
23.		$(1, \pi/2, 1)$
24.		$(-1, \pi/2, -1)$

In Exercises 25–34, translate the equation from the given coordinate system (rectangular, cylindrical) into an equation in the other system. Then identify the figure in space defined by the equation or by the equation and inequality.

25. $r = 0$ **26.** $x^2 + y^2 = 5$

27. $z = 0$ **28.** $z = -2$

29. $x^2 + y^2 + z^2 = 4$ **30.** $x^2 + y^2 + \left(z - \frac{1}{2}\right)^2 = \frac{1}{4}$

31. $r = \csc \theta$ **32.** $r = -3 \sec \theta$

33. $x^2 + y^2 + (z - 1)^2 = 1, z \le 1$

34. $r^2 + z^2 = 4, z \le -\sqrt{2}$

In Exercises 35–38, describe the set of points whose cylindrical coordinates satisfy the given equation. Sketch each set. *Work in groups of two or three.*

35. $r = -2 \sin \theta$ **36.** $r = 2 \cos \theta$

37. $r = 1 - \cos \theta$ **38.** $r = 1 + \sin \theta$

Extending the Ideas

39. Find the Cartesian coordinates of the center of the sphere

$$r^2 + z^2 = 4r \cos \theta + 6r \sin \theta + 2z.$$

40. Find an equation in the form $r = f(\theta)$ in cylindrical coordinates for the plane $ax + by = c$, $c \neq 0$.

41. Writing to Learn *Vertical Planes* Show that planes perpendicular to the x-axis have equations of the form $r = a \sec \theta$ in cylindrical coordinates.

42. Writing to Learn *Vertical Planes* Show that planes perpendicular to the y-axis have equations of the form $r = b \csc \theta$ in cylindrical coordinates.

43. Writing to Learn *Symmetry* What symmetry will you find in a surface that has an equation of the form $r = f(z)$ in cylindrical coordinates?

44. Describe the surface $y - \sqrt{4 - z^2} = 0$.

CAS Explorations

In Exercises 45–48, plot the surface over the indicated domain. If you can, rotate the surface into different viewing positions. Then describe the surface in words.

45. $z = y^2$, $-2 \leq x \leq 2$, $-0.5 \leq y \leq 2$

46. $z = 1 - y^2$, $-2 \leq x \leq 2$, $-2 \leq y \leq 2$

47. $z = \sin x$, $-2\pi \leq x \leq 2\pi$, $-2\pi \leq y \leq 2\pi$

48. $z = x^2 + 2y^2$ over

(a) $-3 \leq x \leq 3$, $-3 \leq y \leq 3$

(b) $-1 \leq x \leq 1$, $-2 \leq y \leq 3$

(c) $-2 \leq x \leq 2$, $-2 \leq y \leq 2$

(d) $-2 \leq x \leq 2$, $-1 \leq y \leq 1$

In Exercise 49, perform the following steps.

(a) Solve the equation for r. Choose the expression for the positive square root and simplify it.

(b) Plot r as a function of θ and z. Use the specified ranges of the variables for your plot.

(c) From your plot in (b), estimate the center and radius of the sphere to the nearest integer value.

(d) Convert your equation to Cartesian coordinates. Simplify the result. You may need to complete the final simplification by hand to obtain an equation for the sphere in the form

$$(x - x_0)^2 + (y - y_0)^2 + (z - z_0)^2 = a^2.$$

Compare the coordinates of the center given by this form with your estimates in (c).

(e) Plot the implicit equation obtained in (d). How does it compare with the plot produced in (b)? Can you explain any discrepancies from the way in which a computer grapher plots surfaces?

49. $r^2 + z^2 = 2r(\cos \theta + \sin \theta) + 2$, $\pi/4 \leq \theta \leq 9\pi/4$, $-2 \leq z \leq 2$

12.6 Quadric Surfaces

What you'll learn about

- Definition of Quadric Surface
- Ellipsoids
- Paraboloids
- Cones
- Hyperboloids
- Liquid Mirror Telescopes

Definition of Quadric Surface

A **quadric surface** is the graph in space of a second-degree equation in x, y, and z. The most general form is

$$Ax^2 + By^2 + Cz^2 + Dxy + Eyz + Fxz + Gx + Hy + Jz + K = 0,$$

where A, B, C, and so on are constants, but the equation can be simplified by translation and rotation, as in the two-dimensional case in Appendix A5.3. We will study only the simpler equations. Although the definition of cylinder did not require it, the cylinders in Figures 12.31–12.34 were also quadric surfaces. We now examine ellipsoids (these include spheres), paraboloids, cones, and hyperboloids.

Ellipsoids

EXAMPLE 1 Graphing Ellipsoids

The **ellipsoid**

$$\frac{x^2}{a^2} + \frac{y^2}{b^2} + \frac{z^2}{c^2} = 1$$

(Figure 12.40) cuts the coordinate axes at $(\pm a, 0, 0)$, $(0, \pm b, 0)$, $(0, 0, \pm c)$. It lies within the rectangular box defined by the inequalities $|x| \le a$, $|y| \le b$, and $|z| \le c$. The surface is symmetric with respect to each of the coordinate planes because the variables in the defining equation are squared.

The curves in which the three coordinate planes cut the surface are ellipses. For example,

$$\frac{x^2}{a^2} + \frac{y^2}{b^2} = 1 \qquad \text{when } z = 0.$$

The section cut from the surface by the plane $z = z_0$, $|z_0| < c$, is the ellipse

$$\frac{x^2}{a^2(1 - (z_0/c)^2)} + \frac{y^2}{b^2(1 - (z_0/c)^2)} = 1.$$

If any two of the semiaxes a, b, and c are equal, the surface is an **ellipsoid of revolution.** If all three are equal, the surface is a sphere.

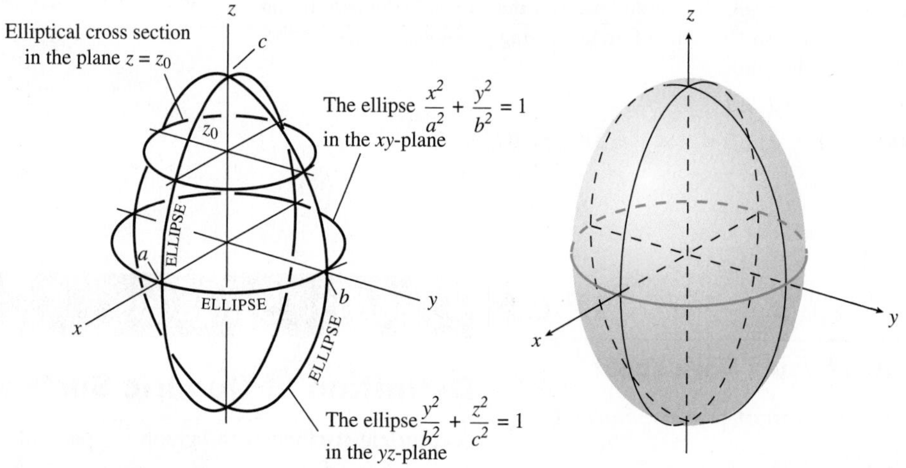

Figure 12.40 The ellipsoid $x^2/a^2 + y^2/b^2 + z^2/c^2 = 1$ in Example 1.

A CAS three-dimensional graphing program can help in visualizing surfaces in space. Many systems can rotate the figure so you can see it as if it were a physical model you could turn in your hand. Hidden-line algorithms (see Exercise 62, Section 12.4) are used to block out portions of the surface that you would not see from your current viewing angle. Most three-dimensional computer graphing programs allow the graph to be displayed in a box as illustrated with the graph of the ellipsoid in Figure 12.41.

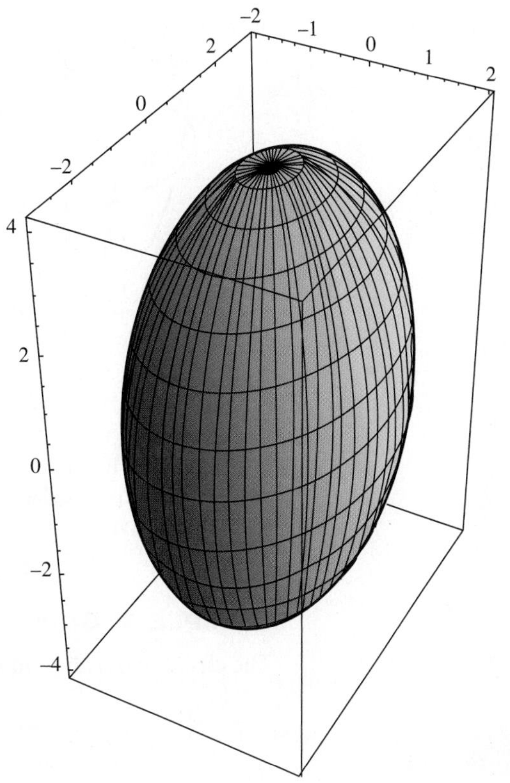

Figure 12.41 The graph of the ellipsoid $x^2/4 + y^2/9 + z^2/16 = 1$ drawn in a box using Mathematica.

Paraboloids

EXAMPLE 2 Graphing an Elliptic Paraboloid

The **elliptic paraboloid**

$$\frac{x^2}{a^2} + \frac{y^2}{b^2} = \frac{z}{c}$$

is symmetric with respect to the planes $x = 0$ and $y = 0$ (Figure 12.42). The only intercept on the axes is the origin. Except for this point, the surface lies above or entirely below the xy-plane, depending on the sign of c. The sections cut by the coordinate planes are

$x = 0$: the parabola $z = \frac{c}{b^2}y^2$

$y = 0$: the parabola $z = \frac{c}{a^2}x^2$

$z = 0$: the point $(0, 0, 0)$

Each plane $z = z_0$ above the xy-plane cuts the surface in the ellipse

$$\frac{x^2}{a^2} + \frac{y^2}{b^2} = \frac{z_0}{c}.$$

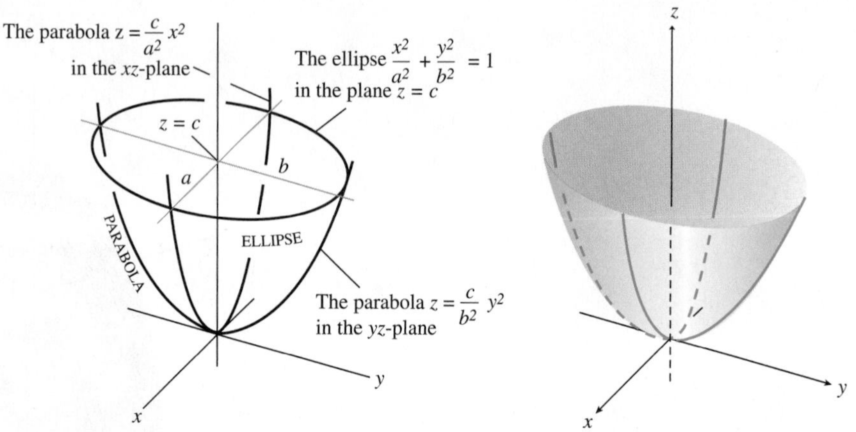

Figure 12.42 The elliptic paraboloid $x^2/a^2 + y^2/b^2 = z/c$ in Example 2, shown for $c > 0$. The cross sections perpendicular to the z-axis above the xy-plane are ellipses. The cross sections in the planes that contain the z-axis are parabolas.

EXAMPLE 3 Graphing a Circular Paraboloid

The **circular paraboloid** or **paraboloid of revolution**

$$\frac{x^2}{a^2} + \frac{y^2}{a^2} = \frac{z}{c}$$

is obtained by taking $b = a$ in the equation for the elliptic paraboloid of Example 2. The cross sections of the surface by planes perpendicular to the z-axis are circles centered on the z-axis. The cross sections by planes containing the z-axis are congruent parabolas with a common focus at the point $(0, 0, a^2/(4c))$.

Shapes cut from circular paraboloids are used for antennas in radio telescopes, satellite trackers, and microwave radio links (Figure 12.43).

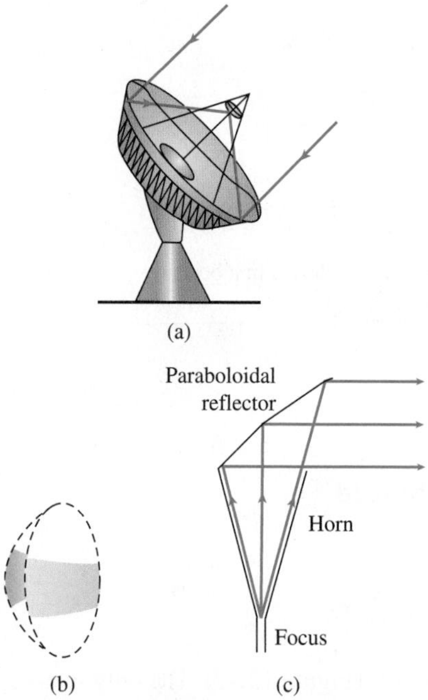

Figure 12.43 Many antennas are shaped like pieces of paraboloids of revolution. (a) Radio telescopes use the same principles as optical telescopes. (b) A "rectangular-cut" radar reflector. (c) The profile of a horn antenna in a microwave radio link.

Cones

EXAMPLE 4 Graphing an Elliptic Cone

The **elliptic cone**

$$\frac{x^2}{a^2} + \frac{y^2}{b^2} = \frac{z^2}{c^2}$$

is symmetric with respect to the three coordinate planes (Figure 12.44). The sections cut by the coordinate planes are

$x = 0$: the lines $z = \pm\frac{c}{b}y$

$y = 0$: the lines $z = \pm\frac{c}{a}x$

$z = 0$ the point $(0, 0, 0)$.

The sections cut by the planes $z = z_0$ above and below the xy-plane are ellipses whose centers lie on the z-axis and whose vertices lie on the above lines.

If $a = b$, the cone is a **right circular cone.**

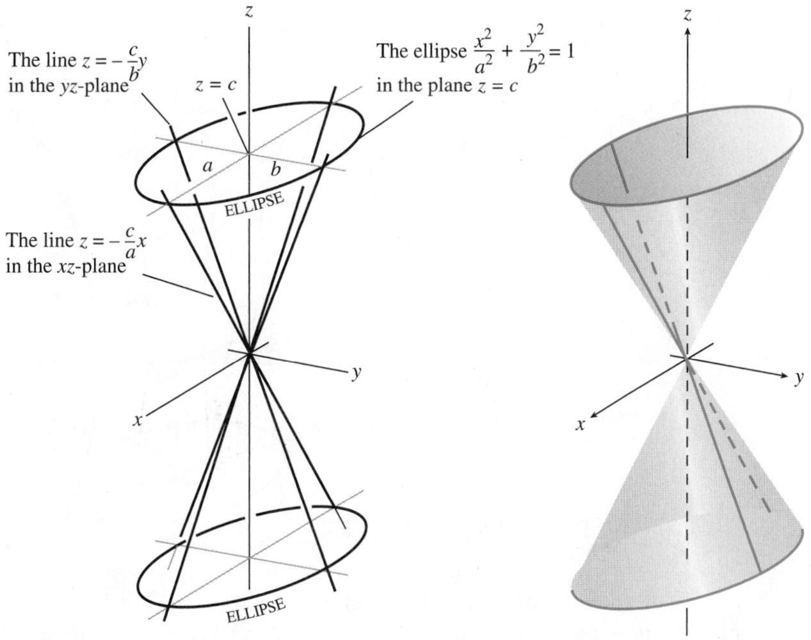

Figure 12.44 The elliptic cone $x^2/a^2 + y^2/b^2 = z^2/c^2$ in Example 4. Planes perpendicular to the z-axis cut the cone in ellipses above and below the xy-plane. Vertical planes that contain the z-axis cut it in a pair of intersecting lines.

Hyperboloids

EXAMPLE 5 Graphing a Hyperboloid of One Sheet

The **hyperboloid of one sheet**

$$\frac{x^2}{a^2} + \frac{y^2}{b^2} - \frac{z^2}{c^2} = 1$$

is symmetric with respect to each of the three coordinate planes (Figure 12.45). The sections cut by the coordinate planes are

$$x = 0: \quad \text{the hyperbola} \quad \frac{y^2}{b^2} - \frac{z^2}{c^2} = 1$$

$$y = 0: \quad \text{the hyperbola} \quad \frac{x^2}{a^2} - \frac{z^2}{c^2} = 1$$

$$z = 0: \quad \text{the ellipse} \quad \frac{x^2}{a^2} - \frac{y^2}{b^2} = 1$$

The plane $z = z_0$ cuts the surface in an ellipse with center on the z-axis and vertices on one of the above hyperbolas.

The surface is connected, meaning that it is possible to travel from one point on it to any other without leaving the surface. For this reason, it is said to have *one sheet,* in contrast to the hyperboloid in the next example, which has two sheets.

If $a = b$, the hyperboloid is a surface of revolution.

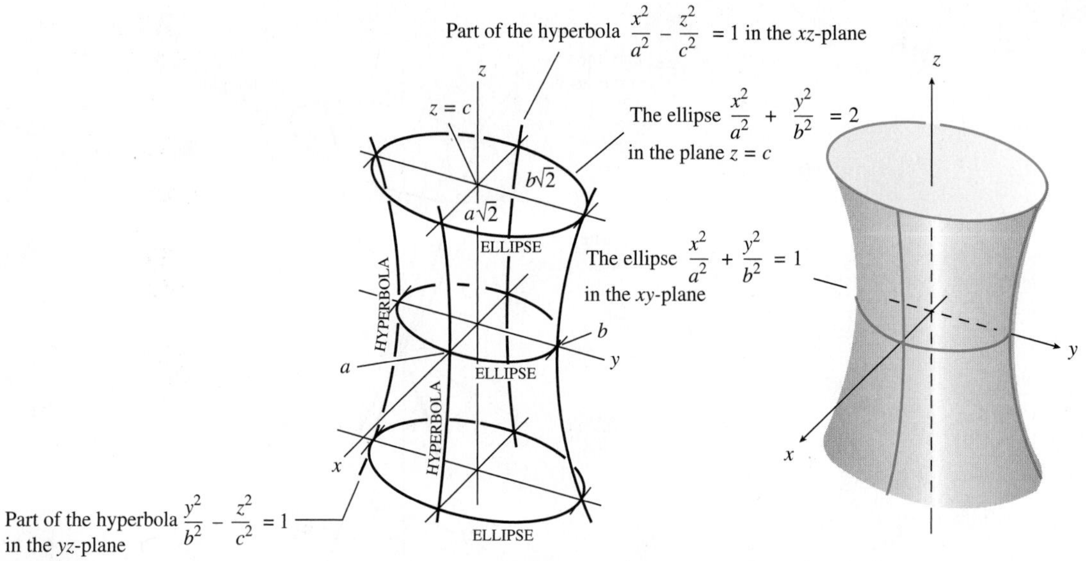

Figure 12.45 The hyperboloid $x^2/a^2 + y^2/b^2 - z^2/c^2 = 1$ in Example 5. Planes perpendicular to the z-axis cut it in ellipses. Vertical planes containing the z-axis cut it in hyperbolas.

EXAMPLE 6 Graphing a Hyperboloid of Two Sheets

The **hyperboloid of two sheets**

$$\frac{z^2}{c^2} - \frac{x^2}{a^2} - \frac{y^2}{b^2} = 1$$

is symmetric with respect to the three coordinate planes (Figure 12.46). The plane $z = 0$ does not intersect the surface; in fact, for a horizontal plane to intersect the surface, we must have $|z| \geq c$. The hyperbolic sections

$$x = 0: \quad \frac{z^2}{c^2} - \frac{y^2}{b^2} = 1$$

$$y = 0: \quad \frac{z^2}{c^2} - \frac{x^2}{a^2} = 1$$

have their vertices and foci on the z-axis. The surface is separated into two portions, one above the plane $z = c$ and the other below the plane $z = -c$. This accounts for its name.

The equation for the hyperboloid of one sheet and the equation for the hyperboloid of two sheets have different numbers of negative terms. The number in each case is the same as the number of sheets of the hyperboloid. If we replace the 1 on the right side of either equation by 0, we obtain the equation

$$\frac{x^2}{a^2} + \frac{y^2}{b^2} = \frac{z^2}{c^2}$$

for an elliptic cone. The hyperboloids are asymptotic to this cone (Figure 12.47) in the same way that the hyperbolas

$$\frac{x^2}{a^2} - \frac{y^2}{b^2} = \pm 1$$

are asymptotic to the lines

$$\frac{x^2}{a^2} - \frac{y^2}{b^2} = 0$$

in the *xy*-plane.

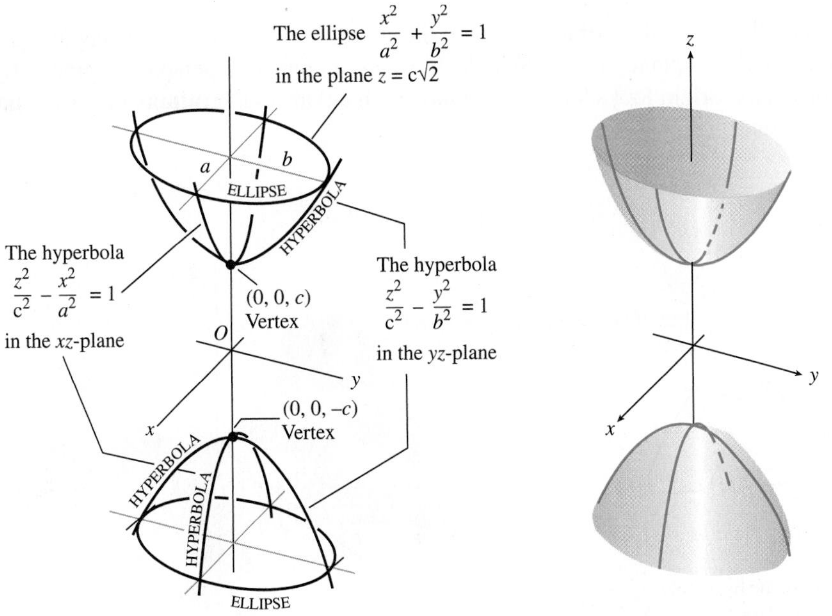

Figure 12.46 The hyperboloid $z^2/c^2 - x^2/a^2 - y^2/b^2 = 1$ in Example 6. Planes perpendicular to the z-axis above and below the vertices cut it in ellipses. Vertical planes containing the z-axis cut it into hyperbolas.

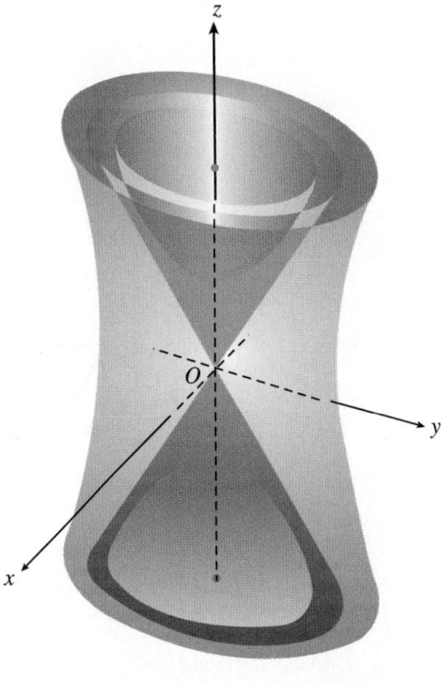

Figure 12.47 Both hyperboloids are asymptotic to the cone. (Example 6)

EXAMPLE 7 Graphing a Hyperbolic Paraboloid

The **hyperbolic paraboloid**

$$\frac{y^2}{b^2} - \frac{x^2}{a^2} = \frac{z}{c}, \qquad c > 0$$

has symmetry with respect to the planes $x = 0$ and $y = 0$ (Figure 12.48). The sections in these planes are

$x = 0$: the parabola $z = \frac{c}{b^2}y^2$

$y = 0$: the parabola $z = -\frac{c}{a^2}x^2.$

In the plane $x = 0$, the parabola opens upward from the origin. The parabola in the plane $y = 0$ opens downward.

If we cut the surface by a plane $z = z_0 > 0$, the section is a hyperbola

$$\frac{y^2}{b^2} - \frac{x^2}{a^2} = \frac{z_0}{c},$$

with its focal axis parallel to the y-axis and its vertices on the parabola

$$z = \frac{c}{b^2}y^2.$$

If z_0 is negative, the focal axis is parallel to the x-axis and the vertices lie on the hyperbola

$$z = -\frac{c}{a^2}x^2.$$

Near the origin, the surface is shaped like a saddle. To a person traveling along the surface in the yz-plane, the origin looks like a minimum. To a person traveling in the xz-plane, the origin looks like a maximum. Such a point is a **minimax** or **saddle point** of a surface.

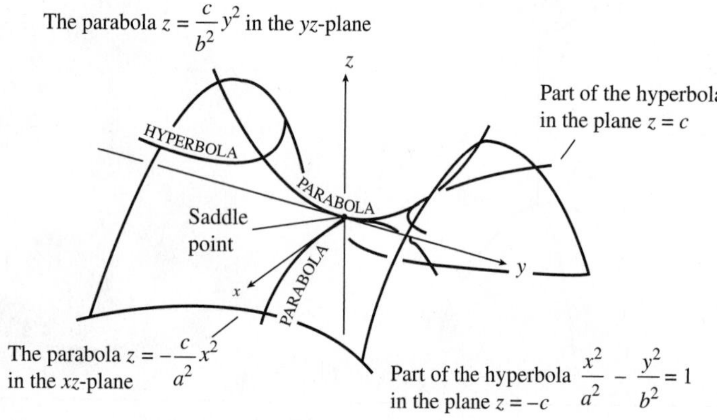

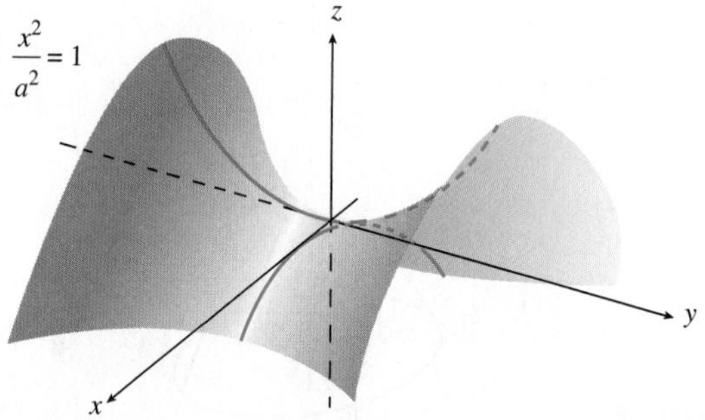

Figure 12.48 The hyperbolic paraboloid $y^2/b^2 - x^2/a^2 = z/c$, $c > 0$ in Example 7. The cross sections in planes perpendicular to the z-axis above and below the xy-plane are hyperbolas. The cross sections in planes perpendicular to the other axes are parabolas.

EXPLORATION 1 **Identifying Shapes of Familiar Objects**

Match each of the familiar objects on the left with its identifying shape of the right. In each case, try to come up with a few other examples of familiar objects having the same identifying shape. (Some shapes are more commonly found than others.)

1. Jelly bean	**A.** Circular paraboloid
2. Reflector in a flashlight	**B.** Ellipsoid of revolution
3. Nuclear plant cooling tower	**C.** Hyperbolic paraboloid
4. Saddle	**D.** Hyperboloid of revolution

Drawing Lesson
How to Draw Quadric Surfaces

$$x^2 + \frac{y^2}{4} + z^2 = 1 \qquad\qquad z = 4 - x^2 - y^2$$

1. Lightly sketch the three coordinate axes.

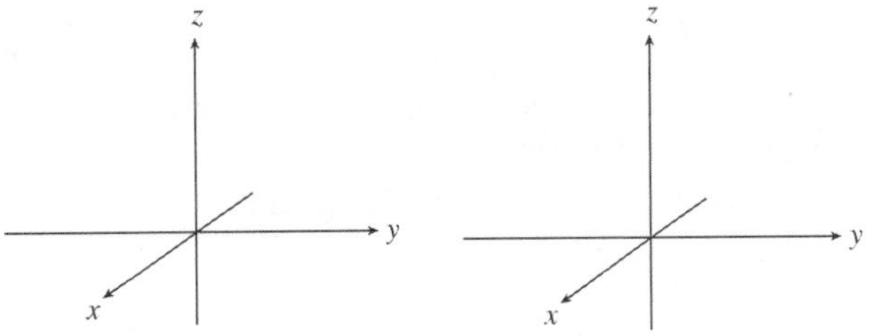

2. Decide on a scale and mark the intercepts on the axes.

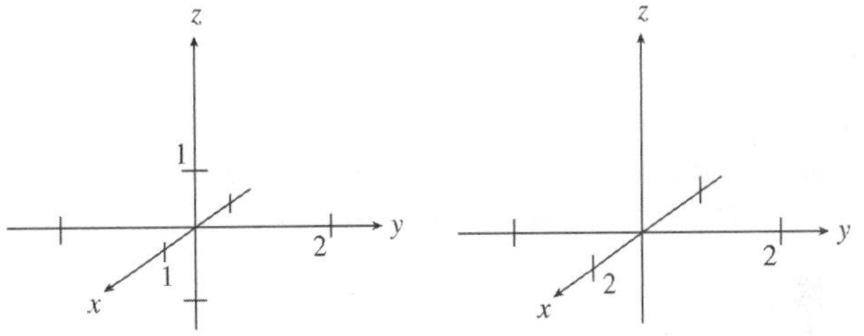

3. Sketch cross sections in the coordinate planes and in a few parallel planes, but don't clutter the picture. Use tangent lines as guides.

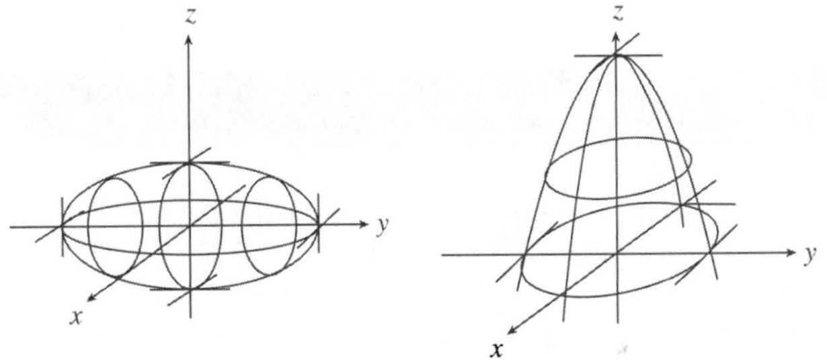

4. If more is required, darken the parts exposed to view. Leave the rest light. Use line breaks when you can.

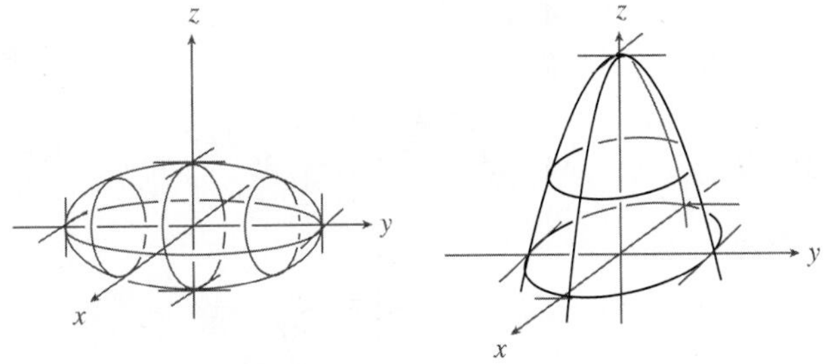

Liquid Mirror Telescopes

When a circular pan of liquid is rotated about its vertical axis, the surface of the liquid does not stay flat. Instead, it assumes the shape of a paraboloid of revolution, exactly what is needed for the primary mirror of a reflecting telescope. At the beginning of the twentieth century, attempts to make reliable mirrors with revolving mercury failed because of surface ripples and focus losses caused by variations in the speed of rotation. Today these difficulties can be overcome with synchronous motors driven by oscillator-stabilized power supplies and checked against constant clocks.

Using the same idea, astronomers at the Steward Observatory's Mirror Laboratory in Tucson, Arizona, have used a large heated spinning turntable to cast borosilicate glass blanks for lightweight mirrors. Spincast mirrors cost less than traditionally cast mirrors and can be made larger. Their shorter focal lengths also allow them to be installed in compact telescope frames that are less expensive to house and less likely to flex in strong winds.

Quick Review 12.6

In Exercises 1 and 2, consider the ellipse

$$\frac{x^2}{4} + \frac{y^2}{9} = 1.$$

1. Solve for y and give the two functions that can be entered into a function grapher to produce the graph of the ellipse.

2. Give parametric equations that will produce the graph of the ellipse.

In Exercises 3 and 4, consider the hyperbola

$$\frac{x^2}{4} - \frac{y^2}{9} = 1$$

3. Solve for y and give the two functions that can be entered into a function grapher to produce the graph of the hyperbola.

4. Give parametric equations that will produce the graph of the hyperbola.

In Exercises 5 and 6, find the x- and y-intercepts of the graph of the equation.

5. $\frac{x^2}{9} + \frac{y^2}{4} = 1$

6. $\frac{x^2}{9} - \frac{y^2}{4} = 1$

In Exercises 7–10, determine whether the graph of the equation is symmetric with respect to the **(a)** x-axis, **(b)** y-axis, **(c)** origin.

7. $\frac{x^2}{25} + \frac{y^2}{16} = 1$

8. $\frac{y^2}{25} - \frac{x^2}{4} = 1$

9. $y = \frac{3}{2}x^2$

10. $x = \frac{4}{3}y^2$

Section 12.6 Exercises

In Exercises 1–10, match the equation with the surface it defines. Also, identify each surface by type (paraboloid, ellipsoid, etc.). The surfaces are labeled (a)–(j).

1. $x^2 + y^2 + 4z^2 = 10$

2. $z^2 + 4y^2 - 4x^2 = 4$

3. $y^2 + z^2 = x^2$

4. $x = y^2 - z^2$

5. $x = -y^2 - z^2$

6. $z^2 + x^2 - y^2 = 1$

7. $x = z^2 - y^2$

8. $z = -4x^2 - y^2$

9. $x^2 + 4z^2 = y^2$

10. $9x^2 + 4y^2 + 2z^2 = 36$

(a)

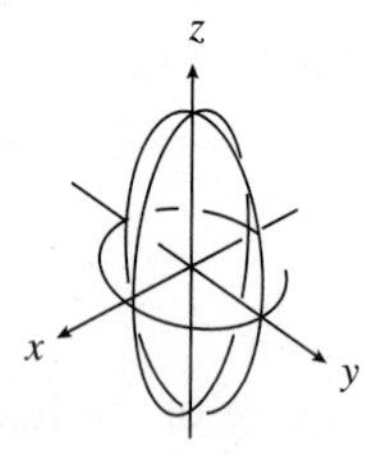

(b)

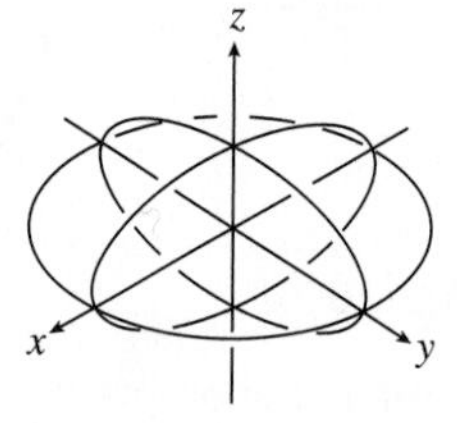

(c)

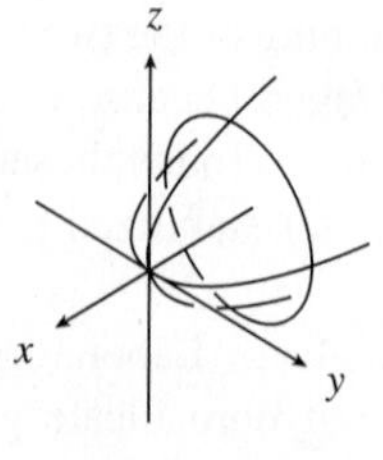

(d)

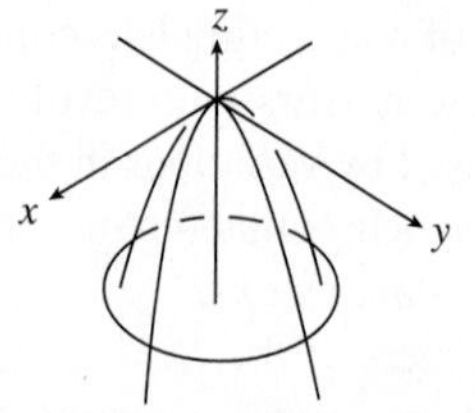

(e)

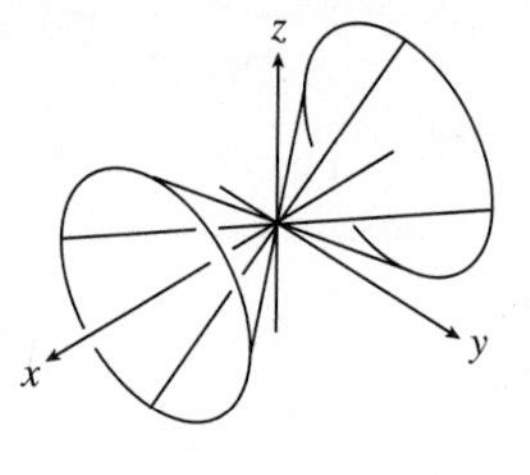

(f)

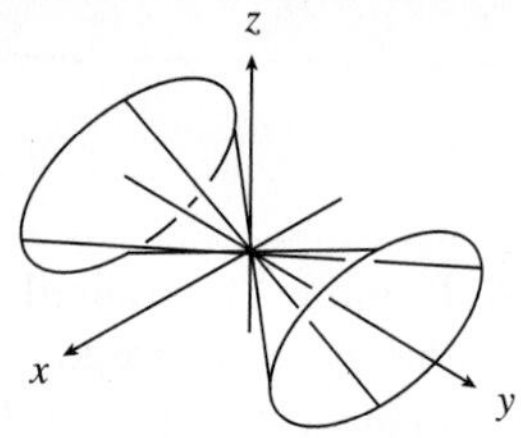

(g)

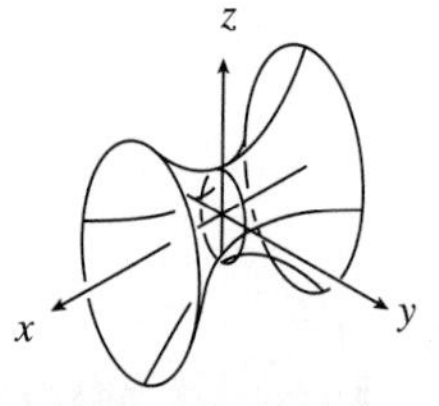

(h)

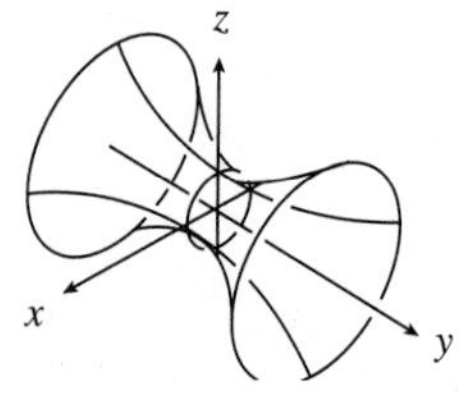

(i)

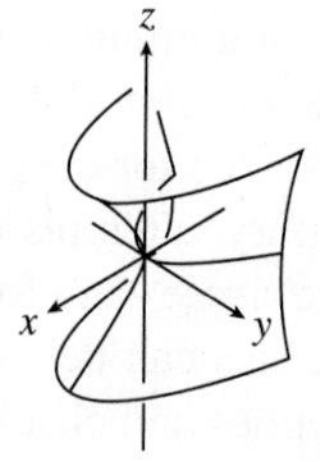

(j)

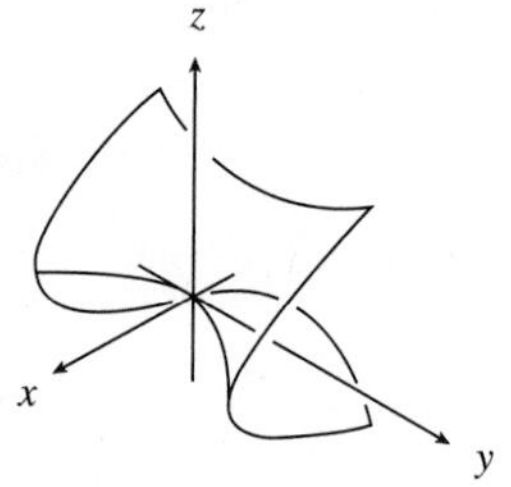

In Exercises 11–14, sketch the ellipsoid.

11. $9x^2 + y^2 + z^2 = 9$

12. $4x^2 + 4y^2 + z^2 = 16$

13. $4x^2 + 9y^2 + 4z^2 = 36$

14. $9x^2 + 4y^2 + 36z^2 = 36$

In Exercises 15–20, sketch the paraboloid.

15. $z = x^2 + 4y^2$

16. $z = x^2 + 9y^2$

17. $z = 8 - x^2 - y^2$

18. $z = 18 - x^2 - 9y^2$

19. $x = 4 - 4y^2 - z^2$

20. $y = 1 - x^2 - z^2$

In Exercises 21–24, sketch the cone.

21. $x^2 + y^2 = z^2$

22. $y^2 + z^2 = x^2$

23. $4x^2 + 9z^2 = 9y^2$

24. $9x^2 + 4y^2 = 36z^2$

In Exercises 25–32, sketch the hyperboloid.

25. $x^2 + y^2 - z^2 = 1$

26. $y^2 + z^2 - x^2 = 1$

27. $\frac{y^2}{4} + \frac{z^2}{9} - \frac{x^2}{4} = 1$

28. $\frac{x^2}{4} + \frac{y^2}{4} - \frac{z^2}{9} = 1$

29. $z^2 - x^2 - y^2 = 1$

30. $\frac{y^2}{4} - \frac{x^2}{4} - z^2 = 1$

31. $x^2 - y^2 - \frac{z^2}{4} = 1$

32. $\frac{x^2}{4} - y^2 - \frac{z^2}{4} = 1$

In Exercises 33 and 34, sketch the hyperbolic paraboloid.

33. $y^2 - x^2 = z$

34. $x^2 - y^2 = z$

In Exercises 35–50, sketch the surface.

35. $x^2 + y^2 + z^2 = 4$

36. $4x^2 + 4y^2 = z^2$

37. $z = 1 + y^2 - x^2$

38. $y^2 - z^2 = 6$

39. $y = -(x^2 + z^2)$

40. $z^2 - 4x^2 - 4y^2 = 4$

41. $x^2 + y^2 - z^2 = 4$

42. $x = 6 - y^2$

43. $x^2 + z^2 = 2$

44. $4x^2 + 4y^2 + z^2 = 4$

45. $16y^2 + 9z^2 = 4x^2$

46. $z = x^2 - y^2 - 1$

47. $z = -(x^2 + y^2)$

48. $y^2 - x^2 - z^2 = 1$

49. $36x^2 + 9y^2 + 4z^2 = 36$

50. $9x^2 + 16y^2 = 4z^2$

Explorations

51. ***Volumes of Ellipsoids*** **(a)** Express the area of the cross section cut from the ellipsoid

$$x^2 + \frac{y^2}{4} + \frac{z^2}{9} = 1$$

by the plane $z = c$ as a function of c. (The area of an ellipse with semiaxes a and b is πab.)

(b) Use slices perpendicular to the z-axis to find the volume of the ellipsoid in (a).

(c) Now find the volume of the ellipsoid

$$\frac{x^2}{a^2} + \frac{y^2}{b^2} + \frac{z^2}{c^2} = 1.$$

Does your formula give the volume of a sphere of radius a if $a = b = c$?

52. ***Volume of a Barrel*** The barrel shown here is shaped like an ellipsoid with equal pieces cut from the ends by planes perpendicular to the z-axis. The cross sections perpendicular to the z-axis are circular. The barrel is $2h$ units high, its midsection radius is R, and its end radii are both r. Find a formula for the barrel's volume. Then check two things. First, suppose the sides of the barrel are straightened to turn the barrel into a cylinder of radius R and height $2h$. Does your formula give the cylinder's volume? Second, suppose $r = 0$ and $h = R$ so the barrel is a sphere. Does your formula give the sphere's volume?

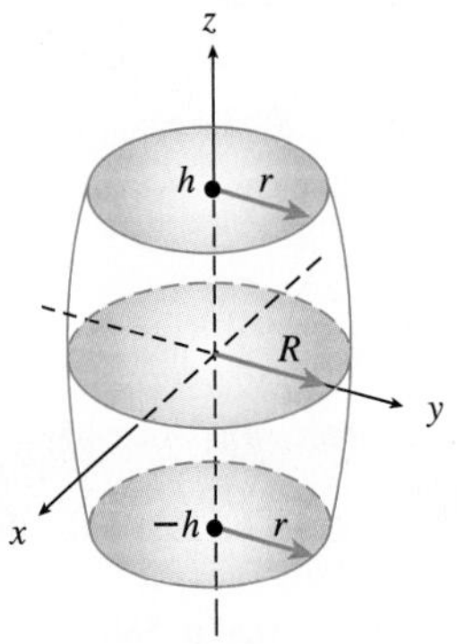

53. Show that the volume of the segment cut from the paraboloid

$$\frac{x^2}{a^2} + \frac{y^2}{b^2} = \frac{z}{c}$$

by the plane $z = h$ equals half the segment's base times its altitude. (Figure 12.42 shows the segment for the special case $h = c$.)

54. **(a)** Find the volume of the solid bounded by the hyperboloid

$$\frac{x^2}{a^2} + \frac{y^2}{b^2} - \frac{z^2}{c^2} = 1$$

and the planes $z = 0$ and $z = h$, $h > 0$.

(b) Express your answer in (a) in terms of h and the areas A_0 and A_h of the regions cut by the hyperboloid from the planes $z = 0$ and $z = h$.

(c) Show that the volume in (a) is also given by the formula

$$V = \frac{h}{6}(A_0 + 4A_m + A_h),$$

where A_m is the area of the region cut by the hyperboloid from the plane $z = h/2$.

55. **Writing to Learn** Every time we found the trace of a quadric surface in a plane parallel to one of the coordinate planes, it turned out to be a conic section. Was this mere coincidence? Did it have to happen? Give reasons for your answer.

56. **Writing to Learn** Suppose you intersect a quadric surface with a plane that is *not* parallel to one of the coordinate planes. What will the trace in the plane be like? Give reasons for your answer.

Extending the Ideas

57. If the hyperbolic paraboloid

$$\frac{y^2}{b^2} - \frac{x^2}{a^2} = \frac{z}{c}$$

is cut by the plane $y = y_1$, the resulting curve is a parabola. Find its vertex and focus.

58. Writing to Learn Suppose you set $z = 0$ in the equation

$$Ax^2 + By^2 + Cz^2 + Dxy + Eyz + Fxz + Gx + Hy + Jz + K = 0$$

to obtain a curve in the xy-plane. What will the curve be like? Give reasons for your answer.

CAS Explorations

In Exercises 59–63, use a CAS to plot the surface. Identify the type of quadric surface from your graph.

59. $\frac{x^2}{9} + \frac{y^2}{36} = 1 - \frac{z^2}{25}$

60. $\frac{x^2}{9} - \frac{z^2}{9} = 1 - \frac{y^2}{16}$

61. $5x^2 = z^2 - 3y^2$

62. $\frac{y^2}{16} = 1 - \frac{x^2}{9} + z$

63. $\frac{x^2}{9} - 1 = \frac{y^2}{16} + \frac{z^2}{2}$

Chapter 12 Key Terms

angle between differentiable curves (p. 588)
angle between intersecting lines (p. 588)
angle between planes (p. 601)
angle between vectors (p. 582)
Cartesian coordinates of a point (p. 571)
circular paraboloid (p. 612)
component equation for a plane (p. 597)
coordinate planes (p. 571)
cross (vector) product (p. 588)
cylinder (p. 602)
cylindrical coordinates of a point (p. 605)
determinant formula for **A** × **B** (p. 591)
direction angles (p. 587)
direction of a nonzero vector (p. 574)
distance between points (p. 575)
distance from point to line (p. 600)
distance from point to plane (p. 600)
dot (scalar) product (inner product) (p. 581)
ellipsoid (p. 610)
ellipsoid of revolution (p. 610)
elliptic cone (p. 612)
elliptic paraboloid (p. 611)
first octant (p. 571)
generating curve for cylinder (p. 602)
hyperbolic paraboloid (p. 615)
hyperboloid of one sheet (p. 613)
hyperboloid of two sheets (p. 614)
inner product (dot product) (p. 581)
magnitude of a vector (p. 573)
midpoint of a line segment (p. 578)
octants (p. 571)
origin (p. 571)
orthogonal (perpendicular) vectors (p. 582)
paraboloid of revolution (p. 612)
parametric equations for a line (p. 596)
perpendicular (orthogonal) vectors (p. 582)
position vector (p. 572)
quadric surface (p. 609)
rectangular coordinates (p. 571)
right circular cone (p. 612)
right-handed coordinate frame (p. 571)
right-hand rule (p. 588)
scalar component of **B** in the direction of **A** (p. 583)
standard equation for a sphere (p. 572)
standard unit vectors (p. 572)
torque (p. 573)
triple scalar (box) product (p. 592)
unit vector (p. 573)
vector as sum of orthogonal vectors (p. 584)
vector (cross) product (p. 588)
vector equation for a line (p. 595)
vector equation for a plane (p. 597)
vector operations (p. 573)
vector projection (p. 583)
work (p. 585)
xy-plane (p. 571)
xz-plane (p. 571)
yz-plane (p. 571)
zero vector (p. 573)

Chapter 12 Review Exercises

In Exercises 1 and 2, express the vector as a product of its length and direction.

1. $2\mathbf{i} - 3\mathbf{j} + 6\mathbf{k}$ **2.** $\mathbf{i} + 2\mathbf{j} - \mathbf{k}$

3. Find a vector 2 units long in the direction of $\mathbf{A} = 4\mathbf{i} - \mathbf{j} + 4\mathbf{k}$.

4. The points $O, A, B, C, D,$ and E are vertices of the rectangular box shown here. Express $\overrightarrow{OD}$ and $\overrightarrow{OE}$ in terms of $\overrightarrow{OA}$, $\overrightarrow{OB}$, and $\overrightarrow{OC}$.

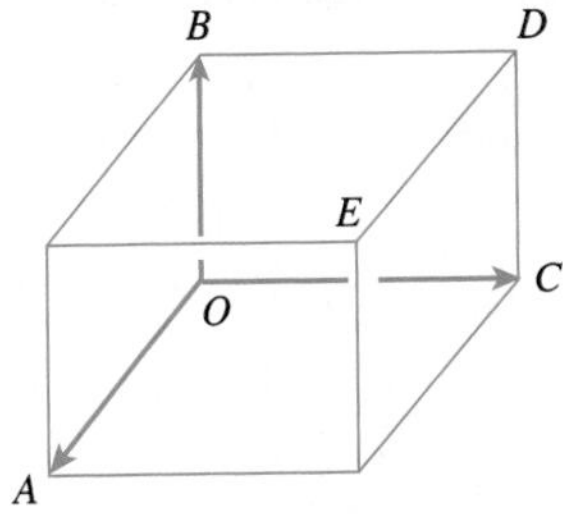

5. Copy the vectors **u** and **v** and sketch the vector projection of **v** onto **u**.

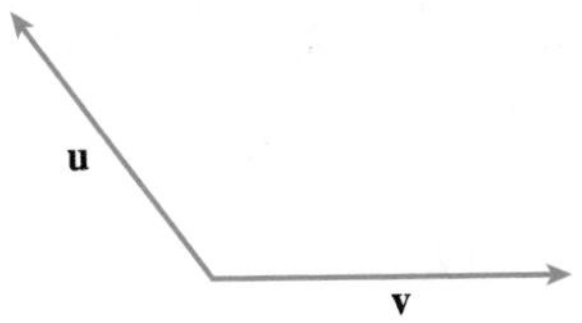

6. Express vectors **a, b,** and **c** in terms of **u** and **v**.

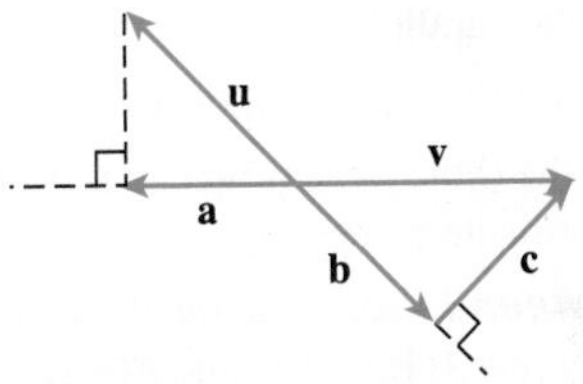

In Exercises 7 and 8, find $|\mathbf{A}|$, $|\mathbf{B}|$, $\mathbf{A} \cdot \mathbf{B}$, $\mathbf{B} \cdot \mathbf{A}$, $\mathbf{A} \times \mathbf{B}$, $\mathbf{B} \times \mathbf{A}$, $|\mathbf{A} \times \mathbf{B}|$, the angle θ between **A** and **B,** the scalar component of **B** in the direction of **A,** and the vector projection of **B** onto **A.**

7. $\mathbf{A} = \mathbf{i} + \mathbf{j}$
$\mathbf{B} = 2\mathbf{i} + \mathbf{j} - 2\mathbf{k}$

8. $\mathbf{A} = \mathbf{i} - \mathbf{j} + 2\mathbf{k}$
$\mathbf{B} = -\mathbf{i} - \mathbf{k}$

In Exercises 9 and 10, write **B** as a sum of a vector parallel to **A** and a vector orthogonal to **A**.

9. $\mathbf{A} = 2\mathbf{i} + \mathbf{j} - \mathbf{k}$
$\mathbf{B} = \mathbf{i} + \mathbf{j} - 5\mathbf{k}$

10. $\mathbf{A} = \mathbf{i} - 2\mathbf{j}$
$\mathbf{B} = \mathbf{i} + \mathbf{j} + \mathbf{k}$

In Exercises 11 and 12, draw coordinate axes and then sketch **A, B,** and $\mathbf{A} \times \mathbf{B}$ as vectors at the origin.

11. $\mathbf{A} = \mathbf{i}, \mathbf{B} = \mathbf{i} + \mathbf{j}$ **12.** $\mathbf{A} = \mathbf{i} - \mathbf{j}, \mathbf{B} = \mathbf{i} + \mathbf{j}$

In Exercises 13 and 14, find the unit vectors that are tangent and normal to the curve at point *P.*

13. $y = \tan x$, $P(\pi/4, 1)$ **14.** $x^2 + y^2 = 25$, $P(3, 4)$

15. For any vectors **A** and **B,** show that $|\mathbf{A} + \mathbf{B}|^2 + |\mathbf{A} - \mathbf{B}|^2 = 2|\mathbf{A}|^2 + 2|\mathbf{B}|^2$.

Exploration

16. Let ABC be the triangle determined by vectors **u** and **v.**

(a) Express the area of ΔABC in terms of **u** and **v.**

(b) Express the triangle's altitude h in terms of **u** and **v.**

(c) Find the area and altitude if $\mathbf{u} = \mathbf{i} - \mathbf{j} + \mathbf{k}$ and $\mathbf{v} = 2\mathbf{i} + \mathbf{k}$.

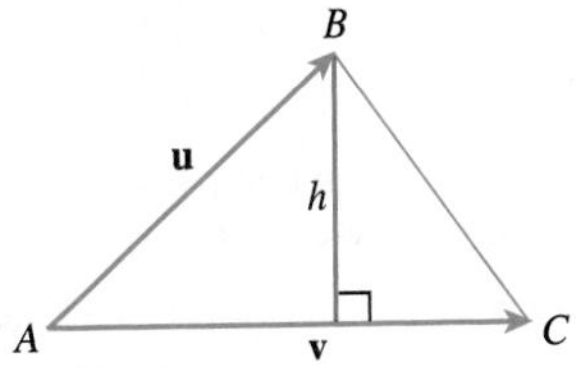

17. If $|\mathbf{v}| = 2$, $|\mathbf{w}| = 3$, and the angle between **v** and **w** is $\pi/3$, find $|\mathbf{v} - 2\mathbf{w}|$.

18. For what value or values of a will the vectors $\mathbf{u} = 2\mathbf{i} + 4\mathbf{j} - 5\mathbf{k}$ and $\mathbf{v} = -4\mathbf{i} - 8\mathbf{j} + a\mathbf{k}$ be parallel?

In Exercises 19 and 20, find **(a)** the area of the parallelogram determined by vectors **A** and **B, (b)** the volume of the parallelepiped determined by the vectors **A, B,** and **C.**

19. $\mathbf{A} = \mathbf{i} + \mathbf{j} - \mathbf{k}$, $\mathbf{B} = 2\mathbf{i} + \mathbf{j} + \mathbf{k}$, $\mathbf{C} = -\mathbf{i} - 2\mathbf{j} + 3\mathbf{k}$

20. $\mathbf{A} = \mathbf{i} + \mathbf{j}$, $\mathbf{B} = \mathbf{j}$, $\mathbf{C} = \mathbf{i} + \mathbf{j} + \mathbf{k}$

21. Writing to Learn Suppose **n** is normal to a plane and **v** is parallel to the plane. Describe how you would find a vector **u** that is both perpendicular to **v** and parallel to the plane.

22. Find a vector in the plane parallel to the line $ax + by = c$.

In Exercises 23 and 24, find the distance from the point to the line.

23. $(2, 2, 0)$; $x = -t$, $y = t$, $z = -1 + t$

24. $(0, 4, 1)$; $x = 2 + t$, $y = 2 + t$, $z = t$

25. Parametrize the line that passes through the point $(1, 2, 3)$ parallel to the vector $\mathbf{v} = -3\mathbf{i} + 7\mathbf{k}$.

26. Parametrize the line segment joining the points $P(1, 2, 0)$ and $Q(1, 3, -1)$.

In Exercises 27 and 28, find the distance from the point to the plane.

27. $(6, 0, -6)$, $x - y = 4$

28. $(3, 0, 10)$, $2x + 3y + z = 2$

29. Find an equation for the plane that passes through the point $(3, -2, 1)$ normal to the vector $\mathbf{n} = 2\mathbf{i} + \mathbf{j} + \mathbf{k}$.

30. Find an equation for the plane that passes through the point $(-1, 6, 0)$ perpendicular to the line $x = -1 + t$, $y = 6 - 2t$, $z = 3t$.

In Exercises 31 and 32, find an equation for the plane through points *P, Q,* and *R.*

31. $P(1, -1, 2)$, $Q(2, 1, 3)$, $R(-1, 2, -1)$

32. $P(1, 0, 0)$, $Q(0, 1, 1)$, $R(0, 0, 1)$

33. Find the points in which the line $x = 1 + 2t$, $y = -1 - t$, $z = 3t$ meets the three coordinate planes.

34. Find the point in which the line through the origin perpendicular to the plane $2x - y - z = 4$ meets the plane $3x - 5y + 2z = 6$.

In Exercises 35 and 36, find the acute angle between the planes.

35. $x = 7, x + y\sqrt{2}z = -3$

36. $x + y = 1, y + z = 1$

37. Find parametric equations for the line in which the planes $x + 2y + z = 1$ and $x - y + 2z = -8$ intersect.

38. Show that the line in which the planes $x + 2y - 2z = 5$ and $5x - 2y - z = 0$ intersect is parallel to the line $x = -3 + 2t$, $y = 3t$, $z = 1 + 4t$.

39. The planes $3x + 6z = 1$ and $2x + 2y - z = 3$ intersect in a line.

(a) Show that the planes are orthogonal.

(b) Find equations for the line of intersection.

40. Find an equation for the plane that passes through the point (1, 2, 3) parallel to $\mathbf{u} = 2\mathbf{i} + 3\mathbf{j} + \mathbf{k}$ and $\mathbf{v} = \mathbf{i} - \mathbf{j} + 2\mathbf{k}$.

41. Writing to Learn Is $\mathbf{v} = 2\mathbf{i} - 4\mathbf{j} + \mathbf{k}$ related in any special way to the plane $2x + y = 5$? Give reasons for your answer.

42. The equation $\mathbf{n} \cdot \overrightarrow{P_0P} = 0$ represents the plane through P_0 normal to $\mathbf{n}$. What set does the inequality $\mathbf{n} \cdot \overrightarrow{P_0P} > 0$ represent?

43. Find the distance from the point $P(1, 4, 0)$ to the plane through $A(0, 0, 0)$, $B(2, 0, -1)$ and $C(2, -1, 0)$.

44. Find the distance from the point (2, 2, 3) to the plane $2x + 3y + 5z = 0$.

45. Find a vector parallel to the plane $2x - y - z = 4$ and orthogonal to $\mathbf{i} + \mathbf{j} + \mathbf{k}$.

46. Find a unit vector orthogonal to $\mathbf{A}$ in the plane of $\mathbf{B}$ and $\mathbf{C}$ if $\mathbf{A} = 2\mathbf{i} - \mathbf{j} + \mathbf{k}$, $\mathbf{B} = \mathbf{i} + 2\mathbf{j} + \mathbf{k}$, and $\mathbf{C} = \mathbf{i} + \mathbf{j} - 2\mathbf{k}$.

47. Find a vector of magnitude 2 parallel to the line of intersection of the planes $x + 2y + z - 1 = 0$ and $x - y + 2z + 7 = 0$.

48. Find the point in which the line through the origin perpendicular to the plane $2x - y - z = 4$ meets the plane $3x - 5y + 2z = 6$.

49. Find the point in which the line through $P(3, 2, 1)$ normal to the plane $2x - y + 2z = -2$ meets the plane.

50. What angle does the line of intersection of the planes $2x + y - z = 0$ and $x + y + 2z = 0$ make with the positive x-axis?

51. The line

$$L\colon x = 3 + 2t, \qquad y = 2t, \qquad z = t$$

intersects the plane $x + 3y - z = -4$ in a point P. Find the coordinates of P and find equations for the line through P perpendicular to L.

52. Show that for every real number k the plane $x - 2y + z + 3 + k(2x - y - z + 1) = 0$ contains the line of intersection of the planes $x - 2y + z + 3 = 0$ and $2x - y - z + 1 = 0$.

53. Find an equation for the plane through $A(-2, 0, -3)$ and $B(1, -2, 1)$ that lies parallel to the line through $C(-2, -13/5, 26/5)$ and $D(16/5, -13/5, 0)$.

54. Writing to Learn Is the line $x = 1 + 2t$, $y = -2 + 3t$, $z = -5t$ related in any way to the plane $-4x - 6y + 10z = 9$? Give reasons for your answer.

In Exercises 55 and 56, *work in groups of two or three.*

55. Which of the following are equations for the plane through the points $P(1, 1, -1)$, $Q(3, 0, 2)$, and $R(-2, 1, 0)$?

(a) $(2\mathbf{i} - 3\mathbf{j} + 3\mathbf{k}) \cdot ((x + 2)\mathbf{i} + (y - 1)\mathbf{j} + z\mathbf{k}) = 0$

(b) $x = 3 - t, y = -11t, z = 2 - 3t$

(c) $(x + 2) + 11(y - 1) = 3z$

(d) $(2\mathbf{i} - 3\mathbf{j} + 3\mathbf{k}) \times ((x + 2)\mathbf{i} + (y - 1)\mathbf{j} + z\mathbf{k}) = \mathbf{0}$

(e) $((2\mathbf{i} - \mathbf{j} + 3\mathbf{k}) \times (-3\mathbf{i} + \mathbf{k})) \cdot ((x + 2)\mathbf{i}(y - 1)\mathbf{j} + z\mathbf{k}) = 0$

56. The parallelogram shown here has vertices at $A(2, -1, 4)$, $B(1, 0, -1)$, $C(1, 2, 3)$, and D. Find

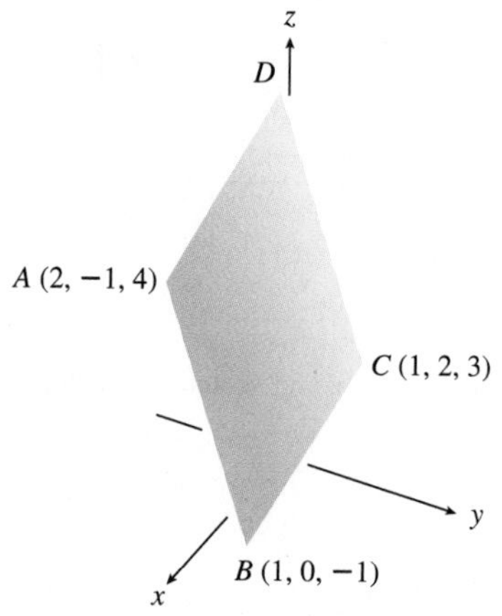

(a) the coordinates of D.

(b) the cosine of the interior angle at B.

(c) the vector projection of $\overrightarrow{BA}$ onto $\overrightarrow{BC}$.

(d) the area of the parallelogram.

(e) an equation for the plane of the parallelogram.

(f) the areas of the orthogonal projections of the parallelogram on the three coordinate planes.

57. *Distance Between Lines* Find the distance between the line L_1 through the points $A(1, 0, -1)$ and $B(-1, 1, 0)$ and the line L_2 through the points $C(3, 1, -1)$ and $D(4, 5, -2)$. The distance is to be measured along the line perpendicular to the two lines. First find a vector $\mathbf{n}$ perpendicular to both lines. Then project $\overrightarrow{AC}$ onto $\mathbf{n}$.

58. *(Continuation of Exercise 57)* Find the distance between the line through $A(4, 0, 2)$ and $B(2, 4, 1)$ and the line through $C(1, 3, 2)$ and $D(2, 2, 4)$.

In Exercises 59 and 60, the equation defines sets both in the plane and in three-dimensional space. Identify both sets.

59. $x = 0$

60. $x + y = 1$

61. Find the center and radius of the sphere

$$2x^2 + 2y^2 + 2z^2 - 12x + 4y - 8z + 10 = 0.$$

62. *Work Pushing a Car* Find the work done in pushing a car 250 m with a force of magnitude 160 N directed at an angle of $\pi/6$ rad downward from the horizontal against the back of the car as shown in the figure.

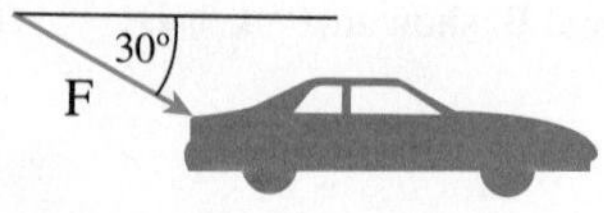

63. *Torque on a Spark Plug* The operator's manual for the Toro® 21-in. lawnmower says "tighten the spark plug to 15 ft-lb (20.4 N · m)." If you are installing the plug with a 10.5-in. socket wrench that places the center of your hand 9 in. from the axis of the spark plug as shown in the figure, about how hard should you pull? Answer in pounds.

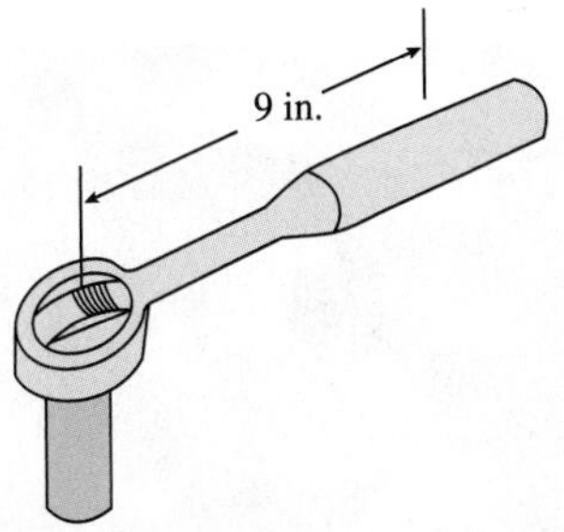

64. In the figure here, D is the midpoint of side AB of triangle ABC and E is one-third of the way between C and B. Use vectors to prove that F is the midpoint of line segment CD.

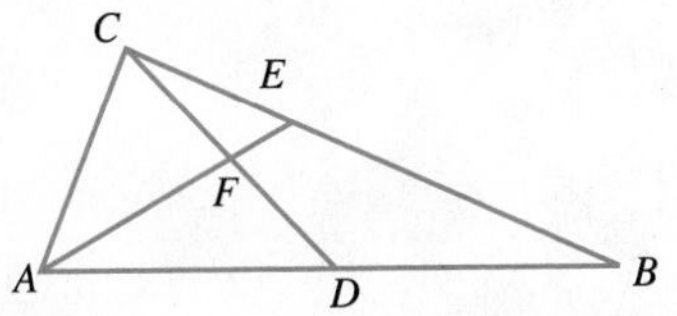

65. *Determinant Equations for Planes* **(a)** Show that

$$\begin{vmatrix} x_1 - x & y_1 - y & z_1 - z \\ x_2 - x & y_2 - y & z_2 - z \\ x_3 - x & y_3 - y & z_3 - z \end{vmatrix} = 0$$

is an equation for the plane through the three noncollinear points $P_1(x_1, y_1, z_1)$, $P_2(x_2, y_2, z_2)$, and $P_3(x_3, y_3, z_3)$.

(b) What set of points in space is described by the equation

$$\begin{vmatrix} x & y & z & 1 \\ x_1 & y_1 & z_1 & 1 \\ x_2 & y_2 & z_2 & 1 \\ x_3 & y_3 & z_3 & 1 \end{vmatrix} = 0?$$

66. *Distance from a Point to a Line* Use vectors to prove that the distance from $P_1(x_1, y_1)$ to the line $ax + by = c$ is

$$d = \frac{|ax_1 + by_1 - c|}{\sqrt{a^2 + b^2}}.$$

In Exercises 67–70, the coordinates of a point in space are given in one of two coordinate systems. Find the coordinates of the point in the other system. There may be more than one answer because points in cylindrical coordinates can have more than one coordinate triple.

	Rectangular (x, y, z)	**Cylindrical** (r, θ, z)
67.		$(1, 0, 0)$
68.		$(1, \pi/2, 0)$
69.	$(-1, 0, -1)$	
70.	$(0, -1, 1)$	

In Exercises 71–74, translate the equation from the given coordinate system (rectangular, cylindrical) into the other system. Identify the set of points in space defined by the equation.

71. $z = 2$

72. $x^2 + y^2 + (z - 3)^2 = 9$

73. $r = 7 \sin \theta$

74. $r = 4 \cos \theta$

In Exercises 75–84, sketch the surface.

75. $x^2 + y^2 + z^2 = 4$

76. $x^2 + (y - 1)^2 + z^2 = 1$

77. $x^2 + z^2 = y^2$

78. $4y^2 + z^2 - 4x^2 = 4$

79. $y^2 - x^2 - z^2 = 1$

80. $z = x^2 + y^2 + 1$

81. $z^2 - \frac{x^2}{4} - y^2 = 1$

82. $9x^2 + 4y^2 + z^2 = 36$

83. $4x^2 + 9z^2 = y^2$

84. $z = 4x^2 + y^2 - 4$

Chapter 13

Vector-Valued Functions and Motion in Space

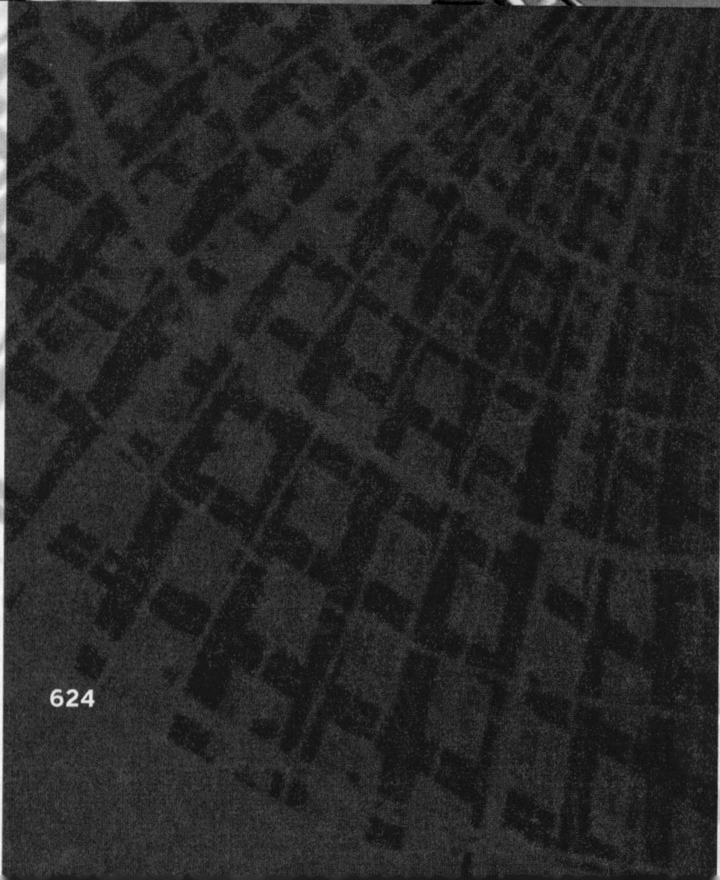

The cars of a looping roller coaster must remain firmly in contact with the track at the top of the loop and must not subject riders to severe *G* forces at the bottom of the loop. A roller coaster design can be analyzed mathematically to determine the distances, accelerations, and forces involved.

The loop of a roller coaster is described by the vector equation

$$\mathbf{r}(t) = (t - 30\cos t)\mathbf{i} + 2t\mathbf{j} + (-45\sin t)\mathbf{k},\quad \pi/2 \le t \le 5\pi/2,$$

where $\mathbf{r}$ is in feet and t is in seconds. Find an integral representing the distance traveled. Then use a calculator to estimate the distance. You will learn the skills to solve this problem in Section 13.2.

Chapter 13 Overview

When a body travels through space, the equations $x = f(t)$, $y = g(t)$, and $z = h(t)$ that give the body's coordinates as functions of time serve as parametric equations for the body's motion and path. With vector notation, we can condense these into a single equation $\mathbf{r}(t) = f(t)\mathbf{i} + g(t)\mathbf{j} + h(t)\mathbf{k}$ that gives the body's position as a vector function of time.

In this chapter, we show how to use calculus to study the paths, velocities, and accelerations of moving bodies. As we go along, we see how our work answers the standard questions about the paths and motions of planets and satellites. In the final section, we use our new vector calculus to derive Kepler's laws of planetary motion from Newton's laws of motion and gravitation.

13.1 Vector-Valued Functions and Space Curves

What you'll learn about

- Space Curves
- Limits and Continuity
- Derivatives and Motion on Smooth Curves
- Differentiation Rules
- Vector Functions of Constant Length
- Integrals of Vector Functions

Space Curves

To track a particle moving in space, we run a vector $\mathbf{r}$ from the origin to the particle (Figure 13.1) and study the changes in $\mathbf{r}$. When a particle moves through space during a time interval I, we think of the particle's coordinates as functions defined on I:

$$x = f(t), \quad y = g(t), \quad z = h(t), \quad t \in I. \tag{1}$$

The points $(x, y, z) = (f(t), g(t), h(t))$, $t \in I$, make up the **curve** in space that is the particle's **path.** The equations and interval in Equation (1) **parametrize** the curve. The vector

$$\mathbf{r}(t) = \overrightarrow{OP} = f(t)\mathbf{i} + g(t)\mathbf{j} + h(t)\mathbf{k} \tag{2}$$

from the origin to the particle's **position** $P(f(t), g(t), h(t))$ at time t is the particle's **position vector**. The functions f, g, and h are the **component functions (components)** of the position vector. We think of the particle's path as the **curve traced by r** (the terminal point of $\mathbf{r}$) during the time interval I.

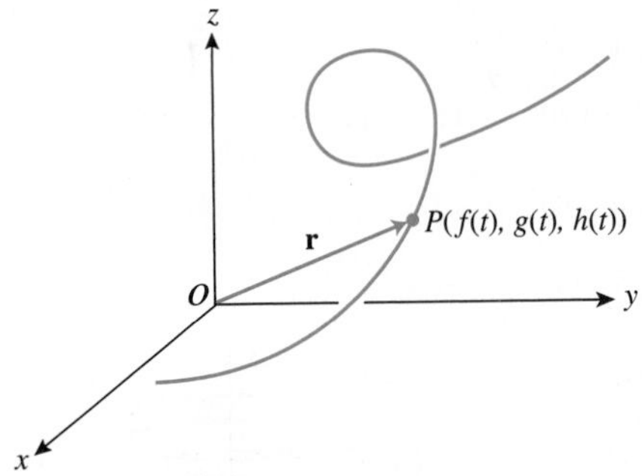

Figure 13.1 The position vector $\mathbf{r}(t) = \overrightarrow{OP}$ of a particle moving through space is a function of time.

Equations (1) and (2) define $\mathbf{r}$ as a vector function of the real variable t on the interval I. More generally, a **vector function** or **vector-valued function** on a domain set D is a rule that assigns a vector in space to each element in D. For now, the domains will be intervals of real numbers. Later, in Chapter 16, the domains will be regions in the plane or space. Vector functions will then be called "vector fields."

We refer to real-valued functions as **scalar functions** to distinguish them from vector functions. The components of $\mathbf{r}$ are scalar functions of t. When we define a vector-valued function by giving its component functions, we assume the vector function's domain to be the common domain of the components. You will find this material to be very similar to the material on planar curves.

EXAMPLE 1 Graphing a Helix

Graph the vector function

$$\mathbf{r}(t) = (\cos t)\mathbf{i} + (\sin t)\mathbf{j} + t\mathbf{k}.$$

SOLUTION

The vector function $\mathbf{r}$ is defined for all real values of t. The curve traced by $\mathbf{r}$ is a **helix** (from an old Greek word for "spiral") that winds around the circular cylinder $x^2 + y^2 = 1$

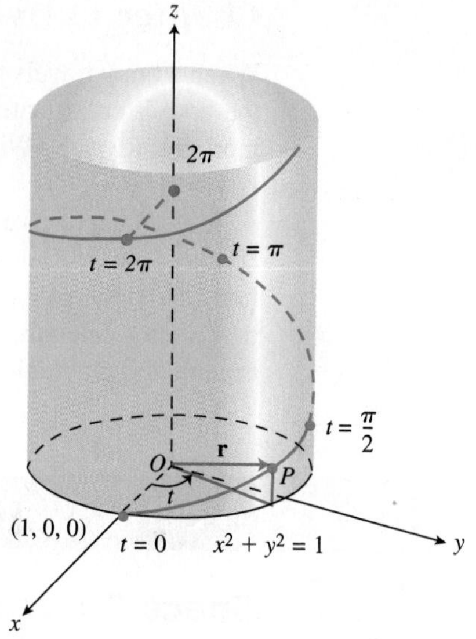

Figure 13.2 The upper half of the helix $\mathbf{r}(t) = (\cos t)\mathbf{i} + (\sin t)\mathbf{j} + t\mathbf{k}$. (Example 1)

(Figure 13.2). The curve lies on the cylinder because the **i**- and **j**-components of **r**, being the x- and y-coordinates of the tip of **r**, satisfy the cylinder's equation:

$$x^2 + y^2 = (\cos t)^2 + (\sin t)^2 = 1.$$

The curve rises as the **k**-component $z = t$ increases. Each time t increases by 2π, the curve completes one turn around the cylinder. The equations

$$x = \cos t, \qquad y = \sin t, \qquad z = t$$

parametrize the helix, the interval $-\infty < t < \infty$ being understood. You will find more helices in Figure 13.3.

Figure 13.4 shows the graph of the vector function of Exercise 12, $\mathbf{r}(t) = (2 \cos 3t)\mathbf{i} + (e^{-1})\mathbf{j} + (2 \sin 3t)\mathbf{k}$.

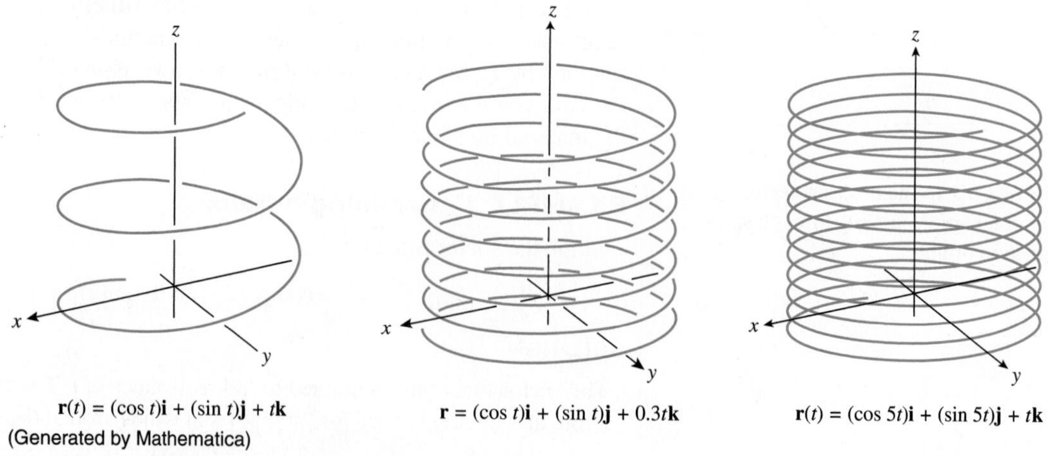

Figure 13.3 Helices drawn by computer.

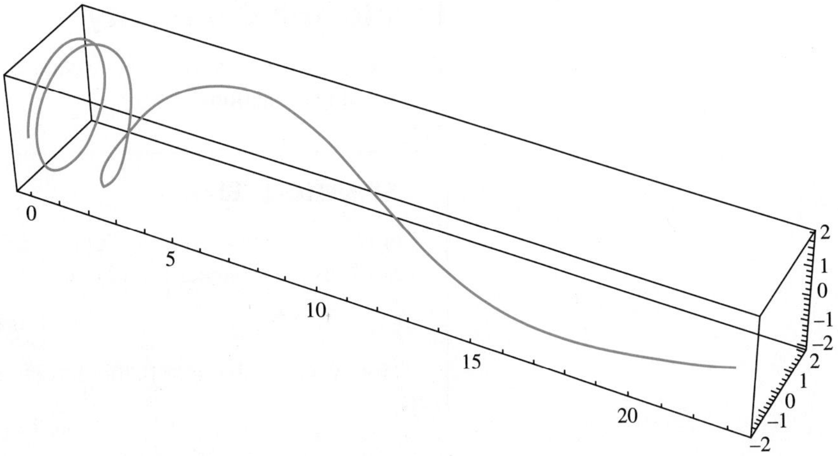

Figure 13.4 The graph of $\mathbf{r}(t) = (2 \cos 3t)\mathbf{i} + (e^{-1})\mathbf{j} + (2 \sin 3t)\mathbf{k}$ obtained parametrically for $-\pi \leq t \leq \pi$ using Mathematica.

EXPLORATION 1 How Vector-Valued Functions in Space Ought to Work

The rules for vector-valued functions in space and vector-valued functions in the plane are so similar you can probably figure them out for yourself. How many of these can you answer before we give you the definitions?

1. If $\mathbf{r}(t) = (t^2 + 3)\mathbf{i} + (\cos t)\mathbf{j} + (\sin t/t)\mathbf{k}$, what is $\lim_{t \to 0} \mathbf{r}(t)$?
2. Is $\mathbf{g}(t) = (e^{3t+1})\mathbf{i} + (|t|)\mathbf{j} + (\tan^2 t)\mathbf{k}$ continuous at $t = 0$? Is it differentiable there?
3. Find $d\mathbf{r}/dt$ if $\mathbf{r}(t) = (t^3)\mathbf{i} + (\ln(t + 3))\mathbf{j} + (\tan t)\mathbf{k}$.
4. Find $\int_0^4 \mathbf{r}(t)\, dt$ if $\mathbf{r}(t) = (t^2)\mathbf{i} + (\sin \pi t)\mathbf{j} + (\sqrt{t})\mathbf{k}$.
5. A particle moves through space with position vector at time t given by $\mathbf{r}(t) = (2t^3)\mathbf{i} + (\sin t)\mathbf{j} + (e^{2t})\mathbf{k}$. Find the velocity vector.
6. Find the acceleration vector for the particle in part (5).
7. Find the speed and direction of motion of the particle in (5) at time $t = 0$.
8. If $\mathbf{u}$ and $\mathbf{v}$ are vectors in three-dimensional space, what is the rule for finding $(d/dt)\,(\mathbf{u} \cdot \mathbf{v})$?
9. If $\mathbf{r}$ is a differentiable function of t and t is a differentiable function of s, what would the Chain Rule say about $d\mathbf{r}/ds$?
10. We did not consider the cross product of two-dimensional vectors, so we have no two-dimensional formula for $(d/dt)\,(\mathbf{u} \times \mathbf{v})$. Nonetheless, what do you suppose the three-dimensional formula for the derivative of a cross product would be?

Limits and Continuity

The way we define limits of vector-valued functions is similar to the way we define limits of real-valued functions.

> **DEFINITION Limit**
>
> Let $\mathbf{r}(t) = f(t)\mathbf{i} + g(t)\mathbf{j} + h(t)\mathbf{k}$ be a vector function and $\mathbf{L}$ a vector. We say that $\mathbf{r}$ has **limit L** as t approaches t_0 and write
>
> $$\lim_{t \to 0} \mathbf{r}(t) = \mathbf{L}$$
>
> if, for every number $\varepsilon > 0$, there exists a corresponding $\delta > 0$ such that for all t
>
> $$0 < |t - t_0| < \delta \Rightarrow |\mathbf{r}(t) - \mathbf{L}| < \varepsilon.$$

If $\mathbf{L} = L_1\mathbf{i} + L_2\mathbf{j} + L_3\mathbf{k}$, then, $\lim_{t \to t_0} \mathbf{r}(t) = \mathbf{L}$ precisely when

$$\lim_{t \to t_0} f(t) = L_1, \qquad \lim_{t \to t_0} g(t) = L_2, \qquad \lim_{t \to t_0} h(t) = L_3.$$

The equation

$$\lim_{t \to t_0} \mathbf{r}(t) = \left(\lim_{t \to t_0} f(t)\right)\mathbf{i} + \left(\lim_{t \to t_0} g(t)\right)\mathbf{j} + \left(\lim_{t \to t_0} h(t)\right)\mathbf{k}$$

provides a practical way to calculate limits of vector functions.

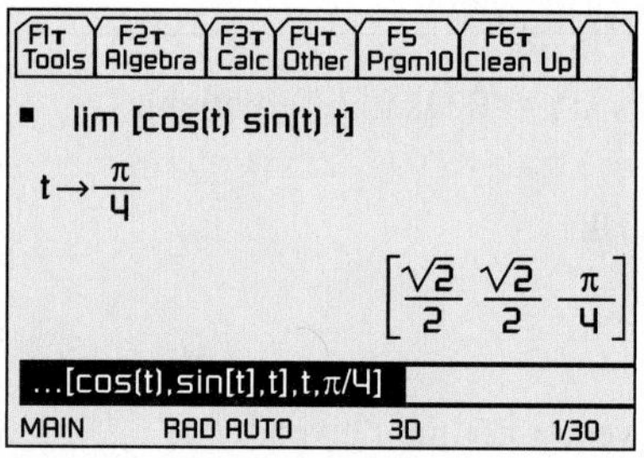

Figure 13.5 Checking the result of Example 2 on a graphing calculator. Notice that the displayed vectors omit the commas.

EXAMPLE 2 Finding Limits of Vector Functions

If $\mathbf{r}(t) = (\cos t)\mathbf{i} + (\sin t)\mathbf{j} + t\mathbf{k}$, then

$$\begin{aligned}\lim_{t \to \pi/4} \mathbf{r}(t) &= \left(\lim_{t \to \pi/4} \cos t\right)\mathbf{i} + \left(\lim_{t \to \pi/4} \sin t\right)\mathbf{j} + \left(\lim_{t \to \pi/4} t\right)\mathbf{k} \\ &= \frac{\sqrt{2}}{2}\mathbf{i} + \frac{\sqrt{2}}{2}\mathbf{j} + \frac{\pi}{4}\mathbf{k}.\end{aligned}$$

Limits can be checked with a CAS. For example, the vector $\mathbf{r}(t)$ of Example 2 is entered as [cos (t), sin (t), t] on the advanced graphing calculator we use. Figure 13.5 shows what Example 2 looks like on this calculator.

We define continuity for vector functions the same way we define continuity for scalar functions.

> **DEFINITION Continuity at a Point**
>
> A vector function $\mathbf{r}(t)$ is **continuous at a point $\mathbf{t} = \mathbf{t}_0$** in its domain if
>
> $$\lim_{t \to t_0} \mathbf{r}(t) = \mathbf{r}(t_0)$$

A vector function $\mathbf{r}(t)$ is **continuous** if it is continuous at every point in its domain. Since limits can be expressed in terms of components, we can test vector functions for continuity by examining their components (Exercise 42).

Component Test for Continuity at a Point

The vector function $\mathbf{r}(t) = f(t)\mathbf{i} + g(t)\mathbf{j} + h(t)\mathbf{k}$ is continuous at $t = t_0$ if and only if f, g, and h are continuous at t_0.

EXAMPLE 3 Finding Points of Continuity and Discontinuity

(a) The function

$$\mathbf{r}(t) = (\cos t)\mathbf{i} + (\sin t)\mathbf{j} + t\mathbf{k}$$

is continuous because $\cos t$, $\sin t$, and t are continuous.

(b) The function

$$\mathbf{g}(t) = (\cos t)\mathbf{i} + (\sin t)\mathbf{j} + (\text{int } t)\mathbf{k}$$

is discontinuous (not continuous) at every integer.

Derivatives and Motion on Smooth Curves

Suppose $\mathbf{r}(t) = f(t)\mathbf{i} + g(t)\mathbf{j} + h(t)\mathbf{k}$ is the position vector of a particle moving along a curve in space and f, g, and h are differentiable functions of t. Then (see Figure 13.6) the difference between the particle's positions at time $t + \Delta t$ and time t is $\Delta\mathbf{r} = \mathbf{r}(t + \Delta t) - \mathbf{r}(t)$. We are led to the following definition.

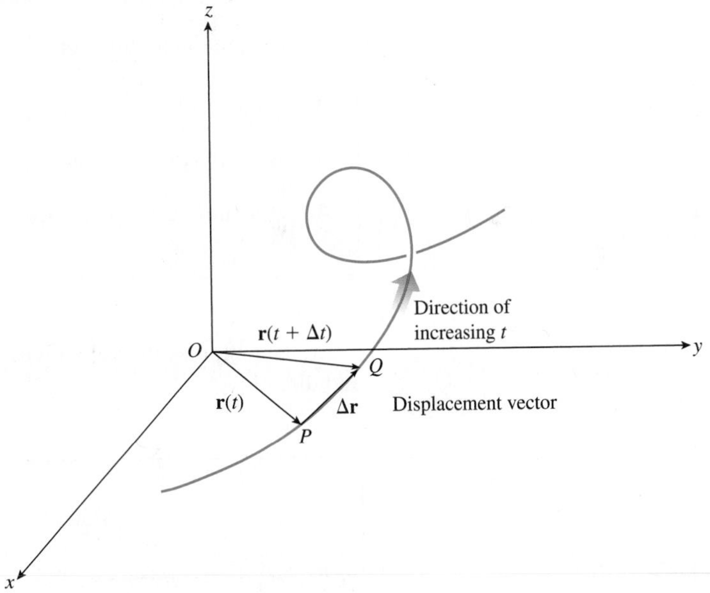

Figure 13.6 Between time t and time $t + \Delta t$, the particle moving along the path shown here undergoes the displacement $\overrightarrow{PQ} = \Delta\mathbf{r}$. The vector sum $\mathbf{r}(t) + \Delta\mathbf{r}$ gives the new position, $\mathbf{r}(t + \Delta t)$.

DEFINITION Derivative at a Point

The vector function $\mathbf{r}(t) = f(t)\mathbf{i} + g(t)\mathbf{j} + h(t)\mathbf{k}$ is **differentiable at $t = t_0$** if f, g, and h are differentiable at t_0. The **derivative** is the vector

$$\frac{d\mathbf{r}}{dt} = \lim_{\Delta t \to 0} \frac{\mathbf{r}(t + \Delta t) - \mathbf{r}(t)}{\Delta t} = \frac{df}{dt}\mathbf{i} + \frac{dg}{dt}\mathbf{j} + \frac{dh}{dt}\mathbf{k}.$$

A vector function **r** is **differentiable** if it is differentiable at every point of its domain. The curve traced by **r** is **smooth** if $d\mathbf{r}/dt$ is continuous and never **0**, that is, if f, g, and h have continuous first derivatives that are not simultaneously 0.

The vector $d\mathbf{r}/dt$, when different from **0**, is also a vector tangent to the curve. The **tangent line** to the curve at a point $(f(t_0), g(t_0), h(t_0))$ is defined to be the line through the point parallel to $d\mathbf{r}/dt$ at $t = t_0$. We require $d\mathbf{r}/dt \neq \mathbf{0}$ for a smooth curve to make sure the curve has a continuously turning tangent at each point. On a smooth curve there are no sharp corners or cusps.

A curve that is made up of a finite number of smooth curves pieced together in a continuous fashion is **piecewise smooth** (Figure 13.7).

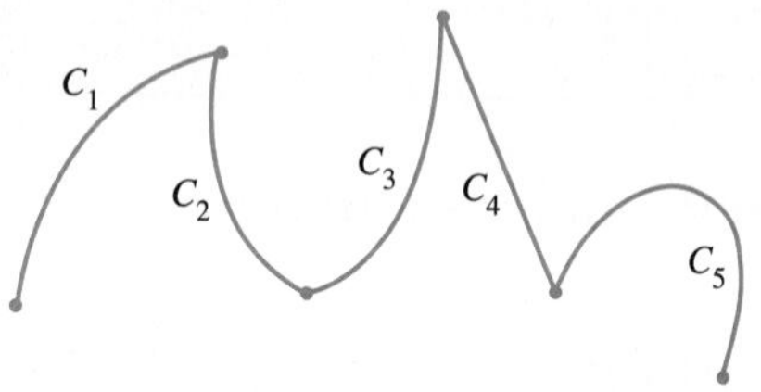

Figure 13.7 A piecewise smooth curve made up of five smooth curves connected end to end in continuous fashion.

We may conclude that the derivative $d\mathbf{r}/dt$ is just what we want for modeling a particle's velocity. It points in the direction of motion and gives the rate of change of position with respect to time. For a smooth curve, the velocity is never zero; the particle does not stop or reverse direction.

DEFINITIONS Velocity, Speed, Acceleration, Direction of Motion

If **r** is the position vector of a particle moving along a smooth curve in space, then at any time t,

1. $\mathrm{v}(t) = \dfrac{d\mathbf{r}}{dt}$, the derivative of position, is the particle's **velocity vector** and is tangent to the curve.
2. $|\mathbf{v}(t)|$, the magnitude of **v**, is the particle's **speed**.
3. $\mathbf{a}(t) = \dfrac{d\mathbf{v}}{dt} = \dfrac{d^2\mathbf{r}}{dt^2}$, the derivative of velocity and the second derivative of position, is the particle's **acceleration vector**.
4. $\dfrac{\mathbf{v}}{|\mathbf{v}|}$, a unit vector, is the **direction of motion**.

We can express the velocity of a smoothly moving particle as the product of its speed and direction.

$$\text{Velocity} = |\mathbf{v}|\left(\frac{\mathbf{v}}{|\mathbf{v}|}\right) = (\text{speed})(\text{direction})$$

EXAMPLE 4 Studying Motion

The vector $\mathbf{r}(t) = (3\cos t)\mathbf{i} + (3\sin t)\mathbf{j} + t^2\mathbf{k}$ gives the position of a moving body at time t. Find

(a) the velocity and acceleration vectors.

(b) the body's speed and direction at $t = 2$.

(c) at what times the body's velocity and acceleration are orthogonal.

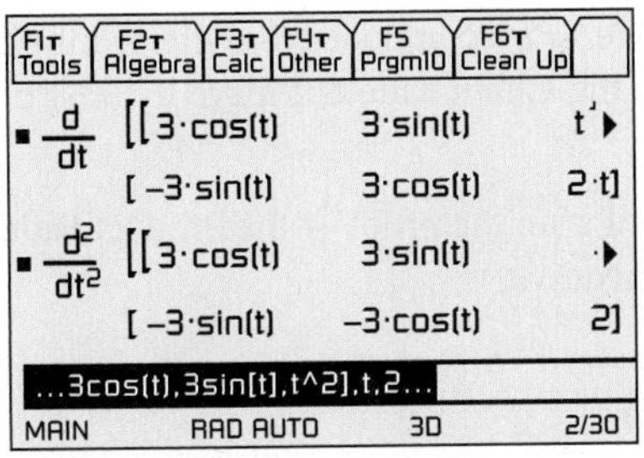

Figure 13.8 The velocity and acceleration of Example 4.

SOLUTION

(a)

$$\mathbf{r} = (3\cos t)\mathbf{i} + (3\sin t)\mathbf{j} + t^2\mathbf{k}$$

$$\mathbf{v} = \frac{d\mathbf{r}}{dt} = -(3\sin t)\mathbf{i} + (3\cos t)\mathbf{j} + 2t\mathbf{k}$$

$$\mathbf{a} = \frac{d^2\mathbf{r}}{dt^2} = -(3\cos t)\mathbf{i} - (3\sin t)\mathbf{j} + 2\mathbf{k}$$

We can also check derivative computations with our advanced graphing calculator. Figure 13.8 shows **v** and **a** computed on our graphing calculator.

(b) At $t = 2$, the body's speed and direction are

$$\text{Speed: } |\mathbf{v}(2)| = \sqrt{(-3\sin 2)^2 + (3\cos 2)^2 + (4)^2} = 5,$$

$$\text{Direction: } \frac{\mathbf{v}(2)}{|\mathbf{v}(2)|} = -\left(\frac{3}{5}\sin 2\right)\mathbf{i} + \left(\frac{3}{5}\cos 2\right)\mathbf{j} + \frac{4}{5}\mathbf{k}.$$

(c) To find the times when **v** and **a** are orthogonal, we look for values of t for which

$$\mathbf{v}\cdot\mathbf{a} = 9\sin t\cos t - 9\cos t\sin t + 4t = 0.$$

The only value is $t = 0$.

Differentiation Rules

Because the derivatives of vector functions may be computed component by component, the rules for differentiating vector functions have the same form as the rules for differentiating scalar functions.

Differentiation Rules for Vector Functions

Let **u** and **v** be differentiable vector functions of t, **C** any constant vector, c any scalar, and f any differentiable scalar function of t.

1. **Constant Function Rule:** $\frac{d}{dt}\mathbf{C} = \mathbf{0}$
2. **Scalar Multiple Rules:** $\frac{d}{dt}(c\mathbf{u}) = c\frac{d\mathbf{u}}{dt}$

   $\frac{d}{dt}(f\mathbf{u}) = \frac{df}{dt}\mathbf{u} + f\frac{d\mathbf{u}}{dt}$
3. **Sum Rule:** $\frac{d}{dt}(\mathbf{u}+\mathbf{v}) = \frac{d\mathbf{u}}{dt} + \frac{d\mathbf{v}}{dt}$
4. **Difference Rule:** $\frac{d}{dt}(\mathbf{u}-\mathbf{v}) = \frac{d\mathbf{u}}{dt} - \frac{d\mathbf{v}}{dt}$
5. **Dot-Product Rule:** $\frac{d}{dt}(\mathbf{u}\cdot\mathbf{v}) = \frac{d\mathbf{u}}{dt}\cdot\mathbf{v} + \mathbf{u}\cdot\frac{d\mathbf{v}}{dt}$
6. **Cross-Product Rule:** $\frac{d}{dt}(\mathbf{u}\times\mathbf{v}) = \frac{d\mathbf{u}}{dt}\times\mathbf{v} + \mathbf{u}\times\frac{d\mathbf{v}}{dt}$
7. **Chain Rule (Short Form):** If **r** is a differentiable function of t and t is a differentiable function of s, then

$$\frac{d\mathbf{r}}{ds} = \frac{d\mathbf{r}}{dt}\frac{dt}{ds}.$$

As an algebraic convenience, we sometimes write the product of a scalar c and a vector **v** as **v**c instead of c**v**. This permits us, for instance, to write the Chain Rule in a familiar form:

$$\frac{d\mathbf{r}}{ds} = \frac{d\mathbf{r}}{dt}\frac{dt}{ds}.$$

The proof of the Dot-Product Rule is very similar (one more component) to the proof on page 535. We will prove the Cross-Product Rule and the Chain Rule but leave the rest of the rules as exercises.

Proof of the Cross-Product Rule We model the proof after the proof of the Product Rule for scalar functions. According to the definition of derivative,

$$\frac{d}{dt}(\mathbf{u} \times \mathbf{v}) = \lim_{h \to 0} \frac{\mathbf{u}(t+h) \times \mathbf{v}(t+h) - \mathbf{u}(t) \times \mathbf{v}(t)}{h}$$

To change this fraction into an equivalent one that contains the difference quotients for the derivatives of **u** and **v**, we subtract and add $\mathbf{u}(t) \times \mathbf{v}(t+h)$ in the numerator. Then

$$\begin{aligned}
&\frac{d}{dt}(\mathbf{u} \times \mathbf{v}) \\
&= \lim_{h \to 0} \frac{\mathbf{u}(t+h) \times \mathbf{v}(t+h) - \mathbf{u}(t) \times \mathbf{v}(t+h) + \mathbf{u}(t) \times \mathbf{v}(t+h) - \mathbf{u}(t) \times \mathbf{v}(t)}{h} \\
&= \lim_{h \to 0} \left[\frac{\mathbf{u}(t+h) - \mathbf{u}(t)}{h} \times \mathbf{v}(t+h) + \mathbf{u}(t) \times \frac{\mathbf{v}(t+h) - \mathbf{v}(t)}{h} \right] \\
&= \lim_{h \to 0} \frac{\mathbf{u}(t+h) - \mathbf{u}(t)}{h} \times \lim_{h \to 0} \mathbf{v}(t+h) + \lim_{h \to 0} \mathbf{u}(t) \times \lim_{h \to 0} \frac{\mathbf{v}(t+h) - \mathbf{v}(t)}{h}.
\end{aligned}$$

The last equality holds because the limit of the cross product of two vector functions is the cross product of their limits if the latter exist (Exercise 43). As h approaches zero, $\mathbf{v}(t+h)$ approaches $\mathbf{v}(t)$ because **v**, being differentiable at t, is continuous at t (Exercise 44). The two fractions approach the values of $d\mathbf{u}/dt$ and $d\mathbf{v}/dt$ at t. In short,

$$\frac{d}{dt}(\mathbf{u} \times \mathbf{v}) = \frac{d\mathbf{u}}{dt} \times \mathbf{v} + \mathbf{u} \times \frac{d\mathbf{v}}{dt}.$$

Proof of the Chain Rule Suppose $\mathbf{r}(t) = f(t)\mathbf{i} + g(t)\mathbf{j} + h(t)\mathbf{k}$ is a differentiable vector function of t and t is a differentiable scalar function of some other variable s. Then f, g, and h are differentiable functions of s, and the Chain Rule for differentiable real-valued functions gives

$$\begin{aligned}
\frac{d\mathbf{r}}{ds} &= \frac{df}{ds}\mathbf{i} + \frac{dg}{ds}\mathbf{j} + \frac{dh}{ds}\mathbf{k} \\
&= \frac{df}{dt}\frac{dt}{ds}\mathbf{i} + \frac{dg}{dt}\frac{dt}{ds}\mathbf{j} + \frac{dh}{dt}\frac{dt}{ds}\mathbf{k} \\
&= \left(\frac{df}{dt}\mathbf{i} + \frac{dg}{dt}\mathbf{j} + \frac{dh}{dt}\mathbf{k}\right)\frac{dt}{ds} \\
&= \frac{d\mathbf{r}}{dt}\frac{dt}{ds}.
\end{aligned}$$

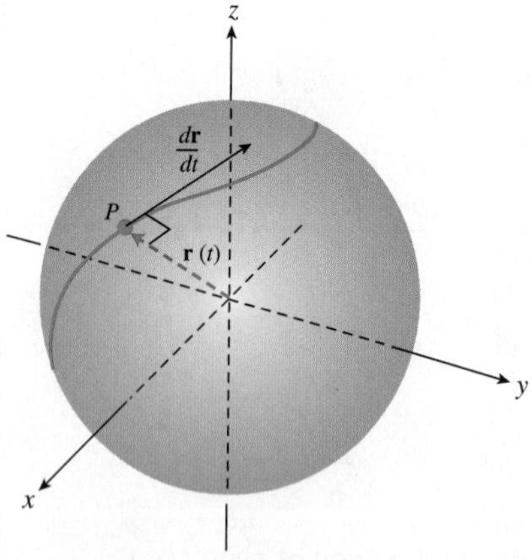

Figure 13.9 If a particle moves on a sphere in such a way that its position **r** is a differentiable function of time, then $\mathbf{r} \cdot (d\mathbf{r}/dt) = 0$.

Vector Functions of Constant Length

When we track a particle moving on a sphere centered at the origin (Figure 13.9), the position vector has a constant length equal to the radius of the sphere. The velocity vector $d\mathbf{r}/dt$, tangent to the path of motion, is tangent to the sphere and hence perpendicular to **r**. This is always the case for a differentiable vector function of constant length: The vector and its first derivative are orthogonal. With the length constant, the change in the function is a change in direction only, and direction changes take place at right angles.

We will use the observation in Equation (3) repeatedly in Section 13.3.

If $\mathbf{u}$ is a differentiable vector function of t of constant length, then

$$\mathbf{u} \cdot \frac{d\mathbf{u}}{dt} = 0. \tag{3}$$

To see why Equation (3) holds, suppose $\mathbf{u}$ is a differentiable function of t and $|\mathbf{u}|$ is constant. Then $\mathbf{u} \cdot \mathbf{u} = |\mathbf{u}^2|$ is constant and we may differentiate both sides of this equation to get

$$\frac{d}{dt}(\mathbf{u} \cdot \mathbf{u}) = \frac{d}{dt}(\text{constant}) = 0$$

$$\frac{d\mathbf{u}}{dt} \cdot \mathbf{u} + \mathbf{u} \cdot \frac{d\mathbf{u}}{dt} = 0 \qquad \text{Dot-Product Rule with } \mathbf{v} = \mathbf{u}$$

$$2\mathbf{u} \cdot \frac{d\mathbf{u}}{dt} = 0 \qquad \text{Dot multiplication is commutative}$$

$$\mathbf{u} \cdot \frac{d\mathbf{u}}{dt} = 0$$

EXAMPLE 5 Supporting Equation (3)

Show that $\mathbf{u}(t) = (\sin t)\mathbf{i} + (\cos t)\mathbf{j} + \sqrt{3}\mathbf{k}$ has constant length and is orthogonal to its derivative.

SOLUTION

$$\mathbf{u}(t) = (\sin t)\,\mathbf{i} + (\cos t)\,\mathbf{j} + \sqrt{3}\,\mathbf{k}$$

$$|\mathbf{u}(t)| = \sqrt{(\sin t)^2 + (\cos t)^2 + (\sqrt{3})^2} = \sqrt{1 + 3} = 2$$

$$\frac{d\mathbf{u}}{dt} = (\cos t)\,\mathbf{i} - (\sin t)\,\mathbf{j}$$

$$\mathbf{u} \cdot \frac{d\mathbf{u}}{dt} = \sin t \cos t - \sin t \cos t = 0$$

Integrals of Vector Functions

A differentiable vector function $\mathbf{R}(t)$ is an **antiderivative** of a vector function $\mathbf{r}(t)$ on an interval I if $d\mathbf{R}/dt = \mathbf{r}$ at each point of I. If $\mathbf{R}$ is an antiderivative of $\mathbf{r}$ on I, it can be shown, working one component at a time, that every antiderivative of $\mathbf{r}$ on I has the form $\mathbf{R} + \mathbf{C}$ for some constant vector $\mathbf{C}$ (Exercise 47).

DEFINITION Indefinite Integral

The **indefinite integral** of $\mathbf{r}$ with respect to t is the set of all antiderivatives of $\mathbf{r}$, denoted by $\int \mathbf{r}(t)\, dt$. If $\mathbf{R}$ is any antiderivative of $\mathbf{r}$, then

$$\int \mathbf{r}(t)\, dt = \mathbf{R}(t) + \mathbf{C}.$$

The usual arithmetic rules for indefinite integrals apply.

We can check evaluation of integrals (both definite and indefinite) with our advanced graphing calculator.

EXAMPLE 6 Finding Antiderivatives

$$\int ((\cos t)\,\mathbf{i} + \mathbf{j} - 2t\mathbf{k})\,dt = \left(\int \cos t\,dt\right)\mathbf{i} + \left(\int dt\right)\mathbf{j} - \left(\int 2t\,dt\right)\mathbf{k} \quad (4)$$

$$= (\sin t + C_1)\,\mathbf{i} + (t + C_2)\,\mathbf{j} - (t^2 + C_3)\,\mathbf{k} \quad (5)$$

$$= (\sin t)\,\mathbf{i} + t\mathbf{j} - t^2\mathbf{k} + \mathbf{C} \qquad \mathbf{C} = C_1\mathbf{i} + C_2\mathbf{j} - C_3\mathbf{k}$$

As in the integration of scalar functions, we recommend that you skip the steps in Equations (4) and (5) and go directly to the final form. Find an antiderivative for each component and add a constant vector at the end.

Definite integrals of vector functions are also defined in terms of components.

DEFINITION Definite Integrals

If the components of $\mathbf{r}(t) = f(t)\mathbf{i} + g(t)\mathbf{j} + h(t)\mathbf{k}$ are integrable over $[a, b]$, then so is $\mathbf{r}$, and the **definite integral** of $\mathbf{r}$ from a to b is

$$\int_a^b \mathbf{r}(t)\,dt = \left(\int_a^b f(t)\,dt\right)\mathbf{i} + \left(\int_a^b g(t)\,dt\right)\mathbf{j} + \left(\int_a^b h(t)\,dt\right)\mathbf{k}.$$

EXAMPLE 7 Evaluating Definite Integrals

$$\int_0^\pi ((\cos t)\,\mathbf{i} + \mathbf{j} - 2t\mathbf{k})\,dt = \left(\int_0^\pi \cos t\,dt\right)\mathbf{i} + \left(\int_0^\pi dt\right)\mathbf{j} - \left(\int_0^\pi 2t\,dt\right)\mathbf{k}$$

$$= (\sin t\,]_0^\pi)\mathbf{i} + (t\,]_0^\pi)\mathbf{j} - (t^2\,]_0^\pi)\mathbf{k}$$

$$= (0 - 0)\mathbf{i} + (\pi - 0)\mathbf{j} - (\pi^2 - 0^2)\mathbf{k}$$

$$= \pi\mathbf{j} - \pi^2\,\mathbf{k}$$

EXAMPLE 8 Finding a Particle's Position Function

The velocity of a particle moving in space is

$$\frac{d\mathbf{r}}{dt} = (\cos t)\mathbf{i} - (\sin t)\mathbf{j} + \mathbf{k}.$$

Find the particle's position function as a function of t if $\mathbf{r} = 2\mathbf{i} + \mathbf{k}$ when $t = 0$.

SOLUTION

Our goal is to solve the initial value problem that consists of

The differential equation: $\dfrac{d\mathbf{r}}{dt} = (\cos t)\mathbf{i} - (\sin t)\mathbf{j} + \mathbf{k}$

The initial condition: $\mathbf{r}(0) = 2\mathbf{i} + \mathbf{k}.$

Integrating both sides of the differential equation with respect to t gives

$$\mathbf{r}(t) = (\sin t)\mathbf{i} + (\cos t)\mathbf{j} + t\mathbf{k} + \mathbf{C}.$$

The initial condition determines the value of **C**:

$$(\sin 0)\mathbf{i} + (\cos 0)\mathbf{j} + (0)\mathbf{k} + \mathbf{C} = 2\mathbf{i} + \mathbf{k} \qquad \mathbf{r}(0) = 2\mathbf{i} + \mathbf{k}$$

$$\mathbf{j} + \mathbf{C} = 2\mathbf{i} + \mathbf{k}$$

$$\mathbf{C} = 2\mathbf{i} - \mathbf{j} + \mathbf{k}.$$

The particle's position as a function of t is

$$\mathbf{r}(t) = (\sin t + 2)\mathbf{i} + (\cos t - 1)\mathbf{j} + (t + 1)\mathbf{k}.$$

To check (always a good idea), we can see from this formula that

$$\frac{d\mathbf{r}}{dt} = (\cos t + 0)\mathbf{i} + (-\sin t - 0)\mathbf{j} + (1 + 0)\mathbf{k}$$

$$= (\cos t)\mathbf{i} - (\sin t)\mathbf{j} + \mathbf{k}$$

and

$$\mathbf{r}(0) = (\sin 0 + 2)\mathbf{i} + (\cos 0 - 1)\mathbf{j} + (0 + 1)\mathbf{k}$$

$$= 2\mathbf{i} + \mathbf{k}.$$

Quick Review 13.1

In Exercises 1–4, let $f(x) = \text{int } x$, the greatest integer function.

1. Find $\lim_{x \to -2^-} \text{int } x$.
2. Find $\lim_{x \to -2^+} \text{int } x$.
3. At what values of x is f continuous?
4. Find the points of discontinuity of f.

In Exercises 5 and 6, let $f(x) = (\cot x)/x$.

5. Find an equation of the line tangent to the graph of f at $x = \pi/4$.
6. Find an equation of the line normal to the graph of f at $x = \pi/4$.
7. Find $\dfrac{d^2y}{dx^2}$ for $y = \dfrac{2x + 1}{x + 3}$.
8. Evaluate $\displaystyle\int \frac{dx}{1 + x}$.
9. Evaluate $\displaystyle\int_0^2 \frac{dx}{1 + x}$.
10. Solve the initial value problem

$$\frac{dy}{dx} = \cos x + \sin x, \quad y\left(\frac{\pi}{2}\right) = 1.$$

Section 13.1 Exercises

In Exercises 1–4, $\mathbf{r}(t)$ is the position of a particle in the xy-plane at time t. Find an equation in x and y whose graph is the path of the particle. Then find the particle's velocity and acceleration vectors at the given value of t.

1. $\mathbf{r}(t) = (t + 1)\mathbf{i} + (t^2 - 1)\mathbf{j}, \quad t = 1$
2. $\mathbf{r}(t) = (t^2 + 1)\mathbf{i} + (2t - 1)\mathbf{j}, \quad t = 1/2$
3. $\mathbf{r}(t) = e^t\mathbf{i} + \frac{2}{9}e^{2t}\mathbf{j}, \quad t = \ln 3$
4. $\mathbf{r}(t) = (\cos 2t)\mathbf{i} + (3\sin 2t)\mathbf{j}, \quad t = 0$

In Exercises 5–8, $\mathbf{r}(t)$ is the position vector of a particle moving along a curve in the xy-plane. Find the particle's velocity and acceleration vectors at the stated times and sketch them as vectors on the curve.

5. ***Motion on the Circle*** $x^2 + y^2 = 1$

   $\mathbf{r}(t) = (\sin t)\mathbf{i} + (\cos t)\mathbf{j}; \quad t = \pi/4$ and $\pi/2$

6. ***Motion on the Circle*** $x^2 + y^2 = 16$

   $\mathbf{r}(t) = \left(4\cos\frac{t}{2}\right)\mathbf{i} + \left(4\sin\frac{t}{2}\right)\mathbf{j}; \quad t = \pi$ and $3\pi/2$

7. ***Motion on the Cycloid*** $x = t - \sin t,\ y = 1 - \cos t$

   $\mathbf{r}(t) = (t - \sin t)\mathbf{i} + (1 - \cos t)\mathbf{j}; \quad t = \pi$ and $3\pi/2$

8. ***Motion on the Parabola*** $y = x^2 + 1$

   $\mathbf{r}(t) = t\mathbf{i} + (t^2 + 1)\mathbf{j}; \quad t = -1, 0,$ and 1

In Exercises 9–12, $\mathbf{r}(t)$ is the position of a particle in space at time t. **(a)** Find the particle's velocity and acceleration vectors. Then **(b)** find the particle's speed and direction of motion at the given value of t. **(c)** Write the particle's velocity at that time as the product of its speed and direction.

9. $\mathbf{r}(t) = (t + 1)\mathbf{i} + (t^2 - 1)\mathbf{j} + 2t\mathbf{k}, \quad t = 1$
10. $\mathbf{r}(t) = (2\cos t)\mathbf{i} + (3\sin t)\mathbf{j} + 4t\mathbf{k}, \quad t = \pi/2$

11. $\mathbf{r}(t) = (\sec t)\mathbf{i} + (\tan t)\mathbf{j} + \frac{4}{3}t\mathbf{k}, \quad t = \pi/6$

12. $\mathbf{r}(t) = (2\cos 3t)\mathbf{i} + (e^{-t})\mathbf{j} + (2\sin 3t)\mathbf{k}, \quad t = 0$

In Exercises 13–16, $\mathbf{r}(t)$ is the position of a particle in space at time t. Find the angle between the velocity and acceleration vectors at time $t = 0$.

13. $\mathbf{r}(t) = (3t + 1)\mathbf{i} + \sqrt{3}t\mathbf{j} + t^2\mathbf{k}$

14. $\mathbf{r}(t) = \left(\frac{\sqrt{2}}{2}t\right)\mathbf{i} + \left(\frac{\sqrt{2}}{2}t - 16t^2\right)\mathbf{j}$

15. $\mathbf{r}(t) = (\ln(t^2 + 1))\mathbf{i} + (\tan^{-1} t)\mathbf{j} + \sqrt{t^2 + 1}\mathbf{k}$

16. $\mathbf{r}(t) = \frac{4}{9}(1 + t)^{3/2}\mathbf{i} + \frac{4}{9}(1 - t)^{3/2}\mathbf{j} + \frac{1}{3}t\mathbf{k}$

In Exercises 17 and 18, $\mathbf{r}(t)$ is the position vector of a particle in space at time t. Find the time or times in the given time interval when the velocity and acceleration vectors are orthogonal.

17. $\mathbf{r}(t) = (t - \sin t)\mathbf{i} + (1 - \cos t)\mathbf{j} + t\mathbf{k}; \quad 0 \le t \le 2\pi$

18. $\mathbf{r}(t) = (\sin t)\mathbf{i} + t\mathbf{j} + (\cos t)\mathbf{k}, \quad t \ge 0$

In Exercises 19–22, evaluate the integral.

19. $\int_0^1 [t^3\mathbf{i} + 7\mathbf{j} + (t + 1)\mathbf{k}]\, dt$

20. $\int_0^{\pi/3} [(\sec t \tan t)\mathbf{i} + (\tan t)\mathbf{j} + (2\sin t \cos t)\mathbf{k}]\, dt$

21. $\int_1^4 \left[\frac{1}{t}\mathbf{i} + \frac{1}{5 - t}\mathbf{j} + \frac{1}{2t}\mathbf{k}\right] dt$

22. $\int_0^1 \left[\frac{2}{\sqrt{1 - t^2}}\mathbf{i} + \frac{\sqrt{3}}{1 + t^2}\mathbf{k}\right] dt$

In Exercises 23–26, solve the initial value problem for $\mathbf{r}$ as a vector function of t.

23. Differential equation: $\frac{d\mathbf{r}}{dt} = \frac{3}{2}(t + 1)^{1/2}\mathbf{i} + e^{-t}\mathbf{j} + \frac{1}{t + 1}\mathbf{k}$

Initial condition: $\mathbf{r}(0) = \mathbf{k}$

24. Differential equation: $\frac{d\mathbf{r}}{dt} = (t^3 + 4t)\mathbf{i} + t\mathbf{j} + 2t^2\mathbf{k}$

Initial condition: $\mathbf{r}(0) = \mathbf{i} + \mathbf{j}$

25. Differential equation: $\frac{d^2\mathbf{r}}{dt^2} = -32\mathbf{k}$

Initial conditions: $\mathbf{r}(0) = 100\mathbf{k}$ and $\left.\frac{d\mathbf{r}}{dt}\right|_{t=0} = 8\mathbf{i} + 8\mathbf{j}$

26. Differential equation: $\frac{d^2\mathbf{r}}{dt^2} = -(\mathbf{i} + \mathbf{j} + \mathbf{k})$

Initial conditions: $\mathbf{r}(0) = 10\mathbf{i} + 10\mathbf{j} + 10\mathbf{k}$ and

$\left.\frac{d\mathbf{r}}{dt}\right|_{t=0} = 0$

In Exercises 27–30, find parametric equations for the line that is tangent to the given curve at the given parameter value $t = t_0$.

27. $\mathbf{r}(t) = (\sin t)\mathbf{i} + (t^2 - \cos t)\mathbf{j} + e^t\mathbf{k}, \quad t_0 = 0$

28. $\mathbf{r}(t) = (2\sin t)\mathbf{i} + (2\cos t)\mathbf{j} + 5t\mathbf{k}, \quad t_0 = 4\pi$

29. $\mathbf{r}(t) = (a\sin t)\mathbf{i} + (a\cos t)\mathbf{j} + bt\mathbf{k}, \quad t_0 = 2\pi$

30. $\mathbf{r}(t) = (\cos t)\mathbf{i} + (\sin t)\mathbf{j} + (\sin 2t)\mathbf{k}, \quad t_0 = \frac{\pi}{2}$

Exploration

31. ***Motion on Circular Paths*** Each of the following equations (a)–(e) describes the motion of a particle having the same path, namely the unit circle $x^2 + y^2 = 1$. Although the path of each particle is the same, the behavior, or "dynamics," of each particle is different. For each particle, answer the following questions.

(i) Does the particle have constant speed? If so, what is its constant speed?

(ii) Is the particle's acceleration vector always orthogonal to its velocity vector?

(iii) Does the particle move clockwise or counterclockwise around the circle?

(iv) Does the particle begin at the point (1, 0)?

(a) $\mathbf{r}(t) = (\cos t)\mathbf{i} + (\sin t)\mathbf{j}, \quad t \ge 0$

(b) $\mathbf{r}(t) = \cos(2t)\mathbf{i} + \sin(2t)\mathbf{j}, \quad t \ge 0$

(c) $\mathbf{r}(t) = \cos\left(t - \frac{\pi}{2}\right)\mathbf{i} + \sin\left(t - \frac{\pi}{2}\right)\mathbf{j}, \quad t \ge 0$

(d) $\mathbf{r}(t) = (\cos t)\mathbf{i} - (\sin t)\mathbf{j}, \quad t \ge 0$

(e) $\mathbf{r}(t) = \cos(t^2)\mathbf{i} + \sin(t^2)\mathbf{j}, \quad t \ge 0$

32. ***Motion Along a Circular Path*** Show that the vector-valued function

$$\mathbf{r}(t) = (2\mathbf{i} + 2\mathbf{j} + \mathbf{k}) + \cos t\left(\frac{1}{\sqrt{2}}\mathbf{i} - \frac{1}{\sqrt{2}}\mathbf{j}\right) + \sin t\left(\frac{1}{\sqrt{3}}\mathbf{i} + \frac{1}{\sqrt{3}}\mathbf{j} + \frac{1}{\sqrt{3}}\mathbf{k}\right)$$

describes the motion of a particle moving on the circle of radius 1 centered at the point (2, 2, 1) and lying in the plane $x + y - 2z = 2$.

33. ***Motion Along a Line*** At time $t = 0$, a particle is located at the point (1, 2, 3). It travels in a straight line toward the point (4, 1, 4) and has speed 2 at (1, 2, 3) and constant acceleration $3\mathbf{i} - \mathbf{j} + \mathbf{k}$. Find an equation for the position vector $\mathbf{r}(t)$ of the particle at time t.

34. ***Motion Along a Line*** A particle traveling in a straight line is located at the point $(1, -1, 2)$ and has speed 2 at time $t = 0$. The particle moves toward the point (3, 0, 3) with constant acceleration $2\mathbf{i} + \mathbf{j} + \mathbf{k}$. Find its position vector $\mathbf{r}(t)$ at time t.

35. ***Motion Along a Parabola*** A particle moves along the top of the parabola $y^2 = 2x$ in the xy-plane from left to right at a constant speed of 5 units per second. Find the velocity of the particle as it moves through the point (2, 2).

36. *Motion Along a Cycloid* A particle moves on a cycloid in the xy-plane in such a way that its position at time t is

$$\mathbf{r}(t) = (t - \sin t)\mathbf{i} + (1 - \cos t)\mathbf{j}.$$

Find the maximum and minimum values of $|\mathbf{v}|$ and $|\mathbf{a}|$. (*Hint*: Find the extreme values of $|\mathbf{v}|^2$ and $|\mathbf{a}|^2$ first and take square roots later.)

37. *Motion Along an Ellipse* A particle moves around the ellipse $(y/3)^3 + (z/2)^2 = 1$ in the yz-plane in such a way that its position at time t is

$$\mathbf{r}(t) = (3 \cos t)\mathbf{j} + (2 \sin t)\mathbf{k}.$$

Find the maximum and minimum values of $|\mathbf{v}|$ and $|\mathbf{a}|$. (See the hint in Exercise 36.)

38. *Orthogonality Implies Constant Length* Let $\mathbf{v}$ be a differentiable vector function of t. Show that if $\mathbf{v} \cdot (d\mathbf{v}/dt) = 0$ for all t, then $|\mathbf{v}|$ is constant.

39. *Constant Function Rule* Prove that if $\mathbf{u}$ is the vector function with the constant value $\mathbf{C}$, then $d\mathbf{u}/dt = \mathbf{0}$.

40. *Scalar Multiple Rules*

(a) Prove that if $\mathbf{u}$ is a differentiable function of t and c is any real number, then

$$\frac{d(c\mathbf{u})}{dt} = c\frac{d\mathbf{u}}{dt}.$$

(b) Prove that if $\mathbf{u}$ is a differentiable function of t and f is a differentiable scalar function of t, then

$$\frac{d}{dt}(f\mathbf{u}) = \frac{df}{dt}\mathbf{u} + f\frac{d\mathbf{u}}{dt},$$

41. *Sum and Difference Rules* Prove that if $\mathbf{u}$ and $\mathbf{v}$ are differentiable functions of t, then

$$\frac{d}{dt}(\mathbf{u} + \mathbf{v}) = \frac{d\mathbf{u}}{dt} + \frac{d\mathbf{v}}{dt}$$

and

$$\frac{d}{dt}(\mathbf{u} - \mathbf{v}) = \frac{d\mathbf{u}}{dt} - \frac{d\mathbf{v}}{dt}.$$

42. *Component Test for Continuity* Show that the vector function $\mathbf{r}$ defined by the rule

$$\mathbf{r}(t) = f(t)\mathbf{i} + g(t)\mathbf{j} + h(t)\mathbf{k}$$

is continuous at $t = t_0$ if and only if f, g, and h are continuous at t_0.

43. *Limits of Cross Products* Suppose that $\mathbf{r}_1(t) = f_1(t)\mathbf{i} + g_1(t)\mathbf{j} + h_1(t)\mathbf{k}$, $\mathbf{r}_2(t) = f_2(t)\mathbf{i} + g_2(t)\mathbf{j} + h_2(t)\mathbf{k}$, $\lim_{t\to t_0} \mathbf{r}_1(t) = \mathbf{A}$, and $\lim_{t\to t_0} \mathbf{r}_2(t) = \mathbf{B}$. Use the determinant formula for cross products and the Limit Product Rule for scalar functions to show that

$$\lim_{t\to t_0}(\mathbf{r}_1(t) \times \mathbf{r}_2(t)) = \mathbf{A} \times \mathbf{B}.$$

44. *Differentiability Implies Continuity* Show that if $\mathbf{r}(t) = f(t)\mathbf{i} + g(t)\mathbf{j} + h(t)\mathbf{k}$ is differentiable at $t = t_0$, then it is continuous at t_0 as well.

45. *Properties of Integrable Vector Functions* Establish the following properties of integrable vector functions.

(a) The *Constant Scalar Multiple Rule*:

$$\int_a^b k\mathbf{r}(t)\,dt = k\int_a^b \mathbf{r}(t)\,dt \quad \text{(any scalar } k\text{)}$$

The Rule for Negatives,

$$\int_a^b (-\mathbf{r}(t))\,dt = -\int_a^b \mathbf{r}(t)\,dt$$

is obtained by taking $k = -1$.

(b) The *Sum and Difference Rules*:

$$\int_a^b (\mathbf{r}_1(t) \pm \mathbf{r}_2(t))\,dt = \int_a^b \mathbf{r}_1(t)\,dt \pm \int_a^b \mathbf{r}_2(t)\,dt$$

(c) The *Constant Vector Multiple Rules*:

$$\int_a^b \mathbf{C} \cdot \mathbf{r}(t)\,dt = \mathbf{C} \cdot \int_a^b \mathbf{r}(t)\,dt \quad \text{(any constant vector } \mathbf{C}\text{)}$$

and

$$\int_a^b \mathbf{C} \times \mathbf{r}(t)\,dt = \mathbf{C} \times \int_a^b \mathbf{r}(t)\,dt \quad \text{(any constant vector } \mathbf{C}\text{)}$$

46. *Products of Scalar and Vector Functions* Suppose the scalar function $u(t)$ and the vector function $\mathbf{r}(t)$ are both defined for $a \le t \le b$.

(a) Show that $u\mathbf{r}$ is continuous on $[a, b]$ if u and $\mathbf{r}$ are continuous on $[a, b]$.

(b) If u and $\mathbf{r}$ are both differentiable on $[a, b]$, show that $u\mathbf{r}$ is differentiable on $[a, b]$ and that

$$\frac{d}{dt}(u\mathbf{r}) = u\frac{d\mathbf{r}}{dt} + \mathbf{r}\frac{du}{dt}.$$

47. *Antiderivatives of Vector Functions*

(a) Use Corollary 2 of the Mean Value Theorem for derivatives of scalar functions to show that if two vector functions $\mathbf{R}_1(t)$ and $\mathbf{R}_2(t)$ have identical derivatives on an interval I, then the functions differ by a constant vector value throughout I.

(b) Use the result in (a) to show that if $\mathbf{R}(t)$ is any antiderivative of $\mathbf{r}(t)$ on I, then every antiderivative of $\mathbf{r}$ on I equals $\mathbf{R}(t) + \mathbf{C}$ for some constant vector $\mathbf{C}$.

48. *Fundamental Theorem of Calculus* The Fundamental Theorem of Calculus for scalar functions of a real variable holds for vector functions of a real variables as well. Prove this by using the theorem for scalar functions to show first that if a vector function $\mathbf{r}(t)$ is continuous for $a \le t \le b$, then

$$\frac{d}{dt}\int_a^b \mathbf{r}(\tau)\,d\pi = \mathbf{r}(t)$$

at every point τ of $[a, b]$. Then use the conclusion in part (b) of Exercise 47 to show that if $\mathbf{R}$ is any antiderivative of $\mathbf{r}$ on $[a, b]$, then

$$\int_a^b \mathbf{r}(t)\,dt = \mathbf{R}(b) - \mathbf{R}(a).$$

49. Writing to Learn Explain why the motion in Exercises 5–8 takes place on the curves indicated in each exercise.

Extending the Ideas

50. *Derivatives of Triple Scalar Products*

(a) Show that if **u**, **v**, and **w** are differentiable vector functions of t, then

$$\frac{d}{dt}(\mathbf{u}\cdot\mathbf{v}\times\mathbf{w})=\frac{d\mathbf{u}}{dt}\cdot\mathbf{v}\times\mathbf{w}+\mathbf{u}\cdot\frac{d\mathbf{v}}{dt}\times\mathbf{w}+\mathbf{u}\cdot\mathbf{v}\times\frac{d\mathbf{w}}{dt}.$$

(b) Show that the equation in part (a) is equivalent to

$$\frac{d}{dt}\begin{vmatrix}u_1 & u_2 & u_3\\ v_1 & v_2 & v_3\\ w_1 & w_2 & w_3\end{vmatrix}=\begin{vmatrix}\frac{du_1}{dt} & \frac{du_2}{dt} & \frac{du_3}{dt}\\ v_1 & v_2 & v_3\\ w_1 & w_2 & w_3\end{vmatrix}$$

$$+\begin{vmatrix}u_1 & u_2 & u_3\\ \frac{dv_1}{dt} & \frac{dv_2}{dt} & \frac{dv_3}{dt}\\ w_1 & w_2 & w_3\end{vmatrix}+\begin{vmatrix}u_1 & u_2 & u_3\\ v_1 & v_2 & v_3\\ \frac{dw_1}{dt} & \frac{dw_2}{dt} & \frac{dw_3}{dt}\end{vmatrix}$$

This equation says that the derivative of a 3 by 3 determinant of differentiable functions is the sum of the three determinants obtained from the original by differentiating one row at a time. The result extends to determinants of any order.

51. *(Continuation of Exercise 50)* Suppose $\mathbf{r}(t)=f(t)\mathbf{i}+g(t)\mathbf{j}+h(t)\mathbf{k}$ and f, g, and h have derivatives through order three. Use the results of Exercise 50 to show that

$$\frac{d}{dt}\left(\mathbf{r}\cdot\frac{d\mathbf{r}}{dt}\times\frac{d^2\mathbf{r}}{dt^2}\right)=\mathbf{r}\cdot\left(\frac{d\mathbf{r}}{dt}\times\frac{d^3\mathbf{r}}{dt^3}\right).$$

(*Hint*: Differentiate on the left and look for vectors whose products are zero.)

CAS Explorations

Tangent Lines

In Exercises 52–55, perform the following steps.

(a) Use a CAS to plot the space curve traced by the position vector **r**.

(b) Find the components of the velocity vector $d\mathbf{r}/dt$.

(c) Evaluate $d\mathbf{r}/dt$ at the given point t_0 and find parametric equations for the line tangent to the curve at $\mathbf{r}(t_0)$.

(d) Use a CAS to plot the tangent line together with the curve over the given interval.

52. $\mathbf{r}(t)=(\sin t-t\cos t)\mathbf{i}+(\cos t+t\sin t)\mathbf{j}+t^2\mathbf{k},\ 0\le t\le 6\pi,$ $t_0=3\pi/2$

53. $\mathbf{r}(t)=\sqrt{2}t\mathbf{i}+e^t\mathbf{j}+e^{-t}\mathbf{k},\quad -2\le t\le 3,\quad t_0=1$

54. $\mathbf{r}(t)=(\sin 2t)\mathbf{i}+(\ln(1+t))\mathbf{j}+t\mathbf{k},\quad 0\le t\le 4\pi,$ $t_0=\pi/4$

55. $\mathbf{r}(t)=(\ln(t^2+2))\mathbf{i}+(\tan^{-1}3t)\mathbf{j}+\sqrt{t^2+1}\mathbf{k},\quad -3\le t\le 5,$ $t_0=3$

Helices

In Exercises 56 and 57, you will use a CAS to explore graphically the behavior of the helix

$$\mathbf{r}(t)=(\cos at)\mathbf{i}+(\sin at)\mathbf{j}+bt\mathbf{k}$$

as you change the values of the constants a and b.

56. Writing to Learn Set $b=1$. Plot the helix $\mathbf{r}(t)$ together with the tangent line to the curve at $t=3\pi/2$ for $a=1, 2, 4$, and 6 over the interval $0\le t\le 4\pi$. Describe in your own words what happens to the graph of the helix and the position of the tangent line as a increases through these positive values.

57. Writing to Learn Set $a=1$. Plot the helix $\mathbf{r}(t)$ together with the tangent line to the curve at $t=3/2$ for $b=1/4, 1/2, 2$, and 4 over the interval $0\le t\le 4\pi$. Describe in your own words what happens to the graph of the helix and the position of the tangent line as b increases through these positive values.

13.2 Arc Length and the Unit Tangent Vector T

What you'll learn about

- Arc Length
- Speed on a Smooth Curve
- The Unit Tangent Vector **T**

Arc Length

One special feature of smooth curves is that they have a measurable length. This enables us to locate points on these curves by giving their directed distances along the curve from some **base point,** the way we locate points on coordinate axes by giving their directed distances from the origin (Figure 13.10). Time is the natural parameter for describing a moving body's velocity and acceleration, but s, the arc length, is the natural parameter for studying a curve's shape. Both parameters appear in analyses of space flight.

To measure distance along a smooth curve in space, we add a z-term to the formula we use for curves in the plane.

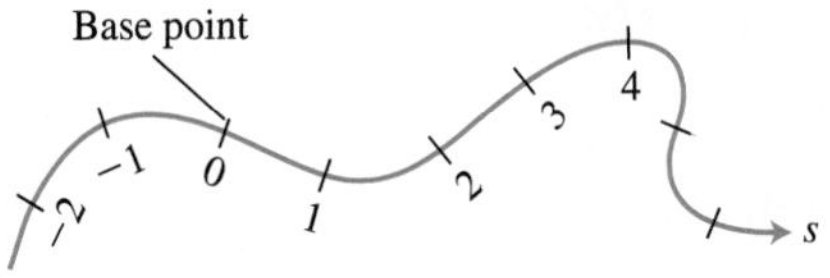

Figure 13.10 Smooth curves can be scaled like number lines, the coordinate of each point being its directed distance from a preselected base point.

DEFINITION Arc Length: Length of a Smooth Curve

The **length** of a smooth curve $\mathbf{r}(t) = f(t)\mathbf{i} + g(t)\mathbf{j} + h(t)\mathbf{k}$, $a \le t \le b$, that is traced exactly once as t increases from $t = a$ to $t = b$ is

$$L = \int_a^b \sqrt{\left(\frac{df}{dt}\right)^2 + \left(\frac{dg}{dt}\right)^2 + \left(\frac{dh}{dt}\right)^2}\, dt$$

$$L = \int_a^b \sqrt{\left(\frac{dx}{dt}\right)^2 + \left(\frac{dy}{dt}\right)^2 + \left(\frac{dz}{dt}\right)^2}\, dt \qquad (1)$$

$$= \int_a^b |\mathbf{v}|\, dt$$

Just as for plane curves, we can calculate the length of a curve in space from any convenient parametrization that meets the stated conditions. We omit the proof.

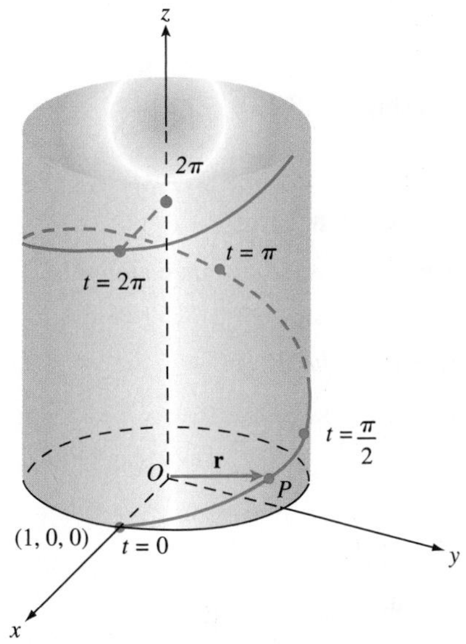

Figure 13.11 The helix $\mathbf{r}(t) = (\cos t)\mathbf{i} + (\sin t)\mathbf{j} + t\mathbf{k}$. (Example 1)

EXAMPLE 1 Applying the Definition of Length

Find the length of one turn of the helix $\mathbf{r}(t) = (\cos t)\mathbf{i} + (\sin t)\mathbf{j} + t\mathbf{k}$.

SOLUTION

The helix makes one full turn as t runs from 0 to 2π (Figure 13.11). The length of this portion of the curve is

$$L = \int_a^b |\mathbf{v}|\, dt = \int_0^{2\pi} \sqrt{(-\sin t)^2 + (\cos t)^2 + (1)^2}\, dt$$

$$= \int_0^{2\pi} \sqrt{2}\, dt = 2\pi\sqrt{2} \text{ units.}$$

This is $\sqrt{2}$ times the length of the circle in the xy-plane over which the helix stands.

If we choose a base point $P(t_0)$ on a smooth curve C parametrized by t, each value of t determines a point $P(t) = (x(t), y(t), z(t))$ on C and a "directed distance"

$$s(t) = \int_{t_0}^{t} |\mathbf{v}(\tau)|\, d\tau,$$

measured along C from the base point (Figure 13.12). If $t > t_0$, $s(t)$ is the distance from $P(t_0)$ to $P(t)$. If $t < t_0$, $s(t)$ is the negative of the distance. Each value of s determines a point on C and this parametrizes C with respect to s. We call s an **arc length parameter** for the curve. The parameter's value increases in the direction of increasing t.

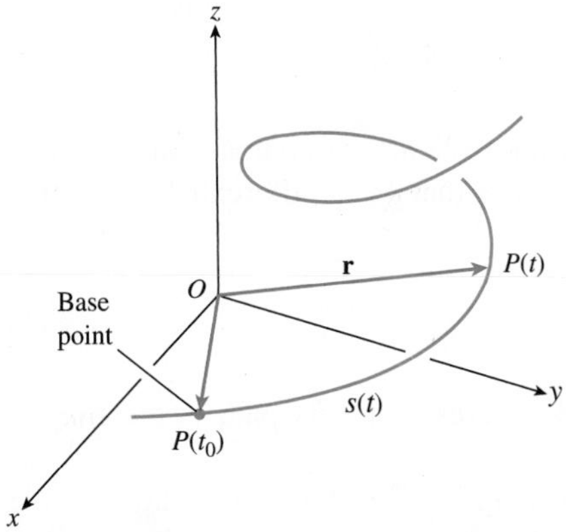

Figure 13.12 The directed distance along the curve from $P(t_0)$ to any point is $P(t)$ is $s(t) = \int_{t_o}^{t} |\mathbf{v}(\tau)|\, d\tau$.

Arc Length Parameter with Base Point $P(t_0)$ on a Smooth Curve

$$s(t) = \int_{t_0}^{t} \sqrt{[x'(\tau)]^2 + [y'(\tau)]^2 + [z'(\tau)]^2}\, d\tau = \int_{t_0}^{t} |\mathbf{v}(\tau)|\, d\tau \qquad (2)$$

We use the Greek letter τ ("tau") as the variable of integration in the integral for s because the letter t is already in use as the upper limit.

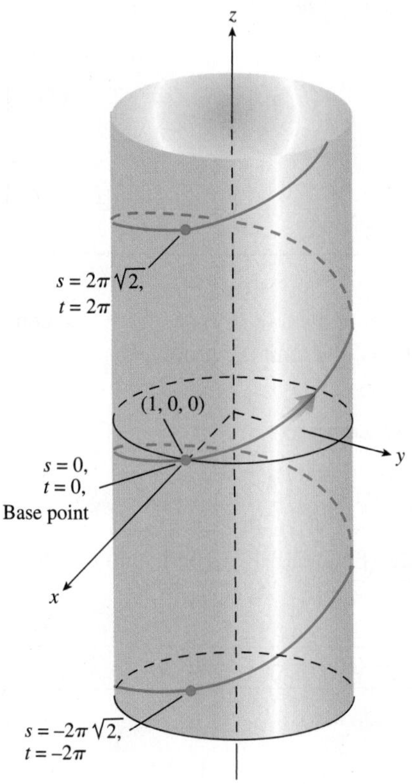

Figure 13.13 Arc length parameter values on the helix $\mathbf{r}(t) = (\cos t)\mathbf{i} + (\sin t)\mathbf{j} + t\mathbf{k}$. (Example 2)

EXAMPLE 2 Finding an Arc Length Parameter

If $t_0 = 0$, the arc length parameter along the helix

$$\mathbf{r}(t) = (\cos t)\mathbf{i} + (\sin t)\mathbf{j} + t\mathbf{k}$$

from t_0 to t is

$$\begin{aligned} s(t) &= \int_{t_0}^{t} |\mathbf{v}(\tau)|\, d\tau && \text{Eq. (2)} \\ &= \int_0^t \sqrt{2}\, d\tau && \text{Value from Example 1} \\ &= \sqrt{2}t. \end{aligned}$$

Thus, $s(2\pi) = 2\pi\sqrt{2}$, $s(-2\pi) = -2\pi\sqrt{2}$, and so on (Figure 13.13).

EXAMPLE 3 Finding Directed Distance Along a Line

Show that if $\mathbf{u} = u_1\mathbf{i} + u_2\mathbf{j} + u_3\mathbf{k}$ is a unit vector, then the directed distance along the line L given by

$$\mathbf{r}(t) = (x_0 + tu_1)\mathbf{i} + (y_0 + tu_2)\mathbf{j} + (z_0 + tu_3)\mathbf{k}$$

from the point $P_0(x_0, y_0, z_0)$ where $t = 0$ is t itself (Figure 13.14).

SOLUTION

$$\begin{aligned} \mathbf{v} &= \frac{d}{dt}(x_0 + tu_1)\mathbf{i} + \frac{d}{dt}(y_0 + tu_2)\mathbf{j} + \frac{d}{dt}(z_0 + tu_3)\mathbf{k} \\ &= u_1\mathbf{i} + u_2\mathbf{j} + u_3\mathbf{k} = \mathbf{u}, \end{aligned}$$

so

$$s(t) = \int_0^t |\mathbf{v}|\, d\tau = \int_0^t |\mathbf{u}|\, d\tau = \int_0^t 1\, d\tau = t.$$

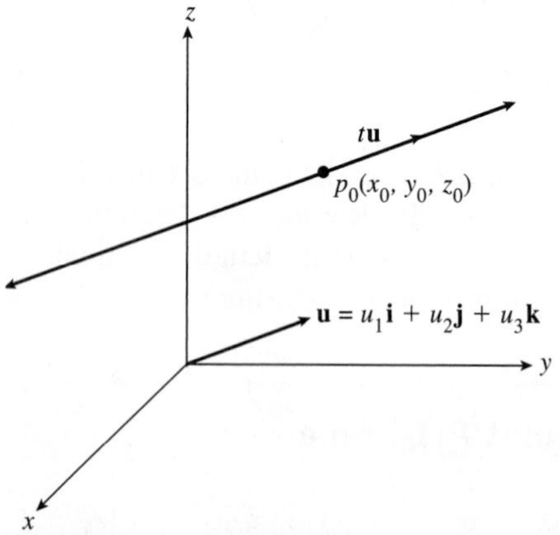

Figure 13.14 The figure for Example 3.

Speed on a Smooth Curve

Since the derivatives beneath the radical in Equation (2) are continuous (the curve is smooth), the Fundamental Theorem of Calculus tells us that s is a differentiable function of t with derivative

$$\frac{ds}{dt} = |\mathbf{v}(t)|. \tag{3}$$

As we expect, the speed with which the particle moves along its path is the magnitude of $\mathbf{v}$.

Although the base point $P(t_0)$ plays a role in defining s in Equation (2), it plays no role in Equation (3). The rate at which a moving particle covers distance along its path has nothing to do with how far away the base point is.

Notice also that $ds/dt > 0$ since $|\mathbf{v}(t)|$ is never zero for a smooth curve. We see once again that s is an increasing function of t.

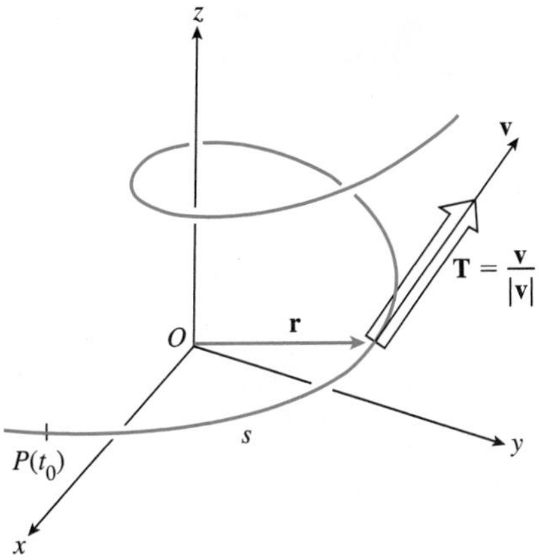

Figure 13.15 We find the unit tangent vector **T** by dividing **v** by $|\mathbf{v}|$.

The Unit Tangent Vector T

Since $ds/dt > 0$ for the curves we are considering, s is one-to-one and has an inverse that gives t as a differentiable function of s (Section 3.8). The derivative of the inverse is

$$\frac{dt}{ds} = \frac{1}{ds/dt} = \frac{1}{|\mathbf{v}|}.$$

This makes $\mathbf{r}$ a differentiable function of s whose derivative can be calculated with the Chain Rule to be

$$\frac{d\mathbf{r}}{ds} = \frac{d\mathbf{r}}{dt}\frac{dt}{ds} = \mathbf{v}\frac{1}{|\mathbf{v}|} = \frac{\mathbf{v}}{|\mathbf{v}|}.$$

This equation says that $d\mathbf{r}/ds$ is a unit vector in the direction of $\mathbf{v}$. The vector $d\mathbf{r}/ds$ is the unit tangent vector of the curve traced by $\mathbf{r}$ and denoted by $\mathbf{T}$ (Figure 13.15).

DEFINITION Unit Tangent Vector

The **unit tangent vector** of a smooth curve $\mathbf{r}(t)$ is

$$\mathbf{T} = \frac{d\mathbf{r}}{ds} = \frac{d\mathbf{r}/dt}{ds/dt} = \frac{\mathbf{v}}{|\mathbf{v}|}. \tag{4}$$

The unit tangent vector $\mathbf{T}$ is a differentiable function of t whenever $\mathbf{v}$ is a differentiable function of t. As we see in Section 13.3, $\mathbf{T}$ is one of three unit vectors in a traveling reference frame that is used to describe the motion of space vehicles and other bodies moving in three dimensions.

EXAMPLE 4 Finding the Unit Tangent Vector T

Find the unit tangent vector of the helix $\mathbf{r}(t) = (\cos t)\mathbf{i} + (\sin t)\mathbf{j} + t\mathbf{k}$.

SOLUTION

$$\mathbf{v} = (-\sin t)\mathbf{i} + (\cos t)\mathbf{j} + \mathbf{k}$$

$$|\mathbf{v}| = \sqrt{(-\sin t)^2 + (\cos t)^2 + (1)^2} = \sqrt{2}$$

$$\mathbf{T} = \frac{\mathbf{v}}{|\mathbf{v}|} = -\frac{\sin t}{\sqrt{2}}\mathbf{i} + \frac{\cos t}{\sqrt{2}}\mathbf{j} + \frac{1}{\sqrt{2}}\mathbf{k}$$

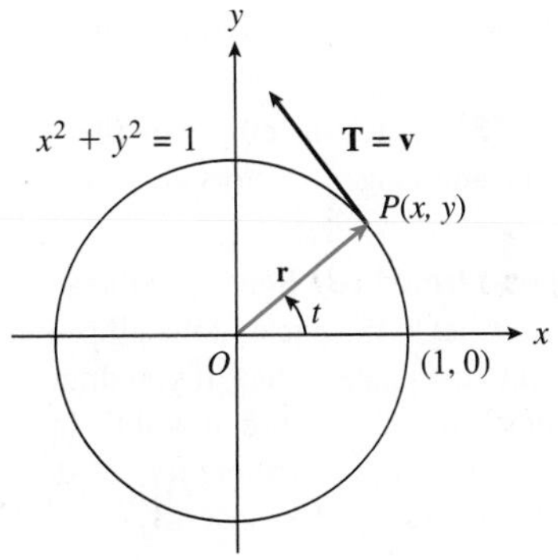

Figure 13.16 The motion $\mathbf{r}(t) = (\cos t)\mathbf{i} + (\sin t)\mathbf{j}$. (Example 5)

EXAMPLE 5 Finding the Unit Tangent Vector T

For the counterclockwise motion $\mathbf{r}(t) = (\cos t)\mathbf{i} + (\sin t)\mathbf{j}$ around the unit circle,

$$\mathbf{v} = (-\sin t)\mathbf{i} + (\cos t)\mathbf{j}$$

is already a unit vector, so $\mathbf{T} = \mathbf{v}$ (Figure 13.16).

Quick Review 13.2

In Exercises 1–4, find an equation for the tangent line to the curve $x^2 + y^2 = 9$ at the indicated point.

1. $(3, 0)$

2. $(0, 3)$

3. $\left(-\frac{3}{\sqrt{2}}, \frac{3}{\sqrt{2}}\right)$

4. $\left(\frac{3}{\sqrt{2}}, \frac{3}{\sqrt{2}}\right)$

5. Let $x = 2 \cos t$ and $y = 3 \sin t$. Find two unit vectors

(a) tangent to the curve at $t = \pi/3$.

(b) normal to the curve at $t = \pi/3$.

6. Find the length of the curve $y = \sin x$ from $x = 0$ to $x = \pi/2$.

7. Find the length of the curve $x = \cos^3 t, \quad y = \sin^3 t, \quad 0 \le t \le \pi$.

In Exercises 8–10, find dy/dx.

8. $y = \int_2^x t \sin t \, dt$

9. $y = \int_0^{x^2} \cos(t^2) \, dt$

10. $y = \int_{\cos x}^{\sin x} \ln(1 + t^2) \, dt$

Section 13.2 Exercises

In Exercises 1–8, find **(a)** the curve's unit tangent vector. Also, find **(b)** the length of the indicated portion of the curve.

1. $\mathbf{r}(t) = (2 \cos t)\mathbf{i} + (2 \sin t)\mathbf{j} + \sqrt{5}t\mathbf{k}, \quad 0 \le t \le \pi$

2. $\mathbf{r}(t) = (6 \sin 2t)\mathbf{i} + (6 \cos 2t)\mathbf{j} + 5t\mathbf{k}, \quad 0 \le t \le \pi$

3. $\mathbf{r}(t) = t\mathbf{i} + (2/3)t^{3/2}\mathbf{k}, \quad 0 \le t \le 8$

4. $\mathbf{r}(t) = (2 + t)\mathbf{i} - (t + 1)\mathbf{j} + t\mathbf{k}, \quad 0 \le t \le 3$

5. $\mathbf{r}(t) = (\cos^3 t)\mathbf{j} + (\sin^3 t)\mathbf{k}, \quad 0 \le t \le \pi/2$

6. $\mathbf{r}(t) = 6t^3\mathbf{i} - 2t^3\mathbf{j} - 3t^3\mathbf{k}, \quad 1 \le t \le 2$

7. $\mathbf{r}(t) = (t \cos t)\mathbf{i} + (t \sin t)\mathbf{j} + (2\sqrt{2}/3)t^{3/2}\mathbf{k}, \quad 0 \le t \le \pi$

8. $\mathbf{r}(t) = (t \sin t + \cos t)\mathbf{i} + (t \cos t - \sin t)\mathbf{j}, \quad \sqrt{2} \le t \le 2$

9. Find the point on the curve

$$\mathbf{r}(t) = (5 \sin t)\mathbf{i} + (5 \cos t)\mathbf{j} + 12t\mathbf{k}$$

at a distance 26π units along the curve from the origin in the direction of increasing arc length.

10. Find the point on the curve

$$\mathbf{r}(t) = (12 \sin t)\mathbf{i} - (12 \cos t)\mathbf{j} + 5t\mathbf{k}$$

at a distance 13π units along the curve from the origin in the direction opposite to the direction of increasing arc length.

In Exercises 11–14, find **(a)** the arc length parameter along the curve from the point where $t = 0$ by evaluating the integral

$$s = \int_0^t |\mathbf{v}(\tau)| \, d\tau.$$

Then find **(b)** the length of the indicated portion of the curve.

11. $\mathbf{r}(t) = (4 \cos t)\mathbf{i} + (4 \sin t)\mathbf{j} + 3t\mathbf{k}, \quad 0 \le t \le \pi/2$

12. $\mathbf{r}(t) = (\cos t + t \sin t)\mathbf{i} + (\sin t - t \cos t)\mathbf{j}, \quad \pi/2 \le t \le \pi$

13. $\mathbf{r}(t) = (e^t \cos t)\mathbf{i} + (e^t \sin t)\mathbf{j} + e^t\mathbf{k}, \quad -\ln 4 \le t \le 0$

14. $\mathbf{r}(t) = (1 + 2t)\mathbf{i} + (1 + 3t)\mathbf{j} + (6 - 6t)\mathbf{k}, \quad -1 \le t \le 0$

15. Find the length of the curve

$$\mathbf{r}(t) = (\sqrt{2}\, t)\mathbf{i} + (\sqrt{2}\, t)\mathbf{j} + (1 - t^2)\mathbf{k}$$

from $(0, 0, 1)$ to $(\sqrt{2}, \sqrt{2}, 0)$.

16. Writing to Learn The length $2\pi\sqrt{2}$ of the turn of the helix of Example 1 is also the length of the diagonal of a square 2π units on a side. Show how to obtain this square by cutting away and flattening a portion of the cylinder around which the helix winds.

Exercises 17–20 refer to the curve $\mathbf{r}(t) = (\cos t)\mathbf{i} + (\sin t)\mathbf{j} + (1 - \cos t)\mathbf{k}, \quad 0 \le t \le 2\pi$.

17. Show that the curve is an ellipse by showing that it is the intersection of a right circular cylinder and a plane. Find equations for the cylinder and plane.

18. ***(Continuation of Exercise 17)*** Sketch the ellipse on the cylinder. Add to your sketch the unit tangent vectors at $t = 0$, $\pi/2$, π, and $3\pi/2$.

19. ***(Continuation of Exercises 17 and 18)*** Show that the acceleration vector always lies parallel to the plane of the ellipse (orthogonal to a vector normal to the plane). Thus, if you draw the acceleration as a vector attached to the ellipse, it will lie in the plane of the ellipse. Add the acceleration vectors for $t = 0$, $\pi/2$, π, and $3\pi/2$ to the sketch you made in Exercise 18.

20. Write and evaluate an integral for the length of the ellipse.

21. Writing to Learn Explain how to use a two-dimensional grapher to graph the curves in Exercises 3, 5, and 12.

Exploration

22. ***Length Is Independent of Parametrization*** To illustrate that the length of a smooth space curve does not depend on the parametrization you use to compute it, calculate the length of one turn of the helix in Example 1 with each of the following parametrizations.

    (a) $\mathbf{r}(t) = (\cos 4t)\mathbf{i} + (\sin 4t)\mathbf{j} + 4t\mathbf{k}, \quad 0 \le t \le \pi/2$

    (b) $\mathbf{r}(t) = [\cos(t/2)]\mathbf{i} + [\sin(t/2)]\mathbf{j} + (t/2)\mathbf{k}, \quad 0 \le t \le 4\pi$

    (c) $\mathbf{r}(t) = (\cos t)\mathbf{i} - (\sin t)\mathbf{j} - t\mathbf{k}, \quad -2\pi \le t \le 0$

Extending the Ideas

23. ***Arc Length in Cylindrical Coordinates***

    (a) Show that when you express $ds^2 = dx^2 + dy^2 + dz^2$ in terms of cylindrical coordinates, you get $ds^2 = dr^2 + r^2\,d\theta^2 + dz^2$.

    (b) Interpret this result geometrically in terms of the edges and diagonal of a box. Sketch the box.

    (c) Use the result in (a) to find the length of the curve $r = e^\theta$, $z = e^\theta$, $0 \le \theta \le \ln 8$.

13.3 Curvature, Torsion, and the TNB Frame

What you'll learn about

- Curvature of a Plane Curve
- The Principal Unit Normal Vector for Plane Curves
- Circle of Curvature and Radius of Curvature
- Curvature and Normal Vectors for Space Curves
- Torsion and the Binormal Vector
- Tangential and Normal Components of Acceleration
- Formulas for Computing Curvature and Torsion

Curvature of a Plane Curve

As a particle moves along a smooth curve in the plane, $\mathbf{T} = d\mathbf{r}/ds$ turns as the curve bends. Since $\mathbf{T}$ is a unit vector, its length remains constant and only its direction changes as the particle moves along the curve. The rate at which the direction changes per unit of length along the curve is the *curvature* (Figure 13.17). The traditional symbol for the curvature is the Greek letter κ ("kappa").

DEFINITION Curvature

If $\mathbf{T}$ is the unit tangent vector of a smooth curve, the **curvature** function of the curve is

$$\kappa = \left|\frac{d\mathbf{T}}{ds}\right|.$$

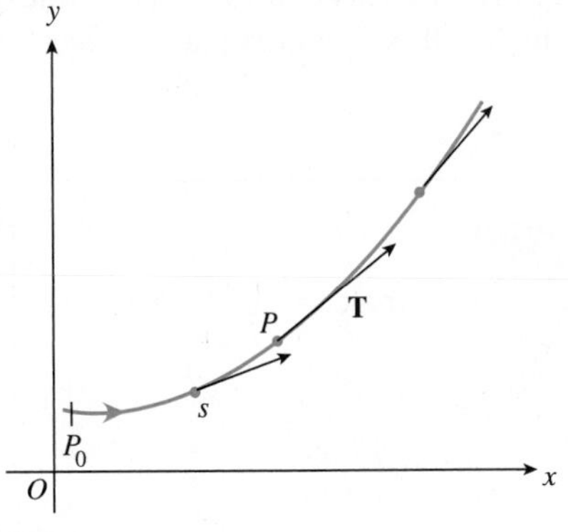

Figure 13.17 As P moves along the curve in the direction of increasing arc length, the unit tangent vector turns. The value of $|d\mathbf{T}/ds|$ is the *curvature* of the curve at P.

The curvature measures how sharply a curve bends at a point. If $|d\mathbf{T}/ds|$ is large, $\mathbf{T}$ turns sharply as the particle passes through P and the curvature at P is large. If $|d\mathbf{T}/ds|$ is close to zero, $\mathbf{T}$ turns more slowly and the curvature at P is smaller. In Figure 13.18, the curvature at Q is greater than the curvature at P.

Testing the definition, we see in Examples 1 and 2 that the curvature is constant for straight lines and circles.

EXAMPLE 1 Finding the Curvature of a Straight Line

Show that the curvature of a straight line is zero.

SOLUTION

On a straight line, the unit tangent vector $\mathbf{T}$ always points in the same direction, so its components are constants. Therefore, $|d\mathbf{T}/ds| = |\mathbf{0}| = 0$ (Figure 13.19).

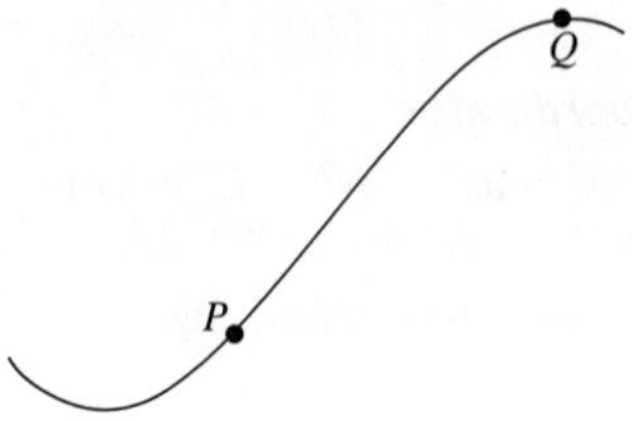

Figure 13.18 The curvature at Q is greater than the curvature at P.

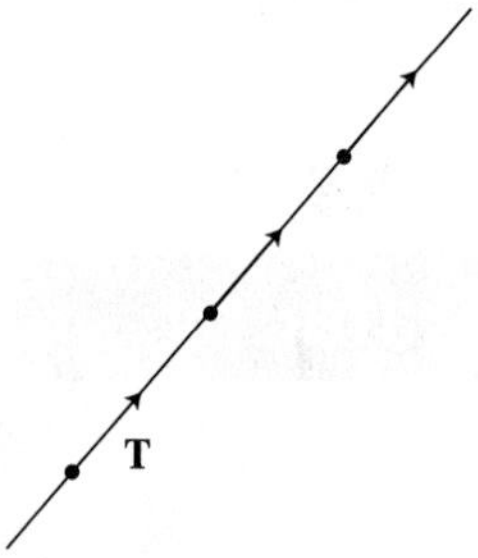

Figure 13.19 Along a straight line, **T** always points in the same direction. The curvature, $|d\mathbf{T}/ds|$, is zero. (Example 1)

EXAMPLE 2 Finding the Curvature of a Circle

Show that the curvature of a circle of radius a is $1/a$.

SOLUTION

To see why (Figure 13.20), start with the parametrization

$$\mathbf{r}(\theta) = (a\cos\theta)\mathbf{i} + (a\sin\theta)\mathbf{j}$$

and substitute $\theta = s/a$ to parametrize in terms of arc length s:

$$\mathbf{r} = \left(a\cos\frac{s}{a}\right)\mathbf{i} + \left(a\sin\frac{s}{a}\right)\mathbf{j}.$$

Then

$$\mathbf{T} = \frac{d\mathbf{r}}{ds} = \left(-\sin\frac{s}{a}\right)\mathbf{i} + \left(\cos\frac{s}{a}\right)\mathbf{j}$$

and

$$\frac{d\mathbf{T}}{ds} = \left(-\frac{1}{a}\cos\frac{s}{a}\right)\mathbf{i} - \left(\frac{1}{a}\sin\frac{s}{a}\right)\mathbf{j}.$$

Hence, for any value of s,

$$\begin{aligned}\kappa &= \left|\frac{d\mathbf{T}}{ds}\right| \\ &= \sqrt{\frac{1}{a^2}\cos^2\left(\frac{s}{a}\right) + \frac{1}{a^2}\sin^2\left(\frac{s}{a}\right)} \\ &= \frac{1}{\sqrt{a^2}} = \frac{1}{|a|} = \frac{1}{a}.\end{aligned}$$

Since $a > 0$, $|a| = a$.

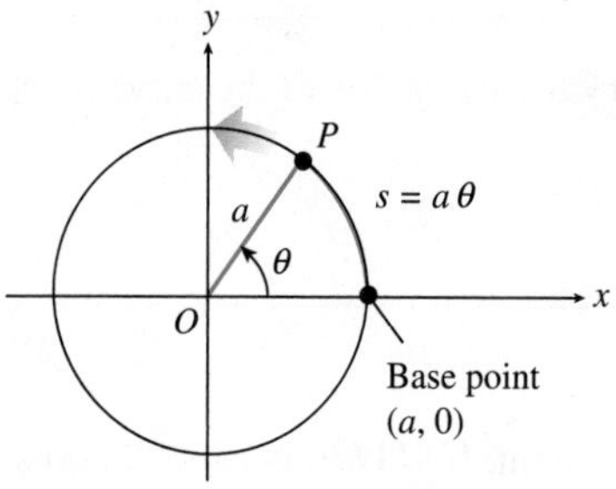

Figure 13.20 The point P has coordinates $(a\cos\theta, a\sin\theta) = (a\cos(s/a), a\sin(s/a))$. (Example 2)

The Principal Unit Normal Vector for Plane Curves

Since **T** has constant length, the vector $d\mathbf{T}/ds$ is orthogonal to **T** (Section 13.1). Therefore, if at a point where $d\mathbf{T}/ds \neq \mathbf{0}$, we divide $d\mathbf{T}/ds$ by its length κ, we obtain a *unit* vector orthogonal to **T** (Figure 13.21).

> **DEFINITION Principal Unit Normal Vector**
>
> At a point where $\kappa \neq 0$, the **principal unit normal vector** for a curve in the plane is
>
> $$\mathbf{N} = \frac{1}{\kappa}\frac{d\mathbf{T}}{ds}.$$

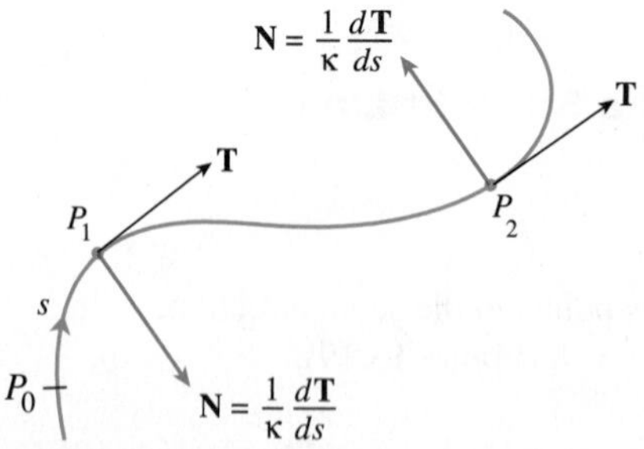

Figure 13.21 The vector $d\mathbf{T}/ds$, normal to the curve, always points in the direction in which **T** is turning. The vector **N** is the direction of $d\mathbf{T}/ds$.

The vector $d\mathbf{T}/ds$ points in the direction in which **T** turns as the curve bends. Therefore, if we face in the direction of increasing arc length, the vector $d\mathbf{T}/ds$ points to the right if **T** turns clockwise and toward the left if **T** turns counterclockwise. In other words, the principal normal vector **N** will point toward the concave side of the curve (Figure 13.21). Exercise 10 illustrates what happens at a point where the concavity changes and **T** momentarily stops turning.

Because the arc length parameter for a smooth curve $\mathbf{r}(t) = f(t)\mathbf{i} + g(t)\mathbf{j}$ is defined with ds/dt positive, $ds/dt = |ds/dt|$, and the Chain Rule gives

$$\begin{aligned}\mathbf{N} &= \frac{d\mathbf{T}/ds}{|d\mathbf{T}/ds|} \\ &= \frac{(d\mathbf{T}/dt)(dt/ds)}{|d\mathbf{T}/dt||dt/ds|} \\ &= \frac{d\mathbf{T}/dt}{|d\mathbf{T}/dt|}. \end{aligned} \tag{1}$$

This formula enables us to find $\mathbf{N}$ without having to find κ and s first.

EXAMPLE 3 Finding T and N

Find $\mathbf{T}$ and $\mathbf{N}$ for the circular motion $\mathbf{r}(t) = (\cos 2t)\mathbf{i} + (\sin 2t)\mathbf{j}$.

SOLUTION

We first find $\mathbf{T}$:

$$\begin{aligned}\mathbf{v} &= -(2\sin 2t)\mathbf{i} + (2\cos 2t)\mathbf{j}, \\ |\mathbf{v}| &= \sqrt{4\sin^2 2t + 4\cos^2 2t} = 2, \\ \mathbf{T} &= \frac{\mathbf{v}}{|\mathbf{v}|} = -(\sin 2t)\mathbf{i} + (\cos 2t)\mathbf{j}.\end{aligned}$$

From this we find

$$\begin{aligned}\frac{d\mathbf{T}}{dt} &= -(2\cos 2t)\mathbf{i} - (2\sin 2t)\mathbf{j}, \\ \left|\frac{d\mathbf{T}}{dt}\right| &= \sqrt{4\cos^2 2t + 4\sin^2 2t} = 2,\end{aligned}$$

and

$$\begin{aligned}\mathbf{N} &= \frac{d\mathbf{T}/dt}{|d\mathbf{T}/dt|} \qquad \text{Eq. (1)} \\ &= -(\cos 2t)\mathbf{i} - (\sin 2t)\mathbf{j}.\end{aligned}$$

Circle of Curvature and Radius of Curvature

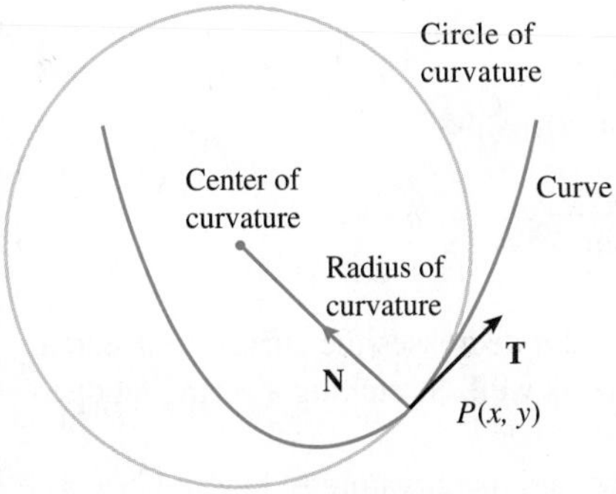

Figure 13.22 The osculating circle at $P(x, y)$ lies toward the inner side of the curve.

The **circle of curvature** or **osculating circle** at a point P on a plane curve where $\kappa \neq 0$ is the circle in the plane of the curve that

1. is tangent to the curve at P (has the same tangent line the curve has);
2. has the same curvature the curve has at P; and
3. lies toward the concave or inner side of the curve (as in Figure 13.22).

The **radius of curvature** of the curve at P is the radius of the circle of curvature, which, according to Example 2, is

$$\text{Radius of curvature} = \rho = \frac{1}{\kappa}. \tag{2}$$

To find ρ, we find κ and take the reciprocal. The **center of curvature** of the curve at P is the center of the circle of curvature.

Curvature and Normal Vectors for Space Curves

Just as it does for a curve in the plane, the arc length parameter s gives the unit tangent vector $\mathbf{T} = d\mathbf{r}/ds$ for a smooth curve in space. We again define the curvature to be

$$\kappa = \left|\frac{d\mathbf{T}}{ds}\right|. \tag{3}$$

The vector $d\mathbf{T}/ds$ is orthogonal to $\mathbf{T}$, and we define the principal unit normal to be

$$\mathbf{N} = \frac{1}{\kappa}\frac{d\mathbf{T}}{ds} = \frac{d\mathbf{T}/dt}{|d\mathbf{T}/dt|}. \tag{4}$$

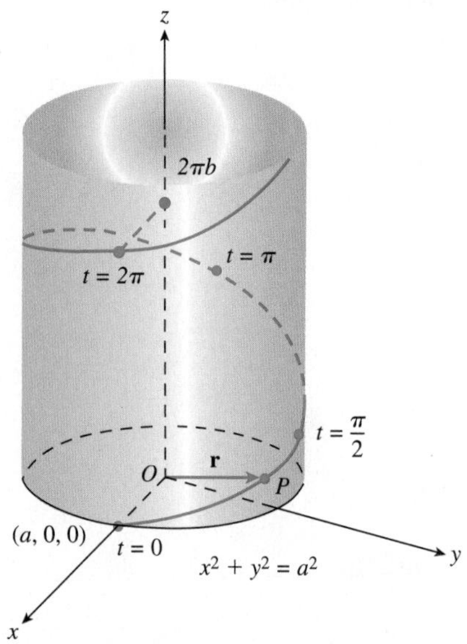

Figure 13.23 The helix $\mathbf{r}(t) = (a\cos t)\mathbf{i} + (a\sin t)\mathbf{j} + bt\mathbf{k}$ drawn with a and b positive and $t \geq 0$. (Example 4)

EXAMPLE 4 Finding Curvature on a Helix

Find the curvature for the helix (Figure 13.23)
$\mathbf{r}(t) = (a\cos t)\mathbf{i} + (a\sin t)\mathbf{j} + bt\mathbf{k}, \qquad a, b \geq 0, \qquad a^2 + b^2 \neq 0.$

SOLUTION

We calculate $\mathbf{T}$ from the velocity vector $\mathbf{v}$:

$$\mathbf{v} = -(a\sin t)\mathbf{i} + (a\cos t)\mathbf{j} + b\mathbf{k},$$

$$|\mathbf{v}| = \sqrt{a^2\sin^2 t + a^2\cos^2 t + b^2} = \sqrt{a^2 + b^2},$$

$$\mathbf{T} = \frac{\mathbf{v}}{|\mathbf{v}|} = \frac{1}{\sqrt{a^2 + b^2}}[-(a\sin t)\mathbf{i} + (a\cos t)\mathbf{j} + b\mathbf{k}].$$

Then, we find $d\mathbf{T}/ds$ as

$$\frac{d\mathbf{T}}{ds} = \frac{d\mathbf{T}}{dt}\frac{dt}{ds} \qquad \text{Chain rule}$$

$$= \frac{d\mathbf{T}}{ds}\cdot\frac{1}{|\mathbf{v}|} \qquad \frac{ds}{dt} = |\mathbf{v}|,\ \text{so}\ \frac{dt}{ds} = \frac{1}{|\mathbf{v}|}$$

$$= \frac{1}{\sqrt{a^2 + b^2}}[-(a\cos t)\mathbf{i} - (a\sin t)\mathbf{j}]\cdot\left(\frac{1}{\sqrt{a^2 + b^2}}\right)$$

$$= \frac{a}{a^2 + b^2}[-(\cos t)\mathbf{i} - (\sin t)\mathbf{j}].$$

Therefore,

$$\kappa = \left|\frac{d\mathbf{T}}{ds}\right| \qquad \text{Eq. (3)}$$

$$= \frac{a}{a^2 + b^2}|-(\cos t)\mathbf{i} - (\sin t)\mathbf{j}|$$

$$= \frac{a}{a^2 + b^2}\sqrt{(\cos t)^2 + (\sin t)^2} = \frac{a}{a^2 + b^2}.$$

From this equation we see that increasing b for fixed a decreases the curvature. Decreasing a for fixed b eventually decreases the curvature as well. Stretching a spring tends to straighten it.

If $b = 0$, the helix reduces to a circle of radius a and its curvature reduces to $1/a$, as it should. If $a = 0$, the helix becomes the z-axis, and its curvature reduces to 0, again as it should.

EXAMPLE 5 Finding the Principal Unit Normal Vector N

Find **N** for the helix in Example 4.

SOLUTION

We have

$$\frac{d\mathbf{T}}{dt} = -\frac{1}{\sqrt{a^2+b^2}}[(a\cos t)\mathbf{i} + (a\sin t)\mathbf{j}], \qquad \text{Example 4}$$

$$\left|\frac{d\mathbf{T}}{dt}\right| = \frac{1}{\sqrt{a^2+b^2}}\sqrt{a^2\cos^2 t + a^2\sin^2 t} = \frac{a}{\sqrt{a^2+b^2}},$$

$$\mathbf{N} = \frac{d\mathbf{T}/dt}{|d\mathbf{T}/dt|} \qquad \text{Eq. (4)}$$

$$= -\frac{\sqrt{a^2+b^2}}{a}\cdot\frac{1}{\sqrt{a^2+b^2}}[(a\cos t)\mathbf{i} + (a\sin t)\mathbf{j}]$$

$$= -(\cos t)\mathbf{i} - (\sin t)\mathbf{j}.$$

Torsion and the Binormal Vector

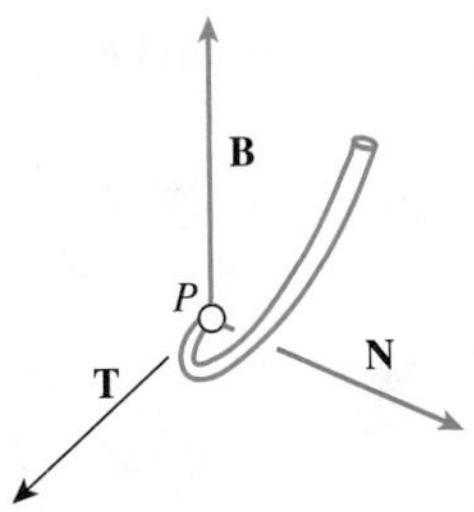

Figure 13.24 The vectors **T, N,** and **B** (in that order) make a right-handed frame of mutually orthogonal unit vectors in space.

The **binormal vector** of a curve in space is $\mathbf{B} = \mathbf{T} \times \mathbf{N}$, a unit vector orthogonal to both **T** and **N** (Figure 13.24). Together **T**, **N**, and **B** define a moving right-handed vector frame that always travels with a body moving along a curve in space. It is the **Frenet** ("fre-nay") **frame** (after Jean-Frédéric Frenet, 1816–1900), or the **TNB frame.** This vector frame plays a significant role in calculating the flight paths of space vehicles.

How does $d\mathbf{B}/ds$ behave in relation to **T, N,** and **B?** From the rule for differentiating a cross product, we have

$$\frac{d\mathbf{B}}{ds} = \frac{d\mathbf{T}}{ds} \times \mathbf{N} + \mathbf{T} \times \frac{d\mathbf{N}}{ds}.$$

Since **N** is the direction of $d\mathbf{T}/ds$, $(d\mathbf{T}/ds) \times \mathbf{N} = \mathbf{0}$ and

$$\frac{d\mathbf{B}}{ds} = \mathbf{0} + \mathbf{T} \times \frac{d\mathbf{N}}{ds} = \mathbf{T} \times \frac{d\mathbf{N}}{ds}.$$

From this we see that $d\mathbf{B}/ds$ is orthogonal to **T** since a cross product is orthogonal to its factors.

Since $d\mathbf{B}/ds$ is also orthogonal to **B** (the latter has constant length), it follows that $d\mathbf{B}/ds$ is orthogonal to the plane of **B** and **T**. In other words, $d\mathbf{B}/ds$ is parallel to **N,** so $d\mathbf{B}/ds$ is a scalar multiple of **N**. In symbols,

$$\frac{d\mathbf{B}}{ds} = -\tau\mathbf{N}.$$

The minus sign in this equation is traditional. The scalar τ is the *torsion* along the curve. Notice that

$$\frac{d\mathbf{B}}{ds}\cdot\mathbf{N} = -\tau\mathbf{N}\cdot\mathbf{N} = -\tau(1) = -\tau,$$

so that

$$\tau = -\frac{d\mathbf{B}}{ds}\cdot\mathbf{N}.$$

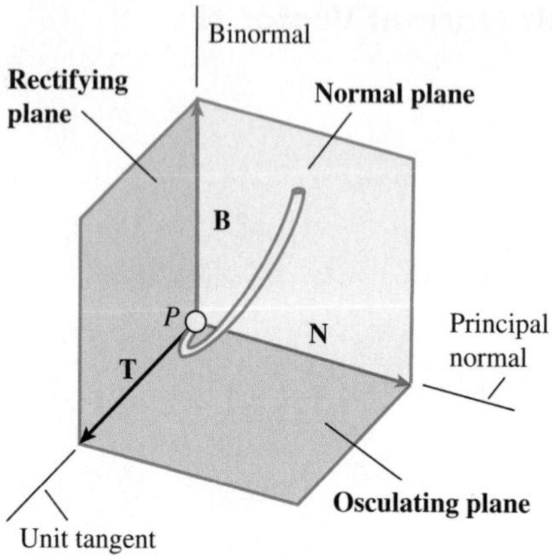

Figure 13.25 The names of the three planes determined by **T, N,** and **B.**

DEFINITION Torsion

Let $\mathbf{B} = \mathbf{T} \times \mathbf{N}$. The **torsion** function of a smooth curve is

$$\tau = -\frac{d\mathbf{B}}{ds} \cdot \mathbf{N}.$$

Unlike the curvature κ, which is never negative, the torsion τ may be positive, negative, or zero.

The three planes determined by **T, N,** and **B** are shown in Figure 13.25. The curvature $\kappa = |d\mathbf{T}/ds|$ can be thought of as the rate at which the normal plane turns as the point P moves along the curve. Similarly, the torsion $\tau = -(d\mathbf{B}/ds) \cdot \mathbf{N}$ is the rate at which the osculating plane turns about **T** as P moves along the curve. Torsion measures how the curve twists.

Tangential and Normal Components of Acceleration

When a body is accelerated by gravity, brakes, a combination of rocket motors, or whatever, we usually want to know how much of the acceleration acts to move the body straight ahead in the direction of motion, in the tangential direction **T.** We can find out if we use the Chain Rule to rewrite **v** as

$$\mathbf{v} = \frac{d\mathbf{r}}{ds} = \frac{d\mathbf{r}}{ds}\frac{ds}{dt} = \mathbf{T}\frac{ds}{dt}$$

and differentiate both ends of this string of equations to get

$$\begin{aligned}\mathbf{a} = \frac{d\mathbf{v}}{dt} &= \frac{d}{dt}\left(\mathbf{T}\frac{ds}{dt}\right) = \frac{d^2s}{dt^2}\mathbf{T} + \frac{ds}{dt}\frac{d\mathbf{T}}{dt} \\ &= \frac{d^2s}{dt^2}\mathbf{T} + \frac{ds}{dt}\left(\frac{d\mathbf{T}}{ds}\frac{ds}{dt}\right) = \frac{d^2s}{dt^2}\mathbf{T} + \frac{ds}{dt}\left(\kappa\mathbf{N}\frac{ds}{dt}\right) \\ &= \frac{d^2s}{dt^2}\mathbf{T} + \kappa\left(\frac{ds}{dt}\right)^2\mathbf{N}.\end{aligned}$$

DEFINITION Tangential and Normal Components of Acceleration

$$\mathbf{a} = a_{\mathrm{T}}\mathbf{T} + a_{\mathrm{N}}\mathbf{N}, \tag{5}$$

where

$$a_{\mathrm{T}} = \frac{d^2s}{dt^2} = \frac{d}{dt}|\mathbf{v}| \quad \text{and} \quad a_{\mathrm{N}} = \kappa\left(\frac{ds}{dt}\right)^2 = \kappa|\mathbf{v}^2| \tag{6}$$

are the **tangential** and **normal** scalar components of acceleration.

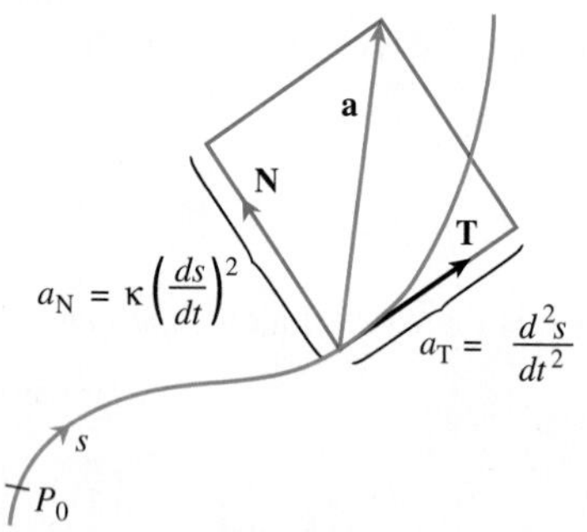

Figure 13.26 The tangential and normal components of acceleration. The acceleration **a** always lies in the plane of **T** and **N,** orthogonal to **B.**

Equation (5) is remarkable in that **B** does not appear. No matter how the path of the moving body we are watching may appear to twist and turn in space, the acceleration **a** *always lies in the plane of* **T** and **N** orthogonal to **B.** The equation also tells exactly how much of the acceleration takes place tangent to the motion (d^2s/dt^2) and how much takes place normal to the motion [$\kappa(ds/dt)^2$] (Figure 13.26).

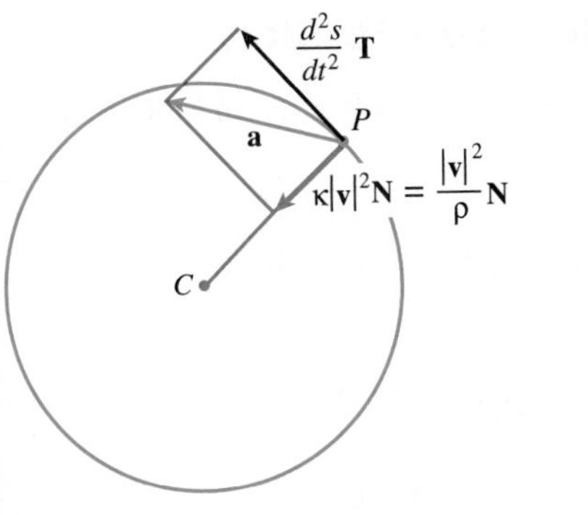

Figure 13.27 The tangential and normal components of the acceleration of a body that is speeding up as it moves counterclockwise around a circle of radius ρ.

What other information can we read from Equation (5)? By definition, the acceleration **a** is the rate of change of velocity **v**, and in general, both length and direction of **v** changes as a body moves along its path. The tangential component of acceleration a_{T} measures the rate of change of the *length* of **v** (that is, the change in speed). The normal component of acceleration a_{N} measures the rate of change of the *direction* of **v.**

Notice that the normal scalar component of the acceleration is the curvature times the *square* of the speed. This explains why you have to hold on when your car makes a sharp (large κ), high-speed (large $|\mathbf{v}|$) turn. If you double the speed of your car, you will experience four times the normal component of acceleration for the same curvature.

If a body moves in a circle at a constant speed, d^2s/dt^2 is zero and all the acceleration points along **N** toward the circle's center. If the body is speeding up or slowing down, **a** has a nonzero tangential component (Figure 13.27).

To calculate a_{N}, we usually use the formula $a_{\mathrm{N}} = \sqrt{|\mathbf{a}|^2 - a_{\mathrm{T}}^2}$, which comes from solving the equation $|\mathbf{a}|^2 = \mathbf{a}\cdot\mathbf{a} = a_{\mathrm{T}}^2 + a_{\mathrm{N}}^2$ for a_{N}. With this formula we find a_{N} without having to calculate κ first.

$$a_{\mathrm{N}} = \sqrt{|\mathbf{a}|^2 - a_{\mathrm{T}}^2} \qquad (7)$$

EXAMPLE 6 Finding an Acceleration Vector

Without finding **T** and **N,** write the acceleration of the motion

$$\mathbf{r}(t) = (\cos t + t\sin t)\mathbf{i} + (\sin t - t\cos t)\mathbf{j}, \qquad t > 0$$

in the form $\mathbf{a} = a_{\mathrm{T}}\mathbf{T} + a_{\mathrm{N}}\mathbf{N}$. (The path of motion is the involute of the circle in Figure 13.28.)

SOLUTION

We use the first of Equations (6) to find a_{T}:

$$\mathbf{v} = \frac{d\mathbf{r}}{dt} = (t\cos t)\mathbf{i} + (t\sin t)\mathbf{j},$$

$$|\mathbf{v}| = \sqrt{t^2\cos^2 t + t^2\sin^2 t} = \sqrt{t^2} = |t| = t, \qquad t > 0$$

$$a_{\mathrm{T}} = \frac{d}{dt}|\mathbf{v}| = 1. \qquad \text{Eq. (6)}$$

Knowing a_{T}, we use Equation (7) to find a_{N}:

$$\mathbf{a} = (\cos t - t\sin t)\,\mathbf{i} + (\sin t + t\cos t)\,\mathbf{j},$$

$$|\mathbf{a}|^2 = t^2 + 1, \qquad \text{After some algebra}$$

$$a_{\mathrm{N}} = \sqrt{|\mathbf{a}|^2 - a_{\mathrm{T}}^2} \qquad \text{Eq. (7)}$$

$$= \sqrt{(t^2+1) - (1)} = \sqrt{t^2} = t.$$

We then use Equation (5) to find **a**:

$$\mathbf{a} = a_{\mathrm{T}}\mathbf{T} + a_{\mathrm{N}}\mathbf{N} = (1)\mathbf{T} + t\mathbf{N}\ \mathbf{T} + t\mathbf{N}.$$

See Figure 13.28.

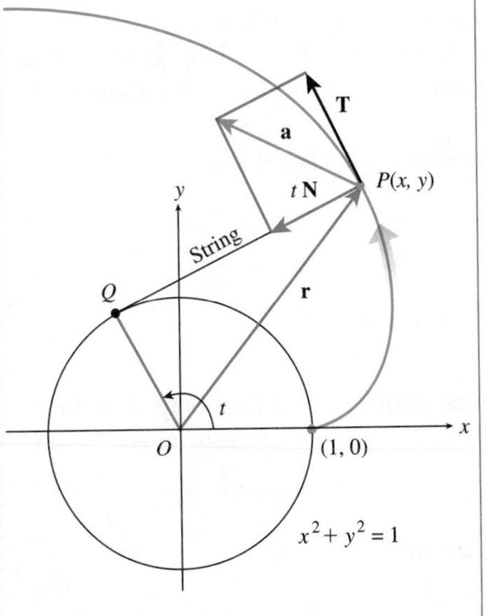

Figure 13.28 The tangential and normal components of the acceleration of the motion $\mathbf{r}(t) = (\cos t + t\sin t)\mathbf{i} + (\sin t - t\cos t)\mathbf{j}$, for $t > 0$. (Example 6)

Formulas for Computing Curvature and Torsion

We now present some easy-to-use formulas for computing the curvature and torsion of a smooth curve. From Equation (5), we have

$$\begin{aligned}\mathbf{v} \times \mathbf{a} &= \left(\frac{ds}{dt}\mathbf{T}\right) \times \left[\frac{d^2s}{dt^2}\mathbf{T} + \kappa\left(\frac{ds}{dt}\right)^2\mathbf{N}\right] \\ &= \left(\frac{ds}{dt}\frac{d^2s}{dt^2}\right)(\mathbf{T} \times \mathbf{T}) + \kappa\left(\frac{ds}{dt}\right)^3(\mathbf{T} \times \mathbf{N}) \\ &= \kappa\left(\frac{ds}{dt}\right)^3\mathbf{B}\end{aligned}$$

From Section 13.2, Eqs. (3) and (4), $|\mathbf{v}|\mathbf{T} = (ds/dt)\mathbf{T}$.

$\mathbf{T} \times \mathbf{T} = \mathbf{0}$ and $\mathbf{T} \times \mathbf{N} = \mathbf{B}$

It follows that

$$|\mathbf{v} \times \mathbf{a}| = \kappa\left|\frac{ds}{dt}\right|^3|\mathbf{B}| = \kappa|\mathbf{v}|^3.$$

$\frac{ds}{dt} = |\mathbf{v}|$ and $|\mathbf{B}| = 1$

Solving for κ gives the following formula.

A Vector Formula for Curvature

$$\kappa = \frac{|\mathbf{v} \times \mathbf{a}|}{|\mathbf{v}|^3} \qquad (8)$$

Equation (8) calculates the curvature, a geometric property of the curve, from the velocity and acceleration of any representation of the curve in which $|\mathbf{v}|$ is different from zero. Take a moment to think about how remarkable this really is: From any formula for motion along a curve, no matter how variable the motion may be (as long as $\mathbf{v}$ is never zero), we can calculate a physical property of the curve that seems to have nothing to do with the way the curve is traversed.

The most widely used formula for torsion, derived in more advanced texts, is

$$\tau = \frac{\begin{vmatrix} \dot{x} & \dot{y} & \dot{z} \\ \ddot{x} & \ddot{y} & \ddot{z} \\ \dddot{x} & \dddot{y} & \dddot{z} \end{vmatrix}}{|\mathbf{v} \times \mathbf{a}|^2} \qquad (\text{if } \mathbf{v} \times \mathbf{a} \neq \mathbf{0}). \qquad (9)$$

This formula calculates the torsion directly from the derivatives of the component functions $x = f(t)$, $y = g(t)$, $z = h(t)$ that make up $\mathbf{r}$. The determinant's first row comes from $\mathbf{v}$, the second row from $\mathbf{a}$, and the third from $\dot{\mathbf{a}} = d\mathbf{a}/dt$.

Newton's Dot Notation for Derivatives

The dots in Equation (9) denote differentiation with respect to t, one derivative for each dot. Thus, $\dot{x}$ ("x dot") means dx/dt, $\ddot{x}$ ("x double dot") means d^2x/dt^2, and $\dddot{x}$ ("x triple dot") means d^3x/dt^3. Similarly, $\dot{y} = dy/dt$, and so on.

EXAMPLE 7 Finding Curvature and Torsion

Use Equations (8) and (9) to find κ and τ for the helix

$$\mathbf{r}(t) = (a \cos t)\mathbf{i} + (a \sin t)\mathbf{j} + bt\mathbf{k}, \qquad a, b \geq 0, \qquad a^2 + b^2 \neq 0.$$

SOLUTION

We calculate the curvature with Equation (8):

$$\begin{aligned}\mathbf{v} &= -(a \sin t)\mathbf{i} + (a \cos t)\mathbf{j} + b\mathbf{k}, \\ \mathbf{a} &= -(a \cos t)\mathbf{i} - (a \sin t)\mathbf{j},\end{aligned}$$

$$\mathbf{v} \times \mathbf{a} = \begin{vmatrix} \mathbf{i} & \mathbf{j} & \mathbf{k} \\ -a \sin t & a \cos t & b \\ -a \cos t & -a \sin t & 0 \end{vmatrix}$$

$$= (ab \sin t)\mathbf{i} - (ab \cos t)\mathbf{j} + a^2\mathbf{k},$$

$$\kappa = \frac{|\mathbf{v} \times \mathbf{a}|}{|\mathbf{v}|^3} = \frac{\sqrt{a^2b^2 + a^4}}{(a^2 + b^2)^{3/2}} = \frac{a\sqrt{a^2 + b^2}}{(a^2 + b^2)^{3/2}} = \frac{a}{a^2 + b^2}. \tag{10}$$

Notice that Equation (10) agrees with the result in Example 4, where we calculated the curvature directly from its definition.

To evaluate Equation (9) for the torsion, we find the entries in the determinant by differentiating $\mathbf{r}$ with respect to t. We already have $\mathbf{v}$ and $\mathbf{a}$, and

$$\dot{\mathbf{a}} = \frac{d\mathbf{a}}{dt} = (a \sin t)\mathbf{i} - (a \cos t)\mathbf{j}.$$

Hence,

$$\tau = \frac{\begin{vmatrix} \dot{x} & \dot{y} & \dot{z} \\ \ddot{x} & \ddot{y} & \ddot{z} \\ \dddot{x} & \dddot{y} & \dddot{z} \end{vmatrix}}{|\mathbf{v} \times \mathbf{a}|^2} = \frac{\begin{vmatrix} -a \sin t & a \cos t & b \\ -a \cos t & -a \sin t & 0 \\ a \sin t & -a \cos t & 0 \end{vmatrix}}{(a\sqrt{a^2 + b^2})^2}$$

Value of $|\mathbf{v} \times \mathbf{a}|$ from Eq. (10)

$$= \frac{b(a^2 \cos^2 t + a^2 \sin^2 t)}{a^2(a^2 + b^2)}$$

$$= \frac{b}{a^2 + b^2}. \tag{11}$$

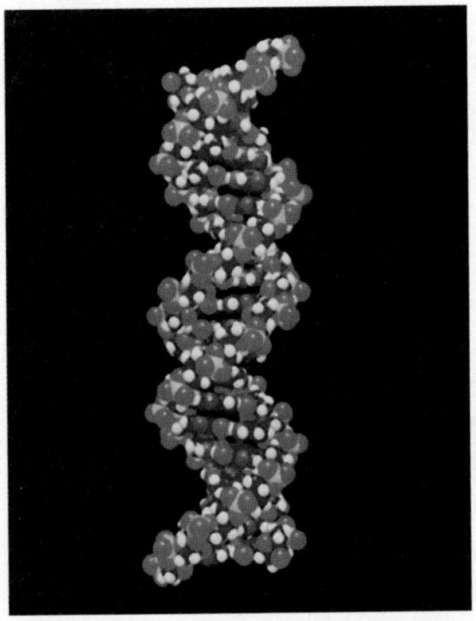

Figure 13.29 The helical shape of a DNA molecule is characterized by its constant curvature and torsion.

From Equation (11), we see that the torsion of a helix about a circular cylinder is constant. In fact, constant curvature and constant torsion characterize the helix among all curves in space.

The DNA molecule, the basic building block of life forms, is designed in the form of two helices winding around each other, a little like the rungs and sides of a twisted rope ladder (Figure 13.29). Not only is the space occupied by the DNA molecule very much smaller than it would be if it were unraveled, but when the molecule is damaged the imperfect piece can be snipped out by a kind of molecular scissors (because the curvature and torsion functions are constant) and the DNA made right again.

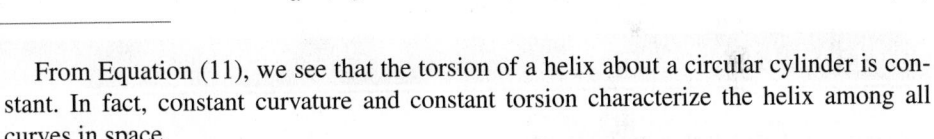

Formulas for Curves in Space

Unit tangent vector: $\mathbf{T} = \dfrac{\mathbf{v}}{|\mathbf{v}|}$

Principal unit normal vector: $\mathbf{N} = \dfrac{d\mathbf{T}/dt}{|d\mathbf{T}/dt|}$

Binormal vector: $\mathbf{B} = \mathbf{T} \times \mathbf{N}$

continued

Curvature:
$$\kappa = \left|\frac{d\mathbf{T}}{ds}\right| = \frac{|\mathbf{v} \times \mathbf{a}|}{|\mathbf{v}|^3}$$

Torsion:
$$\tau = -\frac{d\mathbf{B}}{ds} \cdot \mathbf{N} = \frac{\begin{vmatrix} \dot{x} & \dot{y} & \dot{z} \\ \ddot{x} & \ddot{y} & \ddot{z} \\ \dddot{x} & \dddot{y} & \dddot{z} \end{vmatrix}}{|\mathbf{v} \times \mathbf{a}|^2}$$

Tangential and normal scalar components of acceleration:
$$\mathbf{a} = a_{\mathrm{T}}\mathbf{T} + a_{\mathrm{N}}\mathbf{N}$$
$$a_{\mathrm{T}} = \frac{d}{dt}|\mathbf{v}|$$
$$a_{\mathrm{N}} = \kappa|\mathbf{v}|^2 = \sqrt{|\mathbf{a}|^2 - a_{\mathrm{T}}^2}$$

Quick Review 13.3

In Exercises 1–5, let $\mathbf{u} = \frac{\mathbf{i}+\mathbf{j}}{\sqrt{2}}$, $\mathbf{v} = \frac{\mathbf{i}-\mathbf{j}}{\sqrt{2}}$, and $\mathbf{w} = 5\mathbf{i} - \mathbf{j}$.

1. Show that $\mathbf{u} \cdot \mathbf{v} = 0$.
2. Show that $\mathbf{w} = 2\sqrt{2}\mathbf{u} + 3\sqrt{2}\mathbf{v}$.
3. Show that $\mathbf{w} \cdot \mathbf{u} = 2\sqrt{2}$.
4. Show that $\mathbf{w} \cdot \mathbf{v} = 3\sqrt{2}$.
5. If $\mathbf{w} = a\mathbf{u} + b\mathbf{v}$, show that $a = \mathbf{w} \cdot \mathbf{u}$ and $b = \mathbf{w} \cdot \mathbf{v}$.

In Exercises 6–8, $\mathbf{r}(t) = (\sin t)\mathbf{i} + t\mathbf{j}$ is the position vector of a particle in the plane at time t.

6. Find $\mathbf{v}$.
7. Find $\mathbf{a}$.
8. Find the times t when $\mathbf{v} \cdot \mathbf{a} = 0$ and neither $\mathbf{v}$ nor $\mathbf{a}$ are zero. What are $\mathbf{v}$ and $\mathbf{a}$ and for these values of t?

In Exercises 9 and 10, use determinants to find $\mathbf{u} \times \mathbf{v}$.

9. $\mathbf{u} = 2\mathbf{i} - 3\mathbf{j} - \mathbf{k}$, $\mathbf{v} = -2\mathbf{i} + 7\mathbf{j} - 3\mathbf{k}$
10. $\mathbf{u} = -\mathbf{i} + \mathbf{k}$, $\mathbf{v} = 3\mathbf{j} - 4\mathbf{k}$

Section 13.3 Exercises

In Exercises 1–4, find **T**, **N**, and κ for the plane curve.

1. $\mathbf{r}(t) = t\mathbf{i} + (\ln \cos t)\mathbf{j}$, $\quad -\pi/2 < t < \pi/2$
2. $\mathbf{r}(t) = (\ln \sec t)\mathbf{i} + t\mathbf{j}$, $\quad -\pi/2 < t < \pi/2$
3. $\mathbf{r}(t) = (2t + 3)\mathbf{i} + (5 - t^2)\mathbf{j}$
4. $\mathbf{r}(t) = (\cos t + t \sin t)\mathbf{i} + (\sin t - t \cos t)$, $\quad t > 0$

In Exercises 5 and 6, write **a** in the form $\mathbf{a} = a_{\mathrm{T}}\mathbf{T} + a_{\mathrm{N}}\mathbf{N}$ without finding **T** and **N**.

5. $\mathbf{r}(t) = (2t + 3)\mathbf{i} + (t^2 - 1)\mathbf{j}$
6. $\mathbf{r}(t) = \ln(t^2 + 1)\mathbf{i} + (t - 2\tan^{-1} t)\mathbf{j}$

Explorations

7. ***A Formula for the Curvature of the Graph of a Function in the xy-Plane*** The graph $y = f(x)$ in the xy-plane automatically has the parametrization $x = x$, $y = f(x)$, and the vector formula $\mathbf{r}(x) = x\mathbf{i} + f(x)\mathbf{j}$.

   (a) Use this formula to show that if f is a twice differentiable function of x, then
   $$\kappa(x) = \frac{|f''(x)|}{[1 + (f'(x))^2]^{3/2}}.$$

   (b) Use the formula for κ in (a) to find the curvature of $y = \ln(\cos x)$, $-\pi/2 < x < \pi/2$. Compare your answer with the answer in Exercise 1.

   (c) Show that the curvature is zero at a point of inflection.

8. ***A Formula for the Curvature of a Parametrized Plane Curve*** Let $\mathbf{r}(t) = f(t)\mathbf{i} + g(t)\mathbf{j}$ be a smooth curve defined by the twice-differentiable functions $x = f(t)$ and $y = g(t)$.

   (a) Show that the curvature of **r** is given by the formula
   $$\kappa = \frac{|\dot{x}\ddot{y} - \dot{y}\ddot{x}|}{(\dot{x}^2 + \dot{y}^2)^{3/2}}.$$

   (b) Apply the formula in (a) to find the curvature of
   $$\mathbf{r}(t) = t\mathbf{i} + (\ln \sin t)\mathbf{j},\ 0 < t < \pi.$$

9. ***Normals to Plane Curves***

   (a) Show that $\mathbf{n}(t) = -g'(t)\mathbf{i} + f'(t)\mathbf{j}$ and $-\mathbf{n}(t) = g'(t)\mathbf{i} - f'(t)\mathbf{j}$ are both normal to the curve $\mathbf{r}(t) = f(t)\mathbf{i} + g(t)\mathbf{j}$ at the point $(f(t), g(t))$.

   To obtain **N** for a particular plane curve, we can choose the one of **n** or $-\mathbf{n}$ from part (a) that points toward the concave side of the curve, and make it into a unit vector. (See Figure 13.21.) Apply this method to find **N** for the following curves.

(b) $\mathbf{r}(t) = t\mathbf{i} + e^{2t}\mathbf{j}$

(c) $\mathbf{r}(t) = \sqrt{4 - t^2}\,\mathbf{i} + t\mathbf{j},\ -2 \le t \le 2$

10. ***(Continuation of Exercise 9)***

(a) Use the method of Exercise 9 to find **N** for the curve $\mathbf{r}(t) = t\mathbf{i} + (1/3)t^3\mathbf{j}$ when $t < 0$; when $t > 0$.

(b) Writing to Learn Calculate

$$\mathbf{N} = \frac{d\mathbf{T}/dt}{|d\mathbf{T}/dt|}, \qquad t \neq 0,$$

for the curve in (a). Does **N** exist at $t = 0$? Graph the curve and explain what happens to **N** as t passes from negative to positive values.

In Exercises 11–16, find **T**, **N**, **B**, κ, and τ for the space curve.

11. $\mathbf{r}(t) = (3 \sin t)\mathbf{i} + (3 \cos t)\mathbf{j} + 4t\mathbf{k}$

12. $\mathbf{r}(t) = (\cos t + t \sin t)\mathbf{i} + (\sin t - t \cos t)\mathbf{j} + 3\mathbf{k}, \quad t > 0$

13. $\mathbf{r}(t) = (e^t \cos t)\mathbf{i} + (e^t \sin t)\mathbf{j} + 2\mathbf{k}$

14. $\mathbf{r}(t) = (6 \sin 2t)\mathbf{i} + (6 \cos 2t)\mathbf{j} + 5t\mathbf{k}$

15. $\mathbf{r}(t) = (t^3/3)\mathbf{i} + (t^2/2)\mathbf{j}, \qquad t > 0$

16. $\mathbf{r}(t) = (\cos^3 t)\mathbf{i} + (\sin^3 t)\mathbf{j}, \quad 0 < t < \pi/2$

In Exercises 17 and 18, write **a** in the form $\mathbf{a} = a_T\mathbf{T} + a_N\mathbf{N}$ without finding **T** and **N**.

17. $\mathbf{r}(t) = (a \cos t)\mathbf{i} + (a \sin t)\mathbf{j} + bt\mathbf{k}$

18. $\mathbf{r}(t) = (1 + 3t)\mathbf{i} + (t - 2)\mathbf{j} - 3t\mathbf{k}$

In Exercises 19–22, write **a** in the form $\mathbf{a} = a_T\mathbf{T} + a_N\mathbf{N}$ at the given value of t without finding **T** and **N**.

19. $\mathbf{r}(t) = (t + 1)\mathbf{i} + 2t\mathbf{j} + t^2\mathbf{k}, \qquad t = 1$

20. $\mathbf{r}(t) = (t \cos t)\mathbf{i} + (t \sin t)\mathbf{j} + t^2\mathbf{k}, \qquad t = 0$

21. $\mathbf{r}(t) = t^2\,\mathbf{i} + \left(t + \frac{1}{3}t^3\right)\mathbf{j} + \left(t - \frac{1}{3}t^3\right)\mathbf{k}, \qquad t = 0$

22. $\mathbf{r}(t) = (e^t \cos t)\mathbf{i} + (e^t \sin t)\mathbf{j} + \sqrt{2}e^t\mathbf{k}, \qquad t = 0$

In Exercises 23 and 24, find **r**, **T**, **N**, and **B** at the given value of t. Then find equations for the osculating, normal, and rectifying planes at that value of t (see Figure 13.25 for definitions).

23. $\mathbf{r}(t) = (\cos t)\mathbf{i} + (\sin t)\mathbf{j} - \mathbf{k}, \qquad t = \pi/4$

24. $\mathbf{r}(t) = (\cos t)\mathbf{i} + (\sin t)\mathbf{j} + t\mathbf{k}, \qquad t = 0$

25. Writing to Learn The speedometer on your car reads a steady 35 mph. Could you be accelerating? Explain.

26. Writing to Learn Can anything be said about the acceleration of a particle that is moving at a constant speed? Give reasons for your answer.

27. Writing to Learn Can anything be said about the speed of a particle whose acceleration is always orthogonal to its velocity? Give reasons for your answer.

28. ***Motion Along a Parabola*** An object of mass m travels along the parabola $y = x^2$ with a constant speed of 10 units/sec. What is the force on the object due to its acceleration at (0, 0)? At $(2^{1/2}, 2)$? Write your answers in terms of **i** and **j**. (Remember Newton's law, $\mathbf{F} = m\mathbf{a}$.)

29. ***Curvature in Physics*** **Writing to Learn** The following is a quotation from an article in *The American Mathematical Monthly,* titled "Curvature in the Eighties" by Robert Osserman (October 1990, page 731):

> Curvature also plays a key role in physics. The magnitude of a force required to move an object at constant speed along a curved path is, according to Newton's laws, a constant multiple of the curvature of the trajectories.

Explain mathematically why the second sentence of the quotation is true.

30. ***What happens if*** $a_N = 0$**?** Show that a moving particle will move in a straight line if the normal component of its acceleration is zero.

31. ***Curvature Extremes*** Show that the parabola $y = ax^2$, $a \neq 0$, has its largest curvature at its vertex and has no minimum curvature. (*Note*: Since the curvature of a curve remains the same if the curve is translated or rotated, this result is true for any parabola.)

32. ***Curvature Extremes*** Show that the ellipse $x = a \cos t$, $y = b \sin t$, $a > b > 0$, has its largest curvature on its major axis and its smallest curvature on its minor axis. (As in Exercise 31, the same is true for any ellipse.)

33. ***Maximizing the Curvature of a Helix*** In Example 4, we found the curvature of the helix $\mathbf{r}(t) = (a \cos t)\mathbf{i} + (a \sin t)\mathbf{j} + bt\mathbf{k}$ $(a, b \ge 0)$ to be $\kappa = a/(a^2 + b^2)$. What is the largest value κ can have for a given value of b? Give reasons for your answer.

34. ***A Useful Shortcut to Curvature*** If you already know $|a_N|$ and $|\mathbf{v}|$, then the formula $a_N = \kappa|\mathbf{v}|^2$ gives a convenient way to find the curvature. Use it to find the curvature and radius of curvature of the curve $\mathbf{r}(t) = (\cos t + t \sin t)\mathbf{i} + (\sin t - t \cos t)\mathbf{j}$, $t > 0$. (Take a_N and $|\mathbf{v}|$ from Example 6.)

35. ***Curvature and Torsion for a Line*** Show that κ and τ are both zero for the line $\mathbf{r}(t) = (x_0 + At)\mathbf{i} + (y_0 + Bt)\mathbf{j} + (z_0 + Ct)\mathbf{k}$.

36. ***Total Curvature*** We find the **total curvature** of the portion of a smooth curve that runs from $s = s_0$ to $s = s_1 > s_0$ by integrating κ from s_0 to s_1. If the curve has some other parameter, say t, then the total curvature is

$$K = \int_{s_0}^{s_1} \kappa\, ds = \int_{t_0}^{t_1} \kappa \frac{ds}{dt}\, dt = \int_{t_0}^{t_1} \kappa|\mathbf{v}|\, dt,$$

where t_0 and t_1 correspond to s_0 and s_1. Find the total curvature of the portion on the helix $\mathbf{r}(t) = (3 \cos t)\mathbf{i} + (3 \sin t)\mathbf{j} + t\mathbf{k}$, $0 \le t \le 4\pi$.

37. ***(Continuation of Exercise 36)*** Find the total curvatures of the following curves.

(a) The involute of the unit circle:
$\mathbf{r}(t) = (\cos t + t \sin t)\mathbf{i} + (\sin t - t \cos t)\mathbf{j}$, $a \le t \le b$ $(a > 0)$. (Exercise 34 gives a convenient way to find κ. Use values from Example 6.)

(b) The parabola $y = x^2$, $-\infty < x < \infty$

38. ***Circle of Curvature***

(a) Find an equation for the circle of curvature of the curve $\mathbf{r}(t) = t\mathbf{i} + (\sin t)\mathbf{j}$ at the point $(\pi/2, 1)$. (The curve parametrizes the graph of $y = \sin x$ in the xy-plane.)

(b) Find an equation for the circle of curvature of the curve $\mathbf{r}(t) = (2 \ln t)\mathbf{i} - [t + (1/t)]\mathbf{j}$, $e^{-2} \le t \le e^2$, at the point $(0, -2)$, where $t = 1$.

39. Writing to Learn What can be said about the torsion of a (sufficiently differentiable) plane curve $\mathbf{r}(t) = f(t)\mathbf{i} + g(t)\mathbf{j}$? Give reasons for your answer.

40. *The Torsion of a Helix* In Example 7, we found the torsion of the helix $\mathbf{r}(t) = (a \cos t)\mathbf{i} + (a \sin t)\mathbf{j} + bt\mathbf{k}$, $a, b \ge 0$ to be $\tau = b/(a^2 + b^2)$. What is the largest value τ can have for a given value of a? Give reasons for your answer.

Explorations

Plotting Curvature Functions

In Exercises 41–44, find the curvature of the plane curve $y = f(x)$ using the formula

$$\kappa(x) = \frac{|f''(x)|}{[1 + (f'(x))^2]^{3/2}}$$

derived in Exercise 7. Then graph $f(x)$ together with $\kappa(x)$ over the given interval. You will find some surprises.

41. $y = x^2$, $\quad -2 \le x \le 2$

42. $y = x^4/4$, $\quad -2 \le x \le 2$

43. $y = \sin x$, $\quad 0 \le x \le 2\pi$

44. $y = e^x$, $\quad -1 \le x \le 2$

Extending the Ideas

45. *Differentiable Curves with Zero Torsion Lie in Planes* That a sufficiently differentiable curve with zero torsion lies in a plane is a special case of the fact that a particle whose velocity remains perpendicular to a fixed vector **C** moves in a plane perpendicular to **C**. This, in turn, can be viewed as the solution of the following problem in calculus.

Suppose $\mathbf{r}(t) = f(t)\mathbf{i} + g(t)\mathbf{j} + h(t)\mathbf{k}$ is twice differentiable for all t in an interval $[a, b]$, $\mathbf{r} = \mathbf{0}$ when $t = a$, and $\mathbf{v} \cdot \mathbf{k} = 0$ for all t in $[a, b]$. Then $h(t) = 0$ for all t in $[a, b]$.

Solve this problem. (*Hint*: Start with $\mathbf{a} = d^2\mathbf{r}/dt^2$ and apply the initial conditions in reverse order.)

46. *A Formula That Calculates τ from* B *and* v If we start with the definition $\tau = -(d\mathbf{B}/ds) \cdot \mathbf{N}$ and apply the Chain Rule to rewrite $d\mathbf{B}/ds$ as

$$\frac{d\mathbf{B}}{ds} = \frac{d\mathbf{B}}{dt}\frac{dt}{ds} = \frac{d\mathbf{B}}{dt}\frac{1}{|\mathbf{v}|},$$

we arrive at the formula

$$\tau = -\frac{1}{|\mathbf{v}|}\left(\frac{d\mathbf{B}}{dt} \cdot \mathbf{N}\right).$$

The advantage of this formula over Equation (9) is that it is easier to derive and state. The disadvantage is that it can take a lot of work to evaluate with pencil and paper. Use the new formula to find the torsion of the helix in Example 7.

CAS Explorations

Osculating Circles In Exercises 47–50, you will explore the osculating circle at a point P on a plane curve where $\kappa \ne 0$. Perform the following steps.

(a) Plot the plane curve over the specified interval to see what it looks like.

(b) Calculate the curvature κ of the curve at the given value t_0 using the appropriate formula from Exercise 8.

(c) Find the unit normal vector **N** at t_0. Notice that the signs of the components of **N** depend on whether the unit tangent vector **T** is turning clockwise or counterclockwise at $t = t_0$. (See Exercise 9.)

(d) If $\mathbf{C} = a\mathbf{i} + b\mathbf{j}$ is the vector from the origin to the center (a, b) of the osculating circle, find the center **C** from the vector equation

$$\mathbf{C} = \mathbf{r}(t_0) + \frac{1}{\kappa(t_0)}\mathbf{N}(t_0).$$

The point $P(x_0, y_0)$ on the curve is given by the position vector $\mathbf{r}(t_0)$.

(e) Graph the equation $(x - a)^2 + (y - b)^2 = 1/\kappa^2$ of the osculating circle. Then graph the curve and osculating circle together. You may need to experiment with the size of the viewing window, but be sure it is square.

47. $\mathbf{r}(t) = (3 \cos t)\mathbf{i} + (5 \sin t)\mathbf{j}$, $\quad 0 \le t \le 2\pi$, $\quad t_0 = \pi/4$

48. $\mathbf{r}(t) = (\cos^3 t)\mathbf{i} + (\sin^3 t)\mathbf{j}$, $\quad 0 \le t \le 2\pi$, $\quad t_0 = \pi/4$

49. $\mathbf{r}(t) = t^2\mathbf{i} + (t^3 - 3t)\mathbf{j}$, $\quad -4 \le t \le 4$, $\quad t_0 = 3/5$

50. $\mathbf{r}(t) = (t^3 - 2t^2 - t)\mathbf{i} + \dfrac{3t}{\sqrt{1 + t^2}}\mathbf{j}$, $\quad -2 \le t \le 5$, $t_0 = 1$

13.4 Planetary Motion and Satellites

What you'll learn about

- Motion in Polar and Cylindrical Coordinates
- Planets Move in Planes
- Coordinates and Initial Conditions
- Kepler's First Law (The Conic Section Law)
- Kepler's Second Law (The Equal Area Law)
- Proof of Kepler's First Law
- Kepler's Third Law (The Time–Distance Law)
- Orbit Data

Motion in Polar and Cylindrical Coordinates

When a particle moves along a curve in the polar coordinate plane, we express its position, velocity, and acceleration in terms of the moving unit vectors

$$\mathbf{u}_r = (\cos\theta)\mathbf{i} + (\sin\theta)\mathbf{j}, \qquad \mathbf{u}_\theta = -(\sin\theta)\mathbf{i} + (\cos\theta)\mathbf{j}, \tag{1}$$

shown in Figure 13.30. The vector $\mathbf{u}_r$ points along the position vector $\overrightarrow{OP}$, so $\mathbf{r} = r\mathbf{u}_r$. The vector $\mathbf{u}_\theta$ orthogonal to $\mathbf{u}_r$ points in the direction of increasing θ.

We find from Equations (1) that

$$\frac{d\mathbf{u}_r}{d\theta} = -(\sin\theta)\mathbf{i} + (\cos\theta)\mathbf{j} = \mathbf{u}_\theta,$$

$$\frac{d\mathbf{u}_r}{d\theta} = -(\cos\theta)\mathbf{i} - (\sin\theta)\mathbf{j} = -\mathbf{u}_r. \tag{2}$$

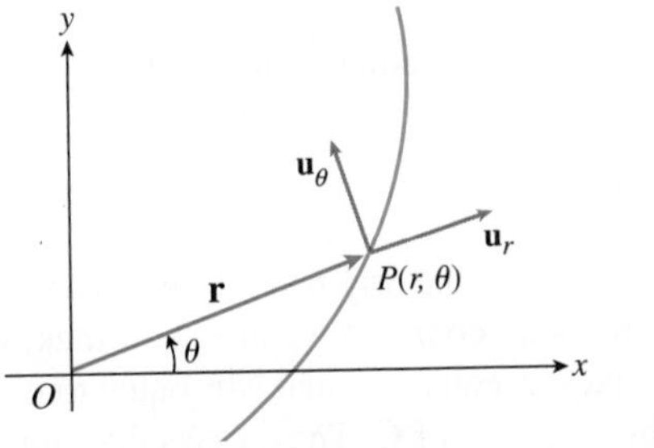

Figure 13.30 The length of $\mathbf{r}$ is the positive polar coordinate r of the point P. Thus, $\mathbf{u}_r$, which is $\mathbf{r}/|r|$, is also $\mathbf{r}/r$.

As in the previous section, we use Newton's dot notation for time derivatives to keep the formulas as simple as we can: $\dot{\mathbf{u}}_r$ means $d\mathbf{u}_r/dt$, $\dot{\theta}$ means $d\theta/dt$, and so on.

When we differentiate $\mathbf{u}_r$ and $\mathbf{u}_\theta$ with respect to t to find how they change with time, the Chain Rule gives

$$\dot{\mathbf{u}}_r = \frac{d\mathbf{u}_r}{d\theta}\dot{\theta} = \dot{\theta}\mathbf{u}_\theta, \qquad \dot{\mathbf{u}}_\theta = \frac{d\mathbf{u}_\theta}{d\theta}\dot{\theta} = -\dot{\theta}\mathbf{u}_r. \tag{3}$$

Hence,

$$\mathbf{v} = \dot{\mathbf{r}} = \frac{d}{dt}(r\mathbf{u}_r) = \dot{r}\mathbf{u}_r + r\dot{\mathbf{u}}_r = \dot{r}\mathbf{u}_r + r\dot{\theta}\mathbf{u}_\theta. \tag{4}$$

See Figure 13.31.

The acceleration is

$$\mathbf{a} = \dot{\mathbf{v}} = (\ddot{r}\mathbf{u}_r + \dot{r}\dot{\mathbf{u}}_r) + (\dot{r}\dot{\theta}\mathbf{u}_\theta + r\ddot{\theta}\mathbf{u}_\theta + r\dot{\theta}\dot{\mathbf{u}}_\theta). \tag{5}$$

When Equations (3) are used to evaluate $\dot{\mathbf{u}}_r$ and $\dot{\mathbf{u}}_\theta$ and the components are separated, the equation for acceleration becomes

$$\mathbf{a} = (\ddot{r} - r\dot{\theta}^2)\mathbf{u}_r + (r\ddot{\theta} + 2\dot{r}\dot{\theta})\mathbf{u}_\theta. \tag{6}$$

To extend these equations of motion to space, we add $z\mathbf{k}$ to the right-hand side of the equation $\mathbf{r} = r\mathbf{u}_r$. Then, in cylindrical coordinates,

$$\begin{aligned}\mathbf{r} &= r\mathbf{u}_r + z\mathbf{k}\\ \mathbf{v} &= \dot{r}\mathbf{u}_r + r\dot{\theta}\mathbf{u}_\theta + \dot{z}\mathbf{k}\\ \mathbf{a} &= (\ddot{r} - r\dot{\theta}^2)\mathbf{u}_r + (r\ddot{\theta} + 2\dot{r}\dot{\theta})\mathbf{u}_\theta + \ddot{z}\mathbf{k}.\end{aligned} \tag{7}$$

The vectors $\mathbf{u}_r$, $\mathbf{u}_\theta$, and $\mathbf{k}$ make a right-handed frame (Figure 13.32) in which

$$\mathbf{u}_r \times \mathbf{u}_\theta = \mathbf{k}, \qquad \mathbf{u}_\theta \times \mathbf{k} = \mathbf{u}_r, \qquad \mathbf{k} \times \mathbf{u}_r = \mathbf{u}_\theta. \tag{8}$$

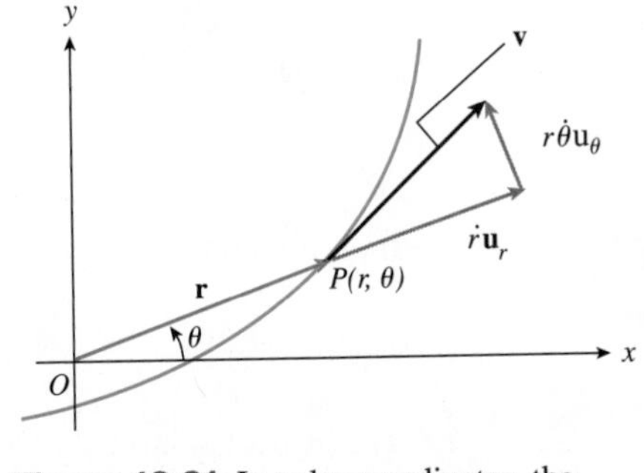

Figure 13.31 In polar coordinates, the velocity vector is $\mathbf{v} = \dot{r}\mathbf{u}_r + r\dot{\theta}\mathbf{u}_\theta$.

Planets Move in Planes

Newton's Law of Gravitation says that if $\mathbf{r}$ is the radius vector from the center of a sun of mass M to the center of a planet of mass m, then the force $\mathbf{F}$ of the gravitational attraction between the planet and sun is

$$\mathbf{F} = -\frac{GmM}{|\mathbf{r}|^2}\frac{\mathbf{r}}{|\mathbf{r}|} \tag{9}$$

Notice that $|\mathbf{r}| \neq r$ if $z \neq 0$.

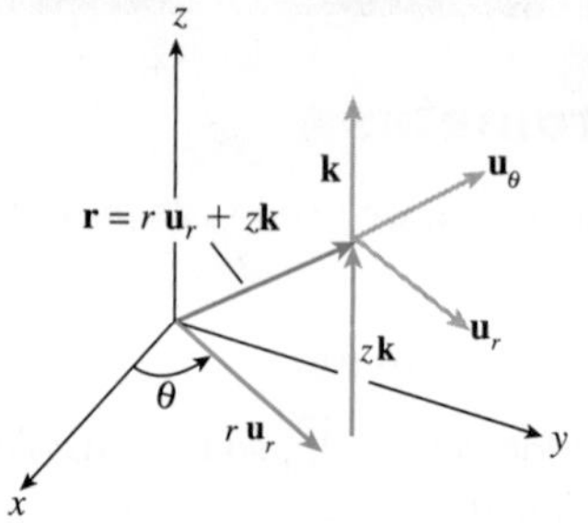

Figure 13.32 Position vector and basic unit vectors in cylindrical coordinates.

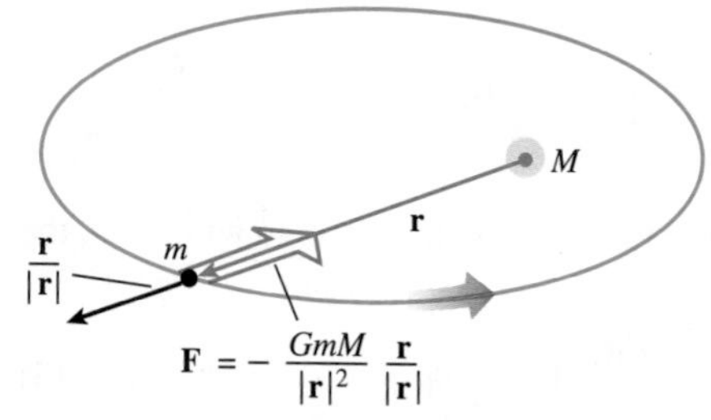

Figure 13.33 The force of gravity is directed along the line joining the centers of mass.

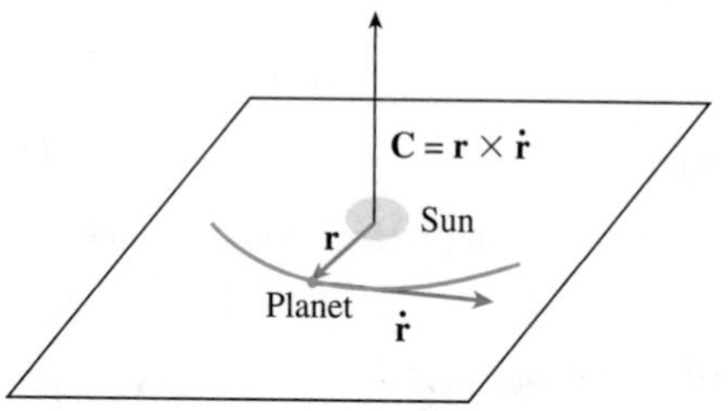

Figure 13.34 A planet that obeys Newton's laws of gravitation and motion travels in the plane through its sun's center of mass perpendicular to $\mathbf{C} = \mathbf{r} \times \dot{\mathbf{r}}$.

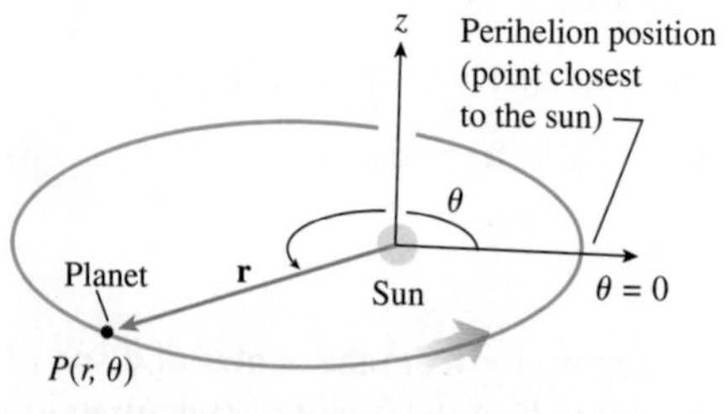

Figure 13.35 The coordinate system for planetary motion. The motion is counterclockwise when viewed from above, as it is here, and $\dot{\theta} > 0$.

(Figure 13.33). The number G is the **universal gravitational constant**. If we measure mass in kilograms, force in newtons, and distance in meters, G is about $6.6720 \times 10^{-11}\ \text{Nm}^2\text{kg}^{-2}$.

Combining Equation (9) with Newton's second law, $\mathbf{F} = m\ddot{\mathbf{r}}$, for the force acting on the planet gives

$$m\ddot{\mathbf{r}} = -\frac{GmM}{|\mathbf{r}|^2}\frac{\mathbf{r}}{|\mathbf{r}|},$$

$$\ddot{\mathbf{r}} = -\frac{GM}{|\mathbf{r}|^2}\frac{\mathbf{r}}{|\mathbf{r}|}. \tag{10}$$

The planet is accelerated toward its sun's center at all times.

Equation (10) says that $\ddot{\mathbf{r}}$ is a scalar multiple of $\mathbf{r}$ at every value of t, so that

$$\mathbf{r} \times \ddot{\mathbf{r}} = \mathbf{0}. \tag{11}$$

A routine calculation shows $\mathbf{r} \times \ddot{\mathbf{r}}$ to be the derivative of $\mathbf{r} \times \dot{\mathbf{r}}$:

$$\frac{d}{dt}(\mathbf{r} \times \dot{\mathbf{r}}) = \underbrace{\dot{\mathbf{r}} \times \dot{\mathbf{r}}}_{\mathbf{0}} + \mathbf{r} \times \ddot{\mathbf{r}} = \mathbf{r} \times \ddot{\mathbf{r}}. \tag{12}$$

Hence Equation (11) is equivalent to

$$\frac{d}{dt}(\mathbf{r} \times \dot{\mathbf{r}}) = \mathbf{0}, \tag{13}$$

which integrates to

$$\mathbf{r} \times \dot{\mathbf{r}} = \mathbf{C} \tag{14}$$

for some constant $\mathbf{C}$.

Equation (14) tells us that $\mathbf{r}$ and $\dot{\mathbf{r}}$ always lie in a plane perpendicular to $\mathbf{C}$. Hence, the planet moves in a fixed plane through the center of its sun (Figure 13.34).

Coordinates and Initial Conditions

We now introduce cylindrical coordinates in a way that places the origin at the sun's center of mass and makes the plane of the planet's motion the polar coordinate plane. This makes $\mathbf{r}$ the planet's polar coordinate position vector and makes $|\mathbf{r}|$ equal to r and $\mathbf{r}/|\mathbf{r}|$ equal to $\mathbf{u}_r$. We also position the z-axis in a way that makes $\mathbf{k}$ the direction of $\mathbf{C}$. Thus, $\mathbf{k}$ has the same right-hand relation to $\mathbf{r} \times \dot{\mathbf{r}}$ that $\mathbf{C}$ does, and the planet's motion is counterclockwise when viewed from the positive z-axis. This makes θ increase with t, so that $\theta > 0$ for all t. Finally, we rotate the polar coordinate plane about the z-axis, if necessary, to make the initial ray coincide with the direction $\mathbf{r}$ has when the planet is closest to the sun. This runs the initial ray through the planet's **perihelion position** (Figure 13.35).

If we measure time so that $t = 0$ at perihelion, we have the following initial conditions for the planet's motion.

1. $r = r_0$, the minimum radius, when $t = 0$.
2. $\dot{r} = 0$ when $t = 0$ (because r has a minimum value then).
3. $\theta = 0$ when $t = 0$.
4. $|\mathbf{v}| = v_0$ when $t = 0$.

Since

$$\begin{aligned}
v_0 &= |\mathbf{v}|_{t=0} \\
&= |\dot{r}\mathbf{u}_r + r\dot{\theta}\mathbf{u}_\theta|_{t=0} && \text{Eq. (4)} \\
&= |r\dot{\theta}\mathbf{u}_\theta|_{t=0} && \dot{r} = 0 \text{ when } t = 0 \\
&= (|r\dot{\theta}||\mathbf{u}_\theta|)_{t=0} \\
&= |r\dot{\theta}|_{t=0} && |\mathbf{u}_\theta| = 1 \\
&= (r\dot{\theta})_{t=0} && r \text{ and } \dot{\theta} \text{ both positive}
\end{aligned}$$

we also know that

5. $r\dot{\theta} = v_0$ when $t = 0$.

Kepler's First Law (The Conic Section Law)

Kepler's first law says that a planet's path is a conic section with the sun at one focus. The eccentricity of the conic is

$$e = \frac{r_0 v_0^{\,2}}{GM} - 1 \tag{15}$$

and the polar equation is

$$r = \frac{(1 + e)r_0}{1 + e\cos\theta} \tag{16}$$

(Appendix A5, Section 4).

The derivation uses Kepler's second law, so we will state and prove the second law before proving the first law.

Kepler's Second Law (The Equal Area Law)

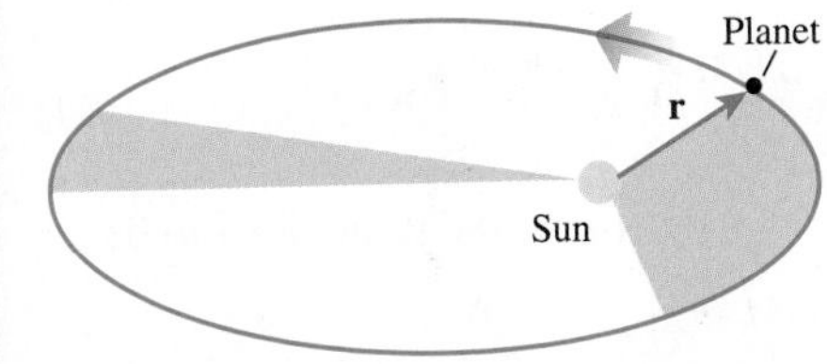

Figure 13.36 The line joining a planet to its sun sweeps over equal areas in equal times.

Kepler's second law says that the radius vector from the sun to a planet (the vector $\mathbf{r}$ in our model) sweeps out equal areas in equal times (Figure 13.36). To derive the law, we use Equation (4) to evaluate the cross product $\mathbf{C} = \mathbf{r} \times \dot{\mathbf{r}}$ from Equation (14):

$$\begin{aligned}
\mathbf{C} &= \mathbf{r} \times \dot{\mathbf{r}} = \mathbf{r} \times \mathbf{v} \\
&= r\mathbf{u}_r \times (\dot{r}\mathbf{u}_r + r\dot{\theta}\mathbf{u}_\theta) && \text{Eq. (4)} \\
&= r\dot{r}\underbrace{(\mathbf{u}_r \times \mathbf{u}_r)}_{\mathbf{0}} + r(r\dot{\theta})\underbrace{(\mathbf{u}_r \times \mathbf{u}_\theta)}_{\mathbf{k}} \\
&= r(r\dot{\theta})\mathbf{k}.
\end{aligned} \tag{17}$$

Setting t equal to zero shows that

$$\mathbf{C} = [r(r\dot{\theta})]_{t=0}\,\mathbf{k} = r_0 v_0 \mathbf{k}. \qquad \text{Init. cond. 5} \tag{18}$$

Substituting this value for $\mathbf{C}$ in Equation (17) gives

$$r_0 v_0 \mathbf{k} = r^2\dot{\theta}\mathbf{k} \qquad \text{or} \qquad r^2\dot{\theta} = r_0 v_0. \tag{19}$$

This is where the area comes in. The area differential in polar coordinates is

$$dA = \frac{1}{2} r^2\, d\theta$$

Accordingly, dA/dt has the constant value

$$\frac{dA}{dt} = \frac{1}{2} r^2 \dot{\theta} = \frac{1}{2} r_0 v_0, \qquad \text{Eq. (19)} \tag{20}$$

which is Kepler's second law.

For Earth, r_0 is about 150,000,000 km, v_0 is about 30 km/sec, and dA/dt is about 2,250,000,000 km^2/sec. Every time your heart beats, Earth advances 30 km along its orbit and the radius joining Earth to the sun sweeps out 2,250,000,000 km^2 of area.

The German astronomer, mathematician, and physicist Johannes Kepler (1571–1630) was the first, and until Descartes, the only scientist to demand physical (as opposed to theological) explanations of celestial phenomena. His three laws of motion, the results of a lifetime of work, changed the course of astronomy forever and played a crucial role in the development of Newton's physics.

Proof of Kepler's First Law

To prove that a planet moves along a conic section with one focus at its sun, we need to express the planet's radius r as a function of θ. This requires a long sequence of calculations and some substitutions that are not altogether obvious.

We begin with the equation that comes from equating the coefficients of $\mathbf{u}_r = \mathbf{r}/|\mathbf{r}|$ in Equations (6) and (10):

$$\ddot{r} - r\dot{\theta}^2 = -\frac{GM}{r^2}. \tag{21}$$

We eliminate θ temporarily by replacing it with $r_0 v_0 / r^2$ from Equation (19) and rearrange the resulting equation to get

$$\ddot{r} = \frac{r_0^2 v_0^2}{r^3} - \frac{GM}{r^2}. \tag{22}$$

We change this into a first-order equation by a change of variable. With

$$p = \frac{dr}{dt}, \quad \frac{d^2 r}{dt^2} = \frac{dp}{dt} = \frac{dp}{dr}\frac{dr}{dt} = p\frac{dp}{dr}, \qquad \text{Chain Rule}$$

Equation (22) becomes

$$p\frac{dp}{dr} = \frac{r_0^2 v_0^2}{r^3} - \frac{GM}{r^2}. \tag{23}$$

Multiplying through by 2 and integrating with respect to r gives

$$p^2 = (\dot{r})^2 = -\frac{r_0^2 v_0^2}{r^2} + \frac{2GM}{r} + C_1. \tag{24}$$

The initial conditions that $r = r_0$ and $\dot{r} = 0$ when $t = 0$ determine the value of C_1 to be

$$C_1 = v_0^2 - \frac{2GM}{r_0}.$$

Accordingly, Equation (24), after a suitable rearrangement, becomes

$$\dot{r}^2 = v_0^2\left(1 - \frac{r_0}{r^2}\right) + 2GM\left(\frac{1}{r} - \frac{1}{r_0}\right). \tag{25}$$

The effect of going from Equation (21) to Equation (25) has been to replace a second-order differential equation in r by a first-order differential equation in r. Our goal is still to express r in terms of θ, so we now bring θ back into the picture. To accomplish this, we divide both sides of Equation (25) by the squares of the corresponding sides of Equation (19), $r^2\dot{\theta} = r_0 v_0$, and use the fact that $\dot{r}/\dot{\theta} = (dr/dt)/(d\theta/dt) = dr/d\theta$ to get

$$\begin{aligned} \frac{1}{r^4}\left(\frac{dr}{d\theta}\right)^2 &= \frac{1}{r_0^2} - \frac{1}{r^2} + \frac{2GM}{r_0^2 v_0^2}\left(\frac{1}{r} - \frac{1}{r_0}\right) \qquad (26) \\ &= \frac{1}{r_0^2} - \frac{1}{r^2} + 2h\left(\frac{1}{r} - \frac{1}{r_0}\right). \qquad h = \frac{GM}{r_0^2 v_0^2} \end{aligned}$$

To simplify further, we substitute

$$u = \frac{1}{r}, \quad u_0 = \frac{1}{r_0}, \quad \frac{du}{d\theta} = -\frac{1}{r^2}\frac{dr}{d\theta}, \quad \left(\frac{du}{d\theta}\right)^2 = \frac{1}{r^4}\left(\frac{dr}{d\theta}\right)^2,$$

obtaining

$$\left(\frac{du}{d\theta}\right)^2 = u_0^2 - u^2 + 2hu - 2hu_0 = (u_0 - h)^2 - (u - h)^2 \tag{27}$$

$$\frac{du}{d\theta} = \pm\sqrt{(u_0 - h)^2 + (u - h)^2} \tag{28}$$

Which sign do we take? We know that $\dot{\theta} = r_0 v_0 / r^2$ is positive. Also, r starts from a minimum value at $t = 0$, so it cannot immediately decrease, and $\dot{r} \geq 0$, at least for early positive values of t. Therefore,

$$\frac{dr}{d\theta} = \frac{\dot{r}}{\dot{\theta}} \geq 0 \quad \text{and} \quad \frac{du}{d\theta} = -\frac{1}{r^2}\frac{dr}{d\theta} \leq 0.$$

The correct sign for Equation (28) is the negative sign. With this determined, we rearrange Equation (28) and integrate both sides with respect to θ:

$$\frac{-1}{\sqrt{(u_0 - h)^2 - (u - h)^2}} \frac{du}{d\theta} = 1 \tag{29}$$

$$\cos^{-1}\left(\frac{u - h}{u_0 - h}\right) = \theta + C_2.$$

The constant C_2 is zero because $u = u_0$ when $\theta = 0$ and $\cos^{-1}(1) = 0$. Therefore,

$$\frac{u - h}{u_0 - h} = \cos\theta$$

and

$$\frac{1}{r} = u = h + (u_0 - h)\cos\theta. \tag{30}$$

A few more algebraic maneuvers produce the final equation

$$r = \frac{(1 + e)r_0}{1 + e\cos\theta}, \tag{31}$$

where

$$e = \frac{1}{r_0 h} - 1 = \frac{r_0 v_0^2}{GM} - 1. \tag{32}$$

Together, Equations (31) and (32) say that the path of the planet is a conic section with one focus at the sun and with eccentricity $(r_0 v_0^2)/(GM) - 1$. This is the modern formulation of Kepler's first law.

Kepler's Third Law (The Time–Distance Law)

The time T it takes a planet to go around its sun once is the planet's **orbital period**. *Kepler's third law* says that T and the orbit's semimajor axis a are related by the equation

$$\frac{T^2}{a^3} = \frac{4\pi^2}{GM}. \tag{33}$$

Since the right-hand side of this equation is constant within a given solar system, the ratio of T^2 to a^3 *is the same for every planet in the system.*

Kepler's third law is the starting point for working out the size of our solar system. It allows the semimajor axis of each planetary orbit to be expressed in astronomical units, Earth's semimajor axis being one unit. The distance between any two planets at any time can then be predicted in astronomical units. All that remains is to find one of these distances in kilometers, which can be done by bouncing radar waves off Venus, for example. The astronomical unit is now known, after a series of such measurements, to be 149,597,870 km.

We derive Kepler's third law by combining two formulas for the area enclosed by the planet's elliptical orbit:

Formula 1: Area $= \pi ab$ — The geometry formula in which a is the semimajor axis and b is the semiminor axis.

$$\begin{aligned}\text{Formula 2:}\quad \text{Area} &= \int_0^T dA \\ &= \int_0^T \frac{1}{2} r_0 v_0 \, dt \qquad \text{Eq. (20)} \\ &= \frac{1}{2} T r_0 v_0.\end{aligned}$$

Equating these gives

$$T = \frac{2\pi ab}{r_0 v_0} = \frac{2\pi a^2}{r_0 v_0}\sqrt{1 - e^2}. \qquad \text{For any ellipse, } b = a\sqrt{1 - e^2}. \tag{34}$$

It remains only to express a and e in terms of r_0, v_0, G, and M. Equation (32) does this for e. For a, we observe that setting θ equal to π in Equation (31) gives

$$r_{max} = r_0 \frac{1 + e}{1 - e}.$$

Hence,

$$2a = r_0 + r_{max} = \frac{2r_0}{1 - e} = \frac{2r_0 GM}{2GM - r_0 v_0^2}. \tag{35}$$

Squaring both sides of Equation (34) and substituting the results of Equations (32) and (35) now produces Kepler's third law (Exercise 15).

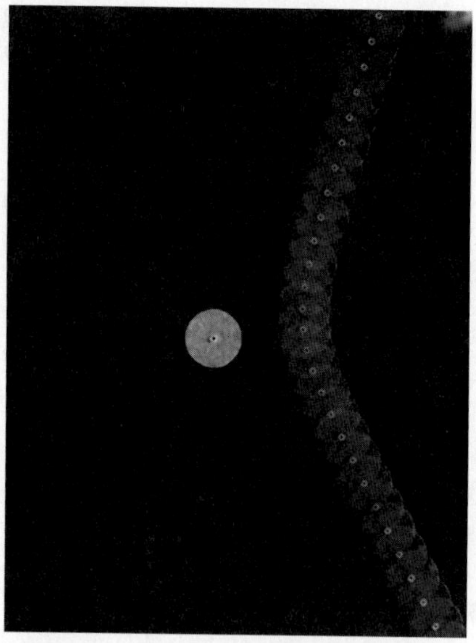

Figure 13.37 This multiflash photograph shows a body being deflected by an inverse square law force. It moves along a hyperbola.

Orbit Data

Although Kepler discovered his laws empirically and stated them only for the six planets known at the time, the modern derivations of Kepler's laws show that they apply to any body driven by a force that obeys an inverse square law. They apply to Halley's comet and the asteroid Icarus. They apply to the moon's orbit about Earth, and they applied to the orbit of the spacecraft *Apollo 8* about the moon. They also applied to the air puck shown in Figure 13.37 being deflected by an inverse square law force; its path is a hyperbola. Charged particles fired at the nuclei of atoms scatter along hyperbolic paths.

Tables 13.1 to 13.3 give additional data for planetary orbits and for orbits of seven of Earth's artificial satellites (Figure 13.38). *Vanguard I* sent back data that revealed differences between the levels of Earth's oceans and provided the first determination of the precise locations of some of the more isolated Pacific islands. The data also verified that the gravitation of the sun and moon would affect the orbits of Earth's satellites and that solar radiation could exert enough pressure to deform an orbit.

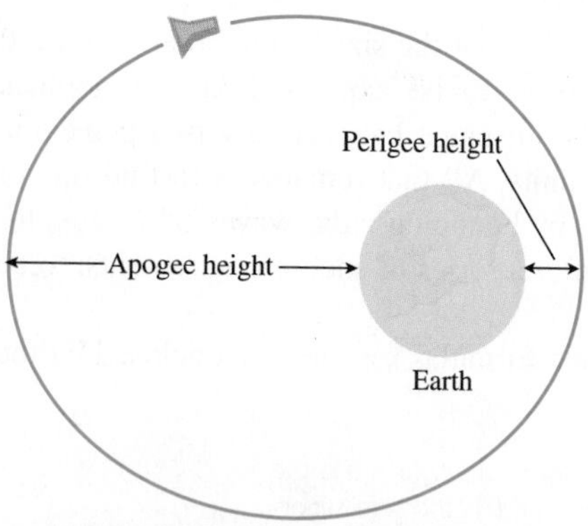

Figure 13.38 The orbit of an Earth satellite: $2a$ = diameter of Earth + perigee height + apogee height.

Table 13.1 Values of *a*, *e*, and *T* for the Major Planets

Planet	Semimajor axis $a^{\dagger}$	Eccentricity e	Period T
Mercury	57.95	0.2056	87.967 days
Venus	108.11	0.0068	224.701 days
Earth	149.57	0.0167	365.256 days
Mars	227.84	0.0934	1.8808 years
Jupiter	778.14	0.0484	11.8613 years
Saturn	1427.0	0.0543	29.4568 years
Uranus	2870.3	0.0460	84.0081 years
Neptune	4499.9	0.0082	164.784 years
Pluto	5909	0.2481	248.35 years

†Millions of kilometers

Table 13.2 Data on Earth's Satellites

Name	Launch date	Time or expected time aloft	Mass at launch (kg)	Period (min)	Perigee height (km)	Apogee height (km)	Semimajor axis ***a*** (km)	Eccentricity
Sputnik 1	Oct. 1957	57.6 days	83.6	96.2	215	939	6,955	0.052
Vanguard 1	March 1958	300 years	1.47	138.5	649	4,340	8,872	0.208
Syncom 3	Aug. 1964	$>10^6$ years	39	1436.2	35,718	35,903	42,189	0.002
Skylab 4	Nov. 1973	84.06 days	13,980	93.11	422	437	6,808	0.001
Tiros 11	Oct. 1978	500 years	734	102.12	850	866	7,236	0.001
GOES 4	Sept. 1980	$>10^6$ years	627	1436.2	35,776	35,800	42,166	0.0003
Intelsat 5	Dec 1980	$>10^6$ years	1,928	1417.67	35,143	35,707	41,803	0.007

Syncom 3 is one of a series of U.S. Department of Defense telecommunications satellites. *Tiros 11* (for "television infrared observation satellite") is one of a series of weather satellites. *GOES 4* (for "geostationary operational environmental satellite") is one of a series of satellites designed to gather information about Earth's atmosphere. Its orbital period, 1436.2 minutes, is nearly the same as Earth's rotational period of 1436.1 minutes, and its orbit is nearly circular ($e = 0.0003$). *Intelsat 5* is a heavy-capacity commercial telecommunications satellite.

Table 13.3 Numerical Data

Universal gravitational constant: $G = 6.6720 \times 10^{-11}\ \text{Nm}^2\text{kg}^{-2}$
(When you use this value of G in a calculation, remember to express force in newtons, distance in meters, mass in kilograms, and time in seconds.)
Sun's mass: 1.99×10^{30} kg
Earth's mass: 5.975×10^{24} kg
Equatorial radius of Earth: 6378.533 km
Polar radius of Earth: 6356.912 km
Earth's rotational period: 1436.1 min
Earth's orbital period: 1 year = 365.256 days

Quick Review 13.4

In Exercises 1–3, find the eccentricity of the conic section.

1. $4x^2 + 9y^2 = 36$ **2.** $12x^2 - 3y^2 = 24$

3. $y^2 + 4y - x + 6 = 0$

In Exercises 4–6, find a polar equation for the conic with focus at (0, 0) and given eccentricity and directrix.

4. $e = 1, \quad x = -2$ **5.** $e = 5/4, \quad x = 4$

6. $e = 2/3, \quad x = -5$

In Exercises 7 and 8, find the endpoints of the major and minor axes of the ellipse.

7. $\dfrac{x^2}{36} + \dfrac{y^2}{64} = 1$ **8.** $\dfrac{x^2}{49} + \dfrac{y^2}{16} = 1$

In Exercises 9 and 10, solve the separable differential equation.

9. $\dfrac{dy}{dx} = 2(x + y^2x)$ **10.** $(y + 1)\dfrac{dy}{dx} = y(x - 1)$

Section 13.4 Exercises

Reminder: When a calculation involves the universal gravitational constant G, express force in newtons, distance in meters, mass in kilograms, and time in seconds.

1. ***Period of Skylab 4*** Because the orbit of *Skylab 4* had a semimajor axis of $a = 6808$ km, Kepler's third law with M equal to Earth's mass should give the period. Calculate it. Compare your result with the value in Table 13.2.

2. ***Earth's Velocity at Perihelion*** Earth's distance from the sun at perihelion is approximately 149,577,000 km, and the eccentricity of Earth's orbit about the sun is 0.0167. Find the velocity v_0 of Earth in its orbit at perihelion. (Use Equation (15).)

3. ***Semimajor Axis of Proton I*** In July 1965, the USSR launched *Proton 1,* weighing 12,200 kg (at launch), with a perigee height of 183 km, an apogee height of 589 km, and a period of 92.25 min. Using the relevant data for the mass of Earth and the gravitational constant G, find the semimajor axis a of the orbit from Equation (33). Compare your answer with the number you get by adding the perigee and apogee heights to the diameter of Earth.

4. ***Semimajor Axis of Viking I*** The *Viking I* orbiter, which surveyed Mars from August 1975 to June 1976, had a period of 1639 min. Use this and the fact that the mass of Mars is 6.418×10^{23} kg to find the semimajor axis of the *Viking I* orbit.

5. ***Average Diameter of Mars*** The *Viking 1* orbiter was 1499 km from the surface of Mars at its closest point and 35,800 km from the surface at its farthest point. Use this information together with the value you obtained in Exercise 4 to estimate the average diameter of Mars.

6. ***Period of Viking 2*** The *Viking 2* orbiter, which surveyed Mars from September 1975 to August 1976, moved in an ellipse whose semimajor axis was 22,030 km. What was the orbital period? (Express your answer in minutes.)

Exploration

7. ***Geosynchronous Orbits*** Several satellites in Earth's equatorial plane have nearly circular orbits whose periods are the same as Earth's rotational period. Such orbits are **geosynchronous** or **geostationary** because they hold the satellite over the same spot on Earth's surface.

   (a) **Writing to Learn** Approximately what is the semimajor axis of a geosynchronous orbit? Give reasons for your answer.

   (b) About how high is a geosynchronous orbit above Earth's surface?

   (c) Which of the satellites in Table 13.2 have (nearly) geosynchronous orbits?

8. **Writing to Learn *Semimajor Axis of Mars's Orbit*** The mass of Mars is 6.418×10^{23} kg. If a satellite of Mars is to hold a stationary orbit (have the same period as the period of Mars's rotation, which is 1477.4 min), what must the semimajor axis of its orbit be? Give reasons for your answer.

9. ***Distance from Earth to the Moon*** The period of the moon's revolution about Earth is 2.36055×10^6 sec. About how far away is the moon?

10. ***Finding Satellite Speed*** A satellite moves around Earth in a circular orbit. Express the satellite's speed as a function of the orbit's radius.

11. ***Finding T^2/a^3*** If T is measured in seconds and a in meters, what is the value of T^2/a^3 for planets in our solar system? For satellites orbiting Earth? For satellites orbiting the moon? (The moon's mass is 7.354×10^{22} kg.)

12. ***Type of Orbit*** For what values of v_0 in Equation (15) is the orbit in Equation (16) a circle? An ellipse? A parabola? A hyperbola?

13. ***Circular Orbits*** Show that a planet in a circular orbit moves with a constant speed. (*Hint*: This is a consequence of one of Kepler's laws.)

14. **Writing to Learn *The Area Derivative in Kepler's Second Law*** Suppose $\mathbf{r}$ is the position vector of a particle moving along a plane curve and dA/dt is the rate at which the vector sweeps out area. Without introducing coordinates, and assuming the necessary derivatives exist, give a geometric argument based on increments and limits for the validity of the equation

$$\frac{dA}{dt} = \frac{1}{2}\left|\mathbf{r} \times \dot{\mathbf{r}}\right|.$$

15. **Writing to Learn *Kepler's Third Law*** Complete the derivation of Kepler's third law (the part following Equation (34)).

16. ***Trouble in River City—The Problem with the Geocentric View*** Two planets, A and B, are orbiting their sun in circular orbits, with A being the inner planet and B being farther away from the sun. Suppose the positions of A and B at time t are

$$\mathbf{r}_A(t) = 2\cos(2\pi t)\mathbf{i} + 2\sin(2\pi t)\mathbf{j}$$

and

$$\mathbf{r}_B(t) = 3\cos(\pi t)\mathbf{i} + 3\sin(\pi t)\mathbf{j},$$

respectively, where the sun is assumed to be located at the origin and distance is measured in astronomical units. (Notice that planet A moves faster than planet B.) The people on planet A regard their planet, not the sun, as the center of their planetary system (their solar system).

   (a) Using planet A as the origin of a new coordinate system, give parametric equations for the location of planet B at time t. Write your answer in terms of $\cos(\pi t)$ and $\sin(\pi t)$.

   (b) Using planet A as the origin, graph the path of planet B.

   This exercise illustrates the difficulty that people before Kepler's time, with an Earth-centered or geocentric (planet A) view of our solar system, had in understanding the motions of the planets (planet B = Mars). See D. G. Saari's article in *The American Mathematical Monthly,* Vol. 97, Feb. 1990, pp. 105–119.

Extending the Ideas

17. **Writing to Learn *Earth Orbit*** Kepler discovered that the path of Earth around the sun is an ellipse with the sun at one of the foci. Let $\mathbf{r}(t)$ be the position vector from the center of the sun to the center of Earth at time t. Let $\mathbf{w}$ be the vector from Earth's South Pole to North Pole. It is known that $\mathbf{w}$ is constant and not orthogonal to the plane of the ellipse (Earth's axis is tilted). In terms of $\mathbf{r}(t)$ and $\mathbf{w}$, give the mathematical meaning of (a) perihelion, (b) **aphelion** (position farthest from the sun), (c) equinox, (d) summer solstice, (e) winter solstice.

Chapter 13 Key Terms

Chapter 13 Review Exercises

In Exercises 1 and 2, graph the curve and sketch its velocity and acceleration vectors at the given value(s) of t. Then write $\mathbf{a}$ in the form $\mathbf{a} = a_T\mathbf{T} + a_N\mathbf{N}$ without finding $\mathbf{T}$ and $\mathbf{N}$, and find the value of κ at the given value(s) of t.

1. $\mathbf{r}(t) = (4\cos t)\mathbf{i} + (\sqrt{2}\sin t)\mathbf{j}$, $t = 0_t$ $t = \pi/4$
2. $\mathbf{r}(t) = (\sqrt{2}\sec t)\mathbf{i} + (\sqrt{2}\tan t)\mathbf{j}$, $t = 0$
3. ***Highest Speed*** The position of a particle in the plane at time t is
$$\mathbf{r} = \frac{1}{\sqrt{1+t^2}}\mathbf{i} + \frac{t}{\sqrt{1+t^2}}\mathbf{j}.$$
Find the particle's highest speed.
4. ***Constant Angle Between Position and Acceleration*** Suppose $\mathbf{r}(t) = (e^t\cos t)\mathbf{i} + (e^t\sin t)\mathbf{j}$. Show that the angle between $\mathbf{r}$ and $\mathbf{a}$ never changes. What is the angle?
5. ***Finding Curvature*** At point P, the velocity and acceleration of a particle moving in the plane are $\mathbf{v} = 3\mathbf{i} + 4\mathbf{j}$ and $\mathbf{a} = 5\mathbf{i} + 15\mathbf{j}$. Find the curvature of the particle's path at P.
6. ***Finding Where the Curvature is Greatest*** Find the point on the curve $y = e^x$ where the curvature is greatest.
7. ***Which Direction Does It Go?*** A particle moves around the unit circle in the xy-plane. Its position at time t is $\mathbf{r} = x\mathbf{i} + y\mathbf{j}$, where x and y are differentiable functions of t. Find dy/dt if $\mathbf{v}\cdot\mathbf{i} = y$. Is the motion clockwise, or counterclockwise?
8. ***Sending a Message through a Tube*** You send a message through a pneumatic tube that follows the curve $9y = x^3$ (distance in meters). At the point (3, 3), $\mathbf{v}\cdot\mathbf{i} = 4$ and $\mathbf{a}\cdot\mathbf{i} = -2$. Find the values of $\mathbf{v}\cdot\mathbf{j}$ and $\mathbf{a}\cdot\mathbf{j}$ at (3, 3).

In Exercises 9 and 10, solve the initial value problem for $\mathbf{r}$ as a vector function of t.

9. Differential equation: $\dfrac{d\mathbf{r}}{dt} = -t\mathbf{i} - t\mathbf{j} - t\mathbf{k}$
Initial condition: $\mathbf{r}(0) = \mathbf{i} + 2\mathbf{j} + 3\mathbf{k}$
10. Differential equation: $\dfrac{d\mathbf{r}}{dt} = (180t)\mathbf{i} + (180t - 16t^2)\mathbf{j}$
Initial condition: $\mathbf{r}(0) = 100\mathbf{j}$
11. ***Velocity Orthogonal to Position*** A particle moves in the plane so that its velocity and position vectors are always orthogonal. Show that the particle moves in a circle centered at the origin.

12. *Radius of Curvature* Show that the radius of curvature of a twice-differentiable plane curve $\mathbf{r}(t) = f(t)\mathbf{i} + g(t)\mathbf{j}$ is given by the formula

$$\rho = \frac{\dot{x}^2 + \dot{y}^2}{\sqrt{\ddot{x}^2 + \ddot{y}^2 - \ddot{s}^2}} \quad \text{where} \quad \dot{s} = \frac{d}{dt}\sqrt{\dot{x}^2 + \dot{y}^2}.$$

In Exercises 13 and 14, find the length of the curve.

13. $\mathbf{r}(t) = (2\cos t)\mathbf{i} + (2\sin t)\mathbf{j} + t^2\mathbf{k}, \quad 0 \le t \le \pi/4$

14. $\mathbf{r}(t) = (3\cos t)\mathbf{i} + (3\sin t)\mathbf{j} + 2t^{3/2}\mathbf{k}, \quad 0 \le t \le 3$

In Exercises 15–18, find **T**, **N**, **B**, κ, and τ at the given value of t.

15. $\mathbf{r}(t) = \frac{4}{9}(1+t)^{3/2}\mathbf{i} + \frac{4}{9}(1-t)^{3/2}\mathbf{j} + \frac{1}{3}t\mathbf{k}, \quad t = 0$

16. $\mathbf{r}(t) = (e^t \sin 2t)\mathbf{i} + (e^t \cos 2t)\mathbf{j} + 2e^t\mathbf{k}, \quad t = 0$

17. $\mathbf{r}(t) = t\mathbf{i} + \frac{1}{2}e^{2t}\mathbf{j}, \quad t = \ln 2$

18. $\mathbf{r}(t) = \frac{3}{2}(e^{2t} + e^{-2t})\mathbf{i} + \frac{3}{2}(e^{2t} - e^{-2t})\mathbf{j} + 6t\mathbf{k}, \quad t = \ln 2$

In Exercises 19 and 20, write **a** in the form $\mathbf{a} = a_T\mathbf{T} + a_N\mathbf{N}$ at $t = 0$ without finding **T** and **N**.

19. $\mathbf{r}(t) = (2 + 3t + 3t^2)\mathbf{i} + (4t + 4t^2)\mathbf{j} - (6\cos t)\mathbf{k}$

20. $\mathbf{r}(t) = (2 + t)\mathbf{i} + (t + 2t^2)\mathbf{j} + (1 + t^2)\mathbf{k}$

21. *Finding Curvature* Express the curvature of the curve

$$\mathbf{r}(t) = \left(\int_0^t \cos\left(\frac{1}{2}\pi\theta^2\right) d\theta\right)\mathbf{i} + \left(\int_0^t \sin\left(\frac{1}{2}\pi\theta^2\right) d\theta\right)\mathbf{j}$$

as a function of the directed distance s measured along the curve from the origin (see figure).

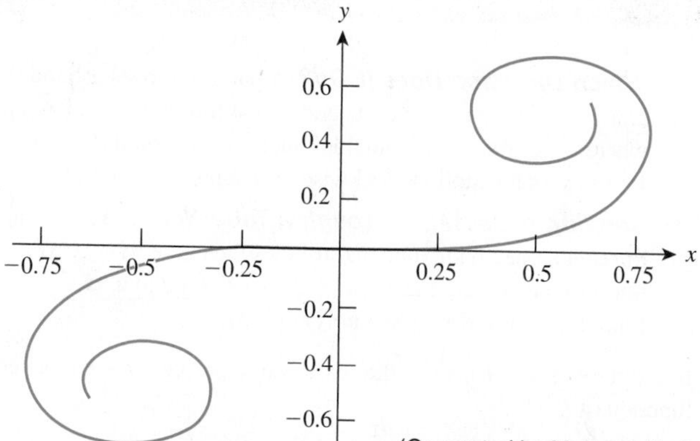

22. *An Alternative Definition of Curvature in the Plane* An alternative definition gives the curvature of a sufficiently differentiable plane curve to be $|d\phi/ds|$, where ϕ is the angle between **T** and **i** (see figure, part (a)). Part (b) of the figure shows the distance s measured counterclockwise around the circle $x^2 + y^2 = a^2$ from the point $(a, 0)$ to a point P, along with the angle ϕ at P. Calculate the circle's curvature using the alternative definition.

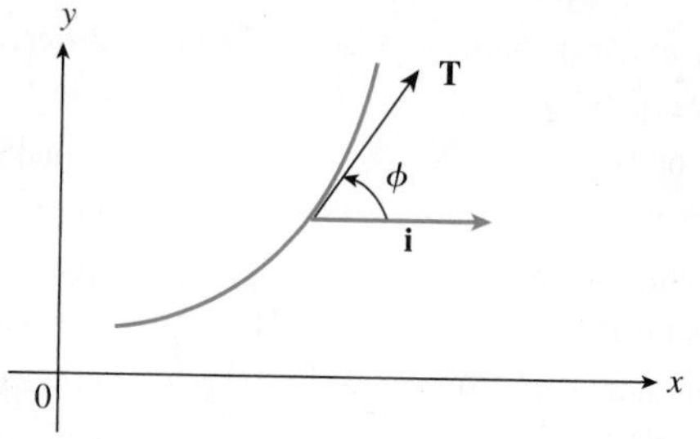

(a)

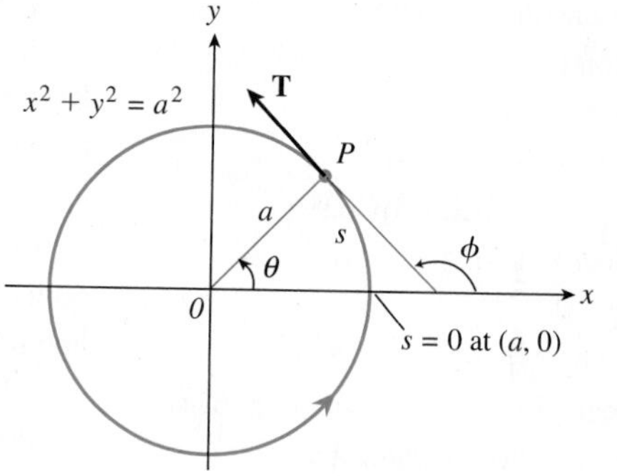

(b)

23. Find **T**, **N**, **B**, κ, and τ as functions of t if $\mathbf{r}(t) = (\sin t)\mathbf{i} + (\sqrt{2}\cos t)\mathbf{j} + (\sin t)\mathbf{k}$.

24. *Velocity and Acceleration Perpendicular* At what times in the interval $0 \le t \le \pi$ are the velocity and acceleration vectors of the motion $\mathbf{r}(t) = \mathbf{i} + (5\cos t)\mathbf{j} + (3\sin t)\mathbf{k}$ orthogonal?

25. The position of a particle moving in space at time $t \ge 0$ is

$$\mathbf{r}(t) = 2\mathbf{i} + \left(4\sin\frac{t}{2}\right)\mathbf{j} + \left(3 - \frac{t}{\pi}\right)\mathbf{k}.$$

Find the first time **r** is orthogonal to the vector $\mathbf{i} - \mathbf{j}$.

26. *Finding Frenet-Frame Planes* Find equations for the osculating, normal, and rectifying planes of the curve $\mathbf{r}(t) = t\mathbf{i} + t^2\mathbf{j} + t^3\mathbf{k}$ at the point $(1, 1, 1)$.

27. *Finding Parametric Equations for a Line* Find parametric equations for the line that is tangent to the curve

$$\mathbf{r}(t) = e^t\mathbf{i} + (\sin t)\mathbf{j} + \ln(1 - t)\mathbf{k} \text{ at } t = 0.$$

28. *Finding Parametric Equations for a Line* Find parametric equations for the line tangent to the helix $\mathbf{r}(t) = (\sqrt{2}\cos t)\mathbf{i} + (\sqrt{2}\sin t)\mathbf{j} + t\mathbf{k}$ at the point where $t = \pi/4$.

29. *The View from Skylab 4* What percentage of Earth's surface area could astronauts see when *Skylab 4* was at its apogee height, 437 km above the surface? To find out, model the visible surface as the surface generated by revolving the circular arc GT, on page 657, about the y-axis. Then carry out the following steps.

(a) Use similar triangles in the figure to show that $y_0/6380 = 6380/(6380 + 437)$. Solve for y_0.

(b) To four significant digits, calculate the visible area as

$$VA = \int_{y_0}^{6380} 2\pi x \sqrt{1 + \left(\frac{dx}{dy}\right)^2}\, dy.$$

(c) Express the result in (b) as a percentage of Earth's surface area.

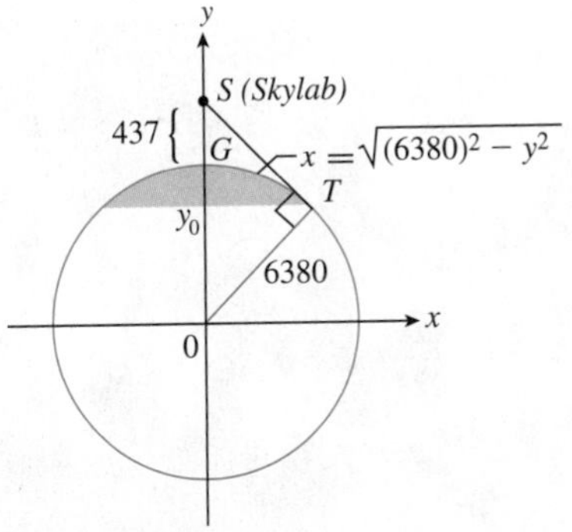

30. *Orbit Equation* Deduce from the orbit equation

$$r = \frac{(1 + e)\, r_0}{1 + e \cos \theta}$$

that a planet is closest to its sun when $\theta = 0$ and show that $r = r_0$ at that time.

31. *A Kepler Equation* The problem of locating a planet in its orbit at a given time and date eventually leads to solving "Kepler" equations of the form

$$f(x) = x - 1 - \frac{1}{2} \sin x = 0.$$

(a) Show that this particular equation has a solution between $x = 0$ and $x = 2$.

(b) Find the solution to as many decimal places as you can.

32. In Section 13.4, we found the velocity of a particle moving in the plane to be

$$\mathbf{v} = \dot{x}\mathbf{i} + \dot{y}\mathbf{j} = \dot{r}\mathbf{u}_r + r\dot{\theta}\mathbf{u}_\theta.$$

(a) Express $\dot{x}$ and $\dot{y}$ in terms of $\dot{r}$ and $r\dot{\theta}$ by evaluating the dot products $\mathbf{v} \cdot \mathbf{i}$ and $\mathbf{v} \cdot \mathbf{j}$.

(b) Express $\dot{r}$ and $r\dot{\theta}$ in terms of $\dot{x}$ and $\dot{y}$ by evaluating the dot products $\mathbf{v} \cdot \mathbf{u}_r$ and $\mathbf{v} \cdot \mathbf{u}_\theta$.

33. *The Curvature of Polar Curves* Express the curvature of a twice-differentiable curve $r = f(\theta)$ in the polar coordinate plane in terms of r and its derivatives.

34. *The Voyage of the Beetle* A slender rod through the origin of the polar coordinate plane rotates (in the plane) about the origin at the rate of 3 rad/min. A beetle starting from the point (2, 0) crawls along the rod toward the origin at the rate of 1 in./min.

(a) Find the beetle's acceleration and velocity in polar form when it is halfway to (1 in. from) the origin.

(b) To the nearest tenth of an inch, what will be the length of the path the beetle has traveled by the time it reaches the origin?

Chapter 14

Multivariable Functions and Their Derivatives

The appearance of a region's landscape is important to its human inhabitants. It is part of their cultural identity and affects the health of their environment and economy. Natural resource planners use 3-D modeling to produce realistic models of current landscapes and to simulate the effects of changes on them.

Using 3-D modeling software, a natural resource planner creates a mountain range with the function $z = f(x, y) = -x^4 - y^4 - 14x^2y^2 + 32x^2 + 128y^2$. Find the highest elevation in the mountain range. You will explore problems of this type in Section 14.7.

Chapter 14 Overview

Functions with two or more independent variables appear in science more often than functions of a single variable, and their calculus is even richer. Their derivatives are more varied and more interesting because of the different ways in which the variables can interact, and their integrals lead to a greater variety of applications. The studies of probability, statistics, fluid dynamics, and electricity, to mention only a few, all lead in natural ways to functions of more than one variable. The mathematics of these functions is one of the finest achievements in science.

As we see in this chapter, the rules of calculus remain essentially the same as we move into higher dimensions. We do not have to reinvent the theory. In higher dimensions the points representing independent variables can move around in a variety of directions instead of just along a line, but this is easily handled with the vector notation of the previous chapters.

14.1 Functions of Several Variables

What you'll learn about

- Functions and Variables
- Domains and Regions
- Graphs and Level Curves of Functions of Two Variables
- Contour Lines
- Level Surfaces of Functions of Three Variables
- Computer Graphing
- An Interesting Application (Optional)

Functions and Variables

Many functions depend on more than one independent variable. The function $V = \pi r^2 h$ calculates the volume of a right circular cylinder from its radius and height. The function $f(x, y) = x^2 + y^2$ calculates the height of the paraboloid $z = x^2 + y^2$ above the point $P(x, y)$ from the two coordinates of P.

The domains of real-valued functions of several independent real variables are sets of ordered pairs (triples, quadruples, whatever) of real numbers. The ranges are sets of real numbers of the kind we have worked with all along.

DEFINITIONS Multivariable Functions

Suppose D is a set of n-tuples of real numbers $(x_1, x_2, \ldots, x_n)$. A **real-valued function** f on D is a rule that assigns a real number

$$w = f(x_1, x_2, \ldots, x_n)$$

to each element in D. The set D is the function's **domain**. The set of w-values taken on by f is the function's **range**. The symbol w is the **dependent variable** of f, and f is a function of the n **independent variables** x_1 to x_n. The x's are the function's **input variables;** w is the function's **output variable**.

If f is a function of two independent variables, we usually call the independent variables x and y and picture the domain of f as a region in the xy-plane. If f is a function of three independent variables, we call the variables x, y, and z and picture the domain as a region in space.

In applications, we tend to use letters that remind us of what the variables stand for. To say that the volume of a right circular cylinder is a function of its radius and height, we might write $V = f(r, h)$. To be more specific, we might replace the notation $f(r, h)$ by the formula that calculates the value of V from the values of r and h and write $V = \pi r^2 h$. In either case, r and h would be the independent variables and V the dependent variable of the function.

As usual, we evaluate functions defined by formulas by substituting the values of the independent variables in the formula and calculating the corresponding value of the dependent variable.

EXAMPLE 1 Finding Distance from the Origin in Space

When we use rectangular coordinates in three-dimensional space, the distance of a point (x, y, z) from the origin is given by the function $D(x, y, z) = \sqrt{x^2 + y^2 + z^2}$. The value of D at the point $(3, 0, 4)$ is $D(3, 0, 4) = \sqrt{3^2 + 0^2 + 4^2} = \sqrt{25} = 5$.

Domains and Regions

In defining functions of more than one variable, we follow the usual practice of excluding inputs that lead to complex numbers or division by zero. If $f(x, y) = \sqrt{y - x^2}$, we do not allow y to be less than x^2. If $f(x, y) = 1/(xy)$, we do not allow x or y to be zero. The domains of functions are otherwise assumed to be the largest sets for which the defining rules generate real numbers.

EXPLORATION 1 Finding Domains and Ranges

For each of the following functions of *two* variables, the *domain* is given. Fill in the *range:*

Function	Domain	Range
$w = \sqrt{y - x^2}$	$y \geq x^2$	
$w = \dfrac{1}{xy}$	$xy \neq 0$	
$w = x \ln y$	Half-plane $y > 0$	
$w = \sqrt{1 - (x^2 + y^2)}$	Disk $x^2 + y^2 \leq 1$	

For each of the following functions of *three* variables, the *range* is given. Fill in the *domain:*

Function	Domain	Range
$w = \sqrt{x^2 + y^2 + z^2}$		$(0, \infty)$
$w = \dfrac{1}{x^2 + y^2 + z^2}$		$(0, \infty)$
$w = \sin xyz$		$[-1, 1]$
$w = \sqrt{4 - x^2 - y^2 - z^2}$		$[0, 2]$

The domains of functions defined on portions of the plane can have interior points and boundary points just the way the domains of functions defined on intervals of the real line can.

DEFINITIONS Interior, Boundary, Open and Closed in the Plane

A point (x_0, y_0) in a region (set) R in the xy-plane is an **interior point** of R if it is the center of a disk that lies entirely in R (Figure 14.1a). A point (x_0, y_0) is a **boundary point** of R if every disk centered at (x_0, y_0) contains points that lie outside of R as well as points that lie inside R (Figure 14.1b). The boundary point itself need not belong to R.

continued

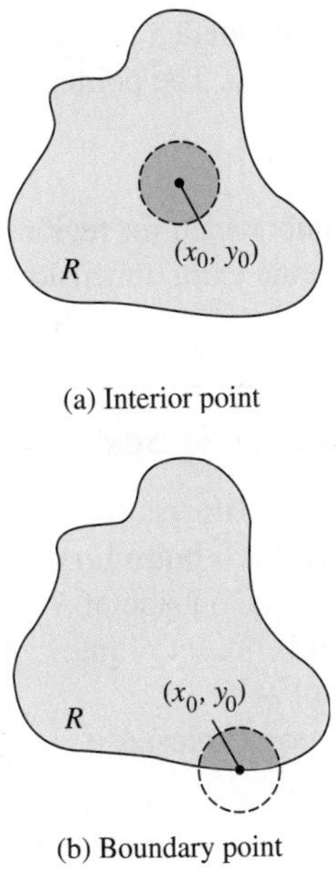

Figure 14.1 Interior points and boundary points of a plane region R. An interior point is necessarily a point of R. A boundary point of R need not belong to R.

The interior points of a region, as a set, make up the **interior** of the region. The region's boundary points make up its **boundary**. A region is **open** if it consists entirely of interior points. A region is **closed** if it contains all its boundary points (Figure 14.2).

As with intervals of real numbers, some regions in the plane are neither open nor closed. If you start with the open disk in Figure 14.2 and add to it some but not all of its boundary points, the resulting set is neither open nor closed. The boundary points that *are* there keep the set from being open. The absence of the remaining boundary points keeps the set from being closed.

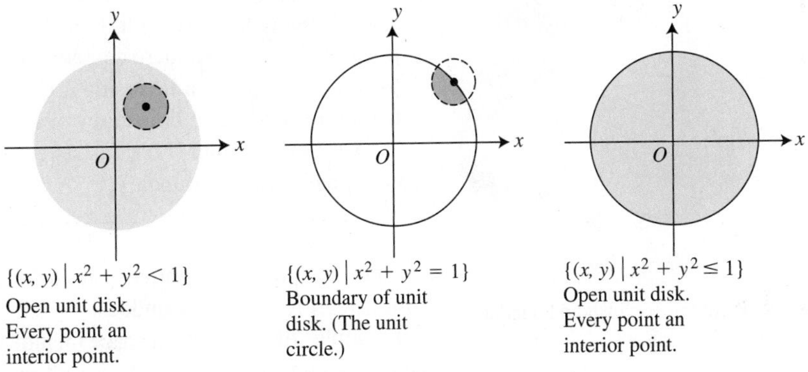

y
x
O
$\{(x, y) \mid x^2 + y^2 < 1\}$
Open unit disk.
Every point an interior point.
y
x
O
$\{(x, y) \mid x^2 + y^2 = 1\}$
Boundary of unit disk. (The unit circle.)
y
x
O
$\{(x, y) \mid x^2 + y^2 \leq 1\}$
Open unit disk.
Every point an interior point.

Figure 14.2 Interior points and boundary points of the unit disk in the plane.

DEFINITIONS Bounded and Unbounded Regions in the Plane

A region in the plane is **bounded** if it lies inside a disk of finite radius. A region is **unbounded** if it is not bounded.

Examples of *bounded* sets in the plane include line segments, triangles, interiors of triangles, rectangles, circles, and disks. Examples of *unbounded* sets in the plane include lines, coordinate axes, the graphs of functions defined on infinite intervals, quadrants, half-planes, and the plane itself.

EXAMPLE 2 Describing the Domain of a Function of Two Variables

Describe the domain of the function $f(x, y) = \sqrt{y - x^2}$.

SOLUTION

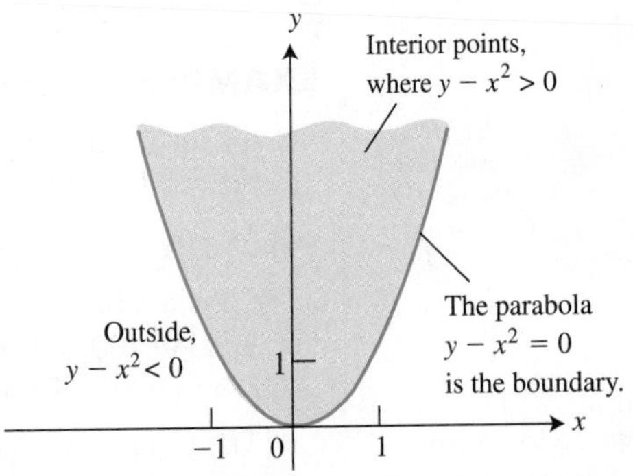

Figure 14.3 The domain of $f(x, y) = \sqrt{y - x^2}$ consists of the shaded region and its bounding parabola $y = x^2$.

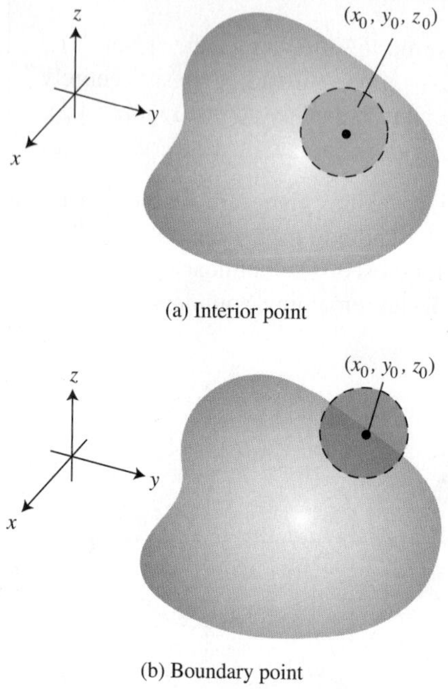

Figure 14.4 Interior points and boundary points of a region in space.

Since f is defined only where $y - x^2 \geq 0$, the domain is the closed, unbounded region shown in Figure 14.3. The parabola $y = x^2$ is the boundary of the domain. The points above the parabola make up the domain's interior.

The definitions of interior, boundary, open, closed, bounded, and unbounded for regions in space are similar to those for regions in the plane. To accommodate the extra dimension, we use solid spheres instead of disks.

DEFINITIONS Interior, Boundary, Open and Closed in Space

A point (x_0, y_0, z_0) in a region R in space is an **interior point** of R if it is the center of a solid sphere that lies entirely in R (Figure 14.4a). A point (x_0, y_0, z_0) is a **boundary point** of R if every sphere centered at (x_0, y_0, z_0) encloses points that lie outside of R as well as points that lie inside R (Figure 14.4b). The **interior** of R is the set of interior points of R. The **boundary** of R is the set of boundary points of R.

A region is **open** if it consists entirely of interior points. A region is **closed** if it contains its entire boundary.

A region in space is **bounded** if it lies inside a sphere of finite radius. A region in space is **unbounded** if it is not bounded.

Examples of *open* sets in space include the interior of a sphere, the open half-space $z > 0$, the first octant (where x, y and z are all positive), and space itself.

Examples of *closed* sets in space include lines, planes, the closed half-space $z \geq 0$, the first octant together with its bounding planes, and space itself (since it has no boundary points).

A solid sphere with part of its boundary removed or a solid cube with one missing face, edge, or corner point would be *neither open nor closed*.

Graphs and Level Curves of Functions of Two Variables

There are two standard ways to picture the values of a function $f(x, y)$. One is to draw and label curves in the domain on which f has a constant value (each of which is a curve in the xy-plane). The other is to sketch the surface $z = f(x, y)$ in space.

DEFINITIONS Level Curve, Graph, Surface (Functions of Two Variables)

The set of points in the plane where a function $f(x, y)$ has a constant value $f(x, y) = c$ is a **level curve** of f. The set of points $(x, y, f(x, y))$ in space for (x, y) in the domain of f is called the **graph** of f. The graph of f is also called the **surface** $z = f(x, y)$.

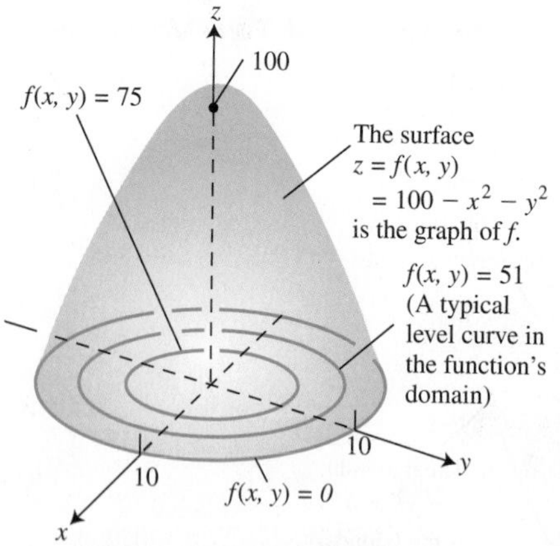

Figure 14.5 The graph and selected level curves of the function $f(x, y) = 100 - x^2 - y^2$.

EXAMPLE 3 Graphing a Function of Two Variables

Graph the function $f(x, y) = 100 - x^2 - y^2$ in space. Also plot the level curves $f(x, y) = 0$, $f(x, y) = 51$, and $f(x, y) = 75$ in the domain of f in the plane.

SOLUTION

The domain of f is the entire xy-plane. The range of f is the set of real numbers less than or equal to 100. The graph is the paraboloid $z = 100 - x^2 - y^2$, a portion of which is shown in Figure 14.5.

The level curve $f(x, y) = 0$ is the set of points in the xy-plane at which

$$f(x, y) = 100 - x^2 - y^2 = 0, \qquad \text{or} \qquad x^2 + y^2 = 100.$$

which is the circle of radius 10 centered at the origin (Figure 14.5). Similarly, the level curves $f(x, y) = 51$ and $f(x, y) = 75$ are the circles

$$f(x, y) = 100 - x^2 - y^2 = 51, \qquad \text{or} \qquad x^2 + y^2 = 49,$$

$$f(x, y) = 100 - x^2 - y^2 = 75, \qquad \text{or} \qquad x^2 + y^2 = 25.$$

The level curve $f(x, y) = 100$ consists of the origin alone. (It is still called a level curve.)

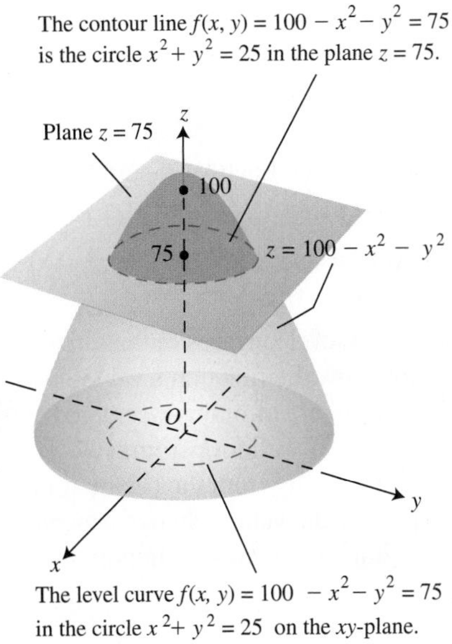
The contour line $f(x, y) = 100 - x^2 - y^2 = 75$ is the circle $x^2 + y^2 = 25$ in the plane $z = 75$.
Plane $z = 75$
z
100
75
$z = 100 - x^2 - y^2$
O
y
x
The level curve $f(x, y) = 100 - x^2 - y^2 = 75$ in the circle $x^2 + y^2 = 25$ on the xy-plane.

Figure 14.6 The graph of $f(x, y) = 100 - x^2 - y^2$ and its intersection with the plane $z = 75$.

Contour Lines

The curve in space in which the plane $z = c$ cuts a surface $z = f(x, y)$ is made up of the points that represent the function value $f(x, y) = c$. It is called the **contour line** $f(x, y) = c$ to distinguish it from the level curve $f(x, y) = c$ in the domain of f. Figure 14.6 shows the contour line $f(x, y) = 75$ on the surface $z = 100 - x^2 - y^2$ defined by the function $f(x, y) = 100 - x^2 - y^2$. The contour line lies 75 units directly above the circle $x^2 + y^2 = 25$, which is the level curve $f(x, y) = 75$ in the function's domain.

Not everyone makes this distinction between level curves and contour lines, but the distinction can be discerned from context. For example, on most maps the curves that represent constant elevation (height above sea level) are called contours, not level curves, even though they are all drawn in the same plane (Figure 14.7).

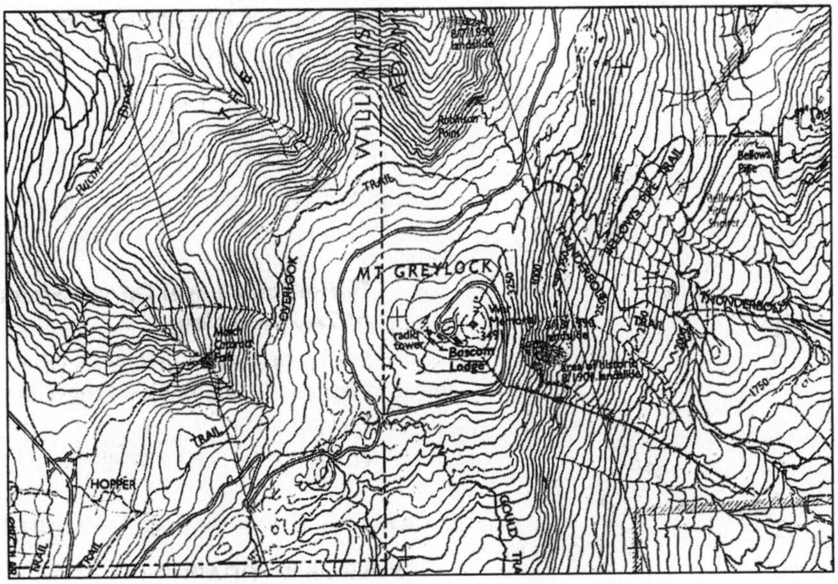
MT GREYLOCK
HOPPER
TRAIL

Figure 14.7 Contours on Mt. Greylock in western Massachusetts.

Level Surfaces of Functions of Three Variables

In the plane, the points where a function of two independent variables has a constant value $f(x, y) = c$ make a curve in the function's domain. In space, the points where a function of three independent variables has a constant value $f(x, y, z) = c$ make a surface in the function's domain.

DEFINITION Level Surface

The set of points (x, y, z) in space where a function of three independent variables has a constant value $f(x, y, z) = c$ is a **level surface** of f.

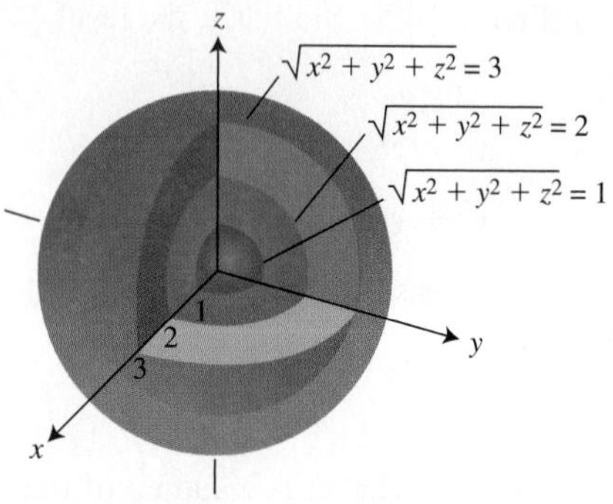

Figure 14.8 The level surfaces of $f(x, y, z) = \sqrt{x^2 + y^2 + z^2}$ are concentric spheres.

Since the graphs of functions of three variables consist of points $(x, y, z, f(x, y, z))$ lying in a four-dimensional space, we cannot sketch them effectively in our three-dimensional frame of reference. We can see how the function behaves, however, by looking at its three-dimensional level surfaces.

EXAMPLE 4 Describing Level Surfaces of a Function of Three Variables

Describe the level surfaces of the function $f(x, y, z) = \sqrt{x^2 + y^2 + z^2}$.

SOLUTION

The value of f is the distance from the origin to the point (x, y, z). Each level surface $\sqrt{x^2 + y^2 + z^2} = c$, $c > 0$, is a sphere of radius c centered at the origin. Figure 14.8 shows a cutaway view of three of these spheres. The level surface $\sqrt{x^2 + y^2 + z^2} = 0$ consists of the origin alone.

We are not graphing the function here; we are looking at level surfaces in the function's three-dimensional domain. The level surfaces show how the function's values change as we move through its domain. If we remain on a sphere of radius c centered at the origin, the function maintains a constant value, namely c. If we move from one sphere to another, the function's value changes. As we move away from the origin, it increases; as we move toward the origin, it decreases. The way the values change depends on the direction we take. The relationship of change in value to direction is important and will be revisited in Section 14.7.

Computer Graphing

Three-dimensional graphing programs for computers make it possible to graph functions of two variables with only a few keystrokes. We can often get information more quickly from a graph than from a formula.

Some graphing calculators have three-dimensional graphing features. At this time, they are not as robust as computer graphing programs. They are slower, are not able to graph parametrically, and do not do a good job with contour plots. For these reasons, and except for an occasional example, we will stick with computer graphing programs for three-dimensional graphing.

Just as in two dimensions, graphing in three dimensions requires *viewing* skills.

EXAMPLE 5 Modeling Temperature Beneath the Earth's Surface

The temperature beneath the earth's surface is a function of x, the depth beneath the surface, and t, the time of the year. If we measure x in feet and t in days elapsed from the average date of the yearly surface high, we can model the variation in temperature with the function

$$w = \cos(1.7 \times 10^{-2}t - 0.2x)e^{-0.2x}.$$

(The temperature at 0 ft is scaled to vary from $+1$ to -1, so that the variation at x feet can be interpreted as a fraction of the variation at the surface.)

(a) Sketch the two-dimensional graphs of one year's temperature variation at depths of 0, 3, and 9 ft.

(b) Interpret these graphs to say what happens to the variation of temperature as depth increases.

(c) Figure 14.9 shows a computer-generated graph of w as a function of x and t. Interpret this graph to say what happens to the variation of temperature as depth increases.

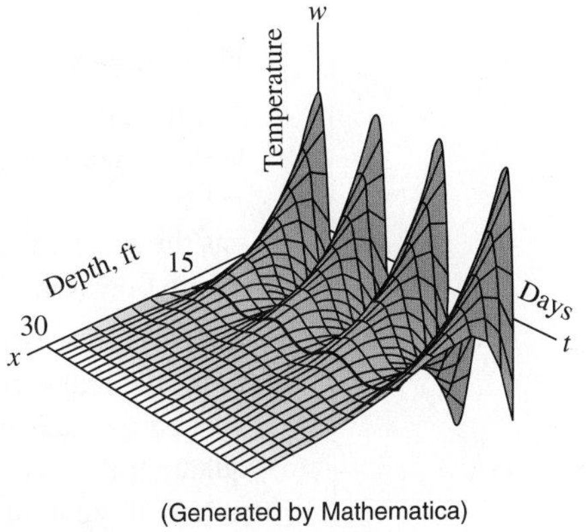

(Generated by Mathematica)

Figure 14.9 This computer-generated graph of $w = \cos(1.7 \times 10^{-2}t - 0.2x)e^{-0.2x}$ shows the seasonal variation of the temperature below ground as a fraction of surface temperature. At $x = 15$ ft, the variation is only 5% of the variation at the surface. At $x = 30$ ft, the variation is less than 0.25% of the surface variation. (Adapted from art provided by Norton Starr for G. C. Berresford, "Differential Equations and Root Cellars," *The UMAP Journal,* Vol. 2, No. 3 [1981], pp. 53–75.)

SOLUTION

(a) Figure 14.10 shows the graphs of $w = \cos(1.7 \times 10^{-2}t - 0.2x)e^{-0.2x}$ for $x = 0$, $x = 3$, and $x = 9$. Each curve shows w as a function of t in the window $[0, 365]$ by $[-1.2, 1.2]$.

(b) From these graphs, it would appear that the variation is greatest at the surface, decreasing in amplitude as the depth increases. It also appears that the wave is undergoing a gradual phase shift to the right as depth increases, indicating that variation lags increasingly behind surface variation as the depth increases.

(c) The computer-generated graph (Figure 14.9) shows how w varies with time and depth simultaneously. The variation in temperature (vertical amplitude in the figure) decreases dramatically as depth increases, decreasing to about 5% of surface variation at 15 ft and to negligible variation at 30 ft. The graph also shows that the temperature 15 ft below the surface is about a half a year out of phase with the surface temperature. (Follow the lines perpendicular to the 15-ft line and see how they go from peaks at 15 ft to valleys at 0 ft.) When the temperature is lowest at the surface (late January, say), it is at its highest 15 ft below. Fifteen feet below the ground, the seasons are reversed!

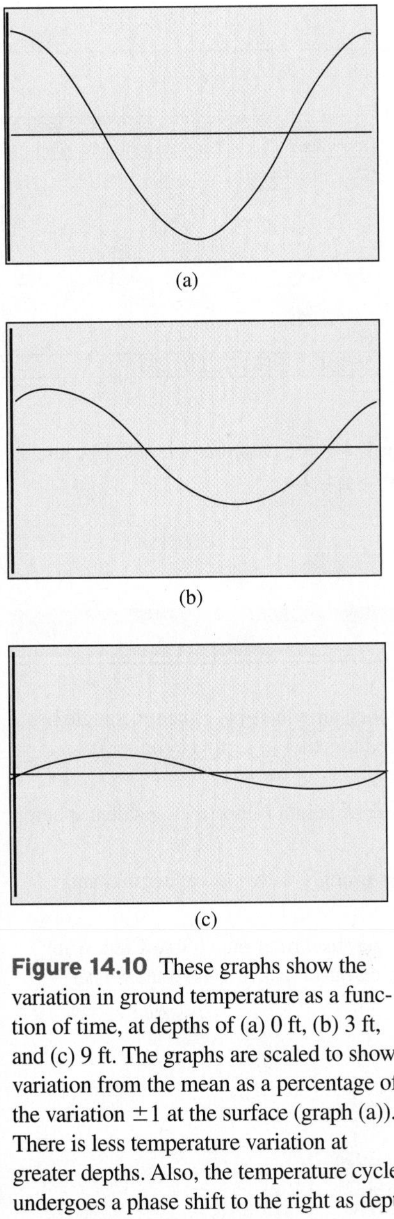

Figure 14.10 These graphs show the variation in ground temperature as a function of time, at depths of (a) 0 ft, (b) 3 ft, and (c) 9 ft. The graphs are scaled to show variation from the mean as a percentage of the variation ± 1 at the surface (graph (a)). There is less temperature variation at greater depths. Also, the temperature cycle undergoes a phase shift to the right as depth increases, indicating that the temperature cycle below the surface lags behind the cycle at ground level. (Example 5)

An Interesting Application (Optional)

Exploration 2 illustrates one way to visualize the complex zeros of any single valued function $f(x)$. You will need a CAS for this exploration.

EXPLORATION 2 Visualizing the Complex Zeros of a Function

Let $f(x)$ be a function of the single variable x. For the complex number $x + yi$, define $g(x, y) = |f(x + yi)|$. The graph of g is sometimes called the *complex modulus surface of f.*

1. Explain why the zeros of f occur where the surface g touches or crosses the xy-plane.
2. Let $f(x) = x^3 + 1$. Use a CAS to show that
$g(x, y) = \sqrt{x^6 + 3x^4y^2 + 2x^3 + 3x^2y^4 - 6xy^2 + y^6 + 1}.$

continued

3. Find the zeros of f (real and nonreal) algebraically. (*Hint:* Factor f.)
4. Use the graph of g to estimate the zeros of f graphically. Compare your graph with the graph in Figure 14.11a. We used the viewing window $-1.5 \leq x \leq 1.5$, $-1.5 \leq y \leq 1.5$, $-1 \leq z \leq 3$. The graph suggests that the surface looks like it has three "teeth" that touch the xy-plane. Of course, we cannot "see" exactly where they touch.
5. Improve your estimate in (4) using contour plots of g. We used Figure 14.11b to "see" the real zero of -1 along the x-axis and estimate that the other two complex zeros are near $0.5 \pm 0.75i$. Figure 14.11c shows a zoom-in view in the first quadrant that with trace allows us to estimate this zero as $0.5 + 0.857i$. Compare with your answer in (3).

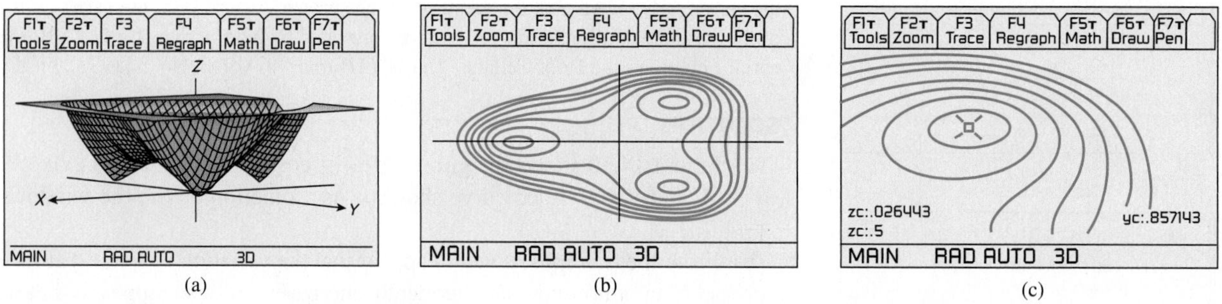

Figure 14.11 The graph of (a) $g(x, y) = |f(x + yi)|$ in $-1.5 \leq x \leq 1.5$, $-1.5 \leq y \leq 1.5$, $-1 \leq z \leq 3$, together with its (b) contour plot in $-1.5 \leq x \leq 1.5$, $-1.5 \leq y \leq 1.5$, and the (c) zoom-in contour plot in $0 \leq x \leq 1.5$, $0 \leq y \leq 1.5$.

Quick Review 14.1

Find a formula for each of the following functions of more than one independent variable:

1. The volume V of a right circular cone with radius r and height h
2. The total surface area S of a closed cylindrical container with radius r and height h
3. The time t required for a car traveling x miles per hour to travel y feet
4. The altitude h to the base b of an isosceles triangle with legs of length a
5. The area A of a triangle in which sides of length a and b meet at a 20° angle
6. The volume of the solid generated by revolving the region enclosed by the graphs of $y^2 = ax$ and the line $x = b$ (where a and b are positive) about the x-axis
7. The volume V enclosed when an x-inch-by-y-inch rectangle has a pair of opposite sides taped together to form a cylinder (two possible formulas)
8. The volume V of a cylinder of height h inscribed inside a sphere of radius r
9. The area A of an isosceles triangle with legs of length a and vertex angle θ
10. The linear velocity v of a carousel rider on a horse k feet from the axis of rotation, if the carousel makes m revolutions per minute

Section 14.1 Exercises

In Exercises 1–8, find the function's domain and range and determine whether the domain is bounded or unbounded.

1. $f(x, y) = y - x$

2. $f(x, y) = \sqrt{y - x}$

3. $f(x, y) = \ln(x^2 + y^2)$

4. $f(x, y) = \cos(x^2 + y^2)$

5. $f(x, y) = xy$

6. $f(x, y) = y/x^2$

7. $f(x, y) = 1/\sqrt{16 - x^2 - y^2}$

8. $f(x, y) = \sqrt{9 - x^2 - y^2}$

In Exercises 9–16, display the values of the functions in two ways: (**a**) by sketching the surface $z = f(x, y)$ and (**b**) by drawing an assortment of level curves in the function's domain. Label each level curve you draw with its function value.

9. $f(x, y) = y^2$

10. $f(x, y) = 4 - y^2$

11. $f(x, y) = x^2 + y^2$

12. $f(x, y) = \sqrt{x^2 + y^2}$

13. $f(x, y) = -(x^2 + y^2)$

14. $f(x, y) = 4 - x^2 - y^2$

15. $f(x, y) = 4x^2 + y^2$

16. $f(x, y) = 4x^2 + y^2 + 1$

Exercises 17–22 show level curves for the functions graphed in (a)–(f). Match each set of level curves with the appropriate function.

17.

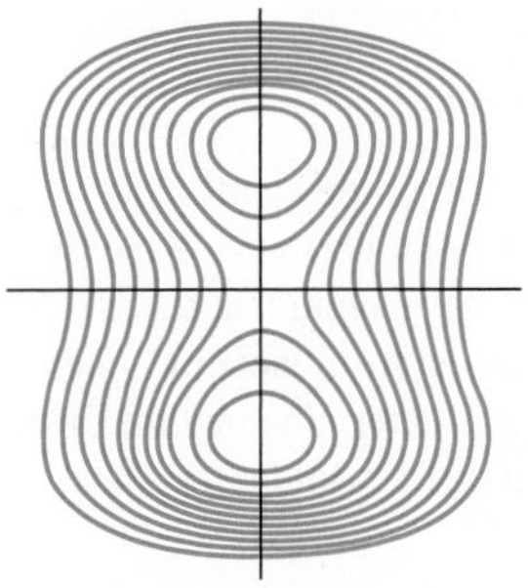

18.

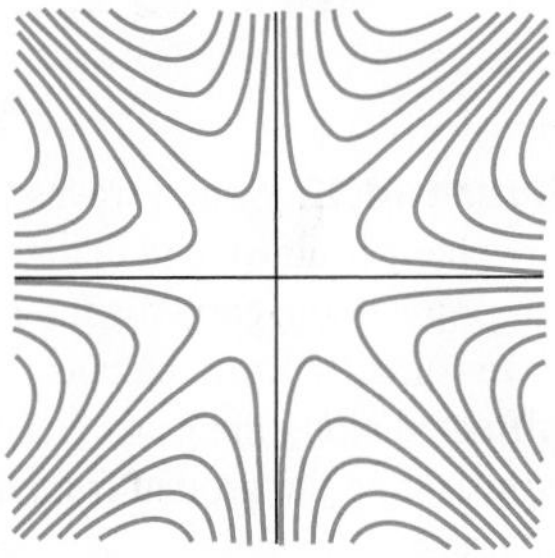

19.

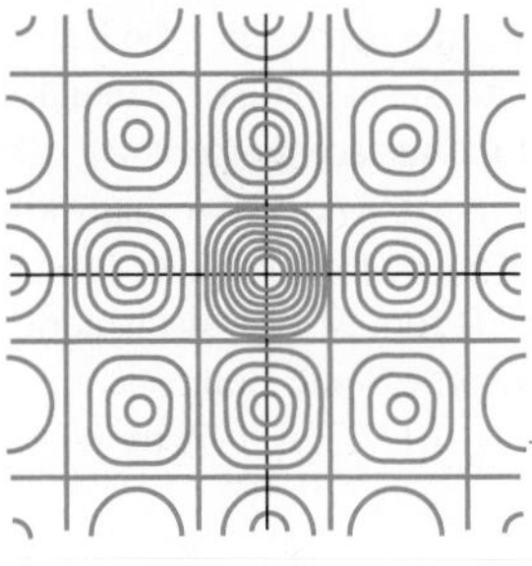

20.

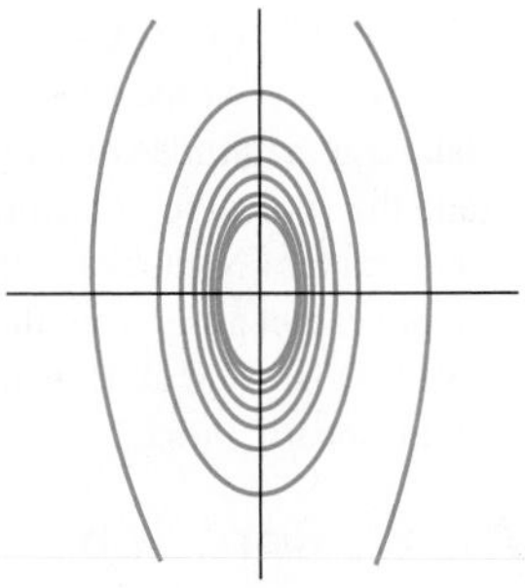

21.

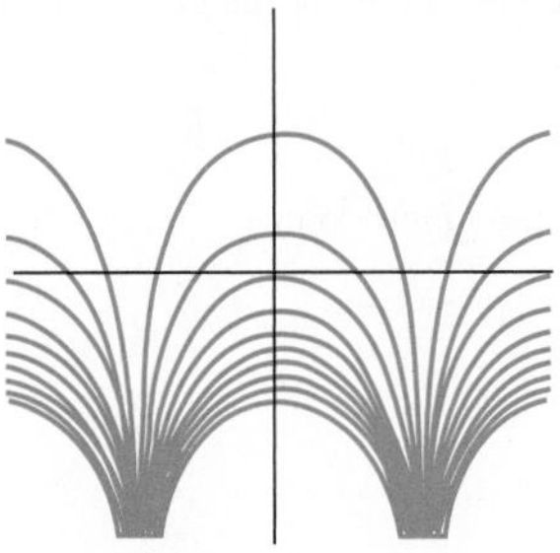

22.

(a)

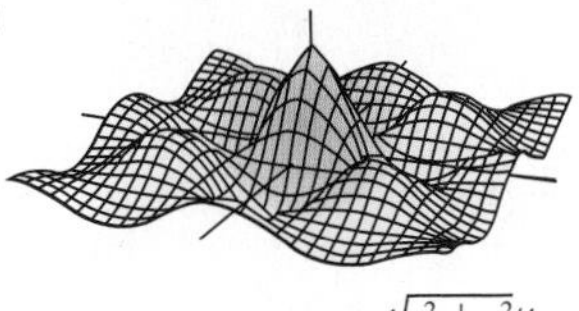

$z = (\cos x)(\cos y)\, e^{-\sqrt{x^2 + y^2}/4}$

(b)

$z = -\dfrac{xy^2}{x^2 + y^2}$

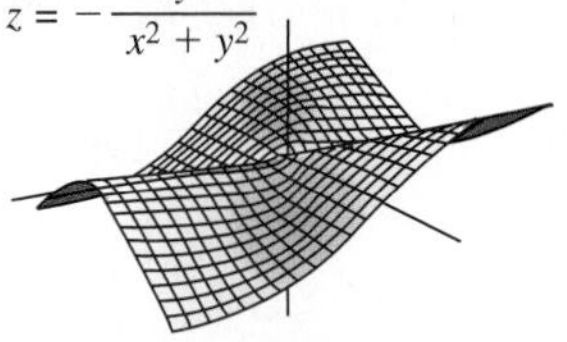

(c)

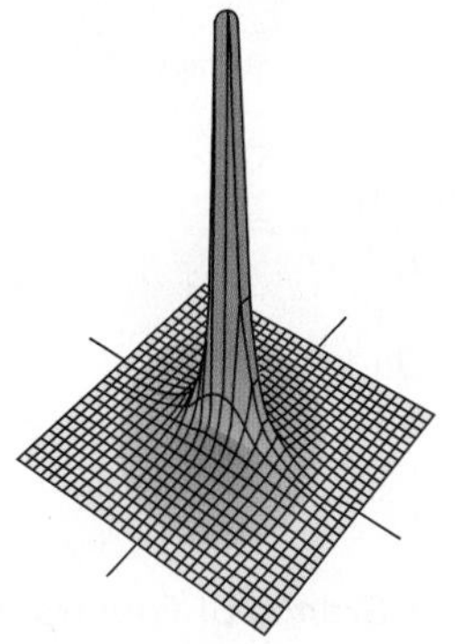

$z = \dfrac{1}{(4x^2 + y^2)}$

(d)

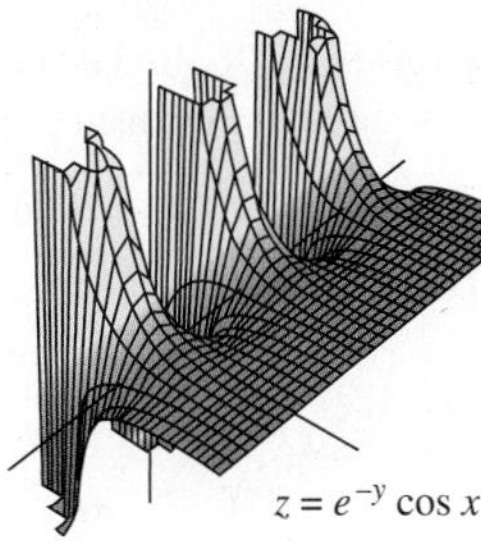

$z = e^{-y} \cos x$

(e)

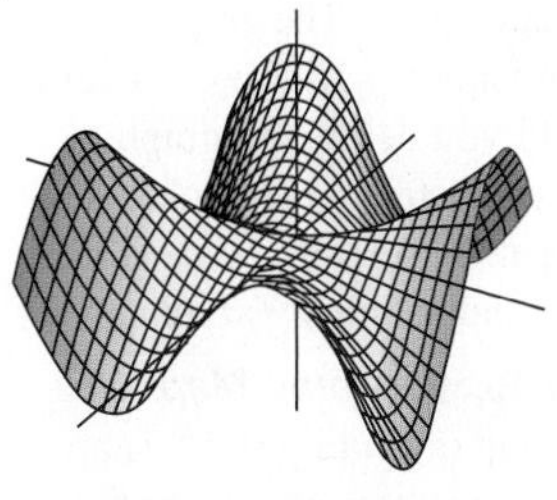

$z = \dfrac{xy(x^2 - y^2)}{(x^2 + y^2)}$

(f)

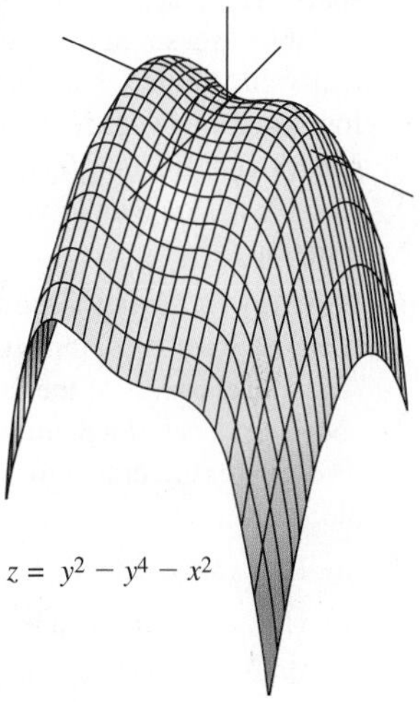

$z = y^2 - y^4 - x^2$

In Exercises 23–30, sketch a typical level surface for the function.

23. $f(x, y, z) = x^2 + y^2 + z^2$

24. $f(x, y, z) = \ln(x^2 + y^2 + z^2)$

25. $f(x, y, z) = x + z$

26. $f(x, y, z) = z$

27. $f(x, y, z) = x^2 + y^2$

28. $f(x, y, z) = y^2 + z^2$

29. $f(x, y, z) = z - x^2 - y^2$

30. $f(x, y, z) = \dfrac{x^2}{25} + \dfrac{y^2}{16} + \dfrac{z^2}{9}$

In Exercises 31–34, find an equation for the level curve of the function $f(x, y)$ that passes through the given point.

31. $f(x, y) = 16 - x^2 - y^2, \quad (2\sqrt{2}, \sqrt{2})$

32. $f(x, y) = \sqrt{x^2 - 1}, \quad (1, 0)$

33. $f(x, y) = \displaystyle\int_x^y \frac{dt}{1 + t^2}, \quad (-\sqrt{2}, \sqrt{2})$

34. $f(x, y) = \displaystyle\sum_{n=0}^{\infty} \left(\frac{x}{y}\right)^n, \quad (1, 2)$

In Exercises 35–38, find an equation for the level surface of the function through the given point.

35. $f(x, y, z) = \sqrt{x - y} - \ln z, \quad (3, -1, 1)$

36. $f(x, y, z) = \ln(x^2 + y + z^2), \quad (-1, 2, 1)$

37. $g(x, y, z) = \displaystyle\sum_{n=0}^{\infty} \frac{(x + y)^n}{n! z^n}, \quad (\ln 2, \ln 4, 3)$

38. $g(x, y, z) = \displaystyle\int_x^y \frac{d\theta}{\sqrt{1 - \theta^2}} + \int_{\sqrt{2}}^z \frac{dt}{t\sqrt{t^2 - 1}}, \quad (0, 1/2, 2)$

39. Writing to Learn *Defining the Graphs of Functions of n Independent Variables* As you know, the graph of a real-valued function of a single variable is a set in two-coordinate space. The graph of a real-valued function of two independent variables is a set in three-coordinate space. The graph of a real-valued function of three independent variables is a set in four-coordinate space. How would you define the graph of a real-valued function $f(x_1, x_2, x_3, x_4)$ of four independent real variables? How would you define the graph of a real-valued function $f(x_1, x_2, x_3, \ldots, x_n)$ of n independent variables?

40. Writing to Learn *Reading a Topographic Map* The "contour lines" on a topographic map (as in Figure 14.7) are really level curves of the function $h(x, y)$ that gives the height above sea level of a point with coordinates (x, y) on the map. The level curves are drawn for h values at regular intervals (for example, 20 ft).

(a) How can you spot a mountain on a topographic map? Explain.

(b) How can you spot a level area on a topographic map? Explain.

(c) Why do rivers and streams usually run perpendicular to contour lines?

(d) What geological formation would be indicated by a series of straight contour lines very close together? Explain.

Explorations

41. *Maximum Value of a Function on a Line in Space* Does the function $f(x, y, z) = xyz$ have a maximum value on the line $x = 20 - t$, $y = t$, $z = 20$? If so, what is it? Give reasons for your answer. (*Hint:* Along the line, $w = f(x, y, z)$ is a differentiable function of the single variable t.)

42. *Minimum Value of a Function on a Line in Space* Does the function $f(x, y, z) = xy - z$ have a minimum value on the line $x = t - 1$, $y = t - 2$, $z = t + 7$? If so, what is it? Give reasons for your answer. (*Hint:* Along the line, $w = f(x, y, z)$ is a differentiable function of the single variable t.)

Extending the Ideas

43. *The Concorde's Sonic Booms* The width w of the region in which people on the ground hear the Concorde's sonic boom directly, not reflected from a layer of the atmosphere, is a function of

T = air temperature at ground level (in degrees Kelvin),

h = the Concorde's altitude (in kilometers), and

d = the vertical temperature gradient (temperature drop in degrees Kelvin per km).

The formula for w is

$$w = 4(Th/d)^{\frac{1}{2}}.$$

See Figure 14.12.

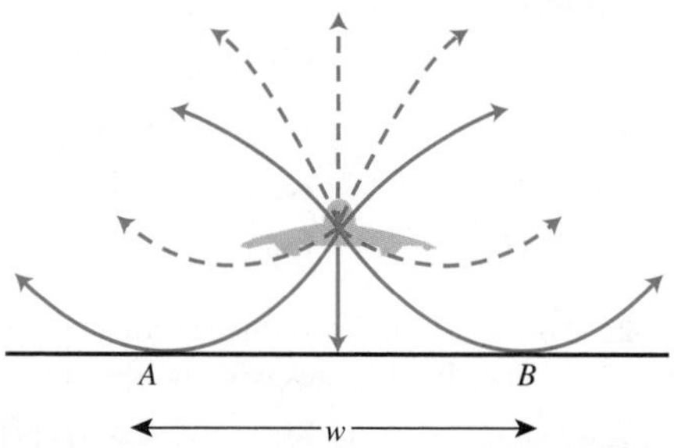

Figure 14.12 Sound waves from the Concorde bend as the temperature changes above and below the altitude at which the plane flies. The sonic boom carpet is the region on the ground that receives shock waves directly from the plane, not reflected from the atmosphere or diffracted along the ground. The carpet is determined by the grazing rays striking the ground from the point directly under the plane. (Exercise 43)

The Washington, D.C.–bound Concorde approaches the United States from Europe on a course that takes it south of Nantucket Island at an altitude of 16.8 km. If the surface temperature is 290 K and the vertical temperature gradient is 5 K/km, how many kilometers south of Nantucket must the plane be flown to keep its sonic boom carpet away from the island? (From N. K. Balachandra, W. L. Donn, and D. H. Rind, "Concorde Sonic Booms as an Atmospheric Probe," *Science,* July 1, 1977, Vol. 197, pp. 47–49.)

CAS Explorations

In Exercises 44–47, perform the following steps for the given function.

(a) Plot the surface over the given rectangle.

(b) Plot several level curves in the rectangle.

(c) Plot the level curve of f through the given point.

44. $f(x, y) = x \sin \dfrac{y}{2} + y \sin 2x, \quad 0 \le x \le 5\pi,$
$0 \le y \le 5\pi, \quad P(3\pi, 3\pi)$

45. $f(x, y) = (\sin x)(\cos y)e^{\sqrt{x^2 + y^2/8}}, \quad 0 \le x \le 5\pi$
$0 \le y \le 5\pi, \quad P(4\pi, 4\pi)$

46. $f(x, y) = \sin(x + 2\cos y), \quad -2\pi \le x \le 2\pi,$
$-2\pi \le y \le 2\pi, \quad P(\pi, \pi)$

47. $f(x, y) = e^{(x^{0.1} - y)} \sin(x^2 + y^2), \quad 0 \le x \le 2\pi,$
$-2\pi \le y \le \pi, \quad P(\pi, -\pi)$

In Exercises 48–51, plot the level surfaces.

48. $4 \ln(x^2 + y^2 + z^2) = 1$

49. $x^2 + z^2 = 1$

50. $x + y^2 - 3z^2 = 1$

51. $\sin\left(\frac{x}{2}\right) - (\cos y)\sqrt{x^2 + z^2} = 2$

Just as you describe curves in the plane parametrically with a pair of equations $x = f(t)$, $y = g(t)$ defined on some parameter interval I, you can sometimes describe surfaces in space with a triple of equations $x = f(u, v)$, $y = g(u, v)$, $z = h(u, v)$ defined on some parameter rectangle $a \le u \le b$, $c \le v \le d$. Many computer algebra systems permit you to plot such surfaces in *parametric mode.* (Parametrized surfaces are discussed in detail in Section 16.6.)

In Exercises 52–55, plot the surfaces. Also plot several level curves in the xy-plane.

52. $x = u\cos v, \quad y = u\sin v, \quad z = u, \quad 0 \le u \le 2,$
$0 \le v \le 2\pi$

53. $x = u\cos v, \quad y = u\sin v, \quad z = v, \quad 0 \le u \le 2,$
$0 \le v \le 2\pi$

54. $x = (2 + \cos u)\cos v, \quad y = (2 + \cos u)\sin v,$
$z = \sin u, \quad 0 \le u \le 2\pi, \quad 0 \le v \le 2\pi$

55. $x = 2\cos u \cos v, \quad y = 2\cos u \sin v, \quad z = 2\sin u,$
$0 \le u \le 2\pi, \quad 0 \le v \le \pi$

In Exercises 56 and 57, find all the zeros of the function.

56. $f(x) = x^5 - 1$

57. $f(x) = x^4 + 1$

14.2 Limits and Continuity in Higher Dimensions

What you'll learn about

- Limits
- Continuity
- The Max-Min Property for Continuous Functions

Limits

If the values of a real-valued function $f(x, y)$ lie close to a fixed real number L for all points (x, y) sufficiently close to the point (x_0, y_0) but not equal to (x_0, y_0), we say that L is the limit of f as (x, y) approaches (x_0, y_0). In symbols, we write

$$\lim_{(x,y)\to(x_0,y_0)} f(x, y) = L,$$

and we say, "the limit of f as (x, y) approaches (x_0, y_0) equals L." This is like the limit of a function of one variable, except that two independent variables are involved instead of one, complicating the issue of "closeness." If (x_0, y_0) is an interior point of f's domain, (x, y) can approach (x_0, y_0) from any direction. To take the added dimension into account, we adjust the definition to measure distances in the domain with the two-dimensional distance formula rather than simple absolute value.

DEFINITION Limit of a Function of Two Independent Variables

The function f **has limit** L as (x, y) approaches (x_0, y_0) if, given any positive number ε, there is a positive number δ such that for all (x, y) in the domain of f,

$$0 < \sqrt{(x - x_0)^2 + (y - y_0)^2} < \delta \Rightarrow |f(x, y) - L| < \varepsilon.$$

We write $\lim_{(x,y)\to(x_0,y_0)} f(x, y) = L$.

Closeness in *both* dimensions in the xy-plane implies closeness in *each* dimension (and vice versa), so we can also use the following, equivalent, definition of limit.

DEFINITION Limit of a Function of Two Independent Variables

The function f **has limit** L as (x, y) approaches (x_0, y_0) if, given any positive number ε, there is a positive number δ such that for all (x, y) in the domain of f,

$$0 < |x - x_0| < \delta \quad \text{and} \quad 0 < |y - y_0| < \delta \Rightarrow |f(x, y) - L| < \varepsilon.$$

We write $\lim_{(x,y)\to(x_0,y_0)} f(x, y) = L$.

These definitions apply to boundary points as well as interior points of the domain of f. The only requirement is that the point (x, y) remain in the domain at all times.

It can be shown, as for functions of a single variable, that

$$\lim_{(x,y)\to(x_0,y_0)} x = x_0$$

$$\lim_{(x,y)\to(x_0,y_0)} y = y_0$$

$$\lim_{(x,y)\to(x_0,y_0)} k = k \quad \text{(any number } k\text{)}.$$

It can also be shown that the limit of the sum of two functions is the sum of their limits (when they both exist), with similar results for the limits of their differences, products, constant multiples, quotients, and powers.

THEOREM 1 Properties of Limits of Functions of Two Variables

If L, M, and k are real numbers and

$$\lim_{(x,y)\to(x_0,y_0)} f(x, y) = L \quad \text{and} \quad \lim_{(x,y)\to(x_0,y_0)} g(x, y) = M,$$

then

1. *Sum Rule:* $\lim_{(x,y)\to(x_0,y_0)} [f(x, y) + g(x, y)] = L + M$
2. *Difference Rule:* $\lim_{(x,y)\to(x_0,y_0)} [f(x, y) - g(x, y)] = L - M$
3. *Product Rule:* $\lim_{(x,y)\to(x_0,y_0)} [f(x, y) \cdot g(x, y)] = L \cdot M$
4. *Constant-Multiple-Rule* $\lim_{(x,y)\to(x_0,y_0)} k \cdot f(x, y) = k \cdot L$ (any number k)
5. *Quotient Rule:* $\lim_{(x,y)\to(x_0,y_0)} \dfrac{f(x, y)}{g(x, y)} = \dfrac{L}{M}$ if $M \neq 0$
6. *Power Rule:* Let $a > 0$. Then

   $$\lim_{(x,y)\to(x_0,y_0)} [f(x, y)]^a = L^a,$$

   provided L^a is a real number.

When we apply Theorem 1 to polynomials and rational functions, we obtain the useful result that the limits of these functions as $(x, y) \to (x_0, y_0)$ can be calculated by evaluating the functions at (x_0, y_0). The only requirement is that the rational functions be defined at (x_0, y_0).

EXAMPLE 1 Calculating Limits of Rational Functions

Find (**a**) $\lim_{(x,y)\to(3,-4)} (x^2 + y^2)$ and (**b**) $\lim_{(x,y)\to(0,1)} \frac{x - xy + 3}{x^2y + 5xy - y^3}$.

SOLUTION

(**a**) $\lim_{(x,y)\to(3,-4)} (x^2 + y^2) = (3)^2 + (-4)^2 = 25$

(**b**) $\lim_{(x,y)\to(0,1)} \frac{x - xy + 3}{x^2y + 5xy - y^3} = \frac{0 - 0 \cdot 1 + 3}{0^2 \cdot 1 + 5 \cdot 0 \cdot 1 - 1^3} = -3$

As in the single-variable case, it is the *continuity* of polynomial and rational functions over their domains that enables us to compute these limits so easily.

EXAMPLE 2 Calculating Limits

Find

$$\lim_{(x,y)\to(0,0)} \frac{x^2 - xy}{\sqrt{x} - \sqrt{y}}.$$

SOLUTION

Since the denominator $\sqrt{x} - \sqrt{y}$ approaches 0 as $(x, y) \to (0, 0)$, we cannot use the Quotient Rule from Theorem 1. However, if we multiply numerator and denominator by $\sqrt{x} + \sqrt{y}$ we produce an equivalent fraction (equivalent for $(x, y) \neq (0, 0)$) whose limit we *can* find:

$$\lim_{(x,y)\to(0,0)} \frac{x^2 - xy}{\sqrt{x} - \sqrt{y}} = \lim_{(x,y)\to(0,0)} \frac{(x^2 - xy)(\sqrt{x} + \sqrt{y})}{(\sqrt{x} - \sqrt{y})(\sqrt{x} + \sqrt{y})}$$

$$= \lim_{(x,y)\to(0,0)} \frac{x(x - y)(\sqrt{x} + \sqrt{y})}{x - y} \qquad \text{Algebra}$$

$$= \lim_{(x,y)\to(0,0)} x(\sqrt{x} + \sqrt{y}) = 0 \qquad \text{Cancel the factor } (x-y).$$

We can cancel the factor $(x - y)$ in Example 2 because the path $y = x$ (along which $x - y = 0$) is *not* in the domain of the function

$$\frac{x^2 - xy}{\sqrt{x} - \sqrt{y}}.$$

Continuity

The definition of continuity for functions of two variables is essentially the same as for functions of a single variable.

DEFINITIONS Continuity at a Point, Continuity

A function $f(x, y)$ is **continuous at the point** (x_0, y_0) if

1. f is defined at (x_0, y_0).
2. $\lim_{(x,y)\to(x_0,y_0)} f(x, y)$ exists.
3. $\lim_{(x,y)\to(x_0,y_0)} f(x, y) = f(x_0, y_0)$.

A function is **continuous** if it is continuous at every point of its domain.

As with the definition of limit, the definition of continuity applies at boundary points as well as interior points of the domain of f. The only requirement is that the point (x, y) remain in the domain at all times.

As you may have guessed, one consequence of Theorem 1 is that algebraic combinations of continuous functions are continuous at every point at which all the functions involved are defined. Hence, sums, differences, products, constant multiples, quotients, and powers of continuous functions are continuous where defined. In particular, polynomials and rational functions of two variables are continuous at every point at which they are defined.

If $z = f(x, y)$ is a continuous function of x and y and if $w = g(z)$ is a continuous function of z, then the composite $w = g(f(x, y))$ is continuous. Thus,

$$e^{x-y}, \qquad \cos\left(\frac{xy}{x^2+1}\right), \qquad \ln(1 + x^2y^2)$$

are all continuous at every point (x, y).

As with functions of a single variable, the general rule is that composites of continuous functions are continuous. The only requirement is that each function be continuous where it is applied.

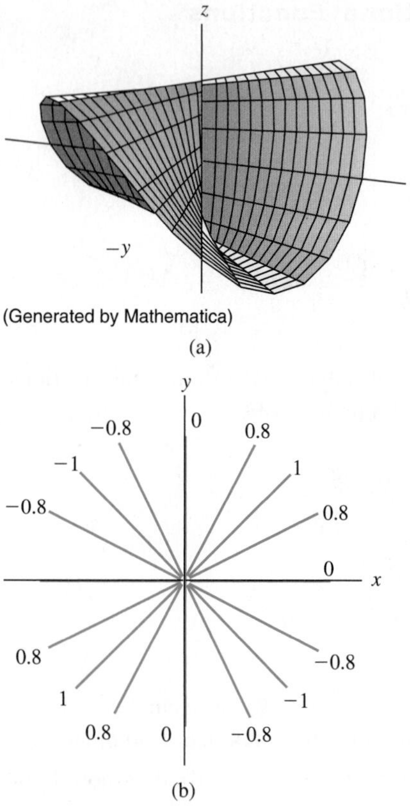

Figure 14.13 (a) The graph of

$$f(x, y) = \begin{cases} \dfrac{2xy}{x^2 + y^2}, & (x, y) \neq (0, 0) \\ 0, & (x, y) = (0, 0) \end{cases}$$

is continuous at every point except the origin. (b) The level curve of f.

EXAMPLE 3 Showing that a Function Has a Single Discontinuity

Show that

$$f(x, y) = \begin{cases} \dfrac{2xy}{x^2 + y^2}, & (x, y) \neq (0, 0) \\ 0, & (x, y) = (0, 0) \end{cases}$$

is continuous at every point except the origin (Figure 14.13).

SOLUTION

The function f is continuous at any point $(x, y) \neq (0, 0)$ because its values are then given by a rational function of x and y.

At $(0, 0)$, the value of f is defined, but f, we claim, has no limit as $(x, y) \to (0, 0)$. The reason is that different paths of approach to the origin can lead to different limits, as we will now see.

For every value of m, the function f has a constant value on the "punctured" line $y = mx$, $x \neq 0$, because

$$f(x, y)\Big|_{y=mx} = \frac{2xy}{x^2 + y^2}\Big|_{y=mx} = \frac{2x(mx)}{x^2 + (mx)^2} = \frac{2m}{1 + m^2}$$

Therefore, f has this number as its limit as (x, y) approaches $(0, 0)$ along the line:

$$\lim_{\substack{\text{along } y=mx \\ (x,y)\to(0,0)}} f(x, y) = \lim_{(x,y)\to(0,0)} \left[f(x, y)\big|_{y=mx}\right] = \frac{2m}{1 + m^2}.$$

The limit changes with m, however. There is therefore no single number we may call the limit of f as (x, y) approaches the origin. The limit fails to exist, and the function is not continuous.

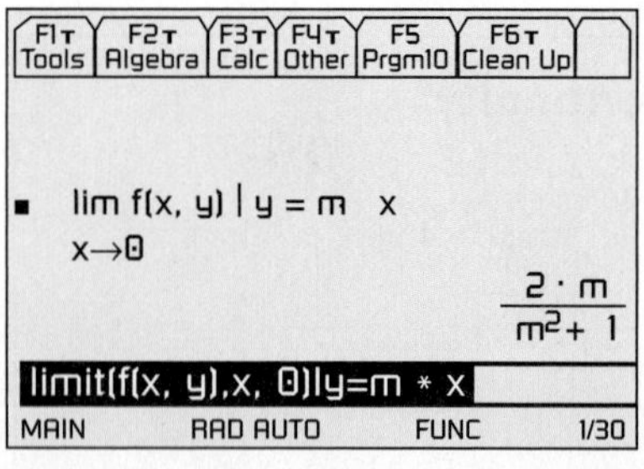

Figure 14.14 Read the expression in the figure as the limit of $f(x, y)$ as $x \to 0$ with the restriction that $y = mx$. The vertical bar translates to "with the restriction that."

We can support the result of Example 3 with CAS as suggested by Figure 14.14.

Example 3 illustrates an important point about the limits of functions of two variables (or even more variables, for that matter). For a limit to exist at a point, the limit must be the same along every approach path. If we ever find paths with different limits, we know that the function has no limit at the point they approach.

The Two-Path Test for Discontinuity

If a function $f(x, y)$ has different limits along two different paths as (x, y) approaches (x_0, y_0), then $\lim_{(x,y)\to(x_0,y_0)} f(x, y)$ does not exist.

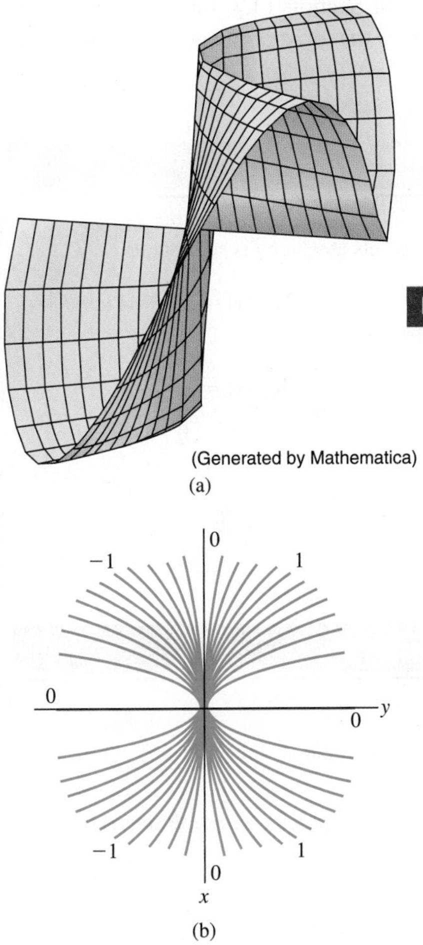

Figure 14.15 (a) The graph of $f(x, y) = 2x^2y/(x^4 + y^2)$. As the graph suggests and the level-curve values in (b) confirm, $\lim_{(x,y)\to(0,0)} f(x, y)$ does not exist.

EXPLORATION 1 **Exploring Pathways to the Origin**

Does the function

$$f(x, y) = \frac{2x^2y}{x^4 + y^2}$$

have a limit as (x, y) approaches $(0, 0)$?

(a) Find $f(x, y)\big|_{y=x^2}$ and compute $\lim_{\substack{(x,y)\to(0,0)\\ \text{along } y=x^2}} f(x, y)$.

(b) Find $f(x, y)\big|_{y=-x^2}$ and compute $\lim_{\substack{(x,y)\to(0,0)\\ \text{along } y=-x^2}} f(x, y)$.

(c) Explain why we can conclude that $\lim_{(x,y)\to(0,0)} f(x, y)$ does not exist.

(d) Show that the values of

$$f(x, y) = \frac{2x^2y}{x^4 + y^2}$$

are *constant* along any parabola of the form $y = kx^2$. Explain why such parabolas are level curves of f.

(e) Several level curves of f are graphed in Figure 14.15. How could we conclude from this graph that $\lim_{(x,y)\to(0,0)} f(x, y)$. does not exist?

The language we use in Exploration 1 showing that f has no limit at the origin might seem contradictory; one could easily argue that f has, in fact, many limits there. But that is just the point. There is no path-independent limit; therefore, by our definition, $\lim_{(x,y)\to(0,0)} f(x, y)$ does not exist. It is our translating this formal statement into the more colloquial "has no limit" that creates the apparent contradiction. The mathematics is fine; the problem arises in how we tend to talk about it. In the crunch, we need the formality to keep things straight.

The Max-Min Property for Continuous Functions

We have seen that a function of a single variable that is continuous throughout a closed, bounded interval takes on an absolute maximum value and an absolute minimum value at least once in that interval. The same is true of a function $z = f(x, y)$ that is continuous on a closed, bounded set R in the plane (like a line segment, a disk, or a filled-in triangle). The function takes on an absolute maximum value at some point in R and an absolute minimum value at some point in R.

The max-min property and other results of this section hold for functions of three or more variables. A continuous function $w = f(x, y, z)$, for example, must take on absolute maximum and minimum values on any closed, bounded set (solid ball or cube, spherical shell, rectangular solid) on which it is defined.

We will learn how to find these extreme values in Section 14.7, but first we need to know about derivatives in higher dimensions, which is the topic of the next section.

Quick Review 14.2

In Exercises 1–5, find the limit.

1. $\lim_{x\to 2} \dfrac{3x^2 - 7x + 5}{x^3 + x^2 - 9}$

2. $\lim_{x\to 0} \sqrt{3 + \sec x}$

3. $\lim_{x\to 4} \dfrac{x + 5}{\sqrt{x^2 + 9}}$

4. $\lim_{x\to 3} \dfrac{2x^2 - 7x + 3}{x^2 - 9}$

5. $\lim_{x\to \pi} \dfrac{\sin x}{x - \pi}$

In Exercises 6–10, find the points at which f is continuous.

6. $f(x) = \dfrac{\sin 4x}{x^2 - 4}$

7. $f(x) = (x^2 + 1) \ln x$

8. $f(x) = \dfrac{|2x + 3|}{2x + 3}$

9. $f(x) = \begin{cases} \dfrac{\sin 2x}{\sin x}, & x \neq 0 \\ 0, & x = 0 \end{cases}$

10. $f(x) = \dfrac{x^2 - 3x - 10}{2 + \sin x}$

Section 14.2 Exercises

In Exercises 1–12, find the limit.

1. $\lim_{(x,y)\to(0,0)} \dfrac{3x^2 - y^2 + 5}{x^2 + y^2 + 2}$

2. $\lim_{(x,y)\to(1,1)} \ln |1 + x^2y^2|$

3. $\lim_{(x,y)\to(0,\,\ln 2)} e^{x-y}$

4. $\lim_{(x,y)\to(0,4)} \dfrac{x}{\sqrt{y}}$

5. $\lim_{(x,y,z)\to(1,3,4)} \sqrt{x^2 + y^2 + z^2 - 1}$

6. $\lim_{(x,y,z)\to(1,2,6)} \left(\dfrac{1}{x} + \dfrac{1}{y} + \dfrac{1}{z}\right)$

7. $\lim_{(x,y)\to(0,\pi/4)} \sec x \tan y$

8. $\lim_{(x,y)\to(0,0)} \cos \dfrac{x^2 + y^2}{x + y + 1}$

9. $\lim_{(x,y)\to(1,1)} \cos \sqrt[3]{|xy| - 1}$

10. $\lim_{(x,y)\to(1,0)} \dfrac{x \sin y}{x^2 + 1}$

11. $\lim_{(x,y)\to(0,0)} \dfrac{e^y \sin x}{x}$

12. $\lim_{(x,y)\to(0,0)} \tan^{-1}(1/\sqrt{x^2 + y^2})$

In Exercises 13–20, find the limit by rewriting the fraction first.

13. $\lim_{\substack{(x,y)\to(1,1)\\ x\neq y}} \dfrac{x^2 - 2xy + y^2}{x - y}$

14. $\lim_{\substack{(x,y)\to(1,1)\\ x\neq y}} \dfrac{x^2 - y^2}{x - y}$

15. $\lim_{\substack{(x,y)\to(1,1)\\ x\neq y}} \dfrac{xy - y - 2x + 2}{x - 1}$

16. $\lim_{\substack{(x,y)\to(2,4)\\ y\neq -4,\, x\neq x^2}} \dfrac{y + 4}{x^2y - xy + 4x^2 - 4x}$

17. $\lim_{\substack{(x,y)\to(0,0)\\ x\neq y}} \dfrac{x - y + 2\sqrt{x} - 2\sqrt{y}}{\sqrt{x} - \sqrt{y}}$

18. $\lim_{\substack{(x,y)\to(2,2)\\ x+y\neq 4}} \dfrac{x + y - 4}{\sqrt{x + y} - 2}$

19. $\lim_{\substack{(x,y)\to(2,0)\\ 2x-y\neq 4}} \dfrac{\sqrt{2x - y} - 2}{2x - y - 4}$

20. $\lim_{\substack{(x,y)\to(4,3)\\ x\neq y+1}} \dfrac{\sqrt{x} - \sqrt{y + 1}}{x - y - 1}$

In Exercises 21–26, find the limit. In each exercise, P stands for the point (x, y, z).

21. $\lim_{P\to(2,3,-6)} \sqrt{x^2 + y^2 + z^2}$

22. $\lim_{P\to(0,-2,0)} \ln \sqrt{x^2 + y^2 + z^2}$

23. $\lim_{P\to(3,3,0)} (\sin^2 x + \cos^2 y + \sec^2 z)$

24. $\lim_{P\to(\pi,0,3)} ze^{-2y} \cos 2x$

25. $\lim_{P\to(-1/4,\pi/2,2)} \tan^{-1} xyz$

26. $\lim_{P\to(1,-1,-1)} \dfrac{2xy + yz}{x^2 + z^2}$

In Exercises 27–30, at what points (x, y) in the plane is the function continuous?

27. **(a)** $f(x, y) = \sin(x + y)$
(b) $f(x, y) = \ln(x^2 + y^2)$

28. **(a)** $f(x, y) = \dfrac{x + y}{x - y}$
(b) $f(x, y) = \dfrac{y}{x^2 + 1}$

29. **(a)** $g(x, y) = \sin \dfrac{1}{xy}$
(b) $g(x, y) = \dfrac{x + y}{2 + \cos x}$

30. **(a)** $g(x, y) = \dfrac{x^2 + y^2}{x^2 - 3x + 2}$
(b) $g(x, y) = \dfrac{1}{x^2 - y}$

In Exercises 31–34, at what points (x, y, z) in space is the function continuous?

31. **(a)** $f(x, y, z) = x^2 + y^2 - 2z^2$
(b) $f(x, y, z) = \sqrt{x^2 + y^2 - 1}$

32. **(a)** $f(x, y, z) = \ln xyz$
(b) $f(x, y, z) = e^{x+y} \cos z$

33. **(a)** $f(x, y, z) = xy \sin (1/z)$

(b) $f(x, y, z) = \dfrac{1}{x^2 + y^2 + z^2 - 1}$

34. **(a)** $f(x, y, z) = \dfrac{1}{|x| + |y| + |z|}$ **(b)** $f(x, y, z) = \dfrac{1}{|xy| + |z|}$

In Exercises 35–42, show that the function has no limit as (x, y) approaches $(0, 0)$ by considering different paths of approach.

35. $f(x, y) = -\dfrac{x}{\sqrt{x^2 + y^2}}$

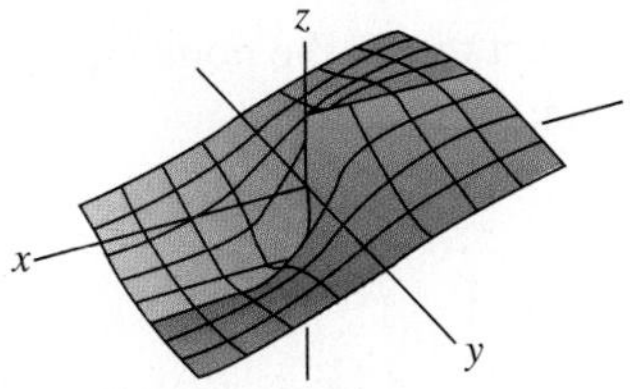

(Generated by Mathematica)

36. $f(x, y) = \dfrac{x^4}{x^4 + y^2}$

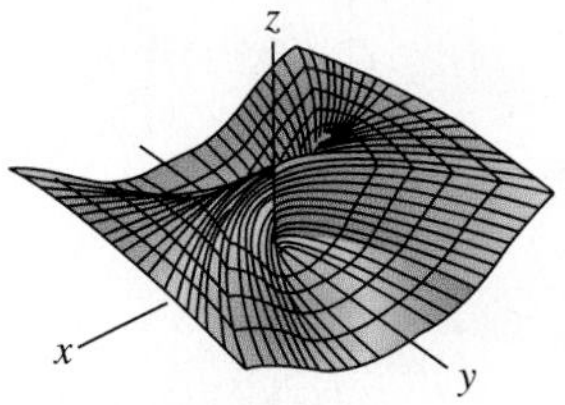

(Generated by Mathematica)

37. $f(x, y) = \dfrac{x^4 - y^2}{x^4 + y^2}$ **38.** $f(x, y) = \dfrac{xy}{|xy|}$

39. $g(x, y) = \dfrac{x - y}{x + y}$ **40.** $g(x, y) = \dfrac{x + y}{x - y}$

41. $h(x, y) = \dfrac{x^2 + y}{y}$ **42.** $h(x, y) = \dfrac{x^2}{x^2 - y}$

43. **Writing to Learn** If $\lim_{(x,y)\to(x_0,y_0)} f(x, y) = L$, must f be defined at (x_0, y_0)? Give reasons for your answer.

44. **Writing to Learn** If $f(x_0, y_0) = 3$, what can you say about $\lim_{(x,y)\to(x_0,y_0)} f(x, y)$ if f is continuous at (x_0, y_0)? If f is not continuous at (x_0, y_0)? Give reasons for your answers.

Explorations

45. *(Continuation of Example 3)*

(a) Reread Example 3. Then substitute $m = \tan \theta$ into the formula

$$f(x, y)\big|_{y=mx} = \frac{2m}{1 + m^2}$$

and simplify the result to show how the value of f varies with the line's angle of inclination.

(b) Use the formula you obtained in (a) to show that the limit of f as $(x, y) \to (0, 0)$ along the line $y = mx$ varies from -1 to 1 depending on the angle of approach.

46. **Removing a Discontinuity in the Plane** Define $f(0, 0)$ in a way that extends.

$$f(x, y) = xy\frac{x^2 - y^2}{x^2 + y^2}$$

to be continuous at the origin.

Extending the Ideas

The *Sandwich Theorem* for functions of two variables states that if $g(x, y) \le f(x, y) \le h(x, y)$ for all $(x, y) \ne (x_0, y_0)$ in a disk centered at (x_0, y_0) and if g and h have the same finite limit L as $(x, y) \to (x_0, y_0)$, then $\lim_{(x,y)\to(x_0,y_0)} f(x, y) = L$. In Exercises 47–50, use this result to support your answers to the question.

47. Does knowing that

$$1 - \frac{x^2y^2}{3} < \frac{tan^{-1} xy}{xy} < 1$$

tell you anything about

$$\lim_{(x,y)\to(0,0)} \frac{\tan^{-1} xy}{xy}?$$

Give reasons for your answer.

48. Does knowing that

$$2|xy| - \frac{x^2y^2}{6} < 4 - 4\cos\sqrt{|xy|} < 2|xy|$$

tell you anything about

$$\lim_{(x,y)\to(0,0)} \frac{4 - 4\cos\sqrt{|xy|}}{|xy|}?$$

Give reasons for your answer.

49. Does knowing that

$$\left|\sin\frac{1}{x}\right| \le 1$$

tell you anything about

$$\lim_{(x,y)\to(0,0)} y\sin\frac{1}{x}?$$

Give reasons for your answer.

50. Does knowing that

$$\left|\cos\frac{1}{y}\right| \le 1$$

tell you anything about

$$\lim_{(x,y)\to(0,0)} x\cos\frac{1}{y}?$$

Give reasons for your answer.

CAS Explorations

51. Explore the graphs of the four functions whose limits you considered in Exercises 47–50. Try to find a view that supports your results in the previous exercises.

14.3 Partial Derivatives

What you'll learn about

- Definitions and Notation
- Calculations
- Functions of More Than Two Variables
- Partial Derivatives and Continuity
- Second-Order Partial Derivatives
- The Mixed Derivative Theorem
- Partial Derivatives of Still Higher Order

Definitions and Notation

When we hold all but one of the independent variables of a function constant and differentiate with respect to that one variable, we get a "partial" derivative. For example, let (x_0, y_0) be some point in the domain of the function $f(x, y)$, and suppose we hold the value of y fixed at y_0. The vertical plane $y = y_0$ will cut the surface $z = f(x, y)$ in the curve $z = f(x, y_0)$ (Figure 14.16). This curve is the graph of the function $z = f(x, y_0)$ in the plane $y = y_0$. The horizontal coordinate in this plane is x; the vertical coordinate is z.

We define the partial derivative of f with respect to x at the point (x_0, y_0) as the ordinary derivative of $f(x, y_0)$ with respect to x at the point $x = x_0$.

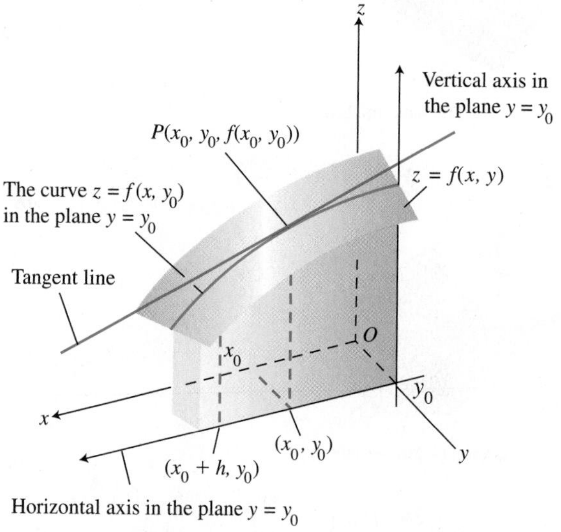

Figure 14.16 The intersection of the plane $y = y_0$ with the surface $z = f(x, y)$, viewed from a point above the first quadrant of the xy-plane.

DEFINITION Partial Derivative with Respect to x

The **partial derivative of $f(x, y)$ with respect to x** at the point (x_0, y_0) is

$$\left.\frac{\partial f}{\partial x}\right|_{(x_0,y_0)} = \left.\frac{d}{dx} f(x, y_0)\right|_{(x_0,y_0)} = \lim_{h\to 0} \frac{f(x_0 + h, y_0) - f(x_0, y_0)}{h},$$

provided the limit exists.

The stylized "∂" is just another kind of "d." It is convenient to have this distinguishable way of extending the Leibniz differential notation into a multivariable context.

The slope of the curve $z = f(x, y_0)$ at the point $P(x_0, y_0, f(x_0, y_0))$ in the plane $y = y_0$ is the value of the partial derivative of f with respect to x at (x_0, y_0). The tangent line to the curve at P is the line in the plane $y = y_0$ that passes through P with this slope. The partial derivative $\partial f/\partial x$ at (x_0, y_0) gives the rate of change of f with respect to x when y is held fixed at the value y_0. Geometrically, this is the rate of change of f in the direction of **i** at (x_0, y_0).

The notation that we use for a partial derivative depends on what aspect of the derivative we want to emphasize:

$\dfrac{\partial f}{\partial x}(x_0, y_0)$ or $f_x(x_0, y_0)$	Partial derivative of f with respect to "x at (x_0, y_0) or "f sub x at (x_0, y_0)." Convenient for stressing the point (x_0, y_0).
$\left.\dfrac{\partial z}{\partial x}\right\rvert_{(x_0, y_0)}$	"Partial derivative of z with respect to x at (x_0, y_0)." Common in science and engineering when you are dealing with variables and do not mention the function explicitly.
f_x, $\dfrac{\partial f}{\partial x}$, z_x, or $\dfrac{\partial z}{\partial x}$	"Partial derivative of f (or z) with respect to x." Convenient when you are treating the partial derivative as a function in its own right.

The definition of the partial derivative of $f(x, y)$ with respect to y at (x_0, y_0) is similar to the definition of the partial derivative of f with respect to x. We hold x fixed at the value x_0 and take the ordinary derivative of $f(x_0, y)$ with respect to y at y_0.

DEFINITION Partial Derivative with Respect to *y*

The **partial derivative of $f(x, y)$ with respect to y** at the point (x_0, y_0) is

$$\left.\frac{\partial f}{\partial x}\right\rvert_{(x_0, y_0)} = \left.\frac{d}{dy} f(x_0, y)\right\rvert_{(x_0, y_0)} = \lim_{h \to 0} \frac{f(x_0, y_0 + h) - f(x_0, y_0)}{h},$$

provided the limit exists.

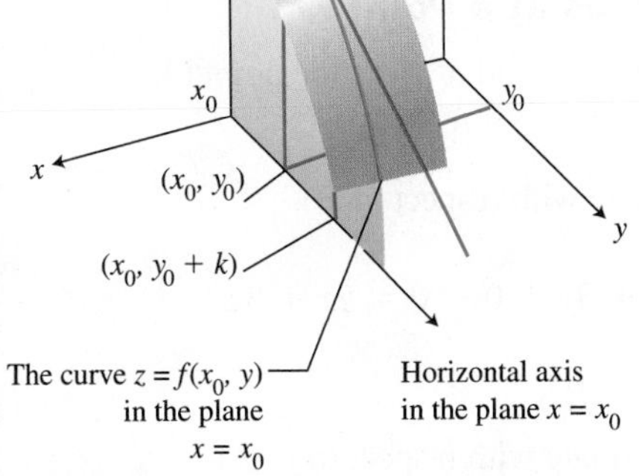

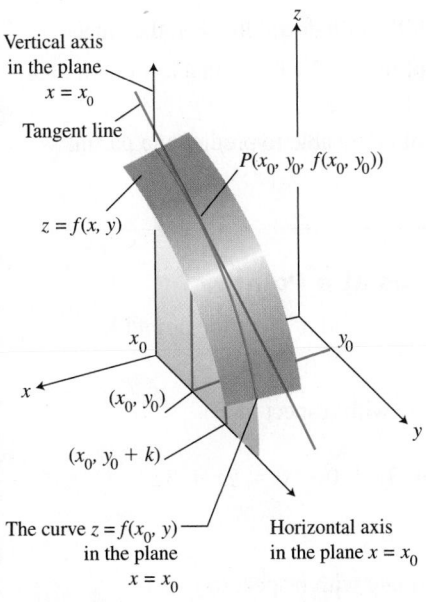

Figure 14.17 The intersection of the plane $x = x_0$ with the surface $z = f(x, y)$, viewed from above the first quadrant of the xy-plane.

The slope of the curve $z = f(x_0, y)$ at the point $P(x_0, y_0, f(x_0, y_0))$ in the plane $x = x_0$ (Figure 14.17) is the value of the partial derivative of f with respect to y at (x_0, y_0). The tangent line to the curve at P is the line in the plane $x = x_0$ that passes through P with this slope. The partial derivative $\partial f/\partial y$ at (x_0, y_0) gives the rate of change of f with respect to y when x is held fixed at the value x_0. Geometrically, this is the rate of change of f in the direction of **j** at (x_0, y_0).

The partial derivative with respect to y is denoted the same way as the partial derivative with respect to x:

$$\frac{\partial f}{\partial y}(x_0, y_0), \quad f_y(x_0, y_0), \quad \frac{\partial f}{\partial y}, \quad f_y.$$

Notice that we now have two tangent lines associated with the surface $z = f(x, y)$ at the point $P(x_0, y_0, f(x_0, y_0))$. (See Figure 14.18.) Is the plane they determine tangent to the surface at P? It would be nice if it were, but we have to learn more about partial derivatives before we can find out.

Calculations

The definitions of $\partial f/\partial x$ and $\partial f/\partial y$ give two different ways to differentiate f at a point: with respect to x in the usual way while treating y as constant and with respect to y in the usual way while treating x as constant. Can one partial derivative be predicted from the other? Before we calculate some partial derivatives, Exploration 1 anticipates the answer to that question.

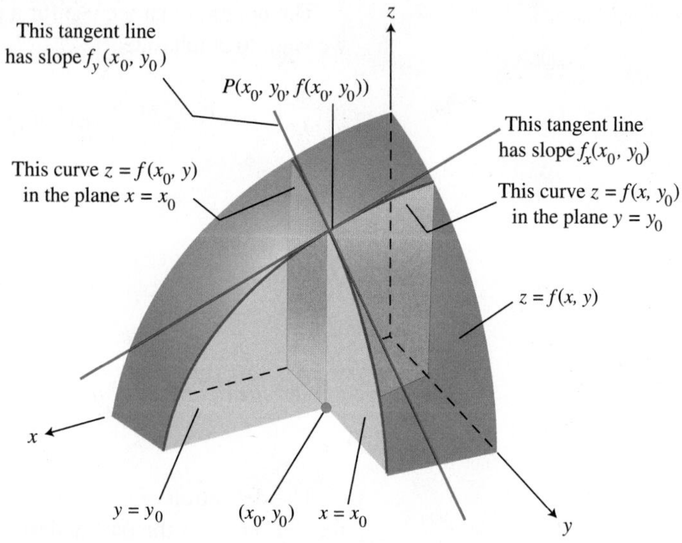

Figure 14.18 Figures 14.14 and 14.15 combined. The tangent lines at the point $P(x_0, y_0, f(x_0, y_0))$ determine a plane that appears (at least in this picture) to be tangent to the surface.

EXPLORATION 1 An Intersection of Two Hiking Paths

On a piece of cardboard or stiff paper, draw two straight lines to represent hiking paths that cross in the woods. Hikers *A* and *B* are headed toward the intersection along different paths. Draw and label a point on each path to represent *A* and *B*, and indicate each hiker's direction of travel with an arrow. Notice that you can change the slope of the "terrain" by tilting the cardboard in various directions.

1. Tilt the cardboard so that both hikers will be hiking uphill when they meet.
2. Tilt the cardboard so that both hikers will be hiking downhill when they meet.
3. Tilt the cardboard so that *A* will be hiking uphill and *B* downhill when they meet.
4. Tilt the cardboard so that *A* will be hiking uphill and *B* will be on a level path when they meet.
5. What do you conclude about the likelihood of being able to predict one partial derivative from knowing the other?

Partial Derivatives with NDER

Most calculators that find numerical derivatives require you to specify the variable of differentiation. Any other variables will be given their previously stored values. This means that NDER will actually compute partial derivatives. Just store the values of x_0 and y_0 into the respective registers for x and y, and then differentiate with respect to x at x_0 or with respect to y at y_0. Computers and calculators with CAS (computer algebra systems) can compute partial derivatives numerically or symbolically, using almost the same commands as in the single-variable case.

EXAMPLE 1 Finding Partial Derivatives at a Point

If $f(x, y) = x^2 + 3xy + y - 1$, find the values of $\partial f/\partial x$ and $\partial f/\partial y$ at the point $(4, -5)$.

SOLUTION

To find $\partial f/\partial x$, we regard y as fixed and differentiate with respect to x:

$$\frac{\partial f}{\partial x} = \frac{\partial}{\partial x}(x^2 + 3xy + y - 1) = 2x + 3y + 0 - 0 = 2x + 3y.$$

The value of $\partial f/\partial x$ at $(4, -5)$ is $2(4) + 3(-5) = -7$.

To find $\partial f/\partial y$, we regard x as fixed and differentiate with respect to y:

$$\frac{\partial f}{\partial y} = \frac{\partial}{\partial y}(x^2 + 3xy + y - 1) = 0 + 3x + 1 - 0 = 3x + 1.$$

The value of $\partial f/\partial y$ at $(4, -5)$ is $3(4) + 1 = 13$.

EXAMPLE 2 Finding a Partial Derivative as a Function

Find $\partial f/\partial y$ if $f(x, y) = y \sin xy$.

SOLUTION

We treat x as a constant and f as a product of y and $\sin xy$:

$$\begin{aligned}\frac{\partial f}{\partial y} &= \frac{\partial}{\partial y}(y \sin xy) = y \cdot \frac{\partial}{\partial y}(\sin xy) + \sin xy \cdot \frac{\partial}{\partial y}(y)\\ &= y \cos xy \cdot \frac{\partial}{\partial y}(xy) + \sin xy = xy \cos xy + \sin xy.\end{aligned}$$

EXAMPLE 3 Partial Derivatives May Be Different Functions

Find $\partial f/\partial x$ and $\partial f/\partial y$ if

$$f(x, y) = \frac{2y}{y + \cos x}.$$

SOLUTION

We apply the Quotient Rule, first with y held constant:

$$\begin{aligned}f_x &= \frac{\partial}{\partial x}\left(\frac{2y}{y + \cos x}\right) = \frac{(y + \cos x)\left(\frac{\partial}{\partial x}\right)(2y) - 2y\left(\frac{\partial}{\partial x}\right)(y + \cos x)}{(y + \cos x)^2}\\ &= \frac{(y + \cos x)(0) - 2y(-\sin x)}{(y + \cos x)^2} = \frac{2y \sin x}{(y + \cos x)^2}\end{aligned}$$

With x held constant, we get

$$\begin{aligned}f_y &= \frac{\partial}{\partial y}\left(\frac{2y}{y + \cos x}\right) = \frac{(y + \cos x)\left(\frac{\partial}{\partial y}\right)(2y) - 2y\left(\frac{\partial}{\partial y}\right)(y + \cos x)}{(y + \cos x)^2}\\ &= \frac{(y + \cos x)(2) - 2y(1)}{(y + \cos x)^2} = \frac{2 \cos x}{(y + \cos x)^2}.\end{aligned}$$

Implicit differentiation works for partial derivatives the way it works for ordinary derivatives, as the next example illustrates.

EXAMPLE 4 Implicit Partial Differentiation

Find $\partial z/\partial x$ if the equation

$$yz - \ln z = x + y$$

defines z as a function of two independent variables x and y and the partial derivative exists.

SOLUTION

We differentiate both sides of the equation with respect to x, holding y constant and treating z as a differentiable function of x:

$$\begin{aligned}\frac{\partial}{\partial x}(yz) - \frac{\partial}{\partial x}(\ln z) &= \frac{\partial x}{\partial x} + \frac{\partial y}{\partial x}\\ y\frac{\partial z}{\partial x} - \frac{1}{z}\frac{\partial z}{\partial x} &= 1 + 0\\ \left(y - \frac{1}{z}\right)\frac{\partial z}{\partial x} &= 1\\ \frac{\partial z}{\partial x} &= \frac{z}{yz - 1}.\end{aligned}$$

With y constant, $\frac{\partial}{\partial x}(yz) = y\frac{\partial z}{\partial x}$.

Functions of More Than Two Variables

The definitions of the partial derivatives of functions of three or more variables are like the definitions for the functions of two variables. They are ordinary derivatives with respect to one variable, taken while the other independent variables are held constant.

EXAMPLE 5 A Function of Three Variables

If x, y, and z are independent variables and $f(x, y, z) = x \sin(y + 3z)$, find $\partial f/\partial z$.

SOLUTION

$$\begin{aligned}\frac{\partial f}{\partial z} &= \frac{\partial}{\partial z}[x \sin(y + 3z)] = x\frac{\partial}{\partial z}\sin(y + 3z)\\ &= x\cos(y + 3z)\frac{\partial}{\partial z}(y + 3z) = 3x\cos(y + 3z)\end{aligned}$$

EXAMPLE 6 Electrical Resistors in Parallel

If resistors of R_1, R_2, and R_3 ohms are connected in parallel to make an R-ohm resistor, the value of R can be found from the equation

$$\frac{1}{R} = \frac{1}{R_1} + \frac{1}{R_2} + \frac{1}{R_3} \qquad \text{(Figure 14.19).}$$

Find the value of $\partial R/\partial R_2$ when $R_1 = 30$, $R_2 = 45$, and $R_3 = 90$ ohms.

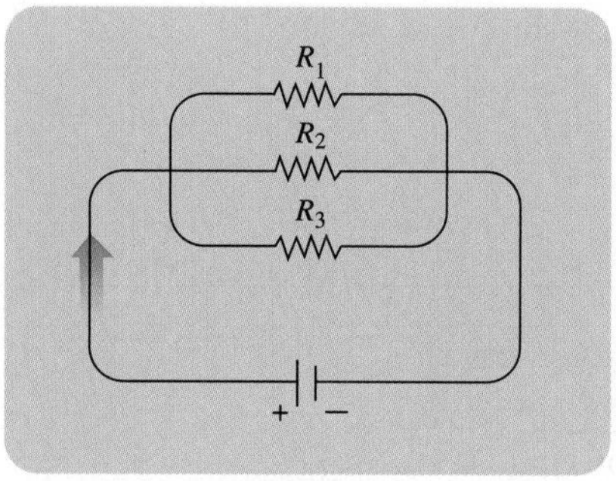

Figure 14.19 Resistors arranged this way are said to be connected in parallel (Example 6). Each resistor lets a portion of the current through. Their combined resistance R is calculated with the formula $1/R = 1/R_1 + 1/R_2 + 1/R_3$.

SOLUTION

To find $\partial R/\partial R_2$, we treat R_1 and R_3 as constants and differentiate with respect to R_2:

$$\begin{aligned}\frac{\partial}{\partial R_2}\left(\frac{1}{R}\right) &= \frac{\partial}{\partial R_2}\left(\frac{1}{R_1} + \frac{1}{R_2} + \frac{1}{R_3}\right)\\ -\frac{1}{R^2}\frac{\partial R}{\partial R_2} &= 0 - \frac{1}{R_2^2} + 0\\ \frac{\partial R}{\partial R_2} &= \frac{R^2}{R_2^2} = \left(\frac{R}{R_2}\right)^2.\end{aligned}$$

When $R_1 = 30$, $R_2 = 45$, and $R_3 = 90$.

$$\frac{1}{R} = \frac{1}{30} + \frac{1}{45} + \frac{1}{90} = \frac{1}{15},$$

so $R = 15$ and

$$\frac{\partial R}{\partial R_2} = \left(\frac{15}{45}\right)^2 = \frac{1}{9}.$$

Partial Derivatives and Continuity

Since the existence of the derivative at a point always implies continuity in the single-variable case, you might be surprised to learn that a function $f(x, y)$ can have partial derivatives with respect to both x and y at a point and yet *fail* to be continuous there. The following example illustrates what can happen.

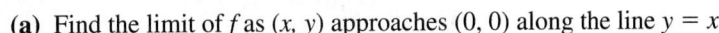

EXAMPLE 7 $\partial f/\partial x$ **and** $\partial f/\partial y$ **Exist But** f **Is Discontinuous**

Let

$$f(x, y) = \begin{cases} 0 & \text{if } xy \neq 0 \\ 1 & \text{if } xy = 0 \end{cases} \qquad \text{(Figure 14.20).}$$

(a) Find the limit of f as (x, y) approaches $(0, 0)$ along the line $y = x$.
(b) Prove that f is not continuous at the origin.
(c) Show that both partial derivatives $\partial f/\partial x$ and $\partial f/\partial y$ exist at the origin.

SOLUTION

(a) Since $f(x, y)$ is constantly zero along the line $y = x$ except at the origin, we have

$$\lim_{(x,y)\to(0,0)} f(x,y)\Big|_{y=x} = \lim_{(x,y)\to(0,0)} 0\Big|_{y=x} = 0.$$

(b) Since $f(0, 0) = 1$, the limit in (a) proves f cannot be continuous at $(0, 0)$.
(c) To find $\partial f/\partial x$ at $(0, 0)$, we hold y fixed at $y = 0$. Then $f(x, y) = 1$ for all x, and the graph of f is the line L_1 in Figure 14.20. The slope of this line at any x is $\partial f/\partial x = 0$. In particular, $\partial f/\partial x = 0$ at $(0, 0)$. Similarly, $\partial f/\partial y$ is the slope of line L_2 at any y, so $\partial f/\partial y = 0$ at $(0, 0)$.

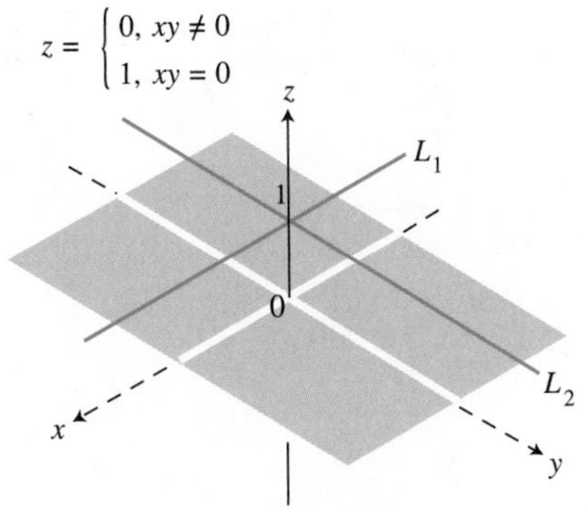

Figure 14.20 The graph of

$$f(x, y) = \begin{cases} 0 & \text{if } xy \neq 0 \\ 1 & \text{if } xy = 0 \end{cases}$$

consists of the lines L_1 and L_2 in the plane $z = 1$ and the four open quadrants of the xy-plane one unit below. The function has partial derivatives at the origin but is not continuous there.

Example 7 notwithstanding, it is still true in higher dimensions that *differentiability* at a point implies continuity. What Example 7 suggests is that we need a stronger requirement for differentiability in higher dimensions than the mere existence of the partial derivatives. We define differentiability for functions of two variables in the next section, at which time we revisit the connection to continuity.

Second-order Partial Derivatives

When we differentiate a function $f(x, y)$ twice, we produce its second-order derivatives. These derivatives are usually denoted by

$\dfrac{\partial^2 f}{\partial x^2}$	"*d* squared *f d x* squared"	or	f_{xx}	"*f* sub *x x*"
$\dfrac{\partial^2 f}{\partial y^2}$	"*d* squared *f d y* squared"		f_{yy}	"*f* sub *y y*"
$\dfrac{\partial^2 f}{\partial x \partial y}$	"*d* squared *f d x d y*"		f_{yx}	"*f* sub *y x*"
$\dfrac{\partial^2 f}{\partial y \partial x}$	"*d* squared *f d y d x*"		f_{xy}	"*f* sub *x y*"

The defining equations are

$$\frac{\partial^2 f}{\partial x^2} = \frac{\partial}{\partial x}\left(\frac{\partial f}{\partial x}\right) \quad \text{or} \quad f_{xx} = (f_x)_x,$$

$$\frac{\partial^2 f}{\partial x \partial y} = \frac{\partial}{\partial x}\left(\frac{\partial f}{\partial y}\right) \quad \text{or} \quad f_{yx} = (f_y)_x,$$

and so on. Notice the order in which the derivatives are taken: both $\partial^2 f/\partial x \partial y$ and f_{yx} mean to differentiate first with respect to y, then with respect to x.

EXAMPLE 8 Finding Second-Order Partial Derivatives

If $f(x, y) = x \cos y + ye^x$, find $\partial^2 f/\partial x^2$, $\partial^2 f/\partial y \partial x$, $\partial^2 f/\partial y^2$, and $\partial^2 f/\partial x \partial y$.

SOLUTION

$$\frac{\partial f}{\partial x} = \frac{\partial}{\partial x}(x \cos y + ye^x)$$

$$= \cos y + ye^x.$$

So

$$\frac{\partial^2 f}{\partial x^2} = \frac{\partial}{\partial x}\left(\frac{\partial f}{\partial x}\right) = ye^x$$

$$\frac{\partial^2 f}{\partial y \partial x} = \frac{\partial}{\partial y}\left(\frac{\partial f}{\partial x}\right) = -\sin y + e^x.$$

$$\frac{\partial f}{\partial y} = \frac{\partial}{\partial y}(x \cos y + ye^x)$$

$$= -x \sin y + e^x.$$

So

$$\frac{\partial^2 f}{\partial y^2} = \frac{\partial}{\partial y}\left(\frac{\partial f}{\partial y}\right) = -x \cos y$$

$$\frac{\partial^2 f}{\partial x \partial y} = \frac{\partial}{\partial x}\left(\frac{\partial f}{\partial y}\right) = -\sin y + e^x.$$

The Mixed Derivative Theorem

You probably noticed in Example 8 that the "mixed" second-order partial derivatives

$$\frac{\partial^2 f}{\partial y \partial x} \quad \text{and} \quad \frac{\partial^2 f}{\partial x \partial y}$$

were equal. This was no mere coincidence; they have to be equal whenever all five of the functions f, f_x, f_y, f_{xy}, and f_{yx} are continuous. That is the assertion of the following theorem, also known as *Euler's Theorem.*

THEOREM 2 The Mixed Derivative Theorem

If $f(x, y)$ and its partial derivatives f_x, f_y, f_{xy}, and f_{yx} are defined throughout an open region containing a point (a, b) and are all continuous at (a, b), then

$$f_{xy}(a, b) = f_{yx}(a, b).$$

Theorem 2 says that to calculate a mixed second-order partial derivative we may normally differentiate in either order. This can work to our advantage, as shown in the following example.

EXAMPLE 9 Choosing the Order of Differentiation

Find $\partial^2 w/\partial x \partial y$ if $w = xy + e^y/(y^2 + 1)$.

SOLUTION

The symbol $\partial^2 w/\partial x \partial y$ tells us to differentiate first with respect to y and then respect to x. If we postpone the differentiation with respect to y and differentiate first with respect to x, however, we get the answer more quickly. In two steps,

$$\frac{\partial w}{\partial x} = y \quad \text{and} \quad \frac{\partial^2 w}{\partial y \partial x} = 1.$$

We are in for significantly more work if we differentiate first with respect to y. (Just try it.)

Partial Derivatives of Still Higher Order

Although we deal mostly with first- and second-order partial derivatives, because they appear the most frequently in applications, there is no theoretical limit to how many times we can differentiate a function as long as the derivatives involved exist. Thus, we get third- and fourth-order derivatives denoted by symbols like

$$\frac{\partial^3 f}{\partial x \partial y^2} = f_{yyx},$$

$$\frac{\partial^4 f}{\partial x^2 \partial y^2} = f_{yyxx},$$

and so on. As with second-order derivatives, the order of differentiation is immaterial as long as the function and its derivatives through the order in question are all continuous.

Quick Review 14.3

In Exercises 1–10, y is given as a function of a *single* variable x. The number k is a constant. Find dy/dx and d^2y/dx^2.

1. $y = kx^2 + 5x$ **2.** $y = \sin kx$

3. $y = 20e^{kx}$ **4.** $y = (x + k)e^x$

5. $y = \tan^{-1}(x\sqrt{k})$ **6.** $y = \ln|x - k| + 3x$

7. $y = k^x$ **8.** $y = e^k \cos(kx)$

9. $y = \dfrac{x}{x - k}$ **10.** $y = \dfrac{k}{k - x}$

Section 14.3 Exercises

In Exercises 1–18, find $\partial f/\partial x$ and $\partial f/\partial y$.

1. $f(x, y) = 2x$ **2.** $f(x, y) = 2x - 3y - 4$

3. $f(x, y) = x(y - 1)$ **4.** $f(x, y) = x^2 + y^2$

5. $f(x, y) = (x^2 - 1)(y + 2)$

6. $f(x, y) = 5xy - 7x^2 - y^2 + 3x - 6y + 2$

7. $f(x, y) = \dfrac{1}{x + y}$ **8.** $f(x, y) = (2x - 3y)^3$

9. $f(x, y) = \sqrt{x^2 + y^2}$ **10.** $f(x, y) = \dfrac{x}{x^2 + y^2}$

11. $f(x, y) = \dfrac{x + y}{xy - 1}$ **12.** $f(x, y) = \sin(x + y)$

13. $f(x, y) = e^x \sin(y + 1)$ **14.** $f(x, y) = \tan^{-1}\left(\dfrac{y}{x}\right)$

15. $f(x, y) = e^{(x+y+1)}$ **16.** $f(x, y) = \ln(x + y)$

17. $f(x, y) = \log_y x$

18. $f(x, y) = \displaystyle\int_x^y g(t)\, dt$ (g continuous for all t)

In Exercises 19–24, find f_x, f_y, and f_z.

19. $f(x, y, z) = xy + yz + xz$ **20.** $f(x, y, z) = (x^2 + y^2 + z^2)^{-1/2}$

21. $f(x, y, z) = 1 + y^2 + 2z^2$ **22.** $f(x, y, z) = \tan(x + y + z)$

23. $f(x, y, z) = \ln(x + 2y + 3z)$ **24.** $f(x, y, z) = \sin(x + yz)$

In Exercises 25–30, find the partial derivative of the function with respect to each variable.

25. $f(t, \alpha) = \cos(2\pi t - \alpha)$ **26.** $g(u, v) = v^2 e^{(2u/v)}$

27. $h(\rho, \phi, \theta) = \rho \sin\phi \cos\theta$

28. $g(r, \theta, z) = r(1 - \cos\theta) - z$

29. ***Work Done by Heart*** (Section 4.5, Exercise 47)

$$W(P, V, \delta, v, g) = PV + \frac{V\delta v^2}{2g}$$

30. ***Wilson Lot Size Formula*** (Section 4.4, Exercise 50)

$$A(c, h, k, m, q) = \frac{km}{q} + cm + \frac{hq}{2}$$

In Exercises 31–36, find the second-order partial derivatives f_{xx}, f_{yy}, f_{xy}, and f_{yx} for the function.

31. $f(x, y) = x + y + xy$ **32.** $f(x, y) = \sin xy$

33. $f(x, y) = x^2y + \cos y + y \sin x$

34. $f(x, y) = xe^y + y + 1$ **35.** $f(x, y) = \ln(x + y)$

36. $f(x, y) = \tan^{-1}(y/x)$

In Exercises 37–40, verify that $w_{xy} = w_{yx}$.

37. $w = \ln(2x + 3y)$ **38.** $w = e^x + x \ln y + y \ln x$

39. $w = xy^2 + x^2y^3 + x^3y^4$ **40.** $w = x \sin y + y \sin x + xy$

Explorations (Order of Differentiation)

Exercises 41 and 42 should be done without writing anything down.

41. Which order of differentiation will calculate f_{xy} faster: x first or y first?

(a) $f(x, y) = x \sin y + e^y$

(b) $f(x, y) = 1/x$

(c) $f(x, y) = y + (x/y)$

(d) $f(x, y) = y + x^2y + 4y^3 - \ln(y^2 + 1)$

(e) $f(x, y) = x^2 + 5xy + \sin x + 7e^x$

(f) $f(x, y) = x \ln xy$

42. The fifth-order partial derivative $\partial^5 f/\partial x^2 \partial y^3$ is zero for each of the following functions. To show this as quickly as possible, which variable would you differentiate with respect to first: x or y?

(a) $f(x, y) = y^2 x^4 e^x + 2$

(b) $f(x, y) = y^2 + y(\sin x - x^4)$

(c) $f(x, y) = x^2 + 5xy + \sin x + 7e^x$ **(d)** $f(x, y) = xe^{y^2/2}$

43. Assume that the equation

$$x^3 z + z^3 x - 2yz = 0$$

defines z as a differentiable function of the two independent variables x and y. Find the value of $\partial z/\partial x$ at the point $(x, y, z) = (1, 1, 1)$.

44. Assume that the equation

$$xz + y \ln x - 9/z = 0$$

defines x as a differentiable function of the two independent variables y and z. Find the value of $\partial x/\partial z$ at the point $(x, y, z) = (1, -1, 3)$.

45. Writing to Learn Let $w = f(x, y, z)$ be a function of three independent variables, and write the formal definition of the partial derivative $\partial f/\partial z$ at (x_0, y_0, z_0). Use this definition to find $\partial f/\partial z$ at $(1, 2, 3)$ for $f(x, y, z) = x^2 yz^2$.

46. Writing to Learn Let $w = f(x, y, z)$ be a function of three independent variables, and write the formal definition of the partial derivative $\partial f/\partial y$ at (x_0, y_0, z_0). Use this definition to find $\partial f/\partial y$ at $(-1, 0, 3)$ for $f(x, y, z) = -2xy^2 + yz^2$.

Extending the Ideas

47. *Laplace Equations* The **three-dimensional Laplace equation**

$$\frac{\partial^2 f}{\partial x^2} + \frac{\partial^2 f}{\partial y^2} + \frac{\partial^2 f}{\partial z^2} = 0$$

is satisfied by steady-state temperature distributions $T = f(x, y, z)$ in space, by gravitational potentials, and by electrostatic potentials. The **two-dimensional Laplace equation**

$$\frac{\partial^2 f}{\partial x^2} + \frac{\partial^2 f}{\partial y^2} = 0,$$

obtained by dropping the $\partial^2 f/\partial z^2$ term, describes potentials and steady-state temperature distributions in a plane (Figure 14.21). Show that each of the following functions satisfies a Laplace equation.

(a) $f(x, y, z) = x^2 + y^2 - 2z^2$

(b) $f(x, y, z) = 2z^3 - 3(x^2 + y^2)z$

(c) $f(x, y) = e^{-2y} \cos 2x$ **(d)** $f(x, y) = \ln \sqrt{x^2 + y^2}$

(e) $f(x, y, z) = (x^2 + y^2 + z^2)^{-1/2}$

(f) $f(x, y, z) = e^{3x+4y} \cos 5z$

48. *The One-Dimensional Wave Equation* If we stand on an ocean shore and take a snapshot of the waves, the picture shows a regular pattern of peaks and valleys in an instant of time (Figure 14.22). Show that the following functions are all solutions of the wave equation.

(a) $w = \sin(x + ct)$ **(b)** $w = \cos(2x + 2ct)$

(c) $w = \sin(x + cy) + \cos(2x + 2ct)$

(d) $w = \ln(2x + 2ct)$ **(e)** $w = \tan(2x - 2ct)$

(f) $w = 5 \cos(3x + 3ct) + e^{x+ct}$

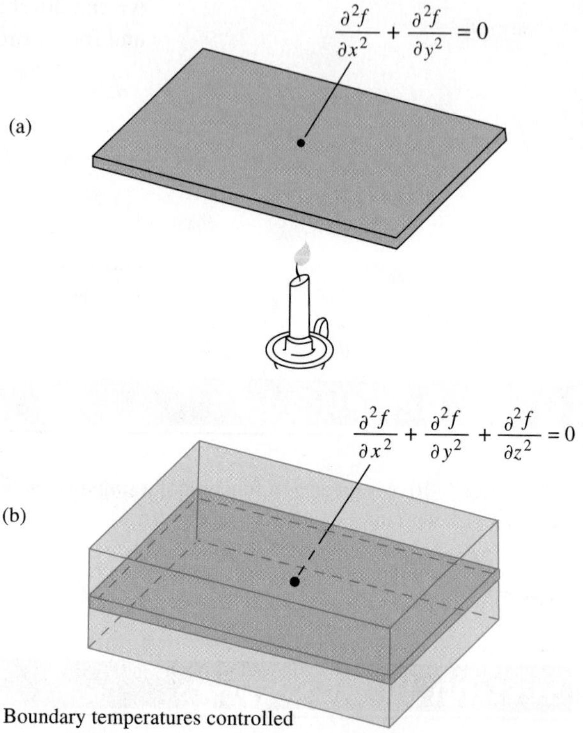

Figure 14.21 Steady-state temperature distributions in planes and solids satisfy Laplace equations. The plane (a) may be treated as a thin slice of the solid (b) perpendicular to the z-axis.

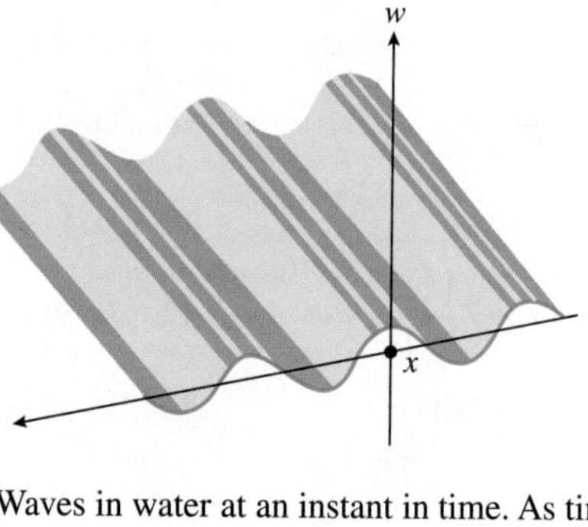

Figure 14.22 Waves in water at an instant in time. As time passes,

$$\frac{\partial^2 w}{\partial t^2} = c^2 \frac{\partial^2 w}{\partial x^2}.$$

We see periodic vertical motion in space with respect to distance. If we stand in the water, we can feel the rise and fall of the water as the waves go by. We see periodic vertical motion in time. In physics, this beautiful symmetry is expressed by the **one-dimensional wave equation**

$$\frac{\partial^2 w}{\partial t^2} = c^2 \frac{\partial^2 w}{\partial x^2},$$

where w is the wave height, x is the distance variable, and c is the velocity with which the waves are propagated.

In our example, x is the distance across the ocean's surface, but in other applications, x might be the distance along a vibrating string, distance through the air (sound waves), or distance through space (light waves). The number c varies with the medium and type of wave.

14.4 Differentiability, Linearization, and Differentials

What you'll learn about

- Differentiability
- Linearization of a Function of Two Variables
- Accuracy of the Standard Linear Approximation
- Predicting Change with Differentials
- Absolute, Relative, and Percentage Change
- Functions of More Than Two Variables

Differentiability

Surprising as it may seem, the starting point for differentiability is not Fermat's difference quotient, but rather the idea of increment. As Example 7 in Section 14.3 demonstrates, differentiability in higher dimensions is complicated because a function $z = f(x, y)$ can actually be *discontinuous* at a point where its first partial derivatives exist. This paradox arises because limits of functions of more than one independent variable cannot be considered one variable at a time as "partial limits." What we need, informally, is a criterion that will guarantee infintesimal smallness in all the variables at once. We find it in the Increment Theorem from advanced calculus.

THEOREM 3 The Increment Theorem for Functions of Two Variables

Suppose the first partial derivatives of $f(x, y)$ are defined throughout an open region R containing the point (x_0, y_0) and f_x and f_y are continuous at (x_0, y_0). Then the change

$$\Delta z = f(x_0 + \Delta x, y_0 + \Delta y) - f(x_0, y_0)$$

in the value of f that results from moving from (x_0, y_0) to another point $(x_0 + \Delta x, y_0 + \Delta y)$ in R satisfies an equation of the form

$$\Delta z = f_x(x_0, y_0)\,\Delta x + f_y(x_0, y_0)\,\Delta y + \varepsilon_1\,\Delta x + \varepsilon_2\,\Delta y,$$

in which $\varepsilon_1, \varepsilon_2 \to 0$ as $\Delta x, \Delta y \to 0$.

The condition on Δz at the end of the Increment Theorem (which generalizes to n dimensions with n epsilons) is exactly the condition that we will require for differentiability. Even without seeing the proof of the Increment Theorem, you can probably appreciate how the combined effect of all those factors approaching zero will guarantee impressive smallness in all the independent variables at once.

DEFINITION Differentiability of a Function of Two Variables

A function $z = f(x, y)$ is **differentiable at** (x_0, y_0) if $f_x(x_0, y_0)$ and $f_y(x_0, y_0)$ exist and Δz satisfies an equation of the form

$$\Delta z = f_x(x_0, y_0)\,\Delta x + f_y(x_0, y_0)\,\Delta y + \varepsilon_1\,\Delta x + \varepsilon_2\,\Delta y,$$

in which $\varepsilon_1, \varepsilon_2 \to 0$ as $\Delta x, \Delta y \to 0$. We call f **differentiable** if it is differentiable at every point in its domain.

In light of this definition, we have the immediate corollary of Theorem 3 that a function is differentiable if its first partial derivatives are *continuous*.

COROLLARY OF THEOREM 3 Continuity of Partial Derivatives Implies Differentiability

If the partial derivatives f_x and f_y of a function $f(x, y)$ are continuous throughout an open region R, then f is differentiable at every point of R.

As we can see from Theorems 3 and 4, a function $f(x, y)$ must be continuous at a point (x_0, y_0) if its partial derivatives f_x and f_y are continuous throughout an open region containing (x_0, y_0). But remember that it is still possible for a function of two variables to be discontinuous at a point where its first partial derivatives exist. We saw this in Section 14.3, Example 7. Existence alone is not enough.

If $z = f(x, y)$ is differentiable, then the definition of differentiability assures that $\Delta z = f(x_0 + \Delta x, y_0 + \Delta y) - f(x_0, y_0)$ approaches 0 as Δx and Δy approach 0. This tells us that a function of two variables is continuous at every point where it is differentiable.

THEOREM 4 Differentiability Implies Continuity

If a function $f(x, y)$ is differentiable at (x_0, y_0), then f is continuous at (x_0, y_0).

Linearization of a Function of Two Variables

Functions of two variables can be complicated, but sometimes we can replace them with simpler ones that give the accuracy required for specific applications without being so hard to work with. We do this in a way that is similar to the way we find linear replacements for functions of a single variable.

Suppose the function we wish to replace is $z = f(x, y)$ and that we want the replacement to be effective near a point (x_0, y_0) at which we know the values of f, f_x, and f_y and at which f is differentiable (Figure 14.23).

Since f is differentiable,

$$\Delta z = f_x(x_0, y_0)\, \Delta x + f_y(x_0, y_0)\, \Delta y + \varepsilon_1\, \Delta x + \varepsilon_2\, \Delta y,$$

where $\varepsilon_1, \varepsilon_2 \to 0$ as $\Delta x, \Delta y \to 0$.

Rewriting Δz, Δx, and Δy, we have

$$f(x, y) - f(x_0, y_0) = f_x(x_0, y_0)(x - x_0) + f_y(x_0, y_0)(y - y_0) + \varepsilon_1\, \Delta x + \varepsilon_2\, \Delta y.$$

If the increments Δx and Δy are small, the products $\varepsilon_1\, \Delta x$ and $\varepsilon_2\, \Delta y$ will eventually be smaller still and we will have

$$f(x, y) \approx \underbrace{f(x_0, y_0) + f_x(x_0, y_0)(x - x_0) + f_y(x_0, y_0)(y - y_0)}_{L(x,\, y)}.$$

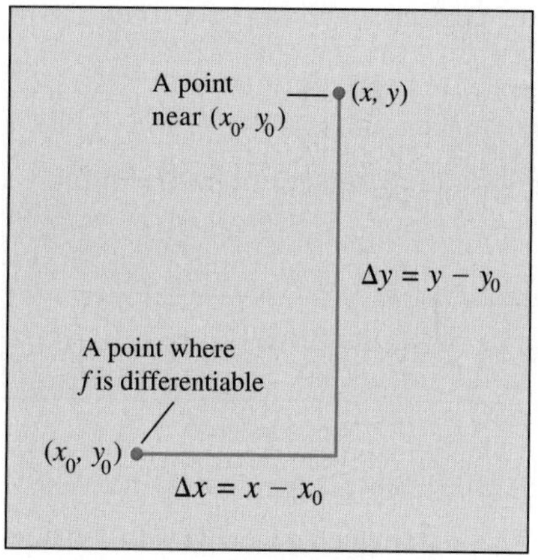

Figure 14.23 If f is differentiable at (x_0, y_0), then the value of f at any point (x, y) nearby is approximately $f(x_0, y_0) + f_x(x_0, y_0)\, \Delta x + f_y(x_0, y_0)\, \Delta y$.

In other words, as long as Δx and Δy are small, f will have approximately the same value as the linear function L. If f is hard to use and if our work can tolerate the error involved, we can safely replace f by L.

DEFINITIONS Linearization, Standard Linear Approximation

The **linearization** of a function $f(x, y)$ at a point (x_0, y_0) where f is differentiable is the function

$$L(x, y) = f(x_0, y_0) + f_x(x_0, y_0)(x - x_0) + f_y(x_0, y_0)(y - y_0).$$

The approximation

$$f(x, y) \approx L(x, y)$$

is the **standard linear approximation** of f at (x_0, y_0).

In Section 14.6, we see that the plane $z = L(x, y)$ is tangent to the surface $z = f(x, y)$ at the point (x_0, y_0). Thus, the linearization of a function of two variables is a tangent-*plane* approximation in the same way that the linearization of a function of a single variable is a tangent-*line* approximation.

EXAMPLE 1 Finding a Linearization

Find the linearization of $f(x, y) = x^2 - xy + \frac{1}{2}y^2 + 3$ at the point (3, 2).

SOLUTION

We first evaluate f, f_x, and f_y at the point (3, 2).

$$f(3, 2) = \left(x^2 - xy + \frac{1}{2}y^2 + 3\right)\Big|_{(3,2)} = 8,$$

$$f_x(3, 2) = \frac{\partial}{\partial x}\left(x^2 - xy + \frac{1}{2}y^2 + 3\right)\Big|_{(3,2)} = (2x - y)\big|_{(3,2)} = 4,$$

$$f_y(3, 2) = \frac{\partial}{\partial y}\left(x^2 - xy + \frac{1}{2}y^2 + 3\right)\Big|_{(3,2)} = (-x + y)\big|_{(3,2)} = -1,$$

getting

$$\begin{aligned} L(x, y) &= f(x_0, y_0) + f_x(x_0, y_0)(x - x_0) + f_y(x_0, y_0)(y - y_0) \\ &= 8 + (4)(x - 3) + (-1)(y - 2) = 4x - y - 2. \end{aligned}$$

Accuracy of the Standard Linear Approximation

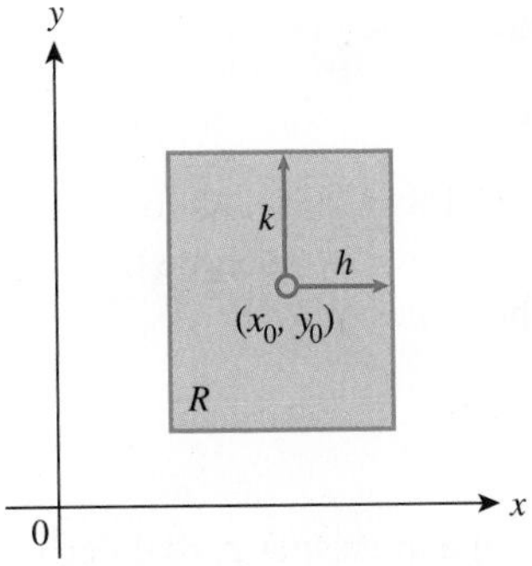

Figure 14.24 The rectangular region R: $|x - x_0| \le h$, $|y - y_0| \le k$ in the xy-plane. On this kind of region, we can find a useful error bound for the standard linear approximation.

Suppose $L(x, y)$ is the linearization of a differentiable function $f(x, y)$ at (x_0, y_0) and we use L to approximate f at points (x, y) close to (x_0, y_0). How accurate can we expect the approximation to be? As you might expect, the closeness of the approximation depends on three things:

1. the closeness of x to x_0,
2. the closeness of y to y_0, and
3. the "curviness" of f near (x_0, y_0), as measured by the magnitude of the second partial derivatives.

In fact, if we can find a common upper bound M for $|f_{xx}|$, $|f_{yy}|$ and $|f_{xy}|$ on a rectangle R containing (x_0, y_0) (Figure 14.24), then we can bound the error throughout R by using a simple formula. The formula is derived from Taylor's Theorem, but we will omit the derivation here.

The Error in the Standard Linear Approximation

If f has continuous first and second partial derivatives throughout an open set containing a rectangle R centered at (x_0, y_0) and if M is an upper bound for the values of $|f_{xx}|$, $|f_{yy}|$, and $|f_{xy}|$ on R, then the error $E(x, y)$ incurred in replacing $f(x, y)$ on R by its linearization

$$L(x, y) = f(x_0, y_0) + f_x(x_0, y_0)(x - x_0) + f_y(x_0, y_0)(y - y_0)$$

satisfies the inequality

$$|E(x, y)| \le \frac{1}{2}M(|x - x_0| + |y - y_0|)^2.$$

When we need to make $|E(x, y)|$ small for a given M, we just make $|x - x_0|$ and $|y - y_0|$ small.

EXAMPLE 2 Bounding the Error in Example 1

In Example 1, we found the linearization of $f(x, y) = x^2 - xy + \frac{1}{2}y^2 + 3$ at the point $(3, 2)$ to be $L(x, y) = 4x - y - 2$. Find an upper bound for the error in the approximation $f(x, y) \approx L(x, y)$ over the rectangle

$$R: |x - 3| \le 0.1, \qquad |y - 2| \le 0.1.$$

Express the upper bound as a percentage of $f(3, 2)$, the value of f at the center of the rectangle.

SOLUTION

We use the inequality $E(x, y)| \le \frac{1}{2}M(|x - x_0| + |y - y_0|)^2$.

To find a suitable value for M, we calculate f_{xx}, f_{yy}, and f_{xy}, finding, after some routine differentiation, that all three derivatives are constant. In terms of magnitude,

$$|f_{xx}| = |2| = |2|, \qquad |f_{xy}| = |-1| = 1, \qquad |f_{yy}| = |1| = 1.$$

The largest of these is 2, so we may safely take M to be 2. With $(x_0, y_0) = (3, 2)$, we know that, throughout R,

$$|E(x, y)| \le \frac{1}{2}(2)(|x - 3| + |y - 2|)^2 = (|x - 3| + |y - 2|)^2.$$

Finally, since $|x - 3| \le 0.1$ and $|y - 2| \le 0.1$ on R, we have

$$|E(x, y| \le (0.1 + 0.1)^2 = 0.04.$$

As a percentage of $f(3, 2) = 8$, the error is no greater than $0.04/8 = 0.5\%$. As long as (x, y) stays in R, the approximation $f(x, y) \approx L(x, y)$ will be in error by no more than 0.04, which is one-half of one percent of the value of f at the center of R.

Predicting Change with Differentials

Suppose we know the value of a differentiable function $f(x, y)$ and its first partial derivatives at a point (x_0, y_0) and we want to predict how much the value of f will change if we move to a point $(x_0 + \Delta x, y_0 + \Delta y)$ nearby. If Δx and Δy are small, f and its linearization at (x_0, y_0) will change by nearly the same amount, so the change in L will give a practical estimate of the change in f. (We used the differential in the same way in Section 4.5.)

The change in f is

$$\Delta f = f(x_0 + \Delta x, y_0 + \Delta y) - f(x_0, y_0).$$

This formula is usually as hard to work with as the formula for f. On the other hand, the change in L is

$$\begin{aligned}\Delta L &= L(x_0 + \Delta x, y_0 + \Delta y) - L(x_0, y_0)\\ &= f(x_0, y_0) + f_x(x_0, y_0)\,\Delta x + f_y(x_0, y_0)\,\Delta y - L(x_0, y_0) && \text{Definition of linearization}\\ &= f_x(x_0, y_0)\,\Delta x + f_y(x_0, y_0)\,\Delta y. && \text{Since } L(x_0, y_0) = f(x_0, y_0)\end{aligned}$$

This is just a known constant times Δx plus a known constant times Δy. Moving to differential notation, we use the more suggestive notation df for ΔL and write

$$df = f_x(x_0, y_0)\,dx + f_y(x_0, y_0)\,dy,$$

in which df denotes the change in the linearization that results from the changes dx and dy in x and y. As usual, we call dx and dy differentials of x and y. We call df the corresponding *total* differential of f.

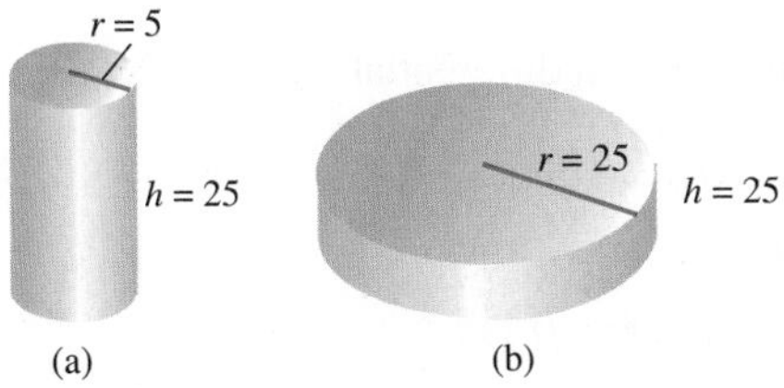

Figure 14.25 The volume of cylinder (a) is more sensitive to a small change in r than it is to an equally small change in h. The volume of cylinder (b) is more sensitive to small changes in h than it is to small changes in r. (Exploration 1)

DEFINITION Total Differential

If we move from (x_0, y_0) to a point $(x_0 + dx, y_0 + dy)$ nearby, the resulting change in the linearization of f is

$$df = f_x(x_0, y_0)\,dx + f_y(x_0, y_0)\,dy.$$

This change in the linearization of f is called the **total differential of f.**

EXPLORATION 1 Sensitivity to Change

Your company manufactures right circular cylindrical molasses storage tanks that are 25 ft high with a radius of 5 ft. How sensitive is the volume of such a tank to small variations in height and radius (Figure 14.25)?

1. Express the volume $V(r, h)$ of the tank as a function of radius r and height h.
2. Find dV at (5, 25) in terms of dr and dh.
3. As a quality control engineer concerned with being sure the tanks have the correct volume, would you be more concerned with variations in their radii or variations in their heights? Explain.
4. Suppose the values of r and h were reversed and your company were producing shorter, wider cylinders of radius 25 and height 5. Would this affect your answer to part 3? Why?
5. Is there a ratio of height to radius that would make the volume of the tank equally sensitive to changes in either variable? If so, what is it?

The general rule to be learned from Exploration 1 is that functions are most sensitive to small changes in the variables that generate the largest partial derivatives.

Absolute Change vs. Relative Change

If you measure a 20-volt potential with an error of 10 volts, your reading is probably too crude to be useful. You are off by 50%. But if you measure a 200,000-volt potential with an error of 10 volts, your reading is within 0.005% of the true value. An absolute error of 10 volts is significant in the first case but of minimal consequence in the second because the relative error is so small.

In other cases, a small relative error—say, traveling a few meters too far in a journey of hundreds of thousands of meters—can have spectacular consequences.

Absolute, Relative, and Percentage Change

When we move from (x_0, y_0) to a point nearby, we can describe the corresponding change in the value of a function $f(x, y)$ in three ways:

	True	**Estimate**
Absolute change:	Δf	df
Relative change:	$\dfrac{\Delta f}{f(x_0, y_0)}$	$\dfrac{df}{f(x_0, y_0)}$
Percentage change:	$\left(\dfrac{\Delta f}{f(x_0, y_0)} \times 100\right)\%$	$\left(\dfrac{df}{f(x_0, y_0)} \times 100\right)\%$

EXAMPLE 3 Estimating Change in Volume

Suppose a cylindrical can is designed to have a radius of 1 in. and a height of 5 in., but the radius and height are off by the amounts $dr = +0.03$ in. and $dh = -0.1$ in. Estimate the resulting absolute, relative, and percentage changes in the volume of the can.

SOLUTION

To estimate the absolute change in V, we evaluate the total differential

$$\begin{aligned} dV &= V_r(r_0, h_0)\, dr + V_h(r_0, h_0)\, dh \\ &= 2\pi r_0 h_0\, dr + \pi r_0^2\, dh \\ &= 2\pi(1)(5)(0.03) + \pi(1)^2(-0.1) \\ &= 0.3\pi - 0.1\pi \\ &= 0.2\pi. \end{aligned}$$

We divide this by $V(r_0, h_0)$ to estimate the relative change:

$$\frac{dV}{V(r_0, h_0)} = \frac{0.2\pi}{\pi(1)^2(5)} = 0.04.$$

The percentage error is

$$\left(\frac{dV}{V(r_0, h_0)} \times 100\right)\% = (0.04 \times 100)\% = 4\%.$$

EXAMPLE 4 Predicting Measurement Error

The volume of a right circular cylinder is to be calculated from measured values of r and h. Suppose r is measured with an error of no more than 2% and h with an error of no more than 0.5%. Estimate the resulting possible percentage error in the calculation of V.

SOLUTION

We write the given conditions in terms of relative errors for the sake of computation:

$$\left|\frac{dr}{r}\right| \le 0.02 \quad \text{and} \quad \left|\frac{dh}{h}\right| \le 0.005.$$

Since

$$\frac{dV}{V} = \frac{2\pi rh\, dr + \pi r^2\, dh}{\pi r^2 h} = \frac{2dr}{r} + \frac{dh}{h},$$

we have

$$\begin{aligned} \left|\frac{dV}{V}\right| &= \left|2\frac{dr}{r} + \frac{dh}{h}\right| \\ &\le \left|2\frac{dr}{r}\right| + \left|\frac{dh}{h}\right| \qquad \text{Property of absolute value} \\ &\le 2(0.02) + 0.005 = 0.045. \end{aligned}$$

We estimate the error in the volume calculation to be at most 4.5%.

How accurately do we have to measure r and h to have a reasonable chance of calculating $V = \pi r^2 h$ with an error of, say, less than 2%? Questions like this can be difficult because there is usually no single right answer. Since

$$\frac{dV}{V} = 2\frac{dr}{r} + \frac{dh}{h},$$

we see that dV/V is controlled by a combination of dr/r and dh/h. If we can measure h with great accuracy, we might come out all right even if we are sloppy about measuring r. On the other hand, our measurement of h might have so large a dh that the resulting dV/V would be too crude an estimate of $\Delta V/V$ to be useful even if dr were zero.

What we do in such cases is look for a reasonable square about the measured values (r_0, h_0) in which V will not vary by more than the allowed amount from $V_0 = \pi r_0^2 h_0$.

EXAMPLE 5 Controlling the Error

Find a reasonable square about the point $(r_0, h_0) = (5, 12)$ in which the value of $V = \pi r^2 h$ will not vary from its value at $(5, 12)$ by more than ± 0.1.

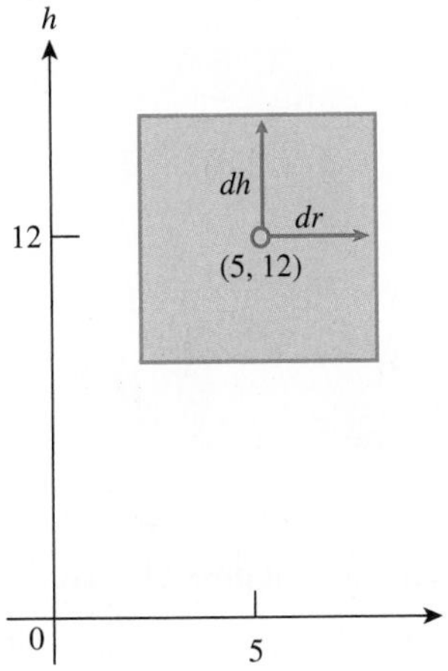

Figure 14.26 A small square about the point (5, 12) in the *rh*-plane. (Example 5)

SOLUTION

We approximate the variation ΔV by the differential

$$\begin{aligned} dV &= 2\pi r_0 h_0 \, dr + \pi r_0^2 \, dh = 2\pi(5)(12) \, dr + \pi(5)^2 \, dh \\ &= 120\pi \, dr + 25\pi \, dh. \end{aligned}$$

Since the region to which we are restricting our attention is a square (Figure 14.26), we may set $dh = dr$ to get

$$dV = 120\pi \, dr + 25\pi \, dr = 145\pi \, dr.$$

We wish to choose dr small enough to ensure that $|dV| \le 0.1$. Writing dV in terms of dr, we have

$$|dV| = |145\pi \, dr| \le 0.1.$$

Solving, we find a corresponding upper bound for dr:

$$|dr| \le \frac{0.1}{145\pi} \approx 2.1 \times 10^{-4}$$ Rounding down to make sure that dr will not accidentally be too big

With $dh = dr$, then, the square we want is described by the inequalities

$$|r - 5| \le 2.1 \times 10^{-4}, \qquad |h - 12| \le 2.1 \times 10^{-4}.$$

As long as (r, h) stays in this square, we may expect $|dV|$ to be less than or equal to 0.1, and we may expect $|\Delta V|$ to be approximately the same size.

Functions of More Than Two Variables

Analogous results hold for differentiable functions of more than two variables; we summarize a few of them here.

1. The **linearization** of $f(x, y, z)$ at a point $P_0(x_0, y_0, z_0)$ is
$L(x, y, z) = f(P_0) + f_x(P_0)(x - x_0) + f_y(P_0)(y - y_0) + f_z(P_0)(z - z_0)$.
2. Suppose R is a closed rectangular solid centered at P_0 and lying in an open region on which the second partial derivatives of f are continuous. Also suppose $|f_{xx}|$, $|f_{yy}|$, $|f_{zz}|$, $|f_{xy}|$, $|f_{xz}|$, and $|f_{yz}|$ are all less than or equal to M throughout R. Then the **error** $E(x, y, z) = f(x, y, z) - L(x, y, z)$ in the approximation of f by L is bounded throughout R by the inequality
$$|E| \le \frac{1}{2} M(|x - x_0| + |y - y_0| + |z - z_0|)^2.$$
3. If the second partial derivatives of f are continuous and if x, y, and z change from x_0, y_0, and z_0 by small amounts dx, dy, and dz, the **total differential**
$$df = f_x(P_0) \, dx + f_y(P_0) \, dy + f_z(P_0) \, dz$$
gives a good approximation of the resulting change in f.

EXAMPLE 6 Linearizing a Function of Three Variables

Find the linearization $L(x, y, z)$ of the function $f(x, y, z) = x^2 - xy + 3 \sin z$ at the point $(2, 1, 0)$, and find an upper bound for the error incurred when L is used to approximate f on the rectangle R:

$$|x - 2| \le 0.01, \qquad |y - 1| \le 0.02, \qquad |z| \le 0.01.$$

SOLUTION

Differentiation and evaluation gives

$$f(2, 1, 0) = 2, \qquad f_x(2, 1, 0) = 3, \qquad f_y(2, 1, 0) = -2, \qquad f_z(2, 1, 0) = 3.$$

Thus,

$$L(x, y, z) = 2 + 3(x - 2) + (-2)(y - 1) + 3(z - 0) = 3x - 2y + 3z - 2.$$

Since

$$f_{xx} = 2, \qquad f_{yy} = 0, \qquad f_{zz} = -3 \sin z,$$
$$f_{xy} = -1, \qquad f_{xz} = 0, \qquad f_{yz} = 0,$$

we may safely take M in the error bound formula to be 3, the maximum possible value of $|-3 \sin z|$. Hence

$$|E| \le \frac{1}{2} 3(0.01 + 0.02 + 0.01)^2 = 0.0024.$$

The error will be no greater than 0.0024.

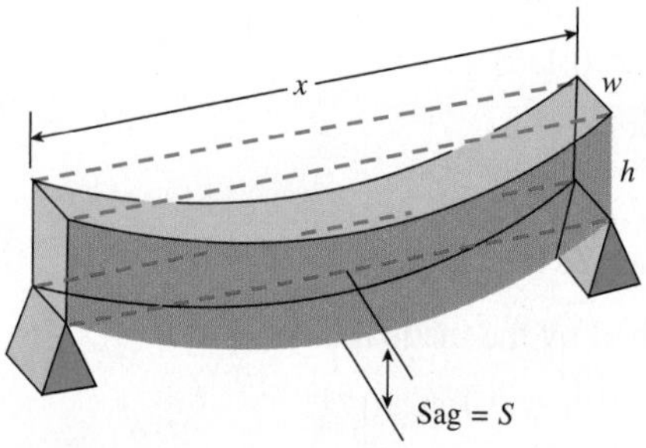

Figure 14.27 A beam supported at its two ends before and after loading. Example 7 shows how the sag S is related to the weight of the load and the dimensions of the beam.

EXAMPLE 7 Finding the Sag in Uniformly Loaded Beams

A horizontal rectangular beam, supported at both ends, will sag when subjected to a uniform load (constant weight per meter of beam length). The amount S of sag (Figure 14.27) is calculated with the formula

$$S = C \frac{px^4}{wh^3}.$$

In this equation,

p = the load (newtons per meter of beam length),
x = the length between supports (meters),
w = the width of the beam (meters),
h = the height of the beam (meters),
C = a constant that depends on the units of measurement and the material from which the beam is made.

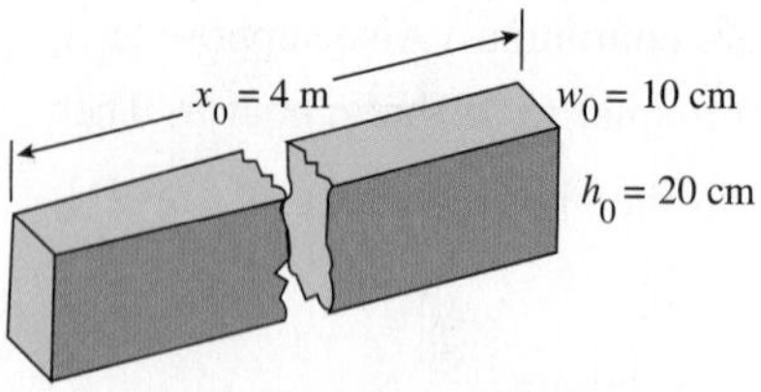

Figure 14.28 The dimensions of the beam in Example 7.

Find dS for a beam 4 m long, 10 cm wide, and 20 cm high that is subjected to a load of 100 N/m (Figure 14.28). What conclusions can be drawn about the beam from the expression for dS?

SOLUTION

Since S is a function of the four independent variables p, x, w, and h, its total differential is

$$dS = S_p\, dp + S_x\, dx + S_w\, dw + S_h\, dh.$$

When we write this out for a particular set of values p_0, x_0, w_0, and h_0 and simplify the result, we find that

$$dS = S_0 \left(\frac{dp}{p_0} + \frac{4dx}{x_0} - \frac{dw}{w_0} - \frac{3dh}{h_0} \right),$$

where

$$S_0 = S(p_0, x_0, w_0, h_0) = C\frac{p_0 x_0^4}{w_0 h_0^3}.$$

If $p_0 = 100$ N/m, $x_0 = 4$ m, $w_0 = 0.1$ m, and $h_0 = 0.2$ m, then

$$dS = S_0\left(\frac{dp}{100} + dx - 10\,dw - 15\,dh\right).$$

Here is what we can learn from this equation for dS:

Since dp and dx appear with positive coefficients, increases in p (load) and x (length) will increase the sag. But dw and dh appear with negative coefficients, so increases in w (width) and h (height) will decrease the sag (make the beam stiffer). The sag is not very sensitive to changes in load because the coefficient of dp is 1/100. The magnitude of the coefficient of dh is greater than the magnitude of the coefficient of dw. Making the beam 1 cm higher will therefore decrease the sag more than making the beam 1 cm wider.

Quick Review 14.4

Let $f(x) = x - \sin 2x + 1$. (Notice that f is a function of a single independent variable.)

1. Find the linearization of f at (0, 1).
2. Use the linearization to estimate $f(0.2)$.
3. With a calculator, find the actual error in the estimate in Exercise 2.
4. Find the relative error in Exercise 2.
5. Find the percentage error in Exercise 2.
6. Using a graphing calculator, find the largest open interval $(-a, a)$ on which the linearization approximates f with an error less than 0.02.
7. Write an equation relating the differentials df and dx.
8. Use the differential formula in Exercise 7 to estimate the change in f when x changes from π to $\pi + 1/2$.
9. Looking at the graph of f near $x = \pi$, why would you expect the estimate in Exercise 8 to be fairly accurate?
10. Looking at the graph of f near $x = 1/2$, why would you expect the differential formula in Exercise 7 to be less accurate in estimating the change in f when x changes from 1/2 to 1?

Section 14.4 Exercises

In Exercises 1–6, find the linearization $L(x, y)$ of the function f at **(a)** the origin and **(b)** the given point.

1. $f(x, y) = x^2 + y^2 + 1$, $\quad (1, 1)$
2. $f(x, y) = (x + y + 2)^2$, $\quad (1, 2)$
3. $f(x, y) = 3x - 4y + 5$, $\quad (1, 1)$
4. $f(x, y) = x^3y^4$, $\quad (1, 1)$
5. $f(x, y) = e^x \cos y$, $\quad (0, \pi/2)$
6. $f(x, y) = e^{2y-x}$, $\quad (1, 2)$

In Exercises 7–10, find the linearization $L(x, y)$ of the function $f(x, y)$ at the given point. Then use the technique of Example 2 to find an upper bound for the magnitude $|E|$ of the error in the approximation $f(x, y) \approx L(x, y)$ over the rectangle R. (Use $|\cos y| \le 1$ and $|\sin y| \le 1$ when estimating E in Exercises 8 and 9.)

7. $f(x, y) = x^2 - 3xy + 5 \quad (2, 1)$

   R: $|x - 2| \le 0.1, \quad |y - 1| \le 0.1$

8. $f(x, y) = 1 + y + x\cos y \quad (0, 0)$

   R: $|x| \le 0.2, \quad |y| \le 0.2$

9. $f(x, y) = e^x \cos y \quad (0, 0)$

   R: $|x| \le 0.1, \quad |y| \le 0.1$

   (Use $e^x \le 1.11$ in estimating E.)

10. $f(x, y) = \ln x + \ln y \quad (1, 1)$

    R: $|x - 1| \le 0.2, \quad |y - 1| \le 0.2$

11. **Writing to Learn** You plan to calculate the area of a long, thin rectangle from measurements of its length and width. Which dimension should you measure more carefully? Give reasons for your answer.

12. **Writing to Learn**

    (a) Around the point (1, 0), is $f(x, y) = x^2(y + 1)$ more sensitive to changes in x or to changes in y? Give reasons for your answer.

    (b) What ratio of dx to dy will make df equal zero at (1, 0)?

13. Suppose T is to be found from the formula $T = x(e^y + e^{-y})$, where x and y are found to be 2 and ln 2, respectively, with maximum possible errors of magnitudes $|dx| = 0.1$ and $|dy| = 0.02$. Estimate the maximum possible error in the computed value of T.

14. About how accurately may $V = \pi r^2 h$ be calculated from measurements of r and h that are in error by 1%?

15. If $r = 5.0$ cm and $h = 12.0$ cm to the nearest millimeter, what should we expect to be the maximum percentage error in calculating $V = \pi r^2 h$?

16. To estimate the volume of a cylinder of radius about 2 m and height about 3 m, about how accurately should the radius and height be measured so that the error in the volume estimate will not exceed 0.1 m^3? Assume that the possible error dr in measuring r is equal to the possible error dh in measuring h.

17. Give a reasonable square centered at (1, 1) over which the value of $f(x, y) = x^3y^4$ will not vary by more than ± 0.1.

18. ***Variation in Electrical Resistance*** The resistance R produced by wiring resistors of R_1 and R_2 ohms in parallel (Figure 14.29) can be calculated from the formula

$$\frac{1}{R} = \frac{1}{R_1} + \frac{1}{R_2}.$$

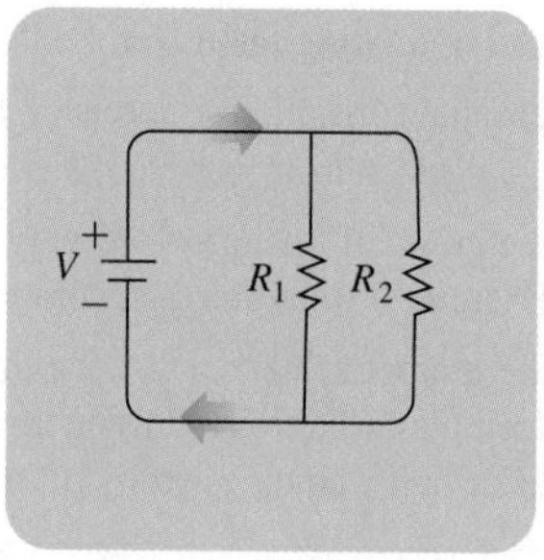

Figure 14.29 The circuit in Exercises 18 and 19.

(a) Show that

$$dR = \left(\frac{R}{R_1}\right)^2 dR_1 + \left(\frac{R}{R_2}\right)^2 dR_2$$

(b) You have designed a two-resistor circuit like the one in Figure 14.29 to have resistances of $R_1 = 100$ ohms and $R_2 = 400$ ohms, but there is always some variation in manufacturing, so the resistors received by your firm will probably not have these exact values. Will the values of R be more sensitive to variations in R_1 or to variations in R_2? Give reasons for your answer.

19. ***(Continuation of Exercise 18)*** In another circuit like the one in Figure 14.29, you plan to change R_1 from 20 to 20.1 ohms and R_2 from 25 to 24.9 ohms. By what percentage will this change R?

20. ***Error Carry-over in Coordinate Changes***

(a) If $x = 3 \pm 0.01$ and $y = 4 \pm 0.01$, as shown here, with approximately what accuracy can you calculate the polar coordinates r and θ of the point $P(x, y)$ from the formulas $r^2 = x^2 + y^2$ and $\theta = \tan^{-1}(y/x)$? Express your estimates as percentage changes of the values that r and θ have at the point (3, 4).

(b) At the point (3, 4), are the values of r and θ more sensitive to changes in x or to changes in y? Give reasons for your answer.

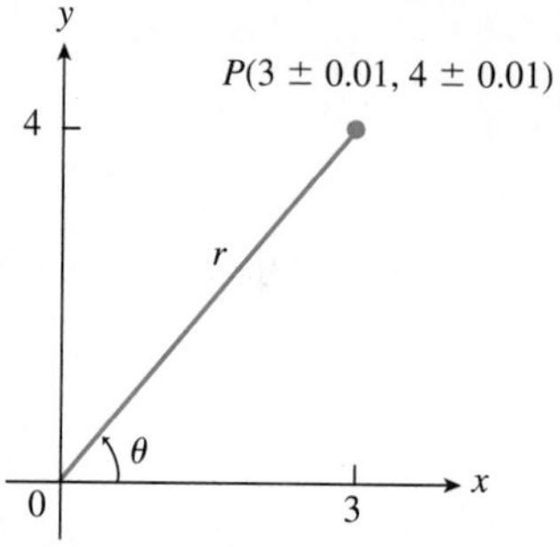

In Exercises 21–26, find the linearization $L(x, y, z)$ of the given function at each of the given points.

21. $f(x, y, z) = xy + yz + xz$ at

(a) (1, 1, 1) **(b)** (1, 0, 0) **(c)** (0, 0, 0)

22. $f(x, y, z) = x^2 + y^2 + z^2$ at

(a) (1, 1, 1) **(b)** (0, 1, 0) **(c)** (1, 0, 0)

23. $f(x, y, z) = \sqrt{x^2 + y^2 + z^2}$ at

(a) (1, 0, 0) **(b)** (1, 1, 0) **(c)** (1, 2, 2)

24. $f(x, y, z) = (\sin xy)/z$ at

(a) $(\pi/2, 1, 1)$ **(b)** (2, 0, 1)

25. $f(x, y, z) = e^x + \cos(y + z)$ at

(a) (0, 0, 0) **(b)** $\left(0, \frac{\pi}{2}, 0\right)$ **(c)** $\left(0, \frac{\pi}{4}, \frac{\pi}{4}\right)$

26. $f(x, y, z) = \tan^{-1}(xyz)$ at

(a) (1, 0, 0) **(b)** (1, 1, 0) **(c)** (1, 1, 1)

In Exercises 27–30, find the linearization $L(x, y, z)$ of the function $f(x, y, z)$ at the given point. Then use the technique of Example 6 to find an upper bound for the magnitude $|E|$ of the error in the approximation $f(x, y, z) \approx L(x, y, z)$ over the rectangle R.

27. $f(x, y, z) = xz - 3yz + 2$ (1, 1, 2)

R: $|x - 1| \le 0.01$, $|y - 1| \le 0.01$, $|z - 2| \le 0.02$

28. $f(x, y, z) = x^2 + xy + yz + \frac{z^2}{4}$ (1, 1, 2)

R: $|x - 1| \le 0.01$, $|y - 1| \le 0.01$, $|z - 2| \le 0.08$

29. $f(x, y, z) = xy + 2yz - 3xz$ (1, 1, 0)

R: $|x - 1| \le 0.01$, $|y - 1| \le 0.01$, $|z| \le 0.01$

30. $f(x, y, z) = \sqrt{2}\cos x \sin(y + z)$ $(0, 0, \pi/4)$

R: $|x| \le 0.01$, $|y| \le 0.01$, $|z - \pi/4| \le 0.01$

31. ***The Sagging Beam Revisited*** The beam of Example 7 is tipped on its side so that $h = 0.1$ m and $w = 0.2$ m.

(a) What is the value of dS now?

(b) Compare the sensitivity of the newly positioned beam to a small change in height with its sensitivity to an equally small change in width.

32. Estimate how strongly simultaneous errors of 2% in a, b, and c might affect the calculation of the product $p(a, b, c) = abc$.

33. Suppose $u = xe^y + y \sin z$ and x, y, and z can be measured with maximum possible errors of ± 0.2, ± 0.6, and $\pm \pi/180$, respectively. Estimate the maximum possible error in calculating u from the measured values $x = 2$, $y = \ln 3$, and $z = \pi/2$.

34. **Writing to Learn** Does a function $f(x, y)$ with continuous first partial derivatives throughout an open region R have to be continuous on R? Give reasons for your answer.

35. **Writing to Learn** If a function $f(x, y)$ has continuous second partial derivatives throughout an open region R, must the first-order partial derivatives of f be continuous on R? Give reasons for your answer.

Explorations

36. ***Designing a Box*** Estimate how much wood it takes to make a hollow rectangular box whose inside measurements are 5 ft long by 3 ft wide by 2 ft deep if the box is to be made of 1/2-in.-thick lumber and is to have no top.

37. ***Designing a Soda Can*** A standard 12-ounce soda can is essentially a cylinder of radius $r = 1$ in. and height $h = 5$ in.

(a) At these dimensions, how sensitive is the can's volume to a small change in the radius versus a small change in the height?

(b) Could you design a soda can that *appears* to hold more soda but in fact holds the same 12 ounces? What might its dimensions be? (There is more than one correct answer.)

38. ***Surveying a Triangular Field*** The area of a triangle is $(1/2)\,ab \sin C$, where a and b are the lengths of two sides of the triangle and C is the measure of the included angle. In surveying a triangular plot, you have measured a, b, and C to be 150 ft, 200 ft, and 60° respectively. By about how much could your area calculation be in error if your values of a and b are off by half a foot each and your measurement of C is off by 2°? (See the figure.) (*Note:* Be sure to use radians.)

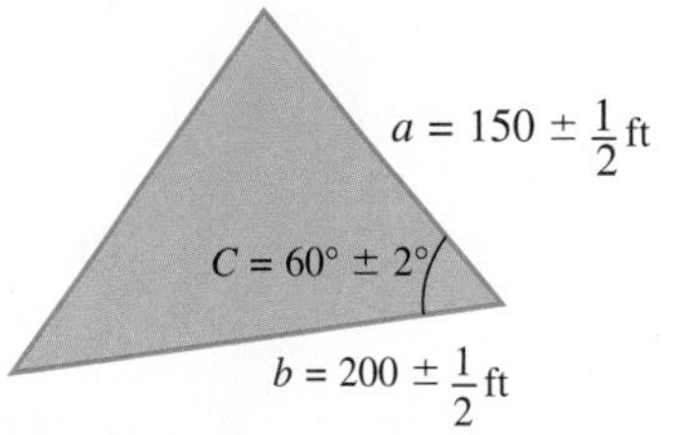

Extending the Ideas

39. ***Determinant of a Matrix*** If $|a|$ is much greater than $|b|$, $|c|$, and $|d|$, is the value of the determinant

$$f(a, b, c, d) = \begin{vmatrix} a & b \\ c & d \end{vmatrix}$$

more sensitive to small changes in a, b, c, or d? Give reasons for your answer.

40. ***The Wilson Lot Size Formula*** The Wilson Lot Size Formula in economics says that the most economical quantity Q of goods (radios, shoes, brooms, whatever) for a store to order is given by the formula $Q = \sqrt{2KM/h}$, where K is the cost of placing the order, M is the number of items sold per week, and h is the weekly holding cost for each item (cost of space, utilities, security, and so on). To which of the variables K, M, and h is Q most sensitive near the point $(K_0, M_0, h_0) = (2, 20, 0.05)$? Give reasons for your answers.

14.5 The Chain Rule

What you'll learn about

- Composite Functions in Higher Dimensions
- Functions of Two Variables
- Functions of Three Variables
- Functions Defined on Surfaces
- Implicit Differentiation Improved
- Functions of Many Variables

Composite Functions in Higher Dimensions

When we are interested in the temperature $w = f(x, y, z)$ at points along a curve $x = g(t)$, $y = h(t)$, $z = k(t)$ in space or in the pressure or density along a path through a gas or fluid, we may think of f as a function of the single variable t. For each value of t, the temperature at the point $(g(t), h(t), k(t))$ is the value of the composite function $f(g(t), h(t), k(t))$. If we then wish to know the rate at which f changes with respect to t along the path, we only have to differentiate this composite function with respect to t, provided, of course, the derivative exists.

Sometimes we can find the derivative by substituting the formulas for g, h, and k into the formula for f and differentiating directly with respect to t. Often, however, we have to work with functions whose formulas are too complicated for convenient substitution or for which formulas are not readily available. To find a function's derivatives under circumstances like these (and to get further insight into how calculus works in higher dimensions), we use a multivariable form of the Chain Rule. The form that the rule takes depends on how many variables are involved, but, except for the presence of additional variables, it works just like the Chain Rule.

Functions of Two Variables

We studied what happened when $w = f(x)$ was a differentiable function of x and $x = g(t)$ was a differentiable function of t. This made w a differentiable function of t, and the Chain Rule said that dw/dt could be calculated with the formula

$$\frac{dw}{dt} = \frac{dw}{dx}\frac{dx}{dt}.$$

The analogous formula for a function $w = f(x, y)$ is given in Theorem 5.

> **THEOREM 5 Chain Rule for Functions of Two Variables**
>
> If $w = f(x, y)$ is differentiable and x and y are differentiable functions of t, then w is a differentiable function of t and
>
> $$\frac{dw}{dt} = \frac{\partial f}{\partial x}\frac{dx}{dt} + \frac{\partial f}{\partial y}\frac{dy}{dt}.$$

Proof of Theorem 5 The proof consists of showing that if x and y are differentiable at $t = t_0$, then w is differentiable at t_0 and

$$\left(\frac{dw}{dt}\right)_{t_0} = \left(\frac{\partial w}{\partial x}\right)_{P_0}\left(\frac{dx}{dt}\right)_{t_0} + \left(\frac{\partial w}{\partial y}\right)_{P_0}\left(\frac{dy}{dt}\right)_{t_0},$$

where $P_0 = (x(t_0), y(t_0))$.

Let Δx, Δy, and Δw be the increments that result from changing t from t_0 to $t_0 + \Delta t$. Since f is differentiable (remember the definition in Section 14.4),

$$\Delta w = \left(\frac{\partial w}{\partial x}\right)_{P_0}\Delta x + \left(\frac{\partial w}{\partial y}\right)_{P_0}\Delta y + \varepsilon_1\,\Delta x + \varepsilon_2\,\Delta y,$$

where $\varepsilon_1, \varepsilon_2 \to 0$ as $\Delta x, \Delta y \to 0$. To find dw/dt, we divide this equation through by Δt and let Δt approach zero. The division gives

$$\frac{\Delta w}{\Delta t} = \left(\frac{\partial w}{\partial x}\right)_{P_0}\frac{\Delta x}{\Delta t} + \left(\frac{\partial w}{\partial y}\right)_{P_0}\frac{\Delta y}{\Delta t} + \varepsilon_1\frac{\Delta x}{\Delta t} + \varepsilon_2\frac{\Delta y}{\Delta t}.$$

Letting Δt approach zero gives

$$\begin{aligned}\left(\frac{dw}{dt}\right)_{t_0} &= \lim_{\Delta t\to 0}\frac{\Delta w}{\Delta t}\\ &= \left(\frac{\partial w}{\partial x}\right)_{P_0}\left(\frac{dx}{dt}\right)_{t_0} + \left(\frac{\partial w}{\partial y}\right)_{P_0}\left(\frac{dy}{dt}\right)_{t_0} + 0\cdot\left(\frac{dx}{dt}\right)_{t_0} + 0\cdot\left(\frac{dy}{dt}\right)_{t_0}\\ &= \left(\frac{\partial w}{\partial x}\right)_{P_0}\left(\frac{dx}{dt}\right)_{t_0} + \left(\frac{\partial w}{\partial y}\right)_{P_0}\left(\frac{dy}{dt}\right)_{t_0}.\end{aligned}$$

The **tree diagram** in the margin provides a convenient way to remember the Chain Rule for functions of two variables. Notice that both partial derivatives and single-variable derivatives are involved. From the diagram you see that when $t = t_0$, the single-variable derivatives dx/dt and dy/dt are evaluated at t_0, whereas the partial derivatives $\partial w/\partial x$ and $\partial w/\partial y$ are evaluated at the point (x_0, y_0) determined by evaluating the differentiable functions x and y at t_0. The "true" independent variable is t, whereas x and y are **intermediate variables** controlled by t. The "true" dependent variable is w.

One way to remember the Chain Rule is to picture the diagram below. To find dw/dt, start at w and read down each route to t, multiplying derivatives along the way. Then add the products.

Chain Rule

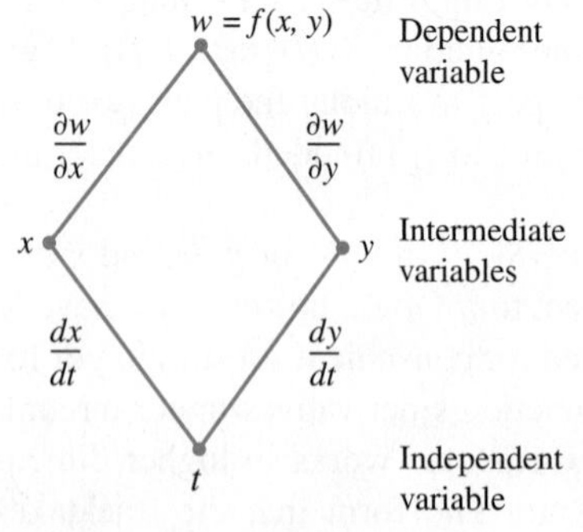

$$\frac{dw}{dt} = \frac{\partial w}{\partial x}\frac{dx}{dt} + \frac{\partial w}{\partial y}\frac{dy}{dt}$$

A more precise notation for the Chain Rule shows how the partial and single-variable derivatives involved are evaluated:

$$\frac{dw}{dt}(t_0) = \frac{\partial f}{\partial x}(x_0, y_0) \cdot \frac{dx}{dt}(t_0) + \frac{\partial f}{\partial y}(x_0, y_0) \cdot \frac{dy}{dt}(t_0).$$

EXAMPLE 1 Applying the Chain Rule

Use the Chain Rule to find the derivative of $w = xy$ with respect to t along the path $x = \cos t$, $y = \sin t$. What is the derivative's value at $t = \pi/2$?

SOLUTION

We apply the Chain Rule to find dw/dt as follows:

$$\begin{aligned}\frac{dw}{dt} &= \frac{\partial w}{\partial x}\frac{dx}{dt} + \frac{\partial w}{\partial y}\frac{dy}{dt} \\ &= \frac{\partial(xy)}{\partial x} \cdot \frac{d}{dt}(\cos t) + \frac{\partial(xy)}{\partial y} \cdot \frac{d}{dt}(\sin t) \\ &= (y)(-\sin t) + (x)(\cos t) \\ &= (\sin t)(-\sin t) + (\cos t)(\cos t) \\ &= -\sin^2 t + \cos^2 t \\ &= \cos(2\,t)\end{aligned}$$

At the given value of t,

$$\left(\frac{dw}{dt}\right)_{t=\frac{\pi}{2}} = \cos\left(2 \cdot \frac{\pi}{2}\right) = -1.$$

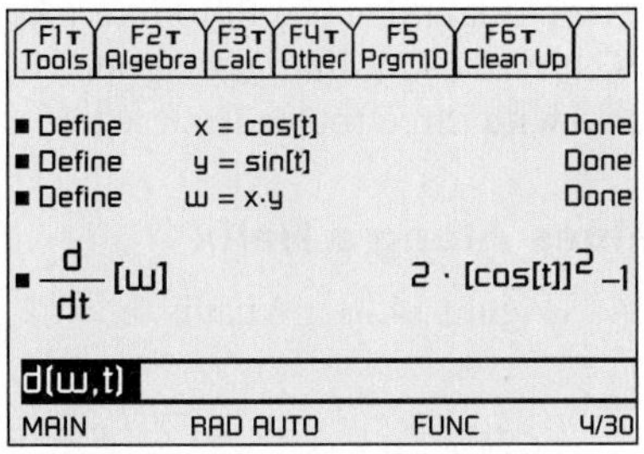

Figure 14.30 We have used the "Define" command to express x, y, and therefore w as functions of t. (Example 1)

Figure 14.30 shows CAS support for the computation of dw/dt in Example 1 because $2\cos^2 t - 1 = \cos(2t)$.

Chain Rule

Here we have three routes from w to t instead of two, but finding dw/dt is still the same. Read down each route, multiplying derivatives along the way; then add.

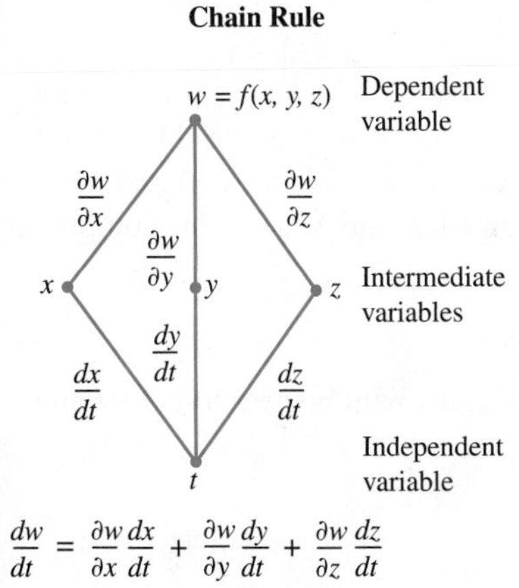

EXPLORATION 1 Bypassing the Chain Rule

Example 1 was intended to illustrate how the Chain Rule works for a function of two variables, but notice that the output of the process was the derivative of w with respect to the single variable t. Could we have done this as a single-variable problem and avoided confronting the multivariable nature of w altogether?

1. Write the function w of Example 1 explicitly as a function of t.
2. Find dw/dt using the techniques of the Chain Rule. Do you get the same function as in the solution to Example 1?
3. Find dw/dt along the same (x, y) path if $w = x^2e^y$. Again, find it in two ways: by using the Chain Rule for functions of two variables and by writing w explicitly as a function of t.
4. Do you think that the two methods will always lead to the same solution?

Exploration 1 suggests that the "new" Chain Rule leads to the same dw/dt that we could have found using the rules. That is an important property of the new rule: It works! Remember that when we differentiated an expression like x^2e^y with respect to t, we were not thinking of it as a function of two independent variables controlled by t (even though it was). As we develop the rules for multivariable derivatives, we must expect them to be consistent with our previous results.

Functions of Three Variables

You can probably predict the Chain Rule for functions of three variables, as it only involves adding the expected third term to the two-variable formula.

> **THEOREM 6 Chain Rule for Functions of Three Variables**
>
> If $w = f(x, y, z)$ is differentiable and x, y, and z are differentiable functions of t, then w is a differentiable function of t and
>
> $$\frac{dw}{dt} = \frac{\partial f}{\partial x}\frac{dx}{dt} + \frac{\partial f}{\partial y}\frac{dy}{dt} + \frac{\partial f}{\partial z}\frac{dz}{dt}.$$

The proof is identical to the proof of Theorem 5, except that there is a third intermediate variable to be dealt with every step of the way. There is also a similar diagram (in the margin) for remembering the new equation, this one with three routes from w to t.

The helix
$\mathbf{r} = (\cos t)\mathbf{i} + (\sin t)\mathbf{j} + t\mathbf{k}$

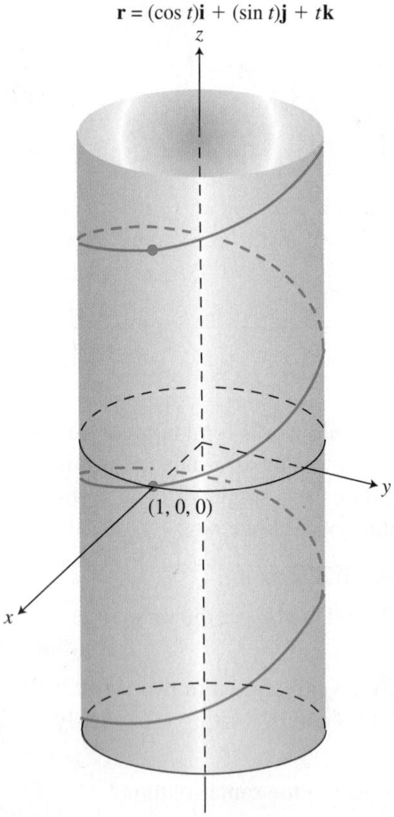

Figure 14.31 Example 2 shows how the values of $w = xy + z$ vary with t along this helix.

EXAMPLE 2 Changes in a Function's Values Along a Helix

Find dw/dt if $w = xy + z$, $x = \cos t$, $y = \sin t$, and $z = t$ (Figure 14.31). What is the derivative's value at $t = 0$?

SOLUTION

$$\begin{aligned}\frac{dw}{dt} &= \frac{\partial w}{\partial x}\frac{dx}{dt} + \frac{\partial w}{\partial y}\frac{dy}{dt} + \frac{\partial w}{\partial z}\frac{dz}{dt}\\ &= (y)(-\sin t) + (x)(\cos t) + (1)(1)\\ &= (\sin t)(-\sin t) + (\cos t)(\cos t) + 1\\ &= -\sin^2 t + \cos^2 t + 1\\ &= 1 + \cos 2t\end{aligned}$$

$$\left(\frac{dw}{dt}\right)_{t=0} = 1 + \cos(0) = 2$$

Functions Defined on Surfaces

If we are interested in the temperature $w = f(x, y, z)$ at points (x, y, z) on a globe in space, we might prefer to think of x, y, and z as functions of the variables r and s that give the points' longitudes and latitudes. If $x = g(r, s)$, $y = h(r, s)$, and $z = k(r, s)$, we could then express the temperature as a function of r and s with the composite function

$$w = f(g(r, s), h(r, s), k(r, s)).$$

Under the right conditions, w would have partial derivatives with respect to both r and s that could be calculated in the following way.

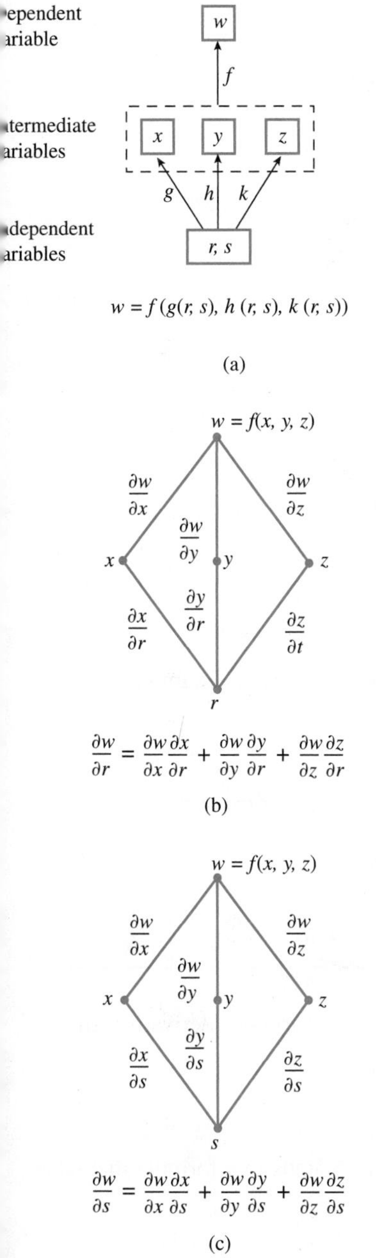

igure 14.32 Composite function and ree diagrams to accompany Theorem 7.

THEOREM 7 Chain Rule for Two Independent Variables and Three Intermediate Variables

Suppose $w = f(x, y, z)$, $x = g(r, s)$, $y = h(r, s)$, and $z = k(r, s)$. If all four functions are differentiable, then w has partial derivatives with respect to r and s, given by the formulas

$$\frac{\partial w}{\partial r} = \frac{\partial w}{\partial x}\frac{\partial x}{\partial r} + \frac{\partial w}{\partial y}\frac{\partial y}{\partial r} + \frac{\partial w}{\partial z}\frac{\partial z}{\partial r},$$

$$\frac{\partial w}{\partial s} = \frac{\partial w}{\partial x}\frac{\partial x}{\partial s} + \frac{\partial w}{\partial y}\frac{\partial y}{\partial s} + \frac{\partial w}{\partial z}\frac{\partial z}{\partial s}.$$

The first of these equations can be derived from the Chain Rule in Theorem 6 by holding s fixed and treating r as t. The second can be derived in the same way, holding r fixed and treating s as t. The tree diagrams for both equations are shown in Figure 14.32.

EXAMPLE 3 Partial Derivatives Using Theorem 7

Express $\partial w/\partial r$ and $\partial w/\partial s$ in terms of r and s if

$$w = x + 2y + z^2, \qquad x = \frac{r}{s}, \qquad y = r^2 + \ln s, \qquad z = 2r.$$

SOLUTION

$$\begin{aligned}\frac{\partial w}{\partial r} &= \frac{\partial w}{\partial x}\frac{\partial x}{\partial r} + \frac{\partial w}{\partial y}\frac{\partial y}{\partial r} + \frac{\partial w}{\partial z}\frac{\partial z}{\partial r}\\ &= (1)\left(\frac{1}{s}\right) + (2)(2r) + (2z)(2)\\ &= \frac{1}{s} + 4r + (4r)(2)\\ &= \frac{1}{s} + 12r\end{aligned}$$

$$\begin{aligned}\frac{\partial w}{\partial s} &= \frac{\partial w}{\partial x}\frac{\partial x}{\partial s} + \frac{\partial w}{\partial y}\frac{\partial y}{\partial s} + \frac{\partial w}{\partial z}\frac{\partial z}{\partial s}\\ &= (1)\left(-\frac{r}{s^2}\right) + (2)\left(\frac{1}{s}\right) + (2z)(0)\\ &= \frac{2}{s} - \frac{r}{s^2}\end{aligned}$$

If f is a function of two variables instead of three, each equation in Theorem 7 becomes correspondingly one term shorter.

If $w = f(x, y)$, $x = g(r, s)$, and $y = h(r, s)$, then

$$\frac{\partial w}{\partial r} = \frac{\partial w}{\partial x}\frac{\partial x}{\partial r} + \frac{\partial w}{\partial y}\frac{\partial y}{\partial r} \quad \text{and} \quad \frac{\partial w}{\partial s} = \frac{\partial w}{\partial x}\frac{\partial x}{\partial s} + \frac{\partial w}{\partial y}\frac{\partial y}{\partial s}.$$

Figure 14.33 shows the tree diagram for the first of these equations. The diagram for the second equation is similar: Just replace r with s.

Chain Rule

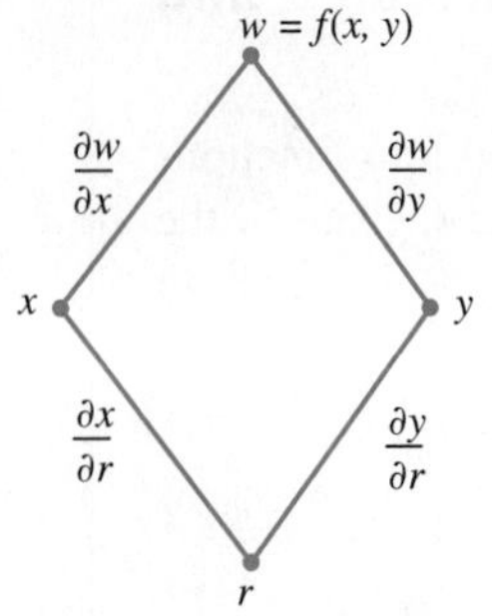

$$\frac{\partial w}{\partial r} = \frac{\partial w}{\partial x}\frac{\partial x}{\partial r} + \frac{\partial w}{\partial y}\frac{\partial y}{\partial r}$$

Figure 14.33 Tree diagram for the equation

$$\frac{\partial w}{\partial r} = \frac{\partial w}{\partial x}\frac{\partial x}{\partial r} + \frac{\partial w}{\partial y}\frac{\partial y}{\partial r}.$$

EXAMPLE 4 More Partial Derivatives

Express $\partial w/\partial r$ and $\partial w/\partial s$ in terms of r and s if

$$w = x^2 + y^2, \qquad x = r - s, \qquad y = r + s.$$

SOLUTION

$$\begin{aligned}\frac{\partial w}{\partial r} &= \frac{\partial w}{\partial x}\frac{\partial x}{\partial r} + \frac{\partial w}{\partial y}\frac{\partial y}{\partial r}\\ &= (2x)(1) + (2y)(1)\\ &= 2(r - s) + 2(r + s)\\ &= 4r\end{aligned}$$

$$\begin{aligned}\frac{\partial w}{\partial s} &= \frac{\partial w}{\partial x}\frac{\partial x}{\partial s} + \frac{\partial w}{\partial y}\frac{\partial y}{\partial s}\\ &= (2x)(-1) + (2y)(1)\\ &= -2(r - s) + 2(r + s)\\ &= 4s\end{aligned}$$

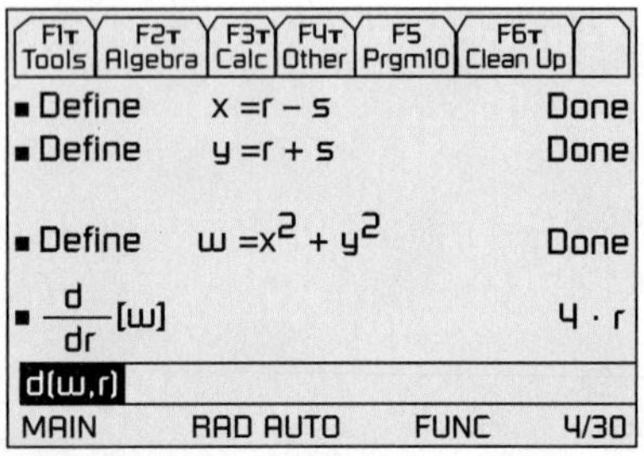

Figure 14.34 This figure illustrates how to use a CAS to write x, y, and therefore w as function of r and s. (Example 4)

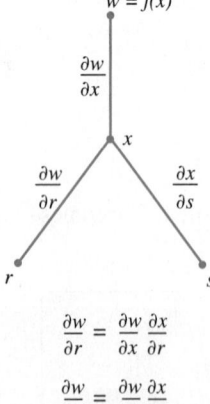

Figure 14.34 shows CAS support for the computation of $\partial w/\partial r$ in Example 4. If you have a CAS available, try providing support for $\partial w/\partial s$.

If f is a function of x alone, our equations become even simpler.

> If $w = f(x)$ and $x = g(r, s)$, then
>
> $$\frac{\partial w}{\partial r} = \frac{dw}{dx}\frac{\partial x}{\partial r} \quad \text{and} \quad \frac{\partial w}{\partial s} = \frac{dw}{dx}\frac{\partial x}{\partial s}.$$

Notice that, in this case, we can use the ordinary (single-variable) derivative, dw/dx. The tree diagram is shown in Figure 14.35.

Chain Rule

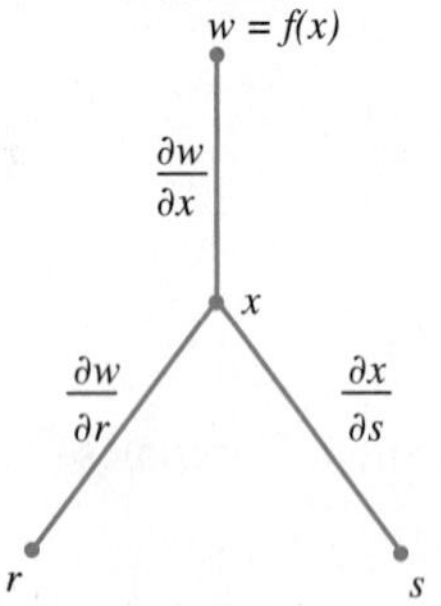

$$\frac{\partial w}{\partial r} = \frac{\partial w}{\partial x}\frac{\partial x}{\partial r}$$

$$\frac{\partial w}{\partial s} = \frac{\partial w}{\partial x}\frac{\partial x}{\partial s}$$

Figure 14.35 Tree diagram for differentiating f as a composite function of r and s with one intermediate variable.

Implicit Differentiation Improved

Believe it or not, the two-variable Chain Rule in Theorem 5 leads to a formula that takes most of the work out of implicit differentiation. Suppose:

1. the function $F(x, y)$ is differentiable, and
2. the equation $F(x, y) = 0$ defines y implicitly as a differentiable function of x, say $y = h(x)$.

Since $w = F(x, y) = 0$, the derivative dw/dx must be zero. Computing the derivative from the Chain Rule (tree diagram in Figure 14.36), we find

$$\begin{aligned}0 = \frac{dw}{dx} &= F_x\frac{dx}{dx} + F_y\frac{dy}{dx}\\ &= F_x \cdot 1 + F_y \cdot \frac{dy}{dx}.\end{aligned}$$

If $F_y = \partial w/\partial y \neq 0$, we can solve this equation for dy/dx to get

$$\frac{dy}{dx} = -\frac{F_x}{F_y}.$$

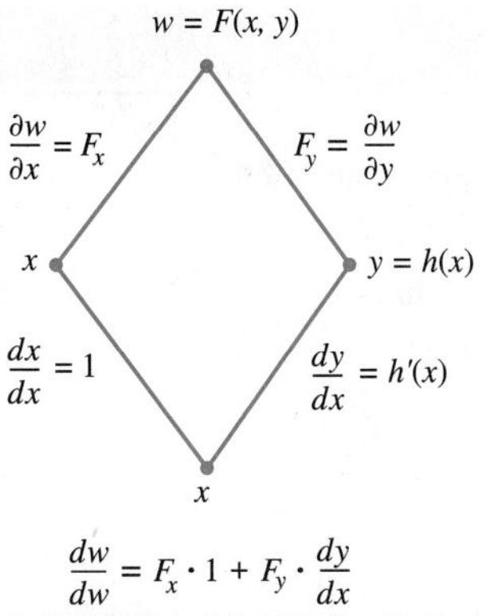

Figure 14.36 Tree diagram for differentiating $w = F(x, y)$ with respect to x. Setting $dw/dx = 0$ leads to a simple computational formula for implicit differentiation. (Theorem 8)

This relationship gives a surprisingly simple shortcut to finding derivatives of implicitly defined functions, which we state here as a theorem.

THEOREM 8 A Formula for Implicit Differentiation

Suppose $F(x, y)$ is differentiable and the equation $F(x, y) = 0$ defines y implicitly as a differentiable function of x. Then, at any point where $F_y \neq 0$,

$$\frac{dy}{dx} = -\frac{F_x}{F_y}.$$

EXAMPLE 5 Speedy Implicit Differentiation

Use Theorem 8 to find dy/dx if $x^2 - xy + y^2 = 7$.

SOLUTION

Take $F(x, y) = x^2 - xy + y^2 - 7$. Then

$$\frac{dy}{dx} = -\frac{F_x}{F_y} = -\frac{2x - y}{-x + 2y} = \frac{y - 2x}{2y - x}.$$

This calculation is significantly shorter than the single-variable calculation with which we found dy/dx.

Functions of Many Variables

We have seen several different forms of the Chain Rule in this section, but you do not have to memorize them all if you can see them as special cases of the same general formula. When solving particular problems, it may help to draw the appropriate tree diagram, placing the dependent variable at the top, the intermediate variables in the middle, and the selected independent variable at the bottom. To find the derivative of the dependent variable with respect to the selected independent variable, start at the dependent variable and read down all the different routes to the independent variable, calculating and multiplying the derivatives along each route. Then add the products you found along the different routes.

In general, suppose $w = f(x, y, \ldots, v)$ is a differentiable function of the variables $x, y, \ldots, v$ (a finite set) and the $x, y, \ldots, v$ are differentiable functions of the variables $p, q, \ldots, t$ (another finite set). Then w is a differentiable function of the variables p through t, and the partial derivatives of w with respect to these variables are given by equations of the form

$$\frac{\partial w}{\partial p} = \frac{\partial w}{\partial x}\frac{\partial x}{\partial p} + \frac{\partial w}{\partial y}\frac{\partial y}{\partial p} + \cdots + \frac{\partial w}{\partial v}\frac{\partial v}{\partial p}.$$

The other equations are obtained by replacing p by $q, \ldots, t$, one at a time.

Another way to remember this equation is to think of the right-hand side as the dot product of two vectors with components

$$\underbrace{\left(\frac{\partial w}{\partial x}, \frac{\partial w}{\partial y}, \ldots, \frac{\partial w}{\partial v}\right)}_{\substack{\text{Derivatives of } w \text{ with} \\ \text{respect to the} \\ \text{intermediate variables}}} \quad \text{and} \quad \underbrace{\left(\frac{\partial x}{\partial p}, \frac{\partial y}{\partial p}, \ldots, \frac{\partial v}{\partial p}\right)}_{\substack{\text{Derivatives of the intermediate} \\ \text{variables with respect to the} \\ \text{selected independent variable}}}.$$

Quick Review 14.5

In Exercises 1–5, find $\partial f/\partial x$ and $\partial f/\partial y$.

1. $f(x, y) = xy + \sin y$
2. $f(x, y) = x^3 - y^2 + 5$
3. $f(x, y) = \tan(x + y)$
4. $f(x, y) = e^{xy} + 10$
5. $f(x, y) = x \sin y - y \cos x$

In Exercises 6–10, find dy/dt at the given value of t.

6. $y = \cos x, \quad x = t^2, \quad t = \sqrt{\pi}$
7. $y = \tan x, \quad x = e^{t/2}, \quad t = 2 \ln \pi$
8. $y = \ln x, \quad x = \cos^2 t, \quad t = \pi/4$
9. $ty - 3t^2 = 5, \quad t = 1$
10. $\tan y = x, \quad t = \sqrt[3]{x}, \quad t = \sqrt{2}$

Section 14.5 Exercises

In Exercises 1–6, **(a)** express dw/dt as a function of t, both by using the Chain Rule and by expressing w in terms of t and differentiating directly with respect to t. Then **(b)** evaluate dw/dt at the given value of t.

1. $w = x^2 + y^2, \quad x = \cos t, \quad y = \sin t; \quad t = \pi$
2. $w = x^2 + y^2, \quad x = \cos t + \sin t, \quad y = \cos t - \sin t;$ $t = 0$
3. $w = \dfrac{x}{z} + \dfrac{y}{z}, \quad x = \cos^2 t, \quad y = \sin^2 t, \quad z = 1/t;$ $t = 3$
4. $w = \ln(x^2 + y^2 + z^2), \quad x = \cos t, \quad y = \sin t,$ $t = 4\sqrt{t}; \quad t = 3$
5. $w = 2ye^x - \ln z, \quad x = \ln(t^2 + 1), \quad y = \tan^{-1} t,$ $z = e^t; \quad t = 1$
6. $w = z - \sin xy, \quad x = t, \quad y = \ln t, \quad z = e^{t-1};$ $t = 1$

In Exercises 7 and 8, **(a)** express $\partial z/\partial r$ and $\partial z/\partial \theta$ as functions of r and θ both by using the Chain Rule and by expressing w directly in terms of r and θ before differentiating. Then **(b)** evaluate $\partial z/\partial r$ and $\partial z/\partial \theta$ at the given point (r, θ).

7. $z = 4e^x \ln y, \quad x = \ln(r \cos \theta), \quad y = r \sin \theta;$ $(r, \theta) = (2, \pi/4)$
8. $z = \tan^{-1}(x/y), \quad x = r \cos \theta, \quad y = r \sin \theta;$ $(r, \theta) = (1.3, \pi/6)$

In Exercises 9 and 10, **(a)** express $\partial w/\partial u$ and $\partial w/\partial v$ as functions of u and v both by using the Chain Rule and by expressing w in terms of u and v before differentiating. Then **(b)** evaluate $\partial w/\partial u$ and $\partial w/\partial v$ at the given point (u, v).

9. $w = xy + yz + xz, \quad x = u + v, \quad y = u - v, \quad z = uv;$ $(u, v) = (1/2, 1)$
10. $w = \ln(x^2 + y^2 + z^2), \quad x = ue^v \sin u, \quad y = ue^v \cos u,$ $z = ue^v; \quad (u, v) = (-2, 0)$

In Exercises 11 and 12, **(a)** express $\partial u/\partial x$, $\partial u/\partial y$, and $\partial u/\partial z$ as functions of x, y, and z both by using the Chain Rule and by expressing u directly in terms of x, y, and z before differentiating. Then **(b)** evaluate $\partial u/\partial x$, $\partial u/\partial y$, and $\partial u/\partial z$ at the given point (x, y, z).

11. $u = \dfrac{p - q}{q - r}, \quad p = x + y + z, \quad q = x - y + z,$ $r = x + y - z; \quad (x, y, z) = (\sqrt{3}, 2, 1)$
12. $u = e^{qr} \sin^{-1} p, \quad p = \sin x, \quad q = z^2 \ln y,$ $r = 1/z; \quad (x, y, z) = (\pi/4, 1/2, -1/2)$

In Exercises 13–24, draw a tree diagram and write a Chain Rule formula for each derivative.

13. $\dfrac{dz}{dt}$ for $z = f(x, y), \quad x = g(t), \quad y = h(t)$
14. $\dfrac{dz}{dt}$ for $z = f(u, v, w), \quad u = g(t), \quad v = h(t),$ $w = k(t)$
15. $\dfrac{\partial w}{\partial u}$ and $\dfrac{\partial w}{\partial v}$ for $w = h(x, y, z), \quad x = f(u, v),$ $y = g(u, v), \quad z = k(u, v)$
16. $\dfrac{\partial w}{\partial x}$ and $\dfrac{\partial w}{\partial y}$ for $w = f(r, s, t), \quad r = g(x, y),$ $s = h(x, y), \quad t = k(x, y)$
17. $\dfrac{\partial w}{\partial u}$ and $\dfrac{\partial w}{\partial v}$ for $w = g(x, y), \quad x = h(u, v), \quad y = k(u, v)$
18. $\dfrac{\partial w}{\partial x}$ and $\dfrac{\partial w}{\partial y}$ for $w = g(u, v), \quad u = h(x, y), \quad v = k(x, y)$
19. $\dfrac{\partial z}{\partial t}$ and $\dfrac{\partial z}{\partial s}$ for $z = f(x, y), \quad x = g(t, s), \quad y = h(t, s)$
20. $\dfrac{\partial y}{\partial r}$ for $y = f(u), \quad u = g(r, s)$
21. $\dfrac{\partial w}{\partial s}$ and $\dfrac{\partial w}{\partial t}$ for $w = g(u), \quad u = h(s, t)$
22. $\dfrac{\partial w}{\partial p}$ for $w = f(x, y, z, v), \quad x = g(p, q) \quad y = h(p, q)$ $z = j(p, q), \quad v = k(p, q)$
23. $\dfrac{\partial w}{\partial r}$ and $\dfrac{\partial w}{\partial s}$ for $w = f(x, y), \quad x = g(r), \quad y = h(s)$
24. $\dfrac{\partial w}{\partial s}$ for $w = g(x, y), \quad x = h(r, s, t), \quad y = k(r, s, t)$

In Exercises 25–28, assume that the equation defines y as a differentiable function of x and use Theorem 8 to find the value of dy/dx at the given point.

25. $x^3 - 2y^2 + xy = 0, \quad (1, 1)$

26. $xy + y^2 - 3x - 3 = 0, \quad (-1, 1)$

27. $x^2 + xy + y^2 - 7 = 0, \quad (1, 2)$

28. $xe^y + \sin xy + y - \ln 2 = 0, \quad (0, \ln 2)$

In Exercises 29–34, find the specified partial derivatives.

29. $\partial w/\partial r$ when $r = 1, s = -1$, if $w = (x + y + z)^2$, $x = r - s$, $y = \cos(r + s)$, $z = \sin(r + s)$

30. $\partial w/\partial v$ when $u = -1, v = 2$, if $w = xy + \ln z$, $x = v^2/u$, $y = u + v$, $z = \cos u$

31. $\partial w/\partial v$ when $u = 0, v = 0$, if $w = x^2 + (y/x)$, $x = u - 2v + 1$, $y = 2u + v - 2$

32. $\partial z/\partial u$ when $u = 0, v = 1$, if $z = \sin xy + x \sin y$, $x = u^2 + v^2$, $y = uv$

33. $\partial z/\partial u$ and $\partial z/\partial v$ when $u = \ln 2, v = 1$, if $z = 5 \tan^{-1} x$, $x = e^u + \ln v$

34. $\partial z/\partial u$ and $\partial z/\partial v$ when $u = 1, v = -2$, if $z = \ln q$, $q = \sqrt{v} = 3 \tan^{-1} u$

35. ***A Function Defined on a Curve in Space*** Let $w = x^2e^{2y} \cos 3z$. Find the value of dw/dt at the point $(1, \ln 2, 0)$ on the curve $x = \cos t$, $y = \ln(t + 2)$, $z = t$.

36. ***Temperature on a Circle*** Let $T = f(x, y)$ be the temperature at the point (x, y) on the circle defined parametrically by

$$x = \cos t, \quad y = \sin t, \quad 0 \le t \le 2\pi,$$

and suppose

$$\frac{\partial T}{\partial x} = 8x - 4y, \qquad \frac{\partial T}{\partial y} = 8y - 4x.$$

(a) Find where the maximum and minimum temperatures on the circle occur by examining the derivatives dT/dt and d^2T/dt^2.

(b) Suppose $T = 4x^2 - 4xy + 4y^2$. Find the maximum and minimum values of T on the circle.

37. ***Temperature on an Ellipse*** Let $T = g(x, y)$ be the temperature at the point (x, y) on the ellipse defined parametrically by

$$x = 2\sqrt{2} \cos t, \quad y = \sqrt{2} \sin t, \quad 0 \le t \le 2\pi,$$

and suppose

$$\frac{\partial T}{\partial x} = y, \qquad \frac{\partial T}{\partial y} = x.$$

(a) Locate the maximum and minimum temperatures on the ellipse by examining dT/dt and d^2T/dt^2.

(b) Suppose $T = xy - 2$. Find the maximum and minimum values of T on the ellipse.

38. **Writing to Learn** ***Narrowing the Search*** Suppose the partial derivatives of a function $f(x, y, z)$ at points on the helix $x = \cos t$, $y = \sin t$, $z = t$ are

$$f_x = \cos t, \quad f_y = \sin t, \quad f_z = t^2 + t - 2.$$

Explain how we can conclude that the points on the curve where f can take on extreme values are $(\cos(-2), \sin(-2), -2)$ and $(\cos 1, \sin 1, 1)$.

Explorations

39. If $f(u, v, w)$ is differentiable and $u = x - y$, $v = y - z$, and $w = z - x$, show that

$$\frac{\partial f}{\partial x} + \frac{\partial f}{\partial y} + \frac{\partial f}{\partial z} = 0.$$

40. ***Changes in an Electric Circuit*** The voltage V in a circuit that satisfies the law $V = IR$ is slowly dropping as the battery wears out. At the same time, the resistance R is increasing as the resistor heats up. Use the equation

$$\frac{dV}{dt} = \frac{\partial V}{\partial I}\frac{dI}{dt} + \frac{\partial V}{\partial R}\frac{dR}{dt}$$

to find how the current is changing at the instant when $R = 600$ ohms, $I = 0.04$ amp, $dR/dt = 0.5$ ohms/sec, and $dV/dt = -0.01$ volt/sec.

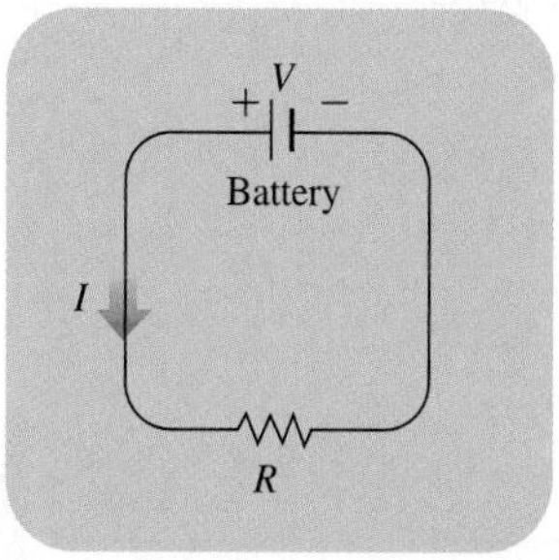

41. ***The Effects of Changing the Dimensions of a Box*** The lengths a, b, and c of the edges of a rectangular box are changing with time. At the instant in question, $a = 1$ m, $b = 2$ m, $c = 3$ m, $da/dt = db/dt = 1$ m/sec, and $dc/dt = -3$ m/sec. At what rates are the box's volume V and surface area S changing at that instant? Are the box's interior diagonals increasing in length, or decreasing? How can you tell?

42. ***Laplace Equations*** Show that if $w = f(u, v)$ satisfies the Laplace equation $f_{uu} + f_{vv} = 0$ and if $u = (x^2 - y^2)/2$ and $v = xy$, then w satisfies the Laplace equation $w_{xx} + w_{yy} = 0$.

43. ***Laplace Equations*** Let $w = f(u) + g(v)$, where $u = x + iy$ and $v = x - iy$ and $i = \sqrt{-1}$. Show that w satisfies the Laplace equation $w_{xx} + w_{yy} = 0$ if all the necessary functions are differentiable.

Extending the Ideas

44. ***Extending Implicit Differentiation to Three Variables*** Theorem 8 can be generalized to functions of three variables and even more. The three-variable version goes like this: If the equation $F(x, y, z) = 0$ determines x as a differentiable function of x and y, then, at points where $F_z \neq 0$,

$$\frac{\partial z}{\partial x} = -\frac{F_x}{F_z} \quad \text{and} \quad \frac{\partial z}{\partial y} = -\frac{F_y}{F_z}.$$

Use these equations to find the values of $\partial z/\partial x$ and $\partial z/\partial y$ at the points given:

(a) $z^3 - xy + yz + y^3 - 2 = 0, \quad (1, 1, 1)$

(b) $\frac{1}{x} + \frac{1}{y} + \frac{1}{z} = 1, \quad (2, 3, 6)$

(c) $\sin(x + y) + \sin(y + z) + \sin(x + z) = 0, \quad (\pi, \pi, \pi)$

(d) $xe^y + ye^z + 2 \ln x - 2 - 3 \ln 2 = 0, \quad (1, \ln 2, \ln 3)$

45. ***Polar Coordinates*** Suppose we substitute polar coordinates $x = r \cos \theta$ and $y = r \sin \theta$ into a differentiable function $w = f(x, y)$.

(a) Show that

$$\frac{\partial w}{\partial r} = f_x \cos \theta + f_y \sin \theta$$

and

$$\frac{1}{r}\frac{\partial w}{\partial \theta} = -f_x \sin \theta + f_y \cos \theta.$$

(b) Solve the equations in (a) simultaneously to express f_x and f_y in terms of $\partial w/\partial r$ and $\partial w/\partial \theta$.

(c) Show that

$$(f_x)^2 + (f_y)^2 = \left(\frac{\partial w}{\partial r}\right)^2 + \frac{1}{r^2}\left(\frac{\partial w}{\partial \theta}\right)^2.$$

46. ***Differentiating Integrals*** Under mild continuity restrictions it is true that if

$$F(x) = \int_a^b g(t, x)\, dt,$$

then

$$F'(x) = \int_a^b g_x(t, x)\, dt.$$

Using this fact and the Chain Rule, we can find the derivative of

$$F(x) = \int_a^{f(x)} g(t, x)\, dt$$

by letting

$$G(u, x) = \int_a^b g(t, x)\, dt,$$

where $u = f(x)$. Find the derivatives of the following functions defined by integrals.

(a) $F(x) = \int_0^{x^2} \sqrt{t^4 + x^3}\, dt$

(b) $F(x) = \int_{x^2}^{1} \sqrt{t^3 + x^2}\, dt$

14.6 Directional Derivatives, Gradient Vectors, and Tangent Plane

What you'll learn about

- Directional Derivatives in the Plane
- Geometric Interpretation of the Directional Derivative
- Calculation
- Properties of Directional Derivatives
- Gradients and Tangents to Level Curves
- Functions of Three Variables
- Tangent Planes and Normal Lines
- Planes Tangent to a Surface $z = f(x, y)$
- Increments and Distance
- Algebra Rules for Gradients

Directional Derivatives in the Plane

Suppose the function $f(x, y)$ is defined throughout a region R in the xy-plane, $P_0(x_0, y_0)$ is a point in R, and $\mathbf{u} = u_1\mathbf{i} + u_2\mathbf{j}$ is a unit vector. Then the equations

$$x = x_0 + su_1, \; y = y_0 + su_2$$

parametrize the line through P_0 parallel to $\mathbf{u}$. The parameter s measures arc length from P_0 in the direction of $\mathbf{u}$. We find the rate of change of f at P_0 in the direction of $\mathbf{u}$ by calculating df/ds at P_0 (Figure 14.37).

DEFINITION Directional Derivative

The derivative of f at $P_0(x_0, y_0)$ in the direction of the unit vector $\mathbf{u} = u_1\mathbf{i} + u_2\mathbf{j}$ is the number

$$\left(\frac{df}{ds}\right)_{\mathbf{u},P_0} = \lim_{s \to 0} \frac{f(x_0 + su_1, y_0 + su_2) - f(x_0, y_0)}{s}, \qquad (1)$$

provided the limit exists.

The directional derivative is also denoted by

$$(D_{\mathbf{u}} f)_{P_0}. \qquad \text{"The derivative of } f \text{ at } P_0 \text{ in the direction of } \mathbf{u}\text{"}$$

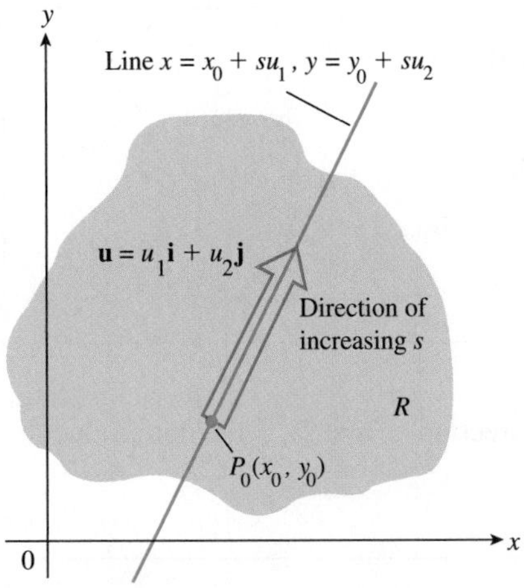

Figure 14.37 The rate of change of f in the direction of $\mathbf{u}$ at a point P_0 is the rate at which f changes along this line at P_0.

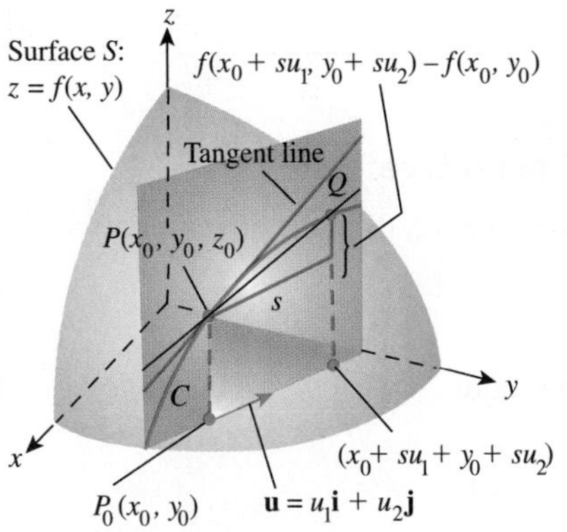

Figure 14.38 The slope of the curve C at P_0 is

$$\lim_{Q\to P} \text{slope } (PQ)$$

$$= \lim_{s\to 0} \frac{f(x_0 + su_1, y_0 + su_2) - f(x_0, y_0)}{s}$$

$$= \left(\frac{df}{ds}\right)_{\mathbf{u}, P_0}$$

EXAMPLE 1 Finding a Directional Derivative

Find the derivative of $f(x, y) = x^2 + xy$ at $P_0(1, 2)$ in the direction of the unit vector $\mathbf{u} = (1/\sqrt{2})\mathbf{i} + (1/\sqrt{2})\mathbf{j}$.

SOLUTION

$$\left(\frac{df}{ds}\right)_{\mathbf{u}, P_0} = \lim_{s\to 0} \frac{f(x_0 + su_1, y_0 + su_2) - f(x_0, y_0)}{s} \qquad \text{Eq. (1)}$$

$$= \lim_{s\to 0} \frac{f\left(1 + s\cdot\frac{1}{\sqrt{2}},\ 2 + s\cdot\frac{1}{\sqrt{2}}\right) - f(1, 2)}{s}$$

$$= \lim_{s\to 0} \frac{\left(1 + \frac{s}{\sqrt{2}}\right)^2 + \left(1 + \frac{s}{\sqrt{2}}\right)\left(2 + \frac{s}{\sqrt{2}}\right) - (1^2 + 1\cdot 2)}{s}$$

$$= \lim_{s\to 0} \frac{\left(1 + \frac{2s}{\sqrt{2}} + \frac{s^2}{2}\right) + \left(2 + \frac{3s}{\sqrt{2}} + \frac{s^2}{2}\right) - 3}{s}$$

$$= \lim_{s\to 0} \frac{\frac{5s}{\sqrt{2}} + s^2}{s} = \lim_{s\to 0}\left(\frac{5}{\sqrt{2}} + s\right) = \frac{5}{\sqrt{2}}.$$

The rate of change of $f(x, y) = x^2 + xy$ at $P_0(1, 2)$ in the direction of $\mathbf{u} = (1/\sqrt{2})\mathbf{i} + (1/\sqrt{2})\mathbf{j}$ is $5\sqrt{2}$.

Geometric Interpretation of the Directional Derivative

The equation $z = f(x, y)$ represents a surface S in space. If $z_0 = f(x_0, y_0)$, then the point $P(x_0, y_0, z_0)$ lies on S. The vertical plane that passes through P and $P_0(x_0, y_0)$ parallel to $\mathbf{u}$ intersects S in a curve C (Figure 14.38). The rate of change of f in the direction of $\mathbf{u}$ is the slope of the tangent to C at P.

Notice that when $\mathbf{u} = \mathbf{i}$, the directional derivative at P_0 is $\partial f/\partial x$ evaluated at (x_0, y_0). When $\mathbf{u} = \mathbf{j}$, the directional derivative at P_0 is $\partial f/\partial y$ evaluated at (x_0, y_0). The directional derivative generalizes the two partial derivatives. We can now ask for the rate of change of f in any direction $\mathbf{u}$, not just the directions $\mathbf{i}$ and $\mathbf{j}$.

Calculation

As you know, it is rarely convenient to calculate a derivative directly from its definition as a limit, and the directional derivative is no exception. We can develop a more efficient formula in the following way. We begin with the line

$$x = x_0 + su_1, \qquad y = y_0 + su_2, \tag{2}$$

through $P_0(x_0, y_0)$, parametrized with the arc length parameter s increasing in the direction of the unit vector $\mathbf{u} = u_1\mathbf{i} + u_2\mathbf{j}$. Then

$$\left(\frac{df}{ds}\right)_{\mathbf{u}, P_0} = \left(\frac{\partial f}{\partial x}\right)_{P_0}\frac{dx}{ds} + \left(\frac{\partial f}{\partial y}\right)_{P_0}\frac{dy}{ds} \qquad \text{Chain Rule}$$

$$= \left(\frac{\partial f}{\partial x}\right)_{P_0}\cdot u_1 + \left(\frac{\partial f}{\partial y}\right)_{P_0}\cdot u_2 \qquad \text{From Eqs. (2), } dx/ds = u_1 \text{ and } dy/ds = u_2.$$

$$= \underbrace{\left[\left(\frac{\partial f}{\partial x}\right)_{P_0}\mathbf{i} + \left(\frac{\partial f}{\partial y}\right)_{P_0}\mathbf{j}\right]}_{\textit{gradient of } f \text{ at } P_0} \cdot \underbrace{[u_1\mathbf{i} + u_2\mathbf{j}]}_{\text{direction } \mathbf{u}} \tag{3}$$

The notation ∇f is read "grad f" as well as "gradient of f" and "del f." The symbol ∇ by itself is read "del." Another notation for the gradient is grad f, read the way it is written.

DEFINITION Gradient Vector or Gradient

The **gradient vector (gradient)** of $f(x, y)$ at a point $P_0(x_0, y_0)$ is the vector

$$\nabla f = \frac{\partial f}{\partial x}\mathbf{i} + \frac{\partial f}{\partial y}\mathbf{j}$$

obtained by evaluating the partial derivatives of f at P_0.

Equation (3) says that the derivative of f in the direction of $\mathbf{u}$ at P_0 is the dot product of $\mathbf{u}$ with the gradient of f at P_0.

THEOREM 9 The Directional Derivative is a Scalar Product

If the partial derivatives of $f(x, y)$ are defined at $P_0(x_0, y_0)$, then

$$\left(\frac{df}{ds}\right)_{\mathbf{u},P_0} = (\nabla f)_{P_0} \cdot \mathbf{u}, \tag{4}$$

the scalar product of the gradient f at P_0 and $\mathbf{u}$.

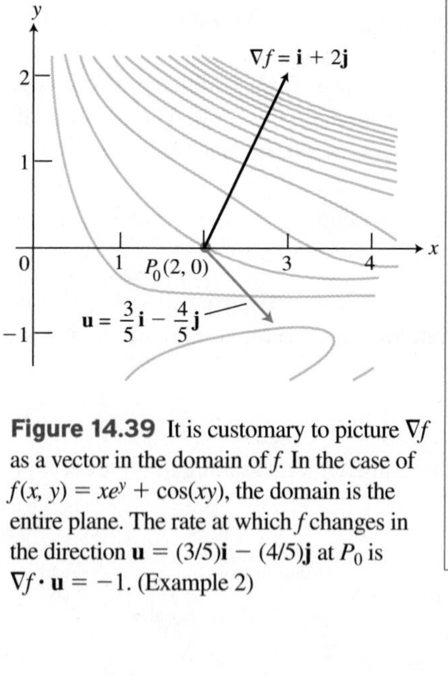

Figure 14.39 It is customary to picture ∇f as a vector in the domain of f. In the case of $f(x, y) = xe^y + \cos(xy)$, the domain is the entire plane. The rate at which f changes in the direction $\mathbf{u} = (3/5)\mathbf{i} - (4/5)\mathbf{j}$ at P_0 is $\nabla f \cdot \mathbf{u} = -1$. (Example 2)

EXAMPLE 2 Finding the Directional Derivative

Find the derivative of $f(x, y) = xe^y + \cos(xy)$ at the point (2, 0) in the direction of $\mathbf{A} = 3\mathbf{i} - 4\mathbf{j}$.

SOLUTION

The direction of $\mathbf{A}$ is obtained by dividing $\mathbf{A}$ by its length

$$\mathbf{u} = \frac{\mathbf{A}}{|\mathbf{A}|} = \frac{\mathbf{A}}{5} = \frac{3}{5}\mathbf{i} - \frac{4}{5}\mathbf{j}.$$

The partial derivatives of f at (2, 0) are

$$f_x(2, 0) = (e^y - y\sin(xy))_{(2,0)} = e^0 - 0 = 1,$$

$$f_y(2, 0) = (xe^y - x\sin(xy))_{(2,0)} = 2e^0 - 2 \cdot 0 = 2.$$

The gradient of f at (2, 0) is

$$\nabla f|_{(2,0)} = f_x(2, 0)\,\mathbf{i} + f_y(2, 0)\,\mathbf{j} = \mathbf{i} + 2\mathbf{j}$$

(Figure 14.39). The derivative of f at (2, 0) in the direction of $\mathbf{A}$ is therefore

$$(D_{\mathbf{u}}f)|_{(2,0)} = \nabla f|_{(2,0)} \cdot \mathbf{u} \qquad \text{Eq. (4)}$$

$$= (\mathbf{i} + 2\mathbf{j}) \cdot \left(\frac{3}{5}\mathbf{i} - \frac{4}{5}\mathbf{j}\right) = \frac{3}{5} - \frac{8}{5} = -1.$$

Properties of Directional Derivatives

Evaluating the dot product in the formula

$$D_{\mathbf{u}}f = \nabla f \cdot \mathbf{u} = |\nabla f||\mathbf{u}|\cos\theta = |\nabla f|\cos\theta,$$

where θ is the angle between the vectors $\mathbf{u}$ and ∇f, reveals the following properties.

Properties of the Directional Derivative

$$D_{\mathbf{u}}f = \nabla f \cdot \mathbf{u} = |\nabla f|\cos\theta$$

1. The function f increases most rapidly when $\cos\theta = 1$ or when $\mathbf{u}$ is the direction of ∇f. That is, at each point P in its domain, f increases most rapidly in the direction of the gradient vector ∇f at P. The derivative in this direction is
$$D_{\mathbf{u}}f = |\nabla f|\cos(0) = |\nabla f|.$$
2. Similarly, f decreases most rapidly in the direction of $-\nabla f$. The derivative in this direction is $D_{\mathbf{u}}f = |\nabla f|\cos(\pi) = -|\nabla f|$.
3. Any direction $\mathbf{u}$ orthogonal to the gradient is a direction of zero change in f because θ then equals $\pi/2$ and
$$D_{\mathbf{u}}f = |\nabla f|\cos(\pi/2) = |\nabla f| \cdot 0 = 0.$$

As we will discuss later, these properties hold in three dimensions as well as two.

EXAMPLE 3 Finding Directions of Maximal, Minimal, and Zero Change

Find the directions in which $f(x, y) = (x^2/2) + (y^2/2)$ **(a)** increases most rapidly and **(b)** decreases most rapidly at the point $(1, 1)$. **(c)** What are the directions of zero change in f at $(1, 1)$?

SOLUTION

(a) The function increases most rapidly in the direction of ∇f at $(1, 1)$. The gradient is

$$(\nabla f)_{(1,1)} = (x\mathbf{i} + y\mathbf{j})_{(1,1)} = \mathbf{i} + \mathbf{j}.$$

Its direction is

$$\mathbf{u} = \frac{\mathbf{i} + \mathbf{j}}{|\mathbf{i} + \mathbf{j}|} = \frac{\mathbf{i} + \mathbf{j}}{\sqrt{(1)^2 + (1)^2}} = \frac{1}{\sqrt{2}}\mathbf{i} + \frac{1}{\sqrt{2}}\mathbf{j}.$$

(b) The function decreases most rapidly in the direction of $-\nabla f$ at $(1, 1)$, which is

$$-\mathbf{u} = -\frac{1}{\sqrt{2}}\mathbf{i} - \frac{1}{\sqrt{2}}\mathbf{j}.$$

(c) The directions of zero change at $(1, 1)$ are the directions orthogonal to ∇f:

$$\mathbf{n} = -\frac{1}{\sqrt{2}}\mathbf{i} + \frac{1}{\sqrt{2}}\mathbf{j} \quad \text{and} \quad -\mathbf{n} = \frac{1}{\sqrt{2}}\mathbf{i} - \frac{1}{\sqrt{2}}\mathbf{j}.$$

See Figure 14.40.

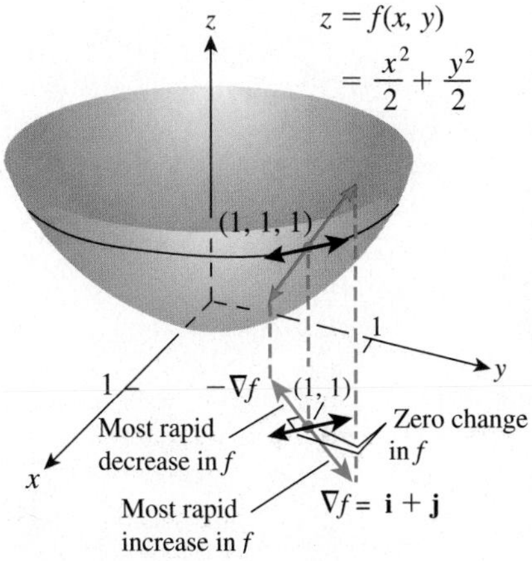

Figure 14.40 The direction in which $f(x, y) = (x^2/2) + (y^2/2)$ increases most rapidly at $(1, 1)$ is the direction of $\nabla f_{(1,1)} = \mathbf{i} + \mathbf{j}$. It corresponds to the direction of steepest ascent on the surface at $(1, 1, 1)$.

Gradients and Tangents to Level Curves

If a differentiable function $f(x, y)$ has a constant value c along a smooth curve $\mathbf{r} = g(t)\mathbf{i} + h(t)\mathbf{j}$ (making the curve a level curve of f), then $f(g(t), h(t)) = c$. Differentiating both sides of this equation with respect to t leads to the equations

$$\frac{d}{dt} f(g(t), h(t)) = \frac{d}{dt}(c),$$

$$\frac{\partial f}{\partial x}\frac{dg}{dt} + \frac{\partial f}{\partial y}\frac{dh}{dt} = 0, \quad \text{Chain Rule}$$

$$\underbrace{\left(\frac{\partial f}{\partial x}\mathbf{i} + \frac{\partial f}{\partial y}\mathbf{j}\right)}_{\nabla f} \cdot \underbrace{\left(\frac{dg}{dt}\mathbf{i} + \frac{dh}{dt}\mathbf{j}\right)}_{\frac{d\mathbf{r}}{dt}} = 0. \qquad (5)$$

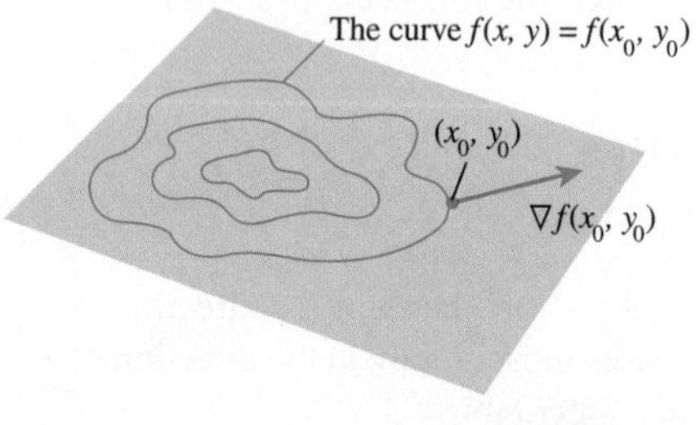

Figure 14.41 The gradient of a differentiable function of two variables at a point is always normal to the function's level curve through the point.

Equation (5) says that ∇f is normal to the tangent vector $d\mathbf{r}/dt$, so it is normal to the curve.

At every point (x_0, y_0) in the domain of $f(x, y)$, the gradient of f is normal to the level curve through (x_0, y_0) (Figure 14.41). This observation enables us to find equations for tangent lines to level curves. They are the lines normal to the gradients. The line through a point $P_0(x_0, y_0)$ normal to a vector $\mathbf{N} = A\mathbf{i} + B\mathbf{j}$ has the equation

$$A(x - x_0) + B(y - y_0) = 0$$

(Exercise 59). If $\mathbf{N}$ is the gradient $(\nabla f)_{(x_0, y_0)} = f_x(x_0, y_0)\mathbf{i} + f_y(x_0, y_0)\mathbf{j}$, the equation becomes

$$f_x(x_0, y_0)(x - x_0) + f_y(x_0, y_0)(y - y_0) = 0. \qquad (6)$$

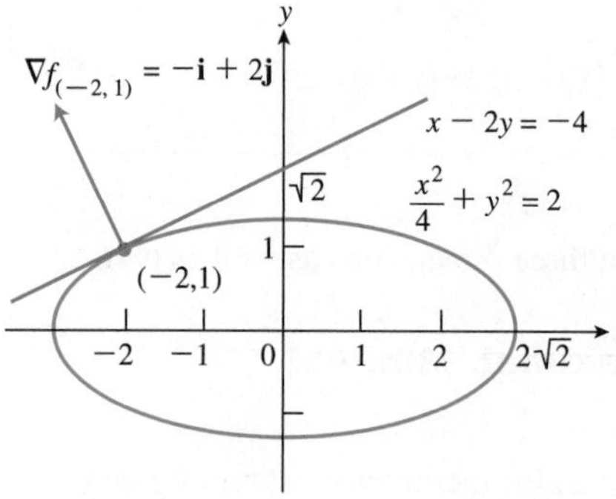

Figure 14.42 We can find the tangent to the ellipse $(x^2/4) + y^2 = 2$ by treating the ellipse as a level curve of the function $f(x, y) = (x^2/4) + y^2$. (Example 4)

EXAMPLE 4 Finding an Equation for a Tangent Line

Find an equation for the line tangent to the ellipse

$$\frac{x^2}{4} + y^2 = 2$$

(Figure 14.42) at the point $(-2, 1)$.

SOLUTION

The ellipse is a level curve of the function

$$f(x, y) = \frac{x^2}{4} + y^2.$$

The gradient of f at $(-2, 1)$ is

$$\nabla f\big|_{(-2,1)} = \left(\frac{x}{2}\mathbf{i} + 2y\mathbf{j}\right)_{(-2,1)} = -\mathbf{i} + 2\mathbf{j}.$$

The tangent (from Equation 6) is the line

$$(-1)(x + 2) + (2)(y - 1) = 0$$

$$x - 2y = -4.$$

Functions of Three Variables

We obtain three-variable formulas by adding the z-terms to the two-variable formulas. For a differentiable function $f(x, y, z)$ and a unit vector $\mathbf{u} = u_1\mathbf{i} + u_2\mathbf{j} + u_3\mathbf{k}$ in space, we have

$$\nabla f = \frac{\partial f}{\partial x}\mathbf{i} + \frac{\partial f}{\partial y}\mathbf{j} + \frac{\partial f}{\partial z}\mathbf{k}$$

and
$$D_{\mathbf{u}}f = \nabla f \cdot \mathbf{u} = \frac{\partial f}{\partial x}u_1 + \frac{\partial f}{\partial y}u_2 + \frac{\partial f}{\partial z}u_3.$$

The directional derivative can once again be written in the form

$$D_{\mathbf{u}}f = \nabla f \cdot \mathbf{u} = |\nabla f||\mathbf{u}| \cos \theta = |\nabla f| \cos \theta,$$

so the properties listed earlier for functions of two variables continue to hold. At any given point, f increases most rapidly in the direction of ∇f and decreases most rapidly in the direction of $-\nabla f$. In any direction orthogonal to ∇f, the derivative is zero.

EXAMPLE 5 Finding Directions of Maximal, Minimal, and Zero Change

(a) Find the derivative of $f(x, y, z) = x^3 - xy^2 - z$ at $P_0(1, 1, 0)$ in the direction of $\mathbf{A} = 2\mathbf{i} - 3\mathbf{j} + 6\mathbf{k}$.

(b) In what directions does f change most rapidly at P_0, and what are the rates of change in these directions?

SOLUTION

(a) The direction of **A** is obtained by dividing **A** by its length:

$$|\mathbf{A}| = \sqrt{(2)^2 + (-3)^2 + (6)^2} = \sqrt{49} = 7$$

$$\mathbf{u} = \frac{\mathbf{A}}{|\mathbf{A}|} = \frac{2}{7}\mathbf{i} - \frac{3}{7}\mathbf{j} + \frac{6}{7}\mathbf{k}.$$

The partial derivatives of f at P_0 are

$$f_x = 3x^2 - y^2\big|_{(1,1,0)} = 2, \qquad f_y = -2xy\big|_{(1,1,0)} = -2, \qquad f_z = -1\big|_{(1,1,0)} = -1.$$

The gradient of f at P_0 is

$$\nabla f\big|_{(1,1,0)} = 2\mathbf{i} - 2\mathbf{j} - \mathbf{k}.$$

The derivative of f at P_0 in the direction of **A** is therefore

$$(D_{\mathbf{u}}f)\big|_{(1,1,0)} = \nabla f\big|_{(1,1,0)} \cdot \mathbf{u} = (2\mathbf{i} - 2\mathbf{j} - \mathbf{k}) \cdot \left(\frac{2}{7}\mathbf{i} - \frac{3}{7}\mathbf{j} + \frac{6}{7}\mathbf{k}\right)$$

$$= \frac{4}{7} + \frac{6}{7} - \frac{6}{7} = \frac{4}{7}.$$

(b) The function increases most rapidly in the direction of $\nabla f = 2\mathbf{i} - 2\mathbf{j} - \mathbf{k}$ and decreases most rapidly in the direction of $-\nabla f$. The rates of change in the directions are, respectively,

$$|\nabla f| = \sqrt{(2)^2 + (-2)^2 + (-1)^2} = \sqrt{9} = 3 \qquad \text{and} \qquad -|\nabla f| = -3.$$

Tangent Planes and Normal Lines

If $\mathbf{r} = g(t)\mathbf{i} + h(t)\mathbf{j} + k(t)\mathbf{k}$ is a smooth curve on the level surface $f(x, y, z) = c$ of a differentiable function f, then $f(g(t), h(t), k(t)) = c$. Differentiating both sides of this equation with respect to t leads to

$$\frac{d}{dt}f(g(t), h(t), k(t)) = \frac{d}{dt}(c),$$

$$\frac{\partial f}{\partial x}\frac{dg}{dt} + \frac{\partial f}{\partial y}\frac{dh}{dt} + \frac{\partial f}{\partial z}\frac{dk}{dt} = 0, \qquad \text{Chain Rule}$$

$$\underbrace{\left(\frac{\partial f}{\partial x}\mathbf{i} + \frac{\partial f}{\partial y}\mathbf{j} + \frac{\partial f}{\partial z}\mathbf{k}\right)}_{\nabla f} \cdot \underbrace{\left(\frac{dg}{dt}\mathbf{i} + \frac{dh}{dt}\mathbf{j} + \frac{dk}{dt}\mathbf{k}\right)}_{d\mathbf{r}/dt} = 0. \tag{7}$$

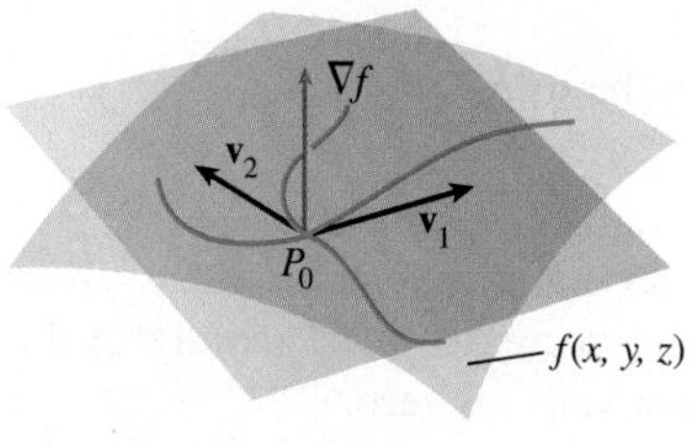

Figure 14.43 ∇f is orthogonal to the velocity vector of every smooth curve in the surface through P_0. The velocity vectors at P_0 therefore lie in a common plane, the tangent plane at P_0.

At every point on the curve, ∇f is orthogonal to the curve's velocity vector.

Now let us restrict our attention to the curves that pass through a fixed point P_0 on the surface (Figure 14.43). All the velocity vectors at P_0 are orthogonal to ∇f at P_0, so the curve's tangent lines all lie in the plane through P_0 normal to ∇f. This is the *tangent plane* of the surface at P_0. The line through P_0 perpendicular to the plane is the surface's *normal line* P_0.

DEFINITIONS Tangent Plane and Normal Line

The **tangent plane** at the point $P_0(x_0, y_0, z_0)$ on the level surface $f(x, y, z) = c$ is the plane through P_0 normal to $\nabla f|_{P_0}$. The **normal line** of the surface at P_0 is the line through P_0 parallel to $\nabla f|_{P_0}$.

Thus, from Section 12.4, the tangent plane and normal line, respectively, have the following equations:

$$f_x(P_0)(x - x_0) + f_y(P_0)(y - y_0) + f_z(P_0)(z - z_0) = 0, \tag{8}$$

$$x = x_0 + f_x(P_0)t, \qquad y = y_0 + f_y(P_0)t, \qquad z = z_0 + f_z(P_0)t. \tag{9}$$

EXAMPLE 6 Finding Tangent Plane and Normal Line

Find the tangent plane and normal line of the surface

$$f(x, y, z) = x^2 + y^2 + z - 9 = 0 \qquad \text{A circular paraboloid}$$

at the point $P_0(1, 2, 4)$.

SOLUTION

The surface is shown in Figure 14.44.

The tangent plane is the plane through P_0 perpendicular to the gradient of f at P_0. The gradient is

$$\nabla f|_{P_0} = (2x\mathbf{i} + 2y\mathbf{j} + \mathbf{k})_{(1,2,4)} = 2\mathbf{i} + 4\mathbf{j} + \mathbf{k}.$$

The plane is therefore the plane

$$2(x - 1) + 4(y - 2) + (z - 4) = 0, \qquad \text{or} \qquad 2x + 4y + z = 14.$$

The line normal to the surface at P_0 is

$$x = 1 + 2t, \qquad y = 2 + 4t, \qquad z = 4 + t.$$

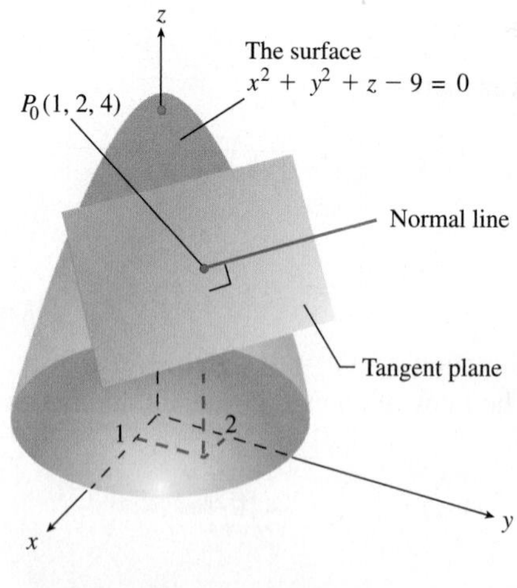

Figure 14.44 The tangent plane and normal line to the surface $x^2 + y^2 + z - 9 = 0$ at $P_0(1, 2, 4)$. (Example 6)

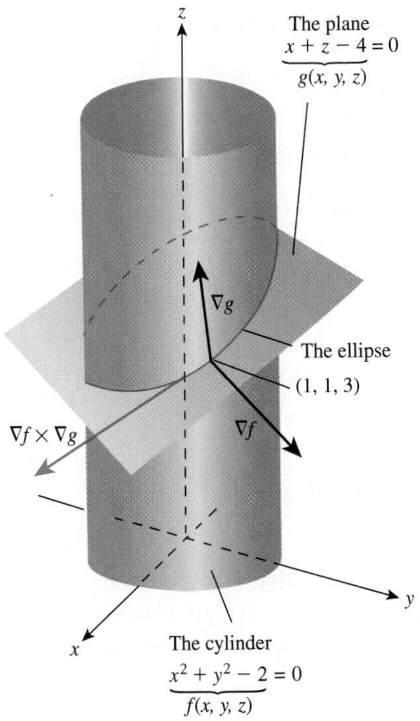

Figure 14.45 The cylinder $f(x, y, z) = x^2 + y^2 - 2 = 0$ and the plane $g(x, y, z) = x + z - 4 = 0$ intersect in an ellipse. (Example 7)

EXAMPLE 7 Finding Parametric Equations for a Line Tangent to a Curve

The surfaces

$$f(x, y, z) = x^2 + y^2 - 2 = 0 \qquad \text{A cylinder}$$

and

$$g(x, y, z) = x + z - 4 = 0 \qquad \text{A plane}$$

meet in an ellipse (Figure 14.45). Find parametric equations for the line tangent to the ellipse at the point $P_0(1, 1, 3)$.

SOLUTION

The tangent line is orthogonal to both ∇f and ∇g at P_0 and is therefore parallel to $\mathbf{v} = \nabla f \times \nabla g$. The components of $\mathbf{v}$ and the coordinates of P_0 give us equations for the line. We have

$$\nabla f_{(1,1,3)} = (2x\mathbf{i} + 2y\mathbf{j})_{(1,1,3)} = 2\mathbf{i} + 2\mathbf{j},$$

$$\nabla g_{(1,1,3)} = (\mathbf{i} + \mathbf{k})_{(1,1,3)} = \mathbf{i} + \mathbf{k},$$

$$\mathbf{v} = (2\mathbf{i} + 2\mathbf{j}) \times (\mathbf{i} + \mathbf{k}) = \begin{vmatrix} \mathbf{i} & \mathbf{j} & \mathbf{k} \\ 2 & 2 & 0 \\ 1 & 0 & 1 \end{vmatrix} = 2\mathbf{i} - 2\mathbf{j} - 2\mathbf{k}.$$

The line is

$$x = 1 + 2t, \qquad y = 1 - 2t, \qquad z = 3 - 2t.$$

Planes Tangent to a Surface $z = f(x, y)$

To find an equation for the plane tangent to a surface $z = f(x, y)$ at a point $P_0(x_0, y_0, z_0)$, where $z_0 = f(x_0, y_0)$, we first observe that the equation $z = f(x, y)$ is equivalent to $f(x, y) - z = 0$. The surface $z = f(x, y)$ is therefore the zero level surface of the function $F(x, y, z) = f(x, y) - z$. The partial derivatives of F are

$$F_x = \frac{\partial}{\partial x}(f(x, y) - z) = f_x - 0 = f_x,$$

$$F_y = \frac{\partial}{\partial y}(f(x, y) - z) = f_y - 0 = f_y,$$

$$F_z = \frac{\partial}{\partial z}(f(x, y) - z) = 0 - 1 = -1.$$

The formula

$$F_x(P_0)(x - x_0) + F_y(P_0)(y - y_0) + F_z(P_0)(z - z_0) = 0 \qquad \text{Eq. (8) restated for } F(x, y, z)$$

for the plane tangent to the level surface at P_0 therefore reduces to

$$f_x(x_0, y_0)(x - x_0) + f_y(x_0, y_0)(y - y_0) - (z - z_0) = 0.$$

Plane Tangent to a Surface $z = f(x, y)$ at $(x_0, y_0, f(x_0, y_0))$

The plane tangent to the surface $z = f(x, y)$ at the point $P(x_0, y_0, z_0) = (x_0, y_0, f(x_0, y_0))$ is

$$f_x(x_0, y_0)(x - x_0) + f_y(x_0, y_0)(y - y_0) - (z - z_0) = 0. \qquad (10)$$

EXAMPLE 8 Finding a Plane Tangent to a Surface $z = f(x, y)$

Find the plane tangent to the surface $z = x\cos y - ye^x$ at (0, 0, 0).

SOLUTION

We calculate the partial derivatives of $f(x, y) = x\cos y - ye^x$ and use Equation (10):

$$f_x(0, 0) = (\cos y - ye^x)_{(0,0)} = 1 - 0 \cdot 1 = 1,$$

$$f_y(0, 0) = (-x\sin y - e^x)_{(0,0)} = 0 - 1 = -1.$$

The tangent plane is therefore

$$1 \cdot (x - 0) - 1 \cdot (y - 0) - (z - 0) = 0, \qquad \text{Eq. (10)}$$

or

$$x - y - z = 0.$$

Increments and Distance

The directional derivative plays the role of an ordinary derivative when we want to estimate how much the value of a function f will change if we move a small distance ds from a point P_0 to another point nearby. If f were a function of a single variable, we would have

$$df = f'(P_0)\,ds. \qquad \text{Ordinary derivative} \times \text{increment}$$

For a function of two or more variables, we use the formula

$$df = (\nabla f|_{P_0} \cdot \mathbf{u})\,ds, \qquad \text{Directional derivative} \times \text{increment}$$

where $\mathbf{u}$ is the direction of the motion away from P_0.

Estimating the Change in f in a Direction $\mathbf{u}$

To estimate the change in the value of a function f when we move a small distance ds from a point P_0 in a particular direction $\mathbf{u}$, use the formula

$$df = \underbrace{(\nabla f|_{P_0} \cdot \mathbf{u})}_{\text{directional derivative}} \cdot \underbrace{ds.}_{\text{distance increment}}$$

EXAMPLE 9 Estimating Change

Estimate how much the value of $f(x, y, z) = xe^y + yz$ will change if the point $P(x, y, z)$ moves 0.1 units from $P_0(2, 0, 0)$ straight toward $P_1(4, 1, -2)$.

SOLUTION

We first find the derivative of f in the direction of

$$\overrightarrow{P_0P_1} = 2\mathbf{i} + \mathbf{j} - 2\mathbf{k}.$$

The direction of this vector is

$$\mathbf{u} = \frac{\overrightarrow{P_0P_1}}{|\overrightarrow{P_0P_1}|} = \frac{\overrightarrow{P_0P}}{3} = \frac{2}{3}\mathbf{i} + \frac{1}{3}\mathbf{j} - \frac{2}{3}\mathbf{k}.$$

The gradient of f at P_0 is

$$\nabla f|_{(2,0,0)} = (e^y\mathbf{i} + (xe^y + z)\mathbf{j} + y\mathbf{k})|_{(2,0,0)} = \mathbf{i} + 2\mathbf{j}.$$

Therefore,

$$\nabla f|_{P_0} \cdot \mathbf{u} = (\mathbf{i} + 2\mathbf{j}) \cdot \left(\frac{2}{3}\mathbf{i} + \frac{1}{3}\mathbf{j} - \frac{2}{3}\mathbf{k}\right) = \frac{2}{3} + \frac{2}{3} = \frac{4}{3}.$$

The change in f that results from moving $ds = 0.1$ unit away from P_0 in the direction of $\mathbf{u}$ is approximately

$$df = (\nabla f|_{P_0} \cdot \mathbf{u})\,(ds) = \left(\frac{4}{3}\right)(0.1) \approx 0.13.$$

Algebra Rules for Gradients

If we know the gradients of two functions f and g, we automatically know the gradients of their constant multiples, sum, difference, product, and quotient.

Algebra Rules for Gradients

1. *Constant Multiple Rule:* $\nabla(kf) = k\nabla f$ (any number k)
2. *Sum Rule:* $\nabla(f + g) = \nabla f + \nabla g$
3. *Difference Rule:* $\nabla(f - g) = \nabla f - \nabla g$
4. *Product Rule:* $\nabla(fg) = f\nabla g + g\nabla f$
5. *Quotient Rule:* $\nabla\left(\frac{f}{g}\right) = \frac{g\nabla f - f\nabla g}{g^2}$

These rules have the same form as the corresponding rules for derivatives, as they should (Exercise 65).

EXAMPLE 10 Illustrating the Gradient Rules

We illustrate the rules with $f(x, y, z) = x - y$, $g(x, y, z) = z$.

SOLUTION

With $\nabla f = \mathbf{i} - \mathbf{j}$ and $\nabla g = \mathbf{k}$, we have

1. $\nabla(2f) = \nabla(2x - 2y) = 2\mathbf{i} - 2\mathbf{j} = 2\nabla f.$
2. $\nabla(f + g) = \nabla(x - y + z) = \mathbf{i} - \mathbf{j} + \mathbf{k} = \nabla f + \nabla g.$
3. $\nabla(f - g) = \nabla(x - y - z) = \mathbf{i} - \mathbf{j} - \mathbf{k} = \nabla f - \nabla g.$
4. $\nabla(fg) = \nabla(xz - yz) = z\mathbf{i} - z\mathbf{j} + (x - y)\mathbf{k} = g\nabla f + f\nabla g.$
5. $\nabla\left(\frac{f}{g}\right) = \nabla\left(\frac{x - y}{z}\right)$

$$= \frac{\partial}{\partial x}\left(\frac{x - y}{z}\right)\mathbf{i} + \frac{\partial}{\partial y}\left(\frac{x - y}{z}\right)\mathbf{j} + \frac{\partial}{\partial z}\left(\frac{x - y}{z}\right)\mathbf{k}$$

$$= \frac{1}{z}\mathbf{i} - \frac{1}{z}\mathbf{j} - \frac{x - y}{z^2}\mathbf{k}$$

$$= \frac{z\mathbf{i} - z\mathbf{j} - (x - y)\mathbf{k}}{z^2} = \frac{g\nabla f - f\nabla g}{g^2}.$$

Quick Review 14.6

In Exercises 1 and 2, let $\mathbf{u} = 2\mathbf{i} - \mathbf{j} + \mathbf{k}$.

1. Find the length of **u**.
2. Find the direction of **u**.

In Exercises 3–6, let $\mathbf{u} = 3\mathbf{i} - \mathbf{j}$ and $\mathbf{v} = -\mathbf{i} + 2\mathbf{j} - \mathbf{k}$.

3. Find $\mathbf{u} \cdot \mathbf{v}$.
4. Find $\mathbf{u} \times \mathbf{v}$.
5. Find a vector perpendicular to the plane determined by **u** and **v**.
6. Find the direction of $\mathbf{u} \times \mathbf{v}$.
7. Find parametric equations for the line through the points $(-1, 2, -1)$ and $(3, 2, 0)$.
8. Find parametric equations for the line through the point $(2, -1, 1)$ and parallel to the vector $3\mathbf{i} - 2\mathbf{j} + \mathbf{k}$.
9. Find an equation for the line through the point $(2, 0, -2)$ perpendicular to the plane $x - 2y + 3z = 1$.
10. Find an equation for the plane through the point $(1, 0, -2)$ normal to the vector $\mathbf{n} = -\mathbf{i} + 3\mathbf{j} - 2\mathbf{k}$.

Section 14.6 Exercises

In Exercises 1–4, find the gradient of the function at the given point. Then sketch the gradient together with the level curve that passes through the point.

1. $f(x, y) = y - x, \quad (2, 1)$
2. $f(x, y) = \ln(x^2 + y^2), \quad (1, 1)$
3. $g(x, y) = y - x^2, \quad (-1, 0)$
4. $g(x, y) = \dfrac{x^2}{2} - \dfrac{y^2}{2}, \quad (\sqrt{2}, 1)$

In Exercises 5–8, find ∇f at the given point.

5. $f(x, y, z) = x^2 + y^2 - 2z^2 + z \ln x, \quad (1, 1, 1)$
6. $f(x, y, z) = 2z^3 - 3(x^2 + y^2)z + \tan^{-1} xz, \quad (1, 1, 1)$
7. $f(x, y, z) = (x^2 + y^2 + z^2)^{-1/2} + \ln(xyz), \quad (-1, 2, -2)$
8. $f(x, y, z) = e^{x+y} \cos z + (y + 1) \sin^{-1} x, \quad (0, 0, \pi/6)$

In Exercises 9–16, find the derivative of the function at P_0 in the direction of **A**.

9. $f(x, y) = 2xy - 3y^2, \quad P_0(5, 5), \quad \mathbf{A} = 4\mathbf{i} + 3\mathbf{j}$
10. $f(x, y) = 2x^2 + y^2, \quad P_0(-1, 1), \quad \mathbf{A} = 3\mathbf{i} - 4\mathbf{j}$
11. $g(x, y) = x - (y^2/x) + \sqrt{3} \sec^{-1} (2xy), \quad P_0(1, 1),$ $\mathbf{A} = 12\mathbf{i} + 5\mathbf{j}$
12. $h(x, y) = \tan^{-1} (y/x) + \sqrt{3} \sin^{-1} (xy/2), \quad P_0(1, 1),$ $\mathbf{A} = 3\mathbf{i} + 2\mathbf{j}$
13. $f(x, y, z) = xy + yz + zx, \quad P_0(1, -1, 2),$ $\mathbf{A} = 3\mathbf{i} + 6\mathbf{j} - 2\mathbf{k}$
14. $f(x, y, z) = x^2 + 2y^2 - 3z^2, \quad P_0(1, 1, 1), \quad \mathbf{A} = \mathbf{i} + \mathbf{j} + \mathbf{k}$
15. $g(x, y, z) = 3e^x \cos yz, \quad P_0(0, 0, 0), \quad \mathbf{A} = 2\mathbf{i} + \mathbf{j} - 2\mathbf{k}$
16. $h(x, y, z) = \cos xy + e^{yz} + \ln zx, \quad P_0(1, 0, 1/2),$ $\mathbf{A} = \mathbf{i} + 2\mathbf{j} + 2\mathbf{k}$

In Exercises 17–22, find the directions in which the function increases and decreases most rapidly at P_0. Then find the derivative of the function in these directions.

17. $f(x, y) = x^2 + xy + y^2, \quad P_0(-1, 1)$
18. $f(x, y) = x^2y + e^{xy} \sin y, \quad P_0(1, 0)$
19. $f(x, y, z) = (x/y) - yz, \quad P_0(4, 1, 1)$
20. $g(x, y, z) = xe^y + z^2, \quad P_0(1, \ln 2, 1/2)$
21. $f(x, y, z) = \ln xy + \ln yz + \ln xz, \quad P_0(1, 1, 1)$
22. $h(x, y, z) = \ln(x^2 + y^2 - 1) + y + 6z, \quad P_0(1, 1, 0)$
23. ***Estimating Change*** By about how much will
$$f(x, y, z) = \ln \sqrt{x^2 + y^2 + z^2}$$
change if the point $P(x, y, z)$ moves from $P_0(3, 4, 12)$ a distance of $ds = 0.1$ units in the direction of $3\mathbf{i} + 6\mathbf{j} - 2\mathbf{k}$?
24. ***Estimating Change*** By about how much will
$$f(x, y, z) = e^x \cos yz$$
change as the point $P(x, y, z)$ moves from the origin a distance of $ds = 0.1$ units in the direction of $2\mathbf{i} + 2\mathbf{j} - 2\mathbf{k}$?
25. ***Estimating Change*** By about how much will
$$g(x, y, z) = x + x \cos z - y \sin z + y$$
change if the point $P(x, y, z)$ moves from $P_0(2, -1, 0)$ a distance of $ds = 0.2$ units toward the point $P_1(0, 1, 2)$?
26. ***Estimating Change*** By about how much will
$$h(x, y, z) = \cos(\pi xy) + xz^2$$
change if the point $P(x, y, z)$ moves from $P_0(-1, -1, -1)$ a distance of $ds = 0.1$ units toward the origin?

In Exercises 27–34, find an equation for the **(a)** tangent plane and **(b)** normal line at the point P_0 on the given surface.

27. $x^2 + y^2 + z^2 = 3, \quad P_0(1, 1, 1)$
28. $x^2 + y^2 - z^2 = 18, \quad P_0(3, 5, -4)$
29. $2z - x^2 = 0, \quad P_0(2, 0, 2)$
30. $x^2 + 2xy - y^2 + z^2 = 7, \quad P_0(1, -1, 3)$
31. $\cos \pi x - x^2y + e^{xz} + yz = 4, \quad P_0(0, 1, 2)$
32. $x^2 - xy - y^2 - z = 0, \quad P_0(1, 1, -1)$
33. $x + y + z = 1, \quad P_0(0, 1, 0)$
34. $x^2 + y^2 - 2xy - x + 3y - z = -4, \quad P_0(2, -3, 18)$

In Exercises 35–38, find an equation for the plane that is tangent to the given surface at the given point.

35. $z = \ln(x^2 + y^2)$, $(1, 0, 0)$

36. $z = e^{-(x^2 + y^2)}$, $(0, 0, 1)$

37. $z = \sqrt{y - x}$, $(1, 2, 1)$

38. $z = 4x^2 + y^2$, $(1, 1, 5)$

In Exercises 39–42, sketch the curve $f(x, y) = c$ together with ∇f and the tangent line at the given point. Then write an equation for the tangent line.

39. $x^2 + y^2 = 4$ $(\sqrt{2}, \sqrt{2})$

40. $x^2 - y = 1$ $(\sqrt{2}, 1)$

41. $xy = -4$, $(2, -2)$

42. $x^2 - xy + y^2 = 7$, $(-1, 2)$ (These are the curve and point in Section 3.7, Example 4.)

In Exercises 43–48, *work in groups of two or three* to find parametric equations for the line tangent to the curve of intersection of the surfaces at the given point.

43. Surfaces: $x + y^2 + 2z = 4$, $x = 1$
Point: $(1, 1, 1)$

44. Surfaces: $xyz = 1$, $x^2 + 2y^2 + 3z^2 = 6$
Point: $(1, 1, 1)$

45. Surfaces: $x^2 + 2y + 2z = 4$, $y = 1$
Point: $(1, 1, 1/2)$

46. Surfaces: $x + y^2 + z = 2$, $y = 1$
Point: $(1/2, 1, 1/2)$

47. Surfaces: $x^3 + 3x^2y^2 + y^3 + 4xy - z^2 = 0$, $x^2 + y^2 + z^2 = 11$
Point: $(1, 1, 3)$

48. Surfaces: $x^2 + y^2 = 4$, $x^2 + y^2 - z = 0$
Point: $(\sqrt{2}, \sqrt{2}, 4)$

49. In what directions is the derivative of $f(x, y) = xy + y^2$ at $P(3, 2)$ equal to zero?

50. In what two directions is the derivative of $f(x, y) = (x^2 - y^2)/(x^2 + y^2)$ at $P(1, 1)$ equal to zero?

51. Writing to Learn Is there a direction **A** in which the rate of change of $f(x, y) = x^2 - 3xy + 4y^2$ at $P(1, 2)$ equals 14? Give reasons for your answer.

52. Writing to Learn Is there a direction **A** in which the rate of change of the temperature function $T(x, y, z) = 2xy - yz$ (temperature in degrees Celsius, distance in meters) at $P(1, -1, 1)$ is -3°C/m? Give reasons for your answer.

53. Writing to Learn The derivative of $f(x, y)$ at $P_0(1, 2)$ in the direction of $\mathbf{i} + \mathbf{j}$ is $2\sqrt{2}$ and in the direction of $-2\mathbf{j}$ is -3. What is the derivative of f in the direction of $-\mathbf{i} - 2\mathbf{j}$? Give reasons for your answer.

54. The derivative of $f(x, y, z)$ at a point P is greatest in the direction of $\mathbf{A} = \mathbf{i} + \mathbf{j} - \mathbf{k}$. In this direction the value of the derivative is $2\sqrt{3}$.

(a) Writing to Learn What is ∇f at P? Give reasons for your answer.

(b) What is the derivative of f at P in the direction of $\mathbf{i} + \mathbf{j}$?

Explorations

55. *Temperature Change Along a Circle* Suppose the Celsius temperature at the point (x, y) in the xy-plane is $T(x, y) = x \sin 2y$ and distance in the xy-plane is measured in meters. A particle is moving *clockwise* around the circle of radius 1 m centered at the origin at the constant rate of 2 m/sec.

(a) How fast is the temperature experienced by the particle changing in °C/m at the point $P(1/2, \sqrt{3}/2)$?

(b) How fast is the temperature experienced by the particle changing in degrees Celsius per second at P?

56. *Change Along the Involute of a Circle* Find the derivative of $f(x, y) = x^2 + y^2$ in the direction of the unit tangent vector of the curve $\mathbf{r}(t) = (\cos t + t \sin t)\mathbf{i} + (\sin t - t \cos t)\mathbf{j}$, $t > 0$ (Figure 14.46).

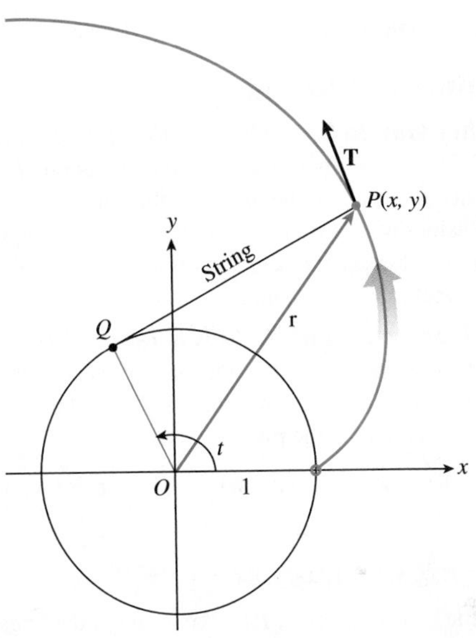

Figure 14.46 If you move along the involute of the unit circle, covering distance along the curve at a constant rate, your distance from the origin will increase at a constant rate as well. (This is how to interpret the result of your calculation in Exercise 56.)

57. *Change Along a Helix* Find the derivative of $f(x, y, z) = x^2 + y^2 + z^2$ in the direction of the unit tangent vector of the helix $\mathbf{r}(t) = (\cos t)\mathbf{i} + (\sin t)\mathbf{j} + t\mathbf{k}$ at the points where $t = -\pi/4$, 0, and $\pi/4$. The function f gives the square of the distance from a point $P(x, y, z)$ on the helix to the origin. The derivatives calculated here give the rates at which the square of the distance is changing with respect to t as P moves through the points where $t = -\pi/4$, 0, and $\pi/4$.

58. *Changing Temperature* The Celsius temperature in a region in space is given by $T(x, y, z) = 2x^2 - xyz$. A particle is moving in this region and its position at time t is given by $x = 2t^2$, $y = 3t$, $z = -t^2$, where time is measured in seconds and distance in meters.

(a) How fast is the temperature experienced by the particle changing in degrees Celsius per meter when the particle is at the point $P(8, 6, -4)$?

(b) How fast is the temperature experienced by the particle changing in degrees Celsius per second at P?

59. *Lines in the xy-Plane* Show that $A(x - x_0) + B(y - y_0) = 0$ is an equation for the line in the xy-plane through the point (x_0, y_0) normal to the vector $\mathbf{N} = A\mathbf{i} + B\mathbf{j}$.

60. *Normal Curves and Tangent Curves* A curve is **normal** to a surface $f(x, y, z) = c$ at a point of intersection if the curve's velocity vector is a scalar multiple of ∇f at the point. The curve is **tangent** to the surface at a point of intersection if its velocity vector is orthogonal to ∇f there.

(a) Show that the curve

$$\mathbf{r}(t) = \sqrt{t}\mathbf{i} + \sqrt{t}\mathbf{j} - \frac{1}{4}(t + 3)\mathbf{k}$$

is normal to the surface $x^2 + y^2 - z = 3$ when $t = 1$.

(b) Show that the curve

$$\mathbf{r}(t) = \sqrt{t}\mathbf{i} + \sqrt{t}\mathbf{j} + (2t - 1)\mathbf{k}$$

is tangent to the surface $x^2 + y^2 - z = 1$ when $t = 1$.

Extending the Ideas

61. *Another Way to See Why Gradients Are Normal to Level Curves* Suppose a differentiable function $f(x, y)$ has a constant value c along the differentiable curve $x = g(t), y = h(t)$ for all values of t. Differentiate both sides of the equation $f(g(t), h(t)) = c$ with respect to t to show that ∇f is normal to the curve's tangent vector at every point.

62. *The Linearization of f(x,y) is a Tangent-Plane Approximation* Show that the tangent plane at the point $P_0(x_0, y_0, f(x_0, y_0))$ on the surface $z = f(x, y)$ defined by a differentiable function f is the plane

$$f_x(x_0, y_0)(x - x_0) + f_y(x_0, y_0)(y - y_0) - (z - f(x_0, y_0)) = 0$$

or

$$z = f(x_0, y_0) + f_x(x_0, y_0)(x - x_0) + f_y(x_0, y_0)(y - y_0).$$

Thus, the tangent plane at P_0 is the graph of the linearization of f at P_0 (Figure 14.47).

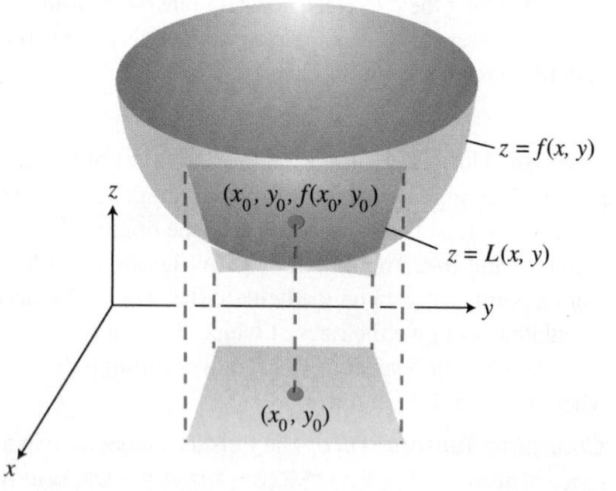

Figure 14.47 The graph of a function $z = f(x, y)$ and its linearization at a point (x_0, y_0). The plane defined by L is tangent to the surface at the point above the point (x_0, y_0). This furnishes a geometric explanation of why the values of L lie close to those of f in the immediate neighborhood of (x_0, y_0). (Exercise 62)

63. *Directional Derivatives and Scalar Components* How is the derivative of a differentiable function $f(x, y, z)$ at a point P_0 in the direction of a unit vector $\mathbf{u}$ related to the scalar component of $(\nabla f)_{P_0}$ in the direction of $\mathbf{u}$? Give reasons for your answer.

64. *Directional Derivatives and Partial Derivatives* Assuming that the necessary derivatives of $f(x, y, z)$ are defined, how are $D_{\mathbf{i}}f$, $D_{\mathbf{j}}f$, and $D_{\mathbf{k}}f$ related to f_x, f_y, and f_z? Give reasons for your answer.

65. *The Algebra Rules for Gradients* Given a constant k and the gradients

$$\nabla f = \frac{\partial f}{\partial x}\mathbf{i} + \frac{\partial f}{\partial y}\mathbf{j} + \frac{\partial f}{\partial z}\mathbf{k}$$

and

$$\nabla g = \frac{\partial g}{\partial x}\mathbf{i} + \frac{\partial g}{\partial y}\mathbf{j} + \frac{\partial g}{\partial z}\mathbf{k},$$

use the scalar equations

$$\frac{\partial}{\partial x}(kf) = k\frac{\partial f}{\partial x},$$

$$\frac{\partial}{\partial x}(f \pm g) = \frac{\partial f}{\partial x} \pm \frac{\partial g}{\partial x},$$

$$\frac{\partial}{\partial x}(fg) = f\frac{\partial g}{\partial x} + g\frac{\partial f}{\partial x},$$

$$\frac{\partial}{\partial x}\left(\frac{f}{g}\right) = \frac{g\frac{\partial f}{\partial x} - f\frac{\partial g}{\partial x}}{g^2},$$

and so on, to establish the following rules:

(a) $\nabla(kf) = k\nabla f$

(b) $\nabla(f + g) = \nabla f + \nabla g$

(c) $\nabla(f - g) = \nabla f - \nabla g$

(d) $\nabla(fg) = f\nabla g + g\nabla f$

(e) $\nabla\left(\frac{f}{g}\right) = \frac{g\nabla f - f\nabla g}{g^2}$

CAS Explorations

66. Draw a graph of the surface and its tangent plane determined in

(a) Exercise 29.

(b) Exercise 32.

(c) Exercise 34.

14.7 Extreme Values and Saddle Points

What you'll learn about

- Behavior on Closed Bounded Regions
- Derivative Tests for Local Extreme Values
- Absolute Extrema on Closed Bounded Regions
- Limitations of Theorem 10
- Summary

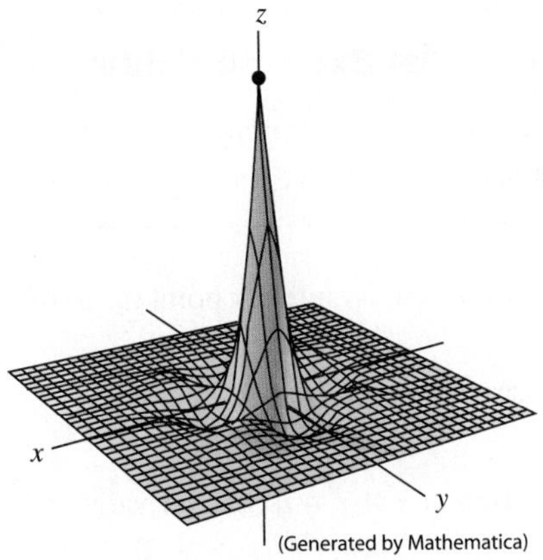

Figure 14.48 The function $z = (\cos x) \cdot (\cos y)e^{-\sqrt{x^2+y^2}}$ has a maximum value of 1 and a minimum value of about -0.067 on the square region $|x| \le 3\pi/2$, $|y| \le 3\pi/2$.

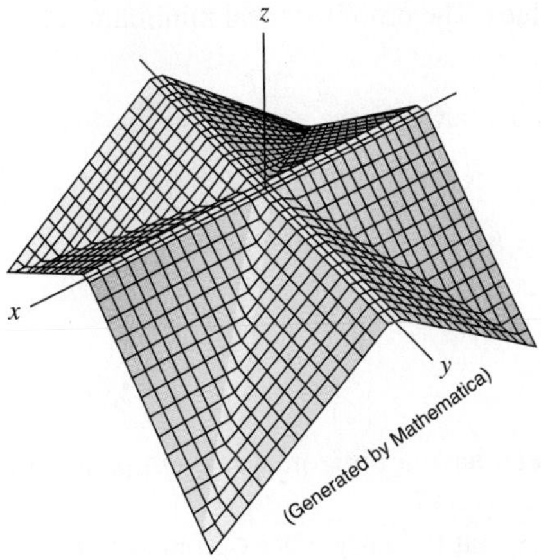

Figure 14.49 The "roof surface" $z = (1/2)(||x| - |y|| - |x| - |y|)$, $|x| \le a$, $|y| \le a$, viewed from the point (10, 15, 20). The defining function has a maximum value of 0 and a minimum value of $-a$.

Behavior on Closed Bounded Regions

As we saw when we were working with functions of a single variable, differentiable functions were just what we wanted for modeling optimization problems. Because these functions were continuous, we knew that on finite closed intervals they did assume both maximum and minimum values. Because they were differentiable, we knew that they would assume these values only at domain endpoints or at interior domain points where the first derivative vanished. Occasionally, we encountered functions that failed to be differentiable at one or more interior domain points and we had to add these points to the list to be investigated as well.

We also saw that the condition that $f'(c) = 0$ did not always signal the presence of an extreme value. At such a point c, the graph might have an inflection point instead of a local maximum or minimum. The graph might rise as it approached c from the left, level off at c, then rise again as it left c. Or, it might fall toward c, level off at c, and then resume falling. That is, the graph might cross its tangent line at $x = c$.

Functions of two variables exhibit similar behavior. As we mentioned in Section 14.2, continuous functions of two variables assume extreme values on closed, bounded domains (see Figures 14.48 and 14.49). As we see in this section, we can narrow the search for these extreme values by examining the functions' first partial derivatives. A function of two variables can assume extreme values only at domain boundary points or at interior domain points where both first partial derivatives are zero or where one or both of the first partial derivatives fails to exist.

Once again, the vanishing of derivatives at an interior point (a, b) does not always signal the presence of an extreme value. Right above (a, b) the surface that is the graph of the function might be shaped like a saddle and cross its tangent plane there. (We will say more about saddle points when the time comes.)

Derivative Tests for Local Extreme Values

For functions of two independent variables, we define local maximum and minimum values in the following way.

> **DEFINITIONS Local Maximum and Local Minimum**
>
> Let $f(x, y)$ be defined on a region R containing the point (a, b). Then
>
> 1. $f(a, b)$ is a **local maximum** value of f if $f(a, b) \ge f(x, y)$ for all domain points (x, y) in an open disk centered at (a, b).
>
> 2. $f(a, b)$ is a **local minimum** value of f if $f(a, b) \le f(x, y)$ for all domain points (x, y) in an open disk centered at (a, b).

Local maxima correspond to mountain peaks on the surface $z = f(x, y)$ and local minima correspond to valley bottoms (Figure 14.50). At such points the tangent planes, when they exist, are horizontal. Local extrema are also called **relative extrema**.

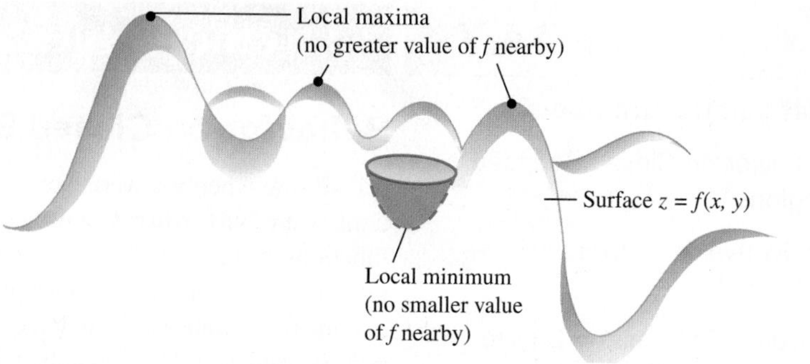

Figure 14.50 A local maximum is a mountain peak, and a local minimum is a valley low.

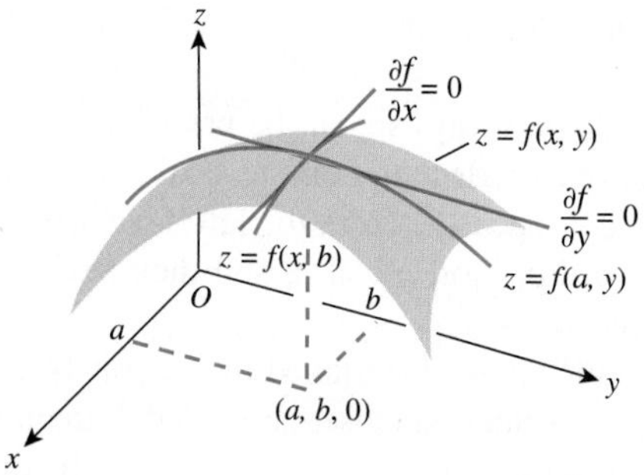

Figure 14.51 The maximum of f occurs at $x = a$, $y = b$.

As with functions of a single variable, the key to identifying the local extrema is a first derivative test.

> **THEOREM 10 First Derivative Test for Local Extreme Values**
>
> If $f(x, y)$ has a local maximum or minimum value at an interior point (a, b) of its domain and if the first partial derivatives exist there, then $f_x(a, b) = 0$ and $f_y(a, b) = 0$.

Proof of Theorem 10 Suppose f has a local maximum at an interior point (a, b) of its domain. Then

1. $x = a$ is an interior point of the domain of the curve $z = f(x, b)$ in which the plane $y = b$ cuts the surface $z = f(x, y)$ (Figure 14.51).
2. The function $z = f(x, b)$ is a differentiable function of x at $x = a$ (the derivative is $f_x(a, b)$).
3. The function $z = f(x, b)$ has a local maximum value at $x = a$.
4. The value of the derivative of $z = f(x, b)$ at $x = a$ is therefore zero (Theorem 2, Section 4.1). Since this derivative is $f_x(a, b)$, we conclude that $f_x(a, b) = 0$.

A similar argument with the function $z = f(a, y)$ shows that $f_y(a, b) = 0$.

This proves the theorem for local maximum values. The proof for local minimum values is left as Exercise 36.

If we substitute the values $f_x(a, b) = 0$ and $f_y(a, b) = 0$ into the equation

$$f_x(a, b)(x - a) + f_y(a, b)(y - b) - (z - f(a, b)) = 0$$

for the tangent plane to the surface $z = f(x, y)$ at (a, b), the equation reduces to

$$0 \cdot (x - a) + 0 \cdot (y - b) - z + f(a, b) = 0$$

or

$$z = f(a, b).$$

Thus, Theorem 10 says that the surface does indeed have a horizontal tangent plane at a local extremum, provided there is a tangent plane there.

As in the single-variable case, Theorem 10 says that the only places a function $f(x, y)$ can ever have an extreme value are

1. interior points where $f_x = f_y = 0$,
2. interior points where one or both of f_x and f_y do not exist, and
3. boundary points of the function's domain.

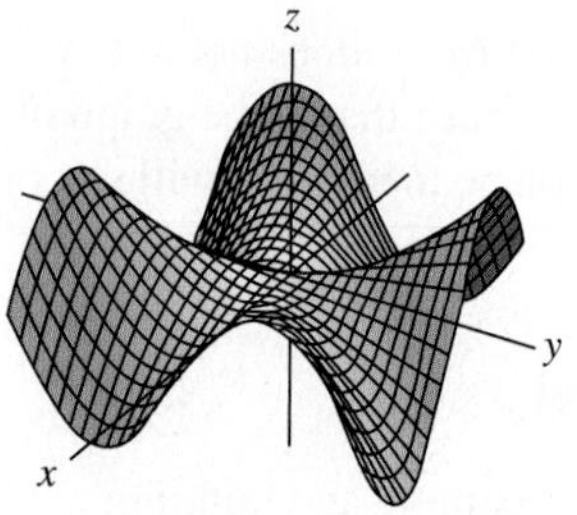

$$z = \frac{xy(x^2 - y^2)}{(x^2 + y^2)}$$

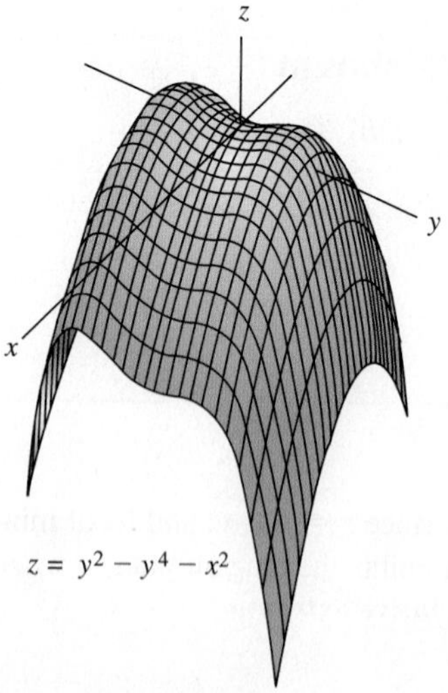

$$z = y^2 - y^4 - x^2$$

(Generated by Mathematica)

Figure 14.52 Saddle points at the origin.

DEFINITION Critical Point

An interior point of the domain of a function $f(x, y)$ where both f_x and f_y are zero or where one or both of f_x and f_y do not exist is a **critical point** of f.

Thus, the only points where a function $f(x, y)$ can assume extreme values are critical points and boundary points. As with differentiable functions of a single variable, not every critical point gives rise to a local extremum. A differentiable function of two variables might have a *saddle point* instead.

DEFINITION Saddle Point

A differentiable function $f(x, y)$ has a **saddle point** at a critical point (a, b) if in every open disk centered at (a, b) there are domain points (x, y), where $f(x, y) > f(a, b)$, and domain points (x, y), where $f(x, y) < f(a, b)$. The corresponding point $(a, b, f(a, b))$ on the surface $z = f(x, y)$ is a saddle point of the surface (Figure 14.52).

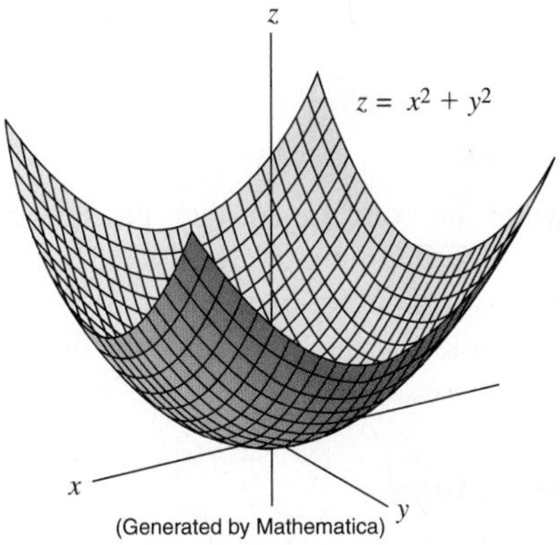

Figure 14.53 The graph of the function $f(x, y) = x^2 + y^2$ is the paraboloid $z = x^2 + y^2$. The function has only one critical point, the origin, which gives rise to a local minimum value of 0. (Example 1)

EXAMPLE 1 Finding Local Extreme Values

Find the local extreme values of $f(x, y) = x^2 + y^2$.

SOLUTION

The domain of f is the entire plane (so there are no boundary points), and the partial derivatives $f_x = 2x$ and $f_y = 2y$ exist everywhere. Therefore, local extreme can occur only where

$$f_x = 2x = 0 \qquad \text{and} \qquad f_y = 2y = 0.$$

The only possibility is the origin, where the value of f is zero. Since f is never negative, we see that the origin gives a local minimum (Figure 14.53).

EXAMPLE 2 Identifying a Saddle Point

Find the local extreme values (if any) of $f(x, y) = y^2 - x^2$.

SOLUTION

The domain of f is the entire plane (so there are no boundary points), and the partial derivatives $f_x = -2x$ and $f_y = 2y$ exist everywhere. Therefore, local extrema can occur only at the origin $(0, 0)$. Along the positive x-axis, however, f has the value $f(x, 0) = -x^2 < 0$; along the positive y-axis, f has the value $f(0, y) = y^2 > 0$. Therefore, every open disk in the xy-plane centered at $(0, 0)$ contains points where the function is positive and points where it is negative. The function has a saddle point at the origin (Figure 14.54) instead of a local extreme value. We conclude that the function has no local extreme values.

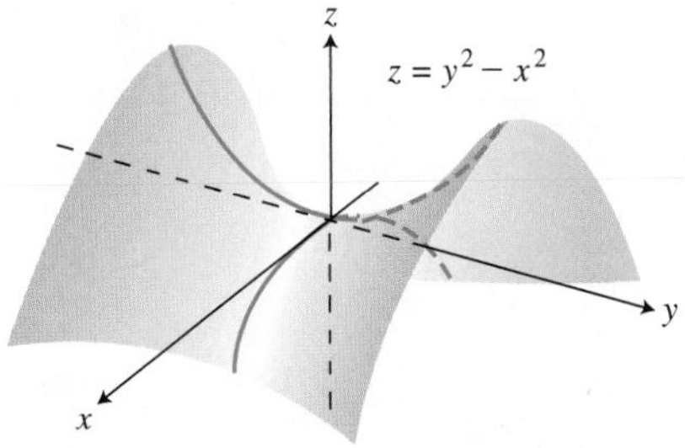

Figure 14.54 The origin is a saddle point of the function $f(x, y) = y^2 - x^2$. There are no local extreme values. (Example 2)

That $f_x = f_y = 0$ at an interior point (a, b) of R does not guarantee a local extreme value at (a, b). If f and its first and second partial derivatives are continuous on R, however, we may be able to learn more from the following theorem, whose proof will be omitted.

THEOREM 11 Second Derivative Test for Local Extreme Values

Suppose $f(x, y)$ and its first and second partial derivatives are continuous throughout a disk centered at (a, b) and $f_x(a, b) = f_y(a, b) = 0$. Then

(i) f has a **local maximum** at (a, b) if $f_{xx} < 0$ and $f_{xx}f_{yy} - f_{xy}^2 > 0$ at (a, b);

(ii) f has a **local minimum** at (a, b) if $f_{xx} > 0$ and $f_{xx}f_{yy} - f_{xy}^2 > 0$ at (a, b);

(iii) f has a **saddle point** at (a, b) if $f_{xx}f_{yy} - f_{xy}^2 < 0$ at (a, b).

(iv) The test is inconclusive at (a, b) if $f_{xx}f_{yy} - f_{xy}^2 = 0$ at (a, b). In this case, we must find some other way to determine the behavior of f at (a, b).

The expression $f_{xx}f_{yy} - f_{xy}^2$ is the **discriminant** of f. It is sometimes easier to remember the determinant form,

$$f_{xx}f_{yy} - f_{xy}^2 = \begin{vmatrix} f_{xx} & f_{xy} \\ f_{xy} & f_{yy} \end{vmatrix}.$$

Theorem 11 says that if the discriminant is positive at the point (a, b), then the surface curves the same way in all directions: downward if $f_{xx} < 0$, giving rise to a local maximum, and upward if $f_{xx} > 0$, giving a local minimum. On the other hand, if the discriminant is negative at (a, b), then the surface curves up in some directions and down in others, so we have a saddle point.

EXAMPLE 3 Identifying Local Extreme Values

Find the local extreme values of $f(x, y) = xy - x^2 - y^2 - 2x - 2y + 4$.

SOLUTION

The function is defined and differentiable for all x and y and its domain has no boundary points. The function has extreme values only at the points where f_x and f_y are simultaneously zero. This leads to

$$f_x = y - 2x - 2 = 0, \qquad f_y = x - 2y - 2 = 0,$$

or

$$x = y = -2.$$

Therefore, the point $(-2, -2)$ is the only point where f may take on an extreme value. To see if it does so, we calculate

$$f_{xx} = -2, \qquad f_{yy} = -2, \qquad f_{xy} = 1.$$

The discriminant of f at $(a, b) = (-2, -2)$ is

$$f_{xx}f_{yy} - f_{xy}^2 = (-2)(-2) - (1)^2 = 3.$$

The combination

$$f_{xx} < 0 \qquad \text{and} \qquad f_{xx}f_{yy} - f_{xy}^2 > 0$$

tells us that f has a local maximum at $(-2, -2)$. The value of f at this point is $f(-2, -2) = 8$.

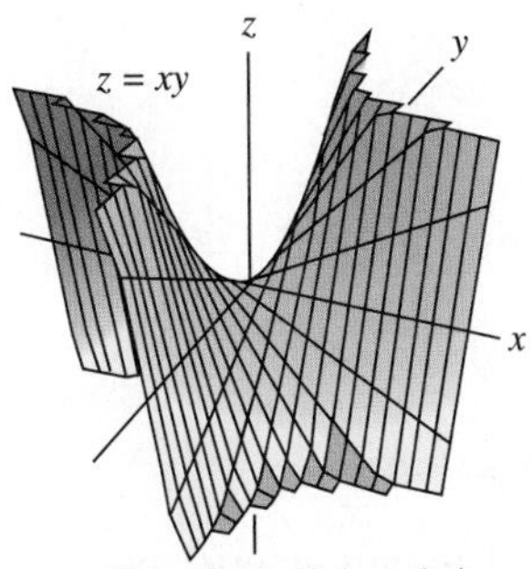

Figure 14.55 The surface $z = xy$ has a saddle point at the origin. (Example 4)

EXAMPLE 4 Searching for Local Extreme Values

Find the local extreme values of $f(x, y) = xy$.

SOLUTION

Since f is differentiable everywhere (Figure 14.55), it can assume extreme values only where

$$f_x = y = 0 \qquad \text{and} \qquad f_y = x = 0.$$

Thus, the origin is the only point where f might have an extreme value. To see what happens there, we calculate

$$f_{xx} = 0, \qquad f_{yy} = 0, \qquad f_{xy} = 1.$$

The discriminant,

$$f_{xx}f_{yy} - f_{xy}^2 = -1,$$

is negative. Therefore, the function has a saddle point at (0, 0). We conclude that $f(x, y) = xy$ has no local extreme values.

Absolute Extrema on Closed Bounded Regions

We organize the search for the absolute extrema of a continuous function $f(x, y)$ on a closed and bounded region R into three steps.

Step 1: *List the interior points* of R where f may have local maxima and minima and evaluate f at these points. These are the points where $f_x = f_y = 0$ or where one or both of f_x and f_y fail to exist (the critical points of f).

Step 2: *List the boundary points* of R where f has local maxima and minima and evaluate f at these points. We show how to do this shortly.

Step 3: *Look through the two lists* for the maximum and minimum values of f. These will be the absolute maxima and minima values of f on R. Since absolute maxima and minima are also local maximum and minima, the absolute maximum and minimum values of f already appear somewhere in the lists made in steps 1 and 2. We have only to glance at the lists to see what they are.

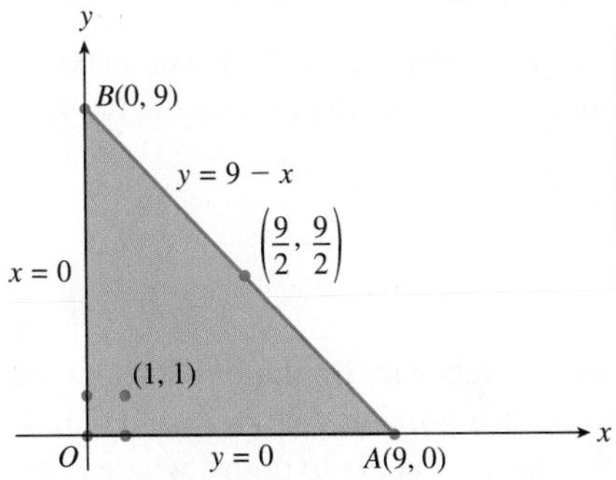

Figure 14.56 This triangular plate is the domain of the function in Example 5.

EXAMPLE 5 Finding Absolute Extrema

Find the absolute maximum and minimum values of

$$f(x, y) = 2 + 2x + 2y - x^2 - y^2$$

on the triangular plate in the first quadrant bounded by the lines $x = 0$, $y = 0$, $y = 9 - x$.

SOLUTION

Since f is differentiable, the only places where f can assume these values are points inside the triangle (Figure 14.56), where $f_x = f_y = 0$ and points on the boundary.

Interior points. For these, we have

$$f_x = 2 - 2x = 0, \qquad f_y = 2 - 2y = 0,$$

yielding the single point $(x, y) = (1, 1)$. The value of f there is

$$f(1, 1) = 4.$$

Boundary points. We take the triangle one side at a time:

1. On the segment OA, $y = 0$. The function

$$f(x, y) = f(x, 0) = 2 + 2x - x^2$$

may now be regarded as a function of x defined on the closed interval $0 \le x \le 9$. Its extreme values may occur at the endpoints

$$x = 0, \quad \text{where} \quad f(0, 0) = 2,$$

$$x = 9, \quad \text{where} \quad f(9, 0) = 2 + 18 - 81 = -61,$$

and at the interior points where $f'(x, 0) = 2 - 2x = 0$. The only interior point where $f'(x, 0) = 0$ is $x = 1$, where

$$f(x, 0) = f(1, 0) = 3.$$

2. On the segment OB, $x = 0$ and

$$f(x, y) = f(0, y) = 2 + 2y - y^2.$$

We know from the symmetry of f in x and y and from the analysis we just carried out that the candidates on this segment are

$$f(0, 0) = 2, \quad f(0, 9) = -61, \quad f(0, 1) = 3.$$

3. We have already accounted for the values of f at the endpoints of AB, so we need only look at the interior points of AB. With $y = 9 - x$, we have

$$f(x, y) = 2 + 2x + 2(9 - x) - x^2 - (9 - x)^2 = -61 + 18x - 2x^2.$$

Setting $f'(x, 9 - x) = 18 - 4x = 0$ gives

$$x = \frac{18}{4} = \frac{9}{2}.$$

At this value of x,

$$y = 9 - \frac{9}{2} = \frac{9}{2} \quad \text{and} \quad f(x, y) = f\left(\frac{9}{2}, \frac{9}{2}\right) = -\frac{41}{2}.$$

Looking through the two lists. The candidates are: 4, 2, −61, 3, −(41/2). The maximum is 4, which f assumes at (1, 1). The minimum is −61, which f assumes at (0, 9) and (9, 0).

Limitations of Theorem 10

Despite the power of Theorem 10, we urge you to remember its limitations. It does not apply to boundary points of a function's domain, where it is possible for a function to have extreme values along with nonzero derivatives, and it does not apply to points where either f_x or f_y fails to exist.

Summary

Summary of Max-Min Tests

The extreme values of $f(x, y)$ can occur only at

(i) **boundary points** of the domain of f and

(ii) **critical points** (interior points where $f_x = f_y = 0$ or points where f_x or f_y fails to exist).

If the first- and second-order partial derivatives of f are continuous throughout a disk centered at a point (a, b) and if $f_x(a, b) = f_y(a, b) = 0$, you may be able to classify $f(a, b)$ with the ***second derivative test:***

(i) $f_{xx} < 0$ and $f_{xx}f_{yy} - f_{xy}^2 > 0$ at $(a, b) \Rightarrow$ **local maximum,**

(ii) $f_{xx} > 0$ and $f_{xx}f_{yy} - f_{xy}^2 > 0$ at $(a, b) \Rightarrow$ **local minimum,**

(iii) $f_{xx}f_{yy} - f_{xy}^2 < 0$ at $(a, b) \Rightarrow$ **saddle point,**

(iv) $f_{xx}f_{yy} - f_{xy}^2 = 0$ at $(a, b) \Rightarrow$ **test is inconclusive.**

Quick Review 14.7

In Exercises 1–4, let $f(x) = x/(x^2 + 1)$

1. Find the critical points of f.

2. Find the local minimum values of f and where they occur.

3. Find the local maximum values of f and where they occur.

4. Find the absolute extrema of f and where they occur.

In Exercises 5–8, let $f(x) = 3 + 2x - x^2, \quad -2 \le x \le 5.$

5. Find the critical points of f.

6. Find the local minimum values of f and where they occur.

7. Find the local maximum values of f and where they occur.

8. Find the absolute extreme of f and where they occur.

In Exercises 9 and 10, solve the system of equations.

9. $-2x + y = 2$
$x - 2y = 2$

10. $3x - 4y = 5$
$2x + y = 1$

Section 14.7 Exercises

In Exercises 1–18, find all the local maxima, local minima, and saddle points of the function.

1. $f(x, y) = x^2 + xy + y^2 + 3x - 3y + 4$

2. $f(x, y) = 2xy - 5x^2 - 2y^2 + 4x + 4y - 4$

3. $f(x, y) = x^2 + xy + 3x + 2y + 5$

4. $f(x, y) = 2xy - x^2 - 2y^2 + 3x + 4$

5. $f(x, y) = 5xy - 7x^2 + 3x - 6y + 2$

6. $f(x, y) = 3x^2 + 6xy + 7y^2 - 2x + 4y$

7. $f(x, y) = 2x^2 + 3xy + 4y^2 - 5x + 2y$

8. $f(x, y) = x^2 - 2xy + 2y^2 - 2x + 2y + 1$

9. $f(x, y) = x^2 - y^2 - 2x + 4y + 6$

10. $f(x, y) = x^3 + 3xy + y^3$

11. $f(x, y) = 6x^2 - 2x^3 + 3y^2 + 6xy$

12. $f(x, y) = x^3 + y^3 + 3x^2 - 3y^2 - 8$

13. $f(x, y) = 4xy - x^4 - y^4$

14. $f(x, y) = x^4 + y^4 + 4xy$

15. $f(x, y) = \dfrac{1}{x^2 + y^2 - 1}$

16. $f(x, y) = \dfrac{1}{x} + xy + \dfrac{1}{y}$

17. $f(x, y) = y \sin x$

18. $f(x, y) = e^{2x} \cos y$

In Exercises 19–26, find the absolute maxima and minima of the function on the given domain.

19. $f(x, y) = 2x^2 - 4x + y^2 - 4y + 1$ on the closed triangular plate bounded by the lines $x = 0$, $y = 2$, $y = 2x$ in the first quadrant

20. $f(x, y) = x^2 + y^2$ on the closed triangular plate bounded by the lines $x = 0$, $y = 0$, $y + 2x = 2$ in the first quadrant

21. $T(x, y) = x^2 + xy + y^2 - 6x + 2$ on the rectangular plate $0 \le x \le 5, -3 \le y \le 0$

22. $f(x, y) = 48xy - 32x^3 - 24y^2$ on the rectangular plate $0 \le x \le 1, 0 \le y \le 1$

23. $f(x, y) = (4x - x^2)\cos y$ on the rectangular plate $1 \le x \le 3,\ -\pi/4 \le y \le \pi/4$ (Figure 14.57)

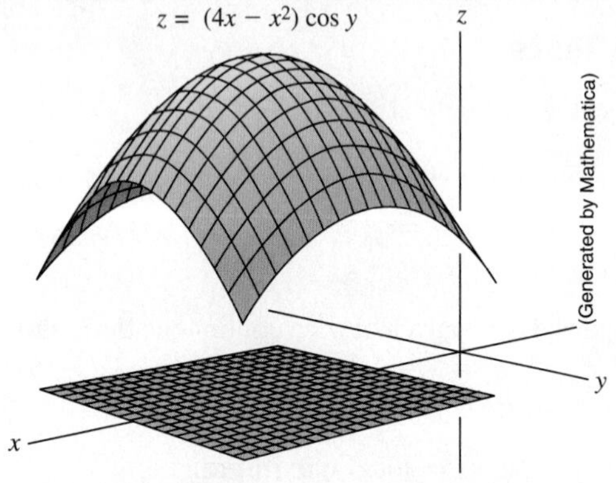

Figure 14.57 The function and domain in Exercise 23.

24. $f(x, y) = 4x - 8xy + 2y + 1$ on the triangular plate bounded by the lines $x = 0$, $y = 0$, $x + y = 1$ in the first quadrant

25. $f(x, y) = x^3 + y^2$ on the closed disk $x^2 + y^2 \le 1$

26. $f(x, y) = 3x^2 + x + y^2 - 1$ on the closed disk $x^2 + y^2 \le 4$

27. ***Maximizing an Integral*** Find two numbers a and b with $a \le b$ such that

$$\int_a^b (6 - x - x^2)dx$$

has its largest value.

28. ***Maximizing an Integral*** Find two numbers a and b with $a \le b$ such that

$$\int_a^b (24 - 2x - x^2)^{1/3}\, dx$$

has its largest value.

29. ***Temperature Extremes*** The flat circular plate in Figure 14.58 has the shape of the region $x^2 + y^2 \le 1$. The plate, including the boundary where $x^2 + y^2 = 1$, is heated so that the temperature at the point (x, y) is

$$T(x, y) = x^2 + 2y^2 - x.$$

Find the temperatures at the hottest and coldest points on the plate.

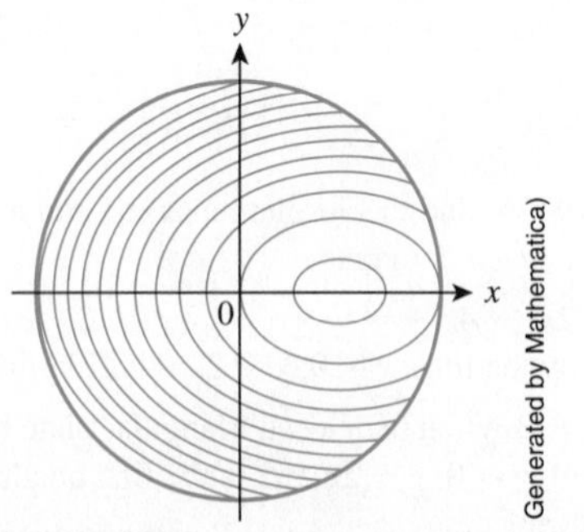

Figure 14.58 Curves of constant temperature are called **isotherms.** The figure shows isotherms of the temperature function $T(x, y) = x^2 + 2y^2 - x$ on the disk $x^2 + y^2 \le 1$ in the xy-plane. Exercise 29 asks you to locate the extreme temperatures.

30. Find the critical points of

$$f(x, y) = xy + 2x - \ln x^2y$$

in the open first quadrant $(x > 0, y > 0)$ and show that f takes on a minimum there (Figure 14.59).

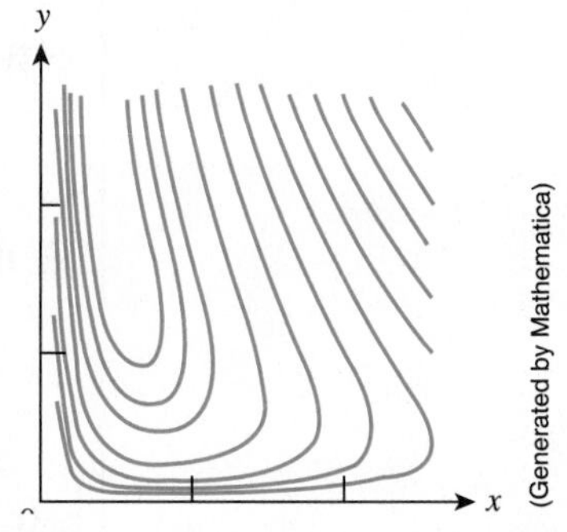

Figure 14.59 The function $f(x, y) = xy + 2x - \ln x^2y$ (selected level curves shown here) takes on a minimum value somewhere in the open first quadrant $x > 0$, $y > 0$. (Exercise 30)

31. **Writing to Learn** Find the maxima, minima, and saddle points of $f(x, y)$, if any, given that

(a) $f_x = 2x - 4y$ and $f_y = 2y - 4x.$

(b) $f_x = 2x - 2$ and $f_y = 2y - 4.$

(c) $f_x = 9x^2 - 9$ and $f_y = 2y + 4.$

Describe your reasoning in each case.

32. **Writing to Learn** ***When the Second Derivative Test is Inconclusive*** The discriminant $f_{xx}f_{yy} - f_{xy}^2$ is zero at the origin for each of the following functions, so the second derivative test fails there. Determine whether the function has a local maximum, a local minimum, or neither at the origin by imagining what the surface $z = f(x, y)$ looks like. Describe your reasoning in each case.

(a) $f(x, y) = x^2y^2$ **(b)** $f(x, y) = 1 - x^2y^2$

(c) $f(x, y) = xy^2$ **(d)** $f(x, y) = x^3y^2$

(e) $f(x, y) = x^3y^3$ **(f)** $f(x, y) = x^4y^4$

33. Show that $(0, 0)$ is a critical point of $f(x, y) = x^2 + kxy + y^2$ no matter what value the constant k has. (*Hint:* Consider two cases: $k = 0$ and $k \ne 0$.)

34. **Writing to Learn** For what values of the constant k does the second derivative test guarantee that $f(x, y) = x^2 + kxy + y^2$ will have a saddle point at $(0, 0)$? A local minimum at $(0, 0)$? For what values of k is the second derivative test inconclusive? Give reasons for your answers.

In Exercises 35–40, *work in groups of two or three* to solve the problem.

35. (a) **Writing to Learn** If $f_x(a, b) = f_y(a, b) = 0$, must f have a local maximum or minimum value at (a, b)? Give reasons for your answer.

(b) **Writing to Learn** Can you conclude anything about $f(a, b)$ if f and its first and second partial derivatives are continuous throughout a disk centered at (a, b) and also $f_{xx}(a, b)$ and $f_{yy}(a, b)$ differ in sign? Give reasons for your answer.

36. Using the proof of Theorem 10 given in the text for the case in which f has a local maximum at (a, b), prove the theorem for the case in which f has a local minimum at (a, b).

37. Among all the points on the graph of $z = 10 - x^2 - y^2$ that lie above the plane $x + 2y + 3z = 0$, find the point farthest from the plane.

38. Find the point on the graph of $z = x^2 + y^2 + 10$ nearest the plane $x + 2y - z = 0$.

39. Writing to Learn The function $f(x, y) = x + y$ fails to have an absolute maximum value in the closed first quadrant $x \geq 0$ and $y \geq 0$. Does this contradict the discussion on finding absolute extrema given in the text? Give reasons for your answer.

40. Consider the function

$$f(x, y) = x^2 + y^2 + 2xy - x - y + 1$$

over the square $0 \leq x \leq 1$ and $0 \leq y \leq 1$.

(a) Show that f has an absolute minimum along the line segment $2x + 2y = 1$ in this square. What is the absolute minimum value?

(b) Find the absolute maximum value of f over the square.

Explorations

Extreme Values on Parametrized Curves To find the extreme values of a function $f(x, y)$ on a curve $x = x(t)$, $y = y(t)$, we treat f as a function of the single variable t and use the Chain Rule to find where df/dt is zero. As in any other single-variable case, the extreme values of f are then found among the values at the

(i) critical points (points where df/dt is zero or fails to exist), and

(ii) endpoints of the parameter domain.

In Exercises 41–44, find the absolute maximum and minimum values of the functions on the given curves.

41. Functions:

(a) $f(x, y) = x + y$ **(b)** $g(x, y) = xy$

(c) $h(x, y) = 2x^2 + y^2$

Curves:

(i) The semicircle $x^2 + y^2 = 4$, $y \geq 0$

(ii) The quarter circle $x^2 + y^2 = 4$, $x \geq 0$, $y \geq 0$

Use the parametric equations $x = 2 \cos t$, $y = 2 \sin t$.

42. Functions:

(a) $f(x, y) = 2x + 3y$ **(b)** $g(x, y) = xy$

(c) $h(x, y) = x^2 + 3y^2$

Curves:

(i) The semi-ellipse $(x^2/9) + (y^2/4) = 1$, $y \geq 0$

(ii) The quarter ellipse $(x^2/9) + (y^2/4) = 1$, $x \geq 0$, $y \geq 0$

Use the parametric equations $x = 3 \cos t$, $y = 2 \sin t$.

43. Function: $f(x, y) = xy$

Curves:

(i) The line $x = 2t$, $y = t + 1$

(ii) The line segment $x = 2t$, $y = t + 1$, $-1 \leq t \leq 0$

(iii) The line segment $x = 2t$, $y = t + 1$, $0 \leq t \leq 1$

44. Functions:

(a) $f(x, y) = x^2 + y^2$ **(b)** $g(x, y) = \dfrac{1}{x^2 + y^2}$

Curves:

(i) The line $x = t$, $y = 2 - 2t$

(ii) The line segment $x = t$, $y = 2 - 2t$, $0 \leq t \leq 1$

Extending the Ideas

CAS Explorations

In Exercises 45–50, you will use a CAS to identify the local extrema of the function. Perform the following steps:

(a) Plot the function over the given rectangle.

(b) Plot some level curves in the rectangle.

(c) Calculate the function's first partial derivatives and find the critical points. How do the critical points relate to the level curves plotted in (b)? Which critical points, if any, appear to give a saddle point? Give reasons for your answer.

45. $f(x, y) = x^2 + y^3 - 3xy$ $\quad -5 \leq x \leq 5, \quad -5 \leq y \leq 5$

46. $f(x, y) = x^3 - 3xy^2 + y^2, \quad -2 \leq x \leq 2, \quad -2 \leq y \leq 2$

47. $f(x, y) = x^4 + y^2 - 8x^2 - 6y + 16, \quad -3 \leq x \leq 3,$ $-6 \leq y \leq 6$

48. $f(x, y) = 2x^4 + y^4 - 2x^2 - 2y^2 + 3, \quad -3/2 \leq x \leq 3/2,$ $-3/2 \leq y \leq 3/2$

49. $f(x, y) = 5x^6 + 18x^5 - 30x^4 + 30xy^2 - 120x^3, \quad -4 \leq x \leq 3,$ $-2 \leq y \leq 2$

50. $f(x, y) = \begin{cases} x^5 \ln(x^2 + y^2), & (x, y) \neq (0, 0) \\ 0, & (x, y) = (0, 0) \end{cases}$,

$-2 \leq x \leq 2, -2 \leq y \leq 2$

51. ***Least Squares and Regression Lines*** When we try to fit a line $y = mx + b$ to a set of numerical data points (x_1, y_1), $(x_2, y_2), \ldots, (x_n, y_n)$ (Figure 14.60) we usually choose the line that minimizes the sum of the squares of the vertical distances from the points to the line. In theory, this means finding the values of m and b that minimize the value of the function

$$w = (mx_1 + b - y_1)^2 + \cdots + (mx_n + b - y_n)^2.$$

Use the first and second derivative tests to show that these values are

$$m = \frac{(\Sigma x_x)(\Sigma y_k) - n\Sigma x_k y_k}{(\Sigma x_k)^2 - n\Sigma x_k^2}$$

$$b = \frac{1}{n}(\Sigma y_k - m\Sigma x_k).$$

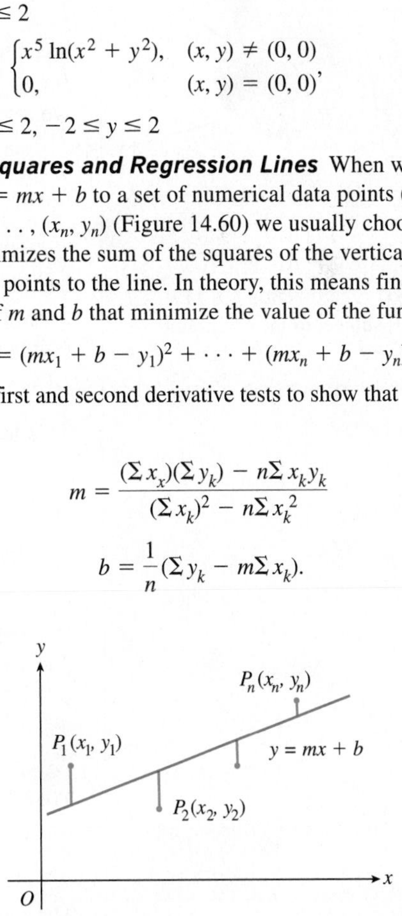

Figure 14.60 To fit a line to noncollinear points, we choose the line that minimizes the sum of the squares of the deviations.

14.8 Lagrange Multipliers

What you'll learn about

- Constrained Maxima and Minima
- The Method of Lagrange Multipliers
- Lagrange Multipliers with Two Constraints

Constrained Maxima and Minima

As we saw in Section 14.7, we sometimes need to find the extreme values of a function whose domain is constrained to lie within some particular subset of the plane, such as a disk or a closed triangular region. But, as Figure 14.61 suggests, a function may be subject to other kinds of constraints as well.

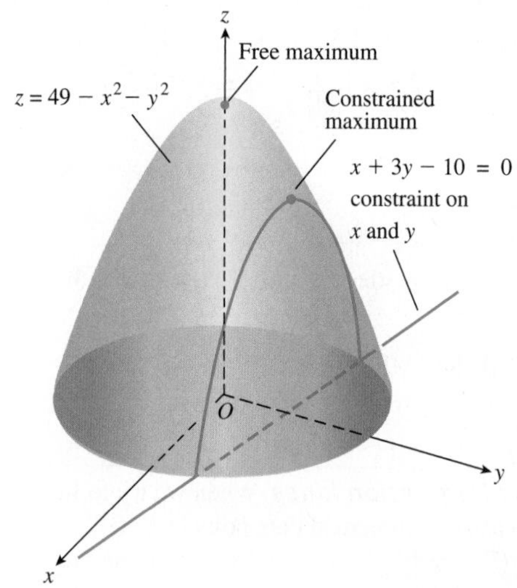

Figure 14.61 The function $f(x, y) = 49 - x^2 - y^2$, subject to the constraint $g(x, y) = x + 3y - 10 = 0$.

EXAMPLE 1 Finding a Minimum with Constraint

Find the point $P(x, y, z)$ closest to the origin on the plane $2x + y - z - 5 = 0$.

SOLUTION

The problem asks us to find the minimum value of the function

$$|\overrightarrow{OP}| = \sqrt{(x-0)^2 + (y-0)^2 + (z-0)^2}$$
$$= \sqrt{x^2 + y^2 + z^2}$$

subject to the constraint that

$$2x + y - z - 5 = 0.$$

Since $|\overrightarrow{OP}|$ has a minimum value wherever the function

$$f(x, y, z) = x^2 + y^2 + z^2$$

has a minimum value, we may solve the problem by finding the minimum value of $f(x, y, z)$ subject to the constraint $2x + y - z - 5 = 0$ (thus avoiding square roots). If we regard x and y as the independent variables in this equation and write z as

$$z = 2x + y - 5,$$

the problem reduces to one of finding the points (x, y) at which the function

$$h(x, y) = f(x, y, 2x + y - 5) = x^2 + y^2 + (2x + y - 5)^2$$

has its minimum value or values. Since the domain of h is the entire xy-plane, the first derivative test of Section 14.7 tells us that any minima that h might have must occur at points where

$$h_x = 2x + 2(2x + y - 5)(2) = 0, \qquad h_y = 2y + 2(2x + y - 5) = 0.$$

This leads to

$$10x + 4y = 20, \qquad 4x + 4y = 10,$$

and the solution

$$x = \frac{5}{3}, \qquad y = \frac{5}{6}.$$

We may apply a geometric argument together with the second derivative test to show that these values minimize h. The z-coordinate of the corresponding point on the plane $z = 2x + y - 5$ is

$$z = 2\left(\frac{5}{3}\right) + \frac{5}{6} - 5 = -\frac{5}{6}.$$

Therefore, the point we seek is

$$\text{Closest point: } P\left(\frac{5}{3}, \frac{5}{6}, -\frac{5}{6}\right).$$

The distance from P to the origin is $5/\sqrt{6} \approx 2.04$.

Attempts to solve a constrained maximum or minimum problem by substitution, as we might call the method of Example 1, do not always go smoothly. This is one of the reasons for learning the new method of this section.

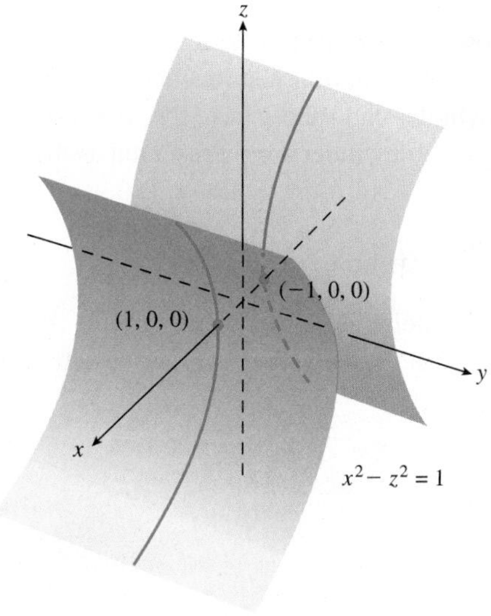

Figure 14.62 The hyperbolic cylinder $x^2 - z^2 - 1 = 0$ in Example 2.

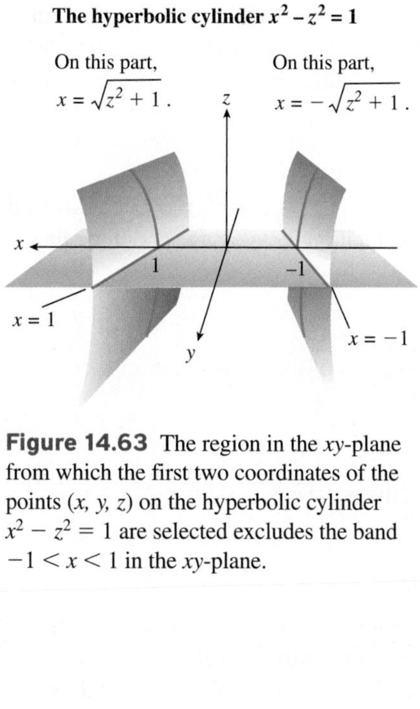

Figure 14.63 The region in the xy-plane from which the first two coordinates of the points (x, y, z) on the hyperbolic cylinder $x^2 - z^2 = 1$ are selected excludes the band $-1 < x < 1$ in the xy-plane.

EXAMPLE 2 Finding a Minimum with Constraint

Find the points closest to the origin on the hyperbolic cylinder

$$x^2 - z^2 - 1 = 0.$$

SOLUTION 1

The cylinder is shown in Figure 14.62. We seek the points on the cylinder closest to the origin. These are the points whose coordinates minimize the value of the function

$$f(x, y, z) = x^2 + y^2 + z^2 \qquad \text{Square of the distance}$$

subject to the constraint that $x^2 - z^2 - 1 = 0$. If we regard x and y as independent variables, the constraint equation is

$$z^2 = x^2 - 1,$$

and the values of $f(x, y, z) = x^2 + y^2 + z^2$ on the cylinder are given by the function

$$h(x, y) = x^2 + y^2 + (x^2 - 1) = 2x^2 + y^2 - 1.$$

To find the points on the cylinder whose coordinates minimize f, we look for the points in the xy-plane whose coordinates minimize h. The only extreme value of h occurs where

$$h_x = 4x = 0 \qquad \text{and} \qquad h_y = 2y = 0,$$

that is, at the point (0, 0). But now we're in trouble—there are no points on the cylinder where both x and y are zero. What went wrong?

What happened was that the first derivative test found (as it should have) the point *in the domain of h* where h has a minimum value. We, on the other hand, want the points *on the cylinder* where h has a minimum value. Although the domain of h is the entire xy-plane, the domain from which we can select the first two coordinates of the points (x, y, z) on the cylinder is restricted to the "shadow" of the cylinder on the xy-plane; it does not include the band between the lines $x = -1$ and $x = 1$ (Figure 14.63).

We can avoid this problem if we treat y and z as independent variables (instead of x and y) and express x in terms of y and z as

$$x^2 = z^2 + 1.$$

With this substitution, $f(x, y, z) = x^2 + y^2 + z^2$ becomes

$$k(y, z) = (z^2 + 1) + y^2 + z^2 = 1 + y^2 + 2z^2$$

and we look for the points where k takes on its smallest value. The domain of k in the yz-plane now matches the domain from which we select the y- and z-coordinates of the points (x, y, z) on the cylinder. Hence, the points that minimize k in the plane will have corresponding points on the cylinder. The smallest values of k occur where

$$k_y = 2y = 0 \qquad \text{and} \qquad k_z = 4z = 0,$$

or where $y = z = 0$. This leads to

$$x^2 = z^2 + 1 = 1, \qquad x = \pm 1.$$

The corresponding points on the cylinder are $(\pm 1, 0, 0)$. We can see from the inequality

$$k(y, z) = 1 + y^2 + 2z^2 \geq 1$$

that the points $(\pm 1, 0, 0)$ give a minimum value for k. We can also see that the minimum distance from the origin to a point on the cylinder is 1 unit.

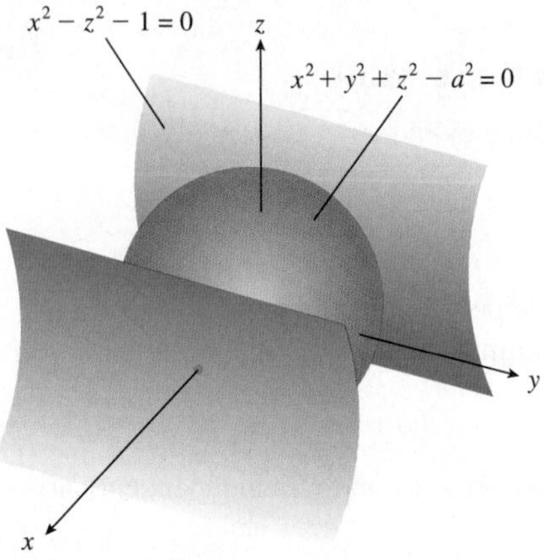

Figure 14.64 A sphere expanding like a soap bubble centered at the origin until it just touches the hyperbolic cylinder $x^2 - z^2 - 1 = 0$. See Solution 2 of Example 2.

SOLUTION 2

Another way to find the points on the cylinder closest to the origin is to imagine a small sphere centered at the origin expanding like a soap bubble until it just touches the cylinder (Figure 14.64). At each point of contact, the cylinder and sphere have the same tangent plane and normal line. Therefore, if the sphere and cylinder are represented as the level surfaces obtained by setting

$$f(x, y, z) = x^2 + y^2 + z^2 - a^2 \quad \text{and} \quad g(x, y, z) = x^2 - z^2 - 1$$

equal to 0, then the gradients ∇f and ∇g will be parallel where the surfaces touch. At any point of contact we should therefore be able to find a scalar λ ("lambda") such that

$$\nabla f = \lambda \nabla g,$$

or

$$2x\mathbf{i} + 2y\mathbf{j} + 2z\mathbf{k} = \lambda(2x\mathbf{i} - 2z\mathbf{k}).$$

Thus, the coordinates x, y, and z of any point of tangency will have to satisfy the three scalar equations

$$2x = 2\lambda x, \qquad 2y = 0, \qquad 2z = -2\lambda z. \tag{1}$$

For what values of λ will a point (x, y, z) whose coordinates satisfy the equations in (1) also lie on the surface $x^2 - z^2 - 1 = 0$? To answer this question, we remember that no point on the surface has a zero x-coordinate and conclude that $x \neq 0$ in the first equation in (1). Thus, $2x = 2\lambda x$ only if

$$2 = 2\lambda, \quad \text{or} \quad \lambda = 1.$$

For $\lambda = 1$, the equation $2z = -2\lambda z$ becomes $2z = -2z$. If this equation is to be satisfied as well, z must be zero. Since $y = 0$ also (from the equation $2y = 0$), we conclude that the points we seek all have coordinates of the form

$$(x, 0, 0).$$

What points on the surface $x^2 - z^2 = 1$ have coordinates of this form? The answer is the points $(x, 0, 0)$ for which

$$x^2 - (0)^2 = 1, \qquad x^2 = 1, \qquad \text{or} \qquad x = \pm 1.$$

The points on the cylinder closest to the origin are the points $(\pm 1, 0, 0)$.

The Method of Lagrange Multipliers

In Solution 2 of Example 2, we solved the problem by the **method of Lagrange multipliers**. In general terms, the method says that the extreme values of a function $f(x, y, z)$ whose variables are subject to a constraint $g(x, y, z) = 0$ are to be found on the surface $g = 0$ at the points where

$$\nabla f = \lambda \nabla g$$

for some scalar λ (called a **Langrange multiplier**).

To explore the method further and see why it works, we first make the following observation, which we state as a theorem.

THEOREM 12 The Orthogonal Gradient Theorem

Suppose $f(x, y, z)$ is differentiable in a region whose interior contains a smooth curve

$$C: \mathbf{r} = g(t)\mathbf{i} + h(t)\mathbf{j} + k(t)\mathbf{k}.$$

If P_0 is a point on C where f has a local maximum or minimum relative to its values on C, then ∇f is orthogonal to C at P_0. At every point on the curve, $\nabla f \cdot \mathbf{v} = 0$.

Proof of Theorem 12 We show that ∇f is orthogonal to the curve's velocity vector at P_0. The values of f on C are given by the composite $f(g(t), h(t), k(t))$, whose derivative with respect to t is

$$\frac{df}{dt} = \frac{\partial f}{\partial x}\frac{dg}{dt} + \frac{\partial f}{\partial y}\frac{dh}{dt} + \frac{\partial f}{\partial z}\frac{dk}{dt} = \nabla f \cdot \mathbf{v}.$$

At any point P_0 where f has a local maximum or minimum relative to its values on the curve, $df/dt = 0$, so

$$\nabla f \cdot \mathbf{v} = 0.$$

By dropping the z-terms in Theorem 12, we obtain a similar result for functions of two variables.

Corollary of Theorem 12

At the points on a smooth curve $\mathbf{r} = g(t)\mathbf{i} + h(t)\mathbf{j}$ where a differentiable function $f(x, y)$ takes on its local maxima and minima relative to its values on the curve, $\nabla f \cdot \mathbf{v} = 0$.

Theorem 12 is the key to the method of Lagrange multipliers. Suppose $f(x, y, z)$ and $g(x, y, z)$ are differentiable and P_0 is a point on the surface $g(x, y, z) = 0$ where f has a local maximum or minimum value relative to its other values on the surface. Then f takes on a local maximum or minimum at P_0 relative to its values on every differentiable curve through P_0 on the surface $g(x, y, z) = 0$. Therefore, ∇f is orthogonal to the velocity vector of every such differentiable curve through P_0. But so is ∇g (because ∇g is orthogonal to the level surface $g = 0$, as we saw in Section 14.6). Therefore, at P_0, ∇f is some scalar multiple λ of ∇g.

The Method of Lagrange Multipliers

Suppose $f(x, y, z)$ and $g(x, y, z)$ are differentiable. To find the local maximum and minimum values of f subject to the constraint $g(x, y, z) = 0$, find the values of $x, y, z,$ and λ that simultaneously satisfy the equations

$$\nabla f = \lambda \nabla g \qquad \text{and} \qquad g(x, y, z) = 0.$$

For functions of two independent variables, the appropriate equations are

$$\nabla f = \lambda \nabla g \qquad \text{and} \qquad g(x, y) = 0.$$

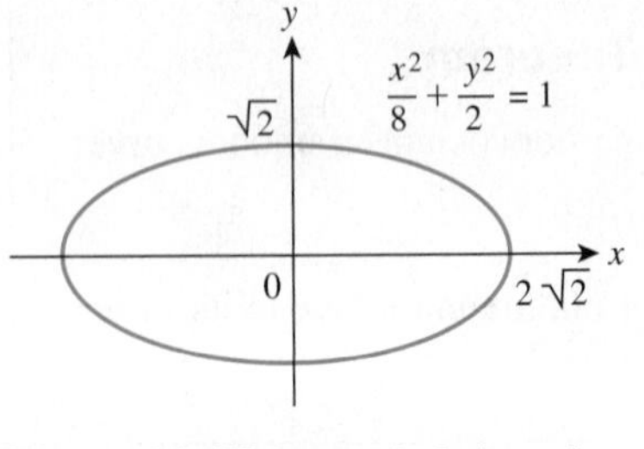

Figure 14.65 Example 3 shows how to find the largest and smallest values of the product xy on this ellipse.

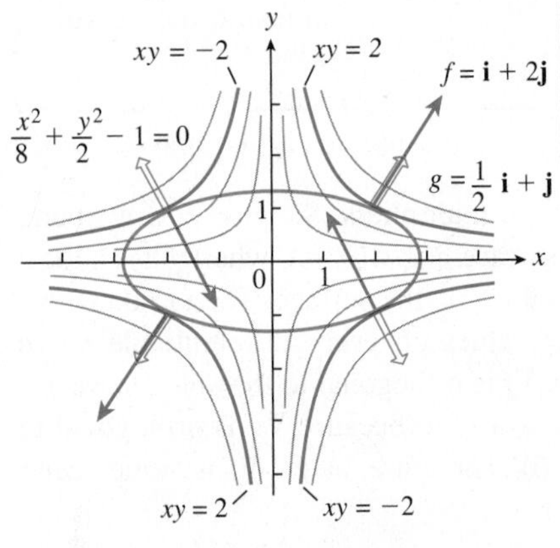

Figure 14.66 When subjected to the constraint $g(x, y) = x^2/8 + y^2/2 - 1 = 0$, the function $f(x, y) = xy$ takes on extreme values at the four points $(\pm 2, \pm 1)$. These are the points on the ellipse where ∇f (red) is a scalar multiple of ∇g (blue). (Example 3)

EXAMPLE 3 Using the Method of Lagrange Multipliers

Find the greatest and smallest values that the function

$$f(x, y) = xy$$

takes on the ellipse (Figure 14.65)

$$\frac{x^2}{8} + \frac{y^2}{2} = 1.$$

SOLUTION

We want to find the extreme values of $f(x, y) = xy$ subject to the constraint

$$g(x, y) = \frac{x^2}{8} + \frac{y^2}{2} - 1 = 0$$

To do so, we first find the values of x, y, and λ for which

$$\nabla f = \lambda \nabla g \qquad \text{and} \qquad g(x, y) = 0.$$

The gradient equation gives

$$y\mathbf{i} + x\mathbf{j} = \frac{\lambda}{4}x\mathbf{i} + \lambda y\mathbf{j},$$

from which we find

$$y = \frac{\lambda}{4}x, \qquad x = \lambda y, \qquad \text{and} \qquad y = \frac{\lambda}{4}(\lambda y) = \frac{\lambda^2}{4}y,$$

so that $y = 0$ or $\lambda = \pm 2$. We now consider these two cases.

Case 1: If $y = 0$, then $x = y = 0$. But $(0, 0)$ is not on the ellipse. Hence, $y \neq 0$.

Case 2: If $y \neq 0$, then $\lambda = \pm 2$ and $x = \pm 2y$. Substituting this in the equation $g(x, y) = 0$ gives

$$\frac{(\pm 2y)^2}{8} + \frac{y^2}{2} = 1, \qquad y^2 + y^2 = 2, \qquad \text{and} \qquad y = \pm 1.$$

The function $f(x, y) = xy$ therefore takes on its extreme values on the ellipse at the four points $(\pm 2, 1)$, $(\pm 2, -1)$. The extreme values are $xy = 2$ and $xy = -2$.

The Geometry of the Solution The level curves of the function $f(x, y) = xy$ are the hyperbolas $xy = c$ (Figure 14.66). The further the hyperbolas lie from the origin, the larger the absolute value of f. We want to find the extreme values of $f(x, y)$, given that the point (x, y) also lies on the ellipse $x^2 + 4y^2 = 8$. Which hyperbolas intersecting the ellipse lie farthest from the origin? The hyperbolas that just graze the ellipse, the ones that are tangent to it. At these points, any vector normal to the hyperbola is normal to the ellipse, so $\nabla f = y\mathbf{i} + x\mathbf{j}$ is a multiple ($\lambda = \pm 2$) of $\nabla g = (x/4)\mathbf{i} + y\mathbf{j}$. At the point $(2, 1)$, for example,

$$\nabla f = \mathbf{i} + 2\mathbf{j}, \qquad \nabla g = \frac{1}{2}\mathbf{i} + \mathbf{j}, \qquad \text{and} \qquad \nabla f = 2\nabla g.$$

At the point $(-2, 1)$,

$$\nabla f = \mathbf{i} - 2\mathbf{j}, \qquad \nabla g = -\frac{1}{2}\mathbf{i} + \mathbf{j}, \qquad \text{and} \qquad \nabla f = -2\nabla g.$$

EXAMPLE 4 Finding Extreme Function Values on a Circle

Find the maximum and minimum values of the function $f(x, y) = 3x + 4y$ on the circle $x^2 + y^2 = 1$.

SOLUTION

We model this as a Lagrange multiplier problem with

$$f(x, y) = 3x + 4y, \qquad g(x, y) = x^2 + y^2 - 1$$

and look for the values of x, y, and λ that satisfy the equations

$$\nabla f = \lambda \nabla g: \qquad 3\mathbf{i} + 4\mathbf{j} = 2x\lambda\mathbf{i} + 2y\lambda\mathbf{j},$$
$$g(x, y) = 0: \qquad x^2 + y^2 - 1 = 0.$$

The gradient equation implies that $\lambda \neq 0$ and gives

$$x = \frac{3}{2\lambda}, \qquad y = \frac{2}{\lambda}.$$

These equations tell us, among other things, that x and y have the same sign. With these values for x and y, the equation $g(x, y) = 0$ gives

$$\left(\frac{3}{2\lambda}\right)^2 + \left(\frac{2}{\lambda}\right)^2 - 1 = 0,$$

so

$$\frac{9}{4\lambda^2} + \frac{4}{\lambda^2} = 1, \quad 9 + 16 = 4\lambda^2, \quad 4\lambda^2 = 25, \quad \text{and} \quad \lambda = \pm\frac{5}{2}.$$

Thus,

$$x = \frac{3}{2\lambda} = \pm\frac{3}{5}, \qquad y = \frac{2}{\lambda} = \pm\frac{4}{5},$$

and $f(x, y) = 3x + 4y$ has extreme values at $(x, y) = \pm(3/5, 4/5)$.

By calculating the value of $3x + 4y$ at the points $\pm(3/5, 4/5)$, we see that its maximum and minimum values on the circle $x^2 + y^2 = 1$ are

$$3\left(\frac{3}{5}\right) + 4\left(\frac{4}{5}\right) = \frac{25}{5} = 5 \quad \text{and} \quad 3\left(-\frac{3}{5}\right) + 4\left(-\frac{4}{5}\right) = -\frac{25}{5} = -5.$$

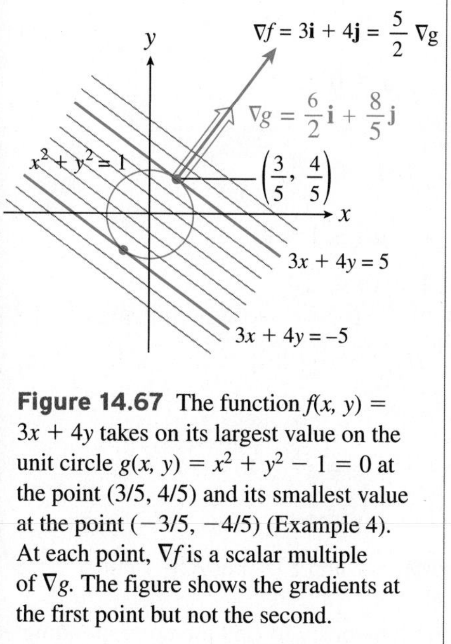

Figure 14.67 The function $f(x, y) = 3x + 4y$ takes on its largest value on the unit circle $g(x, y) = x^2 + y^2 - 1 = 0$ at the point $(3/5, 4/5)$ and its smallest value at the point $(-3/5, -4/5)$ (Example 4). At each point, ∇f is a scalar multiple of ∇g. The figure shows the gradients at the first point but not the second.

The Geometry of the Solution (Figure 14.67) The level curves of $f(x, y) = 3x + 4y$ are the lines $3x + 4y = c$. The further the lines lie from the origin, the larger the absolute value of f. We want to find the extreme values of $f(x, y)$ given that the point (x, y) also lies on the circle $x^2 + y^2 = 1$. Which lines intersecting the circle lie farthest from the origin? The lines tangent to the circle. At the points of tangency, any vector normal to the line is normal to the circle, so the gradient $\nabla f = 3\mathbf{i} + 4\mathbf{j}$ is a multiple ($\lambda = \pm 5/2$) of the gradient $\nabla g = 2x\mathbf{i} + 2y\mathbf{j}$. At the point $(3/5, 4/5)$, for example,

$$\nabla f = 3\mathbf{i} + 4\mathbf{j}, \qquad \nabla g = \frac{6}{5}\mathbf{i} + \frac{8}{5}\mathbf{j}, \quad \text{and} \quad \nabla f = \frac{5}{2}\nabla g.$$

Lagrange Multipliers with Two Constraints

Many problems require us to find the extreme values of a differentiable function $f(x, y, z)$ whose variables are subject to two constraints. If the constraints are

$$g_1(x, y, z) = 0 \quad \text{and} \quad g_2(x, y, z) = 0$$

and g_1 and g_2 are differentiable, with ∇g_1 not parallel to ∇g_2, we find the constrained local maxima and minima of f by introducing two Lagrange multipliers λ and μ (mu, pronounced "mew"). That is, we locate points $P(x, y, z)$ where f takes on its constrained extreme values by finding the values of x, y, z, λ, and μ that simultaneously satisfy the equations

$$\nabla f = \lambda \nabla g_1 + \mu \nabla g_2, \qquad g_1(x, y, z) = 0, \qquad g_2(x, y, z) = 0. \tag{2}$$

The equations in (2) have a nice geometric interpretation. The surfaces $g_1 = 0$ and $g_2 = 0$ (usually) intersect in a smooth curve, say C (Figure 14.68), and along this curve we seek the points where f has local maximum and minimum values relative to its other values on the curve. These are the points where ∇f is normal to C, as we saw in Theorem 12. But ∇g_1 and ∇g_2 are also normal to C at these points because C lies in the surfaces $g_1 = 0$ and $g_2 = 0$. Therefore, ∇f lies in the plane determined by ∇g_1 and ∇g_2, which means that $\nabla f = \lambda \nabla g_1 + \mu \nabla g_2$ for some λ and μ. Since the points we seek also lie in both surfaces, their coordinates must satisfy the equations $g_1(x, y, z) = 0$ and $g_2(x, y, z) = 0$, which are the remaining requirements in Equation (2).

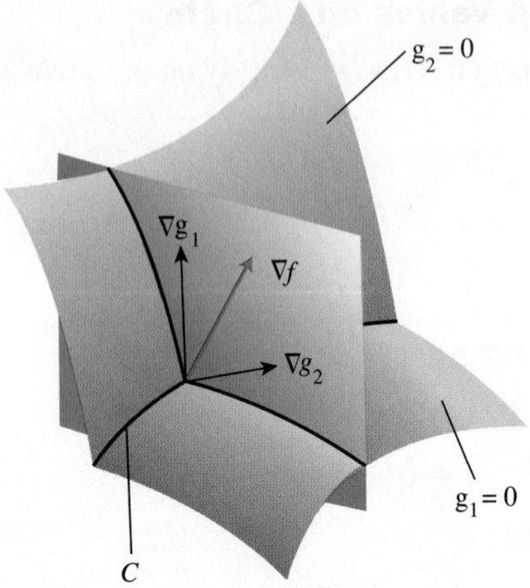

Figure 14.68 The vectors ∇g_1 and ∇g_2 lie in a plane perpendicular to the curve C because ∇g_1 is normal to the surface $g_1 = 0$ and ∇g_2 is normal to the surface $g_2 = 0$.

EXAMPLE 5 Finding Extremes of Distance on an Ellipse

The plane $x + y + z = 1$ cuts the cylinder $x^2 + y^2 = 1$ in an ellipse (Figure 14.69). Find the points on the ellipse that lie closest to and farthest from the origin.

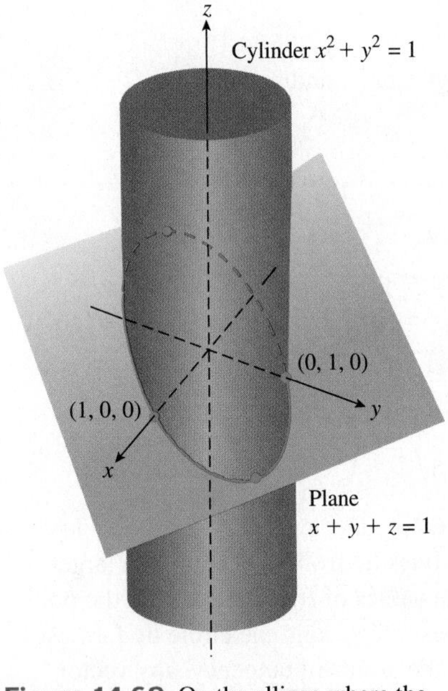

Figure 14.69 On the ellipse where the plane and cylinder meet, what are the points closest to and farthest from the origin? (Example 5)

SOLUTION

We find the extreme values of

$$f(x, y, z) = x^2 + y^2 + z^2$$

(the square of the distance from (x, y, z) to the origin) subject to the constraints

$$g_1(x, y, z) = x^2 + y^2 - 1 = 0 \tag{3}$$

$$g_2(x, y, z) = x + y + z - 1 = 0 \tag{4}$$

The gradient equation in (2) gives

$$\nabla f = \lambda \nabla g_1 + \mu \nabla g_2 \qquad \text{Eq. (2)}$$

$$2x\mathbf{i} + 2y\mathbf{j} + 2z\mathbf{k} = \lambda(2x\mathbf{i} + 2y\mathbf{j}) + \mu(\mathbf{i} + \mathbf{j} + \mathbf{k})$$

$$2x\mathbf{i} + 2y\mathbf{j} + 2z\mathbf{k} = (2\lambda x + \mu)\mathbf{i} + (2\lambda y + \mu)\mathbf{j} + \mu\mathbf{k}$$

or

$$2x = 2\lambda x + \mu, \qquad 2y = 2\lambda y + \mu, \qquad 2z = \mu. \tag{5}$$

The scalar equations in (5) yield

$$\begin{aligned} 2x = 2\lambda x + 2z &\Rightarrow (1 - \lambda)x = z, \\ 2y = 2\lambda y + 2z &\Rightarrow (1 - \lambda)y = z. \end{aligned} \tag{6}$$

Equations (6) are satisfied simultaneously if either $\lambda = 1$ and $z = 0$ or $\lambda \neq 1$ and $x = y = z/(1 - \lambda)$.

If $z = 0$, then solving Equations (3) and (4) simultaneously to find the corresponding points on the ellipse gives two points: (1, 0, 0) and (0, 1, 0). This makes sense when you look at Figure 14.69.

If $x = y$, then Equations (3) and (4) give

$$\begin{aligned} x^2 + x^2 - 1 &= 0 & x + x + z - 1 &= 0 \\ 2x^2 &= 1 & z &= 1 - 2x \\ x &= \pm\frac{\sqrt{2}}{2} & z &= 1 \mp \sqrt{2}. \end{aligned}$$

The corresponding points on the ellipse are

$$P_1 = \left(\frac{\sqrt{2}}{2}, \frac{\sqrt{2}}{2}, 1 - \sqrt{2}\right) \quad \text{and} \quad P_2 = \left(-\frac{\sqrt{2}}{2}, -\frac{\sqrt{2}}{2}, 1 + \sqrt{2}\right).$$

We need to be careful here, however. Although P_1 and P_2 both give local maxima of f on the ellipse, P_2 is farther from the origin than P_1.

The points on the ellipse closest to the origin are (1, 0, 0) and (0, 1, 0). The point on the ellipse farthest from the origin is P_2.

Quick Review 14.8

In Exercises 1–4, find all the local maxima and local minima of the function.

1. $f(x, y) = 2xy - 5x^2 - 2y^2 + 4x - 4$
2. $f(x, y) = 3 + 2x + 2y - 2x^2 - 2xy - y^2$
3. $f(x, y) = x^2 + 3xy + 3y^2 - 6x + 3y - 6$
4. $f(x, y) = 8x^3 + y^3 + 6xy$

In Exercises 5–7, find del (the gradient) of the function.

5. $g(y, z) = 2y^2 - 3z^2$
6. $k(x, y) = 3x^3y - 2xy^3 + \sin xy$
7. $h(x, y, z) = 3x - 2y + 2z^2$

In Exercises 8–10, let $\mathbf{u} = 2\mathbf{i} - 3\mathbf{j} + 4\mathbf{k}$, $\mathbf{v} = \mathbf{i} - 2\mathbf{j} - 2\mathbf{k}$, and $\mathbf{w} = -7\mathbf{i} + 14\mathbf{j} + 14\mathbf{k}$. Decide whether the two vectors listed are parallel, perpendicular, or neither.

8. **u** and **v**
9. **u** and **w**
10. **v** and **w**

Section 14.8 Exercises

In Exercises 1–16, the problem involves a function of two variables with one constraint.

1. Find the points on the ellipse $x^2 + 2y^2 = 1$ where $f(x, y) = xy$ has its extreme values.
2. Find the extreme values of $f(x, y) = xy$ subject to the constraint $g(x, y) = x^2 + y^2 - 10 = 0$.
3. Find the maximum value of $f(x, y) = 49 - x^2 - y^2$ on the line $x + 3y = 10$ (Figure 14.61).
4. Find the local extreme values of $f(x, y) = x^2y$ on the line $x + y = 3$.
5. Find the points on the curve $xy^2 = 54$ nearest the origin.
6. Find the points on the curve $x^2y = 2$ nearest the origin.
7. **Writing to Learn** Use the method of Lagrange multipliers to find

   (a) the minimum value of $x + y$, subject to the constraints $xy = 16, x > 0, y > 0$;

   (b) the maximum value of xy, subject to the constraint $x + y = 16$.

   Comment on the geometry of each solution.
8. Find the points on the curve $x^2 + xy + y^2 = 1$ in the xy-plane that lie nearest to and farthest from the origin.
9. ***Best Cylindrical Can*** Find the dimensions of the closed right circular cylindrical can of smallest surface area whose volume is 16π cm^3.
10. ***Cylinder in a Sphere*** Find the radius and height of the open right circular cylinder of largest surface area that can be inscribed in a sphere of radius a. What is the largest surface area?
11. ***Rectangle of Greatest Area in an Ellipse*** Use the method of Lagrange multipliers to find the dimensions of the rectangle of greatest area that can be inscribed in the ellipse $x^2/16 + y^2/9 = 1$ with sides parallel to the coordinate axes.
12. ***Rectangle of Greatest Perimeter in an Ellipse*** Find the dimensions of the rectangle of largest perimeter that can be inscribed in the ellipse $x^2/a^2 + y^2/b^2 = 1$ with sides parallel to the coordinate axes. What is the largest perimeter?
13. Find the maximum and minimum values of $x^2 + y^2$ subject to the constraint $x^2 - 2x + y^2 - 4y = 0$.
14. Find the maximum and minimum values of $3x - y + 6$ subject to the constraint $x^2 + y^2 = 4$.
15. ***Ant on a Metal Plate*** The temperature at a point (x, y) on a metal plate is $T(x, y) = 4x^2 - 4xy + y^2$. An ant on the plate walks around the circle of radius 5 centered at the origin. What are the highest and lowest temperatures encountered by the ant?
16. ***Storing LPG*** Your firm has been asked to design a storage tank for liquid petroleum gas. The customer's specifications call for a cylindrical tank with hemispherical ends, and the tank is to hold 8000 m^3 of gas. The customer also wants to use the smallest amount of material possible in building the tank. What radius and height do you recommend for the cylindrical portion of the tank?

In Exercises 17–30, the problem involves a function of three variables with one constraint.

17. ***Closest Point*** Find the point on the plane $x + 2y + 3z = 13$ closest to the point $(1, 1, 1)$.

18. ***Farthest Point*** Find the point on the sphere $x^2 + y^2 + z^2 = 4$ which is farthest from the point $(1, -1, 1)$.

19. ***Minimum Distance*** Find the minimum distance from the surface $x^2 - y^2 - z^2 = 1$ to the origin.

20. ***Nearest Point*** Find the point on the surface $z = xy + 1$ nearest the origin.

21. ***Closest Point*** Find the points on the surface $z^2 = xy + 4$ closest to the origin.

22. ***Closest Point*** Find the point(s) on the surface $xyz = 1$ closest to the origin.

23. ***Extreme Values on a Sphere*** Find the maximum and minimum values of

$$f(x, y, z) = x - 2y + 5z$$

on the sphere $x^2 + y^2 + z^2 = 30$.

24. ***Extreme Values on a Sphere*** Find the points on the sphere $x^2 + y^2 + z^2 = 25$ where $f(x, y, z) = x + 2y + 3z$ has its maximum and minimum values.

25. ***Smallest Sum*** Find three real numbers whose sum is 9 and the sum of whose squares is as small as possible.

26. ***Largest Product*** Find the largest product the positive numbers x, y, and z can have if $x + y + z^2 = 16$.

27. ***Largest Box in a Sphere*** Find the dimensions of the closed rectangular box with maximum volume that can be inscribed in the unit sphere.

28. ***Largest Volume*** Find the largest volume a closed rectangular box can have if it lies in the first octant with three faces in the coordinate planes and a vertex on the plane $x/a + y/b + z/c = 1$, where $a > 0$, $b > 0$, and $c > 0$.

29. ***Hottest Point on a Space Probe*** A space probe in the shape of the ellipsoid

$$4x^2 + y^2 + 4z^2 = 16$$

enters the earth's atmosphere and its surface begins to heat. After 1 hour, the temperature at the point (x, y, z) on the probe's surface is

$$T(x, y, z) = 8x^2 + 4yz - 16z + 600.$$

Find the hottest point on the probe's surface.

30. ***Temperature Extremes on a Sphere*** Suppose the Celsius temperature at the point (x, y, z) on the sphere $x^2 + y^2 + z^2 = 1$ is $T = 400xyz^2$. Locate the highest and lowest temperatures on the sphere.

Explorations

31. ***Maximizing a Utility Function. An Example from Economics*** In economics, the usefulness or utility of amounts x and y of two capital goods G_1 and G_2 is sometimes measured by a function $U(x, y)$. For example, G_1 and G_2 might be two chemicals a pharmaceutical company needs to have on hand and $U(x, y)$ the gain from manufacturing a product whose synthesis requires different amounts of the chemicals depending on the process used. If G_1 costs a dollars per kilogram, G_2 costs b dollars per kilogram, and the total amount allocated for the purchase of G_1 and G_2 together is c dollars, then the company's managers want to maximize $U(x, y)$ given that $ax + by = c$. Thus, they need to solve a typical Lagrange multiplier problem.

Suppose

$$U(x, y) = xy + 2x$$

and the equation $ax + by = c$ simplifies to

$$2x + y = 30$$

Find the maximum value of U and the corresponding values of x and y subject to this latter constraint.

32. ***Placing a Radio Telescope on a Newly Discovered Planet*** You are in charge of erecting a radio telescope on a newly discovered planet. To minimize interference, you want to place it where the magnetic field of the planet is weakest. The planet is spherical, with a radius of 6 units. Based on a coordinate system whose origin is at the center of the planet, the strength of the magnetic field is given by $M(x, y, z) = 6x - y^2 + xz + 60$. Where should you locate the radio telescope?

In Exercises 33–40, the problem involves two constraints.

33. Maximize the function $f(x, y, z) = x^2 + 2y - z^2$ subject to the constraints $2x - y = 0$ and $y + z = 0$.

34. Maximize the function $f(x, y, z) = x^2 + y^2 + z^2$ subject to the constraints $x + 2y + 3z = 6$ and $x + 3y + 9z = 9$.

35. Find the point closest to the origin on the line of intersection of the planes $y + 2z = 12$ and $x + y = 6$.

36. Find the maximum value that $f(x, y, z) = x^2 + 2y - z^2$ can have on the line of intersection of the planes $2x - y = 0$ and $y + z = 0$.

37. Find the extreme values of $f(x, y, z) = x^2yz + 1$ on the intersection of the plane $z = 1$ with the sphere $x^2 + y^2 + z^2 = 10$.

38. **(a)** Find the maximum value of $w = xyz$ on the line of intersection of the two planes $x + y + z = 40$ and $x + y - z = 0$.

(b) Writing to Learn Give a geometric argument to support your claim that you have found a maximum, and not a minimum value of w.

39. Find the extreme values of the function $f(x, y, z) = xy + z^2$ on the circle in which the plane $y - x = 0$ intersects the sphere $x^2 + y^2 + z^2 = 4$.

40. Find the point closest to the origin on the curve of intersection of the plane $2y + 4z = 5$ and the cone $z^2 = 4x^2 + 4y^2$.

Extending the Ideas

41. ***The Condition $\nabla f = \lambda \nabla g$ Is Not Sufficient*** Although $\nabla f = \lambda \nabla g$ is a necessary condition for the occurrence of an extreme value of $f(x, y)$ subject to the condition $g(x, y) = 0$, it does not in itself guarantee that an extreme value exists. As a case in point, try using the method of Lagrange multipliers to find a maximum value of $f(x, y) = x + y$ subject to the constraint that $xy = 16$. The method will identify the two points $(4, 4)$ and $(-4, -4)$ as candidates for the location of extreme values. Yet the sum $(x + y)$ has no maximum value on the hyperbola $xy = 16$. The

farther you go from the origin on this hyperbola in the first quadrant, the larger the sum $f(x, y) = x + y$ becomes.

42. ***A Least Squares Plane*** The plane $z = Ax + By + C$ is to be "fitted" to the following points (x_k, y_k, z_k):

$$(0, 0, 0), \quad (0, 1, 1), \quad (1, 1, 1), \quad (1, 0, -1).$$

Find the values of A, B, and C that minimize

$$\sum_{k=1}^{4} (Ax_k + By_k + C - z_k)^2$$

the sum of the squares of the deviations.

43. ***Geometric vs. Arithmetic Means***

(a) Show that the maximum value of $a^2b^2c^2$ on a sphere of radius r centered at the origin of a Cartesian abc-coordinate system is $(r^2/3)^3$.

(b) Using part (a), show that for nonnegative numbers a, b, and c,

$$(abc)^{1/3} \leq \frac{a + b + c}{3}.$$

That is, the *geometric mean* of three numbers is less than or equal to their *arithmetic mean.*

44. Let $a_1, a_2, \ldots, a_n$ be n positive numbers. Find the maximum of $\sum_{i=1}^{n} a_i x_i$ subject to the constraint $\sum_{i=1}^{n} x_i^2 = 1$.

CAS Explorations

In Exercises 45–50, perform the following steps implementing the method of Lagrange multipliers for finding constrained extrema:

(a) Form the function $h = f - \lambda_1 g_1 - \lambda_2 g_2$, where f is the function to optimize subject to the constraints $g_1 = 0$ and $g_2 = 0$.

(b) Determine all the first partial derivatives of h, including the partials with respect to λ_1 and λ_2, and set them equal to 0.

(c) Solve the system of equations found in (b) for all the unknowns, including λ_1 and λ_2.

(d) Evaluate f at each of the solution points found in (c) and select the extreme value subject to the constraints asked for in the exercise.

45. Minimize $f(x, y, z) = xy + yz$ subject to the constraints $x^2 + y^2 - 2 = 0$ and $x^2 + z^2 - 2 = 0$.

46. Minimize $f(x, y, z) = xyz$ subject to the constraints $x^2 + y^2 - 1 = 0$ and $x - z = 0$.

47. Maximize $f(x, y, z) = x^2 + y^2 + z^2$ subject to the constraints $2y + 4z - 5 = 0$ and $4x^2 + 4y^2 - z^2 = 0$.

48. Minimize $f(x, y, z) = x^2 + y^2 + z^2$ subject to the constraints $x^2 - xy + y^2 - z^2 - 1 = 0$ and $x^2 + y^2 - 1 = 0$.

49. Minimize $f(x, y, z, w) = x^2 + y^2 + z^2 + w^2$ subject to the constraints $2x - y + z - w - 1 = 0$ and $x + y - z + w - 1 = 0$.

50. Determine the distance from the line $y = x + 1$ to the parabola $y^2 = x$. (*Hint:* Let (x, y) be a point on the line and (w, z) a point on the parabola. You want to minimize $(x - w)^2 + (y - z)^2$.)

Chapter 14 Key Terms

absolute change (p. 697)
algebra rules for gradients (p. 721)
boundary of a region in space (p. 670)
boundary of a region in the plane (p. 669)
boundary point of a region in space (p. 670)
boundary point of a region in the plane (p. 669)
bounded region in the plane (p. 669)
Chain Rule for functions of three variables (p. 706)
Chain Rule for functions of two variables (p. 704)
closed region in space (p. 670)
closed region in the plane (p. 669)
continuity at a point (p. 679)
continuous function (p. 679)
contour line (p. 671)
critical point (p. 727)
del (p. 725)
dependent variable (p. 667)
differentiable at a point (p. 693)
differentiable function (p. 693)
directional derivative (p. 712)
discriminant of $f(x, y)$ (p. 728)
domain of a multivariable function (p. 667)
error in an approximation (p. 695)
first derivative test for local extrema (p. 726)
formula for implicit differentiation (p. 709)
gradient (p. 714)
gradient vector (p. 714)
graph of $f(x, y)$ (p. 670)
Increment Theorem (p. 693)
independent variables (p. 667)
input variables (p. 667)
interior of a region in space (p. 670)
interior point of a region in the plane (p. 668)
interior of a region in the plane (p. 669)
interior point of a region in space (p. 670)
Lagrange multiplier (p. 736)
Lagrange multiplier method (p. 736)
Laplace equation (p. 692)
level curve (p. 670)
level surface (p. 671)
limit of multivariable function (p. 677)
linearization of a function (p. 694)
local maximum of a multivariable function (p. 725)
local minimum of a multivariable function (p. 725)
Mixed Derivative Theorem (p. 690)
normal line at a point on a surface (p. 718)
open region in space (p. 670)
open region in the plane (p. 669)
Orthogonal Gradient Theorem (p. 737)
output variable (p. 667)
partial derivative of a function (p. 684)
percentage change (p. 697)

Chapter 14 Review Exercises

In Exercises 1–4, find the domain and range of the function and identify its level curves. Sketch a typical level curve.

1. $f(x, y) = 9x^2 + y^2$

2. $f(x, y) = e^{x+y}$

3. $g(x, y) = \dfrac{1}{xy}$

4. $g(x, y) = \sqrt{x^2 - y}$

In Exercise 5–8, find the domain and range of the function and identify its level surfaces. Sketch a typical level surface.

5. $f(x, y, z) = x^2 + y^2 - z$

6. $g(x, y, z) = x^2 + 4y^2 + 9z^2$

7. $h(x, y, z) = \dfrac{1}{x^2 + y^2 + z^2}$

8. $k(x, y, z) = \dfrac{1}{x^2 + y^2 + z^2 + 1}$

In Exercises 9–14, find the limit.

9. $\displaystyle\lim_{(x,y)\to(\pi,\ln 2)} e^y \cos x$

10. $\displaystyle\lim_{(x,y)\to(0,0)} \frac{2 + y}{x + \cos y}$

11. $\displaystyle\lim_{\substack{(x,y)\to(1,1)\\ x\neq y}} \frac{x - y}{x^2 - y^2}$

12. $\displaystyle\lim_{(x-y)\to(1,1)} \frac{x^3y^3 - 1}{xy - 1}$

13. $\displaystyle\lim_{P\to(1,-1,e)} \ln |x + y + z|$

14. $\displaystyle\lim_{P\to(1,-1,-1)} \tan^{-1}(x + y + z)$

In Exercises 15 and 16, show that the limit does not exist by considering different paths of approach.

15. $\displaystyle\lim_{\substack{(x,y)\to(0,0)\\ y\neq x^2}} \frac{y}{x^2 - y}$

16. $\displaystyle\lim_{\substack{(x,y)\to(0,0)\\ xy\neq 0}} \frac{x^2 - y^2}{xy}$

17. (a) Writing to Learn Let $f(x, y) = (x^2 - y^2)/(x^2 + y^2)$ for $(x, y) \neq (0, 0)$. Is it possible to define $f(0, 0)$ in a way that makes f continuous at the origin? Why?

(b) Writing to Learn Let

$$f(x, y) = \begin{cases} \dfrac{\sin(x - y)}{|x| + |y|}, & |x| + |y| \neq 0 \\ 0, & (x, y) = (0, 0). \end{cases}$$

Is f continuous at the origin? Why?

18. Let

$$f(r, \theta) = \begin{cases} \dfrac{\sin 6r}{6r}, & r \neq 0 \\ 1, & r = 0, \end{cases}$$

where r and θ are polar coordinates. Find

(a) $\displaystyle\lim_{r\to 0} f(r, \theta)$ **(b)** $f_r(0, 0)$

(c) $f_\theta(r, \theta)$, $r \neq 0$

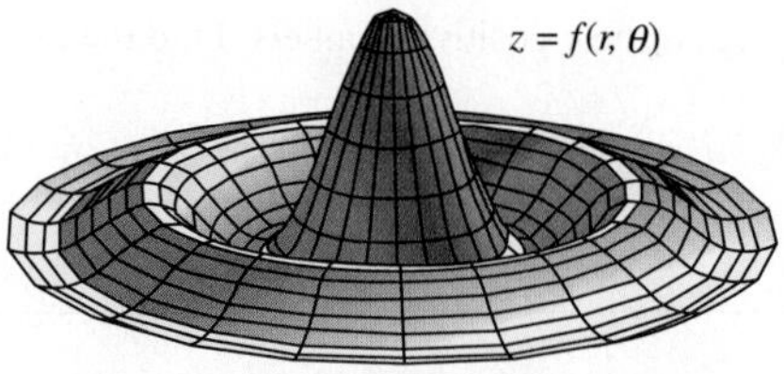

(Generated by Mathematica)

In Exercises 19–24, find the partial derivatives of the function with respect to each variable.

19. $g(r, \theta) = r\cos\theta + r\sin\theta$

20. $f(x, y) = \dfrac{1}{2}\ln(x^2 + y^2) + \tan^{-1}\dfrac{y}{x}$

21. $f(R_1, R_2, R_3) = \dfrac{1}{R_1} + \dfrac{1}{R_2} + \dfrac{1}{R_3}$

22. $h(x, y, z) = \sin(2\pi x + y - 3z)$

23. $P(n, R, T, V) = \dfrac{nRT}{V}$ (the Ideal Gas Law)

24. $f(r, l, T, w) = \dfrac{1}{2rl}\sqrt{\dfrac{T}{\pi w}}$

In Exercises 25–28, find the second-order partial derivatives of the function.

25. $g(x, y) = y + \dfrac{x}{y}$

26. $g(x, y) = e^x + y\sin x$

27. $f(x, y) = x + xy - 5x^3 + \ln(x^2 + 1)$

28. $f(x, y) = y^2 - 3xy + \cos y + 7e^y$

In Exercises 29 and 30, find the linearization $L(x, y)$ of the function $f(x, y)$ at the point P_0. Then find an upper bound for the magnitude of the error E in the approximation $f(x, y) \approx L(x, y)$ over the rectangle R.

29. $f(x, y) = \sin x \cos y, \quad P_0(\pi/4, \pi/4)$

$$R: \left|x - \frac{\pi}{4}\right| \le 0.1, \quad \left|y - \frac{\pi}{4}\right| \le 0.1$$

30. $f(x, y) = xy - 3y^2 + 2, \quad P_0(1, 1)$

$R: |x - 1| \le 0.1, \quad |y - 1| \le 0.2$

In Exercises 31 and 32, find the linearization of the function at the given points.

31. $f(x, y, z) = xy + 2yz - 3xz$ at $(1, 0, 0)$ and $(1, 1, 0)$

32. $f(x, y, z) = \sqrt{2} \cos x \sin (y + z)$ at $(0, 0, \pi/4)$ and $(\pi/4, \pi/4, 0)$

33. Writing to Learn You plan to calculate the volume inside a stretch of pipeline that is about 36 in. in diameter and 1 mi long. With which measurement should you be more careful, the length or the diameter? Why?

34. Writing to Learn Near the point $(1, 2)$, is $f(x, y) = x^2 - xy + y^2 - 3$ more sensitive to changes in x, or to changes in y? How do you know?

35. *Current, Voltage, and Resistance* Suppose the current I (amperes) in an electrical circuit is related to the voltage V (volts) and the resistance R (ohms) by the equation $I = V/R$. If the voltage drops from 24 to 23 volts and the resistance drops from 100 to 80 ohms, will I increase or decrease? By about how much? Express the changes in V and R and the estimated change in I as percentages of their original values.

36. If $a = 10$ cm and $b = 16$ cm to the nearest millimeter, what should you expect the maximum percentage error to be in the calculated area πab of the ellipse $x^2/a^2 + y^2/b^2 = 1$?

37. Let $y = uv$ and $z = u + v$, where u and v are positive independent variables.

(a) If u is measured with an error of 2% and v with an error of 3%, about what is the percentage error in the calculated value of y?

(b) Show that the percentage error in the calculated value of z is less than the percentage error in the value of y.

38. *Cardiac Index* To make different people comparable in studies of cardiac output, researchers divide the measured cardiac output by the body surface area to find the *cardiac index C:*

$$C = \frac{\text{cardiac output}}{\text{body surface area}}$$

The body surface area B is calculated with the formula

$$B = 71.84 w^{0.425} h^{0.725},$$

which gives B in square centimeters when the weight w is measured in kilograms and the height h in centimeters. You are about to calculate the cardiac index of a person with the following measurements:

Cardiac output:	7 L/min
Weight:	70 kg
Height:	180 cm

Which will have a greater effect on the calculation, a 1-kg error in measuring the weight or a 1-cm error in measuring the height?

39. Find dw/dt at $t = 0$ if $w = \sin(xy + \pi)$, $x = e^t$, and $y = \ln(t + 1)$.

40. Find $\partial w/\partial u$ and $\partial w/\partial v$ when $u = v = 0$ if $w = \ln \sqrt{1 + x^2} - \tan^{-1}$ and $x = 2e^a \cos v$.

41. Find the value of the derivative of $f(x, y, z) = xy + yz + xz$ with respect to t on the curve $x = \cos t$, $y = \sin t$, $z = \cos 2t$ at $t = 1$.

42. Show that if $w = f(s)$ is any differentiable function of s and if $s = y + 5x$, then

$$\frac{\partial w}{\partial x} - 5\frac{\partial w}{\partial y} = 0.$$

In Exercises 43 and 44, assume that the equation defines y as a differentiable function of x and find the value of dy/dx at point P.

43. $1 - x - y^2 - \sin xy = 0, \quad P(0, 1)$

44. $2xy + e^{x+y} - 2 = 0, \quad P(0, \ln 2)$

In Exercises 45–48, find the directions in which f increases and decreases most rapidly at P_0 and find the derivative of f in each direction. Also, find the derivative of f at P_0 in the direction of the vector $\mathbf{A}$.

45. $f(x, y) = \cos x \cos y, \quad P_0(\pi/4, \pi/4), \quad \mathbf{A} = 3\mathbf{i} + 4\mathbf{j}$

46. $f(x, y) = x^2e^{-2y}, \quad P_0(1, 0), \quad \mathbf{A} = \mathbf{i} + \mathbf{j}$

47. $f(x, y, z) = \ln(2x + 3y + 6z), \quad P_0(-1, -1, 1),$
$\mathbf{A} = 2\mathbf{i} + 3\mathbf{j} + 6\mathbf{k}$

48. $f(x, y, z) = x^2 + 3xy - z^2 + 2y + z + 4, \quad P_0(0, 0, 0),$
$\mathbf{A} = \mathbf{i} + \mathbf{j} + \mathbf{k}$

49. Find the derivative of $f(x, y, z) = xyz$ in the direction of the velocity vector of the helix

$$\mathbf{r}(t) = (\cos 3t)\mathbf{i} + (\sin 3t)\mathbf{j} + 3t\mathbf{k}$$

at $t = \pi/3$.

50. What is the largest value that the directional derivative of $f(x, y, z) = xyz$ can have at the point $(1, 1, 1)$?

51. At the point $(1, 2)$ the function $f(x, y)$ has a derivative of 2 in the direction toward $(2, 2)$ and derivative of -2 in the direction toward $(1, 1)$.

(a) Find $f_x(1, 2)$ and $f_y(1, 2)$.

(b) Find the derivative of f at $(1, 2)$ in the direction toward the point $(4, 6)$.

52. Which of the following statements are true if $f(x, y)$ is differentiable at (x_0, y_0)?

(a) If $\mathbf{u}$ is a unit vector, the derivative of f at (x_0, y_0) in the direction of $\mathbf{u}$ is $(f_x(x_0, y_0)\mathbf{i} + f_y(x_0, y_0)\mathbf{j}) \cdot \mathbf{u}$.

(b) The derivative of f at (x_0, y_0) in the direction of $\mathbf{u}$ is a vector.

(c) The directional derivative of f at (x_0, y_0) has its greatest value in the direction of ∇f.

(d) At (x_0, y_0), vector ∇f is normal to the curve $f(x, y) = f(x_0, y_0)$.

In Exercises 53 and 54, sketch the surface $f(x, y, z) = c$ together with ∇f at the given points.

53. $x^2 + y + z^2 = 0$; $(0, -1, \pm 1)$, $(0, 0, 0)$

54. $y^2 + z^2 = 4$; $(2, \pm 2, 0)$, $(2, 0, \pm 2)$

In Exercises 55 and 56, find an equation for the plane tangent to the level surface $f(x, y, z) = c$ at the point P_0. Also, find parametric equations for the line that is normal to the surface at P_0.

55. $x^2 - y - 5z = 0$, $P_0(2, -1, 1)$

56. $x^2 + y^2 + z = 4$, $P_0(1, 1, 2)$

In Exercises 57 and 58, find an equation for the plane tangent to the surface $z = f(x, y)$ at the given point.

57. $z = \ln(x^2 + y^2)$, $(0, 1, 0)$

58. $z = 1/(x^2 + y^2)$, $(1, 1, 1/2)$

In Exercises 59 and 60, find equations for the lines that are tangent and normal to the level curve $f(x, y) = c$ at the point P_0. Then sketch the lines and level curve together with ∇f at P_0.

59. $y - \sin x = 1$, $P_0(\pi, 1)$

60. $\dfrac{y^2}{2} - \dfrac{x^2}{2} = \dfrac{3}{2}$, $P_0(1, 2)$

In Exercises 61 and 62, find parametric equations for the line that is tangent to the curve of intersection of the surfaces at the given point.

61. Surfaces: $x^2 + 2y + 2z = 4$, $y = 1$
Point: $(1, 1, 1/2)$

62. Surfaces: $x + y^2 + z = 2$, $y = 1$
Point: $(1/2, 1, 1/2)$

In Exercises 63–68, find the local maxima, local minima, and saddle points of the function. Find the function's values at these points.

63. $f(x, y) = x^2 - xy + y^2 + 2x + 2y - 4$

64. $f(x, y) = 5x^2 + 4xy - 2y^2 + 4x - 4y$

65. $f(x, y) = 2x^3 + 3xy + 2y^3$

66. $f(x, y) = x^3 + y^3 - 3xy + 15$

67. $f(x, y) = x^3 + y^3 + 3x^2 - 3y^2$

68. $f(x, y) = x^4 - 8x^2 + 3y^2 - 6y$

In Exercises 69–76, find the absolute maximum and minimum values of f on the region R.

69. $f(x, y) = x^2 + xy + y^2 - 3x + 3y$
R: The triangular region cut from the first quadrant by the line $x + y = 4$

70. $f(x, y) = x^2 - y^2 - 2x + 4y + 1$
R: The rectangular region in the first quadrant bounded by the coordinates axes and the lines $x = 4$ and $y = 2$

71. $f(x, y) = y^2 - xy - 3y + 2x$
R: The square region enclosed by the lines $x = \pm 2$ and $y = \pm 2$

72. $f(x, y) = 2x + 2y - x^2 - y^2$
R: The square bounded by the coordinate axes and the lines $x = 2$, $y = 2$ in the first quadrant

73. $f(x, y) = x^2 - y^2 - 2x + 4y$
R: The triangular region bounded below by the x-axis, above by the line $y = x + 2$, and on the right by the line $x = 2$

74. $f(x, y) = 4xy - x^4 - y^4 + 16$
R: The triangular region bounded below by the line $y = -2$, above by the line $y = x$, and on the right by the line $x = 2$

75. $f(x, y) = x^3 + y^3 + 3x^2 - 3y^2$
R: The square region enclosed by the lines $x = \pm 1$ and $y = \pm 1$

76. $f(x, y) = x^3 + 3xy + y^3 + 1$
R: The square region enclosed by the lines $x = \pm 1$ and $y = \pm 1$

77. Find the extreme values of $f(x, y) = x^3 + y^2$ on the circle $x^2 + y^2 = 1$.

78. Find the extreme values of $f(x, y) = xy$ on the circle $x^2 + y^2 = 1$.

79. Find the extreme values of $f(x, y) = x^2 + 3y^2 + 2y$ on the unit disk $x^2 + y^2 \leq 1$.

80. Find the extreme values of $f(x, y) = x^2 + y^2 - 3x - xy$ on the disk $x^2 + y^2 \leq 9$.

81. Find the extreme values of $f(x, y, z) = x - y + z$ on the unit sphere $x^2 + y^2 + z^2 = 1$.

82. Find the points on the surface $z^2 - xy = 4$ closest to the origin.

83. A closed rectangular box is to have volume V cm^3. The cost of the material used in the box is a cents/cm^2 for top and bottom, b cents/cm^2 for front and back, and c cents/cm^2 for the remaining sides. What dimensions minimize the total cost of materials?

84. Find the plane $x/a + y/b + z/c = 1$ that passes through the point $(2, 1, 2)$ and cuts off the least volume from the first octant.

85. Find the extreme values of $f(x, y, z) = x(y + z)$ on the curve of intersection of the right circular cylinder $x^2 + y^2 = 1$ and the hyperbolic cylinder $xz = 1$.

86. Find the point closest to the origin on the curve of intersection of the plane $x + y + z = 1$ and the cone $z^2 = 2x^2 + 2y^2$.

87. Let $w = f(r, \theta)$, $r = \sqrt{x^2 + y^2}$ and $\theta = \tan^{-1}(y/x)$. Find $\partial w/\partial x$ and $\partial w/\partial y$ and express your answers in terms of r and θ.

88. Let $z = f(u, v)$, $u = ax + by$, and $v = ax - by$. Express z_x and z_y in terms of f_u, f_v, and the constants a and b.

89. If $w = \ln(x^2 + y^2 + 2z)$, $x = r + s$, $y = r - s$, and $z = 2rs$, find w_r and w_s by the Chain Rule. Then check your answer another way.

90. The equations $e^u \cos v - x = 0$ and $e^u \sin v - y = 0$ define u and v as differentiable functions of x and y. Show that the angle between the vectors

$$\frac{\partial u}{\partial x}\mathbf{i} + \frac{\partial u}{\partial y}\mathbf{j} \quad \text{and} \quad \frac{\partial v}{\partial x}\mathbf{i} + \frac{\partial v}{\partial y}\mathbf{j}$$

is constant.

91. Find the points on the surface

$$(y + z)^2 + (z - x)^2 = 16$$

where the normal line is parallel to the yz-plane.

92. Find the points on the surface

$$xy + yz + zx - x - z^2 = 0$$

where the tangent plane is parallel to the xy-plane.

93. Suppose $\nabla f(x, y, z)$ is always parallel to the position vector $x\mathbf{i} + y\mathbf{j} + z\mathbf{k}$. Show that $f(0, 0, a) = f(0, 0, -a)$ for any a.

94. Show that the directional derivative of

$$f(x, y, z) = \sqrt{x^2 + y^2 + z^2}$$

at the origin equals 1 in any direction but that f has no gradient vector at the origin.

95. Show that the line normal to the surface $xy + z = 2$ at the point $(1, 1, 1)$ passes through the origin.

96. **(a)** Sketch the surface $x^2 - y^2 + z^2 = 4$.

(b) Find a vector normal to the surface at $(2, -3, 3)$. Add the vector to your sketch.

(c) Find the equations for the tangent plane and normal line at $(2, -3, 3)$.

Chapter 15 Multiple Integrals

Magnetic compasses are required equipment in most aircraft, yet they are adversely influenced by vibration, by other metal and electrical components, and during turns and acceleration. Most aircraft are also equipped with a directional gyroscope, which resists changes in direction while the aircraft rotates around it.

One directional gyroscope has a disk with a radius of 6 cm, thickness of 0.5 cm, and a density of 8.9 gm/cm^3, suspended on a weightless axle. If the gyroscope spins at an angular velocity of 1800 radians per second, what is its kinetic energy? Section 15.2 covers the necessary mathematics to solve this problem.

Chapter 15 Overview

The problems we can solve by integrating functions of two and three variables are similar to the problems solved by single-variable integration, but more general. As in the previous chapter, we can perform the necessary calculations by drawing on our experience with functions of a single variable.

15.1 Double Integrals

What you'll learn about

- Double Integrals over Rectangles
- Properties of Double Integrals
- Double Integrals as Volumes
- Fubini's Theorem for Calculating Double Integrals
- Double Integrals over Bounded Nonrectangular Regions
- Finding Limits of Integration

Double Integrals over Rectangles

Suppose $f(x, y)$ is defined on a rectangular region R given by

$$R: \quad a \le x \le b, \qquad c \le y \le d.$$

We imagine R to be covered by a network of lines parallel to the x- and y-axes (Figure 15.1). These lines divide R into small pieces of area $\Delta A = \Delta x\, \Delta y$. We number these in some order $\Delta A_t, \Delta A_2, \ldots, \Delta A_n$, choose a point (x_k, y_k) in each piece ΔA_k, and form the sum

$$S_n = \sum_{k=1}^{n} f(x_k, y_k)\, \Delta A_k. \tag{1}$$

If f is continuous throughout R, then, as we refine the mesh width to make both Δx and Δy go to zero, the sums in Equation (1) approach a limit, the **double integral** of f over R. The notation for it is

$$\iint_R f(x, y)\, dA \quad \text{or} \quad \iint_R f(x, y)\, dx\, dy.$$

Thus,

$$\iint_R f(x, y)\, dA = \lim_{\Delta A \to 0} \sum_{k=1}^{n} f(x_k, y_k)\, \Delta A_k. \tag{2}$$

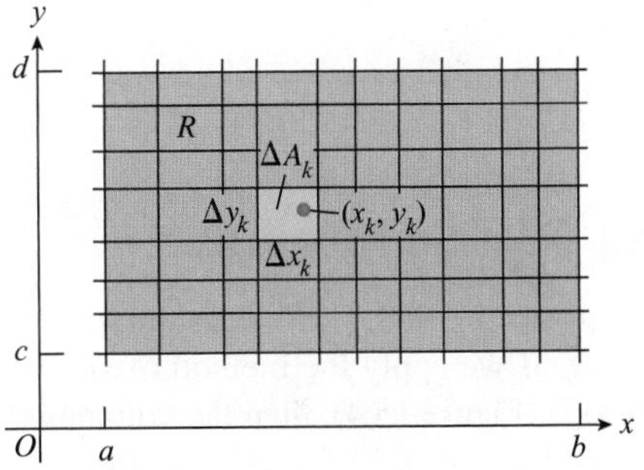

Figure 15.1 Rectangular grid partitioning the region R into small rectangles of area $\Delta A_k = \Delta x_k\, \Delta y_k$.

As with functions of a single variable, the sums approach this limit no matter how the intervals $[a, b]$ and $[c, d]$ that determine R are partitioned, as long as the norms of the partitions both go to zero. The limit in Equation (2) is also independent of the order in which the areas ΔA_k are numbered and independent of the choice of the point (x_k, y_k) within each ΔA_k. The values of the individual approximating sums S_n depend on these choices, but the sums approach the same limit in the end. The proof of the existence and uniqueness of this limit for a continuous function f is given in more advanced texts. The continuity of f is a sufficient condition for the existence of the double integral, but not a necessary one. The limit in question exists for many discontinuous functions as well.

Properties of Double Integrals

Like single integrals, double integrals of continuous functions have algebraic properties that are useful in computations and applications.

Properties of Double Integrals

1. *Constant Multiple:* $\displaystyle\iint_R kf(x, y)\, dA = k \iint_R f(x, y)\, dA$

(any number k)

continued

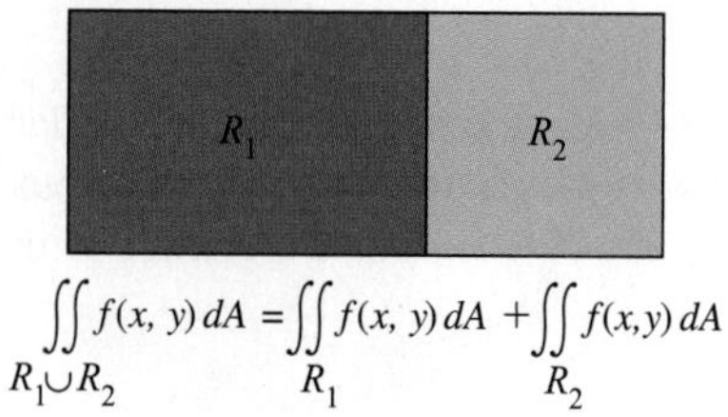

R_1
R_2
$\iint_{R_1 \cup R_2} f(x, y)\, dA = \iint_{R_1} f(x, y)\, dA + \iint_{R_2} f(x, y)\, dA$

Figure 15.2 Double integrals have the same kind of domain additivity property that single integrals have.

2. *Sum and Difference:*

$$\iint_R (f(x, y) \pm g(x, y))\, dA = \iint_R f(x, y)\, dA \pm \iint_R g(x, y)\, dA$$

3. *Domination:*

(a) $\displaystyle\iint_R f(x, y)\, dA \ge 0 \quad \text{if} \quad f(x, y) \ge 0 \text{ on } R$

(b) $\displaystyle\iint_R f(x, y)\, dA \ge \iint_R g(x, y)\, dA \quad \text{if} \quad f(x, y) \ge g(x, y) \text{ on } R$

4. *Additivity:* $\displaystyle\iint_R f(x, y)\, dA = \iint_{R_1} f(x, y)\, dA + \iint_{R_2} f(x, y)\, dA$

if R is the union of two nonoverlapping rectangles R_1 and R_2 (Figure 15.2).

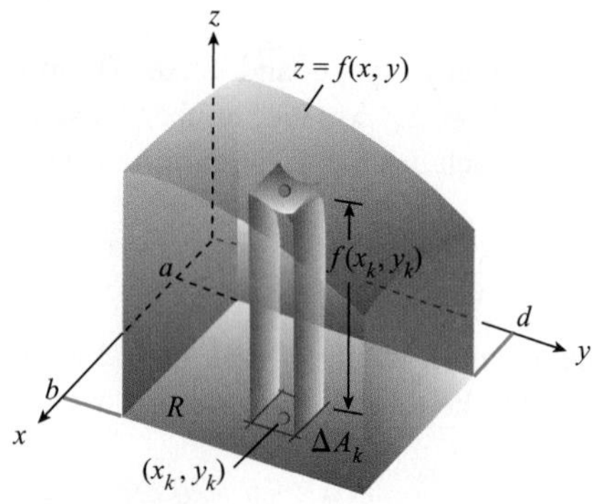

Figure 15.3 Approximating solids with rectangular prisms leads us to define the volumes of more general prisms as double integrals. The volume of the prism shown here is the double integral of $f(x, y)$ over the base region R.

Double Integrals as Volumes

When $f(x, y)$ is positive, we may interpret the double integral of f over a rectangular region R as the volume of the solid prism bounded below by R and above by the surface $z = f(x, y)$ (Figure 15.3). Each term $f(x_k, y_k)\,\Delta A_k$ in the sum $S_n = \sum f(x_k, y_k)\,\Delta A_k$ is the volume of a vertical rectangular prism that approximates the volume of the portion of the solid that stands directly above the base ΔA_k. The sum S_n thus approximates what we want to call the *total volume of the solid.* We define this volume to be

$$\text{Volume} = \lim S_n = \iint_R f(x, y)\, dA. \tag{3}$$

Fubini's Theorem for Calculating Double Integrals

Suppose we wish to calculate the volume under the plane $z = 4 - x - y$ over the rectangular region R: $0 \le x \le 2$, $0 \le y \le 1$ in the xy-plane. If we apply the method of slicing from Section 7.3, with slices perpendicular to the x-axis (Figure 15.4), then the volume is

$$\int_{x=0}^{x=2} A(x)\, dx, \tag{4}$$

where $A(x)$ is the cross-section area at x. For each value of x we may calculate $A(x)$ as the integral

$$A(x) = \int_{y=0}^{y=1} (4 - x - y)\, dy, \tag{5}$$

which is the area under the curve $z = 4 - x - y$ in the plane of the cross section at x. In calculating $A(x)$, x is held fixed and the integration takes place with respect to y. Combining Equations (4) and (5), we see that the volume of the entire solid is

$$\begin{aligned} \text{Volume} &= \int_{x=0}^{x=2} A(x)\, dx = \int_{x=0}^{x=2} \left(\int_{y=0}^{y=1} (4 - x - y)\, dy \right) dx \\ &= \int_{x=0}^{x=2} \left[4y - xy - \frac{y^2}{2} \right]_{y=0}^{y=1} dx = \int_{x=0}^{x=2} \left(\frac{7}{2} - x \right) dx \\ &= \left[\frac{7}{2}x - \frac{x^2}{2} \right]_0^2 = 5 \text{ units cubed.} \end{aligned} \tag{6}$$

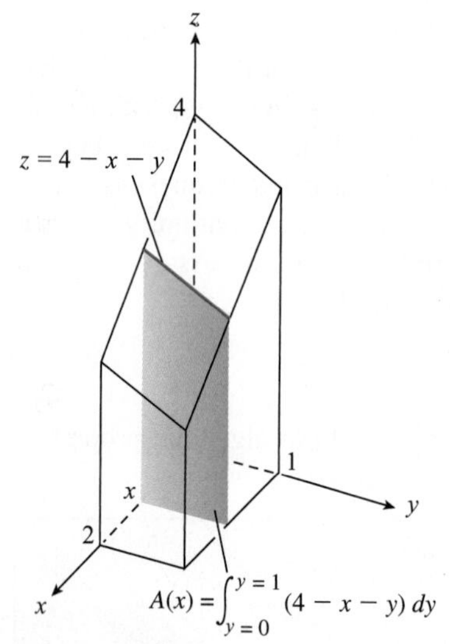

Figure 15.4 To obtain the cross-section area $A(x)$, we hold x fixed and integrate with respect to y.

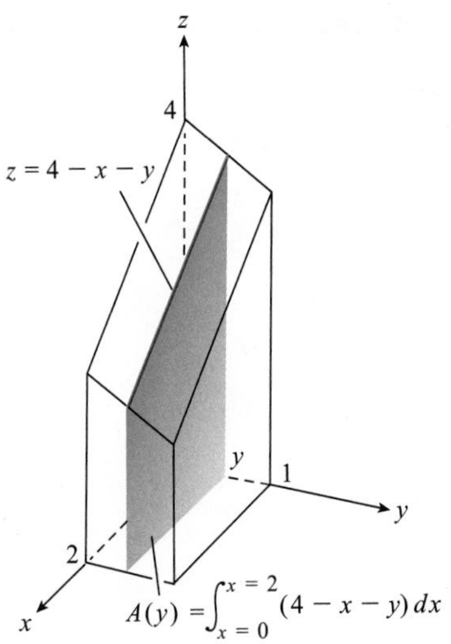

Figure 15.5 To obtain the cross-section area $A(y)$, we hold y fixed and integrate with respect to x.

If we had just wanted to write instructions for calculating the volume, without carrying out any of the integrations, we could write

$$\text{Volume} = \int_0^2 \int_0^1 (4 - x - y)\, dy\, dx.$$

The expression on the right, an **iterated** or **repeated integral,** says that the volume is obtained by integrating $4 - x - y$ with respect to y from $y = 0$ to $y = 1$, holding x fixed, and then integrating the resulting expression in x with respect to x from $x = 0$ to $x = 2$.

What would have happened if we had calculated the volume by slicing with planes perpendicular to the y-axis (Figure 15.5)? As a function of y, the typical cross-section area is

$$A(y) = \int_{x=0}^{x=2} (4 - x - y)\, dx = \left[4x - \frac{x^2}{2} - xy\right]_{x=0}^{x=2} = 6 - 2y. \tag{7}$$

The volume of the entire solid is therefore

$$\text{Volume} = \int_{y=0}^{y=1} A(y)\, dy = \int_{y=0}^{y=1} (6 - 2y)\, dy = [6y - y^2]_0^1 = 5 \text{ cubic units},$$

in agreement with our earlier calculation.

Again, we may give instructions for calculating the volume as an iterated integral by writing

$$\text{Volume} = \int_0^1 \int_0^2 (4 - x - y)\, dx\, dy.$$

The expression on the right says we can find the volume by integrating $4 - x - y$ with respect to x from $x = 0$ to $x = 2$ (as in Equation (7)) and integrating the result with respect to y from $y = 0$ to $y = 1$. In this iterated integral, the order of integration is first x and then y, the reverse of the order in Equation (6).

What do these two volume calculations with iterated integrals have to do with the double integral

$$\iint_R (4 - x - y)\, dA$$

over the rectangle R: $0 \le x \le 2$, $0 \le y \le 1$? The answer is they both give the value of the double integral. A theorem published in 1907 by Guido Fubini (1879–1943) says that the double integral of any continuous function over a rectangle can be calculated as an iterated integral in either order of integration. (Fubini proved his theorem in greater generality, but this is how it translates into what we are doing now.)

THEOREM 1 Fubini's Theorem (First Form)

If $f(x, y)$ is continuous on the rectangular region R: $a \le x \le b$, $c \le y \le d$, then

$$\iint_R f(x, y)\, dA = \int_c^d \int_a^b f(x, y)\, dx\, dy = \int_a^b \int_c^d f(x, y)\, dy\, dx.$$

Fubini's theorem says that double integrals over rectangles can be calculated as iterated integrals. Thus, we can evaluate a double integral by integrating with respect to one variable at a time.

Fubini's theorem also says that we may calculate the double integral by integrating in *either* order, a genuine convenience, as we will see in Example 3. In particular, when we calculate a volume by slicing, we may use planes either perpendicular to the x-axis or to the y-axis.

EXAMPLE 1 Evaluating a Double Integral

Calculate $\displaystyle\iint_R f(x, y)\,dA$ for $f(x, y) = 1 - 6x^2y$ and R: $0 \le x \le 2,\ -1 \le y \le 1$.

SOLUTION

By Fubini's theorem,

$$\iint_R f(x, y)\,dA = \int_{-1}^{1}\int_0^2 (1 - 6x^2y)\,dx\,dy = \int_{-1}^{1} \left[x - 2x^3y\right]_{x=0}^{x=2} dy$$

$$= \int_{-1}^{1} (2 - 16y)\,dy = \left[2y - 8y^2\right]_{-1}^{1} = 4.$$

Reversing the order of integration gives the same answer:

$$\int_0^2\int_{-1}^{1} (1 - 6x^2y)\,dy\,dx = \int_0^2 \left[y - 3x^2y^2\right]_{y=-1}^{y=1} dx$$

$$= \int_0^2 \left[(1 - 3x^2) - (-1 - 3x^2)\right] dx$$

$$= \int_0^2 2\,dx = 4 \text{ cubic units.}$$

Technology *Multiple Integration* Most computer algebra systems (CAS) can calculate both multiple and iterated integrals. The typical procedure is to apply the CAS integrate command in nested iterations according to the order of integration you specify. Figure 15.6 shows how one new advanced graphing calculator with CAS features calculates

$$\iint x^2y\,dx\,dy \quad \text{and} \quad \int_{-\pi/3}^{\pi/4}\int_0^1 x\cos y\,dx\,dy.$$

If a CAS cannot produce an exact value for a definite integral, it can usually find an approximate value numerically.

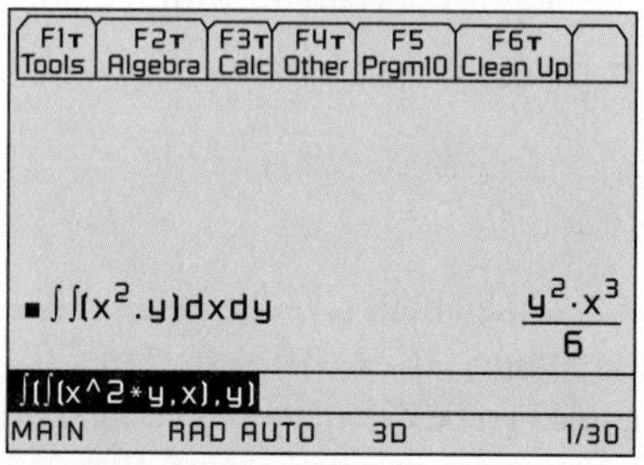

(a)

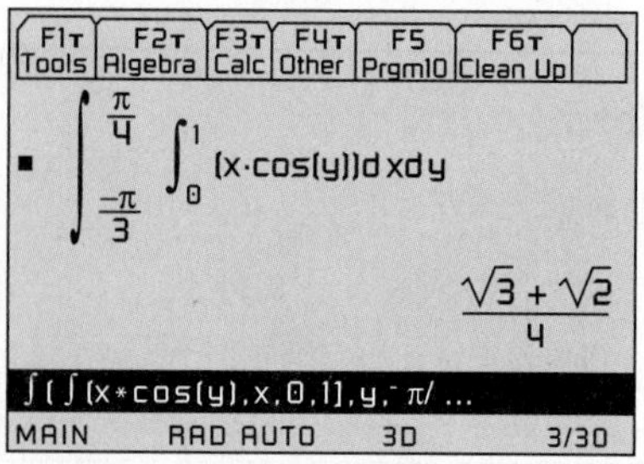

(b)

Figure 15.6 The value of $\displaystyle\iint x^2y\,dx\,dy$ (a) and the value of $\displaystyle\int_{-\pi/3}^{\pi/4}\int_0^1 x\cos y\,dx\,dy$ (b).

Double Integrals over Bounded Nonrectangular Regions

To define the double integral of a function $f(x, y)$ over a bounded nonrectangular region, like the one shown in Figure 15.7, we again imagine R to be covered by a rectangular grid, but we include in the partial sum only the small pieces of area $\Delta A = \Delta x\,\Delta y$ that lie entirely within the region (shaded in the figure). We number the pieces in some order, choose an arbitrary point (x_k, y_k) in each ΔA_k, and form the sum

$$S_n = \sum_{k=1}^{n} f(x_k, y_k)\,\Delta A_k.$$

The only difference between this sum and the one in Equation (1) for rectangular regions is that now the areas ΔA_k may not cover all R. As the mesh becomes increasingly fine and the number of terms in S_n increases, however, more and more of R is included. If f is continuous and the boundary of R is made from the graphs of a finite number of continuous functions of x and/or continuous functions of y joined end to end, then the sums S_n will have a limit as the norms of the partitions that define the rectangular grid independently approach zero. The limit is the **double integral** of f over R:

$$\iint_R f(x, y)\, dA = \lim_{\Delta A \to 0} \sum f(x_k, y_k)\, \Delta A_k.$$

This limit may also exist under less restrictive circumstances.

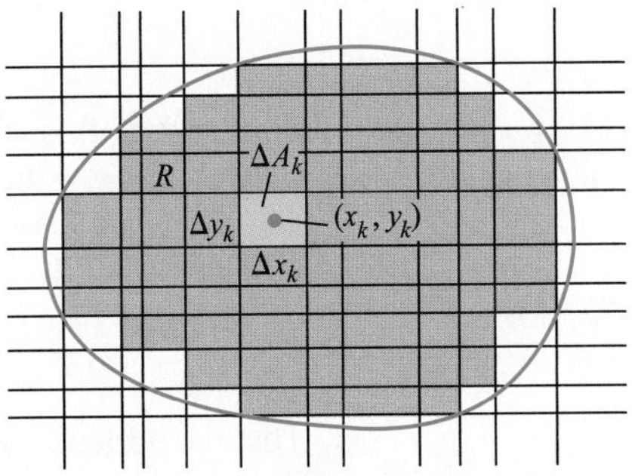

Figure 15.7 A rectangular grid partitioning a bounded nonrectangular region into cells.

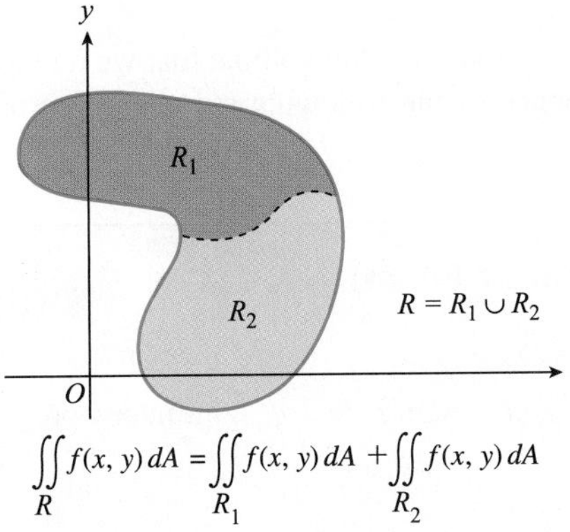

Figure 15.8 The additivity property for rectangular regions holds for regions bounded by continuous curves.

Double integrals of continuous functions over nonrectangular regions have the same algebraic properties as integrals over rectangular regions. The domain additivity property corresponding to property 4 says that if R is decomposed into nonoverlapping regions R_1 and R_2 with boundaries that are again made of a finite number of line segments or smooth curves (see Figure 15.8 for an example), then

$$\iint_R f(x, y)\, dA = \iint_{R_1} f(x, y)\, dA + \iint_{R_2} f(x, y)\, dA.$$

If $f(x, y)$ is positive and continuous over R (Figure 15.9), we define the volume of the solid region between R and the surface $z = f(x, y)$ to be $\iint_R f(x, y)\, dA$, as before.

If R is a region like the one shown in the xy-plane in Figure 15.10, bounded "above" and "below" by the curves $y = g_2(x)$ and $y = g_1(x)$ and on the sides by the lines $x = a$, $x = b$, we

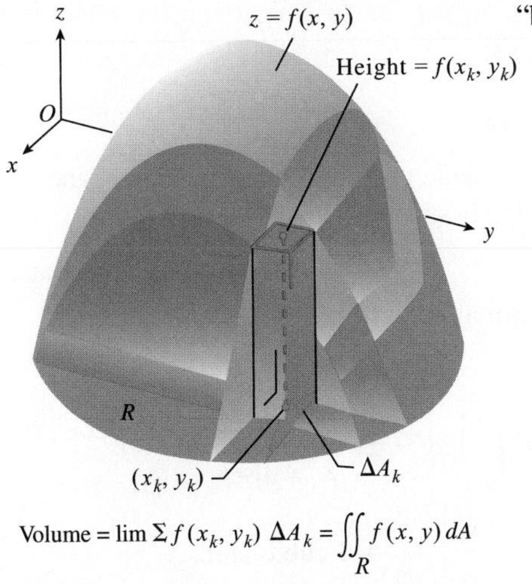

Figure 15.9 We define the volume of solids with curved bases the same way we define the volumes of solids with rectangular bases.

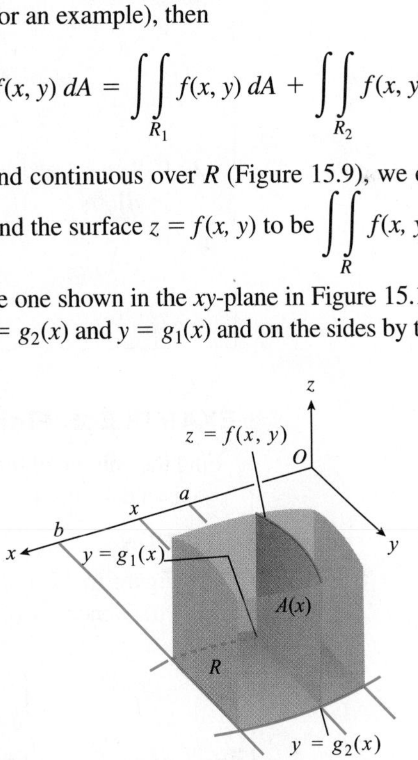

Figure 15.10 The area of the vertical slice shown here is $A(x) = \int_{g_1(x)}^{g_2(x)} f(x, y)\, dy$.

To calculate the volume of the solid, we integrate this area from $x = a$ to $x = b$.

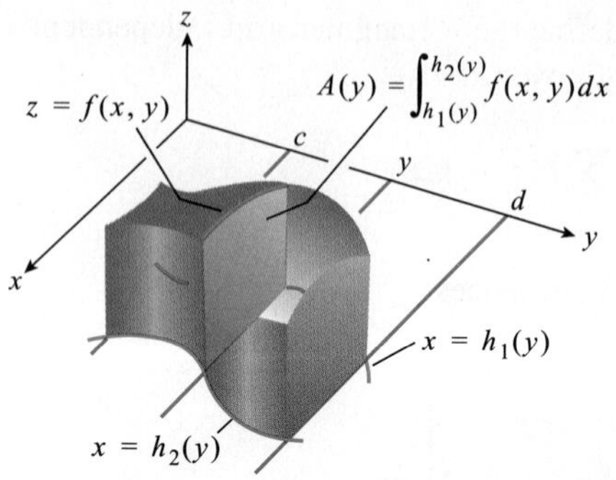

Figure 15.11 The volume of the solid shown here is

$$\int_c^d A(y)\,dy = \int_c^d \int_{h_1(y)}^{h_2(y)} f(x, y)\,dx\,dy.$$

may again calculate the volume by the method of slicing. We first calculate the cross-section area

$$A(x) = \int_{y=g_1(x)}^{y=g_2(x)} f(x, y)\,dy$$

and then integrate $A(x)$ from $x = a$ to $x = b$ to get the volume as an iterated integral:

$$V = \int_a^b A(x)\,dx = \int_a^b \int_{g_1(x)}^{g_2(x)} f(x, y)\,dy\,dx. \tag{8}$$

Similarly, if R is a region like the one shown in Figure 15.11, bounded by the curves $x = h_2(y)$ and $x = h_1(y)$ and the lines $y = c$ and $y = d$, then the volume calculated by slicing is given by the iterated integral

$$\text{Volume} = \int_c^d \int_{h_1(y)}^{h_2(y)} f(x, y)\,dx\,dy. \tag{9}$$

That the iterated integrals in Equations (8) and (9) both give the volume that we define to be the double integral of f over R is a consequence of the following stronger form of Fubini's theorem.

THEOREM 2 Fubini's Theorem (Stronger Form)

Let $f(x, y)$ be continuous on a region R.

1. If R is defined by $a \le x \le b$, $g_1(x) \le y \le g_2(x)$, with g_1 and g_2 continuous on $[a, b]$, then

$$\iint_R f(x, y)\,dA = \int_a^b \int_{g_1(x)}^{g_2(x)} f(x, y)\,dy\,dx.$$

2. If R is defined by $c \le y \le d$, $h_1(y) \le x \le h_2(y)$, with h_1 and h_2 continuous on $[c, d]$, then

$$\iint_R f(x, y)\,dA = \int_c^d \int_{h_1(y)}^{h_2(y)} f(x, y)\,dx\,dy.$$

EXAMPLE 2 Finding Volume

Find the volume of the prism whose base is the triangle in the xy-plane bounded by the x-axis and the lines $y = x$ and $x = 1$ and whose top lies in the plane $z = f(x, y) = 3 - x - y$.

SOLUTION

See Figure 15.12. For any x between 0 and 1, y may vary from $y = 0$ to $y = x$ (Figure 15.12b). Hence,

$$V = \int_0^1 \int_0^x (3 - x - y)\,dy\,dx = \int_0^1 \left[3y - xy - \frac{y^2}{2}\right]_{y=0}^{y=x} dx$$

$$= \int_0^1 \left(3x - \frac{3x^2}{2}\right) dx = \left[\frac{3x^2}{2} - \frac{x^3}{2}\right]_{x=0}^{x=1} = 1 \text{ cubic unit.}$$

When the order of integration is reversed (Figure 15.12c), the integral for the volume is

$$V = \int_0^1 \int_y^1 (3 - x - y)\, dx\, dy = \int_0^1 \left[3x - \frac{x^2}{2} - xy \right]_{x=y}^{x=1} dy$$

$$= \int_0^1 \left(3 - \frac{1}{2} - y - 3y + \frac{y^2}{2} + y^2 \right) dy$$

$$= \int_0^1 \left[\frac{5}{2} - 4y + \frac{3}{2} y^2 \right] dy = \left[\frac{5}{2} y - 2y^2 + \frac{y^3}{2} \right]_{y=0}^{y=1} = 1 \text{ cubic unit.}$$

The two integrals are equal, as they should be.

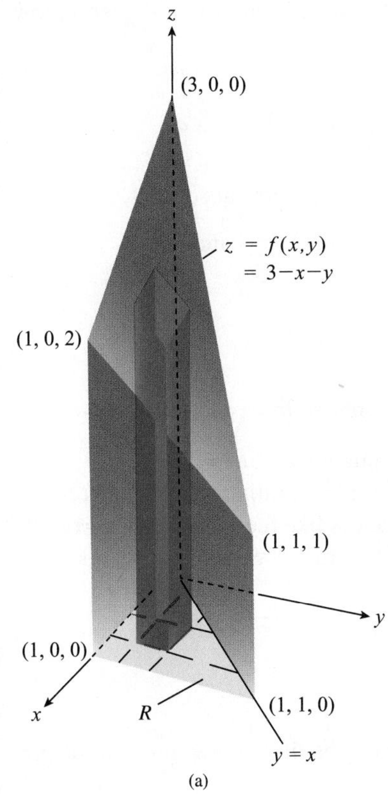

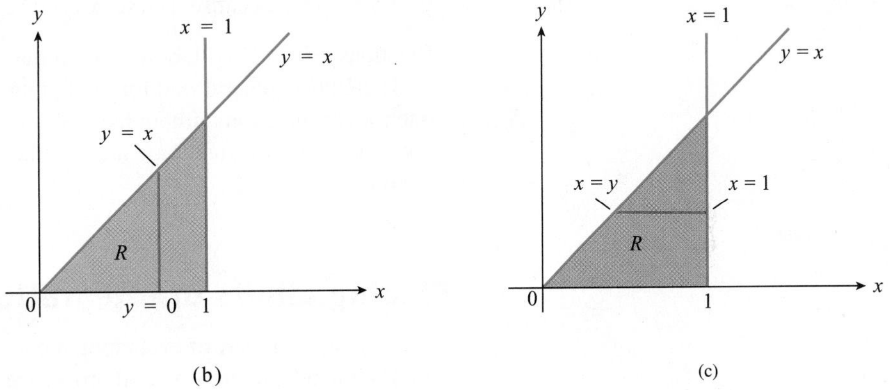

Figure 15.12 (a) Prism with a triangular base in the *xy*-plane. The volume of this prism is defined as a double integral over *R*. To evaluate it as an iterated integral, we may integrate first with respect to *y* and then with respect to *x*, or the other way around (Example 2). (b) Integration limits of $\int_{x=0}^{x=1} \int_{y=0}^{y=x} f(x, y)\, dy\, dx$. If we integrate first with respect to *y*, we integrate along a vertical line through *R* and then integrate from left to right to include all the vertical lines in *R*. (c) Integration limits of $\int_{y=0}^{y=1} \int_{x=y}^{x=1} f(x, y)\, dx\, dy$. If we integrate first with respect to *x*, we integrate along a horizontal line through *R* and then integrate from bottom to top to include all the horizontal lines in *R*.

Although Fubini's theorem assures us that a double integral may be calculated as an iterated integral in either order of integration, the value of one integral may be easier to find than the value of the other. The next example shows how this can happen.

EXAMPLE 3 Evaluating a Double Integral

Calculate

$$\iint_R \frac{\sin x}{x}\, dA,$$

where *R* is the triangle in the *xy*-plane bounded by the *x*-axis, the line $y = x$, and the line $x = 1$.

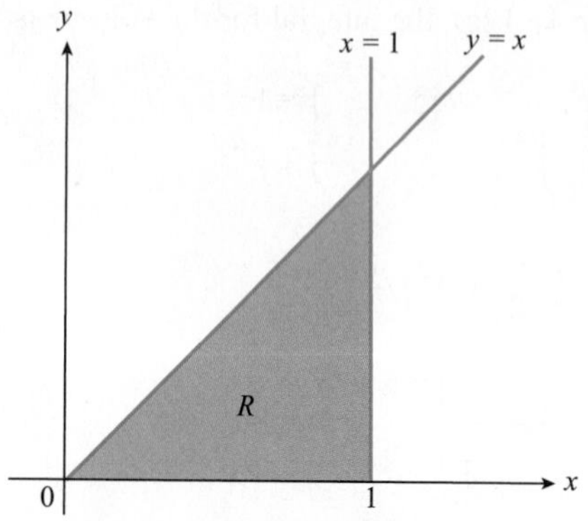

Figure 15.13 The region of integration in Example 3.

SOLUTION

The region of integration is shown in Figure 15.13. If we integrate first with respect to y and then with respect to x, we find

$$\int_0^1 \left(\int_0^x \frac{\sin x}{x}\, dy \right) dx = \int_0^1 \left(y \frac{\sin x}{x} \Big]_{y=0}^{y=x} \right) dx = \int_0^1 \sin x\, dx$$

$$= -\cos(1) + 1 \approx 0.46 \text{ units cubed.}$$

If we reverse the order of integration and attempt to calculate (by hand)

$$\int_0^1 \int_y^1 \frac{\sin x}{x}\, dx\, dy,$$

we are stopped because $\int ((\sin x)/x)\, dx$ cannot be expressed in terms of elementary functions. (A CAS will, however, produce an approximation to the answer.)

There is no general rule for predicting which order of integration will be the good one for computation without technology in circumstances like these, so don't worry about how to start. Just forge ahead, and if the order you first choose doesn't work, try the other.

Finding Limits of Integration

The most difficult part of evaluating a double integral can be finding the limits of integration. Fortunately, there is a good procedure to follow.

Procedure for Finding Limits of Integration

A. To evaluate $\iint_R dA$ over a region R, integrating first with respect to y and then with respect to x, take the following steps:

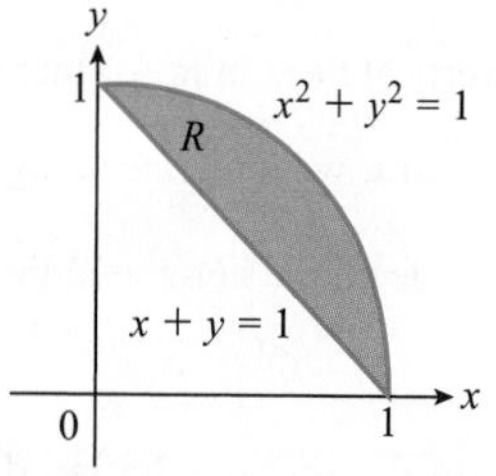

1. *A sketch.* Sketch the region of integration and label the bounding curves.

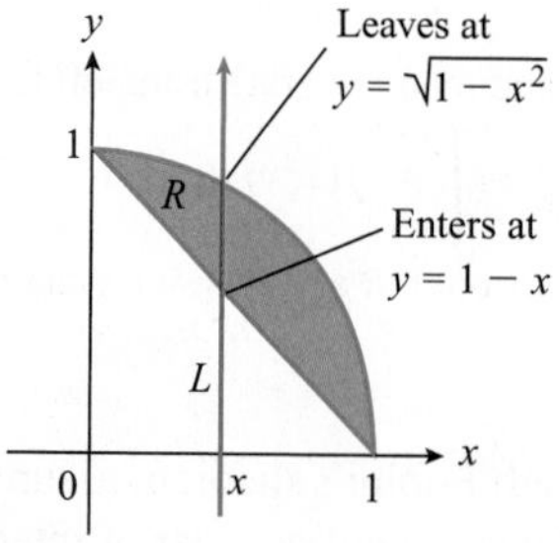

2. *The y-limits of integration.* Imagine a vertical line L cutting through R in the direction of increasing y. Mark the y-values where L enters and leaves. These are the y-limits of integration.

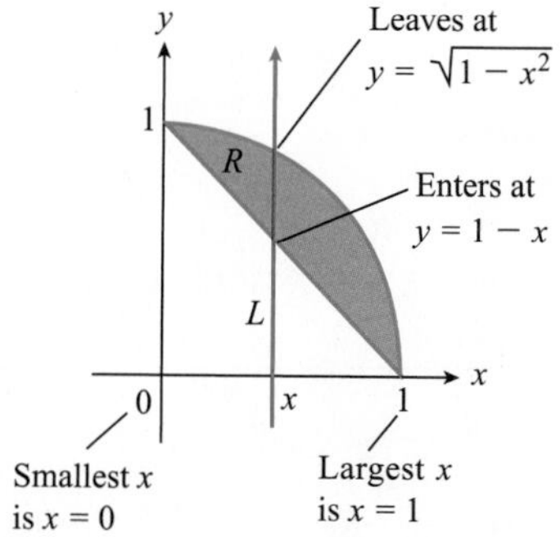

3. *The x-limits of integration.* Choose x-limits that include all the vertical lines through R. The integral is

$$\iint_R f(x, y)\, dA =$$

$$\int_{x=0}^{x=1} \int_{y=1-x}^{y=\sqrt{1-x^2}} f(x, y)\, dy\, dx.$$

B. To evaluate the same double integral as an iterated integral with the order of integration reversed, use horizontal lines instead of vertical lines. The integral is

$$\iint_R f(x, y)\, dA = \int_0^1 \int_{1-y}^{\sqrt{1-y^2}} f(x, y)\, dx\, dy.$$

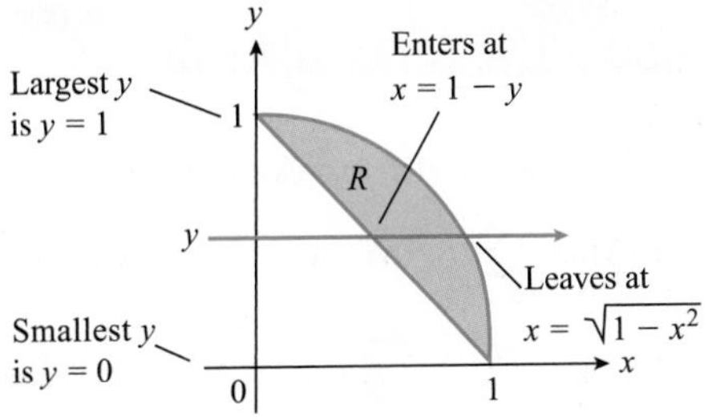

EXAMPLE 4 Reversing Order of Integration

Sketch the region of integration for the integral

$$\int_0^2 \int_{x^2}^{2x} (4x + 2)\, dy\, dx$$

and write an equivalent integral with the order of integration reversed.

SOLUTION

The region of integration is given by the inequalities $x^2 \le y \le 2x$ and $0 \le x \le 2$. It is therefore the region bounded by the curves $y = x^2$ and $y = 2x$ between $x = 0$ and $x = 2$ (Figure 15.14a).

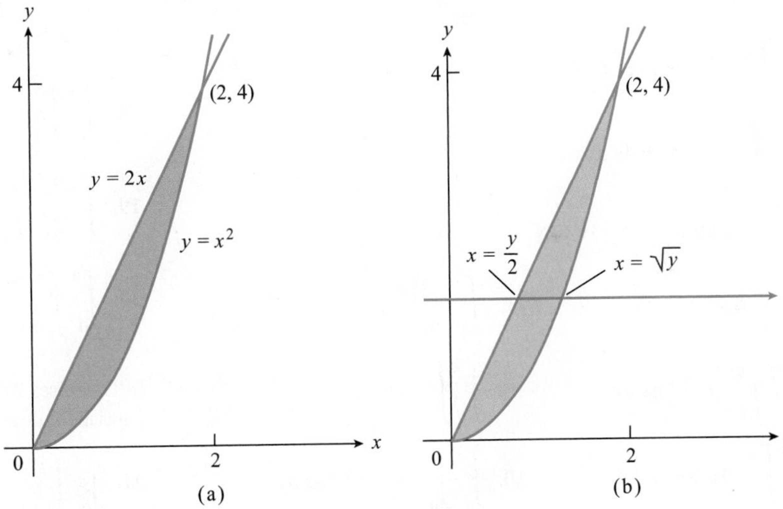

Figure 15.14 Figure for Example 4.

To find limits for integrating in the reverse order, we imagine a horizontal line passing from left to right through the region. It enters at $x = y/2$ and leaves at $x = \sqrt{y}$. To include all such lines, we let y run from $y = 0$ to $y = 4$ (Figure 15.14b). The integral is

$$\int_0^4 \int_{y/2}^{\sqrt{y}} (4x + 2)\, dx\, dy.$$

The common value of these integrals is 8.

Quick Review 15.1

In Exercises 1 and 2, express the limit as a definite integral.

1. $\lim_{\|P\|\to 0} \sum_{k=1}^{n} c_k^3 \, \Delta x_k$, where P is any partition of $[0, 3]$

2. $\lim_{\|P\|\to 0} \sum_{k=1}^{n} \sqrt[3]{2 - c_k^2} \, \Delta x_k$, where P is any partition of $[-1, 1]$

In Exercises 3–8, evaluate the integral.

3. $\int e^{\sin x} \cos x \, dx$

4. $\int \frac{2}{1-x} \, dx$

5. $\int \left(e^x - \frac{5}{x^2}\right) dx$

6. $\int_0^{\pi/4} \sec x \tan x \, dx$

7. $\int_{-2}^{1} (1 + |x|) \, dx$

8. $\int_{-1}^{1} \frac{\sin x}{x} \, dx$

In Exercises 9 and 10, find the volume of the solid.

9. The solid lies between the planes perpendicular to the x-axis at $x = 0$ and $x = 2$. The cross sections perpendicular to the x-axis on the interval $0 \le x \le 2$ are squares whose diagonals run from $y = -\sqrt{x}$ to $y = \sqrt{x}$.

10. The solid lies between planes perpendicular to the x-axis at $x = -2$ and $x = 2$. The cross sections perpendicular to the x-axis are circular disks whose diameters run from the parabola $y = x^2$ to the parabola $y = 8 - x^2$.

Section 15.1 Exercises

In Exercises 1–10, sketch the region of integration and evaluate the integral.

1. $\int_0^3 \int_0^2 (4 - y^2) \, dy \, dx$

2. $\int_0^3 \int_{-2}^0 (x^2 y - 2xy) \, dy \, dx$

3. $\int_{-1}^0 \int_{-1}^1 (x + y + 1) \, dx \, dy$

4. $\int_{\pi}^{2\pi} \int_0^{\pi} (\sin x + \cos y) \, dx \, dy$

5. $\int_0^{\pi} \int_0^{x} x \sin y \, dy \, dx$

6. $\int_0^{\pi} \int_0^{\sin x} y \, dy \, dx$

7. $\int_1^{\ln 8} \int_0^{\ln y} e^{x+y} \, dx \, dy$

8. $\int_1^2 \int_y^{y^2} dx \, dy$

9. $\int_0^1 \int_0^{y^2} 3y^3 e^{xy} \, dx \, dy$

10. $\int_1^4 \int_0^{\sqrt{x}} \frac{3}{2} e^{y/\sqrt{x}} \, dx \, dy$

In Exercises 11–16, integrate f over the given region.

11. $f(x, y) = x/y$ over the region in the first quadrant bounded by the lines $y = x$, $y = 2x$, $x = 1$, $x = 2$

12. $f(x, y) = 1/(xy)$ over the square $1 \le x \le 2$, $1 \le y \le 2$

13. $f(x, y) = x^2 + y^2$ over the triangular region with vertices $(0, 0)$, $(1, 0)$, and $(0, 1)$

14. $f(x, y) = y \cos xy$ over the rectangle $0 \le x \le \pi$, $0 \le y \le 1$

15. $f(u, v) = v - \sqrt{u}$ over the triangular region cut from the first quadrant of the uv-plane by the line $u + v = 1$

16. $f(s, t) = e^s \ln t$ over the region in the first quadrant of the st-plane that lies above the curve $s = \ln t$ from $t = 1$ to $t = 2$

In Exercises 17–20, an integral over a region in a Cartesian coordinate plane is given. Sketch the region and evaluate the integral.

17. $\int_{-2}^0 \int_v^{-v} 2 \, dp \, dv$ (the pv-plane)

18. $\int_0^1 \int_0^{\sqrt{1-s^2}} 8t \, dt \, ds$ (the st-plane)

19. $\int_{-\pi/3}^{\pi/3} \int_0^{\sec t} 3 \cos t \, du \, dt$ (the tu-plane)

20. $\int_0^3 \int_{-2}^{4-2u} \frac{4 - 2u}{v^2} \, dv \, du$ (the uv-plane)

In Exercises 21–30, sketch the region of integration and write an equivalent double integral with the order of integration reversed.

21. $\int_0^1 \int_2^{4-2x} dy \, dx$

22. $\int_0^2 \int_{y-2}^0 dx \, dy$

23. $\int_0^1 \int_y^{\sqrt{y}} dx \, dy$

24. $\int_0^1 \int_{1-x}^{1-x^2} dy \, dx$

25. $\int_0^1 \int_1^{e^x} dy \, dx$

26. $\int_0^{\ln 2} \int_{e^y}^2 dx \, dy$

27. $\int_0^{3/2} \int_0^{9-4x^2} 16x \, dy \, dx$

28. $\int_0^2 \int_0^{4-y^2} y \, dx \, dy$

29. $\int_0^1 \int_{-\sqrt{1-y^2}}^{\sqrt{1-y^2}} 3y \, dx \, dy$

30. $\int_0^2 \int_{-\sqrt{4-x^2}}^{\sqrt{4-x^2}} 6x \, dy \, dx$

In Exercises 31–40, sketch the region of integration, determine an order of integration that will enable you to evaluate the integral analytically, and evaluate the integral.

31. $\int_0^{\pi} \int_x^{\pi} \frac{\sin y}{y}\, dy\, dx$

32. $\int_0^{2} \int_x^{2} 2y^2 \sin xy\, dy\, dx$

33. $\int_0^{1} \int_y^{1} x^2 e^{xy}\, dx\, dy$

34. $\int_0^{2} \int_0^{4-x^2} \frac{xe^{2y}}{4-y}\, dy\, dx$

35. $\int_0^{2\sqrt{\ln 3}} \int_{y/2}^{\sqrt{\ln 3}} e^{x^2}\, dx\, dy$

36. $\int_0^{3} \int_{\sqrt{x/3}}^{1} e^{y^3}\, dy\, dx$

37. $\int_0^{1/16} \int_{y^{1/4}}^{1/2} \cos(16\pi x^5)\, dx\, dy$

38. $\int_0^{8} \int_{\sqrt[3]{x}}^{2} \frac{dy\, dx}{y^4 + 1}$

39. $\iint_R (y - 2x^2)\, dA$, where R is the region inside the square $|x| + |y| = 1$

40. $\iint_R xy\, dA$, where R is the region bounded by the lines $y = x$, $y = 2x$, and $x + y = 2$

In Exercises 41–50, find the volume of the solid.

41. The region that lies under the paraboloid $z = x^2 + y^2$ and above the triangle enclosed by the lines $y = x$, $x = 0$, and $x + y = 2$ in the xy-plane

42. The solid that is bounded above by the cylinder $z = x^2$ and below by the region enclosed by the parabola $y = 2 - x^2$ and the line $y = x$ in the xy-plane

43. The solid whose base is the region in the xy-plane that is bounded by the parabola $y = 4 - x^2$ and the line $y = 3x$, while the top of the solid is bounded by the plane $z = x + 4$

44. The solid in the first octant bounded by the coordinate planes, the cylinder $x^2 + y^2 = 4$, and the plane $z + y = 3$

45. The solid in the first octant bounded by the coordinate planes, the plane $x = 3$, and the parabolic cylinder $z = 4 - y^2$

46. The solid cut from the first octant by the surface $z = 4 - x^2 - y$

47. The wedge cut from the first octant by the cylinder $z = 12 - 3y^2$ and the plane $x + y = 2$

48. The solid cut from the square column $|x| + |y| \le 1$ by the planes $z = 0$ and $3x + z = 3$

49. The solid that is bounded on the front and back by the planes $x = 2$ and $x = 1$, on the sides by the cylinders $y = \pm 1/x$, and above by the planes $z = x + 1$ and $z = 0$

50. The solid that is bounded on the front and back by the planes $x = \pm\pi/3$, on the sides by the cylinders $y = \pm\sec x$, above by the cylinder $z = 1 + y^2$, and below by the xy-plane

In Exercises 51–54, *work in groups of two or three* to evaluate the improper integrals as iterated integrals.

51. $\int_1^{\infty} \int_{e^{-x}}^{1} \frac{1}{x^3 y}\, dy\, dx$

52. $\int_{-1}^{1} \int_{-1/\sqrt{1-x^2}}^{1/\sqrt{1-x^2}} (2y + 1)\, dy\, dx$

53. $\int_{-\infty}^{\infty} \int_{-\infty}^{\infty} \frac{1}{(x^2 + 1)(y^2 + 1)}\, dx\, dy$

54. $\int_0^{\infty} \int_0^{\infty} xe^{-(x+2y)}\, dx\, dy$

Explorations

In Exercises 55 and 56, approximate the double integral of $f(x, y)$ over the region R partitioned by the given vertical lines $x = a$ and horizontal lines $y = c$. In each subrectangle, use (x_k, y_k) as indicated for your approximation.

$$\iint_R f(x, y)\, dA \approx \sum_{k=1}^{n} f(x_k, y_k)\, \Delta A_k$$

55. $f(x, y) = x + y$ over the region R bounded above by the semicircle $y = \sqrt{1 - x^2}$ and below by the x-axis, using the partition $x = -1, -1/2, 0, 1/4, 1/2, 1$ and $y = 0, 1/2, 1$ with (x_k, y_k) the lower left corner in the kth subrectangle

56. $f(x, y) = x + 2y$ over the region R inside the circle $(x - 2)^2 + (y - 3)^2 = 1$ using the partition $x = 1, 3/2, 2, 5/2, 3$ and $y = 2, 5/2, 3, 7/2, 4$ with (x_k, y_k) the center (centroid) in the kth subrectangle

57. Integrate $f(x, y) = \sqrt{4 - x^2}$ over the smaller sector cut from the disk $x^2 + y^2 \le 4$ by the rays $\theta = \pi/6$ and $\theta = \pi/2$.

58. Integrate $f(x, y) = 1/[(x^2 - x)(y - 1)^{2/3}]$ over the infinite rectangle $2 \le x < \infty$, $0 \le y \le 2$

59. A solid right (noncircular) cylinder has its base R in the xy-plane and is bounded above by the paraboloid $z = x^2 + y^2$. The cylinder's volume is

$$V = \int_0^1 \int_0^y (x^2 + y^2)\, dx\, dy + \int_1^2 \int_0^{2-y} (x^2 + y^2)\, dx\, dy$$

Sketch the base region R and express the cylinder's volume as a single iterated integral with the order of integration reversed. Then evaluate the integral to find the volume.

60. Evaluate the integral

$$\int_0^2 (\tan^{-1} \pi x - \tan^{-1} x)\, dx.$$

(*Hint*: Write the integrand as an integral.)

61. Writing to Learn What region R in the xy-plane maximizes the value of

$$\iint_R (4 - x^2 - 2y^2)\, dA?$$

Give reasons for your answer.

62. Writing to Learn What region R in the xy-plane minimizes the value of

$$\iint_R (x^2 + y^2 - 9)\, dA?$$

Give reasons for your answer.

63. Writing to Learn Is it all right to evaluate the integral of a continuous function $f(x, y)$ over a rectangular region in the xy-plane and get different answers depending on the order of integration? Give reasons for your answer.

64. Writing to Learn How would you evaluate the double integral of a continuous function $f(x, y)$ over the region R in the xy-plane enclosed by the triangle with vertices (0, 1), (2, 0), and (1, 2)? Give reasons for your answer.

Extending the Ideas

65. Prove that

$$\int_{-\infty}^{\infty}\int_{-\infty}^{\infty} e^{-x^2-y^2}\,dx\,dy = \lim_{b\to\infty}\int_{-b}^{b}\int_{-b}^{b} e^{-x^2-y^2}\,dx\,dy = 4\left(\int_0^{\infty} e^{-x^2}\,dx\right)^2.$$

66. Evaluate the improper integral

$$\int_0^1\int_0^3 \frac{x^2}{(y-1)^{2/3}}\,dy\,dx.$$

CAS Explorations

In Exercises 67–70, evaluate the integrals.

67. $\displaystyle\int_1^3\int_1^x \frac{1}{xy}\,dy\,dx$

68. $\displaystyle\int_0^1\int_0^1 e^{-(x^2+y^2)}\,dy\,dx$

69. $\displaystyle\int_0^1\int_0^1 \tan^{-1} xy\,dy\,dx$

70. $\displaystyle\int_{-1}^1\int_0^{\sqrt{1-x^2}} 3\sqrt{1-x^2-y^2}\,dy\,dx$

15.2 Areas, Moments, and Centers of Mass

What you'll learn about

- Areas of Bounded Regions in the Plane
- Average Value
- First and Second Moments and Centers of Mass
- Centroids of Geometric Figures

Areas of Bounded Regions in the Plane

If we take $f(x, y) = 1$ in the definition of the double integral over a region R in the preceding section, the partial sums reduce to

$$S_n = \sum_{k=1}^{n} f(x_k, y_k)\,\Delta A_k = \sum_{k=1}^{n} \Delta A_k. \tag{1}$$

This approximates what we would like to call the area of R. As Δx and Δy approach zero, the coverage of R by the ΔA_k's (Figure 15.15) becomes increasingly complete, and we define the *area of R* to be the limit

$$\text{Area} = \lim_{n\to\infty}\sum_{k=1}^{n}\Delta A_k = \iint_R dA. \tag{2}$$

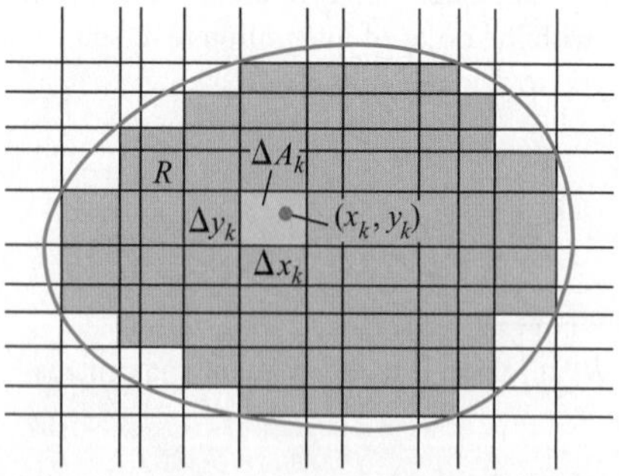

Figure 15.15 The first step in defining the area of a region is to partition the interior of the region into cells.

DEFINITION Area

The **area** of a closed, bounded plane region R is

$$A = \iint_R dA. \tag{3}$$

As with the other definitions in this chapter, the definition here applies to a greater variety of regions than does the earlier single-variable definition of area, but it agrees with the earlier definition on regions to which they both apply.

To evaluate the integral in (3), we integrate the constant function $f(x, y) = 1$ over R.

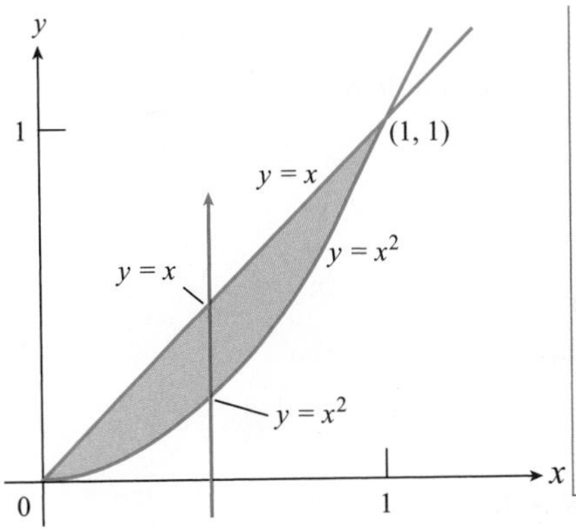

Figure 15.16 The area of the region between the parabola and the line in Example 1 is $\int_0^1 \int_{x^2}^{x} dy\, dx$.

EXAMPLE 1 Finding Area

Find the area of the region R bounded by $y = x$ and $y = x^2$ in the first quadrant.

SOLUTION

We sketch the region (Figure 15.16) and calculate the area as

$$A = \int_0^1 \int_{x^2}^{x} dy\, dx = \int_0^1 [y]_{x^2}^{x}\, dx = \int_0^1 (x - x^2)\, dx$$

$$= \left[\frac{x^2}{2} - \frac{x^3}{3}\right]_0^1 = \frac{1}{6} \text{ square units}$$

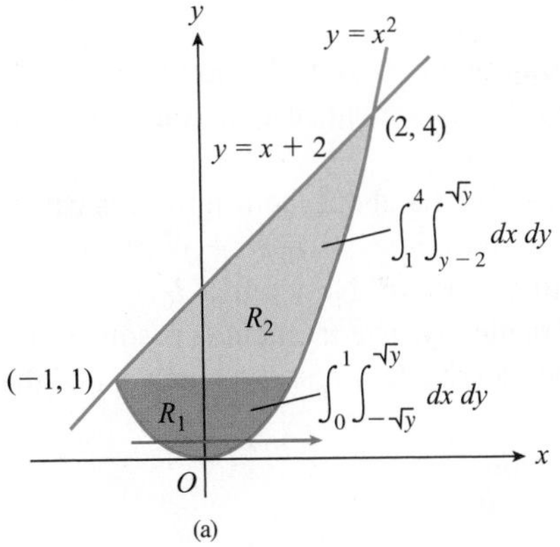

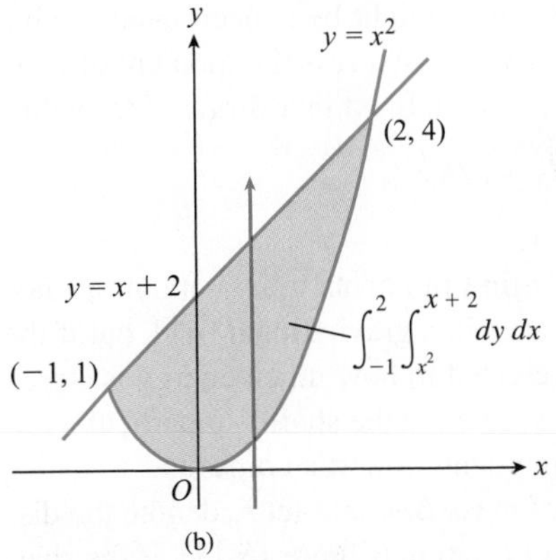

Figure 15.17 Calculating the area takes (a) two double integrals if the first integration is with respect to x, but (b) only one if the first integration is with respect to y. (Example 2)

EXAMPLE 2 Finding Area

Find the area of the region R enclosed by the parabola $y = x^2$ and the line $y = x + 2$.

SOLUTION

If we divide R into the regions R_1 and R_2 shown in Figure 15.17a, we may calculate the area as

$$A = \iint_{R_1} dA + \iint_{R_2} dA = \int_0^1 \int_{-\sqrt{y}}^{\sqrt{y}} dx\, dy + \int_1^4 \int_{y-2}^{\sqrt{y}} dx\, dy.$$

On the other hand, reversing the order of integration (Figure 15.17b) gives

$$A = \int_{-1}^{2} \int_{x^2}^{x+2} dy\, dx.$$

This result is simpler and is the only one we would bother to write down in practice. The area is

$$A = \int_{-1}^{2} [y]_{x^2}^{x+2}\, dx = \int_{-1}^{2} (x + 2 - x^2)\, dx$$

$$= \left[\frac{x^2}{2} + 2x - \frac{x^3}{3}\right]_{-1}^{2} = \frac{9}{2} \text{ square units.}$$

Average Value

The average value of an integrable function of a single variable on a closed interval is the integral of the function over the interval divided by the length of the interval. For an integrable function of two variables defined on a closed and bounded region that has measurable area, the *average value* is the integral over the region divided by the area of the region. If f is the function and R the region, then

$$\textbf{Average value} \text{ of } f \text{ over } R = \frac{1}{\text{area of } R} \iint_R f\, dA. \tag{4}$$

If f is the area density of a thin plate covering R, then the double integral of f over R divided by the area of R is the plate's **average density** in units of mass per unit area. If $f(x, y)$ is the distance from the point (x, y) to a fixed point P, then the average value of f over R is the **average distance** of points in R from P.

EXAMPLE 3 Finding Average Value

Find the average value of $f(x, y) = x \cos xy$ over the rectangle R: $0 \le x \le \pi$, $0 \le y \le 1$.

SOLUTION

The value of the integral of f over R is

$$\int_0^{\pi}\int_0^1 x \cos xy \, dy \, dx = \int_0^{p} \Big[\sin xy\Big]_{y=0}^{y=1} dx$$

$$= \int_0^{\pi} (\sin x - 0)\, dx = -\cos x\Big]_0^{\pi} = 1 + 1 = 2.$$

The area of R is π. The average value of f over R is $2/\pi$.

Global Warming

The "global warming" controversy deals with whether the average air temperature over the surface of Earth is increasing.

First and Second Moments and Centers of Mass

To find the moments and centers of mass of thin sheets and plates, we use formulas. With double integrals, we can accommodate a greater variety of shapes and density functions. The formulas are given in Table 15.1. The examples that follow show how the formulas are used.

The mathematical difference between the **first moments** M_x and M_y and the **moments of inertia**, or **second moments**, I_x and I_y is that the second moments use the *squares* of the "lever-arm" distances x and y.

The moment I_0 is also called the **polar moment** of inertia about the origin. It is calculated by integrating the density $\delta(x, y)$ (mass per unit area) times $r^2 = x^2 + y^2$, the square of the distance from a representative point (x, y) to the origin. Notice that $I_0 = I_x + I_y$; once we find any two of these, we get the third automatically. The moment I_0 is sometimes called I_z, for moment of inertia about the z-axis. The identity $I_z = I_x + I_y$ is then called the **Perpendicular Axis Theorem**.

The **radius of gyration** R_x is defined by the equation

$$I_x = MR_x^2.$$

It tells how far from the x-axis the entire mass of the plate might be concentrated to give the same I_x. The radius of gyration gives a convenient way to express the moment of inertia in terms of a mass and a length. The radii R_y and R_0 are defined in a similar way, with

$$I_y = MR_y^2 \quad \text{and} \quad I_0 = MR_0^2.$$

We take square roots to get the formulas in Table 15.1.

Why the interest in moments of inertia? A body's first moments tell us about balance and about the torque the body exerts about different axes in a gravitational field, but if the body is a rotating shaft, we are more likely to be interested in how much energy is stored in the shaft or about how much energy it will take to accelerate the shaft to a particular angular velocity. This is where the second moment or moment of inertia comes in.

Think of partitioning the shaft into small blocks of mass Δm_k and let r_k denote the distance from the kth block's center of mass to the axis of rotation (Figure 15.18). If the shaft rotates at an angular velocity of $\omega = d\theta/dt$ radians per second, the block's center of mass will trace its orbit at a linear speed of

$$v_k = \frac{d}{dt}(r_k\theta) = r_k\frac{d\theta}{dt} = r_k\omega. \tag{5}$$

The block's kinetic energy will be approximately

$$\frac{1}{2}\Delta m_k v_k^2 = \frac{1}{2}\Delta m_k (r_k\omega)^2 = \frac{1}{2}\omega^2 r_k^2 \, \Delta m_k. \tag{6}$$

Table 15.1 Mass and Moment Formulas for Thin Plates Covering Regions in the *xy*-Plane

Density: $\delta(x, y)$

Mass: $M = \iint \delta(x, y)\, dA$

First moments: $M_x = \iint y\delta(x, y)\, dA, \qquad M_y = \iint x\delta(x, y)\, dA$

Center of mass: $\bar{x} = \dfrac{M_y}{M}, \qquad \bar{y} = \dfrac{M_x}{M}$

Moments of inertia (second moments):

About the x-axis: $I_x = \iint y^2\delta(x, y)\, dA$

About the y-axis: $I_y = \iint x^2\delta(x, y)\, dA$

About the origin **(polar moment):**

$$I_0 = \iint (x^2 + y^2)\delta(x, y)\, dA = I_x + I_y$$

About a line L: $I_L = \iint r^2(x, y)\delta(x, y)\, dA,$ where $r(x, y) =$ distance from (x, y) to L

Radii of gyration:

About the x-axis: $R_x = \sqrt{I_x/M}$

About the y-axis: $R_y = \sqrt{I_y/M}$

About the origin: $R_0 = \sqrt{I_0/M}$

The kinetic energy of the shaft will be approximately

$$\sum \frac{1}{2}\,\omega^2 r_k{}^2\, \Delta m_k. \tag{7}$$

The integral approached by these sums as the shaft is partitioned into smaller and smaller blocks gives the shaft's kinetic energy:

$$\mathrm{KE}_{\text{shaft}} = \int \frac{1}{2}\,\omega^2 r^2\, dm = \frac{1}{2}\,\omega^2 \int r^2\, dm. \tag{8}$$

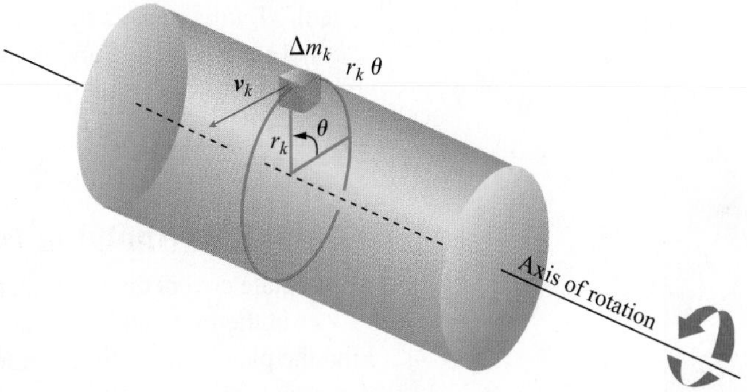

Figure 15.18 To find an integral for the amount of energy stored in a rotating shaft, we first imagine the shaft to be partitioned into small blocks. Each block has its own kinetic energy. We add the contributions of the individual blocks to find the kinetic energy of the shaft.

The factor

$$I = \int r^2\, dm \tag{9}$$

is the moment of inertia of the shaft about its axis of rotation, and we see from Equation (8) that the shaft's kinetic energy is

$$\mathrm{KE}_{\text{shaft}} = \frac{1}{2} I\omega^2. \tag{10}$$

To start a shaft of inertial moment I rotating at an angular velocity ω, we need to provide a kinetic energy of $\mathrm{KE} = (1/2)I\omega^2$. To stop the shaft, we have to take this amount of energy back out. To start a locomotive with mass m and accelerate it to a linear velocity v, we need to provide a kinetic energy of $\mathrm{KE} = (1/2)mv^2$. To stop the locomotive, we have to remove this amount of energy. The shaft's moment of inertia is analogous to the locomotive's mass. What makes the locomotive hard to start or stop is its mass. What makes the shaft hard to start or stop is its moment of inertia. The moment of inertia takes into account not only the mass but also its distribution.

The moment of inertia also plays a role in determining how much a horizontal metal beam will bend under a load. The stiffness of the beam is a constant times I, the polar moment of inertia of a typical cross section of the beam perpendicular to the beam's longitudinal axis. The greater the value of I, the stiffer the beam and the less it will bend under a given load. This is why we use I beams instead of beams whose cross sections are square. The flanges at the top and bottom of the beam hold most of the beam's mass away from the longitudinal axis to maximize the value of I (Figure 15.19).

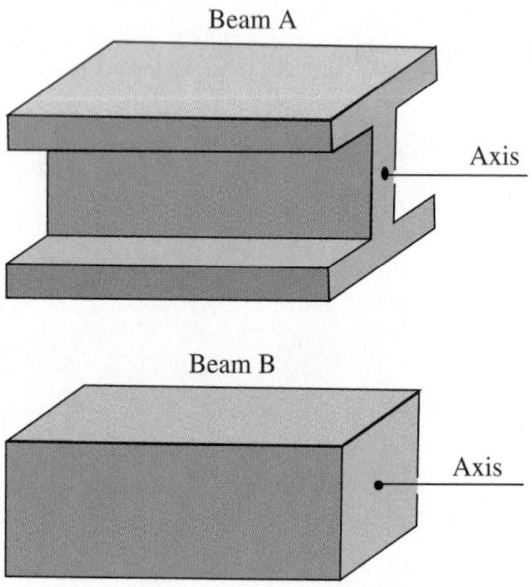

Figure 15.19 The greater the polar moment of inertia of the cross section of a beam about the beam's longitudinal axis, the stiffer the beam. Beams A and B have the same cross-section area, but A is stiffer.

EXPLORATION 1 Seeing Moment of Inertia at Work

If you want to see the moment of inertia at work, try the following experiment.

1. Tape two coins to the ends of a pencil and twiddle the pencil about the center of mass. The moment of inertia accounts for the resistance you feel each time you change the direction of motion.
2. Now move the coins an equal distance toward the center of mass and twiddle the pencil again. The system has the same mass and the same center of mass but now offers less resistance to the changes in motion. The moment of inertia has been reduced.

The moment of inertia is what gives a baseball bat, golf club, or tennis racket its "feel." Tennis rackets that weigh the same, look the same, and have identical centers of mass will feel and behave differently if their masses are not distributed the same way.

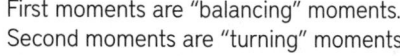

First moments are "balancing" moments. Second moments are "turning" moments.

EXAMPLE 4 Applying Formulas from Table 15.1

A thin plate covers the triangular region bounded by the x-axis and the lines $x = 1$ and $y = 2x$ in the first quadrant. The plate's density at the point (x, y) is $\delta(x, y) = 6x + 6y + 6$. Find the plate's mass, first moments, center of mass, moments of inertia, and radii of gyration about the coordinate axes.

SOLUTION

We sketch the plate and put in enough detail to determine the limits of integration for the integrals we have to evaluate (Figure 15.20).

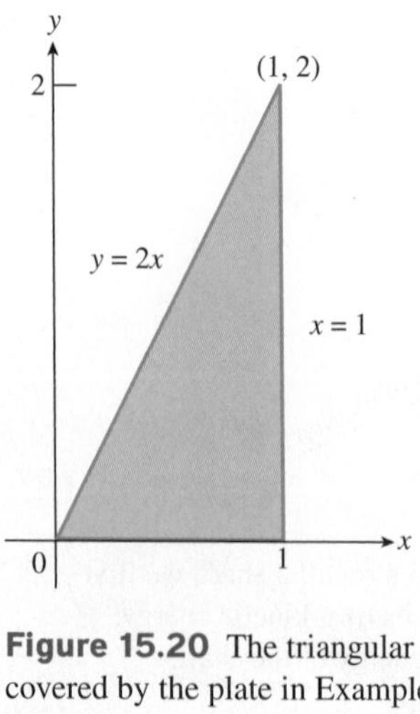

Figure 15.20 The triangular region covered by the plate in Example 4.

The plate's mass is

$$M = \int_0^1 \int_0^{2x} \delta(x, y)\, dy\, dx = \int_0^1 \int_0^{2x} (6x + 6y + 6)\, dy\, dx$$

$$= \int_0^1 \left[6xy + 3y^2 + 6y\right]_{y=0}^{y=2x} dx$$

$$= \int_0^1 (24x^2 + 12x)\, dx = \left[8x^3 + 6x^2\right]_0^1 = 14.$$

The first moment about the x-axis is

$$M_x = \int_0^1 \int_0^{2x} y\delta(x, y)\, dy\, dx = \int_0^1 \int_0^{2x} (6xy + 6y^2 + 6y)\, dy\, dx$$

$$= \int_0^1 \left[3xy^2 + 2y^3 + 3y^2\right]_{y=0}^{y=2x} dx = \int_0^1 (28x^3 + 12x^2)\, dx$$

$$= \left[7x^4 + 4x^3\right]_0^1 = 11.$$

A similar calculation gives

$$M_y = \int_0^1 \int_0^{2x} x\delta(x, y)\, dy\, dx = 10.$$

The coordinates of the center of mass are therefore

$$\bar{x} = \frac{M_y}{M} = \frac{10}{14} = \frac{5}{7}, \qquad \bar{y} = \frac{M_x}{M} = \frac{11}{14}.$$

The moment of inertia about the x-axis is

$$I_x = \int_0^1 \int_0^{2x} y^2\delta(x, y)\, dy\, dx = \int_0^1 \int_0^{2x} (6xy^2 + 6y^3 + 6y^2)\, dy\, dx$$

$$= \int_0^1 \left[2xy^3 + \frac{3}{2}y^4 + 2y^3\right]_{y=0}^{y=2x} dx = \int_0^1 (40x^4 + 16x^3)\, dx$$

$$= \left[8x^5 + 4x^4\right]_0^1 = 12.$$

Similarly, the moment of inertia about the y-axis is

$$I_y = \int_0^1 \int_0^{2x} x^2\delta(x, y)\, dy\, dx = \frac{39}{5}.$$

Since we know I_x and I_y, we do not need to evaluate an integral to find I_0; we can use the equation $I_0 = I_x + I_y$ instead:

$$I_0 = 12 + \frac{39}{5} = \frac{99}{5}.$$

The three radii of gyration are

$$R_x = \sqrt{I_x/M} = \sqrt{12/14} = \sqrt{6/7} \approx 0.93,$$

$$R_y = \sqrt{I_y/M} = \sqrt{\left(\frac{39}{5}\right)/14} = \sqrt{39/70} \approx 0.75,$$

$$R_0 = \sqrt{I_0/M} = \sqrt{\left(\frac{99}{5}\right)/14} = \sqrt{99/70} \approx 1.19.$$

Centroids of Geometric Figures

When the density of an object is constant, it cancels out of the numerator and denominator of the formulas for $\bar{x}$ and $\bar{y}$. As far as $\bar{x}$ and $\bar{y}$ are concerned, δ might as well be 1. Thus, when δ is constant, the location of the center of mass becomes a feature of the object's shape and not of the material of which it is made. In such cases, engineers may call the center of mass the **centroid** of the shape. To find a centroid, we set δ equal to 1 and proceed to find $\bar{x}$ and $\bar{y}$ as before, by dividing first moments by masses.

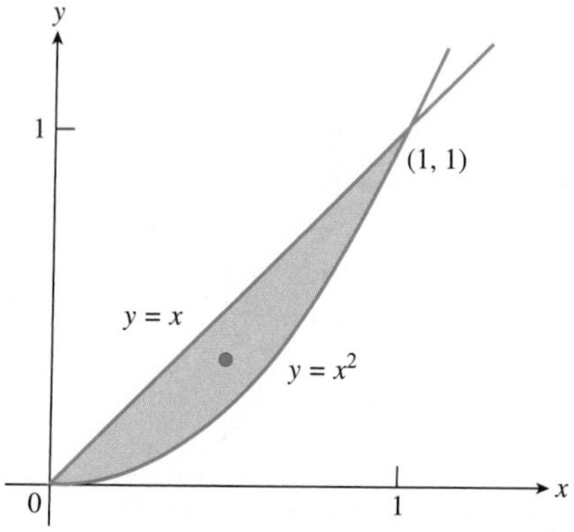

Figure 15.21 Example 5 finds the centroid of the region shown here.

EXAMPLE 5 Finding the Centroid of a Region

Find the centroid of the region in the first quadrant that is bounded above by the line $y = x$ and below by the parabola $y = x^2$.

SOLUTION

We sketch the region and include enough detail to determine the limits of integration (Figure 15.21.). We then set δ equal to 1 and evaluate the appropriate formulas from Table 15.1:

$$M = \int_0^1 \int_{x^2}^{x} dy\, dx = \int_0^1 [y]_{y=x^2}^{y=x}\, dx = \int_0^1 (x - x^2)\, dx$$

$$= \left[\frac{x^2}{2} - \frac{x^3}{3}\right]_0^1 = \frac{1}{6},$$

$$M_x = \int_0^1 \int_{x^2}^{x} y\, dy\, dx = \int_0^1 \left[\frac{y^2}{2}\right]_{y=x^2}^{y=x} dx$$

$$= \int_0^1 \left(\frac{x^2}{2} - \frac{x^4}{2}\right) dx = \left[\frac{x^3}{6} - \frac{x^5}{10}\right]_0^1 = \frac{1}{15},$$

$$M_y = \int_0^1 \int_{x^2}^{x} x\, dy\, dx = \int_0^1 [xy]_{y=x^2}^{y=x}\, dx$$

$$= \int_0^1 (x^2 - x^3)\, dx = \left[\frac{x^3}{3} - \frac{x^4}{4}\right]_0^1 = \frac{1}{12}.$$

From these values of M, M_x, and M_y, we find

$$\bar{x} = \frac{M_y}{M} = \frac{1/12}{1/6} = \frac{1}{2} \quad \text{and} \quad \bar{y} = \frac{M_x}{M} = \frac{1/15}{1/6} = \frac{2}{5}.$$

The centroid is the point $\left(\frac{1}{2}, \frac{2}{5}\right)$.

Quick Review 15.2

In Exercises 1 and 2, find the area of the region between the x-axis and the graph of the given function over the given interval.

1. $y = e^x$ over $[0, 1]$

2. $y = \cos x$ over $[0, \pi/2]$

In Exercises 3 and 4, consider the region between the curve $y = 2 - x^2$ and the line $y = -2$.

3. Find the area of the region by integrating with respect to x.

4. Find the area of the region by integrating with respect to y.

5. Find the average value of $f(x) = \sin x$ on $[0, \pi]$.

6. Find the area of the region enclosed by $y = x^2 - 3$ and $y = 1$.

Suppose we have a finite collection of masses in the coordinate plane, the mass m_k located at the point (x_k, y_k) as shown in the figure.

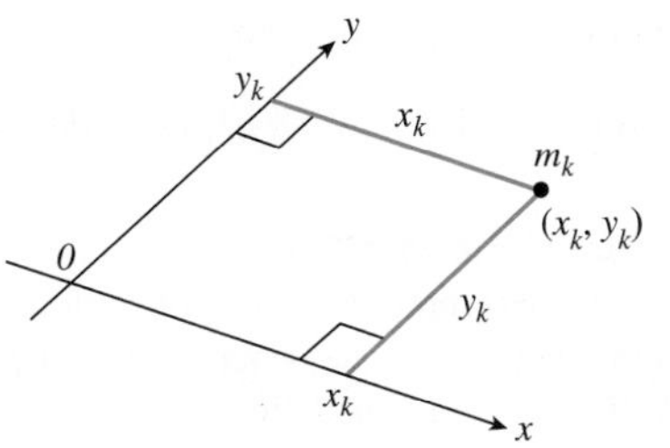

Each mass m_k has **moment $m_k y_k$ about the x-axis** and **moment $m_k x_k$ about the y-axis.** The moments of the entire system about the coordinate axes are

$$\text{Moment about } x\text{-axis:} \quad M_x = \sum m_k y_k,$$

$$\text{Moment about } y\text{-axis:} \quad M_y = \sum m_k x_k.$$

The **center of mass** is $(\bar{x}, \bar{y})$, where

$$\bar{x} = \frac{M_y}{M} = \frac{\sum m_k x_k}{\sum m_k} \quad \text{and} \quad \bar{y} = \frac{M_x}{M} = \frac{\sum m_k y_k}{\sum m_k}.$$

Suppose we have a thin, flat plate occupying a region in the plane.

7. Imagine the region cut into thin strips parallel to the y-axis. Show that

$$\bar{x} = \frac{\int x\, dm}{\int dm},$$

where $dm = \delta\, dA$, δ = density (mass per unit area), and A = area of the region.

8. Imagine the region cut into thin strips parallel to the x-axis. Show that

$$\bar{y} = \frac{\int y\, dm}{\int dm},$$

where $dm = \delta\, dA$, δ = density, and A = area of the region.

In Exercises 9 and 10, use the results of Exercises 7 and 8 to find the center of mass of the region with given density.

9. The region bounded by the parabola $y = x^2$ and the line $y = 4$ with constant density δ

10. The region bounded by the lines $y = x$, $y = -x$, $x = 2$ with constant density δ

Section 15.2 Exercises

In Exercises 1–8, sketch the region bounded by the given lines and curves. Then express the region's area as an iterated double integral and evaluate the integral.

1. The coordinate axes and the line $x + y = 2$

2. The lines $x = 0$, $y = 2x$, and $y = 4$

3. The parabola $x = -y^2$ and the line $y = x + 2$

4. The parabola $x = y - y^2$ and the line $y = -x$

5. The curve $y = e^x$ and the lines $y = 0$, $x = 0$, and $x = \ln 2$

6. The curves $y = \ln x$ and $y = 2 \ln x$ and the line $x = e$, in the first quadrant

7. The parabolas $x = y^2$ and $x = 2y - y^2$

8. The parabolas $x = y^2 - 1$ and $x = 2y^2 - 2$

In Exercises 9–14, the integral or sum of integrals gives the area of a region in the xy-plane. Sketch each region, label each bounding curve with its equation, and give the coordinates of the points where the curves intersect. Then find the area of the region.

9. $\displaystyle\int_0^6 \int_{y^2/3}^{2y} dx\, dy$

10. $\displaystyle\int_0^3 \int_{-x}^{x(2-x)} dy\, dx$

11. $\displaystyle\int_0^{\pi/4} \int_{\sin x}^{\cos x} dy\, dx$

12. $\displaystyle\int_{-1}^2 \int_{y^2}^{y+2} dx\, dy$

13. $\displaystyle\int_{-1}^0 \int_{-2x}^{1-x} dy\, dx + \int_0^2 \int_{-x/2}^{1-x} dy\, dx$

14. $\displaystyle\int_0^2 \int_{x^2-4}^{0} dy\, dx + \int_0^4 \int_0^{\sqrt{x}} dy\, dx$

15. Find the average value of $f(x, y) = \sin(x + y)$ over

(a) the rectangle $0 \le x \le \pi$, $0 \le y \le \pi$.

(b) the rectangle $0 \le x \le \pi$, $0 \le y \le \pi/2$.

16. Which do you think will be larger, the average value of $f(x, y) = xy$ over the square $0 \le x \le 1$, $0 \le y \le 1$, or the average value of f over the quarter circle $x^2 + y^2 \le 1$ in the first quadrant? Calculate them to find out.

17. Find the average height of the paraboloid $z = x^2 + y^2$ over the square $0 \le x \le 2$, $0 \le y \le 2$.

18. Find the **average value** of $f(x, y) = 1/(xy)$ over the square $\ln 2 \le x \le 2 \ln 2$, $\ln 2 \le y \le 2 \ln 2$.

In Exercises 19–30, the density of the region is constant.

19. Find the center of mass of a thin plate of density $\delta = 3$ bounded by the lines $x = 0$, $y = x$, and the parabola $y = 2 - x^2$ in the first quadrant.

20. Find the moments of inertia and radii of gyration about the coordinate axes of a thin rectangular plate of constant density δ bounded by the lines $x = 3$ and $y = 3$ in the first quadrant.

21. Find the centroid of the region in the first quadrant bounded by the x-axis, the parabola $y^2 = 2x$, and the line $x + y = 4$.

22. Find the centroid of the triangular region cut from the first quadrant by the line $x + y = 3$.

23. Find the centroid of the semicircular region bounded by the x-axis and the curve $y = \sqrt{1 - x^2}$.

24. The area of the region in the first quadrant bounded by the parabola $y = 6x - x^2$ and the line $y = x$ is 125/6 square units. Find the centroid.

25. Find the centroid of the region cut from the first quadrant by the circle $x^2 + y^2 = a^2$.

26. Find the moment of inertia about the x-axis of a thin plate of density $\delta = 1$ bounded by the circle $x^2 + y^2 = 4$. Then use your result to find I_y and I_0 for the plate.

27. Find the centroid of the region between the x-axis and the arch $y = \sin x$, $0 \le x \le \pi$.

28. Find the moment of inertia with respect to the y-axis of a thin sheet of constant density $\delta = 1$ bounded by the curve $y = (\sin^2 x)/x^2$ and the interval $\pi \le x \le 2\pi$ of the x-axis.

29. ***Centroid of an Infinite Region*** Find the centroid of the infinite region in the second quadrant enclosed by the coordinate axes and the curve $y = e^x$. (Use improper integrals in the mass-moment formulas.)

30. ***First Moment of an Infinite Plate*** Find the first moment about the y-axis of a thin plate of density $\delta(x, y) = 1$ covering the infinite region under the curve $y = e^{-x^2/2}$ in the first quadrant.

In Exercises 31–40, the density of the region varies throughout the region.

31. Find the moment of inertia and radius of gyration about the x-axis of a thin plate bounded by the parabola $x = y - y^2$ and the line $x + y = 0$ if $\delta(x, y) = x + y$.

32. Find the mass of a thin plate occupying the smaller region cut from the ellipse $x^2 + 4y^2 = 12$ by the parabola $x = 4y^2$ if $\delta(x, y) = 5x$.

33. Find the center of mass of a thin triangular plate bounded by the y-axis and the lines $y = x$ and $y = 2 - x$ if $\delta(x, y) = 6x + 3y + 3$.

34. Find the center of mass and moment of inertia about the x-axis of a thin plate bounded by the curves $x = y^2$ and $x = 2y - y^2$ if the density at the point (x, y) is $\delta(x, y) = y + 1$.

35. Find the center of mass and moment of inertia and radius of gyration about the y-axis of a thin rectangular plate cut from the first quadrant by the lines $x = 6$ and $y = 1$ if $\delta(x, y) = x + y + 1$.

36. Find the center of mass and the moment of inertia and radius of gyration about the y-axis of a thin plate bounded by the line $y = 1$ and the parabola $y = x^2$ if the density is $\delta(x, y) = y + 1$.

37. Find the center of mass and the moment of inertia and radius of gyration about the y-axis of a thin plate bounded by the x-axis, the lines $x = \pm 1$, and the parabola $y = x^2$ if $\delta(x, y) = 7y + 1$.

38. Find the center of mass and the moment of inertia and radius of gyration about the x-axis of a thin rectangular plate bounded by the lines $x = 0$, $x = 20$, $y = -1$, and $y = 1$ if $\delta(x, y) = 1 + (x/20)$.

39. Find the center of mass, the moments of inertia and radii of gyration about the coordinate axes, and the polar moment of inertia and radius of gyration of a thin triangular plate bounded by the lines $y = x$, $y = -x$, and $y = 1$ if $\delta(x, y) = y + 1$.

40. Repeat Exercise 39 for $\delta(x, y) = 3x^2 + 1$.

In Exercises 41 and 42, *work in groups of two or three* to solve the problem.

41. ***Number of Bacteria in a Rectangle*** If $f(x, y) = (10{,}000e^y)/(1 + |x|/2)$ represents the "population density" of a certain bacteria on the xy-plane, where x and y are measured in centimeters, find the total population of bacteria within the rectangle $-5 \le x \le 5$ and $-2 \le y \le 0$.

42. ***Number of People in a Region*** If $f(x, y) = 100(y + 1)$ represents the population density of a planar region on Earth, where x and y are measured in miles, find the number of people in the region bounded by the curves $x = y^2$ and $x = 2y - y^2$.

Explorations

43. ***Appliance Design*** When we design an appliance, one of the concerns is how difficult the appliance will be to tip over. When tipped, it will right itself as long as its center of mass lies on the correct side of the *fulcrum,* the point on which the appliance is riding as it tips. Suppose the profile of an appliance of approximate constant density is parabolic, like an old-fashioned radio. It fills the region $0 \le y \le a(1 - x^2)$, $-1 \le x \le 1$, in the xy-plane (Figure 15.22). What values of a will guarantee that the appliance will have to be tipped more than 45° to fall over?

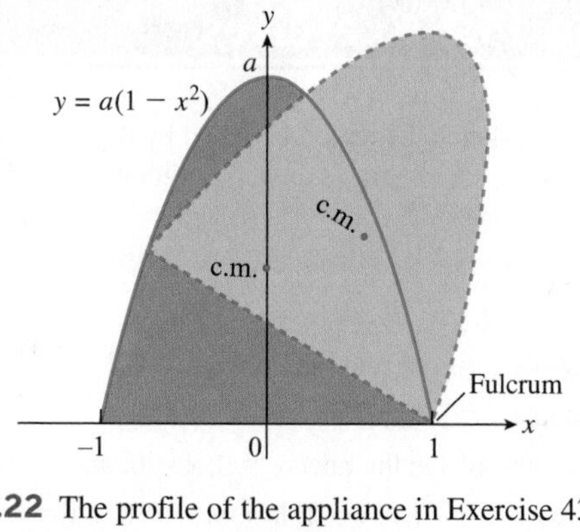

Figure 15.22 The profile of the appliance in Exercise 43.

44. ***Minimizing a Moment of Inertia*** A rectangular plate of constant density $\delta(x, y) = 1$ occupies the region bounded by the lines $x = 4$ and $y = 2$ in the first quadrant. The moment of inertia I_a of the rectangle about the line $y = a$ is given by the integral

$$I_0 = \int_0^4 \int_0^2 (y - a)^2 \, dy \, dx.$$

Find the value of a that minimizes I_a.

45. ***Centroid of an Infinite Region*** Find the centroid of the infinite region in the xy-plane bounded by the curves $y = 1/\sqrt{1 - x^2}$, $y = -1/\sqrt{1 - x^2}$, and the lines $x = 0$, $x = 1$.

46. ***Radii of Gyration*** Find the radius of gyration of a slender rod of constant linear density δ gm/cm and length L cm with respect to an axis

(a) through the rod's center of mass perpendicular to the rod's axis.

(b) perpendicular to the rod's axis at one end of the rod.

47. A thin plate of constant density δ occupies the region R in the xy-plane bounded by the curves $x = y^2$ and $x = 2y - y^2$ (see Exercise 34).

(a) Find δ such that the plate has the same mass as the plate in Exercise 34.

(b) ***Average Density*** Compare the value of δ found in part (a) with the average value of $\delta(x, y) = y + 1$ over R.

48. **Writing to Learn** ***Average Temperature in Texas*** According to the *Texas Almanac,* Texas has 254 counties and a National Weather Service station in each county. Assume that at time t_0 each of the 254 weather stations recorded the local temperature. Find a formula that would give a reasonable approximation to the average temperature in Texas at time t_0. Your answer should involve information that is readily available in the *Texas Almanac.*

Extending the Ideas

The Parallel Axis Theorem

Let $L_{\text{c.m.}}$ be a line in the xy-plane that runs through the center of mass of a thin plate of mass m covering a region in the plane. Let L be a line in the plane parallel to and h units away from $L_{\text{c.m.}}$. The **Parallel Axis Theorem** says that under these conditions, the moments of inertia I_L and $L_{\text{c.m.}}$ of the plate about L and $L_{\text{c.m.}}$ satisfy the equation

$$I_L = I_{\text{c.m.}} + mh^2. \tag{1}$$

This equation gives a quick way to calculate one moment when the other moment and the mass are known.

49. ***Proof of the Parallel Axis Theorem***

(a) Show that the first moment of a thin flat plate about any line in the plane of the plate through the plate's center of mass is zero. (*Hint:* Place the center of mass at the origin with the line along the y-axis. What does the formula $\bar{x} = M_y/M$ then tell you?)

(b) Use the result in (a) to derive the Parallel Axis Theorem. Assume that the plate is coordinatized in a way that makes $L_{\text{c.m.}}$ the y-axis and L the line $x = h$. Then expand the integrand of the integral for I_L to rewrite the integral as the sum of integrals whose values you recognize.

50. ***Applying the Parallel Axis Theorem***

(a) Use the Parallel Axis Theorem and the results of Example 4 to find the moments of inertia of the plate in Example 4 about the vertical and horizontal lines through the plate's center of mass.

(b) Use the results in (a) to find the plate's moments of inertia about the lines $x = 1$ and $y = 2$.

Pappus's Formula

Suppose m_1 and m_2 are the masses of thin plates P_1 and P_2 that cover nonoverlapping regions in the xy-plane. Let $\mathbf{c}_1$ and $\mathbf{c}_2$ be the vectors from the origin to the respective centers of mass of P_1 and P_2. Then the center of mass of the union $P_1 \cup P_2$ of the two plates is determined by the vector

$$\mathbf{c} = \frac{m_1\mathbf{c}_1 + m_2\mathbf{c}_2}{m_1 + m_2} \tag{2}$$

Equation (2) is known as **Pappus's formula**. For more than two nonoverlapping plates, as long as their number is finite, the formula generalizes to

$$\mathbf{c} = \frac{m_1\mathbf{c}_1 + m_2\mathbf{c}_2 + \cdots + m_n\mathbf{c}_n}{m_1 + m_2 + \cdots + m_n}. \tag{3}$$

This formula is especially useful for finding the centroid of a plate of irregular shape that is made up of pieces of constant density whose centroids we know from geometry. We find the centroid of each piece and apply Equation (3) to find the centroid of the plate.

51. Derive Pappus's formula (Equation (2)). (*Hint:* Sketch the plates as regions in the first quadrant and label their centers of mass as $(\bar{x}_1, \bar{y}_1)$ and $(\bar{x}_2, \bar{y}_2)$. What are the moments of $P_1 \cup P_2$ about the coordinate axes?)

52. Use Equation (2) and mathematical induction to show that Equation (3) holds for any positive integer $n > 2$.

53. Let A, B, and C be the shapes indicated in Figure 15.23a. Use Pappus's formula to find the centroid of

(a) $A \cup B$ **(b)** $A \cup C$

(c) $B \cup C$ **(d)** $A \cup B \cup C$

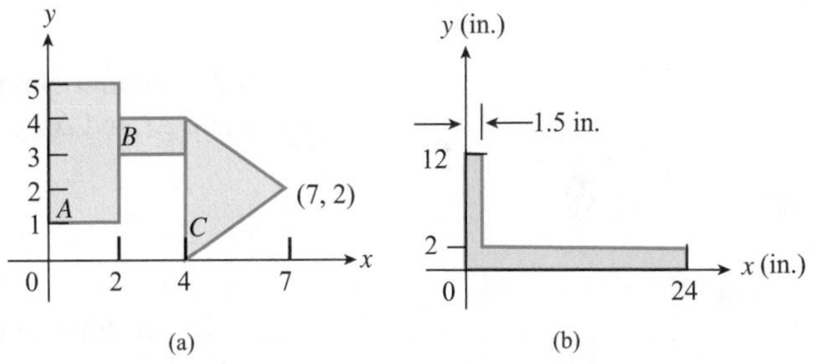

Figure 15.23 The figures for Exercises 53 and 54.

54. ***Center of Mass of a Carpenter's Square*** Locate the center of mass of the carpenter's square in Figure 15.23b.

55. **Writing to Learn** ***Designing a Two-Dimensional Ice Cream Cone*** An isosceles triangle T has base $2a$ and altitude h. The base lies along the diameter of a semicircular disk D of radius a so that the two together make a shape resembling an ice cream cone. What relation must hold between a and h to place the centroid of $T \cup D$ on the common boundary of T and D? inside T?

56. **Writing to Learn** ***Shape Design*** An isosceles triangle T of altitude h has as its base one side of a square Q whose edges have length s. (The square and triangle do not overlap.) What relation must hold between h and s to place the centroid of $T \cup Q$ on the base of the triangle? Compare your answer with the answer to Exercise 55.

15.3 Double Integrals in Polar Form

What you'll learn about

- Integrals in Polar Coordinates
- Finding Limits of Integration
- Changing Cartesian Integrals into Polar Integrals

Integrals in Polar Coordinates

When we defined the double integral of a function over a region R in the xy-plane, we began by cutting R into rectangles whose sides were parallel to the coordinate axes. These were the natural shapes to use because their sides have either constant x-values or constant y-values. In polar coordinates, the natural shapes are "polar rectangles" whose sides have constant r- and θ-values.

Suppose a function $f(r, \theta)$ is defined over a region R that is bounded by the rays $\theta = \alpha$ and $\theta = \beta$ and by the continuous curves $r = g_1(\theta)$ and $r = g_2(\theta)$. Also suppose $0 \le g_1(\theta) \le g_2(\theta) \le a$ for every value of θ between α and β. Then R lies in the fan-shaped region Q defined by the inequalities $0 \le r \le a$ and $\alpha \le \theta \le \beta$. See Figure 15.24.

We cover Q by a grid of circular arcs and rays. The arcs are cut from circles centered at the origin, with radii Δr, $2\,\Delta r, \ldots, m\,\Delta r$, where $\Delta r = a/m$. The rays are given by

$$\theta = \alpha,\ \theta = \alpha + \Delta\theta,\ \theta = \alpha + 2\Delta\theta, \ldots, \theta = \alpha + m'\Delta\theta = \beta,$$

where $\Delta\theta = (\beta - \alpha)/m'$. The arcs and rays partition Q into small patches called "polar rectangles."

We number the polar rectangles that lie inside R (the order does not matter), calling their areas $\Delta A_1, \Delta A_2, \ldots, \Delta A_n$.

We let (r_k, θ_k) be the center of the polar rectangle whose area is ΔA_k. By "center" we mean the point that lies halfway between the circular arcs on the ray that bisects the arcs. We then form the sum

$$S_n = \sum_{k=1}^{n} f(r_k, \theta_k)\,\Delta A_k. \tag{1}$$

If f is continuous throughout R, this sum will approach a limit as we refine the grid to make Δr and $\Delta\theta$ go to zero. This limit is the **double integral of f over R.** In symbols,

$$\lim_{n\to\infty} S_n = \iint_R f(r, \theta)\,dA.$$

To see how to evaluate this limit, we first write the sum S_n in a way that expresses ΔA_k in terms of Δr and $\Delta\theta$. The radius of the inner are bounding ΔA_k is $r_k - (\Delta r/2)$

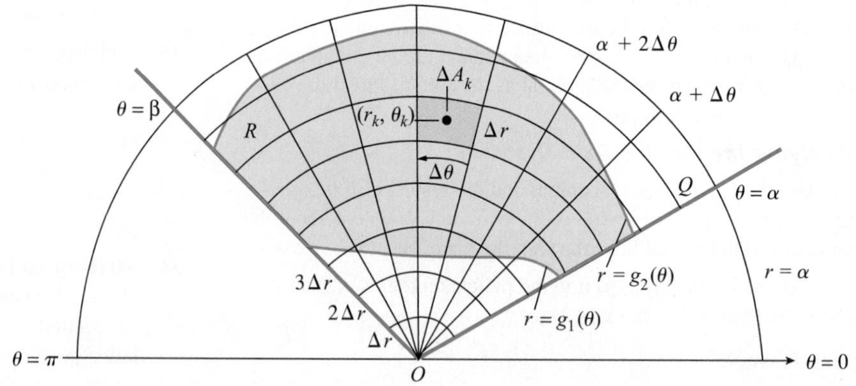

Figure 15.24 The region R: $g_1(\theta) \le r \le g_2(\theta)$, $\alpha \le \theta \le \beta$ is contained in the fan-shaped region Q: $0 \le r \le a$, $\alpha \le \theta \le \beta$. The partition of Q by circular arcs and rays induces a partition of R.

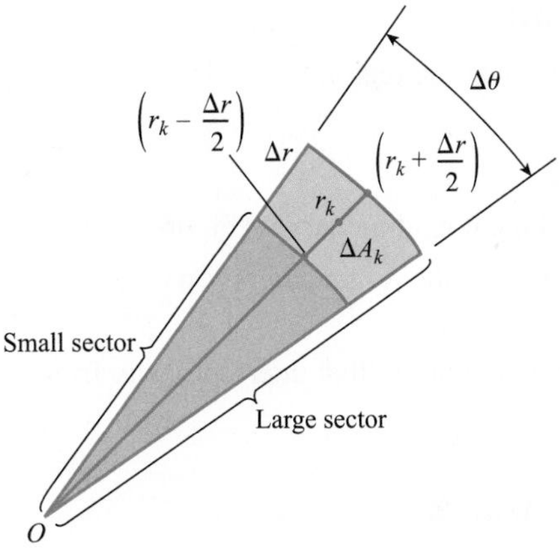

Figure 15.25 The observation that $\Delta A_k = \begin{pmatrix}\text{area of}\\ \text{large sector}\end{pmatrix} - \begin{pmatrix}\text{area of}\\ \text{small sector}\end{pmatrix}$ leads to the formula $\Delta A_k = r_k\,\Delta r\,\Delta\theta$. The text explains why.

(Figure 15.25). The radius of the outer arc is $r_k + (\Delta r/2)$. The areas of the circular sectors subtended by these arcs at the origin are

$$\text{Inner radius: } \frac{1}{2}\left(r_k - \frac{\Delta r}{2}\right)^2 \Delta\theta \qquad \text{Outer radius: } \frac{1}{2}\left(r_k + \frac{\Delta r}{2}\right)^2 \Delta\theta. \tag{2}$$

Therefore,

$$\begin{aligned}\Delta A_k &= \text{area of large sector} - \text{area of small sector}\\ &= \frac{\Delta\theta}{2}\left[\left(r_k + \frac{\Delta r}{2}\right)^2 - \left(r_k - \frac{\Delta r}{2}\right)^2\right] = \frac{\Delta\theta}{2}(2r_k\,\Delta r) = r_k\,\Delta r\,\Delta\theta.\end{aligned}$$

Combining this result with Equation (1) gives

$$S_n = \sum_{k=1}^{n} f(r_k, \theta_k) r_k\,\Delta r\,\Delta\theta. \tag{3}$$

A version of Fubini's theorem now says that the limit approached by these sums can be evaluated by repeated single integration with respect to r and θ as

$$\iint_R f(r, \theta)\,dA = \int_{\theta=\alpha}^{\theta=\beta} \int_{r=g_1(\theta)}^{r=g_2(\theta)} f(r, \theta) r\,dr\,d\theta. \tag{4}$$

Finding Limits of Integration

The procedure for finding limits of integration in rectangular coordinates also works for polar coordinates.

How to Integrate in Polar Coordinates

To evaluate $\iint_R f(r, \theta)\,dA$ over a region R in polar coordinates, integrating first with respect to r and then with respect to θ, take the following steps.

1. *A sketch.* Sketch the region and label the bounding curves.

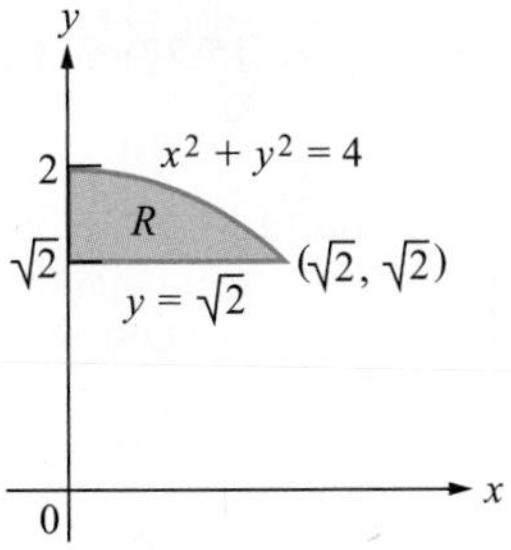

2. *The r-limits of integration.* Imagine a ray L from the origin cutting through R in the direction of increasing r. Mark the r-values where L enters and leaves R. These are the r-limits of integration. They usually depend on the angle θ that L makes with the positive x-axis.

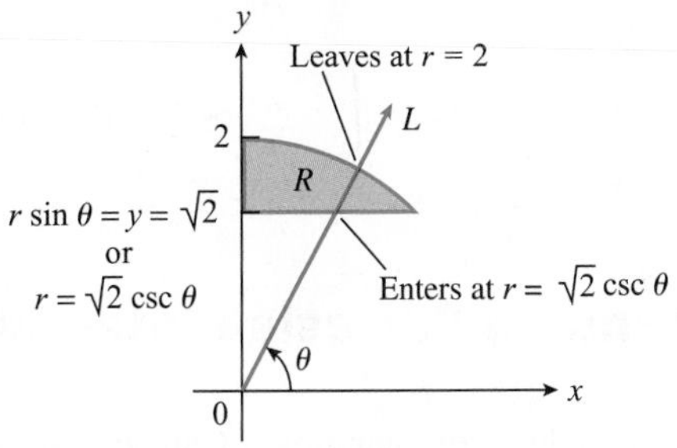

3. *The θ-limits of integration.* Find the smallest and largest θ-values that bound R. These are the θ-limits of integration.

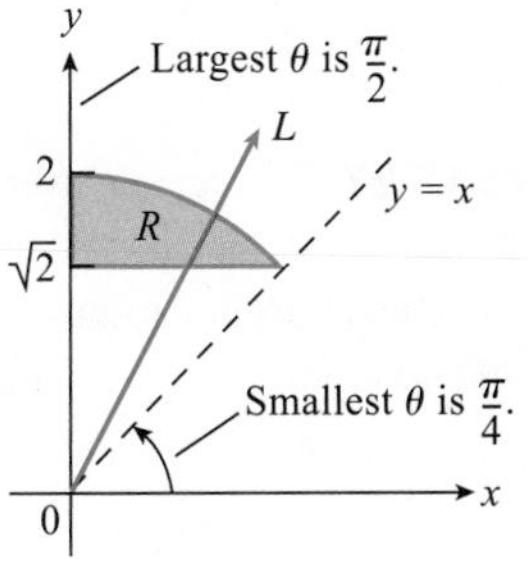

The integral is

$$\iint_R f(r, \theta)\,dA = \int_{\theta=\pi/4}^{\theta=\pi/2} \int_{r=\sqrt{2}\csc\theta}^{r=z} f(r, \theta)\; r\,dr\,d\theta.$$

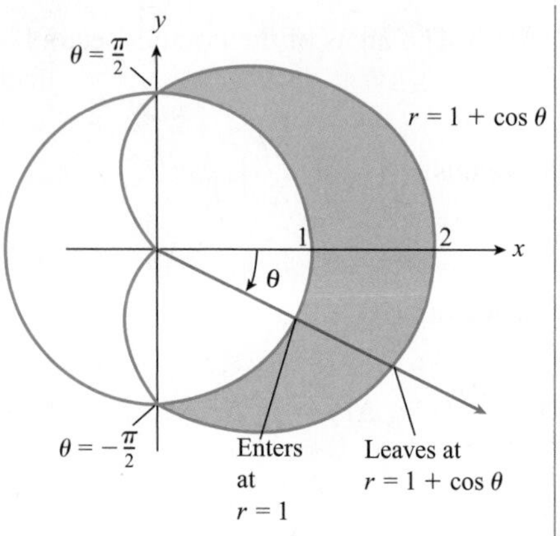

Figure 15.26 The sketch for Example 1.

EXAMPLE 1 Finding Limits of Integration

Find the limits of integration for integrating $f(r, \theta)$ over the region R that lies inside the cardioid $r = 1 + \cos\theta$ and outside the circle $r = 1$.

SOLUTION

Step 1: *A sketch.* We sketch the region and label the bounding curves (Figure 15.26)

Step 2: *The r-limits of integration.* A typical ray from the origin enters R where $r = 1$ and leaves where $r = 1 + \cos\theta$.

Step 3: *The θ-limits of integration.* The rays from the origin that intersect R run from $\theta = -\pi/2$ to $\theta = \pi/2$. The integral is

$$\int_{-\pi/2}^{\pi/2} \int_{1}^{1+\cos\theta} f(r, \theta) r\, dr\, d\theta.$$

If $f(r, \theta)$ is the constant function whose value is 1, then the integral of f over R is the area of R.

Area in Polar Coordinates

The area of a closed and bounded region R in the polar coordinate plane is

$$A = \iint_R r\, dr\, d\theta. \tag{5}$$

As you might expect, this formula for area is consistent with all earlier formulas, although we will not prove this fact.

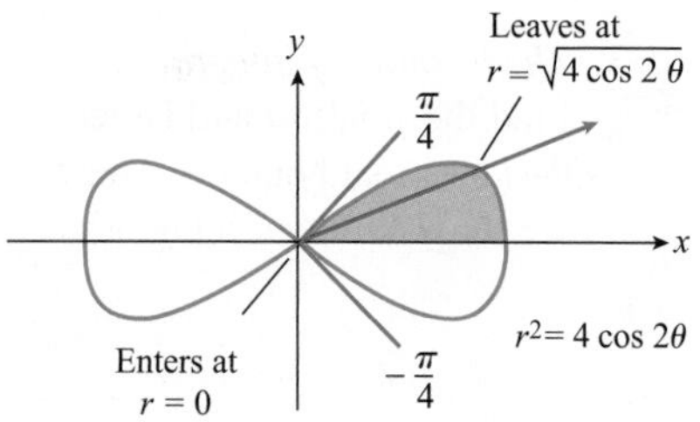

Figure 15.27 To integrate over the shaded region, we run r from 0 to $\sqrt{4\cos 2\theta}$ and θ from 0 to $\pi/4$. (Example 2)

EXAMPLE 2 Finding Area in Polar Coordinates

Find the area enclosed by the lemniscate $r^2 = 4\cos 2\theta$.

SOLUTION

We graph the lemniscate to determine the limits of integration (Figure 15.27) and see that the total area is four times the first-quadrant portion.

$$A = 4\int_0^{\pi/4}\int_0^{\sqrt{4\cos 2\theta}} r\, dr\, d\theta = 4\int_0^{\pi/4}\left[\frac{r^2}{2}\right]_{r=0}^{r=\sqrt{4\cos 2\theta}} d\theta$$

$$= 4\int_0^{\pi/4} 2\cos 2\theta\, d\theta = 4\sin 2\theta\Big]_0^{\pi/4} = 4.$$

Changing Cartesian Integrals into Polar Integrals

The procedure for changing a Cartesian integral $\int_R f(x, y)\, dx\, dy$ into a polar integral has two steps.

Step 1: Substitute $x = r\cos\theta$ and $y = r\sin\theta$, and replace $dx\, dy$ in the Cartesian integral by $r\, dr\, d\theta$.

Step 2: Supply polar limits of integration for the boundary of R.

The Cartesian integral then becomes

$$\iint_R f(x, y)\, dx\, dy = \iint_G f(r\cos\theta, r\sin\theta) r\, dr\, d\theta, \tag{6}$$

where G denotes the region of integration in polar coordinates. This is like the substitution method except that there are now two variables to substitute for instead of one. Notice that $dx\, dy$ is not replaced by $dr\, d\theta$ but by $r\, dr\, d\theta$. We will see why in Section 15.7.

EXAMPLE 3 Changing Cartesian Integrals to Polar

Find the polar moment of inertia about the origin of a thin plate of density $\delta(x, y) = 1$ bounded by the quarter circle $x^2 + y^2 = 1$ in the first quadrant.

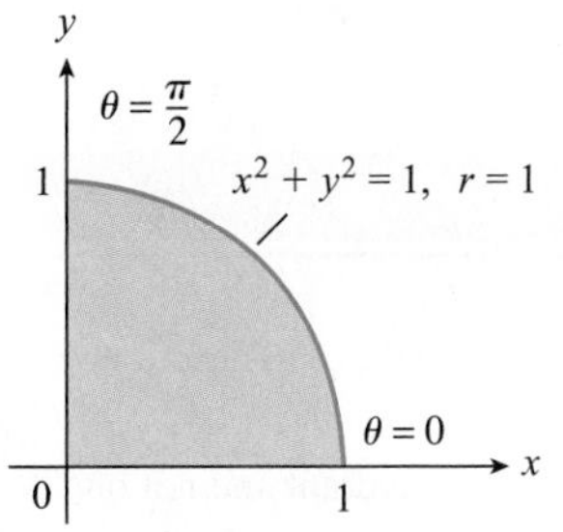

Figure 15.28 In polar coordinates, this region is described by simple inequalities: $0 \le r \le 1$ and $0 \le \theta \le \pi/2$. (Example 3)

SOLUTION

We sketch the plate to determine the limits of integration (Figure 15.28).

In Cartesian coordinates, the polar moment is the value of the integral

$$\int_0^1 \int_0^{\sqrt{1-x^2}} (x^2 + y^2)\, dy\, dx.$$

Integration with respect to y gives

$$\int_0^1 \left(x^2\sqrt{1 - x^2} + \frac{(1 - x^2)^{3/2}}{3} \right) dx,$$

an integral difficult to evaluate without tables or technology.

Things go better if we change the original integral to polar coordinates. Substituting $x = r\cos\theta$, $y = r\sin\theta$ and replacing $dx\, dy$ by $r\, dr\, d\theta$, we get

$$\int_0^1 \int_0^{\sqrt{1-x^2}} (x^2 + y^2)\, dy\, dx = \int_0^{\pi/2} \int_0^1 (r^2) r\, dr\, d\theta$$

$$= \int_0^{\pi/2} \left[\frac{r^4}{4} \right]_{r=0}^{r=1} d\theta = \int_0^{\pi/2} \frac{1}{4}\, d\theta = \frac{\pi}{8}.$$

Why is the polar coordinate transformation so effective here? One reason is that $x^2 + y^2$ simplifies to r^2. Another is that the limits of integration become constants.

EXAMPLE 4 Evaluating Integrals Using Polar Coordinates

Evaluate

$$\iint_R e^{x^2+y^2}\, dy\, dx,$$

where R is the semicircular region bounded by the x-axis and the curve $y = \sqrt{1 - x^2}$ (Figure 15.29).

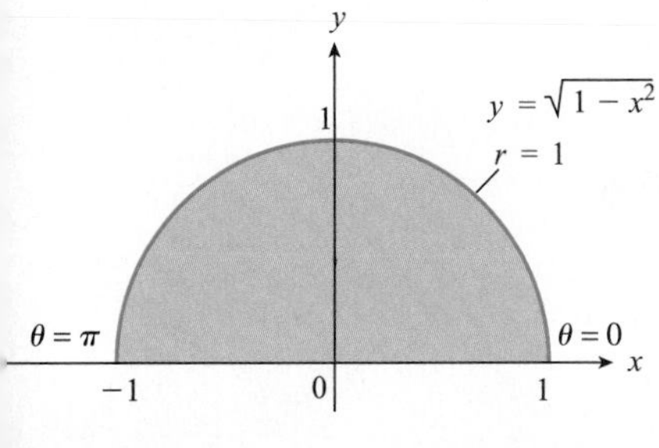

Figure 15.29 The semicircular region in Example 4 is the region $0 \le r \le 1$, $0 \le \theta \le \pi$.

SOLUTION

In Cartesian coordinates, the integral in question is a nonelementary integral and there is no direct way to integrate $e^{x^2+y^2}$ analytically with respect to either x or y. We could use a CAS to get an approximation (2.699) to its value. Let's try polar coordinates.

Substituting $x = r\cos\theta$, $y = r\sin\theta$ and replacing $dy\,dx$ by $r\,dr\,d\theta$ enables us to evaluate the integral as

$$\iint_R e^{x^2+y^2}\,dy\,dx = \int_0^{\pi}\int_0^1 e^{r^2} r\,dr\,d\theta = \int_0^{\pi}\left[\frac{1}{2}e^{r^2}\right]_0^1 d\theta$$

$$= \int_0^{\pi}\frac{1}{2}(e-1)\,d\theta = \frac{\pi}{2}(e-1).$$

The r in the $r\,dr\,d\theta$ was just what we needed to integrate e^{r^2} analytically. Without it, we would have been stuck, as we were at the beginning.

Quick Review 15.3

In Exercises 1–3, replace the Cartesian equation by an equivalent polar equation.

1. $x^2 + y^2 = 9$

2. $x = 3$

3. $x^2 + (y+2)^2 = 4$

In Exercises 4 and 5, replace the polar equation by an equivalent Cartesian equation.

4. $r^2 = 4r\cos\theta$

5. $r = \sec\theta$

In Exercises 6 and 7, use polar coordinate inequalities to describe the region of the plane.

6. The portion of $x^2 + y^2 \le 4$ in the second quadrant and not on the coordinate axes.

7. The portion of $x^2 + y^2 \le 4$ in the third and fourth quadrants and not on the coordinate axes.

In Exercises 8–10, find the area of the region.

8. Inside the cardioid $r = 2(1 + \cos\theta)$

9. Inside the lemniscate $r^2 = 2\cos 2\theta$

10. Shared by the circle $r = 2$ and the cardioid $r = 2(1 + \cos\theta)$

Section 15.3 Exercises

In Exercises 1–16, change the Cartesian integral into an equivalent polar integral. Then evaluate the polar integral.

1. $\displaystyle\int_{-1}^{1}\int_0^{\sqrt{1-x^2}} dy\,dx$

2. $\displaystyle\int_{-1}^{1}\int_{-\sqrt{1-x^2}}^{\sqrt{1-x^2}} dy\,dx$

3. $\displaystyle\int_0^1\int_0^{\sqrt{1-y^2}} (x^2+y^2)\,dx\,dy$

4. $\displaystyle\int_{-1}^{1}\int_{-\sqrt{1-y^2}}^{\sqrt{1-y^2}} (x^2+y^2)\,dx\,dy$

5. $\displaystyle\int_{-a}^{a}\int_{-\sqrt{a^2-x^2}}^{\sqrt{a^2-x^2}} dy\,dx$

6. $\displaystyle\int_0^2\int_0^{\sqrt{4-y^3}} (x^2+y^2)\,dx\,dy$

7. $\displaystyle\int_0^6\int_0^y x\,dx\,dy$

8. $\displaystyle\int_0^2\int_0^x y\,dy\,dx$

9. $\displaystyle\int_{-1}^{0}\int_{-\sqrt{1-x^3}}^{0} \frac{2}{1+\sqrt{x^2+y^2}}\,dy\,dx$

10. $\displaystyle\int_{-1}^{1}\int_{-\sqrt{1-y^2}}^{0} \frac{4\sqrt{x^2+y^2}}{1+x^2+y^2}\,dx\,dy$

11. $\displaystyle\int_0^{\ln 2}\int_0^{\sqrt{(\ln 2)^2-y^2}} e^{\sqrt{x^2+y^2}}\,dx\,dy$

12. $\displaystyle\int_0^1\int_0^{\sqrt{1-x^2}} e^{-(x^2+y^2)}\,dy\,dx$

13. $\displaystyle\int_0^2\int_0^{\sqrt{1-(x-1)^2}} \frac{x+y}{x^2+y^2}\,dy\,dx$

14. $\displaystyle\int_0^2\int_{-\sqrt{1-(y-1)^2}}^{0} xy^2\,dx\,dy$

15. $\displaystyle\int_{-1}^{1}\int_{-\sqrt{1-y^2}}^{\sqrt{1-y^2}} \ln(x^2+y^2+1)\,dx\,dy$

16. $\displaystyle\int_{-1}^{1}\int_{-\sqrt{1-x^2}}^{\sqrt{1-x^2}} \frac{2}{(1+x^2+y^2)^2}\,dy\,dx$

In Exercises 17–22, find the area of the region.

17. The region cut from the first quadrant by the curve $r = 2(2 - \sin 2\theta)^{1/2}$

18. The region that lies inside the cardioid $r = 1 + \cos\theta$ and outside the circle $r = 1$

19. The region enclosed by one leaf of the rose $r = 12\cos 3\theta$

20. The region enclosed by the positive x-axis and spiral $r = 4\theta/3$, $0 \le \theta \le 2\pi$ (the region looks like a snail shell)

21. The region cut from the first quadrant by the cardioid $r = 1 + \sin\theta$

22. The region common to the interiors of the cardioids $r = 1 + \cos\theta$ and $r = 1 - \cos\theta$

23. ***First Moment of a Plate*** Find the first moment about the x-axis of a thin plate of constant density $\delta(x, y) = 3$, bounded below by the x-axis and above by the cardioid $r = 1 - \cos\theta$.

24. ***Inertial and Polar Moments of a Disk*** Find the moment of inertia about the x-axis and the polar moment of inertia about the origin of a thin disk bounded by the circle $x^2 + y^2 = a^2$ if the disk's density at the point (x, y) is $\delta(x, y) = k(x^2 + y^2)$, k a constant.

25. ***Mass*** Find the mass of a thin plate covering the region outside the circle $r = 3$ and inside the circle $r = 6\sin\theta$ if the plate's density function is $\delta(x, y) = 1/r$.

26. ***Polar Moment of a Cardioid Region Outside a Circle*** Find the polar moment of inertia about the origin of a thin plate covering the region that lies inside the cardioid $r = 1 - \cos\theta$ and outside the circle $r = 1$ if the plate's density function is $\delta(x, y) = 1/r^2$.

27. ***Centroid of a Cardioid Region*** Find the centroid of the region enclosed by the cardioid $r = 1 + \cos\theta$.

28. ***Polar Moment of a Cardioid Region*** Find the polar moment of inertia about the origin of a thin plate enclosed by the cardioid $r = 1 + \cos\theta$ if the plate's density function is $\delta(x, y) = 1$.

29. ***Average Height of a Surface*** Find the average height of the hemisphere $z = \sqrt{a^2 - x^2 - y^2}$ above the disk $x^2 + y^2 \le a^2$ in the xy-plane.

30. ***Average Height of a Surface*** Find the average height of the (single) cone $z = \sqrt{x^2 + y^2}$ above the disk $x^2 + y^2 \le a^2$ in the xy-plane.

31. ***Average Distance from the Origin*** Find the average distance from a point $P(x, y)$ in the disk $x^2 + y^2 \le a^2$ to the origin.

32. ***Average Squared Distance*** Find the average value of the *square* of the distance from the point $P(x, y)$ in the disk $x^2 + y^2 \le 1$ to the boundary point $A(1, 0)$.

33. Integrate $f(x, y) = [\ln(x^2 + y^2)]/\sqrt{x^2 + y^2}$ over the region $1 \le x^2 + y^2 \le e$.

34. Integrate $f(x, y) = [\ln(x^2 + y^2)]/(x^2 + y^2)$ over the region $1 \le x^2 + y^2 \le e$.

35. ***Volume*** The region that lies inside the cardioid $r = 1 + \cos\theta$ and outside the circle $r = 1$ is the base of a solid right cylinder. The top of the cylinder lies in the plane $z = x$. Find the cylinder's volume.

36. ***Volume*** The region enclosed by the lemniscate $r^2 = 2\cos 2\theta$ is the base of a solid right cylinder whose top is bounded by the sphere $z = \sqrt{2 - r^2}$. Find the cylinder's volume.

Explorations

37. *The Error Function erf(x)*

(a) The usual way to evaluate the improper integral

$$I = \int_0^\infty e^{-x^2}\,dx \text{ is first to calculate its square:}$$

$$I^2 = \left(\int_0^\infty e^{-x^2}\,dx\right)\left(\int_0^\infty e^{-y^2}\,dy\right) = \int_0^\infty\int_0^\infty e^{-(x^2+y^2)}\,dx\,dy.$$

Evaluate the last integral using polar coordinates and solve the resulting equation for I.

(b) Evaluate

$$\lim_{x\to\infty} \operatorname{erf}(x) = \lim_{x\to\infty} \int_0^x \frac{2e^{-t^2}}{\sqrt{\pi}}\,dt.$$

38. Evaluate the integral

$$\int_0^\infty\int_0^\infty \frac{1}{(1 + x^2 + y^2)^2}\,dx\,dy.$$

In Exercises 39–41, *work in groups of two or three* to solve the problem.

39. **Writing to Learn** Integrate the function $f(x, y) = 1/(1 - x^2 - y^2)$ over the disk $x^2 + y^2 \le 3/4$. Does the integral of $f(x, y)$ over the disk $x^2 + y^2 \le 1$ exist? Give reasons for your answer.

40. Use the double integral in polar coordinates to derive the formula

$$A = \int_\alpha^\beta \frac{1}{2} r^2\,d\theta$$

for the area of the fan-shaped region between the origin and polar curve $r = f(\theta)$, $\alpha \le \theta \le \beta$.

41. ***Average Squared Distance*** Let P_0 be a point inside a circle of radius a and let h denote the distance from P_0 to the center of the circle. Let d denote the distance from an arbitrary point P to P_0. Find the average value of d^2 over the region enclosed by the circle. (*Hint:* Simplify your work by placing the center of the circle at the origin and P_0 on the x-axis.)

Extending the Ideas

CAS Explorations

In Exercises 42–45, perform the following steps.

(a) Plot the Cartesian region of integration in the xy-plane.

(b) Change each boundary curve of the Cartesian region in (a) to its polar representation by solving its Cartesian equation for r and θ.

(c) Plot the polar region of integration in the $r\theta$-plane.

(d) Change the integrand from Cartesian to polar coordinates. Determine the limits of integration from your plot in (c) and evaluate the polar integral.

42. $\displaystyle\int_0^1 \int_x^1 \frac{y}{x^2 + y^2}\, dy\, dx$

43. $\displaystyle\int_0^1 \int_0^{x/2} \frac{x}{x^2 + y^2}\, dy\, dx$

44. $\displaystyle\int_0^1 \int_{-y/3}^{y/3} \frac{y}{\sqrt{x^2 + y^2}}\, dx\, dy$

45. $\displaystyle\int_0^1 \int_y^{2-y} \sqrt{x + y}\, dx\, dy$

15.4 Triple Integrals in Rectangular Coordinates

What you'll learn about

- Triple Integrals
- Properties of Triple Integrals
- Volume of a Region in Space
- Finding Limits of Integration
- Average Value of a Function in Space

Triple Integrals

If $F(x, y, z)$ is a function defined on a closed bounded region D in space—the region occupied by a solid ball, for example, or a lump of clay—then the integral of F over D may be defined in the following way. We partition a rectangular region containing D into rectangular cells by planes parallel to the coordinate planes (Figure 15.30). We number the cells that lie inside D from 1 to n in some order, a typical cell having dimensions Δx_k by Δy_k by Δz_k and volume ΔV_k. We choose a point (x_k, y_k, z_k) in each cell and form the sum

$$S_n = \sum_{k=1}^{n} F(x_k, y_k, z_k)\, \Delta V_k. \tag{1}$$

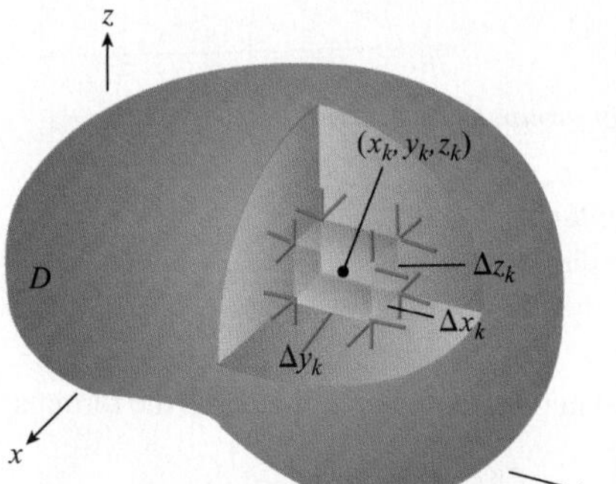

Figure 15.30 Partitioning a solid with rectangular cells of volume ΔV_k.

If F is continuous and the bounding surface of D is made up of smooth surfaces joined along continuous curves, then as Δx_k, Δy_k, and Δz_k approach zero independently, the sums S_n approach a limit

$$\lim_{n\to\infty} S_n = \iiint_D F(x, y, z)\, dV. \tag{2}$$

This limit is the **triple integral of F over D**. The limit also exists for some discontinuous functions.

Properties of Triple Integrals

Triple integrals of continuous functions have the same algebraic properties as double and single integrals.

Properties of Triple Integrals

1. *Constant Multiple:* $\displaystyle\iiint_D kF\, dV = k\iiint_D F\, dV$ (any number k)

2. *Sum and Difference:*

$$\iiint_D (F \pm G)\, dV = \iiint_D F\, dV \pm \iiint_D G\, dV$$

continued

3. *Domination:*

(a) $\displaystyle\iiint_D F\,dV \geq 0 \quad \text{if} \quad F \geq 0 \text{ on } D$

(b) $\displaystyle\iiint_D F\,dV \geq \iiint_D G\,dV \quad \text{if} \quad F \geq G \text{ on } D$

4. *Additivity:*

$$\iiint_D F\,dV = \iiint_{D_1} F\,dV + \iiint_{D_2} F\,dV + \cdots + \iiint_{D_n} F\,dV$$

if D is the union of a finite number of nonoverlapping cells $D_1, D_2, \ldots, D_n$.

Volume of a Region in Space

If F is the constant function whose value is 1, then the sums in Equation (1) reduce to

$$S_n = \sum_{k=1}^{n} F(x_k, y_k, z_k)\,\Delta V_k = \sum_{k=1}^{n} \Delta V_k. \tag{3}$$

As Δx, Δy, and Δz approach zero, the cells ΔV_k become smaller and more numerous and fill up more and more of D. We therefore define the volume of D to be the triple integral

$$\lim_{n\to\infty} \sum_{k=1}^{n} \Delta V_k = \iiint_D dV.$$

DEFINITION Volume

The **volume** of a closed, bounded region in space is

$$V = \iiint_D dV. \tag{4}$$

As we will see in a moment, this integral enables us to calculate the volumes of solids enclosed by curved surfaces.

Finding Limits of Integration

We evaluate triple integrals by applying a three-dimensional version of Fubini's theorem to evaluate them by repeated single integrations. As with double integrals, there is a geometric procedure for finding the limits of integration.

How to Find Limits of Integration in Triple Integrals

To evaluate

$$\iiint_D F(x, y, z)\,dV$$

over a region D, integrating first with respect to z, then with respect to y, finally with x, take the following steps.

1. *A sketch.* Sketch the region D along with its "shadow" R (vertical projection) in the xy-plane. Label the upper and lower bounding surfaces of D and the upper and lower bounding curves of R.

2. *The z-limits of integration.* Draw a line M passing through a typical point (x, y) in R parallel to the z-axis. As z increases, M enters D *at* $z = f_1(x, y)$ and leaves at $z = f_2(x, y)$. These are the z-limits of integration.

3. *The y-limits of integration.* Draw a line L through (x, y) parallel to the y-axis. As y increases, L enters R at $y = g_1(x)$ and leaves at $y = g_2(x)$. These are the y-limits of integration.

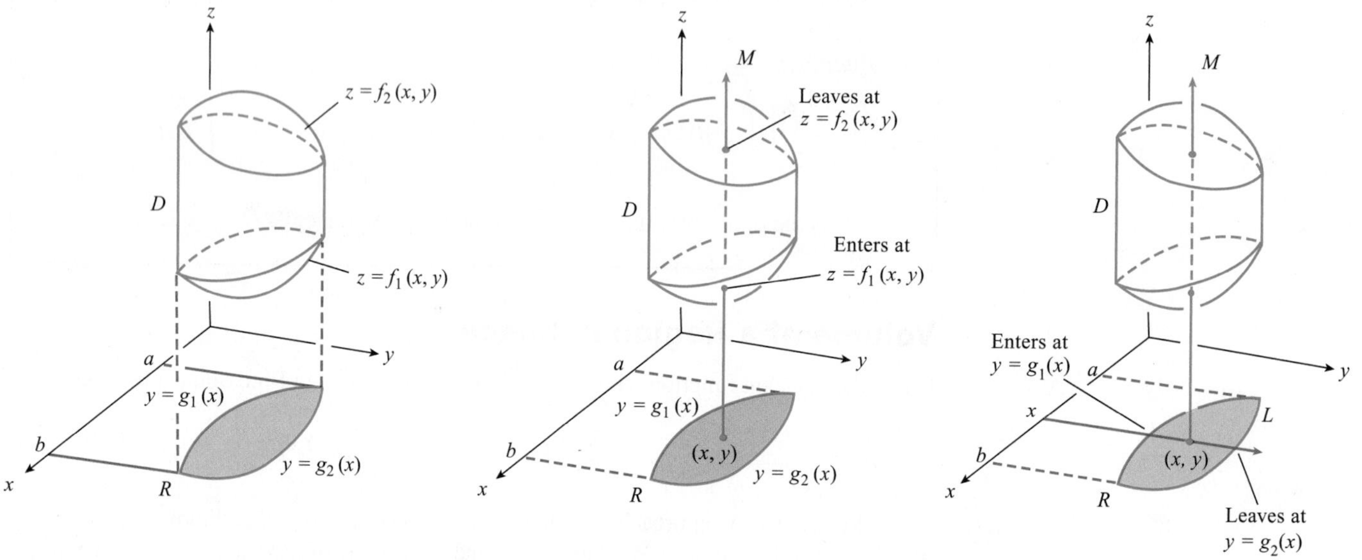

4. *The x-limits of integration.* Choose x-limits that include all lines through R parallel to the y-axis ($x = a$ and $x = b$ in the preceding figure). These are the x-limits of integration. The integral is

$$\int_{x=a}^{x=b} \int_{y=g_1(x)}^{y=g_2(x)} \int_{z=f_1(x,y)}^{z=f_2(x,y)} F(x, y, z)\, dz\, dy\, dx.$$

Follow similar procedures if you change the order of integration. The "shadow" of region D lies in the plane of the last two variables with respect to which the iterated integration takes place.

EXAMPLE 1 Finding Volume

Find the volume of the region D enclosed by the surfaces $z = x^2 + 3y^2$ and $z = 8 - x^2 - y^2$.

SOLUTION

The volume is

$$V = \iiint_D dz\, dy\, dx,$$

the integral of $F(x, y, z) = 1$ over D. To find the limits of integration for evaluating the integral, we take these steps.

Step 1: *A sketch.* The surfaces (Figure 15.31) intersect on the elliptical cylinder $x^2 + 3y^2 = 8 - x^2 - y^2$ or $x^2 + 2y^2 = 4$. The boundary of the region R, the projection of D onto the xy-plane, is an ellipse with the same equation: $x^2 + 2y^2 = 4$. The "upper" boundary of R is the curve $y = \sqrt{(4 - x^2)/2}$. The lower boundary is the curve $y = -\sqrt{(4 - x^2)/2}$.

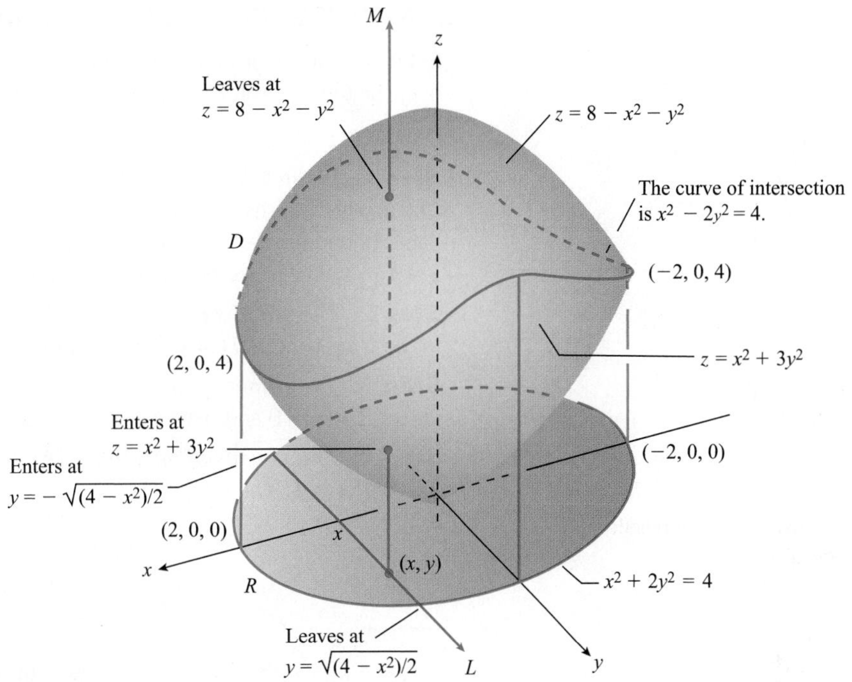

Figure 15.31 The volume of the region enclosed by these two paraboloids is calculated in Example 1.

Step 2: *The z-limits of integration.* The line M passing through a typical point (x, y) in R parallel to the z-axis enters D at $z = x^2 + 3y^2$ and leaves at $z = 8 - x^2 - y^2$.

Step 3: *The y-limits of integration.* The line L through (x, y) parallel to the y-axis enters R at $y = -\sqrt{(4 - x^2)/2}$ and leaves at $y = \sqrt{(4 - x^2)/2}$.

Step 4: *The x-limits of integration.* As L sweeps across R, the values of x vary from $x = -2$ at $(-2, 0, 0)$ to $x = 2$ at $(2, 0, 0)$. The volume of D is

$$V = \iiint_D dz\,dy\,dx$$

$$= \int_{-2}^{2} \int_{-\sqrt{(4-x^2)/2}}^{\sqrt{(4-x^2)/2}} \int_{x^2+3y^2}^{8-x^2-y^2} dz\,dy\,dx$$

$$= \int_{-2}^{2} \int_{-\sqrt{(4-x^2)/2}}^{\sqrt{(4-x^2)/2}} (8 - 2x^2 - 4y^2)\,dy\,dx$$

$$= \int_{-2}^{2} \left[(8 - 2x^2)y - \frac{4}{3}y^3\right]_{y=-\sqrt{(4-x^2)/2}}^{y=\sqrt{(4-x^2)/2}} dx$$

$$= \int_{-2}^{2} \left(2(8 - 2x^2)\sqrt{\frac{4 - x^2}{2}} - \frac{8}{3}\left(\frac{4 - x^2}{2}\right)^{3/2}\right) dx$$

$$= \int_{-2}^{2} \left[8\left(\frac{4 - x^2}{2}\right)^{3/2} - \frac{8}{3}\left(\frac{4 - x^2}{2}\right)^{3/2}\right] = \frac{4\sqrt{2}}{3}\int_{-2}^{2} (4 - x^2)^{3/2}\,dx$$

$$= 8\pi\sqrt{2} \text{ units cubed}$$ After integration with the substitution $x = 2 \sin u$.

In the next example, we project D onto the xz-plane instead of the xy-plane.

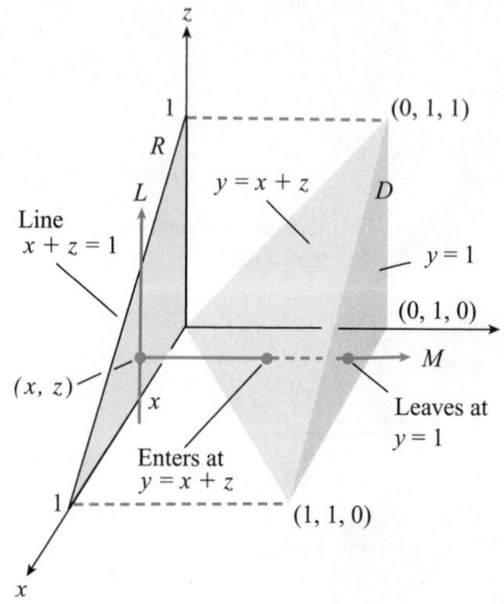

Figure 15.32 The tetrahedron in Example 2.

EXAMPLE 2 Finding Limits of Integration

Set up the limits of integration for evaluating the triple integral of a function $F(x, y, z)$ over the tetrahedron D with vertices $(0, 0, 0)$, $(1, 1, 0)$, $(0, 1, 0)$, and $(0, 1, 1)$.

SOLUTION

Step 1: *A sketch.* We sketch D along with its "shadow" R in the xz-plane (Figure 15.32). The upper (right-hand) bounding surface of D lies in the plane $y = 1$. The lower (left-hand) bounding surface lies in the plane $y = x + z$. The upper boundary of R is the line $z = 1 - x$. The lower boundary is the line $z = 0$.

Step 2: *The y-limits of integration.* The line through a typical point (x, z) in R parallel to the y-axis enters D at $y = x + z$ and leaves at $y = 1$.

Step 3: *The z-limits of integration.* The line L through (x, z) parallel to the z-axis enters R at $z = 0$ and leaves at $z = 1 - x$.

Step 4: *The x-limits of integration.* As L sweeps across R, the value of x varies from $x = 0$ to $x = 1$. The integral is

$$\int_0^1 \int_0^{1-x} \int_{x+z}^{1} F(x, y, z)\, dy\, dz\, dx.$$

As we know, there are sometimes (but not always) two different orders in which the single integrations for evaluating a double integral may be worked. For triple integrals, there could be as many as *six*.

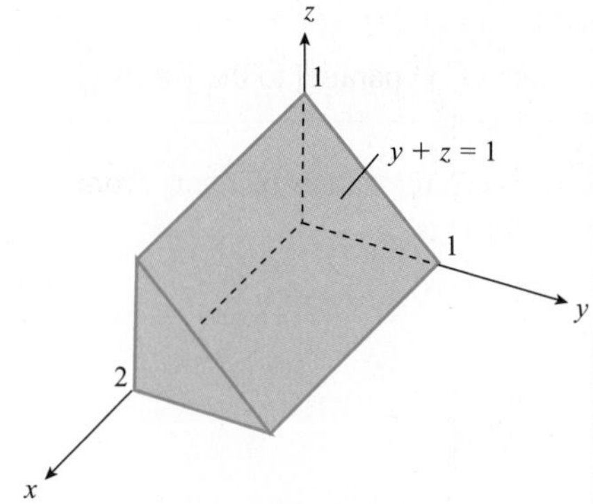

Figure 15.33 Example 3 gives six different iterated triple integrals for the volume of this prism.

EXAMPLE 3 Finding Volume

Each of the following integrals gives the volume of the solid shown in Figure 15.33.

(a) $\displaystyle\int_0^1 \int_0^{1-z} \int_0^{2} dx\, dy\, dz$ **(b)** $\displaystyle\int_0^1 \int_0^{1-y} \int_0^{2} dx\, dz\, dy$

(c) $\displaystyle\int_0^1 \int_0^{2} \int_0^{1-z} dy\, dx\, dz$ **(d)** $\displaystyle\int_0^2 \int_0^{1} \int_0^{1-z} dy\, dz\, dx$

(e) $\displaystyle\int_0^1 \int_0^{2} \int_0^{1-y} dz\, dx\, dy$ **(f)** $\displaystyle\int_0^2 \int_0^{1} \int_0^{1-y} dz\, dy\, dx$

Average Value of a Function in Space

The average value of a function F over a region D in space is defined by the formula

$$\textbf{Average value} \text{ of } F \text{ over } D = \frac{1}{\text{volume of } D} \iiint_D F\, dV. \tag{5}$$

For example, if $F(x, y, z) = \sqrt{x^2 + y^2 + z^2}$, then the average value of F over D is the average distance of points in D form the origin. If $F(x, y, z)$ is the density of a solid that occupies a region D in space, then the average value of F over D is the average density of the solid in units of mass per unit volume.

EXAMPLE 4 Finding Average Value

Find the average value of $F(x, y, z) = xyz$ over the cube bounded by the coordinate planes and the planes $x = 2$, $y = 2$, and $z = 2$ in the first octant.

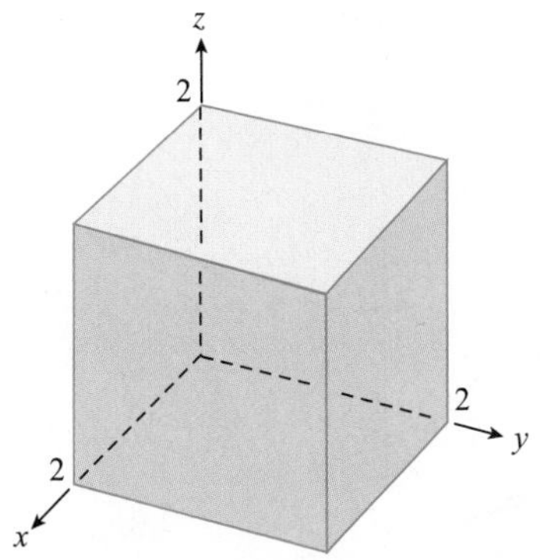

Figure 15.34 The region of integration in Example 4.

SOLUTION

We sketch the cube with enough detail to show the limits of integration (Figure 15.34). We then use Equation (5) to calculate the average value of F over the cube.

The volume of the cube is $(2)(2)(2) = 8$. The value of the integral of F over the cube is

$$\int_0^2\int_0^2\int_0^2 xyz\,dx\,dy\,dz = \int_0^2\int_0^2\left[\frac{x^2}{2}yz\right]_{x=0}^{x=2} dy\,dz = \int_0^2\int_0^2 2yz\,dy\,dz$$

$$= \int_0^2 [y^2z]_{y=0}^{y=2}\,dz = \int_0^2 4z\,dz = [2z^2]_0^2 = 8.$$

With these values, Equation (5) gives

$$\text{Average value of } xyz \text{ over the cube} = \frac{1}{\text{volume}}\iiint_{\text{cube}} xyz\,dV$$

$$= \left(\frac{1}{8}\right)(8) = 1.$$

In evaluating the integral, we choose the order dx, dy, dz, but any of the other five possible orders would have done as well.

Quick Review 15.4

In Exercises 1 and 2, assume $\int_0^3 f(x)\,dx = 2$. Evaluate the integral.

1. $\int_0^3 2f(x)\,dx = 2.$

2. $\int_0^3 (x + f(x))\,dx$

In Exercises 3 and 4, explain, without evaluating the integral, why the inequality is a true statement.

3. $\int_0^3 (x^2 + 4)\,dx \geq 0$

4. $\int_1^4 x(4 - x)\,dx \geq \int_1^4 xe^{-x}\,dx$

In Exercises 5–8, $\int_a^b f(x)\,dx = -2$, $\int_a^b g(x)\,dx = 3$, $\int_b^c f(x)\,dx = 4$, and $\int_b^c g(x)\,dx = -1$. Evaluate the integral.

5. $\int_a^c (f(x) - g(x))\,dx$

6. $\int_a^c (f(x) + g(x))\,dx$

7. $\int_a^c (2f(x) + 3g(x))\,dx$

8. $\int_a^c (rf(x) + sg(x))\,dx$ (r, s constants)

9. Find the average value of $f(x) = \sin x$ over the interval $[0, \pi]$.

10. Find the average value of $f(x, y) = \cos(x + y)$ over the rectangle $0 \leq x \leq \pi$, $0 \leq y \leq \pi$.

Section 15.4 Exercises

1. Find the common value of the integrals in Example 3.

2. Write the six different iterated triple integrals for the volume of the rectangular solid in the first octant bounded by the coordinate planes and the planes $x = 1$, $y = 2$, and $z = 3$. Evaluate one of the integrals.

3. Write six different iterated triple integrals for the volume of the tetrahedron cut from the first octant by the plane $6x + 3y + 2z = 6$. Evaluate one of the integrals.

4. Write six different iterated triple integrals for the volume of the region in the first octant enclosed by the cylinder $x^2 + z^2 = 4$ and the plane $y = 3$. Evaluate one of the integrals.

5. Let D be the region bounded by the paraboloids $z = 8 - x^2 - y^2$ and $z = x^2 + y^2$. Write six different triple iterated integrals for the volume of D. Evaluate one of the integrals.

6. Let D be the region bounded by the paraboloid $z = x^2 + y^2$ and the plane $z = 2y$. Write triple iterated integrals in the order $dz\,dx\,dy$ and $dz\,dy\,dx$ that give the volume of D. Do not evaluate either integral.

In Exercises 7–20, evaluate the integral.

7. $\displaystyle\int_0^1\int_0^1\int_0^1 (x^2 + y^2 + z^2)\,dz\,dy\,dx$

8. $\displaystyle\int_0^{\sqrt{2}}\int_0^{3y}\int_{x^2+3y^2}^{8-x^2-y^2} dz\,dx\,dy$

9. $\displaystyle\int_1^e\int_1^e\int_1^e \frac{1}{xyz}\,dx\,dy\,dz$

10. $\displaystyle\int_0^1\int_0^{3-3x}\int_0^{3-3x-y} dz\,dy\,dx$

11. $\displaystyle\int_0^1\int_0^{\pi}\int_0^{\pi} y\sin z\,dx\,dy\,dz$

12. $\displaystyle\int_{-1}^1\int_{-1}^1\int_{-1}^1 (x + y + z)\,dy\,dx\,dz$

13. $\displaystyle\int_0^3\int_0^{\sqrt{9-x^2}}\int_0^{\sqrt{9-x^2}} dz\,dy\,dx$

14. $\displaystyle\int_0^2\int_{-\sqrt{4-y^2}}^{\sqrt{4-y^2}}\int_0^{2x+y} dz\,dx\,dy$

15. $\displaystyle\int_0^1\int_0^{2-x}\int_0^{2-x-y} dz\,dy\,dx$

16. $\displaystyle\int_0^1\int_0^{1-x^2}\int_3^{4-x^2-y} x\,dz\,dy\,dx$

17. $\displaystyle\int_0^{\pi}\int_0^{\pi}\int_0^{\pi} \cos(u + v + w)\,du\,dv\,dw$ (*uvw*-space)

18. $\displaystyle\int_1^e\int_1^e\int_1^e \ln r \ln s \ln t\,dt\,dr\,ds$ (*rst*-space)

19. $\displaystyle\int_0^{\pi/4}\int_0^{\ln \sec v}\int_{-\infty}^{2t} e^x\,dx\,dt\,dv$ (*tvx*-space)

20. $\displaystyle\int_0^7\int_0^2\int_0^{\sqrt{4-q^2}} \frac{q}{r+1}\,dp\,dq\,dr$ (*pqr*-space)

21. Here is the region of integration of the integral

$$\int_{-1}^1\int_{x^2}^1\int_0^{1-y} dz\,dy\,dx.$$

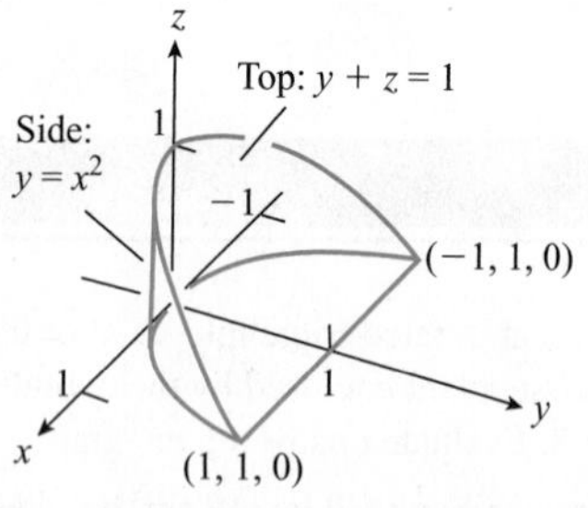

Rewrite the integral as an equivalent iterated integral in the order

(a) $dy\,dz\,dx$ **(b)** $dy\,dx\,dz$
(c) $dx\,dy\,dz$ **(d)** $dx\,dz\,dy$
(e) $dz\,dx\,dy$

22. Here is the region of integration of the integral

$$\int_0^1\int_{-1}^0\int_0^{y^2} dz\,dy\,dx.$$

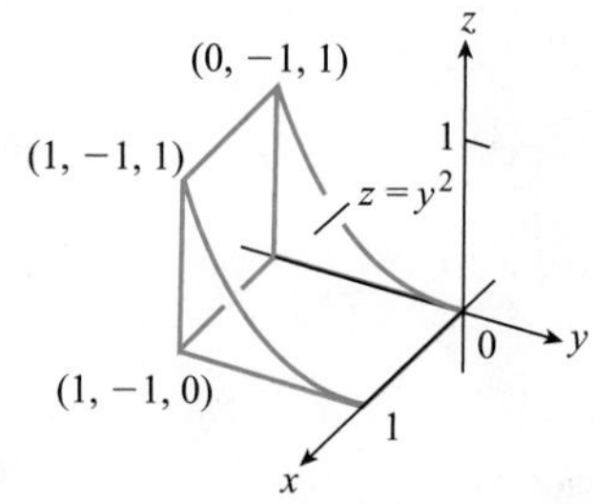

Rewrite the integral as an equivalent iterated integral in the order

(a) $dy\,dz\,dx$ **(b)** $dy\,dx\,dz$
(c) $dx\,dy\,dz$ **(d)** $dx\,dz\,dy$
(e) $dz\,dx\,dy$

In Exercises 23–26, find the volume of the region.

23. The region between the cylinder $z = y^2$ and the xy-plane that is bounded by the planes $x = 0$, $x = 1$, $y = -1$, $y = 1$

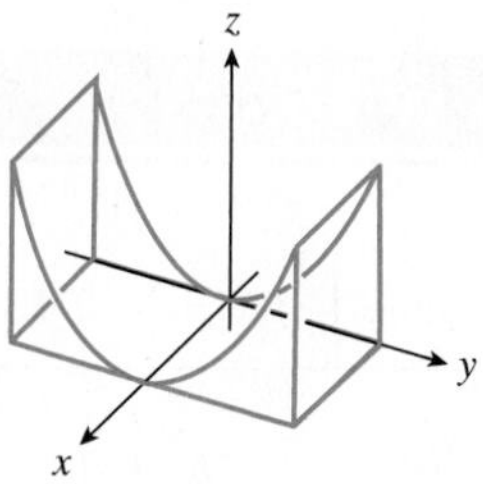

24. The region in the first octant bounded by the coordinate planes and the planes $x + z = 1$, $y + 2z = 2$

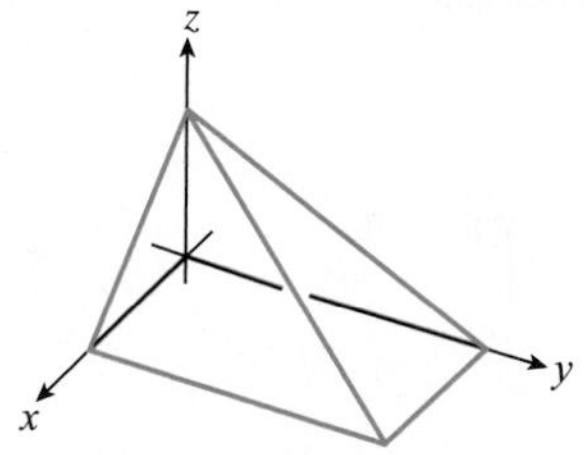

25. The region in the first octant bounded by the coordinate planes, the plane $y + z = 2$, and the cylinder $x = 4 - y^2$

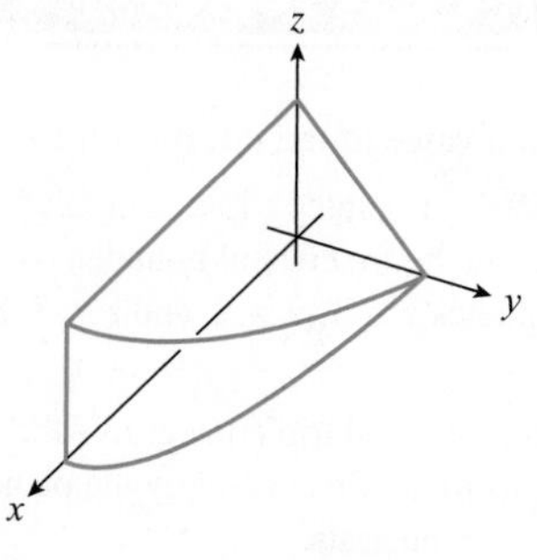

26. The wedge cut from the cylinder $x^2 + y^2 = 1$ by the planes $z = -y$ and $z = 0$

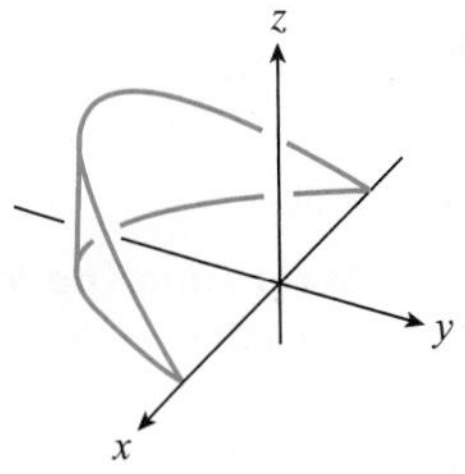

27. The tetrahedron in the first octant bounded by the coordinate planes and the plane $x + y/2 + z/3 = 1$

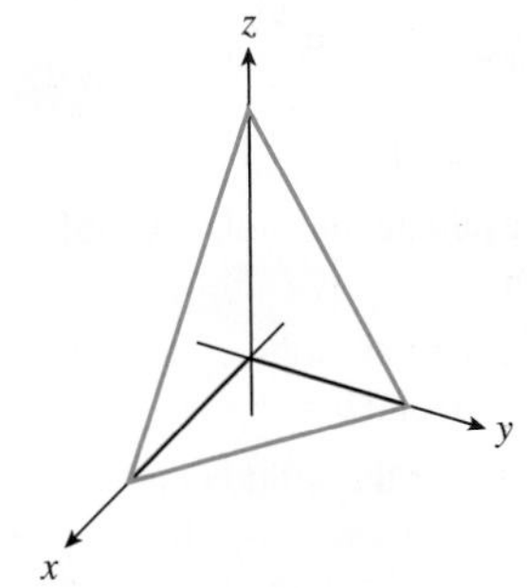

28. The region in the first octant bounded by the coordinate planes, the plane $y = 1 - x$, and the surface $z = \cos(\pi x/2)$, $0 \leq x \leq 1$

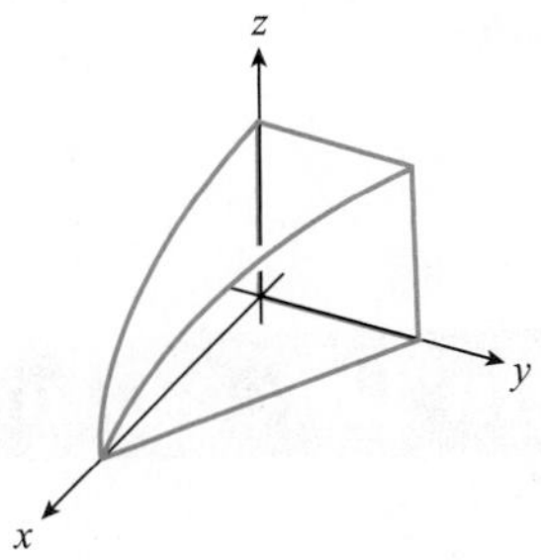

29. The region common to the interiors of the cylinders $x^2 + y^2 = 1$ and $x^2 + z^2 = 1$

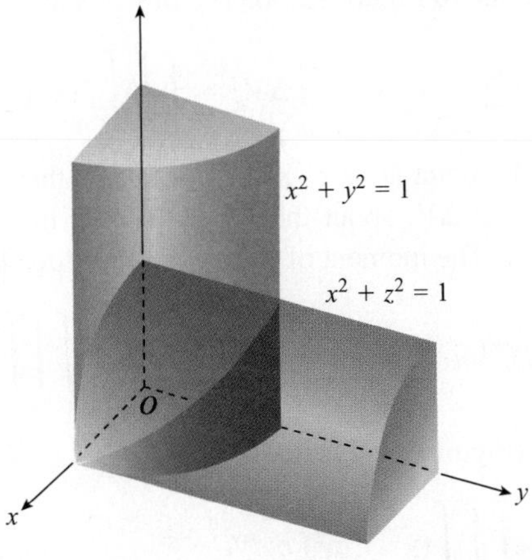

Figure 15.35 One-eighth of the region common to the cylinders $x^2 + y^2 = 1$ and $x^2 + z^2 = 1$ in Exercise 29.

30. The region in the first octant bounded by the coordinate planes and the surface $z = 4 - x^2 - y^2$

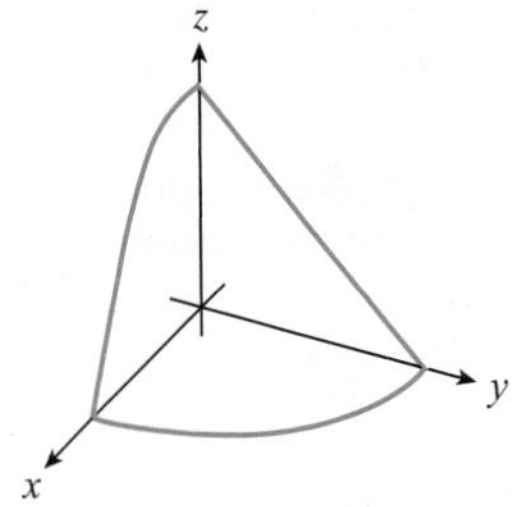

31. The region in the first octant bounded by the coordinate planes, the plane $x + y = 4$, and the cylinder $y^2 + 4z^2 = 16$

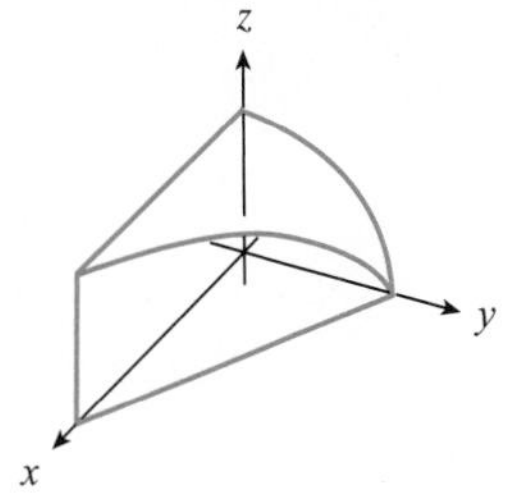

32. The region cut from the cylinder $x^2 + y^2 = 4$ by the plane $z = 0$ and the plane $x + z = 3$

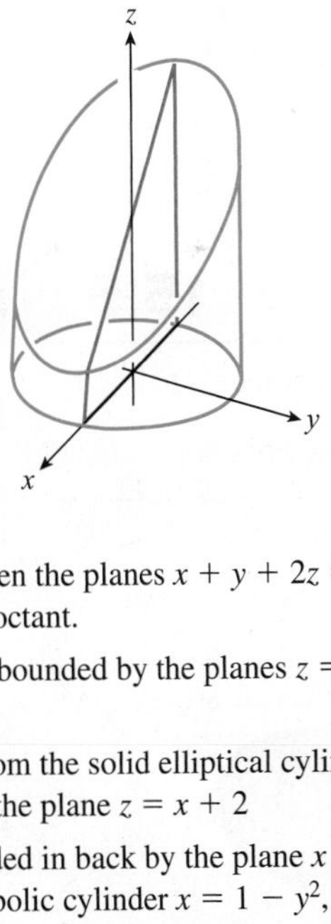

33. The region between the planes $x + y + 2z = 2$ and $2x + 2y + z = 4$ in the first octant.

34. The finite region bounded by the planes $z = x$, $x + z = 8$, $z = y$, $y = 8$, and $z = 0$

35. The region cut from the solid elliptical cylinder $x^2 + 4y^2 \leq 4$ by the xy-plane and the plane $z = x + 2$

36. The region bounded in back by the plane $x = 0$, on the front and sides by the parabolic cylinder $x = 1 - y^2$, on the top by the paraboloid $z = x^2 + y^2$, and on the bottom by the xy-plane

In Exercises 37–40, find the average value of $F(x, y, z)$ over the given region.

37. $F(x, y, z) = x^2 + 9$ over the cube in the first octant bounded by the coordinate planes and the planes $x = 2$, $y = 2$, and $z = 2$

38. $F(x, y, z) = x + y - z$ over the rectangular solid in the first octant bounded by the coordinate planes and the planes $x = 1$, $y = 1$, and $z = 2$

39. $F(x, y, z) = x^2 + y^2 + z^2$ over the cube in the first octant bounded by the coordinate planes and the planes $x = 1$, $y = 1$, and $z = 1$

40. $F(x, y, z) = xyz$ over the cube in the first octant bounded by the coordinate planes and the planes $x = 2$, $y = 2$, and $z = 2$

In Exercises 41–44, *work in groups of two or three* to evaluate the integrals by changing the order of integration in an appropriate way.

41. $\displaystyle\int_0^4 \int_0^1 \int_{2y}^2 \frac{4\cos(x^2)}{2\sqrt{z}}\, dx\, dy\, dz$

42. $\displaystyle\int_0^1 \int_0^1 \int_{x^2}^1 12xze^{zy^2}\, dy\, dx\, dz$

43. $\displaystyle\int_0^1 \int_{\sqrt[3]{z}}^1 \int_0^{\ln 3} \frac{\pi e^{2x} \sin \pi y^2}{y^2}\, dx\, dy\, dz$

44. $\displaystyle\int_0^2 \int_0^{4-x^2} \int_0^x \frac{\sin 2z}{4 - z}\, dy\, dz\, dx$

Explorations

45. Solve for a:

$$\int_0^1 \int_0^{4-a-x^2} \int_a^{4-x^2-y} dz\, dy\, dx = \frac{4}{15}.$$

46. For what value of c is the volume of the ellipsoid $x^2 + (y/2)^2 + z/c)^2 = 1$ equal to 8π?

47. Writing to Learn *Minimizing the Value of an Integral* What domain D in space minimizes the value of the integral

$$\iiint_D (4x^2 + 4y^2 + z^2 - 4)\, dV?$$

Give reasons for your answer.

48. Writing to Learn *Maximizing the Value of an Integral* What domain D in space maximizes the value of the integral

$$\iiint_D (1 - x^2 - y^2 - z^2)\, dV?$$

Give reasons for your answer.

Extending the Ideas

CAS Explorations

In Exercises 49–52, evaluate the triple integral of $F(x, y, z)$ over the specified solid region.

49. $F(x, y, z) = x^2y^2z$ over the solid cylinder bounded by $x^2 + y^2 = 1$ and the planes $z = 0$ and $z = 1$

50. $F(x, y, z) = |xyz|$ over the solid bounded below by the paraboloid $z = x^2 + y^2$ and above by the plane $z = 1$

51. $F(x, y, z) = z/(x^2 + y^2 + z^2)^{3/2}$ over the solid bounded below by the cone $z = \sqrt{x^2 + y^2}$ and above by the plane $z = 1$

52. $F(x, y, z) = x^4 + y^2 + z^2$ over the solid sphere $x^2 + y^2 + z^2 \le 1$

15.5 Masses and Moments in Three Dimensions

What you'll learn about

- Masses and Moments

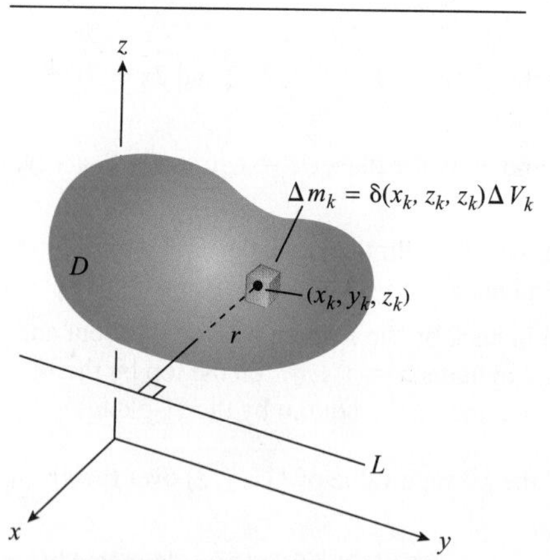

Figure 15.36 To define an object's mass and moment of inertia about a line, we first imagine it to be partitioned into a finite number of mass elements Δm_k.

Masses and Moments

If $\delta(x, y)$ is the density of an object occupying a region D in space (mass per unit volume), the integral of δ over D gives the mass of the object. To see why, imagine partitioning the object into n mass elements like the one in Figure 15.36. The object's mass is the limit

$$M = \lim_{n\to\infty} \sum_{k=1}^{n} \Delta m_k = \lim_{n\to\infty} \sum_{k=1}^{n} \delta(x_k, y_{yk}, z_k)\, \Delta V_k = \iiint_D \delta(x, y, z)\, dV. \qquad (1)$$

If $r(x, y, z)$ is the distance from the point (x, y, z) in D to a line L, then the moment of inertia of the mass $\Delta m_k = \delta(x_k, y_k, z_k)\, \Delta V_k$ about the line L (shown in Figure 15.36) is approximately $\Delta I_k = r^2(x_k, y_k, z_k)\, \Delta m_k$. The moment of inertia of the entire object about L is

$$I_L = \lim_{n\to\infty} \sum_{k=1}^{n} \Delta I_k = \lim_{n\to\infty} \sum r^2(x_k, y_k, z_k)\, \delta(x_k, y_k, z_k)\, \Delta V_k = \iiint_D r^2 \delta\, dV.$$

If L is the x-axis, then $r^2 = y^2 + z^2$ (Figure 15.37) and

$$I_x = \iiint_D (y^2 + z^2)\, \delta\, dV.$$

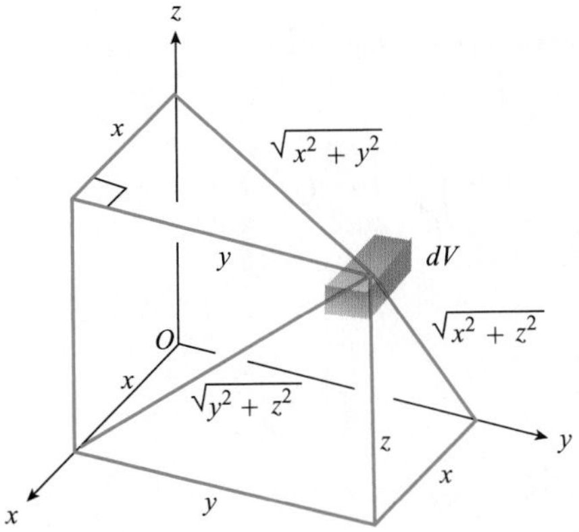

Figure 15.37 Distances from dV to the coordinate planes and axes.

Similarly,

$$I_y = \iiint_D (x^2 + z^2)\,\delta\,dV \qquad \text{and} \qquad I_z = \iiint_D (x^2 + y^2)\,\delta\,dV.$$

These and other useful formulas are summarized in Table 15.2.

Table 15.2 **Mass and Moment Formulas for Objects in Space**

Mass: $M = \iiint_D \delta\,dV \qquad (\delta = \text{density})$

First moments about the coordinate planes:

$$M_{yz} = \iiint_D x\delta\,dV, \qquad M_{xz} = \iiint_D y\delta\,dV, \qquad M_{xy} = \iiint_D z\delta\,dV$$

Center of mass:

$$\bar{x} = \frac{M_{yz}}{M}, \qquad \bar{y} = \frac{M_{xz}}{M}, \qquad \bar{z} = \frac{M_{xy}}{M}$$

Moments of inertia (second moments):

$$I_x = \iiint_D (y^2 + z^2)\delta\,dV$$

$$I_y = \iiint_D (x^2 + z^2)\delta\,dV$$

$$I_z = \iiint_D (x^2 + y^2)\delta\,dV$$

Moment of inertia about a line *L*:

$$I_L = \iiint_D r^2\delta\,dV$$ (where $r(x, y, z)$ = distance from points (x, y, z) to line L)

Radius of gyration about a line *L*:

$$R_L = \sqrt{I_L/M}$$

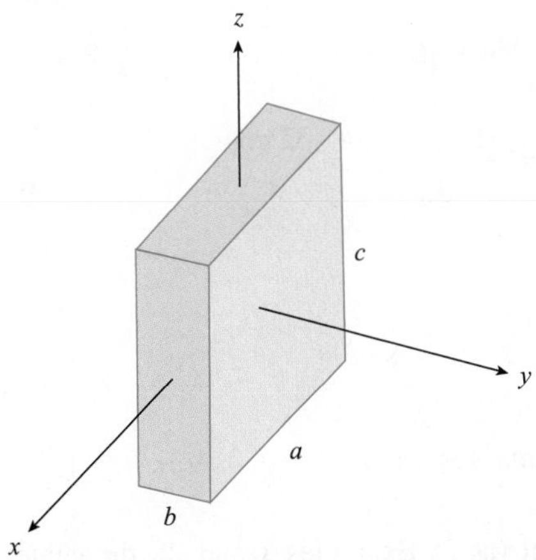

Figure 15.38 Example 1 calculates I_x, I_y, and I_z for the block shown here. The origin lies at the center of the block.

EXAMPLE 1 Finding Moments of Inertia

Find I_x, I_y, and I_z for the rectangular solid of constant density δ shown in Figure 15.38.

SOLUTION

The preceding formula for I_x gives

$$I_x = \int_{-c/2}^{c/2} \int_{-b/2}^{b/2} \int_{-a/2}^{a/2} (y^2 + z^2)\delta\,dx\,dy\,dz. \tag{2}$$

We can avoid some of the work of integration by observing that $(y^2 + z^2)\delta$ is an even function of *x, y, and z* and therefore

$$I_x = 8\int_0^{c/2}\int_0^{b/2}\int_0^{a/2}(y^2 + z^2)\delta\,dx\,dy\,dz = 4a\delta\int_0^{c/2}\int_0^{b/2}(y^2 + z^2)\,dy\,dz$$

$$= 4a\delta\int_0^{c/2}\left[\frac{y^3}{3} + z^2y\right]_{y=0}^{y=b/2}dz$$

$$= 4a\delta\int_0^{c/2}\left(\frac{b^3}{24} + \frac{z^2b}{2}\right)dz$$

$$= 4a\delta\left(\frac{b^3c}{48} + \frac{c^3b}{48}\right) = \frac{abc\delta}{12}(b^2 + c^2)$$

$$= \frac{M}{12}(b^2 + c^2). \qquad M = abc\,\delta$$

Similarly,

$$I_y = \frac{M}{12}(a^2 + c^2) \quad \text{and} \quad I_z = \frac{M}{12}(a^2 + b^2).$$

EXAMPLE 2 Finding Center of Mass

Find the center of mass of a solid of constant density δ bounded below by the disk R: $x^2 + y^2 \le 4$ in the plane $z = 0$ and above by the paraboloid $z = 4 - x^2 - y^2$ (Figure 15.39).

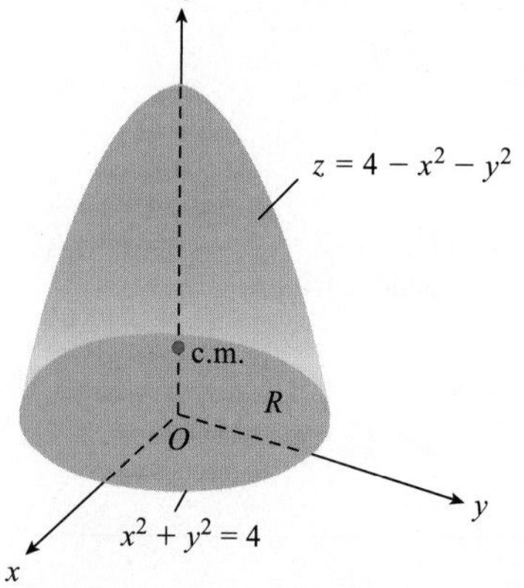

Figure 15.39 Example 2 finds the center of mass of this solid.

SOLUTION

By symmetry, $\bar{x} = \bar{y} = 0$. To find $\bar{z}$, we first calculate

$$M_{xy} = \iint_R\int_{z=0}^{z=4-x^2-y^2} z\delta\,dz\,dy\,dx = \iint_R\left[\frac{z^2}{2}\right]_{z=0}^{z=4-x^2-y^2}\delta\,dy\,dx$$

$$= \frac{\delta}{2}\iint_R(4 - x^2 - y^2)^2\,dy\,dx$$

$$= \frac{\delta}{2}\int_0^{2\pi}\int_0^2(4 - r^2)^2r\,dr\,d\theta \qquad \text{Polar coordinates}$$

$$= \frac{\delta}{2}\int_0^{2\pi}\left[-\frac{1}{6}(4 - r^2)^3\right]_{r=0}^{r=2}d\theta = \frac{16\delta}{3}\int_0^{2\pi}d\theta = \frac{32\pi\delta}{3}.$$

A similar calculation gives

$$M = \iint_R\int_0^{4-x^2-y^2}\delta\,dz\,dy\,dx = 8\pi\delta.$$

Therefore $\bar{z} = (M_{xy}/M) = 4/3$, and the center of mass is $(\bar{x}, \bar{y}, \bar{z}) = (0, 0, 4/3)$.

When the density of a solid object is constant (as in Examples 1 and 2), the center of mass is the **centroid** of the object (as was the case for two-dimensional shapes in Section 15.2).

Quick Review 15.5

In Exercises 1–10, a thin plate of density $\delta = 2$ occupies the region in the xy-plane bounded by the lines $x = 0$, $y = 3x$, and the parabola $y = 4 - x^2$ in the first quadrant. Find the plate's

1. mass.
2. moment about the x-axis.
3. moment about the y-axis.
4. center of mass.
5. moment of inertia about the x-axis.
6. moment of inertia about the y-axis.
7. moment of inertia about the origin.
8. radius of gyration about the x-axis.
9. radius of gyration about the y-axis.
10. radius of gyration about the origin.

Section 15.5 Exercises

In Exercises 1–12, the solid has constant density $\delta = 1$.

1. Evaluate the integral for I_x in Equation (2) in the text directly to show that the shortcut in Example 1 gives the same answer. Use the results in Example 1 to find the radius of gyration of the rectangular solid about each coordinate axis.

2. The coordinate axes in the figure shown here run through the centroid of a solid wedge parallel to the labeled edges. Find I_x, I_y, and I_z, if $a = b = 6$ and $c = 4$.

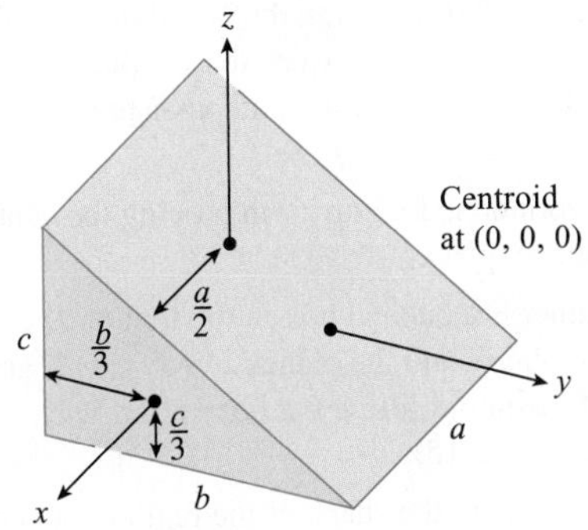

3. Find the moments of inertia of the rectangular solid shown here with respect to its edges by calculating I_x, I_y, and I_z.

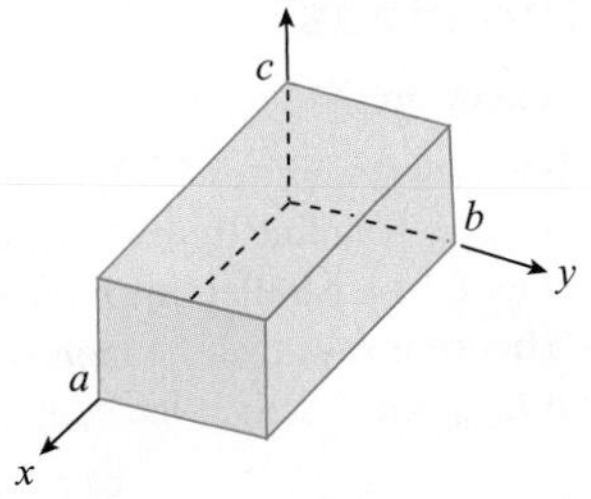

4. **(a)** Find the centroid and the moments of inertia I_x, I_y, and I_z of the tetrahedron whose vertices are the points (0, 0, 0), (1, 0, 0), (0, 1, 0), and (0, 0, 1).

   (b) Find the radius of gyration of the tetrahedron about the x-axis. Compare it with the distance from the centroid to the x-axis.

5. A solid "trough" is bounded below by the surface $z = 4y^2$, above by the plane $z = 4$, and on the ends by the planes $x = 1$ and $x = -1$. Find the center of mass and the moments of inertia with respect to the three axes.

6. A solid is bounded below by the plane $z = 0$, on the sides by the elliptical cylinder $x^2 + 4y^2 = 4$, and above by the plane $z = 2 - x$ (see the figure).

   (a) Find $\bar{x}$ and $\bar{y}$.

   (b) Evaluate the integral

$$M_{xy} = \int_{-2}^{2} \int_{-(1/2)\sqrt{4-x^2}}^{(1/2)\sqrt{4-x^2}} \int_{0}^{2-x} z \, dz \, dy \, dx,$$

   using integral tables or technology to carry out the final integration with respect to x. Then divide M_{xy} by M to verify that $\bar{z} = 5/4$.

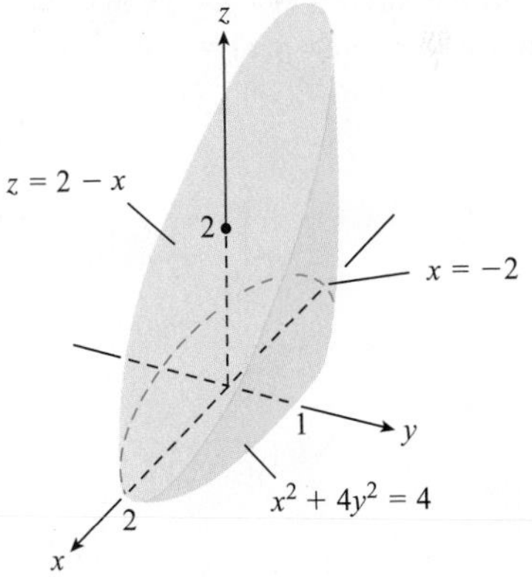

7. **(a)** Find the center of mass of a solid bounded below by the paraboloid $z = x^2 + y^2$ and above by the plane $z = 4$.

   (b) Find the plane $z = c$ that divides the solid into two parts of equal volume. This plane does not pass through the center of mass.

8. A solid cube, 2 units on a side, is bounded by the planes $x = \pm 1$, $z = \pm 1$, $y = 3$, and $y = 5$. Find the center of mass and the moments of inertia and radii of gyration about the coordinate axes.

9. A wedge like the one in Exercise 2 has $a = 4$, $b = 6$, and $c = 3$. Make a quick sketch to check for yourself that the square of the distance from a typical point (x, y, z) of the wedge to the line L: $z = 0, y = 6$ is $r^2 = (y - 6)^2 + z^2$. Then calculate the moment of inertia and radius of gyration of the wedge about L.

10. A wedge like the one in Exercise 2 has $a = 4$, $b = 6$, and $c = 3$. Make a quick sketch to check for yourself that the square of the distance from a typical point (x, y, z) of the wedge to the line L: $x = 4, y = 0$ is $r^2 = (x - 4)^2 + y^2$. Then calculate the moment of inertia and radius of gyration of the wedge about L.

11. A solid like the one in Exercise 3 has $a = 4$, $b = 2$, and $c = 1$. Make a quick sketch to check for yourself that the square of the distance from a typical point (x, y, z) of the wedge to the line L: $y = 2, z = 0$ is $r^2 = (y - 2)^2 + z^2$. Then find the moment of inertia and radius of gyration of the solid about L.

12. A solid like the one in Exercise 3 has $a = 4$, $b = 2$, and $c = 1$. Make a quick sketch to check for yourself that the square of the distance from a typical point (x, y, z) of the wedge to the line L: $x = 4, y = 0$ is $r^2 = (x - 4)^2 + y^2$. Then find the moment of inertia and radius of gyration of the solid about L.

In Exercises 13–18, the solid has variable density. In Exercises 13 and 14, find **(a)** the mass of the solid and **(b)** the center of mass.

13. A solid region in the first octant is bounded by the coordinate planes and the plane $x + y + z = 2$. The density of the solid is $\delta(x, y, z) = 2x$.

14. A solid in the first octant is bounded by the planes $y = 0$ and $z = 0$ and by the surfaces $z = 4 - x^2$ and $x = y^2$ (see the figure). Its density function is $\delta(x, y, z) = kxy$.

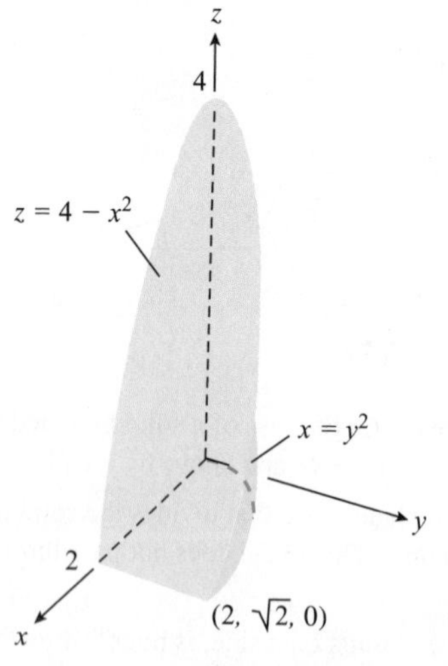

In Exercises 15 and 16, find

(a) the mass of the solid,

(b) the center of mass,

(c) the moments of inertia about the coordinate axes,

(d) the radii of gyration about the coordinate axes.

15. A solid cube in the first octant is bounded by the coordinate planes and by the planes $x = 1$, $y = 1$, and $z = 1$. The density of the cube is $\delta(x, y, z) = x + y + z + 1$.

16. A wedge like the one in Exercise 2 has dimensions $a = 2$, $b = 6$, and $c = 3$. The density is $\delta(x, y, z) = x + 1$. Notice that if the density is constant, the center of mass will be $(0, 0, 0)$.

17. Find the mass of the solid bounded by the planes $x + z = 1$, $x - z = -1$, $y = 0$ and the surface $y = \sqrt{z}$. The density of the solid is $\delta(x, y, z) = 2y + 5$.

18. Find the mass of the solid region bounded by the parabolic surfaces $z = 16 - 2x^2 - 2y^2$ and $z = 2x^2 + 2y^2$ if the density of the solid is $\delta(x, y, z) = \sqrt{x^2 + y^2}$.

Explorations

In Exercises 19 and 20, calculate the following.

(a) Writing to Learn The amount of work done by (constant) gravity g in moving the liquid filling the container to the xy-plane. (*Hint:* Partition the liquid into small volume elements ΔV_i and find the work done (approximately) by gravity on each element. Summation and passage to the limit gives a triple integral to evaluate.)

(b) The work done by gravity in moving the center of mass down to the xy-plane.

19. The container is a cubical box in the first octant bounded by the coordinate planes and the planes $x = 1$, $y = 1$, and $z = 1$. The density of the liquid filling the box is $\delta(x, y, z) = x + y + z + 1$ (refer to Exercise 15).

20. The container is in the shape of the region bounded by $y = 0$, $z = 0$, $z = 4 - x^2$, and $x = y^2$. The density of the liquid filling the region is $\delta(x, y, z) = kxy$ (see Exercise 14).

Extending the Ideas

The Parallel Axis Theorem

The Parallel Axis Theorem (Exercises 15.2) holds in three dimensions as well as in two. Let $L_{\text{c.m.}}$ be a line through the center of mass of a body of mass m and let L be a parallel line h units away from $L_{\text{c.m.}}$. The **Parallel Axis Theorem** says that the moments of inertia $I_{\text{c.m.}}$ and I_L of the body about $L_{\text{c.m.}}$ and L satisfy the equation

$$I_L = I_{\text{c.m.}} + mh^2. \qquad (1)$$

As in the two-dimensional case, the theorem gives a quick way to calculate one moment when the other moment and the mass are known.

21. ***Proof of the Parallel Axis Theorem***

(a) Show that the first moment of a body in space about any plane through the body's center of mass is zero. (*Hint:* Place the body's center of mass at the origin and let the plane be the yz-plane. What does the formula $\bar{x} = M_{yz}/M$ then tell you?)

(b) To prove the Parallel Axis Theorem, place the body with its center of mass at the origin, with the line $L_{\text{c.m.}}$ along the z-axis and the line L perpendicular to the xy-plane at the point $(h, 0, 0)$. Let D be the region of space occupied by the body. Then, in the notation of the figure,

$$I_L = \iiint |\mathbf{v} - h\mathbf{i}|^2\, dm. \tag{2}$$

Expand the integrand in this integral and complete the proof.

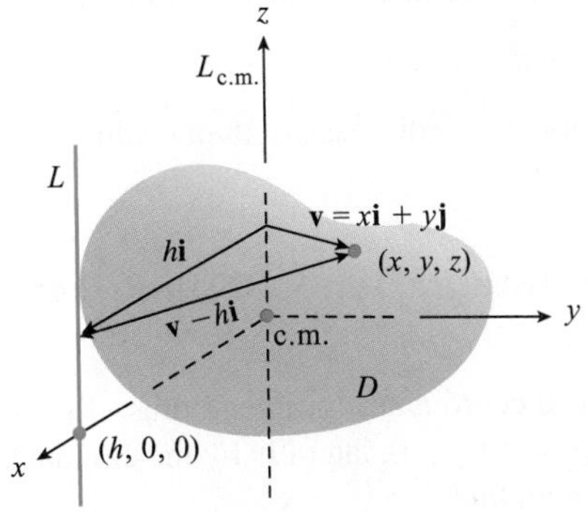

22. ***Using the Parallel Axis Theorem*** The moment of inertia about a diameter of a solid sphere of constant density and radius a is $(2/5)ma^2$, where m is the mass of the sphere. Find the moment of inertia about a line tangent to the sphere.

23. ***Using the Parallel Axis Theorem*** The moment of inertia of the solid in Exercise 3 about the z-axis is $I_z = abc(a^2 + b^2)/3$.

(a) Use Equation (1) to find the moment of inertia and radius of gyration of the solid about the line parallel to the z-axis through the solid's center of mass.

(b) Use Equation (1) and the result in (a) to find the moment of inertia and radius of gyration of the solid about the line $x = 0$, $y = 2b$.

24. ***Using the Parallel Axis Theorem*** If $a = b = 6$ and $c = 4$, the moment of inertia of the solid wedge in Exercise 2 about the x-axis is $I_x = 208$. Find the moment of inertia of the wedge about the line $y = 4$, $z = -4/3$ (the edge of the wedge's narrow end).

Pappus's Formula

Pappus's formula (Exercises 15.2) holds in three dimensions as well as in two. Suppose bodies B_1 and B_2 of mass m_1 and m_2, respectively, occupy nonoverlapping regions in space and $\mathbf{c}_1$ and $\mathbf{c}_2$ are the vectors from the origin to the bodies' respective centers of mass. Then the center of mass of the union $B_1 \cup B_2$ of the two bodies is determined by the vector

$$\mathbf{c} = \frac{m_1\mathbf{c}_1 + m_2\mathbf{c}_2}{m_1 + m_2}. \tag{3}$$

As before, this formula is **Pappus's formula.** As in the two-dimensional case, the formula generalizes to

$$\mathbf{c} = \frac{m_1\mathbf{c}_1 + m_2\mathbf{c}_2 + \cdots + m_n\mathbf{c}_n}{m_1 + m_2 + \cdots + m_n}. \tag{4}$$

for n bodies.

25. ***Deriving Pappus's Formula*** Derive Pappus's formula (Equation (3)). (*Hint:* Sketch B_1 and B_2 as nonoverlapping regions in the first octant and label their centers of mass $(\bar{x}_1, \bar{y}_1, \bar{z}_1)$ and $(\bar{x}_2, \bar{y}_2, \bar{z}_2)$. Express the moments of $B_1 \cup B_2$ about the coordinate planes in terms of the masses m_1 and m_2 and the coordinates of these centers.)

26. ***Applying Pappus's Formula*** The figure shows a solid made from three rectangular solids of constant density $\delta = 1$. Use Pappus's formula to find the center of mass of

(a) $A \cup B$. **(b)** $A \cup C$.

(c) $B \cup C$. **(d)** $A \cup B \cup C$.

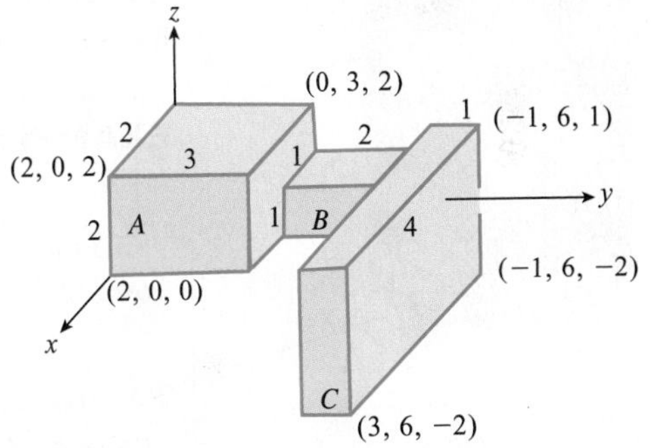

27. **(a)** **Writing to Learn** ***Designing an Ice Cream Cone*** Suppose a solid right circular cone C of base radius a and altitude h is constructed on the circular base of a solid hemisphere S of radius a so that the union of the two solids resembles an ice cream cone. The centroid of a solid cone lies one-fourth of the way from the base toward the vertex. The centroid of a solid hemisphere lies three-eights of the way from the base to the top. What relation must hold between h and a to place the centroid of $C \cup S$ in the common base of the two solids?

(b) If you have not already done so, answer the analogous question about a triangle and a semicircle (Section 15.2, Exercise 55). The answers are not the same.

28. **Writing to Learn** ***Shape Design*** A solid pyramid P with height h and four congruent sides is built with its base as one face of a solid cube C whose edges have length s. The centroid of a solid pyramid lies one-fourth of the way from the base toward the vertex. What relation must hold between h and s to place the centroid of $P \cup C$ in the base of the pyramid? Compare your answer with the answer to Exercise 27. Also compare it to the answer to Exercise 56 in Section 15.2.

15.6 Triple Integrals in Cylindrical and Spherical Coordinates

What you'll learn about

- Integration in Cylindrical Coordinates
- Spherical Coordinates
- Integration in Spherical Coordinates

Integration in Cylindrical Coordinates

Cylindrical coordinates (Figure 15.40) are good for describing cylinders whose axes run along the z-axis and planes that either contain the z-axis or lie perpendicular to the z-axis. As we saw in Section 12.5, surfaces like these have equations of constant coordinate value:

$$r = 4, \qquad \text{Cylinder, radius 4, axis the } z\text{-azis}$$

$$\theta = \frac{\pi}{3}, \qquad \text{Plane containing the } z\text{-axis}$$

$$z = 2. \qquad \text{Plane perpendicular to the } z\text{-azis}$$

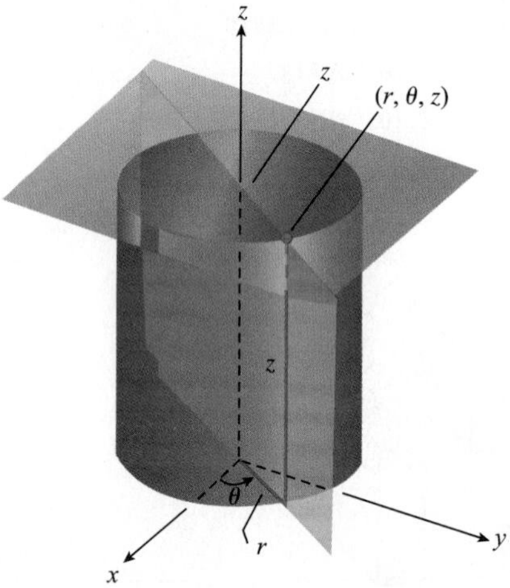

Figure 15.40 Cylindrical coordinates and typical surfaces of constant coordinate value.

The volume element for subdividing a region in space with cylindrical coordinates is

$$dV = dz\, r\, dr\, d\theta \tag{1}$$

(Figure 15.41). Triple integrals in cylindrical coordinates are then evaluated as iterated integrals, as in the following example.

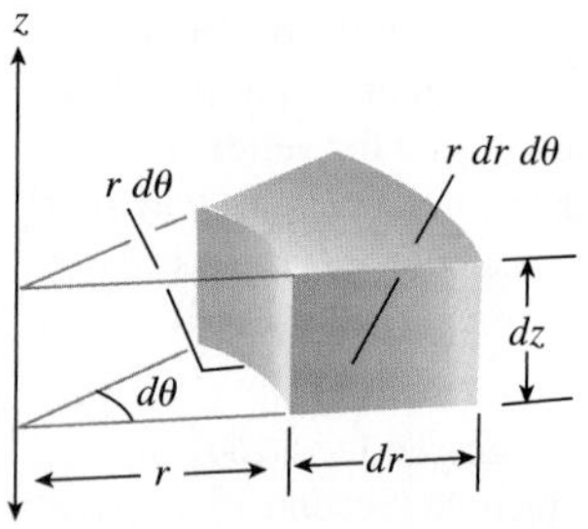

Figure 15.41 The volume element in cylindrical coordinates is $dV = dz\, r\, dr\, d\theta$.

EXAMPLE 1 Finding Limits of Integration in Cylindrical Coordinates

Find the limits of integration in cylindrical coordinates for integrating a function $f(r, \theta, z)$ over the region D bounded below by the plane $z = 0$, laterally by the circular cylinder $x^2 + (y - 1)^2 = 1$, and above by the paraboloid $z = x^2 + y^2$.

SOLUTION

Step 1: *A sketch* (Figure 15.42). The base of D is also the region's projection R on the xy-plane. The boundary of R is the circle $x^2 + (y - 1)^2 = 1$. Its polar coordinate equation is

$$x^2 + (y - 1)^2 = 1$$
$$x^2 + y^2 - 2y + 1 = 1$$
$$r^2 - 2r \sin\theta = 0$$
$$r = 2 \sin\theta.$$

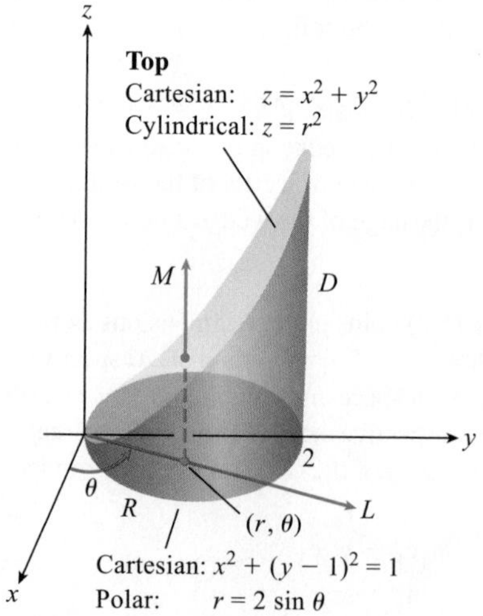

Figure 15.42 The figure for Example 1.

Step 2: *The z-limits of integration.* A line M through a typical point (r, θ) in R parallel to the z-axis enters D at $z = 0$ and leaves at $z = x^2 + y^2 = r^2$.

Step 3: *The r-limits of integration.* A ray L through (r, θ) from the origin enters R at $r = 0$ and leaves at $r = 2 \sin \theta$.

Step 4: *The θ-limits of integration.* As L sweeps across R, the angle θ it makes with the positive x-axis runs from $\theta = 0$ to $\theta = \pi$. The integral is

$$\iiint_D f(r, \theta, z)\, dV = \int_0^{\pi} \int_0^{2 \sin \theta} \int_0^{r^2} f(r, \theta, z)\, dz\, r\, dr\, d\theta.$$

Example 1 illustrates a good procedure for finding limits of integration in cylindrical coordinates. The procedure is summarized below.

How to Integrate in Cylindrical Coordinates

To evaluate

$$\iiint_D f(r, \theta, z)\, dV$$

over a region D in space in cylindrical coordinates, integrating first with respect to z, then with respect to r, and finally with respect to θ, take the following steps.

1. *A sketch.* Sketch the region D along with its projection R on the xy-plane. Label the surfaces and curves that bound D and R.

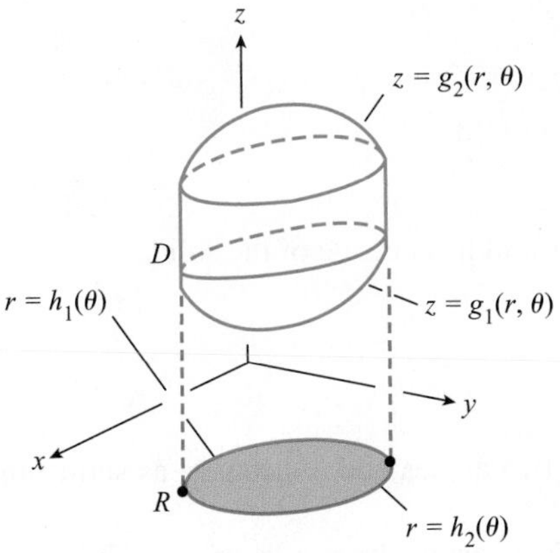

2. *The z-limits of integration.* Draw a line M through a typical point (r, θ) of R parallel to the z-axis. As z increases, M enters D at $z = g_1(r, \theta)$ and leaves at $z = g_2(r, \theta)$. These are the z-limits of integration.

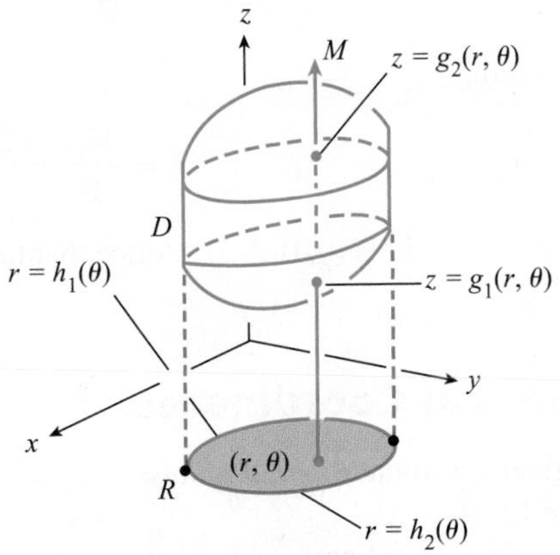

3. *The r-limits of integration.* Draw a ray L through (r, θ) from the origin. The ray enters R at $r = h_1(\theta)$ and leaves at $r = h_2(\theta)$. These are the r-limits of integration.

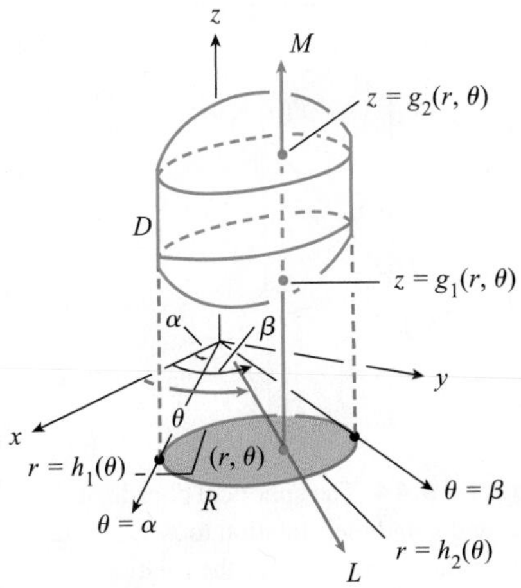

4. *The θ-limits of integration.* As L sweeps across R, the angle θ it makes with the positive x-axis runs from $\theta = \alpha$ to $\theta = \beta$. These are the θ-limits of integration. The integral is

$$\iiint_D f(r, \theta, z)\, dV = \int_{\theta=\alpha}^{\theta=\beta} \int_{r=h_1(\theta)}^{r=h_2(\theta)} \int_{z=g_1(r,\theta)}^{z=g_2(r,\theta)} f(r, \theta, z)\, dz\, r\, dr\, d\theta.$$

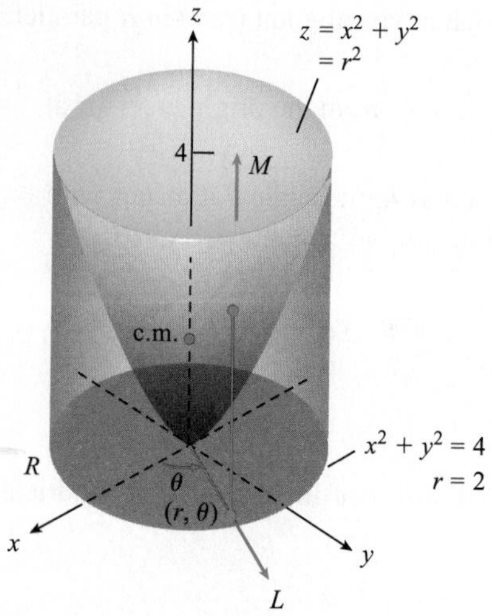

Figure 15.43 Example 2 shows how to find the centroid of this solid.

EXAMPLE 2 Finding a Centroid

Find the centroid ($\delta = 1$) of the solid enclosed by the cylinder $x^2 + y^2 = 4$, bounded above by the paraboloid $z = x^2 + y^2$ and below by the xy-plane.

SOLUTION

Step 1: *A sketch.* We sketch the solid, bounded above by the paraboloid $z = r^2$ and below by the plane $z = 0$ (Figure 15.43). Its base R is the disk $|r| \leq 2$ in the xy-plane.

The solid's centroid $(\bar{x}, \bar{y}, \bar{z})$ lies on its axis of symmetry, here the z-axis. This makes $\bar{x} = \bar{y} = 0$. To find $\bar{z}$, we divide the first moment M_{xy} by the mass M.

To find the limits of integration for the mass and moment integrals, we continue with the four basic steps. We completed step 1 with our initial sketch. The remaining steps give the limits of integration.

Step 2: *The z-limits.* A line M through a typical point (r, θ) in the base parallel to the z-axis enters the solid at $z = 0$ and leaves at $z = r^2$.

Step 3: *The r-limits.* A ray L through (r, θ) from the origin enters R at $r = 0$ and leaves at $r = 2$.

Step 4: *The θ-limits.* As L sweeps over the base like a clock hand moving backward, the angle θ it makes with the positive x-axis runs from $\theta = 0$ to $\theta = 2\pi$. The value of M_{xy} is

$$M_{xy} = \int_0^{2\pi}\int_0^2\int_0^{r^2} z\,dz\,r\,dr\,d\theta = \int_0^{2\pi}\int_0^2\left[\frac{z^2}{2}\right]_0^{r^2} r\,dr\,d\theta$$

$$= \int_0^{2\pi}\int_0^2 \frac{r^5}{2}\,dr\,d\theta = \int_0^{2\pi}\left[\frac{r^6}{12}\right]_0^2 d\theta = \int_0^{2\pi}\frac{16}{3}\,d\theta = \frac{32\pi}{3}.$$

The value of M is

$$M = \int_0^{2\pi}\int_0^2\int_0^{r^2} dz\,r\,dr\,d\theta = \int_0^{2\pi}\int_0^2 [z]_0^{r^2}\,r\,dr\,d\theta$$

$$= \int_0^{2\pi}\int_0^2 r^3\,dr\,d\theta = \int_0^{2\pi}\left[\frac{r^4}{4}\right]_0^2 d\theta = \int_0^{2\pi} 4\,d\theta = 8\pi.$$

Therefore,

$$\bar{z} = \frac{M_{xy}}{M} = \frac{32\pi}{3}\frac{1}{8\pi} = \frac{4}{3},$$

and the centroid is (0, 0, 4/3). Notice that the centroid lies outside of the solid.

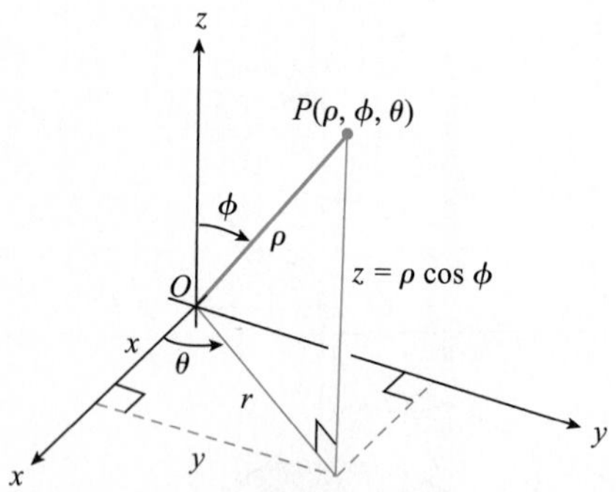

Figure 15.44 The spherical coordinates ρ, ϕ, and θ and their relation to x, y, z, and r. From the figure, we read the relations $r = \rho \sin \phi$, $z = \rho \cos \phi$, $x = r \cos \theta$, $y = r \sin \theta$.

Spherical Coordinates

Spherical coordinates locate points in space with two angles and a distance, as shown in Figure 15.44.

The first coordinate, $\rho = |\overrightarrow{OP}|$, is the point's distance from the origin. Unlike r, *the variable ρ is never negative.* The second coordinate, ϕ, is the angle $\overrightarrow{OP}$ makes with the positive z-axis. It is required to lie in the interval $[0, \pi]$. The third coordinate is the angle θ as measured in cylindrical coordinates.

A few books give spherical coordinates in the order (ρ, θ, ϕ), with θ and ϕ reversed. In some cases, you may also find r being used for ρ. Watch out for this when you read elsewhere.

DEFINITION Spherical Coordinates

Spherical coordinates represent a point P in space by ordered triples (ρ, ϕ, θ) in which

1. ρ is the distance from P to the origin,
2. ϕ is the angle $\overrightarrow{OP}$ makes with the positive z-axis $(0 \le \phi \le \pi)$, and
3. θ is the angle from cylindrical coordinates.

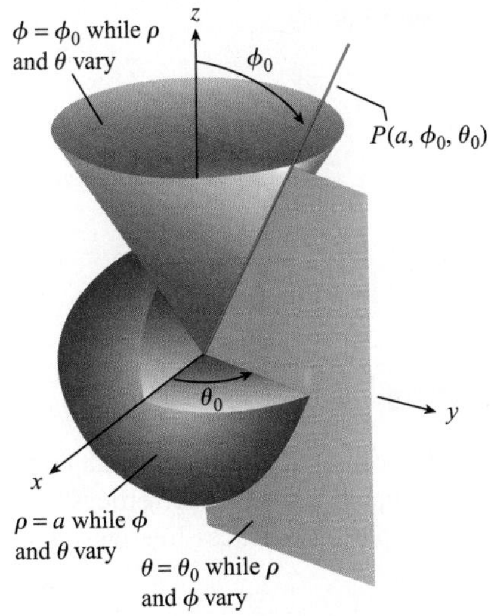

Figure 15.45 Constant-coordinate equations in spherical coordinates yield spheres, single cones, and half-planes.

The equation $\rho = a$ describes the sphere of radius a centered at the origin (Figure 15.45). The equation $\phi = \phi_0$ describes a single cone whose vertex lies at the origin and whose axis lies along the z-axis. (We broaden our interpretation to include the xy-plane as the cone $\phi = \pi/2$.) If ϕ_0 is greater than $\pi/2$, the cone $\phi = \phi_0$ opens downward.

Equations Relating Spherical Coordinates to Cartesian and Cylindrical Coordinates

$$r = \rho \sin \phi, \qquad x = r \cos \theta = \rho \sin \phi \cos \theta,$$
$$z = \rho \cos \phi, \qquad y = r \sin \theta = \rho \sin \phi \sin \theta, \tag{3}$$
$$\rho = \sqrt{x^2 + y^2 + z^2} = \sqrt{r^2 + z^2}$$

EXAMPLE 3 Converting Cartesian to Spherical

Find a spherical coordinate equation for the sphere $x^2 + y^2 + (z - 1)^2 = 1$.

SOLUTION

We use Equations (3) to substitute for x, y, and z:

$$x^2 + y^2 + (z - 1)^2 = 1$$
$$\rho^2 \sin^2 \phi \cos^2 \theta + \rho^2 \sin^2 \phi \sin^2 \theta + (\rho \cos \phi - 1)^2 = 1 \qquad \text{Eqs. (3)}$$
$$\rho^2 \sin^2 \phi \underbrace{(\cos^2 \theta + \sin^2 \theta)}_{1} + \rho^2 \cos^2 \phi - 2\rho \cos \phi + 1 = 1$$
$$\rho^2 \underbrace{(\sin^2 \phi + \cos^2 \phi)}_{1} = 2\rho \cos \phi$$
$$\rho^2 = 2\rho \cos \phi$$
$$\rho = 2 \cos \phi.$$

See Figure 15.46.

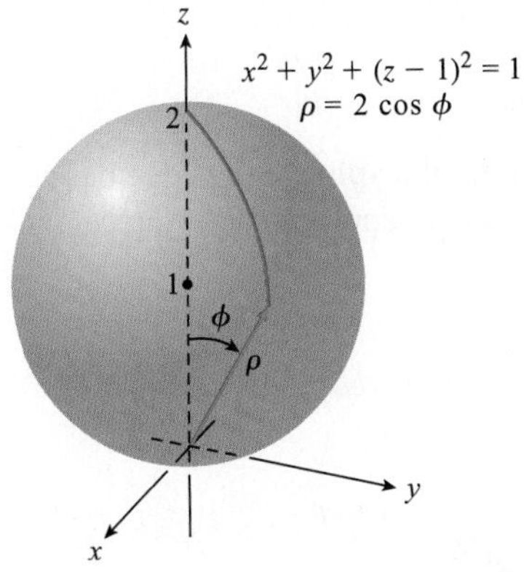

Figure 15.46 The sphere in Example 3.

EXAMPLE 4 Converting Cartesian to Spherical

Find a spherical coordinate equation for the cone $z = \sqrt{x^2 + y^2}$ (Figure 15.47).

SOLUTION 1

Use geometry. The cone is symmetric with respect to the z-axis and cuts the first quadrant of the yz-plane along the line $z = y$. The angle between the cone and the positive z-axis is therefore $\pi/4$ radians. The cone consists of the points whose spherical coordinates have ϕ equal to $\pi/4$, so its equation is $\phi = \pi/4$.

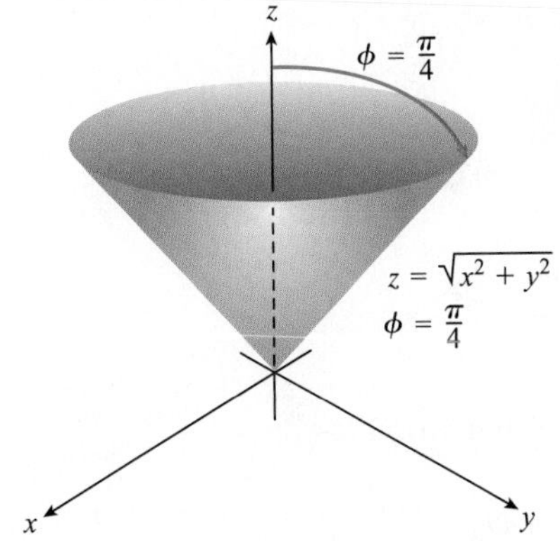

Figure 15.47 The cone in Example 4.

SOLUTION 2

Use algebra. If we use Equations (3) to substitute for x, y, and z, we obtain the same result:

$$z = \sqrt{x^2 + y^2}$$

$$\rho \cos \phi = \sqrt{\rho^2 \sin^2 \phi} \qquad \text{Example 3 details}$$

$$\rho \cos \phi = \rho \sin \phi \qquad \rho \geq 0,\ \sin \phi \geq 0$$

$$\cos \phi = \sin \phi$$

$$\phi = \frac{\pi}{4}. \qquad 0 \leq \phi \leq \pi$$

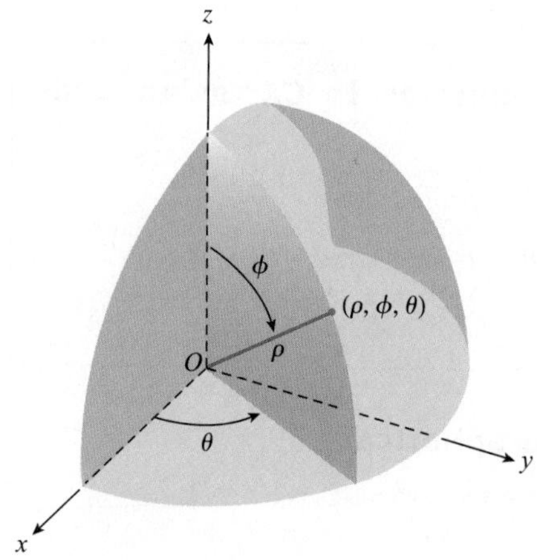

Figure 15.48 Spherical coordinates are measured with a distance and two angles.

Integration in Spherical Coordinates

Spherical coordinates (Figure 15.48) are good for describing spheres centered at the origin, half-planes hinged along the z-axis, and single-napped cones whose vertices lie at the origin and whose axes lie along the z-axis (see Example 4). Surfaces like these have equations of constant coordinate value:

$$\rho = 4, \qquad \text{Sphere, radius 4, center at the origin}$$

$$\phi = \frac{\pi}{3}, \qquad \text{Cone opening up from the origin, making an angle of } \pi/3 \text{ radians with the positive } z\text{-axis}$$

$$\theta = \frac{\pi}{3}. \qquad \text{Half-plane, hinged along the } z\text{-axis, making an angle of } \pi/3 \text{ radians with the positive } x\text{-axis}$$

The volume element in spherical coordinates is the volume of a **spherical wedge** defined by the differentials $d\rho$, $d\phi$, and $d\theta$ (Figure 15.49). The wedge is approximately a rectangu-

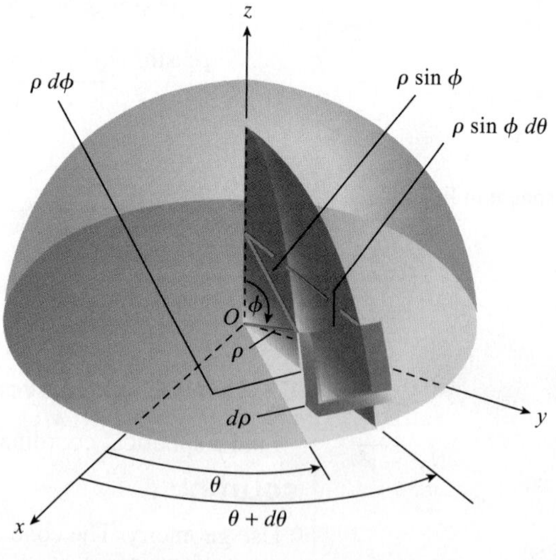

Figure 15.49 The volume element in spherical coordinates is

$$dV = d\rho \cdot \rho\, d\phi \cdot \rho \sin \phi\, d\theta = \rho^2 \sin \phi\, d\rho\, d\phi\, d\theta.$$

lar box with one side a circular arc of length $\rho d\phi$, another side a circular arc of length $\rho \sin \phi \, d\theta$, and thickness $d\rho$. Therefore, the volume element in spherical coordinates is

$$dV = \rho^2 \sin \phi \, d\rho \, d\phi \, d\theta, \tag{4}$$

and triple integrals take the form

$$\iiint F(\rho, \phi, \theta) \, dV = \iiint F(\rho, \phi, \theta) \rho^2 \sin \phi \, d\rho \, d\phi \, d\theta. \tag{5}$$

To evaluate these integrals, we usually integrate first with respect to ρ. The procedure for finding limits of integration follows. We restrict our attention to integrating over domains that are solids of revolution about the z-axis (or portions thereof) and for which the limits for θ and ϕ are constant.

How to Integrate in Spherical Coordinates

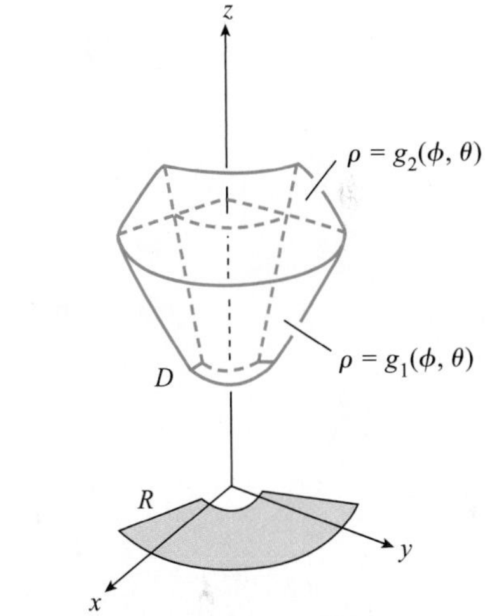

To evaluate

$$\iiint_D f(\rho, \phi, \theta) \, dV$$

over a region D in space in spherical coordinates, integrating first with respect to ρ, then with respect to ϕ, and finally with respect to θ, take the following steps.

1. *A sketch.* Sketch the region D along with its projection R on the xy-plane. Label the surfaces that bound D.
2. *The ρ-limits of integration.* Draw a ray M from the origin making an angle ϕ with the positive z-axis. Also draw the projection of M on the xy-plane (call the projection L). The ray L makes an angle θ with the positive x-axis. As ρ increases, M enters D at $\rho = g_1(\phi, \theta)$ and leaves at $\rho = g_2(\phi, \theta)$. These are the ρ-limits of integration.
3. *The ϕ-limits of integration.* For any given θ, the angle ϕ that M makes with the z-axis runs from $\phi = \phi_{\min}$ to $\phi = \phi_{\max}$. These are the ϕ-limits of integration.
4. *The θ-limits of integration.* The ray L sweeps over R as θ runs from α to β. These are the θ-limits of integration. The integral is

$$\iiint_D f(\rho, \phi, \theta) \, dV = \int_{\theta=\alpha}^{\theta=\beta} \int_{\phi=\phi_{\min}}^{\phi=\phi_{\max}} \int_{\rho=g_1(\phi,\theta)}^{\rho=g_2(\phi,\theta)} f(\rho, \phi, \theta) \, \rho^2 \sin \phi \, d\rho \, d\phi \, d\theta. \tag{6}$$

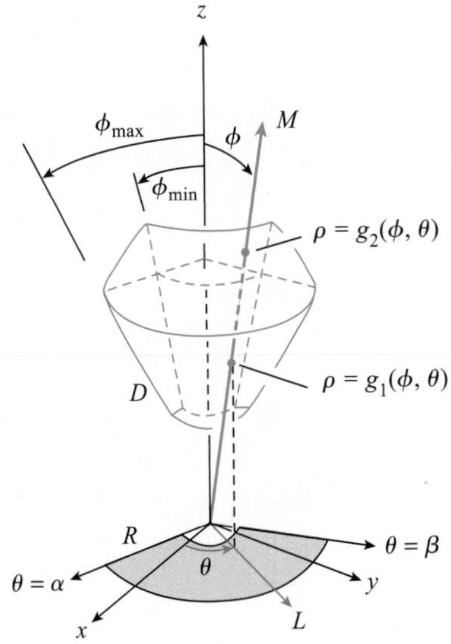

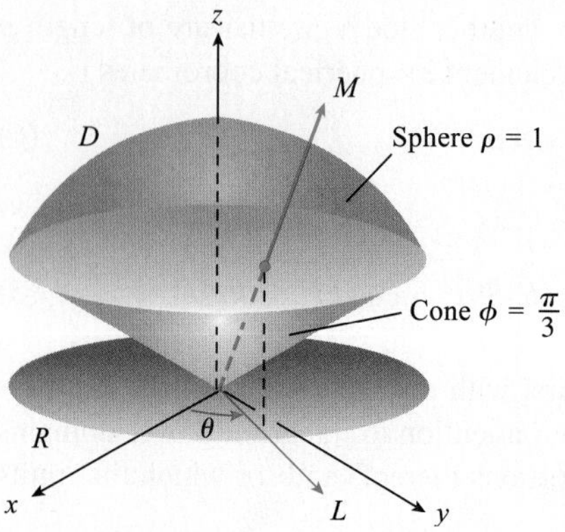

Figure 15.50 The solid in Example 5.

EXAMPLE 5 Finding Volume in Spherical Coordinates

Find the volume of the upper region D cut from the solid sphere $\rho \leq 1$ by the cone $\phi = \pi/3$.

SOLUTION

The volume is $\iiint_D \rho^2 \sin\phi \, d\rho \, d\phi \, d\theta$, the integral of $f(\rho, \phi, \theta) = 1$ over D.

To find the limits of integration for evaluating the integral, we take the following steps.

Step 1: *A sketch.* We sketch D and its projection R on the xy-plane (Figure 15.50).

Step 2: *The ρ-limits of integration.* We draw a ray M from the origin making an angle ϕ with the positive z-axis. We also draw L, the projection of M on the xy-plane, along with the angle θ that L makes with the positive x-axis. Ray M enters D at $\rho = 0$ and leaves at $\rho = 1$.

Step 3: *The ϕ-limits of integration.* The cone $\phi = \pi/3$ makes an angle of $\pi/3$ with the positive z-axis. For any given θ, the angle ϕ can run from $\phi = 0$ to $\phi = \pi/3$.

Step 4: *The θ-limits of integration.* The ray L sweeps over R as θ runs from 0 to 2π. The volume is

$$V = \iiint_D \rho^2 \sin\phi \, d\rho \, d\phi \, d\theta = \int_0^{2\pi} \int_0^{\pi/3} \int_0^1 \rho^2 \sin\phi \, d\rho \, d\phi \, d\theta$$

$$= \int_0^{2\pi} \int_0^{\pi/3} \left[\frac{\rho^3}{3}\right]_0^1 \sin\phi \, d\phi \, d\theta = \int_0^{2\pi} \int_0^{\pi/3} \frac{1}{3} \sin\phi \, d\phi \, d\theta$$

$$= \int_0^{2\pi} \left[-\frac{1}{3}\cos\phi\right]_0^{\pi/3} d\theta = \int_0^{2\pi} \left(-\frac{1}{6} + \frac{1}{3}\right) d\theta = \frac{\pi}{3} \text{ units cubed.}$$

EXAMPLE 6 Finding a Moment of Inertia

A solid of constant density $\delta = 1$ occupies the region D in Example 5. Find the solid's moment of inertia about the z-axis.

SOLUTION

In rectangular coordinates, the moment is

$$I_z = \iiint (x^2 + y^2) \, dV.$$

In spherical coordinates,

$$x^2 + y^2 = (\rho \sin\phi \cos\theta)^2 + (\rho \sin\phi \sin\theta)^2 = \rho^2 \sin^2\phi.$$

Hence,

$$I_z = \iiint (\rho^2 \sin^2\phi) \rho^2 \sin\phi \, d\rho \, d\phi \, d\theta = \iiint \rho^4 \sin^3\phi \, d\rho \, d\phi \, d\theta.$$

For the region in Example 5, this becomes

$$I_z = \int_0^{2\pi}\int_0^{\pi/3}\int_0^1 \rho^4 \sin^3\phi\, d\rho\, d\phi\, d\theta = \int_0^{2\pi}\int_0^{\pi/3}\left[\frac{\rho^5}{5}\right]_0^1 \sin^3\phi\, d\phi\, d\theta$$

$$= \frac{1}{5}\int_0^{2\pi}\int_0^{\pi/3}(1-\cos^2\phi)\sin\phi\, d\phi\, d\theta = \frac{1}{5}\int_0^{2\pi}\left[-\cos\phi + \frac{\cos^3\phi}{3}\right]_0^{\pi/3} d\theta$$

$$= \frac{1}{5}\int_0^{2\pi}\left(-\frac{1}{2} + 1 + \frac{1}{24} - \frac{1}{3}\right) d\theta = \frac{1}{5}\int_0^{2\pi}\frac{5}{24}\, d\theta = \frac{\pi}{12}.$$

Coordinate Conversion Formulas

Cylindrical to Rectangular	Spherical to Rectangular	Spherical to Cylindrical
$x = r\cos\theta$	$x = \rho\sin\phi\cos\theta$	$r = \rho\sin\phi$
$y = r\sin\theta$	$y = \rho\sin\phi\sin\theta$	$z = \rho\cos\phi$
$z = z$	$z = \rho\cos\phi$	$\theta = \theta$

Corresponding volume elements

$$dV = dx\,dy\,dz$$
$$= dz\,r\,dr\,d\theta$$
$$= \rho^2\sin\phi\,d\rho\,d\phi\,d\theta$$

Quick Review 15.6

1. Translate $z = \sqrt{x^2 + y^2}$, $1 \le z \le 2$, into cylindrical coordinates.
2. Translate $z^2 - r^2 = 1$ into rectangular coordinates.

In Exercises 3 and 4, describe the set of points whose cylindrical coordinates satisfy the given equation.

3. $r = 2\sin\theta$
4. $r = 1 + \cos\theta$

In Exercises 5–7, find the trace of the surface $z = x^2 + y^2$ in the given plane.

5. xz-plane
6. yz-plane
7. xy-plane

In Exercises 8–10, find the trace of the surface $z = \sqrt{x^2 + y^2}$ in the given plane.

8. xy-plane
9. yz-plane
10. plane $z = 2$

Section 15.6 Exercises

In Exercises 1–6, the coordinates of a point in space are given in one of two coordinate systems. Find the coordinates of the point in the other system. There may be more than one answer because points in spherical coordinates can have more than one coordinate triple.

	Rectangular (x, y, z)	Spherical (ρ, ϕ, θ)
1.	(0, 0, 0)	
2.	(1, 0, 0)	
3.	(0, 0, 1)	
4.		$(\sqrt{3}, \pi/3, -\pi/2)$
5.		$(2\sqrt{2}, \pi/2, 3\pi/2)$
6.		$(\sqrt{2}, \pi, \pi)$

In Exercises 7–20, translate the equation or the equation and inequality from the given coordinate system (rectangular, cylindrical, spherical) into equations and inequalities in the other two systems. Then identify the figure in space defined by the equation or by the equation and inequality.

7. $r = 0$
8. $x^2 + y^2 = 5$
9. $z = 0$
10. $z = -2$
11. $z = \sqrt{x^2 + y^2}, z \le 1$
12. $\tan^2\phi = 1$
13. $\rho\sin\phi\cos\theta = 0$
14. $x^2 + y^2 + z^2 = 4$
15. $\rho = 5\cos\phi$
16. $\rho = 9\csc\phi$
17. $x^2 + y^2 + (z - 1)^2 = 1, z \le 1$
18. $\rho = 3, \pi/3 \le \phi \le 2\pi/3$

19. $\phi = 3\pi/4,\ 0 \le \rho \le \sqrt{2}$

20. $\phi = \pi/2,\ 0 \le \rho \le \sqrt{7}$

21. Describe the set of points in space whose spherical coordinates satisfy the equation $\rho = 1 - \cos\phi$. Sketch the graph of the equation.

22. ***Horizontal Planes in Cylindrical and Spherical Coordinates***

(a) Show that the plane whose equation is $z = c(c \neq 0)$ in rectangular and cylindrical coordinates has the equation $\rho = c \sec\phi$ in spherical coordinates.

(b) Find an equation for the xy-plane in spherical coordinates.

23. ***Vertical Circular Cylinders in Spherical Coordinates*** Find an equation of the form $\rho = f(\phi)$ for the cylinder $x^2 + y^2 = a^2$.

24. **Writing to Learn *Symmetry*** What symmetry will you find in a surface that has an equation of the form $\rho = f(\phi)$ in spherical coordinates? Give reasons for your answer.

In Exercises 25–28, evaluate the cylindrical coordinate integral.

25. $$\int_0^{2\pi}\int_0^1\int_r^{\sqrt{2-r^2}} dz\, r\, dr\, d\theta$$

26. $$\int_0^{\pi}\int_0^{\theta/\pi}\int_{-\sqrt{4-r^2}}^{3\sqrt{4-r^2}} z\, dz\, r\, dr\, d\theta$$

27. $$\int_0^{2\pi}\int_0^1\int_r^{1/\sqrt{2-r^2}} 3\, dz\, r\, dr\, d\theta$$

28. $$\int_0^{2\pi}\int_0^1\int_{-1/2}^{1/2} (r^2\sin^2\theta + z^2)\, dz\, r\, dr\, d\theta$$

The integrals we have seen so far suggest that there are preferred orders of integration for cylindrical coordinates, but other orders usually work well and are occasionally easier to evaluate. In Exercises 29–32, evaluate the integral.

29. $$\int_0^{2\pi}\int_0^3\int_0^{z/3} r^3\, dr\, dz\, d\theta$$

30. $$\int_{-1}^1\int_0^{2\pi}\int_0^{1+\cos\theta} 4r\, dr\, d\theta\, dz$$

31. $$\int_0^1\int_0^{\sqrt{z}}\int_0^{2\pi} (r^2\cos^2\theta + z^2)\, r\, d\theta\, dr\, dz$$

32. $$\int_0^2\int_{r-2}^{\sqrt{4-r^2}}\int_0^{2\pi} (r\sin\theta + 1)\, r\, d\theta\, dz\, dr$$

In Exercises 33–36, *work in groups of two or three* to solve the problem.

33. Let D be the region bounded below by the plane $z = 0$, above by the sphere $x^2 + y^2 + z^2 = 4$, and on the sides by the cylinder $x^2 + y^2 = 1$. Set up the triple integrals in cylindrical coordinates that give the volume of D using the following orders of integration.

(a) $dz\, dr\, d\theta$ **(b)** $dr\, dz\, d\theta$

(c) $d\theta\, dz\, dr$

34. Let D be the region bounded below by the cone $z = \sqrt{x^2 + y^2}$ and above by the paraboloid $z = 2 - x^2 - y^2$. Set up the triple integrals in cylindrical coordinates that give the volume of D using the following orders of integration.

(a) $dz\, dr\, d\theta$ **(b)** $dr\, dz\, d\theta$

(c) $d\theta\, dz\, dr$

35. Give the limits of integration for evaluating the integral

$$\iiint f(r, \theta, z)\, dz\, r\, dr\, d\theta$$

as an iterated integral over the region that is bounded below by the plane $z = 0$, on the side by the cylinder $r = \cos\theta$, and on top by the paraboloid $z = 3r^2$.

36. Convert the integral

$$\int_{-1}^1\int_0^{\sqrt{1-y^2}}\int_0^z (x^2 + y^2)\, dz\, dx\, dy$$

to an equivalent integral in cylindrical coordinates and evaluate the result.

In Exercises 37–42, set up the iterated integral for evaluating $\iiint_D f(r, \theta, z)\, dz\, r\, dr\, d\theta$ over the given region D.

37. D is the right circular cylinder whose base is the circle $r = 2\sin\theta$ in the xy-plane and whose top lies in the plane $z = 4 - y$ as illustrated in the figure.

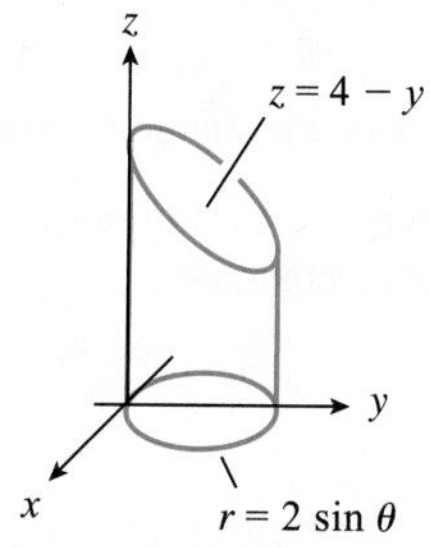

38. D is the right circular cylinder whose base is the circle $r = 3\cos\theta$ and whose top lies in the plane $z = 5 - x$ as illustrated in the figure.

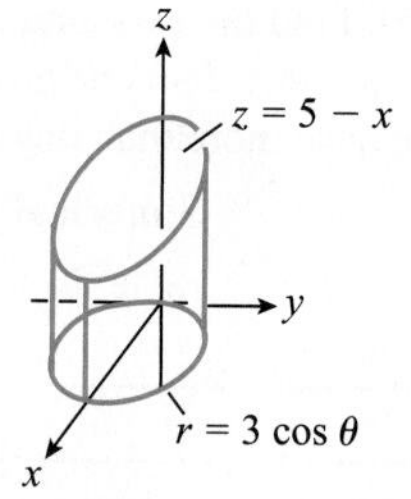

39. D is the solid right cylinder whose base is the region in the xy-plane that lies inside the cardioid $r = 1 + \cos\theta$ and outside the circle $r = 1$ and whose top lies in the plane $z = 4$ as illustrated in the figure.

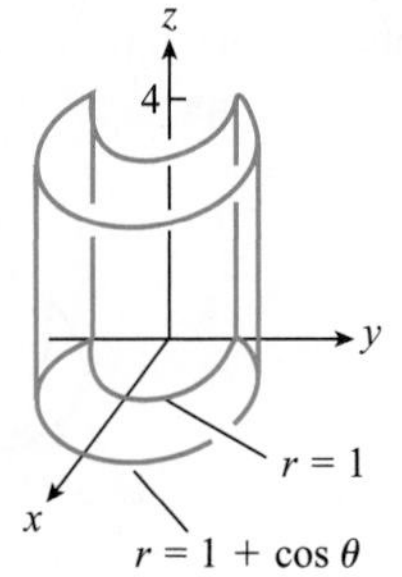

40. D is the solid right cylinder whose base is the region between the circles $r = \cos\theta$ and $r = 2\cos\theta$ and whose top lies in the plane $z = 3 - y$ as illustrated in the figure.

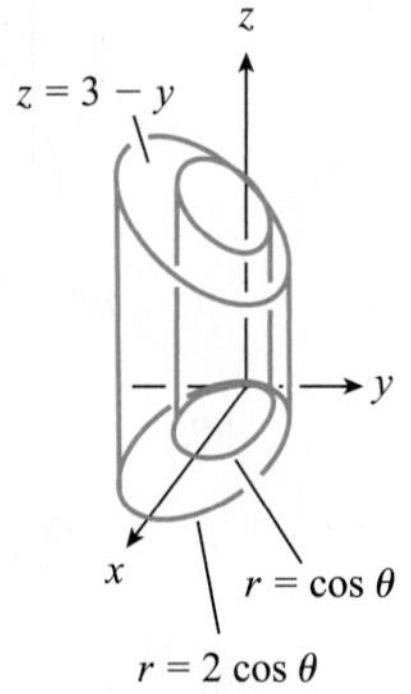

41. D is the prism whose base is the triangle in the xy-plane bounded by the x-axis and the lines $y = x$ and $x = 1$ and whose top lies in the plane $z = 2 - y$ as illustrated in the figure.

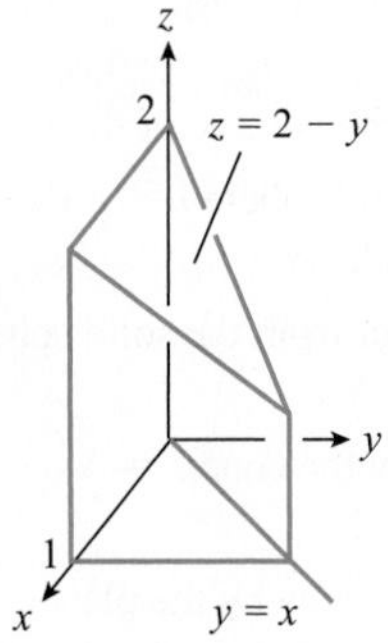

42. D is the prism whose base is the triangle in the xy-plane bounded by the y-axis and the lines $y = x$ and $y = 1$ and whose top lies in the plane $z = 2 - x$ as illustrated in the figure.

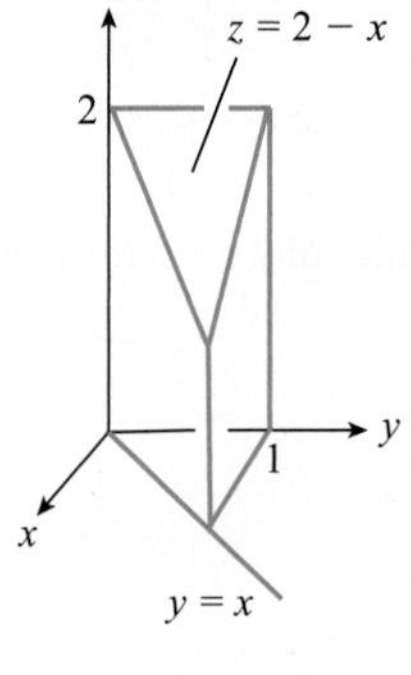

In Exercises 43–46, evaluate the spherical coordinate integral.

43. $\displaystyle\int_0^{\pi}\int_0^{\pi}\int_0^{2\sin\phi} \rho^2 \sin\phi \, d\rho \, d\phi \, d\theta$

44. $\displaystyle\int_0^{2\pi}\int_0^{\pi/4}\int_0^{2} (\rho\cos\phi)\rho^2 \sin\phi \, d\rho \, d\phi \, d\theta$

45. $\displaystyle\int_0^{2\pi}\int_0^{\pi/3}\int_{\sec\phi}^{2} 3\rho^2 \sin\phi \, d\rho \, d\phi \, d\theta$

46. $\displaystyle\int_0^{2\pi}\int_0^{\pi/4}\int_0^{\sec\phi} (\rho\cos\phi)\rho^2 \sin\phi \, d\rho \, d\phi \, d\theta$

While $d\rho\, d\phi\, d\theta$ is the usual order of integration, other orders are possible and occasionally easier to evaluate. In Exercises 47–50, evaluate the integral.

47. $\displaystyle\int_0^{2}\int_{-\pi}^{0}\int_{\pi/4}^{\pi/2} \rho^3 \sin 2\phi \, d\phi \, d\theta \, d\rho$

48. $\displaystyle\int_{\pi/6}^{\pi/3}\int_{\csc\phi}^{2\csc\phi}\int_0^{2\pi} \rho^2 \sin\phi \, d\theta \, d\rho \, d\phi$

49. $\displaystyle\int_0^{1}\int_0^{\pi}\int_0^{\pi/4} 12\rho \sin^3\phi \, d\phi \, d\theta \, d\rho$

50. $\displaystyle\int_{\pi/6}^{\pi/2}\int_{-\pi/2}^{\pi/2}\int_{\csc\phi}^{2} 5\rho^4 \sin^3\phi \, d\rho \, d\theta \, d\phi$

51. Let D be the region in Exercise 33. Set up the triple integrals in spherical coordinates that give the volume of D using the following orders of integration.

(a) $d\rho\, d\phi\, d\theta$ **(b)** $d\phi\, d\rho\, d\theta$

52. Let D be the region bounded below by the cone $z = \sqrt{x^2 + y^2}$ and above by the plane $z = 1$. Set up the triple integrals in spherical coordinates that give the volume of D using the following orders of integration.

(a) $d\rho\, d\phi\, d\theta$ **(b)** $d\phi\, d\rho\, d\theta$

In Exercises 53–58, **(a)** find the spherical coordinate limits for the integral that calculates the volume of the given solid and **(b)** then evaluate the integral.

53. The solid between the sphere $\rho = \cos\phi$ and the hemisphere $\rho = 2$, $z \ge 0$, as illustrated in the figure.

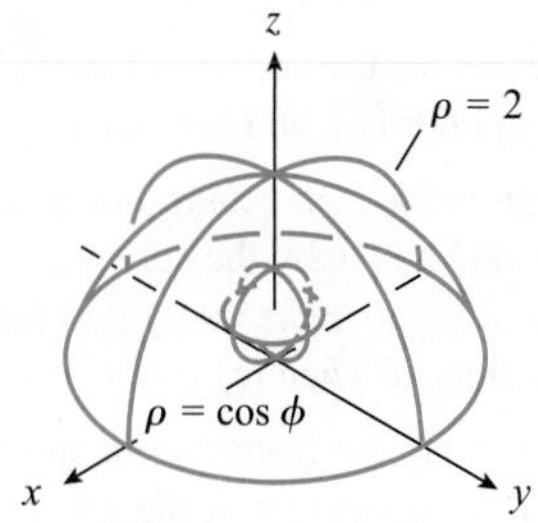

54. The solid bounded below by the hemisphere $\rho = 1$, $z \geq 0$, and above by the cardioid of revolution $\rho = 1 + \cos\phi$ as illustrated in the figure.

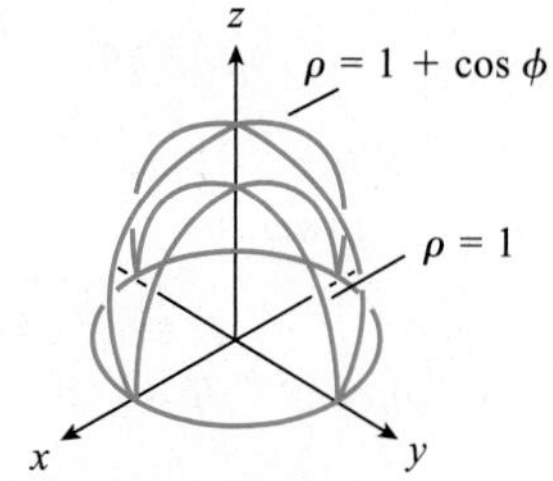

55. The solid enclosed by the cardioid of revolution $\rho = 1 - \cos\phi$.

56. The upper portion cut from the solid in Exercise 55 by the *xy*-plane.

57. The solid bounded below by the sphere $\rho = 2\cos\phi$ and above by the cone $z = \sqrt{x^2 + y^2}$ as illustrated in the figure.

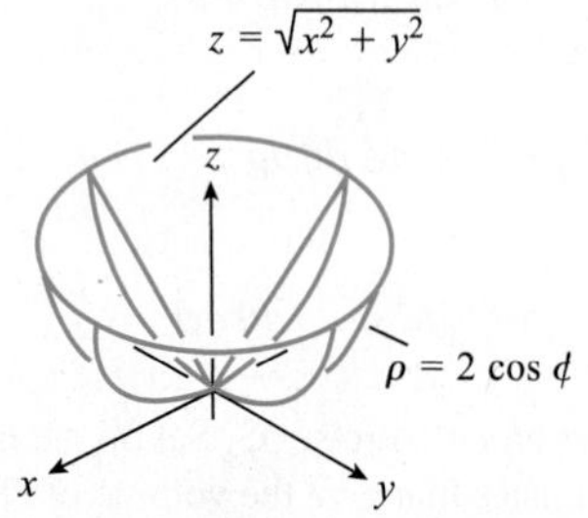

58. The solid bounded below by the *xy*-plane, on the sides by the sphere $\rho = 2$, and above by the cone $\phi = \pi/3$ as illustrated in the figure.

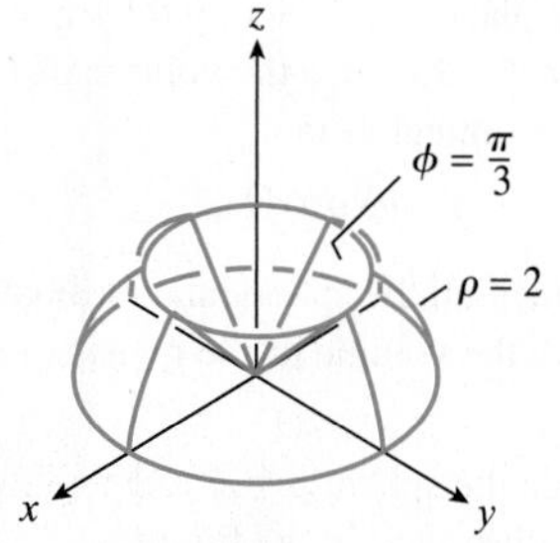

Explorations

59. Set up triple integrals for the volume of the sphere $\rho = 2$ in **(a)** spherical, **(b)** cylindrical, and **(c)** rectangular coordinates.

60. Let D be the region in the first octant that is bounded below by the cone $\phi = \pi/4$ and above by the sphere $\rho = 3$. Express the volume of D as an iterated triple integral in **(a)** cylindrical and **(b)** spherical coordinates. Then **(c)** find V.

61. Let D be the smaller cap cut from a solid sphere of radius 2 units by a plane 1 unit from the center of the sphere. Express the volume of D as an iterated triple integral in **(a)** spherical, **(b)** cylindrical, and **(c)** rectangular coordinates. Then **(d)** find the volume by evaluating one of the three triple integrals.

62. Express the moment of inertia I_z of the solid hemisphere $x^2 + y^2 + z^2 \leq 1$, $z \geq 0$, as an iterated integral in **(a)** cylindrical and **(b)** spherical coordinates. Then **(c)** find I_z.

In Exercises 63–68, find the volume of the solid shown in the figure.

63.

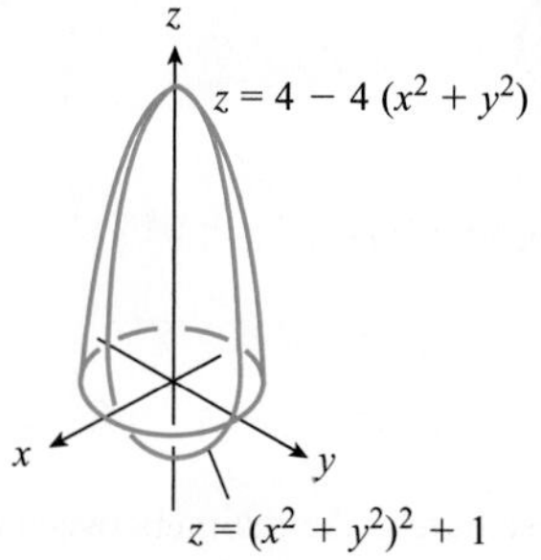

64.

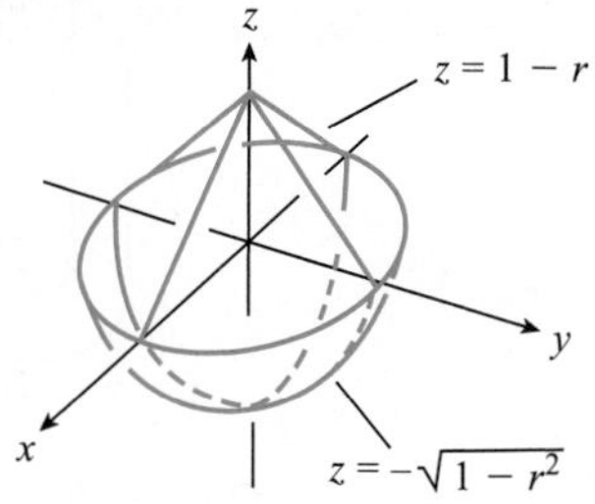

65.

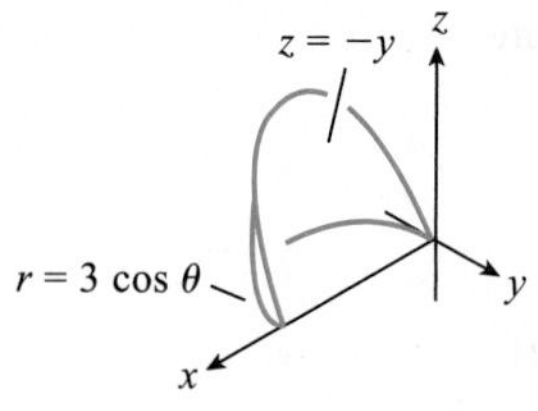

66.

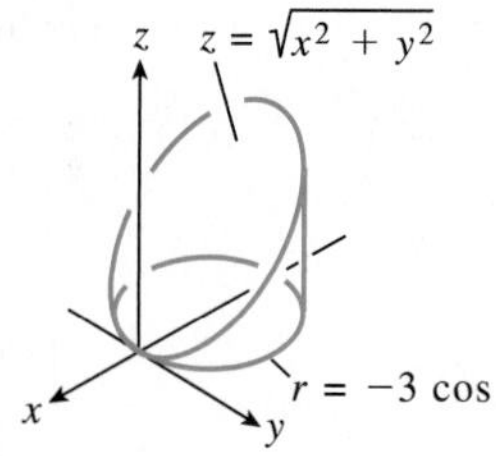

67.

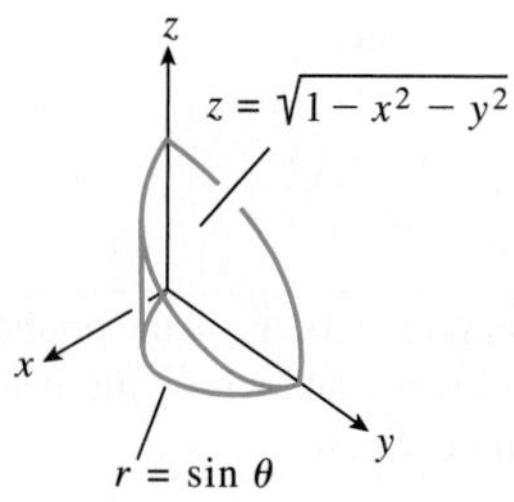

68.

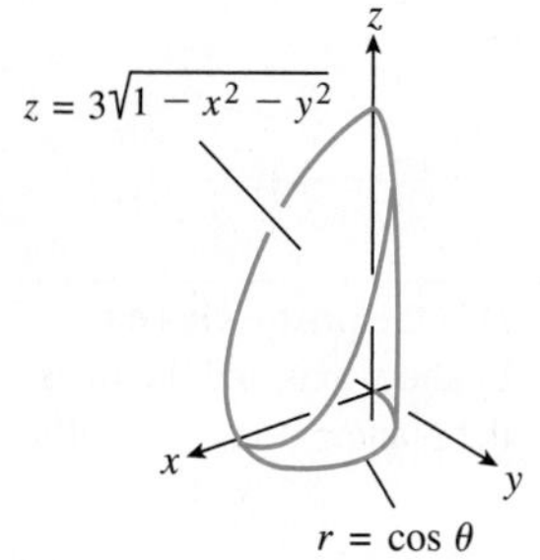

In Exercises 69–76, find the volume of the region.

69. The portion of the solid sphere $\rho \leq a$ that lies between the cones $\phi = \pi/3$ and $\phi = 2\pi/3$

70. The smaller region cut from the solid sphere $\rho \leq 2$ by the plane $z = 1$

71. The solid enclosed by the cone $z = \sqrt{x^2 + y^2}$ between the planes $z = 1$ and $z = 2$

72. The region bounded below by the plane $z = 0$, laterally by the cylinder $x^2 + y^2 = 1$, and above by the paraboloid $z = x^2 + y^2$

73. The solid cut from the thick-walled cylinder $1 \leq x^2 + y^2 \leq 2$ by the cones $z = \pm\sqrt{x^2 + y^2}$

74. The region that lies inside the sphere $x^2 + y^2 + z^2 = 2$ and outside the cylinder $x^2 + y^2 = 1$

75. The region enclosed by the cylinder $x^2 + y^2 = 4$ and the planes $z = 0$ and $y + z = 4$

76. The region cut from the solid cylinder $x^2 + y^2 \leq 1$ by the sphere $x^2 + y^2 + z^2 = 4$

77. ***Average Value*** Find the average value of the function $f(r, \theta, z) = r$ over the region bounded by the cylinder $r = 1$ between the planes $z = -1$ and $z = 1$.

78. ***Average Value*** Find the average value of the function $f(\rho, \phi, \theta) = \rho$ over the solid ball $\rho \leq 1$.

79. ***Center of Mass*** A solid of constant density is bounded below by the plane $z = 0$, above by the cone $z = r$, $r \geq 0$, and on the sides by the cylinder $r = 1$. Find the center of mass.

80. ***Centroid*** Find the centroid of the region in the first octant that is bounded above by the cone $z = \sqrt{x^2 + y^2}$, below by the plane $z = 0$, and on the sides by the cylinder $x^2 + y^2 = 4$ and the planes $x = 0$ and $y = 0$.

81. ***Centroid*** Find the centroid of the solid in Exercise 58.

82. ***Centroid*** Find the centroid of the solid bounded above by the sphere $\rho = a$ and below by the cone $\phi = \pi/4$.

83. ***Centroid*** Find the centroid of the region that is bounded above by the surface $z = \sqrt{r}$, on the sides by the cylinder $r = 4$, and below by the xy-plane.

84. ***Thick-Walled Cylinder*** Find the moment of inertia and radius of gyration about the z-axis of a thick-walled right circular cylinder bounded on the inside by the cylinder $r = 1$, on the outside by the cylinder $r = 2$, and on the top and bottom by the planes $z = 4$ and $z = 0$. (Take $\delta = 1$.)

85. ***Solid Sphere, Constant Density*** Find the moment of inertia of a solid sphere of radius a about a diameter. (Take $\delta = 1$.)

86. ***Solid Sphere, Variable Densities*** A solid sphere is bounded by the sphere $\rho = a$. Find the moment of inertia and radius of gyration about the z-axis if the density is

(a) $\delta(\rho, \phi, \theta) = \rho^2$

(b) $\delta(\rho, \phi, \theta) = r = \rho \sin \phi$.

Extending the Ideas

87. ***Atmospheric Mass*** A spherical planet of radius R has an atmosphere whose density is $\mu = \mu_0 e^{-ch}$, where h is the altitude above the surface of the planet, μ_0 is the density at sea level, and c is a positive constant. Find the mass of the planet's atmosphere.

88. ***Density at the Center of a Planet*** A planet is in the shape of a sphere of radius R and total mass M with spherically symmetric density distribution that increases linearly as one approaches its center. What is the density at the center of this planet if the density at its edge (surface) is taken to be zero?

15.7 Substitutions in Multiple Integrals

What you'll learn about

- Substitutions in Double Integrals
- Substitutions in Triple Integrals

Substitutions in Double Integrals

The polar coordinate substitution of Section 15.3 is a special case of a more general substitution method for double integrals, a method that pictures changes in variables as transformations of regions. As always, the goal of substitution is the transformation of difficult or unfamiliar integrals into integrals we can recognize or handle more easily.

Suppose a region G in the uv-plane is transformed one-to-one into the region R in the xy-plane by equations of the form

$$x = g(u, v), \qquad y = h(u, v),$$

as suggested in Figure 15.51. R is the **image** of G under the transformation, and G is the **preimage** of R. Any function $f(x, y)$ defined on R can be thought of as a function $f(g(u, v), h(u, v))$ defined on G as well. How is the integral of $f(x, y)$ over R related to the integral of $f(g(u, v), h(u, v))$ over G?

Notice the "Reversed" Order

The transforming equations $x = g(u, v)$ and $y = h(u, v)$ go from G to R, but we use them to change an integral over R into an integral over G.

The answer is: If g, h, and f have continuous partial derivatives and $J(u, v)$ (to be discussed in a moment) is zero only at isolated points, if at all, then

$$\iint_R f(x, y)\, dx\, dy = \iint_G f(g(u, v), h(u, v)) \left| J(u, v) \right| du\, dv. \tag{1}$$

The factor $J(u, v)$, whose absolute value appears in Equation (1), is the *Jacobian* of the coordinate transformation, named after the mathematician Carl Jacobi.

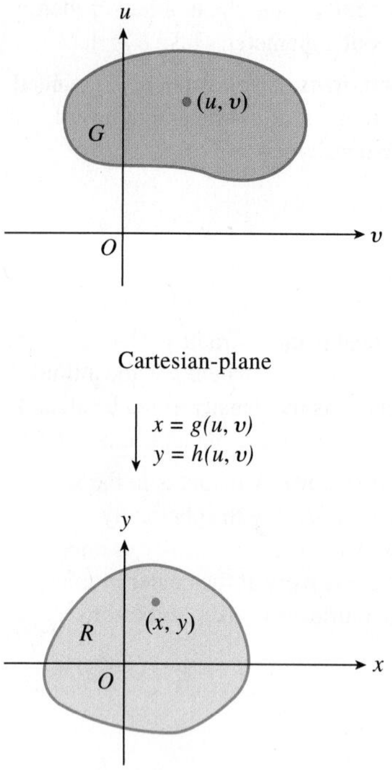

Figure 15.51 The equations $x = g(u, v)$ and $y = h(u, v)$ allow us to change an integral over a region R in the xy-plane into an integral over a region G in the uv-plane.

> **DEFINITION Jacobian Determinant or Jacobian**
>
> The **Jacobian determinant** or **Jacobian** of the coordinate transformation $x = g(u, v)$, $y = h(u, v)$ is
>
> $$J(u, v) = \begin{vmatrix} \dfrac{\partial x}{\partial u} & \dfrac{\partial x}{\partial v} \\ \dfrac{\partial y}{\partial u} & \dfrac{\partial y}{\partial v} \end{vmatrix} = \frac{\partial x}{\partial u}\frac{\partial y}{\partial v} - \frac{\partial y}{\partial u}\frac{\partial x}{\partial v}. \tag{2}$$

The Jacobian is also denoted by

$$J(u, v) = \frac{\partial(x, y)}{\partial(u, v)}$$

to help remember how the determinant in Equation (2) is constructed from the partial derivatives of x and y. The derivation of Equation (1) is intricate and properly belongs to a course in advanced calculus. We will not give the derivation here.

For polar coordinates, we have r and θ in place of u and v. With $x = r\cos\theta$ and $y = r\sin\theta$, the Jacobian is

$$J(r, \theta) = \begin{vmatrix} \dfrac{\partial x}{\partial r} & \dfrac{\partial x}{\partial \theta} \\ \dfrac{\partial y}{\partial r} & \dfrac{\partial y}{\partial \theta} \end{vmatrix} = \begin{vmatrix} \cos\theta & -r\sin\theta \\ \sin\theta & r\cos\theta \end{vmatrix} = r(\cos^2\theta + \sin^2\theta) = r.$$

Hence, Equation (1) becomes

$$\iint_R f(x, y)\, dx\, dy = \iint_G f(r\cos\theta, r\sin\theta)\,|r|\, dr\, d\theta$$

$$= \iint_G f(r\cos\theta, r\sin\theta)\, r\, dr\, d\theta, \qquad \text{If } r \geq 0 \tag{3}$$

which is Equation (6) in Section 15.3.

Figure 15.52 shows how the equations $x = r\cos\theta$, $y = r\sin\theta$ transform the rectangle G: $0 \leq r \leq 1$, $0 \leq \theta \leq \pi/2$ into the quarter circle R bounded by $x^2 + y^2 = 1$ in the first quadrant of the xy-plane.

Notice that the integral on the right-hand side of Equation (3) is not the integral of $f(r\cos\theta, r\sin\theta)$ over a region in the polar coordinate plane. It is the integral of the product of $f(r\cos\theta, r\sin\theta)$ and r over a region G in the *Cartesian* $r\theta$-plane.

Here is an example of another substitution.

EXAMPLE 1 Applying Transformations to Integrate

Evaluate

$$\int_0^4 \int_{x=y/2}^{x=(y/2)+1} \frac{2x - y}{2}\, dx\, dy$$

by applying the transformation

$$u = \frac{2x - y}{2}, \qquad v = \frac{y}{2} \tag{4}$$

and integrating over an appropriate region in the uv-plane.

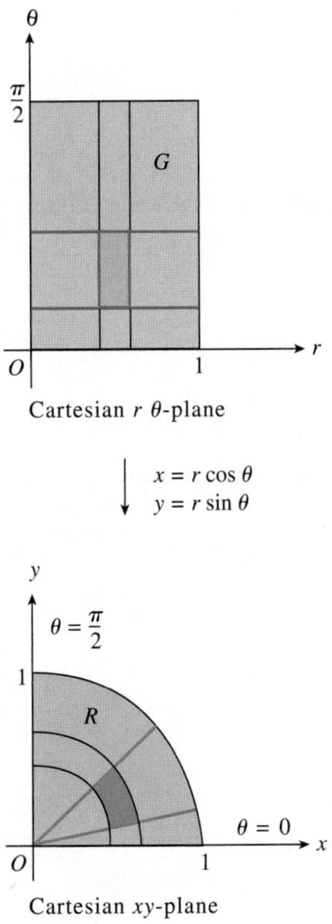

Figure 15.52 The equations $x = r\cos\theta$, $y = r\sin\theta$ transform G into R.

SOLUTION

We sketch the region R of integration in the xy-plane and identify its boundaries (Figure 15.53).

To apply Equation (1), we need to find the corresponding uv-region G and the Jacobian of the transformation. To find them, we first solve Equations (4) for x and y in terms of u and v. Routine algebra gives

$$x = u + v, \qquad y = 2v. \tag{5}$$

We then find the boundaries of G by substituting these expressions into the equations for the boundaries of R (Figure 15.53).

xy-equations for the boundary of R	Corresponding uv-equations for the boundary of G	Simplified uv-equations
$x = y/2$	$u + v = 2v/2 = v$	$u = 0$
$x = (y/2) + 1$	$u + v = (2v/2) + 1 = v + 1$	$u = 1$
$y = 0$	$2v = 0$	$v = 0$
$y = 4$	$2v = 4$	$v = 2$

The Jacobian of the transformation (again from Equations (5)) is

$$J(u, v) = \begin{vmatrix} \dfrac{\partial x}{\partial u} & \dfrac{\partial x}{\partial v} \\ \dfrac{\partial y}{\partial u} & \dfrac{\partial y}{\partial v} \end{vmatrix} = \begin{vmatrix} \dfrac{\partial}{\partial u}(u + v) & \dfrac{\partial}{\partial v}(u + v) \\ \dfrac{\partial}{\partial u}(2v) & \dfrac{\partial}{\partial v}(2v) \end{vmatrix} = \begin{vmatrix} 1 & 1 \\ 0 & 2 \end{vmatrix} = 2.$$

We now have everything we need to apply Equation (1):

$$\int_0^4 \int_{x=y/2}^{x=(y/2)+1} \frac{2x - y}{2}\, dx\, dy$$

$$= \int_{v=0}^{v=2} \int_{u=0}^{u=1} u\left|J(u, v)\right|\, du\, dv$$

$$= \int_0^2 \int_0^1 (u)(2)\, du\, dv = \int_0^2 \left[u^2\right]_0^1 dv = \int_0^2 dv = 2.$$

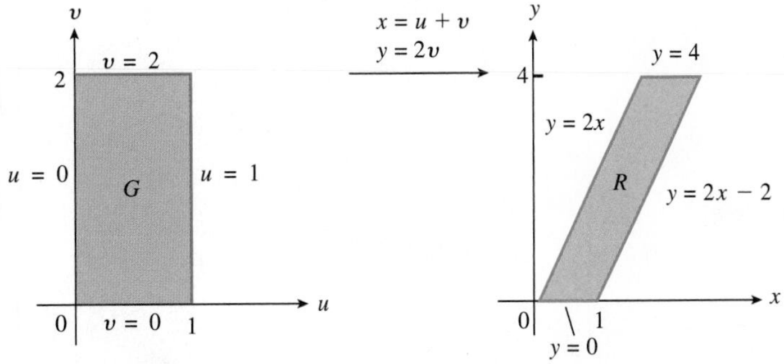

Figure 15.53 The equations $x = u + v$ and $y = 2v$ transform G into R. Reversing the transformation by the equations $u = (2x - y)/2$ and $v = y/2$ transforms R into G. (Example 1)

EXAMPLE 2 Applying Transformations to Integrate

Evaluate $\int_0^1 \int_0^{1-x} \sqrt{x+y}\,(y-2x)^2\,dy\,dx.$

SOLUTION

We sketch the region R of integration in the xy-plane and identify its boundaries (Figure 15.54). The integrand suggests the transformation $u = x + y$ and $v = y - 2x$. Routine algebra produces x and y as functions of u and v:

$$x = \frac{u}{3} - \frac{v}{3}, \qquad y = \frac{2u}{3} + \frac{v}{3} \tag{6}$$

From Equations (6) we can find the boundaries of the uv-region G (Figure 15.54).

xy-equations for the boundary of R	Corresponding uv-equations for the boundary of G	Simplified uv-equations
$x + y = 1$	$\left(\frac{u}{3} - \frac{v}{3}\right) + \left(\frac{2u}{3} + \frac{v}{3}\right) = 1$	$u = 1$
$x = 0$	$\frac{u}{3} - \frac{v}{3} = 0$	$v = u$
$y = 0$	$\frac{2u}{3} + \frac{v}{3} = 0$	$v = -2u$

The Jacobian of the transformation in Equation (6) is

$$J(u, v) = \begin{vmatrix} \frac{\partial x}{\partial u} & \frac{\partial x}{\partial v} \\ \frac{\partial y}{\partial u} & \frac{\partial y}{\partial v} \end{vmatrix} = \begin{vmatrix} \frac{1}{3} & -\frac{1}{3} \\ \frac{2}{3} & \frac{1}{3} \end{vmatrix} = \frac{1}{3}.$$

Applying Equation (1), we evaluate the integral:

$$\begin{aligned}
\int_0^1 \int_0^{1-x} \sqrt{x+y}\,(y-2x)^2\,dy\,dx &= \int_{u=0}^{u=1} \int_{v=-2u}^{v=u} u^{1/2} v^2 \left|J(u, v)\right| dv\,du \\
&= \int_0^1 \int_{-2u}^{u} u^{1/2} v^2 \left(\frac{1}{3}\right) dv\,du \\
&= \frac{1}{3} \int_0^1 u^{1/2} \left[\frac{v^3}{3}\right]_{v=-2u}^{v=u} du \\
&= \frac{1}{9} \int_0^1 u^{1/2} (u^3 + 8u^3)\,du \\
&= \int_0^1 u^{7/2}\,du = \frac{2}{9} u^{9/2} \Big|_0^1 = \frac{2}{9}.
\end{aligned}$$

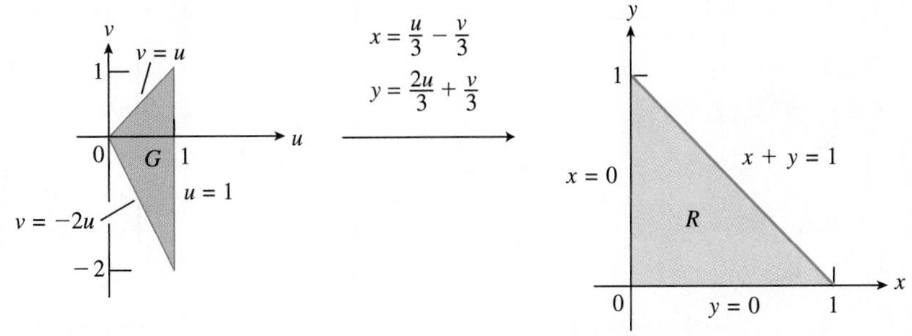

Figure 15.54 The equations $x = (u/3) - (v/3)$ and $y = 2u/3) + (v/3)$ transform G into R. Reversing the transformations by the equations $u = x + y$ and $v = y - 2x$ transforms R into G. (Example 2)

Substitutions in Triple Integrals

The cylindrical and spherical coordinate substitutions in Section 15.6 are special cases of a substitution method that pictures changes of variables in triple integrals as transformations of three-dimensional regions. The method is like the method for double integrals except that now we work in three dimensions instead of two.

Suppose a region G in uvw-space is transformed one-to-one into the region D in xyz-space by differentiable equations of the form

$$x = g(u, v, w), \qquad y = h(u, v, w), \qquad z = k(u, v, w),$$

as suggested in Figure 15.55. Then any function $F(x, y, z)$ defined on D can be thought of as a function

$$F(g(u, v, w), h(u, v, w), k(u, v, w)) = H(u, v, w)$$

defined on G. If g, h, and k have continuous first partial derivatives, then the integral of $F(x, y, z)$ over D is related to the integral of $H(u, v\ w)$ over G by the equation

$$\iiint_D F(x, y, z)\, dx\, dy\, dz = \iiint_G H(u, v, w)\left|J(u, v, w)\right| du\, dv\, dw. \tag{7}$$

The factor $J(u, v\ w)$, whose absolute value appears in this equation, is the **Jacobian determinant**

$$J(u, v, w) = \begin{vmatrix} \dfrac{\partial x}{\partial u} & \dfrac{\partial x}{\partial v} & \dfrac{\partial x}{\partial w} \\ \dfrac{\partial y}{\partial u} & \dfrac{\partial y}{\partial v} & \dfrac{\partial y}{\partial w} \\ \dfrac{\partial z}{\partial u} & \dfrac{\partial z}{\partial v} & \dfrac{\partial z}{\partial w} \end{vmatrix} = \frac{\partial(x, y, z)}{\partial(u, v, w)}. \tag{8}$$

As in the two-dimensional case, the derivation of the change-of-variable formula in Equation (7) is complicated, and we will not go into it here.

For cylindrical coordinates, we have r, θ, and z in place of u, v, and w. The transformation from Cartesian $r\theta z$-space to Cartesian xyz-space is given by the equations

$$x = r\cos\theta, \qquad y = r\sin\theta, \qquad z = z$$

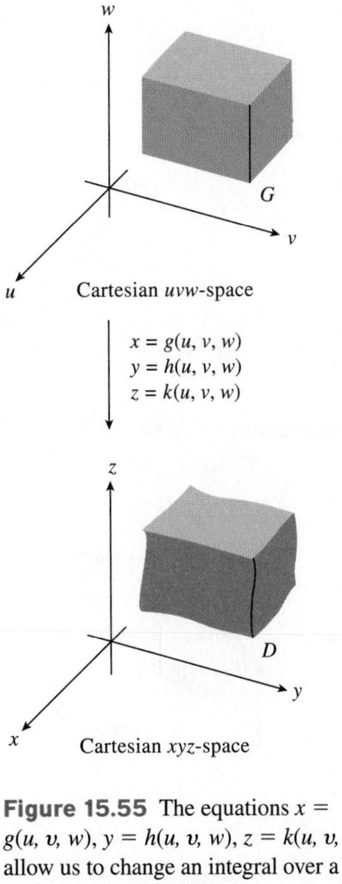

Figure 15.55 The equations $x = g(u, v, w)$, $y = h(u, v, w)$, $z = k(u, v, w)$ allow us to change an integral over a region D in Cartesian xyz-space into an integral over a region G in Cartesian uvw-space.

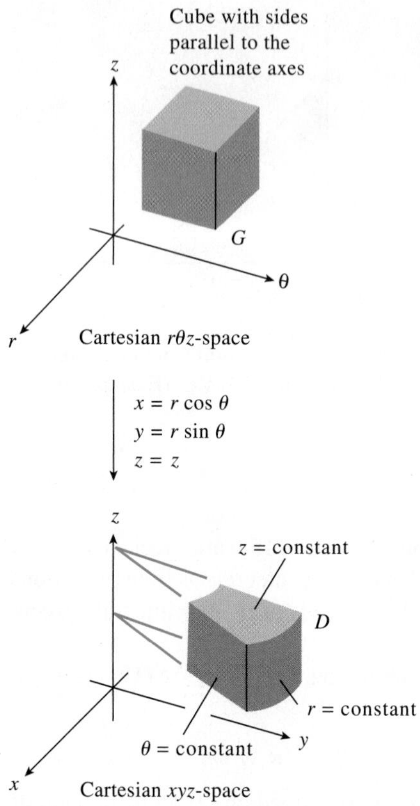

Figure 15.56 The equations $x = r\cos\theta$, $y = r\sin\theta$, and $z = z$ transform G into D.

(Figure 15.56). The Jacobian of the transformation is

$$J(r, \theta, z) = \begin{vmatrix} \dfrac{\partial x}{\partial r} & \dfrac{\partial x}{\partial \theta} & \dfrac{\partial x}{\partial z} \\ \dfrac{\partial y}{\partial r} & \dfrac{\partial y}{\partial \theta} & \dfrac{\partial y}{\partial z} \\ \dfrac{\partial z}{\partial r} & \dfrac{\partial z}{\partial \theta} & \dfrac{\partial z}{\partial z} \end{vmatrix} = \begin{vmatrix} \cos\theta & -r\sin\theta & 0 \\ \sin\theta & r\cos\theta & 0 \\ 0 & 0 & 1 \end{vmatrix}$$

$$= r\cos^2\theta + r\sin^2\theta = r.$$

The corresponding version of Equation (7) is

$$\iiint_D F(x, y, z)\, dx\, dy\, dz = \iiint_G H(r, \theta, z)\, |r|\, dr\, d\theta\, dz. \tag{9}$$

We can drop the absolute value signs whenever $r \geq 0$.

For spherical coordinates, ρ, ϕ, and θ take the place of u, v, and w. The transformation from Cartesian $\rho\phi\theta$-space to Cartesian xyz-space is given by

$$x = \rho\sin\phi\cos\theta, \qquad y = \rho\sin\phi\sin\theta, \qquad z = \rho\cos\phi$$

(Figure 15.57). The Jacobian of the transformation is

$$J(\rho, \phi, \theta) = \begin{vmatrix} \dfrac{\partial x}{\partial \rho} & \dfrac{\partial x}{\partial \phi} & \dfrac{\partial x}{\partial \theta} \\ \dfrac{\partial y}{\partial \rho} & \dfrac{\partial y}{\partial \phi} & \dfrac{\partial y}{\partial \theta} \\ \dfrac{\partial z}{\partial \rho} & \dfrac{\partial z}{\partial \phi} & \dfrac{\partial z}{\partial \theta} \end{vmatrix} = \rho^2\sin\phi \tag{10}$$

(Exercise 17). The corresponding version of Equation (7) is

$$\iiint_D F(x, y, z)\, dx\, dy\, dz = \iiint_G H(\rho, \phi, \theta)\, |\rho^2\sin\phi|\, d\rho\, d\phi\, d\theta. \tag{11}$$

We can drop the absolute value signs because $\sin\phi$ is never negative.

See page 807 for an example of another substitution.

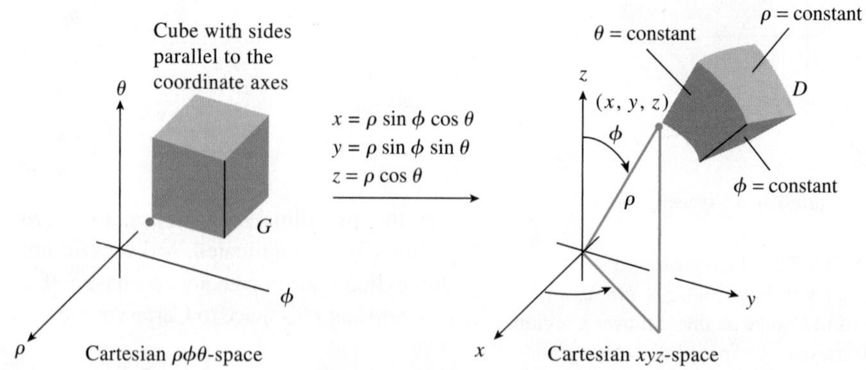

Figure 15.57 The equations $x = \rho\sin\phi\cos\theta$, $y = \rho\sin\phi\sin\theta$, and $z = \rho\cos\phi$ transform G into D.

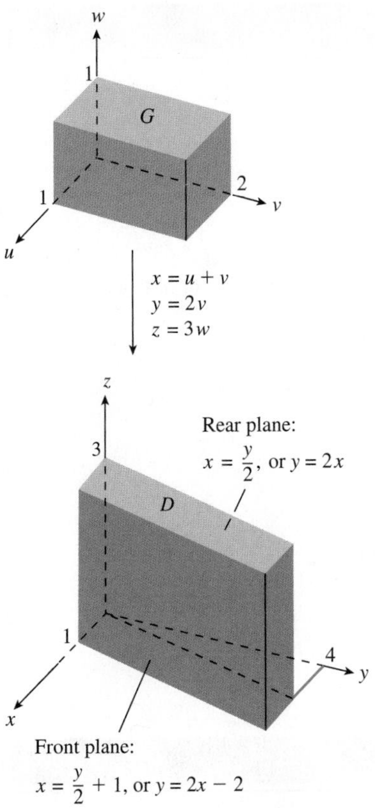

Figure 15.58 The equations $x = u + v$, $y = 2v$, and $z = 3w$ transform G into D. Reversing the transformation by the equations $u = (2x - y)/2$, $v = y/2$, and $w = z/3$ transforms D into G. (Example 3)

EXAMPLE 3 Applying Transformations to Integrate

Evaluate

$$\int_0^3 \int_0^4 \int_{x=y/2}^{x=(y/2)+1} \left(\frac{2x - y}{2} + \frac{z}{3}\right) dx\, dy\, dz$$

by applying the transformation

$$u = (2x - y)/2, \qquad v = y/2, \qquad w = z/3 \tag{12}$$

and integrating over an appropriate region in uvw-space.

SOLUTION

We sketch the region D of integration in xyz-space and identify its boundaries (Figure 15.58). In this case, the bounding surfaces are planes.

To apply Equation (7), we need to find the corresponding uvw-region G and the Jacobian of the transformation. To find them, we first solve Equations (12) for x, y, and z in terms of u, v, and w. Routine algebra gives

$$x = u + v, \qquad y = 2v, \qquad z = 3w. \tag{13}$$

We then find the boundaries of G by substituting these expressions into the equations for the boundaries of D:

xyz-equations for the boundary of D	Corresponding uvw-equations for the boundary of G	Simplified uvw-equations
$x = y/2$	$u + v = 2v/2 = v$	$u = 0$
$x = (y/2) + 1$	$u + v = (2v/2) + 1 = v + 1$	$u = 1$
$y = 0$	$2v = 0$	$v = 0$
$y = 4$	$2v = 4$	$v = 2$
$z = 0$	$3w = 0$	$w = 0$
$z = 3$	$3w = 3$	$w = 1$

The Jacobian of the transformation, again from Equations (13), is

$$J(u, v, w) = \begin{vmatrix} \dfrac{\partial x}{\partial u} & \dfrac{\partial x}{\partial v} & \dfrac{\partial x}{\partial w} \\ \dfrac{\partial y}{\partial u} & \dfrac{\partial y}{\partial v} & \dfrac{\partial y}{\partial w} \\ \dfrac{\partial z}{\partial u} & \dfrac{\partial z}{\partial v} & \dfrac{\partial z}{\partial w} \end{vmatrix} = \begin{vmatrix} 1 & 1 & 0 \\ 0 & 2 & 0 \\ 0 & 0 & 3 \end{vmatrix} = 6.$$

We now have everything we need to apply Equation (7):

$$\int_0^3 \int_0^4 \int_{x=y/2}^{x=(y/2)+1} \left(\frac{2x - y}{2} + \frac{z}{3}\right) dx\, dy\, dz$$

$$= \int_0^1 \int_0^2 \int_0^1 (u + w)\left|J(u, v, w)\right| du\, dv\, dw$$

$$= \int_0^1 \int_0^2 \int_0^1 (u + w)(6)\ du\, dv\, dw = 6\int_0^1 \int_0^2 \left[\frac{u^2}{2} + uw\right]_0^1 dv\, dw$$

$$= 6\int_0^1 \int_0^2 \left(\frac{1}{2} + w\right) dv\, dw = 6\int_0^1 \left[\frac{v}{2} + vw\right]_0^2 dw = 6\int_0^1 (1 + 2w)\, dw$$

$$= 6\left[w + w^2\right]_0^1 = 12.$$

Carl Gustav Jacob Jacobi

Jacobi (1804–1851), one of nineteenth-century Germany's most accomplished scientists, developed the theory of determinants and transformations into a powerful tool for evaluating multiple integrals and solving differential equations. He also applied transformation methods to study nonelementary integrals like the ones that arise in the calculation of arc length. Like Euler, Jacobi was a prolific writer and an even more prolific calculator and worked in a variety of mathematical and applied fields.

Quick Review 15.7

In Exercises 1 and 2, find the value of the determinant.

1. $\begin{vmatrix} 2 & 5 \\ -1 & 6 \end{vmatrix}$

2. $\begin{vmatrix} -3 & 4 & 7 \\ 2 & 0 & 3 \\ 4 & -1 & 2 \end{vmatrix}$

3. Solve for x and y:

$$2x - 3y = 7$$
$$x + 2y = 0$$

4. Solve for x, y, and z:

$$3x - y + 2z = -1$$
$$x + 2y - 3z = -9$$
$$2x + 3y - 4z = -13$$

In Exercises 5–7, solve for x and y in terms of u and v.

5. $3x + 2y = u$
$x - y = v$

6. $2x - y = 2u$
$y = 2v$

7. $x + y = u$
$y - 2x = v$

In Exercises 8 and 9, solve for x, y, and z in terms of u, v, and w.

8. $3x - 2y + z = u + 1$
$2x + y - z = v - 1$
$x + 2y - 3z = w$

9. $2x - y = 2u$
$y = 2v$
$z = 3w$

10. Let $x = u\cos(vw)$ and find

$$\frac{\partial x}{\partial u}, \frac{\partial x}{\partial v}, \frac{\partial x}{\partial w}.$$

Section 15.7 Exercises

In Exercises 1–4, *work in groups of two or three* to solve the problem.

1. **(a)** Solve the system

$$u = x - y, v = 2x + y$$

for x and y in terms of u and v. Then find the value of the Jacobian $\partial(x, y)/\partial(u, v)$.

(b) Find the image under the transformation $u = x - y$, $v = 2x + y$ of the triangular region with vertices (0, 0), (1, 1), and (1, −2) in the xy-plane. Sketch the transformed region in the uv-plane.

2. **(a)** Solve the system

$$u = x + 2y, \qquad v = x - y$$

for x and y in terms of u and v. Then find the value of the Jacobian $\partial(x, y)/\partial(u, v)$.

(b) Find the image under the transformation $u = x + 2y$, $v = x - y$ of the triangular region in the xy-plane bounded by the lines $y = 0$, $y = x$, and $x + 2y = 2$. Sketch the transformed region in the uv-plane.

3. **(a)** Solve the system

$$u = 3x + 2y, \qquad v = x + 4y$$

for x and y in terms of u and v. Then find the value of the Jacobian $\partial(x, y)/\partial(u, v)$.

(b) Find the image under the transformation $u = 3x + 2y$, $v = x + 4y$ of the triangular region in the xy-plane bounded by the x-axis, the y-axis, and the line $x + y = 1$. Sketch the transformed region in the uv-plane.

4. **(a)** Solve the system

$$u = 2x - 3y, \qquad v = -x + y$$

for x and y in terms of u and v. Then find the value of the Jacobian $\partial(x, y)/\partial(u, v)$.

(b) Find the image under the transformation $u = 2x - 3y$, $v = -x + y$ of the parallelogram R in the xy-plane with boundaries $x = -3$, $x = 0$, $y = x$, and $y = x + 1$. Sketch the transformed region in the uv-plane.

5. Find the Jacobian $\partial(x, y)/\partial(u, v)$ for the transformation

(a) $x = u\cos v$, $\quad y = u\sin v$.

(b) $x = u\sin v$, $\quad y = u\cos v$.

6. Find the Jacobian $\partial(x, y, z)/\partial(u, v, w)$ for the transformation

(a) $x = u\cos v$, $\quad y = u\sin v$, $\quad z = w$.

(b) $x = 2u - 1$, $\quad y = 3v - 4$, $\quad z = \frac{1}{2}(w - 4)$.

7. Evaluate the integral

$$\int_0^4 \int_{x=y/2}^{x=(y/2)+1} \frac{2x - y}{2}\, dx\, dy$$

from Example 1 directly by integration with respect to x and y to confirm that its value is 2.

8. Use the transformation in Exercise 1 to evaluate the integral

$$\iint_R (2x^2 - xy - y^2)\, dx\, dy$$

for the region R in the first quadrant bounded by the lines $y = -2x + 4$, $y = -2x + 7$, $y = x - 2$, and $y = x + 1$.

9. Use the transformation in Exercise 3 to evaluate the integral

$$\iint_R (3x^2 + 14xy + 8y^2)\, dx\, dy$$

for the region R in the first quadrant bounded by the lines

$$y = -\frac{3}{2}x + 1, \qquad y = -\frac{3}{2}x + 3,$$

$$y = -\frac{1}{4}x, \qquad \text{and} \qquad y = -\frac{1}{4}x + 1,$$

10. Use the transformation and parallelogram R in Exercise 4 to evaluate the integral

$$\iint_R 2(x - y)\, dx\, dy.$$

11. Let R be the region in the first quadrant of the xy-plane bounded by the hyperbolas $xy = 1$, $xy = 9$ and the lines $y = x$, $y = 4x$. Use the transformation $x = u/v$, $y = uv$ with $u > 0$ and $v > 0$ to rewrite

$$\iint_R \left(\sqrt{\frac{y}{x}} + \sqrt{xy}\right) dx\, dy$$

as an integral over an appropriate region G in the uv-plane. Then evaluate the uv-integral over G.

12. (a) Find the Jacobian of the transformation $x = u$, $y = uv$ and sketch the region G: $1 \le u \le 2$, $1 \le uv \le 2$ in the uv-plane.

(b) Then use Equation (1) to transform the integral

$$\int_1^2 \int_1^2 \frac{y}{x}\, dy\, dx$$

into an integral over G and evaluate both integrals.

Explorations

13. ***Polar Moment of an Elliptical Plate*** A thin plate of constant density covers the region bounded by the ellipse $x^2/a^2 + y^2/b^2 = 1$, $a > 0$, $b > 0$, in the xy-plane. Find the polar moment of the plate about the origin. (*Hint:* Use the transformation $x = ar\cos\theta$, $y = br\sin\theta$.)

14. ***Finding the Area of an Ellipse*** The area πab of the ellipse $x^2/a^2 + y^2/b^2 = 1$ can be found by integrating the function $f(x, y) = 1$ over the region bounded by the ellipse in the xy-plane. Evaluating the integral directly requires a trigonometric substitution. An easier way to evaluate the integral is to use the transformation $x = au$, $y = bv$ and evaluate the transformed integral over the disk G: $u^2 + v^2 \le 1$ in the uv-plane. Find the area this way.

15. Use the transformation in Exercise 2 to evaluate the integral

$$\int_0^{2/3} \int_y^{2-2y} (x + 2y)e^{(y-x)}\, dx\, dy$$

by first writing it as an integral over a region G in the uv-plane.

16. Use the transformation $x = u + (1/2)v$, $y = v$ to evaluate the integral

$$\int_0^2 \int_{y/2}^{(y+4)/2} y^3(2x - y)e^{(2x-y)^2}\, dx\, dy$$

by first writing it as an integral over a region in the uv-plane.

17. Evaluate the determinant in Equation (10) to show that the Jacobian of the transformation from Cartesian $\rho\phi\theta$-space to Cartesian xyz-space is $\rho^2 \sin\phi$.

18. Evaluate the integral in Example 3 by integrating with respect to x, y, and z.

19. ***Volume of an Ellipsoid*** Find the volume of the ellipsoid

$$\frac{x^2}{a^2} + \frac{y^2}{b^2} + \frac{z^2}{c^2} = 1.$$

(*Hint:* Let $x = au$, $y = bv$, and $z = cw$. Then find the volume of an appropriate region in uvw-space.)

20. Evaluate

$$\iiint |xyz|\, dx\, dy\, dz$$

over the solid ellipsoid

$$\frac{x^2}{a^2} + \frac{y^2}{b^2} + \frac{z^2}{c^2} \le 1.$$

(*Hint:* Let $x = au$, $y = bv$, and $z = cw$. Then find the volume of an appropriate region in uvw-space.)

21. Let D be the region in xyz-space defined by the inequalities

$$1 \le x \le 2, \qquad 0 \le xy \le 2, \qquad 0 \le z \le 1.$$

Evaluate

$$\iiint_D (x^2y + 3xyz)\, dx\, dy\, dz$$

by applying the transformation

$$u = x, \qquad v = xy, \qquad w = 3z$$

and integrating over an appropriate region G in uvw-space.

22. ***Centroid of a Solid Semi-ellipsoid*** Assuming the result that the centroid of a solid hemisphere lies on the axis of symmetry three-eighths of the way from the base toward the top, show, by transforming the appropriate integrals, that the centroid of a solid semi-ellipsoid $(x^2/a^2) + (y^2/b^2) + (z^2/c^2) \le 1$, $z \ge 0$, lies on the z-axis three-eighths of the way from the base toward the top. (You can do this without evaluating any of the integrals.)

Extending the Ideas

23. ***Substitutions in Single Integrals*** How can substitutions in single definite integrals be viewed as transformations of regions? What is the Jacobian in such a case? Illustrate with an example.

24. ***Cylindrical Shells*** We learned how to find the volume of a solid of revolution using the shell method, namely if the region between the curve $y = f(x)$ and the x-axis from a to b $(0 < a < b)$ is revolved about the y-axis the volume of the resulting solid is $\int_a^b 2\pi x f(x)\, dx$. Prove that finding volumes by using triple integrals gives the same result. (*Hint*: Use cylindrical coordinates with the roles of y and z changed.)

Chapter 15 Key Terms

Chapter 15 Review Exercises

In Exercises 1–4, sketch the region of integration and evaluate the double integral analytically.

1. $\int_1^{10}\int_0^{1/y} ye^{xy}\, dx\, dy$

2. $\int_0^1\int_0^{x^3} e^{y/x}\, dy\, dx$

3. $\int_0^{3/2}\int_{-\sqrt{9-4t^2}}^{\sqrt{9-4t^2}} t\, ds\, dt$

4. $\int_0^1\int_{\sqrt{y}}^{2-\sqrt{y}} xy\, dx\, dy$

In Exercises 5–8, sketch the region of integration and write an equivalent integral with the order of integration reversed. Then evaluate both integrals analytically.

5. $\int_0^4\int_{-\sqrt{4-y}}^{(y-4)/2} dx\, dy$

6. $\int_0^1\int_{x^2}^{x} \sqrt{x}\, dy\, dx$

7. $\int_0^{3/2}\int_{-\sqrt{9-4y^2}}^{\sqrt{9-4y^2}} y\, dx\, dy$

8. $\int_0^2\int_0^{4-x^2} 2x\, dy\, dx$

In Exercises 9–12, evaluate the integral analytically.

9. $\int_0^1\int_{2y}^{2} 4\cos(x^2)\, dx\, dy$

10. $\int_0^2\int_{y/2}^{1} e^{x^2}\, dx\, dy$

11. $\int_0^8\int_{\sqrt[3]{x}}^{2} \frac{dy\, dx}{y^4+1}$

12. $\int_0^1\int_{\sqrt[3]{y}}^{1} \frac{2\pi \sin \pi x^2}{x^2}\, dx\, dy$

13. ***Area*** Find the area of the region enclosed by the line $y = 2x + 4$ and the parabola $y = 4 - x^2$ in the xy-plane.

14. ***Area*** Find the area of the "triangular" region in the xy-plane that is bounded on the right by the parabola $y = x^2$, on the left by the line $x + y = 2$, and above by the line $y = 4$.

15. ***Volume*** Find the volume under the paraboloid $z = x^2 + y^2$ above the triangle enclosed by the lines $y = x$, $x = 0$, and $x + y = 2$ in the xy-plane.

16. ***Volume*** Find the volume under the parabolic cylinder $z = x^2$ above the region enclosed by the parabola $y = 6 - x^2$ and the line $y = x$ in the xy-plane.

Average Value In Exercises 17 and 18, find the average value of $f(x, y) = xy$ over the given region.

17. The square bounded by the lines $x = 1$, $y = 1$ in the first quadrant

18. The quarter circle $x^2 + y^2 \leq 1$ in the first quadrant

19. ***Centroid*** Find the centroid of the "triangular" region bounded by the lines $x = 2$, $y = 2$ and the hyperbola $xy = 2$ in the xy-plane.

20. ***Centroid*** Find the centroid of the region between the parabola $x + y^2 - 2y = 0$ and the line $x + 2y = 0$ in the xy-plane.

21. ***Polar Moment*** Find the polar moment of inertia about the origin of a thin triangular plate of constant density $\delta = 3$, bounded by the y-axis and the lines $y = 2x$ and $y = 4$ in the xy-plane.

22. ***Polar Moment*** Find the polar moment of inertia about the center of a thin rectangular sheet of constant density $\delta = 1$ bounded by the lines

(a) $x = \pm 2,\ y = \pm 1$ in the xy-plane.

(b) $x = \pm a,\ y = \pm b$ in the xy-plane.

(*Hint*: Find I_x. Then use the formula for I_x to find I_y and add the two to find I_0.)

23. ***Inertial Moment and Radius of Gyration*** Find the moment of inertia and radius of gyration about the x-axis of a thin plate of constant density δ covering the triangle with vertices $(0, 0)$, $(3, 0)$, and $(3, 2)$ in the xy-plane.

24. ***Plate with Variable Density*** Find the center of mass and the moments of inertia and radii of gyration about the coordinate axes of a thin plate bounded by the line $y = x$ and the parabola $y = x^2$ in the xy-plane if the density is $\delta(x, y) = x + 1$.

25. ***Plate with Variable Density*** Find the mass and first moments about the coordinate axes of a thin square plate bounded by the lines $x = \pm 1,\ y = \pm 1$ in the xy-plane if the density is $\delta(x, y) = x^2 + y^2 + 1/3$.

26. ***Triangles with the Same M_x and R_x*** Find the moment of inertia and radius of gyration about the x-axis of a thin triangular plate of constant density δ whose base lies along the interval $[0, b]$ on the x-axis and whose vertex lies on the line $y = h$ above the x-axis. As you will see, it does not matter where on the line this vertex lies. All such triangles have the same moment of inertia and radius of gyration.

In Exercises 27 and 28, evaluate the integral by changing to polar coordinates.

27. $$\int_{-1}^{1}\int_{-\sqrt{1-x^2}}^{\sqrt{1-x^2}} \frac{2\,dy\,dx}{(1 + x^2 + y^2)^2}$$

28. $$\int_{-1}^{1}\int_{-\sqrt{1-y^2}}^{\sqrt{1-y^2}} \ln\,(x^2 + y^2 + 1)\,dx\,dy$$

29. ***Centroid in Polar Coordinates*** Find the centroid of the region in the polar coordinate plane defined by the inequalities $0 \le r \le 3$ and $-\pi/3 \le \theta \le \pi/3$.

30. ***Centroid in Polar Coordinates*** Find the centroid of the region in the first quadrant bounded by the rays $\theta = 0$ and $\theta = \pi/2$ and the circles $r = 1$ and $r = 3$.

31. ***Centroid in Polar Coordinates***

(a) Find the centroid of the region in the polar coordinate plane that lies inside the cardioid $r = 1 + \cos\theta$ and outside the circle $r = 1$.

(b) Sketch the region and show the centroid in your sketch.

32. **(a)** ***Writing to Learn*** Find the centroid of the plane region defined by the polar coordinate inequalities $0 \le r \le a$, $-\alpha \le \theta \le \alpha$ $(0 < \alpha \le \pi)$. How does the centroid move as $\alpha \to \pi^-$?

(b) Sketch the region for $\alpha = 5\pi/6$ and show the centroid in your sketch.

33. Integrate the function $f(x, y) = 1/(1 + x^2 + y^2)^2$ over the region enclosed by one loop of the lemniscate $(x^2 + y^2)^2 - (x^2 - y^2) = 0$.

34. Integrate $f(x, y) = 1/(1 + x^2 + y^2)^2$ over

(a) the triangle with vertices $(0, 0)$, $(1, 0)$, $(1, \sqrt{3})$.

(b) the first quadrant of the xy-plane.

In Exercises 35–38, evaluate the integral analytically.

35. $$\int_0^{\pi}\int_0^{\pi}\int_0^{\pi} \cos(x + y + z)\,dx\,dy\,dz$$

36. $$\int_{\ln 6}^{\ln 7}\int_0^{\ln 2}\int_{\ln 4}^{\ln 5} e^{(x+y+z)}\,dz\,dy\,dx$$

37. $$\int_0^1\int_0^{x^2}\int_0^{x+y} (2x - y - z)\,dz\,dy\,dx$$

38. $$\int_1^e\int_1^x\int_0^z \frac{2y}{z^3}\,dy\,dz\,dx$$

39. ***Volume*** Find the volume of the wedge-shaped region enclosed on the side by the cylinder $x = -\cos y$, $-\pi/2 \le y \le \pi/2$, on the top by the plane $z = -2x$, and below by the xy-plane.

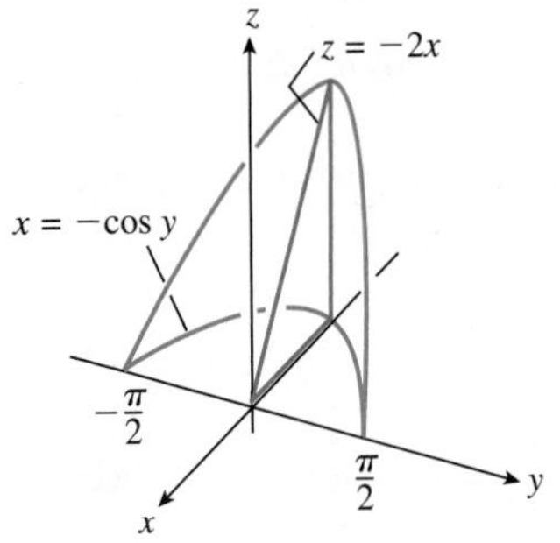

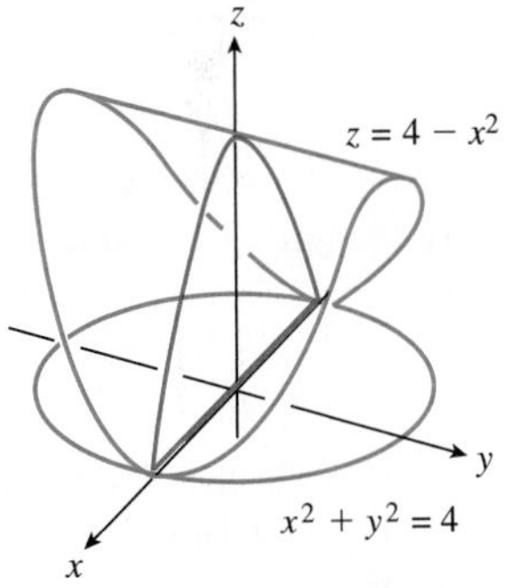

40. ***Volume*** Find the volume of the solid that is bounded above by the cylinder $z = 4 - x^2$, on the sides by the cylinder $x^2 + y^2 = 4$, and below by the xy-plane.

41. ***Average Value (Rectangular Coordinates)*** Find the average value of $f(x, y, z) = 30xz\sqrt{x^2 + y}$ over the rectangular solid in the first octant bounded by the coordinate planes and the planes $x = 1$, $y = 3$, $z = 1$.

42. ***Average Value (Cylindrical Coordinates)*** Find the average value of ρ over the solid sphere $\rho \le a$ (spherical coordinates).

Coordinate Conversions In Exercises 43–46, translate the equation from the given coordinate system (rectangular, cylindrical, spherical) into the other two systems. Identify the set of points defined by the equation.

43. $x^2 + y^2 + (z + 1)^2 = 1$

44. $\rho\cos\phi + \rho^2\sin^2\phi = 1$

45. $r = 4\cos\theta$

46. $\phi = 3\pi/4$

47. Convert

$$\int_0^{2\pi}\int_0^{\sqrt{2}}\int_r^{\sqrt{4-r^2}} 3\,dz\,r\,dr\,d\theta, \qquad r \ge 0$$

to **(a)** rectangular coordinates with the order of integration $dz\,dx\,dy$ and **(b)** spherical coordinates. Then **(c)** evaluate one of the integrals.

48. **(a)** Convert to cylindrical coordinates. Then **(b)** evaluate the new integral.

$$\int_0^1 \int_{-\sqrt{1-x^2}}^{\sqrt{1-x^2}} \int_{-(x^2+y^2)}^{(x^2+y^2)} 21xy^2\, dz\, dy\, dx$$

49. **(a)** Convert to spherical coordinates. Then **(b)** evaluate the new integral.

$$\int_{-1}^1 \int_{-\sqrt{1-x^2}}^{\sqrt{1-x^2}} \int_{\sqrt{x^2+y^2}}^{1} dz\, dy\, dx$$

50. Write an iterated triple integral for the integral of $f(x, y, z) = 6 + 4y$ over the region in the first octant bounded by the cone $z = \sqrt{x^2 + y^2}$, the cylinder $x^2 + y^2 = 1$, and the coordinate planes in **(a)** rectangular coordinates, **(b)** cylindrical coordinates, and **(c)** spherical coordinates. Then **(d)** find the integral of f by evaluating one of the triple integrals.

51. Set up an integral in rectangular coordinates equivalent to the integral

$$\int_0^{\pi/2} \int_1^{\sqrt{3}} \int_1^{\sqrt{4-r^2}} r^3 \sin\theta \cos\theta z^2\, dz\, dr\, d\theta.$$

Arrange the order of integration to be z first, then y, then x.

52. The volume of a solid is

$$\int_0^2 \int_0^{\sqrt{2x-x^2}} \int_{-\sqrt{4-x^2-y^2}}^{\sqrt{4-x^2-y^2}} dz\, dy\, dx.$$

(a) Describe the solid by giving equations for the surfaces that form its boundary.

(b) Convert the integral to cylindrical coordinates but do not evaluate the integral.

53. ***Equivalent Triple Integrals for Volume*** Let D be the smaller spherical cap cut from a solid ball of radius 2 by a plane 1 unit from the center of the sphere. Express the volume of D as an iterated triple integral in **(a)** rectangular, **(b)** cylindrical, and **(c)** spherical coordinates. *Do not evaluate the integrals.*

54. ***Equivalent Triple Integrals for I_z*** Express the moment of inertia I_z of the solid hemisphere bounded below by the plane $z = 0$ and above by the sphere $x^2 + y^2 + z^2 = 1$ as an iterated integral in **(a)** rectangular, **(b)** cylindrical, and **(c)** spherical coordinates. *Do not evaluate the integrals.*

55. ***Spherical vs. Cylindrical Coordinates*** Triple integrals involving spherical shapes do not always require spherical coordinates for convenient evaluation. Some calculations may be accomplished more easily with cylindrical coordinates. As a case in point, find the volume of the region bounded above by the sphere $x^2 + y^2 + z^2 = 8$ and below by the plane $z = 2$ by using **(a)** cylindrical coordinates and **(b)** spherical coordinates.

56. ***Calculating I_z in Spherical Coordinates*** Find the moment of inertia about the z-axis of a solid of constant density $\delta = 1$ that is bounded above by the sphere $\rho = 2$ and below by the cone $\phi = \pi/3$ (spherical coordinates).

57. ***Moment of Inertia of a Thick Sphere*** Find the moment of inertia of a solid of constant density δ bounded by two concentric spheres of radii a and b $(a < b)$ about a diameter.

58. ***Moment of Inertia of an Apple*** Find the moment of inertia about the z-axis of a solid of density $\delta = 1$ enclosed by the spherical coordinate surface $\rho = 1 - \cos\phi$ as illustrated in the figure.

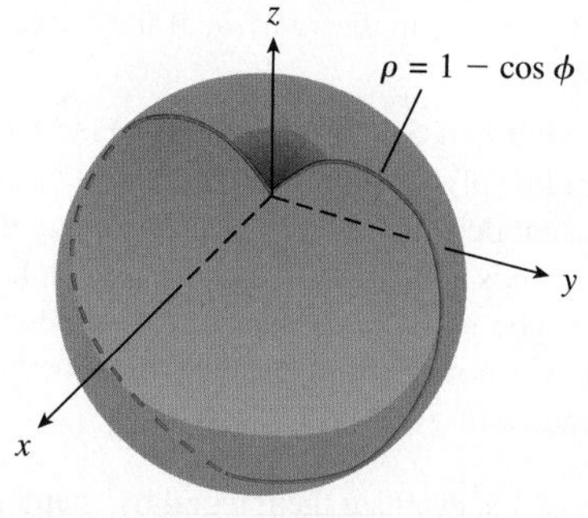

In Exercises 59 and 60, *work in groups of two or three* to solve the problem.

59. Show that if $u = x - y$ and $v = y$, then

$$\int_0^\infty \int_0^x e^{-sx} f(x - y, y)\, dy\, dx = \int_0^\infty \int_0^\infty e^{-s(u+v)} f(u, v)\, du\, dv.$$

60. **Writing to Learn** What relationship must hold between the constants a, b, and c to make

$$\int_{-\infty}^\infty \int_{-\infty}^\infty e^{-(ax^2+2bxy+cy^2)}\, dx\, dy = 1?$$

(*Hint*: Let $s = \alpha x + \beta y$ and $t = \gamma x + \delta y$, where $(\alpha\delta - \beta\gamma)^2 = ac - b^2$. Then $ax^2 + 2bxy + cy^2 = s^2 + t^2$.)

Chapter 16 Integration in Vector Fields

In addition to its use as a sweetener, honey has been used as a medicine, an aphrodisiac, and a wound dressing. Honey reacts with the water molecules in wounds, causing death by dehydration for infection-causing bacteria. It also produces hydrogen peroxide through enzymatic reactions, enhancing its antibacterial properties.

In a bottling facility, honey is forced through a long cylindrical tube of radius 0.5 cm. Its velocity function is given by $\mathbf{v} = 5(0.25 - r^2)\mathbf{k}$ cm/sec, where $r = \sqrt{x^2 + y^2}$ is the distance (in centimeters) from the center of the tube. Find the output of the tube in cubic centimeters per second. This problem can be solved using the ideas in Section 16.5.

Chapter 16 Overview

In this chapter we encounter Green's Theorem, perhaps the most powerful theorem of calculus. It is deep and surprising and has far-reaching consequences. In pure mathematics, it ranks in importance with the Fundamental Theorem of Calculus. In applied mathematics, the generalizations of Green's Theorem provide the foundation for the great vector integral theorems of electricity and magnetism.

The mathematics of this chapter is the mathematics engineers and physicists use to model fluid flow, design underwater transmission cables, explain the distribution of heat in stars, and calculate the work it takes to put satellites into orbit.

16.1 Line Integrals

What you'll learn about

- Definitions and Notation
- Evaluation for Smooth Curves
- Additivity
- Mass and Moment Calculations

Definitions and Notation

Suppose $f(x, y, z)$ is a function whose domain contains the curve $\mathbf{r}(t) = g(t)\mathbf{i} + h(t)\mathbf{j} + k(t)\mathbf{k}$, $a \le t \le b$. The values of f along the curve are given by the composite function $f(g(t), h(t), k(t))$. If we integrate this composite with respect to arc length from $t = a$ to $t = b$, we calculate the **line integral** of f over the curve.

To define this integral, we partition the curve into a finite number of subarcs (Figure 16.1). The typical subarc has length Δs_k. In each subarc, we choose a point (x_k, y_k, z_k) and form the sum

$$S_n = \sum_{k=1}^{n} f(x_k, y_k, z_k)\, \Delta s_k. \tag{1}$$

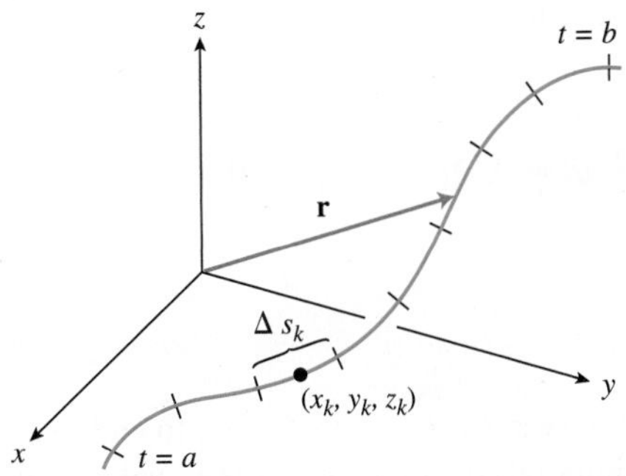

Figure 16.1 The curve $\mathbf{r}(t) = g(t)\mathbf{i} + h(t)\mathbf{j} + k(t)\mathbf{k}$, partitioned into small arcs from $t = a$ to $t = b$. The length of a typical subarc is Δs_k.

If f is continuous and the functions g, h, and k have continuous first derivatives, then the sums in Equation (1) approach a limit as n increases and the lengths Δs_k approach zero. This limit is the **(line) integral of f over the curve from a to b.** If the curve is denoted by a single letter, C for example, the notation for the integral is

$$\int_C f(x, y, z)\, ds. \qquad \text{"The integral of } f \text{ over } C\text{"} \tag{2}$$

Evaluation for Smooth Curves

If $\mathbf{r}(t)$ is smooth for $a \le t \le b$ ($\mathbf{v} = d\mathbf{r}/dt$ is continuous and never $\mathbf{0}$), we can use the equation

$$s(t) = \int_a^t |\mathbf{v}(\tau)|\, d\tau \qquad \text{Eq. (2) of Section 13.2 with } t_0 = a$$

to express ds in Equation (2) as $ds = |\mathbf{v}(t)|\, dt$. A theorem from advanced calculus says we can then evaluate the integral of f over C as

$$\int_C f(x, y, z)\, ds = \int_a^b f(g(t), h(t), k(t))|\mathbf{v}(t)|\, dt.$$

This formula evaluates the integral correctly no matter what parametrization we use, as long as the parametrization is smooth.

How to Evaluate a Line Integral

To integrate a continuous function $f(x, y, z)$ over a curve C:

1. Find a smooth parametrization of C,
$$\mathbf{r}(t) = g(t)\mathbf{i} + h(t)\mathbf{j} + k(t)\mathbf{k}, \qquad a \le t \le b.$$
2. Evaluate the integral as
$$\int_C f(x, y, z)\, ds = \int_a^b f(g(t), h(t), k(t))\left|\mathbf{v}(t)\right|\, dt. \tag{3}$$

If f has the constant value 1, then the integral of f over C gives the length of C.

EXAMPLE 1 Evaluating a Line Integral

Integrate $f(x, y, z) = x - 3y^2 + z$ over the line segment C joining the origin and the point (1, 1, 1) (Figure 16.2).

SOLUTION

We choose the simplest parametrization we can think of:

$$\mathbf{r}(t) = t\mathbf{i} + t\mathbf{j} + t\mathbf{k}, \qquad 0 \le t \le 1.$$

The components have continuous first derivatives and $\left|\mathbf{v}(t)\right| = \sqrt{1^2 + 1^2 + 1^2} = \sqrt{3}$ is never 0, so the parametrization is smooth. The integral of f over C is

$$\begin{aligned}\int_C f(x, y, z)\, ds &= \int_0^1 f(t, t, t) \cdot (\sqrt{3})\, dt && \text{Eq. (3)}\\ &= \int_0^1 (t - 3t^2 + t)\sqrt{3}\, dt\\ &= \sqrt{3}\int_0^1 (2t - 3t^2)\, dt = \sqrt{3}[t^2 - t^3]_0^1 = 0.\end{aligned}$$

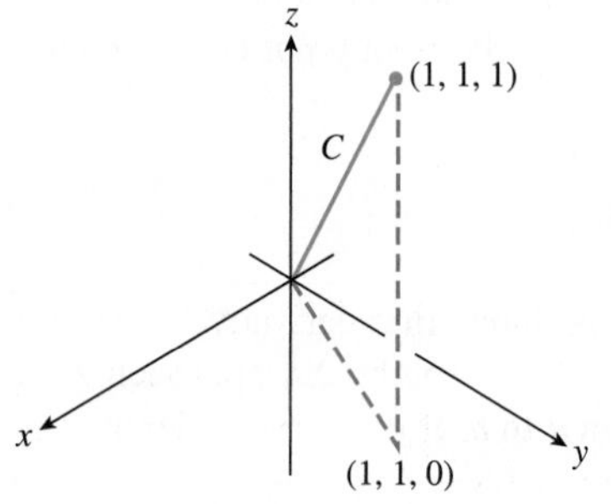

Figure 16.2 The integration path in Example 1.

Additivity

If a curve C is made by joining a finite number of curves $C_1, C_2, \ldots, C_n$ end to end, then the integral of a function over C is the sum of the integrals over the curves that make it up:

$$\int_C f\, ds = \int_{C_1} f\, ds + \int_{C_2} f\, ds + \cdots + \int_{C_n} f\, ds. \tag{4}$$

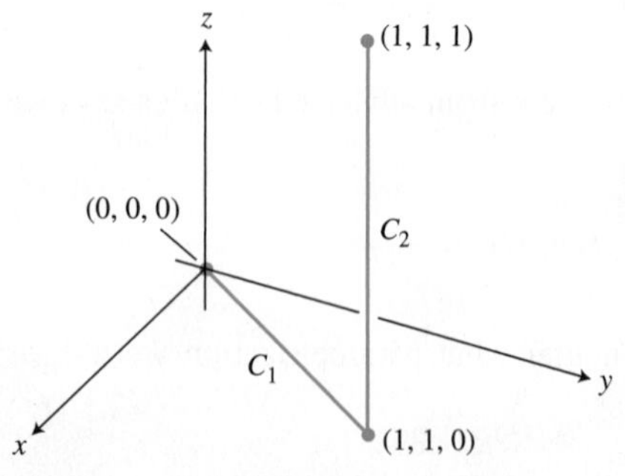

Figure 16.3 The path of integration in Example 2.

EXAMPLE 2 Illustrating Equation (4)

Figure 16.3 shows another path from the origin to (1, 1, 1), the union of line segments C_1 and C_2. Integrate $f(x, y, z) = x - 3y^2 + z$ over $C_1 \cup C_2$.

SOLUTION

We choose the simplest parametrizations for C_1 and C_2 we can think of, checking the lengths of the velocity vectors as we go along:

$$C_1\colon \mathbf{r}(t) = t\mathbf{i} + t\mathbf{j}, \quad 0 \le t \le 1; \qquad \left|\mathbf{v}\right| = \sqrt{1^2 + 1^2} = \sqrt{2},$$
$$C_2\colon \mathbf{r}(t) = \mathbf{i} + \mathbf{j} + t\mathbf{k}, \quad 0 \le t \le 1; \qquad \left|\mathbf{v}\right| = \sqrt{0^2 + 0^2 + 1^2} = 1.$$

With these parametrizations we find

$$\begin{aligned}\int_{C_1\cup C_2} f(x,y,z)\,ds &= \int_{C_1} f(x,y,z)\,ds + \int_{C_2} f(x,y,z)\,ds && \text{Eq. (4)}\\ &= \int_0^1 f(t,t,0)\sqrt{2}\,dt + \int_0^1 f(1,1,t)(1)\,dt && \text{Eq. (3)}\\ &= \int_0^1 (t-3t^2+0)\sqrt{2}\,dt + \int_0^1 (1-3+t)(1)\,dt\\ &= \sqrt{2}\left[\frac{t^2}{2}-t^3\right]_0^1 + \left[\frac{t^2}{2}-2t\right]_0^1 = -\frac{\sqrt{2}}{2}-\frac{3}{2}.\end{aligned}$$

Integral Evaluation

The integrals with respect to t in Examples 1 and 2 were simple enough to do by hand. More complicated integrals might require an integral evaluator like the one in your graphing calculator.

Notice three things about the integrations in Examples 1 and 2. First, as soon as the components of the appropriate curve were substituted into the formula for f, the integration became a standard integration with respect to t. Second, the integral of f over $C_1 \cup C_2$ was obtained by integrating f over each section of the path and adding the results. Third, the integrals of f over C and $C_1 \cup C_2$ had different values. For most functions, the value of the integral along a path joining two points changes if you change the path between them. For a special class of functions, however, the value remains the same, as we see in Section 16.3.

Mass and Moment Calculations

We treat coil springs and wires like masses distributed along smooth curves in space. The distribution is described by a continuous density function $\delta(x, y, z)$ (mass per unit length). The spring's or wire's mass, center of mass, and moments are then calculated with the formulas in Table 16.1. The formulas also apply to thin rods.

Table 16.1 Mass and Moment Formulas for Coil Springs, Thin Rods, and Wires Lying Along a Smooth Curve C in Space

Mass: $M = \int_C \delta(x,y,z)\,ds$

First moments about the coordinate planes:

$$M_{yz} = \int_C x\delta\,ds, \qquad M_{xz} = \int_C y\delta\,ds, \qquad M_{xy} = \int_C z\delta\,ds$$

Coordinates of the center of mass:

$$\bar{x} = M_{yz}/M, \qquad \bar{y} = M_{xz}/M, \qquad \bar{z} = M_{xy}/M$$

Moments of inertia (second moments):

$$I_x = \int_C (y^2+z^2)\delta\,ds, \qquad I_y = \int_C (x^2+z^2)\delta\,ds$$

$$I_z = \int_C (x^2+y^2)\delta\,ds, \qquad I_L = \int_C r^2\delta\,ds$$

$r(x, y, z) =$ distance from point (x, y, z) to line L

Radius of gyration about a line L: $R_L = \sqrt{I_L/M}$

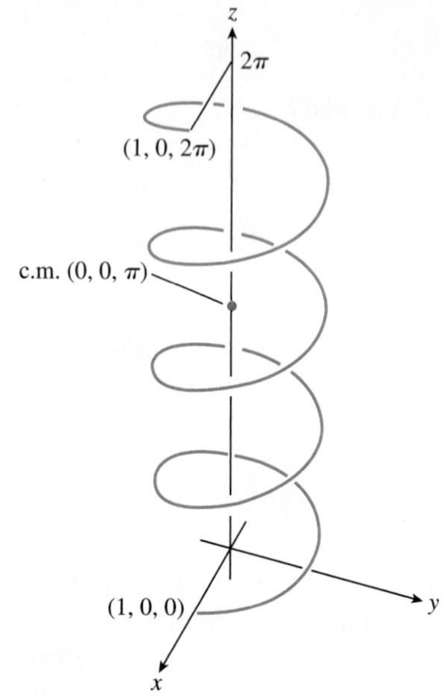

Figure 16.4 The helical spring in Example 3.

EXAMPLE 3 Finding Mass, Center of Mass, Moment of Inertia, and Radius of Gyration

A coil spring lies along the helix

$$\mathbf{r}(t) = (\cos 4t)\mathbf{i} + (\sin 4t)\mathbf{j} + t\mathbf{k}, \qquad 0 \le t \le 2\pi.$$

The spring's density is a constant, $\delta = 1$. Find the spring's mass and center of mass, and its moment of inertia and radius of gyration about the z-axis.

SOLUTION

We sketch the spring (Figure 16.4). The symmetry and constant density put the center of mass at the point $(0, 0, \pi)$ on the z-axis.

For the remaining calculations, we first find $|\mathbf{v}(t)|$:

$$|\mathbf{v}(t)| = \sqrt{\left(\frac{dx}{dt}\right)^2 + \left(\frac{dy}{dt}\right)^2 + \left(\frac{dz}{dt}\right)^2}$$

$$= \sqrt{(-4 \sin 4t)^2 + (4 \cos 4t)^2 + (1)^2} = \sqrt{17}.$$

We then evaluate the formulas from Table 16.1 using Equation (3):

$$M = \int_{\text{Helix}} \delta \, ds = \int_0^{2\pi} (1)\sqrt{17}\, dt = 2\pi\sqrt{17}$$

$$I_z = \int_{\text{Helix}} (x^2 + y^2)\delta \, ds = \int_0^{2\pi} (\cos^2 4t + \sin^2 4t)(1)\sqrt{17}\, dt$$

$$= \int_0^{2\pi} \sqrt{17}\, dt = 2\pi\sqrt{17}$$

$$R_z = \sqrt{I_z/M} = \sqrt{2\pi\sqrt{17}/(2\pi\sqrt{17})} = 1.$$

Notice that the radius of gyration about the z-axis is the radius of the cylinder around which the helix winds.

A Balancing Trick

The center of mass of the arch in Example 4 lies outside the arch. This is the principle behind a neat dinner-table trick. If you overlap the prongs of two forks and insert a half-dollar part way to hold the forks together, you will be able to hold the forks out in space by balancing the coin on the rim of a glass.

EXAMPLE 4 Finding a Center of Mass

A slender metal arch, denser at the bottom than top, lies along the semicircle $y^2 + z^2 = 1$, $z \ge 0$, in the yz-plane (Figure 16.5). Find the center of the arch's mass if the density at the point (x, y, z) on the arch is $\delta(x, y, z) = 2 - z$.

SOLUTION

We know $\bar{x} = 0$ and $\bar{y} = 0$ because the arch lies in the yz-plane with its mass distributed symmetrically about the z-axis. To find $\bar{z}$, we parametrize the semicircle as

$$\mathbf{r}(t) = (\cos t)\mathbf{j} + (\sin t)\mathbf{k}, \qquad 0 \le t \le \pi.$$

For this parametrization,

$$|\mathbf{v}(t)| = \sqrt{\left(\frac{dx}{dt}\right)^2 + \left(\frac{dy}{dt}\right)^2 + \left(\frac{dz}{dt}\right)^2} = \sqrt{(0)^2 + (-\sin t)^2 + (\cos t)^2} = 1,$$

so $ds = vt$. The formulas in Table 16.1 then give

$$M = \int_C \delta \, ds = \int_C (2 - z)\, ds = \int_0^{\pi} (2 - \sin t)\, dt = 2\pi - 2$$

$$M_{xy} = \int_C z\delta \, ds = \int_C z(2 - z)\, ds = \int_0^{\pi} (\sin t)(2 - \sin t)\, dt$$

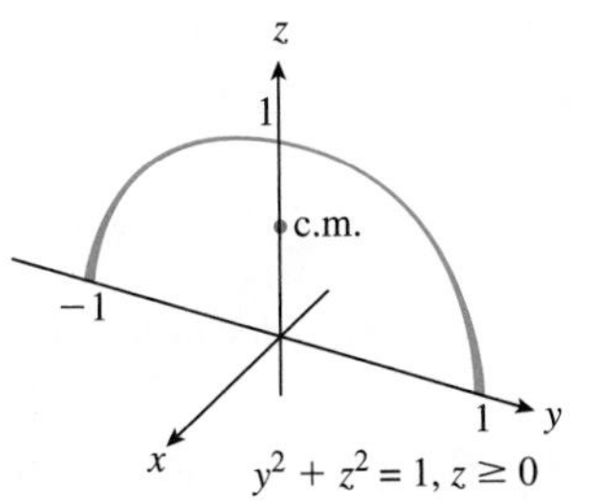

Figure 16.5 Example 4 shows how to find the center of mass of a circular arch of variable density.

$$= \int_0^{\pi} (2 \sin t - \sin^2 t)\, dt = \frac{8 - \pi}{2}$$

$$\bar{z} = \frac{M_{xy}}{M} = \frac{8 - \pi}{2} \cdot \frac{1}{2\pi - 2} = \frac{8 - \pi}{4\pi - 4} \approx 0.57.$$

With $\bar{z}$ to the nearest hundredth, the center of mass is (0, 0, 0.57).

Quick Review 16.1

In Exercises 1–5, evaluate the integrals analytically.

1. $\int \cos 3x\, dx$

2. $\int \sin 2x\, dx$

3. $\int (x^2 - x^3 + 2)\, dx$

4. $\int_{-1}^{2} (x^2 - x^3 + 2)\, dx$

5. $\int_0^{\pi} \cos 3x\, dx$

In Exercises 6–10, parametrize the line segment with the given endpoints.

6. (0, 0), (2, 3)

7. (0, 0), (a, b)

8. (−2, 1), (3, −2)

9. (0, 0, 0), (2, 3, 4)

10. (−1, 1, 2), (3, 3, −2)

Section 16.1 Exercises

In Exercises 1–8, match the vector equation with the graphs in Figure 16.6.

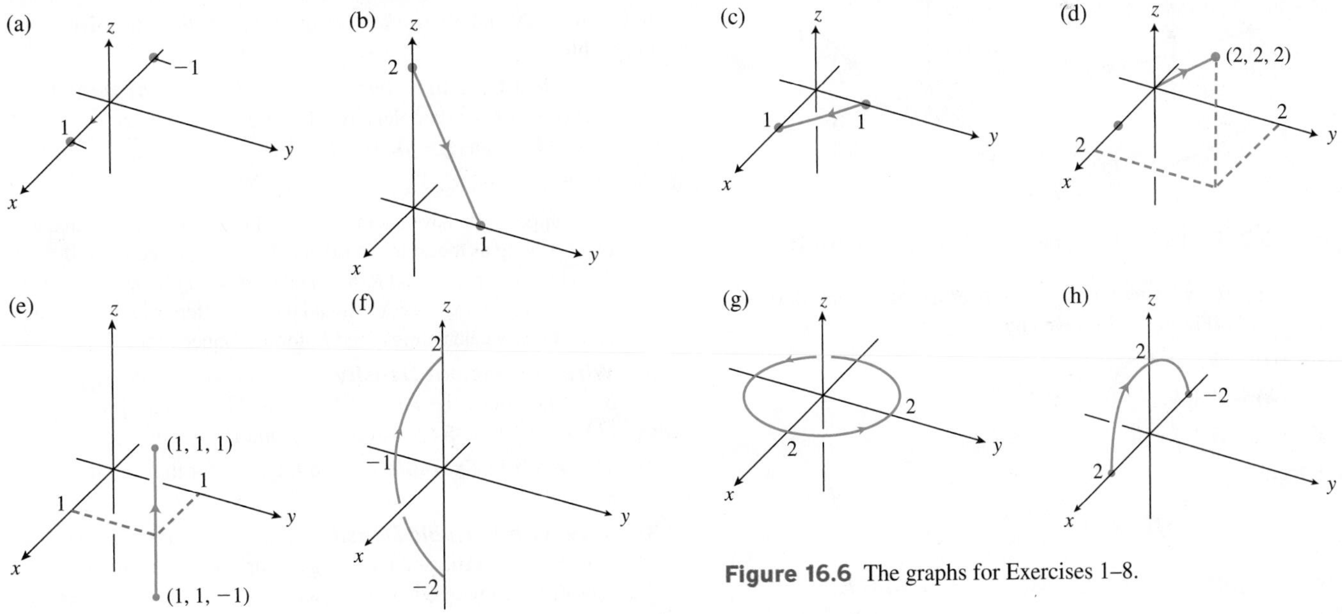

Figure 16.6 The graphs for Exercises 1–8.

1. $\mathbf{r}(t) = t\mathbf{i} + (1 - t)\mathbf{j}, \quad 0 \le t \le 1$

2. $\mathbf{r}(t) = \mathbf{i} + \mathbf{j} + t\mathbf{k}, \quad -1 \le t \le 1$

3. $\mathbf{r}(t) = (2 \cos t)\mathbf{i} + (2 \sin t)\mathbf{j}, \quad 0 \le t \le 2\pi$

4. $\mathbf{r}(t) = t\mathbf{i}, \quad -1 \le t \le 1$

5. $\mathbf{r}(t) = t\mathbf{i} + t\mathbf{j} + t\mathbf{k}, \quad 0 \le t \le 2$

6. $\mathbf{r}(t) = t\mathbf{j} + (2 - 2t)\mathbf{k}, \quad 0 \le t \le 1$

7. $\mathbf{r}(t) = (t^2 - 1)\mathbf{j} + 2t\mathbf{k}, \quad -1 \le t \le 1$

8. $\mathbf{r}(t) = (2 \cos t)\mathbf{i} + (2 \sin t)\mathbf{k}, \quad 0 \le t \le \pi$

9. Evaluate $\int_C (x + y)\,ds$, where C is the straight-line segment $x = t$, $y = (1 - t)$, $z = 0$, from (0, 1, 0) to (1, 0, 0).

10. Evaluate $\int_C (x - y + z - 2)\,ds$, where C is the straight-line segment $x = t$, $y = (1 - t)$, $z = 1$, from (0, 1, 1) to (1, 0, 1).

11. Evaluate $\int_C (xy + y + z)\,ds$ along the curve $\mathbf{r}(t) = 2t\mathbf{i} + t\mathbf{j} + (2 - 2t)\mathbf{k}$, $0 \le t \le 1$.

12. Evaluate $\int_C \sqrt{x^2 + y^2}\,ds$ along the curve $\mathbf{r}(t) = (4\cos t)\mathbf{i} + (4\sin t)\mathbf{j} + 3t\mathbf{k}$, $-2\pi \le t \le 2\pi$.

13. Find the line integral of $f(x, y, z) = x + y + z$ over the straight-line segment from (1, 2, 3) to (0, −1, 1).

14. Find the line integral of $f(x, y, z) = \sqrt{3}/(x^2 + y^2 + z^2)$ over the curve $\mathbf{r}(t) = t\mathbf{i} + t\mathbf{j} + t\mathbf{k}$, $1 \le t \le \infty$.

Explorations

15. Integrate $f(x, y, z) = x + \sqrt{y} - z^2$ over the path from (0, 0, 0) to (1, 1, 1) (Figure 16.7a) given by

C_1: $\mathbf{r}(t) = t\mathbf{i} + t^2\mathbf{j}$, $0 \le t \le 1$,

C_2: $\mathbf{r}(t) = \mathbf{i} + \mathbf{j} + t\mathbf{k}$, $0 \le t \le 1$.

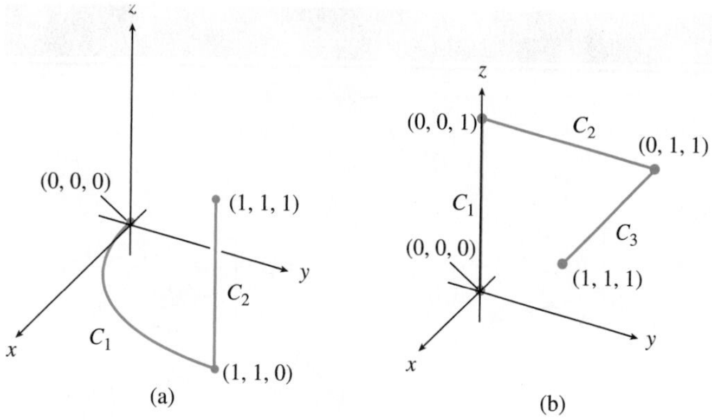

Figure 16.7 The paths of integration for Exercises 15 and 16.

16. Integrate $f(x, y, z) = x + \sqrt{y} - z^2$ over the path from (0, 0, 0) to (1, 1, 1) (Figure 16.7b) given by

C_1: $\mathbf{r}(t) = t\mathbf{k}$, $0 \le t \le 1$,

C_2: $\mathbf{r}(t) = t\mathbf{j} + \mathbf{k}$, $0 \le t \le 1$,

C_3: $\mathbf{r}(t) = t\mathbf{i} + \mathbf{j} + \mathbf{k}$, $0 \le t \le 1$.

17. Integrate

$$f(x, y, z) = \frac{x + y + z}{x^2 + y^2 + z^2}$$

over the path $\mathbf{r}(t) = t\mathbf{i} + t\mathbf{j} + t\mathbf{k}$, $0 < a \le t \le b$.

18. Integrate

$$f(x, y, z) = -\sqrt{x^2 + z^2}$$

over the circle $\mathbf{r}(t) = (a\cos t)\mathbf{j} + (a\sin t)\mathbf{k}$, $0 \le t \le 2\pi$.

In Exercises 19–22, integrate f over the given curve in the xy-plane.

19. $f(x, y) = x^3/y$, C: $y = x^2/2$, $0 \le x \le 2$

20. $f(x, y) = \dfrac{x + y^2}{\sqrt{1 + x^2}}$, C: $y = \dfrac{x^2}{2}$, from (1, 1/2) to (0, 0)

21. $f(x, y) = x + y$, C: $x^2 + y^2 = 4$ in the first quadrant from (2, 0) to (0, 2)

22. $f(x, y) = x^2 - y$, C: $x^2 + y^2 = 4$ in the first quadrant from (0, 2) to $(\sqrt{2}, \sqrt{2})$

23. ***Mass of a Wire*** Find the mass of a wire that lies along the curve $\mathbf{r}(t) = (t^2 - 1)\mathbf{j} + 2t\mathbf{k}$, $0 \le t \le 1$, if the density is $\delta = (3/2)t$.

24. ***Center of Mass of a Curved Wire*** A wire of density $\delta(x, y, z) = 15\sqrt{y + 2}$ lies along the curve $\mathbf{r}(t) = (t^2 - 1)\mathbf{j} + 2t\mathbf{k}$, $-1 \le t \le 1$. Find its center of mass. Then sketch the curve and center of mass together.

25. ***Wire with Different Density Functions*** Find the mass of a thin wire lying along the curve $\mathbf{r}(t) = \sqrt{2}t\mathbf{i} + \sqrt{2}t\mathbf{j} + (4 - t^2)\mathbf{k}$, $0 \le t \le 1$, if the density is **(a)** $\delta = 3t$, **(b)** $\delta = 1$.

26. ***Wire with Variable Density*** Find the center of mass of a thin wire lying along the curve $\mathbf{r}(t) = t\mathbf{i} + 2t\mathbf{j} + (2/3)t^{3/2}\mathbf{k}$, $0 \le t \le 2$, if the density is $\delta = 3\sqrt{5 + t}$.

27. ***A Wire Hoop*** A circular wire hoop of constant density δ lies along the circle $x^2 + y^2 = a^2$ in the xy-plane. Find the hoop's moment of inertia and radius of gyration about the z-axis.

28. ***A Slender Rod*** A slender rod of constant density lies along the line segment $\mathbf{r}(t) = t\mathbf{j} + (2 - 2t)\mathbf{k}$, $0 \le t \le 1$, in the yz-plane. Find the moments of inertia and radii of gyration of the rod about the three coordinate axes.

In Exercises 29 and 30, *work in groups of two or three* to solve the problem.

29. **Writing to Learn** ***Two Springs of Constant Density*** A spring of constant density δ lies along the helix $\mathbf{r}(t) = (\cos t)\mathbf{i} + (\sin t)\mathbf{j} + t\mathbf{k}$, $0 \le t \le 2\pi$.

(a) Find I_z and R_z.

(b) Suppose you have another spring of constant density δ that is twice as long as the spring in (a) and lies along the helix for $0 \le t \le 4\pi$. Do you expect I_z and R_z for the longer spring to be the same as those for the shorter one, or should they be different? Check your prediction by calculating I_z and R_z for the longer spring.

30. ***Wire of Constant Density*** A wire of constant density $\delta = 1$ lies along the curve $\mathbf{r}(t) = (t\cos t)\mathbf{i} + (t\sin t)\mathbf{j} + (2\sqrt{2}/3)t^{3/2}\mathbf{k}$, $0 \le t \le 1$. Find $\bar{z}$, I_z, and R_z.

31. ***The Arch in Example 4*** Find I_x and R_x for the arch in Example 4.

32. ***Wire with Variable Density*** Find the center of mass, and the moments of inertia and radii of gyration about the coordinate axes of a thin wire lying along the curve

$$\mathbf{r}(t) = t\mathbf{i} + \frac{2\sqrt{2}}{3}t^{3/2}\mathbf{j} + \frac{t^2}{2}\mathbf{k}, \quad 0 \le t \le 2,$$

if the density is $\delta = 1/(t + 1)$.

Extending the Ideas

CAS Explorations

In Exercises 33–36, perform the following steps to evaluate the line integral:

(a) Find $ds = |\mathbf{v}(t)|\,dt$ for the path $\mathbf{r}(t) = g(t)\mathbf{i} + h(t)\mathbf{j} + k(t)\mathbf{k}$.

(b) Express the integrand $f(g(t), h(t), k(t))|\mathbf{v}(t)|$ as a function of the parameter t.

(c) Evaluate $\int_C f\,ds$ using Equation (3) in the text.

33. $f(x, y, z) = \sqrt{1 + 30x^2 + 10y}$; $\mathbf{r}(t) = t\mathbf{i} + t^2\mathbf{j} + 3t^2\mathbf{k}$, $0 \le t \le 2$

34. $f(x, y, z) = \sqrt{1 + x^3 + 5y^3}$; $\mathbf{r}(t) = t\mathbf{i} + \frac{1}{3}t^2\mathbf{j} + \sqrt{t}\mathbf{k}$, $0 \le t \le 2$

35. $f(x, y, z) = x\sqrt{y} - 3z^2$; $\mathbf{r}(t) = \cos 2t\mathbf{i} + \sin 2t\mathbf{j} + 5t\mathbf{k}$, $0 \le t \le \pi/2$

36. $f(x, y, z) = \left(1 + \frac{9}{4}z^{1/3}\right)^{1/4}$; $\mathbf{r}(t) = \cos 2t\mathbf{i} + \sin 2t\mathbf{j} + t^{5/2}\mathbf{k}$, $0 \le t \le 2\pi$

16.2 Vector Fields, Work, Circulation, and Flux

What you'll learn about

- Vector Fields
- Gradient Fields
- Work Done by a Force over a Curve in Space
- Notation and Evaluation
- Flow Integrals and Circulation
- Flux Across a Plane Curve

Vector Fields

A **vector field** on a domain in the plane or in space is a function that assigns a vector to each point in the domain. In a typical field of three-dimensional vectors has a formula like

$$\mathbf{F}(x, y, z) = M(x, y, z)\mathbf{i} + N(x, y, z)\mathbf{j} + P(x, y, z)\mathbf{k}.$$

The field is **continuous** if the **component functions** M, N, and P are continuous, **differentiable** if M, N, and P are differentiable, and so on. A typical field of two-dimensional vectors has a formula like

$$\mathbf{F}(x, y) = M(x, y)\mathbf{i} + N(x, y)\mathbf{j}.$$

If we attach a projectile's velocity vector to each point of the projectile's trajectory in the plane of motion, we have a two-dimensional field defined along the trajectory. If we attach the gradient vector of a scalar function to each point of a level surface of the function, we have a three-dimensional field on the surface. If we attach the velocity vector to each point of a flowing fluid, we have a three-dimensional field defined on a region in space. These and other fields are illustrated in Figures 16.8 through 16.16. Some of the illustrations give formulas for the fields as well.

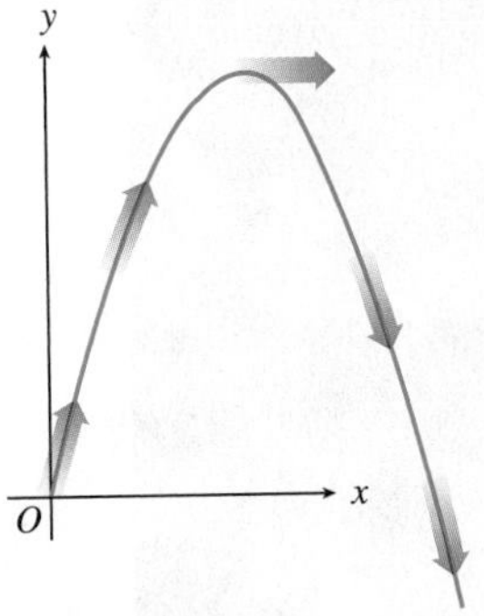

Figure 16.8 The velocity vectors $\mathbf{v}(t)$ of a projectile's motion make a vector field along the trajectory.

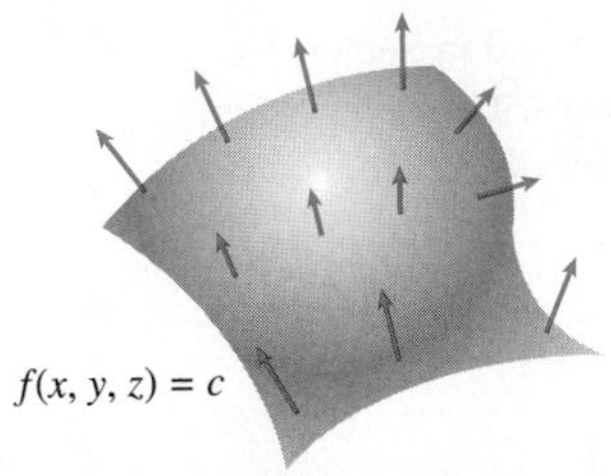

Figure 16.9 The field of gradient vectors ∇f on a surface $f(x, y, z) = c$.

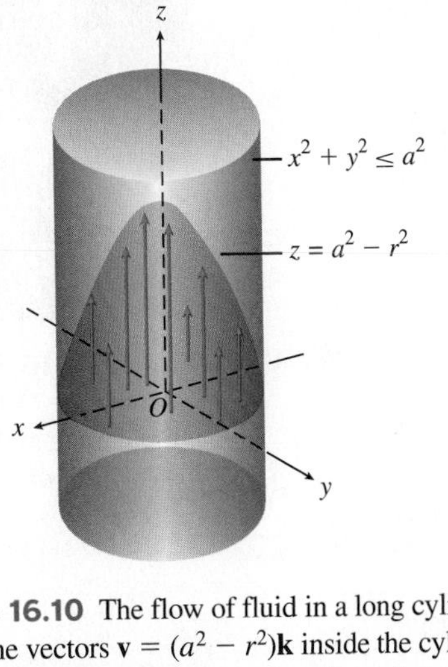

Figure 16.10 The flow of fluid in a long cylindrical pipe. The vectors $\mathbf{v} = (a^2 - r^2)\mathbf{k}$ inside the cylinder that have their bases in the xy-plane have their tips on the paraboloid $z = a^2 - r^2$.

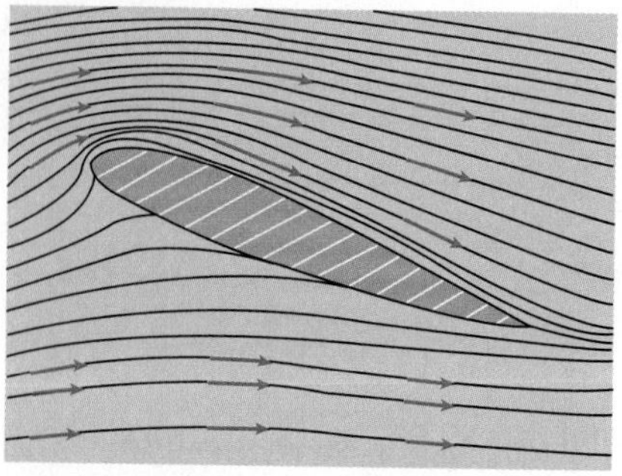

Figure 16.11 Velocity vectors of a flow around an airfoil in a wind tunnel. The streamlines were made visible by kerosene smoke. (Adapted from *NCFMF Book of Film Notes,* 1974, MIT Press with Education Development Center, Inc., Newton, Massachusetts.)

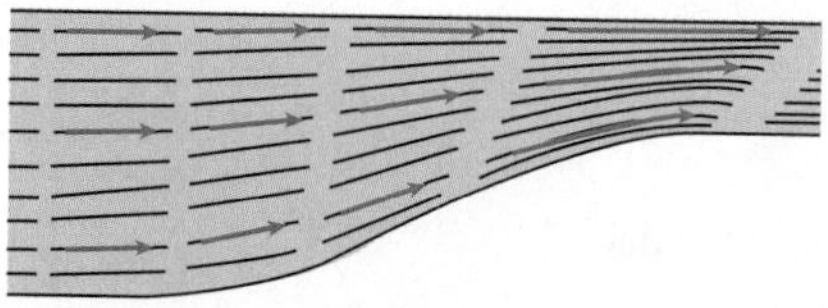

Figure 16.12 Streamlines in a contracting channel. The water speeds up as the channel narrows and the velocity vectors increase in length. (Adapted from *NCFMF Book of Film Notes,* 1974, MIT Press with Education Development Center, Inc., Newton, Massachusetts.)

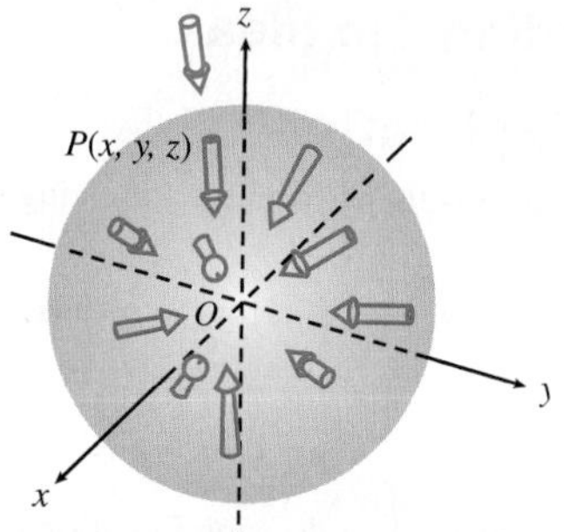

Figure 16.13 Vectors in the gravitational field

$$\mathbf{F} = -\frac{GM(x\mathbf{i} + y\mathbf{j} + z\mathbf{k})}{(x^2 + y^2 + z^2)^{3/2}}.$$

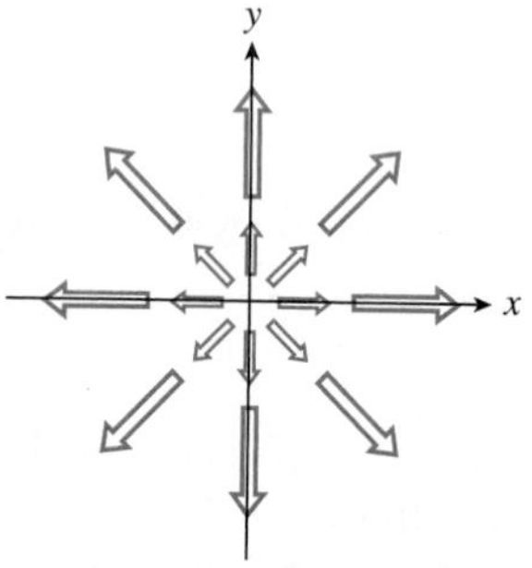

Figure 16.14 The radial field $\mathbf{F} = x\mathbf{i} + y\mathbf{j}$ of position vectors of points in the plane. Notice the convention that an arrow is drawn with its tail, not its head, at the point where $\mathbf{F}$ is evaluated.

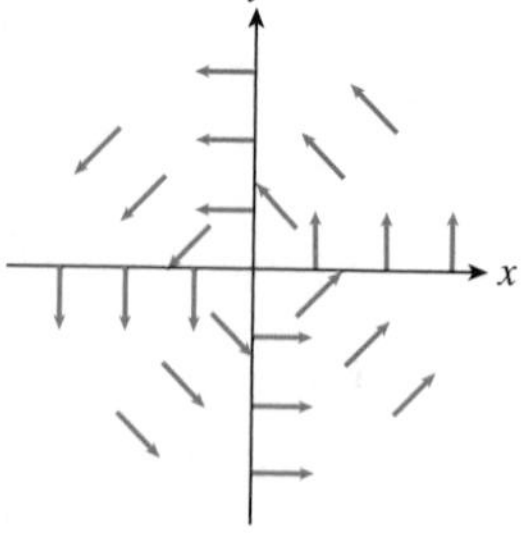

Figure 16.15 The circumferential or "spin" field of unit vectors

$$\mathbf{F} = (-y\mathbf{i} + x\mathbf{j})/(x^2 + y^2)^{1/2}$$

in the plane. The field is not defined at the origin.

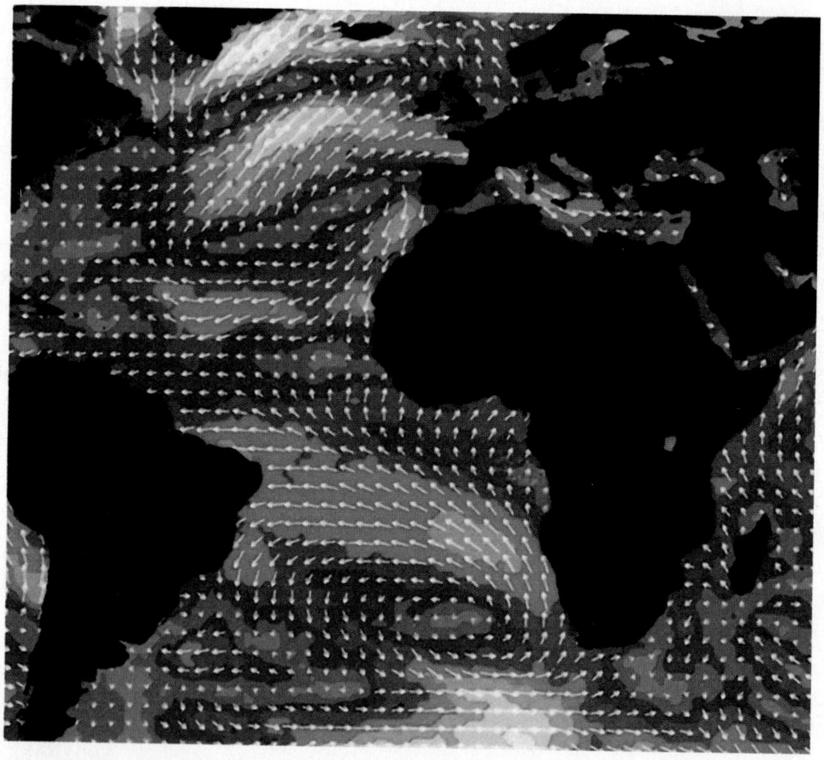

Figure 16.16 NASA's *Seasat* used radar during a three-day period in September 1978 to take 350,000 wind measurements over the world's oceans. The arrows show wind direction; their length and the color contouring indicate speed. Notice the heavy storm south of Greenland.

To sketch the fields that had formulas, we picked a representative selection of domain points and sketched the vectors attached to them. Notice the convention that the arrows representing the vectors are drawn with their tails, not their heads, at the points where the vector functions are evaluated. This is different from the way we drew the position vectors of the planets and projectiles in Chapter 11, with their tails at the origin and their heads at the planet's and projectile's location.

Gradient Fields

DEFINITION Gradient Field

The **gradient field** of a differentiable function $f(x, y, z)$ is the field of gradient vectors

$$\nabla f = \frac{\partial f}{\partial x}\mathbf{i} + \frac{\partial f}{\partial y}\mathbf{j} + \frac{\partial f}{\partial z}\mathbf{k}.$$

EXAMPLE 1 Finding Gradient Fields

Find the gradient field of $f(x, y, z) = xyz$.

SOLUTION

The gradient field of f is the field $\mathbf{F} = \nabla f = yz\mathbf{i} + xz\mathbf{j} + xy\mathbf{k}.$

As we see in Section 16.3, gradient fields play a special role in engineering, mathematics, and physics.

Work Done by a Force over a Curve in Space

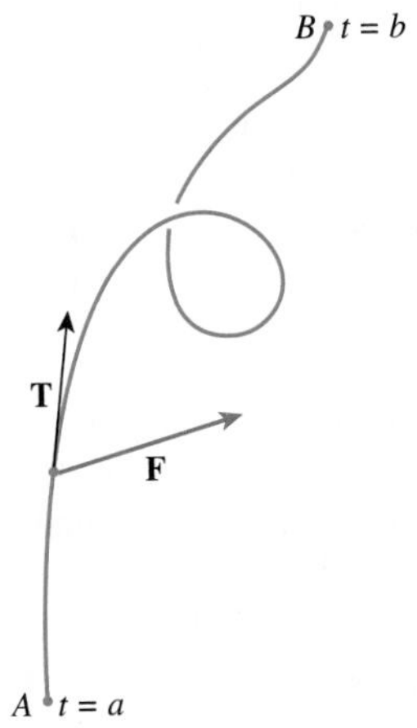

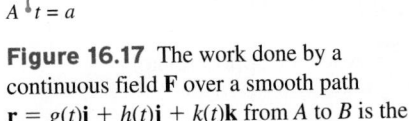

Figure 16.17 The work done by a continuous field $\mathbf{F}$ over a smooth path $\mathbf{r} = g(t)\mathbf{i} + h(t)\mathbf{j} + k(t)\mathbf{k}$ from A to B is the integral of $\mathbf{F} \cdot \mathbf{T}$ over the path from $t = a$ to $t = b$.

Suppose the vector field

$$\mathbf{F} = M(x, y, z)\mathbf{i} + N(x, y, z)\mathbf{j} + P(x, y, z)\mathbf{k}$$

represents a force throughout a region in space (it might be the force of gravity or an electromagnetic force of some kind) and

$$\mathbf{r}(t) = g(t)\mathbf{i} + h(t)\mathbf{j} + k(t)\mathbf{k}, \qquad a \le t \le b,$$

is a smooth curve in the region. Then the integral of $\mathbf{F} \cdot \mathbf{T}$, the scalar component of $\mathbf{F}$ in the direction of the curve's unit tangent vector, over the curve is the *work done by* $\mathbf{F}$ *over the curve* from a to b (Figure 16.17).

DEFINITION Work

The **work** done by a force $\mathbf{F} = M(x, y, z)\mathbf{i} + N(x, y, z)\mathbf{j} + P(x, y, z)\mathbf{k}$ over a smooth curve $\mathbf{r}(t) = g(t)\mathbf{i} + h(t)\mathbf{j} + k(t)\mathbf{k}$ from $t = a$ to $t = b$ is

$$W = \int_{t=a}^{t=b} \mathbf{F} \cdot \mathbf{T}\, ds. \qquad (1)$$

We motivate Equation (1) with the same kind of reasoning we used in Section 7.5 to derive the formula $W = \int_a^b F(x)\,dx$ for the work done by a continuous force of magnitude $F(x)$ directed along an interval of the x-axis. We divide the curve into short segments, apply the constant-force-times-distance formula for work to approximate the work over each curved segment, add the results to approximate the work over the entire curve, and calculate the work as the limit of the approximating sums as the segments become shorter and more numerous. To find exactly what the limiting integral should be, we partition the parameter interval $I = [a, b]$ in the usual way and choose a point c_k in each subinterval $[t_k, t_{k+1}]$. The partition of I determines ("induces," we say) a partition of the curve, with the point P_k being the tip of the position vector $\mathbf{r}$ at $t = t_k$ and Δs_k being the length of the curve segment P_kP_{k+1} (Figure 16.18).

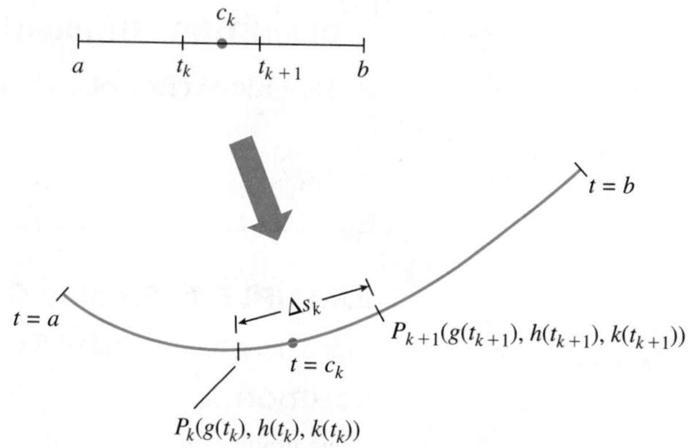

Figure 16.18 Each partition interval $a \le t \le b$ induces a partition of the curve $\mathbf{r} = g(t)\mathbf{i} + h(t)\mathbf{j} + k(t)\mathbf{k}$.

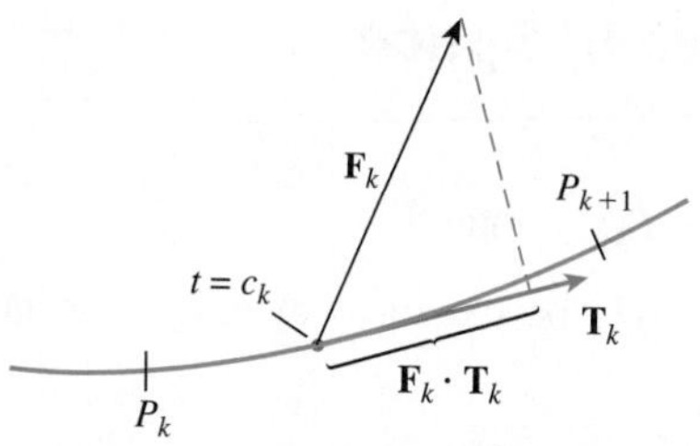

Figure 16.19 An enlarged view of the curve segment P_kP_{k+1} in Figure 16.18, showing the force vector and unit tangent vector at the point on the curve where $t = c_k$.

If $\mathbf{F}_k$ denotes the value of $\mathbf{F}$ at the point on the curve corresponding to $t = c_k$ and $\mathbf{T}_k$ denotes the curve's tangent vector at this point, then $\mathbf{F}_k \cdot \mathbf{T}_k$ is the scalar component of $\mathbf{F}$ in the direction of $\mathbf{T}$ at $t = c_k$ (Figure 16.19). The work done by $\mathbf{F}$ along the curve segment P_kP_{k+1} will be approximately

$$\begin{pmatrix}\text{Force component in}\\ \text{direction of motion}\end{pmatrix} \times \begin{pmatrix}\text{distance}\\ \text{applied}\end{pmatrix} = \mathbf{F}_k \cdot \mathbf{T}_k \, \Delta s_k.$$

The work done by $\mathbf{F}$ along the curve from $t = a$ to $t = b$ will be approximately

$$\sum_{k=1}^{n} \mathbf{F}_k \cdot \mathbf{T}_k \, \Delta s_k.$$

As the norm of the partition of $[a, b]$ approaches zero, the norm of the induced partition of the curve approaches zero and these sums approach the line integral

$$\int_{t=a}^{t=b} \mathbf{F} \cdot \mathbf{T} \, ds.$$

The sign of the number we calculate with this integral depends on the direction in which the curve is traversed as t increases. If we reverse the direction of motion, then we reverse the direction of $\mathbf{T}$ and change the sign of $\mathbf{F} \cdot \mathbf{T}$ and its integral.

Notation and Evaluation

Table 16.2 shows six ways to write the work integral in Equation (1). Despite their variety, the formulas in Table 16.2 are all evaluated the same way.

Table 16.2 Different Ways to Write the Work Integral

$W = \int_{t=a}^{t=b} \mathbf{F}\cdot\mathbf{T}\,ds$	The definition
$= \int_{t=a}^{t=b} \mathbf{F}\cdot d\mathbf{r}$	Compact differential form
$= \int_a^b \mathbf{F}\cdot\frac{d\mathbf{r}}{dt}\,dt$	Expanded to include dt; emphasizes the parameter t and velocity vector $d\mathbf{r}/dt$
$= \int_a^b \left(M\frac{dg}{dt} + N\frac{dh}{dt} + P\frac{dk}{dt}\right)dt$	Emphasizes the component functions
$= \int_a^b \left(M\frac{dx}{dt} + N\frac{dy}{dt} + P\frac{dz}{dt}\right)dt$	Abbreviates the components of $\mathbf{r}$
$= \int_a^b M\,dx + N\,dy + P\,dz$	dt's canceled; the most common form

How to Evaluate a Work Integral

To evaluate the work integral, take these steps:

1. Evaluate $\mathbf{F}$ on the curve as a function of the parameter t.
2. Find $d\mathbf{r}/dt$.
3. Dot $\mathbf{F}$ with $d\mathbf{r}/dt$.
4. Integrate the resulting scalar function from $t = a$ to $t = b$.

EXAMPLE 2 Finding Work Done By a Force

Find the work done by $\mathbf{F} = (y - x^2)\mathbf{i} + (z - y^2)\mathbf{j} + (x - z^2)\mathbf{k}$ over the curve $\mathbf{r}(t) = t\mathbf{i} + t^2\mathbf{j} + t^3\mathbf{k}$, $0 \le t \le 1$, from $(0, 0, 0)$ to $(1, 1, 1)$ (Figure 16.20).

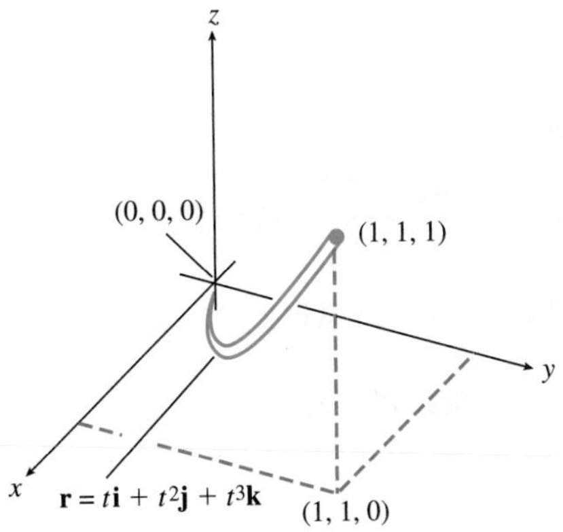

Figure 16.20 The curve in Example 2.

SOLUTION

Step 1: *Evaluate* **F** *on the curve.*

$$\mathbf{F} = (y - x^2)\mathbf{i} + (z - y^2)\mathbf{j} + (x - z^2)\mathbf{k}$$
$$= \underbrace{(t^2 - t^2)}_{0}\mathbf{i} + (t^3 - t^4)\mathbf{j} + (t - t^6)\mathbf{k}$$

Step 2: *Find* $d\mathbf{r}/dt$.

$$\frac{d\mathbf{r}}{dt} = \frac{d}{dt}(t\mathbf{i} + t^2\mathbf{j} + t^3\mathbf{k}) = \mathbf{i} + 2t\mathbf{j} + 3t^2\mathbf{k}$$

Step 3: *Dot* **F** *with* $d\mathbf{r}/dt$.

$$\mathbf{F}\cdot\frac{d\mathbf{r}}{dt} = [(t^3 - t^4)\mathbf{j} + (t - t^6)\mathbf{k}]\cdot(\mathbf{i} + 2t\mathbf{j} + 3t^2\mathbf{k})$$
$$= (t^3 - t^4)(2t) + (t - t^6)(3t^2) = 2t^4 - 2t^5 + 3t^3 - 3t^8$$

Step 4: *Integrate from* $t = 0$ *to* $t = 1$.

$$\text{Work} = \int_0^1 (2t^4 - 2t^5 + 3t^3 - 3t^8)\,dt = \frac{29}{60}$$

In Step 4 of Example 2, you can use your grapher to approximate the value of the integral or a CAS to find the exact value shown.

Flow Integrals and Circulation

Instead of being a force field, suppose $\mathbf{F} = M\mathbf{i} + N\mathbf{j} + P\mathbf{k}$ represents the velocity field of a fluid flowing through a region in space (a tidal basin or the turbine chamber of a hydroelectric generator, for example). Under these circumstances, the integral of $\mathbf{F} \cdot \mathbf{T}$ along a curve in the region gives the *fluid's flow along the curve.*

DEFINITIONS Flow, Flow Integral, and Circulation

If $\mathbf{r}(t) = g(t)\mathbf{i} + h(t)\mathbf{j} + k(t)\mathbf{k}$, $a \le t \le b$, is a smooth curve in the domain of a continuous velocity field $\mathbf{F} = M(x, y, z)\mathbf{i} + N(x, y, z)\mathbf{j} + P(x, y, z)\mathbf{k}$, the **flow** along the curve from $t = a$ to $t = b$ is the integral of $\mathbf{F} \cdot \mathbf{T}$ over the curve from a to b:

$$\text{Flow} = \int_a^b \mathbf{F} \cdot \mathbf{T}\, ds. \qquad (2)$$

The integral in this case is a **flow integral.** If the curve is a closed loop, then the flow is the **circulation** around the curve.

We evaluate flow integrals the same way we evaluate work integrals.

EXAMPLE 3 Finding the Flow

A fluid's velocity field is $\mathbf{F} = x\mathbf{i} + z\mathbf{j} + y\mathbf{k}$. Find the flow along the helix $\mathbf{r}(t) = (\cos t)\mathbf{i} + (\sin t)\mathbf{j} + t\mathbf{k}$, $0 \le t \le \pi/2$.

SOLUTION

Step 1: *Evaluate* $\mathbf{F}$ *on the curve.*

$$\mathbf{F} = x\mathbf{i} + z\mathbf{j} + y\mathbf{k} = (\cos t)\mathbf{i} + t\mathbf{j} + (\sin t)\mathbf{k}$$

Step 2: *Find* $d\mathbf{r}/dt$.

$$\frac{d\mathbf{r}}{dt} = (-\sin t)\mathbf{i} + (\cos t)\mathbf{j} + \mathbf{k}$$

Step 3: *Find* $\mathbf{F} \cdot (d\mathbf{r}/dt)$.

$$\mathbf{F} \cdot \frac{d\mathbf{r}}{dt} = (\cos t)(-\sin t) + (t)(\cos t) + (\sin t)(1)$$

$$= -\sin t \cos t + t \cos t + \sin t$$

Step 4: *Integrate from* $t = a$ *to* $t = b$.

$$\text{Flow} = \int_{t=a}^{t=b} \mathbf{F} \cdot \frac{d\mathbf{r}}{dt}\, dt = \int_0^{\pi/2} (-\sin t \cos t + t \cos t + \sin t)\, dt$$

$$= \frac{\pi}{2} - \frac{1}{2}$$

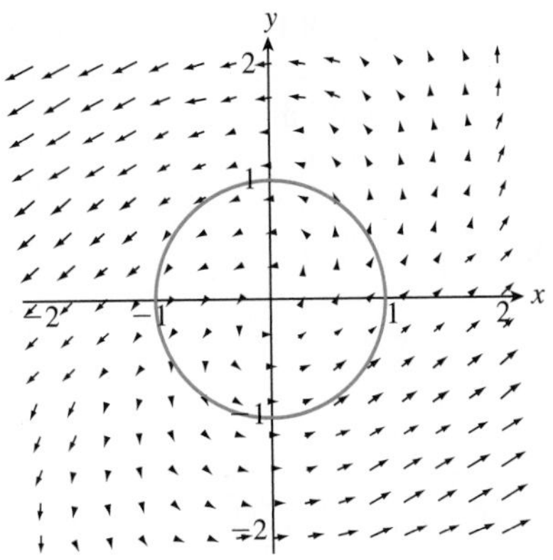

Figure 16.21 This figure suggests that the projections of the vectors of **F** that start on the circle onto the tangent vectors to the circle point in the direction of increasing t. This supports the positive value for circulation found in Example 4.

EXAMPLE 4 Finding Circulation

Find the circulation of the field $\mathbf{F} = (x - y)\mathbf{i} + x\mathbf{j}$ around the circle $\mathbf{r}(t) = (\cos t)\mathbf{i} + (\sin t)\mathbf{j}$, $0 \le t \le 2\pi$.

SOLUTION

1. On the circle, $\mathbf{F} = (x - y)\mathbf{i} + x\mathbf{j} = (\cos t - \sin t)\mathbf{i} + (\cos t)\mathbf{j}$.

2. $\dfrac{d\mathbf{r}}{dt} = (-\sin t)\mathbf{i} + (\cos t)\mathbf{j}$

3. $\mathbf{F} \cdot \dfrac{d\mathbf{r}}{dt} = -\sin t \cos t + \underbrace{\sin^2 t + \cos^2 t}_{1}$

4. $$\text{Circulation} = \int_0^{2\pi} \mathbf{F} \cdot \frac{d\mathbf{r}}{dt}\, dt = \int_0^{2\pi} (1 - \sin t \cos t)\, dt$$
$$= \left[t - \frac{\sin^2 t}{2} \right]_0^{2\pi} = 2\pi$$

Figure 16.21 shows the circulation vector field **F** together with the unit circle $\mathbf{r}(t)$.

Flux Across a Plane Curve

To find the rate at which a fluid is entering or leaving a region enclosed by a smooth curve C in the xy-plane, we calculate the line integral over C of $\mathbf{F} \cdot \mathbf{n}$, the scalar component of the fluid's velocity field in the direction of the curve's outward-pointing normal vector. The value of this integral is the *flux of* **F** *across C*. *Flux* is Latin for *flow,* but many flux calculations involve no motion at all. If **F** were an electric field or a magnetic field, for instance, the integral of $\mathbf{F} \cdot \mathbf{n}$ would still be called the flux of the field across C.

DEFINITION Flux

If C is a smooth closed curve in the domain of a continuous vector field $\mathbf{F} = M(x, y)\mathbf{i} + N(x, y)\mathbf{j}$ in the plane and if $\mathbf{n}$ is the outward-pointing unit normal vector on C, then the **flux** of **F** across C is given by the following line integral:

$$\text{Flux of } \mathbf{F} \text{ across } C = \int_C \mathbf{F} \cdot \mathbf{n}\, ds. \tag{3}$$

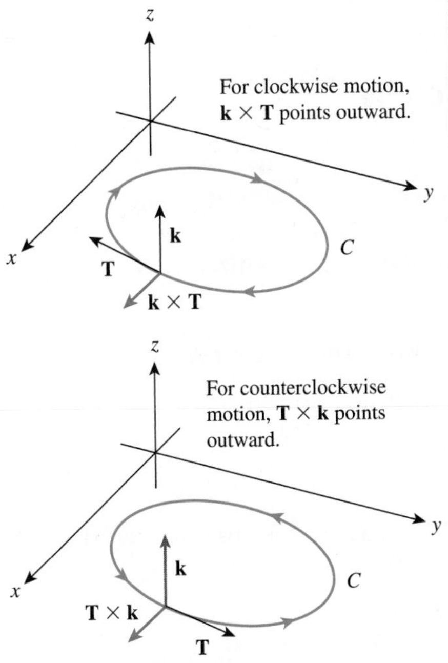

Figure 16.22 To find an outward unit normal vector for a smooth curve C in the xy-plane that is traversed counterclockwise as t increases, we take $\mathbf{n} = \mathbf{T} \times \mathbf{k}$.

Notice the difference between flux and circulation. The flux of **F** across C is the line integral with respect to arc length of $\mathbf{F} \cdot \mathbf{n}$, the scalar component of **F** in the direction of the outward normal. The circulation of **F** around C is the line integral with respect to arc length of $\mathbf{F} \cdot \mathbf{T}$, the scalar component of **F** in the direction of the unit tangent vector. Flux is the integral of the normal component of **F**; circulation is the integral of the tangential component of **F**.

To evaluate the integral in Equation (3), we begin with a parametrization

$$x = g(t), \qquad y = h(t), \qquad a \le t \le b,$$

that traces the curve C exactly once as t increases from a to b. We can find the outward unit normal vector **n** by crossing the curve's unit tangent vector **T** with the vector **k**, but which order do we choose, $\mathbf{T} \times \mathbf{k}$ or $\mathbf{k} \times \mathbf{T}$? Which one points outward? It depends on which way C is traversed as the parameter t increases. If the motion is clockwise, then $\mathbf{k} \times \mathbf{T}$ points outward; if the motion is counterclockwise, then $\mathbf{T} \times \mathbf{k}$ points outward (Figure 16.22). The usual choice is $\mathbf{n} = \mathbf{T} \times \mathbf{k}$, the choice that assumes counterclockwise motion.

Thus, although the value of the arc length integral in the definition of flux in Equation (3) does not depend on which way C is traversed, the formulas we are about to derive for *evaluating* the integral in Equation (3) will assume counterclockwise motion.

In terms of components,

$$\mathbf{n} = \mathbf{T} \times \mathbf{k} = \left(\frac{dx}{ds}\mathbf{i} + \frac{dy}{ds}\mathbf{j}\right) \times \mathbf{k} = \frac{dy}{ds}\mathbf{i} - \frac{dx}{ds}\mathbf{j}.$$

If $\mathbf{F} = M(x, y)\mathbf{i} + N(x, y)\mathbf{j}$, then

$$\mathbf{F} \cdot \mathbf{n} = M(x, y)\frac{dy}{ds} - N(x, y)\frac{dx}{ds}.$$

Hence,

$$\int_C \mathbf{F} \cdot \mathbf{n}\, ds = \int_C \left(M\frac{dy}{ds} - N\frac{dx}{ds}\right) ds = \oint_C M\, dy - N\, dx.$$

We put a directed circle $\circlearrowleft$ on the last integral as a reminder that the integration around the closed curve C is to be in the counterclockwise direction. To evaluate this integral, we express M, dy, N, and dx in terms of t and integrate from $t = a$ to $t = b$. We do not need to know either $\mathbf{n}$ or ds to find the flux.

Formula for Calculating Flux Across a Smooth Closed Plane Curve

$$(\text{Flux of } \mathbf{F} = M\mathbf{i} + N\mathbf{j} \text{ across } C) = \oint_C M\, dy - N\, dx \qquad (4)$$

The integral can be evaluated from any smooth parametrization $x = g(t)$, $y = h(t)$, $a \le t \le b$, that traces C counterclockwise exactly once.

EXAMPLE 5 Finding Flux Across a Circle

Find the flux of $\mathbf{F} = (x - y)\mathbf{i} + x\mathbf{j}$ across the circle $x^2 + y^2 = 1$ in the xy-plane.

SOLUTION

The parametrization $\mathbf{r}(t) = (\cos t)\mathbf{i} + (\sin t)\mathbf{j}$, $0 \le t \le 2\pi$, traces the circle counterclockwise exactly once. We can therefore use this parametrization in Equation (4). With

$$M = x - y = \cos t - \sin t, \qquad dy = d(\sin t) = \cos t\, dt$$

$$N = x = \cos t, \qquad dx = d(\cos t) = -\sin t\, dt,$$

we find

$$\text{Flux} = \oint_C M\, dy - N\, dx = \int_0^{2\pi} (\cos^2 t - \sin t \cos t + \cos t \sin t)\, dt \qquad \text{Eq. (4)}$$

$$= \int_0^{2\pi} \cos^2 t\, dt = \int_0^{2\pi} \frac{1 + \cos 2t}{2} = \pi.$$

The flux of $\mathbf{F}$ across the circle is π. Since the answer is positive, the net flow across the curve is outward. A net inward flow would have given a negative flux.

Quick Review 16.2

1. Let $f(x, y) = x \sin y + y \cos x$. Find $\partial f/\partial x$ and $\partial f/\partial y$.
2. Let $f(x, y, z) = x \sin (yz) + xyz$. Find $\partial f/\partial x$, $\partial f/\partial y$, and $\partial f/\partial z$.

In Exercises 3 and 4, find dy.

3. $y = x^3 - 2 \cos x$
4. $y = x \sin x$
5. Let $x = 2 \cos t$ and $y = 3 \sin t$. Find dy and dx.
6. Let $\mathbf{u} = t\mathbf{i} + t^2\mathbf{j} + (\cos t)\mathbf{k}$ and $\mathbf{v} = (\cos t)\mathbf{i} + (\sin t)\mathbf{j} - t\mathbf{k}$. Compute $\mathbf{u} \cdot \mathbf{v}$.

In Exercises 7–10, identify whether the circle is being traced clockwise or counterclockwise.

7. $x = 2 \cos t, \quad y = 2 \sin t, \quad 0 \le t \le 2\pi$
8. $x = -2 \cos t, \quad y = 2 \sin t, \quad 0 \le t \le 2\pi$
9. $x = -2 \cos t, \quad y = -2 \sin t, \quad 0 \le t \le 2\pi$
10. $x = 2 \sin t, \quad y = 2 \cos t, \quad 0 \le t \le 2\pi$

Section 16.2 Exercises

In Exercises 1–4, find the gradient field of the function.

1. $f(x, y, z) = (x^2 + y^2 + z^2)^{-1/2}$
2. $f(x, y, z) = \ln\sqrt{x^2 + y^2 + z^2}$
3. $g(x, y, z) = e^z - \ln(x^2 + y^2)$
4. $g(x, y, z) = xy + yz + xz$
5. Give a formula $\mathbf{F} = M(x, y)\mathbf{i} + N(x, y)\mathbf{j}$ for the vector field in the plane that has the property that $\mathbf{F}$ points toward the origin with magnitude inversely proportional to the square of the distance from the origin. (The field is not defined at (0, 0).)
6. Give a formula $\mathbf{F} = M(x, y)\mathbf{i} + N(x, y)\mathbf{j}$ for the vector field in the plane that has the property that $\mathbf{F} = \mathbf{0}$ at (0, 0) and that, at any other point (a, b), $\mathbf{F}$ is tangent to the circle $x^2 + y^2 = a^2 + b^2$ and points in the clockwise direction with magnitude $|\mathbf{F}| = \sqrt{a^2 + b^2}$.

In Exercises 7–12, *work in groups of two or three* to find the work done by force $\mathbf{F}$ from (0, 0, 0) to (1, 1, 1) over each of the following paths (Figure 16.23).

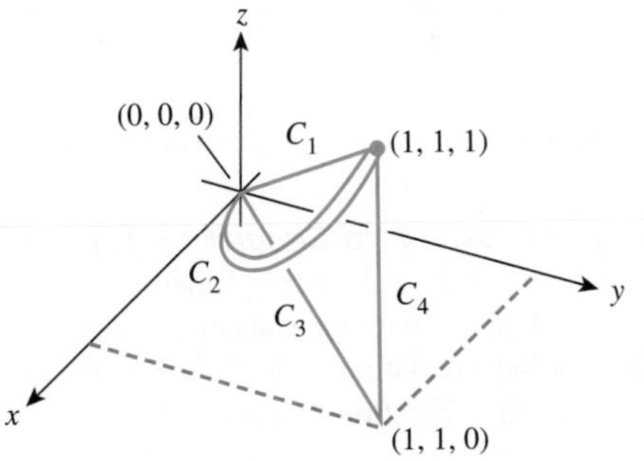

Figure 16.23 The paths from (0, 0, 0) to (1, 1, 1).

(a) The straight-line path C_1: $\mathbf{r}(t) = t\mathbf{i} + t\mathbf{j} + t\mathbf{k}, 0 \le t \le 1$

(b) The curved path C_2: $\mathbf{r}(t) = t\mathbf{i} + t^2\mathbf{j} + t^4\mathbf{k}, 0 \le t \le 1$

(c) The path $C_3 \cup C_4$ consisting of the line segment from (0, 0, 0) to (1, 1, 0) followed by the segment from (1, 1, 0) to (1, 1, 1)

7. $\mathbf{F} = 3y\mathbf{i} + 2x\mathbf{j} + 4z\mathbf{k}$
8. $\mathbf{F} = [1/(x^2 + 1)]\mathbf{j}$
9. $\mathbf{F} = \sqrt{z}\mathbf{i} - 2x\mathbf{j} + \sqrt{y}\mathbf{k}$
10. $\mathbf{F} = xy\mathbf{i} + yz\mathbf{j} + xz\mathbf{k}$
11. $\mathbf{F} = (3x^2 - 3x)\mathbf{i} + 3z\mathbf{j} + \mathbf{k}$
12. $\mathbf{F} = (y + z)\mathbf{i} + (z + x)\mathbf{j} + (x + y)\mathbf{k}$

In Exercises 13–16, find the work done by $\mathbf{F}$ over the curve in the direction of increasing t.

13. $\mathbf{F} = xy\mathbf{i} + y\mathbf{j} - yz\mathbf{k}$
    $\mathbf{r}(t) = t\mathbf{i} + t^2\mathbf{j} + t\mathbf{k}, \quad 0 \le t \le 1$
14. $\mathbf{F} = 2y\mathbf{i} + 3x\mathbf{j} + (x + y)\mathbf{k}$
    $\mathbf{r}(t) = (\cos t)\mathbf{i} + (\sin t)\mathbf{j} + (t/6)\mathbf{k}, \quad 0 \le t \le 2\pi$
15. $\mathbf{F} = z\mathbf{i} + x\mathbf{j} + y\mathbf{k}$
    $\mathbf{r}(t) = (\sin t)\mathbf{i} + (\cos t)\mathbf{j} + t\mathbf{k}, \quad 0 \le t \le 2\pi$
16. $\mathbf{F} = 6z\mathbf{i} + y^2\mathbf{j} + 12x\mathbf{k}$
    $\mathbf{r}(t) = (\sin t)\mathbf{i} + (\cos t)\mathbf{j} + (t/6)\mathbf{k}, \quad 0 \le t \le 2\pi$
17. Evaluate $\int_C xy\,dx + (x + y)\,dy$ along the curve $y = x^2$ in the xy-plane from $(-1, 1)$ to $(2, 4)$.
18. Evaluate $\int_C (x - y)\,dx + (x + y)\,dy$ counterclockwise around the triangle in the xy-plane with vertices (0, 0), (1, 0), and (0, 1).
19. Evaluate $\int_C \mathbf{F} \cdot \mathbf{T}\,ds$ for the vector field $\mathbf{F} = x^2\mathbf{i} - y\mathbf{j}$ along the curve $x = y^2$ from (4, 2) to $(1, -1)$ in the xy-plane.
20. Evaluate $\int_C \mathbf{F} \cdot d\mathbf{r}$ for the vector field $\mathbf{F} = y\mathbf{i} - x\mathbf{j}$ counterclockwise along the unit circle $x^2 + y^2 = 1$ from (1, 0) to (0, 1) in the xy-plane.
21. ***Work*** Find the work done by the force $\mathbf{F} = xy\mathbf{i} + (y - x)\mathbf{j}$ over the straight line from (1, 1) to (2, 3) in the xy-plane.
22. ***Work*** Find the work done by the gradient of $f(x, y) = (x + y)^2$ counterclockwise around the circle $x^2 + y^2 = 4$ from (2, 0) to itself in the xy-plane.

23. ***Circulation and Flux*** Find the circulation and flux of the fields

$$\mathbf{F}_1 = x\mathbf{i} + y\mathbf{j} \quad \text{and} \quad \mathbf{F}_2 = -y\mathbf{i} + x\mathbf{j}$$

around and across each of the following curves in the xy-plane.

(a) The circle $\mathbf{r}(t) = (\cos t)\mathbf{i} + (\sin t)\mathbf{j}, 0 \le t \le 2\pi$

(b) The ellipse $\mathbf{r}(t) = (\cos t)\mathbf{i} + (4 \sin t)\mathbf{j}, 0 \le t \le 2\pi$

24. ***Flux Across a Circle*** Find the flux of the fields $\mathbf{F}_1 = 2x\mathbf{i} - 3y\mathbf{j}$ and $\mathbf{F}_2 = -2x\mathbf{i} + (x - y)\mathbf{j}$ across the circle $\mathbf{r}(t) = (a \cos t)\mathbf{i} + (a \sin t)\mathbf{j}$, $0 \le t \le 2\pi$ in the xy-plane.

In Exercises 25–28, find the circulation and flux of the field $\mathbf{F}$ around and across the closed semicircular path in the xy-plane that consists of the semicircular arch $\mathbf{r}_1(t) = (a \cos t)\mathbf{i} + (a \sin t)\mathbf{j}, 0 \le t \le \pi$, followed by the line segment $\mathbf{r}_2(t) = t\mathbf{i}, -a \le t \le a$.

25. $\mathbf{F} = x\mathbf{i} + y\mathbf{j}$

26. $\mathbf{F} = x^2\mathbf{i} + y^2\mathbf{j}$

27. $\mathbf{F} = -y\mathbf{i} + x\mathbf{j}$

28. $\mathbf{F} = -y^2\mathbf{i} + x^2\mathbf{j}$

29. ***Flow*** Evaluate the flow integral of the velocity field $\mathbf{F} = (x + y)\mathbf{i} - (x^2 + y^2)\mathbf{j}$ along each of the following paths from $(1, 0)$ to $(-1, 0)$ in the xy-plane.

(a) The upper half of the circle $x^2 + y^2 = 1$

(b) The line segment from $(1, 0)$ to $(-1, 0)$

(c) The line segment from $(1, 0)$ to $(0, -1)$ followed by the line segment from $(0, -1)$ to $(-1, 0)$

30. ***Flux*** Find the flux of the field in Exercise 29 outward across the triangle with vertices $(1, 0), (0, 1), (-1, 0)$.

31. ***Spin Field*** Draw the spin field

$$\mathbf{F} = -\frac{y}{\sqrt{x^2 + y^2}}\mathbf{i} + \frac{x}{\sqrt{x^2 + y^2}}\mathbf{j}$$

(see Figure 16.15) along with its horizontal and vertical components at a representative assortment of points on the circle $x^2 + y^2 = 4$ in the xy-plane.

32. ***Radial Field*** Draw the radial field

$$\mathbf{F} = x\mathbf{i} + y\mathbf{j}$$

(see Figure 16.14) along with its horizontal and vertical components at a representative assortment of points on the circle $x^2 + y^2 = 1$ in the xy-plane.

33. ***A Field of Tangent Vectors***

(a) Find a field $\mathbf{G} = P(x, y)\mathbf{i} + Q(x, y)\mathbf{j}$ in the xy-plane with the property that at any point $(a, b) \ne (0, 0)$, $\mathbf{G}$ is a vector of magnitude $\sqrt{a^2 + b^2}$ tangent to the circle $x^2 + y^2 = a^2 + b^2$ and pointing in the counterclockwise direction. (The field is undefined at $(0, 0)$.)

(b) Writing to Learn How is $\mathbf{G}$ related to the spin field $\mathbf{F}$ in Figure 16.15?

34. ***A Field of Tangent Vectors***

(a) Find a field $\mathbf{G} = P(x, y)\mathbf{i} + Q(x, y)\mathbf{j}$ in the xy-plane with the property that at any point $(a, b) \ne (0, 0)$, $\mathbf{G}$ is a unit vector tangent to the circle $x^2 + y^2 = a^2 + b^2$ and pointing in the clockwise direction.

(b) Writing to Learn How is $\mathbf{G}$ related to the spin field $\mathbf{F}$ in Figure 16.15?

35. ***Unit Vectors Pointing Toward the Origin*** Find a field $\mathbf{F} = M(x, y)\mathbf{i} + N(x, y)\mathbf{j}$ in the xy-plane with the property that at each point $(x, y) \ne (0, 0)$, $\mathbf{F}$ is a unit vector pointing toward the origin. (The field is undefined at $(0, 0)$.)

36. ***Two "Central" Fields*** Find a field $\mathbf{F} = M(x, y)\mathbf{i} + N(x, y)\mathbf{j}$ in the xy-plane with the property that at each point $(x, y) \ne (0, 0)$, $\mathbf{F}$ points toward the origin and $|\mathbf{F}|$ is **(a)** the distance from (x, y) to the origin and **(b)** inversely proportional to the distance from (x, y) to the origin. (The field is undefined at $(0, 0)$.)

Flow In Exercises 37–40, $\mathbf{F}$ is the velocity field of a fluid flowing through a region in space. Find the flow along the given curve in the direction of increasing t.

37. $\mathbf{F} = -4xy\mathbf{i} + 8y\mathbf{j} + 2\mathbf{k}$

$\mathbf{r}(t) = t\mathbf{i} + t^2\mathbf{j} + \mathbf{k}, \quad 0 \le t \le 2$

38. $\mathbf{F} = x^2\mathbf{i} + yz\mathbf{j} + y^2\mathbf{k}$

$\mathbf{r}(t) = 3t\mathbf{j} + 4t\mathbf{k}, \quad 0 \le t \le 1$

39. $\mathbf{F} = (x - z)\mathbf{i} + x\mathbf{k}$

$\mathbf{r}(t) = (\cos t)\mathbf{i} + (\sin t)\mathbf{k}, \quad 0 \le t \le \pi$

40. $\mathbf{F} = -y\mathbf{i} + x\mathbf{j} + 2\mathbf{k}$

$\mathbf{r}(t) = (-2 \cos t)\mathbf{i} + (2 \sin t)\mathbf{j} + 2t\mathbf{k}, \quad 0 \le t \le 2\pi$

41. ***Circulation*** Find the circulation of $\mathbf{F} = 2x\mathbf{i} + 2z\mathbf{j} + 2y\mathbf{k}$ around the closed path consisting of the following three curves traversed in the direction of increasing t:

C_1: $\mathbf{r}(t) = (\cos t)\mathbf{i} + (\sin t)\mathbf{j} + t\mathbf{k}, \quad 0 \le t \le \pi/2$

C_2: $\mathbf{r}(t) = \mathbf{j} + (\pi/2)(1 - t)\mathbf{k}, \quad 0 \le t \le 1$

C_3: $\mathbf{r}(t) = t\mathbf{i} + (1 - t)\mathbf{j}, \quad 0 \le t \le 1$

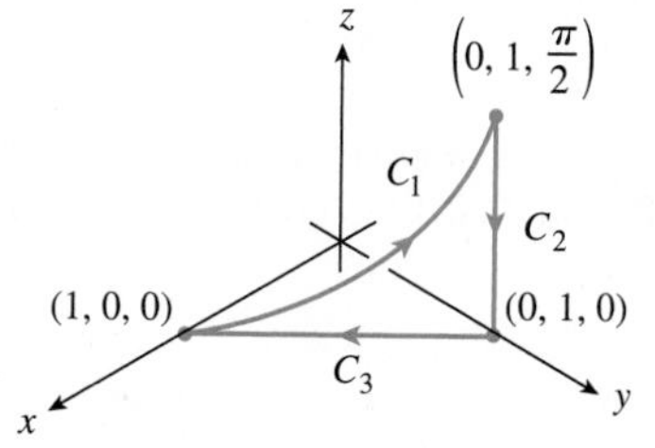

In Exercises 42–44, *work in groups of two or three* to solve the problem.

42. **Writing to Learn** ***Zero Circulation*** Let C be the ellipse in which the plane $2x + 3y - z = 0$ meets the cylinder $x^2 + y^2 = 12$. Show, without evaluating either line integral directly, that the circulation of the field $\mathbf{F} = x\mathbf{i} + y\mathbf{j} + z\mathbf{k}$ around C in either direction is zero.

43. ***Flow Along a Curve*** The field $\mathbf{F} = xy\mathbf{i} + y\mathbf{j} - yz\mathbf{k}$ is the velocity field of a flow in space. Find the flow from $(0, 0, 0)$ to $(1, 1, 1)$ along the curve of intersection of the cylinder $y = x^2$ and the plane $z = x$.

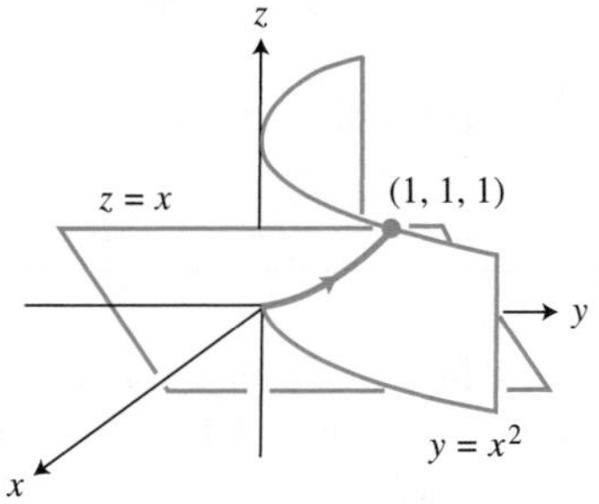

44. ***Flow of a Gradient Field*** Find the flow of the field $\mathbf{F} = \nabla(xy^2z^3)$

(a) once around the curve in Exercise 42, clockwise as viewed from above.

(b) along the line segment from $(1, 1, 1)$ to $(2, 1, -1)$.

Extending the Ideas

45. **Writing to Learn** ***Work and Area*** Suppose $f(t)$ is differentiable and positive for $a \le t \le b$. Let C be the path $\mathbf{r}(t) = t\mathbf{i} + f(t)\mathbf{j}$, and $\mathbf{F} = y\mathbf{i}$. Is there any relation between the value of the work integral

$$\int_C \mathbf{F} \cdot d\mathbf{r}$$

and the area of the region bounded by the t-axis, the graph of f, and the lines $t = a$ and $t = b$? Give reasons for your answer.

46. ***Work Done by a Force Moving a Particle*** A particle in the xy-plane moves along the smooth curve $y = f(x)$ from $(a, f(a))$ to $(b, f(b))$. The force moving the particle has constant magnitude k and always points away from the origin. Show how the work done by the force is

$$\int \mathbf{F} \cdot \mathbf{T}\, ds = k[(b^2 + (f(b))^2)^{1/2} - (a^2 + (f(a))^2)^{1/2}]$$

CAS Explorations

In Exercises 47–52, perform the following steps for finding the work done by force $\mathbf{F}$ over the given path:

(a) Find $d\mathbf{r}$ for the path $\mathbf{r}(t) = g(t)\mathbf{i} + h(t)\mathbf{j} + k(t)\mathbf{k}$.

(b) Evaluate the force $\mathbf{F}$ along the path.

(c) Evaluate $\int_C \mathbf{F} \cdot d\mathbf{r}$.

47. $\mathbf{F} = xy^6\mathbf{i} + 3x(xy^5 + 2)\mathbf{j}$

$\mathbf{r}(t) = (2\cos t)\mathbf{i} + (\sin t)\mathbf{j}, \quad 0 \le t \le 2\pi$

48. $\mathbf{F} = \dfrac{3}{1 + x^2}\mathbf{i} + \dfrac{2}{1 + y^2}\mathbf{j}$

$\mathbf{r}(t) = (\cos t)\mathbf{i} + (\sin t)\mathbf{j}, \quad 0 \le t \le \pi$

49. $\mathbf{F} = (y + yz\cos xyz)\mathbf{i} + (x^2 + xz\cos xyz)\mathbf{j} + (z + xy\cos xyz)\mathbf{k}$

$\mathbf{r}(t) = (2\cos t)\mathbf{i} + (3\sin t)\mathbf{j} + \mathbf{k}, \quad 0 \le t \le 2\pi$

50. $\mathbf{F} = 2xy\mathbf{i} - y^2\mathbf{j} + ze^x\mathbf{k}$

$\mathbf{r}(t) = -t\mathbf{i} + \sqrt{t}\mathbf{j} + 3t\mathbf{k}, \quad 1 \le t \le 4$

51. $\mathbf{F} = (2y + \sin x)\mathbf{i} + (z^2 + (1/3)\cos y)\mathbf{j} + x^4\mathbf{k}$

$\mathbf{r}(t) = (\sin t)\mathbf{i} + (\cos t)\mathbf{j} + (\sin 2t)\mathbf{k}, \quad -\pi/2 \le t \le \pi/2$

52. $\mathbf{F} = (x^2y)\mathbf{i} + \dfrac{1}{3}x^3\mathbf{j} + xy\mathbf{k}$

$\mathbf{r}(t) = (\cos t)\mathbf{i} + (\sin t)\mathbf{j} + (2\sin^2 t - 1)\mathbf{k}, \quad 0 \le t \le 2\pi$

53. Graph the vector field and curve given in

(a) Exercise 37.

(b) Exercise 39.

54. Graph the circulation field $\mathbf{F}$ and curve C_1 given in Exercise 41.

16.3 Path Independence, Potential Functions, and Conservative Fields

What you'll learn about

- Path Independence
- Assumptions Now in Effect
- Line Integrals in Conservative Fields
- Finding Potentials for Conservative Fields
- Exact Differential Forms

Path Independence

If A and B are two points in an open region D in space, the work $\int \mathbf{F} \cdot d\mathbf{r}$ done in moving a particle from A and B by a field defined on D usually depends on the path taken. For some special fields, however, the integral's value is the same for all paths from A to B. If this is true for all points A and B in D, we say that the *integral* $\int \mathbf{F} \cdot d\mathbf{r}$ *is path independent in D* and that $\mathbf{F}$ *is conservative on D.*

DEFINITIONS Path Independence and Conservative Field

Let **F** be a field defined on an open region D in space, and suppose for any two points A and B in D the work $\int_A^B \mathbf{F} \cdot d\mathbf{r}$ done in moving from A to B is the same for all paths from A to B. Then the integral $\int \mathbf{F} \cdot d\mathbf{r}$ is **path independent in D** and the field **F** is **conservative on D.**

Conservative

The word ***conservative*** comes from physics, where it refers to fields in which the principle of conservation of energy holds (it does, in conservative fields).

Under conditions normally met in practice, a field **F** is conservative if and only if it is the gradient field of a scalar function f—that is, if and only if $\mathbf{F} = \nabla f$ for some f. Such a function f is a *potential function* for **F**.

DEFINITION Potential Function

If **F** is a field defined on D and $\mathbf{F} = \nabla f$ for some scalar function f on D, then f is a **potential function** for **F** on D.

An **electric potential** is a scalar function whose gradient field is an electric field, a **gravitational potential** is a scalar function whose gradient field is a gravitational field, and so on. As we will see in a moment, once we have found a potential function f for a field **F**, we can evaluate all the work integrals in the domain of **F** by calculating the potential difference between two end points of the path along which the work is done

$$\int_A^B \mathbf{F} \cdot d\mathbf{r} = \int_A^B \nabla f \cdot d\mathbf{r} = f(B) - f(A). \tag{1}$$

If you think of ∇f for functions of several variables as being something like the derivative f' for functions of a single variable, then you see that Equation (1) is the vector-calculus analogue of the Fundamental Theorem of Calculus formula

$$\int_a^b f'(x)\,dx = f(b) - f(a).$$

Naturally, we need to impose conditions on the curves, fields, and domains to make Equation (1) and its implications hold.

Assumptions Now in Effect

We assume that all curves are *piecewise smooth*—that is, made up of finitely many smooth pieces connected end to end. We also assume that the components of **F** have continuous first partial derivatives. When $\mathbf{F} = \nabla f$, this continuity requirement guarantees that the mixed second derivatives of the potential function f are equal, a result we will find revealing in studying conservative fields **F**.

We assume D to be a *connected open* region in space. Open means that every point in D is the center of a ball that lies entirely in D, and **connected,** in an open region, means that every point can be connected to every other point by a smooth curve lying inside the region.

Line Integrals in Conservative Fields

Here is the theorem that says the value of an integral along a path in a conservative field depends only on the location of the endpoints of the path and not on the specific path taken.

THEOREM 1 The Fundamental Theorem of Line Integrals

1. Let $\mathbf{F} = M\mathbf{i} + N\mathbf{j} + P\mathbf{k}$ be a vector field whose components are continuous throughout an open connected region D in space. Then there exists a differentiable function f such that

$$\mathbf{F} = \nabla f = \frac{\partial f}{\partial x}\mathbf{i} + \frac{\partial f}{\partial y}\mathbf{j} + \frac{\partial f}{\partial z}\mathbf{k}$$

if and only if for all points A and B in D the value of $\int_A^B \mathbf{F}\cdot d\mathbf{r}$ is independent of the path joining A to B in D.

2. If the integral is independent of the path from A to B, its value is

$$\int_A^B \mathbf{F}\cdot d\mathbf{r} = f(B) - f(A).$$

Proof That $\mathbf{F} = \nabla f$ Implies Path Independence of the Integral Suppose A and B are two points in D and that C: $\mathbf{r}(t) = g(t)\mathbf{i} + h(t)\mathbf{j} + k(t)\mathbf{k},\ a \le t \le b,$ is a smooth curve in D joining A and B. Along the curve, f is a differentiable function of t and

$$\frac{df}{dt} = \frac{\partial f}{\partial x}\frac{dx}{dt} + \frac{\partial f}{\partial y}\frac{dy}{dt} + \frac{\partial f}{\partial z}\frac{dz}{dt} \qquad \text{Chain Rule}$$

$$= \nabla f\cdot\left(\frac{dx}{dt}\mathbf{i} + \frac{dy}{dt}\mathbf{j} + \frac{dz}{dt}\mathbf{k}\right) = \nabla f\cdot\frac{d\mathbf{r}}{dt} = \mathbf{F}\cdot\frac{d\mathbf{r}}{dt} \qquad \text{Because } \mathbf{F} = \nabla f \qquad (2)$$

Therefore,

$$\int_C \mathbf{F}\cdot d\mathbf{r} = \int_{t=a}^{t=b} \mathbf{F}\cdot\frac{d\mathbf{r}}{dt}\,dt = \int_a^b \frac{df}{dt}\,dt \qquad \text{Eq. (2)}$$

$$= f(g(t), h(t), k(t))\Big]_a^b = f(B) - f(A).$$

Thus, the value of the work integral depends only on the values of f at A and B and not on the path in between. This proves Part 2 as well as the forward implication in Part 1. We omit the more technical proof of the reverse implication.

EXAMPLE 1 Finding Work Done by a Conservative Field

Find the work done by the conservative field

$$\mathbf{F} = yz\mathbf{i} + xz\mathbf{j} + xy\mathbf{k} = \nabla(xyz)$$

along any smooth curve C joining the point $(-1, 3, 9)$ to $(1, 6, -4)$.

SOLUTION

With $f(x, y, z) = xyz$, we have

$$\int_A^B \mathbf{F}\cdot d\mathbf{r} = \int_A^B \nabla f\cdot d\mathbf{r} \qquad \mathbf{F} = \nabla f$$

$$= f(B) - f(A) \qquad \text{Fundamental Theorem, Part 2}$$

$$= xyz\big|_{(1,6,-4)} - xyz\big|_{(-1,3,9)}$$

$$= (1)(6)(-4) - (-1)(3)(9)$$

$$= -24 + 27 = 3.$$

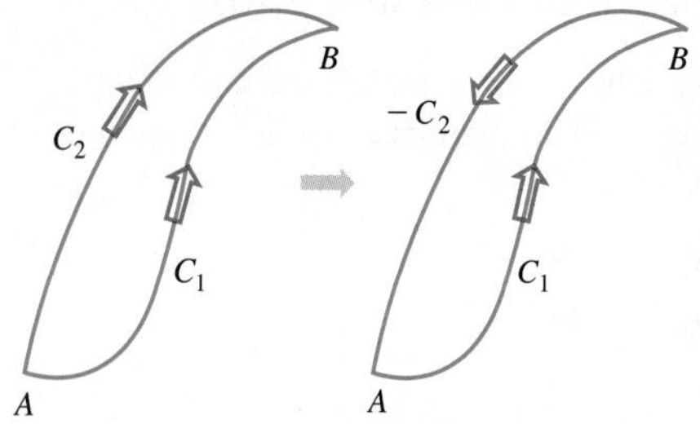

Figure 16.24 If we have two paths from A to B, one of them can be reversed to make a loop.

> **THEOREM 2 Closed-Loop Property of Conservative Fields**
>
> Under the assumptions now in effect, the following statements are equivalent:
>
> **1.** $\oint_C \mathbf{F} \cdot d\mathbf{r} = 0$ around every closed loop in D.
>
> **2.** The field $\mathbf{F}$ is conservative on D.

Proof That (1) ⇒ (2) We want to show that for any two points A and B in D the integral of $\mathbf{F} \cdot d\mathbf{r}$ has the same value over any two paths C_1 and C_2 from A to B. We reverse the direction on C_2 to make a path $-C_2$ from B to A (Figure 16.24). Together C_1 and $-C_2$ make a closed loop C, and

$$\int_{C_1} \mathbf{F} \cdot d\mathbf{r} - \int_{C_2} \mathbf{F} \cdot d\mathbf{r} = \int_{C_1} \mathbf{F} \cdot d\mathbf{r} + \int_{-C_2} \mathbf{F} \cdot d\mathbf{r} = \int_{C} \mathbf{F} \cdot d\mathbf{r} = 0.$$

Thus, the integrals over C_1 and C_2 give the same value.

Proof That (2) ⇒ (1) We want to show that the integral of $\mathbf{F} \cdot d\mathbf{r}$ is zero over any closed loop C. We pick two points A and B on C and use them to break C into two pieces: C_1 from A to B followed by C_2 from B back to A (Figure 16.25). Then

$$\oint_C \mathbf{F} \cdot d\mathbf{r} = \int_{C_1} \mathbf{F} \cdot d\mathbf{r} + \int_{C_2} \mathbf{F} \cdot d\mathbf{r} = \int_A^B \mathbf{F} \cdot d\mathbf{r} - \int_A^B \mathbf{F} \cdot d\mathbf{r} = 0.$$

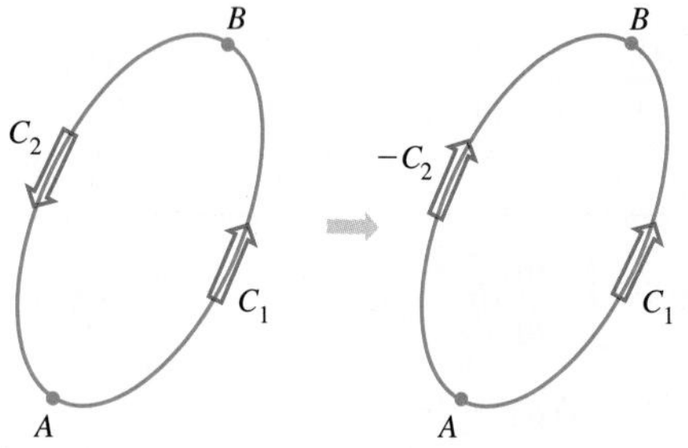

Figure 16.25 If A and B lie on a loop, we can reverse part of the loop to make two paths from A to B.

The following diagram summarizes the results of Theorems 1 and 2.

	Theorem 1		Theorem 2	
$\mathbf{F} = \nabla f$ on D	⇔	$\mathbf{F}$ conservative on D	⇔	$\oint_C \mathbf{F} \cdot d\mathbf{r} = 0$ over any closed path in D

Now that we see how convenient it is to evaluate the line integrals in conservative fields, two questions remain:

1. How do we know when a given field $\mathbf{F}$ is conservative?
2. If $\mathbf{F}$ is in fact conservative, how do we find a potential function for $\mathbf{F}$?

Finding Potential Functions for Conservative Fields

The test for a field's being conservative is the following.

> **Component Test for Conservative Fields**
>
> Let $\mathbf{F} = M(x, y, z)\mathbf{i} + N(x, y, z)\mathbf{j} + P(x, y, z)\mathbf{k}$ be a field whose component functions have continuous first partial derivatives. Then, $\mathbf{F}$ is conservative if and only if
>
> $$\frac{\partial P}{\partial y} = \frac{\partial N}{\partial z}, \quad \frac{\partial M}{\partial z} = \frac{\partial P}{\partial x}, \quad \text{and} \quad \frac{\partial N}{\partial x} = \frac{\partial M}{\partial y}. \tag{3}$$

Proof We show that Equations (3) must hold if $\mathbf{F}$ is conservative. There is a potential function f such that

$$\mathbf{F} = M\mathbf{i} + N\mathbf{j} + P\mathbf{k} = \frac{\partial f}{\partial x}\mathbf{i} + \frac{\partial f}{\partial y}\mathbf{j} + \frac{\partial f}{\partial z}\mathbf{k}.$$

Hence,

$$\begin{aligned}\frac{\partial P}{\partial y} &= \frac{\partial}{\partial y}\left(\frac{\partial f}{\partial z}\right) = \frac{\partial^2 f}{\partial y\,\partial z}\\ &= \frac{\partial^2 f}{\partial z\,\partial y}\\ &= \frac{\partial}{\partial z}\left(\frac{\partial f}{\partial y}\right) = \frac{\partial N}{\partial z}.\end{aligned}$$

Continuity implies that the mixed partial derivatives are equal.

The other two equations in (3) are proved similarly.

The second half of the proof, that Equations (3) imply that **F** is conservative, is a consequence of Stoke's Theorem taken up in Section 16.7.

Once we know **F** is conservative, we usually want to find a potential function for **F**. This requires solving the equation $\nabla f = \mathbf{F}$ or

$$\frac{\partial f}{\partial x}\mathbf{i} + \frac{\partial f}{\partial y}\mathbf{j} + \frac{\partial f}{\partial z}\mathbf{k} = M\mathbf{i} + N\mathbf{j} + P\mathbf{k}$$

for f. We accomplish this by integrating the three equations

$$\frac{\partial f}{\partial x} = M, \qquad \frac{\partial f}{\partial y} = N, \qquad \frac{\partial f}{\partial z} = P.$$

EXAMPLE 2 Finding a Potential Function

Show that $\mathbf{F} = (e^x \cos y + yz)\mathbf{i} + (xz - e^x \sin y)\mathbf{j} + (xy + z)\mathbf{k}$ is conservative and find a potential function for it.

SOLUTION

We apply the test in Equations (3) to

$$M = e^x \cos y + yz, \qquad N = xz - e^x \sin y, \qquad P = xy + z$$

and calculate

$$\frac{\partial P}{\partial y} = x = \frac{\partial N}{\partial z}, \qquad \frac{\partial M}{\partial z} = y = \frac{\partial P}{\partial x}, \qquad \frac{\partial N}{\partial x} = z - e^x \sin y = \frac{\partial M}{\partial y}.$$

Together, these equations tell us that there is a function f with $\nabla f = \mathbf{F}$.

We find f by integrating the equations

$$\frac{\partial f}{\partial x} = e^x \cos y + yz, \qquad \frac{\partial f}{\partial y} = xz - e^x \sin y, \qquad \frac{\partial f}{\partial z} = xy + z. \tag{4}$$

We integrate the first equation with respect to x, holding y and z fixed, to get

$$f(x, y, z) = e^x \cos y + xyz + g(y, z).$$

We write the constant of integration as a function of y and z because its value may change if y and z change. We then calculate $\partial f/\partial y$ from this equation and match it with the expression for $\partial f/\partial y$ in Equations (4). This gives

$$-e^x \sin y + xz + \frac{\partial g}{\partial y} = xz - e^x \sin y,$$

so $\partial g/\partial y = 0$. Therefore, g is a function of z alone, and

$$f(x, y, z) = e^x \cos y + xyz + h(z).$$

We now calculate $\partial f/\partial z$ from this equation and match it to the formula for $\partial f/\partial z$ in Equations (4). This gives

$$xy + \frac{dh}{dz} = xy + z, \qquad \text{or} \qquad \frac{dh}{dz} = z,$$

so

$$h(z) = \frac{z^2}{2} + C.$$

Hence,

$$f(x, y, z) = e^x \cos y + xyz + \frac{z^2}{2} + C.$$

We have found infinitely many potential functions for **F**, one for each value of C.

EXAMPLE 3 Showing a Field is Not Conservative

Show that $\mathbf{F} = (2x - 3)\mathbf{i} - z\mathbf{j} + (\cos z)\mathbf{k}$ is not conservative.

SOLUTION

We apply the component test in Equations (3) and find right away that

$$\frac{\partial P}{\partial y} = \frac{\partial}{\partial y}(\cos z) = 0, \qquad \frac{\partial N}{\partial z} = \frac{\partial}{\partial z}(-z) = -1.$$

The two are unequal, so **F** is not conservative. No further testing is required.

Exact Differential Forms

As we see in the next section and again later on, it is often convenient to express work and circulation integrals in the "differential" form

$$\int_A^B M\,dx + N\,dy + P\,dz$$

mentioned in Section 16.2. Such integrals are relatively easy to evaluate if $M\,dx + N\,dy + P\,dz$ is the differential of a function f. For then

$$\begin{aligned}\int_A^B M\,dx + N\,dy + P\,dz &= \int_A^B \frac{\partial f}{\partial x}dx + \frac{\partial f}{\partial y}dy + \frac{\partial f}{\partial z}dz \\ &= \int_A^B \nabla f \cdot d\mathbf{r} \\ &= f(B) - f(A). \qquad \text{Theorem 1}\end{aligned}$$

Thus,

$$\int_A^B df = f(B) - f(A),$$

just as with differentiable functions of a single variable.

DEFINITIONS Differential Form and Exact Differential Form

The form $M(x, y, z)\,dx + N(x, y, z)\,dy + P(x, y, z)\,dz$ is a **differential form.** A differential form is **exact** on a domain D in space if

$$M\,dx + N\,dy + P\,dz = \frac{\partial f}{\partial x}dx + \frac{\partial f}{\partial y}dy + \frac{\partial f}{\partial z}dz = df$$

for some (scalar) function f throughout D.

Notice that if $M\,dx + N\,dy + P\,dz = df$ on D, then $\mathbf{F} = M\mathbf{i} + N\mathbf{j} + P\mathbf{k}$ is the gradient field of f on D. Conversely, if $\mathbf{F} = \nabla f$, then the form $M\,dx + N\,dy + P\,dz$ is exact. The test for the form's being exact is therefore the same as the test for **F**'s being conservative.

Component Test for Exactness of $M\,dx + N\,dy + P\,dz$

The differential form $M\,dx + N\,dy + P\,dz$ is exact if and only if

$$\frac{\partial P}{\partial y} = \frac{\partial N}{\partial z}, \qquad \frac{\partial M}{\partial z} = \frac{\partial P}{\partial x}, \qquad \text{and} \qquad \frac{\partial N}{\partial x} = \frac{\partial M}{\partial y}. \tag{5}$$

This is equivalent to saying that the field $\mathbf{F} = M\mathbf{i} + N\mathbf{j} + P\mathbf{k}$ is conservative.

EXAMPLE 4 Showing a Differential Form is Exact

Show that $y\,dx + x\,dy + 4\,dz$ is exact and evaluate the integral

$$\int_{(1,1,1)}^{(2,3,-1)} y\,dx + x\,dy + 4\,dz$$

over the line segment from $(1, 1, 1)$ to $(2, 3, -1)$.

SOLUTION

We let $M = y$, $N = x$, $P = 4$ and apply the test of Equations (5):

$$\frac{\partial P}{\partial y} = 0 = \frac{\partial N}{\partial z}, \qquad \frac{\partial M}{\partial z} = 0 = \frac{\partial P}{\partial x}, \qquad \frac{\partial N}{\partial x} = 1 = \frac{\partial M}{\partial y}.$$

These equalities tell us that $y\,dx + x\,dy + 4\,dz$ is exact, so

$$y\,dx + x\,dy + 4\,dz = df$$

for some function f, and the integral's value is $f(2, 3, -1) - f(1, 1, 1)$.

We find f up to a constant by integrating the equations

$$\frac{\partial f}{\partial x} = y, \qquad \frac{\partial f}{\partial y} = x, \qquad \frac{\partial f}{\partial z} = 4. \tag{6}$$

From the first equation we get

$$f(x, y, z) = xy + g(y, z).$$

The second equation tells us that

$$\frac{\partial f}{\partial y} = x + \frac{\partial g}{\partial y} = x, \qquad \text{or} \qquad \frac{\partial g}{\partial y} = 0.$$

Hence, g is a function of z alone, and

$$f(x, y, z) = xy + h(z).$$

The third of Equations (6) tells us that

$$\frac{\partial f}{\partial z} = 0 + \frac{dh}{dz} = 4, \qquad \text{or} \qquad h(z) = 4z + C.$$

Therefore,

$$f(x, y, z) = xy + 4z + C.$$

The value of the integral is

$$f(2, 3, -1) - f(1, 1, 1) = 2 + C - (5 + C) = -3.$$

Quick Review 16.3

In Exercises 1 and 2, compute the indicated value of the $f(x, y, z) = e^{xyz} + \sin(xy + xz)$.

1. $f(0, 1, 2)$
2. $f(1, \pi/2, 0)$

In Exercises 3–7, find the indicated partial derivative of $f(x, y, z) = \cos^{-1}(xyz)$.

3. $\dfrac{\partial f}{\partial x}$
4. $\dfrac{\partial f}{\partial y}$
5. $\dfrac{\partial f}{\partial z}$
6. $\dfrac{\partial^2 f}{\partial y\,\partial x}$
7. $\dfrac{\partial^2 f}{\partial x\,\partial z}$

In Exercises 8–10, let $f(x, y, z) = e^{x^2+y^2+z^2} + xyz + g(x, y, z)$. Determine the most general function g that satisfies the given partial differential equation.

8. $\dfrac{\partial f}{\partial x} = 2xe^{x^2+y^2+z^2} + yz$
9. $\dfrac{\partial f}{\partial y} = 2ye^{x^2+y^2+z^2} + xz + 2y$
10. $\dfrac{\partial f}{\partial z} = 2ze^{x^2+y^2+z^2} + xy + z$

Section 16.3 Exercises

In Exercises 1–6, determine whether the field is conservative or not conservative.

1. $\mathbf{F} = yz\mathbf{i} + xz\mathbf{j} + xy\mathbf{k}$
2. $\mathbf{F} = (y \sin z)\mathbf{i} + (x \sin z)\mathbf{j} + (xy \cos z)\mathbf{k}$
3. $\mathbf{F} = y\mathbf{i} + (x + z)\mathbf{j} - y\mathbf{k}$
4. $\mathbf{F} = -y\mathbf{i} + x\mathbf{j}$
5. $\mathbf{F} = (z + y)\mathbf{i} + z\mathbf{j} + (y + x)\mathbf{k}$
6. $\mathbf{F} = (e^x \cos y)\mathbf{i} - (e^x \sin y)\mathbf{j} + z\mathbf{k}$

In Exercises 7–12, find a potential function f for the field $\mathbf{F}$.

7. $\mathbf{F} = 2x\mathbf{i} + 3y\mathbf{j} + 4z\mathbf{k}$
8. $\mathbf{F} = (y + z)\mathbf{i} + (x + z)\mathbf{j} + (x + y)\mathbf{k}$
9. $\mathbf{F} = e^{y+2z}(\mathbf{i} + x\mathbf{j} + 2x\mathbf{k})$
10. $\mathbf{F} = (y \sin z)\mathbf{i} + (x \sin z)\mathbf{j} + (xy \cos z)\mathbf{k}$
11. $\mathbf{F} = (\ln x + \sec^2(x + y))\mathbf{i} + \left(\sec^2(x + y) + \dfrac{y}{y^2 + z^2}\right)\mathbf{j} + \dfrac{z}{y^2 + z^2}\mathbf{k}$
12. $\mathbf{F} = \dfrac{y}{1 + x^2y^2}\mathbf{i} + \left(\dfrac{x}{1 + x^2y^2} + \dfrac{z}{\sqrt{1 - y^2z^2}}\right)\mathbf{j} + \left(\dfrac{y}{\sqrt{1 - y^2z^2}} + \dfrac{1}{z}\right)\mathbf{k}$

In Exercises 13–22, show that the differential form in the integral is exact. Then evaluate the integral.

13. $\displaystyle\int_{(0,0,0)}^{(2,3,-6)} 2x\,dx + 2y\,dy + 2z\,dz$
14. $\displaystyle\int_{(1,1,2)}^{(3,5,0)} yz\,dx + xz\,dy + xy\,dz$
15. $\displaystyle\int_{(0,0,0)}^{(1,2,3)} 2xy\,dx + (x^2 - z^2)\,dy - 2yz\,dz$
16. $\displaystyle\int_{(0,0,0)}^{(3,3,1)} 2x\,dx - y^2\,dy - \frac{4}{1 + z^2}\,dz$
17. $\displaystyle\int_{(1,0,0)}^{(0,1,1)} \sin y \cos x\,dx + \cos y \sin x\,dy + dz$
18. $\displaystyle\int_{(0,2,1)}^{(1,\pi/2,2)} 2\cos y\,dx + \left(\frac{1}{y} - 2x \sin y\right)dy + \frac{1}{z}\,dz$
19. $\displaystyle\int_{(1,1,1)}^{(1,2,3)} 3x^2\,dx + \frac{z^2}{y}\,dy + 2z \ln y\,dz$
20. $\displaystyle\int_{(1,2,1)}^{(2,1,1)} (2x \ln y - yz)\,dx + \left(\frac{x^2}{y} - xz\right)dy - xy\,dz$
21. $\displaystyle\int_{(1,1,1)}^{(2,2,2)} \frac{1}{y}\,dx + \left(\frac{1}{z} - \frac{x}{y^2}\right)dy - \frac{y}{z^2}\,dz$
22. $\displaystyle\int_{(-1,-1,-1)}^{(2,2,2)} \frac{2x\,dx + 2y\,dy + 2z\,dz}{x^2 + y^2 + z^2}$

In Exercises 23 and 24, *work in groups of two or three* to solve the problem.

23. Evaluate the integral

$$\int_{(1,1,1)}^{(2,3,-1)} y\,dx + x\,dy + 4\,dz$$

from Example 4 by finding parametric equations for the line segment from (1, 1, 1) to (2, 3, −1) and evaluating the line integral of $\mathbf{F} = y\mathbf{i} + x\mathbf{j} + 4\mathbf{k}$ along the segment. Since $\mathbf{F}$ is conservative, the integral is independent of the path.

24. Evaluate $\displaystyle\int_C x^2\,dx + yz\,dy + (y^2/2)\,dz$ along the line segment C joining (0, 0, 0) to (0, 3, 4).

Writing to Learn In Exercises 25 and 26, show that the value of the integral does not depend on the path taken from A to B.

25. $\displaystyle\int_A^B z^2\,dx + 2y\,dy + 2xz\,dz$

26. $\displaystyle\int_A^B \frac{x\,dx + y\,dy + z\,dz}{\sqrt{x^2 + y^2 + z^2}}$

In Exercises 27 and 28, express $\mathbf{F}$ in the form ∇f.

27. $\mathbf{F} = \dfrac{2x}{y}\mathbf{i} + \left(\dfrac{1 - x^2}{y^2}\right)\mathbf{j}$

28. $\mathbf{F} = (e^x \ln y)\,\mathbf{i} + \left(\dfrac{e^x}{y} + \sin z\right)\mathbf{j} + (y \cos z)\,\mathbf{k}$

29. ***Work Along Different Paths*** Find the work done by
$$\mathbf{F} = (x^2 + y)\mathbf{i} + (y^2 + x)\mathbf{j} + ze^z\mathbf{k}$$
over the following paths from $(1, 0, 0)$ to $(1, 0, 1)$.

(a) The line segment $x = 1, y = 0, 0 \le z \le 1$

(b) The helix
$$\mathbf{r}(t) = (\cos t)\,\mathbf{i} + (\sin t)\,\mathbf{j} + \left(\frac{t}{2\pi}\right)\mathbf{k}, \qquad 0 \le t \le 2\pi$$

(c) The x-axis from $(1, 0, 0)$ to $(0, 0, 0)$ followed by the parabola $z = x^2, y = 0$ from $(0, 0, 0)$ to $(1, 0, 1)$

30. ***Work Along Different Paths*** Find the work done by
$$\mathbf{F} = e^{yz}\mathbf{i} + (xze^{yz} + z \cos y)\mathbf{j} + (xye^{yz} + \sin y)\mathbf{k}$$
over the following paths from $(1, 0, 1)$ to $(1, \pi/2, 0)$.

(a) The line segment $x = 1, y = \pi t/2, z = 1 - t, 0 \le t \le 1$

(b) The line segment from $(1, 0, 1)$ to the origin followed by the line segment from the origin to $(1, \pi/2, 0)$

(c) The line segment from $(1, 0, 1)$ to $(1, 0, 0)$, followed by the x-axis from $(1, 0, 0)$ to the origin, followed by the parabola $y = \pi x^2/2, z = 0$

Explorations

31. ***Evaluating a Work Integral Two Ways*** Let $\mathbf{F} = \nabla(x^3y^2)$ and let C be the path in the xy-plane from $(-1, 1)$ to $(1, 1)$ that consists of the line segment from $(-1, 1)$ to $(0, 0)$ followed by the line segment from $(0, 0)$ to $(1, 1)$. Evaluate $\displaystyle\int_C \mathbf{F} \cdot d\mathbf{r}$ in the following two ways.

(a) Find parametrizations for the segments that make up C and evaluate the integral directly.

(b) Use the fact that $f(x, y) = x^3y^2$ is a potential function for $\mathbf{F}$.

32. ***Same Integrand, Different Paths*** Evaluate
$$\int_C 2x \cos y\,dx - x^2 \sin y\,dy$$
along the following paths C in the xy-plane.

(a) The parabola $y = (x - 1)^2$ from $(1, 0)$ to $(0, 1)$

(b) The line segment from $(-1, \pi)$ to $(1, 0)$

(c) The x-axis from $(-1, 0)$ to $(1, 0)$

(d) The astroid $\mathbf{r}(t) = (\cos^3 t)\mathbf{i} + (\sin^3 t)\mathbf{j}, 0 \le t \le 2\pi$, counterclockwise from $(1, 0)$ back to $(1, 0)$

33. ***A Gravitational Field*** Find a potential function for the gravitational field
$$\mathbf{F} = -GmM\frac{x\mathbf{i} + y\mathbf{j} + z\mathbf{k}}{(x^2 + y^2 + z^2)^{3/2}}$$
(G, m, and M are constants).

34. ***(Continuation of Exercise 33)*** Let P_1 and P_2 be points in space at distances s_1 and s_2 from the origin. Show that the work done by the gravitational field in Exercise 33 in moving a particle from P_1 to P_2 is the quantity
$$GmM\left(\frac{1}{s_2} - \frac{1}{s_1}\right).$$

35. **(a)** How are the constants a, b, and c related if the following differential form is exact?
$$(ay^2 + 2czx)\,dx + y(bx + cz)\,dy + (ay^2 + cx^2)\,dz$$

(b) For what values of b and c will
$$\mathbf{F} = (y^2 + 2czx)\mathbf{i} + y(bx + cy)\mathbf{j} + (y^2 + cx^2)\mathbf{k}$$
be a gradient field?

36. Suppose $\mathbf{F} = \nabla f$ is a conservative vector field and
$$g(x, y, z) = \int_{(0,0,0)}^{(x,y,z)} \mathbf{F} \cdot d\mathbf{r}.$$
Show that $\nabla g = \mathbf{F}$.

37. **Writing to Learn** ***Path of Least Work*** You have been asked to find the path along which a force field $\mathbf{F}$ will perform the least work in moving a particle between two locations. A quick calculation on your part shows $\mathbf{F}$ to be conservative. How should you respond? Give reasons for your answer.

38. **Writing to Learn** ***A Revealing Experiment*** By experiment, you find that a force field $\mathbf{F}$ performs only half as much work in moving an object along path C_1 from A to B as it does in moving the object along path C_2 from A to B. What can you conclude about $\mathbf{F}$? Give reasons for your answer.

Extending the Ideas

39. ***Work Done by Gravity on a String*** A string lies along the circle $x^2 + y^2 = 4$ from $(2, 0)$ to $(0, 2)$ in the first quadrant. The density of the string is $\rho(x, y) = xy$.

(a) Partition the string into a finite number of subarcs to show that the work done by gravity to move the string straight down to the x-axis is given by
$$\text{Work} = \lim_{n\to\infty} \sum_{k=1}^{n} gx_k y_k^2\,\Delta s_k = \int_C gxy^2\,ds,$$
where g is the universal gravitational constant.

(b) Find the total work done by evaluating the line integral in part (a).

(c) Show that the total work done equals the work required to move the string's center of mass $(\bar{x}, \bar{y})$ straight down to the x-axis.

CAS Exploration

40. Draw the force field $\mathbf{F}$ and curve $\mathbf{r}(t)$ given in Exercise 29 (b).

16.4 Green's Theorem in the Plane

What you'll learn about

- Flux Density at a Point: Divergence
- Circulation Density at a Point: The **k**-Component of Curl
- Two Forms for Green's Theorem
- Mathematical Assumptions
- Using Green's Theorem to Evaluate Line Integrals
- Proof of Green's Theorem for Special Regions
- Extending the Proof to Other Regions

Flux Density at a Point: Divergence

We need two new ideas for Green's Theorem. The first is the idea of the *flux density* of a vector field at a point, which in mathematics is the *divergence* of the vector field. We obtain it in the following way.

Suppose $\mathbf{F}(x, y) = M(x, y)\mathbf{i} + N(x, y)\mathbf{j}$ is the vector velocity of a fluid flow in the plane and the first partial derivatives of M and N are continuous at each point of a region R. Let (x, y) be a point in R, and let A be a small rectangle with one corner at (x, y) that, along with its interior, lies entirely in R (Figure 16.26). The sides of the rectangle, parallel to the coordinate axes, have lengths of Δx and Δy. The rate at which fluid leaves the rectangle across the bottom edge is approximately.

$$\mathbf{F}(x, y) \cdot (-\mathbf{j})\, \Delta x = -N(x, y)\, \Delta x.$$

This is the scalar component of the velocity at (x, y) in the direction of the outward normal times the length of the segment. If the velocity is in meters per second, for example, the exit rate will be in meters per second times meters or square meters per second. The rates at which the fluid crosses the other three sides in the directions of their outward normals can be estimated in a similar way. All told, we have

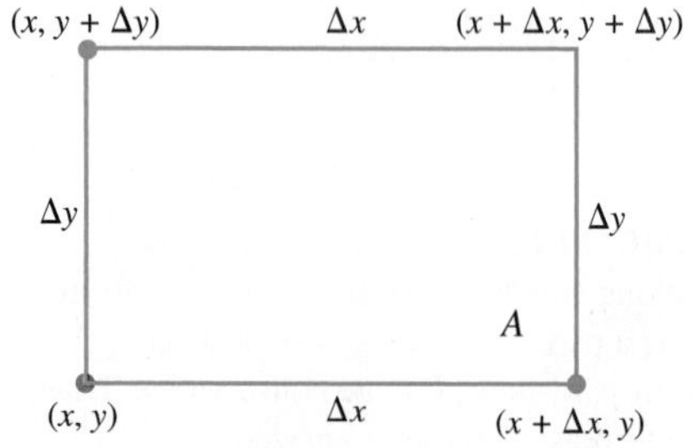

Figure 16.26 The rectangle for defining the flux density (divergence) of a vector field at a point (x, y).

Top: $\quad \mathbf{F}(x, y + \Delta y) \cdot \mathbf{j}\, \Delta x = N(x, y + \Delta y)\, \Delta x$

Bottom: $\quad \mathbf{F}(x, y) \cdot (-\mathbf{j})\, \Delta x = -N(x, y)\, \Delta x$

Right: $\quad \mathbf{F}(x + \Delta x, y) \cdot \mathbf{i}\, \Delta y = M(x + \Delta x, y)\, \Delta y$

Left: $\quad \mathbf{F}(x, y) \cdot (-\mathbf{i})\, \Delta y = -M(x, y)\, \Delta y.$

Combining opposite pairs gives

Top and bottom: $\quad (N(x, y + \Delta y) - N(x, y))\, \Delta x \approx \left(\dfrac{\partial N}{\partial y} \Delta y\right) \Delta x$

Right and left: $\quad (M(x + \Delta x, y) - M(x, y))\, \Delta y \approx \left(\dfrac{\partial M}{\partial x} \Delta x\right) \Delta y.$

Adding these last two approximations gives

$$\text{Flux across rectangle boundary} \approx \left(\frac{\partial M}{\partial x} + \frac{\partial N}{\partial y}\right) \Delta x\, \Delta y.$$

We now divide by $\Delta x\, \Delta y$ to estimate the total flux per unit area or *flux density* for the rectangle:

$$\frac{\text{Flux across rectangular boundary}}{\text{Rectangle area}} \approx \left(\frac{\partial M}{\partial x} + \frac{\partial N}{\partial y}\right).$$

Finally, we let Δx and Δy approach zero to define the *flux density* of $\mathbf{F}$ at the point (x, y).

In mathematics, the *flux density* is the *divergence* of $\mathbf{F}$. The symbol for it is div $\mathbf{F}$, pronounced "divergence of $\mathbf{F}$" or "div $\mathbf{F}$."

DEFINITION Flux Density or Divergence

The **flux density** or **divergence** of a vector field $\mathbf{F} = M\mathbf{i} + N\mathbf{j}$ at the point (x, y) is

$$\operatorname{div} \mathbf{F} = \frac{\partial M}{\partial x} + \frac{\partial N}{\partial y}. \tag{1}$$

Intuitively, if water were flowing into a region through a small hole at the point (x_0, y_0), the lines of flow would diverge there (hence the name) and, since water would be flowing out of a small rectangle about (x_0, y_0), the divergence of $\mathbf{F}$ at (x_0, y_0) would be positive. If the water were draining out instead of flowing in, the divergence would be negative. See Figure 16.27.

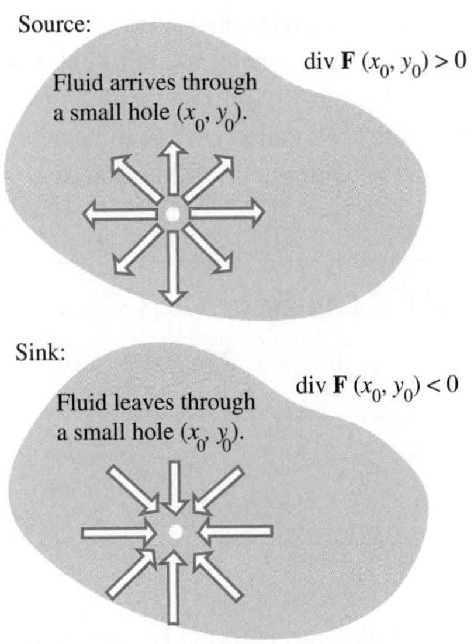

Source:
div F (x0, y0) > 0
Fluid arrives through
a small hole (x0, y0).
Sink:
div F (x0, y0) < 0
Fluid leaves through
a small hole (x0, y0).

Figure 16.27 In the flow of an incompressible fluid across a plane region, the divergence is positive at a "source," a point where fluid enters the system, and negative at a "sink," a point where the fluid leaves the system.

EXAMPLE 1 Finding Divergence

Find the divergence of $\mathbf{F}(x, y) = (x^2 - y)\mathbf{i} + (xy - y^2)\mathbf{j}$.

SOLUTION

We use the formula in Equation (1):

$$\begin{aligned} \operatorname{div} \mathbf{F} &= \frac{\partial M}{\partial x} + \frac{\partial N}{\partial y} = \frac{\partial}{\partial x}(x^2 - y) + \frac{\partial}{\partial y}(xy - y^2) \\ &= 2x + x - 2y = 3x - 2y. \end{aligned}$$

Circulation Density at a Point: The k-Component of Curl

The second of the two new ideas we need for Green's Theorem is the idea of *circulation density* of a vector field $\mathbf{F}$ at a point. To obtain it, we return to the velocity field

$$\mathbf{F}(x, y) = M(x, y)\mathbf{i} + N(x, y)\mathbf{j}$$

and the rectangle A. The rectangle is redrawn here as Figure 16.28.

The counterclockwise circulation of $\mathbf{F}$ around the boundary of A is the sum of flow rates along the sides. For the bottom edge, the flow rate is approximately

$$\mathbf{F}(x, y) \cdot \mathbf{i}\, \Delta x = M(x, y)\, \Delta x.$$

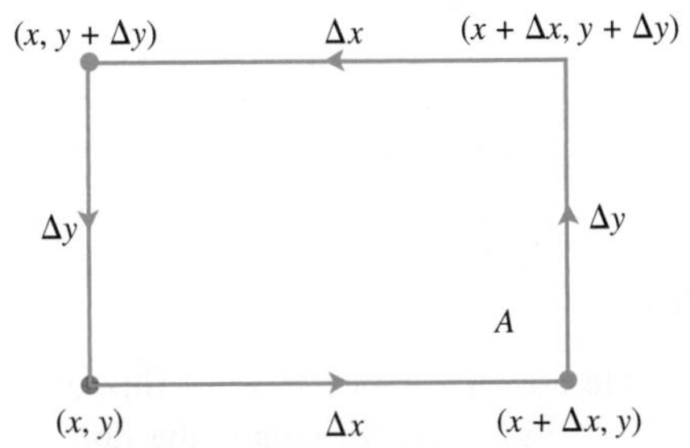

(x, y + Δy)
Δx
(x + Δx, y + Δy)
Δy
Δy
A
(x, y)
Δx
(x + Δx, y)

Figure 16.28 The rectangle for defining the circulation density (curl) of a vector field at a point (x, y).

This is the scalar component of the velocity $\mathbf{F}(x, y)$ in the direction of the tangent vector $\mathbf{i}$ times the length of the segment. The rates of flow along the other sides in the counterclockwise direction are expressed in a similar way. In all, we have

Top: $\quad \mathbf{F}(x, y + \Delta y) \cdot (-\mathbf{i})\, \Delta x = -M(x, y + \Delta y)\, \Delta x$

Bottom: $\quad \mathbf{F}(x, y) \cdot \mathbf{i}\, \Delta x = M(x, y)\, \Delta x$

Right: $\quad \mathbf{F}(x + \Delta x, y) \cdot \mathbf{j}\, \Delta y = N(x + \Delta x, y)\, \Delta y$

Left: $\quad \mathbf{F}(x, y) \cdot (-\mathbf{j})\, \Delta y = -N(x, y)\, \Delta y.$

We add opposite pairs to get

Top and bottom: $\quad -(M(x, y + \Delta y) - M(x, y))\, \Delta x \approx -\left(\frac{\partial M}{\partial y} \Delta y\right) \Delta x$

Right and left: $\quad (N(x + \Delta x, y) - N(x, y))\, \Delta y \approx \left(\frac{\partial N}{\partial x} \Delta x\right) \Delta y.$

Adding these last two approximation and dividing by $\Delta x\, \Delta y$ gives an estimate of the *circulation density* for the rectangle:

$$\frac{\text{Circulation around rectangle}}{\text{Rectangle area}} \approx \frac{\partial N}{\partial x} - \frac{\partial M}{\partial y}.$$

Finally, we let Δx and Δy approach zero to define the circulation density of $\mathbf{F}$ at the point (x, y).

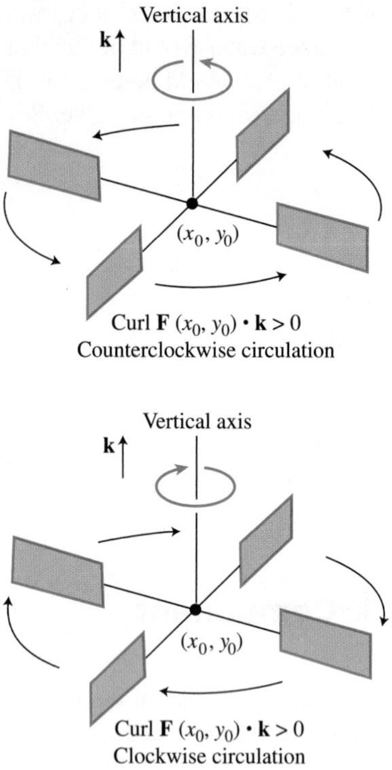

Figure 16.29 In the flow of an incompressible fluid over a plane region, the **k**-component of the curl measures the rate of the fluid's rotation at a point. The **k**-component is positive at points where the rotation is counterclockwise and negative where the rotation is clockwise.

The positive orientation for circulation in the xy-plane is counterclockwise around a vertical axis looking downward on the plane from the tip of the (vertical) unit vector **k** (Figure 16.29). The general density just defined is actually the **k**-component of a more general circulation-density vector we investigate in Section 16.7, called *curl* **F**, the *curl* of the vector field **F**. For Green's Theorem, we need only the **k**-component of this vector.

DEFINITION k-Component of Circulation Density or Curl

The **k**-component of the circulation density or curl of a vector field $\mathbf{F} = M\mathbf{i} + N\mathbf{j}$ at the point (x, y) is the scalar

$$(\text{curl } \mathbf{F}) \cdot \mathbf{k} = \frac{\partial N}{\partial x} - \frac{\partial M}{\partial y}. \tag{2}$$

If water is moving about a region in the xy-plane in a thin layer, then the **k**-component of the circulation, or curl, at a point (x_0, y_0) gives a way to measure how fast and in what direction a small paddle wheel will spin if it is put into the water at (x_0, y_0) with its axis perpendicular to the plane, parallel to the unit vector **k** (Figure 16.29).

EXAMPLE 2 Finding the k-Component of Curl

Find the **k**-component of the curl for $\mathbf{F}(x, y) = (x^2 - y)\mathbf{i} + (xy - y^2)\mathbf{j}$.

SOLUTION

We use the formula in Equation (2):

$$(\text{curl } \mathbf{F}) \cdot \mathbf{k} = \frac{\partial N}{\partial x} - \frac{\partial M}{\partial y} = \frac{\partial}{\partial x}(xy - y^2) - \frac{\partial}{\partial y}(x^2 - y) = y + 1.$$

Two Forms for Green's Theorem

In one form, Green's Theorem says that under suitable conditions the outward flux of a vector field across a simple closed curve in the plane (Figure 16.30) equals the double integral of the divergence of the field over the region enclosed by the curve. Recall the formulas for flux in Equations (3) and (4) in Section 16.2.

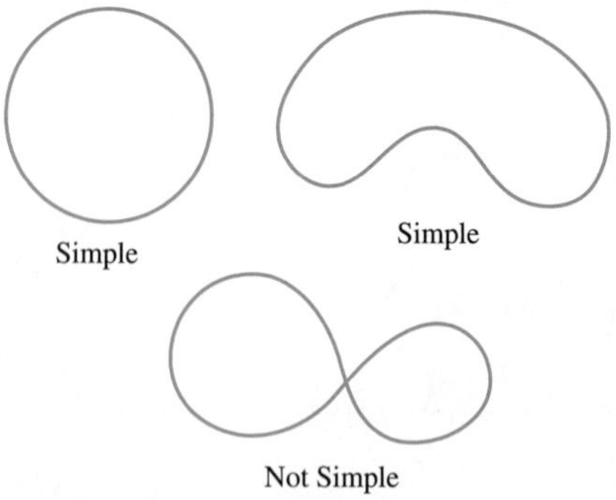

Figure 16.30 In Proving Green's Theorem, we distinguish between two kinds of closed curves, simple and not simple. Simple curves do not cross themselves. A circle is simple; a figure eight is not.

THEOREM 3 Green's Theorem (Flux-Divergence or Normal Form)

The outward flux of a field $\mathbf{F} = M\mathbf{i} + N\mathbf{j}$ across a simple closed curve C equals the double integral of div **F** over the region R enclosed by C.

$$\underbrace{\oint_C \mathbf{F} \cdot \mathbf{n}\, ds}_{\text{outward flux}} = \oint_C M\, dy - N\, dx = \underbrace{\iint_R \left(\frac{\partial M}{\partial x} + \frac{\partial N}{\partial y}\right) dx\, dy}_{\text{divergence integral}} \tag{3}$$

In another form, Green's Theorem says that the counterclockwise circulation of a vector field around a simple closed curve is the double integral of the **k**-component of the curl of the field over the region enclosed by the curve.

For a two-dimensional field $\mathbf{F} = M\mathbf{i} + N\mathbf{j}$, the integral in Equation (2), Section 16.2, for circulation takes the equivalent form

$$\oint_C \mathbf{F} \cdot \mathbf{T}\, ds = \oint_C M\, dx + N\, dy.$$

THEOREM 4 Green's Theorem (Circulation-Curl or Tangential Form)

The counterclockwise circulation of a field $\mathbf{F} = M\mathbf{i} + N\mathbf{j}$ around a simple closed curve C in the plane equals the double integral of $(\text{curl}\ \mathbf{F}) \cdot \mathbf{k}$ over the region R enclosed by C.

$$\underbrace{\oint_C \mathbf{F} \cdot \mathbf{T}\, ds}_{\text{counter clockwise circulation}} = \oint_C M\, dx + N\, dy = \underbrace{\iint_R \left(\frac{\partial N}{\partial x} - \frac{\partial M}{\partial y}\right) dx\, dy}_{\text{curl integral}} \tag{4}$$

The two forms of Green's Theorem are equivalent. We do not need to prove them both. Applying Equation (3) to the field $\mathbf{G}_1 = N\mathbf{i} - M\mathbf{j}$ gives Equation (4), and applying Equation (4) to $\mathbf{G}_2 = -N\mathbf{i} + M\mathbf{j}$ gives Equation (3).

Mathematical Assumptions

We need two kinds of assumptions for Green's Theorem to hold. First, we need conditions on M and N to ensure the existence of the integrals. The usual assumptions are that M, N, and their first partial derivatives are continuous at every point of some open region containing C and R. Second, we need geometric conditions on the curve C. It must be simple, closed, and made up of pieces along which we can integrate M and N. The usual assumptions are that C is piecewise smooth. The proof we give for Green's Theorem, however, assumes things about the shape of R as well. You can find proofs that are less restrictive in more advanced texts. First, let's look at some examples.

EXAMPLE 3 Verifying Green's Theorem

Verify both forms of Green's Theorem for the field $\mathbf{F}(x, y) = (x - y)\mathbf{i} + x\mathbf{j}$ and the region R bounded by the unit circle.

$$C: \quad \mathbf{r}(t) = (\cos t)\mathbf{i} + (\sin t)\mathbf{j}, \qquad 0 \le t \le 2\pi.$$

SOLUTION

We first express all functions, derivatives, and differentials in terms of t:

$$M = \cos t - \sin t, \qquad dx = d(\cos t) = -\sin t\, dt,$$
$$N = \cos t, \qquad dy = d(\sin t) = \cos t\, dt,$$
$$\frac{\partial M}{\partial x} = 1, \qquad \frac{\partial M}{\partial y} = -1, \qquad \frac{\partial N}{\partial x} = 1, \qquad \frac{\partial N}{\partial y} = 0.$$

The two sides of Equation (3) are

$$\begin{aligned}\oint_C M\, dy - N\, dx &= \int_{t=0}^{t=2\pi} (\cos t - \sin t)(\cos t\, dt) - (\cos t)(-\sin t\, dt)\\ &= \int_0^{2\pi} \cos^2 t\, dt = \pi,\end{aligned}$$

$$\begin{aligned}\iint_R \left(\frac{\partial M}{\partial x} + \frac{\partial N}{\partial y}\right) dx\, dy &= \iint_R (1 + 0)\, dx\, dy\\ &= \iint_R dx\, dy = \text{area of unit circle} = \pi.\end{aligned}$$

The two sides of Equation (4) are

$$\oint_C M\,dx + N\,dy = \int_{t=0}^{t=2\pi} (\cos t - \sin t)(-\sin t\,dt) + (\cos t)(\cos t\,dt)$$

$$= \int_0^{2\pi} (-\sin t\cos t + 1)\,dt = 2\pi,$$

$$\iint_R \left(\frac{\partial N}{\partial x} - \frac{\partial M}{\partial y}\right) dx\,dy = \iint_R (1 - (-1))\,dx\,dy = 2\iint_R dx\,dy = 2\pi.$$

Using Green's Theorem to Evaluate Line Integrals

If we construct a closed curve C by piecing a number of different curves end to end, the process of evaluating a line integral over C can be lengthy because there are so many different integrals to evaluate. However, if C bounds a region R to which Green's Theorem applies, we can use Green's Theorem to change the line integral around C into one double integral over R.

EXAMPLE 4 Evaluating a Line Integral Using Green's Theorem

Evaluate the integral

$$\oint_C xy\,dy - y^2\,dx,$$

where C is the square cut from the first quadrant by the lines $x = 1$ and $y = 1$.

SOLUTION

We can use either form of Green's Theorem to change the line integral into a double integral over the square.

1. *With Equation* (3): Taking $M = xy$, $N = y^2$, and C and R as the square's boundary and interior gives

$$\oint_C xy\,dy - y^2\,dx = \iint_R (y + 2y)\,dx\,dy = \int_0^1\int_0^1 3y\,dx\,dy$$

$$= \int_0^1 [3xy]_{x=0}^{x=1}\,dy = \int_0^1 3y\,dy = \frac{3}{2}y^2\Big]_0^1 = \frac{3}{2}.$$

2. *With Equation* (4): Taking $M = -y^2$ and $N = xy$ gives the same result:

$$\oint_C -y^2\,dx + xy\,dy = \iint_R (y - (-2y))\,dx\,dy = \frac{3}{2}.$$

The Green of Green's Theorem

The Green of Green's Theorem was George Green (1793–1841), a self-taught scientist in Nottingham, England. Green's work on the mathematical foundations of gravitation, electricity, and magnetism was published privately in 1828 in a short book entitled *An Essay on the Application of Mathematical Analysis to Electricity and Magnetism.* The book sold all of 52 copies (fewer than 100 were printed), the copies going mostly to Green's patrons and personal friends. A few weeks before Green's death in 1841, Sir William Thomson noticed a reference to Green's book and in 1845 was finally able to locate a copy. Excited by what he read, Thomson shared Green's ideas with other scientists and had the book republished in a series of journal articles. Green's mathematics provided the foundation on which Thomson, Stokes, Rayleigh, and Maxwell built the present-day theory of electromagnetism.

EXAMPLE 5 Finding Outward Flux

Calculate the outward flux of the field $\mathbf{F}(x, y) = x\mathbf{i} + y^2\mathbf{j}$ across the square bounded by the lines $x = \pm 1$ and $y = \pm 1$.

SOLUTION

Calculating the flux with a line integral would take four integrations, one for each side of the square. With Green's theorem, we can change the line integral to one double integral. With $M = x$, $N = y^2$, C the square, and R the square's interior, we have

$$\begin{aligned}\text{Flux} &= \oint_C \mathbf{F}\cdot\mathbf{n}\,ds = \oint_C M\,dy - N\,dx \\ &= \iint_R \left(\frac{\partial M}{\partial x} + \frac{\partial N}{\partial y}\right) dx\,dy \\ &= \int_{-1}^{1}\int_{-1}^{1} (1 + 2y)\,dx\,dy = \int_{-1}^{1} \Big[x + 2xy\Big]_{x=-1}^{x=1} dy \\ &= \int_{-1}^{1} (2 + 4y)\,dy = \Big[2y + 2y^2\Big]_{-1}^{1} = 4.\end{aligned}$$

Proof of Green's Theorem for Special Regions

Let C be a smooth simple closed curve in the xy-plane with the property that lines parallel to the axes cut it in no more than two points. Let R be the region enclosed by C, and suppose M, N, and their first partial derivatives are continuous at every point of some open region containing C and R. We want to prove the circulation-curl form of Green's Theorem.

$$\oint_C M\,dx + N\,dy = \iint_R \left(\frac{\partial N}{\partial x} - \frac{\partial M}{\partial y}\right) dx\,dy. \qquad (5)$$

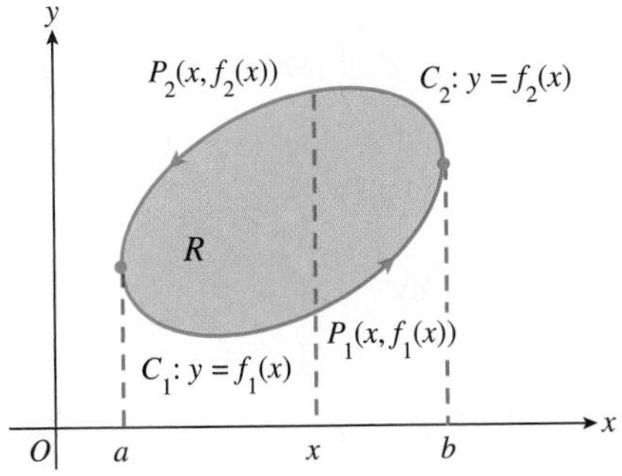

Figure 16.31 The boundary curve C is made up of C_1, the graph of $y = f_1(x)$, and C_2, the graph of $y = f_2(x)$.

Figure 16.31 shows C made up of two directed parts:

$$C_1:\quad y = f_1(x),\quad a \le x \le b, \qquad C_2:\quad y = f_2(x),\quad b \ge x \ge a.$$

For any x between a and b, we can integrate $\partial M/\partial y$ with respect to y from $y = f_1(x)$ to $y = f_2(x)$ and obtain

$$\int_{f_1(x)}^{f_2(x)} \frac{\partial M}{\partial y}\,dy = M(x, y)\Big]_{y=f_1(x)}^{y=f_2(x)} = M(x, f_2(x)) - M(x, f_1(x)).$$

We can then integrate this with respect to x from a to b:

$$\begin{aligned}\int_a^b \int_{f_1(x)}^{f_2(x)} \frac{\partial M}{\partial y}\,dy\,dx &= \int_a^b [M(x, f_2(x)) - M(x, f_1(x))]\,dx \\ &= -\int_b^a M(x, f_2(x))\,dx - \int_a^b M(x, f_1(x))\,dx \\ &= -\int_{C_2} M\,dx - \int_{C_1} M\,dx \\ &= -\oint_C M\,dx.\end{aligned}$$

Therefore,

$$\oint_C M\,dx = \iint_R \left(-\frac{\partial M}{\partial y}\right) dx\,dy. \qquad (6)$$

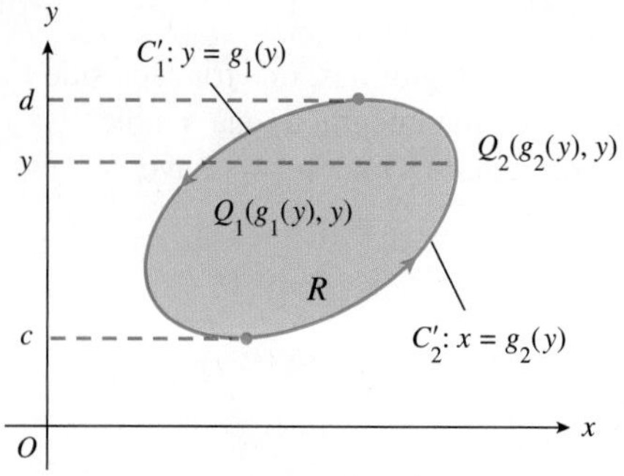

Figure 16.32 The boundary curve C is made up of C'_1, the graph of $x = g_1(y)$, and C'_2, the graph of $x = g_2(y)$.

Equation (6) is half the result we need for Equation (5). We derive the other half by integrating $\partial N/\partial x$ first with respect to x and then with respect to y, as suggested by Figure 16.32. This shows the curve C of Figure 16.31 decomposed into the two directed parts

$$C'_1:\quad x = g_1(y),\qquad d \ge y \ge c,\qquad \text{and}\qquad C'_2:\quad x = g_2(y),\qquad c \le y \le d.$$

The result of this double integration is

$$\oint_C N\,dy = \iint_R \frac{\partial N}{\partial x}\,dx\,dy. \tag{7}$$

Combining Equations (6) and (7) gives Equation (5). This concludes the proof.

Extending the Proof to Other Regions

The argument we just gave does not apply directly to the rectangular region in Figure 16.33 because the lines $x = a$, $x = b$, $y = c$, and $y = d$ meet the region's boundary in more than two points. If we divide the boundary C into four directed line segments, however,

$$C_1:\quad y = c,\qquad a \le x \le b,\qquad C_2:\quad x = b,\qquad c \le y \le d,$$

$$C_3:\quad y = d,\qquad b \ge x \ge a,\qquad C_4:\quad x = a,\qquad d \ge y \ge c,$$

we can modify the argument in the following way.

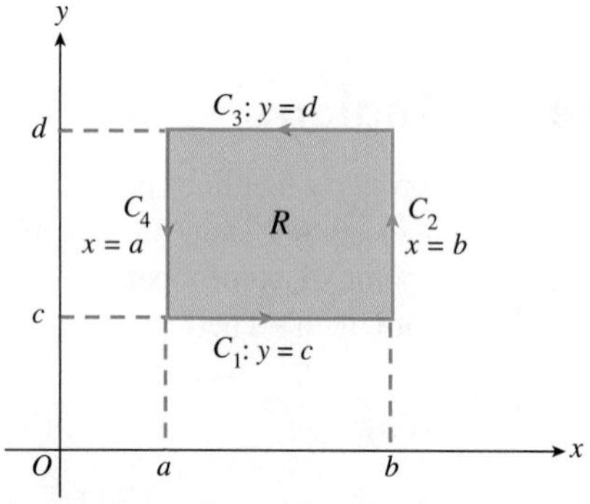

Figure 16.33 To prove Green's Theorem for a rectangle, we divide the boundary into four directed line segments.

Proceeding as in the proof of Equation (7), we have

$$\begin{aligned}
\int_c^d \int_a^b \frac{\partial N}{\partial x}\,dx\,dy &= \int_c^d (N(b, y) - N(a, y))\,dy \\
&= \int_c^d N(b, y)\,dy + \int_d^c N(a, y)\,dy \\
&= \int_{C_2} N\,dy + \int_{C_4} N\,dy.
\end{aligned} \tag{8}$$

Because y is constant along C_1 and C_3, $\int_{C_1} N\,dy = \int_{C_3} N\,dy = 0$, so we can add $\int_{C_1} N\,dy + \int_{C_3} N\,dy$ to the right-hand side of Equation (8) without changing the equality. Doing so, we have

$$\int_c^d \int_a^b \frac{\partial N}{\partial y}\,dx\,dy = \oint_C N\,dy. \tag{9}$$

Similarly, we can show that

$$\int_a^b \int_c^d \frac{\partial M}{\partial y}\,dy\,dx = -\oint_C M\,dx. \tag{10}$$

Subtracting Equation (10) from Equation (9), we again arrive at

$$\oint_C M\,dx + N\,dy = \iint_R \left(\frac{\partial N}{\partial x} - \frac{\partial M}{\partial y}\right) dx\,dy.$$

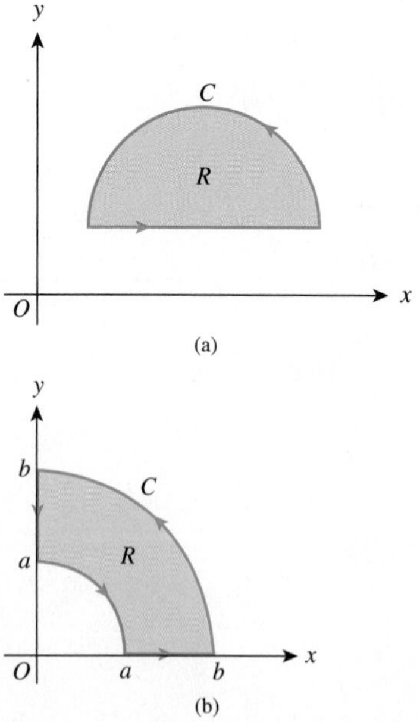

Figure 16.34 Other regions to which Green's Theorem applies.

Regions like those in Figure 16.34 can be handled with no greater difficulty. Equation (5) still applies. It also applies to the horseshoe-shaped region R shown in Figure 16.35, as

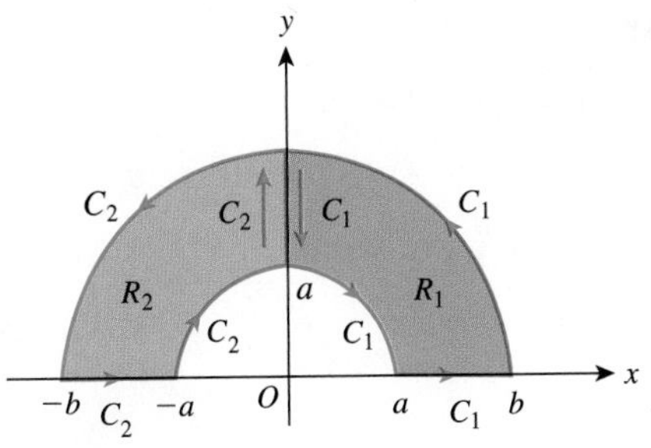

Figure 16.35 A region R that combines regions R_1 and R_2.

we see by putting together the regions R_1 and R_2 and their boundaries. Green's Theorem applies to C_1, R_1, and to C_2, R_2, yielding

$$\int_{C_1} M\,dx + N\,dy = \iint_{R_1} \left(\frac{\partial N}{\partial x} - \frac{\partial M}{\partial y}\right) dx\,dy,$$

$$\int_{C_2} M\,dx + N\,dy = \iint_{R_2} \left(\frac{\partial N}{\partial x} - \frac{\partial M}{\partial y}\right) dx\,dy.$$

When we add these two equations, the line integral along the y-axis from b to a for C_1 cancels the integral over the same segment but in the opposite direction for C_2. Hence,

$$\oint_{C} M\,dx + N\,dy = \iint_{R} \left(\frac{\partial N}{\partial x} - \frac{\partial M}{\partial y}\right) dx\,dy,$$

where C consists of the two segments of the x-axis from $-b$ to $-a$ and from a to b and of the two semicircles and where R is the region inside C.

The device of adding line integrals over separate boundaries to build up an integral over a single boundary can be extended to any finite number of sub-regions. In Figure 16.36a, let C_1 be the boundary, oriented counterclockwise, of the region R_1 in the first quadrant. Similarly for the other three quadrants: C_i is the boundary of the region R_i, $i = 1, 2, 3, 4$. By Green's Theorem,

$$\oint_{C_1} M\,dx + N\,dy = \iint_{R_1} \left(\frac{\partial N}{\partial x} - \frac{\partial M}{\partial y}\right) dx\,dy. \tag{11}$$

We add Equations (11) for $i = 1, 2, 3, 4$ and get (Figure 16.36b):

$$\oint_{r=b} (M\,dx + N\,dy) + \oint_{r=a} (M\,dx + N\,dy) = \iint_{a \le r \le b} \left(\frac{\partial N}{\partial x} - \frac{\partial M}{\partial y}\right) dx\,dy. \tag{12}$$

Equation (12) says that the double integral of $(\partial N/\partial x) - (\partial M/\partial y)$ over the annular ring R equals the line integral of $M\,dx + N\,dy$ over the complete boundary of R in the direction that keeps R on our left as we progress (Figure 16.36b).

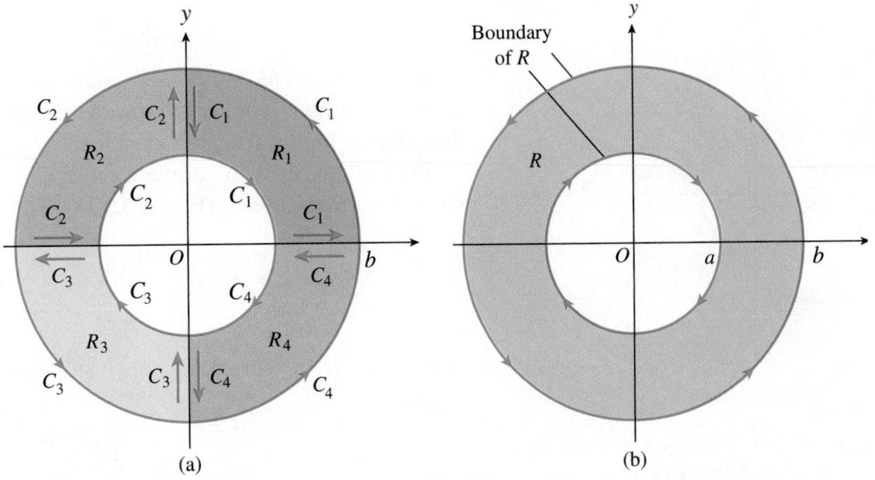

Figure 16.36 The annular region R combines four smaller regions. In polar coordinates, $r = a$ for the inner circle, $r = b$ for the outer circle, and $a \le r \le b$ for the region itself.

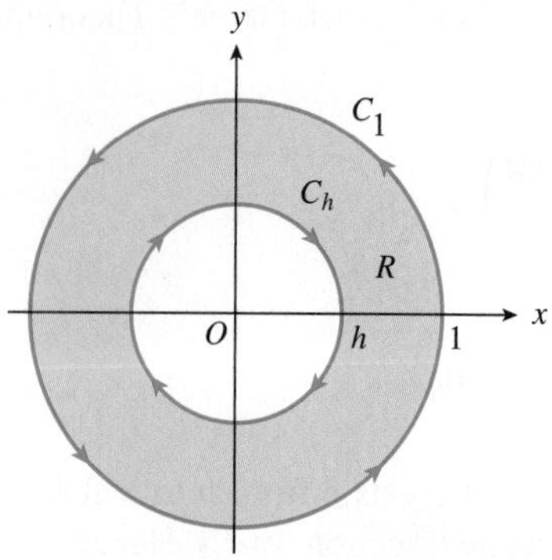

Figure 16.37 Green's Theorem may be applied to the annular region *R* by integrating along the boundaries as shown. (Example 6)

EXAMPLE 6 Verifying Green's Theorem

Verify the circulation form of Green's Theorem (Equation (4)) on the annular ring $R: h^2 \leq x^2 + y^2 \leq 1, 0 < h < 1$ (Figure 16.37), if

$$M = \frac{-y}{x^2 + y^2}, \qquad N = \frac{x}{x^2 + y^2}.$$

SOLUTION

The boundary of *R* consists of the circle

$$C_1: \quad x = \cos t, \qquad y = \sin t, \qquad 0 \leq t \leq 2\pi,$$

traversed counterclockwise as *t* increases and the circle

$$C_h: \quad x = h \cos \theta, \qquad y = -h \sin \theta, \qquad 0 \leq \theta \leq 2\pi,$$

traversed clockwise as θ increases. The functions *M* and *N* and their partial derivatives are continuous throughout *R*. Moreover,

$$\frac{\partial M}{\partial y} = \frac{(x^2 + y^2)(-1) + y(2y)}{(x^2 + y^2)^2}$$

$$= \frac{y^2 - x^2}{(x^2 + y^2)^2} = \frac{\partial N}{\partial x},$$

so

$$\iint_R \left(\frac{\partial N}{\partial x} - \frac{\partial M}{\partial y}\right) dx\, dy = \iint_R 0\, dx\, dy = 0.$$

The integral of $M\,dx + N\,dy$ over the boundary of *R* is

$$\int_C M\,dx + N\,dy = \oint_{C_1} \frac{x\,dy - y\,dx}{x^2 + y^2} + \oint_{C_h} \frac{x\,dy - y\,dx}{x^2 + y^2}$$

$$= \int_0^{2\pi} (\cos^2 t + \sin^2 t)\,dt - \int_0^{2\pi} \frac{h^2(\cos^2 \theta + \sin^2 \theta)}{h^2}\,d\theta$$

$$= 2\pi - 2\pi = 0.$$

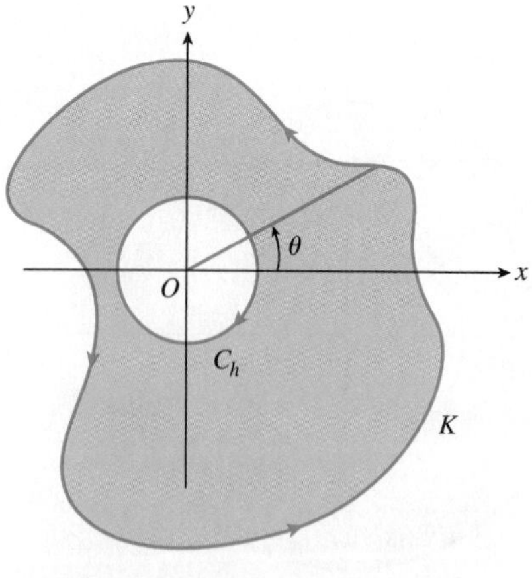

Figure 16.38 The region bounded by the circle C_h and the curve *K*.

The functions *M* and *N* in Example 6 are discontinuous at (0, 0), so we cannot apply Green's Theorem to the circle C_1 and the region inside it. We must exclude the origin. We do so by excluding the points inside C_h.

We could replace the circle C_1 in Example 6 by an ellipse or any other simple closed curve *K* surrounding C_h (Figure 16.38). The result would still be

$$\oint_K (M\,dx + N\,dy) + \oint_{C_h} (M\,dx + N\,dy) = \iint_R \left(\frac{\partial N}{\partial x} - \frac{\partial M}{\partial y}\right) dy\, dx = 0,$$

which leads to the surprising conclusion that

$$\oint_K (M\,dx + N\,dy) = 2\pi$$

for any such curve K. We can explain this result by changing to polar coordinates. With

$$x = r\cos\theta, \qquad y = r\sin\theta,$$

$$dx = -r\sin\theta\,d\theta + \cos\theta\,dr \qquad dy = r\cos\theta\,d\theta + \sin\theta\,dr,$$

we have

$$\frac{x\,dy - y\,dx}{x^2 + y^2} = \frac{r^2(\cos^2\theta + \sin^2\theta)\,d\theta}{r^2} = d\theta,$$

and θ increases by 2π as we traverse K once counterclockwise.

Quick Review 16.4

In Exercises 1–4, parametrize the given straight line segment.

1. C_1 from $(0, 0)$ to $(1, 0)$
2. C_2 from $(1, 0)$ to $(1, 1)$
3. C_3 from $(1, 1)$ to $(0, 1)$
4. C_4 from $(0, 1)$ to $(0, 0)$

In Exercises 5–8, evaluate the line integral $\int_C xy\,dy - y^2\,dx$ for the given curve.

5. $C = C_1$ of Exercise 1
6. $C = C_2$ of Exercise 2
7. $C = C_3$ of Exercise 3
8. $C = C_4$ of Exercise 4

In Exercises 9 and 10, let $M(x, y) = -y/(x^2 + y^2)$.

9. Find $\partial M/\partial x$.
10. Find $\partial M/\partial y$.

Section 16.4 Exercises

In Exercises 1–4, verify Green's Theorem by evaluating both sides of Equations (3) and (4) for the field $\mathbf{F} = M\mathbf{i} + N\mathbf{j}$. Take the domains of integration in each case to be the disk R: $x^2 + y^2 \le a^2$ and its bounding circle C: $\mathbf{r} = (a\cos t)\mathbf{i} + (a\sin t)\mathbf{j}$, $0 \le t \le 2\pi$.

1. $\mathbf{F} = -y\mathbf{i} + x\mathbf{j}$
2. $\mathbf{F} = y\mathbf{i}$
3. $\mathbf{F} = 2x\mathbf{i} - 3y\mathbf{j}$
4. $\mathbf{F} = -x^2y\mathbf{i} + xy^2\mathbf{j}$

In Exercises 5–10, use Green's theorem to find the counterclockwise circulation and outward flux for the field $\mathbf{F}$ and curve C.

5. $\mathbf{F} = (x - y)\mathbf{i} + (y - x)\mathbf{j}$
   C: The square bounded by $x = 0, x = 1, y = 0, y = 1$
6. $\mathbf{F} = (x^2 + 4y)\mathbf{i} + (x + y^2)\mathbf{j}$
   C: The square bounded by $x = 0, x = 1, y = 0, y = 1$
7. $\mathbf{F} = (y^2 - x^2)\mathbf{i} + (x^2 + y^2)\mathbf{j}$
   C: The triangle bounded by $y = 0$, $x = 3$, and $y = x$
8. $\mathbf{F} = (x + y)\mathbf{i} + (x^2 + y^2)\mathbf{j}$
   C: The triangle bounded by $y = 0$, $x = 1$, and $y = x$
9. $\mathbf{F} = (x + e^x \sin y)\mathbf{i} + (x + e^x \cos y)\mathbf{j}$
   C: The right-hand loop of the lemniscate $r^2 = \cos 2\theta$
10. $\mathbf{F} = \left(tan^{-1}\frac{y}{x}\right)\mathbf{i} + \ln(x^2 + y^2)\mathbf{j}$
    C: The boundary of the region defined by the polar coordinate inequalities $1 \le r \le 2$, $0 \le \theta \le \pi$
11. Find the counterclockwise circulation and outward flux of the field $\mathbf{F} = xy\mathbf{i} + y^2\mathbf{j}$ around and over the boundary of the region enclosed by the curves $y = x^2$ and $y = x$ in the first quadrant.
12. Find the counterclockwise circulation and the outward flux of the field $\mathbf{F} = (-\sin y)\mathbf{i} + (x\cos y)\mathbf{j}$ around and over the square cut from the first quadrant by the lines $x = \pi/2$ and $y = \pi/2$.
13. Find the outward flux of the field
    $$\mathbf{F} = \left(3xy - \frac{x}{1 + y^2}\right)\mathbf{i} + (e^x + \tan^{-1} y)\mathbf{j}$$
    across the cardioid $r = a(1 + \cos\theta)$, $a > 0$.
14. Find the counterclockwise circulation of
    $$\mathbf{F} = (y + e^x \ln y)\mathbf{i} + (e^x/y)\mathbf{j}$$
    around the boundary of the region that is bounded above by the curve $y = 3 - x^2$ and below by the curve $y = x^4 + 1$.

In Exercises 15 and 16, find the work done by $\mathbf{F}$ in moving a particle once counterclockwise around the given curve.

15. $\mathbf{F} = 2xy^3\mathbf{i} + 4x^2y^2\mathbf{j}$
    C: The boundary of the "triangular" region in the first quadrant enclosed by the x-axis, the line $x = 1$, and the curve $y = x^3$
16. $\mathbf{F} = (4x - 2y)\mathbf{i} + (2x - 4y)\mathbf{j}$
    C: The circle $(x - 2)^2 + (y - 2)^2 = 4$

In Exercises 17–20, use Green's Theorem to evaluate the integral.

17. $\oint_C (y^2\,dx + x^2\,dy)$

C: The triangle bounded by $x = 0, x + y = 1, y = 0$

18. $\oint_C (3y\,dx + 2x\,dy)$

C: The boundary of $0 \le x \le \pi, 0 \le y \le \sin x$

19. $\oint_C (6y + x)\,dx + (y + 2x)\,dy$

C: The circle $(x - 2)^2 + (y - 3)^2 = 4$

20. $\oint_C (2x + y^2)\,dx + (2xy + 3y)\,dy$

C: Any simple closed curve in the plane for which Green's Theorem holds

Explorations

If a simple closed curve C in the plane and the region R it encloses satisfy the hypotheses of Green's Theorem, the area of R is given by

GREEN'S THEOREM Area Formula

$$\text{Area of } R = \frac{1}{2}\oint_C x\,dy - y\,dx \qquad (13)$$

21. **(a)** Prove Equation (13). (*Hint:* Use Equation (11).)

(b) Use Equation (13) to find the area of the region enclosed by the circle $\mathbf{r}(t) = (a\cos t)\mathbf{i} + (a\sin t)\mathbf{j}, 0 \le t \le 2\pi$.

In Exercises 22–24, use Equation (13) to find the area of the region enclosed by the curve.

22. The ellipse $\mathbf{r}(t) = (a\cos t)\mathbf{i} + (b\sin t)\mathbf{j}, \quad 0 \le t \le 2\pi$

23. The astroid $\mathbf{r}(t) = (\cos^3 t)\mathbf{i} + (\sin^3 t)\mathbf{j}, \quad 0 \le t \le 2\pi$

24. The curve $\mathbf{r}(t) = t^2\mathbf{i} + \left(\frac{t^3}{3} - t\right)\mathbf{j}, \quad -\sqrt{3} \le t \le \sqrt{3}$

25. Let C be the boundary of a region on which Green's Theorem holds. Use Green's Theorem to calculate

(a) $\oint_C f(x)\,dx + g(y)\,dy$.

(b) $\oint_C ky\,dx + hx\,dy$ (k and h constants.)

26. ***Integral Dependent Only On Area*** Show that the value of

$$\oint_C xy^2\,dx + (x^2y + 2x)\,dy$$

around any square depends only on the area of the square and not on its location in the plane.

27. **Writing to Learn** What is special about the integral

$$\oint_C 4x^3y\,dx + x^4\,dy?$$

Give reasons for your answer.

28. **Writing to Learn** What is special about the integral

$$\oint_C -y^3\,dx + x^3\,dy?$$

Give reasons for your answer.

29. ***Area as a Line Integral*** Show that if R is a region in the plane bounded by a piecewise smooth simple closed curve C, then

$$\text{Area of } R = \oint_C x\,dy = -\oint_C y\,dx.$$

30. ***Definite Integral as Line Integral*** Suppose a nonnegative function $y = f(x)$ has a continuous first derivative on $[a, b]$. Let C be the boundary of the region in the xy-plane that is bounded below by the x-axis, above by the graph of f, and on the sides by the lines $x = a$ and $x = b$. Show that

$$\int_a^b f(x)\,dx = -\oint_C y\,dx.$$

31. ***Area and the Centroid***

(a) Let A be the area and $\bar{x}$ the x-coordinate of the centroid of a region R that is bounded by a piecewise smooth simple closed curve C in the xy-plane. Show that

$$\frac{1}{2}\oint_C x^2\,dy = -\oint_C xy\,dy = \frac{1}{3}\oint_C x^2\,dy - xy\,dx = A\bar{x}.$$

(b) What is the analogous statement for A and $\bar{y}$?

32. ***Moment of Inertia*** Let I_y be the moment of inertia about the y-axis of the region in Exercise 31. Show that

$$\frac{1}{3}\oint_C x^3\,dy = -\oint_C x^2y\,dx = \frac{1}{4}\oint_C x^3\,dy - x^2y\,dx = I_y.$$

In Exercises 33–36, *work in groups of two or three* to solve the problem.

33. ***Green's Theorem and Laplace's Equation*** Assuming that all the necessary derivatives exist and are continuous, show that if $f(x, y)$ satisfies the **Laplace equation**

$$\frac{\partial^2 f}{\partial x^2} + \frac{\partial^2 f}{\partial y^2} = 0,$$

then

$$\oint_C \frac{\partial f}{\partial y}\,dx - \frac{\partial f}{\partial x}\,dy = 0$$

for all closed curves to which Green's Theorem applies. (The converse is also true: If the line integral is always zero, then f satisfies the Laplace equation.)

34. *Maximizing Work* Among all smooth simple closed curves in the plane, oriented counterclockwise, find the one along which the work done by

$$\mathbf{F} = \left(\frac{1}{4}x^2y + \frac{1}{3}y^3\right)\mathbf{i} + x\mathbf{j}$$

is greatest. (*Hint:* Where is (curl $\mathbf{F}$) · $\mathbf{k}$ positive?)

35. *Regions with Many Holes* Green's Theorem holds for a region R with any finite number of holes as long as the bounding curves are smooth, simple, and closed and we integrate over each component of the boundary in the direction that keeps R on our immediate left as we go along (Figure 16.39).

(a) Let $f(x, y) = \ln(x^2 + y^2)$ and let C be the circle $x^2 + y^2 = a^2$. Evaluate the flux integral

$$\oint_C \nabla f \cdot \mathbf{n}\, ds.$$

(b) Let K be an arbitrary smooth simple closed curve in the plane that does not pass through (0, 0). Use Green's Theorem to show that

$$\oint_K \nabla f \cdot \mathbf{n}\, ds$$

has two possible values, depending on whether (0, 0) lies inside K or outside K.

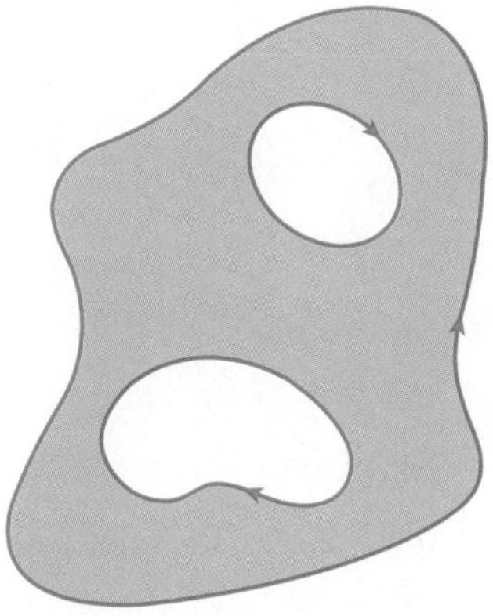

Figure 16.39 Green's Theorem holds for regions with more than one hole. (Exercise 35)

36. *Bendixson's Criterion* The **streamlines** of a planar fluid flow are the smooth curves traced by the fluid's individual particles. The vectors $\mathbf{F} = M(x, y)\mathbf{i} + N(x, y)\mathbf{j}$ of the flow's velocity field are the tangent vectors of the streamlines. Show that if the flow takes place over a *simply connected* region R (no holes or missing points) and that if $M_x + N_y \neq 0$ throughout R, then none of the streamlines in R is closed. In other words, no particle of fluid ever has a closed trajectory in R. The criterion is $M_x + N_y \neq 0$ **Bendixson's criterion** for the nonexistence of closed trajectories.

37. Establish Equation (7) to finish the proof of the special case of Green's Theorem.

38. Establish Equation (10) to complete the argument for the extension of Green's Theorem.

39. Writing to Learn *Curl Components of Conservative Fields* Can anything be said about the curl component of a conservative two-dimensional vector field? Give reasons for your answer.

40. Writing to Learn *The Circulation of a Conservative Field* Does Green's Theorem give any information about the circulation of a conservative field? Does this agree with anything else you know? Give reasons for your answer.

Extending the Ideas

CAS Explorations

In Exercises 41–44, perform the following steps:

(a) Plot C in the xy-plane.

(b) Determine the integrand $\partial N/\partial x - \partial M/\partial y$ for the curl form of Green's Theorem.

(c) Determine the (double integral) limits of integration from your plot in (a) and evaluate the curl integral for the counter-clockwise circulation of the field $\mathbf{F}$ around the curve C.

41. $\mathbf{F} = (2x - y)\mathbf{i} + (x + 3y)\mathbf{j}$
C: The ellipse $x^2 + 4y^2 = 4$

42. $\mathbf{F} = (2x^3 - y^3)\mathbf{i} + (x^3 + y^3)\mathbf{j}$
C: The ellipse $\dfrac{x^2}{4} + \dfrac{y^2}{9} = 1$

43. $\mathbf{F} = x^{-1}e^y\mathbf{i} + (e^y \ln x + 2x)\mathbf{j}$
C: The boundary of the region defined by $y = 1 + x^4$ (below) and $y = 2$ (above)

44. $\mathbf{F} = xe^y\mathbf{i} + 4x^2 \ln y\mathbf{j}$
C: The triangle with vertices (0, 0), (2, 0), and (0, 4)

16.5 Surface Area and Surface Integrals

What you'll learn about

- Surface Area
- A Practical Formula
- Surface Integrals
- Algebraic Properties: The Surface Area Differential
- Orientation
- Surface Integral for Flux
- Moments and Masses of Thin Shells

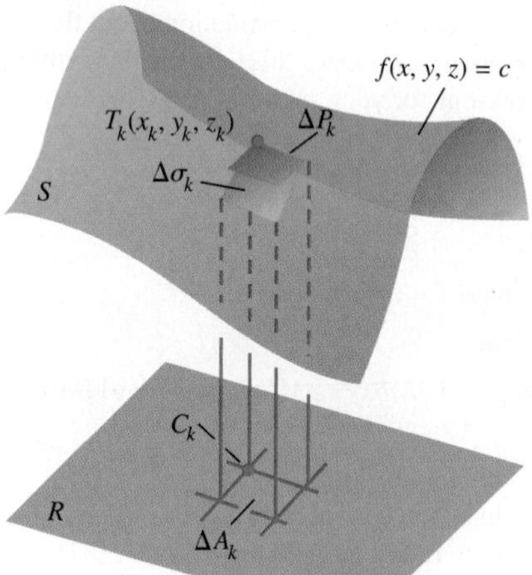

Figure 16.40 A surface S and its vertical projection onto a plane beneath it. You can think of R as the shadow of S on the plane. The tangent plate ΔP_k approximates the surface patch $\Delta\sigma_k$ above ΔA_k.

Surface Area

Figure 16.40 shows a surface S lying above its "shadow" region R in a plane beneath it. The surface is defined by the equation $f(x, y, z) = c$. If the surface is **smooth** (∇f is continuous and never vanishes on S), we can define and calculate its area as a double integral over R.

The first step in defining the area of S is to partition the region R into small rectangles ΔA_k of the kind we would use if we were defining an integral over R. Directly above each ΔA_k lies a patch of surface $\Delta\sigma_k$ that we may approximate with a portion ΔP_k of the tangent plane. To be specific, we suppose ΔP_k is a portion of the plane that is tangent to the surface at the point $T_k(x_k, y_k, z_k)$ directly above the back corner C_k of ΔA_k. If the tangent plane is parallel to R, then ΔP_k will be congruent to ΔA_k. Otherwise, it will be a parallelogram whose area is somewhat larger than the area of ΔA_k.

Figure 16.41 gives a magnified view of $\Delta\sigma_k$ and ΔP_k, showing the gradient vector $\nabla f(x_k, y_k, z_k)$ at T_k and a unit vector $\mathbf{p}$ that is normal to R. The figure also shows the angle γ_k between ∇f and $\mathbf{p}$. The other vectors in the picture, $\mathbf{u}_k$ and $\mathbf{v}_k$, lie along the edges of the patch ΔP_k in the tangent plane. Thus, both $\mathbf{u}_k \times \mathbf{v}_k$ and ∇f are normal to the tangent plane.

We now need from advanced vector geometry that $|(\mathbf{u}_k \times \mathbf{v}_k) \cdot \mathbf{p}|$ is the area of the projection of the parallelogram determined by $\mathbf{u}_k$ and $\mathbf{v}_k$ onto any plane normal to $\mathbf{p}$. In our case, this translates into the statement

$$|(\mathbf{u}_k \times \mathbf{v}_k) \cdot \mathbf{p}| = \Delta A_k. \tag{1}$$

Now, $|\mathbf{u}_k \times \mathbf{v}_k|$ itself is the area ΔP_k (standard fact about cross products), so Equation (1) becomes

$$\underbrace{|\mathbf{u}_k \times \mathbf{v}_k|}_{\Delta P_k}\underbrace{|\mathbf{p}|}_{1}\underbrace{|\cos(\text{angle between } \mathbf{u}_k \times \mathbf{v}_k \text{ and } \mathbf{p})|}_{\substack{\text{same as } |\cos\gamma_k| \text{ because} \\ \nabla f \text{ and } \mathbf{u}_k \times \mathbf{v}_k \text{ are both} \\ \text{normal to the tangent plane}}} = \Delta A_k \tag{2}$$

or

$$\Delta P_k |\cos\gamma_k| = \Delta A_k$$

or

$$\Delta P_k = \frac{\Delta A_k}{|\cos\gamma_k|},$$

provided $\cos\gamma_k \neq 0$. We will have $\cos\gamma_k \neq 0$ as long as ∇f is not parallel to the ground plane and $\nabla f \cdot \mathbf{p} \neq 0$.

Since the patches ΔP_k approximate the surface patches $\Delta\sigma_k$ that fit together to make S, the sum

$$\sum \Delta P_k = \sum \frac{\Delta A_k}{|\cos\gamma_k|} \tag{3}$$

looks like an approximation of what we might like to call the surface area of S. It also looks as if the approximation would improve if we refined the partition of R. In fact, the sums on the right-hand side of Equation (3) are approximating sums for the double integral

$$\iint_R \frac{1}{|\cos\gamma_k|}\, dA. \tag{4}$$

We therefore define the **area** of S to be the value of this integral whenever it exists.

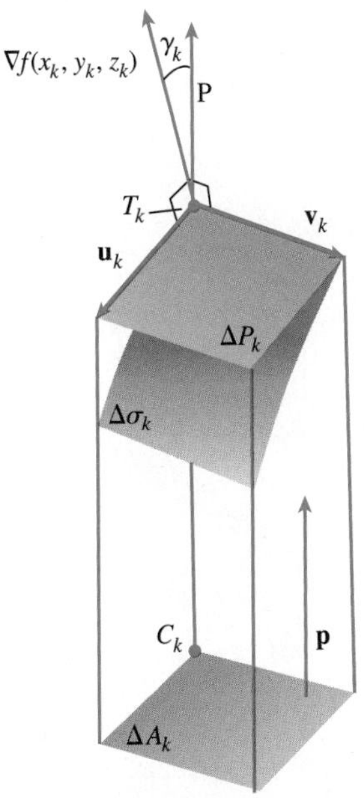

Figure 16.41 Magnified view from Figure 16.40. The vector $\mathbf{u}_k \times \mathbf{v}_k$ (not shown) is parallel to the vector ∇f because both vectors are normal to the plane of ΔP_k.

A Practical Formula

For any surface $f(x, y, z) = c$, we have $|\nabla f \cdot \mathbf{p}| = |\nabla f||\mathbf{p}||\cos\gamma|$, so

$$\frac{1}{|\cos\gamma|} = \frac{|\nabla f|}{|\nabla f \cdot \mathbf{p}|}.$$

This combines with Equation (4) to give a practical formula for area.

> **Formula for Surface Area**
>
> The area of the surface $f(x, y, z) = c$ over a closed and bounded plane region R is
>
> $$\text{Surface area} = \iint_R \frac{|\nabla f|}{|\nabla f \cdot \mathbf{p}|}\, dA, \tag{5}$$
>
> where $\mathbf{p}$ is a unit vector normal to R and $\nabla f \cdot \mathbf{p} \neq 0$.

Thus, the area is the double integral over R of the magnitude of ∇f divided by the magnitude of the scalar component of ∇f normal to R.

We reached Equation (5) under the assumptions that $\nabla f \cdot \mathbf{p} \neq 0$ throughout R and that ∇f is continuous. Whenever the integral exists, however, we define its value to be the area of the portion of the surface $f(x, y, z) = c$ that lies over R.

EXAMPLE 1 Finding Surface Area

Find the area of the surface cut from the bottom of the paraboloid $x^2 + y^2 - z = 0$ by the plane $z = 4$.

SOLUTION

We sketch the surface S and the region R below it in the xy-plane (Figure 16.42). The surface S is part of the level surface $f(x, y, z) = x^2 + y^2 - z = 0$, and R is the disk $x^2 + y^2 \le 4$ in the xy-plane. To get a unit normal to the plane of R, we can take $\mathbf{p} = \mathbf{k}$.

At any point (x, y, z) on the surface, we have

$$\begin{aligned} f(x, y, z) &= x^2 + y^2 - z \\ \nabla f &= 2x\mathbf{i} + 2y\mathbf{j} - \mathbf{k} \\ |\nabla f| &= \sqrt{(2x)^2 + (2y)^2 + (-1)^2} \\ &= \sqrt{4x^2 + 4y^2 + 1} \\ |\nabla f \cdot \mathbf{p}| &= |\nabla f \cdot \mathbf{k}| = |-1| = 1. \end{aligned}$$

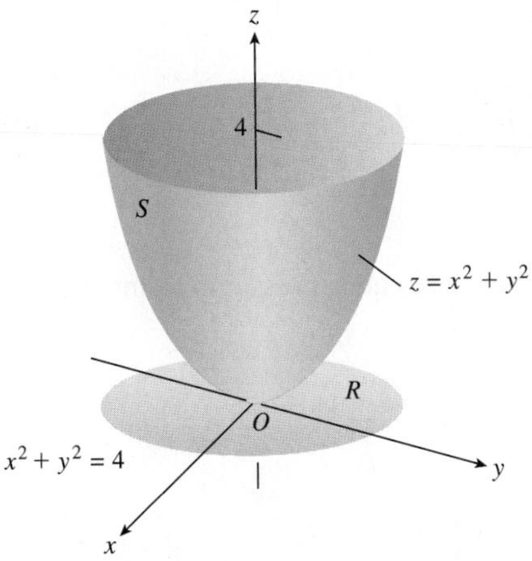

Figure 16.42 The area of this parabolic surface is calculated in Example 1.

In the region R, $dA = dx\,dy$. Therefore,

$$\text{Surface area} = \iint_R \frac{|\nabla f|}{|\nabla f \cdot \mathbf{p}|}\,dA \qquad \text{Eq. (5)}$$

$$= \iint_{x^2+y^2\le 4} \sqrt{4x^2 + 4y^2 + 1}\,dx\,dy$$

$$= \int_0^{2\pi}\int_0^2 \sqrt{4r^2 + 1}\,r\,dr\,d\theta \qquad \text{Polar coordinates}$$

$$= \int_0^{2\pi}\left[\frac{1}{12}(4r^2 + 1)^{3/2}\right]_0^2 d\theta$$

$$= \frac{\pi}{6}(17^{3/2} - 1) \approx 36.177 \text{ units squared.}$$

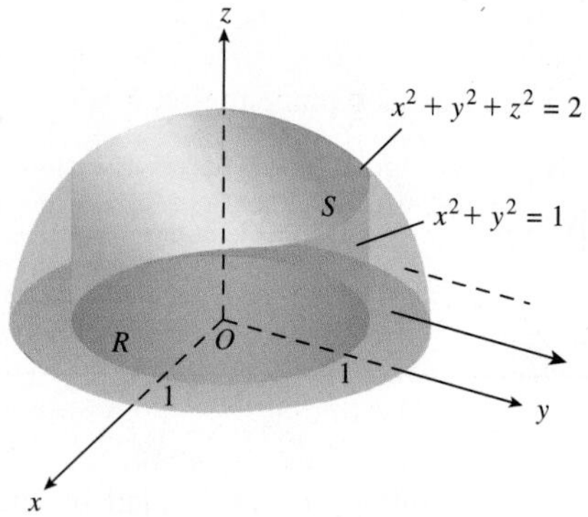

Figure 16.43 The cap cut from the hemisphere by the cylinder projects vertically onto the disk R: $x^2 + y^2 \le 1$. (Example 2)

EXAMPLE 2 Finding Surface Area

Find the area of the cap cut from the hemisphere $x^2 + y^2 + z^2 = 2$, $z \ge 0$, by the cylinder $x^2 + y^2 = 1$ (Figure 16.43).

SOLUTION

The cap S is part of the level surface $f(x, y, z) = x^2 + y^2 + z^2 = 2$. It projects one-to-one onto the disk R: $x^2 + y^2 \le 1$ in the xy-plane. The vector $\mathbf{p} = \mathbf{k}$ is normal to the plane of R.

At any point on the surface,

$$f(x, y, z) = x^2 + y^2 + z^2$$

$$\nabla f = 2x\mathbf{i} + 2y\mathbf{j} + 2z\mathbf{k}$$

$$|\nabla f| = 2\sqrt{x^2 + y^2 + z^2} = 2\sqrt{2} \qquad \text{Because } x^2 + y^2 + z^2 = 2 \text{ at points of } S$$

$$|\nabla f \cdot \mathbf{p}| = |2z| = 2z.$$

Therefore,

$$\text{Surface area} = \iint_R \frac{|\nabla f|}{|\nabla f \cdot \mathbf{p}|}\,dA = \iint_R \frac{2\sqrt{2}}{2z}\,dA = \sqrt{2}\iint_R \frac{dA}{z}. \qquad (6)$$

What do we do about the z?

Since z is the z-coordinate of a point on the sphere, we can express it in terms of x and y as

$$z = \sqrt{2 - x^2 - y^2}.$$

With this substitution, we continue the work of Equation (6):

$$\begin{aligned}\text{Surface area} &= \sqrt{2}\iint_R \frac{dA}{z} = \sqrt{2}\iint_R \frac{dA}{\sqrt{2 - x^2 - y^2}} \\ &= \sqrt{2}\int_0^{2\pi}\int_0^1 \frac{r\,dr\,d\theta}{\sqrt{2 - r^2}} \qquad \text{Polar coordinates} \\ &= \sqrt{2}\int_0^{2\pi} \left[-(2 - r^2)^{1/2}\right]_{r=0}^{r=1} d\theta \\ &= 2\pi(2 - \sqrt{2}).\end{aligned}$$

Surface Integrals

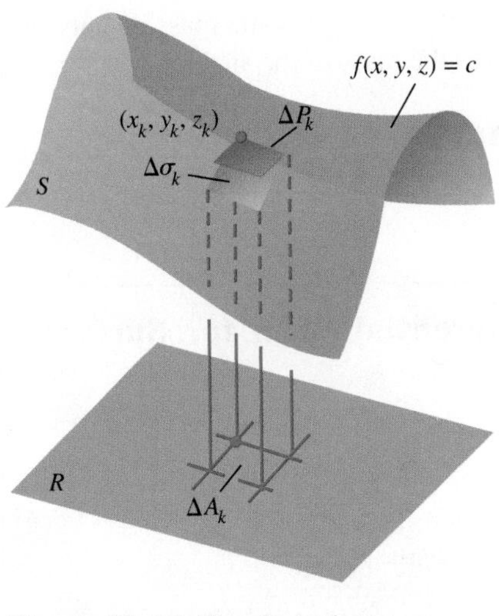

Figure 16.44 If we know how an electrical charge is distributed over a surface, we can find the total charge with a surface integral.

We now show how to integrate a function over a surface, using the ideas just developed for calculating surface area.

Suppose, for example, we have an electrical charge distributed over a surface $f(x, y, z) = c$ like the one in Figure 16.44 and we know the charge density $g(x, y, z)$ (charge per unit area) at each point on S. Then we may calculate the total charge on S in the following way.

We partition the shadow region R on the ground plane beneath S into small rectangles of the kind we would use if we were defining the area of S. Then directly above each ΔA_k lies a patch of surface $\Delta\sigma_k$ that we approximate with a parallelogram-shaped portion of tangent plane, ΔP_k.

Up to this point the construction proceeds as in the definition of surface area, but now we take one additional step: We evaluate g at (x_k, y_k, z_k) and then approximate the total charge on the surface patch $\Delta\sigma_k$ by the product $g(x_k, y_k, z_k)\,\Delta P_k$. The rationale is that when the partition of R is sufficiently fine, the value of g throughout $\Delta\sigma_k$ is nearly constant and ΔP_k is nearly the same as $\Delta\sigma_k$. The total charge over S is then approximated by the sum

$$\text{Total charge} \approx \sum g(x_k, y_k, z_k)\,\Delta P_k = \sum g(x_k, y_k, z_k)\frac{\Delta A_k}{|\cos\gamma_k|}. \tag{7}$$

If f, the function defining the surface S, and its first partial derivatives are continuous and if g is continuous over S, then the sums on the right-hand side of Equation (7) approach the limit

$$\iint_R g(x, y, z)\frac{dA}{|\cos\gamma_k|} = \iint_R g(x, y, z)\frac{|\nabla f|}{|\nabla f \cdot \mathbf{p}|}\,dA \tag{8}$$

as the partition of R is refined in the usual way. This limit is the *integral of g over the surface S* and is calculated as a double integral over R. The value of the integral is the total charge on the surface S.

As you might expect, the formula in Equation (8) defines the integral of *any* function g over the surface S as long as the integral exists.

DEFINITION Integral of g over S and Surface Integral

If R is the shadow region of a surface S defined by the equation $f(x, y, z) = c$ and g is a continuous function defined at the points of S, then the **integral of g over S** is the integral

$$\iint_R g(x, y, z) \frac{|\nabla f|}{|\nabla f \cdot \mathbf{p}|} \, dA, \tag{9}$$

where $\mathbf{p}$ is a unit vector normal to R and $\nabla f \cdot \mathbf{p} \neq 0$. The integral itself is a **surface integral.**

The integral in Equation (9) takes on different meanings in different applications. If g has the constant value 1, the integral gives the area of S. If g gives the mass density of a thin shell of material modeled by S, the integral gives the mass of the shell.

Algebraic Properties; The Surface Area Differential

By writing $d\sigma$ for $(|\nabla f| / |\nabla f \cdot \mathbf{p}|) \, dA$, we can abbreviate the integral in Equation (9).

Surface Area Differential and Differential Form for Surface Integrals

$$d\sigma = \frac{|\nabla f|}{|\nabla f \cdot \mathbf{p}|} \, dA \qquad \iint_S g \, d\sigma \tag{10}$$

surface area differential — differential formula for surface integrals

Surface integrals behave like other double integrals, the integral of the sum of two functions being the sum of their integrals and so on. The domain additivity property takes the form

$$\iint_S g \, d\sigma = \iint_{S_1} g \, d\sigma + \iint_{S_2} d\sigma + \cdots + \iint_{S_n} g \, d\sigma.$$

The idea is that if S is partitioned by smooth curves into a finite number of nonoverlapping smooth patches (i.e., if S is **piecewise smooth**), then the integral over S is the sum of the integrals over the patches. Thus, the integral of a function over the surface of a cube is the sum of the integrals over the faces of the cube. We integrate over a turtle shell of welded plates by integrating one plate at a time and adding the results.

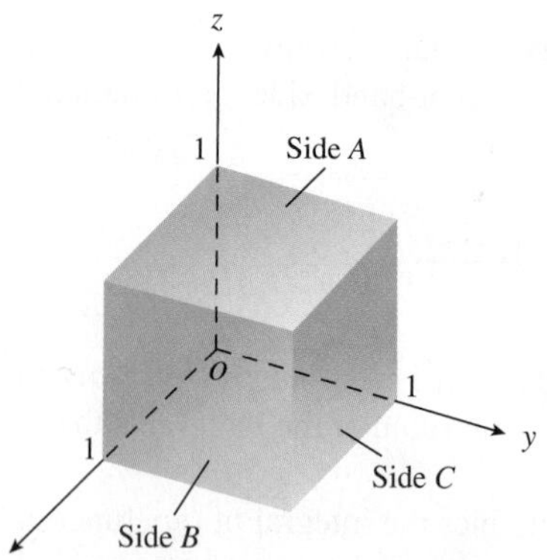

Figure 16.45 To integrate a function over the surface of a cube, we integrate over each face and add the results. (Example 3)

EXAMPLE 3 Integrating Over a Surface

Integrate $g(x, y, z) = xyz$ over the surface of the cube cut from the first octant by the planes $x = 1$, $y = 1$, and $z = 1$ (Figure 16.45).

SOLUTION

We integrate xyz over each of the six sides and add the results. Since $xyz = 0$ on the sides that lie in the coordinate planes, the integral over the surface of the cube reduces to

$$\iint_{\substack{\text{cube}\\\text{surface}}} xyz\, d\sigma = \iint_{\text{side } A} xyz\, d\sigma + \iint_{\text{side } B} xyz\, d\sigma + \iint_{\text{side } C} xyz\, d\sigma.$$

Side A is the surface $f(x, y, z) = z = 1$ over the square region R_{xy}: $0 \le x \le 1,\ 0 \le y \le 1$, in the xy-plane. For this surface and region,

$$\mathbf{p} = \mathbf{k}, \qquad \nabla f = \mathbf{k}, \qquad |\nabla f| = 1, \qquad |\nabla f \cdot \mathbf{p}| = |\mathbf{k} \cdot \mathbf{k}| = 1,$$

$$d\sigma = \frac{|\nabla f|}{|\nabla f \cdot \mathbf{p}|}\, dA = \frac{1}{1}\, dx\, dy = dx\, dy,$$

$$xyz = xy(1) = xy,$$

and

$$\iint_{\text{side } A} xyz\, d\sigma = \iint_{R_{xy}} xy\, dx\, dy = \int_0^1\!\int_0^1 xy\, dx\, dy = \int_0^1 \frac{y}{2}\, dy = \frac{1}{4}.$$

Symmetry tells us that the integrals of xyz over sides B and C are also 1/4. Hence,

$$\iint_{\substack{\text{cube}\\\text{surface}}} xyz\, d\sigma = \frac{1}{4} + \frac{1}{4} + \frac{1}{4} = \frac{3}{4}.$$

Orientation

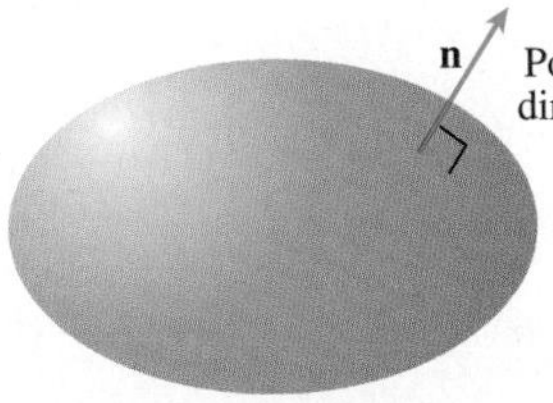

Figure 16.46 Smooth closed surfaces in space are orientable. The outward unit normal vector defines the positive direction at each point.

A smooth surface S is **orientable** or **two-sided** if it is possible to define a field $\mathbf{n}$ of unit normal vectors on S that varies continuously with position. Any patch or subportion of an orientable surface is orientable. Spheres and other smooth closed surfaces in space (smooth surfaces that enclose solids) are orientable. By convention, we choose $\mathbf{n}$ on a closed surface to point outward.

Once $\mathbf{n}$ has been chosen, we have **oriented** the surface, and the surface together with its normal field is an **oriented surface.** The vector $\mathbf{n}$ at any point is the **positive direction** at that point (Figure 16.46).

The Möbius band in Figure 16.47 is not orientable. No matter where you start to construct a continuous unit normal field (shown as the shaft of a thumbtack in the figure), moving the vector continuously around the surface in the manner shown will return it to the starting point with a direction opposite to the one it had when it started out. The vector at that point cannot point both ways and yet it must if the field is to be continuous. We conclude that no such field exists.

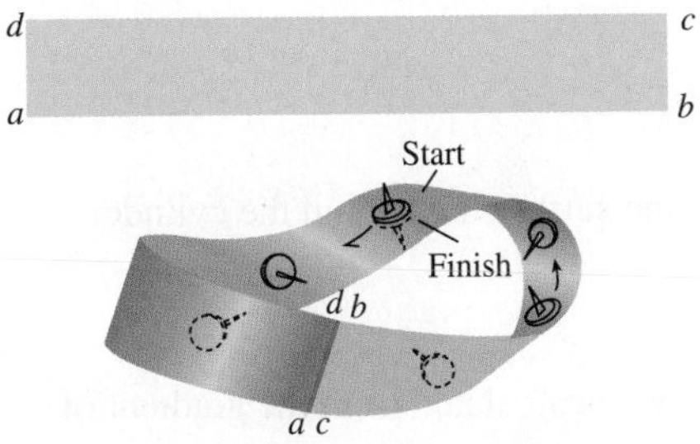

Figure 16.47 To make a Möbius band, take a rectangular strip of paper *abcd,* give the end *bc* a single twist, and paste the ends of the strip together to match *a* with *c* and *b* with *d.* The Möbius band is a nonorientable or one-sided surface.

Surface Integral for Flux

Suppose $\mathbf{F}$ is a continuous vector field defined over an oriented surface S and $\mathbf{n}$ is the chosen unit normal field on the surface. The integral of $\mathbf{F} \cdot \mathbf{n}$ over S is the *flux across S* in the positive direction. Thus, the flux is the integral over S of the scalar component of $\mathbf{F}$ in the direction of $\mathbf{n}$.

DEFINITION Flux

The **flux** of a three-dimensional vector field **F** across an oriented surface S in the direction of **n** is given by the formula

$$\text{Flux} = \iint_S \mathbf{F} \cdot \mathbf{n}\, d\sigma. \tag{11}$$

The definition is analogous to the flux of a two-dimensional field **F** across a plane curve C. In the plane (Section 16.2), the flux is

$$\int_C \mathbf{F} \cdot \mathbf{n}\, ds,$$

the integral of the scalar component of **F** normal to the curve.

If **F** is the velocity field of a three-dimensional fluid flow, then the flux of **F** across S is the net rate at which fluid is crossing S in the chosen positive direction. We discuss such flows in more detail in Section 16.7.

If S is part of a level surface $g(x, y, z) = c$, then **n** may be taken to be one of the two fields

$$\mathbf{n} = \pm \frac{\nabla g}{|\nabla g|}, \tag{12}$$

depending on which one gives the preferred direction. The corresponding flux is

$$\begin{aligned}
\text{Flux} &= \iint_S \mathbf{F} \cdot \mathbf{n}\, d\sigma && \text{Eq. (11)}\\
&= \iint_R \left(\mathbf{F} \cdot \frac{\pm\nabla g}{|\nabla g|}\right) \frac{|\nabla g|}{|\nabla g \cdot \mathbf{p}|}\, dA && \text{Eqs. (12) and (10)}\\
&= \iint_R \mathbf{F} \cdot \frac{\pm\nabla g}{|\nabla g \cdot \mathbf{p}|}\, dA && (13)
\end{aligned}$$

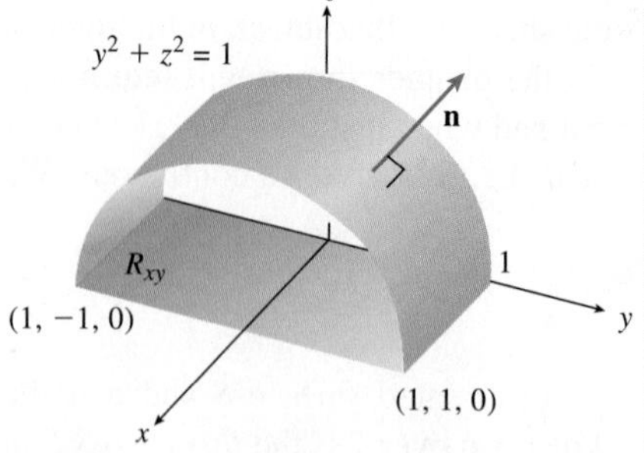

Figure 16.48 Example 4 calculates the flux of a vector field outward through this surface. The area of the shadow region R_{xy} is 2.

EXAMPLE 4 Finding Flux

Find the flux of $\mathbf{F} = yz\mathbf{j} + z^2\mathbf{k}$ outward through the surface S cut from the cylinder $y^2 + z^2 = 1$, $z \geq 0$, by the planes $x = 0$ and $x = 1$.

SOLUTION

The outward normal field on S (Figure 16.48) may be calculated from the gradient of $g(x, y, z) = y^2 + z^2$ to be

$$\mathbf{n} = +\frac{\nabla g}{|\nabla g|} = \frac{2y\mathbf{j} + 2z\mathbf{k}}{\sqrt{4y^2 + 4z^2}} = \frac{2y\mathbf{j} + 2z\mathbf{k}}{2} = y\mathbf{j} + z\mathbf{k}.$$

With $\mathbf{p} = \mathbf{k}$, we also have

$$d\sigma = \frac{|\nabla g|}{|\nabla g \cdot \mathbf{k}|}\, dA = \frac{2}{|2z|}\, dA = \frac{1}{z}\, dA. \qquad |z| = z \text{ because } z \geq 0 \text{ on } S$$

The value of $\mathbf{F} \cdot \mathbf{n}$ on the surface is given by the formula

$$\begin{aligned}\mathbf{F} \cdot \mathbf{n} &= (yz\mathbf{j} + z^2\mathbf{k}) \cdot (y\mathbf{j} + z\mathbf{k}) \\ &= y^2z + z^3 = z(y^2 + z^2) \\ &= z \qquad y^2 + z^2 = 1 \text{ on } S\end{aligned}$$

Therefore, the flux of $\mathbf{F}$ outward through S is

$$\iint_S \mathbf{F} \cdot \mathbf{n}\, d\sigma = \iint_S (z)\left(\frac{1}{z}\, dA\right) = \iint_{R_{xy}} dA = \text{area}\,(R_{xy}) = 2.$$

Moments and Masses of Thin Shells

Thin shells of material like bowls, metal drums, and domes are modeled with surfaces. Their moments and masses are calculated with the formulas in Table 16.3.

Table 16.3 Mass and Moment Formulas for Very Thin Shells

Mass: $M = \iint_S \delta(x, y, z)\, d\sigma \qquad (\delta(x, y, z) = \text{density at } (x, y, z), \text{ mass per unit area})$

First moments about the coordinate planes:

$$M_{yz} = \iint_S x\delta\, d\sigma, \qquad M_{xz} = \iint_S y\delta\, d\sigma, \qquad M_{xy} = \iint_S z\delta\, d\sigma$$

Coordinates of center of mass:

$\bar{x} = M_{yz}/M, \qquad \bar{y} = M_{xz}/M, \qquad \bar{z} = M_{xy}/M$

Moments of inertia:

$$I_x = \iint_S (y^2 + z^2)\,\delta\, d\sigma, \qquad I_y = \iint_S (x^2 + z^2)\,\delta\, d\sigma,$$

$$I_z = \iint_S (x^2 + y^2)\,\delta\, d\sigma, \qquad I_L = \iint_S r^2\,\delta\, d\sigma,$$

$r(x, y, z) = $ distance from point (x, y, z) to line L

Radius of gyration about a line L: $R_L = \sqrt{I_L/M}$

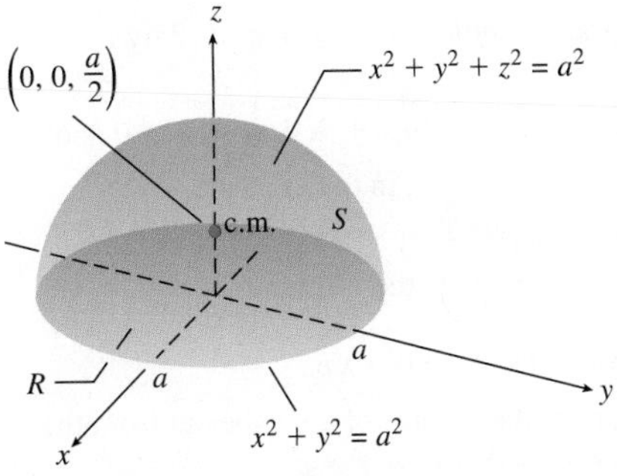

Figure 16.49 The center of mass of a thin hemispherical shell of constant density lies on the axis of symmetry halfway from the base to the top. (Example 5)

EXAMPLE 5 Finding Center of Mass

Find the center of mass of a thin hemispherical shell of radius a and constant density δ.

SOLUTION

We model the shell with the hemisphere

$$f(x, y, z) = x^2 + y^2 + z^2 = a^2, \qquad z \geq 0$$

(Figure 16.49). The symmetry of the surface about the z-axis tells us that $\bar{x} = \bar{y} = 0$. It remains only to find $\bar{z}$ from the formula $\bar{z} = M_{xy}/M$.

The mass of the shell is

$$M = \iint_S \delta\, d\sigma = \delta \iint_S d\sigma = (\delta)(\text{area of } S) = 2\pi a^2 \delta.$$

To evaluate the integral for M_{xy}, we take $\mathbf{p} = \mathbf{k}$ and calculate

$$|\nabla f| = |2x\mathbf{i} + 2y\mathbf{j} + 2z\mathbf{k}| = 2\sqrt{x^2 + y^2 + z^2} = 2a,$$

$$|\nabla f \cdot \mathbf{p}| = |\nabla f \cdot \mathbf{k}| = |2z| = 2z,$$

$$d\sigma = \frac{|\nabla f|}{|\nabla f \cdot \mathbf{p}|}\, dA = \frac{a}{z}\, dA.$$

Then

$$M_{xy} = \iint_S z\delta\, d\sigma = \delta \iint_R z\frac{a}{z}\, dA = \delta a \iint_R dA = \delta a\,(\pi a^2) = \delta\pi a^3,$$

$$\bar{z} = \frac{M_{xy}}{M} = \frac{\pi a^3 \delta}{2\pi a^2 \delta} = \frac{a}{2},$$

The shell's center of mass is the point $(0, 0, a/2)$.

Quick Review 16.5

In Exercises 1–5, let $z = f(x, y) = \sqrt{4 - x^2 - y^2}$ and P_0 be the point $(1, 1, \sqrt{2})$.

1. Evaluate f_x at P_0.
2. Evaluate f_y at P_0.
3. Find a vector perpendicular to the surface $z = f(x, y)$ at P_0.
4. Find an equation for the plane tangent to the surface $z = f(x, y)$ at P_0.
5. Find an equation for the normal line to the surface $z = f(x, y)$ at P_0.

In Exercises 6–10, evaluate the integral.

6. $\displaystyle\int_0^{2\pi}\int_0^2 \sqrt{4r^2 + 1}\, r\, dr\, d\theta$
7. $\displaystyle\int_0^{2\pi}\int_0^1 \frac{r\, dr\, d\theta}{\sqrt{2 - r^2}}$
8. $\displaystyle\int_0^2\int_0^{\sqrt{4-x^2}} dy\, dx$
9. $\displaystyle\int_0^2\int_0^2 e^{x+y}\, dy\, dx$
10. $\displaystyle\int_0^2\int_0^{y/2} y\sin(xy)\, dx\, dy$

Section 16.5 Exercises

In Exercises 1–12, find the area of the surface.

1. The surface cut from the paraboloid $x^2 + y^2 - z = 0$ by the plane $z = 2$
2. The band cut from the paraboloid $x^2 + y^2 - z = 0$ by the planes $z = 2$ and $z = 6$
3. The region cut from the plane $x + 2y + 2z = 5$ by the cylinder whose walls are $x = y^2$ and $x = 2 - y^2$
4. The portion of the surface $x^2 - 2z = 0$ that lies above the triangle bounded by the lines $x = \sqrt{3}$, $y = 0$, and $y = x$ in the xy-plane
5. The portion of the surface $x^2 - 2y - 2x = 0$ that lies above the triangle bounded by the lines $x = 2$, $y = 0$, and $y = 3x$ in the xy-plane
6. The cap cut from the sphere $x^2 + y^2 + z^2 = 2$ by the cone $z = \sqrt{x^2 + y^2}$
7. The ellipse cut from the plane $z = cx$ by the cylinder $x^2 + y^2 = 1$
8. The upper portion of the cylinder $x^2 + y^2 = 1$ that lies between the planes $x = \pm 1/2$ and $y = \pm 1/2$
9. The portion of the paraboloid $x = 4 - y^2 - z^2$ that lies above the ring $1 \le y^2 + z^2 \le 4$ in the yz-plane
10. The surface cut from the paraboloid $x^2 + y + z^2 = 2$ by the plane $y = 0$
11. The portion of the surface $x^2 - 2\ln x + \sqrt{15}y - z = 0$ above the square R: $1 \le x \le 2$, $0 \le y \le 1$, in the xy-plane
12. The portion of the surface $2x^{3/2} + 2y^{3/2} - 3z = 0$ above the square R: $0 \le x \le 1$, $0 \le y \le 1$, in the xy-plane

In Exercises 13–18, integrate g over the surface.

13. $g(x, y, z) = x + y + z$ over the surface of the cube cut from the first octant by the planes $x = a$, $y = a$, $z = a$
14. $g(x, y, z) = y + z$ over the surface of the wedge in the first octant bounded by the coordinate planes and the planes $x = 2$ and $y + z = 1$
15. $g(x, y, z) = xyz$ over the surface of the rectangular solid cut from the first octant by the planes $x = a$, $y = b$, and $z = c$

16. $g(x, y, z) = xyz$ over the surface of the rectangular solid bounded by the planes $x = \pm a$, $y = \pm b$, and $z = \pm c$

17. $g(x, y, z) = x + y + z$ over the portion of the plane $2x + 2y + z = 2$ that lies in the first octant.

18. $g(x, y, z) = x\sqrt{y^2 + 4}$ over the surface cut from the parabolic cylinder $y^2 + 4z = 16$ by the planes $x = 0$, $x = 1$, and $z = 0$

In Exercises 19 and 20, find the flux of the field **F** across the portion of the given surface in the specified direction.

19. $\mathbf{F}(x, y, z) = -\mathbf{i} + 2\mathbf{j} + 3\mathbf{k}$

S: rectangular surface $z = 0$, $\quad 0 \le x \le 2$, $\quad 0 \le y \le 3$, direction **k**

20. $\mathbf{F}(x, y, z) = yx^2\mathbf{i} - 2\mathbf{j} + xz\mathbf{k}$

S: rectangular surface $y = 0$, $\quad -1 \le x \le 2$, $\quad 2 \le z \le 7$, direction $-\mathbf{j}$

In Exercises 21–26, find the flux of the field **F** across the portion of the sphere $x^2 + y^2 + z^2 = a^2$ in the first octant in the direction away from the origin.

21. $\mathbf{F}(x, y, z) = z\mathbf{k}$

22. $\mathbf{F}(x, y, z) = -y\mathbf{i} + x\mathbf{j}$

23. $\mathbf{F}(x, y, z) = y\mathbf{i} - x\mathbf{j} + \mathbf{k}$

24. $\mathbf{F}(x, y, z) = zx\mathbf{i} + zy\mathbf{j} + z^2\mathbf{k}$

25. $\mathbf{F}(x, y, z) = x\mathbf{i} + y\mathbf{j} + z\mathbf{k}$

26. $\mathbf{F}(x, y, z) = \dfrac{x\mathbf{i} + y\mathbf{j} + z\mathbf{k}}{\sqrt{x^2 + y^2 + z^2}}$

27. ***Flux*** Find the flux of the field $\mathbf{F}(x, y, z) = z^2\mathbf{i} + x\mathbf{j} - 3z\mathbf{k}$ upward through the surface cut from the parabolic cylinder $z = 4 - y^2$ by the planes $x = 0$, $x = 1$, and $z = 0$.

28. ***Flux*** Find the flux of the field $\mathbf{F}(x, y, z) = 4x\mathbf{i} + 4y\mathbf{j} + 2\mathbf{k}$ outward (away from the z-axis) through the surface cut from the bottom of the paraboloid $z = x^2 + y^2$ by the plane $z = 1$.

29. ***Flux*** Let S be the portion of the cylinder $y = e^x$ in the first octant that projects parallel to the x-axis onto the rectangle R_{yz}: $1 \le y \le 2$, $0 \le z \le 1$ in the yz-plane (Figure 16.50). Let **n** be the unit vector normal to S that points away from the yz-plane. Find the flux of the field $\mathbf{F}(x, y, z) = -2\mathbf{i} + 2y\mathbf{j} + z\mathbf{k}$ across S in the direction of **n**.

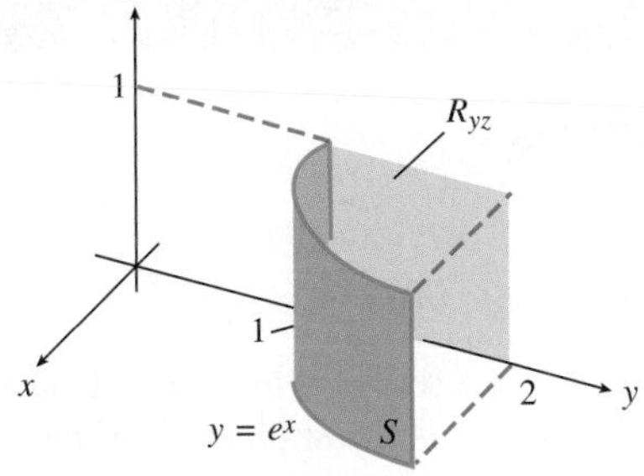

Figure 16.50 The surface and region in Exercise 29.

30. ***Flux*** Let S be the portion of the cylinder $y = \ln x$ in the first octant whose projection parallel to the y-axis onto the xz-plane is the rectangle R_{xz}: $1 \le x \le e$, $0 \le z \le 1$. Let **n** be the unit vector normal to S that points away from the xz-plane. Find the flux of $\mathbf{F} = 2y\mathbf{j} + z\mathbf{k}$ through S in the direction of **n**.

31. ***Flux*** Find the outward flux of the field $\mathbf{F} = 2xy\mathbf{i} + 2yz\mathbf{j} + 2xz\mathbf{k}$ across the surface of the cube cut from the first octant by the planes $x = a$, $y = a$, $z = a$.

32. ***Flux*** Find the outward flux of the field $\mathbf{F} = xz\mathbf{i} + yz\mathbf{j} + \mathbf{k}$ across the surface of the upper cap cut from the solid sphere $x^2 + y^2 + z^2 \le 25$ by the plane $z = 3$.

In Exercises 33–36, *work in groups of two or three* to solve the problem.

33. ***Centroid*** Find the centroid of the portion of the sphere $x^2 + y^2 + z^2 = a^2$ that lies in the first octant.

34. ***Centroid*** Find the centroid of the surface cut from the cylinder $y^2 + z^2 = 9$, $z \ge 0$, by the planes $x = 0$ and $x = 3$ (resembles the surface in Example 4).

35. ***Thin Shell of Constant Density*** Find the center of mass and the moment of inertia and radius of gyration about the z-axis of a thin shell of constant density δ cut from the cone $x^2 + y^2 - z^2 = 0$ by the planes $z = 1$ and $z = 2$.

36. ***Conical Surface of Constant Density*** Find the moment of inertia about the z-axis of a thin shell of constant density δ cut from the cone $4x^2 + 4y^2 - z^2 = 0$, $z \ge 0$, by the circular cylinder $x^2 + y^2 = 2x$ (Figure 16.51).

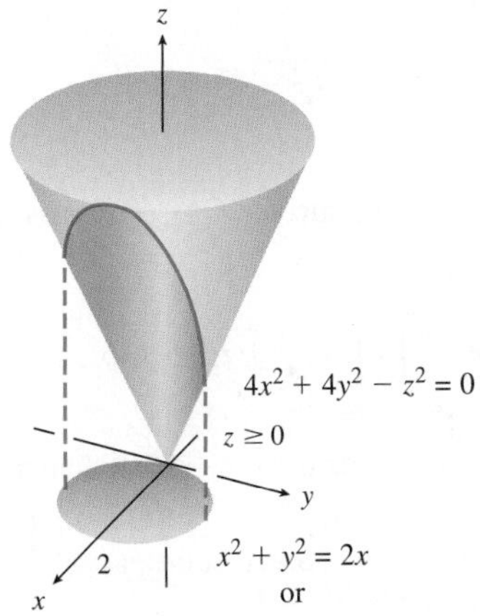

Figure 16.51 The surface in Exercises 36.

Explorations

37. ***Spherical Shells***

(a) Find the moment of inertia about a diameter of a thin spherical shell of radius a and constant density δ. (Work with a hemispherical shell and double the result.)

(b) Use the Parallel Axis Theorem (Exercises 14.5) and the result in (a) to find the moment of inertia about a line tangent to the shell.

38. ***Cones with and without Ice Cream***

(a) Find the centroid of the lateral surface of a solid cone of base radius a and height h (cone surface minus the base).

(b) Use Pappus's formula (Exercises 14.5) and the result in (a) to find the centroid of the complete surface of a solid cone (side plus base).

(c) Writing to Learn A cone of radius a and height h is joined to a hemisphere of radius a to make a surface S that resembles an ice cream cone. Use Pappus's formula and the results in (a) and Example 5 to find the centroid of S. How high does the cone have to be to place the centroid in the plane shared by the bases of the hemisphere and cone?

Extending the Ideas

Specialized Formulas for Surface Area If S is the surface defined by a function $z = f(x, y)$ that has continuous first partial derivatives throughout a region R_{xy} in the xy-plane (Figure 16.52), then S is also the level surface $F(x, y, z) = 0$ of the function $F(x, y, z) = f(x, y) - z$. Taking the unit normal to R_{xy} to be $\mathbf{p} = \mathbf{k}$ then gives

$$|\nabla f| = |f_x\mathbf{i} + f_y\mathbf{j} - \mathbf{k}| = \sqrt{f_x^2 + f_y^2 + 1},$$
$$|\nabla f \cdot \mathbf{p}| = |(f_x\mathbf{i} + f_y\mathbf{j} - \mathbf{k}) \cdot \mathbf{k}| = |-1| = 1,$$

and

$$A = \iint_{R_{xy}} \frac{|\nabla f|}{|\nabla f \cdot \mathbf{p}|}\,dA = \iint_{R_{xy}} \sqrt{f_x^2 + f_y^2 + 1}\,dx\,dy. \qquad (14)$$

Similarly, the area of a smooth surface $x = f(y, z)$ over a region R_{yz} in the yz-plane is

$$A = \iint_{R_{yz}} \sqrt{f_y^2 + f_z^2 + 1}\,dy\,dz, \qquad (15)$$

and the area of a smooth surface $y = f(x, z)$ over a region R_{xz} in the xz-plane is

$$A = \iint_{R_{xz}} \sqrt{f_x^2 + f_z^2 + 1}\,dx\,dz. \qquad (16)$$

In Exercises 39–44, use Equations (14)–(16) to find the areas of the surfaces.

39. The surface cut from the bottom of the paraboloid $z = x^2 + y^2$ by the plane $z = 3$

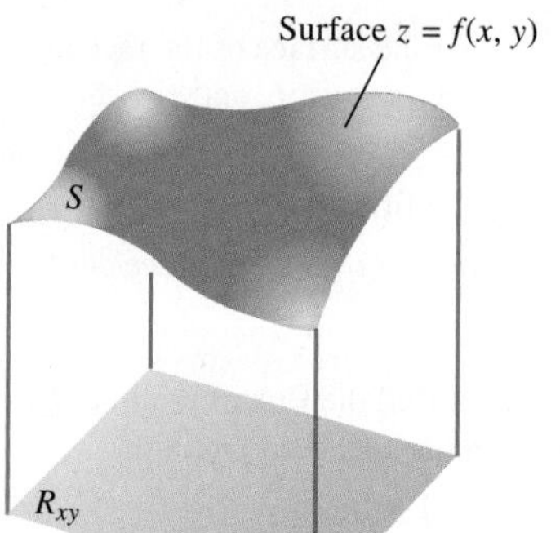

Figure 16.52 For a surface $z = f(x, y)$, the surface area formula in Equation (5) takes the form

$$A = \iint_{R_{xy}} \sqrt{f_x^2 + f_y^2 + 1}\,dx\,dy.$$

40. The surface cut from the "nose" of the paraboloid $x = 1 - y^2 - z^2$ by the yz-plane

41. The portion of the cone $z = \sqrt{x^2 + y^2}$ that lies over the region between the circle $x^2 + y^2 = 1$ and the ellipse $9x^2 + 4y^2 = 36$ in the xy-plane. (*Hint:* Use formulas from geometry to find the area of the region.)

42. The triangle cut from the plane $2x + 6y + 3z = 6$ by the bounding planes of the first octant. Calculate the area three ways, once with each formula.

43. The surface in the first octant cut from the cylinder $y = (2/3)z^{3/2}$ by the planes $x = 1$ and $y = 16/3$

44. The portion of the plane $y + z = 4$ that lies above the region cut from the first quadrant of the xz-plane by the parabola $x = 4 - z^2$

16.6 Parametrized Surfaces

What you'll learn about

- Parametrizations of Surfaces
- Surface Area
- Surface Integrals

Parametrizations of Surfaces

Let

$$\mathbf{r}(u, v) = f(u, v)\mathbf{i} + g(u, v)\mathbf{j} + h(u, v)\mathbf{k} \qquad (1)$$

be a continuous vector function that is defined on a region R in the uv-plane and one-to-one on the interior of R (Figure 16.53). The range of $\mathbf{r}$ is the **surface** S defined or traced by $\mathbf{r}$. Equation (1) and the domain R together constitute a **parametrization** of the surface. The variables u and v are the **parameters,** and R is the **parameter domain.** To simplify our discussion, we will take R to be a rectangle defined by inequalities of the form $a \le u \le b$, $c \le v \le d$. The requirement that $\mathbf{r}$ be one-to-one on the interior of R ensures that S does not cross itself. Notice that Equation (1) is the vector equivalent of *three* parametric equations:

$$x = f(u, v), \qquad y = g(u, v), \qquad z = h(u, v).$$

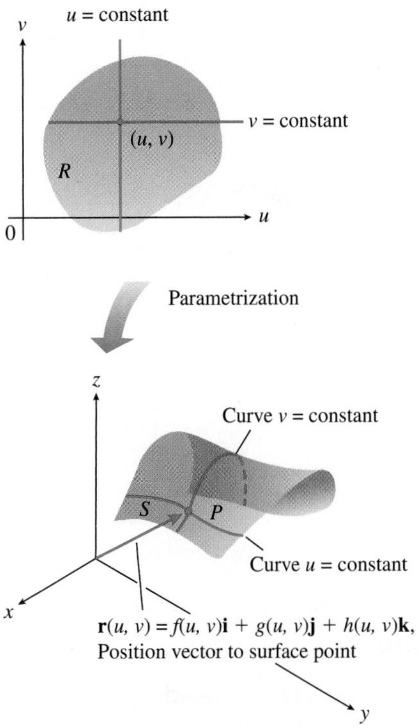

Figure 16.53 A parametrized surface.

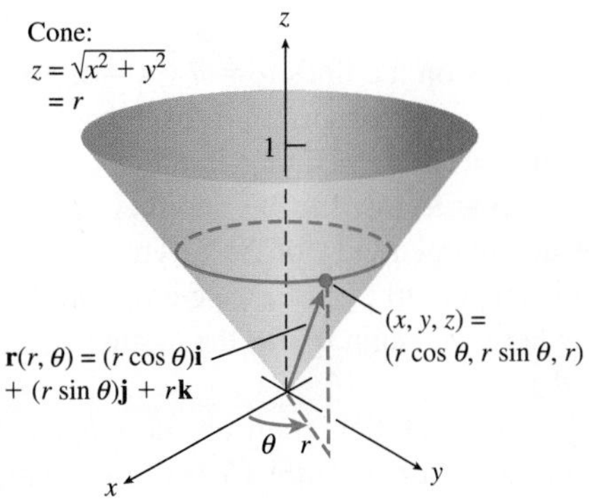

Figure 16.54 The cone in Example 1.

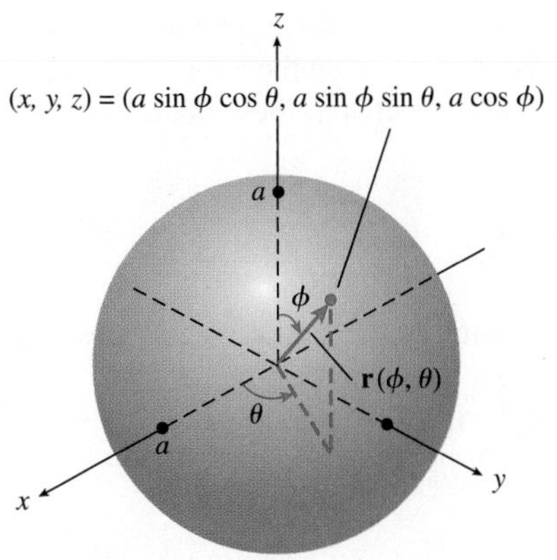

Figure 16.55 The sphere in Example 2.

EXAMPLE 1 Parametrizing a Cone

Find a parametrization of the cone $z = \sqrt{x^2 + y^2}$, $0 \le z \le 1$.

SOLUTION

Here, cylindrical coordinates provide everything we need. A typical point (x, y, z) on the cone (Figure 16.54) has $x = r\cos\theta$, $y = r\sin\theta$, and $z = \sqrt{x^2 + y^2} = r$, with $0 \le r \le 1$ and $0 \le \theta \le 2\pi$. Taking $u = r$ and $v = \theta$ in Equation (1) gives the parametrization

$$\mathbf{r}(r, \theta) = (r\cos\theta)\mathbf{i} + (r\sin\theta)\mathbf{j} + r\mathbf{k}, \qquad 0 \le r \le 1, \qquad 0 \le \theta \le 2\pi.$$

EXAMPLE 2 Parametrizing a Sphere

Find a parametrization of the sphere $x^2 + y^2 + z^2 = a^2$.

SOLUTION

Spherical coordinates provide what we need. A typical point (x, y, z) on the sphere (Figure 16.55) has $x = a\sin\phi\cos\theta$, $y = a\sin\phi\sin\theta$, and $z = a\cos\phi$, $0 \le \phi \le \pi$, $0 \le \theta \le 2\pi$. Taking $u = \phi$ and $v = \theta$ in Equation (1) gives the parametrization

$$\mathbf{r}(\phi, \theta) = (a\sin\phi\cos\theta)\mathbf{i} + (a\sin\phi\sin\theta)\mathbf{j} + (a\cos\phi)\mathbf{k}, \qquad 0 \le \phi \le \pi, \qquad 0 \le \theta \le 2\pi.$$

EXAMPLE 3 Parametrizing a Cylinder

Find a parametrization of the cylinder $x^2 + (y - 3)^2 = 9$, $0 \le z \le 5$.

SOLUTION

In cylindrical coordinates, a point (x, y, z) has $x = r\cos\theta$, $y = r\sin\theta$, and $z = z$. For points on the cylinder $x^2 + (y - 3)^2 = 9$ (Figure 16.56), $r = 6\sin\theta$, $0 \le \theta \le \pi$. A typical point on the cylinder therefore has

$$x = r\cos\theta = 6\sin\theta\cos\theta = 3\sin 2\theta,$$

$$y = r\sin\theta = 6\sin^2\theta,$$

$$z = z.$$

Taking $u = \theta$ and $v = z$ in Equation (1) gives the parametrization

$$\mathbf{r}(\theta, z) = (3\sin 2\theta)\mathbf{i} + (6\sin^2\theta)\mathbf{j} + z\mathbf{k}, \qquad 0 \le \theta \le \pi, \qquad 0 \le z \le 5.$$

Surface Area

Our goal is to find a double integral for calculating the area of a curved surface S based on the parametrization

$$\mathbf{r}(u, v) = f(u, v)\mathbf{i} + g(u, v)\mathbf{j} + h(u, v)\mathbf{k}, \qquad a \le u \le b, \qquad c \le v \le d.$$

We need to assume that S is smooth enough for the construction we are about to carry out. The definition of smoothness involves the partial derivatives of $\mathbf{r}$ with respect to u and v:

$$\mathbf{r}_u = \frac{\partial \mathbf{r}}{\partial u} = \frac{\partial f}{\partial u}\mathbf{i} + \frac{\partial g}{\partial u}\mathbf{j} + \frac{\partial h}{\partial u}\mathbf{k},$$

$$\mathbf{r}_v = \frac{\partial \mathbf{r}}{\partial v} = \frac{\partial f}{\partial v}\mathbf{i} + \frac{\partial g}{\partial v}\mathbf{j} + \frac{\partial h}{\partial v}\mathbf{k}.$$

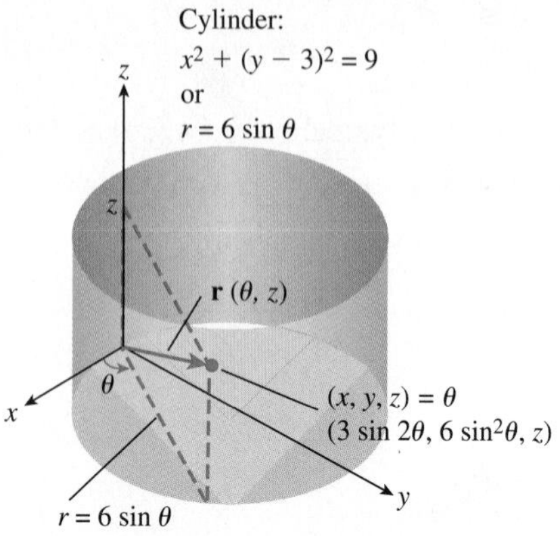

Figure 16.56 The cylinder in Example 3.

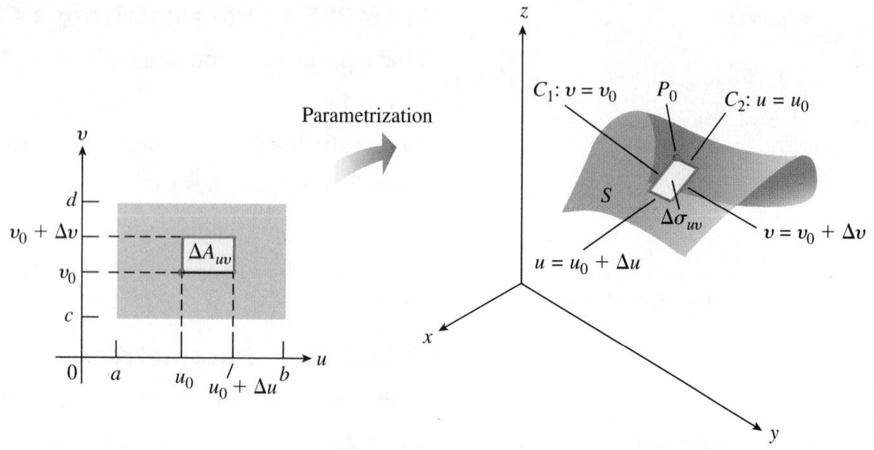

Figure 16.57 A rectangular area element ΔA_{uv} in the uv-plane maps onto a curved area element $\Delta\sigma_{uv}$ on S.

> **DEFINITION Smooth Parametrized Surface**
>
> A parametrized surface $\mathbf{r}(u, v) = f(u, v)\mathbf{i} + g(u, v)\mathbf{j} + h(u, v)\mathbf{k}$ is **smooth** if $\mathbf{r}_u$ and $\mathbf{r}_v$ are continuous and $\mathbf{r}_u \times \mathbf{r}_v$ is never zero on the parameter domain.

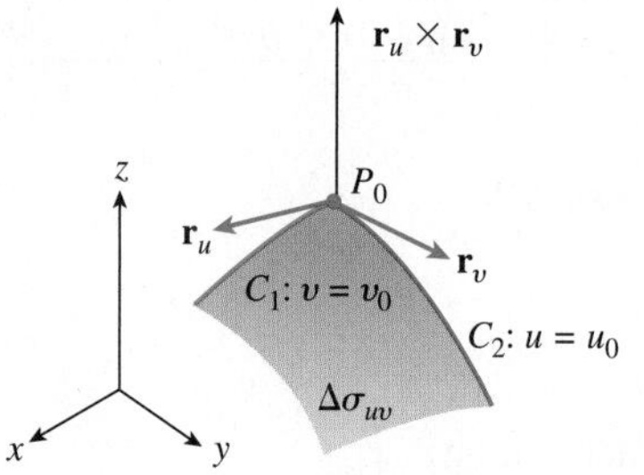

Figure 16.58 A magnified view of a surface area element $\Delta\sigma_{uv}$.

Now consider a small rectangle in ΔA_{uv} in R with sides on the lines $u = u_0$, $u = u_0 + \Delta u$, $v = v_0$, and $v = v_0 + \Delta v$ (Figure 16.57). Each side of ΔA_{uv} maps to a curve on the surface S, and together these four curves bound a "curved area element" $\Delta\sigma_{uv}$. In the notation of the figure, the side $v = v_0$ maps to curve C_1, the side $u = u_0$ maps to C_2, and their common vertex (u_0, v_0) maps to P_0. Figure 16.58 shows an enlarged view of $\Delta\sigma_{uv}$. The vector $\mathbf{r}_u(u_0, v_0)$ is tangent to C_1 at P_0. Likewise, $\mathbf{r}_v(u_0, v_0)$ is tangent to C_2 at P_0. The cross product $\mathbf{r}_u \times \mathbf{r}_v$ is normal to the surface at P_0. (Here is where we begin to use the assumption that S is smooth. We want to be sure that $\mathbf{r}_u \times \mathbf{r}_v \neq \mathbf{0}$.)

We next approximate the surface element $\Delta\sigma_{uv}$ by the parallelogram on the tangent plane whose sides are determined by the vectors $\Delta u\mathbf{r}_u$ and $\Delta v\mathbf{r}_v$ (Figure 16.59). The area of the parallelogram is

$$|\Delta u\mathbf{r}_u \times \Delta v\mathbf{r}_v| = |\mathbf{r}_u \times \mathbf{r}_v|\,\Delta u\,\Delta v. \tag{2}$$

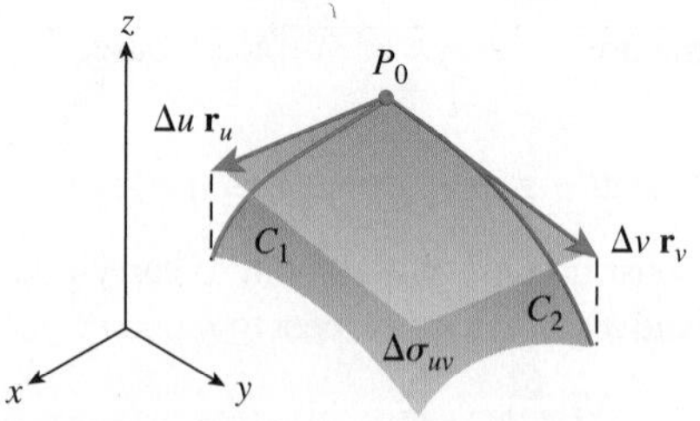

Figure 16.59 The parallelogram determined by the vectors $\Delta u\mathbf{r}_u$ and $\Delta v\mathbf{r}_v$ approximates the surface area element $\Delta\sigma_{uv}$.

A partition of the region R in the uv-plane by rectangular regions ΔA_{uv} generates a partition of the surface S into surface area elements $\Delta\sigma_{uv}$. We approximate the area of each surface element $\Delta\sigma_{uv}$ by the parallelogram area in Equation (2) and sum these areas together to obtain an approximation of the area of S:

$$\sum_u \sum_v |\mathbf{r}_u \times \mathbf{r}_v|\,\Delta u\,\Delta v. \tag{3}$$

As Δu and Δv approach zero independently, the continuity of $\mathbf{r}_u$ and $\mathbf{r}_v$ guarantees that the sum in Equation (3) approaches the double integral $\int_c^d \int_a^b |\mathbf{r}_u \times \mathbf{r}_v|\,du\,dv$. This double integral gives the area of the surface S.

Parametric Formula for Surface Area

The area of the smooth surface

$$\mathbf{r}(u, v) = f(u, v)\mathbf{i} + g(u, v)\mathbf{j} + h(u, v)\mathbf{k}, \qquad a \le u \le b, \qquad c \le v \le d$$

is

$$A = \int_c^d \int_a^b |\mathbf{r}_u \times \mathbf{r}_v| \, du \, dv. \tag{4}$$

As in Section 16.5, we can abbreviate the integral in Equation (4) by writing $d\sigma$ for $|\mathbf{r}_u \times \mathbf{r}_v| \, du \, dv$.

Surface Area Differential and Differential Formula for Surface Area

$$d\sigma = |\mathbf{r}_u \times \mathbf{r}_v| \, du \, dv \qquad \iint_S d\sigma \tag{5}$$

surface are differential — differential formula for surface area

EXAMPLE 4 Finding Surface Area (Cone)

Find the surface area of the cone in Example 1 (Figure 16.54).

SOLUTION

In Example 1, we found the parametrization

$$\mathbf{r}(r, \theta) = (r\cos\theta)\mathbf{i} + (r\sin\theta)\mathbf{j} + r\mathbf{k}, \qquad 0 \le r \le 1, \qquad 0 \le \theta \le 2\pi.$$

To apply Equation (4) we first find $\mathbf{r}_r \times \mathbf{r}_\theta$:

$$\mathbf{r}_r \times \mathbf{r}_\theta = \begin{vmatrix} \mathbf{i} & \mathbf{j} & \mathbf{k} \\ \cos\theta & \sin\theta & 1 \\ -r\sin\theta & r\cos\theta & 0 \end{vmatrix}$$

$$= -(r\cos\theta)\mathbf{i} - (r\sin\theta)\mathbf{j} + \underbrace{(r\cos^2\theta + r\sin^2\theta)}_{r}\mathbf{k}.$$

Thus, $|\mathbf{r}_r \times \mathbf{r}_\theta| = \sqrt{r^2\cos^2\theta + r^2\sin^2\theta + r^2} = \sqrt{2r^2} = \sqrt{2}\,r$. The area of the cone is

$$A = \int_0^{2\pi}\int_0^1 |\mathbf{r}_r \times \mathbf{r}_\theta| \, dr \, d\theta \qquad \text{Eq. (4) with } u = r,\ v = \theta$$

$$= \int_0^{2\pi}\int_0^1 \sqrt{2}\,r \, dr \, d\theta = \int_0^{2\pi} \frac{\sqrt{2}}{2} \, d\theta = \pi\sqrt{2} \text{ units squared.}$$

EXAMPLE 5 Finding Surface Area (Sphere)

Find the surface area of a sphere of radius a.

SOLUTION

We use the parametrization from Example 2:

$$\mathbf{r}(\phi, \theta) = (a \sin \phi \cos \theta)\mathbf{i} + (a \sin \phi \sin \theta)\mathbf{j} + (a \cos \phi)\mathbf{k},$$
$$0 \le \phi \le \pi, \qquad 0 \le \theta \le 2\pi.$$

For $\mathbf{r}_\phi \times \mathbf{r}_\theta$ we get

$$\mathbf{r}_\phi \times \mathbf{r}_\theta = \begin{vmatrix} \mathbf{i} & \mathbf{j} & \mathbf{k} \\ a \cos \phi \cos \theta & a \cos \phi \sin \theta & -a \sin \phi \\ -a \sin \phi \sin \theta & a \sin \phi \cos \theta & 0 \end{vmatrix}$$
$$= (a^2 \sin^2 \phi \cos \theta)\mathbf{i} + (a^2 \sin^2 \phi \sin \theta)\mathbf{j} + (a^2 \sin \phi \cos \phi)\mathbf{k}.$$

Thus,

$$\begin{aligned} |\mathbf{r}_\phi \times \mathbf{r}_\theta| &= \sqrt{a^4 \sin^4 \phi \cos^2 \theta + a^4 \sin^4 \phi \sin^2 \theta + a^4 \sin^2 \phi \cos^2 \phi} \\ &= \sqrt{a^4 \sin^4 \phi + a^4 \sin^2 \phi \cos^2 \phi} \\ &= \sqrt{a^4 \sin^2 \phi (\sin^2 \phi + \cos^2 \phi)} \\ &= a^2 \sqrt{\sin^2 \phi} = a^2 \sin \phi \end{aligned}$$

since $\sin \phi \ge 0$ for $0 \le \phi \le \pi$. Therefore, the area of the sphere is

$$\begin{aligned} A &= \int_0^{2\pi} \int_0^{\pi} a^2 \sin \phi \, d\phi \, d\theta \\ &= \int_0^{2\pi} [-a^2 \cos \phi]_0^{\pi} \, d\theta = \int_0^{2\pi} 2a^2 \, d\theta = 4\pi a^2 \text{ units squared.} \end{aligned}$$

Surface Integrals

Having found the formula for calculating the area of a parametrized surface, we can now integrate a function over the surface using the parametrized form.

DEFINITION Integral of $G(x, y, z)$ over S

If S is a smooth surface defined parametrically as

$$\mathbf{r}(u, v) = f(u, v)\mathbf{i} + g(u, v)\mathbf{j} + h(u, v)\mathbf{k}, \qquad a \le u \le b, \qquad c \le v \le d,$$

and $G(x, y, z)$ is a continuous function defined on S, then the **integral of G over S** is

$$\iint_S G(x, y, z) \, d\sigma = \int_c^d \int_a^b G(f(u, v), g(u, v), h(u, v)) \, |\mathbf{r}_u \times \mathbf{r}_v| \, du \, dv.$$

EXAMPLE 6 Integrating Over a Surface Parametrically

Integrate $G(x, y, z) = x^2$ over the cone $z = \sqrt{x^2 + y^2}, 0 \le z \le 1$.

SOLUTION

Continuing the work in Examples 1 and 4, we have $|\mathbf{r}_r \times \mathbf{r}_\theta| = \sqrt{2}\, r$ and

$$\iint_S x^2\, d\sigma = \int_0^{2\pi}\int_0^1 (r^2 \cos^2\theta)(\sqrt{2}\, r)\, dr\, d\theta$$

$$= \sqrt{2}\int_0^{2\pi}\int_0^1 r^3 \cos^2\theta\, dr\, d\theta$$

$$= \frac{\sqrt{2}}{4}\int_0^{2\pi} \cos^2\theta\, d\theta = \frac{\sqrt{2}}{4}\left[\frac{\theta}{2} + \frac{1}{4}\sin 2\theta\right]_0^{2\pi} = \frac{\pi\sqrt{2}}{4}.$$

EXAMPLE 7 Finding Flux

Find the flux of $\mathbf{F} = yz\mathbf{i} + x\mathbf{j} - z^2\mathbf{k}$ outward through the parabolic cylinder $y = x^2$, $0 \le x \le 1, 0 \le z \le 4$ (Figure 16.60).

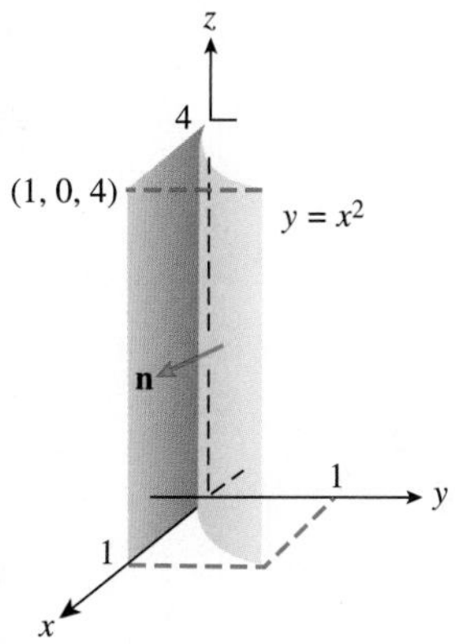

Figure 16.60 The parabolic surface in Example 7.

SOLUTION

On the surface we have $x = x$, $y = x^2$, and $z = z$, so we automatically have the parametrization $\mathbf{r}(x, z) = x\mathbf{i} + x^2\mathbf{j} + z\mathbf{k}$, $0 \le x \le 1, 0 \le z \le 4$. The cross product of tangent vectors is

$$\mathbf{r}_x \times \mathbf{r}_z = \begin{vmatrix} \mathbf{i} & \mathbf{j} & \mathbf{k} \\ 1 & 2x & 0 \\ 0 & 0 & 1 \end{vmatrix} = 2x\mathbf{i} - \mathbf{j}.$$

The unit normal pointing outward from the surface is

$$\mathbf{n} = \frac{\mathbf{r}_x \times \mathbf{r}_z}{|\mathbf{r}_x \times \mathbf{r}_z|} = \frac{2x\mathbf{i} - \mathbf{j}}{\sqrt{4x^2 + 1}}.$$

On the surface, $y = x^2$, so the vector field is

$$\mathbf{F} = yz\mathbf{i} + x\mathbf{j} - z^2\mathbf{k} = x^2 z\mathbf{i} + x\mathbf{j} - z^2\mathbf{k}.$$

Thus,

$$\mathbf{F}\cdot\mathbf{n} = \frac{1}{\sqrt{4x^2 + 1}}\left((x^2 z)(2x) + (x)(-1) + (-z^2)(0)\right)$$

$$= \frac{2x^3 z - x}{\sqrt{4x^2 + 1}}.$$

The flux of $\mathbf{F}$ outward through the surface is

$$\iint_S \mathbf{F}\cdot\mathbf{n}\, d\sigma = \int_0^4\int_0^1 \frac{2x^3 z - x}{\sqrt{4x^2 + 1}}\, |\mathbf{r}_x \times \mathbf{r}_z|\, dx\, dz$$

$$= \int_0^4\int_0^1 \frac{2x^3 z - x}{\sqrt{4x^2 + 1}}\sqrt{4x^2 + 1}\, dx\, dz$$

$$= \int_0^4\int_0^1 (2x^3 z - x)\, dx\, dz = \int_0^4 \left[\frac{1}{2}x^4 z - \frac{1}{2}x^2\right]_{x=0}^{x=1} dz$$

$$= \int_0^4 \frac{1}{2}(z - 1)\, dz = \frac{1}{4}(z - 1)^2\Big]_0^4$$

$$= 2.$$

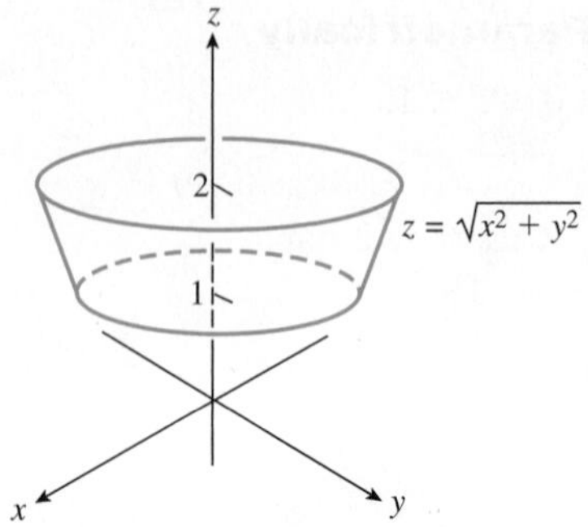

Figure 16.61 The cone frustum in Example 8.

EXAMPLE 8 Finding Center of Mass

Find the center of mass of a thin shell of constant density δ cut from the cone $z = \sqrt{x^2 + y^2}$ by the planes $z = 1$ and $z = 2$ (Figure 16.61).

SOLUTION

The symmetry of the surface about the z-axis tells us that $\bar{x} = \bar{y} = 0$.We find $\bar{z} = M_{xy}/M$. Working as in Examples 1 and 4 we have

$$\mathbf{r}(r, \theta) = (r\cos\theta)\mathbf{i} + (r\sin\theta)\mathbf{j} + r\mathbf{k}, \qquad 1 \le r \le 2, \qquad 0 \le \theta \le 2\pi,$$

and

$$|\mathbf{r}_r \times \mathbf{r}_\theta| = \sqrt{2}r.$$

Therefore,

$$\begin{aligned} M &= \iint_S \delta\, d\sigma = \int_0^{2\pi}\int_1^2 \delta\sqrt{2}\, r\, dr\, d\theta \\ &= \delta\sqrt{2}\int_0^{2\pi}\left[\frac{r^2}{2}\right]_1^2 d\theta = \frac{3}{2}\delta\sqrt{2}\int_0^{2\pi} d\theta \\ &= 3\pi\delta\sqrt{2}, \\ M_{xy} &= \iint_S \delta z\, d\sigma = \int_0^{2\pi}\int_1^2 \delta r\sqrt{2}\, r dr\, d\theta \\ &= \delta\sqrt{2}\int_0^{2\pi}\int_1^2 r^2\, dr\, d\theta = \delta\sqrt{2}\int_0^{2\pi}\left[\frac{r^3}{3}\right]_1^2 d\theta \\ &= \frac{7}{3}\delta\sqrt{2}\int_0^{2\pi} \delta\theta = \frac{14}{3}\pi\delta\sqrt{2} \\ \bar{z} &= \frac{M_{xy}}{M} = \frac{14\pi\delta\sqrt{2}}{3(3\pi\delta\sqrt{2})} = \frac{14}{9}. \end{aligned}$$

The shell's center of mass is the point (0, 0, 14/9).

Quick Review 16.6

In Exercises 1 and 2, the rectangular coordinates of P are (1, 1, 1).

1. Find cylindrical coordinates for P.

2. Find spherical coordinates for P.

In Exercises 3 and 4, consider the rectangular equation $x^2 + (y + 2)^2 = 4$.

3. Describe the surface defined by the equation.

4. Find equivalent equations for the surface in **(a)** cylindrical and **(b)** spherical coordinates.

In Exercises 5 and 6, consider the rectangular equation $x^2 + y^2 + z^2 = 9$.

5. Describe the surface defined by the equation.

6. Find equivalent equations for the surface in **(a)** cylindrical and **(b)** spherical coordinates.

In Exercises 7 and 8, consider the cylindrical equation $r = 2\csc\theta$.

7. Describe the surface defined by the equation.

8. Find equivalent equations for the surface in **(a)** rectangular and **(b)** spherical coordinates.

In Exercises 9 and 10, let $\mathbf{u} = 2\mathbf{i} - 3\mathbf{j} + \mathbf{k}$ and $\mathbf{v} = -2\mathbf{i} + 4\mathbf{j} - 2\mathbf{k}$. Use determinants to find the vector.

9. $\mathbf{u} \times \mathbf{v}$

10. $(\mathbf{u} + \mathbf{v}) \times (\mathbf{u} - \mathbf{v})$

Section 16.6 Exercises

In Exercises 1–16, find a parametrization of the surface. (There are many correct ways to do these, so your answers may not be the same as those in the back of the book.)

1. ***Parabolic Bowl*** The paraboloid $z = x^2 + y^2$, $z \le 4$
2. ***Inverted Parabolic Bowl*** The paraboloid $z = 9 - x^2 - y^2$, $z \ge 0$
3. ***Conical Triangle*** The first-octant portion of the cone $z = \sqrt{x^2 + y^2}/2$ between the planes $z = 0$ and $z = 3$
4. ***Cone Frustum*** The portion of the cone $z = 2\sqrt{x^2 + y^2}$ between the planes $z = 2$ and $z = 4$
5. ***Spherical Cap*** The cap cut from the sphere $x^2 + y^2 + z^2 = 9$ by the cone $z = \sqrt{x^2 + y^2}$
6. ***Spherical Triangle*** The portion of the sphere $x^2 + y^2 + z^2 = 4$ in the first octant between the xy-plane and the cone $z = \sqrt{x^2 + y^2}$
7. ***Spherical Band*** The portion of the sphere $x^2 + y^2 + z^2 = 3$ between the planes and $z = \sqrt{3}/2$ and $z = -\sqrt{3}/2$
8. ***Spherical Mushroom Cap*** The upper portion cut from the sphere $x^2 + y^2 + z^2 = 8$ by the plane $z = -2$
9. ***Parabolic Reflector*** The surface cut from the parabolic cylinder $z = 4 - y^2$ by the planes $x = 0$, $x = 2$, and $z = 0$
10. ***Parabolic Reflector*** The surface cut from the parabolic cylinder $y = x^2$ by the planes $z = 0$, $z = 3$, and $y = 2$
11. ***Circular Cylindrical Band*** The portion of the cylinder $y^2 + z^2 = 9$ between the planes $x = 0$ and $x = 3$
12. ***Half of a Circular Cylindrical Band*** The portion of the cylinder $x^2 + z^2 = 4$ above the xy-plane between the planes $y = -2$ and $y = 2$
13. ***Tilted Plane Inside a Cylinder*** The portion of the plane $x + y + z = 1$
    (a) inside the cylinder $x^2 + y^2 = 9$
    (b) inside the cylinder $y^2 + z^2 = 9$
14. ***Tilted Plane Inside a Cylinder*** The portion of the plane $x - y + 2z = 2$
    (a) inside the cylinder $x^2 + z^2 = 3$
    (b) inside the cylinder $y^2 + z^2 = 2$
15. ***Circular Cylindrical Band*** The portion of the cylinder $(x - 2)^2 + z^2 = 4$ between the planes $y = 0$ and $y = 3$
16. ***Circular Cylindrical Band*** The portion of the cylinder $y^2 + (z - 5)^2 = 25$ between the planes $x = 0$ and $x = 10$

In Exercises 17–26, use a parametrization to express the area of the surface as a double integral. Then evaluate the integral. (There are many correct ways to set up the integrals, so your integrals may not be the same as those in the back of the book. They should have the same values, however.)

17. ***Tilted Plane Inside a Cylinder*** The portion of the plane $y + 2z = 2$ inside the cylinder $x^2 + y^2 = 1$
18. ***Tilted Plane Inside a Cylinder*** The portion of the plane $z = -x$ inside the cylinder $x^2 + y^2 = 4$
19. ***Cone Frustum*** The portion of the cone $z = 2\sqrt{x^2 + y^2}$ between the planes $z = 2$ and $z = 6$
20. ***Cone Frustum*** The portion of the cone $z = \sqrt{x^2 + y^2}/3$ between the planes $z = 1$ and $z = 4/3$
21. ***Circular Cylindrical Band*** The portion of the cylinder $x^2 + y^2 = 1$ between the planes $z = 1$ and $z = 4$
22. ***Circular Cylindrical Band*** The portion of the cylinder $x^2 + z^2 = 10$ between the planes $y = -1$ and $y = 1$
23. ***Parabolic Cap*** The cap cut from the paraboloid $z = 2 - x^2 - y^2$ by the cone $z = \sqrt{x^2 + y^2}$
24. ***Parabolic Band*** The portion of the paraboloid $z = x^2 + y^2$ between the planes $z = 1$ and $z = 4$
25. ***Inverted Spherical Mushroom Cap*** The lower portion cut from the sphere $x^2 + y^2 + z^2 = 2$ by the cone $z = \sqrt{x^2 + y^2}$
26. ***Spherical Band*** The portion of the sphere $x^2 + y^2 + z^2 = 4$ between the planes $z = -1$ and $z = \sqrt{3}$

In Exercises 27–34, integrate the given function over the given surface.

27. ***Parabolic Cylinder*** $G(x, y, z) = x$, over the parabolic cylinder $y = x^2$, $0 \le x \le 2$, $0 \le z \le 3$
28. ***Circular Cylinder*** $G(x, y, z) = z$, over the cylindrical surface $y^2 + z^2 = 4$, $z \ge 0$, $1 \le x \le 4$
29. ***Unit Sphere*** $G(x, y, z) = x^2$, over the unit sphere $x^2 + y^2 + z^2 = 1$
30. ***Hemisphere*** $G(x, y, z) = z^2$, over the hemisphere $x^2 + y^2 + z^2 = a^2$, $z \ge 0$
31. ***Rhombus*** $F(x, y, z) = z$, over the portion of the plane $x + y + z = 4$ that lies above the square $0 \le x \le 1$, $0 \le y \le 1$, in the xy-plane
32. ***Cone*** $F(x, y, z) = z - x$, over the cone $z = \sqrt{x^2 + y^2}$, $0 \le z \le 1$
33. ***Parabolic Dome*** $H(x, y, z) = x^2\sqrt{5 - 4z}$, over the parabolic dome $z = 1 - x^2 - y^2$, $z \ge 0$
34. ***Spherical Cap*** $H(x, y, z) = yz$, over the part of the sphere $x^2 + y^2 + z^2 = 4$ that lies above the cone $z = \sqrt{x^2 + y^2}$

In Exercises 35–44, use a parametrization to find the flux $\iint_S \mathbf{F} \cdot \mathbf{n}\, d\sigma$ across the surface in the given direction.

35. $\mathbf{F} = z^2\mathbf{i} + x\mathbf{j} - 3z\mathbf{k}$ outward (normal away from the x-axis) through the surface cut from the parabolic cylinder $z = 4 - y^2$ by the planes $x = 0$, $x = 1$, and $z = 0$
36. $\mathbf{F} = x^2\mathbf{j} - xz\mathbf{k}$ outward (normal away from the yz-plane) through the surface cut from the parabolic cylinder $y = x^2$, $-1 \le x \le 1$, by the planes $z = 0$ and $z = 2$

37. $\mathbf{F} = z\mathbf{k}$ across the portion of the sphere $x^2 + y^2 + z^2 = a^2$ in the first octant in the direction away from the origin

38. $\mathbf{F} = x\mathbf{i} + y\mathbf{j} + z\mathbf{k}$ across the sphere $x^2 + y^2 + z^2 = a^2$ in the direction away from the origin

39. $\mathbf{F} = 2xy\mathbf{i} + 2yz\mathbf{j} + 2xz\mathbf{k}$ upward across the portion of the plane $x + y + z = 2a$ that lies above the square $0 \le x \le a$, $0 \le y \le a$, in the xy-plane

40. $\mathbf{F} = x\mathbf{i} + y\mathbf{j} + z\mathbf{k}$ outward through the portion of the cylinder $x^2 + y^2 = 1$ cut by the planes $z = 0$ and $z = a$

41. $\mathbf{F} = xy\mathbf{i} - z\mathbf{k}$ outward (normal away from the z-axis) through the cone $z = \sqrt{x^2 + y^2}$, $0 \le z \le 1$

42. $\mathbf{F} = y^2\mathbf{i} + xz\mathbf{j} - \mathbf{k}$ outward (normal away from the z-axis) through the cone $z = 2\sqrt{x^2 + y^2}$, $0 \le z \le 2$

43. $\mathbf{F} = -x\mathbf{i} - y\mathbf{j} + z^2\mathbf{k}$ outward (normal away from the z-axis) through the portion of the cone $z = \sqrt{x^2 + y^2}$ between the planes $z = 1$ and $z = 2$

44. $\mathbf{F} = 4x\mathbf{i} + 4y\mathbf{j} + 2\mathbf{k}$ outward (normal away from the z-axis) through the surface cut from the bottom of the paraboloid $z = x^2 + y^2$ by the plane $z = 1$

In Exercises 45–48, *work in groups of two or three* to find the appropriate center, moment, or radius of gyration.

45. ***A Quarter Dome*** Find the centroid of the portion of the sphere $x^2 + y^2 + z^2 = a^2$ that lies in the first octant.

46. ***A Thin Shell*** Find the center of mass and the moment of inertia and radius of gyration about the z-axis of a thin shell of constant density δ cut from the cone $x^2 + y^2 - z^2 = 0$ by the planes $z = 1$ and $z = 2$.

47. ***A Spherical Shell*** Find the moment of inertia about the z-axis of a thin spherical shell $x^2 + y^2 + z^2 = a^2$ of constant density δ.

48. ***A Conical Shell*** Find the moment of inertia about the z-axis of a thin conical shell $z = \sqrt{x^2 + y^2}$, $0 \le z \le 1$, of constant density δ.

Explorations

Tangent Planes The **tangent plane** at a point

$$P_0(f(u_0, v_0), g(u_0, v_0), h(u_0, v_0))$$

on a parametrized surface

$$\mathbf{r}(u, v) = f(u, v)\mathbf{i} + g(u, v)\mathbf{j} + h(u, v)\mathbf{k}$$

is the plane through P_0 normal to the vector $\mathbf{r}_u(u_0, v_0) \times \mathbf{r}_v(u_0, v_0)$, which is the cross product of the tangent vectors $\mathbf{r}_u(u_0, v_0)$ and $\mathbf{r}_v(u_0, v_0)$ at P_0.

In Exercises 49–52, find an equation for the plane that is tangent to the surface at the given point P_0. Then find a Cartesian equation for the surface and sketch the surface and tangent plane together.

49. ***Cone*** The cone $\mathbf{r}(r, \theta) = (r\cos\theta)\mathbf{i} + (r\sin\theta)\mathbf{j} + r\mathbf{k}$, $r \ge 0$, $0 \le \theta \le 2\pi$, at the point $P_0(\sqrt{2}, \sqrt{2}, 2)$ corresponding to $(r, \theta) = (2, \pi/4)$

50. ***Hemisphere*** The hemisphere surface $\mathbf{r}(\phi, \theta) = (4\sin\phi\cos\theta)\mathbf{i} + (4\sin\phi\sin\theta)\mathbf{j} + (4\cos\phi)\mathbf{k}$, $0 \le \phi \le \pi/2$, $0 \le \theta \le 2\pi$, at the point $P_0(\sqrt{2}, \sqrt{2}, 2\sqrt{3})$ corresponding to $(\phi, \theta) = (\pi/6, \pi/4)$

51. ***Circular Cylinder*** The circular cylinder $\mathbf{r}(\theta, z) = (3\sin 2\theta)\mathbf{i} + (6\sin^2\theta)\mathbf{j} + z\mathbf{k}$, $0 \le \theta \le \pi$, at the point $P_0(3\sqrt{3}/2, 9/2, 0)$ corresponding to $(\theta, z) = (\pi/3, 0)$. (See Example 3.)

52. ***Parabolic Cylinder*** The parabolic cylinder surface $\mathbf{r}(x, y) = x\mathbf{i} + y\mathbf{j} - x^2\mathbf{k}$, $-\infty < x < \infty$, $-\infty < y < \infty$, at the point $P_0(1, 2, -1)$ corresponding to $(x, y) = (1, 2)$

Extending the Ideas

53. ***Torus of Revolution***

(a) A **torus of revolution** (doughnut) is the surface obtained by rotating a circle C in the xz-plane about the z-axis in space. If the radius of C is $r > 0$ and the center is $(R, 0, 0)$, $R > r$, show that a parametrization of the torus is

$\mathbf{r}(u, v) = ((R + r\cos u)\cos v)\mathbf{i} + ((R + r\cos u)\sin v)\mathbf{j} + (r\sin u)\mathbf{k}$,

where $0 \le u \le 2\pi$ and $0 \le v \le 2\pi$ are the angles in Figure 16.62.

(b) Show that the surface area of the torus is $A = 4\pi^2 Rr$.

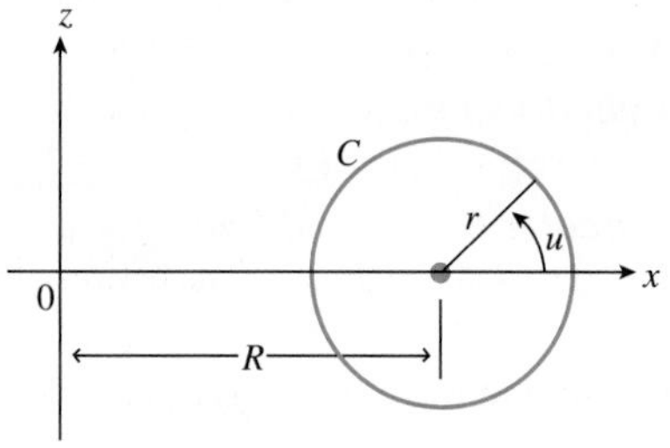

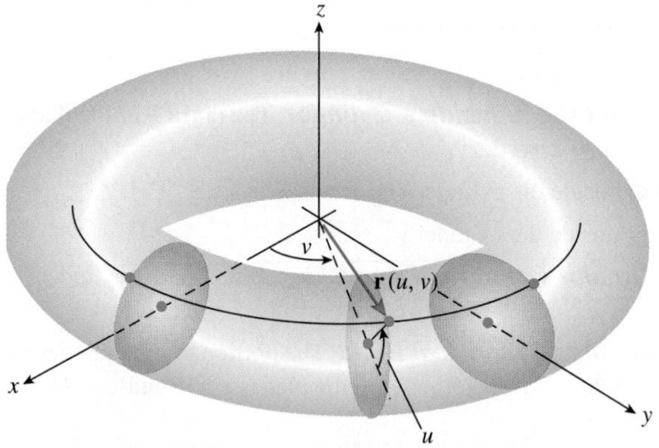

Figure 16.62 The torus surface in Exercise 53.

54. ***Parametrizing a Surface of Revolution*** Suppose the parametrized curve C: $(f(u), g(u))$, $a \le u \le b$, $g(u) \ge 0$, is revolved about the x-axis.

(a) Show that

$$\mathbf{r}(u, v) = f(u)\mathbf{i} + (g(u)\cos v)\mathbf{j} + (g(u)\sin v)\mathbf{k}$$

is a parametrization of the resulting surface of revolution, where $0 \le v \le 2\pi$ is the angle from the xy-plane to the point $\mathbf{r}(u, v)$ on the surface. (See the accompanying figure.) Notice that $f(u)$ measures distance *along* the axis of revolution and $g(u)$ measures distance *from* the axis of revolution

(b) Find a parametrization for the surface obtained by revolving the curve $x = y^2$, $y \ge 0$, about the x-axis.

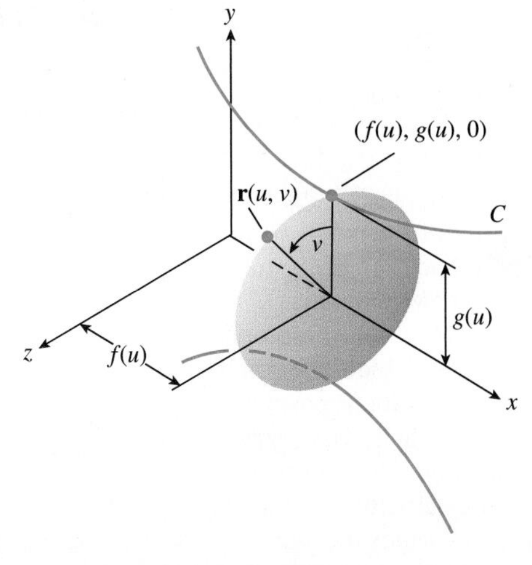

16.7 Stokes's Theorem

What you'll learn about

- Circulation Density: Curl
- Stokes's Theorem
- Getting the Most from a Paddle Wheel
- Proof of Stokes's Theorem for Polyhedral Surfaces
- Stokes's Theorem for Surfaces with Holes
- An Important Identity
- Conservative Fields and Stokes's Theorem

Circulation Density: Curl

As we saw in section 16.4, the $\mathbf{k}$-component of the circulation density or curl of a two-dimensional field $\mathbf{F} = M\mathbf{i} + N\mathbf{j}$ at a point (x, y) is the scalar quantity $(\partial N/\partial x - \partial M/\partial y)$. In three dimensions, the circulation around a point P in a plane is described by a vector normal to the plane of the circulation (Figure 16.63), pointing in the direction that gives it a right-hand relation to the circulation line. The length of the vector gives the rate of the fluid's rotation, which usually varies as the circulation plane is tilted about P. It turns out (Stokes's Theorem) that the vector of greatest circulation in a flow with velocity field $\mathbf{F} = M\mathbf{i} + N\mathbf{j} + P\mathbf{k}$ is

$$\text{curl}\,\mathbf{F} = \left(\frac{\partial P}{\partial y} - \frac{\partial N}{\partial z}\right)\mathbf{i} + \left(\frac{\partial M}{\partial z} - \frac{\partial P}{\partial x}\right)\mathbf{j} + \left(\frac{\partial N}{\partial x} - \frac{\partial M}{\partial y}\right)\mathbf{k}. \tag{1}$$

Notice that $(\text{curl}\,\mathbf{F}) \cdot \mathbf{k}$ equals $\partial N/\partial x - \partial M/\partial y$, consistent with the definition in section 16.4 for $\mathbf{F} = M\mathbf{i} + N\mathbf{j}$.

The formula for curl $\mathbf{F}$ in Equation (1) is usually written using the symbolic operator

$$\nabla = \mathbf{i}\frac{\partial}{\partial x} + \mathbf{j}\frac{\partial}{\partial y} + \mathbf{k}\frac{\partial}{\partial z}. \tag{2}$$

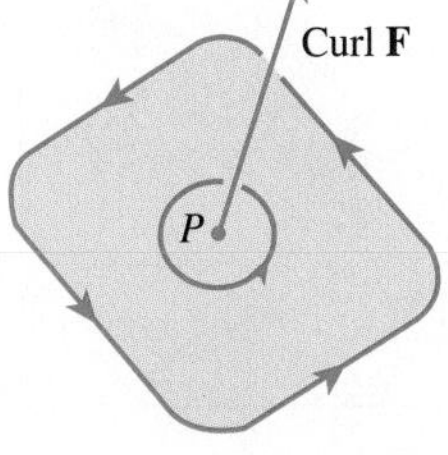

Figure 16.63 The circulation vector at a point P in a plane in a three dimensional fluid flow. Notice its right-hand relation to the circulation line.

The symbol ∇ is pronounced "del." The curl of $\mathbf{F}$ can be found by calculating $\nabla \times \mathbf{F}$:

$$\nabla \times \mathbf{F} = \begin{vmatrix} \mathbf{i} & \mathbf{j} & \mathbf{k} \\ \frac{\partial}{\partial x} & \frac{\partial}{\partial y} & \frac{\partial}{\partial z} \\ M & N & P \end{vmatrix}$$

$$= \left(\frac{\partial P}{\partial y} - \frac{\partial N}{\partial z}\right)\mathbf{i} + \left(\frac{\partial M}{\partial z} - \frac{\partial P}{\partial x}\right)\mathbf{j} + \left(\frac{\partial N}{\partial x} - \frac{\partial M}{\partial y}\right)\mathbf{k} \tag{3}$$

$$= \text{curl}\,\mathbf{F}.$$

$$\text{curl}\,\mathbf{F} = \nabla \times \mathbf{F} \tag{4}$$

George Gabriel Stokes

Sir George Gabriel Stokes (1819–1903), one of the most influential scientific figures of his century, was Lucasian Professor of Mathematics at Cambridge University from 1849 until his death in 1903. His theoretical and experimental investigations covered hydrodynamics, elasticity, light, gravity, sound, heat, meteorology, and solar physics. He left electricity and magnetism to his friend William Thomson, Baron Kelvin of Largs. It is another one of those delightful quirks of history that the theorem we call Stokes's Theorem isn't his theorem at all. He learned of it from Thomson in 1850 and a few years later included it among the questions on an examination he wrote for the Smith Prize. It has been known as Stokes's Theorem ever since. As usual, things have balanced out. Stokes was the original discover of the principles of spectrum analysis that we now credit to Bunsen and Kirchhoff.

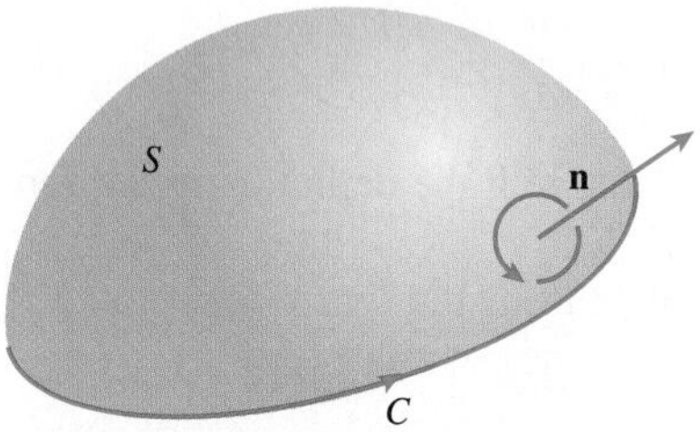

Figure 16.64 The orientation of the bounding curve C gives it a right-handed relation to the normal field **n**.

EXAMPLE 1 Finding Curl

Find the curl of $\mathbf{F} = (x^2 - y)\mathbf{i} + 4z\mathbf{j} + x^2\mathbf{k}$.

SOLUTION

$$\begin{aligned}
\text{curl } \mathbf{F} &= \nabla \times \mathbf{F} \qquad \text{Eq. (4)} \\
&= \begin{vmatrix} \mathbf{i} & \mathbf{j} & \mathbf{k} \\ \dfrac{\partial}{\partial x} & \dfrac{\partial}{\partial y} & \dfrac{\partial}{\partial z} \\ x^2 - y & 4z & x^2 \end{vmatrix} \\
&= \left(\frac{\partial}{\partial y}(x^2) - \frac{\partial}{\partial z}(4z)\right)\mathbf{i} - \left(\frac{\partial}{\partial x}(x^2) - \frac{\partial}{\partial z}(x^2 - y)\right)\mathbf{j} \\
&\qquad + \left(\frac{\partial}{\partial x}(4z) - \frac{\partial}{\partial y}(x^2 - y)\right)\mathbf{k} \\
&= (0 - 4)\,\mathbf{i} - (2x - 0)\,\mathbf{j} + (0 + 1)\,\mathbf{k} \\
&= -4\mathbf{i} - 2x\mathbf{j} + \mathbf{k}
\end{aligned}$$

As we will see, the operator ∇ has a number of other applications. For instance, when applied to a scalar function $f(x, y, z)$, it gives the gradient of f:

$$\nabla f = \frac{\partial f}{\partial x}\mathbf{i} + \frac{\partial f}{\partial y}\mathbf{j} + \frac{\partial f}{\partial z}\mathbf{k}.$$

This may now be read as "del f" as well as "grad f."

Stokes's Theorem

Stokes's Theorem says that, under conditions normally met in practice, the circulation of a vector field around the boundary of an oriented surface in space in the direction counterclockwise with respect to the surface's unit normal vector field **n** (Figure 16.64) equals the integral of the normal component of the curl of the field over the surface.

THEOREM 5 Stokes's Theorem

The circulation of $\mathbf{F} = M\mathbf{i} + N\mathbf{j} + P\mathbf{k}$ around the boundary C of an oriented surface S in the direction counterclockwise with respect to the surface's unit normal vector **n** equals the integral of $\nabla \times \mathbf{F} \cdot \mathbf{n}$ over S.

$$\underbrace{\oint_C \mathbf{F} \cdot d\mathbf{r}}_{\text{counterclockwise circulation}} = \underbrace{\iint_S \nabla \times \mathbf{F} \cdot \mathbf{n}\, d\sigma}_{\text{curl integral}} \qquad (5)$$

Notice from Equation (5) that if two different oriented surfaces S_1 and S_2 have the same boundary C, then their curl integrals are equal:

$$\iint_{S_1} \nabla \times \mathbf{F} \cdot \mathbf{n}_1\, d\sigma = \iint_{S_2} \nabla \times \mathbf{F} \cdot \mathbf{n}_2\, d\sigma.$$

Both curl integrals equal the counterclockwise circulation integral on the left side of Equation (5) as long as the unit normal vectors $\mathbf{n}_1$ and $\mathbf{n}_2$ correctly orient the surfaces.

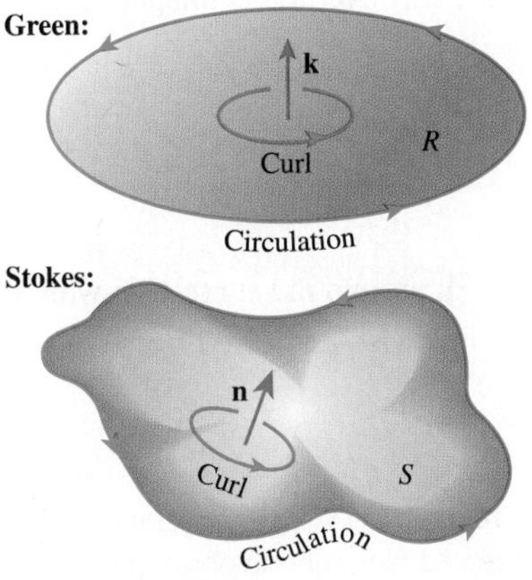

Figure 16.65 Green's Theorem vs. Stokes's Theorem.

Naturally, we need some mathematical restrictions on **F**, C, and S to ensure the existence of the integrals in Stokes's equation. The usual restrictions are that all the functions and derivatives be continuous.

If C is a curve in the xy-plane, oriented counterclockwise, and R is the region in the xy-plane bounded by C, then $d\sigma = dx\,dy$ and

$$(\nabla \times \mathbf{F}) \cdot \mathbf{n} = (\nabla \times \mathbf{F}) \cdot \mathbf{k} = \left(\frac{\partial N}{\partial x} - \frac{\partial M}{\partial y}\right). \tag{6}$$

Under these conditions, Stokes's equation becomes

$$\oint_C \mathbf{F} \cdot d\mathbf{r} = \iint_R \left(\frac{\partial N}{\partial x} - \frac{\partial M}{\partial y}\right) dx\,dy,$$

which is the circulation-curl form of the equation in Green's theorem. Conversely, by reversing these steps we can rewrite the circulation-curl form of Green's Theorem for two-dimensional fields in del notation as

$$\oint_C \mathbf{F} \cdot d\mathbf{r} = \iint_R \nabla \times \mathbf{F} \cdot \mathbf{k}\, dA. \tag{7}$$

See Figure 16.65.

EXAMPLE 2 Verifying Stokes's Equation

Evaluate Equation (5) for the hemisphere S: $x^2 + y^2 + z^2 = 9$, $z \geq 0$, its bounding circle C: $x^2 + y^2 = 9$, $z = 0$, and the field $\mathbf{F} = y\mathbf{i} - x\mathbf{j}$.

SOLUTION

We calculate the counterclockwise circulation around C (as viewed from above) using the parametrization $\mathbf{r}(\theta) = (3\cos\theta)\mathbf{i} + (3\sin\theta)\mathbf{j}$, $0 \leq \theta \leq 2\pi$:

$$d\mathbf{r} = (-3\sin\theta\, d\theta)\mathbf{i} + (3\cos\theta\, d\theta)\mathbf{j}$$

$$\mathbf{F} = y\mathbf{i} - x\mathbf{j} = (3\sin\theta)\mathbf{i} - (3\cos\theta)\mathbf{j}$$

$$\mathbf{F} \cdot d\mathbf{r} = -9\sin^2\theta\, d\theta - 9\cos^2\theta\, d\theta = -9\, d\theta$$

$$\oint_C \mathbf{F} \cdot d\mathbf{r} = \int_0^{2\pi} -9\, d\theta = -18\pi.$$

For the curl integral of **F**, we have

$$\nabla \times \mathbf{F} = \left(\frac{\partial P}{\partial y} - \frac{\partial N}{\partial z}\right)\mathbf{i} + \left(\frac{\partial M}{\partial z} - \frac{\partial P}{\partial x}\right)\mathbf{j} + \left(\frac{\partial N}{\partial x} - \frac{\partial M}{\partial y}\right)\mathbf{k}$$

$$= (0 - 0)\mathbf{i} + (0 - 0)\mathbf{j} + (-1 - 1)\mathbf{k} = -2\mathbf{k},$$

$$\mathbf{n} = \frac{x\mathbf{i} + y\mathbf{j} + z\mathbf{k}}{\sqrt{x^2 + y^2 + z^2}} = \frac{x\mathbf{i} + y\mathbf{j} + z\mathbf{k}}{3},$$ Outer unit normal

$$d\sigma = \frac{3}{z}\, dA,$$ Section 16.5, Example 5, with $a = 3$

$$\nabla \times \mathbf{F} \cdot \mathbf{n} = -\frac{2z}{3}\frac{3}{3}\, dA = -dA,$$

and

$$\iint_S \nabla \times \mathbf{F} \cdot \mathbf{n}\, d\sigma = \iint_{x^2+y^2 \le 9} -2\, dA = -18\pi$$

The circulation around the circle equals the integral of the curl over the hemisphere, as it should.

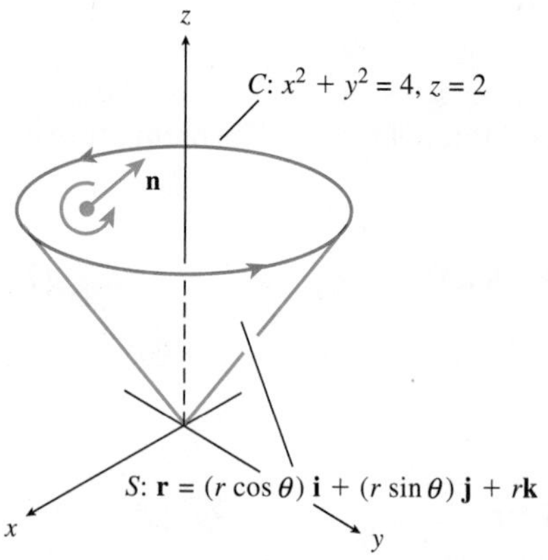

Figure 16.66 The curve C and cone S in Example 3.

EXAMPLE 3 Finding Circulation

Find the circulation of the field $\mathbf{F} = (x^2 - y)\mathbf{i} + 4z\mathbf{j} + x^2\mathbf{k}$ around the curve C in which the plane $z = 2$ meets the cone $z = \sqrt{x^2 + y^2}$, counterclockwise as viewed from above (Figure 16.66).

SOLUTION

Stokes's Theorem enables us to find the circulation by integrating over the surface of the cone. Traversing C in the counterclockwise direction viewed from above corresponds to taking the *inner* normal $\mathbf{n}$ to the cone (which has a positive z-component).

We parametrize the cone as

$$\mathbf{r}(r, \theta) = (r\cos\theta)\mathbf{i} + (r\sin\theta)\mathbf{j} + r\mathbf{k}, \qquad 0 \le r \le 2, \qquad 0 \le \theta \le 2\pi.$$

We then have

$$\mathbf{n} = \frac{\mathbf{r}_r \times \mathbf{r}_\theta}{|\mathbf{r}_r \times \mathbf{r}_\theta|} = \frac{-(r\cos\theta)\mathbf{i} - (r\sin\theta)\mathbf{j} + r\mathbf{k}}{r\sqrt{2}} \qquad \text{Section 16.6, Example 4}$$

$$= \frac{1}{\sqrt{2}}(-(\cos\theta)\mathbf{i} - (\sin\theta)\mathbf{j} + \mathbf{k}),$$

$$d\sigma = r\sqrt{2}\, dr\, d\theta, \qquad \text{Section 16.6, Example 4}$$

$$\nabla \times \mathbf{F} = -4\mathbf{i} - 2x\mathbf{j} + \mathbf{k} \qquad \text{Example 1}$$

$$= -4\mathbf{i} - 2(r\cos\theta)\mathbf{j} + \mathbf{k}. \qquad x = r\cos\theta$$

Accordingly,

$$\nabla \times \mathbf{F} \cdot \mathbf{n} = \frac{1}{\sqrt{2}}(4\cos\theta + 2r\cos\theta\sin\theta + 1)$$

$$= \frac{1}{\sqrt{2}}(4\cos\theta + r\sin 2\theta + 1),$$

and the circulation is

$$\oint_C \mathbf{F} \cdot d\mathbf{r} = \iint_S \nabla \times \mathbf{F} \cdot \mathbf{n}\, d\sigma \qquad \text{Strokes's Theorem}$$

$$= \int_0^{2\pi}\int_0^2 \frac{1}{\sqrt{2}}(4\cos\theta + r\sin 2\theta + 1)(r\sqrt{2}\, dr\, d\theta) = 4\pi.$$

Getting the Most from a Paddle Wheel

Suppose $\mathbf{v}(x, y, z)$ is the velocity of a moving fluid whose density at (x, y, z) is $\delta(x, y, z)$, and let $\mathbf{F} = \delta\mathbf{v}$. Then

$$\oint_C \mathbf{F} \cdot d\mathbf{r}$$

is the circulation of the fluid around the closed curve C. By Stoke's Theorem, the circulation is equal to the flux of $\nabla \times \mathbf{F}$ through a surface spanning C:

$$\oint_C \mathbf{F} \cdot d\mathbf{r} = \iint_S \nabla \times \mathbf{F} \cdot \mathbf{n}\, d\sigma.$$

Suppose we fix a point Q in the domain of $\mathbf{F}$ and a direction $\mathbf{u}$ at Q. Let C be a circle of radius ρ, with center at Q, whose plane is normal to $\mathbf{u}$. If $\nabla \times \mathbf{F}$ is continuous at Q, then the average value of the $\mathbf{u}$-component of $\nabla \times \mathbf{F}$ over the circular disk S bounded by C approaches the $\mathbf{u}$-component of $\nabla \times \mathbf{F}$ at Q as $\rho \to 0$:

$$(\nabla \times \mathbf{F} \cdot \mathbf{u})_Q = \lim_{\rho \to 0} \frac{1}{\pi\rho^2} \iint_S \nabla \times \mathbf{F} \cdot \mathbf{u}\, d\sigma. \tag{8}$$

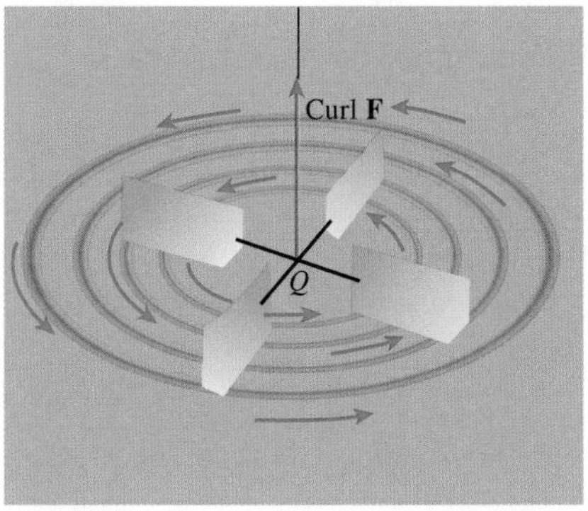

Figure 16.67 The paddle interpretation of curl **F**.

If we replace the double integral in Equation (8) by the circulation, we get

$$(\nabla \times \mathbf{F} \cdot \mathbf{u})_Q = \lim_{\rho \to 0} \frac{1}{\pi\rho^2} \oint_C \mathbf{F} \cdot d\mathbf{r}. \tag{9}$$

The left-hand side of Equation (9) has its maximum value when $\mathbf{u}$ is the direction of $\nabla \times \mathbf{F}$. When ρ is small, the limit on the right-hand side of Equation (9) is approximately

$$\frac{1}{\pi\rho^2} \oint_C \mathbf{F} \cdot d\mathbf{r},$$

which is the circulation around C divided by the area of the disk (the circulation density). Suppose a small paddle wheel of radius ρ is introduced into the fluid at Q, with its axle directed along $\mathbf{u}$. The circulation of the fluid around C will affect the rate of spin of the paddle wheel. The wheel will spin fastest when the circulation integral is maximized; therefore, it will spin fastest when the axle of the paddle wheel points in the direction of $\nabla \times \mathbf{F}$ (Figure 16.67).

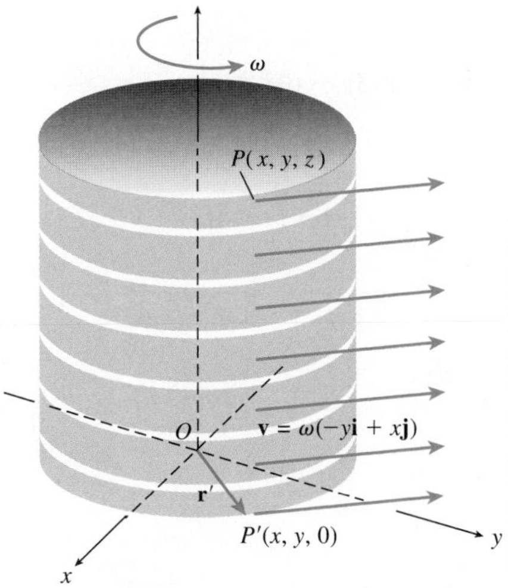

Figure 16.68 A steady rotational flow parallel to the xy-plane, with constant angular velocity ω in the positive (counterclockwise) direction.

EXAMPLE 4 Relating $\nabla \times \mathbf{F}$ to Circulation Density

A fluid of constant density rotates around the z-axis with velocity $\mathbf{v} = \omega(-y\mathbf{i} + x\mathbf{j})$, where ω is a positive constant called the *angular velocity* of the rotation (Figure 16.68). If $\mathbf{F} = \mathbf{v}$, find $\nabla \times \mathbf{F}$ and relate it to the circulation density.

SOLUTION

With $\mathbf{F} = \mathbf{v} = -\omega y\mathbf{i} + \omega x\mathbf{j}$,

$$\begin{aligned}\nabla \times \mathbf{F} &= \left(\frac{\partial P}{\partial y} - \frac{\partial N}{\partial z}\right)\mathbf{i} + \left(\frac{\partial M}{\partial z} - \frac{\partial P}{\partial x}\right)\mathbf{j} + \left(\frac{\partial N}{\partial x} - \frac{\partial M}{\partial y}\right)\mathbf{k} \\ &= (0 - 0)\mathbf{i} + (0 - 0)\mathbf{j} + (\omega - (-\omega))\mathbf{k} = 2\omega\mathbf{k}.\end{aligned}$$

By Stoke's Theorem, the circulation of **F** around a circle C of radius ρ bounding a disk S in a plane normal to $\nabla \times \mathbf{F}$, say the xy-plane, is

$$\oint_C \mathbf{F} \cdot d\mathbf{r} = \iint_S \nabla \times \mathbf{F} \cdot \mathbf{n}\, d\sigma = \iint_S 2\omega\mathbf{k} \cdot \mathbf{k}\, dx\, dy = (2\omega)(\pi\rho^2).$$

Thus,

$$(\nabla \times \mathbf{F}) \cdot \mathbf{k} = 2\omega = \frac{1}{\pi\rho^2} \oint_C \mathbf{F} \cdot d\mathbf{r},$$

in agreement with Equation (9) with $\mathbf{u} = \mathbf{k}$.

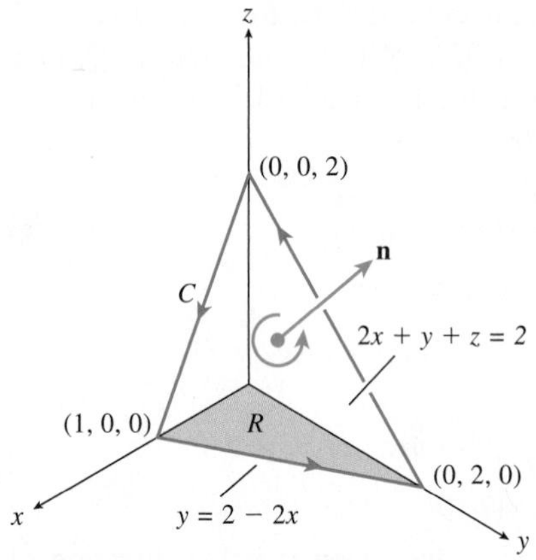

Figure 16.69 The planar surface in Example 5.

EXAMPLE 5 Applying Stokes's Theorem

Use Stokes's Theorem to evaluate $\int_C \mathbf{F} \cdot d\mathbf{r}$, if $\mathbf{F} = xz\mathbf{i} + xy\mathbf{j} + 3xz\mathbf{k}$ and C is the boundary of the portion of the plane $2x + y + z = 2$ in the first octant, traversed counterclockwise as viewed from above (Figure 16.69).

SOLUTION

The plane is the level surface $f(x, y, z) = 2$ of the function $f(x, y, z) = 2x + y + z$. The unit normal vector

$$\mathbf{n} = \frac{\nabla f}{|\nabla f|} = \frac{2\mathbf{i} + \mathbf{j} + \mathbf{k}}{|2\mathbf{i} + \mathbf{j} + \mathbf{k}|} = \frac{1}{\sqrt{6}}(2\mathbf{i} + \mathbf{j} + \mathbf{k})$$

is consistent with the counterclockwise motion around C. To apply Stokes's Theorem, we find

$$\text{curl}\, \mathbf{F} = \nabla \times \mathbf{F} = \begin{vmatrix} \mathbf{i} & \mathbf{j} & \mathbf{k} \\ \dfrac{\partial}{\partial x} & \dfrac{\partial}{\partial y} & \dfrac{\partial}{\partial z} \\ xz & xy & 3xz \end{vmatrix} = (x - 3z)\mathbf{j} + y\mathbf{k}.$$

On the plane, z equals $2 - 2x - y$, so

$$\nabla \times \mathbf{F} = (x - 3(2 - 2x - y))\mathbf{j} + y\mathbf{k} = (7x + 3y - 6)\mathbf{j} + y\mathbf{k}$$

and

$$\nabla \times \mathbf{F} \cdot \mathbf{n} = \frac{1}{\sqrt{6}}(7x + 3y - 6 + y) = \frac{1}{\sqrt{6}}(7x + 4y - 6).$$

The surface area element is

$$d\sigma = \frac{|\nabla f|}{|\nabla f \cdot \mathbf{k}|}\, dA = \frac{\sqrt{6}}{1}\, dx\, dy.$$

The circulation is

$$\oint_C \mathbf{F} \cdot d\mathbf{r} = \iint_S \nabla \times \mathbf{F} \cdot \mathbf{n}\, d\sigma \qquad \text{Stokes's Theorem}$$

$$= \int_0^1 \int_0^{2-2x} \frac{1}{\sqrt{6}}(7x + 4y - 6)\sqrt{6}\, dy\, dx$$

$$= \int_0^1 \int_0^{2-2x} (7x + 4y - 6)\, dy\, dx = -1.$$

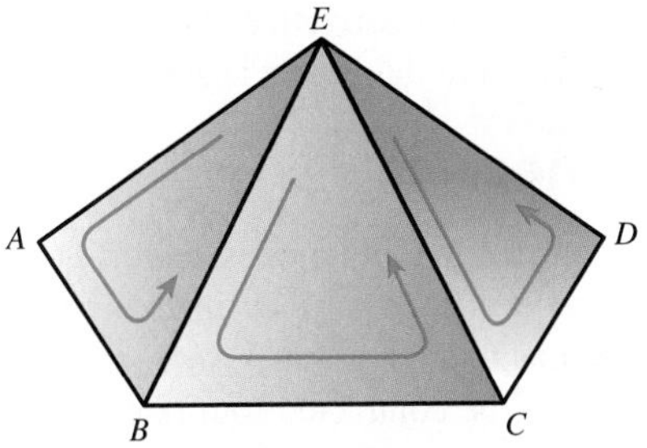

Figure 16.70 Part of a polyhedral surface.

Proof of Stokes's Theorem for Polyhedral Surfaces

Let S be a polyhedral surface consisting of a finite number of plane regions. (Think of one of Buckminster Fuller's geodesic domes.) We apply Green's theorem to each separate panel of S. There are two types of panels:

1. those that are surrounded on all sides by other panels and
2. those that have one or more edges that are not adjacent to other panels.

The boundary Δ of S consists of edges of panels of the second type that are not adjacent to other panels. In Figure 16.70, the triangles EAB, BCE, and CDE represent a part of S, with $ABCD$ part of the boundary Δ. Applying Green's Theorem to the three triangles in turn and adding the results, we get

$$\left(\oint_{EAB} + \oint_{BCE} + \oint_{CDE}\right) \mathbf{F} \cdot d\mathbf{r} = \left(\iint_{EAB} + \iint_{BCE} + \iint_{CDE}\right) \nabla \times \mathbf{F} \cdot \mathbf{n}\, d\sigma. \quad (10)$$

The three line integrals on the left-hand side of Equation (10) combine into a single line integral taken around the periphery $ABCDE$ because the integrals along interior segments cancel in pairs. For example, the integral along segment BE in triangle ABE is opposite in sign to the integral along the same segment in triangle EBC. The same holds for segment CE. Hence, Equation (10) reduces to

$$\oint_{ABCDE} \mathbf{F} \cdot d\mathbf{r} = \iint_{ABCDE} \nabla \times \mathbf{F} \cdot \mathbf{n}\, d\sigma.$$

When we apply Green's Theorem to all the panels and add the results, we get

$$\oint_{\Delta} \mathbf{F} \cdot d\mathbf{r} = \iint_{S} \nabla \times \mathbf{F} \cdot \mathbf{n}\, d\sigma. \quad (11)$$

This is Stokes's Theorem for a polyhedral surface S. You can find proofs for more general surfaces in advanced calculus texts.

Stokes's Theorem for Surfaces with Holes

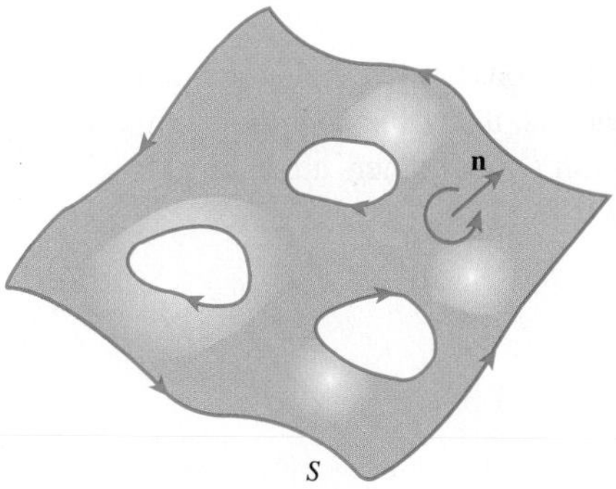

Figure 16.71 Stokes's Theorem also holds for oriented surfaces with holes.

Stokes's Theorem can be extended to an oriented surface S that has one or more holes (Figure 16.71), in a way analogous to the extension of Green's Theorem: The surface integral over S of the normal component of $\nabla \times \mathbf{F}$ equals the sum of the line integrals around all the boundary curves of the tangential component of $\mathbf{F}$, where the curves are to be traced in the direction induced by the orientation of S.

An Important Identity

The following identity arises frequently in mathematics and the physical sciences.

$$\text{curl grad } f = \mathbf{0} \quad \text{or} \quad \nabla \times \nabla f = \mathbf{0} \quad (12)$$

This identity holds for any function $f(x, y, z)$ whose second partial derivatives are continuous. The proof goes like this:

$$\nabla \times \nabla f = \begin{vmatrix} \mathbf{i} & \mathbf{j} & \mathbf{k} \\ \frac{\partial}{\partial x} & \frac{\partial}{\partial y} & \frac{\partial}{\partial z} \\ \frac{\partial f}{\partial x} & \frac{\partial f}{\partial y} & \frac{\partial f}{\partial z} \end{vmatrix} = (f_{zy} - f_{yz})\mathbf{i} - (f_{zx} - f_{xz})\mathbf{j} + (f_{yx} - f_{xy})\mathbf{k}.$$

If the second partial derivatives are continuous, the mixed second derivatives in parentheses are equal (The Mixed Derivative Theorem, Section 13.3) and the vector is zero.

Conservative Fields and Stokes's Theorem

In Section 16.3, we found that saying that a field $\mathbf{F}$ is conservative in an open region D in space is equivalent to saying that the integral of $\mathbf{F}$ around every closed loop in D is zero. This, in turn, is equivalent in *simply connected* open regions to saying that $\nabla \times \mathbf{F} = \mathbf{0}$. A region D is **simply connected** if every closed path in D can be contracted to a point in D without ever leaving D. If D consisted of space with a line removed, for example, D would not be simply connected. There would be no way to contract a loop around the line to a point without leaving D. On the other hand, space itself is simply connected (Figure 16.72).

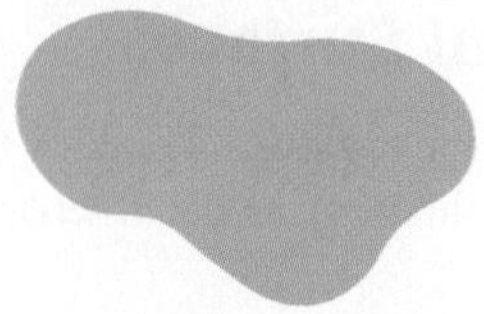

Connected and simply connected.

Connected but not simply connected.

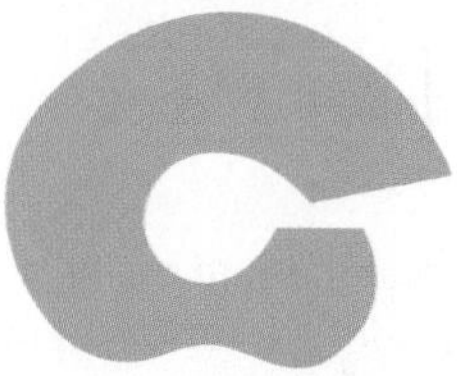

Connected and simply connected.

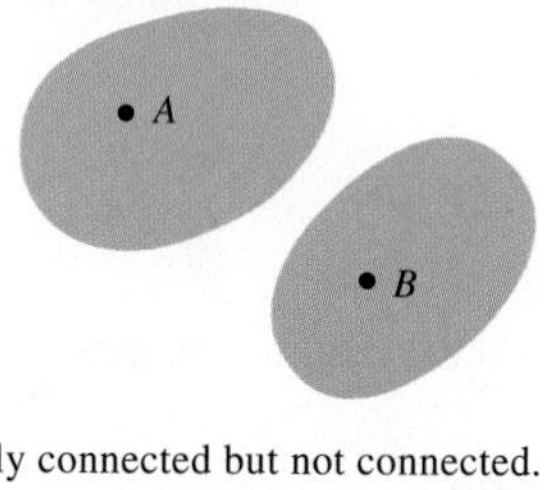

Simply connected but not connected.
No path from A to B lies entirely in the region.

Figure 16.72 Connectivity and simple connectivity are not the same. Neither implies the other, as these pictures of plane regions illustrate. To make three dimensional regions with these properties, thicken the plane regions into cylinders.

THEOREM 6 Zero Curl Implies Path Independence

If $\nabla \times \mathbf{F} = \mathbf{0}$ at every point of a simply connected open region D in space, then on any piecewise smooth closed path C in D.

$$\oint_C \mathbf{F} \cdot d\mathbf{r} = 0.$$

Sketch of a Proof Theorem 6 is usually proved in two steps. The first step is for simple closed curves. A theorem from topology, a branch of advanced mathematics, states that every differentiable simple closed curve C in a simply connected open region D is the boundary of a smooth two-sided surface S that also lies in D. Hence, by Stokes's Theorem,

$$\oint_C \mathbf{F} \cdot d\mathbf{r} = \iint_S \nabla \times \mathbf{F} \cdot \mathbf{n}\, d\sigma = 0.$$

The second step is for curves that cross themselves, like the one in Figure 16.73. The idea is to break these into simple loops spanned by orientable surfaces, apply Stokes's Theorem one loop at a time, and add the results.

The following diagram summarizes the results for conservative fields defined on connected, simply connected open regions. In such regions, under the conditions imposed on $\mathbf{F}$ and C in Section 16.3, the properties in the diagram's four corners are equivalent.

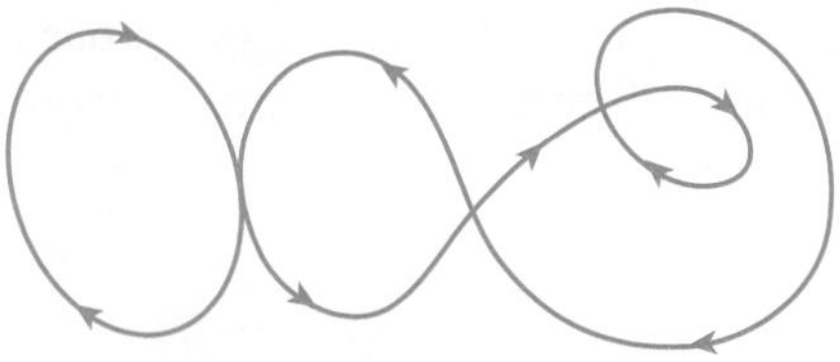

Figure 16.73 In a simply connected open region in space, differentiable curves that cross themselves can be divided into loops to which Stokes's Theorem applies.

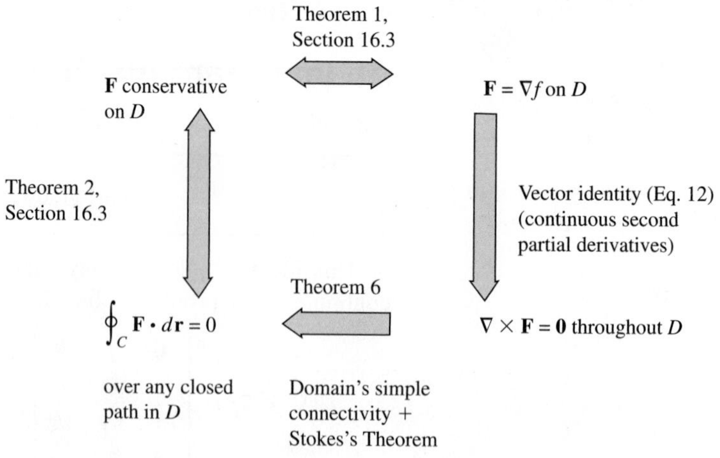

Quick Review 16.7

In Exercises 1–6, let $f(x, y, z) = e^{-xyz} \ln(x + y + z)$. Compute the indicated partial derivative.

1. f_x
2. f_z
3. f_{xy}
4. f_{yx}
5. f_{yz}
6. f_{zy}

In Exercises 7 and 8, let $\mathbf{u} = x\mathbf{i} + y\mathbf{j} - z\mathbf{k}$ and $\mathbf{v} = a\mathbf{i} + b\mathbf{j} + c\mathbf{k}$. Use determinants to compute the vector.

7. $\mathbf{u} \times \mathbf{v}$
8. $\mathbf{v} \times \mathbf{u}$

9. Find ∇f if $f(x, y, z) = x \sin(y + z)$.

10. Solve for x:

$$\begin{vmatrix} 1 & x & x^2 \\ 2 & 3 & -1 \\ 1 & 0 & 1 \end{vmatrix} = 0.$$

Section 16.7 Exercises

In Exercises 1–6, use the surface integral in Stokes's Theorem to calculate the circulation of the field $\mathbf{F}$ around the curve C in the indicated direction.

1. $\mathbf{F} = x^2\mathbf{i} + 2x\mathbf{j} + z^2\mathbf{k}$

   C: The ellipse $4x^2 + y^2 = 4$ in the xy-plane, counterclockwise when viewed from above

2. $\mathbf{F} = 2y\mathbf{i} + 3x\mathbf{j} - 1/z^2\mathbf{k}$

   C: The circle $x^2 + y^2 = 9$ in the xy-plane, counterclockwise when viewed from above

3. $\mathbf{F} = y\mathbf{i} + xz\mathbf{j} + x^2\mathbf{k}$

   C: The boundary of the triangle cut from the plane $x + y + z = 1$ by the first octant, counterclockwise when viewed from above

4. $\mathbf{F} = (y^2 + z^2)\mathbf{i} + (x^2 + z^2)\mathbf{j} + (x^2 + y^2)\mathbf{k}$

   C: The boundary of the triangle cut from the plane $x + y + z = 1$ by the first octant, counterclockwise when viewed from above

5. $\mathbf{F} = (y^2 + z^2)\mathbf{i} + (x^2 + y^2)\mathbf{j} + (x^2 + y^2)\mathbf{k}$

   C: The square bounded by the lines $x = \pm 1$ and $y = \pm 1$ in the xy-plane, counterclockwise when viewed from above

6. $\mathbf{F} = x^2y^3\mathbf{i} + \mathbf{j} + z\mathbf{k}$

   C: The intersection of the cylinder $x^2 + y^2 = 4$ and the hemisphere $x^2 + y^2 + z^2 = 16$, $z \geq 0$

7. Let $\mathbf{n}$ be the outer unit normal of the elliptical shell

   $$S\colon 4x^2 + 9y^2 + 36z^2 = 36, \qquad z \geq 0,$$

   and let

   $$\mathbf{F} = y\mathbf{i} + x^2\mathbf{j} + (x^2 + y^4)^{3/2} \sin e^{\sqrt{xyz}}\,\mathbf{k}.$$

   Find the value of

   $$\iint_S \nabla \times \mathbf{F} \cdot \mathbf{n}\, d\sigma.$$

   (*Hint:* One parametrization of the ellipse at the base of the shell is $x = 3\cos t$, $y = 2\sin t$, $0 \leq t \leq 2\pi$.)

8. Let $\mathbf{n}$ be the outer normal (normal away from the origin) of the parabolic shell

   $$S\colon 4x^2 + y + z^2 = 4, \qquad y \geq 0$$

   and let

   $$\mathbf{F} = \left(-z + \frac{1}{2 + x}\right)\mathbf{i} + (\tan^{-1} y)\,\mathbf{j} + \left(x + \frac{1}{4 + z}\right)\mathbf{k}.$$

   Find the value of

   $$\iint_S \nabla \times \mathbf{F} \cdot \mathbf{n}\, d\sigma.$$

9. Let S be the cylinder $x^2 + y^2 = a^2$, $0 \leq z \leq h$, together with its top, $x^2 + y^2 \leq a^2$, $z = h$. Let $\mathbf{F} = -y\mathbf{i} + x\mathbf{j} + x^2\mathbf{k}$. Use Stokes's Theorem to calculate the flux of $\nabla \times \mathbf{F}$ outward through S.

10. Evaluate

    $$\iint_S \nabla \times (y\mathbf{i}) \cdot \mathbf{n}\, d\sigma,$$

    where S is the hemisphere $x^2 + y^2 + z^2 = 1$, $z \geq 0$.

11. Show that

    $$\iint_S \nabla \times \mathbf{F} \cdot \mathbf{n}\, d\sigma$$

    has the same value for all oriented surfaces that span C and that induce the same positive direction on C.

12. **Writing to Learn** Let $\mathbf{F}$ be a differentiable vector field defined on a region containing a smooth closed oriented surface S and its interior. Let $\mathbf{n}$ be the unit normal vector field on S. Suppose S is the union of two surfaces S_1 and S_2 joined along a smooth simple closed curve C. Can anything be said about

    $$\iint_S \nabla \times \mathbf{F} \cdot \mathbf{n}\, d\sigma?$$

    Give reasons for your answer.

In Exercises 13–18, use the surface integral in Stokes's Theorem to calculate the flux of the curl of the field **F** across the surface *S* in the direction of the outward unit normal **n**.

13. $\mathbf{F} = 2z\mathbf{i} + 3x\mathbf{j} + 5y\mathbf{k}$

S: $\mathbf{r}(r, \theta) = (r\cos\theta)\mathbf{i} + (r\sin\theta)\mathbf{j} + (4 - r^2)\mathbf{k}$, $0 \le r \le 2$, $0 \le \theta \le 2\pi$

14. $\mathbf{F} = (y - z)\mathbf{i} + (z - x)\mathbf{j} + (x + z)\mathbf{k}$

S: $\mathbf{r}(r, \theta) = (r\cos\theta)\mathbf{i} + (r\sin\theta)\mathbf{j} + (9 - r^2)\mathbf{k}$, $0 \le r \le 3$, $0 \le \theta \le 2\pi$

15. $\mathbf{F} = x^2y\mathbf{i} + 2y^3z\mathbf{j} + 3z\mathbf{k}$

S: $\mathbf{r}(r, \theta) = (r\cos\theta)\mathbf{i} + (r\sin\theta)\mathbf{j} + r\mathbf{k}$, $0 \le r \le 1$, $0 \le \theta \le 2\pi$

16. $\mathbf{F} = (x - y)\mathbf{i} + (y - z)\mathbf{j} + (z - x)\mathbf{k}$

S: $\mathbf{r}(r, \theta) = (r\cos\theta)\mathbf{i} + (r\sin\theta)\mathbf{j} + (5 - r)\mathbf{k}$, $0 \le r \le 5$, $0 \le \theta \le 2\pi$

17. $\mathbf{F} = 3y\mathbf{i} + (5 - 2x)\mathbf{j} + (z^2 - 2)\mathbf{k}$

S: $\mathbf{r}(r, \theta) = (\sqrt{3}\sin\phi\cos\phi)\mathbf{i} + (\sqrt{3}\sin\phi\sin\theta)\mathbf{j} + (\sqrt{3}\cos\phi)\mathbf{k}$, $0 \le \theta \le \pi/2$, $0 \le \theta \le 2\pi$

18. $\mathbf{F} = y^2\mathbf{i} + z^2\mathbf{j} + x\mathbf{k}$

S: $\mathbf{r}(\phi, \theta) = (2\sin\phi\cos\theta)\mathbf{i} + (2\sin\phi\sin\theta)\mathbf{j} + (2\cos\phi)\mathbf{k}$, $0 \le \phi \le \pi/2$, $0 \le \theta \le 2\pi$

Explorations

19. Use the identity $\nabla \times \nabla f = \mathbf{0}$ (Equation (12) in the text) and Stokes's Theorem to show that the circulation of the following fields around the boundary of any smooth orientable surface in space are zero.

(a) $\mathbf{F} = 2x\mathbf{i} + 2y\mathbf{j} + 2z\mathbf{k}$

(b) $\mathbf{F} = \nabla(xy^2z^3)$

(c) $\mathbf{F} = \nabla \times (x\mathbf{i} + y\mathbf{j} + z\mathbf{k})$

(d) $\mathbf{F} = \nabla f$

20. Let $f(x, y, z) = (x^2 + y^2 + z^2)^{-1/2}$. Show that the clockwise circulation of the field $\mathbf{F} = \nabla f$ around the circle $x^2 + y^2 = a^2$ in the *xy*-plane is zero

(a) by taking $\mathbf{r} = (a\cos t)\mathbf{i} + (a\sin t)\mathbf{j}$, $0 \le t \le 2\pi$, and integrating $\mathbf{F} \cdot d\mathbf{r}$ over the circle.

(b) by applying Stokes's Theorem.

In Exercises 21–24, *work in groups of two or three* to solve the problem.

21. Let *C* be a simple closed smooth curve in the plane $2x + 2y + z = 2$, oriented as shown here. Show that

$$\oint_C 2y\,dx + 3z\,dy - x\,dz$$

depends only on the area of the region enclosed by *C* and not on the position or shape of *C*.

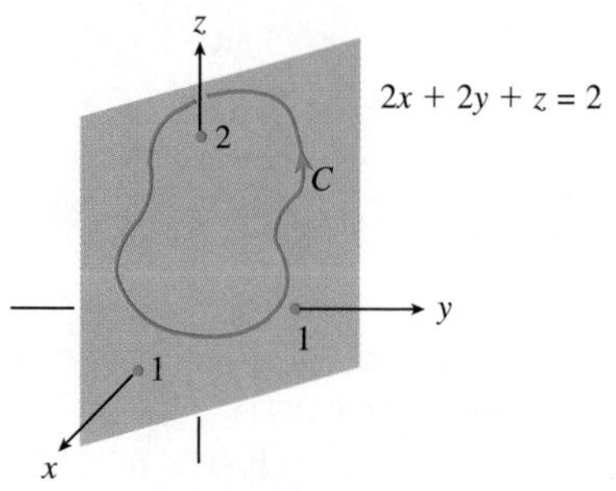

22. Show that if $\mathbf{F} = x\mathbf{i} + y\mathbf{j} + z\mathbf{k}$, then $\nabla \times \mathbf{F} = \mathbf{0}$.

23. Find a vector field with twice-differentiable components whose curl is $x\mathbf{i} + y\mathbf{j} + z\mathbf{k}$ or prove that no such field exists.

24. Writing to Learn Does Stokes's Theorem say anything about circulation in a field whose curl is zero? Give reasons for your answer.

Extending the Ideas

25. Let *R* be a region in the *xy*-plane that is bounded by a piecewise smooth simple closed curve *C*, and suppose the moments of inertia of *R* about the *x*- and *y*-axes are known to be I_x and I_y. Evaluate the integral

$$\oint_C \nabla(r^4) \cdot \mathbf{n}\,ds,$$

where $r = \sqrt{x^2 + y^2}$, in terms of I_x and I_y.

26. *Zero Curl, Yet Not Conservative* Show that the curl of

$$\mathbf{F} = \frac{-y}{x^2 + y^2}\mathbf{i} + \frac{x}{x^2 + y^2}\mathbf{j} + z\mathbf{k}$$

is zero but that

$$\oint_C \mathbf{F} \cdot d\mathbf{r}$$

is not zero if *C* is the circle $x^2 + y^2 = 1$ in the *xy*-plane. (Theorem 6 does not apply here because the domain of **F** is not simply connected. The field **F** is not defined along the *z*-axis so there is no way to contract *C* to a point without leaving the domain of **F**.)

16.8 The Divergence Theorem and a Unified Theory

What you'll learn about

- Divergence in Three Dimensions
- The Divergence Theorem
- Proof of the Divergence Theorem for Special Regions
- The Divergence Theorem for Other Regions
- Gauss's Law: One of the Four Great Laws of Electromagnetic Theory
- Continuity Equation of Hydrodynamics
- Unifying the Integral Theorems

Divergence in Three Dimensions

The **divergence** of a vector field

$$\mathbf{F} = M(x, y, z)\mathbf{i} + N(x, y, z)\mathbf{j} + P(x, y, z)\mathbf{k}$$

is the scalar function

$$\text{div}\,\mathbf{F} = \nabla \cdot \mathbf{F} = \frac{\partial M}{\partial x} + \frac{\partial N}{\partial y} + \frac{\partial P}{\partial z}. \tag{1}$$

The symbol "div **F**" is read as "divergence of **F**" or "div **F**." The notation $\nabla \cdot \mathbf{F}$ is read "del dot **F**."

Div **F** has the same physical interpretation in three dimensions that it does in two. If **F** is the velocity field of a fluid flow, the value of div **F** at a point (x, y, z) is the rate at which fluid is being piped in or drained away at (x, y, z). The divergence is the flux per unit volume or flux density at the point.

EXAMPLE 1 Finding Divergence

Find the divergence of $\mathbf{F} = 2xz\mathbf{i} - xy\mathbf{j} - z\mathbf{k}$.

SOLUTION

The divergence of **F** is

$$\nabla \cdot \mathbf{F} = \frac{\partial}{\partial x}(2xz) + \frac{\partial}{\partial y}(-xy) + \frac{\partial}{\partial z}(-z) = 2z - x - 1.$$

The Divergence Theorem

The Divergence Theorem says that under suitable conditions the outward flux of a vector field across a closed surface (oriented outward) equals the triple integral of the divergence of the field over the region enclosed by the surface.

THEOREM 7 Divergence Theorem

The flux of a vector field $\mathbf{F} = M\mathbf{i} + N\mathbf{j} + P\mathbf{k}$ across a closed oriented surface S in the direction of the surface's outward unit normal field **n** equals the integral of $\nabla \cdot \mathbf{F}$ over the region D enclosed by the surface:

$$\underbrace{\iint_S \mathbf{F} \cdot \mathbf{n}\, d\sigma}_{\text{outward flux}} = \underbrace{\iiint_D \nabla \cdot \mathbf{F}\, dV}_{\text{divergence integral}}. \tag{2}$$

Divergence Theorem

Mikhail Vassilievich Ostrogradsky (1801–1862) was the first mathematician to publish a proof of the Divergence Theorem. Upon being denied his degree at Kharkhov University by the minister for religious affairs and national education (for atheism), Ostrogradsky left Russia for Paris in 1822, attracted by the presence of Laplace, Legendre, Fourier, Poisson, and Cauchy. While working on the theory of heat in the mid-1820s, he formulated the Divergence Theorem as a tool for converting volume integrals to surface integrals.

Carl Friedrich Gauss (1777–1855) had already proved the theorem while working on the theory of gravitation, but his notebooks were not to be published until many years later. (The theorem is sometimes called Gauss's Theorem.) The list of Gauss's accomplishments in science and mathematics is truly astonishing, ranging from the co-invention of the electric telegraph with Wilhelm Weber in 1833 to the development of a wonderfully accurate theory of planetary orbits and to work in non-Euclidean geometry that later became fundamental to Einstein's general theory of relativity.

EXAMPLE 2 Verifying the Divergence Theorem

Evaluate both sides of Equation (2) for the field $\mathbf{F} = x\mathbf{i} + y\mathbf{j} + z\mathbf{k}$ over the sphere $x^2 + y^2 + z^2 = a^2$.

SOLUTION

The outer normal to S, calculated from the gradient of $f(x, y, z) = x^2 + y^2 + z^2 - a^2$, is

$$\mathbf{n} = \frac{2(x\mathbf{i} + y\mathbf{j} + z\mathbf{k})}{\sqrt{4(x^2 + y^2 + z^2)}} = \frac{x\mathbf{i} + y\mathbf{j} + z\mathbf{k}}{a}$$

Hence,

$$\mathbf{F} \cdot \mathbf{n}\, d\sigma = \frac{x^2 + y^2 + z^2}{a}\, d\sigma = \frac{a^2}{a}\, d\sigma = a\, d\sigma$$

because $x^2 + y^2 + z^2 = a^2$ on the surface. Therefore,

$$\iint_S \mathbf{F} \cdot \mathbf{n}\, d\sigma = \iint_S a\, d\sigma = a(4\pi a^2) = 4\pi a^3.$$

The divergence of $\mathbf{F}$ is

$$\nabla \cdot \mathbf{F} = \frac{\partial}{\partial x}(x) + \frac{\partial}{\partial y}(y) + \frac{\partial}{\partial z}(z) = 3,$$

so

$$\iiint_D \nabla \cdot \mathbf{F}\, dV = \iiint_D 3\, dV = 3\left(\frac{4}{3}\pi a^3\right) = 4\pi a^3.$$

EXAMPLE 3 Finding Flux

Find the flux of $\mathbf{F} = xy\mathbf{i} + yz\mathbf{j} + xz\mathbf{k}$ outward through the surface of the cube cut from the first octant by the planes $x = 1$, $y = 1$, and $z = 1$.

SOLUTION

Instead of calculating the flux as a sum of six separate integrals, one for each face of the cube, we can calculate the flux by integrating the divergence

$$\nabla \cdot \mathbf{F} = \frac{\partial}{\partial x}(xy) + \frac{\partial}{\partial y}(yz) + \frac{\partial}{\partial z}(xz) = y + z + x$$

over the cube's interior:

$$\text{Flux} = \iint_{\substack{S\\ \text{cube}\\ \text{surface}}} \mathbf{F} \cdot \mathbf{n}\, d\sigma = \iiint_{\substack{D\\ \text{cube}\\ \text{interior}}} \nabla \cdot \mathbf{F}\, dV \qquad \text{Divergence Theorem}$$

$$= \int_0^1 \int_0^1 \int_0^1 (x + y + z)\, dx\, dy\, dz = \frac{3}{2} \qquad \text{Routine integration}$$

Proof of the Divergence Theorem for Special Regions

To prove the Divergence Theorem, we assume that the components of **F** have continuous first partial derivatives. We also assume that D is a convex region with no holes or bubbles, such as a solid sphere, cube, or ellipsoid, and that S is a piecewise smooth surface. In addition, we assume that any line perpendicular to the xy-plane at an interior point of the region R_{xy} that is the projection of D on the xy-plane intersects the surface S in exactly two points, producing surfaces

$$S_1: \quad z = f_1(x, y), \qquad (x, y) \text{ in } R_{xy}$$

$$S_2: \quad z = f_2(x, y), \qquad (x, y) \text{ in } R_{xy}$$

with $f_1 \le f_2$. We make similar assumptions about the projection of D onto the other two coordinate planes. See Figure 16.74.

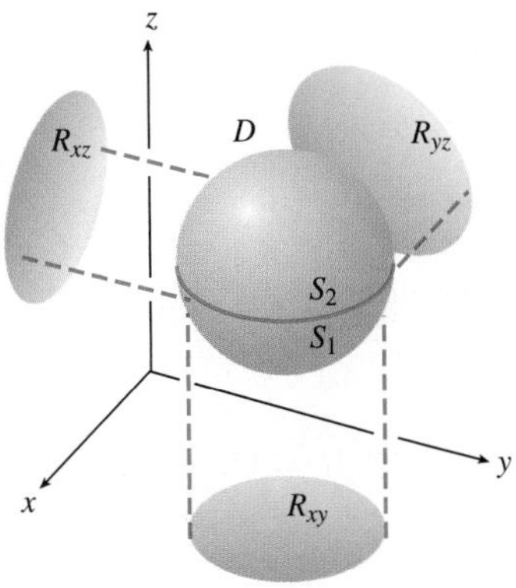

Figure 16.74 We first prove the Divergence Theorem for the kind of three-dimensional region shown here. We then extend the theorem to other regions.

The components of the unit normal vector $\mathbf{n} = n_1\mathbf{i} + n_2\mathbf{j} + n_3\mathbf{k}$ are the cosines of the angles α, β, and γ that **n** makes with **i**, **j**, and **k** (Figure 16.75). This is true because all the vectors involved are unit vectors. We have

$$n_1 = \mathbf{n} \cdot \mathbf{i} = |\mathbf{n}||\mathbf{i}| \cos \alpha = \cos \alpha,$$

$$n_2 = \mathbf{n} \cdot \mathbf{j} = |\mathbf{n}||\mathbf{j}| \cos \beta = \cos \beta,$$

$$n_3 = \mathbf{n} \cdot \mathbf{k} = |\mathbf{n}||\mathbf{k}| \cos \gamma = \cos \gamma.$$

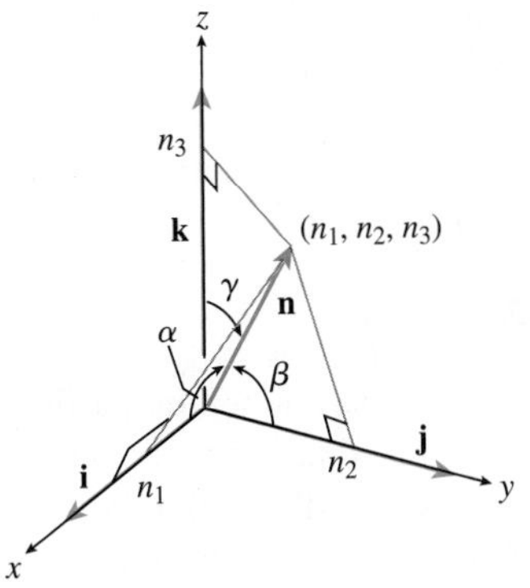

Figure 16.75 The scalar components of a unit normal vector **n** are the cosines of the angles α, β, and γ that it makes with **i**, **j**, and **k**.

Thus,

$$\mathbf{n} = (\cos \alpha)\mathbf{i} + (\cos \beta)\mathbf{j} + (\cos \gamma)\mathbf{k}$$

and

$$\mathbf{F} \cdot \mathbf{n} = M \cos \alpha + N \cos \beta + P \cos \gamma.$$

In component form, the Divergence Theorem states that

$$\iint_S (M \cos \alpha + N \cos \beta + P \cos \gamma)\, d\sigma = \iiint_D \left(\frac{\partial M}{\partial x} + \frac{\partial N}{\partial y} + \frac{\partial P}{\partial z} \right) dx\, dy\, dz.$$

We prove the theorem by proving the three equalities:

$$\iint_S M \cos \alpha \, d\sigma = \iiint_D \frac{\partial M}{\partial x}\, dx\, dy\, dz, \tag{3}$$

$$\iint_S N \cos \beta \, d\sigma = \iiint_D \frac{\partial N}{\partial y}\, dx\, dy\, dz, \tag{4}$$

$$\iint_S P \cos \gamma \, d\sigma = \iiint_D \frac{\partial P}{\partial z}\, dx\, dy\, dz. \tag{5}$$

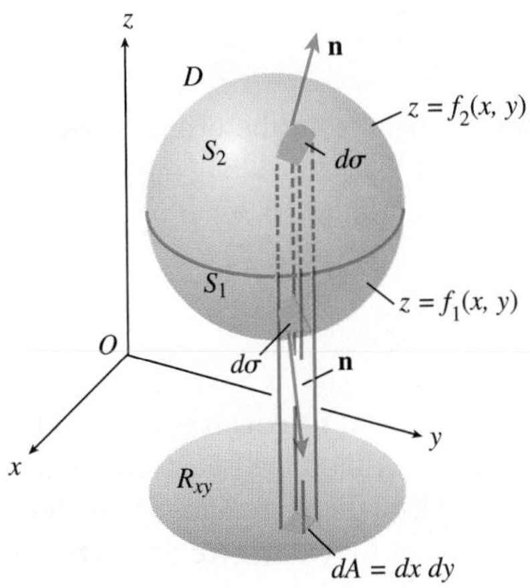

Figure 16.76 The three-dimensional region D enclosed by the surfaces S_1 and S_2 shown here projects vertically onto a two-dimensional region R_{xy} in the xy-plane.

We prove Equation (5) by converting the surface integral on the left to a double integral over the projection R_{xy} of D on the xy-plane (Figure 16.76). The surface S consists of an upper part S_2 whose equation is $z = f_2(x, y)$ and a lower part S_1 whose equation is $z = f_1(x, y)$. On S_2, the outer normal **n** has a positive **k**-component and

$$\cos \gamma \, d\sigma = dx\, dy \quad \text{because} \quad d\sigma = \frac{dA}{|\cos \gamma|} = \frac{dx\, dy}{\cos \gamma}.$$

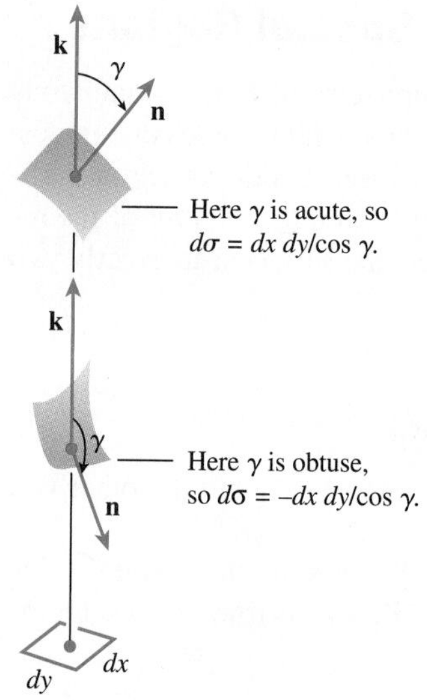

Figure 16.77 An enlarged view of the area patches in Figure 16.75. The relations $d\sigma = \pm dx\, dy/\cos\gamma$ are derived in Section 16.5.

See Figure 16.77. On S_1, the outer normal $\mathbf{n}$ has a negative $\mathbf{k}$-component and

$$\cos\gamma\, d\sigma = -dx\, dy.$$

Therefore,

$$\begin{aligned}
\iint_S P\cos\gamma\, d\sigma &= \iint_{S_2} P\cos\gamma\, d\sigma + \iint_{S_1} P\cos\gamma\, d\sigma \\
&= \iint_{R_{xy}} P(x, y, f_2(x, y))\, dx\, dy - \iint_{R_{xy}} P(x, y, f_1(x, y))\, dx\, dy \\
&= \iint_{R_{xy}} P(x, y, f_2(x, y)) - P(x, y, f_1(x, y))\, dx\, dy \\
&= \iint_{R_{xy}} \left[\int_{f_1(x, y)}^{f_2(x, y)} \frac{\partial P}{\partial z}\, dz \right] dx\, dy = \iiint_D \frac{\partial P}{\partial z}\, dz\, dx\, dy.
\end{aligned}$$

This proves Equation (5).

The proofs for Equations (3) and (4) follow the same pattern, or just permute $x, y, z; M, N, P; \alpha, \beta, \gamma$, in order, and get those results from Equation (5).

The Divergence Theorem for Other Regions

The Divergence Theorem can be extended to regions that can be partitioned into a finite number of simple regions of the type just discussed and to regions that can be defined as limits of simpler regions in certain ways. For example, suppose D is the region between two concentric spheres and $\mathbf{F}$ has continuously differentiable components throughout D and on the bounding surfaces. Split D by an equatorial plane and apply the Divergence Theorem to each half separately. The bottom half, D_1, is shown in Figure 16.78. The surface S_1 that bounds D_1 consists of an outer hemisphere, a plane washer-shaped base, and an inner hemisphere. The Divergence Theorem says that

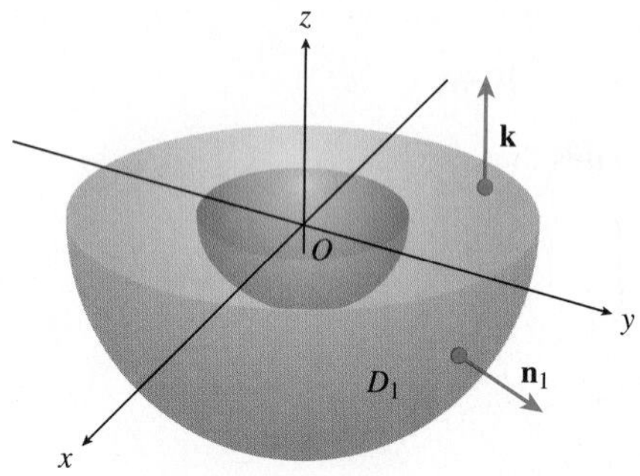

Figure 16.78 The lower half of the solid region between two concentric spheres.

$$\iint_{S_1} \mathbf{F}\cdot\mathbf{n}_1\, d\sigma_1 = \iiint_{D_1} \nabla\cdot\mathbf{F}\, dV_1. \tag{6}$$

The unit normal $\mathbf{n}_1$ that points outward from D_1 points away from the origin along the outer surface, equals $\mathbf{k}$ along the flat base, and points toward the origin along the inner surface. Next apply the Divergence Theorem to D_2, as shown in Figure 16.79:

$$\iint_{S_2} \mathbf{F}\cdot\mathbf{n}_2\, d\sigma_2 = \iiint_{D_2} \nabla\cdot\mathbf{F}\, dV_2. \tag{7}$$

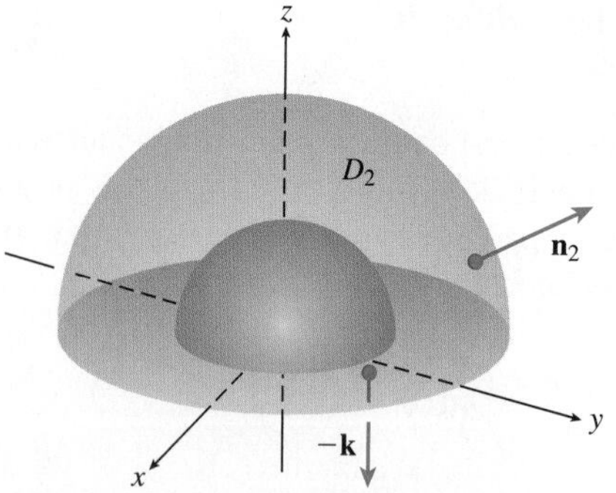

Figure 16.79 The upper half of the solid region between two concentric spheres.

As we follow $\mathbf{n}_2$ over S_2, pointing outward from D_2, we see that $\mathbf{n}_2$ equals $-\mathbf{k}$ along the washer-shaped base in the xy-plane, points away from the origin on the outer sphere, and points toward the origin on the inner sphere. When we add Equations (6) and (7), the integrals over the flat base cancel because of the opposite signs of $\mathbf{n}_1$ and $\mathbf{n}_2$. We thus arrive at the result

$$\iint_S \mathbf{F}\cdot\mathbf{n}\, d\sigma_2 = \iiint_D \nabla\cdot\mathbf{F}\, dV,$$

with D the region between the spheres, S the boundary of D consisting of two spheres, and $\mathbf{n}$ the unit normal to S directed outward from D.

EXAMPLE 4 Finding Outward Flux

Find the net outward flux of the field

$$\mathbf{F} = \frac{x\mathbf{i} + y\mathbf{j} + z\mathbf{k}}{\rho^3}, \qquad \rho = \sqrt{x^2 + y^2 + z^2}$$

across the boundary of the region D: $0 < a^2 \le x^2 + y^2 + z^2 \le b^2$.

SOLUTION

The flux can be calculated by integrating $\nabla \cdot \mathbf{F}$ over D. We have

$$\frac{\partial \rho}{\partial x} = \frac{1}{2}(x^2 + y^2 + z^2)^{-1/2}(2x) = \frac{x}{\rho}$$

and

$$\frac{\partial M}{\partial x} = \frac{\partial}{\partial x}(x\rho^{-3}) = \rho^{-3} - 3x\rho^{-4}\frac{\partial \rho}{\partial x} = \frac{1}{\rho^3} - \frac{3x^2}{\rho^5}.$$

Similarly,

$$\frac{\partial N}{\partial y} = \frac{1}{\rho^3} - \frac{3y^2}{\rho^5} \quad \text{and} \quad \frac{\partial P}{\partial z} = \frac{1}{\rho^3} - \frac{3z^2}{\rho^5}.$$

Hence,

$$\operatorname{div} \mathbf{F} = \frac{3}{\rho^3} - \frac{3}{\rho^5}(x^2 + y^2 + z^2) = \frac{3}{\rho^3} - \frac{3\rho^2}{\rho^5} = 0$$

and

$$\iiint_D \nabla \cdot \mathbf{F}\, dV = 0.$$

So the integral of $\nabla \cdot \mathbf{F}$ over D is zero and the net outward flux across the boundary of D is zero, but there is more to learn from this example. The flux leaving D across the inner sphere S_a is the negative of the flux leaving D across the outer sphere S_b (because the sum of these fluxes is zero). Hence, the flux of $\mathbf{F}$ across S_a in the direction away from the origin equals the flux of $\mathbf{F}$ across S_b in the direction away from the origin. Thus, the flux of $\mathbf{F}$ across a sphere centered at the origin is independent of the radius of the sphere. What is this flux?

To find it, we evaluate the flux integral directly. The outward unit normal on the sphere of radius a is

$$\mathbf{n} = \frac{x\mathbf{i} + y\mathbf{j} + z\mathbf{k}}{\sqrt{x^2 + y^2 + z^2}} = \frac{x\mathbf{i} + y\mathbf{j} + z\mathbf{k}}{a}.$$

Hence, on the sphere,

$$\mathbf{F} \cdot \mathbf{n} = \frac{x\mathbf{i} + y\mathbf{j} + z\mathbf{k}}{a^3} \cdot \frac{x\mathbf{i} + y\mathbf{j} + z\mathbf{k}}{a} = \frac{x^2 + y^2 + z^2}{a^4} = \frac{a^2}{a^4} = \frac{1}{a^2}$$

and

$$\iint_{S_a} \mathbf{F} \cdot \mathbf{n}\, d\sigma = \frac{1}{a^2}\iint_{S_a} d\sigma = \frac{1}{a^2}(4\pi a^2) = 4\pi.$$

The outward flux of $\mathbf{F}$ across any sphere centered at the origin is 4π.

Gauss's Law: One of the Four Great Laws of Electromagnetic Theory

There is more to be learned from Example 4. In electromagnetic theory, the electric field created by a point charge q located at the origin is the inverse square field

$$\mathbf{E}(x, y, z) = \frac{1}{4\pi\varepsilon_0}\frac{q}{|\mathbf{r}|^2}\left(\frac{\mathbf{r}}{|\mathbf{r}|}\right) = \frac{q}{4\pi\varepsilon_0}\frac{\mathbf{r}}{|\mathbf{r}|^3} = \frac{q}{4\pi\varepsilon_0}\frac{x\mathbf{i} + y\mathbf{j} + z\mathbf{k}}{\rho^3},$$

where ε_0 is a physical constant, $\mathbf{r}$ is the position vector of the point (x, y, z), and $\rho = |\mathbf{r}| = \sqrt{x^2 + y^2 + z^2}$. In the notation of Example 4,

$$\mathbf{E} = \frac{q}{4\pi\varepsilon_0}\mathbf{F}.$$

The calculations in Example 4 show that the outward flux of $\mathbf{E}$ across any sphere centered at the origin is q/ε_0, but this result is not confined to spheres. The outward flux of $\mathbf{E}$ across any closed surface S that encloses the origin (and to which the Divergence Theorem applies) is also q/ε_0. To see why, we have only to imagine a large sphere S_a centered at the origin and enclosing the surface S. Since

$$\nabla \cdot \mathbf{E} = \nabla \cdot \frac{q}{4\pi\varepsilon_0}\mathbf{F} = \frac{q}{4\pi\varepsilon_0}\nabla \cdot \mathbf{F} = 0$$

when $\rho > 0$, the integral of $\nabla \cdot \mathbf{E}$ over the region D between S and S_a is zero. Hence, by the Divergence Theorem,

$$\iint_{\substack{\text{boundary}\\ \text{of } D}} \mathbf{E} \cdot \mathbf{n}\, d\sigma = 0,$$

and the flux of $\mathbf{E}$ across S in the direction away from the origin must be the same as the flux of $\mathbf{E}$ across S_a in the direction away from the origin, which is $4\pi q$. This statement, called *Gauss's law,* also applies to charge distributions that are more general than the one assumed here, as you will see in nearly any physics text.

$$\text{Guass's Law: } \iint_S \mathbf{E} \cdot \mathbf{n}\, d\sigma = \frac{q}{\varepsilon_0}$$

Continuity Equation of Hydrodynamics

Let D be a region in space bounded by a closed oriented surface S. If $\mathbf{v}(x, y, z)$ is the velocity field of a fluid flowing smoothly through D, $\delta = \delta(t, x, y, z)$ is the fluid's density at (x, y, z) at time t, and $\mathbf{F} = \delta\mathbf{v}$, then the **continuity equation** of hydrodynamics states that

$$\nabla \cdot \mathbf{F} + \frac{\partial \delta}{\partial t} = 0.$$

If the functions involved here have continuous first partial derivatives, the equation evolves naturally from the Divergence Theorem, as we will now see. First, the integral

$$\iint_S \mathbf{F} \cdot \mathbf{n}\, d\sigma$$

is the rate at which mass leaves D across S (leaves because $\mathbf{n}$ is the outer normal). To see why, consider a patch of area $\Delta\sigma$ on the surface (Figure 16.80). In a short time interval Δt, the volume ΔV of fluid that flows across the patch is approximately equal to the volume of

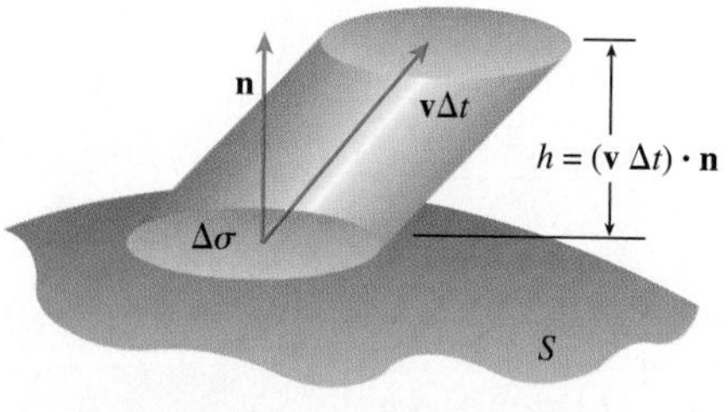

Figure 16.80 The fluid that flows upward through the patch $\Delta\sigma$ in a short time Δt fills a "cylinder" whose volume is approximately base × height $\mathbf{v} \cdot \mathbf{n}\, \Delta\sigma\, \Delta t$.

a cylinder with base area $\Delta\sigma$ and height $(\mathbf{v}\,\Delta t)\cdot\mathbf{n}$, where $\mathbf{v}$ is a velocity vector rooted at a point of the patch:

$$\Delta V \approx \mathbf{v}\cdot\mathbf{n}\,\Delta\sigma\,\Delta t.$$

The mass of this volume of fluid is about

$$\Delta m \approx \delta\,\mathbf{v}\cdot\mathbf{n}\,\Delta\sigma\,\Delta t,$$

so the rate at which mass is flowing out of D across the patch is about

$$\frac{\Delta m}{\Delta t} \approx \delta\,\mathbf{v}\cdot\mathbf{n}\,\Delta\sigma.$$

This leads to the approximation

$$\sum\frac{\Delta m}{\Delta t} \approx \sum\delta\,\mathbf{v}\cdot\mathbf{n}\,\Delta\sigma$$

as an estimate of the average rate at which mass flows across S. Finally, letting $\Delta\sigma \to 0$ and $\Delta t \to 0$ gives the instantaneous rate at which mass leaves D across S as

$$\frac{dm}{dt} = \iint_S \delta\,\mathbf{v}\cdot\mathbf{n}\,d\sigma,$$

which for our particular flow is

$$\frac{dm}{dt} = \iint_S \mathbf{F}\cdot\mathbf{n}\,d\sigma.$$

Now let B be a solid sphere centered at a point Q in the flow. The average value of $\nabla\cdot\mathbf{F}$ over B is

$$\frac{1}{\text{volume of } B}\iiint_B \nabla\cdot\mathbf{F}\,dV.$$

It is a consequence of the continuity of the divergence that $\nabla\cdot\mathbf{F}$ actually takes on this value at some point P in B. Thus,

$$(\nabla\cdot\mathbf{F})_P = \frac{1}{\text{volume of } B}\iiint_B \nabla\cdot\mathbf{F}\,dV = \frac{\iint_S \mathbf{F}\cdot\mathbf{n}\,d\sigma}{\text{volume of } B}$$

$$= \frac{\text{rate at which mass leaves } B \text{ across its surfaces}}{\text{volume of } B}. \qquad (8)$$

The fraction on the right describes the decrease in mass per unit volume.

Now let the radius of B approach zero while the center Q stays fixed. The left-hand side of Equation (8) converges to $(\nabla\cdot\mathbf{F})_Q$, the right side to $(-\partial\delta/\partial t)_Q$. The equality of these two limits is the continuity equation

$$\nabla\cdot\mathbf{F} = -\frac{\partial\delta}{\partial t}.$$

The continuity equation "explains" $\nabla\cdot\mathbf{F}$: The divergence of $\mathbf{F}$ at a point is the rate at which the density of the fluid is decreasing there.

The Divergence Theorem

$$\iint_S \mathbf{F} \cdot \mathbf{n}\, d\sigma = \iiint_D \nabla \cdot \mathbf{F}\, dV$$

now says that the net decrease in density of the fluid in region D is accounted for by the mass transported across the surface S. In this context, the theorem becomes a statement about conservation of mass.

Unifying the Integral Theorems

If we think of a two-dimensional field $\mathbf{F} = M(x, y)\mathbf{i} + N(x, y)\mathbf{j}$ as a three-dimensional field whose $\mathbf{k}$-component is zero, then $\nabla \cdot \mathbf{F} = (\partial M/\partial x) + (\partial N/\partial y)$ and the normal form of Green's Theorem can be written as

$$\oint_C \mathbf{F} \cdot \mathbf{n}\, ds = \iint_R \left(\frac{\partial M}{\partial x} + \frac{\partial N}{\partial y}\right) dx\, dy = \iint_R \nabla \cdot \mathbf{F}\, dA.$$

Similarly, $\nabla \times \mathbf{F} \cdot \mathbf{k} = (\partial N/\partial x) - (\partial M/\partial y)$, so the tangential form of Green's Theorem can be written as

$$\oint_C \mathbf{F} \cdot d\mathbf{r} = \iint_R \left(\frac{\partial N}{\partial x} - \frac{\partial M}{\partial y}\right) dx\, dy = \iint_R \nabla \times \mathbf{F} \cdot \mathbf{k}\, dA.$$

With the equations of Green's Theorem now in del notation, we can see their relationship to the equations in Stokes's Theorem and the Divergence Theorem.

Green's Theorem and its Generalization to Three Dimensions

Normal form of Green's Theorem:	$\oint_C \mathbf{F} \cdot \mathbf{n}\, ds = \iint_R \nabla \cdot \mathbf{F}\, dA$
Divergence Theorem:	$\iint_S \mathbf{F} \cdot \mathbf{n}\, d\sigma = \iiint_D \nabla \cdot \mathbf{F}\, dV$
Tangential form of Green's Theorem:	$\oint_C \mathbf{F} \cdot d\mathbf{r} = \iint_R \nabla \cdot \mathbf{F} \cdot \mathbf{k}\, dA$
Stokes's Theorem:	$\oint_C \mathbf{F} \cdot d\mathbf{r} = \iint_S \nabla \cdot \mathbf{F} \cdot \mathbf{n}\, d\sigma$

Stokes's Theorem generalizes the tangential (curl) form of Green's Theorem from a flat surface in the plane to a surface in three-dimensional space. In each theorem, the integral of the normal component of curl $\mathbf{F}$ over the interior of the surface equals the circulation of $\mathbf{F}$ around the boundary.

Likewise, the Divergence Theorem generalizes the normal (flux) form of Green's Theorem from a two-dimensional region in the plane to a three-dimensional region in space. In each case, the integral of $\nabla \cdot \mathbf{F}$ over the interior of the region equals the total flux of the field across the boundary.

There is still more to be learned here. All these results can be viewed as forms of a *single fundamental theorem.* The Fundamental Theorem of Calculus says that if $f(x)$ is differentiable on $[a, b]$, then

$$\int_a^b \frac{df}{dx}\,dx = f(b) - f(a).$$

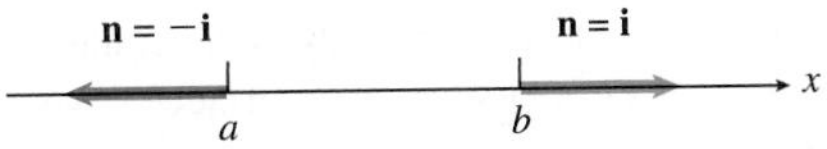

Figure 16.81 The outward unit normals at the boundary of $[a, b]$ in one dimensional space.

If we let $\mathbf{F} = f(x)\mathbf{i}$ throughout $[a, b]$, then $(df/dx) = \nabla \cdot \mathbf{F}$. If we define the unit vector $\mathbf{n}$ normal to the boundary of $[a, b]$ to be $\mathbf{i}$ at b and $-\mathbf{i}$ at a (Figure 16.81), then

$$\begin{aligned} f(b) - f(a) &= f(b)\mathbf{i} \cdot (\mathbf{i}) + f(a)\mathbf{i} \cdot (-\mathbf{i}) \\ &= \mathbf{F}(b) \cdot \mathbf{n} + \mathbf{F}(a) \cdot \mathbf{n} \\ &= \text{total outward flux of } \mathbf{F} \text{ across the boundary of } [a, b]. \end{aligned}$$

The Fundamental Theorem now says that

$$\int_{[a,b]} \nabla \cdot \mathbf{F}\,dx = \text{total outward flux of } \mathbf{F} \text{ across the boundary.}$$

The Fundamental Theorem of Calculus, the flux form of Green's Theorem, and the Divergence Theorem all say that the integral of the differential operator $\nabla \cdot$ operating on a field $\mathbf{F}$ over a region equals the sum of the normal field components over the boundary of the region.

Stokes's Theorem and the circulation form of Green's Theorem say that, when things are properly oriented, the integral of the normal component of the curl operating on a field over a region equals the sum of the tangential field components on the boundary of the region.

The beauty of these interpretations is the observance of a marvelous underlying principle, which we might state as follows.

> The integral of a differential operator acting on a field over a region equals the sum of the field components appropriate to the operator over the boundary of the region.

Quick Review 16.8

In Exercises 1–4, evaluate the integral.

1. $\displaystyle\int_0^2 \int_0^{2-x} \int_0^{2-x-y} dz\,dy\,dx$

2. $\displaystyle\int_0^2 \int_0^{2-x} \int_0^{2-x-y} x\,dz\,dy\,dx$

3. $\displaystyle\int_0^2 \int_0^{2-x} \int_0^{2-x-y} y\,dz\,dy\,dx$

4. $\displaystyle\int_0^2 \int_0^{2-x} \int_0^{2-x-y} z\,dz\,dy\,dx$

In Exercises 5–8, rewrite the integral $\displaystyle\int_0^1 \int_0^1 \int_0^{y^2} dz\,dy\,dx$ as an iterated integral in the given order.

5. $dy\,dz\,dx$

6. $dy\,dx\,dz$

7. $dx\,dy\,dz$

8. $dx\,dz\,dy$

In Exercises 9 and 10, find the angle that the vector $\mathbf{i} + \mathbf{j} + \mathbf{k}$ makes with the indicated axis.

9. x-axis

10. y-axis

Section 16.8 Exercises

In Exercises 1–4, find the divergence of the field.

1. The spin field in Figure 16.15
2. The radial field in Figure 16.14
3. The gravitational field in Figure 16.13
4. The velocity field in Figure 16.10

In Exercises 5–16, use the Divergence Theorem to find the outward flux of $\mathbf{F}$ across the boundary of the region D.

5. $\mathbf{F} = (y - x)\mathbf{i} + (z - y)\mathbf{j} + (y - x)\mathbf{k}$
   D: The cube bounded by the planes $x = \pm 1$, $y = \pm 1$, and $z = \pm 1$
6. $\mathbf{F} = x^2\mathbf{i} + y^2\mathbf{j} + z^2\mathbf{k}$
   (a) D: The cube cut from the first octant by the planes $x = 1$, $y = 1$, and $z = 1$
   (b) D: The cube bounded by the planes $x = \pm 1$, $y = \pm 1$, and $z = \pm 1$
   (c) D: The region cut from the solid cylinder $x^2 + y^2 \le 4$ by the planes $z = 0$ and $z = 1$
7. $\mathbf{F} = y\mathbf{i} + xy\mathbf{j} - z\mathbf{k}$
   D: The region inside the solid cylinder $x^2 + y^2 \le 4$ between the planes $z = 0$ and the paraboloid $z = x^2 + y^2$
8. $\mathbf{F} = x^2\mathbf{i} + xz\mathbf{j} + 3z\mathbf{k}$
   D: the solid sphere $x^2 + y^2 + z^2 \le 4$
9. $\mathbf{F} = x^2\mathbf{i} - 2xy\mathbf{j} + 3xz\mathbf{k}$
   D: The region cut from the first octant by the sphere $x^2 + y^2 + z^2 = 4$
10. $\mathbf{F} = (6x^2 + 2xy)\mathbf{i} + (2y + x^2z)\mathbf{j} + 4x^2y^3\mathbf{k}$
    D: The region cut from the first octant by the cylinder $x^2 + y^2 = 4$ and the plane $z = 3$
11. $\mathbf{F} = 2xz\mathbf{i} - xy\mathbf{j} - z^2\mathbf{k}$
    D: The wedge cut from the first octant by the plane $y + z = 4$ and the elliptical cylinder $4x^2 + y^2 = 16$
12. $\mathbf{F} = x^3\mathbf{i} + y^3\mathbf{j} + z^3\mathbf{k}$
    D: The solid sphere $x^2 + y^2 + z^2 \le a^2$
13. $\mathbf{F} = \sqrt{x^2 + y^2 + z^2}\,(x\mathbf{i} + y\mathbf{j} + z\mathbf{k})$
    D: The region $1 \le x^2 + y^2 + z^2 \le 2$
14. $\mathbf{F} = (x\mathbf{i} + y\mathbf{j} + z\mathbf{k})/\sqrt{x^2 + y^2 + z^2}$
    D: The region $1 \le x^2 + y^2 + z^2 \le 4$
15. $\mathbf{F} = (5x^3 + 12xy^2)\mathbf{i} + (y^3 + e^y \sin z)\mathbf{j} + (5z^3 + e^y \cos z)\mathbf{k}$
    D: The solid region between the spheres $x^2 + y^2 + z^2 = 1$ and $x^2 + y^2 + z^2 = 2$
16. $\mathbf{F} = \ln(x^2 + y^2)\mathbf{i} - \left(\dfrac{2z}{x}\tan^{-1}\dfrac{y}{x}\right)\mathbf{j} + z\sqrt{x^2 + y^2}\,\mathbf{k}$
    D: The thick-walled cylinder $1 \le x^2 + y^2 \le 2$, $-1 \le z \le 2$

Explorations

17. ***div (curl G)*** $= 0$
    (a) Show that if the necessary partial derivatives of the components of the field $\mathbf{G} = M\mathbf{i} + N\mathbf{j} + P\mathbf{k}$ are continuous, then $\nabla \cdot \nabla \times \mathbf{G} = 0$.
    (b) Writing to Learn What, if anything, can you conclude about the flux of the field $\nabla \times \mathbf{G}$ across a closed surface? Give reasons for your answer.
18. ***Identities*** Let $\mathbf{F}_1$ and $\mathbf{F}_2$ be differentiable vector fields, and let a and b be arbitrary real constants. Verify the following identities.
    (a) $\nabla \cdot (a\mathbf{F}_1 + b\mathbf{F}_2) = a\nabla \cdot \mathbf{F}_1 + b\nabla \cdot \mathbf{F}_2$
    (b) $\nabla \times (a\mathbf{F}_1 + b\mathbf{F}_2) = a\nabla \times \mathbf{F}_1 + b\nabla \times \mathbf{F}_2$
    (c) $\nabla \cdot (\mathbf{F}_1 \times \mathbf{F}_2) = \mathbf{F}_2 \cdot \nabla \times \mathbf{F}_1 - \mathbf{F}_1 \cdot \nabla \times \mathbf{F}_2$
19. ***Identities*** Let $\mathbf{F}$ be a differentiable vector field and let $g(x, y, z)$ be a differentiable scalar function. Verify the following identities.
    (a) $\nabla \cdot (g\mathbf{F}) = g\nabla \cdot \mathbf{F} + \nabla g \cdot \mathbf{F}$
    (b) $\nabla \times (g\mathbf{F}) = g\nabla \times \mathbf{F} + \nabla g \times \mathbf{F}$
20. ***Identities*** If $\mathbf{F} = M\mathbf{i} + N\mathbf{j} + P\mathbf{k}$ is a differentiable vector field, we define the notation $\mathbf{F} \cdot \nabla$ to mean
    $$M\frac{\partial}{\partial x} + N\frac{\partial}{\partial y} + P\frac{\partial}{\partial z}.$$
    For differentiable vector fields $\mathbf{F}_1$ and $\mathbf{F}_2$ verify the following identities.
    (a) $\nabla \times (\mathbf{F}_1 \times \mathbf{F}_2) = (\mathbf{F}_2 \cdot \nabla)\mathbf{F}_1 - (\mathbf{F}_1 \cdot \nabla)\mathbf{F}_2 + (\nabla \cdot \mathbf{F}_2)\mathbf{F}_1 - (\nabla \cdot \mathbf{F}_1)\mathbf{F}_2$
    (b) $\nabla(\mathbf{F}_1 \cdot \mathbf{F}_2) = (\mathbf{F}_1 \cdot \nabla)\mathbf{F}_2 + (\mathbf{F}_2 \cdot \nabla)\mathbf{F}_1 + \mathbf{F}_1 \times (\nabla \times \mathbf{F}_2) + \mathbf{F}_2 \times (\nabla \times \mathbf{F}_1)$

In Exercises 21–24, *work in groups of two or three* to solve the problem.

21. **Writing to Learn** Let $\mathbf{F}$ be a field whose components have continuous first partial derivatives throughout a portion of space containing a region D bounded by a smooth closed surface S. If $|\mathbf{F}| \le 1$, can any bound be placed on the size of
    $$\iiint_D \nabla \cdot \mathbf{F}\, dV?$$
    Give reasons for your answer.
22. **Writing to Learn** The base of the closed cubelike surface shown here is the unit square in the xy-plane. The four sides lie in the planes $x = 0$, $x = 1$, $y = 0$, and $y = 1$. The top is an arbitrary smooth surface whose identity is unknown. Let $\mathbf{F} = x\mathbf{i} - 2y\mathbf{j} + (z + 3)\mathbf{k}$, and suppose the outward flux of $\mathbf{F}$ through side

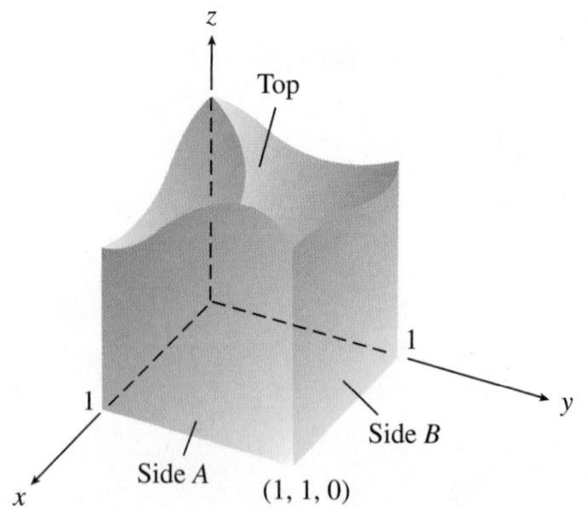

A is 1 and through side B is -3. Can you conclude anything about the outward flux through the top? Give reasons for your answer.

23. **(a)** Show that the flux of the position vector field $\mathbf{F} = x\mathbf{i} + y\mathbf{j} + z\mathbf{k}$ outward through a smooth closed surface S is three times the volume of the region enclosed by the surface.

(b) Let $\mathbf{n}$ be the outward unit normal vector field on S. Show that it is not possible for $\mathbf{F}$ to be orthogonal to $\mathbf{n}$ at every point of S.

24. Among all rectangular solids defined by the inequalities $0 \le x \le a$, $0 \le y \le b$, $0 \le z \le 1$, find the one for which the total flux of $\mathbf{F} = (-x^2 - 4xy)\mathbf{i} - 6yz\mathbf{j} + 12z\mathbf{k}$ outward through the six sides is greatest. What is the greatest flux?

25. Let $\mathbf{F} = x\mathbf{i} + y\mathbf{j} + z\mathbf{k}$, and suppose the surface S and region D satisfy the hypotheses of the Divergence Theorem. Show that the volume of D is given by the formula

$$\text{Volume of } D = \frac{1}{3}\iint_S \mathbf{F}\cdot\mathbf{n}\,d\sigma.$$

26. Show that the outward flux of a constant vector field $\mathbf{F} = \mathbf{C}$ across any closed surface to which the Divergence Theorem applies is zero.

27. ***Harmonic Functions*** A function $f(x, y, z)$ is **harmonic** in a region D in space if it satisfies the Laplace equation

$$\nabla^2 f = \nabla\cdot\nabla f = \frac{\partial^2 f}{\partial x^2} + \frac{\partial^2 f}{\partial y^2} + \frac{\partial^2 f}{\partial z^2} = 0$$

throughout D.

(a) Suppose f is harmonic throughout a bounded region D enclosed by a smooth surface S and $\mathbf{n}$ is the chosen unit normal vector on S. Show that the integral over S of $\nabla f\cdot\mathbf{n}$, the derivative of f in the direction of $\mathbf{n}$, is zero.

(b) Show that if f is harmonic on D, then

$$\iint_S f\nabla f\cdot\mathbf{n}\,d\sigma = \iiint_D |\nabla f|^2\,dV.$$

28. Let S be the surface of the portion of the solid sphere $x^2 + y^2 + z^2 \le a^2$ that lies in the first octant and let $f(x,y,z) = \ln\sqrt{x^2 + y^2 + z^2}$. Calculate

$$\iint_S \nabla f\cdot\mathbf{n}\,d\sigma.$$

($\nabla f\cdot\mathbf{n}$ is the derivative of f in the direction of $\mathbf{n}$.)

29. ***Green's First Formula*** Suppose f and g are scalar functions with continuous first- and second-order partial derivatives throughout a closed region D that is bounded by a piecewise smooth surface S. Show that

$$\iint_S f\,\nabla g\cdot\mathbf{n}\,d\sigma = \iiint_D (f\nabla^2 g + \nabla f\cdot\nabla g)\,dV. \qquad (9)$$

Equation (9) is **Green's first formula.** (*Hint:* Apply the Divergence Theorem to the field $\mathbf{F} = f\nabla g$.)

30. ***Green's Second Formula (Continuation of Exercise 29)*** Interchange f and g in Equation (9) to obtain a similar formula. Then subtract this formula from Equation (9) to show that

$$\iint_S (f\nabla g - g\nabla f)\cdot\mathbf{n}\,d\sigma = \iiint_D (f\nabla^2 g - g\nabla 2f)\,dV. \qquad (10)$$

This equation is **Green's second formula.**

Extending the Ideas

31. ***Conservation of Mass*** Let $\mathbf{v}(t, x, y, z)$ be a continuously differentiable vector field over the region D in space and let $p(t, x, y, z)$ be a continuously differentiable scalar function. The variable t represents the time domain. The Law of Conservation of Mass asserts that

$$\frac{d}{dt}\iiint_D p(t, x, y, z)\,dV = -\iint_S p\mathbf{v}\cdot\mathbf{n}\,d\sigma,$$

where S is the surface enclosing D.

(a) Give a physical interpretation of the conservation of mass law if $\mathbf{v}$ is a velocity flow field and p represents the density of the fluid at point (x, y, z) at time t.

(b) Use the Divergence Theorem and Leibniz's rule,

$$\frac{d}{dt}\iiint_D p(t, x, y, z)\,dV = \iiint_D \frac{\partial p}{\partial t}\,dV,$$

to show that the Law of Conservation of Mass is equivalent to the continuity equation,

$$\nabla\cdot p\mathbf{v} + \frac{\partial p}{\partial t} = 0.$$

(In the first term, $\nabla\cdot p\mathbf{v}$, the variable t is held fixed, and in the second term, $\partial p/\partial t$, it is assumed that the point (x, y, z) in D is held fixed.)

32. ***General Diffusion Equation*** Let $T(t, x, y, z)$ be a function with continuous second derivatives giving the temperature at time t at the point (x, y, z) of a solid occupying a region D in space. If the solid's specific heat and mass density are denoted by the constants c and ρ respectively, the quantity $c\rho T$ is the solid's **heat energy per unit volume.**

(a) Explain why $-\nabla T$ points in the direction of heat flow.

(b) Let $-k\nabla T$ denote the **energy flux vector.** (Here the constant k is the **conductivity.**) Assuming the Law of Conservation of Mass with $-k\nabla T = \mathbf{v}$ and $c\rho T = p$ in Exercise 31, derive the **diffusion** (heat) **equation.**

Chapter 16 Key Terms

Bendixson's criterion (p. 851)
center of mass (p. 818)
circulation around a curve (p. 826)
circulation density (p. 841)
component functions (p. 821)
component test for conservative fields (p. 834)
conductivity (p. 891)
connected region (p. 832)
conservative field (p. 832)
continuity equation (p. 886)
continuous field (p. 821)
curl (p. 841)
differentiable field (p. 821)
differential form (p. 836)
diffusion equation (p. 891)
diffusivity constant (p. 891)
divergence (p. 840)
divergence of a vector field (p. 881)
Divergence Theorem (p. 881)
energy flux vector (p. 891)
exact differential form (p. 836)
first moments (p. 817)
flow along a curve (p. 826)
flow integral (p. 826)
flux across a curve (p. 827)
flux across a surface (p. 858)
flux density (p. 840)
Fundamental Theorem of Line Integrals (p. 833)
Gauss's Law (p. 886)
gradient field (p. 823)
Green's first formula (p. 891)
Green's second formula (p. 891)
Green's Theorem (normal form) (p. 842)
Green's Theorem (tangential form) (p. 843)
harmonic function (p. 891)
heat energy per unit volume (p. 891)
integral over a curve (p. 815)
integral over a surface (p. 852)
Laplace equation (p. 850)
line integral (p. 815)
mass (p. 817)
moment of inertia (p. 817)
orientable (p. 857)
oriented surface (p. 857)
parameter domain (p. 862)
parameters (p. 862)
parametric formula for surface area (p. 865)
parametrization of a surface (p. 862)
path independent integral (p. 833)
piecewise smooth (p. 856)
positive direction (p. 857)
potential function (p. 832)
radius of gyration (p. 817)
simply connected (p. 878)
smooth parametrized surface (p. 864)
smooth surface (p. 852)
Stokes's Theorem (p. 872)
streamlines (p. 851)
surface (p. 862)
surface area (p. 852)
surface area differential (p. 856)
surface integral (p. 856)
tangent plane at a point (p. 870)
test for exactness (p. 837)
torus of revolution (p. 870)
two-sided surface (p. 857)
vector field (p. 821)
work done by a force (p. 823)

Chapter 16 Review Exercises

In Exercises 1–4, evaluate the line integral over the indicated paths.

1. Figure 16.82 shows two polygonal paths in space joining the origin to the point (1, 1, 1). Integrate $f(x, y, z) = 2x - 3y^2 - 2z + 3$ over each path.

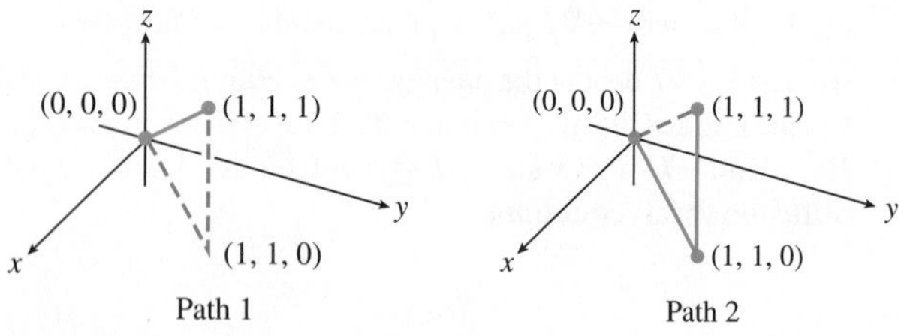

Figure 16.82 The paths in Exercise 1.

2. Figure 16.83 shows three polygonal paths joining the origin to the point (1, 1, 1). Integrate $f(x, y, z) = x^2 + y - z$ over each path.

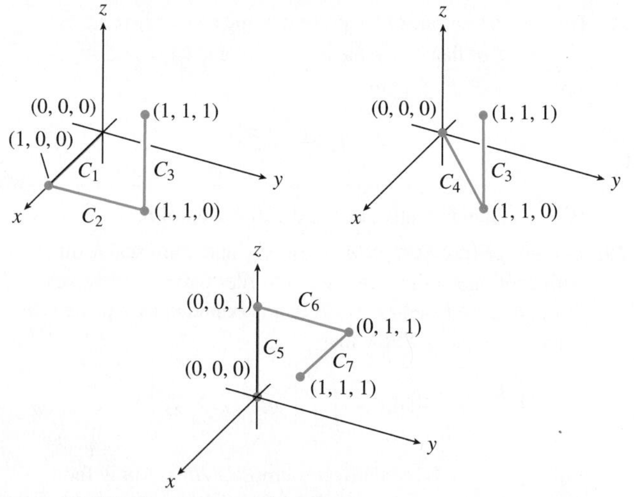

Figure 16.83 The paths in Exercise 2.

3. Integrate $f(x, y, z) = \sqrt{x^2 + z^2}$ over the circle $\mathbf{r}(t) = (a \cos t)\mathbf{j} + (a \sin t)\mathbf{k}, 0 \le t \le 2\pi$.

4. Integrate $f(x, y, z) = \sqrt{x^2 + z^2}$ over the curve $\mathbf{r}(t) = (\cos t + t \sin t)\mathbf{i} + (\sin t - t \cos t)\mathbf{j}, 0 \le t \le \sqrt{3}$.

In Exercises 5 and 6, evaluate the integral.

5. $\displaystyle\int_{(-1,1,1)}^{(4,-3,0)} \frac{dx + dy + dz}{\sqrt{x + y + z}}$

6. $\displaystyle\int_{(1,1,1)}^{(10,3,3)} dx - \sqrt{\frac{z}{y}}\,dy - \sqrt{\frac{y}{z}}\,dz$

7. Integrate $\mathbf{F} = (y \sin z)\mathbf{i} + (x \sin z)\mathbf{j} + (xy \cos z)\mathbf{k}$ around the circle cut from the sphere $x^2 + y^2 + z^2 = 5$ by the plane $z = -1$, clockwise as viewed from above.

8. Integrate $\mathbf{F} = 3x^2y\mathbf{i} + (x^3 + 1)\mathbf{j} + 9z^2\mathbf{k}$ around the circle cut from the sphere $x^2 + y^2 + z^2 = 9$ by the plane $x = 2$.

In Exercises 9 and 10, evaluate the line integral.

9. $\displaystyle\int_C 8x \sin y\, dx - 8y \cos x\, dy$

C is the square cut from the first quadrant by the lines $x = \pi/2$ and $y = \pi/2$.

10. $\displaystyle\int_C y^2\, dx + x^2\, dy$

C is the circle $x^2 + y^2 = 4$.

11. Find the area of the elliptical region cut from the plane $x + y + z = 1$ by the cylinder $x^2 + y^2 = 1$.

12. Find the area of the cap cut from the paraboloid $y^2 + z^2 = 3x$ by the plane $x = 1$.

13. Find the area of the cap cut from the top of the sphere $x^2 + y^2 + z^2 = 1$ by the plane $z = \sqrt{2}/2$.

14. **(a)** Find the area of the surface cut from the hemisphere $x^2 + y^2 + z^2 = 4, z \ge 0$, by the cylinder $x^2 + y^2 = 2x$.

(b) Find the area of the portion of the cylinder that lies inside the hemisphere. (*Hint:* Project onto the xz-plane. Or, evaluate the integral $\int h\, ds$, where h is the altitude of the cylinder and ds is the element of arc length on the circle $x^2 + y^2 = 2x$ in the xy-plane.)

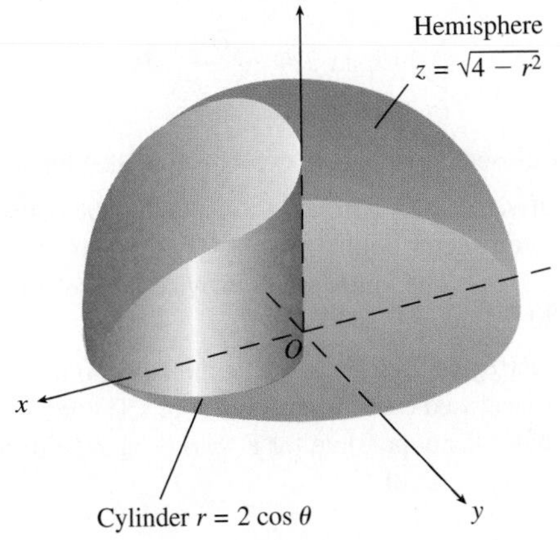

15. Find the area of the triangle in which the plane $(x/a) + (y/b) + (z/c) = 1$ $(a, b, c > 0)$ intersects the first octant. Check your answer with an appropriate vector calculation.

16. Integrate

(a) $g(x, y, z) = \dfrac{yz}{\sqrt{4y^2 + 1}}$

(b) $g(x, y, z) = \dfrac{z}{\sqrt{4y^2 + 1}}$

over the surface cut from the parabolic cylinder $y^2 - z = 1$ by the planes $x = 0, x = 3$, and $z = 0$.

17. Integrate $g(x, y, z) = x^4 y(y^2 + z^2)$ over the portion of the cylinder $y^2 + z^2 = 25$ that lies in the first octant between the planes $x = 0$ and $x = 1$ and above the plane $z = 3$.

18. ***Area of Wyoming*** The state of Wyoming is bounded by the meridians 111°3′ and 104°3′ west longitude and by the circles 41° and 45° north latitude. Assuming that Earth is a sphere of radius $R = 3959$ mi, find the area of Wyoming.

In Exercises 19–24, find a parametrization for the surface. (There are many ways to do these, so your answers may not be the same as those in the back of the book.)

19. The portion of the sphere $x^2 + y^2 + z^2 = 36$ between the planes $z = -3$ and $z = 3\sqrt{3}$

20. The portion of the paraboloid $z = -(x^2 + y^2)/2$ above the plane $z = -2$

21. The cone $z = 1 + \sqrt{x^2 + y^2}, z \le 3$

22. The portion of the plane $4x + 2y + 4z = 12$ that lies above the square $0 \le x \le 2, 0 \le y \le 2$ in the first quadrant

23. The portion of the paraboloid $y = 2(x^2 + z^2), y \le 2$, that lies above the xy-plane

24. The portion of the hemisphere $x^2 + y^2 + z^2 = 10, y \ge 0$, in the first octant

25. Find the area of the surface $\mathbf{r}(u, v) = (u + v)\mathbf{i} + (u - v)\mathbf{j} + v\mathbf{k}$, $0 \le u \le 1, 0 \le v \le 1$.

26. Integrate $f(x, y, z) = xy - z^2$ over the surface in Exercise 25.

27. ***Area of a Helicoid*** Find the surface area of the helicoid $\mathbf{r}(r, \theta) = r \cos \theta\mathbf{i} + r \sin \theta\mathbf{j} + \theta\mathbf{k}, 0 \le \theta \le 2\pi$ and $0 \le r \le 1$, in the accompanying figure.

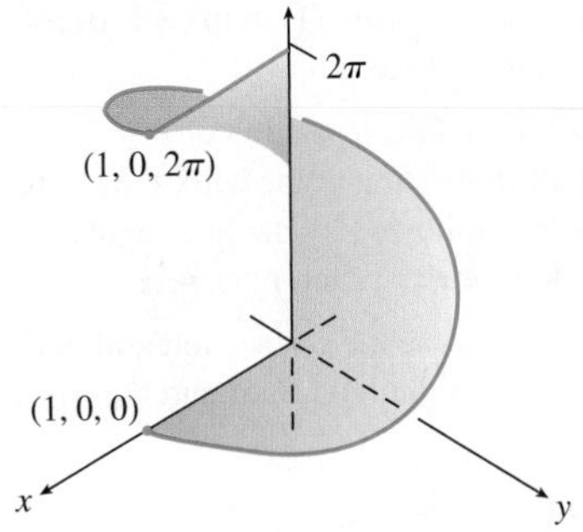

28. *Integrating over a Helicoid* Evaluate the integral

$$\iint_S \sqrt{x^2 + y^2 + 1}\, d\sigma,$$ where S is the helicoid in Exercise 27.

In Exercises 29–32, identify whether the field is conservative or not conservative.

29. $\mathbf{F} = x\mathbf{i} + y\mathbf{j} + z\mathbf{k}$

30. $\mathbf{F} = (x\mathbf{i} + y\mathbf{j} + z\mathbf{k})/(x^2 + y^2 + z^2)^{3/2}$

31. $\mathbf{F} = xe^y\mathbf{i} + ye^x\mathbf{j} + ze^x\mathbf{k}$

32. $\mathbf{F} = (\mathbf{i} + z\mathbf{j} + y\mathbf{k})/(x + yz)$

In Exercises 33 and 34, find a potential function for the field.

33. $\mathbf{F} = 2\mathbf{i} + (2y + z)\mathbf{j} + (y + 1)\mathbf{k}$

34. $\mathbf{F} = (z \cos xz)\mathbf{i} + e^y\mathbf{j} + (x \cos xz)\mathbf{k}$

In Exercises 35 and 36, find the work done by the field along the paths from (0, 0, 0) to (1, 1, 1) in Figure 16.82.

35. $\mathbf{F} = 2xy\mathbf{i} + \mathbf{j} + x^2\mathbf{k}$ **36.** $\mathbf{F} = 2xy\mathbf{i} + x^2\mathbf{j} + \mathbf{k}$

In Exercises 37–40, *work in groups of two or three* to solve the problem.

37. *Finding Work Two Ways* Find the work done by

$$\mathbf{F} = \frac{x\mathbf{i} + y\mathbf{j}}{(x^2 + y^2)^{3/2}}$$

over the plane curve $\mathbf{r}(t) = (e^t \cos t)\mathbf{i} + (e^t \sin t)\mathbf{j}$ from the point $(1, 0)$ to the point $(e^{2\pi}, 0)$ in two ways:

(a) by using the parametrization of the curve to evaluate the work integral.

(b) by evaluating a potential function for **F**.

38. *Flows* Find the flow of the field $\mathbf{F} = \nabla(x^2ze^y)$

(a) once around the ellipse C in which the plane $x + y + z = 1$ intersects the cylinder $x^2 + z^2 = 25$, clockwise as viewed from the positive y-axis.

(b) along the curved boundary of the helicoid in Exercise 27 from $(1, 0, 0)$ to $(1, 0, 2\pi)$.

39. *Flows* Suppose $\mathbf{F}(x, y) = (x + y)\mathbf{i} - (x^2 + y^2)\mathbf{j}$ is the velocity field of a fluid flowing across the xy-plane. Find the flow along each of the following paths from $(1, 0)$ to $(-1, 0)$.

(a) The upper half of the circle $x^2 + y^2 = 1$

(b) The line segment from $(1, 0)$ to $(-1, 0)$

(c) The line segment from $(1, 0)$ to $(-1, 0)$ followed by the line segment from $(0, -1)$ to $(-1, 0)$

40. *Circulation* Find the circulation of $\mathbf{F} = 2x\mathbf{i} + 2z\mathbf{j} + 2y\mathbf{k}$ along the closed path consisting of the helix $\mathbf{r}_1(t) = (\cos t)\mathbf{i} + \sin t)\mathbf{j} + t\mathbf{k}$, $0 \le t \le \pi/2$, followed by the line segments $\mathbf{r}_2(t) = \mathbf{j} + (\pi/2)(1 - t)\mathbf{k}$, $0 \le t \le 1$, and $\mathbf{r}_3(t) = t\mathbf{i} + (1 - t)\mathbf{j}$, $0 \le t \le 1$.

In Exercises 41 and 42, use the surface integral in Stokes's Theorem to find the circulation of the field **F** around the curve C in the indicated direction.

41. $\mathbf{F} = y^2\mathbf{i} - y\mathbf{j} + 3z^2\mathbf{k}$

C: The ellipse in which the plane $2x + 6y - 3z = 6$ meets the cylinder $x^2 + y^2 = 1$, counterclockwise as viewed from above

42. $\mathbf{F} = (x^2 + y)\mathbf{i} + (x + y)\mathbf{j} + (4y^2 - z)\mathbf{k}$

C: The circle in which the plane $z = -y$ meets the sphere $x^2 + y^2 + z^2 = 4$, counterclockwise as viewed from above

43. *Mass of a Wire* Find the mass of a thin wire lying along the curve $\mathbf{r}(t) = \sqrt{2}\,t\mathbf{i} + \sqrt{2}\,t\mathbf{j} + (4 - t^2)\mathbf{k}$, $0 \le t \le 1$, if the density at t is **(a)** $\delta = 3t$ and **(b)** $\delta = 1$.

44. *Center of Mass of a Curved Wire* Find the center of mass of a thin wire lying along the curve $\mathbf{r}(t) = t\mathbf{i} + 2t\mathbf{j} + (2/3)t^{2/3}\mathbf{k}$, $0 \le t \le 2$, if the density at t is $\delta = 3\sqrt{5 + t}$.

45. *Center of Mass, Moments, and Radii of Gyration* Find the center of mass and the moments of inertia and radii of gyration about the coordinate axes of a thin wire lying along the curve

$$\mathbf{r}(t) = t\mathbf{i} + \frac{2\sqrt{2}}{3}t^{3/2}\mathbf{j} + \frac{t^2}{2}\mathbf{k},\ 0 \le t \le 2,$$

if the density is $\delta = 1/(t + 1)$.

46. *A Metal Arch* A slender metal arch lies along the semicircle $y = \sqrt{a^2 - x^2}$ in the xy-plane. The density at the point (x, y) on the arch is $\delta(x, y) = 2a - y$. Find the center of mass.

47. *Wire of Constant Density* A wire of constant density $\delta = 1$ lies along the curve $\mathbf{r}(t) = (e^t \cos t)\mathbf{i} + (e^t \sin t)\mathbf{j} + e^t\mathbf{k}$, $0 \le t \le \ln 2$. Find $\bar{z}$, I_z, and R_z.

48. *Wire of Constant Density* Find the mass and center of mass of a wire of constant density δ that lies along the helix $\mathbf{r}(t) = (2 \sin t)\mathbf{i} + (2 \cos t)\mathbf{j} + 3t\mathbf{k}$, $0 \le t \le 2\pi$.

49. *Thin Shell of Variable Density* Find I_z, R_z, and the center of mass of a thin shell of density $\delta(x, y, z) = z$ cut from the upper portion of the sphere $x^2 + y^2 + z^2 = 25$ by the plane $z = 3$.

50. *Moment of Inertia of a Cube about One Edge* Find the moment of inertia about the z-axis of the surface of the cube cut from the first octant by the planes $x = 1$, $y = 1$, and $z = 1$ if the density is $\delta = 1$.

In Exercises 51 and 52, use Green's Theorem to find the counterclockwise circulation and outward flux for the given field and curve.

51. $\mathbf{F} = (2xy + x)\mathbf{i} + (xy - y)\mathbf{j}$

C: The square bounded by $x = 0$, $x = 1$, $y = 0$, $y = 1$

52. $\mathbf{F} = (y - 6x^2)\mathbf{i} + (x + y^2)\mathbf{j}$

C: The triangle made by the lines $y = 0$, $y = x$, and $x = 1$.

53. Show that

$$\oint_C \ln x \sin y\, dy - \frac{\cos y}{x}\, dx = 0$$

for any closed curve C to which Green's Theorem applies.

54. (a) *Outward Flux and Area* Show that the outward flux of the position vector field $\mathbf{F} = x\mathbf{i} + y\mathbf{j}$ across any closed curve to which Green's Theorem applies is twice the area of the region enclosed by the curve.

(b) *Writing to Learn* Let $\mathbf{n}$ be the outward unit normal vector to a closed curve to which Green's Theorem applies. Show that it is not possible for $\mathbf{F} = x\mathbf{i} + y\mathbf{j}$ to be orthogonal to $\mathbf{n}$ at every point of C.

In Exercises 55–58, find the outward flux of **F** across the boundary of D.

55. $\mathbf{F} = 2xy\mathbf{i} + 2yz\mathbf{j} + 2xz\mathbf{k}$

D: The cube cut from the first octant by the planes $x = 1$, $y = 1$, $z = 1$

56. $\mathbf{F} = xz\mathbf{i} + yz\mathbf{j} + \mathbf{k}$

D: The entire surface of the upper cap cut from the solid sphere $x^2 + y^2 + z^2 \leq 25$ by the plane $z = 3$

57. $\mathbf{F} = -2x\mathbf{i} - 3y\mathbf{j} + z\mathbf{k}$

D: The upper region cut from the solid sphere $x^2 + y^2 + z^2 \leq 2$ by the paraboloid $z = x^2 + y^2$

58. $\mathbf{F} = (6x + y)\mathbf{i} - (x + z)\mathbf{j} + 4yz\mathbf{k}$

D: The region in the first octant bounded by the cone $z = \sqrt{x^2 + y^2}$, the cylinder $x^2 + y^2 = 1$, and the coordinate planes

59. ***Flux*** Let S be the surface that is bounded on the left by the hemisphere $x^2 + y^2 + z^2 = a^2$, $y \leq 0$, in the middle by the cylinder $x^2 + z^2 = a^2$, $0 \leq y \leq a$, and on the right by the plane $y = a$. Find the flux of the field $\mathbf{F} = y\mathbf{i} + z\mathbf{j} + x\mathbf{k}$ outward across S.

60. ***Flux*** Find the outward flux of the field $\mathbf{F} = 3xz^2\mathbf{i} + y\mathbf{j} - z^3\mathbf{k}$ across the surface of the solid in the first octant that is bounded by the cylinder $x^2 + 4y^2 = 16$ and the planes $y = 2x$, $x = 0$, and $z = 0$.

61. ***Flux*** Use the Divergence Theorem to find the flux of $\mathbf{F} = xy^2\mathbf{i} + x^2y\mathbf{j} + y\mathbf{k}$ outward through the surface of the region enclosed by the cylinder $x^2 + y^2 = 1$ and the planes $z = 1$ and $z = -1$.

62. ***Finding Flux Two Ways*** Find the flux of $\mathbf{F} = (3z + 1)\mathbf{k}$ upward across the hemisphere $x^2 + y^2 + z^2 = a^2$, $z \geq 0$ **(a)** with the Divergence Theorem and **(b)** by evaluating the flux integral directly.

Appendices

A1 Formulas from Precalculus Mathematics

What you'll learn about

- Algebra
- Geometry
- Trigonometry

. . . and why

These basic ideas and formulas from precalculus are useful in calculus.

Algebra

1. Laws of Exponents

$$a^m a^n = a^{m+n}, \quad (ab)^m = a^m b^m, \quad (a^m)^n = a^{mn}, \quad a^{m/n} = \sqrt[n]{a^m}$$

If $a \neq 0$, $\quad \dfrac{a^m}{a^n} = a^{m-n}, \quad a^0 = 1, \quad a^{-m} = \dfrac{1}{a^m}$

2. Zero Division by zero is not defined.

If $a \neq 0$: $\quad \dfrac{0}{a} = 0, \quad a^0 = 1, \quad 0^a = 0$

For any number a: $\quad a \cdot 0 = 0 \cdot a = 0$

3. Fractions

$$\frac{a}{b} + \frac{c}{d} = \frac{ad + bc}{bd}, \quad \frac{a}{b} \cdot \frac{c}{d} = \frac{ac}{bd}, \quad \frac{a/b}{c/d} = \frac{a}{b} \cdot \frac{d}{c}, \quad \frac{-a}{b} = -\frac{a}{b} = \frac{a}{-b},$$

$$\frac{(a/b) + (c/d)}{(e/f) + (g/h)} = \frac{(a/b) + (c/d)}{(e/f) + (g/h)} \cdot \frac{bdfh}{bdfh} = \frac{(ad + bc)fh}{(eh + fg)bd}$$

4. The Binomial Theorem
For any positive integer n,

$$(a + b)^n = a^n + na^{n-1}b + \frac{n(n-1)}{1 \cdot 2}a^{n-2}b^2 + \frac{n(n-1)(n-2)}{1 \cdot 2 \cdot 3}a^{n-3}b^3 + \cdots + nab^{n-1} + b^n.$$

For instance,

$$(a + b)^1 = a + b,$$
$$(a + b)^2 = a^2 + 2ab + b^2,$$
$$(a + b)^3 = a^3 + 3a^2b + 3ab^2 + b^3,$$
$$(a + b)^4 = a^4 + 4a^3b + 6a^2b^2 + 4ab^3 + b^4.$$

5. Differences of Like Integer Powers, $n > 1$

$$a^n - b^n = (a - b)(a^{n-1} + a^{n-2}b + a^{n-3}b^2 + \cdots + ab^{n-2} + b^{n-1})$$

For instance,

$$a^2 - b^2 = (a - b)(a + b),$$
$$a^3 - b^3 = (a - b)(a^2 + ab + b^2),$$
$$a^4 - b^4 = (a - b)(a^3 + a^2b + ab^2 + b^3).$$

6. Completing the Square

If $a \neq 0$, we can rewrite the quadratic $ax^2 + bx + c$ in the form $au^2 + C$ by a process called completing the square:

$$ax^2 + bx + c = a\left(x^2 + \frac{b}{a}x\right) + c \qquad \text{Factor } a \text{ from the first two terms.}$$

$$= a\left(x^2 + \frac{b}{a}x + \frac{b^2}{4a^2} - \frac{b^2}{4a^2}\right) + c \qquad \text{Add and subtract the square of half the coefficient of } x.$$

$$= a\left(x^2 + \frac{b}{a}x + \frac{b^2}{4a^2}\right) + a\left(-\frac{b^2}{4a^2}\right) + c \qquad \text{Bring out the } -\frac{b^2}{4a^2}.$$

$$= \underbrace{a\left(x^2 + \frac{b}{a}x + \frac{b^2}{4a^2}\right)}_{\text{This is } \left(x + \frac{b}{2a}\right)^2.} + \underbrace{c - \frac{b^2}{4a}}_{\text{Call this part } C.}$$

$$= au^2 + C \qquad u = x + \frac{b}{2a}$$

7. The Quadratic Formula

By completing the square on the first two terms of the equation

$$ax^2 + bx + c = 0$$

and solving the resulting equation for x (details omitted), we obtain

$$x = \frac{-b \pm \sqrt{b^2 - 4ac}}{2a}.$$

This equation is the **quadratic formula**.

The solutions of the equation $2x^2 + 3x - 1 = 0$ are

$$x = \frac{-3 \pm \sqrt{(3)^2 - 4(2)(-1)}}{2(2)} = \frac{-3 \pm \sqrt{9 + 8}}{4}$$

or

$$x = \frac{-3 + \sqrt{17}}{4} \quad \text{and} \quad x = \frac{-3 - \sqrt{17}}{4}.$$

Geometry

(A = area, B = area of base, C = circumference, h = height, S = lateral area or surface area, V = volume)

1. Triangle

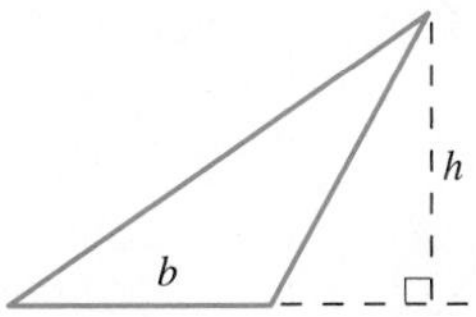

$$A = \frac{1}{2}bh$$

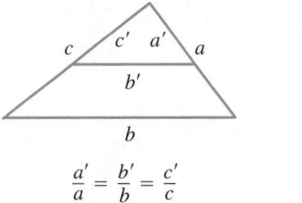

2. Similar Triangles

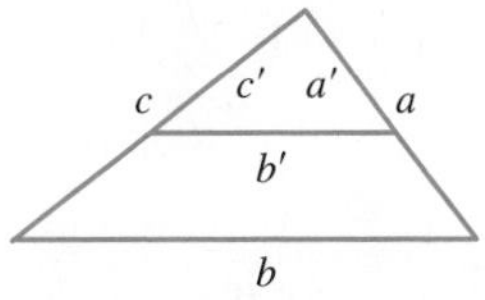

$$\frac{a'}{a} = \frac{b'}{b} = \frac{c'}{c}$$

3. Pythagorean Theorem

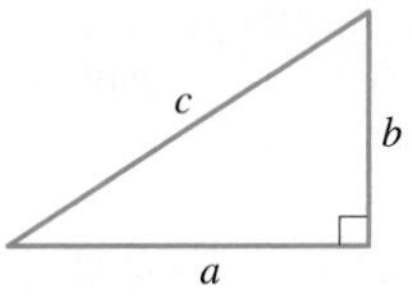

$$a^2 + b^2 = c^2$$

4. Parallelogram

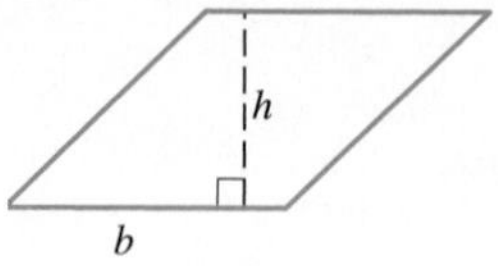

$A = bh$

5. Trapezoid

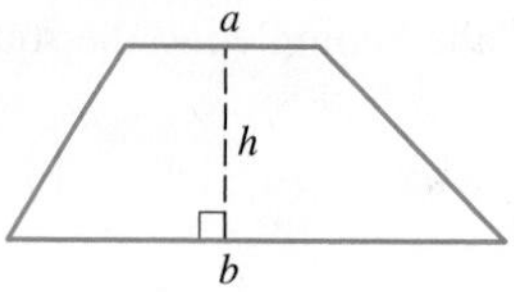

$A = \frac{1}{2}(a + b)h$

6. Circle

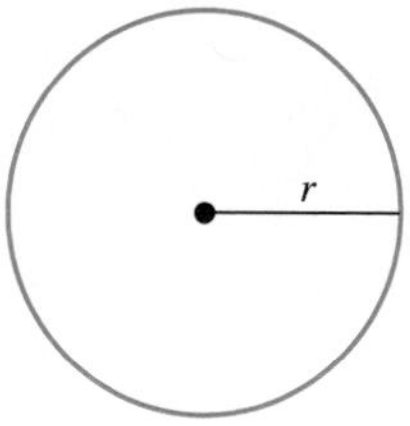

$A = \pi r^2$,
$C = 2\pi r$

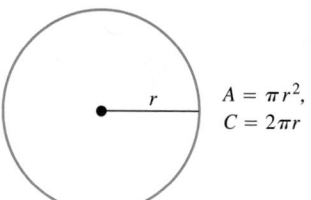

7. Any Cylinder or Prism with Parallel Bases

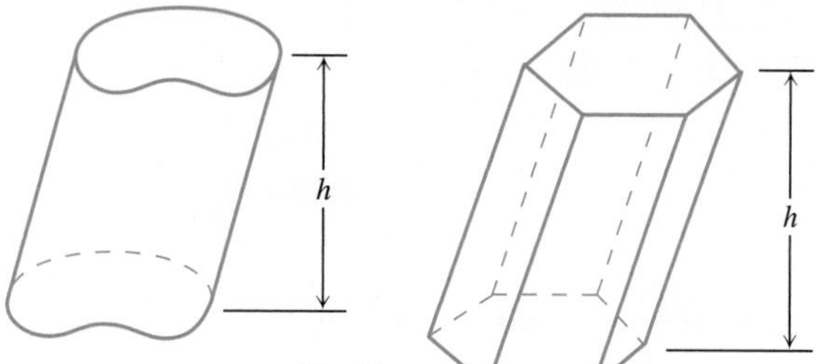

$V = Bh$

8. Right Circular Cylinder

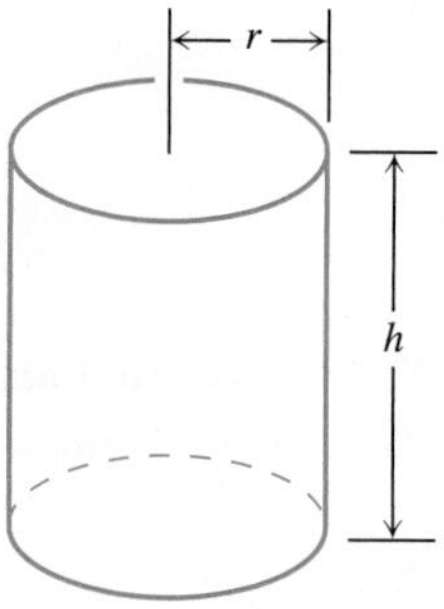

$V = \pi r^2 h,\ S = 2\pi rh$

9. Any Cone or Pyramid

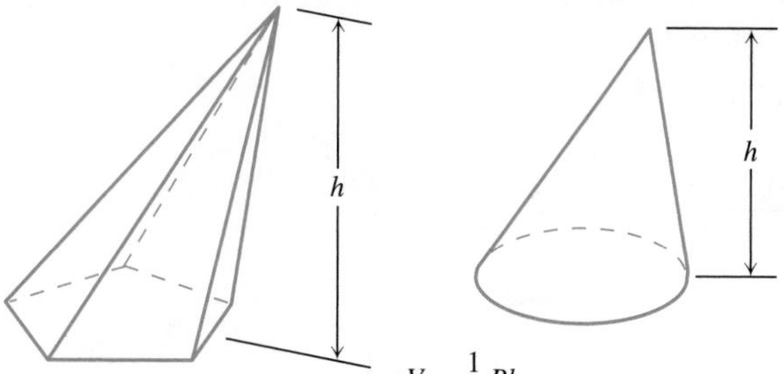

$V = \frac{1}{3}Bh$

10. Right Circular Cone

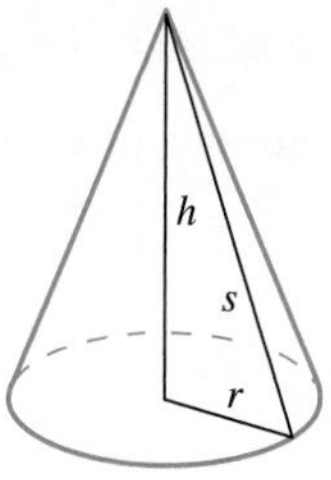

$V = \frac{1}{3}\pi r^2 h,\ S = \pi rs$

11. Sphere

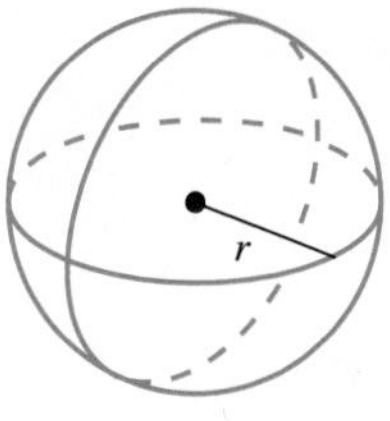

$V = \frac{4}{3}\pi r^3,\ S = 4\pi r^2$

Trigonometry

1. Definitions of Fundamental Identities

Sine: $\sin\theta = \dfrac{y}{r} = \dfrac{1}{\csc\theta}$

Cosine: $\cos\theta = \dfrac{x}{r} = \dfrac{1}{\sec\theta}$

Tangent: $\tan\theta = \dfrac{y}{x} = \dfrac{1}{\cot\theta}$

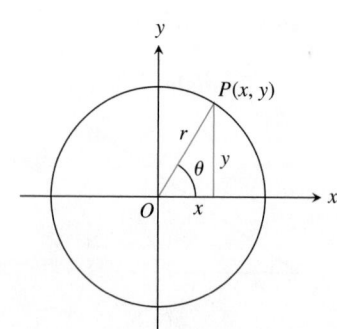

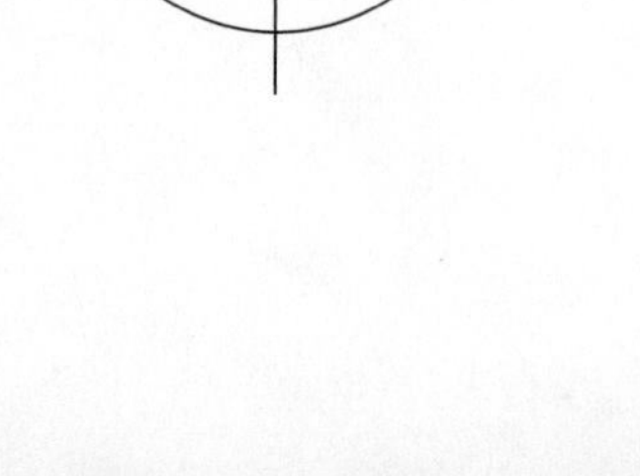

2. Identities

$$\sin(-\theta) = -\sin\theta, \qquad \cos(-\theta) = \cos\theta,$$

$$\sin^2\theta + \cos^2\theta = 1, \qquad \sec^2\theta = 1 + \tan^2\theta, \qquad \csc^2\theta = 1 + \cot^2\theta$$

$$\sin 2\theta = 2\sin\theta\cos\theta, \qquad \cos 2\theta = \cos^2\theta - \sin^2\theta$$

$$\cos^2\theta = \frac{1 + \cos 2\theta}{2}, \qquad \sin^2\theta = \frac{1 - \cos 2\theta}{2}$$

$$\sin(A + B) = \sin A\cos B + \cos A\sin B \qquad \tan(A + B) = \frac{\tan A + \tan B}{1 - \tan A\tan B}$$

$$\sin(A - B) = \sin A\cos B - \cos A\sin B$$

$$\cos(A + B) = \cos A\cos B - \sin A\sin B \qquad \tan(A - B) = \frac{\tan A - \tan B}{1 + \tan A\tan B}$$

$$\cos(A - B) = \cos A\cos B + \sin A\sin B$$

$$\sin\left(A - \frac{\pi}{2}\right) = -\cos A, \qquad \cos\left(A - \frac{\pi}{2}\right) = \sin A$$

$$\sin\left(A + \frac{\pi}{2}\right) = \cos A, \qquad \cos\left(A + \frac{\pi}{2}\right) = -\sin A$$

$$\sin A\sin B = \frac{1}{2}\cos(A - B) - \frac{1}{2}\cos(A + B)$$

$$\cos A\cos B = \frac{1}{2}\cos(A - B) + \frac{1}{2}\cos(A + B)$$

$$\sin A\cos B = \frac{1}{2}\sin(A - B) + \frac{1}{2}\sin(A + B)$$

$$\sin A + \sin B = 2\sin\frac{1}{2}(A + B)\cos\frac{1}{2}(A - B)$$

$$\sin A - \sin B = 2\cos\frac{1}{2}(A + B)\sin\frac{1}{2}(A - B)$$

$$\cos A + \cos B = 2\cos\frac{1}{2}(A + B)\cos\frac{1}{2}(A - B)$$

$$\cos A - \cos B = -2\sin\frac{1}{2}(A + B)\sin\frac{1}{2}(A - B)$$

3. Common Reference Triangles

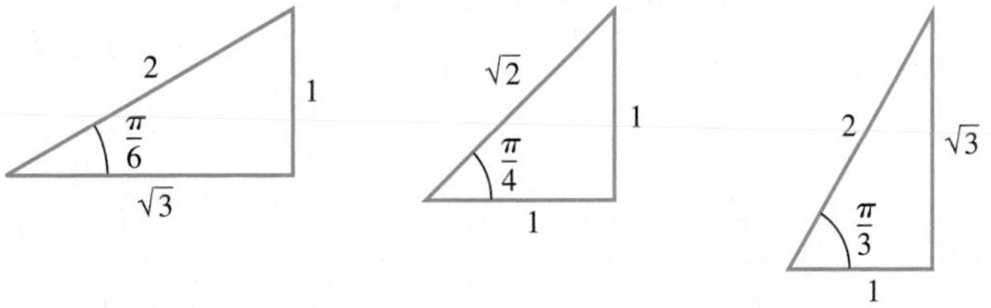

4. Angles and Sides of a Triangle

Law of cosines: $c^2 = a^2 + b^2 - 2ab\cos C$

Law of sines: $\dfrac{\sin A}{a} = \dfrac{\sin B}{b} = \dfrac{\sin C}{c}$

Area $= \dfrac{1}{2}bc\sin A = \dfrac{1}{2}ac\sin B = \dfrac{1}{2}ab\sin C$

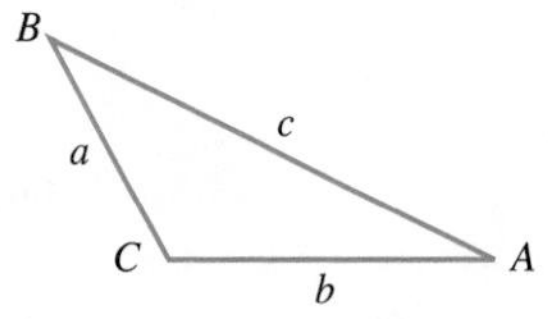

A2 Mathematical Induction

What you'll learn about

- Mathematical Induction Principle
- Other Starting Integers

. . . and why

Mathematical induction is an important method to provide proofs.

Mathematical Induction Principle

Many formulas, like

$$1 + 2 + \cdots + n = \frac{n(n+1)}{2},$$

can be shown to hold for every positive integer n by applying an axiom called the *mathematical induction principle.* A proof that uses this axiom is a *proof by mathematical induction* or a *proof by induction.*

The steps in proving a formula by induction are the following.

Step 1: Check that the formula holds for $n = 1$.

Step 2: Prove that if the formula holds for any positive integer $n = k$, then it also holds for the next integer, $n = (k + 1)$.

Once these steps are completed (the axiom says), we know that the formula holds for all positive integers n. By step 1 it holds for $n = 1$. By step 2 it holds for $n = 2$, and therefore by step 2 also for $n = 3$, and by step 2 again for $n = 4$, and so on. If the first domino falls, and the kth domino always knocks over the $(k + 1)$st when it falls, all the dominoes fall.

From another point of view, suppose we have a sequence of statements $S_1, S_2, \ldots,$ $S_n, \ldots,$ one for each positive integer. Suppose we can show that assuming any one of the statements to be true implies that the next statement in line is true. Suppose that we can also show that S_1 is true. Then we may conclude that the statements are true from S_1 on.

EXAMPLE 1 Sum of the First *n* Positive Integers

Show that for every positive integer n,

$$1 + 2 + \cdots + n = \frac{n(n+1)}{2}.$$

SOLUTION

We accomplish the proof by carrying out the two steps.

Step 1: The formula holds for $n = 1$ because

$$1 = \frac{1(1+1)}{2}.$$

Step 2: If the formula holds for $n = k$, does it hold for $n = (k + 1)$? The answer is yes, and here's why: If

$$1 + 2 + \cdots + k = \frac{k(k+1)}{2},$$

then

$$\begin{aligned} 1 + 2 + \cdots + k + (k+1) &= \frac{k(k+1)}{2} + (k+1) \\ &= \frac{k^2 + k + 2k + 2}{2} \\ &= \frac{(k+1)(k+2)}{2} = \frac{(k+1)((k+1)+1)}{2}. \end{aligned}$$

The last expression in this string of equalities is the expression $n(n + 1)/2$ for $n = (k + 1)$.

continued

The mathematical induction priniciple now guarantees the original formula for all positive integers n. All *we* have to do is carry out steps 1 and 2. The mathematical induction principle does the rest. *Now try Exercise 1.*

EXAMPLE 2 Sums of Powers of 1/2

Show that for all positive integers n,

$$\frac{1}{2^1} + \frac{1}{2^2} + \cdots + \frac{1}{2^n} = 1 - \frac{1}{2^n}.$$

SOLUTION

We accomplish the proof by carrying out the two steps of mathematical induction.

Step 1: The formula holds for $n = 1$ because

$$\frac{1}{2^1} = 1 - \frac{1}{2^1}.$$

Step 2: If

$$\frac{1}{2^1} + \frac{1}{2^2} + \cdots + \frac{1}{2^k} = 1 - \frac{1}{2^k},$$

then

$$\begin{aligned}\frac{1}{2^1} + \frac{1}{2^2} + \cdots + \frac{1}{2^k} + \frac{1}{2^{k+1}} &= 1 - \frac{1}{2^k} + \frac{1}{2^{k+1}} \\ &= 1 - \frac{1 \cdot 2}{2^k \cdot 2} + \frac{1}{2^{k+1}} \\ &= 1 - \frac{2}{2^{k+1}} + \frac{1}{2^{k+1}} \\ &= 1 - \frac{1}{2^{k+1}}.\end{aligned}$$

Thus, the original formula holds for $n = (k + 1)$ whenever it holds for $n = k$.

With these steps verified, the mathematical induction principle now guarantees the formula for every positive integer n. *Now try Exercise 5.*

Other Starting Integers

Instead of starting at $n = 1$, some induction arguments start at another integer. The steps for such an argument are as follows.

Step 1: Check that the formula holds for $n = n_1$ (the first appropriate integer).

Step 2: Prove that if the formula holds for any integer $n = k \geq n_1$, then it also holds for $n = (k + 1)$.

Once these steps are completed, the mathematical induction principle guarantees the formula for all $n \geq n_1$.

EXAMPLE 3 Factorial Exceeding Exponential

Show that $n! > 3^n$ if n is large enough.

continued

SOLUTION

How large is large enough? We experiment:

n	1	2	3	4	5	6	7
$n!$	1	2	6	24	120	720	5040
3^n	3	9	27	81	243	729	2187

It looks as if $n! > 3^n$ for $n \geq 7$. To be sure, we apply mathematical induction. We take $n_1 = 7$ in step 1 and try for step 2.

Suppose $k! > 3^k$ for some $k \geq 7$. Then

$$(k+1)! = (k+1)(k!) > (k+1)3^k > 7 \cdot 3^k > 3^{k+1}.$$

Thus, for $k \geq 7$,

$$k! > 3^k \quad \Rightarrow \quad (k+1)! > 3^{k+1}.$$

The mathematical induction principle now guarantees $n! > 3^n$ for all $n \geq 7$.

Now try Exercise 7.

Section A2 Exercises

1. ***General Triangle Inequality*** Assuming that the triangle inequality $|a + b| \leq |a| + |b|$ holds for any two numbers a and b, show that

$$|x_1 + x_2 + \cdots + x_n| \leq |x_1| + |x_2| + \cdots + |x_n|$$

for any n numbers.

2. ***Partial Sums of Geometric Series*** Show that if $r \neq 1$, then

$$1 + r + r^2 + \cdots + r^n = \frac{1 - r^{n+1}}{1 - r}$$

for every positive integer n.

3. ***Positive Integer Power Rule*** Use the Product Rule,

$$\frac{d}{dx}(uv) = u\frac{dv}{dx} + v\frac{du}{dx},$$

and the fact that

$$\frac{d}{dx}(x) = 1$$

to show that

$$\frac{d}{dx}(x^n) = nx^{n-1}$$

for every positive integer n.

4. ***Products into Sums*** Suppose that a function $f(x)$ has the property that $f(x_1x_2) = f(x_1) + f(x_2)$ for any two positive numbers x_1 and x_2. Show that

$$f(x_1x_2 \ldots x_n) = f(x_1) + f(x_2) + \cdots + f(x_n)$$

for the product of any n positive numbers $x_1, x_2, \ldots, x_n$.

5. Show that

$$\frac{2}{3^1} + \frac{2}{3^2} + \cdots + \frac{2}{3^n} = 1 - \frac{1}{3^n}$$

for all positive integers n.

6. Show that $n! > n^3$ if n is large enough.

7. Show that $2^n > n^2$ if n is large enough.

8. Show that $2^n \geq 1/8$ for $n \geq -3$.

9. ***Sums of Squares*** Show that the sum of the squares of the first n positive integers is

$$\frac{n\left(n + \frac{1}{2}\right)(n+1)}{3}.$$

10. ***Sums of Cubes*** Show that the sum of the cubes of the first n positive integers is $(n(n+1)/2)^2$.

11. ***Rules for Finite Sums*** Show that the following finite sum rules hold for every positive integer n.

(a) $\sum_{k=1}^{n} (a_k + b_k) = \sum_{k=1}^{n} a_k + \sum_{k=1}^{n} b_k$

(b) $\sum_{k=1}^{n} (a_k - b_k) = \sum_{k=1}^{n} a_k - \sum_{k=1}^{n} b_k$

(c) $\sum_{k=1}^{n} ca_k = c \cdot \sum_{k=1}^{n} a_k$ (Any number c)

(d) $\sum_{k=1}^{n} a_k = n \cdot c$, if a_k has the constant value c.

12. ***Absolute Values*** Show that $|x^n| = |x|^n$ for every positive integer n and every real number x.

A3 Using the Limit Definition

What you'll learn about

- Limit Definition
- Finding Deltas for Given Epsilons
- Proving Limit Theorems

. . . and why

This section provides practice using the formal definition of limit.

Limit Definition

We begin by setting the stage for the definition of limit. Recall that the limit of f of x as x approaches c equals L ($\lim_{x \to c} f(x) = L$) means that the values $f(x)$ of the function f approach or equal L as the values of x approach (but do not equal) c. Suppose we are watching the values of a function $f(x)$ as x approaches c (without taking on the value of c itself). Certainly we want to be able to say that $f(x)$ stays within one-tenth of a unit of L as soon as x stays within some distance δ of c (Figure A3.1). But that in itself is not enough, because as x continues on its course toward c, what is to prevent $f(x)$ from jittering about within the interval from $L - 1/10$ to $L + 1/10$ without tending toward L?

We can insist that $f(x)$ stay within 1/100 or 1/1000 or 1/100,000 of L. Each time, we find a new δ-interval about c so that keeping x within that interval keeps $f(x)$ within $\epsilon = 1/100$ or 1/1000 or 1/100,000 of L. And each time the possibility exists that c jitters away from L at the last minute.

Figure A3.2 illustrates the problem. You can think of this as a quarrel between a skeptic and a scholar. The skeptic presents ϵ-challenges to prove that the limit does not exist or, more precisely, that there is room for doubt, and the scholar answers every challenge with a δ-interval around c.

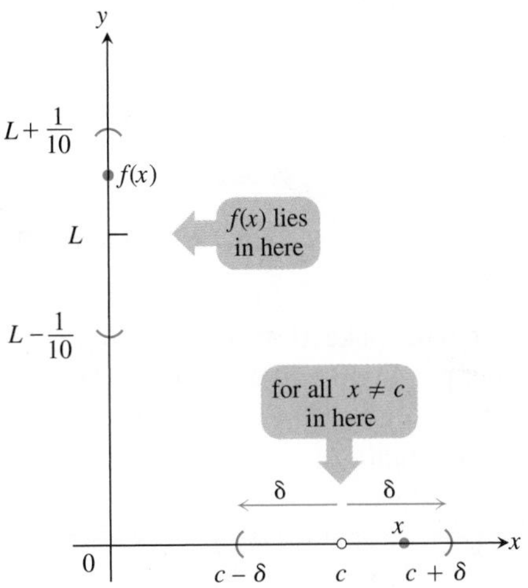

Figure A3.1 A preliminary stage in the development of the definition of limit.

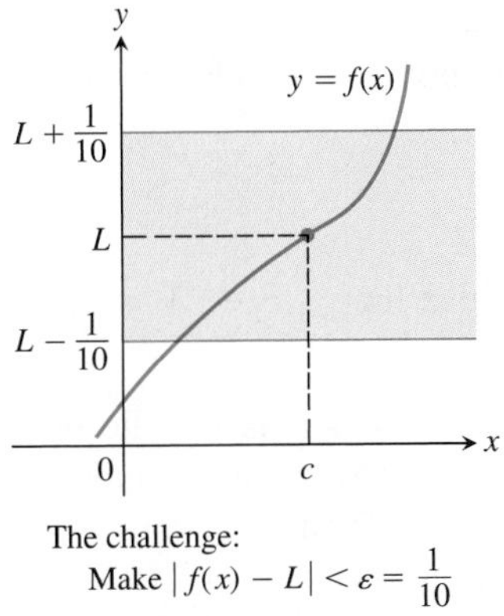

Figure A3.2 The first of a possibly endless sequence of challenges.

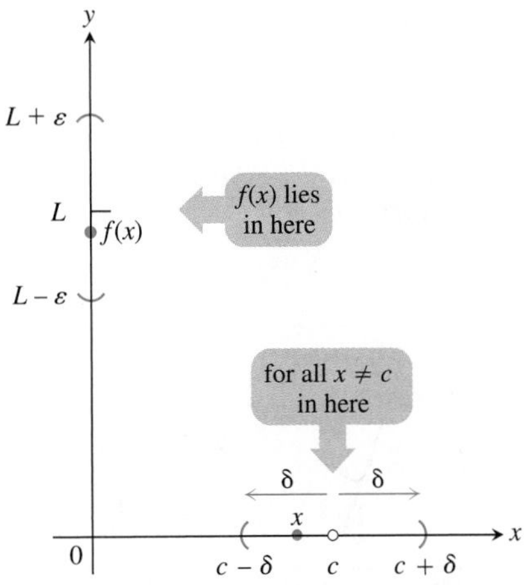

Figure A3.3 The relation of the δ and ϵ in the definition of limit.

How do we stop this seemingly endless sequence of challenges and responses? By proving that for every ϵ-distance that the challenger can produce, we can find, calculate, or conjure a matching δ-distance that keeps x "close enough" to c to keep $f(x)$ within that distance of L (Figure A3.3).

The following definition that we made in Section 2.1 provides a mathematical way to say that the closer x gets to c, the closer $f(x)$ must get to L.

DEFINITION Limit

Let c and L be real numbers. The function **f has limit L as x approaches c** if, given any positive number ϵ, there is a positive number δ such that for all x

$$0 < |x - c| < \delta \quad \Rightarrow \quad |f(x) - L| < \epsilon.$$

We write

$$\lim_{x \to c} f(x) = L.$$

Finding Deltas for Given Epsilons

From our work in Chapter 2 we know that $\lim_{x\to1}(5x-3)=2$. In Example 1, we confirm this result using the definition of limit.

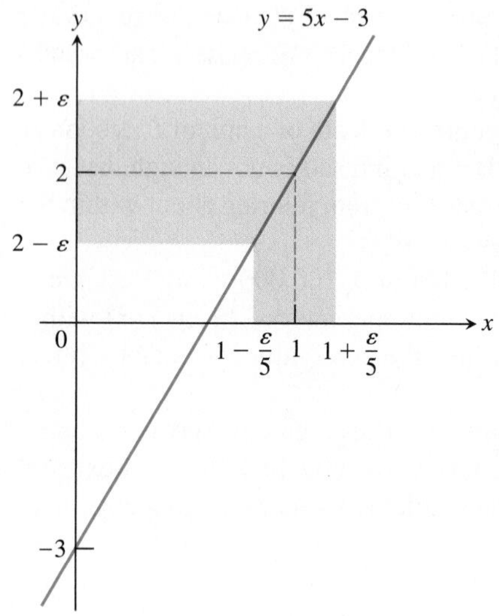

Figure A3.4 If $f(x)=5x-3$, then $0<|x-1|<\epsilon/5$ guarantees that $|f(x)-2|<\epsilon$. (Example 1)

EXAMPLE 1 Using the Definition of Limit

Show that $\lim_{x\to1}(5x-3)=2$.

SOLUTION

Set $c=1$, $f(x)=5x-3$, and $L=2$ in the definition of limit. For any given $\epsilon>0$ we have to find a suitable $\delta>0$ so that if $x\neq1$ and x is within distance δ of $c=1$, that is, if

$$0<|x-1|<\delta,$$

then $f(x)$ is within distance ϵ of $L=2$, that is,

$$|f(x)-2|<\epsilon.$$

We find δ by working backward from the ϵ-inequality:

$$|(5x-3)-2|=|5x-5|<\epsilon$$
$$5|x-1|<\epsilon$$
$$|x-1|<\epsilon/5$$

Thus we can take $\delta=\epsilon/5$ (Figure A3.4). If $0<|x-1|<\delta=\epsilon/5$, then

$$|(5x-3)-2|=|5x-5|$$
$$=5|x-1|<5(\epsilon/5)=\epsilon.$$

This proves that $\lim_{x\to1}(5x-3)=2$. *Now try Exercise 5.*

The value of $\delta=\epsilon/5$ is not the only value that will make $0<|x-1|<\delta$ imply $|f(x)-2|=|5x-5|<\epsilon$ in Example 1. Any smaller positive δ will do as well. The definition does not ask for a "best" positive δ, just one that will work.

We can use graphs to find a δ for a specific ϵ as in Example 2.

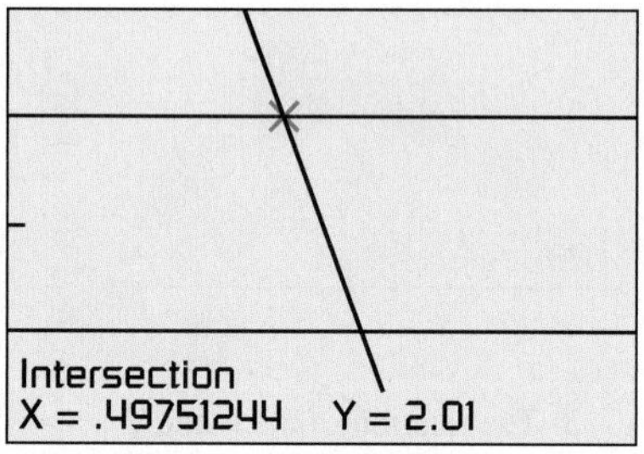

[0.48, 0.52] by [1.98, 2.02]

(a)

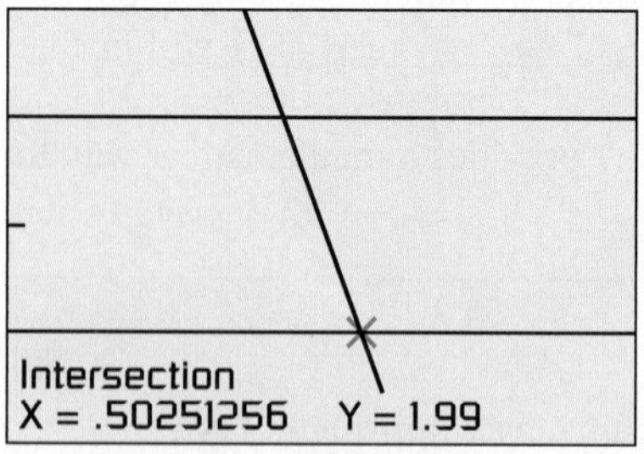

[0.48, 0.52] by [1.98, 2.02]

(b)

Figure A3.5 We can see from the two graphs that if $0.498<x<0.502$, then $1.99<f(x)<2.01$. (Example 2)

EXAMPLE 2 Finding a δ Graphically

For the limit $\lim_{x\to0.5}(1/x)=2$, find a δ that works for $\epsilon=0.01$. That is, find a $\delta>0$ such that for all x

$$0<|x-0.5|<\delta \Rightarrow |f(x)-2|<0.01.$$

SOLUTION

Here $f(x)=1/x$, $c=0.5$, and $L=2$. Figure A3.5 shows the graphs of f and the two horizontal lines

$$y=L-\epsilon=2-0.01=1.99 \quad\text{and}\quad y=L+\epsilon=2+0.01=2.01.$$

Figure A3.5a shows that the graph of f intersects the horizontal line $y=2.01$ at about (0.49751244, 2.01), and Figure A3.5b shows that the graph of f intersects the horizontal line $y=1.99$ at about (0.50251256, 1.99). It follows that

$$0<|x-0.5|<0.002 \Rightarrow |f(x)-2|<0.01.$$

Thus, $\delta=0.002$ works. *Now try Exercise 3.*

EXAMPLE 3 Finding δ Algebraically

Prove that $\lim_{x\to 2} f(x) = 4$ if

$$f(x) = \begin{cases} x^2, & x \neq 2 \\ 1, & x = 2. \end{cases}$$

SOLUTION

Our task is to show that given $\epsilon > 0$ there exists a $\delta > 0$ such that for all x

$$0 < |x - 2| < \delta \quad \Rightarrow \quad |f(x) - 4| < \epsilon.$$

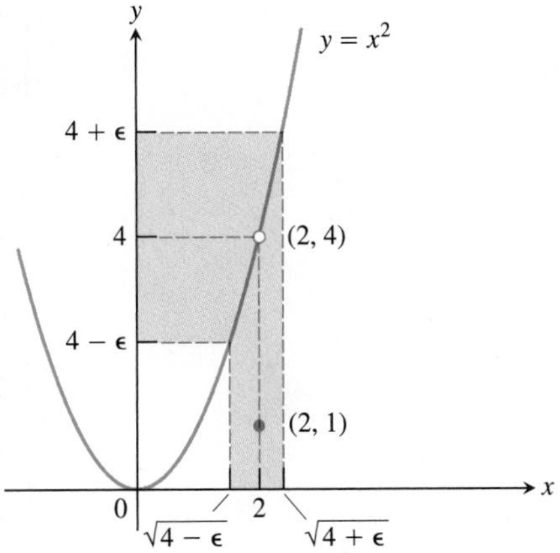

Figure A3.6 The function in Example 3.

Step 1: Solve the inequality $|f(x) - 4| < \epsilon$ to find an open interval about $c = 2$ on which the inequality holds for all $x \neq c$.

For $x \neq c = 2$, we have $f(x) = x^2$, and the inequality to solve is $|x^2 - 4| < \epsilon$:

$$|x^2 - 4| < \epsilon$$
$$-\epsilon < x^2 - 4 < \epsilon$$
$$4 - \epsilon < x^2 < 4 + \epsilon$$
$$\sqrt{4 - \epsilon} < |x| < \sqrt{4 + \epsilon} \qquad \text{Assume } \epsilon < 4.$$
$$\sqrt{4 - \epsilon} < x < \sqrt{4 + \epsilon} \qquad \text{An open interval about 2 that solves the inequality}$$

The inequality $|f(x) - 4| < \epsilon$ holds for all $x \neq 2$ in the open interval $(\sqrt{4 - \epsilon}, \sqrt{4 + \epsilon})$ (Figure A3.6).

Step 2: Find a value of $\delta > 0$ that places the *centered* interval $(2 - \delta, 2 + \delta)$ inside the open interval $(\sqrt{4 - \epsilon}, \sqrt{4 + \epsilon})$.

Take δ to be the distance from $c = 2$ to the nearer endpoint of $(\sqrt{4 - \epsilon}, \sqrt{4 + \epsilon})$. In other words, take

$$\delta = \min\{2 - \sqrt{4 - \epsilon}, \sqrt{4 + \epsilon} - 2\},$$

the *minimum* (the smaller) of the two numbers $2 - \sqrt{4 - \epsilon}$ and $\sqrt{4 + \epsilon} - 2$. If δ has this or any smaller positive value, the inequality

$$0 < |x - 2| < \delta$$

will automatically place x between $\sqrt{4 - \epsilon}$ and $\sqrt{4 + \epsilon}$ to make

$$|f(x) - 4| < \epsilon.$$

For all x,

$$0 < |x - 2| < \delta \quad \Rightarrow \quad |f(x) - 4| < \epsilon.$$

This completes the proof. ***Now try Exercise 13.***

Why was it all right to assume $\epsilon < 4$ in Example 3? Because, in finding a δ such that, for all x, $0 < |x - 2| < \delta$ implied $|f(x) - 4| < \epsilon < 4$, we found a δ that would work for any larger ϵ as well.

Finally, notice the freedom we gained in letting

$$\delta = \min\{2 - \sqrt{4 - \epsilon}, \sqrt{4 + \epsilon} - 2\}.$$

We did not have to spend time deciding which, if either, number was the smaller of the two. We just let δ represent the smaller and went on to finish the argument.

Proving Limit Theorems

We use the limit definition to prove parts 1, 3, and 5 of Theorem 1 (Properties of Limits) from Section 2.1.

THEOREM 1 Properties of Limits

If L, M, c, and k are real numbers and

$$\lim_{x\to c} f(x) = L \quad \text{and} \quad \lim_{x\to c} g(x) = M, \quad \text{then}$$

1. *Sum Rule:* $\lim_{x\to c} (f(x) + g(x)) = L + M$

2. *Difference Rule:* $\lim_{x\to c} (f(x) - g(x)) = L - M$

3. *Product Rule:* $\lim_{x\to c} (f(x) \cdot g(x)) = L \cdot M$

4. *Constant Multiple Rule:* $\lim_{x\to c} k \cdot f(x) = k \cdot L$

5. *Quotient Rule:* $\lim_{x\to c} \frac{f(x)}{g(x)} = \frac{L}{M}, \quad M \neq 0$

6. *Power Rule:* If r and s are integers, $s \neq 0$, then
$$\lim_{x\to c} (f(x))^{r/s} = L^{r/s}$$
provided $L^{r/s}$ is a real number.

Proof of the Limit Sum Rule We need to show that for any $\epsilon > 0$, there is a $\delta > 0$ such that for all x in the common domain D of f and g,

$$0 < |x - c| < \delta \quad \Rightarrow \quad |f(x) + g(x) - (L + M)| < \epsilon.$$

Regrouping terms, we get

$$\begin{aligned} |f(x) + g(x) - (L + M)| &= |(f(x) - L) + (g(x) - M)| \\ &\leq |f(x) - L| + |g(x) - M|. \qquad |a + b| \leq |a| + |b| \end{aligned}$$

Here we have applied the triangle inequality, which states that for all real numbers a and b, $|a + b| \leq |a| + |b|$. Since $\lim_{x\to c} f(x) = L$, there exists a number $\delta_1 > 0$ such that for all x in D

$$0 < |x - c| < \delta_1 \quad \Rightarrow \quad |f(x) - L| < \epsilon/2.$$

Similarly, since $\lim_{x\to c} g(x) = M$, there exists a number $\delta_2 > 0$ such that for all x in D

$$0 < |x - c| < \delta_2 \quad \Rightarrow \quad |g(x) - M| < \epsilon/2.$$

Let $\delta = \min\{\delta_1, \delta_2\}$, the smaller of δ_1 and δ_2. If $0 < |x - c| < \delta$ then

$$0 < |x - c| < \delta_1, \quad \text{so} \quad |f(x) - L| < \epsilon/2,$$

and

$$0 < |x - c| < \delta_2, \quad \text{so} \quad |g(x) - M| < \epsilon/2.$$

Therefore, $|f(x) + g(x) - (L + M)| < \frac{\epsilon}{2} + \frac{\epsilon}{2} = \epsilon.$

This shows that $\lim_{x\to c} (f(x) + g(x)) = L + M.$ ■

Proof of the Limit Product Rule We show that for any $\epsilon > 0$, there is a $\delta > 0$ such that for all x in the common domain D of f and g,

$$0 < |x - c| < \delta \quad \Rightarrow \quad |f(x)g(x) - LM| < \epsilon.$$

Write $f(x)$ and $g(x)$ as $f(x) = L + (f(x) - L)$, $g(x) = M + (g(x) - M)$.

Multiply these expressions together and subtract LM:

$$\begin{aligned} f(x) \cdot g(x) - LM &= (L + (f(x) - L))(M + (g(x) - M)) - LM \\ &= LM + L(g(x) - M) + M(f(x) - L) + (f(x) - L)(g(x) - M) - LM \qquad (1) \\ &= L(g(x) - M) + M(f(x) - L) + (f(x) - L)(g(x) - M) \end{aligned}$$

Since f and g have limits L and M as $x \to c$, there exist positive numbers δ_1, δ_2, δ_3, and δ_4 such that for all x in D

$$\begin{aligned} 0 < |x - c| < \delta_1 &\quad \Rightarrow \quad |f(x) - L| < \sqrt{\epsilon/3} \\ 0 < |x - c| < \delta_2 &\quad \Rightarrow \quad |g(x) - M| < \sqrt{\epsilon/3} \\ 0 < |x - c| < \delta_3 &\quad \Rightarrow \quad |f(x) - L| < \frac{\epsilon}{3(1 + |M|)} \qquad (2) \\ 0 < |x - c| < \delta_4 &\quad \Rightarrow \quad |g(x) - M| < \frac{\epsilon}{3(1 + |L|)}. \end{aligned}$$

If we take δ to be the smallest of the numbers δ_1 through δ_4, the inequalities on the right-hand side of (2) will hold simultaneously for $0 < |x - c| < \delta$. Then, applying the triangle inequality to Equation 1, we have for all x in D, $0 < |x - c| < \delta$ implies

$$\begin{aligned} &|f(x) \cdot g(x) - LM| \\ &\quad \le |L||g(x) - M| + |M||f(x) - L| + |f(x) - L||g(x) - M| \\ &\quad \le (1 + |L|)|g(x) - M| + (1 + |M|)|f(x) - L| + |f(x) - L||g(x) - M| \\ &\quad \le \frac{\epsilon}{3} + \frac{\epsilon}{3} + \sqrt{\frac{\epsilon}{3}}\sqrt{\frac{\epsilon}{3}} = \epsilon. \qquad \text{Values from (2)} \end{aligned}$$

This completes the proof of the Limit Product Rule. ■

Proof of the Limit Quotient Rule We show that $\lim_{x \to c} (1/g(x)) = 1/M$. We can then conclude that

$$\lim_{x \to c} \frac{f(x)}{g(x)} = \lim_{x \to c} \left(f(x) \cdot \frac{1}{g(x)} \right) = \lim_{x \to c} f(x) \cdot \lim_{x \to c} \frac{1}{g(x)} = L \cdot \frac{1}{M} = \frac{L}{M}$$

by the Limit Product Rule.

Let $\epsilon > 0$ be given. To show that $\lim_{x \to c} (1/g(x)) = 1/M$, we need to show that there exists a $\delta > 0$ such that for all x

$$0 < |x - c| < \delta \quad \Rightarrow \quad \left| \frac{1}{g(x)} - \frac{1}{M} \right| < \epsilon.$$

Since $|M| > 0$, there exists a positive number δ_1 such that for all x

$$0 < |x - c| < \delta_1 \quad \Rightarrow \quad |g(x) - M| < \frac{|M|}{2}. \qquad (3)$$

continued

For any numbers A and B it can be shown that

$$|A| - |B| \leq |A - B| \quad \text{and} \quad |B| - |A| \leq |A - B|,$$

from which it follows that $||A| - |B|| \leq |A - B|$. With $A = g(x)$ and $B = M$, this becomes

$$||g(x)| - |M|| \leq |g(x) - M|,$$

which can be combined with the inequality on the right in (3) to get, in turn,

$$\begin{aligned} ||g(x)| - |M|| &< \frac{|M|}{2} \\ -\frac{|M|}{2} < |g(x)| - |M| &< \frac{|M|}{2} \\ \frac{|M|}{2} < |g(x)| &< \frac{3|M|}{2} \\ \frac{1}{|g(x)|} < \frac{2}{|M|} &< \frac{3}{|g(x)|}. \quad \text{Multiply by } 2/(|M||g(x)|). \qquad (4) \end{aligned}$$

Therefore, $0 < |x - c| < \delta$ implies that

$$\begin{aligned} \left|\frac{1}{g(x)} - \frac{1}{M}\right| = \left|\frac{M - g(x)}{Mg(x)}\right| &\leq \frac{1}{|M|} \cdot \frac{1}{|g(x)|} \cdot |M - g(x)| \\ &< \frac{1}{|M|} \cdot \frac{2}{|M|} \cdot |M - g(x)|. \quad \text{Inequality (4)} \qquad (5) \end{aligned}$$

Since $(1/2)|M|^2\epsilon > 0$, there exists a number $\delta_2 > 0$ such that for all x in D

$$0 < |x - c| < \delta_2 \quad \Rightarrow \quad |M - g(x)| < \frac{\epsilon}{2}|M|^2. \qquad (6)$$

If we take δ to be the smaller of δ_1 and δ_2, the conclusions in (5) and (6) both hold for all x such that $0 < |x - c| < \delta$. Combining these conclusions gives

$$0 < |x - c| < \delta_2 \quad \Rightarrow \quad \left|\frac{1}{g(x)} - \frac{1}{M}\right| < \epsilon.$$

This completes the proof of the Limit Quotient Rule. ■

The last proof we give is of the Sandwich Theorem (Theorem 4) of Section 2.1.

THEOREM 4 The Sandwich Theorem

If $g(x) \leq f(x) \leq h(x)$ for all $x \neq c$ in some interval about c, and

$$\lim_{x \to c} g(x) = \lim_{x \to c} h(x) = L,$$

then

$$\lim_{x \to c} f(x) = L.$$

Proof for Right-hand Limits Suppose that $\lim_{x \to c^+} g(x) = \lim_{x \to c^+} h(x) = L$. Then for any $\epsilon > 0$ there exists a $\delta > 0$ such that for all x the inequality $c < x < c + \delta$ implies

$$L - \epsilon < g(x) < L + \epsilon \quad \text{and} \quad L - \epsilon < h(x) < L + \epsilon.$$

continued

These inequalities combine with the inequality $g(x) \le f(x) \le h(x)$ to give

$$L - \epsilon < g(x) \le f(x) \le h(x) < L + \epsilon,$$
$$L - \epsilon < f(x) < L + \epsilon,$$
$$-\epsilon < f(x) - L < \epsilon.$$

Thus, for all x, the inequality $c < x < c + \delta$ implies $|f(x) - L| < \epsilon$. Therefore, $\lim_{x\to c^+} f(x) = L$.

Proof for Left-hand Limits Suppose that $\lim_{x\to c^-} g(x) = \lim_{x\to c^-} h(x) = L$. Then for any $\epsilon > 0$ there exists a $\delta > 0$ such that for all x the inequality $c - \delta < x < c$ implies

$$L - \epsilon < g(x) < L + \epsilon \quad \text{and} \quad L - \epsilon < h(x) < L + \epsilon.$$

We conclude as before that for all x, $c - \delta < x < c$ implies $|f(x) - L| < \epsilon$. Therefore, $\lim_{x\to c^-} f(x) = L$.

Proof for Two-sided Limits If $\lim_{x\to c} g(x) = \lim_{x\to c} h(x) = L$, then $g(x)$ and $h(x)$ both approach L as $x\to c^+$ and $x\to c^-$; so $\lim_{x\to c^+} f(x) = L$ and $\lim_{x\to c^-} f(x) = L$. Hence $\lim_{x\to c} f(x)$ exists and equals L. ∎

Section A3 Exercises

In Exercises 1 and 2, sketch the interval (a, b) on the x-axis with the point c inside. Then find a value of $\delta > 0$ such that for all x,

$$0 < |x - c| < \delta \Rightarrow a < x < b.$$

1. $a = 4/9, \quad b = 4/7, \quad c = 1/2$

2. $a = 2.7591, \quad b = 3.2391, \quad c = 3$

In Exercises 3 and 4, use the graph to find a $\delta > 0$ such that for all x $0 < |x - c| < \delta \Rightarrow |f(x) - L| < \epsilon$.

3.

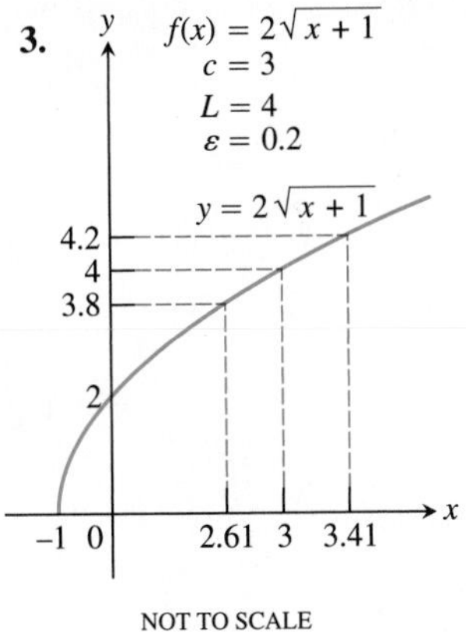

4.

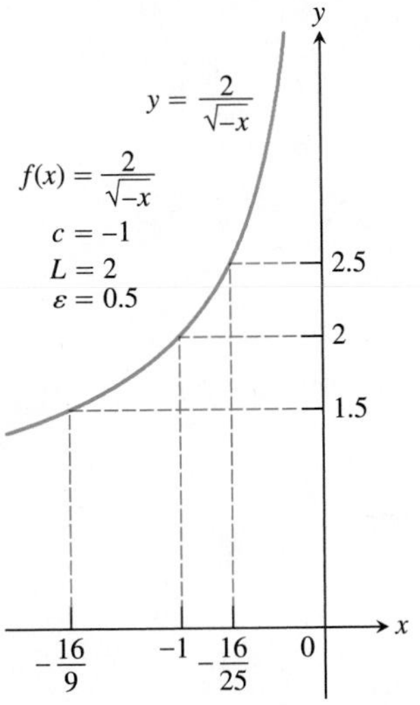

Exercises 5–8 give a function $f(x)$ and numbers L, c, and ϵ. Find an open interval about c on which the inequality $|f(x) - L| < \epsilon$ holds. Then give a value for $\delta > 0$ such that for all x satisfying $0 < |x - c| < \delta$ the inequality $|f(x) - L| < \epsilon$ holds. Use algebra to find your answers.

5. $f(x) = 2x - 2, \quad L = -6, \quad c = -2, \quad \epsilon = 0.02$

6. $f(x) = \sqrt{x + 1}, \quad L = 1, \quad c = 0, \quad \epsilon = 0.1$

7. $f(x) = \sqrt{19 - x}, \quad L = 3, \quad c = 10, \quad \epsilon = 1$

8. $f(x) = x^2, \quad L = 4, \quad c = -2, \quad \epsilon = 0.5$

Exercises 9–12 give a function $f(x)$, a point c, and a positive number ϵ. **(a)** Find $L = \lim_{x\to c} f(x)$. Then **(b)** find a number $\delta > 0$ such that for all x

$$0 < |x - c| < \delta \Rightarrow |f(x) - L| < \epsilon.$$

9. $f(x) = \dfrac{x^2 + 6x + 5}{x + 5}, \quad c = -5, \quad \epsilon = 0.05$

10. $f(x) = \begin{cases} 4 - 2x, & x < 1, \\ 6x - 4, & x \ge 1, \end{cases} \quad c = 1, \quad \epsilon = 0.5$

11. $f(x) = \sin x, \quad c = 1, \quad \epsilon = 0.01$

12. $f(x) = \dfrac{x}{x^2 - 4}, \quad c = -1, \quad \epsilon = 0.1$

In Exercises 13 and 14, use the definition of limit to prove the limit statement.

13. $\lim_{x\to 1} f(x) = 1$ if $f(x) = \begin{cases} x^2, & x \neq 1 \\ 2, & x = 1 \end{cases}$

14. $\lim_{x\to\sqrt{3}} \frac{1}{x^2} = \frac{1}{3}$

15. ***Relating to Limits*** Given $\epsilon > 0$, **(a)** find an interval $I = (5, 5 + \delta)$, $\delta > 0$, such that if x lies in I, then $\sqrt{x-5} < \epsilon$. **(b)** What limit is being verified?

16. ***Relating to Limits*** Given $\epsilon > 0$, **(a)** find an interval $I = (4 - \delta, 4)$, $\delta > 0$, such that if x lies in I, then $\sqrt{4-x} < \epsilon$. **(b)** What limit is being verified?

17. Prove the Constant Multiple Rule for limits.

18. Prove the Difference Rule for limits.

19. ***Generalized Limit Sum Rule*** Suppose that functions $f_1(x)$, $f_2(x)$, and $f_3(x)$ have limits L_1, L_2, and L_3, respectively, as $x \to c$. Show that their sum has limit $L_1 + L_2 + L_3$. Use mathematical induction (Appendix A2) to generalize this result to the sum of any finite number of functions.

20. ***Generalized Limit Product Rule*** Use mathematical induction and the Limit Product Rule in Theorem 1 to show that if functions $f_1(x), f_2(x), \ldots, f_n(x)$ have limits $L_1, L_2, \ldots, L_n$, respectively, as $x \to c$, then

$$\lim_{x\to c} (f_1(x) \cdot f_2(x) \cdot \cdots \cdot f_n(x)) = L_1 \cdot L_2 \cdot \cdots \cdot L_n.$$

21. ***Positive Integer Power Rule*** Use the fact that $\lim_{x\to c} x = c$ and the result of Exercise 20 to show that $\lim_{x\to c} x^n = c^n$ for any integer $n > 1$.

22. ***Limits of Polynomials*** Use the fact that $\lim_{x\to c} k = k$ for any number k together with the results of Exercises 19 and 21 to show that $\lim_{x\to c} f(x) = f(c)$ for any polynomial function

$$f(x) = a_n x^n + a_{n-1}x^{n-1} + \cdots + a_1 x + a_0.$$

23. ***Limits of Rational Functions*** Use Theorem 1 and the result of Exercise 22 to show that if $f(x)$ and $g(x)$ are polynomial functions and $g(c) \neq 0$, then

$$\lim_{x\to c} \frac{f(x)}{g(x)} = \frac{f(c)}{g(c)}.$$

24. ***Composites of Continuous Functions*** Figure A3.7 gives the diagram for a proof that the composite of two continuous functions is continuous. Reconstruct the proof from the diagram. The statement to be proved is this: If f is continuous at $x = c$ and g is continuous at $f(c)$, then $g \circ f$ is continuous at c.

Assume that c is an interior point of the domain of f and that $f(c)$ is an interior point of the domain of g. This will make the limits involved two-sided. (The argument for the cases that involve one-sided limits are similar.)

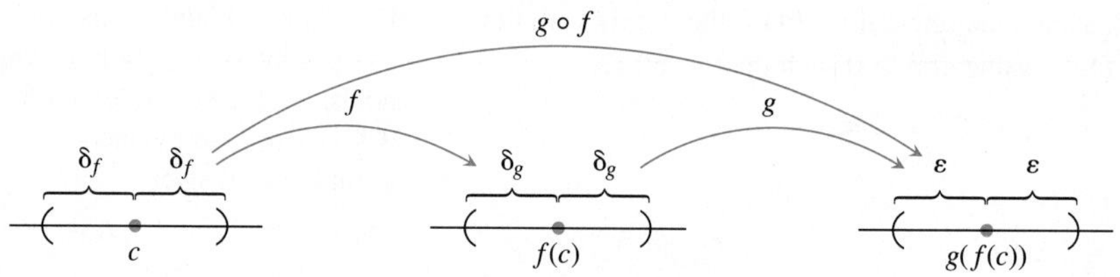

Figure A3.7 The continuity of composites holds for any finite number of functions. The only requirement is that each function be continuous where it is applied. Here, f is to be continuous at c and g at $f(c)$.

A4 Proof of the Chain Rule

What you'll learn about

- Error in the Approximation $\Delta f \approx df$
- The Proof

. . . and why

This section helps explain approximating change in function values.

Error in the Approximation $\Delta f \approx df$

Let $f(x)$ be differentiable at $x = a$ and suppose that Δx is an increment of x. We know that the differential $df = f'(a)\Delta x$ is an approximation for the change $\Delta f = (f(a + \Delta x) - f(a))$ in f as x changes from a to $(a + \Delta x)$. How well does df approximate Δf?

We measure the approximation error by subtracting df from Δf:

$$\text{Approximation error} = \Delta f - df = \Delta f - f'(a)\Delta x$$

$$= \underbrace{f(a + \Delta x) - f(a)}_{\Delta f} - f'(a)\Delta x \qquad \Delta f = f(a + \Delta x) - f(a)$$

$$= \underbrace{\left(\frac{f(a + \Delta x) - f(a)}{\Delta x} - f'(a)\right)}_{\text{Call this part } \epsilon.} \cdot \Delta x = \epsilon \cdot \Delta x$$

As $\Delta x \to 0$, the difference quotient $(f(a + \Delta x) - f(a))/\Delta x$ approaches $f'(a)$ (remember the definition of $f'(a)$), so the quantity in parentheses becomes a very small number (which is why we called it ϵ). In fact, $\epsilon \to 0$ as $\Delta x \to 0$. When Δx is small, the **approximation error** $\epsilon \Delta x$ is smaller still.

$$\underbrace{\Delta f}_{\text{true change}} = \underbrace{f'(a)\Delta x}_{\text{estimated change}} + \underbrace{\epsilon \Delta x}_{\text{error}} \qquad (1)$$

The Proof

We want to show if $f(u)$ is a differentiable function of u and $u = g(x)$ is a differentiable function of x, then $y = f(g(x))$ is a differentiable function of x. More precisely, if g is differentiable at a and f is differentiable at $g(a)$, then the composite is differentiable at a and

$$\left.\frac{dy}{dx}\right|_{x=a} = f'(g(a)) \cdot g'(a).$$

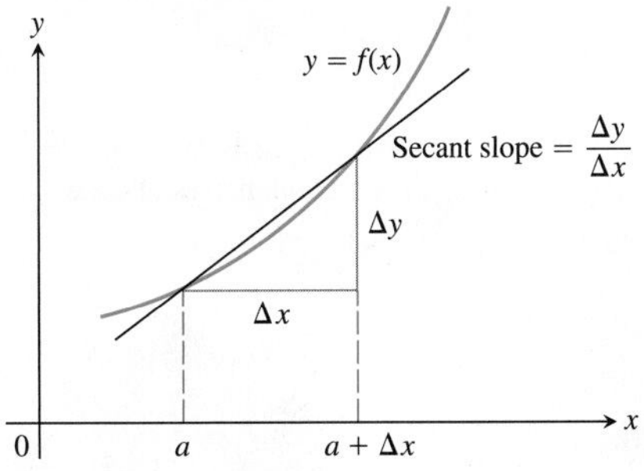

Figure A4.1 The graph of y as a function of x. The derivative of y with respect to x at $x = a$ is $\lim_{\Delta x \to 0} (\Delta y/\Delta x)$.

Let Δx be an increment in x and let Δu and Δy be the corresponding increments in u and y. As you can see in Figure A4.1,

$$\left.\frac{dy}{dx}\right|_{x=a} = \lim_{\Delta x \to 0} \frac{\Delta y}{\Delta x},$$

so our goal is to show that the limit is $f'(g(a)) \cdot g'(a)$.

By Equation 1,

$$\Delta u = g'(a)\Delta x + \epsilon_1 \Delta x = (g'(a) + \epsilon_1)\Delta x,$$

where $\epsilon_1 \to 0$ as $\Delta x \to 0$. Similarly, since f is differentiable at $g(a)$,

$$\Delta y = f'(g(a))\Delta u + \epsilon_2 \Delta u = (f'(g(a)) + \epsilon_2)\Delta u,$$

where $\epsilon_2 \to 0$ as $\Delta u \to 0$. Notice also that $\Delta u \to 0$ as $\Delta x \to 0$. Combining the equations for Δu and Δy gives $\Delta y = (f'(g(a)) + \epsilon_2)(g'(a) + \epsilon_1)\Delta x$, so

$$\frac{\Delta y}{\Delta x} = f'(g(a))g'(a) + \epsilon_2 g'(a) + f'(g(a))\epsilon_1 + \epsilon_2 \epsilon_1.$$

Since ϵ_1 and ϵ_2 go to zero as Δx goes to zero, three of the four terms on the right vanish in the limit, leaving

$$\lim_{\Delta x \to 0} \frac{\Delta y}{\Delta x} = f'(g(a))g'(a).$$

This concludes the proof. ■

A5 Conic Sections

What you'll learn about

- Circles
- Interiors and Exteriors of Circles
- Parabolas
- Ellipses
- Axes of an Ellipse
- Hyperbolas
- Asymptotes and Drawing
- Reflective Properties
- Other Applications

. . . and why

This section provides some basic information about equations of conic sections and how to sketch their graphs.

Overview

Conic sections are the paths traveled by planets, satellites, and other bodies (even electrons) whose motions are driven by inverse-square forces. Once we know that the path of a moving body is a conic section, we immediately have information about the body's velocity and the force that drives it. In this appendix, we study the connections between conic sections and quadratic equations and classify conic sections by eccentricity (Pluto's orbit is highly eccentric while Earth's is nearly circular).

A5.1 Conic Sections and Quadratic Equations

Circles

The Greeks of Plato's time defined conic sections as the curves formed by cutting through a double cone with a plane (Figure A5.1). Today, we define conic sections with the distance function in the coordinate plane.

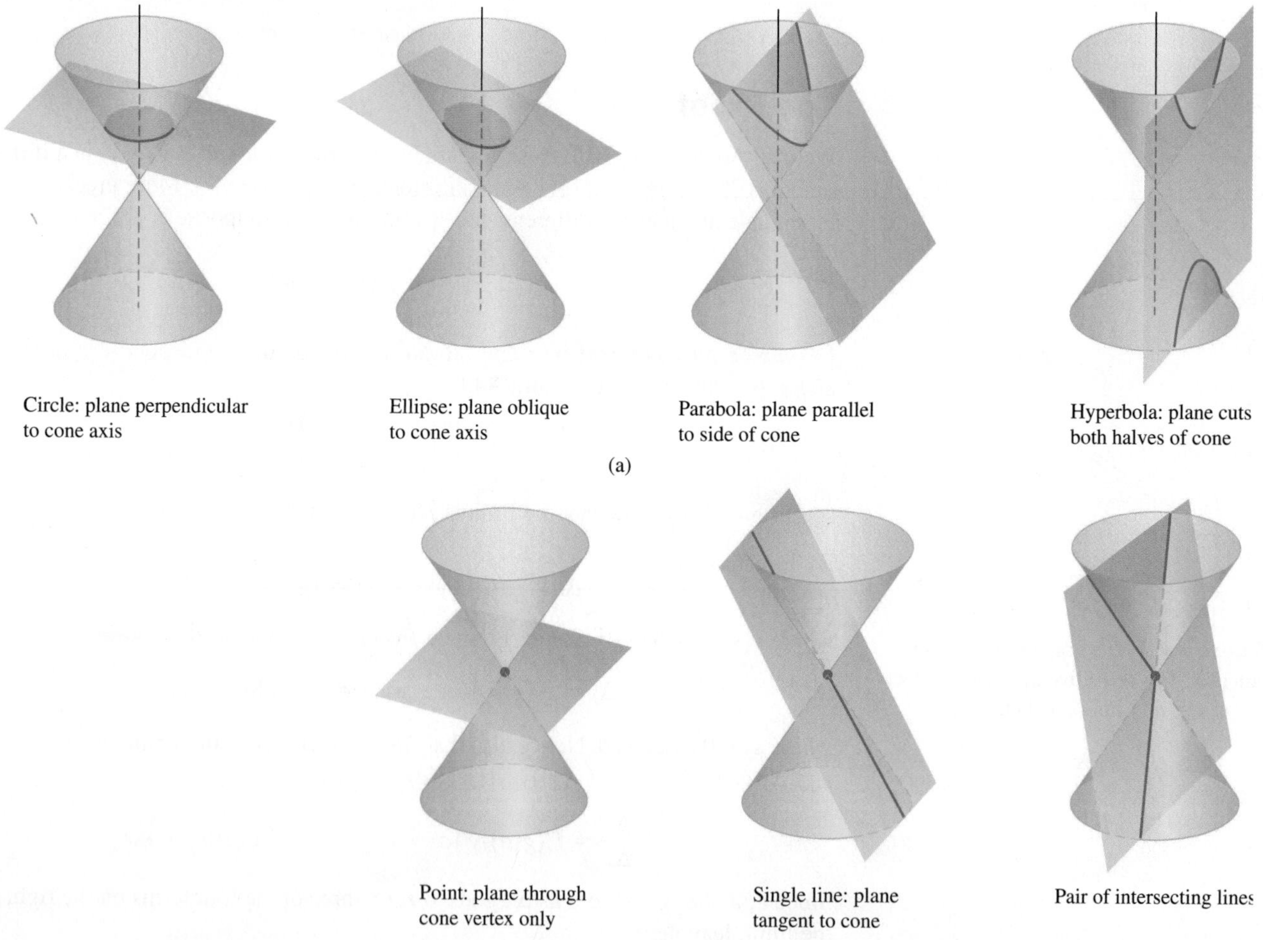

Figure A5.1 The standard conic sections (a) are the curves in which a plane cuts a double cone. Hyperbolas come in two parts, called *branches*. The point and lines obtained by passing the plane through the cone's vertex (b) are *degenerate* conic sections.

DEFINITION Circle

A **circle** is the set of points in a plane whose distance from a given fixed point in the plane is constant. The fixed point is the **center** of the circle; the constant distance is the **radius**.

If $a > 0$, the equation $x^2 + y^2 = a^2$ represents all the points (x, y) in the plane whose distance from the origin is

$$\sqrt{(x-0)^2 + (y-0)^2} = \sqrt{x^2 + y^2} = \sqrt{a^2} = a.$$

These are the points of the circle of radius a centered at the origin. If we shift the circle to place its center at the point (h, k), its equation becomes $(x - h)^2 + (y - k)^2 = a^2$.

Circle of Radius *a* Centered at (*h*, *k*)

$$(x - h)^2 + (y - k)^2 = a^2$$

EXAMPLE 1 Finding Center and Radius

Find the center and radius of the circle

$$x^2 + y^2 + 4x - 6y - 3 = 0.$$

SOLUTION

We convert the equation to standard form by completing the squares in x and y:

$$x^2 + y^2 + 4x - 6y - 3 = 0$$ Start with the given equation.

$$(x^2 + 4x) + (y^2 - 6y) = 3$$ Gather terms. Move the constant to the right-hand side.

$$\left(x^2 + 4x + \left(\frac{4}{2}\right)^2\right) + \left(y^2 - 6y + \left(\frac{-6}{2}\right)^2\right) = 3 + \left(\frac{4}{2}\right)^2 + \left(\frac{-6}{2}\right)^2$$ Add the square of half the coefficient of x to each side of the equation. Do the same for y. The parenthetical expressions on the left-hand side are now perfect squares.

$$(x^2 + 4x + 4) + (y^2 - 6y + 9) = 3 + 4 + 9$$

$$(x + 2)^2 + (y - 3)^2 = 16$$ Write each quadratic as a squared linear expression.

With the equation now in standard form, we read off the center's coordinates and the radius: $(h, k) = (-2, 3)$ and $a = 4$. ***Now try Exercise 3.***

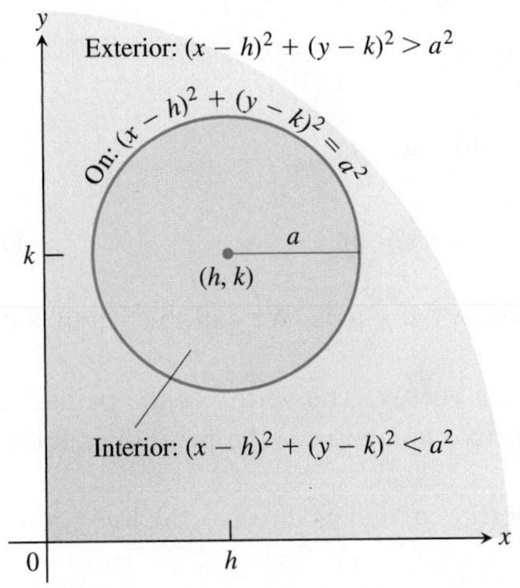

Figure A5.2 The interior and exterior of the circle $(x - h)^2 + (y - k)^2 = a^2$.

Interiors and Exteriors of Circles

The points that lie inside the circle $(x - h)^2 + (y - k)^2 = a^2$ are the points less than a units from (h, k). They satisfy the inequality

$$(x - h)^2 + (y - k)^2 < a^2.$$

They make up the region we call the **interior** of the circle (Figure A5.2).

The circle's **exterior** consists of the points that lie more than a units from (h, k). These points satisfy the inequality

$$(x - h)^2 + (y - k)^2 > a^2.$$

EXAMPLE 2 Interpreting Inequalities

Inequality	Region
$x^2 + y^2 < 1$	Interior of the unit circle
$x^2 + y^2 \le 1$	Unit circle plus its interior
$x^2 + y^2 > 1$	Exterior of the unit circle
$x^2 + y^2 \ge 1$	Unit circle plus its exterior

Now try Exercise 5.

Parabolas

DEFINITION Parabola

A set that consists of all the points in a plane equidistant from a given fixed point and a given fixed line in the plane is a **parabola**. The fixed point is the **focus** of the parabola. The fixed line is the **directrix**.

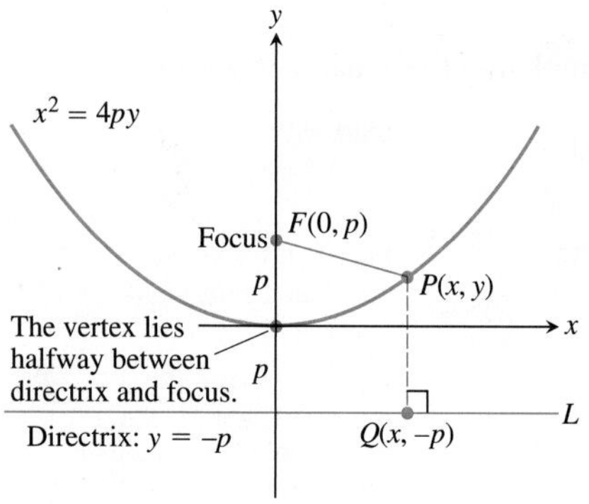

Figure A5.3 The parabola $x^2 = 4py$.

If the focus F lies on the directrix L, the parabola is the line through F perpendicular to L. We consider this to be a degenerate case and assume henceforth that F does not lie on L.

A parabola has its simplest equation when its focus and directrix straddle one of the coordinate axes. For example, suppose that the focus lies at the point $F(0, p)$ on the positive y-axis and that the directrix is the line $y = -p$ (Figure A5.3). In the notation of the figure, a point $P(x, y)$ lies on the parabola if and only if $PF = PQ$. From the distance formula,

$$PF = \sqrt{(x - 0)^2 + (y - p)^2} = \sqrt{x^2 + (y - p)^2}$$

$$PQ = \sqrt{(x - x)^2 + (y - (-p))^2} = \sqrt{(y + p)^2}.$$

When we equate these expressions, square, and simplify, we get

$$y = \frac{x^2}{4p} \quad \text{or} \quad x^2 = 4py. \quad \text{Standard form} \tag{1}$$

These equations reveal the parabola's symmetry about the y-axis. We call the y-axis the **axis** of the parabola (short for "axis of symmetry").

The point where a parabola crosses its axis is the **vertex**. The vertex of the parabola $x^2 = 4py$ lies at the origin (Figure A5.3). The positive number p is the parabola's **focal length**.

If the parabola opens downward, with its focus at $(0, -p)$ and its directrix the line $y = p$, Equations 1 become

$$y = -\frac{x^2}{4p} \quad \text{or} \quad x^2 = -4py$$

(Figure A5.4). We obtain similar equations for parabolas opening to the right or to the left (Figure A5.5 and Table A5.1).

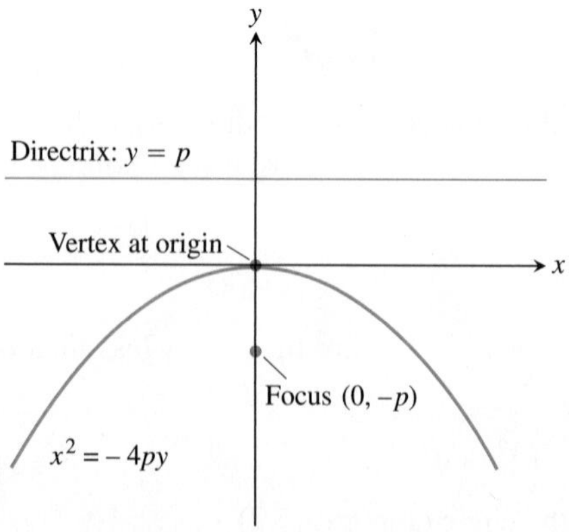

Figure A5.4 The parabola $x^2 = -4py$.

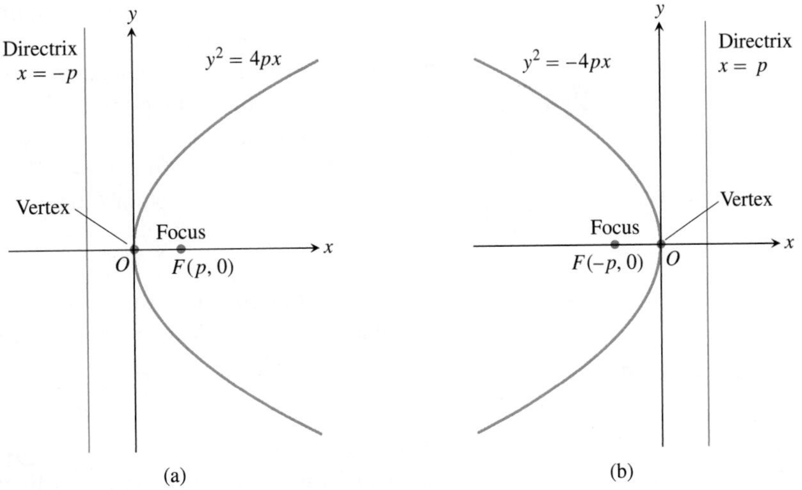

Figure A5.5 (a) The parabola $y^2 = 4px$. (b) The parabola $y^2 = -4px$.

Table A5.1 Standard-form equations for parabolas with vertices at the origin ($p > 0$)

Equation	Focus	Directrix	Axis	Opens
$x^2 = 4py$	$(0, p)$	$y = -p$	y-axis	Up
$x^2 = -4py$	$(0, -p)$	$y = p$	y-axis	Down
$y^2 = 4px$	$(p, 0)$	$x = -p$	x-axis	To the right
$y^2 = -4px$	$(-p, 0)$	$x = p$	x-axis	To the left

EXAMPLE 3 Finding Focus and Directrix

Find the focus and directrix of the parabola $y^2 = 10x$.

SOLUTION

We find the value of p in the standard equation $y^2 = 4px$:

$$4p = 10, \quad \text{so} \quad p = \frac{10}{4} = \frac{5}{2}.$$

Then we find the focus and directrix for this value of p:

$$\text{Focus:} \quad (p, 0) = \left(\frac{5}{2}, 0\right)$$

$$\text{Directrix:} \quad x = -p \quad \text{or} \quad x = -\frac{5}{2}.$$

Now try Exercise 7.

Ellipses

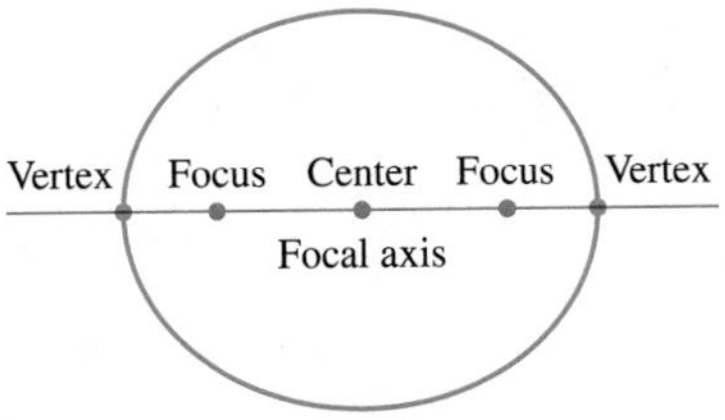

Figure A5.6 Points on the focal axis of an ellipse.

DEFINITION Ellipse

An **ellipse** is the set of points in a plane whose distances from two fixed points in the plane have a constant sum. The fixed points are the **foci** of the ellipse. The line through the foci is the **focal axis.** The point on the axis halfway between the foci is the **center.** The points where the focal axis and ellipse cross are the **vertices** (Figure A5.6).

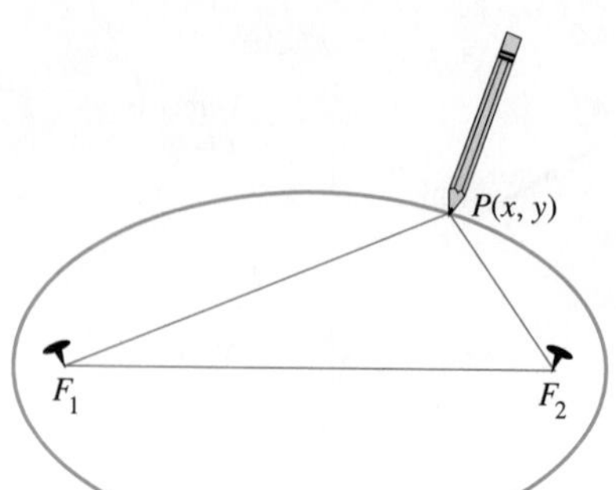

Figure A5.7 How to draw an ellipse.

The quickest way to construct an ellipse uses the definition. Put a loop of string around two tacks F_1 and F_2, pull the string taut with a pencil point P, and move the pencil around to trace a closed curve (Figure A5.7). The curve is an ellipse because the sum $PF_1 + PF_2$, being the length of the loop minus the distance between the tacks, remains constant. The ellipse's foci lie at F_1 and F_2.

If the foci are $F_1(-c, 0)$ and $F_2(c, 0)$ (Figure A5.8) and $PF_1 + PF_2$ is denoted by $2a$, then the coordinates of a point P on the ellipse satisfy the equation

$$\sqrt{(x+c)^2 + y^2} + \sqrt{(x-c)^2 + y^2} = 2a.$$

To simplify this equation, we move the second radical to the right-hand side, square, isolate the remaining radical, and square again, obtaining

$$\frac{x^2}{a^2} + \frac{y^2}{a^2 - c^2} = 1. \tag{2}$$

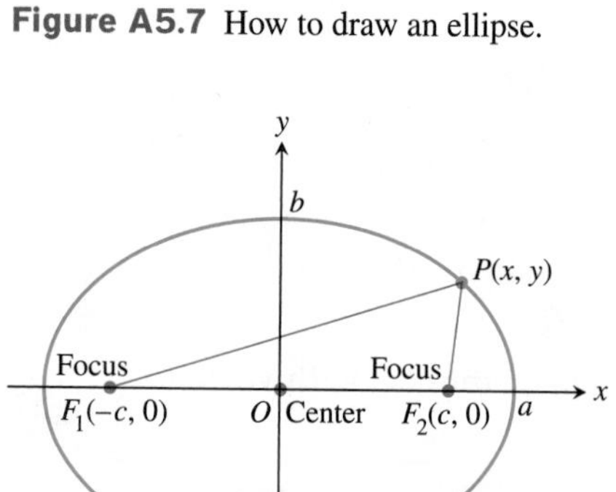

Figure A5.8 The ellipse defined by the equation $PF_1 + PF_2 = 2a$ is the graph of the equation $(x^2/a^2) + (y^2/b^2) = 1$.

Since $PF_1 + PF_2$ is greater than the length F_1F_2 (triangle inequality for triangle PF_1F_2), the number $2a$ is greater than $2c$. Accordingly, $a > c$ and the number $a^2 - c^2$ in Equation 2 is positive.

The algebraic steps leading to Equation 2 can be reversed to show that every point P whose coordinates satisfy an equation of this form with $0 < c < a$ also satisfies the equation $PF_1 + PF_2 = 2a$. A point therefore lies on the ellipse if and only if its coordinates satisfy Equation 2.

If

$$b = \sqrt{a^2 - c^2}, \tag{3}$$

then $a^2 - c^2 = b^2$ and Equation 2 takes the form

$$\frac{x^2}{a^2} + \frac{y^2}{b^2} = 1. \tag{4}$$

Equation 4 reveals that this ellipse is symmetric with respect to the origin and both coordinate axes. It lies inside the rectangle bounded by the lines $x = \pm a$ and $y = \pm b$. It crosses the axes at the points $(\pm a, 0)$ and $(0, \pm b)$. The tangents at these points are perpendicular to the axes because

$$\frac{dy}{dx} = -\frac{b^2 x}{a^2 y} \qquad \text{Obtained from Eq. 4 by implicit differentiation}$$

is zero if $x = 0$ and infinite if $y = 0$.

Axes of an Ellipse

The **major axis** of the ellipse in Equation 4 is the line segment of length $2a$ joining the points $(\pm a, 0)$. The **minor axis** is the line segment of length $2b$ joining the points $(0, \pm b)$. The number a itself is the **semimajor axis**, the number b the **semiminor axis**. The number c found from Equation 3 as

$$c = \sqrt{a^2 - b^2},$$

is the **center-to-focus** distance of the ellipse.

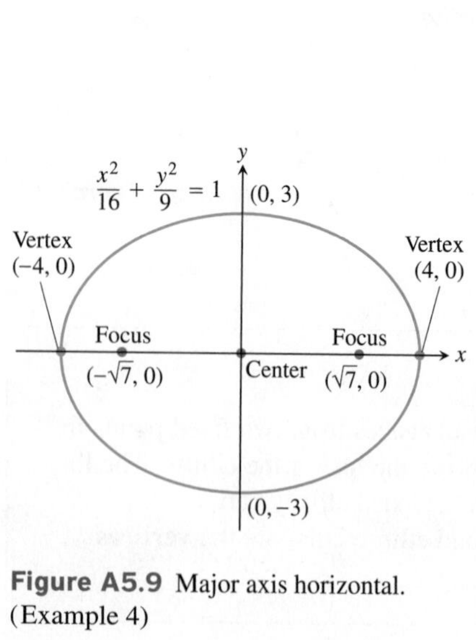

Figure A5.9 Major axis horizontal. (Example 4)

EXAMPLE 4 Major Axis Horizontal

The ellipse

$$\frac{x^2}{16} + \frac{y^2}{9} = 1 \tag{5}$$

(Figure A5.9) has

Semimajor axis: $a = \sqrt{16} = 4$

Semiminor axis: $b = \sqrt{9} = 3$

continued

Center-to-focus distance:	$c = \sqrt{16 - 9} = \sqrt{7}$
Foci:	$(\pm c, 0) = (\pm\sqrt{7}, 0)$
Vertices:	$(\pm a, 0) = (\pm 4, 0)$
Center:	$(0, 0)$.

Now try Exercise 13.

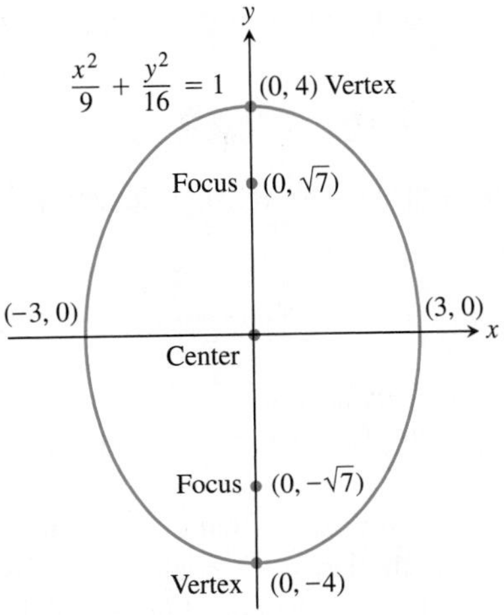

Figure A5.10 Major axis vertical. (Example 5)

EXAMPLE 5 Major Axis Vertical

The ellipse

$$\frac{x^2}{9} + \frac{y^2}{16} = 1, \qquad (6)$$

obtained by interchanging x and y in Equation 5, has its major axis vertical instead of horizontal (Figure A5.10). With a^2 still equal to 16 and b^2 equal to 9, we have

Semimajor axis:	$a = \sqrt{16} = 4$
Semiminor axis:	$b = \sqrt{9} = 3$
Center-to-focus distance:	$c = \sqrt{16 - 9} = \sqrt{7}$
Foci:	$(0, \pm c) = (0, \pm\sqrt{7})$
Vertices:	$(0, \pm a) = (0, \pm 4)$
Center:	$(0, 0)$.

Now try Exercise 17.

There is never any cause for confusion in analyzing equations like (5) and (6). We simply find the intercepts on the coordinate axes; then we know which way the major axis runs because it is the longer of the two axes. The center always lies at the origin and the foci lie on the major axis.

Standard-Form Equations for Ellipses Centered at the Origin

Foci on the x-axis: $\frac{x^2}{a^2} + \frac{y^2}{b^2} = 1 \quad (a > b)$

Center-to-focus distance:	$c = \sqrt{a^2 - b^2}$
Foci:	$(\pm c, 0)$
Vertices:	$(\pm a, 0)$

Foci on the y-axis: $\frac{x^2}{b^2} + \frac{y^2}{a^2} = 1 \quad (a > b)$

Center-to-focus distance:	$c = \sqrt{a^2 - b^2}$
Foci:	$(0, \pm c)$
Vertices:	$(0, \pm a)$

In each case, a is the semimajor axis and b is the semiminor axis.

Hyperbolas

DEFINITION Hyperbola

A **hyperbola** is the set of points in a plane whose distances from two fixed points in the plane have a constant difference. The two fixed points are the **foci** of the hyperbola.

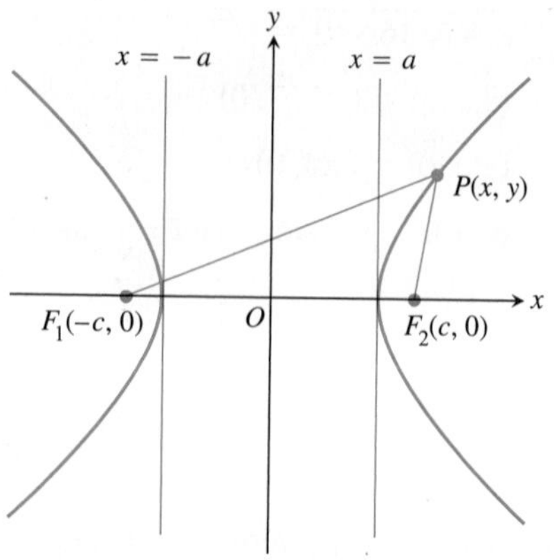

Figure A5.11 Hyperbolas have two branches. For points on the right-hand branch of the hyperbola shown here, $PF_1 - PF_2 = 2a$. For points on the left-hand branch, $PF_2 - PF_1 = 2a$.

If the foci are $F_1(-c, 0)$ and $F_2(c, 0)$ (Figure A5.11) and the constant difference is $2a$, then a point (x, y) lies on the hyperbola if and only if

$$\sqrt{(x+c)^2 + y^2} - \sqrt{(x-c)^2 + y^2} = \pm 2a. \tag{7}$$

To simplify this equation, we move the second radical to the right-hand side, square, isolate the remaining radical, and square again, obtaining

$$\frac{x^2}{a^2} + \frac{y^2}{a^2 - c^2} = 1. \tag{8}$$

So far, this looks just like the equation for an ellipse. But now $a^2 - c^2$ is negative because $2a$, being the difference of two sides of triangle PF_1F_2 is less than $2c$, the third side.

The algebraic steps leading to Equation 8 can be reversed to show that every point P whose coordinates satisfy an equation of this form with $0 < a < c$ also satisfies Equation 7. A point therefore lies on the hyperbola if and only if its coordinates satisfy Equation 8.

If we let b denote the positive square root of $c^2 - a^2$,

$$b = \sqrt{c^2 - a^2}, \tag{9}$$

then $a^2 - c^2 = -b^2$ and Equation 8 takes the more compact form

$$\frac{x^2}{a^2} - \frac{y^2}{b^2} = 1. \tag{10}$$

The differences between Equation 10 and the equation for an ellipse (Equation 4) are the minus sign and the new relation

$$c^2 = a^2 + b^2. \quad \text{From Eq. 9}$$

Like the ellipse, the hyperbola is symmetric with respect to the origin and coordinate axes. It crosses the x-axis at the points $(\pm a, 0)$. The tangents at these points are vertical because

$$\frac{dy}{dx} = \frac{b^2 x}{a^2 y} \quad \text{Obtained from Eq. 10 by implicit differentiation}$$

is infinite when $y = 0$. The hyperbola has no y-intercepts; in fact, no part of the curve lies between the lines $x = -a$ and $x = a$.

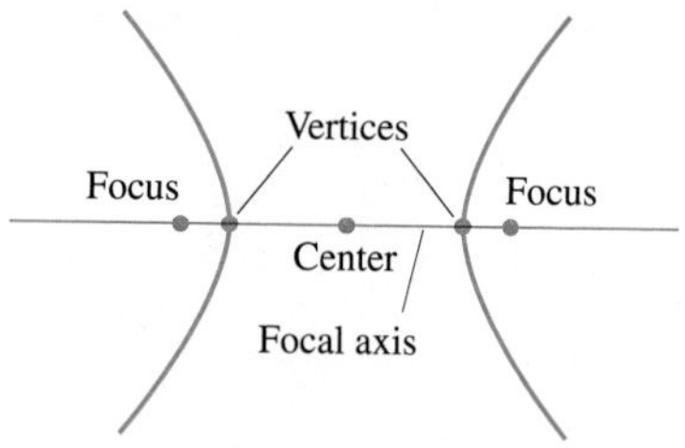

Figure A5.12 Points on the focal axis of a hyperbola.

> **DEFINITION Parts of a Hyperbola**
>
> The line through the foci of a hyperbola is the **focal axis.** The point on the axis halfway between the foci is the hyperbola's **center.** The points where the focal axis and hyperbola cross are the **vertices** (Figure A5.12).

Asymptotes and Drawing

The hyperbola

$$\frac{x^2}{a^2} - \frac{y^2}{b^2} = 1 \tag{11}$$

has two asymptotes, the lines

$$y = \pm\frac{b}{a}x.$$

The asymptotes give the guidance we need to draw hyperbolas quickly. (See the drawing lesson.) The fastest way to find the equations of the asymptotes is to replace the 1 in Equation 11 by 0 and solve the new equation for y:

$$\underbrace{\frac{x^2}{a^2} - \frac{y^2}{b^2} = 1}_{\text{hyperbola}} \quad \Rightarrow \quad \underbrace{\frac{x^2}{a^2} - \frac{y^2}{b^2} = 0}_{\text{0 for 1}} \quad \Rightarrow \quad \underbrace{y = \pm\frac{b}{a}x.}_{\text{asymptotes}}$$

Standard-Form Equations for Hyperbolas Centered at the Origin

Foci on the x-axis: $\frac{x^2}{a^2} - \frac{y^2}{b^2} = 1$

Center-to-focus distance: $c = \sqrt{a^2 + b^2}$

Foci: $(\pm c, 0)$

Vertices: $(\pm a, 0)$

Asymptotes: $\frac{x^2}{a^2} - \frac{y^2}{b^2} = 0$ or $y = \pm\frac{b}{a}x$

Foci on the y-axis: $\frac{y^2}{a^2} - \frac{x^2}{b^2} = 1$

Center-to-focus distance: $c = \sqrt{a^2 + b^2}$

Foci: $(0, \pm c)$

Vertices: $(0, \pm a)$

Asymptotes: $\frac{y^2}{a^2} - \frac{x^2}{b^2} = 0$ or $y = \pm\frac{a}{b}x$

Notice the difference in the asymptote equations (b/a in the first, a/b in the second).

DRAWING LESSON How to Graph the Hyperbola $\frac{x^2}{a^2} - \frac{y^2}{b^2} = 1$

1. Mark the points $(\pm a, 0)$ and $(0, \pm b)$ with line segments and complete the rectangle they determine.
2. Sketch the asymptotes by extending the rectangle's diagonals.
3. Use the rectangle and asymptotes to guide your drawing.

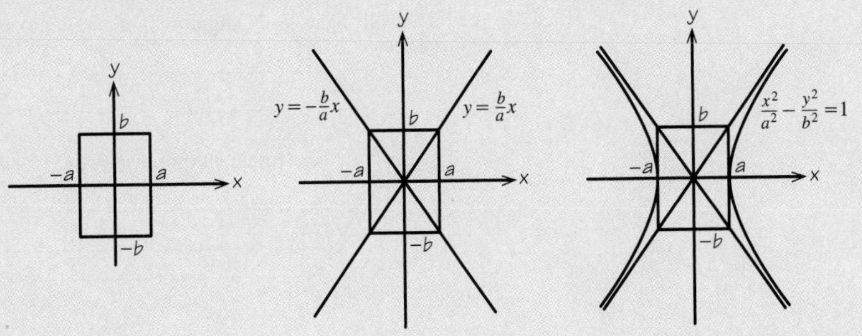

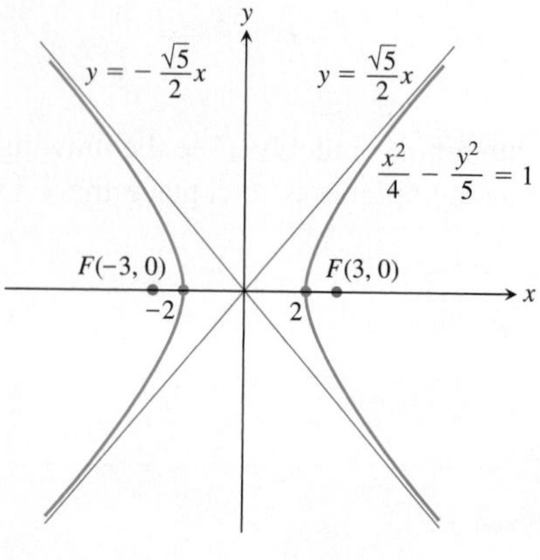

Figure A5.13 The hyperbola in Example 6.

EXAMPLE 6 Foci on the *x*-Axis

The equation

$$\frac{x^2}{4} - \frac{y^2}{5} = 1 \tag{12}$$

is Equation 10 with $a^2 = 4$ and $b^2 = 5$ (Figure A5.13). We have

Center-to-focus distance: $c = \sqrt{a^2 + b^2} = \sqrt{4 + 5} = 3$

Foci: $(\pm c, 0) = (\pm 3, 0)$

Vertices: $(\pm a, 0) = (\pm 2, 0)$

Center: $(0, 0)$

Asymptotes: $\frac{x^2}{4} - \frac{y^2}{5} = 0$ or $y = \pm\frac{\sqrt{5}}{2}x.$

Now try Exercise 21.

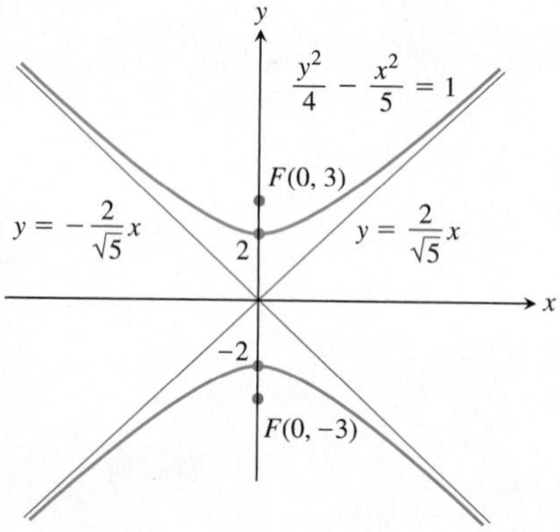

Figure A5.14 The hyperbola in Example 7.

EXAMPLE 7 Foci on the *y*-Axis

The hyperbola

$$\frac{y^2}{4} - \frac{x^2}{5} = 1,$$

obtained by interchanging x and y in Equation 12, has its vertices on the y-axis instead of the x-axis (Figure A5.14). With a^2 still equal to 4 and b^2 equal to 5, we have

Center-to-focus distance: $c = \sqrt{a^2 + b^2} = \sqrt{4 + 5} = 3$

Foci: $(0, \pm c) = (0, \pm 3)$

Vertices: $(0, \pm a) = (0, \pm 2)$

Center: $(0, 0)$

Asymptotes: $\frac{y^2}{4} - \frac{x^2}{5} = 0$ or $y = \pm\frac{2}{\sqrt{5}}x.$

Now try Exercise 23.

Reflective Properties

The chief applications of parabolas involve their use as reflectors of light and radio waves. Rays originating at a parabola's focus are reflected out of the parabola parallel to the parabola's axis (Figure A5.15).

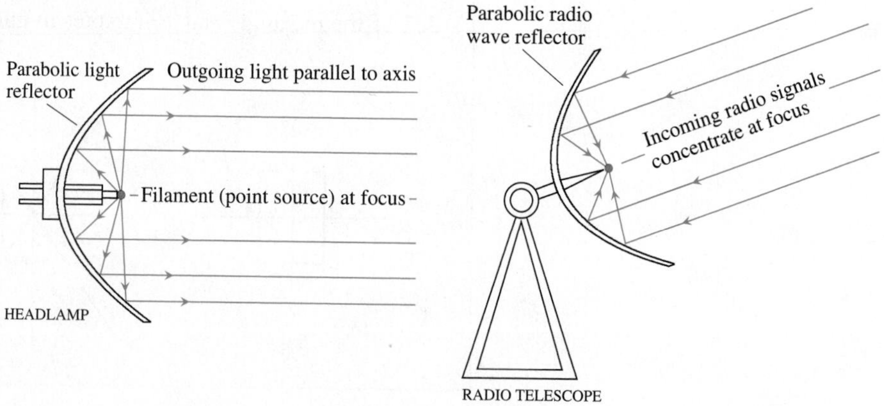

Figure A5.15 Two of the many uses of parabolic reflectors.

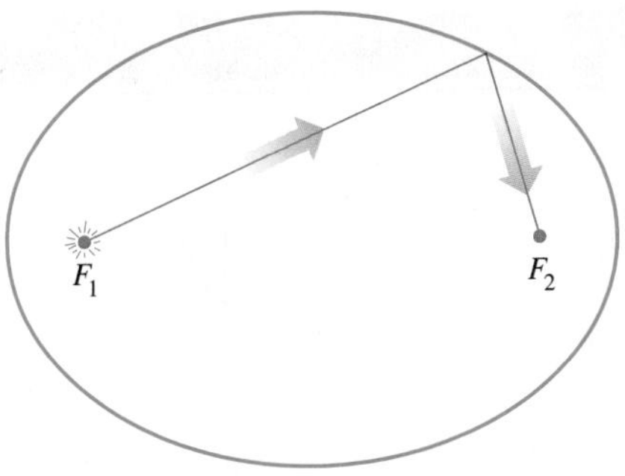

Figure A5.16 An elliptical mirror (shown here in profile) reflects light from one focus to the other.

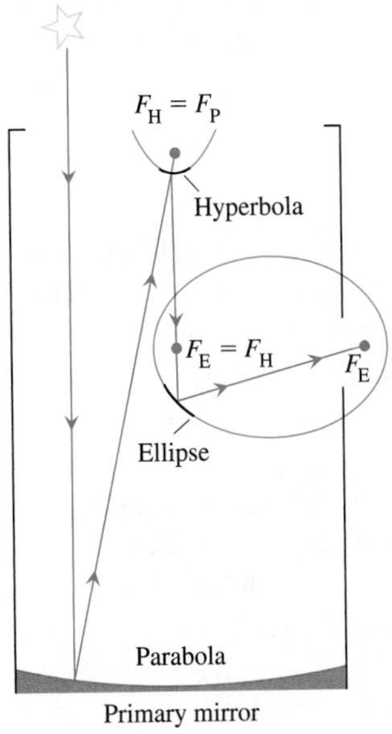

Figure A5.17 Schematic drawing of a reflecting telescope.

This property is used by flashlight, headlight, and spotlight reflectors and by microwave broadcast antennas to direct radiation from point sources into narrow beams. Conversely, electromagnetic waves arriving parallel to a parabolic reflector's axis are directed toward the reflector's focus. This property is used to intensify signals picked up by radio telescopes and television satellite dishes, to focus arriving light in telescopes, and to concentrate sunlight in solar heaters.

If an ellipse is revolved about its major axis to generate a surface (a surface called an *ellipsoid*) and the interior is silvered to produce a mirror, light from one focus will be reflected to the other focus (Figure A5.16). Ellipsoids reflect sound the same way, and this property is used to construct *whispering galleries,* rooms in which a person standing at one focus can hear a whisper from the other focus. Statuary Hall in the U.S. Capitol building is a whispering gallery. Ellipsoids also appear in instruments used to study aircraft noise in wind tunnels (sound at one focus can be received at the other focus with relatively little interference from other sources).

Light directed toward one focus of a hyperbolic mirror is reflected toward the other focus. This property of hyperbolas is combined with the reflective properties of parabolas and ellipses in designing modern telescopes. In Figure A5.17 starlight reflects off a primary parabolic mirror toward the mirror's focus F_P. It is then reflected by a small hyperbolic mirror, whose focus is $F_H = F_P$, toward the second focus of the hyperbola, $F_E = F_H$. Since this focus is shared by an ellipse, the light is reflected by the elliptical mirror to the ellipse's second focus to be seen by an observer.

As past experience with NASA's Hubble space telescope shows, the mirrors have to be nearly perfect to focus properly. The aberration that caused the malfunction in Hubble's primary mirror (now corrected with additional mirrors) amounted to about half a wavelength of visible light, no more than $1/50$ the width of a human hair.

Other Applications

Water pipes are sometimes designed with elliptical cross sections to allow for expansion when the water freezes. The triggering mechanisms in some lasers are elliptical, and stones on a beach become more and more elliptical as they are ground down by waves. There are also applications of ellipses to fossil formation. The ellipsolith, once thought to be a separate species, is now known to be an elliptically deformed nautilus.

Hyperbolic paths arise in Einstein's theory of relativity and form the basis for the (unrelated) LORAN radio navigation system. (LORAN is short for "long range navigation.") Hyperbolas also form the basis for a new system the Burlington Northern Railroad developed for using synchronized electronic signals from satellites to track freight trains. Computers aboard Burlington Northern locomotives in Minnesota can track trains to within one mile per hour of their speed and to within feet of their actual location.

Section A5.1 Exercises

In Exercises 1 and 2, find an equation for the circle with center $C(h, k)$ and radius a. Sketch the circle in the xy-plane. Label the circle's center and x- and y-intercepts (if any) with their coordinate pairs.

1. $C(0, 2),\quad a = 2$ **2.** $C(-1, 5),\quad a = \sqrt{10}$

In Exercises 3 and 4, find the center and radius of the circle. Then sketch the circle.

3. $x^2 + y^2 + 4x - 4y + 4 = 0$ **4.** $x^2 + y^2 - 4x + 4y = 0$

In Exercises 5 and 6, describe the regions defined by the inequalities and pairs of inequalities.

5. $(x - 1)^2 + y^2 \le 4$

6. $x^2 + y^2 > 1,\quad x^2 + y^2 < 4$

Match the parabolas in Exercises 7–10 with the following equations:

$$x^2 = 2y,\quad x^2 = -6y,\quad y^2 = 8x,\quad y^2 = -4x.$$

Then find the parabola's focus and directrix.

7.

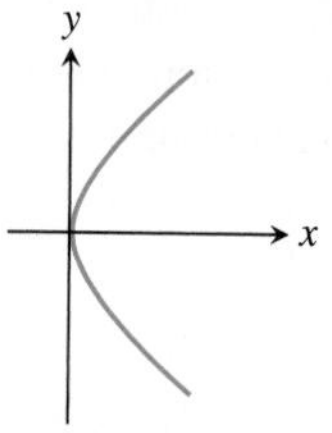

8.

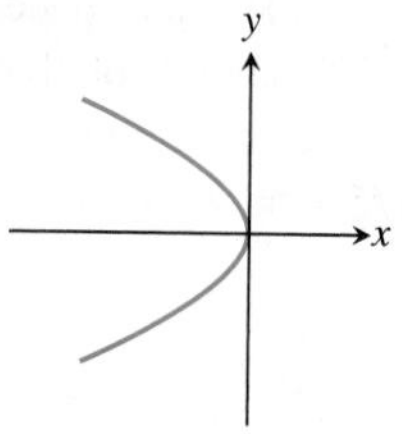

9.

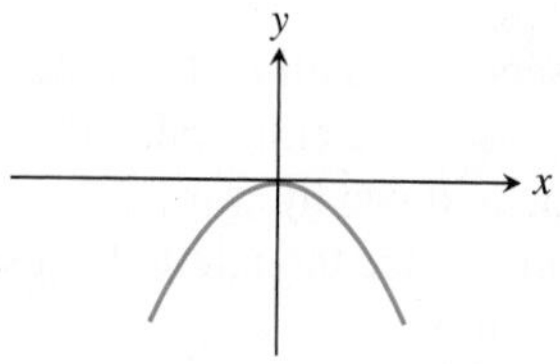

10.

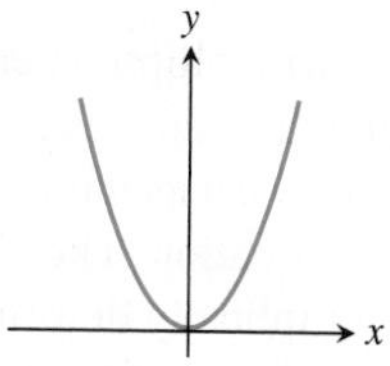

Match each conic section in Exercises 11–14 with one of these equations:

$$\frac{x^2}{4} + \frac{y^2}{9} = 1,\quad \frac{x^2}{2} + y^2 = 1,$$

$$\frac{y^2}{4} - x^2 = 1,\quad \frac{x^2}{4} - \frac{y^2}{9} = 1.$$

Then find the conic section's foci and vertices. If the conic section is a hyperbola, find its asymptotes as well.

11.

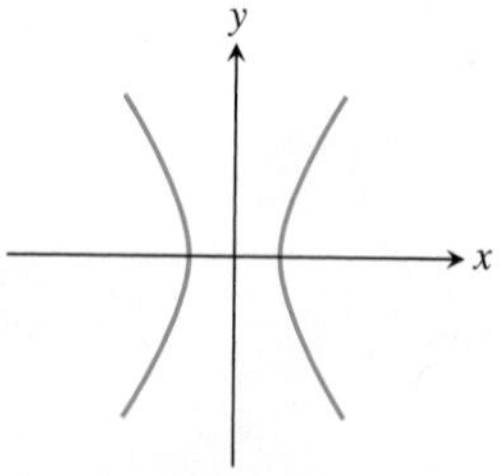

12.

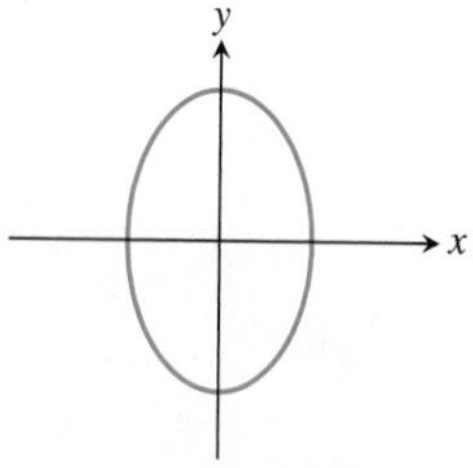

13.

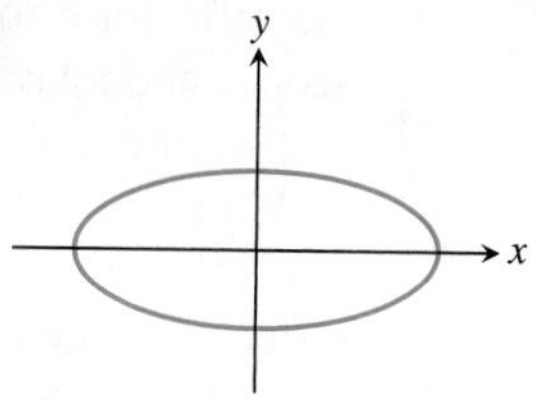

14.

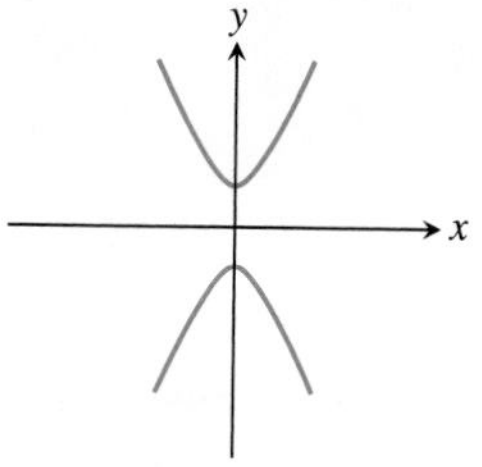

Exercises 15 and 16 give equations of parabolas. Find each parabola's focus and directrix. Then sketch the parabola. Include the focus and directrix in your sketch.

15. $y^2 = 12x$ **16.** $y = 4x^2$

Exercises 17 and 18 give equations for ellipses. Put each equation in standard form. Then sketch the ellipse. Include the foci in your sketch.

17. $16x^2 + 25y^2 = 400$

18. $3x^2 + 2y^2 = 6$

Exercises 19 and 20 give information about the foci and vertices of ellipses centered at the origin of the xy-plane. In each case, find the ellipse's standard-form equation from the given information.

19. Foci: $(\pm\sqrt{2}, 0)$
Vertices: $(\pm 2, 0)$

20. Foci: $(0, \pm 4)$
Vertices: $(0, \pm 5)$

Exercises 21 and 22 give equations for hyperbolas. Put each equation in standard form and find the hyperbola's asymptotes. Then sketch the hyperbola. Include the asymptotes and foci in your sketch.

21. $x^2 - y^2 = 1$ **22.** $8y^2 - 2x^2 = 16$

Exercises 23 and 24 give information about the foci, vertices, and asymptotes of hyperbolas centered at the origin of the xy-plane. In each case, find the hyperbola's standard-form equation from the information given.

23. Foci: $(0, \pm\sqrt{2})$
Asymptotes: $y = \pm x$

24. Vertices: $(\pm 3, 0)$
Asymptotes: $y = \pm\frac{4}{3}x$

25. The parabola $y^2 = 8x$ is shifted down 2 units and right 1 unit to generate the parabola $(y + 2)^2 = 8(x - 1)$.
(a) Find the new parabola's vertex, focus, and directrix.
(b) Plot the new vertex, focus, and directrix, and sketch in the parabola.

26. The ellipse $x^2/16 + y^2/9 = 1$ is shifted 4 units to the right and 3 units up to generate the ellipse

$$\frac{(x - 4)^2}{16} + \frac{(y - 3)^2}{9} = 1.$$

(a) Find the foci, vertices, and center of the new ellipse.

(b) Plot the new foci, vertices, and center, and sketch in the new ellipse.

27. The hyperbola $x^2/16 - y^2/9 = 1$ is shifted 2 units to the right to generate the hyperbola

$$\frac{(x-2)^2}{16} - \frac{y^2}{9} = 1.$$

(a) Find the center, foci, vertices, and asymptotes of the new hyperbola. **(b)** Plot the new center, foci, vertices, and asymptotes, and sketch in the hyperbola.

Exercises 28–31 give equations for conic sections and tell how many units up or down and to the right or left each is to be shifted. Find an equation for the new conic section and find the new vertices, foci, directrices, center, and asymptotes, as appropriate.

28. $y^2 = 4x$, left 2, down 3

29. $\frac{x^2}{6} + \frac{y^2}{9} = 1$, left 2, down 1

30. $\frac{x^2}{4} - \frac{y^2}{5} = 1$, right 2, up 2

31. $y^2 - x^2 = 1$, left 1, up 1

Find the center, foci, vertices, asymptotes, and radius, as appropriate, of each conic section in Exercises 32–36.

32. $x^2 + 4x + y^2 = 12$

33. $2x^2 + 2y^2 - 28x + 12y + 114 = 0$

34. $x^2 + 2x + 4y - 3 = 0$

35. $x^2 + 5y^2 + 4x = 1$

36. $x^2 - y^2 - 2x + 4y = 4$

37. ***Archimedes' Formula for the Volume of a Parabolic Solid*** The region enclosed by the parabola $y = (4h/b^2)x^2$ and the line $y = h$ is revolved about the y-axis to generate the solid shown here. Show that the volume of the solid is $3/2$ the volume of the corresponding cone.

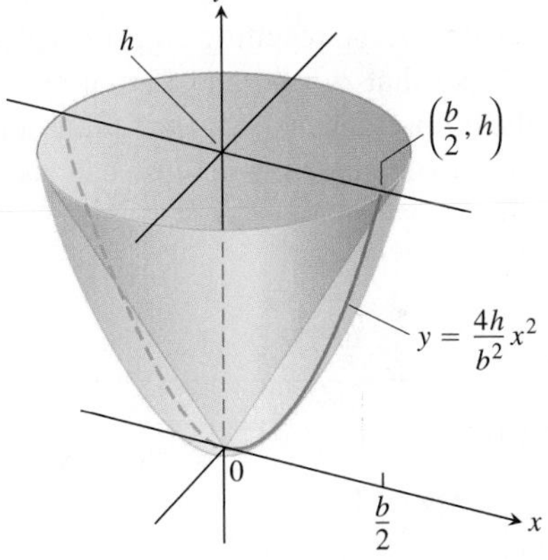

38. ***Comparing Volumes*** If lines are drawn parallel to the coordinate axes through a point P on the parabola $y^2 = kx$, $k > 0$, the parabola partitions the rectangular region bounded by these lines and the coordinate axes into two smaller regions, A and B.

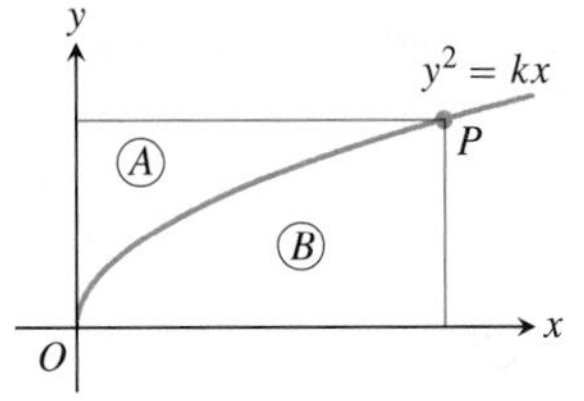

(a) If the two smaller regions are revolved about the y-axis, show that they generate solids whose volumes have the ratio 4:1.

(b) What is the ratio of the volumes of the solids generated by revolving the regions about the x-axis?

39. ***Perpendicular Tangents*** Show that the tangents to the curve $y^2 = 4px$ from any point on the line $x = -p$ are perpendicular.

40. ***Maximizing Area*** Find the dimensions of the rectangle of largest area that can be inscribed in the ellipse $x^2 + 4y^2 = 4$ with its sides parallel to the coordinate axes. What is the area of the rectangle?

41. ***Volume*** Find the volume of the solid generated by revolving the region enclosed by the ellipse $9x^2 + 4y^2 = 36$ about the **(a)** x-axis, **(b)** y-axis.

42. ***Volume*** The "triangular" region in the first quadrant bounded by the x-axis, the line $x = 4$, and the hyperbola $9x^2 - 4y^2 = 36$ is revolved about the x-axis to generate a solid. Find the volume of the solid.

43. ***Volume*** The region bounded on the left by the y-axis, on the right by the hyperbola $x^2 - y^2 = 1$, and above and below by the lines $y = \pm 3$ is revolved about the y-axis to generate a solid. Find the volume of the solid.

Extending the Ideas

44. ***Suspension Bridge Cables*** The suspension bridge cable shown here supports a uniform load of w pounds per horizontal foot. It can be shown that if H is the horizontal tension of the cable at the origin, then the curve of the cable satisfies the equation

$$\frac{dy}{dx} = \frac{w}{H}x.$$

Show that the cable hangs in a parabola by solving this differential equation subject to the initial condition that $y = 0$ when $x = 0$.

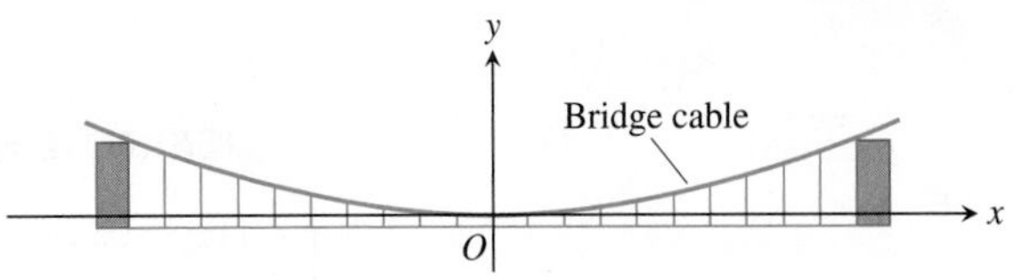

45. ***Ripple Tank*** Circular waves were made by touching the surface of a ripple tank, first at a point A and shortly thereafter at a nearby point B. As the waves expanded, their points of intersection appeared to trace a hyperbola. Did they really do that? To find out, we can model the waves with circles in the plane centered at nearby points labeled A and B as in the accompanying figure.

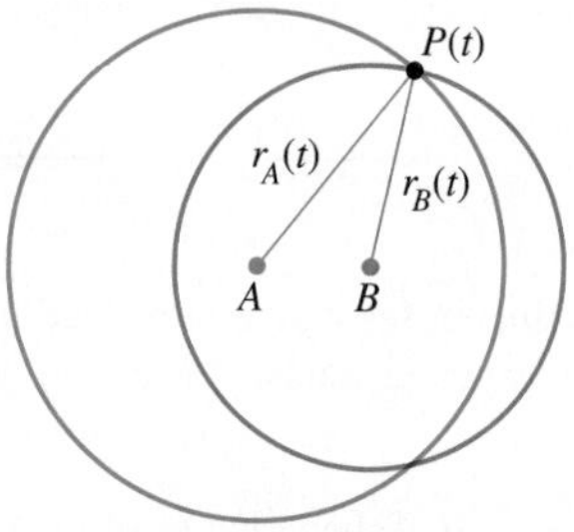

At time t, the point P is $r_A(t)$ units from A and $r_B(t)$ units from B. Since the radii of the circles increase at a constant rate, the rate at which the waves are traveling is

$$\frac{dr_A}{dt} = \frac{dr_B}{dt}.$$

Conclude from this equation that $r_A - r_B$ has a constant value, so that P must lie on a hyperbola with foci at A and B.

46. ***How the Astronomer Kepler Used String to Draw Parabolas*** Kepler's method for drawing a parabola (with more modern tools) requires a string the length of a T square and a table whose edge can serve as the parabola's directrix. Pin one end of the string to the point where you want the focus to be and the other end to the upper end of the T square. Then, holding the string taut against the T square with a pencil, slide the T square along the table's edge. As the T square moves, the pencil will trace a parabola. Why?

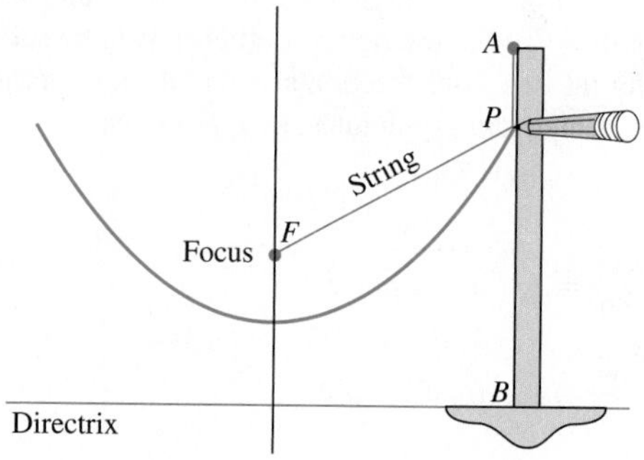

What you'll learn about

- Ellipses and Orbits
- Hyperbolas
- Focus-Directrix Equation

. . . and why

This section provides basic information about eccentricity of conic sections.

A5.2 Classifying Conic Sections by Eccentricity

Ellipses and Orbits

We now associate with each conic section a number called the eccentricity. The eccentricity tells whether the conic is a circle, ellipse, parabola, or hyperbola, and, in the case of ellipses and hyperbolas, describes the conic's proportions. We begin with the ellipse.

Although the center-to-focus distance c does not appear in the equation

$$\frac{x^2}{a^2} + \frac{y^2}{b^2} = 1, \quad (a > b)$$

for an ellipse, we can still determine c from the equation

$$c = \sqrt{a^2 - b^2}.$$

If we fix a and vary c over the interval $0 \le c \le a$, the resulting ellipses will vary in shape (Figure A5.18). They are circles if $c = 0$ (so that $a = b$) and flatten as c increases. If $c = a$, the foci and vertices overlap and the ellipse degenerates into a line segment.

We use the ratio of c to a to describe the various shapes the ellipse can take. We call this ratio the ellipse's eccentricity.

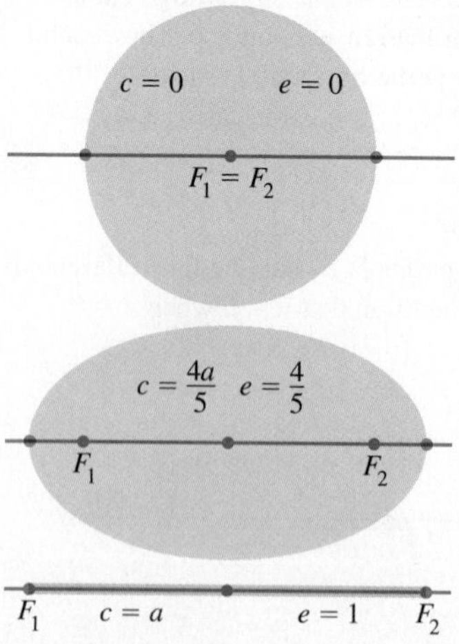

Figure A5.18 The ellipse changes from a circle to a line segment as c increases from 0 to a.

DEFINITION Eccentricity of Ellipse

The **eccentricity** of the ellipse $x^2/a^2 + y^2/b^2 = 1$ $(a > b)$ is

$$e = \frac{c}{a} = \frac{\sqrt{a^2 - b^2}}{a}.$$

Table A5.2 Eccentricities of planetary orbits

Mercury	0.21
Venus	0.01
Earth	0.02
Mars	0.09
Jupiter	0.05
Saturn	0.06
Uranus	0.05
Neptune	0.01
Pluto	0.25

The planets in the solar system revolve around the sun in elliptical orbits with the sun at one focus. Most of the orbits are nearly circular, as can be seen from the eccentricities in Table A5.2. Pluto has a fairly eccentric orbit, with $e = 0.25$, as does Mercury, with $e = 0.21$. Other members of the solar system have orbits that are even more eccentric. Icarus, an asteroid about 1 mile wide that revolves around the sun every 409 Earth days, has an orbital eccentricity of 0.83 (Figure A5.19).

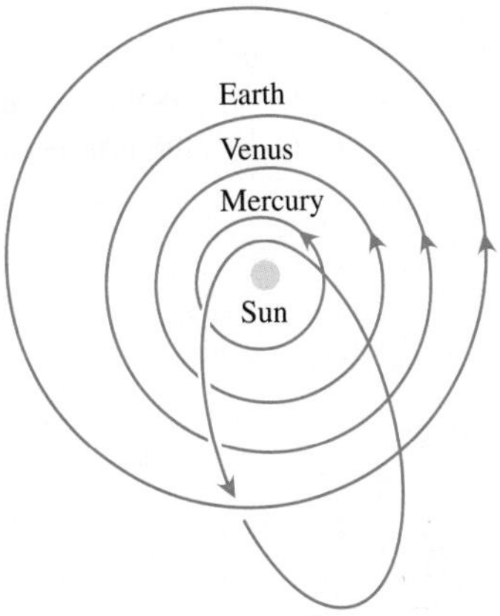

Figure A5.19 The orbit of the asteroid Icarus is highly eccentric. Earth's orbit is so nearly circular that its foci lie inside the sun.

Halley's comet

Edmund Halley (1656–1742; pronounced "*haw*-ley"), British biologist, geologist, sea captain, pirate, spy, Antarctic voyager, astronomer, adviser on fortifications, company founder and director, and the author of the first actuarial mortality tables, was also the mathematician who pushed and harried Newton into writing his *Principia*. Despite these accomplishments, Halley is known today chiefly as the man who calculated the orbit of the great comet of 1682: "wherefore if according to what we have already said [the comet] should return again about the year 1758, candid posterity will not refuse to acknowledge that this was first discovered by an Englishman." Indeed, candid posterity did not refuse—ever since the comet's return in 1758, it has been known as Halley's comet.

Last seen rounding the sun during the winter and spring of 1985–1986, the comet is due to return in the year 2062. The comet has made about 2000 cycles so far with about the same number to go before the sun erodes it away.

EXAMPLE 1 Finding the Eccentricity of an Orbit

The orbit of Halley's comet is an ellipse 36.18 astronomical units long by 9.12 astronomical units wide. (One *astronomical unit* [AU] is 149,597,870 km, the semimajor axis of Earth's orbit.) Its eccentricity is

$$e = \frac{\sqrt{a^2 - b^2}}{a} = \frac{\sqrt{(36.18/2)^2 - (9.12/2)^2}}{(1/2)(36.18)}$$

$$= \frac{\sqrt{(18.09)^2 - (4.56)^2}}{18.09}$$

$$\approx 0.97.$$

Now try Exercise 1.

EXAMPLE 2 Locating Vertices

Locate the vertices of an ellipse of eccentricity 0.8 whose foci lie at the points $(0, \pm 7)$.

SOLUTION

Since $e = c/a$, the vertices are the points $(0, \pm a)$ where

$$a = \frac{c}{e} = \frac{7}{0.8} = 8.75,$$

or $(0, \pm 8.75)$.

Now try Exercise 5.

Whereas a parabola has one focus and one directrix, each ellipse has two foci and two **directrices.** These are the lines perpendicular to the major axis at distances $\pm a/e$ from the center. The parabola has the property that

$$PF = 1 \cdot PD \tag{1}$$

for any point P on it, where F is the focus and D is the point nearest P on the directrix. For an ellipse, it can be shown that the equations that replace (1) are

$$PF_1 = e \cdot PD_1, \quad PF_2 = e \cdot PD_2. \tag{2}$$

Here, e is the eccentricity, P is any point on the ellipse, F_1 and F_2 are the foci, and D_1 and D_2 are the points on the directrices nearest P (Figure A5.20).

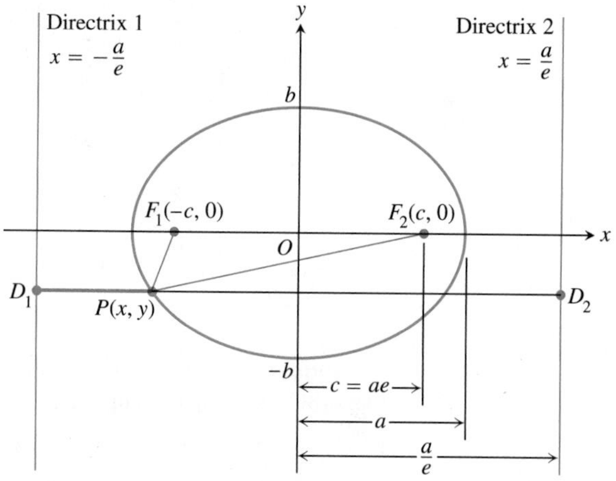

Figure A5.20 The foci and directrices of the ellipse $x^2/a^2 + y^2/b^2 = 1$. Directrix 1 corresponds

In each equation in (2) the directrix and focus must correspond; that is, if we use the distance from P to F_1, we must also use the distance from P to the directrix at the same end of the ellipse. The directrix $x = -a/e$ corresponds to $F_1(-c, 0)$, and the directrix $x = a/e$ corresponds to $F_2(c, 0)$.

Hyperbolas

The eccentricity of a hyperbola is also $e = c/a$, only in this case c equals $\sqrt{a^2 + b^2}$ instead of $\sqrt{a^2 - b^2}$. In contrast to the eccentricity of an ellipse, the eccentricity of a hyperbola is always greater than 1.

DEFINITION Eccentricity of Hyperbola

The **eccentricity** of the hyperbola $x^2/a^2 - y^2/b^2 = 1$ is

$$e = \frac{c}{a} = \frac{\sqrt{a^2 + b^2}}{a}.$$

In both ellipse and hyperbola, the eccentricity is the ratio of the distance between the foci to the distance between the vertices (because $c/a = 2c/2a$).

$$\text{Eccentricity} = \frac{\text{distance between foci}}{\text{distance between vertices}}$$

In an ellipse, the foci are closer together than the vertices and the ratio is less than 1. In a hyperbola, the foci are farther apart than the vertices and the ratio is greater than 1.

EXAMPLE 3 Finding Eccentricity

Find the eccentricity of the hyperbola $9x^2 - 16y^2 = 144$.

SOLUTION

We divide both sides of the hyperbola's equation by 144 to put it in standard form, obtaining

$$\frac{9x^2}{144} - \frac{16y^2}{144} = 1 \quad \text{or} \quad \frac{x^2}{16} - \frac{y^2}{9} = 1.$$

With $a^2 = 16$ and $b^2 = 9$, we find that $c = \sqrt{a^2 + b^2} = \sqrt{16 + 9} = 5$, so

$$e = \frac{c}{a} = \frac{5}{4}.$$

Now try Exercise 15.

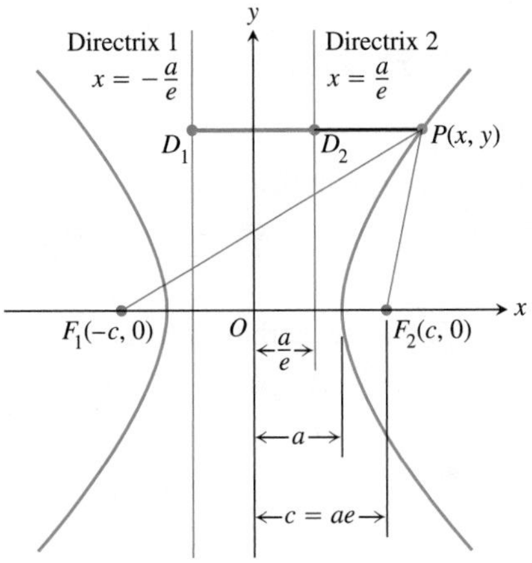

Figure A5.21 The foci and directrices of the hyperbola $x^2/a^2 - y^2/b^2 = 1$. No matter where P lies on the hyperbola, $PF_1 = e \cdot PD_1$, and $PF_2 = e \cdot PD_2$.

As with the ellipse, it can be shown that the lines $x = \pm a/e$ act as **directrices** for the hyperbola and that

$$PF_1 = e \cdot PD_1 \quad \text{and} \quad PF_2 = e \cdot PD_2. \tag{3}$$

Here P is any point on the hyperbola, F_1 and F_2 are the foci, and D_1 and D_2 are the points nearest P on the directrices (Figure A5.21).

Focus-Directrix Equation

To complete the picture, we define the eccentricity of a parabola to be $e = 1$. Equations 1–3 then have the common form $PF = e \cdot PD$.

DEFINITION Eccentricity of Parabola

The **eccentricity** of a parabola is $e = 1$.

The **focus-directrix equation** $PF = e \cdot PD$ unites the parabola, ellipse, and hyperbola in the following way. Suppose that the distance PF of a point P from a fixed point F (the focus) is a constant multiple of its distance from a fixed line (the directrix). That is, suppose

$$PF = e \cdot PD, \tag{4}$$

where e is the constant of proportionality. Then the path traced by P is

(a) a *parabola* if $e = 1$,

(b) an *ellipse* of eccentricity e if $e < 1$, and

(c) a *hyperbola* of eccentricity e if $e > 1$.

Equation 4 may not look like much to get excited about. There are no coordinates in it and when we try to translate it into coordinate form it translates in different ways, depending on the size of e. At least, that is what happens in Cartesian coordinates. However, in polar coordinates, the equation $PF = e \cdot PD$ translates into a single equation regardless of the value of e, an equation so simple that it has been the equation of choice of astronomers and space scientists for nearly 300 years.

Given the focus and corresponding directrix of a hyperbola centered at the origin and with foci on the x-axis, we can use the dimensions shown in Figure A5.21 to find e. Knowing e, we can derive a Cartesian equation for the hyperbola from the equation $PF = e \cdot PD$, as in the next example. We can find equations for ellipses centered at the origin and with foci on the x-axis in a similar way, using the dimensions shown in Figure A5.20.

EXAMPLE 4 Using Focus and Directrix

Find a Cartesian equation for the hyperbola centered at the origin that has a focus at $(3, 0)$ and the line $x = 1$ as the corresponding directrix.

SOLUTION

We first use the dimensions shown in Figure A5.21 to find the hyperbola's eccentricity. The focus is

$$(c, 0) = (3, 0), \quad \text{so} \quad c = 3.$$

The directrix is the line

$$x = \frac{a}{e} = 1, \quad \text{so} \quad a = e.$$

When combined with the equation $e = c/a$ that defines eccentricity, these results give

$$e = \frac{c}{a} = \frac{3}{e}, \quad \text{so} \quad e^2 = 3 \quad \text{and} \quad e = \sqrt{3}.$$

Knowing e, we can now derive the equation we want from the equation $PF = e \cdot PD$. In the notation of Figure A5.22, we have

$$PF = e \cdot PD \qquad \text{Eq. 4}$$

$$\sqrt{(x-3)^2 + (y-0)^2} = \sqrt{3}|x-1| \qquad e = \sqrt{3}$$

$$x^2 - 6x + 9 + y^2 = 3(x^2 - 2x + 1)$$

$$2x^2 - y^2 = 6$$

$$\frac{x^2}{3} - \frac{y^2}{6} = 1.$$

Now try Exercise 19.

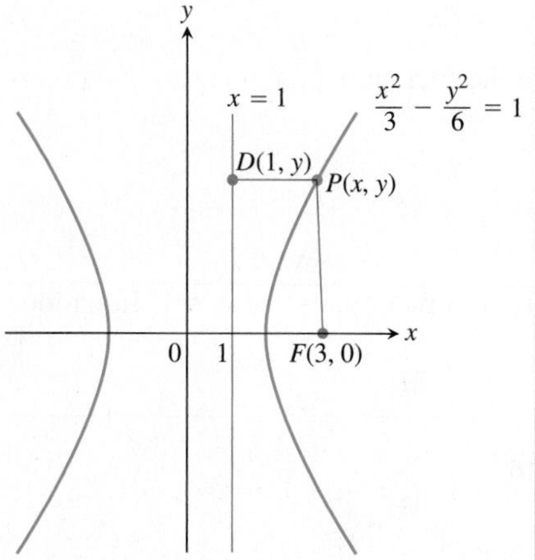

Figure A5.22 The hyperbola in Example 4.

Section A5.2 Exercises

In Exercises 1–4, find the eccentricity, foci, and directrices of the ellipse.

1. $16x^2 + 25y^2 = 400$
2. $2x^2 + y^2 = 2$
3. $3x^2 + 2y^2 = 6$
4. $6x^2 + 9y^2 = 54$

Exercises 5–8 give the foci or vertices and the eccentricities of ellipses centered at the origin of the xy-plane. In each case, find the ellipse's standard-form equation.

5. Foci: $(0, \pm 3)$
   Eccentricity: 0.5
6. Foci: $(\pm 8, 0)$
   Eccentricity: 0.2
7. Vertices: $(\pm 10, 0)$
   Eccentricity: 0.24
8. Vertices: $(0, \pm 70)$
   Eccentricity: 0.1

Exercises 9 and 10 give foci and corresponding directrices of ellipses centered at the origin of the xy-plane. In each case, use the dimensions in Figure A5.20 to find the eccentricity of the ellipse. Then find the ellipse's standard-form equation.

9. Focus: $(\sqrt{5}, 0)$

Directrix: $x = \frac{9}{\sqrt{5}}$

10. Focus: $(-4, 0)$

Directrix: $x = -16$

11. Draw an ellipse of eccentricity 4/5. Explain your procedure.

12. Draw the orbit of Pluto (eccentricity 0.25) to scale. Explain your procedure.

13. The endpoints of the major and minor axes of an ellipse are $(1, 1)$, $(3, 4)$, $(1, 7)$, and $(-1, 4)$. Sketch the ellipse, give its equation in standard form, and find its foci, eccentricity, and directrices.

14. Find an equation for the ellipse of eccentricity 2/3 that has the line $x = 9$ as a directrix and the point $(4, 0)$ as the corresponding focus.

In Exercises 15–18, find the eccentricity, foci, and directrices of the hyperbola.

15. $9x^2 - 16y^2 = 144$

16. $y^2 - x^2 = 8$

17. $8x^2 - 2y^2 = 16$

18. $8y^2 - 2x^2 = 16$

Exercises 19 and 20 give the eccentricities and the vertices or foci of hyperbolas centered at the origin of the xy-plane. In each case, find the hyperbola's standard-form equation.

19. Eccentricity: 3

Vertices: $(0, \pm 1)$

20. Eccentricity: 3

Foci: $(\pm 3, 0)$

Exercises 21 and 22 give foci and corresponding directrices of hyperbolas centered at the origin of the xy-plane. In each case, find the hyperbola's eccentricity. Then find the hyperbola's standard-form equation.

21. Focus: $(4, 0)$

Directrix: $x = 2$

22. Focus: $(-2, 0)$

Directrix: $x = -\frac{1}{2}$

23. A hyperbola of eccentricity 3/2 has one focus at $(1, -3)$. The corresponding directrix is the line $y = 2$. Find an equation for the hyperbola.

Explorations

24. ***The Effect of Eccentricity on a Hyperbola's Shape*** What happens to the graph of a hyperbola as its eccentricity increases? To find out, rewrite the equation $x^2/a^2 - y^2/b^2 = 1$ in terms of a and e instead of a and b. Graph the hyperbola for various values of e and describe what you find.

25. ***Determining Constants*** What values of the constants a, b, and c make the ellipse

$$4x^2 + y^2 + ax + by + c = 0$$

lie tangent to the x-axis at the origin and pass through the point $(-1, 2)$? What is the eccentricity of the ellipse?

Extending the Ideas

26. ***The Reflective Property of Ellipses*** An ellipse is revolved about its major axis to generate an ellipsoid. The inner surface of the ellipsoid is silvered to make a mirror. Show that a ray of light emanating from one focus will be reflected to the other focus. Sound waves also follow such paths, and this property is used in constructing "whispering galleries." (*Hint:* Place the ellipse in standard position in the xy-plane and show that the lines from a point P on the ellipse to the two foci make congruent angles with the tangent to the ellipse at P.)

27. ***The Reflective Property of Hyperbolas*** Show that a ray of light directed toward one focus of a hyperbolic mirror, as in the accompanying figure, is reflected toward the other focus. (*Hint:* Show that the tangent to the hyperbola at P bisects the angle made by segments PF_1 and PF_2.)

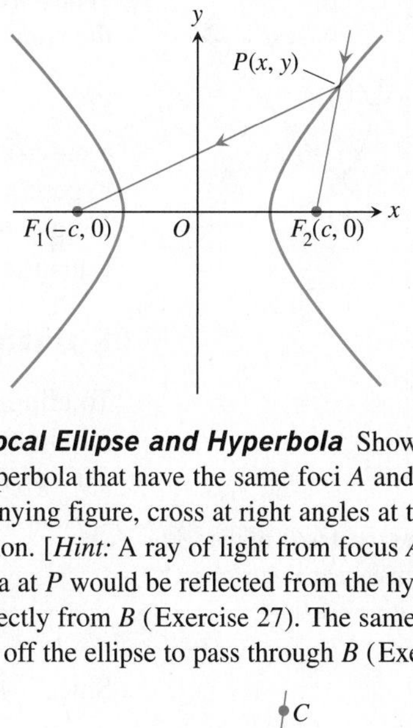

28. ***A Confocal Ellipse and Hyperbola*** Show that an ellipse and a hyperbola that have the same foci A and B, as in the accompanying figure, cross at right angles at their points of intersection. [*Hint:* A ray of light from focus A that met the hyperbola at P would be reflected from the hyperbola as if it came directly from B (Exercise 27). The same ray would be reflected off the ellipse to pass through B (Exercise 26).]

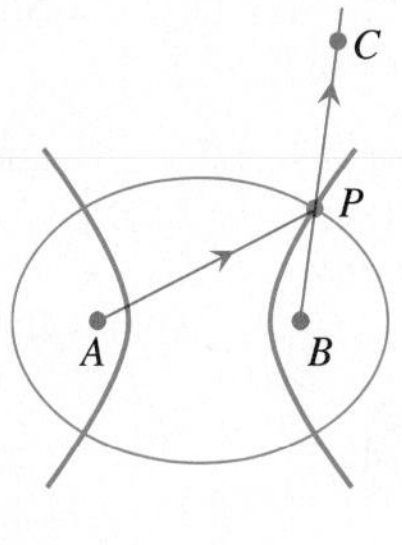

What you'll learn about

- Quadratic Curves
- Cross Product Term
- Rotating Axes to Eliminate *Bxy*
- Possible Graphs of Quadratic Equations
- Discriminant Test
- Technology Application

. . . and why

This section provides basic information about general quadratic equations in two variables and their graphs.

A5.3 Quadratic Equations and Rotations

Quadratic Curves

In this section, we examine one of the most amazing results in analytic geometry, which is that the Cartesian graph of any equation

$$Ax^2 + Bxy + Cy^2 + Dx + Ey + F = 0, \tag{1}$$

in which A, B, and C are not all zero, is nearly always a conic section. The exceptions are the cases in which there is no graph at all or the graph consists of two parallel lines. It is conventional to call all graphs of Equation 1, curved or not, **quadratic curves.**

Cross Product Term

You may have noticed that the term Bxy did not appear in the equations for the conic sections in Section A5.1. This happened because the axes of the conic sections ran parallel to (in fact, coincided with) the coordinate axes.

To see what happens when the parallelism is absent, let us write an equation for a hyperbola with $a = 3$ and foci at $F_1(-3, -3)$ and $F_2(3, 3)$ (Figure A5.23). The equation $|PF_1 - PF_2| = 2a$ becomes $|PF_1 - PF_2| = 2(3) = 6$ and

$$\sqrt{(x+3)^2 + (y+3)^2} - \sqrt{(x-3)^2 + (y-3)^2} = \pm 6.$$

When we transpose one radical, square, solve for the remaining radical and square again, the equation reduces to

$$2xy = 9, \tag{2}$$

a case of Equation 1 in which the cross product term is present. The asymptotes of the hyperbola in Equation 2 are the x- and y-axes, and the focal axis makes an angle of $\pi/4$ radians with the positive x-axis. As in this example, the cross product term is present in Equation 1 only when the axes of the conic are tilted.

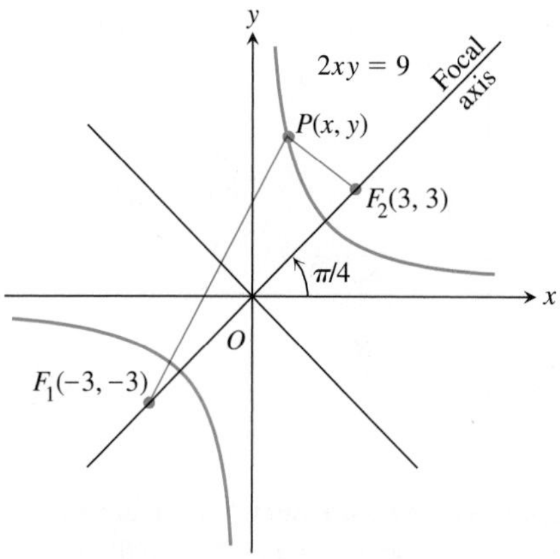

Figure A5.23 The focal axis of the hyperbola $2xy = 9$ makes an angle of $\pi/4$ radians with the positive x-axis.

Rotating Axes to Eliminate *Bxy*

To eliminate the xy-term from the equation of a conic, we rotate the coordinate axes to eliminate the "tilt" in the axes of the conic. The equations for the rotations we use are derived in the following way. In the notation of Figure A5.24, which shows a counterclockwise rotation about the origin through an angle α,

$$\begin{aligned} x &= OM = OP\cos(\theta + \alpha) = OP\cos\theta\cos\alpha - OP\sin\theta\sin\alpha \\ y &= MP = OP\sin(\theta + \alpha) = OP\cos\theta\sin\alpha + OP\sin\theta\cos\alpha. \end{aligned} \tag{3}$$

Since

$$OP\cos\theta = OM' = x'$$

and

$$OP\sin\theta = M'P = y',$$

the equations in (3) reduce to the following.

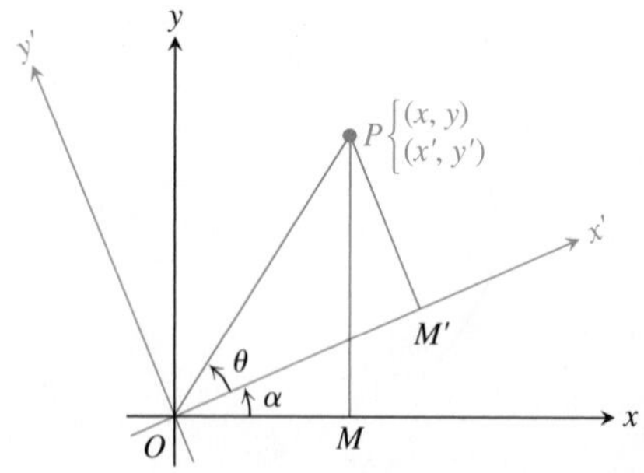

Figure A5.24 A counterclockwise rotation through angle α about the origin.

Equations for Rotating Coordinate Axes

$$\begin{aligned} x &= x'\cos\alpha - y'\sin\alpha \\ y &= x'\sin\alpha + y'\cos\alpha \end{aligned} \tag{4}$$

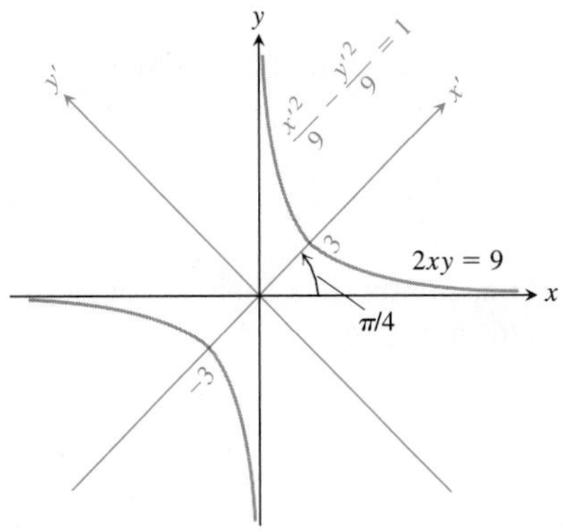

Figure A5.25 The hyperbola in Example 1 (x' and y' are the new coordinates).

EXAMPLE 1 Changing an Equation

The x- and y-axes are rotated through an angle of $\pi/4$ radians about the origin. Find an equation for the hyperbola $2xy = 9$ in the new coordinates.

SOLUTION

Since $\cos \pi/4 = \sin \pi/4 = 1/\sqrt{2}$, we substitute

$$x = \frac{x' - y'}{\sqrt{2}}, \quad y = \frac{x' + y'}{\sqrt{2}}$$

from Equations 4 into the equation $2xy = 9$, obtaining

$$2\left(\frac{x' - y'}{\sqrt{2}}\right)\left(\frac{x' + y'}{\sqrt{2}}\right) = 9$$

$$x'^2 - y'^2 = 9$$

$$\frac{x'^2}{9} - \frac{y'^2}{9} = 1.$$

See Figure A5.25. ***Now try Exercise 35.***

If we apply Equations 4 to the quadratic Equation 1, we obtain a new quadratic equation

$$A'x'^2 + B'x'y' + C'y'^2 + D'x' + E'y' + F' = 0. \tag{5}$$

The new and old coefficients are related by the equations

$$\begin{aligned}
A' &= A\cos^2\alpha + B\cos\alpha\sin\alpha + C\sin^2\alpha \\
B' &= B\cos 2\alpha + (C - A)\sin 2\alpha \\
C' &= A\sin^2\alpha - B\sin\alpha\cos\alpha + C\cos^2\alpha \\
D' &= D\cos\alpha + E\sin\alpha \\
E' &= -D\sin\alpha + E\cos\alpha \\
F' &= F.
\end{aligned} \tag{6}$$

Equations 6 show, among other things, that if we start with an equation for a curve in which the cross product term is present ($B \neq 0$), we can find a rotation angle α that produces an equation in which no cross product term appears ($B' = 0$). To find α, we set $B' = 0$ in the second equation in (6) and solve the resulting equation,

$$B\cos 2\alpha + (C - A)\sin 2\alpha = 0,$$

for α. In practice, this means determining α from one of the two equations.

$$\cot 2\alpha = \frac{A - C}{B} \quad \text{or} \quad \tan 2\alpha = \frac{B}{A - C}. \tag{7}$$

EXAMPLE 2 Eliminating a Cross Product Term

The coordinate axes are to be rotated through an angle α to produce an equation for the curve

$$2x^2 + \sqrt{3}xy + y^2 - 10 = 0$$

that has no cross product term. Find a suitable α and the corresponding new equation. Identify the curve.

continued

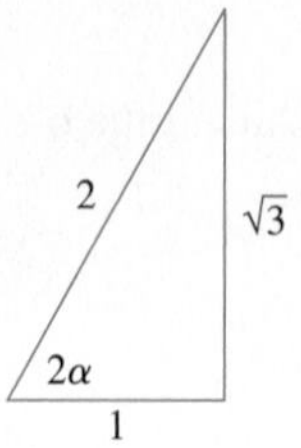

Figure A5.26 This triangle identifies $2\alpha = \cot^{-1}(1/\sqrt{3})$ as $\pi/3$. (Example 2)

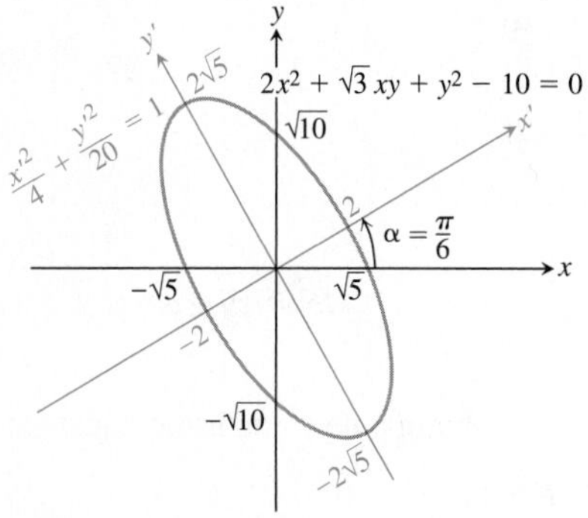

Figure A5.27 The conic section in Example 2.

SOLUTION

The equation $2x^2 + \sqrt{3}xy + y^2 - 10 = 0$ has $A = 2$, $B = \sqrt{3}$, and $C = 1$. We substitute these values into Equation 7 to find α:

$$\cot 2\alpha = \frac{A - C}{B} = \frac{2 - 1}{\sqrt{3}} = \frac{1}{\sqrt{3}}.$$

From the right triangle in Figure A5.26, we see that one appropriate choice of angle is $2\alpha = \pi/3$, so we take $\alpha = \pi/6$. Substituting $\alpha = \pi/6$, $A = 2$, $B = \sqrt{3}$, $C = 1$, $D = E = 0$, and $F = -10$ into Equations 6 gives

$$A' = \frac{5}{2}, \quad B' = 0, \quad C' = \frac{1}{2}, \quad D' = E' = 0, \quad F' = -10.$$

Equation 5 then gives

$$\frac{5}{2}x'^2 + \frac{1}{2}y'^2 - 10 = 0, \quad \text{or} \quad \frac{x'^2}{4} + \frac{y'^2}{20} = 1.$$

The curve is an ellipse with foci on the new y'-axis (Figure A5.27).

Now try Exercise 21.

Possible Graphs of Quadratic Equations

We now return to the graph of the general quadratic equation.

Since axes can always be rotated to eliminate the cross product term, there is no loss of generality in assuming that this has been done and that the equation has the form

$$Ax^2 + Cy^2 + Dx + Ey + F = 0. \tag{8}$$

Equation 8 represents

(a) a *circle* if $A = C \neq 0$ (special cases: the graph is a point or there is no graph at all);

(b) a *parabola* if Equation 8 is quadratic in one variable and linear in the other;

(c) an *ellipse* if A and C are both positive or both negative (special cases: circles, a single point, or no graph at all);

(d) a *hyperbola* if A and C have opposite signs (special case: a pair of intersecting lines);

(e) a *straight line* if A and C are zero and at least one of D and E is different from zero;

(f) *one or two straight lines* if the left-hand side of Equation 8 can be factored into the product of two linear factors.

See Table A5.3 (on page 600) for examples.

Discriminant Test

We do not need to eliminate the xy-term from the equation

$$Ax^2 + Bxy + Cy^2 + Dx + Ey + F = 0 \tag{9}$$

to tell what kind of conic section the equation represents. If this is the only information we want, we can apply the following test instead.

As we have seen, if $B \neq 0$, then rotating the coordinate axes through an angle α that satisfies the equation

$$\cot 2\alpha = \frac{A - C}{B} \tag{10}$$

will change Equation 9 into an equivalent form

$$A'x'^2 + C'y'^2 + D'x' + E'y' + F' = 0 \tag{11}$$

without a cross product term.

Now, the graph of Equation 11 is a (real or degenerate)

(a) *parabola* if A' or $C' = 0$; that is, if $A'C' = 0$;

(b) *ellipse* if A' and C' have the same sign; that is, if $A'C' > 0$;

(c) *hyperbola* if A' and C' have opposite signs; that is, if $A'C' < 0$.

It can also be verified from Equations 6 that for any rotation of axes,

$$B^2 - 4AC = B'^2 - 4A'C'. \tag{12}$$

This means that the quantity $B^2 - 4AC$ is not changed by a rotation. But when we rotate through the angle α given by Equation 10, B' becomes zero, so

$$B^2 - 4AC = -4A'C'.$$

Since the curve is a parabola if $A'C' = 0$, an ellipse if $A'C' > 0$, and a hyperbola if $A'C' < 0$, the curve must be a parabola if $B^2 - 4AC = 0$, an ellipse if $B^2 - 4AC < 0$, and a hyperbola if $B^2 - 4AC > 0$. The number $B^2 - 4AC$ is called the **discriminant** of Equation 9.

Discriminant Test

With the understanding that occasional degenerate cases may arise, the quadratic curve $Ax^2 + Bxy + Cy^2 + Dx + Ey + F = 0$ is

(a) a **parabola** if $B^2 - 4AC = 0$,

(b) an **ellipse** if $B^2 - 4AC < 0$,

(c) a **hyperbola** if $B^2 - 4AC > 0$.

EXAMPLE 3 Applying the Discriminant Test

(a) $3x^2 - 6xy + 3y^2 + 2x - 7 = 0$ represents a parabola because

$$B^2 - 4AC = (-6)^2 - 4 \cdot 3 \cdot 3 = 36 - 36 = 0.$$

(b) $x^2 + xy + y^2 - 1 = 0$ represents an ellipse because

$$B^2 - 4AC = (1)^2 - 4 \cdot 1 \cdot 1 = -3 < 0.$$

(c) $xy - y^2 - 5y + 1 = 0$ represents a hyperbola because

$$B^2 - 4AC = (1)^2 - 4(0)(-1) = 1 > 0.$$

Now try Exercise 15.

Technology Application

How Some Calculators Use Rotations to Evaluate Sines and Cosines

Some calculators use rotations to calculate sines and cosines of arbitrary angles. The procedure goes something like this: The calculator has, stored,

1. ten angles or so, say

$$\alpha_1 = \sin^{-1}(10^{-1}), \quad \alpha_2 = \sin^{-1}(10^{-2}), \quad \ldots, \quad \alpha_{10} = \sin^{-1}(10^{-10}),$$

and

2. twenty numbers, the sines and cosines of the angles $\alpha_1, \alpha_2, \ldots, \alpha_{10}$.

To calculate the sine and cosine of an arbitrary angle θ, we enter θ (in radians) into the calculator. The calculator substracts or adds multiples of 2π to θ to replace θ by the angle between 0 and 2π that has the same sine and cosine as θ (we continue to call the angle θ).

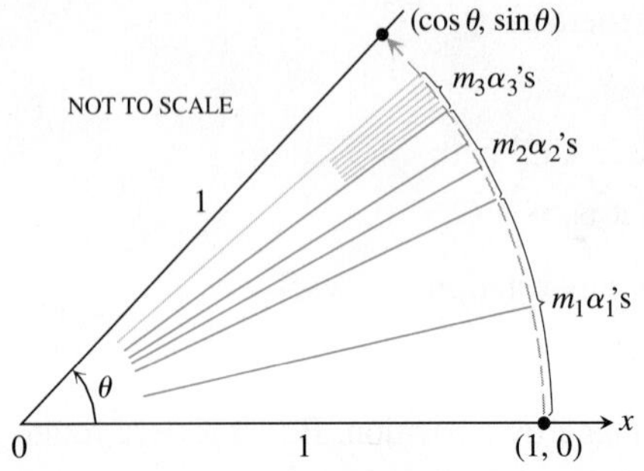

Figure A5.28 To calculate the sine and cosine of an angle θ between 0 and 2π, the calculator rotates the point (1, 0) to an appropriate location on the unit circle and displays the resulting coordinates.

The calculator then "writes" θ as a sum of multiples of α_1 (as many as possible without overshooting) plus multiples of α_2 (again, as many as possible), and so on, working its way to α_{10}. This gives

$$\theta \approx m_1\alpha_1 + m_2\alpha_2 + \cdots + m_{10}\alpha_{10}.$$

The calculator then rotates the point (1, 0) through m_1 copies of α_1 (through α_1, m_1 times in succession), plus m_2 copies of α_2, and so on, finishing off with m_{10} copies of α_{10} (Figure A5.28). The coordinates of the final position of (1, 0) on the unit circle are the values the calculator gives for ($\cos\theta$, $\sin\theta$).

Table A5.3 Examples of quadratic curves

$Ax^2 + Bxy + Cy^2 + Dx + Ey + F = 0$

	A	*B*	*C*	*D*	*E*	*F*	Equation	Remarks
Circle	1		1			−4	$x^2 + y^2 = 4$	$A = C$; $F < 0$
Parabola			1	−9			$y^2 = 9x$	Quadratic in y, linear in x
Ellipse	4		9			−36	$4x^2 + 9y^2 = 36$	A, C have same sign, $A \neq C$; $F < 0$
Hyperbola	1		−1			−1	$x^2 - y^2 = 1$	A, C have opposite signs
One line (still a conic section)	1						$x^2 = 0$	y-axis
Intersecting lines (still a conic section)		1		1	−1	−1	$xy + x - y - 1 = 0$	Factors to $(x - 1)(y + 1) = 0$, so $x = 1$, $y = -1$
Parallel lines (not a conic section)	1			−3		2	$x^2 - 3x + 2 = 0$	Factors to $(x - 1)(x - 2) = 0$, so $x = 1$, $x = 2$
Point	1		1				$x^2 + y^2 = 0$	The origin
No graph	1					1	$x^2 = -1$	No graph

Section A5.3 Exercises

Use the discriminant $B^2 - 4AC$ to decide whether the equations in Exercises 1–16 represent parabolas, ellipses, or hyperbolas.

1. $x^2 - 3xy + y^2 - x = 0$

2. $3x^2 - 18xy + 27y^2 - 5x + 7y = -4$

3. $3x^2 - 7xy + \sqrt{17}y^2 = 1$

4. $2x^2 - \sqrt{15}xy + 2y^2 + x + y = 0$

5. $x^2 + 2xy + y^2 + 2x - y + 2 = 0$

6. $2x^2 - y^2 + 4xy - 2x + 3y = 6$

7. $x^2 + 4xy + 4y^2 - 3x = 6$

8. $x^2 + y^2 + 3x - 2y = 10$

9. $xy + y^2 - 3x = 5$

10. $3x^2 + 6xy + 3y^2 - 4x + 5y = 12$

11. $3x^2 - 5xy + 2y^2 - 7x - 14y = -1$

12. $2x^2 - 4.9xy + 3y^2 - 4x = 7$

13. $x^2 - 3xy + 3y^2 + 6y = 7$

14. $25x^2 + 21xy + 4y^2 - 350x = 0$

15. $6x^2 + 3xy + 2y^2 + 17y + 2 = 0$

16. $3x^2 + 12xy + 12y^2 + 435x - 9y + 72 = 0$

In Exercises 17–26, rotate the coordinate axes to change the given equation into an equation that has no cross product (xy) term. Then identify the graph of the equation. (The new equations will vary with the size and direction of the rotation you use.)

17. $xy = 2$

18. $x^2 + xy + y^2 = 1$

19. $3x^2 + 2\sqrt{3}xy + y^2 - 8x + 8\sqrt{3}y = 0$

20. $x^2 - \sqrt{3}xy + 2y^2 = 1$

21. $x^2 - 2xy + y^2 = 2$

22. $3x^2 - 2\sqrt{3}xy + y^2 = 1$

23. $\sqrt{2}x^2 + 2\sqrt{2}xy + \sqrt{2}y^2 - 8x + 8y = 0$

24. $xy - y - x + 1 = 0$

25. $3x^2 + 2xy + 3y^2 = 19$

26. $3x^2 + 4\sqrt{3}xy - y^2 = 7$

27. Find the sine and cosine of an angle through which the coordinate axes can be rotated to eliminate the cross product term from the equation

$$14x^2 + 16xy + 2y^2 - 10x + 26{,}370y - 17 = 0.$$

Do not carry out the rotation.

28. Find the sine and cosine of an angle through which the coordinate axes can be rotated to eliminate the cross product term from the equation

$$4x^2 - 4xy + y^2 - 8\sqrt{5}x - 16\sqrt{5}y = 0.$$

Do not carry out the rotation.

The conic sections in Exercises 17–26 were chosen to have rotation angles that were "nice" in the sense that once we knew $\cot 2\alpha$ or $\tan 2\alpha$ we could identify 2α and find $\sin\alpha$ and $\cos\alpha$ from familiar triangles. The conic sections encountered in practice may not have such nice rotation angles, and we may have to use a calculator to determine α from the value of $\cot 2\alpha$ or $\tan 2\alpha$.

In Exercises 29–34, use a calculator to find an angle α through which the coordinate axes can be rotated to change the given equation into a quadratic equation that has no cross product term. Then find $\sin\alpha$ and $\cos\alpha$ to two decimal places and use Equations 6 to find the coefficients of the new equation to the nearest decimal place. In each case, say whether the conic section is an ellipse, hyperbola, or parabola.

29. $x^2 - xy + 3y^2 + x - y - 3 = 0$

30. $2x^2 + xy - 3y^2 + 3x - 7 = 0$

31. $x^2 - 4xy + 4y^2 - 5 = 0$

32. $2x^2 - 12xy + 18y^2 - 49 = 0$

33. $3x^2 + 5xy + 2y^2 - 8y - 1 = 0$

34. $2x^2 + 7xy + 9y^2 + 20x - 86 = 0$

35. ***The Hyperbola*** $xy = a$ The hyperbola $xy = 1$ is one of many hyperbolas of the form $xy = a$ that appear in science and mathematics.

(a) Rotate the coordinate axes through an angle of 45° to change the equation $xy = 1$ into an equation with no xy-term. What is the new equation?

(b) Do the same for the equation $xy = a$.

36. Writing to Learn Can anything be said about the graph of the equation $Ax^2 + Bxy + Cy^2 + Dx + Ey + F = 0$ if $AC < 0$? Give reasons for your answer.

37. Writing to Learn Does any nondegenerate conic section $Ax^2 + Bxy + Cy^2 + Dx + Ey + F = 0$ have all of the following properties?

(a) It is symmetric with respect to the origin.

(b) It passes through the point $(1, 0)$.

(c) It is tangent to the line $y = 1$ at the point $(-2, 1)$.

Give reasons for your answer.

38. ***When A = C*** Show that rotating the axes through an angle of $\pi/4$ radians will eliminate the xy-term from Equation 1 whenever $A = C$.

39. ***Identifying a Conic Section***

(a) What kind of conic section is the curve $xy + 2x - y = 0$?

(b) Solve the equation $xy + 2x - y = 0$ for y and sketch the curve as the graph of a rational function of x.

(c) Find equations for the lines parallel to the line $y = -2x$ that are normal to the curve. Add the lines to your sketch.

40. ***Sign of AC*** Prove or find counterexamples to the following statements about the graph of

$$Ax^2 + Bxy + Cy^2 + Dx + Ey + F = 0.$$

(a) If $AC > 0$, the graph is an ellipse.

(b) If $AC > 0$, the graph is a hyperbola.

(c) If $AC < 0$, the graph is a hyperbola.

Explorations

41. ***90° Rotations*** What effect does a 90° rotation about the origin have on the equations of the following conic sections? Give the new equation in each case.

(a) The ellipse $x^2/a^2 + y^2/b^2 = 1 \quad (a > b)$

(b) The hyperbola $x^2/a^2 - y^2/b^2 = 1$

(c) The circle $x^2 + y^2 = a^2$

(d) The line $y = mx$

(e) The line $y = mx + b$

42. ***180° Rotations*** What effect does a 180° rotation about the origin have on the equations of the following conic sections? Give the new equation in each case.

(a) The ellipse $x^2/a^2 + y^2/b^2 = 1 \quad (a > b)$

(b) The hyperbola $x^2/a^2 - y^2/b^2 = 1$

(c) The circle $x^2 + y^2 = a^2$

(d) The line $y = mx$

(e) The line $y = mx + b$

Extending the Ideas

43. ***Degenerate Conic Section***

(a) Decide whether the equation

$$x^2 + 4xy + 4y^2 + 6x + 12y + 9 = 0$$

represents an ellipse, a parabola, or a hyperbola.

(b) Show that the graph of the equation in part (a) is the line $2y = -x - 3$.

44. ***Degenerate Conic Section***

(a) Decide whether the conic section with equation

$$9x^2 + 6xy + y^2 - 12x - 4y + 4 = 0$$

represents a parabola, an ellipse, or a hyperbola.

(b) Show that the graph of the equation in part (a) is the line $y = -3x + 2$.

45. ***A Nice Area Formula for Ellipses*** When $B^2 - 4AC$ is negative, the equation

$$Ax^2 + Bxy + Cy^2 = 1$$

represents an ellipse. If the ellipse's semi-axes are a and b, its area is πab (a standard formula). Show that the area is also $2\pi/\sqrt{4AC - B^2}$. (*Hint:* Rotate the coordinate axes to eliminate the xy-term and apply Equation 12 to the new equation.)

46. ***Other Rotation Invariants*** We describe the fact that $B'^2 - 4A'C'$ equals $B^2 - 4AC$ after a rotation about the origin by saying that the discriminant of a quadratic equation is an **invariant** of the equation. Use Equations 6 to show that the numbers **(a)** $A + C$ and **(b)** $D^2 + E^2$ are also invariants, in the sense that

$$A' + C' = A + C \quad \text{and} \quad D'^2 + E'^2 = D^2 + E^2.$$

We can use these equalities to check against numerical errors when we rotate axes. They can also be helpful in shortening the work required to find values for the new coefficients.

What you'll learn about

- The Problem with Rectangular Coordinates
- Lines
- Circles
- Ellipses, Parabolas, and Hyperbolas from One Simple Equation

A5.4 Polar Equations for Conic Sections

The Problem with Rectangular Coordinates

One problem with using rectangular coordinates in astronomy and astronautical engineering is that in rectangular coordinates we need three different kinds of equations for modeling the paths along which celestial objects move when subject to the inverse-square force of gravitation. We need one kind of equation for objects whose paths are ellipses (planetary orbits), another kind for objects that trace hyperbolas (certain comets and other one-time visitors from outside the solar system), and still another for parabolas not seen in practice, perhaps, but useful to the theory). With a shift to polar coordinates, however, we find that all these different orbits can be described with one simple equation (which is why polar and cylindrical coordinates are used so extensively today in the study of motion in space). We develop that equation here.

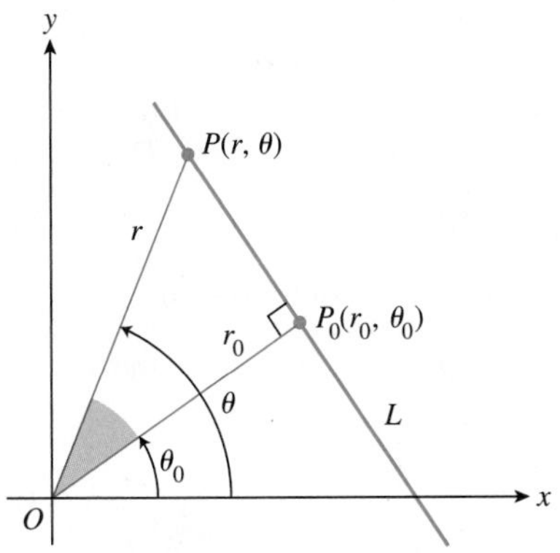

A5.29 We obtain a polar equation for line L by reading the relation $r_0/r = \cos(\theta - \theta_0)$ from triangle OP_0P.

Since it is also useful from time to time to be able to produce polar equations for lines, we begin our treatment with them.

Lines

Suppose the perpendicular from the origin to line L meets L at the point $P_0(r_0, \theta_0)$, with $r_0 \geq 0$ (Figure A5.29). Then, if $P(r, \theta)$ is any other point on L, the points P, P_0, and O are the vertices of a right triangle, from which we can read the relation

$$\frac{r_0}{r} = \cos(\theta - \theta_0)$$

or

$$r\cos(\theta - \theta_0) = r_0$$

> **The Standard Polar Equation for Lines**
>
> If the point $P_0(r_0, \theta_0)$ is the foot of the perpendicular from the origin to the line L and if $r_0 \geq 0$, then an equation for L is
>
> $$r\cos(\theta - \theta_0) = r_0. \qquad (1)$$

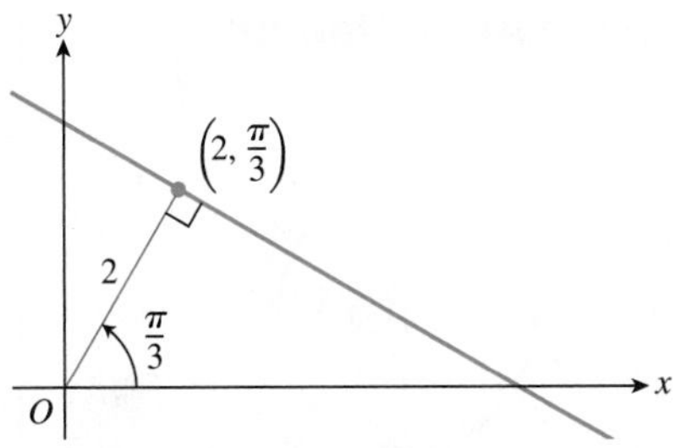

A5.30 The standard polar equation of this line is

$$r\cos\left(\theta - \frac{\pi}{3}\right) = 2.$$

(Example 1)

EXAMPLE 1 Applying Equation (1)

Find an equation for the line in Figure A5.30.

SOLUTION

From the figure, we see that the foot of the perpendicular from the origin to the line is the point $(2, \pi/3)$. With $\theta = \pi/3$ and $r_0 = 2$, Equation (1) becomes

$$r\cos\left(\theta - \frac{\pi}{3}\right) = 2.$$

EXAMPLE 2 Converting from Polar to Cartesian

Use the identity $\cos(A - B) = \cos A \cos B + \sin A \sin B$ to find a Cartesian equation for the line in Example 1.

SOLUTION

$$r\cos\left(\theta - \frac{\pi}{3}\right) = 2$$

$$r\left(\cos\theta\cos\frac{\pi}{3} + \sin\theta\sin\frac{\pi}{3}\right) = 2$$

$$\frac{1}{2}r\cos\theta + \frac{\sqrt{3}}{2}r\sin\theta = 2$$

$$\frac{1}{2}x + \frac{\sqrt{3}}{2}y = 2$$

$$x + \sqrt{3}y = 4$$

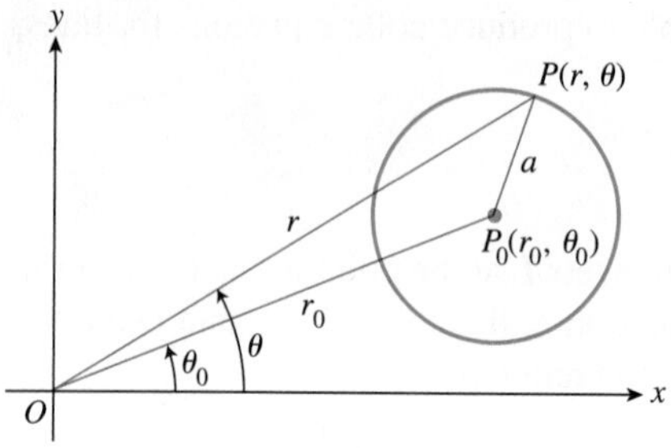

A5.31 We can get a polar equation for this circle by applying the Law of Cosines to triangle OP_0P.

Circles

To find a polar equation for the circle of radius a centered at $P_0(r_0, \theta_0)$, we let $P(r, \theta)$ be a point on the circle and apply the Law of Cosines to triangle OP_0P (Figure A5.31). This gives

$$a^2 = r_0{}^2 + r^2 - 2r_0 r \cos(\theta - \theta_0). \tag{2}$$

If the circle passes through the origin, then $r_0 = a$ and Equation (2) simplifies to

$$\begin{aligned} a^2 &= a^2 + r^2 - 2ar\cos(\theta - \theta_0) && \text{Eq. (2) with } r_0 = a \\ r^2 &= 2ar\cos(\theta - \theta_0) \\ r &= 2a\cos(\theta - \theta_0). && (3) \end{aligned}$$

If the circle's center lies on the positive x-axis, $\theta_0 = 0$ and Equation (3) becomes

$$r = 2a\cos\theta. \tag{4}$$

If the center lies on the positive y-axis, $\theta = \pi/2$, $\cos(\theta - \pi/2) = \sin\theta$, and Equation (3) becomes

$$r = 2a\sin\theta. \tag{5}$$

Equations for circles through the origin centered on the negative x- and y-axes can be obtained from Equations (4) and (5) by replacing r with $-r$.

Polar Equations for Circles Through the Origin Centered On the *x*- and *y*-Axes, Radius *a*

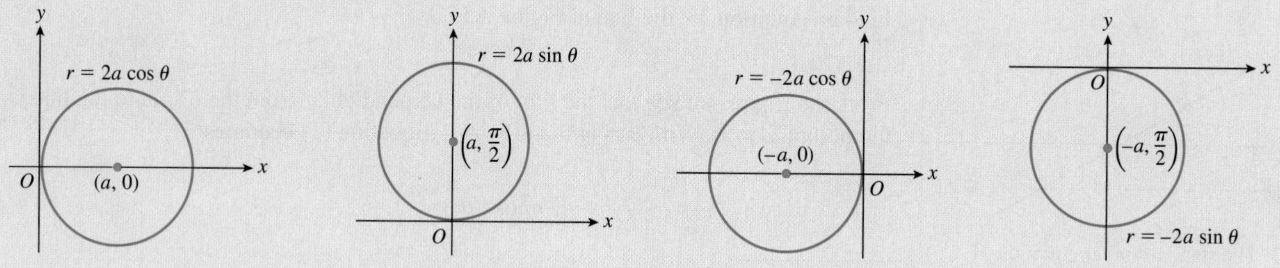

EXAMPLE 3 Circles Through the Origin

Radius	Center (polar coordinates)	Equation
3	(3, 0)	$r = 6\cos\theta$
2	$(2, \pi/2)$	$r = 4\sin\theta$
1/2	(− 1/2, 0)	$r = -\cos\theta$
1	$(-1, \pi/2)$	$r = -2\sin\theta$

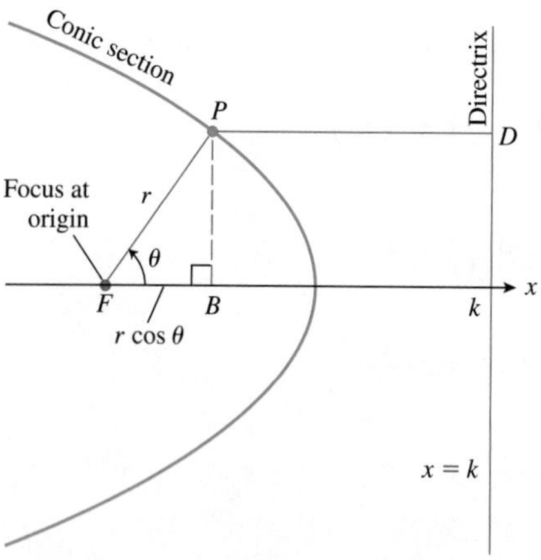

A5.32 If a conic section is put in this position, then $PF = r$ and $PD = k - r\cos\theta$.

Ellipses, Parabolas, and Hyperbolas from One Simple Equation

To find polar equation for ellipses, parabolas, and hyperbolas, we place one focus at the origin and the corresponding directrix to the right of the origin along the vertical line $x = k$ (Figure A5.32). This makes

$$PF = r$$

and

$$PD = k - FB = k - r\cos\theta.$$

Table A5.4 Equations for conic sections ($e > 0$)

A. $r = \dfrac{ke}{1 + e\cos\theta}$

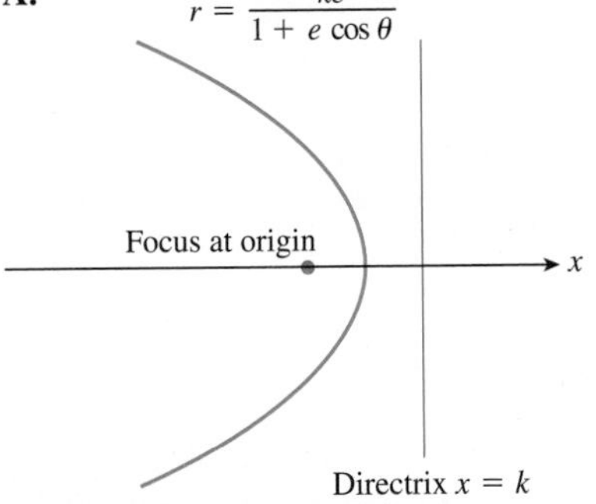

B. $r = \dfrac{ke}{1 + e\cos\theta}$

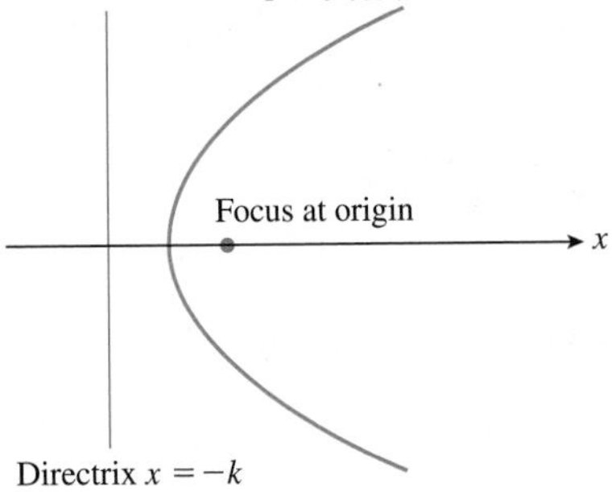

C. $r = \dfrac{ke}{1 + e\sin\theta}$

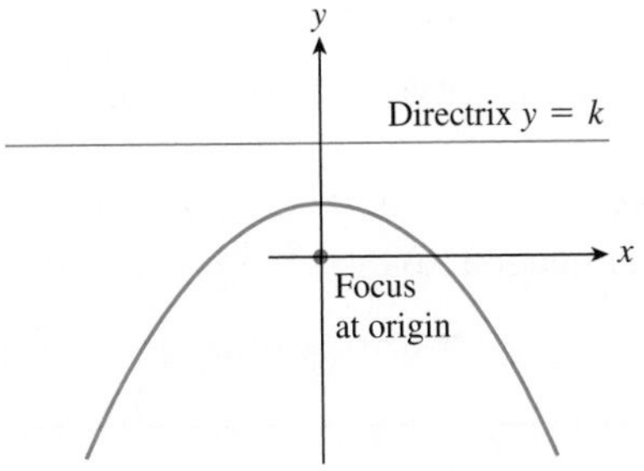

D. $r = \dfrac{ke}{1 - e\sin\theta}$

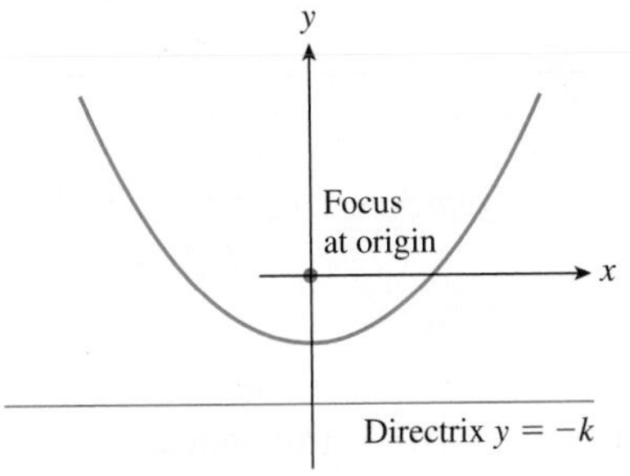

The conic's focus-directrix equation $PF = e \cdot PD$ then becomes

$$r = e(k - r\cos\theta).$$

which can be solved for r to obtain

$$r = \frac{ke}{1 + e\cos\theta}. \qquad (6)$$

Equation (6) represents an ellipse if $0 < e < 1$, a parabola if $e = 1$, and a hyperbola if $e > 1$. And there we have it: ellipses, parabolas, and hyperbolas from one simple equation.

EXAMPLE 4 Conics From Equation (6)

$e = \dfrac{1}{2}$:	ellipse	$r = \dfrac{k}{2 + \cos\theta}$
$e = 1$:	parabola	$r = \dfrac{k}{1 + \cos\theta}$
$e = 2$:	hyperbola	$r = \dfrac{2k}{1 + 2\cos\theta}$

You may see variations of Equation (6) from time to time, depending on the location of the directrix. If the directrix is the line $x = -k$ to the left of the origin (the origin is still a focus), we replace Equation (6) by

$$r = \frac{ke}{1 - e\cos\theta}.$$

The denominator now has a $(-)$ instead of a $(+)$. If the directrix is either of the lines $y = k$ or $y = -k$, the equations we get have sines in them instead of cosines, as shown in Table A5.4.

EXAMPLE 5 Finding An Equation for a Hyperbola

Find an equation for the hyperbola with eccentricity 3/2 and directrix $x = 2$.

SOLUTION

We use Equation (A) in Table A5.4 with $k = 2$ and $e = 3/2$ to get

$$r = \frac{2(3/2)}{1 + (3/2)\cos\theta} \quad \text{or} \quad r = \frac{6}{2 + 3\cos\theta}.$$

EXAMPLE 6 Finding the Directrix of a Parabola

Find the directrix of the parabola

$$r = \frac{25}{10 + 10\cos\theta}.$$

continued

SOLUTION

We divide the numerator and denominator by 10 to put the equation in standard form:

$$r = \frac{5/2}{1 + \cos\theta}.$$

This is the equation

$$r = \frac{ke}{1 + e\cos\theta}.$$

with $k = 5/2$ and $e = 1$. The equation of the directrix is $x = 5/2$.

From the ellipse diagram in Figure A5.33, we see that k is related to the eccentricity e and the semimajor axis a by the equation

$$k = \frac{a}{e} - ea. \tag{7}$$

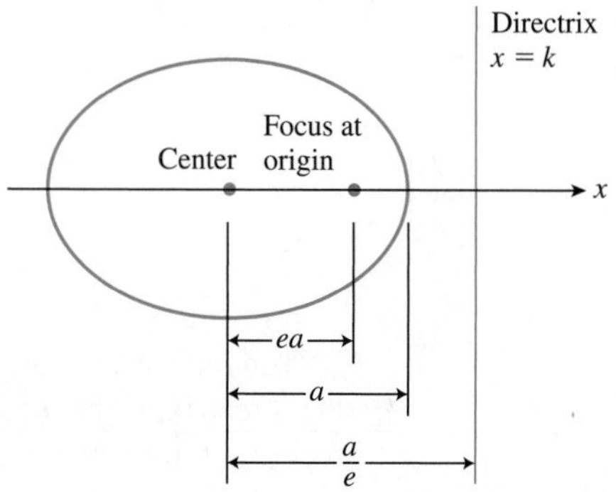

A5.33 In an ellipse with semimajor axis a, the focus–directrix distance is $k = (a/e) - ea$, so $ke = a(1 - e^2)$.

From this, we find that $ke = a(1 - e^2)$. Replacing ke in Equation (6) by $a(1 - e^2)$ gives the standard polar equation for an ellipse.

Ellipse with Eccentricity *e* and Semimajor Axis *a*

$$r = \frac{a(1 - e^2)}{1 + e\cos\theta} \tag{8}$$

Notice that when $e = 0$, Equation (8) becomes $r = a$, which represents a circle. Equation (8) is the starting point for calculating planetary orbits.

EXAMPLE 7 Finding a Planetary Orbit

Find a polar equation for an ellipse with semimajor axis 39.44 AU (astronomical units) and eccentricity 0.25. This is the approximate size of Pluto's orbit around the sun.

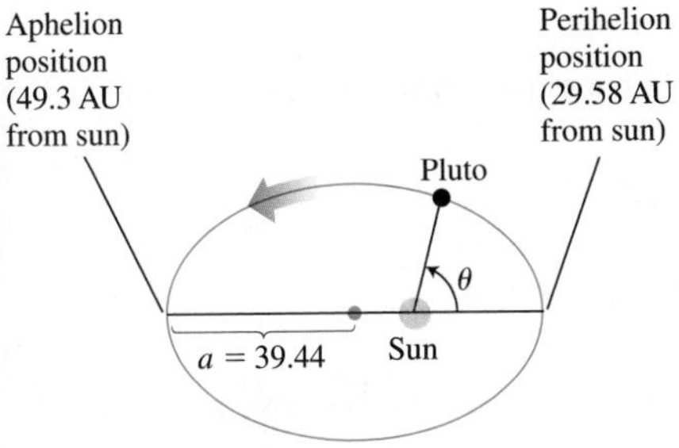

A5.34 The orbit of Pluto. (Example 7)

SOLUTION

We use Equation (8) with $a = 39.44$ and $e = 0.25$ to find

$$r = \frac{39.44(1 - (0.25)^2)}{1 + 0.25 \cos \theta} = \frac{147.9}{4 + \cos \theta}.$$

At its point of closest approach (perihelion), Pluto is

$$r = \frac{147.9}{4 + 1} = 29.58 \text{ AU}$$

from the sun. At its most distant point (aphelion), Pluto is

$$r = \frac{147.9}{4 - 1} = 49.3 \text{ AU}$$

from the sun (Figure A5.34).

EXAMPLE 8 Finding a Focus-to-Directrix Distance

Find the distance from one focus of the ellipse in Example 7 to the associated directrix.

SOLUTION

We use Equation (7) with $a = 39.44$ and $e = 0.25$ to find

$$k = 39.44\left(\frac{1}{0.25} - 0.25\right) = 147.9 \text{ AU}.$$

Section A5.4 Exercises

In Exercises 1–4, find polar and Cartesian equations for the line.

1.

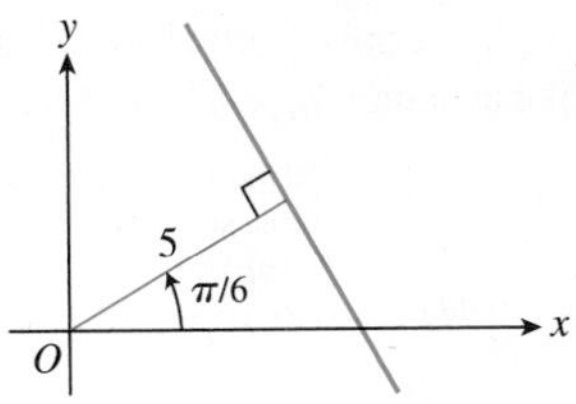

2.

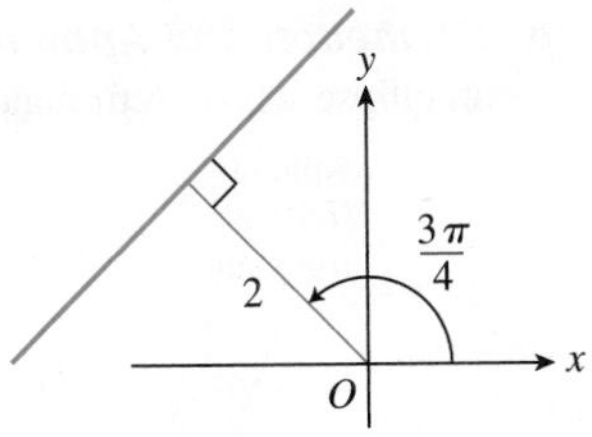

3.

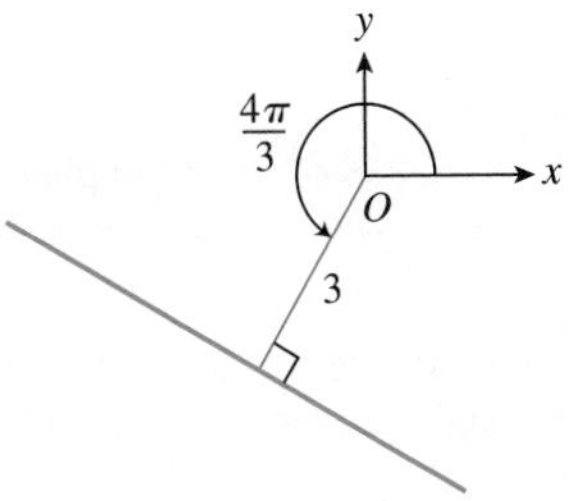

4.

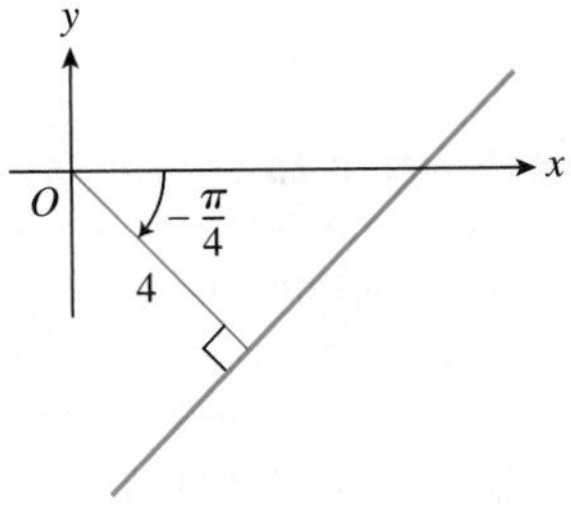

In Exercises 5–8, sketch the line and find a Cartesian equation for it.

5. $r \cos\left(\theta - \frac{\pi}{4}\right) = \sqrt{2}$

6. $r \cos\left(\theta + \frac{3\pi}{4}\right) = 1$

7. $r \cos\left(\theta - \frac{2\pi}{3}\right) = 3$

8. $r \cos\left(\theta + \frac{\pi}{3}\right) = 2$

In Exercises 9–12, find a polar equation in the form $r \cos(\theta - \theta_0) = r_0$ for the line.

9. $\sqrt{2}x + \sqrt{2}y = 6$

10. $\sqrt{3}x - y = 1$

11. $y = -5$

12. $x = -4$

In Exercises 13–16, find a polar equation for the circle.

13.

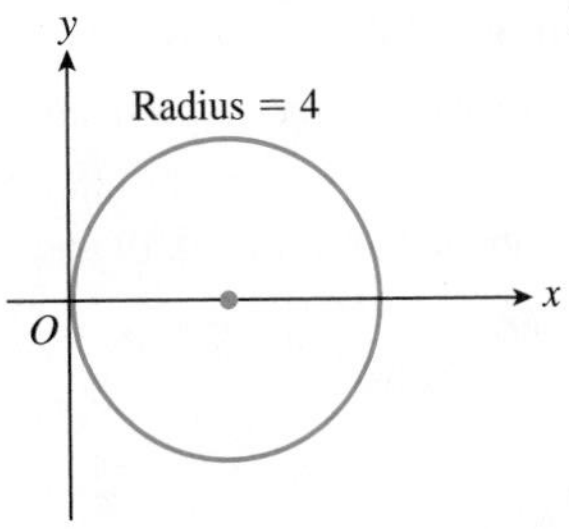

14.

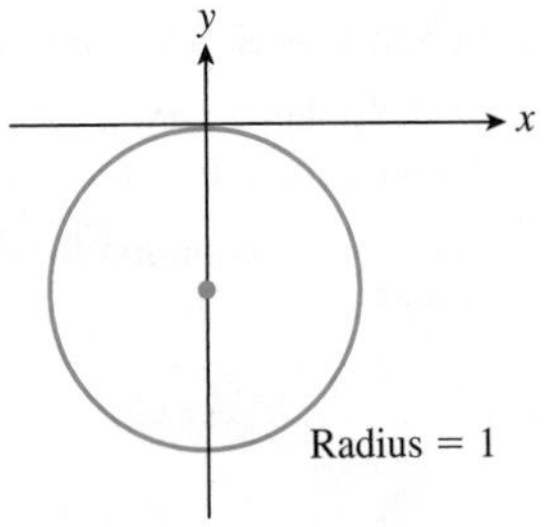

15.

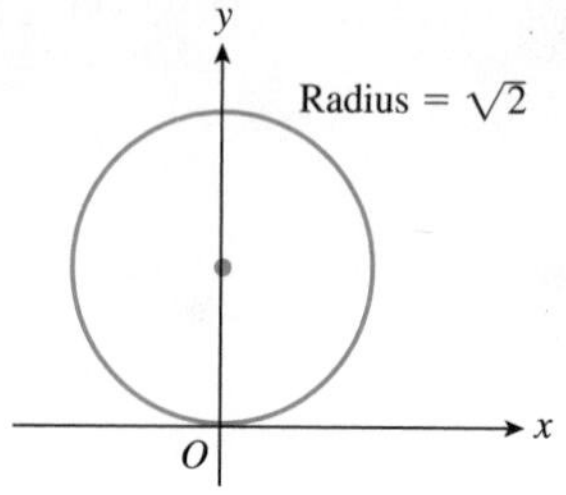

16.

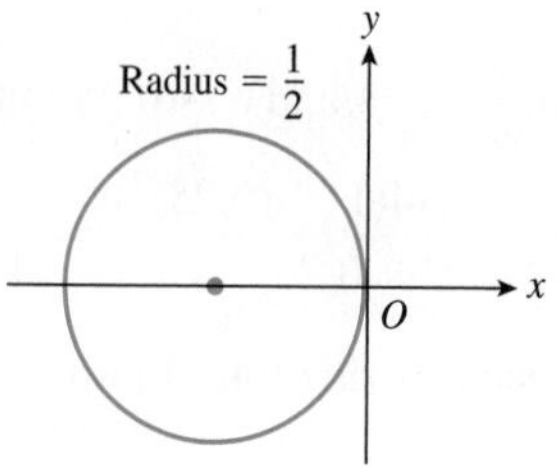

In Exercises 17–20, sketch the circle. Give polar coordinates for the center and identify the radius.

17. $r = 4 \cos \theta$

18. $r = 6 \sin \theta$

19. $r = -2 \cos \theta$

20. $r = -8 \sin \theta$

In Exercises 21–24, find a polar equation for the circle. Sketch the circle in the coordinate plane and label it with both its Cartesian and polar equations.

21. $(x - 6)^2 + y^2 = 36$

22. $x^2 + (y - 5)^2 = 25$

23. $x^2 + 2x + y^2 = 0$

24. $x^2 + y^2 + y = 0$

Exercises 25–32 give the eccentricities of conic sections with one focus at the origin, along with the directrix corresponding to that focus. Find a polar equation for each conic section.

25. $e = 1, \quad x = 2$

26. $e = 1, \quad y = 2$

27. $e = 5, \quad y = -6$

28. $e = 2, \quad x = 4$

29. $e = 1/2, \quad x = 1$

30. $e = 1/4, \quad x = -2$

31. $e = 1/5, \quad y = -10$

32. $e = 1/3, \quad y = 6$

In Exercises 33–40, sketch the parabola or ellipse. Include the directrix that corresponds to the focus at the origin. Label the vertices with appropriate polar coordinates. Label the center of the ellipse as well. Support with a grapher.

33. $r = \dfrac{1}{1 + \cos \theta}$

34. $r = \dfrac{6}{2 + \cos \theta}$

35. $r = \dfrac{25}{10 - 5 \cos \theta}$

36. $r = \dfrac{4}{2 - 2 \cos \theta}$

37. $r = \dfrac{400}{16 + 8 \sin \theta}$

38. $r = \dfrac{12}{3 + 3 \sin \theta}$

39. $r = \dfrac{8}{2 - 2 \sin \theta}$

40. $r = \dfrac{4}{2 - \sin \theta}$

41. **(a)** Find Cartesian equations for the curves $r = 4 \sin \theta$ and $r = \sqrt{3} \sec \theta$.

(b) Sketch the curves together and label their points of intersection in both Cartesian and polar coordinates.

42. Repeat Exercise 41 for $r = 8 \cos \theta$ and $r = 2 \sec \theta$.

43. Find a polar equation for the parabola with focus (0, 0) and directrix $r \cos \theta = 4$.

44. Find a polar equation for the parabola with focus (0, 0) and directrix $r \cos (\theta - \pi/2) = 2$.

Explorations

45. Writing to Learn In the same viewing window, graph the conics

$$r = \frac{e}{1 + e \cos \theta}$$

for $e = 0.1, 0.2, 0.3, 0.4, 0.5, 0.6, 0.7, 0.8$, and 0.9. Explain the effects of the parameter e.

46. Writing to Learn In the same viewing window, graph the conics

$$r = \frac{e}{1 + e \cos \theta}$$

for $e = 1.1, 1.2, 1.3, 1.4, 1.5, 2, 2.5, 3$, and 10. Explain the effect of the parameter e.

47. Writing to Learn In the same viewing window, graph the conics

$$r = \frac{k}{1 + \cos \theta}$$

for $k = -8, -4, -3, -2, -1, 0, 1, 2, 3, 4$, and 8. Explain the effect of the parameter k.

48. Writing to Learn In the same viewing window, graph the conics

$$r = \frac{k}{1 - \sin \theta}$$

for $k = -8, -4, -3, -2, -1, 0, 1, 2, 3, 4$, and 8. Explain the effect of the parameter k.

Extending the Ideas

Graphing Inequalities In Exercises 49 and 50, sketch the region defined by the inequality.

49. $0 \le r \le 2 \cos \theta$

50. $-3 \cos \theta \le r \le 0$

51. ***Perihelion and Aphelion.*** A planet travels about its sun in an ellipse whose semimajor axis has length a.

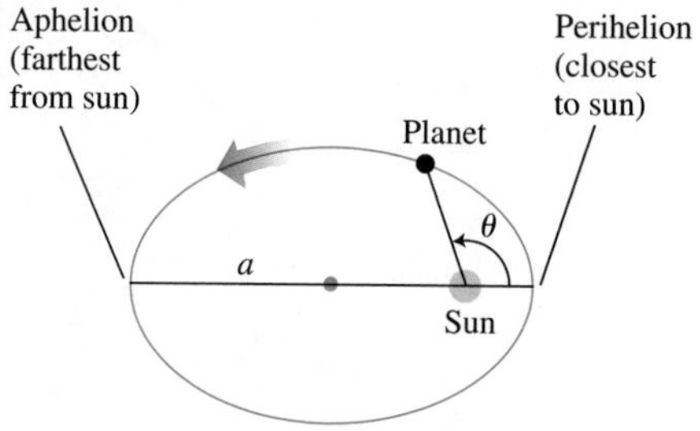

(a) **Writing to Learn** Show that $r = a(1 - e)$ when the planet is closest to the sun and that $r = a(1 + e)$ when the planet is farthest from the sun.

(b) Use the data in Table 5.5 to find how close each planet in our solar system comes to the sun and how far away each planet gets from the sun.

52. ***Planetary Orbits.*** In Example 7, we drew the orbit of Pluto.

(a) Use the data in Table A5.5 to find polar equations for the orbits of the other planets. Draw the orbits in the same viewing window for Mercury through Mars. Then draw the orbits in the same viewing window for Jupiter through Pluto. Explain why it was necessary to use two viewing windows.

(b) Study the orbits of Neptune and Pluto together. The right side of the viewing window suggests an astronomical event that occurred on January 21, 1979 and March 14, 1999, and will not happen again until September 2226. The behavior that better identifies the event is hidden. Make a conjecture about what the event is. Zoom in to help you decide that the event is indeed possible.

Table A5.5 Semimajor axes and eccentricities of the planets in our solar system

Planet	Semimajor axis (astronomical units)	Eccentricity
Mercury	0.3871	0.2056
Venus	0.7233	0.0068
Earth	1.000	0.0167
Mars	1.524	0.0934
Jupiter	5.203	0.0484
Saturn	9.539	0.0543
Uranus	19.18	0.0460
Neptune	30.06	0.0082
Pluto	39.44	0.2481

53. **Writing to Learn** ***The Space Engineer's Formula for Eccentricity*** The space engineer's formula for the eccentricity of an elliptical orbit is

$$e = \frac{r_{\text{max}} - r_{\text{min}}}{r_{\text{max}} + r_{\text{min}}},$$

where r is the distance from the space vehicle to the attracting focus of the ellipse along which it travels. Why does the formula work?

(b) **Writing to Learn** ***Drawing the Orbit of Mercury*** You have a string with a knot in each end that can be pinned to a drawing board. The string is 10 in. long from the center of one knot to the center of the other. How far apart should the pins be to use the method illustrated in Figure A5.7 (Section A5.1) to draw an ellipse of eccentricity 0.2? The resulting ellipse would resemble the orbit of Mercury.

54. ***Halley's Comet*** (See Section A5.2, Example 1.)

(a) ***Orbit Equation*** Write an equation for the orbit of Halley's comet in a coordinate system in which the sun lies at the origin and the other focus lies on the negative x-axis, scaled in astronomical units.

(b) ***Perihelion*** How close does the comet come to the sun in astronomical units? In kilometers?

(c) ***Aphelion*** What is the farthest the comet gets from the sun in astronomical units? In kilometers?

A6 Hyperbolic Functions

What you'll learn about

- Background
- Definitions
- Identities
- Derivatives and Integrals
- Inverse Hyperbolic Functions
- Identities for $\text{sech}^{-1} x$, $\text{csch}^{-1} x$, $\coth^{-1} x$
- Derivatives of Inverse Hyperbolic Functions; Associated Integrals

. . . and why

This section provides basic information about hyperbolic functions and their derivatives and integrals.

Background

Suspension cables like those of the Golden Gate Bridge, which support a constant load per horizontal foot, hang in parabolas (Section A5.1, Exercise 44). Cables like power line cables, which hang freely, hang in curves called hyperbolic cosine curves.

Besides describing the shapes of hanging cables, hyperbolic functions describe the motions of waves in elastic solids, the temperature distributions in metal cooling fins, and the motions of falling bodies that encounter air resistance proportional to the square of the velocity. If a hanging cable were turned upside down (without changing shape) to form an arch, the internal forces, then reversed, would once again be in equilibrium, making the inverted hyperbolic cosine curve the ideal shape for a self-standing arch. The center line of the Gateway Arch to the West in St. Louis follows a hyperbolic cosine curve.

Definitions

The hyperbolic cosine and sine functions are defined by the first two equations in Table A6.1. The table also defines the hyperbolic tangent, cotangent, secant, and cosecant. As we will see, the hyperbolic functions bear a number of similarities to trigonometric functions after which they are named.

Table A6.1 The six basic hyperbolic functions

Hyperbolic cosine of x:	$\cosh x = \dfrac{e^x + e^{-x}}{2}$
Hyperbolic sine of x:	$\sinh x = \dfrac{e^x - e^{-x}}{2}$
Hyperbolic tangent:	$\tanh x = \dfrac{\sinh x}{\cosh x} = \dfrac{e^x - e^{-x}}{e^x + e^{-x}}$
Hyperbolic cotangent:	$\coth x = \dfrac{\cosh x}{\sinh x} = \dfrac{e^x + e^{-x}}{e^x - e^{-x}}$
Hyperbolic secant:	$\text{sech}\, x = \dfrac{1}{\cosh x} = \dfrac{2}{e^x + e^{-x}}$
Hyperbolic cosecant:	$\text{csch}\, x = \dfrac{1}{\sinh x} = \dfrac{2}{e^x - e^{-x}}$

See Figure A6.1 for graphs.

Pronouncing "cosh" and "sinh"

"Cosh" is often pronounced "kosh," rhyming with "gosh" or "gauche." "Sinh" is pronounced as if spelled "cinch" or "shine."

Identities

Hyperbolic functions satisfy the identities in Table A6.2. Except for differences in sign, these are identities we already know for trigonometric functions.

Table A6.2 Identities for hyperbolic functions

$$\sinh 2x = 2 \sinh x \cosh x$$
$$\cosh 2x = \cosh^2 x + \sinh^2 x$$
$$\cosh^2 x = \frac{\cosh 2x + 1}{2}$$
$$\sinh^2 x = \frac{\cosh 2x - 1}{2}$$
$$\cosh^2 x - \sinh^2 x = 1$$
$$\tanh^2 x = 1 - \text{sech}^2 x$$
$$\coth^2 x = 1 + \text{csch}^2 x$$

Derivatives and Integrals

The six hyperbolic functions, being rational combinations of the differentiable functions e^x and e^{-x}, have derivatives at every point at which they are defined (Table A6.3 on the following page). Again, there are similarities with trigonometric functions. The derivative formulas in Table A6.3 lead to the integral formulas seen there.

Table A6.3 **Derivatives and companion integrals**

$\frac{d}{dx}(\sinh u) = \cosh u \frac{du}{dx}$	$\int \sinh u\, du = \cosh u + C$
$\frac{d}{dx}(\cosh u) = \sinh u \frac{du}{dx}$	$\int \cosh u\, du = \sinh u + C$
$\frac{d}{dx}(\tanh u) = \text{sech}^2\, u \frac{du}{dx}$	$\int \text{sech}^2\, u\, du = \tanh u + C$
$\frac{d}{dx}(\coth u) = -\text{csch}^2\, u \frac{du}{dx}$	$\int \text{csch}^2\, u\, du = -\coth u + C$
$\frac{d}{dx}(\text{sech}\, u) = -\text{sech}\, u \tanh u \frac{du}{dx}$	$\int \text{sech}\, u \tanh u\, du = -\text{sech}\, u + C$
$\frac{d}{dx}(\text{csch}\, u) = -\text{csch}\, u \coth u \frac{du}{dx}$	$\int \text{csch}\, u \coth u\, du = -\text{csch}\, u + C$

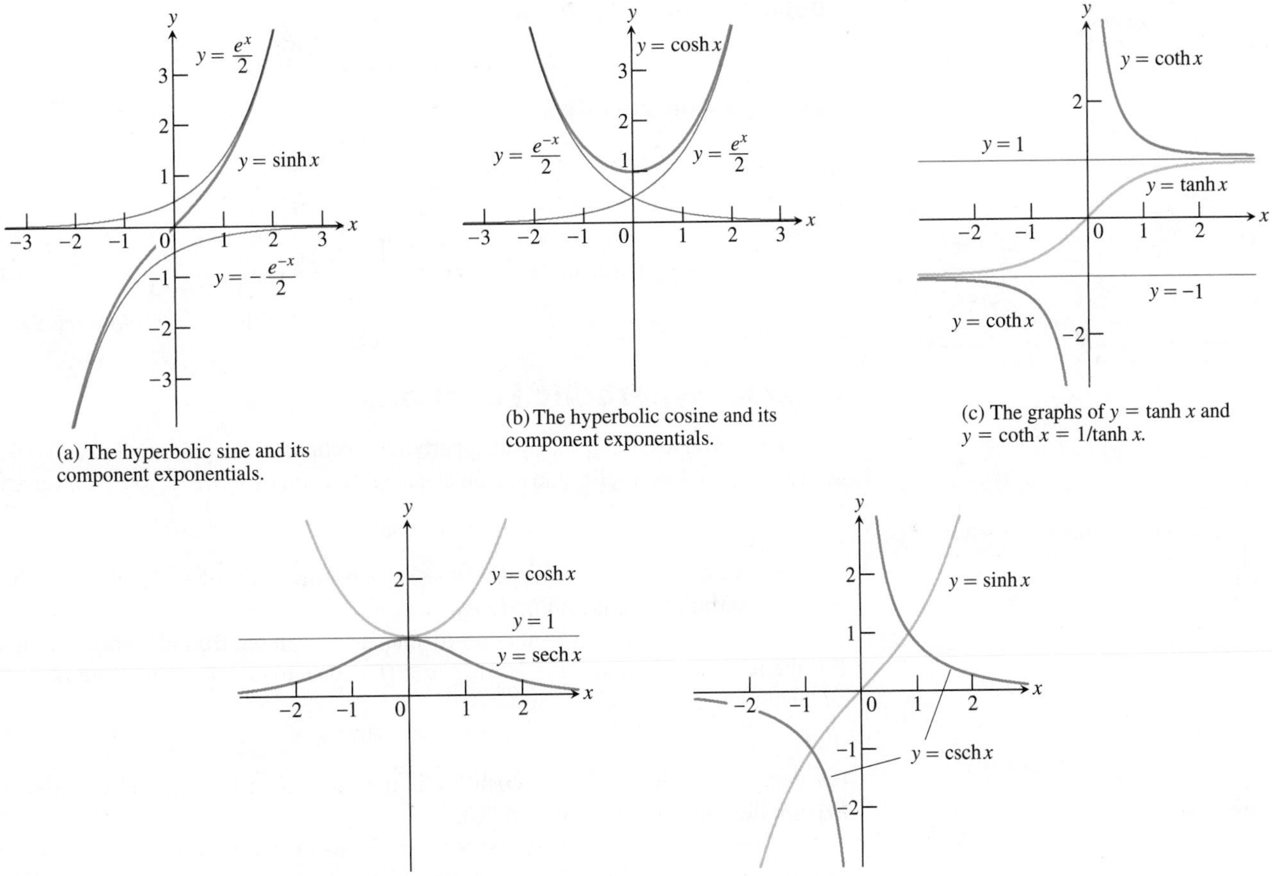

(a) The hyperbolic sine and its component exponentials.

(b) The hyperbolic cosine and its component exponentials.

(c) The graphs of $y = \tanh x$ and $y = \coth x = 1/\tanh x$.

(d) The graphs of $y = \cosh x$ and $y = \text{sech}\, x = 1/\cosh x$.

(e) The graphs of $y = \sinh x$ and $y = \text{csch}\, x = 1/\sinh x$.

Figure A6.1 The graphs of the six hyperbolic functions.

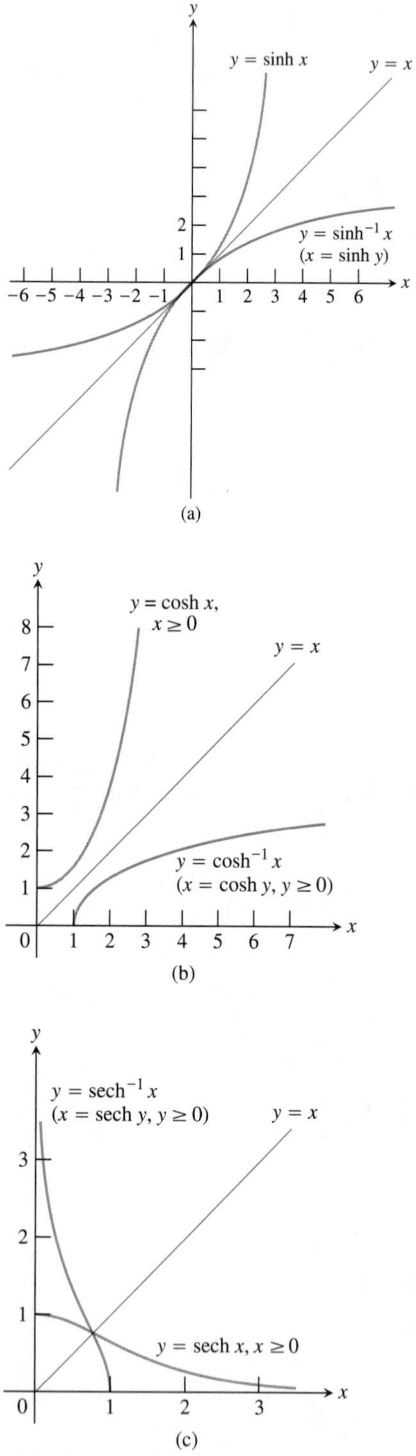

Figure A6.2 The graphs of the inverse hyperbolic sine, cosine, and secant of x. Notice the symmetries about the line $y = x$.

EXAMPLE 1 Finding a Derivative

$$\frac{d}{dt}(\tanh \sqrt{1 + t^2}) = \text{sech}^2 \sqrt{1 + t^2} \cdot \frac{d}{dt}(\sqrt{1 + t^2})$$

$$= \frac{t}{\sqrt{1 + t^2}} \text{sech}^2 \sqrt{1 + t^2}$$

Now try Exercise 13.

EXAMPLE 2 Integrating a Hyperbolic Cotangent

$$\int \coth 5x\, dx = \int \frac{\cosh 5x}{\sinh 5x} dx = \frac{1}{5} \int \frac{du}{u} \qquad u = \sinh 5x,\ du = 5 \cosh 5x\, dx$$

$$= \frac{1}{5} \ln |u| + C = \frac{1}{5} \ln |\sinh 5x| + C$$

Now try Exercise 41.

EXAMPLE 3 Using an Identity to Integrate

Evaluate $\displaystyle\int_0^1 \sinh^2 x\, dx.$

SOLUTION

Solve Numerically To five decimal places,

$$\text{NINT}((\sinh x)^2, x, 0, 1) = 0.40672.$$

Confirm Analytically

$$\int_0^1 \sinh^2 x\, dx = \int_0^1 \frac{\cosh 2x - 1}{2} dx \qquad \text{Table A6.2}$$

$$= \frac{1}{2} \int_0^1 (\cosh 2x - 1)\, dx = \frac{1}{2}\left[\frac{\sinh 2x}{2} - x\right]_0^1 = \frac{\sinh 2}{4} - \frac{1}{2} \approx 0.40672$$

Now try Exercise 47.

Inverse Hyperbolic Functions

We use the inverses of the six basic hyperbolic functions in integration. Since $d(\sinh x)/dx = \cosh x > 0$, the hyperbolic sine is an increasing function of x. We denote its inverse by

$$y = \sinh^{-1} x.$$

For every value of x in the interval $-\infty < x < \infty$, the value of $y = \sinh^{-1} x$ is the number whose hyperbolic sine is x (Figure A6.2a).

The function $y = \cosh x$ is not one-to-one, as we can see from the graph in Figure A6.1. But the restricted function $y = \cosh x$, $x \geq 0$, is one-to-one and therefore has an inverse, denoted by

$$y = \cosh^{-1} x.$$

For every value of $x \geq 1$, $y = \cosh^{-1} x$ is the number in the interval $0 \leq y < \infty$ whose hyperbolic cosine is x (Figure A6.2b).

Like $y = \cosh x$, the function $y = \text{sech}\, x = 1/\cosh x$ fails to be one-to-one, but its restriction to nonnegative values of x does have an inverse, denoted by

$$y = \text{sech}^{-1} x.$$

For every value of x in the interval $(0, 1]$, $y = \text{sech}^{-1} x$ is the nonnegative number whose hyperbolic secant is x (Figure A6.2c).

The hyperbolic tangent, cotangent, and cosecant are one-to-one on their domains and therefore have inverses, denoted by

$$y = \tanh^{-1} x, \qquad y = \coth^{-1} x, \qquad y = \operatorname{csch}^{-1} x$$

(Figure A6.3).

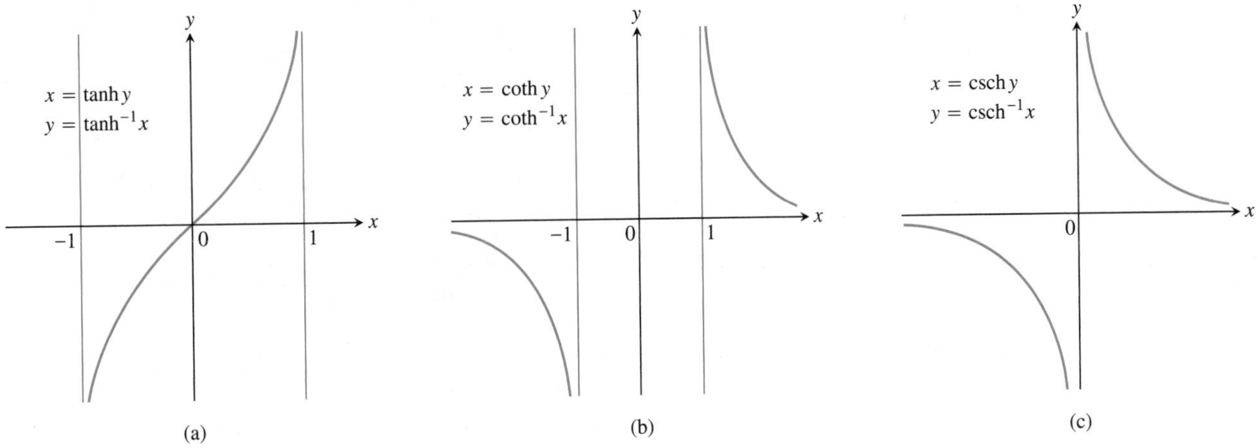

Figure A6.3 The graphs of the inverse hyperbolic tangent, cotangent, and cosecant of x.

EXPLORATION 1 Viewing Inverses

Let $x_1(t) = t, y_1(t) = t,$

$$x_2(t) = t, \qquad y_2(t) = 1/\cosh t,$$

$$x_3(t) = y_2(t), \quad y_3(t) = x_2(t).$$

1. Graph the parametric equations simultaneously in a square viewing window that contains $0 \le x \le 6$, $0 \le y \le 4$. Set tMin $= 0$, tMax $= 6$, and t-step $= 0.05$. Explain what you see. Explain the domain of each function.
2. Let $x_4(t) = t$, $y_4(t) = \cosh^{-1}(1/t)$. Graph and compare (x_3, y_3) and (y_4, x_4). Predict what you should see, and explain what you do see.

Table A6.4 **Identities for inverse hyperbolic functions**

$\operatorname{sech}^{-1} x = \cosh^{-1} \dfrac{1}{x}$
$\operatorname{csch}^{-1} x = \sinh^{-1} \dfrac{1}{x}$
$\coth^{-1} x = \tanh^{-1} \dfrac{1}{x}$

Identities for $\operatorname{sech}^{-1} x$, $\operatorname{csch}^{-1} x$, $\coth^{-1} x$

We use the identities in Table A6.4 to calculate the values of $\operatorname{sech}^{-1} x$, $\operatorname{csch}^{-1} x$, and $\coth^{-1} x$ on calculators that give only $\cosh^{-1} x$, $\sinh^{-1} x$, and $\tanh^{-1} x$.

Derivatives of Inverse Hyperbolic Functions; Associated Integrals

The chief use of inverse hyperbolic functions lies in integrations that reverse the derivative formulas in Table A6.5.

Table A6.5 **Derivatives of inverse hyperbolic functions**

$$\frac{d(\sinh^{-1} u)}{dx} = \frac{1}{\sqrt{1 + u^2}} \frac{du}{dx}$$

$$\frac{d(\cosh^{-1} u)}{dx} = \frac{1}{\sqrt{u^2 - 1}} \frac{du}{dx}, \quad u > 1$$

$$\frac{d(\tanh^{-1} u)}{dx} = \frac{1}{1 - u^2} \frac{du}{dx}, \quad |u| < 1$$

$$\frac{d(\coth^{-1} u)}{dx} = \frac{1}{1 - u^2} \frac{du}{dx}, \quad |u| > 1$$

$$\frac{d(\operatorname{sech}^{-1} u)}{dx} = \frac{-du/dx}{u\sqrt{1 - u^2}}, \quad 0 < u < 1$$

$$\frac{d(\operatorname{csch}^{-1} u)}{dx} = \frac{-du/dx}{|u|\sqrt{1 + u^2}}, \quad u \neq 0$$

The restrictions $|u| < 1$ and $|u| > 1$ on the derivative formulas for $\tanh^{-1} u$ and $\coth^{-1} u$ come from the natural restrictions on the values of these functions. (See Figures A6.3a and b.) The distinction between $|u| < 1$ and $|u| > 1$ becomes important when we convert the derivative formulas into integral formulas. If $|u| < 1$, the integral of $1/(1 - u^2)$ is $\tanh^{-1} u + C$. If $|u| > 1$, the integral is $\coth^{-1} u + C$.

With appropriate substitutions, the derivative formulas in Table A6.5 lead to the integral formulas in Table A6.6.

Table A6.6 **Integrals leading to inverse hyperbolic functions**

1. $$\int \frac{du}{\sqrt{a^2 + u^2}} = \sinh^{-1}\left(\frac{u}{a}\right) + C, \quad a > 0$$

2. $$\int \frac{du}{\sqrt{u^2 - a^2}} = \cosh^{-1}\left(\frac{u}{a}\right) + C, \quad u > a > 0$$

3. $$\int \frac{du}{a^2 - u^2} = \begin{cases} \frac{1}{a}\tanh^{-1}\left(\frac{u}{a}\right) + C & \text{if } u^2 < a^2 \\ \frac{1}{a}\coth^{-1}\left(\frac{u}{a}\right) + C & \text{if } u^2 > a^2 \end{cases}$$

4. $$\int \frac{du}{u\sqrt{a^2 - u^2}} = -\frac{1}{a}\operatorname{sech}^{-1}\left(\frac{u}{a}\right) + C, \quad 0 < u < a$$

5. $$\int \frac{du}{u\sqrt{a^2 + u^2}} = -\frac{1}{a}\operatorname{csch}^{-1}\left|\frac{u}{a}\right| + C, \quad u \neq 0$$

EXAMPLE 4 Using Table A6.6

Evaluate $\int_0^1 \frac{2\,dx}{\sqrt{3+4x^2}}$.

SOLUTION

Solve Analytically

The indefinite integral is

$$\int \frac{2\,dx}{\sqrt{3+4x^2}} = \int \frac{du}{\sqrt{a^2+u^2}} \qquad u = 2x,\ du = 2\,dx,\ a = \sqrt{3}$$

$$= \sinh^{-1}\left(\frac{u}{a}\right) + C \qquad \text{Formula from Table A6.6}$$

$$= \sinh^{-1}\left(\frac{2x}{\sqrt{3}}\right) + C.$$

Therefore,

$$\int_0^1 \frac{2\,dx}{\sqrt{3+4x^2}} = \sinh^{-1}\left(\frac{2x}{\sqrt{3}}\right)\Big]_0^1 = \sinh^{-1}\left(\frac{2}{\sqrt{3}}\right) - \sinh^{-1}(0)$$

$$= \sinh^{-1}\left(\frac{2}{\sqrt{3}}\right) - 0 \approx 0.98665.$$

Support Numerically

To five decimal places,

$$\text{NINT}\,(2/\sqrt{3+4x^2}, x, 0, 1) = 0.98665.$$

Now try Exercise 37.

Section A6 Exercises

In Exercises 1–4, find the values of the remaining five hyperbolic functions.

1. $\sinh x = -\frac{3}{4}$

2. $\sinh x = \frac{4}{3}$

3. $\cosh x = \frac{17}{15},\quad x > 0$

4. $\cosh x = \frac{13}{5},\quad x > 0$

In Exercises 5–10, rewrite the expression in terms of exponentials and simplify the results as much as you can. Support your answers graphically.

5. $2\cosh(\ln x)$

6. $\sinh(2\ln x)$

7. $\cosh 5x + \sinh 5x$

8. $\cosh 3x - \sinh 3x$

9. $(\sinh x + \cosh x)^4$

10. $\ln(\cosh x + \sinh x) + \ln(\cosh x - \sinh x)$

11. Use the identities

$$\sinh(x+y) = \sinh x \cosh y + \cosh x \sinh y$$
$$\cosh(x+y) = \cosh x \cosh y + \sinh x \sinh y$$

to show that

(a) $\sinh 2x = 2\sinh x \cosh x$;

(b) $\cosh 2x = \cosh^2 x + \sinh^2 x$.

12. Use the definitions of $\cosh x$ and $\sinh x$ to show that

$$\cosh^2 x - \sinh^2 x = 1.$$

In Exercises 13–24, find the derivative of y with respect to the appropriate variable.

13. $y = 6\sinh\frac{x}{3}$

14. $y = \frac{1}{2}\sinh(2x+1)$

15. $y = 2\sqrt{t}\tanh\sqrt{t}$

16. $y = t^2\tanh\frac{1}{t}$

17. $y = \ln(\sinh z)$

18. $y = \ln(\cosh z)$

19. $y = \operatorname{sech} \theta(1 - \ln \operatorname{sech} \theta)$ **20.** $y = \operatorname{csch} \theta(1 - \ln \operatorname{csch} \theta)$

21. $y = \ln \cosh x - \frac{1}{2} \tanh^2 x$ **22.** $y = \ln \sinh x - \frac{1}{2} \coth^2 x$

23. $y = (x^2 + 1) \operatorname{sech} (\ln x)$ (*Hint:* Before differentiating, express in terms of exponentials and simplify.)

24. $y = (4x^2 - 1) \operatorname{csch} (\ln 2x)$

In Exercises 25–36, find the derivative of y with respect to the appropriate variable.

25. $y = \sinh^{-1} \sqrt{x}$

26. $y = \cosh^{-1} (2\sqrt{x + 1})$

27. $y = (1 - \theta) \tanh^{-1} \theta$

28. $y = (\theta^2 + 2\theta) \tanh^{-1} (\theta + 1)$

29. $y = (1 - t) \coth^{-1} \sqrt{t}$

30. $y = (1 - t^2) \coth^{-1} t$

31. $y = \cos^{-1} x - x \operatorname{sech}^{-1} x$

32. $y = \ln x + \sqrt{1 - x^2} \operatorname{sech}^{-1} x$

33. $y = \operatorname{csch}^{-1} \left(\frac{1}{2}\right)^{\theta}$

34. $y = \operatorname{csch}^{-1} 2^{\theta}$

35. $y = \sinh^{-1} (\tan x)$

36. $y = \cosh^{-1} (\sec x), \quad 0 < x < \pi/2$

Verify the integration formulas in Exercises 37–40.

37. **(a)** $\int \operatorname{sech} x\, dx = \tan^{-1} (\sinh x) + C$

(b) $\int \operatorname{sech} x\, dx = \sin^{-1} (\tanh x) + C$

38. $\int x \operatorname{sech}^{-1} x\, dx = \frac{x^2}{2} \operatorname{sech}^{-1} x - \frac{1}{2}\sqrt{1 - x^2} + C$

39. $\int x \coth^{-1} x\, dx = \frac{x^2 - 1}{2} \coth^{-1} x + \frac{x}{2} + C$

40. $\int \tanh^{-1} x\, dx = x \tanh^{-1} x + \frac{1}{2} \ln (1 - x^2) + C$

Evaluate the integrals in Exercises 41–50.

41. $\int \sinh 2x\, dx$ **42.** $\int \sinh \frac{x}{5}\, dx$

43. $\int 6 \cosh \left(\frac{x}{2} - \ln 3\right) dx$ **44.** $\int 4 \cosh (3x - \ln 2)\, dx$

45. $\int \tanh \frac{x}{7}\, dx$ **46.** $\int \coth \frac{\theta}{\sqrt{3}}\, d\theta$

47. $\int \operatorname{sech}^2 \left(x - \frac{1}{2}\right) dx$ **48.** $\int \operatorname{csch}^2 (5 - x)\, dx$

49. $\int \frac{\operatorname{sech} \sqrt{t} \tanh \sqrt{t}\, dt}{\sqrt{t}}$

50. $\int \frac{\operatorname{csch} (\ln t) \coth (\ln t)\, dt}{t}$

Evaluate the integrals in Exercises 51–60 analytically and support with NINT.

51. $\int_{\ln 2}^{\ln 4} \coth x\, dx$ **52.** $\int_{0}^{\ln 2} \tanh 2x\, dx$

53. $\int_{-\ln 4}^{-\ln 2} 2e^{\theta} \cosh \theta\, d\theta$ **54.** $\int_{0}^{\ln 2} 4e^{-\theta} \sinh \theta\, d\theta$

55. $\int_{-\pi/4}^{\pi/4} \cosh (\tan \theta) \sec^2 \theta\, d\theta$

56. $\int_{0}^{\pi/2} 2 \sinh (\sin \theta) \cos \theta\, d\theta$

57. $\int_{1}^{2} \frac{\cosh (\ln t)}{t}\, dt$ **58.** $\int_{1}^{4} \frac{8 \cosh \sqrt{x}}{\sqrt{x}}\, dx$

59. $\int_{-\ln 2}^{0} \cosh^2 \left(\frac{x}{2}\right) dx$ **60.** $\int_{0}^{\ln 10} 4 \sinh^2 \left(\frac{x}{2}\right) dx$

In Exercises 61 and 62, find the volume of the solid generated by revolving the shaded region about the x-axis.

61.

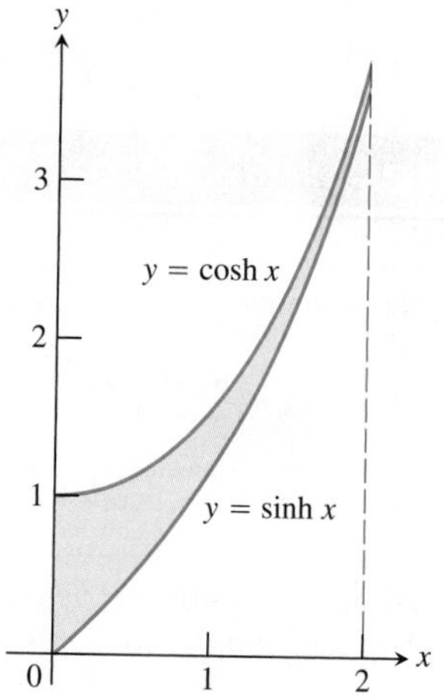

62.

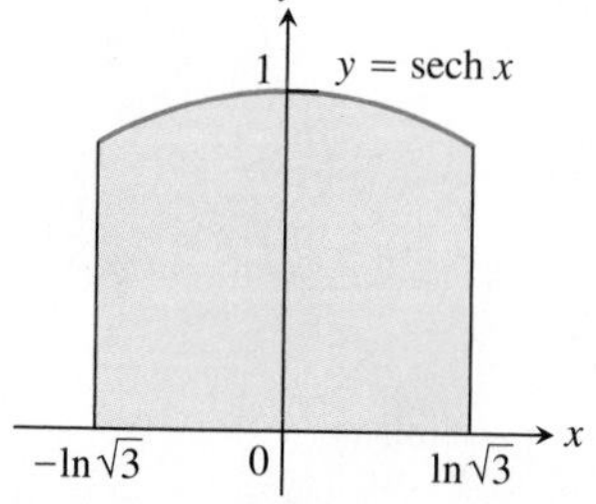

63. Find the volume of the solid generated by revolving the shaded region about the line $y = 1$.

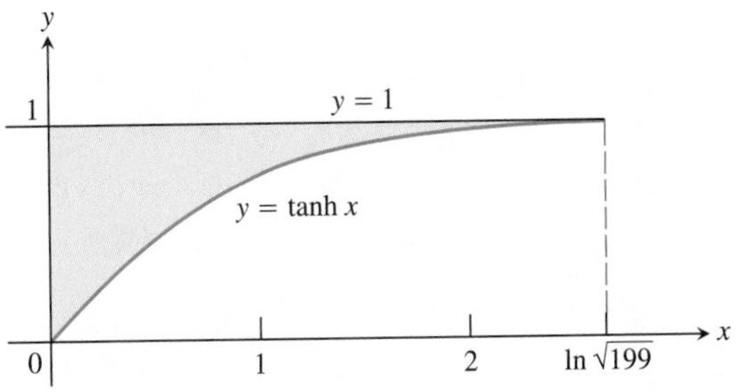

64. **(a)** Find the length of the curve $y = (1/2)\cosh 2x$, $0 \le x \le \ln\sqrt{5}$.

(b) Find the length of the curve $y = (1/a)\cosh ax$, $0 \le x \le b$.

Extending the Ideas

65. ***Even-Odd Decompositions***

(a) Show that if a function f is defined on an interval symmetric about the origin (so that f is defined at $-x$ whenever it is defined at x), then

$$f(x) = \frac{f(x)+f(-x)}{2} + \frac{f(x)-f(-x)}{2}. \qquad (1)$$

Then show that

$$\frac{f(x)+f(-x)}{2} \quad \text{is even}$$

and

$$\frac{f(x)-f(-x)}{2} \quad \text{is odd.}$$

(b) In Equation 1, set $f(x) = e^x$. Identify the even and odd parts of f.

66. **Writing to Learn** ***(Continuation of Exercise 65)*** Equation 1 in Exercise 65 simplifies considerably if f itself is **(a)** even or **(b)** odd. What are the new equations? Explain.

67. ***Skydiving*** If a body of mass m falling from rest under the action of gravity encounters an air resistance proportional to the square of the velocity, then the body's velocity t seconds into the fall satisfies the differential equation

$$m\frac{dv}{dt} = mg - kv^2,$$

where k is a constant that depends on the body's aerodynamic properties and the density of the air. (We assume that the fall is short enough so that variation in the air's density will not affect the outcome.)

Show that

$$v = \sqrt{\frac{mg}{k}}\tanh\left(\sqrt{\frac{gk}{m}}\,t\right)$$

satisfies the differential equation and the initial condition that $v = 0$ when $t = 0$.

68. ***Accelerations Whose Magnitudes Are Proportional to Displacement*** Suppose that the position of a body moving along a coordinate line at time t is

(a) $s = a\cos kt + b\sin kt$,

(b) $s = a\cosh kt + b\sinh kt$.

Show in both cases that the acceleration d^2s/dt^2 is proportional to s but that in the first case it is directed toward the origin while in the second case it is directed away from the origin.

69. ***Tractor Trailers and the Tractrix*** When a tractor trailer turns into a cross street or driveway, its rear wheels follow a curve like the one shown here. (This is why the rear wheels sometimes ride up over the curb.)

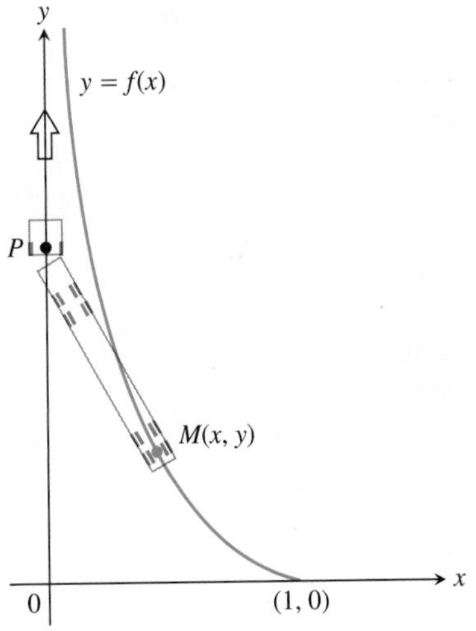

We can find an equation for the curve if we picture the rear wheels as a mass M at the point $(1, 0)$ on the x-axis attached by a rod of unit length to a point P representing the cab at the origin. As P moves up the y-axis, it drags M along behind it. The curve traced by M, called a *tractrix* from the Latin word *tractum* for "drag," can be shown to be the graph of the function $y = f(x)$ that solves the initial value problem

Differential equation: $\dfrac{dy}{dx} = -\dfrac{1}{x\sqrt{1-x^2}} + \dfrac{x}{\sqrt{1-x^2}}$,

Initial condition: $y = 0$ when $x = 1$.

Solve the initial value problem to find an equation for the curve. (You need an inverse hyperbolic function.)

70. ***A Minimal Surface*** Find the area of the surface swept out by revolving the curve $y = 4\cosh(x/4)$, $-\ln 16 \le x \le \ln 81$, about the x-axis. See the accompanying figure at the top of the next page.

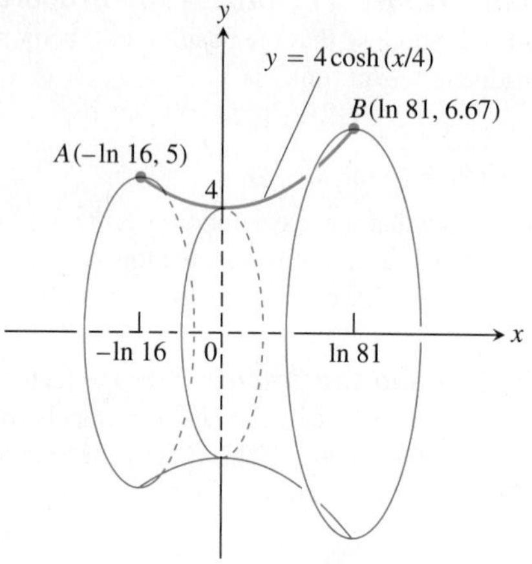

It can be shown that, of all continuously differentiable curves joining points A and B in the figure, the curve $y = 4\cosh(x/4)$ generates the surface of least area. If you made a rigid wire frame of the end-circles through A and B and dipped them in a soap-film solution, the surface spanning the circles would be the one generated by the curve.

71. *Hanging Cables* Show that the function $y = a\cosh(x/a)$ solves the initial value problem

$$y'' = (1/a)\sqrt{1 + (y')^2}, \quad y'(0) = 0, \quad y(0) = a.$$

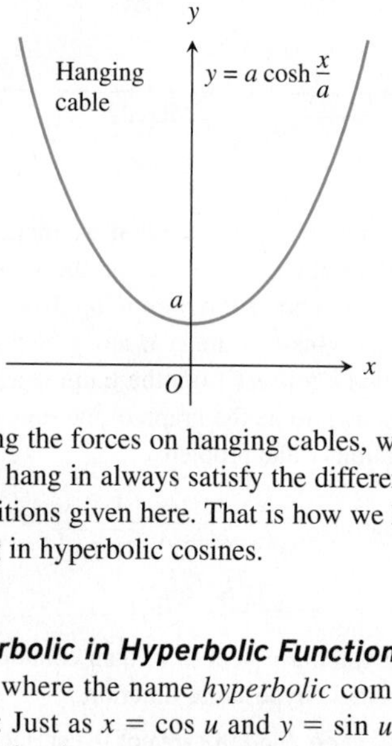

By analyzing the forces on hanging cables, we can show that the curves they hang in always satisfy the differential equation and initial conditions given here. That is how we know that hanging cables hang in hyperbolic cosines.

72. *The Hyperbolic in Hyperbolic Functions* In case you are wondering where the name *hyperbolic* comes from, here is the answer: Just as $x = \cos u$ and $y = \sin u$ are identified with points (x, y) on the unit circle, the functions $x = \cosh u$ and $y = \sinh u$ are identified with points (x, y) on the right-hand branch of the unit hyperbola $x^2 - y^2 = 1$ (Figure A6.4).

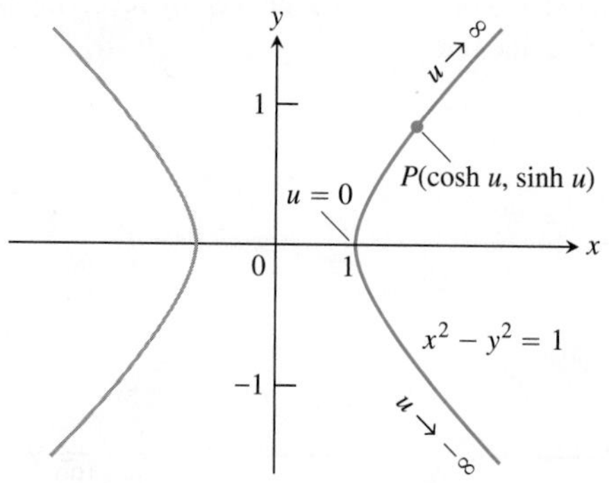

Figure A6.4 Since $\cosh^2 u - \sinh^2 u = 1$, the point $(\cosh u, \sinh u)$ lies on the right-hand branch of the hyperbola $x^2 - y^2 = 1$ for every value of u (Exercise 72).

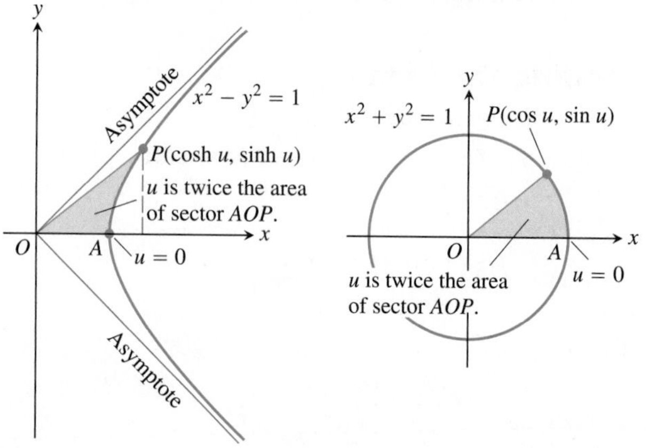

Figure A6.5 One of the analogies between hyperbolic and circular functions is revealed by these two diagrams (Exercise 72).

Another analogy between hyperbolic and circular functions is that the variable u in the coordinates $(\cosh u, \sinh u)$ for the points of the right-hand branch of the hyperbola $x^2 - y^2 = 1$ is twice the area of the sector AOP pictured in Figure A6.5. To see why, carry out the following steps.

(a) Let $A(u)$ be the area of sector AOP. Show that

$$A(u) = \frac{1}{2}\cosh u \sinh u - \int_1^{\cosh u} \sqrt{x^2 - 1}\, dx.$$

(b) Differentiate both sides of the equation in (a) with respect to u to show that

$$A'(u) = \frac{1}{2}.$$

(c) Solve the equation in (b) for $A(u)$. What is the value of $A(0)$? What is the value of the constant of integration C in your solution? With C determined, what does your solution say about the relationship of u to $A(u)$?

A7 A Brief Table of Integrals

The formulas below are stated in terms of constants a, b, c, m, n, and so on. These constants can usually assume any real value and need not be integers. Occasional limitations on their values are stated with the formulas. Formula 5 requires $n \neq -1$, for example, and Formula 11 requires $n \neq -2$. The formulas also assume that the constants do not take on values that require dividing by zero or taking even roots of negative numbers. For example, Formula 8 assumes $a \neq 0$, and Formula 13(a) cannot be used unless b is negative.

1. $\displaystyle\int u\,dv = uv - \int v\,du$

2. $\displaystyle\int a^u\,du = \frac{a^u}{\ln a} + C, \quad a \neq 1, \quad a > 0$

3. $\displaystyle\int \cos u\,du = \sin u + C$

4. $\displaystyle\int \sin u\,du = -\cos u + C$

5. $\displaystyle\int (ax+b)^n\,dx = \frac{(ax+b)^{n+1}}{a(n+1)} + C, \quad n \neq -1$

6. $\displaystyle\int (ax+b)^{-1}\,dx = \frac{1}{a}\ln|ax+b| + C$

7. $\displaystyle\int x(ax+b)^n\,dx = \frac{(ax+b)^{n+1}}{a^2}\left[\frac{ax+b}{n+2} - \frac{b}{n+1}\right] + C, \quad n \neq -1, -2$

8. $\displaystyle\int x(ax+b)^{-1}\,dx = \frac{x}{a} - \frac{b}{a^2}\ln|ax+b| + C$

9. $\displaystyle\int x(ax+b)^{-2}\,dx = \frac{1}{a^2}\left[\ln|ax+b| + \frac{b}{ax+b}\right] + C$

10. $\displaystyle\int \frac{dx}{x(ax+b)} = \frac{1}{b}\ln\left|\frac{x}{ax+b}\right| + C$

11. $\displaystyle\int (\sqrt{ax+b})^n\,dx = \frac{2}{a}\frac{(\sqrt{ax+b})^{n+2}}{n+2} + C, \quad n \neq -2$

12. $\displaystyle\int \frac{\sqrt{ax+b}}{x}\,dx = 2\sqrt{ax+b} + b\int \frac{dx}{x\sqrt{ax+b}}$

13. (a) $\displaystyle\int \frac{dx}{x\sqrt{ax+b}} = \frac{2}{\sqrt{-b}}\tan^{-1}\sqrt{\frac{ax+b}{-b}} + C, \quad \text{if } b < 0$

(b) $\displaystyle\int \frac{dx}{x\sqrt{ax+b}} = \frac{1}{\sqrt{b}}\ln\left|\frac{\sqrt{ax+b}-\sqrt{b}}{\sqrt{ax+b}+\sqrt{b}}\right| + C, \quad \text{if } b > 0$

14. $\displaystyle\int \frac{\sqrt{ax+b}}{x^2}\,dx = -\frac{\sqrt{ax+b}}{x} + \frac{a}{2}\int \frac{dx}{x\sqrt{ax+b}} + C$

15. $\displaystyle\int \frac{dx}{x^2\sqrt{ax+b}} = -\frac{\sqrt{ax+b}}{bx} - \frac{a}{2b}\int \frac{dx}{x\sqrt{ax+b}} + C$

16. $\displaystyle\int \frac{dx}{a^2+x^2} = \frac{1}{a}\tan^{-1}\frac{x}{a} + C$

17. $\displaystyle\int \frac{dx}{(a^2+x^2)^2} = \frac{x}{2a^2(a^2+x^2)} + \frac{1}{2a^3}\tan^{-1}\frac{x}{a} + C$

18. $\displaystyle\int \frac{dx}{a^2-x^2} = \frac{1}{2a}\ln\left|\frac{x+a}{x-a}\right| + C$

19. $\displaystyle\int \frac{dx}{(a^2-x^2)^2} = \frac{x}{2a^2(a^2-x^2)} + \frac{1}{2a^2}\int \frac{dx}{a^2-x^2}$

20. $\displaystyle\int \frac{dx}{\sqrt{a^2+x^2}} = \sinh^{-1}\frac{x}{a} + C = \ln\left(x + \sqrt{a^2+x^2}\right) + C$

21. $\int \sqrt{a^2 + x^2}\, dx = \frac{x}{2}\sqrt{a^2 + x^2} + \frac{a^2}{2} \ln (x + \sqrt{a^2 + x^2}) + C$

22. $\int x^2\sqrt{a^2 + x^2}\, dx = \frac{x}{8}(a^2 + 2x^2)\sqrt{a^2 + x^2} - \frac{a^4}{8} \ln (x + \sqrt{a^2 + x^2}) + C$

23. $\int \frac{\sqrt{a^2 + x^2}}{x}\, dx = \sqrt{a^2 + x^2} - a \ln \left| \frac{a + \sqrt{a^2 + x^2}}{x} \right| + C$

24. $\int \frac{\sqrt{a^2 + x^2}}{x^2}\, dx = \ln (x + \sqrt{a^2 + x^2}) - \frac{\sqrt{a^2 + x^2}}{x} + C$

25. $\int \frac{x^2}{\sqrt{a^2 + x^2}}\, dx = -\frac{a^2}{2} \ln (x + \sqrt{a^2 + x^2}) + \frac{x\sqrt{a^2 + x^2}}{2} + C$

26. $\int \frac{dx}{x\sqrt{a^2 + x^2}} = -\frac{1}{a} \ln \left| \frac{a + \sqrt{a^2 + x^2}}{x} \right| + C$

27. $\int \frac{dx}{x^2\sqrt{a^2 + x^2}} = -\frac{\sqrt{a^2 + x^2}}{a^2 x} + C$

28. $\int \frac{dx}{\sqrt{a^2 - x^2}} = \sin^{-1} \frac{x}{a} + C$

29. $\int \sqrt{a^2 - x^2}\, dx = \frac{x}{2}\sqrt{a^2 - x^2} + \frac{a^2}{2} \sin^{-1} \frac{x}{a} + C$

30. $\int x^2\sqrt{a^2 - x^2}\, dx = \frac{a^4}{8} \sin^{-1} \frac{x}{a} - \frac{1}{8}x\sqrt{a^2 - x^2}(a^2 - 2x^2) + C$

31. $\int \frac{\sqrt{a^2 - x^2}}{x}\, dx = \sqrt{a^2 - x^2} - a \ln \left| \frac{a + \sqrt{a^2 - x^2}}{x} \right| + C$

32. $\int \frac{\sqrt{a^2 - x^2}}{x^2}\, dx = -\sin^{-1} \frac{x}{a} - \frac{\sqrt{a^2 - x^2}}{x} + C$

33. $\int \frac{x^2}{\sqrt{a^2 - x^2}}\, dx = \frac{a^2}{2} \sin^{-1} \frac{x}{a} - \frac{1}{2}x\sqrt{a^2 - x^2} + C$

34. $\int \frac{dx}{x\sqrt{a^2 - x^2}} = -\frac{1}{a} \ln \left| \frac{a + \sqrt{a^2 - x^2}}{x} \right| + C$

35. $\int \frac{dx}{x^2\sqrt{a^2 - x^2}} = -\frac{\sqrt{a^2 - x^2}}{a^2 x} + C$

36. $\int \frac{dx}{\sqrt{x^2 - a^2}} = \cosh^{-1} \frac{x}{a} + C = \ln \left| x + \sqrt{x^2 - a^2} \right| + C$

37. $\int \sqrt{x^2 - a^2}\, dx = \frac{x}{2}\sqrt{x^2 - a^2} - \frac{a^2}{2} \ln \left| x + \sqrt{x^2 - a^2} \right| + C$

38. $\int \left(\sqrt{x^2 - a^2}\right)^n dx = \frac{x\left(\sqrt{x^2 - a^2}\right)^n}{n + 1} - \frac{na^2}{n + 1} \int \left(\sqrt{x^2 - a^2}\right)^{n-2} dx, \quad n \neq -1$

39. $\int \frac{dx}{\left(\sqrt{x^2 - a^2}\right)^n} = \frac{x\left(\sqrt{x^2 - a^2}\right)^{2-n}}{(2 - n)a^2} - \frac{n - 3}{(n - 2)a^2} \int \frac{dx}{\left(\sqrt{x^2 - a^2}\right)^{n-2}}, \quad n \neq 2$

40. $\int x\left(\sqrt{x^2 - a^2}\right)^n dx = \frac{\left(\sqrt{x^2 - a^2}\right)^{n+2}}{n + 2} + C, \quad n \neq -2$

41. $\int x^2\sqrt{x^2 - a^2}\, dx = \frac{x}{8}(2x^2 - a^2)\sqrt{x^2 - a^2} - \frac{a^4}{8} \ln \left| x + \sqrt{x^2 - a^2} \right| + C$

42. $\int \frac{\sqrt{x^2 - a^2}}{x}\, dx = \sqrt{x^2 - a^2} - a \sec^{-1} \left| \frac{x}{a} \right| + C$

43. $\int \frac{\sqrt{x^2 - a^2}}{x^2}\, dx = \ln\left|x + \sqrt{x^2 - a^2}\right| - \frac{\sqrt{x^2 - a^2}}{x} + C$

44. $\int \frac{x^2}{\sqrt{x^2 - a^2}}\, dx = \frac{a^2}{2} \ln\left|x + \sqrt{x^2 - a^2}\right| + \frac{x}{2}\sqrt{x^2 - a^2} + C$

45. $\int \frac{dx}{x\sqrt{x^2 - a^2}} = \frac{1}{a} \sec^{-1}\left|\frac{x}{a}\right| + C = \frac{1}{a} \cos^{-1}\left|\frac{a}{x}\right| + C$

46. $\int \frac{dx}{x^2\sqrt{x^2 - a^2}} = \frac{\sqrt{x^2 - a^2}}{a^2 x} + C$

47. $\int \frac{dx}{\sqrt{2ax - x^2}} = \sin^{-1}\left(\frac{x - a}{a}\right) + C$

48. $\int \sqrt{2ax - x^2}\, dx = \frac{x - a}{2}\sqrt{2ax - x^2} + \frac{a^2}{2} \sin^{-1}\left(\frac{x - a}{a}\right) + C$

49. $\int \left(\sqrt{2ax - x^2}\right)^n dx = \frac{(x - a)\left(\sqrt{2ax - x^2}\right)^n}{n + 1} + \frac{na^2}{n + 1}\int \left(\sqrt{2ax - x^2}\right)^{n-2} dx$

50. $\int \frac{dx}{\left(\sqrt{2ax - x^2}\right)^n} = \frac{(x - a)\left(\sqrt{2ax - x^2}\right)^{2-n}}{(n - 2)a^2} + \frac{(n - 3)}{(n - 2)a^2}\int \frac{dx}{\left(\sqrt{2ax - x^2}\right)^{n-2}}$

51. $\int x\sqrt{2ax - x^2}\, dx = \frac{(x + a)(2x - 3a)\sqrt{2ax - x^2}}{6} + \frac{a^3}{2} \sin^{-1}\left(\frac{x - a}{a}\right) + C$

52. $\int \frac{\sqrt{2ax - x^2}}{x}\, dx = \sqrt{2ax - x^2} + a \sin^{-1}\left(\frac{x - a}{a}\right) + C$

53. $\int \frac{\sqrt{2ax - x^2}}{x^2}\, dx = -2\sqrt{\frac{2a - x}{x}} - \sin^{-1}\left(\frac{x - a}{a}\right) + C$

54. $\int \frac{x\, dx}{\sqrt{2ax - x^2}} = a \sin^{-1}\left(\frac{x - a}{a}\right) - \sqrt{2ax - x^2} + C$

55. $\int \frac{dx}{x\sqrt{2ax - x^2}} = -\frac{1}{a}\sqrt{\frac{2a - x}{x}} + C$

56. $\int \sin ax\, dx = -\frac{1}{a} \cos ax + C$

57. $\int \cos ax\, dx = \frac{1}{a} \sin ax + C$

58. $\int \sin^2 ax\, dx = \frac{x}{2} - \frac{\sin 2ax}{4a} + C$

59. $\int \cos^2 ax\, dx = \frac{x}{2} + \frac{\sin 2ax}{4a} + C$

60. $\int \sin^n ax\, dx = -\frac{\sin^{n-1} ax \cos ax}{na} + \frac{n - 1}{n}\int \sin^{n-2} ax\, dx$

61. $\int \cos^n ax\, dx = \frac{\cos^{n-1} ax \sin ax}{na} + \frac{n - 1}{n}\int \cos^{n-2} ax\, dx$

62. (a) $\int \sin ax \cos bx\, dx = -\frac{\cos (a + b)x}{2(a + b)} - \frac{\cos (a - b)x}{2(a - b)} + C, \quad a^2 \neq b^2$

(b) $\int \sin ax \sin bx\, dx = \frac{\sin (a - b)x}{2(a - b)} - \frac{\sin (a + b)x}{2(a + b)} + C, \quad a^2 \neq b^2$

(c) $\int \cos ax \cos bx\, dx = \frac{\sin (a - b)x}{2(a - b)} + \frac{\sin (a + b)x}{2(a + b)} + C, \quad a^2 \neq b^2$

63. $$\int \sin ax \cos ax \, dx = -\frac{\cos 2ax}{4a} + C$$

64. $$\int \sin^n ax \cos ax \, dx = \frac{\sin^{n+1} ax}{(n+1)a} + C, \quad n \neq -1$$

65. $$\int \frac{\cos ax}{\sin ax} \, dx = \frac{1}{a} \ln |\sin ax| + C$$

66. $$\int \cos^n ax \sin ax \, dx = -\frac{\cos^{n+1} ax}{(n+1)a} + C, \quad n \neq -1$$

67. $$\int \frac{\sin ax}{\cos ax} \, dx = -\frac{1}{a} \ln |\cos ax| + C$$

68. $$\int \sin^n ax \cos^m ax \, dx = -\frac{\sin^{n-1} ax \cos^{m+1} ax}{a(m+n)} + \frac{n-1}{m+n} \int \sin^{n-2} ax \cos^m ax \, dx, \quad n \neq -m \quad (\text{If } n = -m, \text{ use No. 86.})$$

69. $$\int \sin^n ax \cos^m ax \, dx = \frac{\sin^{n+1} ax \cos^{m-1} ax}{a(m+n)} + \frac{m-1}{m+n} \int \sin^n ax \cos^{m-2} ax \, dx, \quad m \neq -n \quad (\text{If } m = -n, \text{ use No. 87.})$$

70. $$\int \frac{dx}{b + c \sin ax} = \frac{-2}{a\sqrt{b^2 - c^2}} \tan^{-1} \left[\sqrt{\frac{b-c}{b+c}} \tan \left(\frac{\pi}{4} - \frac{ax}{2} \right) \right] + C, \quad b^2 > c^2$$

71. $$\int \frac{dx}{b + c \sin ax} = \frac{-1}{a\sqrt{c^2 - b^2}} \ln \left| \frac{c + b \sin ax + \sqrt{c^2 - b^2} \cos ax}{b + c \sin ax} \right| + C, \quad b^2 < c^2$$

72. $$\int \frac{dx}{1 + \sin ax} = -\frac{1}{a} \tan \left(\frac{\pi}{4} - \frac{ax}{2} \right) + C$$

73. $$\int \frac{dx}{1 - \sin ax} = \frac{1}{a} \tan \left(\frac{\pi}{4} + \frac{ax}{2} \right) + C$$

74. $$\int \frac{dx}{b + c \cos ax} = \frac{2}{a\sqrt{b^2 - c^2}} \tan^{-1} \left[\sqrt{\frac{b-c}{b+c}} \tan \frac{ax}{2} \right] + C, \quad b^2 > c^2$$

75. $$\int \frac{dx}{b + c \cos ax} = \frac{1}{a\sqrt{c^2 - b^2}} \ln \left| \frac{c + b \cos ax + \sqrt{c^2 - b^2} \sin ax}{b + c \cos ax} \right| + C, \quad b^2 < c^2$$

76. $$\int \frac{dx}{1 + \cos ax} = \frac{1}{a} \tan \frac{ax}{2} + C$$

77. $$\int \frac{dx}{1 - \cos ax} = -\frac{1}{a} \cot \frac{ax}{2} + C$$

78. $$\int x \sin ax \, dx = \frac{1}{a^2} \sin ax - \frac{x}{a} \cos ax + C$$

79. $$\int x \cos ax \, dx = \frac{1}{a^2} \cos ax + \frac{x}{a} \sin ax + C$$

80. $$\int x^n \sin ax \, dx = -\frac{x^n}{a} \cos ax + \frac{n}{a} \int x^{n-1} \cos ax \, dx$$

81. $$\int x^n \cos ax \, dx = \frac{x^n}{a} \sin ax - \frac{n}{a} \int x^{n-1} \sin ax \, dx$$

82. $$\int \tan ax \, dx = \frac{1}{a} \ln |\sec ax| + C$$

83. $$\int \cot ax \, dx = \frac{1}{a} \ln |\sin ax| + C$$

84. $$\int \tan^2 ax \, dx = \frac{1}{a} \tan ax - x + C$$

85. $$\int \cot^2 ax \, dx = -\frac{1}{a} \cot ax - x + C$$

86. $$\int \tan^n ax \, dx = \frac{\tan^{n-1} ax}{a(n-1)} - \int \tan^{n-2} ax \, dx, \quad n \neq 1$$

87. $$\int \cot^n ax \, dx = -\frac{\cot^{n-1} ax}{a(n-1)} - \int \cot^{n-2} ax \, dx, \quad n \neq 1$$

88. $$\int \sec ax \, dx = \frac{1}{a} \ln |\sec ax + \tan ax| + C$$

89. $$\int \csc ax \, dx = -\frac{1}{a} \ln |\csc ax - \cot ax| + C$$

90. $$\int \sec^2 ax \, dx = \frac{1}{a} \tan ax + C$$

91. $$\int \csc^2 ax \, dx = -\frac{1}{a} \cot ax + C$$

92. $\int \sec^n ax\,dx = \frac{\sec^{n-2} ax \tan ax}{a(n-1)} + \frac{n-2}{n-1}\int \sec^{n-2} ax\,dx, \quad n \neq 1$

93. $\int \csc^n ax\,dx = -\frac{\csc^{n-2} ax \cot ax}{a(n-1)} + \frac{n-2}{n-1}\int \csc^{n-2} ax\,dx, \quad n \neq 1$

94. $\int \sec^n ax \tan ax\,dx = \frac{\sec^n ax}{na} + C, \quad n \neq 0$

95. $\int \csc^n ax \cot ax\,dx = -\frac{\csc^n ax}{na} + C, \quad n \neq 0$

96. $\int \sin^{-1} ax\,dx = x \sin^{-1} ax + \frac{1}{a}\sqrt{1 - a^2x^2} + C$

97. $\int \cos^{-1} ax\,dx = x \cos^{-1} ax - \frac{1}{a}\sqrt{1 - a^2x^2} + C$

98. $\int \tan^{-1} ax\,dx = x \tan^{-1} ax - \frac{1}{2a}\ln(1 + a^2x^2) + C$

99. $\int x^n \sin^{-1} ax\,dx = \frac{x^{n+1}}{n+1}\sin^{-1} ax - \frac{a}{n+1}\int \frac{x^{n+1}\,dx}{\sqrt{1 - a^2x^2}}, \quad n \neq -1$

100. $\int x^n \cos^{-1} ax\,dx = \frac{x^{n+1}}{n+1}\cos^{-1} ax + \frac{a}{n+1}\int \frac{x^{n+1}\,dx}{\sqrt{1 - a^2x^2}}, \quad n \neq -1$

101. $\int x^n \tan^{-1} ax\,dx = \frac{x^{n+1}}{n+1}\tan^{-1} ax - \frac{a}{n+1}\int \frac{x^{n+1}\,dx}{1 + a^2x^2}, \quad n \neq -1$

102. $\int e^{ax}\,dx = \frac{1}{a}e^{ax} + C$

103. $\int b^{ax}\,dx = \frac{1}{a}\frac{b^{ax}}{\ln b} + C, \quad b > 0, \quad b \neq 1$

104. $\int xe^{ax}\,dx = \frac{e^{ax}}{a^2}(ax - 1) + C$

105. $\int x^n e^{ax}\,dx = \frac{1}{a}x^n e^{ax} - \frac{n}{a}\int x^{n-1}e^{ax}\,dx$

106. $\int x^n b^{ax}\,dx = \frac{x^n b^{ax}}{a \ln b} - \frac{n}{a \ln b}\int x^{n-1}b^{ax}\,dx, \quad b > 0, \quad b \neq 1$

107. $\int e^{ax} \sin bx\,dx = \frac{e^{ax}}{a^2 + b^2}(a \sin bx - b \cos bx) + C$

108. $\int e^{ax} \cos bx\,dx = \frac{e^{ax}}{a^2 + b^2}(a \cos bx + b \sin bx) + C$

109. $\int \ln ax\,dx = x \ln ax - x + C$

110. $\int x^n(\ln ax)^m\,dx = \frac{x^{n+1}(\ln ax)^m}{n+1} - \frac{m}{n+1}\int x^n(\ln ax)^{m-1}\,dx, \quad n \neq -1$

111. $\int x^{-1}(\ln ax)^m\,dx = \frac{(\ln ax)^{m+1}}{m+1} + C, \quad m \neq -1$

112. $\int \frac{dx}{x \ln ax} = \ln|\ln ax| + C$

113. $\int \sinh ax\,dx = \frac{1}{a}\cosh ax + C$

114. $\int \cosh ax\,dx = \frac{1}{a}\sinh ax + C$

115. $\int \sinh^2 ax\,dx = \frac{\sinh 2ax}{4a} - \frac{x}{2} + C$

116. $\int \cosh^2 ax\,dx = \frac{\sinh 2ax}{4a} + \frac{x}{2} + C$

117. $\int \sinh^n ax\,dx = \frac{\sinh^{n-1} ax \cosh ax}{na} - \frac{n-1}{n}\int \sinh^{n-2} ax\,dx, \quad n \neq 0$

118. $\displaystyle\int \cosh^n ax\,dx = \frac{\cosh^{n-1} ax \sinh ax}{na} + \frac{n-1}{n}\int \cosh^{n-2} ax\,dx, \quad n \neq 0$

119. $\displaystyle\int x \sinh ax\,dx = \frac{x}{a}\cosh ax - \frac{1}{a^2}\sinh ax + C$

120. $\displaystyle\int x \cosh ax\,dx = \frac{x}{a}\sinh ax - \frac{1}{a^2}\cosh ax + C$

121. $\displaystyle\int x^n \sinh ax\,dx = \frac{x^n}{a}\cosh ax - \frac{n}{a}\int x^{n-1}\cosh ax\,dx$

122. $\displaystyle\int x^n \cosh ax\,dx = \frac{x^n}{a}\sinh ax - \frac{n}{a}\int x^{n-1}\sinh ax\,dx$

123. $\displaystyle\int \tanh ax\,dx = \frac{1}{a}\ln(\cosh ax) + C$

124. $\displaystyle\int \coth ax\,dx = \frac{1}{a}\ln|\sinh ax| + C$

125. $\displaystyle\int \tanh^2 ax\,dx = x - \frac{1}{a}\tanh ax + C$

126. $\displaystyle\int \coth^2 ax\,dx = x - \frac{1}{a}\coth ax + C$

127. $\displaystyle\int \tanh^n ax\,dx = -\frac{\tanh^{n-1} ax}{(n-1)a} + \int \tanh^{n-2} ax\,dx, \quad n \neq 1$

128. $\displaystyle\int \coth^n ax\,dx = -\frac{\coth^{n-1} ax}{(n-1)a} + \int \coth^{n-2} ax\,dx, \quad n \neq 1$

129. $\displaystyle\int \operatorname{sech} ax\,dx = \frac{1}{a}\sin^{-1}(\tanh ax) + C$

130. $\displaystyle\int \operatorname{csch} ax\,dx = \frac{1}{a}\ln\left|\tanh\frac{ax}{2}\right| + C$

131. $\displaystyle\int \operatorname{sech}^2 ax\,dx = \frac{1}{a}\tanh ax + C$

132. $\displaystyle\int \operatorname{csch}^2 ax\,dx = -\frac{1}{a}\coth ax + C$

133. $\displaystyle\int \operatorname{sech}^n ax\,dx = \frac{\operatorname{sech}^{n-2} ax \tanh ax}{(n-1)a} + \frac{n-2}{n-1}\int \operatorname{sech}^{n-2} ax\,dx, \quad n \neq 1$

134. $\displaystyle\int \operatorname{csch}^n ax\,dx = -\frac{\operatorname{csch}^{n-2} ax \coth ax}{(n-1)a} - \frac{n-2}{n-1}\int \operatorname{csch}^{n-2} ax\,dx, \quad n \neq 1$

135. $\displaystyle\int \operatorname{sech}^n ax \tanh ax\,dx = -\frac{\operatorname{sech}^n ax}{na} + C, \quad n \neq 0$

136. $\displaystyle\int \operatorname{csch}^n ax \coth ax\,dx = -\frac{\operatorname{csch}^n ax}{na} + C, \quad n \neq 0$

137. $\displaystyle\int e^{ax}\sinh bx\,dx = \frac{e^{ax}}{2}\left[\frac{e^{bx}}{a+b} - \frac{e^{-bx}}{a-b}\right] + C, \quad a^2 \neq b^2$

138. $\displaystyle\int e^{ax}\cosh bx\,dx = \frac{e^{ax}}{2}\left[\frac{e^{bx}}{a+b} + \frac{e^{-bx}}{a-b}\right] + C, \quad a^2 \neq b^2$

139. $\displaystyle\int_0^\infty x^{n-1}e^{-x}\,dx = (n-1)!, \quad n > 0$

140. $\displaystyle\int_0^\infty e^{-ax^2}\,dx = \frac{1}{2}\sqrt{\frac{\pi}{a}}, \quad a > 0$

141. $$\int_0^{\pi/2} \sin^n x\,dx = \int_0^{\pi/2} \cos^n x\,dx = \begin{cases} \dfrac{1\cdot 3\cdot 5\cdots(n-1)}{2\cdot 4\cdot 6\cdots n}\cdot\dfrac{\pi}{2}, & \text{if } n \text{ is an even integer} \geq 2 \\[2ex] \dfrac{2\cdot 4\cdot 6\cdots(n-1)}{3\cdot 5\cdot 7\cdots n}, & \text{if } n \text{ is an odd integer} \geq 3 \end{cases}$$

A8 Determinants and Cramer's Rule

What you'll learn about

- Matrices
- Determinants
- Minors and Cofactors
- Expanding by Columns or by Other Rows
- Useful Facts about Determinants
- Cramer's Rule

Matrices

A rectangular array of numbers like

$$A = \begin{bmatrix} 2 & 1 & 3 \\ 1 & 0 & -2 \end{bmatrix}$$

is called a **matrix.** We call A a 2 by 3 matrix because it has two rows and three columns. An m by n matrix has m rows and n columns, and the **entry** or **element** (number) in the ith row and jth column is denoted by a_{ij} (Figure A8.1). The matrix

$$A = \begin{bmatrix} 2 & 1 & 3 \\ 1 & 0 & -2 \end{bmatrix}$$

has

$$a_{11} = 2, \quad a_{12} = 1, \quad a_{13} = 3,$$
$$a_{21} = 1, \quad a_{22} = 0, \quad a_{23} = -2.$$

A matrix with the same number of rows as columns is a **square matrix.** It is a **matrix of order *n*** if the number of rows and columns is n.

Determinants

The vertical bar in the notation $|a_{ij}|$ does not mean absolute value.

With each square matrix A we associate a number det A or $|a_{ij}|$, called the **determinant** of A, calculated from the entries of A in the following way. For $n = 1$ and $n = 2$, we define

$$\det[a] = a, \tag{1}$$

$$\det \begin{bmatrix} a_{11} & a_{12} \\ a_{21} & a_{22} \end{bmatrix} = a_{11}a_{22} - a_{21}a_{12}. \tag{2}$$

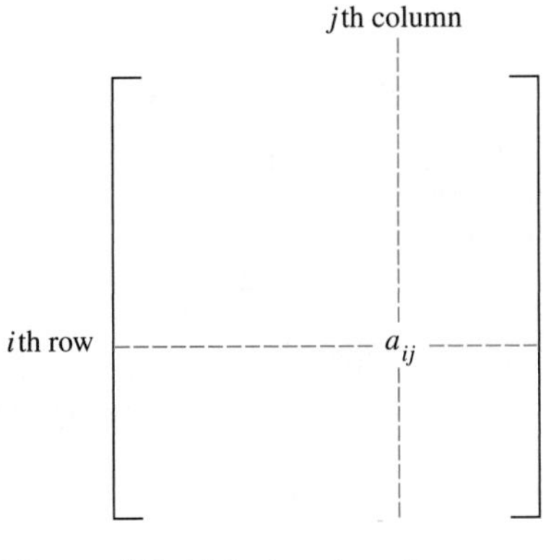

Figure A8.1 The location of entry a_{ij}.

For a matrix of order 3, we define

$$\det A = \det \begin{bmatrix} a_{11} & a_{12} & a_{13} \\ a_{21} & a_{22} & a_{23} \\ a_{31} & a_{32} & a_{33} \end{bmatrix} = \begin{array}{l}\text{sum of all signed products} \\ \text{of the form } \pm a_{1i}a_{2j}a_{3k},\end{array} \tag{3}$$

where i, j, k is a permutation of 1, 2, 3 in some order. There are $3! = 6$ such permutations, so there are six terms in the sum. The sign is positive when the index of the permutation is even and negative when the index is odd.

> **DEFINITION Index of a Permutation**
>
> Given any permutation of the numbers $1, 2, 3, \ldots, n$, denote the permutation by $i_1, i_2, i_3, \ldots, i_n$. In this arrangement, some of the numbers following i_1 may be less than i_1, and the number of these is called the **number of inversions** in the arrangement pertaining to i_1. Likewise, there are a number of inversions pertaining to each of the other i's; it is the number of indices that come after that particular i in the arrangement and are less than it. The **index** of the permutation is the sum of all the numbers of inversions pertaining to the separate indices.

EXAMPLE 1 Finding the Index of a Permutation

Find the index of the permutation

$$5 \quad 3 \quad 1 \quad 2 \quad 4$$

of the numbers 1, 2, 3, 4, and 5.

SOLUTION

The permutation

$$5 \quad 3 \quad 1 \quad 2 \quad 4$$

has four inversions pertaining to the first element, 5, two inversions pertaining to the second element, 3, and no further inversions, so the index is $4 + 2 = 6$.

The following table shows the permutations of 1, 2, 3, the index of each permutation, and the signed product in the determinant of Equation (3).

Permutation	Index	Signed product
1 2 3	0	$+a_{11}a_{22}a_{33}$
1 3 2	1	$-a_{11}a_{23}a_{32}$
2 1 3	1	$-a_{12}a_{21}a_{33}$
2 3 1	2	$+a_{12}a_{23}a_{31}$
3 1 2	2	$+a_{13}a_{21}a_{32}$
3 2 1	3	$-a_{13}a_{22}a_{31}$

The sum of the six signed products is

$$a_{11}(a_{22}a_{33} - a_{23}a_{32}) - a_{12}(a_{21}a_{33} - a_{23}a_{31}) + a_{13}(a_{21}a_{32} - a_{22}a_{31})$$

$$= a_{11}\begin{vmatrix} a_{22} & a_{23} \\ a_{32} & a_{33} \end{vmatrix} - a_{12}\begin{vmatrix} a_{21} & a_{23} \\ a_{31} & a_{33} \end{vmatrix} + a_{13}\begin{vmatrix} a_{21} & a_{22} \\ a_{31} & a_{32} \end{vmatrix} = \begin{vmatrix} a_{11} & a_{12} & a_{13} \\ a_{21} & a_{22} & a_{23} \\ a_{31} & a_{32} & a_{33} \end{vmatrix}$$

The formula

$$\begin{vmatrix} a_{11} & a_{12} & a_{13} \\ a_{21} & a_{22} & a_{23} \\ a_{31} & a_{32} & a_{33} \end{vmatrix} = a_{11}\begin{vmatrix} a_{22} & a_{23} \\ a_{32} & a_{33} \end{vmatrix} - a_{12}\begin{vmatrix} a_{21} & a_{23} \\ a_{31} & a_{33} \end{vmatrix} + a_{13}\begin{vmatrix} a_{21} & a_{22} \\ a_{31} & a_{32} \end{vmatrix} \quad (4)$$

reduces the calculation of a 3 by 3 determinant to the calculation of three 2 by 2 determinants.

Many people prefer to remember the following scheme for calculating the six signed products in the determinant of a 3 by 3 matrix:

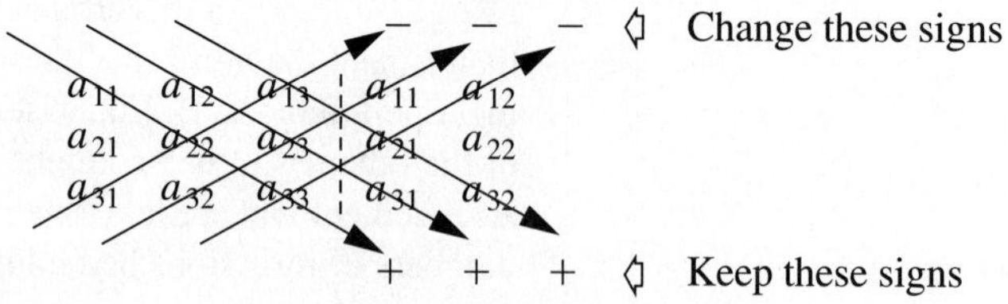

(5)

Minors and Cofactors

The second-order determinants on the right-hand side of Equation (4) are the **minors** (short for "minor determinants") of the entries they multiply. Thus,

$$\begin{vmatrix} a_{22} & a_{23} \\ a_{32} & a_{33} \end{vmatrix} \text{ is the minor of } a_{11}, \qquad \begin{vmatrix} a_{21} & a_{23} \\ a_{31} & a_{33} \end{vmatrix} \text{ is the minor of } a_{12},$$

and so on. The minor of the element a_{ij} in a matrix A is the determinant of the matrix that remains after we delete the row and column containing a_{ij}:

$$\begin{vmatrix} a_{11} & a_{12} & a_{13} \\ a_{21} & a_{22} & a_{23} \\ a_{31} & a_{32} & a_{33} \end{vmatrix}. \qquad \text{The minor of } a_{22} \text{ is } \begin{vmatrix} a_{11} & a_{13} \\ a_{31} & a_{33} \end{vmatrix}.$$

$$\begin{vmatrix} a_{11} & a_{12} & a_{13} \\ a_{21} & a_{22} & a_{23} \\ a_{31} & a_{32} & a_{33} \end{vmatrix}. \qquad \text{The minor of } a_{23} \text{ is } \begin{vmatrix} a_{11} & a_{12} \\ a_{31} & a_{32} \end{vmatrix}.$$

The **cofactor** A_{ij} of a_{ij} is $(-1)^{i+j}$ times the minor of a_{ij}. Thus,

$$A_{22} = (-1)^{2+2} \begin{vmatrix} a_{11} & a_{13} \\ a_{31} & a_{33} \end{vmatrix} = \begin{vmatrix} a_{11} & a_{13} \\ a_{31} & a_{33} \end{vmatrix},$$

$$A_{23} = (-1)^{2+3} \begin{vmatrix} a_{11} & a_{12} \\ a_{31} & a_{32} \end{vmatrix} = -\begin{vmatrix} a_{11} & a_{12} \\ a_{31} & a_{32} \end{vmatrix}.$$

The factor $(-1)^{i+j}$ changes the sign of the minor when $i + j$ is odd. There is a checkerboard pattern for remembering these changes:

$$\begin{matrix} + & - & + \\ - & + & - \\ + & - & + \end{matrix}$$

In the upper left corner, $i = 1$, $j = 1$, and $(-1)^{1+1} = +1$. In going from any cell to an adjacent cell in the same row or column, we change i by 1 or j by 1, but not both, so we change the exponent from even to odd or from odd to even, which changes the sign from $+$ to $-$ or from $-$ to $+$.

When we rewrite Equation (4) in terms of cofactors we get

$$\det A = a_{11}A_{11} + a_{12}A_{12} + a_{13}A_{13}. \tag{6}$$

EXAMPLE 2 Finding a Determinant Two Ways

Find the determinant of

$$A = \begin{vmatrix} 2 & 1 & 3 \\ 3 & -1 & -2 \\ 2 & 3 & 1 \end{vmatrix}.$$

SOLUTION

Using Equation (6): The cofactors are

$$A_{11} = (-1)^{1+1} \begin{vmatrix} -1 & -2 \\ 3 & 1 \end{vmatrix}, \qquad A_{12} = (-1)^{1+2} \begin{vmatrix} 3 & -2 \\ 2 & 1 \end{vmatrix},$$

$$A_{13} = (-1)^{1+3} \begin{vmatrix} 3 & -1 \\ 2 & 3 \end{vmatrix}.$$

continued

To find det A, we multiply each element of the first row of A by its cofactor and add:

$$\det A = 2\begin{vmatrix} -1 & -2 \\ 3 & 1 \end{vmatrix} + (-1)\begin{vmatrix} 3 & -2 \\ 2 & 1 \end{vmatrix} + 3\begin{vmatrix} 3 & -1 \\ 2 & 3 \end{vmatrix}$$

$$= 2(-1+6) - 1(3+4) + 3(9+2) = 10 - 7 + 33 = 36.$$

SOLUTION

Using the scheme in Equation (5): From Equation (5) we find

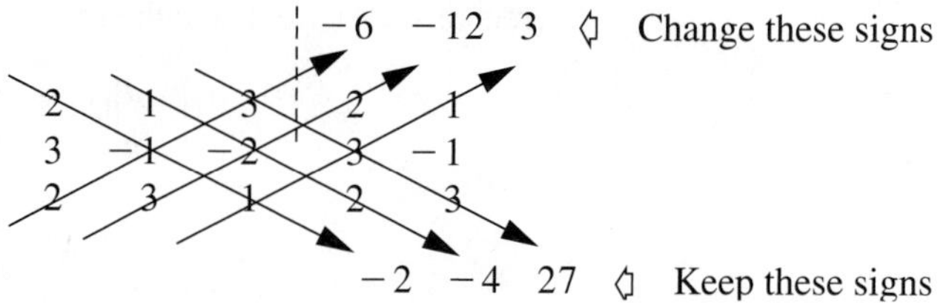

$$\det A = -(-6) - (-12) - 3 + (-2) + (-4) + 27 = 36.$$

Expanding by Columns or by Other Rows

The determinant of a square matrix can be calculated from the cofactors of any row or any column.

If we were to expand the determinant in Example 2 by cofactors according to elements of its third column, say, we would still get 36:

$$+3\begin{vmatrix} 3 & -1 \\ 2 & 3 \end{vmatrix} - (-2)\begin{vmatrix} 2 & 1 \\ 2 & 3 \end{vmatrix} + 1\begin{vmatrix} 2 & 1 \\ 3 & -1 \end{vmatrix}$$

$$= 3(9+2) + 2(6-2) + 1(-2-3) = 33 + 8 - 5 = 36.$$

Useful Facts about Determinants

Fact 1: If two rows (or columns) are identical, then the determinant is zero.

Fact 2: Interchanging two rows (or columns) changes the sign of the determinant.

Fact 3: The determinant is the sum of the products of the elements of the ith row (or column) by their cofactors, for any i.

Fact 4: The determinant of the transpose of a matrix is the same as the determinant of the original matrix. (The **transpose** of a matrix is obtained by writing the rows as columns. The first row becomes the first column, the second row the second column, and so on.)

Fact 5: Multiplying each element of some row (or column) by a constant c multiplies the determinant by c.

Fact 6: If all elements above the main diagonal (or all below it) are zero, then the determinant is the product of the elements on the main diagonal. (The **main diagonal** is the diagonal from upper left to lower right.)

EXAMPLE 3 Illustrating Fact 6

$$\begin{vmatrix} 3 & 4 & 7 \\ 0 & -2 & 5 \\ 0 & 0 & 5 \end{vmatrix} = (3)(-2)(5) = -30$$

Fact 7: If the elements of any row are multiplied by the cofactors of the corresponding elements of a different row and these products are summed, then the sum is zero.

EXAMPLE 4 Illustrating Fact 7

If A_{11}, A_{12}, A_{13} are the cofactors of the elements of the first row of $A = (a_{ij})$, then the sums

$$a_{21}A_{11} + a_{22}A_{12} + a_{23}A_{13}$$

(elements of second row times cofactors of elements of first row) and

$$a_{31}A_{11} + a_{32}A_{12} + a_{33}A_{13}$$

are both zero.

Fact 8: If the elements of any column are multiplied by the cofactors of the corresponding elements of a different column and these products are summed, then the sum is zero.

Fact 9: f each element of a row is multiplied by a constant c and the results added to a different row, then the determinant is not changed. A similar result holds for columns.

EXAMPLE 5 Adding a Multiple of One Row to Another Row

If we start with

$$A = \begin{bmatrix} 2 & 1 & 3 \\ 3 & -1 & -2 \\ 2 & 3 & 1 \end{bmatrix}$$

and add -2 times row 1 to row 2 (subtract 2 times row 1 from row 2), we get

$$B = \begin{bmatrix} 2 & 1 & 3 \\ -1 & -3 & -8 \\ 2 & 3 & 1 \end{bmatrix}.$$

Since $\det A = 36$ (Example 2), we should find that $\det B = 36$ as well. Indeed we do, as the following calculation shows:

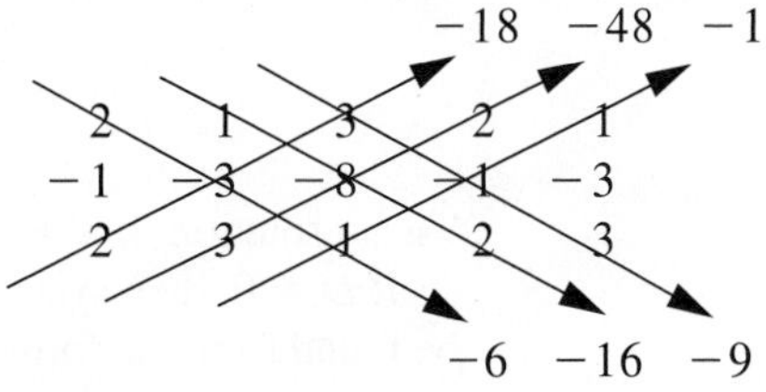

$$\det B = -(-18) - (-48) - (-1) + (-6) + (-16) + (-9)$$
$$= 18 + 48 + 1 - 6 - 16 - 9 = 67 - 31 = 36.$$

EXAMPLE 6 Transforming a Fourth-Order Determinant to Make it Easier to Evaluate

Evaluate the fourth-order determinant

$$D = \begin{vmatrix} 1 & -2 & 3 & 1 \\ 2 & 1 & 0 & 2 \\ -1 & 2 & 1 & -2 \\ 0 & 1 & 2 & 1 \end{vmatrix}.$$

continued

SOLUTION

We subtract 2 times row 1 from row 2 and add row 1 to row 3 to get

$$D = \begin{vmatrix} 1 & -2 & 3 & 1 \\ 0 & 5 & -6 & 0 \\ 0 & 0 & 4 & -1 \\ 0 & 1 & 2 & 1 \end{vmatrix}.$$

We then multiply the elements of the first column by their cofactors to get

$$D = (1)\begin{vmatrix} 5 & -6 & 0 \\ 0 & 4 & -1 \\ 1 & 2 & 1 \end{vmatrix} = 5(4 + 2) - (-6)(0 + 1) + 0 = 36.$$

Cramer's Rule

If the determinant $D = \det A = \begin{vmatrix} a_{11} & a_{12} \\ a_{21} & a_{22} \end{vmatrix} = 0$, then the system

$$\begin{aligned} a_{11}x + a_{12}y &= b_1 \\ a_{21}x + a_{22}y &= b_2 \end{aligned} \qquad (7)$$

has either infinitely many solutions or no solution at all. The system

$$\begin{aligned} x + y &= 0, \\ 2x + 2y &= 0 \end{aligned}$$

whose determinant is

$$D = \begin{vmatrix} 1 & 1 \\ 2 & 2 \end{vmatrix} = 2 - 2 = 0$$

has infinitely many solutions. We can find an x to match any given y. The system

$$\begin{aligned} x + y &= 0, \\ 2x + 2y &= 2 \end{aligned}$$

has no solution. If $x + y = 0$, then $2x + 2y = 2(x + y)$ cannot be 2.

If $D \neq 0$, then system (7) has a unique solution, and **Cramer's Rule** states that it may be found from the formulas

$$x = \frac{\begin{vmatrix} b_1 & a_{12} \\ b_2 & a_{22} \end{vmatrix}}{D}, \qquad y = \frac{\begin{vmatrix} a_{11} & b_1 \\ a_{21} & b_2 \end{vmatrix}}{D}. \qquad (8)$$

The numerator in the formula for x comes from replacing the first column in A (the x-column) by the column of constants b_1 and b_2 (the b-column). Replacing the y-column by the b-column gives the numerator of the y-solution.

EXAMPLE 7 Applying Cramer's Rule

Solve the system

$$\begin{aligned} 3x - y &= 9 \\ x + 2y &= -4. \end{aligned}$$

continued

SOLUTION

We use Equations (8). The determinant of the coefficient matrix is

$$D = \begin{vmatrix} 3 & -1 \\ 1 & 2 \end{vmatrix} = 6 + 1 = 7.$$

Hence,

$$x = \frac{\begin{vmatrix} 9 & -1 \\ -4 & 2 \end{vmatrix}}{D} = \frac{18 - 4}{7} = \frac{14}{7} = 2,$$

$$y = \frac{\begin{vmatrix} 3 & 9 \\ 1 & -4 \end{vmatrix}}{D} = \frac{-12 - 9}{7} = \frac{-21}{7} = -3.$$

Systems of three equations in three unknowns work the same way. If

$$D = \det A = \begin{vmatrix} a_{11} & a_{12} & a_{13} \\ a_{21} & a_{22} & a_{23} \\ a_{31} & a_{32} & a_{33} \end{vmatrix} = 0,$$

the system

$$\begin{aligned} a_{11}x + a_{12}y + a_{13}z &= b_1, \\ a_{21}x + a_{22}y + a_{23}z &= b_2, \\ a_{31}x + a_{32}y + a_{33}z &= b_3, \end{aligned} \tag{9}$$

has either infinitely many solutions or no solution at all. If $D \neq 0$, then the system has a unique solution, given by Cramer's Rule:

$$x = \frac{1}{D}\begin{vmatrix} b_1 & a_{12} & a_{13} \\ b_2 & a_{22} & a_{23} \\ b_3 & a_{32} & a_{33} \end{vmatrix}, \qquad y = \frac{1}{D}\begin{vmatrix} a_{11} & b_1 & a_{13} \\ a_{21} & b_2 & a_{23} \\ a_{31} & b_3 & a_{33} \end{vmatrix}.$$

$$z = \frac{1}{D}\begin{vmatrix} a_{11} & a_{12} & b_1 \\ a_{21} & a_{22} & b_2 \\ a_{31} & a_{32} & b_3 \end{vmatrix}.$$

The pattern continues in higher dimensions.

Section A8 Exercises

In Exercises 1–4, evaluate the determinant.

1. $\begin{vmatrix} 2 & 3 & 1 \\ 4 & 5 & 2 \\ 1 & 2 & 3 \end{vmatrix}$

2. $\begin{vmatrix} 2 & -1 & -2 \\ -1 & 2 & 1 \\ 3 & 0 & -3 \end{vmatrix}$

3. $\begin{vmatrix} 1 & 2 & 3 & 4 \\ 0 & 1 & 2 & 3 \\ 0 & 0 & 2 & 1 \\ 0 & 0 & 3 & 2 \end{vmatrix}$

4. $\begin{vmatrix} 1 & -1 & 2 & 3 \\ 2 & 1 & 2 & 6 \\ 1 & 0 & 2 & 3 \\ -2 & 2 & 0 & -5 \end{vmatrix}$

In Exercises 5–8, evaluate the determinant by expanding according to the cofactors of (a) the third row and (b) the second column.

5. $\begin{vmatrix} 2 & -1 & 2 \\ 1 & 0 & 3 \\ 0 & 2 & 1 \end{vmatrix}$

6. $\begin{vmatrix} 1 & 0 & -1 \\ 0 & 2 & -2 \\ 2 & 0 & 1 \end{vmatrix}$

7. $\begin{vmatrix} 1 & 1 & 0 & 0 \\ 0 & 0 & -2 & 1 \\ 0 & -1 & 0 & 7 \\ 3 & 0 & 2 & 1 \end{vmatrix}$

8. $\begin{vmatrix} 0 & 1 & 0 & 0 \\ 0 & 1 & 1 & 0 \\ 1 & 1 & 1 & 1 \\ 1 & 1 & 0 & 0 \end{vmatrix}$

In Exercises 9–16, solve the system of equations by Cramer's Rule.

9. $x + 8y = 4$
$3x - y = -13$

10. $2x + 3y = 5$
$3x - y = 2$

11. $4x - 3y = 6$
$3x - 2y = 5$

12. $x + y + z = 2$
$2x - y + z = 0$
$x + 2y - z = 4$

13. $2x + y - z = 2$
$x - y + z = 7$
$2x + 2y + z = 4$

14. $2x - 4y = 6$
$x + y + z = 1$
$5y + 7z = 10$

15. $x - z = 3$
$2y - 2z = 2$
$2x + z = 3$

16. $x_1 + x_2 - x_3 + x_4 = 2$
$x_1 - x_2 + x_3 + x_4 = -1$
$x_1 + x_2 + x_3 - x_4 = 2$
$x_1 + x_3 + x_4 = -1$

Explorations

17. Find values of h and k for which the system

$$2x + hy = 8,$$
$$x + 3y = k$$

has **(a)** infinitely many solutions and **(b)** no solution at all.

18. For what value of x will

$$\begin{vmatrix} x & x & 1 \\ 2 & 0 & 5 \\ 6 & 7 & 1 \end{vmatrix} = 0?$$

Extending the Ideas

19. Writing to Learn Suppose u, v, and w are twice-differentiable functions of x that satisfy the relation $au + bv + cw = 0$, where a, b, and c are constants, not all zero. Show that

$$\begin{vmatrix} u & v & w \\ u' & v' & w' \\ u'' & v'' & w'' \end{vmatrix} = 0.$$

20. *Partial Fractions.* Expanding the quotient

$$\frac{ax + b}{(x - r_1)(x - r_2)}$$

by partial fractions calls for finding the values of C and D that make the equation

$$\frac{ax + b}{(x - r_1)(x - r_2)} = \frac{C}{x - r_1} + \frac{D}{x - r_2}$$

hold for all x.

(a) Find a system of linear equations that determines C and D.

(b) Writing to Learn Under what circumstances does the system of equations in part (a) have a unique solution? That is, when is the determinant of the coefficient matrix of the system different from zero?

Glossary

Absolute convergence: If the series $\sum|a_n|$ of absolute values converges, then $\sum a_n$ is said to converge absolutely.

Absolute error: |(true value) − (approximate value)|

Absolute maximum: The function f has an absolute maximum value $f(c)$ at a point c in its domain D if and only if $f(x) \le f(c)$ for all x in D.

Absolute minimum: The function f has an absolute minimum value $f(c)$ at a point c in its domain D if and only if $f(x) \ge f(c)$ for all x in D.

Absolute, relative, and percentage change: As we move from $x = a$ to a nearby point $a + dx$, we can describe the corresponding change in the value of a function $f(x)$ three ways:

Absolute change: $\Delta f = f(a + dx) - f(a)$

Relative change: $\Delta f / f(a)$

Percentage change: $(\Delta f / f(a)) \times 100$.

Absolute value function: The function $f(x) = |x|$ is

$$|x| = \begin{cases} -x, & x < 0 \\ x, & x \ge 0. \end{cases}$$

Acceleration: The derivative of a velocity function with respect to time.

Acceleration vector: If $<x(t), y(t)>$ is the position vector of a particle moving along a smooth curve in the plane, then $<x''(t), y''(t)>$

$$\mathbf{a} = \frac{d^2\mathbf{r}}{dt^2}$$

is the particle's acceleration vector.

Algebraic function: A function $y = f(x)$ that satisfies an equation of the form $P_n y^n + \cdots + P_1 y + P_0 = 0$ in which the P's are polynomials in x with rational coefficients. The function $y = 1/\sqrt{x+1}$ is algebraic, for example, because it satisfies the equation $(x + 1)y^2 - 1 = 0$. Here, $P_2 = x + 1$, $P_1 = 0$, and $P_0 = -1$. All polynomials and rational functions are algebraic.

Alternating harmonic series: The series

$$\sum_{n=1}^{\infty} \frac{(-1)^{n-1}}{n}.$$

Alternating series: A series in which the terms are alternately positive and negative.

Amplitude: Of a periodic function $f(x)$ continuous for all real x, the number

$$\frac{(\text{absolute max of } f) - (\text{absolute min of } f)}{2},$$

is called the amplitude.

The amplitude of the sine function

$$f(x) = A \sin\left[\frac{2\pi}{B}(x - C)\right] + D,$$

is $|A|$.

Angle between curves: At a point of intersection of two differentiable curves, the angle between their tangent lines at the point of intersection.

Angle between vectors u and v: The angle

$$\theta = \cos^{-1}\left(\frac{\mathbf{u} \cdot \mathbf{v}}{|\mathbf{u}||\mathbf{v}|}\right).$$

Antiderivative: A function $F(x)$ is an antiderivative of a function $f(x)$ if $F'(x) = f(x)$ for all x in the domain of f. A vector function $\mathbf{R}(t)$ is an antiderivative of a vector function $\mathbf{r}(t)$ on an internal I if $d\mathbf{R}/dt = \mathbf{r}(t)$ at each point of I.

Antidifferentiation: The process of finding an antiderivative.

Antidifferentiation by partial fractions: A method for integrating a rational function by writing it as a sum of proper fractions, called partial fractions, with linear or quadratic denominators.

Antidifferentiation by parts: A method of integration in which $\int u\,dv$ is written as $uv - \int v\,du$.

Antidifferentiation by substitution: A method of integration in which $\int f(g(x)) \cdot g'(x)\,dx$ is rewritten as $\int f(u)\,du$ by substituting $u = g(x)$ and $du = g'(x)\,dx$.

Arbitrary constant: See *Constant of integration.*

Arc length: The length

$$\int_a^b \sqrt{1 + \left(\frac{dy}{dx}\right)^2}\,dx$$

of a smooth curve (y a function of x and dy/dx continuous) beginning at $x = a$ and ending at $x = b$.

For a smooth plane curve $y = f(x)$, $a \le x \le b$, the number

$$L = \int_a^b \sqrt{1 + \left(\frac{dy}{dx}\right)^2}\,dx.$$

For a smooth space curve $\mathbf{r}(t) = f(t) = \mathbf{i} + g(t)\mathbf{j} + h(t)\mathbf{k}$, $a \le t \le b$, the number

$$L = \int_a^b \sqrt{\left(\frac{df}{dt}\right)^2 + \left(\frac{dg}{dt}\right)^2 + \left(\frac{dh}{dt}\right)^2}\,dt.$$

Arc length parameter: The signed distance s measured from a base point on a smooth curve C that determines a point on the curve.

Arccosine or inverse cosine function: The inverse of the cosine function with restricted domain $[0, \pi]$.

Arcsine or inverse sine function: The inverse of the sine function with restricted domain $[-\pi/2, \pi/2]$.

Arctangent or inverse tangent function: The inverse of the tangent function with restricted domain $(-\pi/2, \pi/2)$.

Area of a closed bounded plane region *R*:

$$A = \iint_R dA,$$

or, in polar coordinates,

$$A = \iint_R r\,dr\,d\theta.$$

Arithmetic sequence: A sequence that can be written in the form $\{a, a + d, a + 2d, \ldots, a + (n - 1)d, \ldots\}$ for some common difference d.

Asymptote: The line $y = b$ is a horizontal asymptote of the graph of a function $y = f(x)$ if either

$$\lim_{x\to\infty} f(x) = b \quad \text{or} \quad \lim_{x\to-\infty} f(x) = b.$$

The line $x = a$ is a vertical asymptote of the graph of a function $y = f(x)$ if either

$$\lim_{x\to a^+} f(x) = \pm\infty \quad \text{or} \quad \lim_{x\to a^-} f(x) = \pm\infty.$$

Average rate of change of a quantity over a period of time: The amount of change divided by the time it takes.

Average value of a continuous function *f* on [*a*, *b*]:

$$\frac{1}{b - a}\int_a^b f(x)\,dx.$$

of a function on a region *D* in space:

$$\frac{1}{\text{volume of } D}\iiint_D F(\mathbf{x}, \mathbf{y}, \mathbf{z})\,dV$$

of a function on a region *R* in the plane:

$$\frac{1}{\text{area of } R}\iint_R f(\mathbf{x}, \mathbf{y})\,dA.$$

Average velocity: Displacement (change in position) divided by time traveled.

Axis of revolution: The line about which a solid of revolution is generated. See also *Solid of revolution.*

Base (exponential and logarithm): See *Exponential function with base a; Logarithm function with base a.*

Basic trigonometric functions: When an angle of measure θ is placed in standard position in the coordinate plane and (x, y) is the point in which its terminal ray intersects a circle with center $(0, 0)$ and radius r, the values of the six basic trigonometric functions of θ are

Sine: $\sin\theta = \dfrac{y}{r}$	Cosecant: $\csc\theta = \dfrac{r}{y}$
Cosine: $\cos\theta = \dfrac{x}{r}$	Secant: $\sec\theta = \dfrac{r}{x}$
Tangent: $\tan\theta = \dfrac{y}{x}$	Cotangent: $\cot\theta = \dfrac{x}{y}$

Big-oh notation: If functions f and g are positive for x sufficiently large, then f is big-oh of g (written $f = O(g)$) if there exists a positive integer M such that

$$\frac{f(x)}{g(x)} \le M$$

for x sufficiently large.

Binomial series: The Maclaurin series for $f(x) = (1 + x)^m$.

Binormal vector of a curve in space: The vector $\mathbf{B} = \mathbf{T} \times \mathbf{N}$, where $\mathbf{T}$ and $\mathbf{N}$ are the unit tangent and normal vectors.

Boundary point of a region *R* in the plane: A point (x_0, y_0) such that every disk centered at (x_0, y_0) contains points that lie outside of R as well as points that lie in R. The region's boundary points make up its *boundary.*

Boundary point of a region *D* in space: A point (x_0, y_0, z_0) such that every sphere centered at (x_0, y_0, z_0) contains points that lie outside of D as well as points that lie in D. The region's boundary points make up its *boundary.*

Bounded: A function f is bounded on a given domain if there are numbers m and M such that $m \le f(x) \le M$ for any x in the domain of f. The number m is a lower bound, and the number M is an upper bound for f.

Bounded (from) above: A function f is bounded (from) above on a given domain if there is a number M such that $f(x) \le M$ for all x in the domain.

Bounded (from) below: A function f is bounded (from) below on a given domain if there is a number m such that $m \le f(x)$ for all x in the domain.

Bounded region: In the plane, a region that lies inside a disk of finite radius. In space, a region that lies inside a sphere of finite radius.

Cardioid: Any of the heart-shaped polar curves $r = a(1 - \cos\theta)$ or $r = a(1 - \sin\theta)$, $a \ne 0$ a constant.

Cartesian coordinates of a point in space: The ordered triple (x, y, z).

Center of curvature: See *Circle of curvature.*

Center of a power series: See *Power series.*

Centroid: The center of mass of a shape with constant density.

Chain Rule: If $y = f(u)$ is differentiable at the point $u = g(x)$, and g is differentiable at x, then the composite function $(f \circ g)(x) = f(g(x))$ is differentiable at x, and

$$(f \circ g)'(x) = f'(g(x)) \cdot g'(x), \quad \text{or} \quad \frac{dy}{dx} = \frac{dy}{du} \cdot \frac{du}{dx},$$

where dy/du is evaluated at $u = g(x)$.

Chain Rule for differentiating vector functions (short form): If $\mathbf{r}$ is a differentiable function of t and t is a differentiable function of s, then

$$\frac{d\mathbf{r}}{ds} = \frac{d\mathbf{r}}{dt}\frac{dt}{ds}.$$

Chain Rule for functions of three variables: If $w = f(x, y, z)$ is differentiable and x, y, and z are differentiable functions of t, then w is a differentiable function of t and

$$\frac{dw}{dt} = \frac{\partial f}{\partial x}\frac{dx}{dt} + \frac{\partial f}{\partial y}\frac{dy}{dt} + \frac{\partial f}{\partial z}\frac{dz}{dt}.$$

There are similar rules for functions of other numbers of variables.

Circular functions: The functions cos x and sin x with reference to their function values corresponding to points (cos x, sin x), x in radians, on the unit circle. More generally, the six basic trigonometric functions.

Circle of curvature: At a point P on a plane curve where the curvature κ is not zero, the circle that

1. is tangent to the curve at P,

2. has the same curvature the curve has at P, and

3. lies toward the concave or inner side of the curve.

The *radius of curvature* of the curve at P is $\rho = 1/\kappa$, the reciprocal of the curvature at P. The *center of curvature* is the center of the circle of curvature.

Circular paraboloid: A surface generated by revolving a paraboloid in space about its axis. A typical equation (axis the z-axis) is

$$\frac{x^2}{a^2} + \frac{y^2}{a^2} = \frac{z}{c}.$$

Circulation around a curve: The flow along a closed loop.

Circulation density: See *Curl.*

Closed interval $[a, b]$: The set of all real numbers x with $a \le x \le b$.

Closed region in the plane or space: A region that contains all its boundary points.

Common difference: The diffference between two consecutive terms of an arithmetic sequence.

Common ratio: The quotient of any term of a geometric sequence and its preceding term. 7

Comparison Test (Direct, for improper integrals): For f and g continuous on $[a, \infty)$ with $0 \le f(x) \le g(x)$ for all $x \ge a$,

(1) $\int_a^\infty f(x)\,dx$ converges if $\int_a^\infty g(x)\,dx$ converges;

(2) $\int_a^\infty g(x)\,dx$ diverges if $\int_a^\infty f(x)\,dx$ diverges.

Comparison Test (Direct, for infinite series): Let $\sum a_n$ be a series with no negative terms. Then

(1) $\sum a_n$ converges if there is a convergent series $\sum c_n$ with $a_n \le c_n$ for all $n > N$ for some integer N;

(2) $\sum a_n$ diverges if there is a divergent series $\sum d_n$ of nonnegative terms with $a_n \ge d_n$ for all $n > N$ for some integer N.

Comparison Test (Limit, for improper integrals): If the positive functions f and g are continuous on $[a, \infty)$ and if

$$\lim_{x\to\infty} \frac{f(x)}{g(x)} = L, \qquad 0 < L < \infty,$$

then $\displaystyle\int_a^\infty f(x)\,dx$ and $\displaystyle\int_a^\infty g(x)\,dx$ both converge or both diverge.

Comparison Test (Limit, for infinite series): Suppose that $a_n > 0$ and $b_n > 0$ for all $n \ge N$, N an integer.

(1) if

$$\lim_{n\to\infty} \frac{a_n}{b_n} = c, \quad 0 < c < \infty,$$

then $\sum a_n$ and $\sum b_n$ both converge or both diverge;

(2) if

$$\lim_{n\to\infty} \frac{a_n}{b_n} = 0$$

and $\sum b_n$ converges, then $\sum a_n$ converges;

(3) if

$$\lim_{n\to\infty} \frac{a_n}{b_n} = \infty$$

and $\sum b_n$ diverges, then $\sum a_n$ diverges.

Complex number: An expression of the form $a + bi$ where a and b are real numbers and i is defined $\sqrt{-1}$.

Component equation for a plane: The component equation for the plane through $P_0(x_0, y_0, z_0)$ normal to $\mathbf{n} = A\mathbf{i} + B\mathbf{j} + C\mathbf{k}$ is $A(x - x_0) + B(y - y_0) + C(z - z_0) = 0$ or $Ax + By + Cz = D$, where $D = Ax_0 + By_0 + Cz_0$. 9

Component functions: Of a parametrized curve $x = f(t)$, $y = g(t)$, $t \in I$, the functions f and g. Of a vector function $\mathbf{r}(t) = f(t)\mathbf{i} + g(t)\mathbf{j}$, the functions f and g. Similarly in three dimensions.

Component form of a vector: If $\mathbf{v}$ is a vector in the plane equal to the vector with initial point (0, 0) and terminal point (v_1, v_2), the component form of $\mathbf{v}$ is $\mathbf{v} = \langle v_1, v_2\rangle$.

Components of a vector: See *Component form of a vector.*

Component test for conservative fields: If $\mathbf{F} = M\mathbf{i} + N\mathbf{j} + P\mathbf{k}$ is a field whose component functions have continuous first partial derivatives, then $\mathbf{F}$ is conservative if and only if

$$\frac{\partial P}{\partial y} = \frac{\partial N}{\partial z}, \quad \frac{\partial M}{\partial z} = \frac{\partial P}{\partial x}, \quad \text{and} \quad \frac{\partial N}{\partial x} = \frac{\partial M}{\partial y}.$$

Composite function $f \circ g$: The function $(f \circ g)(x) = f(g(x))$.

Concave down: The graph of a differentiable function $y = f(x)$ is concave down on an open interval I if y' is decreasing on I.

Concave up: The graph of a differentiable function $y = f(x)$ is concave up on an open interval I if y' is increasing on I.

Conditional convergence: An infinite series is conditionally convergent if it is convergent but not absolutely convergent.

Conic Section Law: See *Kepler's first law.*

Connected open region: An open region in which each point can be connected to any other point by a smooth curve lying in the region.

Conservative field: A vector field $\mathbf{F}$ in an open region D in which the work done in moving from any one point to another is the same for all paths between those two points. The integral

$\int \mathbf{F} \cdot d\mathbf{r}$ of such a field is said to be *path independent* in D.

Constant function: A function that assigns the same value to every element in its domain.

Constant of integration: The arbitrary constant C in $\int f(x)\,dx = F(x) + C$, where F is any antiderivative of f.

Continuity at an endpoint: A function $f(x)$ is continuous at a left endpoint a of its domain if $\lim_{x\to a^+} f(x) = f(a)$. The function is continuous at a right endpoint b of its domain if $\lim_{x\to b^-} f(x) = f(b)$.

Continuity at an interior point: A function $f(x)$ is continuous at an interior point c of its domain if $\lim_{x\to c} f(x) = f(c)$.

Continuity equation of hydrodynamics: If $\mathbf{v}$ is velocity field of a fluid flowing smoothly through a region D in space and $\delta(t, x, y, z)$ is the fluid's density at the point $P(x, y, z)$ at time t, then at each point of D,

$$\nabla \cdot (\delta\mathbf{v}) = -\frac{\partial \delta}{\partial t}.$$

Continuity of vector functions: A vector function $\mathbf{r}(t)$ is continuous at $t = c$ if $\lim_{t\to c} \mathbf{r}(t) = \mathbf{r}(c)$ (use appropriate one-sided limits at endpoints). In terms of components, $\mathbf{r}(t) = f(t)\mathbf{i} + g(t)\mathbf{j} + h(t)\mathbf{k}$ is continuous at $t = c$ if and only if f, g and h are continuous at $t = c$.

Continuity on an interval: A function is continuous on an interval if and only if it is continuous at each point of the interval.

Continuous extension of a function f: A function identical to f except that it is continuous at one or more points where f is not.

Continuous function: A function that is continuous at each point of its domain.

Contour line: The curve in space in which the plane $z = c$ cuts a surface $z = f(x, y)$

Convergent improper integral: An improper integral whose related limit(s) is (are) finite.

Convergent sequence: A sequence converges if it has a limit. See also *Limit at infinity.*

Convergent series: An infinite series converges if its sequence of partial sums has a finite limit.

Coordinate planes: The planes $x = 0$, $y = 0$, and $z = 0$ that divide space into eight **octants.** The octant in which all coordinates are nonnegative is called the *first octant.*

Cosecant function: See *Basic trigonometric functions.*

Cosine function: See *Basic trigonometric functions.*

Cotangent function: See *Basic trigonometric functions.*

Critical point: A point (value) in the interior of the domain of a function f at which $f' = 0$ or f' does not exist. An interior point of the domain of a function $f(x, y)$ where both first partial derivatives are zero or where one or both of the first partial derivatives do not exist.

Critical value: See *Critical point (value).*

Cross-product rule for differentiating vector functions:

$$\frac{d}{dt}(\mathbf{u} \times \mathbf{v}) = \mathbf{u} \times \frac{d\mathbf{v}}{dt} + \frac{d\mathbf{u}}{dt} \times \mathbf{v}$$

Cross section area: The area of a cross section of a solid.

Cross (vector) product: The cross (vector) product $\mathbf{A} \times \mathbf{B}$ of two nonparallel vectors $\mathbf{A}$ and $\mathbf{B}$ is the vector $\mathbf{A} \times \mathbf{B} = (|\mathbf{A}||\mathbf{B}| \sin \theta)\mathbf{n}$, where $\mathbf{n}$ is a unit vector normal to the plane determined by $\mathbf{A}$ and $\mathbf{B}$.

Curl: In a three-dimensional vector field $\mathbf{F}$, curl $\mathbf{F} = \nabla \times \mathbf{F}$.

Curvature: The curvature function of a smooth curve with unit tangent vector $\mathbf{T}$ is $\kappa = \left|\frac{d\mathbf{T}}{ds}\right|$.

Curve traced by a vector function: The curve traced by $\mathbf{r}(t) = f(t)\mathbf{i} + g(t)\mathbf{j} + h(t)\mathbf{k}$, $t \in I$, is the parametrized curve $x = f(t)$, $y = g(t)$, $z = h(t)$, $t \in I$.

Cylinder: A surface composed of the lines that pass through a given plane curve parallel to a given line in space. The curve is a *generating curve* for the cylinder.

Cylindrical coordinates of a point: Ordered triples (r, θ, z) in which r and θ are polar coordinates for the vertical projection of P on the xy-plane and z is the standard rectangular vertical coordinate.

Decay models: See *Exponential growth and decay.*

Decreasing function: Let f be a function defined on an interval I. Then f decreases on I if, for any two points x_1 and x_2 in I,

$$x_1 < x_2 \Rightarrow f(x_1) > f(x_2).$$

Decreasing on an interval: See *Decreasing function.*

Definite integral of a vector function $\mathbf{r}(t) = f(t)\mathbf{i} + g(t)\mathbf{j} + h(t)\mathbf{k}$ from a to b: The vector

$$\int_a^b \mathbf{r}(t)\,dt = \left(\int_a^b f(t)\,dt\right)\mathbf{i} + \left(\int_a^b g(t)\,dt\right)\mathbf{j} + \left(\int_a^b h(t)\,dt\right)\mathbf{k}$$

Definite integral of f over an interval $[a, b]$: For any partition P of $[a, b]$, let a number c_k be chosen arbitrarily in each subinterval $[x_{k-1}, x_k]$, and let $\Delta x_k = x_k - x_{k-1}$. If there exists a number I such that

$$\lim_{\|P\|\to 0} \sum_{k=1}^{n} f(c_k)\,\Delta x_k = I$$

no matter how P and the c_k's are chosen, then I is the definite integral of f over $[a, b]$.

Delta notation (Δ): See *Increment.*

Density: See *Mass.*

Density function: See *Mass.*

Derivative of a function f at a point a:

$$\lim_{h\to 0} \frac{f(a+h) - f(a)}{h},$$

provided the limit exists. 9

Derivative of a function f with respect to x: The function f' whose value at x is

$$\lim_{h\to 0} \frac{f(x+h) - f(x)}{h},$$

provided the limit exists. Alternatively,

$$\lim_{x\to a} \frac{f(x) - f(a)}{x - a},$$

provided the limit exists.

Derivative of a vector function at a point: The vector function $\mathbf{r}(t) = f(t)\mathbf{i} + g(t)\mathbf{j} + h(t)\mathbf{k}$ is differentiable at $t = t_0$ if f, g, and h are differentiable at t_0. The derivative is the vector

$$\frac{df}{dt}\mathbf{i} + \frac{dg}{dt}\mathbf{j} + \frac{dh}{dt}\mathbf{k}.$$

Determinant formula for $\mathbf{A} \times \mathbf{B}$: If $\mathbf{A} = a_1\mathbf{i} + a_2\mathbf{j} + a_3\mathbf{k}$ and $\mathbf{B} = b_1\mathbf{i} + b_2\mathbf{j} + b_3\mathbf{k}$, then

$$\mathbf{A} \times \mathbf{B} = \begin{vmatrix} \mathbf{i} & \mathbf{j} & \mathbf{k} \\ a_1 & a_2 & a_3 \\ b_1 & b_2 & b_3 \end{vmatrix}.$$

Difference quotient of the function f at a:

$$\frac{f(a+h) - f(a)}{h}.$$

Alternatively,

$$\frac{f(x) - f(a)}{x - a}.$$

Difference rule for differentiating vector functions:

$$\frac{d}{dt}(\mathbf{u} - \mathbf{v}) = \frac{d\mathbf{u}}{dt} - \frac{d\mathbf{v}}{dt}.$$

Differentiability: If $f'(x)$ exists, the function f is differentiable at x. A function that is differentiable at every point of its domain is a differentiable function.

Differentiable curve: The graph of a differentiable function; also, a parametrized curve whose component functions are differentiable at every parameter value.

Differentiable vector function: $\mathbf{r}(t) = f(t)\mathbf{i} + g(t)\mathbf{j} + h(t)\mathbf{k}$ is differentiable at t if f, g, and h are differentiable at t, and is differentiable if f, g, and h are differentiable. Its derivative is the vector

$$\frac{d\mathbf{r}}{dt} = \frac{df}{dt}\mathbf{i} + \frac{dg}{dt}\mathbf{j} + \frac{dh}{dt}\mathbf{k}$$

Differential: If $y = f(x)$ is a differentiable function, the differential dx is an independent variable and the differential dy is $dy = f'(x)\,dx$.

Differential calculus: The branch of mathematics that deals with derivatives.

Differential equation: An equation containing a derivative.

Differential form: $M(x, y, z)\,dx + N(x, y, z)\,dy + P(x, y, z)\,dz$ is a differential form. A differential form is *exact* on a domain D in space if

$$Mdx + Ndy + Pdz = \frac{\partial f}{\partial x}dx + \frac{\partial f}{\partial y}dy + \frac{\partial f}{\partial z}dz = df$$

for some (scalar) function f throughout D.

Differentiation: The process of taking a derivative.

Directional derivative: The rate of change $D_u f = \nabla f \cdot \mathbf{u}$ of a function $f(x, y, z)$ at a point P_0 in the direction of a unit vector $\mathbf{u} = u_1\mathbf{i} + u_2\mathbf{j} + u_3\mathbf{j}$.

Direction field: See *Slope field.*

Direction angle of a vector: The smallest nonnegative angle formed with the positive x-axis as the initial ray and the vector as the terminal ray.

Direction of a nonzero vector A: The vector $\mathbf{A}/|\mathbf{A}|$.

Direction of motion: $\mathbf{v}/|\mathbf{v}|$, where $\mathbf{v}$ is the (nonzero) velocity vector of the motion.

Discontinuity: If a function f is not continuous at a point c, then c is a point of discontinuity of f.

Disk method: A method for finding the volume of a solid of revolution by evaluating $\int_a^b A(x)\,dx$, where $A(x)$ is the area of the disk cut by a cross section of the solid perpendicular to the axis of revolution at x.

Distance between points in space: The distance between $P_1(x_1, y_1, z_1)$ and $P_2(x_2, y_2, z_2)$ is

$$|\overrightarrow{P_1P_2}| = \sqrt{(x_2 - x_1)^2 + (y_2 - y_1)^2 + (z_2 - z_1)^2}.$$

Distance traveled (from velocity): The integral of the absolute value of a velocity function with respect to time.

Divergence of a three-dimensional vector field: $\text{div}\,\mathbf{F} = \nabla \cdot \mathbf{F}$.

Divergence of a two-dimensional vector field: Given a vector field $\mathbf{F} = M\mathbf{i} + N\mathbf{j}$,

$$\text{div}\,\mathbf{F} = \frac{\partial M}{\partial x} + \frac{\partial N}{\partial y}.$$

Also called the *flux density of* **F**.

Divergence Theorem: Under suitable conditions, the outward flux of a vector field across a closed surface (oriented outward) equals the triple integral of the divergence of the field over the region enclosed by the surface.

Divergent improper integral: An improper integral for which at least one of the defining limits does not exist.

Divergent sequence: An infinite sequence that has no limit as $n \to \infty$.

Divergent series: An infinite series whose sequence of partial sums diverges.

Domain of a function: See *Function* and *Multivariable function.*

Domination: A function f dominates a function g on a domain D if $f(x) \geq g(x)$ for all x in D. A sequence $\{a_n\}$ dominates a sequence $\{b_n\}$ if $a_n \geq b_n$ for all n. An infinite series $\sum a_n$ dominates an infinite series $\sum b_n$ if $a_n \geq b_n$ for all n.

Dot (inner) product: Of vectors $\mathbf{u} = \langle u_1, u_2 \rangle$ and $\mathbf{v} = \langle v_1, v_2 \rangle$, the number $\mathbf{u} \cdot \mathbf{v} = u_1v_1 + u_2v_2$. Of vectors $\mathbf{A} = a_1\mathbf{i} + a_2\mathbf{j} + a_3\mathbf{k}$ and $\mathbf{B} = b_1\mathbf{i} + b_2\mathbf{j} + b_3\mathbf{k}$, the number $\mathbf{A} \cdot \mathbf{B} = a_1b_1 + a_2b_2 + a_3b_3$. It can also be written as $|\mathbf{A}||\mathbf{B}| \cos \theta$, where θ is the angle between **A** and **B**.

Dot product rule for differentiating vector functions:

$$\frac{d}{dt}(\mathbf{u} \cdot \mathbf{v}) = \mathbf{u} \cdot \frac{d\mathbf{v}}{dt} + \frac{d\mathbf{u}}{dt} \cdot \mathbf{v}$$

Double integral of f over a region R in the plane:

$$\iint_R f(x, y)\,dA = \lim_{\Delta A \to 0} \sum_{k=1}^{n} f(x_k, y_k)\,\Delta A_k,$$

or, in polar form,

$$\iint_R f(r, \theta)\,dA = \lim_{n \to \infty} \sum_{k=1}^{n} f(r_k, \theta_k)\,\Delta A_k.$$

Dummy variable of integration: In $\int_a^b f(x)\,dx$, the variable x. It could be any other letter without changing the value of the integral.

$\frac{dy}{dx}$**:** The derivative of y with respect to x.

***e* (the number):** To 9 decimal places, $e = 2.718281828$. More formally,

$$e = \lim_{x \to \infty} \left(1 + \frac{1}{x}\right)^x.$$

Ellipsoid: A surface defined by an equation of the form

$$\frac{x^2}{a^2} + \frac{y^2}{b^2} + \frac{z^2}{c^2} = 1.$$

Ellipsoid of revolution: An ellipsoid in which any two of the semiaxes a, b, and c are equal.

Elliptic cone: A surface defined by an equation of the form

$$\frac{x^2}{a^2} + \frac{y^2}{b^2} = \frac{z^2}{c^2}.$$

Elliptic paraboloid: A surface defined by an equation of the form

$$\frac{x^2}{a^2} + \frac{y^2}{b^2} = \frac{z}{c}.$$

End behavior model: The function g is

(1) a right end behavior model for f if and only if

$$\lim_{x \to \infty} \frac{f(x)}{g(x)} = 1;$$

(2) a left end behavior model for f if and only if

$$\lim_{x \to -\infty} \frac{f(x)}{g(x)} = 1;$$

(3) an end behavior model for f if it is both a left end and a right end behavior model for f.

Equal area law: See *Kepler's second law.*

Euler's method: A method using linearizations to approximate the solution of an initial value problem.

Even function: A function f for which $f(-x) = f(x)$ for every x in the domain of f.

Exact differential form: See *Differential form.*

Exponential change: See *Law of exponential change.*

Exponential function with base *a*: The function $f(x) = a^x$, $a > 0$ and $a \neq 1$.

Exponential growth and decay: Growth and decay modeled by the functions $y = k \cdot a^x$, $k > 0$, with $a > 1$ for growth and $0 < a < 1$ for decay.

Extreme value: See *Extremum.*

Extremum: A maximum or minimum value (extreme value) of a function on a set. See also *Absolute maximum; Absolute minimum; Local maximum; Local minimum.*

First derivative test for extreme values, multivariable: If $f(x, y)$ has a local maximum or minimum value at an interior point (a, b) of its domain and if the first partial derivatives exist there, then $f_x(a, b) = 0$ and $f_y(a, b) = 0$.

First derivative test (for local extrema): For a continuous function f,

(1) if f' changes sign from positive to negative at a critical point c, then f has a local maximum value at c;

(2) if f' changes sign from negative to positive at a critical point c, then f has a local minimum value at c;

(3) if f' does not change sign at a critical point c, then f has no local extreme value at c;

(4) if $f' < 0$ $(f' > 0)$ for $x > a$ where a is a left endpoint in the domain of f, then f has a local maximum (minimum) value at a;

(5) if $f' < 0$ $(f' > 0)$ for $x < b$ where b is a right endpoint in the domain of f, then f has a local minimum (maximum) value at b.

Finite sequence: A sequence whose domain has a finite number of elements.

First moments:

For a thin plate covering a region R in the xy-plane, about the x- and y-axis:

$$M_x = \iint_R y\delta(x, y)\, dA, \qquad M_y = \iint_R x\delta(x, y)\, dA.$$

For a solid object occupying a region D in space, about the yz-, xz-, xy-planes,

$$M_{yz} = \iiint_D x\delta\, dV, \quad M_{xz} = \iiint_D y\delta\, dV, \quad M_{xy} = \iiint_D z\delta\, dV.$$

For coil springs, thin rods, and wires lying along a smooth curve C in space,

$$M_{yz} = \int_C x\delta\, ds, \qquad M_{xz} = \int_C y\delta\, ds, \qquad M_{xy} = \int_C z\delta\, ds.$$

For a thin shell modeled by a surface S:

$$M_{yz} = \iint_S x\delta\, d\sigma, \quad M_{xz} = \iint_S y\delta\, d\sigma, \quad M_{xy} = \iint_S z\delta\, d\sigma.$$

First octant: See *Coordinate planes.*

Flow along a curve: The integral with respect to arc length over the curve of the dot product of a fluid's velocity field and the curve's unit tangent vector.

Flow integral: Flow $= \displaystyle\int_a^b \mathbf{F} \cdot \mathbf{T}\, ds.$

Flux across a smooth closed curve C: $\displaystyle\int_C \mathbf{F} \cdot \mathbf{n}\, ds$, where $\mathbf{n}$ is the outward-pointing unit normal vector on C.

Flux across a surface S in the direction of the chosen unit normal field $\mathbf{n}$: $\displaystyle\iint_S \mathbf{F} \cdot \mathbf{n}\, d\sigma.$

Flux density: See *Divergence.*

Free fall equation: When air resistance is absent or insignificant and the only force acting on a falling body is the force of gravity, we call the way the body falls *free fall.* In a free fall short enough for the acceleration of gravity to be assumed constant, call it g, the position of a body released to fall from position s_0 at time $t = 0$ with velocity v_0 is modeled by the equation $s(t) = (1/2)gt^2 + v_0 t + s_0$.

Frequency of a periodic function: The reciprocal of the period of the function, or the number of cycles or periods per unit time. The function $\sin x$, with x in seconds, has period 2π seconds and completes $1/2\pi$ cycles per second (has frequency $1/2\pi$).

Frenet (TNB) frame: See TNB *frame.*

Fubini's theorem: Under favorable conditions (normally met in practice), the double integral of a continuous function over a region in the plane can be evaluated as an iterated integral.

Function: A rule that assigns a unique element in a set R to each element in a set D. The set D is the *domain* of the function. The set of elements assigned from R is the *range* of the function.

Fundamental Theorem of Calculus, Part 1: If f is continuous on $[a, b]$, then the function $F(x) = \int_a^x f(t)\, dt$ has a derivative with respect to x at every point in $[a, b]$ and

$$\frac{dF}{dx} = \frac{d}{dx}\int_a^x f(t)\, dt = f(x).$$

Fundamental Theorem of Calculus, Part 2: If f is continuous on $[a, b]$, and F is any antiderivative of f on $[a, b]$, then

$$\int_a^b f(x)\, dx = F(b) - F(a).$$

Fundamental Theorem of Line Integrals: If $\mathbf{F}$ is a continuous vector field throughout an open connected region D in space, then there exists a differentiable function f such that

$$\mathbf{F} = \nabla f = \frac{\partial f}{\partial x}\mathbf{i} + \frac{\partial f}{\partial y}\mathbf{j} + \frac{\partial f}{\partial z}\mathbf{k}$$

if and only if for all points A and B in D the value of $\int_A^B \mathbf{F} \cdot d\mathbf{r}$ is independent of the path joining A to B in D. If the integral is independent of the path from A to B, its value is

$$\int_A^B \mathbf{F} \cdot d\mathbf{r} = f(B) - f(A).$$

Gaussian curve: See *Normal probability density function.*

Gauss's law: The total electric flux out of any closed surface is proportional to the total electric charge inside the surface.

General linear equation: $Ax + By = C$ (A and B not both 0).

Generating curve for a cylinder: See *Cylinder.*

Geometric sequence: A sequence of the form $a, ar, ar^2, \ldots, ar^n, \ldots$, in which each term after the first term is obtained by multiplying its preceding term by the same number r. The number r is the *common ratio* of the sequence.

Geometric series: A series of the form

$$a + ar + ar^2 + \cdots + ar^n + \cdots = \sum_{n=1}^{\infty} ar^{n-1},$$

in which each term after the first term is obtained by multiplying its preceding term by the same number r. The number r is the *common ratio* of the series.

Global maximum: See *Absolute maximum.*

Global minimum: See *Absolute minimum.*

Gradient field: The field of gradient vectors

$$\nabla f = \frac{\partial f}{\partial x}\mathbf{i} + \frac{\partial f}{\partial y}\mathbf{j} + \frac{\partial f}{\partial z}\mathbf{k}$$

of a differentiable function $f(x, y, z)$.

Gradient vector (gradient) of $f(x, y, z)$ at P_0: The vector

$$\nabla f = \frac{\partial f}{\partial x}\mathbf{i} + \frac{\partial f}{\partial y}\mathbf{j} + \frac{\partial f}{\partial z}\mathbf{k}$$

obtained by evaluating the partial derivatives of f at a point P_0.

Graph of a function $f(x)$: The set of points (x, y) in the coordinate plane whose coordinates are the input-output pairs of the function.

Graph of a function $f(x, y)$: The set of all points $(x, y, f(x, y))$ in space for (x, y) in the domain of f. The graph is also called the *surface* $z = f(x, y)$.

Gravitational constant: See *Universal gravitation constant.*

Green's Theorem (normal form): Under suitable conditions, the outward flux of a vector field across a simple closed curve in the plane equals the double integral of the divergence of the field over the region enclosed by the curve.

Green's Theorem (tangential form): Under suitable conditions, the counterclockwise circulation of a vector field around a simple closed curve is the double integral of the k-component of the curl of the field over the region enclosed by the curve.

Growth models: See *Exponential growth and decay; Logistic growth.*

Growth constant: For a population modeled by a differentiable function $P(t)$ giving the number of individuals at time t, the product $\frac{1}{P}\left(\frac{dP}{dt}\right)$.

Growth rate: See *Relative growth rate.*

Half-life of a radioactive element: The time required for half of the radioactive nuclei present in a sample to decay.

Harmonic series: The series

$$1 + \frac{1}{2} + \frac{1}{3} + \frac{1}{4} + \cdots + \frac{1}{n} + \cdots = \sum_{n=1}^{\infty} \frac{1}{n}.$$

Helix: A spiral with equally spaced coils that winds around a circular cylinder.

Hooke's Law: When a force is applied to stretch or compress a spring, the magnitude F of the force in the direction of motion is proportional to the distance x that the spring is stretched or compressed. In symbols, $F \sim x$ or $F = kx$, where k is the *constant of proportionality*. This relationship is *Hooke's Law.* If an elastic material is stretched too far, it becomes distorted and will not return to its original state. The distance beyond which distortion occurs is the material's *elastic limit.* Hooke's Law holds only as long as the material is not stretched past its elastic limit.

Horizontal line: In the Cartesian coordinate plane, a line parallel to the x-axis.

Hyperbolic paraboloid: A surface defined by an equation of the form

$$\frac{y^2}{b^2} - \frac{x^2}{a^2} = \frac{z}{c}, \; c > 0.$$

Hyperboloid of one sheet: A surface defined by an equation of the form

$$\frac{x^2}{a^2} + \frac{y^2}{b^2} - \frac{z^2}{c^2} = 1.$$

Hyperboloid of two sheets: A surface defined by an equation of the form

$$\frac{z^2}{c^2} - \frac{x^2}{a^2} - \frac{y^2}{b^2} = 1.$$

Imaginary number: A complex number of the form $0 + bi$. See also *Complex number.*

Implicit differentiation: A process for finding dy/dx when y is implicitly defined as a function of x by an equation of the form $f(x, y) = 0$.

Improper integral: An integral on an infinite interval or on a finite interval containing one or more points of infinite discontinuity of the integrand. Its value is found as a limit or sum of limits.

Increasing function: Let f be a function defined on an interval I. Then f increases on I if, for any two points x_1 and x_2 in I,

$$x_1 < x_2 \Rightarrow f(x_1) < f(x_2).$$

Increasing on an interval: See *Increasing function.*

Increment: If coordinates change from (x_1, y_1) to (x_2, y_2), the increments in the coordinates are $\Delta x = x_2 - x_1$ and $\Delta y = y_2 - y_1$. The symbols Δx and Δy are read "delta x" and "delta y."

Indefinite integral of a function f: The set of all antiderivatives of f, denoted by $\int f(x)\, dx$.

Indefinite integral of a vector function r(t): The set of all antiderivatives of **r**, denoted by $\int \mathbf{r}(t)\, dt$.

Indeterminate form: A nonnumeric expression of the form $0/0$, ∞/∞, $0 \cdot \infty$, $\infty - \infty$, 1^∞, ∞^0, or 0^0 obtained when trying substitution to evaluate a limit. The expression reveals nothing about the limit but does suggest that l'Hôpital's Rule may be applied to help find the limit.

Infinite discontinuity: A point of discontinuity where one or both of the one-sided limits are infinite.

Infinite limit: If the values of a function $f(x)$ outgrow all positive bounds as x approaches a finite number a, we say

$$\lim_{x \to a} f(x) = \infty.$$

If the values of f become large and negative, exceeding all negative bounds as $x \to a$, we say

$$\lim_{x \to a} f(x) = -\infty.$$

Infinite sequence: A sequence whose domain is an infinite subset of the positive integers.

Infinite series: An expression of the form

$$a_1 + a_2 + a_3 + \cdots + a_n + \cdots = \sum_{k=1}^{\infty} a_k.$$

The numbers $a_1, a_2, \ldots$ are the *terms* of the series; a_n is the nth term. The *partial sums* of the series form a sequence

$$s_1 = a_1$$
$$s_2 = a_1 + a_2$$
$$s_3 = a_1 + a_2 + a_3$$
$$\vdots$$
$$s_n = a_1 + a_2 + a_3 + \cdots + a_n$$

of numbers, each defined as a finite sum. If the sequence of partial sums has a limit S as $n \to \infty$, the series *converges* to the *sum S.* A series that fails to converge *diverges.*

Inflection point: A point where the graph of a function has a tangent line and the concavity changes.

Initial condition: See *Initial value problem.*

Initial value problem: For a first-order differential equation, the problem of finding the solution that has a particular value at a given point. The condition that the solution have this value at the point is called the *initial condition* of the problem.

Inner product: See *Dot (inner) product.*

Instantaneous rate of change of f with respect to x at a: The derivative

$$f'(a) = \lim_{h \to 0} \frac{f(a + h) - f(a)}{h},$$

provided the limit exists.

Instantaneous velocity: The derivative of a position function with respect to time.

Integrable function on $[a, b]$: A function for which the definite integral over $[a, b]$ exists.

Integral calculus: The branch of mathematics that deals with integrals.

Integral over a curve: See *Line integral.*

Integral over a surface: See *Surface integral.*

Integrand: $f(x)$ in $\int f(x)\, dx$ or in $\int_a^b f(x)\, dx$.

Integration: The evaluation of a definite integral, an indefinite integral, or an improper integral.

Integration by parts: See *Antidifferentiation by parts.*

Intermediate Value Theorem for Continuous Functions: A function $y = f(x)$ that is continuous on a closed interval $[a, b]$ takes on every y-value between $f(a)$ and $f(b)$.

Intermediate Value Theorem for Derivatives: If a and b are any two points in an interval on which f is differentiable, then f' takes on every value between $f'(a)$ and $f'(b)$.

Interior point of a region in space: A point (x_0, y_0, z_0) in a region R that lies at the center of a solid sphere that lies entirely in R. The interior points of the region, as a set, make up the *interior of the region.*

Interior point of a region in the plane: A point (x_0, y_0) in a region R that lies at the center of a disk that lies entirely in R. The interior points of the region, as a set, make up the *interior of the region.*

Interval: A subset of the number line formed by any of the following: (1) two points and the points in between; (2) only the points in between two points; (3) the points in between two points and one of the two points; (4) one point and the points to one side of it; (5) only the points to one side of a given point. The real line is also considered to be an interval.

Interval of convergence: The interval of x-values for which a power series converges. See also *Power series.*

Inverse function f^{-1}: The function obtained by reversing the ordered pairs of a one-to-one function f.

Iterated integral: A multiple integral that is evaluated by repeated single-variable integrations.

Jacobian determinant (Jacobian): The Jacobian determinant of the coordinate transformation $x = g(u, v)$, $y = h(u, v)$ is

$$J(u, v) = \begin{vmatrix} \frac{\partial x}{\partial u} & \frac{\partial x}{\partial v} \\ \frac{\partial y}{\partial u} & \frac{\partial y}{\partial v} \end{vmatrix} = \frac{\partial x}{\partial u}\frac{\partial y}{\partial v} - \frac{\partial y}{\partial u}\frac{\partial x}{\partial v}.$$

Jerk: The derivative of an acceleration function with respect to time.

Jump discontinuity: A point of discontinuity where the one-sided limits exist but have different values. At such a point, the function jumps from one value to another.

Kepler's first law (the Conic Section Law): A planet's path about its sun is a conic section with the sun at one focus.

Kepler's second law (the Equal Area Law): The radius vector from a sun to one of its planets sweeps out equal areas in equal times.

Kepler's third law (the Time Distance Law): A planet's orbital period T about a sun of mass M is related to the orbit's semimajor axis a by the equation $T^2/a^3 = 4\pi^2/GM$ where G is the universal gravitational constant.

Kilogram: See *Mass.*

Lagrange error bound: A bound for truncation error obtained from the Lagrange form of the remainder for a Taylor series.

Lagrange form of the remainder: The formula

$$\frac{f^{n+1}(c)}{(n+1)!}(x - a)^{n+1}$$

for the remainder in Taylor's Theorem.

Lagrange multiplier method: A method for finding extreme values of a function $f(x, y, z)$ whose variables are subject to a constraint $g(x, y, z) = 0$. The extreme values of f are found at points on the surface $g(x, y, z) = 0$ where ∇f is a scalar multiple λ of ∇g. The multiplier λ in the equation $\nabla f = \lambda \nabla g$ is called a **Lagrange multiplier,** after Joseph Louis Lagrange (1736-1813).

Law of exponential change: If a quantity y changes at a rate proportional to the amount present ($dy/dt = ky$) and $y = y_0$ when $t = 0$, then

$$y = y_0 e^{kt},$$

where $k > 0$ represents growth and $k < 0$ represents decay. The number k is the *rate constant.*

Left end behavior model: See *End behavior model.*

Left-hand derivative: The derivative defined by a left-hand limit.

Left-hand limit: The limit of f as x approaches c from the left, or $\lim_{x\to c^-} f(x)$.

Length (magnitude) of a vector: The length (magnitude) of $\mathbf{v} = \langle v_1, v_2 \rangle$ is $|\mathbf{v}| = \sqrt{v_1^2 + v_2^2}$.

Level curve: A set of points in the plane where a function $f(x, y)$ has a constant value $f(x, y) = c$.

L'Hôpital's Rule: Suppose that $f(a) = g(a) = 0$, that f and g are differentiable on an open interval I containing a, and that $g'(x) \neq 0$ on I if $x \neq a$. Then

$$\lim_{x\to a} \frac{f(x)}{g(x)} = \lim_{x\to a} \frac{f'(x)}{g'(x)},$$

provided the limit exists (or is $\pm\infty$). L'Hôpital's Rule also applies to quotients that lead to ∞/∞. If $f(x)$ and $g(x)$ both approach ∞ as $x \to a$, then

$$\lim_{x\to a} \frac{f(x)}{g(x)} = \lim_{x\to a} \frac{f'(x)}{g'(x)},$$

provided the latter limit exists (or is $\pm\infty$). In this case, a may itself be either finite or infinite.

Limit: The function f has limit L as x approaches c if, given any positive number ε, there exists a positive number δ such that for all x,

$$0 < |x - c| < \delta \quad \Rightarrow \quad |f(x) - L| < \varepsilon.$$

This is represented as $\lim_{x\to c} f(x) = L$.

Limit at infinity: The function f has limit L as x approaches ∞ if, given any positive number ε, there exists a positive number N such that for all $x > N$, $|f(x) - L| < \varepsilon$. This is represented as $\lim_{x\to\infty} f(x) = L$.

The function f has limit L as x approaches $-\infty$ if, given any positive number ε, there is a negative number N such that for all x with $x < N$, $|f(x) - L| < \varepsilon$. This is represented as $\lim_{x\to-\infty} f(x) = L$.

The sequence $f(n) = x_n$ has limit L, if $\lim_{n\to\infty} f(n) = L$.

Limit of a sequence: See *Limit at infinity.*

Limit of a vector function: If $\lim_{t \to c} f(t) = L_1$, $\lim_{t \to c} g(t) = L_2$, $\lim_{t \to c} h(t) = L_3$, and $\mathbf{r}(t) = f(t)\mathbf{i} + g(t)\mathbf{j} + h(t)\mathbf{k}$, then $\lim_{t \to c} \mathbf{r}(t) = L_1\mathbf{i} + L_2\mathbf{j} + L_3\mathbf{k}$.

Limit of a function of two independent variables: The function $f(x, y)$ has limit L as (x, y) approaches (x_0, y_0) if, given any positive number ε, there exist a positive number δ such that for all(x, y) in the domain of f, $0 < \sqrt{(x - x_0)^2 + (y - y_0)^2} < \delta \Rightarrow |f(x, y) - L| < \varepsilon$. We write $\lim_{(x, y) \to (x_0, y_0)} f(x, y) = L$. Similar definitions hold for functions if three and more independent variables.

Limits of integration: a and b in $\int_a^b f(x)\,dx$.

Linear approximation (standard) of *f* at *a*: The approximation $f(x) \approx L(x)$, where $L(x)$ is the linearization of f at a.

Linear equation: See *General linear equation.*

Linear function: A function that can be expressed in the form $f(x) = mx + b$.

Linearization of *f* at *a*: The approximating function $L(x) = f(a) + f'(a)(x - a)$ when f is differentiable at $x = a$.

Local extrema: See *Local maximum; Local minimum.*

Local linearity: If a function $f(x)$ is differentiable at $x = a$, then, close to a, its graph resembles the tangent line at a.

Local linearization: See *Linearization of f at a.*

Local maximum: The function f has a local maximum value $f(c)$ at a point c in the interior of its domain if and only if $f(x) \le f(c)$ for all x in some open interval containing c. The function has a local maximum value at an endpoint c if the inequality holds for all x in some half-open domain interval containing c.

Local minimum: The function f has a local minimum value $f(c)$ at a point c in the interior of its domain if and only if $f(x) \ge f(c)$ for all x in some open interval containing c. The function has a local minimum value at an endpoint c if the inequality holds for all x in some half-open domain interval containing c.

Logarithm function with base *a*: The function $y = \log_a x$, which is the inverse of the exponential function $y = a^x$, $a > 0$, $a \ne 1$.

Logarithmic differentiation: The process of taking the natural logarithm of both sides of an equation, differentiating, and then solving for the desired derivative.

Logistic curve: A solution curve of the logistic differential equation. It describes population growth that begins slowly when the population is small, speeds up as the number of reproducing individuals increases and nutrients are still plentiful, and slows down again as the population reaches the carrying capacity of its environment.

Logistic differential equation:

$$\frac{dP}{dt} = kP(M - P),$$

where P is current population, t is time, M is the carrying capacity of the environment, and k is a positive proportionality constant.

Logistic growth model: The solution

$$P = \frac{M}{1 + Ae^{-(Mk)t}},$$

to the logistic differential equation, A an arbitrary constant. This model assumes that the relative growth rate of a population is positive but decreases as the population increases due to environmental and economic factors. See also *Logistic differential equation.*

Lower bound: See *Bounded.*

LRAM: Left-hand endpoint rectangular approximation method. The method of approximating a definite integral over an interval using the function values at the left-hand endpoints of the subintervals determined by a partition.

Maclaurin series: See *Taylor series.*

Magnitude: Of a number, its absolute value; of a vector, its length.

Mass: When a body is acted upon by no force or by a zero resultant force (the applied forces cancel), it moves with a constant velocity and zero acceleration. But what happens when the resultant force is not zero? If the body is initially at rest, it starts to move. If it is initially moving, the force may speed it up, slow it down, or change direction of its velocity. In each case, the body undergoes an acceleration (velocity change). We want to know the relation of the acceleration to the force, and that is what Newton's second law of motion, $F = ma$, is about.

Experiments with pucks on air-hockey tables show that if we apply a horizontal force at constant magnitude, the body's velocity changes at a constant rate during the time the force is applied. If we double the force, the velocity changes at twice the rate. If we halved the force, the velocity changes at half the rate. For a given body, the ratio F/a of the force to the acceleration it produces is constant, regardless of the magnitude of the force. We call this ratio the **mass** of the body. If we denote the mass by m, then $m = F/a$, or $F = ma$. If a large force is needed to give a body a certain acceleration (think of pushing a car), the mass is large. When only a small force is needed to give a body the same acceleration (think of pushing a bicycle), the mass is small. The mass is a quantitative measure of the body's inertia, its tendency to remain at rest or to keep moving once it is set in motion.

The SI unit of mass is the **kilogram,** officially defined to be the mass of a block of platinum-iridium alloy kept in a vault near Paris, France. This standard kilogram and the equation $F = ma$ are used to define the **newton,** one newton being the amount of force that gives an acceleration of one meter per second squared to a body with a mass of one kilogram. It takes a force of about one newton to lift an apple from a table.

In many bodies, the mass is not evenly distributed but varies from place to place. Snow in the mountains packs down during the winter to become heavier at the bottom than at the surface. We describe this situation by saying that the snow becomes denser as you go down, that its **density** (mass per unit volume) is greater at the bottom than at the top. (The densities of metal plates are measured in units of mass per unit area. The densities of wires, springs, and slender rods are measured in units of mass per unit length.)

The function that gives a body's density at each point is called its **density function.** Once we know this function, we can calculate the body's mass by integrating the function over the region occupied by the body.

Maximum: See *Absolute maximum; Local maximum.*

Mean value: See *Average value of a continuous function on [a, b].*

Mean Value Theorem for Definite Integrals: If f is continuous on $[a, b]$, then at some point c in $[a, b]$,

$$f(c) = \frac{1}{b-a}\int_a^b f(x)\,dx.$$

Mean Value Theorem for Derivatives: If $y = f(x)$ is continuous at every point of the closed interval $[a, b]$ and differentiable at every point of its interior (a, b), then there is at least one point c in (a, b) at which

$$f'(c) = \frac{f(b) - f(a)}{b - a}.$$

Midpoint of a line segment: In space, the midpoint of the line segment joining points $P_1(x_1, y_1, z_1)$ and $P_2(x_2, y_2, z_2)$ is the point

$$\left(\frac{x_1 + x_2}{2}, \frac{y_1 + y_2}{2}, \frac{z_1 + z_2}{2}\right).$$

Minimum: See *Absolute minimum; Local minimum.*

Mixed derivative theorem (Euler's Theorem): If f_x, f_y, f_{xy}, and f_{yx} are defined throughout an open region containing a point (a, b) and are all continuous at (a, b), then $f_{xy}(a, b) = f_{yx}(a, b)$.

Moment of inertia (second moment): For thin plates covering a region R in the xy-plane:

About the x-axis:

$$I_x = \iint_R y^2 \delta(x, y)\,dA.$$

About the y-axis:

$$I_y = \iint_R x^2(x, y)\,dA.$$

About the origin (polar moment):

$$I_0 = \iint_R (x^2 + y^2)\,\delta(x, y)\,dA = I_x + I_y.$$

About a line L:

$$I_L = \iint_R r^2(x, y)\,\delta(x, y)\,dA,$$

where $r(x, y)$ is the distance from (x, y) to L. There are similar formulas for moments of inertia of solids, curves, and thin shells in space.

Monotonic (monotone) function: A function that is always increasing on an interval or always decreasing on an interval. .

Monotonic sequence: See *Monotonic function.*

MRAM: Midpoint rectangular approximation method. The method of approximating a definite integral over an interval using the function values at the midpoints of the subintervals determined by a partition.

Multivariable function: If D is a set of n-tuples $(x_1, x_2, \ldots, x_n)$, a *real-valued function* $w = f(x_1, x_2, \ldots, x_n)$ that assigns a real number to each element in D is called a multivariable function with domain D. The range is the set of w-values taken on by f. The dependent or output variable is w, and x_1 to x_n are the independent or input variables.

Natural logarithm: a is the natural logarithm of b if and only if $b = e^a$. The natural logarithm function $y = \ln x$ is the inverse of the exponential function $y = e^x$.

NDER($f(x)$, a): The numerical derivative of f at $x = a$.

Newton (unit of force): See *Mass.*

Newton's dot notation: $\dot{x}$ means dx/dt, $\ddot{x}$ means d^2x/dt^2, $\dddot{x}$ *means* d^3x/dt^3, and so on.

NINT($f(x)$, x, a, b): The numerical integral of f with respect to x, from $x = a$ to $x = b$.

Nonremovable discontinuity: A discontinuity that is not removable. See also *Removable discontinuity.*

Norm of a partition: The longest subinterval length, denoted $\|P\|$, for a partition P.

Normal component of acceleration:

$$a_N = \kappa\left(\frac{ds}{dt}\right)^2 = \kappa|\mathbf{v}|^2.$$

Normal curve: The graph of a normal probability density function.

Normal line to a curve at a point: The line perpendicular to the tangent at that point.

Normal line at point on surface: The line through P_0 parallel to $\nabla f|_{P_0}$.

Normal plane: The plane determined by **N** and **B.**

Normal probability density function: The normal probability density function for a population with *mean* μ and *standard deviation* σ is

$$f(x) = \frac{1}{\sigma\sqrt{2\pi}}e^{-(x-\mu)^2/(2\sigma^2)}.$$

The mean μ represents the average value of the variable x. The standard deviation σ measures the "scatter" around the mean.

Numerical derivative: An approximation of the derivative of a function using a numerical algorithm.

Numerical integration: Approximating the integral of a function using a numerical algorithm.

Numerical method: A method for generating a numerical solution of a problem. For example, a method for estimating the value of a definite integral, for estimating the zeros of a function or solutions of an equation, or for estimating values of the function that solves an initial value problem.

Numerical solution: Of an equation $f(x) = 0$, an estimate of one or more of its roots; of an initial value problem, a table of estimated values of the solution function.

Octants: See *Coordinate planes.*

Odd function: A function f for which $f(-x) = -f(x)$ for every x in the domain of f.

One-sided limit: See *Left-hand limit; Right-hand limit.*

One-to-one function: A function f for which $f(a) \neq f(b)$ whenever $a \neq b$.

Open interval (a, b): All numbers x with $a < x < b$.

Open region in plane or space: A region that consists entirely of interior points.

Optimization: In an application, maximizing or minimizing some aspect of the system being modeled.

Orbital period: The time it takes a planet to go around its sun once.

Order of a derivative: If y is a function of x, $y' = dy/dx$ is the first order, or first, derivative of y with respect to x; $y'' = d^2y/dx^2$ is the second order, or second, derivative of y; $y^{(n)} = dy^{(n-1)}/dx$ is the nth order, or nth, derivative of y.

Order of a differential equation: The order of the highest order derivative in the equation.

Orientable surface: A smooth surface S is orientable or two-sided if it is possible to define a field $\mathbf{n}$ of unit normal vectors on S that varies continuously with position. Once $\mathbf{n}$ is chosen, the surface is *oriented* and the surface together with its normal field is an *oriented surface.* The vector $\mathbf{n}$ at any point is the *positive direction* at that point.

Origin: The point (0, 0) in the Cartesian coordinate plane; the point (0, 0) in the polar coordinate plane. The point (0, 0, 0) in three-dimensional space.

Orthogonal curves: See *Perpendicular curves.*

Orthogonal Gradient Theorem: If $f(x, y, z)$ is differentiable in a region whose interior contains a smooth curve C and P_0 is a point of C where f has a local maximum or minimum relative to its values on C, then ∇f is orthogonal (normal) to C at P_0.

Orthogonal vectors: Vectors making a 90° angle.

Oscillating discontinuity: A point near which the function values oscillate too much for the function to have a limit.

Osculating circle: See *Circle of curvature.*

Osculating plane: The plane determined by **N** and **T.**

Paraboloid of revolution: See *Circular paraboloid.*

Parallel curves: In the plane, curves that differ from one another by a vertical translation (shift).

Parameter: See *Parametric equations.*

Parameter domain: See *Parametrization of a surface.*

Parameter interval: See *Parametric equations.*

Parametric equations: If x and y are given as functions $x = f(t)$, $y = g(t)$, over an interval of t-values, then the set of points $(x, y) = (f(t), g(t))$ defined by these equations is a *parametric curve*; the equations are *parametric equations* for the curve; the variable t is the *parameter* for the curve; and the interval of allowable t-values is the *parameter interval.*

Parametric equations for a line: The standard parametrization of the line through $P_0(x_0, y_0, z_0)$ parallel to the vector $\mathbf{v} = A\mathbf{i} + B\mathbf{j} + C\mathbf{k}$ is $x = x_0 + tA$, $y = y_0 + tB$, $z = z_0 + tC$, $-\infty < t < \infty$. 8

Parametric formula for surface area: See *Surface area.*

Parametrization of a curve: The parametric equations and parameter interval describing a curve.

Parametrization of a surface: If $\mathbf{r}(u, v) = f(u, v)\mathbf{i} + g(u, v)\mathbf{j} + h(u, v)\mathbf{k}$ is a continuous vector function that is defined on a region R in the uv-plane and one-to-one on the interior of R, then the range of $\mathbf{r}$ is the *surface S* defined or traced by $\mathbf{r}$. The equation and the domain R together constitute a *parametrization* of the surface. The variables u and v are the *parameters,* and R is the *parameter domain.*

Partial derivative of a function: The partial derivative of $f(x, y)$ with respect to x at the point (x_0, y_0) is

$$\left.\frac{\partial f}{\partial x}\right|_{(x_0,y_0)} = \left.\frac{d}{dx} f(x, y_0)\right|_{(x_0,y_0)} = \lim_{h\to 0} \frac{f(x_0 + h, y_0) - f(x_0, y_0)}{h},$$

provided the limit exists. The partial derivative with respect to y has a similar definition.

Partial fractions: See *Antidifferentiation by partial fractions.*

Partial sum: See *Infinite series.*

Particular solution: The unique solution of a differential equation satisfying given initial condition or conditions.

Partition of an interval $[a, b]$: A set

$$\{x_0 = a, x_1, x_2, \dots, x_n = b\}$$

of points in $[a, b]$ numbered in order from left to right.

Path independent integral: See *Conservative field.*

Percentage change: See *Absolute, relative, and percentage change.*

Percentage error:

$$\frac{|\text{approximate value} - \text{exact value}|}{|\text{exact value}|} \times 100.$$

Perihelion position: The position of a planet in which it is closest to its sun.

Period of a periodic function *f*: The smallest positive number p for which $f(x + p) = f(x)$ for every value of x. See also *Periodic function.*

Periodic function: A function f for which there is a positive number p such that $f(x + p) = f(x)$ for every value of x.

Perpendicular Axis Theorem: The moment of inertia about the z-axis can be calculated as I_z, $I_z = I_x + I_y$.

Perpendicular (orthogonal) curves: Two curves are said to be perpendicular (orthogonal) at a point of intersection if their tangents at that point are perpendicular.

Perpendicular vectors: See *Orthogonal vectors.*

Piecewise-defined function: A function that is defined by applying different formulas to different parts of its domain.

Piecewise smooth curve: A curve made from a finite number of smooth curves pieced together in a continuous fashion.

Polar coordinates: Each point P in the polar coordinate plane has polar coordinates (r, θ), where r gives the directed distance from the origin O to P and θ gives a directed angle from the initial ray to ray OP.

Pole: In the polar coordinate plane, the origin.

Polynomial: An expression of the form

$$a_n x^n + a_{n-1}x^{n-1} + \cdots + a_1 x + a_0.$$

Position function: A function f that gives the position $f(t)$ of a body on a coordinate axis at time t.

Position vector: The vector $\langle a, b\rangle$ is the position vector of the point (a, b). Of a point $P(x, y, z)$ in space, the vector $\mathbf{r} = \overrightarrow{OP} = x\mathbf{i} + y\mathbf{j} + z\mathbf{k}$. Of a particle $P(f(t), g(t), h(t))$ moving along a parametrized curve $x = f(t)$, $y = g(t)$, $z = h(t)$ in space, the vector $\mathbf{r} = \overrightarrow{OP} = f(t)\mathbf{i} + g(t)\mathbf{k} + h(t)\mathbf{k}$.

Potential function: If $\mathbf{F}$ is a vector field defined on a region D, and if $\mathbf{F} = \nabla f$ for some scalar function f on D, then f is a potential function for $\mathbf{F}$.

Power series: An expression of the form

$$c_0 + c_1 x + c_2 x^2 + \cdots + c_n x^n + \cdots = \sum_{n=0}^{\infty} c_n x^n$$

is a power series centered at $x = 0$. An expression of the form

$$c_0 + c_1(x - a) + c_2(x - a)^2 + \cdots + c_n(x - a)^n + \cdots = \sum_{n=0}^{\infty} c_n(x - a)^n$$

is a power series centered at $x = a$. The number a is the *center* of the series.

Prime notation ($f'(x)$): If $y = f(x)$, then both y' and $f'(x)$ denote the derivative of the function with respect to x.

Principal unit normal vector N: At a point on a smooth curve where $\kappa \neq 0$,

$$\mathrm{N} = \frac{1}{\kappa}\frac{d\mathbf{T}}{ds}.$$

Probability: See *Probability density function.*

Probability density function (pdf): A function $f(x)$ such that $f(x) \geq 0$ for all x and $\int_{-\infty}^{\infty} f(x)\,dx = 1$. The *probability* associated with the interval $[a, b]$ is $\int_a^b f(x)\,dx$.

Product Rule: The product of two differentiable functions u and v is differentiable, and

$$\frac{d}{dx}(uv) = u\frac{dv}{dx} + v\frac{du}{dx}.$$

***p*-series:** A series of the form

$$\sum_{n=1}^{\infty} \frac{1}{n^p}, \quad p \text{ a nonzero constant.}$$

Quadric surface: The graph in space of a second-degree equation in x, y, z. The most general form is

$$Ax^2 + By^2 + Cz^2 + Dxy + Eyz + Fxz + Gx + Hy + Jz + K = 0.$$

Quotient Rule: At a point where $v \neq 0$, the quotient $y = u/v$ of two differentiable functions is differentiable, and

$$\frac{d}{dx}\left(\frac{u}{v}\right) = \frac{v\dfrac{du}{dx} - u\dfrac{dv}{dx}}{v^2}.$$

Radian measure: If a central angle of a circle of radius r intercepts an arc of length s on the circle, the radian measure of the angle is s/r.

Radius of convergence: In general, the positive number R for which the power series

$$\sum_{n=0}^{\infty} c_n(x - a)^n$$

converges when $|x - a| < R$ and diverges when $|x - a| > R$. If the series converges only for $x = a$, then $R = 0$. If the series converges for every x, then $R = \infty$.

Radius of curvature: See *Circle of curvature.*

Radius of gyration: The radius of gyration R_L of an object of mass M about a line L is defined by the equation $I_L = MR_L^2$. It tells how far from L the entire mass might be concentrated to give the same moment of inertia I_L. The radius of gyration gives a convenient way to express the moment of inertia in terms of a mass and a length.

Range of a function: See *Function* and *Multivariable function.*

Rate constant: See *Law of exponential change.*

Rate of change: See *Average rate of change of a quantity over a period of time; Instantaneous rate of change of f with respect to x at a.*

Ratio Test: Let $\sum a_n$ be a series with positive terms and with

$$\lim_{n\to\infty} \frac{a_{n+1}}{a_n} = L.$$

Then (1) the series converges if $L < 1$; (2) the series diverges if $L > 1$; (3) the test is inconclusive if $L = 1$.

Rational function: A function that can be expressed as the quotient of two polynomial functions.

Rectifying plane: The plane determined by **B** and **T.**

Regression analysis: The process of finding a curve to fit data.

Regular partition: A partition in which consecutive points are equally spaced.

Related rate equation: An equation involving two or more variables that are differentiable functions of time that can be used to find an equation relating the corresponding rates.

Relative change: See *Absolute, relative, and percentage change.*

Relative extrema: Same as *Local extrema.*

Relative maximum: Same as *Local maximum.*

Relative minimum: Same as *Local minimum.*

Remainder of order *n*: The remainder

$$R_n(x) = \frac{f^{(n+1)}(c)}{(n+1)!}(x-a)^{n+1},$$

in Taylor's Theorem.

Removable discontinuity: A discontinuity c of the function f for which $f(c)$ can be (re)defined so that $\lim_{x\to c} f(x) = f(c)$.

Repeated integral: See *Iterated integral.*

Resultant vector: The vector that results from adding or subtracting two vectors.

Riemann sum: A sum of the form

$$\sum_{k=1}^{n} f(c_k) \cdot \Delta x_k,$$

where f is a continuous function on a closed interval $[a, b]$, c_k is some point in, and Δx_k is the length of the kth subinterval in some partition of $[a, b]$.

Right end behavior model: See *End behavior model.*

Right-hand derivative: The derivative defined by a right-hand limit.

Right-handed coordinate frame: A three-dimensional coordinate system with x-, y-, and z-axes such that when the right hand is held so that the fingers curl from the positive x-axis toward the positive y-axis, the thumb points along the positive z-axis.

Right-hand limit: The limit of f as x approaches c from the right, or $\lim_{x\to c^+} f(x)$.

Right-hand rule: The selection of a unit normal vector **n** to a plane determined by two vectors **A** and **B** in space such that **n** points the way a right thumb points when the fingers are curled through the angle from **A** to **B.**

Root of an equation: See *Zero of a function.*

Roundoff error: Error due to rounding.

RRAM: Right-hand endpoint rectangular approximation method. The method of approximating a definite integral over an interval using the function values at the right-hand endpoints of the subintervals determined by a partition.

Saddle point: A point on a surface that can look like a local minimum from one perspective and a local maximum from another perspective. It is sometimes called a *minimax* of the surface. For a surface $z = f(x, y)$, there is a saddle point at a critical point (a, b) if in every open disk centered at (a, b) there are domain points at which $f(x, y) > f(a, b)$ and domain points at which $f(x, y) < f(a, b)$.

Scalar: In the context of vectors, scalars are real numbers that behave like scaling factors.

Scalar component of B in the direction of A: The dot product of **B** with the direction of **A.**

Scalar function: Name used for real-valued functions to distinguish them from vector-valued functions.

Scalar multiple of a vector: $k\mathbf{u} = \langle ku_1, ku_2\rangle$, where k is a scalar (real number) and $\mathbf{u} = \langle u_1, u_2\rangle$.

Scalar product: See *Dot (inner) product*

Secant function: See *Basic trigonometric functions.*

Secant line to a curve: A line through two points on the curve.

Second derivative: If y is a function of x and $y' = dy/dx$ is the first derivative of y with respect to x, then $y'' = dy'/dx = d^2y/dx^2$ is the second derivative of y with respect to x.

Second derivative test for extreme values for functions of two variables: If $f(x, y)$ and its first and second partial derivatives are continuous throughout a disk centered at (a, b) and the first partial derivatives of f at (a, b) are 0, then

(1) f has a local maximum at (a, b) if $f_{xx} < 0$ and $f_{xx}f_{yy} - f_{xy}^2 > 0$ at (a, b);

(2) f has a local minimum at (a, b) if $f_{xx} > 0$ and $f_{xx}f_{yy} - f_{xy}^2 > 0$ at (a, b);

(3) f has a saddle point at (a, b) if $f_{xx}f_{yy} - f_{xy}^2 < 0$ at (a, b); and (4) the test is inconclusive at (a, b) if $f_{xx}f_{yy} - f_{xy}^2 = 0$ at (a, b).

Second derivative test for local extrema: If $f'(c) = 0$ and $f''(c) < 0$, then f has a local maximum at $x = c$. If $f'(c) = 0$ and $f''(c) > 0$, then f has a local minimum at $x = c$.

Second moment: See *Moment of inertia.*

Second-order partial derivatives: Derivatives obtained from a function by two successive partial differentiations.

Separable differential equation: A differential equation $y' = f(x, y)$ in which f can be expressed as a product of a function of x and a function of y.

Separating the variables: For a separable differential equation $y' = f(x, y)$, the process of combining all the y-terms with y' on one side of the equation and putting all the x-terms on the other side.

Sequence: A function whose domain is the set of positive integers.

Sigma notation: Notation using the Greek letter capital sigma, Σ, for writing lengthy sums in compact form.

Simple harmonic motion: Periodic motion, like the vertical motion of a weight bobbing up and down at the end of a spring, that can be modeled with a sinusoidal position function.

Simply connected region: A region D in which every closed path in D can be contracted to a point in D without ever leaving the region.

Sine function: See *Basic trigonometric functions.*

Slope field: A slope field for the first-order differential equation $dy/dx = f(x, y)$ is a plot of short line segments with slopes $f(x, y)$ at a lattice of points (x, y) in the plane.

Slope of a curve: The slope of a curve $y = f(x)$ at the point $(a, f(a))$ is $f'(a)$, provided f is differentiable at a.

Smooth curve: The graph of a smooth function.

Smooth function: A real-valued function $y = f(x)$ with a continuous first derivative. A vector function whose first derivative is continuous and never zero.

Smooth parametrized curve: A plane curve $x = f(t)$, $y = g(t)$ for which the derivatives f' and g' are continuous and not simultaneously zero. A space curve $x = f(t)$, $y = g(t)$, $z = h(t)$ for which f', g' and h' are continuous and not simultaneously zero.

Smooth parametrized surface: A parametrized surface $\mathbf{r}(u, v) = f(u, v)\mathbf{i} + g(u, v)\mathbf{j} + h(u, v)\mathbf{k}$ whose partial derivatives $\mathbf{r}_u$ and $\mathbf{r}_v$ are continuous and whose cross-product $\mathbf{r}_u \times \mathbf{r}_v$ is never zero on the parameter domain.

Smooth surface: A surface $f(x, y, z) = c$ on which ∇f is continuous and never vanishes.

Smooth vector curve: Curve traced by a smooth vector function. See also *Smooth function.*

Solid of revolution: A solid generated by revolving a plane region about a line in the plane.

Solution of a differential equation: Any function that together with its derivatives satisfies the equation. When we find all such functions, we have *solved* the differential equation.

Space curve: When a particle $P(x, y, z)$ moves through space, we think of the particle's coordinates as functions $x = f(t)$, $y = g(t)$, $z = h(t)$ defined on some interval I. The curve traced by P as the parameter t runs through I is called a space curve.

Speed: The absolute value, or magnitude, of velocity.

Spherical coordinates: Coordinates of the point P in the form (ρ, ϕ, θ), where ρ is the distance from the origin to the point, ϕ is the angle $\overrightarrow{OP}$ makes with the positive z-axis $(0 \leq \phi \leq \pi)$. and θ is the angle from cylindrical coordinates.

Spherical wedge: The three-dimensional figure, shaped like a slice of pie, defined by spherical coordinate differentials $d\rho$, $d\phi$, and $d\theta$.

Standard equation for a sphere: The standard equation for a sphere of radius a and center (x_0, y_0, z_0) is $(x - x_0)^2 + (y - y_0)^2 + (z - z_0)^2 = a^2$.

Standard linear approximation: The standard linear approximation of f at (x_0, y_0) is the function $L(x, y) = f(x_0, y_0) + f_x(x_0, y_0)(x - x_0) + f_y(x_0, y_0)(y - y_0)$.

Standard position of a vector: The representative vector with initial point at the origin.

Standard unit vectors: In the plane, the vectors $\mathbf{i} = \langle 1, 0 \rangle$, $\mathbf{j} = \langle 0, 1 \rangle$. In space, the vectors **i, j,** and **k** defined by the directed line segments from the origin to the points (1, 0, 0), (0, 1, 0), and (0, 0, 1), respectively.

Stokes's Theorem: The circulation of a vector field around the boundary of an oriented surface in space in the direction counterclockwise with respect to the surface's unit normal vector field equals the integral of the normal component of the curl of the field over the surface.

Sum of a series: See *Infinite series.*

Sum of vectors:

$$\mathbf{v} + \mathbf{u} = \langle v_1, v_2 \rangle + \langle u_1, u_2 \rangle = \langle v_1 + u_1, v_2 + u_2 \rangle$$

Surface: See *Parametrization of a surface* and *Graph of a function (x, y).*

Surface area

Gradient formula: The area of the surface $f(x, y, z) = c$ defined over a closed and bounded plane region R is

$$\iint_R \frac{|\nabla f|}{|\nabla f \cdot \mathbf{p}|}\, dA,$$

where $\mathbf{p}$ is a unit vector normal to R and $\nabla f \cdot \mathbf{p} \neq 0$.

Parametric formula: The area of the smooth surface $\mathbf{r}(u, v) = f(u, v)\mathbf{i} + g(u, v)\mathbf{j} + h(u, v)\mathbf{k},\ a \le u \le b,\ c \le v \le d$, is

$$A = \int_c^d \int_a^b |\mathbf{r}_u \times \mathbf{r}_v|\, du\, dv.$$

Surface area differential:

$$d\sigma = \frac{|\nabla f|}{|\nabla f \cdot \mathbf{p}|}\, dA,$$

or, for a parametrized surface,

$$d\sigma = |\mathbf{r}_u \times \mathbf{r}_v|\, du\, dv.$$

Surface integral: The integral of a function g over a surface S.

Symmetric difference quotient: The quotient

$$\frac{f(a + h) - f(a - h)}{2h}$$

that a graphing calculator uses to calculate NDER$(f(x), a)$, the numerical derivative of f at $x = a$.

Symmetry: For a curve to have

(1) symmetry about the x-axis, the point (x, y) must lie on the curve if and only if $(x, -y)$ lies on the curve;

(2) symmetry about the y-axis, the point (x, y) must lie on the curve if and only if $(-x, y)$ lies on the curve;

(3) symmetry about the origin, the point (x, y) must lie on the curve if and only if $(-x, -y)$ lies on the curve.

Tabular integration: A time-saving way to organize the work of repeated integrations by parts.

Tangent function: See *Basic trigonometric functions.*

Tangential component of acceleration:

$$a_{\mathrm{T}} = \frac{d^2 s}{dt^2} = \frac{d}{dt}|\mathbf{v}|.$$

Tangent line: To the graph of a function $y = f(x)$ at a point $x = a$ where f' exists, the line through $(a, f(a))$ with slope $f'(a)$.

To a parametrized curve at a point P where $dx/dt \neq 0$, the line through P with slope equal to the value of $(dy/dt)/(dx/dt)$ at P.

To a curve traced by a vector function $\mathbf{r}(t)$ at a point P where $\mathbf{v} \neq \mathbf{0}$, the line through P parallel to $\mathbf{v}$.

Tangent plane at a point on a surface: The plane tangent to a surface $f(x, y, z) = c$ at point P_0 is the plane through P_0 normal to $\nabla f|_{P_0}$.

Taylor polynomial: Let f be a function with derivatives through order n throughout some open interval containing 0. Then

$$P_n(x) = \sum_{k=0}^{n} \frac{f^{(k)}(0)}{k!} x^k$$

is the Taylor polynomial of order n for f at $x = 0$.

If f is a function with derivatives through order n throughout some open interval containing the point $x = a$, then

$$P_n(x) = \sum_{k=0}^{n} \frac{f^{(k)}(a)}{k!} (x - a)^k$$

is the Taylor polynomial of order n for f at $x = a$.

Taylor series: Let f be a function with derivatives of all orders throughout some open interval containing 0. Then

$$f(0) + f'(0)x + \frac{f''(0)}{2!}x^2 + \cdots + \frac{f^{(n)}(0)}{n!}x^n + \cdots = \sum_{k=0}^{\infty} \frac{f^{(k)}(0)}{k!}x^k,$$

is the Taylor series generated by f at $x = 0$. This series is also called the *Maclaurin series* generated by f.

If f is a function with derivatives of all orders throughout some open interval containing the point $x = a$, then

$$f(a) + f'(a)(x - a) + \frac{f''(a)}{2!}(x - a)^2 + \cdots + \frac{f^{(n)}(a)}{n!}(x - a)^n + \cdots,$$

$$\text{or } \sum_{k=0}^{\infty} \frac{f^{(k)}(a)}{k!}(x - a)^k,$$

is the Taylor series generated by f at $x = a$.

Term of a sequence or series: For the sequence

$$a_1, a_2, a_3, \ldots, a_n, \ldots,$$

or for the series

$$a_1 + a_2 + a_3 + \cdots + a_n + \cdots,$$

a_n is the nth term.

Time Distance Law: See *Kepler's third law.*

TNB (Frenet) frame: The right-handed frame made by the mutually orthogonal unit vectors **T**, **N**, and **B** (in that order).

Torque: When we turn a threaded bolt with a wrench, the resulting force *along the axis of that bolt* is called a torque.

Torsion: The torsion function of a smooth curve is

$$\tau = -\frac{d\mathbf{B}}{ds} \cdot \mathbf{N}.$$

Total differential: The change $df = f_x(x_0, y_0)\, dx + f_y(x_0, y_0)\, dy$ in the value of the linearization of $f(x, y)$ when the point of evaluation moves from (x_0, y_0) to $(x_0 + dx, y_0 + dy)$. Analogous definitions hold for functions of more than two independent variables.

Transcendental function: A function that is not algebraic. (See *Algebraic function.*) The six basic trigonometric functions are transcendental as are the inverse trigonometric functions and the exponential and logarithmic functions studied in this book.

Trapezoidal Rule: To approximate $\int_a^b f(x)\,dx$, use

$$T = \frac{h}{2}(y_0 + 2y_1 + 2y_2 + \cdots + 2y_{n-1} + y_n),$$

where $[a, b]$ is partitioned into n subintervals of equal length $h = (b - a)/n$ and y_i is the value of f at each partition point x_i.

Trigonometric function: See *Basic trigonometric functions.*

Triple integral of $F(x, y, z)$ over D:

$$\lim_{n\to\infty} \sum_{k=1}^{n} F(x_k, y_k, z_k)\,\Delta V_k = \iiint_D F(x, y, z)\,dV.$$

Triple scalar (box) product: A product of the form $(\mathbf{A} \times \mathbf{B}) \cdot \mathbf{C}$, where $\mathbf{A}, \mathbf{B}, \mathbf{C}$ are vectors in space.

Truncation error: The error incurred in using a finite partial sum to estimate the sum of an infinite series.

Two-sided limit: Limit at an interior point of a function's domain. See also *Limit.*

Two sided surface: See *Orientable surface.*

Unbounded region: A region that is not bounded.

Unit circle: The circle of radius 1 centered at the origin.

Unit tangent vector T: Every smooth curve $\mathbf{r} = f(t)\mathbf{i} + g(t)\mathbf{j} + h(t)\mathbf{k}$ has a unit tangent vector $\mathbf{T}$ defined by the equation

$$\mathbf{T} = \frac{d\mathbf{r}}{ds} = \frac{d\mathbf{r}/dt}{ds/dt} = \frac{\mathbf{v}}{|\mathbf{v}|}.$$

Unit vector: A vector with magnitude 1. See also *Standard unit vectors.*

Universal gravitational constant: The constant $G = 6.6720 \times 10^{-11}\ \mathrm{Nm^2\,kg^{-2}}$ in Newton's Law of Gravitation.

Upper bound: See *Bounded.*

***u*-substitution:** See *Antidifferentiation by substitution.*

Value of an improper integral: See *Improper integral.*

Variable of integration: In $\int f(x)\,dx$ or $\int_a^b f(x)\,dx$, the variable x.

Vector (cross) product: See *Cross (vector) product.*

Vector equation for a line: The vector equation for the line through $P_0(x_0, y_0, z_0)$ parallel to $\mathbf{v}$ is $\overrightarrow{PP_0} = t\mathbf{v}$, $-\infty < t < \infty$.

Vector equation for a plane: A point P lies in the plane through P_0 normal to $\mathbf{n}$ if and only if $\mathbf{n} \cdot \overrightarrow{PP_0} = 0$.

Vector field: A function on a domain in the plane or in space that assigns a vector to each point in the domain. The field is continuous if its component functions are continuous, differentiable if its component functions are differentiable, and so on.

Vector in the plane: A directed line segment in the plane, with the understanding that two such vectors are equal if they have the same length and direction.

Vector projection: A vector projection of a vector $\mathbf{B} = \overrightarrow{PQ}$ onto a nonzero vector $\mathbf{A} = \overrightarrow{PS}$ is the vector $\overrightarrow{PR}$ determined by dropping a perpendicular from Q to the point R on the line PS. If $\mathbf{B}$ represents a force, then $\overrightarrow{PR}$ represents the effective force in the direction of A.

Vector-valued function on a domain D: A rule that assigns a vector in space to each element of D.

Vector (vector-valued) function: The equation $\mathbf{r}(t) = f(t)\mathbf{i} + g(t)\mathbf{j} + h(t)\mathbf{k}$, $t \in I$, defines $\mathbf{r}$ as a vector function of t on the interval I. See also *Vector field.*

Velocity: The rate of change of position with respect to time. See also *Average velocity; Instantaneous velocity; Velocity vector.*

Velocity vector: If $<x(t), y(t)>$ is the position vector of a particle moving along a smooth curve in the plane, then at any time t, then $<x'(t), y'(t)>$ is the particle's velocity vector.

Vertical line: In the Cartesian coordinate plane, a line parallel to the y-axis.

Viewing window: On a graphing calculator, the portion of the coordinate plane displayed on the screen.

Volume by slicing: A method for finding the volume of a solid by evaluating $\int_a^b A(x)\,dx$, where $A(x)$ (assumed integrable) is the solid cross section area at x.

Work: The definite integral of force times the distance over which the force is applied.

In everyday life, *work* means an activity that requires muscular or mental effort. In science, the term refers specifically to a force $\mathbf{F}$ acting on a body and the body's subsequent displacement.

The work done by a force $\mathbf{F}$ along a smooth path C in space is the integral of $\mathbf{F} \cdot \mathbf{T}$, the effective force in the direction of motion at each point, over the length of the path: $W = \int_C \mathbf{F} \cdot \mathbf{T}\,ds$

This formula simplifies to $W = \mathbf{F} \cdot \mathbf{D}$ for a constant force $\mathbf{F}$ acting through a displacement $\mathbf{D} = \overrightarrow{PQ}$. It simplifies still further to $W = Fd$ for a force of constant magnitude F acting in the direction of the displacement over a distance d.

***x*-intercept:** The x-coordinate of the point where a curve intersects the x-axis.

***xy*-plane:** The plane in space whose standard equation is $z = 0$.

xz-plane: The plane in space whose standard equation is $y = 0$.

y-intercept: The y-coordinate of the point where a curve intersects the y-axis.

yz-plane: The plane in space whose standard equation is $x = 0$.

Zero of a function: A solution of the equation $f(x) = 0$ is a zero of the function f or a *root* of the equation.

Zero vector: The vector <0, 0>, which has zero length and no direction. In the plane, the vector $\mathbf{0} = 0\mathbf{i} + 0\mathbf{j}$. In space, the vector $\mathbf{0} = 0\mathbf{i} + 0\mathbf{j} + 0\mathbf{k}$.

Answers to Odd-Numbered Questions

CHAPTER 1

Section 1.1

Exercises 1.1

1. -2 **3.** -1 **5. (a)** Yes **(b)** No

7. $\sqrt{2}$ **9.** $y = \frac{4}{3}x - \frac{7}{3}$

Exercises 1.1

1. $\Delta x = -2, \Delta y = -3$ **3.** $\Delta x = -5, \Delta y = 0$

5. (a) and **(c)**, **(b)** 3

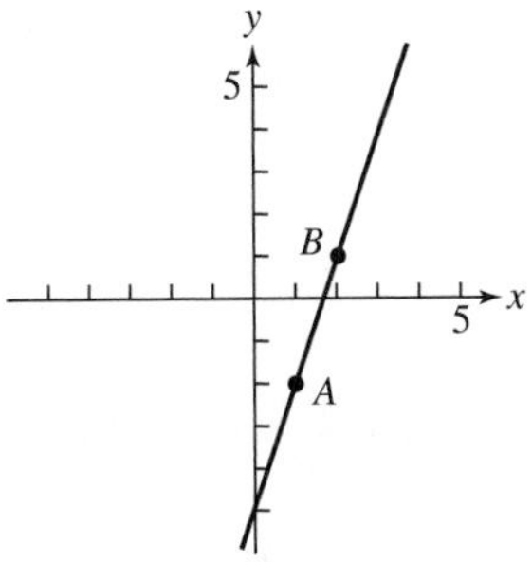

7. (a) and **(c)**, **(b)** 0

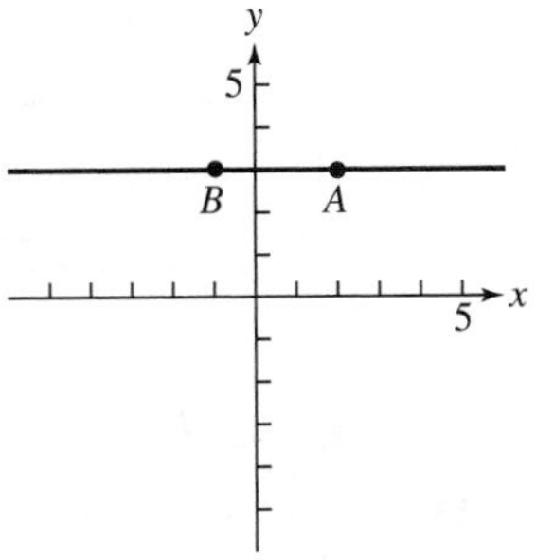

9. $x = 3; y = 2$ **11.** $x = 0; y = -\sqrt{2}$ **13.** $y = 1(x - 1) + 1$

15. $y = 2(x - 0) + 3$ **17.** $y = 3x - 2$

19. $y = -\frac{1}{2}x - 3$ **21.** $3x - 2y = 0$

23. $x = -2$ **25.** $y = \frac{5}{2}x$

27. (a) $-\frac{3}{4}$ **(b)** 3

(c)

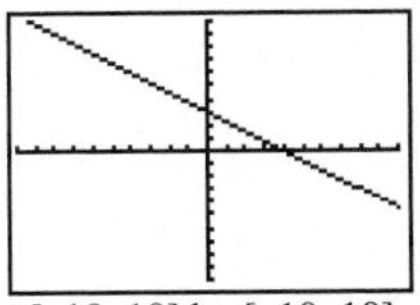

[−10, 10] by [−10, 10]

29. (a) $-\frac{4}{3}$ **(b)** 4 **(c)**

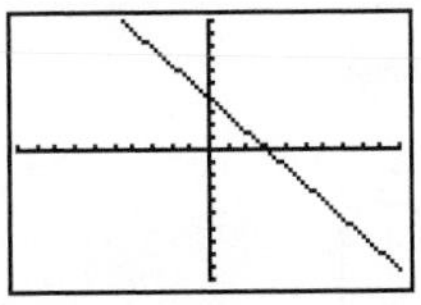

[−10, 10] by [−10, 10]

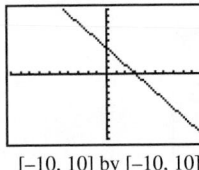

31. (a) $y = -x$ **(b)** $y = x$ **33. (a)** $x = -2$ **(b)** $y = 4$

35. $m = \frac{7}{2}, b = -\frac{3}{2}$ **37.** $y = -1$

39. $y = 1(x - 3) + 4$
$y = x - 3 + 4$
$y = x + 1$, which is the same equation.

41. (a) $k = 2$ **(b)** $k = -2$

43. 5.97 atmospheres ($k = 0.0994$)

45. (a) $y = 2216.2x - 4387470.6$

(b) 2216.2; it represents the approximate rate of increase in earnings in dollars per year.

(c)

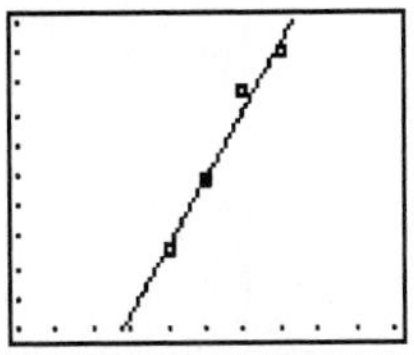

[1995, 2005] by [40000, 50000]

(d) about $62,659

47. False. A vertical line has no slope.

49. A **51.** D

53. (a) $y = 5980x - 11{,}810{,}220$

(b) The rate at which the median price is increasing in dollars per year

(c) $y = 21650x - 43{,}105{,}030$

(d) South: $5,980 per year, West: $21,650 per year; more rapidly in the West

55. The coordinates of the three missing vertices are $(5, 2)$, $(-1, 4)$ and $(-1, -2)$.

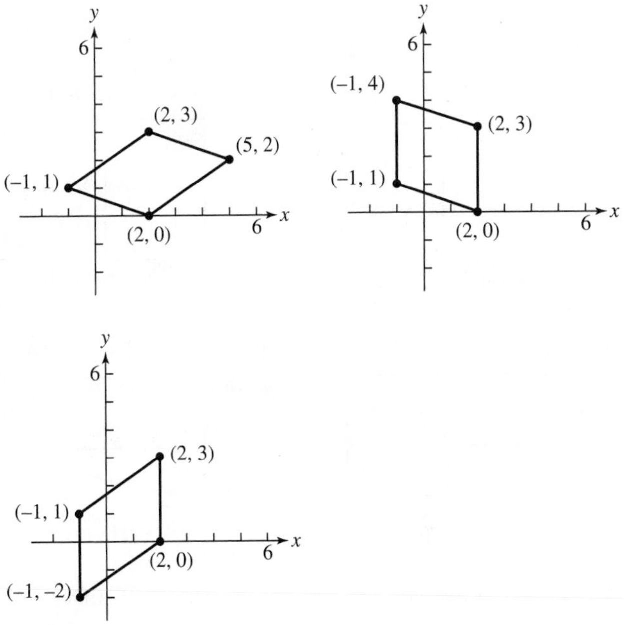

57. $y = -\frac{3}{4}(x - 3) + 4$ or $y = -\frac{3}{4}x + \frac{25}{4}$

Section 1.2

Exercises 1.2

1. $[-2, \infty)$ **3.** $[-1, 7]$ **5.** $(-4, 4)$

7. Translate the graph of f 2 units left and 3 units downward.

9. (a) $x = -3, 3$ **(b)** No real solution

11. (a) $x = 9$ **(b)** $x = -6$

Exercises 1.2

1. (a) $A(d) = \pi\left(\frac{d}{2}\right)^2$ **(b)** $A(4) = 4\pi \text{ in}^2$

3. (a) $S(e) = 6e^2$ **(b)** $S(5) = 150 \text{ ft}^2$

5. (a) $(-\infty, \infty); (-\infty, 4]$

(b)

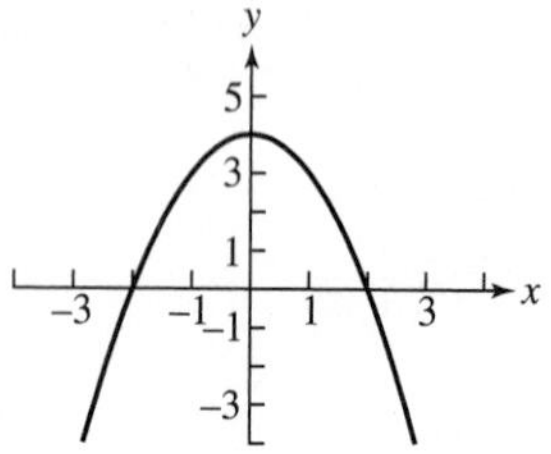

7. (a) $[1, \infty); [2, \infty)$

(b)

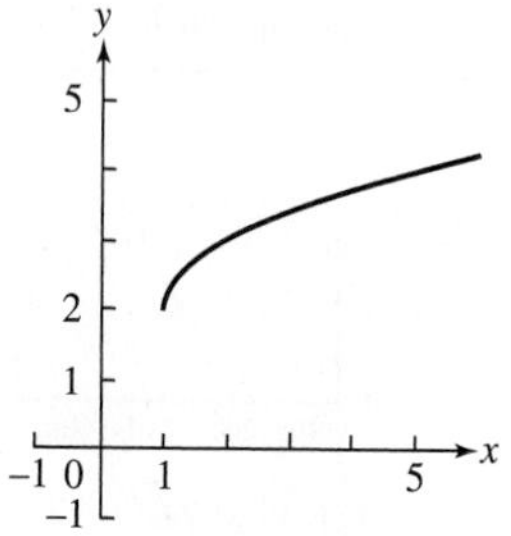

9. (a) $(-\infty, 2) \cup (2, \infty);$ $(-\infty, 0) \cup (0, \infty)$

(b)

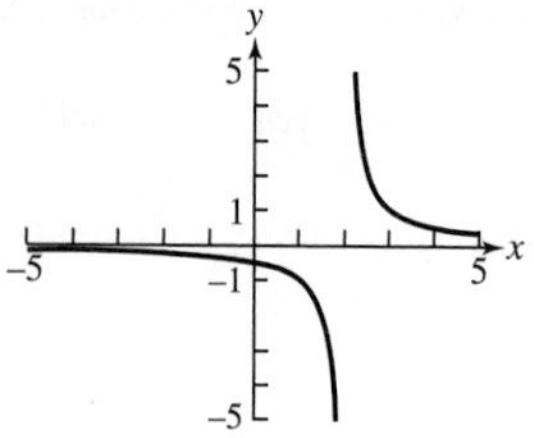

11. (a) $(-\infty, 0) \cup(0, \infty);$ $(-\infty, 1)\cup (1, \infty)$

(b)

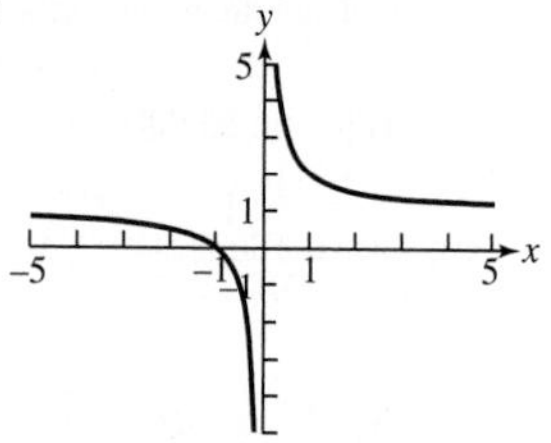

13. (a) $(-\infty, \infty); (-\infty, \infty)$

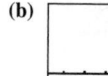

(b)

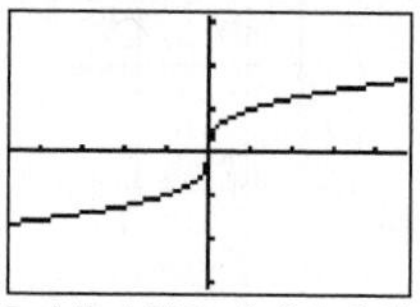

[–4.7, 4.7] by [–3.1, 3.1]

15. (a) $(-\infty, \infty); (-\infty, 1]$

(b)

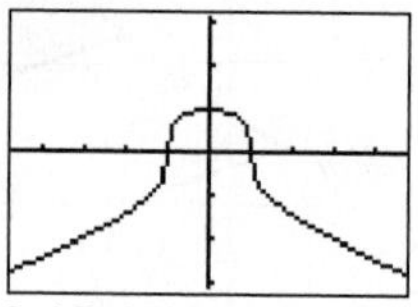

[–4.7, 4.7] by [–3.1, 3.1]

17. (a) $(-\infty, \infty); [0, \infty)$

(b)

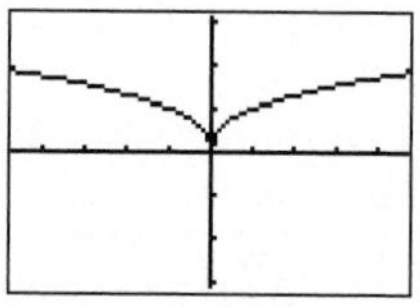

[–4.7, 4.7] by [–3.1, 3.1]

19. (a) $(-\infty, \infty); (-\infty; \infty)$

(b)

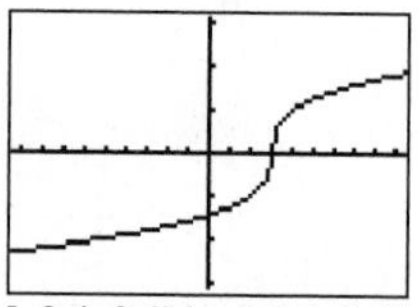

[–9.4, 9.4] by [–3.1, 3.1]

21. Even **23.** Neither **25.** Even **27.** Odd **29.** Neither

31.

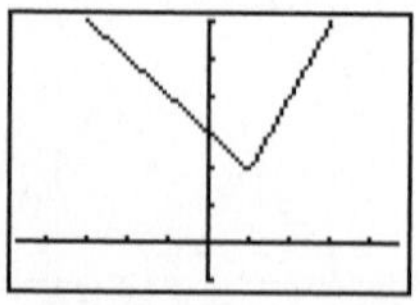

[–4.7, 4.7] by [–1, 6]

33.

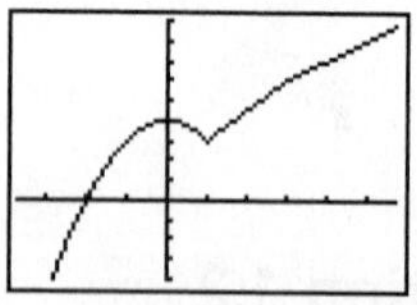

[–3.7, 5.7] by [–4, 9]

35. Because if the vertical line test holds, then for each x-coordinate, there is at most one y-coordinate giving a point on the curve. This y-coordinate would correspond to the value assigned to the x-coordinate. Since there's only one y-coordinate, the assignment would be unique.

37. No **39.** Yes

41. $f(x) = \begin{cases} x, & 0 \le x \le 1 \\ 2 - x, & 1 < x \le 2 \end{cases}$

43. $f(x) = \begin{cases} 2 - x, & 0 < x \le 2 \\ \frac{5}{3} - \frac{x}{3}, & 2 < x \le 5 \end{cases}$

45. $f(x) = \begin{cases} -x, & -1 \le x < 0 \\ 1, & 0 < x \le 1 \\ \frac{3}{2} - \frac{x}{2}, & 1 < x < 3 \end{cases}$

47. $f(x) = \begin{cases} 0, & 0 \le x \le \frac{T}{2} \\ \frac{2}{T}x - 1, & \frac{T}{2} < x \le T \end{cases}$

49. (a)

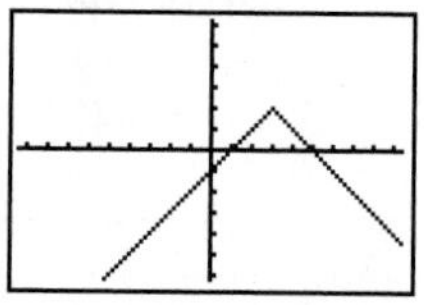

[–9.4, 9.4] by [–6.2, 6.2]

(b) All reals **(c)** $(-\infty, 2]$

51. (a) $x^2 + 2$ **(b)** $x^2 + 10x + 22$ **(c)** 2 **(d)** 22 **(e)** -2 **(f)** $x + 10$

53. (a) $g(x) = x^2$ **(b)** $g(x) = \frac{1}{x - 1}$ **(c)** $f(x) = \frac{1}{x}$ **(d)** $f(x) = x^2$

55. (a) Because the circumference of the original circle was 8π and a piece of length x was removed. **(b)** $r = \frac{8\pi - x}{2\pi} = 4 - \frac{x}{2\pi}$

(c) $h = \sqrt{16 - r^2} = \frac{\sqrt{16\pi x - x^2}}{2\pi}$

(d) $V = -\frac{1}{3}\pi r^2 h = \frac{(8\pi - x)^2\sqrt{16\pi x - x^2}}{24\pi^2}$

57. False. $f(-x) \ne f(x)$ **59.** B **61.** D

63. (a) For $f \circ g$:

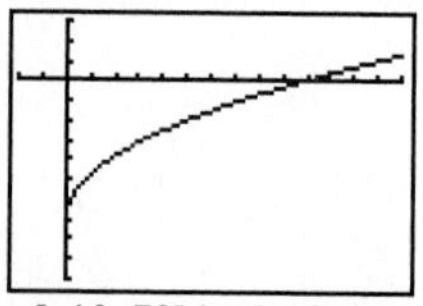

[–10, 70] by [–10, 3]

Domain: $[0, \infty)$; Range: $[-7, \infty)$

For $g \circ f$:

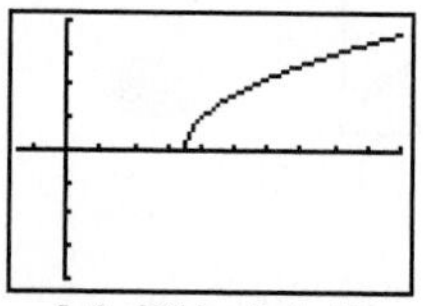

[–3, 20] by [–4, 4]

Domain: $[7, \infty)$; Range: $[0, \infty)$

(b) $(f \circ g)(x) = \sqrt{x} - 7;$
$(g \circ f)(x) = \sqrt{x - 7}$

65. (a) For $f \circ g$:

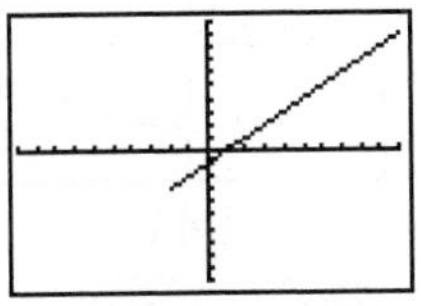

[–10, 10] by [–10, 10]

Domain: $[-2, \infty)$; Range: $[-3, \infty)$

For $g \circ f$:

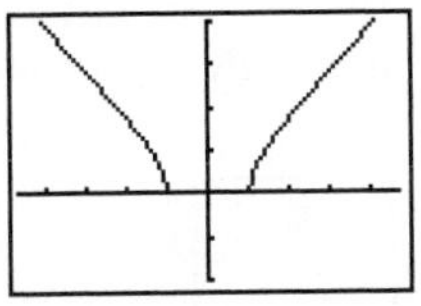

[–4.7, 4.7] by [–2, 4]

Domain: $(-\infty, -1] \cup [1, \infty)$; Range: $[0, \infty)$

(b) $(f \circ g)(x) = (\sqrt{x+2})^2 - 3$
$= x - 1, x \geq -2$
$(g \circ f)(x) = \sqrt{x^2 - 1}$

67. (a)

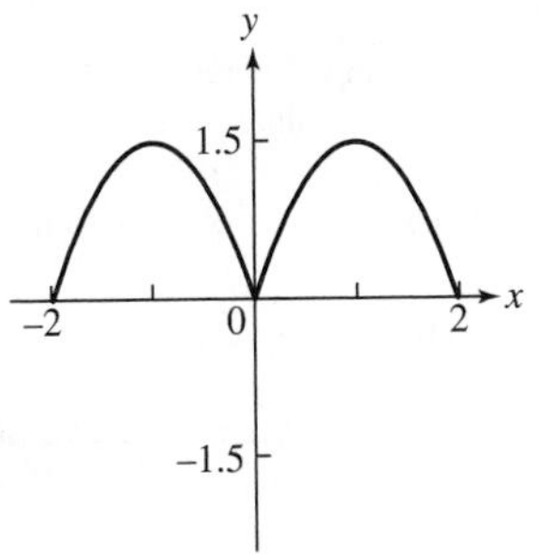

(b)

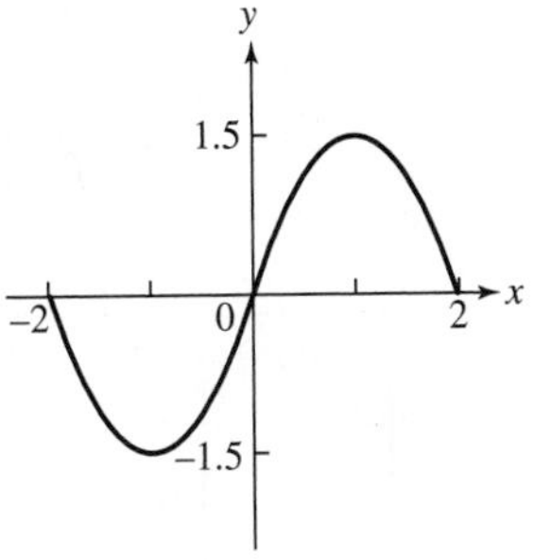

69. (a)

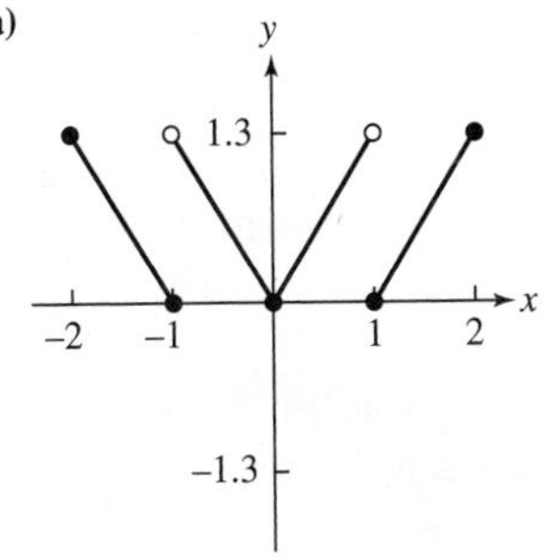

(b)

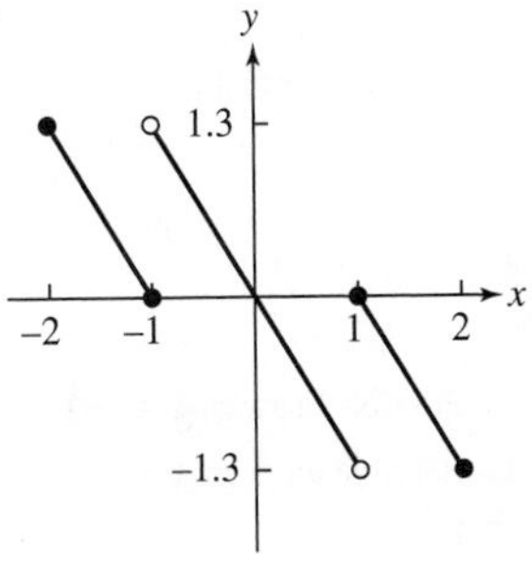

71. (a)

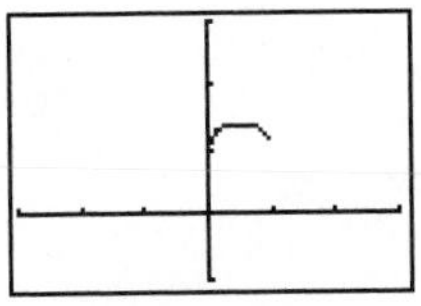

[–3, 3] by [–1, 3]

(b) Domain of y_1: $[0, \infty)$
Domain of y_2: $(-\infty, 1]$
Domain of y_3: $[0, 1]$

(c) The results for $y_1 - y_2$, $y_2 - y_1$, and $y_1 \cdot y_2$ are the same as for $y_1 + y_2$ above.

Domain of $\frac{y_1}{y_2}$: $[0, 1)$ Domain of $\frac{y_2}{y_1}$: $(0, 1]$

(d) The domain of a sum, difference, or product of two functions is the intersection of their domains.
The domain of a quotient of two functions is the intersection of their domains with any zeros of the denominator removed.

Section 1.3

Quick Review 1.3

1. 2.924 **3.** 0.192

5. 1.8882 **7.** \$630.58

9. $x^{-18}y^{-5} = \frac{1}{x^{18}y^5}$

Exercises 1.3

1.

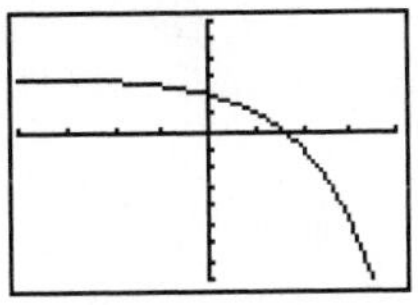

[–4, 4] by [–8, 6]

Domain: All reals Range: $(-\infty, 3)$

3.

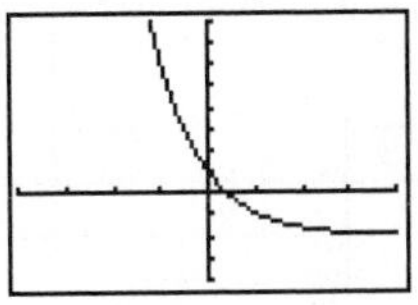

[–4, 4] by [–4, 8]

Domain: All reals Range: $(-2, \infty)$

5. 3^{4x} **7.** 2^{-6x} **9.** ≈ 2.322 **11.** ≈ -0.631

13. (a) **15.** (e) **17.** (b)

19. (a) 1.032, 1.041, 1.034, 1.034, 1.029

(b) One possibility is $2168(1.034)^n$.

(c) 3348 thousand, or 3,348,000

21. After 19 years

23. (a) $A(t) = 6.6\left(\frac{1}{2}\right)^{t/14}$

(b) About 38.1145 days later

25. ≈ 11.433 years **27.** ≈ 11.090 years

29. ≈ 19.108 years **31.** $2^{48} \approx 2.815 \times 10^{14}$

33.

x	y	Δy
1	–1	
2	1	2
3	3	2
4	5	2

35.

x	y	Δy
1	1	
2	4	3
3	9	5
4	16	7

37. Since $\Delta x = 1$, the corresponding value of Δy is equal to the slope of the line. If the changes in x are constant for a linear function, then the corresponding changes in y are constant as well.

39. (a) $y = 14153.84(1.01963)^x$

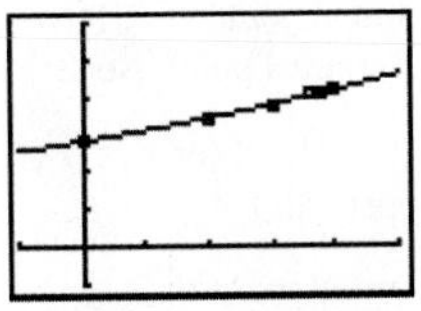

[–5, 25] by [–5000, 30000]

(b) Estimate: 22,133,000; the estimate exceeds the actual by 14,000.

(c) ≈ 0.020 or 2%

41. False. It is positive 1/9

43. D **45.** B

47. (a)

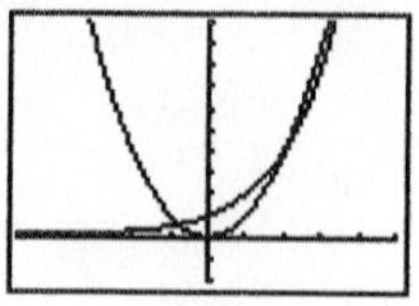

[−5, 5] by [−2, 10]

In this window, it appears they cross twice, although a third crossing off-screen appears likely.

(b)

x	change in $Y1$	change in $Y2$
1		
	3	2
2		
	5	4
3		
	7	8
4		

(c) $x = -0.7667, x = 2, x = 4$ **(d)** $(-0.7667, 2) \cup (4, \infty)$

49. $a = 0.5, k = 3$

Quick Quiz (Sections 1.1–1.3)

1. C **3.** E

Section 1.4

Quick Review 1.4

1. $y = -\frac{5}{3}x + \frac{29}{3}$ **3.** $x = 2$

5. x-intercepts: $x = -4$ and $x = 4$ y-intercepts: none

7. (a) Yes **(b)** No **(c)** Yes

9. (a) $t = \frac{-2x - 5}{3}$ **(b)** $t = \frac{3y + 1}{2}$

Exercises 1.4

1. Graph (c). Window: $[-4, 4]$ by $[-3, 3]$, $0 \le t \le 2\pi$

3. Graph (d). Window: $[-10, 10]$ by $[-10, 10]$, $0 \le t \le 2\pi$

5. (a)

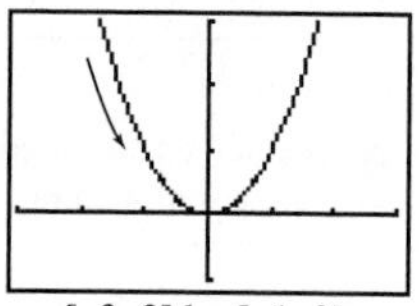

[−3, 3] by [−1, 3]

No initial or terminal point

(b) $y = x^2$; all

7. (a)

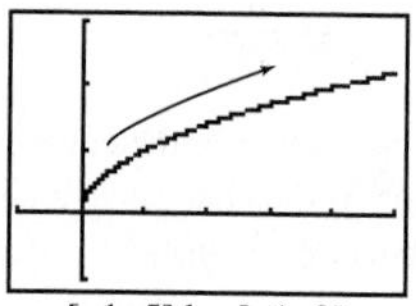

[−1, 5] by [−1, 3]

Initial point: $(0, 0)$
Terminal point: None

(b) $y = \sqrt{x}$; all (or $x = y^2$; upper half)

9. (a)

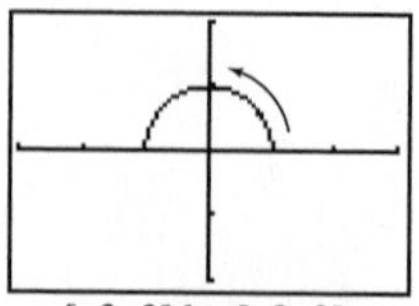

[−3, 3] by [−2, 2]

Initial point: $(1, 0)$
Terminal point: $(-1, 0)$

(b) $x^2 + y^2 = 1$; upper half (or $y = \sqrt{1 - x^2}$; all)

11. (a)

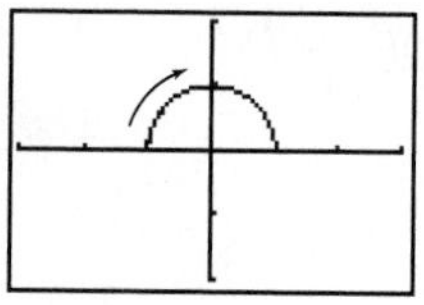

[−3, 3] by [−2, 2]

Initial point: $(-1, 0)$
Terminal point: $(0, 1)$

(b) $x^2 + y^2 = 1$; upper half (or $y = \sqrt{1 - x^2}$; all)

13. (a)

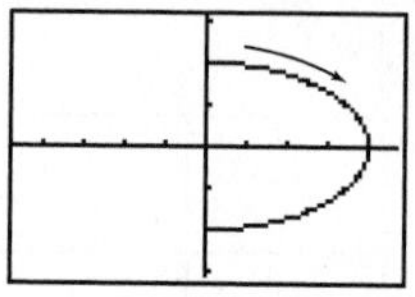

[−4.7, 4.7] by [−3.1, 3.1]

Initial point: $(0, 2)$
Terminal point: $(0, -2)$

(b) $\left(\frac{x}{4}\right)^2 + \left(\frac{y}{2}\right)^2 = 1$; right half (or $x = 2\sqrt{4 - y^2}$; all)

15. (a)

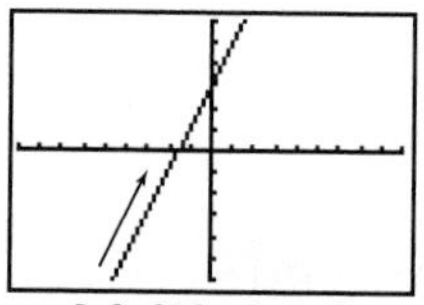

[−9, 9] by [−6, 6]

Initial and terminal point: $(0, 5)$

(b) $y = 2x + 3$; all

17. (a)

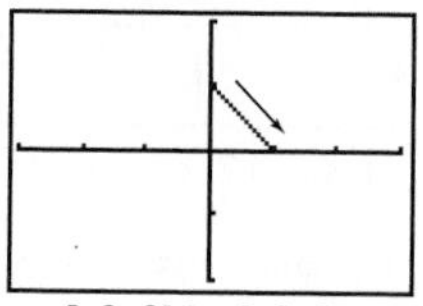

[−3, 3] by [−2, 2]

Initial point: $(0, 1)$
Terminal point: $(1, 0)$

(b) $y = -x + 1$; $(0, 1)$ to $(1, 0)$

19. (a)

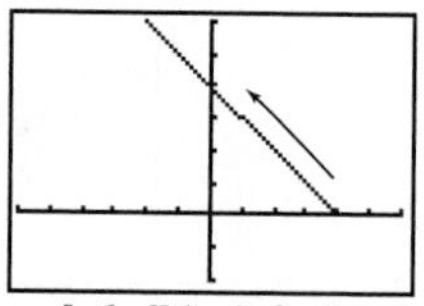

[−6, 6] by [−2, 6]

Initial point: $(4, 0)$
Terminal point: None

(b) $y = -x + 4$; $x \le 4$

21. (a)

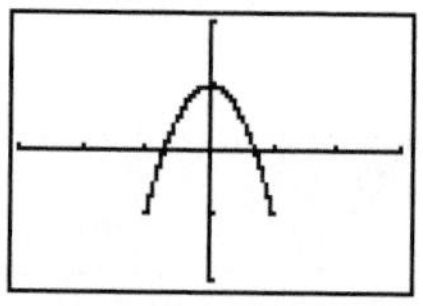

[−3, 3] by [−2, 2]

The curve is traced and retraced in both directions, and there is no initial or terminal point.

(b) $y = -2x^2 + 1$; $-1 \le x \le 1$

23. Possible answer: $x = -1 + 5t, y = -3 + 4t, 0 \le t \le 1$

25. Possible answer: $x = t^2 + 1, y = t, t \le 0$

27. Possible answer: $x = 2 - 3t, y = 3 - 4t, t \ge 0$

29. $1 < t < 3$ **31.** $-5 \le t < -3$

33. Possible answer: $x = t, y = t^2 + 2t + 2, t > 0$

35. Possible answers:
(a) $x = a\cos t, y = -a\sin t, 0 \le t \le 2\pi$
(b) $x = a\cos t, y = a\sin t, 0 \le t \le 2\pi$
(c) $x = a\cos t, y = -a\sin t, 0 \le t \le 4\pi$
(d) $x = a\cos t, y = a\sin t, 0 \le t \le 4\pi$

37. False. It is an ellipse.

39. D **41.** A

43. (a) The resulting graph appears to be the right half of a hyperbola in the first and fourth quadrants. The parameter a determines the x-intercept. The parameter b determines the shape of the hyperbola. If b is smaller, the graph has less steep slopes and appears "sharper." If b is larger, the slopes are steeper and the graph appears more "blunt."
(b) This appears to be the left half of the same hyperbola.
(c) Because both sec t and tan t are discontinuous at these points. This might cause the grapher to include extraneous lines (the asymptotes to the hyperbola) in its graph.

(d) $\left(\frac{x}{a}\right)^2 - \left(\frac{y}{b}\right)^2 = (\sec t)^2 - (\tan t)^2 = 1$

by a standard trigonometric identity.

(e) This changes the orientation of the hyperbola. In this case, b determines the y-intercept of the hyperbola, and a determines the shape. The parameter interval $\left(-\frac{\pi}{2}, \frac{\pi}{2}\right)$ gives the upper half of the hyperbola. The parameter interval $\left(\frac{\pi}{2}, \frac{3\pi}{2}\right)$ gives the lower half. The same values of t cause discontinuities and may add extraneous lines to the graph.

45. (a)

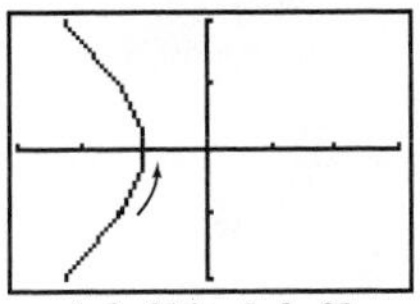

[–3, 3] by [–2, 2]

No initial or terminal point

(b) $x^2 - y^2 = 1$; left branch

(or $x = -\sqrt{y^2 + 1}$; all)

47. $x = 2 \cot t$, $y = 2 \sin^2 t$, $0 < t < \pi$

Section 1.5

Quick Review 1.5

1. 1 **3.** $x^{2/3}$

5. Possible answer: $x = t$, $y = \frac{1}{t - 1}$, $t \geq 2$

7. (4, 5)

9. (a) (1.58, 3) **(b)** No intersection

Exercises 1.5

1. No **3.** Yes **5.** Yes **7.** Yes **9.** No **11.** No

13. $f^{-1}(x) = \frac{x - 3}{2}$

15. $f^{-1}(x) = (x + 1)^{1/3}$ or $\sqrt[3]{x + 1}$

17. $f^{-1}(x) = -x^{1/2}$ or $-\sqrt{x}$

19. $f^{-1}(x) = 2 - (-x)^{1/2}$ or $2 - \sqrt{-x}$

21. $f^{-1}(x) = \frac{1}{x^{1/2}}$ or $\frac{1}{\sqrt{x}}$

23. $f^{-1}(x) = \frac{1 - 3x}{x - 2}$

25.

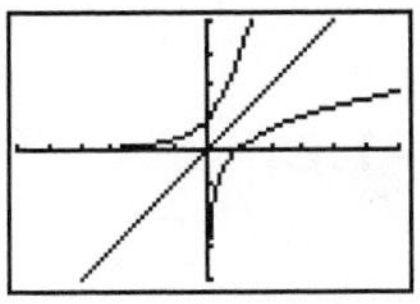

[–6, 6] by [–4, 4]

27.

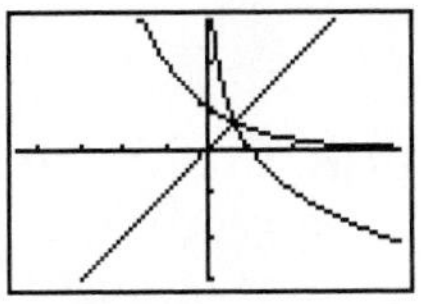

[–4.5, 4.5] by [–3, 3]

29.

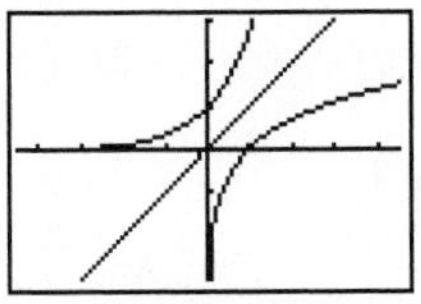

[–4.5, 4.5] by [–3, 3]

31.

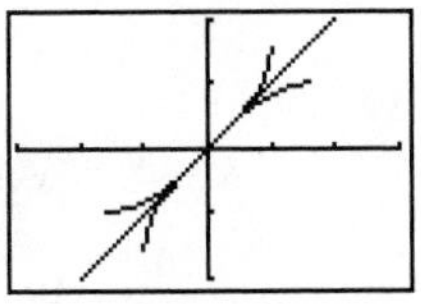

[–3, 3] by [–2, 2]

33. $t = \frac{\ln 2}{\ln 1.045} \approx 15.75$

35. $x = \ln\left(\frac{3 \pm \sqrt{5}}{2}\right) \approx -0.96$ or 0.96

37. $y = e^{2t+4}$

39.

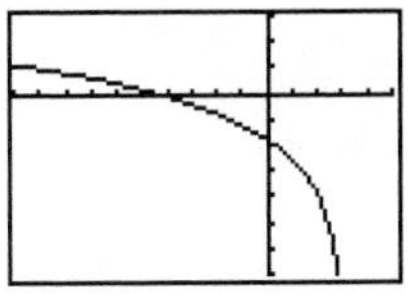

[–10, 5] by [–7, 3]

Domain: $(-\infty, 3)$;
Range: all reals

41.

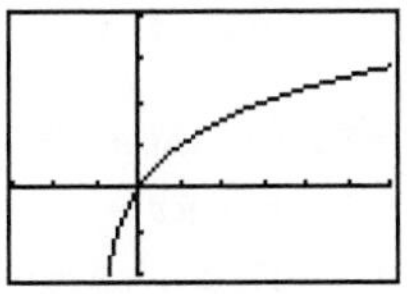

[–3, 6] by [–2, 4]

Domain: $(-1, \infty)$;
Range: all reals

43. $f^{-1}(x) = \log_2\left(\frac{x}{100 - x}\right)$

45. (a) $f(f(x)) = \sqrt{1 - (f(x))^2}$
$= \sqrt{1 - (1 - x^2)}$
$= \sqrt{x^2}$
$= x$, since $x \geq 0$

(b) $f(f(x)) = f\left(\frac{1}{x}\right) = \frac{1}{1/x} = x$ for all $x \neq 0$

47. About 14.936 years. (If the interest is only paid annually, it will take 15 years.)

49. (a) $y = 1.758 + 1.076 \ln(x)$

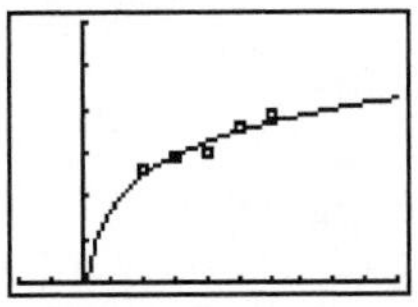

[–2, 10] by [0, 6]

(b) 4 trillion cubic feet
(c) Sometime during 2009

51. (a) Suppose that $f(x_1) = f(x_2)$. Then $mx_1 + b = mx_2 + b$, which gives $x_1 = x_2$ since $m \neq 0$.
(b) $f^{-1}(x) = \frac{x - b}{m}$; the slopes are reciprocals.
(c) They are also parallel lines with nonzero slope.
(d) They are also perpendicular lines with nonzero.

53. False. Consider $f(x) = x^2$, $g(x) = \sqrt{x}$. Notice that $(f \circ g)(x) = x$ but f is not one-to-one.

55. A **57.** B

59. If the graph of $f(x)$ passes the horizontal line test, so will the graph of $g(x) = -f(x)$ since it's the same graph reflected about the x-axis.

61. (a) Domain: All reals
Range: If $a > 0$, then (d, ∞)
If $a < 0$, then $(-\infty, d)$
(b) Domain: (c, ∞)
Range: All reals

Section 1.6

Quick Review 1.6

1. 60° 3. $-\frac{2\pi}{9}$ **5.** $x \approx 0.6435$, $x \approx 2.4981$

7. $x \approx 0.7854\left(\text{or } \frac{\pi}{4}\right)$, $x \approx 3.9270\left(\text{or } \frac{5\pi}{4}\right)$

9. $f(-x) = (-x)^3 - 3(-x) = -x^3 + 3x$
$= -(x^3 - 3x) = -f(x)$
The graph is symmetric about the origin because if a point (a, b) is on the graph, then so is the point $(-a, -b)$.

Exercises 1.6

1. $\frac{5\pi}{4}$ **3.** $\frac{1}{2}$ radian or $\approx 28.65°$ **5.** Even **7.** Odd

9. $\sin\theta = 8/17$, $\tan\theta = -8/15$, $\csc\theta = 17/8$, $\sec\theta = -17/15$, $\cot\theta = -15/8$

11. (a) $\frac{2\pi}{3}$

(b) $x \neq \frac{k\pi}{3}$, for integers k

(c) $(-\infty, -5] \cup [1, \infty)$

(d)

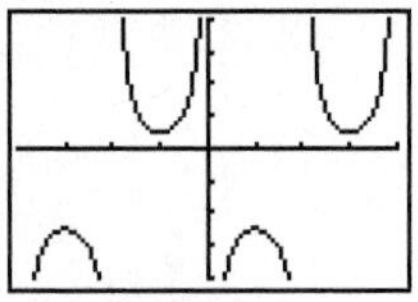

$\left[-\frac{2\pi}{3}, \frac{2\pi}{3}\right]$ by $[-8, 8]$

13. (a) $\frac{\pi}{3}$

(b) $x \neq \frac{k\pi}{6}$, for odd integers k

(c) All reals

(d)

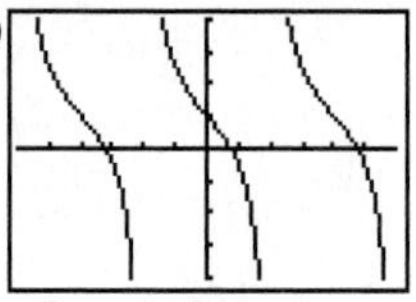

$\left[-\frac{\pi}{2}, \frac{\pi}{2}\right]$ by $[-8, 8]$

15. Possible answers are:
(a) $[0, 4\pi]$ by $[-3, 3]$ **(b)** $[0, 4\pi]$ by $[-3, 3]$
(c) $[0, 2\pi]$ by $[-3, 3]$

17. (a) π **(b)** 1.5 **(c)** $[-2\pi, 2\pi]$ by $[-2, 2]$

19. (a) π **(b)** 3 **(c)** $[-2\pi, 2\pi]$ by $[-4, 4]$

21. (a) 6 **(b)** 4 **(c)** $[-3, 3]$ by $[-5, 5]$

23. (a) $y = 1.543 \sin(2468.635x - 0.494) + 0.438$

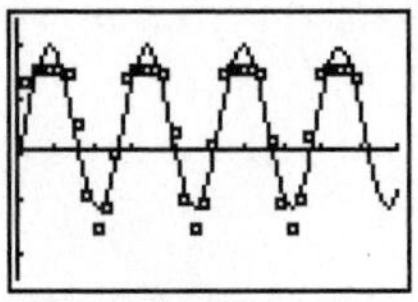

[0, 0.01]by [–2.5, 2.5]

(b) Frequency = 392.9, so it must be a "G."

25. The portion of the curve $y = \cos x$ between $0 \leq x \leq \pi$ passes the horizontal line test so it is one-to-one.

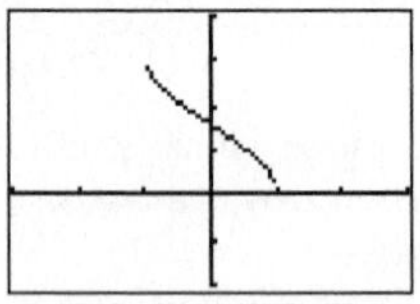

[–3, 3] by [–2, 4]

27. $\frac{\pi}{6}$ radian or 30° **29.** ≈ -1.3734 radians or $-78.6901°$

31. $x \approx 1.190$ and $x \approx 4.332$ **33.** $x = \frac{\pi}{6}$ and $x = \frac{5\pi}{6}$

35. $x = \frac{7\pi}{6} + 2k\pi$ and $x = \frac{11\pi}{6} + 2k\pi$, k any integer

37. $\cos\theta = \frac{15}{17}$ $\sin\theta = \frac{8}{17}$ $\tan\theta = \frac{8}{15}$
$\sec\theta = \frac{17}{15}$ $\csc\theta = \frac{17}{8}$ $\cot\theta = \frac{15}{8}$

39. $\cos\theta = -\frac{3}{5}$ $\sin\theta = \frac{4}{5}$ $\tan\theta = -\frac{4}{3}$
$\sec\theta = -\frac{5}{3}$ $\csc\theta = \frac{5}{4}$ $\cot\theta = -\frac{3}{4}$

41. $\frac{\sqrt{72}}{11} \approx 0.771$

43. (a) 37 **(b)** 365 **(c)** 101 **(d)** 25
(e) $f(x) = 37 \sin\left[\frac{2\pi}{365}(x - 101)\right] + 25$

45. (a) $\cot(-x) = \frac{\cos(-x)}{\sin(-x)} = \frac{\cos(x)}{-\sin(x)} = -\cot(x)$

(b) Assume that f is even and g is odd.
Then $\frac{f(-x)}{g(-x)} = \frac{f(x)}{-g(x)} = -\frac{f(x)}{g(x)}$ so $\frac{f}{g}$ is odd.
The situation is similar for $\frac{g}{f}$.

47. Assume that f is even and g is odd.
Then $f(-x)\,g(-x) = f(x)[-g(x)] = -f(x)g(x)$ so fg is odd.

49. (a) $y = 3.0014 \sin(0.9996x + 2.0012) + 2.9999$
(b) $y = 3\sin(x + 2) + 3$

51. False. The amplitude is 1/2.

53. B **55.** A

57. (a) $\sqrt{2}\sin\left(ax + \frac{\pi}{4}\right)$ **(b)** See part **(a)**.

(c) It works.

(d) $\sin\left(ax + \frac{\pi}{4}\right)$
$= \sin(ax) \cdot \frac{1}{\sqrt{2}} + \cos(ax) \cdot \frac{1}{\sqrt{2}}$
$= \frac{1}{\sqrt{2}}(\sin ax + \cos ax)$
So, $\sin(ax) + \cos(ax) = \sqrt{2}\sin\left(ax + \frac{\pi}{4}\right)$.

59. Since $\sin(x)$ has period 2π, $(\sin(x + 2\pi))^3 = (\sin(x))^3$. This function has period 2π. A graph shows that no smaller number works for the period.

61. One possible graph:

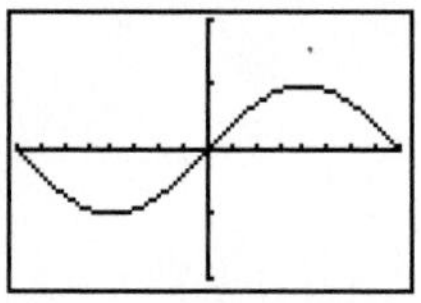

$\left[-\frac{\pi}{60}, \frac{\pi}{60}\right]$ by $[-2, 2]$

Quick Quiz (Sections 1.4–1.6)

1. C **3.** E

Review Exercises

1. $y = 3x - 9$ **2.** $y = -\frac{1}{2}x + \frac{3}{2}$ **3.** $x = 0$ **4.** $y = -2x$

5. $y = 2$ **6.** $y = -\frac{2}{5}x + \frac{21}{5}$ **7.** $y = -3x + 3$ **8.** $y = 2x - 5$

9. $y = -\frac{4}{3}x - \frac{20}{3}$ **10.** $y = -\frac{5}{3}x - \frac{19}{3}$ **11.** $y = \frac{2}{3}x + \frac{8}{3}$

12. $y = \frac{5}{3}x - 5$ **13.** $y = -\frac{1}{2}x + 3$ **14.** $y = -\frac{2}{7}x - \frac{6}{7}$
15. Origin **16.** y-axis **17.** Neither **18.** y-axis
19. Even **20.** Odd **21.** Even **22.** Odd **23.** Odd
24. Neither **25.** Neither **26.** Even

27. (a) Domain: all reals
(b) Range: $[-2, \infty)$
(c)
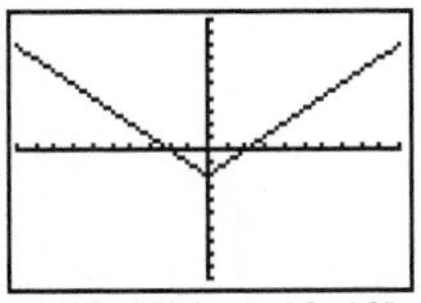
[–10, 10] by [–10, 10]

28. (a) Domain: $(-\infty\ 1]$
(b) Range $[-2, \infty)$
(c)
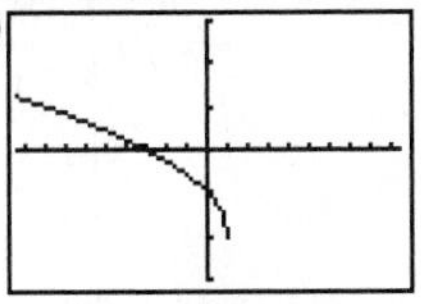
[–9.4, 9.4] by [–3, 3]

29. (a) Domain: $[-4, 4]$
(b) Range: $[0, 4]$
(c)
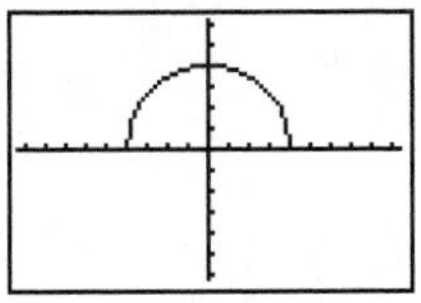
[–9.4, 9.4] by [–6.2, 6.2]

30. (a) Domain: all reals
(b) Range: $(1, \infty)$
(c)
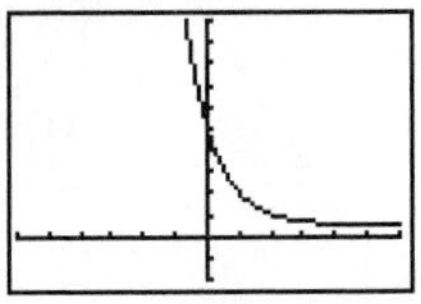
[–6, 6] by [–4, 20]

31. (a) Domain: all reals
(b) Range: $(-3, \infty)$
(c)
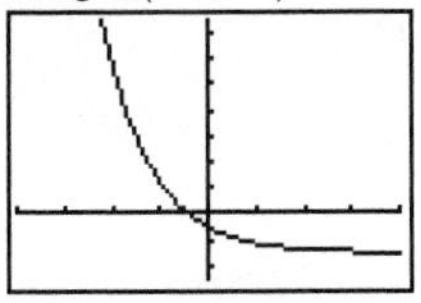
[–4, 4] by [–5, 15]

32. (a) Domain: $x \neq \frac{k\pi}{4}$, for odd integers k
(b) Range: all reals
(c)
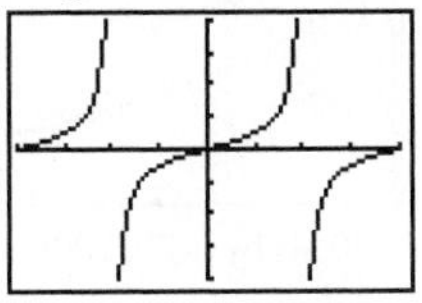
$\left[-\frac{\pi}{2}, \frac{\pi}{2}\right]$ by [–8, 8]

33. (a) Domain: all reals
(b) Range: $[-3, 1]$
(c)
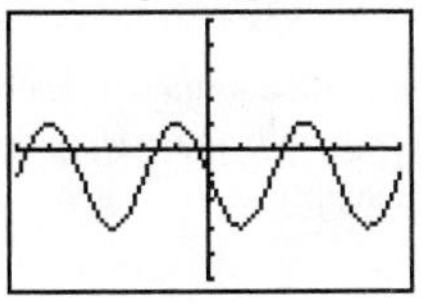
[$-\pi$, π] by [–5, 5]

34. (a) Domain: all reals
(b) Range: $[0, \infty)$
(c)
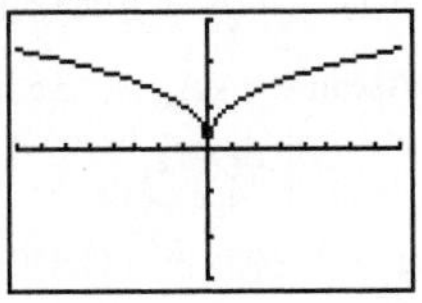
[–8, 8] by [–3, 3]

35. (a) Domain: $(3, \infty)$
(b) Range: all reals
(c)
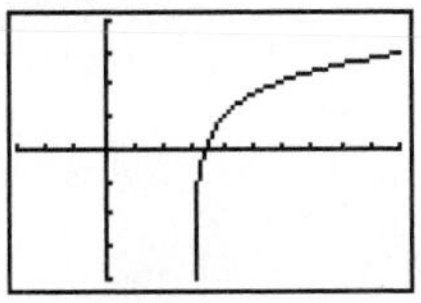
[–3, 10] by [–4, 4]

36. (a) Domain: all reals
(b) Range: all reals
(c)
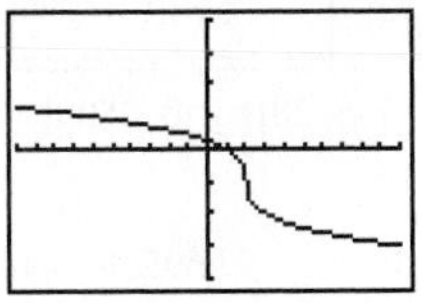
[–10, 10] by [–4, 4]

37. (a) Domain: $[-4, 4]$
(b) Range: $[0, 2]$
(c)
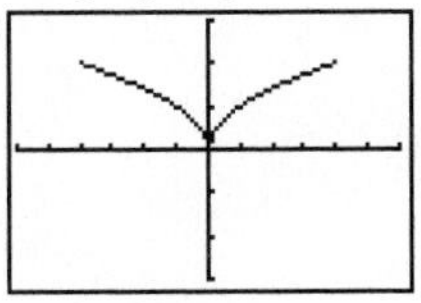
[–6, 6] by [–3, 3]

38. (a) Domain: $[-2, 2]$
(b) Range: $[-1, 1]$
(c)
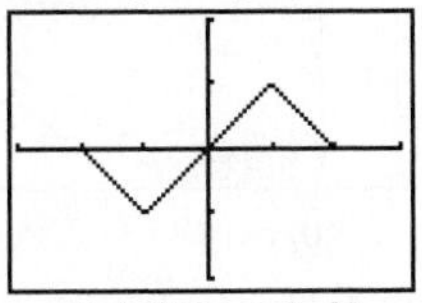
[–3, 3] by [–2, 2]

39. $f(x) = \begin{cases} 1 - x, & 0 \le x < 1 \\ 2 - x, & 1 \le x \le 2 \end{cases}$

40. $f(x) = \begin{cases} \frac{5x}{2}, & 0 \le x < 2 \\ -\frac{5}{2}x + 10, & 2 \le x \le 4 \end{cases}$

41. (a) 1 **(b)** $\frac{1}{\sqrt{2.5}}\left(= \sqrt{\frac{2}{5}}\right)$ **(c)** $x, x \neq 0$ **(d)** $\frac{1}{\sqrt{1/\sqrt{x+2} + 2}}$

42. (a) 2 **(b)** 1 **(c)** x **(d)** $\sqrt[3]{\sqrt[3]{x+1} + 1}$

43. (a) $(f \circ g)(x) = -x, x \ge -2$
$(g \circ f)(x) = \sqrt{4 - x^2}$
(b) Domain $(f \circ g)$: $[-2, \infty)$
Domain $(g \circ f)$: $[-2, 2]$
(c) Range $(f \circ g)$: $(-\infty, 2]$
Range $(g \circ f)$: $[0, 2]$

44. (a) $(f \circ g)(x) = \sqrt[4]{1 - x}$
$(g \circ f)(x) = \sqrt{1 - \sqrt{x}}$
(b) Domain $(f \circ g)$: $(-\infty, 1]$
Domain $(g \circ f)$: $[0, 1]$
(c) Range $(f \circ g)$: $[0, \infty)$
Range $(g \circ f)$: $[0, 1]$

45. (a)
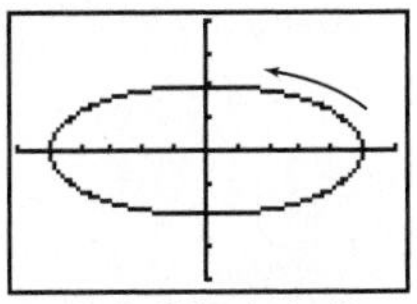
[–6, 6] by [–4, 4]

Initial point: $(5, 0)$
Terminal point: $(5, 0)$
(b) $\left(\frac{x}{5}\right)^2 + \left(\frac{y}{2}\right)^2 = 1$; all

46. (a)
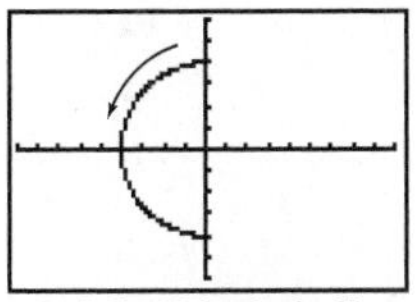
[–9, 9] by [–6, 6]

Initial point: $(0, 4)$
Terminal point: $(0, -4)$
(b) $x^2 + y^2 = 16$; left half

47. (a)
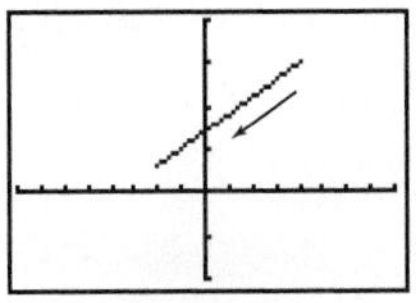
[–8, 8] by [–10, 20]

Initial point: $(4, 15)$
Terminal point: $(-2, 3)$
(b) $y = 2x + 7$; from $(4, 15)$ to $(-2, 3)$

48. (a)
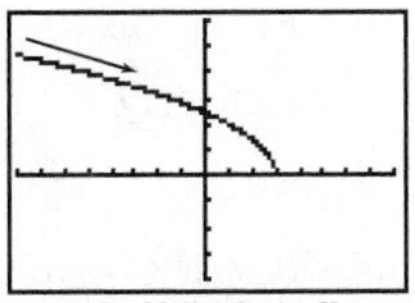
[–8, 8] by [–4, 6]

Initial point: None
Terminal point: $(3, 0)$
(b) $y = \sqrt{6 - 2x}$; all

49. Possible answer: $x = -2 + 6t, y = 5 - 2t, 0 \le t \le 1$

50. Possible answer: $x = -3 + 7t, y = -2 + t, -\infty < t < \infty$

51. Possible answer: $x = 2 - 3t, y = 5 - 5t, 0 \le t$

52. Possible answer: $x = t, y = t(t - 4), t \le 2$

53. (a) $f^{-1}(x) = \frac{2 - x}{3}$
(b)
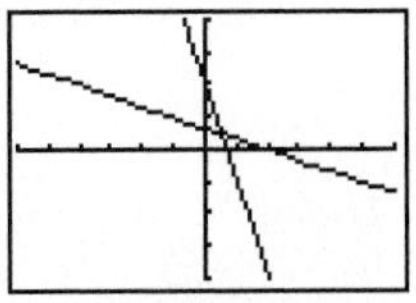
[–6, 6] by [–4, 4]

54. (a) $f^{-1}(x) = \sqrt{x} - 2$
(b)
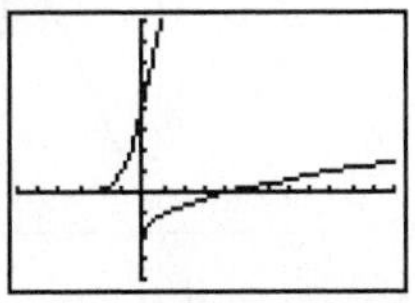
[–6, 12] by [–4, 8]

55. ≈ 0.6435 radians or $36.8699°$

56. ≈ -1.1607 radians or $-66.5014°$

57. $\cos\theta = \dfrac{3}{7}$ $\quad \sin\theta = \dfrac{\sqrt{40}}{7}$ $\quad \tan\theta = \dfrac{\sqrt{40}}{3}$

$\sec\theta = \dfrac{7}{3}$ $\quad \csc\theta = \dfrac{7}{\sqrt{40}}$ $\quad \cot\theta = \dfrac{3}{\sqrt{40}}$

58. **(a)** $x \approx 3.3430$ and $x \approx 6.0818$

(b) $x \approx 3.3430 + 2k\pi$ and $x \approx 6.0818 + 2k\pi$, k any integer

59. $x = -5 \ln 4$

60. **(a)**

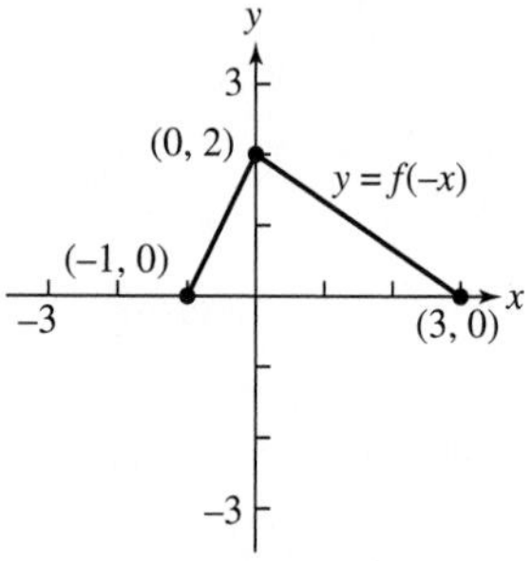

(b)

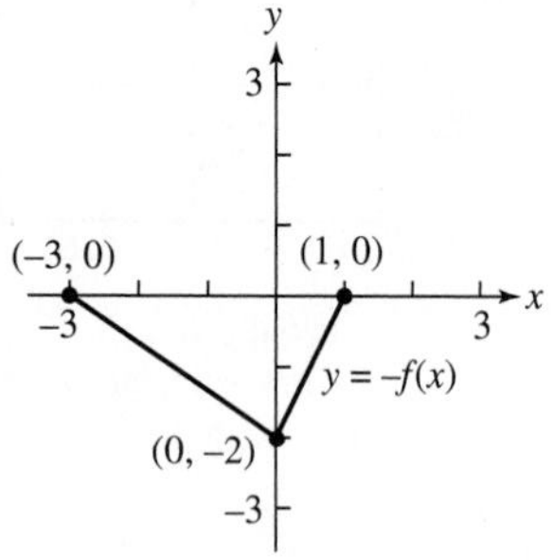

(c)

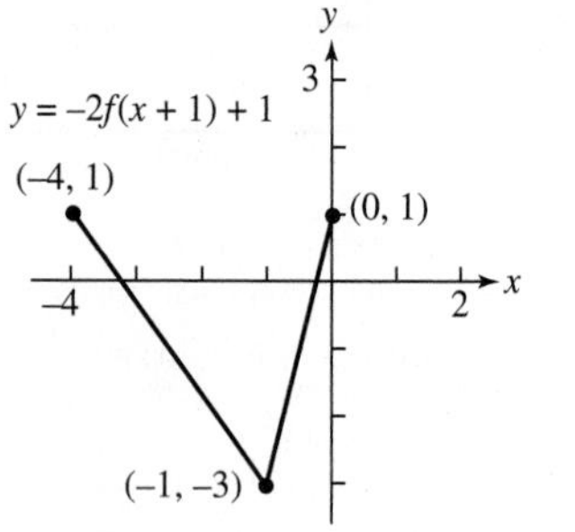

(d)

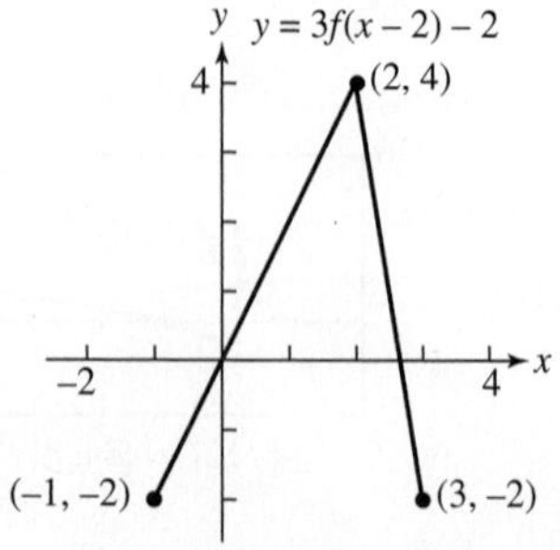

61. **(a)**

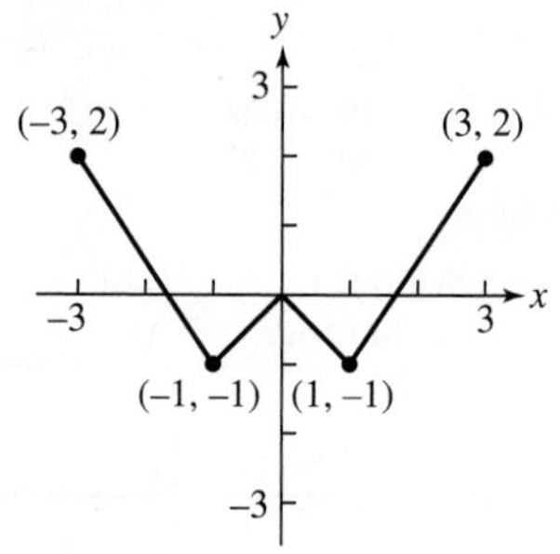

(b)

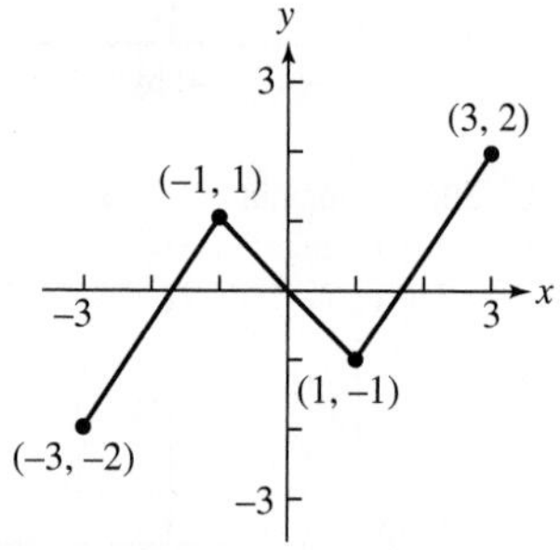

62. **(a)** $V = 100{,}000 - 10{,}000x$, $0 \le x \le 10$ **(b)** After 4.5 years

63. **(a)** 90 units **(b)** $90 - 52 \ln 3 \approx 32.8722$ units

(c)

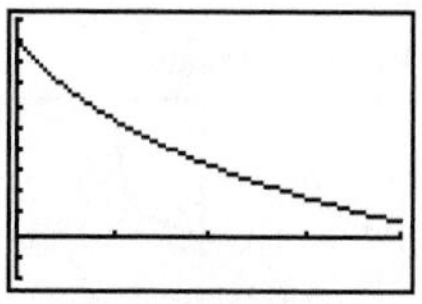

[0, 4] by [–20, 100]

64. After $\dfrac{\ln(10/3)}{\ln 1.08} \approx 15.6439$ years

(If the bank only pays interest at the end of the year, it will take 16 years.)

65. **(a)** $N = 4 \cdot 2^t$ **(b)** 4 days: 64; 1 week: 512

(c) After $\dfrac{\ln 500}{\ln 2} \approx 8.9658$ days, or after nearly 9 days

(d) Because it suggests the number of guppies will continue to double indefinitely and become arbitrarily large, which is impossible due to the finite size of the tank and the oxygen supply in the water.

66. **(a)** $y = 72.695x - 143{,}940.564$

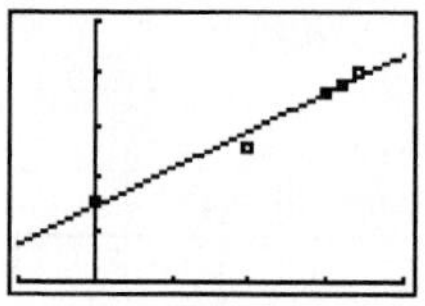

[–5, 20] by [0, 2500]

(b) 2103

(c) Slope $= 72.695$. It represents the number of doctoral degrees earned per year.

67. **(a)** $y = 19{,}092(1.0025)^x$.

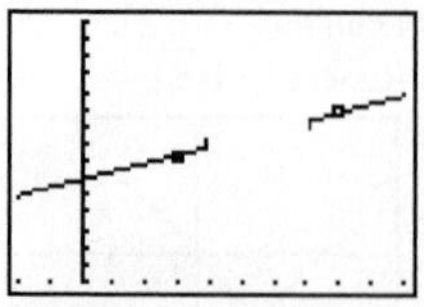

[–2, 10] by [18500, 20000]

(b) 19,526 thousand or 19,526,000

(c) 0.0025 or 0.25%.

68. **(a)** $m = -1$ **(b)** $y = -x - 1$ **(c)** $y = x + 3$ **(d)** 2

69. **(a)** $(2, \infty)$ **(b)** $(-\infty, \infty)$ **(c)** $x = 2 + e \approx 4.718$

(d) $f^{-1}(x) = 2 + e^{1-x}$

(e) $(f \circ g^{-1})(x) = f(f^{-1}(x)) = f(2 + e^{1-x}) = 1 - \ln(2 + e^{1-x} - 2)$
$= 1 - \ln(e^{1-x})$
$= 1 - (1 - x)$
$= x$

$(f^{-1} \circ g)(x) = f^{-1}(f(x)) = f^{-1}(1 - \ln(x - 2)) = 2 + e^{1-(1-\ln(x-2))}$
$= 2 + e^{\ln(x-2)}$
$= 2 + (x - 2)$
$= x$

70. **(a)** $(-\infty, \infty)$ **(b)** $[-2, 4]$ **(c)** π **(d)** Even **(e)** $x \approx 2.526$

CHAPTER 2

Section 2.1

Quick Review 2.1

1. 0 **3.** 0 **5.** $-4 < x < 4$

7. $-1 < x < 5$ **9.** $x - 6$

Exercises 2.1

1. 48 ft/sec **3.** 96 ft/sec

5. $2c^3 - 3c^2 + c - 1$

7. $-\frac{3}{2}$ **9.** -15 **11.** 0 **13.** 4

15. **(a)**

x	-0.1	-0.01	-0.001	-0.0001
$f(x)$	1.566667	1.959697	1.995997	1.999600

(b)

x	0.1	0.01	0.001	0.0001
$f(x)$	2.372727	2.039703	2.003997	2.000400

The limit appears to be 2.

17. **(a)**

x	-0.1	-0.01	-0.001	-0.0001
$f(x)$	-0.054402	-0.005064	-0.000827	-0.000031

(b)

x	0.1	0.01	0.001	0.0001
$f(x)$	-0.054402	-0.005064	-0.000827	-0.000031

The limit appears to be 0.

19. **(a)**

x	-0.1	-0.01	-0.001	-0.0001
$f(x)$	2.0567	2.2763	2.2999	2.3023

(b)

x	0.1	0.01	0.001	0.0001
$f(x)$	2.5893	2.3293	2.3052	2.3029

The limit appears to be approximately 2.3.

21. Expression not defined at $x = -2$. There is no limit.

23. Expression not defined at $x = 0$. There is no limit.

25. $\frac{1}{2}$ **27.** $-\frac{1}{2}$ **29.** 12 **31.** -1 **33.** 0

35. Answers will vary. One possible graph is given by the window $[-4.7, 4.7]$ by $[-15, 15]$ with Xscl = 1 and Yscl = 5.

37. 0 **39.** 0 **41.** 1

43. **(a)** True **(b)** True
(c) False **(d)** True
(e) True **(f)** True
(g) False **(h)** False
(i) False **(j)** False

45. **(a)** 3 **(b)** -2
(c) No limit **(d)** 1

47. **(a)** -4 **(b)** -4
(c) -4 **(d)** -4

49. **(a)** 4 **(b)** -3
(c) No limit **(d)** 4

51. **(c)** **53.** **(d)**

55. **(a)** 6 **(b)** 0
(c) 9 **(d)** -3

57. **(a)**

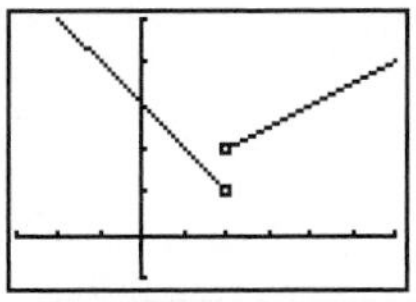

[–3, 6] by [–1, 5]

(b) Right-hand: 2 Left-hand: 1
(c) No, because the two one-sided limits are different

59. **(a)**

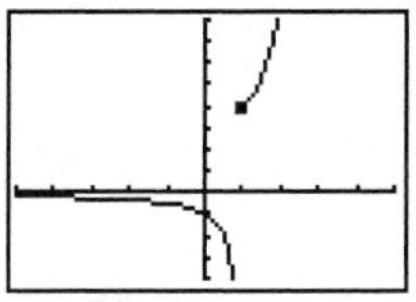

[–5, 5] by [–4, 8]

(b) Right-hand: 4
Left-hand: no limit
(c) No, because the left-hand limit doesn't exist

61. **(a)**

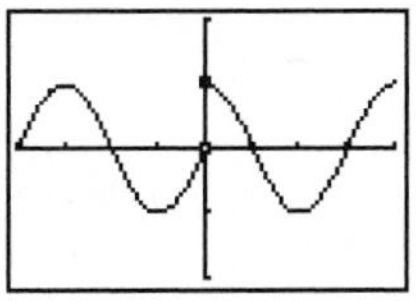

[–2π, 2π] by [–2, 2]

(b) $(-2\pi, 0) \cup (0, 2\pi)$
(c) $c = 2\pi$ **(d)** $c = -2\pi$

63. **(a)**

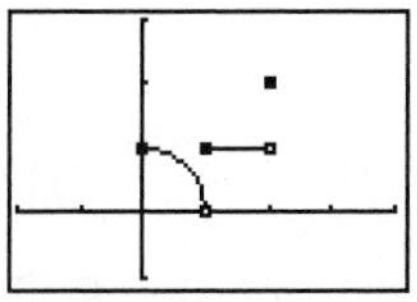

[–2, 4] by [–1, 3]

(b) $(0, 1) \cup (1, 2)$ **(c)** $c = 2$
(d) $c = 0$

65. 0

67. 0

69. **(a)** 14.7 m/sec
(b) 29.4 m/sec

71. True. Definition of limit.

73. C **75.** E

77. **(a)** Because the right-hand limit at zero depends only on the values of the function for positive x-values near zero

(b) Use: area of triangle $= \left(\frac{1}{2}\right)$(base)(height)

area of circular sector $= \frac{(\text{angle})(\text{radius})^2}{2}$

(c) This is how the areas of the three regions compare.
(d) Multiply by 2 and divide by $\sin\theta$.
(e) Take reciprocals, remembering that all of the values involved are positive.
(f) The limits for $\cos\theta$ and 1 are both equal to 1. Since $\frac{\sin\theta}{\theta}$ is between them, it must also have a limit of 1.

(g) $\dfrac{\sin(-\theta)}{-\theta} = \dfrac{-\sin(\theta)}{-\theta} = \dfrac{\sin(\theta)}{\theta}$

(h) If the function is symmetric about the y-axis, and the right-hand limit at zero is 1, then the left-hand limit at zero must also be 1.

(i) The two one-sided limits both exist and are equal to 1.

79. (a) $f\left(\dfrac{\pi}{6}\right) = \dfrac{1}{2}$

(b) One possible answer: $a = 0.305$, $b = 0.775$

(c) One possible answer: $a = 0.513$, $b = 0.535$

Section 2.2

Quick Review 2.2

1. $f^{-1}(x) = \dfrac{x+3}{2}$

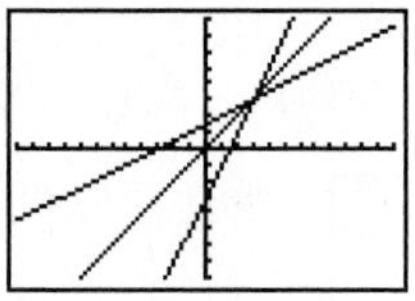

[–12, 12] by [–8, 8]

3. $f^{-1}(x) = \tan(x)$, $-\dfrac{\pi}{2} < x < \dfrac{\pi}{2}$

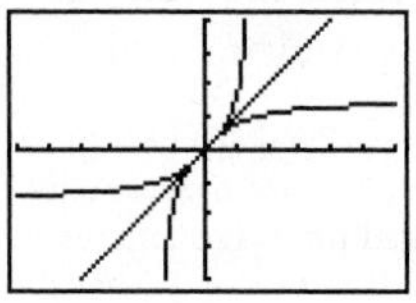

[–6, 6] by [–4, 4]

5. $q(x) = \dfrac{2}{3}$

$r(x) = -3x^2 - \left(\dfrac{5}{3}\right)x + \dfrac{7}{3}$

7. (a) $f(-x) = \cos x$ **(b)** $f\left(\dfrac{1}{x}\right) = \cos\left(\dfrac{1}{x}\right)$

9. (a) $f(-x) = -\dfrac{\ln(-x)}{x}$ **(b)** $f\left(\dfrac{1}{x}\right) = -x \ln x$

Exercises 2.2

1. (a) 1 **(b)** 1 **(c)** $y = 1$

3. (a) 0 **(b)** $-\infty$ **(c)** $y = 0$

5. (a) 3 **(b)** -3 **(c)** $y = 3, y = -3$

7. (a) 1 **(b)** -1 **(c)** $y = 1, y = -1$

9. 0 **11.** 0

13. ∞ **15.** $-\infty$ **17.** 0 **19.** ∞ **21.** Both are 1.

23. Both are 1. **25.** Both are 0.

27. (a) $x = -2, x = 2$

(b) Left-hand limit at -2 is ∞.
Right-hand limit at -2 is $-\infty$.
Left-hand limit at 2 is $-\infty$.
Right-hand limit at 2 is ∞.

29. (a) $x = -1$

(b) Left-hand limit at -1 is $-\infty$.
Right-hand limit at -1 is ∞.

31. (a) $x = k\pi$, k any integer

(b) At each vertical asymptote:
Left-hand limit is $-\infty$.
Right-hand limit is ∞.

33. Vertical asymptotes at $a = (4k+1)\dfrac{\pi}{2}$ and $b = (4k+3)\dfrac{\pi}{2}$, k any integer.

$\lim_{x\to a^-} f(x) = \infty$, $\lim_{x\to a^+} f(x) = -\infty$, $\lim_{x\to b^-} f(x) = -\infty$, $\lim_{x\to b^+} f(x) = \infty$

35. (a) **37. (d)**

39. (a) $3x^2$ **(b)** None

41. (a) $\dfrac{1}{2x}$ **(b)** $y = 0$

43. (a) $4x^2$ **(b)** None

45. (a) e^x **(b)** $-2x$

47. (a) x **(b)** x

49. At ∞: ∞ At $-\infty$: 0

51. At ∞: 0 At $-\infty$: 0

53. (a) 0 **(b)** -1 **(c)** $-\infty$ **(d)** -1

55. One possible answer:

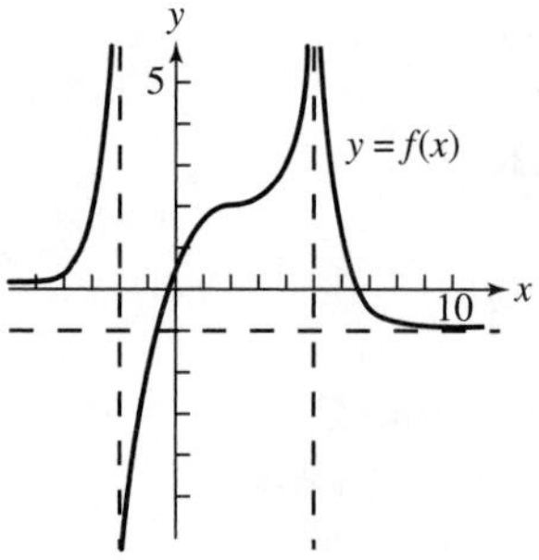

57. $\dfrac{f_1(x)/f_2(x)}{g_1(x)/g_2(x)} = \dfrac{f_1(x)/g_1(x)}{f_2(x)/g_2(x)}$ As x goes to infinity, $\dfrac{f_1}{g_1}$ and $\dfrac{f_2}{g_2}$ both approach 1. Therefore, using the above equation, $\dfrac{f_1/f_2}{g_1/g_2}$ must also approach 1.

59. True. For example, $f(x) = \dfrac{x}{\sqrt{x^2+1}}$ has $y = \pm 1$ as horizontal asymptotes.

61. A **63.** C

65. (a) $f \to -\infty$ as $x \to 0^-$, $f \to \infty$ as $x \to 0^-$, $g \to 0$, $fg \to 1$

(b) $f \to \infty$ as $x \to 0^-$, $f \to -\infty$ as $x \to 0^+$, $g \to 0$, $fg \to -8$

(c) $f \to -\infty$ as $x \to 2^-$, $f \to \infty$ as $x \to 2^+$, $g \to 0$, $fg \to 0$

(d) $x \to \infty$, $g \to 0$, $fg \to \infty$

(e) Nothing—you need more information to decide.

67. For $x > 0$, $0 < e^{-x} < 1$, so $0 < \dfrac{e^{-x}}{x} < \dfrac{1}{x}$.

Since both 0 and $\dfrac{1}{x}$ approach zero as $x \to \infty$, the Sandwich Theorem states that $\dfrac{e^{-x}}{x}$ must also approach zero.

69. Limit $= 2$, because $\dfrac{\ln x^2}{\ln x} = \dfrac{2\ln x}{\ln x} = 2$.

71. Limit $= 1$. Since $\ln(x+1) = \ln x\left(1 + \dfrac{1}{x}\right) = \ln x + \ln\left(1 + \dfrac{1}{x}\right)$,

$\dfrac{\ln(x+1)}{\ln x} = \dfrac{\ln x + \ln(1 + 1/x)}{\ln x} = 1 + \dfrac{\ln(1+1/x)}{\ln x}$. But as $x \to \infty$, $1 + \dfrac{1}{x}$ approaches 1, so $\ln\left(1 + \dfrac{1}{x}\right)$ approaches $\ln(1) = 0$.

Also, as $x \to \infty$, $\ln x$ approaches infinity. This means the second term above approaches 0 and the limit is 1

Quick Quiz (Sections 2.1 and 2.2)

1. D

3. E

Section 2.3

Quick Review 2.3

1. 2
3. **(a)** 1 **(b)** 2 **(c)** No limit **(d)** 2
5. $g(x) = \sin x, x \geq 0 \quad (f \circ g)(x) = \sin^2 x, x \geq 0$
7. $x = \frac{1}{2}, -5$ **9.** $x = 1$

Exercises 2.3

1. $x = -2$, infinite discontinuity
3. None
5. All points not in the domain, i.e., all $x < -3/2$
7. $x = 0$, jump discontinuity
9. $x = 0$, infinite discontinuity
11. **(a)** Yes **(b)** Yes **(c)** Yes **(d)** Yes
13. **(a)** No **(b)** No
15. 0
17. No, because the right-hand and left-hand limits are not the same at zero
19. **(a)** $x = 2$ **(b)** Not removable; the one-sided limits are different.
21. **(a)** $x = 1$ **(b)** Not removable; it's an infinite discontinuity.
23. **(a)** All points not in the domain along with $x = 0, 1$
(b) $x = 0$ is a removable discontinuity; assign $f(0) = 0$, $x = 1$ is not removable; the two-sided limits are different.
25. $y = x - 3$
27. $y = \begin{cases} \dfrac{\sin x}{x}, & x \neq 0 \\ 1, & x = 0 \end{cases}$
29. $y = \sqrt{x} + 2$
31. The domain of f is all real numbers $x \neq 3$. f is continuous at all those points, so f is a continuous function.
33. f is the composite of two continuous functions $g \circ h$ where $g(x) = \sqrt{x}$ and $h(x) = \dfrac{x}{x+1}$.
35. f is the composite of three continuous functions $g \circ h \circ k$ where $g(x) = \cos x$, $h(x) = \sqrt[3]{x}$, and $k(x) = 1 - x$.
37. Assume $y = x$, constant functions, and the square root function are continuous.
Use the sum, composite, and quotient theorems.
Domain: $(-2, \infty)$
39. Assume $y = x$ and the absolute value function are continuous.
Use the product, constant multiple, difference, and composite theorems.
Domain: $(-\infty, \infty)$
41. One possible answer:

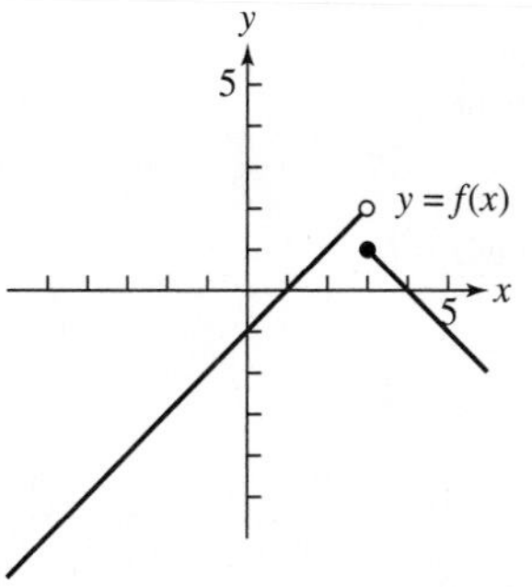

43. One possible answer:

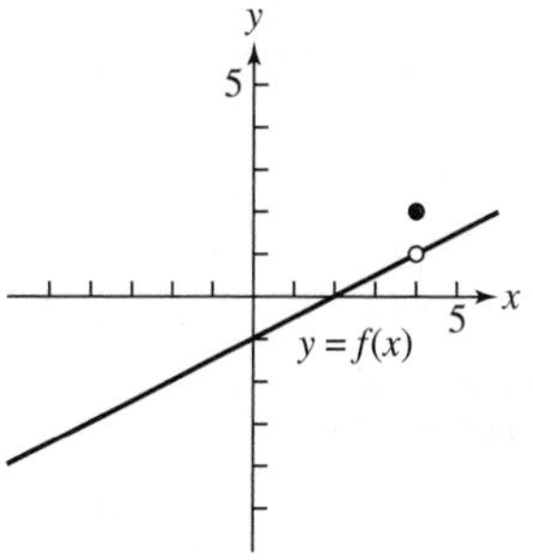

45. $x \approx -0.724$ and $x \approx 1.221$
47. $a = \frac{4}{3}$ **49.** $a = 4$
51. Consider $f(x) = x - e^{-x}$, f is continuous, $f(0) = -1$, and $f(1) = 1 - \frac{1}{e} > 0.5$. By the Intermediate Value Theorem, for some c in $(0, 1)$, $f(c) = 0$ and $e^{-c} = c$.
53. **(a)** $f(x) = \begin{cases} -1.10 \text{ int } (-x), & 0 \leq x \leq 6 \\ 7.25, & 6 < x \leq 24 \end{cases}$
(b)

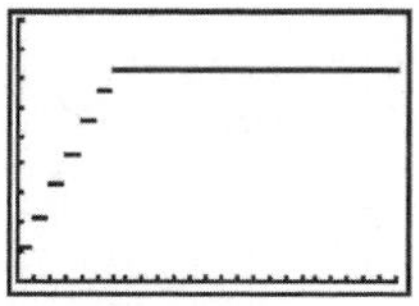

[0, 24] by [0, 9]

This is continuous at all values of x in the domain $[0, 24]$ except for $x = 0, 1, 2, 3, 4, 5, 6$.
55. False. If f has a jump discontinuity at $x = a$, then $\lim_{x\to a^-} f(x) \neq \lim_{x\to a} f(x)$ so f is not continuous at $x = a$.
57. E **59.** E
61. This is because $\lim_{h\to 0} f(a + h) = \lim_{x\to a} f(x)$.
63. Since the absolute value function is continuous, this follows from the theorem about continuity of composite functions.

Section 2.4

Quick Review 2.4

1. $\Delta x = 8, \ \Delta y = 3$
3. Slope $= -\frac{4}{7}$
5. $y = \frac{3}{2}x + 6$
7. $y = -\frac{3}{4}x + \frac{19}{4}$
9. $y = \frac{2}{-3}x + \frac{7}{3}$

Exercises 2.4

1. **(a)** 19 **(b)** 1
3. **(a)** $\dfrac{1 - e^{-2}}{2} \approx 0.432$ **(b)** $\dfrac{e^3 - e}{2} \approx 8.684$
5. **(a)** $-\dfrac{4}{\pi} \approx -1.273$ **(b)** $-\dfrac{3\sqrt{3}}{\pi} \approx -1.654$

7. Using $Q_1 = (10, 225)$, $Q_2 = (14, 375)$, $Q_3 = (16.5, 475)$, $Q_4 = (18, 550)$, and $P = (20, 650)$

(a)

Secant	Slope
PQ_1	43
PQ_2	46
PQ_3	50
PQ_4	50

Units are meters/second

(b) Approximately 50 m/sec

9. (a) -4 **(b)** $y = -4x - 4$

(c) $y = \frac{1}{4}x + \frac{9}{2}$

(d)

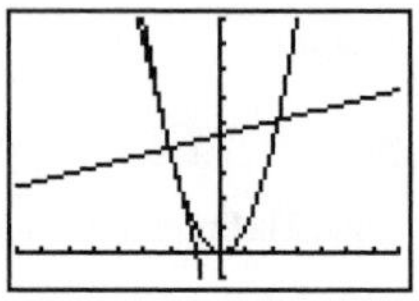

[–8, 7] by [–1, 9]

11. (a) -1 **(b)** $y = -x + 3$

(c) $y = x - 1$

(d)

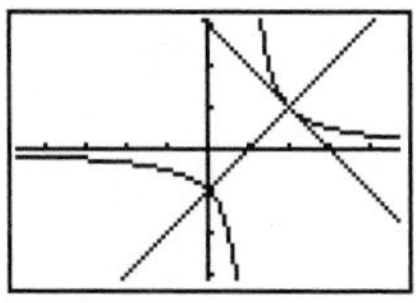

[–4.7, 4.7] by [–3.1, 3.1]

13. (a) 1 **(b)** -1

15. No. Slope from the left is -2; slope from the right is 2. The two-sided limit of the difference quotient doesn't exist.

17. Yes. The slope is $-\frac{1}{4}$.

19. (a) $2a$ **(b)** The slope of the tangent steadily increases as a increases.

21. (a) $-\dfrac{1}{(a-1)^2}$

(b) The slope of the tangent is always negative. The tangents are very steep near $x = 1$ and nearly horizontal as a moves away from the origin.

23. 3 ft/sec **25.** $-1/4$ ft/sec **27.** 19.6 m/sec

29. 6π in^2/in. **31.** 3.72 m/sec

33. $(-2, -5)$

35. (a) At $x = 0$: $y = -x - 1$

At $x = 2$: $y = -x + 3$

(b) At $x = 0$: $y = x - 1$ At $x = 2$: $y = x - 1$

37. (a)

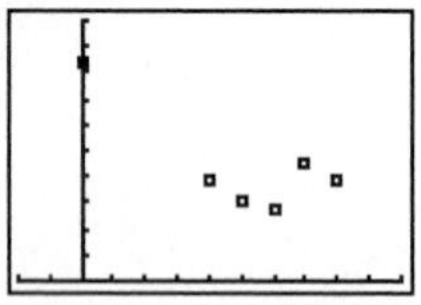

[–2, 10] by [0, 1000]

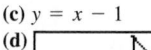

(b) Slope of $PQ_1 = 2$, slope of $PQ_2 = 25.33$, slope of $PQ_3 = -59$.

39. True. The normal line is perpendicular to the tangent line at the point.

41. D **43.** C

45. (a) $\dfrac{e^{1+h} - e}{h}$ **(b)** Limit ≈ 2.718 **(c)** They're about the same.

(d) Yes, it has a tangent whose slope is about e.

47. No **49.** Yes

51. This function has a tangent with slope zero at the origin. It is sandwiched between two functions, $y = x^2$ and $y = -x^2$, both of which have slope zero at the origin.

Looking at the difference quotient, $-h \le \dfrac{f(0+h) - f(0)}{h} \le h$, so the Sandwich Theorem tells us that the limit is 0.

53. Slope ≈ 0.540

55. If $x = a + h$, then $x - a = h$. Replacing $f(a + h)$ by $f(x)$ and h by $x - a$ turns the first expression given for the difference quotient into the second expression.

Quick Quiz (Sections 2.3 and 2.4)

1. D **3.** B

Review Exercises

1. -15 **2.** $\frac{5}{21}$

3. No limit **4.** No limit

5. $-\frac{1}{4}$ **6.** $\frac{2}{5}$

7. $+\infty, -\infty$ **8.** $\frac{1}{2}$

9. 2 **10.** 0 **11.** 6 **12.** 5

13. 0 **14.** 1 **15.** Limit exists

16. Limit exists **17.** Limit exists

18. Doesn't exist **19.** Limit exists

20. Limit exists

21. Yes **22.** No

23. No **24.** Yes

25. (a) 1 **(b)** 1.5 **(c)** No

(d) g is discontinuous at $x = 3$ (and points not in domain).

(e) Yes, can remove discontinuity at $x = 3$ by assigning the value 1 to $g(3)$.

26. (a) 1.5 **(b)** 0 **(c)** 0 **(d)** No

(e) k is discontinuous at $x = 1$ (and points not in domain).

(f) Discontinuity at $x = 1$ is not removable because the two one-sided limits are different.

27. (a) Vertical Asymp.: $x = -2$

(b) Left-hand limit $= -\infty$

Right-hand limit $= \infty$

28. (a) Vertical Asymp.: $x = 0$ and $x = -2$

(b) At $x = 0$:

Left-hand limit $= -\infty$

Right-hand limit $= -\infty$

At $x = -2$:

Left-hand limit $= -\infty$

Right-hand limit $= -\infty$

29. (a) At $x = -1$:

Left-hand limit $= 1$

Right-hand limit $= 1$

At $x = 0$:

Left-hand limit $= 0$

Right-hand limit $= 0$

At $x = 1$:

Left-hand limit $= -1$

Right-hand limit $= 1$

(b) At $x = -1$:

Yes, the limit is 1.

At $x = 0$:

Yes, the limit is 0.

At $x = 1$:

No, the limit doesn't exist because the two one-sided limits are different.

(c) At $x = -1$:
Continuous because $f(-1) =$ the limit.
At $x = 0$:
Discontinuous because $f(0) \neq$ the limit.
At $x = 1$:
Discontinuous because limit doesn't exist.

30. **(a)** Left-hand limit $= 3$ Right-hand limit $= -3$
(b) No, because the two one-sided limits are different
(c) Every place except for $x = 1$
(d) At $x = 1$

31. $x = -2$ and $x = 2$

32. There are no points of discontinuity.

33. **(a)** $2/x$ **(b)** $y = 0$ (x-axis)

34. **(a)** 2 **(b)** $y = 2$

35. **(a)** x^2 **(b)** None

36. **(a)** x **(b)** None

37. **(a)** e^x **(b)** x

38. **(a)** $\ln |x|$ **(b)** $\ln |x|$

39. $k = 8$ **40.** $k = \frac{1}{2}$

41. One possible answer:

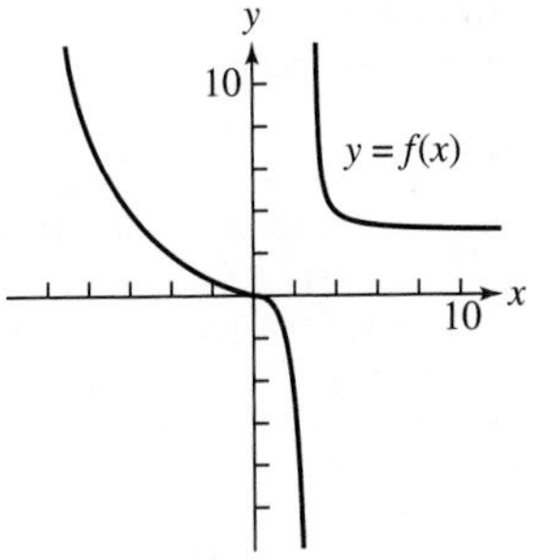

42. One possible answer:

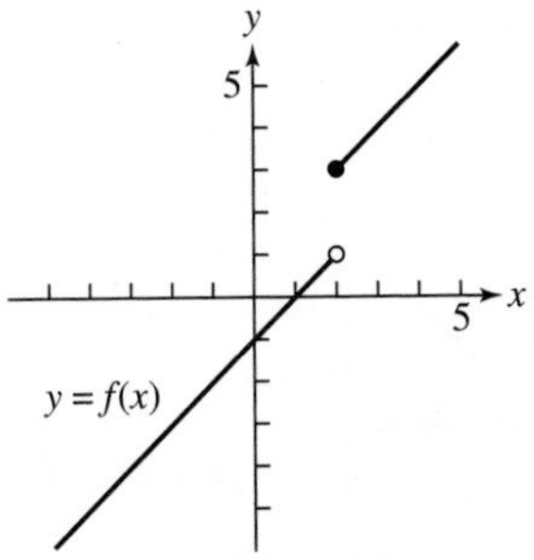

43. $\frac{2}{\pi}$ **44.** $\frac{2}{3}\pi aH$ **45.** $12a$ **46.** $2a - 1$

47. **(a)** -1 **(b)** $y = -x - 1$ **(c)** $y = x - 3$

48. $\left(\frac{3}{2}, -\frac{9}{4}\right)$

49. **(a)** Perhaps this is the number of bears placed in the reserve when it was established.
(b) 200

49. **(c)** Perhaps this is the maximum number of bears that the reserve can support due to limitations of food, space, or other resources. Or, perhaps the number is capped at 200 and excess bears are moved to other locations.

50. **(a)** $\begin{cases} f(x)3.20 - 1.35 \cdot \text{int}(-x + 1), & 0 < x \leq 20 \\ 0, & x = 0 \end{cases}$

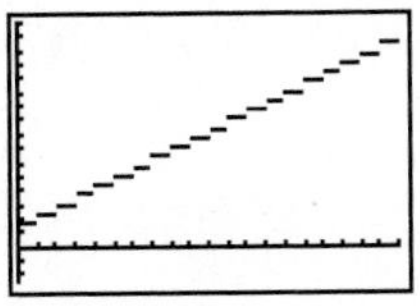

[0, 20] by [–5, 32]

(b) f is discontinuous at integer values of x: 0, 1, 2, . . . , 19

51. **(a)**

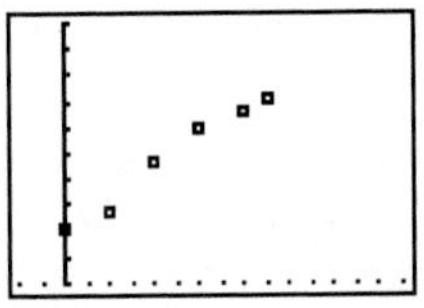

[–2, 15] by [15000, 20000]

(b) Slope of $PQ_1 = 313.857$; slope of $PQ_2 = 244.8$; slope of $PQ_3 = 210$
(c) Answers are the same as in part (b) but with *people per year* added.
(d) Answers will vary.
(e) Answers will vary.

52. $\lim_{x \to c} f(x) = 3/2$; $\lim_{x \to c} g(x) = 1/2$

53. **(a)** All real numbers except 3 or -3.
(b) $x = -3$ and $x = 3$ **(c)** $y = 0$
(d) Odd, because $f(-x) = \dfrac{-x}{|(-x)^2 - 9|} = \dfrac{x}{|x^2 - 9|} = -f(x)$ for all x in the domain.
(e) $x = -3$ and $x = 3$. Both are nonremovable.

54. **(a)** $\lim_{x \to 2^-} f(x) = \lim_{x \to 2^-} (x^2 - a^2x) = 4 - 2a^2$.
(b) $\lim_{x \to 2^+} f(x) = \lim_{x \to 2^+} (4 - 2x^2) = -4$
(c) For $\lim_{x \to 2} f(x)$ to exist, we must have $4 - 2a^2 = -4$, so $a = \pm 2$. If $a = \pm 2$, then $\lim_{x \to 2^-} f(x) = \lim_{x \to 2^+} f(x) = f(2) = -4$, making f continuous at 2 by definition.

55. **(a)** The zeros of $f(x) = \dfrac{x^3 - 2x^2 + 1}{x^2 + 3}$ are the same as the zeros of the polynomial $x^3 - 2x^2 + 1$. By inspection, one such zero is $x = 1$. Divide $x^3 - 2x^2 + 1$ by $x - 1$ to get $x^2 - x^2 - 1$, which has zeros $\dfrac{1 \pm \sqrt{5}}{2}$ by the quadratic formula. Thus, the zeros of f are 1, $\dfrac{1 + \sqrt{5}}{2}$, and $\dfrac{1 - \sqrt{5}}{2}$.

(c) $\lim_{x \to \infty} f(x) = +\infty$ and $\lim_{x \to \infty} \dfrac{f(x)}{g(x)} = \lim_{x \to \infty} \dfrac{x^3 - 2x^2 + 1}{x^3 + 3x} = 1.$

CHAPTER 3

Section 3.1

Quick Review 3.1

1. 4 **3.** -1 **5.** 0

7. $\lim_{x \to 1^+} f(x) = 0$; $\lim_{x \to 1^-} f(x) = 3$

9. No, the two one-sided limits are different.

Exercises 3.1

1. $-1/4$ **3.** 2 **5.** $-1/4$ **7.** $1/4$

9. $f'(x) = 3$ **11.** $2x$ **13.** **(b)** **15.** **(d)**

17. **(a)** $y = 5x - 7$ **(b)** $y = -\frac{1}{5}x + \frac{17}{5}$

19. **(a)** $y = 3x - 2$ **(b)** $y = -\frac{1}{3}x + \frac{4}{3}$

21. **(a)** Sometime around April 1. The rate then is approximately $1/6$ hour per day.
(b) Yes. Jan. 1 and July 1
(c) Positive: Jan 1, through July 1 Negative: July 1 through Dec. 31

23. **(a)** 0 and 0 **(b)** 1700 and 1300 **25.** (iv)

27.

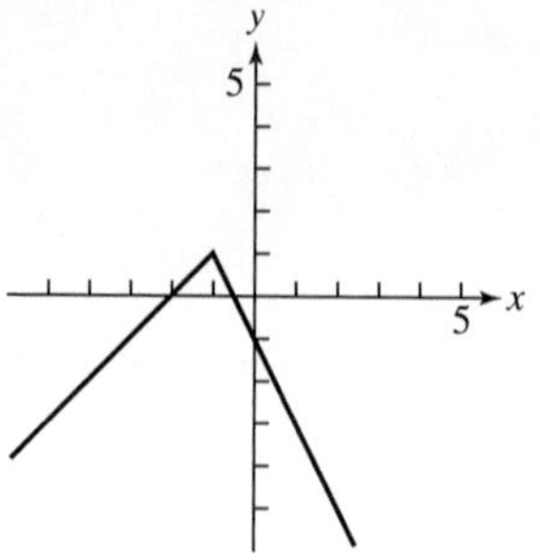

29. Graph of derivative:

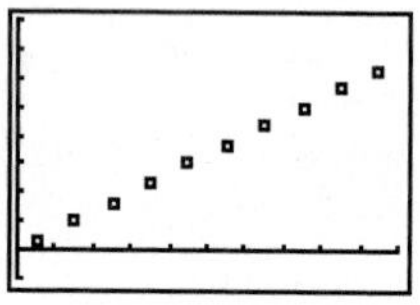

[0,10] by [-10,80]

(a) The speed of the skier **(b)** Feet per second
(c) Approximately $D = 6.65t$

31. We show that the right-hand derivative at $x = 1$ does not exist:

$$\lim_{h\to 0^+} \frac{f(1+h) - f(1)}{h} = \lim_{h\to 0^+} \frac{3(1+h) - 2 - 2}{h}$$
$$= \lim_{h\to 0^+} \frac{3h - 1}{h} = -\infty$$

33.

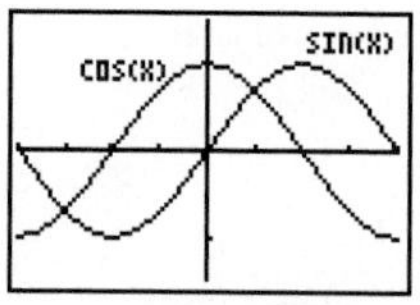

$[-\pi, \pi]$ by $[-1.5, 1.5]$

Cosine could be the derivative of sine. The values of cosine are positive where sine is increasing, zero where sine has horizontal tangents, and negative where sine is decreasing.

35. Two parabolas are parallel if they have the same derivative at every value of x. This means their tangent lines are parallel at each value of x. Two such parabolas are given by $y = x^2$ and $y = x^2 + 4$. They are graphed below.

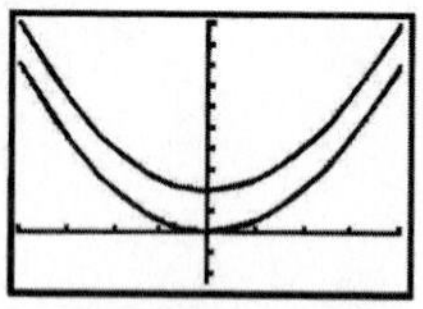

[−4, 4] by [−5, 20]

The parabolas are "everywhere equidistant," as long as the distance between them is always measured along a vertical line.

37. False. Let $f(x) = |x|$. The left hand derivative at $x = 0$ is -1 and the right hand derivative at $x = 0$ is 1. $f'(0)$ does not exist.

39. A **41.** C

43. **(e)** The y-intercept is $b - a$.

45. **(a)** 0.992 **(b)** 0.008
(c) If P is the answer to (b), then the probability of a shared birthday when there are four people is

$$1 - (1 - P)\frac{362}{365} \approx 0.016.$$

(d) No. Clearly, February 29th is a much less likely birth date. Furthermore, census data do not support the assumption that the other 365 birth dates are equally likely. However, this simplifying assumption may still give us some insight into this problem even if the calculated probabilities aren't completely accurate.

Section 3.2

Quick Review 3.2

1. Yes **3.** Yes **5.** No
7. $[0, \infty)$ **9.** 3.2

Exercises 3.2

1. Left-hand derivative $= 0$
Right-hand derivative $= 1$
Differentiable at all other points

3. Left-hand derivative $= \frac{1}{2}$
Right-hand derivative $= 2$
Differentiable at all other points

5. **(a)** All points in $[-3, 2]$ **(b)** None **(c)** None
7. **(a)** All points in $[-3, 3]$ except $x = 0$ **(b)** None **(c)** $x = 0$
9. **(a)** All points in $[-1, 2]$ except $x = 0$ **(b)** $x = 0$ **(c)** None
11. Discontinuity **13.** Corner **15.** Corner
17. 4, yes **19.** 2, yes **21.** 8.000001, yes **23.** 0, no **25.** 0, no

27.

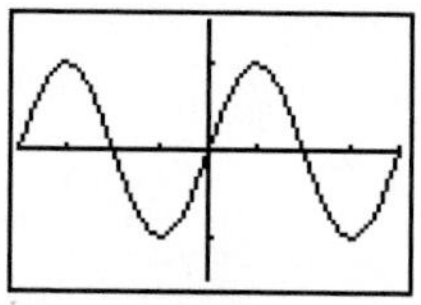

$[-2\pi, 2\pi]$ by $[-1.5, 1.5]$

$\frac{dy}{dx} = \sin x$

29.

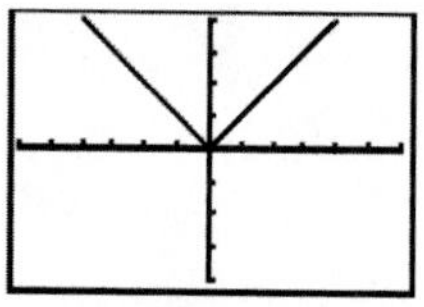

[−6, 6] by [-4, 4]

$dy/dx = \text{abs}(x)$ or $|x|$

31. All reals except $x = -1, 5$
33. All reals except $x = 0$
35. All reals except $x = 3$
37. The function $f(x)$ does not have the Intermediate Value Property. Choose some a in $(-1, 0)$ and b in $(0, 1)$. Then $f(a) = 0$ and $f(b) = 1$, but f does not take on any value between 0 and 1.
39. **(a)** $a + b = 2$ **(b)** $a = -3$ and $b = 5$
41. False. The function $f(x) = |x|$ is continuous at $x = 0$ but is not differentiable at $x = 0$.
43. A **45.** C
47. **(a)**

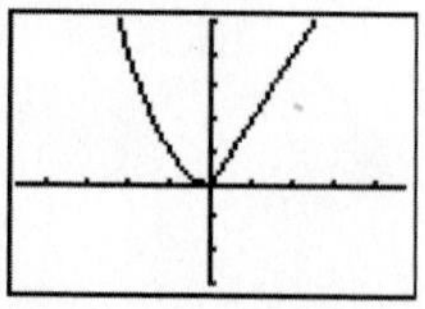

[-4.7, 4.7] by [-3, 5]

(b) See Exercise 46.

(c)

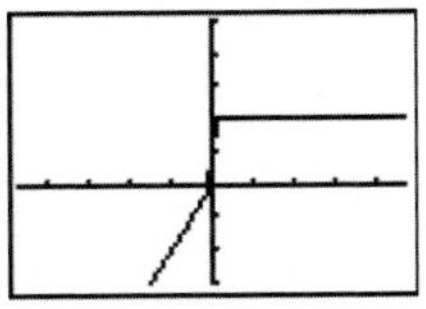

(d) NDER(Y1, x, -0.1) $= -0.2$, NDER(Y1, x, 0) $= 0.9995$, NDER(Y1, x, 0.1) $= 2$.

Section 3.3

Quick Review 3.3

1. $x + x^2 - 2x^{-1} - 2$

3. $3x^2 - 2x^{-1} + 5x^{-2}$ **5.** $x^{-3} + x^{-1} + 2x^{-2} + 2$

7. Root: $x \approx 1.173$, $500x^6 \approx 1305$ Root: $x \approx 2.394$, $500x^6 \approx 94,212$

9. (a) 0 **(b)** 0 **(c)** 0

Exercises 3.3

1. $dy/dx = -2x$ **3.** $dy/dx = 2$

5. $dy/dx = x^2 + x + 1$ **7.** At $x = 1/3, 1$

9. At $x = 0, \pm\sqrt{2}$ **11.** At $x = -1, 0, 1$

13. (a) $3x^2 + 2x + 1$ **(b)** $3x^2 + 2x + 1$

15. $7x^6 + 10x^4 + 4x^3 + 6x^2 + 2x + 1$

17. $-\dfrac{19}{(3x-2)^2}$ **19.** $\dfrac{3}{x^4}$

21. $\dfrac{x^4 + 2x}{(1 - x^3)^2}$

23. (a) 13 **(b)** -7 **(c)** $\dfrac{7}{25}$ **(d)** 20

25. (iii) **27.** $y = \dfrac{1}{2}x + \dfrac{1}{2}$

29. $-8x^{-3} - 8$ **31.** $\dfrac{1}{\sqrt{x}(\sqrt{x} + 1)^2}$

33. $y' = 4x^3 + 3x^2 - 4x + 1$, $y'' = 12x^2 + 6x - 4$, $y''' = 24x + 6$, $y^{(iv)} = 24$

35. $y' = -x^{-2} + 2x$, $y'' = 2x^{-3} + 2$, $y''' = -6x^{-4}$, $y^{(iv)} = 24x^{-5}$

37. $y = -\dfrac{1}{9}x + \dfrac{29}{9}$

39. $(-1, 27)$ and $(2, 0)$

41. At $(0, 0)$: $y = 4x$
At $(1, 2)$: $y = 2$

43. (a) Let $f(x) = x$,

$$\lim_{h\to0} \frac{f(x+h) - f(x)}{h} = \lim_{h\to0} \frac{(x+h) - x}{h}$$

$$= \lim_{h\to0} \frac{h}{h} = \lim_{h\to0} (1) = 1$$

(b) Note that $u = u(x)$ is a function of x,

$$\lim_{h\to0} \frac{-u(x+h) - [-u(x)]}{h}$$

$$= \lim_{h\to0} \left(-\frac{u(x+h) - u(x)}{h}\right)$$

$$= -\lim_{h\to0} \frac{u(x+h) - u(x)}{h} = -\frac{du}{dx}$$

45. $-\dfrac{f''(x)}{[f(x)]^2}$ **47.** $\dfrac{ds}{dt} = 9.8t$, $\dfrac{d^2s}{dt^2} = 9.8$

49. If the radius of a circle is changed by a very small amount Δr, the change in the area can be thought of as a very thin strip with length given by the circumference, $2\pi r$, and width Δr. Therefore, the change in the area can be thought of as $(2\pi r)(\Delta r)$, which means that the change in the area divided by the change in the radius is just $2\pi r$.

51. 390 bushels of annual production per year.

53. False. π^3 is a constant so $d/dx\,(\pi^3) = 0$.

55. B **57.** E

59. (a) It is insignificant in the limiting case and can be treated as zero (and removed from the expression).

(b) It was "rejected" because it is incomparably smaller than the other terms: $v\,du$ and $u\,dv$.

(c) The product rule given in the text.

(d) Because dx is "infinitely small," and this could be thought of as dividing by zero.

(e) $d\left(\dfrac{u}{v}\right) = \dfrac{u + du}{v + dv} - \dfrac{u}{v}$

$$= \frac{(u + du)v - u(v + dv)}{(v + dv)v}$$

$$= \frac{uv + vdu - uv - udv}{v^2 + vdv}$$

$$= \frac{vdu - udv}{v^2}$$

Quick Quiz (Sections 3.1–3.3)

1. D **3.** C

Section 3.4

Quick Review 3.4

1. Downward **3.** x-intercepts $= 2, 8$

5. $(5, 144)$ **7.** $x = \dfrac{15}{8}$

9. 64

Exercises 3.4

1. (a) $V = x^3$ **(b)** $\dfrac{dV}{ds} = 3s^2$

(c) 3, 75 **(d)** in^3/in.

3. (a) $A = \dfrac{\sqrt{3}}{4}s^2$ **(b)** $\dfrac{dA}{ds} = \dfrac{\sqrt{3}}{2}s$

(c) $\sqrt{3}, 5\sqrt{5}$ **(d)** in^2/in.

5. (a)

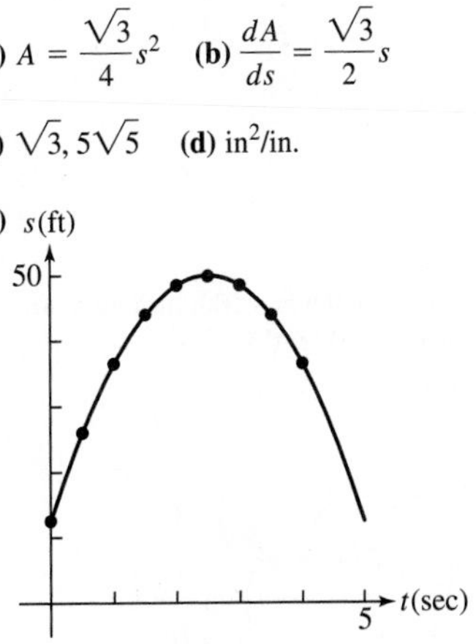

(b) $s'(1) = 18$, $s'(2.5) = 0$, $s'(3.5) = -12$

7. (a) p' **(slope)**

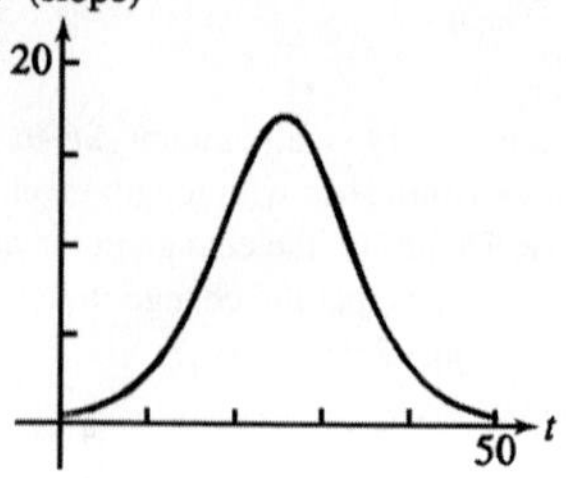

horizontal axis: Days
vertical axis: Flies per day

(b) Fastest: Around the 25th day
Slowest: Day 50 or day 0

9. (a) Move forward: $0 \le t < 1$ and $5 < t < 7$
move backward: $1 < t < 5$
speed up: $1 < t < 2$ and $5 < t < 6$
slow down: $0 \le t < 1, 3 < t < 5$, and $6 < t < 7$

(b) Positive: $3 < t < 6$
negative: $0 \le t < 2$ and $6 < t < 7$
zero: $2 < t < 3$ and $7 < t \le 9$

(c) At $t = 0$ and $2 < t < 3$

(d) $7 < t \le 9$

11. (a) At $t = 2$ and $t = 7$ **(b)** Between $t = 3$ and $t = 6$

(c) Speed(m/sec)

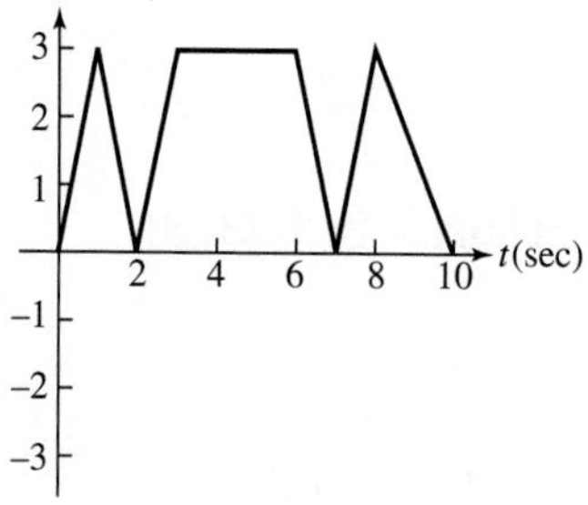

(d) Acceleration (m/sec^2)

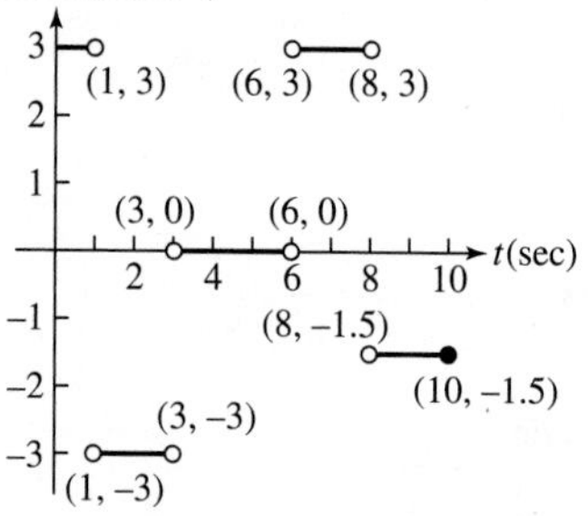

12. (a) 135 seconds

(b) $\frac{5}{73} \approx 0.068$ furlongs/sec

(c) $\frac{1}{13} \approx 0.077$ furlongs/sec

(d) During the last furlong (between the 9th and 10th furlong markers)

(e) During the first furlong (between markers 0 and 1)

13. (a) $\text{vel}(t) = 24 - 1.6t$ m/sec, $\text{accel}(t) = -1.6$ m/sec^2

(b) 15 seconds

(c) 180 meters

(d) About 4,393 seconds

(e) 30 seconds

15. About 29.388 meters

17. For the moon:
$x_1(t) = 3(t < 160) + 3.1(t \ge 160)$
$y_1(t) = 832t - 2.6t^2$
t-values: 0 to 320
window: $[0, 6]$ by $[-10{,}000, 70{,}000]$

For Earth:
$x_1(t) = 3(t < 26) + 3.1(t \ge 26)$
$y_1(t) = 832t - 16t^2$
t-values: 0 to 52
window: $[0, 6]$ by $[-1000, 11{,}000]$

19. (a) 10 m

(b) 2 m/sec

(c) 5 m/sec

(d) 2 m/sec^2

(e) At $t = \frac{3}{2}$ sec

(f) At $s = -\frac{1}{4}$ m

21. (a) $v(t) = 3t^2 - 16t + 20 = (t - 2)(3t - 10)$

(b) $a(t) = 6t - 16$

(c) $t = 2, 10/3$

(d) The particle starts at the point $s = -16$ when $t = 0$ and moves right until it stops at $s = 0$ when $t = 2$, then it moves left to the point $s = -1.185$ when $t = 10/3$ where it stops again, and finally continues right from there on.

23. At $t = 1$: -6 m/sec^2; At $t = 3$: 6 m/sec^2

25. (a) $\frac{dy}{dt} = \frac{t}{12} - 1$

(b) Fastest: at $t = 0$ slowest:
at $t = 12$; at $t = 0$: $\frac{dy}{dt} = -1$;
at $t = 12$: $\frac{dx}{dt} = 0$

(c)

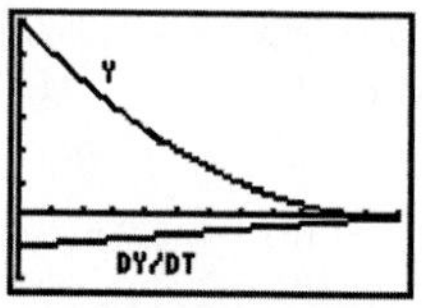

[0, 12] by [−2, 6]

y is decreasing and $\frac{dy}{dt}$ is negative over the entire interval. y decreases more rapidly early in the interval, and the magnitude of $\frac{dy}{dt}$ is larger then. $\frac{dy}{dt}$ is 0 at $t = 12$, where y seems to have a horizontal tangent.

27. (a) \$110 per machine

(b) \$80 per machine

(c) \$79.90 for the 101st machine

29. (a)

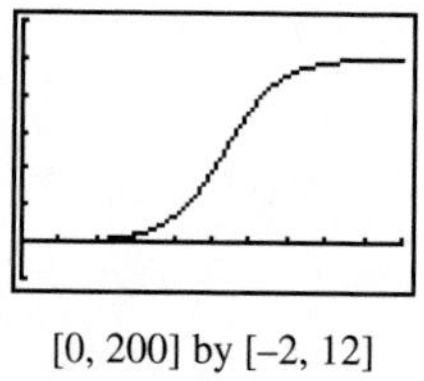

[0, 200] by [–2, 12]

(b) $x \ge 0$ (whole numbers)

(c)

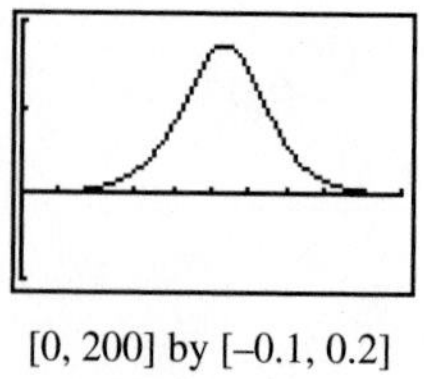

[0, 200] by [–0.1, 0.2]

P seems to be relatively sensitive to changes in x between approximately $x = 60$ and $x = 160$.

(d) The maximum occurs when $x \approx 106.44$. Since x must be an integer, $P(106) \approx 4.924$ thousand dollars or \$4924.

(e) \$13 per package sold, \$165 per package sold, \$118 per package sold, \$31 per package sold, \$6 per package sold, $P'(300) \approx 0$ (on the order of 10^{-6}, or \$0.001 per package sold)

(f) The limit is 10. Maximum possible profit is \$10,000 monthly.

(g) Yes. In order to sell more and more packages, the company might need to lower the price to a point where they won't make any additional profit.

31. Graph C is position, graph A is velocity, and graph B is acceleration. A is the derivative of C because it is positive, negative, and zero where C is increasing, decreasing, and has horizontal tangents, respectively. The relationship between B and A is similar.

33. Possible answer:

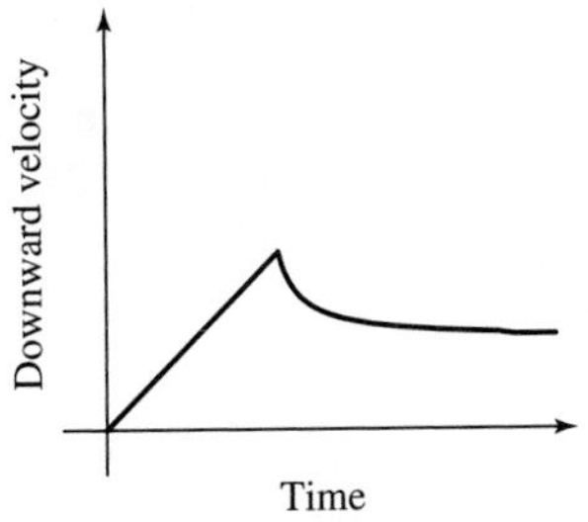

35. Exit velocity $\approx$ 348.712 ft/sec $\approx$ 237.758 mi/h

37. (a) It begins at the point $(-5, 2)$ moving in the positive direction. After a little more than one second, it has moved a bit past $(6, 2)$ and it turns back in the negative direction for approximately 2 seconds. At the end of that time, it is near $(-2, 2)$ and it turns back again in the positive direction. After that, it continues moving in the positive direction indefinitely, speeding up as it goes.

(b) Speeds up: $[1.153, 2.167]$ and $[3.180, \infty]$ slows down: $[0, 1.153]$ and $[2.167, 3.180]$

(c) At $t \approx 1.153$ sec and $t \approx 3.180$ sec

(d) At $t \approx 1.153$ sec and $t \approx 3.180$ sec "instantaneously"

(e) The velocity starts out positive but decreasing, it becomes negative, then starts to increase, and becomes positive again and continues to increase. The speed is decreasing, reaches 0 at $t \approx 1.5$ sec, then increases until $t \approx 2.17$ sec, decreases until $t \approx 3.18$ sec when it is 0 again, then increases after that.

(f) At about 0.745 sec, 1.626 sec, 4.129 sec

39. Since profit = revenue − cost, using Rule 4 (the "difference rule"), and taking derivatives, we see that marginal profit = marginal revenue – marginal cost.

41. True. The acceleration is the first derivative of the velocity which, in turn, is the first derivative of the position function.

43. D **45.** C

47. (a) $g'(x) = h'(x) = t'(x) = 3x^2$

(b)

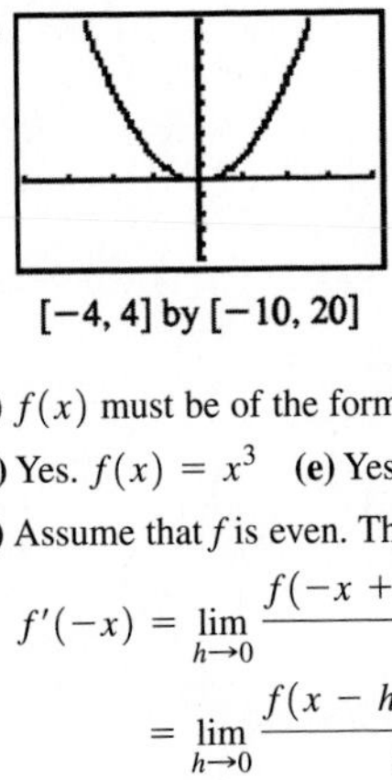

$[-4, 4]$ by $[-10, 20]$

(c) $f(x)$ must be of the form $f(x) = x^3 + c$, where c is a constant.

(d) Yes. $f(x) = x^3$ **(e)** Yes. $f(x) = x^3 + 3$

49. (a) Assume that f is even. Then,

$$f'(-x) = \lim_{h\to 0} \frac{f(-x+h) - f(-x)}{h} = \lim_{h\to 0} \frac{f(x-h) - f(x)}{h},$$

and substituting $k = -h$,

$$= \lim_{k\to 0} \frac{f(x+k) - f(x)}{-k} = -\lim_{k\to 0} \frac{f(x+k) - f(x)}{k} = -f'(x)$$

So, f' is an odd function.

(b) Assume that f is odd. Then,

$$f'(-x) = \lim_{h\to 0} \frac{f(-x+h) - f(-x)}{h} = \lim_{h\to 0} \frac{-f(x-h) + f(x)}{h}$$

and substituting $k = -h$,

$$= \lim_{k\to 0} \frac{-f(x+k) + f(x)}{-k} = \lim_{k\to 0} \frac{f(x+k) - f(x)}{k} = f'(x)$$

So, f' is an even function.

Section 3.5

Quick Review 3.5

1. $3\pi/4 \approx 2.356$

3. $\sqrt{3}/2$

5. Domain: $x \neq k\dfrac{\pi}{2}$, where k is an odd integer; range: all reals

7. $\pm 1/\sqrt{2}$

9. $y = 12x - 35$

Exercises 3.5

1. $1 + \sin x$ **3.** $-\dfrac{1}{x^2} + 5\cos x$

5. $-x^2 \cos x - 2x \sin x$ **7.** $4 \sec x \tan x$

9. $-\dfrac{\csc^2 x}{(1 + \cot x)^2} = -\dfrac{1}{(\sin x + \cos x)^2}$

11. $v = 5\cos t$, $a = -5\sin t$
The weight starts at 0, goes to 5, and then oscillates between 5 and −5. The period of the motion is 2π. The speed is greatest when $\cos t = \pm 1$ $(t = k\pi)$, zero when $\cos t = 0$ $(t = k\pi/2$, k odd$)$. The acceleration is greatest when $\sin t = \pm 1 (t = k\pi/2$, k odd$)$, zero when $\sin t = 0$ $(t = k\pi)$.

13. (a) $v = 3\cos t$, speed $= |3\cos t|$, $a = -3\sin t$
(b) $v = 3\sqrt{2}/2$, speed $= 3\sqrt{2}/2$, $a = -3\sqrt{2}/2$
(c) The body starts at 2, goes up to 5, goes down to −1, and then oscillates between −1 and 5. The period of the motion is 2π.

15. (a) $v = 2\cos t - 3\sin t$,
speed $= |2\cos t - 3\sin t|$,
$a = -2\sin t - 3\cos t$
(b) $v = -\sqrt{2}/2$,
speed $= \sqrt{2}/2$, $a = -5\sqrt{2}/2$
(c) The body starts at 3, goes up to 3.606 $(\sqrt{13})$, down to −3.606 $(-\sqrt{13})$, and then oscillates between −3.606 and 3.606. The period of the motion is 2π.

17. $2\sin t$ **19.** $-\cos t - \sin t$

21. tangent: $y = -x + \pi + 3$, normal: $y = x - \pi + 3$

23. tangent: $y = -8.063x + 25.460$, normal: $y = 0.124x + 0.898$

25. (a)
$$\frac{d}{dx}\tan x = \frac{d}{dx}\frac{\sin x}{\cos x} = \frac{(\cos x)(\cos x) - (\sin x)(-\sin x)}{(\cos x)^2} = \frac{\cos^2 x + \sin^2 x}{\cos^2 x} = \frac{1}{\cos^2 x} = \sec^2 x$$

(b) $\frac{d}{dx}\sec x = \frac{d}{dx}\frac{1}{\cos x}$

$= \frac{(\cos x)(0) - (1)(-\sin x)}{(\cos x)^2}$

$= \frac{\sin x}{(\cos x)^2} = \sec x \tan x$

27. $d/dx\,(\sec x) = \sec x \tan x$, which is 0 at $x = 0$, so the slope of the tangent line is 0.
$d/dx\,(\cos x) = -\sin x$, which is 0 at $x = 0$, so the slope of the tangent line is 0.

29. Tangent: $y = -x + \frac{\pi}{4} + 1$

normal: $y = x + 1 - \frac{\pi}{4}$

31. **(a)** $y = -x + \frac{\pi}{2} + 2$ **(b)** $y = 4 - \sqrt{3}$

33. **(a)** Velocity: $-2\cos t$ m/sec
Speed: $|2\cos t|$ m/sec
Accel.: $2\sin t$ m/sec^2
Jerk: $2\cos t$ m/sec^3
(b) Velocity: $-\sqrt{2}$ m/sec
Speed: $\sqrt{2}$ m/sec
Accel.: $\sqrt{2}$ m/sec^2
Jerk: $\sqrt{2}$ m/sec^3
(c) The body starts at 2, goes to 0, and then oscillates between 0 and 4.
Speed: *Greatest* when $\cos t = \pm 1$ (or $t = k\pi$), at the center of the interval of motion.
Zero when $\cos t = 0\left(\text{or } t = \frac{k\pi}{2}, k \text{ odd}\right)$, at the endpoints of the interval of motion.
Acceleration: *Greatest* (in magnitude) when
$\sin t = \pm 1\left(\text{or } t = \frac{k\pi}{2}, k \text{ odd}\right)$
Zero when $\sin t = 0(\text{or } t = k\pi)$
Jerk: *Greatest* (in magnitude) when $\cos t = \pm 1$ (or $t = k\pi$)
Zero when $\cos t = 0\left(\text{or } t = \frac{k\pi}{2}, k \text{ odd}\right)$

35. $y'' = \csc^3 x + \csc x \cot^2 x$

37. Continuous if $b = 1$, because this makes the two one-sided limits equal. Differentiable: No, because for $b = 1$, the left-hand derivative is 1 and the right-hand derivative is 0. (The left-hand derivative does not exist for other values of b.)

39. $\cos x$

41. **(a)** 0.12
(b) $\sin(0.12) \approx 0.1197122$ The approximation is within 0.0003 of the actual value.

43. $\frac{d}{dx}\cos 2x = \frac{d}{dx}[(\cos x)(\cos x) - (\sin x)(\sin x)]$

$= [2(\cos x)(-\sin x) - 2(\sin x)(\cos x)]$

$= -4(\sin x)(\cos x) = -2(2\sin x \cos x)$

$= -2\sin 2x$

45. False. The velocity is negative and the speed is positive at $t = \pi/4$.

47. B **49.** C

51. $\lim_{h\to 0}\frac{\cos h - 1}{h} = \lim_{h\to 0}\frac{(\cos h - 1)(\cos h + 1)}{h(c}$

$= \lim_{h\to 0}\frac{\cos^2 h - 1}{h(\cos h + 1)}$

$= \lim_{h\to 0}\frac{-\sin^2 h}{h(\cos h + 1)}$

$= -\left(\lim_{h\to 0}\frac{\sin h}{h}\right)\left(\lim_{h\to 0}\frac{\sin h}{\cos h + 1}\right)$

$= -(1)\left(\frac{0}{2}\right) = 0$

Quick Quiz (Sections 3.4–3.6)

1. C **3.** D

Review Exercises

1. $5x^4 - \frac{x}{4} + \frac{1}{4}$

2. $-21x^2 + 21x^6$

3. $-2\cos^2 x + 2\sin^2 x = 2\cos 2x$

4. $-\frac{4}{(2x - 1)^2}$

5. $4t^3$

6. $\frac{4t}{(1 - t^2)^2}$

7. $\frac{1}{2\sqrt{x}} - \frac{1}{2x^{3/2}}$

8. $5x^4(3x^2 - x) + (6x - 1)(x^5 + 1)$

9. $10\theta \sec\theta + 5\theta^2 \sec\theta \tan\theta$

10. $\frac{\sec^2\theta(\theta^3 + \theta + 1) - \tan\theta(3\theta^2 + 1)}{(\theta^3 + \theta + 1)^2}$

11. $(x^2 + 1)\cos x + x\sin x$

12. $(x^2 - 1)\cos x + 3x\sin x$

13. $\frac{x\sec^2 x - 3\tan x}{2x^4}$

14. $\sec^2 x + \csc^2 x$

15. $\frac{\sin x - \cos x}{(\sin x + \cos x)^2}$

16. $\sec x \tan x - \csc x \cot x$

17. $4\pi r^2 + 16\pi r$

18. $\left(\frac{\sqrt{3}}{2} + \frac{3\pi}{4}\right)s$

19. $\frac{\cos t(1 + \tan t) - \sec^2 t(1 + \sin t)}{(1 + \tan t)^2}$

20. $\frac{\cos t + \sin t + 1}{(1 + \cos t)^2}$

21. $2t + 1$

22. $\frac{12 - 2x\cos x - x^2\sin x}{x^4}$

23. 0 **24.** 0 **25.** $6x^2 - 2$ **26.** $4 - 24x$

27. $\frac{2t}{\pi^3} + \frac{3\pi^2}{t^4}$ **28.** $\frac{3t^2}{\pi^2} + \frac{2\pi^3}{t^3}$

29. $\sec^2 x$ **30.** 0

31. For all $x \neq 0$

32. For all real x

33. For all $x \neq 2$

34. For all $x \neq \frac{7}{2}$

35. 0 **36.** 1 **37.** $\frac{1}{\pi^2}$ **38.** $\frac{1}{\pi}$

39. $\dfrac{\sin^2 x + 1}{\cos^3 x}$ **40.** $\dfrac{\cos^2 x + 1}{\sin^3 x}$

41. $2\cos x - x \sin x$

42. $x \cos x + 2 \sin x$

43. $y' = 2x^3 - 3x - 1$, $y'' = 6x^2 - 3$, $y''' = 12x$, $y^{(4)} = 12$, and the rest are all zero.

44. $y' = \dfrac{x^4}{24}$, $y'' = \dfrac{x^3}{6}$, $y''' = \dfrac{x^2}{2}$, $y^{(4)} = x$, $y^{(5)} = 1$, and the rest are all zero.

45. (a) $y - 2 = -2(x - 2)$ **(b)** $y - 2 = \dfrac{1}{2}(x - 2)$

46. (a) $y = -x + \dfrac{\pi}{2} + 2$ **(b)** $y = x - \dfrac{\pi}{2} + 2$

47. (a) $y = \sqrt{2}$ **(b)** $x = \dfrac{\pi}{4}$

48. (a) $y = 3$ **(b)** $x = 1$

49. $(1, 2)$ and $(-1, -2)$

50. $(3, 9/2)$ and $(-2, -14/3)$

51. $(0, 0)$ and $(-2, 12)$

52. none

53. (a)

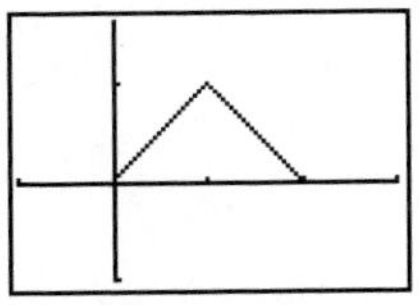

[-1, 3] by [-1, 5/3]

(b) Yes, because both of the one-sided limits as $x \to 1$ are equal to $f(1) = 1$.
(c) No, because the left-hand derivative at $x = 1$ is $+1$ and the right-hand derivative at $x = 1$ is -1.

54. (a) For all m, since $y = \sin 2x$ and $y = mx$ are both continuous on their domains, and they link up at the origin, where $\lim_{x\to 0^-} \sin 2x = \lim_{x \to 0^+} mx = 0$, regardless of the value of m.
(b) For $m = 2$ only, since the left-hand derivative at 0 (which is $2 \cos 0 = 2$) must match the right-hand derivative at 0 (which is m).

55. (a) For all $x \neq 0$ **(b)** At $x = 0$ **(c)** Nowhere

56. (a) For all $x \neq 0$ **(b)** At $x = 0$ **(c)** Nowhere

57. (a) $[-1, 0) \cup (0, 4]$
(b) At $x = 0$
(c) Nowhere in its domain

58. (a) $[-2, 0) \cup (0, 2]$
(b) Nowhere
(c) Nowhere in its domain

59.

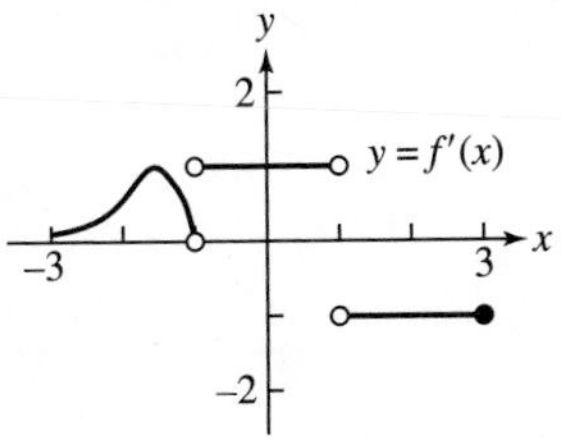

60.

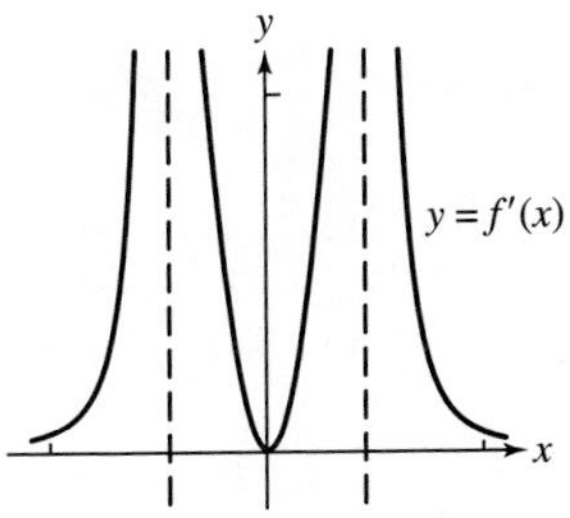

61. (a) iii **(b)** i **(c)** ii

62.

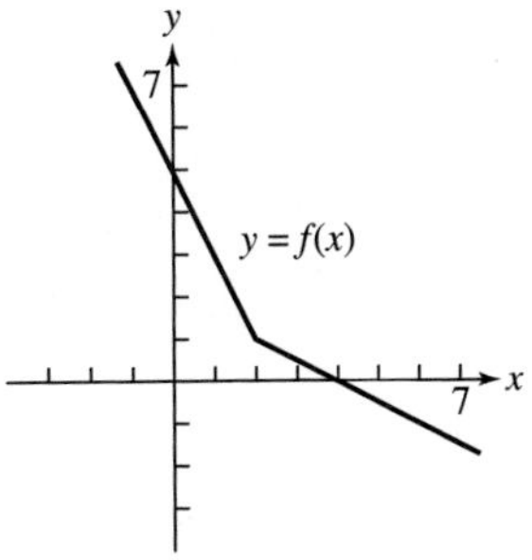

63.

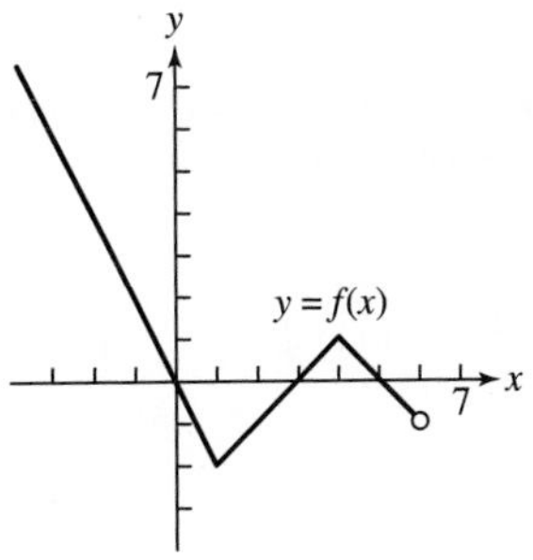

64. Answer is **D**: **i** and **iii** only could be true

65. (a)

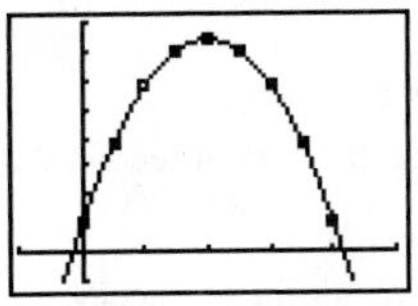

[-1, 5] by [-10,80]

(b)

t interval	avg. vel.
$[0, 0.5]$	56
$[0.5, 1]$	40
$[1, 1.5]$	24
$[1.5, 2]$	8
$[2. 2.5]$	-8
$[2.5, 3]$	-24
$[3, 3.5]$	-40
$[3.5, 4]$	-56

(c)

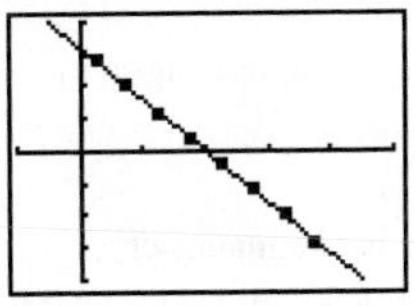

[-1, 5] by [-80, 80]

(d) Average velocity is a good approximation to velocity.

66. $(x^n)' = nx^{n-1}$; $(x^n)'' = n(n-1)x^{n-2}$; $(x^n)''' = n(n-1)(n-2)x^{n-3}$; $\ldots$; and $\dfrac{d^n}{dx^n}(x^n) = n(n-1)(n-2)(n-3)\cdots 2 \cdot 1\, x^0 = n!$

67. (a) 12 **(b)** 1 **(c)** -2 **(d)** 7 **(e)** -1 **(f)** -36

68. (a) 5 **(b)** 2 **(c)** -2 **(d)** $\dfrac{10}{9}$ **(e)** -2 **(f)** 6

69. Yes. The slope of $f + g$ at $x = 0$ is $(f + g)'(0) = f'(0) + g'(0)$. The sum of two positive numbers must also be positive.

70. No; it depends on the values of $f(0)$ and $g(0)$. For example, let $f(x) = x$ and $g(x) = x - 1$. Both lines have positive slope everywhere, but $(f \cdot g)(x) = x^2 - x$ has a negative slope at $x = 0$.

71. (a) $\frac{ds}{dt} = 64 - 32t \quad \frac{d^2s}{dt^2} = -32$
(b) 2 sec **(c)** 64 ft/sec
(d) $\frac{64}{5.2} \approx 12.3$ sec; $s\left(\frac{64}{5.2}\right) \approx 393.8$ ft

72. (a) $\frac{4}{7}$ sec; 280 cm/sec
(b) 560 cm/sec; 980 cm/sec^2

73. $\pi(20x - x^2)$

74. (a) $r(x) = \left(3 - \frac{x}{40}\right)^2 x = 9x - \frac{3}{20}x^2 + \frac{1}{1600}x^3$
(b) 40 people; \$4.00
(c) One possible answer: Probably not, since the company charges less overall for 60 passengers than it does for 40 passengers.

75. (a) -0.6 km/sec **(b)** $18/\pi \approx 5.73$ revolutions/min

76. (a) The derivative of y_1 is y_2. **(b)** Let $y_2 = \frac{|\cos(x)|}{\cos(x)}$.

77. $a = \frac{3\sqrt[4]{2}}{8}$

78. $a = \sqrt{2}$

79. (a) $x \neq k\frac{\pi}{4}$, where k is an odd integer
(b) $(-\pi/2, \pi/2)$
(c) Where it's not defined, at $x = k\frac{\pi}{4}$, k an odd integer
(d) It has period $\pi/2$ and continues to repeat the pattern seen in this window.

80. $y'(r) = -\frac{1}{2r^2l}\sqrt{\frac{T}{\pi d}}$, so increasing r decreases the frequency.

$y'(l) = -\frac{1}{2rl^2}\sqrt{\frac{T}{\pi d}}$, so increasing l decreases the frequency.

$y'(d) = -\frac{1}{4rl}\sqrt{\frac{T}{\pi d^3}}$, so increasing d decreases the frequency.

$y'(T) = -\frac{1}{4rl\sqrt{\pi T d}}$, so increasing I increases the frequency.

81. (a) $v(t) = x'(t) = 3t^2 - 12$
(b) $a(t) = v'(t) = 6t$
(c) The particle is at rest when $3t^2 - 12 = 0$; that is, at $t = 2$.
(d) $a(t) = 6t = 0$ when $t = 0$, at which point the speed is $|v(0)| = |-12| = 12$.
(e) The position at $t = 3$ is $x(3) = -4$, and the velocity is $v(3) = 15$. Since the particle is to the left of the origin and moving to the right, it is moving toward the origin.

82. (a) $y - 3 = 5(x - 4)$
(b) Yes. Since f is differentiable at $x = 3$, it is continuous at $x = 3$.
(c) Yes. Since f is continuous on $[2, 4]$, it takes on all values between $f(2) = -1$ and $f(4) = 3$ (Intermediate Value Theorem).
(d) $g'(2) = \frac{d}{dx}\left(\frac{f(x)}{f(x) - 3}\right)\Big|_{x=2}$

$$= \frac{f'(2)(f(2) - 3) - (f'(2) - 0)f(2)}{(f(2) - 3)^2} = -\frac{9}{16}.$$

(e) Since $f(4) - 3 = 0$, the function g is not defined at $x = 4$.

83. (a)

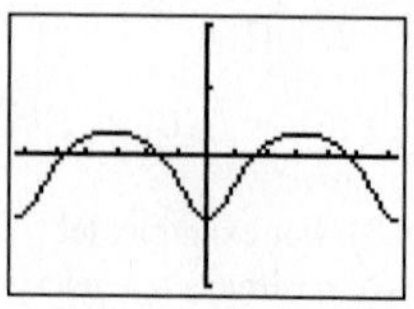

$[-2\pi, 2\pi]$ by $[-2, 2]$

(b) $f'(x) = \frac{2 \sin x}{(\cos x - 2)^2}$ **(c)** $0, \pm\pi, \pm 2\pi$

(d) The low turning points are $f(0) = f(\pm 2\pi) = \frac{1}{1 - 2} = -1$, and the high turning points are

$f(\pm\pi) = \frac{-1}{-1 - 2} = \frac{1}{3}$. The range is the interval $\left[-1, \frac{1}{3}\right]$.

CHAPTER 4

Section 4.1

Quick Review 4.1

1. $\sin(x^2 + 1)$ **3.** $49x^2 + 1$
5. $\sin \frac{x^2 + 1}{7x}$ **7.** $g(h(f(x)))$
9. $f(h(h(x)))$

Exercises 4.1

1. $3\cos(3x + 1)$
3. $-\sqrt{3}\sin(\sqrt{3}x)$
5. $\frac{2 \sin x}{(1 + \cos x)^2}$
7. $-\sin(\sin x)\cos x$
9. $3 \sin\left(\frac{\pi}{2} - 3t\right)$
11. $\frac{4}{\pi}\cos 3t - \frac{4}{\pi}\sin 5t$
13. $-2(x + \sqrt{x})^{-3}\left(1 + \frac{1}{2\sqrt{x}}\right)$
15. $-5\sin^{-6}x\cos x + 3\cos^2 x \sin x$
17. $4\sin^3 x \sec^2 4x + 3\sin^2 x \cos x \tan 4x$
19. $-3(2x + 1)^{-3/2}$
21. $6\sin(3x - 2)\cos(3x - 2) = 3\sin(6x - 4)$
23. $-42(1 + \cos^2 7x)^2 \cos 7x \sin 7x$
25. $-\sec^2(2 - \theta)$
27. $\frac{\theta\cos\theta + \sin\theta}{2\sqrt{\theta}\sin\theta}$
29. $2\sec^2 x \tan x$
31. $18\csc^2(3x - 1)\cot(3x - 1)$
33. $5/2$
35. $-\pi/4$
37. 0
39. (a) $-6\sin(6x + 2)$
(b) $-6\sin(6x + 2)$
41. $y = -x + 2\sqrt{2}$
43. $y = -\frac{1}{2}x - \frac{1}{2}$
45. $y = x + \frac{1}{4}$
47. $y = \sqrt{3}x + 2 - \frac{\pi}{\sqrt{3}}$

49. (a) $\frac{\cos t}{2t+1}$

(b) $\frac{d}{dt}\left(\frac{dy}{dx}\right) = -\frac{(2t+1)(\sin t) + 2\cos t}{(2t+1)^2}$

(c) $\frac{d}{dx}\left(\frac{dy}{dx}\right) = -\frac{(2t+1)(\sin t) + 2\cos t}{(2t+1)^3}$

(d) part (c)

51. 5

53. $\frac{1}{2}$

55. Tangent $y = \pi x - \pi + 2$: Normal: $y = -\frac{1}{\pi}x + \frac{1}{\pi} + 2$

57. $\frac{d}{dx}\cos(x°) = \frac{d}{dx}\cos\left(\frac{\pi x}{180}\right) = -\frac{\pi}{180}\sin\left(\frac{\pi x}{180}\right) = -\frac{\pi}{180}\sin(x°)$

59. The slope of $y = \sin(2x)$ at the origin is 2. The slope of $y = -\sin\frac{x}{2}$ at the origin is $-\frac{1}{2}$. So the lines tangent to the two curves at the origin are perpendicular.

61. The amplitude of the velocity is doubled.
The amplitude of the acceleration is quadrupled.
The amplitude of the jerk is multiplied by 8.

63. Velocity $= \frac{2}{5}$ m/sec

acceleration $= -\frac{4}{125}$ m/sec^2

65. Given: $v = \frac{k}{\sqrt{s}}$

acceleration: $= \frac{dv}{dt} = \frac{dv}{ds}\frac{dv}{dt} = \frac{dv}{ds}v$

$= \frac{-k}{2s^{3/2}}\frac{k}{\sqrt{s}} = -\frac{k^2}{2s^2}$

67. $\frac{dT}{du} = \frac{dT}{dL}\frac{dL}{du}$

$= \frac{\pi}{\sqrt{gL}}kL = k\pi\sqrt{\frac{L}{g}} = \frac{kT}{2}$

69. Yes. Either the graph of $y = g(x)$ must have a horizontal tangent at $x = 1$, or the graph of $y = f(u)$ must have a horizontal tangent at $u = g(1)$. This is because $\frac{d}{dx}f(g(x)) = f'(g(x))\,g'(x)$, so the slope of the tangent to the graph of $y = f(g(x))$ at $x = 1$ is given by $f'(g(1))\,g'(1)$. If this product is zero, then at least one of its factors must be zero.

71. False. It is $+1$

73. C

75. B

77. As $h \to 0$, the second curve (the difference quotient) approaches the first $(y = -2x\sin(x^2))$. This is because $-2x\sin(x^2)$ is the derivative of $\cos(x^2)$, and the second curve is the difference quotient used to define the derivative of $\cos(x^2)$. As $h \to 0$, the difference quotient expression should be approaching the derivative.

79. $\frac{dG}{dx} = \frac{d}{dx}\sqrt{uv} = \frac{d}{dx}\sqrt{x^2+cx} = \frac{2x+c}{2\sqrt{x^2+cx}}$

$= \frac{x + \frac{c}{2}}{\sqrt{x^2+cx}}$

$= \frac{A}{G}$, since $A = x + \frac{c}{2}$.

Section 4.2

Quick Review 4.2

1. $y_1 = \sqrt{x}, y_2 = -\sqrt{x}$

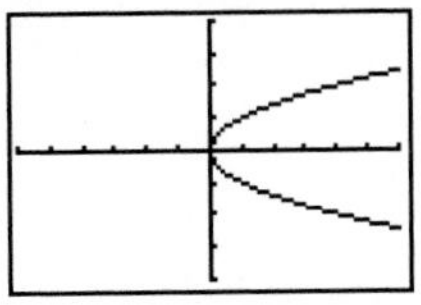

[-6, 6] by [-4, 4]

3. $y_1 = \frac{x}{2}, y_2 = -\frac{x}{2}$

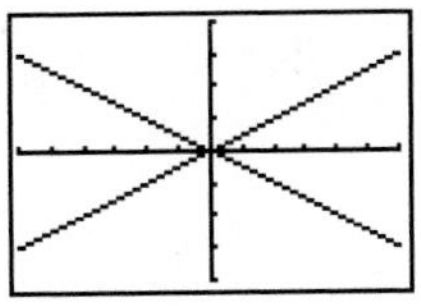

[-6, 6] by [-4, 4]

5. $y_1 = \sqrt{2x+3-x^2}, y_2 = -\sqrt{2x+3-x^2}$

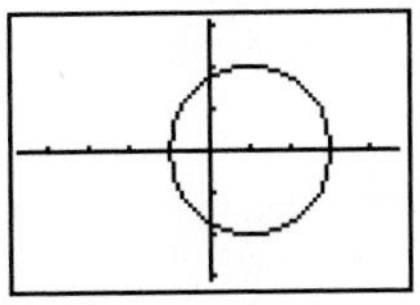

[-4.7, 4.7] by [-3.1, 3.1]

7. $y' = \frac{y + y\cos x}{\sin x - y}$

9. $x^{3/2} - x^{5/6}$

Exercises 4.2

1. $-\frac{2xy + y^2}{2xy + x^2}$

3. $\frac{1}{y(x+1)^2}$

5. $\cos^2 y$

7. $-\frac{1}{x}\cos^2(xy) - \frac{y}{x}$

9. $\frac{dy}{dx} = -\frac{x}{y}$, 2/3

11. $\frac{dy}{dx} = -\frac{x-1}{y-1}$, $-2/3$

13. $\frac{dy}{dx} = \frac{2xy - y^2}{2xy - x^2}$, defined at every point except where $x = 0$ or $y = x/2$

15. $\frac{dy}{dx} = \frac{3x^2 - y}{x - 3y^2}$, defined at every point except where $y^2 = x/3$

17. (a) $y = \frac{7}{4}x - \frac{1}{2}$ **(b)** $y = -\frac{4}{7}x + \frac{29}{7}$

19. (a) $y = 3x + 6$ **(b)** $y = -\frac{1}{3}x + \frac{8}{3}$

21. (a) $y = \frac{6}{7}x + \frac{6}{7}$

(b) $y = -\frac{7}{6}x - \frac{7}{6}$

23. **(a)** $y = -\frac{\pi}{2}x + \pi$ **(b)** $y = \frac{2}{\pi}x - \frac{2}{\pi} + \frac{\pi}{2}$

25. **(a)** $y = 2\pi x - 2\pi$ **(b)** $y = -\frac{x}{2\pi} + \frac{1}{2\pi}$

27. $\frac{dy}{dx} = -\frac{x}{y}$

$\frac{d^2y}{dx^2} = -\frac{(x^2 + y^2)}{y^3} = -\frac{1}{y^3}$

29. $\frac{dy}{dx} = \frac{x + 1}{y}$

$\frac{d^2y}{dx^2} = -\frac{y^2 - (x + 1)^2}{y^3} = -\frac{1}{y^3}$

31. $(9/4)x^{5/4}$

33. $(1/3)x^{-2/3}$

35. $-(2x + 5)^{-3/2}$

37. $x^2(x^2 + 1)^{-1/2} + (x^2 + 1)^{1/2}$

39. $-\frac{1}{4}(1 - x^{1/2})^{-1/2}x^{-1/2}$

41. $-\frac{9}{2}(\csc x)^{3/2}\cot x$

43. **(b)**, **(c)**, and **(d)**

45. **(a)** At $\left(\frac{\sqrt{3}}{4}, \frac{\sqrt{3}}{2}\right)$: Slope $= -1$;

at $\left(\frac{\sqrt{3}}{4}, \frac{1}{2}\right)$: Slope $= \sqrt{3}$

(b)

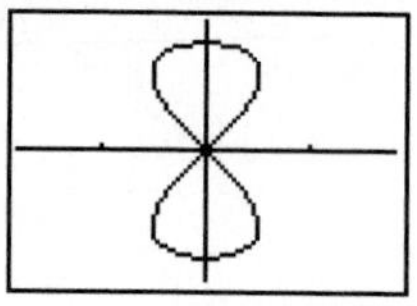

[-1.8, 1.8] by [-1.2, 1.2]

Parameter interval:
$-1 \le t \le 1$

47. **(a)** $(-1)^3(1)^2 = \cos(\pi)$ is true since both sides equal: -1.

(b) The slope is 3/2.

49. The points are $(\pm\sqrt{7}, 0)$

$\frac{dy}{dx} = -\frac{2x + y}{2y + x}$

At both points, $\frac{dy}{dx} = -2$

51. First curve: $\frac{dy}{dx} = -\frac{2x}{3y}$

second curve: $\frac{dy}{dx} = \frac{3x^2}{2y}$

At $(1, 1)$, the slopes are $-\frac{2}{3}$ and $\frac{3}{2}$ respectively.

At $(1, -1)$, the slopes are $\frac{2}{3}$ and $-\frac{3}{2}$ respectively.

In both cases, the tangents are perpendicular.

53. Acceleration $= \frac{dv}{dt} = 4(s - t)^{-1/2}(v - 1)$

$= 32$ ft/sec^2

55. **(a)** At $(4, 2)$: $\frac{5}{4}$; at $(2, 4)$: $\frac{4}{5}$

(b) At $(3\sqrt[3]{2}, 3\sqrt[3]{4}) \approx (3.780, 4.762)$

(c) At $(3\sqrt[3]{4}, 3\sqrt[3]{2}) \approx (4.762, 3.780)$

57. At $(-1, -1)$: $y = -2x - 3$; at $(3, -3$: $y = -2x + 3$

59. False. It is equal to -2.

61. A **63.** E

65. **(a)** $\frac{dy}{dx} = -\frac{b^2x}{a^2y}$

The tangent line is $y - y_1 = -\frac{b^2x_1}{a^2y_1}(x - x_1)$.

This gives: $a^2y_1y - a^2y_1^2 = -b^2x_1x + b^2x_1^2$,

$a^2y_1y + b^2x_1x = a^2y_1^2 + b^2x_1^2$.

But $a^2y_1^2 + b^2x_1^2 = a^2b^2$ since (x_1, y_1) is on the ellipse.

Therefore, $a^2y_1y + b^2x_1x = a^2b^2$, and dividing by a^2b^2 gives $\frac{x_1x}{a^2} + \frac{y_1y}{b^2} = 1$. **(b)** $\frac{x_1x}{a^2} - \frac{y_1y}{b^2} = 1$.

Quick Quiz (Sections 4.1–4.2)

1. B **3.** C

Section 4.3

Quick Review 4.3

1. Domain: $[-1, 1]$; Range: $[-\pi/2, \pi/2]$ At 1: $\pi/2$

3. Domain: all reals Range: $(-\pi/2, \pi/2)$ At 1: $\pi/4$

5. Domain: all reals; Range: all reals At 1: 1

7. $f^{-1}(x) = x^3 - 5$

9. $f^{-1}(x) = \frac{2}{3 - x}$

Exercises 4.3

1. $-\frac{2x}{\sqrt{1 - x^4}}$ **3.** $\frac{\sqrt{2}}{\sqrt{1 - 2t^2}}$

5. $-\frac{6}{t\sqrt{t^4 - 9}}$ **7.** $\sin^{-1} x$

9. $\sqrt{7}/7$ **11.** 1/5

13. $\frac{1}{|2s + 1|\sqrt{s^2 + s}}$

15. $-\frac{2}{(x^2 + 1)\sqrt{x^2 + 2}}$

17. $-\frac{1}{\sqrt{1 - t^2}}$ **19.** $-\frac{1}{2t\sqrt{t - 1}}$

21. $0, x > 1$ **23.** $y = 0.289x + 0.470$

25. $y = 0.378x - 0.286$

27. **(a)** $y = 2x - \frac{\pi}{2} + 1$

(b) $y = \frac{1}{2}x - \frac{1}{2} + \frac{\pi}{4}$

29. **(a)** $f'(x) = 3 - \sin x$ and $f'(x) \neq 0$. So f has a differentiable inverse by Theorem 3.

(b) $f(0) = 1, f'(0) = 3$

(c) $f^{-1}(1) = 0, (f^{-1})'(1) = \frac{1}{3}$

31. (a) $v(t) = \frac{dx}{dt} = \frac{1}{1+t^2}$ which is always positive.

(b) $a(t) = \frac{dv}{dt} = -\frac{2t}{(1+t^2)^2}$ which is always negative.

(c) $\frac{\pi}{2}$

33. $\frac{d}{dx}\cot^{-1} x = \frac{d}{dx}\left(\frac{\pi}{2} - \tan^{-1} x\right)$

$= 0 - \frac{d}{dx}\tan^{-1} x$

$= -\frac{1}{1+x^2}$

35. True. By definition of the function.

37. E **39.** A

41. (a) $y = \pi/2$ **(b)** $y = -\pi/2$ **(c)** None

43. (a) $y = \pi/2$ **(b)** $y = \pi/2$ **(c)** None

45. (a) None **(b)** None **(c)** None

47. (a)

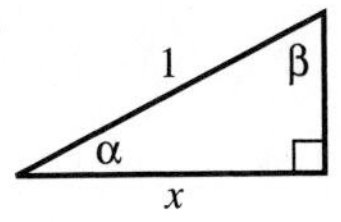

$\alpha = \cos^{-1} x, \beta = \sin^{-1} x$

So $\pi/2 = \alpha + \beta = \cos^{-1} x + \sin^{-1} x.$

(b)

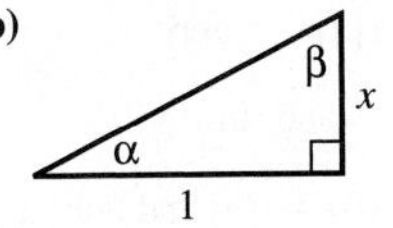

$\alpha = \tan^{-1} x, \beta = \cot^{-1} x$

So $\pi/2 = \alpha + \beta = \tan^{-1} x + \cot^{-1} x.$

(c)

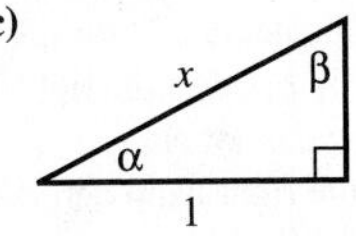

$\alpha = \sec^{-1} x, \beta = \csc^{-1} x$

So $\pi/2 = \alpha + \beta = \sec^{-1} x + \csc^{-1} x.$

49. If s is the length of a side of the square, and let α, β, γ denote the angles labeled $\tan^{-1} 1$, $\tan^{-1} 2$, and $\tan^{-1} 3$, respectively.

$\tan\alpha = \frac{s}{s} = 1$, so $\alpha = \tan^{-1} 1$ and

$\tan\beta = \frac{s}{s/2} = 2$, so $\beta = \tan^{-1} 2$.

$\gamma = \pi - \alpha - \beta = \pi - \tan^{-1} 1 - \tan^{-1} 2$

$= \tan^{-1} 3.$

Section 4.4

Quick Review 4.4

1. $\frac{\ln 8}{\ln 5}$ **3.** $\tan x$

5. $3x - 15$ **7.** $\ln(4x^4)$

9. $t = \frac{\ln 18 - \ln(\ln 5)}{\ln 5} \approx 1.50$

Exercises 4.4

1. $2e^x$ **3.** $-e^{-x}$

5. $\frac{2}{3}e^{2x/3}$ **7.** $e^2 - e^x$

9. $e^{\sqrt{x}}/(2\sqrt{x})$ **11.** $8^x \ln 8$

13. $-3^{\csc x}(\ln 3)(\csc x \cot x)$

15. $\frac{2}{x}$ **17.** $-\frac{1}{x}, x > 0$

19. $\frac{1}{x \ln x}$ **21.** $\frac{2}{x \ln 4} = \frac{1}{x \ln 2}$

23. $-\frac{1}{x \ln 2}, x > 0$ **25.** $\frac{1}{x}, x > 0$

27. $\frac{1}{\ln 10}$ **29.** $\approx(1.379, 5.551)$

31. $2e^{-1}$

33. $\pi x^{\pi - 1}$

35. $-\sqrt{2}x^{-\sqrt{2}-1}$

37. $\frac{1}{x+2}, x > -2$

39. $\frac{\sin x}{2 - \cos x}$, all reals

41. $\frac{3}{(3x+1)\ln 2}, x > -1/3$

43. $(\sin x)^x\,[x \cot x + \ln(\sin x)]$

45. $\left(\frac{(x-3)^4(x^2+1)}{(2x+5)^3}\right)^{1/5}\left(\frac{4}{5(x-3)} + \frac{2x}{5(x^2+1)} - \frac{6}{5(2x+5)}\right)$

47. $\frac{2x^{\ln x}(\ln x)}{x}$

49. $y = ex$

51. (a) 18

(b) 52 students per day

(c) After 4 days; 52 students per day

53. rate $\approx$ 0.098 grams/day

55. (a) ln 2

(b) $f'(0) = \lim_{h \to 0} \frac{2^h - 1}{h}$

(c) ln 2

(d) ln 7

57. False. It is $(\ln 2)2^x$.

59. B

61. A

63. (a) The graph of y_4 is a horizontal line at $y = a$.

(b) The graph of y_3 is a horizontal line at $y = \ln a$.

(c) $\frac{d}{dx}a^x = a^x$ if and only if $y_3 = \frac{y_2}{y_1} = 1$.

So if $y_3 = \ln a$, then $\frac{d}{dx}a^x$ will equal a^x if and only if $\ln a = 1$, or $a = e$.

(d) $y_2 = \frac{d}{dx}a^x = a^x \ln a$. This will equal $y_1 = a^x$ if and only if $\ln a = 1$, or $a = e$.

65. (a) $y = \frac{1}{e}x$

(b) Because the graph of $\ln x$ lies below the graph of the tangent line for all positive $x \neq e$.

(c) Multiplying by e, $e(\ln x) < x$, or $\ln x^e < x$.

(d) Exponentiate both sides of the inequality in part (c).

(e) Let $x = \pi$ to see that $\pi^e < e^\pi$.

Quick Quiz (Sections 4.3–4.4)

1. A

3. C

Review Exercises

1. $3e^{3x-7}$ **2.** $e^x \sec^2(e^x)$ **3.** $3\sin^2 x \cos x$

4. $-\cot x$ **5.** $2\sin(1-2t)$ **6.** $\frac{2}{t^2}\csc^2\frac{2}{t}$

7. $-\dfrac{\sin x}{2\sqrt{1+\cos x}}$

8. $\dfrac{3x+1}{\sqrt{2x+1}}$

9. $3\sec(1+3\theta)\tan(1+3\theta)$

10. $-4\theta\tan(3-\theta^2)\sec^2(3-\theta^2)$

11. $-5x^2\csc 5x\cot 5x + 2x\csc 5x$

12. $\frac{1}{2x}, x > 0$ **13.** $\dfrac{e^x}{1+e^x}$

14. $-xe^{-x}+e^{-x}$ **15.** e

16. $\cot x$, where x is an interval of the form $(k\pi, (k+1)\pi)$, k even

17. $-\dfrac{1}{\cos^{-1}x\sqrt{1-x^2}}$

18. $\dfrac{2}{\theta\ln 2}$

19. $\dfrac{1}{(t-7)\ln 5}, t > 7$

20. $-8^{-t}\ln 8$

21. $\dfrac{2(\ln x)x^{\ln x}}{x}$

22. $\dfrac{(2\cdot 2^x)[x^3\ln 2 + x\ln 2 + 1]}{(x^2+1)^{3/2}}$ or

$\dfrac{(2x)2^x}{\sqrt{x^2+1}}\left(\dfrac{1}{2}+\ln 2-\dfrac{x}{x^2+1}\right)$

23. $\dfrac{e^{\tan^{-1}x}}{1+x^2}$

24. $-\dfrac{u}{\sqrt{u^2-u^4}} = -\dfrac{u}{|u|\sqrt{1-u^2}}$

25. $\dfrac{t}{|t|\sqrt{t^2-1}} + \sec^{-1}t - \dfrac{1}{2t}$

26. $-\dfrac{2+2t^2}{1+4t^2} + 2t\cot^{-1}2t$

27. $\cos^{-1}z$

28. $-\dfrac{1}{x} + \dfrac{\csc^{-1}\sqrt{x}}{\sqrt{x-1}}$

29. -1

30. $2\left(\dfrac{1+\sin\theta}{1-\cos\theta}\right)\left(\dfrac{\cos\theta-\sin\theta-1}{(1-\cos\theta)^2}\right)$

31. For all $x \neq 0$

32. For all real x

33. For all $x < 1$

34. For all $x \neq 0$

35. $-\dfrac{y+2}{x+3}$

36. $-\frac{1}{3}(xy)^{-1/5}$

37. $-\dfrac{y}{x}$ or $-\dfrac{1}{x^2}$

38. $\dfrac{1}{2y(x+1)^2}$

39. $-\dfrac{2x}{y^5}$ **40.** $\dfrac{1+2xy^2}{x^4y^3}$

41. $-2\dfrac{(3y^2+1)^2\cos x + 12y\sin^2 x}{(3y^2+1)^3}$

42. $\frac{2}{3}x^{-4/3}y^{1/3} + \frac{2}{3}x^{-5/3}y^{2/3} = \frac{8}{3}x^{-5/3}y^{1/3}$

43. $32e^{\sqrt[8]{2x}}$

44. $y = 32\sin(\sqrt[8]{2x})$

45. **(a)** $y = \dfrac{2}{\sqrt{3}}x - \sqrt{3}$ **(b)** $y = -\dfrac{\sqrt{3}}{2}x + \dfrac{5\sqrt{3}}{2}$

46. **(a)** $y + \sqrt{3} = 8\left(x - \dfrac{\pi}{3}\right)$ **(b)** $y + \sqrt{3} = -\dfrac{1}{8}\left(x - \dfrac{\pi}{3}\right)$

47. **(a)** $y = -\dfrac{1}{4}x + \dfrac{9}{4}$ **(b)** $y = 4x - 2$

48. **(a)** $y = -\dfrac{5}{4}x + 6$ **(b)** $y = \dfrac{4}{5}x - \dfrac{11}{5}$

49. $y = x - 2\sqrt{2}$

50. $y = \dfrac{4}{3}x + 4\sqrt{2}$

51. $y = \dfrac{10}{3}x - 5\sqrt{3}$

52. $y = (1+\sqrt{2})x - \sqrt{2} - 1 - \dfrac{\pi}{4}$ or $y \approx 2.414x - 3.200$

53. **(a)** $\lim_{x\to 0^-} f(x) = \lim_{x\to 0^-}(\sin ax + b\cos x) = b$ and $\lim_{x\to 0^+} f(x) = \lim_{x\to 0^+}(5x+3) = 3$. Thus $\lim_{x\to 0} f(x) = f(0) = 3$ if and only if $b = 3$

(b) $f'(x) = \begin{cases} a\cos ax - b\sin x, & x < 0 \\ 5, & x > 0 \end{cases}$. The slopes match at $x = 0$ if and only if $a = 5$.

(c) No. Although the slopes match, the function is not continuous.

54. **(a)** The function is continuous for all values of m, because the right-hand limit as $x \to 0$ is equal to $f(0) = 0$ for any value of m.

(b) The left-hand derivative at $x = 0$ is 2, and the right-hand derivative at $x = 0$ is m, so in order for the function to be differentiable at $x = 0$, m must be 2.

55. **(a)** For all $x \neq 1$ **(b)** At $x = 1$ **(c)** Nowhere

56. **(a)** For all x **(b)** Nowhere **(c)** Nowhere

57. **(a)** $[-1, 1) \cup (1, 3]$ **(b)** At $x = 1$ **(c)** Nowhere

58. **(a)** $[-3, 3]$ **(b)** Nowhere **(c)** Nowhere

59. **(a)** $-\cos x$ **(b)** $14x - 13$ **(c)** $2t - 3$ **(d)** $2t - 30t^5$

60. **(a)** $\dfrac{2}{2x+7} - \dfrac{3}{3x+2}$ **(b)** 1

(c) $-2t$ **(d)** $\dfrac{80}{3\sqrt[6]{t}}$

61. **(a)** $y - 4 = -\frac{1}{3}(x-2)$

(b) $y - 2 = \frac{1}{3}(x-4)$

(c) $y - 2 = \frac{1}{2}(x-2)$

62. **(a)** $y - 3 = \frac{1}{2}(x-1)$

(b) $y - 1 = -\frac{1}{2}(x-3)$

(c) $y - 3 = -4(x-1)$

63. $\dfrac{dy}{dx} = \dfrac{(x+2)^5(2x-3)^4}{(x+17)^2}\left(\dfrac{5}{x+2} + \dfrac{8}{2x+3} - \dfrac{2}{x+17}\right)$

64. $\dfrac{dy}{dx} = (x^2+2)^{x+5}\left(\ln(x^2+2) + \dfrac{2x^2+10x}{x^2+2}\right)$

65. (a) $f(x) = \dfrac{x^2}{2}$ or $f(x) = \dfrac{x^2}{2} + C$
(b) $f(x) = e^x$ or $f(x) = Ce^x$
(c) $f(x) = e^{-x}$ or $f(x) = Ce^{-x}$
(d) $f(x) = e^x$ or $f(x) = e^{-x}$ or $f(x) = Ce^x + De^{-x}$
(e) $f(x) = \sin x$ or $f(x) = \cos x$ or $f(x) = C\sin x + D\cos x$

66. (a) $-13/10$ **(b)** $-1/3$
(c) $1/10$ **(d)** -1
(e) $-2/3$ **(f)** -12

67. (a) 5 **(b)** 0
(c) 8 **(d)** 2
(e) 4 **(f)** -1

68. $\sqrt{3}$ **69.** $-1/6$

70. (a) One possible answer:
$x(t) = 10\cos\left(t + \dfrac{\pi}{4}\right)$
$y(t) = 0$
(b) $5\sqrt{2}$
(c) $s = -10$ and $s = 10$
(d) At $t = \pi/4$:
Velocity $= -10$
Speed $= 10$
Acceleration $= 0$

71. (a) $A(-1, 1)$; $B(1, -1)$
(b) $C(-0.5, 2)$; $D(0.5, -2)$

72. (a) $A(-\sqrt{2}, -2\sqrt{2})$; $B(\sqrt{2}, 2\sqrt{2})$
(b) $C(-2, -2)$; $D(2, 2)$

73. (a) $A(-2, -2)$
(b) $B(-1, -3)$

74. At y-intercept $(0, 2\sqrt{2})$ the slope is $\dfrac{2+\sqrt{2}}{2}$.

At y-intercept $(0, -2\sqrt{2})$ the slope is $\dfrac{2-\sqrt{2}}{2}$.

At x-intercept $(2+2\sqrt{3}, 0)$ the slope is $\dfrac{\sqrt{3}}{\sqrt{3}+1}$.

At x-intercept $(2-2\sqrt{3}, 0)$ the slope is $\dfrac{\sqrt{3}}{\sqrt{3}-1}$.

75. 6

76. Every sinusoid with amplitude A and period p is the graph of some equation of the form $y = A\sin\left(\dfrac{2\pi}{p}x + k\right) + D$. The slope at any x is $\dfrac{dy}{dx} = A\cdot\dfrac{2\pi}{p}\cos\left(\dfrac{2\pi}{p}x + k\right)$. Since the maximum value of cosine is 1, the maximum slope is $\dfrac{2\pi A}{p}$.

77. Yes

78. (a) $P(0) \approx 1.339$, so initially, one student was infected
(b) 200
(c) After 5 days, when the rate is 50 students/day

79. (a) $-\dfrac{2}{3}$
(b) $-\dfrac{5}{27}$

80. $-1/(3\sqrt{3})$

81. (a) $g'(x) = k\cdot e^{kx} + f'(x)$, so $g'(0) = k + 3$.
$g''(x) = k^2\cdot e^{kx} + f''(x)$, so $g''(0) = k^2 - 1$.
(b) $h'(x) = b\sin(bx)f(x) + f'(x)\cos(bx)$, so $h'(0) = b\cdot\sin(0) + 3\cdot\cos(0) = 3$. Note that $h(0) = \cos(0)\cdot f(0) = 1\cdot 2 = 2$, so the tangent line has equation $y - 2 = 3(x - 0)$.

82. (a) $\dfrac{dy}{dx} = \dfrac{e^x - e^{-x}}{2}$
(b) $\dfrac{d^2y}{dx^2} = \dfrac{e^x + e^{-x}}{2}$
(c) At $x = 1$, $\dfrac{dy}{dx} = \dfrac{e^1 - e^{-1}}{2} = 1.175$ and $y = \dfrac{e^1 + e^{-1}}{2} = 1.543$. The tangent line has equation $y - 1.543 = 1.175(x - 1)$.
(d) The normal line has equation $y - 1.543 = -0.851(x - 1)$.
(e) The tangent line is horizontal where $dy/dx = 0$; that is, where $e^x = e^{-x}$. This is true only at $x = 0$.

83. (a) The domain of f is the interval $(-1, 1)$.
(b) $f'(x) = \dfrac{-2x}{1-x^2} = \dfrac{2x}{x^2-1}$ on the domain $(-1, 1)$.
(c) The domain of f' is the interval $(-1, 1)$.
(d) $f''(x) = \left(\dfrac{2x}{x^2-1}\right)' = \dfrac{2(x^2-1) - 2x(2x)}{(x^2-1)^2} = \dfrac{-2(x^2+1)}{(x^2-1)^2} < 0$
for all x in the domain of f, since $\dfrac{x^2+1}{(x^2-1)^2} > 0$ for all x between -1 and 1.

CHAPTER 5

Section 5.1

Quick Review 5.1

1. $\dfrac{-1}{2\sqrt{4-x}}$ **3.** $\dfrac{\sin(\ln x)}{x}$

5. (c) **7.** (d) **9.** ∞

11. (a) 1 **(b)** 1 **(c)** Undefined

Exercises 5.1

1. Minima at $(-2, 0)$ and $(2, 0)$, maximum at $(0, 2)$

3. Maximum at $(0, 5)$

5. Maximum at $x = b$, minimum at $x = c_2$; Extreme Value Theorem applies, so both the max and min exist.

7. Maximum at $x = c$, no minimum; Extreme Value Theorem doesn't apply, since the function isn't defined on a closed interval.

9. Maximum at $x = c$, minimum at $x = a$; Extreme Value Theorem doesn't apply, since the function isn't continuous.

11. Maximum value is $\dfrac{1}{4} + \ln 4$ at $x = 4$; minimum value is 1 at $x = 1$; local maximum at $\left(\dfrac{1}{2}, 2 - \ln 2\right)$

13. Maximum value is $\ln 4$ at $x = 3$; minimum value is 0 at $x = 0$.

15. Maximum value is 1 at $x = \dfrac{\pi}{4}$; minimum value is -1 at $x = \dfrac{5\pi}{4}$; local minimum at $\left(0, \dfrac{1}{\sqrt{2}}\right)$; local maximum at $\left(\dfrac{7\pi}{4}, 0\right)$

17. Maximum value is $3^{2/5}$ at $x = -3$; minimum value is 0 at $x = 0$. [(0, 0) is not a stationary point]

19. Min value 1 at $x = 2$

21. Local max at $(-2, 17)$: local min at $\left(\frac{4}{3}, -\frac{41}{27}\right)$

23. Min value 0 at $x = -1, 1$

25. Min value 1 at $x = 0$

27. Max value 2 at $x = 1$; min value 0 at $x = -1, 3$

29. Maximum value is $\frac{1}{2}$ at $x = 1$;

minimum value is $-\frac{1}{2}$ at $x = -1$.

31. Maximum value is 11 at $x = 5$;
minimum value is 5 on the interval $[-3, 2]$;
local maximum at $(-5, 9)$

33. Maximum value is 5 on the interval $[3, \infty)$;
minimum value is -5 on the interval $(-\infty, -2]$.

35.

crit. pt.	derivative	extremum	value
$x = -\frac{4}{5}$	0	local max	$\frac{12}{25}10^{1/3}$
$x = 0$	undefined	local min	0

$(0, 0)$ is not a stationary point.

37.

crit. pt.	derivative	extremum	value
$x = -2$	undefined	local max	0
$x = -\sqrt{2}$	0	minimum	-2
$x = \sqrt{2}$	0	maximum	2
$x = 2$	undefined	local min	0

$(-2, 0)$ and $(2, 0)$ are not stationary points.

39.

crit. pt.	derivative	extremum	value
$x = 1$	undefined	minimum	2

$(1, 2)$ is not a stationary point.

41.

crit. pt.	derivative	extremum	value
$x = -1$	0	maximum	5
$x = 1$	undefined	local min	1
$x = 3$	0	maximum	5

$(1, 1)$ is not a stationary point.

43. (a) Max value is 144 at $x = 2$. **(b)** The largest volume of the box is 144 cubic units and it occurs when $x = 2$.

45. False. For example, the maximum could occur at a corner, where $f'(c)$ would not exist.

47. E **49.** B

51. (a) No
(b) The derivative is defined and nonzero for $x \neq 2$. Also, $f(2) = 0$, and $f(x) > 0$ for all $x \neq 2$.
(c) No, because $(-\infty, \infty)$ is not a closed interval.
(d) The answers are the same as (a) and (b) with 2 replaced by a.

53. (a) $f'(x) = 3ax^2 + 2bx + c$ is a quadratic, so it can have 0, 1, or 2 zeros, which would be the critical points of *f*. Examples:

The function $f(x) = x^3 - 3x$ has two critical points at $x = -1$ and $x = 1$.

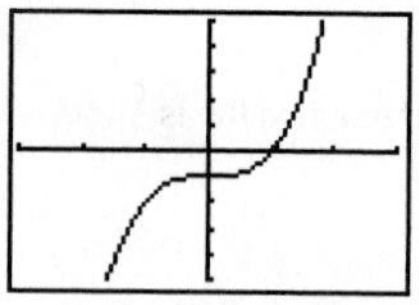

[–3, 3] by [–5, 5]

The function $f(x) = x^3 - 1$ has one critical point at $x = 0$.

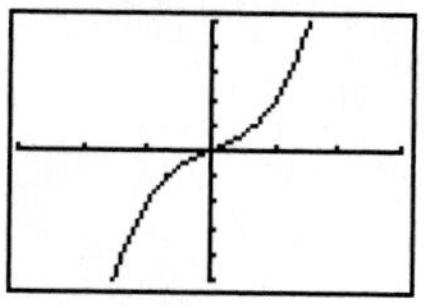

[–3, 3] by [–5, 5]

The function $f(x) = x^3 + x$ has no critical points.

(b) Two or none.

55. (a)

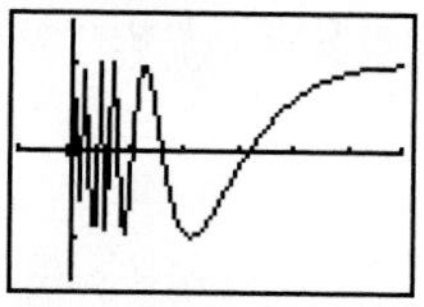

[–0.1, 0.6] by [–1.5, 1.5]

$f(0) = 0$ is not a local extreme value because in any open interval containing $x = 0$, there are infinitely many points where $f(x) = 1$ and where $f(x) = -1$.

(b) One possible answer, on the interval $[0, 1]$:

$$f(x) = \begin{cases} (1 - x)\cos\dfrac{1}{1 - x}, & 0 \le x < 1 \\ 0, & x = 1 \end{cases}$$

This function has no local extreme value at $x = 1$. Note that it is continuous on $[0, 1]$.

Section 5.2

Quick Review 5.2

1. $(-\sqrt{3}, \sqrt{3})$

3. $[-2, 2]$

5. On $(-2, 2)$

7. For all x in its domain, or, for all $x \neq \pm 1$

9. $C = 3$

Exercises 5.2

1. (a) Yes. **(b)** $2c + 2 = \frac{2 - (-1)}{1 - 0} = 3$, so $c = \frac{1}{2}$

3. No. There is a vertical tangent at $x = 0$.

5. (a) Yes.

(b) $\frac{1}{\sqrt{1 - c^2}} = \frac{(\pi/2) - (-\pi/2)}{1 - (-1)}$
$= \frac{\pi}{2}$, so $c = \sqrt{1 - 4/\pi^2} \approx 0.771$.

7. No. The split function is discontinuous at $x = \frac{\pi}{2}$.

9. (a) $y = \frac{5}{2}$ **(b)** $y = 2$

11. Because the trucker's average speed was 79.5 mph, and by the Mean Value Theorem, the trucker must have been going that speed at least once during the trip.

13. Because its average speed was approximately 7.667 knots, and by the Mean Value Theorem, it must have been going that speed at least once during the trip.

15. (a) Local maximum at $\left(\frac{5}{2}, \frac{25}{4}\right)$

(b) On $\left(-\infty, \frac{5}{2}\right]$

(c) On $\left[\frac{5}{2}, \infty\right)$

17. **(a)** None **(b)** None **(c)** On $(-\infty, 0)$ and $(0, \infty)$
19. **(a)** None **(b)** On $(-\infty, \infty)$ **(c)** None
21. **(a)** Local maximum at $(-2, 4)$ **(b)** None **(c)** On $[-2, \infty)$
23. **(a)** Local max at $\left(8/3, \frac{16\sqrt{3}}{9}\right)$; local min at $(4, 0)$
(b) On $(-\infty, 8/3]$ **(c)** On $[8/3, 4]$
25. **(a)** Local max at $(-2, 1/4)$;
local min at $(2, -1/4)$
(b) On $(-\infty, -2]$ and $[2, \infty)$
(c) On $[-2, 2]$
27. **(a)** Local maximum at $\approx (-1.126, -0.036)$;
local minimum at $\approx (0.559, -2.639)$
(b) On $(-\infty, -1.126]$ and $[0.559, \infty)$
(c) On $[-1.126, 0.559]$
29. $\frac{x^2}{2} + C$
31. $x^3 - x^2 + x + C$
33. $e^x + C$
35. $\frac{1}{x} + \frac{1}{2}, x > 0$
37. $\ln(x + 2) + 3$
39. Possible answers:
(a)

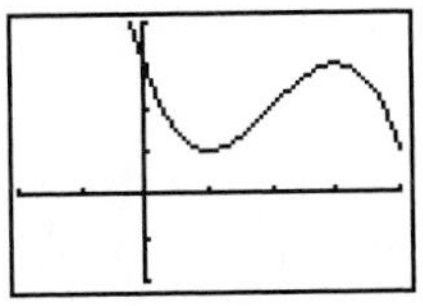

[–2, 4] by [–2, 4]

(b)

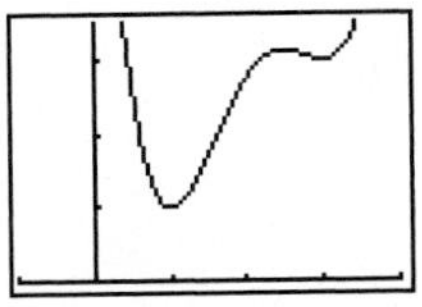

[–1, 4] by [0, 3.5]

(c)

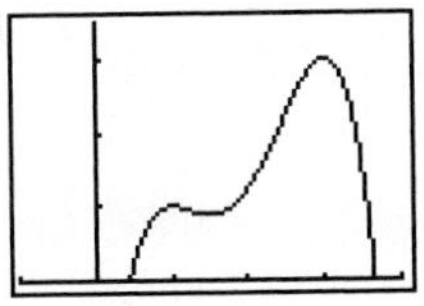

[–1, 4] by [0, 3.5]

41. One possible answer:

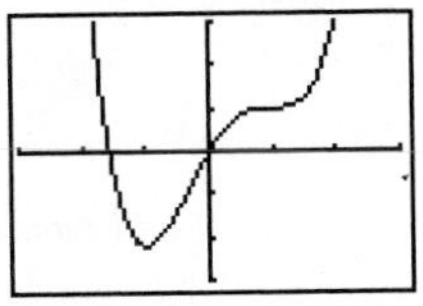

[–3, 3] by [–15, 15]

43. **(a)** 48 m/sec
(b) 720 meters
(c) After about 27.604 seconds, and it will be going about 48.166 m/sec
45. Because the function is not continuous on $[0, 1]$
47. $f(x)$ must be zero at least once between a and b by the Intermediate Value Theorem.
Now suppose that $f(x)$ is zero twice between a and b. Then by the Mean Value Theorem, $f'(x)$ would have to be zero at least once between the two zeros of $f(x)$, but this can't be true since we are given that $f'(x) \neq 0$ on this interval.
Therefore, $f(x)$ is zero once and only once between a and b.
49. Let $f(x) = x + \ln(x + 1)$. Then $f(x)$ is continuous and differentiable everywhere on $[0, 3]$. $f'(x) = 1 + \frac{1}{x+1}$, which is never zero on $[0, 3]$. Now $f(0) = 0$, so $x = 0$ is one solution of the equation. If there were a second solution, $f(x)$ would be zero twice in $[0, 3]$, and by the Mean Value Theorem, $f'(x)$ would have to be zero somewhere between the two zeros of $f(x)$. But this can't happen, since $f'(x)$ is never zero on $[0, 3]$. Therefore, $f(x) = 0$ has exactly one solution in the interval $[0, 3]$.
51. **False.** For example, the function x^3 is increasing on $(-1, 1)$, but $f'(0) = 0$.
53. A **55.** E
57. **(a)** Increasing: $[-2, -1.3]$ and $[1.3, 2]$;
decreasing: $[-1.3, 1.3]$;
local max: $x \approx -1.3$
local min: $x \approx 1.3$
(b) Regression equation: $y = 3x^2 - 5$

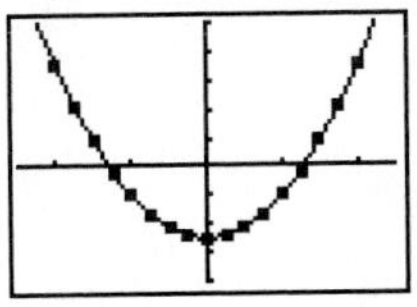

[–2.5, 2.5] by [–8, 10]

(c) $f(x) = x^2 - 5x$
59. $\frac{f(b) - f(a)}{b - a} = \frac{\frac{1}{b} - \frac{1}{a}}{b - a} = -\frac{1}{ab}$
$f'(c) = -\frac{1}{c^2}$, so $-\frac{1}{c^2} = -\frac{1}{ab}$ and $c^2 = ab$.
Thus, $c = \sqrt{ab}$.
61. By the Mean Value Theorem, $\sin b - \sin a = (\cos c)(b - a)$ for some c between a and b. Taking the absolute value of both sides and using $|\cos c| \leq 1$ gives the result.
63. Let $f(x)$ be a monotonic function defined on an interval D. For any two values in D, we may let x_1 be the smaller value and let x_2 be the larger value, so $x_1 < x_2$. Then either $f(x_1) < f(x_2)$ (if f is increasing), or $f(x_1) > f(x_2)$ (if f is decreasing), which means $f(x_1) \neq f(x_2)$. Therefore, f is one-to-one.

Section 5.3

Quick Review 5.3

1. $(-3, 3)$ **3.** f: all reals f': all reals **5.** $f: x \neq 2$ $f': x \neq 2$
7. $y = 0$ **9.** $y = 0$ and $y = 200$

Exercises 5.3

1. Local minimum at $\left(\frac{1}{2}, -\frac{5}{4}\right)$: $-\frac{5}{4}$ is an absolute minimum.
3. Local maximum: $(0, 1)$; local minima: $(-1, -1)$ and $(1, -1)$; -1 is an absolute minimum.
5. Local maxima: $(-\sqrt{8}, 0)$ and $(2, 4)$; local minima: $(-2, -4)$ and $(\sqrt{8}, 0)$; 4 is an absolute maximum and -4 is an absolute minimum.
7. **(a)** $(-7/4, \infty)$ **(b)** $(-\infty, -7/4)$
9. **(a)** $(-\infty, 0)$ **(b)** $(0, \infty)$
11. **(a)** None **(b)** $(1, \infty)$ **13.** $(-2, -2/e^2)$
15. $(0, 0)$ **17.** $(0, 0)$ and $(-2, 6\sqrt[3]{2})$ **19.** $(1,1)$
21. **(a)** Zero: $x = \pm 1$; positive; $(-\infty, -1)$ and $(1, \infty)$; negative: $(-1, 1)$
(b) Zero: $x = 0$; positive: $(0, \infty)$; negative: $(-\infty, 0)$
23. **(a)** $(-\infty, -2]$ and $[0, 2]$
(b) $[-2, 0]$ and $[2, \infty)$
(c) Local maxima: $x = -2$ and $x = 2$; local minimum: $x = 0$

25. (a) $v(t) = 2t - 4$ **(b)** $a(t) = 2$
(c) It begins at position 3 moving in a negative direction. It moves to position -1 when $t = 2$, and then changes direction, moving in a positive direction thereafter.

27. (a) $v(t) = 3t^2 - 3$ **(b)** $a(t) = 6t$
(c) It begins at position 3 moving in a negative direction. It moves to position 1 when $t = 1$, and then changes direction, moving in a positive direction thereafter.

29. (a) $t = 2.2, 6, 9.8$ □**(b)** $t = 4, 8, 11$

31. Some calculators use different logistic regression equations, so answers may vary.

(a) $y = \dfrac{12655.179}{1 + 12.871e^{-0.0326x}}$

(b)

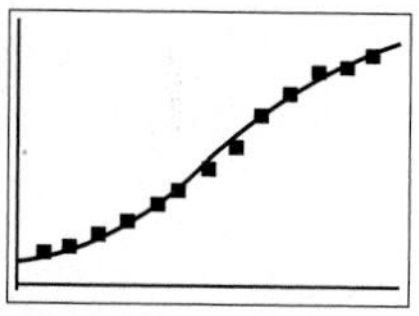

[0, 140] by [–200, 12000]

(c) The regression equation predicts a population of 12,209,870. (This is remarkably close to the 2000 census number of 12,281,054.)
(d) The second derivative has a zero at about 78, indicating that the population was growing the fastest in 1898. This corresponds to the inflection point on the regression curve.
(e) The regression equation predicts a population limit of about 12,655,179.

33. $y' = 3 - 3x^2$ and $y'' = -6x$.
$y' = 0$ at ± 1. $y''(-1) > 0$ and $y''(1) < 0$, so there is a local minimum at $(-1, 3)$ and a local maximum at $(1, 7)$.

35. $y' = 3x^2 + 6x$ and $y'' = 6x + 6$.
$y' = 0$ at -2 and 0. $y''(-2) < 0$ and $y''(0) > 0$, so there is a local maximum at $(-2, 2)$ and a local minimum at $(0, -2)$.

37. $y' = (x + 1)e^x$ and $y'' = (x + 2)e^x$.
$y' = 0$ at -1 and $y''(-1) > 0$, so there is a local minimum at $(-1, -1/e)$.

39. (a) None **(b)** At $x = 2$ **(c)** At $x = 1$ and $x = \dfrac{5}{3}$

41.

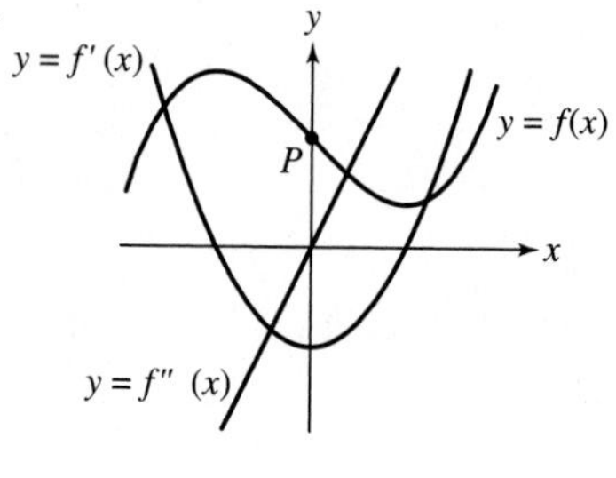

43. No. f must have a horizontal tangent line at that point, but it could be increasing (or decreasing) on both sides of the point, and there would be no local extremum.

45. One possible answer:

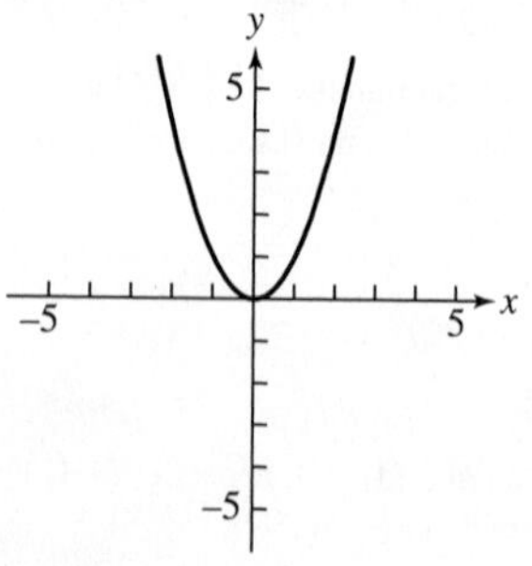

47. One possible answer:

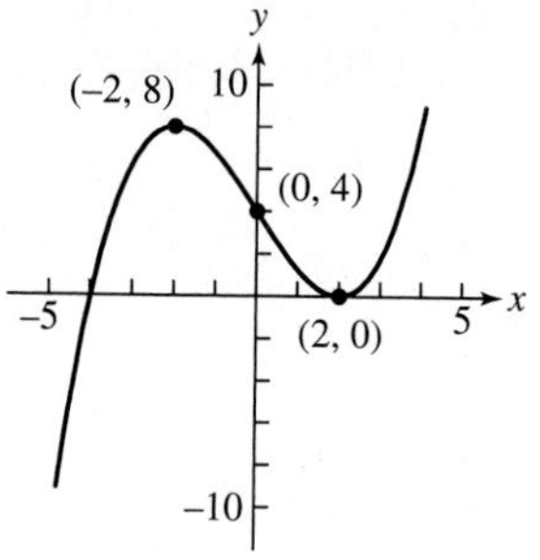

49. (a) $[0, 1]$, $[3, 4]$, and $[5.5, 6]$
(b) $[1, 3]$ and $[4, 5.5]$
(c) Local maxima: $x = 1$, $x = 4$ (if f is continuous at $x = 4$), and $x = 6$; local minima: $x = 0$, $x = 3$, and $x = 5.5$

51. (a) Absolute maximum at $(1, 2)$; absolute minimum at $(3, -2)$
(b) None
(c) One possible answer:

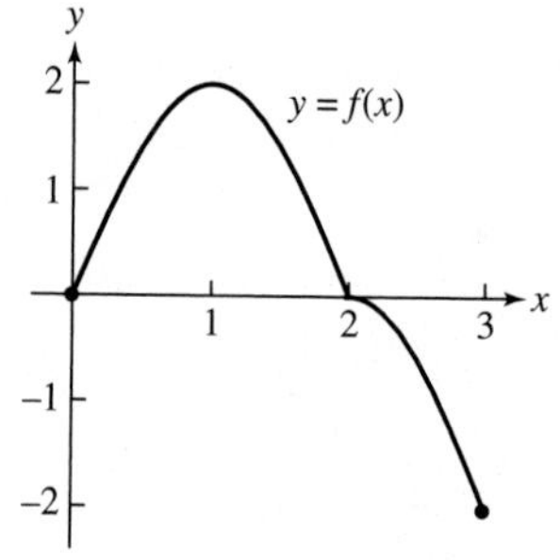

53.

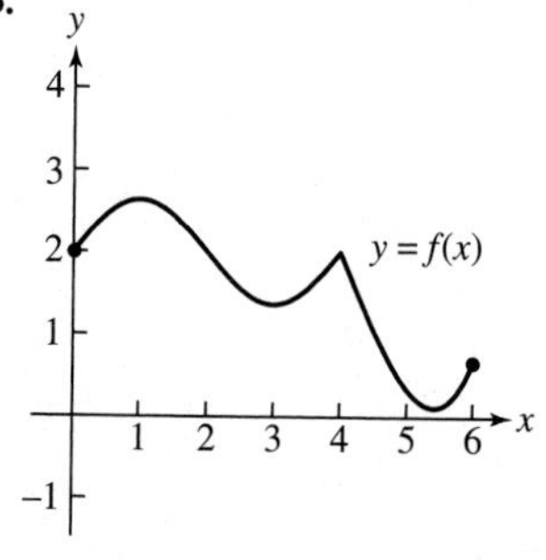

55. False. For example, consider $f(x) = x^4$ at $c = 0$.

57. A **59.** C

61. (a) In Exercise 7, $a = 4$ and $b = 21$, so $-\dfrac{b}{3a} = -\dfrac{7}{4}$, which is the x-value where the point of inflection occurs. The local extrema are at $x = -2$ and $x = -\dfrac{3}{2}$, which are symmetric about $x = -\dfrac{7}{4}$.
(b) In Exercise 2, $a = -2$ and $b = 6$, so $-\dfrac{b}{3a} = 1$, which is the x-value where the point of inflection occurs. The local extrema are at $x = 0$ and $x = 2$, which are symmetric about $x = 1$.
(c) $f'(x) = 3ax^2 + 2bx + c$ and $f''(x) = 6ax + 2b$. The point of inflection will occur where $f''(x) = 0$, which is at $x = -\dfrac{b}{3a}$.
If there are local extrema, they will occur at the zeros of $f'(x)$. Since $f'(x)$ is quadratic, its graph is a parabola and any zeros will be symmetric about the vertex, which will also be where $f''(x) = 0$.

63. (a) Since $f''(x)$ is quadratic it must have 0, 1, or 2 zeros. If $f''(x)$ has 0 or 1 zeros, it will not change sign and the concavity of $f(x)$ will not change, so there is no point of inflection. If $f''(x)$ has 2 zeros, it will change sign twice, and $f(x)$ will have 2 points of inflection.
(b) $f(x)$ has two points of inflection if and only if $3b^2 > 8ac$.

Quick Quiz (Sections 5.1–5.3)

1. C **3.** B

Section 5.4

Quick Review 5.4

1. None
3. $\frac{200\pi}{3}\ \text{cm}^3$
5. $-\sin\alpha$ **7.** $\sin\alpha$
9. $x = 1$ and $y = \sqrt{3}$, or, $x = -1$ and $y = -\sqrt{3}$

Exercises 5.4

1. (a) As large as possible: 0 and 20; as small as possible: 10 and 10
(b) As large as possible: $\frac{79}{4}$ and $\frac{1}{4}$; as small as possible: 0 and 20
3. Smallest perimeter = 16 in., dimensions are 4 in. by 4 in.
5. (a) $y = 1 - x$
(b) $A(x) = 2x(1 - x)$
(c) Largest area $= \frac{1}{2}$, dimensions are 1 by $\frac{1}{2}$
7. Largest volume is $\frac{2450}{27} \approx 90.74\ \text{in}^3$; dimensions: $\frac{5}{3}$ in. by $\frac{14}{3}$ in. by $\frac{35}{3}$ in.
9. Largest area = 80,000 m^2; dimensions: 200 m (perpendicular to river) by 400 m (parallel to river)
11. (a) 10 ft by 10 ft by 5 ft **(b)** Assume that the weight is minimized when the total area of the bottom and the 4 sides is minimized.
13. 18 in. high by 9 in. wide
15. $\theta = \frac{\pi}{2}$
17. $\frac{8}{\pi}$ to 1
19. (a) $V(x) = 2x(24 - 2x)(18 - 2x)$

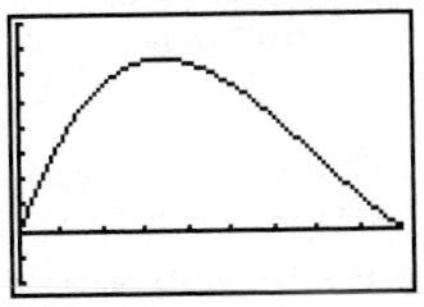

[0, 9] by [–400, 1600]

(b) Domain: $(0, 9)$
(c) Maximum volume $\approx 1309.95\ \text{in}^3$ when $x \approx 3.39$ in.
(d) $V'(x) = 24x^2 - 336x + 864$, so the critical point is at $x = 7 - \sqrt{13}$, which confirms the result in part (c).
(e) $x = 2$ in. or $x = 5$ in.
(f) The dimensions of the resulting box are $2x$ in., $(24 - 2x)$ in., and $(18 - 2x)$ in. Each of these measurements must be positive, so that gives the domain of $(0, 9)$.
21. Dimensions: width ≈ 3.44, height ≈ 2.61; maximum area ≈ 8.98
23. Set $r'(x) = c'(x)$: $4x^{-1/2} = 4x$. The only positive critical value is $x = 1$, so profit is maximized at a production level of 1000 units. Note that $(r - c)''(x) = -2(x)^{-3/2} - 4 < 0$ for all positive x, so the Second Derivative Test confirms the maximum.
25. Set $c'(x) = c(x)/x$: $3x^2 - 20x + 30 = x^2 - 10x + 30$. The only positive solution is $x = 5$, so average cost is minimized at a production level of 5000 units. Note that $\frac{d^2}{dx^2}\left(\frac{c(x)}{x}\right) = 2 > 0$ for all positive x, so the Second Derivative Test confirms the minimum.
27. 67 people
29. (a) $f'(x)$ is a quadratic polynomial, and as such it can have 0, 1, or 2 zeros. If it has 0 or 1 zeros, then its sign never changes, so $f(x)$ has no local extrema.
If $f'(x)$ has 2 zeros, then its sign changes twice, and $f(x)$ has 2 local extrema at those points.
(b) Possible answers:
No local extrema: $y = x^3$;
2 local extrema: $y = x^3 - 3x$
31. (a) $x = 12$ cm and $y = 6$ cm **(b)** $x = 12$ cm and $y = 6$ cm
33. (a) $a = 16$ **(b)** $a = -1$
35. (a) $a = -3$ and $b = -9$ **(b)** $a = -3$ and $b = -24$
37. (a) $4\sqrt{3}$ in. wide by $4\sqrt{6}$ in. deep
(b)

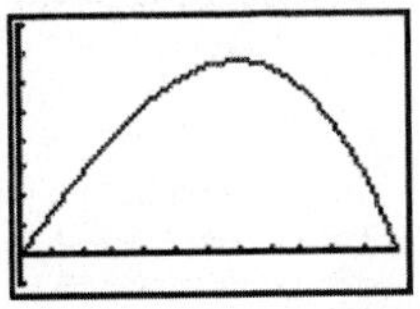

[0, 12] by [−100, 800]

(c)

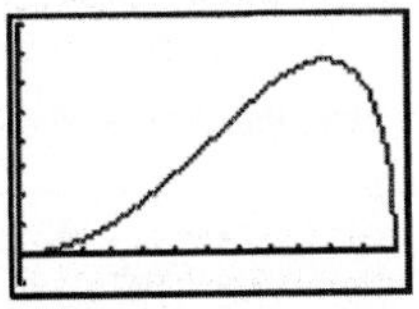

[0, 12] by [−100, 800]

Changing the value of k changes the maximum strength, but not the dimensions of the strongest beam. The graphs for different values of k look the same except that the vertical scale is different.

39. (a) Maximum speed $= 10\pi$ cm/sec;
maximum speed is at $t = \frac{1}{2}, \frac{3}{2}, \frac{5}{2}, \frac{7}{2}$ seconds;
position at those times is $s = 0$ cm (rest position); acceleration at those times is 0 cm/sec^2
(b) The magnitude of the acceleration is greatest when the cart is at positions $s = \pm 10$ cm; The speed of the cart is 0 cm/sec at those times.
41. The minimum distance is $\frac{\sqrt{5}}{2}$
43. No. It has an absolute minimum at the point $\left(\frac{1}{2}, \frac{3}{4}\right)$.
45. (a) Whenever t is an integer multiple of π sec
(b) The greatest distance is $3\sqrt{3}/2$ m when $t = 2\pi/3$ and $4\pi/3$ sec.
47. $\theta = \frac{\pi}{6}$
49. $M = \frac{C}{2}$
51. True. This is guaranteed by the Extreme Value Theorem (Section 5.1).
53. D **55.** B
57. Let P be the foot of the perpendicular from A to the mirror, and Q be the foot of the perpendicular from B to the mirror. Suppose the light strikes the mirror at point R on the way from A to B. Let:
a = distance from A to P
b = distance from B to Q
c = distance from P to Q
x = distance from P to R

To minimize the time is to minimize the total distance the light travels going from A to B. The total distance is

$$D(x) = (x^2 + a^2)^{1/2} + ((c - x)^2 + b^2)^{1/2}.$$

Then $D'(x) = 0$ and $D(x)$ has it minimum when

$x = \frac{ac}{a + b}$, or, $\frac{x}{a} = \frac{c}{a + b}$. It follows that

$c - x = \frac{bc}{a + b}$, or $\frac{c - x}{b} = \frac{c}{a + b}$. This means that the two triangles APR and BQR are similar, and the two angles must be equal.

59. **(a)** $\frac{dv}{dr} = cr(2r_0 - 3r)$ which is zero when $r = \frac{2}{3}r_0$.

(b)

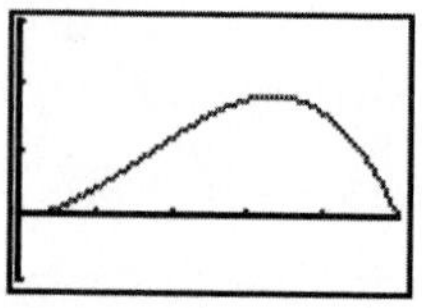

[0, 0.5] by [−0.01, 0.03]

61. $p(x) = 6x - (x^3 - 6x^2 + 15x)$, $x \geq 0$. This function has its maximum value at the points $(0, 0)$ and $(3, 0)$.

63. **(a)** $y'(0) = 0$ **(b)** $y'(-L) = 0$

(c) $y(0) = 0$, so $d = 0$. $y'(0) = 0$, so $c = 0$.
Then $y(-L) = -aL^3 + bL^2 = H$ and
$y'(-L) = 3aL^2 - 2bL = 0$.

Solving, $a = 2\frac{H}{L^3}$ and $b = 3\frac{H}{L^2}$, which gives the equation shown.

65. **(a)** The x- and y-intercepts of the line through R and T are $x - \frac{a}{f'(x)}$ and $a - xf'(x)$ respectively.

The area of the triangle is the product of these two values.

(b) Domain: $(0, 10)$

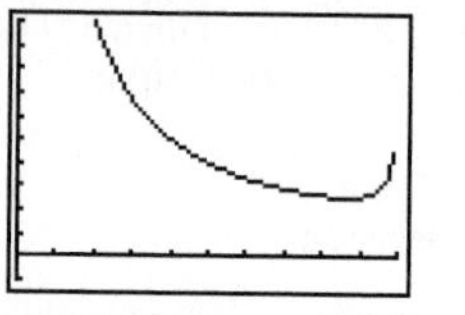

[0, 10] by [−100, 1000]

The vertical asymptotes at $x = 0$ and $x = 10$ correspond to horizontal or vertical tangent lines, which do not form triangles.

(c) Height $= 15$, which is 3 times the y-coordinate of the center of the ellipse.

(d) Part (a) remains unchanged.

The domain is $(0, C)$ and the graph is similar.

The minimum area occurs when $x^2 = \frac{3C^2}{4}$. From this, it follows that the triangle has minimum area when its height is $3B$.

Section 5.5

Quick Review 5.5

1. $2x\cos(x^2 + 1)$

3. $x \approx -0.567$

5. $y = x + 1$

7. **(a)** $x = -1$ **(b)** $x = -\frac{e + 1}{2e} \approx -0.684$

9.

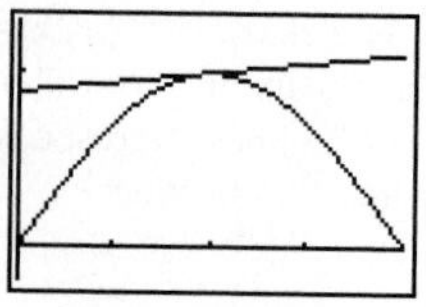

[0, π] by [−0.2, 1.3]

Exercises 5.5

1. **(a)** $L(x) = 10x - 13$

(b) Differs from the true value in absolute value by less than 10^{-1}

3. **(a)** $L(x) = 2$

(b) Differs from the true value in absolute value by less than 10^{-2}

5. **(a)** $L(x) = x - \pi$

(b) Differs from the true value in absolute value by less than 10^{-3}

7. $f(0) = 1$. Also, $f'(x) = k(1 + x)^{k-1}$, so $f'(0) = k$. This means the linearization at $x = 0$ is $L(x) = 1 + kx$.

9. **(a)** $1 - 6x$ **(b)** $2 + 2x$ **(c)** $1 - \frac{x}{2}$

11. $y = 10 + 0.05(x - 10)$, so $y = 10.05$

13. $y = 10 + (1/300)(x - 1000)$, so $y = 10 - 1/150 = 9.99\overline{3}$

15. **(a)** $dy = (3x^2 - 3)\,dx$

(b) $dy = 0.45$ at the given values

17. **(a)** $dy = (2x\ln x + x)\,dx$

(b) $dy = 0.01$ at the given values

19. **(a)** $dy = (\cos x)\,e^{\sin x}\,dx$

(b) $dy = 0.1$ at the given values

21. **(a)** $dy = \frac{dx}{(x + 1)^2}$

(b) $dy = 0.01$ at the given values

23. $-\frac{x}{\sqrt{1 - x^2}}\,dx$

25. $\frac{4}{1 + 16x^2}\,dx$

27. **(a)** 0.21 **(b)** 0.2 **(c)** 0.01

29. **(a)** $-\frac{2}{11}$ **(b)** $-\frac{1}{5}$ **(c)** $-\frac{1}{55}$

31. $\Delta V \approx 4\pi a^2 dr = 20\pi$ cm^3

33. $\Delta V \approx 3a^2\,dx = 15$ cm^3

35. $\Delta V \approx 2\pi ah\,dr = \pi h$ cm^3

37. $2\pi(10)(0.1) \approx 6.3$ in^2

39. $3(15)^2(0.2) \approx 135$ cm^3

41. **(a)** $x + 1$ **(b)** $f(0.1) \approx 1.1$

(c) The actual value is less than 1.1, since the derivative is decreasing over the interval $[0, 0.1]$.

43. The diameter grew $\frac{2}{\pi} \approx 0.6366$ in. The cross-section area grew about 10 in^2.

45. The side should be measured to within 1%.

47. $V = \pi r^2 h$ (where h is constant), so $\frac{dV}{V} = \frac{2\pi rh\,dr}{\pi r^2 h} = 2\frac{dr}{r} = 0.2\%$

49. Since $V = \frac{4}{3}\pi r^3$, we have $dV = 4\pi r^2 dr = 4\pi r^2\left(\frac{1}{16\pi}\right) = \frac{r^2}{4}$.

The volume error in each case is simply $\frac{r^2}{4}$ in^3.

Sphere Type	True Radius	Tape Error	Radius Error	Volume Error
Orange	2″	1/8″	$1/16\pi''$	1 in^3
Melon	4″	1/8″	$1/16\pi''$	4 in^3
Beach Ball	7″	1/8″	$1/16\pi''$	12.25 in^3

51. About 37.87 to 1

53. $x \approx 0.682328$

55. $x \approx 0.386237, 1.961569$

57. True. A look at the graph reveals the problem. The graph decreases after $x = 1$ toward a horizontal asymptote of $x = 0$, so the x-intercepts of the tangent lines keep getting bigger without approaching a zero.

59. B

61. D

63. If $f'(x_1) \neq 0$, then x_2 and all later approximations are equal to x_1.

65. $x_2 = -2$, $x_3 = 4$, $x_4 = -8$, and $x_5 = 16$; $|x_n| = 2^{n-1}$.

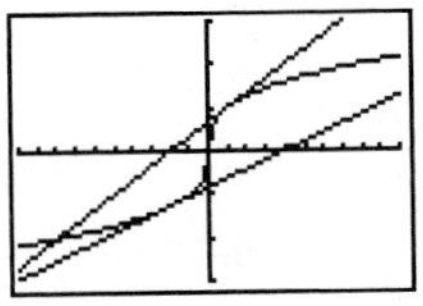

[−10, 10] by [−3, 3]

67. Finding a zero of $\sin x$ by Newton's method would use the recursive formula $x_{n+1} = x_n - \dfrac{\sin(x_n)}{\cos(x_n)} = x_n - \tan x_n$, and that is exactly what the calculator would be doing. Any zero of $\sin x$ would be a multiple of π.

69.
$$\lim_{x\to 0}\frac{\tan x}{x} = \lim_{x\to 0}\frac{\sin x/\cos x}{x} = \lim_{x\to 0}\left(\frac{1}{\cos x}\cdot\frac{\sin x}{x}\right) = \left(\lim_{x\to 0}\frac{1}{\cos x}\right)\left(\lim_{x\to 0}\frac{\sin x}{x}\right) = (1)(1) = 1.$$

71. The linearization is $1 + \dfrac{3x}{2}$. It is the sum of the two individual linearizations.

Section 5.6

Quick Review 5.6

1. $\sqrt{74}$

3. $\dfrac{1 - 2y}{2x + 2y - 1}$

5. $2x\cos^2 y$

7. One possible answer: $x = -2 + 6t$, $y = 1 - 4t$, $0 \le t \le 1$.

9. One possible answer: $\pi/2 \le t \le 3\pi/2$

Exercises 5.6

1. $\dfrac{dA}{dt} = 2\pi r\dfrac{dr}{dt}$

3. (a) $\dfrac{dV}{dt} = \pi r^2\dfrac{dh}{dt}$

(b) $\dfrac{dV}{dt} = 2\pi rh\dfrac{dr}{dt}$

(c) $\dfrac{dV}{dt} = \pi r^2\dfrac{dh}{dt} + 2\pi rh\dfrac{dr}{dt}$

5. $\dfrac{ds}{dt} = \dfrac{x\dfrac{dx}{dt} + y\dfrac{dy}{dt} + z\dfrac{dz}{dt}}{\sqrt{x^2 + y^2 + z^2}}$

7. (a) 1 volt/sec **(b)** $-\dfrac{1}{3}$ amp/sec **(c)** $\dfrac{dV}{dt} = I\dfrac{dR}{dt} + R\dfrac{dI}{dt}$

(d) $\dfrac{dR}{dt} = \dfrac{3}{2}$ ohms/sec. R is increasing since $\dfrac{dR}{dt}$ is positive.

9. (a) $\dfrac{dA}{dt} = 14$ cm²/sec **(b)** $\dfrac{dP}{dt} = 0$ cm/sec **(c)** $\dfrac{dD}{dt} = -\dfrac{14}{13}$ cm/sec

(d) The area is increasing, because its derivative is positive. The perimeter is not changing, because its derivative is zero. The diagonal length is decreasing, because its derivative is negative.

11. (a) 1 ft/min **(b)** 40π ft²/min

13. $\dfrac{dx}{dt} = \dfrac{3000}{\sqrt{51}}$ mph ≈ 420.084 mph

15. $\dfrac{19\pi}{2500} \approx 0.0239$ in³/min

17. (a) $\dfrac{32}{9\pi} \approx 1.13$ cm/min **(b)** $-\dfrac{80}{3\pi} \approx -8.49$ cm/min

19. (a) 12 ft/sec **(b)** $-\dfrac{119}{2}$ ft²/sec **(c)** -1 radian/sec

21. (a) $\dfrac{5}{2}$ ft/sec **(b)** $-\dfrac{3}{20}$ radian/sec

23. (a) $\dfrac{24}{5}$ cm/sec **(b)** 0 cm/sec

(c) $-\dfrac{1200}{160.801} \approx -0.00746$ cm/sec

25. 1 radian/sec

27. 1.6 cm²/min

29. -3 ft/sec

31. In front: 2 radians/sec; Half second later: 1 radian/sec

33. 7.1 in./min **35.** 29.5 knots

37. **False.** Since $\dfrac{dA}{dt} = 2\pi r\dfrac{dr}{dt}$, the value of $\dfrac{dA}{dt}$ depends on r.

39. E **41.** B

43. (a) $\dfrac{dc}{dt} = 0.3$ $\dfrac{dr}{dt} = 0.9$ $\dfrac{dp}{dt} = 0.6$ $\dfrac{dc}{dt} = -1.5625$

(b) $\dfrac{dr}{dt} = 3.5$ $\dfrac{dp}{dt} = 5.0625$

45. (a) The point being plotted would correspond to a point on the edge of the wheel as the wheel turns.

(b) One possible answer: $\theta = 16\pi t$, where t is in seconds.

(c) Assuming counterclockwise motion, the rates are as follows.

$\theta = \dfrac{\pi}{4}$: $\dfrac{dx}{dt} \approx -71.086$ ft/sec

$\dfrac{dy}{dt} \approx 71.086$ ft/sec

$\theta = \dfrac{\pi}{2}$: $\dfrac{dx}{dt} \approx -100.531$ ft/sec

$\dfrac{dy}{dt} = 0$ ft/sec

$\theta = \pi$: $\dfrac{dx}{dt} = 0$ ft/sec

$\dfrac{dy}{dt} \approx -100.531$ ft/sec

47. (a) 9% per year **(b)** Increasing at 1% per year

Quick Quiz (Sections 5.4–5.6)

1. B **3.** A

Review Exercises

1. Maximum: $\dfrac{4\sqrt{6}}{9}$ at $x = \dfrac{4}{3}$; minimum: -4 at $x = -2$

2. No global extrema

3. (a) $[-1, 0)$ and $[1, \infty)$

(b) $(-\infty, 1]$ and $(0, 1]$

(c) $(-\infty, 0)$ and $(0, \infty)$

(d) None

(e) Local minima at $(1, e)$ and $(-1, e)$

(f) None

4. **(a)** $[-\sqrt{2}, \sqrt{2}]$
(b) $[-2, -\sqrt{2}]$ and $[\sqrt{2}, 2]$
(c) $(-2, 0)$
(d) $(0, 2)$
(e) Local max: $(-2, 0)$ and $(\sqrt{2}, 2)$; local min: $(2, 0)$ and $(-\sqrt{2}, -2)$

5. **(a)** Approximately $(-\infty, 0.385]$
(b) Approximately $[0.385, \infty)$
(c) None **(d)** $(-\infty, \infty)$
(e) Local maximum at $\approx (0.385, 1.215)$
(f) None

6. **(a)** $[1, \infty)$ **(b)** $(-\infty, 1]$
(c) $(-\infty, \infty)$ **(d)** None
(e) Local minimum at $(1, 0)$
(f) None

7. **(a)** $[0, 1)$ **(b)** $(-1, 0]$
(c) $(-1, 1)$ **(d)** None
(e) Local minimum at $(0, 1)$
(f) None

8. **(a)** $(-\infty, -2^{-1/3}] \approx (-\infty, -0.794]$
(b) $[-2^{-1/3}, 1) \approx [-0.794, 1)$ and $(1, \infty)$
(c) $(-\infty, -2^{1/3}) \approx (-\infty, -1.260)$ and $(1, \infty)$
(d) $(-1.260, 1)$
(e) Local maximum at

$$\left(-2^{-1/3}, \frac{2}{3} \cdot 2^{-1/3}\right) \approx (-0.794, 0.529)$$

(f) $\left(-2^{1/3}, \frac{1}{3} \cdot 2^{1/3}\right) \approx (-1.260, 0.420)$

9. **(a)** None
(b) $[-1, 1]$
(c) $(-1, 0)$
(d) $(0, 1)$
(e) Local maximum at $(-1, \pi)$; local minimum at $(1, 0)$
(f) $\left(0, \frac{\pi}{2}\right)$

10. **(a)** $[-\sqrt{3}, \sqrt{3}]$
(b) $(-\infty, -\sqrt{3}]$ and $[\sqrt{3}, \infty)$
(c) Approximately $(-2.584, -0.706)$ and $(3.290, \infty)$
(d) Approximately $(-\infty, -2.584)$ and $(-0.706, 3.290)$
(e) Local maximum at

$$\left(\sqrt{3}, \frac{\sqrt{3}-1}{4}\right) \approx (1.732, 0.183);$$

local minimum at

$$\left(-\sqrt{3}, \frac{-\sqrt{3}-1}{4}\right) \approx (-1.732, -0.683)$$

(f) $\approx (-2.584, -0.573)$, $(-0.706, -0.338)$, and $(3.290, 0.161)$

11. **(a)** $(0, 2]$ **(b)** $[-2, 0)$
(c) None **(d)** $(-2, 0)$ and $(0, 2)$
(e) Local maxima at $(-2, \ln 2)$ and $(2, \ln 2)$
(f) None

12. **(a)** Approximately $[0, 0.176]$, $\left[0.994, \frac{\pi}{2}\right]$, $[2.148, 2.965]$, $\left[3.834, \frac{3\pi}{2}\right]$, and $\left[5.591, 2\pi\right]$

(b) Approximately $[0.176, 0.994]$, $\left[\frac{\pi}{2}, 2.148\right]$, $[2.965, 3.834]$, and $\left[\frac{3\pi}{2}, 5.591\right]$

(c) Approximately $(0.542, 1.266)$, $(1.876, 2.600)$, $(3.425, 4.281)$, and $(5.144, 6.000)$

(d) Approximately $(0, 0.542)$, $(1.266, 1.876)$, $(2.600, 3.425)$, $(4.281, 5.144)$, and $(6.000, 2\pi)$

(e) Local maxima at $\approx (0.176, 1.266)$, $\left(\frac{\pi}{2}, 0\right)$ and $(2.965, 1.266)$, $\left(\frac{3\pi}{2}, 2\right)$, and $(2\pi, 1)$;
local minima at $\approx (0, 1)$, $(0.994, -0.513)$, $(2.148, -0.513)$, $(3.834, -1.806)$, and $(5.591, -1.806)$
Note that the local extrema at $x \approx 3.834$, $x = \frac{3\pi}{2}$, and $x \approx 5.591$ are also absolute extrema.

(f) $\approx (0.542, 0.437)$, $(1.266, -0.267)$, $(1.876, -0.267)$, $(2.600, 0.437)$, $(3.425, -0.329)$, $(4.281, 0.120)$, $(5.144, 0.120)$, and $(6.000, -0.329)$

13. **(a)** $\left(0, \frac{2}{\sqrt{3}}\right]$
(b) $(-\infty, 0]$ and $\left[\frac{2}{\sqrt{3}}, \infty\right)$
(c) $(-\infty, 0)$
(d) $(0, \infty)$
(e) Local maximum at

$$\left(\frac{2}{\sqrt{3}}, \frac{16}{3\sqrt{3}}\right) \approx (1.155, 3.079)$$

(f) None

14. **(a)** Approximately $[-0.578, 1.692]$
(b) Approximately $(-\infty, -0.578]$ and $[1.692, \infty)$
(c) Approximately $(-\infty, 1.079)$
(d) Approximately $(1.079, \infty)$
(e) Local maximum at $\approx (1.692, 20.517)$; local minimum at $\approx (-0.578, 0.972)$
(f) $\approx (1.079, 13.601)$

15. **(a)** $\left[0, \frac{8}{9}\right]$ **(b)** $(-\infty, 0]$ and $\left[\frac{8}{9}, \infty\right)$
(c) $\left(-\infty, -\frac{2}{9}\right)$ **(d)** $\left(-\frac{2}{9}, 0\right)$ and $(0, \infty)$
(e) Local maximum at $\approx (0.889, 1.011)$; local minimum at $(0, 0)$
(f) $\approx \left(-\frac{2}{9}, 0.667\right)$

16. **(a)** Approximately $(-\infty, 0.215]$
(b) Approximately $[0.215, 2)$ and $(2, \infty)$
(c) Approximately $(2, 3.710)$
(d) $(-\infty, 2)$ and approximately $(3.710, \infty)$
(e) Local maximum at $\approx (0.215, -2.417)$
(f) $\approx (3.710, -3.420)$

17. **(a)** None **(b)** At $x = -1$ **(c)** At $x = 0$ and $x = 2$

18. **(a)** At $x = -1$ **(b)** At $x = 2$ **(c)** At $x = \frac{1}{2}$

19. $f(x) = -\frac{1}{4}x^{-4} - e^{-x} + C$

20. $f(x) = \sec x + C$

21. $f(x) = 2 \ln x + \frac{1}{3}x^3 + x + C$

22. $f(x) = \frac{2}{3}x^{3/2} + 2x^{1/2} + C$

23. $f(x) = -\cos x + \sin x + 2$

24. $f(x) = \frac{3}{4}x^{4/3} + \frac{x^3}{3} + \frac{x^2}{2} + x - \frac{31}{12}$

25. $s(t) = 4.9t^2 + 5t + 10$

26. $s(t) = 16t^2 + 20t + 5$

27. $L(x) = 2x + \frac{\pi}{2} - 1$

28. $L(x) = \sqrt{2}x - \frac{\pi\sqrt{2}}{4} + \sqrt{2}$

29. $L(x) = -x + 1$

30. $L(x) = 2x + 1$

31. Global minimum value of $\frac{1}{2}$ at $x = 2$

32. **(a)** T **(b)** P

33. **(a)** $(0, 2]$ **(b)** $[-3, 0)$
(c) Local maxima at $(-3, 1)$ and $(2, 3)$

34. The 24th day

35.

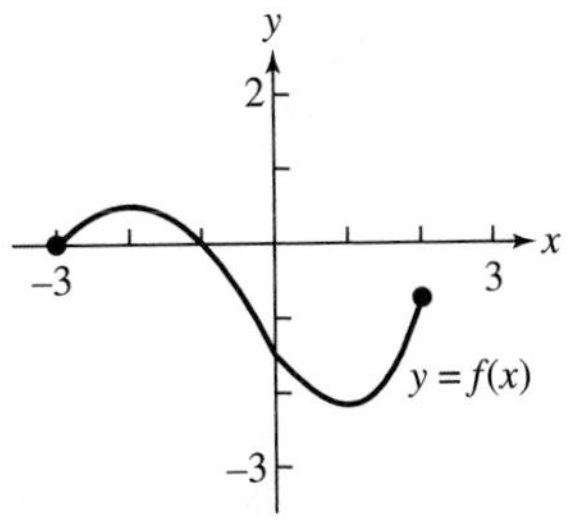

36. **(a)** Absolute minimum is -2 at $x = 1$; absolute maximum is 3 at $x = 3$
(b) None
(c)

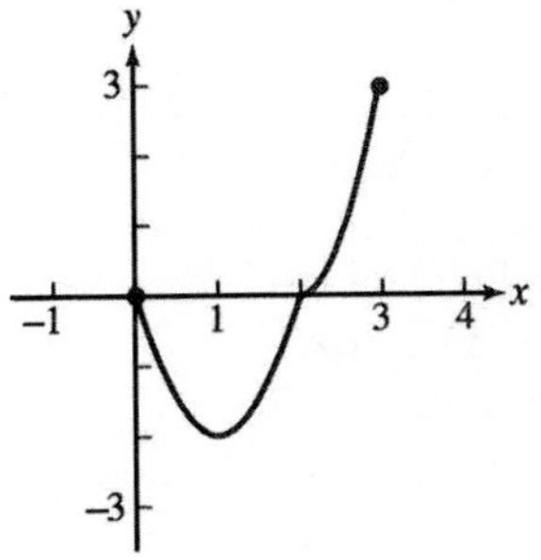

37. **(a)** $f(x)$ is continuous on $[0.5, 3]$ and differentiable on $(0.5, 3)$.
(b) $c \approx 1.579$
(c) $y \approx 1.457x - 1.075$
(d) $y \approx 1.457x - 1.579$

38. **(a)** $v(t) = -3t^2 - 6t + 4$
(b) $a(t) = -6t - 6$
(c) The particle starts at position 3 moving in the positive direction, but decelerating. At approximately $t = 0.528$, it reaches position 4.128 and changes direction, beginning to move in the negative direction. After that, it continues to accelerate while moving in the negative direction.

39. **(a)** $L(x) = -1$
(b) Using the linearization. $f(0, 1) \approx -1$
(c) Greater than the approximation in (b), since $f'(x)$ is actually positive over the interval $(0, 0.1)$ and the estimate is based on the derivative being 0.

40. **(a)** $dy = (2x - x^2)e^{-1}dx$ **(b)** $dy \approx 0.00368$

41. **(a)** With some rounding, $y = \frac{502191.397}{1 + 8.215\,e^{-0.021x}}$
(b) The regression fit looks very good:

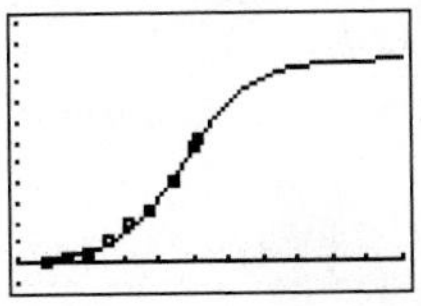

[1750, 2300] by [–50000, 600000]

(c) 393,709,000 million
(d) About 1987; a point of inflection.
(e) The U.S. population levels off and never exceeds about 502,200,000 million.
(f) No

42. $x \approx 0.828361$

43. 1200 m/sec

44. 1162.5 m

45. $r = 25$ ft and $s = 50$ ft

46. 54 square units

47. Base is 6 ft by 6 ft, height = 3 ft

48. Base is 4 ft by 4 ft; height = 2 ft.

49. Height = 2, radius = $\sqrt{2}$

50. $r = h = 4$ ft

51. **(a)** $V(x) = x(15 - 2x)(5 - x)$
(b) $0 < x < 5$

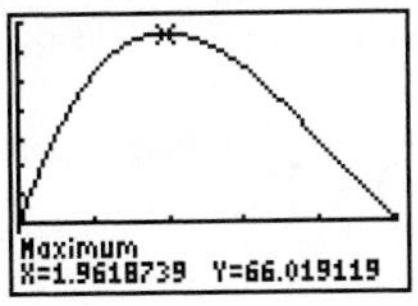

$[0, 5]$ by $[-10, 70]$

(c) Maximum volume ≈ 66.019 in^3 when $x \approx 1.962$ in.
(d) $V'(x) = 6x^2 - 50x + 75$, which is zero at $x = \frac{25 - 5\sqrt{7}}{6} \approx 1.962$.

52. 29.925 square units

53. $x = \frac{48}{\sqrt{7}} \approx 18.142$ mi and $y = \frac{36}{\sqrt{7}} \approx 13.607$ mi

54. $x = 100$ m and $r = \frac{100}{\pi}$ m

55. 276 grade A and 553 grade B tires

56. **(a)** 0.765 unit
(b) When $t = \frac{7\pi}{8} \approx 2.749$ (plus multiples of π if they keep going)

57. Dimensions: base is 6 in. by 12 in., height = 2 in.; maximum volume = 144 in^3

58. -40 m^2/sec

59. 5 m/sec **60.** Increasing 1 cm/min

61. $\frac{dx}{dt} = 4$ units/second **62.** **(a)** $h = \frac{5r}{2}$
(b) $\frac{125}{144\pi} \approx 0.276$ ft/min

63. 5 radians/sec **64.** Not enough speed. Duck!

65. $dV \approx \frac{2\pi ah}{3}\,dr$

66. **(a)** Within 1% **(b)** Within 3%

67. **(a)** Within 4% **(b)** Within 8% **(c)** Within 12%

68. Height = 14 feet, estimated error = $\pm\frac{2}{45}$ feet

69. $\frac{dy}{dx} = 2 \sin x \cos x - 3$.
Since $\sin x$ and $\cos x$ are both between 1 and -1, $2 \sin x \cos x$ is never greater than 2, and therefore $\frac{dy}{dx} \le 2 - 3 = -1$ for all values of x.

70. **(a)** The only x-value for which f has a relative maximum is $x = -2$. That is the only place where the derivative of f goes from positive to negative.
(b) The only x-value for which f has a relative minimum is $x = 0$. That is the only place where the derivative of f goes from negative to positive.
(c) The graph of f is concave up on $(-1, 1)$ and on $(2, 3)$. Those are the intervals on which the derivative of f is increasing.

(d)

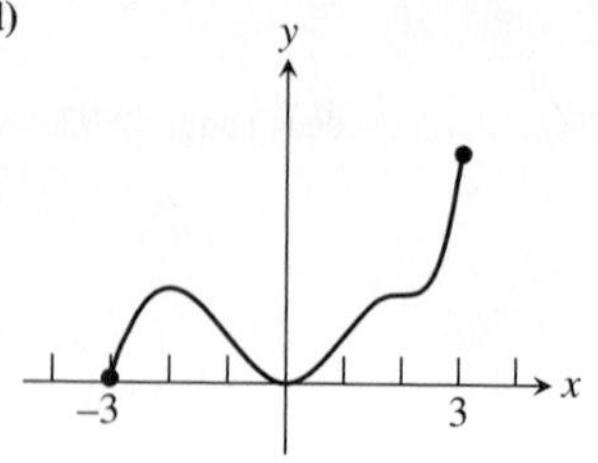

71. The volume V of a cone $(V = \frac{1}{3}\pi r^2 h)$ is increasing at the rate of 4π cubic inches per second. At the instant when the radius of the cone is 2 inches, its volume is 8π cubic inches and the radius is increasing at 1/3 inch per second.

(a) $A = \pi r^2$, so $\frac{dA}{dt} = 2\pi r \frac{dr}{dt} = 2\pi(2)\left(\frac{1}{3}\right) = \frac{4\pi}{3}$ in²/sec.

(b) $V = \frac{1}{3}\pi r^2 h$, so $\frac{dV}{dt} = \frac{1}{3}\left(2\pi r \frac{dr}{dt} h + \pi r^2 \frac{dh}{dt}\right)$. Plugging in the known values, we have $4\pi = \frac{1}{3}\left(2\pi \cdot 2 \cdot \frac{1}{3} \cdot 6 + \pi \cdot 2^2 \cdot \frac{dh}{dt}\right)$.

From this we get $\frac{dh}{dt} = 1$ in/sec.

(c) $\frac{dA}{dh} = \frac{dA/dt}{dh/dt} = \frac{4\pi/3}{1} = \frac{4\pi}{3}$ in²/in.

72. (a) $V = \pi a^2 b$, and $b = \frac{60 - 2a}{4} = 15 - \frac{a}{2}$, so $V = 15\pi a^2 - \frac{\pi a^3}{2}$.

Thus $\frac{dV}{da} = 30\pi a - \frac{3\pi a^2}{2} = \frac{3}{2}\pi a(20 - a)$. The domain of consideration for a in this problem is $(0, 30)$, so $a = 20$ is the only critical number. The cylinder of maximum volume is formed when $a = 20$ and $b = 5$.

(b) The sign graph for the derivative $\frac{dV}{da} = \frac{3}{2}\pi a(20 - a)$ on the interval $(0, 30)$ is as follows:

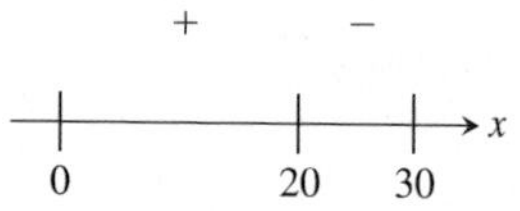

By the First Derivative Test, there is a maximum at $x = 20$.

CHAPTER 6

Section 6.1

Quick Review 6.1

1. 400 miles
3. 100 ft/sec ≈ 68.18 mph
5. 28 miles
7. −3°
9. 17,500 people

Exercises 6.1

1. Compute the area of the rectangle under the curve to find the particle is at $x = 20$.

3. Each rectangle has base 1. The area under the curve is approximately $1\left(\frac{5}{4} + \frac{13}{4} + \frac{29}{4} + \frac{53}{4}\right) = 25$, so the particle is close to $x = 25$.

5. (a)

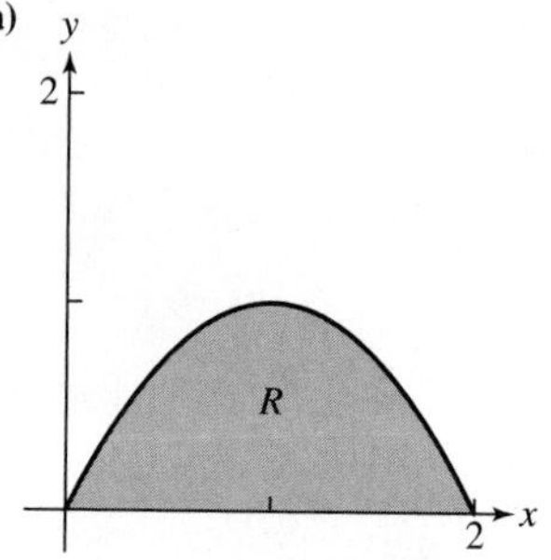

(b)

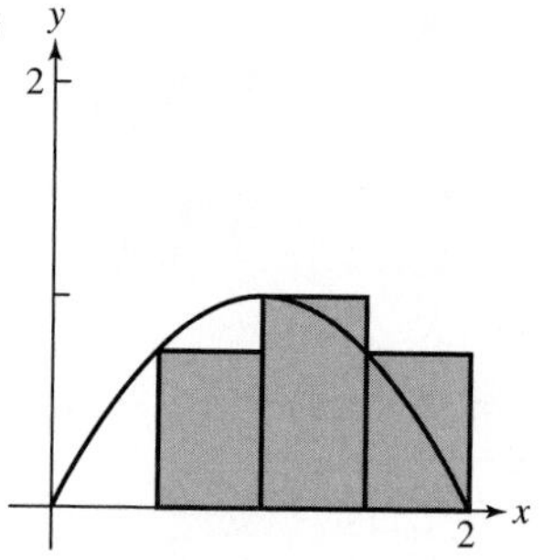

LRAM = 1.25

7.

n	$LRAM_n$	$MRAM_n$	$RRAM_n$
10	1.32	1.34	1.32
50	1.3328	1.3336	1.3328
100	1.3332	1.3334	1.3332
500	1.333328	1.333336	1.333328

9. 13.5 **11.** 0.8821

13.

n	MRAM
10	526.21677
20	524.25327
40	523.76240
80	523.63968
160	523.60900

15. ≈44.8; ≈6.7 L/min
17. (a) 5220 m **(b)** 4920 m
19. (a) 0.969 mi **(b)** 0.006 h = 21.6 sec; 116 mph
21. (a) $S_8 \approx 120.95132$ Underestimate **(b)** 10%
23. (a) 15.465 ft³ **(b)** 16.515 ft³
25. 39.26991
27. (a) 240 ft/sec **(b)** 1520 ft with RRAM and $n = 5$
29. (a) Upper: 60.9 tons; lower: 46.8 tons
(b) By the end of October
31. True. Because the graph rises from left to right, the left-hand rectangles will all lie under the curve.
33. E **35.** C
37. (a) 2 **(b)** $2\sqrt{2} \approx 2.828$ **(c)** $8 \sin\left(\frac{\pi}{8}\right) \approx 3.061$
(d) Each area is less than the area of the circle, π. As n increases, the polygon area approaches π.
39. $RRAM_n f = LRAM_n f + f(x_n)\Delta x - f(x_0)\Delta x$
Since $f(a) = f(b)$, or $f(x_0) = f(x_n)$, we have $RRAM_n f = LRAM_n f$.

Section 6.2

Quick Review 6.2

1. 55 **3.** 5500 **5.** $\sum_{k=0}^{25} 2k$

7. $\sum_{x=1}^{50}(2x^2+3x)$ **9.** $\sum_{k=0}^{n}(-1)^k = 0$ if n is odd.

Exercises 6.2

1. $\int_0^2 x^2\,dx$ **3.** $\int_1^4 \frac{1}{x}\,dx$

5. $\int_0^1 \sqrt{4-x^2}\,dx$

7. 15 **9.** −480 **11.** 2.75 **13.** 21

15. $\frac{9\pi}{2}$ **17.** $\frac{5}{2}$ **19.** 3 **21.** $\frac{3\pi^2}{2}$

23. $\frac{1}{2}b^2$ **25.** $b^2 - a^2$ **27.** $\frac{3}{2}a^2$

29. $\int_8^{11} 87\,dt = 261$ miles **31.** $\int_6^{7.5} 300\,dt = 450$ calories

33. ≈ 0.9905 **35.** $\frac{32}{3}$

37. **(a)** 0 **(b)** 1 **39.** **(a)** −1 **(b)** $-\frac{7}{2}$

41. False. Consider the function in the graph below.

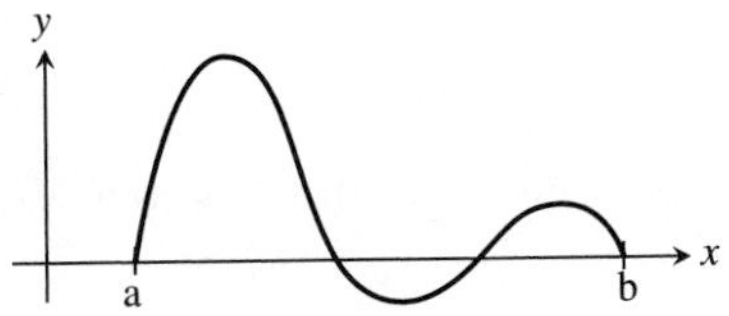

43. E **45.** C **47.** 0

49. $\frac{1}{4}$ **51.** $\frac{3}{4}$

53. $\frac{1}{2}$ **55.** $-\frac{3}{4}$

57. **(a)** $f \to +\infty$

(b) Using right endpoints we have

$$\int_0^1 \frac{1}{x^2}\,dx = \lim_{n\to\infty}\sum_{k=1}^{n}\frac{1}{n}\frac{n^2}{k^2}$$

$$= \lim_{n\to\infty}\sum_{k=1}^{n}\frac{n}{k^2} = \lim_{n\to\infty} n\left[1+\frac{1}{2^2}+\cdots+\frac{1}{n^2}\right].$$

$$n\left(1+\frac{1}{2^2}+\cdots+\frac{1}{n^2}\right) > n \text{ and } n\to\infty$$

$$\text{so } n\left(1+\frac{1}{2^2}+\cdots+\frac{1}{n^2}\right)\to\infty.$$

Section 6.3

Quick Review 6.3

1. $\sin x$ **3.** $\tan x$
5. $\sec x$ **7.** x^n

9. $xe^x + e^x$

Exercises 6.3

1. **(a)** 0 **(b)** −8 **(c)** −12 **(d)** 10 **(e)** −2 **(f)** 16

3. **(a)** 5 **(b)** $5\sqrt{3}$ **(c)** −5 **(d)** −5

5. **(a)** 4 **(b)** −4

7. $0 \le \int_0^1 \sin(x^2)\,dx \le \sin(1) < 1$

9. $0 \le (b-a)\min f(x) \le \int_a^b f(x)\,dx$

11. 0, at $x = 1$

13. −2, at $x = \frac{1}{\sqrt{3}}$

15. $\frac{3}{2}$

17. 0

19. $-\cos(2\pi) + \cos\pi = -2$

21. $e^1 - e^0 = e - 1$

23. $4^2 - 1^2 = 15$

25. $5(6) - 5(-2) = 40$

27. $\tan^{-1}(1) - \tan^{-1}(-1) = \pi/2$

29. $\ln e - \ln 1 = 1$

31. $2/\pi$

33. $4/\pi$

35. 4

37. $\frac{1}{2} \le \int_0^1 \frac{1}{1+x^4}\,dx \le 1$

39. Yes; $av(f) = \frac{1}{b-a}\int_a^b f(x)\,dx$, therefore

$$\int_a^b f(x)\,dx = av(f)(b-a) = \int_a^b av(f)\,dx.$$

41. Avg rate $= \frac{\text{total amount released}}{\text{total time}}$

$$= \frac{2000\text{ m}^3}{100\text{ min} + 50\text{ min}} = 13\tfrac{1}{3}\text{ m}^3/\text{min}$$

43. $\frac{7}{6}$

45. False. For example, $\sin 0 = \sin\pi = 0$, but the average value of $\sin x$ on $[0, \pi]$ is greater than 0.

47. A **49.** B

51. **(a)** $A = \frac{1}{2}(b)(h) = \frac{1}{2}bh$

(b) $\frac{h}{2b}x^2 + C$

(c) $\int_0^b y(x)\,dx = \frac{h}{2b}x^2\Big]_0^b = \frac{hb^2}{2b} = \frac{1}{2}bh$

53. $\int_a^b F'(x)\,dx = \int_a^b G'(x)\,dx \to F(b) - F(a) = G(b) - G(a)$

Quick Quiz (Sections 6.1–6.3)

1. D **3.** C

Section 6.4

Quick Review 6.4

1. $2x\cos x^2$ **3.** 0 **5.** $2^x \ln 2$

7. $\frac{-x\sin x - \cos x}{x^2}$ **9.** $\frac{y+1}{2y-x}$

Exercises 6.4

1. $\sin^2 x$
3. $(x^3 - x)^5$
5. $\tan^3 x$
7. $\dfrac{1 + x}{1 + x^2}$
9. $2xe^{x^4}$
11. $\dfrac{\sqrt{1 + 25x^2}}{x}$
13. $-\ln(1 + x^2)$
15. $-\dfrac{3x^2 \cos x^3}{x^6 + 2}$
17. $\dfrac{dy}{dx} = \sin(x^2) - \dfrac{\sin x}{2\sqrt{x}}$
19. $3x^2 \cos(2x^2) - 2x \cos(2x^2)$
21. $y = \int_5^x \sin^3 t\, dt$
23. $y = \int_2^x \ln(\sin t + 5)\, dt + 3$
25. $y = \int_7^x \cos^2 5t\, dt - 2$
27. $5 - \ln 6 \approx 3.208$
29. 1
31. $\dfrac{5}{2}$
33. 2
35. $2\sqrt{3}$
37. 0
39. $\dfrac{8}{3}$
41. $\dfrac{5}{2}$
43. $\dfrac{1}{2}$
45. $\dfrac{5}{6}$
47. π
49. ≈ 3.802
51. ≈ 8.886
53. $x \approx 0.699$
55. $-3/2$
57. **(a)** 0 **(b)** H is increasing on $[0, 6]$ where $H'(x) = f(x) > 0$.
(c) H is concave up on $(9, 12)$ where $H''(x) = f'(x) > 0$.
(d) $H(12) = \int_0^{12} f(t)\, dt > 0$ because there is more area above the x-axis than below for $y = f(x)$.
(e) $x = 6$ since $H'(6) = f(6) = 0$ and $H''(6) = f'(6) < 0$.
(f) $x = 0$ since $H(x) > 0$ on $(0, 12]$.
59. **(a)** $s'(3) = f = 0$ **(b)** $s''(3) = f'(3) > 0$
(c) $s(3) = \int_0^3 f(x)\, dx = -\frac{1}{2}(3)(6) = -9$ units
(d) $s(t) = 0$ at $t = 6$ sec because $\int_0^6 f(x)\, dx = 0$
(e) $s''(t) = f'(t) = 0$ at $t = 7$ sec
(f) $0 < t < 3$: $s < 0$, $s' < 0 \Rightarrow$ away
$3 < t < 6$: $s < 0$, $s' > 0 \Rightarrow$ toward
$t > 6$: $s > 0$, $s' > 0 \Rightarrow$ away
(g) The positive side
61. $L(x) = 2 + 10x$
63. $\displaystyle\int_0^{\pi/k} \sin kx\, dx = \frac{2}{k}$
65. True. The Fundamental Theorem of Calculus guarantees that F is differentiable on I, so it must be continuous on I.
67. D **69.** E
71. **(a)** $f(t)$ is even, so $\displaystyle\int_0^x f(t)\, dt = \int_{-x}^0 f(t)\, dt$,
so $\displaystyle -\int_0^x f(t)\, dt = \int_{-x}^0 f(t)\, dt = \int_0^{-x} f(t)\, dt.$
(b) 0 **(c)** $k\pi$, $k = \pm 1, \pm 2, \ldots$
(d)

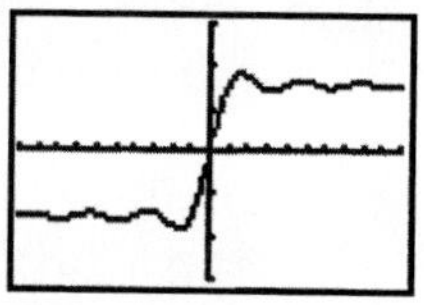

$[-20, 20]$ by $[-3, 3]$

73. \$4500
75. **(a)** True, $h'(x) = f(x) \Rightarrow h''(x) = f'(x)$
(b) True, h and h' are both differentiable.
(c) $h'(1) = f(1) = 0$
(d) True, $h''(1) = f'(1) < 0$ and $h'(1) = 0$
(e) False, $h''(1) = f'(1) < 0$
(f) False, $h''(1) = f'(1) \neq 0$
(g) True, $\dfrac{dh}{dx} = f(x) = 0$ at $x = 1$ and $h'(x) = f(x)$ is a decreasing function.
77. Using area, $\displaystyle\int_0^x f(t)\, dt = \int_{-x}^0 f(t)\, dt = -\int_0^{-x} f(t)\, dt$
79. $x \approx 1.0648397$. $\displaystyle\lim_{t\to\infty} \frac{\sin t}{t} = 0$. Not enough area between x-axis and $\dfrac{\sin x}{x}$ for $x > 1.0648397$ to get $\displaystyle\int_0^x \frac{\sin t}{t}\, dt$ back to 1.
or: $\mathrm{Si}(x)$ doesn't decrease enough (for $x > 1.0648397$) to get back to 1.

Section 6.5

Quick Review 6.5

1. Concave down **3.** Concave down
5. Concave up **7.** Concave up **9.** Concave down

Exercises 6.5

1. **(a)** 2 **(b)** Exact **(c)** 2
3. **(a)** 4.25 **(b)** Over **(c)** 4
5. **(a)** 5.146 **(b)** Under **(c)** $\dfrac{16}{6}$
7. $\frac{1}{2}(12 + 2(10) + 2(9) + 2(11) + 2(13) + 2(16) + 18) = 74$
9. 15,990 ft^3
11. $\displaystyle\frac{1}{60 \times 60}\left[\frac{2}{2}(0 + 30) + \frac{1.2}{2}(30 + 40) + \cdots + \frac{4.6}{2}(120 + 130)\right] \approx$ 0.633 mi $\approx$ 3340 ft.
13. **(a)** $\left(\frac{1/2}{3}\right)\left(0 + 4\left(\frac{1}{2}\right) + 2(1) + 4\left(\frac{3}{2}\right) + 2\right) = 2$
(b) 2
15. **(a)** $\left(\frac{1/2}{3}\right)\left(0^3 + 4\left(\frac{1}{2}\right)^3 + 2(1)^3 + 4\left(\frac{3}{2}\right)^3 + 2^3\right) = 4$
(b) 4
17. **(a)** $\left(\frac{1}{3}\right)\left(\sqrt{0} + 4(\sqrt{1}) + 2(\sqrt{2}) + 4(\sqrt{3}) + (\sqrt{4})\right) \approx 5.2522$
(b) 16/3

19. **(a)** 12 **(b)** 12, $|E_S| = 0$

(c) $f^{(4)}(x) = 0$ for $f(x) = x^3 - 2x$, so $M_{f^{(4)}} = 0$.

(d) Simpson's Rule will always give the exact value for cubic polynomials.

21. **(b)** We are approximating the area under the temperature graph. Doubling the endpoints increases the error in the first and last trapezoids.

23. The exact value is π. $S_{50} \approx 3.1379$, $S_{100} \approx 3.14029$

25. $S_{50} \approx 1.3706$, $S_{100} = 1.3706$ using $a = 0.0001$ as lower limit
$S_{50} = 1.37076$, $S_{100} = 1.37076$ using $a = 0.000000001$ as lower limit

27. **(a)** $T_{10} = 1.983523538$. $T_{100} = 1.999835504$
$T_{1000} = 1.999998355$

(b)

n	$\lvert E_T \rvert$
10	$0.016476462 = 1.6476462 \times 10^{-2}$
100	1.64496×10^{-4}
1000	1.645×10^{-6}

(c) $|E_{T_{10n}}| \approx 10^{-2} \times |E_{T_n}|$

(d) $|E_{T_n}| \le \frac{\pi^3 M}{12n^2} \cdot |E_{T_{10n}}| \le \frac{\pi^3 M}{12(10n)^2}$

$= \frac{\pi^3 M}{12n^2} \times 10^{-2}$

29. 466.67 in^2

31. False. The Trapezoidal Rule will overestimate the integral if the curve is concave up.

33. A

35. C

37. **(a)** $f''(x) = 2\cos(x^2) - 4x^2 \sin(x^2)$

(b)

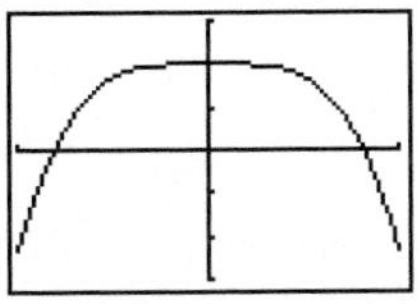

$[-1, 1]$ by $[-3, 3]$

(c) The graph shows that $-3 \le f''(x) \le 2$ for $-1 \le x \le 1$.

(d) $|E_T| \le \frac{1-(-1)}{12}(h^2)(3) = \frac{h^2}{2}$

(e) $|E_T| \le \frac{h^2}{2} \le \frac{0.1^2}{2} < 0.1$

(f) $n \ge 20$

39. Each quantity is equal to

$\frac{h}{2}(y_0 + 2y_1 + 2y_2 + \cdots + 2y_{n-1} + y_n)$.

Quick Quiz (Sections 6.4 and 6.5)

1. C **3.** C

Review Exercises

1.

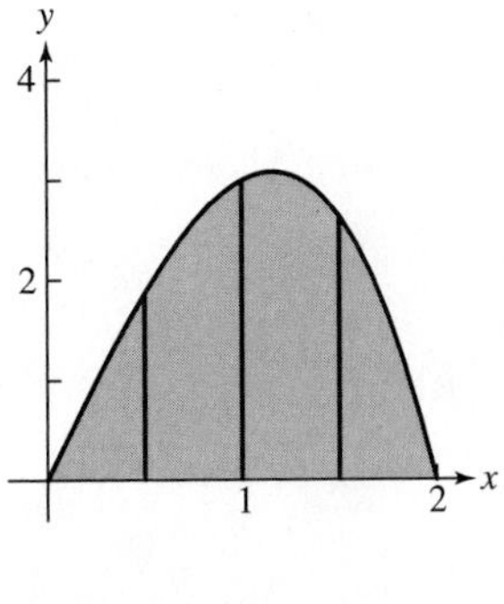

2. 3.75

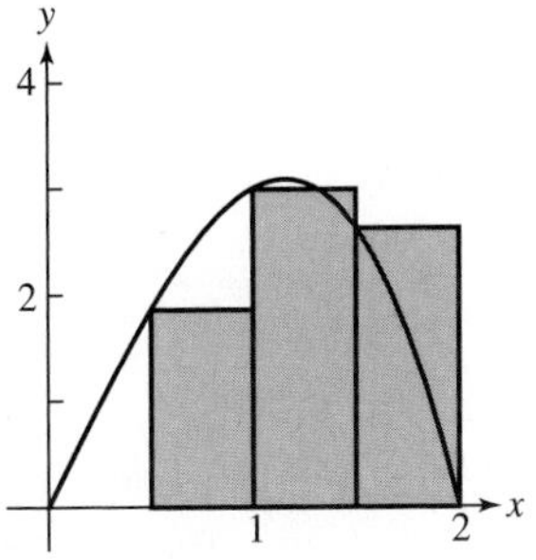

3. 4.125

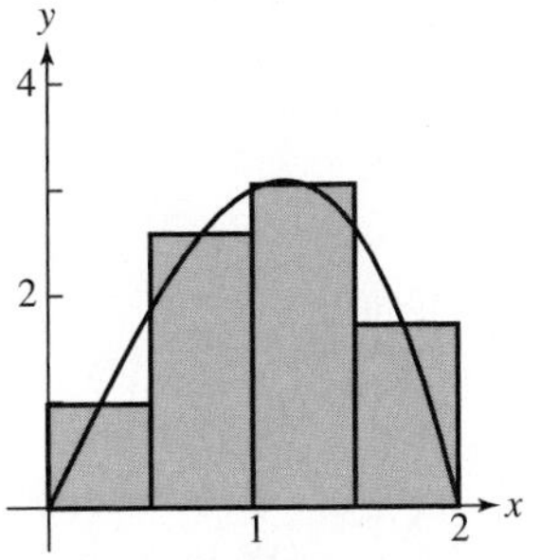

4. 3.75

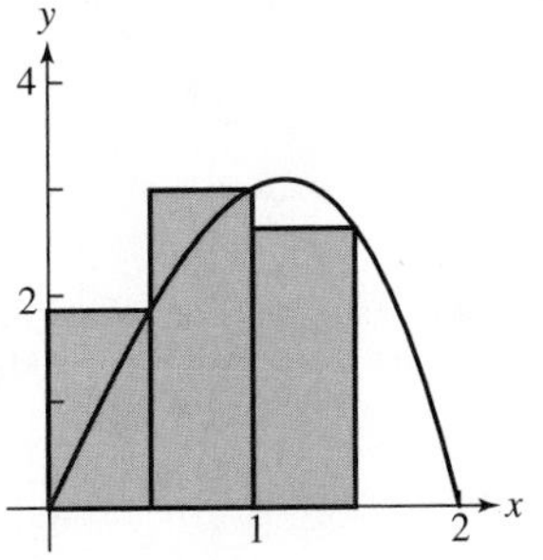

5. 3.75

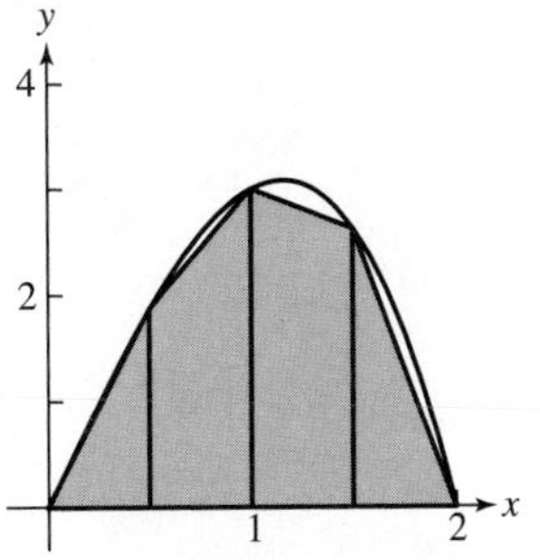

6. 4

7.

n	LRAM_n	MRAM_n	RRAM_n
10	1.78204	1.60321	1.46204
20	1.69262	1.60785	1.53262
30	1.66419	1.60873	1.55752
50	1.64195	1.60918	1.57795
100	1.62557	1.60937	1.59357
1000	1.61104	1.60944	1.60784

8. ln 5 **9.** **(a)** True **(b)** True **(c)** False

10. **(a)** $V = \lim_{n\to\infty} \sum_{i=1}^{n} \pi \sin^2(m_i)\Delta x$ **(b)** 4.9348

11. **(a)** 26.5 m

(b)

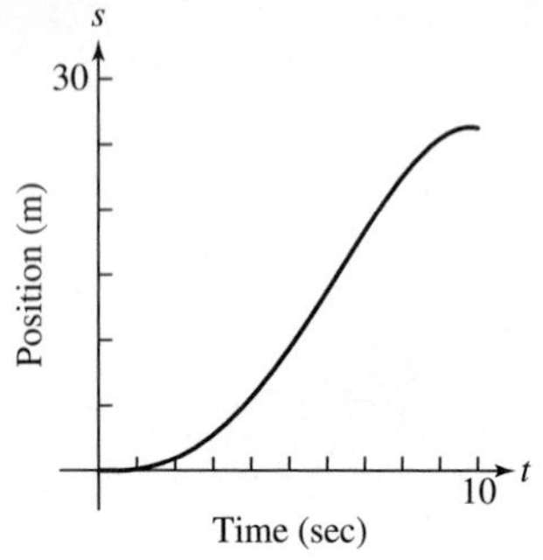

12. **(a)** $\int_0^{10} x^3\,dx$ **(b)** $\int_0^{10} x \sin x\,dx$

(c) $\int_0^{10} x(3x-2)^2\,dx$ **(d)** $\int_0^{10} (1+x^2)^{-1}\,dx$

(e) $\int_0^{10} \pi\left(9 - \sin^2\frac{\pi x}{10}\right)dx$

13. 10 **14.** 2 **15.** 20 **16.** 42 **17.** $\frac{\sqrt{2}}{2}$ **18.** 16

19. 3 **20.** 2 **21.** 2 **22.** 1 **23.** $\sqrt{3}$ **24.** 1 **25.** 8

26. 2 **27.** −1 **28.** 0 **29.** 2 ln 3 **30.** π **31.** 40 **32.** 64π

33. **(a)** Upper = 4.392 L; lower = 4.008 L.

(b) 4.2 L

34. **(a)** Lower = 87.15 ft; upper = 103.05 ft

(b) 95.1 ft

35. One possible answer:

The dx is important because it corresponds to actual physical quantity Δx in a Riemann sum. Without the Δx, our integral approximations would be way off.

36. $\frac{16}{3}$ **37.** $1 \le \sqrt{1+\sin^2 x} \le \sqrt{2}$

38. **(a)** $\frac{4}{3}$ **(b)** $\frac{2}{3}a^{3/2}$ **39.** $\sqrt{2+\cos^3 x}$

40. $14x\sqrt{2+\cos^3(7x^2)}$ **41.** $\frac{-6}{3+x^4}$

42. $\frac{2}{4x^2+1} - \frac{1}{x^2+1}$ **43.** \$230

44. $av(I)$ = 4800 cases; average holding cost = \$192 per day

45. $x \approx 1.63052$ or $x \approx -3.09131$

46. **(a)** True **(b)** True **(c)** True **(d)** False **(e)** True **(f)** False **(g)** True

47. $F(1) - F(0)$

48. $y = \int_5^x \frac{\sin t}{t}\,dt + 3$ **49.** Use the fact that $y' = 2x + \frac{1}{x}$.

50. (b); $\frac{dy}{dx} = 2x \to y = x^2 + c;\ y(1) = 4 \to c = 3$

51. **(a)** ≈2.42 gal **(b)** ≈24.83 mpg

52. **(a)** 6144 ft **(b)** 4296 ft **(c)** B

53. **(a)** $h(y_1 + y_3) + 2(2hy_2) = h(y_1 + 4y_2 + y_3)$

(b) $\frac{1}{3}[h(y_0 + 4y_1 + y_2) + h(y_2 + 4y_3 + y_4) + \cdots + h(y_{2n-2} + 4y_{2n-1} + y_{2n}).]$

54. **(a)** 0 **(b)** −1 **(c)** $-\pi$ **(d)** $x = 1$ **(e)** $y = 2x + 2 - \pi$

(f) $x = -1, x = 2$ **(g)** $[-2\pi, 0]$

55. **(a)** NINT $(e^{-x^2/2}, x, -10, 10) \approx 2.506628275$

(b) The area is $\sqrt{2\pi}$. NINT $(e^{-x^2/2}, x, -20, 20) \approx 2.506628275$

56. ≈1500 yd^3

57. **(a)** $(V^2)_{av} = \frac{(V_{max})^2}{2}$, $V_{rms} = \frac{V_{max}}{\sqrt{2}}$

(b) ≈339 volts

58. **(a)** $\int_0^{24} R(t)\,dt \approx \frac{4}{2}(9.6 + 2(10.3) + 2(10.9) + 2(11.1) + 2(10.9) + 2(10.5) + 9.6) = 253.2$

This is the total number of gallons of water that flowed through the pipe during the 24-hour period.

(b) Yes. Because $R(0) = R(24)$, the Mean Value Theorem guarantees that there is a number c between 0 and 24 such that $R'(c) = 0$.

(c) Average rate $= \frac{1}{24-0}\int_0^{24} Q(t)dt = 10.58$ gallons per hour

59. Since $f'(x) = ax^2 + bx$, $f'(1) = a + b$. Also $f''(x) = 2ax + b$, so $f''(1) = 2a + b$. Applying property (ii), we have $a + b = -6$ and $2a + b = 6$. Solve these two equations simultaneously to get $a = 12$ and $b = -18$. Then

$f'(x) = 12x^2 - 18x$

$f(x) = 4x^3 - 9x^2 + C$ for some constant C

$\int_1^2 (4x^3 - 9x^2 + C)\,dx = x^4 - 3x^3 + Cx\Big|_1^2 = 16 - 24 + 2C - (1 - 3 + C) = -6 + C$

So $-6 + C = 14$, and $C = 20$. Putting it all together, $f(x) = 4x^3 - 9x^2 + 20$.

60. **(a)** Find these integrals using signed areas.

$g(4) = \int_1^4 f(t)\,dt = 1\left(\frac{3+1}{2}\right) + \frac{1}{2} + \left(-\frac{1}{2}\right) = 2$

$g(-2) = -\frac{1}{2}(3)(3) = -\frac{9}{2}$

(b) By the Fundamental Theorem of Calculus, $g'(2) = f(2) = 1$

(c) Since $g'(x) = f(x)$ is positive on $(-2, 3)$ and negative on $(3, 4)$, the minimum value of g occurs at one of the two endpoints. Comparing the two values in part (a), we see that the minimum value is $g(-2) = -\frac{9}{2}$.

(d) There is a point of inflection at $x = 1$ because $f = g'$ changes direction (from increasing to decreasing). There is no such change of direction at $x = 2$, so no point of inflection there.

CHAPTER 7

Section 7.1

Quick Review 7.1

1. Yes **3.** No **5.** No
7. Yes **9.** -5 **11.** 3

Exercises 7.1

1. $y = x^5 - \tan x + C$
3. $y = -\cos x + e^{-x} + 2x^4 + C$
5. $y = 5^x + \tan^{-1} x + C$
7. $y = \sin(t^3) + C$
9. $u = \tan(x^5) + C$
11. $y = -3\cos x + 5$
13. $u = x^7 - x^3 + 5x - 4$
15. $y = x^{-1} + x^{-3} + 12x - 11\ (x > 0)$
17. $y = \tan^{-1}t + 2^t + 2$
19. $v = 4\sec t + e^t + 3t^2(-\pi/2 < t < \pi/2)$ (Note that $C = 0$.)
21. $y = \int_1^x \sin(t^2)\,dt + 5$
23. $F(x) = \int_2^x e^{\cos t}\,dt + 9$
25. Graph (b) **27.** Graph (a)

29.

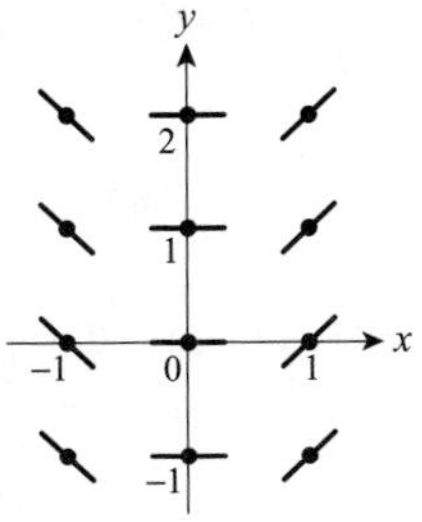

31.

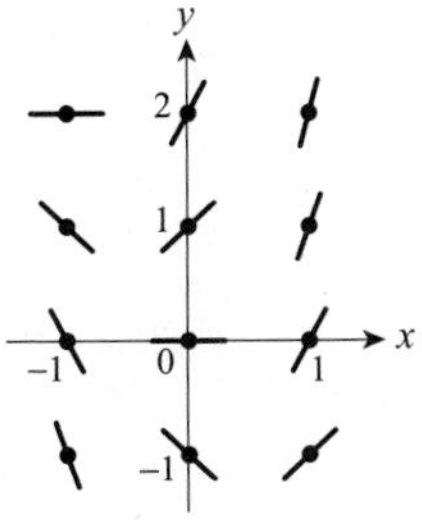

33.

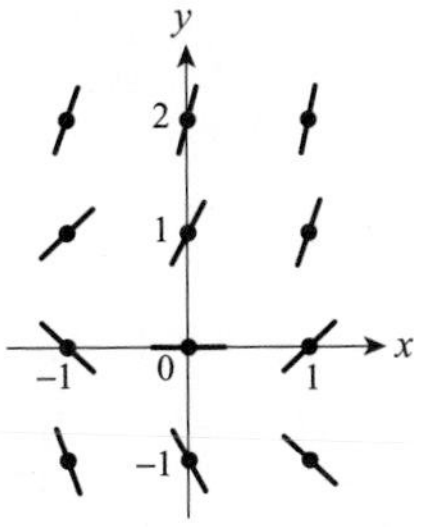

35. Graph (c)

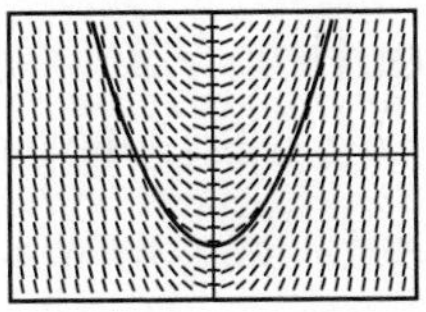

37. Graph (a)

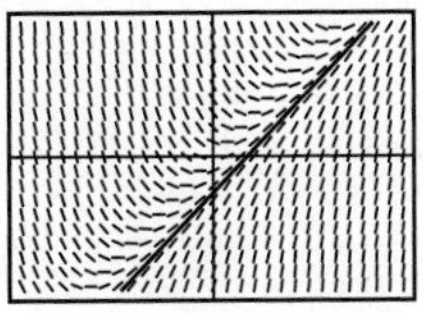

39. Graph (b)

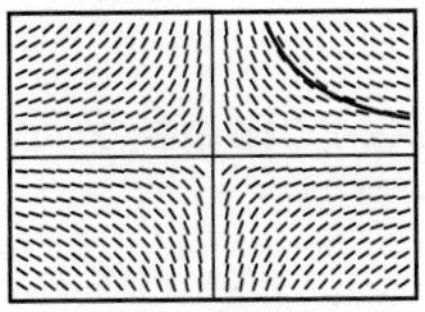

41. (d)

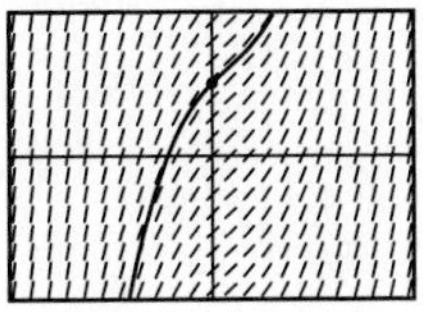

43. (c)

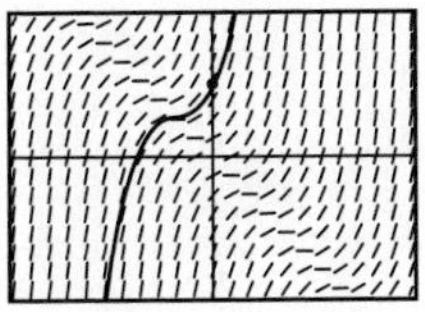

45. (b)

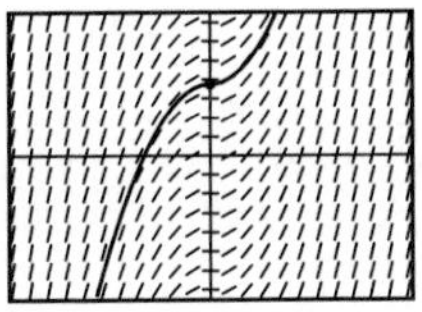

47. (a)

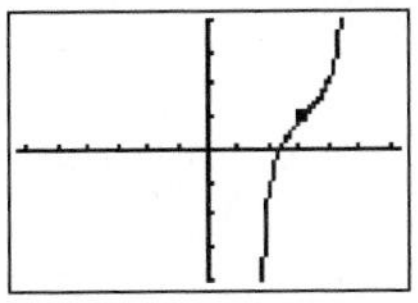

$[-2\pi, 2\pi]$ by $[-4, 4]$

(b) The solution to the initial value problem includes only the continuous portion of the function $y = \tan x + 1$ that passes through the point $(\pi, 1)$.

49. The correct graph is (c) since $\frac{dy}{dx} = 2y + x = 0$ at the point $(-2, 1)$. The line through $(2, 1)$ will have slope 4.

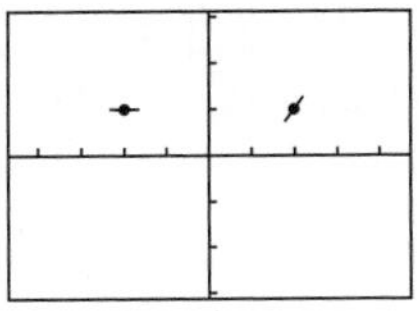

51. 2.03 **53.** 2.3
55. 0.97 **57.** 2.031
59. (a) Graph (b)
(b) The slope is always positive, so graphs (a) and (c) can be ruled out.
61. For one thing, there are positive slopes in the second quadrant of the slope field. The graph of $y = x^2$ has negative slopes in the second quadrant.
63. Euler's Method gives an estimate $f(1.4) \approx 4.32$. The solution to the initial value problem is $f(x) = x^2 + x + 1$, from which we get $f(1.4) = 4.36$. The percentage error is thus $(4.36 - 4.32)/4.36 = 0.9\%$.
65. At every point (x, y), $(e^{(x-y)/2})(-e^{(y-x)/2}) = -e^{(x-y)/2+(y-x)/2} = -e^0 = -1$, so the slopes are negative reciprocals. The slope lines are therefore perpendicular.
67. The perpendicular slope field would be produced by $dy/dx = -\sin x$, so $y = \cos x + C$ for any constant C.
69. True. They are all lines of the form $y = 5x + C$.
71. C **73.** B
75. **(a)** $y = \frac{x^2}{2} + \frac{1}{x} + \frac{1}{2}, x > 0$
(b) $y = \frac{x^2}{2} + \frac{1}{x} + \frac{3}{2}, x < 0$
(c) $y' = \begin{cases} x - 1/x^2, & x < 0 \\ x - 1/x^2 & x > 0 \end{cases}$
(d) $C_1 = \frac{3}{2}, C_2 = \frac{1}{2}$
(e) $C_1 = \frac{1}{2}, C_2 = -\frac{7}{2}$
77. **(a)** $y = 2x^3 + 2x^2 + C_1x + C_2$
(b) $y = e^x - \sin x + C_1x + C_2$
(c) $y = \frac{x^5}{20} + \frac{x^{-1}}{2} + C_1x + C_2$
79. **(a)** $y = \frac{x^2}{2} + C$ **(b)** $y = -\frac{x^2}{2} + C$
(c) $y = Ce^x$ **(d)** $y = Ce^{-x}$
(e) $y = Ce^{x^2/2}$

Section 7.2

Quick Review 7.2

1. $32/5$ **3.** 3^x **5.** $4(x^3 - 2x^2 + 3)^3(3x^2 - 4x)$

7. $-\tan x$ **9.** $\sec x$

Exercises 7.2

1. $\sin x - x^3 + C$

3. $t^3/3 + t^{-1} + C$

5. $(3/5)x^5 + x^{-2} + \tan x + C$

7. $(-\cot u + C)' = -(-\csc^2 u) = \csc^2 u$

9. $\left(\frac{1}{2}e^{2x} + C\right)' = \frac{1}{2}e^{2x}\cdot 2 = e^{2x}$

11. $(\tan^{-1}u + C)' = \dfrac{1}{1 + u^2}$

13. $\int f(u)\,du = \int \sqrt{u}\,du = (2/3)u^{3/2} + C = (2/3)x^3 + C$

$\int f(u)\,dx = \int \sqrt{u}\,dx = \int \sqrt{x^2}\,dx = \int x\,dx = (1/2)x^2 + C$

15. $\int f(u)\,du = \int e^u\,du = e^u + C = e^{7x} + C$

$\int f(u)\,dx = \int e^u\,du = \int e^{7x}\,dx = (1/7)e^{7x} + C$

17. $-\frac{1}{3}\cos 3x + C$ **19.** $\frac{1}{2}\sec 2x + C$

21. $(1/3)\tan^{-1}(x/3) + C$ **23.** $\frac{2}{3}\left(1 - \cos\frac{t}{2}\right)^3 + C$

25. $\dfrac{1}{1 - x} + C$ **27.** $\frac{2}{3}(\tan x)^{3/2} + C$

29. $-(1/4)\ln|\cos(4x + 2)| + C$ or $(1/4)\ln|\sec(4x + 2)| + C$

31. $\frac{1}{3}\sin(3z + 4) + C$ **33.** $\frac{1}{7}(\ln x)^7 + C$

35. $\frac{3}{4}\sin(s^{4/3} - 8) + C$ **37.** $(1/2)\sec(2t + 1) + C$

39. $\ln(\ln x) + C$ **41.** $(1/2)\ln(x^2 + 1) + C$

43. $\frac{1}{3}\ln|\sec(3x)| + C = -\frac{1}{3}\ln|\cos(3x)| + C$

45. $\ln|\sec x + \tan x| + C$

47. $\dfrac{\cos^3 2x}{6} - \dfrac{\cos 2x}{2} + C$

49. $x - \dfrac{\sin 2x}{2} + C$

51. $\frac{1}{3}\tan^3 x - \tan x + x + C$

53. $14/3$ **55.** $-1/2$

57. $10/3$ **59.** $2\sqrt{3}$ **61.** 1.504

63. -0.693 **65.** 0.805

67. (a) $\frac{1}{2}\sqrt{10} - \frac{3}{2} \approx 0.081$

(b) $\frac{1}{2}\sqrt{10} - \frac{3}{2} \approx 0.081$

69. Note that $dy/dx = \tan x$ and $y(3) = 5$.

71. False. The interval of integration should change from $[0, \pi/4]$ to $[0, 1]$, resulting in a different numerical answer.

73. D **75.** B

77. (a) $\frac{d}{dx}\left(\frac{2}{3}(x + 1)^{3/2} + C\right) = \sqrt{x + 1}$

(b) Because $dy_1/dx = \sqrt{x + 1}$ and $dy_2/dx = \sqrt{x + 1}$ **(c)** $4\frac{2}{3}$

(d) $C = y_1 - y_2 = \int_0^x \sqrt{x + 1}\,dx - \int_3^x \sqrt{x + 1}\,dx$

$= \int_0^x \sqrt{x + 1}\,dx + \int_x^3 \sqrt{x + 1}\,dx = \int_0^3 \sqrt{x + 1}\,dx$

79. (a) $\int 2\sin x\cos x\,dx = \int 2u\,du = u^2 + C = \sin^2 x + C$

(b) $\int 2\sin x\cos x\,dx = -\int 2u\,du = -u^2 + C = -\cos^2 x + C$

(c) Since $\sin^2 x - (-\cos^2 x) = 1$, the two answers differ by a constant (accounted for in the constant of integration).

81. (a) $\int \dfrac{dx}{\sqrt{1 - x^2}} = \int \dfrac{\cos u\,du}{\sqrt{1 - \sin^2 u}} = \int \dfrac{\cos u\,du}{\sqrt{\cos^2 u}} = \int 1\,du.$

(Note $\cos u > 0$, so $\sqrt{\cos^2 u} = |\cos u| = \cos u$.)

(b) $\int \dfrac{dx}{\sqrt{1 - x^2}} = \int 1\,du = u + C = \sin^{-1}x + C$

83. (a) $\int_0^{1/2} \dfrac{\sqrt{x}\,dx}{\sqrt{1 - x}} = \int_{\sin^{-1}\sqrt{0}}^{\sin^{-1}\sqrt{1/2}} \dfrac{\sin y\cdot 2\sin y\cos y\,dy}{\sqrt{1 - \sin^2 y}}$

$= \int_0^{\pi/4} \dfrac{2\sin^2 y\cos y\,dy}{\cos y} = \int_0^{\pi/4} 2\sin^2 y\,dy$

(b) $\int_0^{1/2} \dfrac{\sqrt{x}\,dx}{\sqrt{1 - x}} = \int_0^{\pi/4} 2\sin^2 y\,dy$

$= \int_0^{\pi/4} (1 - \cos 2y)\,dy = [y - (1/2)\sin 2y]\Big|_0^{\pi/4}$

$= (\pi - 2)/4$

Section 7.3

Quick Review 7.3

1. $2x^3\cos 2x + 3x^2\sin 2x$

3. $\dfrac{2}{1 + 4x^2}$ **5.** $x = \frac{1}{3}\tan y$

7. $\dfrac{2}{\pi}$ **9.** $y = \frac{1}{2}x^2 - \cos x + 3$

Exercises 7.3

1. $-x\cos x + \sin x + C$

3. $\frac{3}{2}te^{2t} - \frac{3}{4}e^{2t} + C$

5. $x^2\sin x + 2x\cos x - 2\sin x + C$

7. $\frac{3}{2}x^2e^{2x} - \frac{3}{2}xe^{2x} + \frac{3}{4}e^{2x} + C$

9. $\frac{y^2}{2}\ln y - \frac{y^2}{4} + C$

11. $-(x + 2)\cos x + \sin x + 4$

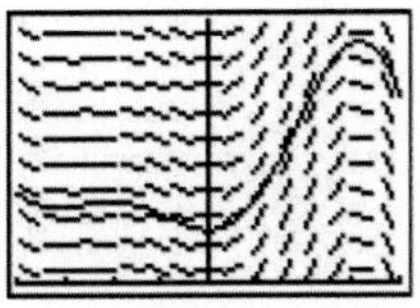

[–4, 4] by [0, 10]

13. $u = x \tan x + \ln|\cos x| + 1$

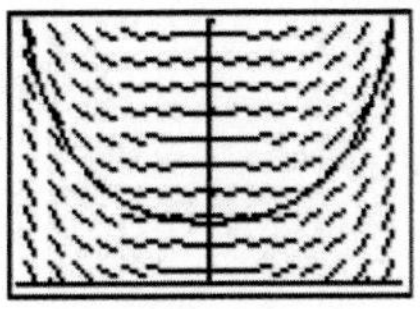

[–1.2, 1.2] by [0, 3]

15. $y = \frac{2x}{3}(x - 1)^{3/2} - \frac{4}{15}(x - 1)^{5/2} + 2$

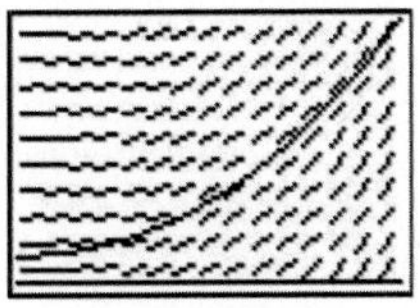

[1, 5] by [0, 20]

17. $\frac{e^x}{2}(\sin x - \cos x) + C$

19. $\frac{e^x}{5}(2 \sin 2x + \cos 2x) + C$

21. $(-x^4 - 4x^3 - 12x^2 - 24x - 24)e^{-x} + C$

23. $\left(-\frac{x^3}{2} - \frac{3x^2}{4} - \frac{3x}{4} - \frac{3}{8}\right)e^{-2x} + C$

25. $\frac{\pi^2}{8} - \frac{1}{2} \approx 0.734$

27. $\frac{1}{13}[e^6(2\cos 9 + 3\sin 9) - e^{-4}(2\cos 6 - 3\sin 6)] \approx -18.186$

29. $y = \left(\frac{x^2}{4} - \frac{x}{8} + \frac{1}{32}\right)e^{4x} + C$

31. $y = \frac{\theta^2}{2}\sec^{-1}\theta - \frac{1}{2}\sqrt{\theta^2 - 1} + C$

33. **(a)** π **(b)** 3π **(c)** 4π

35. $\frac{1 - e^{-2\pi}}{2\pi} \approx 0.159$

37. True. Use parts, letting $u = x^2$, $dv = g(x)dx$, and $v = f(x)$.

39. B **41.** C

43. $-2(\sqrt{x}\cos\sqrt{x} - \sin\sqrt{x}) + C$

45. $\frac{(x^6 - 3x^4 + 6x^2 - 6)e^{x^2}}{2} + C$

47. $u = x^n$, $dv = \cos x\, dx$

49. $u = x^n$, $dv = e^{ax}\, dx$

51. **(a)** Let $y = f^{-1}(x)$. Then $x = f(y)$, so $dx = f'(y)\, dy$. Substitute directly.
(b) $u = y$, $dv = f'(y)\, dy$

53. **(a)** $\int \sin^{-1} x\, dx = x \sin^{-1} x \cos(\sin^{-1} x) + C$
(b) $\int \sin^{-1} x\, dx = x \sin^{-1} x + \sqrt{1 - x^2} + C$
(c) $\cos(\sin^{-1} x) = \sqrt{1 - x^2}$

55. **(a)** $\int \cos^{-1} x\, dx = x \cos^{-1} x - \sin(\cos^{-1} x) + C$
(b) $\int \cos^{-1} x\, dx = x \cos^{-1} x - \sqrt{1 - x^2} + C$
(c) $\sin(\cos^{-1} x) = \sqrt{1 - x^2}$

57. $\int \sec^3 x\, dx = \frac{1}{2}(\sec x \tan x + \ln|\sec x + \tan x|) + C$

Quick Quiz (Sections 7.1–7.3)

1. E **3.** A

Section 7.4

Quick Review 7.4

1. $a = e^b$ **3.** $x = e^2 - 3$

5. $x = \frac{\ln 2.5}{\ln 0.85} \approx -5.638$

7. $t = \frac{\ln 10}{\ln 1.1} \approx 24.159$

9. $y = -1 + e^{2x-3}$

Exercises 7.4

1. $y = \sqrt{x^2 + 3}$, valid for all real numbers

3. $y = x$, valid on the interval $(0, \infty)$

5. $y = 6e^{x^2/2+2x} - 5$, valid for all real numbers

7. $y = -\ln(2 - e^{\sin x})$, valid for all real numbers

9. $y = (x^2 + 3)^{-1}$, valid for all real numbers

11. $y(t) = 100e^{1.5t}$

13. $y(t) = 50(2^{t/5}) = 50e^{(0.2 \ln 2)t}$

15. 8.06 yr doubling time; \$13,197.14 in 30 yr

17. \$600 initially; 13.2 yr doubling time

19. **(a)** 14.94 yr **(b)** 14.62 yr **(c)** 14.68 yr **(d)** 14.59 yr

21. 90 years

23. **(a)** 2.8×10^{14} bacteria
(b) The bacteria reproduce fast enough that even if many are destroyed, there are enough left to make the person sick.

25. 0.585 day

27. $y \approx 2e^{0.4581t}$

29. $y = y_0e^{-kt} = y_0e^{-k(3/k)} = y_0e^{-3} < 0.05y_0$

31. **(a)** 17.53 minutes longer **(b)** 13.26 minutes

33. **(a)** $T - T_s = 79.47(0.932^t)$
(b) $T = 10 + 79.47(0.932^t)$

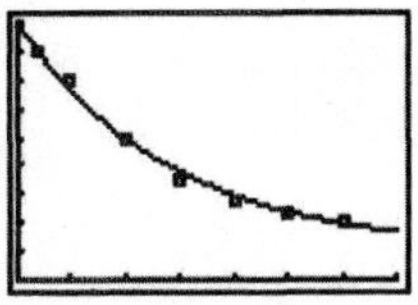

[0, 35] by [0, 90]

(c) 52.5 seconds **(d)** 89.47°C

35. 6658 years

37. 3.15 years

39. 585.4 kg

41. **(a)** $p = 1013e^{-0.121h}$ **(b)** 2.383 millibars **(c)** 0.977 km

43. **(a)** $V = V_0e^{-t/40}$ **(b)** 92.1 seconds

45. **(a)** $\frac{\ln 90}{100} \approx 0.045$ or 4.5% **(b)** $\frac{\ln 131}{100} \approx 0.049$ or 4.9%

47. False. The correct solution is $|y| = e^{kx+C}$, which can be written (with a new C) as $y = Ce^{kx}$.

49. D **51.** D

53. **(a)** Since acceleration is $\frac{dv}{dt}$, we have Force $= m\frac{dv}{dt} = -kv$.

(b) From $m\frac{dv}{dt} = -kv$, we get $\frac{dv}{dt} = -\frac{k}{m}v$, which is the differential equation for exponential growth modeled by $v = Ce^{-(k/m)t}$. Since $v = v_0$ at $t = 0$, it follows that $C = v_0$.

(c) In each case, we would solve $2 = e^{-(k/m)t}$. If k is constant, an increase in m would require an increase in t. The object of larger mass takes longer to slow down. Alternatively, one can consider the equation $\frac{dv}{dt} = -\frac{k}{m}v$ to see that v changes more slowly for larger values of m.

55. $s(t) = 1.32(1 - e^{-0.606t})$

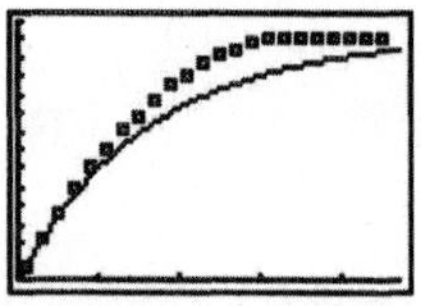

[0, 4.7] by [0, 1.4]

57. **(a)**

x	$\left(1 + \frac{1}{x}\right)^x$
10	2.5937
100	2.7048
1000	2.7169
10,000	2.7181
100,000	2.7183

$e \approx 2.7183$

(b) $r = 2$

x	$\left(1 + \frac{2}{x}\right)^x$
10	6.1917
100	7.2446
1000	7.3743
10,000	7.3876
100,000	7.3889

$e^2 \approx 7.389$

$r = 0.5$

x	$\left(1 + \frac{0.5}{x}\right)^x$
10	1.6289
100	1.6467
1000	1.6485
10,000	1.6487
100,000	1.6487

$e^{0.5} \approx 1.6487$

(c) As we compound more times the increment of time between compounding approaches 0. Continuous compounding is based on an instantaneous rate of change which is a limit of average rates as the increment in time approaches 0.

Section 7.5

Quick Review 7.5

1. $x + 1 + \frac{1}{x - 1}$

3. $1 + \frac{3}{x^2 + x - 2}$

5. $(-\infty, \infty)$ **7.** 0

9. $y = 0, y = 60$

Exercises 7.5

1. $A = 3, B = -2$

3. $A = 2, B = -3$

5. $\ln \frac{|x|^3}{(x - 4)^2} + C$

7. $x^2 + \ln (x^2 - 4)^4 + C$

9. $2 \tan^{-1} x + C$

11. $\ln \left|\frac{x - 3}{2x + 1}\right| + C$

13. $\ln (|1x + 1|^3|2x - 3|) + C$

15. $y = \ln \left|\frac{x^3}{x - 2}\right| + C,$

17. $F(x) = \ln \frac{|x^2 - 1|}{x^2} + C,$

19. $\ln |x^2 - 4| + C$

21. $x + \ln |x^2 - x| + C$

23. **(a)** 200 individuals **(b)** 100 individuals **(c)** 60 individuals per year

25. **(a)** 1200 individuals **(b)** 600 individuals **(c)** 72 individuals per year

27. $P = \frac{200}{1 + 24e^{-1.2t}}$

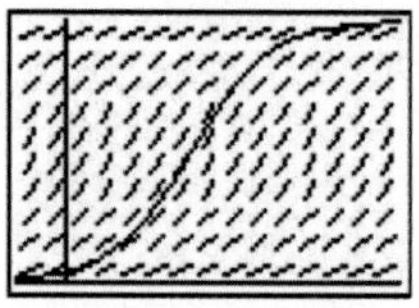

[–1, 7] by [0, 200]

29. $P = \frac{1200}{1 + 59e^{-0.24t}}$

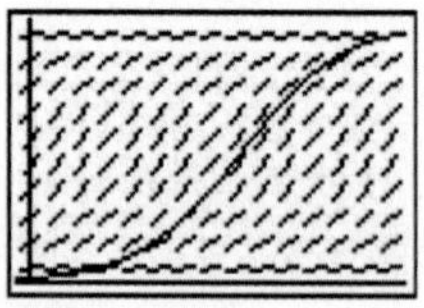

[–1, 30] by [0, 1200]

31. **(a)** $k = 0.0007$; $M = 1000$

(b) $P(0) \approx 8$; Initially there are 8 rabbits.

33. **(a)** $P(t) = \frac{150}{1 + 24e^{-0.225t}}$

(b) About 17.21 weeks; 21.28 weeks

35. Separate the variables and solve:

$$\frac{dP}{P(M-P)} = k\,dt$$

$$\frac{M\,dP}{P(M-P)} = Mk\,dt \qquad \text{Multiply by } M.$$

$$\left(\frac{1}{P} + \frac{1}{M-P}\right)dP = Mk\,dt \qquad \text{Partial fractions}$$

$$\left(\frac{1}{P-M} - \frac{1}{P}\right)dP = Mk\,dt \qquad \text{Multiply by } -1.$$

$$\ln\left|\frac{P-M}{P}\right| = -Mkt + C$$

$$\left|1 - \frac{M}{P}\right| = e^{-Mkt}\cdot e^{C}$$

$$\frac{M}{P} = e^{-Mkt}\cdot A + 1 \qquad \text{Let } A = \pm e^{C}$$

$$\frac{P}{M} = \frac{1}{1 + Ae^{-Mkt}} \qquad \text{Reciprocate both sides.}$$

$$P = \frac{M}{1 + Ae^{-Mkt}}$$

37. (a) The regression equation is $P = \dfrac{232739.9}{1 + 14.582e^{-0.101t}}$.

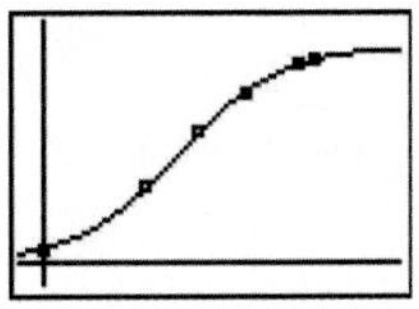

[–5, 70] by [–24000, 260000]

(b) Approximately 232,740 people

(c) Sometime in the 60th year, that is, in 2010

(d) $dP/dt = (4.352 \times 10^{-7})\,P(232739.9 - P)$

39. False. It does look exponential, but it resembles the solution to $dP/dt = kP(100 - 10) = (90k)P$

41. D **43.** D

45. (a) dP/dt has the same sign as $(M - P)(P - m)$.

(b) $P(t) = \dfrac{1200Ae^{11\,kt/12} + 100}{1 + Ae^{11\,kt/12}}$

(c) $P(t) = \dfrac{300(8e^{11\,kt/12} + 3)}{9 + 2e^{11\,kt/12}}$

(d)

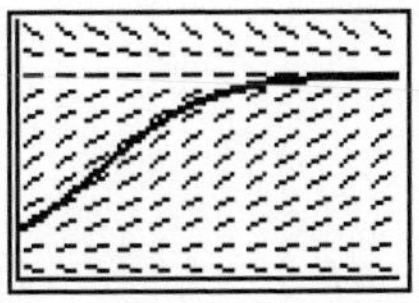

[0, 75] by [0, 1500]

(e) $P(t) = \dfrac{AMe^{(M-m)kt/M} + m}{1 + Ae^{(M-m)kt/M}}$, where $A = \dfrac{P(0) - m}{M - P(0)}$

47. (a) $5\ln|x+3| + \dfrac{15}{x+3} + C$ **(b)** $-\dfrac{5}{x+3} + \dfrac{15}{2(x+3)^2} + C$

Quick Quiz (Sections 7.4 and 7.5)

1. C **3.** A

Review Exercises

1. $\sqrt{3}$ **2.** 2 **3.** 8

4. 0 **5.** 2

6. 147/8 **7.** $e - 1$ **8.** $\dfrac{2}{3}$

9. $\ln(64/9) - \ln(27/4) = \ln(256/243)$

10. $\ln(1/4) - \ln 16 = -6\ln 2$

11. $-\ln|2 - \sin x| + C$

12. $\dfrac{1}{2}(3x+4)^{2/3} + C$

13. $\dfrac{1}{2}\ln(t^2 + 5) + C$

14. $-\sec\dfrac{1}{\theta} + C$

15. $-\ln|\cos(\ln y)| + C$

16. $\ln|\sec(e^x) + \tan(e^x)| + C$

17. $\ln|\ln x| + C$

18. $-\dfrac{2}{\sqrt{t}} + C$

19. $x^3\sin x + 3x^2\cos x - 6x\sin x - 6\cos x + C$

20. $\dfrac{x^5\ln x}{5} - \dfrac{x^5}{25} + C$

21. $\left(\dfrac{3\sin x}{10} - \dfrac{\cos x}{10}\right)e^{3x} + C$

22. $\left(-\dfrac{x^2}{3} - \dfrac{2x}{9} - \dfrac{2}{27}\right)e^{-3x} + C$

23. $\dfrac{5}{2}\ln\left|\dfrac{x-5}{x+5}\right| + C$

24. $\dfrac{1}{2}\ln|(2x-1)^3(x+1)^2| + C$

25. $y = \dfrac{x^3}{6} + \dfrac{x^2}{2} + x + 1$

26. $y = \dfrac{x^3}{3} + 2x - \dfrac{1}{x} - \dfrac{1}{3}$

27. $y = \ln(t+4) + 2$

28. $y = -\dfrac{1}{2}\csc 2\theta + \dfrac{3}{2}$

29. $y = \dfrac{x^3}{3} + \ln x - x + \dfrac{2}{3}$

30. $r = \sin t - \dfrac{t^2}{2} - 2t - 1$

31. $y = 4e^x - 2$

32. $y = 2e^{x^2+x} - 1$

33. $y = \dfrac{1}{1 + 9e^{-t}}$

34. $y = \dfrac{100}{1 + 19e^{-0.1x}}$

35. $y = \displaystyle\int_4^x \sin^3 t\,dt + 5$

36. $y = \displaystyle\int_1^x \sqrt{1 + t^4}\,dt + 2$

37.

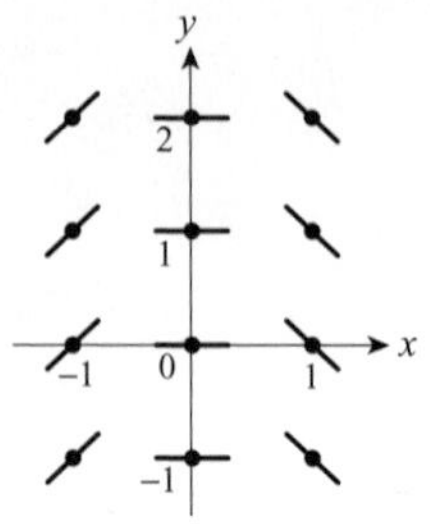

38.

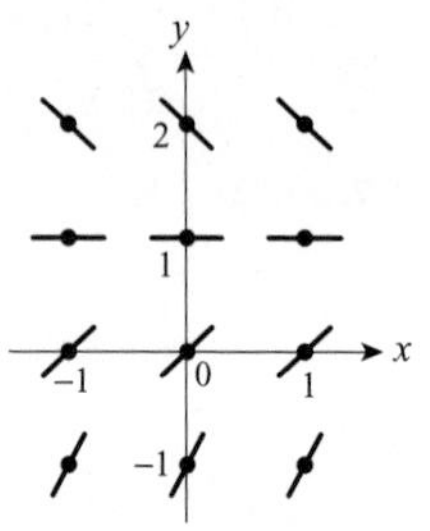

39. Graph (b) **40.** Graph (d) **41.** Graph (c) **42.** Graph (a)
43. 1.362 **44.** 2.362 **45.** Graph (b) **46.** Graph (d)
47. **iv.** since the given graph looks like $y = x^2$, which satisfies $dy/dx = 2x$ and $y(1) = 1$.
48. Yes, $y = x$ is a solution. **49.** **(a)** $v = 2t + 3t^2 + 4$ **(b)** 6 m
50.

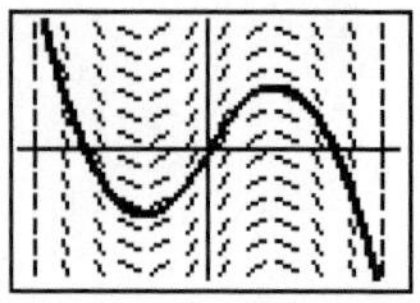

[–10, 10] by [–10, 10]

51. **(a)** $k \approx 0.262059$
(b) About 3.81593 years

52. About 92 minutes **53.** $-3°C$ **54.** About 41.2 years
55. About 18,935 years old **56.** About 5.3% **57.** About 59.8 ft
58. **(a)** $y = c + (y_0 - c)e^{-(kA/V)t}$ **(b)** c
59. **(a)** $k = \frac{1}{150}$, carrying capacity $= 150$
(b) ≈ 2; Initially there were 2 infected students.
(c) About 6 days
60. Use the Fundamental Theorem of Calculus to obtain $y' = \sin(x^2) + 3x^2 + 1$. Then differentiate again and also verify the initial conditions.
61. $P = \dfrac{800}{1 + 15e^{-0.002t}}$
62. Method 1—Compare graph of $y_1 = x^2 \ln x$ with

$$y_2 = \text{NDER}\left(\frac{x^3 \ln x}{3} - \frac{x^3}{9}\right).$$

Method 2—Compare graph of $y_1 = \text{NINT}(x^2 \ln x)$ with $y_2 = \dfrac{x^3 \ln x}{3} - \dfrac{x^3}{9}$.

63. **(a)** About 11.3 years **(b)** About 11 years

64. **(a)** $$\frac{d}{dx}\int_0^x u(t)\,dt = u(x)$$
$$\frac{d}{dx}\int_3^x u(t)\,dt = u(x)$$
(b) $C = \displaystyle\int_0^3 u(t)\,dt$

65. **(a)** The regression equation is $y = \dfrac{272286.4}{1 + 302.69e^{-0.2095t}}$. The graph is shown below.

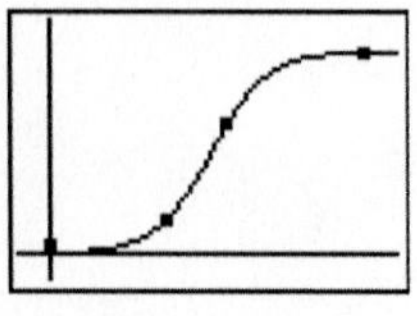

(b) 272,286 people
(c) $dP/dt = 7.694 \times 10^{-7}\,P(272286.4 - P)$
(d) The carrying capacity drops to 267,312.6, which is below the actual 2003 population. The logistic regression is strongly affected by points at the extremes of the data, especially when there are so few data points being used. While the fit may be more dramatic for a small data set, the equation is not as reliable.

66. **(a)** $T = 79.961(0.9273)^t$

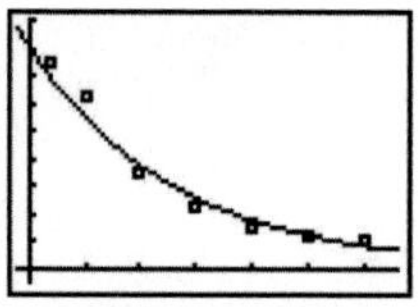

[–1, 33] by [–5, 90]

(b) About 9.2 sec
(c) About 79.96° C

67. **(a)** 1/2 **(b)** Separate the variables to get $\dfrac{dy}{y(1-y)} = 1.2\,dt$. Solve the differential equation using the same steps as in Example 5 in Section 7.5 to obtain $y = \dfrac{1}{1 + 9e^{-1.2t}}$.
(c) Set $\dfrac{1}{2} = \dfrac{1}{1 + 9e^{-1.2t}}$ and solve for t to obtain $t = \dfrac{5 \ln 3}{3} \approx 1.83$ days.

68. **(a)** $dP/dt = k(600 - P)$. Separate the variables to obtain

$$\frac{dP}{600 - P} = k\,dt$$
$$\frac{dP}{P - 600} = -k\,dt$$
$$\ln|P - 600| = -kt + C_1$$
$$P - 600 = Ce^{-kt}$$
$$200 - 600 = Ce^0 \Rightarrow C = -400$$
$$P - 600 = -400e^{-kt}$$
$$P(t) = 600 - 400e^{-kt}$$

(b) $500 = 600 - 400e^{-k \cdot 2}$
$1/4 = e^{-2k}$
$k = \ln 2 \approx 0.693$
(c) $\lim_{t\to\infty}(600 - 400e^{-0.693t}) = 600$

69. **(a)** Separate the variables to obtain

$$\frac{dv}{v + 17} = -2dt$$
$$\ln|v + 17| = -2t + C_1$$
$$v + 17 = Ce^{-2t}$$
$$-47 + 17 = Ce^0 \Rightarrow C = -30$$
$$v + 17 = -30e^{-2t}$$
$$v = -30e^{-2t} - 17$$

(b) $\lim_{t\to\infty}(-30e^{-2t} - 17) = -17$ feet per second
(c) $-20 = -30e^{-2t} - 17$
$t = \dfrac{\ln 10}{2} \approx 1.151$ seconds

CHAPTER 8

Section 8.1

Quick Review 8.1

1. Changes sign at $-\frac{\pi}{2}, 0, \frac{\pi}{2}$

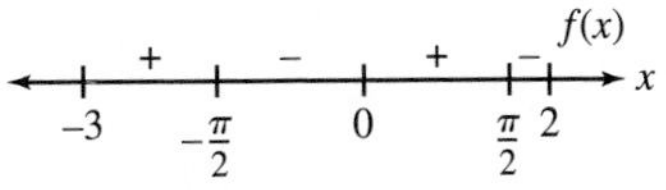

3. Always positive

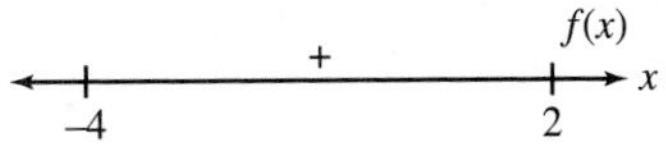

5. Changes sign at $\frac{\pi}{4}, \frac{3\pi}{4}, \frac{5\pi}{4}$

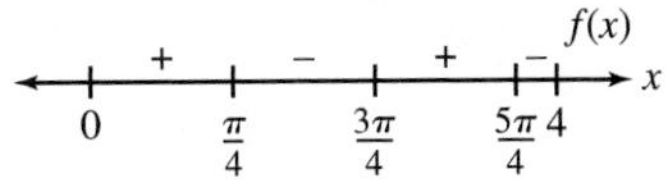

7. Changes sign at 0

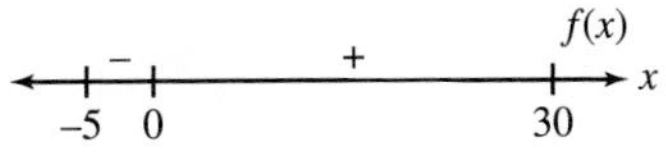

9. Changes sign at $0.9633 + k\pi$
$2.1783 + k\pi$
where k is an integer

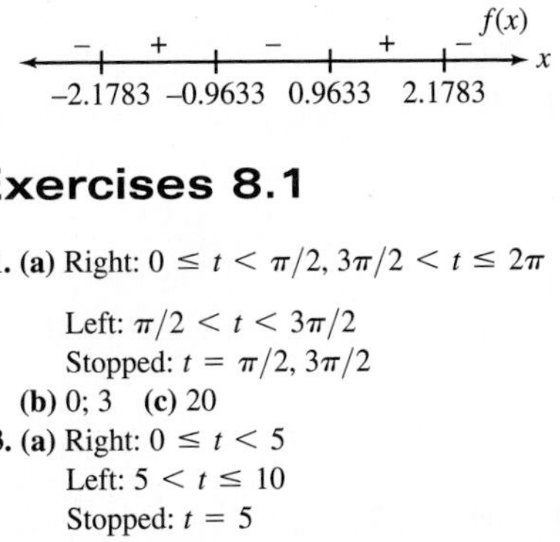

Exercises 8.1

1. **(a)** Right: $0 \le t < \pi/2, 3\pi/2 < t \le 2\pi$
Left: $\pi/2 < t < 3\pi/2$
Stopped: $t = \pi/2, 3\pi/2$
(b) 0; 3 **(c)** 20

3. **(a)** Right: $0 \le t < 5$
Left: $5 < t \le 10$
Stopped: $t = 5$
(b) 0; 3 **(c)** 245

5. **(a)** Right: $0 < t < \pi/2, 3\pi/2 < t < 2\pi$
Left: $\pi/2 < t < \pi, \pi < t < 3\pi/2$
Stopped: $t = 0, \pi/2, \pi, 3\pi/2, 2\pi$
(b) 0; 3 **(c)** 20/3

7. **(a)** Right: $0 \le t < \pi/2, 3\pi/2 < t \le 2\pi$
Left: $\pi/2 < t < 3\pi/2$
Stopped: $t = \pi/2, 3\pi/2$
(b) 0; 3 **(c)** $2e - (2/e) \approx 4.7$

9. **(a)** 63 mph **(b)** 344.52 feet

11. **(a)** −6 ft/sec **(b)** 5.625 sec **(c)** 0 **(d)** 253.125 feet

13. 33 cm

15. $t = a$

17. **(a)** 6 **(b)** 4 meters

19. **(a)** 5 **(b)** 7 meters

21. ≈332.965 billion barrels

23. **(a)** 2 miles **(b)** $2\pi r \Delta r$
(c) Population = Population density × Area **(d)** ≈83,776

25. **(a)** 797.5 thousand **(b)** $B(x) = 1.6x^2 + 2.3x + 5.0$ **(c)** ≈904.02
(d) The answer in (a) corresponds to the area of left-hand rectangles. These rectangles lie under the curve $B(x)$. The answer in (c) corresponds to the area under the curve. This area is greater than the area of the rectangles.

27. 1156.5

29. **(a)** 18 N **(b)** 81 N · cm

31. False. The displacement is the integral of the velocity from $t = 0$ to $t = 5$ and is positive.

33. C **35.** B

37. 0.04875

39. (a, b) Take $dm = \delta\, dA$ as m_k and let $dA \to 0, k \to$ in the center of mass equations.

41. $\bar{x} = 4/3, \bar{y} = 0$

Section 8.2

Quick Review 8.2

1. 2 **3.** 2

5. $9\pi/2$ **7.** (0, 1)

9. (−1, −1); (0, 0); (1, 1)

Exercises 8.2

1. $\pi/2$ **3.** 1/12

5. 128/15 **7.** ≈1.670

9. 5/6 **11.** ≈7.542

13. 16 **15.** $10\frac{2}{3}$

17. 4 **19.** $\frac{2}{3}a^3$

21. $21\frac{1}{3}$ **23.** $30\frac{3}{8}$

25. 8/3 **27.** 8

29. $6\sqrt{3}$ **31.** $\frac{4 - \pi}{\pi} \approx 0.273$

33. $4 - \pi \approx 0.858$

35. ≈4.333

37. 1/2

39. $\sqrt{2} - 1 \approx 0.414$

41. **(a)** $(-\sqrt{c}, c)$; $(\sqrt{c}, c)$

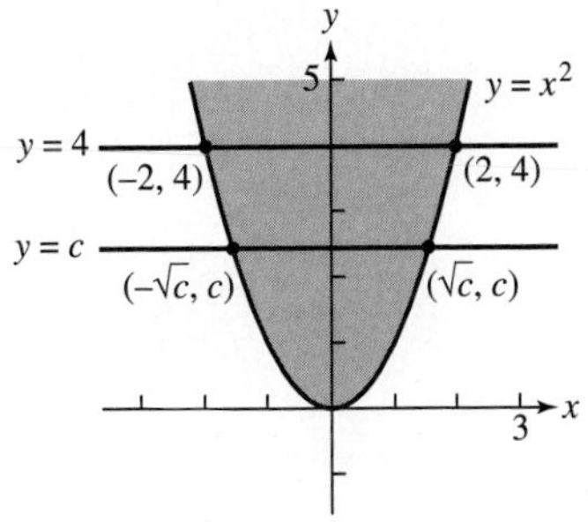

(b) $\int_0^c \sqrt{y}\, dy = \int_c^4 \sqrt{y}\, dy \Rightarrow c = 2^{4/3}$

(c) $\int_0^{\sqrt{c}} (c - x^2)\, dx = (4 - c)\sqrt{c} + \int_{\sqrt{c}}^4 (4 - x^2)\, dx \Rightarrow c = 2^{4/3}$

43. 3/4
45. Neither; both are zero.
47. $\ln 4 - (1/2) \approx 0.886$
49. $k \approx 1.8269$
51. False. It is $\int_0^{0.739} (\cos x - x)\, dx$.
53. E **55.** A
57. Since $f(x) - g(x)$ is the same for each region where $f(x)$ and $g(x)$ represent the upper and lower edges, area $= \int_a^b [f(x) - g(x)]\, dx$ will be the same for each.

Section 8.3

Quick Review 8.3

1. x^2 **3.** $\pi x^2/2$
5. $(\sqrt{3}/4)x^2$
7. $x^2/4$ **9.** $6x^2$

Exercises 8.3

1. (a) $\pi(1 - x^2)$ **(b)** $4(1 - x^2)$
(c) $2(1 - x^2)$ **(d)** $\sqrt{3}(1 - x^2)$
3. 16 **5.** 16/3
7. $2\pi/3$ **9.** $4 - \pi$ **11.** $32\pi/5$
13. 36π **15.** $2\pi/3$
17. $117\pi/5$ **19.** $\pi^2 - 2\pi$
21. 2.301 **23.** 2π
25. $4\pi/3$ **27.** 8π
29. (a) 8π **(b)** $32\pi/5$ **(c)** $8\pi/3$ **(d)** $224\pi/15$
31. (a) $16\pi/15$ **(b)** $56\pi/15$ **(c)** $64\pi/15$
33. (a) $6\pi/5$ **(b)** $4\pi/5$ **(c)** 2π **(d)** 2π
35. 8π **37.** $128\pi/5$
39. (a) $2\sqrt{3}$ **(b)** 8 **41.** 8π
43. The volumes are equal by Cavalieri's Theorem.
45. (a) $512\pi/21$ **(b)** $832\pi/21$
47. (a) $11\pi/48$ **(b)** $11\pi/48$
49. (a) $36\pi/5$ cm^3 **(b)** 192.3 g
51. (a) $32\pi/3$ **(b)** The answer is independent of *r*.
53. 5 **55.** ≈ 13.614 **57.** ≈ 16.110
59. ≈ 53.226 **61.** ≈ 6.283
63. True, by definition.
65. A **67.** B
69. (a) $\dfrac{2}{\pi}, \dfrac{\pi^2 - 8}{2}$ **(b)** 0
(c) $V = \dfrac{\pi(2c^2\pi - 8c + \pi)}{2}$

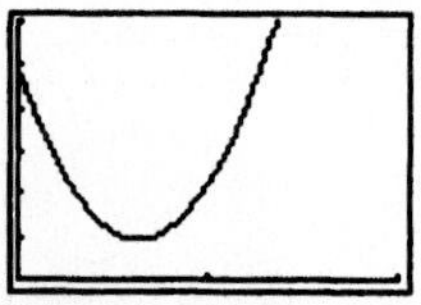

[0, 2] by [0, 6]
Volume $\rightarrow \infty$

71. Hemisphere cross-sectional area:
$\pi(\sqrt{R^2 - h^2})^2 = A_1$
Right circular cylinder with cone removed cross-sectional area:
$\pi R^2 - \pi h^2 = A_2$
Since $A_1 = A_2$, the two volumes are equal by Cavalieri's theorem.
Thus, volume of hemisphere = volume of cylinder − volume of cone
$$= \pi R^3 - \frac{1}{3}\pi R^3 = \frac{2}{3}\pi R^3.$$
73. (a) $\pi h^2(3a - h)/3$ **(b)** $1/(120\pi)$ m/sec

Quick Quiz (Sections 8.1 and 8.3)

1. C **3.** D

Section 8.4

Quick Review 8.4

1. $x + 1$ **3.** $\sec x$ **5.** $\sqrt{2}\cos x$ **7.** 0 **9.** 2

Exercises 8.4

1. (a) $\displaystyle\int_{-1}^{2} \sqrt{1 + 4x^2}\, dx$
(b)

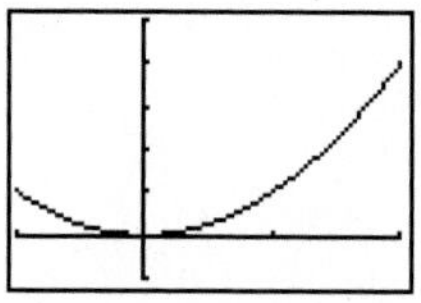

[−1, 2] by [−1, 5]

(c) ≈ 6.126

3. (a) $\displaystyle\int_{0}^{\pi} \sqrt{1 + \cos^2 y}\, dy$
(b)

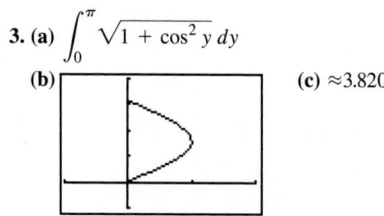

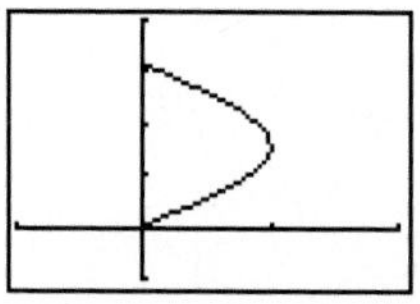

[−1, 2] by [−1, 4]

(c) ≈ 3.820

5. (a) $\displaystyle\int_{-1}^{7} \sqrt{1 + \frac{1}{2x + 2}}\, dx$
(b)

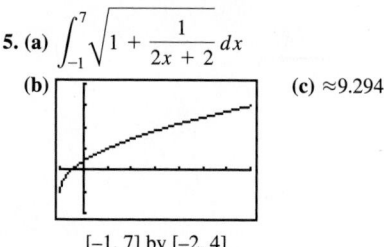

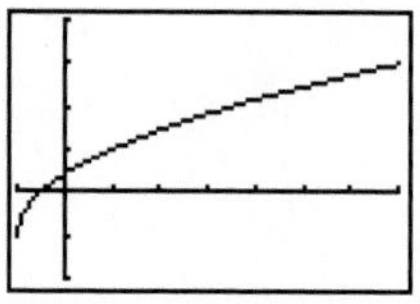

[−1, 7] by [−2, 4]

(c) ≈ 9.294

7. (a) $\displaystyle\int_{0}^{\pi/6} \sqrt{1 + \tan^2 x}\, dx$
(b)

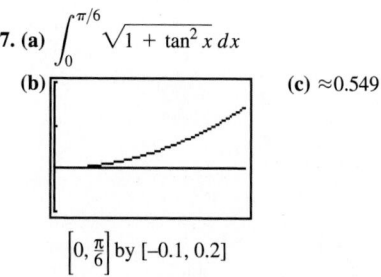

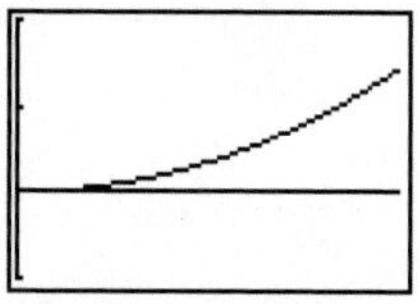

$\left[0, \frac{\pi}{6}\right]$ by [−0.1, 0.2]

(c) ≈ 0.549

9. (a) $\displaystyle\int_{-\pi/3}^{\pi/3} \sqrt{1 + \sec^2 x \tan^2 x}\, dx$
(b)

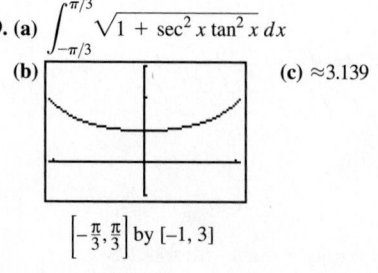

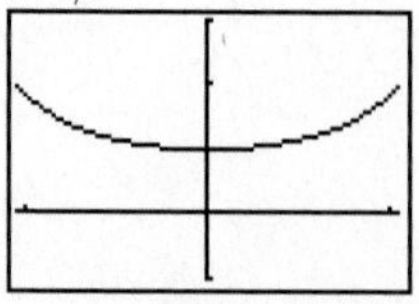

$\left[-\frac{\pi}{3}, \frac{\pi}{3}\right]$ by [−1, 3]

(c) ≈ 3.139

11. 12 **13.** 53/6
15. 17/12 **17.** 2
19. **(a)** $y = \sqrt{x}$ **(b)** Two. We know the absolute value of the derivative of the function and the value of the function at one value of x.
21. 1 **23.** ≈21.07 inches
25. ≈3.6142 **27.** ≈13.132
29. ≈16.647
31. No. Consider the curve $y = \frac{1}{3}\sin\left(\frac{1}{x}\right) + 0.5$ for $0 < x < 1$.
33. True, by definition.
35. C **37.** A
39. **(a)** The fin is the hypotenuse of a right triangle with leg lengths Δx_k and $\left.\frac{df}{dx}\right|_{x=x_{k-1}} \Delta x_k = f'(x_{k-1})\Delta x_k$.

(b) $$\lim_{n\to\infty} \sum_{k=1}^{n} \sqrt{(\Delta x_k)^2 + (f'(x_{k-1})\Delta x_k)^2}$$
$$= \lim_{n\to\infty} \sum_{k=1}^{n} \Delta x_k \sqrt{1 + (f'(x_{k-1}))^2}$$
$$= \int_a^b \sqrt{1 + (f'(x))^2}\, dx$$

Section 8.5

Quick Review 8.5

1. **(a)** $1 - (1/e)$ **(b)** ≈0.632
3. **(a)** $\frac{\sqrt{2}}{2}$ **(b)** ≈0.707
5. **(a)** $(1/3)\ln(9/2)$ **(b)** ≈0.501
7. $\int_0^7 (1 - x^2)(2\pi x)\, dx$
9. $\int_0^7 \pi(y/2)^2 (10 - y)\, dy$

Exercises 8.5

1. ≈4.4670 J **3.** 9 J
5. 4900 J **7.** 1944 ft-lb
9. **(a)** 7238 lb/in. **(b)** ≈905 in.-lb and ≈2714 in.-lb
11. 780 J
13. **(b)** 1123.2 lb
15. **(b)** 3705 lb
17. **(a)** 1,497,600 ft-lb **(b)** ≈100 min
(d) 1,494,240 ft-lb, ≈100 min; 1,500,000 ft-lb, 100 min
19. Through valve: ≈84,687.3 ft-lb Over the rim: ≈98,801.8 ft-lb
Through a hose attached to a valve in the bottom is faster, because it takes more time to do more work.
21. ≈53,482.5 ft-lb
23. ≈967,611 ft-lb, yes
25. **(a)** ≈209.73 lb **(b)** ≈838.93 lb; the fluid force doubles.
27. 1/3 **29.** 68%
31. **(a)** 0.5 (50%) **(b)** ≈0.24 (24%) **(c)** ≈0.0036 (0.36%) **(d)** 0
33. The proportion of lightbulbs that last between 100 and 800 hours.
35. True. The force against each vertical side is 842.4 lb.
37. D **39.** E
41. **(a)** 1.15×10^{-28} J
(b) ≈7.6667×10^{-29} J
43. 50 ft-lb **45.** 122.5 ft-lb
47. ≈109.7 ft-lb **49.** 4.5 ft

Quick Quiz (Sections 8.4 and 8.5)

1. A **3.** C

Review Exercises

1. ≈10.417 ft **2.** ≈31.361 gal **3.** ≈1464
4. 14 g **5.** 14,400 **6.** 1
7. $\frac{9}{2}$ **8.** 1/6 **9.** 18 **10.** 30.375
11. ≈0.0155 **12.** 4 **13.** ≈8.9023
14. ≈2.1043 **15.** $2\sqrt{3} - 2\pi/3 \approx 1.370$
16. $2\sqrt{3} + 4\pi/3 \approx 7.653$
17. ≈1.2956 **18.** ≈5.7312
19. 4π **20.** 2π
21. **(a)** $32\pi/3$ **(b)** $128\pi/15$ **(c)** $64\pi/5$ **(d)** $32\pi/3$
22. **(a)** 4π **(b)** πk^2 **(c)** $1/\pi$
23. $88\pi \approx 276$ in.^{3} **24.** $\pi^2/4$ **25.** $\pi(2 - \ln 3)$
26. $28\pi/3$ ft^3 ≈ 29.3215 ft^3
27. ≈19.4942 **28.** ≈5.2454
29. 2.296 sec **30.** (a) is true **31.** 39
32. **(a)** 4000 J **(b)** 640 J **(c)** 4640 J
33. 22,800,000 ft-lb **34.** 12 J, ≈213.3 J
35. No, the work going uphill is positive, but the work going downhill is negative.
36. ≈113.097 in.-lb **37.** ≈426.67 lb
38. base ≈ 6.6385 lb, front and back: 5.7726 lb, sides ≈ 9.4835 lb
39. 14.4 **40.** ≈0.2051 (20.5%)
41. Answers will vary.
42. **(a)** ≈0.6827 (68.27%) **(b)** 0.9545 (95.45%); 0.9973 (99.73%)
43. The probability that the variable has some value in the range of all possible values is 1.
44. π **45.** 3π **46.** $2\pi^2$ **47.** $16\pi/3$ **48.** ≈9.7717
49. **(a)** $y = 5 - \frac{5}{4}x^2$ **(b)** ≈335.1032 in.^{3}
50. $f(x) = \frac{x^2 - 2\ln x + 3}{4}$ **51.** ≈3.84 **52.** ≈5.02
53. **(a)** The two curves intersect at $x = 1.2237831$. Store this value as A.
$$\text{Area} = \int_0^A (2 + \sin x - \sec x)\, dx = 1.366.$$
(b) $$\text{Volume} = \int_0^A \pi((2 + \sin x)^2 - (\sec x)^2)\, dx = 16.404.$$
(c) $$\text{Volume} = \int_0^A (2 + \sin x - \sec x)^2\, dx = 1.629.$$
54. **(a)** $$\text{Average temp} = \frac{1}{14 - 6}\int_6^{14} \left(80 - 10\cos\left(\frac{\pi t}{12}\right)\right) dt \approx 87°\text{F}.$$
(b) $F(t) = 80 - 10\cos\left(\frac{\pi t}{12}\right) \geq 78$ for $5.2308694 \leq t \leq 18.766913$.
Store these two values as A and B.
(c) $$\text{Cost} = 0.05\int_A^B \left(80 - 10\cos\left(\frac{\pi t}{12}\right) - 78\right) dt \approx 5.10$$
The cost was about \$5.10.
55. **(a)** $$\int_9^{17} \frac{15600}{(t^2 - 24t + 160)}\, dt \approx 6004 \text{ people.}$$
(b) $$15\int_9^{17} \frac{15600}{(t^2 - 24t + 160)}\, dt + 11\int_{17}^{23} \frac{15600}{(t^2 - 24t + 160)}\, dt \approx$$
104,048 dollars
(c) $H'(17) = E(17) - L(17) \approx -380$ people. $H(17)$ is the number of people in the park at 5:00, and $H'(17)$ is the rate at which the number of people in the park is changing at 5:00.
(d) When $H'(t) = E(t) - L(t) = 0$; that is, at $t = 15.795$.

CHAPTER 9

Section 9.1

Quick Review 9.1

1. 5/8 **3.** 1 **5.** 12
7. 0 **9.** 1

Exercises 9.1

1. 1/2, 2/3, 3/4, 4/5, 5/6, 6/7; 50/51
3. 2, 9/4, 64/27, 625/256, 7776/3125 $\approx$ 2.48832. 117649/46656 $\approx$ 2.521626; $(51/50)^{50} \approx 2.691588$
5. 3, 1, −1, −3: −11
7. 2, 4, 8, 16: 256
9. 1, 1, 2, 3; 21
11. **(a)** 3 **(b)** 19 **(c)** $a_n = a_{n-1} + 3$ **(d)** $a_n = 3n - 5$
13. **(a)** 1/2 **(b)** 9/2 **(c)** $a_n = a_{n-1} + 1/2$ **(d)** $a_n = (n + 1)/2$
15. **(a)** 1/2 **(b)** $8(1/2)^8 = 0.03125$ **(c)** $a_n = (1/2)a_{n-1}$ **(d)** $a_n = 8(1/2)^{n-1} = 2^{4-n}$
17. **(a)** −3 **(b)** $(-3)^9 = -19.683$ **(c)** $a_n = (-3)a_{n-1}$ **(d)** $a_n = (-3)(-3)^{n-1} = (-3)^n$
19. $-5, a_n = a_{n-1} + 3$ for all $n \geq 2$
21. $a_1 = 3.01, r = 10.\ a_n = 3.01(10)^{n-1}, n \geq 1$

23.
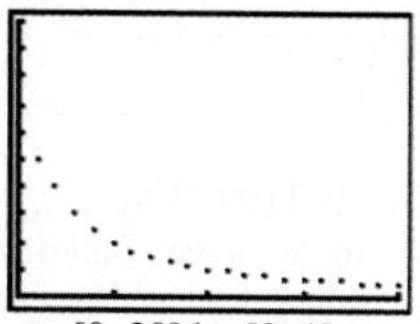
[0, 20] by [0, 1]

25.
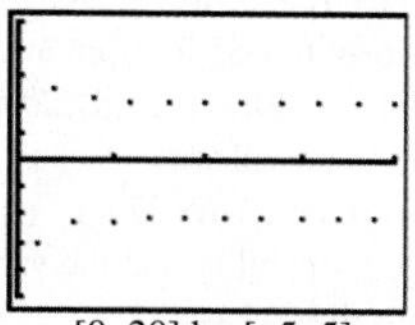
[0, 20] by [−5, 5]

27.
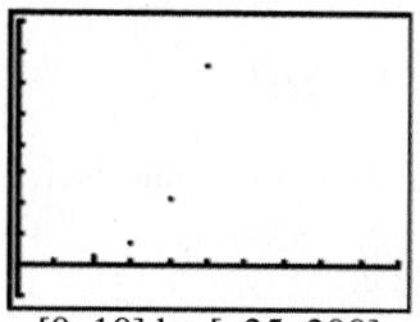
[0, 10] by [−25, 200]

29.
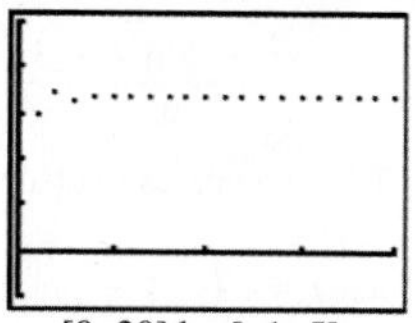
[0, 20] by [−1, 5]

31. converges, 3 **33.** converges, 2/5
35. diverges **37.** diverges
39. converges, 1 **41.** 0
43. 0, (Note: $\dfrac{1}{n!} \leq \dfrac{1}{n}$ for $n \geq 1$)
45. Graph (b) **47.** Table (d)
49. False. Consider the sequence with nth term $a_n = -5 + 2(n - 1)$. Here $a_1 = -5$, $a_2 = -3$, $a_3 = -1$, and $a_4 = 1$.
51. C **53.** D **55.** **(b)** 2π
57. $a_n = ar^{n-1}$ implies that $\log a_n = \log a + (n - 1)\log r$. Thus $\{\log a_n\}$ is an arithmetic sequence with first term $\log a$ and common ratio $\log r$.
59. Given $\epsilon > 0$ choose $M = 1/\epsilon$. Then $\left|\dfrac{1}{n} - 0\right| < \epsilon$ if $n > M$.

Section 9.2

Quick Review 9.2

1. 1.1052 **3.** 1
5. 2 **7.** 3
9. $y = \dfrac{\sin h}{h}$

Exercises 9.2

1. Appears to be about 1/4; 1/4 by l'Hôpital's Rule
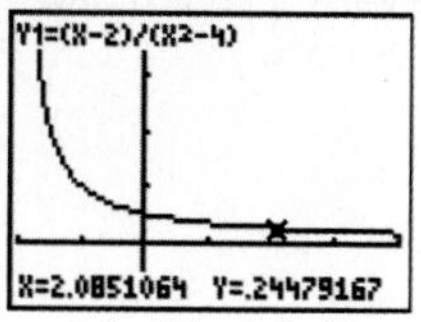

[−2, 4] by [−1, 4]

3. Appears to be about 1/4; 1/4 by l'Hôpital's Rule
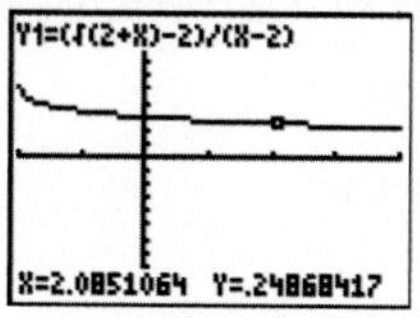

[−2, 4] by [−1, 1]

5. 1/2 **7.** −1

9.
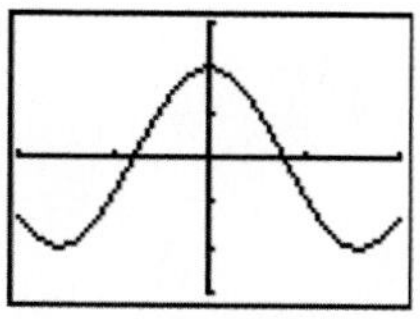
[−2, 2] by [−3, 3]

(a) 2 **(b)** 2

11.
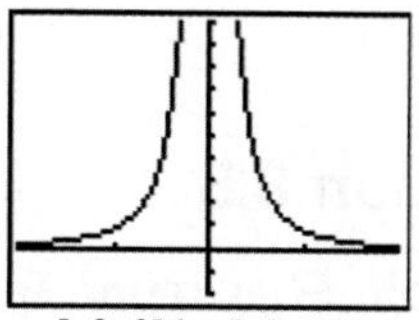
[−2, 2] by [−2, 10]

(a) ∞ **(b)** ∞

13.
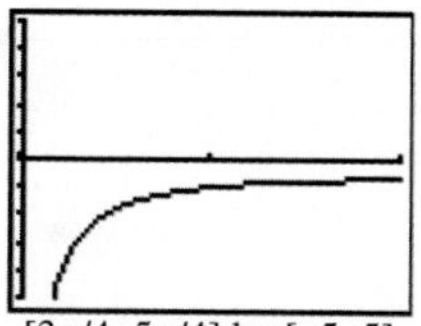
[3π/4, 5π/4] by [−5, 5]

Left $(\infty)/(-\infty)$, right $(-\infty)/(\infty)$, limit $= -1$

15.
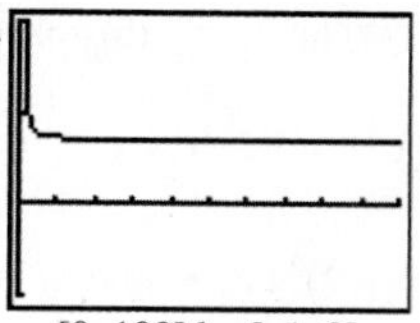
[0, 100] by [−1, 2]

$(\infty)/(\infty)$, limit $= \ln 2$

17. $\infty \cdot 0$, 0 **19.** $\infty - \infty$, 1
21. 1^∞, e^2 **23.** 0^0, 1 **25.** ∞^0, 1
27. **(a)**

x	10	10^2	10^3	10^4	10^5
$f(x)$	1.1513	0.2303	0.0354	0.0046	0.00058

Estimated limit = 0
(b) Note $\ln x^5 = 5 \ln x$.

$$\lim_{x\to\infty} \frac{5 \ln x}{x} = \lim_{x\to\infty} \frac{5/x}{1} = \frac{0}{1} = 0$$

29. 3/4 **31.** 1 **33.** 0
35. ln 3/ln 2 **37.** 1 **39.** ∞
41. 0 **43.** $e^{1/2}$ **45.** e **47.** e^{-1}
49. 3/11 **51.** (cos 1)/2
53. **(a)** L'Hôpital's Rule does not help because applying l'Hôpital's Rule to this quotient essentially "inverts" the problem by interchanging the numerator and denominator. It is still essentially the same problem and one is no closer to a solution. Applying l'Hôpital's Rule a second time returns to the original problem.
(b), (c) 3
55. $c = 27/10$, because this is the limit of $f(x)$ as x approaches 0.

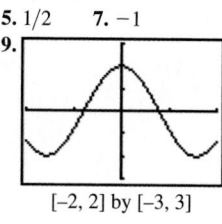

57. **(a)** $\ln\left(1+\frac{r}{k}\right)^{kt} = kt\ln\left(1+\frac{r}{k}\right)$. And, as $k \to \infty$,

$$\lim_{k\to\infty} kt\ln\left(1+\frac{r}{k}\right) = \lim_{k\to\infty}\frac{t\ln\left(1+\frac{r}{k}\right)}{\frac{1}{k}}$$

$$= \lim_{k\to\infty}\frac{t\left(\frac{-r}{k^2}\right)\left(1+\frac{r}{k}\right)^{-1}}{\frac{-1}{k^2}}.$$

$$= \lim_{k\to\infty}\frac{rt}{1+\frac{r}{k}} = rt.$$

Hence, $\lim_{k\to\infty} A_0\left(1+\frac{r}{k}\right)^{kt} = A_0e^{rt}$.

(b) Part (a) shows that as the number of compoundings per year increases toward infinity, the limit of interest compounded k times per year is interest compounded continuously.

59. **(a)** 1 **(b)** $\pi/2$ **(c)** π

61. **(a)** $(-\infty, -1)\cup(0, \infty)$ **(b)** ∞ **(c)** e

63. False. The limit is 1. **65.** D **67.** E

69. Possible answers: **(a)** $f(x) = 3x + 1$, $g(x) = x$
(b) $f(x) = x + 1$, $g(x) = x^2$
(c) $f(x) = x^2$, $g(x) = x + 1$

71. **(a)** $c = 1/3$ **(b)** $c = \pi/4$

Quick Quiz (Sections 9.1 and 9.2)

1. C **3.** B

Section 9.3

Quick Review 9.3

1. 0 **3.** ∞ **5.** $-3x^4$

7. $\lim_{x\to\infty}\frac{f(x)}{g(x)} = \lim_{x\to\infty}\left(1+\frac{1}{x}\right) = 1 + 0 = 1$

9. **(a)** Local minimum at $(0, 1)$ Local minimum at $\approx(2, 1.541)$ **(b)** $[0, 2]$
(c) $(-\infty, 0]$ and $[2, \infty)$

Exercises 9.3

1. $\lim_{x\to\infty}\frac{e^x}{x^3 - 3x + 1} = \infty$

3. $\lim_{x\to\infty}\frac{e^x}{e^{\cos x}} = \infty$

5. $\lim_{x\to\infty}\frac{\ln x}{x - \ln x} = 0$

7. $\lim_{x\to\infty}\frac{\ln x}{\sqrt[3]{x}} = 0$

9. $\lim_{x\to\infty}\frac{x^2 + 4x}{x^2} = 1$

11. $\lim_{x\to\infty}\frac{\sqrt{x^6 + x^2}}{x^2} = 1$

13. $\lim_{x\to\infty}\frac{\log\sqrt{x}}{\ln x} = \frac{1}{2\ln 10}$

15. Slower **17.** Slower

19. Slower **21.** Faster

23. Slower **25.** Same rate

27. Slower **29.** $e^{x/2}$, e^x, $(\ln x)^x$, x^x

31. $\lim_{x\to\infty}\frac{f_2(x)}{f_1(x)} = \sqrt{10}$ and $\lim_{x\to\infty}\frac{f_3(x)}{f_1(x)} = 1$, so f_2 and f_3 also grow at the same rate.

33. $\lim_{x\to\infty}\frac{f_2(x)}{f_1(x)} = 1$ and $\lim_{x\to\infty}\frac{f_3(x)}{f_1(x)} = 1$, so f_2 and f_3 also grow at the same rate.

35. f grows faster than and g

37. f and g grow at the same rate

39. **(a)** The nth derivative of x^n is $n!$, which is a constant. Therefore n applications of l'Hôpital's Rule give

$$\lim_{x\to\infty}\frac{e^x}{x^n} = \cdots = \lim_{x\to\infty}\frac{e^x}{n!} = \infty.$$

(b) In this case, n applications of l'Hôpital's Rule give

$$\lim_{x\to\infty}\frac{a^x}{x^n} = \cdots = \lim_{x\to\infty}\frac{a^x(\ln a)^n}{n!} = \infty$$

41. **(a)** $\lim_{x\to\infty}\frac{\ln x}{x^{1/n}} = \lim_{x\to\infty}\frac{1/x}{\left[\frac{x^{(1/n)-1}}{n}\right]} = \lim_{x\to\infty}\frac{n}{x^{1/n}} = 0$

(b) $\lim_{x\to\infty}\frac{\ln x}{x^a} = \lim_{x\to\infty}\frac{1/x}{ax^{a-1}} = \lim_{x\to\infty}\frac{1}{ax^a} = 0$

43. The one which is $O(n\log_2 n)$ is likely the most efficient, because of the three given functions; it grows the most slowly as $n \to \infty$.

45. **(a)** The limit will be the ratio of the leading coefficients of the polynomials.
(b) The limit will be the same as in part (a).

47. False. They grow at the same rate.

49. A **51.** D

53. (a) and (b) both follow from the fact that if f and g are negative, then

$$\lim_{x\to\infty}\left|\frac{f(x)}{g(x)}\right| = \lim_{x\to\infty}\frac{-f(x)}{-g(x)} = \lim_{x\to\infty}\frac{f(x)}{g(x)}$$

Section 9.4

Quick Review 9.4

1. $\ln 2$ **3.** $\frac{1}{2}\tan^{-1}\frac{x}{2} + C$

5. $(-3, 3)$ **7.** Because $-1 \le \cos x \le 1$ for all x

9. $\lim_{x\to\infty}\frac{4e^x - 5}{3e^x + 7} = \frac{4}{3}$

Exercises 9.4

1. **(a)** $\lim_{b\to\infty}\int_0^b \frac{2x}{x^2 + 1}\,dx$ **(b)** ∞, diverges

3. **(a)** $\lim_{b\to-\infty}\int_b^0 \frac{2x}{(x^2 + 1)^2}\,dx + \lim_{b\to\infty}\int_0^b \frac{2x}{(x^2 + 1)^2}\,dx$ **(b)** 0 converges

5. 1/3 **7.** diverges **9.** 1 **11.** ln (3) **13.** ln (2)

15. diverges **17.** $(3/4)\,e^{-2}$

19. diverges **21.** 2 **23.** $\pi/2$

25. **(a)** The integral has an infinite discontinuity at the interior point $x = 1$.
(b) diverges

27. **(a)** The integral has an infinite discontinuity at the endpoint $x = 0$.
(b) $\sqrt{3}$

29. **(a)** The integral has an infinite discontinuity at the endpoint $x = 0$.
(b) $-1/4$

31. $0 \le \frac{1}{1 + e^x} \le \frac{1}{e^x}$ on $[1, \infty)$, converges because $\int_1^\infty \frac{1}{e^x}\,dx$ converges

33. $0 \le \frac{1}{x} \le \frac{2 + \cos x}{x}$ on $[\pi, \infty)$, diverges because $\int_{\pi}^{\infty} \frac{1}{x}\,dx$ diverges

35. diverges **37.** π **39.** $2\pi^2$ **41.** diverges **43.** 1

45. **(a)** Since f is an even function, the substitution

$$u = -x \text{ gives } \int_{-\infty}^{0} f(x)\,dx = \int_{0}^{\infty} f(u)\,du.$$

(b) Since f is an odd function, the substitution

$$u = -x \text{ gives } \int_{-\infty}^{0} f(x)\,dx = -\int_{0}^{\infty} f(u)\,du.$$

47. 6 **49.** True. See Theorem 6. **51.** B **53.** C

55. **(a)** $A(x) = (\pi/4)\,e^{2x}$ **(b)** $V = \int_{-\infty}^{\ln 2} A(x)dx = \int_{-\infty}^{\ln 2} (\pi/4)\,e^{2x}\,dx$

(c) $\pi/2$

57. **(a)** For $x \ge 6$, $x^2 \ge 6x$, and therefore, $e^{-x^2} \le e^{-6x}$. The inequality for the integrals follows. The value of the second integral is $e^{-36}/6$, which is less than 4×10^{-17}.

(b) The error in the estimate is the integral over the interval $[6, \infty)$, and we have shown that it is bounded by 4×10^{-17} in part (a).

(c) 0.13940279264 (This agrees with Figure 9.19.)

(d) $\int_{0}^{\infty} e^{-x^2}\,dx = \int_{0}^{\infty} e^{-x^2}\,dx + \int_{3}^{\infty} e^{-x^2}\,dx.$

The error in the approximation is

$$\int_{3}^{\infty} e^{-x^2}\,dx \le \int_{3}^{\infty} e^{-3x}\,dx < 0.000042.$$

59. **(a)** $n = 0$: integral $= 1$
$n = 1$: integral $= 1$
$n = 2$: integral $= 2$

(b) Integration by parts gives

$$\int x^n e^{-x}\,dx = -x^n e^{-x} + n\int x^{n-1} e^{-x}\,dx + C.$$

Since the term $(-x^n e^{-x})$ has value 0 at $x = 0$ and has limit equal to 0 as $x \to \infty$, when the above equation is evaluated "from 0 to infinity," it gives $f(n+1) = nf(n)$.

(c) This follows from the formula $f(n+1) = nf(n)$ by an induction argument. In fact, it follows that $\int_0^{\infty} x^n e^{-x}\,dx = n!$.

61. **(a)** $\int_{-\infty}^{1} \frac{dx}{1+x^2} = \frac{3\pi}{4}$, $\int_{1}^{\infty} \frac{dx}{1+x^2} = \frac{\pi}{4}$

$$\int_{-\infty}^{\infty} \frac{dx}{1+x^2} = \frac{3\pi}{4} + \frac{\pi}{4} = \pi$$

(b) $\int_{-\infty}^{c} f(x)\,dx = \int_{-\infty}^{0} f(x)\,dx + \int_{0}^{c} f(x)\,dx$

$$\int_{c}^{\infty} f(x)\,dx = \int_{c}^{0} f(x)\,dx + \int_{0}^{\infty} f(x)\,dx$$

Thus,

$$\int_{-\infty}^{c} f(x)\,dx + \int_{c}^{\infty} f(x)\,dx$$

$$= \int_{-\infty}^{0} f(x)\,dx + \int_{0}^{c} f(x)\,dx + \int_{c}^{0} f(x)\,dx + \int_{0}^{\infty} f(x)\,dx$$

$$= \int_{-\infty}^{0} f(x)\,dx + \int_{c}^{\infty} f(x)\,dx,$$

because

$$\int_{0}^{c} f(x)\,dx + \int_{c}^{0} f(x)\,dx = 0.$$

Quick Quiz (Sections 9.3 and 9.4)

1. E **3.** B

Review Exercises

1. $-1/2, 3/5, -2/3, 5/7$; $a_{40} = 41/43$

2. $-3, -6, -12, -24$; $a_{40} = -3(2^{39})$

3. **(a)** 3/2 **(b)** 25/2 **(c)** $a_n = \frac{3n - 5}{2}$

4. **(a)** -4 **(b)** 2048 **(c)** $a_n = (-1)^{n-1}\,(2^{2n-3})$

5.

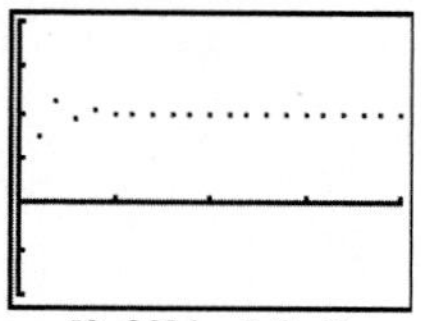

[0, 20] by [–2, 4]

6.

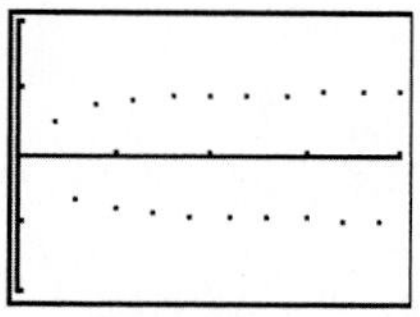

[0, 20] by [–2, 2]

7. converges, 3/2 **8.** diverges **9.** The limit doesn't exist

10. 3/5 **11.** 2 **12.** $1/e$ **13.** 1 **14.** e^3 **15.** 0

16. -1 **17.** $-1/2$ **18.** 1 **19.** 1 **20.** ∞ **21.** ∞ **22.** 0

23. Same rate, because $\lim_{x\to\infty} \frac{f(x)}{g(x)} = \frac{1}{5}$

24. Same rate, because $\lim_{x\to\infty} \frac{f(x)}{g(x)} = \frac{\ln 3}{\ln 2}$

25. Same rate, because $\lim_{x\to\infty} \frac{f(x)}{g(x)} = 1$

26. Faster, because $\lim_{x\to\infty} \frac{f(x)}{g(x)} = \infty$

27. Faster, because $\lim_{x\to\infty} \frac{f(x)}{g(x)} = \infty$

28. Same rate, because $\lim_{x\to\infty} \frac{f(x)}{g(x)} = 1$

29. Slower, because $\lim_{x\to\infty} \frac{f(x)}{g(x)} = 0$

30. Slower, because $\lim_{x\to\infty} \frac{f(x)}{g(x)} = 0$

31. Same rate, because $\lim_{x\to\infty} \frac{f(x)}{g(x)} = \frac{1}{2}$

32. Slower, because $\lim_{x\to\infty} \frac{f(x)}{g(x)} = 0$

33. Same rate, because $\lim_{x\to\infty} \frac{f(x)}{g(x)} = 1$

34. Faster, because $\lim_{x\to\infty} \frac{f(x)}{g(x)} = \infty$.

35. **(a)** $\lim_{x\to 0} = \ln 2$
(b) Define $f(0) = \ln 2$

36. **(a)** $\lim_{x\to 0^+} f(x) = 0$
(b) Define $f(0) = 0$

37. 2 **38.** $\ln(5/4)$ **39.** $-2\ln(2)$ **40.** $\pi/2$ **41.** -1

42. 6 **43.** 0 **44.** $\ln(3)$ **45.** 2 **46.** $-1/9$ **47.** $\pi/2$

48. π **49.** diverges **50.** converges

51. **(a)** -6 **(b)** 1/2 **(c)** $a_n = -3(2^{2-n})$

52. **(a)** 13 **(b)** -1.5 **(c)** $a_n = -1.5n + 14.5$

53. **(a)** $\lim_{b\to-\infty} \int_{b}^{0} e^{2x}\,dx + \lim_{b\to\infty} \int_{0}^{b} e^{-2x}\,dx$ **(b)** 1

54. 2π **55.** 1

56. (a) $\int_0^{\infty} xe^{-x/2}\,dx$ **(b)** $\lim_{b\to\infty}\int_0^b xe^{-x/2}\,dx$

(c) Note that $\int xe^{-x/2}\,dx$ can be found by parts:

$$\int xe^{-x/2}\,dx = x(-2e^{-x/2}) - \int(-2e^{-x/2})dx = -2xe^{-x/2} - 4e^{-x/2} + C.$$

Area =

$$\lim_{b\to\infty}\int_0^b xe^{-x/2}dx = \lim_{b\to\infty}\Big[-2xe^{-x/2} - 4e^{-x/2}\Big]_0^b$$
$$= \lim_{b\to\infty}(-2be^{-b/2} - 4e^{-b/2} + 0 + 4) = 4.$$

57. (a) $\int_0^{\infty} \pi x^2\,dy = \pi\int_0^{\infty}\frac{dy}{(y+1)^2}$

(b) $\lim_{b\to\infty}\pi\int_0^b \frac{dy}{(y+1)^2}$

(c) Volume $= \lim_{b\to\infty}\pi\int_0^b\frac{dy}{(y+1)^2} = \lim_{b\to\infty}\pi\Big[-(y+1)^{-1}\Big]_0^b$
$$= \lim_{b\to\infty}\pi\left(-\frac{1}{b+1}+1\right) = \pi$$

58. Note that $\int xe^{-x}\,dx$ can be found by parts:

$$\int xe^{-x}\,dx = x(-e^{-x}) - \int(-e^{-x})\,dx = -xe^{-x} - e^{-x} + C.$$

So,

$$\int_0^{\infty} xe^{-x}\,dx = \lim_{k\to\infty}\int_0^k xe^{-x}\,dx = \lim_{k\to\infty}\Big[-xe^{-x} - e^{-x}\Big]_0^k$$
$$= \lim_{k\to\infty}\left(-\frac{k}{e^k} - \frac{1}{e^k} + 1\right)$$

By l'Hôpital's rule, $\lim_{k\to\infty}\left(-\frac{k}{e^k}\right) = \lim_{k\to\infty}\left(-\frac{1}{e^k}\right) = 0$. Therefore,

$$\int_0^{\infty} xe^{-x}\,dx = \lim_{k\to\infty}\left(-\frac{k}{e^k} - \frac{1}{e^k} + 1\right) = 0 - 0 + 1 = 1.$$

The integral converges to 1.

CHAPTER 10

Section 10.1

Quick Review 10.1

1. 4/3, 1, 4/5, 2/3, 1/8

3. (a) 3 **(b)** 39,366 **(c)** $a_n = 2(3^{n-1})$

5. (a)

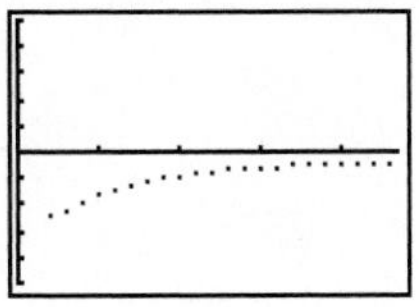

[0, 25] by [–0.5, 0.5]

(b) 0

7. (a)

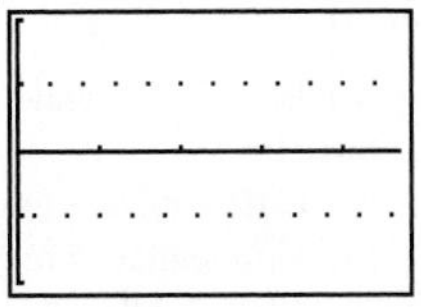

[0, 23.5] by [–2, 2]

(b) The limit does not exist.

9. (a)

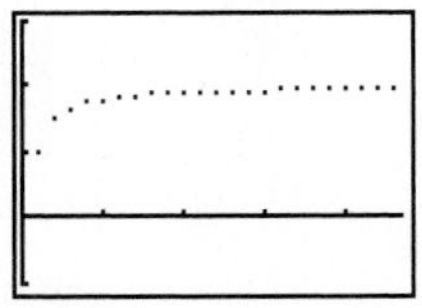

[0, 23.5] by [–1, 3]

(b) 2

Exercises 10.1

1. (a) $* = n^2$ **(b)** $* = (n+1)^2$ **(c)** $* = 3$

3. Different **5.** Same

7. Diverges

9. Converges

11. Converges; sum = 3

13. Converges; sum = 15/4

15. Diverges

17. Converges; sum = $2 - \sqrt{2}$

19. Converges; sum = $\frac{e}{\pi - e}$

21. Interval: $-\frac{1}{2} < x < \frac{1}{2}$; function: $f(x) = \frac{1}{1-2x}$

23. Interval: $1 < x < 5$; function: $f(x) = \frac{2}{x-1}$

25. Converges for all values of x except odd integer multiples of $\frac{\pi}{2}$;
function: $f(x) = \frac{1}{1-\sin x}$

27. $f'(x) = \frac{2}{(2x-1)^2} = \sum_{n=1}^{\infty} 2^n\, nx^{n-1}, -\frac{1}{2} < x < \frac{1}{2}$

29. $f'(x) = -\frac{2}{(x-1)^2} = \sum_{n=1}^{\infty}\left(-\frac{1}{2}\right)^n n(x-3)^{n-1}, 1 < x < 5$

31. $\int_0^x \frac{1}{1-2t}\,dt = -\frac{1}{2}\ln(|2x-1|) = \sum_{n=0}^{\infty}\frac{2^n}{n+1}x^{n+1}, -\frac{1}{2} < x < \frac{1}{2}$

33. $\int_3^x \frac{2}{t-1}\,dt = 2\ln\left(\frac{|x-1|}{2}\right) = \sum_{n=0}^{\infty}\left(-\frac{1}{2}\right)^n\frac{(x-3)^{n+1}}{n+1}, 1 < x < 5$

35. (a) The partial sums tend toward infinity.
(b) The partial sums are alternately 1 and 0.
(c) The partial sums alternate between positive and negative while their magnitude increases toward infinity.

37. $x = 19/20$

39. (a) $\sum_{n=1}^{\infty} 2\left(\frac{3}{5}\right)^{n-1}$ **(b)** $\sum_{n=1}^{\infty}\frac{13}{2}\left(-\frac{3}{10}\right)^{n-1}$

41. Let $a = 234/1000$ and $r = 1/1000$, giving
$(0.234) + (0.234)(0.001) + (0.234)(0.001)^2 + (0.234)(0.001)^3 + \cdots$
The sum is 26/111.

43. $d/9$ **45.** 157/111

47. 22/7 **49.** 7.113 seconds **51.** $\pi/2$

53. For $r \neq 1$, the result follows from:
If $|r| < 1$, $r^n \to 0$ as $n \to \infty$, and if $|r| > 1$ or $r = -1$, r^n has no finite limit as $n \to \infty$.
When $r = 1$, the nth partial sum is na, which goes to $\pm\infty$.

55. Series: $x + 2x^2 + 4x^3 + \cdots + 2^{n-1}x^n + \cdots$
Interval: $-1/2 < x < 1/2$

57. Series: $1 - (x-4) + (x-4)^2 - (x-4)^3 + \cdots + (-1)^n(x-4)^n + \cdots$
Interval: $3 < x < 5$

59. One possible series:
$1 + (x-1) + (x-1)^2 + \cdots + (x-1)^n + \cdots$
Interval: $0 < x < 2$

61. (a) 2 **(b)** $t > -1/2$ **(c)** $t > 9$

63. $(x-1) - \frac{(x-1)^2}{2} + \frac{(x-1)^3}{3} - \cdots + \frac{(-1)^{n-1}(x-1)^n}{n} + \cdots$

65. (a) No, because if you differentiate it again, you would have the original series for *f*, but by Theorem 1, that would have to converge for $-2 < x < 2$, which contradicts the assumption that the original series converges only for $-1 < x < 1$.

(b) No, because if you integrate it again, you would have the original series for f, but by Theorem 2, that would have to converge for $-2 < x < 2$, which contradicts the assumption that the original series converges only for $-1 < x < 1$.

67. False. It converses because it is a geometric series with ratio $1/2$ that is less than 1.

69. A **71.** D

73. Let $L = \lim_{n\to\infty} a_n$. Then by definition of convergence, for $\frac{\epsilon}{2}$ there corresponds an N such that for all m and n, $n, m > N \Rightarrow |a_m - L| < \frac{\epsilon}{2}$ and $|a_n - L| < \frac{\epsilon}{2}$.

Now,

$|a_m - a_n| = |a_m - L + L - a_n| \le |a_m - L| + |a_n - L|$

$< \frac{\epsilon}{2} + \frac{\epsilon}{2} = \epsilon$ whenever $m > N$ and $n > N$.

75. Consider the two subsequences $a_{k(n)}$ and $a_{i(n)}$, where $\lim_{n\to\infty} a_{k(n)} = L_1$, $\lim_{n\to\infty} a_{i(n)} = L_2$, and $L_1 \neq L_2$. Given an $\epsilon > 0$ there corresponds an N_1 such that for $k(n) > N_1$, $|a_{k(n)} - L_1| < \epsilon$, and an N_2 such that for $i(n) > N_2$, $|a_{i(n)} - L_2| < \epsilon$. Assume a_n converges. Let $N = \max\{N_1, N_2\}$. Then for $n > N$, we have that $|a_n - L_1| < \epsilon$ and $|a_n - L_2| < \epsilon$ for infinitely many n. This implies that $\lim_{n\to\infty} a_n = L_1$ and $\lim_{n\to\infty} a_n = L_2$ where $L_1 \neq L_2$. Since the limit of a sequence is unique (by Exercise 74), a_n does not converge and hence diverges.

Section 10.2

Quick Review 10.2

1. $2^n e^{2x}$ **3.** $3^x(\ln 3)^n$

5. $n!$ **7.** $\dfrac{2n(x-a)^{n-1}}{(n-1)!}$

9. $\dfrac{(x+a)2^{n-1}}{(2n-1)!}$

Exercises 10.2

1. $P_4(x) = -\frac{1}{8}x^4 + \frac{1}{2}x^2 + 1$

3. $P_5(x) = -\frac{x^5}{2^6} + \frac{x^4}{2^5} - \frac{x^3}{2^4} + \frac{x^2}{2^3} - \frac{x}{2^2} + \frac{1}{2}, \sum_{n=0}^{\infty}(-1)^n\frac{x^n}{2^{n+1}}$

5. $2x - \frac{4x^3}{3} + \frac{4x^5}{15} - \cdots + (-1)^n\frac{(2x)^{2n+1}}{(2n+1)!} + \cdots$ converges for all real x

7. $x^2 - \frac{x^6}{3} + \frac{x^{10}}{5} - \cdots + (-1)^n\frac{x^{4n+2}}{2n+1} + \cdots$ converges for $-1 \le x \le 1$

9. $1 - \frac{x^2}{2^2 2!} + \frac{x^4}{2^4 4!} - \frac{x^6}{2^6 6!} + \cdots + (-1)^n\frac{x^{2n}}{2^{2n}(2n)!} + \cdots$ The series converges for all real x.

11. $x + x^4 + x^7 + \cdots + x^{3n+1} + \cdots$ converges for $-1 < x < 1$

13. $\sum_{n=0}^{\infty}(-1)^n\frac{(x-2)^n}{3^{n+1}} = \frac{1}{3} - \frac{x-2}{3^2} + \frac{(x-2)^2}{3^3} - \frac{(x-2)^3}{3^4} + \cdots$

15. (a) $4 - 2x + x^3$

(b) $3 + (x-1) + 3(x-1)^2 + (x-1)^3$

17. (a) 0

(b) $1 + 4(x-1) + 6(x-1)^2 + 4(x-1)^3$

19. $P_0(x) = \frac{\sqrt{2}}{2}$

$P_1(x) = \frac{\sqrt{2}}{2} + \left(\frac{\sqrt{2}}{2}\right)\left(x - \frac{\pi}{4}\right)$

$P_2(x) = \frac{\sqrt{2}}{2} + \left(\frac{\sqrt{2}}{2}\right)\left(x - \frac{\pi}{4}\right) - \left(\frac{\sqrt{2}}{4}\right)\left(x - \frac{\pi}{4}\right)^2$

$P_3(x) = \frac{\sqrt{2}}{2} + \left(\frac{\sqrt{2}}{2}\right)\left(x - \frac{\pi}{4}\right) - \left(\frac{\sqrt{2}}{4}\right)\left(x - \frac{\pi}{4}\right)^2 - \left(\frac{\sqrt{2}}{12}\right)\left(x - \frac{\pi}{4}\right)^3$

21. $P_0(x) = 2$

$P_1(x) = 2 + \frac{x-4}{4}$

$P_2(x) = 2 + \frac{x-4}{4} - \frac{(x-4)^2}{64}$

$P_3(x) = 2 + \frac{x-4}{4} - \frac{(x-4)^2}{64} + \frac{(x-4)^3}{512}$

23. (a) $P_3(x) = 4 - (x-1) + \frac{3}{2}(x-1)^2 + \frac{1}{3}(x-1)^3$

$f(1.2) \approx P_3(1.2) \approx 3.863$

(b) For f', $P_2(x) = -1 + 3(x-1) + (x-1)^2$

$f'(1.2) \approx P_2(1.2) = -0.36$

25. (a) $1 + \frac{x}{2} + \frac{x^2}{8} + \cdots + \frac{x^n}{2^n \cdot n!} + \cdots$

(b) $1 + \frac{x}{2!} + \frac{x^2}{3!} + \cdots + \frac{x^n}{(n+1)!} + \cdots$

(c) $g'(1) = 1$ and from the series,

$g'(1) = \frac{1}{2!} + \frac{2}{3!} + \frac{3}{4!} + \cdots + \frac{n}{(n+1)!} + \cdots = \sum_{n=1}^{\infty}\frac{n}{(n+1)!}$

27. (a) $1 + \frac{x}{2} - \frac{x^2}{8} + \frac{x^3}{16}$

(b) $1 + \frac{x^2}{2} - \frac{x^4}{8} + \frac{x^6}{16}$

(c) $5 + x + \frac{x^3}{6} - \frac{x^5}{40}$

29. 27 terms (or, up to and including the 52nd-degree term)

31. (1) $\sin x$ is odd and $\cos x$ is even

(2) $\sin 0 = 0$ and $\cos 0 = 1$

33. 1/24

35. (a)

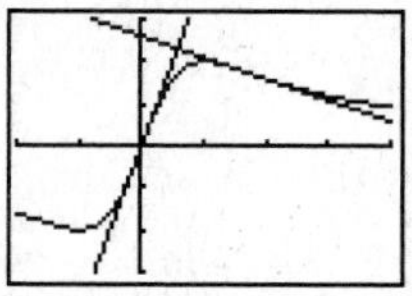

[–2, 4] by [–3, 3]

(b) $f''(a)$ must be 0 because of the inflection point, so the second degree term in the Taylor series of f at $x = a$ is zero.

37. True. The constant term is $f(0)$.

39. E **41.** C

43. (a) $1 - \frac{x^2}{3!} + \frac{x^4}{5!} - \cdots + \frac{(-1)^n x^{2n}}{(2n+1)!} + \cdots$

(b) Because f is undefined at $x = 0$

(c) $k = 1$

45. (a) Differentiate 3 times.

(b) Differentiate k times and let $x = 0$.

(c) $\dfrac{m(m-1)(m-2)\cdots(m-k+1)}{k!}$

(d) $f(0) = 1$, $f'(0) = m$, and we're done by part (c).

Section 10.3

Quick Review 10.3

1. 2 **3.** 1 **5.** 7

7. No **9.** Yes

Exercises 10.3

1. $1 - 2x + 2x^2 - \frac{4}{3}x^3 + \frac{2}{3}x^4$; $f(0.2) \approx 0.6704$

3. $-5x + \frac{5}{6}x^3$; $f(0.2) \approx -0.9933$

5. $1 + 2x + 3x^2 + 4x^3 + 5x^4$; $f(0.2) \approx 1.56$

7. $x + x^2 + \frac{x^3}{2!} + \frac{x^4}{3!} + \cdots + \frac{x^{n+1}}{n!} + \cdots$

9. $x^2 - \frac{x^4}{3} + \frac{2x^6}{45} - \cdots + (-1)^n \frac{2^{2n+1}x^{2n+2}}{(2n+2)!} + \cdots$

11. $P_7(x)$ 13. $\frac{(2|x|)^7}{1 - 2x}$

15. If $M = 1$ and $r = 1$ then $|\cos^{(n+1)}(t)| \le Mr^{n+1} = 1$ for all t, since all derivatives of the cosine function are sine or cosine functions bounded between -1 and 1.

17. If $M = 1$ and $r = 8$, then $|f^{(n+1)}(t)| \le Mr^{n+1} = 8^{n+1}$ for all t. since the $(n + 1)$st derivatives of f is a sine or cosine function (bounded between -1 and 1), times 8^{n+1} (the result of $(n + 1)$ applications of the Chain Rule).

19. Using the theorem, $-0.56 < x < 0.56$ Graphically, $-0.57 < x < 0.57$

21. $|\text{Error}| < 1.67 \times 10^{-10}$ $x < \sin x$ for negative values of x.

23. $|\text{Error}| < 1.842 \times 10^{-4}$

25. All of the derivatives of $\cosh x$ are either $\cosh x$ or $\sinh x$. For any real x, $\cosh x$ and $\sinh x$ are both bounded by $e^{|x|}$. So for any real x, let $M = e^{|x|}$ and $r = 1$ in the Remainder Estimation Theorem. It follows that the series converges to $\cosh x$ for all real values of x.

27. **(a)** 0
(b) $-x^2/2$
(c) The graphs of the linear and quadratic approximations fit the graph of the function near $x = 0$.

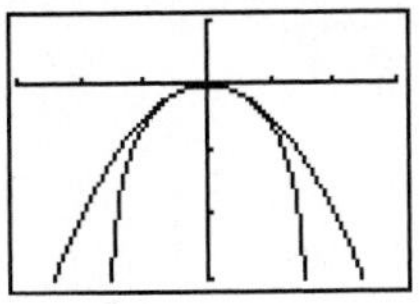

[–3, 3] by [–3, 1]

29. **(a)** 1
(b) $1 + \frac{x^2}{2}$
(c) The graphs of the linear and quadratic approximations fit the graph of the function near $x = 0$.

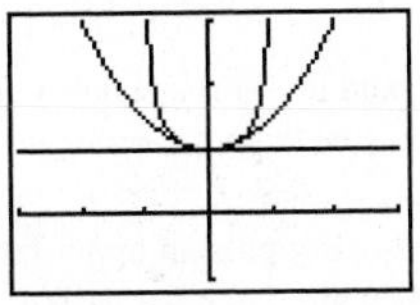

[–3, 3] by [–1, 3]

31. **(a)** x **(b)** x
(c) The graphs of the linear and quadratic and approximations fit the graph of the function near $x = 0$.

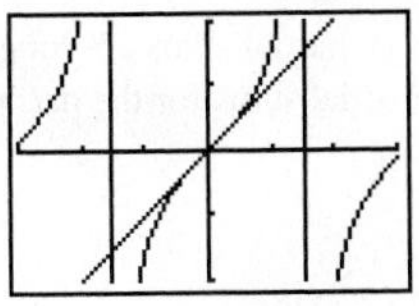

[–3, 3] by [–2, 2]

33. $|\text{Error}| < 4.61 \times 10^{-6}$, by Remainder Estimation Theorem (actual maximum error is $\approx 4.251 \times 10^{-6}$)

35. **(a)** No
(b) Yes. $2 + x - \frac{x^3}{3} + \frac{x^5}{10} - \cdots + \frac{(-1)^{n+1}x^{2n-1}}{[(2n-1)(n-1)!]} + \cdots$
(c) For all real values of x. This is assured by Theorem 2 of Section 10.1, because the series for e^{-x^2} converges for all real values of x.

37. **(a)** $\tan x$ **(b)** $\sec x$

39. True. The coefficient of x is $f'(0)$.

41. E 43. A

45. **(a)** It works.
(b) Let $P = \pi + x$ where x is the error in the original estimate. Then
$$P + \sin P = (\pi + x) + \sin(\pi + x)$$
$$= (\pi + x) - \sin x = \pi + (x - \sin x)$$
But by the Remainder Estimation Theorem, $|x - \sin x| < \frac{|x|^3}{6}$.
Therefore, the difference between the new estimate $P + \sin P$ and π is less than $\frac{|x|^3}{6}$.

47. Note that $f(-1) = \frac{1}{2}$. The partial sums of the Maclaurin series $\sum_{n=0}^{\infty} (-1)^n$ are 1, 0, 1, 0, 1, and so on, so the remainders are $-\frac{1}{2}, \frac{1}{2}, -\frac{1}{2}, \frac{1}{2}$, and so on. Thus
$$R_n(-1) = \frac{(-1)^{n+1}}{2}, \text{ and } \lim_{n\to\infty}\left(\frac{(-1)^{n+1}}{2}\right) \ne 0.$$

49. The derivative is $(ae^{ax})(\cos bx + i \sin bx) + (e^{ax})(-b \sin bx + ib \cos bx)$
$= a[e^{ax}(\cos bx + i \sin bx)] + ib[e^{ax}(\cos bx + ib \sin bx)]$
$= (a + ib)e^{(a+ib)x}$.

Quick Quiz (Sections 10.1 and 10.3)

1. D 3. E

Section 10.4

Quick Review 10.4

1. $|x|$ 3. 0

5. $\frac{|2x + 1|}{2}$

7. $a_n = 5^n$, $b_n = n^5$, $N = 6$

9. $a_n = \frac{1}{10^n}$, $b_n = \frac{1}{n!}$, $N = 25$

Exercises 10.4

1. $-6 < x < -4$; The graph of the function $y = \frac{-1}{x + 4}$ and $P_5(x)$ illustrates the support.

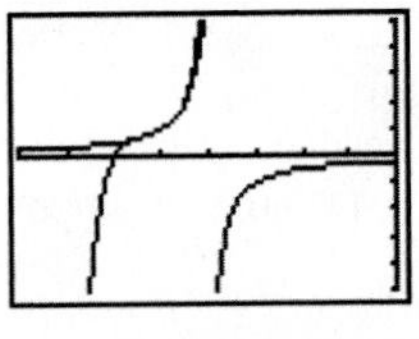

[−8, 0] by [−5, 5]

3. $\frac{x^{3n}}{2n! + 1} \le \frac{x^{3n}}{n!} \le \frac{(x^3)^n}{n!}$ and $\sum_{n=0}^{\infty} \frac{(x^3)^n}{n!}$ is the Taylor series for e^{x^3} which converges for all x.

5. $\left|\frac{(\cos x)^n}{n!+1}\right| \le \left|\frac{(\cos x)^n}{n!}\right| \le \frac{1}{n!}$ and $\sum_{n=0}^{\infty}\frac{1}{n!}$ converges to e.

7. 1 **9.** 1/4 **11.** 10 **13.** 3

15. 5 **17.** 0

19. 1/2 **21.** 1

23. Interval: $-1 < x < 3$ Sum: $-\frac{4}{x^2 - 2x - 3}$

25. Interval: $0 < x < 16$ Sum: $\frac{2}{4 - \sqrt{x}}$

27. Interval: $-2 < x < 2$ Sum: $\frac{3}{4 - x^2}$

29. Diverges (nth-Term Test)

31. Converges (Ratio Test)

33. Converges (Ratio Test, Direct Comparison Test)

35. Converges (Ratio Test)

37. Converges (Ratio Test)

39. Converges (geometric series)

41. Diverges (nth-Term Test, Ratio Test)

43. Converges (Ratio Test)

45. One possible answer:

$\sum \frac{1}{n}$ diverges (see Exploration 1 in this section) even though $\lim_{n\to\infty} \frac{1}{n} = 0$.

47. Almost, but the Ratio Test won't determine whether there is convergence or divergence at the endpoints of the interval.

49. 3 **51.** 1

53. $-1/\ln 2$

55. True. See Theorem 8.

57. B **59.** E

61. **(a)** For $k \le N$, it's obvious that

$$a_1 + \cdots + a_k \le a_1 + \cdots + a_N + \sum_{n=N+1}^{\infty} c_n$$

For all $k > N$,

$$\begin{aligned} a_1 + \cdots + a_k &= a_1 + \cdots + a_N + a_{N+1} + \cdots + a_k \\ &\le a_1 + \cdots + a_N + c_{N+1} + \cdots + c_k \\ &\le a_1 + \cdots + a_N + \sum_{n=N+1}^{\infty} c_n. \end{aligned}$$

(b) Since all of the a_n are nonnegative, the partial sums of the series form a nondecreasing sequence of real numbers. Part (a) shows that the sequence is bounded above, so it must converge to a limit.

63. Answers will vary.

Section 10.5

Quick Review 10.5

1. Converges, $p > 1$

3. Diverges, comparison test with integral of $1/x$

5. Diverges, limit comparison test with integral of $1/\sqrt{x}$

7. Yes **9.** No

Exercises 10.5

1. Use $f(x) = 1/\sqrt[3]{x}$, diverges

3. $S_1 = 1, S_2 = 3/2, S_3 = 11/6, S_4 = 25/12, S_5 = 137/60$. $S_6 = 49/20$

5. Diverges, compare with $\sum_{n=1}^{\infty}(3/n)$

7. Diverges **9.** Diverges

11. Diverges **13.** Diverges

15. Converges **17.** Diverges

19. Diverges **21.** Diverges

23. Converges conditionally; 0.0101

25. Converges conditionally; ≈ 0.00217

27. Diverges

29. Converges conditionally

31. Converges conditionally

33. The positive terms $2 + \frac{4}{3^2} + \frac{6}{5^2} + \cdots + \frac{2n+2}{(2n+1)^2} + \cdots$ diverge to ∞ and the negative term $-\frac{3}{2^2} - \frac{5}{4^2} - \frac{7}{6^2} - \cdots - \frac{2n+1}{(2n)^2} - \cdots$ diverge to $-\infty$.

Answers will vary. Here is one possibility.

(a) Add positive terms until the partial sum is greater than 2. Then add negative terms until the partial sum is less than -2. Then add positive terms until the partial sum is greater than 4. Then add negative terms until the partial sum is less than -4. Repeat this process so that the partial sums swing arbitrarily far in both directions.

(b) Add positive terms until the partial sum is greater than 4. Then add negative terms until the partial sum is less than 4. Continue in this manner indefinitely, always closing in on 4.

35. **(a)** $(-1, 1)$ **(b)** $(-1, 1)$ **(c)** None

37. **(a)** $(-1/2, 0)$ **(b)** $(-1/2, 0)$ **(c)** None

39. **(a)** $(-8, 12)$ **(b)** $(-8, 12)$ **(c)** None

41. **(a)** $[-3, 3]$ **(b)** $[-3, 3]$ **(c)** None

43. **(a)** $(-8, 2)$ **(b)** $(-8, 2)$ **(c)** None

45. **(a)** $(-3, 3)$ **(b)** $(-3, 3)$ **(c)** None

47. **(a)** $(1/2, 3/2)$ **(b)** $(1/2, 3/2)$ **(c)** None

49. **(a)** $(-\pi - 1, -\pi + 1)$ **(b)** $(-\pi - 1, -\pi + 1)$ **(c)** At $x = -\pi - 1$

51. $40.554 < \text{sum} < 41.555$

53.

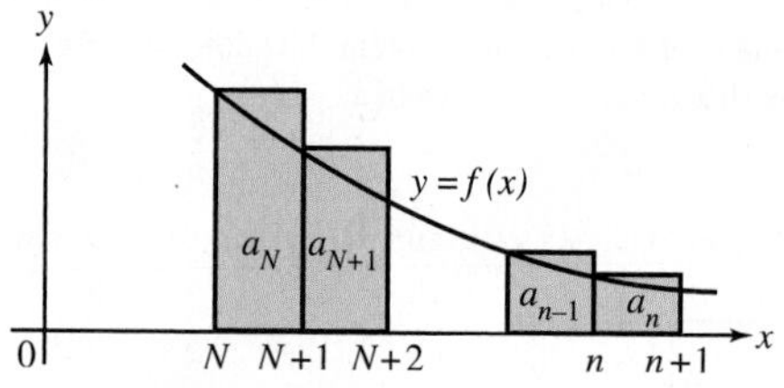

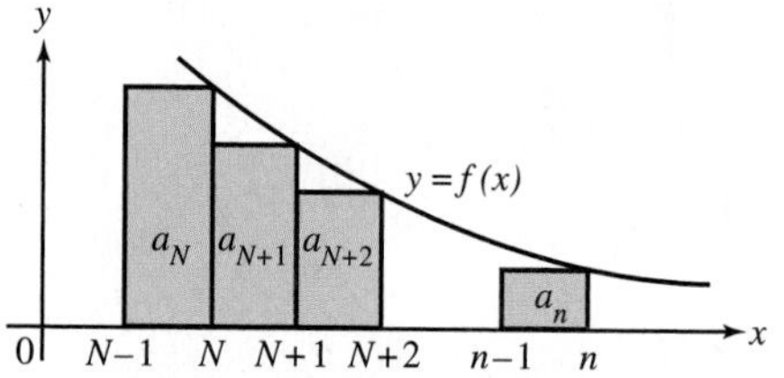

Comparing areas in the figures, we have for all $n \ge N$,

$$\int_N^{n+1} f(x)\,dx < a_N + \cdots + a_n < a_N + \int_N^n f(x)\,dx.$$

If the integral diverges, it must go to infinity, and the first inequality forces the partial sums of the series to go to infinity as well, so the series is divergent.

If the integral converges, then the second inequality puts an upper bound on the partial sums of the series, and since they are a nondecreasing sequence, they must converge to a finite sum for the series.

55. Radius is $\frac{3}{e}$ (about 1.104).

57. Possible answer: $\sum \frac{1}{n \ln n}$

This series diverges by the Integral Test, but its partial sums are roughly $\ln(\ln n)$, so they are much smaller than the partial sums for the harmonic series, which are about $\ln n$.

59. **(a)** Diverges

(b) $S = \sum_{n=1}^{\infty}\frac{3n}{3n^3 + n} = \sum_{n=1}^{\infty}\frac{3}{3n^2+1}$ which converges.

61. Convergent for $-1/2 \le x < 1/2$. Use the Ratio Test, Direct Comparison Test, and Alternating Series Test.

63. Use the Alternating Series Test.

65. (a) It fails to satisfy $u_n \ge u_{n+1}$ for all $n \ge N$.
(b) The sum is $-1/2$.

67. True. The term $a_{101} = \dfrac{(-1)^{101}}{(101)^2}$ is negative.

69. A **71.** B

73. (a) Converges **(b)** Converges **(c)** Converges

Quick Quiz (Sections 10.4 and 10.5)

1. E **3.** D

Review Exercises

1. (a) ∞ **(b)** All real numbers **(c)** All real numbers **(d)** None
2. (a) 3 **(b)** $[-7, -1]$ **(c)** $(-7, -1)$ **(d)** At $x = -7$
3. (a) $\dfrac{3}{2}$ **(b)** $(-1/2, 5/2)$ **(c)** $(-1/2, 5/2)$ **(d)** None
4. (a) ∞ **(b)** All real numbers **(c)** All real numbers **(d)** None
5. (a) $1/3$ **(b)** $[0, 2/3]$ **(c)** $[0, 2/3]$ **(d)** None
6. (a) 1 **(b)** $(-1, 1)$ **(c)** $(-1, 1)$ **(d)** None
7. (a) 1 **(b)** $(-3/2, 1/2)$ **(c)** $(-3/2, 1/2)$ **(d)** None
8. (a) ∞ **(b)** All real numbers **(c)** All real numbers **(d)** None
9. (a) 1 **(b)** $[-1, 1)$ **(c)** $(-1, 1)$ **(d)** At $x = -1$
10. (a) $1/e$ **(b)** $[-1/e, 1/e]$ **(c)** $[-1/e, 1/e]$ **(d)** None
11. (a) $\sqrt{3}$ **(b)** $(-\sqrt{3}, \sqrt{3})$ **(c)** $(-\sqrt{3}, \sqrt{3})$ **(d)** None
12. (a) 1 **(b)** $[0, 2]$ **(c)** $(0, 2)$ **(d)** At $x = 0$ and $x = 2$
13. (a) 0 **(b)** $x = 0$ only **(c)** $x = 0$ **(d)** None
14. (a) $1/10$ **(b)** $[-1/10, 1/10)$ **(c)** $(-1/10, 1/10)$ **(d)** At $x = -1/10$
15. (a) 0 **(b)** $x = 0$ only **(c)** $x = 0$ **(d)** None
16. (a) $\sqrt{3}$ **(b)** $(-\sqrt{3}, \sqrt{3})$ **(c)** $(-\sqrt{3}, \sqrt{3})$ **(d)** None
17. $f(x) = 1/(1 + x)$ evaluated at $x = 1/4$; Sum $= 4/5$
18. $f(x) = \ln(1 + x)$ evaluated at $x = 2/3$; Sum $= \ln(5/3)$.
19. $f(x) = \sin x$ evaluated at $x = \pi$; Sum $= 0$.
20. $f(x) = \cos x$ evaluated at $x = \pi/3$; Sum $= 1/2$.
21. $f(x) = e^x$ evaluated at $x = \ln 2$; Sum $= 2$.
22. $f(x) = \tan^{-1} x$ evaluated at $x = 1/\sqrt{3}$; Sum $= \pi/6$.
23. $1 + 6x + 36x^2 + \cdots + (6x)^n + \cdots$
24. $1 - x^3 + x^6 - \cdots + (-1)^n x^{3n} + \cdots$
25. $1 - 2x^2 + x^9$
26. $4x + 4x^2 + 4x^3 + \cdots + 4x^{n+1} + \cdots$
27. $\pi x - \dfrac{(\pi x)^3}{3!} + \dfrac{(\pi x)^5}{5!} - \cdots + (-1)^n \dfrac{(\pi x)^{2n+1}}{(2n+1)!} + \cdots$
28. $\dfrac{-2x}{3} + \dfrac{4x^3}{81} - \dfrac{4x^5}{3645} + \cdots + \dfrac{(-1)^{n+1}}{(2n+1)!}\left(\dfrac{2x}{3}\right)^{2n+1} + \cdots$
29. $-\dfrac{x^3}{3!} + \dfrac{x^5}{5!} - \dfrac{x^7}{7!} + \cdots + (-1)^n \dfrac{x^{2n+1}}{(2n+1)!} + \cdots$
30. $1 + \dfrac{x^2}{2!} + \dfrac{x^4}{4!} + \cdots + \dfrac{x^{2n}}{(2n)!} + \cdots$
31. $1 - \dfrac{5x}{2!} + \dfrac{(5x)^2}{4!} - \cdots + (-1)^n \dfrac{(5x)^n}{(2n)!} + \cdots$
32. $1 + \dfrac{\pi x}{2} + \dfrac{\pi^2 x^2}{8} + \cdots + \dfrac{1}{n!}\left(\dfrac{\pi x}{2}\right)^n + \cdots$
33. $x - x^3 + \dfrac{x^5}{2!} - \dfrac{x^7}{3!} + \cdots + (-1)^n \dfrac{x^{2n+1}}{n!} + \cdots$
34. $3x - \dfrac{(3x)^3}{3} + \dfrac{(3x)^5}{5} - \cdots + (-1)^n \dfrac{(3x)^{2n+1}}{2n+1} + \cdots$
35. $-2x - 2x^2 - \dfrac{8x^3}{3} - \cdots - \dfrac{(2x)^n}{n} - \cdots$
36. $-x^2 - \dfrac{x^3}{2} - \dfrac{x^4}{3} - \cdots - \dfrac{x^{n+1}}{n} - \cdots$
37. $1 + (x - 2) + (x - 2)^2 + (x - 2)^3 + \cdots + (x - 2)^n + \cdots$
38. $2 + 7(x + 1) - 5(x + 1)^2 + (x + 1)^3$
(Finite. General term for $n \ge 4$ is 0)
39. $\dfrac{1}{3} - \dfrac{x - 3}{9} + \dfrac{(x - 3)^2}{27} - \dfrac{(x - 3)^3}{81} + \cdots + (-1)^n \dfrac{(x - 3)^n}{3^{n+1}} + \cdots$
40. $-(x - \pi) + \dfrac{(x - \pi)^3}{3!} - \dfrac{(x - \pi)^5}{5!} + \dfrac{(x - \pi)^7}{7!} - \cdots$
$+ (-1)^{n+1} \dfrac{(x - \pi)^{2n+1}}{(2n + 1)!} + \cdots$
41. Diverges. It is -5 times the harmonic series.
42. Converges conditionally. Alternating Series Test and $p = 1/2$.
43. Converges absolutely. Direct Comparison Test with $1/n^2$.
44. Converges absolutely. Ratio Test
45. Converges conditionally. Alternating Series Test and Direct Comparison Test with $1/n$.
46. Converges absolutely. Integral Test
47. Converges absolutely. Ratio Test
48. Converges absolutely. nth-Root Test or Ratio Test.
49. Diverges. nth-Term Test for Divergence
50. Converges absolutely. Direct Comparison Test with $1/n^{3/2}$.
51. Converges absolutely. Limit Comparison Test with $1/n^2$.
52. Diverges. nth-Term Test for Divergence
53. $1/6$ **54.** -1
55. (a) $P_3(x) = 1 + 4(x - 3) + 3(x - 3)^2 + 2(x - 3)^3$
$f(3.2) \approx P_3(3.2) = 1.936$
(b) For f': $P_2(x) = 4 + 6(x - 3) + 6(x - 3)^2$
$f'(2.7) \approx P_2(2.7) = 2.74$
(c) It underestimates the values, since the graph of f is concave up near $x = 3$.
56. (a) $f(4) = 7$ and $f'''(4) = -12$
(b) For f': $P_2(x) = -3 + 10(x - 4) - 6(x - 4)^2$
$f'(4.3) \approx P_2(4.3) = -0.54$
(c) $7(x - 4) - \dfrac{3}{2}(x - 4)^2 + \dfrac{5}{3}(x - 4)^3 - \dfrac{1}{2}(x - 4)^4$
(d) No. One would need the entire Taylor series for $f(x)$, and it would have to converge to $f(x)$ at $x = 3$.
57. (a) $\dfrac{5x}{2} - \dfrac{5x^3}{48} + \dfrac{x^5}{768} - \cdots + (-1)^n \dfrac{5}{(2n + 1)!}\left(\dfrac{x}{2}\right)^{2n+1} + \cdots$
(b) All real numbers. Use the Ratio Test.
(c) Note that the absolute value of $f^{(n)}(x)$ is bounded by $5/2^n$ for all x and all $n = 1, 2, 3, \ldots$ So if $-2 < x < 2$, the truncation error using P_n is bounded by $\dfrac{5}{2^{n+1}} \cdot \dfrac{2^{n+1}}{(n + 1)!} = \dfrac{5}{(n + 1)!}$. To make this less than 0.1 requires $n \ge 4$. So, two nonzero terms (up through degree 4) are needed.
58. (a) $1 + 2x + 4x^2 + 8x^3 + \cdots + (2x)^n + \cdots$
(b) $(-1/2, 1/2)$. The series for $1/(1 - t)$ is known to converge for $-1 < t < 1$, so by substituting $t = 2x$, we find the resulting series converges for $-1 < 2x < 1$.
(c) Possible answer:
$f(-1/4) = 2/3$, so one percent is approximately 0.0067. It takes 7 terms (up through degree 6). This can be found by trial and error.
59. (a) $1/e$ **(b)** $-5/18 \approx -0.278$
(c) By the Alternating Series Estimation Theorem, the error is bounded by the size of the next term, which is $32/243$, or about 0.132.
60. (a) $1 - (x - 3) + (x - 3)^2 - (x - 3)^3 + \cdots + (-1)^n (x - 3)^n + \cdots$
(b) $(x - 3) - \dfrac{(x - 3)^2}{2} + \dfrac{(x - 3)^3}{3} - \dfrac{(x - 3)^4}{4} + \cdots$
$+ (-1)^n \dfrac{(x - 3)^{n+1}}{n + 1} + \cdots$

(c) Evaluate at $x = 3.5$. This is an alternating series. By the Alternating Series Estimation Theorem, since the size of the third term is $1/24 < 0.05$, the first two terms will suffice. The estimate for $\ln(3/2)$ is 0.375.

61. (a) $1 - 2x^2 + 2x^4 - \frac{4x^6}{3} + \cdots + (-1)^n \frac{2^n x^{2n}}{n!} + \cdots$
(b) All real numbers. Use the Ratio Test.
(c) This is an alternating series. The difference will be bounded by the magnitude of the fifth term, which is $\frac{(2x^2)^4}{4!} = \frac{2x^8}{3}$.
Since $-0.6 \le x \le 0.6$, this term is less than $\frac{2(0.6)^8}{3}$ which is less than 0.02.

62. (a) $x^2 - x^3 + x^4 - x^5 + \cdots + (-1)^n x^{n+2} + \cdots$
(b) No. The partial sums form the sequence 1, 0, 1, 0, 1, 0, ... which has no limit.

63. (a) $\frac{x^3}{3} - \frac{x^7}{7(3!)} + \frac{x^{11}}{11(5!)} + \cdots + \frac{(-1)^n x^{4n+3}}{(4n+3)(2n+1)!} + \cdots$
(b) The first two nonzero terms suffice (through degree 7).
(c) 0.31026830
(d) Within 1.5×10^{-7}

64. (a) 0.88566
(b) $41/60 \approx 0.68333$
(c) Since f is concave up, the trapezoids used to estimate the area lie above the curve, and the estimate is too large.
(d) Since all the derivatives are positive (and $x > 0$), the remainder, $R_n(x)$, must be positive. This means that $P_n(x)$ is smaller than $f(x)$.
(e) $e - 2 \approx 0.71828$

65. (a) Because $[\$1000(1.08)^{-n}](1.08)^n = \$1000$ will be available after n years.
(b) Assume that the first payment goes to the charity at the end of the first year. Then, $1000(1.08)^{-1} + 1000(1.08)^{-2} + 1000(1.08)^{-3} + \cdots$
(c) This is a geometric series with sum equal to \$12,500. This represents the amount which must be invested today in order to completely fund the perpetuity forever.

66. \$16,666.67 [Again, assuming first payment at end of year.]

67. (a) $0\left(\frac{1}{2}\right) + 1\left(\frac{1}{2}\right)^2 + 2\left(\frac{1}{2}\right)^3 + 3\left(\frac{1}{2}\right)^4 + \cdots$
(b) $1 + 2x + 3x^2 + 4x^3 + \cdots$
(c) $x^2 + 2x^3 + 3x^4 + 4x^5 + \cdots$
(d) The expected payoff of the game is \$1.

68. (a) $\frac{b^2\sqrt{3}}{4} + \frac{3b^2\sqrt{3}}{4^2} + \frac{3^2b^2\sqrt{3}}{4^3} + \cdots$
(b) $b^2\sqrt{3}$. Note that this is the same as the area of the original triangle!
(c) No. For example, let $b = 1/2$ and set the base of the triangle along the x-axis from (0, 0) to (1, 0). The points removed by the construction are all of the form $(k/2^n, 0)$ so points of the form $(x, 0)$ with x irrational (among others) still remain. The same sort of thing is happening along the other two sides of the triangle (and, in fact, along any of the sides of any of the smaller blue triangles in the figure). While there are infinitely many points remaining throughout the triangle, they paradoxically take up zero area. (This figure, the Sierpinski triangle, is well known to students of fractal geometry.)

69. $\frac{1}{(1-x)^2} = 1 + 2x + 3x^2 + 4x^3 + 5x^4 + \cdots$; Substitute $x = 1/2$ to get the desired result.

70. (b) Solve $x = \frac{2x^2}{(x-1)^3}$, $x \approx 2.769$.

71. (a) Computing the coefficients,
$f(1) = \frac{1}{2}$
$f'(x) = -(x+1)^{-2}$, so $f'(1) = -\frac{1}{4}$
$f''(x) = 2(x+1)^{-3}$, so $\frac{f''(1)}{2!} = \frac{1}{8}$
$f'''(x) = -6(x+1)^{-4}$, so $\frac{f'''(1)}{3!} = -\frac{1}{16}$
In general, $f^{(n)}(x) = \frac{(-1)^n n!}{(x+1)^{n+1}}$, so $\frac{f^{(n)}}{n!} = \frac{(-1)^n}{2^{n+1}}$
So $f(x) = \frac{1}{2} - \frac{x-1}{4} + \frac{(x-1)^2}{8} + \cdots + (-1)^n \frac{(x-1)^n}{2^{n+1}} + \cdots$
(b) Ratio Test for absolute convergence:
$\lim_{n\to\infty} \frac{|x-1|^{n+1}}{2^{n+2}} \cdot \frac{2^{n+1}}{|x-1|^n} = \frac{|x-1|}{2}$
$\frac{|x-1|}{2} < 1 \Rightarrow -1 < x < 3$. The series converges absolutely on $(-1, 3)$.
At $x = -1$, the series is $\sum_{n=0}^{\infty} \frac{1}{2}$, which diverges by the nth-Term Test.
At $x = 3$, the series is $\sum_{n=0}^{\infty} (-1)^n \frac{1}{2}$, which diverges by the nth-Term Test.
The interval of convergence is $(-1, 3)$.
(c) $P_3(x) = \frac{1}{2} - \frac{x-1}{4} + \frac{(x-1)^2}{8} - (x-1)^{3/16}$
$P_3(0.5) = \frac{1}{2} - \frac{0.5-1}{4} + \frac{(0.5-1)^2}{8} - \frac{(0.5-1)^3}{16}$
$= 0.664025$

72. (a) Ratio test for absolute convergence:
$\lim_{n\to\infty} \frac{(n+1)|x|^{n+1}}{2^{n+1}} \cdot \frac{2^n}{n|x|^n} = \lim_{n\to\infty} \frac{n+1}{n} \cdot \frac{|x|}{2} = \frac{|x|}{2}$
$\frac{|x|}{2} < 1 \Rightarrow -2 < x < 2$
The series converges absolutely on $(-2, 2)$.
The series diverges at both endpoints by the nth-Term Test, since $\lim_{n\to\infty} n \ne 0$ and $\lim_{n\to\infty} (-1)^n n \ne 0$.
The interval of convergence is $(-2, 2)$.
(b) The series converges at -1 and forms an alternating series: $-\frac{1}{2} + \frac{2}{4} - \frac{3}{8} + \frac{4}{16} + \cdots (-1)^n \frac{n}{2^n} + \cdots$. The nth term of this series decreases in absolute value to 0, so the truncation error after 9 terms is less than the absolute value of the 10th term. Thus error $< \frac{10}{2^{10}} < 0.01$.

73. (a) $P_1(x) = -1 + 2x$ **(b)** $P_2(x) = -1 + 2x - \frac{3}{2}x^2$
(c) $P_3(x) = -1 + 2x - \frac{3}{2}x^2 + \frac{2}{3}x^3$ **(d)** -0.106

CHAPTER 11

Section 11.1

Quick Review 11.1

1. $y = 2x + 1$ **3.** $x^2 + y^2 = 1$
5. $y^2 = 1 + x^2$
7. $y = 2x^2 - 1$
9. $y = \sqrt{1 - x^2}$

Exercises 11.1

1. Yes, y is a function of x.
$y = 2x - 9$

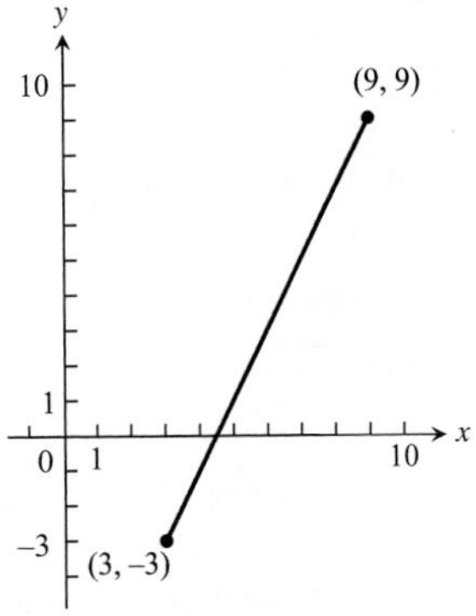

3. Yes, y is a function of x.
$y = \sqrt{x^2 + 1}$

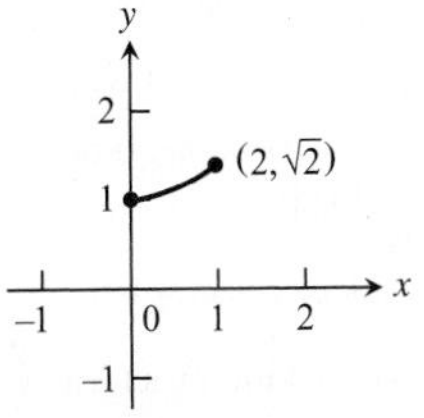

5. Yes, y is a function of x.
$y = 1 - 2x^2$

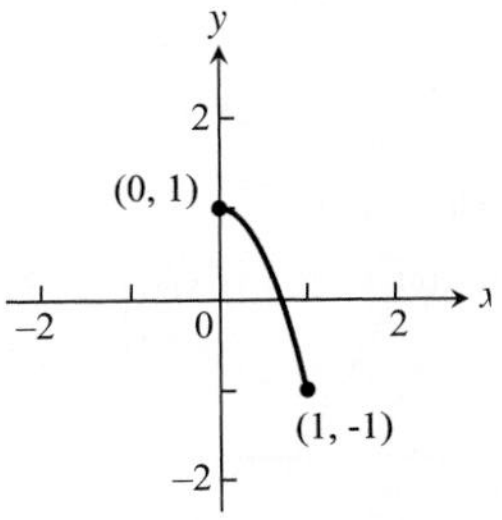

7. (a) $-\dfrac{1}{2}\tan t$ **(b)** $-\dfrac{1}{8}\sec^3 t$ **9. (a)** $\sqrt{3 + \dfrac{3}{t}}$ **(b)** $-\dfrac{\sqrt{3}}{t^{3/2}}$

11. (a) $\dfrac{3t^2}{2t - 3}$ **(b)** $\dfrac{6t^2 - 18t}{(2t - 3)^3}$ **13. (a)** $\sin t$ **(b)** $\cos^3 t$ **15. (a)** 4 **(b)** 0

17. (a)

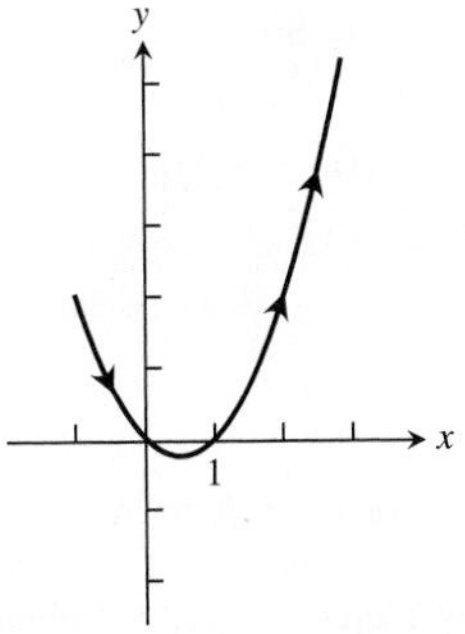

(b) $(0.5, -20.25)$

(c) We seek to minimize y as a function of t, so we compute $dy/dt = 2t + 1$, which is negative for $-2 \le t < -0.5$ and positive for $-0.5 < t \le 2$. There is a relative minimum at $t = -0.5$, where $(x, y) = (0.5, -0.25)$.

19. (a)

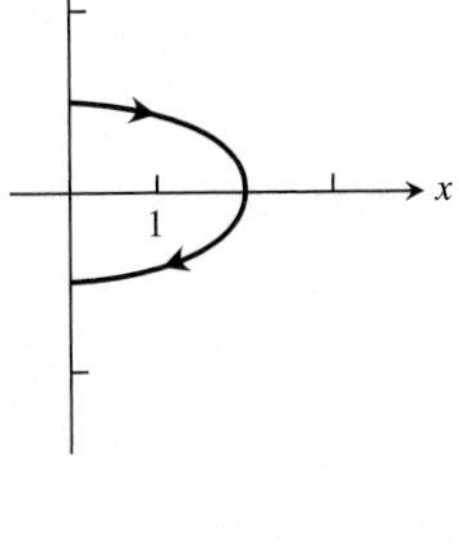

(b) $(2, 0)$

(c) We seek to maximize x as a function of t, so we compute $dx/dt = 2\cos t$, which is positive for $0 \le t < \pi/2$ and negative for $\pi/2 < t \le \pi$. There is a relative maximum at $t = \pi/2$, where $(x, y) = (2, 0)$.

21. (a)

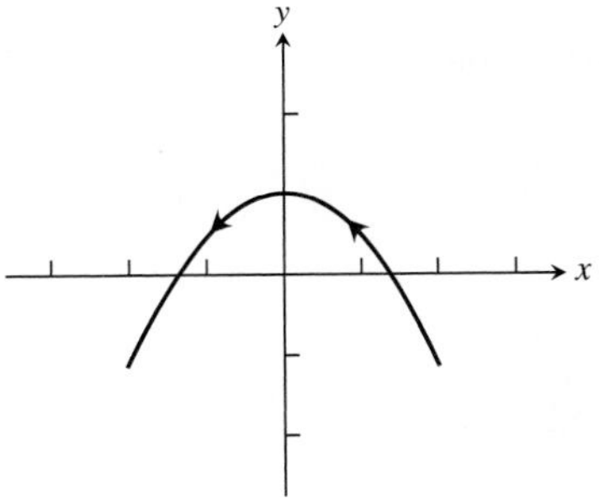

(b) $(0, 1)$

(c) We seek to maximize y as a function of t, so we compute $dy/dt = -2\sin(2t)$, which is positive for $1.5 \le t < \pi$ and negative for $\pi < t \le 4.5$. There is a relative maximum at $t = \pi$, where $(x, y) = (0, 1)$.

23. (a) $(2, 0)$ and $(2, -2)$ **(b)** $(1, -1)$ and $(3, -1)$

25. (a) At $t = \pm\dfrac{2}{\sqrt{3}}$, or $\approx (0.845, -3.079)$ and $(3.155, 3.079)$

(b) Nowhere

27. 2π **29.** π^2

31. $21/2$ **33.** $\dfrac{2\sqrt{2} - 1}{3} \approx 0.609$

35. (a) π **(b)** π

37. Just substitute x for t and note that $dx/dx = 1$.

39. $3\pi a^2$

41. $x = at - b\sin t$ and $y = a - b\cos t$ $(0 < a < b)$

43. 21.010

45. False. Indeed, y may not even be a function of x. (See Example 1.)

47. B **49.** C

51. (a) $x = \cos t + t\sin t$, $y = \sin t - t\cos t$ **(b)** $2\pi^2$

53. (a) ≈ 461.749 ft **(b)** ≈ 41.125 ft

55. (a) ≈ 840.421 ft **(b)** $16{,}875/64 \approx 263.672$ ft

57. $8\pi^2$ **59.** 178.561

Section 11.2

Quick Review 11.2

1. $\sqrt{17}$ **3.** $b = 5/2$

5. $a = 4$

7. $v(t) = \sin t + t\cos t$; $a(t) = 2\cos t - t\sin t$

9. 32

Exercises 11.2

1. $\langle 2, 3\rangle$ **3.** $\langle 1, -4\rangle$

5. $\sqrt{8}$, 45°

7. 2, 30° **9.** 5, 180°

11. $\langle -4, 0\rangle$

13. $\langle -0.868, 4.924\rangle$

15. $\langle 3, 3\rangle$

17. (a) $\langle 9, -6\rangle$ **(b)** $3\sqrt{13}$

19. (a) $\langle 1, 3\rangle$ **(b)** $\sqrt{10}$

21. (a) $\langle 12, -19\rangle$ **(b)** $\sqrt{505}$

23. (a) $\langle 1/5, 14/5\rangle$ **(b)** $\sqrt{197}/5$

25. Speed $\approx$ 346.735 mph direction $\approx$ 14.266° east of north

27. $\mathbf{v}(t) = \langle 6t, 6t^2\rangle$, $\mathbf{a}(t) = \langle 6, 12t\rangle$

29. $\mathbf{v}(t) = \langle e^{-t} - te^{-t}, -e^{-t}\rangle$, $\mathbf{a}(t) = \langle -2e^{-t} + te^{-t}, e^{-t}\rangle$

31. $\mathbf{v}(t) = \langle 2t + 2\cos 2t, 2t + 2\sin 2t\rangle$,
$\mathbf{a}(t) = \langle 2 - 4\sin 2t, 2 + 4\cos 2t\rangle$

33. **(a)** $\langle 90t\cos 55°, 90t\sin 55° - 16t^2\rangle$
(b) $\langle 90\cos 55°, 90\sin 55° - 32t\rangle$
(c) No, the ball hits the fence.

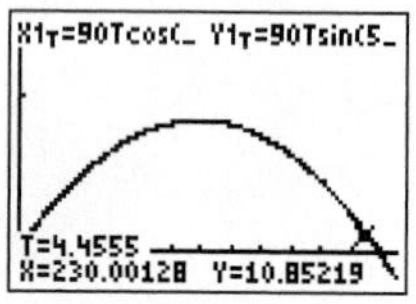

(d) About 4.456 seconds
(e) About 86.055 ft/sec

35. Velocity: $\langle -3\sin 3t, 2\cos 2t\rangle$; acceleration: $\langle -9\cos 3t, -4\sin 2t\rangle$

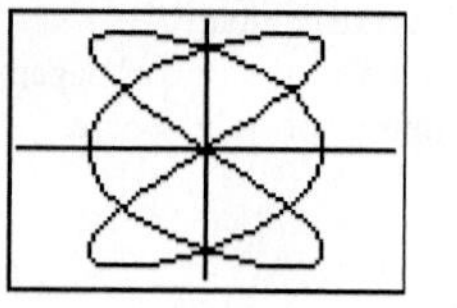

[–1.6, 1.6] by [–1.1, 1.1]
$0 \le t \le 2\pi$

37. **(a)** Velocity: $\langle 4\cos 4t\cos t - \sin t\sin 4t, 2\cos 2t\rangle|_{t=5\pi/4} = \langle 2\sqrt{2}, 0\rangle$; speed: $2\sqrt{2}$
(b)

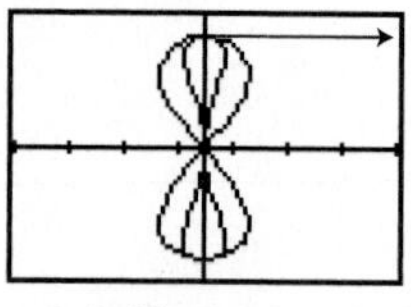

[–4, 4] by [–1.2, 1.2]
$0 \le t \le 2\pi$

(c) To the right

39. **(a)** $(20, 9)$ **(b)** 19.343

41. **(a)** $(3 + \ln 4, -1.7)$ **(b)** 1.419

43. The parametric equations are $x = t^3 - t^2 + 2$ and $y = t + \sin(\pi t)/\pi + 6$.

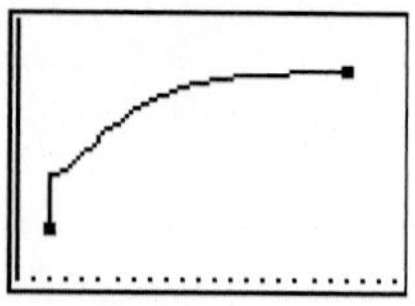

[0, 23] by [5, 10]
$0 \le t \le 3$

45. **(a)** $\pi\sqrt{7/12} \approx 2.399$ **(b)** $\langle -5\pi^2/72, -\pi^2\sqrt{3}/24\rangle$ **(c)** $\dfrac{x^2}{25} + \dfrac{y^2}{9} = 1$

47. **(a)** $\left\langle -\dfrac{4t}{(1 + t^2)^2}, \dfrac{2 - 2t^2}{(1 + t^2)^2}\right\rangle$
(b) No. The x-component of velocity is zero only if $t = 0$, while the y-component of velocity is zero only if $t = 1$. At no time will the velocity be $(0, 0)$.
(c) $\lim_{t\to\infty}\left\langle \dfrac{1 - t^2}{1 + t^2}, \dfrac{2t}{1 + t^2}\right\rangle = \langle -1, 0\rangle$

49. **(a)** $\left.\dfrac{e^t\cos t - e^t\sin t}{e^t\sin t + e^t\cos t}\right|_{t=\pi/2} = -1$

51. **(a)** $3 + \displaystyle\int_2^4 (2 + \sin(t^2))\,dt \approx 3.942$ **(b)** $y - 5 = \dfrac{-6}{2 + \sin 4}(x - 3)$
(c) $\sqrt{(2 + \sin 4)^2 + (-6)^2} \approx 6.127$
(d) $\langle 8\cos 16, 2(2 + \sin 16) + 7(8)\cos 16\rangle \approx \langle -7.661, -50.205\rangle$

53. False. For example, $\mathbf{u}$ and $-1(\mathbf{u})$ have opposite directions.

55. E **57.** B

59. The velocity vector is $\langle -x, \sqrt{1 - x^2}\rangle$, which has slope $-\dfrac{\sqrt{1 - x^2}}{x}$.
The acceleration vector is $\left\langle \dfrac{d}{dt}(-x), \dfrac{d}{dt}(\sqrt{1 - x^2})\right\rangle$
$= \left\langle -\dfrac{dx}{dt}, \dfrac{-2x}{\sqrt{1 - x^2}}\dfrac{dx}{dt}\right\rangle$
$= \left\langle x, \dfrac{x^2}{\sqrt{1 - x^2}}\right\rangle$, which has slope $\dfrac{x}{\sqrt{1 - x^2}}$. Since the slopes are negative reciprocals of each other, the vectors are orthogonal.

61. **(a)** The particles collide when $t = 2$.
(b) First particle: $v_1(2) = \langle 1, -2\rangle$, so the direction unit vector is $\langle 1/\sqrt{5}, -2/\sqrt{5}\rangle$.
Second particle: $v_2(t) = \langle 3/2, 3/2\rangle$, so the direction unit vector is $\langle 1/\sqrt{2}, 1/\sqrt{2}\rangle$.

63.

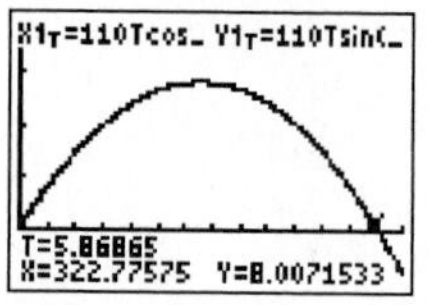

A closer view:

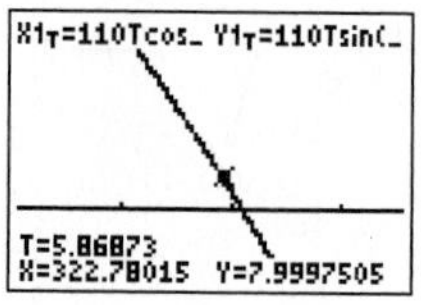

65. **(a)** The diagram shows, by vector addition, that $\mathbf{v} + \mathbf{w} = \mathbf{u}$, so $\mathbf{w} = \mathbf{u} - \mathbf{v}$.
(b) This is just the Law of Cosines applied to the triangle, the sides of which are the magnitudes of the vectors.
(c) By the HMT Rule, $\mathbf{w} = \langle u_1 - v_1, u_2 - v_2\rangle$. So

$$\begin{aligned}|\mathbf{u}|^2 + |\mathbf{v}|^2 - |\mathbf{w}|^2 &= (u_1^2 + u_2^2) + (v_1^2 + v_2^2) \\ &\quad - [(u_1 - v_1)^2 + (u_2 - v_2)^2] \\ &= u_1^2 + u_2^2 + v_1^2 + v_2^2 - [u_1^2 - 2u_1v_1 + v_1^2 \\ &\quad + u_2^2 - 2u_2v_2 + v_2^2] \\ &= 2u_1v_1 + 2u_2v_2 \\ &= 2(u_1v_1 + u_2v_2)\end{aligned}$$

(d) From part (b), $|\mathbf{w}|^2 = |\mathbf{u}|^2 + |\mathbf{v}|^2 - 2|\mathbf{u}||\mathbf{v}|\cos\theta$, so $|\mathbf{u}|^2 + |\mathbf{v}|^2 - |\mathbf{w}|^2 = 2|\mathbf{u}||\mathbf{v}|\cos\theta$.
From part (c), $|\mathbf{u}|^2 + |\mathbf{v}|^2 - |\mathbf{w}|^2 = 2(u_1v_1 + u_2v_2)$. Substituting, we get $2(u_1v_1 + u_2v_2) = 2|\mathbf{u}||v|\cos\theta$, so $\mathbf{u}\cdot\mathbf{v} = u_1v_1 + u_2v_2 = |\mathbf{u}||\mathbf{v}|\cos\theta$.

Section 11.3

Quick Review 11.3

1. $\langle 2\sqrt{3}, 2\rangle$ **3.** 4π

5. Graph $y = \left(\dfrac{4 - x^2}{3}\right)^{1/2}$ and $y = -\left(\dfrac{4 - x^2}{3}\right)^{1/2}$.

7. $-\dfrac{5}{3}\cot 2 \approx 0.763$ **9.** $(3, 0)$ and $(-3, 0)$

Exercises 11.3

1.

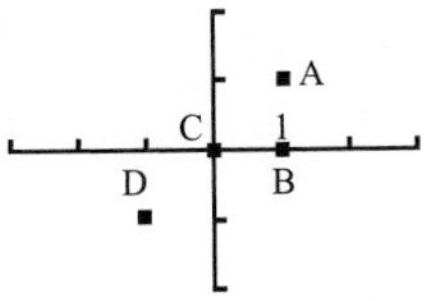

(a) $(1, 1)$ **(b)** $(1, 0)$
(c) $(0, 0)$ **(d)** $(-1, -1)$

3.

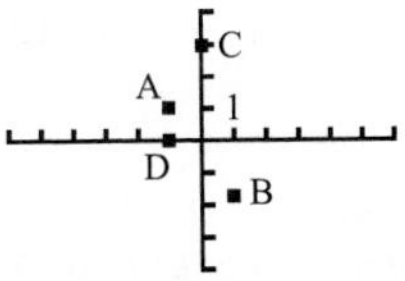

(a) $(\sqrt{2}, 3\pi/4)$ or $(\sqrt{2}, -5\pi/4)$
(b) $(2, -\pi/3)$ or $(-2, 2\pi/3)$
(c) $(3, \pi/2)$ or $(3, 5\pi/2)$
(d) $(1, \pi)$ or $(-1, 0)$

5.

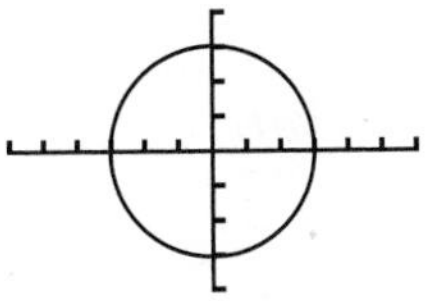

$0 \le \theta \le 2\pi$

7.

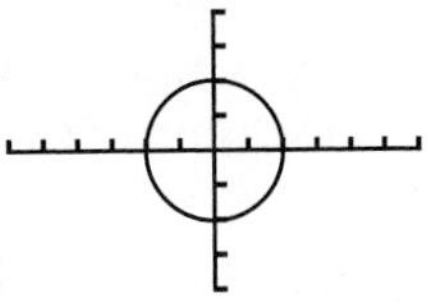

$0 \le \theta \le 2\pi$

9.

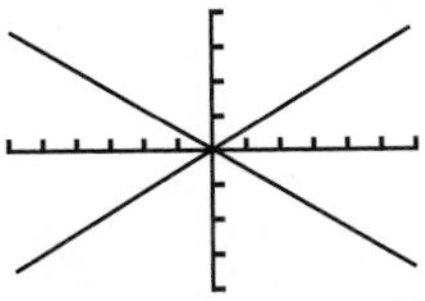

11.

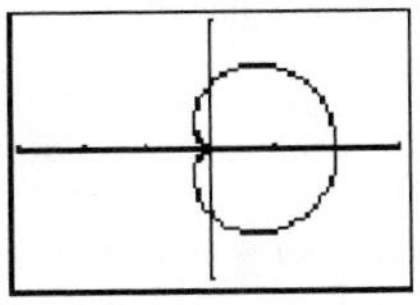

[–3, 3] by [–2, 2]

$0 \le \theta \le 2\pi$

cardioid

13.

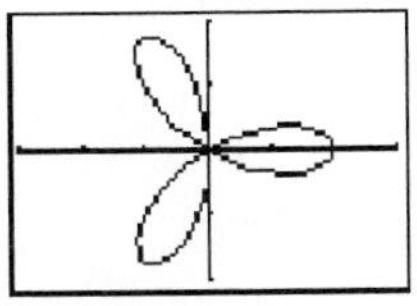

[–3, 3] by [–2, 2]

$0 \le \theta \le \pi$

rose

15.

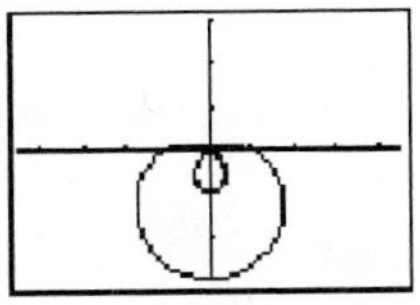

[–4.5, 4.5] by [–3, 3]

$0 \le \theta \le 2\pi$

limaçon

17.

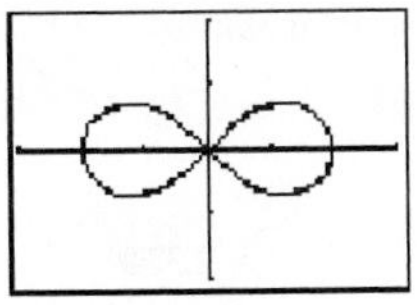

[–3, 3] by [–2, 2]

$-\pi/4 \le \theta \le \pi/4$

lemniscate

19.

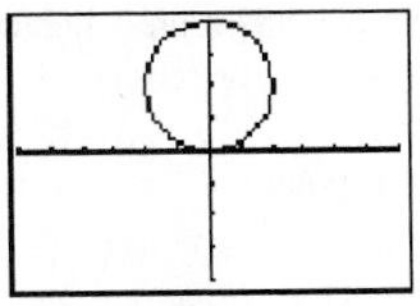

[–6, 6] by [–4, 4]

$0 \le \theta \le \pi$

circle

21. $y = 4$, a horizontal line
23. $x + y = 1$, a line (slope $= -1$, y-intercept $= 1$)
25. $y - 2x = 5$, a line (slope $= 2$, y-intercept $= 5$)
27. $x^2 = y^2$, the union of two lines: $y = \pm x$
29. $x^2 + (y - 4)^2 = 16$, a circle (center $= (0, 4)$, radius $= 4$)

31.

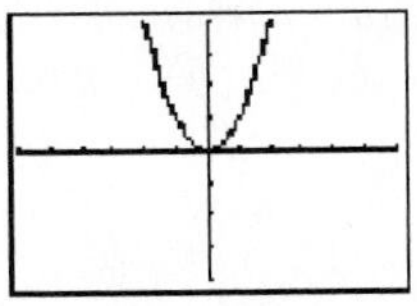

[–6, 6] by [–4, 4]

$0 \le \theta \le 2\pi$

It is a parabola.

33.

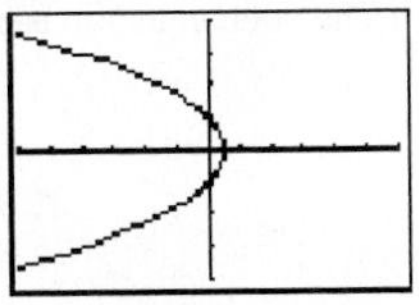

[–6, 6] by [–4, 4]

$0 \le \theta \le 2\pi$

It is a parabola.

35.

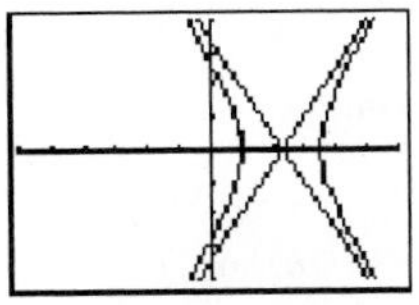

[–6, 6] by [–4, 4]

$0 \le \theta \le 2\pi$

It is a hyperbola.

37.

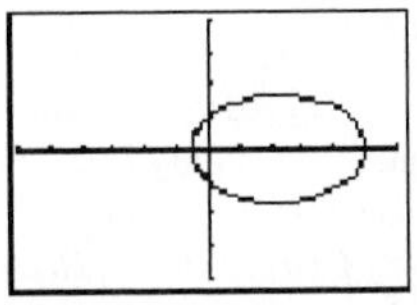

[–6, 6] by [–4, 4]

$0 \le \theta \le 2\pi$

It is an ellipse.

39. At $\theta = 0$: -1: At $\theta = \pi$: 1
41. At $(2, 0)$: $-2/3$ At $(-1: \pi/2)$: 0
At $(2, \pi)$: $2/3$ At $(5, 3\pi/2)$: 0
43. 18π **45.** $\pi/8$ **47.** 2 **49.** 11π
51. $(\pi/2) - 1$ **53.** $5\pi - 8$ **55.** $8 - \pi$

57.

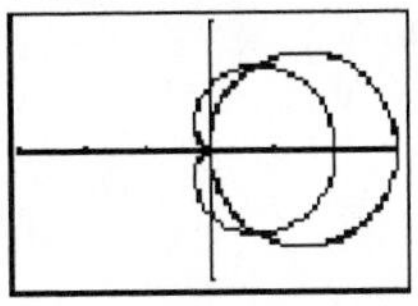

[–3, 3] by [–2, 2]

$0 \le \theta \le \pi$ for the circle
$0 \le \theta \le 2\pi$ for the cardioid

$$\int_{-\pi/3}^{\pi/3} \frac{1}{2}\left((3\cos\theta)^2 - (1 + \cos\theta)^2\right) d\theta = \pi$$

59.

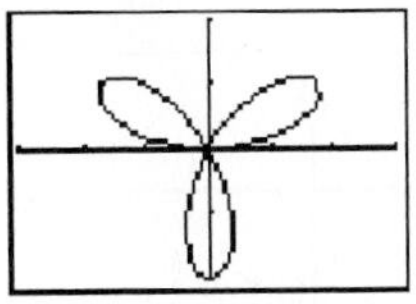

[–3, 3] by [–2, 2]

$0 \le \theta \le \pi$

$$\text{Area} = \int_0^{\pi} \frac{1}{2}(2\sin 3\theta)^2 d\theta = \pi$$

$$\text{Slope} = \left.\frac{d/d\theta(2\sin 3\theta \sin\theta)}{d/d\theta(2\sin 3\theta \cos\theta)}\right|_{\theta=\pi/4} = \frac{1}{2}$$

61. True. Polar coordinates determine a unique point.
63. D **65.** B

67. (a)

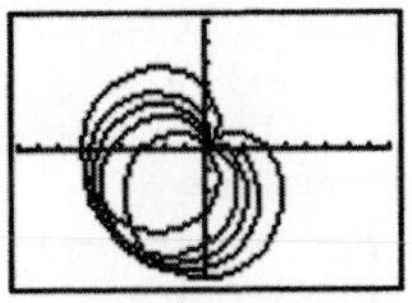

[–9, 9] by [–6, 6]

(b)

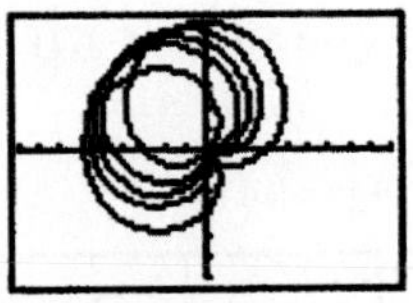

[–9, 9] by [–6, 6]

(c) The graph of r_2 is the graph of r_1 rotated counterclockwise about the origin by the angle α.

69. (a)

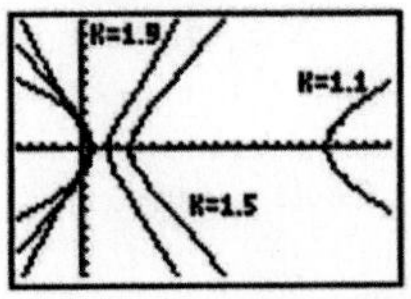

[–5, 25] by [–10, 10]

The graphs are hyperbolas.

(b) As $k \to 1^+$, the right branch of the hyperbola goes to infinity and "disappears." The left branch approaches the parabola $y^2 = 4 - 4x$.

71. $d = [(x_2 - x_1)^2 + (y_2 - y_1)^2]^{1/2}$
$= [(r_2 \cos\theta_2 - r_1 \cos\theta_1)^2 + (r_2 \sin\theta_2 - r_1 \sin\theta_1)^2]^{1/2}$
and then simplify using trigonometric identities.

73. $(dx/d\theta)^2 + (dy/d\theta)^2$
$= (f'(\theta)\cos\theta - f(\theta)\sin\theta)^2 + (f'(\theta)\sin\theta + f(\theta)\cos\theta)^2$
$= (f'(\theta)\cos\theta)^2 + (f(\theta)\sin\theta)^2 + (f'(\theta)\sin\theta)^2 + (f(\theta)\cos\theta)^2$
$= (f(\theta))^2(\sin^2\theta + \cos^2\theta) + (f'(\theta))^2(\cos^2\theta + \sin^2\theta)$
$= (f(\theta))^2 + (f'(\theta))^2 = r^2 + (dr/d\theta)^2$

Quick Quiz (Sections 11-1–11-3)

1. A **3.** D

Review Exercises

1. (a) $\langle -17, 32\rangle$ **(b)** $\sqrt{1313}$ **2. (a)** $\langle -1, -1\rangle$ **(b)** $\sqrt{2}$
3. (a) $\langle 6, -8\rangle$ **(b)** 10 **4. (a)** $\langle 10, -25\rangle$ **(b)** $\sqrt{725} = 5\sqrt{29}$
5. $\langle -\sqrt{3}/2, -1/2\rangle$ [assuming counterclockwise]
6. $\langle \sqrt{3}/2, 1/2\rangle$ **7.** $\langle 8/\sqrt{17}, -2/\sqrt{17}\rangle$
8. $\langle -3, -4\rangle$ **9. (a)** $y = \dfrac{\sqrt{3}}{2}x + \dfrac{1}{4}$ **(b)** 1/4
10. (a) $y = -3x + \dfrac{13}{4}$ **(b)** $\sqrt{6}$
11. (a) $(0, 1/2)$ and $(0, -1/2)$ **(b)** Nowhere
12. (a) $(0, 2)$ and $(0, -2)$ **(b)** $(-2, 0)$ and $(2, 0)$
13. (a) $(0, 0)$ **(b)** Nowhere
14. (a) $(0, 9)$ and $(0, -9)$ **(b)** $(-4, 0)$ and $(4, 0)$

15.
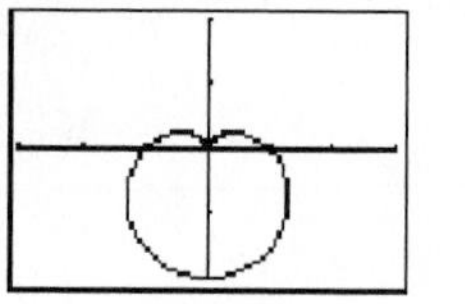
[-3, 3] by [-2, 2]
$0 \le \theta \le 2\pi$
Cardioid

16.
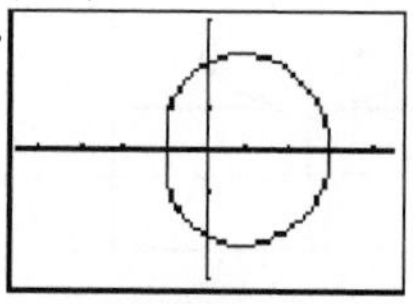
[-4.5, 4.5] by [-3, 3]
$0 \le \theta \le 2\pi$
Convex limaçon

17. (a)
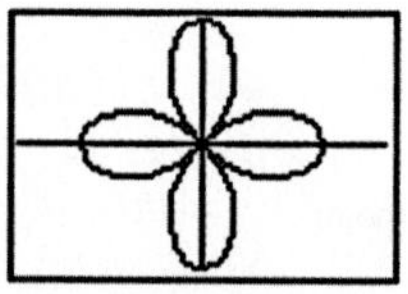
[-1.5, 1.5] by [-1, 1]
$0 \le \theta \le 2\pi$
4-petaled rose

18. (a)
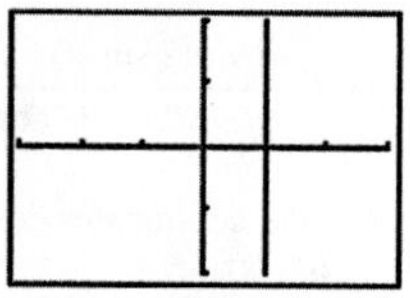
[-3, 3] by [-2, 2]
$-\pi/2 \le \theta \le \pi/2$
Vertical line

19. (a)
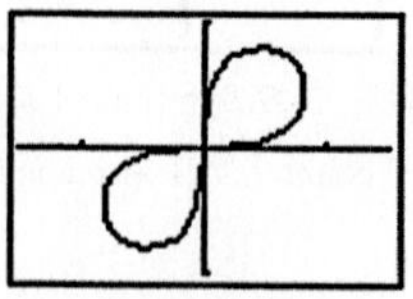
[-1.5, 1.5] by [-1, 1]
$0 \le \theta \le \pi/2$
Lemniscate

20. (a)
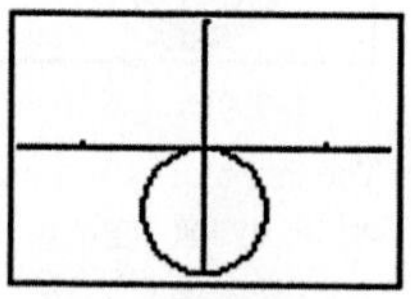
[-1.5, 1.5] by [-1, 1]
$0 \le \theta \le \pi$
Circle

21. 4.041 **22.** 0.346
23. Horizontal: $y = 0, y \approx \pm 0.443, y \approx \pm 1.739$
Vertical: $x = 2, x \approx 0.067, x \approx -1.104$
24. Horizontal: $y = 1/2, y = -4$
Vertical: $x = 0, x \approx \pm 2.598$
25. $y = \pm x + \sqrt{2}$ and $y = \pm x - \sqrt{2}$

26. $y = x - 1$ and $y = -x - 1$ **27.** $x = y$, a line
28. $x^2 + y^2 = 3x$, a circle $\left(\text{center} = \left(\dfrac{3}{2}, 0\right), \text{radius} = \dfrac{3}{2}\right)$
29. $x^2 = 4y$, parabola **30.** $x - \sqrt{3}y = 4\sqrt{3}$ or $y = \dfrac{x}{\sqrt{3}} - 4$, a line
31. $r = -5\sin\theta$ **32.** $r = 2\sin\theta$
33. $r^2\cos^2\theta + 4r^2\sin^2\theta = 16$, or
$$r^2 = \frac{16}{\cos^2\theta + 4\sin^2\theta}$$
34. $(r\cos\theta + 2)^2 + (r\sin\theta - 5)^2 = 16$
35. $9\pi/2$ **36.** $\pi/12$ **37.** $(\pi/4) + 2$ **38.** 5π
39. (a) $\mathbf{v}(t) = \langle -4\sin t, \sqrt{2}\cos t\rangle$ and $\mathbf{a}(t) = \langle -4\cos t, -\sqrt{2}\sin t\rangle$
(b) 3
40. (a) $\mathbf{v}(t) = \langle \sqrt{3}\sec t\tan t, \sqrt{3}\sec^2 t\rangle$ and
$\mathbf{a}(t) = \langle \sqrt{3}(\sec t\tan^2 t + \sec^3 t), 2\sqrt{3}\sec^2 t\tan t\rangle$
(b) $\sqrt{3}$
41. $$\text{Speed} = |\mathbf{v}(t)| = \sqrt{\left(-\frac{t}{(1+t^2)^{3/2}}\right)^2 + \left(\frac{1}{(1+t^2)^{3/2}}\right)^2} = \frac{1}{1+t^2}$$
The maximum value of $\dfrac{1}{1+t^2}$ is 1, when $t = 0$.
42. $\mathbf{r}(t) = \langle e^t\cos t, e^t\sin t\rangle$, with slope $\dfrac{e^t\sin t}{e^t\cos t} = \tan t$.
$\mathbf{v}(t) = \langle e^t\cos t - e^t\sin t, e^t\sin t + e^t\cos t\rangle$
$\mathbf{a}(t) = \langle -2e^t\sin t, 2e^t\cos t\rangle$, with slope $\dfrac{2e^t\cos t}{-2e^t\sin t} = -\dfrac{1}{\tan t}$
Since the slopes are negative reciprocals, the angle is always 90°.
43. $\mathbf{r}(t) = \langle \cos t - 1, \sin t + 1\rangle$ **44.** $\mathbf{r}(t) = \langle \tan^{-1} t + 1, \sqrt{t^2 + 1}\rangle$
45. $\mathbf{r}(t) = \langle 1, t^2\rangle$ **46.** $\mathbf{r}(t) = \langle -t^2 + 6t - 2, -t^2 + 2t + 2\rangle$
47. (a) $\dfrac{\pi\sqrt{17}}{4} \approx 3.238$ **(b)** x-component: $\dfrac{3\pi^2}{16\sqrt{2}}$
y-component: $-\dfrac{5\pi^2}{16\sqrt{2}}$ **(c)** $\dfrac{x^2}{9} + \dfrac{y^2}{25} = 1$
48. (a) 1 **(b)** $e^3\sqrt{2}$ **(c)** $(e^3 - 1)\sqrt{2}$
49. (a) 104/5 **(b)** 4144/135 **(c)** $\dfrac{dy}{dx} = \dfrac{3}{5}\sqrt{x + 2}$
50. Speed ≈ 591.982 mph: Direction ≈ 8.179° north of east
51. (a) $\mathbf{r}(t) = \langle t^2 + \pi, \cos(t^2 + \pi)\rangle$
(b) At this point $t^2 + \pi = 4$, so $t = \sqrt{4 - \pi}$.
Speed $= \sqrt{(2t)^2 + (2t(-\sin(t^2 + \pi)))^2}\big|_{t=\sqrt{4-\pi}} = 2.324$
52. (a) $\mathbf{v}_A(t) = \langle 1, 2\rangle$ and $\mathbf{v}_B(t) = \langle 3/2, 3/2\rangle$
(b) $\displaystyle\int_0^3 \sqrt{1 + (2t - 4)^2}\, dt = 6.126$
(c) Setting $x_A = x_B$, we find that $t = 4$. Plugging $t = 4$ into y_A and y_B, we find that both values are the same (4). Thus, the particles collide when $t = 4$. (*Note*: If you graph both paths, they will cross at $(-1, 1)$. However, the particles are there at different times.)
53. (a) $$\text{Area} = \int_0^{\pi} \frac{1}{2}\left(\frac{4}{1 + \sin\theta}\right)^2 d\theta = \frac{32}{3}$$
(b) The polar equation is equivalent to $r + r\sin\theta = 4$. Thus,
$$r = 4 - r\sin\theta$$
$$r^2 = (4 - r\sin\theta)^2$$
$$x^2 + y^2 = (4 - y)^2$$
$$x^2 + y^2 = 16 - 8y + y^2$$
$$8y = 16 - x^2$$
(c) $\text{Area} = \displaystyle\int_{-4}^{4}\left(2 - \frac{x^2}{8}\right)dx$, which, indeed, is $\dfrac{32}{3}$.

CHAPTER 12

Section 12.1

Quick Review

1. $5\sqrt{2}$ **2.** $(3/2, 5/2)$ **3.** $\sqrt{13}$ **4.** $\frac{2}{\sqrt{13}}\mathbf{i} + \frac{3}{\sqrt{13}}\mathbf{j}$

5. $-\frac{6}{\sqrt{13}}\mathbf{i} - \frac{9}{\sqrt{13}}\mathbf{j}$

6. Ellipse, center $(0, 0)$, x-intercepts: $(\pm 2, 0)$, vertices: $(0, \pm 3)$
7. Ellipse plus interior, center $(0, 0)$, x-intercepts: $(\pm 2, 0)$, vertices: $(0, \pm 3)$
8. $(x - 2)^2 + (y + 3)^2 = 9$ **9.** Center: $(-3, 1)$, radius $= 2$
10. $5\mathbf{i} - 4\mathbf{j}$

Exercises

1. The line through $(2, 3, 0)$ parallel to the z-axis **3.** The x-axis
5. The circle $x^2 + y^2 = 4$ in the plane $z = -2$
7. The circle $y^2 + z^2 = 1$ in the yz-plane
9. The circle $x^2 + y^2 = 16$ in the xy-plane
11. **(a)** The first quadrant of the xy-plane
(b) The fourth quadrant of the xy-plane
13. **(a)** The ball of radius 1 centered at the origin
(b) All points at distance greater than 1 unit from the origin
15. **(a)** The upper hemisphere of radius 1 centered at the origin
(b) The solid upper hemisphere of radius 1 centered at the origin
17. **(a)** $x = 3$ **(b)** $y = -1$ **(c)** $z = -2$
19. **(a)** $z = 1$ **(b)** $x = 3$ **(c)** $y = -1$
21. **(a)** $x^2 + (y - 2)^2 = 4, z = 0$
(b) $(y - 2)^2 + z^2 = 4, x = 0$
(c) $x^2 + z^2 = 4, y = 2$
23. **(a)** $y = 3, z = -1$ **(b)** $x = 1, z = -1$ **(c)** $x = 1, y = 3$
25. $x^2 + y^2 + z^2 = 25, z = 3$ **27.** $0 \le z \le 1$ **29.** $z \le 0$
31. **(a)** $(x - 1)^2 + (y - 1)^2 + (z - 1)^2 < 1$
(b) $(x - 1)^2 + (y - 1)^2 + (z - 1)^2 > 1$

33. $2\mathbf{i} + \mathbf{j} - 2\mathbf{k} = 3\left(\frac{2}{3}\mathbf{i} + \frac{1}{3}\mathbf{j} - \frac{2}{3}\mathbf{k}\right)$ **35.** $5\mathbf{k} = 5(\mathbf{k})$

37. $\frac{1}{\sqrt{6}}\mathbf{i} - \frac{1}{\sqrt{6}}\mathbf{j} - \frac{1}{\sqrt{6}}\mathbf{k} = \sqrt{\frac{1}{2}}\left(\frac{1}{\sqrt{3}}\mathbf{i} - \frac{1}{\sqrt{3}}\mathbf{j} - \frac{1}{\sqrt{3}}\mathbf{k}\right)$

39. **(a)** $2\mathbf{i}$ **(b)** $-\sqrt{3}\,\mathbf{k}$ **(c)** $\frac{3}{10}\mathbf{j} + \frac{2}{5}\mathbf{k}$ **(d)** $6\mathbf{i} - 2\mathbf{j} + 3\mathbf{k}$

41. $\frac{7}{13}(12\,\mathbf{i} - 5\,\mathbf{k})$

43. **(a)** $5\sqrt{2}$ **(b)** $\frac{3}{5\sqrt{2}}\mathbf{i} + \frac{4}{5\sqrt{2}}\mathbf{j} - \frac{1}{\sqrt{2}}\mathbf{k}$ **(c)** $\left(\frac{1}{2}, 3, \frac{5}{2}\right)$

45. **(a)** $\sqrt{3}$ **(b)** $-\frac{1}{\sqrt{3}}\mathbf{i} - \frac{1}{\sqrt{3}}\mathbf{j} - \frac{1}{\sqrt{3}}\mathbf{k}$ **(c)** $\left(\frac{5}{2}, \frac{7}{2}, \frac{9}{2}\right)$

47. Center $(-2, 0, 2)$, radius $2\sqrt{2}$
49. $(x - 1)^2 + (y - 2)^2 + (z - 3)^2 = 14$
51. Center $(-2, 0, 2)$, radius $\sqrt{8}$

53. Center $\left(-\frac{1}{4}, -\frac{1}{4}, -\frac{1}{4}\right)$, radius $\frac{5\sqrt{3}}{4}$ **55.** $A = (4, -3, 5)$

57. **(a)** $\sqrt{y^2 + z^2}$ **(b)** $\sqrt{x^2 + z^2}$ **(c)** $\sqrt{x^2 + y^2}$

59. Let $A = (a_1, a_2, a_3)$, $B = (b_1, b_2, b_3)$, $C = (c_1, c_2, c_3)$, and $D = (d_1, d_2, d_3)$. The midpoints of the sides are

$$M_{AB} = \left(\frac{a_1 + b_1}{2}, \frac{a_2 + b_2}{2}, \frac{a_3 + b_3}{2}\right),$$

$$M_{BC} = \left(\frac{b_1 + c_1}{2}, \frac{b_2 + c_2}{2}, \frac{b_3 + c_3}{2}\right),$$

$$M_{CD} = \left(\frac{c_1 + d_1}{2}, \frac{c_2 + d_2}{2}, \frac{c_3 + d_3}{2}\right),$$

$$M_{AD} = \left(\frac{a_1 + d_1}{2}, \frac{a_2 + d_2}{2}, \frac{a_3 + d_3}{2}\right),$$

The midpoint of the segment joining M_{AB} and M_{CD} and the midpoint of the segment joining M_{BC} and M_{AD} have coordinates $\frac{a_i + b_i + c_i + d_i}{4}$ for $i = 1, 2, 3$.

61. $\overrightarrow{P_1P_2} = \mathbf{i} + 2\mathbf{j} + 3\mathbf{k} = \overrightarrow{P_4P_3}$ and $\overrightarrow{P_2P_3} = 2\mathbf{i} + 3\mathbf{j} + 4\mathbf{k} = \overrightarrow{P_1P_4}$. As vectors the opposite sides are represented by equal vectors. Therefore, they are parallel and have the same length, and the figure is a parallelogram.

63. **(a)** $x = -1$: $y^2 + z^2 = 8$, $x = 0$: $y^2 + z^2 = 9$, $x = 2$: $y^2 + z^2 = 5$
(b)

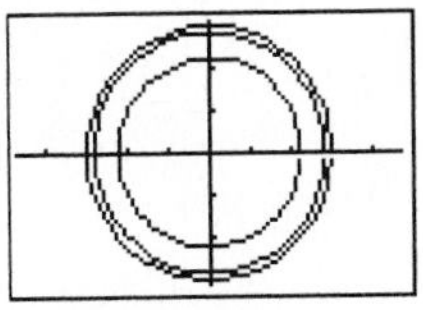

$[-4.7, 4.7]$ by $[-3.1, 3.1]$

(c) If $0 \le |c| \le 3$, then for $x = c$ graph $r = \sqrt{9 - c^2}$ in polar coordinate mode. If $|c| > 3$, then there is no graph.
(d) If $|x| \le 3$, then $A_x = \pi(9 - x^2)$. **(e)** It is the volume of the sphere.

65. $\frac{2}{3}\mathbf{i} + \frac{2}{3}\mathbf{j} + \frac{4}{3}\mathbf{k}$

Section 12.2

Quick Review

1. 0 **2.** $\pi/2$ **3.** 1 **4.** $x + y = 5$ **5.** $x - y = 1$

6. $\pm\left(\frac{2}{\sqrt{7}}\mathbf{i} + \sqrt{\frac{3}{7}}\mathbf{j}\right)$ **7.** $\pm\left(\sqrt{\frac{3}{7}}\mathbf{i} - \frac{2}{\sqrt{7}}\mathbf{j}\right)$ **8.** $\pm\left(\frac{5}{\sqrt{34}}\mathbf{i} + \frac{3}{\sqrt{34}}\mathbf{j}\right)$

9. $\pm\left(\frac{3}{\sqrt{34}}\mathbf{i} - \frac{5}{\sqrt{34}}\mathbf{j}\right)$ **10.** $250\ \mathrm{N \cdot m}$, assuming distance in meters (m)

Exercises

1. **(a)** $\mathbf{A} \cdot \mathbf{B} = -25$, $|\mathbf{A}| = 5$, $|\mathbf{B}| = 5$ **(b)** π **(c)** -5 **(d)** $-2\mathbf{i} + 4\mathbf{j} - \sqrt{5}\mathbf{k}$
3. **(a)** $\mathbf{A} \cdot \mathbf{B} = 25$, $|\mathbf{A}| = 15$, $|\mathbf{B}| = 5$ **(b)** $\cos^{-1}(1/3) \approx 1.23$ rad **(c)** $5/3$
(d) $\frac{1}{9}(10\mathbf{i} + 11\mathbf{j} - 2\mathbf{k})$
5. **(a)** $\mathbf{A} \cdot \mathbf{B} = 2$, $|\mathbf{A}| = \sqrt{34}$, $|\mathbf{B}| = \sqrt{3}$ **(b)** $\cos^{-1}(2/\sqrt{102}) \approx 1.37$ rad
(c) $2/\sqrt{34}$ **(d)** $\frac{1}{17}(5\mathbf{j} - 3\mathbf{k})$

7. $\mathbf{B} = \left(\frac{3}{2}\mathbf{i} + \frac{3}{2}\mathbf{j}\right) + \left(-\frac{3}{2}\mathbf{i} + \frac{3}{2}\mathbf{j} + 4\mathbf{k}\right)$

9. $\mathbf{B} = \left(\frac{14}{3}\mathbf{i} + \frac{28}{3}\mathbf{j} - \frac{14}{3}\mathbf{k}\right) + \left(\frac{10}{3}\mathbf{i} - \frac{16}{3}\mathbf{j} - \frac{22}{3}\mathbf{k}\right)$

11. The sum of two vectors is *always* orthogonal to their difference: $(\mathbf{v}_1 + \mathbf{v}_2) \cdot (\mathbf{v}_1 - \mathbf{v}_2) = 0$.
15. $\theta = \cos^{-1}(2/\sqrt{6}) \approx 0.62\text{ rad} \approx 35.26°$ **17.** a
19. **(a)** $|\mathbf{D}| = \sqrt{70}$ **(b)** $|\mathbf{D}| = \sqrt{568}$ **21.** $5\ \mathrm{N \cdot m}$ or 5 J
23. $3464.10\ \mathrm{N \cdot m} = 3464.10$ J
25. Slope of $\mathbf{v} = a\mathbf{i} + b\mathbf{j}$ is b/a, slope of $ax + by = c$ is $-a/b$

27. $x + 2y = 4$

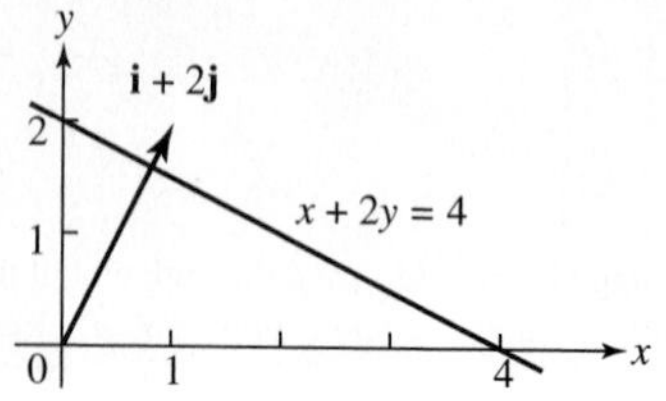

29. $-2x + y = -3$

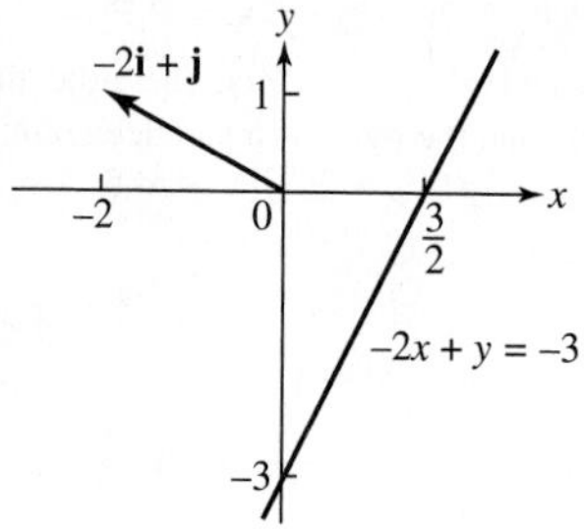

31. $x + y = -1$

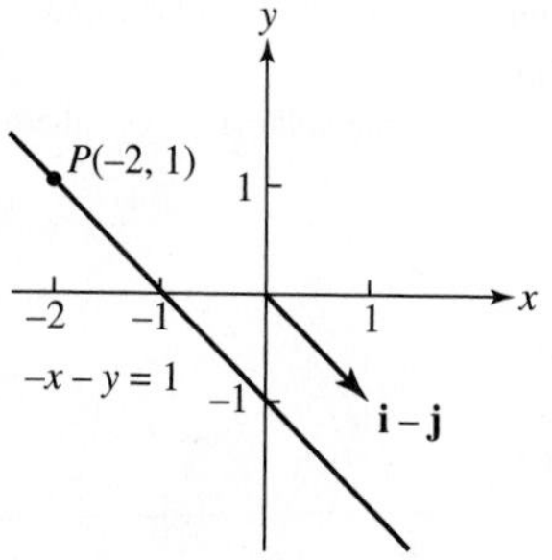

33. $2x - y = 0$

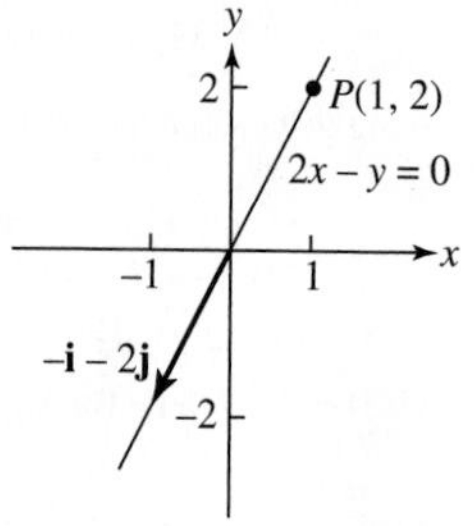

35. $\pi/4$ **37.** $\pi/6$ **39.** $\cos^{-1}\left(\frac{7}{5\sqrt{2}}\right) \approx 0.14$ rad

41. $\pi/3$ and $2\pi/3$ at each point

43. The angle at (0, 0) is $\pi/2$; the angles at (1, 1) are $\pi/4$ and $3\,\pi/4$.

47. $(x\mathbf{i} + y\mathbf{j}) \cdot \mathbf{v} = |x\mathbf{i} + y\mathbf{j}||\mathbf{v}| \cos\theta \le 0$ when $\pi/2 \le \theta \le \pi$. This means (x, y) has to be a point whose position vector makes an angle with $\mathbf{v}$ that is a right angle or bigger.

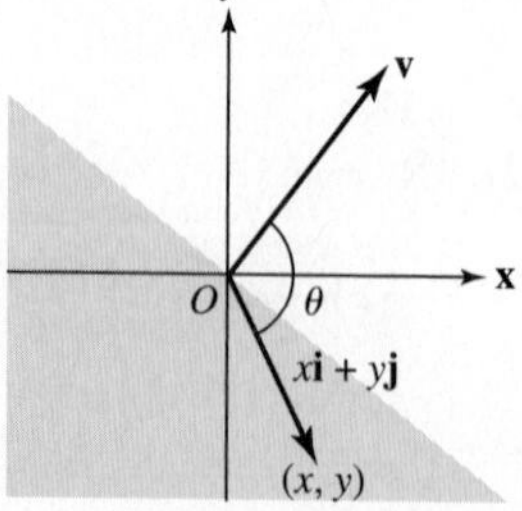

Section 12.3

Quick Review

1. Slope of AB = slope of DC = 3/2, slope of AD = slope of BC = 1/2, so opposite sides are parallel

2. 8

3. $\angle A$ and $\angle C$: $\cos^{-1}\left(\frac{14}{\sqrt{20}\sqrt{13}}\right) \approx 29.74°$

$\angle B$ and $\angle D$: $\cos^{-1}\left(\frac{14}{\sqrt{20}\sqrt{13}}\right) \approx 150.26°$

4. $x = 0, \pi/2, \pi, 3\pi/2, 2\pi$ **5.** $x = \pi/4, 3\pi/4, 5\pi/4, 7\pi/4$

6. 5 **7.** −3 **8.** 35 **9.** 3 **10.** 0

Exercises

1. $\mathbf{A} \times \mathbf{B}$: length = 3, direction = $\frac{2}{3}\mathbf{i} + \frac{1}{3}\mathbf{j} + \frac{2}{3}\mathbf{k}$

$\mathbf{B} \times \mathbf{A}$: length = 3, direction = $-\frac{2}{3}\mathbf{i} - \frac{1}{3}\mathbf{j} - \frac{2}{3}\mathbf{k}$

3. $\mathbf{A} \times \mathbf{B}$: length = 0, has no direction
$\mathbf{B} \times \mathbf{A}$: length = 0, has no direction

5. $\mathbf{A} \times \mathbf{B}$: length = 6, direction = $-\mathbf{k}$
$\mathbf{B} \times \mathbf{A}$: length = 6, direction = $\mathbf{k}$

7. $\mathbf{A} \times \mathbf{B}$: length = $6\sqrt{5}$, direction = $\frac{1}{\sqrt{5}}\mathbf{i} - \frac{2}{\sqrt{5}}\mathbf{k}$

$\mathbf{B} \times \mathbf{A}$: length = $6\sqrt{5}$.

direction = $-\frac{1}{\sqrt{5}}\mathbf{i} + \frac{2}{\sqrt{5}}\mathbf{k}$

9. $\mathbf{A} \times \mathbf{B} = \mathbf{k}$

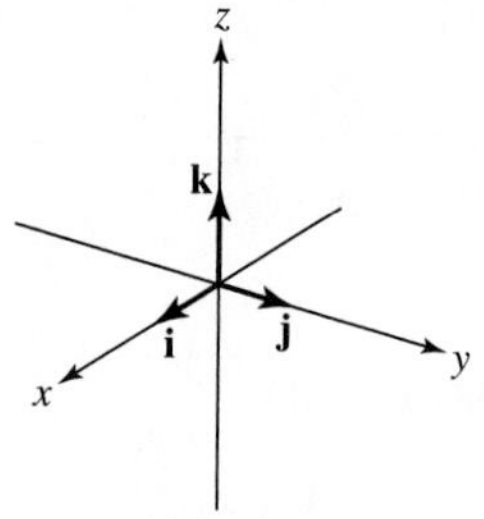

11. $\mathbf{A} \times \mathbf{B} = \mathbf{i} - \mathbf{j} + \mathbf{k}$

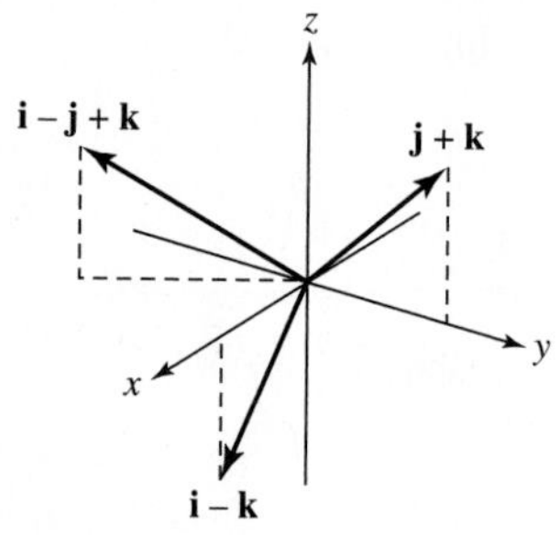

13. $\mathbf{A} \times \mathbf{B} = -2\mathbf{k}$

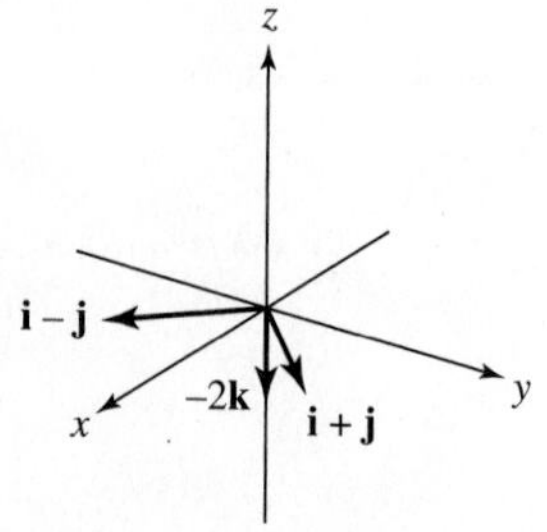

15. **(a)** $2\sqrt{6}$ **(b)** $\pm\frac{1}{\sqrt{6}}(2\mathbf{i}+\mathbf{j}+\mathbf{k})$ **17.** **(a)** $\sqrt{2}/2$ **(b)** $\pm\frac{1}{\sqrt{2}}(\mathbf{i}-\mathbf{j})$

19. **(a)** None **(b)** **A** and **C** are parallel because $\mathbf{A}\times\mathbf{C}=\mathbf{0}$.

21. $10\sqrt{3}$ ft · lb **23.** 8 **25.** 7

27. **(a)** True, $|\mathbf{A}| = \sqrt{a_1^2+a_2^2+a_3^2} = \sqrt{\mathbf{A}\cdot\mathbf{A}}$

(b) Not always true, $\mathbf{A}\cdot\mathbf{A} = |\mathbf{A}|^2$

(c) True, $\mathbf{A}\times\mathbf{0} = \begin{vmatrix} \mathbf{i} & \mathbf{j} & \mathbf{k} \\ a_1 & a_2 & a_3 \\ 0 & 0 & 0 \end{vmatrix} = \mathbf{0}$

(d) True, $\mathbf{A}\times(-\mathbf{A}) = \begin{vmatrix} \mathbf{i} & \mathbf{j} & \mathbf{k} \\ a_1 & a_2 & a_3 \\ -a_1 & -a_2 & -a_3 \end{vmatrix} = \mathbf{0}$

(e) Not always true, $\mathbf{i}\times\mathbf{j}=\mathbf{k}\neq-\mathbf{k}=\mathbf{j}\times\mathbf{i}$ for example

(f) True, Equation (3) **(g)** True, $(\mathbf{A}\times\mathbf{B})\cdot\mathbf{B} = \mathbf{A}\cdot(\mathbf{B}\times\mathbf{B}) = \mathbf{A}\cdot\mathbf{0} = 0$

(h) True, Equation (5)

29. **(a)** $\text{proj}_{\mathbf{B}}\mathbf{A} = \left(\frac{\mathbf{A}\cdot\mathbf{B}}{\mathbf{B}\cdot\mathbf{B}}\right)\mathbf{B}$ **(b)** $\pm(\mathbf{A}\times\mathbf{B})$

(c) $\pm(\mathbf{A}\times\mathbf{B})\times\mathbf{C}$ **(d)** $|(\mathbf{A}\times\mathbf{B})\cdot\mathbf{C}|$

31. **(a)** Yes, $\mathbf{A}\times\mathbf{B}$ and **C** are both vectors

(b) No, **A** is a vector but $\mathbf{B}\cdot\mathbf{C}$ is a scalar

(c) Yes, **A** and $\mathbf{B}\times\mathbf{C}$ are both vectors

(d) No, **A** is a vector but $\mathbf{B}\cdot\mathbf{C}$ is a scalar

33. 2 **35.** 13 **37.** 11/2 **39.** 25/2

41. $\frac{1}{2}|\mathbf{A}\times\mathbf{B}| = \pm\frac{1}{2}\begin{vmatrix} a_1 & a_2 \\ b_1 & b_2 \end{vmatrix}$. The applicable sign (+) is the acute angle from **A** to **B** runs counterclockwise in the xy-plane and (−) if it runs clockwise, because the area must be a nonnegative number.

43. No. For example, $\mathbf{i}+\mathbf{j}\neq-\mathbf{i}+\mathbf{j}$, but $\mathbf{i}\times(\mathbf{i}+\mathbf{j}) = \mathbf{i}\times(-\mathbf{i}+\mathbf{j}) = \mathbf{k}$.

Section 12.4

Quick Review

1. **(a)** Yes **(b)** No **(c)** No **(d)** No

2. $x=-2+5t,\ y=-3+4t,\ -\infty<t<\infty$

3. $x=-2+5t,\ y=-3+4t,\ 0\le t\le 1$

4. $x=1+3t,\ y=2-2t,\ -\infty<t<\infty$

5. $x=3/5,\ y=4/5$ **6.** $x=1/17,\ y=7/17$

7. $-\frac{2}{3}\mathbf{i}+\frac{1}{3}\mathbf{j}+\frac{2}{3}\mathbf{k}$ **8.** $\mathbf{u}=3\mathbf{i}+5\mathbf{j}+\mathbf{k},\ \mathbf{w}=-3\mathbf{i}-5\mathbf{j}-\mathbf{k}$

9. $\mathbf{u}\cdot\mathbf{v}_1 = 9-10+1=0,\ \mathbf{w}\cdot\mathbf{v}_1=-9+10-1=0$

10. $\mathbf{u}\cdot\mathbf{v}_2 = -3+5-2=0,\ \mathbf{w}\cdot\mathbf{v}_2=3-5+2=0$

Exercises

1. $x=3+t,\ y=-4+t,\ z=-1+t$ **3.** $x=-2+5t,\ y=5t,\ z=3-5t$

5. $x=3+2t,\ y=-2-t,\ z=1+3t$ **7.** $x=2+3t,\ y=4+7t,\ z=5-5t$

9. $x=2-2t,\ y=3+4y,\ z=-2t$

11. $x=t,\ y=t,\ z=\frac{3}{2}t,\ 0\le t\le 1$

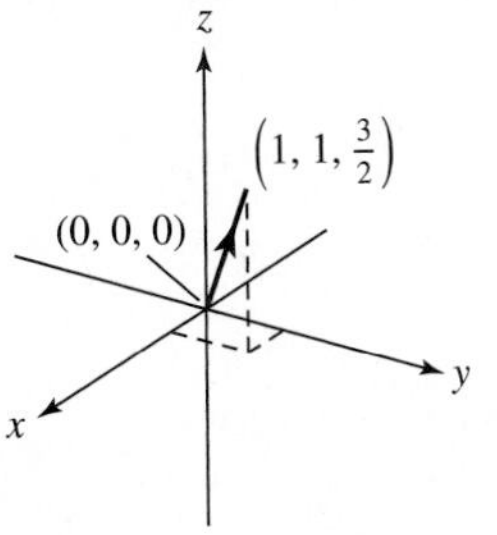

13. $x=0,\ y=1-2t,\ z=1,\ 0\le t\le 1$

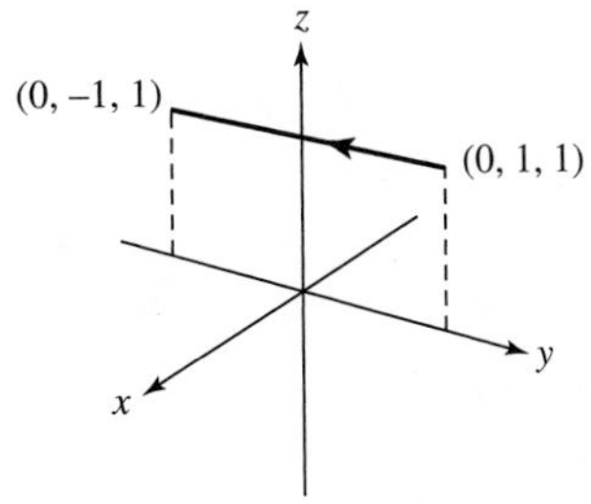

15. $3x-2y-z=-3$ **17.** $7x-5y-4z=6$ **19.** $x+3y+4z=34$

21. $(1, 2, 3);\ -20x+12y+z=7$ **23.** $y+z=3$ **25.** $x-y+z=0$

29. 0 **33.** 19/5 **35.** $9/\sqrt{41}$ **39.** $\cos^{-1}\left(\frac{5}{3\sqrt{6}}\right)\approx 0.82$ rad

41. $\left(\frac{3}{2}, -\frac{3}{2}, \frac{1}{2}\right)$ **43.** (1, 1, 0) **45.** $x=1-t,\ y=1+t,\ z=-1$

47. $x=4,\ y=3+6t,\ z=1+3t$

49. L_1 and L_2 intersect at (5, 3, 1), L_2 and L_3 are parallel, L_1 and L_3 are skew

51. $x=2+2t,\ y=-4-t,\ z=7+3t;$

$x=-2-t,\ y=-2+\frac{1}{2}t,\ z=1-\frac{3}{2}t$

53. yz-plane: $(0, -1/2, -3/2)$ (set $x=0$); xz-plane: $(-1, 0, -3)$ (set $y=0$); xy-plane: $(1, -1, 0)$ (set $z=0$)

55. No, because the line and plane intersect in the point $(-1, 7, -3)$

57. There are many possible answers. $x+y=3$ and $2y+z=7$ are two such planes.

59. All planes except those through the origin or parallel to a coordinate axis

61. **(a)** $\overrightarrow{EP} = c\overrightarrow{EP_1};\ y=cy_1$ and $z=cz_1$

(b) At $x_1=0$: $c=1,\ y=y_1,\ z=z_1$; at $x_1=x_0$: $x_0=0,\ y=0,\ z=0$;

$\lim_{x_0\to\infty} c = \lim_{x_0\to\infty}\frac{-x_0}{x_1-x_0} = \lim_{x_0\to\infty}\frac{-1}{-1} = 1$, so $c\to 1$ and $y\to y_1$ and $z\to z_1$

Section 12.5

Quick Review

1. **(a)** Circle, center = $(-1, 0)$, radius = 1

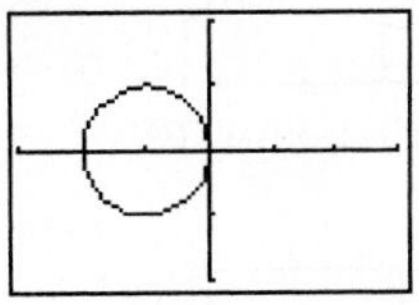

[–3, 3] by [–2, 2]

(b) Circle, center = (0, 2), radius = 2

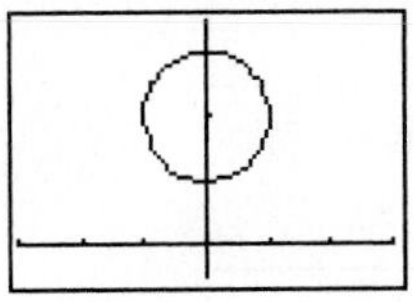

[–3, 3] by [–0.5, 3.5]

2. **(a)** Ellipse, center = (0, 0), vertices: $(\pm\sqrt{2}, 0)$, y-intercepts: $(0, \pm 2)$

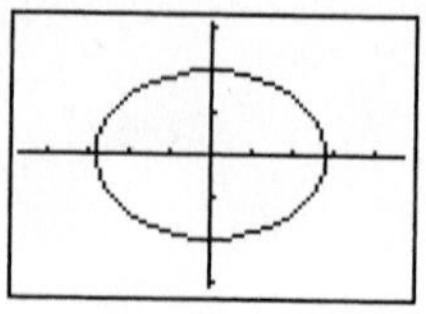

[−4.7, 4.7] by [−3.1, 3.1]

(b) Ellipse, center = (0, 0), x-intercepts: $(\pm 3, 0)$, vertices: $(0, \pm 6)$

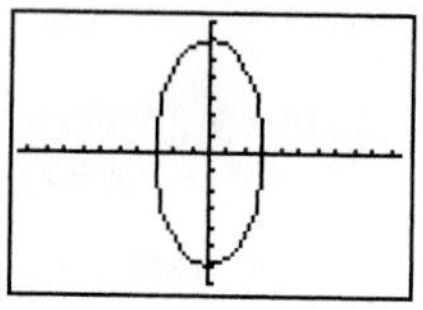

[−10.5, 10.5] by [−7, 7]

3. **(a)** Hyperbola, center = (0, 0)

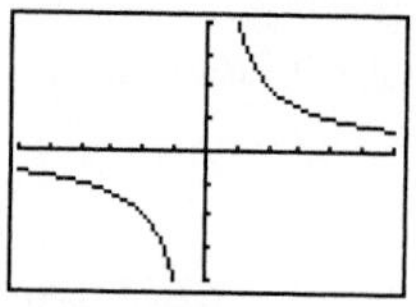

[−6, 6] by [−4, 4]

(b) Hyperbola, center = (0, 0), vertices $(\pm 6, 0)$

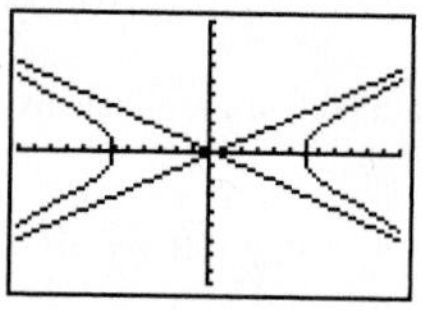

[−12, 12] by [−9, 9]

4. **(a)** Parabola, x-intercepts: $(\pm 1, 0)$, vertex: $(0, -1)$

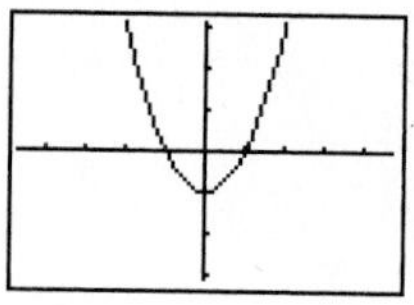

[−4.7, 4.7] by [−3.1, 3.1]

(b) Parabola, vertex: (4, 0), y-intercepts: $(0, \pm 2)$

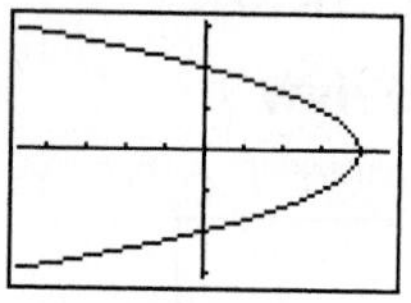

[−4.7, 4.7] by [−3.1, 3.1]

5. $r = 3$

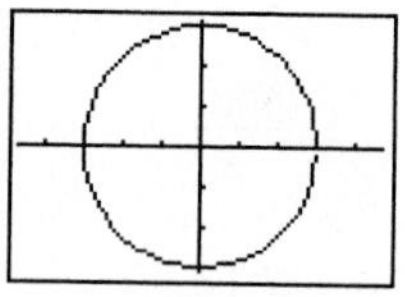

[−4.7, 4.7] by [−3.1, 3.1]

6. $r = 2 \cos \theta$

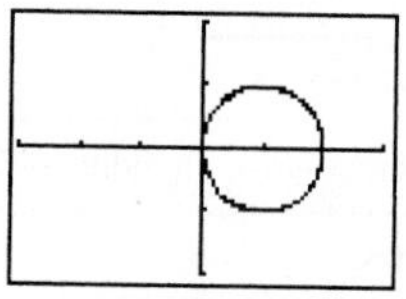

[−3, 3] by [−2, 2]

7. $r = -4 \sin \theta$

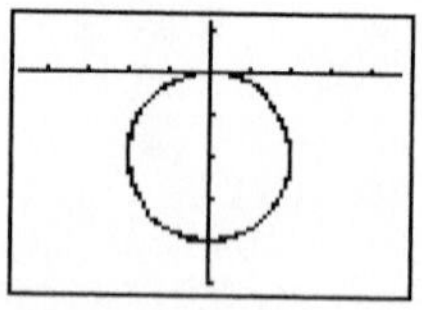

[−4.7, 4.7] by [−5, 1.2]

8. $r = -6 \cos \theta$

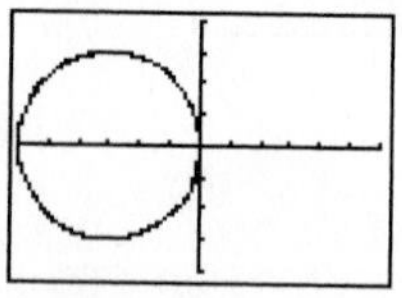

[−6, 6] by [−4, 4]

9. **(a)** Cardioid

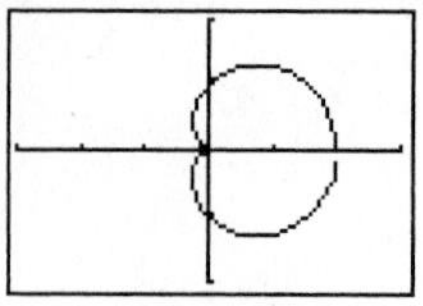

[−3, 3] by [−2, 2]

(b) Cardioid

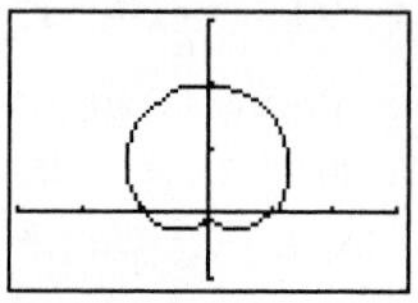

[−3, 3] by [−1, 3]

10. **(a)** Horizontal line $y = 2$

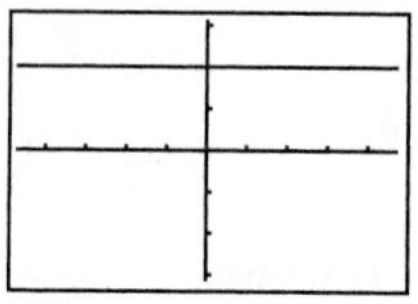

[−4.7, 4.7] by [−3.1, 3.1]

(b) Vertical line $x = -1$

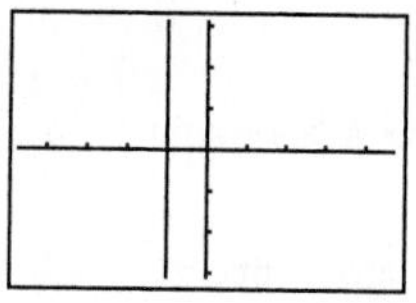

[−4.7, 4.7] by [−3.1, 3.1]

Exercises

1. a, elliptical cylinder

3.

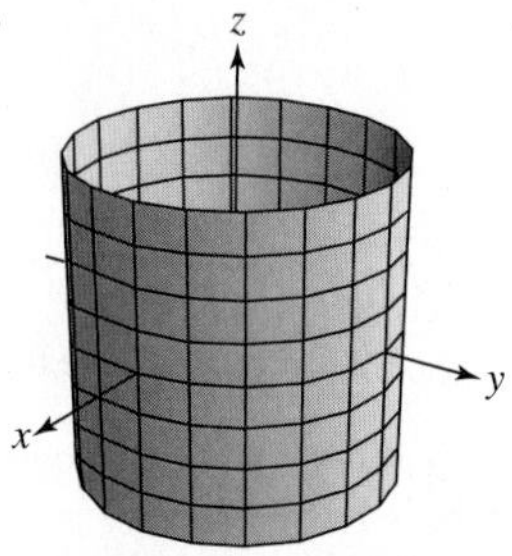

5.

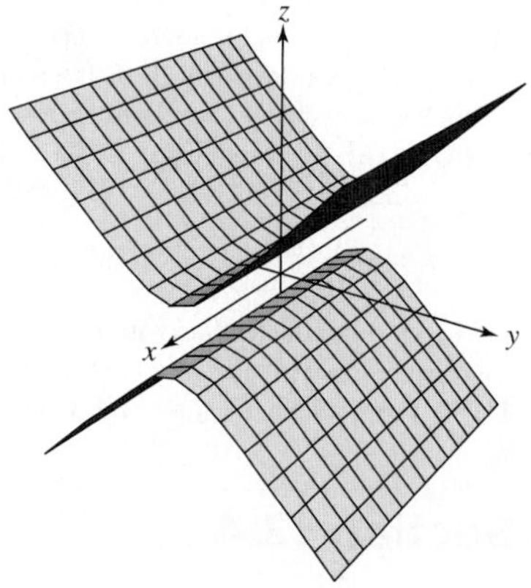

7.

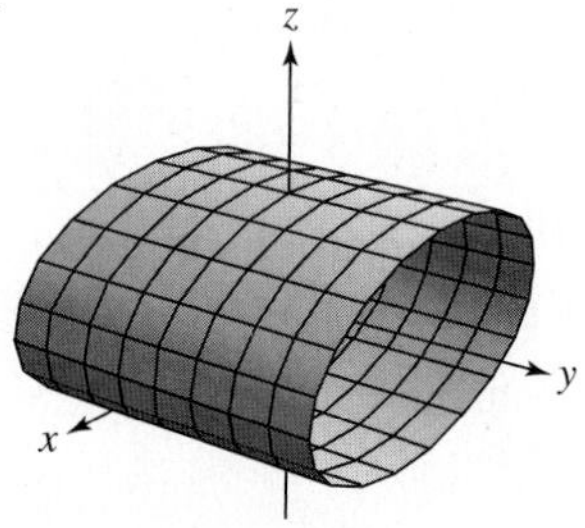

9.

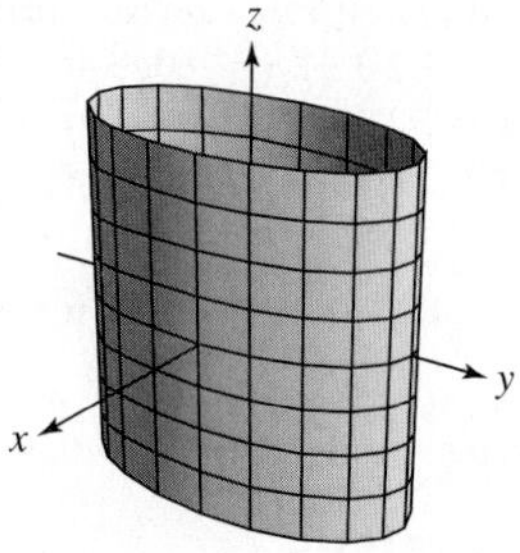

11.

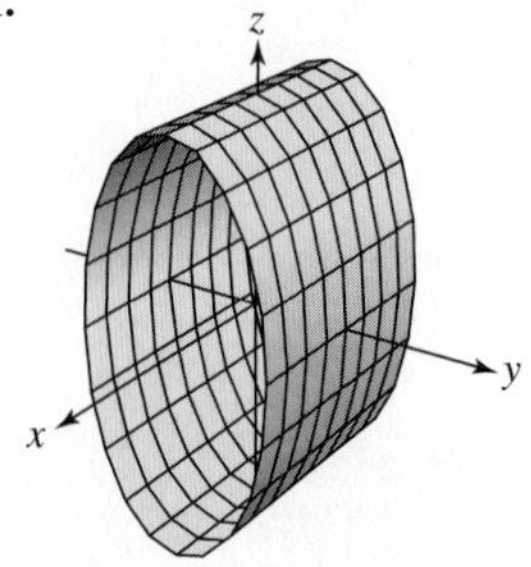

13. d **15.** a **17.** (0, 0, 0) **19.** $(1, \pi/2, 0)$ **21.** (1, 0, 0)
23. (0, 1, 1) **25.** $x^2 + y^2 = 0$, the z-axis **27.** $z = 0$, the xy-plane
29. $r^2 + z^2 = 4$, a sphere of radius 2 centered at the origin
31. $y = 1$, the plane $y = 1$
33. $r^2 + z^2 = 2z$, $z \le 1$, the lower half (hemisphere) of the sphere of radius 1 centered at (0, 0, 1) (rectangular)
35. Right circular cylinder parallel to the z-axis

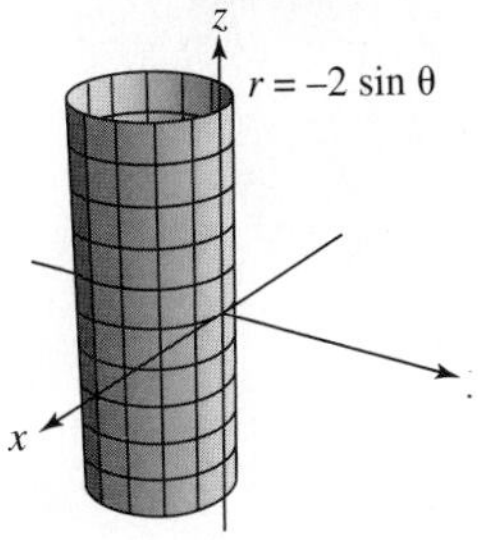

37. Cylinder parallel to the z-axis

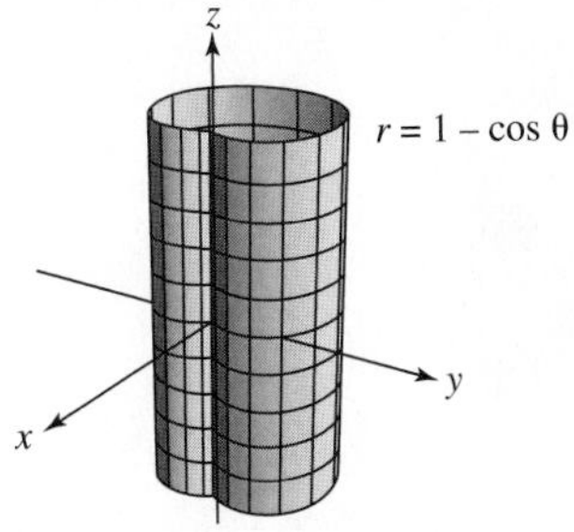

39. (2, 3, 1)
43. The surface is symmetric with respect to the z-axis.
45. Parabolic cylinder

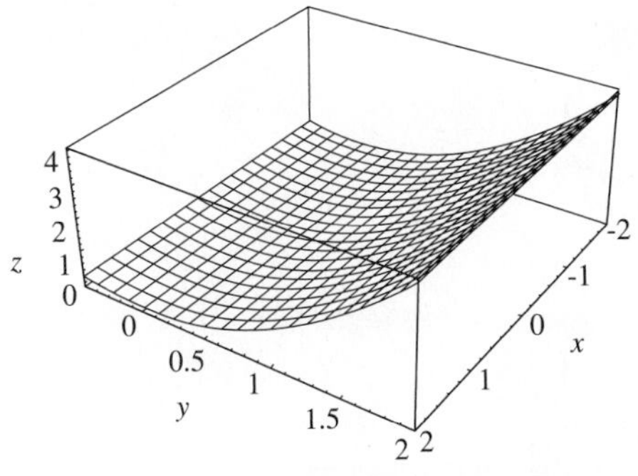

47. Sinusoidal cylinder

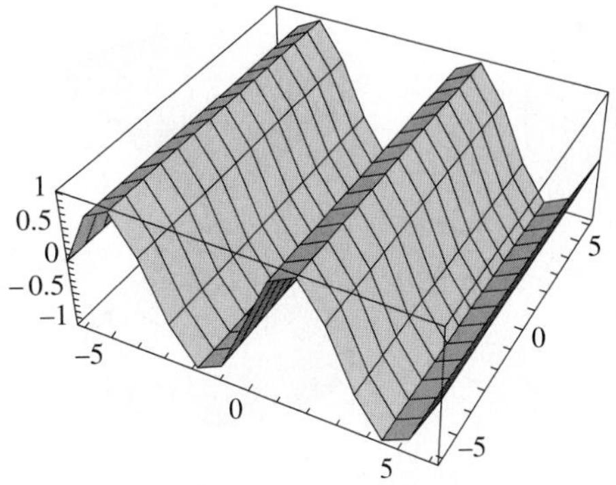

Section 12.6

Quick Review

1. $y = \pm 3\sqrt{1 - \dfrac{x^2}{4}}$; $y_1 = 3\sqrt{1 - \dfrac{x^2}{4}}$; $y_2 = -3\sqrt{1 - \dfrac{x^2}{4}}$

2. $x = 2\cos t$, $y = 3\sin t$, $0 \le t \le 2\pi$ **3.** $y = \pm 3\sqrt{\dfrac{x^2}{4} - 1}$

4. $x = 2\sec t$, $y = 3\tan t$, $0 \le t \le 2\pi$ **5.** $(\pm 3, 0)$, $(0, \pm 2)$ **6.** $(\pm 3, 0)$
7. (a) Yes **(b)** Yes **(c)** Yes **8. (a)** Yes **(b)** Yes **(c)** Yes
9. (a) No **(b)** Yes **(c)** No **10. (a)** Yes **(b)** No **(c)** No

Exercises

1. b, ellipsoid **3.** e, cone **5.** c, paraboloid
7. i, hyperbolic paraboloid **9.** f, cone

11.

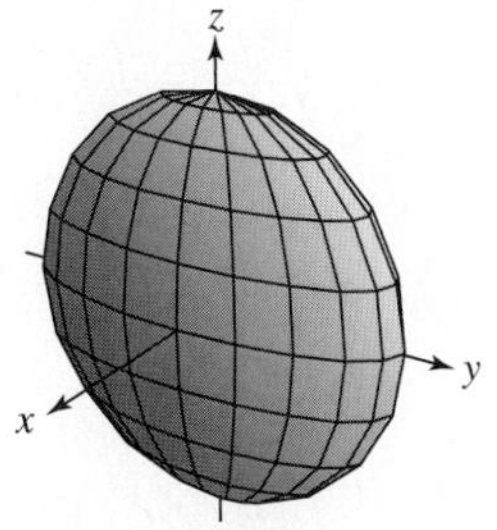

13.

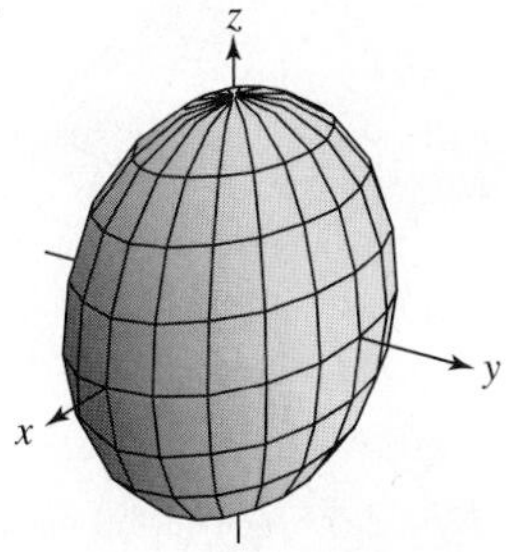

15.

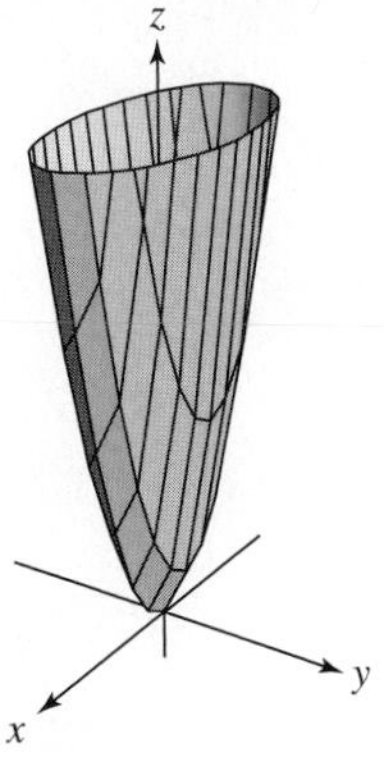

17.

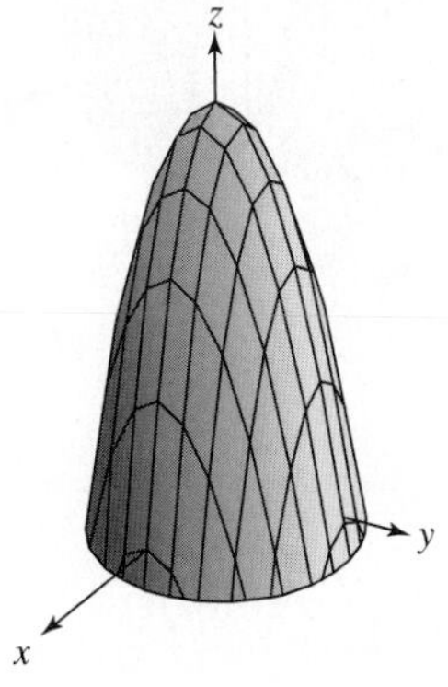

19.

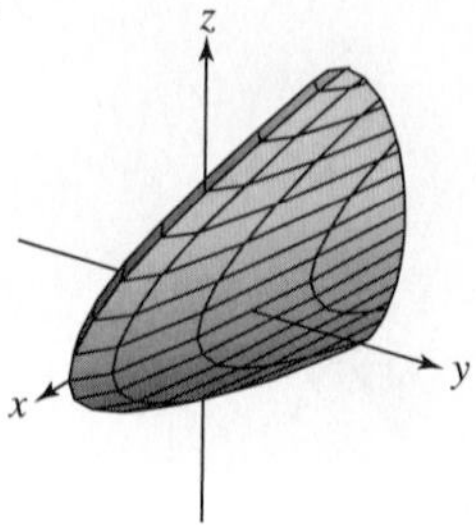

21.

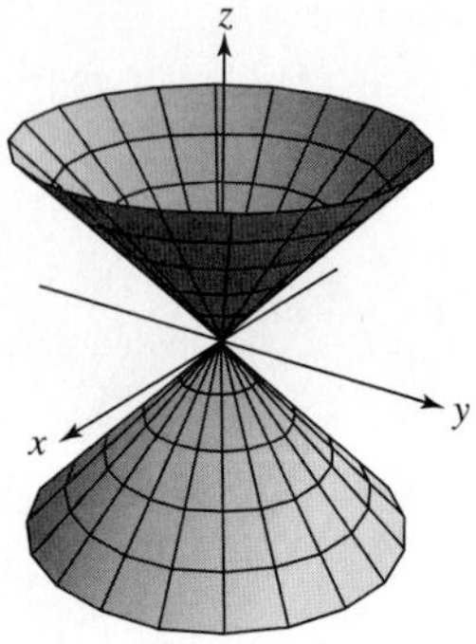

23.

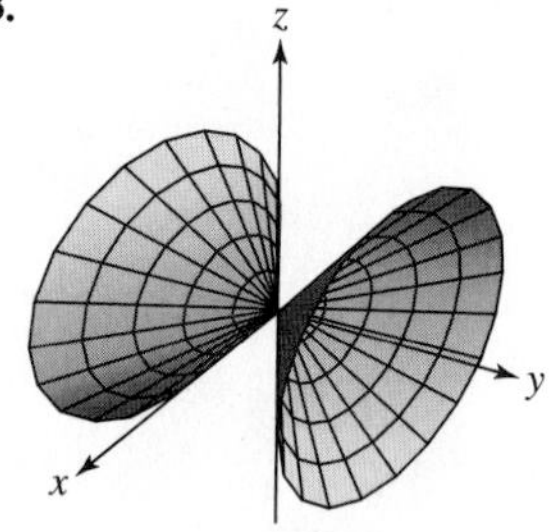

25.

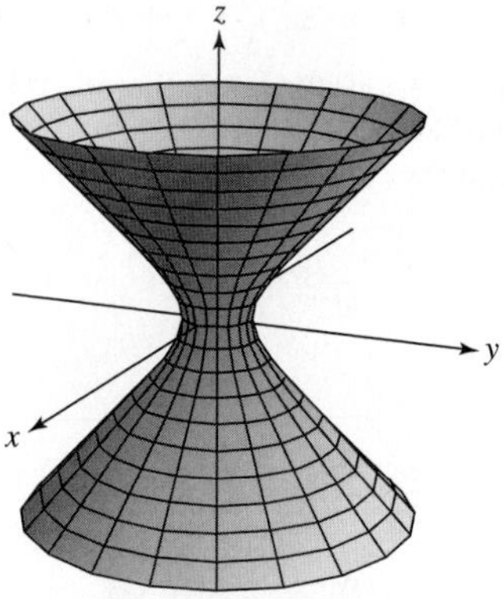

27.

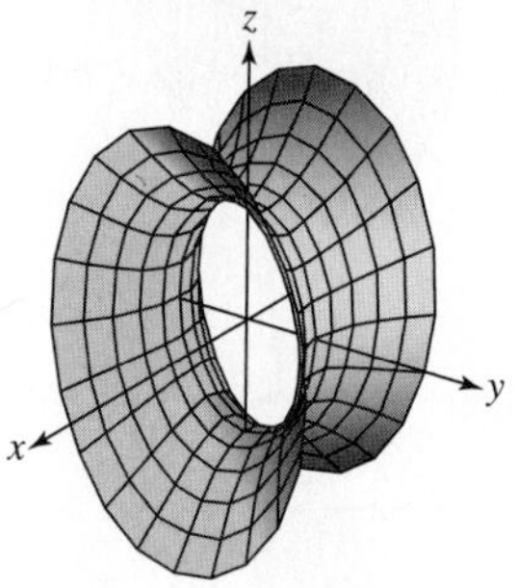

29.

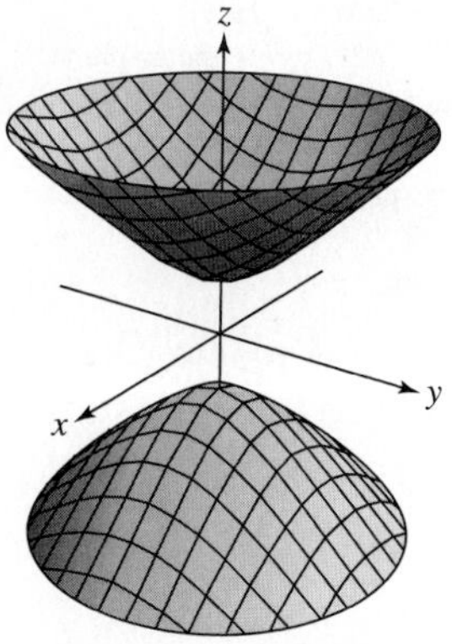

31.

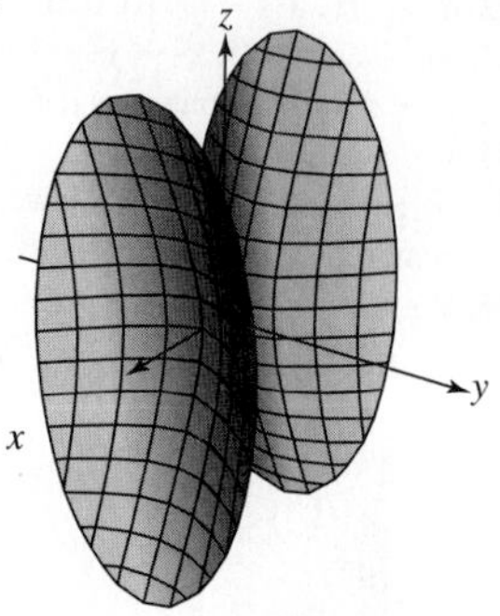

33.

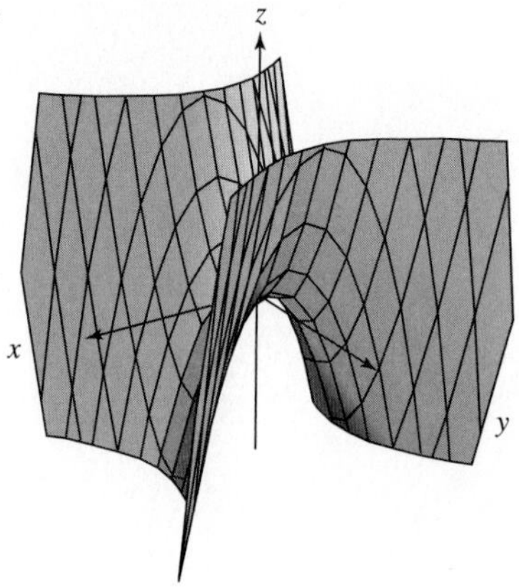

35.

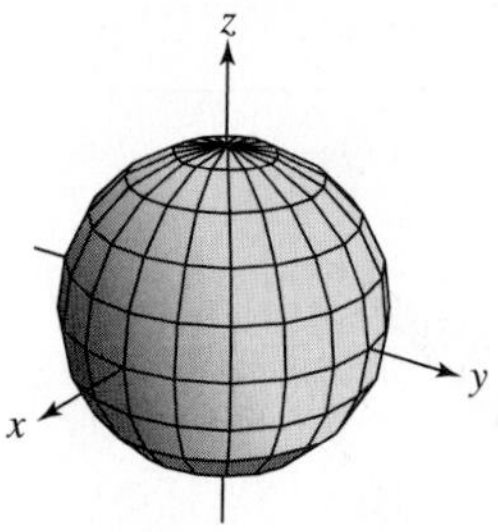

37.

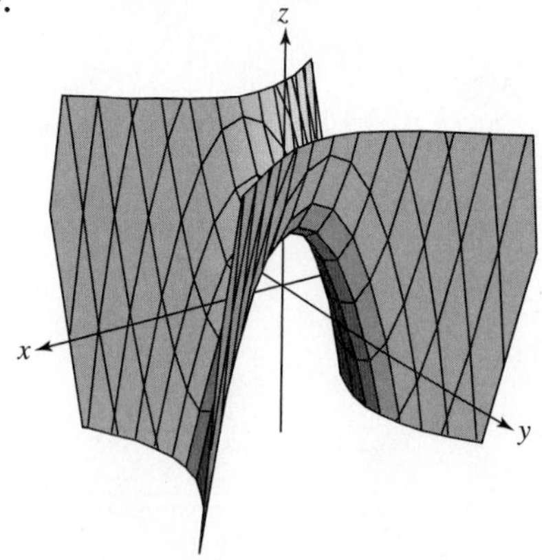

39.

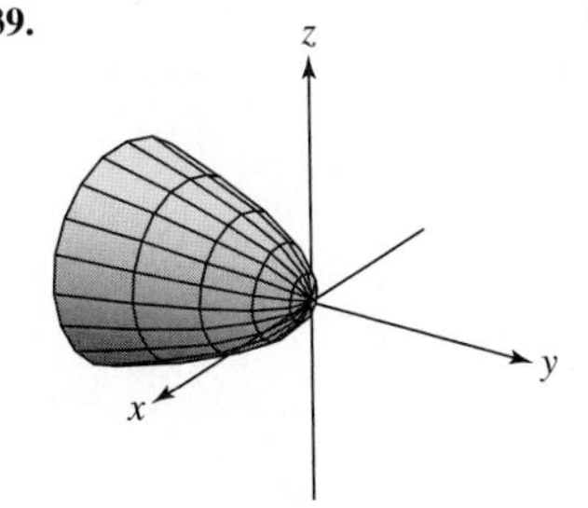

41.

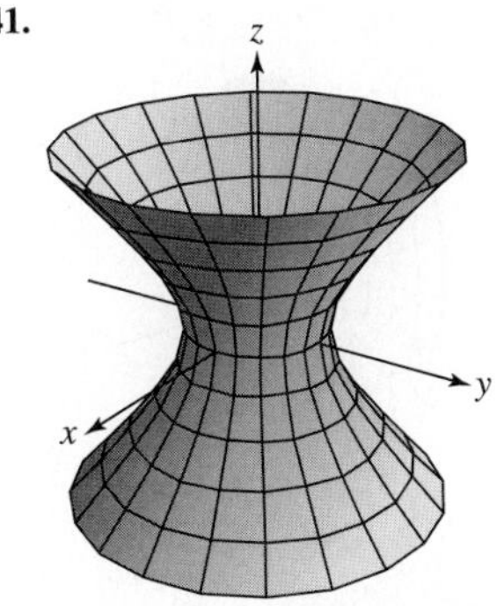

43.

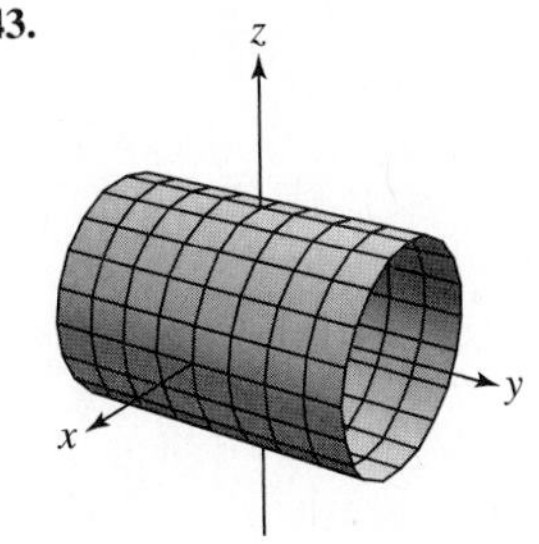

45.

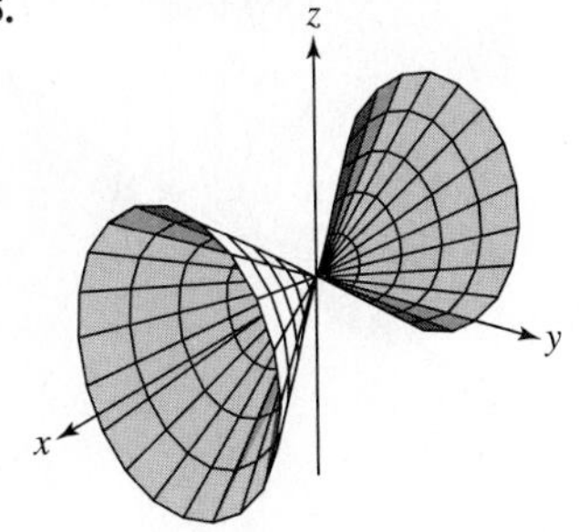

47.

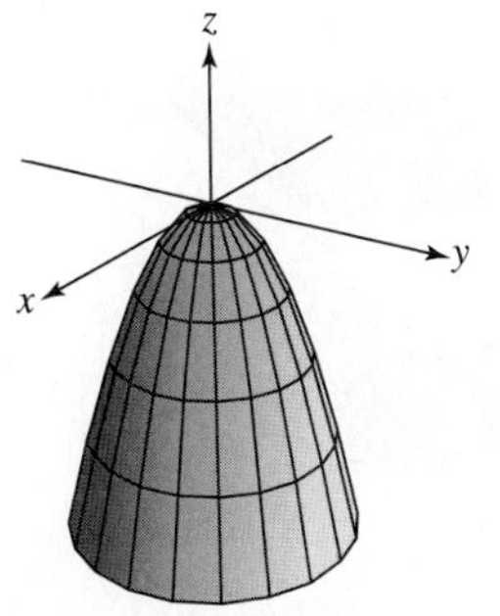

49.

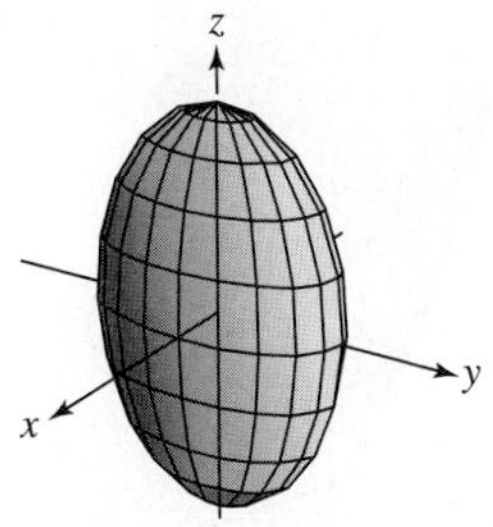

51. (a) $\frac{2\pi(9-c^2)}{9}$ (b) 8π (c) $\frac{4\pi abc}{3}$, yes $V = \frac{4\pi r^3}{3}$

53. Volume of segment: $V = \frac{\pi abh^2}{c}$; area of elliptic base when $z = h$: $A = \frac{\pi abh}{c}$; $V = \frac{1}{2}Ah$

57. Vertex: $\left(0, y_1, \frac{cy_1^2}{b^2}\right)$, focus: $\left(0, y_1, \frac{cy_1^2}{b^2} - \frac{a^2}{4c}\right)$

Chapter 12 Review Exercises

1. $2\mathbf{i} - 3\mathbf{j} + 6\mathbf{k} = 7\left(\frac{2}{7}\mathbf{i} - \frac{3}{7}\mathbf{j} + \frac{6}{7}\mathbf{k}\right)$

2. $\mathbf{i} + 2\mathbf{j} - \mathbf{k} = \sqrt{6}\left(\frac{1}{\sqrt{6}}\mathbf{i} + \frac{2}{\sqrt{6}}\mathbf{j} - \frac{1}{\sqrt{6}}\mathbf{k}\right)$

3. $\frac{8}{\sqrt{33}}\mathbf{i} - \frac{2}{\sqrt{33}}\mathbf{j} + \frac{8}{\sqrt{33}}\mathbf{k}$

4. $\overrightarrow{OD} = \overrightarrow{OC} + \overrightarrow{OB}$, $\overrightarrow{OE} = \overrightarrow{OC} + \overrightarrow{OA} + \overrightarrow{OB}$

5.

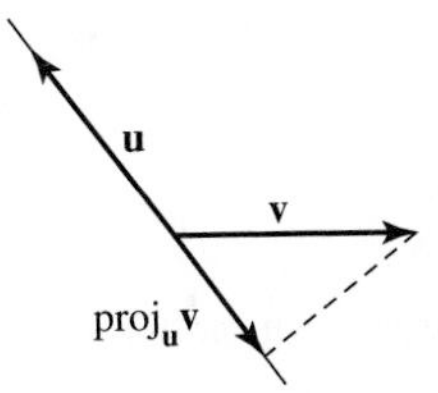

6. $\mathbf{a} = \text{proj}_\mathbf{v}\,\mathbf{u}$, $\mathbf{b} = \text{proj}_\mathbf{u}\,\mathbf{v}$, $\mathbf{c} = \mathbf{v} - \text{proj}_\mathbf{u}\,\mathbf{v}$

7. $|\mathbf{A}| = \sqrt{2}$, $|\mathbf{B}| = 3$, $\mathbf{A}\cdot\mathbf{B} = 3$, $\mathbf{B}\cdot\mathbf{A} = 3$, $\mathbf{A}\times\mathbf{B} = -2\mathbf{i} + 2\mathbf{j} - \mathbf{k}$, $\mathbf{B}\times\mathbf{A} = 2\mathbf{i} - 2\mathbf{j} + \mathbf{k}$, $|\mathbf{A}\times\mathbf{B}| = 3$, $\theta = \pi/4$, $|\mathbf{B}|\cos\theta = 3/\sqrt{2}$, $\text{proj}_\mathbf{A}\,\mathbf{B} = \frac{3}{2}(\mathbf{i} + \mathbf{j})$

8. $|\mathbf{A}| = \sqrt{6}$, $|\mathbf{B}| = \sqrt{2}$, $\mathbf{A}\cdot\mathbf{B} = -3$, $\mathbf{B}\cdot\mathbf{A} = -3$, $\mathbf{A}\times\mathbf{B} = -\mathbf{i} - \mathbf{j} + \mathbf{k}$, $\mathbf{B}\times\mathbf{A} = \mathbf{i} + \mathbf{j} - \mathbf{k}$, $|\mathbf{A}\times\mathbf{B}| = \sqrt{3}$, $\theta = 5\pi/6$, $|\mathbf{B}|\cos\theta = -\sqrt{3/2}$, $\text{proj}_\mathbf{A}\,\mathbf{B} = -\frac{1}{2}(\mathbf{i} + \mathbf{j} + \mathbf{k})$

9. $\mathbf{B} = \frac{4}{3}(2\mathbf{i} + \mathbf{j} - \mathbf{k}) - \frac{1}{3}(5\mathbf{i} + \mathbf{j} + 11\mathbf{k})$

10. $\mathbf{B} = -\frac{1}{5}(\mathbf{i} - 2\mathbf{j}) + \left(\frac{6}{5}\mathbf{i} + \frac{3}{5}\mathbf{j} + \mathbf{k}\right)$

11. $\mathbf{A}\times\mathbf{B} = \mathbf{k}$

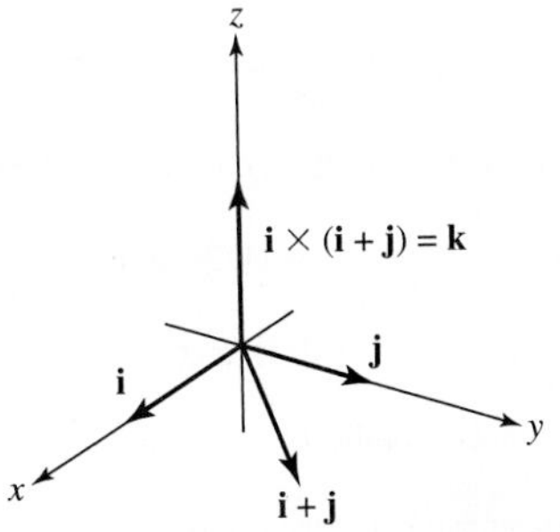

12. $\mathbf{A}\times\mathbf{B} = 2\mathbf{k}$

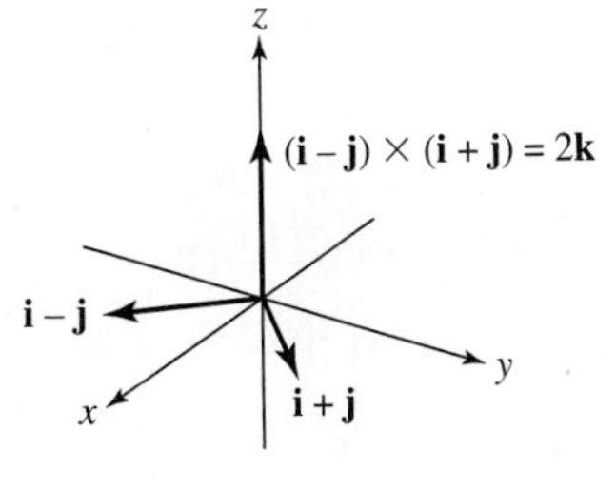

13. Tangent: $\pm\left(\frac{1}{\sqrt{5}}\mathbf{i} + \frac{2}{\sqrt{5}}\mathbf{j}\right)$, normal: $\pm\left(-\frac{2}{\sqrt{5}}\mathbf{i} + \frac{1}{\sqrt{5}}\mathbf{j}\right)$

14. Tangent: $\pm\frac{1}{5}(4\mathbf{i} - 3\mathbf{j})$, normal: $\pm\frac{1}{5}(3\mathbf{i} + 4\mathbf{j})$

16. (a) $\frac{1}{2}|\mathbf{u}\times\mathbf{v}|$ (b) $h = \frac{|\mathbf{u}\times\mathbf{v}|}{|\mathbf{v}|}$ (c) Area: $\sqrt{6}/2$, h: $\sqrt{6/5}$

17. $2\sqrt{7}$ **18.** $a = 10$ **19.** (a) $\sqrt{14}$ (b) 1 **20.** (a) 1 (b) 1

21. $\mathbf{n}\times\mathbf{v}$ or $\mathbf{v}\times\mathbf{n}$ **22.** $b\mathbf{i} - a\mathbf{j}$ **23.** $\sqrt{78}/3$ **24.** $\sqrt{78}/3$

25. $x = 1 - 3t$, $y = 2$, $z = 3 + 7t$ **26.** $x = 1$, $y = 2 + t$, $z = -t$; $0 \le t \le 1$

27. $\sqrt{2}$ **28.** $\sqrt{14}$ **29.** $2x + y - z = 3$ **30.** $x - 2y + 3z = -13$

31. $-9x + y + 7z = 4$ **32.** $x + y + z = 1$

33. $x = 0$: $(0, -1/2, -3/2)$, $y = 0$: $(-1, 0, -3)$, $z = 0$: $(1, -1, 0)$

34. $(4/3, -2/3, -2/3)$ **35.** $\pi/3$ **36.** $\pi/3$

37. $x = -5 + 5t,\ y = 3 - t,\ z = -3t$

39. (a) Normals: $\mathbf{n}_1 = 3\mathbf{i} + 6\mathbf{k},\ \mathbf{n}_2 = 2\mathbf{i} + 2\mathbf{j} - \mathbf{k}$, and $\mathbf{n}_1 \cdot \mathbf{n}_2 = 0$

(b) $x = -12t,\ y = \dfrac{19}{12} + 15t$, and $z = \dfrac{1}{6} + 6t$

40. $7x - 3y - 5z = -14$

42. The half-space of points lying on one side of the plane in the direction of **n**

43. 3 **44.** $25/\sqrt{38}$ **45.** $-3\mathbf{j} + 3\mathbf{k}$ **6.** $\dfrac{1}{\sqrt{14}}(-2\mathbf{i} - 3\mathbf{j} + \mathbf{k})$

47. $\dfrac{2}{\sqrt{35}}(5\mathbf{i} - \mathbf{j} - 3\mathbf{k})$ **48.** $(4/3, -2/3, -2/3)$ **49.** $(11/9, 26/9, -7/9)$

50. $\cos^{-1}\left(\dfrac{3}{\sqrt{35}}\right) \approx 59.5°$

51. $(1, -2, 1)$; $x = 1 - 5t,\ y = -2 + 3t$, and $z = -1 + 4t$

53. $2x + 7y + 2z + 10 = 0$

55. (a) No **(b)** No **(c)** No **(d)** No **(e)** Yes

56. (a) $(2, 1, 8)$ **(b)** $\cos\theta = 3/\sqrt{15}$ **(c)** $\dfrac{9}{5}(\mathbf{j} + 2\mathbf{k})$ **(d)** $6\sqrt{6}$

(e) $7x + 2y - z = 8$ **(f)** yz-plane: 14, xz-plane: 4, xy-plane: 2

57. $11/\sqrt{107}$ **58.** $12/\sqrt{62}$

59. The y-axis in the xy-plane; the yz-plane in three-dimensional space

60. The line $x + y = 1$ in the xy-plane; the plane $x + y = 1$ in three-dimensional space

61. Center: $(3, -1, 2)$, radius: $3\sqrt{2}$ **62.** $20{,}000\sqrt{3} \approx 34{,}641$ J

63. 20 lb

65. (b) All points in the plane determined by $P_1(x_1, y_1, z_1)$, $P_2(x_2, y_2, z_2)$, and $P_3(x_3, y_3, z_3)$

67. $(1, 0, 0)$ **68.** $(0, 1, 0)$ **69.** $(1, \pi, -1)$ **70.** $(1, 3\pi/2, 1)$

71. $z = 2$, a plane parallel to the xy-plane

72. $r^2 + z^2 = 6z$, a sphere of radius 3 centered at $(0, 0, 3)$ (rectangular)

73. $x^2 + \left(y - \dfrac{7}{2}\right)^2 = \dfrac{49}{4}$, a circular cylinder parallel to the z-axis

74. $(x - 2)^2 + y^2 = 4$, a circular cylinder parallel to the z-axis

75.

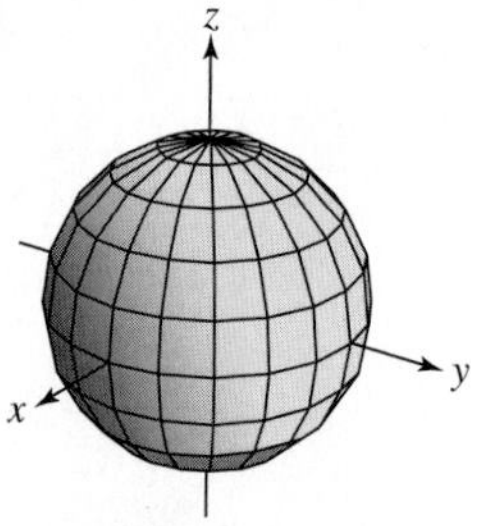

76.

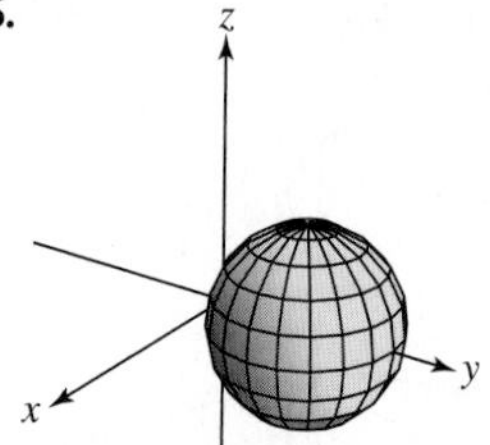

77.

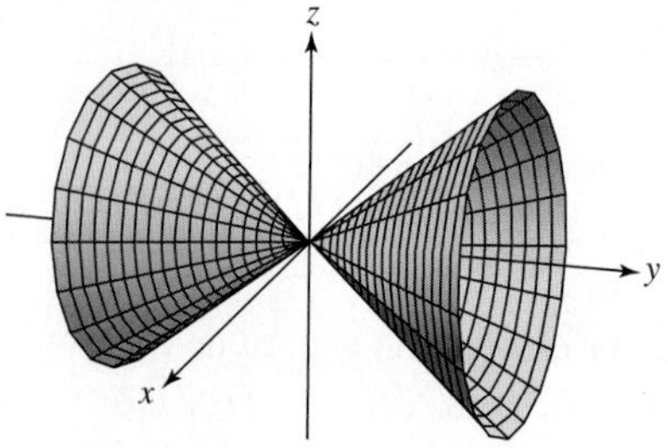

78.

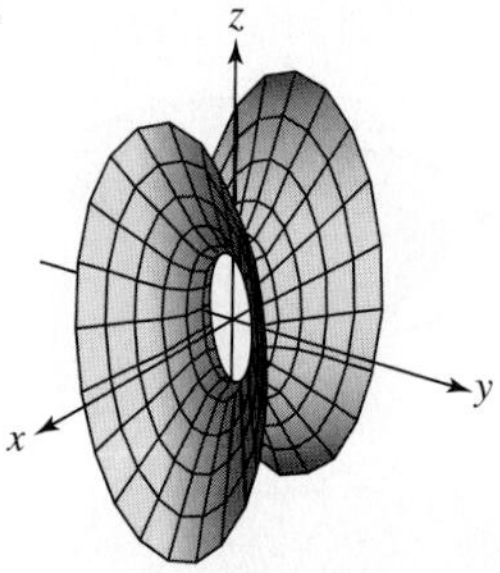

79.

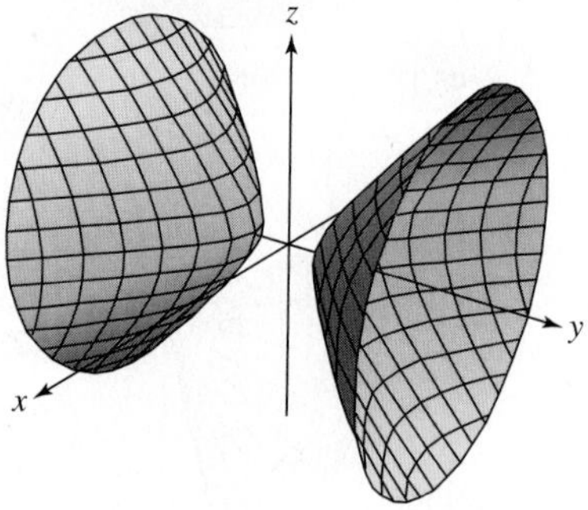

80.

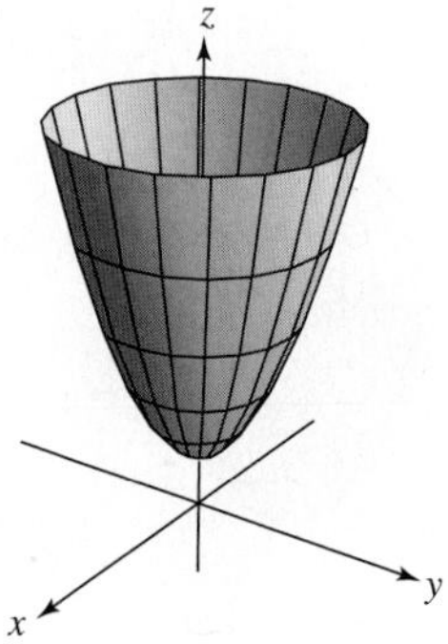

81.

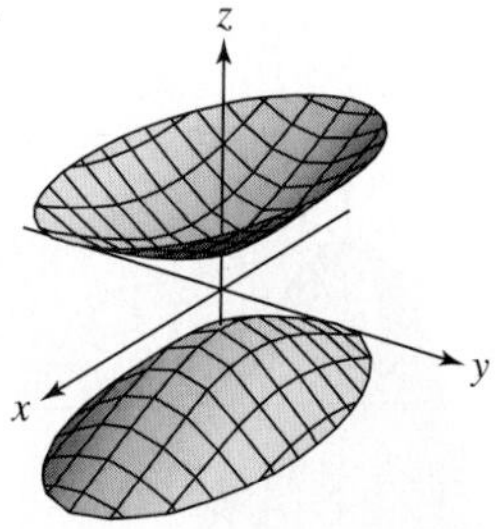

82.

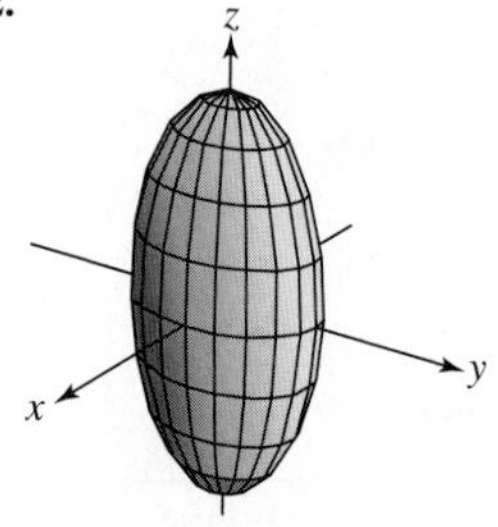

83.

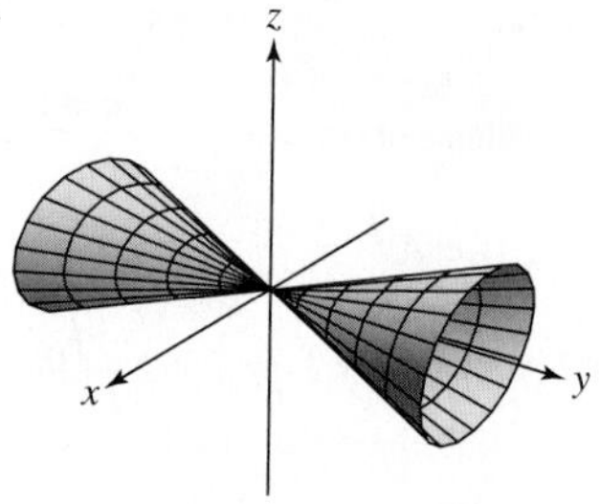

84.

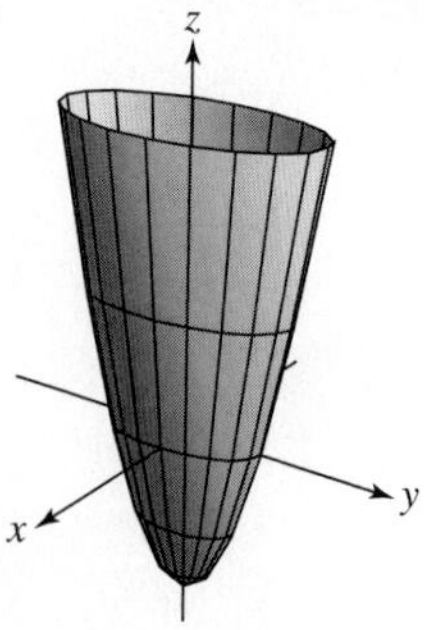

CHAPTER 13

Section 13.1

Quick Review

1. -3 **2.** -2 **3.** At all noninteger values of x **4.** At every integer

5. $y - \dfrac{4}{\pi} = -\dfrac{8(\pi+2)}{\pi^2}\left(x - \dfrac{\pi}{4}\right)$

6. $y - \dfrac{4}{\pi} = \dfrac{\pi^2}{8(\pi+2)}\left(x - \dfrac{\pi}{4}\right)$

7. $-\dfrac{10}{(x+3)^3}$ **8.** $\ln(|x+1|) + C$ **9.** $\ln 3$ **10.** $y = \sin x - \cos x$

Exercises

1. $y = x^2 - 2x$, $\mathbf{v} = \mathbf{i} + 2\mathbf{j}$, $\mathbf{a} = 2\mathbf{j}$ **3.** $y = \dfrac{2}{9}x^2$, $\mathbf{v} = 3\mathbf{i} + 4\mathbf{j}$, $\mathbf{a} = 3\mathbf{i} + 8\mathbf{j}$

5. $\mathbf{v}\left(\dfrac{\pi}{4}\right) = \dfrac{\sqrt{2}}{2}\mathbf{i} - \dfrac{\sqrt{2}}{2}\mathbf{j}$, $\mathbf{a}\left(\dfrac{\pi}{4}\right) = -\dfrac{\sqrt{2}}{2}\mathbf{i} - \dfrac{\sqrt{2}}{2}\mathbf{j}$,

$\mathbf{v}\left(\dfrac{\pi}{2}\right) = -\mathbf{j}$, $\mathbf{a}\left(\dfrac{\pi}{2}\right) = -\mathbf{i}$

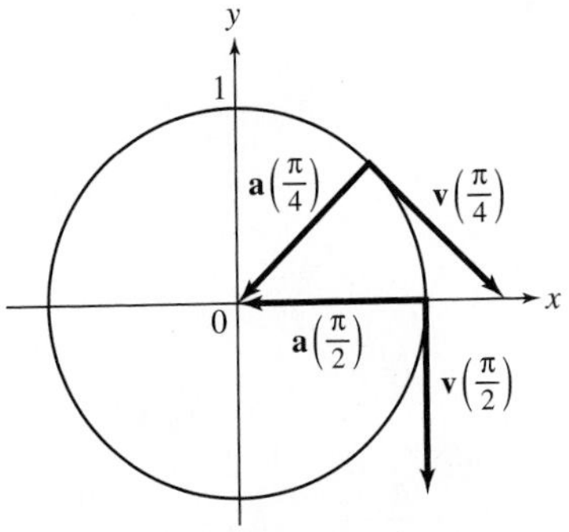

7. $\mathbf{v}(\pi) = 2\mathbf{i}$, $\mathbf{a}(\pi) = -\mathbf{j}$, $\mathbf{v}\left(\dfrac{3\pi}{2}\right) = \mathbf{i} - \mathbf{j}$, $\mathbf{a}\left(\dfrac{3\pi}{2}\right) = -\mathbf{i}$

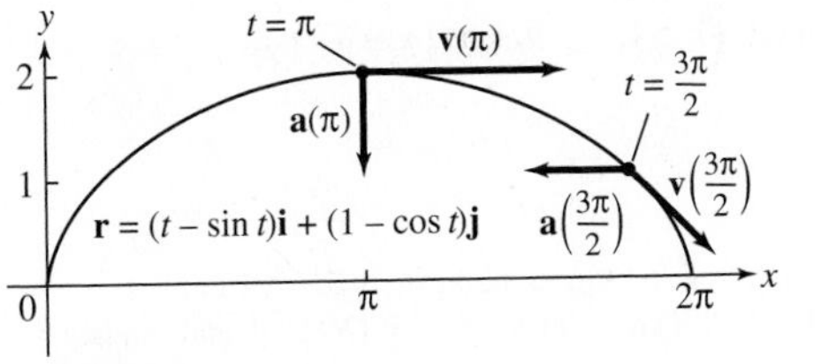

9. (a) $\mathbf{v} = \mathbf{i} + 2t\mathbf{j} + 2\mathbf{k}$, $\mathbf{a} = 2\mathbf{j}$ **(b)** Speed: 3; direction: $\dfrac{1}{3}\mathbf{i} + \dfrac{2}{3}\mathbf{j} + \dfrac{2}{3}\mathbf{k}$

(c) $\mathbf{v}(1) = 3\left(\dfrac{1}{3}\mathbf{i} + \dfrac{2}{3}\mathbf{j} + \dfrac{2}{3}\mathbf{k}\right)$

11. (a) $\mathbf{v} = (\sec t \tan t)\mathbf{i} + (\sec^2 t)\mathbf{j} + \dfrac{4}{3}\mathbf{k}$,

$\mathbf{a} = (\sec t \tan^2 t + \sec^3 t)\mathbf{i} + (2\sec^2 t \tan t)\mathbf{j}$

(b) Speed: 2; direction: $\dfrac{1}{3}\mathbf{i} + \dfrac{2}{3}\mathbf{j} + \dfrac{2}{3}\mathbf{k}$

(c) $\mathbf{v}\left(\dfrac{\pi}{6}\right) = 2\left(\dfrac{1}{3}\mathbf{i} + \dfrac{2}{3}\mathbf{j} + \dfrac{2}{3}\mathbf{k}\right)$

13. $\pi/2$ **15.** $\pi/2$ **17.** $t = 0, \pi$, or 2π

19. $\dfrac{1}{4}\mathbf{i} + 7\mathbf{j} + \dfrac{3}{2}\mathbf{k}$ **21.** $(\ln 4)\mathbf{i} + (\ln 4)\mathbf{j} + (\ln 2)\mathbf{k}$

23. $\mathbf{r} = [(t+1)^{3/2} - 1]\mathbf{i} + (1 - e^{-t})\mathbf{j} + [1 + \ln(t+1)]\mathbf{k}$

25. $\mathbf{r} = 8t\mathbf{i} + 8t\mathbf{j} + (100 - 16t^2)\mathbf{k}$ **27.** $x = t$, $y = -1$, $z = 1 + t$

29. $x = at$, $y = a$, $z = 2\pi b + bt$

31. (a) (i) Constant speed 1 **(ii)** Yes **(iii)** Counterclockwise **(iv)** Yes
(b) (i) Constant speed 2 **(ii)** Yes **(iii)** Counterclockwise **(iv)** Yes
(c) (i) Constant speed 1 **(ii)** Yes **(iii)** Counterclockwise **(iv)** No, starts at $(0, -1)$
(d) (i) Constant speed 1 **(ii)** Yes **(iii)** Clockwise **(iv)** Yes
(e) (i) Variable speed **(ii)** No **(iii)** Counterclockwise **(iv)** Yes

33. $\mathbf{r}(t) = \left(\dfrac{1}{2}t^2 + \dfrac{2}{\sqrt{11}}t\right)(3\mathbf{i} - \mathbf{j} + \mathbf{k}) + (\mathbf{i} + 2\mathbf{j} + 3\mathbf{k})$

35. $\mathbf{v} = 2\sqrt{5}\,\mathbf{i} + \sqrt{5}\,\mathbf{j}$

37. $\max|\mathbf{v}| = 3$, $\min|\mathbf{v}| = 2$, $\max|\mathbf{a}| = 3$, $\min|\mathbf{a}| = 2$

49. Show that the components of $\mathbf{r}(t)$ satisfy the corresponding equation.

Section 13.2

Quick Review

1. $x = 3$ **2.** $y = 3$ **3.** $y = x + 3\sqrt{2}$ **4.** $y = -x + 3\sqrt{2}$

5. (a) $\pm\left(\dfrac{2\sqrt{7}}{7}\mathbf{i} - \dfrac{\sqrt{21}}{7}\mathbf{j}\right)$ **(b)** $\pm\left(\dfrac{\sqrt{21}}{7}\mathbf{i} + \dfrac{2\sqrt{7}}{7}\mathbf{j}\right)$

6. ≈ 1.91 **7.** 3 **8.** $x \sin x$ **9.** $2x\cos(x^4)$

10. $(\cos x)\ln(1 + \sin^2 x) + (\sin x)\ln(1 + \cos^2 x)$

Exercises

1. (a) $\left(-\dfrac{2}{3}\sin t\right)\mathbf{i} + \left(\dfrac{2}{3}\cos t\right)\mathbf{j} + \dfrac{\sqrt{5}}{3}\mathbf{k}$ **(b)** 3π

3. (a) $\dfrac{1}{\sqrt{1+t}}\mathbf{i} + \dfrac{\sqrt{t}}{\sqrt{1+t}}\mathbf{k}$ **(b)** 52/3

5. (a) $(-\cos t)\mathbf{j} + (\sin t)\mathbf{k}$ **(b)** 3/2

7. (a) $\left(\dfrac{\cos t - \sin t}{t+1}\right)\mathbf{i} + \left(\dfrac{\sin t + t\cos t}{t+1}\right)\mathbf{j} + \left(\dfrac{\sqrt{2t}}{t+1}\right)\mathbf{k}$ **(b)** $\dfrac{\pi^2}{2} + \pi$

9. $(5, 0, 24\pi)$ **11. (a)** $s = 5t$ **(b)** $5\pi/2$

13. (a) $s = \sqrt{3}e^t - \sqrt{3}$ **(b)** $3\sqrt{3}/4$ **15.** $\sqrt{2} + \ln(1 + \sqrt{2}) \approx 2.30$

17. Cylinder: $x^2 + y^2 = 1$, plane: $x + z = 1$

19.

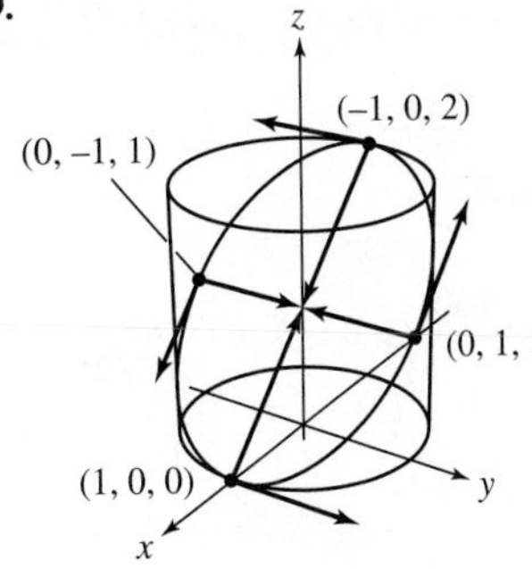

21. Graph parametrically. For example, use $x = t,\ y = (2/3)t^{3/2},\ 0 \le t \le 8$ for Exercise 3.

23. (b)

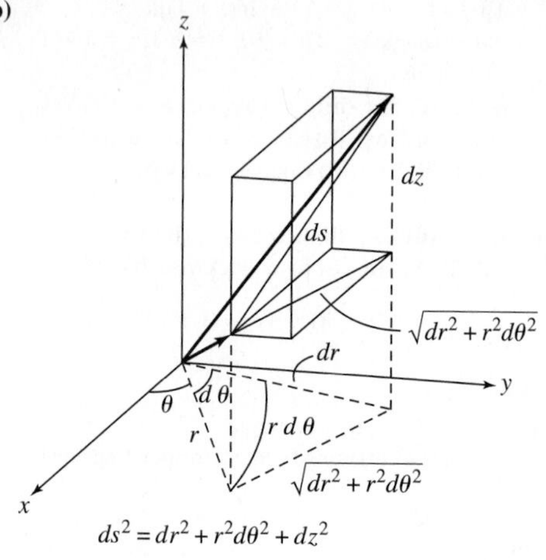

(c) $7\sqrt{3}$

25. Yes **27.** Speed is constant. **33.** $\kappa(b) = \dfrac{1}{2b}$ **37. (a)** $b - a$ **(b)** π

39. Torsion is zero.

41. $\kappa = \dfrac{2}{(1 + 4x^2)^{3/2}}$

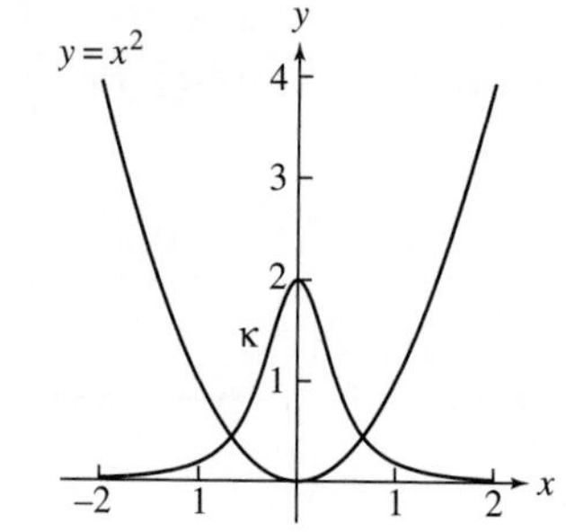

43. $\kappa = \dfrac{|\sin x|}{(1 + \cos^2 x)^{3/2}}$

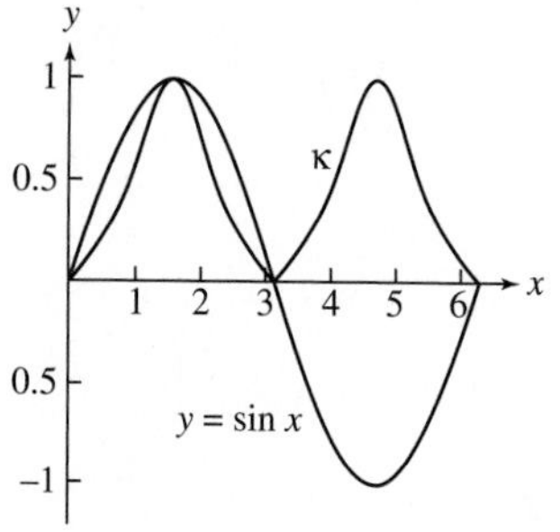

Section 13.3

Quick Review

6. $(\cos t)\mathbf{i} + \mathbf{j}$ **7.** $-(\sin t)\mathbf{i}$

8. $t = (2k + 1)\dfrac{\pi}{2}$: $\mathbf{v} = \mathbf{j},\ \mathbf{a} = \begin{cases} -\mathbf{i}, & \text{if } k \text{ is even,} \\ \mathbf{i}, & \text{if } k \text{ is odd} \end{cases}$

9. $16\mathbf{i} + 8\mathbf{j} + 8\mathbf{k}$ **10.** $-3\mathbf{i} - 4\mathbf{j} - 3\mathbf{k}$

Exercises

1. $\mathbf{T} = (\cos t)\mathbf{i} - (\sin t)\mathbf{j},\ \mathbf{N} = -(\sin t)\mathbf{i} - (\cos t)\mathbf{j},\ \kappa = \cos t$

3. $\mathbf{T} = \dfrac{1}{\sqrt{1 + t^2}}\mathbf{i} - \dfrac{t}{\sqrt{1 + t^2}}\mathbf{j},\ \mathbf{N} = \dfrac{-t}{\sqrt{1 + t^2}}\mathbf{i} - \dfrac{1}{\sqrt{1 + t^2}}\mathbf{j},$

$\kappa = \dfrac{1}{2}(1 + t^2)^{-3/2}$

5. $\mathbf{a} = \dfrac{2t}{\sqrt{1 + t^2}}\mathbf{T} + \dfrac{2}{\sqrt{1 + t^2}}\mathbf{N}$ **7. (b)** $\kappa = \cos t$

9. (a) Form the dot product with the tangent vector $\mathbf{v}$.

(b) $\mathbf{N} = \dfrac{-2e^{2t}}{\sqrt{1 + 4e^{4t}}}\mathbf{i} + \dfrac{1}{\sqrt{1 + 4e^{4t}}}\mathbf{j}$ **(c)** $\mathbf{N} = -\dfrac{1}{2}(\sqrt{4 - t^2}\,\mathbf{i} + t\mathbf{j})$

11. $\mathbf{T} = \left(\dfrac{3}{5}\cos t\right)\mathbf{i} - \left(\dfrac{3}{5}\sin t\right)\mathbf{j} + \dfrac{4}{5}\mathbf{k},\ \mathbf{N} = -(\sin t)\,\mathbf{i} - (\cos t)\,\mathbf{j},$

$\mathbf{B} = \left(\dfrac{4}{5}\cos t\right)\mathbf{i} - \left(\dfrac{4}{5}\sin t\right)\mathbf{j} - \dfrac{3}{5}\mathbf{k},\ \kappa = 3/25,\ \tau = -4/25$

13. $\mathbf{T} = \left(\dfrac{\cos t - \sin t}{\sqrt{2}}\right)\mathbf{i} + \left(\dfrac{\sin t + \cos t}{\sqrt{2}}\right)\mathbf{j},$

$\mathbf{N} = -\left(\dfrac{\cos t + \sin t}{\sqrt{2}}\right)\mathbf{i} + \left(\dfrac{-\sin t + \cos t}{\sqrt{2}}\right)\mathbf{j},\ \mathbf{B} = \mathbf{k},\ \kappa = \dfrac{1}{e^t\sqrt{2}},\ \tau = 0$

15. $\mathbf{T} = \dfrac{t}{\sqrt{t^2 + t}}\mathbf{i} + \dfrac{t}{\sqrt{t^2 + t}}\mathbf{j},\ \mathbf{N} = \dfrac{1}{\sqrt{t^2 + 1}}\mathbf{i} - \dfrac{t}{\sqrt{t^2 + 1}}\mathbf{j},$

$\mathbf{B} = -\mathbf{k},\ \kappa = \dfrac{1}{t(t^2 + 1)^{3/2}},\ \tau = 0$

17. $\mathbf{a} = (0)\mathbf{T} + |a|\mathbf{N} = |a|\mathbf{N}$ **19.** $\mathbf{a}(1) = \dfrac{4}{3}\mathbf{T} + \dfrac{2\sqrt{5}}{3}\mathbf{N}$

21. $\mathbf{a}(0) = (0)\mathbf{T} + 2\mathbf{N} = 2\mathbf{N}$

23. $\mathbf{r}\left(\dfrac{\pi}{4}\right) = \dfrac{1}{\sqrt{2}}\mathbf{i} + \dfrac{1}{\sqrt{2}}\mathbf{j} - \mathbf{k},\ \mathbf{T}\left(\dfrac{\pi}{4}\right) = -\dfrac{\sqrt{2}}{2}\mathbf{i} + \dfrac{\sqrt{2}}{2}\mathbf{j},$

$\mathbf{N}\left(\dfrac{\pi}{4}\right) = -\dfrac{\sqrt{2}}{2}\mathbf{i} - \dfrac{\sqrt{2}}{2}\mathbf{j},\ \mathbf{B}\left(\dfrac{\pi}{4}\right) = \mathbf{k}$, osculating plane: $z = -1$,

normal plane: $-x + y = 0$, rectifying plane. $x + y = \sqrt{2}$

Section 13.4

Quick Review

1. $\sqrt{5}/3$ **2.** $\sqrt{5}$ **3.** 1 **4.** $r = \dfrac{2}{1 - \cos\theta}$ **5.** $r = \dfrac{20}{4 + 5\cos\theta}$

6. $r = \dfrac{10}{3 - 2\cos\theta}$ **7.** Major: $(0, \pm 8)$, minor: $(\pm 6, 0)$

8. Major: $(\pm 7, 0)$, minor: $(0, \pm 4)$ **9.** $\tan^{-1} y = x^2 + C$

10. $y + \ln(|y|) = \dfrac{x^2}{2} - x + C$

Exercises

1. $T \approx 93.2$ min **3.** $a \approx 6763$ km; 6765 km **5.** 6501 km

7. (a) 42,167 km **(b)** 35,788 km **(c)** *Syncom 3, GOES 4,* and *Intelsat 5*

9. 376,821 km

11. Solar system: $\approx 2.97 \times 10^{-19}$ sec²/m³; Earth: 0.903×10^{-14} sec²/m³; Moon: 8.046×10^{-12} sec²/m³

17. (i) When $|\mathbf{r}(t)|$ is a minimum **(ii)** When $|\mathbf{r}(t)|$ is a maximum **(iii)** When $\mathbf{r}(t) \cdot \mathbf{w} = 0$ **(iv)** When angles between $\mathbf{r}(t)$ and $\mathbf{w}$ is a maximum **(v)** When angles between $\mathbf{r}(t)$ and $\mathbf{w}$ is a minimum

Chapter Review

1. $\mathbf{v}(0) = \sqrt{2}\,\mathbf{j},\ \mathbf{a}(0) = -4\mathbf{i},\ \mathbf{v}\left(\dfrac{\pi}{4}\right) = -2\sqrt{2}\mathbf{i} + \mathbf{j},$

$\mathbf{a}\left(\dfrac{\pi}{4}\right) = -2\sqrt{2}\mathbf{i} - \mathbf{j}$; at $t = 0$: $\mathbf{a} = 4\mathbf{N}$,

$\kappa = 2$; at $t = \dfrac{\pi}{4}$: $\mathbf{a} = \dfrac{7}{3}\mathbf{T} + \dfrac{4\sqrt{2}}{3}\mathbf{N},\ \kappa = \dfrac{4\sqrt{2}}{27}$

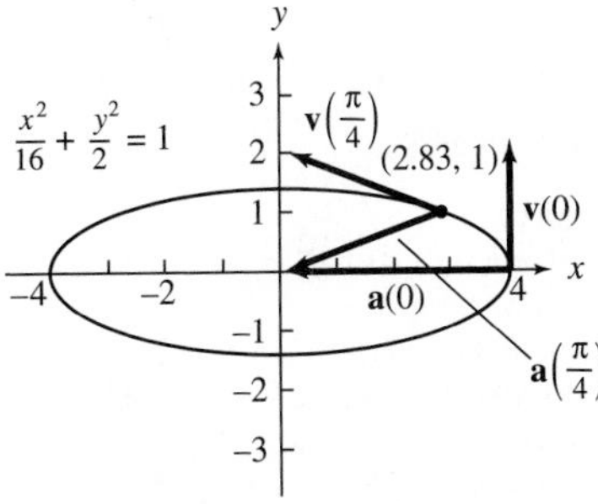

2. $\mathbf{v}(0) = \sqrt{3}\mathbf{j}$, $\mathbf{a}(0) = \sqrt{3}\mathbf{i}$; at $t = 0$: $\mathbf{a} = \sqrt{3}\mathbf{N}$, $\kappa = 1/\sqrt{3}$

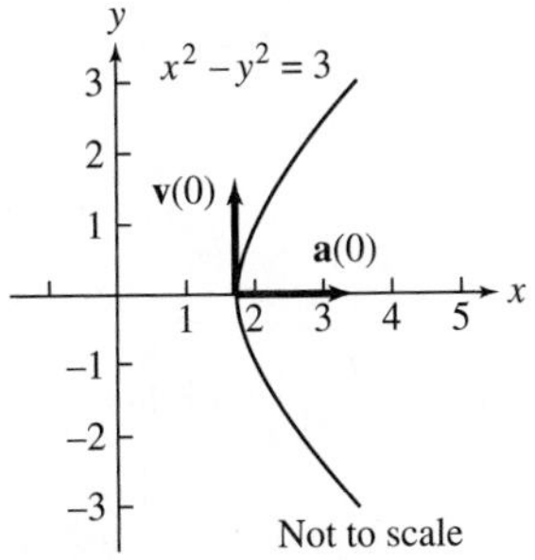

3. $|\mathbf{v}| = 1$ at $t = 0$ **4.** $\pi/2$ **5.** $\kappa = 1/5$ **6.** $\left(-\ln\sqrt{2}, \frac{1}{\sqrt{2}}\right)$

7. $\frac{dy}{dt} = -x$, clockwise **8.** $\mathbf{v}\cdot\mathbf{j} = 12$, $\mathbf{a}\cdot\mathbf{j} = 26$

9. $\mathbf{r} = \left(-\frac{t^2}{2} + 1\right)\mathbf{i} + \left(-\frac{t^2}{2} + 2\right)\mathbf{j} + \left(-\frac{t^2}{2} + 3\right)\mathbf{k}$

10. $\mathbf{r} = 90t^2\mathbf{i} + \left(90t^2 - \frac{16}{3}t^3 + 100\right)\mathbf{j}$

13. $\frac{\pi}{4}\sqrt{1 + \frac{\pi^2}{16}} + \ln\left(\frac{\pi}{4} + \sqrt{1 + \frac{\pi^2}{16}}\right) \approx 1.72$ **14.** 14

15. $\mathbf{T}(0) = \frac{2}{3}\mathbf{i} - \frac{2}{3}\mathbf{j} + \frac{1}{3}\mathbf{k}$, $\mathbf{N}(0) = \frac{1}{\sqrt{2}}\mathbf{i} + \frac{1}{\sqrt{2}}\mathbf{j}$,
$\mathbf{B}(0) = -\frac{1}{3\sqrt{2}}\mathbf{i} + \frac{1}{3\sqrt{2}}\mathbf{j} + \frac{4}{3\sqrt{2}}\mathbf{k}$, $\kappa(0) = \frac{\sqrt{2}}{3}$, $\tau(0) = 1/6$

16. $\mathbf{T}(0) = \frac{2}{3}\mathbf{i} + \frac{1}{3}\mathbf{j} + \frac{2}{3}\mathbf{k}$, $\mathbf{N}(0) = \frac{1}{\sqrt{5}}\mathbf{i} - \frac{2}{\sqrt{5}}\mathbf{j}$,
$\mathbf{B}(0) = \frac{4}{3\sqrt{5}}\mathbf{i} + \frac{2}{3\sqrt{5}}\mathbf{j} - \frac{5}{3\sqrt{5}}\mathbf{k}$, $\kappa(0) = \frac{2\sqrt{5}}{9}$, $\tau(0) = -4/9$

17. $\mathbf{T}(\ln 2) = \frac{1}{\sqrt{17}}\mathbf{i} + \frac{4}{\sqrt{17}}\mathbf{j}$, $\mathbf{N}(\ln 2) = -\frac{4}{\sqrt{17}}\mathbf{i} + \frac{1}{\sqrt{17}}\mathbf{j}$, $\mathbf{B}(\ln 2) = \mathbf{k}$,
$\kappa(\ln 2) = \frac{8}{17\sqrt{17}}$, $\tau(\ln 2) = 0$

18. $\mathbf{T}(\ln 2) = -\frac{15}{17\sqrt{2}}\mathbf{i} + \frac{1}{\sqrt{2}}\mathbf{j} + \frac{8}{17\sqrt{2}}\mathbf{k}$, $\mathbf{N}(\ln 2) = \frac{8}{17}\mathbf{i} - \frac{15}{17}\mathbf{k}$,
$\mathbf{B}(\ln 2) - \frac{15}{17\sqrt{2}}\mathbf{i} + \frac{1}{\sqrt{2}}\mathbf{j} - \frac{8}{17\sqrt{2}}\mathbf{k}$, $\kappa(\ln 2) = 32/867$, $\tau(\ln 2) = 32/867$

19. $\mathbf{a}(0) = 10\mathbf{T} + 6\mathbf{N}$ **20.** $\mathbf{a}(0) = 2\sqrt{2}\mathbf{T} + 2\sqrt{3}\mathbf{N}$

21. $\kappa = \pi s$ **22.** $\kappa = 1/a$

23. $\mathbf{T} = \left(\frac{1}{\sqrt{2}}\cos t\right)\mathbf{i} - (\sin t)\mathbf{j} + \left(\frac{1}{\sqrt{2}}\cos t\right)\mathbf{k}$,
$\mathbf{N} = \left(-\frac{1}{\sqrt{2}}\sin t\right)\mathbf{i} - (\cos t)\mathbf{j} - \left(\frac{1}{\sqrt{2}}\sin t\right)\mathbf{k}$,
$\mathbf{B} = \frac{1}{\sqrt{2}}\mathbf{i} - \frac{1}{\sqrt{2}}\mathbf{k}$, $\kappa = 1/\sqrt{2}$, $\tau = 0$

24. $t = 0, \pi/2$, or π **25.** $t = \pi/3$

26. Osculating plane: $3x - 3y + z = 1$, normal plane: $x + 2y + 3z = 6$, rectifying plane: $11x + 8y - 9z = 10$

27. $x = 1 + t, y = t, z = -t$ **28.** $x = 1 - t, y = 1 + t, z = \frac{\pi}{4} + t$

29. (a) $y_0 \approx 5971$ km **(b)** 1.639×10^7 km^2 **(c)** 3.21%

31. (b) ≈ 1.498701134

32. (a) $\dot{x} = \dot{r}\cos\theta - r\dot{\theta}\sin\theta$, $\dot{y} = \dot{r}\sin\theta + r\dot{\theta}\cos\theta$
(b) $\dot{r} = \dot{x}\cos\theta + \dot{y}\sin\theta$, $r\dot{\theta} = -\dot{x}\sin\theta + \dot{y}\cos\theta$

33. $\kappa = \frac{f^2 - ff'' + 2(f')^2}{[(f')^2 + f^2]^{3/2}}$

34. (a) $\mathbf{v}(1) = -\mathbf{u}_r + 3\mathbf{u}_\theta$, $\mathbf{a}(1) = -9\mathbf{u}_r - 6\mathbf{u}_\theta$ **(b)** 6.5 in.

CHAPTER 14

Section 14.1

Quick Review

1. $V = \frac{1}{3}\pi r^2 h$ **2.** $S = 2\pi rh + 2\pi r^2$ **3.** $t = \frac{y}{5280x}$

4. $h = \sqrt{a^2 - \frac{b^2}{4}}$ **5.** $A = \frac{1}{2}ab\sin 20°$ **6.** $V = \frac{1}{2}\pi ab^2$

7. $V = \frac{x^2y}{4\pi}$ or $V = \frac{xy^2}{4\pi}$ **8.** $V = \frac{4\pi r^2h - \pi h^3}{4} = \frac{\pi h}{4}(4r^2 - h^2)$

9. $A = \frac{1}{2}a^2\sin\theta$ **10.** $v = 2\pi mk$ ft/min

Exercises

1. Domain: all points in the xy-plane, range: all real numbers, domain unbounded

3. Domain: all $(x, y) \neq (0, 0)$, range:all real numbers, domain unbounded

5. Domain: all points in the xy-plane, range:all real numbers, domain unbounded

7. Domain: all (x, y) satisfying $x^2 + y^2 < 16$, range: $z \geq 1/4$, domain bounded

9. (a)

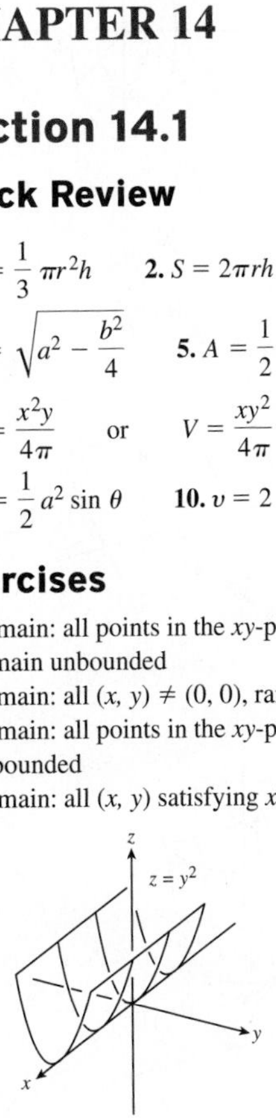

(b)

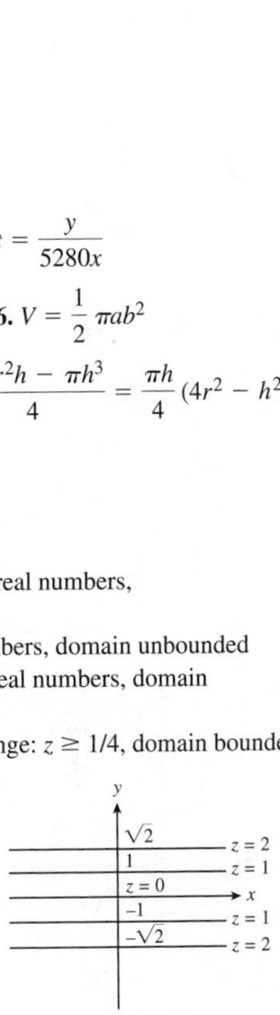

11. (a)

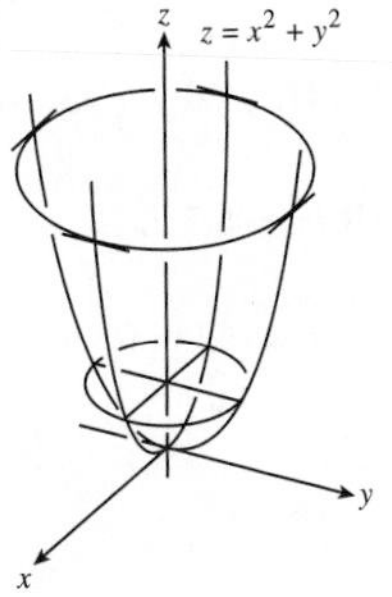

(b)

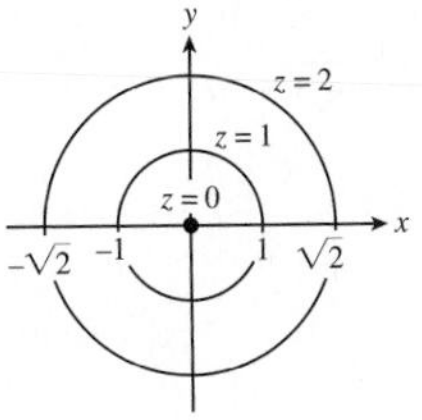

13. (a)

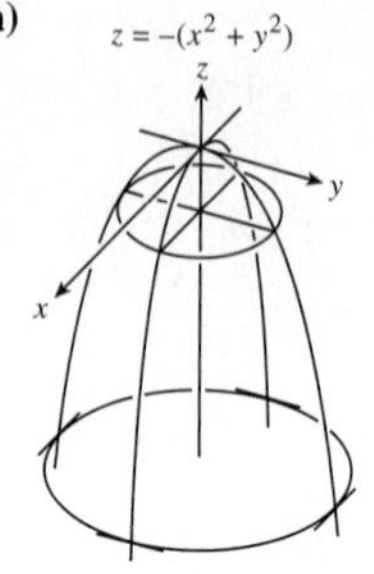

(b)

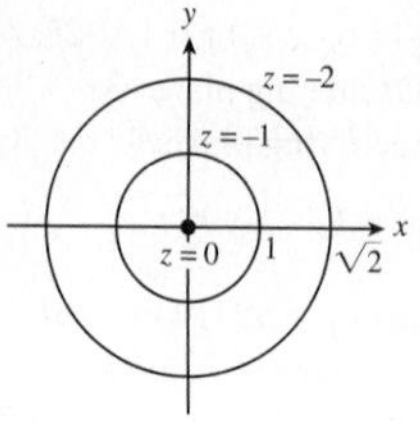

15. (a)

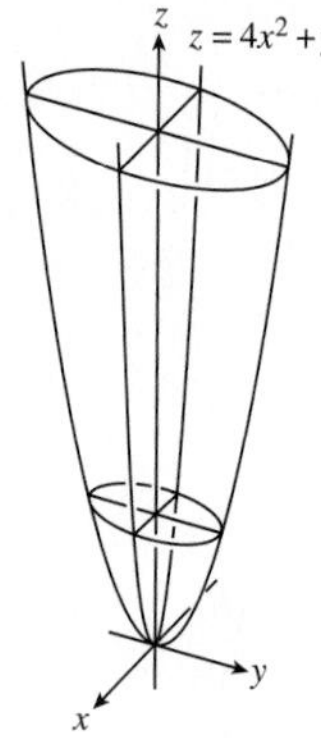

(b)

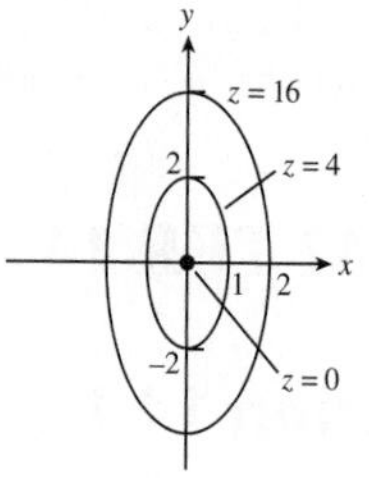

17. f **19.** a **21.** d

23.

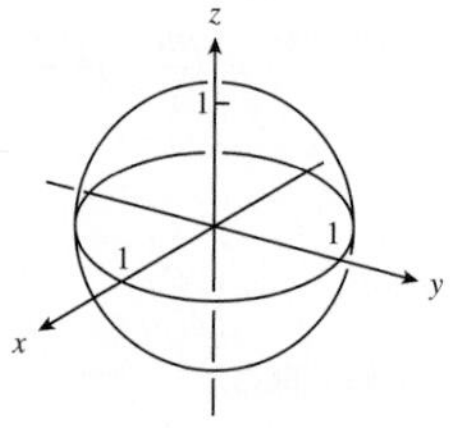

$f(x, y, z) = x^2 + y^2 + z^2 = 1$

25.

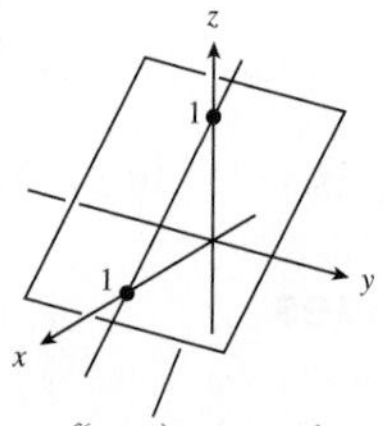

$f(x, y, z) = x + z = 1$

27.

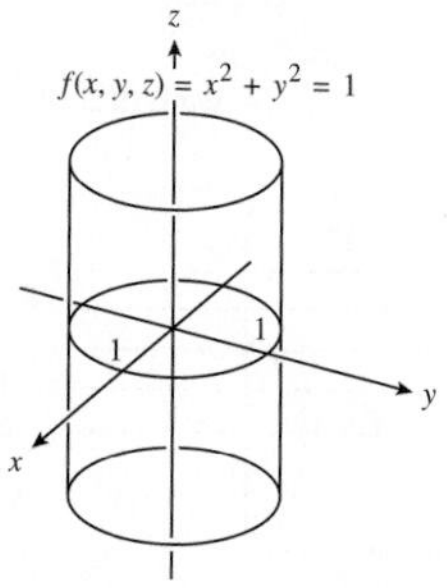

29.

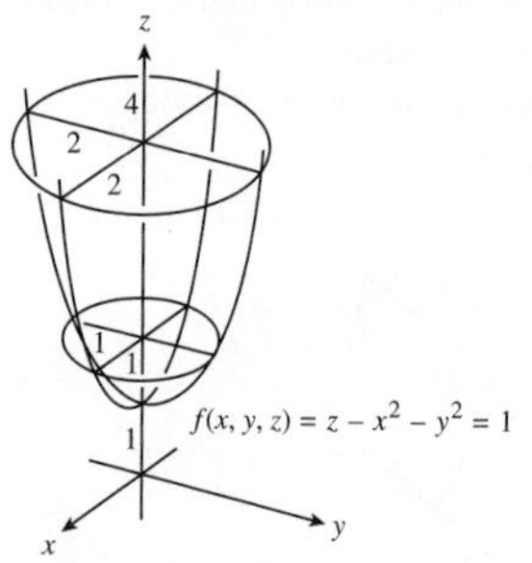

31. $x^2 + y^2 = 10$ **33.** $\tan^{-1} y - \tan^{-1} x = 2 \tan^{-1} \sqrt{2}$

35. $\sqrt{x - y} - \ln z = 2$ **37.** $\dfrac{x + y}{z} = \ln 2$ **41.** 2000 **43.** ≈63 km

57. $\dfrac{\sqrt{2}}{2} + \dfrac{\sqrt{2}}{2} i \approx 0.71 + 0.71i$, $\dfrac{\sqrt{2}}{2} - \dfrac{\sqrt{2}}{2} i \approx 0.71 - 0.71i$,

$-\dfrac{\sqrt{2}}{2} + \dfrac{\sqrt{2}}{2} i \approx -0.71 + 0.71i$, $-\dfrac{\sqrt{2}}{2} - \dfrac{\sqrt{2}}{2} i \approx -0.71 - 0.71i$

Section 14.2

Quick Review

1. 1 **2.** 2 **3.** 1/5 **4.** 5/6 **5.** −1 **6.** All $x \neq \pm 2$
7. All $x > 0$ **8.** All $x \neq -3/2$ **9.** All $x \neq 0$ **10.** All real numbers

Exercises

1. 5/2 **3.** 1/2 **5.** 5 **7.** 1 **9.** 1 **11.** 1 **13.** 0 **15.** −1

17. 2 **19.** 1/4 **21.** 7 **23.** 2 **25.** $\tan^{-1}\left(-\dfrac{\pi}{4}\right) \approx -0.67$

27. (a) All (x, y) **(b)** All $(x, y) \neq (0, 0)$
29. (a) All (x, y) except where $x = 0$ or $y = 0$ **(b)** All (x, y)
31. (a) All (x, y, z)
(b) All (x, y, z) except the interior of the cylinder $x^2 + y^2 = 1$
33. (a) All (x, y, z) where $z \neq 0$ **(b)** All (x, y, z) where $x^2 + y^2 + z^2 \neq 1$
35. Consider paths along $y = x$, $x > 0$, and along $y = x$, $x < 0$
37. Consider the path $y = kx^2$, k a constant
39. Consider the paths $y = kx$, $k \neq -1$ **41.** Consider the path $y = kx^2$, $k \neq 0$
43. No **45. (a)** $f(x, y)|_{y=mx} = \sin 2\theta$ where $\tan \theta = m$
47. The limit is 1. **49.** The limit is 0.

Section 14.3

Quick Review

1. $\dfrac{dy}{dx} = 2kx + 5, \dfrac{d^2y}{dx^2} = 2k$ **2.** $\dfrac{dy}{dx} = k \cos kx, \dfrac{d^2y}{dx^2} = -k^2 \sin kx$

3. $\dfrac{dy}{dx} = 20ke^{kx}, \dfrac{d^2y}{dx^2} = 20k^2e^{kx}$

4. $\dfrac{dy}{dx} = (x + k + 1)e^x, \dfrac{d^2y}{dx^2} = (x + k + 2)e^x$

5. $\dfrac{dy}{dx} = \dfrac{\sqrt{k}}{1 + kx^2}, \dfrac{d^2y}{dx^2} = -\dfrac{2k^{3/2}x}{(1 + kx^2)^2}$

6. $\dfrac{dy}{dx} = \dfrac{1}{x - k} + 3, \dfrac{d^2y}{dx^2} = -\dfrac{1}{(x - k)^2}$ **7.** $\dfrac{dy}{dx} = k^x \ln k, \dfrac{d^2y}{dx^2} = k^x (\ln k)^2$

8. $\dfrac{dy}{dx} = -ke^k \sin (kx), \dfrac{d^2y}{dx^2} = -k^2e^k \cos (kx)$

9. $\dfrac{dy}{dx} = -\dfrac{k}{(x - k)^2}, \dfrac{d^2y}{dx^2} = \dfrac{2k}{(x - k)^3}$ **10.** $\dfrac{dy}{dx} = \dfrac{k}{(k - x)^2}, \dfrac{d^2y}{dx^2} = \dfrac{2k}{(k - x^3)}$

Exercises

1. $\dfrac{\partial f}{\partial x} = 2, \dfrac{\partial f}{\partial y} = 0$ **3.** $\dfrac{\partial f}{\partial x} = y - 1, \dfrac{\partial f}{\partial y} = x$

5. $\dfrac{\partial f}{\partial x} = 2x(y + 2), \dfrac{\partial f}{\partial y} = x^2 - 1$ **7.** $\dfrac{\partial f}{\partial x} = -\dfrac{1}{(x + y)^2}, \dfrac{\partial f}{\partial y} = -\dfrac{1}{(x + y)^2}$

9. $\dfrac{\partial f}{\partial x} = \dfrac{x}{\sqrt{x^2 + y^2}}, \dfrac{\partial f}{\partial y} = \dfrac{x}{\sqrt{y^2 + y^2}}$

11. $\dfrac{\partial f}{\partial x} = \dfrac{-y^2 - 1}{(xy - 1)^2}, \dfrac{\partial f}{\partial y} = \dfrac{-x^2 - 1}{(xy - 1)^2}$

13. $\dfrac{\partial f}{\partial x} = e^x \sin (y + 1), \dfrac{\partial f}{\partial y} = e^x \cos (y + 1)$

15. $\dfrac{\partial f}{\partial x} = e^{(x+y+1)}, \dfrac{\partial f}{\partial y} = e^{(x+y+1)}$ **17.** $\dfrac{\partial f}{\partial x} = \dfrac{1}{x \ln y}, \dfrac{\partial f}{\partial y} = \dfrac{-\ln x}{y(\ln y)^2}$

19. $f_x = y + z, f_y = x + z, f_z = y + x$ **21.** $f_x = 0, f_y = 2y, f_z = 4z$

23. $f_x = \dfrac{1}{x + 2y + 3z}, f_y = \dfrac{2}{x + 2y + 3z}, f_z = \dfrac{3}{x + 2y + 3z}$

25. $\dfrac{\partial f}{\partial t} = -2\pi \sin (2\pi t - \alpha), \dfrac{\partial f}{\partial \alpha} = \sin (2\pi t - \alpha)$

27. $\dfrac{\partial h}{\partial \rho} = \sin \phi \cos \theta, \dfrac{\partial h}{\partial \phi} = \rho \cos \phi \cos \theta, \dfrac{\partial h}{\partial \theta} = -\rho \sin \phi \sin \theta$

29. $W_P = V, W_V = P + \dfrac{\delta v^2}{2g}, W_\delta = \dfrac{Vv^2}{2g}, W_v = \dfrac{V\delta v}{g}, W_g = -\dfrac{V\delta v^2}{2g^2}$

31. $f_{xx} = 0, f_{yy} = 0, f_{xy} = f_{yx} = 1$
33. $f_{xx} = 2y - y \sin x, f_{yy} = -\cos y, f_{xy} = f_{yx} = 2x + \cos x$
35. $f_{xx} = -\dfrac{1}{(x+y)^2}, f_{yy} = -\dfrac{1}{(x+y)^2}, f_{xy} = f_{yx} = -\dfrac{1}{(x+y)^2}$
37. $w_{xy} = w_{yx} = -\dfrac{6}{(2x+3y)^2}$
39. $w_{xy} = w_{yx} = 2y + 6xy^2 + 12x^2y^3$
41. (a) x first **(b)** y first **(c)** x first **(d)** x first **(e)** y first **(f)** y first
43. -2 **45.** $\dfrac{\partial f}{\partial z}(x_0, y_0, z_0) = \lim\limits_{h \to 0} \dfrac{f(x_0, y_0, z_0 + h) - f(x_0, y_0, z_0)}{h}$; 12

Section 14.4

Quick Review

1. $y = 1 - x$ **2.** 0.8 **3.** 0.01058 **4.** 0.013 **5.** 1.3%
6. Graph the error $y = |x - \sin(2x) + 1 - (1 - x)|$, along with the line $y = 0.02$ in $[-0.3, 0.3]$ by $[-0.01, 0.03]$.

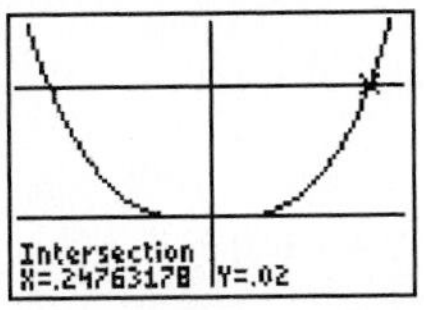

Interval: $\approx (-0.2476, 0.2476)$
7. $df = (1 - 2\cos(2x))\,dx$ **8.** $-1/2$
9. The graph is quite straight near $x = \pi$, so the linearization at $x = \pi$ should be quite close to the graph of f.
10. The graph is turning around near $x = 1/2$, so a straight-line approximation will be less accurate.

Exercises

1. (a) $L(x, y) = 1$ **(b)** $L(x, y) = 2x + 2y - 1$
3. (a) $L(x, y) = 3x - 4y + 5$ **(b)** $L(x, y) = 3x - 4y + 5$
5. (a) $L(x, y) = x + 1$ **(b)** $L(x, y) = -y + \dfrac{\pi}{2}$
7. $L(x, y) = x - 6y + 7$; $|E(x, y)| \le 0.06$
9. $L(x, y) = x + 1$; $|E(x, y)| \le 0.0222$
11. width (smaller dimension) **13.** 0.31 **15.** $\pm 2.415\%$
17. $|x - 1| \le 0.014$ and $|y - 1| \le 0.014$ **19.** $\approx 0.1\%$
21. (a) $L(x, y, z) = 2x + 2y + 2z - 3$ **(b)** $L(x, y, z) = y + z$ **(c)** $L(x, y, z) = 0$
23. (a) $L(x, y, z) = x$
(b) $L(x, y, z) = \dfrac{1}{\sqrt{2}}x + \dfrac{1}{\sqrt{2}}y$
(c) $L(x, y, z) = \dfrac{1}{3}x + \dfrac{2}{3}y + \dfrac{2}{3}z$
25. (a) $L(x, y, z) = 2 + x$
(b) $L(x, y, z) = x - y - z + \dfrac{\pi}{2} + 1$
(c) $L(x, y, z) = x - y - z + \dfrac{\pi}{2} + 1$
27. $L(x, y, z) = 2x - 6y - 2z + 6$; $|E(x, y, z)| \le 0.0024$
29. $L(x, y, z) = x + y - z - 1$; $|E(x, y, z)| \le 0.00135$
31. (a) $dS = S_0\left(\dfrac{1}{100}dp + dx - 5dw - 30dh\right)$
(b) More sensitive to a change in height
33. 4.8 **35.** Yes
37. (a) The volume is about 10 times more sensitive to a change in r.
(b) One solution is $dh = 1.5$, $dr = -0.15$, $h = 0.85$ in., $r = 0.85$ in.
39. d

Section 14.5

Quick Review

1. $\dfrac{\partial f}{\partial x} = y$; $\dfrac{\partial f}{\partial y} = x + \cos y$ **2.** $\dfrac{\partial f}{\partial x} = 3x^2$; $\dfrac{\partial f}{\partial y} = -2y$
3. $\dfrac{\partial f}{\partial x} = \sec^2(x + y)$; $\dfrac{\partial f}{\partial y} = \sec^2(x + y)$ **4.** $\dfrac{\partial f}{\partial x} = ye^{xy}$; $\dfrac{\partial f}{\partial y} = xe^{xy}$
5. $\dfrac{\partial f}{\partial x} = \sin y + y \sin x$; $\dfrac{\partial f}{\partial y} = x \cos y - \cos x$ **6.** 0 **7.** $\pi/2$ **8.** -2
9. -2 **10.** 2/3

Exercises

1. (a) $\dfrac{dw}{dt} = 0$ **(b)** $\dfrac{dw}{dt}(\pi) = 0$ **3. (a)** $\dfrac{dw}{dt} = 1$ **(b)** $\dfrac{dw}{dt}(3) = 1$
5. (a) $\dfrac{dw}{dt} = 4t\tan^{-1} t + 1$ **(b)** $\dfrac{dw}{dt}(1) = \pi + 1$
7. (a) $\dfrac{\partial z}{\partial r} = (4\cos\theta)\ln(r\sin\theta) + 4\cos\theta$,
$\dfrac{\partial z}{\partial \theta} = (-4r\sin\theta)\ln(r\sin\theta) + \dfrac{4r\cos^2\theta}{\sin\theta}$
(b) At $(2, \pi/4)$: $\dfrac{\partial z}{\partial r} = \sqrt{2}(\ln 2 + 2)$, $\dfrac{\partial z}{\partial \theta} = -2\sqrt{2}\ln 2 + 4\sqrt{2}$
9. (a) $\dfrac{\partial w}{\partial u} = 2u + 4uv$, $\dfrac{\partial w}{\partial v} = -2v + 2u^2$
(b) At $(1/2, 1)$: $\dfrac{\partial w}{\partial u} = 3$, $\dfrac{\partial w}{\partial v} = -3/2$
11. (a) $\dfrac{\partial u}{\partial x} = 0$, $\dfrac{\partial u}{\partial y} = \dfrac{z}{(z-y)^2}$, $\dfrac{\partial u}{\partial z} = -\dfrac{y}{(z-y)^2}$
(b) At $(\sqrt{3}, 2, 1)$: $\dfrac{\partial u}{\partial x} = 0$, $\dfrac{\partial u}{\partial y} = 1$, $\dfrac{\partial u}{\partial z} = -2$
13. $\dfrac{dz}{dt} = \dfrac{\partial z}{\partial x}\dfrac{dx}{dt} + \dfrac{\partial z}{\partial y}\dfrac{dy}{dt}$

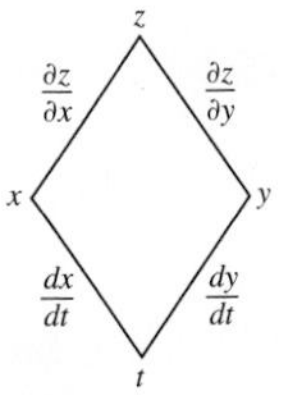

15. $\dfrac{\partial w}{\partial u} = \dfrac{\partial w}{\partial x}\dfrac{\partial x}{\partial u} + \dfrac{\partial w}{\partial y}\dfrac{\partial y}{\partial u} + \dfrac{\partial w}{\partial z}\dfrac{\partial z}{\partial u}$

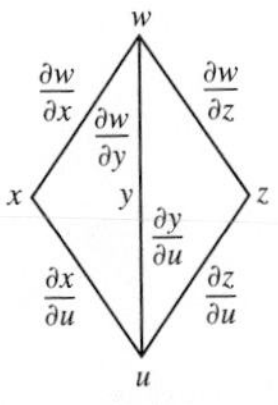

$\dfrac{\partial w}{\partial v} = \dfrac{\partial w}{\partial x}\dfrac{\partial x}{\partial v} + \dfrac{\partial w}{\partial y}\dfrac{\partial y}{\partial v} + \dfrac{\partial w}{\partial z}\dfrac{\partial z}{\partial v}$

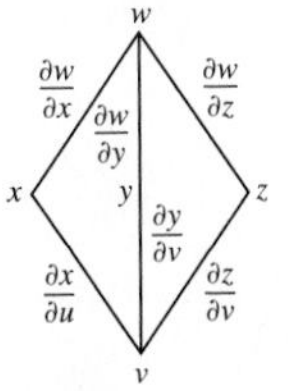

17. $\dfrac{\partial w}{\partial u} = \dfrac{\partial w}{\partial x}\dfrac{\partial x}{\partial u} + \dfrac{\partial w}{\partial y}\dfrac{\partial y}{\partial u}$

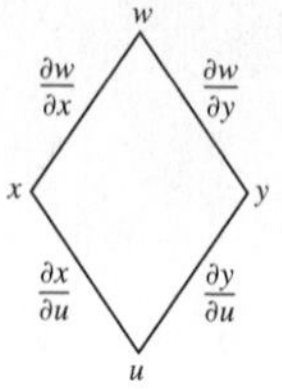

$\dfrac{\partial w}{\partial v} = \dfrac{\partial w}{\partial x}\dfrac{\partial x}{\partial v} + \dfrac{\partial w}{\partial y}\dfrac{\partial y}{\partial v}$

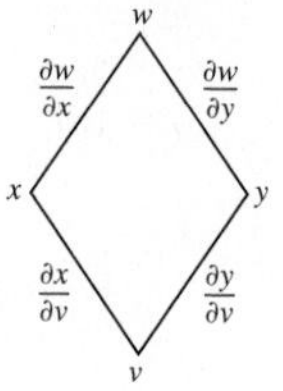

19. $\dfrac{\partial z}{\partial t} = \dfrac{\partial z}{\partial x}\dfrac{\partial x}{\partial t} + \dfrac{\partial z}{\partial y}\dfrac{\partial y}{\partial t}$

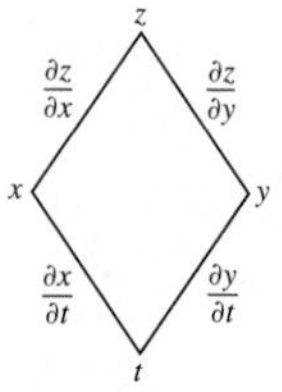

$\dfrac{\partial z}{\partial s} = \dfrac{\partial z}{\partial x}\dfrac{\partial x}{\partial s} + \dfrac{\partial z}{\partial y}\dfrac{\partial y}{\partial s}$

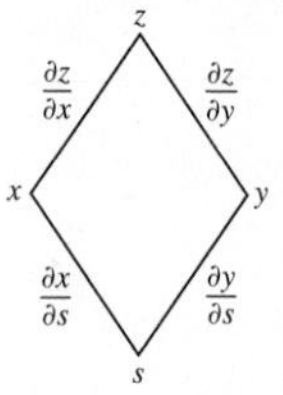

21. $\dfrac{\partial w}{\partial s} = \dfrac{dw}{du}\dfrac{\partial u}{\partial s}$

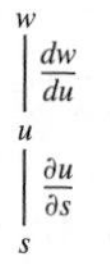

$\dfrac{\partial w}{\partial t} = \dfrac{dw}{du}\dfrac{\partial u}{\partial t}$

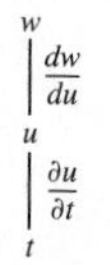

23. $\dfrac{\partial w}{\partial r} = \dfrac{\partial w}{\partial x}\dfrac{dx}{dr} + \dfrac{\partial w}{\partial y}\dfrac{dy}{dr} = \dfrac{\partial w}{\partial x}\dfrac{dx}{dr}$ since $\dfrac{dy}{dr} = 0$

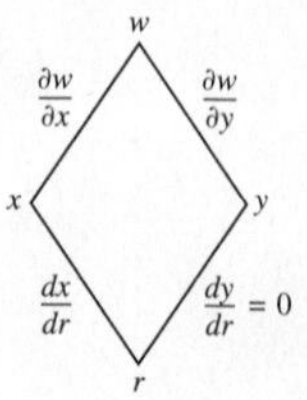

$\dfrac{\partial w}{\partial s} = \dfrac{\partial w}{\partial y}\dfrac{dy}{ds}$

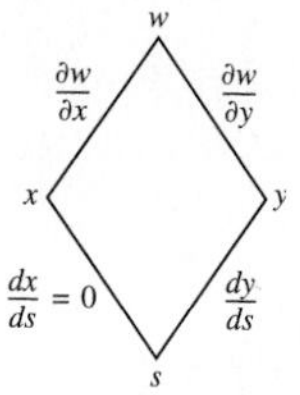

25. 4/3 **27.** $-4/5$ **29.** 12 **31.** -7 **33.** $\partial z/\partial u = 2$, $\partial z/v = 1$
35. 4
37. (a) Minimum: $(-2, 1)$, $(2, -1)$, maximum: $(2, 1)$, $(-2, -1)$
(b) Maximum 0, minimum -4
41. Volume is increasing at 3 m^3/sec, surface area is not changing, diagonals are decreasing in length.
45. (b) $f_x = (\cos\theta)\dfrac{\partial w}{\partial r} - \left(\dfrac{\sin\theta}{r}\right)\dfrac{\partial w}{\partial \theta}$, $f_y = (\sin\theta)\dfrac{\partial w}{\partial r} + \left(\dfrac{\cos\theta}{r}\right)\dfrac{\partial w}{\partial \theta}$

Section 14.6

Quick Review

1. $\sqrt{6}$ **2.** $\dfrac{2}{\sqrt{6}}\mathbf{i} - \dfrac{1}{\sqrt{6}}\mathbf{j} + \dfrac{1}{\sqrt{6}}\mathbf{k}$ **3.** -5 **4.** $\mathbf{i} + 3\mathbf{j} + 5\mathbf{k}$

5. $\mathbf{u} \times \mathbf{v} = \mathbf{i} + 3\mathbf{j} + 5\mathbf{k}$ **6.** $\dfrac{1}{\sqrt{35}}\mathbf{i} + \dfrac{3}{\sqrt{35}}\mathbf{j} + \dfrac{5}{\sqrt{35}}\mathbf{k}$

7. $x = -1 + 4t$, $y = 2$, $z = -1 + t$ **8.** $x = 2 + 3t$, $y = -1 - 2t$, $z = 1 + t$
9. $x = 2 + t$, $y = -2t$, $z = -2 + 3t$ **10.** $x - 3y + 2z = -3$

Exercises

1. $\nabla f = -\mathbf{i} + \mathbf{j}$, level curve: $y - x = -1$

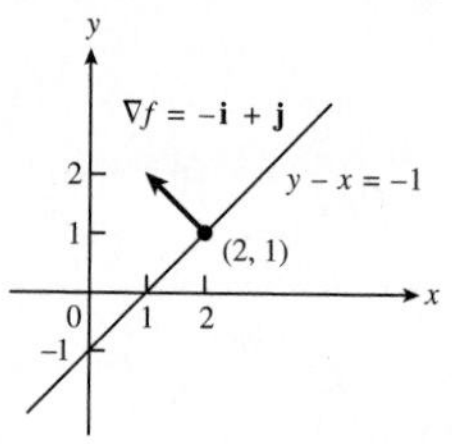

3. $\nabla g = 2\mathbf{i} + \mathbf{j}$, level curve: $y - x^2 = -1$

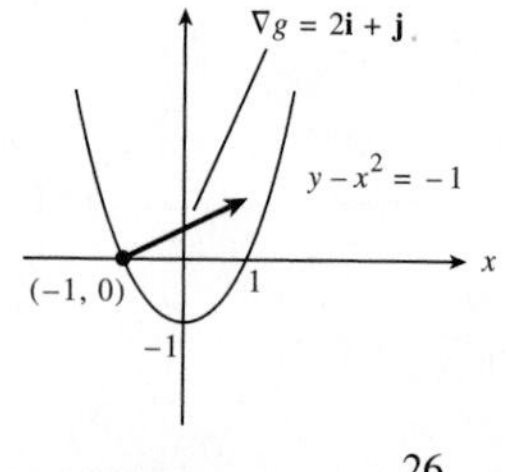

5. $3\mathbf{i} + 2\mathbf{j} - 4\mathbf{k}$ **7.** $-\dfrac{26}{27}\mathbf{i} + \dfrac{23}{54}\mathbf{j} - \dfrac{23}{54}\mathbf{k}$ **9.** -4 **11.** 31/13

13. 3 **15.** 2

17. Increases: $\mathbf{u} = -\dfrac{1}{\sqrt{2}}\mathbf{i} + \dfrac{1}{\sqrt{2}}\mathbf{j}$, $(D_{\mathbf{u}}f)_{P_0} = \sqrt{2}$;
decreases: $-\mathbf{u} = \dfrac{1}{\sqrt{2}}\mathbf{i} - \dfrac{1}{\sqrt{2}}\mathbf{j}$, $(D_{-\mathbf{u}}f)_{P_0} = -\sqrt{2}$

19. Increases: $\mathbf{u} = \dfrac{1}{3\sqrt{3}}\mathbf{i} - \dfrac{5}{3\sqrt{3}}\mathbf{j} - \dfrac{1}{3\sqrt{3}}\mathbf{k}$, $(D_{\mathbf{u}}f)_{P_0} = 3\sqrt{3}$;
decreases: $-\mathbf{u} = -\dfrac{1}{3\sqrt{3}}\mathbf{i} + \dfrac{5}{3\sqrt{3}}\mathbf{j} + \dfrac{1}{3\sqrt{3}}\mathbf{k}$, $(D_{-\mathbf{u}}f)_{P_0} = -\sqrt{2}$

21. Increases: $-\mathbf{u} = \frac{1}{\sqrt{3}}\mathbf{i} + \frac{1}{\sqrt{3}}\mathbf{j} + \frac{1}{\sqrt{3}}\mathbf{k}$, $(D_{\mathbf{u}}f)_{P_0} = 2\sqrt{3}$;

decreases: $-\mathbf{u} = -\frac{1}{\sqrt{3}}\mathbf{i} - \frac{1}{\sqrt{3}}\mathbf{j} - \frac{1}{\sqrt{3}}\mathbf{k}$, $(D_{-\mathbf{u}}f)_{P_0} = -2\sqrt{3}$

23. 0.000760 **25.** 0

27. (a) $x + y + z = 3$ **(b)** $x = 1 + 2t$, $y = 1 + 2t$, $z = 1 + 2t$

29. (a) $2x - z = 2$ **(b)** $x = 2 - 4t$, $y = 0$, $z = 2 + 2t$

31. (a) $2x + 2y + z = 4$ **(b)** $x = 2t$, $y = 1 + 2t$, $z = 2 + t$

33. (a) $x + y + z = 1$ **(b)** $x = t$, $y = 1 + t$, $z = t$

35. $2x - z = 2$ **37.** $x - y + 2z = 1$

39.

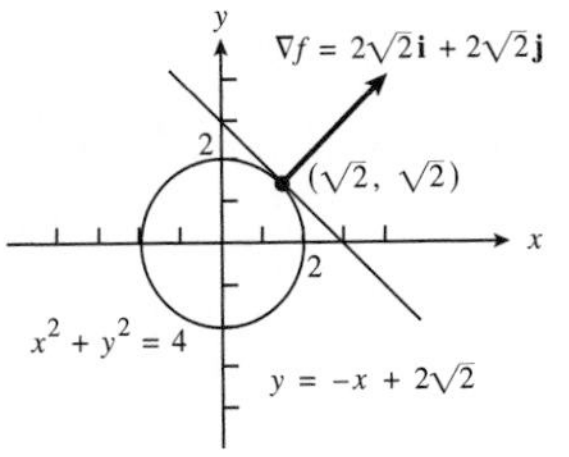

41.

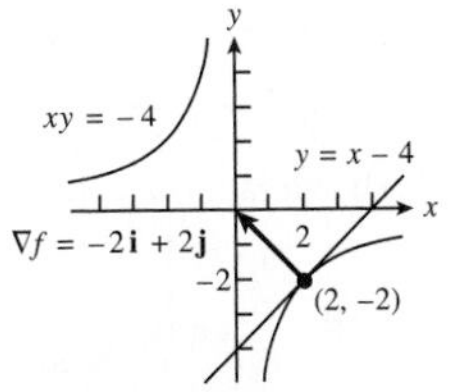

43. $x = 1$, $y = 1 + 2t$, $z = 1 - 2t$ **45.** $x = 1 - 2t$, $y = 1$, $z = \frac{1}{2} + 2t$

47. $x = 1 + 90t$, $y = 1 - 90t$, $z = 3$

49. $\mathbf{u} = \frac{7}{\sqrt{53}}\mathbf{i} - \frac{2}{\sqrt{53}}\mathbf{j}$, $-\mathbf{u} = -\frac{7}{\sqrt{53}}\mathbf{i} + \frac{2}{\sqrt{53}}\mathbf{j}$ **51.** No

53. $-7/\sqrt{5}$ **55. (a)** 0.935° C/m **(b)** 1.87° C/sec

57. $t = -\frac{\pi}{4}: \frac{-\pi}{2\sqrt{2}}$; $t = 0$: 0; $t = \frac{\pi}{4}: \frac{\pi}{2\sqrt{2}}$ **63.** $\nabla f \cdot \mathbf{u} = (D_{\mathbf{u}}f)_{P_0}$

Section 14.7

Quick Review

1. (1, 1/2), (−1, −1/2) **2.** −1/2 at $x = -1$ **3.** 1 at $x = 1$

4. Absolute maximum of 1/2 at $x = 1$, absolute minimum of −1/2 at $x = -1$

5. (1, 4) **6.** −5 at $x = -2$, −12 at $x = 5$ **7.** 4 at $x = 1$

8. Absolute maximum of 4 at $x = 1$, absolute minimum of −12 at $x = 5$

9. $x = -2$, $y = -2$ **10.** $x = 9/11$, $y = -7/11$

Exercises

1. Local minimum of −5 at (−3, 3) **3.** Saddle point at (−2, 1)

5. Saddle point at (6/5, 69/25) **7.** Local minimum of −6 at (2, −1)

9. Saddle point at (1, 2)

11. Local minimum of 0 at (0, 0), saddle point at (1, −1)

13. Local maximum of 2 at (1, 1) and (−1, −1), saddle point at (0, 0)

15. Local maximum of −1 at (0, 0)

17. Saddle points at $(n\pi, 0)$ for every integer n

19. Absolute maximum of 1 at (0, 0), absolute minimum of −5 at (1, 2)

21. Absolute maximum of 11 at (0, −3), absolute minimum of −10 at (4, −2)

23. Absolute maximum of 4 at (2, 0), absolute minimum of $3\sqrt{2}/2$ at $(3, \pm\pi/4)$ and $(1, \pm\pi/4)$

25. Absolute maximum of 1 at (1, 0), (0, 1), and (0, −1), absolute minimum of −1 at (−1, 0)

27. $a = -3$ and $b = 2$

29. Hottest: $2\frac{1}{4}°$ at $(-1/2, \pm\sqrt{3}/2)$, coldest: $-\frac{1}{4}°$ at (1/2, 0)

31. (a) Saddle point at (0, 0)
(b) Local minimum at (1, 2)
(c) Local minimum at (1, −2), saddle point at (−1, −2)

35. (a) No **(b)** Saddle point at (a, b)

37. (1/6, 1/3, 355/36) **39.** No

41. (a) (i) Absolute minimum of −2 at (−2, 0) when $t = \pi$; absolute maximum of $2\sqrt{2}$ at $(\sqrt{2}, \sqrt{2})$ when $t = \pi/4$
(ii) Absolute minimum of 2 at (2, 0) and (0, 2) when $t = 0, \pi/2$, respectively; absolute maximum of $2\sqrt{2}$ at $(\sqrt{2}, \sqrt{2})$ when $t = \pi/4$
(b) (i) Absolute minimum of −2 at $(-\sqrt{2}, \sqrt{2})$ when $t = 3\pi/4$; absolute maximum of 2 at $(\sqrt{2}, \sqrt{2})$ when $t = \pi/4$
(ii) Absolute minimum of 0 at (2, 0) and (0, 2) when $t = 0, \pi/2$, respectively; absolute maximum of 2 at $(\sqrt{2}, \sqrt{2})$ when $t = \pi/4$
(c) (i) Absolute minimum of 4 at (0, 2) when $t = \pi/2$; absolute maximum of 8 at (2, 0) and (−2, 0) when $t = 0, \pi$, respectively
(ii) Absolute minimum of 4 at (0, 2) when $t = \pi/2$; absolute maximum of 8 at (2, 0) when $t = 0$

43. (i) Absolute minimum of −1/2 at (−1, 1/2) when $t = -1/2$; no absolute maximum
(ii) Absolute minimum of −1/2 at (−1, 1/2) when $t = -1/2$; absolute maximum of 0 at (0, 1) and (−2, 0) when $t = -1, 0$, respectively
(iii) Absolute minimum of 0 at (0, 1) when $t = 0$; absolute maximum of 4 at (2, 2) when $t = 1$

Section 14.8

Quick Review

1. Local maximum of −28/9 at (4/9, 2/9) **2.** Local maximum of 4 at (0, 1)

3. Local minimum of −63 at (15, −8)

4. Local maximum of 1 at (−1/2, −1) [(0, 0) is a saddle point]

5. $\nabla g = 4y\mathbf{j} - 6z\mathbf{k}$

6. $\nabla k = (9x^2y - 2y^3 + y\cos xy)\mathbf{i} + (3x^3 - 6xy^2 + x\cos xy)\mathbf{j}$

7. $\nabla h = 3\mathbf{i} - 2\mathbf{j} + 4z\mathbf{k}$ **8.** Perpendicular **9.** Perpendicular

10. Parallel

Exercises

1. $(\pm\sqrt{2}, \pm 1/2)$ **3.** 39 **5.** $(3, \pm 3\sqrt{2})$

7. (a) Minimum value of 8 at (4, 4) **(b)** Maximum value of 64 at (8, 8)

9. $r = 2$ cm, $h = 4$ cm, area $= 24\pi$ cm² **11.** $4\sqrt{2}$ by $3\sqrt{2}$

13. Maximum of 20 at (2, 4), minimum of 0 at (0, 0)

15. Maximum of 125° at $(2\sqrt{5}, -\sqrt{5})$ and $(-2\sqrt{5}, \sqrt{5})$, minimum of 0° at $(\sqrt{5}, 2\sqrt{5})$ and $(-\sqrt{5}, -2\sqrt{5})$

17. (3/2, 2, 5/2) **19.** Minimum distance is 1 at (±1, 0, 0)

21. (0, 0, 2), (0, 0, −2)

23. Maximum value of 30 at (1, −2, 5), minimum value of −30 at (−1, 2, −5)

25. 3, 3, and 3 **27.** $2/\sqrt{3}$ by $2/\sqrt{3}$ by $2/\sqrt{3}$

29. (±4/3, −4/3, −4/3), temperature $= 642\frac{2}{3}°$ **31.** \$128 at (8, 14)

33. Maximum value of 4/3 at (2/3, 4/3, −4/3) **35.** (2, 4, 4)

37. Maximum of $1 + 6\sqrt{3}$ at $(\pm\sqrt{6}, \sqrt{3}, 1)$ minimum of $1 - 6\sqrt{3}$ at $(\pm\sqrt{6}, -\sqrt{3}, 1)$

39. Maximum value of 4 at (0, 0, ±2), minimum value of 2 at $(\pm\sqrt{2}, \pm\sqrt{2}, 0)$

42. $A = -1/2$, $B = 3/2$, $C = -1/4$

Chapter 14 Review Exercises

1. Domain: all (x, y); range: $z \geq 0$; level curves are ellipses with major axis along the y-axis and minor axis along the x-axis

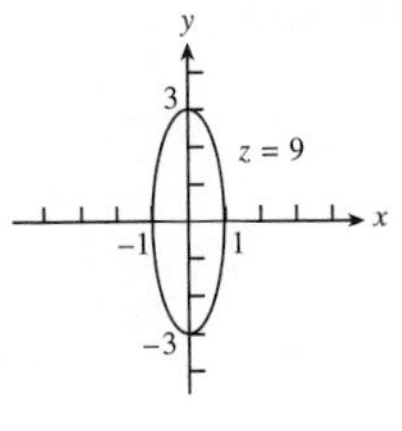

2. Domain: all (x, y); range: $0 < z < \infty$; level curves are the straight lines $x + y = \ln z$ with slope -1 and $z > 0$

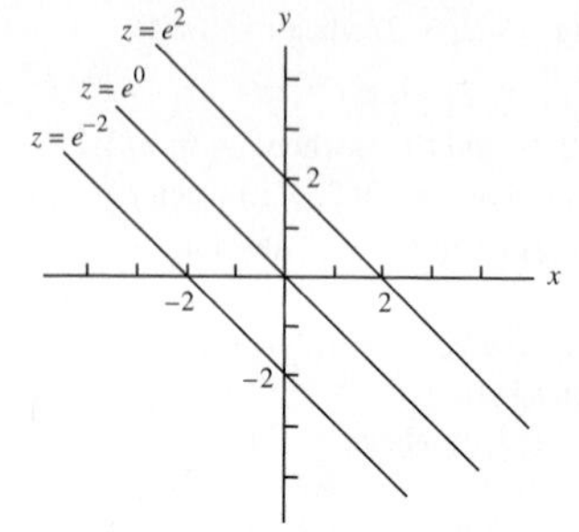

3. Domain: all (x, y) such that $x \neq 0$ and $y \neq 0$; range: $z \neq 0$; level curves are hyperbolas with the x- and y-axis as asymptotes

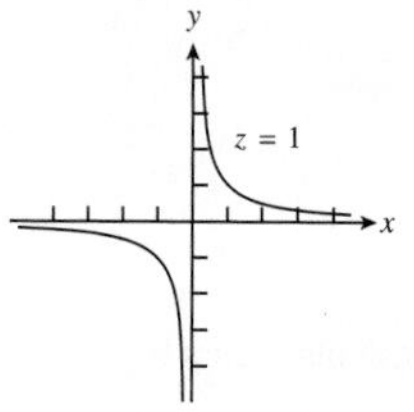

4. Domain: all (x, y) such that $x^2 - y \geq 0$; range: $z \geq 0$; level curves are the parabolas $y = x^2 - c$, $c \geq 0$

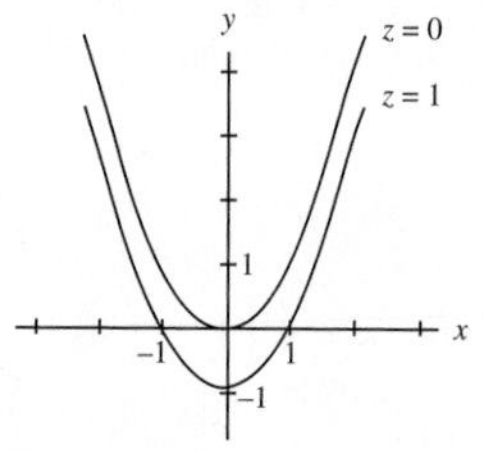

5. Domain: all (x, y, z); range: all real numbers; level curves are paraboloids of revolutions with the z-axis as axis

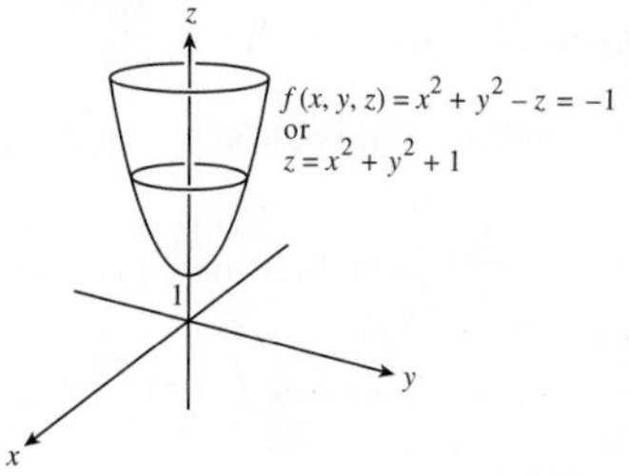

6. Domain: all (x, y, z); range: all nonnegative real numbers; level curves are ellipsoids with center $(0, 0, 0)$

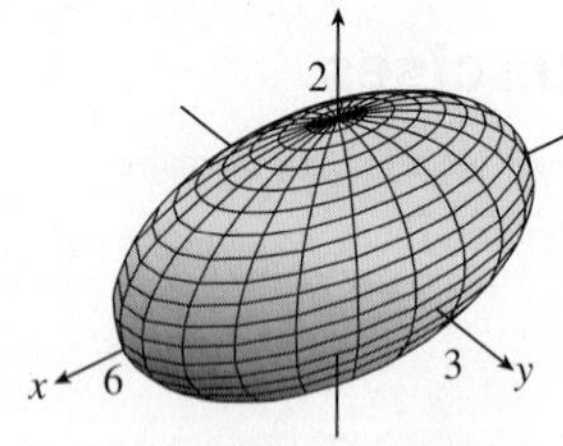

$g(x, y, z) = x^2 + 4y^2 + 9z^2 = 36$

7. Domain: all $(x, y, z) \neq (0, 0, 0)$; range: all positive real numbers; level curves are spheres with center $(0, 0, 0)$ and radius $r > 0$

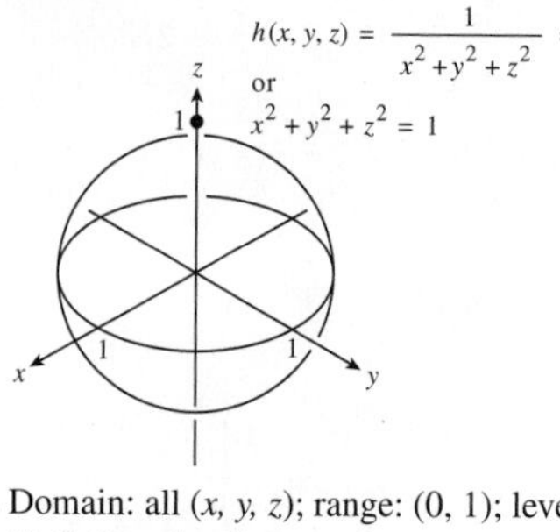

8. Domain: all (x, y, z); range: $(0, 1)$; level curves are spheres with center $(0, 0, 0)$ and radius $r > 0$

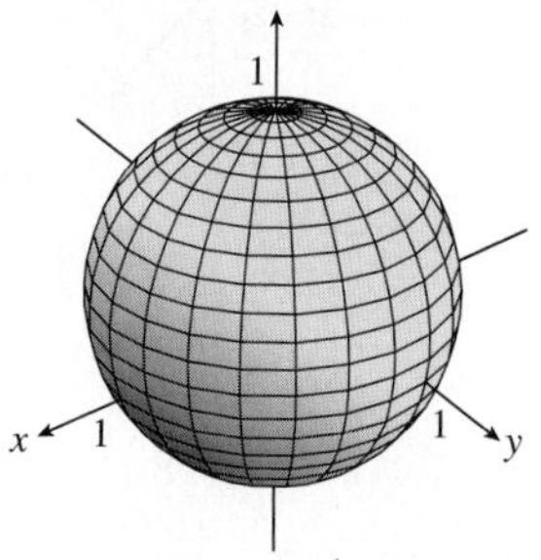

$k(x, y, z) = \dfrac{1}{x^2 + y^2 + z^2 + 1} = \dfrac{1}{2}$

or $x^2 + y^2 + z^2 = 1$

9. -2 **10.** 2 **11.** 1/2 **12.** 3 **13.** 1 **14.** $-\pi/4$

17. (a) No **(b)** No **18. (a)** 1 **(b)** 0 **(c)** 0

19. $\dfrac{\partial g}{\partial r} = \cos\theta + \sin\theta,\ \dfrac{\partial g}{\partial \theta} = -r\sin\theta + r\cos\theta$

20. $\dfrac{\partial f}{\partial x} = \dfrac{x - y}{x^2 + y^2},\ \dfrac{\partial f}{\partial y} = \dfrac{x + y}{x^2 + y^2}$

21. $\dfrac{\partial f}{\partial R_1} = -\dfrac{1}{R_1^2},\ \dfrac{\partial f}{\partial R_2} = -\dfrac{1}{R_2^2},\ \dfrac{\partial f}{\partial R_3} = -\dfrac{1}{R_3^2}$

22. $\dfrac{\partial h}{\partial x} = 2\pi\cos(2\pi x + y - 3z),\ \dfrac{\partial h}{\partial y} = \cos(2\pi x + y - 3z),$

$\dfrac{\partial h}{\partial z} = -3\cos(2\pi x + y - 3z)$

23. $\dfrac{\partial P}{\partial n} = \dfrac{RT}{V},\ \dfrac{\partial P}{\partial R} = \dfrac{nT}{V},\ \dfrac{\partial P}{\partial T} = \dfrac{nR}{V},\ \dfrac{\partial P}{\partial V} = -\dfrac{nRT}{V^2}$

24. $\dfrac{\partial f}{\partial r} = -\dfrac{1}{2r^2 l}\sqrt{\dfrac{T}{\pi w}},\ \dfrac{\partial f}{\partial l} = -\dfrac{1}{2rl^2}\sqrt{\dfrac{T}{\pi w}},$

$\dfrac{\partial f}{\partial T} = \dfrac{1}{4rlT}\sqrt{\dfrac{T}{\pi w}},\ \dfrac{\partial f}{\partial w} = -\dfrac{1}{4rlw}\sqrt{\dfrac{T}{\pi w}}$

25. $\dfrac{\partial^2 g}{\partial x^2} = 0,\ \dfrac{\partial^2 g}{\partial y^2} = \dfrac{2x}{y^3},\ \dfrac{\partial^2 g}{\partial y \partial x} = \dfrac{\partial^2 g}{\partial x \partial y} = -\dfrac{1}{y^2}$

26. $\dfrac{\partial^2 g}{\partial x^2} = e^x - y\sin x,\ \dfrac{\partial^2 g}{\partial y^2} = 0,\ \dfrac{\partial^2 g}{\partial y \partial x} = \dfrac{\partial^2 g}{\partial x \partial y} = \cos x$

27. $\dfrac{\partial^2 f}{\partial x^2} = -30x + \dfrac{2 - 2x^2}{(x^2 + 1)^2},\ \dfrac{\partial^2 f}{\partial y^2} = 0,\ \dfrac{\partial^2 f}{\partial y \partial x} = \dfrac{\partial^2 f}{\partial x \partial y} = 1$

28. $\dfrac{\partial^2 f}{\partial x^2} = 0,\ \dfrac{\partial^2 f}{\partial y^2} = 2 - \cos y + 7e^y,\ \dfrac{\partial^2 f}{\partial y \partial x} = \dfrac{\partial^2 f}{\partial x \partial y} = -3$

29. $L(x, y) = \dfrac{1}{2} + \dfrac{1}{2}x - \dfrac{1}{2}y$. Upper bound for E depends on the bound M used for $|f_{xx}|$, $|f_{xy}|$, and $|f_{yy}|$. With $M = \sqrt{2}/2$, $|E| \leq 0.0142$; with $M = 1$, $|E| \leq 0.02$.

30. $L(x, y) = x - 5y + 4$. Maximum of $|f_{xx}|$, $|f_{xy}|$, and $|f_{yy}|$ is 6, so $|E| \le 0.27$.

31. $L(x, y, z) = y - 3z$ at $(1, 0, 0)$; $L(x, y, z) = x + y - z - 1$ at $(1, 1, 0)$

32. $L(x, y, z) = 1 + y + z - \pi/4$ at $(0, 0, \pi/4)$;
$L(x, y, z) = \frac{\sqrt{2}}{2} - \frac{\sqrt{2}}{2}x + \frac{\sqrt{2}}{2}y + \frac{\sqrt{2}}{2}z$ at $(\pi/4, \pi/4, 0)$

33. Diameter **34.** y

35. I increases by 0.038 amp; % change in V about -4.17%; % change in R is -20%; % change in I about 15.83%

36. $\approx 0.8125\%$ **37. (a)** 5% **38.** A 1-cm error in height **39.** -1

40. $\frac{\partial w}{\partial u} = \frac{2}{5}, \frac{\partial w}{\partial v} = 0$ at $u = v = 0$

41. $-(\sin 1 + \cos 2)(\sin 1) + (\cos 1 + \cos 2)(\cos 1) - 2(\sin 1 + \cos 1)(\sin 2) \approx -2.80$

43. -1 **44.** $-(\ln 2 + 1)$

45. Increases most rapidly: $\mathbf{u} = -\frac{\sqrt{2}}{2}\mathbf{i} - \frac{\sqrt{2}}{2}\mathbf{j}$;
decreases most rapidly: $-\mathbf{u} = \frac{\sqrt{2}}{2}\mathbf{i} + \frac{\sqrt{2}}{2}\mathbf{j}$;
$(D_{\mathbf{u}}f)_{P_0} = \sqrt{2}/2$; $(D_{-\mathbf{u}}f)_{P_0} = -\sqrt{2}/2$; with
$\mathbf{u}_1 = \frac{\mathbf{A}}{|\mathbf{A}|}$, $(D_{\mathbf{u}_1}f)_{P_0} = -7/10$

46. Increases most rapidly: $\mathbf{u} = \frac{1}{\sqrt{2}}\mathbf{i} - \frac{1}{\sqrt{2}}\mathbf{j}$;
decreases most rapidly: $-\mathbf{u} = -\frac{1}{\sqrt{2}}\mathbf{i} + \frac{1}{\sqrt{2}}\mathbf{j}$;
$(D_{\mathbf{u}}f)_{P_0} = 2\sqrt{2}$; $(D_{-\mathbf{u}}f)_{P_0} = -2\sqrt{2}$; with $\mathbf{u}_1 = \frac{\mathbf{A}}{|\mathbf{A}|}$, $(D_{\mathbf{u}_1}f)_{P_0} = 0$

47. Increases most rapidly: $\mathbf{u} = \frac{2}{7}\mathbf{i} + \frac{3}{7}\mathbf{j} + \frac{6}{7}\mathbf{k}$;
decreases most rapidly: $-\mathbf{u} = -\frac{2}{7}\mathbf{i} - \frac{3}{7}\mathbf{j} - \frac{6}{7}\mathbf{k}$;
$(D_{\mathbf{u}}f)_{P_0} = 7$: $(D_{-\mathbf{u}}f)_{P_0} = -7$; with $\mathbf{u}_1 = \frac{\mathbf{A}}{|\mathbf{A}|}$, $(D_{\mathbf{u}_1}f)_{P_0} = 7$

48. Increases most rapidly: $\mathbf{u} = \frac{2}{\sqrt{5}}\mathbf{j} + \frac{1}{\sqrt{5}}\mathbf{k}$;
decreases most rapidly: $-\mathbf{u} = -\frac{2}{\sqrt{5}}\mathbf{j} - \frac{1}{\sqrt{5}}\mathbf{k}$;
$(D_{\mathbf{u}}f)_{P_0} = \sqrt{5}$; $(D_{-\mathbf{u}}f)_{P_0} = -\sqrt{5}$; with $\mathbf{u}_1 = \frac{\mathbf{A}}{|\mathbf{A}|}$, $(D_{\mathbf{u}_1}f)_{P_0} = \sqrt{3}$

49. $\pi/\sqrt{2}$ **50.** $\sqrt{3}$ **51. (a)** $f_x(1, 2) = f_y(1, 2) = 2$ **(b)** 14/5

52. (a) True **(b)** False **(c)** True **(d)** True

53.

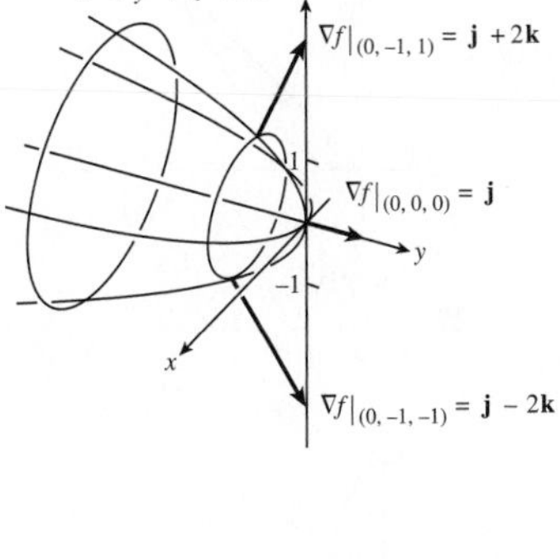

54.

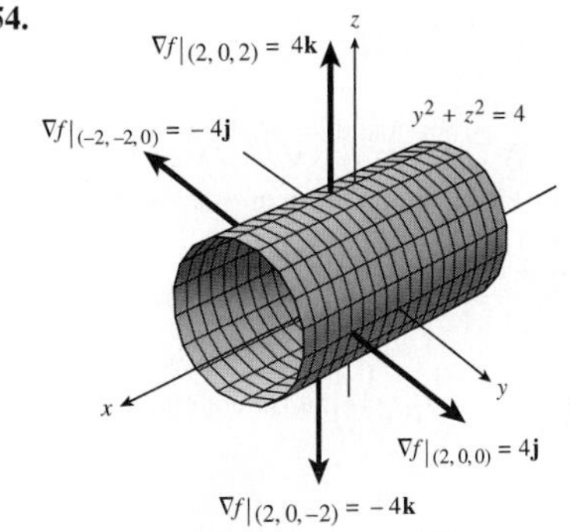

55. $4x - y - 5z = 4$; $x = 2 + 4t$, $y = -1 - t$, $z = 1 - 5t$

56. $2x + 2y + z = 6$; $x = 1 + 2t$, $y = 1 + 2t$, $z = 2 + t$

57. $2y - z = 2$ **58.** $x + y + 2z = 3$

59. Tangent line: $x + y = \pi + 1$; normal line: $y = x - \pi + 1$

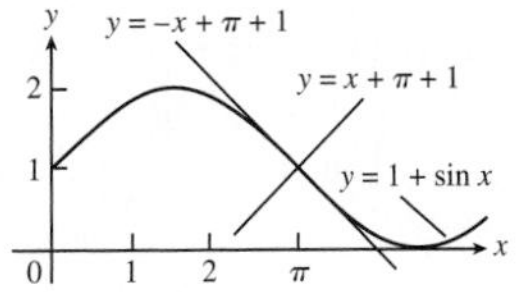

60. Tangent line: $y = \frac{1}{2}x + \frac{3}{2}$; normal line: $y = -2x + 4$

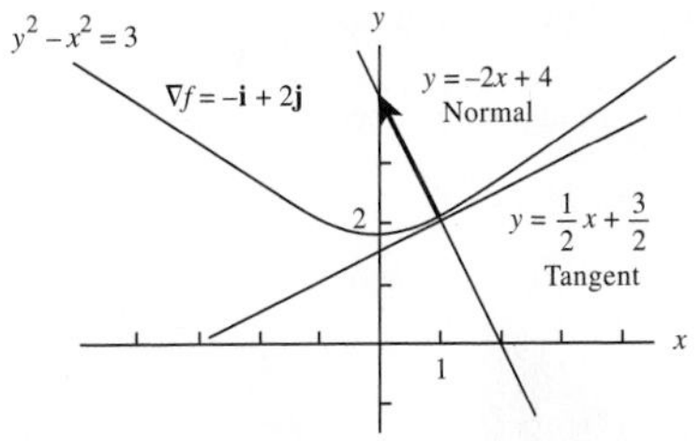

61. $x = 1 - 2t$, $y = 1$, $z = \frac{1}{2} + 2t$ **62.** $x = \frac{1}{2} - t$, $y = 1$, $z = \frac{1}{2} + t$

63. Local minimum of -8 at $(-2, -2)$

64. Saddle point at $(0, -1)$ with $f(0, -1) = 2$

65. Saddle point at $(0, 0)$ with $f(0, 0) = 0$; local maximum of 1/4 at $(-1/2, -1/2)$

66. Saddle point at $(0, 0)$ with $f(0, 0) = 15$; local minimum of 14 at $(1, 1)$

67. Saddle points at $(0, 0)$ and $(-2, 2)$ with $f(0, 0) = f(-2, 2) = 0$; local minimum of -4 at $(0, 2)$; local maximum value of 4 at $(-2, 0)$

68. Saddle point at $(0, 1)$ with $f(0, 1) = -3$; local minimum of -19 at $(2, 1)$ and $(-2, 1)$

69. Absolute maximum of 28 at $(0, 4)$; absolute minimum of $-9/4$ at $(3/2, 0)$

70. Absolute maximum of 13 at $(4, 2)$; absolute minimum of 0 at $(1, 0)$

71. Absolute maximum of 18 at $(2, -2)$; absolute minimum of $-17/4$ at $(-2, 1/2)$

72. Absolute maximum of 2 at $(1, 1)$; absolute minimum of 0 at $(0, 0)$, $(0, 2)$, $(2, 2)$ and $(2, 0)$

73. Absolute maximum of 8 at $(-2, 0)$; absolute minimum of -1 at $(1, 0)$

74. Absolute maximum of 18 at $(1, 1)$ and $(-1, -1)$; absolute minimum of -32 at $(2, -2)$

75. Absolute maximum of 4 at $(1, 0)$; absolute minimum of -4 at $(0, -1)$

76. Absolute maximum of 6 at $(1, 1)$; absolute minimum of -2 at $(1, -1)$ and $(-1, 1)$

77. Absolute maximum of 1 at $(0, \pm 1)$ and $(1, 0)$; absolute minimum of -1 at $(-1, 0)$

78. Absolute maximum of 1/2 at $\left(\frac{1}{\sqrt{2}}, \frac{1}{\sqrt{2}}\right)$ and $\left(-\frac{1}{\sqrt{2}}, -\frac{1}{\sqrt{2}}\right)$; absolute minimum of $-1/2$ at $\left(-\frac{1}{\sqrt{2}}, \frac{1}{\sqrt{2}}\right)$ and $\left(\frac{1}{\sqrt{2}}, -\frac{1}{\sqrt{2}}\right)$

79. Absolute maximum of 5 at (0, 1); absolute minimum of $-1/3$ at $(0, -1/3)$

80. Absolute maximum of $9 + \frac{27\sqrt{3}}{4} \approx 20.69$ at $\left(-\frac{3\sqrt{3}}{2}, \frac{3}{2}\right)$; absolute minimum of -3 at (2, 1)

81. Absolute maximum of $\sqrt{3}$ at $\left(\frac{1}{\sqrt{3}}, -\frac{1}{\sqrt{3}}, \frac{1}{\sqrt{3}}\right)$; absolute minimum of $-\sqrt{3}$ at $\left(-\frac{1}{\sqrt{3}}, \frac{1}{\sqrt{3}}, -\frac{1}{\sqrt{3}}\right)$

82. $(0, 0, -2)$, $(0, 0, 2)$

83. Width $= \left(\frac{c^2V}{ab}\right)^{1/3}$, depth $= \left(\frac{b^2V}{ac}\right)^{1/3}$, height $= \left(\frac{a^2V}{bc}\right)^{1/3}$

84. $x + 2y + z = 6$

85. Absolute maximum of 3/2 at $\left(\frac{1}{\sqrt{2}}, \frac{1}{\sqrt{2}}, \sqrt{2}\right)$ and $\left(-\frac{1}{\sqrt{2}}, -\frac{1}{\sqrt{2}}, -\sqrt{2}\right)$; absolute minimum of 1/2 at $\left(-\frac{1}{\sqrt{2}}, \frac{1}{\sqrt{2}}, -\sqrt{2}\right)$ and $\left(\frac{1}{\sqrt{2}}, -\frac{1}{\sqrt{2}}, \sqrt{2}\right)$

86. (1/4, 1/4, 1/2)

87. $\frac{\partial w}{\partial x} = (\cos\theta)\frac{\partial w}{\partial r} - \left(\frac{\sin\theta}{r}\right)\frac{\partial w}{\partial \theta}, \frac{\partial w}{\partial y} = (\sin\theta)\frac{\partial w}{\partial r} + \left(\frac{\cos\theta}{r}\right)\frac{\partial w}{\partial \theta}$

88. $z_x = af_u + af_v$, $z_y = bf_u - bf_v$ **89.** $W_r = W_s = \frac{2}{r+s}$

90. Angle is $\pi/2$ **91.** $(t, -t \pm 4, t)$, t a real number

92. $(-1/2, 1/2, 1/2)$, $(0, 1, 0)$

96. (a)

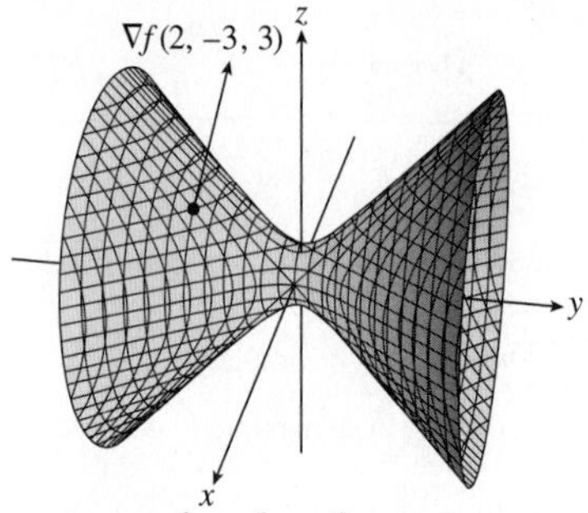

$x^2 + y^2 + z^2 = 4$

(b) $\nabla f = 4\mathbf{i} + 6\mathbf{j} + 6\mathbf{k}$

(c) $2x + 3y + 3z = 4$; $x = 2 + 4t$, $y = -3 + 6t$, $z = 3 + 6t$

CHAPTER 15

Section 15.1

Quick Review

1. $\int_0^3 x^3\,dx$ **2.** $\int_{-1}^1 \sqrt[3]{2 - x^2}\,dx$ **3.** $e^{\sin x} + C$

4. $-2\ln(|x - 1|) + C$ **5.** $e^x + \frac{5}{x} + C$ **6.** $\sqrt{2} - 1$ **7.** 11/2

8. ≈ 1.89 **9.** 4 **10.** $512\pi/15 \approx 107.23$

Exercises

1. 16

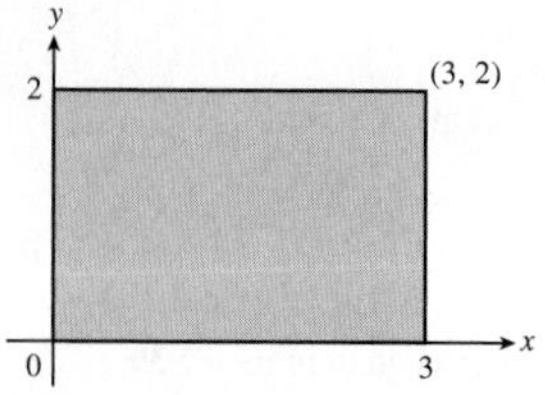

3. 1

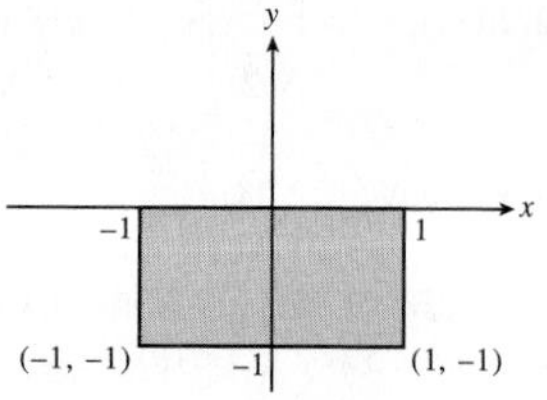

5. $\frac{\pi^2}{2} + 2$

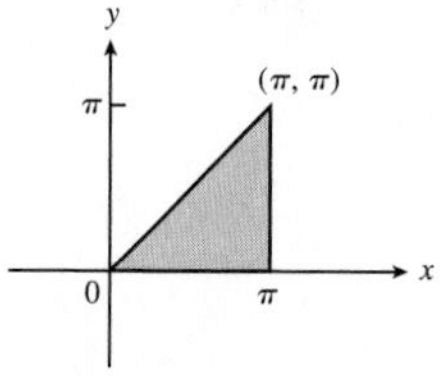

7. $8\ln 8 - 16 + e \approx 3.35$

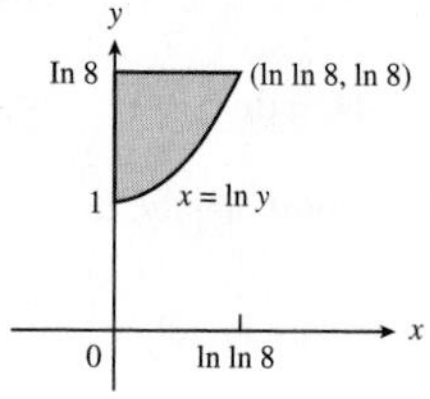

9. $e - 2$

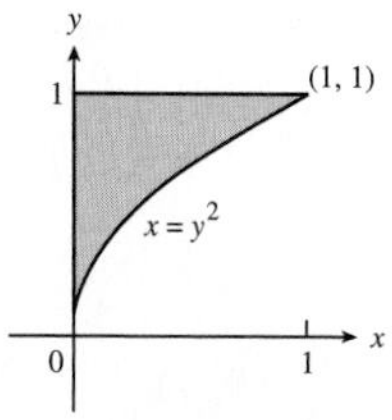

11. $\frac{3}{2}\ln 2$ **13.** 1/6 **15.** $-1/10$

17. 8

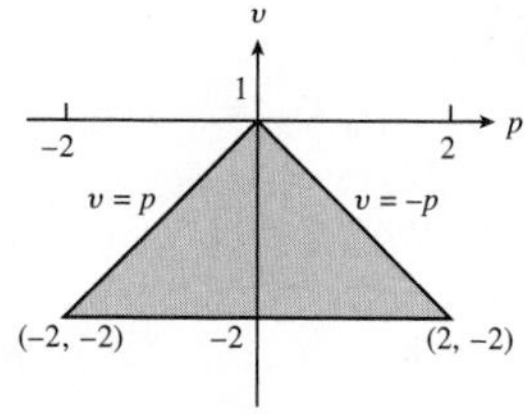

19. 2π

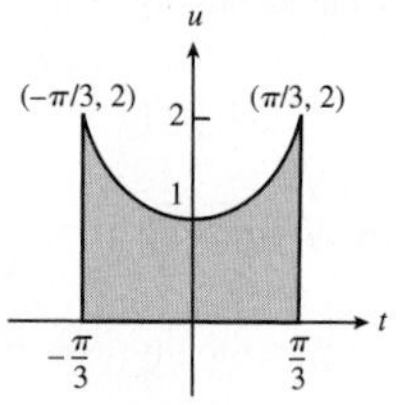

21. $\int_2^4 \int_0^{(4-y)/2} dx\,dy$

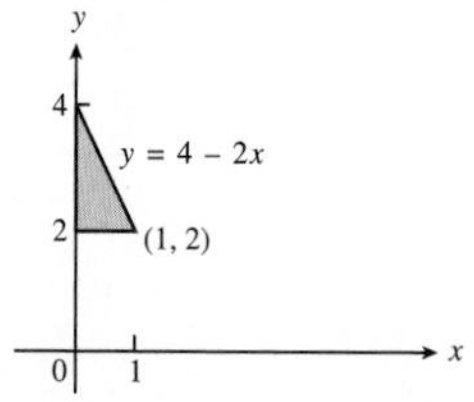

23. $\int_0^1 \int_{x^2}^{x} dy\,dx$

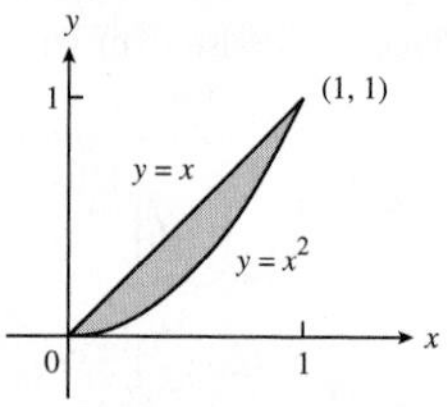

25. $\int_1^e \int_{\ln y}^{1} dx\,dy$

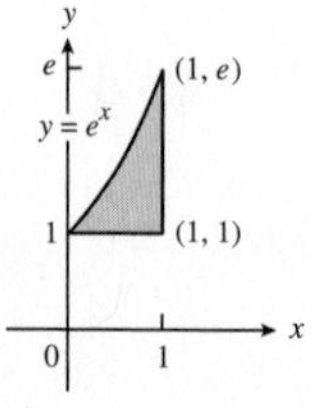

27. $\int_0^9 \int_0^{\frac{1}{2}\sqrt{9-y}} 16x\,dx\,dy$

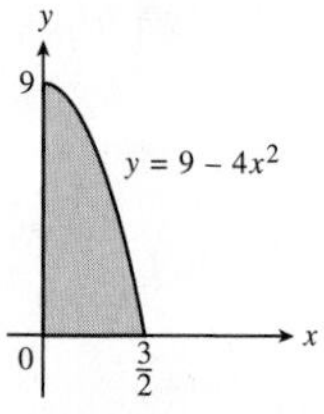

29. $\int_{-1}^{1}\int_{0}^{\sqrt{1-x^2}} 3y\,dy\,dx$

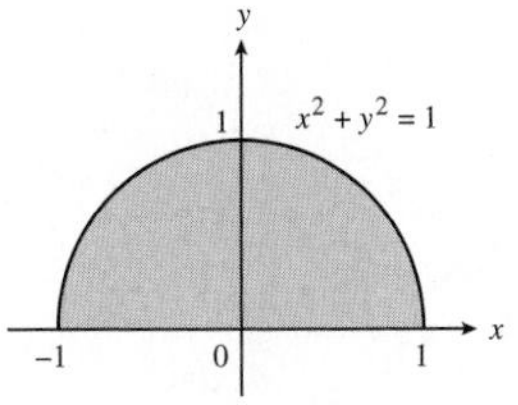

31. 2

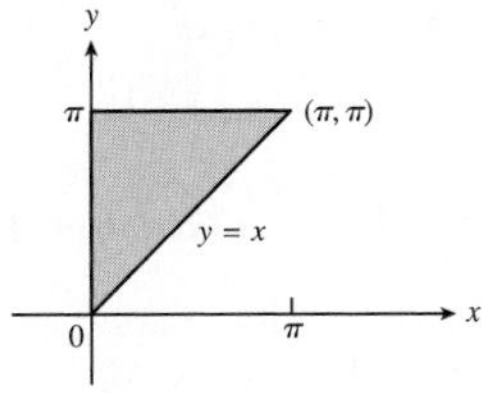

33. $\frac{e-2}{2}$

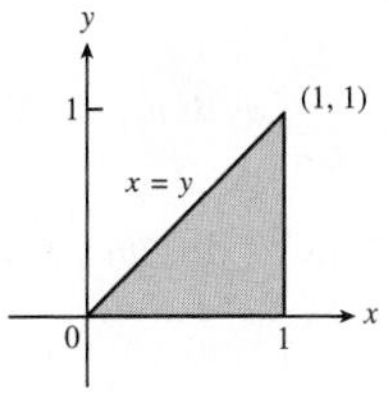

35. 2

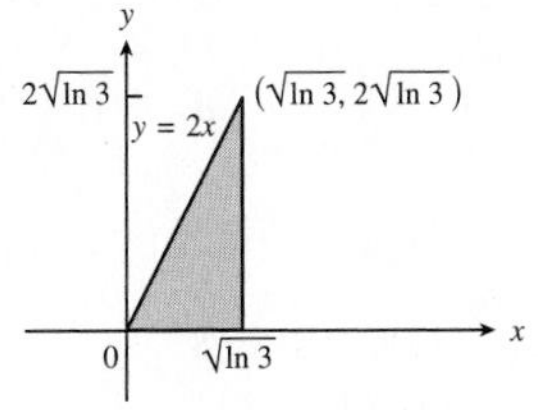

37. $\frac{1}{80\pi}$

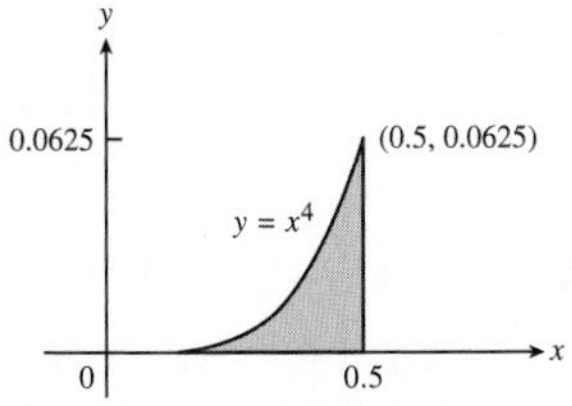

39. −2/3

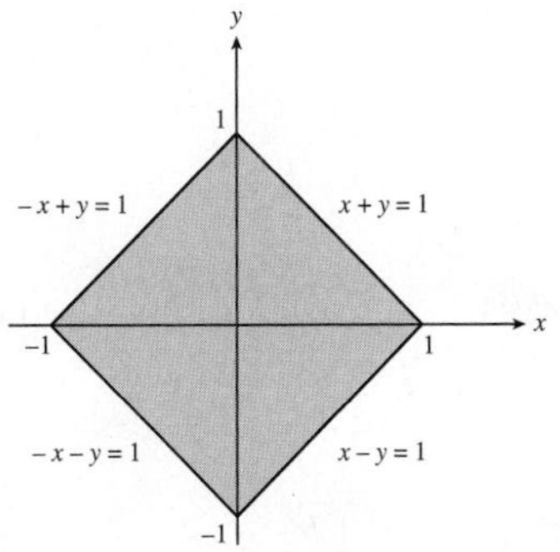

41. 4/3 **43.** 625/12 **45.** 16 **47.** 20 **49.** $2(1 + \ln 2) \approx 3.39$

51. 1 **53.** π^2 **55.** 1/16 **57.** $20\sqrt{3}/9 \approx 3.85$

59. $\int_{0}^{1}\int_{x}^{2-x} (x^2 + y^2)\,dy\,dx = 4/3$

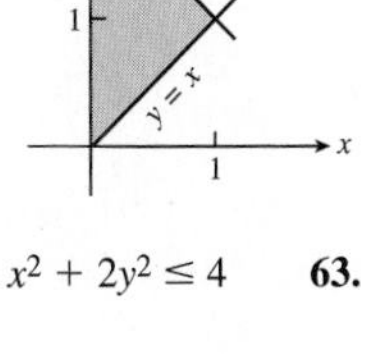

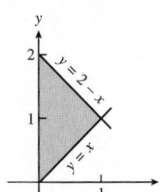

61. $x^2 + 2y^2 \le 4$ **63.** No **67.** ≈0.60 **69.** ≈0.23

Section 15.2

Quick Review

1. $e - 1$ **2.** 1 **3.** $\int_{-2}^{2} (2 - x^2 + 2)\,dx = 32/3$

4. $\int_{-2}^{2} 2\sqrt{2 - y}\,dy = 32/3$ **5.** $2/\pi \approx 0.64$ **6.** 32/3

9. $\bar{x} = 0, \bar{y} = 12/5$ **10.** $\bar{x} = 4/3, \bar{y} = 0$

Exercises

1. $\int_{0}^{2}\int_{0}^{2-x} dy\,dx = \int_{0}^{2}\int_{0}^{2-y} dx\,dy = 2$

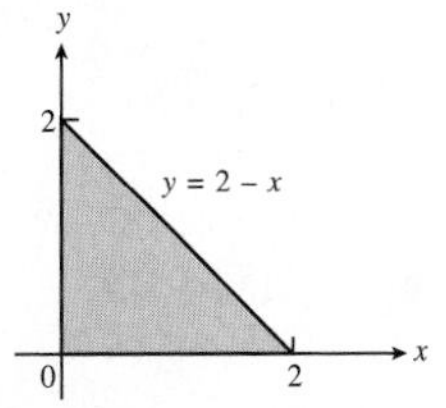

3. $\int_{-2}^{1}\int_{y-2}^{-y^2} dx\,dy = 9/2$

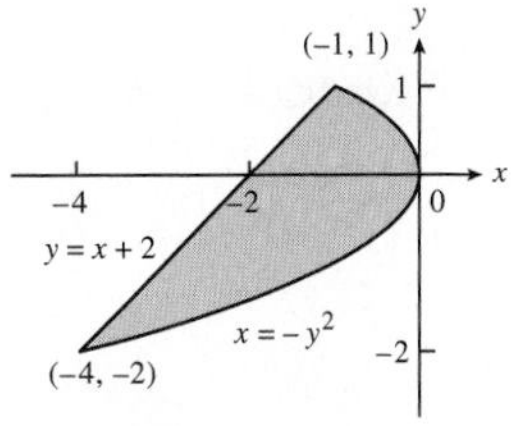

5. $\int_{0}^{\ln 2}\int_{0}^{e^x} dy\,dx = 1$

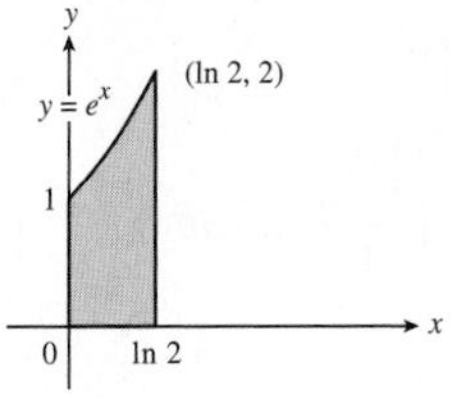

7. $\int_{0}^{1}\int_{y^2}^{2y-y^2} dx\,dy = 1/3$

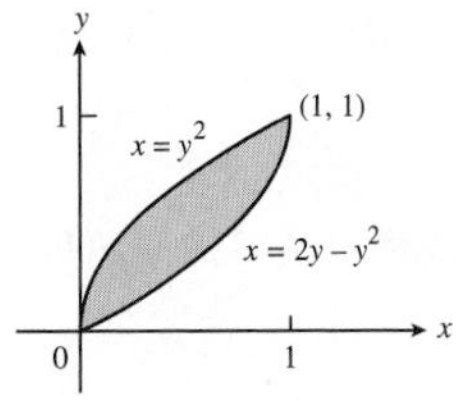

9. 12

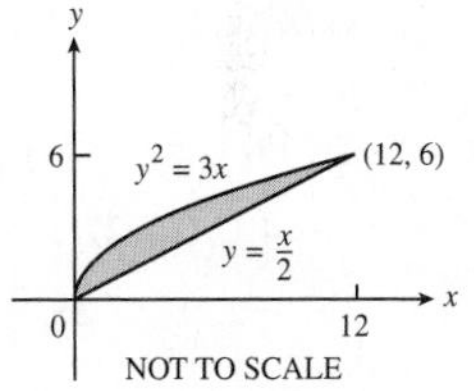

11. $\sqrt{2} - 1$

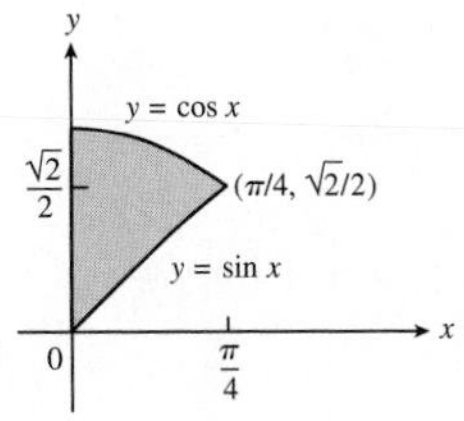

13. 3/2

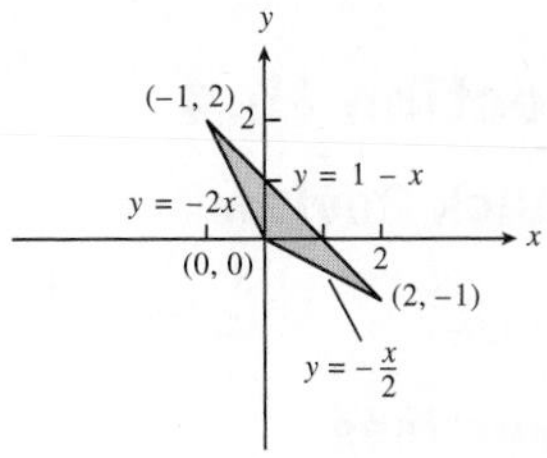

15. (a) 0 **(b)** $4/\pi^2$ **17.** 8/3 **19.** $\bar{x} = 5/14, \bar{y} = 38/35$

21. $\bar{x} = 64/35, \bar{y} = 5/7$ **23.** $\bar{x} = 0, \bar{y} = \frac{4}{3\pi}$ **25.** $\bar{x} = \bar{y} = \frac{4a}{3\pi}$

27. $\bar{x} = \pi/2, \bar{y} = \pi/8$ **29.** $\bar{x} = -1, \bar{y} = 1/4$

31. $I_x = 64/105, R_x = 2\sqrt{\frac{2}{7}}$ **33.** $\bar{x} = 3/8, \bar{y} = 17/16$

35. $\bar{x} = 11/3, \bar{y} = 14/27, I_y = 432, R_y = 4$
37. $\bar{x} = 0, \bar{y} = 13/31, I_y = 7/5, R_y = \sqrt{21/31}$
39. $\bar{x} = 0, \bar{y} = 7/10, I_x = 9/10, R_x = 3\sqrt{6}/10,$
$I_y = 3/10, R_y = 3\sqrt{2}/10, I_0 = 6/5, R_0 = 3\sqrt{2}/5$
41. $\approx 43{,}329$ **43.** $0 < a \le 5/2$ **45.** $\bar{x} = 2/\pi, \bar{y} = 0$
47. **(a)** 3/2 **(b)** Values are the same
53. **(a)** $\bar{x} = 7/5, \bar{y} = 31/10$ **(b)** $\bar{x} = 19/7, \bar{y} = 18/7$
(c) $\bar{x} = 9/2, \bar{y} = 19/8$ **(d)** $\bar{x} = 11/4, \bar{y} = 43/16$
55. On common boundary: $h = a\sqrt{2}$; inside T: $h > a\sqrt{2}$

Section 15.3

Quick Review

1. $r^2 = 9$ **2.** $r\cos\theta = 3$ **3.** $r = -4\sin\theta$ **4.** $(x-2)^2 + y^2 = 4$
5. $x = 1$ **6.** $0 < r \le 2, \frac{\pi}{2} < \theta < \pi$
7. $0 < r \le 2, \pi < \theta < 2\pi, \theta \ne \frac{3\pi}{2}$ **8.** 6π **9.** 2 **10.** $5\pi - 8$

Exercises

1. $\int_0^{\pi}\int_0^1 r\,dr\,d\theta = \frac{\pi}{2}$ **3.** $\int_0^{\pi/2}\int_0^1 r^3\,dr\,d\theta = \frac{\pi}{8}$
5. $\int_0^{2\pi}\int_0^a r\,dr\,d\theta = \pi a^2$ **7.** $\int_{\pi/4}^{\pi/2}\int_0^{6\csc\theta} r^2\cos\theta\,dr\,d\theta = 36$
9. $\int_{\pi}^{3\pi/2}\int_0^1 \frac{2r}{1+r}\,dr\,d\theta = (1 - \ln 2)\pi \approx 0.96$
11. $\int_0^{\pi/2}\int_0^{\ln 2} re^r\,dr\,d\theta = \frac{\pi}{2}(2\ln 2 - 1) \approx 0.61$
13. $\int_0^{\pi/2}\int_0^{2\cos\theta} (\cos\theta + \sin\theta)\,dr\,d\theta = \frac{\pi}{2} + 1$
15. $4\int_0^{\pi/2}\int_0^1 \ln(r^2+1)\,r\,dr\,d\theta = \pi(\ln 4 - 1) \approx 1.21$
17. $2(\pi - 1)$ **19.** 12π **21.** $\frac{3\pi}{8} + 1 \approx 2.18$ **23.** 4
25. $6\sqrt{3} - 2\pi \approx 4.11$ **27.** $\bar{x} = 5/6, \bar{y} = 0$ **29.** $2a/3$ **31.** $2a/3$
33. $2\pi(2 - \sqrt{e}) \approx 2.21$ **35.** $\frac{4}{3} + \frac{5\pi}{8} \approx 3.30$
37. **(a)** $I = \frac{\sqrt{\pi}}{2} \approx 0.89$ **(b)** 1 **39.** $\pi\ln 4$, no **41.** $\frac{1}{2}(a^2 + 2h^2)$

Section 15.4

Quick Review

1. 4 **2.** 13/2 **5.** 0 **6.** 4 **7.** 10 **8.** $2r + 2s$ **9.** $2/\pi$
10. $-4/\pi^2$

Exercises

1. 1
3. $\int_0^1\int_0^{2-2x}\int_0^{3-3x-3y/2} dz\,dy\,dx = 1, \int_0^2\int_0^{1-y/2}\int_0^{3-3x-3y/2} dz\,dx\,dy,$
$\int_0^1\int_0^{3-3x}\int_0^{2-2x-2z/3} dy\,dz\,dx, \int_0^3\int_0^{1-z/3}\int_0^{2-2x-2z/3} dy\,dx\,dz,$
$\int_0^2\int_0^{3-3y/2}\int_0^{1-y/2-z/3} dx\,dz\,dy, \int_0^3\int_0^{2-2z/3}\int_0^{1-y/2-z/3} dx\,dy\,dz$
5. $\int_{-2}^2\int_{-\sqrt{4-x^2}}^{\sqrt{4-x^2}}\int_{x^2+y^2}^{8-x^2-y^2} dz\,dy\,dx = 16\pi,$
$\int_{-2}^2\int_{-\sqrt{4-y^2}}^{\sqrt{4-y^2}}\int_{x^2+y^2}^{8-x^2-y^2} dz\,dx\,dy,$
$\int_{-2}^2\int_{y^2}^4\int_{-\sqrt{z-y^2}}^{\sqrt{z-y^2}} dx\,dz\,dy + \int_{-2}^2\int_4^{8-y^2}\int_{-\sqrt{8-z-y^2}}^{\sqrt{8-z-y^2}} dx\,dz\,dy,$
$\int_0^4\int_{-\sqrt{z}}^{\sqrt{z}}\int_{-\sqrt{z-y^2}}^{\sqrt{z-y^2}} dx\,dy\,dz + \int_4^8\int_{-\sqrt{8-z}}^{\sqrt{8-z}}\int_{-\sqrt{8-z-y^2}}^{\sqrt{8-z-y^2}} dx\,dy\,dz,$
$\int_{-2}^2\int_{x^2}^4\int_{-\sqrt{z-x^2}}^{\sqrt{z-x^2}} dy\,dz\,dx + \int_{-2}^2\int_4^{8-x^2}\int_{-\sqrt{8-z-x^2}}^{\sqrt{8-z-x^2}} dy\,dz\,dx,$
$\int_0^4\int_{-\sqrt{z}}^{\sqrt{z}}\int_{-\sqrt{z-x^2}}^{\sqrt{z-x^2}} dy\,dx\,dz + \int_4^8\int_{-\sqrt{8-z}}^{\sqrt{8-z}}\int_{-\sqrt{8-z-x^2}}^{\sqrt{8-z-x^2}} dy\,dx\,dz$
7. 1 **9.** 1 **11.** $\frac{\pi^3}{2}(1 - \cos 1) \approx 7.13$ **13.** 18 **15.** 7/6
17. 0 **19.** $1/2 - \pi/8$
21. **(a)** $\int_{-1}^1\int_0^{1-x^2}\int_{x^2}^{1-z} dy\,dz\,dx$ **(b)** $\int_0^1\int_{-\sqrt{1-z}}^{\sqrt{1-z}}\int_{x^2}^{1-z} dy\,dx\,dz$
(c) $\int_0^1\int_0^{1-z}\int_{-\sqrt{y}}^{\sqrt{y}} dx\,dy\,dz$ **d)** $\int_0^1\int_0^{1-y}\int_{-\sqrt{y}}^{\sqrt{y}} dx\,dz\,dy$
(e) $\int_0^1\int_{-\sqrt{y}}^{\sqrt{y}}\int_0^{1-y} dz\,dx\,dy$
23. 2/3 **25.** 20/3 **27.** 1 **29.** 16/3 **31.** $8\pi - \frac{32}{2} \approx 14.47$
33. 2 **35.** 4π **37.** 31/3 **39.** 1 **41.** $2\sin 4 \approx -1.51$ **43.** 4
45. 13/3 or 3 **47.** $4x^2 + 4y^2 + z^2 \le 4$ **49.** $\pi/48 \approx 0.07$ **51.** ≈ 1.84

Section 15.5

Quick Review

1. 13/3 **2.** 158/15 **3.** 3/2 **4.** $\bar{x} = \frac{9}{26}, \bar{y} = \frac{158}{65}$
5. 6091/210 **6.** 23/30 **7.** 1042/35 **8.** $\sqrt{6091/910}$ **9.** $\sqrt{23/130}$
10. $\sqrt{3126/455}$

Exercises

1. $R_x = \sqrt{\frac{b^2+c^2}{12}}, R_y = \sqrt{\frac{a^2+c^2}{12}}, R_z = \sqrt{\frac{a^2+b^2}{12}}$
3. $I_x = \frac{abc(b^2+c^2)}{3}, I_y = \frac{abc(a^2+c^2)}{3}, I_z = \frac{abc(a^2+b^2)}{3}$
5. $\bar{x} = \bar{y} = 0, \bar{z} = 12/5, I_x = 7904/105, I_y = 4832/63, I_z = 256/45$
7. **(a)** $\bar{x} = \bar{y} = 0, \bar{z} = 8/3$ **(b)** $2\sqrt{2}$
9. $I_L = 1386, R_L = \sqrt{77/2}$ **11.** $I_L = 40/3, R_L = \sqrt{5/3}$
13. **(a)** 4/3 **(b)** $\bar{x} = 4/5, \bar{y} = \bar{z} = 2/5$
15. **(a)** 5/2 **(b)** $\bar{x} = \bar{y} = \bar{z} = 8/15$ **(c)** $I_x = I_y = I_z = 11/6$
(d) $R_x = R_y = R_z = \sqrt{11/15}$
17. 3 **19.** **(a)** $\frac{4}{3}g$ **(b)** $\frac{4}{3}g$
23. **(a)** $I_{\text{c.m.}} = \frac{abc(a^2+b^2)}{12}, R_{\text{c.m.}} = \sqrt{\frac{a^2+b^2}{12}}$
(b) $I_L = \frac{abc(a^2+7b^2)}{3}, R_L = \sqrt{\frac{a^2+7b^2}{3}}$
27. **(a)** $h = a\sqrt{3}$ **(b)** $h = a\sqrt{2}$

Section 15.6

Quick Review

1. $z = r,\ 1 \le r \le 2$ **2.** $z^2 - x^2 - y^2 = 1$
3. Right circular cylinder parallel to the z-axis generated by the circle $r = 2 \sin \theta$ in the $r\theta$-plane
4. Cylinder of lines parallel to the z-axis generated by the cardioid $r = 1 + \cos \theta$
5. $z = x^2$ **6.** $z = y^2$ **7.** The origin $(0, 0)$ **8.** $z = |x|$ **9.** $z = |y|$
10. Circle with radius 2 and center $(0, 0, 2)$ in the plane $z = 2$

Exercises

1. $(0, 0, 0)$ **3.** $(1, 0, 0)$ **5.** $(0, -2\sqrt{2}, 0)$
7. Rectangular: $x^2 + y^2 = 0$; spherical: $\phi = 0$ or $\phi = \pi$; the z-axis
9. Cylindrical or rectangular: $z = 0$; spherical: $\phi = \pi/2$; the xy-plane
11. Cylindrical: $z = r,\ 0 \le r \le 1$; spherical: $\phi = \pi/4,\ 0 \le \rho \le \sqrt{2}$; a (finite) cone
13. Rectangular: $x = 0$; cylindrical: $\theta = \pi/2$; the yz-plane
15. Rectangular: $x^2 + y^2 + (z - 5/2)^2 = 25/4$; cylindrical: $r^2 + z^2 = 5z$; a sphere of radius 5/2 centered at $(0, 0, 5/2)$ (rectangular)
17. Cylindrical: $r^2 + z^2 = 2z,\ z \le 1$; spherical: $\rho = 2 \cos \phi,\ \pi/4 \le \phi \le \pi/2$; the lower half (hemisphere) of the sphere of radius 1 centered at $(0, 0, 1)$ (rectangular)
19. Rectangular: $z = -\sqrt{x^2 + y^2},\ -1 \le z \le 0$; cylindrical: $r = -z$; a cone with vertex at the origin and base the circle $x^2 + y^2 = 1$ in the plane $z = -1$
21. Cardioid of revolution symmetric about the z-axis, cusp at the origin pointing down

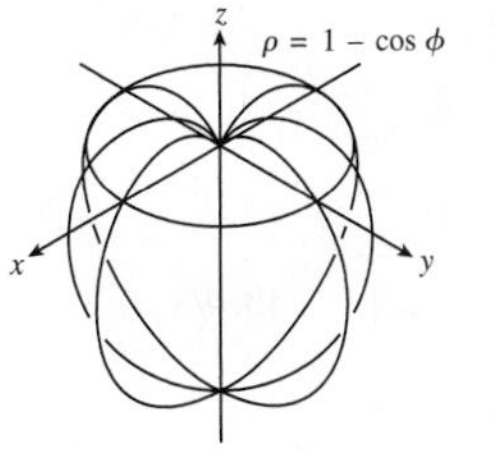

23. $\rho \sin \theta = a$ **25.** $\dfrac{4\pi(\sqrt{2} - 1)}{3} \approx 1.74$ **27.** $\pi(6\sqrt{2} - 8) \approx 1.52$

29. $3\pi/10$ **31.** $\pi/3$

33. (a) $\displaystyle\int_0^{2\pi}\int_0^1\int_0^{\sqrt{4-r^2}} dz\, r\, dr\, d\theta$

(b) $\displaystyle\int_0^{2\pi}\int_0^{\sqrt{3}}\int_0^1 r\, dr\, dz\, d\theta + \int_0^{2\pi}\int_{\sqrt{3}}^2\int_0^{\sqrt{4-z^2}} r\, dr\, dz\, d\theta$

(c) $\displaystyle\int_0^1\int_0^{\sqrt{4-r^2}}\int_0^{2\pi} r\, d\theta\, dz\, dr$

35. $\displaystyle\int_{-\pi/2}^{\pi/2}\int_0^{\cos\theta}\int_0^{3r^2} f(r, \theta, z)\, dz\, r\, dr\, d\theta$

37. $\displaystyle\int_0^{\pi}\int_0^{2\sin\theta}\int_0^{4-r\sin\theta} f(r, \theta, z)\, dz\, r\, dr\, d\theta$

39. $\displaystyle\int_{-\pi/2}^{\pi/2}\int_1^{1+\cos\theta}\int_0^4 f(r, \theta, z)\, dz\, r\, dr\, d\theta$

41. $\displaystyle\int_0^{\pi/4}\int_0^{\sec\theta}\int_0^{2-r\sin\theta} f(r, \theta, z)\, dz\, r\, dr\, d\theta$ **43.** π^2 **45.** 5π

47. 2π **49.** $\dfrac{(4\sqrt{2} - 5)\pi}{\sqrt{2}} \approx 1.46$

51. (a) $\displaystyle\int_0^{2\pi}\int_0^{\pi/6}\int_0^2 \rho^2 \sin\phi\, d\rho\, d\phi\, d\theta + \int_0^{2\pi}\int_{\pi/6}^{\pi/2}\int_0^{\csc\phi} \rho^2 \sin\phi\, d\rho\, d\phi\, d\theta$

(b) $\displaystyle\int_0^{2\pi}\int_1^2\int_{\pi/6}^{\sin^{-1}(1/\rho)} \rho^2 \sin\theta\, d\phi\, d\rho\, d\theta + \int_0^{2\pi}\int_0^2\int_0^{\pi/6} \rho^2 \sin\phi\, d\phi\, d\rho\, d\theta$

53. (a) $\displaystyle\int_0^{2\pi}\int_0^{\pi/2}\int_{\cos\phi}^2 \rho^2 \sin\phi\, d\rho\, d\phi\, d\theta$ **(b)** $31\pi/6 \approx 16.23$

55. (a) $\displaystyle\int_0^{2\pi}\int_0^{\pi}\int_0^{1-\cos\theta} \rho^2 \sin\phi\, d\rho\, d\phi\, d\theta$ **(b)** $8\pi/3 \approx 8.38$

57. (a) $\displaystyle\int_0^{2\pi}\int_{\pi/4}^{\pi/2}\int_0^{2\cos\phi} \rho^2 \sin\phi\, d\rho\, d\phi\, d\theta$ **(b)** $\pi/3$

59. (a) $\displaystyle 8\int_0^{\pi/2}\int_0^{\pi/2}\int_0^2 \rho^2 \sin\phi\, d\rho\, d\phi\, d\theta$

(b) $\displaystyle 8\int_0^{\pi/2}\int_0^2\int_0^{\sqrt{4-r^2}} dz\, r\, dr\, d\theta$

(c) $\displaystyle 8\int_0^2\int_0^{\sqrt{4-x^2}}\int_0^{\sqrt{4-x^2-y^2}} dz\, dy\, dx$

61. (a) $\displaystyle\int_0^{\pi/2}\int_0^{\pi/3}\int_{\sec\phi}^2 \rho^2 \sin\phi\, d\rho\, d\phi\, d\theta$ **(b)** $\displaystyle\int_0^{2\pi}\int_0^{\sqrt{3}}\int_1^{\sqrt{4-r^2}} dz\, r\, dr\, d\theta$

(c) $\displaystyle\int_{-\sqrt{3}}^{\sqrt{3}}\int_{-\sqrt{3-x^2}}^{\sqrt{3-x^2}}\int_1^{\sqrt{4-x^2-y^2}} dz\, dy\, dx$ **(d)** $5\pi/3$

63. $8\pi/3$ **65.** $9/4$ **67.** $\dfrac{3\pi - 4}{18} \approx 0.30$ **69.** $2\pi a^3/3$ **71.** $7\pi/3$

73. $\dfrac{4\pi(2\sqrt{2} - 1)}{3} \approx 7.66$ **75.** 16π **77.** $2/3$

79. $\bar{x} = \bar{y} = 0,\ \bar{z} = 3/8$ **81.** $\bar{x} = \bar{y} = 0,\ \bar{z} = 3/8$

83. $\bar{x} = \bar{y} = 0,\ \bar{z} = 5/6$ **85.** $I_z = 8\pi a^5/15$ **87.** $4\pi\mu_0\left(\dfrac{R^2}{c} + \dfrac{2R}{c^2} + \dfrac{2}{c^3}\right)$

Section 15.7

Quick Review

1. 17 **2.** 9 **3.** $x = 2,\ y = -1$ **4.** $x = -2,\ y = 1,\ z = 3$

5. $x = \dfrac{u + 2v}{5},\ y = \dfrac{u - 3v}{5}$ **6.** $x = u + v,\ y = 2v$

7. $x = \dfrac{u - v}{3},\ y = \dfrac{2u + v}{3}$

8. $x = \dfrac{u + 4v - w - 3}{10},\ y = \dfrac{-u + 2v - w - 3}{2},$
$z = \dfrac{-3u + 8v - 7w - 11}{10}$

9. $x = u + v,\ y = 2v,\ z = 3w$

10. $\dfrac{\partial x}{\partial u} = \cos(vw),\ \dfrac{\partial x}{\partial v} = -uw \sin(vw),\ \dfrac{\partial x}{\partial w} = -uv \sin(vw)$

Exercises

1. (a) $x = \frac{1}{3}(u + v),\ y = \frac{1}{3}(-2u + v),\ \frac{\partial(x, y)}{\partial(u, v)} = \frac{1}{3}$

(b)

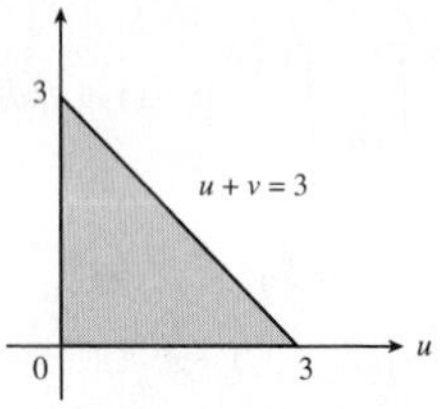

3. (a) $x = \frac{1}{5}(2u - v),\ y = \frac{1}{10}(-u + 3v),\ \frac{\partial(x, y)}{\partial(u, v)} = \frac{1}{10}$

(b)

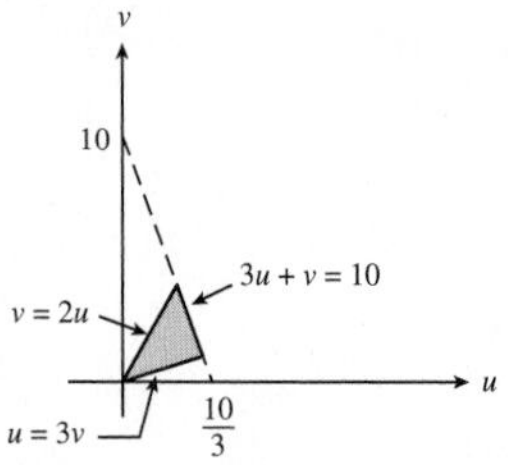

5. (a) u **(b)** $-u$ **9.** 64/5

11. $\int_1^3 \int_1^2 (v + u)\left(\frac{2u}{v}\right) dv\, du = 8 + \frac{52}{3}\ln 2 \approx 20.01$ **13.** $\frac{ab\pi(a^2 + b^2)}{4}$

15. $\int_0^2 \int_0^u ue^{-v}\left|-\frac{1}{3}\right| dv\, du = \frac{1}{3}(3e^{-2} + 1) \approx 0.47$ **19.** $4\pi abc/3$

21. $2 + \ln 8 \approx 4.08$

Chapter 15 Review Exercises

1. $9e - 9 \approx 15.46$ **2.** $\frac{e - 2}{2} \approx 0.36$

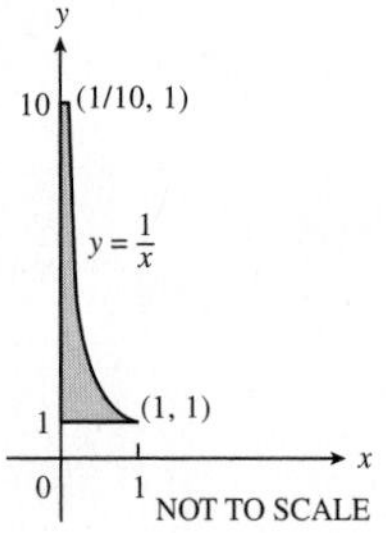

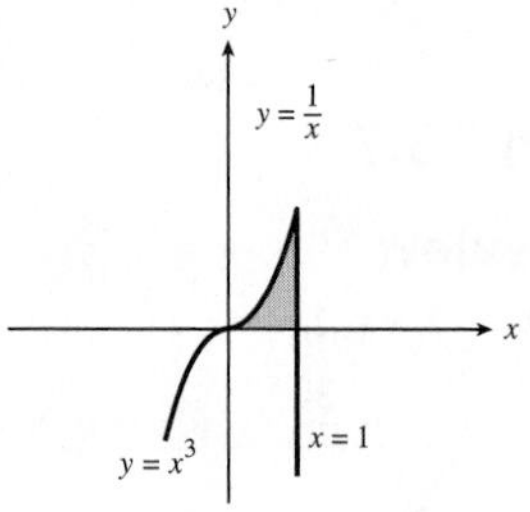

3. 9/2

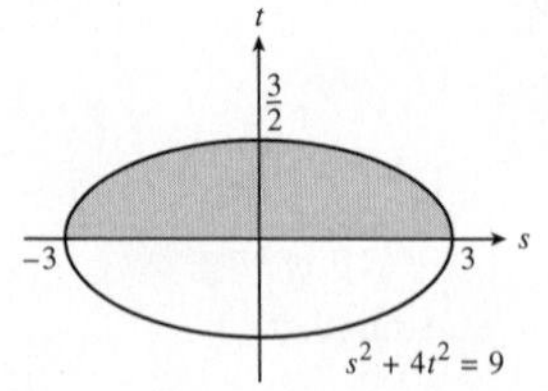

4. 1/5

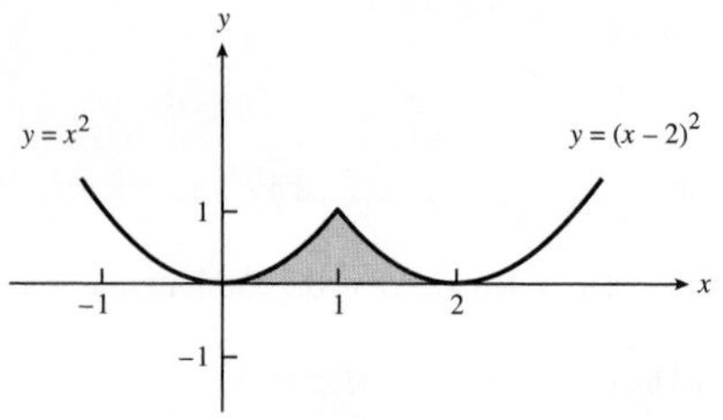

5. $\int_{-2}^{0} \int_{2x+4}^{4-x^2} dy\, dx = 4/3$ **6.** $\int_0^1 \int_y^{\sqrt{y}} dx\, dy = 4/35$

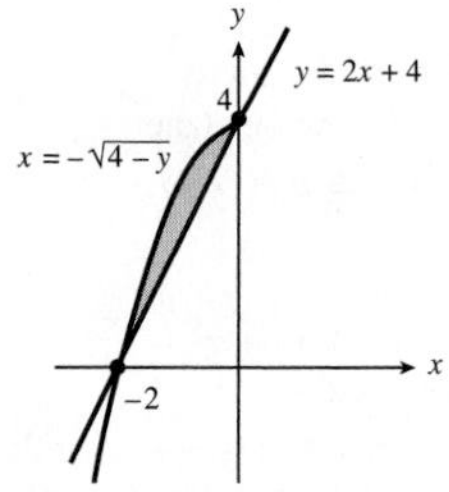

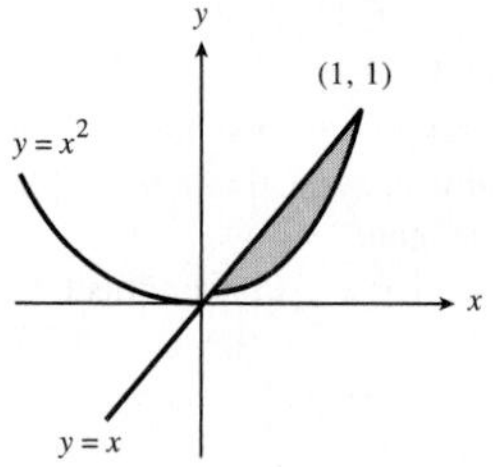

7. $\int_{-3}^{3} \int_0^{(1/2)\sqrt{9-x^2}} y\, dy\, dx = 9/2$ **8.** $\int_0^4 \int_0^{\sqrt{4-y}} 2x\, dx\, dy = 8$

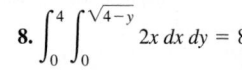

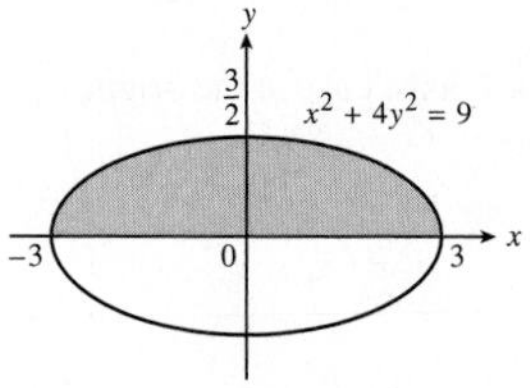

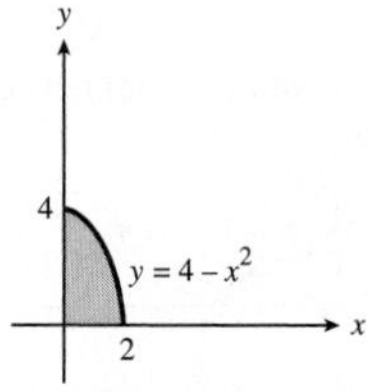

9. sin 4 **10.** $e - 1$ **11.** $\frac{\ln 17}{4} \approx 0.71$ **12.** 2 **13.** 4/3

14. 37/6 **15.** 4/3 **16.** 125/4 **17.** 1/4 **18.** $\frac{1}{2\pi}$

19. $\bar{x} = \bar{y} = \frac{1}{2 - \ln 4} \approx 1.63$ **20.** $\bar{x} = -12/5,\ \bar{y} = 2$ **21.** 104

22. (a) 40/3 **(b)** $\frac{4ab(b^2 + a^2)}{3}$ **23.** $I_x = 2\delta,\ R_x = \sqrt{2/3}$

24. $\bar{x} = 8/15,\ \bar{y} = 13/30;\ I_x = 17/280;\ R_x = \sqrt{17/70};$
$I_y = 1/12;\ R_y = \sqrt{1/3}$

25. $M = 4;\ M_x = 0;\ M_y = 0$ **26.** $I_x = \delta bh^3/12;\ R_x = h/\sqrt{6}$ **27.** π

28. $(\ln 4 - 1)\pi \approx 1.21$ **29.** $\bar{x} = 3\sqrt{3}/\pi,\ \bar{y} = 0$ **30.** $\bar{x} = \bar{y} = \frac{13}{3\pi}$.

31. (a) $\bar{x} = \frac{15\pi + 32}{6\pi + 48} \approx 1.18,\ \bar{y} = 0$

(b)

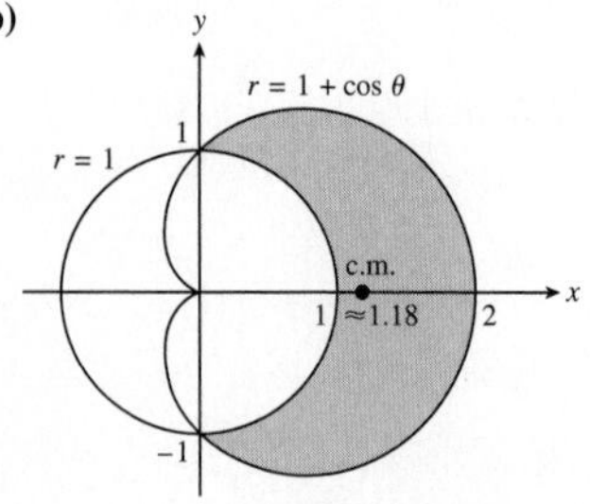

32. (a) $\bar{x} = \dfrac{2a \sin \alpha}{3\alpha}, \bar{y} = 0; \lim_{\alpha \to \pi^-} \bar{x} = 0$

(b) $\bar{x} = \dfrac{2a}{5\pi}, \bar{y} = 0$

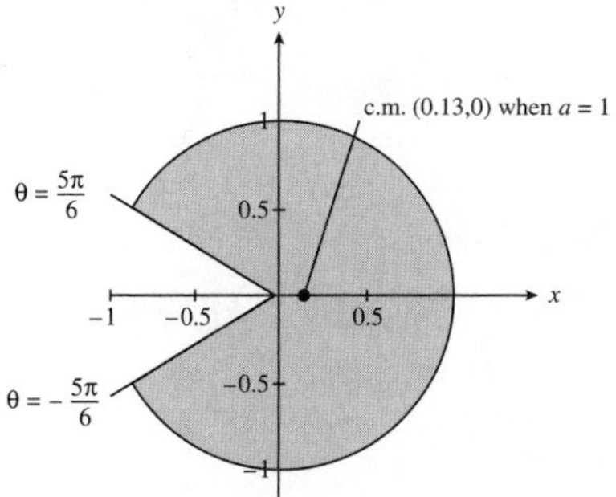

33. $\dfrac{\pi - 2}{4}$ **34. (a)** $\dfrac{\sqrt{2}}{4} \tan^{-1} \sqrt{\dfrac{3}{2}} \approx 0.31$ **(b)** $\pi/4$ **35.** 0 **36.** 1

37. 8/35 **38.** 1 **39.** $\pi/2$ **40.** 12π **41.** $\dfrac{1}{3}[2(31 - 3^{5/2})] \approx 10.27$

42. $3a/4$

43. Cylindrical: $r^2 + z^2 = -2z$; spherical: $\rho = -2 \cos \phi$; a sphere of radius 1 centered at $(0, 0, -1)$ (rectangular)

44. Cylindrical: $z = 1 - r^2$; rectangular: $z = 1 - x^2 - y^2$; a circular paraboloid opening downward from the point $(0, 0, 1)$ (rectangular), axis along the z-axis

45. Rectangular: $(x - 2)^2 + y^2 = 4$; spherical: $\rho \sin \phi = 4 \cos \theta$; a circular cylinder parallel to the z-axis generated by the circle $(x - 2)^2 + y^2 = 4$ in the xy-plane

46. Cylindrical: $z = -r, r \geq 0$; rectangular: $z = -\sqrt{x^2 + y^2}$; the lower nappe of a cone making an angle of $3\pi/4$ with the positive z-axis and having vertex at the origin

47. (a) $\displaystyle\int_{-\sqrt{2}}^{\sqrt{2}} \int_{-\sqrt{2-y^2}}^{\sqrt{2-y^2}} \int_{\sqrt{x^2+y^2}}^{\sqrt{4-x^2-y^2}} 3\, dz\, dx\, dy$

(b) $\displaystyle\int_0^{2\pi} \int_0^{\pi/4} \int_0^2 3\rho^2 \sin \phi\, d\rho d\phi d\theta$ **(c)** $2\pi(8 - 4\sqrt{2}) \approx 14.72$

48. (a) $\displaystyle\int_{-\pi/2}^{\pi/2} \int_0^1 \int_{-r^2}^{r^2} 21r^3 \cos \theta \sin^2 \theta\, dz\, r\, dr\, d\theta$ **(b)** 4

49. (a) $\displaystyle\int_0^{2\pi} \int_0^{\pi/4} \int_0^{\sec \phi} \rho^2 \sin \phi\, d\rho d\phi d\theta$ **(b)** $\pi/3$

50. (a) $\displaystyle\int_0^1 \int_0^{\sqrt{1-x^2}} \int_0^{\sqrt{x^2+y^2}} (6 + 4y)\, dz\, dy\, dx$

(b) $\displaystyle\int_0^{\pi/2} \int_0^1 \int_0^r (6 + 4r \sin \theta)\, dz\, r\, dr\, d\theta$

(c) $\displaystyle\int_0^{\pi/2} \int_{\pi/4}^{\pi/2} \int_0^{\csc \theta} (6 + 4\rho \sin \phi \sin \theta) \cdot (\rho^2 \sin \phi)\, d\rho\, d\phi\, d\theta$

(d) $\pi + 1$

51. $\displaystyle\int_0^1 \int_{\sqrt{1-x^2}}^{\sqrt{3-x^2}} \int_1^{\sqrt{4-x^2-y^2}} z^2 yx\, dz\, dy\, dx$

$\displaystyle+ \int_1^{\sqrt{3}} \int_0^{\sqrt{3-x^2}} \int_1^{\sqrt{4-x^2-y^2}} z^2 yx\, dz\, dy\, dx$

52. (a) Bounded on the top and bottom by the sphere $x^2 + y^2 + z^2 = 4$, on the right by the right circular cylinder $(x - 1)^2 + y^2 = 1$, on the left by the plane $y = 0$

(b) $\displaystyle\int_0^{\pi/2} \int_0^{2 \cos \theta} \int_{-\sqrt{4-r^2}}^{\sqrt{4-r^2}} dz\, r\, dr\, d\theta$

53. (a) $\displaystyle\int_{-\sqrt{3}}^{\sqrt{3}} \int_{-\sqrt{3-x^2}}^{\sqrt{3-x^2}} \int_1^{\sqrt{4-x^2-y^2}} dz\, dy\, dx$

(b) $\displaystyle\int_0^{2\pi} \int_0^{\sqrt{3}} \int_1^{\sqrt{4-r^2}} dz\, r\, dr\, d\theta$

(c) $\displaystyle\int_0^{2\pi} \int_0^{\pi/3} \int_{\sec \phi}^2 \rho^2 \sin \phi\, d\rho d\phi d\theta$

54. (a) $\displaystyle\int_{-1}^1 \int_{-\sqrt{1-x^2}}^{\sqrt{1-x^2}} \int_0^{\sqrt{1-x^2-y^2}} (x^2 + y^2)\, dz\, dy\, dx$

(b) $\displaystyle\int_0^{2\pi} \int_0^1 \int_0^{\sqrt{1-r^2}} r^3\, dz\, dr\, d\theta$

(c) $\displaystyle\int_0^{2\pi} \int_0^{\pi/2} \int_0^1 \rho^4 \sin^3 \phi\, d\rho d\phi d\theta$

55. (a) and **(b)** $\dfrac{8\pi(4\sqrt{2} - 5)}{3} \approx 5.50$ **56.** $8\pi/3$ **57.** $\dfrac{8\pi\delta(b^5 - a^5)}{15}$

58. $64\pi/35$ **60.** $ac - b^2 = \pi^2$

CHAPTER 16

Section 16.1

Quick Review

1. $\dfrac{1}{3} \sin 3x + C$ **2.** $-\dfrac{1}{2} \cos 2x + C$ **3.** $-\dfrac{x^4}{4} + \dfrac{x^3}{3} + 2x + C$

4. 21/4 **5.** 0 **6.** $x = 2t, y = 3t, 0 \leq t \leq 1$

7. $x = at, y = bt, 0 \leq t \leq 1$ **8.** $x = -2 + 5t, y = 1 - 3t, 0 \leq t \leq 1$

9. $x = 2t, y = 3t, z = 4t, 0 \leq t \leq 1$

10. $x = -1 + 4t, y = 1 + 2t, z = 2 - 4t, 0 \leq t \leq 1$

Exercises

1. c **3.** g **5.** d **7.** f **9.** $\sqrt{2}$ **11.** 13/2 **13.** $3\sqrt{14}$

15. $\dfrac{5}{3}\sqrt{5} + \dfrac{4}{3} \approx 5.06$ **17.** $\sqrt{3} \ln \left(\dfrac{b}{a}\right)$ **19.** $\dfrac{10\sqrt{5} - 2}{3} \approx 6.79$

21. 8 **23.** $2\sqrt{2} - 1 \approx 1.83$

25. (a) $4\sqrt{2} - 2 \approx 3.66$ **(b)** $\sqrt{2} + \ln(1 + \sqrt{2}) \approx 2.30$

27. $I_z = 2\pi\delta a^3, R_z = a$

29. (a) $I_z = 2\pi\delta\sqrt{2}, R_z = 1$ **(b)** $I_z = 4\pi\delta\sqrt{2}, R_z = 1$

31. $I_x = 2\pi - 2, R_x = 1$ **33.** 326/3 **35.** $-\dfrac{25\pi^3\sqrt{29}}{8} \approx -521.79$

Section 16.2

Quick Review

1. $\dfrac{\partial f}{\partial x} = \sin y - y \sin x, \dfrac{\partial f}{\partial y} = x \cos y + \cos x$

2. $\dfrac{\partial f}{\partial x} = \sin(yz) + yz, \dfrac{\partial f}{\partial y} = xz \cos(yz) + xz, \dfrac{\partial f}{\partial z} = xy \cos(yz) + xy$

3. $(3x^2 + 2 \sin x)\, dx$ **4.** $(\sin x + x \cos x)\, dx$

5. $dy = 3 \cos t, dt, dx = -2 \sin t\, dt$ **6.** $t^2 \sin t$ **7.** Counterclockwise

8. Clockwise **9.** Counterclockwise **10.** Clockwise

Exercises

1. $\nabla f = \frac{-x\mathbf{i} - y\mathbf{j} - z\mathbf{k}}{(x^2 + y^2 + z^2)^{3/2}}$

3. $\nabla g = -\left(\frac{2x}{x^2 + y^2}\right)\mathbf{i} - \left(\frac{2y}{x^2 + y^2}\right)\mathbf{j} + e^z\mathbf{k}$

5. $\mathbf{F} = -\frac{kx}{(x^2 + y^2)^{3/2}}\mathbf{i} - \frac{ky}{(x^2 + y^2)^{3/2}}\mathbf{j},\ k > 0$

7. (a) 9/2 (b) 13/3 (c) 9/2 **9.** (a) 1/3 (b) $-1/5$ (c) 0
11. (a) 2 (b) 3/2 (c) 1/2 **13.** 1/2 **15.** $-\pi$ **17.** 69/4
19. $-39/2$ **21.** 25/6
23. (a) $\text{Circ}_1 = 0$, $\text{Circ}_2 = 2\pi$, $\text{Flux}_1 = 2\pi$, $\text{Flux}_2 = 0$
(b) $\text{Circ}_1 = 0$, $\text{Circ}_2 = 8\pi$, $\text{Flux}_1 = 8\pi$, $\text{Flux}_2 = 0$
25. Circ = 0, Flux = $a^2\pi$ **27.** Circ = $a^2\pi$, Flux = 0
29. (a) $-\pi/2$ (b) 0 (c) 1
31.

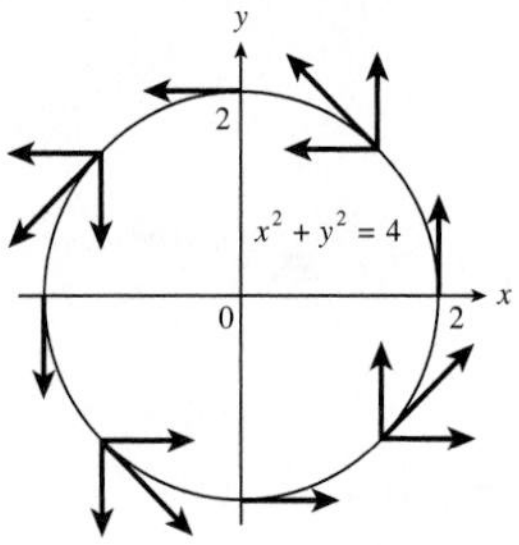

33. (a) $\mathbf{G} = -y\mathbf{i} + x\mathbf{j}$ (b) $\mathbf{G} = (\sqrt{x^2 + y^2})\mathbf{F}$ **35.** $\mathbf{F} = -\frac{x\mathbf{i} + y\mathbf{j}}{\sqrt{x^2 + y^2}}$
37. 48 **39.** π **41.** 0 **43.** 1/2 **45.** Yes, work and area are equal.
47. 12π **49.** -6π **51.** $\pi/2$

Section 16.3

Quick Review

1. 1 **2.** 2 **3.** $-\frac{yz}{\sqrt{1 - x^2y^2z^2}}$ **4.** $-\frac{xz}{\sqrt{1 - x^2y^2z^2}}$

5. $-\frac{xy}{\sqrt{1 - x^2y^2z^2}}$

6. $-\frac{z}{\sqrt{1 - x^2y^2z^2}} - \frac{x^2y^2z^3}{(1 - x^2y^2z^2)^{3/2}}$

7. $-\frac{y}{\sqrt{1 - x^2y^2z^2}} - \frac{x^2y^3z^2}{(1 - x^2y^2z^2)^{3/2}}$

8. $g(x, y, z) = h(y, z)$, $h(y, z)$ and function of y and z
9. $g(x, y, z) = y^2 + h(x, z)$, $h(x, z)$ any function of x and z
10. $g(x, y, z) = \frac{z^2}{2} + h(x, y)$, $h(x, y)$ any function of x and y

Exercises

1. Conservative **3.** Not conservative **5.** Not conservative
7. $x^2 + \frac{3}{2}y^2 + 2z^2 + C$ **9.** $xe^{y + 2z} + C$
11. $\frac{1}{2}\ln(y^2 + z^2) + x\ln x - x + \tan(x + y) + C$ **13.** 49 **15.** -16
17. 1 **19.** 9 ln 2 **21.** 0 **27.** $\mathbf{F} = \nabla\left(\frac{x^2 - 1}{y}\right)$
29. (a) 1 (b) 1 (c) 1 **31.** (a) 2
33. $\frac{GmM}{(x^2 + y^2 + z^2)^{1/2}}$ **35.** (a) $b = c = 2a$ (b) $a = 1, b = c = 2$
37. The path will not matter. **39.** (b) $\frac{16}{3}g$

Section 16.4

Quick Review

1. $x = t,\ y = 0,\ 0 \le t \le 1$ **2.** $x = 1,\ y = t,\ 0 \le t \le 1$
3. $x = 1 - t,\ y = 1,\ 0 \le t \le 1$ **4.** $x = 0,\ y = 1 - t,\ 0 \le t \le 1$
5. 0 **6.** 1/2 **7.** 1 **8.** 0 **9.** $\frac{2xy}{(x^2 + y^2)^2}$ **10.** $\frac{y^2 - x^2}{(x^2 + y^2)^2}$

Exercises

5. Circ = 0, Flux = 2 **7.** Circ = 9, Flux = -9
9. Circ = $\frac{1}{2}$, Flux = $\frac{1}{2}$ **11.** Circ = $-\frac{1}{12}$, Flux = $\frac{1}{5}$ **13.** 0
15. 2/33 **17.** 0 **19.** -16π **21.** (b) πa^2 **23.** $3\pi/8$
25. (a) 0 (b) $(h - k)$ (area of the region)
27. Its zero for any simple closed curve C.
31. (b) $-\frac{1}{2}\oint_C y^2\,dx = \oint_C xy\,dy = \frac{1}{3}\oint xy\,dy - y^2\,dx = A\bar{y}$
35. (a) 0 (b) 0 when (0, 0) is in the region; 4π when (0, 0) is not in the region
39. Its zero.

Section 16.5

Quick Review

1. $-\frac{\sqrt{2}}{2}$ **2.** $-\frac{\sqrt{2}}{2}$ **3.** $\frac{\sqrt{2}}{2}\mathbf{i} + \frac{\sqrt{2}}{2}\mathbf{j} + \mathbf{k}$ **4.** $x + y + \sqrt{2}z = 4$
5. $x = 1 + \frac{\sqrt{2}}{2}t,\ y = 1 + \frac{\sqrt{2}}{2}t,\ z = \sqrt{2} + t$
6. $\frac{(17\sqrt{17} - 1)\pi}{6} \approx 36.18$ **7.** $2(\sqrt{2} - 1)\pi \approx 2.60$ **8.** π
9. $(e^2 - 1)^2 \approx 40.82$ **10.** ≈ 0.66

Exercises

1. $13\pi/3$ **3.** 4 **5.** $6\sqrt{6} - 2\sqrt{2} \approx 11.87$ **7.** $\pi\sqrt{c^2 + 1}$
9. $\frac{\pi}{6}(17\sqrt{17} - 5\sqrt{5}) \approx 30.85$ **11.** $3 + 2\ln 2 \approx 4.39$ **13.** $9a^3$
15. $\frac{abc(ab + ac + bc)}{4}$ **17.** 2 **19.** 18 **21.** $\pi a^3/6$ **23.** $\pi a^2/4$
25. $\pi a^3/2$ **27.** -32 **29.** -4 **31.** $3a^4$ **33.** $\bar{x} = \bar{y} = \bar{z} = a/2$
35. $\bar{x} = \bar{y} = 0$, $\bar{z} = 14/9$, $I_z = 15\pi\delta\sqrt{2}/2$, $R_z = \sqrt{10}/2$
37. (a) $8\pi a^4\delta/3$ (b) $20\pi a^4\delta/3$ **39.** $\frac{\pi}{6}(13\sqrt{13} - 1) \approx 24.02$
41. $5\pi\sqrt{2}$ **43.** $\frac{2}{3}(5\sqrt{5} - 1) \approx 6.79$

Section 16.6

Quick Review

1. $(\sqrt{2}, \pi/4, 1)$
2. $\left(\sqrt{3}, \frac{\pi}{2} - \tan^{-1}\left(\frac{1}{\sqrt{2}}\right), \frac{\pi}{4}\right)$ and $\frac{\pi}{2} - \tan^{-1}\left(\frac{1}{\sqrt{2}}\right) \approx 54.74°$
3. Right circular cylinder parallel to the z-axis generated by the circle $x^2 + (y + 2)^2 = 4$ in the xy-plane
4. (a) $r = -4\sin\theta$ (b) $\rho\sin\phi + 4\sin\theta = 0$
5. The sphere with center at the origin and radius 3
6. (a) $r^2 + z^2 = 9$ (b) $\rho = 3$ **7.** The plane $y = 2$
8. (a) $y = 2$ (b) $\rho\sin\phi\sin\theta = 2$ **9.** $2\mathbf{i} + 2\mathbf{j} + 2\mathbf{k}$
10. $-4\mathbf{i} - 4\mathbf{j} - 4\mathbf{k}$

Exercises

1. $\mathbf{r}(r, \theta) = (r\cos\theta)\mathbf{i} + (r\sin\theta)\mathbf{j} + r^2\,\mathbf{k},\ 0 \le r \le 2,\ 0 \le \theta \le 2\pi$

3. $\mathbf{r}(r, \theta) = (r\cos\theta)\mathbf{i} + (r\sin\theta)\mathbf{j} + \left(\dfrac{r}{2}\right)\mathbf{k},\ 0 \le r \le 6,\ 0 \le \theta \le \pi/2$

5. $\mathbf{r}(r, \theta) = (r\cos\theta)\mathbf{i} + (r\sin\theta)\mathbf{j} + \sqrt{9 - r^2}\,\mathbf{k},\ 0 \le r \le 3/\sqrt{2},\ 0 \le \theta \le 2\pi$

7. $\mathbf{r}(\phi, \theta) = (\sqrt{3}\sin\phi\cos\theta)\mathbf{i} + (\sqrt{3}\sin\phi\sin\theta)\mathbf{j} + (\sqrt{3}\cos\phi)\mathbf{k},$

$\dfrac{\pi}{3} \le \phi \le \dfrac{2\pi}{3},\ 0 \le \theta \le 2\pi$

9. $\mathbf{r}(x, y) = x\mathbf{i} + y\mathbf{j} + (4 - y^2)\mathbf{k},\ -2 \le y \le 2,\ 0 \le x \le 2$

11. $\mathbf{r}(u, v) = u\mathbf{i} + (3\cos v)\mathbf{j} + (3\sin v)\mathbf{k},\ 0 \le u \le 3,\ 0 \le v \le 2\pi$

13. (a) $\mathbf{r}(r, \theta) = (r\cos\theta)\mathbf{i} + (r\sin\theta)\mathbf{j} + (1 - r\cos\theta - r\sin\theta)\mathbf{k},\ 0 \le \theta \le 2\pi,\ 0 \le r \le 3$

(b) $\mathbf{r}(u, v) = (1 - u\cos v - u\sin v)\mathbf{i} + (u\cos v)\mathbf{j} + (u\sin v)\mathbf{k},\ 0 \le u \le 3,\ 0 \le v \le 2\pi$

15. $\mathbf{r}(u, v) = (4\cos^2 v)\mathbf{i} + u\mathbf{j} + (4\cos v\sin v)\mathbf{k},\ -\dfrac{\pi}{2} \le v \le \dfrac{\pi}{2},\ 0 \le u \le 3$

17. $\displaystyle\int_0^{2\pi}\int_0^1 \frac{\sqrt{5}}{2}\, r\,dr\,d\theta = \pi\frac{\sqrt{5}}{2} \approx 3.51$

19. $\displaystyle\int_0^{2\pi}\int_1^3 r\sqrt{5}\,dr\,d\theta = 8\pi\sqrt{5} \approx 56.20$ **21.** $\displaystyle\int_0^{2\pi}\int_1^4 dr\,d\theta = 6\pi$

23. $\displaystyle\int_0^{2\pi}\int_0^1 r\sqrt{4r^2 + 1}\,dr\,d\theta = \frac{\pi}{6}(5\sqrt{5} - 1) \approx 5.33$

25. $\displaystyle\int_0^{2\pi}\int_{\pi/4}^{\pi} 2\sin\phi\,d\phi\,d\theta = (4 + 2\sqrt{2})\,\pi \approx 21.45$

27. $\dfrac{17\sqrt{17} - 1}{4} \approx 17.27$ **29.** $4\pi/3$ **31.** $3\sqrt{3}$ **33.** $11\pi/12 \approx 2.88$

35. -32 **37.** $\pi a^3/6$ **39.** $13a^4/6$ **41.** $2\pi/3$ **43.** $-73\pi/6 \approx -38.22$

45. $\bar{x} = \bar{y} = \bar{z} = a/2$ **47.** $I_z = 8\delta\pi a^4/3$

49. Tangent plane: $x + y - \sqrt{2}z = 0$; surface: $z = \sqrt{x^2 + y^2}$

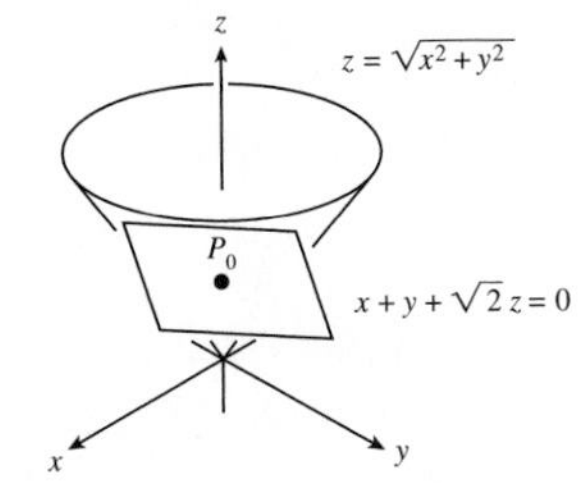

51. Tangent plane: $\sqrt{3}x + y = 9$; surface: $x^2 + (y - 3)^2 = 9$

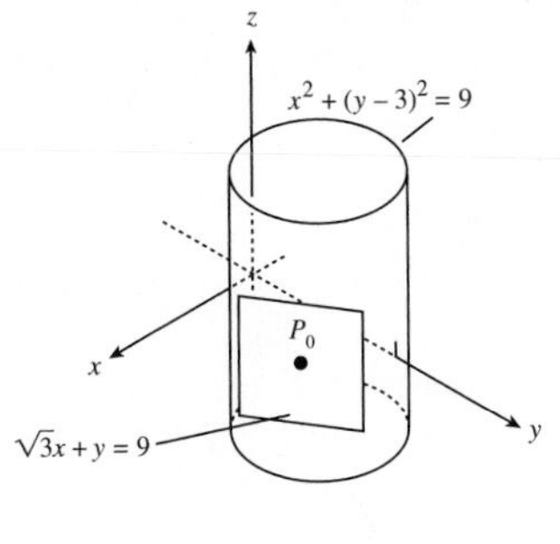

Section 16.7

Quick Review

1. $\dfrac{e^{-xyz}}{x + y + z} - yze^{-xyz}\ln(x + y + z)$

2. $\dfrac{e^{-xyz}}{x + y + z} - xye^{-xyz}\ln(x + y + z)$

3. $(xyz^2 - z)e^{-xyz}\ln(x + y + z) - \dfrac{(y^2z + 2xyz + yz^2 + x^2z + xz^2 + 1)e^{-xyz}}{(x + y + z)^2}$

4. $(xyz^2 - z)e^{-xyz}\ln(x + y + z) - \dfrac{(y^2z + 2xyz + yz^2 + x^2z + xz^2 + 1)e^{-xyz}}{(x + y + z)^2}$

5. $(x^2yz - x)e^{-xyz}\ln(x + y + z) - \dfrac{(xz^2 + x^2z + 2xyz + x^2y + xy^2 + 1)e^{-xyz}}{(x + y + z)^2}$

6. $(x^2yz - x)e^{-xyz}\ln(x + y + z) - \dfrac{(xz^2 + x^2z + 2xyz + x^2y + xy^2 + 1)e^{-xyz}}{(x + y + z)^2}$

7. $(cy + bz)\mathbf{i} - (cx + az)\mathbf{j} + (bx - ay)\mathbf{k}$

8. $-(cy + bz)\mathbf{i} + (cx + az)\mathbf{j} - (bx - ay)\mathbf{k}$

9. $\nabla f = (\sin(y + z))\mathbf{i} + (x\cos(y + z))\mathbf{j} + (x\cos(y + z))\mathbf{k}$

10. $\dfrac{-1 \pm \sqrt{5}}{2}$

Exercises

1. 4π **3.** $-5/6$ **5.** 0 **7.** -6π **9.** $2\pi a^2$ **13.** 12π **15.** $-\pi/4$

17. -15π **21.** Its value is -2 times the area of the region.

23. No such field exists. **25.** $16I_y + 16I_x$

Section 16.8

Quick Review

1. $4/3$ **2.** $2/3$ **3.** $2/3$ **4.** $2/3$ **5.** $\displaystyle\int_0^1\int_0^1\int_{\sqrt{z}}^1 dy\,dz\,dx$

6. $\displaystyle\int_0^1\int_0^1\int_{\sqrt{z}}^1 dy\,dx\,dz$ **7.** $\displaystyle\int_0^1\int_{\sqrt{z}}^1\int_0^1 dx\,dy\,dz$

8. $\displaystyle\int_0^1\int_0^{y^2}\int_0^1 dx\,dz\,dy$ **9.** $\cos^{-1}\left(\dfrac{1}{\sqrt{3}}\right) \approx 54.74°$

10. $\cos^{-1}\left(\dfrac{1}{\sqrt{3}}\right) \approx 54.74°$

Exercises

1. 0 **3.** 0 **5.** -16 **7.** -8π **9.** 3π **11.** $-40/3$ **13.** 12π

15. $(48\sqrt{2} - 12)\pi \approx 175.56$ **17. (b)** Its value is zero.

21. Its value never exceeds the surface area of S.

31. (a) $\displaystyle\iiint_D p(t, x, y, z)\,dV$ represents the mass of the fluid at any time t, and the instantaneous rate of change of mass is flux of the fluid through the surface S.

Chapter 16 Review Exercises

1. Path 1: $2\sqrt{3}$; path 2: $3\sqrt{2}+1$

2. Path 1: 10/3; path 2: $\dfrac{5\sqrt{2}+9}{6} \approx 2.68$; path 3: $-2/3$ **3.** $4a^2$ **4.** 7/3

5. 0 **6.** 5 **7.** 0 **8.** 0 **9.** 0 **10.** 0 **11.** $\pi\sqrt{3}$

12. $\dfrac{\pi}{6}(7\sqrt{21}-9) \approx 12.08$ **13.** $2\pi\left(1-\dfrac{1}{\sqrt{2}}\right) \approx 1.84$

14. **(a)** $4\pi - 8$ **(b)** 8 **15.** $\dfrac{1}{2}abc\sqrt{\dfrac{1}{a^2}+\dfrac{1}{b^2}+\dfrac{1}{c^2}}$

16. **(a)** 0 **(b)** -4 **17.** 50 **18.** $\approx$97,751 square miles

19. $\mathbf{r}(\phi, \theta) = (6\sin\phi\cos\theta)\mathbf{i} + (6\sin\phi\sin\theta)\mathbf{j} + (6\cos\phi)\mathbf{k}$, $\dfrac{\pi}{6} \le \phi \le \dfrac{2\pi}{3}, 0 \le \theta \le 2\pi$

20. $\mathbf{r}(r, \theta) = (r\cos\theta)\mathbf{i} + (r\,sin\,\theta)\mathbf{j} - \left(\dfrac{r^2}{2}\right)\mathbf{k}, 0 \le r \le 2, 0 \le \theta \le 2\pi$

21. $\mathbf{r}(r, \theta) = (r\cos\theta)\mathbf{i} + (r\sin\theta)\mathbf{j} + (1+r)\mathbf{k}, 0 \le r \le 2, 0 \le \theta \le 2\pi$

22. $\mathbf{r}(x, y) = x\mathbf{i} + y\mathbf{j} + \left(3 - x - \dfrac{y}{2}\right)\mathbf{k}, 0 \le x \le 2, 0 \le y \le 2$

23. $\mathbf{r}(u, v) = (u\cos v)\mathbf{i} + 2u^2\mathbf{j} + (u\sin v)\mathbf{k}, 0 \le u \le 1, 0 \le v \le \pi$

24. $\mathbf{r}(\phi, \theta) = (\sqrt{10}\sin\phi\cos\theta)\mathbf{i} + (\sqrt{10}\sin\phi\sin\theta)\mathbf{j} + (\sqrt{10}\cos\phi)\mathbf{k}$, $0 \le \phi \le \dfrac{\pi}{2}, 0 \le \theta \le \dfrac{\pi}{2}$

25. $\sqrt{6}$ **26.** $-\sqrt{2/3}$ **27.** $\pi(\sqrt{2} + \ln(1+\sqrt{2})) \approx 7.21$

28. $8\pi/3$ **29.** Conservative **30.** Conservative **31.** Not conservative

32. Conservative **33.** $2x + y^2 + zy + z + C$ **34.** $\sin(xz) + e^y + C$

35. Path 1: 2; Path 2: 8/3 **36.** Path 1: 2; Path 2: 2

37. **(a)** $1 - e^{-2\pi} \approx 1.00$ **(b)** $1 - e^{-2\pi} \approx 1.00$ **38.** **(a)** 0 **(b)** 2π

39. **(a)** $-\pi/2$ **(b)** 0 **(c)** 1 **40.** 0 **41.** 0 **42.** 0

43. **(a)** $4\sqrt{2} - 2 \approx 3.66$ **(b)** $\sqrt{2} + \ln(1+\sqrt{2}) \approx 2.30$

44. $\bar{x} = 19/18, \bar{y} = 19/9, \bar{z} = 4\sqrt{2}/7$

45. $\bar{x} = 1, \bar{y} = 16/15, \bar{z} = 2/3, I_x + 232/45, I_y = 64/15, I_z = 56/9$, $R_x = \sqrt{116/45}, R_y = \sqrt{32/15}, R_z = \sqrt{28/9}$

46. $\bar{x} = 0, \bar{y} = \dfrac{8a - a\pi}{4\pi - 4a}, \bar{z} = 0$ **47.** $\bar{z} = 3/2, I_z = 7\sqrt{3}/3, R_z = \sqrt{7/3}$

48. $M = 2\pi\delta\sqrt{13}, \bar{x} = \bar{y} = 0, \bar{z} = 3\pi$

49. $\bar{x} = \bar{y} = 0, \bar{z} = 49/12, I_z = 640\pi, R_z = 2\sqrt{2}$ **50.** 14/3 **51.** Circ $= -1/2$, Flux $=$ 3/2 **52.** Circ $= 0$, Flux $= -11/3$ **55.** 3

56. 128π **57.** $\dfrac{2}{3}\pi(7 - 8\sqrt{2}) \approx -9.03$ **58.** $\pi + 1$ **59.** 0

60. 8/3 **61.** π **62.** **(a)** $2\pi a^3$ **(b)** $2\pi a^3$

Appendix A3

1.

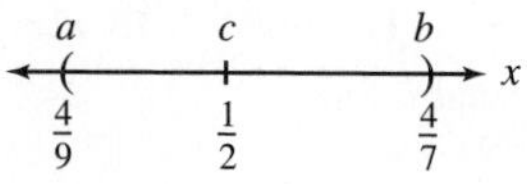

$\delta = 1/18$

3. $\delta = 0.39$ **5.** $(-2.01, -1.99)$; $\delta = 0.01$ **7.** $(3, 15)$; $\delta = 5$

9. **(a)** -4 **(b)** $\delta = 0.05$ **11.** **(a)** $\sin 1 \approx 0.841$ **(b)** $\delta = 0.018$

13. $\delta = \min\{1 - \sqrt{1-\varepsilon}, \sqrt{1+\varepsilon} - 1\}$

15. **(a)** $I = (5, 5 + \varepsilon^2)$ **(b)** $\lim_{x\to 5^+} \sqrt{x-5} = 0$

Appendix A5.1

1. $x^2 + (y-2)^2 = 4$

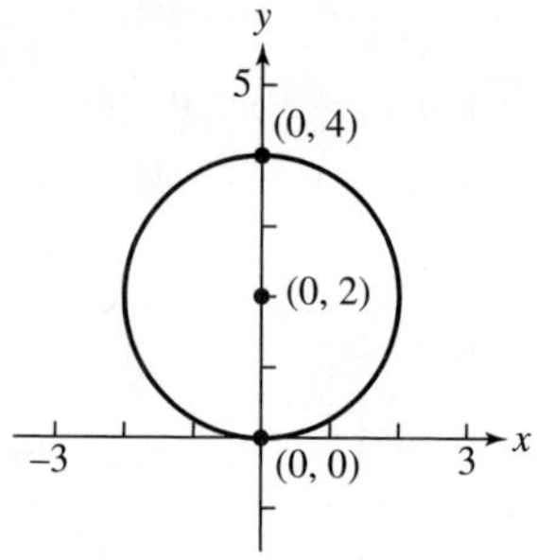

3. Center $= (-2, 2)$; radius $= 2$

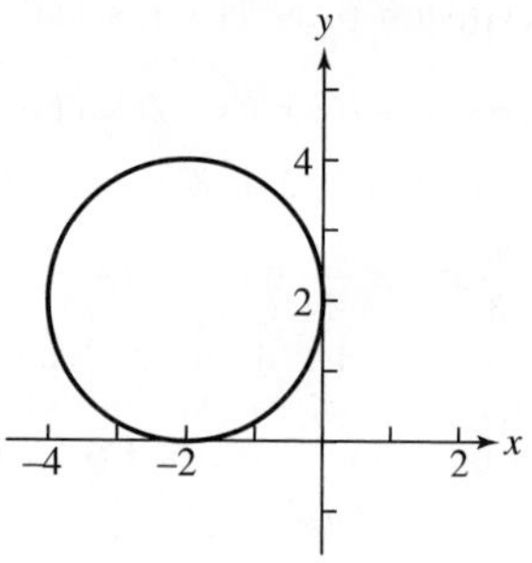

5. The circle with center at (1, 0) and radius 2 plus its interior.

7. $y^2 = 8x$; focus is (2, 0); directrix is $x = -2$

9. $x^2 = -6y$; focus is $(0, -3/2)$; directrix is $y = 3/2$

11. $\dfrac{x^2}{4} - \dfrac{y^2}{9} = 1$; foci are $(\pm\sqrt{13}, 0)$; vertices are $(\pm 2, 0)$; asymptotes are $y = \pm\dfrac{3}{2}x$

13. $\dfrac{x^2}{2} + y^2 = 1$; foci are $(\pm 1, 0)$; vertices are $(\pm\sqrt{2}, 0)$

15. Focus is (3, 0); directrix is $x = -3$

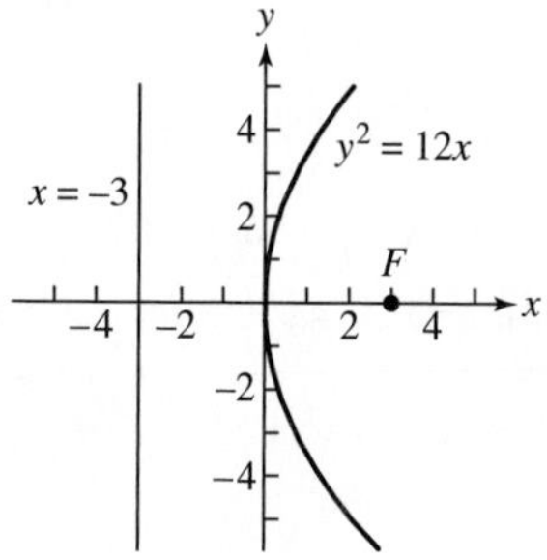

17. $\dfrac{x^2}{25} + \dfrac{y^2}{16} = 1$; foci are $(\pm 3, 0)$

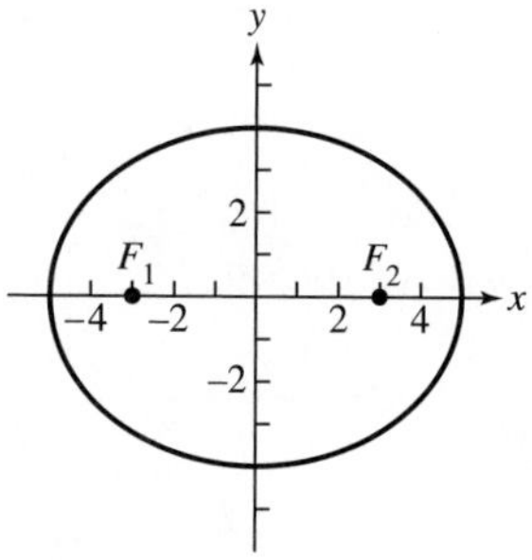

19. $\dfrac{x^2}{4} + \dfrac{y^2}{2} = 1$

21. $x^2 - y^2 = 1$; asymptotes are $y = \pm x$; foci are $(\pm\sqrt{2}, 0)$

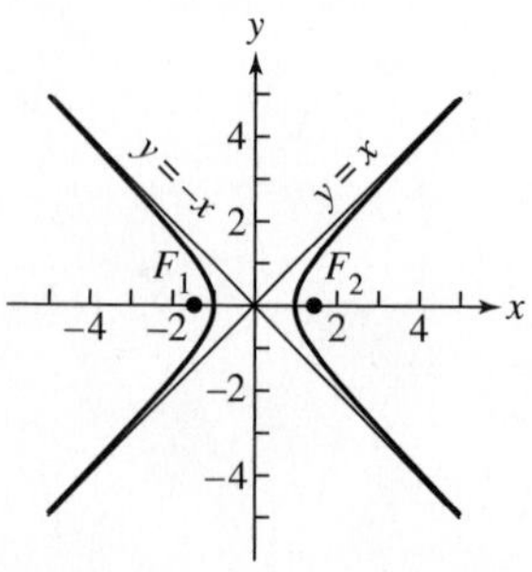

23. $y^2 - x^2 = 1$

25. **(a)** Vertex is $(1, -2)$; focus is $(3, -2)$; directrix is $x = -1$

(b)

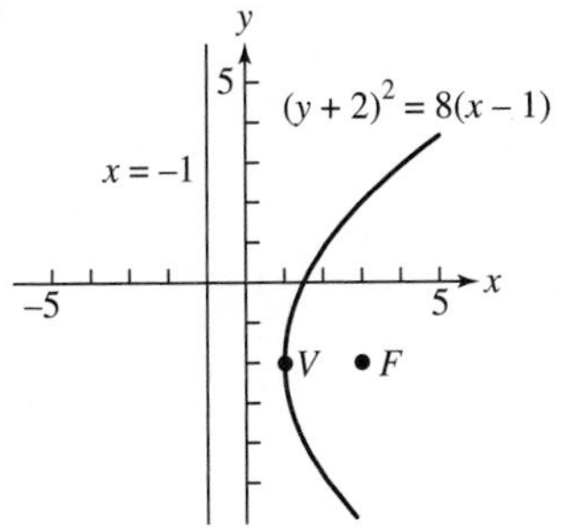

27. **(a)** Center is $(2, 0)$; foci are $(-3, 0)$ and $(7, 0)$; asymptotes are $y = \pm\dfrac{3(x-2)}{4}$; vertices are $(-2, 0)$ and $(6, 0)$

(b)

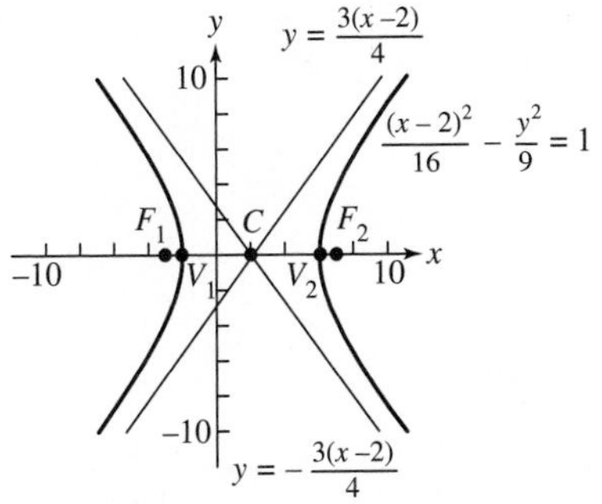

29. $\dfrac{(x+2)^2}{6} + \dfrac{(y+1)^2}{9} = 1$; vertices are $(-2, 2)$ and $(-2, -4)$; foci are $(-2, -1 \pm \sqrt{3})$; center is $(-2, -1)$

31. $(y-1)^2 - (x+1)^2 = 1$; vertices are $(-1, 2)$ and $(-1, 0)$; foci are $(-1, 1 \pm \sqrt{2})$; center is $(-1, 1)$; asymptotes are $y = \pm(x + 1) \quad + 1$

33. Circle; center is $(7, -3)$; radius is 1

35. Ellipse; center is $(-2, 0)$; foci are $(-4, 0)$ and $(0, 0)$; vertices are $(-2 \pm \sqrt{5}, 0)$

37. Volume of the parabolic solid is $V_1 = \dfrac{\pi h b^2}{8}$; volume of the cone is $V_2 = \dfrac{\pi h b^2}{12}$; $\dfrac{V_1}{V_2} = \dfrac{3}{2}$

39. The slopes of the two tangents to $y^2 = 4px$ from the point $(-p, a)$ are $m_1 = \dfrac{2p}{a + \sqrt{a^2 + 4p^2}}$ and $m_2 = \dfrac{2p}{a - \sqrt{a^2 + 4p^2}}$, and $m_1 m_2 = -1$.

41. **(a)** 24π **(b)** 16π **43.** 24π

45. $\dfrac{dr_A}{dt} = \dfrac{dr_B}{dt} \Rightarrow \dfrac{d}{dt}(r_A - r_B) = 0$
$\Rightarrow r_A - r_B =$ a constant

Appendix A5.2

1. $e = 3/5$; foci are $(\pm 3, 0)$; directrices are $x = \pm 25/3$

3. $e = 1/\sqrt{3}$; foci are $(0, \pm 1)$; directrices are $y = \pm 3$

5. $\dfrac{x^2}{27} + \dfrac{y^2}{36} = 1$ **7.** $\dfrac{x^2}{100} + \dfrac{y^2}{94.24} = 1$ **9.** $e = \dfrac{\sqrt{5}}{3}$; $\dfrac{x^2}{9} + \dfrac{y^2}{4} = 1$

11. Take $c = 4$ and $a = 5$, then $e = \dfrac{c}{a} = \dfrac{4}{5}$ and $b = 3$. The equation is $\dfrac{x^2}{25} + \dfrac{y^2}{9} = 1$.

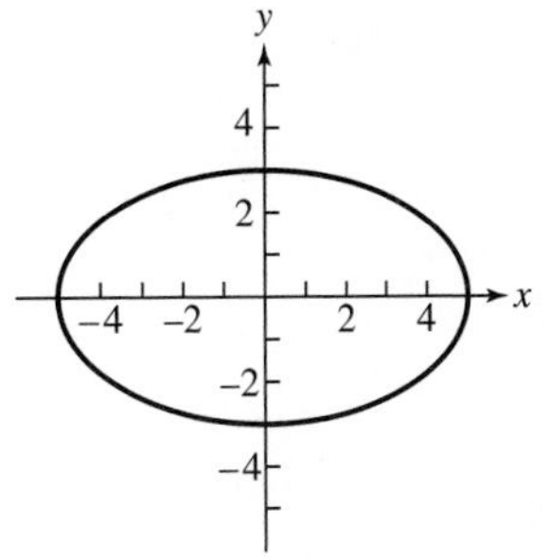

13. $\dfrac{(x-1)^2}{4} + \dfrac{(y-4)^2}{9} = 1$; foci are $(1, 4 \pm \sqrt{5})$; $e = \dfrac{\sqrt{5}}{3}$; directrices are $y = 4 \pm \dfrac{9\sqrt{5}}{5}$.

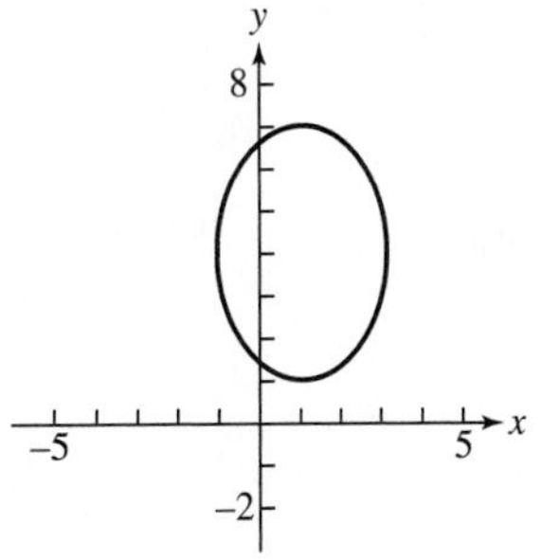

15. $e = 5/4$; foci are $(\pm 5, 0)$; directrices are $x = \pm 16/5$

17. $e = \sqrt{5}$; foci are $(\pm\sqrt{10}, 0)$; directrices are $x = \pm\sqrt{10}/5$

19. $y^2 - \dfrac{x^2}{8} = 1$ **21.** $e = \sqrt{2}$; $\dfrac{x^2}{8} - \dfrac{y^2}{8} = 1$

23. $\dfrac{(y-6)^2}{36} - \dfrac{(x-1)^2}{45} = 1$

25. $a = 0, b = -4, c = 0$; $e = \sqrt{3}/2$

Appendix A5.3

1. Hyperbola **3.** Ellipse **5.** Parabola **7.** Parabola

9. Hyperbola **11.** Hyperbola **13.** Ellipse **15.** Ellipse

17. $(x')^2 - (y')^2 = 4$; hyperbola **19.** $4(x')^2 + 16y' = 0$; parabola

21. $(y')^2 = 1$; parallel horizontal lines **23.** $(x')^2 + 4y' = 0$; parabola

25. $4(x')^2 + 2(y')^2 = 19$; ellipse

27. $\sin\alpha = \dfrac{1}{\sqrt{5}}$, $\cos\alpha = \dfrac{2}{\sqrt{5}}$; or $\sin\alpha = -\dfrac{2}{\sqrt{5}}$, $\cos\alpha = \dfrac{1}{\sqrt{5}}$

29. $\sin\alpha \approx 0.23$, $\cos\alpha \approx 0.97$; $A' \approx 0.88$, $B' \approx 0.00$, $C' \approx 3.12$, $D' \approx 0.74$, $E' \approx -1.20$, $F' = -3$; $0.88(x')^2 + 3.12(y')^2 + 0.74x' - 1.20y' - 3 = 0$; ellipse

31. $\sin\alpha \approx 0.45$, $\cos\alpha \approx 0.89$; $A' \approx 0.00$, $B' \approx 0.00$, $C' \approx 5.00$, $D' = 0$, $E' = 0$, $F' = -5$; $5.00(y')^2 - 5 = 0$ or $y' = \pm 1.00$; parallel lines

33. $\sin\alpha \approx 0.63$, $\cos\alpha \approx 0.77$; $A' \approx 5.05$, $B' \approx 0.00$, $C' \approx -0.05$, $D' \approx -5.07$, $E' \approx -6.19$, $F' = -1$; $5.05(x')^2 - 0.05(y')^2 - 5.07\,x' - 6.19\,y' - 1 = 0$; hyperbola

35. **(a)** $(x')^2 - (y')^2 = 2$ **(b)** $(x')^2 - (y')^2 = 2a$

37. Yes, $x^2 + 4xy + 5y^2 - 1 = 0$

39. (a) Hyperbola

(b) $y = -\dfrac{2x}{x-1}$

(c) At $(3, -3)$: $y = -2x + 3$;
At $(-1, -1)$: $y = -2x - 3$

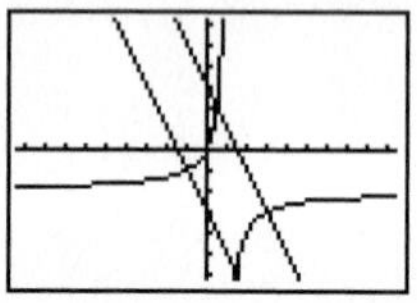

$[-9.4, 9.4]$ by $[-6.2, 6.2]$

41. (a) $\dfrac{(x')^2}{b^2} + \dfrac{(y')^2}{a^2} = 1$ **(b)** $\dfrac{(y')^2}{a^2} - \dfrac{(x')^2}{b^2} = 1$

(c) $(x')^2 + (y')^2 = a^2$ **(d)** $y' = -\dfrac{1}{m}x'$ **(e)** $y' = -\dfrac{1}{m}x' + \dfrac{b}{m}$

43. (a) Parabola

(b) The equation can be written in the form $(x + 2y + 3)^2 = 0$.

Appendix A5.4

1. $r \cos\left(\theta - \dfrac{\pi}{6}\right) = 5$; $y = -\sqrt{3}x + 10$

3. $r \cos\left(\theta - \dfrac{4\pi}{3}\right) = 3$; $y = -\dfrac{\sqrt{3}}{3}x - 2\sqrt{3}$

5. $y = 2 - x$

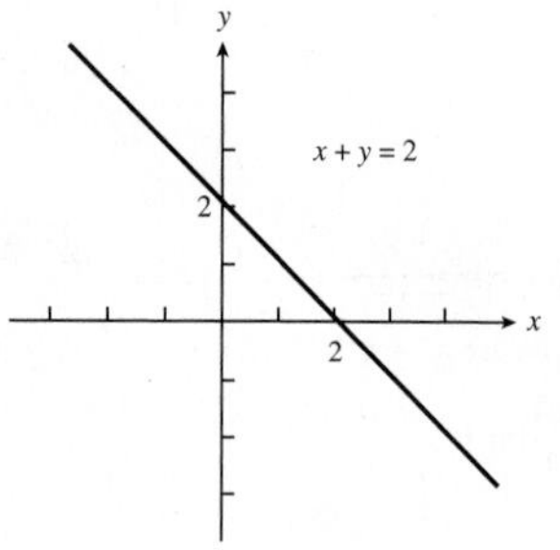

7. $y = \dfrac{\sqrt{3}}{3}x + 2\sqrt{3}$

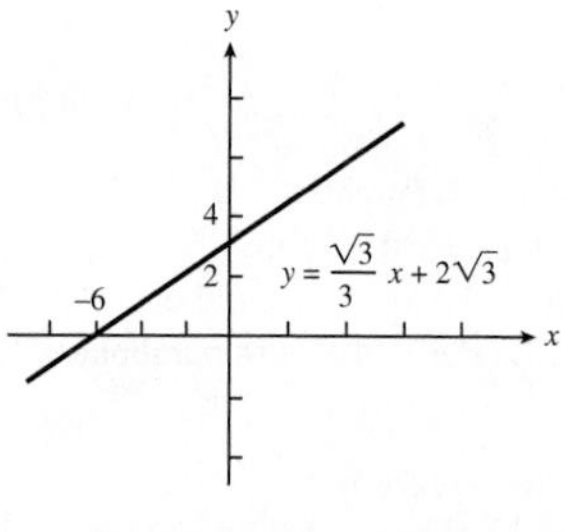

9. $r \cos\left(\theta - \dfrac{\pi}{4}\right) = 3$ **11.** $r \cos\left(\theta + \dfrac{\pi}{2}\right) = 5$

13. $r = 8 \cos\theta$ **15.** $r = 2\sqrt{2} \sin\theta$

17.

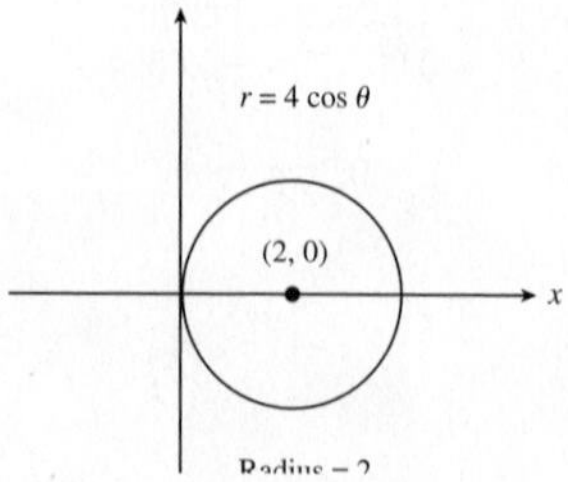

19.

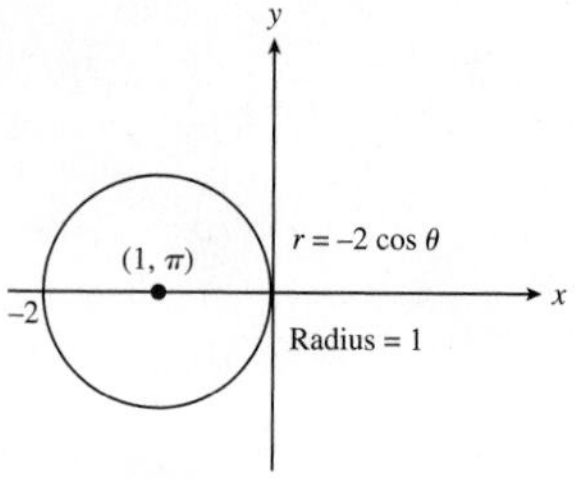

21.

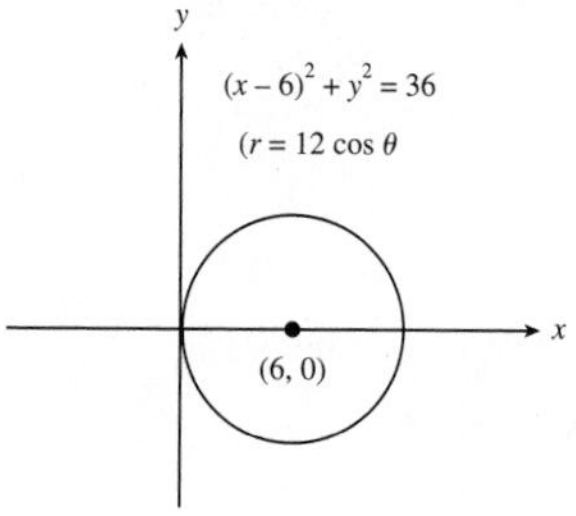

23.

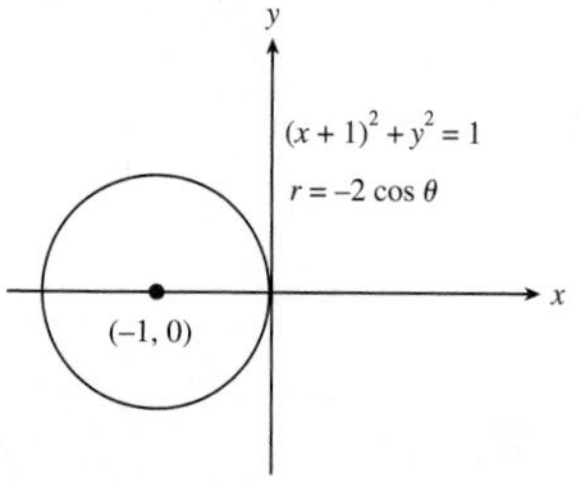

25. $r = \dfrac{2}{1 + \cos\theta}$ **27.** $r = \dfrac{30}{1 - 5\sin\theta}$ **29.** $r = \dfrac{1}{2 + \cos\theta}$

31. $r = \dfrac{10}{5 - \sin\theta}$

33.

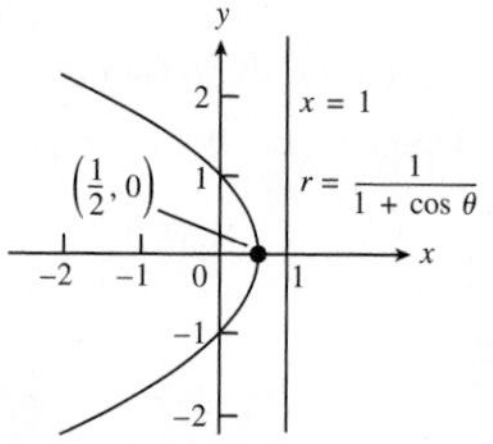

35.

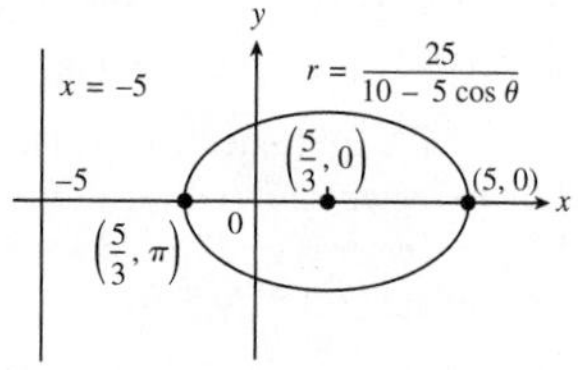

37.

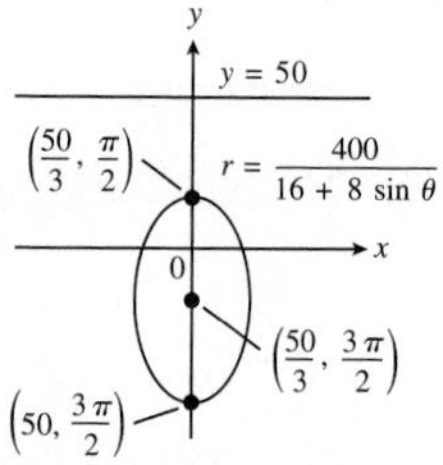

39.

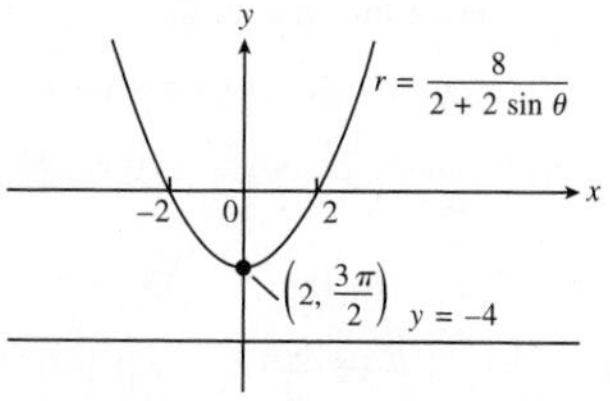

41. (a) $x^2 + y^2 = 4y$; $x = \sqrt{3}$

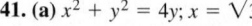

(b)

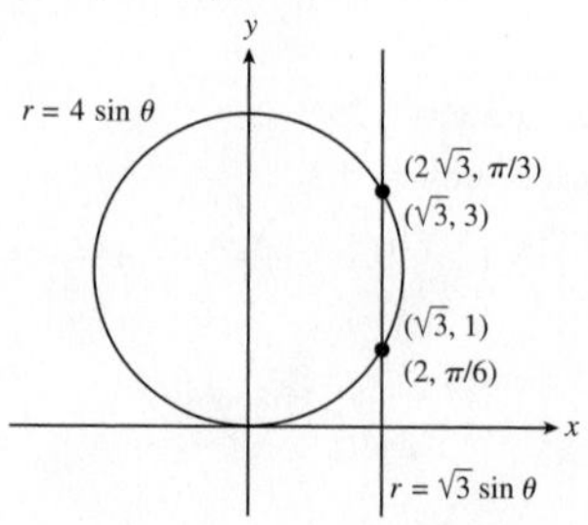

43. $r = \dfrac{4}{1 + \cos\theta}$

49.

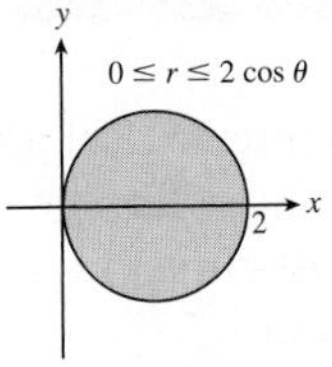

51. (b)

Planet	Perihelion	Aphelion
Mercury	0.3075 AU	0.4667 AU
Venus	0.7184 AU	0.7282 AU
Earth	0.9833 AU	1.0167 AU
Mars	1.3817 AU	1.6663 AU
Jupiter	4.9512 AU	5.4548 AU
Saturn	9.0210 AU	10.0570 AU
Uranus	18.2977 AU	20.0623 AU
Neptune	29.8135 AU	30.3065 AU
Pluto	29.6549 AU	49.2251 AU

53. (b) 2 in. apart

Appendix A6

1. $\cosh x = \frac{5}{4}$; $\tanh x = -\frac{3}{5}$; $\coth x = -\frac{5}{3}$; $\text{sech}\, x = \frac{4}{5}$; $\text{csch}\, x = -\frac{4}{3}$

3. $\sinh x = \frac{8}{15}$; $\tanh x = \frac{8}{17}$; $\coth x = \frac{17}{8}$; $\text{sech}\, x = \frac{15}{17}$; $\text{csch}\, x = \frac{15}{8}$

5. $x + \frac{1}{x}$ **7.** e^{5x} **9.** e^{4x} **13.** $\frac{dy}{dx} = 2\cosh\frac{x}{3}$

15. $\frac{dy}{dt} = \text{sech}^2\sqrt{t} + \frac{\tanh\sqrt{t}}{\sqrt{t}}$ **17.** $\frac{dy}{dz} = \coth z$

19. $\frac{dy}{d\theta} = (\text{sech}\,\theta \tanh\theta)(\ln \text{sech}\,\theta)$ **21.** $\frac{dy}{dx} = \tanh^3 x$

23. $y = 2x$; $\frac{dy}{dx} = 2$ **25.** $\frac{dy}{dx} = \frac{1}{2\sqrt{x}(1+x)}$

27. $\frac{dy}{d\theta} = \frac{1}{1+\theta} - \tanh^{-1}\theta$ **29.** $\frac{dy}{dt} = \frac{1}{2\sqrt{t}} - \coth^{-1}\sqrt{t}$

31. $\frac{dy}{dx} = -\text{sech}^{-1} x$ **33.** $\frac{dy}{d\theta} = \dfrac{\ln 2}{\sqrt{1 + \left(\frac{1}{2}\right)^{2\theta}}}$ **35.** $\frac{dy}{dx} = |\sec x|$

37. (a) $\frac{d}{dx}(\tan^{-1}(\sinh x) + C) = \text{sech}\, x$

(b) $\frac{d}{dx}(\sin^{-1}(\tanh x) + C) = \text{sech}\, x$

39. $\frac{d}{dx}\left(\frac{x^2-1}{2}\coth^{-1} x + \frac{x}{2} + C\right) = x\coth^{-1} x$

41. $\frac{\cosh 2x}{2} + C$ **43.** $12\sinh\left(\frac{x}{2} - \ln 3\right) + C$

45. $7\ln\left|\cosh\frac{x}{7}\right| + C$ **47.** $\tanh\left(x - \frac{1}{2}\right) + C$

49. $-2\,\text{sech}\sqrt{t} + C$ **51.** $\ln(5/2) \approx 0.916$

53. $(3/32) + \ln 2 \approx 0.787$ **55.** $e - e^{-1} \approx 2.350$

57. 3/4 **59.** $(3/8) + \ln\sqrt{2} \approx 0.722$ **61.** 2π

63. $\left(2\ln\frac{199}{100} - \frac{99}{100}\right)\pi \approx 1.214$

65. (a) If $g(x) = \frac{f(x) + f(-x)}{2}$, then

$g(-x) = \frac{f(-x) + f(x)}{2} = g(x)$. Thus,

$\frac{f(x) + f(-x)}{2}$ is even. If $h(x) = \frac{f(x) - f(-x)}{2}$,

then $h(-x) = \frac{f(-x) - f(x)}{2} = -\frac{f(x) - f(-x)}{2} = -h(x)$.

Thus $\frac{f(x) - f(-x)}{2}$ is odd.

(b) Even part: $\frac{e^x + e^{-x}}{2} = \cosh x$

Odd part: $\frac{e^x - e^{-x}}{2} = \sinh x$

69. $y = \text{sech}^{-1}(x) - \sqrt{1 - x^2}$

Appendix A8

1. -5 **3.** 1 **5.** -7 **7.** 38 **9.** $x = -4, y = 1$

11. $x = 3, y = 2$ **13.** $x = 3, y = -2, z = 2$ **15.** $x = 2, y = 0, z = -1$

17. (a) $h = 6, k = 4$ **(b)** $h = 6, k \neq 4$

Applications Index

Note: Numbers in parentheses refer to exercises on the pages indicated.

Education

Growth and Decay. *See also* Population Modeling and Life Science

Home and Community

Interest, Investment, Financial Assistance

Life Science and Medicine

Linear Motion (acceleration, distance, height, position, time, velocity)

Physical Science and Engineering

Population Modeling and Demographics. *See also* Life Science and Medicine

Sports. *See also* Projectile Motion

Miscellaneous

Subject Index

Note: Numbers in parentheses refer to exercises on the pages indicated.

A

B

C

D

G

J

K

L

M

N

O

Q

R

S

T

Credits

Illustrations

Chapter 13, p. 651, Figure 13.29 © 1994 Nelson L. Max, University of California/Biological Photo Service.

Chapter 14, p. 671, Figure 14.7 Appalachian Mountain Club.

Chapter 16, p. 822, Figure 16.11 Adapted from *NCFMF Book of Film Notes,* 1974, MIT Press with Education Development Center, Inc.; p. 822 Figure 16.12 Adapted from *NCFMF Book of Film Notes,* 1974, MIT Press with Education Development Center, Inc.

Appendix A, p. 916, Figures A5.1 (a) and (b) © THOMAS' CALCULUS: Chapter 10, p. 686, Figures 10 (a) and (b).

Appendix A, p. 917, Figure A5.2 © THOMAS' CALCULUS: Chapter 1, p. 14, Figure 1.18.

Appendix A, p. 927, figure accompanying exercise 37 © THOMAS' CALCULUS: Chapter 10, p. 695, figure accompanying exercise 75.

Technical illustrative and technical artwork for this edition was produced by Tech-Graphics.

Photographs

Page 2, Martin D. Vonka/Shutterstock; **Page 12,** Royal Institution of Great Britain/Science Photo Library/Photo Researchers, Inc.; **Page 32,** Science Source, Photo Researchers, Inc.; **Page 58,** Fong Kam Yee/Shutterstock; **Page 78,** John Elk, Bruce Coleman, Inc.; **Page 80,** AP Photo/Jim McKnight; **Page 87,** Courtesy of author; **Page 89,** World History Archive/Alamy; **Page 93,** Jet Propulsion Labs/NASA; **Page 98,** Dirk Wiersma/Photo Researchers, Inc.; **Page 103,** Courtesy of David H. Blackwell; **Page 119,** Jacques Boyer/Roger-Viollet/The Image Works; **Page 139,** *PSSC Physics,* second edition. DC Heath & Co. with Education Development Center, Inc.; **Page 159,** Jenny Thomas/Addison Wesley/Pearson Education; **Page 163,** JSC/NASA; **Page 190,** Konstantin Sutyagin/ Shutterstock; **Page 207,** PhotoDisc; **Page 240,** Courtesy of Dr Fan Chung Graham; **Page 248,** NASA; **Page 266,** Brian P. Gielczyk/Shutterstock; **Page 273,** The Granger Collection; **Page 280,** The Granger Collection; **Page 298,** Library of Congress Prints and Photographs Division [LC-USZ62-101363]; **Page 317,** Marshall Henrichs/Addison Wesley/Pearson Education; **Page 324,** Undersea Discoveries/Shutterstock; **Page 348,** Moviestore collection Ltd/Alamy; **Page 358,** PhotoDisc; **Page 359,** Courtesy of J. Ernest Wilkins, Jr.; **Page 365,** Digital Vision; **Page 382,** Mikhail Olykainen/Shutterstock; **Page 408,** Giovanni Dall'Orto; **Page 421,** Jenny Thomas/Addison Wesley/Pearson Education; **Page 425,** Corbis/Bettmann; **Page 438,** NASA/JPL; **Page 448,** NASA; **Page 449,** The Granger Collection; **Page 457,** Michael Flynn/Navy Visual News Service; **Page 460,** George Doyle/Stockbyte/Getty Images; **Page 476,** Studio 37/Shutterstock; **Page 486,** *PSSC Physics,* second edition. DC Heath & Co. with Education Development Center, Inc.; **Page 503,** SPL/Photo Researchers, Inc.; **Page 508,** Pearson Education; **Page 518,** Medioimages/Photodisc/Getty Images; **Page 536,** Creatas/PhotoLibrary **Page 570** © 1999 PhotoDisc **Page 624** © 1998 Tony Stone Images; **Page 660** Figure 12.37 from *PSSC Physics,* 2/e, 1965; D.C. Heath & Co. with Education Development Center, Inc., Newton, MA. Reprinted with permission. **Page 666** © 1999 PhotoDisc; **Page 697** AIT 13.1 Roger-Viollet **Page 748** © 1999 PhotoDisc **Page 814** © 1999 PhotoDisc; **Page 822** Figure 15.16 InterNetwork, Inc., and NASA/Jet Propulsion Laboratory.